PHILIP'S

ESSENTIAL
ENCYCLOPEDIA

Published in Great Britain by
George Philip Limited, Michelin House,
81 Fulham Road, London SW3 6RB

First published 1997
Second edition (revised and updated) 1998

EDITOR
Steve Luck

ART EDITOR
Mike Brown

TEXT EDITORS
Chris Humphries
Frances Adlington

PRODUCTION
Claudette Morris

Reproduction by Colourpath Ltd, London

A CIP catalogue record for this book is available from the British Library.

ISBN 0–540–07525–6

Printed in China

PHILIP'S

ESSENTIAL ENCYCLOPEDIA

The *Philip's Essential Encyclopedia* has been created as a stimulating reference source for everyday family use - as a study aid for secondary school students, a first stop for general enquiries and puzzle answers, and a treasure-trove for browsers. The 10,000 alphabetically organized entries provide clear, essential information on a vast variety of subjects, from world affairs to science and the arts. The 16-page world atlas, and 16 pages of colour illustration covering technology, the human body, the arts, Earth science and natural history, convey visual information far beyond the descriptive power of many thousands of words.

When choosing a single-volume encyclopedia, the most important consideration for the user is the criteria by which the articles have been selected. *Philip's Essential Encyclopedia* has been created with secondary school students in mind. Core subjects have been given the greatest attention. The articles, compatible with and complementary to what is learned in the classroom, have been written with exceptional clarity so that even complex concepts can be understood by readers as young as thirteen or fourteen. This second edition has been fully revised and updated, with particular attention being paid to international and national contemporary political and social events.

An encyclopedia, however, must contain more than just a comprehensive coverage of core subjects. Equally full in their treatment are the articles that cover leisure interests, such as sports and popular music, animals and plants, cinema and current affairs, making this encyclopedia ideal for home reference as well as an important resource at school or college.

Cross-references

The *Philip's Essential Encyclopedia* has more than 20,000 individual cross-references, indicated by SMALL CAPITAL letters, which take the reader from one article to other articles that provide useful related information. For example, contained within the "pancreas" article are cross-references to SMALL INTESTINE, AMYLASE, TRYPSIN, INSULIN and DIABETES.

Alphabetical order

The order of articles is strictly alphabetical, except that Mc is treated as if it were spelt Mac, and abbreviations as if spelt out in full, thus St is treated as Saint. Articles that have more than one word in the heading, such as "Panama Canal", are ordered as if there were no space between the words. Articles that share the same main heading follow the basic hierarchy of people, places and things – for example:

> Washington, Booker T. (Taliaferro)
> Washington, George
> Washington
> Washington, D.C.

The hierarchy for biographical entries is: saints, popes, emperors, kings, queens, princes, dukes, knights, commoners. However, when popes, emperors, kings and queens share the same name, they are collected together by country and then follow in chronological order. Thus Henry I, Henry II, Henry III, etc. (of England) are grouped together, followed by Henry II, Henry III, Henry IV (of France).

Places that share a name are ordered by the alphabetical order of the country. Foreign place names have been anglicized, with the local spelling in brackets, for example, Florence (Firenze); Moscow (Moskva).

Alternative spellings

For Chinese spellings, the Pinyin system of transliteration is generally preferred, with cross-references from the Wade-Giles system where appropriate, for example, Peking *See* Beijing. Wade-Giles transliterations have also been retained where they remain in common use, for example, Chiang Kai-shek.

Alternative spellings and names of headwords are followed in parenthesis, for example, Dalai Lama (Grand Lama).

International coverage

The importance of cultures beyond the English-speaking world is deliberately emphasized. In an age when international barriers are being steadily removed, the *Philip's Essential Encyclopedia* has thousands of articles on peoples, cultures, religions and beliefs.

Science

In keeping with the methods taught in schools and colleges, modern scientific names have been used. For example information on "acetaldehyde" will be found under "ethanal". Where less well-known modern names are used, cross-references from the old names will take the reader to the new headings.

Metric units have been used throughout with corresponding imperial measurements following in brackets.

A/a, first letter of the Roman alphabet. It evolved from the Egyptian hieroglyph representing the head of an ox through the Hebrew word aleph, meaning ox, to the Greek alpha.

Aachen (Aix-la-Chapelle) City in SW North Rhine-Westphalia, W Germany. It was the site of medieval imperial diets and the coronations of the monarchs of the Holy Roman Empire from 1349–1531. Industries: iron, steel, machinery, textiles. Pop. (1993) 246,100.

Aalto, Alvar (1898–1976) Finnish architect and furniture designer, famous for his imaginative handling of floor levels and use of natural materials and irregular forms. *See also* INTERNATIONAL STYLE

aardvark Nocturnal, bristly haired mammal of central and S Africa. It feeds on termites and ants, which it scoops up with its sticky 30cm (12in) tongue. Length: up to 1.5m (5ft); weight: up to 70kg (154lb). It is the only representative of the order *Tubulidentata*.

Aaron Brother of MOSES chosen by God to be the first Jewish high priest. According to the biblical book of Exodus, he helped to obtain the release of the Israelites from slavery in Egypt. He lapsed into idolatry and made a golden calf for the people to worship, but he was later restored to divine favour.

abacus Archaic mathematical tool used in ancient times in the Middle and Far East for addition and subtraction. One form of abacus consists of beads strung on wires and arranged in columns.

abalone Seashore MOLLUSC with a single flattened spiral shell perforated by a row of respiratory holes. It is found on Mediterranean, Atlantic and N Pacific shores and off the coasts of South Africa and Australia. Length: to 30cm (12in). Family Haliotidae

Abbas I (the Great) (1571–1629) Shah of Persia (1588–1629). The outstanding ruler of the SAFAVID dynasty, he restored Persia as a great power, waging war successfully against the invading Uzbeks and Ottoman Turks and recapturing Hormuz from the Portuguese. Tolerant in religion, he encouraged Dutch and English merchants and admitted Christian missionaries. He made ISFAHAN his capital, turning it into one of the world's most beautiful cities.

Abbasid Muslim CALIPH dynasty (750–1258). They traced their descent from al-Abbas, the uncle of MUHAMMAD, and came to power by defeating the UMAYYADS. The Abbasids moved the caliphate from Damascus to Baghdad in 862, where it achieved great splendour. From the 10th century, Abbasid caliphs ceased to exercise political power, becoming religious figureheads. After the family's downfall in 1258, following the fall of Baghdad to the Mongols, one member was invited by the Mameluke sultan to Cairo, where the dynasty was recognized until the 16th century.

abbey Complex of buildings that constitute a religious community, the centre of which is the abbey church. Since the decline of MONASTICISM often only the church remains.

abdomen In VERTEBRATES, portion of the body between the chest and the pelvis, containing the abdominal cavity and abdominal viscera, including most of the digestive organs. In ARTHROPODS, it is the posterior part of the body, containing the reproductive organs and part of the digestive system.

Abélard, Pierre (1079–1142) French philosopher noted for his application of logic to theological questions. In *Sic et Non* he attempted to reconcile differences between the Fathers of the Church by using the Aristotelian method of DIALECTIC. His views were condemned by the Council of Sens (1140). He is perhaps best known for his tragic love affair with his young female pupil Héloïse. The affair scandalized Abélard's contemporaries. He was castrated and became a monk, while Héloïse was forced to enter a convent. These events inspired his *Historia Calamitatum Mearum*.

Aberdeen City and seaport in NE Scotland, called "the Granite City" after its famous grey granite architecture. Aberdeen has gained in importance since the development of the North Sea oilfields in the late 1970s and is also the centre of the waning Scottish fishing industry. Pop. (1991) 204,885.

aberration In physics, defect in LENS and mirror images arising when the incident light is not at or near the centre of the lens or mirror. **Spherical aberration** occurs when rays falling on the periphery of a lens or mirror are not brought to the same focus as light at the centre; the image is blurred. **Chromatic aberration** occurs when the wavelengths of the dispersed light are not brought to the same focus; the image is falsely coloured.

Abidjan Former capital of the Ivory Coast (and the largest city in W Africa), situated on the Ebrié Lagoon, inland from the Gulf of Guinea. It is Ivory Coast's cultural and economic centre. Industries: textile manufactures and sawmilling. Pop. (1988) 1,929,079.

Abkhazia Autonomous republic on the Black Sea coast of Georgia; the capital is Sukhumi. The area was conquered by Romans, Byzantines, Arabs and Turks before becoming a Russian protectorate in 1910. It was made a Soviet republic in 1921 and an autonomous republic within Georgia in 1930. After the establishment of an independent Georgia, the Abkhazian parliament declared independence in 1992. In 1993 Abkhazian forces seized the capital. In May 1994 a cease-fire deployed 2,500 peacekeeping Russian soldiers, and in November a new constitution proclaimed Abkhazian sovereignty. Its independent status was confirmed by a new Georgian constitution in 1995. Tobacco, tea, grapes and citrus fruits are the main crops. Area 8,600sq km (3,320sq mi). Pop. (1990) 537,500.

aborigines Indigenous inhabitants of a country. The term usually applies to NATIVE AUSTRALIANS.

abortion Loss of a fetus before it is sufficiently advanced to survive outside the womb; commonly called a miscarriage. A medical abortion is the termination of pregnancy by drugs or surgery. The rights of the fetus and the mother's right to choose provoke much political and ethical debate.

Abraham In the Old Testament, progenitor of the Hebrews and founder of Judaism. God tested his loyalty by demanding he sacrifice his son, ISAAC. He is esteemed by Muslims who regard him as the ancestor, through his son ISHMAEL, of the Arabs.

abrasives Rough substances used to grind and polish surfaces. Some abrasives are used as fine powders, others in larger fragments with sharp cutting edges. Most natural abrasives are minerals.

Absalom In the Old Testament, third and favourite son of King DAVID. He murdered his brother Amnon, led a rebellion against David and was routed. Trapped in flight when his hair became entangled in the branches of an oak, he was killed by David's general Joab.

abscess Collection of pus anywhere in the body, contained in a cavity of inflamed tissue. It is caused by bacterial infection.

absolute zero Temperature at which all parts of a system are at the lowest energy permitted by the laws of QUANTUM MECHANICS; zero on the kelvin temperature scale, which is $-273.16°C$ ($-459.67°F$). At this temperature the system's ENTROPY, its energy available for useful work, is also zero, although the total energy of the system may not be zero.

absolution Formal rite carried out by a Christian priest in which repentant sinners are forgiven the sins they have confessed. The rite is based on the authority given by Christ to his apostles to forgive sins (John 20). See also CONFESSION; PENANCE

absorption Taking up chemically or physically of molecules of one substance into another. The absorbed matter permeates all of the absorber. This includes a gas taken in by a liquid and a liquid or gas absorbed by a solid. The process is often utilized commercially, such as the purification of natural gas by the absorption of hydrogen sulphide in aqueous ethanolamine. See also ADSORPTION

abstract art Art in which recognizable objects are reduced to schematic marks. The movement became established in the early 20th century. Art historians often credit Wassily KANDINSKY with being the first to explore expressionist abstraction in 1910. Geometrical abstraction found its most adept, early exponents in Russia in c.1913. Pioneers included Kasimir MALEVICH, who invented SUPREMATISM, and LISSITZKY, a leading proponent of CONSTRUCTIVISM. The French *Section d'Or* worked in parallel to the Russians. Other geometric abstract artists include Piet MONDRIAN, Naum GABO and Ben NICHOLSON. Influential movements include De STIJL and Concrete Art.

abstract expressionism Mainly US art movement in which the creative process itself is examined and explored. It is neither wholly abstract nor wholly expressionist. One of the most influential of all 20th-century North American art movements, the term originally applied to paintings created in 1945–55 by artists from the New York School. In the early 1950s, two distinct groups emerged with Willem DE KOONING and Jackson POLLOCK heading the most aggressive trend, which involved dripping or throwing paint onto canvas. Barnett Newman and Mark ROTHKO were more contemplative. See also ACTION PAINTING

Absurd, Theatre of the Dramatic and literary critical term developed from the philosophy of Albert CAMUS to describe discordant human experience in an inhuman world. It was first applied in 1961 to describe contemporary drama which depicted the irrationality of life in an unconventional dramatic style. Exponents include Samuel BECKETT, Eugène IONESCO, Jean GENET and Edward ALBEE. Beckett's play *Waiting for Godot* is a classic of the genre.

Abu Bakr (573–634) First Muslim CALIPH. One of the earliest converts to Islam, Abu Bakr was chief adviser to the Prophet MUHAMMAD. After Muhammad's death he was elected leader of the Muslim community. During his short reign (632–34), he defeated the tribes that had revolted against Muslim rule in Medina after the death of Muhammad and restored them to Islam. By invading the Byzantine Christian provinces of Syria and Palestine and the Iranian province of Iraq, he launched the series of Holy Wars through which the first major expansion of Islam was accomplished.

Abu Dhabi (Abu Zaby) Largest and wealthiest of the seven UNITED ARAB EMIRATES, lying on the S coast of the Persian Gulf. Also the name of its capital city (1984 pop. 242,975), federal capital of the UAE. Since the late 1950s, Abu Dhabi's economy has been based almost entirely on crude oil production. Area: 67,340sq km (26,000sq mi). Pop. (1985) 670,125.

Abuja Nigeria's administrative capital since December 1991. The new city was designed by the Japanese architect Kenzo Tange, and work began in 1976. Government offices began moving in the 1980s to relieve pressure on the infrastructure of LAGOS. Pop. (1992 est.) 305,900.

Abu Simbel Ancient Egyptian village on the W bank of the River Nile, near the border with Sudan, and location of two rock-cut sandstone temples built (c.1292–1225 BC) by RAMSES II. In 1963–66 the temples and statuary were moved further inland to prevent their disappearance under the waters of Lake Nasser, created by the construction of the new ASWAN High Dam.

abyssal zone Division of the ocean that begins at about the 2,000-m (6,600-ft) depth and includes the rest of the deep ocean. The water temperature ranges from $-1°C$ to $5°C$ (30–40°F). The zone has no light so there are no seasons and no plants, but there are many forms of life, such as glass sponges, crinoids (sea lilies), and brachiopods (lamp shells). The bottom is covered by deposits of biogenic oozes formed by the remains of microscopic plankton, and non-biogenic sediments (red clays).

acacia (mimosa) Evergreen shrubs and trees widely distributed in tropical and subtropical regions, especially Australia. They have compound leaves made up of many small leaflets, and yellow or white flowers. Height: 1.2–18m (4–59ft). Family Leguminosae; genus *Acacia*.

Académie Française Official French literary society, now part of the Institut de France. Originating as a private discussion group whose members were persuaded by Cardinal RICHELIEU to become an official body in 1635, the society is the guardian of the French language and of literary conventions.

Academy Award *See* OSCAR

acanthus PERENNIAL plant with thistle-like leaves, found in Africa, the Mediterranean region, India and Malaysia. It has lobed, often spiny leaves and white or coloured flower spikes. The pattern of the leaves is a common classical architectural motif.

Acapulco (Acapulco de Juárez) City on the SW coast of Mexico. Founded in 1550, it was for 250 years an important port on the Manila galleon-route linking Spain and the Philippines. Now Mexico's most famous Pacific resort, it is noted for beautiful scenery, deep-sea fishing and luxurious hotels. The port exports cotton, fruit, hides and tobacco. Pop. (1990) 593,212.

acceleration Amount by which the VELOCITY of an object increases in a certain time. It can be found by applying the equation acceleration = (change in velocity)/(time taken for change). It is measured in metres per second per second (m/s^2).

accelerator, particle Machine for increasing the energy of charged particles by increasing their speed. Accelerators are used mostly in PARTICLE PHYSICS' experiments, in which high-energy particles are forced to collide with other particles. The way the fragments of particles behave following the collision provides physicists with information on the forces found within atoms. In a **linear** accelerator, the particles travel in a straight line. In a **cyclotron**, particles are accelerated in a spiral path between pairs of D-shaped magnets with an alternating electric field between them. A **synchrotron** synchronizes the accelerating electric current to the time it takes to make one revolution. The CERN synchrotron accelerator in Geneva, Switzerland has a circumference of 27km (16.7mi).

accordion Musical instrument of the reed organ type. It has an organ-like tone produced by air from the bellows vibrating reeds. It was invented in 1822 and is widely used in folk music.

Accra Capital and largest city of Ghana, on the Gulf of Guinea. Occupied by the Ga people since the 15th century, it became the capital of Britain's Gold Coast colony in 1875. Today it is a major port

and economic centre, the site of the University of Ghana (1948), and headquarters of the Defence Commission of the Organization of African Unity. Industries: engineering, timber, textiles. Main export is cacao. Pop. (1988 est.) 949,113.

accumulator (secondary cell, storage battery) Voltaic cell (BATTERY) that can be recharged. The most commonly used car battery is a lead-acid accumulator.

acetaldehyde *See* ETHANAL

acetate (ethanoate) Salt or ester of acetic (ethanoic) acid. It is used in synthetic acetate fibres, in lacquers and in acetate film.

acetone (propanone) Colourless flammable liquid (CH_3COCH_3) made by oxidizing propan–2–ol. It is a raw material for the manufacture of many organic chemicals and is a widely used solvent. Properties: r.d. 0.79; m.p. $-94.8°C$ ($-138.6°F$); b.p. $56.2°C$ ($133.2 °F$).

acetylene *See* ETHYNE

Achaemenids Ruling dynasty of the first PERSIAN empire, which stretched from the River Nile as far E as modern Afghanistan. The dynasty was founded by CYRUS THE GREAT (r.559–529 BC) and named after his ancestor, Achaemenes. Its last ruler, DARIUS III (r.336–330 BC), was defeated by Alexander the Great.

Achilles In the Greek epic tradition, the most fearless Greek fighter of the Trojan War and the hero of Homer's *Iliad*. Legend held him invulnerable from weapons because he had been dipped in the River Styx at birth, except for the heel by which he was held. Achilles died at TROY, when an arrow shot by PARIS struck his heel.

Achilles tendon Strong band of elastic connective tissue at the back of the ankle. One of the largest tendons in the body. It connects the calf muscles to the heel bone. The spring provided by this tendon is very important in walking and running.

acid Chemical compound containing hydrogen that can be replaced by a metal or other positive ION to form a SALT. Acids dissociate in water to yield aqueous hydrogen ions (H^+), thus acting as proton donors. The solutions are corrosive, have a sour taste and have a pH below 7. *See also* BASE

acid rain Rain that is highly acidic because of sulphur oxides, nitrogen oxides, and other air pollutants dissolved in it. Acid rain may have a pH value as low as 2.8. Acid rain can severely damage both plant and animal life. Certain lakes, for example, have lost all fish and plant life because of acid rain.

acne Inflammatory disorder of the sebaceous (oil-producing) glands of the SKIN resulting in skin eruptions such as blackheads and infected spots; it is seen mostly on the face, neck, back and chest. Acne is extremely common in both sexes at PUBERTY, but is usually more pronounced in boys. It does not usually persist beyond early adulthood.

Aconcagua Mountain in the ANDES range on the border between Argentina and Chile. It is the highest peak in the Western Hemisphere, at 22,834ft

3

(6,969m). A snow-capped, extinct volcano, it was first climbed in 1897 by Edward Fitzgerald. The w slopes are in Chile, but the summit is in Argentina.

acorn Fruit of an OAK tree.

acoustics Study of the behaviour of sound waves. Experts apply acoustics in the design of concert and lecture halls, loudspeakers and musical instruments. Audiologists use acoustics to assess degrees of abnormality in the hearing of their patients. *See also* ANECHOIC CHAMBER

Acquired Immune Deficiency Syndrome (AIDS) Fatal disease caused by a RETROVIRUS called Human Immunodeficiency Virus (HIV), which renders the body's IMMUNE SYSTEM incapable of resisting infection. The first diagnosis was in New York in 1979. In 1983–84 scientists at the Pasteur Institute in France and the National Cancer Institute in the USA isolated HIV as the cause of the disease. The virus can remain dormant in infected cells for up to 10 years. Initial AIDS-related complex (ARC) symptoms include severe weight loss and fatigue. It may develop into the AIDS syndrome, characterized by secondary infections, neurological damage and cancers. AIDS is transmitted only by a direct exchange of body fluids. Transmission is most commonly through sexual intercourse, the sharing of contaminated needles by intravenous drug users, and from the uterus of infected mothers to their babies. In the USA and Europe, over 90% of victims have been homosexual or bisexual men. However, 90% of reported cases are in the developing world and many victims are heterosexual. Recent combinations of drugs have met with some success in controlling symptoms. By 1996 over 6.4 million people had died from AIDS.

acropolis Hill-top fortress of an ancient Greek city. The earliest known examples were fortified castles built for the Mycenaean kings, and it was only later that they became the symbolic homes of the gods. The most famous acropolis, in Athens, had walls by the 13th century BC, but the Persians destroyed the complex and the surviving buildings date from the late 5th century BC. They include the PARTHENON, the Erechtheion, the Propylaea and the Temple of Athena Nike.

acrylic Type of plastic, one of a group of synthetic, short-chain, unsaturated carboxylic acid derivatives. Variations include hard and transparent, soft and resilient, or liquid forms. They are used for moulded structural parts, adhesives and paints.

actinide series Group of radioactive elements with similar chemical properties. Their atomic numbers range from 89 to 103. Each element is analogous to the corresponding LANTHANIDE SERIES (rare-earth) group. The most important of the group is uranium. Those having atomic numbers greater than 92 are called TRANSURANIC ELEMENTS.

actinium Radioactive metallic element (symbol Ac), the first of the ACTINIDE SERIES, discovered in 1899. It is found associated with uranium ores. Ac^{227}, a decay product of U^{235}, emits beta particles (electrons) during disintegration. Properties: at.no.89; r.d.10.07 (calc.); m.p.1,100°C (1,900°F); b.p. 3,200°C (5,800°F); most stable isotope Ac^{227} (half-life 21.8 yr).

action painting Act and result of applying paint spontaneously. From 1952, painters such as Willem DE KOONING and Jackson POLLOCK moved away from ABSTRACT EXPRESSIONISM to make dynamic pictures with spontaneous gestures such as dripping and pouring paint onto their canvases.

action potential Change that occurs in the electrical potential between the outside and the inside of a nerve fibre or muscle fibre when stimulated by the transmission of a nerve impulse. At rest the fibre is electrically negative inside and positive outside. When the nerve or muscle is stimulated, the charges are momentarily reversed.

Actium, Battle of (31 BC) Naval battle in which the fleet of Octavian (later Emperor AUGUSTUS), commanded by Marcus Vipsanius AGRIPPA, defeated the fleets of Mark ANTONY and CLEOPATRA. Mark Antony's army surrendered a week later, and Octavian became sole ruler of the Roman empire.

active transport Energy-requiring process by which molecules or ions are transported across the membranes of living cells against a concentration gradient. It is particularly important in the uptake of food across the gut lining, in the reabsorption of water and salts from the urine in the kidney before excretion, and in the uptake of minerals by the plant root. Active transport enables cells to maintain an internal chemical environment which is of a different composition from that of their surroundings.

act of Parliament Statute created in Britain when a bill, having passed through a variety of stages in both the House of Commons and House of Lords, receives the royal assent. Embodying the supreme force of British law, an act remains in force until it is repealed by Parliament.

Act of Union *See* UNION, ACTS OF

Acts of the Apostles Book of the New Testament describing the spread of the Gospel of Christ immediately after his death and resurrection. It mainly focuses on St PETER and St PAUL. The book was probably written *c*.65 AD by the author of St LUKE's gospel.

acupuncture System of medical treatment in which long needles are inserted into the body to assist healing, relieve pain or for anaesthetic purposes. Of ancient Chinese origin, it enables surgery to be done with the patient conscious and free of pain. It has so far defied scientific explanation.

Adam In the Old Testament (Genesis 2), first man and progenitor of all mankind, created from dust by God in his own image. He and his wife EVE were cast out of the Garden of EDEN to become mortal after they ate forbidden fruit from the Tree of the Knowledge of Good and Evil.

Adam, Robert (1728–92) Scottish architect. The greatest British architect of the late-18th century, his refined neo-classical style was widely influential.

He was equally brilliant as an interior decorator and furniture designer. The Adelphi Complex, London (1768) was his most ambitious project; his interior designs include Kenwood House, London (1767) and Syon House, Middlesex (1762–69).

Adams, Gerry (1948–) Northern Irish politician, president of SINN FÉIN (1983–). Adams was interned (1972–78) by the British government for IRISH REPUBLICAN ARMY (IRA) involvement. He was elected as an MP to Westminster (1983–92, 1997–). Adams' negotiations with John HUME led to the IRA cease-fire (1994). He headed the Sinn Féin delegation in the 1997 peacetalks.

Adams, John (1735–1826) Second US President (1797–1801). Influenced by his radical cousin Samuel Adams, he helped to draft the DECLARATION OF INDEPENDENCE (1776) and the Treaty of Paris (1783), which ended the AMERICAN REVOLUTION. Adams was George WASHINGTON's vice president (1789–97). He assumed a moderate Federalist position.

Adams, John Quincy (1767–1848) Sixth US President (1825–29), son of John ADAMS. Adams served in his father's administration, before becoming (1803–08) a FEDERALIST PARTY representative in the US senate. Adams acted as secretary of state (1817–24) for James MONROE. He was largely responsible for formulating the MONROE DOCTRINE. Adams became president without an electoral majority, his appointment decided by the House of Representatives.

adaptation Adjustment by a living organism to its surroundings. Animals and plants adapt to changes in their environment through variations in structure, reproduction or organization within communities. Some such changes are temporary (acclimatization), while others may involve changes in the genetic material (DNA) and be inherited by offspring (EVOLUTION). The word is also used to describe a particular characteristic, of body size, shape, colour, physiology or behaviour, that fits an organism to survive in its environment.

adaptive radiation In biology, the EVOLUTION of different forms of living organisms from a common ancestral stock, as different populations adapt to different environmental conditions or modes of life. Eventually the populations may become so different that they constitute separate species. Examples are the many different kinds of finches in the GALÁPAGOS ISLANDS, which diversified to specialize in different kinds of food, feeding methods and HABITATS. *See also* ADAPTATION

adder Any of several snakes in various parts of the world, some poisonous and others harmless. The European viper (*Vipera berus*) is called an adder in Britain. The puff adder (*Bitis arietans*) is a large African viper, and the death adder (*Acanthophis antarcticus*) is a dangerous Australian elapid.

addiction Inability to control the use of a particular substance, resulting in physiological or psychological dependence. It is most frequently associated with DRUG ADDICTION. In a medical context, addiction requires a physical dependence. When the dose of a drug is reduced or withdrawn from the user, the addict experiences withdrawal syndromes.

Addis Ababa (Amheric, new flower) Capital and largest city in Ethiopia, situated on a plateau at *c*.2,440m (8,000ft) in the highlands of Shewa province. Addis Ababa was made capital of Ethiopia in 1889. It is the headquarters of the ORGANIZATION OF AFRICAN UNITY (OAU). It is the main centre for the country's vital coffee trade. Industries: food, tanning, textiles and wood products. Pop. (1990 est.) 1,700,000.

addition reaction Chemical reaction in which two substances combine to form a third substance, with no other substance being produced. Addition reactions are most commonly used in ORGANIC CHEMISTRY, particularly by adding a simple molecule across a carbon-carbon double bond in an UNSATURATED COMPOUND. *See also* SUBSTITUTION

Adelaide Capital of the state of SOUTH AUSTRALIA, situated at the mouth of the Torrens River. Founded in 1836 and named after William IV's wife, the port exports wool, fruit, wine and wheat. Industries: oil refining, machinery, motor vehicle assembly, electronics, chemicals, textiles. Pop. (1994) 1,076,400.

Aden Commercial capital and largest city of the Yemen, historic capital of the Aden Protectorate (1937–67) and the former (southern) People's Democratic Republic of Yemen (1967–90). With the opening of the SUEZ CANAL in 1869, its importance increased. It was made a crown colony in 1937. In 1970 Aden became the sole capital of the new People's Democratic Republic of Yemen. When the (northern) Yemen Arab Republic and the (southern) People's Democratic Republic of Yemen combined to form a united Republic of Yemen in 1990, SANA'A became the official capital. Industries: cigarette manufacture, oil and salt refining. Pop. (1995) 562,000.

Adenauer, Konrad (1876–1967) German statesman, first chancellor of the Federal Republic of Germany (1949–63). He was Lord Mayor of Cologne (1917–33) and was twice imprisoned by the Nazis. He helped to create the Christian Democratic Union (CDU), West Germany's dominant post-war party, and was its leader (1946–66). As chancellor, he led West Germany into NATO (1955) and campaigned for the establishment of the European Economic Community.

adenoids Masses of LYMPH tissue in the upper part of the PHARYNX (throat) behind the NOSE; part of a child's defences against disease, they normally disappear by the age of ten.

adhesion Attraction of molecules of one substance to the molecules of another. GUM, GLUE and paste use the property of adhesion to join substances together. *See also* COHESION

adipose tissue (fatty tissue) Connective tissue made up of body cells that store globules of fat.

Adler, Alfred (1870–1937) Austrian psychiatrist. After working with Sigmund FREUD (1902–11), Adler broke away to found his own school of "individual psychology". He believed that striving for social success and power was fundamental in human motivation. According to his theory, individuals develop problems when they cannot surmount feelings of inferiority acquired in childhood.

administrative law Regulates the powers, procedures and acts of administrative agencies of the executive branch of government.

Adonis In Phoenician and Greek myth, a youth of remarkable beauty, loved by PERSEPHONE and APHRODITE. Adonis was gored to death by a boar, and during his afterlife Zeus decided that Adonis should spend part of the year with Persephone, queen of the underworld, and part with Aphrodite.

adrenal gland One of a pair of small endocrine glands situated on top of the KIDNEYS. They produce many STEROIDS, which regulate the blood's salt and water balance and are concerned with the METABOLISM of carbohydrates, proteins and fats, and the HORMONES ADRENALINE and noradrenaline. *See also* ENDOCRINE SYSTEM

adrenaline HORMONE secreted by the ADRENAL GLANDS, important in preparing the body's response to stress. It has widespread effects in the body, increasing the strength and rate of heartbeat and the rate and depth of BREATHING, diverting blood from the SKIN and DIGESTIVE SYSTEM to the heart and muscles, and stimulating the release of GLUCOSE from the LIVER to increase energy supply by promoting increased RESPIRATION. Adrenaline is used medicinally, especially in the resuscitation of patients in shock or following cardiac arrest.

Adrian IV (c.1100–59) Pope (1154–59), b. Nicholas Breakspear, the only English pope. In 1155 he crowned emperor FREDERICK I, Barbarossa.

Adriatic Sea Shallow arm of the Mediterranean Sea, separated from the Ionian Sea by the Strait of Otranto, between Albania and the "heel" of Italy. Lobsters and sardines are the chief catches of local fisheries. Length: *c.*800km (500mi); Max. depth: 1,230m (4,035ft).

adsorption Attraction of a gas or liquid to the surface of a solid or liquid. It involves attraction of molecules at the surface, unlike ABSORPTION that implies incorporation. The amounts adsorbed and the rate of adsorption depend on the structure exposed, the chemical identities and concentrations of the substances involved, and the temperature.

advent Liturgical season preceding Christmas. It begins on the Sunday nearest 30 November (St Andrew's Day). Advent refers both to Christ's birth and to his coming in glory as judge at the end of history.

Adventists Christians belonging to any of a group of churches whose distinctive belief concerns the imminent Second Coming of Christ. William Miller (1782–1849) formed the first organized Adventist movement in the USA in 1831.

Christ's failure to return on dates forecast by Miller led to splits in the movement. The largest group to emerge was the SEVENTH-DAY ADVENTISTS.

Aegean civilization Bronze Age cultures, chiefly MINOAN and MYCENAEAN, of Greece and the Aegean islands *c.*3000–1100 BC.

Aegean Sea Part of the Mediterranean Sea between Greece and Turkey, bounded by Crete to the S and connected to the Black Sea and the Sea of Marmara by the Dardanelles to the NE. Oil and natural gas have been discovered in the area, but the principal income is derived from tourism, fishing and crops such as citrus fruits, olives and grapes.

Aeneas In Greek mythology, the son of Anchises and APHRODITE. Active in the defence of TROY, he led the Trojans to Italy. The Romans acknowledged Aeneas and his Trojan company as their ancestors.

Aeneid Poem written by VIRGIL between 30–19 BC. Written in 12 books, the *Aeneid* recounts the legendary founding of the town of Lavinium and the Roman state by the Trojan AENEAS.

aerial (antenna) Conductor component of radio and television systems for the broadcast and transmission of signals. An aerial's design usually depends on the wavelength of the signal.

aerobic Connected with or dependent on the presence of free oxygen or air. An aerobic organism can only survive in the presence of oxygen and depends on it for breaking down GLUCOSE and other foods to release energy. This process is called aerobic RESPIRATION. *See also* ANAEROBIC

aerodynamics Science of gases in motion and the forces acting on objects, such as aircraft, in motion through the air. An aircraft designer must consider four main factors and their interrelationships: weight of the aircraft and the load it will carry; lift to overcome the pull of gravity; drag, or the forces that retard motion; and thrust, the driving force. Air resistance (drag) increases as the square of an object's speed and is minimized by streamlining. Engineers use the WIND TUNNEL and computer systems to predict aerodynamic performance.

aerofoil Any shape or surface, such as a wing, tail or propeller blade on an aircraft, that has as its major function the deflection of airflow to produce a pressure differential or LIFT. A typical aerofoil has a leading and trailing edge, and an upper and lower camber.

aeronautics Study of flight and the control of AIRCRAFT involving AERODYNAMICS, aircraft structures and methods of propulsion. Aeronautics started with the study of the BALLOON, which mainly concerned the raising of a load by means of BUOYANCY. It later included the heavier-than-air flight of gliders, planes, helicopters and rockets. A HELICOPTER utilizes LIFT provided by a rotor. Gliders and planes use wings to provide lift, but a minimum forward speed is essential to maintain height. A plane is pulled forward by propeller, or is pushed by the reaction forces of expanding gases from one or more jet or rocket engines. The increased speeds of modern aircraft to supersonic (speeds in excess of that of sound, *c.*1,225km/h or 760mph) and the accompanying shock waves this produces have brought changes in wing and fuselage designs to improve streamlining. Hypersonic speeds (in excess of five times the speed of sound or Mach 5) require further fundamental changes.

aeroplane *See* AIRCRAFT

aerosol Suspension of liquid or solid particles in a gas. Fog – millions of tiny water droplets suspended in air – is a liquid-based example; airborne dust or smoke is a solid-based equivalent. Manufactured aerosols are used in products such as deodorants, cosmetics, paints and household sprays. *See also* CHLOROFLUOROCARBONS (CFCs)

Aeschylus (525–456 BC) Greek dramatist. The earliest of the great Greek playwrights. He is said to have been responsible for the development of TRAGEDY as a dramatic form through his addition of a second actor and the reduced role of the chorus. He was also the first to introduce scenery. His best-known work is the trilogy *Oresteia*, comprising *Agamemnon*, *The Choephori* and *The Eumenides*.

Aesir Primary group of Nordic gods who lived in Asgard. Woden (ODIN), THOR (Donar) and Tyr (Tiw), with a few others, were the object of a cult that extended throughout the lands inhabited by Germanic peoples.

Aesop (620–560 BC) Greek fabulist. According to one tradition, he was a former slave, the reputed creator of numerous short tales about animals, all illustrating human virtues and failings (they were almost certainly written by several people).

aesthetic movement Late 19th-century English cult of beauty. It grew out of a more widespread philosophy called aestheticism, which spread across Europe from the early 19th century as a reaction against industrialization and utilitarian philosophies. The main protagonists were Aubrey Beardsley, J.M. WHISTLER, Oscar WILDE and Walter Pater.

aesthetics Philosophy of beauty and taste. Deriving from the Greek word meaning perception, the term appeared in Germany during the mid-18th century. GOETHE, HEGEL and KANT popularized the concept in the late 18th and early 19th centuries, while in the 20th century, theories of aesthetics have been modified, such that what was considered as inherent beauty, may merely be perceived beauty. These changes had revolutionary implications for the development of modern art.

affidavit Formal written statement testifying on oath that a specified fact or account is true. Countersigned (usually with an official seal) by a witness of juridical authority, affidavits may be used as evidence in court and tribunal proceedings, or to guarantee the identity of a person claiming legal rights.

Afghanistan Landlocked country in S Asia bordered by Turkmenistan, Uzbekistan, Tajikistan, China, Pakistan and Iran; the capital is KABUL. **Land and climate** The central highlands reach a height of more than 7,600m (24,900ft) in the E and

AFGHANISTAN	
AREA: 652,090sq km (251,773sq mi)	
POPULATION: 19,062,000	
CAPITAL (POPULATION): Kabul (700,000)	
GOVERNMENT: Islamic republic	
ETHNIC GROUPS: Pathan (Pashtun) 52%, Tajik 20%, Uzbek 9%, Hazara 9%, Chahar 3%, Turkmen 2%, Baluchi 1%	
LANGUAGES: Pashto, Dari (Persian) both official	
RELIGIONS: Islam (Sunni Muslim 74%, Shiite Muslim 25%)	
CURRENCY: Afghani = 100 puls	

make up nearly 75% of Afghanistan. The main range is the HINDU KUSH, which is cut by fertile valleys. North of the highlands are broad plateaus and hilly areas. To the S are lowlands, consisting largely of semi-desert. In winter, N winds bring cold weather to the mountains, but summers are hot and dry. To the S rainfall decreases and temperatures are higher. Grassland covers much of the N; conifers grow on the higher mountain slopes. **Economy** Afghanistan is one of the world's poorest countries, depending heavily on agriculture, which employs *c.*60% of the workforce. Many people are semi-nomadic herdspeople, while wheat is the chief crop of the settled farmers in the valleys. Afghanistan has many mineral deposits, but most are undeveloped. Natural gas is produced, together with some coal, copper, gold, precious stones and salt. Afghanistan has few manufacturing industries. The main exports are karakul skins, cotton, fruit and nuts. **History** In ancient times, Afghanistan was invaded by Aryans, Persians, Greeks, Macedonians and warrior armies from central Asia. Arab armies introduced Islam in the late 7th century. AHMAD SHAH founded the Durrani dynasty and established the first unified state in 1747. The dynasty's collapse in 1818 created a power vacuum, which Russia and Britain struggled to fill. British troops invaded in 1839–42 and 1878. The dominance of British interests was recognized in the Anglo-Russian Agreement (1907). In 1921 Afghanistan became fully independent. In 1973 an army coup overthrew the monarchy and established a republic. In 1978 the military government was deposed in a Marxist coup, backed by the Soviet Union. The costly Afghanistan War (1979–89) was fought between government-backed Soviet troops and Mujaheddin guerrillas. In 1988–89 Soviet troops withdrew, but the civil war raged on. In 1992 Mujaheddin forces captured Kabul and set up a moderate Islamic government. Fundamentalist Muslims continued to agitate. In 1996 the radical TALIBAN, based in KANDAHAR, captured much of Afghanistan, including Kabul, and formed an interim government. Rival factions mounted a joint offensive against the Taliban and fighting continued throughout 1997.

Africa Second-largest continent (after Asia), straddling the Equator and lying largely within the tropics. **Land** Africa forms a plateau between the Atlantic and Indian oceans. Its highest features include the ATLAS and Ahaggar mountains in the NW, the Ethiopian Highlands in the E, and the Drakensberg Mountains in the S. Lake Assal in the Afar Depression of Djibouti is the lowest point at −153m (−502ft). The huge sunken strip in the E is the African section of the Great RIFT VALLEY. The SAHARA stretches across the N and the KALAHARI and NAMIB are smaller deserts in the S and SW. MADAGASCAR lies off the SE coast. **Structure and geology** Africa is composed largely of ancient metamorphic rocks overlain with tertiary Mesozoic and Palaeozoic sediments. The mountains of the NW are folded sedimentary material, roughly contemporaneous with the Alps. The Great Rift Valley, formed by the progressive movement of the Arabian Peninsula away from Africa, is mainly igneous in the N and older pre-Cambrian in the S. **Lakes and rivers** The Rift Valley contains the lakes ALBERT, MALAWI and TANGANYIKA. Lake VICTORIA to the E is Africa's largest; Lake CHAD lies in the S Sahara. Rivers include the NILE, NIGER, CONGO and ZAMBEZI. **Climate and vegetation** Much of the continent is hot and (outside the desert areas) humid. The belt along the equator receives more than 254cm (100in) of precipitation a year and is covered by tropical rainforest. The forest gives way both in the N and S to areas of acacia and brush and then through savanna grassland to desert. The N strip of the continent and the area around the Cape have a Mediterranean climate. **Peoples** Africa is home to over 13% of the world's population, divided into more than 700 culturally distinct tribes and groups. N of the Sahara, Arabs and Berbers predominate, while to the S some of the many black tribes include the FULANI, GALLA, HAUSA, HOTTENTOTS, IGBO, MASAI, MOSSI, SAN, YORUBA and ZULU. Indians and Europeans also form significant minorities. Africa is relatively thinly populated and c.75% of the population is rural. **Economy** Agriculture is restricted in central Africa by the large expanse of tropical rainforest, though cash crops such as cocoa, rubber and groundnuts are grown on plantations. Along the N coast, crops such as citrus fruits, olives and cereals are grown. The Sahara is largely unproductive, supporting only a nomadic herding community. East and S Africa are the richest agricultural areas, containing large mixed farms and cattle ranching. Apart from South Africa, the entire continent is industrially underdeveloped. Mining is most important. Zambia contains the world's largest deposits of copper ore; bauxite is extracted in W Africa; and oil is produced in Libya, Algeria and Nigeria. South Africa is extremely rich in minerals; gold, diamonds and coal being the most important. **Recent History** Before the 1880s Europeans were, except in South Africa, largely confined to the coastal regions. By the end of the 19th century the whole continent, except for Liberia and Ethiopia, was under foreign domination, either by European powers or (in the N) by the Ottoman empire. Beginning in the 1950s, the former colonies secured their independence within the space of 40 years, but rapid decolonization brought unrest and instability to many parts of the continent. A major factor in this unrest was the artificial boundaries created by colonialism. Lasting democracy has proved difficult to achieve in many countries and military rule is prevalent, often based on pre-colonial tribal divisions of power. Area: c.30,000,000sq km (11,700,000sq mi) *Highest mountain* Kilimanjaro (Tanzania) 5,895m (19,340ft) *Longest river* Nile 6,670km (4,140mi) *Population* (1990 est.) 647,518,000 *Largest cities* CAIRO (6,663,000); KINSHASA (3,804,000); ALEXANDRIA (3,170,000); CAPE TOWN (2,350,000) *See also* individual countries

African National Congress (ANC) South African political party. It was formed in 1912 with the aim of securing racial equality and full political rights for non-whites. By the 1950s it had become the principal opposition to the APARTHEID regime. A military wing was set up in the aftermath of the SHARPEVILLE Massacre. It engaged in economic and industrial sabotage. In 1961 the ANC was banned, and in 1964 its leaders, Nelson MANDELA and Walter SISULU, began long terms as political prisoners. Finally, in 1990, the party was legalized, Mandela was released, and many of the legislative pillars of apartheid were removed. In 1994, in South Africa's first multiracial elections, the ANC gained over 60% of the popular vote. Nelson Mandela became the first post-apartheid president of South Africa.

Afrikaans One of 11 official languages of the Republic of South Africa. Derived from the language spoken by the original Dutch settlers of the 17th century, it quickly evolved to become a distinct language. Afrikaans is regarded as a cultural focal point by South Africans of Dutch origin. It is the everyday means of communication for some three million speakers of European, African and mixed descent.

Afrika Korps German armoured force in World War 2 that operated in N Africa. Under its commander General ROMMEL it had spectacular but transient success against the British in 1941–42.

Afrikaner Descendant of the predominantly Dutch settlers in South Africa. Known as Boers ("farmers"), Afrikaners first settled around the Cape region in the 17th century. To avoid British control, the Afrikaners spread N and E from the Cape in the GREAT TREK and founded the independent South African Republic (TRANSVAAL) and Orange Free State. Defeat in the South African, or Boer, War (1899–1902) led to the republics merging in the Union of South Africa (1910). *See also* CAPE PROVINCE; SOUTH AFRICAN WARS

Agadir Seaport in SW Morocco, on the Atlantic coast. In 1960 the town suffered a disastrous earthquake, but it was rebuilt with tourism in mind and is now a popular all-year destination for Europeans. Fishing is the other main economic activity. Pop. (1990) 439,000.

Aga Khan Name of the leaders of the sect of Ishmaili Muslims. Aga Khan III (1877–1957) is the best known. He headed the All-India Muslim League in support of British rule in 1906. He moved to Europe and was known for his enormous wealth and love of racehorses. His son, Prince Karim, became Aga Khan IV in 1957.

Agamemnon In Greek mythology, king of Mycenae, and brother of Menelaus. According to Homer's *Iliad*, he led the Greeks at the siege of TROY. When Troy fell, Agamemnon returned home but was murdered by his wife CLYTEMNESTRA and her lover Aegisthus.

agar Complex substance extracted from seaweed; its powder forms a "solid" gel in solution. It is used as a thickening agent in foods; an adhesive; as a medium for growing bacteria, MOULD, YEAST and other microorganisms; as a medium for TISSUE CULTURE; and as a gel for ELECTROPHORESIS.

agaric Order of fungi that includes edible mushrooms, ink caps and the poisonous AMANITA. Their spores are borne on the surface of gills or pores on the under-surface of the cap.

agate Microcrystalline form of quartz with parallel bands of colour. It is regarded as a semiprecious stone and is used for making ornaments. Hardness *c.*6.5; s.g. *c.*2.6.

agave Succulent, flowering plant found in tropical, subtropical and temperate regions. Agaves have narrow, lance-shaped leaves clustered at the base, and many have large flower clusters. The flower of the century plant (*Agave americana*) of sw North America grows up to 7.6m (25ft) in one season. The century plant flowers every 20–30 years. Other species are SISAL (*A. sisalana*) and mescal (*Lophophora williamsii*), whose fermented sap forms the basis of the liqueur tequila. Family Agavaceae.

agglutination Clumping of BACTERIA or red blood cells by ANTIBODIES that react with ANTIGENS on the cell surface.

Agincourt Village in Pas de Calais, NE France. It is the site of the English King HENRY V's victory over the French in 1415 during the HUNDRED YEARS WAR. Poor French tactics and the superior rate of fire of the English longbow over the French crossbow contributed to the English victory against a superior French force.

Agni Fire-god in Vedic mythology, revered as god of the home and appearing in lightning and the Sun as a nature deity.

agnosticism Philosophical viewpoint according to which it is impossible either to demonstrate or refute the existence of a supreme being or ultimate cause on the basis of available evidence. It was particularly associated with English rationalist Thomas HUXLEY (1825–95), and is used as a reasoned basis for the rejection of both Christianity and atheism.

Agra City in in Uttar Pradesh state, and site of the TAJ MAHAL, N central India. It was founded in 1566 by the Mogul emperor AKBAR I. An important rail junction and commercial and administrative centre, its products include glass, shoes and textiles. Agra's fine Mogul architecture make it a major tourist destination in India. Pop. (1991) 892,200.

Agricultural Revolution Series of changes in farming practice in the 18th and early 19th centuries. The main changes comprised crop rotation, new machinery, increased capital investment, scientific breeding, land reclamation and enclosure of common lands. Originating in Britain, these advances led to greatly increased agricultural productivity in Europe.

agriculture Practice of cultivating crops and raising livestock. Originally people hunted animals and gathered roots, berries and fruits. Later a knowledge of husbandry and crop farming enabled them to produce food on a small scale. Modern archaeological dating techniques suggest that the production of CEREALS and the domestication and breeding of animals were widespread throughout E Mediterranean countries by *c.*7000 BC. The Egyptians and Mesopotamians (*c.*3000 BC) were the earliest peoples to organize agriculture on a large scale, using irrigation techniques and manure as fertilizer. Soon after, farming formed the foundations of societies in China, India, Europe, Mexico and Peru. The development of agriculture took place much later in some areas but, by Roman times (200 BC–AD 400), crop farming and the domestication of animals were commonplace in w Europe. In 17th- and 18th-century Europe, selective breeding improved milk and meat yields. The use of the four-field system of crop rotation meant that fields could be used continuously for production with no deterioration in yield or quality of the crops. The AGRICULTURAL REVOLUTION began with industrial growth in the 18th century. Many items of farm machinery were introduced in the 19th century. This equipment became widespread in the UK in the 1840s. In Western Europe and North America, mechanization has advanced greatly and a large proportion of agricultural production is now carried out by FACTORY FARMING, involving the battery production of livestock, especially pigs and poultry. The enormous food-producing regions of the American Midwest and the Russian steppes consist largely of farms given over to the production of either grain or livestock. In much of the underdeveloped world, agriculture, especially RICE production, is still labour intensive. 75% of the world's labour force is engaged in farming. Shifting agriculture of the slash and burn method is still practised in some regions.

Agrippa, Marcus Vipsanius (b.63 BC) Roman general, adviser to Octavian (later AUGUSTUS). He helped Octavian to power by winning naval battles against Sextus Pompeius in 36 BC and helping to defeat MARK ANTONY at ACTIUM in 31 BC.

agronomy Science of soil management and

9

improvement in the interests of agriculture. It includes the studies of particular plants and soils and their interrelationships. Agronomy involves disease-resistant plants, selective breeding and the development of chemical fertilizers.

Ahern, Bertie (1951–) Irish statesman, taoiseach (1997–). Ahern was first elected to the Dáil Éireann in 1977. He served as vice president (1983–94) of FIANNA FÁIL, before becoming leader. He succeeded John BRUTON as taoiseach.

Ahimsa Non-violence or non-injury to both people and animals. A central concept of JAINISM and BUDDHISM, it is also important in HINDUISM. It inspired the passive resistance of Mahatma GANDHI.

Ahmadabad (Ahmedabad) City on the Sabarmati River, W India. Founded in 1411 by Ahmad Shah, the Muslim ruler of Gujarat, it is the cultural, commercial and transport centre of the state, with many magnificent mosques, temples and tombs. It is the headquarters of the Indian National CONGRESS PARTY movement. The city's principal industry is cotton. Pop. (1991) 2,954,526.

Ahmad Shah Durrani (1722–73) Emir of Afghanistan (1747–73) and founder of the Durrani dynasty. He united the Afghan tribes and is sometimes known as the founder of modern Afghanistan.

Ahura Mazdah (Ormazd or Ormuzd) In ZOROASTRIANISM, the religion of ancient Persia, the supreme deity and the god of light and wisdom. Ahura Mazdah created the universe and the twin spirits of good and evil. He later became identified with the good spirit, who was in constant conflict with Ahriman, the evil spirit and god of darkness.

Aidan, Saint (d.651) Irish monk from Iona who brought Christianity to NE England. He became the first Bishop of Lindisfarne, where he established a monastery and sent out missionaries all over N England. His feast day is 31 August.

AIDS Acronym for ACQUIRED IMMUNE DEFICIENCY SYNDROME

aileron Hinged control surface on the outer trailing edge of each wing of an AIRCRAFT. By moving down or up in opposite directions, ailerons cause the aeroplane to roll or bank.

Ainu Aboriginal people of Hokkaidō (N Japan), Sakhalin and the Kuril islands. Traditionally hunters, fishers and trappers, they practise ANIMISM and are famed for their bear cult.

aircraft Any vehicle capable of travelling in the Earth's atmosphere. By far the most common aircraft is the aeroplane. This is a heavier-than-air flying machine that depends upon fixed wings for LIFT in the air, as it moves under the THRUST of its engines. This thrust may be provided by an airscrew (propeller) turned by a piston or turbine engine, or by the exhaust gases of a JET engine or rocket motor. Gliders differ from planes only in their dependence upon air currents to keep them airborne. The main body of a plane is the fuselage, to which are attached the wings and tail assembly. Engines may be incorporated into or slung below the wings, but

are sometimes mounted on the fuselage towards the tail or built into the fuselage near the wings. The landing gear or undercarriage, with its heavy wheels and stout shock absorbers, is usually completely retractable into the wings or fuselage. Wing design varies with the type of plane: high-speed fighters have slim, often swept-back or adjustable wings that create minimal air resistance (DRAG) at high speeds. At the other extreme, heavy air freighters need broader wings in order to achieve the necessary lift at take-off. A delta wing is a broad wing, or fuselage extension, that is aerodynamically suited for both large and small high-speed planes. A plane is steered by the pilot moving flaps and AILERONS on the wings and rudder and elevators on the tail assembly. This deflects the pressure of air on the AEROFOIL surfaces, causing the plane to rise or descend, to bank (tilt) or swing and turn in the air. RADAR systems aid navigation, an AUTOPILOT keeps the aircraft steady on a fixed course, and pressurized cabins allow passenger planes to fly at heights exceeding 10,000m (32,800ft). *See also* AIRSHIP; AERODYNAMICS; BALLOON; GLIDING; HELICOPTER

aircraft carrier Military vessel with a wide open deck that serves as a runway for the launching and landing of aircraft. A modern nuclear-powered carrier may have a flight deck about 300m (1,000ft) long, a displacement of about 75,000 tonnes, a 4,000-man crew and carry 90 aircraft of various types. Some carriers have large, angled decks to permit launching and landing simultaneously.

air-cushion vehicle (ACV) Vehicle, such as a HOVERCRAFT, that is lifted from the ground by air as it is forced out from under the craft.

air force Military air power, first used in World War 1. In 1918 the British government formed the Royal AIR FORCE (RAF). The United States Air Force (USAF) was created in 1947.

Air Force, Royal (RAF) Youngest of the British armed services, formed in 1918 by the amalgamation of the Royal Naval Air Service and the Royal Flying Corps. It was controlled by the Air Ministry from 1919–64, when it was merged into the Ministry of Defence. Total personnel (1996): 68,164.

airship (dirigible) Powered lighter-than-air craft able to control its direction of motion. A gas that is less dense than air, nowadays helium, provides lift. A rigid airship, or Zeppelin, maintains its form with a framework of girders covered by fabric or aluminium alloy. Non-rigid airships, or blimps, have no internal structure. They rely on the pressure of the contained gas to maintain the shape.

Aix-en-Provence City in SE France, 27km (17 mi) N of Marseilles. It is a cultural centre with a university (1409), an 11th–13th-century cathedral and several art galleries. Industries: wine-making equipment and electrical apparatus. Agricultural products: olives, almonds. Pop. (1990) 123,842.

Aix-la-Chapelle, Treaty of (1748) Diplomatic agreement, principally between France and Britain, that ended the War of the AUSTRIAN SUC-

CESSION (1740–48). The treaty provided for the restitution of conquests made during the war, contributed to the rise of Prussian power and confirmed British control of the slave trade to Spanish America. An earlier treaty signed at Aix-la-Chapelle ended the War of Devolution (1668).

Ajax In Greek mythology, name given to two heroes who fought for Greece against TROY. The Greater Ajax is depicted in Homer's *Iliad* as a courageous warrior who led the troops of Salamis against Troy. The Lesser Ajax was shipwrecked by ATHENA for raping CASSANDRA.

Akbar I (the Great) (1542–1605) Emperor of India (1556–1605). Generally regarded as the greatest of his dynasty, he assumed personal control in 1560 and set out to establish Mogul rule throughout India, extending his authority as far S as Ahmadnagar. Building a new capital at Fatehpur Sikri, he endeavoured to unify the empire by conciliatory policies towards Hindus.

Akhnaten (d.1362 BC) Ancient Egyptian king of the 18th dynasty (r. *c*.1379–1362 BC). He succeeded his father, AMENHOTEP III, as Amenhotep IV. In an attempt to overthrow the influence of the priests of the temple of AMUN at LUXOR, he renounced the old gods and introduced an almost monotheistic worship of the sun god, Aten. He adopted the name Akhnaten and established a new capital at Akhetaten (modern Tell el-Amarna). After his death TUTANKHAMUN reinstated Amun as national god, and the capital reverted to Luxor.

Akiba Ben Joseph (50–135) Jewish rabbi and martyr in Palestine. He developed a new method of interpreting the Halakah, Hebrew oral laws, and supported a revolt (132) against the Roman emperor, Hadrian. He was imprisoned by the Romans and tortured to death.

Akihito (1933–) Emperor of Japan. He succeeded his father, Hirohito, in 1989. In 1959 he married a commoner, Michiko Shoda, the first such marriage in the history of the imperial dynasty.

Alabama State in SE USA in the chief cotton-growing region; the state capital is MONTGOMERY. Birmingham is the largest city and a leading iron and steel centre. In the 1960s it was a centre of the CIVIL RIGHTS movement. The N of the state lies in the Appalachian Highlands, which have coal, iron ore and other mineral deposits, and the rest consists of the Gulf coastal plain, crossed by a wide strip of fertile soil. The Mobile River and its tributaries form the chief river system. Principal crops: peanuts, soya beans and maize, with cotton now less important. Industries: chemicals, textiles, electronics, metal products. Area: 133,915sq km (51,705sq mi). Pop. (1992) 4,137,511.

alabaster Fine-grained, massive variety of GYPSUM, snow-white and translucent in its natural form. It can be dyed or made opaque by heating and is used for making statues and other ornaments.

Alaric (370–410) King and founder of a group of GOTHS called the Visigoths (395–410). His forces ravaged Thrace, Macedonia and Greece and occupied Epirus (395–96). He besieged and sacked (410) Rome when the emperor Honorius would not grant him a position at court.

Alaska State of the USA in NW North America, separated from the rest of continental USA by the province of British Columbia, Canada, and from Russia by the Bering Strait. The capital is JUNEAU. The largest city is ANCHORAGE on the S coast. It became the 49th state of the Union in 1959. About 25% of Alaska lies inside the Arctic Circle. The main Alaska Range includes Mount MCKINLEY, the highest peak in North America. The chief river is the YUKON. The economy is based on oil, fish, natural gas, timber and quartz. Area: 1,530,700sq km (591,004sq mi). Pop. (1992) 587,766.

Alban, Saint First British martyr, from the Roman town of Verulamium (now St Albans). He was killed for hiding a Christian priest from the Romans. In 797 King Offa founded an abbey on the site of Alban's execution. His feast day is 22 June.

Albania Balkan republic; the capital is TIRANË. **Land and climate** About 70% of the country is mountainous; rising to Mount Korab at 2,764m (9,068ft) on the Macedonian border. Most Albanians live in the farming regions of the W coastal lowlands. Albania is subject to severe earthquakes. The coastal regions of Albania have a typical Mediterranean climate, with fairly dry, sunny summers and cool, moist winters, while the mountains have a severe climate, with heavy winter snowfalls. Maquis covers much of the unfarmed lowlands. **Economy** Albania is Europe's poorest country, 56% of the population are engaged in agriculture. Crops include fruits, maize, olives, potatoes, sugar beet, vegetables and wheat. Livestock farming is also important. The country has some mineral reserves, such as chromite, copper and nickel, which are exported, and also some oil, brown coal and hydroelectricity. Albania's heavy industry has caused severe pollution in some areas. **History** In ancient times, Albania was part of ILLYRIA, and in 167 BC became part of the ROMAN EMPIRE. In the 15th century Scanderbeg successfully led the Albanians against the invading Turks. After his death in

ALBANIA
AREA: 28,750sq km (11,100sq mi)
POPULATION: 3,363,000
CAPITAL (POPULATION): Tiranë (251,000)
GOVERNMENT: Multiparty republic
ETHNIC GROUPS: Albanian 98%, Greek 1.8%, Macedonian, Montenegrin, Gypsy
LANGUAGES: Albanian (official)
RELIGIONS: Many people say they are non-believers; of the believers, 65% follow Islam, and 33% Christianity (Orthodox 20%,Roman Catholics 13%)
CURRENCY: Lek = 100 qindars (official)

1468 the Turks took over, and Albania remained part of the OTTOMAN EMPIRE until 1912. Italy invaded Albania in 1939, and German forces occupied Albania in 1943. In 1944 Albanian Communists, led by Enver HOXHA, took power. In the early 1960s, Albania broke with the Soviet Union after Soviet criticism of the Chinese COMMUNIST PARTY, to which it was allied until the late 1970s. **Politics** In the early 1990s, the Albanian government introduced reforms, permitting opposition parties. In 1996 the Democratic Party, headed by Sali Berisha, won a sweeping victory. In 1997 the collapse of huge pyramid finance schemes sparked a large-scale rebellion in s Albania. A state of emergency was proclaimed. In negotiation with opposition leaders, Berisha formed a government of national reconciliation and agreed to hold a general election in June. The former communist Socialist Party of Albania was victorious, and its secretary-general, Rexhep Mejdani, replaced Berisha as president.

Albany Capital of New York state, on the Hudson River. Industries: paper, brewing, machine tools, metal products, textiles. Pop. (1992) 99,708.

albatross Large, migratory oceanic bird of the Southern Hemisphere, famed for its effortless gliding flight. There are 13 species. The wandering albatross has a long, hooked bill, short tail, webbed toes and the greatest wing span of any living bird – 3.5m (11.5ft) or more. Length: 0.7–1.4m (2.3–4.4ft). Family Diomedeidae.

albedo Fraction of light or other radiation that is reflected from a surface. An ideal reflector has an albedo of 1; those of real reflectors are less, that of the Earth, viewed from satellites, is 0.35.

Albee, Edward Franklin (1928–) US playwright. Associated both with social criticism and the Theatre of the ABSURD, his best-known play is *Who's Afraid of Virginia Woolf?* (1962), an intense portrait of a destructive marriage. Other works include *The Ballad of the Sad Cafe* (1963); both *A Delicate Balance* (1966) and *Seascape* (1975) won Pulitzer prizes.

Albéniz, Isaac (1860–1909) Spanish composer and pianist. The majority of his compositions are for piano. He often used Spanish folk elements in his compositions, notably in the piano suite *Iberia* (1906–09), creating a distinctively Spanish style.

Albert, Lake Lake in the RIFT VALLEY of E central Africa on the border between Zaïre and Uganda. It is fed by the Semliki River and the Victoria Nile and drained by the Albert Nile (*Bahr el Jebel*). Ugandans call it Lake Nyanza and the Zaïrians named it Lake Mobuto Sese Seko. Length: 160km (100mi). Width: 35km (22mi). Maximum depth: 51m (168ft). Area: 5,350 sq km (2,065sq mi).

Alberta Province of w Canada bounded on the w mainly by the Rocky Mountains and in the s by the USA; the capital is EDMONTON. Other major cities include CALGARY. Most of Alberta is prairie. The principal rivers are the Athabasca, Peace, North and South Saskatchewan, and Milk. Lesser Slave Lake

is the largest of the many lakes. The fertile plains support wheat farming and livestock. Major resources are oil and natural gas, coal, minerals and wood. Industries: petroleum products, metals, chemicals, wood products. Area: 661,188sq km (255,285sq mi). Pop. (1991) 2,545,553.

Alberti, Leon Battista (1404–72) Italian architect, humanist and writer. The first major art theorist of the RENAISSANCE, he influenced its painters, sculptors and architects with his theories in *On Painting* (1435). His buildings include the Rucellai Palace, Florence, the Tempio Malatestiano, Rimini, and the church of San Andrea, Mantua.

Albigenses (Cathars) Members of a heretical religious sect that existed in s France from the 11th to the early 14th centuries and took its name from the French city of Albi. Pope Innocent III ordered a crusade against them in 1200, which saw much destruction in Languedoc and Provence.

albino Person or animal with a rare hereditary absence of pigment from the skin, hair and eyes. The hair is white and the skin and eyes are pink because, in the absence of pigment, the blood vessels are visible. The eyes are abnormally sensitive to light and vision is often poor.

Albinoni, Tomaso (1671–1750) Italian violinist and composer. He worked mainly in Venice, where he was a friend of Vivaldi. He was one of the first composers of CONCERTOS for a solo instrument; he also wrote nearly 50 operas.

Albright, Madeleine Korbel (1937–) US stateswoman, secretary of state (1997–), b. Czechoslovakia. Following Bill Clinton's re-election (1996), Albright became the the first female secretary of state. She has a reputation as a staunch anti-communist and hawkish advocate of US military involvement in international crises, such as the GULF WAR and the civil war in BOSNIA.

albumin (albumen) Type of water-soluble PROTEIN occurring in animal tissues and fluids. Principal forms are egg albumin (egg white), milk albumin and blood albumin. In a healthy human, it constitutes *c*.5% of body weight. It is composed of a colourless fluid (plasma) in which are suspended ERYTHROCYTES (red blood cells), LEUCOCYTES (white blood cells) and PLATELETS.

alchemy Primitive form of chemistry practised in Western Europe from early Christian times until the 17th century. It was popularly supposed to involve a search for the Philosopher's Stone – capable of transmuting base metals into gold – and the elixir of life. It actually involved a combination of practical chemistry, astrology, philosophy and mysticism. Similar movements existed in China and India.

Alcock, Sir John William (1892–1919) Pioneer British aviator who, together with Arthur Whitten-Brown, was the first to fly non-stop across the Atlantic Ocean (14 June 1919).

alcohol Organic compound having a hydroxyl (-OH) group bound to a carbon atom. ETHANOL, the alcohol found in alcoholic drinks, has the formula C_2H_5OH. Alcohols are used to make dyes and perfumes and as SOLVENTS in varnishes.

Aldrin, "Buzz" (Edwin) (1930–) US astronaut. Aldrin piloted the Gemini XII orbital-rendezvous space flight (November 1966) and the lunar module for the first Moon landing (20 July 1969). He followed Neil ARMSTRONG to become the second man on the Moon.

Aleppo (Halab) City in NW Syria, the country's second largest city. Like the capital DAMASCUS, it claims to be the world's oldest continually inhabited city. Industries: cotton, silk weaving, dried nuts and fruit. Pop. (1993) 1,494,000.

Aleut Branch of the Eskimo people who occupy the ALEUTIAN ISLANDS and Alaska Peninsula. They are divided into two major language groups, the Unalaska and Atka. About 4,000 Aleuts live in scattered villages throughout SW Alaska.

Aleutian Islands Volcanic island chain, separating the Bering Sea from the Pacific Ocean. They were purchased with Alaska by the USA in 1867. The islands have several US military bases and wildlife reserves. Industries: fishing, furs. Area: 17,666sq km (6,821sq mi). Pop. (1990) 11,942.

A-level See GENERAL CERTIFICATE OF EDUCATION

Alexander III (c.1105–81) Pope (1159–81). His election to the papacy was opposed by the Holy Roman emperor FREDERICK I, who had an antipope, Victor IV, elected. The ensuing schism ended 17 years later with the victory of the LOMBARD LEAGUE over Frederick at the Battle of Legnano.

Alexander I (1777–1825) Russian tsar (1801–25). After repulsing Napoleon's attempt to conquer Russia (1812), he led his troops across Europe and into Paris (1814). Under the influence of various mystical groups, he helped form the Holy Alliance with other European powers. He was named constitutional monarch of Poland in 1815 and also annexed Finland, Georgia and Bessarabia to Russia.

Alexander II (1818–81) Russian tsar (1855–81). He was known as the "Tsar Liberator" for his emancipation of the serfs in 1861. He warred with Turkey (1877–78) and gained much influence in the Balkans. He sold Alaska (1867), but expanded the eastern part of the empire. He brutally put down a revolt in Poland (1863). In 1881 he was assassinated by revolutionaries.

Alexander III (1845–94) Russian tsar (1881–94). He introduced reactionary measures limiting local government; censorship of the press was enforced and arbitrary arrest and exile became common. Ethnic minorities were persecuted. Toward the end of his career, he formed an alliance with France.

Alexander Nevski, Saint (1220–63) Russian ruler, Grand Duke of Novgorod and Grand Duke of Vladimir. He submitted to Mongol rule following their invasion of Russia, and the Great Khan appointed him Grand Duke of Kiev. He defeated the Swedes on the River Neva in 1240 (hence the name "Nevski") and the Teutonic Knights on the

frozen Lake Peipus in 1242. He was canonized by the Russian Orthodox Church in 1547.

Alexander the Great (356–323 BC) King of Macedonia (336–323 BC), considered the greatest conqueror of classical times. Son of PHILIP II of Macedonia and tutored by ARISTOTLE, he rapidly consolidated Macedonian power in Greece. In 334 BC he began his destruction of the vast Achaemenid Persian empire, conquering W Asia Minor and storming Tyre in 332 BC. He subdued Egypt and occupied Babylon, marching N in 330 BC to Media and then conquering central Asia in 328 BC. In 327 BC he invaded India but was prevented from advancing beyond the Punjab by the threat of mutiny. He died in Babylon, planning new conquests in Arabia. Although his empire did not outlive him, he was responsible for the spread of Greek civilization in the Mediterranean and W Asia.

Alexandria Chief port and second largest city of Egypt, situated on the W extremity of the Nile delta. Founded by ALEXANDER THE GREAT in 332 BC, it became a great centre of Greek (and Jewish) culture. An offshore island housed the 3rd-century BC Pharos lighthouse, one of the SEVEN WONDERS OF THE WORLD, and the city contained a great library (founded by Ptolemy I and said to contain 700,000 volumes). Today it is a deepwater port handling over 75% of Egypt's trade. The main industries are oil refining, cotton textiles, plastics and paper. Alexandria is the Middle East headquarters for the WORLD HEALTH ORGANIZATION (WHO). Pop. (1990 est.) 3,170,000.

Alexius I (1048–1118) (Alexius Comnenus) Byzantine emperor (1081–1118), founder of the Comnenian dynasty. He held off the Normans, who threatened Constantinople and turned the Western armies of the First CRUSADE to his own advantage by using them to reconquer parts of Anatolia.

alfalfa (lucerne) Leguminous, perennial plant with spiral pods and purple, clover-like flowers. Like other legumes, it enriches the soil with nitrogen and is often grown by farmers and then ploughed in. It is a valuable fodder plant. Height: 0.5–1.2m (1.5–4ft). Species Medicago sativa. Family Leguminosae. See also NITROGEN FIXATION

Alfonso Name of a number of rulers of Spanish kingdoms. **Alfonso V** (994–1028) became king of León and Asturias after his supporters took the city of León in 999. He was killed in battle against the MOORS. **Alfonso VIII** (1155–1214) was king of Castile (1158–1214). He succeeded his father Sancho III at the age of three. He took control of the kingdom in 1166 and at first opposed both Moors and fellow-Christian kings. In 1212 he forged a coalition with the Christian rulers and won a major victory over the ALMOHADS at Las Navas de Tolosa. **Alfonso X** (1221–84), king of Castile and León (1252–84), was the son and successor of Ferdinand III. He continued his father's wars against the Moors but his chief ambition was to become Holy Roman emperor. **Alfonso XIII**

(1886–1941), king of Spain (1886–1931), was born after the death of his father, Alfonso XII. His mother acted as regent until 1902. Although personally popular, he could not satisfy the conflicting demands of the nationalists, socialists and republicans. In 1923 he supported the establishment of a military dictatorship under PRIMO DE RIVERA. It fell in 1930 and a republic was proclaimed in 1931.

Alfred the Great (849–99) King of Wessex (871–99). A warrior and scholar, Alfred saved Wessex from the Danes and laid the foundations of a united English kingdom. After the Danish invasion of 878, he escaped to Athelney in Somerset, returning to defeat the Danes at Edington and recover the kingdom. By a pact with the Danish leader, Guthrum, England was roughly divided in two, with the Danelaw occupying the NE. Although Alfred controlled only Wessex and part of Mercia, his leadership was widely recognized throughout England after his capture of London (886). To strengthen Wessex against future attack, he built a fleet of ships, constructed forts and reorganized the army.

algae Large group of essentially aquatic photosynthetic organisms found in salt- and freshwater worldwide. Algae are a primary source of food for molluscs, fish and other aquatic animals. Algae are important to humans as food and as FERTILIZERS. They range in size from unicellular microscopic organisms to huge brown SEAWEEDS more than 45m (150ft) long. Algae belong to the kingdom PROTOCTISTA. *See also* GREEN ALGAE; RED ALGAE; PHOTOSYNTHESIS

Algarve Southernmost province of Portugal, and the most popular of the country's tourist areas. The capital is Faro. Irrigated orchards produce almonds, oranges, figs and olives, and the main fish catches are tuna and sardines. Area: 4,986sq km (1,925sq mi). Pop. (1994 est.) 344,300.

algebra Form of arithmetic in which symbols replace numbers. Thus $3 + 5 = 8$ is a statement in arithmetic; $x + y = 8$ is one in algebra, involving the VARIABLES x and y. Boolean algebra (an example of a higher algebra) can be applied to sets and to logical propositions. Algebraic operations are the arithmetical operations addition, subtraction, multiplication and division. Operations that involve infinite series and functions such as $\log x$ are not algebraic as they depend on the use of limits. *See also* MATHEMATICS

Algeria Second-largest country in N Africa; the capital is ALGIERS. **Land and climate** Most of the population lives in the N, on the fertile coastal plains and hills and in ALGIERS and ORAN. S of this region are high plateaus and ranges of the ATLAS Mountains, but over 80% of Algeria lies in the SAHARA. Algiers has warm, dry summers and mild, moist winters. The N highlands have colder winters and warmer summers. Annual rainfall is less than 200mm (8in). The N has areas of scrub and farmland. The Sahara contains regions of erg (sand

ALGERIA	
AREA: 2,381,700sq km (919,590sq mi)	
POPULATION: 26,346,000	
CAPITAL (POPULATION): Algiers (2,168,000)	
GOVERNMENT: Socialist republic	
ETHNIC GROUPS: Arab, Berber, French	
LANGUAGES: Arabic (official), Berber, French	
RELIGIONS: Sunni Muslim 98%, Christianity (Roman Catholic)	
CURRENCY: Algerian dinar = 100 centimes	

dunes), but most of the desert is gravel-strewn plains and areas of bare rock. **Economy** Algeria is a developing country. Its natural gas reserves are among the largest in the world, and gas and oil account for more than 90% of the country's exports. Other manufactured products include cement, iron and steel, textiles and vehicles. Although arable land accounts for only 3% of the country's land area, farming employs *c.*14% of the workforce. Barley, citrus fruits, dates, grapes, olives, potatoes and wheat are the major crops. Cattle, goats and sheep are raised by BERBER nomads. **History** By the 4th century BC, Algeria was an integral part of the Roman empire. In the late 7th century Arabs conquered Algeria and converted the local population to Islam. In the early 10th century the FATIMIDS built an empire from their base in NE Algeria. In the late 15th century, the Spanish gained control of coastal Algeria but were ousted by the Ottomans. In 1830 France invaded Algeria and rapidly began the process of colonization. In 1954 the National Liberation Front (FLN) launched a nationwide revolt against French rule. By 1962 the war had claimed *c.*250,000 lives. Despite the opposition of the one million French colonists (*colons*) and a section of the French army (the OAS), Charles DE GAULLE persisted with an accord to grant Algeria independence. On 3 July 1962 France declared Algeria independent. Ahmed Ben Bella became president of the newly reformed republic. In 1965 Ben Bella was overthrown in a military coup. A revolutionary council, led by the authoritarian Colonel Houari Boumédienne, ruled until 1978, when Chadli Benjedid became president. Prolonged anti-government demonstrations led to the legalization of opposition parties in 1989. In January 1992, with the opposition Islamic Salvation Front (FIS) on course for electoral victory, Benjedid cancelled the second round of voting and declared a national state of emergency. He was forced to resign and a military government took charge. The FIS was banned and many of its leaders were arrested and imprisoned. In 1992 Benjedid's successor, Muhammad Boudiaf, was assassinated as part of a terrorist campaign launched by anti-Western Muslim fundamentalists. In 1995 the election of General Liamine Zeroual held out hope of a peaceful settlement, but the terrorist campaign continued. Between 1992 and 1997 it is estimated that the civil war has claimed 100,000 civilian lives. In 1997 the terrorist campaign intensified.

Algiers Capital and largest city of Algeria, on the Bay of Algiers, N Africa's chief port on the Mediterranean. Founded by the Phoenicians, it suffered a succession of invasions and acted as the capital of the French colony of Algeria (1830–1962). Industries: oil refining, phosphates, wine, metallurgy, cement and tobacco. Pop. (1995) 2,168,000.

algorithm Step-by-step set of instructions needed to obtain some result from given starting data. The term is also used in computer science for the method of a computer in following an established series of steps in the solution of a problem.

Alhambra Spanish citadel of the sultans of Granada. Standing on a plateau overlooking Granada, S Spain, it is one of the most beautiful and well-preserved examples of medieval ISLAMIC ART AND ARCHITECTURE. Most of the complex dates from 1238–1358, when the Nasrid dynasty was in power.

Ali (600–61) Fourth Muslim CALIPH (656–61), cousin and son-in-law of the Prophet MUHAMMAD. Ali was married to FATIMA. He is regarded by the SHIITES as the first Imam and rightful heir of Muhammad. Ali succeeded Othman as caliph, despite opposition from Aishah and Muawiya. After Ali's assassination, his first son, Hasan, abdicated in favour of Muawiya, who founded the UMAYYAD dynasty. His second son, Husayn, led the insurrection against the Umayyads, but was defeated and killed. The division in Islam between the SUNNIS and Shiites dates from this time.

Ali, Muhammad (1942–) US boxer, b. Cassius Clay. He won the Olympic light-heavyweight championship in 1960 and then beat Sonny Liston for the world heavyweight championship in 1964. He regained the title from George Foreman in 1974 and for a third time in 1978. Ali is regarded as the most skilful and stylish heavyweight boxer ever. He now suffers from Parkinson's disease.

alienation Term used in PSYCHOLOGY to mean a feeling of estrangement and separation from other people. In existential psychology, it is extended to include the perception that one is estranged from one's "real self" because of social conformity.

alimentary canal Digestive tract of an animal. It begins with the MOUTH, continues through the OESOPHAGUS to the STOMACH and INTESTINES, and ends at the anus. It is about 9m (30ft) long in humans. *See also* DIGESTIVE SYSTEM

aliphatic compound Any organic chemical compound whose carbon atoms are linked in straight chains, not closed rings. They include the ALKANES, ALKENES and ALKYNES.

alkali Soluble BASE that reacts with an ACID to form a SALT and water. A solution of an alkali has a pH greater than 7. Alkali solutions are used as cleaning materials. Strong alkalis include the hydroxides of the ALKALI METALS and ammonium hydroxide. The carbonates of these metals are weak alkalis.

alkali metals Univalent metals forming Group I of the periodic table: lithium, sodium, potassium, rubidium, caesium and francium. They are soft silvery-white metals that tarnish rapidly in air and react violently with water to form hydroxides.

alkaline-earth metals Bivalent metals forming Group II of the periodic table: beryllium, magnesium, calcium, strontium, barium and radium. They are all light, soft and highly reactive. All, except beryllium and magnesium, react with cold water to form hydroxides (though magnesium reacts with hot water). Radium is important for its radioactivity.

alkaloid Member of a class of complex nitrogen-containing organic compounds found in certain plants. They are sometimes bitter and highly poisonous substances, used as DRUGS. Examples include codeine, morphine, nicotine and quinine.

alkane HYDROCARBON compound with the general formula C_nH_{2n+2}. Alkanes have a single carbon-carbon bond and form an homologous series whose first members are METHANE, ETHANE, PROPANE and BUTANE. Because alkanes are SATURATED COMPOUNDS they are relatively unreactive. Alkanes are used as fuels. *See also* PARAFFIN

alkene (olefin) Unsaturated HYDROCARBON compound with the general formula C_nH_{2n}. Alkenes have a carbon-carbon double bond and form an homologous series whose first members are ETHENE and PROPENE. They are reactive, particularly in ADDITION reactions. Alkenes are made by the dehydration of alcohols. They are used as fuels and to make POLYMERS.

alkyne (acetylene) Unsaturated HYDROCARBON compound with the general formula C_nH_{2n-2}. Alkynes have a carbon-carbon triple bond and form an homologous series whose first members are ETHYNE and propene.

Allah One and only God of ISLAM. Unreserved surrender to Allah, as preached in the KORAN, is the very heart of the Islamic faith.

Allahabad City in N central India, in Uttar Pradesh state, at the confluence of the Ganges and Yamuna rivers. A pilgrimage centre for Hindus, the city hosts the Kumbh Mela fair, a religious celebration, every 12 years. It has one of the oldest universities in India (1887). Pop. (1991) 806,000.

allegory Literary work in either prose or verse in which more than one level of meaning is expressed simultaneously. The fables of AESOP and LA FONTAINE are examples of simple allegory. *Pilgrim's Progress* (1684) by John BUNYAN is a sophisticated religious allegory.

allele One of two or more alternative forms of a particular GENE. Different alleles may give rise to different forms of the characteristic for which the gene codes. Different flower colour in peas is due to the presence of different alleles of a single gene.

Allen, Woody (1935–) US film director, writer and actor, b. Allen Stewart Konigsberg. He made his film debut as an actor and screenwriter in *What's New Pussycat?* (1965). His debut as a director was

Take the Money and Run (1969). *Annie Hall* (1977) won an Academy Award for Best Picture and Allen was voted Best Director. *Zelig* (1983) and *The Purple Rose of Cairo* (1985) gained praise for their inventiveness. Allen won a Best Screenplay Oscar for *Hannah and Her Sisters* (1986). After a damaging break-up from Mia Farrow, Allen returned to his best form with *Mighty Aphrodite* (1996).

Allende Gossens, Salvador (1908–73) President of Chile (1970–73). He was the first democratically elected Marxist head of state in Latin America. His socialist reforms antagonized powerful elements in Chile, and he incurred the hostility of the US. He died in a military coup backed by the US Central Intelligence Agency.

allergy Disorder in which the body mounts a hypersensitive reaction to one or more substances (allergens) not normally considered harmful. Typical allergic reactions are sneezing (HAY FEVER), "wheezing" and difficulty in breathing (ASTHMA) and skin eruptions and itching (ECZEMA). A tendency to allergic reactions is often hereditary.

Allies Term used in WORLD WAR 1 and WORLD WAR 2 for the forces that fought the CENTRAL POWERS and AXIS POWERS respectively. In World War 1 they numbered 23 and included Belgium, Britain and its Commonwealth, France, Italy, Japan, Russia and the USA. In World War 2 the 49 Allies included Belgium, Britain and the Commonwealth, France, Netherlands, Soviet Union and the USA.

alligator Broad-snouted crocodilian reptile found only in the USA and China. The American alligator, *Alligator mississippiensis*, is found in the SE USA; it grows up to 5.8m (19ft) long. The almost extinct smaller Chinese alligator, *A. sinensis*, is restricted to the Yangtze-Kiang river basin. Length: up to 1.5m (5ft). Family Alligatoridea.

allotropy Property of some chemical elements that enables them to exist in two or more distinct physical forms. Each form (allotrope) can have different chemical properties but can be changed into another allotrope. Examples of allotropes are molecular oxygen and ozone; white and yellow phosphorous; and graphite and diamond (carbon).

alloy Combination of two or more metals. An alloy's properties are different from those of its constituent elements. Alloys are generally harder and stronger, and have lower melting points. Most alloys are prepared by mixing when molten. Some mixtures that combine a metal with a non-metal, such as STEEL, are also referred to as alloys.

All Saints' Day In the Christian liturgical calendar, the day on which all the saints are commemorated. The feast is observed on 1 November in the West and on the first Sunday after Pentecost (Whitsun) in the East. The eve of the day is celebrated in some western countries as Hallowe'en.

All Souls' Day Day of remembrance and prayer for the dead. Observed by Roman Catholics and High Church Anglicans on 2 November, or on 3 November if the former falls on a Sunday.

allspice (pimento) Aromatic tree native to the West Indies and Central America. The fruits are used as a spice, in perfume and in medicine. Height: up to 12m (40ft). Family Myrtaceae; species *Pimenta officinalis*

alluvial fan Generally fan-shaped area of ALLUVIUM (water-borne sediment) deposited by a river when the stream reaches a plain on lower ground, and the water velocity is abruptly reduced. Organic matter is also transported, making the soil highly fertile. Valuable minerals such as cassiterite (tin ore, SnO_2), diamonds, gold and platinum are often found in alluvial fans.

alluvium Sediments (sand, silt and mud) deposited by flowing water along the banks, delta or flood-plain of a river or stream. Fine textured sediments that contain organic matter form soil.

Almaty Largest city and, until 2000, capital of Kazakstan, in the far SE of the country near the border with Kyrgyzstan. In 1991 (as Alma-Ata) it hosted the meeting of 11 former Soviet republics that created the COMMONWEALTH OF INDEPENDENT STATES (CIS). In 1993 it became Almaty, closer to the Kazak form of the name. In 1995 AQMOLA was made capital-designate. Pop. (1991) 1,515,300.

Almohad BERBER Muslim dynasty (1145–1269) in North Africa and Spain, the followers of a reform movement within ISLAM. It was founded by Muhammad ibn Tumart, who set out from the Atlas Mountains to purify Islam and oust the ALMORAVIDS from Morocco and eventually Spain. In 1212 Alfonso VIII of Castile routed the Almohads, and in 1269 their capital, MARRAKESH, fell to the Marinids.

almond Small tree native to the E Mediterranean region and SW Asia; also the seed of its nut-like fruit. Family Rosaceae; species *Prunus dulcis*.

Almoravid BERBER Muslim dynasty (1054–1145) in Morocco and Spain. They rose to power under Abdullah ibn Yasin who converted Saharan tribes in a religious revival. Abu Bakr founded Marrakesh as their capital in 1070; his brother Yusuf ibn Tashufin defeated Alfonso VI of Castile in 1086. Almoravid rule was ended by the rise of the ALMOHADS.

aloe Genus of South African plants with spiny-edged, fleshy leaves. The plants grow in dense rosettes and have drooping red, orange or yellow flower clusters. Family Liliaceae.

alpaca *See* LLAMA

alphabet System of letters representing the sounds of speech. The word alphabet is derived from the first two letters of the Greek alphabet, *alpha* and *beta*. The most important alphabets in use today are Roman, CYRILLIC, GREEK, ARABIC, HEBREW and Devanagari. The Latin alphabet developed from the Greek. It was perfected *c.*AD 100 and is the foundation on which Western alphabets are based. In some alphabets, such as the Devanagari of India, each character represents a syllable. BRAILLE and MORSE code are alphabets invented to meet special needs.

Alpha Centauri Brightest star in the constellation Centaurus, and the third-brightest star in the sky. It is a visual BINARY.

alpha particles (alpha rays) Stable, positively charged particles emitted spontaneously from the nuclei of certain radioactive isotopes undergoing alpha decay. They consist of two protons and two neutrons and are identical to the nuclei of helium atoms. Their penetrating power is low compared with that of beta particles (ELECTRONS) but they cause intense ionization along their track. This ionization is used to detect them. *See also* RADIOACTIVITY; Ernest RUTHERFORD

Alps Mountain system in S central Europe, extending *c.*1,200km (750mi) in a broad arc from near the Gulf of Genoa on the Mediterranean Sea through France, Italy, Switzerland, Liechtenstein, Austria, Germany and Slovenia. The system was formed by the collision of the European and African tectonic plates. The highest peak is MONT BLANC at 4,807m (15,771ft).

Alsace Region in E France, comprising the départements of Bas-Rhin and Haut-Rhin. It is separated from Germany by the RHINE. Industries: steel, textiles, chemicals; wine-making. STRAS-BOURG is the leading city. Area: 8,280sq km (3,197sq mi). Pop. (1990) 1,624,400.

Altai (Altajsk) Complex mountain system in central Asia stretching from Kazakstan into N China and W Mongolia, and from S Siberia to the Gobi Desert. The highest peak is Mount Belukha, on the Kazakstan-Russia border, at 4,506m (14,783ft).

Altaic languages Family of languages spoken by about 80 million people in Turkey, Iran, the Soviet Union, Mongolia, and parts of China. It consists of three branches: the Turkic languages, the Mongolian languages, and the Tungusic languages. They are named after the ALTAI Mountains.

Altair Star Alpha Aquilae, whose luminosity is ten times that of the Sun. Characteristics: apparent mag. 0.77; spectral type A7; distance 16 light-years.

Altamira World heritage site of notable Palaeolithic cave paintings and engravings (*c.*14,000–9,500 BC) near Santander, N Spain. The roof of the lateral chamber is covered with paintings of animals, including boars, deer, horses and particularly bison, as well as eight engraved anthropomorphic figures.

alternating current (AC) *See* ELECTRIC CURRENT

alternation of generations Two generation cycle by which plants and some algae reproduce. The asexual diploid SPOROPHYTE form produces haploid SPORES that grow into the sexual (GAMETO-PHYTE) form. The gametophyte produces the egg cell that is fertilized by a male gamete to produce a diploid zygote that grows into another sporophyte.

alternative energy *See* RENEWABLE ENERGY

alternator Electrical generator that produces an alternating ELECTRIC CURRENT.

altimeter Instrument for measuring altitude. The simplest type is a form of aneroid BAROMETER. As height increases, air pressure decreases, so the barometer scale can be calibrated to show altitude.

Some aircraft have a radar altimeter, which measures the time taken to bounce a radar signal off the ground and thus calculates altitude.

Altiplano High plain in the South American Andes of Peru and W Bolivia, at an elevation of about 3,650m (12,000ft).

altitude In astronomy, the angular distance of a celestial body above the observer's horizon. It is measured in degrees from 0 (on the horizon) to 90 (at the zenith) along the GREAT CIRCLE passing through the body and the zenith. If the object is below the horizon, the altitude is negative.

alto In singing, the highest male voice, also called COUNTERTENOR; or the lowest female voice, also called CONTRALTO. It is also used to describe that member of a family of instruments with a range that corresponds to the alto voice; for example, an alto FLUTE is a fourth lower than a standard one.

alumina (aluminium oxide, Al_2O_3) Mineral used as an abrasive, electrical insulator and furnace lining. Other forms of alumina include corundum, two impure varieties of which are the gemstones SAPPHIRE and RUBY.

aluminium Metallic silvery white element (symbol Al) of group III of the periodic table. It is the most common metal in the Earth's crust; the chief ore is BAUXITE from which the metal is extracted by electrolysis. Alloyed with other metals, it is extensively used in machined and moulded articles, particularly where lightness is important, as in aircraft. It is protected from oxidation (corrosion) by a thin, natural layer of oxide. Properties: at.no. 13; r.a.m. 26.98; r.d. 2.69; m.p. 660.2°C (1,220.38°F); b.p. 1800°C (3272°F); most common isotope Al^{27}. *See also* ANODIZING

alveolus One of a cluster of microscopic air-sacs that open out from the alveolar ducts at the far end of each bronchiole in the LUNGS. The alveolus is the site for the exchange of gases between the air and the bloodstream, and is covered in a network of CAPILLARY blood vessels. *See also* GAS EXCHANGE; RESPIRATORY SYSTEM

Alzheimer's disease Degenerative condition characterized by progressive mental impairment; it is the commonest cause of DEMENTIA. Sometimes seen in middle years, Alzheimer's becomes increasingly common with advancing age. The cause of the disease is unknown.

AM Abbreviation of AMPLITUDE MODULATION

Amal Lebanese Muslim Shiite political movement. Backed variously by Syria and the Palestinian Liberation Organization (PLO), its members have perpetrated a number of terrorist outrages since the 1980s.

amalgam Solid or liquid alloy of mercury with other metals. Dentists once filled teeth with amalgams usually containing copper and zinc. Most metals dissolve in mercury, although iron and platinum are exceptions.

amanita Large, widely distributed genus of fungi. Amanitas usually have distinct stalks and the prominent remains of a veil in a fleshy ring under the cap and at the bulbous base. They include some of the most poisonous fungi known, such as the DEATH CAP. *See also* FLY AGARIC

Amaterasu Sun goddess of the SHINTO pantheon, considered to be the ancestor of the Japanese imperial clan.

Amati Family of Italian violin-makers in Cremona in the 16th and 17th centuries. They included Andrea (*c.*1520–78), the founder of the Cremona school of violin-making; his two sons Antonio (*c.*1550–1638) and Girolamo (1551–1635); and Girolamo's son Nicolo (1596–1684) and grandson Girolamo (1649–1740).

Amazon Second-longest river in the world, draining the vast Amazon RAINFOREST basin of N South America. It carries by far the greatest volume of water of any river in the world: the average rate of discharge is about 95,000m^3 (3,355,000ft^3) every second, nearly three times as much as its nearest rival, the Congo. The flow is so great that its silt discolours the water up to 200km (125mi) into the Atlantic. Length: *c.*6,430km (3,990mi).

Amazon In Greek mythology, a race of female warriors who lived in a totally matriarchal society. Heracles, Theseus and other Greek heroes challenged the Amazons. As allies of the Trojans, they took part in the defence of TROY, where their queen Penthesilea was slain by ACHILLES after she had killed many Greek warriors.

amber Hard, yellow or brown, translucent fossil resin, mainly from pine trees. Amber is most often found in alluvial soils, in lignite beds or around sea-shores, especially near the BALTIC SEA. The resin sometimes occurs with embedded fossil insects or plants. Amber can be polished to a high degree and is used to make jewellery.

ambergris Musky, waxy solid formed in the intestine of a SPERM WHALE. It is used in perfumes as a fixative for the scent.

Ambrose, Saint (339–97) Roman cleric who, as Bishop of Milan from 374, resisted demands to surrender Milan's churches to the Arians and refused to compromise his orthodox position. He was the author of works on theology and ethics that greatly influenced the thought of the Western church. His feast day is 7 December. *See also* ARIANISM

Amenhotep III (*c.*1417–*c.*1379 BC) Ancient Egyptian king. He succeeded his father, Thutmose IV. The 18th dynasty was at its height during his reign. He maintained peace throughout the empire and undertook extensive building works. His wife, Queen Tiy, played an important role in state affairs. He was succeeded by his son, who took the name AKHNATEN.

Amenhotep IV *See* AKHNATEN

America Western hemisphere, consisting of the continents of NORTH AMERICA and SOUTH AMERICA, joined by the isthmus of CENTRAL AMERICA. It extends from N of the Arctic Circle to 56° S, separating the Atlantic Ocean from the Pacific.

NATIVE AMERICANS settled the entire continent by 8,000 BC. Norsemen were probably the first Europeans to explore America in the 8th century, but Christopher COLUMBUS is popularly credited with the first European discovery in 1492. America was first applied to the lands in 1507 and derives from Amerigo Vespucci, a Florentine navigator who was falsely believed to be the first European to set foot on the mainland.

American Indians Alternative name for NATIVE AMERICANS

American literature English explorers and early colonists produced literary accounts of North America. The first English language work published in New England was the *Bay Psalm Book* (1640). Early colonial literature was often an expression of Puritan piety. Many of the leading figures in the AMERICAN REVOLUTION, such as Thomas PAINE and Benjamin FRANKLIN, produced important literary works. Early 19th-century writers, such as Washington IRVING and James Fenimore COOPER, were influenced by European ROMANTICISM. The pre-eminent US romantic poet was Henry Wadsworth LONGFELLOW. TRANSCENDENTALISM was the first distinctive national literary movement. Leading writers included Henry David Thoreau, Ralph Waldo EMERSON, Oliver Wendell Holmes and Louisa May Alcott. Walt WHITMAN's free-verse epic *Leaves of Grass* (1855–92) is perhaps the most fully realized poetic expression of transcendentalism. The 1840s and 1850s produced American fiction classics, such as Herman MELVILLE's *Moby Dick* (1851) and Nathaniel HAWTHORNE's *The Scarlet Letter* (1850). Harriet Beecher STOWE's anti-slavery story *Uncle Tom's Cabin* (1852) was the best-selling novel of the 19th century. Henry JAMES and Mark TWAIN were the precursors of a new realism: while James embraced psychological realism in *Portrait of a Lady* (1881), Twain used regional dialects in humorous classics such as *Huckleberry Finn* (1885). Realism fed into NATURALISM, producing writers who either focused on the development of cities (Theodore DRIESER and Edith WHARTON), or those who concentrated on a hostile wilderness (Jack LONDON). Stephen CRANE's *Red Badge of Courage* (1895) was groundbreaking in its naturalistic treatment of the Civil War. Emily DICKINSON was finally published posthumously in 1890. In the early 20th century many US writers went into exile. Gertrude STEIN held court in Paris over the "Lost Generation", a group of emigrés that included Ernest HEMINGWAY and Henry MILLER. T.S. ELIOT and Ezra POUND led the search for experimental poetic forms. Eliot's fragmentary poem *The Wasteland* (1922) is often viewed as the archetype of high MODERNISM. Wallace Stevens and William Carlos WILLIAMS developed the new poetry. William FAULKNER was one of the leading modernist novelists. The HARLEM RENAISSANCE saw the emergence of African-American writers, such as

Langston Hughes. The "jazz age" in 1920s New York was captured by F. Scott FITZGERALD in *The Great Gatsby* (1925). Writers such as John STEINBECK, Carson MCCULLERS and Eudora Welty emerged in the 1930s. The first great American dramatist was Eugene O'NEILL. In the 1950s, dramatists such as Arthur MILLER, Edward ALBEE and Sam Shepard developed American theatre. African-American writers, such as Ralph Ellison and James Baldwin, dealt with racial inequality and violence in US society. Maya ANGELOU and Toni MORRISON focused on the history of African-American women. During the 1960s novelists such as Saul BELLOW, Philip ROTH and Joseph HELLER explored the Jewish urban intellectual approach to American society. Humour was also a major outlet for writers such as John UPDIKE, Kurt VONNEGUT and Thomas PYNCHON. Norman MAILER used a more muscular, Hemingway-like approach. The BEAT MOVEMENT (including Jack KEROUAC, Allen GINSBERG) rejected the establishment and embraced alternative values. A major trend in American poetry was the "confessional" style of poets such as Robert LOWELL and Sylvia PLATH.

American Revolution (1775–83) (American War of Independence) Successful revolt by the THIRTEEN COLONIES in North America against British rule. A number of issues provoked the conflict, including restrictions on trade and manufacturing, restrictions on land settlement in the West, and attempts to raise revenue in America by such means as the STAMP ACT (1765) and the Tea Act (1773), which led to the BOSTON TEA PARTY. "No taxation without representation" became the colonial radicals' rallying cry. On 4 July 1776 the DECLARATION OF INDEPENDENCE made the break with Britain decisive. The colonists, under WASHINGTON were supported by France from 1777. In 1781, surrounded by American forces and the French navy, England, under Lord Cornwallis, were forced to surrender at Yorktown. The war was formally ended by the Peace of Paris (1783), which recognized the independence of the USA.

American Samoa US-administered group of five volcanic islands and two coral atolls of the SAMOA island chain in the S Pacific, *c.*650mi NE of Fiji. The principal islands are Tutuila, the Manu'a group and Aun'u. Rose Island (uninhabited) and Swain's Island are coral atolls. The population is largely Polynesian, who are considered US nationals. The US government and the tuna fish canning industry are the main sources of employment. Pop. (1990) 46,773.

americium Radioactive metallic element (symbol Am) of the ACTINIDE SERIES, first made in 1944 by Glenn Seaborg and others by neutron bombardment of plutonium. It is used in home smoke detectors, and Am^{241} is a source of gamma rays. Properties: at.no. 95; r.a.m. 243.13; r.d. 13.67; m.p. 995°C (1,821°F); b.p. unknown; most stable isotope Am^{243} (half-life 7,650 yr).

amethyst Transparent, violet variety of crystallized QUARTZ, containing more iron oxide than other varieties. It is found mainly in Brazil, Uruguay, Ontario, Canada and North Carolina, USA. Amethyst is valued as a semi-precious gem.

Amin, Idi (1925–) Ugandan statesman, president (1971–79). He gained power by a military coup in 1971, overthrowing Milton OBOTE. He established a dictatorship marked by atrocities, and expelled about 80,000 Asian Ugandans in 1972. When Tanzanian forces joined rebel Ugandans in a march on KAMPALA, Amin fled to Libya.

amine Any of a group of organic compounds derived from AMMONIA by replacing hydrogen atoms with alkyl groups. Methylamine (CH_3NH_2) has one hydrogen replaced. Replacement of two hydrogens gives a secondary amine and of three hydrogens, a tertiary amine. Amines are produced in the putrefaction of organic matter and are weakly basic. *See also* ALKALOID

amino acid Organic acid containing at least one carboxyl group (COOH) and at least one amino group (NH_2). Amino acids are of great biological importance because they combine together to form PROTEIN. Amino acids form PEPTIDES by the reaction of adjacent amino and carboxyl groups. Proteins are polypeptide chains consisting of hundreds of amino acids. About 20 amino acids occur in proteins; not all organisms are able to synthesize all of them. Essential amino acids are those that an organism has to obtain ready-made from its environment.

Amis, Sir Kingsley (1922–95) British novelist, father of Martin AMIS. Amis' debut novel, *Lucky Jim* (1954), a sparkling satire on academia, is a classic of post-1945 British fiction. *The Old Devils* won the 1986 Booker Prize.

Amis, Martin (1949–) British novelist and journalist, son of Kingsley AMIS. His debut novel, *The Rachel Papers* (1974), won the Somerset Maugham Award. A highly respected modern writer, his work is darkly humorous. His more recent novels include *Money* (1984), *London Fields* (1989), *Time's Arrow* (1991) and *Night Train* (1997).

Amman Capital and largest city of Jordan, 80km (50 mi) ENE of Jerusalem. It became the capital of Trans-Jordan in 1921. From 1948 it grew rapidly, partly as a result of the influx of Palestinian refugees. Industries: cement, textiles, tobacco, leather. Pop. (1994 est.) 1,300,042.

ammeter Instrument for measuring ELECTRIC CURRENT in AMPERES. An ammeter is connected in series in a circuit. In the moving-coil type for direct current (DC), the current to be measured passes through a coil suspended in a magnetic field and deflects a needle attached to the coil. In the moving-iron type for both direct and alternating current (AC), current through a fixed coil magnetizes two pieces of soft iron that repel each other and deflect the needle. Digital ammeters are now also commonly used.

19

ammonia Colourless nonflammable pungent gas (NH$_3$) manufactured by the HABER PROCESS. It is used to make nitrogenous fertilisers. Ammonia solutions are used in cleaning and bleaching. The gas is extremely soluble in water, forming an alkaline solution of ammonium hydroxide (NH$_4$OH) that can give rise to ammonium salts containing the ion NH$_4^+$. Chief properties: r.d. 0.59; m.p. -77.7 °C (-107.9°F); b.p. -33.4 °C (-28.1 °F).

ammonite Any of an extinct group of shelled cephalopod MOLLUSCS. Most ammonites had a spiral shell, and they are believed to be related to the nautiloids – the only surviving form being the pearly NAUTILUS. They are common as FOSSILS in marine rocks.

Amnesty International Human rights organization, founded in 1961. It campaigns on behalf of prisoners of conscience. Advocating non-violence, and politically impartial, it opposes the use of torture and the death penalty. The organization was awarded the Nobel Peace Prize in 1977.

amnion Membrane or sac that encloses the EMBRYO of a reptile, bird or mammal. The embryo floats in the amniotic fluid within the sac.

amoeba Microscopic, almost transparent, single-celled protozoan animal that has a constantly changing, irregular shape. Found in ponds, damp soil and animal intestines, it consists of a thin outer cell membrane, a large nucleus, food and contractile vacuoles, and fat globules. It reproduces by binary fission. Length: up to 3mm (0.1in). Class Sarcodina; species include the common *Amoeba proteus* and *Entamoeba histolytica*, which causes amoebic DYSENTERY.

Amos (active *c*.750 BC) Old Testament prophet. He was named as the author of the Book of Amos, the third of the 12 books of the Minor Prophets.

ampere SI unit of ELECTRIC CURRENT (symbol A). It is defined as the current in a pair of straight, parallel conductors of infinite length and 1m (39in) apart in a vacuum that produces a force of 2×10^{-7} newton per metre in their length. This force may be measured on a current balance instrument, the standard against which current meters, such as an AMMETER, are calibrated.

Ampère, André Marie (1775–1836) French physicist and mathematician. He founded electrodynamics (now called ELECTROMAGNETISM) and performed numerous experiments to investigate the magnetic effects of electric currents. He devised techniques for detecting and measuring currents, and constructed an early type of galvanometer. Ampère's law – proposed by him – is a mathematical description of the magnetic force between two electric currents. His name is also commemorated in the fundamental unit of current, the AMPERE (A). *See also* ELECTRIC CURRENT

amphetamine DRUG that stimulates the CENTRAL NERVOUS SYSTEM. These drugs (known as "pep pills" or "speed") can lead to drug abuse and dependence. They can induce a temporary sense of well-being, often followed by fatigue and depression. *See also* ADDICTION

amphibian Class of egg-laying VERTEBRATES, whose larval stages (tadpoles) are usually spent in water but whose adult life is normally spent on land. Amphibians have smooth, moist skin and are cold-blooded. Larvae breathe through gills; adults usually have lungs. All adults are carnivorous but larvae are frequently herbivorous. There are three living orders: Urodela (NEWTS and SALAMANDERS); Anura (FROGS and TOADS) and Apoda or CAECILIANS.

amphibole Any of a large group of complex rock-forming minerals characterized by a double-chain silicate structure (Si$_4$O$_{11}$). They all contain water as OH$^-$ ions and usually calcium, magnesium and iron. Found in IGNEOUS and METAMORPHIC rocks, they form wedge-shaped fragments on cleavage. Crystals are orthorhombic or monoclinic.

amphitheatre In ancient Rome and the Roman empire, a large circular or oval building with the performance space surrounded by tiered seating. It was used as a theatre for gladiatorial contests, wild-animal shows and similar events. Many ruined amphitheatres remain; the best-known being the COLOSSEUM in Rome. The term is now used generically to refer to any open, banked arena.

amplifier Device for changing the magnitude (size) of a signal, such as voltage or current, but not the way it varies. Amplifiers are used in radio and television transmitters and receivers, and in audio equipment. *See also* THERMIONICS

amplitude modulation (AM) Form of RADIO transmission. Broadcasts on the short-, medium- and long-wave bands are transmitted by amplitude modulation. The sound signals to be transmitted are superimposed on a constant-amplitude radio signal called the carrier. The resulting modulated signal varies in amplitude according to the strength of the signal. *See also* FREQUENCY MODULATION (FM)

Amritsar City in Punjab state, NW India, founded in 1577. Religious centre of SIKHISM, and site of its holiest shrine, the Golden Temple. Industries: textiles, silk weaving and food processing. Pop. (1991) 709,000.

Amsterdam Capital and largest city in the Netherlands, on the River Amstel and linked to the North Sea by the North Sea Canal. Canals crisscross the city, which is a major European port and leading financial and cultural centre, with an important stock exchange and diamond-cutting industry. Other industries: iron and steel, oil refining, rolling stock, chemicals, glass and shipbuilding. Pop. (1994) 724,096.

Amun (Amon) Ancient Egyptian deity of reproduction or the animating force. The "invisible one", Amun is commonly represented as a human being wearing ram's horns and a twin-feathered crown. His cult temple was at Weset (LUXOR).

Amundsen, Roald (1872–1928) Norwegian explorer and discoverer of the South Pole. From 1903–06 he sailed through the NORTHWEST PAS-

SAGE and was able to locate the exact position of the North Magnetic Pole. His next expedition took him to ANTARCTICA, and in December 1911 (one month ahead of SCOTT) he reached the South Pole. In 1925–26, he conducted an exploration of the north polar regions by air.

amylase Digestive enzyme secreted by the SALIVARY GLANDS (salivary amylase) and the PANCREAS (pancreatic amylase. It aids digestion by breaking down starch into MALTOSE (a disaccharide) and then GLUCOSE (a monosaccharide).

Anabaptists Protestant sects founded c.1525 by followers of various "radicals" of the REFORMATION in Switzerland, Germany, Moravia and the Netherlands. Believing that infants, unaware of good and evil, were not punishable for sin, they insisted on adult baptism as an act of free choice. They were persecuted by the authorities and rejected by many other reformers.

anabolic steroid Any of a group of hormones that stimulate the growth of tissue. Synthetic versions are used in medicine to treat OSTEOPOROSIS and some types of ANAEMIA; they may also be prescribed to aid weight gain in severely ill or elderly patients. These drugs are associated with a number of side-effects, including acne, fluid retention, liver damage and masculinization in women. Some athletes have been known to abuse anabolic steroids in order to increase muscle bulk.

anabolism See METABOLISM

anaconda Large constricting SNAKE of South America, the heaviest snake in the world. It feeds mainly on birds and small mammals. Females give birth to up to 75 live young. Species *Eunectes murinus*. Length: up to 9m (30ft).

anaemia Condition in which there is a shortage of HAEMOGLOBIN, the oxygen-carrying pigment contained in ERYTHROCYTES (red blood cells). Symptoms include weakness, breathlessness, faintness, palpitations and lowered resistance. It may be due to a decrease in the production of haemoglobin or excessive destruction of red blood cells or blood loss. Worldwide, iron deficiency is the commonest cause of anaemia.

anaerobic Connected with the absence of oxygen or air, or not dependent on oxygen or air for survival. An anaerobic organism, or anaerobe, is a microorganism that can survive by releasing energy from GLUCOSE and other foods in the absence of oxygen. The process by which it does so is called anaerobic respiration. Most anaerobes can survive in oxygen but do not need it for RESPIRATION. *See also* AEROBIC

anaesthesia State of insensibility or loss of sensation produced by disease or by various anaesthetic drugs used during surgical procedures. During general, or total, anaesthesia the entire body becomes insensible and the individual sleeps; in local anaesthesia only a specific part of the body is rendered insensible or numb and the patient remains conscious.

analgesic DRUG that relieves or prevents pain without causing loss of consciousness. It does not cure the cause of the pain, but helps to deaden the sensation. Some analgesics are also NARCOTICS, and many have valuable anti-inflammatory properties. Common analgesics include aspirin, codeine and morphine. *See also* ANAESTHESIA

analogue signal In telecommunications and electronics, transmission of information by means of variation in a continuous waveform. An analogue signal varies (usually in AMPLITUDE or FREQUENCY) in direct proportion to the information content of the signal.

anarchy Absence of standard forms of government. The philosophy of anarchism maintains that people will be better off if governments are abolished. The natural goodness of people will then prevail, and they can use voluntary associations to deal with any problems that may arise. Some anarchists advocate violence to overthrow and eliminate the state.

Anatolia See ASIA MINOR

anatomy Branch of biological science that studies the structure of an organism. The study of anatomy can be divided in several ways. On the basis of size, there is **gross** anatomy, which is studying structures with the naked eye; **microscopic** anatomy, studying finer detail with a light microscope; **submicroscopic** anatomy, studying even finer structural detail with an electron microscope; and **molecular** anatomy, studying with sophisticated instruments the molecular make-up of an organism. Microscopic and submicroscopic anatomy involve two closely related sciences: HISTOLOGY and CYTOLOGY. Anatomy can also be classified according to the type of organism studied: plant, invertebrate, vertebrate or human anatomy. *See also* PHYSIOLOGY

Anaximander (611–547 BC) Ancient Greek scientist and philosopher. His fame rests on his doctrine of a single world principle: a non-perceivable substance, which he called *apeiron* (Gr. infinite), that was the starting point and origin of the cosmic process. He is said to have made the first map of the world, which he conceived of as an immobile cylindrical object at the centre of the universe.

ancestor worship Any of various religious beliefs and practices found in societies where kinship is strong. The spirits of dead ancestors or tribal members, believed capable of good or harm, are propitiated by prayers and sacrifices. It is practised chiefly in sub-Saharan Africa and Melanesia.

Anchorage City in S central Alaska. Founded as a railway town in 1914, it became the supply centre for the gold- and coal-mining regions to the N. It suffered a severe earthquake in 1964. By far Alaska's largest city, its industries include oil and natural gas. Tourism is increasingly important. Pop. (1992) 245,866.

anchovy Commercially valuable food marine fish found worldwide in shoals in temperate and tropical seas. There are more than 100 species, including the European anchovy *Engraulis encrasicholus*. Length: 10–25cm (4–10in). Family Engraulidae.

ancien régime Term used to describe the political, legal and social system in France before the FRENCH REVOLUTION of 1789. It was characterized by a rigid social order, a fiscal system weighted in favour of the rich, and an absolutist monarchy.

Andalusia (Andalucía) Largest, most populous and southernmost region of Spain, crossed by the Guadalquivir River, and comprising eight provinces. The capital is SEVILLE; other major cities include MÁLAGA, GRANADA and CÓRDOBA. In the N are the Sierra Morena mountains, which are rich in minerals. In the S are the Sierra Nevada, rising to Mulhacén (Spain's highest point), at 3,378m (11,411ft). Farms in the low-lying sw raise horses and cattle (including fighting bulls) and grow most of the country's cereals; other important crops are citrus fruits, olives, sugar and grapes. Sherry is made from grapes grown in the neighbourhood of Jerez de la Frontera, near Cádiz. Area: 87,268sq km (33,707sq mi). Pop. (1991) 6,940,522.

Andaman and Nicobar Islands Territory of India comprising two chains of islands in the Bay of Bengal. The capital is Port Blair (on South Andaman). The main exports are timber, coffee, coconuts and copra. Total area: 8,300sq km (3,200sq mi). Pop. (1991) 280,661.

Andean Indians *See* NATIVE AMERICANS

Andersen, Hans Christian (1805–1875) Danish writer of some of the best-loved fairy tales. His humorous, delicate, but frequently also melancholy stories were first published in 1835. They include *The Ugly Duckling*, *The Little Mermaid*, *The Little Match Girl* and *The Emperor's New Clothes*.

Anderson, Elizabeth Garrett (1836–1917) British physician and pioneer of women's rights. She had to overcome intense prejudice against female doctors to become one of the first English women to practise. Later she became England's first female mayor.

Andes Chain of mountains in South America, extending along the whole length of the w coast. The longest mountain range in the world, they stretch for 8,900km (5,500mi). At their widest they are about 800km (500mi) across. There are more than 50 peaks over 6,700m (21,980ft) high. They contain many active volcanoes, including COTOPAXI in Ecuador. Earthquakes are common, and cities such as LIMA, Callao and VALPARAÍSO have been severely damaged. The highest peak is ACONCAGUA, rising 6,960m (22,834ft) in Argentina. Lake TITICACA (the highest lake in the world) lies in the Andes at 3,810m (12,500ft) above sea-level on the Peru-Bolivia border.

Andhra Pradesh State in SE India on the Bay of Bengal; the capital is HYDERABAD. It was created in 1953 from part of MADRAS, and in 1956 incorporated the princely state of Hyderabad. Though mountainous to the NE, most of the region is flat coastal plain. Products include rice and groundnuts; coal, chrome and manganese are mined. The principal language is Telugu. Area: 276,814sq km (106,878sq mi). Pop. (1991) 66,508,008.

Andorra Small independent state situated in the E Pyrenees between France and Spain. The main sources of income include stock rearing and agriculture; the sale of water and hydroelectricity to Catalonia; and tourism, particularly skiing. Area: 453sq km (175sq mi). Pop. (1993) 61,599.

Andrea del Sarto (1486–1531) (Andrea d'Agnolo di Francesco) Florentine artist. A contemporary of MICHELANGELO and RAPHAEL, he was one of the outstanding painters and draughtsmen of the High RENAISSANCE. He was an excellent portraitist, a master of composition, and he produced many frescos and altarpieces.

Andrew, Saint In the New Testament, brother of Simon PETER and one of the original 12 DISCIPLES of JESUS. According to tradition, he was crucified on an X-shaped cross. He is patron saint of Scotland and Russia; his feast day is 30 November.

Androcles In Roman legend, a slave who ran away from his master. Androcles removed a thorn from the paw of a suffering lion. When he later faced the same lion in the Roman Arena, the lion refused to harm him.

androgen General name for male sex HORMONES, such as TESTOSTERONE.

Andromeda In Greek mythology, daughter of Cepheus and Cassiopea, king and queen of Ethiopia. When her country was under threat from a sea dragon, Andromeda was offered as a sacrifice and chained to a rock by the sea. She was saved by PERSEUS.

Andromeda Large constellation of the northern hemisphere, adjoining the Square of Pegasus. The main stars lie in a line leading away from Pegasus, and the star Alpha Andromedae actually forms one corner of the Square. The most famous object in the constellation is the ANDROMEDA GALAXY

Andromeda Galaxy Spiral GALAXY 2.2 million light years away in the constellation ANDROMEDA, the most distant object visible to the naked eye. The Andromeda Galaxy has a mass of over 300,000 million Suns. Its diameter is about 150,000 light years, somewhat larger than our own Galaxy.

Andropov, Yuri Vladimirovich (1914–84) Soviet statesman, president of the Soviet Union (1983–84), general secretary of the Communist Party (1982–84). Andropov first gained attention for his role in the suppression of the Hungarian uprising (1956). As head (1967–82) of the KGB, Andropov took a hardline against political dissidence, supporting Soviet intervention in Czechoslovakia (1968) and Poland (1981). He joined the Politburo in 1973. Andropov succeeded Leonid BREZHNEV as leader. Perhaps his most significant decision was the promotion of GORBACHEV.

anechoic chamber (dead room) Room designed to be echo-free so that it can be used in acoustic laboratories to measure sound reflection and transmission, and to test audio equipment. The walls, floor and ceiling must be insulated and all surfaces covered with an absorbent material such as rubber, often over inward-pointing pyramid shapes to reduce reflection. The room is usually asymmetrical to reduce stationary waves. *See also* ACOUSTICS

anemometer Instrument using pressure tubes or rotating cups, vanes or propellers to measure the speed or force of the wind.

anemone (windflower) Perennial plant found worldwide. Anemones have sepals resembling petals, and numerous stamens and pistils covering a central knob; two or three deeply toothed leaves appear in a whorl midway up the stem. Many are wild flowers, such as the wood anemone (*Anemone nemorosa*), common in Britain and Europe. There are 120 species. Family Ranunculaceae. *See also* BUTTERCUP; SEA ANEMONE

angel Spiritual being superior to man but inferior to God. In the Bible, angels appear on earth as messengers and servants of God (the word "angel" derives from the Greek word for "messenger"). Angels also form an integral part of Judaism and Islam. In Christian theology, there is a hierarchy of angels consisting of nine orders: Seraphim, Cherubim, Thrones, Dominations, Virtues, Powers, Principalities, Archangels and Angels.

Angel Falls Waterfall in SE Venezuela, in the Guiana Highlands. Part of the Caroní river, the waterfall was discovered in 1935.

angelfish Tropical fish found in the Atlantic and Indo-Pacific oceans, popular as an aquarium fish because of its graceful, trailing fins and beautiful markings. Length: 2–10cm (0.75–4in). Family Cichlidae.

Angelico, Fra (1400–1455) (Guido di Pietro) Florentine painter and Dominican friar. Angelico and his assistants painted a cycle of some 50 devotional frescos in the friary of San Marco, Florence (*c.*1438–45). These pictures show great technical skill and are the key to Angelico's reputation as an artist of extraordinary sweetness and serenity. His style showed a marked change towards narrative detail in frescos carried out for Pope Nicholas V's Vatican chapel (1447–50).

Angelou, Maya (1928–) US writer, editor and entertainer. She is best known for five volumes of autobiography, starting with *I Know Why the Caged Bird Sings* (1970). The fourth volume, *The Heart of a Woman*, deals with her involvement in the 1960s CIVIL RIGHTS movement as the Northern Coordinator for Martin Luther KING.

Angevins English royal dynasty named after King Henry II, son of the Count of Anjou (and grandson of Henry I), who ascended the throne in 1154. The Angevins, who later became the PLANTAGENET royal line, retained the crown until 1485.

angina Pain in the chest due to insufficient blood supply to the heart, usually associated with diseased coronary arteries. Generally induced by exertion or stress, it is treated with drugs, such as glyceryl trinitrate, or surgery.

angiosperm Plants with true flowers, as distinct from GYMNOSPERM and other non-flowering plants. They include most trees, bushes and non-woody herbs. There are two main groups: monocotyledons, such as grasses and daffodils (which have one seed-leaf) and DICOTYLEDONS, such as peas and oak (which have two seed-leaves).

angle Measure of the inclination of two straight lines or planes to each other. One complete revolution is divided into 360 degrees or 2π radians. One degree may be subdivided into 60 minutes, and one minute into 60 seconds.

Angles Germanic tribe from a district of Schleswig-Holstein now called Angeln. In the 5th century they invaded England with neighbouring tribes, JUTES, SAXONS and others. They settled mainly in Northumbria and East Anglia. The name England (Angle-land) derives from them.

Anglican Communion Worldwide fellowship of independent national or regional churches tracing their origin to the CHURCH OF ENGLAND and in communion with the See of CANTERBURY, SE England. The Anglican Communion does not proclaim any distinctive doctrines of its own; instead it claims to hold fast to the faith and order of the primitive, undivided church of the first centuries. By the mid-1990s the total number of Anglicans in the world was about 70 million, organized into about 30,000 parishes and 35 self-governing provinces.

Anglicanism Beliefs in accordance with the teachings of the CHURCH OF ENGLAND. Developing since Henry VIII's separation from the Roman Catholic Church (1534), it is based on scriptural and ecclesiastical authority. Elements of both Catholicism and Protestantism are contained in the theology. Recently many Anglican provinces have decided to ordain women, often causing sharp divisions within the church. In 1982 diplomatic ties with the Catholic Church were restored.

angling Popular freshwater or marine sport. The two basic types of freshwater fishing are game fishing and coarse fishing. **Game** fishing uses artificial bait, such as spinning lures and flies (imitation insects), and is undertaken in fast-moving water where salmon and trout can be found. **Coarse** fishing takes place in slow-moving water in which fish are caught using either live bait, such as maggots and worms, or cereal bait, such as sweetcorn. **Saltwater** fishing requires heavier rods and reels, and includes trolling and big-game fishing. Flatfish, mackerel and sea bass are among the more common seafish caught, while tuna, swordfish, marlin, sailfish and shark are taken in big-game fishing. *See also* FISHING

Anglo-Irish Agreement (1985) (Hillsborough Agreement) Agreement on the status of Northern Ireland, signed by Margaret Thatcher and Garret Fitzgerald. It gave Ireland the right of consultation; it asserted that future changes would have to be ratified by a majority of the people of Northern Ireland; and it set up the Anglo-Irish Intergovernmental Conference (AIIC) to promote cooperation. The agreement was denounced by Northern Irish Unionists.

Anglo-Saxon art and architecture Style of art and architecture produced in Britain following the invasions by the ANGLO-SAXONS from the 5th to the 11th centuries. The most famous archaeological find is the pagan ship-burial at SUTTON HOO. Anglo-Saxon art is predominantly Christian, consisting of stone crosses, ivory carvings and illuminated manuscripts (the most important being the LINDISFARNE GOSPELS). Anglo-Saxon churches are characterized by square apses, aisles or side chambers called *porticus*, pilaster strips and distinctive timber work.

Anglo-Saxons People of Germanic origin – the ANGLES, SAXONS and other tribes who invaded England from the mid-5th century, when Roman power was in decline. By 600 they were established in most of England. They were converted to Christianity in the 7th century. Early tribal groups were led by warrior lords whose thegns (noblemen) provided military service in exchange for rewards and protection. The tribal groups eventually developed into larger kingdoms, such as Northumbria and WESSEX. The term Anglo-Saxon became synonymous with "English". The Anglo-Saxon period ended with the NORMAN CONQUEST (1066).

Angola Country on the SW coast of Africa; the capital is LUANDA. **Land and climate** Most of Angola is part of the plateau that makes up the interior of S Africa, with a narrow coastal plain in the W. In the NE, several rivers flow N to the River CONGO. In the S some rivers, including the Cubango and the Cuanda, flow SE into the interior of Africa. Angola has a tropical climate with temperatures of over 20°C (68°F) throughout the year, though the highest areas are cooler. Grasslands cover much of the country. The S is a desert region that merges into the NAMIB DESERT. Some rainforest grows in N Angola towards Zaïre. **Economy** Angola is a poor, developing country, where more than 70% of the people make a meagre living by farming. The main food crops are cassava, maize and coffee. However,

Angola has huge economic potential: it has large oil reserves near Luanda, and in the CABINDA enclave, oil is by far the leading export. The country is a major diamond producer and has reserves of copper, manganese and phosphates. Angola also has a growing manufacturing sector, much of it based on hydroelectric power. **History and politics** Bantu-speaking people from the N settled in Angola around 2,000 years ago. In the early 1600s Angola became important as a source of slaves for Brazil, Portugal's huge colony in South America. After the decline of the slave trade, Portuguese settlers began to develop the land, and the Portuguese population increased greatly in the 20th century. In the 1950s, local nationalists began to demand independence and, in 1956, the Popular Movement for the Liberation of Angola (MPLA) was founded, drawing support from the Mbundu tribe and *mestizos* (people of African and European descent). The MPLA led a revolt in Luanda in 1961, but it was put down by Portuguese troops. Other opposition movements developed. In the N, the Kongo set up the Front for the Liberation of Angola (FNLA), and in 1966 southern peoples, including many of the Ovimbundu, formed the National Union for the Total Independence of Angola (UNITA). The Portuguese granted independence in 1975, but a power struggle developed among rival nationalist forces. The MPLA formed the government but UNITA troops, opposed to the MPLA's austere Marxist policies, began a civil war. After 16 crippling years of war a peace treaty was signed in 1991 and multiparty elections were held in 1992. After a victory for the MPLA, which had renounced its Socialist policies, civil strife resumed when UNITA refused to abide by the result. A new peace accord was signed in Lusaka in 1994, which provided for the formation of a government of national unity and reconciliation, bringing together UNITA and MPLA politicians. In April 1997 this government was finally inaugurated, with DOS SANTOS remaining as president. UNITA leader SAVIMBI rejected the vice presidency and was offered a post with "special status". The political climate remains unstable, with violence between UNITA and government forces.

Angora *See* ANKARA

Angstrom Obsolete unit of length, equal to 10^{-10} m or 0.1nm (nanometre). It is used to express the wavelength of light and ultraviolet radiation, interatomic and intermolecular distances. Symbol: Å.

Anguilla Island in the West Indies, most northerly of the Leeward Islands. Settled in the 17th century by English colonists, it became part of the St Kitts-Nevis-Anguilla group. Declared independent in 1967, it re-adopted British colonial status in 1980, and is now a self-governing dependency. The economy is based on fishing and tourism. Area: 91sq km (35sq mi). Pop. (1992) 8,960.

aniline (phenylamine) Highly poisonous, colourless oily liquid ($C_6H_5NH_2$) made by the reduction of nitrobenzene. It is an important material for mak-

---

ANGOLA

AREA: 1,246,700sq km (481,351sq mi)
POPULATION: 10,609,000
CAPITAL (POPULATION): Luanda (1,544,000)
GOVERNMENT: Multiparty republic
ETHNIC GROUPS: Ovimbundu 37%, Mbundu 22%, Kongo 13%, Luimbe-Nganguela 5%, Nyaneka-Humbe 5%, Chokwe, Luvale, Luchazi
LANGUAGES: Portuguese (official)
RELIGIONS: Christianity (Roman Catholic 69%, Protestant 20%), traditional beliefs 10%
CURRENCY: Kwanza = 100 lwe

ing organic compounds such as drugs, explosives and dyes. Properties: r.d. 1.02; m.p. −6.2°C (20.8°F); b.p. 184.1°C (363.4°F). *See also* AMINE

animal Living organism of the animal kingdom, usually distinguishable from members of the plant kingdom by its power of locomotion (at least during some stage of its existence); a well-defined body shape; limited growth; its feeding exclusively on organic matter; the production of two different kinds of sex cells; and the formation of an embryo or larva during the developmental stage. Higher animals, such as the VERTEBRATES, are easily distinguishable from plants, but the distinction becomes blurred with the lower forms. Some one-celled organisms could easily be assigned to either category. Scientists have classified about a million different kinds of animals in more than twenty phyla. The simplest (least highly evolved) animals include the PROTOZOA, SPONGES, JELLYFISH and WORMS. Other invertebrate phyla include ARTHRO-PODS (arachnids, crustaceans and insects), MOL-LUSCS (shellfish, octopus and squid) and ECHINO-DERMS (sea urchins and starfish). Vertebrates belong to the CHORDATA phylum, which includes fish, amphibians, reptiles, birds and mammals.

animal rights Freedom from subjection to pain and distress, especially applied to those animals used in scientific experimentation. Animal rights campaigners wish to extend animal rights further to include all farm animals kept, transported or slaughtered in inhumane conditions.

animism Belief that within every animal, plant or inanimate object dwells a spirit capable of governing its existence and influencing human affairs. Natural objects and phenomena are regarded as possessing life, consciousness and a spirit. These beliefs are widespread among tribal peoples and were once thought to represent the beginnings of organized religion.

anion Negative ION attracted to the ANODE during electrolysis.

Ankara Capital of Turkey, at the confluence of the Cubuk and Ankara rivers. In ancient times it was known as Ancyra. It replaced Istanbul as capital in 1923, changing its name to Ankara in 1930. It is noted for its angora wool and mohair products. Pop. (1990) 2,541,899.

Annam Former kingdom on E coast of Indochina, now in Vietnam; the capital was Hué. The ancient empire fell to China in 214 BC. It regained independence in 939, but was briefly ruled by China again from 1407–28. The French obtained missionary and trade agreements in 1787, and a protectorate was established (1883–84). During World War 2 it was occupied by the Japanese; in 1949 it was incorporated into the Republic of VIETNAM.

Annan, Kofi (1938–) Ghanaian diplomat, seventh secretary-general of the UN (1996–). Annan became the first black African secretary-general. In 1993 he was elected under-secretary-general for peacekeeping. His efficient handling of the

removal of UN troops from Bosnia earnt him the support of the USA and Britain.

Annapolis Seaport capital of Maryland, USA, on the S bank of the Severn River on Chesapeake Bay. It is the seat of the US Naval Academy (founded 1845). Industries include: boatyards and seafood packing. Pop. (1992) 34,070.

Annapurna Mountain massif in the HIMALAYAS, in N central Nepal, notoriously dangerous to climbers. It has two of the world's highest peaks: Annapurna 1 in the W rises to 8,078m (26,504ft); Annapurna 2 in the E rises to 7,937m (26,041ft).

Anne (1665–1714) Queen of Great Britain and Ireland (1702–14). The second daughter of James II, she was the last STUART sovereign, and after the Act of UNION (1707) the first monarch of the United Kingdom of England and Scotland. She presided over an age of military success and cultural distinction. Despite 18 pregnancies, no child survived her.

annealing Slow heating and cooling of a metal, alloy or glass to relieve internal stresses and make up dislocations or vacancies introduced during mechanical shaping, such as rolling or extruding (ejection). Annealing increases the material's workability and durability.

Anne Boleyn *See* BOLEYN, ANNE

annelid Animal phylum of segmented WORMS. All have encircling grooves usually corresponding to internal partitions of the body. A digestive tube, nerves and blood vessels run through the entire body, but each segment has its own set of internal organs. Annelids form an important part of the diets of many animals. The three main classes are: Polychaeta, marine worms; Oligochaeta, freshwater or terrestrial worms and Hirudinea (LEECHES).

Anne of Austria (1601–66) Daughter of Philip III of Spain, wife of LOUIS XIII of France and mother of LOUIS XIV. Her husband died in 1643, and she ruled France as regent in close alliance with Cardinal MAZARIN until her death. The era was immortalized by Alexandre Dumas in his novels, *The Three Musketeers* and *Twenty Years After*.

Anne of Cleves (1515–57) Fourth wife of HENRY VIII of England. Her marriage (1540) was a political alliance joining Henry with the German Protestants, and was never consummated, being declared null after only six months.

annual Plant that completes its life cycle in one growing season, such as the sweet pea, sunflower, wheat. Annual plants overwinter as seeds. *See also* BIENNIAL; PERENNIAL

annual ring (growth ring) Concentric circles visible in cross-sections of woody stems or trunks. Each year the CAMBIUM layer produces a layer of XYLEM, the vessels of which are large and thin-walled in the spring and smaller and thick-walled in the summer, creating the contrast between the rings. Used to determine the age of trees, the thickness of these rings also reveals environmental conditions during a tree's lifetime.

Annunciation Announcement made to the Virgin Mary by the Angel GABRIEL that she was to be the mother of Christ (Luke 1). In many Christian churches the Feast of the Annunciation is kept on 25 March, a date often called "Lady Day". The Annunciation was a common subject for painters during medieval and Renaissance times.

anode Positive electrode of an electrolytic cell that attracts ANIONS during ELECTROLYSIS.

anodizing Electrolytic process to coat ALUMINIUM or MAGNESIUM with a thin layer of oxide to help prevent corrosion. The process makes the metal the ANODE in an acid solution. The protective coating, steamed to seal the pores, is insoluble and a good insulator. It can be dyed bright colours, many of which are resistant to sunlight.

anorexia nervosa Abnormal loss of the desire to eat. A pathological condition, it is seen mainly in young females anxious to lose weight. It can result in severe emaciation and in rare cases can be life-threatening.

Anouilh, Jean (1910–87) French playwright and screenwriter. A major dramatist of the mid-20th century, he was influenced by neo-classicism. He often reinterpreted Greek myth as a means of exploring oppression, notably in *Antigone* (1944), perhaps his most celebrated play. The underlying theme of many of his plays is the contrast between innocence and bitter experience. Other works include *Becket* (1959).

Anschluss Unification of Austria and Germany in 1938. Prohibited by treaty at the end of World War I, expressly to limit the strength of Germany, Anschluss was nevertheless favoured by many Germans and Austrians. Unification finally took place through a show of force under HITLER. It was dissolved by the Allies in 1945.

Anselm of Canterbury, Saint (1033–1109) English theologian, b. Italy. He was an early scholastic philosopher and became Archbishop of Canterbury in 1093. His belief in the rational character of Christian belief led him to propose an ontological argument for the existence of God. His feast day is 21 April. *See also* ONTOLOGY

ant Social insect belonging to a family that also includes the BEE and WASP. A typical ant colony consists of one or more queens (fertile females), workers (sterile females) and winged males. Some species also have a caste of soldier ants, which guard the colony. Ants range in length from 2–25mm (0.08–1.0in) and are found worldwide except Antarctica. They typically feed on plants, nectar and other insects. Most ants are wingless except at times of dispersal. Family Formicidae.

Antarctica Fifth-largest continent, covering *c.*9.5% of the world's land area. Surrounding the South Pole, it is bordered by the Antarctic Ocean and the S sections of the Atlantic, Pacific and Indian oceans. Almost entirely within the Antarctic Circle, it holds strategic and scientific interest for the rest of the world. No people live here permanently, although scientists frequently stay for short periods for purposes of research and exploration. Seven nations lay claim to sectors of it. Covered by an ice-sheet with an average thickness of about 1,800m (5,900ft), it contains *c.*90% of the world's ice and over 70% of its freshwater. **Land** The continent is a snowy desert covering *c.*14,200,000sq km (5,500,000sq mi). The land is a high plateau, having an average elevation of 1,800m (6,000ft) and rising to 5,140m (16,860ft) in the Vinson Massif. Mountain ranges occur near the coasts. The interior, or South Polar Plateau, lies beneath *c.*2,000m (6,500ft) of snow, accumulated over tens of thousands of years. Mineral deposits exist in the mountains, but their recovery has not become practicable. Coal may be plentiful, but the value of known deposits of copper, nickel, gold and iron will not repay the expenses of extracting and exporting them. **Seas and glaciers** Antarctic rivers are frozen, inching towards the sea, and instead of lakes there are large bodies of ice along the coasts. The great Beardmore Glacier creeps down from the South Polar Plateau and eventually becomes part of the Ross Ice Shelf. The southernmost part of the Atlantic is the portion of the Antarctic Ocean known as the Weddell Sea. **Climate and vegetation** Antarctica remains cold all year, with only a few coastal areas being free from snow or ice in summer (December to February). On most of the continent the temperature remains below freezing, and in August it has been recorded at nearly −90°C (−130°F). Precipitation generally amounts to 17.5–38cm (7–15in) of snow a year, but melting is less than that, resulting in a build-up over the centuries. Nevertheless, mosses manage to survive on rocks along the outer rim of the continent. Certain algae grow on the snow, and others appear in pools of freshwater when melting occurs. **History** Islands associated with the continent were sighted in the 18th century. Between 1838–40 the US explorer Charles Wilkes discovered enough of the coast to prove that a continent existed, and James Clark Ross of Britain made coastal maps. Towards the end of the 19th century, exploration reached inland developing into a race for the SOUTH POLE. Roald AMUNDSEN of Norway won, reaching the Pole on 14 December 1911, a month before Robert Falcon SCOTT. The aeroplane brought a new era of exploration, and Richard E. BYRD became the best known of the airborne polar explorers. In 1991 the Antarctic Treaty of 1959, which pledged international scientific co-operation, was renewed and extended, banning commercial exploitation of the area.

Antarctic Circle Southernmost of the Earth's parallels, 66.5° s of the Equator. At this latitude the sun neither sets on the day of summer SOLSTICE (December 22) nor rises on the day of winter solstice (June 21). *See also* ARCTIC CIRCLE

anteater Toothless, mainly nocturnal, insect-eating mammal that lives in the swamps and savannas of tropical America. It has a long, sticky tongue and powerful claws. Length: up to 152cm (60in). Family Myrmecophagidae. *See also* EDENTATE

antelope Hollow-horned, speedy RUMINANT found throughout the Old World except in Madagascar, Malaya and Australasia; most antelopes occur in Africa. They range in size from that of a rabbit to that of an ox. In some species both sexes bear horns of varied shapes and sizes; in others, only the males are horned. Family Bovidae.

anthem Choral composition in Anglican and other English-language church services analogous to the Roman Catholic MOTET in Latin. Developed in the 16th century as a verse anthem with soloists, the anthem was later performed with orchestral accompaniment and by a choir without soloists. Composers of anthems include Henry PURCELL and Ralph VAUGHAN WILLIAMS.

anther In botany, the fertile part of a male sex organ in a flower. The anther produces and distributes pollen, and together with its connecting filament forms a STAMEN.

Anthony, Saint (250–355) Egyptian saint and first Christian monk. He withdrew into complete solitude at the age of 20 to practise ascetic devotion. The monastic ideal, outlined in the *Life of St Anthony* attracted many. By the time of St Anthony's death, Christian monasticism was well established. His feast day is 17 January.

anthracite Form of COAL consisting of more than 90% CARBON, relatively hard, black and with a metallic lustre. It burns with the hot pale-blue flame of complete combustion. It is the final form in the series of fuels: PEAT, lignite, bituminous COAL and black coal.

anthrax Contagious disease, chiefly of livestock, caused by the microbe *Bacillus anthracis*. Human beings can catch anthrax from contact with infected animals or their hides.

anthropoidea Suborder of primates including monkeys, apes and human beings. Anthropoids have flatter, more human-like faces, larger brains and are larger in size than prosimian PRIMATES.

anthropology Scientific study of human development and how different societies are interrelated. It is concerned with the chronological and geographical range of human societies. Public interest in cultural evolution followed the publication of *On the Origin of Species* by Charles DARWIN (1859). **Physical** anthropologists are concerned with the history of human evolution in its biological sense. **Social** anthropologists study living societies in order to learn about cultural and social evolution. **Applied** anthropology is the specific study of a particular community and its collective and individual relationships. *See also* ETHNOGRAPHY; ETHNOLOGY

antibiotic Substance that is capable of stopping the growth of (or destroying) BACTERIA and other microorganisms. Many antibiotics are themselves produced by microorganisms. Antibiotics are GERMICIDES that are safe enough to be eaten or injected into the body. The introduction of antibiotics post-

1945 has revolutionized medical science, making possible the virtual elimination of once widespread and often fatal diseases, including TYPHOID FEVER, PLAGUE and CHOLERA. Important antibiotics are PENICILLIN, the first widely used antibiotic, streptomycin and the tetracyclines. Some bacteria have developed antibiotic resistance. *See also* ANTISEPTIC

antibody PROTEIN synthesized in the BLOOD in response to the entry of "foreign" substances or organisms into the body. Each episode of bacterial or viral infection prompts the production of a specific antibody to fight the disease in question. After the infection has cleared, the antibody remains in the blood to fight off any future invasion.

Antichrist Term loosely referring to the supreme enemy of Christ. It is used in the letters of St JOHN to refer to a force that will appear at the end of time. Martin LUTHER and other leaders of the REFORMATION applied it to the PAPACY.

anticline Arch-shaped fold in rock strata. Unless the formation has been overturned, the oldest rocks are found in the centre with younger rocks symmetrically on each side of it.

Anti-Corn Law League Organization formed in Manchester, England (1839), to agitate for the removal of import duties on grain. It was led by Richard COBDEN and John BRIGHT. By holding mass meetings, distributing pamphlets and contesting elections it helped bring about the repeal of the CORN LAWS in 1846.

anticyclone Area of high atmospheric pressure around which air circulates. The direction of air circulation is clockwise in the Northern hemisphere and anticlockwise in the Southern hemisphere. Anticyclones are often associated with settled weather conditions. In middle latitudes, they bring periods of hot, dry weather in summer and cold, often foggy, weather in winter.

antifreeze Substance dissolved in a liquid to lower its freezing point. Ethylene glycol (ethane diol, HOC_2H_4OH), is used in car radiators.

antigen Any substance or organism that induces the production of an ANTIBODY, part of the body's defence mechanism against disease.

Antigonus I (382–301 BC) General of ALEXANDER THE GREAT. He became governor of Phrygia in 333 BC and, in the struggles over the regency, he defeated challengers to gain control of Mesopotamia, Syria and Asia Minor. At Salamis in 306 BC he defeated his former ally, Ptolemy I, but was himself killed at Ipsus.

Antigua and Barbuda Caribbean islands in the LEEWARD ISLANDS group, part of the Lesser ANTILLES; the capital is St John's (on Antigua). **Antigua** is atypical of the Leeward Islands in that, despite its height – rising to 405m (1,328ft) – it has no rivers or forests; **Barbuda**, by contrast, is a well-wooded low coral atoll. Only 1,400 people live on the game reserve island of Barbuda, where lobster fishing is the main occupation, and none on the rocky island of Redondo. Antigua and Barbuda were linked by Britain after 1860, gained internal self-government in 1967 and independence in 1981. Both islands rely heavily on tourism. Other activities include livestock rearing, mixed market gardening and fishing. Area: 440sq km (170sq mi). Pop. (1994) 65,000.

antihistamine Any one of certain DRUGS that counteracts or prevents the effects of histamine, a substance released by the body in response to injury, or more often as part of an allergic reaction. Histamine can produce symptoms such as sneezing, running nose and burning eyes. *See also* HAY FEVER

Antilles Collective name for the two major island groups in the West Indies archipelago, between the Atlantic Ocean and the Caribbean Sea, stretching in an arc from Puerto Rico to the N coast of Venezuela. The Greater Antilles (larger of the two groups) includes CUBA, HISPANIOLA, JAMAICA, PUERTO RICO and the CAYMAN ISLANDS. The Lesser Antilles comprises mainly the British VIRGIN ISLANDS, the US VIRGIN ISLANDS, the LEEWARD ISLANDS and WINDWARD ISLANDS, plus small islands off the coast of South America.

antimatter Matter made up of antiparticles, identical to ordinary particles in every way except that charge, SPIN and magnetic moment are reversed. When an antiparticle, such as a positron (anti-electron), antiproton or antineutron meets its respective particle, both are annihilated. Since a PHOTON is its own antiparticle the possibility exists that there are stars or galaxies composed entirely of antimatter. *See also* SUBATOMIC PARTICLES

antimony Toxic semimetallic element (symbol Sb) of group V of the PERIODIC TABLE. Stibnite (a sulphide) is its commonest ore. It is used in some alloys, particularly in hardening lead for batteries, and in semiconductors. It has two allotropes. Properties: at.no. 51; r.a.m. 121.75; r.d. 6.68; m.p. 630.5°C (1,166.9°F); b.p. 1,750°C (3,182°F); most common isotope Sb^{121} (57.25%).

Antiochus III (242–187 BC) King of Syria (223–187 BC), son of Seleucus II. After his defeat at Rafa (217 BC) by Ptolemy IV, he invaded Egypt (212–202 BC), seizing land from Ptolemy V. He recaptured Palestine, Asia Minor and the Thracian Cheronese. The Romans overwhelmed him at Thermopylae (191 BC) and at Magnesia (190 BC). The rebuilt SELEUCID empire shrank when he gave up all possessions W of the Taurus. Seleucus IV succeeded him.

antiphon Alternate short verses or phrases (usually of a psalm or canticle) sung by two spatially separated halves of a choir. More generally, antiphon refers to a short piece of plainsong during the recitation of divine office.

antipope Name given to rivals of legitimately elected popes, generally "appointed" by unauthorized religious factions. The most famous were the AVIGNON popes, who rivalled those of ROME during the Great Schism of 1378–1417.

antiseptic Chemicals that destroy or stop the growth of many microorganisms. Antiseptics are weak germicides that can be used on the skin. LISTER pioneered the use of antiseptics in 1867. One commonly used is ALCOHOL. *See also* ANTIBIOTIC

antitoxin ANTIBODY produced by the body in response to a TOXIN. It is specific in action and neutralizes the toxin. Antitoxin sera are used to treat and prevent bacterial diseases such as TETANUS and DIPHTHERIA.

antler Bony outgrowth on the skulls of male DEER (and female reindeer). In temperate-zone species, antlers begin to grow in early summer. They are soft, well supplied with blood and covered with velvety skin. Later, the blood recedes and the dried skin is rubbed off. Antlers then serve as sexual ornaments and weapons until they are shed the following spring. More branches are added each year until maturity is reached.

Antofagasta Seaport and rail centre on the coast of N Chile, the capital of Antofagasta province. Built in 1870 to provide port facilities for the nitrate and copper deposits in the ATACAMA DESERT, it has both ore refining and concentrating plants. The Chuquicamata open-cast copper mine, 220km (135mi) to the NE, is the world's largest. Pop. (1992) 226,749.

Antonello da Messina (1430–79) Sicilian artist. A pioneer of oil painting in Italy, he probably learned the oil technique in Naples, a centre for Dutch artists. His work married Netherlandish taste for detail with Italian clarity. Apart from religious paintings such as *Salvator Mundi* (1465) and *Ecce Homo* (1470), he produced some remarkable male portraits. His knowledge of oil glazes had a great influence on Venetian painters, notably Giovanni BELLINI.

Antony, Mark (82–30 BC) (Marcus Antonius) Roman general and statesman. Antony fought in Julius CAESAR's campaign in Gaul. After Caesar's assassination, Antony inspired the mob to drive the conspirators, BRUTUS and CASSIUS, from Rome. Antony, Octavian (later Emperor AUGUSTUS) and Lepidus formed the Second Triumverate, which divided up the ROMAN EMPIRE. Antony received Asia. He and CLEOPATRA, queen of Egypt, became lovers. In 40 BC Antony married Octavian's sister Octavia, but relations with Octavian continued to deteriorate. Antony continued to live with Cleopatra in Alexandria and became isolated from Rome. In 32 BC the Senate deprived Antony of his posts. Antony was defeated at the Battle of ACTIUM. He and Cleopatra committed suicide.

Antrim County in Northern Ireland, bounded N by the Atlantic Ocean and NE and E by the North Channel. The capital is BELFAST. Other notable centres are Ballymena, Antrim (on the N shore of Lough NEAGH) and Larne. Noted for the GIANT'S CAUSEWAY, Antrim is chiefly an agricultural region; cereals and livestock are most important. Industries: linen and shipbuilding. Area: 3,043sq km (1,175sq mi). Pop. (1991) 665,013.

Antwerp (Flemish *Antwerpen* Fr. *Anvers*) Port city on the River Scheldt, capital of Antwerp province and Belgium's second-largest city. Industries include: oil refining, food processing, tobacco and diamond cutting. Though heavily bombed during World War 2, it retains many attractive old buildings. Pop. (1993 est.) 462,880.

Anubis In Egyptian mythology, a jackal-headed god. He conducted the souls of the dead to the underworld and presided over funerals.

ANZAC (acronym for Australian and New Zealand Army Corps) Volunteer force of 30,000 men which spearheaded the disastrous GALLIPOLI CAMPAIGN in World War 1. Troops landed at Gallipoli on 25 April 1915. Anzac Day (25 April) is a public holiday in Australia and New Zealand. About 8,500 Anzac troops were killed during World War 1.

aorta Principal ARTERY in the body. Carrying oxygenated blood, the aorta leaves the left ventricle of the HEART and descends the length of the trunk, dividing to form the two main arteries that serve the legs. *See also* CIRCULATORY SYSTEM; HEART

Apache Athabascan-speaking tribe of Native North Americans that live in Arizona, New Mexico and Colorado. Their earlier nomadic raiding customs, brought them into military conflict with Mexico and the USA during the 19th century. The total population is now *c.*11,000.

apartheid Policy of racial segregation practised by the South African government from 1948–90. Racial inequality and restricted rights for non-whites was institutionalized when the Afrikaner-dominated National Party came to power in 1948. Officially a framework for "separate development" of races, in practice apartheid confirmed white-minority rule. It was based on segregation in all aspects of life including residence, land ownership and education. Non-whites, around 80% of the population, were also given separate political structures, quasi-autonomous homelands or bantustans. The system was underpinned by extensive repression, and measures such as pass laws which severely restricted the movements of non-whites. Increasingly isolated internationally and beset by economic difficulties and domestic unrest, the government pledged to dismantle the system in 1990. The transition to nonracial democracy was completed with the presidential and general elections of April 1994. *See also* AFRICAN NATIONAL CONGRESS (ANC)

ape Term usually applied to the anthropoid apes (PRIMATES) that are the closest relatives of humans. There are three great apes – CHIMPANZEE, GORILLA and ORANGUTAN – and one lesser, the GIBBON. An ape differs from a MONKEY in being larger, having no visible tail and in possessing a more complex brain. Two monkeys are also called "apes" – the BARBARY APE of N Africa and Gibraltar, and the black ape of Celebes.

Apennines (Appennino) Mountain range extending the length of Italy, a continuation of the Pennine Alps. The "backbone" of Italy, stretching *c.*1,350km (840mi) from the Genoese Riviera to the tip of the country's "toe". The highest point is Mount Corno, at 2,914m (9,560ft).

aperture In photography, a hole which allows light to pass through the lens onto the film. Modern cameras usually have a diaphragm aperture which works like the iris of a human eye to control the diameter of the aperture.

aphasia Group of disorders of language arising from disease of or damage to the brain. In aphasia, a person has problems formulating or comprehending speech and difficulty in reading and writing. *See also* BRAIN DISORDERS

aphid (plant louse) Winged or wingless, soft-bodied insect found worldwide. It transmits virus diseases of plants when sucking plant juices. Females reproduce with or without mating, producing one to several generations annually. Common species are also known as blackfly and greenfly. Length: to 5mm (0.2in). Family Aphididae.

Aphrodite Greek goddess of love, beauty and fruitfulness, identified by the Romans as VENUS. She was the daughter of Zeus and Dione. Her husband was HEPHAESTUS (in Roman mythology, VULCAN). Among her many lovers were ARES, ADONIS (whose death left her brokenhearted) and Anchises, the father of AENEAS. Statues of her include the Venus de Milo (Paris) and Aphrodite of Cnidus (Rome).

Apocrypha Certain books included in the Bible as an appendix to the OLD TESTAMENT in the SEPTUAGINT and in St Jerome's Vulgate translation but not forming part of the Hebrew canon. Nine books are accepted as canonical by the Roman Catholic Church. They are: Tobit, Judith, Wisdom, Ecclesiasticus, Baruch (including the Letter to Jeremiah), 1 and 2 Maccabees, and parts of Esther and Daniel.

Apollinaire, Guillaume (1880–1918) (Wilhelm Apollinaris de Kostrowitzky) French experimental poet, essayist and playwright. One of the most extraordinary artists of early 20th-century Paris, his *Peintres Cubistes* (1913) was the first attempt to define CUBISM. He also experimented with typography and in his poetry collection, *Calligrammes* (1918), he designed the text to represent the subject on the page. His masterpiece was the wholly unpunctuated *Alcools* (1913), in which he relived the wild romances of his youth.

Apollo In Greek mythology, god of the Sun, archery and prophecy; patron of musicians, poets and physicians; founder of cities and giver of laws. He was the son of Zeus and Leto, twin to ARTEMIS. In the Trojan War he sided with Troy, sending a plague against the Greeks.

Apollonius of Perga (*c.*262–190 BC) Greek mathematician and astronomer. He built on the foundations laid by EUCLID. In *Conics*, he showed that an ELLIPSE, a PARABOLA and a HYPERBOLA can be obtained by taking plane sections at different angles through a cone. In astronomy, he described the motion of the planets in terms of epicycles which remained the basis of the system used until the time of COPERNICUS.

Apollo program US space project. Initiated in May 1961 by President Kennedy, it achieved its objective on 20 July 1969, when Neil ARMSTRONG set foot on the Moon. The programme terminated with the successful Apollo-Soyuz link-up in space during July 1975. It placed more than 30 astronauts in space and 12 on the Moon.

Apostle Missionary sent out and empowered by divine authority to preach the gospel and heal the sick. Jesus commissioned his 12 original DISCIPLES to carry out the purpose of God for man's salvation (Mark 3, Matthew 10, Luke 6). The first qualification for being an apostle was to have "seen the Lord". The 12 disciples thus became the first and original Apostles. The term is also applied in the New Testament to St PAUL. In modern usage it is sometimes given to the leader of the first Christian mission to a country. For example, St PATRICK is described as the "Apostle of Ireland".

Apostles' Creed Statement of Christian faith. The last section affirms the tradition of the "holy Catholic Church; the communion of saints; the forgiveness of sins; the resurrection of the body; and the life everlasting". The text evolved gradually, and its present form was fixed by the early 7th century. It is used widely in private and public worship in all the major Churches in the West. *See also* NICENE CREED

Appalachians Mountain system stretching 2,570km (1,600mi) from E Canada to Alabama, USA.

appeasement Policy in which one government grants unilateral concessions to another to forestall a political, economic or military threat. The 1938 MUNICH AGREEMENT is considered a classic example of appeasement.

appendicitis Inflammation of the APPENDIX caused by obstruction and infection. Symptoms include severe pain in the central abdomen, nausea and vomiting. Acute appendicitis is generally treated by surgery. A ruptured appendix can cause peritonitis and even death.

appendix In some mammals, finger-shaped organ, *c.*10cm (4in) long, located near the junction of the small and large intestines, usually in the lower right part of the abdomen. It has no known function in humans but can become inflamed or infected (APPENDICITIS).

apple Common name for the most widely cultivated fruit tree of temperate climates. Developed from a tree native to Europe and SW Asia, apple trees are propagated by budding or grafting. From the flowers, which require cross-pollination to produce a desirable fruit, the fleshy fruit grows in a variety of sizes, shapes and acidities; it is generally roundish, 5–10cm (2–4in) in diameter, and a shade of yellow, green or red. A mature tree may yield up to 1cu m (30 bushels) of fruit in a single

growing season. Europe produces 50–60% of the world's annual crop, and the USA 16–20%. The alcoholic drink CIDER is made from fermented apple juice. Family Rosaceae; genus *Malus*.

apricot Tree cultivated throughout temperate regions, believed to have originated in China. The large, spreading tree with dark green leaves and white blossoms bears yellow or yellowish-orange edible fruit, with a large stone. Family Rosaceae; species *Prunus armeniaca*.

Aqaba, Gulf of NE arm of the Red Sea between the Sinai Peninsula and Saudi Arabia. AQABA and ELAT lie at the N end of the Gulf. The gulf has played an important role in ARAB-ISRAELI WARS. It was blockaded by the Arabs 1949–56, and again in 1967, when Israel held strategic points along the Strait of Tiran to guarantee open passage for ships. The Gulf has excellent coral and rich marine life.

Aqmola (Akmola, formerly Akmolinsk) Capital-designate of Kazakstan. Aqmola lies on Ishim River in the steppes of N central Kazakstan. Under Soviet rule, Aqmola functioned as capital of the Virgin Lands. From 1961–93 it was known as Tselinograd. Pop. (1990) 281,400.

aqualung Alternative name for self-contained underwater breathing apparatus. *See* SCUBA DIVING

aquamarine *See* BERYL

Aquarius (water-bearer) Constellation of the zodiac, represented by a figure pouring water from a jar.

aquatint Method of engraving on metal plates. The process was invented in the mid-18th century to imitate the effect of brush drawing or watercolour. By sprinkling a plate with fine grains of acid-resistant resin, fusing the resin to the metal (modern enamel sprays avoid this step) and letting acid bite around and through some of the grains, printmakers can achieve extremely varied effects depending on the thickness of the resin and the immersion time. GOYA and PICASSO used aquatint.

aqueduct Man-made channel for conducting water from its source to its distribution point. While the ancient Romans were not the first to build these conduits, their aqueducts are the most famous because of their graceful architectural structures. One of their most extensive water systems, which served Rome itself, consisted of 11 aqueducts and took 500 years to complete. California has the world's largest man-made conduit system: it carries water over a distance of more than 800km (500mi).

aquifer Rock, often sandstone or limestone, which is capable of both storing and transmitting water owing to its porosity and permeability. Much of the world's human population depends on aquifers for its water supply. They may be directly exploited by sinking wells.

Aquinas, Saint Thomas (1225–74) Italian theologian and philosopher. He was the greatest figure of 13th-century SCHOLASTICISM, and founded one of the main traditions of medieval theology. Aquinas argued that faith and reason did not conflict since though separate, both rested on the one absolute truth of the existence of God. Canonized in 1323, his feast day is 7 March.

Aquino, Cory (Maria Corazon) (1933–) Philippine stateswoman, president (1986–92), b. Maria Corazon. In 1954 she married Benigno Aquino (1932–83), an outspoken opponent of the MARCOS regime. Benigno's assassination by Marcos' agents propelled Cory into a political career. Cory claimed to have defeated Marcos in the 1986 presidential election and accused the government of vote-rigging. A rapid, bloodless "people's revolution" forced Marcos into exile. Aquino's administration was beset by economic obstacles, and she survived a coup attempt with the help of the USA (1989). She declined to run for re-election in 1992.

Arab Peoples of many nationalities, found predominantly in the Middle East and North Africa, who share a common heritage in the religion of Islam and their language (ARABIC). The patriarchal family is the basic social unit in a strongly traditional culture that has been little affected by external influences. Wealth from oil has brought rapid modernization in some Arab countries, but a great deal of economic inequality exists.

Arabia Peninsular region of SW Asia bordered by the Persian Gulf (E), the Arabian Sea (S), the Syrian Desert (N) and the Red Sea (W). The original homeland of the ARABS, it is the world's largest peninsula. It is mostly desert, including the vast Rub al Khali ("Empty Quarter") in the S and the An Nafud in the N. The area was unified by the Muslims in the 7th century, and dominated by Ottoman Turks after 1517. Hussein ibn Ali led a successful revolt against the Turks and founded an independent state in 1916. He was subsequently defeated by the SAUD family, who founded Saudi Arabia in 1925. After World War 2 independent Arab states emerged, many of them exploiting the peninsula's vast reserves of oil. Area: *c.*2,600,000sq km (1,000,000sq mi).

Arabic Language originating in the Arabian Peninsula and now spoken in a variety of dialects throughout North Africa and the Middle East. It is a Semitic language, belonging to a major subfamily of Afro-Asiatic languages. Classical Arabic is the language of the KORAN. It spread during Islamic expansion in the 7th and 8th centuries. It is now spoken by more than 100 million people.

Arab-Israeli Wars (1948–49, 1956, 1967, 1973–74) Conflicts between Israel and the Arab states. After Israeli independence (14 May 1948), troops from Egypt, Iraq, Lebanon, Syria and Transjordan (modern Jordan) invaded the country. Initial Arab gains were halted and armistices arranged at Rhodes (January–July 1949). UN security forces upheld the truce until October 1956, when Israeli forces under Moshe DAYAN attacked the SINAI PENINSULA, with support from France and Britain, alarmed at Egypt's nationalization of the SUEZ CANAL. International opinion forced a cease-fire in November. In 1967 guerrilla raids led to Israeli mobilization, and in the ensuing SIX DAY WAR

Israel captured Sinai, the GOLAN HEIGHTS (on the Syrian border) and the Old City of JERUSALEM. In the October War of 1973 (after intermittent hostilities) Egypt and Syria invaded on the Jewish holiday of YOM KIPPUR (6 October); Israel pushed back their advance after severe losses. Fighting lasted 18 days. Subsequent disengagement agreements were supervised by the UN. In 1979 Israel signed a peace treaty with Egypt, but relations with other Arab states remained hostile. Israeli forces invaded Lebanon in 1982 in an effort to destroy bases of the PALESTINE LIBERATION ORGANIZATION (PLO). They were withdrawn (1984) after widespread international criticism. After 1988 the PLO renounced terrorism and gained concessions, including limited autonomy in parts of the occupied territories.

Arab League Organization formed in 1945 to give a collective political voice to the Arab nations. Its members include Syria, Lebanon, Iraq, Jordan, Sudan, Algeria, Kuwait, Saudi Arabia, Libya, Morocco, Tunisia, the Yemen, Qatar and the United Arab Emirates. It has often been divided, notably by the Egyptian peace treaty with Israel (1979) and over the GULF WAR (1991), and has been politically less effective than its founders hoped. In 1997 it met to discuss the apparent breakdown of the Israeli-Palestinian Accord.

arachnid Arthropod of the class Arachnida, which includes the SPIDER, TICK, MITE, SCORPION and HARVESTMAN. Arachnids have four pairs of jointed legs, two distinct body segments (cephalothorax and abdomen), and chelicerate jaws (consisting of clawed pincers). They lack antennae and wings.

Arafat, Yasir (1929–) Palestinian statesman, first president of Palestine (1994–), leader of the PALESTINE LIBERATION ORGANIZATION (PLO). The longtime leader of the anti-Israel guerrilla organization, al-Fatah, he sought the abolition of Israel and the creation of a secular Palestinian state. After the INTIFADA in the occupied territories (GAZA and the WEST BANK), he persuaded the PLO to renounce terrorism and recognize Israel as a legitimate state. After the ISRAELI-PALESTINIAN ACCORD, which acknowledged the PLO as the representative of the Palestinian people, Arafat headed the Palestinian National Authority, which, from 1994, began to exercise control of areas of the occupied territories relinquished by the Israelis. NETANYAHU's election (1996) threatened to halt the peace process, and Arafat has been a leading figure in negotiations to keep the process alive.

Aragón Autonomous region in NE Spain, comprising the provinces of Huesca, Teruel and Zaragoza. In 1479 the Kingdom of Aragón became part of Spain, but retained its own government and military forces until the early 18th century. It produces grapes, wheat and sugar beet. Industries: textiles, chemicals, iron ore, marble, limestone. Area: 47,670sq km (18,500sq mi). Pop. (1991) 1,188,817.

Aral Sea (Aralskoye More) Inland sea in central Asia, SW Kazakstan and NW Uzbekistan. Once the world's fourth largest inland body of water, it has no outlet, contains many small islands and is fed by the rivers Syrdarya in the NE and Amudarya (Oxus) in the S. It is generally shallow and only slightly saline. The diversion of the rivers for irrigation by the Soviet government led to a disastrous drop in the water level and the area of the lake shrunk by more than a third in area between 1960–95. Many fishing communities were left literally stranded. Area: 68,681sq km (26,518sq mi).

Aramaic Ancient Semitic language spoken in Palestine and other parts of the Middle East at the time of Christ. During the late 2nd millennium BC, it became the common spoken and written language of the Middle East under the Persian empire until replaced by ARABIC.

Ararat, Mount (Ağri Daği) Two extinct volcanic peaks in the E extremity of Turkey. The highest peaks in Turkey, they are just N of where, biblically, Noah's Ark is said to have come to rest (Genesis 8). There are two peaks: Great Ararat, 5,165m (16,945ft), (last eruption 1840), and Little Ararat, 3,925m (12,877ft).

Arawak Largest and most widely spread Native South American language family, at one time spoken from the Caribbean to the GRAN CHACO. Some 40 Arawak tribes remain in Brazil today.

arbitration Resolution of a dispute by an unbiased referee (arbiter) chosen by the parties in conflict. In some countries the arbiter's ruling or decision may be enforced by government. While arbitration may be utilized by individuals in conflict, the procedure is most commonly applied in commercial and industrial disputes and overseen by independent bodies such as the Advisory, Conciliation and Arbitration Service (ACAS) in the UK.

arbor vitae Common name for five species of trees or shrubs of the genus *Thuja*, resinous, evergreen conifers of the cypress family native to North America and E Asia. They have thin outer bark, fibrous inner bark, and characteristically flattened branches. Family Cupressaceae.

Arc de Triomphe TRIUMPHAL ARCH in the Place Charles de Gaulle, Paris. The Arc de Triomphe is a generalized copy of the triumphal arches erected in ancient Rome. Napoleon I commissioned J.F. Chalgrin to design this version, completed in 1836.

arch Upward-pointing or curving arrangement of masonry blocks or other load-bearing materials, also used in architectural decoration. The ancient Romans invented traditional masonry arches but later cultures extended their repertoire to include many different and sometimes quite elaborate shapes. The basic structure of a masonry arch consists of wedge-shaped blocks ("voussoirs") placed on top of each other and a central keystone which holds them together at the top. The form of an arch helps to date a building. *See also* VAULT

Archaean Sub-division of pre-Cambrian geological time. It ended about 2,500 million years ago.

archaebacteria Sub-kingdom of the kingdom

PROKARYOTAE, which on the basis of both RNA and DNA composition and biochemistry differ significantly from other BACTERIA. They are thought to resemble ancient bacteria that arose in extreme environments such as sulphur-rich deep sea vents. Archaebacteria have unique protein-like cell walls and cell membrane chemistry, and distinctive RIBOSOMES. They include methane-producing bacteria, which use simple organic compounds such as methanol and acetate as food, combining them with carbon dioxide and hydrogen gas from the air, and releasing methane as a by-product. The bacteria of hot springs and saline areas have a variety of ways of obtaining food and energy, including the use of minerals instead of organic compounds. Some taxonomists consider archaebacteria to be so different from other organisms that they constitute a higher grouping called a DOMAIN. *See also* TAXONOMY

archaeology Scientific study of former human life and activities through material remains such as artefacts and buildings. An archaeologist excavates and retrieves remains from the ground or seabed; recording and interpreting the circumstances in which objects were found, such as their level in the soil and association with other objects. This information can then be used to build a picture of the culture that produced the objects.

archaeopteryx First known bird. About the size of a crow and fully feathered, its fossilized skeleton is more like that of a reptile than a modern bird, and its beak had pronounced jaws with teeth. It was capable probably only of weak, flapping flight.

Archangel (Archangel'sk) City and major port on the North Dvina delta, NW Russia. The city was opened to European trade in c.1600 and prospered as Russia's only port until 1703. In the winter, icebreakers keep the large harbour clear, but the port remains ice-free for about six months, a crucial factor for commerce in N European Russia. Timber and wood products are the main exports, shipbuilding and paper the main industries. Pop. (1994) 407,000.

archery Target sport that makes use of a bow and arrow or a crossbow and bolt. Commonly, archers use a longbow to shoot arrows from specified distances at a target that consists of concentric scoring rings of five colours. The three other divisions of archery are field, flight and crossbow. Since 1931 the sport's world authority has been the Fédération Internationale de Tir à l'Arc (FITA), based in Milan, Italy.

Archimedes (287–212 BC) Greek mathematician and engineer. He developed a method for expressing large numbers and made outstanding discoveries about the determination of areas and volumes, which led to a new accurate method of measuring π (pi). In his work *On Floating Bodies* he stated ARCHIMEDES' PRINCIPLE. He also invented the ARCHIMEDES' SCREW.

Archimedes' principle ARCHIMEDES observed that a body immersed in a FLUID is pushed up by a force equal to the weight of the displaced fluid.

Archimedes' screw Machine used for raising water, thought to have been invented by Archimedes in the 3rd century BC. The most common form of the machine is a cylindrical pipe enclosing a helix, inclined at a 45° angle to the horizontal with its lower end in the water. When the machine rotates, water rises through the pipe.

architecture Art and science of designing permanent buildings for human use. Architecture can express aesthetic ideas from the most restrained UTILITARIANISM to ornate GOTHIC decoration. Apart from the stylistic and historical periods (*see* individual articles), architecture falls under such broad categories as civic, commercial, religious, recreational and domestic. Key figures in the development of western architectural theory include VITRUVIUS, who believed that architecture was merely a form of applied mathematics, and ALBERTI whose pioneering treatise *De re Aedificatoria* (1485) introduced the idea that architecture was an art form. After the 18th century, European architects regarded "building" as a cheap substitute for their profession and something that engineers carried out. Architects began to swing back in the other direction with the arrival of the ARTS AND CRAFTS MOVEMENT, and the introduction of efficient, mass-produced materials. The 20th-century modernists, such as Walter GROPIUS, believed that the form of a building should follow its function. The relationship between the two extremes is continually changing.

arc Portion of a curve. For a circle, the length (s) of an arc is found either by $2 \times r \times \pi \times \theta / 360$ or the product of the radius (r) and the angle (θ), measured in RADIANS, that it subtends at the centre: that is, $s = r\theta$.

Arctic Vast region of icy seas and cold lands around the NORTH POLE, often defined as extending from the Pole to the ARCTIC CIRCLE. In areas N of latitude 66° 30'N, the sun does not set during the height of summer, nor rise during the depths of winter. Many place the S limit of the Arctic proper at the northern boundary of forest growth, others make the limit the summer isotherm of 18°C (50°F). The more southerly areas are frequently referred to as the subarctic. At the centre of the Arctic is the ARCTIC OCEAN, with its many seas and inlets. In the region around the North Pole, the waters of the Arctic are permanently covered with sheet ice or a floating mass of ice debris called the ice pack, but some parts of the ocean are frozen only in winter. When the ice starts to melt in the spring it disintegrates into floes and drifting pack ice. Icebergs have their origins in freshwater glaciers flowing into the ocean from the surrounding lands. **Lands and climate** Bordering the Arctic Ocean are the most northerly lands of Asia, Europe and North America. By far the greater part of the huge frozen island of GREENLAND lies N of the Arctic Circle. Five-sixths of Greenland's surface is always hidden by a thick ice-cap. Arctic lands generally have a summer free from ice and snow. Most of the Arctic tundra is flat and marshy in summer but the subsoil is PERMAFROST. For most of the year Arctic temperatures are below freezing point. In spring the sun appears, and some Arctic lands have sunshine every day from March or April to September. **People** Despite the severity of the climate and the restricted food resources, many peoples live in the Arctic. The most scattered are the *c*.60,000 ESKIMOS spread across polar North America, Greenland, and NE Siberia. Several culturally separate groups of people live in N Siberia. In the European part of Russia there are the numerous Zyryans, and in LAPPLAND the LAPPS. Most of these peoples follow ancient, traditional patterns of life, but the discovery of great mineral wealth, especially in Alaska and Russia, has brought huge change to their homelands. **History** The region was first explored by Norsemen as early as the 9th century. The search for the NORTHWEST PASSAGE gave impetus to further explorations in the 16th and 17th centuries, though a route was not found until the early 1900s. The North Pole was first reached in 1909 by the American Robert Peary, and the first crossing of the Arctic Ocean under the polar ice-cap was made in 1958–59.

Arctic Circle Northernmost of the Earth's parallels, 66.5° N of the equator. At this latitude the sun neither sets on the day of summer SOLSTICE (June 21) nor rises on the day of winter solstice (December 22). *See also* ANTARCTIC CIRCLE

Arctic Ocean Ocean N of the Arctic Circle, between North America and Eurasia. Almost totally landlocked and the Earth's smallest ocean, it is bordered by Greenland, Canada, Alaska, Russia, and Norway. Connected to the Pacific Ocean by the Bering Strait, and to the Atlantic Ocean by the Davis Strait and Greenland Sea, it includes the Barents, Beaufort, Chukchi, Greenland and Norwegian seas. There is animal life (plankton) in all Arctic water and polar bears, seals, and gulls up to about 88° N. Area: 13,986,000sq km (5,400,000sq mi).

Arctic tern Sea bird whose migrations are the longest of any bird – from summer breeding areas in the far N to wintering areas in Antarctica, a round trip of *c*.35,500km (22,000mi). It has grey, black and white feathers and a reddish bill and feet. It nests in colonies and lays one to four eggs in a sandy scrape nest. Length: 38cm (15in). Species *Sterna paradisaea*.

Ardennes (Forest of Ardennes) Sparsely populated wooded plateau in SE Belgium, N Luxembourg and the Ardennes département of N France. The capital is Charleville-Mézières. It was the scene of heavy fighting in both world wars; notably in the Battle of the BULGE. In the well-preserved forest regions wild game is abundant and cleared areas support arable and dairy farming.

area Two-dimensional measurement of a plane figure or body (such as this page) given in square units, such as cm^2 or m^2. The area of a rectangle of sides a and b is ab; the areas of triangles and other polygons can be determined using TRIGONOMETRY.

Areas of curved figures and surfaces can be determined by integral CALCULUS.

Ares In Greek mythology, the god of war, identified with the Roman god MARS. He was the son of Zeus and HERA and lover of APHRODITE. In the Trojan War he sided with the Trojans.

Argentina Second-largest country in South America and the eighth-largest in the world; the capital is BUENOS AIRES. **Land and climate** The high ANDES Mountains in the w contain ACONCAGUA, the highest peak outside Asia. In s Argentina, the Andes overlook PATAGONIA, a plateau region. In east-central Argentina lies a fertile plain called the Pampas; the NE also contains lowland plains. The GRAN CHACO lies w of the River PARANÁ, while Mesopotamia is another fertile plain between the Paraná and the Uruguay rivers. Argentina's climates range from sub-tropical in the N to temperate in the s, with extremely harsh conditions in the high Andes. The rainfall is abundant in the NE, but less to the w and s. Though dry, Patagonia is crossed by rivers rising in the Andes. The Gran Chaco is a forested region, known for quebracho trees. Mesopotamia and the Pampas are grassy regions, and large areas are farmed. Patagonia is too dry for crops; the main activity on the grassy tablelands is sheep raising. **Economy** Argentina is an upper-middle income developing country. It has large areas of fertile farmland and its main products are beef, maize and wheat. Wool, citrus fruits, cotton, grapes, sorghum, soya beans, sugar cane and tea are also produced. Almost 90% of the people live in cities and towns, where many factories process farm products. Other industries include the manufacture of cars, electrical equipment and textiles. The main exports remain agricultural: meat, wheat, maize, vegetable oils, hides and skins, and wool. **History and politics** Spanish explorers reached the coast in 1516, and settlers followed in search of silver and gold. Spanish rule continued until revolutionaries in Buenos Aires, led by General Belgrano, overthrew the viceroy in 1810. By 1816 liberation was complete and Argentina declared independence. A long civil war ensued between centralizers and federalists. Following General Juan Manuel de Rosas' dictatorship (1835–52), Argentina adopted a federal constitution (1853). The presidency of General Julio Roca (1880–86, 1898–1904) saw the triumph of federalism and the development of Argentina's trading economy. For much of World War 2 Argentina was a pro-Axis "neutral" power. In 1944 Ramón Castillo was overthrown by a military coup led by Juan PERÓN, and Argentina switched to the Allies. With the aid of his wife, Eva, Perón established a popular dictatorship. In 1955 Perón was overthrown by a military coup and Perónism was suppressed. Political instability dominated the 1960s, with the military seeking to dampen Perónist support. In 1973 an ailing Perón returned from exile to head a civilian government. He was succeeded (1974) by his third wife, Isabel Martinez Perón, who was in turn deposed by a military coup (1976). Military rule (1976–83) was characterized by the so-called "Dirty War". Torture, "disappearances" and wrongful imprisonment were commonplace. In 1982 Argentina invaded the FALKLAND ISLANDS, precipitating the FALKLANDS WAR. Britain quickly recaptured the islands, and in 1983 the junta was forced to hold elections. Civilian government was restored, but rampant inflation and high unemployment persisted. In 1989 the Perónist candidate Carlos MENEM was elected president. He was re-elected in 1995, but in 1997 parliamentary elections the Perónists lost their majority in the lower house. Menem will have to negotiate with the opposition for the remainder of his presidential term.

argon Monatomic (single-atom), colourless and odourless gaseous element (symbol Ar), the most abundant NOBLE GAS. Argon was discovered in 1894 in air by the British chemists Lord RAYLEIGH and Sir William RAMSAY. It makes up 0.93% of the atmosphere by volume. Obtained commercially by the fractionation of liquid air, it is used in electric light bulbs, fluorescent tubes, argon lasers, arc welding and semiconductor production. The element has no known true compounds. Properties: at.no. 18; r.a.m. 39.948; r.d. 1.78; m.p. $-189.4°C$ ($-308.9°F$); b.p. $-185.9\ °C$ ($-302.6°F$).

Argonauts In Greek legend, 50 heroes, including HERACLES, ORPHEUS, and CASTOR AND POLLUX, who sailed the ship *Argo* to Colchis, a kingdom at the E end of the Black Sea, in search of the GOLDEN FLEECE. Their leader was JASON, husband of MEDEA. Many adventures and tragedies relate to their wanderings.

aria Solo song with instrumental accompaniment, or a lyrical instrumental piece. An important element of operas, cantatas and oratorios, the aria form originated in the 17th century.

Ariadne In Greek mythology, Cretan princess (daughter of MINOS) who fell in love with THESEUS but was abandoned by him after saving him from the MINOTAUR.

Arianism Theological school based on the teachings of Arius (c.AD 250–336), considered heretical by orthodox Christianity. Arius taught that Christ was a created being, and that the Son, though divine, was neither equal nor co-eternal with the

---

ARGENTINA

AREA: 2,766,890sq km (1,068,296sq mi)
POPULATION: 33,101,000
CAPITAL (POPULATION): Buenos Aires (11,662,050)
GOVERNMENT: Federal republic
ETHNIC GROUPS: European 85%, Mestizo, Native American
LANGUAGES: Spanish (official)
RELIGIONS: Christianity (Roman Catholic 92%)
CURRENCY: Peso = 100 centavos

Father. Arianism was condemned by the first Council of NICAEA (325).

Aries (Ram) First constellation of the zodiac. In mythology, it represents the lamb with the golden fleece.

Aristarchus of Samos (310–230 BC) Greek mathematician and astronomer. He tried to calculate the distances of the Sun and Moon from Earth, as well as their sizes. Although his method was sound, the results were inaccurate. He was the first to propose that the Sun is the centre of the Universe (heliocentric theory); the idea was not taken up because it did not seem to make the calculation of planetary positions any easier.

Aristophanes (448–380 BC) Greek writer of comedies. Of his 40 or so plays, only 11 survive, the only extant comedies of the period. All follow the same basic plan: caricatures of contemporary Athenians become involved in absurd situations. A conservative, Aristophanes parodied EURIPIDES' innovations in drama, and satirized the philosophical radicalism of SOCRATES and Athens' expansionist policies. The importance of the chorus in his early works is reflected in titles, such as *The Frogs* (405), *The Birds* (414) and *The Wasps* (422). Other plays include *Lysistrata* (411) and *The Clouds* (423).

Aristotle (384–322 BC) Greek philosopher and scientist, founder of the science of LOGIC, and alongside PLATO the greatest intellectual of ancient Greece. In 367 BC Aristotle entered Plato's Academy in Athens and stayed for the next 20 years. After Plato's death, he travelled, founding academies at Asus and Myrilene, and tutored the young ALEXANDER THE GREAT. From 335–323 BC he lived in Athens, where he founded the Lyceum. In 323 BC he retired to Chalcis on the island of Euboea, where he died. In direct opposition to Plato's IDEALISM, Aristotle's philosophy is based on the principle that all knowledge and theorizing must proceed directly from observation. He covered nearly every branch of study, from statecraft to astronomy. Among his works are the *Organon,* in which he defines logic; *Politics,* on the conduct of the state; *Poetics,* in which he analyses poetry and drama; and *Nicomachean Ethics,* a description of the virtuous life. His work served as the basis for medieval SCHOLASTICISM.

arithmetic Calculations and reckoning using numbers and such operations as addition, subtraction, multiplication and division. The study of arithmetic traditionally involved learning procedures for operations such as long division and extraction of square roots. The procedures of arithmetic were put on a formal axiomatic basis by Giuseppe Peano in the late 19th century. Using certain postulates, including that there is a unique natural number, 1, it is possible to give formal definition of the set of natural numbers and the arithmetical operations. Thus, addition is interpretable in terms of combining sets: in $2 + 7 = 9$, 9 is the cardinal number of a set produced by combining sets of 2 and 7. Multiplication can be thought of as repeated additions: subtraction

and division are the inverse operations of addition and multiplication.

arithmetic progression Sequence of numbers in which each term is produced by adding a constant term (the common difference d) to the preceding one. It has the form $a, a + d, a + 2d$, and so on. An example is the sequence 1, 3, 5, ... The sum of such a progression, $a + (a + d) + (a + 2d) +$ ... is an arithmetic series. For n terms, it has a value $\frac{1}{2}n\,[2a + 0.5(n-1)d]$.

Arizona State in SW USA, bordering on Mexico. The capital is PHOENIX; other cities include Tucson and Mesa. The Colorado Plateau occupies the N part of the state; it is cut by many steep canyons, notably the GRAND CANYON, through which the COLORADO RIVER flows. Arizona's mineral resources, grazing and farmland have long been mainstays of the economy. Area: 295,025sq km (113,909sq mi). Pop. (1992) 3,832,368.

ark According to Genesis 6, the floating house NOAH was ordered to build and live in with his family and one pair of each living creature during the FLOOD. As the flood waters receded, it came to rest on a mountain top, believed to be Mount ARARAT.

Arkansas State in S central USA, bounded on the E by the Mississippi River. The capital (and only large city) is LITTLE ROCK. In the E and S the land is low, providing farmland for cotton, rice and soya beans. The principal waterway is the Arkansas River, which (like all Arkansas' rivers) drains into the Mississippi. The NW of the state, including part of the Ozarks, is higher land. Forests are extensive. Industries: bauxite processing, timber, chemicals. Area: 137,539sq km (53,104sq mi). Pop. (1992) 2,394,253.

Ark of the Covenant In Jewish tradition, a gold-covered chest of acacia that contained the stone tablets on which the TEN COMMANDMENTS were inscribed. It rested in the Holy of Holies within the tabernacle. Only the high priest could look upon the Ark and no one could touch it. In Palestine, the Israelites set up a permanent resting place for the ark in Shiloh. In the 10th century BC, the Ark was moved to the temple built by King SOLOMON in Jerusalem. After the destruction of Solomon's temple in 587 BC, there is no further record of the Ark's location. In today's synagogues, the Ark of the Covenant is a closet or recess in which the sacred scrolls of the congregation are kept.

Arkwright, Sir Richard (1732–92) British inventor and industrialist. He introduced powered machinery to the textile industry with his water-driven frame for spinning; he started work on the machine in 1764 and patented his invention in 1769. He opened textile factories in Nottingham.

Armada, Spanish (1588) Fleet launched by the Catholic PHILIP II of Spain against England to overthrow the Protestant ELIZABETH I. Though a blow to Spanish prestige, the defeat of the Armada had little real effect on the balance of naval power.

armadillo Nocturnal burrowing mammal found

from Texas to Argentina, noted for the armour of bony plates that protect its back and sides. When attacked, some species roll into a defensive ball. It eats insects, carrion and plants. Length: 130–150cm (50–59in). Family Dasypodidae.

Armageddon Place referred to in Revelation 16, where the final battle between the demonic kings of the Earth and the forces of God will be fought at the end of the world. The name is derived from the Hebrew *har megiddo* ("hill of MEGIDDO").

Armagh City and county in SE Northern Ireland, between Lough Neagh and the border with the Republic. The town became an ecclesiastical centre in the 5th century (founded, in legend, by St Patrick) and is now the seat of Roman Catholic and Protestant archbishops. It was settled by Protestants in the 16th century. The county is low-lying in the N and hilly in the S. Much of the land is used for farming and the town is a market centre for agricultural produce. Lurgan and Portadown are centres for textiles and various light industries. Area: 676sq km (261sq mi). Pop. (county, 1991) 67,128; (town, 1991) 14, 625.

Armenia Republic in the S Caucasus; the capital is YEREVAN. **Land and climate** Armenia is a mountainous republic, the highest peak is Mount Aragats, 4,090m (13,420ft). Armenia has many fast-flowing rivers, which have cut deep gorges in the plateau. The largest lake is Lake Sevan, containing 90% of all Armenia's standing water. The major river is the Araks. Vegetation ranges from semi-desert to grassy steppe, forest, mountain pastures and treeless tundra at the highest levels. **Economy** Armenia is a lower-middle income economy. It has been badly hit by the conflict with Azerbaijan in the early 1990s and is in a state of transition. Since 1991, the government has embarked on free-market reforms, selling farmland and state-owned businesses. Armenia is highly industrialized, and production is dominated by mining and chemicals. Agriculture (centred around the Araks River) is the second-largest sector, with cotton, tobacco, fruit and rice the main products. Despite significant increases in production, Armenia is still dependent on food imports. **History and politics** Armenia was an advanced ancient kingdom, and in AD 303 became the first

country to adopt Christianity as its state religion. From 886–1046 Armenia was an independent kingdom. From the 11th–15th centuries the Mongols were the greatest power in the region. By the 16th century Armenia was controlled by the Ottoman empire. Despite religious discrimination, the Armenians generally prospered under their rule. Eastern Armenia was the battleground between the rival Ottoman and Persian empires. In 1828 Russia acquired Persian Armenia, and (with promises of religious toleration) many Armenians moved into the Russian-controlled area. In Turkish Armenia, nationalist movements were encouraged by British promises of protection. The Turkish response was uncompromising and it is estimated that 200,000 Armenians were killed in 1896 alone. In the Russian sector, a process of Russification was enforced. During World War 1, Armenia was the battleground for the Turkish and Russian armies; over 600,000 Armenians were killed by Turkish troops, and 1.75 million were deported to Syria and Palestine. In 1918 Russian Armenia became the Armenian Autonomous Republic, the W part remained part of Turkey and the NW part of Iran. In 1922 Armenia, Azerbaijan and Georgia were federated to form the Transcaucasian Soviet Socialist Republic (one of the four original republics in the Soviet Union). In 1936 Armenia became a separate republic. Earthquakes in 1984 and 1988 destroyed many cities and killed over 80,000 people. In 1988 war broke out between Armenia and Azerbaijan over NAGORNO-KARABAKH (an Armenian enclave in Azerbaijan). In 1990 the Armenian parliament voted to break from the Soviet Union, and in 1991 joined the Commonwealth of Independent States (CIS). In 1992 Armenia invaded Azerbaijan and occupied Nagorno-Karabakh. In 1994, an uneasy ceasefire left Armenia in control of *c.*20% of Azerbaijan.

Arminius, Jacobus (1560–1609) Dutch theologian whose system of beliefs, especially concerning salvation, became widespread and was later known as Arminianism. He rejected the notion of PREDESTINATION developed by John CALVIN, in favour of a more liberal concept of conditional election and universal redemption. Arminius believed that God will elect to everlasting life those who are prepared to respond in faith to the offer of divine salvation. Arminianism, though at first bitterly rejected, finally achieved official recognition in the Netherlands in 1795. It was a major influence on METHODISM.

Armistice Day Day of remembrance for the dead of the two world wars, held on 11 November, the day World War 1 ended in 1918.

arms control Activity undertaken by powerful nations to prevent mutual destruction in warfare, especially nuclear weapons. The nations attempt to maintain a balance of power by regulating each other's stockpile of weapons. *See also* DISARMAMENT; STRATEGIC ARMS LIMITATION TALKS (SALT)

ARMENIA
AREA: 29,800sq km (11,506sq mi)
POPULATION: 3,667,000
CAPITAL (POPULATION): Yerevan (1,254,000)
GOVERNMENT: Multiparty republic
ETHNIC GROUPS: Armenian 93%, Azerbaijani 3%, Russian, Kurd
LANGUAGES: Armenian (official)
RELIGIONS: Christianity (mainly Armenian Apostolic)
CURRENCY: Dram = 100 couma

arms race Rivalry between states or blocs of states to achieve supremacy in military strength. The first modern instance was the race between Germany and Britain to build up their navies before World War 1. The term refers principally to the race in nuclear weapons between the Soviet Union and the USA after World War 2, during the COLD WAR. Examples of arms races at regional level are that of Israel and the Arab states in the Middle East, which started in the 1950s, and of Iran and Iraq since the 1980s.

Armstrong, (Daniel) Louis (1900–71) US jazz trumpeter, singer and bandleader. Armstrong was the greatest early jazz virtuoso and one of the most distinctive sounds in 20th-century music. In the 1930s, he became a bandleader, and gained popular success with his deep, bluesy voice on tunes like *Mack the Knife*. He also appeared in films such as *Pennies from Heaven* (1936), *New Orleans* (1947) and *High Society* (1956).

Armstrong, Neil Alden (1930–) US astronaut. He was chosen as a NASA astronaut in 1962 and was the command pilot for the Gemini 8 orbital flight in 1966. On 20th July 1969 he became the first man to walk on the Moon.

army Organized group of soldiers trained to fight on land, usually rigidly hierarchical in structure. The first evidence of an army comes from Sumer in the 3rd millennium BC. The use of cavalry was a Hittite development and the Assyrians added archers and developed siege machines. In the Middle Ages armies used improved armour and weapons. The short-term feudal levy by which these armies were raised proved inflexible, and this led to the use of mercenaries. Heavy cavalry was replaced by a combination of infantry and archery. The end of the Hundred Years War saw the inception of royal standing armies and an end to the chaos caused by mercenary armies. Muskets and bayonets replaced the combinations of longbow, pike and infantry, and ARTILLERY was much improved. In the French Revolutionary Wars a citizen army was raised by CONSCRIPTION and contained various specialist groups. Other European armies followed suit and the age of the mass national army began. The invention of the MACHINE GUN brought about the deadlocked trench warfare of World War 1, which was broken by the TANK. World War 2 saw highly mechanized and mobile armies whose logistics of supply and support demanded an integration of land, sea and air forces. Since World War 2 nuclear weapons have been deployed both tactically and strategically, and again the nature of weaponry has determined an army's structure.

Army, British Ground service of the UK armed forces. In 1994, Regular Army personnel numbered *c.* 160,000, including *c.*6,000 women and *c.* 10,000 personnel overseas. Since 1945 it has formed part of NORTH ATLANTIC TREATY ORGANIZATION (NATO) forces and maintained overseas garrisons in such areas as the Falklands, Cyprus and Gibraltar. There are three main sections of the British Army: **staff**, who plan and organize operations; **fighting troops**, which include the Household Cavalry, Royal Armoured Corps, Royal Regiment of Artillery, Corps of Royal Engineers, Royal Corp of Signals and Infantry and Army Air Corp; and **administrative troops**, who provide essential services such as medical attention, engineering and technical support. These include Royal Army Medical Corps; Royal Military Police and Royal Electrical and Mechanical Engineers. The monarch is the official head of the British Army. Control of all British armed forces is exercised by the Ministry of Defence, headed by the secretary of state for defence. General supervision of the Army is conducted by the chief of the general staff, who heads an army council. In addition to the Regular Army there is a reserve force of *c.*230,000, over 80,000 of which are in the Territorial Army and the remainder in the Regular Army Reserve. The end of the Cold War and financial pressures have seen a large reduction in conventional forces.

Army, U.S. Ground service of the US armed forces. In 1994 active army personnel numbered 560,000, 32% stationed overseas.

Arnhem City in E central Netherlands. An important trading centre since medieval times, Arnhem was almost destroyed by an abortive Allied airborne attack in 1944. Industries: metallurgy, textiles, electrical equipment, chemicals. Pop. (1994 est.) 133,670.

Arnold, Matthew (1822–88) British poet and critic. He held the Oxford chair in poetry (1857–67). A school inspector (1851–86), his writings include literary criticism, such as *Essays in Criticism* (series 1, 1865; series 2, 1888), and social commentary, such as *Culture and Anarchy* (1869), as well as such classic Victorian poems as *Dover Beach* and *The Scholar Gypsy*. His theories about the social and moral benefits of culture are largely responsible for the establishment of English Literature as a "core" subject in schools and universities.

Arp, Jean (Hans) (1887–1966) Alsatian sculptor, painter and poet. He founded the Zurich DADA movement with the Romanian artists Tristan Tzara, Marcel Janco and others during World War 1. He worked briefly with the Blaue Reiter group, and in the 1920s joined the SURREALISM movement. His sculpture spans the divide between Dada humour and the purity of non-iconic ABSTRACT ART.

arsenic Semimetallic element (symbol As) of group V of the periodic table, probably obtained in 1250 by Albertus Magnus. Compounds containing arsenic are used as a poison, and to harden lead and make semiconductors. Three allotropes are known: white arsenic, black arsenic and a yellow nonmetallic form. Properties: at.no. 33; r.a.m. 74.9216; r.d. 5.7; sublimes 613°C (1,135°F); most common isotope As^{75} (100%).

Artaud, Antonin (1896–1948) French drama theorist and director. His most significant contribution was his concept of the Theatre of CRUELTY. He proposed a physical theatre based on unconscious myth and symbol rather than narrative and psychological realism. His most important work was the essay volume *The Theatre and its Double* (1938).

art deco Fashionable style of design and interior decoration in the 1920s and 1930s. It took its name from the *Exposition Internationale des Arts Décoratifs et Industriels Modernes* held in Paris in 1925. The art deco style is characterized by sleek forms, simplified lines and geometric patterns.

Artemis In Greek mythology, the goddess of hunting and light, identified as DIANA by the Romans. She was the daughter of Zeus and Leto, and twin sister of APOLLO. Associated with the Moon, she was a virgin who assisted in childbirth and protected infants and animals.

arteriosclerosis Blanket term for degenerative diseases of the arteries, in particular atherosclerosis (hardening of the arteries). It is caused by deposits of fatty materials and scar tissue on the ARTERY walls, which narrow the channel and restrict blood flow causing an increased risk of heart disease, stroke or gangrene. Risk factors include cigarette smoking, inactivity, obesity and a diet rich in animal fats and refined sugar. Treatment is by drugs and, in some cases, surgery to replace a diseased length of artery.

artery One of the BLOOD VESSELS that carry BLOOD away from the HEART. The pulmonary artery carries deoxygenated blood from the heart to the lungs, but all other arteries carry oxygenated blood to the body's tissues. An artery's walls are thick, elastic and muscular and pulsate as they carry the blood. A severed artery causes major HAEMORRHAGE.

artesian well Well from which water is forced out naturally under pressure. Artesian wells are bored where water in a layer of porous rock is sandwiched between two layers of impervious rock. The water-filled layer is called an AQUIFER. Water flows up to the surface because distant parts of the aquifer are higher than the well-head.

arthritis Inflammation of the joints, with pain and restricted mobility. The most common forms are osteoarthritis and rheumatoid arthritis. **Osteoarthritis**, common among the elderly, occurs with erosion of joint cartilage and degenerative changes in the underlying bone. **Rheumatoid** arthritis, more common in women, is generally more disabling. It is an autoimmune disease which may disappear of its own accord but is usually slowly progressive. *See also* RHEUMATISM

arthropod Member of the largest animal phylum, Arthropoda. Living forms include CRUSTACEA, ARACHNID, CENTIPEDE, MILLIPEDE and INSECT. The species are thought to have evolved from ANNELIDS. All have a hard outer skin of CHITIN that is attached to the muscular system on the inside. The body is divided into segments, with each segment originally carrying a pair of jointed legs. In some animals some of the legs have evolved into jaws, sucking organs or weapons. Arthropods have well-developed digestive, circulatory and nervous systems. Land forms use tracheae for respiration.

Arthur Legendary British king who was said to rule the Knights of the Round Table. Two medieval chroniclers, Gildas and Nennius, tell of Arthur's fighting against the invading West Saxons and his final defeat of them at Mount Badon (possibly Badbury Hill, Dorset) in the early 6th century. A modern view is that Arthur was a professional soldier in service to the British kings after the Roman occupation.

artichoke (globe artichoke) Tall, thistle-like perennial plant with large, edible flower heads, native to the Mediterranean region. It has spiny leaves and blue flowers. Height: 0.9–1.5m (3–5ft). Family Asteraceae/Compositae; species *Cynara scolymus*. A different plant, the Jerusalem artichoke, is grown for its edible tubers. Family Asteraceae/Compositae; species *Helianthus tuberosus*.

Articles of Confederation (1781) First Federal constitution of the USA, drafted by the CONTINENTAL CONGRESS in 1777. Distrust of central authority and state rivalries produced a weak central government. The CONSTITUTIONAL CONVENTION met in 1787 to draft a new constitution.

artificial insemination Method of inducing PREGNANCY without sexual intercourse by injecting SPERM into the female genital tract. Used extensively in livestock farming, artificial insemination allows proven sires to breed with many females at low cost.

artificial intelligence (AI) Science concerned with developing computers that model high-level human intelligence. A computer may be programmed to answer questions on a specialized subject. Such "expert systems" are said to display the human ability to perform reasoning tasks. A branch of cognitive science termed "artificial life" is concerned with more low-level intelligence. For example, a ROBOT may be programmed to find its way around a maze, displaying the basic ability to physically interact with its surroundings.

artificial selection Breeding of plants and animals in which the parents are individually selected in order to perpetuate certain desired traits and eliminate others from the captive population. By this means, most of our domestic crops, livestock and pets have arisen. Artificial selection can be accelerated by techniques such as plant TISSUE CULTURE and the ARTIFICIAL INSEMINATION of livestock. *See also* CLONE; GENETIC ENGINEERING

artillery Projectile-firing weapons with a carriage or mount. An artillery piece is generally one of four types: gun, howitzer, mortar, or missile launcher. Modern artillery is classified according to calibre; ranging from under 105mm for light artillery to more than 155mm for heavy. Artillery changed the whole strategy and tactics of siege warfare. Advances in the 19th century such as smokeless powder, elongated shells, rifling and rapid-fire breach loading, made artillery indispensable in battle. *See also* CANNON

art nouveau Ornamental style that flourished in most of central and W Europe and the USA from *c.*1890 to World War 1. The idea originated in England with the ARTS AND CRAFTS MOVEMENT. Focusing mainly on the decorative arts, its most characteristic forms come from sinuous distortions of plant forms and asymmetrical lines. It is sometimes known in France by its English name, the "Modern Style". Outstanding art nouveau graphic artists included Beardsley, TIFFANY and Mucha. Charles Rennie MACKINTOSH, Antonio GAUDI and Victor Horta were among its most gifted architects.

Arts and Crafts Movement Late 19th- and early 20th-century British movement led by artists who wanted to revitalize the decorative arts by returning to the ideals of medieval craftsmanship. Inspired by William MORRIS, the movement contributed to European ART NOUVEAU, but was eventually transformed by the acceptance of modern industrial methods.

Arunachal Pradesh State of the E Himalayas in the far NE of India; the capital is Itanagar. Once a district of ASSAM, it was invaded by the Chinese in 1962, but returned to India in 1963. It became a union territory in 1972 and the 24th state of India in 1986. Most of the state is mountainous forest and jungle. Its main products are coffee, rubber, fruit, spices and rice. It is India's least densely populated state. Area: 81,426sq km (31,438sq mi). Pop. (1991) 864,558.

Aryan Language of an ancient people in the region between the Caspian Sea and Hindu Kush mountains. In about 1500 BC one branch entered India, introducing the Sanskrit language; another branch migrated to Europe. In their 1930s racist propaganda, the Nazis traced German descent from Aryans.

asbestos Group of fibrous, naturally occurring, silicate minerals used in insulating, brake lining and in astronaut suits. Several types exist, the most common is white asbestos. Many countries have banned the use of asbestos, as it can cause lung cancer and asbestosis, a lung disease.

Ascension Island in the S Atlantic Ocean, a UK dependency administered from the colony of ST HELENA. Discovered by the Portuguese (reputedly on Ascension Day 1501), it was occupied by Britain in the early 19th century. It now serves as an Anglo-American intercontinental telecommunications centre, and was an important base for British forces and supplies during the FALKLANDS WAR. Area: 88sq km (34sq mi). Pop. (1993) 1,117.

Ascension Day (formerly Holy Thursday) Christian feast day that commemorates Christ's ascension into heaven, 40 days after his resurrection. It falls on a Thursday, the 40th day after EASTER.

ascorbic acid *See* VITAMIN

asexual reproduction Type of reproduction in organisms that does not involve the union of male and female reproductive cells. It occurs in several forms: FISSION, BUDDING and VEGETATIVE REPRODUCTION. *See also* CLONE; SEXUAL REPRODUCTION

ash Group of mainly deciduous trees of the genus *Fraxinus* growing in temperate regions. They usually have leaves made up of many small leaflets, and winged fruits. The wood is elastic, strong and shock-resistant, and is widely used for furniture. Species include manna ash, *F. ornus*, the flowering ash of S Europe and Asia Minor; the European ash, *F. excelsior*, which grows to 45m (148ft) tall; and *F. floribunda*, a native of the Himalayas. Family Oleaceae. The mountain ash of Europe and Asia (*Sorbus aucuparia*) comes from a different family.

Ashanti Administrative region and ethnic group of central Ghana, W Africa; the capital is KUMASI. The Ashanti people (a matrilineal society) established a powerful empire based on the slave trade with the British and Dutch. Conflicts with the British throughout the 19th century were finally resolved in 1902, when the Ashanti territories (a British protectorate since 1896) were declared a crown colony. The society is traditionally agricultural. The region is the main area of Ghana's vital cocoa production. The Ashanti are renowned for their crafts, including high-quality goldwork and weaving. Today Ashanti is the most populous of Ghana's ten regions. Area: 24,390 (9,414sq mi). Pop. (1984) 2,090,100.

Ashdown, Paddy (Jeremy John Durham) (1941–) British politician, first leader of the Social and LIBERAL DEMOCRATS (1988–), b. India. Ashdown was a commander in the Royal Marines (1960–72), before becoming a diplomat. In 1983 he entered parliament as a LIBERAL PARTY MP and quickly became a leading spokesman for the party. Ashdown succeeded David STEEL, who stood down as Liberal leader when the merger with the SOCIAL DEMOCRATIC PARTY (SDP) was formalized. Ashdown's active image helped to boost the party's electoral base in S England.

Ashes, The Cricket trophy nominally held by the winners of the Test series between England and Australia. The actual trophy, an urn containing the ashes of a burned bail, is always kept at Lord's Cricket Ground, London.

Ashgabat (formerly Ashkhabad) Capital of the central Asian republic of Turkmenistan. The city was known as Poltaratsk from 1919–27 and Ashkabad from 1927–92. Its present name was adopted after the republic attained independence from the former Soviet Union. Its factories produce textiles, carpets, silk, metalware, glass and light machinery. Pop. (1990) 411,000.

Ashkenazim Jews who originally settled in NW Europe, as distinguished from the SEPHARDIM, who settled in Spain and Portugal.

Ashkenazy, Vladimir (1937–) Icelandic pianist and conductor, b. Russia. He studied at the Central Music School of Moscow and the Conservatoire, Moscow. Since 1980 he has concentrated on conducting, winning respect for his varied and adventurous programming.

Ashoka (c.271–238 BC) Indian emperor (r.264–238 BC). The greatest emperor of the MAURYA EMPIRE, he at first fought to expand his empire. He was revolted by the bloodshed of war and, renouncing conquest by force, embraced BUDDHISM. He became one of its most fervent supporters and spread its ideas through missionaries to neighbouring countries and through edicts engraved on pillars. His empire encompassed most of India and large areas of Afghanistan.

Ashton, Sir Frederick (1904–88) British choreographer and ballet director. In 1935 he joined the Sadler's Wells Ballet (now the Royal Ballet) in London and was its chief choreographer until 1963, then its director 1963–70. His gifted work for dancers such as Margot FONTEYN and Ninette de VALOIS earned him a reputation as Britain's greatest choreographer. His major pieces include *Cinderella* (1948), *Ondine* (1958) and *Marguèrite and Armand* (1963).

Ashurbanipal (d. c.626 BC) (Assurbanipal) Last great king of ASSYRIA (r.669–633 BC). During his reign, Assyria reached its largest extent, reaching into Upper Egypt, before a rapid decline. Excavations at NINEVEH after 1850 revealed an advanced civilization.

Ash Wednesday First day of LENT

Asia World's largest continent. Entirely in the Eastern Hemisphere, it extends from N of the Arctic Circle in Russia to S of the Equator in Indonesia. **Land** On the W, Asia's boundary with Europe follows a line through the Ural Mountains, W of the CASPIAN SEA and along the Caucasus. Geographically, Europe and Asia are one enormous continent (Eurasia) but historically they have always been regarded as separate continents. Asia has six regions. Northern Asia includes the massive inhospitable region of SIBERIA. A large part lies within the Arctic Circle, forming a cold, treeless plain (tundra) where the soil, except on the surface, is permanently frozen to depths exceeding 700m (2,000ft). Southern Siberia includes great coniferous forests (taiga) and the Russian steppes. Its S boundary runs through the TIAN SHAN and Yablonovy mountains and Lake BAIKAL. The high plateau area of Central Asia extends S to the Himalayas and includes the W Chinese provinces of TIBET and XINKIANG as well as MONGOLIA. This is a region of low rainfall and very low winter temperatures. Much of the area is desert, the largest being the GOBI. The Tibetan plateau is mostly barren. Eastern Asia lies between the plateaus of Central Asia and the Pacific. It is a region of highlands and plains, watered by broad rivers. Off the E coast there are many islands, the most important being the Japanese islands of HOKKAIDŌ, HONSHŪ and KYŪSHŪ, and the Chinese island of TAIWAN. Southeast Asia includes the INDOCHINA peninsula, part of which forms the MALAY PENINSULA, BURMA and many islands,

among which the PHILIPPINES and INDONESIA are the most important. The N of this region is mountainous and the S low-lying. Southern Asia consists of the Indian subcontinent and the island of SRI LANKA. In the N it is bounded by the HINDU KUSH, Pamir, KARAKORAM and Himalayan mountains. In the HIMALAYAS lies Mount EVEREST, the world's highest mountain. To the S of the mountains lie wide plains, crossed by rivers. Farther S is the DECCAN plateau, which rises on its E and W edges to the GHATS. South-west Asia includes most of the MIDDLE EAST. It is made up of two peninsulas: Anatolia (Asia Minor) and the Arabian Peninsula. It is also a region of large inland seas: the Aral, Caspian, Dead and Black seas. **Structure and geology** The most striking feature of the continent is the massive range of Himalayan fold mountains that were formed when the Indo-Australian and Eurasian tectonic plates collided in the Mesozoic era. Most of China and S central Asia is composed of folded Palaeozoic and Mesozoic sediments, and large expanses of central Siberia consist of flat-lying sediments of the same age. The Indian subcontinent is largely pre-Cambrian except for the Deccan Plateau, which is a complex series of lava flows. **Lakes and rivers** Most of the major Asian lakes are found in the centre of the continent, and include the Caspian Sea (the largest landlocked body of water in the world), the ARAL SEA and Lake BALKHASH. The YANGTZE River in China is Asia's longest. The HUANG HE River is China's other major river and, until control measures were taken, it flooded regularly. Like these rivers, the three principal waterways of SE Asia (IRRAWADDY, SALWEEN, MEKONG) rise on the Tibetan plateau but flow S instead of E. The INDUS, BRAHMAPUTRA and GANGES are the largest rivers of the Indian subcontinent, and the OB, YENISEI and LENA are the continent's major N-flowing rivers, emptying into the Arctic Ocean. **Climate and vegetation** Except for the climate found on W temperate seaboards, all the world's major climatic divisions (with local variations) are represented in the continent. The monsoon climates of India and W Southeast Asia are peculiar to these regions and, apart from extremes of heat and cold, typify the continent. Large expanses are covered by desert and semi-arid grassland, with belts of coniferous forest to the N and tropical forest to the S. **People** Asians constitute half the world's population. The main language groups are Indo-Aryan, Sino-Tibetan, Ural-Altaic, Malayan and Semitic. Mandarin Chinese is the most numerous (if not the most widespread) language. HINDUISM is the religion with the most adherents, although it is confined to India and SE Asia. ISLAM, CONFUCIANISM, BUDDHISM, SHINTO, CHRISTIANITY, TAOISM and JUDAISM are also important, with the Islamic influence stretching from Turkey to Indonesia. **Economy** Agriculture is important, although less than 10% of the continent is cultivated. Asia produces more than 90% of the world's rice, rubber, cotton and tobacco. Rice is the major crop in the E and S, wheat and barley are grown in the W and N. China, Japan and Russia are the most highly industrialized countries in terms of traditional heavy materials. Since the 1960s there has been dramatic commercial growth in several countries of SE and E Asia based on a combination of household and high-tech products. Following Japan's example, South Korea, Taiwan, Hong Kong, Singapore, Malaysia and Thailand form the "tiger" economies, so successful in global markets that they invest in Europe and North America. Oil is the most important export of many Middle East countries. **Recent history** Since World War 2, the history of Asia has been dominated by three main themes: the legacy of COLONIALISM; the growth and demise of COMMUNISM; and the rise of Islamic FUNDAMENTALISM. Total area: 44,391,206sq km (17,139,445sq mi) *Highest mountain* Mount Everest (Nepal) 8,848m (29,029ft) *Longest river* Yangtze (China) 5,980km (3,716 mi) *Population* 3,193,000,000 *Largest cities* SHANGHAI (8,760,000); TOKYO (7,927,000); BEIJING (6,560,000) *See also* articles on individual countries

Asia Minor (Anatolia) Great peninsula of W Asia making up most of modern Turkey. The Bosporus, the Sea of Marmara and the Dardanelles divide both Turkey and Europe from Asia. Apart from a narrow coastal plain, the area is a high, arid plateau. In the SE, the Taurus Range rises to more than 3,750m (12,000ft). The area has been inhabited since the Bronze Age. In the 13th–15th centuries it was conquered by the Ottoman Turks and remained part of the Ottoman empire until the establishment of the Republic of Turkey in 1923.

Asimov, Isaac (1920–92) US author and scientist, b. Russia. Although he published several serious scientific works, he is best known for his science fiction novels, including *I, Robot* (1950) and *The Foundation Trilogy* (1951–53).

Asmara (Asmera) Capital of Eritrea, NE Africa. Occupied by Italy in 1889, it was their colonial capital and base for their invasion of Ethiopia (1935–36). In 1993 Asmara became the capital of independent ERITREA. Though ravaged by drought, famine and war, it began a strong recovery based on numerous light industries, including ceramics, footwear and textiles. Pop. (1991) 367,300.

asp Popular name for two species of VIPER: the asp viper of S Europe (*Vipera aspis*); and the Egyptian asp, a horned, side-winding viper of N Africa (*Ceraste cerastes*). Both are weakly venomous and eat small animals. Family: Viperidae.

aspen One of three species of trees of the genus *Populus*, with toothed, rounded leaves. Closely related to poplars, they are native to temperate Eurasia, North Africa and North America. They grow up to 30m (100ft). Family Salicaceae.

asphalt Naturally occurring, black or brown, semi-solid BITUMEN, used mainly for road covering and roofing. Asphalt deposits occur in many parts of the world, including Trinidad, Venezuela,

Alabama and Texas. Asphalt also occurs in petroleum, and it is extracted in oil refineries.

aspirin (acetylsalicylic acid) DRUG widely used to reduce fever, and as an ANALGESIC to relieve minor pain. Recent evidence indicates aspirin can inhibit the formation of blood clots and in low doses can reduce the danger of heart attack and stroke. Aspirin can irritate the stomach and in overdose is toxic.

Asquith, Herbert Henry, 1st Earl of Oxford and Asquith (1852–1928) British statesman, last Liberal prime minister (1908–16). Asquith became an MP in 1886 and served as GLADSTONE's home secretary (1892–95). He was chancellor of the exchequer (1906–08) under Sir Henry Campbell-Bannerman, whom he succeeded as prime minister. Asquith's administration was notable for its social welfare legislation, such as the introduction of old age pensions (1908) and unemployment insurance (1911). David LLOYD GEORGE's radical budget (1909) to finance these reforms was rejected by the House of Lords. Asquith responded by passing the Parliament Act (1911), which ended the Lords' power of veto over Commons legislation. Asquith took Britain into WORLD WAR 1, and in 1915 he formed a coalition government with the Conservative Party. He was replaced as prime minister in a cabinet coup led by Lloyd George. Asquith stayed on as Liberal Party leader until 1926. He was ennobled in 1925.

ass Wild, speedy, long-eared member of the HORSE family found in African and Asian desert and mountain areas. Smaller than the horse, it has a short mane and tail, small hoofs and dorsal stripes. The three African races (species *Equus asinus*) are the Nubian, North African and the rare Somali. Height: 90–150cm (3–5ft) at shoulder. Asian races are the kiang and the ONAGER. Family Equidae.

Assad, Hafez al- (1928–) Syrian statesman, president (1970–). Assad served as minister of defence (1965–70), before seizing power in a military coup. He was elected president in 1971. Initially, Assad took a hardline stance against Israel, and Syrian troops participated in the 1973 ARAB-ISRAELI WAR. Assad was accused of harbouring terrorists. In 1976 Assad deployed troops in the Lebanese civil war, and in 1987 his troops helped to restore order. In the mid-1990s, Assad's stance towards Israel softened, and he played an important role in the Israeli-Palestinian peace negotiations.

Assam State in NE India, almost separated from the rest of the country by Bangladesh. The capital is Dispur and the largest city is Guwahati. Assam's main products are tea, jute, timber and oil. Area: 78,438sq km (30,277sq mi). Pop. (1991) 22,414,322.

Assassin Name given to a Muslim sect of ISMAILIS, founded *c.*1090 by Hasan ibn al-Sabbah. They fought against orthodox Muslims and Christian Crusaders, and committed many political murders, until their defeat in the 13th century.

assay Test to determine the amount of a metal present in a sample of material such as ores and alloys. The term is normally reserved for finding the proportion of gold, silver or platinum present.

asset Anything owned by a person or a company that has a money value. Current assets, can be easily liquidated to produce their cash value. Fixed assets include buildings, machinery and land. Goodwill and PATENTS are described as intangible assets, because they have potential, rather than actual, money value. Asset stripping is the practice of taking over a business and selling off its assets.

assimilation Process by which an organism uses substances taken in from its surroundings to make new living protoplasm or to provide energy for metabolic processes. It includes the incorporation of the products of food digestion into living tissues in animals, and the synthesis of new organic material by a plant during photosynthesis.

Association of Southeast Asian Nations (ASEAN) Regional alliance formed in 1967 to promote economic cooperation. Its members are Indonesia, Malaysia, Philippines, Singapore, Thailand, Brunei and Vietnam. Based in Jakarta, Indonesia, it took over the non-military aspects of the SOUTHEAST ASIA TREATY ORGANISATION (SEATO) in 1975.

associative law Rule of combination in mathematics, in which the result of two or more operations on terms does not depend on the way in which they are grouped. Thus, normal addition and multiplication of numbers follows the associative law, since $a + (b + c) = (a + b) + c$, and $a \times (b \times c) = (a \times b) \times c$.

Assumption In the Roman Catholic Church, principal feast of the Blessed Virgin Mary. It is celebrated on 15 August, and marks the occasion when she was taken up into heaven at the end of her life on Earth.

Assyria Ancient empire of the Middle East. It took its name from the city of Ashur (Assur) on the River Tigris near modern Mosul, Iraq. The Assyrian empire was established in the 3rd millennium BC and reached its zenith between the 9th and 7th centuries BC, when it extended from the Nile to the Persian Gulf and N into Anatolia. Thereafter it declined and was absorbed by the Persian empire. Under ASHURBANIPAL, art and learning reached their peak at NINEVEH. The capture of Nineveh in 612 BC marked the terminal decline of Assyria.

Astaire, Fred (1899–1987) US dancer, actor and choreographer. Astaire's sparkling, improvised solo dances redefined the musical with their energy and zany sophistication. In 1933 cinema's greatest partnership was formed, when he starred opposite Ginger Rogers in *Flying Down to Rio*, the first of ten films together. Classics include *Top Hat* (1935) and *Easter Parade* (1948, with Judy GARLAND). In 1949 he received a special Academy Award for his contribution to film.

astatine Semimetallic radioactive element (symbol At), one of the HALOGENS (group VII of the PERIODIC TABLE). It is rare in nature, and is found in radioactive decay. At^{211} will collect in the thyroid gland and is used in medicine as a radioactive tracer. Properties: at.no. 85; r.a.m. 211; m.p. 302°C (575.6°F); b.p. 377°C (710.6°F); most stable isotope At^{210} (half-life 8.3hr).

aster Genus of mostly perennial, leafy stemmed plants native to the Americas and Eurasia. Asters are popular garden plants and most bear daisy-like flowers. Family Asteraceae/Compositae.

asteroid Small body in an independent orbit around the Sun. The majority move between the orbits of Mars and Jupiter, in the main asteroid belt. The largest asteroid (and the first to be discovered) was CERES, with a diameter of 913km (567mi). There are thought to be a million asteroids with a diameter greater than 1km (0.6mi); below this, they decrease in size to dust particles. Some very small objects find their way to Earth as METEORITES. So far nearly 6,000 asteroids have been catalogued and have had their orbits calculated. This figure is increasing by several hundred a year. At least 10,000 more have been observed, but not often enough for an orbit to be calculated. Some of the larger asteroids are spherical, but most are irregularly shaped, and a wide variety of compositional types have been identified. Asteroids almost certainly originate from the time of the formation of the SOLAR SYSTEM and are not remnants of a large planet that disintegrated, as was once thought.

asthma Disorder of the respiratory system in which the bronchi (air passages) of the LUNGS go into spasm, making breathing difficult. It can be triggered by infection, air pollution, allergy, certain drugs, exertion or emotional stress. Allergic asthma may be treated by injections aimed at lessening sensitivity to specific allergens. Otherwise treatment is with bronchodilators to relax the bronchial muscles and ease breathing; in severe asthma, inhaled steroids may be given. Children often outgrow asthma, while some people suddenly acquire the disease in middle age. *See also* BRONCHITIS; EMPHYSEMA

astigmatism Defect of vision in which the curvature of the lens differs from one perpendicular plane to another. It can be compensated for by use of corrective lenses.

Aston, Francis William (1877–1945) British physicist awarded the 1922 Nobel Prize for chemistry for his work on ISOTOPES. He developed the MASS SPECTROGRAPH that separates isotopes, and used it to identify 212 naturally occurring isotopes.

Astor, Nancy Witcher (Langhorne), Viscountess (1879–1964) British politician, b. USA, the first woman elected to the House of Commons (1919–45). A Conservative, she advocated temperance, educational reform, women's and children's welfare. In the 1930s she and her husband William Waldorf Astor (Viscount Astor) were at the centre of a group of influential proponents of APPEASEMENT toward Nazi Germany.

Astrakhan (Astrachan) City in s Russia, a port on the Caspian Sea. It was developed by the Mongols in the 13th century. A railway, airline and oil shipping terminal, it is also an important trade centre. Industries: fishing, shipbuilding, engineering and oil-refining. Pop. (1992) 512,000.

astrolabe Early astronomical instrument for showing the appearance of the celestial sphere at a given moment, and for determining the altitude of celestial bodies. The basic form consisted of two concentric disks, one with a star map and one with a scale of angles around its rim, joined and pivoted at their centres (rather like a modern planisphere), with a sighting device attached. Astrolabes were used from the time of the ancient Greeks until the 17th century for navigation, measuring time, and terrestrial measurement of height and angles.

astrology Study of the influence supposedly exerted by stars and planets on the natures and lives of human beings. Western astrology draws specifically on the movements of the Sun, Moon and major planets of the Solar System in relation to the stars that make up the 12 constellations known as the ZODIAC. Astrology originated in ancient Babylon and Persia about 3,900 years ago, and rapidly spread through Europe, the Middle East and Asia. In Europe the growing influence of Christianity saw the demise of astrologers. Popular HOROSCOPES still appear in some daily newspapers.

astronaut (Rus. *cosmonaut*) Person who navigates or rides in a space vehicle. The first man to orbit the Earth was the Russian Yuri GAGARIN in 1961. The first man to walk on the Moon was the American Neil ARMSTRONG in 1969. The first woman in space was the Russian Valentina Tereshkova in 1963.

astronomical unit (AU) Mean distance between the Earth and the Sun, used as a fundamental unit of distance, particularly for distances in the Solar System. It is equal to 149,598,000km (92,956,000mi).

astronomy Branch of science studied since ancient times and concerned with the universe and its components in terms of the relative motions of celestial bodies, their positions on the celestial sphere, physical and chemical structure, evolution and the phenomena occurring on them. It includes celestial mechanics, ASTROPHYSICS, COSMOLOGY and astrometry. Waves in all regions of the ELECTROMAGNETIC SPECTRUM can now be studied either with ground-based instruments or, where no atmospheric window exists, by observations and measurements made from satellites, space probes and rockets. **History** Astronomy was first practically used to develop a CALENDAR, the units of which were determined by observing the heavens. The Chinese had a calendar in the 14th century BC. The Greeks developed astronomy significantly between 600 BC and AD 200.The system devised by PTOLEMY was a geometrical representation of the SOLAR SYSTEM that predicted the motions of the planets with great accuracy. From then on astrono-

my remained dormant until the scientific revolution of the 16th and 17th centuries, when COPERNICUS stated his theory that the Earth rotates on its axis and, with all the other planets, revolves round the Sun. This had a profound effect upon contemporary religion and philosophy. KEPLER and his laws of planetary motion refined the theory of heliocentric motion, and his contemporary, GALILEO, made use of the TELESCOPE and discovered the moons of JUPITER. Isaac NEWTON combined the sciences of astronomy and physics. His laws of motion and universal theory of GRAVITATION provided a physical basis for Kepler's laws and the work of many astronomers from then on, such as the prediction of HALLEY'S COMET and the discovery of the planets URANUS, NEPTUNE and PLUTO. By the early 19th century the science of celestial mechanics, the study of the motions of bodies in space as they move under the influence of their mutual gravitation, had become highly advanced and new mathematical techniques permitted the solution of the remaining problems of classical gravitation theory as applied to the Solar System. In the second half of the nineteenth century astronomy was revolutionized by the introduction of techniques based on photography and SPECTROSCOPY. These encouraged investigation into the physical composition of stars, rather than their position. Ejnar HERTZSPRUNG and H.N. Russell studied the relationship between the colour of a star and its luminosity. By this time larger telescopes were being constructed, which extended the limits of the universe known to man. Harlow SHAPLEY determined the shape and size of our galaxy and E.P. HUBBLE's study of distant galaxies led to his theory of an expanding universe. BIG BANG and STEADY STATE THEORY of the origins of the universe were formulated. In recent years, space exploration and observation in different parts of the electromagnetic spectrum have contributed to the discovery and postulation of such phenomena as the QUASAR, PULSAR and BLACK HOLE. There are various branches of modern astronomy: **Optical** astronomy is the oldest branch, which studies sources of light in space. Light rays can penetrate the atmosphere but, because of disturbances, many observations are now made from above the atmosphere. **Gamma-ray**, INFRARED, **ultraviolet** and **x-ray** astronomy are branches which study the emission of radiation (at all wavelengths) from astronomical objects. Higher wavelengths can be studied from the ground while studying lower wavelengths requires the use of satellites and balloons. Other branches within astronomy include RADAR ASTRONOMY and RADIO ASTRONOMY.

astrophysics Branch of ASTRONOMY that studies the physical and chemical nature of celestial bodies and their evolution. Many branches of physics, including nuclear physics, plasma physics, relativity and SPECTROSCOPY, are used to predict properties of stars, planets and other celestial bodies. Astrophysicists also interpret the information obtained from astronomical studies of the electromagnetic spectrum, including light, x-rays and radio waves.

Asturias Region in NW Spain, bordering the Bay of Biscay and traversed by the Cantabrian Mountains. The capital is Oviedo. Industries: coal, manganese, mining, steel and nonferrous metal production, fishing and fruit. Pop. (1991) 1,093,937.

Asunción Capital, chief port and largest city of Paraguay, located on the E bank of the River Paraguay. It is an administrative, industrial and cultural centre. Industries: vegetable oil mills, textiles. Pop. (1992) 637,737.

Aswan City on the E bank of the River Nile, just above Lake Nasser, SE Egypt. Aswan was important to the Egyptians and Greeks because it controlled all shipping and communications above the first cataract of the NILE. The modern city is a commercial and resort centre. It has benefited from the construction of the Aswan High Dam (1960–70), which established flood control on the Nile. Industries: copper, steel, textiles. Pop. (1992) 220,000.

Atacama Desert Desert of N Chile, stretching c.1,000km (620mi) S from the Peru border. Despite its proximity to the Pacific Ocean, it is considered to be the most arid in the world; some areas had no recorded rainfall in the 400 years to 1971. Except where it is artificially irrigated, it is devoid of vegetation. There are large deposits of copper and other minerals; nitrates and iodine are extracted from the salt basins.

Atahualpa (1502–33) (Atabalipa) Last Inca ruler of Peru. In 1532 Atahualpa defeated his half-brother, Huáscar, to control the whole kingdom. In 1532 Spanish conquistadores arrived; Francisco PIZARRO captured Atahualpo and he was later executed.

Atatürk, (Mustafa) Kemal (1881–1938) Turkish general and statesman, first president (1923–38) of the Turkish republic. He joined the YOUNG TURKS and was chief of staff to ENVER PASHA in the revolution (1908). During World War 1 he led resistance to the Allies' GALLIPOLI CAMPAIGN. The defeat of the OTTOMAN EMPIRE persuaded Mustafa Kemal to organize the Turkish Nationalist Party (1919) and set up a rival government. The Treaty of Sèvres pushed him into attack. His expulsion of the Greeks from ASIA MINOR (1921–22) forced the sultan to flee Istanbul. The Treaty of Lausanne (1923) saw the creation of a independent republic. His dictatorship undertook sweeping reforms, which transformed Turkey into a secular, industrial nation. In 1934 he adopted the title Atatürk (Turkish, father of the Turks).

ataxia In medicine, a condition where muscles are uncoordinated. It results in clumsiness, irregular and uncontrolled movements, and difficulties with speech. It may be caused by physical injury to the brain or nervous system, by a STROKE, or by disease.

Athanasian Creed Christian profession of faith, probably written in the 6th century, that explains the teachings of the Church on the Trinity and the incarnation. The Roman Catholic and some Protestant Churches accept its authority.

Athanasius, Saint (d.373) Early Christian leader. As patriarch of Alexandria he confuted ARIANISM, and in various writings defended the teaching that the Son and the Holy Spirit were of equal divinity with God the Father and so shared a threefold being. He is no longer considered the author of the ATHANASIAN CREED. His feast day is 2 May.

atheism Denial of the existence of God or any supernatural or spiritual being. The first Christians were called atheists because they denied Roman religions but the term now indicates the denial of Christian theism. *See also* AGNOSTICISM

Athena In Greek mythology, goddess of war, wisdom and patroness of the arts and industry, identified with MINERVA. Athena emerged from the head of ZEUS fully grown and armed. She received special worship at Athens, where her main temples were the PARTHENON and the Erechtheum.

Athens (Athínai) Capital and largest city of Greece, situated on the Saronic Gulf. The ancient city was built around the Acropolis, a fortified citadel, and was the greatest artistic and cultural centre in ancient Greece, gaining importance after the PERSIAN WARS (500–449 BC). The most noted artistic treasures are the PARTHENON (438 BC), the Erechtheum (406 BC) and the Theatre of Dionysus (c.500 BC, the oldest of the Greek theatres). Modern Athens and its port of PIRAEUS form a major Mediterranean transport and economic centre. Industries: shipbuilding, paper, steel machinery, textiles, pottery, brewing, chemicals, glass. Pop. (1991) 3,072,922.

athletics (track and field) Composite sport that includes running and hurdling events on the track, jumping and throwing field events, cross-country and long-distance road running, and walking.

Atlanta Capital of Georgia, USA, in the NW centre of the state. Industries: textiles, chemicals, iron and steel, electronics. Pop. (1992) 394,848.

Atlantic, Battle of the (1939–43) Campaign for control of the Atlantic sea routes waged by air and naval forces during World War 2. The Germans hoped to starve Britain into submission by U-boat attacks on merchant shipping, and later to prevent US reinforcements reaching the Mediterranean and Europe. More than 14 million tonnes of shipping were destroyed.

Atlantic Charter Joint declaration of peace aims issued in August 1941 by US President Franklin D. ROOSEVELT and British Prime Minister Winston CHURCHILL. It affirmed the right of all nations to choose their own form of government, promised to restore sovereignty to all nations that had lost it, and advocated the disarmament of aggressor nations.

Atlantic Ocean World's second-largest ocean, stretching from the Arctic Circle in the N to the Antarctic Ocean in the S. Its name derives from the ATLAS Mountains, which, for the ancient Greeks, marked the western boundary between the known and the unknown world. Its most striking feature is the MID-ATLANTIC RIDGE, which runs N–S for its entire length. At the crest, the ridge is cleft by a deep RIFT VALLEY, which is frequently offset by E–W transform faults. The age of the crust steadily increases with distance from the central rift, and so there is little doubt that the rift has evolved by sea-floor spreading and is associated with the movement of the Americas away from Europe and Africa at a rate of 2–4cm (0.8–1.6in) a year. The average depth of the Atlantic is 3,700m (12,100ft). The greatest known depth is the Milwaukee Deep in the Puerto Rico Trench, which has a depth of 8,650m (28,370ft). The N clockwise gyre is dominated by the fast-flowing GULF STREAM, travelling at speeds of up to 130km (80mi) a day, and forming the W boundary current of the gyre. The S anti-clockwise gyre is atypical in having a weak western boundary current, the Brazil Current. Apart from oil (found mainly in the Gulf of Guinea), sand and gravel are the most important minerals from the Atlantic. Valuable diamond deposits occur off the coast of Namibia. The North Atlantic contains the most valuable fishing grounds in the world, namely the cod fisheries around Iceland, S Greenland and the Grand Banks of Newfoundland. Area: 82 million sq km (32 million sq mi).

Atlantis Mythical island in the Atlantic Ocean from which, according to Plato, a great empire tried to subdue the Mediterranean countries. It has been identified by some with the Greek island of Thera, destroyed by an earthquake c.1450 BC.

Atlas Mountain system in NW Africa, comprising several folded and roughly parallel chains extending 2,415km (1,500mi) from the coast of SW Morocco to the coast of N Tunisia. North Africa's highest peak, Djebel Toubkal, 4,170m (13,671ft), is found in the Grand Atlas range in W Morocco.

Atlas In Greek mythology, one of the TITANS, brother of PROMETHEUS. Having fought against Zeus, he was condemned to hold up the heavens.

atman Human soul or self in Hindu religion. *See* BRAHMAN

atmosphere Envelope of gases surrounding the Earth. It shields the planet from the harsh environment of space; the gases it contains are vital to life. About 95% by weight of the Earth's atmosphere lies below the 25km (15mi) altitude; the mixture of gases in the lower atmosphere is commonly called air. The atmosphere's composition by weight is: nitrogen 78.09%, oxygen 20.9%, argon 0.93%, carbon dioxide 0.03%, plus 0.05% of hydrogen, the inert gases and varying amounts of water vapour. The atmosphere can be conceived as concentric shells; the innermost is the **troposphere**, in which dust and water vapour create the clouds and weather. The **stratosphere** extends from 10–55km (8–36mi) and is cooler and clearer and contains OZONE. Above, to a height of 70km (43mi), is the **mesosphere**, in which chemical reactions occur,

powered by sunlight. The temperature climbs steadily in the **thermosphere**, which gives way to the **exosphere** at about 400km (250mi), where helium and hydrogen may be lost into space. The **ionosphere** ranges from about 50km (30mi) out into the VAN ALLEN RADIATION BELTS.

atmospheric pressure Pressure exerted by the atmosphere because of its WEIGHT (gravitational attraction to the Earth or other body), measured by barometers and usually expressed in units of mercury. Standard atmospheric pressure at sea level is 760mm (29.92in) of mercury. The column of air above each cm^2 of Earth's surface weighs about 1kg (2.2 lb) the column above each in^2 weighs about 6.7kg (14.7lb).

atoll Ring-shaped REEF of CORAL enclosing a shallow LAGOON. An atoll begins as a reef surrounding a slowly subsiding island, usually volcanic. As the island sinks the coral continues to grow upwards until eventually the island is below sea level and only a ring of coral is left at the surface.

atom Smallest particle of matter that can take part in a chemical reaction, every element having its own characteristic atoms. The atom, once thought indivisible, consists of a central, positively charged NUCLEUS orbited by negatively charged ELECTRONS. The nucleus (identified in 1911 by Ernest RUTHERFORD) is composed of tightly packed PROTONS and NEUTRONS. It occupies a small fraction of the atomic space but accounts for almost all of the mass of the atom. In 1913 Niels BOHR suggested that electrons moved in fixed orbits. The study of QUANTUM MECHANICS has since modified the concept of orbits: the Heisenberg UNCERTAINTY PRINCIPLE says it is impossible to know the exact position and MOMENTUM of a SUBATOMIC PARTICLE. The number of electrons in an atom and their configuration determine its chemical properties. Adding or removing one or more electrons produces an ION.

atomic bomb *See* NUCLEAR WEAPON

atomic clock Most accurate of terrestrial clocks. It is an electric clock regulated by such natural periodic phenomena as emitted radiation or atomic vibration; the atoms of CAESIUM are most commonly used. Clocks that run on radiation from hydrogen atoms lose one second in 1,700,000 years.

atomic energy *See* NUCLEAR ENERGY

atomic mass number (nucleon number) Number of NUCLEONS (protons and neutrons) in the nucleus of an atom. It is represented by the symbol A. In nuclear notation, such as $^7_3$ Li, the mass number is the upper number and the ATOMIC NUMBER (the number of protons) is the lower one. ISOTOPES of an element have different mass numbers but identical atomic numbers.

atomic mass unit (amu) Unit of mass used to compare RELATIVE ATOMIC MASSES, defined as 1/12th the mass of the most abundant isotope of carbon, carbon-12 (6 electrons, 6 protons and 6 neutrons). One amu is equal to 1.66033×10^{-27} kg.

atomic number (proton number) Number of

protons in the nucleus of an atom of an element, which is equal to the number of electrons moving around that nucleus. It is abbreviated to at.no. and represented by the symbol Z. The atomic number determines the chemical properties of an element and its position in the PERIODIC TABLE. ISOTOPES of an element all have the same atomic number but a different ATOMIC MASS NUMBER.

atonality Musical composition without reference to traditional KEYS and HARMONY. Examples include *Pierrot Lunaire* (1912) by Arnold SCHOENBERG.

atonement In religion, process by which a sinner seeks forgiveness from and reconciliation with God, through an act of expiation such as prayer, fasting or good works. In Christian theology, Jesus Christ atoned for the sins of the world by his sacrifice on the cross. Jews observe YOM KIPPUR, their most sacred feast, as a day of repentance.

atrophy In medicine, shrinking or wastage of tissues or organs. It may be associated with disease, malnutrition, or, as in muscle atrophy, with disuse.

atropine Poisonous ALKALOID drug ($C_{17}H_{23}NO_3$) obtained from plants such as DEADLY NIGHTSHADE. Atropine is used medicinally to regularize the heartbeat during anaesthesia, to dilate the pupil of the eye and to treat motion sickness.

Attila (406–453) King of the HUNS ($c.$439–53), co-ruler with his elder brother until 445. Attila defeated the Eastern Roman emperor Theodosius II, extorting land and tribute, and invaded Gaul in 451. He invaded Italy in 452, but disease forced his withdrawal. Attila has a reputation as a fierce warrior, but was fair to his subjects and encouraged learning. On his death the empire fell apart.

Attlee, Clement Richard, 1st Earl (1883–1967) British statesman, prime minister (1945–51). Attlee became an MP in 1922 and leader of the Labour Party in 1935. During World War 2, he served in Winston CHURCHILL's cabinet, first as Dominions Secretary (1942–43) and then as deputy prime minister (1942–45). Attlee won a landslide victory in the 1945 general election. His administration introduced important social reforms, such as the NATIONAL HEALTH SERVICE (NHS), and the nationalization of the power industries, the railways and the BANK OF ENGLAND. He also granted independence to India (1947) and Burma (1948). Attlee was re-elected in 1950, but was defeated by Winston Churchill in 1951.

attorney general Principal law officer. In the USA, the attorney general is the highest law officer of the government, head of the department of justice, and advises the president and heads of the executive department. In the UK, it is the chief law officer of the crown and head of the English bar, and also legal advisor to the House of Commons and the government.

Atwood, Margaret Eleanor (1939–) Canadian novelist, poet and critic. Best known for her novels, she has also published numerous volumes of poetry. Her novels include *Surfacing* (1972),

the award-winning *The Handmaid's Tale* (1985), *The Robber Bride* (1993) and *Alias Grace* (1996).

Auber, Daniel-François-Esprit (1782–1871) French composer. He wrote more than 40 operas, often collaborating with the librettist Scribe. His operas include *La Muette de Portici* (or *Masaniello*) and *Fra Diavolo*. He is regarded as the founder of French grand opera.

aubergine (eggplant) Tropical member of the potato (and nightshade) family. The fruit is eaten as a vegetable. A bushy perennial native to the New World, it is widely cultivated in temperate regions. Family Solanaceae; species *Solanum melongena*.

Auckland Largest city and chief port of New Zealand, lying on an isthmus on NW North Island. The port, built on land purchased from the Maoris in 1840, handles around 60% of New Zealand's trade. Industries: vehicle assembly, boatbuilding, footwear, food canning, chemicals. Auckland has the largest Polynesian population ($c.$65,000) of any city in the world. Pop. (1994) 929,300.

Auden, W.H. (Wystan Hugh) (1907–73) British poet. He came to prominence during the late 1920s as one of a group of left-wing writers, which included Stephen SPENDER, Louis MACNEICE, Cecil DAY-LEWIS and Christopher ISHERWOOD, with whom he collaborated on plays such as *The Ascent of F6* (1936). He moved to the USA in 1939. One of the greatest English-language poets of the 20th century, Auden was a brilliant technician, and his formal dexterity, together with his development towards a more Christian outlook, is evident in his *Collected Poems* (1976).

auditory canal Tube leading from the outer EAR to the eardrum. It is about 2.5cm (1in) long.

Audubon, John James (1785–1851) US ornithologist and artist. His remarkable series of some 400 watercolours of birds, often in action, was published in *Birds of America* (1827–38).

Augsburg City on the River Lech, Bavaria. Founded by the Romans ($c.$15 BC) and named after Augustus, it became a free imperial city in 1276 and was a prosperous banking and commercial centre in the 15th and 16th centuries. Industries: textiles, engineering, motor vehicles. Pop. (1993) 265,000.

Augsburg Confession (1530) Summation of the Lutheran faith, presented to Emperor Charles V at the Diet of Augsburg. Its 28 articles were formulated from earlier Lutheran statements principally by Philip MELANCHTHON. It was denounced by the Roman Catholic Church, but became a model for later Protestant creeds.

Augsburg, Peace of (1555) Agreement reached by the Diet of the Holy Roman Empire in Augsburg ending the conflict between Roman Catholics and Lutherans in Germany. It established the right of each prince to decide on the nature of religious practice in his lands, *cuius regio, cuius religio*. The exclusion of other Protestant sects such as Calvinism proved to be a source of future conflict.

Augusta State capital of Maine, USA, on the

Kennebec River, 72km (45mi) from the Atlantic Ocean. Industries: tourism, textiles, paper and steel. Pop. (1990) 21,325.

Augustine of Canterbury, Saint (d.604) First Archbishop of CANTERBURY. He was sent from Rome in 596 by Pope GREGORY I, at the head of a 40-strong mission. Arriving in Kent in 597, Augustine converted King ETHELBERT and introduced Roman ecclesiastical practices into England. This brought him into conflict with the Celtic monks of Britain and Ireland whose traditions had developed in isolation from the continent. The Synod of Whitby (663) settled disputes in favour of Roman custom. St Augustine's feast day is 28 May (26 May in England and Wales).

Augustine of Hippo, Saint (354–430) Christian theologian and philosopher. Augustine's *Confessions* provide an intimate psychological self-portrait of a spirit in search of ultimate purpose. Bishop of Hippo, North Africa (396–430), in his *Enchiridion* (421) he tended to emphasize the corruption of human will and the freedom of the divine gift of grace. *The City of God* (426) is a model of Christian apologetic literature. Of the Four Fathers of the Latin Church, AMBROSE, JEROME and GREGORY I, Augustine is considered the greatest. His feast day is 28 August.

Augustinian Name of two distinct and long-established Christian orders. The order of Augustinian Canons was founded in the 11th century. Based on the recommendations of St AUGUSTINE OF HIPPO, its discipline was milder than those of full monastic orders. The mendicant order of Augustinian Hermits or Friars was founded in the 13th century and modelled on the DOMINICANS.

Augustus (27 BC–AD 14) (Gaius Julius Caesar Octavianus) First Roman emperor, also called Octavian. Nephew and adopted heir of Julius CAESAR, he formed the Second Triumvirate with Mark ANTONY and Lepidus after Caesar's assassination. They defeated BRUTUS and CASSIUS at Philippi in 42 BC and divided the empire between them. Rivalry between Antony and Octavian was resolved by the defeat of Antony at ACTIUM in 31 BC. While preserving the form of the republic, Octavian held supreme power, and was officially called Imperator Caesar Augustus. He introduced peace and prosperity after years of civil war. He built up the power and prestige of Rome, encouraging patriotic literature and rebuilding much of the city in marble. He extended the frontiers and fostered colonization, took general censuses, and tried to make taxation more equitable. He tried to arrange the succession to avoid future conflicts, though had to acknowledge an unloved stepson, TIBERIUS, as his successor.

auk Squat-bodied sea bird of colder Northern Hemisphere coastlines. The flightless great auk (*Pinguinus impennis*), or the Atlantic penguin, became extinct in the 1840s; height: 76cm (30in). The razorbill auk (*Alca torda*) is the largest of living species. Family Alcidae.

Aung San (1914–47) Burmese politician who opposed British rule. Initially collaborating with the Japanese (1942), he later helped expel the invaders. He was assassinated shortly after his appointment as deputy chairman of the executive council.

Aung San Suu Kyi, Daw (1945–) Burmese civil rights activist. The daughter of AUNG SAN, she was placed under house arrest (1989–95) for leadership of the National League for Democracy, a coalition opposed to Myanmar's oppressive military junta. In 1991 she was awarded the Nobel Peace Prize and the European Parliament's Sakharov Prize (for human rights).

Aurangzeb (1619–1707) Emperor of India (1659–1707). The last of the great MOGUL emperors, he seized the throne from his enfeebled father, SHAH JEHAN, and reigned over an even greater area, spending most of his reign defending it. He was a zealous Muslim, intolerant of Hindus, which provoked long wars with the MARATHA. The empire was already breaking up before his death.

Aurelian (*c.*215–75) Roman emperor. Having risen through the army ranks, he succeeded Claudius II in 270. His victories against the Goths, reconquest of Palmyra and recovery of Gaul and Britain earned him the title "Restorer of the World". He built the Aurelian Wall to protect Rome and was assassinated in an obscure military plot.

Aurelius, Marcus *See* MARCUS AURELIUS (ANTONINUS)

aurochs (urus) Extinct European wild ox, the long-horned ancestor of modern domesticated cattle. Once found throughout the forests of Europe and central and SE Asia, it became extinct in 1627. A dark, shaggy animal, it stood up to 2m (7ft) tall at the shoulder. Family Bovidae; species *Bos primigenius*. *See also* BISON

Aurora In Roman mythology, the goddess of dawn, equivalent to the Greek goddess EOS.

aurora Sporadic, radiant display of coloured light in the night sky, caused by charged particles from the Sun interacting with air molecules in the Earth's magnetic field. Auroras occur in polar regions and are known as **aurora borealis** in the N, and **aurora australis** in the S.

Auschwitz (Pol. *Oświęcim*) Town in Poland. It was the site of a German CONCENTRATION CAMP during World War 2. Auschwitz was Hitler's most "efficient" extermination centre. Between June 1940–January 1945 more than 4 million people were executed here, mostly Jews, of about 40 different nationalities, principally Polish. The buildings have been preserved as the National Museum of Martyrology.

Austen, Jane (1775–1817) English novelist. She completed six novels of great art, insight and wit, casting an ironic but ultimately sympathetic light on the society of upper-middle-class England. In order of composition they are: *Northanger Abbey* (1818), a parody on the contemporary Gothic novel; *Sense and Sensibility* (1811); *Pride* *and Prejudice* (1813); *Mansfield Park* (1814); *Emma* (1816); and *Persuasion* (1818). Not particularly successful in their time, they have since established their place among the most popular and well-crafted works in English literature.

Austerlitz, Battle of Fought in Bohemia, 2 December 1805. The French under NAPOLEON defeated the Austrians and Russians under Mikhail Kutuzov. One of Napoleon's greatest victories, it was also called the Battle of the Three Emperors.

Austin Capital of Texas, on the Colorado River, USA. The main industries are high-tech electronics, furniture, machinery, building materials and food processing. Pop. (1992) 492,329.

Australasia Region that includes Australia, New Zealand and Papua New Guinea.

Australia Earth's smallest continent, between the Pacific and Indian Oceans. Combined with the island of TASMANIA, it forms the independent Commonwealth country of Australia, the world's sixth largest country; the capital is CANBERRA. **Land and climate** The main highland zone is the GREAT DIVIDING RANGE in the E, which contains the country's highest peak, Mount KOSCIUSKO, in NEW SOUTH WALES. The range extends from the Cape York peninsula to VICTORIA; the mountains of Tasmania are a southerly extension. These mountains separate the E coastal plains from the Central Lowlands. The SE lowlands are drained by the MURRAY and Darling, Australia's two longest rivers. Lake EYRE, in the desert to the W, is the continent's largest lake, though it is a dry salt flat for most of the time. The huge Western Plateau, which makes up two-thirds of Australia, is flat with a few low mountain ranges. Only 10% of Australia has an average annual rainfall of more than 1,000mm (39in). These areas include some of the tropical N, where Darwin is situated, the NE coast and the SE. The coasts are usually warm and many parts of the S and SW, including PERTH, enjoy a Mediterranean climate of dry summers and moist winters. The interior is dry and water is quickly evaporated, making many of the rivers only seasonal. Much of the Western Plateau is desert, although areas of grass and low shrubs are found on the desert mar-

gins. The Central Lowlands are grasslands used to raise farm animals, taking their water from artesian wells that tap underground rock stratas The N has areas of savanna and rainforest. In dry areas, acacias are common, while in wetter areas eucalyptus trees are found. **Economy** Australia is a prosperous country. Its economy was originally based on agriculture, although crops can be grown on only 6% of the land. The country remains a major producer and exporter of farm products, particularly cattle, wheat and wool, followed by dairy products, various kinds of fruits and sugar-cane. Grapes grown for wine-making are also important. Australia is also rich in natural resources and is a major producer of minerals, including bauxite, coal, copper, diamonds, gold, iron ore, manganese, nickel, silver, tin, tungsten and zinc. Australia also produces some oil and natural gas. The majority of Australia's imports are manufactured products. They include machinery and other capital goods required by factories. The country has a highly developed manufacturing sector; the major products include consumer goods, notably foodstuffs and household articles. **History and politics** NATIVE AUSTRALIANS (Aborigines) entered the continent from Southeast Asia more than 50,000 years ago. They settled throughout the country and remained isolated from the rest of the world until the first European explorers, the Dutch, arrived in the 17th century. The Dutch did not settle, but in 1770 Britain's Captain Cook explored the E coast. In 1788 the first British settlement was established (for convicts) on the site of present-day Sydney. The first free settlers arrived three years later. In the 19th century, the economy developed rapidly, based on mining and and sheep-rearing. The continent was divided into colonies, which later became states. In 1901 the states of QUEENSLAND, Victoria, Tasmania, New South Wales, SOUTH AUSTRALIA and WESTERN AUSTRALIA, united to create the Commonwealth of Australia. Northern Territory joined the federation in 1911. The federal capital was established at Canberra, in Australian Capital Territory, in 1927. Australia fought as a member of the Allies in both world wars. Post-1945 Australia has steadily realigned itself with its Asian neighbours. Robert MENZIES, Australia's longest-serving prime minister, oversaw many economic and social policy changes and sent Australian troops to the Vietnam War. In 1977 Prime Minister Gough WHITLAM was removed from office by the governor-general. In the early 1990s, Paul Keating proposed that Australia should become a republic by the year 2001. Opinion polls suggest that the majority of Australians share this view. In the 1996 elections, Keating was defeated by a coalition led by John HOWARD. In 2000 Sydney will host the Olympic Games and 2001 is the centenary of their nationhood. The historic mistreatment of Native Australians remains a contentious political issue. In 1993 the government passed the Native Title Act

AUSTRALIA
AREA: 7,686,850sq km (2,967,893sq mi)
POPULATION: 17,529,000
CAPITAL (POPULATION): Canberra (324,600)
GOVERNMENT: Federal constitutional monarchy
ETHNIC GROUPS: White 95%, Aboriginal 1.5%, Asian 1.3%
LANGUAGES: English (official)
RELIGIONS: Christianity (Roman Catholic 26%, Anglican 24%, others 20%), Islam, Buddhism, Judaism
CURRENCY: Australian dollar = 100 cents

which restored to Native Australians land rights over their traditional hunting and sacred areas.

Australopithecus *See* HUMAN EVOLUTION

Austria Landlocked country in the heart of Europe; the capital is VIENNA. **Land and climate** About 75% of the land is mountainous. Northern Austria contains the valley of the River DANUBE, which rises in Germany and flows to the BLACK SEA, and the Vienna Basin, the main farming region. Southern Austria contains ranges of the E ALPS, which rise to Gross Glockner, at 3,979m (12,457ft). The climate is influenced by westerly and easterly winds. Westerlies bring rain, snow and also moderate temperatures, but the dry easterlies bring cold weather in winter and hot weather in summer. Thus E Austria has a more continental climate than the W parts of the country. **Economy** Austria is a prosperous country, with plenty of hydroelectric power, some oil and gas, and reserves of lignite, although fossil fuels are imported. The country's leading economic activity is manufacturing metals and metal products, including iron and steel, vehicles and machines. Vienna is the main industrial centre. Craft industries are important, producing glassware, jewellery and porcelain. Crops are grown on 18% of the land, and another 24% is pasture. Dairy and livestock farming are leading activities; barley, potatoes, rye, sugar beet and wheat are major crops. Tourism, based on winter sports and in Vienna, SALZBURG (especially during the music festival) and INNSBRUCK, is a major industry. **History** Austria was once part of the HOLY ROMAN EMPIRE and, under HABSBURG rulers, it became the most important state in the empire. When the empire dissolved in 1806, the Habsburg ruler became emperor of Austria. In 1867 Austria and Hungary set up a powerful dual monarchy, the AUSTRO-HUNGARIAN EMPIRE, which finally collapsed in 1918 following World War 1. In 1938 Germany annexed Austria and Austria fought alongside Germany in World War 2. In 1945 the Allies partitioned Austria, but the occupation ended in 1955 when Austria became a neutral federal republic. In 1994 Austrians voted in favour of joining the European Union and Austria became a member on 1 January 1995. In 1997 Viktor Klima succeeded Franz Vranitzky as chancellor.

AUSTRIA

AREA: 83,850sq km (32,347sq mi)
POPULATION: 7,884,000
CAPITAL (POPULATION): Vienna (1,589,052)
GOVERNMENT: Federal republic
ETHNIC GROUPS: Austrian 93%, Slav 2%, Turkish, German
LANGUAGES: German (official)
RELIGIONS: Christianity (Roman Catholic 78%, Protestant 6%), Islam
CURRENCY: Schilling = 100 Groschen

Austrian Succession, War of the (1740–48) Overall name for several related wars. They included the war for the Austrian succession itself, in which France supported Spain's claim to part of the HABSBURG domains; the first and second Silesian wars, in which FREDERICK II of Prussia took Silesia from Austria; and the war between France and Britain over colonial possessions, known in North America as King George's War.

Austro-Hungarian empire (1867–1918) Organization of the old Austrian empire into the kingdom of Hungary and the empire of Austria, also known as the "Dual Empire". The emperor of Austria and king of Hungary were the same person, but each nation had its own parliament and controlled its internal affairs. This arrangement ignored other nationalist minorities and pleased neither the Hungarians, who wanted greater autonomy, nor the Austrians, many of whom wanted a realignment with other German states. After World War 1 Hungary and Czechoslovakia declared their independence, the Emperor Charles abdicated and Austria became a republic.

Austronesian languages (Malayo-Polynesian) Family that includes Malay, Indonesian, Tagalog, Malagasy, and numerous other languages spoken in Indonesia, the Philippines and the islands of the Pacific Ocean. There are four branches: Indonesian, Melanesian (which includes Fijian), Micronesian (which includes Chamorro, spoken on Guam), and the Polynesian languages, which include Maori, Tongan, Tahitian and Samoan. There are about 175 million speakers in all.

authoritarianism System of government that concentrates power in the hands of one person or small group of people not responsible to the population as a whole. Freedom of the press and of political organization are suppressed. Many authoritarian regimes arise from military takeovers.

autism Disorder, usually first appearing in early childhood, characterized by a withdrawal from social behaviour, communication difficulties and ritualistic behaviour. Autistic people have difficulty understanding themselves or others as agents with varying beliefs and desires. The causes of autism may originate in genetics, brain damage or psychology.

autobiography Narrative account of a person's life, written by the subject. The modern autobiography has become a distinctive literary form. The first important example of the genre was the 4th-century *Confessions* of AUGUSTINE OF HIPPO, but the modern, introspective autobiography, dealing frankly with all aspects of life, is usually dated from the remarkable *Confessions* of ROUSSEAU (written 1765–72; pub. 1782). *See also* BIOGRAPHY

autochrome Method developed by the LUMIÈRE brothers for colour photography, first marketed in 1907. In widespread use for over 30 years, it was an improvement of the 3-colour screen method, and the first process that enabled colour photography.

autocracy System of government in which a single person or small group of people wields absolute power. Now rarely used, the term is applied to those regimes which came before the development of modern technology and state institutions which made TOTALITARIANISM possible.

autoimmune disease Any one of a group of disorders caused by the body's production of antibodies which attack the body's own tissues. One example of such an autoimmune disease is systemic LUPUS ERYTHEMATOSUS (SLE), an inflammation of the connective tissue occuring most often in young women. The occasional presence of so-called auto-antibodies in an individual does not necessarily indicate autoimmune disease.

Autolycus In Greek mythology, son of Hermes and Chione. He received from his father the gift of making whatever he touched invisible. He was thus able to commit numerous thefts until one day he was caught by SISYPHUS, whose oxen he had stolen.

automation Use of self-governing machines to carry out manufacturing, distribution and other processes automatically. By using FEEDBACK, sensors check a system's operations and send signals to a computer that automatically regulates the process. *See also* MASS PRODUCTION; ROBOT

automobile Road vehicle which first appeared in the 19th century. The first cars were propelled by steam, but were not a success. The age of the motor car really dates from the introduction (1885–86) of the petrol-driven carriages of Gottlieb DAIMLER and Karl BENZ. The INTERNAL COMBUSTION ENGINE for these cars had been developed earlier by several engineers (most notably Nikolaus Otto in 1876). The main components of a motor car remain unchanged. A body (**chassis**) to which are attached all other parts including: an **engine** or power plant; a **transmission** system for transferring the drive to the wheels, and steering, braking and suspension for guiding, stopping and supporting the car. Early cars were assembled by a few experts, but modern mass-production began in the early 1900s by Henry FORD and R. E. Olds in the USA. In most modern motor factories, component parts are put together on assembly lines. Recent technology has seen the introduction of robots (properly, robotic arms secured to the workshop floor) on the assembly line. They are usually used for welding and painting. Increasing concern over the environmental impact of the car (such as congestion, pollution and energy consumption) has encouraged governments to examine alternative forms of mass transport, oil companies to produce cleaner fuels and car manufacturers to look at alternative power plants (such as electric- or gas-powered motors).

autonomic nervous system Part of the body's nervous system that regulates involuntary functions. It helps to regulate the body's internal environment by controlling the rate of heart beat, PERISTALSIS and sweating. *See also* INVOLUNTARY MUSCLE; HOMEOSTASIS

autopilot (automatic pilot) Electronic and mechanical control system that ensures an aircraft follows a pre-programmed flight plan. It monitors the course and speed of the aircraft and corrects any deviations from the flight plan. Systems range from simple wing-levellers in light aircraft to computer-operated units consisting of: a GYROSCOPE; an electric SERVOMECHANISM unit and an accelerometer, which measures the acceleration of the aircraft.

Auvergne Region and former province of S France, comprising the départements of Allier, Puy-de-Dôme, Cantal and Haute-Loire. The capital is Clermont-Ferrand. Running N–S are the Auvergne Mountains, a scenic chain of extinct volcanoes, with the highest peak at Puy de Sancy, 1,886m (6,188ft). Area: 26,013sq km (10,047sq mi). Pop. (1990) 1,321,200.

auxin (plant hormone) Produced mainly in the growing tips of plant stems. Auxins accelerate plant growth by stimulating cell division and enlargement and by interacting with other hormones. Actions include the elongation of cells (by increasing the elasticity of cell walls, allowing the cells to take up more water) in geotropism and PHOTOTROPISM and fruit drop and leaf fall. *See also* GIBBERELLIN

Avalokitesvara In Buddhism, one of the most distinguished of the bodhisattvas (enlightened beings). He is noted for his compassion and mercy, and has remained on Earth in order to bring help to the suffering and knowledge to those who have not yet been converted.

avant-garde Term applied to innovators in the arts, particularly those whose artistic audacity surprises their contemporaries. The word comes from the French for "advance guard", deriving from the military concept for "vanguard", and has radical political overtones.

Avatar In Hinduism, an incarnation of a god in human or animal form that occasionally appears on Earth to combat evil and restore virtue. In Hindu tradition there have been nine incarnations of VISHNU, including BUDDHA, KRISHNA and RAMA, and a tenth is yet to come.

average In statistics, the one score that most typifies an entire set of scores. It is the MEAN of the scores. Other calculations also used to express what is typical in a set of scores are the mode (the one score that occurs most often), and the median (the middle score in a range which thus divides the set of scores into upper and lower halves).

Averröes (Abu-al-Walid Ibn-Rushd) (1126–98) Leading Islamic philosopher in Spain. He served as a judge after 1169 and became physician to the Caliph of Marrakesh in 1182. He was banished in 1195 to Lucena near Seville for advocating reason over religion. His major work, *Incoherence of the Incoherence*, defends Neoplatonism and ARISTOTLE. He exercised a powerful influence on Christian thought that persisted into the Renaissance.

Avicenna (979–1037) (Abu Ali al-Husayn ibn

abd Allah ibn Sina) Iranian (Persian) physician and philosopher whose work influenced the science of medicine for many centuries. He was the greatest philosopher and scientist of the golden age of Islamic learning. His *Canon Medicinae* became a standard work. He also made enduring contributions in the field of Aristotelian philosophy.

Avignon City at the confluence of the Rhône and Durance rivers, in the Vaucluse *département* of Provence, SE France. A thriving city under Roman rule, it was the seat of the popes during their exile from Rome in the 14th century. There is a Papal Palace (1316) and a Romanesque cathedral. The papacy held Avignon until 1791, when it was annexed to France by the revolutionary authorities. Industries: tourism, soap, wine, grain, leather. Pop. (1990) 83,939.

avocado Evergreen, broad-leafed tree native to the tropical New World. The name is extended to its green to dark purple, pear-shaped fruit. Avocados have a high oil content and a nutty flavour. Weight: 200g (7oz) but exceptionally up to 2kg (4.4lb). Family Lauraceae; species *Persea americana*.

Avogadro, Amedeo, Conte di Quaregna (1776–1856) Italian physicist and chemist. His hypothesis, *Avogadro's law* (1811), states that equal volumes of gases at the same pressure and temperature contain an equal number of molecules. This led later physicists to determine that the number of molecules in one MOLE (the relative molecular mass expressed in grams) is constant for all gases. This number, called Avogadro's number, equals 6.02257×10^{23}. It is both the ratio of the universal gas constant to Boltzmann's constant and of Faraday's constant to the charge of the electron.

Avon Former county in SW England. It was created in 1974 from areas of Gloucestershire and Somerset. It was replaced in 1996 by the unitary authorities of BATH and North-East SOMERSET, BRISTOL, North-West Somerset and South GLOUCESTERSHIRE.

Avon Name of four British rivers. The Bristol (**Lower**) Avon rises in the Cotswold Hills in Gloucestershire and flows S and then W through Bristol, entering the Severn estuary at Avonmouth. Length: 121km (75mi). The Warwickshire (**Upper**) Avon rises in Northamptonshire, and flows SW through Stratford upon Avon to join the River Severn at Tewkesbury. Length: 155km (96mi). The Wiltshire (**East**) Avon rises near Devizes and flows S into the English Channel. Length: 77km (48mi). The **Scottish** Avon flows E into the Firth of Forth. Length: 29km (18mi).

axiom Assumption used as a basis for deductive reasoning. The axiomatic method is fundamental to the philosophy of modern mathematics: it was used by the Greeks and formalized early in the 20th century by David Hilbert (1862–1943). In an axiomatic system, certain undefined entities (terms) are taken and described by a set of axioms.

Other, often unsuspected, relationships (theorems) are then deduced by logical reasoning.

axis Imaginary straight line about which a body rotates. In mechanics an axis runs longitudinally through the centre of an axle or rotating shaft. In geography and astronomy, it is a line through the centre of a planet or star, about which the planet or star rotates. The Earth's axis between the North and South geographic poles is 12,700km (7,900mi) long and is inclined at an angle of 66.5° to the plane in which the Earth orbits the Sun. A mathematical axis is a fixed line, such as the x, y or z axis.

Axis Powers Term applied to Germany and Italy after they signed the Rome-Berlin Axis in October 1936. It included Japan after it joined them in the Tripartite Pact (September 1940). Other states that joined the Axis were Hungary and Romania (1940) and Bulgaria (1941).

ayatollah ("gift of God" or "reflection of God") Honorific title bestowed upon a Muslim leader who has distinction and, often, political influence. *See also* KHOMEINI, AYATOLLAH RUHOLLAH.

aye-aye (aare) Primitive, squirrel-like LEMUR of Madagascar. Nocturnal and tree-dwelling, it has dark shaggy fur and an elongated third finger with which it scrapes insects and pulp from bamboo canes. Length: 40cm (16in) excluding tail. Species *Daubentonia madagascariensis*.

Ayer, Sir A.J. (Alfred Jules) (1910–1989) British philosopher. Building on the ideas of the Vienna Circle of positivists and of George Berkeley, David HUME, Bertrand RUSSELL and Ludwig WITTGENSTEIN, he introduced LOGICAL POSITIVISM into British and US philosophy. His works include *Language, Truth and Logic* (1936) and *Philosophy and Language* (1960).

Ayers Rock Outcrop of rock, 448km (280mi) SW of Alice Springs, Northern Territory, Australia. Named after the prominent South Australian politician Sir Henry Ayers (1821–97), it remained undiscovered by Europeans until 1872. It stands 348m (1,142ft) high, and is the largest single rock in the world – the distance around its base is about 10km (6mi). The rock, caves of which are decorated with ancient paintings, is of great religious significance to Native Australians. It is known to them as Uluru.

Aymará Major tribe of Native South Americans who live in the highlands of Bolivia and Peru. By 1500 they had been brought into the INCA empire, which was subsequently conquered by the Spanish. Today the Aymará number *c.*1,360,000. The Ayamará language is spoken by about a million people in Bolivia and 3 million people in Peru.

Ayub Khan, Muhammad (1907–74) Pakistani general and statesman, president (1958–69). After independence and partition of British India, Ayub Khan assumed control of the army in East Pakistan. In 1951 he became commander in chief of the army and served as defence minister (1954–56). In 1958 he led the military coup that overthrew Iskander Mirza. He was confirmed as president in a 1960 referendum. His administration was notable for its economic modernization plans and political reforms. The failure of his regime to deal with poverty and social inequality forced him to resign.

Ayurveda System of medicine practised by the ancient Hindus and derived from the VEDAS. It is still practised in India.

azalea Name given to certain shrubs and small trees of the genus *Rhododendron*, from temperate regions of Asia and North America. Mostly deciduous, they have leathery leaves and funnel-shaped red, pink, magenta, orange, yellow or white flowers, sometimes variegated. Family Ericaceae.

Azerbaijan Country in the SW of Asia, bordering the Caspian Sea to the E; the capital is BAKU. **Land and climate** The CAUCASUS Mountains are in the N and another highland region, including the Little Caucasus Mountains and part of the rugged Armenian plateau, is in the SW. Between these regions lies a broad plain drained by the River Kura, its eastern part S of BAKU lies below sea level. The country also includes the NAKHICHEVAN Autonomous Republic on the Iran frontier, which is totally cut off from the rest of Azerbaijan by Armenian territory. Azerbaijan has hot summers and cool winters. **Economy** With its economy in disarray since the break-up of the Soviet Union, Azerbaijan now ranks among the world's lower-middle income countries. Its chief resource is oil from the Baku region, both on the shore of the CASPIAN SEA and in the sea itself. In 1994 Western oil companies were invited to develop and exploit the offshore deposits. Manufacturing, including oil refining and the production of chemicals, machinery and textiles, is the most valuable activity. Crops include cotton, fruit, grains, tea, tobacco and vegetables. Fishing is still important, although the Caspian Sea has become increasingly polluted. **History** In ancient times the area now called Azerbaijan was invaded many times. Arab armies introduced Islam in 642, but most modern Azerbaijanis are descendants of Persians and Turkic peoples who migrated to the area from the E by the 9th century. The area later came under the MONGOLS between the 13th and 15th centuries and was then ruled by the Persian SAFAVID dynasty. By the early 19th century Azerbaijan was under Russian rule. After the Russian Revolution of 1917, attempts were made to form a Transcaucasian Federation made up of Armenia, Azerbaijan and Georgia. When these attempts failed, Azerbaijanis set up an independent state, but Russian forces again occupied the area in 1920. In 1922 the Russians set up the Soviet Republic of TRANSCAUCASIA, but in 1936 the three areas became separate socialist republics within the SOVIET UNION. In 1991, with the demise of the Soviet Union, Azerbaijan became an independent nation. Economic progress was slow, partly because of civil unrest in NAGORNO-KARABAKH, a large enclave of mainly Christian Armenians. In 1992 Armenia occupied the area between its E border and Nagorno-Karabakh, while ethnic Armenians took over Nagorno-Karabakh itself. A cease-fire was agreed in 1994, with about 20% of Azerbaijan territory under Armenian control. There was little sign of a long-term solution to the dispute, with further outbreaks of fighting in 1997.

azimuth Angle between the vertical plane through a celestial body and the N–S direction. Astronomers measure the angle eastwards from the N point of the observer's horizon. Navigators and surveyors measure it westwards from the S point. Altitude and azimuth form an astronomical co-ordinate system for defining position.

Azores Portuguese island group in the N Atlantic Ocean, 1,290km (800mi) W of Portugal. The capital and chief port is Ponta Delgada (on São Miguel). Although they were known to early explorers, such as the Phoenicians and the Norsemen, they were first settled by the Portuguese in the 15th century. Volcanic in origin, they consist of nine main islands, divided into three groups. The islands' economy, dependent on small-scale farming and fishing, has improved with tourist development. Since 1976 the islands have formed an autonomous region of Portugal. Area: 2,247sq km (868sq mi). Pop. (1994 est.) 239,900.

Azov, Sea of (Azovskoye More) Northern arm of the Black Sea. A shallow sea with only slight salinity, it has fishing ports on its E and S coasts. The marshes and lagoons at the W (Crimean peninsula) end were so noxious that the sea was known as *Sivash* (putrid lake). Area: 37,607sq km (14,520sq mi).

Aztec Native American civilization that dominated the central valley of Mexico in *c*.AD 1450. A war-like group, the Aztec (or Tenochca) settled near Lake Texcoco in *c*.1325, where they founded their capital Tenochtitlan (now Mexico City). They established an empire that included most of modern Mexico and extended S to Guatemala. The Aztec built temples, pyramids and palaces and adorned them with stone images and symbolic carvings. At the time of the Spanish conquest, Aztec society was based on the exploitation of labour. As a result Hernán CORTÉS used disaffected tribesmen to help him defeat the Aztec in 1521. *See also* CENTRAL AND SOUTH AMERICAN MYTHOLOGY

AZERBAIJAN
AREA: 86,600sq km (33,436sq mi)
POPULATION: 7,398,000
CAPITAL (POPULATION): Baku (1,100,000)
GOVERNMENT: Federal multiparty republic
ETHNIC GROUPS: Azerbaijani 83%, Russian 6%, Armenian 6%, Lezgin, Avar, Ukrainian, Tatar
LANGUAGES: Azerbaijani (official)
RELIGIONS: Islam (Shiite Muslim)
CURRENCY: Manat = 100 gopik

B/b is probably derived from an Egyptian hieroglyph for a house, which entered the Semitic alphabet 1500 years later as the letter beth. It then emerged in Greece as beta.

Ba'ath Party Arab political party, founded in 1943. Its major objectives were socialism and Arab unity. It was strongest in Iraq and Syria, and militaristic elements of the Ba'ath Party seized power in those countries in 1968 and 1970 respectively. *See also* HUSSEIN, SADDAM

Babbage, Charles (1791–1871) British mathematician. He compiled the first actuarial tables and planned a mechanical calculating machine, the forerunner of the modern computer.

Babbitt, Milton (1916–) US composer, musicologist and teacher. He studied with Roger Sessions and had a mathematical background that influenced his musical style. He systematized the analysis of TWELVE-TONE MUSIC. His compositions include vocal, piano and chamber music, as well as much electronic music.

Babel, Tower of Tower begun on the plain of Shinar, in Babylonia, by the descendants of NOAH as a means of reaching heaven (Genesis 11). God prevented its completion by confusing the speech of the people and scattering them throughout the world. The Genesis story was probably inspired by a ZIGGURAT in Babylon, seven storeys high and with a shrine to the god Marduk on its top.

Babi faith *See* BAHA'I FAITH

baboon Large African MONKEY with a dog-like face, which walks on all fours. Its buttocks have callous-like pads surrounded by brilliantly coloured skin. Baboons are ground dwellers and are active by day, travelling in families and larger troops led by old males, usually in open, rocky country. Their diet consists of plants, insects and small animals. They can carry food in their cheek pouches. The males have large canine teeth up to 5cm (2in) long. Weight: 14–41kg (30–90lb). Genus *Chaeropithecus* (or *Papio*).

Babur (1483–1530) (Turkish, tiger) First MOGUL emperor of India (1526–30), b. Zahir ud-Din Muhammad. He became ruler of Fergana in 1495 and engaged in a long conflict for control of Samarkand, but ultimately lost both territories. Raising an army, he captured KABUL and carved out a new kingdom for himself in Afghanistan. From here he invaded India, gaining Delhi (1526), Agra (his future capital) (1527) and conquering N India as far as Bengal. He was also a distinguished poet.

Babylon Ancient city on the River Euphrates in MESOPOTAMIA, capital of the empire BABYLONIA. It was rebuilt after being destroyed by ASSYRIA *c.*689 BC, and its new buildings included the HANGING GARDENS, one of the SEVEN WONDERS OF THE WORLD.

Babylonia Ancient region and empire of MESOPOTAMIA, based on the city of BABYLON. The Babylonian empire was first established in the early 18th century BC by HAMMURABI the Great, but declined under the impact of HITTITES and Kassites in *c.*1595 BC. After a long period of weakness and confusion, the empire eventually fell to ASSYRIA in the 8th century BC. Babylon's greatness was restored and in *c.*625 BC its independence was won by Nabopolassar, who captured the Assyrian capital of NINEVEH. This New Babylonian (Chaldaean) empire defeated Egypt and took the Jews to captivity in Babylon in 586 BC. In 538 BC it fell to the Persians.

Babylonian Captivity Deportation of the Jews to BABYLON between the capture of JERUSALEM in 586 BC by NEBUCHADNEZZAR and the reformation of a Palestinian Jewish state (*c.*538 BC) by CYRUS THE GREAT. *See also* DIASPORA; GREAT SCHISM

Bacchus In Roman mythology, the god of wine and fertility, identified with the Greek god DIONYSUS.

Bach, C.P.E. (Carl Philipp Emanuel) (1714–88) German composer and second surviving son of J.S. BACH. The most prolific and famous of Bach's sons, he wrote over 150 keyboard sonatas, 20 symphonies, about 50 harpsichord concertos, numerous chamber works, much sacred music and about 300 songs. Widely esteemed as a keyboard player, he became a leading theorist of his time with his *Essay on the True Art of Keyboard Playing* (1753–62).

Bach, J.C. (Johann Christian) (1735–82) German composer, youngest son of J.S. BACH. He was organist at Milan cathedral and composed operas that were staged in Turin and Naples. He moved to London, and in 1763 he was made music-master to Queen Charlotte. Besides 11 operas, he wrote many instrumental and vocal works.

Bach, Johann Sebastian (1685–1750) Prolific German Baroque composer. He held a series of court positions as organist and music director and had 20 children, four of whom were also composers. Bach brought contrapuntal forms to their highest expression and is unrivaled in his ability to interweave melodies with the exacting rules of Baroque harmony and counterpoint. His greatest works include masterpieces for the organ (chorale preludes, fugues, toccatas); the six *Brandenburg Concertos* for chamber orchestra; over 200 cantatas; church music, such as the *Mass in B Minor*; violin sonatas and concertos; and numerous works for the harpsichord, such as *The Well-Tempered Clavier*, six *Partitas*, and *The Art of Fugue*, incomplete at his death.

bacillus Genus of rod-like BACTERIA present in the air and soil. One example of a species that is pathogenic in man is *Bacillus anthracis*, which causes ANTHRAX.

background radiation Radiation that is normally present in an environment. Such radiation must be taken into account when measuring radiation from a particular source. On Earth, background radiation is caused by the decay of naturally occurring radioactive substances in surface rocks. In space, so-called "microwave background" is attributed to the BIG BANG.

Bacon, Francis (1561–1626) British philosopher, statesman and early advocate of the scientific method. He was also an important essayist. Successively attorney-general, lord keeper and lord chancellor, he was forced to resign his offices in 1621 when found guilty of venality.

Bacon, Francis (1909–1992) British painter, one of the most controversial artists of his generation. He changed the face of English painting in 1945 when he exhibited his TRIPTYCH, *Three Studies for Figures at the Base of a Crucifixion*. The shock of the distorted representations of grieving people in his work stems from his violent handling of paint as much as from the subjects. For much of his life Bacon was shunned by the critical establishment.

bacteria Simple unicellular microscopic organisms. They lack a clearly defined nucleus and most are without CHLOROPHYLL. Many are motile, swimming about by means of whip-like flagella. Most multiply by FISSION. Under adverse conditions many can remain dormant inside highly resistant SPORE with thick protective coverings. Bacteria may be AEROBIC or ANAEROBIC. Although pathogenic bacteria are a major cause of human disease, many bacteria are harmless or even beneficial to humans by providing an important link in FOOD CHAINS, such as in decomposing plant and animal tissue, and in converting free nitrogen and sulphur into AMINO ACIDS and other compounds that plants and animals can use. Bacteria belong to the kingdom PROKARYOTAE. *See also* ARCHAEBACTERIA; EUBACTERIA

bacteriophage VIRUS that lives on and infects BACTERIA. It has a protein head containing a core of DNA and a protein tail. Discovered in 1915, it is important in the study of GENETICS.

Baden-Powell, Robert Stephenson Smyth, Baron of Gilwell (1857–1941) British soldier and founder of the Scout movement. In the second South African war, he held Mafeking against the Boers (1899–1900). From 1910 he devoted his life to the BOY SCOUTS. His sister Agnes (1858–1945) founded the GIRL GUIDES (1910). His wife, Lady Olave (1889–1977), also did much to promote these movements worldwide.

Baden-Württemberg Federal state in SW Germany; the capital is STUTTGART. Formed in 1952 by the merger of Baden, Württemberg-Baden and Württemberg-Hohenzollern, it is a forested and fertile region drained by the Rhine and Danube rivers. Chief manufactures include electrical goods, machinery and vehicle-assembly at the industrial centres of Stuttgart, MANNHEIM and Karlsruhe. Area: 35,750sq km (13,803sq mi). Pop. (1993) 10,234,000.

badger Burrowing, nocturnal mammal that lives in Eurasia, North America and Africa. It has a stocky body with short legs and tail. Eurasian badgers (*Meles meles*) have grey bodies with black-and-white striped heads. American badgers (*Taxidea taxus*) are smaller and have grey-brown to red fur with a white head stripe. Length: 41–71cm (16–28in); weight: 10–20kg (22–44lb). Family Mustelidae.

badminton Court game for two or four players, popular in England from the 1870s. The rules were drawn up in Pune, India, and codified with the formation of the Badminton Association (1893). The object is to use light rackets to volley a shuttlecock over a net until missed or hit out of bounds by an opponent. Only the player serving can score a point, games are played to 15 points.

Baekeland, Leo Hendrik (1863–1944) US chemist, b. Belgium. He invented a type of photographic paper, Velox, capable of being developed under artificial light. He also invented the first thermosetting plastic, BAKELITE, a substance that led to the development of the plastics industry.

Baffin, William (1584–1622) English navigator and explorer. He took part in several expeditions (1612–16) in search of the NORTHWEST PASSAGE. He discovered the Canadian Arctic seaways, the island now named after him, and Lancaster Sound. An outstanding navigator, he published a method of determining longitude by the stars, using nautical tables.

Bagehot, Walter (1826–77) British economist and writer. Editor of *The Economist* (1860–77) he is chiefly remembered for his influential treatise *The English Constitution* (1867).

Baghdad Capital of Iraq, on the River Tigris. Established in 762 as capital of the ABBASID caliphate, it became a centre of Islamic civilization and a focus of caravan routes between Asia and Europe. In 1921 Baghdad became the capital of newly independent Iraq. Industries: building materials, textiles, tanning, bookbinding. Pop. (1987 est.) 3,850,000.

bagpipes Musical instrument with reed pipes connected to a windbag held under the arm and filled by mouth or bellows. The chanter pipe has finger-holes for melody, while drone pipes produce monotone accompaniment.

Baha'i Religion founded in the 1860s by Bahaullah as an outgrowth of the Babi faith. Its headquarters are in HAIFA, Israel, but it has centres worldwide. It seeks world peace through the unification of all religions and stresses a simple life dedicated to serving others. It recognizes Bahaullah as the latest prophet of God.

Bahamas Small independent state in the West Indies, in the W Atlantic, SE of Florida. It consists of about 700 islands, 2,000 cays and numerous coral reefs. The largest island is Grand Bahama; the capital is NASSAU (on New Providence). The islands consist mainly of limestone and coral, and the rocky terrain provides little chance for agricultural development. Most of the islands are low, flat and riverless with mangrove swamps. The climate is subtropical, with temperatures averaging between 21–32°C (70–90°F). Having been discovered by Columbus in his quest of the New World (1492), the islands were partially settled by England's Eleutherian Adventurers (1648). Held briefly by Spain (1782) during the American Revolution, the islands were given back to England by the Treaty of Versailles (1783) in exchange for E Florida. In 1834 slavery was abolished. In 1962 the Bahamian political parties demanded a degree of independence, and by 1963 a new constitution had been drawn up providing for a parliamentary form of government. In 1973 the Bahamas became an independent nation. The main industry is tourism; commercial fishing, salt, rum and handicrafts are also important. Area: 13,860sq km (5,350sq mi). Pop. (1992 est.) 264,000.

Bahrain Emirate archipelago in the Persian (Arabian) Gulf, SW Asia. The capital is MANAMA. Comprising 34 small islands and the largest island of Bahrain, oil was discovered in 1932 and the sheikhdom led the regional development of oil production. It is a hot, desert kingdom linked by a causeway to the Saudi Arabian mainland. From 1861–1971 the country was a British protectorate. Since the late 18th century Bahrain has been governed by the Khalifa family. Despite diversification into aluminum smelting, banking, leisure and communications sectors, oil still accounts for 80% of Bahrain's exports and 20% of its GDP. Bahrain is a predominantly Muslim nation. Tensions exist between the SUNNI and majority SHIITE population, the latter pressing for an Islamic republic. During the IRAN-IRAQ WAR Bahrain supported Iraq, prompting Iran to reiterate its territorial claims to the archipelago. Bahrain also has a long-standing dispute with QATAR over a cluster of oil-rich islands and reefs. Area: 678sq km (262sq mi). Pop. (1995 est.) 558,000.

Baikal, Lake (Baykal) World's deepest lake and the largest freshwater feature in Asia, in S Siberia, Russia. Fed by numerous small rivers, its outlet is the ANGARA River. Framed by the Vostochnyy Sayan and Yablonovy Khrebet mountains, it has rich fish stocks and includes the only freshwater seal species. Area: 31,494sq km (12,160sq mi). Max. depth: 1,743m (5,714ft).

Baird, John Logie (1888–1946) Scottish electrical engineer, inventor of TELEVISION. In 1926 he demonstrated the first working television to members of the Royal Institution, London. In 1928 he transmitted to a ship at sea, and in 1929 was granted experimental broadcasting facilities by the BRITISH BROADCASTING CORPORATION (BBC). His 240-line, part-mechanical, television system was used for the world's first public television service

by the BBC in 1936. In 1937 it was superseded by MARCONI's fully electronic scanning.

Bakelite Trade name (coined by Leo BAEKELAND) for a thermosetting PLASTIC used for insulating purposes and in making paint. It was the first plastic made by the process of condensation, in which many molecules of two chemicals (in this case phenol and formaldehyde) are joined together to form large polymer molecules, by splitting off water molecules.

Baker, Josephine (1906–75) US dancer and singer. After a sensational 1925 Paris debut in *La Revue Nègre*, she became internationally famous for her jazz singing and dancing. Her outrageous art-deco costumes and regal stage act made her one of the most photographed stars of the era.

Baku Capital of Azerbaijan, a port on the W coast of the Caspian Sea. A trade and craft centre in the Middle Ages, commercial oil production began in the 1870s. At the beginning of the 20th century Baku lay at the centre of the world's largest oil field. Its industries include oil processing and equipment, shipbuilding, electrical machinery and chemicals. Pop. (1993) 1,100,000.

Balaclava (Balaklava) Town in the Crimea, site of an inconclusive battle (1854) during the CRIMEAN WAR. The British, French and Turks held a Russian attack on their supply port of Balaclava. The battle is famous for a disastrous charge by Lord Cardigan's Light Brigade to capture Russian guns as described in a poem by Alfred TENNYSON.

balalaika Triangular musical instrument popular in Russia. Strings (usually three) are fingered on a fretted neck and may be picked, or plucked with the fingers. It sounds similar to the MANDOLIN.

balance of payments Overall surplus or deficit that occurs as a result of the exchange of all goods and services between one nation and the rest of the world. A country with a balance of payments deficit must finance it by borrowing from other countries, the INTERNATIONAL MONETARY FUND (IMF), or by using foreign currency reserves. Such deficits, if frequent, can lead to economic pressure for DEVALUATION in order to correct the imbalance. A country with a surplus is in a favourable position, but may come under international pressure to revalue its currency.

Balanchine, George (1904–83) US choreographer and ballet dancer. One of the greatest artists in 20th-century ballet. In 1924 he defected from Russia to work as principal dancer and choreographer for DIAGHILEV and the Ballets Russes. He moved to the USA in 1933, established the School of American Ballet and was director of the Metropolitan Opera ballet (1934–37). Credited with creating US neoclassical ballet, he also undertook film choreography for the Ziegfeld and Goldwyn Follies.

Balaton Largest lake in central Europe, SW of Budapest, central Hungary. Rich in fish, it has many holiday resorts and vineyards line its shores. Area: 600sqkm (232sq mi).

Balboa, Vasco Núñez de (1475–1519) Spanish conquistador, the first European to see the Pacific Ocean. He went to Hispaniola in 1500 and to Darién (Panama) ten years later. With a group of local people he crossed the isthmus and saw the Pacific, which he called the South Sea, in September 1513. He was later executed on a false charge by the governor.

Baldwin, Stanley, 1st Earl Baldwin of Bewdley (1867–1947) British Conservative statesman, prime minister (1923–24, 24–29, 35–37). He entered Parliament in 1908, became chancellor of the exchequer (1922–23), and then succeeded BONAR LAW as prime minister. Baldwin responded to the General Strike (1926) by passing the Trades Disputes Acts (1927), which made any subsequent general strikes illegal. His administration introduced universal adult suffrage. As leader of the national government, he dealt with the abdication of EDWARD VIII (1936). He is often criticized for having failed to prepare Britain for World War 2.

Balearic Islands Group of Spanish islands in the W Mediterranean, off the E coast of Spain; the capital is PALMA. The islands were successively occupied by all the great Mediterranean civilizations of antiquity. In the 11th century a Moorish kingdom used them as a base for piracy. The chief islands are MAJORCA, Minorca and IBIZA. Industries: tourism, silverworking, olive oil, wine, fruit. Area: 5,014sq km (1,936sq mi). Pop. (1991) 709,138.

Balfour, Arthur James Balfour, 1st Earl of (1848–1930) British Conservative statesman, prime minister (1902–05), b. Scotland. As prime minister, he achieved progressive domestic reforms, despite party fractures, until his government was brought down over the tariff reforms proposed by Joseph CHAMBERLAIN. As foreign minister, he issued the BALFOUR DECLARATION (1917). He represented Britain at the VERSAILLES peace conference (1919) and at the first meeting of the LEAGUE OF NATIONS.

Balfour Declaration (1917) Letter written by British foreign minister Arthur BALFOUR to the British Zionist Federation pledging cooperation for the settlement of Jews in PALESTINE. Jews were admitted to the area when it became a British mandate under the League of Nations after World War 1.

Bali Island province of Indonesia, off the E tip of Java, between the Bali Sea and the Indian Ocean. The main town is Denpasar. Under Javanese control from the 10th century, Bali was a Dutch possession from 1908–49, and was occupied by the Japanese during World War 2. It is the centre of Majaphit Hinduism. The island is fertile and densely populated. Industries: rice, sweet potatoes, cassava, copra and meat processing. Area: 5,561sq km (2,147sq mi). Pop. (1990) 2,777,811.

Balkan states Group of countries in the Balkan Peninsula, in SE Europe, consisting of ALBANIA, BOSNIA-HERZEGOVINA, BULGARIA, CROATIA, GREECE, MACEDONIA, ROMANIA, SERBIA and European TURKEY. From the 3rd century AD the region was ruled by Byzantium. It was later invaded by Slav peoples, and then for 500 years formed part of the Ottoman empire. The individual countries regained their independence in the 19th century.

ballad (Lat. *ballare*, to dance) Form of popular poetry which is regularly sung, narrative in style with simple metre, rhyme and often a refrain. The first surviving examples date from medieval times, and typically consist of four-line stanzas. Subjects include historical events, folklore and love. The late-18th-century revival of the ballad was central to the rise of ROMANTICISM. It has also been used by SWINBURNE, LONGFELLOW, Sir Walter SCOTT and KIPLING.

Ballard, J.G. (James Graham) (1930–) British novelist and short-story writer. He was initially associated with sophisticated science fiction through novels such as *The Wind from Nowhere* (1962), *The Drought* (1965), *The Crystal World* (1966) and *Crash* (1973). A larger audience was gained for his semi-autobiographical novel *Empire of the Sun* (1984), dealing with his childhood experiences of a World War 2 prisoner of war camp.

Ballesteros, Severiano (1957–) Spanish golfer. He won the Spanish Young Professional title (1974), the British Open (1979), and in 1980 was the youngest player to win the US Masters. Regarded as one of the most exciting golfers of his era, his success continued into the 1990s. In 1997 he was captain of the victorious European Ryder Cup team.

ballet Theatrical dance form set to music, which, combined with stage design, lighting and costume, conveys a story. Evolving from court spectacle during the Renaissance, the first formal ballet, *Ballet comique de la Reine*, was performed at the court of Catherine de' Medici (1581). Louis XIV founded the French Royal Academy of Dance in 1661. The 1832 performance of *Les Sylphides* set the choreographic model for 19th-century romantic ballets, stressing the role of the prima ballerina. Dancing on the toes (sur les pointes) was introduced. At the end of the 19th century Russian ballet emphasized technique and virtuosity. Subsequently, Sergei DIAGHILEV and his Ballets Russes revolutionized ballet with dynamic choreography and dancing. The preeminence of Russian ballet is maintained by the KIROV and Bolshoi companies. In 1930 Dame Marie RAMBERT founded the first English ballet school, and in 1931 Dame Ninette de VALOIS established the Sadler's Wells Ballet (now the Royal Ballet). Rudolf NUREYEV's influential work for the Royal Ballet enlarged the role and dramatic range of the male dancer. In 1934 the first major US ballet school was instituted under the direction of George BALANCHINE.

balloon Unsteerable, lighter-than-air craft, usually made of nylon. Balloons are used for recreation, scientific and military purposes. A gas that is lighter than air lifts the balloon from the ground. The first balloons to fly were of the open-necked hot-air type. The first human flight was in a hot-air balloon piloted by Jacques and Joseph MONT-GOLFIER (21 November 1783). This type of balloon uses propane gas to inflate it. Controlled descent is achieved through regulated deflation. Unmanned military, or scientific balloons are usually filled with hydrogen which is dangerously flammable. Manned balloons are generally filled with safer helium gas, or hot-air.

ballot Object used to cast a vote or process of voting in an election. The word derives from the Italian *ballotta* (little ball). Since 5th-century BC Athens, balls have been used to cast votes, white for yes, black for no. Today the ballot is a sheet (or sheets) of paper, although in some countries voting machines are used to register votes.

balsam Aromatic RESIN obtained from plants; or healing preparations, especially those with benzoic and cinnamic acid added to the resin; or balsam-yielding trees, such as the balsam fir and balsam poplar. The name is also given to numerous species of the family Balsaminaceae that are plants of moist areas, with pendent flowers. *See also* IMPATIENS

Baltic Sea Part of the Atlantic extending past Denmark, along the N coasts of Germany and Poland, and the E coasts of the BALTIC STATES, separating Sweden from Russia and Finland. The sea extends N–S with an arm reaching out to the E. The N part is the Gulf of Bothnia, the E part the Gulf of Finland. The Baltic is the largest body of brackish water in the world. Its low salinity (due to its large catchment area, about four times the area of the sea) accounts for the ease with which the Gulf of Bothnia freezes in the winter. Area: 414,400sq km (160,000sq mi).

Baltic states Countries of ESTONIA, LATVIA and LITHUANIA, on the E coast of the Baltic Sea. The region was settled by various tribes in the 7th century AD but until the 20th century, remained mostly under Danish, Russian or Polish rule. Following the Russian Revolution in 1917, each state became independent, but came under the control of the Soviet Union in 1940. They regained their independence following the break-up of the Soviet Union in 1991.

Baluchistan Region and province in central and SW Pakistan, bordered by Iran (W), Afghanistan (N) and the Arabian Sea (S). Quetta is the capital. The boundaries with Iran and Afghanistan were settled in 1885–96. The region became part of Pakistan in 1947. The terrain is mostly hilly desert, and is inhabited by nomadic tribes such as the Baluchi. Much of the population is employed in sheep raising. Some cotton is grown, and fishing is the chief occupation on the coast. Natural gas is extracted and exported, along with salt and fish. Area: 347,190sq km (134,102sq mi). Pop. (1985 est.) 4,908,000.

Balzac, Honoré de (1799–1850) French novelist. One of the greatest novelists of the 19th century, Balzac's first success was *Les Chouans* (1829). More than 90 novels and short stories followed

during a lifetime of extraordinary creative effort. He organized these works into a grand fictional scheme, intended as a detailed, realistic study of the whole of contemporary French society, which he called *La Comédie Humaine* (*The Human Comedy*). Among his best-known novels are *Eugénie Grandet* (1833), *Le Pére Goriot* (1834–5) and *La Cousine Bette* (1846).

Bamako Capital of Mali, on the River Niger 145km (90mi) NE of the border with Guinea, W Africa. Once a centre of Muslim learning (11th–15th centuries), it was occupied by the French in 1883 and became capital of the French Sudan (1908). Industries: shipping, groundnuts, meat, metal products. Pop. (1990 est.) 646,000.

bamboo Tall, tree-like GRASS native to tropical and subtropical regions. The hollow, woody stems grow in branching clusters from a thick rhizome and the leaves are stalked blades. It is used in house construction and for household implements. Some bamboo shoots are eaten. The pulp and fibre may form a basis for paper production. Height: to 40m (131ft). There are 1,000 species. Family Poaceae/Gramineae; genus *Bambusa*.

banana Long, curved, yellow or reddish fruit of the tree of the same name. It has soft, creamy flesh. A spike of yellow, clustered flowers grows from the centre of the crown of the tree and bends downwards and develops into bunches of 50–150 fruits in "hands" of 10–20. More than 100 varieties are cultivated. Fruits used for cooking are called plantains. Height: 3–9m (10–30ft). Family Musaceae; genus *Musa*.

band Instrumental ensemble, usually consisting of wind and percussion instruments. A **big band** performs swing music and has about 16 musicians in four sections: trumpets, trombones, saxophones and a rhythm section. A **brass band** contains only brass and percussion instruments. A **dance band** has a rhythm section to provide the strict beat and melody instruments such as saxophone and violin to play the tunes. A **jazz band** varies according to the style of JAZZ: a traditional jazz band usually has a clarinet, trumpet, trombone and a rhythm section, a modern jazz quartet may feature saxophone, piano, drums and bass. A **military (marching) band** contains brass and woodwind instruments with percussion. A ROCK band has a core of electric guitar, bass guitar and drums to which singers and other instruments may be added.

Banda, Hastings Kamuzu (1902–) Malawian politician, the country's first president (1966–94). He guided Nyasaland to independence as MALAWI (1964) establishing an autocratic regime. He was named president for life in 1971. He was the only African leader to maintain friendly relations with the South African apartheid regime. After two years of political unrest and economic crisis, he was forced to allow multiparty elections in 1994, which he and his Malawi Congress Party lost.

Bandaranaike, Sirimavo Ratwatte Dias

(1916–) Sri Lankan politician, prime minister (1960–65, 1970–77). The world's first woman prime minister, she led the Sri Lanka Freedom Party after her husband, Solomon BANDARANAIKE, was assassinated. As prime minister, she changed the country's name to Sri Lanka and promoted a new constitution.

Bandaranaike, Solomon West Ridgeway Dias (1899–1959) Prime Minister of Ceylon (now Sri Lanka) from 1956–59. He made Sinhalese the official language and founded the Sri Lanka Freedom Party to unite nationalists and socialists. Following his assassination by a dissident Buddhist monk, his wife, Sirimavo BANDARANAIKE, succeeded him as prime minister.

Bandar Seri Begawan (formerly, Brunei Town) Capital of BRUNEI, Borneo, SE Asia. The town port was superseded in 1972 by a new deepwater harbour at Maura. Pop. (1991) 45,867.

bandicoot Australian MARSUPIAL about the size of a rabbit and with similarly long ears, hopping gait and burrowing habits. It eats insects rather than vegetation, and its long pointed snout is probably an adaptation for its insectivorous diet. Genus *Perameles.*

Bandung Capital of West Java province, Indonesia. Founded in 1810, it was the administrative centre of the Dutch East Indies, and is now the third-largest city in Indonesia. A centre for Sundanese culture; educational institutions include the Bandung Institute of Technology and two universities. Industries: canning, chemicals, quinine, textiles. Pop. (1990) 2,026,893.

Bangalore (Bangalur) Capital of Karnataka state, s central India. Established in 1537 by the Mysore Dynasty, the city was retained by Britain as a military headquarters until 1947. It is the sixth-largest city in India, and an important industrial and communications centre. Industries: aircraft and machine tools. Pop. (1991) 3,302,296.

Bangkok Capital and chief port of Thailand, on the E bank of the River Menam (Chao Phraya). The port handles most of the country's imports and exports. Industries: building materials, rice processing, textiles, jewellery. Pop. (1993) 5,572,712

Bangladesh Republic in s Asia. It is the world's most densely populated country; the capital is DHAKA. **Land and climate** Apart from hilly regions in the far NE and SE, most of the land is flat and covered by fertile alluvium spread over the land by the Ganges, Brahmaputra and Meghna rivers. These rivers overflow when they are swollen by the annual monsoon rains. Although most of Bangladesh is low and cultivated, forests cover about 16% of the land, notably the large areas of mahogany forests and rubber plantations on the Burmese border. **Economy** Bangladesh is one of the world's poorest countries and its economy depends mainly on agriculture, which employs more than half of the people. Rice is the chief crop, but jute, sugar cane, tobacco and wheat are also

---

BANGLADESH
AREA: 144,000sq km (55,598sq mi)
POPULATION: 119,288,000
CAPITAL (POPULATION): Dhaka (Dacca, 3,397,187)
GOVERNMENT: Multiparty republic
ETHNIC GROUPS: Bengali 98%, tribal groups
LANGUAGES: Bengali (official)
RELIGIONS: Islam (Sunni Muslim) 87%, Hinduism 12%, Buddhism, Christianity
CURRENCY: Taka = 100 paisa

---

grown. Manufactured products include leather, paper and textiles. Some 60% of internal trade is by boat, although this is becoming difficult as the delta silts up. **History and politics** Islam, the chief religion today, was introduced into Bengal in the 13th century. In 1576 Bengal became part of the MOGUL EMPIRE. European influence increased in the 16th century and, in 1858, Bengal became part of British India. In 1947 British India was partitioned between the mainly Hindu India and Muslim Pakistan. Pakistan consisted of two parts, West and East Pakistan, separated by about 1,600km (1,000mi) of Indian territory. Differences developed between the West and East "wings" and in 1971 the East Pakistanis, claiming both ethnic and economic discrimination, rebelled against Islamabad. After a bitter nine-month civil war, they declared East Pakistan to be a separate nation called Bangladesh. Bangladesh became a one-party state in 1975, but military leaders seized control and dissolved parliament. Several military coups have occurred since. In 1991 the Bangladesh National Party (BNP) gained the majority in the first free elections since independence. In 1994 the opposition parties resigned, and in a general election in June 1996, the Awami League gained the majority.

Bangui Capital of the Central African Republic, on the Ubangi River, near the Zaïre border. Founded in 1889 by the French, it is the nation's chief port for international trade. Industries: textiles, food processing, beer, soap. Pop. (1988) 451,690.

banjo Musical instrument with four to nine strings, a body of stretched parchment on a metal hoop, and a long, fretted neck. It is played with a plectrum or the fingers. Probably of African origin, it was taken to the USA by slaves. It is most often used in Dixieland jazz and folk-music.

Banjul (Bathurst) Capital of Gambia, w Africa, on St Mary's Island, where the River Gambia enters the Atlantic Ocean. Founded as a trading post by the British in 1816, it is the country's chief port and commercial centre. Industries: groundnut processing, tourism. Pop. (1983) 44,188.

banking Commercial process providing a wide range of financial services such as holding and transferring money, providing loans and giving stability to the financial sector of the economy. There are a variety of sectors in the banking industry. **Clearing** banks in the UK and **commercial** banks in the USA deal with the general public, as well as with small and medium-sized businesses and corporations; MERCHANT BANKS or investment banks provide services to business and industry, such as investment loans or share flotations. In many countries there are other providers of banking services, such as insurance companies and credit card issuers, as well as BUILDING SOCIETIES in the UK and SAVINGS AND LOAN ASSOCIATIONS in the USA. A country's CENTRAL BANK, sometimes under government control, is the bankers' bank and can be used as an economic regulator.

Bank of England Britain's central banking institution, founded in 1694 by a group of London merchants. Nationalized in 1946, it regulates foreign exchange, issues bank notes, advises the government on monetary matters and acts as the government's financial agent. Since 1997, following legislation put forward by the Labour chancellor Gordon BROWN, the Bank has the power to set national interest rates. It is situated in Threadneedle Street, City of London. The governor of the Bank of England is appointed by the government.

banksia Any of about 70 species of flowering shrubs and small trees found in Australia and New Guinea that belong to the genus *Banksia*. Their evergreen leaves are long and leathery, and they bear tube-shaped heads of yellowish or reddish flowers. The genus was discovered by Sir Joseph Banks. Most banksias are pollinated by birds, but some are pollinated by the honey possum, a small mouse-like marsupial that feeds on their nectar and pollen. Family Proteaceae.

Bannister, Sir Roger Gilbert (1929–) British athlete. The first man to run a mile in less than four minutes (on 6 May 1954 in 3min. 59.4sec.).

Bannockburn Town and moor in central Scotland, scene of a Scottish victory over the English in 1314.

Banting, Sir Frederick Grant (1891–1941) Canadian physician. He shared, with J.J.R. Macleod, the 1923 Nobel Prize for physiology or medicine for his work in extracting the hormone INSULIN from the PANCREAS. This made possible the effective treatment of DIABETES.

Bantu Group of African languages generally considered as forming part of the Benue-Congo branch of the Niger-Congo family. Among the most widely spoken of the several hundred tongues used from the Congo Basin to South Africa are Swahili, Xhosa and Zulu. There are more than 70 million speakers of Bantu languages, and they are widely used in schools. They are almost all tone languages.

banyan Evergreen tree of E India. The branches send down aerial shoots that take root, forming new trunks. Such trunks from a single tree may form a circle up to 100m (330ft) across. Height: to 30m (100ft). Family Moraceae; species *Ficus benghalensis*.

baobab Tropical tree native to Africa. It has a stout trunk containing water storage tissue, and stubby branches with sparse foliage. Fibre from its bark is used for rope. Its fruit has edible pulp. Height: to 18m (60ft); trunk diameter: to 12m (40ft). Family Bombacaceae; species *Adansonia digitata*.

baptism Pouring of water on a person's forehead or the immersion of the body in water, used as a rite of initiation into the Christian church. Baptism is one of the SACRAMENTS of the Christian church. The water symbolizes regeneration. Total immersion is practised by the BAPTISTS. In churches that practise infant baptism, the rite is usually referred to as christening and is the occasion when a child is given its names.

Baptist Member of various Protestant and Evangelical sects who practise BAPTISM of believers and regard immersion as the only legitimate form sanctioned by the New Testament. They generally reject the practice of infant baptism, insisting that initiates must have freedom of thought and expression and must already be believers. Baptists originated among English dissenters of the 17th century, but have spread worldwide through emigration and missionary work. There is no official creed, no hierarchy, and individual churches are autonomous. In the mid-1990s, Baptists worldwide numbered about 31 million.

bar Unit of pressure, the pressure created by a column of mercury 75.007cm high. It is equal to 10^5 pascals. Standard atmospheric pressure (at sea level) is 1.01325 bars, or 1,013.25 millibars.

Barabbas In the New Testament, convicted criminal or terrorist who was in prison at the time of JESUS CHRIST's trial before PONTIUS PILATE. In accordance with a PASSOVER custom, Pilate offered to release a prisoner. The Jerusalem mob, given the choice of which prisoner should be allowed to go free, nominated Barabbas and called for Christ to be crucified (Matthew 27, Mark 15, Luke 23, John 18).

Barbados Island state in the Windward Islands, West Indies; the capital is BRIDGETOWN. Barbados' warm climate has encouraged the growth of its two largest industries: sugar cane and tourism. Barbados was settled by the British in 1627, and dominated by British plantation owners (using African slave labour until the abolition of slavery) for the next three hundred years. It was not until 1966 that it gained its independence. Area: 430sq km (166sq mi). Pop. (1993) 263,900.

Barbary ape Tailless, yellowish-brown, apelike MONKEY native to Algeria, Morocco and introduced into Gibraltar. It is the size of a small dog. The Gibraltar Barbary apes are the only wild monkeys in Europe. Species *Macaca sylvana*. *See also* MACAQUE; PRIMATE

barbel (barb) CARP-like freshwater fish of W Asia and S central Europe. A game and food fish, it has an elongated body, flattened underside and two pairs of fleshy mouth whiskers (barbels). It is a strong swimmer, well adapted to fast-flowing rivers. Length: 50–90cm (19.7–35.4in); weight: 16kg (35lb). Family Cyprinidae; species *Barbus barbus*.

Barbie, Klaus (1913–91) Nazi chief of the German Gestapo in France during World War 2. He was known as the "Butcher of Lyon" for his persecution and murder of French Resistance fighters and Jews. He sent thousands of people to AUSCHWITZ. After the war, he worked for US counter-intelligence before escaping to Bolivia in 1951. He was captured in 1987, brought back to Lyon and sentenced to life imprisonment.

barbiturate DRUG used as sedative or to induce sleep. Highly addictive and dangerous in high doses, or in combination with other drugs such as alcohol, most barbiturates are no longer prescribed. Short-acting barbiturates are used in surgery to induce general anaesthesia; long-acting formulations are prescribed for epilepsy.

Barcelona City and Mediterranean port in NE Spain, capital of CATALONIA and Spain's second-largest city. It is the focus of radical political and Catalan separatist movements. Modern Barcelona is the cosmopolitan, cultural capital of Spain with a number of historic buildings and important shipping, banking and financial businesses. Industries include vehicles, textiles, machinery, petrochemicals and electrical goods. Pop. (1991) 1,625,542.

bar code Coded information consisting of thick and thin lines, and designed for computer recognition. At supermarket checkouts, a laser beam scans the bar code and a light-sensitive detector picks up the reflected signal, which consists of a pattern of pulses. The store's computer translates this into information, including the product's name, weight or size. The computer refers to a price list data file to see how much to charge the customer.

Bardeen, John (1908–91) US physicist known for his research into SEMICONDUCTORS. He worked with the Bell Telephone Laboratories (1945–51) and was professor of physics at Illinois University (1951–75). He was the first person to win the Nobel Prize twice in the same field, physics: in 1956 he shared it with William SHOCKLEY and Walter BRATTAIN, for their joint invention of the TRANSISTOR, and in 1972 with Leon Cooper and John Schrieffer, for their theory of SUPERCONDUCTIVITY.

Barents, Willem (d.1597) Dutch navigator and explorer. He made three expeditions in search of the NORTHEAST PASSAGE (1594–97). On his third voyage he discovered SVALBARD and, crossing the sea now named after him, reached NOVAYA ZEMLYA. The ship was trapped by ice and the Dutch sailors built a shelter; most survived until the following year, when they escaped, but Barents died before they reached safety.

barium Metallic element (symbol Ba) of the alkaline-earth group, discovered in 1808 by Sir Humphry DAVY. It is a soft, silvery-white metal whose chief sources are heavy spar (barium sulphate) and witherite (barium carbonate). Barium compounds are used as rodent poison, pigments for paints and as drying agents. Barium sulphate ($BaSO_4$) is swallowed to allow x-ray examination of the stomach and intestines because barium atoms are opaque to x-rays. Properties: at.no. 56; r.a.m. 137.34; r.d. 3.51; m.p. 725°C (1,337°F); b.p. 1,640°C (2,984°F); most common isotope Ba^{138} (71.66%).

bark Outer protective covering of a woody plant stem. It is made up of several layers. The CORK layer, waxy and waterproof, is the thickest and hardens into the tough, fissured outer covering. Lenticels (pores) in the bark allow GAS EXCHANGE between the stem and the atmosphere. *See also* CAMBIUM

barley Cereal GRASS native to Asia and Ethiopia, cultivated perhaps since 5000 BC. Three cultivated species are: *Hordeum distichum*, commonly grown in Europe; *H. vulgare*, favoured in the USA; and *H. irregulare*, grown in Ethiopia. Barley is eaten by humans and animals, and is used to make malt beverages.Family Poaceae/Gramineae.

bar mitzvah Jewish ceremony in which a young male is initiated into the religious community. At the ceremony, which traditionally takes place when he is aged 13 years and 1 day, he reads a portion of the TORAH in a synagogue. The religious rite is followed by a social celebration.

Barnabas, Saint Early Christian apostle, originally named Joseph, who was a companion of St PAUL. He travelled with Paul on two proselytizing missions to Cyprus and the European mainland. His feast day is 11 June.

barnacle Crustacean that lives mostly on rocks and floating timber. Some barnacles live on whales, turtles and fish, without being parasitic, although there are also parasitic species. The larvae swim freely until ready to become adults, when they settle permanently on their heads; their bodies become covered with calcareous plates. The adult uses its feathery appendages to scoop food into its mouth. Two main types are those with stalks (goose barnacles) and those without (acorn barnacles). Subclass Cirripedia.

Barnard, Christiaan (1922–) South African surgeon. He was the first to perform a human heart transplant (3 December 1967). In 1974 he was the first to implant a second heart in a patient and to link the circulations of the hearts so that they worked together as one.

Barnardo, Thomas John (1845–1905) British philanthropist who founded the Dr Barnardo homes for destitute children. In 1867 he founded the East End Mission for orphan children, the first of his famous homes. These spread rapidly through the UK and still flourish today.

Barnum, Phineas Taylor (1810–91) US showman. He established the American Museum in New York City (1842), where he presented the "dwarf" Tom Thumb, the Fijian mermaid and other "freaks". In 1847 he introduced the Swedish soprano Jenny LIND to US audiences. In 1871 he opened his circus, billed as "The Greatest Show on Earth". He merged with rival James Bailey in 1881, to form Barnum and Bailey's Circus.

barometer Instrument for measuring atmospheric pressure. Mercury and aneroid (non-liquid) barometers are the two basic types. A **mercury barometer** has a vertical column of mercury that changes length with changes in atmospheric pressure. An **aneroid barometer** has a chamber containing a partial vacuum, and the chamber changes shape with changes in pressure. Barometers are used in WEATHER FORECASTING to predict local weather changes: a rising barometer (increasing pressure) indicates dry weather; a falling barometer indicates wet weather. In a **barograph**, the pointer of an aneroid barometer is replaced by a pen that traces variations in pressure on a revolving cylindrical chart. A barometer can also be used in an ALTIMETER to measure altitude by indicating changes in atmospheric pressure. *See also* BAR

baroque Term (perhaps derived from the Portuguese *barroca*, a misshapen pearl) applied to the style of art and architecture prevalent in Europe in the 17th and early 18th centuries. Baroque was at its height in the Rome of BERNINI, BORROMINI and Pietro de Cortona (*c*.1630–80) and in S Germany with Balthazar Neumann and Fischer von Erlach (*c*.1700–50). High baroque at its best was a union of architecture, painting and sculpture in a blend of light, colour and movement calculated to overwhelm the spectator by a direct emotional appeal. Paintings contained visual illusions; sculpture exploited the effect of light on surface and contour. Architecture was created in a series of geometrically controlled spaces (squares, circles, ovals and triangles) which enclosed, adjoined and superimposed each other to create the illusion of rhythmic movement. Buildings were heavily decorated with stucco ornament and free-standing sculpture. Baroque was closely linked to the COUNTER-REFORMATION and was therefore strongest in Roman Catholic countries. Baroque became increasingly florid before merging with the lighter style of ROCOCO. The term is often used to describe the period as well as the style. In music, the period is notable for several stylistic developments, culminating in the masterpieces of J.S. BACH and HANDEL. Many purely instrumental forms, such as fugue, sonata, concerto, suite, toccata, passacaglia and chaconne, emerged and became popular and increasingly virtuosic.

barracuda Marine fish found in tropical Atlantic and Pacific waters. Known to attack people, it has a large mouth with many large, razorsharp teeth. It is long, slender and olive green. Length: usually 1.2–1.8m (4–6ft); weight: 1.4–22.7kg (3–50lb). The great barracuda of the Florida coast grows to 2.5m (8ft). Family Sphyraenidae; there are 20 species.

barrier reef Long, narrow CORAL REEF lying some distance from and roughly parallel to the shore, but separated from it by a lagoon. The GREAT BARRIER REEF is the most famous.

Barrie, Sir James Matthew (1860–1937) Scottish dramatist and novelist. He is chiefly remembered as the writer of *Peter Pan* (1904), an ever-popular play about a boy who refuses to grow up. Although criticized for his sentimentality, his best works are clever, romantic fantasies. His other plays include *The Admirable Crichton* (1902), and *What Every Woman Knows* (1908).

barrow In archaeology, a prehistoric burial mound. Various types of barrow are found, but in Europe they are usually either long or round. Long barrows were built in the NEOLITHIC period, and consisted of a long vault built of huge stones, roofed with stone slabs and covered with soil or chalk. Round barrows primarily date to the early BRONZE AGE, but some in England were built as late as Roman and Saxon times. Usually containing a single body, round barrows vary in diameter from 1.5–50m (4.5–160ft).

Barry, Sir Charles (1795–1860) British architect. He redesigned the HOUSES OF PARLIAMENT in London in a Gothic style after the original building was burnt down in 1834. He worked on the project with PUGIN who was responsible for much of the exterior and interior decoration.

Barthes, Roland (1915–80) French academic, writer and cultural critic. A leading proponent of STRUCTURALISM and SEMIOTICS, his notion of the literary text as a "system of signs" was informed by the linguistics of Ferdinand de SAUSSURE. Perhaps his best-known contribution to literary theory was the notion of the "death of the author" in which the meaning of a text is generated by the reader, rather than by reference to biographical detail. At the time of his death, Barthes was Professor at the Collège de France. His diverse works include *Writing Degree Zero* (1953), *Mythologies* (1957), *S/Z* (1970) and *Camera Lucida* (1980).

Bartholdi, Frédéric Auguste (1834–1904) French sculptor. His most famous piece is *Liberty Enlightening the World* (Statue of Liberty) in New York harbour, which was dedicated in 1886. The colossal *Lion of Belfort* at Belfort, France, is considered his best work.

Bartók, Béla (1881–1945) Hungarian composer and pianist. With Zoltán KODÁLY, Bartók amassed a definitive collection of Hungarian folk music that became the basis of many of his compositions. His orchestral works include *Music for Strings, Percussion, and Celesta* (1936), two violin concertos (1908 and 1938) and Concerto for Orchestra (1943). He wrote one opera, *Bluebeard's Castle* (1911). He also composed three piano concertos and six five-string quartets. His compositional style combines folk music idioms with dissonance and great rhythmic energy.

Bartolommeo, Fra (1457–1517) (Bartolommeo

della Porta) Florentine painter, draughtsman and Domincan friar. In parallel with RAPHAEL, he contributed to the development of a new type of Madonna with Saints, specific to the High RENAISSANCE, in which the Madonna acts as a central point for the whole composition. Bartolommeo's characteristic style is one of restraint combined with monumentality, as exemplified in *The Mystical Marriage of St. Catherine* (1511).

baryon Any elementary particle affected by the strong interaction of nuclear force. The baryon consists of three QUARKS. Baryons are subclasses of HADRONS. The only stable baryons are the PROTON and (provided it is inside a nucleus) the NEUTRON. Heavier baryons are called hyperons. *See also* LEPTON; MESON

Baryshnikov, Mikhail (1948–) US ballet dancer, b. Russia. A member of the KIROV BALLET from 1969–74, he then defected to the West. He was associated with the American Ballet Theater as principal dancer (1974–78) and as artistic director (1980–89).

basal metabolic rate (BMR) Minimum amount of energy required by the body to sustain basic life processes, including breathing, circulation and tissue repair. It is calculated by measuring oxygen consumption. Metabolic rate increases well above basal metabolic rate (BMR) during vigorous physical activity or fever or under the influence of some DRUGS (including CAFFEINE). It falls below BMR during sleep, general ANAESTHESIA or starvation. BMR is higher in children and decreases with age.

basalt Hard, fine-grained, basic IGNEOUS ROCK, which may be intrusive or extrusive. Its colour can be dark green, brown, dark grey or black. It can have a glassy appearance. There are many types of basalt with different proportions of elements. It may be compact or vesicular (porous) because of gas bubbles contained in the lava while it was cooling. If the vesicles are subsequently filled with secondary minerals, such as quartz or calcite, it is called amygdaloidal basalt. Basalts are the main rocks of ocean floors, and form the world's major lava flows, such as the Deccan Trap in India.

base In mathematics, the number of units in a number system that is equivalent to one unit in the next higher counting place. Thus 10 is the base of the decimal system: only the ten digits 0–9 can be used in the units, tens, hundreds, and so on. Each number system has a number of symbols equal to its base. In the BINARY SYSTEM (base 2) there are two symbols, 0 and 1.

base Chemical compound that accepts protons. A base will neutralize an ACID to form a SALT and water. Most are oxides or hydroxides of metals; others, such as ammonia, are compounds that yield hydroxide IONS in water. Soluble bases are called ALKALIS. Strong bases are fully dissociated into ions; weak bases are partially dissociated in solution. *See also* NEUTRALIZATION

baseball National summer sport of the USA, now also popular in Japan and developing in Latin America, Australia and parts of Europe. A baseball pitch comprises a field featuring a diamond-shape configuration of a batting plate and four bases. It is played by two opposing teams of nine players. One run is scored every time a batter completes the circuit of bases.

Basel (Bâle or Basle) City and river port on the River Rhine; capital of Basel-Stadt canton, NW Switzerland. It joined the Swiss Confederation in 1501. It is an economic, financial and historically important cultural centre. It is the centre of the Swiss chemical and pharmaceutical industries. Other industries: publishing, silk, electrical engineering, food processing, metal goods. Pop. (1992) 173,800.

BASIC (**B**eginners' **A**ll-purpose **S**ymbolic **I**nstruction **C**ode) Computer programming language. BASIC is easy to learn and uses many ordinary English words and simple mathematical expressions. Many low-cost home computers accept programs written in BASIC. A device called an interpreter translates the BASIC COMPUTER PROGRAM into a machine code required by a computer's MICROPROCESSOR.

Basil II (*c.*958–1025) Byzantine emperor (976–1025), surnamed Bulgaroctonus ("Bulgarslayer"). One of Byzantium's ablest rulers, Basil reigned during the heyday of the BYZANTINE EMPIRE. He is best known for his military victory over the Bulgarian tsar Samuel in 1014, which brought the entire Balkan peninsula under Byzantine control. During Basil's reign, the Byzantium's sphere of influence was extended by the conversion of Kievan Russia to Orthodox Christianity.

basil Common name for a tropical plant of the MINT family, whose dried leaves are used for flavouring. It has white or purple flowers. Family Lamiaceae/Labiatae. Species *Ocimum basilicum*.

basilica Roman colonnaded hall used for public business; also an early Christian church based on this design. The main characteristics of a basilica church, established by the 4th century AD, were a rectangular plan with a longitudinal axis, a wooden roof and an E end that was either rectangular or contained a semicircular apse. The body of the church usually had a central nave and two flanking aisles, lower and narrower than the nave.

basilisk Semi-aquatic LIZARD found in trees near streams of tropical America. It has a compressed greenish body, whip-like tail, a crest along its back and an inflatable pouch on its head. It can run over water for short distances on its hindlegs, and eats plants and insects. Length: up to 61cm (2ft). Family Iguanidae; genus *Basiliscus*. Basilisk is also a legendary serpent with the body of a cockerel.

Basil the Great, Saint (329–79) One of the most important of the early Church Fathers. He founded a monastic community, and in 370 was ordained a bishop. He wrote a number of books on theology and was a fierce opponent of Arianism. He is thought to have composed the *Liturgy of St Basil*, which is still used in the Eastern Orthodox Church. His feast day is 2 January in the West; 1 January in the East.

basketball Game that originated in the USA, but is now played worldwide. Devised in 1891 by Dr James Naismith, it has been an Olympic sport since 1936. It is played by two teams of five people, usually indoors, on a court up to 27.8m (91ft) long and 15m (49ft) wide. At each end of the court is a backboard on which a bottomless netting basket hangs 3m (10ft) above the floor. The object of the game is to get the ball to drop down through the opposing team's basket, thus scoring a goal.

Basle *See* BASEL

Basov, Nikolai Gennadiyevich (1922–) Soviet physicist. He developed the MASER, which amplifies microwaves, and the LASER, which amplifies light. For these contributions, Basov and his co-worker Alexander PROKHOROV shared the 1964 Nobel Prize for physics with the US physicist Charles Townes (who had made similar discoveries independently).

Basque Country Region of the W Pyrenees in both Spain and France, consisting of the provinces of Alava, Guipúzcoa, part of Navarra and Vizcaya in Spain and Basse-Navarre, Labourd and Soule in France. The main towns are BILBAO and San Sebastián. The region is populated by the BASQUES. It lost its autonomy in the late 18th and early 19th centuries. Separatist movements were formed in response.

Basques Indigenous people of the western Pyrenees in N Spain and SW France, numbering *c*.3,900,000. Their language is not related to any other European tongue. Throughout history they have tenaciously maintained their cultural identity. Basque separatists ETA continue to agitate for an independent state.

Basra (Al-Basrah) City and chief port in Iraq, on the River Shatt al-Arab; capital of Basra province. An ancient centre of Arabic learning, it was captured by the Turks in 1668. In the early 20th century, large oilfields were discovered nearby, resulting in Basra's revival as a commercial and industrial centre. It suffered serious damage during the Iran-Iraq and Gulf wars. Industries: oil refining, flour milling, wool. Agricultural crops include dates, maize and rice. Pop. (1992 est.) 746,000.

bass Any of several bony fishes, both freshwater and marine, and not all closely related. Together they make up a valuable commercial and sport fish. They include the white, black, striped, rock and calico basses. The two main bass families are Serranidae and Centrarchidae.

bass Term denoting low or deep pitch. It is used of the lowest-pitched part of a composition, or the lowest-pitched member of a family of instruments. It applies to the deepest male singing voice. The bass line in a composition is the bottom note of a chord or the lowest line in polyphony, and plays an important role in the harmonic structure of the piece.

Basseterre Capital and chief port of the federated state of ST KITTS-NEVIS, on the SW coast of St Kitts, in the Leeward Islands group, E Caribbean. Founded in 1627, it is an important commercial centre. The main industry is sugar-refining. Pop. (1990) 14,283.

bassoon Bass WOODWIND instrument with a range of three octaves, corresponding to that of the CELLO. It has a double-reed mouthpiece and a conical bore, the tube bending back on itself to reduce the instrument's length. Bassoons are used in symphonic and chamber music. The double bassoon or contrabassoon is the lowest-pitched woodwind instrument, sounding an octave below the bassoon. It consists of a tube 5m (16ft) long, doubled back on itself four times. The modern form of the instrument dates from the late 19th century.

Bastille Fortress and prison in Paris, built in the late 14th century and destroyed during the FRENCH REVOLUTION. Political prisoners were incarcerated here, and it became a symbol of royal oppression. On 14 July 1789, now a national holiday in France, a revolutionary mob stormed it, captured the ammunition store and released its seven prisoners. The Bastille was pulled down soon afterwards.

bat Only MAMMAL that has true flight (although a few others can glide). Bats are nocturnal and found in all tropical and temperate regions. Most are brown, grey or black. A bat's wing is formed by a sheet of skin stretched over a frame of greatly elongated bones. Bats are able to navigate in complete darkness by means of a kind of SONAR, which uses echoes of the bat's own supersonic squeaks to locate obstacles and prey. Many bats live largely on insects, some are carnivorous, some drink blood, some live on nectar and pollen and one group – flying foxes – subsist on fruit. Most are small, although they range in wingspan from 25cm–147cm (10–58in). The 178 genera of bats make up the order Chiroptera.

Bates, H.E. (Herbert Ernest) (1905–74) British novelist, playwright and short-story writer. His novels include *Fair Stood the Wind for France* (1944), *The Jacaranda Tree* (1949), and a popular series featuring the Larkin family, including *The Darling Buds of May* (1958).

Bath Spa city on the River Avon, in SW England. The centre of the new unitary authority of Bath and North-East Somerset, Bath has been designated a world heritage site. Its hot springs were discovered in the 1st century AD by the Romans, who named the city *Aquae Sulis* (waters of the sun). The bathing complex and temple are the finest Roman remains in Britain. In the 18th century (under the direction of Beau Nash) the city became a fashionable resort. John Wood transformed the city into a showcase for Georgian architecture. The Royal Crescent, Queen Square and the Circus are among his notable achievements. Industries: tourism, printing, bookbinding, engineering and clothing. Pop. (1991) 79,900.

batholith Huge mass of IGNEOUS ROCK that cooled and solidified below the Earth's surface. Originating as intrusive igneous structures, they can be seen at the surface when the overlying rocks are eroded. Most batholiths consist of granite rock types, and are associated with the mountain building phases of PLATE TECTONICS.

batik Method of decorating textiles, practised for centuries in Indonesia and introduced into Europe by Dutch traders. Molten wax is applied to the parts of a fabric that are to remain undyed, before the fabric is dipped into cool vegetable dye. The fabric is then dipped in hot water to remove the wax from the undyed areas. The process may be repeated, using different coloured dyes to form intricate patterns.

Batista y Zaldívar, Fulgencio (1901–73) Cuban political leader, president (1940–44, 1952–59). A sergeant in the army, he led a successful coup in 1933, and until 1940 ruled through figurehead presidents. In 1940 he was elected president. He retired in 1944 and moved to Florida, but in 1952 a military coup returned him to power. In 1959 his repressive regime was overthrown by Fidel CASTRO.

battery Collection of voltaic cells that convert chemical energy into direct current (DC) electricity. The term is also commonly used for a single cell, particularly a dry cell as used in portable electronic equipment. Most primary cell batteries are not rechargeable; some types of primary cell – such as nickelcadmium (Nicad) batteries and all accumulators (storage batteries) – can be recharged when a current passed through them in the reverse direction restores the original chemical state.

Baudelaire, Charles Pierre (1821–67) French poet and critic. His collection of poems, *Les Fleurs du Mal* (1857), is one of the highest achievements of 19th-century French poetry. His exploration of the correspondences between scent, sound and colour influenced the SYMBOLISM movement.

Bauhaus German school for architecture and the applied arts. It played an important role in developing links between design and industry. Founded by Walter GROPIUS in 1919, it aimed to combine great craftsmanship with an ideal of an all-embracing modern art in which the division beween monumental and decorative elements would no longer exist. Although Bauhaus specialized in architecture and design, several progressive painters, including KANDINSKY and KLEE, taught there.

bauxite Rock from which most aluminium is extracted. Bauxite is a mixture of several minerals, such as diaspore, gibbsite, boehmite and iron. It is formed by prolonged weathering and leaching of rocks containing aluminium silicates.

Bavaria (Bayern) Largest state in Germany; the capital is MUNICH. Part of the Roman empire until

the 6th century, it was taken by CHARLEMAGNE in 788, forming part of the Holy Roman Empire until the 10th century. Incorporated into Germany in 1871, it remained a kingdom until 1918, becoming a state within the German Federal Republic in 1946. Industries: glass, porcelain and brewing. Area: 70,553sq km (27,256sq mi). Pop. (1993) 11,863,313.

Bayeux tapestry (*c*.1080) Strip of linen embroidered in wool, which measures 70m×48cm (231ft×19in), and depicts (in more than 70 scenes) the life of HAROLD II of England and the NORMAN CONQUEST. An unfounded tradition attributes its design to Matilda, wife of WILLIAM I (THE CONQUERER), but it was probably commissioned by William's half-brother Odo, Bishop of Bayeux. It is now in a museum in Bayeux, N France.

Bay of Pigs (17 April 1961) Unsuccessful effort by Cuban exiles (aided by the USA) to overthrow Fidel CASTRO by invading Cuba near the Bay of Pigs. About 1,500 Cubans, trained, equipped and transported by the US government, were involved. The invasion was badly planned and the Cuban army defeated the exiles within three days. *See also* CUBAN MISSILE CRISIS

Bayreuth City in Bavaria, West Germany, where an annual festival is held, staging exclusively the work of composer Richard WAGNER. The festivals are held in the *Festspielhaus*, built to Wagner's specifications for the performance of great German theatre. The first festival was held in 1876.

BBC *See* BRITISH BROADCASTING CORPORATION

BCG (Bacille Calmette Guérin) Vaccine against tuberculosis. It was named after its discoverers, the French bacteriologists Albert Calmette and Camille Guérin.

bean Plant grown for its edible seeds and seed pods; species include broad, string, kidney and runner beans. The broad bean (*Vicia faba*) is native to N Africa. The string bean (*Phaseolus vulgaris*) is native to tropical South America, and is common in the USA; several varieties are cultivated. Its long pods or kidney-shaped seeds are eaten as vegetables. The runner (*Phaseolus coccineus*) has scarlet, rather than white or lilac flowers, and shorter, broader seeds. *See also* SOYA BEAN

bear Large, omnivorous mammal with a stocky body, thick coarse fur and a short tail. Bears are native to the Americas and Eurasia. The sun bear is the smallest species, the Kodiak brown bear the largest. Bears have poor sight and only fair hearing, but an excellent sense of smell. Except for polar bear which live almost exclusively on fish, walruses and seals, bears eat a wide variety of plant and animal foods. They kill prey with a blow from their powerful fore-paws. In cold regions most bears become dormant or hibernate in winter. Length: 1.3–3m (4–10ft); weight: 45–725kg (100–1,600lb). Order Carnivora; family Ursidae; there are approximately nine species.

beatitudes Blessings spoken by Jesus at the

opening of his SERMON ON THE MOUNT upon those worthy of admission to the Kingdom of God. (Luke 6, Matthew 5).

Beatles, The British rock group, perhaps the most influential band in the history of 20th-century popular music. Formed in Liverpool in 1960, it initially consisted of John Lennon (1940–80), Paul McCartney (1942–), George Harrison (1943–) and Pete Best (1941–). In 1962 Best was replaced by Ringo Starr (Richard Starkey) (1940–). The Beatles' early style was US-derivative rhythm and blues blended with Lennon and McCartney's song-writing talent and attractive harmonies. From 1964–70 they dominated pop music with 18 albums, including *Rubber Soul* (1965), *Revolver* (1966) and *Sgt. Pepper's Lonely Hearts Club Band* (1967). After 1966 they never publicly performed live. The group also made four feature films and supplied the soundtrack for the cartoon *Yellow Submarine* (1968). The group disbanded in 1970 to pursue individual careers. In 1980 Lennon was murdered by a fan, Mark Chapman. Their influence on contemporary British popular music is undiminished.

beat movement Term derived from John Clellon Holme's novel *Go* (1952) and applied to a group of US writers in the 1950s, who rejected middle-class values and commercialism. They also experimented with different states of perception through drugs and meditation. The group included the poets Allen GINSBERG and Lawrence Ferlinghetti, and novelists Jack KEROUAC and William BURROUGHS.

Beaton, Sir Cecil Walter Hardy (1904–80) British photographer, costume and stage designer, and writer. He began his career as a fashion photographer in the 1920s, and took up stage design in the 1930s. His World War 2 photographs recorded the endurance of wartime hardship by the British people. His film and stage designs include *Gigi* (film, 1951), *My Fair Lady* (stage, 1956; film, 1964) and *Coco* (1969). Beaton's books include *The Wandering Years* (1962).

Beaufort wind scale Range of numbers from 0–17 representing the force of winds, together with descriptions of the corresponding land or sea effects. The Beaufort number 0 means calm wind less than 1km/h (0.6214mph), with smoke rising vertically. Beaufort 3 means light breeze, 12–19km/h (8–12mph), with leaves in constant motion. Beaufort 11 is a storm, 103–116km/h (64–72mph) and Beaufort 12–17 is a hurricane, 117.5–219+km/h (73–136+mph), with devastation. The scale is named after its inventor, Admiral Sir Francis Beaufort (1774–1857).

Beauharnais, Joséphine de *See* JOSÉPHINE

Beaumarchais, Pierre Augustin Caron de (1732–99) French dramatist. Beaumarchais' principal plays were the related court satires, *The Barber of Seville* (1775) and *The Marriage of Figaro*. Both were transformed into operas by ROSSINI and MOZART respectively.

Beauvoir, Simone de (1908–86) French novelist, essayist and critic. Her novels *She Came to Stay* (1943) and *The Mandarins* (1954) are portraits of the existentialist intellectual circle of which she and her lifelong companion, Jean-Paul SARTRE, were members. Her best-known work remains the feminist treatise *The Second Sex* (1949). Other significant works include *The Prime of Life* (1960), *A Very Easy Death* (1964) and *Old Age* (1970).

beaver Large RODENT with fine brown to black fur, webbed hind feet, and a broad scaly tail; it lives in streams and lakes of Europe, North America and Asia. Beavers build "lodges" of branches above water-level and dam streams and rivers with stones, sticks and mud. In many places they are hunted for fur. Length: to 1.2m (4ft); weight: up to 32kg (70lb). Family Castoridae; species *Castor fiber*.

bebop (bop) Form of jazz with subtle harmonies and shifting rhythms. It arose in the late 1940s as a development from the simpler SWING style. Involving the extensive use of improvisation, the movement was pioneered by musicians such as Charlie PARKER and Dizzy GILLESPIE.

Becker, Boris (1967–) German tennis player. In his first two years as a professional he rose from obscurity to win the Wimbledon singles title in 1985. He won his second Wimbledon title in 1986 and again in 1989. He also won the US Open in 1989 and the Australian Open in 1991 and 1996. He retired from playing major tournaments at the end of 1997.

Becket, Saint Thomas à (1118–70) English church leader. He was appointed chancellor of England (1155) and became a friend of HENRY II. In 1162 Henry made him archbishop of Canterbury, hoping for his support in asserting royal control, but Becket devoted his loyalty to the church. His defence of clerical privileges against the crown led to fierce conflict. Becket spent six years in exile. Reconciliation was short-lived, as Becket turned on those, including the king, who had violated his rights during his exile. Four of Henry's knights, assuming wrongly they would gain the king's gratitude, killed Becket in Canterbury Cathedral. Henry did penance, and Becket was acclaimed a martyr, canonized in 1173.

Beckett, Samuel (1906–89) Irish playwright and novelist. One of the most influential European writers of the 20th century, he wrote in both French and English. He left Dublin for Paris in the 1920s and became an assistant to James JOYCE. His first published work was a volume of verse *Whoroscope* (1930). His first published novel was *Murphy* (1938). His reputation is largely due to his three full-length plays, *Waiting for Godot* (1952), *Endgame* (1957) and *Happy Days* (1961), which explore notions of suffering, paralysis and survival. His work is often linked to the Theatre of the ABSURD. His other novels include the French trilogy *Molloy* (1951), *Malone Dies* (1951) and *The Unnameable* (1953). He was awarded the 1969 Nobel Prize for literature.

Beckmann, Max (1884–1950) German expressionist painter. He was disturbed by his experiences as a medical orderly in World War 1 and changed his painting style to reflect his awareness of the brutality of life. His EXPRESSIONISM often took the form of allegory, and he drew inspiration from German Gothic art.

Becquerel, Antoine Henri (1852–1908) French physicist. In 1896 he discovered RADIOACTIVITY in uranium salts, for which he shared the 1903 Nobel Prize in physics with Pierre and Marie CURIE. The Becquerel standard unit for measuring radioactivity, which has replaced the CURIE, was named after him. *See also* BETA PARTICLE

Bede, Saint (673–735) (the Venerable Bede) English monk and scholar. He spent his life in the Northumbrian monasteries of Wearmouth and Jarrow. His most important work is the *Ecclesiastical History of the English Nation*, which remains an indispensable primary source for English history from 54 BC–AD 697. His works were profoundly influential across early medieval Europe.

Bedfordshire County in central S England; the county town is Bedford, other major towns include Luton and Dunstable. There are traces of early Bronze Age settlements. The land is mostly flat with low chalk hills, the Chilterns, in the S. The region (drained by the River Ouse) is fertile, and agriculture is the chief economic activity. This includes the growing of cereal crops, cattle raising and market gardening. Industries: motor vehicle manufacture, electrical equipment and precision instruments. Area: 1,235sq km (477sq mi). Pop. (1991) 524,105.

Bedouin Nomadic, desert-dwelling ARAB peoples of the Middle East and followers of ISLAM. Traditionally they live in tents, moving with their herds of camels, goats, sheep and sometimes cattle across vast areas of arid land in search of the sparse grazing. Their society is patrilineal and they are renowned for their hospitality, honesty and fierce independence. In the 20th century many Bedouin have been forced to abandon the nomadic way of life and work in agriculture or in towns.

bee Insect distinguished from other members of the order Hymenoptera, such as ants and wasps, by the presence of specially adapted hairs, with which they collect POLLEN; all bees feed their young NECTAR and pollen. The body is usually quite hairy and the hairs are multi-branched (plumose). Although the honeybee and BUMBLE-BEE are social insects living in well-organized colonies, many other bees are solitary, and some species even live in the colonies of other bees. Found throughout the world, except in polar regions, they are important pollinators of flowers. Entomologists recognize about 12,000 species, but only the honeybee provides the HONEY that we eat. It builds combs of six-sided cells with wax from glands on its abdomen. A honeybee colony may have up to 60,000 individuals, consisting mainly of infertile female workers, with a few male drones and one egg-laying queen.

beech Deciduous tree native to the Northern Hemisphere. Beeches have wide spreading branches, smooth grey bark and alternate, coarse-toothed leaves. Male flowers hang from thin stems; pairs of female flowers hang on hairy stems and develop into triangular, edible nuts enclosed by burs. The American beech (*Fagus grandifolia*) and the European beech (*F. sylvatica*) are important timber trees used for furniture and tool handles. Height: to 36m (117ft). Family Fagaceae; there are 10 species. All belong to the genus *Nothofagus*.

bee-eater Tropical BIRD of the E hemisphere that catches flying bees and wasps. It has a long, curved beak, bright, colourful plumage and a long tail. It nests in large colonies and builds a tunnel to its egg chamber. Length: 15–38cm (6–15in). Family Meropidae.

Beelzebub Name used for Satan or the Devil. The word was originally *Beelzebul* ("Lord of demons") but was corrupted deliberately in Syrian texts and the (Latin) Vulgate to *Beelzebub* ("Lord of flies") as a gesture of contempt. Originally an aspect of Baal, it was used in its present sense in the New Testament (Matthew 10, Mark 3 and Luke 11).

beer Alcoholic beverage produced by the soaking, boiling and fermentation of a cereal extract (often malted barley) flavoured with a bitter substance (hops). Other ingredients are water, sugar and yeast. The alcohol content of beer ranges from *c.*2.5% to 12%, with the majority between 3% and 6%.

Beersheba (Be'er Sheva) Chief city of the Negev region, S Israel. It was the most S point of biblical PALESTINE. It flourished under Byzantine rule, but declined thereafter until restored by the Ottoman Turks *c.*1900. Industries: chemicals, textiles, ceramics. Pop. (1992 est.) 128,400.

beet Vegetable native to Europe and parts of Asia, and cultivated in most cool regions. Its leaves are green or red and edible, although it is generally grown for its thick red or golden root. Some varieties are eaten as a vegetable, others as a source of sugar and some are used as fodder. Family Chenopodiaceae; species *Beta vulgaris See also* SUGAR BEET

Beethoven, Ludwig van (1770–1827) German composer, a profound influence on the development of musical styles. Despite his deafness, which eventually became total, he wrote many masterpieces. He provides a link between the formal CLASSICAL style of HAYDN and MOZART and the ROMANTICISM of WAGNER, BRAHMS and BRUCKNER. Born in Bonn, Beethoven visited Vienna in 1787 and was taught briefly by Mozart; he made Vienna his home from 1792 and took lessons from Haydn. He composed nine symphonies, five piano concertos, a violin concerto, one opera (*Fidelio*), 32 piano sonatas and a sizeable body of chamber music. He made the symphony a dramatic form; he also expanded the size of the orchestra and wrote compositions considered lengthy by contemporaries.

beetle Insect characterized by horny front wings that serve as protective covers for the membranous hind wings. These protective sheaths are often brightly coloured. Beetles are usually stout-bodied, and their mouthparts are adapted for biting and chewing. They are poor fliers, but (like all insects) are protected from injury and drying up by an EXOSKELETON. Beetles are the most numerous of the insects. More than 250,000 species are known, and new ones are still being discovered. They include SCARAB BEETLES, LADYBIRDS and WEEVILS. Most feed on plants, some prey on small animals, including other insects, whereas others are scavengers. Beetles undergo complete METAMORPHOSIS. Their larvae (grubs) usually have three pairs of legs and distinct heads, usually dark in colour. Length: 0.5mm– 6cm (0.02–6.3in). Order Coleoptera.

Begin, Menachem (1913–92) Israeli politician, prime minister (1977–83). A Polish-born Zionist, as commander of the paramilitary *Irgun Zeva'i Leumi*, he led the fight against British rule until Israeli independence in 1948. As leader of the Freedom Party (Herut), Begin was involved in an ongoing political conflict with David BEN-GURION that was finally resolved with the need for unity during the SIX DAY WAR (1967). In 1973 Begin became leader of the Likud coalition, and in 1977, prime minister. Although a fervent nationalist, he sought reconciliation with Egypt, and signed a peace treaty with SADAT in 1979. In recognition of their efforts they shared the 1978 Nobel Peace Prize. Winning re-election by a narrow margin in 1981, Begin maintained a hard line on Israel's security interests.

behaviourism School of psychology that seeks to explain all animal and human behaviour primarily in terms of observable and measurable responses to stimuli. Its method of research often involves laboratory experiments. PAVLOV'S work on conditioned reflexes was a source for the early behaviourists such as J.B. WATSON. They rejected the evidence introspection gives of conscious feelings, motives and will. Later behaviourists such as B.F. SKINNER explain learning and development by "operant conditioning". *See also* DEVELOPMENTAL PSYCHOLOGY

Behn, Aphra (1640–89) English playwright, poet and novelist. The first English professional female writer. She produced 15 risqué comic plays, the most well-known being *The Rover* (1677). She is principally remembered for the first English philosophical novel, *Oroonoko* (1688).

Behring, Emil Adolph von (1854–1917) German bacteriologist and pioneer immunologist. In 1901 he was awarded the first Nobel Prize in physiology or medicine for his work on serum therapy, developing immunization against DIPHTHERIA (1890) and TETANUS (1892) by injections of antitoxins. His discoveries led to the treatment of many childhood diseases.

Beijing (Peking) Capital of the People's Republic of CHINA, on a vast plain between the Pei and Hun Rivers in NE China. The city comprises two walled sections: the Inner (Tatar) City, which houses the Forbidden City (imperial palace complex), and the Outer (Chinese) city. Beijing is the political, cultural, educational, financial and transport centre of China. Since 1949 heavy industry has been introduced, and textiles, iron and steel are now produced. Pop. (1993 est.) 6,560,000.

Beirut (Bayrūt) Capital and chief port of Lebanon, on the Mediterranean coast at the foot of the Lebanon Mountains. In 1920 it became capital of Lebanon under French mandate. With the creation of Israel, thousands of Arabs sought refuge in the city. During the 1950s and 1960s Beirut was a popular tourist destination. In 1976 the civil war began and Beirut rapidly fractured along religious lines. In 1982 West Beirut was devastated by an Israeli invasion in the war against the Palestine Liberation Organization (PLO). Following a series of atrocities, the Israelis began a phased withdrawal in 1985, and in 1987 Syrian troops entered Beirut as part of an Arab peacekeeping force. In 1990 Syrian troops dismantled the "Green Line" separating Muslim West from Christian East Beirut and reopened the Beirut-Damascus highway. By 1991 all militias had withdrawn from the city and restoration work began. The infrastructure, economy and culture of the city has suffered terribly during the civil war, only small-scale industries remain. Pop. (1993 est.) 1,500,000.

Belarus (Belorussia) Landlocked republic in NE Europe, formerly part of the Soviet Union; the capital is MINSK. **Land and climate** The land is low-lying and mostly flat and, in the S, much of the land is marshy. This area contains Europe's largest marsh and peat bog, the Pripet Marshes. A hilly region, extending from NE to SW through the centre of the country, includes the highest point in Belarus, a hill near Minsk, which reaches a height of 346m (1,135ft). Winters are cold and summers warm. Forests cover about a third of Belarus. **Economy** Belarus is an upper-middle-income economy. Like several former republics of the

---

BELARUS
AREA: 207,600sq km (80,154sq mi)
POPULATION: 10,297,000
CAPITAL (POPULATION): Minsk (1,633,600)
GOVERNMENT: Multiparty republic
ETHNIC GROUPS: Belarussian 80%, Russian, Polish, Ukrainian, Jewish
LANGUAGES: Belarussian, Russian (both official)
RELIGIONS: Christianity (mainly Belarussian Orthodox, with Roman Catholics in the w and Evangelicals in the sw)
CURRENCY: Belarussian rouble = 100 kopecks

Soviet Union, it has faced drastic problems in the transition from a state-run economy to a "free market". Farming is important and major products include barley, flax, rye, sugar beet, meat, eggs, potatoes and other vegetables. Leading exports include machinery and transport equipment, chemicals and food products. **History** In the 9th century the area became part of the first East Slavic state, Kievan Rus. In the 13th century Mongol armies overran the area and, later, Belarus became part of Lithuania. In 1569 Lithuania, including Belarus, became part of Poland. In the 18th century, Russia took over most of E Poland, including Belarus. In 1918 Belarus became an independent republic; however, Russia invaded the country and, in 1919, a communist state was established. In 1922 Belarus became a founder republic of the Soviet Union. **Recent events** In 1991, after the breakup of the Soviet Union, Belarus again became independent, though it retained ties with Russia through the Commonwealth of Independent States (CIS), whose administrative centre is located in Minsk. In 1997, despite opposition from Belarusian nationalists, Belarus signed a Union Treaty with Russia, committing the countries to future integration.

Belau (formerly, Palau) Self-governing island group in the Caroline Islands of the W Pacific, consisting of about 200 islands, eight of which are inhabited. The capital is Koror. A Spanish possession from 1710–1898, Belau was then held by Germany until 1914, when Japan occupied it. At the end of World War 2 control passed to the USA, which administered them as part of the US Trust Territory of the Pacific Islands. Self-government was instituted in 1981, and full independence followed in 1994. Most of the inhabitants are Micronesian, engaged in subsistence agriculture. Commercial fishing and copra processing are important economic activities. Area: 460sq km (189sq mi). Pop. (1986) 13,870.

Belfast Capital of Northern Ireland, at the mouth of the River Legan on Belfast Lough. The city was founded in 1177 but did not develop until after the Industrial Revolution. Belfast is now the centre for the manufacture of Irish linen. Since the 19th century, religious and political differences between Protestants and Catholics have been a source of tension. In the late 1960s these differences erupted into violence and civil unrest. Shipbuilding is a major industry and Belfast's harbour includes the Harland and Wolff yard, which has produced many of the world's largest liners. Other industries include aircraft, machinery, tobacco. Pop. (1991) 283,746.

Belgium Kingdom in NW Europe.; the capital is BRUSSELS. **Land and climate** Behind the North Sea coastline, which extends for about 63km (39mi), are low-lying coastal plains. Central Belgium consists of low plateaus and the only hilly region is the Ardennes, in the SE. The chief rivers, are the Schelde in the W and the Sambre and Meuse flowing between the central plateau and the Ardennes.

BELGUIM
AREA: 30,510sq km (11,780sq mi)
POPULATION: 9,998,000
CAPITAL (POPULATION): Brussels (Brussel, Bruxelles, 949,070)
GOVERNMENT: Federal constitutional monarchy
ETHNIC GROUPS: Belgian 91% (Fleming 55%, Walloon 34%), Italian, French, Dutch, Turkish, Moroccan
LANGUAGES: Dutch, French, German (all official)
RELIGIONS: Christianity (Roman Catholic 72%)
CURRENCY: Belgian franc = 100 centimes

Belgium has a cool temperate climate. Farmland and pasture cover c.50% of Belgium. **Economy** Belgium is a major trading nation (Antwerp is the chief port) with a highly developed economy. It has coal reserves, though most of its mines have been closed over the last 30 years because they are uneconomic. While Belgium has to import many raw materials and fuels, its leading activity is manufacturing, the main products including steel, chemicals and processed foods. The other main industries are oil-refining, textiles, diamond cutting and glassware. Agriculture employs only 3% of the people, but Belgian farmers produce most of the basic foods needed by the population. Brussels has provided the headquarters of the European Union since its inception and is also the site of the headquarters of the North Atlantic Treaty Organization (NATO). **History and politics** In the Middle Ages, Belgium was split into small states, but the country was united by the dukes of Burgundy in the 14th and 15th centuries. It later came, at various times, under Austrian, Spanish and French rule. In 1815 Belgium and the Netherlands united as the Low Countries, but Belgium became independent in 1830. In 1885 Belgium became a colonial power when the Congo Free State (now Zaïre) became a Belgian possession. Belgium's economy was weakened by German invasions in both world wars, but the country recovered quickly post-1945 – initially through collaboration with the Netherlands and Luxembourg in a customs union called Benelux, and later through its membership of the European Community. A central political issue in Belgium has been the tensions between Dutch-speaking Flemings and French-speaking Walloons. In the 1970s, the government divided the country into three economic regions: Flanders, Wallonia and bilingual Brussels. **Recent events** In 1993 Belgium adopted a federal system of government, and each of the regions now has its own parliament, which is responsible for local matters. Elections under this new system were held in 1995. During 1996 Belgium was shocked by a large-scale child abuse scandal.

Belgrade (Beograd) Capital of Serbia, situated at the confluence of the Sava and Danube rivers. In the 12th century it became the capital of Serbia but was later ruled by the Ottoman Turks. It was incorporated into the area that came to be known as Yugoslavia in 1929, and suffered much damage under German occupation in World War 2. In 1996 Belgrade witnessed huge demonstrations against the government. Industries: chemicals, metals, machine tools, textiles. Pop. (1991) 1,168,454.

Belize (formerly, British Honduras) Republic in Central America, on the Caribbean Sea; the capital is Belmopan. **Land and climate** Swamp vegetation and rainforest cover large areas. N Belize is mostly low-lying and swampy. Behind the swampy coastal plain in the S, the land rises to 1,122m (3,681ft) at Victoria Peak in the Maya Mountains. Belize has a humid tropical climate, with high temperatures throughout the year. **Economy** Belize is a lower-middle-income developing country. The economy is based on agriculture; sugar cane is the chief commercial crop. Other crops include bananas, beans, citrus fruits, maize and rice. Forestry, fishing and tourism are important activities. **History** Between c.300 BC and AD 1000, Belize was part of the MAYA empire, which had declined long before Spanish explorers reached the coast in the early 16th century. Spain claimed the area but did not settle. Shipwrecked British sailors founded the first European settlement in 1638. Over the next 150 years Britain gradually took control of Belize and established sugar plantations using slave labour. In 1862 Belize became the colony of British Honduras. In 1973 it became known as Belize and achieved independence in 1981. **Recent events** Guatemala has claimed Belize since the early 19th century and objected to its newly independent status. British troops remained in Belize to prevent a possible invasion. In 1983 Guatemala reduced its claim to the S fifth of Belize. In 1992 Guatemala recognized Belize's independence, and in 1993 Britain began to withdraw its troops.

Bell, Alexander Graham (1847–1922) Scottish-born scientist, inventor of the TELEPHONE. He first worked with his father, inventor of a system for educating the deaf. The family moved to Canada in 1870, and Bell taught speech at Boston University (1873–77). His work on the transmission of sound by electricity led to the first demonstration of the telephone in 1876.

belladonna See ATROPINE; NIGHTSHADE

Bellini, Giovanni (c.1430–1516) Italian painter, from a famous artistic family. Giovanni's father, **Jacopo** (c.1400– c.1470), was a pupil of Gentile da Fabriano. His major surviving works are two sketchbooks, the source of many works by his son-in-law Andrea MANTEGNA and his two sons Giovanni and **Gentile** (c.1429–1507). **Giovanni** was the greatest painter of the family and single-handedly transformed Venice into a great centre of the RENAISSANCE.

Bellini, Vincenzo (1801–35) Italian composer of operas. His most notable works are *Norma* and *La Sonnambula* (both 1831) and *I Puritani* (1835). His characteristically flowing melodies require great vocal skill. Popular during the 19th century, these *bel canto* operas have recently regained favour.

Bellow, Saul (1915–) US writer, b. Canada. His work demonstrates intense moral preoccupation with the plight of the individual in modern society. His first novel, *The Dangling Man*, appeared in 1944, and later novels include *The Adventures of Augie March* (1953), and *The Dean's December* (1982). Awarded the 1976 Nobel Prize for literature, he has also written plays and short stories. His recent work includes *Something to Remember Me By* (1991).

Belmopan Capital of Belize, Central America, on the Belize River, 80km (50mi) upstream from Belize City. It replaced Belize City as capital in 1970, the latter having been largely destroyed by a hurricane in 1961. The building of Belmopan began in 1966. Pop. (1991) 3,558.

Belsen Village in Lower Saxony, Germany, site of a CONCENTRATION CAMP established by the Nazi government during World War 2. Originally it housed Jews to be exchanged for German prisoners of war, but an estimated 30,000 people were murdered or died here of starvation and disease before the camp was liberated in April 1945.

Belshazzar In the Old Testament, the son of Nebuchadnezzar and last king of BABYLON. The Book of DANIEL relates how Belshazzar organized a great feast during which a disembodied hand wrote upon the wall, "Mene, mene tekel upharsin". Daniel translated it as "Thou art weighed in the balance and found wanting", and said it signified Babylon's downfall.

beluga (white whale) Small, toothed Arctic WHALE that is a milky white colour when mature. It preys on fish, squid and crustacean and is valued by Eskimos for its meat, hide and blubber. Length: c.4m (13ft). Species: *Delphinapterus leucas*. Beluga is also a type of STURGEON.

Benares See VARANASI

bends (decompression sickness) Syndrome, mostly seen in divers, featuring pain in the joints, dizziness, nausea and paralysis. It is caused by the

BELIZE
AREA: 22,960sq km (8,865sq mi)
POPULATION: 198,000
CAPITAL (POPULATION): Belmopan (3,558)
GOVERNMENT: Constitutional monarchy
ETHNIC GROUPS: Mestizo (Spanish-Indian) 44%, Creole (mainly African-American) 30%, Mayan Indian 11%, Garifuna (Black-Carib Indian) 7%, White 4%, East Indian 3%
LANGUAGES: English (official)
RELIGIONS: Christianity (Roman Catholic 58%, Protestant 29%), Hinduism 2%
CURRENCY: Belize dollar = 100 cents

release of nitrogen into the tissues and blood. This occurs if there is a too rapid return to normal atmospheric pressure after a period of breathing high-pressure air (when the body absorbs more nitrogen). Treatment involves gradual decompression in a hyperbaric chamber.

Benedict (of Nursia), Saint (480–547) Roman Christian figure, founder of Western monasticism and of the BENEDICTINE order. St Benedict was of noble birth and educated in Rome. Shocked by the city's lawlessness, he retired to a cave above Subiaco, where he acquired a reputation for austerity and sanctity. A community grew up round him and he established 12 monasteries. His feast day is 11 July.

Benedict XV (1854–22) Pope (1914–22), b. Giacomo della Chiesa. During World War 1, he strove for peace among nations, stressing pacifist idealism. He tried to unite all Roman Catholics, made changes in the Curia, and published a new Code of Canon Law.

Benedictine Monks and nuns of the monastic Order of St Benedict, who follow the Rule laid down by St BENEDICT OF NURSIA in the 6th century. The order played a leading role in bringing Christianity and civilization to western Europe in the 7th century, and in preserving the traditions of Christianity throughout the medieval period. During the REFORMATION most Benedictine monasteries and nunneries in Europe, including 300 in England, were suppressed. The order revived in France and Germany during the 17th century. Benedictine monks and nuns returned to England in the late 19th century, and the Benedictine Order also spread to North and South America.

Beneš, Eduard (1884–1948) Czech statesman, president (1935–38, 1946–48). A disciple of Tomáš MASARYK, he promoted Czech independence while abroad during World War 1. He became the first foreign minister of Czechoslovakia (1918–35). He was president from 1935–38, and resigned in protest at the MUNICH AGREEMENT. Re-elected in 1946, he resigned in 1948 after the Communist takeover.

Bengal Former province of India. Now a region of the Indian subcontinent that includes WEST BENGAL state in India, and East Bengal, which is part of BANGLADESH. Much of Bengal lies in the deltas of the Ganges and Brahmaputra rivers. The Mogul emperor, Akbar, ruled in the 16th century and Bengal became the richest region in his empire. Conquered by the British in 1757, Bengal became the centre of the Indian Empire, with CALCUTTA as the capital. It was made an autonomous region in 1937, and the present boundaries were fixed in 1947. Area: 200,575sq km (77,442sq mi).

Bengal, Bay of NE Gulf of the Indian Ocean, bounded by India and Sri Lanka (W), India and Bangladesh (N), Burma (E) and the Indian Ocean (S). Many rivers empty into the Bay, including the Ganges, Brahmaputra, Krishna and Mahānadi. The chief ports of the area are MADRAS, CALCUTTA, Chittagong and Trincomalee.

Bengali Major language of the Indian subcontinent. It is spoken by virtually all of the 85 million inhabitants of Bangladesh, and by 45 million in the Indian province of West Bengal. Bengali belongs to the Indic branch of the Indo-European family of languages.

Benghazi (Banghazi) City on the NE shore of the Gulf of Sidra, Libya. Founded by the Greeks in the 6th century BC, the Italians captured it in 1911 and, during the 1930s, developed the air and naval facilities. Libya's second-largest city, Benghazi contains several government offices, and is a commercial and industrial centre for Cyrenaica province. Industries: salt processing, shipping and oil refining. Pop. (1988 est.) 446,250.

Ben-Gurion, David (1886–1973) Israeli statesman, prime minister (1948–53, 1955–63), one of the founders of the state of Israel. Born in Poland, he became leader of the Zionist labour movement in Palestine, founder of the Mapai (Labour) Party (1930) and, after World War 2, leader of the campaign for an independent Jewish state. In 1948 Ben-Gurion became Israel's first prime minister. *See also* ZIONISM

Benin Republic in W Africa, the capital is PORTO-NOVO. **Land and climate** Benin is one of Africa's smallest countries, extending N–S about 620km (390mi). The country has no natural harbours and the one at COTONOU, Benin's main port and biggest city, is artificial. Porto-Novo is further E. Behind the lagoons is a flat plain partly covered by rainforests, while about 80km (50mi) inland there is a large marshy depression. In central Benin the land rises to low plateaus, with the highest land in the NW. Northern Benin is covered by savanna (grassland with scattered trees), the habitat of such animals as water buffaloes, elephants and lions. The N has two national parks, the Penjari and the "W", which Benin shares with Burkina Faso and Niger. Benin has a hot, wet climate, with an average annual temperature on the coast of about 25°C (77°F) and an average rainfall around 1,330mm (52in). The inland plains are wetter than the coast, but the rainfall decreases to the N, which is hot throughout the year, with a rainy summer season and a very dry winter. **Economy** Benin is a developing country and about 70% of the people earn their living by farming.

BENIN
AREA: 112,620sq km (43,483sq mi)
POPULATION: 4,889,000
CAPITAL (POPULATION): Porto-Novo (208,258)
GOVERNMENT: Multiparty republic
ETHNIC GROUPS: Fon, Adja, Bariba, Yoruba, Fulani, Somba
LANGUAGES: French (official)
RELIGIONS: Traditional beliefs 60%, Christianity 23%, Islam 15%
CURRENCY: CFA franc = 100 centimes

Many farmers live at subsistence level, however, growing little more than they need to feed their families. Major food crops include beans, cassava, maize, millet, rice, sorghum and yams, while the chief cash crops grown for export are cotton, palm oil and palm kernels. Forestry is an important activity. Benin also produces oil and limestone, but there is little manufacturing **History and politics** The ancient kingdom of Dahomey had its capital at Abomey. In the 17th century the kings of Dahomey became involved in supplying slaves to European traders including the Portuguese, who shipped Dahomeans to the Americas, and particularly to Portugal's huge territory of Brazil. After slavery was ended in the 19th century, the French began to gain influence in the area. Around 1851 France signed a treaty with the kingdom of Dahomey and, in the 1890s, they proclaimed Dahomey a colony. From 1904 they ruled the area as part of a region called French West Africa, a giant federation that also included the territories now comprising Burkina Faso, Guinea, the Ivory Coast, Mauritania, Mali, Niger and Senegal. Benin became self-governing in 1958 and fully independent in 1960. After much instability and many changes of government, a military coup took place in 1972. Renamed Benin, after the 13th-century kingdom centred on the Nigerian city of that name, the country became a one-party Socialist state. In 1989 Communist policies were dropped and multiparty elections were held in 1991 and 1996.

Ben Nevis Highest peak in the British Isles, in the Highlands region of w central Scotland. Ben Nevis is in the central Grampian Mountain range (overlooking Glen Nevis), near Fort William. It rises to 1,343m (4,406ft).

Bentham, Jeremy (1748–1832) British philosopher, jurist and social reformer. Bentham developed the theory of UTILITARIANISM based on the premise that "the greatest happiness of the greatest number" should be the object of individual and government action. This philosophy was defined in his *Introduction to the Principles of Morals and Legislation* (1789). His followers were responsible for much of England's early reform legislation.

Benz, Karl (1844–1929) German pioneer of the INTERNAL COMBUSTION ENGINE. After some success with an earlier TWO-STROKE ENGINE, he built a FOUR-STROKE ENGINE in 1885 that was first applied to a tricycle. Benz achieved great success when he installed the new engine in a four-wheel vehicle in 1893. Benz was the first to make and sell light, self-propelled vehicles built to a standardized pattern.

benzene Colourless, volatile, sweet smelling flammable liquid HYDROCARBON (C_6H_6), a product of petroleum refining. A benzene molecule is a hexagonal ring of six unsaturated carbon atoms (benzene ring). It is a raw material for manufacturing many organic chemicals and plastics, drugs and dyes. Properties: r.d. 0.88; m.p. 5.5°C (41.9°F); b.p.

80.1°C (176.2°F). Benzene is carcinogenic and should be handled with caution.

Beowulf Oldest English epic poem, dating from c.8th century, and the most important example of Anglo-Saxon verse. It tells how the young prince, Beowulf, slays the monster Grendel and his vengeful mother. Some 50 years later, Beowulf (now king of the Geats) fights and slays a fire-breathing dragon but dies from his wounds. The poem ends with Beowulf's funeral and a lament.

Berbers Caucasian Muslim people of N Africa and the Sahara Desert. Some are herdsmen and subsistence farmers; others, like the TUAREG, roam the desert with their great animal herds. The farmers live in independent villages, governed by meetings of male tribesmen. Their remarkably stable culture dates back to before 2400 BC. After the Arab conquest of the 7th century, there were Berber empires in the 11th and 12th century. Berber languages are spoken by more than 10 million people.

Berg, Alban (1885–1935) Austrian composer. A student of Arnold SCHOENBERG, he composed his later works in a complex, highly individualized style based on Schoenberg's TWELVE-TONE MUSIC technique. His *Wozzeck* (1925) is regarded as one of the masterpieces of 20th-century opera.

Bergen Port on the N Atlantic Ocean; capital of Hordaland county, SW Norway. Founded in the 11th century, Bergen was Norway's chief city and the residence of several medieval kings. Industries include shipbuilding, textiles, fish processing and electrical equipment. Pop. (1990) 212,944.

Bergman, Ingmar (1918–) Swedish stage and film writer-director. With a versatile company of artists and a strong personal vision, he has created dark allegories, satires on sex, and complex studies of human relationships. The intimate and poignant *Fanny and Alexander* (1983) was considered his finest achievement.

Bergman, Ingrid (1915–82) Swedish actress, whose acclaimed stage performances led to a long and varied Hollywood film career. The co-star of *Casablanca* (1942), she won Academy Awards for *Gaslight* (1944), *Anastasia* (1956) and *Murder on the Orient Express* (1974). Married (1950–58) to the director Roberto ROSSELLINI, her last film role was in *Autumn Sonata* (1978).

Bergson, Henri (1859–1941) French philosopher of evolution. He saw existence as a struggle between man's life-force (*élan vital*) and the material world. Man perceives the material world through the use of his intellect, whereas the life-force is perceived through intuition. Bergson received the Nobel Prize for literature in 1927. His works include *Time and Free Will* (1889) and *Creative Evolution* (1907).

Beria, Lavrenti Pavlovich (1899–1953) Head of the secret police (NKVD) in the Soviet Union under Stalin. A communist since the Russian Revolution, he headed the Cheka, predecessor of the NKVD, in Transcaucasia in the 1920s. He took part in Stalin's purges and ruthlessly controlled internal security as NKVD chief (1938–53). When Stalin died he was arrested and executed for treason.

Bering, Vitus Jonassen (1680–1741) Danish naval officer and explorer, in Russian service, who gave his name to the Bering Strait and Bering Sea. In 1728 he sailed N from Kamchatka, NE Siberia, to the Bering Strait to discover whether Asia and North America were joined. He turned back before he was certain, incurring some criticism in St Petersburg. He set out again in 1741, this time reaching Alaska. Returning, he was shipwrecked and died on what is now Bering Island.

Bering Sea Northernmost reach of the Pacific Ocean, bounded by Siberia (NW), Alaska (NE); separated from the Pacific by the ALEUTIAN ISLANDS. Area: c.2,292,000sq km (885,000sq mi).

Bering Strait Strait at the N end of the BERING SEA, separating W Alaska from E Siberia and connecting the Bering Sea to the ARCTIC OCEAN. Min. width: 85km (53mi).

Berkeley, Sir Lennox Randal Francis (1903–1989) English composer. He was a pupil (1927–33) of Nadia BOULANGER in Paris. His early works, such as *Serenade for Strings* and *Symphony* (1939–40), show the influence of Parisian trends and Igor STRAVINSKY. His major choral work is the *Stabat Mater* (1946); he also wrote four operas, including *Nelson* (1954), four symphonies, sacred and chamber music.

berkelium Radioactive metallic element (symbol Bk) of the ACTINIDE SERIES. It does not occur in nature and was first made in 1949 by alpha-particle bombardment of americium-241 at the University of California at Berkeley (after which it is named). Nine isotopes are known. Properties: at.no. 97; r.d. (calculated) 14; m.p. 986°C (1,807°F); most stable isotope Bk^{247} (half-life 1.4×10^3 yr).

Berkshire County in S central England, almost entirely within the River Thames basin, which marks the N border; the county town is Reading. The Berkshire Downs run across the county. It is an agricultural area; dairy cattle and poultry are important, and barley is the main crop. Industries include nuclear research. Area: 1,255sq km (485sq mi). Pop. (1991) 734,246.

Berlin, Irving (1888–1989) US songwriter and composer. A prolific artist, his output approached 1,000 songs. His most popular include *Alexander's Ragtime Band*, *God Bless America* and *There's No Business Like Show Business*. His successful Broadway musicals include *Annie Get Your Gun* (1946) and *Call Me Madam* (1950). He composed the scores for the films *Easter Parade* (1948) and *White Christmas* (1954).

Berlin Capital of Germany, lying on the River Spree, in the NE of the country. Berlin was founded in the 13th century. It became the residence of the Hohenzollerns and the capital of Brandenburg (later Prussia) and of the newly formed state of Germany in 1871. In the early 20th century Berlin was the second-largest city in Europe. Virtually destroyed at the end of WORLD WAR 2, the city was divided into four sectors; British, French, US and Soviet. On the formation of East Germany, the Soviet sector became East Berlin and the rest West Berlin. The BERLIN WALL was erected in 1961 by the East Germans; it separated the two parts of the city until 1989. On the reunification of Germany in 1990, East and West Berlin were amalgamated. Industries: chemicals and electronics. Pop. (1993) 3,466,000.

Berlin Wall Heavily fortified and defended wall, 49km (30mi) long, that divided East and West BERLIN. It was built in 1961 by the East Germans to stop refugees fleeing to West Germany. Some individuals succeeded in crossing it, others were killed in the attempt. After the collapse of the Communist regime in 1989, it was dismantled.

Berlioz, (Louis) Hector (1803–69) French composer. He is noted for his innovative, progressive orchestral writing, the use of large forces, and the emphasis he laid on orchestral colour. His best-known works include the *Symphonie Fantastique* (1830), *Harold in Italy* for viola and orchestra (1834), the operas *Benvenuto Cellini* (1838) and *The Trojans* (1855–58), and the *Requiem* (1837). He also wrote an extremely influential treatise on orchestration (1844).

Bermuda (formerly, Somers Island) British colony, consisting of about 300 islands in the W Atlantic Ocean, 940km (580mi) E of North Carolina; the capital is Hamilton (Bermuda Island). Discovered c.1503, the islands were claimed for Britain by Sir George Somers in the early 17th century. They became a crown colony in 1684, eventually achieving internal self-government in 1968. Tourism is important. Agricultural products include vegetables, bananas and citrus fruits. Area: 53sq km (21sq mi). Pop. (1994 est.) 60,500.

Bern (Berne) Capital of Switzerland, on the River Aare in the Bern region. Founded in 1191 as a military post, it became part of the Swiss Confederation in 1353. Industries: precision instruments, chemicals, textiles, chocolate manufacture, tourism. Pop. (1992) 135,600.

Bernard of Clairvaux, Saint (1090–1153) French mystic and religious leader. He was abbot of the Cistercian monastery of Clairvaux from 1115 until his death. Under his direction nearly 100 new monasteries were founded. He was canonized in 1174. His feast day is 20 August.

Bernhardt, Sarah (1845–1923) French actress of legendary stature. The greatest tragedienne of the late 19th century, she rose to prominence in the Comédie Française (1872–80). In the 1880s, she gained international fame touring Europe and the USA. In 1899 she founded and managed the Théatre Sarah Bernhardt in Paris, where she played the lead in *Hamlet* (1899) and *L'Aiglon*. She also appeared in silent films.

Bernini, Gianlorenzo (1598–1680) Italian architect and sculptor. The outstanding personality of the Italian BAROQUE, his work combines astonishing, flamboyant energy with great clarity of detail. He was also a skilful painter. His architecture was splendid in conception, lavish in use of marble and dramatic lighting, and often grand in scale. His large-scale commissions in and around St Peter's include the baldacchino (canopy) above the high altar (1633), Barbarini Palace (1638), Cathedra Petri (1657–66) and (from 1656 onwards) the great elliptical piazza and enclosing colonnades in front of St Peter's. Bernini, more than any other architect, gave Rome its Baroque character.

Bernoulli, Daniel (1700–82) Swiss mathematician and physicist. His work on hydrodynamics demonstrated that pressure in a FLUID decreases as the velocity of fluid flow increases. This fact, which explains the lift of an aircraft wing, has become known as Bernoulli's principle. Bernoulli also formulated BERNOULLI'S LAW and made the first statement of the KINETIC THEORY of gases.

Bernoulli's law For a steadily flowing fluid, the sum of the pressure, kinetic energy and potential energy per unit volume is constant at any point in the fluid. Using this relationship, formulated by Daniel BERNOULLI, it is possible to measure the velocity of a liquid by measuring its pressure at two points, with a manometer or Pitot tube.

Bernstein, Leonard (1918–90) US conductor, composer and pianist. He was a conductor of the New York Philharmonic (1957–58) and then musical director (1958–69), winning large audiences and world fame through his recordings. His compositions include three symphonies, the oratorio *Kaddish* (1963), ballets, and music for the shows *Candide* (1956) and *West Side Story* (1957).

Bertolucci, Bernardo (1940–) Italian film director. A film-maker of spectacular, poetic epics, often dealing with the conflict between the personal and the political. His full directorial debut was *The Grim Reaper* (1962). His most influential film was probably *The Conformist* (1969). His two greatest commercial successes were *Last Tango in Paris* (1972) and *The Last Emperor* (1987), a Chinese dynastic saga that gained Bertolucci Oscars for Best Director and Best Film.

beryl Mineral, beryllium silicate. Its crystals are usually prisms of the hexagonal system. Gemstone varieties are aquamarine (pale blue-green) from Brazil; emerald (deep green) from Colombia; and morganite (pink) from Madagascar. Cut stones have little brilliance, but are valued for their intense colour. Hardness 8; s.g. 2.6–2.8.

beryllium Strong, light, silver-grey, metallic ALKALINE-EARTH element (symbol Be), first isolated in 1828 by Friedrich Wöhler and A.A.B. Bussy. It occurs in many minerals, notably BERYL, and is used in alloys that combine lightness with rigidity. Properties: at.no. 4; r.a.m. 9.012; r.d. 1.85; m.p. 1,285°C (2,345°F); b.p. 2,970 °C (5,378°F); most common isotope Be^9 (100%).

Berzelius, Jöns Jakob, Baron (1779–1848) Swedish chemist, one of the founders of modern chemistry. His accomplishments include the discovery of cerium, selenium and thorium; the isolation of the elements silicon, zirconium and titanium; the determination of relative atomic masses; and the devising of a modern system of chemical symbols. He prepared the first PERIODIC TABLE of relative atomic masses and contributed to the founding of the theory of radicals.

Bessel, Friedrich Wilhelm (1784–1846) German astronomer and mathematician. He devised a system for analysing and reducing astronomical observations and made the first accepted measurements of the distance of a star (61 Cygni). His observations led him to predict accurately that SIRIUS and Procyon are binary stars. He devised Bessel functions, a type of mathematical function, after observing perturbations of the planets.

Bessemer process First method for the mass production of steel. The process was patented in 1856 by the British engineer and inventor Sir Henry Bessemer (1813–98). In a Bessemer converter, cast iron is converted into steel by blowing air through the molten iron to remove impurities. Precise amounts of carbon and metals are then added to give the desired properties to the steel.

Best, Charles Herbert (1899–1978) Canadian physiologist. He and F.G. BANTING discovered INSULIN in 1921. Best was head of the department of physiology at the University of Toronto (1929–65) and chief of the Banting-Best department of medical research there after Banting's death.

beta-blocker Any of a class of DRUGS that block impulses to beta nerve receptors in various tissues throughout the body, including the heart, airways and periperhal arteries. These drugs are mainly prescribed to regulate the heartbeat, reduce blood pressure, relieve ANGINA and improve survival following a heart attack. However, they are also being used in an increasingly wide range of other conditions, including GLAUCOMA, liver disease, thyrotoxicosis, MIGRAINE and anxiety states. Beta-blockers are not suitable for all heart patients and are not used for patients with asthma or severe lung disease.

beta particle Energetic electron emitted spontaneously by certain radioactive ISOTOPES. Beta decay results from the breakdown of a neutron into a proton, electron and antineutrino. *See also* RADIOACTIVITY

Betelgeuse (Alpha Orionis) Red supergiant star, the second-brightest in the constellation of Orion. It is a pulsating variable whose diameter fluctuates between 300–400 times that of the Sun. Characteristics: apparent mag. 0.85 (mean); absolute mag. −5.5 (mean); spectral type M2; distance 500 light years.

Bethe, Hans Albrecht (1906–) US nuclear physicist, b. Germany. He left Germany when Hitler came to power, going first to Britain and then to the USA to become professor of theoretical physics at Cornell University (1935–75). He worked on stellar energy processes and helped develop the atomic bomb. He is noted for his theories on atomic and nuclear properties and was awarded the 1967 Nobel Prize in physics for his work on the origin of solar and stellar energy.

Bethlehem (Bayt Lahm) Town on the w bank of the River Jordan, 8km (5mi) ssw of Jerusalem, since 1994 administered by the Palestinian authority. The birthplace of JESUS CHRIST, it was the home of King David and the site of the biblical Massacre of the Innocents. The Church of the Nativity, built by Constantine (AD 330), is the oldest Christian church still in use. Pop. (1993 est.) 20,300.

Betjeman, Sir John (1906–84) English poet. Traditional in form, accessible in sentiment, and often apparently parochial in his concern with the details and oddities of English social and domestic life. The seriousness of Betjeman's poetry has often been obscured by its popularity. Poet Laureate from 1972–84, Betjeman was a familiar broadcaster and an idiosyncratic architectural critic.

Bevan, Aneurin (1897–1960) British socialist politician. A former active trade unionist, he entered Parliament in 1929. A stirring orator, he assumed leadership of the Labour Party's left wing, whose views he expressed as editor (1940–45) of *Tribune* magazine. As minister of health (1945–51) he introduced the NATIONAL HEALTH SERVICE (1946).

Beveridge, William Henry, Baron (1879–1963) British academic and social reformer. A director of the labour exchanges (1909–16), he later became director of the London School of Economics (1919–37) and master of University College, Oxford (1937–45). As chairman of the Committee on Social Insurance and Allied Services (1941–42), he wrote the "Beveridge Report", the basis for the post-war creation of the British WELFARE STATE.

Bevin, Ernest (1881–1951) British trade unionist and Labour politician. As general secretary of the Transport and General Workers' Union (TGWU) (1922–40), Bevin helped to plan the GENERAL STRIKE (1926). He was minister of labour and national service in the wartime coalition government (1940–45). As foreign minister in the ATTLEE government (1945–51), he helped to establish the NORTH ATLANTIC TREATY ORGANIZATION (NATO).

Bhagavad Gita (Hindi, Song of the Lord) Popular episode in the sixth book of the Hindu epic, the MAHABHARATA. It presents Krishna as an incarnation of the god Vishnu who, if worshipped, will save men.

Bhopal State capital of MADHYA PRADESH, central India. Founded in 1728, it is noted for its terraced lakes, mosques and prehistoric paintings. In 1984 poisonous gas from the Union Carbide insecticide plant killed 2,500 people, the world's worst industrial disaster. Bhopal is an industrial and trade centre with food processing, electrical engineering, flour milling and cotton textile industries. Pop. (1991) 1,063,000.

Bhutan Kingdom in the Himalayas, on the NE border of India and the s border of China; the capital is Thimbu. Bhutan's economy is based on agriculture and craft industries. Area: 47,000sq km (18,147sq mi). Pop. (1991 est.) 700,000.

Bhutto, Benazir (1953–) Pakistani stateswoman and prime minister (1988–90, 1993–96). The daughter of Zulfikar Ali BHUTTO, she was long considered the leader of the Pakistani People's Party, but was subject to house arrest and forced into exile. Her return in 1986 was marked by intense jubilation and violence. In 1988 Bhutto proclaimed a people's revolution and became the first Pakistani woman prime minister. Amidst charges of corruption, she was removed from office by the president in 1990. Re-elected in 1993, further accusations of corruption led to her removal in 1996.

Bhutto, Zulfikar Ali (1928–79) Pakistani political leader. As leader of the Pakistan People's Party from 1967, he refused to cooperate with the East Pakistani Awami League, which had won a majority in 1970. After BANGLADESH gained independence in the ensuing civil war, Bhutto became president of Pakistan (1971) and prime minister (1973). Disorderly elections in 1977 prompted a military coup. Bhutto was imprisoned and hanged on a murder charge. His daughter, Benazir BHUTTO, inherited his political mantle.

Biafra Former state in w Africa, formed from the E region of Nigeria. It was established in 1967 when the IGBO attempted to secede from Nigeria. A bitter civil war ensued, ending in 1970 when Biafra surrendered and was reincorporated into Nigeria.

Bible Sacred scriptures of Judaism and Christianity. Partly a history of the tribes of Israel, it is regarded as a source of divine revelation and of prescriptions and prohibitions for moral living. The Bible, in the form in which it has developed up to the present day, consists of two main sections. The OLD TESTAMENT, excluding the APOCRYPHA, is accepted as sacred by both Jews and Christians. The Roman Catholic and Eastern Orthodox churches accept parts of the Apocrypha as sacred and include them in the Old Testament. Jews and Protestants for the most part reject them. The NEW TESTAMENT is accepted as sacred only by Christians.

bicycle Two-wheeled vehicle propelled by the rider. The earliest design dates from about 1790. Karl von Drais of Germany developed an improved version around 1816. An Englishman, J. Starley, demonstrated the first successful chain drive in 1871. Bicycles have been a popular means of transport and recreation in many countries since the late 1800s. *See also* CYCLING

biennial Plant that completes its life cycle in two years, producing flowers and seed during the second year, such as an onion. This distinguishes it from an ANNUAL and a PERENNIAL.

Big Bang Theory advanced to explain the origin of the Universe. It states that a giant explosion 10 to 20 thousand million years ago began the expansion of the Universe, which still continues. Everything in the Universe once constituted an exceedingly hot and compressed gas with a temperature exceeding 10,000 million degrees. When the Universe was only a few minutes old, its temperature would have been 1,000 million degrees. As it cooled, nuclear reactions took place that led to material emerging from the fireball consisting of about 75% hydrogen and 25% helium by mass, the composition of the Universe as we observe it today. There were local fluctuations in the density or expansion rate. Slightly denser regions of gas whose expansion rate lagged behind the mean value collapsed to form galaxies when the Universe was perhaps 10% of its present age. The cosmic microwave background radiation detected in 1965 is considered to be the residual radiation of the Big Bang explosion.

Big Ben Bell in the clock tower forming part of the Houses of Parliament at Westminster, London. Its name comes from Sir Benjamin Hall who was commissioner of works (1859) when the bell was installed. The name can refer to the whole tower.

Bihar State in NE India. The capital is Patna. Bihar was a centre of Indian civilization from the 6th century BC to the 7th century AD. It became a province in the Mogul empire. A rich agricultural region, drained by the River Ganges, it produces more than 40% of India's total mineral output. Principal industries include mica, coal and copper and iron ore. Area: 173,877sq km (57,160sq mi). Pop. (1994 est.) 93,080,000.

Bikini Atoll Group of 36 islands in the W central Pacific and part of the US-administered MARSHALL ISLANDS. The USA used the area to conduct atomic weapons tests (1946–56). The islands were affected by fallout and (although considered safe in 1969) were re-evacuated in 1978. Area: 5sq km (2sq mi).

bilberry (blueberry or whortleberry) Deciduous evergreen shrub native to N Europe and E North America, which produces a small, dark purple fruit. Family Ericaceae; genus *Vaccinium*.

bile Bitter yellow, brown or green alkaline fluid, secreted by the LIVER and stored in the GALL BLADDER. Important in digestion, it enters the duodenum via the bile duct. The bile salts it contains emulsify fats (allowing easier digestion and absorption) and neutralize stomach acids.

Bill of Rights (1689) British statute enshrining the constitutional principles won during the GLORIOUS REVOLUTION. It confirmed the abdication of James II and bestowed the throne on William III and Mary II. It excluded Roman Catholics from the succession and outlawed certain of James' abuses of the royal prerogative, such as his manipulation of the legal system and use of a standing army. In general, its provisions hastened the trend towards the supremacy of Parliament over the crown.

Bill of Rights Name given to the first ten amendments to the US Constitution, ratified 1791. The main rights confirmed were: freedom of worship, of speech, of the press, and of assembly; the right to bear arms; freedom from unreasonable search and seizure; the right to a speedy trial by jury; and protection from self-incrimination. Powers not granted specifically to the federal government were reserved for the states.

binary star Two stars in orbit around a common centre of mass. **Visual binaries** can be seen as separate stars with the naked eye or through a telescope. In an **eclipsing binary**, one star periodically passes in front of the other, so that the total light output appears to fluctuate. Most eclipsing binaries are also spectroscopic binaries. A **spectroscopic binary** is a system too close for their separation to be measured visually and must be measured spectroscopically.

binary system In mathematics, number system having a BASE of 2 (the decimal system has a base of 10). It is most appropriate to computers since it is simple and corresponds to the open (0), and the closed (1) states of switch, or logic gate, on which computers are based.

Binet, Alfred (1857–1911) French psychologist. His best-known achievement was the first practical intelligence tests (1905–11), which profoundly influenced the assessment of abilities in psychology and education. *See also* APTITUDE TEST

binoculars Optical instrument that produces a magnified image of a distant object or scene. It consists of a pair of identical telescopes, one for each eye, both containing an objective lens, an eyepiece lens and an optical system (usually prisms), to form an upright image.

binomial nomenclature System of categorizing organisms by giving them a two-part Latin name. The first part of the name is the GENUS and the second the SPECIES. *Homo sapiens* is the binomial name for humans. The system was developed by the botanist Carolus LINNAEUS. *See also* TAXONOMY

binomial theorem Mathematical rule for expanding (as a series) an algebraic expression of the form $(x + y)^n$, where x and y are numerical quantities and n is a positive integer. For $n = 2$, its expansion is given by $(x + y)^2 = x^2 + 2xy + y^2$

biochemistry Science of the CHEMISTRY of life. It attempts to use the methods and concepts of organic and physical chemistry to investigate living matter and systems. Biochemists study both the structure and properties of all the constituents of living matter, such as FATS, PROTEINS, ENZYMES, HORMONES, VITAMINS, DNA, CELLS, MEMBRANES and ORGANS – together with the complex reactions and pathways of these in METABOLISM.

biodegradable Property of a substance that enables it to be decomposed by microorganisms. The end result of decay is stable, simple compounds (such as water and carbon dioxide). This property has been designed into materials such as plastics to aid refuse disposal and reduce pollution.

bioengineering Application of engineering techniques to medical and biological problems such as devices to aid or replace defective or inadequate body organs, as in the production of artificial limbs and hearing aids.

biofeedback In alternative medicine, the use of monitoring systems to provide information about body processes to enable them to be controlled voluntarily. By observing data on events which are normally involuntary, such as breathing and the heartbeat, many people learn to gain control over them to some extent in order to improve well-being. The technique has proved helpful in a number of conditions, including headaches and hypertension.

biogenesis Biological principle maintaining that all living organisms derive from parent(s) generally similar to themselves. This long-held principle was originally established in opposition to the idea of SPONTANEOUS GENERATION of life. On the whole, it still holds good, despite variations in individuals caused by mutations, hybridization and other genetic effects. *See also* GENETICS

biogenetic law (recapitulation theory) Principle that the stages an organism goes through during embryonic development reflect the stages of that organism's evolutionary development.

biography Literary form which describes the events of a person's life. The first known biographies were *Lives* by PLUTARCH in the 1st century. In English literature the first biographies appeared in the 17th century, notably *Lives* (1640–70) by Izaak Walton and *Lives of Eminent Men* (1813) by John AUBREY. The first modern biography was the monumental *Life of Samuel Johnson* (1791) by BOSWELL, which is rich in detail and first-hand recollections. Since its inception, the biography has evolved into a sophisticated and popular form of literature, aiming at a critically balanced assessment of its subject's life. *See also* AUTOBIOGRAPHY

biological clock Internal system in organisms that relates behaviour to natural rhythms. Functions, such as growth, feeding, or reproduction, coincide with certain external events, including day and night, tides, and seasons. This sense of timing makes some animals feed during the day when food is available and they can see best. These "clocks" seem to be set by environmental conditions, but if organisms are isolated from these conditions, they still function according to the usual rhythm. If conditions change gradually, the organisms adjust their behaviour gradually.

biological warfare Use of disease microbes and their toxins in warfare. The extensive use of mustard gas during World War 1, prompted the prohibition of biological warfare by the GENEVA CONVENTION (1925). However, many nations have maintained costly research programmes for the production of harmful microorganisms and discovery of more effective antidotes to their pathogenic effects. These microbes include plant pathogens for the destruction of food crops. None

has yet been used, although US forces employed a variety of biological warfare, such as the use of the defoliant Agent Orange during the VIETNAM WAR.

biology Science of life and living organisms. Its branches include BOTANY, ZOOLOGY, ECOLOGY, PHYSIOLOGY, CYTOLOGY, GENETICS, TAXONOMY, EMBRYOLOGY and MICROBIOLOGY. These sciences deal with the origin, history, structure, development and function of living organisms, their relationships to each other and their environment, and the differences between living and non-living organisms.

bioluminescence Production of light, with very little heat, by some living organisms. Its biological function is varied: in some species, such as fireflies, it is a recognition signal in mating; in others, such as squids, it is a method of warding off predators and in anglerfish it is used to attract prey. The light-emitting substance (luciferin) in most species is an organic molecule that emits light when it is oxidized by molecular oxygen in the presence of an enzyme (luciferase). Each species has different forms of luciferin and luciferase.

biomass Total mass (excluding water content) of the plants and/or animals in a particular place. The term is often used to refer to the totality of living things on Earth; or those occupying a part of the Earth, such as the oceans. It may also refer to plant material that can be exploited, either as fuel or as raw material for an industrial or chemical process.

biome Extensive community of animals and plants whose make-up is determined by soil type and climate. There is generally distinctive, dominant vegetation, and characteristic climate and animal life in each biome. The Earth has ten biomes.

biophysics Study of biological phenomena in terms of the laws and techniques of physics. Techniques include x-ray diffraction and SPECTROSCOPY. Subjects studied include the structure and function of molecules, the conduction of electricity by nerves, the visual mechanism, the transport of molecules across cell membranes, muscle contraction (using electron microscopy) and energy transformations in living organisms.

biopsy Removal of a small piece of tissue from a patient for examination for evidence of disease. An example is the cervical biopsy ("smear test"), performed in order to screen for pre-cancerous changes which can lead to cervical cancer.

biosphere Portion of the Earth from its crust to the surrounding atmosphere, encompassing and including all living organisms, animal and vegetable. It is self-sufficient except for energy and extends a few kilometres above and below sea-level.

biosynthesis Process in living cells by which complex chemical substances, such as PROTEIN, are made from simpler substances. A GENE "orders" a molecule of RNA to be made, which carries the genetic instructions from the DNA. On the RIBOSOMES of the cell, the protein is built up from molecules of AMINO ACIDS, in the order determined by the genetic instructions carried by the RNA.

biotechnology Use of biological processes for medical, industrial and manufacturing purpose. Humans have long used yeast for brewing and bacteria for products such as cheese and yoghurt. Biotechnology now enjoys a wider application. By growing microorganisms in the laboratory, new drugs and chemicals are produced. GENETIC ENGINEERING techniques of cloning, splicing and mixing genes facilitate, for example, the growing of crops outside their normal environment, and the production of vaccines that fight specific diseases. Hormones are also produced, such as INSULIN for treating diabetes.

birch Any of about 40 species of trees and shrubs native to cooler areas of the Northern Hemisphere. The double-toothed leaves are oval or triangular with blunt bases and are arranged alternately along branches. The smooth resinous bark peels off in papery sheets. Male catkins droop, whereas smaller female catkins stand upright and develop into cone-like clusters with tiny one-seeded nuts. Well-known species include the grey, silver, sweet and yellow birches. Height: up to 30m (98ft). Family Betulaceae; genus *Betula*.

bird Any one of about 8,600 species of feathered vertebrates that occupy most natural habitats from deserts and tropics to polar wastes. Birds are warm-blooded and have forelimbs modified as wings, hind-limbs for walking, and jaws elongated into a toothless beak. They lay eggs (usually in nests), incubate the eggs and care for young. As a group they feed on seeds, nectar, fruit and carrion, and hunt live prey ranging from insects to small mammals, although individual species may be very specialized in their diet. Sight is the dominant sense, smell the poorest. Size ranges from the bee hummingbird, 6.4cm (2.5in), to the wandering albatross, whose wingspread reaches 3.5m (11.5ft). Of the 27 orders of birds, the perching birds (Passeriformes) include more species than all others combined. A bird's body is adapted primarily for flight, with all its parts modified accordingly. There are several groups of large flightless land birds, including the ostrich, rhea, emu, cassowary, kiwi and penguin. Birds are descended from Theocodonts (reptiles), and the first fossil bird, ARCHAEOPTERYX, dates from late Jurassic times. Class Aves.

bird of prey Bird that usually has a sharp, hooked beak and curved talons with which it captures its prey. Two orders of birds fit this description: the hawks, falcons, eagles, vultures and secretary bird (order Falconiformes); and the owls (order Strigiformes).

Birmingham Britain's second-largest city, in the West Midlands, England. A small town in the Middle Ages, during the Industrial Revolution it became one of Britain's chief manufacturing cities. Industries: car manufacture, mechanical and electrical engineering, machine tools, metallurgy. Pop. (1990) 961,041.

Birmingham Six Six Irishmen convicted by an English court in 1974 of carrying out terrorist bombings in two public houses in Birmingham, England. Their life sentences were quashed in 1991. The Court of Appeal ruled that methods used by the police in producing some written statements were inappropriate. Their case became notorious as a modern miscarriage of British justice.

birth, Caesarian Delivery of a baby by a surgical incision made through the abdomen and womb of the mother. It is carried out for various medical reasons; the mother usually recovers quickly, without complications. The procedure is named after Julius Caesar, who is reputed to have been born this way.

birth control Alternative term for CONTRACEPTION

Birtwistle, Harrison (1934–) English composer. Influenced by Igor Stravinsky and by medieval and Renaissance music, he has written a wide variety of works consolidating his position as a leading modern composer. His pieces include the instrumental motet *The World is Discovered* (1960), and the operas *The Mask of Orpheus* (performed 1986), *Gawain* (1991) and *The Second Mrs Kong* (1995).

Biscay, Bay of Inlet of the Atlantic Ocean, W of France and N of Spain. It is noted for its strong currents, sudden storms and sardine fishing grounds. The chief ports are BILBAO, San Sebastián and Santander in Spain, and LA ROCHELLE, Bayonne and St-Nazaire in France.

Bismarck, Otto von (1815–98) German statesman responsible for German unification. He was born into a wealthy Prussian family and made an impression during the revolution of 1848 as a diehard reactionary. In 1862 WILLIAM I named him chancellor of Prussia. Victory in the FRANCO-PRUSSIAN WAR (1870–71) brought the S German states into the Prussian-led North German Confederation, and in 1871 Bismarck became the first chancellor of the empire. Bismarck encouraged industry and a paternalist programme of social welfare at home and colonization overseas. He found it difficult to work with WILLIAM II, and in 1890 the "Iron Chancellor" was forced to resign.

Bismarck State capital of North Dakota, USA, overlooking the Missouri River. Industries: livestock raising, dairying, woodworking. Pop. (1990) 49,256.

bismuth Metallic silvery-white element (symbol Bi) of group V of the PERIODIC TABLE, first identified as a separate element in 1753. The chief ores are bismite (Bi_2O_3) and bismuthnite (Bi_2S_3). A poor heat conductor, it is put into low-melting alloys used in automatic sprinkler systems. Bismuth is also used in insoluble compounds to treat gastric ulcers and skin injuries. It expands when it solidifies, a property exploited in several bismuth alloys for castings. Properties: at.no. 83; r.a.m. 208.98; r.d. 9.75; m.p. 271.3°C (520.3 °F); b.p. 1,560°C (2,840°F); most common isotope Bi^{209} (100%).

bison Two species of wild oxen formerly ranging over the grasslands and open woodlands of most of North America and Europe. Once numbered in millions, the American bison (often incorrectly called BUFFALO) is now almost extinct in the wild. The wisent (European bison) was reduced to two herds by the 18th century. Both species now survive in protected areas. Length: to 3.5m (138in); height: to 3m (118in); weight: to 1,350kg (2,976lb). Family Bovidae; species American *Bison bison*; wisent *Bison bonasus*.

Bissau Capital of Guinea-Bissau, near the mouth of the Geba River, W Africa. Established in 1687 by the Portuguese as a slave-trading centre, it became a free port in 1869. It replaced Bonama as capital in 1941. The port facilities have recently been improved. Oil processing is the principal industry. Pop. (1985 est.) 126,900.

bit Abbreviation for binary digit, a 1 or 0 used in binary arithmetic. In computing, a bit is the smallest element of storage. Groups of bits form a BYTE of binary code representing letters and other characters. Binary code is used in computing because it is easy to represent each 1 or 0 by the presence or absence of an electrical voltage. The code is also easy to store on disk as a magnetic or optical pattern.

bittern Solitary heron-like wading bird with a characteristic booming call found in marshes worldwide. A heavy-bodied bird, it is brownish with streaks and spots that help to hide it in swamplands. The female lays 3–6 brownish eggs. Length: 25–90cm (10in–3ft). Family Ardeidae, species *Botaurus stellaris*.

bittersweet *See* NIGHTSHADE

bitumen (asphalt) Material used for roadmaking and for proofing timber against rot. It consists of a mixture of hydrocarbons and other organic chemical compounds. Some bitumen occurs naturally in pitch lakes, notably in Trinidad. The material is also made by distilling tar from coal or wood, and a little is obtained during the refining of petroleum.

bivalve Animal that has a shell with two halves or parts hinged together. The term most usually applies to a class of MOLLUSCS – Pelecypoda or Lamellibranchiata – with left and right shells, such as clams, cockles, mussels and oysters. It also refers to animals of the phylum BRACHIOPODA (lamp shells) with dorsal and ventral shells. Length: 2mm–1.2m (0.17in–4ft).

Bizet, Georges (1838–75) French romantic composer. His opera *Carmen* (1875), although a failure at its first performance, has become one of the most popular operas of all time. Bizet also composed other operas, notably *Les pêcheurs de perles* (1863), and orchestral works, including the Symphony in C (1855) and *L'arlésienne* suites (1872).

Black, Joseph (1728–99) British chemist and physicist. Rediscovering "fixed air" (carbon dioxide), he found that this gas is produced by respiration, burning of charcoal and FERMENTATION, that it behaves as an ACID, and that it is found in the atmosphere. He also discovered hydrogen carbonates (bicarbonates). He investigated LATENT HEAT and specific heat but was unable to reconcile them with the PHLOGISTON theory.

blackbird Songbird of the THRUSH family, common in gardens and woodland throughout most of Europe, the Near East, Australia and New Zealand. The male has jet-black plumage and a bright orange bill. The female is brown, with a brown bill. Length: to 25cm (10in). Species *Turdus merula*.

black body In physics, an ideal body that absorbs all incident radiation and reflects none. Such a body would look "perfectly" black. The study of black bodies has been important in the history of physics. Wien's law, Stefan's law and PLANCK's law of black body radiation grew out of this study, as did Planck's discoveries in quantum mechanics.

Black Death (1348–50) Epidemic of PLAGUE, both bubonic and pneumonic, that killed about one-third of the population of Europe in two years. It was first carried to Mediterranean ports from the Crimea and spread throughout Europe, carried by fleas infesting rats. Plague recurred less severely in 1361 and other years, until the 18th century.

blackfly *See* APHID

Blackfoot Nomadic, warlike Native North American tribes. They are made up of three Algonquin-speaking tribes: the Siksika, or Blackfeet proper; the Kainah; and the Pikuni (Piegan).

Black Forest (Schwarzwald) Mountainous region between the rivers Rhine and Neckar, Baden-Württemburg, SW Germany. It is heavily forested in the higher areas, particularly around the sources of the Danube and Neckar. The highest peak is Feldberg, 1,493m (4,898ft). Industries: tourism, timber, mechanical toys, clocks. Area: *c*.6,000sq km (2,320sq mi).

black hole Postulated end-product of the total gravitational collapse of a massive star into itself following exhaustion of its nuclear fuel; the matter inside is crushed to unimaginably high density. It is an empty region of distorted space-time that acts as a centre of gravitational attraction; matter is drawn towards it and once inside nothing can escape. Its boundary (the event horizon) is a demarcation line, rather than a material surface. Black holes can have an immense range of sizes. Since no light or other radiation can escape from black holes, they are extremely difficult to detect. Not all black holes result from stellar collapse. During the BIG BANG, some regions of space might have become so compressed that they formed so-called primordial black holes. Such black holes would not be completely black, because radiation could still "tunnel out" of the event horizon at steady rate, leading to the evaporation of the hole. Primordial black holes could therefore be very hot. *See also* HAWKING, STEPHEN WILLIAM

Black Muslims African-American nationalist movement in the USA. It aims to establish a separatist black Muslim state. Founded in Detroit by Wallace D. Farad in 1930, it was led by Elijah

MUHAMMAD from 1934–75. The movement grew rapidly from 1945–60, helped by the rhetorical power of the preacher MALCOLM X. In 1976 the movement split into the American Muslim Mission and the Nation of Islam. The former (led by Elijah's son, Wallace D. Muhammad) preach a more integrationist message and align themselves with other Islamic organizations worldwide. The Nation of Islam, led by Louis FARRAKHAN, claims to uphold the true doctrines of Elijah Muhammad, and preaches a more racially exclusive message. During the 1980s and 1990s, the Nation of Islam has gained greater popularity in the USA. Total membership is *c*.10,000.

Black Panthers Revolutionary party of African-Americans in the 1960s and 1970s. It was founded by Huey Newton and Bobby Seale in 1966. They called for the establishment of an autonomous black state, armed resistance to white repression, and the provision of social welfare organizations. Leadership conflicts and the decline of black militancy reduced their influence.

Blackpool Town on the Irish Sea, Lancashire, NW England. One of Britain's most popular resorts. It has 11km (7mi) of sandy beaches, a 158m (520ft) tower (built 1895), many indoor and outdoor entertainments, and a promenade that is illuminated every autumn. Industries: confectionery, tourism. Pop. (1991) 146,069.

Black Sea (Kara Sea) Inland sea between Europe and Asia, connected to the Aegean Sea by the Bosporus, the Sea of Marmara and the Dardanelles. It receives many rivers (including the Danube) and is a major outlet for Russian shipping. Area: 413,365sq km (159,662sq mi).

blackthorn Tree or shrub of the rose family which bears white flowers early in the year and has small plum-like fruits (sloes) and long black thorns that give it its name. The flowers appear before the leaves in spring. Family Rosaceae; species *Prunus spinosa*.

black widow Common name for a small SPIDER found in many warm regions of the world. It is black and has red hour-glass-shaped marks on the underside. Its bite is poisonous, though rarely fatal to humans. Length: 25mm (1in); the male is smaller. Family Theridiidae; genus *Latrodectus*.

bladder Large, elastic-walled organ in the lower abdomen in which URINE is stored. Urine passes from each KIDNEY by way of two narrow tubes (ureters) to the bladder, where it is stored until it can be voided. When pressure in the bladder becomes too great, nervous impulses signal the need for emptying. Urine leaves the bladder through a tube called the URETHRA.

bladderwort Mat-like, aquatic INSECTIVOROUS PLANT found in bogs and ponds. It has thread-like leaves with small bladders in which insects and other small creatures are trapped and drowned. Upright stems bear purple or dark pink flowers. Family Lentibulariaceae; genus *Utricularia*.

Blair, Tony (Anthony Charles Lynton) (1953–) British statesman, prime minister (1997–). Blair became a Labour MP in 1983 and joined the shadow cabinet in 1988. He was elected party leader on the death of John SMITH (1994), and rapidly established himself as a modernizer. His redefinition of Labour's basic principles ("new Labour") did much to increase the party's popularity in the centre ground of British politics, and led to a landslide victory in the 1997 general election. His early reforms included giving the Bank of England independence in the setting of interest rates and winning referenda on devolution for Scotland and Wales.

Blake, William (1757–1827) British poet, philosopher and artist, one of the most extraordinary personalities of ROMANTICISM. He attempted to create a visual symbolism to represent his spiritual visions. He worked as a commercial engraver in the 1780s, but from *c*.1787 he began printing his own illustrated poems in colour. The first example was *Songs of Innocence* (1789). Blake's two patrons, Thomas Butts and John Linnell, enabled him to pursue his individual path as a poet-illustrator, producing notable engravings for *Jerusalem* (1804–20). Blake was extremely prolific: among his other productions were *Songs of Experience* (1794) and illustrations to the *Divine Comedy* by DANTE.

Blanc, Mont *See* MONT BLANC

blank verse Unrhymed verse, especially iambic pentameter or unrhymed heroic couplets, widely used in English dramatic and epic poetry. Henry Howard introduced blank verse into England in the 16th century with his translation of Virgil's *Aeneid*. A highly adaptable form, Christopher MARLOWE and William SHAKESPEARE transformed it into the characteristic medium of Elizabethan and Jacobean drama. John MILTON employed it in *Paradise Lost*, and William WORDSWORTH used it notably in his long autobiography *The Prelude*. It continues to be popular as a form and technical device.

blasphemy Speech or action manifesting contempt for God or religion. Severe penalties were prescribed for it in the Old Testament and also by medieval CANON LAW. Jesus Christ was crucified for blasphemy against Judaism. The statute books of many secular countries still include laws against blasphemy. Britain retains its law, although it is rarely invoked, and at present only applies to Christianity.

blast furnace Cylindrical smelting furnace. It is used in the extraction of metals, mainly iron and copper, from their ores. The ore is mixed with coke and a FLUX (limestone in the case of iron ore). A blast of hot compressed air is piped in at the bottom of the furnace to force up temperatures to where the reduction of the oxide ore to impure metal occurs. The molten metal sinks to the bottom and is tapped off. Waste "slag" floats to the top of the metal and is piped off. *See also* OXIDATION-REDUCTION

79

blastula Stage in the development of the EMBRYO in animals. The blastula consists of a hollow cavity (blastocoel) surrounded by one or more spherical layers of cells. Commonly called the hollow ball of cells stage, it occurs at or near the end of cleavage and precedes the gastrulation stage.

Blériot, Louis (1872–1936) French aircraft designer and aviator. In 1909 he became the first man to fly an aircraft across the English Channel. The flight from Calais to Dover took 37 minutes. As a designer, Blériot was responsible for various innovations, including a system by which the pilot could operate ailerons by remote control.

Bleuler, Paul Eugen (1857–1939) Swiss psychiatrist, pioneer in the diagnosis and treatment of PSYCHOSIS. He coined the term SCHIZOPHRENIA and, unlike his predecessors, attributed the symptoms to psychological rather than physiological origins.

Bligh, William (1754–1817) British naval officer. He was captain of the *Bounty* in 1789, when his mutinous crew cast him adrift. With a few loyal companions, he sailed nearly 6,500km (4,000mi) to Timor. While governor of New South Wales (1805–08) he was imprisoned by mutineers led by his deputy and sent back to England under arrest, though later he was exonerated.

blight Yellowing, browning and withering of plant tissues caused by various diseases; alternatively, the diseases themselves. Blights may be caused by microorganisms, such as bacteria and fungi, or by environmental factors such as drought. Common blights induced by microorganisms include fire, bean, late and potato blight. They typically affect leaves more severely than other parts.

blindness Severe impairment (or complete absence of) vision. It may be due to heredity, accident, disease or old age. Worldwide, the commonest cause of blindness is TRACHOMA. In developed countries, it is most often due to severe DIABETES, GLAUCOMA, CATARACT or degenerative changes associated with ageing.

Bliss, Sir Arthur (1891–1975) English composer. He was a pupil of Charles Villiers Stanford, Ralph Vaughan Williams and Gustav Holst. His works include the *Colour Symphony* (1932), quintets for oboe (1927) and clarinet (1931), a piano concerto (1938), two operas and a number of choral works. From 1953 he was Master of the Queen's Music.

Blitz Name used by the British to describe the night bombings of British cities by the German Luftwaffe (air force) in 1940–41. It is an abbreviation of *Blitzkrieg* (lightning-war); the name used by the German army to describe hard-hitting, surprise attacks on enemy forces.

Blixen, Karen *See* DINESEN, ISAK

Bloemfontein City and judicial capital of South Africa; capital of FREE STATE. Dutch farmers settled here in the early 19th century. The modern city is an important educational centre. Industries: furniture, glassware. Pop. (1991) 300,150.

blood Fluid circulating in the body that transports oxygen and nutrients to all the cells and removes wastes such as carbon dioxide. In a healthy human, it constitutes about 5% of the body's total weight; by volume, it comprises about 5.5l (9.7 pints). It is composed of a colourless, transparent fluid called plasma in which are suspended microscopic ERYTHROCYTES, LEUCOCYTES and PLATELETS.

blood clotting Protective mechanism that prevents excessive blood loss after injury. A mesh of tight fibres (of insoluble FIBRIN) coagulates at the site of injury through a complex series of chemical reactions. This mesh traps blood cells to form a clot which dries to form a scab. This prevents further loss of blood, and also prevents bacteria getting into the wound. Normal clotting takes place within five minutes. The clotting mechanism is impaired in some diseases such as HAEMOPHILIA.

blood group Type into which blood is classified according to which ANTIGENS are present on the surface of its red cells. There are four major types: A, B, AB and O. Each group in the ABO system may also contain the rhesus factor (Rh), in which case it is Rh-positive; otherwise it is Rh-negative. Such typing is essential before BLOOD TRANSFUSION. *See also* LANDSTEINER, KARL

blood poisoning (septicaemia) Presence in the blood of bacteria or their toxins in sufficient quantity to cause illness. Symptoms include chills and fever, sweating and collapse. It is most often seen in people who are already in some way vulnerable, such as the young or old, the critically ill or injured or those whose immune systems have been suppressed.

blood pressure Force exerted by circulating BLOOD on the walls of blood vessels due to the pumping action of the HEART. This is measured, using a gauge known as a SPHYGMOMANOMETER. It is greatest when the heart contracts and lowest when it relaxes. High blood pressure is associated with an increased risk of heart attacks and strokes; abnormally low blood pressure is mostly seen in people in shock or following excessive loss of fluid or blood.

blood transfusion Transfer of blood or a component of blood from one body to another to make up for a deficiency. This is possible only of the BLOOD GROUPS of the donor and recipient are compatible. It is often done to counteract life-threatening SHOCK following excessive blood loss. Donated blood is scrutinized for readily transmissible diseases such as HEPATITIS B and ACQUIRED IMMUNE DEFICIENCY SYNDROME (AIDS).

blood vessels Closed channels that carry blood throughout the body. An ARTERY carries oxygenated blood away from the heart; these give way to smaller arterioles and finally to tiny capillaries deep in the tissues, where oxygen and nutrients are exchanged for cellular wastes. The deoxygenated blood is returned to the heart by way of the VEINS.

Bloomsbury Group Intellectuals who met in Bloomsbury, London from about 1907. They included the art critics Roger Fry and Clive Bell; novelists E.M. FORSTER and Virginia WOOLF; her husband Leonard, a publisher; economist John Maynard KEYNES; and biographer Lytton STRACHEY. The group's attitudes were influenced by the empiricist philosopher G.E. Moore, and are encapsulated in his statement: "the rational ultimate end of human progress consists in the pleasures of human intercourse and the enjoyment of beautiful objects."

bluebell Spring-flowering blue flower, native to Europe. It grows from a bulb, especially in woodlands, and bears a drooping head of bell-shaped flowers. Height: 20–50cm (8–20in). Family Liliaceae; species *Hyacinthoides non-scripta*.

blueberry *See* BILBERRY

blue-green algae *See* CYANOBACTERIA

blues Form of African-American music, originating in the late 19th-century folk traditions of the American South. It evolved from gospel and work songs. The standard verse pattern is the 12-bar blues: three sets of four bars, the second set being a repetition of the first. Hugely influential in the development of jazz and pop music, the syncopated melodic structure uses microtonal "blue" notes (flattened thirds and sevenths).

blue shift In astronomy, an effect in which the lines in the SPECTRUM of a celestial object are displaced towards the blue end of the spectrum. It results from the DOPPLER EFFECT because the object and the observer are moving towards each other. The closing speed can be calculated from the extent of the shift. *See also* RED SHIFT

blue whale Largest animal ever to have lived on Earth, related to the rorquals. It has been overhunted and is now in danger of extinction. Species *Balaenoptera musculus*.

Blunt, Anthony (1907–83) English art historian. Blunt joined the Courtauld Institute of Art, London, holding the post of Director (1947–1974). He was Surveyor of the King's (later Queen's) Pictures (1945–1972). In 1979 it was disclosed that he had been a Soviet spy during World War 2. Blunt was a formidable scholar, earning particular praise for his work on Nicolas POUSSIN.

boa Large constricting SNAKE which gives birth to live young. The boa constrictor (*Constrictor constrictor*) of the American tropics can grow to 3.7m (12ft) in length. The iridescent rainbow boa, the emerald tree boa and the rosy boa are smaller species. Most boas are tree-dwellers, but the rubber boa of the W USA is a burrowing species. Family Boidae.

Boadicea (d. AD 62) Queen of the ICENI in East Britain. She was the wife of King Prasutagus who, on his death, left his daughters and the Roman emperor as co-heirs. The Romans seized his domain and Boadicea led a revolt against them. After initial successes, she was eventually defeated and poisoned herself. *See also* ROMAN BRITAIN

boar Male domestic pig (particularly one that has not been castrated) or, more specifically, the wild pig of Europe, Africa and Asia. In almost all its habitats it is hunted, either for food or for sport. The European wild boar is species *Sus scrofa*.

boat people Refugees that flee their country by sea to avoid political persecution, or to find greater economic opportunities. The term is closely associated with South Vietnamese refugees, of whom, since 1975, some 150,000 have sailed to Hong Kong and other Southeast Asian countries. Other boat people include Cubans fleeing to the USA, and Asians ferried by racketeers into the E coast of England from Germany and Holland.

Boccaccio, Giovanni (1313–75) Italian poet, prose writer and scholar, considered to be one of the founders of the Italian RENAISSANCE. He is best known for his masterpiece the *Decameron* (1348–58), a series of prose stories of contemporary mores, which exercised a tremendous influence on the development of Renaissance literature. His poetry includes *Il Filostrato* (*c*.1338) and *Il Ninfale Fiesolano* (*c*.1344–45).

Bode's law In astronomy, empirical numerical relationship for the mean distances of the planets from the Sun, named after the German astronomer Johann Bode (1747–1826). If 4 is added to the sequence 0, 3, 6, 12, 24, 48, 96 and 192, the result corresponds reasonably with the mean planetary distances, Earth's distance being equal to 10. This aided the discovery of Uranus (1781), but does not work for Neptune.

Bodhidharma (active 6th century AD) Indian Buddhist monk who travelled to China and there founded ZEN (or Ch'an) Buddhism.

bodhisattva (bodhista) In THERAVADA Buddhism, an individual who is about to reach NIRVANA. In MAHAYANA Buddhism, the term is used to denote an individual on the verge of enlightenment who delays his salvation in order to help mankind.

Bodin, Jean (1530–96) French lawyer and political philosopher. In *Six Books of the Republic* (1576) he treated anarchy as the supreme political evil and order as the supreme human need. He supported absolute monarchy and an unrestricted secular sovereignty residing in the state.

Boer (Afrikaans, farmer) Dutch or French Huguenot settler. From 1652 the Boers settled in the area that is now the Republic of South Africa. *See also* AFRIKANER

Boer Wars *See* SOUTH AFRICAN WARS

Boethius (*c*.480–524) (Anicius Manlius Severinus) Roman statesman and philosopher under the Emperor Theodoric. Imprisoned on a charge of conspiracy at Pavia, where he was subsequently executed, he wrote *On the Consolation of Philosophy* (523), a dialogue based on neo-Platonist and Aristotelian principles. Next to the Bible, this was medieval Europe's most influential book.

bog Spongy wet soil consisting of decayed vegetable matter; often called a peat bog. It develops in a depression with little or no drainage, where the water is cold and acidic and almost devoid of oxygen and nitrogen. A bog rarely has standing water like a MARSH, but plants such as cranberry and the carnivorous SUNDEW readily grow there.

Bogart, Humphrey DeForest (1899–1957) US film actor, often cast as a cynical, wisecracking anti-hero who finally does the right thing. In 1941 an association with film noir and John Huston began with roles in *High Sierra* and *The Maltese Falcon*. He starred in *Casablanca* (1942). In 1945 he married Lauren Bacall; their sexual magnetism evident in the noir classic *The Big Sleep* (1946). He won a Best Actor Oscar for *The African Queen* (1951).

Bogotá Capital of Colombia, on a fertile plateau in the centre of the country. It was founded in 1538 by the Spanish on the site of a CHIBCHA Indian settlement. Industries: tobacco, sugar, flour, textiles, engineering, chemicals. Pop. (1992) 4,921,264.

Bohemia Historic region which (with MORAVIA) now comprises the CZECH REPUBLIC. Bohemia was first unified in the 10th century when it became part of the Holy Roman Empire, coming under Habsburg control in 1526. It was the centre of occasional religious or nationalistic revolts against Austrian rule, including that of the Hussites and the episode that sparked the Thirty Years War (1618). It became part of CZECHOSLOVAKIA in 1918 and the Czech Republic in 1992.

Bohr, Aage Niels (1922–) Danish physicist, son of Neils BOHR. With Benjamin Mottelson and James Rainwater he shared the 1975 Nobel Prize for physics for devising a "collective model" of the atomic nucleus that assumes the collective vibration of all nucleons and their individual motion.

Bohr, Niels Henrik David (1885–1962) Danish physicist, major contributor to QUANTUM THEORY and the first person to apply it successfully to atomic structure. Bohr used the quantum theory to explain the spectrum of hydrogen and in the 1920s helped develop the "standard model" of the quantum theory, known as the Copenhagen Interpretation. He was awarded the 1922 Nobel Prize for physics for his work on atomic structure, and in 1957 received the first Atoms for Peace Award.

boil (furuncle) Small, pus-filled swelling on the skin, often occurring around a hair follicle or SEBACEOUS GLAND. Most boils are caused by infection by a bacterium called a STAPHYLOCOCCUS.

boiling point Temperature at which a substance changes phase (state) from a liquid to a vapour or gas. The boiling point increases as the external pressure increases and falls as pressure decreases. It is usually measured at standard pressure of one atmosphere (760mm of mercury). The boiling point of pure water at standard pressure is 100°C (212°F).

Boise Capital and largest city of Idaho, USA, in the valley of the Boise River. Industries: steel, sheet metal, furniture, electrical equipment, timber products. Pop. (1990) 125,738.

Bokassa, Jean Bédel (1921–96) Emperor of the Central African Empire (1977–79). Bokassa came to power in 1966 in a military coup. After serving as president (1966–77), he crowned himself emperor. His regime was brutal. A 1979 coup (with French military aid) removed Bokassa, replacing him with his cousin David Dacko.

boletus Genus of terrestrial fungi, whose spore-bearing parts are tubes instead of the usual gills. There are many species, all of which have a fleshy cap on a central stem and many of which are edible. Some poisonous kinds have red tube mouths. The edible ceps is *Boletus edulis*.

Boleyn, Anne (1507–1536) Second wife of HENRY VIII and mother of ELIZABETH I. They were married in 1533, when his first marriage, to Catherine of Aragon, had been annulled. Henry was desperate for a male heir and following the birth of a stillborn boy (1536), she was accused of adultery and executed for treason. It is thought that Anne's Protestant sympathies, besides Henry's need for a divorce, pushed the king towards the break with Rome that unleashed the English REFORMATION.

Bolingbroke *See* HENRY IV (of England)

Bolívar, Simón (1783–1830) Latin American revolutionary leader, known as "the Liberator". His experiences in Napoleonic Europe influenced his untiring attempts to free South America from Spanish rule. He achieved no real success until 1819, when his victory at Boyacá led to the liberation of New Granada (later Colombia) in 1821. The liberation of Venezuela (1821), Ecuador (1822), Peru (1824) and Upper Peru (1825) followed, the latter renaming itself Bolivia in his honour. Despite the removal of Spanish hegemony from the continent, his hopes of uniting South America into one confederation were dashed by rivalry between the new states.

Bolivia Landlocked republic in w central South America. The administrative capital is LA PAZ; the legal capital is SUCRE. **Land and climate** Bolivia can be divided into two regions. The w is dominated by two parallel ranges of the ANDES Mountains. Between the two, lies the ALTIPLANO. The site of famous ruins, it includes La Paz, close to Lake TITICACA. Sucre lies in the Andean foothills. The E is a

BOLIVIA
AREA: 1,098,580sq km (424,162sq mi)
POPULATION: 7,832,000
CAPITAL (POPULATION): La Paz (1,126,000), Sucre (103,952)
GOVERNMENT: Multiparty republic
ETHNIC GROUPS: Mestizo 31%, Quechua 25%, Aymará 17%, White 15%
LANGUAGES: Spanish, Aymará, Quechua (all official)
RELIGIONS: Christianity (Roman Catholic 94%)
CURRENCY: Boliviano = 100 centavos

region of lush, tropical rainforest. In the SE lies the GRAN CHACO. **Climate and Vegetation** Bolivia's climate varies greatly according to altitude. The highest Andean peaks are permanently covered in snow, while the E plains have a humid climate. The main rainy season is between December and February. The windswept Altiplano is a grassland region. The semi-arid Gran Chaco is a vast lowland plain, drained by the River Madeira, a tributary of the AMAZON. **Economy** Bolivia is the poorest nation in South America (1992 GDP per capita, US$2,410). It is the world's sixth-largest producer of tin, which accounts for nearly a third of all exports. The collapse in world tin prices led many people into coca production, which experts believe may be Bolivia's largest (unofficial) export. Agriculture employs 47% of the workforce. **History and politics** The Altiplano was the site of one of the great pre-Columbian civilizations. At the time of the Spanish conquest (1532), the AYMARÁ had been subsumed into the INCA empire by the Quechua. The Spanish exploited the Andean silver mines with native forced labour. In 1824 the Spanish were expelled with the victory of Antonio José de Sucre, Simón BOLÍVAR's general. For the next century, the new nation of Bolivia was plagued by corruption and instability. War (1932–35) with Paraguay led to the loss of most of the Gran Chaco. During World War 2, the need for tin provided a respite for Bolivia's ravaged economy. In 1941 Victor Paz Estenssoro founded the pro-miner National Revolutionary Movement (MNR), which seized power in 1943 and 1952. Paz nationalized the mines and instituted land reforms for the Native Americans. In 1964 the MNR government was overthrown in a military coup. Guerrilla leader Che GUEVARA was killed in 1967. From 1964 to 1982, Bolivia was ruled by a succession of repressive military regimes. In 1982 civilian rule was restored. In 1997 Banzer became president, promising to maintain, with US support, the war against the growing of coca.

Bologna City in N central Italy, at the foot of Apennines; capital of Bologna and Emilia-Romagna province. It has an 11th-century university, the incomplete Church of San Petronio (1390) and the Palazzo Comunale. Industries: mechanical and electrical engineering, agricultural machinery, publishing, chemicals. Pop. (1992) 401,308.

Bolsheviks (Rus. majority) Marxist revolutionaries led by LENIN who seized power in the RUSSIAN REVOLUTION of 1917. They narrowly defeated the MENSHEVIKS at the Second Congress of the All-Russian Soviet Democratic Workers' Party in London (1903). The split, on tactics as much as doctrine, centred on the means of achieving revolution. The Bolsheviks believed it could be obtained only by professional revolutionaries leading the PROLETARIAT. The Bolsheviks were able to overthrow the Provisional government of KERENSKY through their support in the soviets of Moscow and Petrograd. *See also* MARXISM

Boltzmann, Ludwig (1844–1906) Austrian physicist, acclaimed for his major contribution to statistical mechanics and to the kinetic theory of gases. His research extended the ideas of James MAXWELL. Boltzmann's general law asserts that a system will approach a state of thermodynamic equilibrium because that is the most probable state. He introduced the "Boltzmann equation" (1877) relating the kinetic energy of a gas atom or molecule to temperature. The gas constant per molecule (symbol K) is called the "Boltzmann constant". In 1884 he derived a law, termed the "Stefan-Boltzmann law", for BLACK BODY radiation discovered by his Viennese teacher, Josef Stefan (1835–93). After being attacked for his belief in the atomic theory of matter, Boltzmann committed suicide.

Bombay (Mumbai) Largest city in India, situated on an island off the W coast; capital of Maharashtra state. It is a cultural, educational, trade and financial centre, and the site of the world's largest film industry. It is India's second-largest port (after Calcutta). Industries: chemicals, textiles, oil refining, motor vehicles. Pop. (1991) 9,925,891.

Bonaparte, Joseph (1768–1844) King of Spain, b. Corsica. He was the eldest brother of NAPOLEON I, who made him king of Naples in 1806, and king of Spain from 1808–13. After Napoleon's defeat at Waterloo, he resided in the USA (1815–32).

Bonaparte, Louis (1778–1846) King of Holland (1806–10), brother of Napoleon Bonaparte and father of Charles Louis Napoleon, later Napoleon III of France. Forced by Napoleon to take the Dutch throne, he worked to restore its economy and welfare, but the French Continental System was ruinous to Dutch trade. Napoleon felt he was too lenient and the conflict led Louis to abdicate.

Bonaparte, Napoleon *See* NAPOLEON I

Bonar Law, Andrew *See* LAW, ANDREW BONAR

bond Promissory note guaranteeing the repayment of a specific amount of money on a particular date at a particular fixed rate of interest. Bonds may be issued by corporations, states, cities or the federal government. The quality of the bond, and the interest rate paid on it, is determined by the period of the outstanding loan and the risk involved. Thus the US federal government normally pays a lower rate of interest than cities because US bonds are relatively risk-free. Bonds pay out fixed amounts of interest on a regular basis, and appeal to investors seeking a regular income.

bone CONNECTIVE TISSUE that forms the skeleton of the body, protects its internal organs, serves as a lever during locomotion and when lifting objects, and stores calcium and phosphorus. Bone is composed of a strong, compact layer of COLLAGEN and calcium phosphate and a lighter, porous inner spongy layer containing MARROW, in which ERYTHROCYTES and some LEUCOCYTES are produced.

bone china Hard-paste PORCELAIN, consisting of kaolin, china stone and bone ash. Josiah

SPODE perfected the manufacture of bone china in the 19th century and was largely responsible for its popularity.

Bonhoeffer, Dietrich (1906–45) German theologian. A Lutheran pastor, he opposed the rise of National Socialism in Germany. Arrested by the Nazis in 1943, he was executed for treason after documents linked him with a failed conspiracy to assassinate Hitler in 1944. Among his works, most published posthumously, are *Letters from Prison* (1953) and *Christology* (1966).

Boniface, Saint (675–754) English missionary. He left England in 716 to convert the pagan Germans. For his success he was rewarded with the Archbishopric of Mainz in 751. In 754 he was martyred by pagans in Friesland. He is buried in Fulda, Bavaria, and is venerated as the Apostle of Germany. His feast day is 5 June.

bonito Speedy streamlined tuna-like fish found in all warm and temperate waters, usually in schools. Bonitos are blue, black and silver and highly valued as food and game fish. The ocean bonito (*Katsuwonus pelamis*) is also called skipjack tuna or bluefin. Family Scombridae.

Bonn City and capital of former West Germany, on the River Rhine, 26km (16mi) SSE of Cologne. It was capital of West Germany from 1949 until German reunification in 1990. Pop. (1990) 297,400.

Bonnard, Pierre (1867–1947) French painter and graphic artist. Together with his life-long friend, Jean-Edouard Vuillard, he adapted the traditions of IMPRESSIONISM to create a repertoire of sensuous domestic interiors. Known as *intimiste*, his paintings are drenched in gorgeous colours and generate an atmosphere of exuberant well-being. Notable examples include *The Terrasse Family*, *Luncheon* (1922) and *Martha in a Red Blouse* (1928).

Bonnie Prince Charlie See STUART, CHARLES EDWARD

bonsai Japanese art of dwarfing woody plants and shrubs by pruning and restraining root growth; they are primarily outdoor plants and occur naturally in cliff areas. This art, which has been practised for centuries in the East, is most successful with plants that have a substantial tapering trunk, naturally twisted branches and small leaves. Bonsais can be 5–60cm (2–24in) tall, depending on the plant used.

booby See GANNET

boogie-woogie Type of JAZZ popular in the 1930s. It has a rapid, driving beat, uses BLUES themes and is generally played on the piano.

book Primarily a bound volume of printed pages, it may also be a division within a book (as in the Bible) or a statement of accounts. The earliest books were Egyptian writings on papyrus, of which the BOOK OF THE DEAD is often considered the first. Roman books were mostly in the form of rolls, although the Roman period also saw the emergence of the codex, the forerunner of the paged book. In the Middle Ages, vellum, a fine parchment made

from animals' skins, became the standard material for books, but by the 15th century they were often written on paper. Modern printed books date from the revolutionary invention of moveable metal type in 1454 by GUTENBERG, and the first printed book was a German Latin Bible of 1455.

Booker Prize British literary prize. The Booker is the most prestigious award for new English-language novels published by UK, Commonwealth or Irish writers.

book-keeping Regular and systematic recording in ledgers of the amounts of money involved in business transactions. These records provide the basis for ACCOUNTANCY.

Book of Common Prayer See COMMON PRAYER, BOOK OF

Boole, George (1815–64) English mathematician. Largely self-taught, he was appointed professor of mathematics of Cork University in 1849. He is remembered for his invention of **Boolean algebra**, a set of symbols which can be manipulated to represent logical operations. It is commonly used in computing.

boomslang Venomous snake of the savannas of Africa. It is green or brown with a slender body and a small head. Commonly found in trees or bushes, it lies in wait for lizards and small birds, often with the front portion of its body extended motionless in mid-air. Length: to 1.5m (4.9ft). Species *Dispholidus typus*.

Booth, John Wilkes (1838–65) US actor and assassin of Abraham LINCOLN. He was a Confederate sympathizer. On 14 April 1865, during a performance at Ford's Theater in Washington, D.C., he shot Lincoln, who died the next day.

Booth, William (1829–1912) English religious leader, founder and first general of the SALVATION ARMY. He started his own revivalist movement, which undertook evangelistic and social work among the poor. It became known as the Salvation Army in 1878 and spread to many countries..

bootlegging Illegal supply and sale of goods that are subject to government prohibition or taxation. Bootleg also refers to unlicensed copies or cheap imitations of goods that are packaged to deceive the buyer into thinking they are the original. The name is said to derive from the practice of American frontiersmen who carried bottles of illicit liquor in the tops of their boots, for sale to Native Americans. In its original sense, bootlegging blossomed during the PROHIBITION era in the USA (1920–33), and helped to create powerful gang bosses.

borage Hairy annual plant native to S Europe. It has rough oblong leaves and drooping clusters of pale blue flowers and is cultivated as a food and flavouring. Height: up to 60cm (2ft). Family Boraginaceae; species *Borago officinalis*.

borax Most common borate mineral (hydrated sodium borate, $Na_2B_4O_7.10H_2O$), used to make heat-resistant glass, pottery glaze, water softeners in washing powders, fertilisers, and pharmaceuticals. It is found in large deposits in dried-up alkaline lakes in arid regions as crusts or masses of crystals. It may be colourless or white, transparent or opaque.

Bordeaux City and port on the River Garonne; capital of Gironde département, sw France. Bordeaux is a good deepwater inland port, and serves an area famous for its fine wines and brandies. Industries: shipbuilding, oil refining, pharmaceuticals, flour, textiles, glass. Pop. (1990) 210,336.

Borders Region of se Scotland, its s boundary forms the border between Scotland and England. The Rivers Tweed and Teviot flow e through the region and meet near Kelso. The Cheviot Hills form most of its s border, and the Southern Uplands its e border with STRATHCLYDE and DUMFRIES AND GALLOWAY. Area: 4,714sq km (1,820sq mi). Pop. (1991) 103,881.

Borg, Björn (1956–) Swedish professional tennis player. The dominant figure in men's tennis from the mid-1970s, he is particularly noted for winning five consecutive men's singles titles at Wimbledon (1976–80). Borg earned his "Iceman" nickname from his expressionless consistency on court. He retired in 1983.

Borges, Jorge Luis (1899–86) Argentinian short-story writer, poet and critic. Borges is best known for his short-story collections *Dreamtigers* (1960), *The Book of Imaginary Beings* (1967) and *Dr Brodie's Report* (1970). Dream-like and poetic, they often use intellectual puzzles to dramatize the extreme difficulty of achieving knowledge, and established Borges as one of the most significant literary talents of the century.

Borgia, Cesare (1475–1507) Italian general and political figure. He was made a cardinal (1493) by his father, Pope Alexander VI, but forsook the church to embark on a military campaign (1498–1503) to establish his dominion in central Italy. His ruthless campaigns lend credence to the theory that he was the model for Machiavelli's *The Prince*. His political fortunes collapsed with Alexander's death (1503). Imprisoned by Pope Julius II, he escaped to Spain, where he was killed in battle.

boric acid (boracic acid) Soft white crystalline solid ($H_3 BO_3$) which occurs naturally in certain volcanic hot springs. It is used as a metallurgical flux, preservative, antiseptic, and an insecticide for ants and cockroaches.

Born, Max (1882–1970) German-British physicist. He was professor of physics at Göttingen University from 1921 but left Germany in 1933, teaching at the universities of Cambridge (1933–36) and Edinburgh (1936–53). He returned to Germany in 1954. For his work in QUANTUM MECHANICS, he shared the 1954 Nobel Prize in physics with Walther BOTHE.

Borneo Island in the Malay Archipelago, 640km (400mi) e of Singapore, se Asia. Mostly undeveloped, Borneo is the world's third largest island,

and is divided into four political regions: SARAWAK (w) and SABAH (N) are states of Malaysia; BRUNEI (NW) is a former British protectorate; KALIMANTAN (E, central and s), covers 70% of the island and forms part of Indonesia. Industries: timber, fishing, oil and coal extraction. Area: 743,330sq km (287,000sq mi).

Borodin, Alexander Porfirevich (1833–87) Russian composer and chemist, one of the RUSSIAN FIVE group of composers. His most popular works include the tone poem *In the Steppes of Central Asia* (1880) and the *Polovtsian Dances* from his opera *Prince Igor* (completed after his death by GLAZUNOV and RIMSKY-KORSAKOV). He incorporated Russian folk-song into his compositions.

boron Nonmetallic element (symbol B) of group III of the PERIODIC TABLE, first isolated in 1808 by Sir Humphry DAVY. It occurs in several minerals, notably kernite (its chief ore) and BORAX. It has two allotropes: amorphous boron is an impure brown powder; metallic boron is a black to silver-grey hard crystalline material. The element is used in semiconductor devices and the stable isotope B^{10} is a good neutron absorber, used in nuclear reactors and particle counters. Properties: at.no. 5; r.a.m. 10.81; r.d. 2.34 (cryst.), 2.37 (amorph.); m.p. 2,079°C (3,774°F); sublimes 2,550°C (4,622°F); most common isotope B^{11} (80.22%).

Borromini, Francesco (1599–1667) Italian Baroque architect. He was the most inventive figure of the three masters (BERNINi and Pietro da Cortona) of Roman Baroque. His hallmark was a dynamic hexagonal design based on intersecting equilateral triangles and circles, such as the spectacular Sant'Ivo della Sapienza (begun 1642). His masterpieces include San Carlo alle Quattro Fontane (1638–41) and Sant'Agnese in Piazza Navona (1653–55).

Bosch, Hieronymus (*c*.1450–1516) Flemish painter, b. Jerome van Aken, in 'sHertogenbosch. His paintings of grotesque and fantastic visions based on religious themes led to accusations of heresy and greatly influenced 20th-century SURREALISM. The majority of his pictures explore the distressing consequences of human sin and innocent figures besieged by horrifying physical torments. He had a superb painting technique and used vivid colours. About 40 examples of his work survive, but his most famous themes are *The Temptation of St. Anthony*, *The Garden of Earthly Delights* (often considered his masterpiece) and *Adoration of the Magi*.

Bosnia-Herzegovina One of the five republics that emerged from the former Federal People's Republic of Yugoslavia; the capital is SARAJEVO.
Land and climate Much of the country is mountainous or hilly, with an arid limestone plateau in the sw. The River Sava, which forms most of the N border with Croatia, is a tributary of the Danube. The coastline is limited to a short stretch of 20km (13mi) on the Adriatic Sea coast. A Mediterranean climate,

BOSNIA-HERZEGOVINA

AREA: 51,129sq km (19,745 sq mi)
POPULATION: 4,366,000
CAPITAL (POPULATION): Sarajevo (526,000)
GOVERNMENT: Transitional
ETHNIC GROUPS: Muslim 49%, Serb 31%, Croat 17%
LANGUAGES: Serbo-Croatian
RELIGIONS: Islam 40%, Christianity (Serbian Orthodox 31%, Roman Catholic 15%, Protestant 4%)
CURRENCY: Dinar = 100 paras

with dry, sunny summers and mild, moist winters prevails near the coast. Inland the weather becomes more severe. **Economy** Excluding Macedonia, Bosnia was the least developed of the former republics of Yugoslavia. Its economy has been shattered by the war. Before the war, manufactures were the main exports. Many foodstuffs have to be imported. **History and politics** Slavs settled in the region c.1,400 years ago. Bosnia was settled by Serbs in the 7th century and conquered by Ottoman Turks in 1463. The persistence of serfdom led to a peasant revolt (1875). The Congress of Berlin (1878) handed Bosnia-Herzegovina to the AUSTRO-HUNGARIAN EMPIRE. Serbian nationalism intensified and in 1914 Archduke Franz Ferdinand was assassinated in Sarajevo, precipitating World War 1. In 1918 Bosnia-Herzegovina was annexed to Serbia and incorporated into YUGOSLAVIA in 1929. In World War 2 the region became part of the German puppet state of Croatia. In 1946 Bosnia-Herzegovina became a constituent republic of TITO's socialist federal republic. In 1991 the republic disintegrated with the secession of Croatia, Slovenia and Macedonia. Fearing the creation of a Greater Serbia, Croats and Muslims pushed for independence. In March 1992 a referendum, boycotted by Serbian parties, voted for independence. Alija IZETBEGOVIĆ became president of the new state. War broke out between Bosnian government forces and the Serb-dominated Federal Yugoslav Army (JNA). The JNA overran the republic and besieged the government in Sarajevo. International pressure forced the JNA to withdraw. The JNA handed its weapons to Bosnian Serbs, who established a separate Serb republic led by Radovan KARADŽIĆ (August 1992). Bosnian Serbs controlled 70% of the territory and Croats a further 20%. Muslims were forced from their villages in a deliberate act of "ethnic cleansing". In late 1992 the UN deployed peacekeeping forces to distribute humanitarian aid to the starved capital of Sarajevo. In 1993 the UN declared a number of "safe areas" – government-held enclaves where Muslims would not be shelled or persecuted. In February 1994 Bosnian Serbs attacked the enclaves of Sarajevo and Gorazde, prompting UN air-strikes. The governments of Bosnia and Bosnian

Croats announced a cease-fire and the formation of a Muslim-Croat Federation. In 1995 the Federation launched a major offensive, forcing Bosnian Serbs to negotiate. The Dayton Peace Treaty (December 1995) agreed to preserve Bosnia-Herzegovina as a single state, but partitioned it between the Muslim-Croat Federation (51%) and Bosnian Serbs (Republika Srpska, 49%). The agreement deployed 60,000 NATO troops as part of a Peace Implementation Force (IFOR). Karadžić and the Bosnian Serb army leader Ratko Mladić were indicted for war crimes and forced to resign. In 1996 elections Izetbegović was re-elected and Biljana Plavsic became president of Republika Srpska. NATO troops remained as a "stabilizing" force.

boson ELEMENTARY PARTICLE that has an integer SPIN. Bosons are those particles not covered by the EXCLUSION PRINCIPLE. This means that the number of bosons occupying the same quantum state is not restricted. Bosons are force-transmitting particles, such as PHOTONS and gluons (the particles that hold QUARKS together). *See also* FERMION

Bosporus (Karadeniz Bogazi) Narrow strait joining the Sea of Marmara with the Black Sea, and separating European and Asiatic Turkey. It is an important strategic and commercial waterway. Length: 30km (19mi).

Boston State capital and seaport of Massachusetts, USA, at the mouth of the Charles River, on Massachusetts Bay. A cultural centre, Boston is the home of many important educational establishments, including Boston University and Harvard Medical School. HARVARD UNIVERSITY and the Massachusetts Institute of Technology (MIT) are situated nearby. Industries: publishing, banking and insurance, shipbuilding, electronics, fishing, clothing manufacture. Pop. (1990) 574,283.

Boston Tea Party (1773) Protest by a group of Massachusetts colonists, disguised as Mohawks and led by Samuel Adams, against the Tea Act and, more generally, against "taxation without representation". The Tea Act, passed by the British Parliament in 1773, withdrew duty on tea exported to the colonies. It enabled the EAST INDIA COMPANY to sell tea directly to the colonies without first going to Britain and resulted in colonial merchants being undersold. The protesters boarded three British ships and threw their cargo of tea into Boston harbour. The British retaliated by closing the harbour.

Boswell, James (1740–95) Scottish biographer and author. He travelled widely in Europe, meeting VOLTAIRE and Jean-Jacques ROUSSEAU. Boswell found his vocation as the friend and biographer of Samuel JOHNSON. His monumental *Life of Samuel Johnson* (1791) is his masterpiece and one of the greatest biographies in English.

Bosworth Field English battleground, 19km (12mi) W of Leicester, England, where RICHARD III was defeated by Henry Tudor (1485). Henry, who claimed to represent the Lancastrian royal house, which had competed with the Yorkists during the Wars of the ROSES, invaded England from France. Richard was killed and Henry claimed the throne as HENRY VII.

botany Study of plants and algae, including their classification, structure, physiology, reproduction and evolution. The discipline used to be studied in two halves: lower (non-flowering) plants, which included the ALGAE (now in the kingdom PROTOCTISTA), MOSS and FERNS; and higher (seed-bearing) plants, including most flowers, trees and shrubs.

Botany Bay Large, shallow inlet immediately s of Port Jackson, Sydney Harbour, New South Wales, Australia. It was visited in 1700 by Captain James COOK, who named it because of its flora. It is fed by the Georges and Woronora rivers, and is c.1.6km (1mi) wide at its mouth.

Botha, Louis (1862–1919) South African political and military leader, prime minister (1910–19). During the SOUTH AFRICAN WAR (1899–1902) he was an outstanding commander and led the TRANSVAAL delegation at the peace conference. As premier of Transvaal (1907–10), he advocated reconciliation with the British and in 1910 became first prime minister of the Union of SOUTH AFRICA.

Botha, P.W. (Pieter Willem) (1916–) South African politician, prime minister (1978–84), president (1984–89). The longest-serving member of the APARTHEID regime, he entered parliament in 1948. As defence minister (1966–78), he increased South Africa's armed forces and was responsible for the military involvement in Angola. As prime minister, he undertook limited reform of apartheid. In 1980 he established the Southwest Africa Territorial Force as part of a destabilization policy of South Africa's neighbours. He became the state's first president in 1984. In 1989 he resigned and was replaced by the more liberal, F.W. DE KLERK.

Botham, Ian Terence (1955–) English cricketer. An extrovert show-stealer, he was one of the greatest all–rounders, with 14 test centuries (5,200 runs) and 373 test wickets. In 1979, at Bombay, he became the first player to score a century and take 10 wickets in a test. In 1981 he almost single-handedly helped England regain the Ashes. In 1996 he was appointed as an England coach.

Botswana Landlocked republic in the heart of s Africa; the capital is GABORONE. **Land and climate** Most of the land is flat or gently rolling, with an average height of about 1,000m (3,280ft). The KALAHARI covers much of Botswana. Most of the s has no permanent streams, but large depressions form inland drainage basins in the N, such as the swamps of the Okavango River delta. **Economy** In 1966 Botswana was one of Africa's poorest countries (depending on meat and live cattle for its exports). The discovery of minerals (including coal, cobalt, copper, diamonds and nickel) has boosted the economy. More than 40% of the people still work as farmers, raising cattle and growing crops. Botswana has some food processing plants, and

BOTSWANA
AREA: 581,730sq km (224,606sq mi)
POPULATION: 1,373,000
CAPITAL (POPULATION): Gaborone (138,471)
GOVERNMENT: Multiparty republic
ETHNIC GROUPS: Tswana 75%, Shona 12%, San (Bushmen) 3%
LANGUAGES: English (official), Setswana (national language)
RELIGIONS: Traditional beliefs 49%, Christianity 50%
CURRENCY: Pula = 100 thebe

manufacturing industries (such as soap and textiles). **History** The earliest inhabitants of the region were the nomadic SAN. The Tswana now form the majority population and are traditionally cattle owners. Today, the San form a tiny minority of the population, and many live in permanent settlements. Britain ruled the area as the Bechuanaland Protectorate between 1885 and 1966, when the country became the republic of Botswana. Botswana remains a stable multiparty democracy.

Botticelli, Sandro (1444–1510) (Alessandro di Mariano Filipepi) Florentine RENAISSANCE painter. Loved by the PRE-RAPHAELITE BROTHERHOOD and an important influence on ART NOUVEAU, he was part of a late 15th-century movement that admired the ornamental, linear qualities of Gothic design. He is best known for his mythological allegories *Primavera* (c.1478), *The Birth of Venus* and *Pallas and the Centaur*. Botticelli was one of the privileged few to decorate the Sistine Chapel in Rome (1481) and, at the height of his career, was the most popular painter in Florence. He made a series of delicate pen drawings for a copy of Dante's *Divine Comedy*.

botulism Rare but potentially lethal form of food poisoning caused by a toxin produced by the bacterium *Clostridium botulinum*. The toxin attacks the nervous system, causing paralysis and cessation of breathing. The most likely source of botulism is imperfectly canned meat. Botulinum toxin is used medicinally as a treatment for some neuromuscular disorders.

Bougainville, Louis Antoine de (1729–1811) French maritime explorer. A veteran of the French and Indian Wars, a diplomat, mathematician and soldier, he commanded the frigate *La Boudeuse* on the first French voyage around the world (1766–69). It included a long interlude in Tahiti, which, among other Pacific islands, he claimed for France. Important botanical and astronomical studies were made during the voyage, of which Bougainville published an account in 1771–72.

Bougainville Volcanic island in the sw Pacific Ocean, E of New Guinea; a territory of Papua New Guinea. It was discovered in 1768 by Louis de BOUGAINVILLE. The island was under German control from 1884, and then under Australian administration after 1914 and again in 1945 (after the Japanese wartime occupation). It has been the scene of guerrilla warfare since the late 1980s. Kieta is the chief port. Industries: copper mining, copra, cocoa, timber. Area: 10,049sq km (3,880sq mi). Pop. (1990 est.) 128,000.

bougainvillea Tropical, flowering woody vine native to S America, often grown in warm climates. Its inconspicuous flowers have showy purple or red bracts. It was named after Louis de BOUGAINVILLE. Family Nyctaginaceae; genus *Bougainvillea*.

Boulanger, Nadia (1887–1979) French music teacher. She was one of the foremost teachers of composition in the 20th century. Pupils included Aaron COPLAND, Darius MILHAUD and Jean Français. In the 1930s she became the first woman to conduct the Boston Symphony Orchestra and the New York Philharmonic. Her sister Lili Boulanger (1893–1918) was an accomplished composer.

Boulez, Pierre (1925–) French conductor and composer. Influenced by Olivier MESSIAEN and Anton von WEBERN, he aimed to extend serialism into all aspects of a composition, including rhythm and dynamics. His works for voice and orchestra have received much attention, especially *Le Marteau sans maître* (1954) and *Pli selon pli* (1960). Renowned for conducting complex 20th-century works, Boulez became director of the French Institute for Acoustic and Musical Research (IRCAM) in 1975.

Boulle (Buhl), André Charles (1642–1732) French cabinet-maker, one of a number of skilled craftsmen maintained in the Louvre Palace by Louis XIV to design for the court. Boulle created a distinctive marquetry of tortoiseshell and gilded brass, to which he gave his name. There are examples of his output at Versailles and in the Louvre.

Bourbons European dynastic family, descendants of the CAPETIANS. The ducal title was created in 1327 and continued until 1527. A cadet branch, the Bourbon-Vendôme line, won the kingdom of Navarre. From 1589 (when Henry of Navarre became HENRY IV) until 1789, the Bourbons were France's ruling family. Two members of the family, Louis XVIII and CHARLES X, ruled from 1814–30. The Bourbons became the ruling family of Spain in 1700 when PHILIP V, grandson of LOUIS XIV of France, assumed the throne. His descendants mostly continued to rule Spain until 1931, when the Second Republic was declared. Juan Carlos I, a Bourbon, was restored to the Spanish throne in 1975.

Bourguiba, Habib (1903–) Tunisian statesman, president (1957–87). In 1934 he founded the nationalist Destour Socialist Party. In 1954 he began negotiations that culminated in Tunisia's independence in 1956. He became prime minister and, after the abolition of the monarchy in 1957, was elected Tunisia's first president. In 1975 he was proclaimed president for life. He

maintained a pro-French, autocratic rule until, old and ill, he was removed from power in 1987.

Boutros-Ghali, Boutros (1922–) Egyptian politician, sixth secretary-general of the United Nations (1992–96). As Egypt's foreign affairs minister (1977–91), he was involved in much of the Middle East peace negotiations. He briefly served as Egypt's prime minister (1991–92), before becoming the first African secretary-general of the UN. Early in his term he faced civil war crises in the Balkans, Somalia and Rwanda. A fiercely independent secretary-general, he managed to alienate US opinion and was blamed for the failure of UN peacekeeping in Somalia and Bosnia.

bovine spongiform encephalopathy (BSE) In cattle, degeneration of the brain caused by infectious particles or PRIONS, which may be transmitted by feeding infected meat. It is also known as "mad cow disease". *See also* CREUTZFELD-JAKOB DISEASE (CJD)

bowerbird Forest bird of New Guinea and Australia. The male builds a simple but brightly ornamented bower to attract the female. After mating, the female lays 1–3 eggs in a cup-shaped nest. Adults, mainly terrestrial, have short wings and legs, and variously coloured plumage. Length: 25–38 cm (10–15in). Family Ptilonorhynchidae.

bowls Game popular in Britain and Commonwealth countries, in which a series of bowls (woods) are delivered underarm to stop as close as possible to a small white target ball (jack). A point is scored for each bowl closer to the jack than the best opposition bowl. Variations depend on the playing surface, such as lawn, crown green and indoor.

box Evergreen tree or shrub found in tropical and temperate regions in Europe, North America and W Asia. The shrub is popular for topiary, and box wood is used for musical instruments. The 100 species include English or common *Buxus sempervirens* and larger *Buxus balearica* that grows to 24m (80ft). Family *Buxaceae*.

boxer Smooth-haired working DOG bred originally in Germany. It has a broad head with a deep, short, square muzzle, and its deep-chested body is set on strong, medium-length legs. The tail is commonly docked, and its coat is generally red or brown, with black and white markings. Height: to 61cm (24in) at the shoulder.

Boxer Rebellion (1900) European name for a Chinese revolt aimed at ousting foreigners from China. Forces led by the Society of Righteous and Harmonious Fists (hence the "Boxers"), with tacit support from the Dowager Empress, attacked Europeans and Chinese Christians and besieged Peking's foreign legations enclave for two months. An international expeditionary force relieved the legations in August and suppressed the rising. China agreed to pay an indemnity.

boxing Sport of fist fighting between two people wearing padded gloves within a roped-off ring. A fight is controlled by a referee in the ring and ends when there is a knock-down (a boxer is unable to get to his feet by a count of ten) or a technical knockout (one fighter is seriously injured). If both boxers finish the scheduled number of rounds, the winner is determined by a ringside referee or three judges. Boxing emerged from bareknuckle fighting with the introduction of the Marquess of QUEENSBERRY's rules in 1866.

boycott Refusal to deal with a person, organization or country, either in terms of trade or other activities such as sport. The term originated in 1880 when Irish tenant farmers refused to work for, supply or speak with Captain Charles Boycott, an agent of their landlord. Boycotts can be powerful protest tools, if they have sufficient support.

Boyle, Robert (1627–91) Anglo-Irish scientist, often regarded as the father of modern chemistry. In 1662 he invented an efficient vacuum pump, which enabled him to reduce pressures to levels never before achieved and to formulate BOYLE'S LAW. He also formulated the chemical definitions of an element and a reaction. He was a founding Fellow of the ROYAL SOCIETY.

Boyle's law Volume of a gas at constant temperature is inversely proportional to the pressure. This means that as pressure increases, the volume of a gas at constant temperature decreases. First stated by Robert BOYLE in 1662, Boyle's law is a special case of the IDEAL GAS LAW (involving a hypothetical gas that perfectly obeys the gas laws).

Boyne, Battle of the (1690) Engagement near Drogheda, Ireland, which confirmed the Protestant succession to the English throne. The forces of the Protestant WILLIAM III of England defeated those of the Catholic JAMES II. The battle led to the restoration of English power in Ireland.

Boy Scouts Worldwide social organization for boys that stresses outdoor knowledge and good citizenship. It was founded (1908) in Britain by Lord BADEN-POWELL with the motto, "Be prepared". A companion organization, the GIRL GUIDES, was founded in 1910. In 1967 the movement was officially renamed the Scout Association. By the 1990s it had *c*.14 million members (including the Cubs and Brownies) in over 100 countries.

Brabant Province of central Belgium; the capital is BRUSSELS. Mainly Flemish-speaking, it is a densely populated and fertile agricultural region. Industries: chemicals, metallurgy, food processing. Area: 3,372sq km (1,302sq mi). Pop. (1970 est.) 2,178,000.

brachiopoda (lamp shells) Phylum of *c*.260 species of small, bottom-dwelling, marine invertebrates. They are similar in outward appearance to BIVALVE MOLLUSCS, having a shell composed of two valves; however, unlike bivalves, there is a line of symmetry running through the valves. They live attached to rocks by a pedicle (stalk), or buried in mud or sand. There are 75 genera including *Lingula*, the oldest known animal genus. Most modern brachiopods are less than 5cm (2in) across. More than 30,000 fossil species have been found and described.

bracken Persistent weedy FERN found throughout the world. It has an underground stem that can travel 1.8m (6ft) and sends up fronds that may reach 4.6m (15ft) in some climates. The *typica* variety is widespread in Britain. Family Dennstaedtiaceae; species *Pteridium aquilinum*.

bracket fungus (shelf fungus) Any of a large family (Polyporaceae) of common arboreal fungi that have spore-bearing tubes under the cap. Bracket fungi are usually hard and leathery or wood-like and have no stems. They often cover old logs and their parasitic activity may kill living trees. Some are edible when young.

bract Modified leaf found on a flower stalk or the flower base. Bracts are usually small and scalelike. In some species they are large and brightly coloured, such as DOGWOOD and POINSETTIA.

Bradbury, Ray Douglas (1920–) US novelist and short-story writer. Best known for his imaginative science fiction, Bradbury's most celebrated work includes *The Martian Chronicles* (1950), a collection of connected short stories; *Fahrenheit 451* (1953), a dystopic vision of a book-burning future world; and the fantasy *Something Wicked This Way Comes* (1962). He has also written plays, poetry, children's stories, screenplays, and volumes of essays such as *Journey to Far Metaphor* (1994).

Bradford City in the Aire Valley, West Yorkshire, N England. Since the 14th century it has been a centre for woollen and worsted manufacturing, but industry has recently greatly diversified. The city is home to one of England's largest Asian communities. It has a university (established 1966). Industries: textiles, textile engineering, electrical engineering, micro-electronics. Pop. (1991) 457,344.

Bradman, Sir Don (Donald George) (1908–) Australian cricketer and sports administrator, regarded as the finest batsmen the game has ever known. He played for Australia from 1928 and was captain from 1936–48. His test record was 6,996 runs in 52 games (an average of 99.94), including 29 centuries and a highest score of 334 (against England at Leeds in 1930). During his first-class career he made a total of 28,067 runs (averaging 95.14), including 117 centuries.

Braganza Ruling dynasty of Portugal (1640–1910). The dynasty was founded by the Duke of Braganza, who ruled as John IV (1640–56). During the NAPOLEONIC WARS, the royal family fled to Brazil, then a Portuguese colony. A branch of the house ruled as emperors of Brazil from 1822–89.

Brahe, Tycho (1546–1601) Danish astronomer. Under the patronage of King Frederick II of Denmark he became the most skilled observer of the pre-telescope era, expert in making accurate naked-eye measurements of the stars and planets.

He built an observatory on the island of Hven (1576) and calculated the orbit of the comet seen in 1577. This, together with his study of the supernova, showed that ARISTOTLE was wrong in picturing an unchanging heaven. Brahe could not, however, accept the world system put forward by COPERNICUS. In his own planetary theory (the Tychonian system), the planets move around the Sun, and the Sun itself, like the Moon, moves round the stationary Earth. In 1597 he settled in Prague, where Johann KEPLER became his assistant.

Brahma Creator god in HINDUISM, later identified as one of the three gods in the Trimurti. Brahma is usually thought equal to the gods VISHNU and SHIVA, but later myths tell of him being born from Vishnu's navel. There is only one major temple to Brahma, located at Pushkar, Rajasthan, NW India.

Brahman (Atman) In HINDUISM the supreme soul of the universe. The omnipresent Brahman sustains the earth. According to the UPANISHADS, the individual soul is identified with Brahman. Brahman is not God, but rather is *neti neti* (not this, not that) or indescribable.

Brahmanism Term denoting an early phase of HINDUISM. It was characterized by acceptance of the VEDAS as divine revelation. The Brahmanas, the major text of Brahmanism, are the ritualistic books comprising the greater portion of Vedic literature. They were complemented by the UPANISHADS. In the course of time deities of post-Vedic origin began to be worshipped and the influence of Brahmanist priests declined. This led to a newer, popular form of Hinduism.

Brahmaputra River in S Asia. Rising in SW Tibet, it flows E into China, then S into India and WSW across India into Bangladesh (where it becomes the River YAMUNA). Before emptying into the Bay of BENGAL, it forms (with the GANGES and Meghna rivers) a vast delta. Length: *c*.2,900km (1,800mi).

Brahms, Johannes (1833–97) German composer. He used classical forms rather than the less-strict programmatic style that was becoming popular, and was a master of contrapuntal HARMONY. He composed in all major musical genres except opera. Among his major works are the *German Requiem* (1868), the *Variations on the St Antony Chorale* (1863), the Violin Concerto in D (1878), four symphonies (1876–1885) and two piano concertos (1858 and 1881). His best-known music includes the orchestral *Hungarian Dances* (1873).

Braille System of reading and writing for the blind. It was invented by Louis Braille (1809–52), who lost his sight at the age of three. Braille was a scholar, and later a teacher, at the National Institute of Blind Youth, Paris. He developed a system of embossed dots to enable blind people to read by touch. This was first published in 1829, and a more complete form appeared in 1837. There are also Braille codes for music and mathematics.

brain Mass of nerve tissue which regulates all physical and mental activity; it is continuous with the spinal cord. Weighing about 1.5kg (3.3lb) in the adult (about 2% of body weight), the human brain has three parts: the hindbrain, where basic physiological processes such as breathing and the heartbeat are coordinated; the midbrain links the hindbrain and the forebrain, which is the seat of all higher functions and attributes (personality, intellect, memory, emotion), as well as being involved in sensation and initiating voluntary movement. *See also* CENTRAL NERVOUS SYSTEM

brain damage Result of any harm done to brain tissue causing the death of nerve cells. It may arise from a number of causes, such as oxygen deprivation, brain or other disease or head injury. Sudden failure of the oxygen supply to the brain may result in widespread (global) damage, whereas a blow to the head may affect only one part of the brain (local damage). Common effects of brain damage include weakness of one or more limbs, impaired balance, memory loss and personality change; epilepsy may develop.

brain stem Stalk-like portion of the BRAIN in vertebrates that includes everything except the CEREBELLUM and the CEREBRAL HEMISPHERES. It provides a channel for all signals passing between the spinal cord and the higher parts of the brain. It also controls automatic functions such as breathing and heartbeat.

brake Device for slowing the speed of a vehicle or machine. Braking can be accomplished by a mechanical, hydraulic (liquid) or pneumatic (air) system that presses a non-rotating part into contact with a rotating part, so that friction stops the motion. In a car, the non-rotating part is called a shoe or pad, and the rotating part is a disc or drum attached to a wheel. Some vehicles use electromagnetic effects to oppose the motion and cause braking. A "power" brake utilizes a vacuum system.

Bramante, Donato (1444–1514) Italian architect and painter. He is best known as the greatest exponent of High RENAISSANCE architecture. His first building, Santa Maria presso San Satiro in Milan (*c*.1481), uses perspective to give an illusion of deeply receding space in the choir. In 1506, he started rebuilding St. Peter's in Rome. His influence was enormous and many Milanese painters took up his interest in perspective and *trompe l'oeil*.

bramble *See* BLACKBERRY

Brancusi, Constantin (1876–1957) French sculptor. His primitive style is revealed in a series of wooden sculptures, including *Prodigal Son* (1914), *Sorceress* (1916), and *Chimera* (1918). In 1919, his *Bird in Space* was not permitted into the USA as a work of art, but was taxed on its value as raw metal. This decision was reversed in a suit filed by Brancusi, and the sculpture is now housed in the Museum of Modern Art, New York City. Other works include *The Kiss* (1908), *Prometheus* (1911), *Sculpture for the Blind* (1924), and *Flying Turtle* (1943).

Brandenburg State in NE Germany; the capital is POTSDAM. The region formed the nucleus for the kingdom of Prussia. The March of Brandenburg was founded in 1134 by Albert I (the Bear). It came under the rule of the Hohenzollerns in 1411, and in 1417 Frederick I became the first elector of Brandenburg. Frederick II became the first king of Prussia in 1701. Pop. (1993 est.) 2,543,000

Brando, Marlon (1924–) US film actor. A brooding presence with an inimitable mumbling vocal style, he trained at the Actors' Studio. In 1951 his performance in the film *A Streetcar Named Desire* earned him the first of four consecutive Oscar nominations. He finally won his first Best Actor Oscar as the isolated docker in *On the Waterfront* (1954). By the end of the 1950s he was the first actor to command a million dollar appearance fee. He was awarded a second Best Actor Oscar for his lead performance in *The Godfather* (1971), but refused the award in protest against the persecution of Native Americans. The following year he received another Oscar nomination for his role in *The Last Tango in Paris*. Other notable supporting credits include *Missouri Breaks* (1976), *Apocalypse Now* (1979), and an Oscar-nominated performance in *A Dry White Season* (1989).

Brandt, Bill (1904–1983) British photographer. He assisted Man RAY in Paris (1929–30), before returning to London where he developed a reputation as a social commentator, as shown in his collection *The English at Home* (1936). During the war he documented life during the Blitz in a series of atmospheric wartime landscapes. He is perhaps better known for his nudes, many of which can be found in his book *Perspective of Nudes* (1961).

Brandt, Willy (1913–1992) German politician, chancellor of West Germany from 1969–74, b. Karl Herbert Frahm. An active Social Democrat, he fled to Norway and then Sweden during the Nazi era. He returned to Germany after World War 2 and was elected mayor of West Berlin in 1957. In nationwide politics he became foreign minister in 1966. As chancellor from 1969, he initiated a programme of cooperation with the Communist bloc states, for which he was awarded the Nobel Peace Prize in 1971. He resigned after a close aide was exposed as an East German spy. He chaired the Brandt Commission on international development issues, which published *North-South: A Programme for Survival* (1980) and *Common Crisis* (1983).

Braque, Georges (1882–1963) French painter who created CUBISM with PICASSO. Having tried FAUVISM without success, Braque's interest in analytical painting was sparked by CÉZANNE's 1907 memorial show. *Head of a Woman* (1909), *Violin and Palette* (1909–10) and *The Portuguese* (1911) show his transition through the early, analytical phases of cubism. Braque was badly wounded in World War 1 and afterwards evolved a gentler style of painting, which earned him enormous prestige. He concentrated on still-life subjects but also produced book illustrations, stage sets and decorative ceramics.

Brasília Capital of Brazil, in w central Brazil. Although the city was originally planned in 1891, building did not start until 1956. The city was laid out in the shape of an aircraft, and Oscar Niemeyer designed the modernist public buildings. It was inaugurated as the capital in 1960, in order to develop Brazil's interior. Pop. (1991) 1,596,274.

brass Alloy of mainly copper (55%–95%) and zinc (5%–45%). Brass is yellowish or reddish, malleable and ductile, and can be hammered, machined or cast. Its properties can be altered by varying the amounts of copper and zinc, or by adding other metals, such as tin, lead and nickel. Brass is widely used for pipe and electrical fittings, ornamental metalwork and musical instruments.

brass Family of musical wind instruments made of metal and played by means of a cupped or funnel-shaped mouthpiece. Simple brass instruments, such as the BUGLE, produce a limited range of HARMONICS corresponding to the length of the tube. In most other brass instruments, the length of the air column can be altered by valves or slides to produce the full range of notes. The chief brass instruments of a symphony orchestra are the TRUMPET, FRENCH HORN, TROMBONE and TUBA.

brassica Genus of plants with edible roots or leaves. It includes cabbages, cauliflowers, Brussels sprouts (all subspecies of *Brassica oleracea*), turnip (*B.rapa*) and swede (*B.napobrassica*). Some, such as broccoli, have edible flowerheads. Family Brassicaceae/Cruciferae.

Bratislava Capital of Slovakia on the River Danube, w Slovakia. It became part of Hungary after the 13th century, and was the Hungarian capital from 1526–1784. Incorporated into Czechoslovakia in 1918, it become the capital of Slovakia in 1992. Industries: oil refining, textiles, chemicals, electrical goods, food processing. Pop. (1990) 440,421.

Braun, Wernher von (1912–77) US rocket engineer, b. Germany. He perfected the V-2 rocket missiles in the early 1940s. In 1945 he went to the USA, becoming a US citizen in 1955. In 1958, von Braun was largely responsible for launching the first US satellite, *Explorer 1*. He later worked on the development of the *Saturn* rocket (for the Apollo program) and was deputy associate administrator of NATIONAL AERONAUTICS AND SPACE ADMINISTRATION (NASA) (1970–72).

Brazil The world's fifth-largest country, accounting for 48% of South America; the capital is BRASÍLIA. **Land and climate** Brazil contains three main regions. The AMAZON basin, which is drained by a river system that carries a fifth of the world's running water, covers more than half of the country. Brazil's second region is the NE. The third region is made up of the plateaus in the SE and covers about a quarter of the entire country. It is the most developed and densely populated part of Brazil, and includes the cities of SÃO PAULO, RIO DE JANEIRO, SALVADOR, Belo Horizonte and Brasília. Its main

BRAZIL
AREA: 8,511,970sq km (3,286,472sq mi)
POPULATION: 156,275,000
CAPITAL (POPULATION): Brasília (1,596,274)
GOVERNMENT: Federal republic
ETHNIC GROUPS: White 53%, Mulatto 22%, Mestizo 12%, African American 11%, Japanese 1%, Native American 0.1%
LANGUAGES: Portuguese (official)
RELIGIONS: Christianity (Roman Catholic 88%, Protestant 6%)
CURRENCY: Cruzeiro real

river is the PARANÁ, which flows s through Argentina. Brazil lies almost entirely within the tropics and the average monthly temperatures are high, over 20°C (68°F), with little seasonal variation. The Amazon basin contains the world's largest RAINFORESTS, the selvas. The forests contain a huge variety of plant and animal species, but many species are threatened by loggers, ranchers, mining companies, government hydroelectric schemes and even landless migrants, all of them wanting to exploit the region. The SE contains fertile farmland and large ranches. A large, swampy area is located along Brazil's borders with Bolivia and Paraguay, s of the MATO GROSSO. **Economy** The United Nations has described Brazil as a "rapidly industrializing country" (RIC). Its total volume of production is one of the largest in the world, but most of its people, including poor farmers and residents of the favelas (city slums), do not share in the country's fast economic growth. High rates of inflation and unemployment have caused widespread poverty and serious social and political problems, including, in 1997, large protests organized by the Landless Workers Movement. Brazil is among the world's top producers of bauxite, chrome, diamonds, gold, iron ore, manganese and tin. It is also a major manufacturing country, the products including aircraft, cars, chemicals, raw sugar, iron and steel, paper and textiles. Brazil is one of the world's leading farming countries, and agriculture employs 28% of the workforce. It is the world's largest coffee producer and a major exporter. Forestry is a major industry, though many people fear that the exploitation of the rainforests is an environmental disaster. **History** The Portuguese explorer Pedro Alvarez CABRAL claimed Brazil for Portugal in 1500. With Spain occupied in w South America, the Portuguese began to develop their colony, which was more than 90 times bigger than Portugal. Brazil declared itself an independent empire in 1822. During the reign of PEDRO II slavery was abolished in 1888. Brazil adopted a federal system of government in 1881. In 1889 it became a republic and began a programme of economic development. **Politics** From the 1930s, Brazil faced many political problems, including social unrest, corruption and frequent

spells of dictatorial government by military leaders. A new constitution, which came into force in 1988, took powers from the president and transferred many of them to Congress (the parliament, consisting of an elected Senate and Chamber of Deputies). This constitution paved the way for a return to a shaky democracy in 1990.
Brazil nut Seed of an evergreen tree, which has leathery leaves and grows to 41m (135ft) tall. Its flowers produce thick-walled fruit 10–30.5cm (4–12in) in diameter that contain 25–40 large seeds. Family Lecythidaceae; species *Bertholletia excelsa*.
Brazzaville Capital and largest city of the Congo, w Africa, on the River Congo. Founded in 1880, it was capital of French Equatorial Africa (1910–58). It is a major port, connected by rail to the Atlantic seaport of Pointe-Noire. Industries: foundries, chemicals, shipyards. Pop. (1992) 937,579.
bread Staple food made by mixing flour (containing a little yeast, salt and sugar) with water to make a dough, allowing the yeast to ferment carbohydrates in the mixture (thus providing carbon dioxide gas which leavens the bread), and finally baking in an oven. Yeast fermentation not only lightens the texture of the bread but also adds to its taste. Bicarbonate of soda ($NaHCO_3$) may be used instead of yeast. Unleavened bread, favoured in many Asian countries, is flat in shape and heavy in texture by comparison.
Breakspear, Nicholas *See* ADRIAN IV
bream Freshwater fish of E and N Europe. Its stocky body is green-brown and silver, and anglers prize it for its tasty flesh. Length: 30–50cm (12–20in); weight: 4–6kg (9–13lb). Family Cyprinidae; species *Abramis brama*.
breast (mammary gland) Organ of a female mammal that secretes milk to nourish new-born young. In males the glands are rudimentary and nonfunctional. The human female breast, which develops during puberty, is made up of about 15–20 irregularly shaped lobes separated by connective and fat tissues. Lactiferous ducts lead from each lobe to the nipple, a small cone-shaped structure in the centre of the breast.
breathing Process by which air is taken into and expelled from the LUNGS for the purpose of gas exchange. During inhalation, the intercostal muscles raise the ribs, increasing the volume of the THORAX and drawing air into the lungs. During exhalation, the ribs are lowered, and air is forced out through the nose, and sometimes also the mouth.
breccia Rock formed by the cementation of sharp-angled fragments in a finer matrix of the same or different material. It is formed either inside the Earth by movements of the crust, from scree slopes, or from volcanic material. *See also* CONGLOMERATE
Brecht, Bertolt (1898–1956) German playwright, poet and drama theorist. One of the most influential dramatists of the 20th century. In the 1920s, Brecht developed his distinctive, politicized theory of "epic" theatre. An attempt to move away

from Western theatrical realism, it encouraged audiences to see theatre as staged illusion via a range of "alienation" techniques. Music played an important part in this foregrounding of artifice. Brecht's major works were written in collaboration with composers such as Kurt WEILL, famously, *The Threepenny Opera* (1928). With the rise of Hitler in 1933, Brecht's Marxist views forced him into exile. While in the USA, he wrote *Mother Courage and Her Children* (1941) and *The Good Woman of Setzuan* (1943). In 1949 Brecht returned to East Germany to direct the Berliner Ensemble.

breeding Process of producing offspring, specifically the science of changing or promoting certain genetic characteristics in animals and plants. This is done through careful selection and combination of the parent stock. Breeding may involve CROSS-BREEDING or INBREEDING to produce the desired characteristics in the offspring. Scientific breeding has resulted in disease-resistant strains of crops, and in animals that give improved food yields. *See also* GENE; GENETIC ENGINEERING

Bremen City on the River Weser; capital of Bremen state, N Germany. The city suffered severe damage during World War 2, but many of its original buildings (including the Gothic city hall) survived. Industries: shipbuilding, electrical equipment, textiles. Pop. (1990) 553,200.

Brest City and port on the Atlantic coast of Brittany, w France. An important naval base, the town was severely damaged in World War 2, when used as a German submarine base. Industries: shipbuilding and repair, chemical manufacture, electronic equipment, wine, fruit, coal and timber. Pop. (1990) 147,956.

Brest-Litovsk, Treaty of (March 1918) Peace treaty between Russia and the CENTRAL POWERS, confirming Russian withdrawal from World War 1. The Ukraine and Georgia became independent and Russian territory was surrendered to Germany and Austria-Hungary. The treaty was declared void when the war ended in November.

Breton, André (1896–1966) French poet and theorist. A founder and poet of the SURREALISM movement, he wrote *Manifeste du surréalisme* (1924) and *Le Surréalisme et la Peinture* (1928). His fictional works, an autobiographical novel *Nadja* (1928), *Les Vases Communicants* (1932), *L'Amour Fou* (1937) and *Poèmes* (1948) reflect surrealist theories.

Breton Celtic language spoken in Brittany, on the NW coast of France. It is a descendant of British, an old Celtic language, and is closely related to Welsh. Its approximately half a million users usually also speak French, which is rapidly replacing it.

Breuer, Marcel (1902–81) US architect and designer, b. Hungary. One of the great innovators of modern furniture design, he studied and taught at the BAUHAUS (1920–28), where he created his famous tubular steel chair. In 1937, he settled in the USA and subsequently worked with Walter GROPIUS as a partner in architectural projects. He designed Whitney Museum of American Art in New York City (1966).

brewing Preparation of beer and stout by using yeast as a catalyst in the alcoholic fermentation of liquors containing malt and hops. In beer brewing, a malt liquor (wort) is made from crushed germinated barley grains. Hops are added to the boiling wort both to impart a bitter flavour, and also to help to clarify the beer and keep it free from spoilage by microbes. The clear, filtered wort is cooled and inoculated with brewer's yeast, which ferments part of the sugar from malt into alcohol.

Brezhnev, Leonid Ilyich (1906–82) Soviet politician and effective ruler from the mid-1960s until his death. He became secretary to the central committee of the Soviet Communist Party (1952) and a member of the presidium (later politburo) (1957). In 1964 he helped plan the downfall of Nikita KHRUSHCHEV and became party general secretary, at first sharing power with prime minister Alexei KOSYGIN. In 1977 he became president of the Soviet Union. He pursued a hard line against reforms at home and in Eastern Europe but also sought to reduce tensions with the West. After the Soviet invasion of CZECHOSLOVAKIA (1968), he promulgated the "Brezhnev Doctrine" confirming Soviet domination of satellite states.

Briand, Aristide (1862–1932) French political leader. A moderate, he was premier of 11 governments between 1909–29. He advocated international cooperation and was one of the instigators of the LOCARNO PACT (1925), for which he shared the Nobel Peace Prize with Gustav STRESEMANN in 1926. He was also one of the authors of the KELLOGG-BRIAND PACT of 1928, and favoured a form of European union.

brick Hardened block of clay used for building and paving. Usually rectangular, bricks are made in standard sizes by machines that either mould bricks or cut off extruded sections of stiff clay which are conveyed into a continuously operating kiln where they are baked at temperatures of up to 1,300°C. The first, sun-dried, bricks were used in the Tigris-Euphrates basin c.5,000 years ago.

bridge Structure providing a continuous passage over a body of water, roadway or valley. Bridges are built for people, vehicles, pipelines or power transmission lines. Bridges are prehistoric in origin, the first probably being merely logs over rivers or chasms. Modern bridges take a great variety of forms including beams, arches, cantilevers, suspension bridges and cable-stayed bridges. They can also be movable or floating pontoons. They can be made from a variety of materials, including brick or stone (for arches), steel or concrete.

Bridgetown Capital and port of Barbados, in the West Indies. Founded in 1628, it is the seat of the parliament and has a college of the University of the West Indies. Industries: rum distilling, sugar processing, tourism. Pop. (1990 est.) 6,720.

93

Bright, John (1811–89) British parliamentary reformer. A Quaker and mill owner, he and his fellow radical, Richard COBDEN, were leaders of the ANTI-CORN LAW LEAGUE (founded 1839). First elected to Parliament in 1843, he subsequently represented Manchester, the home of FREE TRADE. After the repeal of the Corn Laws (1846), Bright worked in the cause of parliamentary reform.

Brighton Resort town on the English Channel, East Sussex, s England. Originally a fishing village, it was popularized as a resort by the Prince Regent (George IV), who had the Royal Pavilion rebuilt here in oriental style by John NASH. It is the seat of the University of Sussex (1961) and the University of Brighton (1992). Industries: food processing, furniture, tourism. Pop. (1991) 143,582.

Brindley, James (1716–72) British engineer and pioneer canal-builder who constructed the first major canal in England, from Worsley, Lancashire to Manchester. He was responsible for a network of about 565km (350mi) of canals, an advancement which hastened the INDUSTRIAL REVOLUTION.

Brisbane City and seaport on the Brisbane River; capital of Queensland, E Australia. First settled in 1824 as a penal colony, it became state capital in 1859. It is the location of Parliament House (1869) and the University of Queensland (1909), and is a major shipping and rail centre. Industries: oil refining, shipbuilding, car assembly, railway engineering, chemicals. Pop. (1993 est.) 1,421,600.

bristle tail *See* SILVERFISH

Bristol City and unitary authority at the confluence of the rivers Avon and Frome, sw England. An important seaport and trade centre since achieving city status in 1155, it was a major centre for the wool and cloth industry. From the 15th–18th century, it was England's second city and the base for many New World explorations. The 19th century witnessed a gradual decline in the city's economy due to competition from LIVERPOOL. The city suffered intensive bombing during World War 2. The main port facilities are now at Avonmouth. Industries: aircraft engineering, chemicals, tobacco. Pop. (1991) 376,146.

Britain (Great Britain) Island kingdom in NW Europe, officially the UNITED KINGDOM of Great Britain and NORTHERN IRELAND. It is made up of ENGLAND, SCOTLAND, WALES and NORTHERN IRELAND, the CHANNEL ISLANDS and the Isle of MAN.

Britain, Ancient British history from PREHISTORY to ROMAN BRITAIN. During the NEOLITHIC age, hunter-gatherers gradually turned to sedentary farming. Old STONE AGE remains have been found at Cheddar Gorge, Somerset, s England. There are numerous examples of New Stone Age burial mounds. During the BRONZE AGE (c.2300 BC) the Beaker built an advanced civilization, producing the stone circles at STONEHENGE and Avebury, s England. The IRON AGE was dominated by the CELTS. Julius Caesar invaded Britain in 54 BC, and the Roman conquest began in earnest from 43 BC.

Britain, Battle of (1940) Series of air battles fought over Britain. Early in World War 2 (as a prelude to invasion) the Germans hoped to destroy Britain's industrial and military infrastructure and civilian morale by a sustained series of bombing raids. Failure to eliminate the fighters of the Royal Air Force in August–September resulted in the abandonment of the plans for invasion, though bombing raids continued.

British Antarctic Territory British colony in Antarctica comprising the mainland and islands within a triangular area bounded by latitude 50°s and longitudes 20° and 80°w. It includes the South Shetland Islands, South Orkney Islands and Graham Land. Formerly part of the Falkland Islands, the territory became a British Crown colony in 1962, although today Argentina and Chile claim parts of it. There are no permanent settlements, but teams of scientists occupy meteorological stations and other establishments of the British Antarctic Survey. Area: 1,725,000sq km (666,000sq mi).

British Broadcasting Corporation (BBC) UK state-financed radio and television network. Its directors are appointed by the government but, in terms of policy and content, the BBC is largely independent. It receives its finances from a licence fee. The BBC was set up in 1927 to replace the British Broadcasting Company, which had been in operation since 1922. Its first director-general (1927–38) was Lord Reith, whose philosophy of the BBC as an instrument of education and civilization greatly shaped the corporation's policies. The current director-general is John Birt (1992–). His controversial policies have included rationalizing the BBC, exposing it to the influence of market forces and developing the use of independent production companies.

British Columbia Province of w Canada, on the Pacific coast, bounded N by Alaska, s by Washington state. The Rocky Mountains run N to s through the province. The capital is Victoria, other major cities include VANCOUVER. The region was first sighted by Sir Francis DRAKE in 1578. Captain COOK landed here in 1778, and George Vancouver took possession of the island that bears his name for Britain in 1794. In 1846 the border with the USA was finally settled. Completion of the Canadian Pacific Railway in 1885 spurred the development of the province. The many rivers (principal of which is the Fraser) provide hydroelectric power. Three-quarters of the land is forested,. Mineral deposits include copper, silver, gold, lead, zinc and asbestos. Dairying and fruit-growing are the chief farming activities, practised mainly in the s. Industries: fishing, paper, tourism, transport equipment and chemicals. Area: 948,600sq km (366,255sq mi). Pop. (1991) 3,282,061.

British empire Overseas territories ruled by Britain from the 16th to the 20th century. Historians distinguish two empires. The first, based mainly on commercial ventures (such as sugar and tobacco plantations), missionary activities and slave trading resulted in the creation of British colonies in the Caribbean and North America in the 17th century. This "First Empire" was curtailed by the loss of 13 US colonies, at the end of the AMERICAN REVOLUTION (1775–81). The "Second Empire" was created in the 19th century, with Queen VICTORIA its empress. British colonial expansion was predominantly in the Far East, Australia (initially with the penal colonies), Africa and India (the "jewel" of the empire). By 1914 the empire comprised about 25% of the Earth's land surface and population. Virtually all the constituent members gained independence in the period after World War 2. Most subsequently became members of the COMMONWEALTH.

British Empire, Order of the (OBE) Military and civil order or knighthood bestowed as a reward for public service to the Commonwealth of Nations. Created in 1917, it has five different classes for men and women: Knights (or Dames) Grand Cross, Knights (or Dames) Commander, Commanders, Officers and Members.

British Honduras See BELIZE

British Indian Ocean Territory British colony in the Indian Ocean comprising the islands of the Chagos Archipelago, 1,900km (1,200mi) NE of Mauritius. In 1814 France ceded the territory to Britain and it was administered by MAURITIUS. In 1965 Britain bought it from Mauritius in order to build a joint US/UK naval base on Diego Garcia island. In 1976 the islands of Aldabra, Farquhar and Desroches reverted to SEYCHELLES administration.

British Isles Group of islands off the NW coast of Europe, made up of the UNITED KINGDOM of Great Britain and Northern IRELAND, and the Republic of IRELAND. It also includes the Isle of MAN in the Irish Sea (a self-governing island but part of the United Kingdom) and the CHANNEL ISLANDS in the English Channel (also self-governing, but a British crown dependency).

British Legion Organization of ex-service men and women for helping disabled and unemployed war veterans, their widows and families. Each year during the week preceding Remembrance Day (the Sunday nearest to 11 November) millions of artificial poppies are sold to commemorate the dead of two World Wars and raise funds for the Legion.

British Medical Association (BMA) UK professional body founded in 1832; 66% of all doctors in Britain are members. The BMA was set up to advance the medical sciences. Since the establishment of the NATIONAL HEALTH SERVICE (NHS) in 1948, it has also negotiated over pay and conditions for hospital doctors and general practitioners.

British Museum One of the world's greatest public collections of art, ethnography and archaeology (established 1753). Its first displays came from a private collection purchased from the naturalist, Sir Hans Sloane. Later additions included the ROSETTA

STONE and the ELGIN MARBLES. The present building by Sir Robert Smirke was completed in 1847. The museum contains several separate departments, including the Museum of Mankind and the Department of Prints and Drawings, which houses works by Rembrandt, Rubens and Michelangelo, as well as many examples of Oriental art.

Brittany (Bretagne) Former duchy and province in NW France, forming the peninsula between the Bay of Biscay and the English Channel. Under Roman rule from 56 BC to the 5th century AD, it was later inhabited by CELTS who gave it its name, language (BRETON) and distinctive costume and culture. It was formally incorporated within France in 1532, and the years that followed saw the deliberate suppression of Breton culture. In more recent times, the French government has improved the region's infrastructure. Pop. (1990) 2,795,600.

Britten, (Edward) Benjamin (1913–76) English composer. He is best known for his operas, which rank him among the foremost opera composers of the 20th century. He also wrote numerous songs, many especially for Peter PEARS. Britten's operas include *Peter Grimes* (1945), *Billy Budd* (1951), *The Turn of the Screw* (1954), *A Midsummer Night's Dream* (1960) and *Death in Venice* (1973). Other significant works include the *War Requiem* (1962). In 1948 he established the music festival held annually at his home town of Aldeburgh, on the E coast of England. He was made a peer shortly before his death.

brittle star (serpent star) Marine ECHINODERM with a small central disc body and up to twenty (though typically five) long, sinuous arms; these break off easily and are replaced by regeneration. Class Ophiuroidea; genera include the phosphorescent *Amphiopholis* and *Ophiactis*.

Brno (Brünn) Capital city of central Jihomoravský (MORAVIA) region, SE Czech Republic. Founded in the 10th century, it has a 15th-century cathedral. The Bren Gun was designed here. Industries: armaments, engineering, textiles, chemicals. Pop. (1990 est.) 391,000.

broadcasting Transmission of sound or images by radio waves or through cables to a widely dispersed audience. The first US commercial RADIO company, KDKA, began broadcasting in Pittsburgh in 1920. In the UK, the BBC began radio transmission; there are now four national BBC radio stations. UK public TELEVISION broadcasting began in 1936 from Alexandra Palace, London. The BBC transmitted on one channel. A second channel, *ITV*, run by Independent Television, was set up in 1955. *BBC2* started broadcasting in 1964, *Channel 4* commenced transmission in 1982, and *Channel 5* in 1997. In 1962 Telstar delivered the first transatlantic, SATELLITE TELEVISION broadcast. Rupert MURDOCH's *Sky Television* satellite service began broadcasting in 1989, since when CABLE TELEVISION has also become popular. Further developments include the introduction of digital television.

Broads, Norfolk Region of shallow lakes and waterways in E England, connected by the rivers Waveney, Yare and Bure, between Norwich and the coast. It is a wildlife sanctuary and a popular sailing area, with 320km (200mi) of waterways.

Broglie, Prince Louis Victor de (1892–87) French physicist who theorized that all ELEMENTARY PARTICLES have an associated wave. He devised the formula that predicts this wavelength, and its existence was proven in 1927. Broglie developed this form of QUANTUM MECHANICS, called WAVE MECHANICS, for which he was awarded the 1929 Nobel Prize in physics. Erwin SCHRÖDINGER advanced Broglie's ideas with his equation that describes the wave function of a particle.

bromeliad Any of the 1,700 species of the pineapple family (Bromeliaceae). Most are native to the tropics and subtropics and, beside the PINEAPPLE, include many of the larger EPIPHYTES of trees of the rainforests.

bromide Salt of hydrobromic acid or certain organic compounds containing bromine. The bromides of ammonium, sodium, potassium and certain other metals were once extensively used medically as sedatives. Silver bromide is light-sensitive and is used in photography.

bromine Volatile liquid element (symbol Br) of the halogen group (elements in group VII of the PERIODIC TABLE), first isolated in 1826 by the French chemist A. J. Balard. Bromine is the only liquid form of a nonmetallic element. It is extracted by treating seawater or natural brines with chlorine. A reddish-brown fuming liquid having an unpleasant odour, it is used in commercially useful compounds, such as those used to manufacture photographic film and additives for petrol. Chemically it resembles CHLORINE but is less reactive. Properties: at.no. 35; r.a.m 79.904; r.d. 3.12; m.p. $-7.2°C$ $(19.04°F)$; b.p. $58.8°C$ $(137.8°F)$; the most common isotope is Br^{79} (50.54%).

bronchitis Inflammation of the bronchial tubes most often caused by a viral infection such as the common cold or influenza but exacerbated by environmental pollutants. Symptoms include coughing and the production of large quantities of mucus. It can be acute (sudden and short-lived) or chronic (persistent), especially in those who smoke.

bronchus (pl. bronchi) One of two branches into which the TRACHEA or windpipe divides, with one branch leading to each of the LUNGS. The bronchus divides into smaller and smaller branches, called bronchioles, which extend throughout the lung, opening into the air sacs or ALVEOLI. The bronchi are supported and kept open by rings of CARTILAGE.

Brontë, Anne (1820–49) English novelist and poet. The youngest of the Brontë sisters, she became a governess, an experience reflected in *Agnes Grey* (1847). All of her work was published under the male pseudonym Acton Bell and her best-known novel is *The Tenant of Wildfell Hall* (1848).

Brontë, Charlotte (1816–55) English novelist and poet. Her personal life was unhappy and she persistently suffered from ill-health. Born into genteel poverty, her mother, four sisters, and dissolute brother Branwell died early. Her four novels, *The Professor* (1846), *Jane Eyre* (1847), *Shirley* (1849), and *Villette* (1853) are works of remarkable passion and imagination. Her writings initially appeared under the male pseudonym Currer Bell.

Brontë, Emily (1818–48) English novelist and poet. Like her sisters she wrote under a male pseudonym, Ellis Bell. Her love for her native Yorkshire moors and insight into human passion are manifested in her poetry and her only novel, *Wuthering Heights* (1847).

brontosaurus Former name of apatosaurus, a DINOSAUR of the Jurassic and early Cretaceous periods. It had a long neck and tail, and a small head with the eyes and nostrils on the top so that it could remain presumably almost completely immersed in water. Length: 21m (70ft); weight: to 30 tonnes.

bronze Traditionally an ALLOY of COPPER and no more than 33% tin. It is hard and resistant to corrosion, but easy to work. It has long been used in sculpture and bell-casting. Other metals are often added for specific properties and uses, such as aluminium in aircraft parts and tubing, silicon in marine hardware and chemical equipment, and phosphorus in springs, gunmetal parts and electrical parts.

Bronze Age Period in human cultural development between the introduction of bronze tools and the discovery of iron-working techniques. In Mesopotamia, the Bronze Age began *c.*3200 BC and lasted until *c.*1100 BC. In Britain bronze was used after 2000 BC, and iron technology did not become widespread until *c.*500 BC.

Brooke, Rupert Chawner (1887–1915) English poet. He wrote some of the most anthologized poems in the English language, including *The Soldier* and *The Old Vicarage, Grantchester*, but the romantic image created by his early death during World War 1 has tended to distort his status as a fairly typical poet of the Georgian school.

broom Any of various deciduous shrubs of the PEA family (Fabaceae/Leguminosae). They have yellow, purple or white flowers, usually in clusters. Many belong to the genus *Genista*, which gave its name to the Plantagenet kings of England (from the Latin *Planta genista*), who used the broom as their emblem.

Brown, "Capability" (Lancelot) (1715–83) English landscape gardener who revolutionized garden and parkland layout in the 1700s. He designed or remodelled nearly 150 estates, including gardens at Blenheim and Kew. He worked to achieve casual effects, with scattered groups of trees and gently rolling hills. He earned his nickname from a habit of saying that a place had "capabilities of improvement".

Brown, Ford Madox (1821–93) English painter, closely associated with (although not a member of) the PRE-RAPHAELITE BROTHERHOOD. A meticulous draughtsman, the Pre-Raphaelite influence can be seen in *The Last of England* (1855) and *Work* (1852–63). Late in his career he produced a cycle of paintings on the history of Manchester for the city's town hall (1878–93). He was the grandfather of the writer Ford Madox FORD.

Brown, Gordon (1951–) British statesman, chancellor of the exchequer (1997–), b. Scotland. Brown became a Labour MP in 1983, joining the shadow cabinet in 1987. Under the leadership of John SMITH, Brown was shadow chancellor, a post he continued to hold under Tony BLAIR's leadership. Brown's promise to freeze income tax rates for the lifetime of a parliament did much to secure Labour's victory in the 1997 general election. His first job as chancellor was to give the BANK OF ENGLAND independence in interest rate policy.

Brown, John (1800–59) US anti-slavery agitator, hero of the song *John Brown's Body*. Hoping to start a slave revolt, he led 21 men who captured the US arsenal at Harper's Ferry, Virginia, in 1859. Driven out next day by troops under General Robert E. LEE, Brown was captured, charged with treason and hanged. The trial aggravated North-South tensions.

Brownian movement Random movement of particles suspended in a fluid. It is caused by the unequal bombardment of the larger particles by the smaller molecules of the fluid. The movement is named after Robert Brown, who in 1827 observed the movement of plant spores floating in water.

Browning, Elizabeth Barrett (1806–61) English poet, regarded as the pre-eminent English woman poet of her age. In 1846 she secretly married Robert BROWNING. *The Seraphim and Other Poems* (1838) and *Poems* (1844) established her popularity, later confirmed by her collection of 1850, which included *Sonnets from the Portuguese*. Her last important work was *Aurora Leigh* (1857).

Browning, Robert (1812–89) English poet. Works such as *My Last Duchess* and *Soliloquy of the Spanish Cloister*, both published in *Bells and Pomegranates* (1846), display his characteristic use of dramatic monologue. In 1846 he and Elizabeth Barrett (BROWNING) secretly married and moved to Florence, Italy. He published *Christmas Eve and Easter Day* (1850) and *Men and Women* (1855) before returning to London after her death. One of the foremost poets of the 19th century, Browning is also at times one of the most obscure.

Bruch, Max (1838–1920) German composer and conductor. He wrote three operas but is best remembered for orchestral works, notably his first violin concerto, the *Scottish Fantasy* for violin and orchestra, and the *Kol Nidrei* for cello and orchestra.

Brücke, Die (1905–1913) (The Bridge) First group of German expressionist painters. Founded in Dresden by E.L. KIRCHNER, the group chose their name because they wanted their work to form a bridge with the art of the future. They produced paintings and drawings, but their greatest strength

was the woodcut. Members of the group included Emil NOLDE, Karl Schmidt-Rottluff, Max Pechstein and Erich Heckel. Their work was characterized by jagged edges, harshly distorted figures and a simplification of colour and form. *See also* EXPRESSIONISM

Bruckner, Anton (1824–96) Austrian composer. An intensely pious man, he wrote a great deal of church music – cantatas, masses and a *Te Deum* (1881–84) – and nine symphonies. His compositions are noted for their massive scale: the symphonies are lengthy, monumental creations.

Bruegel, Pieter the Elder (1525–69) Netherlandish landscape painter and draughtsman, the greatest 16th-century Dutch artist. Profoundly influenced by a journey through the Alps, he produced a series of drawings of the region. In 1563 he moved to Brussels and concentrated on painting. His early, characteristically rural scenes, crowded with tiny peasant figures, gave way during his last six years to paintings with larger figures that illustrated proverbs. His son, Pieter the Younger (1564–1637), sometimes copied his work. Another son, Jan (1568–1625), specialized in highly detailed flower paintings, earning the nickname "Velvet Bruegel" for his skill in depicting delicate textures.

Bruges (Brugge) City 88km (55mi) WNW of Brussels; capital of West Flanders province, NW Belgium. Built on a network of canals, it was a trading centre in the 15th century. Its importance declined after 1500, but trade revived when the Zeebrugge ship canal was opened in 1907. It has many medieval buildings. Industries: engineering, brewing, lace, textiles, tourism. Pop. (1993 est.) 116,724.

Brunei Sultanate in N Borneo, SE Asia; the capital is BANDAR SERI BEGAWAN. Bounded in the NW by the South China Sea, Brunei rises from humid plains to forested mountains running along its S border with Malaysia. Oil and gas are the main source of income, accounting for 70% of GDP. During the 16th century Brunei ruled over the whole of Borneo and parts of the Philippines, but gradually lost its influence in the region. It became a British protectorate in 1888. Brunei acheived independence in 1983. The Sultan has executive authority over a council of cabinet ministers, a religious council and a privy council. Area: 5,765sq km (2,225sq mi). Pop. (1993) 276,300.

Brunel, Isambard Kingdom (1806–59) British marine and railway engineer. A man of remarkable foresight, imagination and daring, he revolutionized British engineering. In 1829 he designed the Clifton Suspension Bridge (completed 1864) in Bristol. He is also famous for his ships: *Great Western* (designed 1837), the first trans-Atlantic wooden steamship; *Great Britain* (1843), the first iron-hulled screw-driven steamship; and *Great Eastern* (1858), a steamship powered by screws and paddles which was the largest vessel of its time.

Brunelleschi, Filippo (1377–1446) Florentine architect, first of the great RENAISSANCE architects and a pioneer of perspective. He influenced many later architects, including MICHELANGELO. In 1420 he began to design the dome of Florence Cathedral, the largest since the HAGIA SOPHIA. Other works include the Ospedale degl'Innocenti (1419–26), the Basilica of San Lorenzo (begun 1421) and the Pazzi Chapel (c.1440), all in Florence.

Brussels (Bruxelles) Capital of Belgium and of Brabant province, central Belgium. During the Middle Ages it achieved prosperity through the wool trade and became capital of the Spanish Netherlands. In 1830 it became capital of newly independent Belgium. It has many fine buildings including a 13th-century cathedral, the town hall, splendid art nouveau period buildings and academies of fine arts. The main commercial, financial, cultural and administrative centre of Belgium, it is also the headquarters of the EUROPEAN COMMUNITY (EC) and of the NORTH ATLANTIC TREATY ORGANIZATION (NATO). Industries: textiles, chemicals, electronic equipment, electrical goods, brewing. Pop. (1993 est.) 949,070.

Brussels, Treaty of (1948) Agreement signed by Britain, France and the Low Countries for cooperation in defence, politics, economics and cultural affairs for 50 years. The defence agreement was merged into the NORTH ATLANTIC TREATY ORGANIZATION (NATO) in 1950. In 1954 Italy and West Germany joined the original signatories, and the name was changed to the Western European Union. It was a forerunner of the EUROPEAN COMMUNITY (EC).

brutalism Architectural movement of the 1950s and early 1960s. It took its inspiration from LE CORBUSIER's pilgrimage chapel at Ronchamp and his High Court building at CHANDIGARH, India. Corbusier designed both buildings as a reaction to the sterility of the INTERNATIONAL STYLE. The Brutalists was the name given to a number of young architects, such as Paul Rudolph, James Stirling and Kenzo Tange, who tried to extend Le Corbusier's experiments in aggressive and chunky designs of their own. It should not be confused with the 1950s British movement of **new brutalism**, in which Alison and Peter Smithson adopted the uncompromising simplicity of MIES VAN DER ROHE.

Bruton, John Gerard (1947–) Irish prime minister (1995–97). Bruton was elected to the Dáil (parliament) in 1969. A member of the FINE GAEL party, he rose steadily through the ministerial ranks, earning a reputation as a right-winger. He became leader of Fine Gael in 1990 and prime minister in 1995. In the 1997 general election, his Fine Gael coalition was narrowly defeated.

Brutus (85–42 BC) (Marcus Junius Brutus) Roman republican leader, one of the principal assassins of Julius CAESAR. Brutus sided first with POMPEY against Caesar, but Caesar forgave him and made him governor of Cisalpine Gaul in 46 BC and city praetor in 44 BC. After taking part in Caesar's assassination, Brutus raised an army in Greece but, defeated at Philippi by Mark ANTONY and AUGUSTUS, he committed suicide.

bryophyte Group of small, green, rootless non-VASCULAR PLANTS (phylum Bryophyta), including MOSS and LIVERWORT. Bryophytes grow on damp surfaces exposed to light, including rocks and tree bark, almost everywhere from the Arctic to the Antarctic. There are about 24,000 species. *See also* ALTERNATION OF GENERATIONS

BSE Abbreviation of BOVINE SPONGIFORM ENCEPHALOPATHY

bubonic plague *See* PLAGUE

Buchan, John, 1st Baron Tweedsmuir (1875–1940) British author and politician. He was famous for his adventure novels, such as *The Thirty-Nine Steps* (1915). He also wrote a four-volume history of World War 1 (1915–19) and biographies of Julius Caesar, Walter Scott (1932) and Oliver Cromwell (1934). He was governor-general of Canada (1935–40).

Buchanan, James (1791–1868) 15th US President (1857–1861). A Pennsylvania lawyer, he was elected to Congress in 1820 and was a supporter of Andrew JACKSON. He gained the Democratic nomination for president at the second attempt in 1856, after a spell as ambassador to Britain. His administration was unpopular, as sectional conflicts increased and Buchanan's efforts at compromise failed. The Democratic Party split, Abraham LINCOLN won the 1860 election and the Southern states seceded before Buchanan, who had not been renominated, left office.

Bucharest (Bucuresti) Capital and largest city of Romania, on the River Dimbovita, in the S of the country. Founded in the 14th century on an important trade route, it became capital in 1862 and was occupied by Germany in both World Wars. It is an industrial, commercial and cultural centre. The seat of the patriarch of the Romanian Orthodox Church, it has notable churches, museums and galleries. There are also two universities. Industries: oil refining, chemicals, textiles. Pop. (1992) 2,350,984.

Buchenwald Site of a Nazi concentration camp, near Weimar, Germany. Established in 1937, it became notorious, especially for the medical experiments conducted on its inmates, of whom about 50,000 died. It was liberated by US forces in 1945.

Buckingham Palace London residence of British sovereigns since 1837. Formerly owned by the dukes of Buckingham, it was purchased by George III in 1761 and remodelled into a 600-room palace by John NASH in 1825. Sir Aston Webb redesigned the E front in 1913. The changing of the guard takes place here daily.

Buckinghamshire County in SE central England; the county town is Aylesbury. In the Vale of Aylesbury to the N, cereal crops and beans are grown; livestock and poultry are raised in the S. Industries: furniture, printing, building materials. Area: 1,877sq km (725sq mi). Pop. (1991) 632,487.

bud In plants, a small swelling or projection consisting of a short stem with overlapping, immature leaves covered by scales. Leaf buds develop into leafy twigs, and flower buds develop into blossoms. A bud at the tip of a twig is a terminal bud and contains the growing point; lateral buds develop in leaf axils along a twig.

Budapest Capital of Hungary, on the River Danube. It was created in 1873 by uniting the towns of Buda (capital of Hungary since the 14th century) and Pest on the opposite bank. It became one of the two capitals of the AUSTRO-HUNGARIAN EMPIRE. Budapest was the scene of a popular uprising against the Soviet Union in 1956. The old town contains a remarkable collection of buildings including: Buda Castle; the 13th-century Matthias Church; the Parliament Building; and the National Museum. Industries: iron and steel, chemicals, textiles. Pop. (1993 est.) 2,009,000.

Buddha (Enlightened One) Title adopted by Gautama Siddhartha (*c*.563– *c*.483 BC), the founder of BUDDHISM. Born at Lumbini, Nepal, Siddhartha was son of the ruler of the Sakya tribe, and his early years were spent in luxury. At the age of 29, he realized that human life is little more than suffering. He gave up his wealth and comfort, deserted his family, and took to the road as a wandering ascetic. He travelled south and sought truth in a six-year regime of austerity. After abandoning asceticism as futile, he sought his own middle way towards enlightenment. The moment of truth came *c*.528 BC, as he sat beneath a banyan tree in the village of Buddha Gaya, Bihar, India. After this incident, he taught others about his way to truth. The title *buddha* applies to those who have achieved perfect enlightenment. Buddhists believe that there have been several buddhas before Siddhartha, and there will be many to come. The term also serves to describe a variety of Buddha images.

Buddhism Religion and philosophy founded in India *c*.528 BC by Gautama Siddhartha, the BUDDHA. Buddhism is based on Four Noble Truths: existence is suffering; the cause of suffering is desire; the end of suffering comes with the achievement of NIRVANA; Nirvana is attained through the Eightfold Path: right views, right resolve, right speech, right action, right livelihood, right effort, right mindfulness and right concentration. There are no gods in Buddhism. Alongside the belief in the Four Noble Truths exists *karma*, one of Buddhism's most important concepts: good actions are rewarded and evil ones are punished, either in this life or throughout a long series of lives resulting from *samsara*, the cycle of death and rebirth produced by reincarnation. The achievement of Nirvana breaks the cycle. Buddhism is a worldwide religion. Its main divisions are THERAVADA, or *Hinayana*, in SE Asia, MAHAYANA in N Asia, Lamaism or TIBETAN BUDDHISM in Tibet, and ZEN in Japan. The total number of Buddhists in the world in the mid-1990s was estimated at nearly 250 million.

budding Method of asexual reproduction that produces a new organism from an outgrowth of the parent. Hydras, for example, often bud in spring and summer. A small bulge appears on the parent and grows until it breaks away as a new individual.

Budge, (John) Don (Donald) (1915–) US tennis player. Regarded by many experts as one of the two greatest players of all time (with Bill TILDEN), he was the first man to complete the Grand Slam of the four major singles (Wimbledon, USA, Australia, France) in one year (1938), after which he turned professional. He was Wimbledon champion three times, and US champion in both 1937 and 1938.

budgerigar (parakeet) Small, brightly coloured seed-eating PARROT native to Australia, and a popular pet. It can be taught to mimic speech. The sexes look alike but the coloration of the cere (a waxy membrane at the base of the beak) may vary seasonally. Size: 19cm (7.5in) long. Species *Melopsittacus undulatus*.

budget Plan for the financial expenditure of an individual, a corporation or a government, matching it against expected income. National budgets determine the level of direct and indirect taxation against projected expenditure and economic growth. The complexity of modern trade and finance has sometimes forced governments to make two or more budgets in a single year.

Buenos Aires Capital of Argentina, on the estuary of the Río de la Plata, 240km (150mi) from the Atlantic Ocean. It became a separate federal district and capital of the country in 1880. Industries: meat processing, flour milling, textiles, metal works, car assembly, oil refining. Pop. (1992 est.) 11,662,050.

buffalo Any of several horned mammals and a misnomer for the North American BISON. The massive ox-like Indian, or water, buffalo (*Bubalus bubalis*) is often domesticated for milk and hides. Height: 1.5m (5ft). Family Bovidae.

buffer solution Solution to which a moderate quantity of a strong acid or a strong base can be added without making a significant change to its pH value (acidity or alkalinity). Buffer solutions usually consist of either a mixture of a weak acid and one of its salts, a mixture of an acid salt and its normal salt or a mixture of two acid salts.

bug Any member of the insect order Hemiptera, although in the USA any insect is commonly called a bug. True bugs are flattened insects which undergo gradual or incomplete metamorphosis, have two pairs of wings and use piercing and sucking mouthparts. Most feed on plant juices, such as the greenfly, although a number attack animals and are carriers of disease.

bugle Brass wind instrument resembling a small TRUMPET without valves, capable of playing notes of only one harmonic series. Because its penetrating tones carry great distances, it was often used for military signalling.

Buhl, André Charles *See* BOULLE (BUHL), ANDRÉ CHARLES

building society In the UK, a financial institution primarily for providing mortgage loans to house-buyers. The money lent by a building society comes from savings invested by the public in deposits and shares. Since the Building Societies Act (1986), they have been allowed to offer a wider range of financial services, putting them in direct competition with banks. They are comparable to savings and loan associations in the USA.

Bujumbura (formerly, Usumbura) Capital and chief port of Burundi, E central Africa, at NE end of Lake TANGANYIKA. Founded in 1899 as part of German East Africa, it was the capital of the Belgian trust territory of Ruanda-Urundi after World War 1 and remained capital of Burundi when the country achieved independence in 1962.

Bukhara (Buchara) Ancient city in W Uzbekistan, capital of the Bukhara region. Founded *c.*1st century AD, it was ruled by Arabs (7th–9th century), by Turks and Mongols (12th–15th century) and annexed to Russia in 1868; it was included in Uzbekistan (1924). It is an important Asian trade and cultural centre. Industries: silk processing, rugs, handicrafts, textiles. Pop. (1990) 246,200.

Bukharin, Nikolai Ivanovich (1888–1938) Russian communist political theorist. After the 1917 Revolution he became a leading member of the COMMUNIST INTERNATIONAL (Comintern) and editor of *Pravda*. In 1924 he became a member of the politburo. He opposed agricultural collectivization and was executed for treason by STALIN.

Bulawayo City in SW Zimbabwe, SE Africa; capital of Matabeleland North province. It was founded by the British in 1893 and was the site of the Matabele revolt in 1896. It is the second-largest city in the country. Industries: textiles, motor vehicles, cement, electrical equipment. Pop. (1992) 620,936.

bulb In botany, a food storage organ consisting of a short stem and swollen scale leaves. Food is stored in the scales, which are either layered in a series of rings, as in the onion, or loosely attached to the stem, as in some lilies. Small buds between the scale leaves give rise to new shoots each year. New bulbs are produced in the axils of the outer scale leaves. *See also* ASEXUAL REPRODUCTION

Bulgaria Balkan republic in SE Europe bordering the Black Sea; the capital is SOFIA. **Land and climate** Northern Bulgaria consists of a plateau falling to the valley of the River DANUBE, which forms most of Bulgaria's N frontier with Romania. The heart of Bulgaria is mountainous and the main ranges include the Balkan Mountains (Stara Planina) and the Rhodope Mountains. Between them is the River Maritsa valley, which forms an E–W route between the coast and the interior. Bulgaria has hot summers and cold winters, with moderate rainfall. More than half of Bulgaria is under crops or pasture, while forests, including beech and spruce, cover about 35% of the country. **Economy** Accord-

---

BULGARIA

AREA: 110,910sq km (42,822sq mi)
POPULATION: 8,963,000
CAPITAL (POPULATION): Sofia (1,141,142)
GOVERNMENT: Multiparty republic
ETHNIC GROUPS: Bulgarian 86%, Turkish 10%, Gypsy 3%, Macedonian, Armenian, Romanian, Greek
LANGUAGES: Bulgarian (official)
RELIGIONS: Christianity (Eastern Orthodox 87%), Islam 13%
CURRENCY: Lev = 100 stotinki

---

ing to the World Bank, Bulgaria in the 1990s was a "lower-middle-income" developing country. It has limited deposits of minerals, including brown coal, manganese and iron ore, but manufacturing is the leading economic activity. The main products are chemicals, metal products, machinery and textiles. Manufactured goods are the leading exports. Wheat and maize are the principal crops, and fruit, oilseeds, tobacco and vegetables are also economically important. The valleys of the Maritsa plains are ideal for vines, plums, cotton and tobacco. Livestock farming, especially the rearing of dairy and beef cattle, sheep and pigs, is also important. **History** A powerful Bulgar kingdom was set up in 681, but the country became part of the BYZANTINE EMPIRE in the 11th century. OTTOMAN Turks ruled Bulgaria from 1396 and ethnic Turks still comprise a sizeable minority. In 1879 Bulgaria became a monarchy and, in 1908, it achieved full independence. Bulgaria was an ally of Germany in both World Wars. In 1944 Soviet troops invaded Bulgaria and, after the war, the monarchy was abolished and the country became a subservient Communist ally of the Soviet Union **Politics** In the late 1980s, reforms in the Soviet Union led Bulgaria's government to introduce a multiparty system in 1990. A Socialist government, elected the following year in the first free elections in 44 years, was in effect the former Communist Party, retaining power against confused and raw opposition by promising reforms. Later the new parties did take control, but they faced huge problems in trying to transform the old centralized state-run economy into one based on private enterprise. In early 1997 virtual economic collapse prompted widespread anti-government demonstrations. A general election was called, which was won by a centre-right coalition.

Bulgars Ancient Turkic people originating in the region N and E of the Black Sea. In about AD 650 they split into two groups. The western group moved to Bulgaria, where they became assimilated into the Slavic population and adopted Christianity. The other group moved to the VOLGA region and set up a Bulgar state, eventually converting to Islam. The Volga Bulgars were conquered by the Kievan Rus in the 10th century.

bulimia nervosa EATING DISORDER that takes the form of compulsive eating then purging by induced vomiting or the use of a LAXATIVE or DIURETIC. Confined predominantly to girls and women, the disorder most often results from an underlying psychological problem. An obsession with body image may be reinforced by Western media stereotypes of slimas beautiful.

bulldog English bull-baiting breed of DOG with a distinctive large head, short upturned muzzle and a projecting lower jaw. The body is large, with muscular shoulders, a broad chest and short stout legs; the tail is short. The smooth coat may be white, tan or brindle. Height: (at shoulder) up to 38cm (15in).

bullfighting National sport of Spain and also popular in Latin America and s France. Classically there are six bulls and three matadors who are assigned two bulls each. The matador makes several passes with his red cape (*muleta*) before attempting to kill the bull by thrusting a sword between its shoulder blades.

bullfinch Northern European and Asian finch, with a stout, rounded beak. Males have a crimson and grey body and a black head; females have duller colours. It grows to 14cm (5.5in) long; species *Pyrrhula pyrrhula*.

bull terrier Strong sporting DOG, originating from England; it has a large oval head with small erect ears. The broad-chested body is set on strong legs and the tail is short. The "coloured" variety can be any colour, but the "white" is pure white, often with darker head markings. Height (at shoulder): up to 56cm (22in).

bulrush Grass-like plant of the SEDGE family found in marshes or beside water in Europe, Africa and North America. The common British bulrush (reed mace), *Typha latifolia*, reaches 1.8–2.1m (6–7ft) and bears both male and female flowers. Family Cyperaceae.

bumblebee (humble bee) Robust hairy black BEE with broad yellow or orange stripes. The genus *Bombus* live in organized groups in ground or tree nests, where the fertile queen lays her first eggs after the winter hibernation. These become worker bees. Later, the queen lays eggs to produce drones (males) and new queens which develop before the colony dies. The cycle is then repeated. The genus *psithyrus*, or cuckoo bee, lays its eggs in the nests of *Bombus*, which rear them. Length: up to 2.5cm (1in). Order Hymenoptera; family Apidae.

Bunsen, Robert Wilhelm (1811–99) German chemist, professor at Heidelberg (1852–99). He did important work with organo-arsenic compounds and discovered an arsenic poisoning antidote and evolved a method of gas analysis. With Gustav KIRCHHOFF, he used spectroscopy to discover two new elements (caesium and rubidium). He invented various kinds of laboratory equipment, including the Bunsen burner.

bunting FINCH found throughout most of the world. Males of the genus *Passerina* are brightly coloured, whereas the females are smaller and duller. Members of the genus *Emberiza* are larger and dull coloured, although the snow bunting is almost white. Family Fringillidae.

Buñuel, Luis (1900–83) Spanish film-maker. His films were harsh and ferociously critical of the church and social hypocrisy. His primary concern was the content rather than the form of his films. Among his major works are *Un Chien Andalou* (1928), *Viridiana* (1961), *Belle de Jour* (1966) and *The Phantom of Liberty* (1974).

Bunyan, John (1628–88) English preacher and author. During the English Civil War (1642–52) he fought as a Parliamentarian. He set himself up as a puritan preacher in 1655, and was twice imprisoned for his nonconformist religious activities. His writings, which were popular and colloquial in style, include the Christian allegory *The Pilgrim's Progress* (1684).

buoyancy Upward pressure exerted on an object by the fluid in which it is immersed. The object is subjected to pressure from all sides. The result of all these pressures is a force acting upwards that is equal to the weight of the fluid displaced. *See also* ARCHIMEDES' PRINCIPLE

burdock Oil-yielding weed found throughout Europe, North Africa and North America. It has large basal leaves and thistle-like purple flower heads covered by stiff, hooked bracts. Common burdock, *Arctium pubens*, is biennial and grows to 0.9m (3ft). Family Asteraceae/Compositae.

Burgess, Anthony (1917–93) English novelist. His novels demonstrate an interest in social trends, linguistic effects and religious symbolism. His best-known work is *A Clockwork Orange* (1962), a nightmare vision of a modern dystopia in which he deploys a macabre, invented language. *Earthly Powers* (1980) and *The Kingdom of the Wicked* (1985) are among his most ambitious later novels.

Burghley, William Cecil, 1st Baron (1520–98) English statesman and chief minister of ELIZABETH I of England. He was secretary of state (1550–53) under Edward VI but failed to win Mary I's favour on her accession to the throne. On Mary's death Elizabeth I made him secretary of state (1558–72) and then lord high treasurer (1572–98). An able administrator, he helped steer a moderate course between Catholicism and Protestantism. In 1587 he was responsible for ordering the execution of MARY, QUEEN OF SCOTS.

Burgos Capital city of Burgos province, N Spain. Founded in the 9th century, it was the capital of the former kingdom of Castile. During the Spanish Civil War it was General Franco's headquarters. Sites includes the fine Gothic cathedral (1221) and the burial place of El Cid. It is an important trade and tourist centre. Pop. (1991) 160,381.

Burgundy Historical region and former duchy of E central France that now includes the départements of Yonne, Côte-d'Or, Saône et Loire, Ain and Nièvre. Dijon is the historical capital. Burgundy's golden age began in 1364 Philip the Bold, became duke of Burgundy. His successors created a state that extended across the Rhine and included the Low Countries. It was divided up after the death of Charles the Bold (r.1467–77) with most going to France. It is a rich agricultural region renowned for its wine. Pop. (1990) 1,609,400.

Burke, Edmund (1729–97) British statesman and writer, b. Ireland. He played a major part in the reduction of royal influence in the House of Commons and sought better treatment for Catholics and American colonists. He was involved in the impeachment of Warren HASTINGS in an attempt to reform India's government in 1788. Burke deplored the excesses of the FRENCH REVOLUTION in his most famous work, *Reflections on the Revolution in France* (1790).

Burkina Faso Land-locked republic in w Africa; the capital is OUAGADOUGOU. **Land and climate** Burkina Faso consists of a plateau, between about 200–700m (650–2,300ft) above sea level. It is cut by several rivers, most of which flow s into Ghana or E into the Niger River. It is hot throughout the year, with most rain occurring between May and September, when it is often humid. Rainfall is erratic, however, and droughts are common. The N the country is covered by savanna, consisting of grassland with stunted trees and shrubs. In part of the SAHEL, where the land merges northwards into the Sahara, overgrazing, deforestation and the consequent soil erosion are common problems. Large areas of woodland border the rivers and parts of the SE are swampy. **Economy** Burkina Faso is one of the world's 20 poorest countries and has become dependent on foreign aid. Nearly 90% of the people earn their living by subsistence farming or raising livestock; grazing land covers about 37% of the land and farmland 10% The country's main food crops are beans, maize, millet and sorghum. Cotton, groundnuts and shea nuts, whose seeds produce a fat used to make cooking oil and soap, are grown for sale abroad. There are some deposits of manganese, zinc, lead and nickel in the N of the country, but there is not yet a good enough transport route to exploit them adequately. **History** The people of Burkina Faso are divided into two main groups. The first is the Voltaic,

which includes the Mossi and the smaller Bobo. The second is the Mande family. The French conquered the Mossi capital of Ouagadougou in 1897 and made the area a protectorate. In 1919 the area became the French colony of Upper Volta, remaining under French rule until 1960, when it became an independent republic. **Politics** After independence, Upper Volta became a one-party state, but it suffered from instability. Military groups seized control several times and political killings were common. In 1984 the country's name was changed to Burkina Faso. Elections were held in 1991 for the first time in more than ten years, but 20 opposition parties joined forces to boycott what they regarded as an unfair vote, and the military recorded a hollow victory.

burlesque (It. ridicule) Form of literary or dramatic entertainment that achieves its effect by caricature, ridicule and distortion, often of celebrated literary genres or works. A later form, in the USA, became synonymous with strip shows.

Burlington, Richard Boyle, 3rd Earl of (1694–1753) English architect. He was an important exponents of the PALLADIANISM style in England. He promoted the style through his own buildings, such as his villa at Chiswick, London. He also published drawings by PALLADIO and Inigo JONES.

Burma Republic in SE Asia and officially called the Union of Myanmar since 1989; the capital is RANGOON. **Land and climate** Mountains border the country in the E and w, but the highest mountains are in the N, including Hkakabo Razi at 5,881m (19,294ft). Between these ranges is central Burma, which contains the fertile valleys of the IRRAWADDY and Sittang rivers and MANDALAY, Burma's second-largest city (after Rangoon). The Irrawaddy Delta on the Bay of Bengal is one of the world's leading rice-growing areas. Burma also includes the long Tenasserim coast in the SE. Rangoon lies on the coast and Mandalay is in the interior. Burma has a tropical monsoon climate. Rainfall varies across the country, with the coastal areas being wetter than the interior plains. About 50% of the country is forested. Tropical trees, such as teak, grow on low-lying areas, with mangrove swamps on the coast. **Economy** Burma's internal

---

BURKINA FASO
AREA: 274,200sq km (105,869 sq mi)
POPULATION: 9,490,000
CAPITAL (POPULATION): Ouagadougou (442,223)
GOVERNMENT: Multiparty republic
ETHNIC GROUPS: Mossi 48%, Mande 9%, Fulani 8%, Bobo 7%
LANGUAGES: French (official)
RELIGIONS: Traditional beliefs 45%, Islam 43%, Christianity 12%
CURRENCY: CFA franc = 100 centimes

BURMA
AREA: 676,577 sq km (261,228 sq mi)
POPULATION: 43,668,000
CAPITAL (POPULATION): Rangoon (Yangon, 2,458,712)
GOVERNMENT: Military regime
ETHNIC GROUPS: Burman 69%, Shan 9%, Karen 6%, Rakhine 5%, Mon 2%, Kachin 1%
LANGUAGES: Burmese (official)
RELIGIONS: Buddhism 89%, Christianity 5%, Islam 4%
CURRENCY: Kyat = 100 pyas

political problems have made it one of the world's poorest countries. Agriculture is the main activity, employing 64% of the workforce. The chief crop is rice, and others include maize, sugar cane, pulses, oilseeds, rubber and tobacco. Forestry is important. Teak and rice together make up about two-thirds of the total value of exports. Burma has many mineral resources, mostly undeveloped. It is famous for its precious stones, especially rubies. Manufacturing is predominantly on a small scale.

History and Politics Many groups settled in Burma in ancient times. The ancestors of the main group today, the Burmese, arrived in the 9th century At the end of the 13th century, Burma was conquered by Kublai Khan. A series of wars between Britain and the Konbaung dynasty (1826–85) resulted in British subjugation of the country into a province of British India. In 1937 the British granted Burma limited self-government. Japan conquered the country in 1942, but was driven out in 1945 by Allied forces and internal resistance forces led by AUNG SAN. Burma achieved independence in 1948. In 1962 Ne Win established a military dictatorship and, in 1974, a one-party state. Attempts to control minority liberation movements and the warlords who run the opium trade led to increasingly repressive rule. Elections held in 1990 were won by the opposition National League for Democracy, led by AUNG SAN SUU KYI. The military ignored the result, placing Aung San Suu Kyi under house arrest until 1995. The ruling military junta (the State Law and Order Restoration Council) has continued to rule oppressively, earning Burma the reputation of having one of the world's worst records on human rights.

Burmese Official language of Burma, spoken by 75% of the population, or 25 million people. It belongs to the Tibeto-Burman branch of the Sino-Tibetan family of languages.

burn Injury caused by exposure to flames, scalding liquids, caustic chemicals, acids, electric current or ionizing radiation. Its severity depends on the extent of SKIN loss and the depth of tissue damage. A superficial burn, involving only the EPIDERMIS, causes redness, swelling and pain; it heals within a few days. A partial thickness burn (epidermis and DERMIS) causes intense pain, with mottling and blistering of the skin; it takes a couple of weeks to heal. In a full thickness burn, involving both the skin and the underlying flesh, there is charring, and the damaged flesh looks dry and leathery; there is no pain because the nerve endings have been destroyed. Such a burn, serious in itself, is associated with life-threatening complications, including dehydration and infection. Treatment includes fluid replacement and antibiotics; skin grafting may be necessary.

Burne-Jones, Sir Edward Coley (1833–98) English painter and designer. He was influenced by Dante Gabriel ROSSETTI and William MORRIS, and was also associated with PRE-RAPHAELITE BROTHERHOOD's romanticism and escapism. He often depicted scenes from Arthurian and similar legends and was considered an outstanding designer of stained glass.

Burnett, Frances (1849–1924) US author, b. England. She is chiefly remembered as the author of the children's classics *Little Lord Fauntleroy* (1886), *The Little Princess* (1905) and *The Secret Garden* (1911), although she also wrote adult novels and plays.

Burney, Fanny (1752–1840) English novelist, dramatist and diarist. The daughter of the musicologist Dr Charles Burney, she came to fame with her first novel, *Evelina* (1778), a semi-satirical, semi-sentimental look at polite society through the eyes of a young innocent. This was followed by similar works, such as *Cecilia* (1782), *Camilla* (1796) and *The Wanderer* (1814). Her writings greatly influenced Jane AUSTEN.

Burns, Robert (1759–96) Scottish poet. The success of *Poems, Chiefly in the Scottish Dialect* (1786), which includes *The Holy Fair* and *To a Mouse*, enabled him to move to Edinburgh, where he was admired as "the heaven-taught ploughman". Scotland's unofficial national poet, his works include *Tam o'Shanter* (1790) and the song *Auld Lang Syne*. An annual Burn's night is held on his birthday, 25 January.

Burroughs, Edgar Rice (1875–1950) US author of adventure novels. A prolific writer, he is best known as the creator of the apeman Tarzan, who featured in a series of books, beginning with *Tarzan of the Apes* (1912).

Burroughs, William S. (Seward) (1914–97) US novelist, regarded as one of the founders of the BEAT MOVEMENT. His most notable work, *Naked Lunch* (1959), deals in part with his heroin addiction. Other works, experimental in style, include *The Ticket That Exploded* (1962), *The Wild Boys* (1971) and *The Western Lands* (1987).

bursitis Inflammation of the fluid-filled sac (bursa) surrounding a joint. It is characterized by pain, swelling and restricted movement. Treatment generally includes rest, heat and gentle exercise. "Housemaid's knee", "tennis elbow" and bunions are common forms of bursitis.

Burton, Sir Richard Francis (1821–90) British explorer and scholar. In 1853 he travelled in disguise to Medina and Mecca, one of the first Europeans to visit the holy cities. On his second trip to E Africa, with John SPEKE in 1857, he discovered Lake Tanganyika. A prolific author he was best known for his translation of the *Arabian Nights*.

Burton, Richard (1925–84) Welsh stage and film actor, remembered for his deep, passionate and fiery voice. By the 1950s he had a reputation as a leading Shakespearian actor. From 1952 he concentrated on cinema, appearing in such films as *The Robe* (1953), *Look Back in Anger* (1959) and *Becket* (1964). He made a number of films with Elizabeth Taylor, notably *Who's Afraid of Virginia Woolf?*

103

BURUNDI
AREA: 27,830 sq km (10,745 sq mi)
POPULATION: 5,786,000
CAPITAL (POPULATION): Bujumbura (300,000)
GOVERNMENT: Republic
ETHNIC GROUPS: Hutu 85%, Tutsi 14%, Twa (pygmy) 1%
LANGUAGES: French and Kirundi (both official)
RELIGIONS: Christianity 85% (Roman Catholic 78%), traditional beliefs 13%
CURRENCY: Burundi franc = 100 centimes

(1966). The couple had a tempestuous relationship and several marriages.

Burundi Republic in E central Africa; the capital is BUJUMBURA. **Land and Climate** Part of the Great RIFT VALLEY lies in w Burundi. East of the Rift Valley are high mountains, reaching 2,760m (8,760ft), composed partly of volcanic rocks. In central and E Burundi, the land descends in a series of grassy plateaus. Bujumbura lies on the shore of Lake TANGANYIKA and has a warm climate. A dry season occurs from July to September, but the other months are fairly rainy. Grasslands cover much of Burundi. Once mainly forest, the land has been cleared of trees by farmers. In some areas, new forests are being planted to protect the soil against the rain and wind, because soil erosion is a serious problem. **Economy** Burundi is one of the world's ten poorest countries. About 92% of the people are farmers, who mostly grow little more than they need to feed their families. The main cash crops are coffee, which accounts for 80–90% of the exports, tea and cotton. **History and politics** The Twa, a pygmy people, were the first known inhabitants of Burundi. About 1,000 years ago the Hutu gradually began to settle in the area, pushing the Twa into more remote areas. From the 15th century the Tutsi, a tall, cattle-owning people from the NE, gradually took over the country. The Hutu, although greatly outnumbering the Tutsi, were forced into serfdom, serving the Tutsi overlords. Germany conquered the area that is now Burundi and RWANDA in the 1890s. The area, called Ruanda-Urundi, was then taken by Belgium during World War 1. In 1961 the people of Urundi voted to become a monarchy, while the people of Ruanda voted to become a republic. In 1962 the two territories became fully independent as Burundi and Rwanda. After 1962 the rivalries between the Hutu and Tutsi led to periodic outbreaks of fighting. The Tutsi monarchy was overthrown in 1966 and Burundi became a republic. Instability continued with four coups between 1976 and 1996. Burundi has been affected by the violence in neighbouring ZAÏRE and Rwanda as Tutsis and Hutus fight for power, and there have been periodic massacres.

Bush, George Herbert Walker (1924–) 41st

US President (1989–93). Bush was elected to the House of Representatives from Texas in 1966. Losing a campaign for the Senate in 1970, he was appointed US ambassador to the United Nations by NIXON. Bush was head of the CIA (1976–77) before returning to private industry. In 1980, after campaigning unsuccessfully against Ronald REAGAN for the Republican presidential nomination, he was elected vice-president. As president, Bush worked to further programs instituted by Reagan. His period in office was notable for the invasion of Panama (1989), and for the United Nations (UN)-sanctioned invasion of Kuwait (1990). He was an unpopular president. His failure to improve the economy and his conservative stance on education and abortion led to his defeat by the Democrat Bill CLINTON.

bushido (way of the samurai) Moral discipline important in Japan between 1603–1868. It arose from a fusion of Confucian ethics and Japanese feudalism. Requiring loyalty, courage, honour, politeness and benevolence, Bushido paralleled European chivalry. Although not a religion, Bushido involved family worship and SHINTO rites.

bushmaster Largest pit VIPER, found in central USA and N South America. It has long fangs and large venom glands, and is pinkish and brown with a diamond pattern. Length: up to 3.7m (12ft). Family Viperidae; subfamily Crotalidae.

bustard Large bird found in arid areas of the Eastern Hemisphere. Its plumage is grey, black, brown and white and its neck and legs are long; in appearance it is quite ostrich-like. A swift runner and a strong, though reluctant flier, it feeds on small animals and lays up to five eggs. Family Otidae. Height: 1.3m (4.3ft).

butane Colourless flammable gas (C_4H_{10}), the fourth member of the ALKANE series of HYDROCARBONS. It has two ISOMERS: n-butane is obtained from natural gas; isobutane is a by-product of PETROLEUM refining. Butane can be liquefied under pressure at normal temperatures and is used in the manufacture of fuel gas and synthetic rubber. Properties: b.p. (n-butane) $-0.3°C$ (31.5°F) and (isobutane) $-10.3°C$ (13.46°F).

Buthelezi, Mangusuthu Gatsha (1928–) ZULU chief and politician. Buthelezi was installed as chief of the Buthelezi tribe in 1953 and became chief minister of KwaZulu, a black homeland within APARTHEID South Africa in 1970. In 1975 he founded the Inkatha "freedom" party. Despite factional violence between Inkatha and the rival AFRICAN NATIONAL CONGRESS (ANC) in the early 1990s, Buthelezi became minister for home affairs in the MANDELA government (1994).

butter Edible fat made from milk. A churning process changes the milk from a water-in-oil emulsion to an oil-in-water emulsion. The fat (oil) globules of the milk collide and coalesce, losing their protective shield of protein and turning into butter, thus separating out from the more watery whey. Commercial butter contains about 80% fat, 1– 3% added salt, 1% milk solids and 16% water.

butterfly Day-flying INSECT of the order Lepidoptera. The adult has two pairs of scale-covered wings that are often brightly coloured. The female lays eggs on a selected food source and the (CATERPILLAR) larvae emerge within days or hours. The larvae have chewing mouth-parts and often do great damage to crops until they reach the "resting phase" of the life cycle, the pupa (chrysalis). Within the pupa, the adult (imago) is formed with wings, wing muscles, antennae, a slender body and sucking mouthparts. The adults mate soon after emerging from the chrysalis, and the four-stage life cycle begins again. *See also* METAMORPHOSIS

butterwort Large group of carnivorous bog plants that trap and digest insects in a sticky secretion on their leaves. They bear single white, purple or yellow flowers on a leafless stalk. The sides of the leaves roll over to enclose the insect while it is digested. Family Lentibulariaceae; species *Pinguicula. See also* INSECTIVOROUS PLANT

buzzard Slow-flying bird with broad rounded wings, fan-shaped tail, sharp hooked beak and sharp talons. It is used in reference to many BIRD OF PREY types. Family Accipitridae; genus *Buteo.*

Byatt, A.S. (Antonia Susan) (1936–) British novelist and critic. An academic for much of her career, Byatt was best known as a literary scholar until 1978 when she published her third novel, *The Virgin in the Garden. Possession* (1990) won the Booker Prize. Her recent work includes the novellas *Angels and Insects* (1993) and *The Djinn in the Nightingale's Eye* (1994).

Byrd, Richard Evelyn (1888–1957) US polar explorer. A naval officer and aviator, Byrd led five major expeditions to the Antarctic (1928–57), surveying more than 2,200,000sq km (845,000sq mi) of the continent. Among other feats, he claimed to be the first man to fly over both the North Pole (1926) and the South Pole (1929).

Byrd, William (1543–1623) English composer. He was appointed by Elizabeth I to be joint organist of the Chapel Royal with Thomas TALLIS. With Tallis, he was granted England's first monopoly to print music. Byrd was a master of all the musical forms of his day, and was especially celebrated for his madrigals and church music.

Byron, George Gordon Noel Byron, 6th Baron (1788–1824) British poet. The first two cantos of *Childe Harold's Pilgrimage* (1812) made Byron famous. His romantic image and reputation for dissolute living and numerous sexual affairs vied with his poetic reputation. By 1816 he was a social outcast and went into permanent exile. Abroad, Byron wrote Cantos III and IV of *Childe Harold* (1816, 1818) and *Don Juan*

(1819–24), an epic satire often regarded as his masterpiece. In 1823 he travelled to Greece to fight for Greek independence against the Turks and died of fever at Missolonghi.

byte Binary number used to represent the letters, numbers and other characters in a computer system. Each byte consists of the same number of bits (binary digits). Each BIT has two possible states, represented by the binary numbers 0 and 1. Byte is a contraction of "by eight", and originally meant an eight-bit byte, such as 01101010 (representing j). A typical personal computer memory can store up to 4Mb (4 Megabytes, or 4 million bytes).

Byzantine art and architecture Art produced in the Roman empire E of the Balkans. Its greatest achievements fall within three periods. The first Golden Age coincided with the reign of Justinian (527–65) and saw the construction of the HAGIA SOPHIA. The second Golden Age refers to the artistic revival, which occurred during the time of the Macedonian emperors (867–1057) and which followed the terrible destruction caused by the Iconoclastic Controversy. Finally, the last years of the empire, under the rule of the Palaeologans (1261–1453), are often referred to as the Byzantine Renaissance. Most Byzantine art was religious in subject matter and combined Christian imagery with an oriental expressive style. The MOSAIC and ICON were the most common forms. Byzantine church architecture is typically central rather than longitudinal, and the central dome (surrounded by groupings of smaller or semi-domes) is supported by means of pendentives. Construction is of brick arranged in decorative patterns and mortar. Interiors are faced with marble slabs, coloured glass mosaics, gold leaf and fresco decoration.

Byzantine empire Christian, Greek-speaking, Eastern Roman empire, which outlasted the Roman empire in the West by nearly 1,000 years. Constantinople (Byzantium or Istanbul) was established by the Roman emperor CONSTANTINE I in AD 330. The area of the Byzantine empire varied greatly and its history from *c.*600 was marked by continual military crisis and heroic recovery. At its height under JUSTINIAN I in the 6th century, it controlled, besides Asia Minor and the Balkans, much of the Near East and the Mediterranean coastal regions of Europe and North Africa. Of its many enemies, the most formidable were the Arabs, who overran the Near Eastern provinces in the 7th century; the Slavs and BULGARS, who captured most of the Balkans; and the Seljuk Turks. From 1204–1261 it was controlled by Crusaders from W Europe and, although Constantinople was recovered, Byzantine territory shrank under pressure from the West and from the Ottoman Turks, who finally captured Constantinople in 1453, extinguishing the Byzantine empire.

C/c is derived from the Greek gamma and the Semitic gimel. It originally had a hard sound (like k), but before e, i, or y took on a sibilant sound, or had an h added to create the ch sound.

cabbage white butterfly Butterfly, the green caterpillar of which is a common pest on cabbage plants. The female adult is almost completely white except for black spots on its wing; the male has no forewing spots. Species *Pieris brassicae*.

Caballé, Montserrat (1933–) Spanish soprano. She made her debut as Mimì in Puccini's *La Bohème* (1957). She specializes in Verdi and Donizetti.

cabbage Low, stout vegetable of the genus *Brassica*. Members include Brussels sprouts, cauliflowers, broccoli, kohlrabi and turnips. They are all biennials that produce "heads" one year and flowers the next. They grow in temperate regions. Family Brassicaceae/Cruciferae.

cabbala (kabbala) Form of Jewish mysticism. It holds that every word, letter, number, even accent of the Bible contains mysteries to be interpreted, often in the form of codes for YAHWEH. Cabbalism spread throughout Europe in the 13th century, and is still practised by some Hasidic Jews.

Cabeza de Vaca, Álvar Núñez (1490–1557) Spanish explorer. In 1528 he was shipwrecked off the Texas coast. He and three fellow survivors became the first Europeans to explore the American Southwest, eventually settling in Mexico (1536).

Cabinda Province of Angola, SW Africa, N of Congo River, bounded W by the Atlantic Ocean and separated from the rest of Angola by Zaïre; the seaport and chief town is Cabinda. The 1885 Simulambuco Treaty politically unified Cabinda with Angola. Cabinda refuses to recognize the treaty and claims independence from Angola. There are important offshore oilfields. Industries: oil refining, palm, timber, cacao. Area: 7,270sq km (2,808sq mi). Pop. (1992 est.) 152,100.

cabinet Body of people collectively responsible to the legislature for government in a parliamentary system. Most cabinet ministers have individual responsibility for the management of a department of state. In the UK, cabinet ministers are chosen by the prime minister. A cabinet minister need not sit in either House of Parliament, but usually sits in the House of Commons. In a presidential system, cabinets may be formed out of heads of major departments, but have only advisory status.

cable Wire for mechanical support, for conducting electricity or carrying signals. In civil and mechanical engineering, a cable is made of twisted strands of steel wire. In electrical engineering, a cable is a conductor consisting of one or more insulated wires, which may be either single- or multi-stranded. In a **coaxial** cable one conductor is cylindrical and surrounds the other. FIBRE OPTIC cables carry signals in the form of coded pulses of light.

cable television Generally refers to community antenna TELEVISION. CATV picks up signals at a central antenna and delivers them to individual subscribers via coaxial cables.

Cabot, John (*c.*1450–98) Italian navigator in English service. Supported by Henry VII, he sailed in search of a western route to India, and reached Newfoundland (1497). His discovery served as the basis for English claims in North America.

Cabral, Pedro Alvares (1467–1520) Portuguese navigator who discovered Brazil. In 1500 he led an expedition to the East Indies on the route pioneered by Vasco da GAMA. To avoid contrary winds and currents, he took a westward course in the Atlantic and touched on the coast of Brazil, which he claimed for Portugal.

cacao *See* COCOA

Caccini, Giulio (1550–1618) Italian composer, one of the Florentine *camerata* group that pioneered OPERA. His opera *Euridice* was the first to be printed (probably 1601), and his *Le Nuove Musiche* (1602) was one of the most influential collections of vocal music in the new monodic style.

cactus Any of more than 2,000 species of succulent plants, found particularly in hot desert regions of the Western Hemisphere. Cactus' long roots are adapted to absorb moisture from desert terrains and the fleshy green stem is adapted to water storage. Their height ranges from less than 2.5cm (1in) to more than 15m (50ft). *See also* XEROPHYTE

caddis fly Any of several moth-like insects of the order Trichoptera. Adults have long, many-jointed antennae, hold their wings tent-like over the body and usually grow about 25mm (1in) long.

cadence In music, ending of a melodic phrase and/or its accompanying CHORD progression. In Western classical theory, the main kinds of chordal cadence are: **perfect** (dominant to tonic chords); **imperfect** (tonic or other chord to dominant); **plagal** (subdominant to tonic); and **interrupted** (dominant to chord other than tonic, often submediant).

cadmium Silvery-white metallic element (symbol Cd) in group II of the PERIODIC TABLE, first isolated in 1817. Cadmium is mainly obtained as a by-product in the extraction of zinc and lead. Malleable and ductile, it is used in electroplating, as an absorber of neutrons in nuclear reactors and in nickelcadmium batteries. Properties: at.no. 48; r.a.m. 112.4; r.d. 8.65; m.p. 320.9°C (609.6°F); b.p. 765°C (1,409°F); most common isotope Cd^{114} (28.86%).

caecum Dilated pouch at the junction of the small and large intestines, terminating in the APPENDIX. It has no known function in humans. In rabbits and horses, the caecum contains microorganisms that help to break down the cellulose cell walls of the plants they eat.

Caedmon Earliest known English poet, dating from around the 7th century. His only surviving work is the fragmentary *Hymn on the Creation.*

Caernarvon (Caernarfon) Market town on the Menai Strait, Gwynedd, NW Wales. It has a 13th-century castle built by Edward I. The Princes of Wales are now invested here. The principal industry is tourism. Pop. (1992 est.) 9,600.

Caesar Name of a powerful family of ancient Rome. The name became the title for the Roman emperor in 27 BC on the accession of Octavius (later AUGUSTUS). *Tsar* and *kaiser* are derived from it.

Caesar, (Gaius) Julius (100–44 BC) Roman general and statesman. After the death of SULLA, Caesar became military tribune. He formed the First Triumvirate in 60 BC with POMPEY and CRASSUS, instituted agrarian reforms and created a patrician-plebeian alliance. He conquered Gaul for Rome (58–49 BC) and invaded Britain (54 BC). Refusing Senate demands to disband his army, he provoked civil war with Pompey. Caesar defeated Pompey at Pharsalus (48 BC) and pursued him to Egypt, where he made CLEOPATRA queen. He returned to Rome in 45 BC and was dictator for life. He introduced popular reforms, but his growing power aroused resentment. He was assassinated in the Senate on 15 March by a conspiracy led by CASSIUS and BRUTUS.

caesium Rare silvery-white metallic element (symbol Cs) in group I of the PERIODIC TABLE; the most alkaline and electropositive element. Discovered in 1860 by Robert BUNSEN and Gustav KIRCHHOFF, caesium is ductile and used commercially in photoelectric cells. The decay rate of its most common isotope Cs^{133} is the standard for measuring time. Properties: at.no. 55; r.a.m. 132.9055; r.d. 1.87; m.p. 28.4°C (83.1°F); b.p. 678°C (1,252.4°F). *See also* ALKALI METALS; ATOMIC CLOCK

caffeine ($C_8H_{10}N_4O_2$) White, bitter substance that occurs in coffee, tea and other substances, such as cocoa and ilex plants. It acts as a mild, harmless stimulant and DIURETIC, although an excessive dose can cause insomnia and delirium.

Cage, John (1912–92) US avant-garde composer. He experimented with new sound sources, including noise and silence. *Reunion* (1968) consists of electronic sounds created by chess moves on an electric board. *4'33"* (1952) has no sound, except for the environment in which it is performed. He invented the "prepared piano".

Cain First-born son of ADAM and EVE, brother of ABEL. His story is recounted in Genesis 4. God accepted Abel's offering in preference to Cain's and Cain murdered Abel in anger. Cain was driven out from the Garden of EDEN.

Cairngorms Range of mountains in NE central Scotland, in the Grampian region.

Cairo (Al-Qahirah) Capital of Egypt and port on the River Nile. The largest city in Africa, Cairo was founded in AD 969 by the Fatimid dynasty. Medieval Cairo became capital of the MAMELUKE

empire. During the 20th century it grew dramatically in population and area. Industries: tourism, textiles, leather, iron and steel, sugar refining. Pop. (1992 est.) 6,663,000.

Cajun French-speaking settlers in Louisiana. They were driven from Nova Scotia by the British in the 18th century.

calabash gourd (bottle gourd) Tropical vine with oval leaves and white flowers. It grows to 9–12m (30–40ft). Its smooth, hard fruit is bottle-shaped and grows to 180cm (6ft) long. Family Cucurbitaceae; species *Lagenaria vulgaris.*

Calabria Region in S Italy, including the provinces of Catanzaro, Cosenza and Reggio di Calabria. The capital is Reggio di Calabria. The local economy is almost exclusively agricultural. Area: 15,080sq km (5,822sq mi). Pop. (1992) 2,074,763.

Calais City and seaport on the Strait of Dover, N France. A major commercial centre and port since the Middle Ages, much of its fine architecture was destroyed during World War 2. Industries: lace making, chemicals, paper. Pop. (1990) 75,309.

calcium Common silvery-white metallic element (symbol Ca) of the ALKALINE-EARTH METALS; first isolated in 1808 by Sir Humphry DAVY. It occurs in many rocks and minerals, notably LIMESTONE and GYPSUM, and in bones. Calcium helps regulate the heartbeat and is essential for strong bones and teeth. The metal, which is soft and malleable, has few commercial applications but its compounds are widely used. It is a reactive element, combining readily with oxygen, nitrogen and other non-metals. Properties: at.no. 20; r.a.m. 40.08; r.d. 1.55; m.p. 839°C (1,542°F); b.p. 1,484°C (2,703°F); most common isotope Ca^{40} (96.95%). *See also* HARDNESS OF WATER

calcium carbide (calcium acetylide) Chemical (CaC_2) made commercially by heating coke and calcium oxide (CaO). It reacts with water to yield ETHYNE. Calcium carbide is also used to manufacture ETHANOIC ACID and ETHANAL.

calcium carbonate White compound ($CaCO_3$), insoluble in water, that occurs naturally as MARBLE, CHALK, LIMESTONE and calcite. Calcium carbonate is used in the manufacture of cement, iron, steel and lime, to neutralize soil acidity and as a constituent of antacids. Properties: r.d. 2.7 (calcite).

calcium oxide (quicklime) White solid (CaO) made by heating CALCIUM CARBONATE ($CaCO_3$) at high temperatures. It is used industrially to treat acidic soil and to make porcelain and glass, bleaching powder, caustic soda, mortar and cement.

calculus Topic in mathematics involving (among others) the operations of differentiation and integration. Differential calculus is used to find slopes of curves and rates of change of a given quantity with respect to another; INTEGRAL CALCULUS is used to find the areas enclosed by curves.

Calcutta City on the Hooghly River, E India; capital of West Bengal state. It was the capital of India under British rule (1772–1912). It is the major port and industrial centre of E India. Industries: jute milling, electrical equipment, chemicals, paper, cotton textiles. Pop. (1991) 4,309,819.

Calder, Alexander (1898–1976) US sculptor. Calder created both mobiles, a type of delicate, colourful, kinetic sculpture, and non-moving sculptures called "stabiles".

calendar Way of reckoning time for regulating religious, commercial and civil life, and for dating events in the past and future. The Western Gregorian or New Style calendar was based on the Julian or Old Style solar calendar introduced by Julius Caesar in the 1st century BC.

Calgary City at the confluence of the Bow and Elbow rivers, S Alberta, Canada. Industries: flour milling, timber, brick, cement, oil refining. Pop. (1991) 710,677.

California State in W USA, on the Pacific coast; the largest state by population and the third largest in area. The capital is SACRAMENTO. Other major cities include LOS ANGELES, SAN FRANCISCO, SAN DIEGO and Oakland. The first European settlement was in 1769, when Spaniards founded a Franciscan mission at San Diego. The area became part of Mexico. Settlers came from the USA and, during the Mexican War, US forces occupied California (1846); it was ceded to the USA at the war's end. After gold was discovered in 1848, the GOLD RUSH swelled the population from 15,000 to 250,000 in four years. In 1850 California joined the Union. In the 20th century, the discovery of oil and development of service industries attracted further settlers. Mineral deposits include oil, natural gas, and a variety of ores valuable in manufacturing (the largest economic sector). Industries: agriculture, timber, aircraft, aerospace equipment, electronic components, missiles, wine, tourism. Area: 403,971sq km (155,973sq mi). Pop. (1990) 29,760,021.

californium Radioactive metallic element (symbol Cf) of the ACTINIDE SERIES, first made in 1950 at the University of California, Berkeley, by alpha-particle bombardment of the curium isotope Cm^{242}. One microgram releases 170 million neutrons a minute. Properties: at.no. 98; most stable isotope Cf^{251} (half-life 800yr).

Caligula (AD 12–41) (Gaius Caesar) Roman emperor (37–41). Son of Germanicus Caesar, he became emperor after the death of TIBERIUS. He was highly autocratic and was said to be insane. He was murdered by an officer of the Praetorian Guard and succeeded by his uncle, CLAUDIUS I.

caliph Leader of the Muslim community. After the death of MUHAMMAD, ABU BAKR was chosen to be his caliph (successor). The role was originally elective but later became hereditary. The title remained with the Ottoman sultans (1517–1924), after which it was abolished.

Callaghan, (Leonard) James, Baron (1912–) British statesman, prime minister (1976–79). He became a Labour MP in 1945 and was elected leader of the Labour Party in 1976. He is the only prime minister in British history to have held all three major offices of state: chancellor of the exchequer (1964–67), home secretary (1967–70) and foreign secretary (1974–76). His tenure was marked by delicate negotiations with David STEEL in the Lib-Lab Pact, and strife with the trade unions.

Callas, Maria (1923–77) Greek soprano. Her successes at LA SCALA, Milan and the ROYAL OPERA HOUSE, Covent Garden, established her reputation as a leading singing actress. She was particularly admired in the Italian repertoire.

Callisto Second-largest and outermost of Jupiter's GALILEAN SATELLITES, with a diameter of 4,800km (2,980mi). It is the most heavily cratered object known.

callus In botany, a protective mass of undifferentiated plant cells formed at the site of a wound in a woody plant. Callus tissue is also formed at the base of cuttings as they start to take root.

calorie Unit of heat. A calorie is the amount of heat required to raise one gram of water one degree CELSIUS from 14.5–15.5°C (58.1–59.9°F). The SI system of units uses the JOULE (1 calorie = 4.184 joules) instead of the calorie. A dietitian's "calorie" is the kilocalorie, 1,000 times larger than a calorie.

Calvin, John (1509–64) French theologian of the REFORMATION. He prepared for a career in the Roman Catholic Church but in c.1533 became a Protestant and began work on his *Institutes of the Christian Religion*, which presented the basics of CALVINISM. To avoid persecution, he went to live in Geneva, Switzerland (1536), where he advanced the Reformation.

Calvin, Melvin (1911–) US chemist. He tracked the process by which plants turned carbon dioxide into glucose by means of PHOTOSYNTHESIS. The series of reactions that take place during photosynthesis is known as the Calvin cycle. Calvin received the Nobel Prize for chemistry in 1961.

Calvinism Set of doctrines and attitudes derived from the Protestant theologian John CALVIN. Rejecting papal authority and relying on the Bible as the source of religious truth, Calvinism stresses the sovereignty of God and PREDESTINATION. Calvinism usually subordinates state to church, and cultivates austere morality, family piety, business enterprise, education and science. Important Calvinist leaders include John KNOX and Jonathan Edwards.

cambium In botany, layer of cells parallel to the surface of stems and roots of plants that divides to produce new cells to allow for growth in diameter of the stem and roots. There are two main types of cambium. **Vascular** cambium produces new phloem on the outside and xylem on the inside, leaving narrow bands of thin-walled cells of nutrients and gases to diffuse to the centre of the plant. **Cork** cambium forms a cylinder just below the epidermis, and produces cork cells to replace the epidermis, which ruptures as the stem and root expand, forming the bark and corky outer layer of the older root. *See also* MERISTEM

Cambodia Kingdom in SE Asia; the capital is PHNOM PENH. **Land and climate** Cambodia is bordered by low mountains except in the SE. Most of the country consists of plains drained by the River MEKONG. Cambodia has a tropical monsoon climate, with constant high humidity and temperatures. The dry season runs from November–April. Forests cover about 75% of Cambodia. **Economy** Cambodia is a poor economy, wrecked by war. Until the 1970s the country was agriculturally self-sufficient, but by 1986 it was only able to supply 80% of its needs. Farming is the principal activity; rice, rubber and maize are the major products. **History and politics** From 802–1432, the Khmer people controlled a great empire, with its capital at Angkor. The Hindu stone temples built at Angkor and Angkor Wat form the world's largest group of religious buildings. Cambodia was ruled by France from 1863–1954 when the country became independent. During the VIETNAM WAR North Vietnamese troops used Cambodia as a base, leading to bombing raids by the US and South Vietnamese. Many innocent civilians were killed. Public support rallied to the Cambodian Communists (KHMER ROUGE). In October 1970 the Khmer Republic was declared. Civil War broke out. Despite US bombing campaigns and other military aid, government forces continued to lose ground. In 1973 the US Congress halted air attacks. In 1975 the Khmer Rouge (led by POL POT) seized Phnom Penh. Cambodia was renamed **Kampuchea**. A brutal form of peasant politics was pursued, and a series of purges left between 1–4 million people dead. **Recent events** In 1979 combined Vietnamese and Cambodian troops overthrew Pol Pot's government. Fighting continued between several factions. Elections were held in May 1993 (without the participation of the Khmer Rouge) and a coalition government of the Cambodian People's Party and the royalist Funcinpec was formed. In 1994 the Khmer Rouge was banned. In 1997, after increasing tension between the coalition partners and outbreaks of fighting, Hun Sen ousted his co-premier, Norodom Ranariddh, claiming that Norodom had been negotiating with the Khmer Rouge.

Cambrian Earliest period of the PALAEOZOIC era, lasting from c. 590 million to 505 million years ago.

Cambrian rocks are the earliest to preserve the hard parts of animals as FOSSILS. The commonest animal forms were TRILOBITES, BRACHIOPODS, sponges and snails. Plant life consisted mainly of seaweeds.

Cambridge City on the River Cam, county town of Cambridgeshire, E England. It has one of the world's leading universities. Industries: precision engineering, electronics, printing and publishing. Pop. (1991) 91,933.

Cambridge, University of Founded in 1209 (with claims for an earlier origin), it is one of the oldest scholarly establishments in England. It has a collegiate system, the oldest college being Peterhouse (1284).

Cambridgeshire County in E central England; the county town is CAMBRIDGE. The area is mainly fenland and is drained by the Ouse and Nene rivers. Agriculture is the main economic activity. Area: 3,400sq km (1,312sq mi). Pop. (1990) 645,125.

camel Large, hump-backed, UNGULATE mammal of the family Camelidae. There are two species – the two-humped Bactrian of central Asia and the single-humped Arabian dromedary. Its ability to travel long periods without water makes the camel a perfect desert animal. Genus *Camelus*.

Camelot In English mythology, the seat chosen by King ARTHUR for his court. Its site is not known, although many believe it was Cadbury Castle, Somerset, SW England.

cameo Relief carving, usually on striated gemstones, semi-precious stones or shell. The decoration is often a portrait head. Cameos originated from the carved stone seals bearing the mystic symbol of the scarab beetle used by Ancient Egyptians, Greeks and Etruscans.

camera Apparatus for taking photographs, consisting essentially of a light-proof box containing photographic film. When a shutter is opened, usually briefly, light from the scene is focused by a lens system onto the film. The amount of light falling on the film is controlled by the shutter speed, and by the diameter of the lens APERTURE.

Cameroon Republic in W Africa; the captial is YAOUNDÉ. **Land and climate** Behind the narrow coastal plains on the Gulf of Guinea, the land rises in a series of plateaus. In the N the land slopes down towards the Lake CHAD basin. The mountainous SW region rises to the active volcano, Mount Cameroon at 4,070m (13,354ft). Cameroon has one of the wettest climates on Earth; the rain is heaviest in the hot and humid SW between July and September. The far N has a hot, dry climate. Rainforests flourish in the S. Inland, the forests give way to savanna. **Economy** Cameroon's economy is dominated by agriculture. It is self-sufficient in foodstuffs. Major crops include cassava, maize, millet and yams. Oil accounts for nearly 50% of Cameroon's exports. Other mineral resources include gold and bauxite. **History and politics** Cameroon is a diverse nation, with more than 160 ethnic groups. Bantu-

CAMBODIA
AREA: 181,040sq km (69,900sq mi)
POPULATION: 9,054,000
CAPITAL (POPULATION): Phnom Penh (920,000)
GOVERNMENT: Constitutional monarchy
ETHNIC GROUPS: Khmer 94%, Chinese 3%, Cham 2%, Thai, Lao, Kola, Vietnamese
LANGUAGES: Khmer (official)
RELIGIONS: Buddhism 88%, Islam 2%
CURRENCY: Riel = 100 sen

CAMEROON

AREA: 475,440sq km (183,567sq mi)
POPULATION: 12,198,000
CAPITAL (POPULATION): Yaoundé (750,000)
GOVERNMENT: Multiparty republic
ETHNIC GROUPS: Fang 20%, Bamileke and Bamum 19%, Douala, Luanda and Basa 15%, Fulani 10%
LANGUAGES: French and English (both official)
RELIGIONS: Christianity (Roman Catholic 35%, Protestant 18%), traditional beliefs 25%, Islam 22%
CURRENCY: CFA franc = 100 centimes

speakers predominate in coastal areas, such as DOUALA. Islam is the dominant force in the N, major tribal groupings include the FULANI. In 1472 Portuguese explorers (seeking a sea route to Asia) reached the Cameroon coast. From the 17th century, S Cameroon was a centre of the slave trade. In the early nineteenth century SLAVERY was replaced by the ivory trade, led by Britain. In 1884 Cameroon became a German protectorate. In 1916 the country was captured by Allied troops. After World War 1 Cameroon was divided in two, and ruled by Britain and France. In 1960, following civil unrest, French Cameroon became an independent republic. In 1961 N British Cameroon voted to join the Cameroon Republic, forming the Federal Republic of Cameroon, while S British Cameroon joined Nigeria. In 1966 a one-party state was created, and in 1972 the federation became a unitary state. In 1984 a failed coup led to many executions, and Cameroon became a republic. Biya was re-elected in 1992, but his increasingly autocratic rule is regularly accused of torture and the creation of a police state. In 1995, partly to satisfy its English-speaking community, it became the 52nd member of the COMMONWEALTH OF NATIONS.

Camões, Luís vaz de (1524–80) Portuguese poet and soldier. In 1572 he published *The Lusiads*, which established him as the country's greatest national poet. He also wrote highly accomplished love lyrics and a few comic dramas.

Campaign for Nuclear Disarmament (CND) Movement in Britain, founded by Bertrand RUSSELL and Canon John Collins (1958). Membership and activities declined in the 1970s, but CND revived in the early 1980s in response to the escalation of the East-West nuclear arms race. The end of the COLD WAR and disarmament treaties between the USA and the former Soviet Union lessened CND's political prominence.

Campania Region of SW Italy on the Tyrrhenian Sea, including the provinces of Avellino, Benevento, Caserta, Napoli and Salerno. The capital is NAPLES. It is a mountainous area with fertile plains. Area: 13,595sq km (5,249sq mi). Pop. (1992) 5,668,895.

campanulaceae Bellflower family of herbaceous flowering plants. There are *c.* 300 species, cultivated for their delicate blossoms.

Campbell, Donald Malcolm (1921–67) British speed record holder. Son of Sir Malcolm Campbell (1885-1948) who also a world speed record holder. He set seven new world records on water. He died trying to set a new record. As with his father, all his vehicles were called *Bluebird*. In 1984 his daughter Gina set a new women's water speed record.

Camp David Agreement Significant step towards Arab-Israeli reconciliation. The agreement resulted from a meeting between Anwar SADAT of Egypt and Menachem BEGIN of Israel, mediated by US President Jimmy CARTER in September 1978. Condemned by other Arab leaders, the agreement formed the basis for a 1979 treaty between Egypt and Israel.

Campese, David Ian (1962–) Australian rugby football player. He holds the world record for the number of tries scored in international rugby (63). He retired from international rugby in 1996, after over 100 test appearances.

camphor Organic chemical compound ($C_{10}H_{16}O$). It has a strong odour. Camphor is used in medicine for liniments, in the manufacture of celluloid, lacquers and explosives, and as an ingredient of mothballs.

Campion, Jane (1955–) New Zealand film director and screenwriter. Her films include *Sweetie* (1989), the acclaimed *The Piano* (1993), which shared the Palme d'Or and won her an Oscar for Best Screenplay, and *Portrait of a Lady* (1997).

Camus, Albert (1913–60) French novelist, playwright and essayist. He achieved recognition with his first novel *The Outsider* (1942), a work permeated with the sense of individual alienation that underlies much of his writing including *The Plague* (1947) and *The Fall* (1956). He was awarded the 1957 Nobel Prize for literature.

Canaan Historical region occupying the land between the Mediterranean and the Dead Sea. The Canaanites were a Semitic people, identified with the Phoenicians from *c.*1200 BC. Canaan was the Promised Land of the Israelites, who settled here on their return from Egypt.

Canada Federation in N North America; the captital is OTTAWA. **Land and climate** Canada is the world's second largest country (after Russia), and is thinly populated. Much of the land is too cold or mountainous for human settlement and most Canadians live within 300km (186mi) of its S border. Western Canada has the most rugged terrain, including the Pacific ranges and the mighty ROCKY MOUNTAINS. Mount LOGAN is Canada's highest peak, 6,050m (19,850ft). E of the Rockies are the interior plains of Canada's Prairie Provinces (S ALBERTA, MANITOBA and SASKATCHEWAN). In the N are the bleak Arctic islands. South of the Canadian

Shield lie Canada's most populous regions, the lowlands N of Lakes ERIE and ONTARIO and the ST LAWRENCE RIVER valley. Canada has a cold climate, with winter temperatures below freezing point throughout most of the country. Western Canada has plenty of rainfall but the prairies are dry with 250–500mm (10–20in) of rain annually. SE Canada has a moist climate. Forests of cedar, hemlock and other trees grow on the W mountains, with firs and spruces at higher levels. The interior plains were once grassy prairies, but today are used mainly for farming and ranching. The SE lowlands contain forests of deciduous trees, such as beech, oak and walnut. **Economy** Canada is a highly developed and prosperous country. It is one of the world's leading producers of barley, meat, milk and wheat. Fishing is important in both Atlantic and Pacific waters. Forestry is a major industry and the availability of cheap hydroelectric power has encouraged the development of huge wood pulp and paper industries. Canada is rich in mineral resources producing oil, copper, gold, iron ore, uranium and zinc. Manufacturing is highly developed, especially in the cities, where 77% of the population live. Canada produces cars, chemicals, electronic goods, machinery, telecommunications equipment and timber. Canada and the USA have the largest bilateral trade flow in the world. Since 1 January 1994, Canada, Mexico and the USA have been linked through the NORTH AMERICAN FREE TRADE AGREEMENT (NAFTA). **History** Canada's first people arrived in North America from Asia c.40,000 years ago. Later arrivals were the INUIT, also from Asia. John CABOT was the first European to reach the Canadian coast in 1497. A race began between France and Britain for the riches in this new land. The French established the first European settlement in 1605 and founded Quebec in 1608. French settlement in the W was generally much slower than English development on the Atlantic coast. The FRENCH AND INDIAN WARS (1689–1763) were a protracted battle for colonial domination of Canada. In 1759 Quebec was captured by Britain, and France

surrendered all of its Canadian lands in the Treaty of Paris (1763). During the American Revolution, Canada remained loyal to the English crown, and American attempts to capture it failed. The Constitutional Act (1791) divided Canada along linguistic and religious lines: Upper Canada (now Ontario) was English and Protestant; Lower Canada (now Quebec) was French and Catholic. Border disputes with the USA (such as the WAR OF 1812) continued into the 19th century. Large-scale immigration from Ireland and Scotland increased conflict between the English-speaking majority and the French-speaking minority. In 1867 the British passed the British North American Act establishing the Dominion of Canada. The Dominion's first prime minister (1867–73, 1878–91) was Sir John A. MACDONALD. In 1949 Canada was a founding member of NATO. Under the leadership of W.L. Mackenzie KING, national unity was strengthened and industry developed. Pierre TRUDEAU's first administration (1968–79) was faced with violent separatist demands for Quebec's independence and martial law was imposed in 1970. In Trudeau's second administration, Quebec voted to remain part of the federation (1980). **Politics** Jean CHRÉTIEN was elected prime minister in 1993 and reelected in 1997. In 1995 a referendum on sovereignty for Quebec was narrowly defeated by 50.6% to 49.4%. This issue seems unlikely to disappear. Canada's new constitution has enabled Native Americans to press for land claims. In 1999 NORTHWEST TERRITORIES will become the Inuit territory of Nunavut.

Canadian literature Literary work can be divided into two distinct (yet interrelated) traditions, reflecting Canada's dual French and English linguistic and cultural history. A French language tradition really began in opposition to English colonialism and cultural dominance. The first English language works were accounts of the Canadian landscape by explorers. At the turn of the 19th century prose tended to pastoral romanticism, such as L.M. Montgomery's classic *Anne of Green Gables*. Post-1945 literature reflected and nurtured a burgeoning national consciousness. Recent novelists include Margaret ATWOOD, Robertson DAVIES and Mordecai Richler. Canada also has a healthy tradition of literary criticism; major figures include Northrop Frye and Marshall McLUHAN.

canal Artificial waterway for irrigation, drainage and navigation. The first were built more than 4000 years ago in MESOPOTAMIA.

Canaletto (1697–1768) (Giovanni Antonio Canal) Italian painter of the VENETIAN SCHOOL, famous for his perspectival views of Venice. His early work is more dramatic and free-flowing than his smoother, accurate mature style. He used a camera obscura to make his paintings more precise, sometimes making the finished work seem stiff and mannered. Canaletto managed to infuse his best work with energy, light and colour.

canary Popular cage-bird that lives wild in the

CANADA
AREA: 9,976,140sq km (3,851,788sq mi)
POPULATION: 27,562,000
CAPITAL (POPULATION): Ottawa (313,987)
GOVERNMENT: Federal multiparty constitutional monarchy
ETHNIC GROUPS: British 34%, French 26%, German 4%, Italian 3%, Ukrainian 2%, Native American (Amerindian/Inuit) 1.5%, Chinese, Dutch
LANGUAGES: English and French (both official)
RELIGIONS: Christianity (Roman Catholic 47%, Protestant 41%, Eastern Orthodox 2%), Judaism, Islam, Hinduism, Sikhism
CURRENCY: Canadian dollar = 100 cents

Azores, Canary and Madeira islands. These yellowish FINCHES feed on fruit, seeds and insects, and lay spotted greenish-blue eggs. Family Fringillidae; species *Serinus canarius*.

Canary Islands Group of islands in the N Atlantic Ocean, *c.*113km (70mi) off the NW coast of Africa; they constitute two provinces of Spain, Las Palmas and SANTA CRUZ DE TENERIFE. Under Spanish rule since the 16th century, the islands are mountainous and the climate warm, with little rainfall. Industries: agriculture, fishing and tourism.

Canberra Capital of Australia on the Molonglo River, Australian Capital Territory, SE Australia. Settled in the early 1820s, it was chosen in 1908 as the new site for Australia's capital (succeeding MELBOURNE). The transfer of all governmental agencies was completed after World War 2. Pop. (1993 est.) 324,600.

Cancer Northern constellation between Gemini and Leo. It contains two open clusters: M44, the Praesepe or Beehive Nebula (NGC 2632), and M67 (NGC 2692). The brightest star is Beta Cancri.

cancer Group of diseases featuring the uncontrolled proliferation of cells (tumour formation). Malignant (cancerous) cells spread (metastasize) from their original site to other parts of the body. Known causative agents (carcinogens) include smoking, certain industrial chemicals, asbestos dust and radioactivity. Viruses are implicated in the causation of some cancers. Treatments include surgery, chemotherapy with cell-destroying drugs and radiotherapy (or sometimes a combination of all three).

Cancer, Tropic of Line of latitude, *c.* 23.5° N of the Equator, which marks the N boundary of the tropics. It indicates the farthest N position at which the Sun appears directly overhead at noon.

candela SI unit of luminous intensity (symbol, cd). It is defined as 1/60 of the luminous intensity of a BLACK BODY at atmospheric pressure and the temperature of solidification of platinum, 1,772°C (3,222°F).

Canetti, Elias (1905–94) British writer, b. Bulgaria. His first-hand experiences of violent antisemitism in 1930s Europe inspired his masterpiece, *Crowds and Power* (1960). He won the Nobel Prize for literature in 1981.

Canis Major (Great Dog) Southern constellation situated S of Monoceros. It contains the bright

open cluster M41 (NGC 2287). The brightest star is Alpha Canis Majoris or Sirius (Dog Star), the brightest star in the sky

cannabis Resin from the leaves or stem of the Indian hemp plant, *Cannabis sativa* (family Cannabidaceae). It is smoked or eaten as a psychotropic drug in many parts of the world, producing a NARCOTIC effect.

Cannes Resort on the French Riviera, SE France. An international film festival is held here each spring. Industries: tourism, flowers, textiles. Pop. (1990) 68,676).

Canning, Charles John, Earl (1812–62) British imperial administrator. Son of George CANNING, he served in government before becoming governor general of India (1856–58). He repressed the INDIAN MUTINY and became the first viceroy of India (1858–62).

Canning, George (1770–1827) British politician, prime minister (1827). As Tory foreign minister (1807–10, 1822–24), he favoured vigorous measures against Napoleon. He became prime minister, in coalition with the Whigs, but died four months later. His liberalism, such as support for South American independence, made him a maverick among Tories.

cannon ARTILLERY piece, consisting of a metal tube, used to aim and fire missiles propelled by the explosion of gunpowder in the closed end of the cylinder.

canon In music, form of COUNTERPOINT using strict imitation. All the voices or parts have the same melody, but each voice starts at a different time, at the same or a different pitch.

canon Term used in Christian religion. The basic meaning is a rule or standard. In this sense, a canon is something accepted or decreed as a rule or regulation, such as the official list of saints or the list of books accepted as genuine parts of the BIBLE. Initially a canon was also a priest in a cathedral or collegiate church, whose life was regulated by canon law. They were distinct from secular canons, who lived outside the cathedral and, although ordained, played a largely administrative role.

canonization Official action by which a member of a Christian church is created a cult figure or SAINT and added to the CANON.

canon law In the Roman Catholic, Anglican and Orthodox churches, a body of ecclesiastical laws relating to faith, morals and discipline.

Canopus (Alpha Carinae) Second-brightest star in the sky. Its luminosity and distance are not accurately known, but one estimate classifies it as a bright giant, 800 times as luminous as the Sun, and 74 light years away.

Canova, Antonio (1757–1822) Italian sculptor. His work expresses the elegance and allusions to antique art that characterize NEO-CLASSICISM. Two important pieces of the 1780s, *Theseus and the Minotaur* and Pope Clement XIV's tomb, catapulted Canova into the limelight.

CANARY ISLANDS
AREA: 7,273 sq km (2,807 sq mi)
POPULATION: 1,493,784
CAPITAL (POPULATION): Santa Cruz (189,317) / Las Palmas (372,000)
GOVERNMENT: Spanish autonomous region
ETHNIC GROUPS: Spanish
LANGUAGES: Spanish
RELIGIONS: Christianity (mainly Roman Catholic)
CURRENCY: Spanish currency

cantata Musical work consisting of vocal solos and choruses, often alternating with passages of recitative, and accompanied by an orchestra. It was a popular form in the 17th and 18th centuries, when Alessandro Scarlatti and J.S. Bach wrote numerous cantatas, both secular and religious.

Canterbury City on the Great Stour River in Kent, SE England. It is the seat of the archbishop and primate of the Anglican Church. Tourism is a major industry. Pop. (1991) 123,947.

Canterbury, Archbishop of Primate of all England and spiritual leader of the worldwide ANGLICAN COMMUNION. The archbishopric was established in 597. St AUGUSTINE was the first Archbishop of Canterbury. The Archbishop of Canterbury traditionally crowns British monarchs and officiates at other religious ceremonies of national importance. He presides over the Lambeth Conference of worldwide Anglicanism, but exercises no jurisdiction outside his own ecclesiastical province.

cantilever bridge BRIDGE in which each half of the main span is rigidly supported at one end only. The other ends are joined in the middle of the bridge, where there is no supporting structure.

Canton *See* GUANGZHOU

Cantona, Eric (1966–) French football player. Cantona began his career playing for Auxerre (1980–88). In 1992 he moved to Leeds United and was transferred to Manchester United (1993). His career was a mixture of controversy and success, and he retired in 1997.

Cantonese One of the major languages of China. Within the Chinese People's Republic it is spoken by *c.* 50 million people, mainly in the extreme southern provinces. It is also spoken by most Chinese in Southeast Asia and the USA.

Canute II (c.994–1035) King of Denmark (1014–28), England (1017–35) and Norway (1028–29). He invaded England (1015) and divided it (1016) with the English king Edmund Ironside. He was accepted as king after Edmund's death. His rule was a just and peaceful one. He restored the church and codified English law. His reign in Scandinavia was more turbulent.

canyon Deep, narrow depression in the Earth's crust. Land canyons are the result of erosion by rivers flowing through arid terrain. Marine canyons may be formed when a river bed and the surrounding terrain is submerged, or by turbulence produced by deep water currents.

capacitance Property of an electrical circuit or component (symbol C) that describes its ability to store charge in its CAPACITOR. Capacitance is measured in farads: 1 farad is a capacitance needing a charge of 1 coulomb to raise its potential by 1 volt.

capacitor (condenser) Electrical circuit component that stores charge. It has at least two metal plates and is used principally in alternating current (AC) circuits.

Cape Canaveral Low sandy promontory in E Florida, USA, extending E into the Atlantic Ocean.

It is the site of the John F. Kennedy Space Center which, since 1950, has been NASA's main US launch site for space flights and long-range missiles.

Cape Horn Southernmost point of South America in S Chile. It was sighted by Francis Drake in 1578, and first rounded in 1616 by Cornelis van Schouten.

Cape of Good Hope Peninsula, 48km (30mi) S of Cape Town, South Africa. The first European to sail around it was Bartholomeu Diaz in 1488. The Cape sea route between India and Europe was established by Vasco da Gama in 1497–99.

Cape Province Formerly the largest province in South Africa. In 1994 it was divided into the separate provinces of EASTERN CAPE, WESTERN CAPE and NORTHERN CAPE. The first colony was established by the Dutch EAST INDIA COMPANY in 1652. The BOER settlers' expansion led to territorial wars with indigenous tribes. In 1806 Britain established control. The new British settlers clashed with the Boers, precipitating the GREAT TREK (1835). Diamonds were discovered near KIMBERLEY in 1867. The British attempt to incorporate TRANSVAAL and Orange FREE STATE into a single state with NATAL and Cape Colony resulted in the SOUTH AFRICAN WARS (1899–1902). In 1910 the colony became a province of the Union of South Africa.

Capetians French royal family forming the third dynasty, providing France with 15 kings. It began with Hugh Capet, Duke of Francia (987) following the CAROLINGIANS, and ended with Charles IV (1328), succeeded by PHILIP VI of the House of Valois.

Cape Town City and seaport at the foot of Table Mountain, South Africa. It is South Africa's legislative capital and the capital of WESTERN CAPE province. Industries: clothing, engineering equipment, motor vehicles, wine. Pop. (1991) 2,350,157.

Cape Verde Republic in the E Atlantic Ocean. It is made up of 15 volcanic islands divided into two groups (WINDWARD and LEEWARD). The capital is Praia on São Tiago. An overseas province of Portugal, the islands became independent in 1975. Industries: coffee, tobacco, sugar cane, salt and coal mining. Area: 4,033sq km (1,557sq mi). Pop. (1993 est.) 350,000.

capillary Smallest of BLOOD VESSELS, connecting arteries and veins. Capillary walls consist of only a single layer of cells.

capital In architecture, the block of masonry at the top of a column, often elaborately carved. The design of the capital is characteristic of the ORDERS OF ARCHITECTURE.

capital In ECONOMICS, different forms of wealth. Fixed capital refers to such things as buildings, tools and equipment; working capital (variable or circulating capital) includes raw materials, stock and cash. In accounting, capital includes not only the owner's contribution but also the profits retained within the business for future use.

capitalism Economic system in which property and the means of production are privately owned.

Its development in modern times dates from the INDUSTRIAL REVOLUTION. Capitalism is based on profit motive, individual enterprise and efficiency through competition. In practice, capitalist governments participate in economic regulation, although to a lesser extent than a government within COMMUNISM or SOCIALISM.

capital punishment Punishing a criminal offence by death. Usual methods of execution include hanging, electrocution, lethal injection, lethal gas or firing squad. The death penalty has been abolished in many Western countries. The use of capital punishment is the subject of much debate: supporters claim that such punishment can be deserved and has a deterrent effect, while opponents state that it is inhuman, does not deter and that miscarriages of justice cannot be rectified.

Capone, Al (Alphonse) (1899–1947) US gangster of the PROHIBITION era, b. Italy. He was suspected of involvement in many brutal crimes, but ironically was only ever convicted and imprisoned for income tax evasion (1931).

Capote, Truman (1924–84) US author. His works, typified by keen social observation and characters on the fringes of society, include *Breakfast at Tiffany's* (1958), *The Grass Harp* (1951) and volumes of shorter pieces such as *Music for Chameleons* (1980).

Capra, Frank (1897–1991) US film director, b. Italy. His comedies include *Platinum Blonde* (1931), *It Happened One Night* (1934) and *You Can't Take It With You* (1938). He is best known for *It's a Wonderful Life* (1946).

Capricorn, Tropic of Line of latitude, *c*.23.54° S of the Equator, which marks the S boundary of the tropics. It indicates the farthest S position at which the Sun appears directly overhead at noon.

Capricornus (Sea Goat) One of the less prominent zodiacal constellations. Representing a goat, it has been identified with the Greek god PAN.

capsicum *See* PEPPER

capuchin Small diurnal monkey found in South and Central America. It is generally brown or black and is a tree-dweller. Omnivorous, but preferring fruit, it may grow to 55cm (22in), with a furry, prehensile tail of similar length. Family Cebidae.

Capuchins (officially, Friars Minor of St Francis Capuchin) Roman Catholic religious order, founded in 1525 as an offshoot of the FRANCISCANS. Capuchins are so-called because of the pointed cowl (*capuche*) that forms part of their habit. They re-emphasized Franciscan ideals of poverty and austerity and played an important role in the COUNTER REFORMATION.

capybara Largest living RODENT, native to Central and South America; it is semi-aquatic with webbed feet, a large, nearly hairless, body, short legs and a tiny tail. Length: 1.2m (4ft). Species *Hydrochoerus hydrochoeris*.

car *See* AUTOMOBILE

Caracas Capital of Venezuela, on the Guaire River. The city was under Spanish rule until 1821. It grew after 1930, encouraged by the exploitation of oil. Industries: motor vehicles, oil, brewing, chemicals, rubber. Pop. (1990) 1,824,892.

Caravaggio, Michelangelo Merisi da (1571–1610) Italian painter, the most influential and original painter of the 17th century. Caravaggio's early works were mainly experimental and include the erotic half-length figures of *The Young Bacchus* and *Boy with a Fruit Basket* (both *c*.1595). His mature phase (1599–1606) began with two large-scale religious paintings of St Matthew. The dramatic shadows in the pictures, and the use of a living model, show his revolutionary approach to religious themes. *The Crucifixion of St Peter* and *The Conversion of St Paul* (both 1600–01) are masterpieces of psychological realism.

caraway Biennial herb native to Eurasia and cultivated for its small seed-like fruits used for flavouring foods. It has feathery leaves and white flowers. Family Apiaceae/Umbelliferae; species *Carum carvi*.

carbide Inorganic compound of carbon with metals or other more electropositive elements. Many transition metals form carbides, in which carbon atoms occupy spaces between adjacent atoms in the metal lattice. Some electropositive metals form ionic carbon compounds; the best known is CALCIUM CARBIDE. Carbides are used as abrasives.

carbohydrate Organic compound of carbon, hydrogen and oxygen, a constituent of many foodstuffs. The simplest carbohydrates are SUGARS. STARCH and CELLULOSE are polysaccharides – carbohydrates consisting of hundreds of glucose molecules linked together. *See also* SACCHARIDE

carbon Common nonmetallic element (symbol C) of group IV of the periodic table. Carbon forms a vast number of compounds, which form the basis of organic CHEMISTRY. There are three crystalline ALLOTROPES: GRAPHITE and DIAMOND and "bucky balls". Various amorphous (noncrystalline) forms of carbon also exist, such as coal, coke and charcoal. Properties: at.no. 6; r.a.m. 12.011; r.d. 1.9–2.3 (graphite), 3.15–3.53 (diamond); m.p. *c*.3,550°C (6,422°F); graphite sublimes at 3,367°C (6,093°F); b.p. *c*.4,200°C (7,592°F); most common isotope C^{12} (98.89%).

carbonate Salt of carbonic acid, formed when carbon dioxide (CO_2) dissolves in water. Carbonic acid is an extremely weak and unstable acid. Large parts of the Earth's crust are made up of carbonates, such as CALCIUM CARBONATE and DOLOMITE.

carbon cycle Circulation of carbon in the biosphere. It is a complex chain of events. The most important elements are the taking up of carbon dioxide (CO_2) by green plants during PHOTOSYNTHESIS, and the return of CO_2 to the atmosphere by the respiration and eventual decomposition of the animals that eat the plants.

carbon dating (radiocarbon dating) Method of determining the age of organic materials by measuring the amount of radioactive decay of an ISOTOPE of carbon, carbon-14 (C^{14}). This radio-isotope decays to form nitrogen, with a half-life of 5,730 years. When a living organism dies the amount of C^{14} it contains is fixed relative to its total weight. Over the centuries, this quantity steadily diminishes. The exact amount remaining indicates the age of a specimen.

carbon dioxide (CO_2) Colourless, odourless gas that occurs in the atmosphere (0.03%) and is produced by the combustion of fossil fuels and the exhalation of animals. In its solid form (dry ice) it is used in refrigeration; as a gas it is used in carbonated beverages and fire extinguishers. Properties: m.p. $-56.6°C$ ($-69.9°F$); sublimes $-78.5°C$ ($-109.3°F$).

Carboniferous Fifth geologic division of the PALAEOZOIC era, lasting from 360 to 286 million years ago. It is often called the "Age of Coal" because of its extensive swampy forests that turned into most of today's coal deposits. Amphibians flourished, marine life abounded and the first reptiles appeared.

carbon monoxide Colourless, odourless poisonous gas (CO) formed during the incomplete combustion of fossil fuels, occurring for example in coal gas and the exhaust fumes of cars. Carbon monoxide poisons by combining with the HAEMOGLOBIN in red blood cells and thus preventing them from carrying oxygen round the body. It is used as a reducing agent in metallurgy. Properties: density 0.968 (air = 1); m.p. $-205°C$ ($-337°F$); b.p. $-191.5°C$ ($-312.7°F$).

carcinogen External substance or agent that causes CANCER, including chemicals, such as the tar present in cigarette smoke, large doses of radiation and some viruses, such as polyoma.

carcinoma Form of CANCER arising from the epithelial cells present in skin and the membranes lining the internal organs. It is a malignant growth that tends to invade surrounding tissues, giving rise to metastases (secondary cancers).

cardamom Pungent spice made from seeds of a plant of the GINGER family. Species *Elettaria cardamomum*.

cardiac muscle See MUSCLE

Cardiff (Caerdydd) Capital of Wales and port on the River Severn estuary, at the mouth of the rivers Taff, Rhymney and Ely, S Glamorgan. The construction of docks in 1839 led to the rapid growth of the city, and until the beginning of the 20th century, it was a major coal exporting centre. Industries: steel manufacturing, engineering, chemicals, food processing. Pop. (1991) 279,055.

cardinal Priest of the highest rank in the hierarchy of the Roman Catholic Church after the pope. They are nominated by the pope, who they advise. On the death of a pope they meet in secret conclave to elect his successor.

cardinal (redbird) North American songbird . The male has bright red plumage and crest and a thick orange-red bill. They feed on seeds, fruits, and insects. Length: to 9in (23cm). Family Fringillidae; species *Richmondena cardinalis*.

cardiology Branch of medicine that deals with the diagnosis and treatment of the diseases and disorders of the HEART and vascular system.

Carew, Thomas (1595–1639) English poet. His poetry was largely influenced by Ben JONSON and John DONNE, to whom he wrote an elegy. His work includes *A Rapture* and the MASQUE *Coelum Britannicum*.

Carey, George Leonard (1935–) Anglican Archbishop of CANTERBURY and primate of all England (1991–). Carey belongs to the evangelical wing of the CHURCH OF ENGLAND. He favours the ordination of women priests and supports environmental conservation. *See also* EVANGELICALISM

Caribbean Community and Common Market (CARICOM) Caribbean economic union. CARICOM was formed in 1973 to coordinate economic and foreign policy in the WEST INDIES. The headquarters is in Georgetown, Guyana.

Caribbean Sea Extension of the N Atlantic Ocean linked to the Gulf of Mexico by the Yucatán Channel and to the Pacific Ocean by the Panama Canal. From the 16th century it became notorious for piracy, particularly after other European powers established colonies in the WEST INDIES. With the opening of the Panama Canal (1914) its strategic importance increased. Area: *c.*2,640,000sq km (1,020,000sq mi).

caribou *See* REINDEER

caricature Painting or drawing in which a person is presented in a comic, often ridiculous, light by the distortion of their features. Caricature may be used to interpret the character of a person, event or age. The genre first appeared in the late 16th century.

caries Decay and disintegration of teeth or BONE substance. Caries are caused by acids produced when bacteria present in the mouth break down sugars in food.

Carlists Reactionary Spanish political faction in the 19th century. They favoured the royal claims of Don CARLOS and his successors, and figured in several rebellions, sometimes in alliance with BASQUES and CATALANS. The remnants of the Carlists eventually merged with the fascist FALANGE in 1937.

Carlos (1788–1855) Spanish prince and pretender to the throne. His elder brother, Ferdinand VII, changed Spanish law so that his daughter Isabella II succeeded him (1833). Carlos was proclaimed king by the CARLISTS, and civil war ensued. Isabella won (1840), and Carlos went into exile.

Carlson, Chester (1906–68) US physicist, inventor of XEROGRAPHY (1938). He patented it in 1940. In 1947 he signed an agreement with the Haloid Company (now Rank Xerox). His royalties made him a multi-millionaire.

Carlyle, Thomas (1795–1881) Scottish philosopher, critic and historian. His most successful work, *Sartor Resartus* (1836), combined philosophy and autobiography. His histories include *The French Revolution* (1837). Influenced by Goethe and the German Romantics, he was a powerful advocate of the significance of great leaders in history. He was also an energetic social critic and a proponent of moral values.

Carmelites (officially, Order of Our Lady of Mount Carmel) Order founded by St Berthold in Palestine *c*.1154. The Carmelites devote themselves to contemplation and missionary work.

carnation Slender-stemmed herbaceous plant native to Europe. It has narrow leaves, characteristic swollen stem joints, and produces several dense blooms with serrated (pinked) petals that range from white to yellow, pink and red. Family Caryophyllaceae; species *Dianthus caryophyllus*.

Carnegie, Andrew (1835–1919) US industrialist and philanthropist, b. Scotland. He started the Keystone Bridge Company. From 1873 he concentrated on steel, pioneering mass production techniques. By 1901 the Carnegie Steel Company was producing 25% of US steel. Carnegie donated more than $350 million to charitable foundations.

carnivore Any member of the order of flesh-eating mammals. Mustelids – weasels, martens, minks and the wolverine – make up the largest family. The cats are the most specialized killers among the carnivores. Distantly related to living land carnivores are the seals, sea lions and walruses; they evolved from ancient land carnivores.

carnivorous plant *See* INSECTIVOROUS PLANT

Carnot, Lazare Nicolas Marguerite (1753–1823) French general. He was the outstanding commander of the FRENCH REVOLUTIONARY WARS. Ousted in 1797, he was recalled by Napoleon (1800), who made him minister of war.

Carnot, Marie François Sadi (1837–94) French political leader, president of the Third Republic (1887–94). After quashing the anti-republican movement, he successfully defended the regime during the Panama Canal scandal (1892). He was stabbed to death by an Italian anarchist.

Carnot, Nicolas Léonard Sadi (1796–1832) French engineer and physicist whose work laid the foundation for the science of thermodynamics. His major work, *Réflexions sur la puissance motrice du feu* (1824), provided the first theoretical background for the steam engine and introduced the concept of the second law of thermodynamics.

carnot cycle In thermodynamics, a cycle of events that demonstrates the impossibility of total efficiency in heat engines.

Caro, Anthony (1924–) British sculptor. He is best known for distinctive "structures" made from "found" metal objects, which are welded together in such a way that they keep their original identity but also create a definite mood.

carob Plant of the E Mediterranean. It belongs to the pea family (Fabaceae/Leguminosae) and bears leguminous fruits. Its seeds are used as a substitute for coffee beans. Species *Ceratonia siliqua*.

carol Traditional song usually of religious joy, and associated with Christmas. Earliest examples date to the 14th century.

Carol I (1839–1914) Prince of Romania (1866–81); first king (1881–1914). He aided Russia in the first Russo-Turkish War (1877–78). Romanian independence and Carol's sovereignty were recognized by the Congress of Berlin (1878). He preserved the neutrality of Romania at the start of World War 1, but sympathized with Germany.

Carol II (1893–1953) King of Romania (1930–40). He aimed to become dictator, but German pressure forced him to abdicate in favour of his son Michael in 1940, leaving power in the hands of the Romanian fascist leader, Ion Antonescu.

Caroline Islands Archipelago of *c*.600 volcanic islands, coral islets and reefs in the W Pacific Ocean, N of the Equator; part of the US Trust Territory of the Pacific Islands. In 1979 all the islands except the BELAU group became the Federated States of MICRONESIA. Area: 1,130sq km (450sq mi).

Carolingian renaissance Cultural revival in France and Italy under the encouragement of CHARLEMAGNE. He promoted Catholicism, art and learning by founding abbeys and encouraging church building. He imposed a new culture in Europe, combining Christian, Roman and Frankish elements.

Carolingians Second Frankish dynasty of early medieval Europe. Founded in the 7th century, it rose to power under the MEROVINGIANS. In 732 Charles Martel defeated the Muslims at Poitiers; in 751 his son PEPIN III (THE SHORT) deposed the last Merovingian and became king of the Franks. The dynasty reached its peak under Pepin's son CHARLEMAGNE (after whom the dynasty is called). His empire was later subdivided and broken up by civil wars. Carolingian rule finally ended in 987.

Carothers, Wallace Hume (1896–1937) US chemist who discovered the synthetic polyamide fibre now called NYLON.

carp Freshwater fish native to temperate waters of Asia. Introduced to the USA and Europe, it is an important food fish. It is brown or golden and has four fleshy mouth whiskers called barbels. Length: to 1m (3.2ft). Family Cyprinidae; species *Cyprinus carpio*.

Carpathian Mountains Mountain range in central and E Europe, extending NE from the central Czech Republic to the Polish-Czech border and into Romania and the Ukraine. The highest peak is Gerlachovka, 2,655m (8,711ft). Industries: timber, mining, tourism. Length: 1,530km (950mi).

carpel Female reproductive part of a flowering plant. A carpel consists of a STIGMA, a STYLE and an OVARY. A group of carpels make up the **gynoecium**, the complete female reproductive structure within a flower.

carpetbaggers Term used after the US CIVIL WAR to refer to Northern whites who entered the South as Republicans. They were regarded by many white Southerners as opportunists, seeking political office with the aid of the votes of former slaves for the sake of economic gain.

Carreras, José Maria (1946–) Spanish tenor. He made his début in Barcelona (1970), going on to sing in opera houses worldwide. At the height of his career he developed leukemia. He became a household name as one of the Three Tenors, with Placido DOMINGO and Luciano PAVAROTTI.

Carroll, Lewis (1832–98) (Charles Lutwidge Dodgson) British mathematician, photographer and writer. An Oxford don, much of whose output consisted of mathematical textbooks, he is remembered for *Alice's Adventures in Wonderland* (1865) and its sequel, *Through the Looking Glass* (1872).

carrot Herbaceous, generally BIENNIAL root vegetable, cultivated widely as a food crop. The edible orange taproot is topped by delicate fern-like leaves and white or pink flower clusters. Family UMBELLIFERAE; Species *Daucus carota*.

Carson, Edward Henry (1854–1935) Irish political leader. A famous barrister and powerful orator, he was the leader of resistance to Irish Home Rule. Organizing the paramilitary Ulster Volunteers (1912), he forced the British government to exclude the Protestant provinces from the Home Rule Agreement of 1914.

Cartagena City and port in NW Colombia, on the Bay of Cartagena in the Caribbean Sea; capital of the department of Bolívar. It is the principal oil port of Colombia. Industries: oil refining, sugar, tobacco, textiles, tourism. Pop. (1992) 688,306.

Cartagena Major seaport in SE Spain, on the Mediterranean Sea. Founded in *c.*255 BC by the Carthaginians, the settlement later fell to the Romans. Moors captured it in the 8th century but it was retaken by Spaniards in the 13th century. Industries: shipbuilding, lead, zinc, iron. Pop. (1991) 166,736.

Carte, Richard D'Oyly (1844–1901) English impresario and producer of the operas of GILBERT and SULLIVAN.

cartel Formal agreement among the producers of a product to fix the price and divide the market among themselves. It usually results in higher prices for consumers and extra profits for the producers. Cartels are illegal in many countries.

Carter, Angela (1940–92) British novelist and short-story writer. She is closely associated with MAGIC REALISM. Her writing draws on legend and myth, and mixes past and present. Novels include *Nights at the Circus* (1984), whose central character is half-woman, half-bird, *The Magic Toyshop* (1967) and *The Passion of New Eve* (1977).

Carter, Elliott Cook Jr (1908–) US composer. His works are notable for elaborate COUNTERPOINT, complex structures and use of tempo as an aspect of form. His compositions include a piano (1946) and a cello (1948) sonata, *Variations* (1953–55) and *Concerto* (1970) for orchestra, and four string quartets (1951, 1959, 1971, 1986).

Carter, Jimmy (James Earl Jr) (1924–) 39th US president (1977–81). A Democrat, he was the first president since the Civil War to come from the "Old South". Unable to control a variety of economic problems at home or to secure the release of US hostages held in Iran, he was defeated by Ronald REAGAN in the 1980 election. Since then he has sought to promote human rights.

Cartesian coordinate system System in which the position of a point is specified by its distances from intersecting lines (axes). In the simplest type – rectangular coordinates are used at right angles: y and x. The position of a point is then given by a pair of numbers (x, y).

Carthage Ancient port on the Bay of Tunis, N Africa. It was founded in the 9th century BC by Phoenician colonists. It became a great commercial city and imperial power, controlling an empire in North Africa, S Spain and islands of the W Mediterranean. The PUNIC WARS with Rome ended with the defeat and destruction of Carthage. It was resettled as a Roman colony, and in the 5th century AD it was the capital of the VANDALS.

Carthusian Monastic order founded by St Bruno in 1084. It is based at the Grande Chartreuse monastery near Grenoble, France. It is a mainly contemplative order, in which monks and nuns solemnly vow to live in silence and solitude.

Cartier, Jacques (1491–1557) French explorer. He laid the basis for French settlements in Canada.

cartilage Flexible supporting tissue made up of COLLAGEN. In the vertebrate EMBRYO, the greater part of the SKELETON consists of cartilage, which is gradually replaced by BONE. In humans, cartilage is also present in the larynx, nose and external ear.

cartoon Originally a preparatory drawing. Italian Renaissance painters made very thorough cartoons. Its more common, modern usage in reference to a humorous drawing or satirical picture is derived from a 19th-century competition for fresco designs for Parliament parodied in *Punch* magazine.

Cartwright, Edmund (1743–1823) British inventor of the power loom. It was patented in 1785, but not used commercially until the early 19th century.

Caruso, Enrico (1873–1921) Italian tenor, one of the most widely acclaimed opera singers of all time. He made his debut in Naples in 1894.

Carver, George Washington (1864–1943) US agricultural chemist. He is best known for his scientific research on the peanut, from which he derived more than 300 products. Born into an African-American slave family, his chief motive was to benefit the impoverished farmers of the South.

Carver, Raymond (1938–88) US short-story writer and poet. His fiction depicts, often bleakly, the lives of US citizens. he is best known for his short stories, collected in *Will You Please Be Quiet, Please?* (1976), *What We Talk About When We Talk About Love* (1981) and *Cathedral* (1983).

Cary, (Arthur) Joyce (Lunel) (1888–1957)

British novelist. His experiences in colonial service in Nigeria (1914–20) are reflected in novels, such as *Mister Johnson* (1939). His best-known novel is *The Horse's Mouth* (1944).

Casablanca (Dar el-Beida) City in w Morocco, on Africa's Atlantic coast. Today it is a thriving commercial centre, exporting phosphates and importing petroleum products. Local industries include tourism, textiles and fishing. Pop. (1992 est.) 2,700,000.

Casals, Pablo (Pau) (1876–1973) Spanish (Catalan) cellist and conductor. He organized his own orchestra in Barcelona in 1919. The Casals Festival in Puerto Rico has been held annually since 1957.

Casanova de Seingalt, Giovanni Giacomo (1725–98) Italian libertine and adventurer. From 1750 he travelled through Europe leading a dissolute existence. His exploits are recounted in his *Memoirs*, which were not published in unexpurgated form until 1960. His name is synonymous with the amorous adventurer.

Cascade Range Mountain range in w North America, extending from NE California across Oregon and Washington into Canada. The Cascade Tunnel, at 13km (8mi) the longest rail tunnel in the USA, passes through them. Crater Lake National Park is in the Cascades. The highest peak is Mount RAINIER, 4,395m (14,410ft). The range also includes Mount ST HELENS, 2,549m (8,363ft).

casein Principal protein in milk, containing about 15 amino acids. It is used to make plastics, cosmetics, paper coatings, adhesives, paints, textile sizing, cheeses and animal feed.

Casement, Sir Roger David (1864–1916) Irish humanitarian and revolutionary. While a British consul (1895–1912), he exposed the exploitation of rubber-gatherers in the Belgian Congo and similar iniquities in South America. During World War 1 he sought aid for an Irish nationalist uprising and was executed for treason.

cash crop Agricultural crop cultivated for its commercial value, as opposed to one grown for subsistence. Cash crops, such as coffee, sugar or cotton, were introduced into Africa, Asia and the Americas as part of the colonialist project and were intensively farmed via plantation systems.

cashew Evergreen shrub or tree grown in the tropics, important for its nuts. The wood is used for boxes and boats. Height: to 12m (39ft). Family Anacardiaceae; species *Anacardium occidentale*.

cashmere Woolly hair of a goat native to Kashmir, India. The warm but lightweight wool is woven for clothing.

Caspian Sea Shallow salt lake, the world's largest inland body of water. The Caspian Sea is enclosed by Russia, Kazakstan, Turkmenistan, Azerbaijan and Iran. It is fed mainly by the Volga River. The chief ports are BAKU and ASTRAKHAN. It still has important fisheries and a seal trade. Area: *c.*371,000sq km (143,000sq mi).

Cassandra In Greek mythology, the daughter of PRIAM, skilled in the art of prophecy but condemned by APOLLO never to be taken seriously. Her warning that the Greeks would capture Troy went unheeded. She was carried off as a concubine by AGAMEMNON; they were both murdered by his wife CLYTEMNESTRA.

Cassatt, Mary (1845–1926) French painter and printmaker, b. USA. She was influenced by DEGAS and IMPRESSIONISM. Her finest paintings include *The Bath* (1892).

cassava (manioc) Tapioca plant native to Brazil. A valuable cereal substitute is made from the tuberous roots. Height: up to 2.7m (9ft). Family Euphorbiaceae; species *Manihot esculenta*.

Cassini, Giovanni Domenico (1625–1712) French astronomer. He was the first to measure accurately the dimensions of the SOLAR SYSTEM, and discovered the division in the rings of SATURN that now bear his name, and also four satellites.

Cassiopeia Northern constellation, representing the mother of ANDROMEDA. The five leading stars make up a "W" or "M" pattern.

Cassius Longinus (Gaius) (d.42 BC) Roman general who led the plot to assassinate Julius CAESAR. He sided with POMPEY during the war against Caesar but was pardoned after Caesar defeated Pompey. After the assassination of Caesar in 44 BC he left for Sicily. Believing he had lost the battle against Mark ANTONY and Octavian (AUGUSTUS) at Philippi, Cassius committed suicide.

cassowary Flightless bird of rainforests in Australia and Malaysia. It has coarse black plumage, a horny crest on its brightly coloured head, large feet and sharp claws. Height: to 1.6m (65in). Family Casuariidae; species *Casuarius casuarius*.

caste Formal system of social stratification based on race, gender or religious heritage, and sanctioned by tradition. It is most prevalent in Hindu society.

Castile Region and former kingdom in central Spain. In the 16th century Castile became the most influential power in Spain and the core of the Spanish monarchy.

Castile-La Mancha Region in central Spain; it includes the provinces of Albacete, Ciudad Real, Cuenca, Guadalajara and Toledo; the capital is TOLEDO. Chief products are olive oil and grapes. Area: 79,226sq km (30,590sq mi). Pop. (1991) 1,658,446.

Castile-León Region in N Spain; it includes the provinces of Ávila, Burgos, León, Palencia, Salamanca, Segovia, Soria, Valladolid and Zamora; the capital is Valladolid. Formerly part of the kingdom of León, Castile and ARAGÓN were united in 1479. Extreme climate and poor soil allow limited grain growing and sheep raising. Area: 94,147sq km (36,350sq mi). Pop. (1991) 2,545,926.

casting Forming objects by pouring molten metal into moulds and allowing it to cool and solidify.

Castlereagh, Robert Stewart, 2nd Viscount (1769–1822) British politician. He was chief secretary of Ireland (1799–1801) and helped secure the passage of the Act of Union with Britain in 1800. He was a brilliant foreign secretary (1812–22), backing WELLINGTON in war and helping to secure long-term peace in Europe at the Congress of Vienna (1814–15).

Castor and Pollux (Greek Polydeuces) In Greek mythology, the twin sons of LEDA. Zeus transformed them into the Gemini constellation after Castor died and Pollux refused to be parted from him.

castration Removal of the sexual glands (testes or ovaries) from an animal or human.

castrato Male voice in the soprano or mezzo-soprano register, produced in adult males by CASTRATION during boyhood. Castratos were much used in operas in the 17th and 18th centuries and in music for the Roman Catholic Church. *See also* COUNTERTENOR

Castro, Fidel Ruz (1926–) Cuban revolutionary leader and politician, premier since 1959. In 1953 he was sentenced to 15 years' imprisonment after an unsuccessful coup against the BATISTA regime. Two years later he was granted an amnesty and exiled to Mexico. In January 1959 his guerrilla forces overthrew the regime. He quickly instituted radical reforms, such as collectivizing agriculture, dispossessing foreign companies, forming alliances with the Soviet Union and developing socialist states. Castro has recently introduced cautious economic reforms. *See also* CUBA

cat Carnivorous, often solitary and nocturnal mammal of the family Felidae, ranging in size from the rare Siberian tiger to the domestic cat. It has specialized teeth and claws for hunting, a keen sense of smell, acute hearing, sensitive vision, and balances well with its long tail. One of the first animals to be domesticated, cats have appeared frequently in myth and religion. Order Carnivora.

catabolism *See* METABOLISM

Catalan Romance language spoken mainly in NE Spain, in parts in the Balearic Islands, Andorra and southern France. There are *c*.6 million speakers.

Catalonia (Cataluña) Region in NE Spain, extending from the French border to the Mediterranean Sea. The capital is BARCELONA. Catalonia includes the provinces of Barcelona, Gerona, Lérida and Tarragona. United with ARAGÓN in 1137, it retained its own laws and language. During the Spanish Civil War it was a Loyalist stronghold. It has recently been a focus of separatist movements. Products: grain, fruit, olive oil, wool, wine. Area: 31,932sq km (12,329sq mi). Pop. (1990) 6,059,454.

catalyst Substance that speeds up the rate of a chemical reaction without itself being consumed. Many industrial processes rely on catalysts, such as the HABER PROCESS for manufacturing AMMONIA. The METABOLISM of all living organisms depends on biological catalysts called ENZYMES.

catalytic converter Anti-pollution device used in internal combustion engines. It consists of a bed of catalytic agents through which flow the gaseous exhaust of fuel combustion. Converters located in mufflers reduce harmful unburned hydrocarbons and carbon monoxide.

catalytic cracking *See* CRACKING

Catania Port near Mount Etna, E Sicily, Italy, capital of Catania province. Ancient Catania was founded by the Greeks in 729 BC. Industries: chemicals, cement, textiles. Pop. (1992) 329,898.

cataract Opacity in the lens of an eye, causing blurring of vision. Most cases are due to degenerative changes in old age, but it can also be congenital, or be the result of damage to the lens or a metabolic disorder such as diabetes. Treatment is by removal of the cataract and implanting an artificial lens.

catechism Manual of instruction in Christian church teachings for use by the young or by any candidate preparing for admission to membership of a church. A catechism often takes the form of question and answer.

caterpillar Worm-like larva of a butterfly or moth; it has a segmented body, short antennae, simple eyes, three pairs of true legs and chewing mouthparts. Nearly all caterpillars feed voraciously on plants and are serious crop pests.

catfish Any member of a large family of slow-swimming, scaleless fish found in tropical and subtropical waters; it has fleshy barbels on the upper jaw, sometimes with venomous spines. Most species live in freshwater and can be farmed. Length: up to 3.3m (10ft). Order Siluriformes.

cathedral (Gk. *kathedra*, throne or seat) Main church of a bishop's province, containing his throne. In the ROMANESQUE period, cathedrals started to become very large and many cathedrals are gigantic structures. Among the most remarkable of the great cathedrals of W Europe are CHARTRES (begun 1194) in France, COLOGNE cathedral in Germany, and MILAN cathedral (begun 1386) in Italy. Some of the finest English examples, such as CANTERBURY and YORK, combine Romanesque and Gothic features. In Latin America, cathedrals are often of Portuguese or Spanish RENAISSANCE and BAROQUE origin. The Episcopal Cathedral of St John the Divine in New York is the world's largest Gothic cathedral. *See also* GOTHIC ART AND ARCHITECTURE; BYZANTINE ART AND ARCHITECTURE

Catherine II (the Great) (1729–96) Empress of Russia (1762–96). A German princess, she married Peter III in 1745 and succeeded him after he was murdered. Her economic improvements, patronage of the arts and vast extension of Russian territory raised national prestige, but did little for Russian peasants. After the revolt of 1773–74, led by the Cossack Pugachev, she became increasingly conservative.

Catherine de' Medici (1519–89) Queen of France, wife of HENRY II and daughter of Lorenzo de' MEDICI. She exerted considerable political influence after she became regent for her second son, CHARLES IX, and she remained principal adviser until his death (1574). Her initial tolerance of the HUGUENOTS turned to enmity at the beginning of the French Wars of RELIGION. Her concern for preserving the power of the monarchy led to a dependence on the Catholic House of GUISE. She planned the SAINT BARTHOLOMEW'S DAY MASSACRE (1572).

Catherine of Aragon (1485–1536) Daughter of FERDINAND V and ISABELLA I, she was the first queen of HENRY VIII (1509). Her only surviving child was a daughter (MARY I).

cathode In chemistry, the negative electrode of an electrolytic cell or electron tube. It attracts positive ions (cations) during ELECTROLYSIS.

cathode rays Radiation emitted by the cathode of a thermionic electron valve containing a gas at low pressure. The rays were identified in 1897 by J. J. THOMSON as streams of charged, elementary particles having extremely low mass, later called ELECTRONS.

cathode-ray tube Evacuated electron tube used for television picture tubes, oscilloscopes and display screens in radar sets and computers. An electron gun shoots a beam of electrons, focused by a grid. The electrons strike a fluorescent screen and produce a spot of light. In a television tube, an electrostatic or magnetic field deflects the beam so that it scans a number of lines on the screen, controlled by the incoming picture signals.

Catholic Church Term used in Christianity with one of several connotations. Since the REFORMATION, the term has usually been used to denote the ROMAN CATHOLIC CHURCH, although the ANGLICAN COMMUNION and the OLD CATHOLICS use it to cover themselves as well.

Catholic Emancipation, Act of (1829) Measure by which the statutes (dating back to the REFORMATION) barring Roman Catholics in Britain from holding civil office or sitting in Parliament were repealed. Emancipation was achieved through a series of acts. In 1778 restrictions against land purchase and inheritance were lifted. In 1791 further restrictions were removed, and by 1793 Catholics were allowed in the services, universities and judiciary. The final concession allowing them to sit in Parliament was wrung from the government of the Duke of WELLINGTON, who was concerned by civil unrest in Ireland, led by Daniel O'CONNELL.

cation Positive ION, which is attracted to the CATHODE during ELECTROLYSIS.

Cato the Elder (234–149 BC) (Marcus Porcius) Roman leader. As censor from 184 BC, his constant urging in the Senate that CARTHAGE should be destroyed helped to initiate the Third PUNIC WAR.

Cato the Younger (95–46 BC) (Marcus Porcius Cato Uticensis) Roman politician, great-grandson of CATO THE ELDER. A firm supporter of the republic, he opposed Julius CAESAR and forced the creation of the First Triumvirate. He favoured POMPEY in the civil war against Caesar (49 BC), and, when Caesar emerged victorious, committed suicide.

CAT scan (computerized axial tomography) X-ray technique for displaying images of cross-sections through the human body.

cattle Large ruminant mammals of the family Bovidae, including all the varieties of modern domestic cattle (*Bos taurus*), the brahman (*Bos indicus*) and hybrids of these two. The family also includes the YAK, the wild GAUR, the wild banteng and the kouprey. Horns, sometimes appearing only on the male, are permanent, hollow and unbranched. Domestic cattle are raised for meat, milk and other dairy products. Leather, glue, gelatin and fertilizers are made from the carcasses.

Catullus (Gaius Valerius) (84–54 BC) Roman lyric poet. He is best known for his short love lyrics. His longer works are the poems *Attis* and *The Marriage of Peleus and Thetis*.

Caucasus (Bol'šoj Kavkaz) Mountain region in SE Europe, Russia, Georgia, Armenia and Azerbaijan. The system includes two major regions: N Caucasia (steppes) and TRANSCAUCASIA. It forms a natural barrier between Asia and Europe. There are deposits of oil, iron and manganese, and cotton, fruit and cereal crops are grown. The highest peak is Mount ELBRUS, 5,637m (18,493ft). Length: 1,210km (750mi).

cauliflower Form of CABBAGE, with a short thick stem, large lobed leaves and edible white or purplish flower clusters that form tightly compressed heads. Family Brassicaceae; species *Brassica oleracea botrytis*.

caustic soda (sodium hydroxide, NaOH) Strong ALKALI prepared industrially by the ELECTROLYSIS of salt (sodium chloride, NaCl). It is a white solid. Caustic soda is used in many industries, such as soap-making and in bauxite processing to manufacture ALUMINIUM.

Cavalier (Fr. *chevalier*) Name adopted by the Royalists during the English CIVIL WAR in opposition to the ROUNDHEADS (Parliamentarians). The court party retained the name after the RESTORATION until superseded by the name TORY.

cavalry Mounted troops. Cavalry were first employed by the ancient Egyptians; the first use of cavalry in Europe dates from the invasions of the Huns, Magyars and Mongols. The last prominent use of cavalry occurred in the American CIVIL WAR.

cave Natural underground cavity. The largest caves are formed in carbonate rocks such as limestone.

Cavendish, Henry (1731–1810) British chemist and physicist. He discovered hydrogen and the compositions of water and air. He estimated the Earth's mass and density by a method now known as the "Cavendish experiment".

caviar Roe (eggs) of a STURGEON and three less common fish (also occasionally a salmon), which, salted and seasoned, is a gastronomic delicacy, especially in Russia. The roe is extracted from the fish before it can spawn.

Cavour, Camillo Benso, Conte di (1810–61) Piedmontese politician. From 1852 he was prime minister under VICTOR EMMANUEL II. He engineered Italian liberation from Austria, expelled the French, and neutralized Garibaldi's influence. This led to the formation of the kingdom of Italy (1861).

cavy (wild guinea pig) Herbivorous South American rodent from which domestic GUINEA PIGS are descended. Small with dark fur, cavies live in burrows and often form large colonies for protection. Family Caviidae; species *Cavia aperea*.

Caxton, William (1422–91) First English printer. He set up his own press in 1476 at Westminster. Among his most influential publications were editions of CHAUCER, GOWER and MALORY.

Cayley, Sir George (1773–1857) British inventor who founded the science of AERODYNAMICS. He built the first glider to carry a man successfully and invented a caterpillar tractor.

Cayman Islands British dependency in the West Indies, comprising Grand Cayman, Little Cayman and Cayman Brac, *c.*325km (200mi) NW of Jamaica, in the Caribbean Sea. The capital is Georgetown. Industries: tourism, international finance, turtle and shark fishing, timber, coconuts, oil trans-shipment. Area: 259sq km (100sq mi). Pop. (1989) 25,355.

Cayuga Major branch of the Five Nations of the Iroquois Confederacy, originally living around Lake Cayuga, New York, and the Grand River in Ontario, Canada. Today there are *c.*550 in Oklahoma and 400 Cayuga in New York.

CBI Abbreviation of the CONFEDERATION OF BRITISH INDUSTRY

CD-ROM (compact disc read-only memory) Optical storage device for computer data and programs. A COMPACT DISC, a CD-ROM can store more data and allows faster access than a MAGNETIC DISK.

Ceauşescu, Nicolae (1918–89) Romanian politician, the country's effective ruler from 1965–89. He became a member of the politburo in 1955, general secretary of the Romanian Communist Party in 1965 and head of state in 1967. He promoted Romanian nationalism, pursued an independent foreign policy, but instituted repressive domestic policies. He was deposed and executed in the December 1989 revolution.

Cecil, Robert, 1st Earl of Salisbury (1563–1612) English statesman, son of Lord BURGHLEY. He became secretary of state to ELIZABETH I on his father's retirement in 1596. He was chiefly responsible for negotiating the accession of JAMES I (1603).

cedar Evergreen tree native to the Mediterranean and Asia, but found in warm temperate regions worldwide; it has clustered needle-like leaves and fragrant, durable wood. Height: 30–55m (98–180ft). Family Pinaceae; genus *Cedrus*.

Celebes Former name of SULAWESI, Indonesia

celery Biennial plant, native to the Mediterranean and widely cultivated for its long stalks used as a vegetable. Family Apiaceae/Umbelliferae; species *Apium graveolens*.

celestial mechanics Branch of ASTRONOMY concerned with the relative motions of stars and planets that are associated in systems (such as the Solar System or a binary star system) by gravitational fields. It was introduced by Isaac NEWTON in the 17th century.

celestial sphere Imaginary sphere of infinite radius used to define the positions of celestial bodies as seen from Earth, the centre of the sphere. The position of a celestial body is the point at which a radial line through it meets the surface of the sphere. The position is defined in terms of coordinates.

celibacy Commitment to a lifelong abstention from sexual relations. The status of celibacy as a religious obligation is found in Christianity and Buddhism. From the 4th century, it gradually became compulsory for Roman Catholic priests, monks and nuns.

cell Basic biological unit of which all plant and animal tissues are composed. The cell is the smallest unit of life that can exist independently, with its own self-regulating chemical system. Most cells consist of a MEMBRANE surrounding jelly-like CYTOPLASM with a central NUCLEUS. The nucleus is the main structure in which DNA is stored in CHROMOSOMES. More advanced cells (those that have nuclei) often have other membrane-bounded structures inside the cell, such as MITOCHONDRIA and CHLOROPLASTS. *See also* EUKARYOTE; PROKARYOTAE

cell, electrochemical Device from which electricity is obtained due to a chemical reaction. A cell consists of two electrodes (a positive ANODE and a negative CATHODE) immersed in a solution (electrolyte). A chemical reaction takes place between the electrolyte and one of the electrodes. *See also* BATTERY

cell division Process by which living CELLS reproduce and enable an organism to grow. In EUKARYOTE cells, a single cell splits in two, first by division of the NUCLEUS (occurring by MITOSIS or MEIOSIS), then by fission of the CYTOPLASM.

cello (violoncello) Musical instrument, member of the violin family. It has a soft, mellow tone, one octave below the viola. It is played with a bow and supported by the knees of a seated player. Among the most important players of the 20th century are Pablo CASALS and Jacqueline DU PRÉ.

cellophane Flexible, transparent film made of regenerated CELLULOSE and used mostly as a wrapping material.

celluloid Hard plastic invented in the USA in 1869 by John Hyatt. When heated it can be moulded into a variety of shapes and hardens on cooling. It was the first major plastic and was used for early motion pictures. It is highly flammable.

cellulose POLYSACCHARIDE CARBOHYDRATE $(C_6H_{10}O_5)_n$ that is the structural constituent of the cell walls of plants and algae. Consisting of parallel unbranched chains of GLUCOSE units cross-linked together into a stable structure, it forms the basic material of the paper and textile industries.

Celsius Temperature scale devised in 1742 by the Swedish astronomer Anders Celsius. On this scale the freezing point is 0°C and the boiling point is 100°C.

Celt Person who speaks a CELTIC LANGUAGE or is descended from a Celtic language area. After 2000 BC early Celts spread from E France and W Germany over much of W Europe, including Britain. They developed a village-based, heirarchical society headed by nobles and DRUIDS. Conquered by the Romans, the Celts were pushed into Ireland, Wales, Cornwall and Brittany by Germanic peoples.

Celtic art Artworks produced by Celtic peoples in Europe. Its chief characteristic was swirling, abstract design, which found its fullest expression in metalwork and jewellery. The term is sometimes also applied to the early Christian art of western Europe, such as The Book of Kells.

Celtic languages Group of languages spoken in parts of Britain, Ireland and France, forming a division within the Italo-Celtic subfamily of Indo-European languages. There are two branches of Celtic languages: Brittonic, which includes WELSH, BRETON and Cornish; and Goidelic, including Irish and Scots GAELIC and MANX.

Celtic mythology Legends of local deities of the Celtic tribes scattered throughout Europe and the British Isles. The gods' world was seen as a reflection of the world of men, while female divinities were more closely identified with nature.

Cenozoic Most recent era of geological time, beginning about 65 million years ago and extending up to the present. It is subdivided into the TERTIARY and QUATERNARY periods. It is the period during which present geographical features and plants and animals developed.

censor Public official of ancient Rome, from 443–22 BC. Two censors were elected for 18-month terms. Besides taking the census, they supervised public works, finance and morals, and filled senatorial vacancies.

censorship System whereby a government-appointed body or official claims the right to protect the public interest by influencing the release of any item of mass communication. Censorship usually falls into four broad categories – politics, religion, pornography or violence.

centaur In Greek mythology, a creature half-human and half-horse. Their debauched behaviour was exacerbated by wine. See also CHIRON

Centaurus (Centaur) Brilliant southern constellation representing a centaur. The brightest star in Centaurus is ALPHA CENTAURI.

centigrade Former name for CELSIUS

centipede (lit. hundred-legged) Common name for many arthropods of the class Chilopoda. Found in warm and temperate regions, they have flattened, segmented bodies. Most centipedes have about 70 legs (one pair per segment). Fast-moving predators, they eat small insects and other invertebrates.

Central Administrative region of central Scotland; the capital is STIRLING. Major towns include Falkirk, Alloa, Grangemouth and Dunblane. In the N lie the foothills of the Highlands. The S is drained chiefly by the River Forth and is the region's industrial base. Industries: brewing and distilling. Area: 2,635sq km (913sq mi) Pop: 267,492.

Central African Republic Landlocked nation in central Africa; the capital is BANGUI. **Land and climate** It lies on a plateau, mostly between 600–800m (1,970–2,620 ft) above sea level. In the S, the rivers flow into the navigable Ubangi River (a tributary of the CONGO River). In the N, most rivers are headwaters of the Chari River, which flows into Lake CHAD to the N. Wooded savanna covers much of the country, with open grasslands in the N. About 6% of the land is protected in national parks and reserves. **Economy** About 10% of the land is cultivated, and over 80% of the population is engaged in subsistence agriculture. The main food crops are bananas, maize, manioc, millet and yams. Coffee, cotton, timber and tobacco are the main cash crops. Diamonds (the only major mineral resource) are the most valuable single export. **History and politics** Little is known of the country's early history. Between the 16th–19th centuries, the population was greatly reduced by slavery, and the country is still thinly populated. France first occupied the area in 1887. In 1906 the colony was united with CHAD, and in 1910 was subsumed into French Equatorial Africa (which included Chad, Congo and Gabon). Post-1945 the colony received representation in the French parliament. In 1958 the colony voted to become a self-governing republic within the French community, and became the Central African Republic. In 1960 it declared independence, but the next six years saw a deterioration in the economy, and increasing government corruption and inefficiency. In 1966 Colonel Jean Bédel BOKASSA assumed power in a bloodless coup. In 1976 Bokassa transformed the republic into an empire and proclaimed himself Emperor Bokassa I. In 1979 he was deposed in a French-backed coup. The country adopted a new, multiparty constitution in 1991. Elections were held in 1993, none of the political parties won an overall majority. An army rebellion

---

CENTRAL AFRICAN REPUBLIC
AREA: 622,980sq km (240,533sq mi)
POPULATION: 3,173,000
CAPITAL (POPULATION): Bangui (451,690)
GOVERNMENT: Multiparty republic
ETHNIC GROUPS: Banda 29%, Baya 25%, Ngbandi 11%, Azande 10% Sara 7%, Mbaka 4%, Mbum 4%
LANGUAGES: French (official), Sango (most common)
RELIGIONS: Traditional beliefs 57%, Christianity 35%, Islam 8%
CURRENCY: CFA franc = 100 centimes

was put down in 1996 with the assistance of French troops.

Central America Geographical term for the narrow strip of land that connects NORTH AMERICA to SOUTH AMERICA and divides the Caribbean Sea from the Pacific Ocean; it consists of GUATEMALA, EL SALVADOR, HONDURAS, NICARAGUA, COSTA RICA, BELIZE and PANAMA. Highly developed by the Mayas, the region (excluding Panama) was conquered and ruled by the Spanish from the 16th century until 1821. In 1823 the Central American Federation was formed, but broke up in 1838, the individual states (except Belize) declaring themselves independent. Spanish is the main language. Area: 715,876sq km (276,400sq mi).

Central and South American mythology Traditional beliefs of the native peoples of Mexico and Central and South America. The AZTECS believed that there had been four eras (suns) before the one in which they were living, and that each sun had ended in universal destruction. They expected that their own era, the fifth, would end with an earthquake. The Aztec pantheon was headed by HUITZILOPOCHTLI. Other important deities included QUETZALCÓATL, Tezcatlipoca (god of the night sky) and Tlaloc (rain-god). Human sacrifice was a central feature of Aztec culture. They believed that the Sun would cease to rise unless constantly supplied with human blood. The MAYAS had a god of creation, Hunab Ku, remote from human affairs. His son, Itzamna, usually depicted as a toothless old man, was the inventor of drawing and writing, and also offered help to the sick. Another important god was Cukulan, the bird snake. The vast INCA empire of Peru worshiped Inti, the sun god and ancestor of the ruling dynasty. Another important deity was Viracocha, the creator god. Ancestor worship played a central role in Inca religious observances.

central bank Institution that regulates and sets policy for a nation's banking system. In the UK it is the BANK OF ENGLAND.

Central Criminal Court In the UK, CROWN COURT of central London, housed in the OLD BAILEY. The Central Criminal Court is responsible for trying all serious offences in the City of London and Greater London area.

Central Intelligence Agency (CIA) US government agency established to coordinate the intelligence activities of government departments and agencies responsible for US national security. It is directed by the National Security Council (NSC).

central nervous system (CNS) Term embracing the brain and spinal cord, as distinct from the PERIPHERAL NERVOUS SYSTEM. The CNS coordinates all nervous activity. *See also* NERVOUS SYSTEM

Central Powers Alliance of Germany and Austria-Hungary (plus Bulgaria and Turkey) during World War 1. The name distinguished them from their opponents (Britain, France and Belgium) in the W, plus Russia and others in the E.

central processing unit (CPU) Part of a digital computer circuit that controls all operations. In most modern computers, the CPU consists of one complex INTEGRATED CIRCUIT (IC), a chip called a MICROPROCESSOR. A CPU contains temporary storage circuits that hold data and instructions; an arithmetic and logic unit (ALU) that works out problems; and a control unit that organizes operations.

centre of gravity Point at which the WEIGHT of a body is considered to be concentrated and around which its weight is evenly balanced. In a uniform gravitational field, the centre of gravity is the same as the CENTRE OF MASS.

centre of mass Point at which the whole MASS of an object or group of objects is considered to be concentrated. A centre of mass would therefore exist for colliding elementary particles.

centrifugal force Force that is equal in magnitude and opposite in direction to the CENTRIPETAL FORCE.

centrifuge Rotating device used for separating substances. The denser substance is forced to the outside of a rotating container. A spin dryer uses this principle to remove water from clothes.

centripetal force In circular or curved motion, the force acting on an object that keeps it moving in a circular path. For example, if an object attached to a rope is swung in a circular motion above a person's head, the centripetal force acting on the object is the tension in the rope. The centripetal force acting on the Earth as it orbits the Sun is gravity.

cephalopoda Advanced class of predatory marine molluscs, including SQUID, NAUTILUS, OCTOPUS and CUTTLEFISH. Each has eight or more arms surrounding the mouth, which has a parrot-like beak. The nervous system is well developed, permitting great speed and alertness; the large eyes have an image-forming ability equal to that of vertebrates. Most squirt an inky fluid to alarm attackers. Cephalopods move by squirting water from their mantle edge. Members of this class vary dramatically in size. There are more than 600 species.

cephalosporin Class of ANTIBIOTIC drugs derived from fungi of the genus *Cephalosporium*. Similar to PENICILLIN, they are effective against a wide spectrum of BACTERIA.

cepheid variable One of an important class of variable stars that pulsate in a regular manner, accompanied by changes in luminosity. Cepheids can expand and contract up to 30% in each cycle.

ceramics Objects made of moistened clay that are shaped and then baked. Earthenware, terracotta, brick, tile, faience, majolica, stoneware and PORCELAIN are all ceramics. Glaze, a silicate preparation applied to the clay surface and fused to it during firing, is used to make the pottery non-porous and give it a smooth, colourful, decorative surface.

cereal Any grain of the grass family (Gramineae) grown as a food crop. Wheat, corn, rye, oats and barley are grown in temperate regions. Rice, millet, sorghum and maize require more tropical climates. Cereal cultivation was the basis of early civilizations, and with the development of high-yielding strains, remains the world's most important food source.

cerebellum Part of the brain located at the base of the CEREBRUM. It is involved in maintaining muscle tone, balance and finely coordinated movement.

cerebral cortex Deeply fissured outer layer of the CEREBRUM. The cortex (grey matter) is the most sophisticated part of the brain, responsible for the appreciation of sensation, initiating voluntary movement, emotions and intellect.

cerebral haemorrhage Form of stroke in which there is bleeding from a blood vessel in the BRAIN into the surrounding tissue. It is usually caused by ARTERIOSCLEROSIS and high blood pressure. Symptoms may vary from temporary numbness and weakness down one side of the body to deep coma.

cerebral hemispheres Lateral halves of the CEREBRUM, the largest parts of the BRAIN and the sites of higher thought.

cerebral palsy Disorder mainly of movement and coordination caused by damage to the BRAIN during or soon after birth. It may feature muscular spasm and weakness, lack of coordination and impaired movement or paralysis and deformities of the limbs.

cerebrospinal fluid Clear fluid that cushions the brain and spinal cord, giving some protection against shock. It is found between the two innermost meninges (membranes), in the four ventricles of the brain and in the central canal of the spinal cord.

cerebrum Largest and most highly developed part of the BRAIN, consisting of the CEREBRAL HEMISPHERES separated by a central fissure. It is covered by the CEREBRAL CORTEX. It coordinates all higher functions and voluntary activity.

Cerenkov radiation Light emitted when energetic particles travel through a transparent medium, such as water, at a speed higher than the velocity of light in that medium. This action is called the Cerenkov effect. It is named after Russian physicist Pavel Cerenkov who discovered it in 1934.

Ceres Largest ASTEROID and the first to be discovered (1801). Ceres' diameter measures 913km (567mi). It orbits in the main asteroid belt, at an average distance from the Sun of 414 million km (257 million mi).

cerium Soft, ductile, iron-grey metallic element (symbol Ce), the most abundant of the LANTHANIDE SERIES group, first isolated in 1803. The chief ore is monazite. It is used in alloys, catalysts, nuclear fuels, glass and as the core of carbon electrodes in arc lamps. Properties: at.no. 58; r.a.m. 140.12; r.d. 6.77; m.p. 798°C (1,468°F); b.p. 3,257°C (5,895 °F). The most common isotope is Ce^{140} (88.48%).

Cervantes, Miguel de (1547–1616) Spanish novelist, poet and dramatist. Cervantes published two volumes of his masterpiece *Don Quixote de la Mancha* (1605; 1615). Other works include two surviving plays and a collection of short stories, *Novelas Ejemplares* (1613).

cervical smear (pap test) Test for CANCER of the CERVIX. In this diagnostic procedure, a small sample of tissue is removed from the cervix and examined under a microscope for the presence of abnormal, pre-cancerous cells.

cervix Neck of the WOMB (uterus), projecting downwards into the VAGINA.

Ceylon *See* SRI LANKA

Cézanne, Paul (1839–1906) French painter. Cézanne exhibited at the first impressionist show in 1874. He later developed away from IMPRESSIONISM in favour of a deeper, more analytical approach using colour to model and express form. Figure paintings, such as *The Card Players* (1890–92), and *The Bathers* (1895–1905), as well as landscapes, such as *Mont Sainte Victoire* (1904–06), were painted on this principle. *See also* CUBISM, POST-IMPRESSIONISM

Chad Republic in N central Africa; the capital is NDJAMENA. **Land and climate** Chad is Africa's fifth largest country. Southern Chad is crossed by rivers that flow into Lake CHAD, on the W border with Nigeria. NE of Lake Chad, the Tibesti Mountains rise steeply from the sands of the SAHARA Desert. Central Chad has a hot tropical climate, with a marked dry season between November and April. The S is wetter. The far S contains forests, while central Chad is a region of SAVANNA, merging into the dry grasslands of the SAHEL. Long droughts, over-grazing and felling for firewood is turning the SAHEL into desert. This S creeping process of the Sahara is called DESERTIFICATION. **Economy** Hit by drought and civil war, Chad is one of the world's poorest countries. Subsistence agriculture employs 83% of the population. Groundnuts, millet, rice and sorghum are major crops in the wetter S. The most valuable crop is cotton, accounting for *c*.50% of Chad's exports. **History** North African nomads founded the Kanem empire here in about AD 700. In the 13th century the Islamic state of Bornu was established. In the late 19th century the region fell to Sudan. The French defeated the Sudanese in 1900, and in 1908 Chad became the largest province of French Equatorial Africa. In 1920 it became a separate colony. In 1960 Chad achieved full independence. Divisions between N and S rapidly surfaced.

CHAD
AREA: 1,284,000sq km (495,752sq mi)
POPULATION: 5,961,000
CAPITAL (POPULATION): Ndjamena (529,555)
GOVERNMENT: Transitional
ETHNIC GROUPS: Bagirmi, Kreish and Sara 31%, Sudanic Arab 26%, Teda 7%, Mbum 6%
LANGUAGES: French and Arabic (both official)
RELIGIONS: Islam 40%, Christianity 33%, traditional beliefs 27%
CURRENCY: CFA franc = 100 centimes

Rebellions have frequently rocked the country. Libya occupied the country in the early 1980s. A ceasefire took effect in 1987. In 1996 a new democratic constitution was adopted and multiparty elections were held.

Chad, Lake (Tchad) Lake in N central Africa, lying mainly in the Republic of Chad and partly in Nigeria, Cameroon and Niger. The chief tributary is the Chari River; the lake has no outlet. Depending on the season, the area of the surface varies from c.10,000–26,000sq km (3,850–10,000sq mi). Max. depth: 7.6m (25ft).

Chadwick, Sir James (1891–1974) British physicist who discovered and named the NEUTRON. Chadwick worked on radioactivity with Ernest RUTHERFORD at the Cavendish Laboratory, Cambridge. He received the 1935 Nobel Prize in physics. During World War 2, he moved to the USA to head British research for the Manhattan Project to develop the atomic bomb.

chaffinch Small songbird common throughout Europe. The male has blue and buff colours and a pink breast. Family Fringillidae; species *Fringilla coelebs.*

Chagall, Marc (1887–1985) Russian-French painter. His paintings, with their dreamlike imagery, considerably influenced SURREALISM. He worked in ceramics, mosaics, tapestry and theatre design.

Chain, Sir Ernst Boris (1906–79) British biochemist, b. Germany. He shared the 1945 Nobel Prize in physiology or medicine with Howard FLOREY and Alexander FLEMING for the isolation and development of penicillin as an antibiotic.

chain reaction Self-sustaining nuclear reaction in which one reaction is the cause of a second, the second of a third and so on.. The initial quantity of fissionable material must exceed the CRITICAL MASS. The explosion of an atom bomb is an uncontrolled chain reaction.

Chalcedon, Council of (451) Meeting of all the bishops of the Christian church in the city of Chalcedon, Asia Minor. It reaffirmed the doctrine of two natures (divine and human) in Christ and condemned NESTORIANISM.

chalcedony Microcrystalline form of quartz. When cut and polished, it is used by gem engravers. Some varieties contain impurities giving a distinctive appearance, such as AGATE (coloured bands), ONYX (striped) and bloodstone (dark green with red flecks).

chalcopyrite (copper pyrites) Opaque, brass-coloured, copper iron sulphide ($CuFeS_2$); the most important copper ore. It is found in sulphide veins and in igneous and contact metamorphic rocks. The crystals are tetragonal but often occur in masses. Hardness 3.5–4; s.g. 4.2.

chalk Mineral, mainly calcium carbonate ($CaCO_3$), formed from the shells of minute marine organisms. It is used in making putty, plaster and cement, and harder forms are occasionally used for building. Blackboard chalk is now made from calcium sulphate ($CaSO_4$) or chemically produced calcium carbonate.

Challenger expedition (1872–76) British expedition in oceanographic research. Six naturalists sailed nearly 128,000km (69,000 nautical mi) making studies of the life, water and seabed in the three main oceans.

Chamberlain, Joseph (1836–1914) British political leader. He entered Parliament as a Liberal in 1876. In 1880 he became president of the board of trade. In 1886 he resigned over GLADSTONE's Home Rule Bill and was leader of the Liberal Unionists from 1889. In 1895 he returned to government as colonial secretary, where his aggressive imperialist stance helped provoke the SOUTH AFRICAN WAR (1899). He resigned again in 1903 in order to freely argue for tariff reforms.

Chamberlain, (Arthur) Neville (1869–1940) British prime minister (1937–40). Son of Joseph CHAMBERLAIN. He entered Parliment in 1918 and later became Conservative prime minister. He confronted the threat to European peace posed by Hitler with a policy of APPEASEMENT and signed the MUNICH AGREEMENT (1938). After Hitler's invasion of Poland, Chamberlain declared war in September 1939. He was replaced by Winston CHURCHILL in May 1940.

chamber music Music intended for performance in intimate surroundings rather than a concert hall. It is usually written for two to eight instruments (or voices). The string quartet (two violins, viola and cello) is the most common arrangement.

chameleon Arboreal LIZARD, found chiefly in Madagascar, Africa and Asia, notable for its ability to change colour. The compressed body has a curled tail and bulging eyes. Length: 17–60cm (7–24in). Family Chamaeleontidae; genus *Chamaeleo.*

chamois Nimble, goat-like RUMINANT that lives in mountain ranges of Europe and W Asia. It has coarse, reddish-brown fur with a black tail and horns. Its skin is made into chamois leather. Length: up to 1.3m (50in); weight: 25–50kg (55–110lb). Family Bovidae; species *Rupicapra rupicapra*

chamomile (camomile) Low-growing, yellow- or white-flowered herb. Flowers of the European camomile (*Chamaemelum nobile*) are used to make herbal tea. Family Asteraceae; genus *Chamaemelum.*

Chamorro, Violeta Barrios de (1939–) Nicaraguan stateswoman, president (1990–96). She entered politics in 1978. In 1989, supported by the USA, she became leader of the right-wing coalition, the National Opposition Union (UNO). In February 1990 elections the UNO defeated the incumbent SANDINISTA government, and Chamorro became president.

Champagne District in NE France, made up of the Aube, Marne, Haute-Marne and Ardennes départements. The major city is REIMS. It is an arid region, renowned for its champagne, a sparkling white

125

wine that can only be produced in the district. Area: 25,606sq km (9,886sq mi). Pop. (1990) 1,347,800.

Champaigne, Philippe de (1602–74) French painter, b. Flanders. He was the greatest French portraitist of the 17th century and a remarkable religious painter. After 1643 his beliefs in JANSENISM produced religious paintings characterized by a serene realism.

Champlain, Samuel de (1567–1635) French explorer, founder of New France (Canada). Following the discoveries of CARTIER, he made 12 visits to New France. Besides seeking a NORTH-WEST PASSAGE, he encouraged settlement and the fur trade, established friendly relations with ALGO-NQUIN peoples and increased geographical knowledge. In 1608, he founded Quebec.

Champlain, Lake Lake that lies on the border of New York State and Vermont, USA, and extends into Quebec, Canada. It serves as a link in the Hudson-St Lawrence waterway. Area: 1,101sq km (435sq mi).

chancellor of the exchequer British minister responsible for national finances. The office evolved from the 13th-century clerk of the court of exchequer. Until the mid-19th century the office was inferior to the first lord of the treasury. Since the 1850s it has been probably the second most high-profile cabinet office (after the prime minister).

Chancery In England, court developed in the 15th century for the lord chancellor to deal with petitions from aggrieved persons for redress when no remedy was available in the COMMON LAW courts. By the mid-17th century, Chancery had become a second system of law (equity) rather than a reforming agency. By the Supreme Court of Judicature Act (1925) the court of Chancery was merged into the HIGH COURT OF JUSTICE, of which it is now known as the Chancery Divison.

Chandigarh City in NW India, at the foot of the Siwalik Hills, the joint capital of Punjab and Haryana states. It was designed by LE CORBUSIER and built in the 1950s. Pop. (1991) 511,000.

Chandler, Raymond Thornton (1888–1959) US crime writer. Many of his novels featuring the tough private eye Philip Marlowe, such as *The Big Sleep* (1939), *Farewell, My Lovely* (1940) and *The Long Goodbye* (1953), have been made into successful films.

Chandragupta Founder of the Maurya empire in India (r. c.321–297 BC) and grandfather of ASHOKA. He seized the throne of Magadha and defeated SELEUCUS, gaining dominion over most of N India and part of Afghanistan. His reign was characterized by religious tolerance.

Chandrasekhar, Subrahmanyan (1910–95) US astrophysicist, b. India. He formulated theories about the creation, life and death of stars, and calculated the maximum mass of a white dwarf star before it becomes a neutron star; the Chandrasekhar limit. He shared the 1983 Nobel Prize in physics with William Fowler.

Channel Islands Group of islands at the SW end of the English Channel, c.16km (10mi) off the W coast of France. The main islands are Jersey, Guernsey, Alderney and Sark; the chief towns are St. Helier on Jersey and St. Peter Port on Guernsey. A dependency of the British crown since the Norman Conquest, they were under German occupation during World War 2. They are divided into the administrative bailiwicks of Guernsey and Jersey, each with its own legislative assembly. The islands have a warm, sunny climate and fertile soil. The major industries are tourism and agriculture. Area: 194sq km (75sq mi). Pop. (1991) 142,949.

Channel Tunnel (Chunnel) Railway tunnel under the English Channel, 49km (31mi) long. In 1985 Eurotunnel, a joint French-English private company, were granted a 55-year concession to finance and operate the tunnel. The tunnel became operational in 1994. It consists of two railway tunnels and one service tunnel, and links Folkestone, S England, with Calais, N France.

chant Unaccompanied liturgical singing, especially of PSALMS. Anglican chant developed from the earlier Gregorian tones, which were melody formulas defining pitch relationships only. Later, harmonies were added to the melodies and note values designated to English texts of the psalms.

chaos theory Theory that attempts to describe and explain the highly complex behaviour of apparently chaotic or unpredictable systems which show an underlying order. The behaviour of some physical systems is impossible to describe using the standard laws of physics. They include complex machines, electrical circuits, and natural phenomena such as the weather. Chaos theory provides mathematical methods needed to describe chaotic systems, and even allows some general prediction of a systems' behaviour.

chapel Place of worship, such as a small church or separate area having its own altar within a church or cathedral. Many state and civic buildings, monasteries and convents often have chapels for worship. A chapel also denotes a place of worship subordinate to a larger parish church, or a building used for services by nonconformists.

Chaplin, Charlie (Sir Charles Edward Spencer) (1889–1977) British actor and filmmaker, often considered the greatest silent film comedian. In films such as *The Immigrant* (1917), he developed his tramp character; a figure of pathos in baggy trousers and bowler hat. Major films include *The Kid* (1920), *The Gold Rush* (1924), *City Lights* (1931), *Modern Times* (1936), *The Great Dictator* (1940) and *Limelight* (1952).

Chapman, George (1560–1634) English poet, dramatist and translator. His works include the poem *The Shadow of Night* (1594), the plays *The Blind Beggar of Alexandria* (1598) and *Bussy D'Ambois* (1604), and translations of Homer's *Iliad* (1611) and *Odyssey* (1614–15).

charcoal Porous form of CARBON, made traditionally by heating wood in the absence of air. Today charcoal is chiefly used for its absorptive properties, to decolourize food liquids such as syrups, and to separate chemicals.

Charcot, Jean Martin (1825–93) French physician and founder of neurology. He made classical studies of HYPNOSIS and HYSTERIA, and taught Pierre Janet and Sigmund FREUD. His work centred on discovering how behavioural symptoms of patients relate to neurological disorders.

charge-coupled device (CCD) Type of silicon CHIP designed to capture images. CCDs are found in video cameras, fax machines and digital cameras.

Charge of the Light Brigade (25 October 1854) British cavalry charge in the CRIMEAN WAR. It stemmed from Lord Lucan's misreading of an ambiguous order by the British commander, Lord Raglan. As a result, Lord Cardigan led the unsupported Light Brigade straight at a battery of Russian guns. More than 600 men took part, nearly half of whom were casualties.

charismatic movement Movement within the Christian church. It emphasizes the presence of the Holy Spirit in the life of an individual and in the work of the church. It is particularly associated with PENTECOSTAL CHURCHES.

Charlemagne (742–814) (lit. Charles the Great) King of the Franks (768–814) and Holy Roman emperor (800–14). The eldest son of PEPIN III (THE SHORT), he inherited half the Frankish kingdom (768), annexed the remainder on his brother Carloman's death (771), and built a large empire. In 800 he was consecrated as emperor by Pope Leo II, thus reviving the concept of the Roman empire. Charlemagne encouraged the intellectual awakening of the CAROLINGIAN RENAISSANCE, set up a strong central authority and maintained provincial control through court officials.

Charles II (the Bald) (823–77) King of the West Franks (843–77) and Holy Roman emperor (875–77). Younger son of Emperor LOUIS I, he was involved in the ambitious disputes of his elder brothers. The Treaty of Verdun (843) made him king of the West Franks, in effect the first king of France. Continuing family conflict, rebellion and Viking attacks resulted in territorial losses.

Charles IV (1316–78) Holy Roman emperor (1355–78) and king of Bohemia (1347–78). A skilful diplomat, he blocked or appeased his Wittelsbach and Habsburg rivals and improved relations with the papacy. In 1356 he introduced a stable system of imperial government. He ruled from PRAGUE, where he founded Charles University (1348) and built the Charles Bridge. Czech culture reached a peak under his patronage.

Charles V (1500–58) Holy Roman emperor (1519–56) and king of Spain, as Charles I (1516–56). He ruled the Spanish kingdoms, s Italy, the Netherlands and the Austrian Habsburg lands by inheritance, and, when elected emperor in succession to his grandfather, MAXIMILIAN I, he

headed the largest European empire since CHARLEMAGNE. In addition, the Spanish CONQUISTADORES made him master of a New World empire. In Germany, Charles, who saw himself as the defender of the Catholic Church, nevertheless recognized the need for reform, but other commitments prevented him following a consistent policy, and LUTHERANISM expanded.

Charles VI (1685–1740) Holy Roman emperor (1711–40) and king of Hungary as Charles III. His claim to the Spanish throne against the grandson of LOUIS XIV, PHILIP V, supported by the powers opposed to Louis, caused the War of the SPANISH SUCCESSION. After his election as emperor (1711), he gave up his Spanish claim as international support for it fell away.

Charles I (1887–1922) Austrian Emperor (1916–18) and king (as Charles IV) of Hungary (1916–18). When Hungary and Czechoslovakia declared their independence and Austria became a republic in 1918, Charles, the last HABSBURG emperor, was forced into exile in Switzerland.

Charles I (1600–49) King of England, Scotland and Ireland (r.1625–49). Although he accepted the PETITION OF RIGHT, Charles' insistence on the "divine right of kings" provoked conflict with Parliament and led him to rule without it for 11 years (1629–40). Relations steadily worsened, and Charles' attempt to arrest five leading opponents in the Commons precipitated the English CIVIL WAR. After the defeat of the Royalists, attempts by the parliamentary and army leaders to reach a compromise with the king failed, and he was tried and executed in January 1649.

Charles II (1630–85) King of England, Scotland and Ireland (1660–85). After the English CIVIL WAR (1642–51) he fled to France, but in 1650 was invited to Scotland by the COVENANTERS and crowned king in 1651. Charles' attempted invasion of England was repulsed by CROMWELL, and he was forced back into exile. In 1660 Charles issued the Declaration of Breda, in which he promised religious toleration and an amnesty for his enemies. Parliament agreed to the Declaration and Charles was crowned king in May 1660, ushering in the RESTORATION. Charles' support of LOUIS XIV led to a war with the Netherlands (1672–74). He clashed with Parliament, over both the war and his support of the Catholics. Unable to resolve his differences with Parliament, Charles dissolved it and ruled with financial support from Louis XIV. Known as the Merry Monarch, Charles had many mistresses (including Nell Gwyn), but left no legitimate heir.

Charles V (the Wise) (1337–80) King of France (1364–80). He regained most of the territory previously lost to the English during the HUNDRED YEARS WAR, stabilized the coinage, and endeavoured to suppress anarchy and revolt. He encouraged literature and art, and built the BASTILLE.

Charles VI (the Mad) (1368–1422) King of

127

France (1380–1422). After ruling effectively for four years, Charles suffered recurrent bouts of insanity. English victories at Agincourt (1415) and elsewhere forced Charles to sign the Treaty of Troyes (1420), acknowledging HENRY V of England as his successor.

Charles VII (1403–61) King of France (1422–61). The son of CHARLES VI, he was excluded from the throne by the Treaty of Troyes, but gained power as dauphin s of the River Loire when Charles VI died, while the N remained in English hands. With the support of JOAN OF ARC, he checked the English at Orléans and was crowned king at Reims (1429). The Treaty of Arras (1435) ended the hostility of Burgundy, and by 1453 the English had been driven out of most of France.

Charles VIII (1470–98) King of France (1483–98). Obsessed with gaining the kingdom of NAPLES, he invaded Italy in 1494, beginning the long Italian Wars, and in 1495 he entered Naples. A league of Italian states, the Papacy and Spain forced him to retreat.

Charles IX (1550–74) King of France (1560–74). Charles succeeded his brother FRANCIS II in 1560, and his mother CATHERINE DE' MEDICI became regent. Her authority waned when, in 1571, the young king fell under the influence of Gaspard de Coligny, leader of the HUGUENOTS. Coligny and thousands of his followers were slain in the SAINT BARTHOLOMEW'S DAY MASSACRE (1572), ordered by Charles at the instigation of his mother.

Charles X (1757–1836) King of France (1824–30). Brother of LOUIS XVI and Louis XVIII, he fled France at the outbreak of the FRENCH REVOLUTION (1789). He remained in England until the BOURBON restoration (1814). In 1825 he signed a law indemnifying émigrés for land confiscated during the Revolution. In 1830 he issued the July Ordinance, which restricted suffrage and press freedom, and dissolved the newly elected chamber of deputies. The people rebelled and Charles was forced to abdicate.

Charles III (1716–88) King of Spain (1759–88) and of Naples and Sicily (1735–59), the son of PHILIP V and Elizabeth Farnese. He conquered Naples and Sicily in 1734, and inherited the Spanish crown in 1759 from his half-brother Ferdinand VI. Allied with France in the SEVEN YEARS WAR, he received LOUISIANA in 1763.

Charles X (1622–60) King of Sweden (1654–60). His efforts to complete Swedish diminution of the Baltic resulted in a reign of continuous military activity. He invaded Poland unsuccessfully and twice invaded Denmark. He established the natural frontiers in Scandinavia, recovering the s provinces of Sweden from Denmark.

Charles XII (1682–1718) King of Sweden (1697–1718). Charles XII was one of the greatest military leaders in European history. He defeated Denmark, Poland, Saxony and Russia in a series of brilliant campaigns. Leading the battle, he destroyed the army of PETER I (THE GREAT) at Narva (1700). In 1708 he renewed his assault on Russia, but his army, depleted by the severe winter, was decisively defeated at Poltava (1709). Weakened by war and opposed by numerous enemies, he was killed while fighting in Norway.

Charles XIV (1763–1844) (Jean Baptiste Bernadotte) King of Sweden (1810–44), b. France. He fought in the French Revolution and was chosen by the Swedish legislature in 1810 to succeed Charles XIII. In the Treaty of Kiel, he forced Denmark to cede Norway to Sweden, and became king of Norway as Charles III John (1818–44). He joined the Allies against Napoleon at the Battle of Leipzig (1814). His subsequent reign brought peace and prosperity to Sweden.

Charles Edward Stuart See STUART, CHARLES EDWARD

Charles (Prince of Wales) (1948–) Eldest son of Elizabeth II and heir to the British throne. He married Lady DIANA Spencer in 1981. A fairy-tale marriage rapidly and publicly disintegrated. Their eldest son, Prince William (b.1982), is second in line to the throne. Prince Charles is well-known for his work with charities such as the Prince's Trust and his advocacy of COMMUNITY ARCHITECTURE.

Charles' law Volume of a gas at constant pressure is directly proportional to its absolute temperature. As temperature increases, the volume of a gas also increases at a constant pressure. The relationship was discovered by a French scientist Jacques Charles in 1787. Joseph GAY-LUSSAC established it more accurately in 1802.

Charlton, Sir Bobby (Robert) (1937–) Manchester United and England footballer. In 1966 he was voted European Footballer of the Year and was a member of England's World Cup winning team. He won 106 international caps, scoring an English record of 49 goals. His older brother, Jack (1935–), also a member of England's World Cup winning squad, went into club management and led the Republic of Ireland national team to remarkable success before retiring in 1996.

Charon In Greek mythology, boatman of the Lower World who ferried the souls of the dead across the STYX to HADES.

Charpentier, Gustave (1860–1956) French composer. His best-known compositions are the operas *Louise* (1900) and *Julien* (1913), and the orchestral *Impressions d'Italie*.

Chartism (1838–48) British working class movement for political reform. Combining the discontent of industrial workers with the demands of radical artisans, the movement adhered to the People's Charter (1838), which demanded electoral reform, including universal male suffrage. As well as local riots and strikes, the Chartists organized mass petitions (1839, 1842, 1848). The movement faded away after a major demonstration in 1848.

Chartres Town on the Eure River, NW France; capital of Eure-et-Loire département. The stained glass and sculptures in the 12th–13th century gothic Cathedral of Notre Dame make it one of Europe's finest cathedrals. It is a world heritage site. Industries: brewing, leather, agricultural equipment, radio and television parts. Pop. (1990) 41,850.

Charybdis In Greek mythology, a female monster of the Straits of Messina, opposite SCYLLA. Daughter of Poseidon and Gaea, Zeus hurled her into the sea for stealing Heracles' cattle. A whirlpool formed where she lay under water.

Chateaubriand, François René, Vicomte de (1768–1848) French writer and diplomat, whose works contributed to French ROMANTICISM. *The Genius of Christianity* (1802) was a reaction to ENLIGHTENMENT attacks on Catholicism and established his literary reputation. *Atala* (1801) and *René* (1805) are tragic love stories set in the American wilderness. After 1803 he held important diplomatic posts for both Napoleon and the Bourbons and was minister of foreign affairs (1823–24).

Chatterton, Thomas (1752–70) English poet and forger of antiquities. He achieved posthumous fame for poems such as *Bristowe Tragedie* and *Mynstrelles Songe*, supposedly composed by Thomas Rowley, an imaginary 15th-century monk. An erratic talent, his early suicide established him as a hero for the Romantic movement.

Chaucer, Geoffrey (1346–1400) English medieval poet. His writings are remarkable for their range, narrative sense, power of characterization and humour. They include *The Book of the Duchess* (1369), *The House of Fame* (*c*.1375), *The Parliament of Fowls* and *Troilus and Criseyde* (both *c*.1385). His most famous and popular work is *The Canterbury Tales* (*c*.1387–1400), an extraordinarily varied collection of narrative poems, each told by one of a group of pilgrims while travelling to the shrine of Thomas á Becket.

Chávez, Cesar Estrada (1927–93) US labour leader. Born of Mexican-American parents, Chavez migrated to California as a field worker. In 1962 he founded the National Farm Workers Association (NFWA), which in 1966 merged with the Agricultural Workers Organizing Committee of the AFL-CIO, to become the United Farm Workers Organizing Committee. In 1968–70 he led a successful national boycott of California grapes, and later a lettuce boycott.

Chechenya (formerly, Checheno-Ingush Republic) Republic of the Russian Federation, in the N Caucasus; the capital is GROZNY. Chechen people, who are Sunni Muslims, constitute 50% of the population and 40% live in urban areas. Grozny oil field is a major source of Russian oil. The Chechen people fiercely resisted tsarist Russia's conquest of the Caucasus, even after absorption in 1859. In the 1920s separate autonomous regions were created by the Soviet Union for the Chechen and Ingush peoples. In 1934 the two were united to form a single republic. The republic was dissolved in 1943–44 because of alleged collaboration with the

German occupying forces in World War 2 butwas reconstituted in 1957. In 1991 the Checheno-Ingush Republic split in two. A declaration of independence from the Russian Federation was not recognized by the Russian government. In December 1994, following a period of bloody internal strife, Russia invaded but met fierce resistance. In February 1995, Russian troops completed the capture of Grozny after almost 25,000 civilian deaths. A protracted guerrilla war, hostage-taking and civilian casualties continued. Industries: oil refining and equipment, chemicals. Area: 19,301sq km (7,452sq mi). Pop. (1992) 1,308,000.

cheese Food made by curdling milk and then processing the curd. The commonest source is cows' milk. Blue cheeses are pierced in order to channel air to a reactive fungus previously introduced. The simplest product is cottage cheese, formed when skimmed milk coagulates.

cheetah Spotted large CAT found in hot, arid areas of Africa, the Middle East and India. It has a tawny brown coat with round black spots. Capable of running at more than 95km/h (60mph), it hunts gazelles and antelopes by sight. Length: body: 140–150cm (55–60in); tail: 75–80cm (30–32in); weight: 60kg (132lb). Family Felidae; subfamily Acinonchinae; species *Acinonyx jubatus*.

Cheever, John (1912–82) US short-story writer and novelist. His works satirize the morals of American suburban life, particularly 1940s Manhattan. His novel *The Wapshot Chronicle* (1957) won a National Book award and its sequel, *The Wapshot Scandal* (1964), was also well-received. His short-story collection *The Stories of John Cheever* (1978) won a Pulitzer Prize.

Cheka First secret police force in the Soviet Union. Formed shortly after the Russian Revolution (1917), it had a wide-ranging role during the ensuing civil war. A ferocious reign of terror alienated many Bolshevik organizations and it was disbanded in 1922, replaced first by the GPU and then the KGB.

Chekhov, Anton Pavlovich (1860–1904) Russian dramatist, who worked closely with Konstantin STANISLAVSKY at the MOSCOW ART THEATRE. His major plays, *The Seagull* (1896), *Uncle Vanya* (1897), *The Three Sisters* (1901) and *The Cherry Orchard* (1904), display a deep understanding of human nature and a fine blend of comedy and tragedy. Characters often reveal as much by what they leave unsaid as the subtleties of the dialogue reveal.

chemical bonds Mechanisms that hold together atoms to form molecules. There are several types which arise either from the attraction of unlike charges or from the formation of stable configurations through electron-sharing. The main types are IONIC, COVALENT, metallic and HYDROGEN bonds.

chemical engineering Application of engineering principles to the making of chemical products on an industrial scale. Unit processes of chemical engineering include oxidation and reduction, nitration and sulphonation, electrolysis, polymerization, ion exchange and fermentation.

chemical equation Set of symbols used to represent a CHEMICAL REACTION. Equations show how atoms are rearranged as a result of a reaction, with reactants on the left-hand side and products on the right-hand side.

chemical equilibrium Balance in a REVERSIBLE REACTION, when two opposing reactions proceed at constant equal rates with no net change in the system.

chemical reaction Change or process in which chemical substances convert into other substances. This involves the breaking and formation of CHEMICAL BONDS. Reaction mechanisms include endothermic, exothermic, replacement, combination, decomposition and oxidation reactions.

chemical warfare Use of chemical weapons such as poison and nerve gases, defoliants and herbicides. *See also* BIOLOGICAL WARFARE

chemistry Branch of science concerned with the properties, structure and composition of substances and their reactions with one another. The major division in chemistry is between organic and inorganic. **Inorganic** chemistry studies the preparation, properties and reactions of all chemical elements and their compounds, except those of CARBON. **Organic** chemistry studies the reactions of carbon compounds, which are *c.*100 times more numerous than nonorganic ones. **Analytical** chemistry deals with the composition of substances. PHYSICAL CHEMISTRY deals with the physical properties of substances, such as their boiling and melting points.

chemoreceptor Tiny region on the outer membrane of some biological cells that is sensitive to chemical stimuli. The chemoreceptor transforms a stimulus from an external molecule into a sensation, such as smell or taste.

chemotherapy Treatment of a disease (usually cancer) by a combination of chemical substances, or DRUGS, that kill or impair disease-producing cells or organisms in the body. Specific drug treatment was first introduced in the early 1900s by Paul EHRLICH.

Chernobyl (Ukrainian, Chornobyl) City on the Pripyat River, N central Ukraine. It is 20km (12mi) from the Chernobyl power plant. On 26 April 1986 an explosion in one of the reactors released 8 tonnes of radioactive material into the atmosphere. Fallout spread across E and N Europe, contaminating much agricultural produce. Data on the long-term effects of contamination are inconclusive, though 25,000 local inhabitants have died prematurely.

Chernomyrdin, Viktor (1938–) Russian politician, prime minister (1992–). A member of the Central Committee of the Communist Party (1986–90), he became prime minister despite the

objections of Boris YELTSIN. Chernomyrdin broadly supported economic reform, but was critical of the pace of privatization.

Cherokee Largest tribe of Native Americans in the USA, members of the Iroquoian language family. They migrated S into the Appalachian region of Tennessee, Georgia and the Carolinas. Today, *c.*47,000 Cherokee descendants now live in Oklahoma and *c.*3,000 in North Carolina.

cherry Widely grown fruit tree of temperate regions, probably native to W Asia and E Europe. Various types are grown for their edible fruit – round yellow, red or almost black with a single round stone. The wood is used in furniture. Height: to 30m (100ft). Family Rosaceae; genus *Prunus*; there are about 50 species.

Cheshire County in NW England, bounded W by Wales and N by Greater Manchester and Merseyside. The county town is CHESTER. Cheshire is drained by the Mersey, Weaver and Dee rivers. It is an important industrial and dairy farming region, noted for its cheese. Industries: salt mining, chemicals, textiles, motor vehicles, oil refining. Area: 2,331sq km (900sq mi). Pop. (1991) 956,616.

chess Board game of strategic attack and defence, played on a 64-square chequered board. Two players start with 16 pieces each, white or black, set out along the outer two ranks (rows) of the board. With a black square in the left corner, white's pieces are set out: rook (castle), knight, bishop, queen, king, bishop, knight, rook. Black's pieces align directly opposite. Pawns stand on the second rank. Chess originated in ancient India. Modern chess is a high-profile, international game.

Chester City and county district on the River Dee, NW England, Cheshire. A Roman garrison town, it has been of strategic importance throughout British history. It was a major port until the Dee became silted and Liverpool's port facilities were expanded. Industries: tourism, engineering. Area: 448sq km (173sq mi). Pop. (1991) 115,971.

Chesterton, G.K. (Gilbert Keith) (1874–1936) British essayist, novelist, biographer and poet. Best known for his *Father Brown* stories, which began in 1911, he also wrote literary criticism and essays on social and political themes. His novels include *The Napoleon of Notting Hill* (1904) and *The Man who was Thursday* (1908).

chestnut Deciduous tree native to temperate areas of the Northern Hemisphere. It has lance-shaped leaves and furrowed bark. Male flowers hang in long catkins, females are solitary or clustered at the base of catkins. The prickly husked fruits open to reveal two or three edible nuts. Family Fagaceae; genus *Castanea*; there are four species. *See also* HORSE CHESTNUT

Cheyenne Native North American tribe. Tribal competition forced them to migrate W from Minnesota along the Cheyenne River. The tribe split in *c.*1830, with the Northern Cheyenne remaining near the Platte River, and the Southern Cheyenne settling near the Arkansas River. War broke out following a US army massacre of Cheyenne (1864). General CUSTER crushed Southern Cheyenne resistance, but the Northern Cheyenne helped in his defeat at the Battle of Little Bighorn. They eventually surrendered in 1877, and were forced to move to Oklahoma, then to Montana, where c.2,000 Cheyenne remain.

Cheyenne State capital of Wyoming. Founded in 1867, it became a leading town in the Old West, famous for its lawlessness and connections with figures such as Buffalo Bill, Calamity Jane and Wild Bill Hickok. Industries: packing plants, oil refineries. Pop. (1990) 50,008.

Chiang Kai-shek (1887–1975) (Jiang Jieshi) Chinese nationalist leader. After taking part in resistance against the QING dynasty, he joined the KUOMINTANG, succeeding SUN YAT-SEN as leader (1925). From 1927 he purged the party of communists and headed a Nationalist government in Nanking. Chiang was elected president of China (1948), but in 1949 the victorious communists led by MAO ZEDONG drove his government into exile in TAIWAN, where he remained president until his death.

Chiangmai City in NW Thailand. Founded in the 13th century, it is the commercial, cultural and religious centre of N Thailand. It has air, rail and road links with BANGKOK and is an export point for local produce. The city's own manufactures include pottery, silk and wooden articles. Pop. (1991 est.) 161,541.

chiaroscuro Term for the opposition of light and dark in painting and drawing. CARAVAGGIO and REMBRANDT were masters of the dramatic use of chiaroscuro.

Chibcha (Muisca) Late prehistoric culture in South America. Bogotá and Tunja were the main centres. The Chibcha culture flourished between 1000–1541 and rivalled the INCA in political sophistication. The inhabitants, c.750,000, developed remarkable city-states. The Chibcha were conquered by the Spanish (1536–41). In modern times, Chibcha refers to a Native American language family, whose speakers inhabit S Panama and N Colombia.

Chicago City on the SW shore of Lake Michigan. NE Illinois, USA. In the late 18th century it was a trading post. With the construction of the Erie Canal and railways, and the opening up of the prairies, Chicago attracted settlers and industry. It is the major industrial, commercial, cultural and shipping centre of the Midwest. The world's first skyscraper was built here in 1885. Industries: steel, chemicals, machinery, food processing, metal working. Pop. (1990) 2,783,726.

Chichester, Sir Francis (1901–72) English yachtsman and aviator. He embarked on a solo flight between England and Australia in a Gypsy Moth biplane (1929). He began ocean sailing in the 1950s and won his first solo transatlantic race

in 1960. In 1966–67 in *Gypsy Moth IV* he circumnavigated the globe single-handed.

Chickasaw Muskogean-speaking NATIVE AMERICANS, who originated in Mississippi-Tennessee. In the 1830s the Chickasaw were resettled in Indian Territory (now Oklahoma) when their numbers were c.5,000. Pop. (1995) c.9,000.

chicken *See* POULTRY

chickenpox (varicella) Infectious disease of childhood caused by a virus of the HERPES group. After an incubation period of two to three weeks, a fever develops and red spots (which later develop into blisters) appear on the trunk, face and limbs. Recovery is usual within a week, although the possibility of contagion remains until the last scab has been shed.

chickpea (dwarf pea, garbanzo, chich or gram) Bushy annual plant cultivated from antiquity in S Europe and Asia for its pea-like seeds. It is now also grown widely in the Western Hemisphere. The seeds are boiled or roasted before eating. Family Fabaceae/Leguminosae; species *Cicer arietinum*.

chicory Perennial weedy plant whose leaves are cooked and eaten, or served raw in salads. The fleshy roots are dried and ground for mixing with (or a substitute for) COFFEE. Height: 1.5m (5ft). Family Asteraceae/Compositae; species *Chichorium intybus*.

chigger (harvest mite or red bug) Tiny, red larva of some kinds of MITES found worldwide. Adults lay eggs on plants and hatched larvae find an animal host. On humans their bites cause a severe rash and itching. Length: 0.1–16mm (0.004–0.6in). Order Acarina; family Trombiculidae.

childbirth *See* LABOUR

child psychology *See* DEVELOPMENTAL PSYCHOLOGY

Children's Crusade Name given to two 13th-century CRUSADES by children. One group of French children were offered free transport from Marseilles to the Holy Land, but were sold as slaves in North Africa. Another group of German children bound for the Holy Land travelled to Italy, where the crusade floundered, many dying of starvation and disease.

Chile Republic in SW South America; the capital is SANTIAGO. **Land and climate** Chile stretches c.4,260km (2,650mi) from N to S, while the maximum E-W distance is only about 430km (267mi). The high Andes mountains form the country's E borders with Argentina and Bolivia. To the W are basins and valleys, and natural uplands overlooking the shore. EASTER ISLAND lies 3,500km (2,200mi) off Chile's W coast. The Central Valley, which contains Santiago, Valparaiso and Concepción, is by far the most densely populated region. In the far S, the Strait of MAGELLAN separates the Chilean mainland from TIERRA DEL FUEGO, a bleak group of islands divided between Chile and Argentina. Punta Arenas is the world's southern-

CHILE
AREA: 756,950sq km (292,258sq mi)
POPULATION: 13,599,000
CAPITAL (POPULATION): Santiago (4,385,381)
GOVERNMENT: Multiparty republic
ETHNIC GROUPS: Mestizo 92%, Native American 7%
LANGUAGES: Spanish (official)
RELIGIONS: Christianity (Roman Catholic 81%, Protestant 6%)
CURRENCY: Peso = 100 centavos

most city. Chile's great N-S extent, ranging from the tropics in the N to 55°50' S at Cape HORN, gives it a variety of climates. Industrial growth has led to widespread deforestation. **Economy** Chile is a lower-middle income developing country. Mining is important. Chile is the world's largest producer of copper ore. The industry is based in N Chile. Minerals dominate exports, but the most valuable activity is manufacturing and the main products include iron and steel, wood products, transport equipment, cement and textiles. Agriculture employs 18% of the population; the chief crop is wheat. Climate and landscape combine to make Chile dependent on imports for over 50% of its food consumption. Yet Chile's wine industry is expanding rapidly, and its fishing industry is the world's fifth largest. Chile's economy has become one of the strongest in Latin America. **History and politics** ARAUCANICIANS reached the S tip of South America at least 8,000 years ago. In 1520 the Portuguese navigator Ferdinand MAGELLAN became the first European to sight Chile. In 1541 Pedro de Valdiva founded Santiago. Chile became a Spanish colony. In 1818 Bernado O'HIGGINS proclaimed Chile's independence. In the late 19th century, Chile's economy rapidly industrialized but a succession of autocratic regimes and its dependence on nitrate exports hampered growth. In 1964 Eduardo Frei of the Christian Democratic Party was elected. He embarked on a process of reform. In 1970 Salvador ALLENDE was elected president. He introduced many socialist policies, such as land reform and the nationalization of industries. In 1973 soaring inflation and public disturbances led to a military coup, with covert US support. Allende and many of his supporters were executed. General Augusto PINOCHET assumed control and instigated a series of sweeping market reforms and pro-Western foreign policy initiatives. His regime was characterized by repression and human-rights violations. Free elections were held in 1989. Patricio Aylwyn was elected president, but Pinochet remained important as commander of the armed forces. **Recent events** During the 1990s Chile's economy has improved and a process of social liberalization continues. Pinochet remained commander-in-chief until 1997, and tension between government and army continues.

chilli (chili) Hot red PEPPER. It is an annual with oval leaves and white or greenish-white flowers that produce red or green seedpods. Cayenne pepper comes from the same plant. Height: 2– 2.5m (6–8ft). Family Solanaceae; species *Capsicum annuum*.

Chimera In Greek mythology, a female monster with a lion's head, goat's body and dragon's tail. She was the sister of Cerberus, Hydra and the SPHINX, and slain by Bellerophon.

chimpanzee Intelligent great APE of tropical Africa. Chimpanzees are mostly black and powerfully built. A smaller chimpanzee of the Congo region is sometimes classified as a separate species. Chimpanzees often nest in trees, but spend most of their day searching for fruit and nuts. They are communicative and highly social. Height: *c*.1.3m (4.5ft); weight: *c*.68kg (150lb). Species *Pan troglodytes*, Congo *Pan paniscus*. Family Pongidae. *See also* PRIMATES

Ch'in Alternative transliteration for the QIN dynasty

China Republic in E Asia; the capital is BEIJING. **Land and climate** China is the world's third-largest country (after Russia and Canada). Most people live on the E coastal plains, in the highlands and the fertile river valleys of the HUANG HE and YANGTZE, Asia's longest river, 6,380km (3,960mi). Western China includes the bleak Tibetan plateau, bounded by the HIMALAYAS (the world's highest mountain range). EVEREST, the world's highest peak, lies on the Nepal-Tibet border. Other ranges include the TIAN SHAN and Kunlun Shan. China also has deserts, such as the GOBI on the Mongolian border. BEIJING in NE China has cold winters and warm summers, with moderate rainfall. SHANGHAI, in the E central region, has milder winters and more rain. The SE region has a wet, subtropical climate. In the W, the climate is severe. **Economy** China has one of the world's largest economies. Agriculture employs *c*.70% of the population. It has vast mineral resources and a huge steel industry. **History and politics** The first documented dynasty was the SHANG (*c*.1523–*c*.1027 BC), when bronze casting was perfected. The ZHOU dynasty (*c*.1030–221 BC) was the age of Chinese classical literature, in particular CONFUCIUS and LAO TZU. China was unified by QIN SHIHUANGDI, whose tomb near XIAN contains the famous Terracotta Army. The QIN dynasty (221–206 BC) also built the majority of the GREAT WALL. The HAN dynasty (202 BC–AD 220) developed the empire, a bureaucracy based on CONFUCIANISM, and introduced BUDDHISM. The T'ANG dynasty (618–907) was a golden era of artistic achievement in CHINESE ART and CHINESE LITERATURE. GENGHIS KHAN conquered most of China in the 1210s and established the MONGOL empire; KUBLAI KHAN founded the YÜAN dynasty (1271–1368), a period of dialogue with Europe. The MING dynasty (1368–1644) reestablished Chinese rule and is famed for its fine porcelain. The

Manchu QING dynasty (1644–1911) began by vastly extending the empire, but the 19th century was marked by foreign interventions, such as the OPIUM WAR (1839–42). Popular disaffection culminated in the BOXER REBELLION (1900). The last emperor (Henry PU YI) was overthrown in a revolution led by SUN YAT-SEN and a republic established. China rapidly fragmented between a Beijing government supported by warlords, and Sun Yat-sen's nationalist KUOMINTANG government in GUANGZHOU. The COMMUNIST PARTY OF CHINA initially allied with the nationalists. In 1926 CHIANG KAI-SHEK's nationalists emerged victorious and turned on their communist allies. In 1930 a rival communist government was established, but was uprooted by Kuomintang troops and began the LONG MARCH (1934). Japan, taking advantage of the turmoil, established the puppet state of MANCHUKUO (1932) under Henry Pu Yi. Chiang was forced into an alliance with the communists. Japan launched a full-scale invasion in 1937 and conquered much of N and E China. From 1941 Chinese forces, with Allied support, began to regain territory. At the end of World War 2, civil war resumed. The communists, with greater popular support, triumphed and the Kuomintang fled to TAIWAN. MAO ZEDONG established the People's Republic of China on 1 October 1949. Mao began to collectivize agriculture and nationalize industry. In 1958 the GREAT LEAP FORWARD was a five-year plan to revolutionize industrial production. The CULTURAL REVOLUTION (1966–76) mobilized Chinese youth against bourgeois and bureaucratic culture. By 1971 China had become a world power with a seat on the UN security council and its own nuclear capability. Following Mao's death (1976), a power struggle developed within the party leadership between the GANG OF FOUR and moderates led by DENG XIAOPING; the latter emerged victorious. Deng began a process of modernization, forging closer links with the West. **Recent events** In 1979 special economic zones were created to encourage inward investment. In 1989 student demands for greater liberal reforms were ruthlessly crushed in TIANANMEN SQUARE. In 1997 JIANG ZEMIN succeeded Deng as paramount leader.

CHINA
AREA: 9,596,960 sq km (3,705,386 sq mi)
POPULATION: 1,187,997,000
CAPITAL (POPULATION): Beijing (6,560,000)
GOVERNMENT: Single-party Communist republic
ETHNIC GROUPS: Han (Chinese) 92%, 55 minority groups
LANGUAGES: Mandarin Chinese (official)
RELIGIONS: The government encourages atheism, though Confucianism, Buddhism, Taoism and Islam are practised
CURRENCY: Renminbi (yuan) = 10 jiao = 100 fen

China Sea Western part of the Pacific Ocean, divided by Taiwan into the SOUTH CHINA SEA and the EAST CHINA SEA.

chinchilla Genus of small, furry RODENTS native to South America. Chinchillas were hunted almost to extinction. They are now bred in captivity for their long, close-textured and soft fur, the most expensive of all animal furs. Length: 23–38cm (9–15in); weight; 450–900g (1–2lb). Family Chinchillidae.

Chinese Group of languages spoken by c.95% of the population of China and by millions more in Taiwan, Hong Kong, Southeast Asia, and other countries. There are six major languages, which are not mutually intelligible; the most numerous is MANDARIN, spoken by c.66% of the Chinese population. All Chinese languages are written in a common non-alphabetic script, whose characters number in the thousands.

Chinese architecture Style that as early as the Neolithic period used columns to support roofs, faced houses south, and used bright colours. The characteristic Chinese roof with wide overhang and upturned eaves was probably developed in the ZHOU period. A walled complex with a central axis for temples and palaces was established in the HAN dynasty. The pagoda derives from Buddhist influences and dates from the 6th century.

Chinese art Longest pedigree of any school in world art, its earliest artefacts (painted pottery) date back to the late Neolithic period. By the time of the SHANG dynasty, native craftsmen were proficient at casting bronze and making jade carvings. Painting and sculpture were established during the HAN dynasty. The T'ANG dynasty marked China's artistic zenith. The SUNG dynasty saw the introduction of the first true porcelain. Important technical advances, most notably in the application of coloured ENAMELS, took place during the MING period. Chinese porcelain became highly valuable in European markets, a trend which accelerated under the QING dynasty. The advent of communism created a rift in this long tradition, as artists adopted Soviet-inspired, SOCIALIST REALISM.

Chinese literature Earliest literary texts date from the ZHOU dynasty. This period produced the canonical writings of CONFUCIANISM. During the HAN dynasty, elaborate *fu* prose poems praising the dynasty flourished. The T'ANG dynasty marked the golden age of Chinese literature. Li Po, Tu Fu and Wang Wei were the outstanding poets of the period. In the SUNG dynasty, the novel and drama came into being. From the late 17th to early 19th century, much emphasis was placed on formal technique. The lyric poem has been the dominant form in Chinese literature. It is normally philosophical, with a quietness of tone and an emphasis on simple experiences. In the first half of the 20th century, Chinese literature greatly modernized. During the CULTURAL REVOLUTION, strict censorship was imposed. Recent years have seen a slight liberalization.

Chinese mythology During the SHANG dynasty,

133

a supreme god, Shang Ti, ruled in heaven as Chinese sovereigns did on earth. During the ZHOU dynasty, Shang Ti was replaced by T'ien ("Heaven"). The emperor, the "Son of Heaven", was responsible for maintaining harmony on earth and assumed the role of both priest and monarch. Later, in conjunction with popular mythology, there existed a formal Chinese pantheon ruled by a father-god, the August Personage of Jade. His heavenly court was a replica of the imperial court at BEIJING.

Chinese theatre Traditional theatre is highly stylised and the symbolism of the various dramatic parts, the actors' costumes, make-up and gestures are considered of far greater importance than the dialogue. Although much recent Chinese theatre has become Westernised, the old dramatic tradition remains enormously popular.

Ch'ing Alternative transliteration for the QING dynasty.

chip Piece of SILICON etched to carry tiny electrical circuits. Silicon chips are at the heart of most electronic equipment. Chips are etched, layer by layer, onto slivers of extremely pure silicon. Each layer is "doped" to give it particular electrical properties, and the combination of different layers form components such as TRANSISTORS and DIODES. *See also* CHARGE-COUPLED DEVICE (CCD)

chipmunk Small, ground-dwelling SQUIRREL native to North America and Asia. It carries nuts, berries and seeds in cheek pouches, to store underground. Most chipmunks are brown with one or more black-bordered, light stripes. Length: 13–15cm (5–6in) excluding the tail. Family Sciuridae; genera *Eutamias* and *Tamias*.

Chippendale, Thomas (1718–79) British furniture designer. Much of his fame rested upon the wide circulation of his *The Gentleman and Cabinet Maker's Directory* (1754–62), a trade catalogue illustrating the designs of his factory. Many of Chippendale's finest pieces were marquetry and inlaid items in neo-Classical vein.

Chirac, Jacques (1932–) French statesman, president (1995–). Elected to the National Assembly in 1967, he held a number of ministerial posts. In 1974 he was appointed prime minister by GISCARD D'ESTAING. In 1977 he became mayor of Paris. After the 1986 election, he was again prime minister, this time under MITTERRAND. Despite losing the 1988 presidential election, he successfully reran in 1995.

Chirico, Giorgio de (1888–1978) Italian painter, b. Greece. He painted still lifes and empty, dream-like landscapes in exaggerated perspective. In the 1930s he repudiated all modern art in favour of paintings in the style of the Old Masters. *See also* SURREALISM

Chiron In Greek mythology, wisest and most famous CENTAUR. He taught many of the lesser gods and heroes, including ACHILLES, and was accidently killed by Hercules with a poisoned arrow. He was placed among the stars by ZEUS.

chiropractic Non-orthodox medical practice based on the theory that the nervous system integrates all of the body's functions, including defence against disease. Chiropractors aim to remove nerve interference by manipulations of the affected musculo-skeletal parts, particularly in the spinal region.

Chisinau (Kishinev) Capital of Moldova, in the centre of the country, on the Byk River. Founded in the early 15th century, it came under Turkish and then Russian rule. Romania held the city from 1918–40 when it was annexed by the Soviet Union. Industries: plastics, rubber, textiles, tobacco. Pop. (1994) 700,000.

chitin Hard, tough substance that occurs widely in nature, particularly in the hard shells (exoskeletons) of arthropods such as crabs, insects and spiders. The walls of hyphae (microscopic tubes of fungi) are composed of slightly different chitin. Chemically chitin is a polysaccharide, derived from glucose.

Chittagong Seaport on the Karnaphuli River, near the Bay of Bengal, SE Bangladesh. It is Bangladesh's chief port. Industries: jute, tea, oil, engineering, cotton, iron and steel. Pop. (1991) 1,363,998.

chive Perennial herb whose long hollow leaves have an onion-like flavour used for seasoning. The flowers grow in rose-purple clusters. Family Liliaceae; species *Allium schoenoprasum*.

chlamydia Small, virus-like BACTERIA that live as PARASITES in animals and cause disease. One strain, *C. trachomatis*, is responsible for TRACHOMA and is also a major cause of pelvic inflammatory disease (PID) in women. *C. psittaci* causes PSITTACOSIS. Chlamydial infection is the most common SEXUALLY TRANSMITTED DISEASE in many developed countries.

chloride Salt of HYDROCHLORIC ACID or some organic compounds containing CHLORINE, especially those with the negative ion Cl⁻. The best-known example is common salt, sodium chloride (NaCl). Most chlorides are soluble in water, except mercurous and silver chlorides.

chlorine Common nonmetallic element (symbol Cl) that is one of the HALOGENS. It occurs in common salt (NaCl). It is a greenish-yellow poisonous gas extracted by the electrolysis of brine (salt water) and is widely used to disinfect drinking water and swimming pools, to bleach wood pulp and in the manufacture of plastics, chloroform and pesticide. Chemically it is a reactive element, and combines with most metals. Properties: at.no. 17; r.a.m. 35.453; m.p. 101°C (149.8°F); b.p. 34.6 °C (30.28°F). The most common isotope is Cl³⁵ (75.53%).

chlorofluorocarbon (CFC) Chemical compound in which hydrogen atoms of a hydrocarbon, such as an alkane, are replaced by atoms of fluorine, chlorine, carbon and sometimes bomine. CFCs are inert, stable at high temperatures and are odourless, colourless, nontoxic, noncorrosive and nonflammable. CFCs were widely used in aerosols, fire-extinguishers, refrigerators, and in the manufacture of foam plastics. CFCs slowly drift into the stratosphere and are broken down by the Sun's ultraviolet radiation into chlorine atoms that destroy the OZONE LAYER. Growing environmental concern led to a 1990 international agreement to reduce and eventually phase out the use of CFCs.

chloroform (trichloromethane) Colourless, volatile, sweet-smelling liquid ($CHCl_3$) prepared by the chlorination of methane. Formerly a major anaesthetic, it is used in the manufacture of fluoro-carbons, in cough medicines, for insect bites and as a solvent. Properties: r.d. 1.48; m.p. 63.5°C (82.3°F); b.p. 61.2°C (142.2°F).

chlorophyll Group of green pigments present in the CHLOROPLASTS of plants and ALGAE that absorb light for PHOTOSYNTHESIS. There are five types. Chlorophyll is similar in structure to HAEMOGLOBIN, with a magnesium atom replacing an iron atom.

chloroplast Microscopic green structure within a plant cell in which PHOTOSYNTHESIS takes place. The chloroplast contains internal membranes in which molecules of the light-absorbing pigment CHLOROPHYLL are embedded.

chocolate Originally a drink (introduced to Europe in the 1500s) produced from the seeds of the tropical tree *Theobroma cacao*. The seeds do not have the flavour or colour of chocolate until they have been fermented and roasted. The beans are then ground up to make chocolate powder. The first chocolate bar was produced in the late 1700s.

Choctaw One of the largest tribes of Musko-gean-speaking Native North Americans, located in SE Mississippi and part of Alabama. They are generally at peace with the settlers. A majority of the Choctaw moved to Oklahoma in 1830, where some 40,000 of their descendents still reside.

choir Group of singers who perform together as a musical unit. The earliest choirs were ecclesiastical and sang the PLAINSONG in church services. The beginnings of OPERA marked the development of the secular choir, or CHORUS.

Choiseul, Etienne François, Duc de (1719–85) French statesman, LOUIS XV's chief minister (1758–1770). As minister of foreign affairs, he negotiated the Family Compact (1761), allying the BOURBON rulers of France and Spain, and the Treaty of Paris (1763), in which France was forced to surrender French Canada and India to Britain.

cholera Infectious disease caused by the bacteri-um *Vibrio cholerae*, transmitted in contaminated water. Cholera, prevalent in many tropical regions, produces diarrhoea often accompanied by vomiting and muscle cramps. Untreated it can be fatal, but proper treatment, including fluid replacement and antibiotics, results in a high recovery rate. There is a vaccine.

cholesterol White, fatty STEROID, occurring in large concentrations in the brain, spinal cord and liver. It is synthesized in the liver, intestines and skin and is an intermediate in the synthesis of vit-amin D and many hormones.

Chomsky, (Avram) Noam (1928–) US pro-fessor of LINGUISTICS. He developed the concept of a transformational generative grammar. Chomsky believes that the human capacity for language is partially innate, unlike supporters of BEHAV-IOURISM. He has been a consistent critic of US imperialist tendencies and is the author of several books on politics and international relations.

Chopin, Frédéric François (1810–49) Polish composer for the piano. He studied in Warsaw, moving to Paris in 1831. He wrote two piano con-certos and three piano sonatas but is best known for his numerous short solo pieces.

choral music Music written for several voices. Choral compositions were originally religious, CAN-TATA and ORATORIO being the most usual forms. The foremost composer of cantatas was J.C. BACH and of oratorios HANDEL. Choral music varies greatly in size and style, from the small-scale, secular MADRI-GALS of the 16th century to the large-scale works of the 19th and 20th centuries, such as VERDI's *Requiem* (1874), ELGAR's *Dream of Gerontius* (1900) and the choral symphonies of MAHLER.

chord In music, the simultaneous occurrence of three or more musical tones of different pitch. *See also* HARMONY

chordata Name of a large phylum of VERTE-BRATES and some marine invertebrates, which, at some stage in their lives, have rod-like, cartilagi-nous supporting structures (NOTOCHORDS).

chorus In Greek tragedy, the *choros* danced and chanted commentary. Today, a chorus refers to a group of voices. *See also* CHOIR

Chou Alternative transliteration for the ZHOU dynasty.

Chrétien, Jean (Joseph-Jacques) (1934–) Canada's 20th prime minister (1993–). He became a member of Parliament in 1963 and held cabinet offices in Pierre TRUDEAU's government. In 1990 he became leader of the Liberal Party. His main challenge has been to reduce unemployment. He was reelected in 1997.

Chrétien de Troyes (active 1160–85) Romance writer of N France, noted for his tales of King Arthur. He influenced Geoffrey CHAUCER and Thomas MALORY, and wrote at least five romances, including *Lancelot*, *Yvain* and *Perceval*.

Christ (Gk. *christos*, anointed one) Epithet for the Messiah in Old Testament prophecies. Later applied to JESUS.

Christchurch City on South Island, New Zealand; main town of Canterbury. It was founded as a Church of England settlement (1850). Indus-tries: fertilizers, rubber, woollen goods, electrical goods, furniture. Pop. (1993) 312,600.

christening *See* BAPTISM

Christian Name by which a follower of JESUS CHRIST is known. The major Christian Churches regard belief in the divinity of Christ and the Holy TRINITY as the minimum requirement for a Christian.

Christian IV (1577–1648) King of Denmark and Norway (1588–1648). Despite a costly war with Sweden (1611–13) and his disastrous participation (1625–29) in the THIRTY YEARS WAR, he was a popular monarch. His reign brought economic prosperity, culture and he founded OSLO, Norway.

Christian X (1870–1947) King of Denmark (1912–47) and Iceland (1919–44). During his reign universal suffrage was established (1915) and social welfare policies consolidated. He tried to remain neutral during World War I and defied the Germans during occupation, 1940–45.

Christian Democrats Political group combining Christian conservative principles with progressive social responsibility. Christian Democrats have achieved power in many European countries, notably Germany and Italy. Its political principles include: individual responsibility allied with collective action; social equality within a welfare state; and progress through evolutionary change.

Christianity Religion based on faith in JESUS CHRIST as the Son of God. The orthodox Christian faith affirms belief in the TRINITY and in Christ's incarnation, atoning death on the cross, resurrection and ascension. The history of Christianity has been turbulent and often sectarian. The first major schism took place in 1054, when the eastern and western churches separated. The next occurred in the 16th-century REFORMATION, with the split of PROTESTANTISM and the ROMAN CATHOLIC CHURCH. The number of Christians in the world was estimated at more than 1,000 million (mid-1990s).

Christian Science (officially Church of Christ Scientist) Religious sect founded in 1879 by Mary Baker EDDY. Its followers believe that physical illness and moral problems can only be cured by spiritual and mental activity. Divine Mind is used as a synonym for God.

Christie, Dame Agatha Mary Clarissa (1891–1976) British author of detective stories. *The Mysterious Affair at Styles* (1920) introduced her most famous character, the detective Hercule Poirot. Other novels include *Murder on the Orient Express* (1934) and *And Then There Were None* (1939). Her plays include *The Mousetrap* (1952).

Christie, Linford (1960–) British athlete, b. Jamaica. He won 100m gold medals in the European championships (1986, 1990). He was awarded further gold medals for 100m, 200m and sprint relay in the European Cup in 1987, 1991, 1992 and 1994. In the 1992 Olympic Games, he won the 100m gold medal. In 1993 he won another gold in the world championship. His tally also includes golds in the Commonwealth Games (1990, 1994). He retired in 1997.

Christina (1626–89) Queen of Sweden (1632–54). She brought foreign scholars, such as DESCARTES, to her court. Ruling a Lutheran country, she abdicated to become a Roman Catholic.

Christmas Feast in celebration of the birth of JESUS CHRIST, common in Christendom since the 4th century. Although the exact date of Christ's birth is unknown, the feast takes place on 25 December within all Christian churches. Christmas is also a secular holiday, marked by the exchange of presents.

Christmas Island *See* KIRITIMATI

Christophe, Henri (1767–1820) Haitian revolutionary leader, president (1806–11) and king (1811–20). Born a free black on the island of Grenada, he participated in the armed struggle against the French in Haiti and fought a civil war with the partisans of the mulatto Pétion.

Christopher, Saint Patron saint of ferrymen and travellers. His feast day, 25 July, was omitted from the Roman Catholic calendar of 1969 and is no longer officially recognized.

chromatic Musical term used in melodic and harmonic analysis to refer to notes that do not occur in the scale of the KEY of a passage. Such notes are marked with accidentals; the chords in which they occur are termed chromatic.

chromatography Techniques of chemical analysis by which substances are separated from one another, identified and measured.

chromium Dull grey metal (symbol Cr), one of the TRANSITION ELEMENTS, first isolated in 1797. Its chief ore is CHROMITE. It is used as an electroplated coating. It is also an ingredient of many special steels. Properties: at.no. 24; r.a.m. 51.996; r.d. 7.19; m.p. 1,890°C (3,434°F); b.p. 2,672°C (4,842°F); most common isotope Cr^{52} (83.76%).

chromosome Structure carrying the genetic information of an organism, found only in the cell nucleus of EUKARYOTES. Thread-like and composed of DNA, chromosomes carry a specific set of GENES. Most cells have a DIPLOID number of chromosomes. GAMETES carry a HAPLOID number of chromosomes. *See also* HEREDITY

chromosphere Layer of the Sun's atmosphere between the PHOTOSPHERE and the CORONA. It is about 10,000km (6000mi) thick and is normally invisible because of the glare of the photosphere. At its base the temperature of the chromosphere is about 4,000K, rising to 100,000K at the top.

Chronicles Two historical books of the OLD TESTAMENT. They trace the history of Israel and Judah from the Creation to the return of the Jews from exile in Babylon (538 BC).

chrysalis Intermediate or pupal stage in the life cycle of all insects that undergo complete METAMORPHOSIS. The chrysalis is usually covered with a hard case, but some pupae, such as the silk moth, spin a silk cocoon.

chrysanthemum Large, widely-cultivated genus of annual and perennial plants native to temperate Eurasia. Centuries of selective breeding have modified the original plain flowers, and most species have large white, yellow, bronze, pink or red flower-heads. Family Asteraceae/COMPOSITAE.

chub Freshwater CARP found in flowing waters. It has a large head, wide mouth and is grey-brown. Length 10–60cm (4–25in). Family Cyprinidae. Chub is also the name of a marine fish of warm seas – oval-shaped with a small mouth and bright colours. Family Kyphosidae.

Chungking (Chongqing, Ch'ung-ch'ing) City on the YANGTZE River, S China. It was the wartime capital of China (1937–45). It is a transport and shipping centre with chemicals, steel, iron, silk, cotton textiles and plastics industries. Pop. (1993 est.) 3,780,000.

church Community of believers. Although adopted by non-Christian movements such as SCIENTOLOGY, it is usually used in reference to CHRISTIANITY. The church is also the name of the building used for worship by Christians.

Church of England Christian Church in England, established by law in the 16th century. During the reign of King HENRY VIII, a process of separation from the Roman Catholic Church began. By the Act of Supremacy (1534), the English monarch became head of the church. As the REFORMATION extended to England, the Church of England adopted the Elizabethan Settlement. This agreement, while espousing Protestantism, aimed at preserving religious unity by shaping a national church acceptable to all persons of moderate theological views. The liturgy of the Church of England is contained in the Book of COMMON PRAYER (1662). The church is episcopally governed, but priests and laity share in all major decisions by virtue of their representation in the General Synod. Territorially the church is divided into two provinces, Canterbury and York. The overseas expansion of the Church of England resulted in the gradual development of the worldwide ANGLICAN COMMUNION.

Church of Ireland Anglican Church in Ireland. It claims to be heir to the ancient Church of the island of Ireland. It is territorially divided into two provinces, Armagh and Dublin. The Church of Ireland was the legally established Church until 1869.

Church of Scotland National non-episcopal form of CHRISTIANITY in Scotland, adopting PRESBYTERIANISM by constitutional act in 1689. The church arose as a separate entity during the REFORMATION. Under the leadership of John KNOX, it abolished papal authority and accepted many of the teachings of John CALVIN. The Disruption of 1843 led to about one-third of its ministers and members leaving to form the FREE CHURCH OF SCOTLAND. The spiritual independence of the Church was recognized by an act of Parliament in 1921.

Churchill, Lord Randolph Henry Spencer (1849–95) British politician, secretary of state for India (1885–86) and chancellor of the exchequer (1886). He attempted widespread Party reform, in particular encouraging mass participation in the Conservative Associations. His first budget as chancellor proposed deep cuts in military expenditure and was defeated. Churchill was forced to resign. .

Churchill, Sir Winston Leonard Spencer (1874–1965) British statesman, prime minister (1940–45, 1951–55). Son of Lord Randolph CHURCHILL, he was elected to Parliament in 1900 as a Conservative. He joined the Liberals in 1904 and served in a succession of government posts. He resumed allegiance to the Conservatives in 1924. Out of office from 1929–39, he spoke out against the rising threat of Nazi Germany. He became first lord of the admiralty on the outbreak of WORLD WAR 2, and replaced Neville CHAMBERLAIN as prime minister in 1940. He proved an inspiring war leader. He was the principal architect of the grand alliance of Britain, the USA and Soviet Union, which eventually defeated the Germans. Rejected by a reform-hungry electorate in 1945, he was prime minister again 1951–55. His extensive writings include a history of World War 2 and the *History of the English-Speaking Peoples* (1956–58). He was awarded the Nobel Prize for literature in 1953.

CIA Abbreviation of CENTRAL INTELLIGENCE AGENCY

cicada GRASSHOPPER-like insect found in most parts of the world. Males make a loud sound by the vibration of a pair of plates in their abdomen. Length: up to 5cm (2in).

Cicero (106–43 BC) (Marcus Tullius Cicero) Roman politician, philosopher and orator. A leader of the Senate, he exposed Catiline's conspiracy (63 BC). He criticized Mark ANTONY in the Senate, and when Octavian came to power Antony persuaded him to have Cicero executed. Cicero's fame rests largely on his political philosophy and oratory.

CID Abbreviation of the CRIMINAL INVESTIGATION DEPARTMENT

Cid, El (1043–99) (Rodrigo Díaz de Vivar) Spanish national hero. He was a knight in the service of the king of Castile. His greatest achievement was the conquest of Valencia (1094), which he ruled until his death. His exploits have been romanticized in Spanish legend.

cilia Small hair-like filaments on cell walls whose wafting motion is used for propulsion or moving matter along a surface. Cilia are present in great quantities on some lining cells of the body, such as those along the respiratory tract. Cilia are also found on single-celled PROTOZOA known as CILIATES.

ciliate One of a large class of PROTOZOA found in freshwater, characterized by hair-like CILIA used for locomotion and food collecting. Subclasses include the Holotrichs (*Paramecium*); Spirotrichs (*Stentor*); and Peritrichs (*Vorticella*).

Cimabue, Giovanni 13th-century Florentine painter. His best-known work is *Madonna and Child Enthroned*. Cimabue is said to have taught GIOTTO.

Cimarosa, Domenico (1749–1801) Italian composer. He wrote more than 60 operas, his most famous being *Il matrimonio segreto*, which was first performed in Vienna in 1792. He also wrote seven cantatas and six oratorios.

cinchona Genus of evergreen trees native to the Andes and grown in South America, Indonesia and Zaïre. The dried bark of the trees is a source of QUININE and other medicinal products. Family Rubiaceae.

Cincinnati City on the Ohio River, sw Ohio, USA. It grew around Fort Washington (established 1789). Development was spurred by steamboat trade on the river. The completion of the Miami and Erie Canal in 1832 made the city a shipping centre for farm produce. It built its railway in 1880. Industries: machine tools, brewing, meat packing, aircraft engines, metal goods. Pop. (1990) 364,040.

cine camera Apparatus that takes a number of consecutive still photographs or frames on film. The illusion of motion is created when the developed film is projected on to a screen. *See also* CINEMA; VIDEO RECORDING

cinema Motion pictures as an industry and artistic pursuit. For much of its history cinema has been commercially dominated by HOLLYWOOD. Public showings of silent moving pictures, with live musical accompaniment, began in the 1890s, but speech was not heard in a full-length film until *The Jazz Singer* (1927). The 1930s saw the widespread introduction of colour. The growth of television in the USA during the 1940s profoundly altered film economics. Fewer but more spectacular films were produced. In post-war Europe film-makers explored social and psychological themes with often disturbing candour. *See also* CINE CAMERA

cinematography Technique of taking and projecting cine film, the basis of the CINEMA industry. Based on the experiments and inventions pioneered during the 1880s and 1890s by Thomas EDISON in the USA and the LUMIÈRE brothers in France, cinematography was applied professionally to the taking and showing of films soon after the turn of the century.

cinéma vérité Style of film-making, popular during the 1960s. It attempted to record truthful action, employing a documentary-like style, often using 16mm cameras. The style was also used in dramas, particularly by TRUFFAUT and GODARD.

cinnamon Light-brown SPICE made from the dried inner bark of the cinnamon tree. Its delicate aroma and sweet flavour make it a common ingredient in food. The tree is a bushy evergreen native to India and Burma and cultivated in the West Indies and South America. Family Lauraceae; species *Cinnamomum zeylanicum*.

cipher *See* CRYPTOGRAPHY

circadian rhythm Internal "clock" mechanism found in most organisms, which normally corresponds with the 24-hour day. It relates most obviously to the cycle of waking and sleeping, but is also involved in other cyclic variations, such as body temperature, hormone levels and metabolism.

Circe In Greek mythology, enchantress whose spells could change men into animals. Mistress of the island of Aeaea, she kept Odysseus with her for a year, changing his men into pigs.

circle Plane geometric figure that is the locus of points equidistant from a fixed point (the centre). This distance is the radius (r). The area of a circle is πr^2 and its perimeter (circumference) is $2\pi r$.

circuit System of electric conductors, appliances or electronic components connected together so that they form a continuously conducting path. In modern electronic devices, circuits are often printed in copper on a plastic card (printed circuit). *See also* CAPACITOR; CHIP; INTEGRATED CIRCUIT; TRANSISTOR

circulation, atmospheric Flow of the atmosphere around the Earth. The poleward circulation due to CONVECTION gives rise to large-scale eddies, such as the CYCLONE and ANTICYCLONE, low-pressure troughs and high-pressure ridges. The eddies are also caused by the Earth's rotation maintaining easterly winds towards the Equator and westerly winds towards the poles.

circulatory system Means by which oxygen and nutrients are carried to the body's tissues, and carbon dioxide and other waste products are removed. It consists of BLOOD VESSELS that carry the BLOOD, propelled by the pumping action of the HEART. Humans and other mammals have a double circulatory system, as the blood is pumped first to the lungs, and then to the rest of the body. In fish and many other animals, there is a single circulatory system, with blood passing through the GILLS and on to the rest of the body without an extra boost from the heart. Both these circulatory systems are closed; the blood remains confined within the blood vessels. Insects and many other invertebrates have an open circulatory system, where the blood flows freely within the body cavity, but passes through a series of open blood vessels and heart(s), whose pumping maintains a directional flow.

circumcision Operation of removing part or the whole of the foreskin of the penis or of removing the clitoris. Male circumcision is ritual in some groups, notably Jews and Muslims, and is said to have sanitary benefits. Female circumcision is intended to reduce sexual pleasure and has no medical benefit.

circumference Distance round the boundary of a plane geometric figure, such as a CIRCLE.

cirrhosis Degenerative disease in which there is excessive growth of fibrous tissue in an organ, most often the LIVER, causing inflammation and scarring. Cirrhosis of the liver may be caused by viral hepatitis, prolonged obstruction of the common bile duct, chronic abuse of alcohol or other drugs, blood disorder, heart failure or malnutrition.

Cistercian Religious order of monks founded by St Robert of Molesme (1098), based on ideals of strict Benedictinism. A community dedicated to contemplation, the Cistercians were noted agricultural pioneers. *See also* BENEDICTINE; TRAPPISTS

citric acid Colourless crystalline solid ($C_6H_8O_7$) with a sour taste. It is found in a free form in citrus fruits such as lemons and oranges, and is used for flavouring, in effervescent salts, and as a mordant (colour-fixer) in dyeing. Properties: r.d. 1.54; m.p. 153°C (307.4°F).

citrus Important group of trees and shrubs of the genus *Citrus* in the rue family. They include GRAPEFRUIT, kumquat, LEMON, LIME, ORANGE, tangerine and ugli. They are native to subtropical regions. The stems are usually thorny, the leaves bright green, shiny and pointed. The flowers are usually white, waxy and fragrant. The fruit (hesperidium) is usually ovoid with a thick, aromatic rind. The inside of the fruit is pulpy and juicy and is divided into segments that contain the seeds. Most citrus fruits contain significant amounts of vitamin C. Family Rutaceae.

civet (civet cat) Small, nocturnal, carnivorous mammal, related to the GENET and MONGOOSE, found in Africa, Asia and s Europe. It has a narrow body set on long legs, and its coat is grey-yellow with black markings. There are some 20 species. Length: (overall) 53–150cm (21–59in). Family Viverridae.

civil engineering Field of engineering dealing with large structures and systems. Civil engineers provide facilities for living, industry and transportation, such as roads, bridges, airports, dams, harbours and tunnels.

civil law Legal system derived from ROMAN LAW. It is different from COMMON LAW, the system generally adhered to in England and other English-speaking countries. Civil law is based on a system of codes Thus the civil law judge follows the evidence and is bound by the conditions of the written law and not by previous judicial interpretation. It is prevalent in continental Europe, Louisiana (USA), Quebec (Canada) and Latin America.

civil liberties Basic rights that every citizen possesses and governments must respect in a democracy. In some countries, the courts ensure freedom from government control or restraint, except as the public good may require. *See also* CIVIL RIGHTS

civil list Annual grant of money voted by Parliament to supply the expenses of the royal establishment in Britain. In February 1993 the number of royal family members on the civil list was reduced to the Queen, the Duke of Edinburgh and the Queen Mother.

civil rights Rights conferred legally upon the individual by the state. There is no universal conception of civil rights. The modern use of the phrase is most common in the USA, where it refers to relations between individuals as well as between individuals and the state. It is especially associated with the movement to achieve equal rights for African-Americans.

Civil Rights Acts (1866, 1870, 1875, 1957, 1960, 1964, 1968) US legislation. The Civil Rights Act of 1866 gave African-Americans citizenship and extended civil rights to all persons born in the USA (except Native Americans). The 1870 Act was passed to re-enact the previous measure, which was considered to be of dubious constitutionality. The 1870 law was declared unconstitutional by the US Supreme Court in 1883. The 1875 Act was passed to outlaw discrimination in public places because of race or previous servitude. The act was declared unconstitutional by the Supreme Court (1883–85), which stated that the 14th Amendment, the constitutional basis of the act, protected individual rights against infringement by the states, not by other individuals. The 1957 act established the Civil Rights Commission to investigate violations of the 15th Amendment. The 1960 Act enabled court-appointed federal officials to protect black voting rights. An act of violence to obstruct a court order became a federal offence. The 1964 Act established as law equal rights for all citizens in voting, education, public accommodations and in federally assisted programmes. The 1968 Act guaranteed equal treatment in housing and real estate to all citizens.

civil service Administrative establishment for carrying on the work of government. In Britain the modern service was developed between 1780–1870, as the weight of Parliamentary business became too heavy for ministers to attend to both policy-making and departmental administration. The civil service has grown from its centre in Whitehall, London and now has many regional offices.

Civil War, American (1861–65) War fought in the USA between the northern states (the Union) and the forces of the 11 southern states which seceeded from the Union to form the CONFEDERATE STATES OF AMERICA (Confederacy). Its immediate cause was the determination of the southern states to withdraw from a Union which the northern states regarded as indivisible. The more general cause was the question of slavery, a well-established institution in the South but one which the northern ABOLITIONISTS opposed. The Unionists had superior numbers, greater economic power and command of the seas. The Confederates had passionate conviction and superior generals, such as Robert E. LEE and "Stonewall" Jackson. The war began on 12 April 1861 when Confederate forces attacked FORT SUMTER, South Carolina. The Union victory in the Battle of GETTYSBURG (June–July 1863) was a turning point. The first big Union victory was at Fort Donelson on the Tennessee River (February 1862) under the command of Ulysses S. GRANT. The war ended with Lee's surrender to Grant at Appomattox in April 1865. The South was economically ruined by the war, and RECONSTRUCTION policies poisoned relations between North and South for a century.

Civil War, English (1642–51) Conflict between King CHARLES I and Parliament. Following years of dispute between the king and state essentially over the power of the crown, war began when the king raised his standard at Nottingham. Royalist forces were at first successful at Edgehill (1642) but there were no decisive engagements, and Parliament's position was stronger, as it controlled the SE, and London, the navy, and formed an alliance with Scotland. Parliament's victory at Marston Moor (1644) was a turning point, and in 1645 FAIRFAX and CROMWELL won a decisive victory at Naseby with their NEW MODEL ARMY. Charles surrendered in 1646. While negotiating with Parliament, he secretly secured an agreement with the Scots that led to what is usually called the second civil war (1648). A few local Royalist risings came to nothing, and the Scots, invading England, were swiftly defeated. The execution of Charles I (1649) provoked further conflict in 1650, in which Scots and Irish Royalists supported the future Charles II. Cromwell suppressed the Irish and the Scots, the final battle being fought at Worcester (1651).

Civil War, Spanish (1936–39) Conflict developing from a military rising against the republican government in Spain. The revolt began in Spanish Morocco, led by General FRANCO. It was supported by conservatives and reactionaries of many kinds, collectively known as the Nationalists and including the fascist FALANGE. The leftist, POPULAR FRONT government was supported by republicans, socialists and a variety of leftist groups, collectively known as Loyalists or Republicans. The Nationalists swiftly gained control of most of rural W Spain but not the main industrial regions. The war, fought with great savagery, became a serious international issue, representing the first major clash between the forces of the extreme right and the extreme left in Europe. Franco received extensive military support from MUSSOLINI and HITLER. The Soviet Union provided more limited aid for the Republicans. Liberal and socialist sympathizers from Britain and France fought as volunteers for the Republicans. The Nationalists extended their control in 1937, while the Republicans were weakened by internal quarrels. The fall of Madrid, after a long siege, in March 1939 brought the war to an end, with Franco supreme.

clam Bivalve mollusc found mainly in marine waters. It is usually partly buried in sand or mud. With a large foot for burrowing, its soft, flat body lies between two muscles for opening and closing the shells. Clams feed on PLANKTON. Class Pelecypoda.

Clapham Sect (c.1790–c.1830) Group of British evangelical reformers. Many of them, including William WILBERFORCE, lived in Clapham, S London, and several were members of Parliament. Originally known as the "Saints", they were especially influential in the abolition of SLAVERY and in prison reform.

Clare, John (1793–1864) British poet. His works include *Poems Descriptive of Rural Life*

and Scenery (1820), *The Village Minstrel* (1821), *The Shepherd's Calendar* (1827) and *The Rural Muse* (1835). Briefly lionized as a "peasant" poet, he was declared insane in 1837 and spent most of the rest of his life in asylums.

Clare County between Galway Bay and the River Shannon estuary, Munster province, W Republic of Ireland. Ennis is the county town. The area is hilly and infertile. The chief crops are oats and potatoes. Sheep, cattle, pigs and poultry are raised, and fishing is important. Area: 3,188sq km (1,231sq mi). Pop. (1991) 90,918.

Clarendon, Edward Hyde, 1st Earl of (1609–74) English statesman and historian. He negotiated the RESTORATION (1660). As chief minister to Charles II, he initiated the Clarendon Code, which restricted gatherings of PURITANS and Nonconformists, and the movement of their ministers. In addition, municipal and church officers were required to be professed Anglicans, and all ministers were forced to use the Anglican Book of COMMON PRAYER. Following disagreements with Charles II he was impeached and forced into exile in 1667. *See also* NONCONFORMISM

Clarendon, Constitutions of (1164) Sixteen articles issued by HENRY II of England to limit the temporal and judicial powers of the church. The most controversial article required clergy who had been convicted in church courts to be punished by royal courts. They played a significant role in the dispute between Henry and Thomas à BECKET.

clarinet Single-reed WOODWIND instrument. It is commonly pitched in B flat (also A) and has a range of over 3 OCTAVES. Other members of the family include the alto clarinet in E flat, the bass in B flat and the high sopranino in E flat.

Clarke, Arthur C. (Charles) (1917–) British science-fiction writer. He is noted for the scientific realism in his works, such as *Childhood's End* (1953), and *Voices from the Sky* (1965). Stanley Kubrick's film *2001: A Space Odyssey* (1969) was based on his short story *The Sentinel* (1951).

Clarke, Kenneth Harry (1940–) British politician, chancellor of the exchequer (1993–97). He became an MP in 1970 and joined THATCHER's cabinet in 1985. From 1988–90 he was secretary of state for health. Before becoming chancellor, he was briefly home secretary. A Europhile, he was defeated in the 1997 Tory leadership contest.

classical Term used in many different and apparently conflicting ways. Literally, it refers to the period between the Archaic and the HELLENISTIC AGE phases of ancient Greek culture. It is used more generally to mean the opposite of ROMANTICISM, or to refer to the artistic styles whose origins can be traced in ancient Greece or Rome.

classical economics Term applied to the work of British economists from the late-18th–mid-19th centuries. Classical economists range from Adam SMITH to John Stuart MILL. They maintained that if left to their own devices, without the interference of government, markets would find a natural equilibrium. *See also* MALTHUS, THOMAS

Classical music Music composed from *c.*1750–1820, whose style is characterized by emotional restraint, the dominance of homophonic melodies (melodies with accompaniment), and clear structures and forms underlying the music. The Classical period saw the development of the concerto, sonata, symphony and string quartet, and the piano replace the harpsichord as the most popular keyboard instrument. The greatest composers of this period were HAYDN, MOZART and BEETHOVEN.

classicism Art history term used to describe both an aesthetic attitude and an artistic tradition. The artistic tradition refers to the classical antiquity of Greece and Rome, its art, literature and criticism, and the subsequent periods that looked back to Greece and Rome for their prototypes, such as the CAROLINGIAN RENAISSANCE, RENAISSANCE, and NEO-CLASSICISM. Its aesthetic use suggests the classical characteristics of clarity, order, balance, unity, symmetry and dignity.

classification *See* TAXONOMY

Claude Lorrain (*c.*1604–82) (Claude Gellée) French landscape painter. He developed a style that combined poetic idealism inspired by antique models and his own observations. His mature style evolved between 1640–60, when he explored the natural play of light on different textures.

Claudius I (10 BC–AD 54) (Tiberius Claudius Nero Germanicus) Roman emperor (AD 41–54). The nephew of TIBERIUS, he was the first emperor chosen by the army. He had military successes in Germany and conquered Britain in AD 43. Agrippina (his fourth wife) poisoned him and made her son, NERO, emperor.

Clausius, Rudolf Julius Emanuel (1822–88) German physicist, regarded as the founder of THERMODYNAMICS. Using the work of Nicholas CARNOT, Clausius was the first to formulate the second law of thermodynamics, which states that heat cannot pass from a colder to a hotter object. He also introduced the term ENTROPY.

clavichord Earliest stringed instrument with mechanical action controlled by a keyboard. Possibly originating in the 13th century, it was used extensively from the 16th–18th centuries. It was superseded by the HARPSICHORD and then the PIANO.

clavicle (collarbone) Thin, slightly curved bone attached by ligaments to the top of the STERNUM (breast-bone). The clavicle and shoulder-blade make up the SHOULDER girdle, linking the arms to the axis of the body.

Clay, Cassius Marcellus Former name of Muhammad ALI

clay Group of hydrous silicates of aluminium and magnesium, including kaolinite and halloysite, usually mixed with some quartz, calcite or gypsum. It is formed by the weathering of surface granite or the chemical decomposition of feldspar.

Soft when wet, it hardens on firing and is used to make ceramics, pipes and bricks.

cleavage In embryology, progressive series of cell divisions that transform a fertilized egg into the earliest embryonic stage (BLASTULA). The egg is divided into blastomeres (smaller cells), each containing a DIPLOID number of chromosomes.

cleavage, rock Formation of definite planes through a rock. It is caused by compression associated with folding and metamorphism, and it results in the rock splitting easily parallel to the cleavage. The line of cleavage follows the alignment of minerals within the rock.

cleft palate Congenital deformity in which there is an opening in the roof of the mouth, causing direct communication between the nasal and mouth cavities. It is often associated with HARELIP and makes normal speech difficult. Usual treatment includes surgical correction, followed by special dental care and speech therapy if necessary.

clematis Genus of perennial, mostly climbing shrubs found worldwide. Many have attractive deep blue, violet, white, pink or red flowers or flower clusters. The leaves are usually compound. Family Ranunculaceae.

Clemenceau, Georges (1841–1929) French statesman, prime minister (1906–09, 1917–20). A moderate republican, he served in the Chamber of Deputies from 1876–1893, attempted compromise during the revolt of the PARIS COMMUNE (1871), and strongly supported Dreyfus. He returned to the Senate in 1902 and was twice prime minister. He led the French delegation at the VERSAILLES peace conference. *See also* DREYFUS AFFAIR

Clement I (d. *c.*97) (Saint Clement of Rome) Pope (88–97) and saint. He was executed for refusing to pledge allegiance to the Roman emperor. His feast day is 23 November.

Clement VII (1478–1534) Pope (1523–34), b. Giulio de Medici. He sided with FRANCIS I in the League of Cognac, thus opposing the Holy Roman emperor CHARLES V. The imperial troops attacked Rome, and a compromise was won. He was unable to deal with the rise of Protestantism and his indecisiveness over the divorce of Catherine of Aragon and Henry VIII is thought to have hastened the REFORMATION.

Cleopatra (69–30 BC) Queen of Egypt (51–30 BC). In 48 BC she overthrew her husband, brother and co-ruler Ptolemy XIII with the aid of Julius CAESAR, who became her lover. She went to Rome with Caesar, but after his assassination in 44 BC she returned to Alexandria, once again becoming queen. Mark ANTONY followed her to Egypt and they married (37 BC). The marriage infuriated Octavian (later AUGUSTUS). Rome declared war on Egypt in 31 BC and defeated Antony and Cleopatra's forces at the Battle of ACTIUM. Mark Antony committed suicide and Cleopatra surrendered to Octavian and later killed herself.

clergy Collective organization of ordained or

consecrated priests and ministers, especially of the Christian church. In the Roman Catholic, Orthodox and Anglican churches, the clergy comprises the orders of bishop, priest and deacon, and may also include members of religious orders. In non-episcopal Protestant churches, the clergy consists of pastors and ministers. Functions of the clergy include administration of the sacrament, preaching and the exercise of spiritual guidance. *See also* ORDINATION OF WOMEN

Cleveland, Stephen Grover (1837–1908) 22nd and 24th US President (1885–89 and 1893–97). He rose to national prominence as the reforming Democratic mayor of Buffalo (1881–82) and governor of New York (1883–84). The first Democratic president since the Civil War, Cleveland's attempts at reform had mixed success, and his attempted reduction of the tariff probably contributed to his failure to be renominated in 1888. In his second term, tariff reform again failed, but he secured repeal of the Sherman Silver Purchase Act of 1890.

Cleveland City and port on Lake Erie, NE Ohio, USA. Founded in 1796 by Moses Cleaveland, it grew rapidly with the opening of the Ohio and Erie Canal and the arrival of the railway in 1851. John D. Rockefeller founded Standard Oil Company here in 1870. Cleveland has a symphony orchestra, three universities and an art institute. It is a major Great Lakes shipping port, and an important iron and steel centre. NASA maintains a research centre here. Industries: chemicals, oil refining, engineering, electronics. Pop. (1990) 505,616.

click language Any of several southern African languages belonging chiefly to the Khoisan group and characterized by the use of suction speech sounds called clicks. Several clicks can be distinguished, each being a distinct consonant. Clicks are also found in some Bantu languages.

client-server Type of relationship between computers in a COMPUTER NETWORK. A client computer makes requests of a designated server computer. The server performs the requested functions and delivers the results to the client.

climate Weather conditions of a place or region prevailing over a long time. The major factors influencing climate are temperatures, air movements, incoming and outgoing radiation and moisture movements. Climates are defined on different scales, ranging from macroclimates that cover the broad climatic zones of the globe, down to microclimates that refer to the conditions in a small area, such as a wood or a field.

climatology Scientific study of the Earth's climates. Physical climatology investigates relationships between temperature, pressure, winds, precipitation, and other weather phenomena. Regional climatology considers latitude and other geographical factors, such as the influence of large land masses, in the climatic study of a particular place or region.

clinical psychology Field of psychology concerned with diagnosis and treatment of behavioural disorders. Clinical psychologists are engaged in diagnosis of disorders and in treatment including behaviour therapy and other forms of psychotherapy.

Clinton, Bill (William Jefferson) (1946–) 42nd US president (1993–). Educated at Georgetown University, Oxford University (Rhodes scholar) and Yale University Law School (graduated 1973), he joined the Democratic Party at an early age and directed all of his ambitions to political life. In 1978 he was elected governor of Arkansas, the youngest-ever US governor. Unseated in 1980, Clinton was re-elected in 1982. In the 1992 presidential elections, he defeated George BUSH. Clinton's concrete-plan approach to unemployment, health care and education was the cornerstone of his winning platform. As president, he made health-care reform an immediate priority, appointing his wife, Hillary Rodham Clinton (1947–), to head a commission with that objective. She was soon removed from the position, and many of the reforms were not realized. Although his term in office was dogged by the Whitewater investigations, and the blocking of his reforms and governmental appointments by the Republican-dominated Senate and House of Representatives, he remained unchallenged as the Democratic candidate for the 1996 presidential elections. He won with a strong majority.

Clive, Robert, Baron Clive of Plassey (1725–74) British soldier and administrator. He went to India as an official of the British EAST INDIA COMPANY (1743), and successfully resisted growing French power. He was governor of Bengal (1757–60, 1765–67). He returned to England in 1773 and was charged with but acquitted of embezzling state funds. He committed suicide.

cloaca Cavity into which intestinal, urinary and genital tracts open in fish, reptiles, birds and some primitive mammals.

clock Instrument for measuring time. The earliest timekeeping instruments had no moving parts, being designed to measure the movements of the Sun, Moon and stars. The ancient Egyptians used water clocks, pottery bowls bearing graduated time-marks from which water slowly leaked. Candle clocks and sandglasses were later types of non-mechanical clocks. The central feature of all mechanical clocks is an escapement mechanism, which enables a clock to tick off time at discrete intervals. This movement is transmitted through a series of gears to the hands, which are pushed forward a small distance with every escapement movement. Motive power for mechanical clocks has been provided variously by falling weights, pendulums and coiled springs. Other modern clocks include those using an electrically oscillated quartz crystal as the basis of time-division. Atomic clocks rely upon the natural oscillations of atoms.

cloisonné Enamelling technique in which the

design is constructed out of wires soldered to a plate, and the cells (cloisons) thus formed are filled with coloured ENAMEL paste and fired. It was popular in Byzantine art of the 10th and 11th centuries. It flourished in China during the Ming and Qing dynasties and was also adopted in Japan.

clone Set of organisms obtained from a single original parent through some form of ASEXUAL REPRODUCTION or by ARTIFICIAL SELECTION. Clones are genetically identical and may arise naturally from PARTHENOGENESIS in animals. Cloning is often used in plant propagation (including TISSUE CULTURE) to produce new plants from parents with desirable qualities. It is now possible to produce animal clones from tissue culture. *See also* GENETIC ENGINEERING

cloud Masses of water particles or ice crystals suspended in the lower atmosphere. Clouds are formed when water from the Earth's surface becomes vapour through EVAPORATION. As the water vapour rises, it cools and condenses around microscopic salt and dust particles, forming droplets. Where the atmosphere is below the freezing temperature of water the droplets turn to ice. There are ten different classifications of clouds: cirrus are high, white and thread-like; cirrocumulus are thin sheets; cirrostratus are white and almost transparent; altocumulus are greyish-white; altostratus are grey and streaky, often covering the sky; nimbostratus are thick and dark, and usually shed rain or snow; stratocumulus are masses of cloud; stratus are low-lying and grey; cumulus are white and fluffy-looking; and cumulonimbus are towering, dark clouds that generally produce thunderstorms.

cloud chamber Instrument used to detect and identify charged particles, invented in the 1880s by C.T.R. WILSON to study atomic radiation. The chamber is filled with air supersaturated with water or alcohol vapour. As charged particles pass through the chamber, droplets form on the ions produced, thus revealing the tracks of the particles. The tracks can be deflected by a magnetic field and photographed for analysis.

clove Tall, aromatic, evergreen tree native to the Moluccan Islands. The small purple flowers appear in clusters; the dried flower buds are widely used in cookery. Oil of cloves is distilled from the stems. Height: to 12m (40ft). Family Myrtaceae; species *Syzygium aromaticum*.

clover Low-growing annual, biennial and perennial plants, native to temperate regions of Europe, but now found throughout warmer regions of the N Hemisphere. Most species are good nitrogen-fixers. Family Fabaceae/Leguminosae; genus *Trifolium*. *See also* NITROGEN CYCLE; NITROGEN FIXATION

Clovis I (465–511) Frankish king of the MEROVINGIAN dynasty. He overthrew the Romanized kingdom of Soissons and conquered the Alemmani near Cologne. He and his army later converted to Christianity in fulfilment of a promise made before the battle. In 507 he defeated the Visigoths under Alaric II near Poitiers. By the time he died he controlled most of GAUL.

club moss Any of about 200 species of small evergreen spore-bearing plants that, unlike the more primitive true MOSSES, have specialized tissues for transporting water, food and minerals. They are related to FERNS and HORSETAILS. Millions of years ago their ancestors formed the large trees that dominated CARBONIFEROUS coal forests. Phylum LYCOPODOPHYTA, Family Lycopodiaceae.

cluster, stellar *See* OPEN CLUSTER; GLOBULAR CLUSTER

clutch, electromagnetic Device that uses magnetic attraction to connect two rotating shafts. Forms include disc clutches with energized coils and magnetic clutch plates. Eddy current clutches induce rotational movement in the shaft to be engaged and rotated. Hysteresis clutches also transmit rotation without slip. Other electromagnetic clutches employ magnetic metal particles to induce torque.

Clwyd County in N Wales, bordered by the Irish Sea, Cheshire, Shropshire, Powys and Gwynedd. The county town is Mold. The Vale of Clwyd is a rich agricultural region. Industries: iron and steel, tourism, chemicals, quarrying. Area: 2,426sq km (937sq mi). Pop. (1991) 408,090.

Clyde River in SW Scotland. It rises in the Southern Uplands, flows N, then NW, passing over the Falls of Clyde (which provide hydroelectric power) near Lanark and widening into the Firth of Clyde at Dumbarton. Clydebank, below GLASGOW, was Scotland's main shipbuilding region. Length: 170km (106mi).

Clytemnestra In Greek legend, the unfaithful wife of AGAMEMNON, king of Mycenae, and mother of his son ORESTES. On Agamemnon's return from TROY he was murdered by Clytemnestra and her lover Aegisthus.

CND Abbreviation of CAMPAIGN FOR NUCLEAR DISARMAMENT

cnidaria *See* COELENTERATE

coal Blackish, solid fuel formed from the remains of fossil plants. In the carboniferous and tertiary periods, swamp vegetation subsided to form PEAT bogs. Sedimentary deposits buried the bogs, and the resultant increase in pressure and heat produced lignite (brown coal), then bituminous coal, and ANTHRACITE if temperature increased sufficiently.

coal tar By-product from the manufacture of coke. Coal tar comes from bituminous coal used in the distillation process. It is a volatile substance, important for its organic chemical constituents (coal-tar crudes), which are extracted by further distillation. These are the basic ingredients for the synthesis of many products, such as explosives, drugs, dyes and perfumes.

coaxial cable Communications CABLE consisting of a central conductor with surrounding insulator and tubular shield.

143

cobalt Metallic element (symbol Co), a transition metal. It is mostly obtained as a by-product during the processing of other ores. Cobalt is a constituent of vitamin B_{12}. It is used in high-temperature steel, artists' colours (cobalt blue), jet engine manufacture, cutting tools and magnets. Co^{60} (half-life 5.26yr) is an artificial isotope used as a source of gamma rays in radiotherapy and tracer studies. Properties: at.no. 27; r.a.m. 58.9332; r.d. 8.9; m.p. 1,495°C (2,723°F); b.p. 2,870°C (5,198°F); most common isotope Co^{59} (100 %).

Cobbett, William (1763–1835) British political essayist and reformer, who founded the influential *Cobbett's Weekly Political Register* (1802). His dislike of industrialization led to his tours, published as *Rural Rides* (1830), in which he championed the yeoman society that was wanning as a result of technology. He was an active member of Parliament in the Reformed Parliament of 1832.

Cobden, Richard (1804–65) British Radical politician. With John BRIGHT he led the campaign for the repeal of the CORN LAWS and was the chief spokesman in Parliament (1841–57, 1859–65) for the "Manchester School" of free trade.

COBOL (Common Business-Oriented Language) Widely-used COMPUTER LANGUAGE developed in 1959 for processing business data.

cobra Any of several highly poisonous snakes in the family Elapidae, including the MAMBA, coral snake, kraits and true cobras. It can expand its neck ribs to form a characteristic hood. Found primarily in Africa and Asia, they feed on rats, toads and small birds. The king cobra (*Ophiophagus hannah*) reaches 5.5m (18ft) in length, and is the largest venomous snake in the world.

coca Shrub native to Colombia and Peru that contains the ALKALOID drug COCAINE. Native Americans chew the leaves for pleasure, to quell hunger and to stimulate the nervous system. Height: *c*.2.4m (8ft). Family Erythroxylaceae; species *Erythroxylon coca*.

cocaine White crystalline ALKALOID extracted from the leaves of the coca plant. Once used as a local anaesthetic, it is now primarily an illegal narcotic, with stimulant and hallucinatory effects. It is psychologically habit-forming. Habitual use of cocaine results in physical and nervous deterioration, and withdrawal results in severe depression. *See also* CRACK

coccus Small spherical or spheroid bacterium. Average diameter, 0.5–1.25 micrometres. Some, such as *Streptococcus* and *Staphylococcus*, are common causes of infection.

cochlea Fluid-filled structure in the inner EAR that is essential to hearing. It has a shape like a coiled shell, and is lined with hair cells that move in response to incoming sound waves, stimulating nerve cells to transmit impulses to the BRAIN.

cockatoo Large PARROT with a long, erectile crest. Cockatoos live mainly in Australia and sw Asia. Most are predominantly white, tinged with pink or yellow. They feed on fruit and seeds. Females lay 1–4 white eggs in a tree hole nest. Length: 38cm (15in). Family Psittacidae.

Cockcroft, Sir John Douglas (1897–1967) British physicist who, with Ernest WALTON, was the first person to split the ATOM. He and Walton constructed a particle ACCELERATOR, and created the first man-made nuclear reaction by bombarding lithium atoms with protons (1932). They shared the 1951 Nobel Prize for physics for their use of particle accelerators to study atomic nuclei.

cockle Bivalve mollusc found in marine waters. Its varicoloured, heart-shaped shell has 20–24 strong, radiating ribs. There are *c*.200 species, many of which are edible. Average length: 4–8cm (1.5–3in). Class Bivalvia; family Cardiidae; species include *Cardium aculeatum*.

cockroach (roach) Member of a group of insects with long antennae and a flat, soft body. It is found worldwide, but mostly in the tropics. Its head is hidden under a shield (pronotum) and it may be winged or wingless. Some species are serious household pests. Length: 13–50mm (0.5–2in). Family Blattidae.

cocoa Drink obtained from the seeds of the tropical American evergreen tree *Theobroma cacao*. The seeds are crushed and some fatty substances are removed to produce cocoa powder. Cocoa is the basic ingredient of CHOCOLATE. The Ivory Coast is one of the world's largest producers. Family Sterculiaceae.

coconut palm (copra plant) Tall palm tree native to the shores of the Indo-Pacific region and the Pacific coast of South America; commercially the most important of all palms. Growing to 30.5m (100ft) tall, it has a leaning trunk and a crown of feather-shaped leaves. Copra, the dried kernel of the coconut fruit, is a valuable source of oil used in the manufacture of margarine and soap. The fibrous husk is used for matting as well as a peat substitute (coir) in horticultural composts. Family Arecacae/Palmae; species *Cocos nucifera*.

cocoon Case or wrapping produced by larval forms of animals (such as some MOTHS, BUTTERFLIES and WASPS) for the resting or pupal stage in their life cycle. Most cocoons are made of SILK, and those of the domestic silkworm provide most of the world's commercial silk. *See also* CHRYSALIS; PUPA.

Cocteau, Jean (1889–1963) French writer and AVANT-GARDE film-maker. He was associated with many leading artistic figures of the 1920s, such as APOLLINAIRE, PICASSO, DIAGHILEV and STRAVINSKY. His successful works of surrealist fantasy include the novel *Les enfants terribles* (1929; filmed, 1950); the play *Orphée* (1926; filmed, 1950); and the film *Le sang d'un poète* (1930).

cod Bottom-dwelling, marine fish found in cold to temperate waters of the Northern Hemisphere. It is grey, green, brown or red with darker speckled markings. Cod is one of the chief food fishes. Length: up to 1.8m (6ft). Family Gadidae.

code *See* CRYPTOGRAPHY

codeine White crystalline ALKALOID extracted from OPIUM by the methylation of MORPHINE, and with the properties of weak morphine. It is used in medicine as an analgesic to treat mild to moderate pain, as a cough suppressant and to treat diarrhoea.

Coe, Sebastian Newbold (1956–) English runner. In the 1980 and 1984 Olympic Games, he won gold medals in the 1500m and silver medals in the 800m. His world record time of 1min 41.73sec stood for 16 years. He retired from athletics in 1990, and in 1992 became a Conservative MP. He lost his seat in 1997.

coefficient Term multiplying a specified unknown quantity in an algebraic expression. In the expression $1 + 5x + 2x^2$: 5 and 2 are the coefficients of x and x^2 respectively. In physics, it is a ratio that yields a pure number or a quantity with dimensions.

coelacanth Bony fish of the genus *Latimeria*. Thought to have become extinct, it was found in deep waters off the African coast in 1938. It is grey-brown with lobed fins that have fleshy bases. The scales and bony plates are unlike those of modern fish. Length: 1.5m (5ft). Order Crossopterygii; species *Latimeria chalumnae.*

coelenterate Alternative name for members of the phylum Cnidaria – aquatic animals that include the JELLYFISH, SEA ANEMONE, CORAL and hydroids. Characterized by a digestive cavity that forms the main body, they may have been the first animal group to reach the tissue level of organization. Coelenterates are radially symmetrical, jelly-like and have a nerve net and one body opening. There are *c.*9,000 species.

Coetzee, J.M. (John Michael) (1940–) South African novelist and critic. His novels deal with life under forms of imperialism, including the South African apartheid system in *In the Heart of the Country* (1977) and *Age of Iron* (1990).

coffee Plant and the popular CAFFEINE beverage produced from its seeds (coffee beans). Originally native to Ethiopia, they are now cultivated in the tropics, especially Brazil (the world's biggest producer), Colombia and the Ivory Coast. Family Rubiaceae.

cognitive psychology Broad area of psychology concerned with perceiving, thinking and knowing. It investigates such matters as the way in which people perceive by sight or hearing; how they organize, remember and use information; and the use they make of language.

cognitive therapy Form of PSYCHOTHERAPY that aims to treat psychological problems through changing patients' attitudes and beliefs. It is based on the theory that behaviour is learned and beliefs and attitudes that lead to negative behaviour can be altered by CONDITIONING.

cohesion Mutual attraction between the component atoms, ions or molecules of a substance. Weak cohesive forces permit the fluidity of liquids; those of solids are much stronger.

coin Stamped metal discs of standard sizes used as tokens of money in commercial transactions. The earliest coins date from the 7th century BC. Ancient coins usually contained a specific quantity of precious metal, often gold or silver, and were stamped with the symbol of the issuing authority. With the introduction of banknotes in the late 17th century, and the gradual decline of the quantity of precious metal in each coin, the role of coins changed. They acquired only notional value and became used for smaller money transactions.

Coke, Sir Edward (1552–1634) English jurist. As chief justice of the King's Bench (1613), he championed the COMMON LAW, and after 1620 developed it in Parliament to oppose the king's assumption of "divine right". He helped to draft a declaration of civil liberties, *Petition of Right* (1628), and wrote the influential *Institutes of the Laws of England* (1628).

Colbert, Jean Baptiste (1619–83) French statesman, the principal exponent of MERCANTILISM. From 1661 Colbert controlled most aspects of government: reforming taxation and manufacturing, reducing tariffs, establishing commercial companies and strengthening the navy.

Colchester Town on the River Colne, Essex, SE England. The first Roman colony in Britain was settled here in AD 43 and attacked by Boadicea in AD 61. It is a market centre. Pop. (1991) 142,515.

colchicine *See* COLCHICUM

colchicum Genus of about 30 species of flowering plants, including *C. autumnale*. Species grow throughout Eurasia. The flowers bloom during the autumn. The CORM contains colchicine, an ALKALOID used to treat rheumatism and gout. Colchicine's ability to inhibit MITOSIS make it a valuable IMMUNOSUPPRESSIVE DRUG and aid to cancer research. Family Liliaceae.

cold-blooded *See* POIKILOTHERMAL

Cold War Political, ideological and economic confrontation between the USA and the Soviet Union and their allies from the end of World War 2 until the late 1980s. Despite incidents such as the Berlin Airlift (1948–49) and the CUBAN MISSILE CRISIS (1962), and many threats of retaliatory war by both sides, open warfare never occurred between the NORTH ATLANTIC TREATY ORGANIZATION (NATO) and the WARSAW PACT. It ended with the collapse of communism in the late 1980s and the dissolution of the Warsaw Pact in 1990.

Cole, Nat King (Nathaniel Adams) (1917–65) US singer and pianist. He was a jazz pianist in the King Cole Trio from 1939, but achieved popularity as a singer. Cole's hit songs include *Unforgettable, When I Fall in Love, Mona Lisa* and *Nature Boy*.

Coleridge, Samuel Taylor (1772–1834) British poet and critic. His literary output was mainly criticism, political journalism and philosophy, but he is chiefly remembered for poems, such as *The Rime of the Ancient Mariner, Kubla Khan,*

Christabel and *Frost at Midnight*. In 1798, he and WORDSWORTH published *Lyrical Ballads*, a fundamental work of the English Romantic movement.

Colette (1873–1954) French novelist. Her early works, including the first four *Claudine* novels (1900–03), were published under her first husband's pseudonym, Willy. Among her best-known works are *Chéri* (1920), *The Last of Chéri* (1926) and *Gigi* (1944).

colitis Inflammation of the lining of the colon, or large intestine, that produces bowel changes, usually diarrhoea and cramp-like pains. In severe chronic ulcerative colitis, the colon lining ulcerates and bleeds.

collage Composition made up of various materials (such as cardboard, string and fabric) pasted on to a canvas or other background. Cubist artists developed it into a serious art form. Collage was also used by members of the DADA movement.

collagen Protein substance that is the main constituent of bones, tendons, cartilage, connective tissue and skin. It is made up of inelastic fibres.

collective unconscious According to JUNG's psychological theory, the inherited aspect of the UNCONSCIOUS that is common to all members of the human race. The collective unconscious has evolved over many centuries and contains images (archetypes) that are found in dreams and numerous religious and mystical symbols.

collectivism Political and economic theory, opposed to individualism. It emphasizes the need to replace competition with cooperation. SOCIALISM and COMMUNISM are both expressions of the collectivist idea.

collectivization Agricultural policy enforced in the SOVIET UNION under STALIN in 1929, and adopted by China after the communist takeover in 1949. With the object of modernizing agriculture and making it more efficient, small peasant holdings were combined and agriculture brought under state control.

Collins, Michael (1890–1922) Irish revolutionary. He fought in the EASTER RISING in 1916, and helped to establish the Irish Assembly (Dáil) in 1918. He was one of the negotiators of the treaty that created the Irish Free State in 1921 and was killed in the ensuing civil war.

Collins, (William) Wilkie (1824–89) British novelist. He made important contributions to the development of DETECTIVE FICTION, especially in *The Woman in White* (1860) and *The Moonstone* (1868). He collaborated with Charles DICKENS in writing plays and stories.

colloid Substance composed of fine particles that can be readily dispersed throughout a second substance.

Cologne (Köln) City on the River Rhine, Nordrhein Westfalen, W Germany. The Romans established a fortress at Cologne in AD 50. It enjoyed great influence during the Middle Ages. It was heavily bombed during World War 2. Cologne is a

COLOMBIA
AREA: 1,138,910sq km (439,733sq mi)
POPULATION: 33,424,000
CAPITAL (POPULATION): Bogotá (4,921,000)
GOVERNMENT: Multiparty republic
ETHNIC GROUPS: Mestizo 58%, White 20%, Mulatto 14%, Black 4%, mixed Black and Indian 3%, Native American 1%
LANGUAGES: Spanish (official)
RELIGIONS: Christianity (Roman Catholic 93%)
CURRENCY: Peso = 100 centavos

commercial, industrial and transport centre. Industries: oil refining, petrochemicals, chemicals, engineering, textiles. Pop. (1990) 958,600.

Colombia Republic in NW South America; the capital is BOGOTÁ. **Land and climate** Colombia is the only country in the continent to have coastlines on both the Pacific Ocean and the Caribbean Sea. Colombia contains the three northernmost ranges of the ANDES Mountains. The fertile valleys between the ranges contain about 75% of Colombia's population. East of the Andes lie plains drained by headwaters of the AMAZON and ORINOCO rivers: this area covers about 66% of the country but less than 2% of the population live here. West of the mountains lie the Caribbean lowlands in the N and the Pacific lowlands in the W. The lowlands have a tropical climate, but altitude greatly affects the climate of the highlands. Rainfall is heavy, especially on the Pacific coast, though the Caribbean lowlands and the Andean Magdalena valley have dry seasons. **Economy** Agriculture is important with coffee the leading export. Other crops include bananas, cocoa and maize. Colombia also exports coal, oil, emeralds and gold. Manufacturing is based mainly in Bogotá, Cali and MEDELLÍN. **History and politics** The advanced, pre-Colombian CHIBCHA civilization lived undisturbed in the E cordillera for thousands of years. In 1525 the Spanish established the first European settlement at Santa Marta. Colombia became part of the New Kingdom of Granada, whose territory also included Ecuador, Panama and Venezuela. In 1819 Simón BOLÍVAR liberated the land and established Greater Colombia. In 1830 Ecuador and Venezuela became independent nations. The first civil war (1899–1902) killed nearly 100,000 people. In 1903, aided by the USA, Panama achieved independence. The second civil war, *La Violencia* (1949–1957), was even more bloody. During the 1980s drug lords became a destabilizing force. Armed cartels (such as the Cali) have grown wealthy on the illegal trade in cocaine. Political and media assassinations were frequent. Guerrilla groups fought for social and economic justice. In 1990 elections, a former guerrilla movement, M19, gained 30% of the popular vote. A new constitution was promulgated in 1991. In 1994 Ernesto Samper was elected president.

Colombo Capital and chief seaport of Sri Lanka, on the SW coast. Settled in the 6th century BC, it was taken by Portugal in the 16th century and later by the Dutch. In 1796 it was captured by the British, and it gained its independence in 1948. Apart from shipping, the city has light industries. Pop. (1992 est.) 684,000.

Colombo Plan International organization with headquarters in COLOMBO, Sri Lanka, which seeks to promote economic and social development in S and SE Asia. Initiated by the Commonwealth of Nations (1951), it now includes 26 states including Canada, Japan, UK and the USA.

colon Part of the large INTESTINE. The colon absorbs water from digested food and allows bacterial action for the formation of faeces. *See also* DIGESTIVE SYSTEM

colonialism Control by one country over a dependent area or people. Although associated with modern political history, the practice is ancient. After World War 2, colonialist exploitation was widely recognized, and colonial powers conceded, willingly or not, independence to their colonies. *See also* IMPERIALISM

Colorado State in W USA; the state capital is DENVER. It is the highest state in the nation, with an average elevation of 2,073m (6,800ft). In the W half are the ranges of the ROCKY MOUNTAINS, and in the E the GREAT PLAINS. Major rivers are the COLORADO, RIO GRANDE, Arkansas and South Platte. The USA acquired the E of the state from France in the LOUISIANA PURCHASE (1803). The remainder was ceded by Mexico after the MEXICAN WAR (1848). It achieved statehood in 1876. The most important agricultural activity is the raising of sheep and cattle on the Plains. Industries: tourism, transport and electrical equipment, mining, chemicals, timber. Area: 268,658sq km (103,729sq mi). Pop. (1990) 3,294,394.

Colorado River Major river in SW USA, which rises in the Rocky Mountains of N Colorado, and flows generally SW into the Gulf of California, passing through the GRAND CANYON. Length: 2,333km (1,450mi).

Colosseum Ampitheatre in Rome built AD 72–81 by the Emperor Vespasian. It measures 189×156m (620×513ft) by 45.7m (150ft) high, and seated *c.*50,000 people. Roman citizens came to watch gladiatorial contests and, according to tradition, the martyrdom of Christians.

Colossians, Epistle to the Book of the New Testament in the form of a letter written by either St PAUL or a disciple to the Church at Colossae, a city in SW Phrygia (now central Turkey). The letter is a warning to the Colossians not to adopt ideas from other faiths and philosophies that may undermine the supremacy of JESUS CHRIST.

Colossus of Rhodes One of the SEVEN WONDERS OF THE WORLD, a bronze statue of the Sun god overlooking the harbour at Rhodes. It stood more than 30.5m (100ft) high. It was built

between *c.*292 BC–*c.*280 BC and was destroyed by an earthquake in *c.*224 BC.

colostomy Operation to bring the COLON out through the wall of the abdomen in order to bypass the lower section of the bowel. An artificial opening is created so that faecal matter is passed into a bag, worn outside the body.

colour Sensation experienced when light of sufficient brightness and of a particular wavelength strikes the retina of the eye. Daylight (white light) is made up of a SPECTRUM of colours, each a different wavelength. A pure spectral colour is called a **hue**. Any colour is perceived as a mixture of three primary colours: red, green and blue.

colour blindness General term for various disorders of colour vision. The most common involves red-green vision, a hereditary defect almost exclusively affecting males, in which the person cannot tell red from green. Total colour blindness, an inherited disorder in which the person sees only black, white and grey, is rare.

Coltrane, John William (1926–67) US jazz saxophonist, one of the leading innovators of the 1950s and 1960s. He established a reputation as an intense musician and technical virtuoso. *A Love Supreme* is his masterpiece.

Colum, Padraic (1881–1972) Irish author. A key figure in the Irish literary renaissance, he was an associate of James JOYCE (of whom he wrote a memoir) and author of many poems. From 1914 he lived mainly in the USA, where he developed an interest in myth and folklore. His output includes many plays and a novel *The Flying Swans* (1957).

Columba, Saint (521–97) Irish Christian missionary in Ireland and Scotland. He founded several monasteries throughout Ireland. In 563 he left Ireland and founded an important monastery on the island of Iona. As Abbot of Iona, he strove to convert the PICTS of N Scotland to Christianity. His feast day is 9 June.

Columbia, District of *See* WASHINGTON, D.C.

Columbia River River in SW Canada and NW USA. It flows from Columbia Lake in British Columbia, Canada, through Washington and Oregon, USA, and enters the Pacific Ocean N of Portland. It has one of the largest drainage basins on the continent, *c.*668,220sq km (258,000sq mi). Length: 1,953km (1,214mi).

columbium *See* NIOBIUM

Columbia State capital of South Carolina, USA. Founded in 1786, it was nearly destroyed in the American Civil War. Industries: textiles, printing, electronic equipment. Pop. (1990) 98,052.

columbine Any of *c.*100 species of perennial herbaceous plant native to cool climates of the Northern Hemisphere. They have spurred flowers and notched leaflets. Height: to 90cm (3ft). Family Ranunculaceae; genus *Aquilegia*.

Columbus, Christopher (1451–1506) Italian explorer credited with the discovery of America.

He believed he could establish a route to China and the East Indies by sailing across the Atlantic. He secured Spanish patronage from Ferdinand and Isabella. He set out with three ships (*Niña*, *Pinta* and *Santa Maria*) in 1492 and made landfall in the Bahamas, the first European to reach the Americas since the Vikings. On a second, larger expedition (1493), a permanent colony was established in Hispaniola. He made two more voyages (1498 and 1502), exploring the Caribbean region without reaching the North American mainland. His discoveries laid the basis for the Spanish empire in the Americas.

Columbus State capital of Ohio, USA. Founded in 1812, it grew rapidly after the arrival of the railway in 1850. It is now a major transport, industrial and trading centre for a rich agricultural region. Industries: machinery, aircraft, printing and publishing. Pop. (1990) 632,910.

column In architecture, a vertical post, supporting part of a building. A column may be freestanding, with a capital, base and shaft, or it may be partly attached to a wall. Triumphal columns had narrative reliefs to depict battle victories. *See also* ORDERS OF ARCHITECTURE

coma State of unconsciousness brought about by a head injury, brain disease, drugs or lack of blood supply to the BRAIN.

Comanche Shoshonean-speaking Native American nation that separated from the parent SHOSHONE in the distant past and migrated from E Wyoming into Kansas. Numbering *c*.15,000, they were daring horsemen and introduced the horse to the Northern Plains tribes. Conflict with US forces resulted in their near extinction by 1874. Today *c*.4,500 Comanche live on reservations in sw Oklahoma.

Combination Acts British acts of Parliament of 1799 and 1800 making combinations (or trade unions) of workers illegal. Trade unions nevertheless multiplied after 1815, and in 1824 the acts were repealed. A later Combination Act (1825) restricted the right to strike and, as the TOLPUDDLE MARTYRS (1834) demonstrated, trade-union organizers could still be prosecuted.

combustion Burning, usually in oxygen. The combustion of fuels is used to produce heat and light. An example is a fire.

COMECON Acronym for the COUNCIL FOR MUTUAL ECONOMIC ASSISTANCE.

Comédie-Française French national theatre, founded in 1680. It is organized according to a charter first granted by Louis XIV.

comedy One of the two main types of DRAMA. It differs from TRAGEDY in its lightness of style and theme and its tendency to resolve happily. It originated in early Greek fertility rites and, in modern usage, refers not only to a humorous play or film, but also to the growing tradition of stand-up routines. *See also* ARISTOPHANES

comet Small, icy solar system body in an independent orbit around the Sun. The solid nucleus of a comet is small and comprises rock and dust particles embedded in ice. As the comet approaches the Sun and gets warmer, evaporation begins, and jets of gas and dust form the luminous, spherical coma. Later, radiation pressure from the Sun and the solar wind may send dust and gas streaming away as a tail. Comets are thought to originate outside the solar system.

comfrey Any plant of the genus *Symphytum* of the BORAGE family (Boraginaceae), native to Eurasia. Comfreys have small yellow or purple flowers and hairy leaves. Boiled concoctions of *S. officinale* were once used to treat wounds.

comic opera Musico-dramatic work with some spoken dialogue and a light or amusing plot. The term is used indiscriminately and includes musical comedy and OPERETTA. In operatic works, it approximates most closely to early 18th-century Italian OPERA BUFFA (notably the operas of PERGOLESI), but bears little relation to the French OPÉRA COMIQUE.

Comintern *See* COMMUNIST INTERNATIONAL

Commedia dell' arte Style of Italian comedy, popular from the mid-16th to late-18th century, which spread throughout Europe. Plays were comic, often coarse, and crudely improvised on briefly outlined scenarios. Commedia produced several (now standard) masked characters: Harlequin (clown), Capitano (braggart soldier), Pantalone (deceived father or cuckolded husband), Colombina (maid) and Inamorato (lover).

commensalism Situation in nature in which two species live in close association but only one partner benefits. One of the species (the commensal) may gain from increased food supply, or by procuring shelter, support or means of locomotion, but the other (the host) neither gains nor loses from the relationship. *See also* MUTUALISM; SYMBIOSIS

commodity market A market in which goods or services are bought and sold. Commodities are raw materials such as tea, rubber, tin or copper, which generally need processing to reach their final state. The actual commodities are seldom present, and what is traded is their ownership. The largest commodity exchange in the world is in Chicago, Illinois, USA.

Common Agricultural Policy (CAP) System of support for agriculture within the EUROPEAN COMMUNITY (EC). If prices fall to a level known as intervention prices, the EC buys up surplus product, creating the so-called "beef mountains" and "wine lakes". In 1988, to prevent over-production, the EC introduced a policy of paying farmers to set aside part of their land as fallow. Prices for imports from outside the EC are kept above target by means of levies. By 1994 the CAP was absorbing 51% of the total EC budget, having soared to 75% in the 1970s.

common law Legal system developed in England and adopted in most English-speaking countries. Distinguished from CIVIL LAW, its chief characteristics are judicial precedents, trial by jury and the doctrine of the supremacy of law. It dates to the constitutions of CLARENDON (1164). It is the customary and traditional element in the law accumulating from court decisions. *See also* ROMAN LAW

Common Market *See* EUROPEAN UNION (EU)

Common Prayer, Book of Official liturgy of the ANGLICAN COMMUNION. It was prepared originally as a reformed version of the old Roman Catholic liturgy for Henry VIII by Thomas CRANMER in 1549. Three years later it underwent revision under the Protestant government of Edward VI. The final version (1559), a combination of the two, was produced by Elizabeth I's Archbishop of Canterbury, Matthew Parker. The Prayer Book was further revised in 1662 after the RESTORATION of Charles II.

Commons, House of Lower chamber of the UK PARLIAMENT.

Commonwealth (1649–60) Official name of the republic established in England after the execution of CHARLES I. After a series of unsuccessful attempts to find a suitable constitution, the PROTECTORATE was set up in 1653, in which Oliver CROMWELL was given almost regal powers. The Commonwealth ended with the RESTORATION of CHARLES II.

Commonwealth Games Sporting event originating as the British Empire Games (1930). Competitors are members of the COMMONWEALTH OF NATIONS. Based on the Olympic Games, they are held every four years.

Commonwealth of Independent States (CIS) Alliance of 12 former republics of the SOVIET UNION. The CIS was formed in 1991 with ARMENIA, AZERBAIJAN, BELARUS, GEORGIA, KAZAKSTAN, KYRGYZSTAN, MOLDOVA, RUSSIA, TAJIKISTAN, TURKMENISTAN, UKRAINE and UZBEKISTAN. The BALTIC STATES did not join. All members except Ukraine signed a treaty of economic union in 1993, creating a free trade zone. Russia is the dominant power, with overall responsibility for defence.

Commonwealth of Nations Voluntary association of 53 states, consisting of English-speaking countries formerly part of the BRITISH EMPIRE. Headed by the British sovereign, it exists largely as a forum for discussion.

communications Processes for sharing information and ideas. Facial expressions, hand signals, writing and speech are examples. The 15th-century invention of the printing press revolutionized communications. The 20th century has witnessed a communications revolution, primarily in terms of increased access. TELECOMMUNICATIONS inventions have facilitated rapid, global, mass communication. The INTERNET is the latest in a long line of technological innovations.

Communications Satellite (COMSAT) A private company that provides worldwide SATELLITE communications systems. COMSAT, established by the US Congress, began with the launch of the Early Bird satellite in 1965. Many other nations now participate in COMSAT projects.

communism Political outlook based on the principle of communal ownership of property. The theory is derived from the interpretation placed by Karl MARX and Friedrich ENGELS on the course of human history. Marx asserted that social and political relations depend ultimately upon relations of economic production. All value (and so wealth) is produced by labour (the labour theory of value), yet in a capitalist system, workers' salaries do not represent the full value of their labour, because some of it goes to the owners of the means of production and is appropriated by them in the form of profits. Thus the working class (proletariat) and the class that is in control of capital and production (bourgeoisie) have conflicting interests. Conflicting interests within CAPITALISM would inevitably lead to the overthrow of the bourgeoisie by the proletariat and so the collapse of the system itself. This would be replaced, first by SOCIALISM and eventually by a communist society in which production and distribution would be democratically controlled. A socialist experiment was attempted in Russia following the revolution (1917). Stalin turned communism into an ideology to justify the use of dictatorial state power to drive rapid economic development of a largely agricultural economy. This process was used as a model for other communist countries, such as China, Indonesia and Cuba.

Communist International (Comintern, Third International) Communist organization founded by LENIN in 1919. The Comintern was made up mainly of Russians, and failed to organize a successful revolution in Europe in the 1920s and 1930s. The Soviet Union abolished the Comintern in 1943 to placate its World War 2 allies.

Communist Party, Chinese Political organization established in July 1921 by Li Ta-chao and Ch'en Tu-hsiu. The party was strengthened by its alliance (1924) with CHIANG KAI-SHEK's nationalist KUOMINTANG, but virtually shattered when the Communists were expelled from Chiang's group in 1927. MAO ZEDONG was the guiding force in revitalizing the party in the early 1930s. The Party achieved complete political and military power. Its structure and hierarchy were nearly destroyed during the CULTURAL REVOLUTION, but re-established after Mao's death by DENG XIAOPING. The May 1989 events in Tiananmen Square led to the declaration of martial law. The 1990s has seen a continued swing away from reforms and a consolidation of hardline conservatives in powerful positions. However, the Party has shown a flexible approach to economic reform, which has enabled it to survive the collapse of Soviet COMMUNISM. JIANG ZEMIN became president in 1993. The National People's Congress is the supreme legislative body and nominally elects the highest officers of state. The party has over 40 million members (1995).

Communist Party of the Soviet Union (CPSU) Former ruling party of the SOVIET UNION. It wielded all effective political power in the country and, via the COMMUNIST INTERNATIONAL, had considerable influence over Communist parties in other countries. Party organization paralleled the hierarchy of local government administration, thus enabling party control of every level of government. After the break up of the Soviet Union in 1991, the party was dissolved following a number of decrees by Boris YELTSIN. There remains a strong traditional conservative power base of ex-party members who are politically active in Russia. See also COMMUNISM; LENIN; individual party leaders

community architecture Schemes, mainly for housing, that involve a study of the prevailing social conditions and consultation with the people who are going to use them. In Britain, the idea developed during the 1970s as a reaction to mass housing developments. Its most famous supporter is Charles, Prince of Wales.

commutative law Rule of combination in mathematics; it requires that an operation on two terms is independent of the order of the terms. Addition and multiplication of numbers is commutative, since $a + b = b + a$ and $ab = ba$.

Comoros (Comores) Independent republic off the E coast of Africa between Mozambique and Madagascar in the Indian Ocean, made up of a group of volcanic islands. The three major islands are Grande Comore (home of the capital, Moroni), Anjouan and Mohéli. The islands are mountainous, the climate tropical and the soil fertile. Farming is the chief occupation. Coconuts, copra, vanilla, cocoa and sisal are the main crops and exports. Area: 1,862sq km (719sq mi). Pop. (1994) 535,600.

compact disc (CD) Disc used for high-quality digital sound reproduction. It is a plastic disc with a shiny metal layer and a transparent protective plastic coating. The sound signal consists of millions of minute pits, pressed into one side of the metal. On replay, a narrow laser beam is reflected from the rotating disc's surface. A sensor detects changes in the beam, and forms an electrical signal of pulses. This is processed and decoded to form a sound signal that can be amplified for reproduction on loudspeakers. See also CD-ROM

company Group of people who agree to work together as a firm or business. The legal responsibility of running a company rests with its board of directors which, if the business has raised finance by selling shares in the company, has to account to its shareholders. In a **private** company, the directors sell shares to whomever they please (sometimes the only shareholders are the directors). The shares of a **public** company can be bought and sold by anyone through a STOCK EXCHANGE. In a **public limited company (plc)**, the legal liability of its shareholders is limited to the value of their shares. See also CORPORATION

compass Direction-finding instrument also used to show direction of a magnetic field. It is a horizontal magnetic needle on a vertical pivot whose north-seeking end can turn to point towards mag-

netic N. The compass has been in use since the 12th century. In navigation today, the magnetic compass is often replaced by the motor-driven GYROCOMPASS.

compiler Computer program that translates the symbols of a programming language into instructions readable directly by a computer. Most programs are written in high-level languages, which are made up of words and symbols easily comprehended by humans. A compiler renders them into a form that is readable by the circuits of the computer.

complex number Number of the form $a + b$i, where $i = \sqrt{-1}$, and a and b are REAL NUMBERS. To obtain a solution to the equation $x^2 + 1 = 0$, we need to introduce a new number i, such that $i^2 = -1$. The solutions to similar equations then give rise to a set of numbers of the general form $a + b$ i. These are known as the complex numbers. Since b can be equal to zero, the set of complex numbers includes the real numbers.

Compositae Family of nearly 20,000 species of plants in which the "flower" is actually a composite flower-head consisting of a cluster of many, usually tiny, individual flowers (florets). Composites make up by far the largest family of plants. The Compositae are often known as the Asteraceae.

compound Substance formed by chemical combination of two or more elements that cannot be separated by physical means. Compounds are produced by the rearrangement of valency electrons (outer electrons of an atom) seeking to attain more stable configurations. They usually have properties quite different from those of their constituent elements. See also MOLECULE

Compromise of 1850 Set of balanced resolutions by Senator Henry CLAY to prevent civil war. The US Congress agreed to admit California as a free state, organize New Mexico and Utah as territories without mention of slavery, provide for a tougher fugitive slave law, abolish the slave trade in Washington, D.C., and assume the Texas national debt.

Compton, Arthur Holly (1892–1962) US physicist. He discovered that wavelengths of x-rays increase when the rays collide with electrons (the Compton effect). This helped prove that x-rays could act as particles. He was awarded the 1927 Nobel Prize in physics jointly with the British physicist C.T.R. WILSON.

computer Device that processes data (information) by following a set of instructions called a PROGRAM. All digital computers work by manipulating data represented as numbers. Stages in the long-term development of electronic digital computers are termed **computer generations**. A first generation computer was developed by engineers at the University of Pennsylvania in 1946. The 30-ton machine called ENIAC (Electronic Numerical Indicator and Computer). used electronic VALVES instead of relays. John von NEUMANN helped to develop techniques for storing programs in code.

In 1951, UNIVAC 1 became the first second-generation computer offered for general sale. This second generation computer used a TRANSISTOR to perform the same role as valves. In the 1960s, a third generation of computers appeared with the invention of INTEGRATED CIRCUITS. Fourth generation computers, developed in the 1980s, are even smaller, utilizing powerful MICROPROCESSORS. Fifth generation computers using very large-scale integration (VLSI) chips will utilize the developments of ARTIFICIAL INTELLIGENCE (AI) and may be controlled by spoken commands.

computer-aided design (CAD) Use of COMPUTER GRAPHICS to assist the design of, for example, fabrics, electronic circuits, buildings and vehicles. With CAD, designers can make alterations and analyse their effect.

computer graphics Illustrations produced on computer. Simple diagrams and shapes may be produced by typing on the keyboard. Complex images require a mouse, painting or drawing SOFTWARE and often special graphics HARDWARE.

computerized axial tomography (CAT) Method of taking x-rays that provides images of "slices" through the body. Inside a CAT scanner is an x-ray source, which produces a narrow beam of radiation. This passes through a patient's body and is detected by an electronic sensor. The x-ray source and detector are rotated around the patient's body so that views are taken from all angles. A computer analyses the output of the sensor from each of these angles, and uses the information to build up a picture of the slice of the body.

computer language System of words and rules, based on normal language, in which a computer PROGRAM is written.

computer network Number of computers linked together for COMMUNICATIONS purposes. A typical local area network (LAN) links computers within the same building, enabling staff to exchange data and share printers. A wide area network (WAN) covers longer distances and may link LANs. *See also* INTERNET; MODEM

computer program *See* PROGRAM

computer virus COMPUTER PROGRAM designed to disrupt the operation of a computer. Viruses in widely circulated free software may infect computers worldwide. A virus may remain undetected for months and then suddenly activate.

COMSAT *See* COMMUNICATIONS SATELLITE (COMSAT)

Comte, Auguste (1798–1857) French philosopher, the founder of POSITIVISM. He proposed the law of the three stages (theological, metaphysical and positive) that represent the development of the human race. In the first two stages the human mind finds religious or abstract causes to explain phenomena, while in the third, explanation of a phenomenon is found in a scientific law.

Conakry Capital city of Guinea, W Africa, on Tombo Island, in the Atlantic Ocean. Founded in 1884, it is a major port and the administrative and commercial centre of Guinea. It has an airport. It exports alumina and bananas. Pop. (1983) 705,300.

concentration camp Detention centre for military or political prisoners. The first camps were set up by the British during the SOUTH AFRICAN WARS (1899-1902). The most notorious were those established in Central Europe by the Nazis in the 1930s. Over 6 million people (mostly Jews) were exterminated in the Polish camps. Gulags were widely employed by Stalin, and "reeducation" camps were used in the Chinese CULTURAL REVOLUTION and by the KHMER ROUGE in Cambodia.

conceptualism Philosophical theory in which the universal is found in the particular, a position between NOMINALISM and REALISM. It asserts that the mind is the individual that universalizes by experiencing particulars, finding common factors in them, and conceptualizing these common factors as universals.

concerto Musical work for instrumental soloists accompanied by orchestra. The earliest concertos are the 17th century *Concerto grosso*. J.S. BACH's Brandenburg Concertos are fine examples of this form. VIVALDI composed most of his concertos for one soloist and orchestra and used the three-movement form (fast-slow-fast) which was to become standard, such as the concertos of MOZART and BEETHOVEN. In the 19th century, concertos involved increasing virtuousity, particularly in the works of LISZT and RACHMANINOV.

Concord State capital of New Hampshire, USA, on the Merrimack River. Founded as a trading post in 1660, it was settled in 1727. It was the scene of New Hampshire's ratification of the Constitution as the ninth and deciding state on June 21, 1788, and was designated state capital in 1808. Quarries N of the city produce the famous white granite used for the Library of Congress (Washington, D.C.) and the Museum of Modern Art (New York City). It is an industrial and financial centre. Industries: electrical equipment, printing. Pop. (1992) 36,364.

concordat Agreement between church and state, regulating relations between them on matters of common concern. The term is usually applied to treaties between individual states and the VATICAN.

Concorde Supersonic passenger aircraft. British Aircraft Corporation and Aerospatiale of France jointly developed and built Concorde. Passenger services started in 1976.

concrete Hard, strong building material made by mixing Portland CEMENT, sand, gravel and water. It is an important building material. Its modern use dates from the early 19th century, although the Romans made extensive use of concrete.

Condé (1530–1830) Junior branch of the French royal house of BOURBON. Notable members of the line included Louis I, Prince of Condé (1530–69), a HUGUENOT leader. Louis II, the Great Condé (1621–86), was a famous general.

condensation Formation of a liquid from a gas or vapour, caused by cooling or an increase in pressure. More particularly, it is the changing of water vapour in the air into water droplets, forming mist, cloud, rain, or drops on cold surfaces.

condenser *See* CAPACITOR

conditioning In experimental psychology, learning in which human or animal subjects learn to respond in a certain way to a stimulus. Most of the procedures and terminology of classical conditioning stem from the work of Ivan PAVLOV and B.F. SKINNER.

condor Common name for two species of the American VULTURE: the black Andean condor (*Vultur gryphus*) and the rare grey-brown California condor (*Gymnogyps californianus*). They are two of the largest flying birds and feed on partly rotted carrion. Length: up to 127cm (50in). Wingspan: up to 3.5m (10ft).

conductance Ability of a material to conduct electricity. In a direct current (DC) circuit, it is the reciprocal of electrical resistance. In an alternating current (AC) circuit, it is the resistance divided by the square of impedance (the opposition of a circuit to the passage of a current). SI units of conductance are siemens (symbol S). *See also* ELECTRIC CURRENT

conduction Transfer of heat within a body. If one end of a metal rod is placed in a flame, the heat energy received causes increased vibratory motion of the molecules in that end. These molecules bump into others farther along the rod, and the increased motion is passed along until finally the end not in the flame becomes hot.

conductivity Measure of the ease with which a material allows electricity or heat to pass through it. For a solid substance, the electrical conductivity is the CONDUCTANCE. *See also* ELECTRIC CURRENT

conductor In music, a person who coordinates the performance of a band, orchestra or choir and directs and inspires the interpretation of the music. Before the 19th century a harpsichordist or first violinist "directed" orchestral playing.

conductor Substance or object that allows easy passage of free electrons. Conductors have a low electrical RESISTANCE. Metals are the best conductors.

cone Solid geometric figure swept out by a line (generator) that joins a point moving in a closed curve in a plane, to a fixed point (vertex) outside the plane.

Confederate States of America (1861–65) (Confederacy) Southern states that seceded from the Union, following the election of Abraham LINCOLN. South Carolina left in December 1860, and was followed closely by Alabama, Florida, Georgia, Louisiana, Mississippi and Texas. When the US CIVIL WAR began, Arkansas, North Carolina, Tennessee and Virginia joined.

Confederation, Articles of *See* ARTICLES OF CONFEDERATION

Confederation of British Industry (CBI) UK organization founded in 1965 to promote the prosperity and interests of British industry. it is financed by *c.* 250,000 member companies.

confirmation Sacrament of the Christian Church by which the relationship between God and an individual, established by BAPTISM, is confirmed or strengthened in faith. Candidates for confirmation take the baptismal vows previously made on their behalf by godparents, and confirm the intention to keep them.

Confucianism Philosophy that dominated China until the early 20th century and still has many followers, mainly in Asia. It is based on the *Analects*, sayings attributed to CONFUCIUS. An ethical system to ensure a smooth-running society, it gradually acquired quasi-religious characteristics. Confucianism views man as potentially the most perfect form of *li*, the ultimate embodiment of good. It stresses the responsibility of sovereign to subject, of family members to one another, and of friend to friend.

Confucius (551–479 BC) (K'ung-fu-tzu) Founder of CONFUCIANISM. Born in Lu, he was an excellent scholar and became an influential teacher of the sons of wealthy families. In his later years he sought a return to the political morality of the early ZHOU dynasty.

congenital disorder Abnormal condition present from birth caused by faulty development, infection, or the mother's exposure to drugs or other toxic substances during pregnancy.

conglomerate In geology, a sedimentary rock made up of rounded pebbles embedded in a fine matrix of sand or silt, commonly formed along beaches or on river beds.

Congo Equatorial republic in w central Africa; the capital is BRAZZAVILLE. The main port, Pointe Noire on the Gulf of Guinea. **Land and climate** Congo generally has a hot, wet equatorial climate. Its narrow, treeless coastal plain is dry and cool. Inland the River Niari has carved a fertile valley through the forested highlands. Central Congo consists of luxuriant savanna with valley forests. The N contains large swampy areas in the tributary valleys of the Zaïre and Ubangi rivers. **Economy** More than 60% of the population is engaged in subsistence agriculture. Major food crops include

---

CONGO
AREA: 342,000sq km (132,046sq mi)
POPULATION: 2,368,000
CAPITAL (POPULATION): Brazzaville (937,579)
GOVERNMENT: Multiparty republic
ETHNIC GROUPS: Kongo 52%, Teke 17%, Mboshi 12%, Mbete 5%
LANGUAGES: French (official)
RELIGIONS: Christianity (Roman Catholics 54%, Protestants 25%, African Christians 14%), traditional beliefs 5%
CURRENCY: CFA franc = 100 centimes

bananas, cassava, maize and rice while cash crops are coffee and cocoa. Congo's main exports are oil (70% of the total) and timber. **History and politics** From the 15th–18th centuries, much of Congo probably belonged to the huge Kongo kingdom. The Congo coast became a centre of the European slave trade. The area came under French protection in 1880 and remained under French control until 1960. Congo became a one-party state in 1964, and a military junta took control in 1968. In 1970 Congo declared itself Communist. In 1990 the government officially abandoned its Communist policies. Multi-party elections were held in 1992 and 1993. In the run up to 1997 presidential elections, factional tensions increased until heavy fighting broke out between rival militias.

Congo (Zaïre River) River in central and w Africa; the second-longest in the continent. It rises in s Zaïre and flows in a curve to the Atlantic Ocean for 4,670km (2,900mi). The chief ocean port is Matadi, the major river ports are KINSHASA and KISANGANI.

Congo, Democratic Republic of New name (1997) for ZAÏRE.

congregationalism Christian church denomination in which local churches are autonomous; members have been called Brownists, Separatists and Independents. It is based on the belief that Christ is the head of the church and all members are God's priests. Modern Congregationalism began in England in *c*.1580. In the UK the Congregational Church in England and Wales merged with others to form the United Reformed Church (1972).

Congress Legislative branch of the US federal government established by the US CONSTITUTION (1789). Congress comprises the SENATE and the HOUSE OF REPRESENTATIVES. The main powers of Congress include the right to assess and collect taxes, introduce legislation, regulate commerce, propose Constitutional amendments, mint money, raise and maintain armed forces, establish lower courts, and declare war. Legislation must be passed by both houses and the president to become law. If the president uses his power of veto, Congress can still pass the bill with a two-thirds majority in each house.

Congress Party (officially Indian National Congress) Oldest political party in India, whose fortunes have often been intertwined with the Nehru dynasty. It was founded in 1885, but was not prominent until after World War 1, when Mahatma GANDHI transformed it into a mass independence movement. Jawaharlal NEHRU became president of the Congress in 1929. At independence (1947), Nehru became prime minister. Nehru's daughter Indira GANDHI became prime minister in 1966. In 1984 (after Indira's assassination) her son Rajiv GANDHI became leader, securing the party's re-election in that year. Congress were defeated in 1989.

congress system Attempt during the early 19th century to conduct diplomacy through regular conferences between the European allies that had

defeated Napoleonic France. It originated in the Treaty of PARIS (1815). The four powers (Austria, Britain, Prussia and Russia) met in 1818, 1820 and 1821. Britain withdrew in 1822. Differences between the three remaining powers in 1825 caused the abandonment of the system.

Congreve, William (1670–1729) English dramatist. His comedies include *Love for Love* (1695) and *The Way of the World* (1700). His elegant satire represents the peak of RESTORATION THEATRE. He also wrote a tragedy, *The Mourning Bride* (1697).

conic (conic section) Curve found by the intersection of a plane with a cone. Circles, ellipses, parabolas or hyperbolas are conic sections. Alternatively a conic is the locus of a point that moves so that the ratio of its distances from a fixed point (the focus) and a fixed line (the directrix) is constant. This ratio is called the eccentricity (e): $e = 1$ gives a parabola, $e > 1$ a hyperbola, $e < 1$ an ellipse, and $e = 0$ a circle.

conifer Cone-bearing trees, generally evergreen, such as pines, firs and redwoods. Some are the Earth's largest plants, reaching heights of up to 99m (325ft). They are a major natural resource of the Northern Hemisphere. *See also* GYMNOSPERM

Connecticut State in NE USA; its state capital and largest city is HARTFORD. One of the original 13 colonies, Connecticut was first settled by the English in the 1630s. The Connecticut River valley separates the w and E highlands. The state economy is based on manufacturing. Industries: transport equipment, machinery, chemicals, metallurgy. Area 12,549sq km (4,845sq mi). Pop. (1990) 3,287,116.

connective tissue Supporting and packing tissue that helps to maintain the body's shape and hold it together. Bones, ligaments, cartilage and skin are all types of connective tissue.

Connery, Sean (1930–) Scottish film actor, well known for his role as James Bond. These films include *Dr No* (1962) and *Diamonds are Forever* (1971). He has since become a seasoned and respected actor, playing mature roles, and has won Academy awards for *The Name of the Rose* (1986) and *The Untouchables* (1987). He also had success with *The Hunt for Red October* (1990).

Connolly, James (1870–1916) Irish nationalist leader. He organized the Belfast dock workers and the Dublin transport workers' strike in 1913. He was a leader in the EASTER RISING of 1916 and was executed by the British authorities.

conquistador Leader of the Spanish conquest of the New World in the 16th century. The most famous were CORTÉS and PIZARRO.

Conrad, Joseph (1857–1924) British novelist and short-story writer, b. Poland. His eventful years as a ship's officer informed the exotic settings of many of his novels. His major works include *Lord Jim* (1900), *Heart of Darkness* (1902), *Nostromo* (1904), *The Secret Agent* (1907) and *Victory* (1915).

conscription (military draft) Compulsory enlistment of people for service in the armed forces. In Britain, conscription was used in both World Wars and continued in peacetime as National Service until 1962.

conservation Preservation of nature and natural resources. Conservation includes protecting the landscape from change due to natural erosion; using soil conditioners and artificial fertilizers to maintain soil fertility; replacing topsoil and landscaping spoiled land, and protecting threatened species.

conservation, laws of Physical laws stating that some property of a closed system is unaltered by change in the system; it is conserved. The most important are the laws of conservation of matter and energy.

conservatism Political stance seeking to preserve the historic continuity of a society's laws, customs, social structure and institutions. Rather than an abstract notion of human rights and the application of radical reform, conservatives favour gradual piecemeal changes which address practical grievances. *See also* CHRISTIAN DEMOCRATS; CONSERVATIVE PARTY

Conservative Party (officially Conservative and Unionist Party) Oldest political party in Britain. Its origins lie in the transformation of the early 19th-century TORY PARTY into the Conservative Party under Sir Robert PEEL in the 1830s. Until late in the 19th century it was mainly a party of landed interests and depended electorally on the county constituencies. It held power for 31 of the 71 years between 1834 and 1905 and for most of the 1920s and 30s, either alone or in coalition. Since 1945 it has held office from 1951–64 and 1970–74. From 1979, the party swung further to the right under the leadership of Margaret THATCHER (1975–90) and, securing significant working-class support, it won four consecutive elections before losing in 1997.

Constable, John (1776–1837) British painter, a leading Western landscapist. He studied every effect of clouds and light on water,. His first success came when *The Haywain* (1821) and *View on the Stour* (1817) were shown at the 1824 Paris Salon, although recognition in England only came after his death.

Constance, Council of (1414–18) Ecumenical council that ended the GREAT SCHISM. It was convoked by the antipope John XXIII. Martin V was elected as a new pope in 1417. The Council also attempted to combat heresy, notably that of Jan HUS.

constant In mathematics, a quantity or factor that does not change. It may be universal, such as the ratio of the circumference of a circle to its diameter, or it may be particular, such as a symbol that has a fixed value in an algebraic equation.

Constanta City in E Romania, on the Black Sea. Founded in the 7th century BC as a Greek colony, it was taken by the Romans in 72 BC. It is Romania's chief port and a major trade centre. Industries: shipbuilding, oil refining, textiles. Pop. (1992) 350,476.

Constantine I (285–337) Roman emperor (305–37), called the Great. The first Christian emperor and founder of Constantinople (modern ISTANBUL). In 324 he won sole control of the empire, and in 325 presided over the first council of the Christian church at NICAEA.

Constantinople Former name of ISTANBUL

constellation Grouping of stars, forming an imaginary figure traced on the sky. The groupings have no physical basis as each star is a different distance from Earth. There are 88 constellations that have been assigned boundaries on the CELESTIAL SPHERE by the International Astronomical Union in 1930.

constitution Code of laws or collection of customary practices delineating the powers and organization of the various organs of government within a nation, and some of the rights and obligations of its citizens. *See also* CONSTITUTIONAL LAW

Constitutional Convention (1787) Meeting of delegates, in Philadelphia, from 12 of the 13 US states (Rhode Island abstained), which resulted in the creation of the US Constitution. The Convention was called to revise the ARTICLES OF CONFEDERATION and to redress the lack of power wielded by the existing government structure.

Constitutional Law Procedures and doctrines defining the operation of the constitution of a state. In states with a written constitution, courts often have specific powers relating to the constitution and likely points of conflict. In countries without a written constitution, such as Britain, constitutional law is more imprecise and problems are addressed within the political process.

Constitution of the United States Fundamental laws and basis of government of the USA. It was designed to create a system of "checks and balances" to prevent one branch of government gaining dominance over others. Ten amendments, collectively known as the BILL OF RIGHTS, were later added to the Constitution to protect the rights of the individual. The US Constitution was designed not as a code of laws, but as a statement of principles to which laws should adhere, thus allowing considerable flexibility in judicial interpretation.

constructivism Russian abstract art movement founded *c.*1913 by the sculptor Vladimir TATLIN. Other leading members were the brothers Naum GABO and Antoine PEVSNER, who were nfluenced by CUBISM and FUTURISM. Constructivism influenced modern European architecture and sculpture.

consul One of the two chief magistrates of ancient Rome. Consuls were elected each year to administer civil and military matters. After 367 BC, one consul was a PATRICIAN, the other a PLEBEIAN, each having the power to veto the other's decisions.

consumerism Belief that consumers should influence the policies and practices regulating the standards and methods of manufacturers, advertisers and sellers. Interest in consumerism first arose in the 1960s.

consumption *See* TUBERCULOSIS

contact lens Lens worn on the CORNEA to aid defective vision. Early contact lenses were made of glass, but since 1938 plastic has been used.

contempt In law, disorderly conduct in a court or legislative body, or action performed elsewhere that tends to obstruct the work of a court or legislative body, or bring it into disrepute.

continent Large land masses on the Earth's surface. The continents are EUROPE and ASIA (or Eurasia), AFRICA, NORTH AMERICA, SOUTH AMERICA, AUSTRALIA and ANTARCTICA. They cover about 30% of the Earth above sea level and extend below sea level forming continental shelves. The continental crust is composed of rocks that are less dense than the basaltic rocks in ocean basins, moving position over the surface of the Earth very slowly by CONTINENTAL DRIFT. *See also* PLATE TECTONICS

Continental Congress (1774–89) Federal legislature of the American colonies during the American Revolution and the period of Confederation. Its first meeting, at Philadelphia in September 1774, resulted in unified opposition to British rule, and agreed on a boycott of trade with Britain. In July 1776 the Second Congress adopted the DECLARATION OF INDEPENDENCE and drafted the ARTICLES OF CONFEDERATION.

continental drift Theory that the continents change position very slowly, moving over the Earth's surface at a rate of a few centimetres per year, adding up to thousands of kilometres over GEOLOGICAL TIME. Early supporters claimed that the shapes of the present day continents could be pieced together to form an ancient land mass that had split and drifted apart. Evidence included matching the outlines of continents, rock types, geological structures and fossils. Continental movement can be measured by global positioning satellites.

Continental margin Region of the ocean floor that lies between the shoreline and the abyssal ocean floor. It includes the continental shelf, the continental slope and the continental rise. The continental shelf slopes gently seawards, between the shoreline and the top of the continental slope. Between the continental shelf and the continental rise is the continental slope, which leads into deeper water. The continental rise, at the foot of the slope, is an area of thick deposits of sediments.

Contra Right-wing Nicaraguan revolutionary group active 1979–90. The Contra aimed to overthrow the elected, left-wing SANDINISTA Government and received financial and military assistance from the US government. Elections were held in 1990, at which the political wing of the Contra was victorious. *See also* IRAN-CONTRA AFFAIR

contraception (birth control) Use of devices or techniques to prevent pregnancy. The PILL is a hormone preparation that prevents the release of an egg (OVUM) and thickens the cervical mucus. The intrauterine device (IUD) is a small spring made from plastic or metal inserted into the womb. It stops the fertilized egg embedding itself in the uterine lining.

Barrier methods include the male and female condom and the diaphragm. Devices such as diaphragms or caps cover the cervix thus preventing sperm entering the womb. Less effective is the "rhythm method", which involves the avoidance of sex on days when conception is most likely (during ovulation). Emergency contraception, known as the "morning-after pill", can be taken up to 72 hours after unprotected sexual intercourse; it prevents the fertilized ovum embedding itself in the womb.

contract In law, an agreement between parties that can be legally enforced. A contract creates rights and obligations enforced by law.

contralto Lowest range (below SOPRANO and MEZZO-SOPRANO) of the female singing voice. A male voice in this range is called a COUNTERTENOR.

convection Transfer of heat by flow of currents within fluids (gases or liquids). Warm fluids have a natural tendency to rise (because they are less dense), whereas cooler fluids tend to fall. This movement subsides when all areas of the fluid are at the same temperature.

convection current Heat generated from radioactivity deep within the Earth's MANTLE causing rock to flow towards the CRUST. At the top of the mantle the rising rock is deflected laterally below the crust before sinking. This mantle convection is thought to be the process driving PLATE TECTONICS.

convulsion Intense, involuntary contraction of the muscles, sometimes accompanied by loss of consciousness. A seizure may indicate EPILEPSY although there are other causes, including intoxication, brain abscess or HYPOGLYCAEMIA.

Cook, James (1728–79) British naval officer and explorer. He charted the approaches to Quebec during the Seven Years War. In 1768–71 he led an expedition to Tahiti. He conducted a survey of the unknown coasts of New Zealand, and charted the E coast of Australia, naming it New South Wales and claiming it for Britain. On a second expedition to the S Pacific (1772–75), Cook charted much of the Southern Hemisphere and circumnavigated Antarctica. On his last voyage (1776–79) he discovered the Sandwich (Hawaiian) Islands, where he was killed in a dispute with the inhabitants.

Cook, Robin (1946–) British statesman, foreign secretary (1997–). Cook entered parliament in 1974. A skilful parliamentary speaker, he held various posts in Labour's shadow cabinet (1987–97). As foreign secretary, Cook announced Labour's intention to pursue an ethics-based foreign policy.

Cook Islands Group of about 15 islands in the S Pacific Ocean, NE of New Zealand, consisting of the Northern (Manihiki) Cook Islands and the Southern (Lower) Cook Islands; a self-governing territory in free association with New Zealand. Discovered by Captain James Cook in 1773, the islands became a British protectorate in 1888 and were annexed to New Zealand in 1901. They achieved self-governing status in 1965. Products: copra, citrus fruits. Area: 293sq km (113sq mi). Pop. (1986) 17,463.

Coolidge, (John) Calvin (1872–1933) 30th US President (1923–29). As vice president, he became president on the death of Warren HARDING, and was re-elected in 1924. His administration was characterized by minimal government interference in business and commerce.

cooperative movement Variety of organizations founded to provide mutual assistance in economic enterprises for the benefit of their members. They include agriculture, manufacturing (in which the workers own and manage their own plant), retailing, and banking and finance. *See also* OWEN, ROBERT; COOPERATIVE PARTY

Cooperative Party British political party, formed in 1917 as the political wing of the Cooperative Union. It is associated with the LABOUR PARTY and since 1946 all its parliamentary candidates have stood for election jointly as Labour cooperative candidates. Since 1959 it has limited the number of its candidates to 30.

Cooper, James Fenimore (1789–1851) US novelist. His most successful works were the romantic Leatherstocking Tales about the frontier, of which the best known are *The Pioneers* (1823), *The Last of the Mohicans* (1826) and *The Deerslayer* (1841). He also wrote a number of novels about life at sea.

coordinate geometry (algebraic geometry) Branch of mathematics combining the methods of pure GEOMETRY with those of ALGEBRA. Any geometrical point can be given an algebraical value by relating it to coordinates, marked off from a frame of reference. Thus, if a point is marked on a square grid so that it is x_1 squares along the x axis and y_1 squares along the y axis, it has the coordinates (x_1, y_1). Polar coordinates can also be used. It was first introduced in the 17th century by René DESCARTES. *See* CARTESIAN COORDINATE SYSTEM

coot Aquatic bird of freshwater marshes. Related to the RAIL, it is a strong swimmer and diver and feeds in or near water. All coots have white bills and foreheads. Family Rallidae; genus *Fulica*.

Copenhagen (København) Capital and chief port of Denmark, on E Sjaelland and N Amager Island, in the Øresund. A trading and fishing centre by the early 12th century, it became Denmark's capital in 1443. The commercial and cultural centre of the nation, it has shipbuilding, chemical and brewing industries. Pop. (1994) 620,970.

Copernicus, Nicolas (1473–1543) (Mikotay Kopernik) Polish astronomer. Through his study of planetary motions, Copernicus developed a heliocentric (Sun-centred) theory of the universe in opposition to the accepted geocentric (Earth-centred) theory conceived by PTOLEMY nearly 1,500 years before. *See also* GALILEO; KEPLER

Copland, Aaron (1900–90) US composer, especially known for combining folk and jazz elements with 20th-century symphonic techniques. His ballet music includes *Billy the Kid* (1938), *Rodeo* (1942) and *Appalachian Spring* (1944), which won a Pulitzer prize. He wrote symphonies, chamber music and patriotic pieces. He also experimented with SERIAL MUSIC, as in *Piano Fantasy* (1957).

Copley, John Singleton (1738–1815) US artist who produced some ground-breaking historical paintings. His notable paintings include *Colonel Epes Sargent* (c.1760), *The Boy with a Squirrel* (1765), and the history paintings *Brook Watson and the Shark* (1778) and *The Death of Major Peirson* (1783).

copper Metallic element (symbol Cu), one of the TRANSITION ELEMENTS. Reddish copper occurs native (free or uncombined) and in several ores including cuprite (an oxide) and chalcopyrite (a sulphide). The metal is extracted by smelting and is purified by ELECTROLYSIS. It is malleable, a good thermal and electrical conductor, and is extensively used in boilers, pipes, electrical equipment and alloys, such as brass and bronze. Properties: at.no. 29; r.a.m. 63.546; r.d. 8.92; m.p. 1,083°C (1,981°F); b.p. 2,567°C (4,652°F).

Coppola, Francis Ford (1939–) US film director, producer and screenwriter. He won a Best Picture Oscar for *The Godfather* (1972), the first in the epic Corleone mafia trilogy. *Apocalypse Now* (1975) was a creative updating of the Joseph CONRAD novel *Heart of Darkness* and an expression of the horrors of the VIETNAM WAR. His credits include *Rumble Fish* (1983), *Peggy Sue Got Married* (1986) and *Dracula* (1992).

Coptic Church Ancient Christian church of Egypt and Ethiopia. Its members form 5–10% of Egypt's population. The majority adhere to the Monophysite creed, declared heretical in 451, which denies the humanity of Christ.

copyright Legal authority protecting an individual's or company's works of art, literature, music and computer programs from reproduction or publication without the consent of the owner of the copyright. Since the Universal Copyright Convention (1952) works must carry the copyright symbol (©) followed by the owner's name and the first year of publication.

coral Small coelenterate marine animal of class Anthozoa, often found in colonies. The limestone skeletons secreted by each animal polyp accumulate to form a coral reef. Reef-building corals are found only in waters with temperatures in excess of 20°C (68°F).

Coral Sea Arm of the SW Pacific Ocean between the Great Barrier Reef off the E coast of Australia, Vanuatu (E) and New Guinea (NW). It was the scene of a US naval victory over the Japanese in 1942.

cor anglais (English horn) Reed instrument of the OBOE family. Longer than the oboe, its range is a fifth lower. Its bell is pear-shaped and its double reed is inserted in a curved mouthpiece. Parts have been scored for it in 19th-century works, especially those of BERLIOZ and WAGNER.

Corbusier, Le *See* LE CORBUSIER

Córdoba (Cordova) City on the Guadalquivir

River, s Spain; capital of Córdoba province. A flourishing centre of learning under Abd ar-Rahman III (first caliph of Córdoba), it was captured by Ferdinand III of Castile in 1236. Industries: tourism, coal and lead mining, engineering, textiles, olive oil. Pop. (1991) 300,229.

core Central area of the Earth from a depth of 2,885km (1,790mi). It accounts for 16% of the Earth's volume and 31% of its mass. The outer part of the core is liquid whereas the inner core from 5,150km (3,200mi) to the centre of the Earth is solid. The core is thought to be composed of iron-nickel alloy (90% iron, 10% nickel). Temperature estimates for the core vary from 4,000–7,000°C (7,200–12,600°F). Convection in the iron liquid outer core is thought to produce the Earth's magnetic field.

Corelli, Arcangelo (1653–1713) Italian BAROQUE composer. He achieved early distinction as a violinist under the guidance of Giovanni Benvenuti. He helped to develop the CONCERTO grosso, composed many sonatas and did much to consolidate the principles behind modern violin playing.

Corfu (Kérkyra) Island in NW Greece, second largest of the Ionian island group; the major town is Corfu. The island was allied with Athens in 433 BC against Corinth. The Romans held Corfu from 229 BC, and it was part of the Byzantine empire until the 11th century. It was occupied by the Venetians from 1386–1797, and then fell under British protection from 1809–64, when it passed to Greece. Industries: tourism,fishing, olives, fruit, livestock, wine. Area: 593sq km (229sq mi). Pop. (1991) 107,592.

coriander (cilandro) Herb of the CARROT family native to the Mediterranean and Near East. Oil from the seeds is used as an aromatic flavouring in foods, medicines and spirits (gin); the leaves are used in cooking. Family Apiaceae/Umbelliferae; species *Coriandrum sativum.*

Corinth (Kórinthos) Capital of Corinth department, NE Peloponnesos, at the SW tip of the Isthmus of Corinth, Greece. One of the largest and most powerful cities of ancient Greece, it was allied with Sparta in the Peloponnesian War (431–404 BC). Ruled by the Venetians from 1687–1715, then by the Turks, it became part of Greece in 1822. The modern city is 5km (3mi) NE of ancient Corinth, which was destroyed by an earthquake in 1858. It is a major transport centre and has chemical and winemaking industries. Pop. (1991 est.) 29,000.

Corinthian order One of the five Classical ORDERS OF ARCHITECTURE

Corinthians, Epistles to the Two books of the New Testament that are two letters of St PAUL addressed to the Christian Church in Corint, Greece. The letters centre on the teething troubles of the newly founded Christian community.

Coriolis effect (force) Apparent force on particles or objects due to the rotation of the Earth under them. The motion of particles or objects is deflected towards the right in the Northern Hemisphere and towards the left in the Southern Hemisphere. The direction of water swirling round in a drain demonstrates this force.

Cork County and county town in s Republic of Ireland, in Munster province. The largest of the Irish counties, it has a rugged terrain with fertile valleys. The chief occupations are farming and fishing along the rocky coastline. In the 9th century the Danes occupied Cork, but were driven out in 1172. Oliver Cromwell occupied Cork in 1649. Many public buildings were destroyed in nationalist uprisings in 1920. The largest export is farm produce. Area: 7,462sq km (2,881sq mi). Pop. (1991) 410,369.

cork Outer dead, waterproof layer of the BARK of woody plants. The bark of the cork oak, native to Mediterranean countries, is the chief source of commercial cork. Family Fagaceae; species *Quercus ruber*

corm Fleshy underground stem that produces a plant. In most plants, new corms form on top of old ones, which last for one season.

cormorant Bird found in coastal and inland waters throughout the world. It has a hooked bill, a black body and webbed feet. It dives well. There are 30 species. Length: to 1m (3.3ft). Family Phalacrocoracidae; genus *Phalacrocorax.*

corncrake Bird of the RAIL family common in grain fields of N Europe. It has a brown body and a short bill, and its specific name describes its call. Family Rallidae; species *Crex crex.*

cornea Transparent membrane at the front of the EYE. It is curved and acts as a fixed LENS, so that light entering the eye is to some extent focused before it reaches the lens.

Corneille, Pierre (1606–84) First of the great French classical dramatists. His plays include the tragedy *Médée* (1635), the epic *Le Cid* (1637) and a comedy *Le Menteur* (1643). He was elected to the French Academy in 1647.

cornet Brass musical instrument similar to a trumpet. It was one of the first brass instruments to have valves and, therefore, capable of playing a full range of notes. Its range is about the same as a trumpet's, but its tone is mellower and less penetrating.

Corn Laws Series of acts regulating the import and export of grain in Britain. The act of 1815 prevented the import of wheat until the domestic price exceeded a certain figure. The result was to keep the price of bread high. Opposition led to repeal by the ANTI-CORN LAW LEAGUE (1846).

Cornwall County in sw England, on a peninsula bounded by the Atlantic Ocean, the English Channel and Devon; the county town is Bodmin. Major towns include Truro, St Austell and Penzance. A rocky coast with hills and moors inland, it is drained by the Camel, Fowey, Tamar and Fal rivers. It is a popular tourist region. Area: (including Scilly Isles) 3,512sq km (1,356sq mi). Pop. (1991) 468,425.

corona Outermost layer of the Sun's atmosphere, extending for many millions of kilometres into space. The corona emits strongly in the x-ray region, and has been studied by x-ray satellites. The corona has a temperature of 1–2 million K.

Coronado, Francisco Vásquez de (1510–54) Spanish explorer. He went to Mexico in 1535, and in 1540 he headed an expedition to locate the seven cities of Cibola, reportedly the repositories of untold wealth. He explored the W coast of Mexico, discovered the Colorado River and the Grand Canyon, followed the route of the Rio Grande, and then headed N through the Texas Panhandle, Oklahoma and E Kansas.

coronary artery disease Disease of the coronary blood vessels, particularly the aorta and arteries supplying blood to the heart tissue. *See also* ARTERIOSCLEROSIS; ANGINA

coronary thrombosis Formation of a blood clot in one or other of the coronary arteries supplying the HEART, preventing blood (and with it oxygen and nutrients) from reaching the heart. It leads to death of part of the heart muscle – a HEART ATTACK.

coronation Ceremony of crowning a monarch. The form of coronation used in Britain was first drafted by St Dunstan, who crowned King Edgar in 973. Since 1066, British sovereigns have been crowned in Westminster Abbey, London.

coroner Public official who inquires into deaths that have apparent unnatural causes by means of an inquest and/or post-mortem. The office dates to 12th-century England. Coroners in Britain also inquire into cases of "treasure trove" (coins, gold, silver or bullion with no known owner).

Corot, Jean-Baptiste Camille (1796–1875) French painter, a leading 19th-century landscapists. After 1827 he gained success at the Paris Salon with traditionally romantic paintings executed in a soft-edged style, unlike the precisely observed scenes of his earlier work. .

corporation Business organization that is legally a separate entity, which gives it limited liability. The owners or shareholders are not individually responsible for the legal dealings of the corporation, except in the extent of their holdings. The corporation form is most usual in large organizations.

Correggio (*c.*1490–1534) (Antonio Allegri) Italian painter. His oil paintings and frescos produced daring (although anatomically exact) foreshortening effects inspired by those of MICHELANGELO and RAPHAEL. He was one of the first painters to experiment with the dramatic effects of artificial light.

correlation In STATISTICS, a number that summarizes the direction and degree of relationship between two or more dimensions or variables. Correlations range between 0 (no relationship) and 1.00 (a perfect relationship), and may be positive (as one variable increases, so does the other) or negative (as one variable increases, the other decreases).

corrosion Gradual tarnishing of surface or major structural decomposition by chemical action on solids, especially metals and alloys. It commonly appears as a greenish deposit on copper and brass, RUST on iron, or a grey deposit on aluminium, zinc and magnesium.

Corsica (Corse) Mountainous island in the Mediterranean Sea, *c.*160km (100mi) SE of the French coast. It is a region of France comprising two départements. The capital is Ajaccio. It was a Roman colony, before passing into the hands of a series of Italian rulers. In 1768 France purchased all rights to the island. Products: grapes, olives, mutton, cheese, wool, fish. Area: 8,681sq km (3,352sq mi). Pop. (1990) 250,400.

Cortés, Hernán (1485–1547) Spanish CONQUISTADOR and conqueror of Mexico. Cortés captured Tenochtitlan (Mexico City) after a three-month siege in 1521, gaining the Aztec empire for Spain.

cortex In animal and plant anatomy, outer layer of a gland or tissue. Examples are the cerebral cortex or outer layer of the brain and the cortical layers of tissue in plant roots and stems lying between the bark or EPIDERMIS and the hard wood or conducting tissues.

cortisone HORMONE produced by the cortex of the ADRENAL GLANDS and essential for carbohydrate, protein and fat metabolism, kidney function and disease resistance.

corundum Translucent to transparent mineral in many hues, aluminium oxide (Al_2O_3). It is found in igneous, pegmatitic and metamorphic rocks. It is the hardest natural substance after DIAMOND. Gemstone varieties are sapphire and ruby. Hardness 9; s.g. 4.

Cosby, Bill (1937–) US comedian, actor and writer. The first leading African-American man in a television series (*I Spy*, 1965–68), he established one of the most successful situation comedies in television history, *The Cosby Show* (1984–).

cosecant In TRIGONOMETRY, ratio of the length of the hypotenuse to the length of the side opposite an acute angle in a right-angled triangle.

cosine In TRIGONOMETRY, ratio of the length of the side adjacent to an acute angle to the length of the hypotenuse in a right-angled triangle.

cosmology Branch of scientific study that brings together astronomy, mathematics and physics in an effort to understand the make-up and evolution of the Universe. Once considered the province of theologians and philosophers, it is now an all-embracing science, which has made great strides in the 20th century.

Cossacks Bands of Russian adventurers who undertook the conquest of Siberia in the 17th century. Of ethnically mixed origins, they were escaped serfs, renegades and vagabonds who formed independent, semi-military groups on the fringe of society. After the Russian Revolution (1917), the Cossacks opposed the BOLSHEVIKS and strongly resisted collectivization.

Costa Rica Republic in Central America; the capital is SAN JOSÉ. **Land and climate** Central Costa Rica consists of mountain ranges and plateaus with many volcanoes. In the SE, the densely populated Meseta Central and Valle del General have rich volcanic soils. San José stands at c.1,170m (3,840ft) above sea-level, and has a pleasant climate with an average annual temperature of 20°C (68°F), compared with more than 27°C (81°F) on the coast. The NE trade winds bring heavy rains to the Caribbean coast. Evergreen forests cover about 50% of Costa Rica. **Economy** Costa Rica is one of the most prosperous developing countries in Central America. Agriculture employs 24% of the population. Major crops include coffee, bananas and sugar (all of which are exported). Other crops include beans, citrus fruits, cocoa, maize, potatoes and vegetables. Cattle ranching is important. Costa Rica has rich timber resources. Developing industries include tourism, cement, clothing and fertilizers. **History** Spain ruled the country until 1821; in 1822 Spain's Central American colonies broke away to join Mexico. In 1823 the Central American states broke from Mexico and set up the Central American Federation. This large union gradually disintegrated and Costa Rica achieved full independence in 1838. From the late 19th century, Costa Rica experienced a number of revolutions. In 1948 a revolt led to the abolition of the armed forces. Since then, Costa Rica has been a stable democracy.

Costner, Kevin (1955–) US film actor and director. He established himself as a leading Hollywood actor in the late 1980s. He made his directorial debut with *Dances With Wolves* (1990) and won Academy Awards as Best Director and Best Actor. Other acting credits include *The Untouchables* (1987), *JFK* (1991) and *Tin Cup* (1996).

cotangent Ratio of the length of the side adjacent to an acute angle, to the length of the side opposite the angle in a right-angled triangle.

Cotman, John Sell (1782–1842) British landscape painter and etcher, co-founder (with John CROME) of the Norwich School. He was one of Britain's most important 19th-century watercolourists. His paintings include *Greta Bridge* (c.1805) and *Chirk Aqueduct*.

cotoneaster Genus of about 50 species of deciduous shrubs of the ROSE family (Rosaceae), mostly

native to China. They have small white flowers and small, red or black, round, berry-like fruit, and are often cultivated as ornamental plants.

Cotonou City in S Benin, W Africa. The former capital and largest city in Benin, it is an important port and distribution centre for the offshore oil industry. Industries: textiles, brewing. Pop. (1982) 487,020.

Cotopaxi Active volcano in N central Ecuador, 65km (40mi) S of Quito, in the Andes Mountains. It is the highest continually active volcano in the world and its frequent eruptions have caused severe damage. Height: 5,896m (19,344ft).

Cotswolds Range of limestone hills in W England lying mainly in Gloucestershire, and extending 80km (50mi) NE from Bath.

cotton Annual shrub native to subtropical regions. Most cotton is grown for the fibres that envelop the seeds and are made into fabric. Family Malvaceae; genus *Gossypium*.

cotton gin Machine for separating cotton lint from seeds, a task previously done by hand. It was patented in 1794 by Eli Whitney. It contributed to the prosperity of US cotton plantations and to the industrialization of the textile industry.

cottonmouth *See* WATER MOCCASIN

cotyledon First leaf or pair of leaves produced by the embryo of a flowering plant. It stores and digests food for the embryo plant, and, if it emerges above ground, photosynthesizes for seedling growth. *See also* DICOTYLEDON; MONOCOTYLEDON

cougar *See* PUMA

Coulomb, Charles Augustin de (1736–1806) French physicist. He invented the torsion balance which led to experiments in electrostatics and the discovery of Coulomb's law: the force between two point electric charges is proportional to the product of the charges, and inversely proportional to the square of the distance between them. The SI unit of electric charge is the coulomb.

Council for Mutual Economic Assistance (COMECON) International organization (1949–91) aimed at the coordination of economic policy among communist states. Led by the Soviet Union, its original members were Bulgaria, Czechoslovakia, East Germany, Hungary, Poland and Romania; later joined by Cuba, Mongolia and Vietnam. Cooperation took the form of bilateral trade agreements.

Council of Europe European organization that was founded in 1949 with the aim of strengthening pluralist democracy, human rights, and promoting European cultural identity. It has adopted around 150 conventions, the most important of which is the EUROPEAN CONVENTION ON HUMAN RIGHTS. The organization is based in Strasbourg, France.

council tax Tax levied on British households to pay for local services. Introduced in 1993, it was the successor to community charge (POLL TAX). The level of tax paid is assessed with reference to a range of eight price bands based on house value.

COSTA RICA

AREA: 51,100sq km (19,730sq mi)
POPULATION: 3,099,000
CAPITAL (POPULATION): San José (303,000)
GOVERNMENT: Multiparty republic
ETHNIC GROUPS: White 85%, Mestizo 8%, Black and Mulatto 3%, East Asian (mostly Chinese) 3%
LANGUAGES: Spanish (official)
RELIGIONS: Christianity (Roman Catholic 81%)
CURRENCY: Colón = 100 céntimos

counterpoint In music, technique in composition involving independent melodic lines that are sung or played simultaneously to produce HARMONY. Counterpoint (contrapuntal) writing reached its height in the 16th century, the organ compositions of J.S. Bach in the 18th century, and in the late works of Beethoven.

Counter Reformation Revival of the Roman Catholic Church in Europe during the 16th and early 17th centuries. It began as a reaction to the Protestant REFORMATION. A leading part was played in the movement by new monastic orders, particularly the Society of Jesus (JESUITS). The Council of TRENT (1545–63) clarified Roman Catholic teaching on the major theological controversies of the period and initiated internal reforms.

countertenor Male voice of the same register as the female CONTRALTO

country and western Popular music originally associated with rural areas of S USA. The music typically features sentimental lyrics and instrumental music played with stringed instruments such as the guitar, banjo or fiddle. Its origins were in the folk music of British immigrants (although in Texas, the blues were also an influence).

county One of the main administrative divisions of local government. Counties are usually responsible for policing, local judicial administration, maintaining public roads, and other public facilities, such as a fire service, and keeping record offices. *See also* LOCAL GOVERNMENT

coup d'état Swift stroke of policy, either against the ruling power of a state or by the state against an element within it. Of the former, the most usual is a military takeover of civilian government.

Couperin, Francois (1668–1733) French composer. He was organist and harpsichordist at the court of Louis XIV. "Le Grand", as he was known, is now principally remembered for his many harpsichord pieces. His book on the technique of harpsichord-playing, *L'art de toucher le clavecin* (1716), was highly influential.

Courbet, Gustave (1819–77) French painter, the leading exponent of REALISM. He rejected traditional subject matter and instead painted peasant groups and scenes from life in Paris. His nudes shocked contemporary society. Courbet's rejection of both romantic and classical ideals prepared the way for IMPRESSIONISM.

Court, Margaret (1942–) Australian tennis player. In singles she won the US amateur title (1962, 1965, 1968–69), the US Open (1969–70; 1973), Wimbledon (1963, 1965, 1970), the Australian Open (1960–66; 1969–71) and the French Open (1962, 1964, 1969–70). She won more Grand Slam titles (66) than any player.

Courtauld, Samuel (1793–1881) British industrialist. He founded the firm of Courtaulds in 1816. From 1904 it developed the production of viscose rayon, nylon and other man-made fibres. In 1931 he bequeathed his collection of 19th-century French painting to the University of London (the Courtauld Institute).

court martial Court of the armed services for trial of service persons accused of breaking military law. Court martials do not utilize the JURY system. Members of the court martial are serving officers, in certain cases advised by a judge advocate.

courts of law Judicial assemblies established to try legal cases and to impose punishment for wrongdoing or to remedy a damage. The history of the court system lies in the English assumption of COMMON LAW as its legal basis as opposed to ROMAN LAW. In the UK, courts are hierarchically organized, and try suits of two different types, CIVIL or CRIMINAL. In the UK, civil law cases are heard by county courts and the HIGH COURT OF JUSTICE, while those of criminal law are heard by CROWN COURTS or MAGISTRATES' court. Serious criminal offences are referred from magistrates' courts to a crown court. The Court of Appeal is divided into civil and criminal divisions and hears appeals from crown courts, county courts and the High Court. Appeals from the High Court are heard by the HOUSE OF LORDS, the Supreme Court of Appeal.

Cousteau, Jacques Yves (1910–97) French oceanographer. The co-inventor of the AQUALUNG, he also invented a process of underwater television. Many expeditions made by his ship *Calypso* were filmed for television.

covalent bond Chemical bond in which two atoms share a pair of electrons, one from each atom. Covalent bonds with one shared pair of electrons are called single bonds; double and triple bonds also exist. The molecules tend to have low melting and boiling points and to be soluble in nonpolar solvents. Covalent bonding is most common in organic compounds.

Covenanters Scottish Presbyterians pledged by the National Covenant (1638) to uphold their religion. They opposed CHARLES I's efforts to impose an Anglican episcopal system and supported Parliament in the English CIVIL WAR, in exchange for a promise to introduce Presbyterianism in England and Ireland. The Scots changed sides when this promise was broken, but were defeated by Oliver CROMWELL. Presbyterianism was restored in Scotland in 1688.

Coventry City and county district in West Midlands, central England. An important weaving centre in the Middle Ages, it later became known for its clothing manufacture. The city was badly damaged by bombing during World War 2. Industries: motor vehicles, telecommunications, mechanical and electrical engineering. Pop. (1991) 294,387.

Coverdale, Miles (1488–1569) English cleric who issued the first printed English Bible (1535) and the "Great Bible" (1539). Influenced by the REFORMATION, he helped William TYNDALE on his Bible translation.

Coward, Sir Noel Pierce (1899–1973) British playwright, composer and performer. He is best known for his urbane comedies such as *Hay Fever* (1925), *Private Lives* (1930) and *Blithe Spirit* (1941). His plays frequently lampooned drab high-society etiquette. Other works include the films *In Which We Serve* (1942) and *Brief Encounter* (1945). He also composed hundreds of songs, including *Mad Dogs and Englishmen* and *Mad About the Boy*.

cow Name for mature female CATTLE that have borne at least one calf. It is also applied to other female mammals, such as elephants and seals.

Cowell, Henry Dixon (1887–1965) US composer, influenced by non-Western music. He created "tone clusters" (dissonances produced by striking piano keys with the fist or forearm), used in such pieces as *Advertisement* (1914). Other piano pieces are played directly on the strings by plucking or striking. His output includes over 20 symphonies, many concertos and operas.

Cowper, William (1731–1800) British poet and hymn writer. His poetry often draws engagingly on the countryside or the details of domestic life, as in the long blank-verse poem *The Task* (1785). Some of his contributions to *Olney Hymns* have become standards of the Anglican church.

cowrie (cowry) Gastropod MOLLUSC identified by an ovoid, highly polished shell with a long toothed opening and varied markings. It is found on tropical coral shores. Length: 8.3–152mm (0.33–6in). Family Cypraeidae; more than 160 species.

cowslip Herb of the PRIMROSE family (Primulaceae), with a hanging yellow flower head; species *Primula veris*.

coyote Wild DOG originally native to w North America. Coyotes have moved into many E areas of the USA formerly inhabited by wolves. Usually greyish-brown, they have pointed muzzles, big ears and bushy tails. Length: 90cm (35in); weight: *c.*12kg (26lb). Species *Canis latrans*.

coypu Large aquatic RODENT, native to South America. It now also lives in North America and parts of Europe, both wild and on fur farms. Coypus have brown outer fur and soft grey underfur (nutria). Overall length: 1m (3.5ft); weight: 8kg (20lb). Species *Myocastor coypus*.

crab Flattened, triangular, or oval ten-legged crustacean covered with a hard shell. Primarily marine, some crabs are found in freshwater and a few are terrestrial. Most have a pair of large foreclaws, a pair of movable eyestalks and a segmented mouth. Crabs usually move sideways. Size: pea-sized to 3m (12ft). Order Decapoda.

Crabbe, George (1754–1832) British poet. His poetry is imbued with the atmosphere of his native Suffolk and is unflinchingly anti-sentimental, as in *The Village* (1783) and *The Borough* (1810), the basis for Benjamin Britten's opera *Peter Grimes*.

crab nebula NEBULA located about 6,500 light years away in Taurus. It is the remnant of a supernova noted by Chinese astronomers in July 1054. The nebula was discovered in the 18th century.

crack Street DRUG that is a COCAINE derivative. It is supplied in the form of hard, crystalline lumps, which are heated to produce smoke inhaled for its stimulant effects.

cracking Stage in oil-refining during which the products of the first distillation are treated to break up large hydrocarbons into smaller molecules by the controlled use of heat, catalysts and often pressure. The cracking of petroleum yields heavy oils, petrol, and gases such as ethane, ethylene and propene (propylene), which are used in the manufacture of plastics, textiles, detergents and agricultural chemicals. Cracking is a means of yielding greater amounts of the lighter hydrocarbons, which are in greater demand, from heavier fractions such as lubricating oil.

Craig, James (1871–1940) Northern Irish soldier and politician, first prime minister of Northern Ireland (1921–40). He was an extreme Unionist and helped Sir Edward CARSON to keep the province in Britain.

crake *See* RAIL

Cranach, Lucas, the Elder (1472–1553) German painter and engraver. A friend and follower of Martin Luther, Cranach designed many propaganda woodcuts for the Protestant cause. He also produced some of the first full-length portraits and developed a style of painting female nudes in a unique, enamel-like finish.

cranberry Plant of the HEATH family, distributed widely in N temperate regions. It is a creeping or trailing shrub and bears red berries with an acid taste used to make sauce and juice. Family Ericaceae; Genus *Vaccinium*.

Crane, Stephen (1871–1900) US writer, poet and war correspondent. His best known work is *The Red Badge of Courage* (1895), a grimly realistic story of an American Civil War soldier. Other works include a novel *Maggie: A Girl of the Streets* (1893) and a collection of short stories.

crane Any of several species of tall wading birds found in most parts of the world except S America. It has brownish, greyish or white plumage with a bright ornamental head and feeds on almost anything. Height: to 150cm (60in). Family Gruidae.

crane fly True fly of the order Diptera. It has a slender body, long fragile legs and one pair of wings. The larvae, leatherjackets, live in the soil where they feed on plant roots and stems, frequently becoming agricultural pests. Family Tipulidae; species *Tipula simplex*. Length: to 3cm (1.2in). The name is also given to the HARVESTMAN.

cranesbill Common name for certain species of wild GERANIUM. Some species are cultivated for ornamental ground cover.

cranium Dome-shaped part of the SKULL that protects the brain. It is composed of eight bones that are fused together.

Cranmer, Thomas (1489–1556) English prelate and religious reformer. He was appointed Archbishop of Canterbury by HENRY VIII in 1533. He secured the annulment of Henry's marriage to Catherine of Aragon, despite opposition from the pope. A friend of Thomas CROMWELL, he promoted the introduction of Protestantism into England and compiled the first Book of COMMON PRAYER in 1549. Following the accession of the Roman Catholic MARY I in 1553, Cranmer's reforms were halted. He was burnt at the stake.

Crassus, Marcus Licinius (115–53 BC) Roman political and military leader. He commanded an army for Sulla in 83 BC, and led the troops who defeated the slave rebellion of Spartacus in 71. With POMPEY and Julius CAESAR he formed the First Triumvirate in 60 BC. He was governor of Syria in 54 BC.

crater Roughly circular depression found in the surface of some planets, usually with steep sides. It is formed either by meteoric impact, or at the vent of a volcano.

crater lake Accumulation of water, usually by precipitation of rain or snow but sometimes ground water, in a volcanic crater (caldera). Should an eruption occur, the resulting mud flow (lahar) is often more destructive than a lava flow, owing to its greater speed. Crater Lake in Crater Lake Park, Oregon, USA, was formed by precipitation and the waters are maintained solely by rain and snow. It is the second deepest lake in North America.

Crawford, Joan (1904–77) US film star, b. Lucille Fay le Sueur. Major films include *Our Dancing Daughters* (1928), *Grand Hotel* (1932), *The Women* (1939) and *Mildred Pierce* (1945).

crayfish Edible, freshwater, ten-legged crustacean that lives in rivers and streams of temperate regions. Smaller than lobsters, crayfish burrow into the banks of streams and feed on animal and vegetable matter. Length: normally 8–10cm (3–4in). Families Astacidae (Northern Hemisphere), Parastacidae (Southern Hemisphere), Austroastacidae (Australia).

Crazy Horse (1842–77) Chief of the Oglala SIOUX. He was a leader of Sioux resistance to the advance of white settlers in the Black Hills, and assisted SITTING BULL in the destruction of General CUSTER at the Battle of Little Bighorn in 1876. Persuaded to surrender, he was killed a few months later, allegedly while trying to escape.

creation myth In most mythologies and religions, an account of the origin of the world, as well as of the human race and all the other creatures on Earth. There is a remarkable similarity in the creation stories as recounted in the holy books of major religions, and in the myths and legends of ethnic groups.

Crécy, Battle of (1346) First major battle of the HUNDRED YEARS WAR. The English led by EDWARD III and his son, the Black Prince, defeated the French of PHILIP VI. The English longbow, as well as superior tactics, accounted for their victory.

Cree People belonging to the Algonquin language family of Native Americans. They served as guides and hunters for French and British fur traders. Many of the Plains Cree intermarried with the French. The current population is *c*.130,000.

Creek Confederation of NATIVE AMERICANS, part of the Muskogean-language group. One of the largest groups of SE USA, they ranged from Georgia to Alabama. They formed a settled, agricultural society, with land owned communally. Within the confederacy, individual settlements had a degree of autonomy. After the Creek Wars (1813–14), they were removed to Oklahoma, where *c*.60,000 remain today.

cremation Ritual disposal of a corpse by burning. It was a common custom in parts of the ancient civilized world and is still the only funeral practice among Hindus and Buddhists. Early Christians rejected cremation because of their belief in the physical resurrection of the body. It was not until the 19th century that it was revived in the Western world.

creole Person born in the West Indies, Latin America or S USA but of foreign or mixed descent. Generally a Creole's ancestors were either African slaves or French, Spanish or English settlers.

cress Any of several small, pungent-leaved plants of the mustard family (Brassicaceae/Cruciferae), used in salads and as garnishes. The best known is WATERCRESS. Species *Nasturtium officinale*.

Cretaceous Last period of the MESOZOIC era, lasting from 144 –65 million years ago. Dinosaurs became extinct at the end of this period. The first true placental and MARSUPIAL mammals appeared and modern flowering plants were common.

Crete (Kreti, Kríti) Largest island of Greece, in the E Mediterranean Sea, SSE of the Greek mainland; the capital is IRÁKLION. Minoan civilization flourished on Crete from 2000 BC. Crete was conquered by Rome in 68–67 BC and later came under Byzantine (395), Arab (826) and Venetian (1210) rule. In 1669 Crete fell to Turkey. It was eventually united with Greece (1908). Crete has a mountainous terrain upon which sheep and goats are raised. The mild climate supports the cultivation of cereals, grapes, olives and oranges. Products: wool, hides, cheese, olive oil, wine. Tourism is important. Area: 8,336sq km (3,218sq mi). Pop. (1991) 540,054.

Creutzfeld-Jakob disease (CJD) Rare degenerative brain disease that results in dementia and death. It is believed to be caused by an infective agent, possibly a slow virus. Some scientists believe that CJD can be acquired by eating meat products from cattle infected with BOVINE SPONGIFORM ENCEPHALOPATHY (BSE).

Crick, Francis Harry Compton (1916–) British biophysicist. In the 1950s, with James WATSON and Maurice Wilkins, he established the double-helix molecular structure of deoxyribonucleic acid (DNA). The three were jointly awarded the Nobel Prize for physiology or medicine in 1962.

cricket Brown to black insect with long antennae and hind legs adapted for jumping, found worldwide. Males produce a chirping sound by rubbing their wings together. Length: 3–50mm (0.8–2in). Family Gryllidae.

cricket Bat and ball game popular in Britain and other Commonwealth nations originating c.1700. Two teams of 11 players compete on an oval or round pitch. The game revolves around two wickets, each comprising of three wooden stumps connected at the top with two small cross-pieces (bails). Leading nations compete against each other in a series of test matches. Since the 1960s, one-day or "limited overs" cricket has become increasingly popular. A test match is held over a maximum of five days and two innings per side. In an innings all the players of one team bat once, while the other team fields, providing the bowlers and a wicket-keeper. A bowler is allowed to bowl six consecutive overarm deliveries (an over) at the wicket defended by a batsman; this is followed by another over from the opposite end of the pitch by a different bowler. A run is usually scored by a batsman making contact with the ball and running between the wickets with his partner before the ball can be returned to either wicket. If the ball reaches the boundary of the pitch it scores four, or six runs if it does not bounce.

Crimea (Krym) Peninsula in s Ukraine that extends into the Black Sea, w of the Azov Sea. Simferopol is the capital. It was colonized by the Greeks and then by Romans, Ostrogoths, Huns, Mongols, Byzantines and Turks, before being annexed to Russia in 1783. In 1921 it became an autonomous republic of Russia, and in 1954 was transferred to the Ukraine as the Krymskaya oblast. In 1991 it was made an autonomous republic of an independent Ukraine. The region has many mineral resources, notably iron and gypsum, and intensive agriculture. Area: c.27,000sq km (10,425sq mi). Pop. (1991 est.) 2,549,800.

Crimean War (1853–56) Fought by Britain, France and the Ottoman Turks against Russia. In 1853 Russia occupied Turkish territory and France and Britain, determined to preserve the Ottoman empire, invaded the Crimea (1854) to attack SEV-ASTOPOL. The war was marked on both sides by incompetent leadership and organization. The CHARGE OF THE LIGHT BRIGADE is the best-known example. Sevastopol was eventually captured (1855). At the Treaty of Paris (1856) Russia surrendered its claims on the Ottoman empire.

Criminal Investigation Department (CID) Non-uniformed branch of the London Metropolitan Police (founded 1878) dealing with the prevention and investigation of crime, and with the preparation of information on criminal trends. There are c.1,600 CID officers, whose headquarters are at New Scotland Yard.

criminal law Body of law that defines crimes, lays down rules of procedure for dealing with them and establishes penalties for those convicted. Broadly, a crime is distinguished from a TORT by being deemed injurious to the state. In many countries the criminal law has been codified. Criminal law remains a part of COMMON LAW, although since the 18th century it has been greatly added to by statute law.

Cripps, Sir (Richard) Stafford (1889–1952) British socialist politician. He belonged to the left wing of the Labour Party. As chancellor of the exchequer (1947–50) in the reforming government of ATTLEE, he played a significant part in the post-war reconstruction of the economy.

critical angle Angle at which a significant transition occurs. In optics, it is the angle of incidence with a medium at which total internal REFLECTION occurs. In telecommunications, it is the angle radio waves are reflected by the IONOSPHERE.

critical mass Minimum mass of fissionable material required in a fission bomb or nuclear reactor to sustain a CHAIN REACTION. The fissionable material of a fission bomb is divided into portions less than the critical mass; when brought together at the moment of detonation they exceed the critical mass. *See also* FISSION, NUCLEAR

Croatia Balkan republic in SE Europe; the capital is ZAGREB. **Land and climate** Croatia was one of the six republics that made up the former republic of YUGOSLAVIA. It achieved independence in 1991. It chiefly consists of the fertile Pannonian plains, drained by two main rivers, the Drava and the Sava. The coastal area has a typical Mediterranean climate, with hot, dry summers and mild, moist winters. Inland, the climate becomes more continental. Farmland, including pasture, covers 70% of Croatia, with forest and woodland occupying only 15%. **Economy** The wars of the early 1990s disrupted Croatia's relatively prosperous economy. Before the crisis, DALMATIA had been a major European tourist destination. Croatia has a wide range of manufacturing industries, such as steel, chemicals, oil refining and wood products. Agriculture remains the principal employer. Crops include maize, soya beans, sugar beet and wheat. **History and politics** Slav people settled in the area around 1,400 years ago. In 803 Croatia became part of the Holy Roman Empire. It was an

---

CROATIA
AREA: 56,538sq km (21,824sq mi)
POPULATION: 4,764,000
CAPITAL (POPULATION): Zagreb (726,770)
GOVERNMENT: Multiparty republic
ETHNIC GROUPS: Croat 78%, Serb 12%, Bosnian, Hungarian, Slovene
LANGUAGES: Croatian
RELIGIONS: Christianity (Roman Catholic 77%, Eastern Orthodox 11%), Islam 1%
CURRENCY: Kuna

independent kingdom in the 10th and 11th centuries. In 1102 an 800-year union of the Hungarian and Croatian crowns was formed. In 1526 part of Croatia came under the Turkish OTTOMAN EMPIRE, while the rest of Croatia came under the Austrian HABSBURGS. In 1699 all of Croatia came under Habsburg rule. Following the defeat of Austria-Hungary in World War 1, Croatia became part of the new Kingdom of the Serbs, Croats and Slovenes, renamed Yugoslavia (1929). Germany occupied Yugoslavia during World War 2, and Croatia was proclaimed independent, although it was really a pro-Nazi puppet state (Utashe). After the war, the Communist Party, led by Josip TITO, took power. Tito held Yugoslavia together until his death (1980). In the 1990s Yugoslavia split into five separate nations. A 1991 referendum saw an overwhelming majority in favour of Croatia becoming an independent republic. The Yugoslav National Army was deployed and Serb-dominated areas took up arms in favour of remaining in the federation. War broke out between SERBIA and Croatia. Croatia lost more than 30% of its territory. In 1992 United Nations peacekeeping troops were deployed to maintain an uneasy cease-fire. In August 1992 Franjo TUDJMAN became the republic's first president. In 1992 war broke out in BOSNIA-HERZEGOVINA and Bosnian Croats occupied parts of Croatia. In 1993 Croatian Serbs in E Slavonia voted to establish the separate republic of Krajina. In 1995 Croatian government forces seized Krajina and 150,000 Serbs fled. An agreement between the Croatian government and Croatian Serb leaders provided for the eventual reintegration of Krajina into Croatia. Postponed from 1997, this reintegration is due to take place in 1998. In 1996 Croatia and Yugoslavia formally established diplomatic relations.

Croce, Benedetto (1866–1952) Italian idealist philosopher and politician. He was a senator (1910–20) and minister of education (1920–21). When MUSSOLINI came to power, Croce retired from politics in protest against fascism. He re-entered politics in 1943. As leader of the Liberal Party, he played a prominent role in resurrecting Italy's democratic institutions.

Crockett, Davy (David) (1786–1836) US politician and frontiersman. He served in the Tennessee legislature (1821–26) and the US Congress (1827–31, 1833–35). A Whig, he opposed the policies of Andrew JACKSON and the Democrats. He died at the battle of the Alamo.

crocodile Carnivorous lizard-like REPTILE found in warm parts of every continent except Europe. Most crocodiles have a longer snout than ALLIGATORS. Length: up to 7m (23ft). There are about 12 species. Family Crocodylidae.

crocus Hardy perennial flowering plant. It is low growing with a single tubular flower and grass-like leaves rising from an underground corm. Family Iridaceae; genus *Crocus*.

Croesus King of Lydia in Asia Minor (r. c.560–546 BC). Renowned for his wealth, he was overthrown by CYRUS THE GREAT of Persia.

Cro-Magnon Tall, Upper Paleolithic race of humans, possibly the earliest form of modern *Homo sapiens*. Cro-Magnon people settled in Europe c.35,000 years ago. They manufactured a variety of sophisticated flint tools, as well as bone, shell and ivory jewellery and artifacts. Cro-Magnon artists produced the cave paintings of France and N Spain.

Crompton, Richmal (1890–1969) British writer. She created William, the scruffy, prankish schoolboy. The stories were first collected as *Just William* (1922), and more than 30 William novels followed.

Crompton, Samuel (1753–1827) British inventor of a spinning machine. His "spinning mule" of 1779 reduced the amount of thread-breakage and made possible the production of very fine yarn.

Cromwell, Oliver (1599–1658) Ruler of England as Lord Protector (1653–58). He entered Parliament in 1628. A committed Puritan, he raised troops for Parliament at the outbreak of the English CIVIL WAR and was the outstanding parliamentary commander. He failed to reach a compromise with CHARLES I. The loyalty of Cromwell's troops made him powerful in the subsequent quarrels between Parliament and army. When parliamentary government failed in 1653, army officers made Cromwell "Lord Protector". As ruler, he pursued a dynamic, anti-Spanish foreign policy while endeavouring to restore social stability at home. Although offered the crown by Parliament, he refused. *See also* RUMP PARLIAMENT

Cromwell, Richard (1626–1712) Lord Protector of England (1658–59). Son of Oliver CROMWELL, Richard lacked his father's qualities of leadership. He was ousted from power after eight months.

Cromwell, Thomas, Earl of Essex (1485–1540) English statesman. He was secretary to Cardinal WOLSEY and succeeded him as Henry VIII's chief minister in 1531. He was chiefly responsible for the acts of the REFORMATION Parliament, which set up the CHURCH OF ENGLAND and carried out reforms of administration and finance. He fell from power after the failure of Henry's marriage to ANNE OF CLEVES, which he had promoted, and was executed.

Cronin, A.J. (Archibald Joseph) (1896–1981) Scottish novelist. He was a medical inspector of mines and a physician until the success of his first work, *Hatter's Castle* (1931). Many novels, such as *The Stars Look Down* (1935), *The Citadel* (1937), *The Keys of the Kingdom* (1942) and *The Green Years* (1944), were filmed.

Crookes, Sir William (1832–1919) British chemist and physicist. He invented the radiometer (which measures ELECTROMAGNETIC RADIATION) and the Crookes tube, which led to the discovery of the electron by J.J. THOMSON. He was the first to suggest that CATHODE RAYS consist of negatively charged particles. He also discovered THALLIUM.

crop rotation Practice of successively growing different crops on the same field. Rotated crops generally complement each other, each providing nutrients required by the others.

croquet Lawn game, in which wooden balls are hit with wooden mallets through a series of six wire hoops towards a peg. The first player to complete all 12 hoops (each hoop in both directions) and reach the peg wins the game. Croquet developed in France in the 17th century.

Crosby, "Bing" (Harry Lillis) (1904–77) US popular singer and actor. He became one of the most successful "crooners" in the USA. He won an Academy Award for the film *Going My Way* (1944). His recording of the Irving BERLIN hit *White Christmas* (1942) is the best-selling record of all time.

cross Ancient symbol with different significance to many cultures. In Christianity, it is associated with Christ's sacrificial death by crucifixion for the redemption of mankind. As a religious symbol the cross existed in one form or another in ancient Egypt, Babylonia, and Assyria.

crossbow *See* ARCHERY

croup Respiratory disorder of small children caused by inflammation of the LARYNX and airways. It is mostly triggered by viral infection. Symptoms are a harsh cough, difficult breathing, restlessness and fever.

Crow Large tribe of Siouan-speaking Native Americans who separated in the early 18th century from the HIDATSA. Today they occupy a large reservation area in Montana where they were settled in 1868.

crow Large, black bird found in many temperate woodlands and farm areas worldwide. Living in large flocks, crows prey on small animals and eat plants and carrion. They can be crop pests. They are intelligent birds and can sometimes be taught to repeat phrases. Family Corvidae. *See also* JAY; MAGPIE; RAVEN; ROOK

crown courts In England, courts established in 1971 to replace the assize courts and courts of quarter session. They are superior courts with a general jurisdiction, presided over by High Court judges.

Cruelty, Theatre of French dramatic movement of the late 1920s. It developed under the influence of Antonin ARTAUD, who advocated a physical theatre expressing stark emotions rather than complex dialogue. Violence was used as a theatrical device to disturb audience perception.

Cruikshank, George (1792–1878) British illustrator and cartoonist, well known for his political and theatrical illustrations. He first gained fame with his caricatures of the leading figures in George IV's divorce proceedings. He also illustrated over 800 books, of which the best-known are Dickens' *Sketches by Boz* and *Oliver Twist*.

Cruise, Tom (1962–) US film actor. His career began in teenage films, such as *Risky Business* (1983). Other credits include: *The Color of Money*

(1986), Rain Man (1988), *Born on the Fourth of July* (1989) and *Mission Impossible* (1996).

cruise missile Self-propelled MISSILE that travels, generally at low altitudes, following the contours of the terrain. It is able to fly low enough to avoid conventional radar defences. .

cruiser Warship smaller, lighter and faster than a BATTLESHIP, ranging in size from 7,500–21,000 tonnes. After World War 1, arms limitation treaties restricted its guns to 200mm (8in).

Crusades Military expeditions from Christian Europe to recapture the Holy Land (Palestine) from the Muslims in the 11th–14th centuries. Among the motives for the Crusades were rising religious fervour, protection of pilgrims to the Holy Land and aid for the BYZANTINE EMPIRE against the Seljuk Turks. The First Crusade (1096–99), initiated by Pope URBAN II, captured Jerusalem and created several Christian states. Later crusades had the additional objective of supporting or regaining these states. The Third Crusade (1189–91) was a response to the victories of SALADIN. Although crusader states survived for another 100 years, later crusades were less successful. In the 13th century the church sponsored crusades against other foes, such as the heretical ALBIGENSES in France. *See also* CHILDREN'S CRUSADES

crust In geology, the thin outermost solid layer of the Earth. The crust represents less than 1% of the Earth's volume and varies in thickness from about 5km (3mi) beneath the oceans to *c*.70km (45mi) beneath mountain chains such as the Himalayas. *See also* MOHO

crustacea Class of *c*.30,000 species of ARTHROPODS. The class includes the decapods (crabs, lobsters, shrimps and crayfish), isopods (pill millipedes and woodlice) and many varied forms. Most crustaceans are aquatic and breathe through gills or the body surface. They are typically covered by a hard exoskeleton. They range in size from the Japanese spider crab, up to 3m (12ft) across, to the ocean plankton, as little as 1mm (0.04in) in diameter.

cryogenics Branch of physics that studies materials and effects at temperatures approaching ABSOLUTE ZERO. Some materials exhibit highly unusual properties such as SUPERCONDUCTIVITY or SUPERFLUIDITY at such temperatures. Cryogenics has been used to freeze human bodies in the uncertain hope that future technology may be able to revive the subjects.

cryptography Form of written message in which the original text (plaintext) is replaced by a series of other signs according to a prearranged system, in order to keep the message confidential. Unlike a **code**, in which each letter of the plaintext is replaced by another sign, a **cipher** cannot be "cracked" without a key. Typically, a key is a complex pattern of letters or symbols forming the basis upon which the plaintext is enciphered. The receiver reverses this process to decipher the message. Ciphers were used by the ancient Greeks and were employed widely for military and diplomatic messages during the medieval and Renaissance periods. Mechanical devices for producing complex ciphers were developed between the two World Wars. The best-known cypher machine was the German Enigma device. Modern fast computers are today used by intelligence services for constructing and breaking constantly changing complex ciphers. The same system is used for keeping credit card information secret.

crystal Solid with a regular geometrical form and with characteristic angles between its faces, having limited chemical composition. The structure of a crystal is based upon a regular 3–D arrangement of atoms, ions or molecules. Crystals are produced when a substance passes from a gaseous or liquid phase to a solid state, or comes out of solution by evaporation or precipitation. Slow cooling produces large crystals, whereas fast cooling produces small crystals.

crystallography Study of the formation and structure of crystalline substances. In particular, crystallography is concerned with the internal structure of CRYSTALS. *See also* X-RAY CRYSTALLOGRAPHY

Crystal Palace First building of its size, 124×564m (408×1,850ft), to be made of glass and iron. Sir Joseph Paxton designed it for the Great Exhibition held in Hyde Park, London (1851). It was the first building prefabricated in sections and assembled on site. After the exhibition it was dismantled and re-erected on Sydenham Hill, SE London, where it stood until accidentally destroyed by fire in 1936.

Cuba Caribbean island republic, at the entrance to the Gulf of Mexico; the capital is HAVANA. **Land and climate** The Republic of Cuba, largest and most westerly of the WEST INDIES archipelago, consists of one large island, Cuba, together with the *Isla de la Juventud* (Isle of Youth) and many small islets. The highest mountain range, the Sierra Maestra in the SE, reaches 2,000m (6,562ft) at Pico Turquino. The rest of the land consists of gently rolling hills or coastal plains. Cuba has a semi-tropical climate. Farmland covers about 50% of Cuba and 66% of this is given over to sugar cane. **Economy** Despite major advances in health-care and

education, Cuba's economy has been devastated by the dissolution of the Soviet Union, its primary market and source of aid. The tightening of US trade sanctions since 1992 has also worsened Cuba's economic situation. Sugar accounts for 75% of Cuba's export earnings. Other exports include nickel ore, cigars, fish and rum. **History** When Christopher Columbus discovered Cuba in 1492, it was inhabited by Native Americans. The first Spanish colony was established in 1511. The indigenous population was quickly killed, replaced by African slave labour. Cuba formed a base for Spanish exploration of the American mainland. Discontent at Spanish rule erupted into war in 1868. In 1895 a second war of independence was led by José Martí. In 1898 the sinking of the US battleship *Maine* precipitated the Spanish-American War. From 1898–1902 Cuba was under US military occupation before becoming an independent republic. From 1933–59 Fulgencio BATISTA ruled Cuba, maintaining good relations with the USA. In 1952 he imposed martial law. After an abortive coup attempt in 1953, Fidel CASTRO, supported by Che GUEVARA, launched a revolution in 1956. In 1959 Castro became premier. Castro's brand of revolutionary socialism included the nationalization of many US-owned industries. In 1961 the USA broke off diplomatic ties and imposed a trade embargo. Castro turned to the Soviet Union. Cuban exiles, supported by the US government, launched the disastrous BAY OF PIGS invasion. In 1962 the potential siting of Soviet missiles on Cuba fuelled the CUBAN MISSILE CRISIS. Castro's early attempts to export revolution to the rest of Latin America ended in diplomatic alienation. Cuba turned to acting as a leader of developing nations and providing support for revolutionary movements. Between 1965–73, over 250,000 Cubans became exiles. Emigration was legalized in 1980 and many disaffected Cubans chose to leave.

Cuban Missile Crisis (October 1962) US and Soviet Union confrontation over the installation of Soviet nuclear rockets in Cuba. John F. KENNEDY warned KHRUSHCHEV that any missile launched from Cuba would be met by a full-scale nuclear strike on the Soviet Union. On 24 October, Cuba-bound Soviet ships bearing missiles turned back and Khrushchev ordered the bases to be dismantled.

cube In mathematics, the result of multiplying a given number by itself twice. Thus the cube of a is $a \times a \times a$, written a^3. A cube is also described as the third power of a number. A cube is a regular six-sided solid figure (all its edges are equal in length and all its faces are squares).

cubism Revolutionary, 20th-century art movement. It originated in *c*.1907 with PICASSO and BRAQUE. Abandoning traditional methods of creating pictures with one-point PERSPECTIVE, they built up three-dimensional images on the canvas using fragmented solids and volumes. The initial experimental, "analytical", phase (1907–12) was

CUBA
AREA: 110,860sq km (42,803sq mi)
POPULATION: 10,822,000
CAPITAL (POPULATION): Havana (2,096,054)
GOVERNMENT: Socialist republic
ETHNIC GROUPS: White 66%, Mulatto 22%, Black 12%
LANGUAGES: Spanish (official)
RELIGIONS: Christianity (Roman Catholic 40%, Protestant 3%)
CURRENCY: Cuban peso = 100 centavos

inspired mainly by African sculpture and the later works of CÉZANNE. They treated their subjects in muted grey and beige so as not to distract attention from the new concept. The "synthetic" phase (1912–14) introduced much more colour and decoration. Cubism attracted many painters as well as sculptors. These included LÉGER, Robert DELAUNAY and Sonia DELAUNAY-TERK and Frantisek KUPKA. The most important cubist sculptors were ARCHIPENKO, LIPCHITZ and Ossip Zadkine. It is probably the most important single influence on 20th-century progressive art.

cuckoo Widely distributed forest bird. True Old World cuckoos are generally brownish, although a few species are brightly coloured and notable for parasitic behaviour. Their chief food is insects. Length: 15–75cm (6–30in). Family Cuculidae; genus *Cuculus*.

cucumber Trailing annual vine covered in coarse hairs; it has yellowish flowers and the immature fruit is eaten raw or pickled. Family Cucurbitaceae; species *Cucumis sativus*.

Culloden, Battle of (1746) Decisive battle of the JACOBITE rising of 1745. The Jacobites, led by Charles Edward STUART were defeated near Inverness by government forces under the Duke of Cumberland, son of George II. Culloden ended Stuart attempts to regain the throne by force. The battle was followed by ruthless subjugation of the Highland clans.

cult System of religious beliefs, rites and observances connected with a divinity or group of divinities, or the sect devoted to such a system. Within a religion such as HINDUISM, many gods have their own cults, notably SHIVA.A deified human being or sacred animal may also be the object of worship. In the 20th century a cult often denotes a quasi-religious organization that controls its followers by means of psychological manipulation.

Cultural Revolution (officially, Great Proletarian Cultural Revolution) Campaign initiated in 1966 by MAO ZEDONG to purge the Chinese Communist Party of his opponents and to instil correct revolutionary attitudes. Senior party officials were removed from their posts, intellectuals and others suspected of revisionism were victimized and humiliated. A new youth corps, the RED GUARDS, staged protests, held rallies and violently attacked reactionistic ideas. By 1968 China was approaching civil war. The Red Guards were disbanded and the army restored order.

culture In ANTHROPOLOGY, knowledge that is acquired by human beings by virtue of their membership of a society. A culture incorporates the shared knowledge, expectations and beliefs of a group.

Cumbria County in NW England, bounded by the Solway Firth (N) and the Irish Sea (W); the county town is CARLISLE. The region includes the LAKE DISTRICT and the Cumbrian Mountains. Area: 6,808sq km (2,629sq mi). Pop. (1991) 483,163.

cummings, e.e. (edward estlin) (1894–1962) US poet. His reputation rests on his poetry, which usually exhibits sentimental emotion and/or cynical realism. It is famously characterized by unconventional spelling, punctuation and typography.

cuneiform System of writing developed in Mesopotamia around 3000 BC. The system consists of wedge-shaped strokes, derived from the practice of writing on soft clay with a triangular stylus as a "pen". Cuneiform developed from pictograms. The pictograms came to serve as an "alphabet", eventually consisting of more than 500 characters.

Cunningham, Merce (1919–) US modern dancer and choreographer. In 1952 he formed the much-acclaimed Merce Cunningham Dance Company. His productions are highly experimental and controversial and include *Antic Meet* (1958) and *How to Pass, Kick, Fall and Run* (1965).

Cupid In Roman mythology, god of love, equivalent to the Greek god EROS.

cuprite Reddish-brown, brittle, translucent oxide mineral, cuprous oxide (Cu_2O). Formed by the oxidation of other ores, such as copper sulphide, it is an important source of copper.

Curaçao Largest island of the NETHERLANDS ANTILLES in the West Indies, in the S Caribbean Sea; the capital is Willemstad. Curaçao derives most of its income from tourism and oil-refining. Products: groundnuts, tropical fruits, Curaçao liqueur, phosphates. Area: 444sq km (171sq mi). Pop. (1993 est.) 146,828.

curare Poisonous resinous extract obtained from various tropical South American plants of the genera *Chondodendron* and *Strychnos*. Causing muscle paralysis, it is used on the poisoned arrows of Native South Americans. It is also used as a muscle relaxant in abdominal surgery and setting fractures.

curate (Lat. *cura*, charge) Clergyman who assists the incumbent priest of a parish in the performance of his duties. The term was originally used to denote a priest who had the charge of a parish.

Curia Romana Official administrative body of the Roman Catholic Church. It is based in the VATICAN and consists of a court of officials through which the pope governs the Church.

Curie, Marie (1867–1934) Polish scientist, who specialized in work on RADIATION. Marie and her husband Pierre Curie worked together on a series of radiation experiments. In 1898 they discovered RADIUM and POLONIUM. In 1903 they shared the Nobel Prize in physics with A.H. BECQUEREL. In 1911 Marie became the first person to be awarded a second Nobel Prize (this time in chemistry), for her work on radium and its compounds.

curie Unit (symbol *Ci*) formerly used to measure the activity of a radioactive substance. It is defined as the quantity of a radioactive isotope that decays at the rate of 3.7×10^{10} disintegrations per second. The curie has been replaced by an SI unit, the becquerel (symbol *Bq*).

167

curium Synthetic radioactive metallic element (symbol Cm) of the ACTINIDE SERIES. It was first made in 1944 by the alpha particle bombardment of plutonium-239 in a cyclotron. Silvery in colour, curium is chemically reactive, intensely radioactive and is toxic if absorbed by the body. It provides power for orbiting satellites. Properties: at.no. 96; r.d. (calculated) 13.51; m.p. 1,340°C (2,444°F); 14 isotopes, most stable Cm^{247} (half-life 1.6×10^7 yr).

curlew Long-legged wading bird with a down-curved bill and mottled brown plumage. Often migrating long distances, it feeds on small animals, insects and seeds, and nests on the ground, laying two to four eggs. Length: to 48–62cm (19–25in). Species *Numenius arquata*.

curling Game resembling bowls on ice that is a major winter sport of Scotland, and is popular in Canada, N USA and Nordic countries. The game is played by two teams of four players. At each end of the ice is a circular target with a central area known as the tee. One player sends his stone towards the tee and teammates use brooms to sweep the surface in front of it to give it a smoother surface over which to glide. One point is scored for each stone lying nearer the tee than an opponent's stone.

current *See* OCEANIC CURRENT

Curzon, George Nathaniel, 1st Marquess of Kedleston (1859–1925) British Conservative statesman. He entered Parliament in 1886 and became Viceroy of India (1899–1905). He resigned as a result of an argument with Lord KITCHENER. He served in the war cabinet (1915–19) and as foreign secretary (1919–24).

Cushing, Harvey (1869–1939) US surgeon. His pioneering techniques for surgery on the brain and spinal cord helped advance neurosurgery. He first described the syndrome produced by over-secretion of adrenal hormones that is now known as Cushing's syndrome. It is characterized by weight-gain in the face and trunk, high blood pressure, excessive growth of facial and body hair, and diabetes-like effects.

Custer, George Armstrong (1839–76) US general. Following the US Civil War he was posted to the frontier and led attacks on the CHEYENNE. In 1876, at the Battle of the Little Bighorn, his force was ambushed by the SIOUX and every man killed.

cuticle Exposed outer layer of an animal. In humans this refers to the EPIDERMIS, especially the dead skin at the edge of fingers. In botany, it refers to the waxy layer on the outer surface of epidermal cells of leaves and stems of vascular plants. It helps to prevent excessive water loss.

cuttlefish Cephalopod MOLLUSC related to the SQUID and OCTOPUS. Like squid, cuttlefish swim rapidly by the propulsion of a jet of water forced out through a siphon. Their flattened bodies contain the familiar chalky cuttle-bone. Family Sepiidae; species *Sepia officinalis*.

Cuvier, Georges, Baron de (1769–1832) French geologist and zoologist, a founder of comparative anatomy and palaeontology. His scheme of classification stressed the form of organs and their correlation within the body. He applied this system of classification to fossils, and came to reject the theory of gradual evolution, favouring instead a theory of catastrophic changes.

Cuzco City in S central Peru; capital of Cuzco department. An ancient capital of the Inca empire from *c.*1200, it fell to the Spaniards in 1533. Cuzco was destroyed by earthquakes in 1650 and then rebuilt. Pop. (1993) 255,568.

cyanide Salt or ester of hydrocyanic acid (prussic acid, HCN). The most important cyanides are sodium cyanide (NaCN) and potassium cyanide (KCN), both of which are deadly poisonous. Cyanides have many industrial uses – in electroplating, for the heat treatment of metals, in the extraction of silver and gold, in photography, and in insecticides and pigments.

cyanobacteria (formerly, blue-green algae) One of the major BACTERIA phyla, distinguished by the presence of the green pigment CHLOROPHYLL and the blue pigment phycocyanin. Many cyanobacteria perform NITROGEN FIXATION. They occur in soil, mud and deserts; they are most abundant in lakes, rivers and oceans. Some produce toxic blooms.

cybernetics Study of communication and control systems in animals, organizations and machines. It makes analogies between the brain and nervous system, and computers and other electronic systems. Cybernetics combines aspects of mathematics, neurophysiology, computer technology, INFORMATION THEORY and psychology.

cyberspace Popular term for the perceived "virtual" space within computer memory or networks, especially if rendered graphically. The term is a product of science fiction. During the mid-1990s the term was common, used in reference to the INTERNET and the worldwide web.

cycad Phylum (Cycadophyta) of primitive palm-like shrubs and trees that grow in tropical and subtropical regions. Although they are GYMNOSPERMS, they have feathery palm- or fern-like leaves at the top of stout stems. In addition to their main roots they also have special roots containing CYANOBACTERIA. These plants first flourished about 225 million years ago. Most of the 100 or so surviving species are less than 6.1m (20ft) tall.

cyclamen Genus of 20 species of low-growing perennial herbs, native to central Europe and the Mediterranean region. They have swollen, tuberous corms, and heart- or kidney-shaped leaves. The drooping blooms are white, pink, lilac or crimson. Family Primulaceae.

cycle In physics, series of changes through which any system passes that brings it back to its original state. For example, alternating current starts from zero voltage, rises to a maximum, declines through zero to a minimum and rises again to zero.

In the INTERNAL COMBUSTION ENGINE, the two-stroke engine completes one cycle each downward plunge and return; the four-stroke cycle takes two such movements.

cycling Sport for individuals and teams competing on BICYCLES. Now a regular event at the Olympic Games, cycle racing first became popular following the invention of the pneumatic tyre (1888). The most famous cycle race is the TOUR DE FRANCE (inaugurated 1903).

cyclone System of winds, or storm, that rotates inwards around a centre of low atmospheric pressure (depression). The winds flow anti-clockwise in the Northern Hemisphere and clockwise in the Southern Hemisphere.

Cyclopes In Greek mythology, three demons, each having one eye in the centre of its forehead. They forged the thunderbolts of ZEUS.

cygnus One of the most distinctive constellations, often nicknamed the Northern Cross.

cylinder Solid figure or surface formed by rotating a rectangle using one side as an axis. If the vertical height is h and the radius of the base r, then the volume is $\pi r^2 h$ and the curved surface area $2\pi r h$.

Cymbeline (Cunobelinus) (d. $c.$AD 42) Ancient British king. An ally of the Romans, he was king of the Catuvellauni tribe. After conquering the Trinovantes, he became the strongest ruler of S Britain.

Cynewulf English poet of the early 8th century, presumed to be the author of *Elene*, *The Fates of the Apostles*, *The Ascension* and *Juliana*.

Cynic Philosophical way of life begun by Antisthenes, a pupil of SOCRATES. This goal of life requires self-sufficiency. With the succession of individuals who "lived" its precepts, great variation developed in its interpretation.

cypress Tall, evergreen tree native to North America and Eurasia. It has scale-like leaves, roundish cones and a distinctive symmetrical shape. Height: 6–24m (20–80ft). Family Cupressaceae; genus *Cupressus*. There are about 20 species.

Cyprus Island republic in the NE Mediterranean Sea; the capital is NICOSIA. **Land and climate** Cyprus has scenic mountain ranges, the Kyrenia and the Troodos. The island's fertile lowlands are used extensively for agriculture. It has a Mediterranean climate. **Economy** Industry employs 37% of the workforce and manufactures include cement, footwear, tiles and wine. Farming employs 14% and crops include barley, citrus fruits, grapes, olives, potatoes and wheat. The most valuable activity is tourism. The economy of the Turkish Cypriot N lags behind that of the Greek Cypriot S. **History** Greeks settled on Cyprus $c.$3,200 years ago. From AD 330 the island was part of the Byzantine empire. In the 1570s it became part of the Ottoman empire. Turkish rule continued until 1878 when Cyprus was leased to Britain. Britain annexed the island in 1914, proclaiming it a colony in 1925. In the 1950s Greek Cypriots, who made up 80% of the population, began a campaign for *enosis* (union)

CYPRUS
AREA: 9,250 sq km (3,571 sq mi)
POPULATION: 725,000
CAPITAL (POPULATION): Nicosia (177,451)
GOVERNMENT: Multiparty republic
ETHNIC GROUPS: Greek Cypriot 81%, Turkish Cypriot 19%
LANGUAGES: Greek and Turkish (both official)
RELIGIONS: Christianity (Greek Orthodox), Islam
CURRENCY: Cyprus pound = 100 cents

with Greece. Cyprus became an independent country in 1960. **Politics** The constitution of independent Cyprus provided for power-sharing between the Greek and Turkish Cypriots. It proved unworkable, however, and fighting broke out between the two communities. In 1979 Turkish N Cyprus was proclaimed to be a self-governing region. In 1983 the Turkish Cypriots declared the N to be an independent state called the Turkish Republic of Northern Cyprus; the only country to recognize it is Turkey. The UN regards Cyprus as a single nation under the Greek Cypriot government in the S. Border clashes continued in the 1990s. In mid-1997, UN-sponsored peace negotiations led to the first meeting between the two presidents in three years.

Cyrano de Bergerac, Savinien (1619–55) French writer. His novels and plays combine free thinking, humour and burlesque romance. He is best known for two prose fantasies, *Journey to the Moon* (1656) and *The Comical Tale of the States and Empires of the Sun* (1662). He is perhaps equally famous as the eponymous hero of the popular but historically inaccurate play by Edmond ROSTAND.

Cyrillic ALPHABET based on Greek letter forms that is now used for writing several Slavic languages, most notably Russian and Serbian.

Cyrus the Great (600–529 BC) King of Persia, founder of the ACHAEMENID Persian empire. He overthrew the Medes, then rulers of Persia, in 549 BC, defeated King CROESUS of Lydia ($c.$546 BC), captured BABYLON (539 BC) and the Greek cities in Asia Minor. Though he failed to conquer Egypt, his empire stretched from the Mediterranean to India. He delivered the Jews from their BABYLONIAN CAPTIVITY, sending them home to Palestine.

cystic fibrosis Hereditary glandular disease in which the body produces abnormally thick mucus that obstructs the breathing passages, causing chronic lung disease. The disease is treated with antibiotics, pancreatic enzymes and a high-protein diet; sufferers must undergo vigorous physiotherapy to keep the chest as clear as possible.

cystitis Inflammation of the urinary bladder, usually caused by bacterial infection. It is more common in women. Symptoms include frequent and painful urination, low back pain and slight fever.

cytokinin (kinetin or kinin) Any of a group of

plant hormones that stimulate cell division. Cytokinins work in conjunction with AUXINS to promote swelling and division in the plant cells, producing lateral buds. They can also slow down the aging process in plants, encourage seeds to germinate and plants to flower, and are involved in plant responses to drought and water-logging.

cytology Study of living CELLS and their structure, behaviour and function. Cytology began with Robert HOOKE's microscopic studies of cork in 1665, and the microscope is still the main tool. Recently cytochemistry has focused on the study of the chemistry of cell components.

cytoplasm Jelly-like matter inside a CELL and surrounding the NUCLEUS. Cytoplasm has a complex constituency and contains various bodies known as organelles, with specific metabolic functions. The proteins needed for cell growth and repair are produced in the cytoplasm.

Czech Language spoken in the Czech Republic (Bohemia and Moravia) by c.10 million people. A Slavic language, it is closely related to SLOVAK.

Czechoslovakia Former federal state in central Europe. Formed after World War 1 from parts of the old AUSTRO-HUNGARIAN EMPIRE, Czechoslovakia was formally recognized as a new republic by the Treaty of St Germain (1918). Nationalist tensions caused unrest: the SLOVAKS had long wanted autonomy and the large German population in the N wanted to join with Germany. Hitler's rise to power and annexation of Austria led to the Munich Agreement (1938), which ceded Czech land to Germany. Poland and Hungary also acquired territory. Hitler occupied the country in 1939. In 1945 the country was liberated by Soviet and US troops. A 1946 election gave the Communists a majority in the coalition. By 1948 they had assumed complete control. Czechoslovakia became a Soviet-style state with greatly reduced political and cultural freedom. The PRAGUE SPRING of 1968 with the reforms of Alexander DUBČEK was crushed by Soviet troops and all reforms were reversed. When democratic reforms were introduced in the Soviet Union in the late 1980s, CZECHS also demanded reforms. In 1989 non-communists came to power and the "Velvet Revolution" was complete when Vaclav HAVEL became president. Free elections were held in 1990, but differences between the Czechs and Slovaks led to the partitioning of the country on 1 January 1993. The break was peaceful and the two new nations, the CZECH REPUBLIC and the SLOVAK REPUBLIC have retained many ties. *See also* BOHEMIA; MORAVIA

Czech Republic Republic in central Europe; the capital is PRAGUE. **Land and climate** The Czech Republic lies in central E Europe and contains

---

CZECH REPUBLIC
AREA: 78,864sq km (30,449sq mi)
POPULATION: 10,310,000
CAPITAL (POPULATION): Prague (1,216,005)
GOVERNMENT: Multiparty republic
ETHNIC GROUPS: Czech 81%, Moravian 13%, Slovak 3%, Polish, German, Silesian, Gypsy, Hungarian, Ukrainian
LANGUAGES: Czech (official)
RELIGIONS: Christianity (Roman Catholic 39%, Protestant 4%)
CURRENCY: Czech koruna = 100 halura

---

two regions: the plateau of BOHEMIA in the W, and the lowland of MORAVIA in the E. Prague and Plzen are Bohemia's largest cities; BRNO is the major Moravian city, Mountains form most of the N border. Rivers are vital to this landlocked republic. Some rivers, such as the ELBE, Oder and Vltava flow N into Germany, while others in the S flow into the DANUBE basin. The climate is continental. Many forests have been cut down to create farmland. **Economy** Manufacturing employs 40% of the workforce. Industries include chemicals, beer, iron and steel and machinery. Light industries include glassware and textiles. The Czech Republic is mainly self-sufficient in food. Private ownership of land is gradually being restored. Agriculture employs 12% of the workforce. Livestock raising is important. Crops include grains, fruit, and hops for brewing. **History** CZECHS began to settle in the area c.1,500 years ago. Bohemia became important in the 10th century as a kingdom within the Holy Roman Empire. In 1526 the Austrian Habsburgs assumed control, but a Czech rebellion in 1618 led to the THIRTY YEARS' WAR. German culture dominated the area until the late 18th century. Austria continued to rule Bohemia and Moravia, throughout the 19th and 20th centuries. After World War 1 CZECHOSLOVAKIA was created. Germany occupied the country in World War 2. In 1946 Eduard BENES became president. By 1948 the Communist Party had assumed absolute control. Democratic reforms culminated in the PRAGUE SPRING of 1968. Warsaw Pact troops invaded to crush the liberals. In 1989 mass demonstrations resulted in the "Velvet Revolution". Free elections were held in 1991 resulting in the re-election of Vaclav HÁVEL. In 1992 the government agreed to the secession of the SLOVAK REPUBLIC, and on 1 January 1993 the Czech Republic was created. The break of CZECHOSLOVAKIA was peaceful and the two new nations retain many ties.

D/d is derived from the Semitic daleth and the Greek delta, receiving its present form from the Romans. In Roman numerals, D stands for 500.

dace Any of several small freshwater fish of the CARP family, Cyprinidae. The common European dace (*Leuciscus leuciscus*) is silvery and may grow 30cm (12in) long. The Moapa dace (*Moapa coriacea*) is an endangered species.

Dachau Town in Bavaria, SW Germany, site of the first Nazi CONCENTRATION CAMP established in March 1933. Up to 70,000 people died or were killed here before liberation in 1945. The site is preserved as a memorial.

Dada (Dadaism) Movement in literature and the visual arts, started in Zürich (1915). Members included Jean ARP and Tristan Tzara. The group, repelled by war and bored with CUBISM, promulgated complete nihilism and embraced satire. Dadaists planned irreverent art events, designed to shock a complacent public. They stressed the absurd and the importance of the unconscious. In the early 1920s, conflicts of interest led to the demise of Dadaism. A number of its former adherents, particularly André BRETON, developed SURREALISM.

daddy-longlegs European name for the CRANE FLY

Daedalus In Greek mythology, a masterly architect and sculptor. He constructed the LABYRINTH for King MINOS of Crete. When denied permission to leave the island, he made wings of wax and feathers to escape with his son ICARUS.

daffodil Long-leaved, bulbous plant. The single flowers are yellow or yellow and white, with a bell-like central cup and oval petals. Height: to 45cm (18in). Family Amaryllidaceae Genus *Narcissus*.

Dagestan Republic in the Russian Federation, bounded on the E by the CASPIAN SEA, SE European Russia; the capital is Makhachkala. Islam was introduced in the 7th century, and the majority of the present population is Muslim. Annexed by Russia in the early 19th century, autonomy was granted in 1921. In 1991 it gained full republic status. The region is dominated by the CAUCASUS mountains. The N lowlands are fertile. The rivers Samur and Sulak provide hydroelectric power. Difficulty of access has left mineral resources untapped. Industries: engineering, oil, and chemicals. Area: 50,300sq km (19,416sq mi). Pop. (1994) 1,953,000.

Daguerre, Louis Jacques Mandé (1789–1851) French painter and inventor. In 1829 Daguerre co-invented an early photographic process (daguerreotype) in which a unique image is produced on a copper plate without an intervening negative. Their process was announced in 1839, shortly before William FOX TALBOT developed the calotype.

Dahl, Roald (1913–90) British writer. He is remembered for his witty children's fiction. His books, such as *James and the Giant Peach* (1961) and *Charlie and the Chocolate Factory* (1964), are popular with all ages. His adult stories often feature a grotesque, moral twist, such as *Someone Like You* (1953) and *Kiss, Kiss* (1959). *Boy* (1984) and *Going Solo* (1986) are volumes of autobiography.

dahlia Genus of perennial plants with tuberous roots and large flowers. The common garden dahlia (*Dahlia pinnata*) has been developed into more than 2,000 varieties. Height: to 1.5m (5ft). Family Asteraceae/Compositae.

daisy Any of several members of the family Asteraceae/Compositae, especially the common English garden daisy, *Bellis perennis*. It has basal leaves and long stalks bearing solitary flower heads, each of which has a large, yellow, central disc and small radiating white petal-like florets.

Dakar Capital and largest city of Senegal, W Africa. Founded in 1857, Dakar later became capital of French West Africa. There is a Roman Catholic cathedral and a Presidential Palace. Dakar has excellent educational and medical facilities, including the Pasteur Institute. Industries: textiles, oil refining, brewing. Pop. (1992 est.) 1,729,823.

Dakota *See* NORTH DAKOTA and SOUTH DAKOTA

Daladier, Édouard (1884–1970) French statesman. Leader of the Radicals, he was prime minister (1933, 1934, 1938–40). He signed the Munich Pact (1938) but declared war on Germany in 1939. He was displaced after failing to aid Finland. In 1942 he was interned by the VICHY GOVERNMENT, deported to Germany and released in 1945.

Dalai Lama (Grand Lama) Supreme head of the Yellow Hat Buddhist monastery at Lhasa, TIBET. The title was bestowed upon the third Grand Lama by the Mongol ruler Altan Khan (d.1583). In 1642 the Mongols installed the fifth Dalai Lama as political and spiritual ruler of Tibet. Spiritual supremacy was later shared with the PANCHEN LAMA. In 1950–51, Tenzin Gyatso (1935–), 14th Dalai Lama, temporarily fled Tibet after it was annexed by China. Following a brutally suppressed uprising (1959), he went into exile in N India. In TIBETAN BUDDHISM, the Dalai Lama is revered as the BODHISATTVA *Avalokitesvara*.

Dali, Salvador (1904–89) Spanish artist. His style, a blend of meticulous realism and hallucinatory transformations of form and space, made him an influential exponent of SURREALISM. His dream-like paintings exploit the human fear of distortion, such as *The Persistence of Memory* (1931).

Dallapiccola, Luigi (1904–75) Italian composer. He was the first Italian composer to adopt the TWELVE-TONE system of SCHOENBERG. The opera *Volo di notte* (1940) is a fine example. Persecuted by Mussolini, he wrote many pieces concerned with freedom, notably *Canti di Prigonia* (1941).

Dallas City in NE Texas, USA. First settled in the 1840s, Dallas expanded with the 20th-century development of its oilfields. President Kennedy was assassinated here on 22 November 1963. A leading commercial and transport centre of SW USA, it has many educational and cultural institutions. Industries: oil refining, electronic equipment, clothing and aircraft. Pop. (1990) 1,006,877.

Dalmatia Region of Croatia on the E coast of the ADRIATIC SEA; the capital is SPLIT. From the 10th century it was divided N and S between Croatia and Serbia. The Treaty of Campo Formio (1797) ceded the region to Austria. After World War 1 it became part of Yugoslavia. The coastline stretches from Rijeka to the Montenegro border, and is a popular tourist area. Most of the interior is mountainous. In 1991, following Croatia's secession from the Yugoslav Federation, Dalmatia was the scene of heavy fighting between Croats and Serbs. Other major cities include Zadar (historic capital) and DUBROVNIK.

dalmatian Dog characterized by its white coat with black or brown spots. It has a long flat head with long muzzle and high-set ears. Its powerful body is set on strong legs and the tail is long and tapered. Height: to 58cm (23in) at the shoulder.

Dalton, John (1766–1844) British chemist, physicist and meteorologist. He researched TRADE WINDS, the AURORA borealis, and COLOUR BLINDNESS. His study of gases led to Dalton's law of partial pressures: the total pressure of a gas mixture is equal to the sum of the partial pressures of the individual gases, provided no chemical reaction occurs. His atomic theory states that each element is made up of indestructible, small particles. He also constructed a table of relative atomic masses.

dam Barrier built to confine water (or check its flow) for irrigation, flood control or electricity generation. The first dams were probably constructed by the Egyptians 4,500 years ago. **Gravity** dams are anchored by their own weight. **Single-arch** dams are convex to the water they retain, supported at each end by river banks. Multiple-arch and **buttress** dams are supported by buttresses rooted in the bedrock. HYDROELECTRICITY is made possible by dams, such as the ASWAN High Dam, Egypt.

Damascus Capital of Syria, on the Barada River, SW Syria. Said to be the oldest continuously occupied city in the world. It was held by the Ottoman Turks for 400 years, and after World War 1 came under French administration. It became capital of independent Syria in 1941. Damascus has many historic sites, such as the Great Mosque and the Citadel. It is Syria's administrative and financial centre. Industries: damask fabric, metalware, leather goods and sugar. Pop. (1993 est.) 1,497,000.

Damocles In Greek history, a courtier of Dionysius I of Syracuse (Sicily). Dionysius suspended a sword by a thread above Damocles' head to make him realize that wealth and power were transient.

damselfly Delicate insect resembling the DRAG-

ONFLY. Almost all have a slender, elongated, blue abdomen and a pair of membranous wings. Length: to 5cm (2in). Order Odonata.

damson Small tree and its edible fruit; often applied to varieties of PLUM (*Prunus domestica*), especially *P.d. insititia*. The fleshy DRUPE is generally borne in clusters, has a tart flavour and is made into jam. Family Rosaceae. The damson-plum of tropical America is a separate species, *Chrysophyllum oliviforme*, Family Sapotaceae.

dance Ancient art of ordered, stylized body movements, normally performed to the accompaniment of music or voices. In its most primitive form, dance was probably part of courtship and religious ritual. In China, Japan, and India, graceful MIME is the distinctive feature, whereas the dances of Africa are characterized by rapid, athletic movements. In 18th-century Europe, Bach and Handel, among others, composed music for formal courtly dances, such as the gavotte and minuet. Ballroom dances, such as the waltz, foxtrot, tango and quickstep, became popular in the 19th and early 20th centuries. In the 1950s, dances such as the jive and twist were introduced. Many different styles have emerged from MODERN DANCE. *See also* BALLET; FOLK DANCE

dandelion Widespread perennial weed, with basal leaves and yellow composite flowers. It reproduces by means of parachute seeds. The leaves are used in salads, the flowers in wine-making. Family Asteraceae (COMPOSITAE); species *Taraxacum officinale*.

Daniel Legendary Jewish hero and visionary of the 6th century BC, who was at the court of the Babylonian kings, NEBUCHADNEZZAR and BELSHAZZAR. The OLD TESTAMENT Book of Daniel, probably written *c.*165 BC, relates events in Daniel's life during the BABYLONIAN CAPTIVITY. The book also gives an account of Belshazzar's Feast. The last six of its 12 chapters consist of visions and prophesies.

D'Annunzio, Gabriele (1863–1938) Italian poet, novelist, and playwright. His rhetoric greatly influenced early 20th-century Italian poetry. His poems include *Alcyone* (1904), and novels *The Triumph of Death* (1896) and *The Child of Pleasure* (1898). Of his many plays, *La Figlia di Jorio* (1904) is considered the best. He became a national hero when he seized and ruled TRIESTE from 1919–21.

Dante Alighieri (1265–1321) Italian poet. In his early years Dante wrote many *canzoni* to Beatrice Portinari, who remained the inspiration for much of his life's work. In 1300 he became one of the rulers of Florence, but was exiled in 1302 after a feud between the White and Black GUELPHS. He never returned to Florence, and died impoverished in Ravenna. His writings include *The New Life* (*c.*1293), *Banquet* (*c.*1304–07), *On Monarchy* (*c.*1313), and *De Vulgari Eloquentia* (1304–07). His masterpiece, *The Divine Comedy*, a three-book epic in *terza rima*, is one of the greatest achievements of European literature.

Danton, Georges Jacques (1759–94) French politician and leader of the French REVOLUTION. A moderator in the turbulent 1790s, he sought conciliation between the GIRONDINS and Montagnards. Briefly head of the JACOBINS in 1793 and a member of the Committee of Public Safety, he was arrested during the Reign of Terror and guillotined.

Danube (Donau) River in central and SE Europe. Europe's second-longest river, it rises in SW Germany, flows NE then SE across Austria to form the border between Slovakia and Hungary. It then flows S into Serbia, forming part of Romania's borders with Serbia and Bulgaria. It continues N across SE Romania to the Black Sea. An international waterway, it is controlled by the Danube Commission. Length: c.2,859km (1,770mi).

Danzig See GDAŃSK

Daphne Nymph in GREEK MYTHOLOGY. APOLLO, struck by a gold-tipped arrow of EROS, fell in love with Daphne. She had been shot with one of Eros' leaden points, and so scorned all men. To protect her from Apollo, she was transformed by the Gods into a laurel tree.

Dardanelles (Çanakkale Bogazi, ancient Hellespont) Narrow strait between the Sea of Marmara and the Aegean Sea, separating Çanakkale in Asian Turkey from GALLIPOLI in European Turkey. Throughout the Byzantine and Ottoman empires and both World Wars it was of strategic importance in the defence of Constantinople (ISTANBUL). Since the early 14th century it has been almost continuously controlled by Turkey. The strait was the scene of the GALLIPOLI CAMPAIGN in World War 1. The 1920 Treaty of Sévres demilitarized the straits, but by 1936 Turkey had remilitarized the zone. Length: 61km (38 mi). Width: 1.2–6km (0.75–4mi).

Dar es Salaam Former capital of Tanzania, on the Indian Ocean, E Tanzania. Founded in the 1860s by the sultan of Zanzibar, it was capital of German East Africa (1891–1916) and of Tanganyika (1916–74). It is Tanzania's commercial centre, largest city and port. Industries: textiles, chemicals, and oil products. Pop. (1988 est.) 1,360,850.

Darius I (c.558–486BC) ACHAEMENID king of Persia (521–486BC). Troubled by revolts, particularly in BABYLON, he restored order by dividing the empire into provinces, allowing some local autonomy and tolerating religious diversity. He also fixed an annual taxation and developed commerce. He was defeated at Marathon in 490 BC.

Darjeeling City at the foot of the HIMALAYAS, West Bengal, NE India. A former British hill station, it is noted for its teas and views of KANCHENJUNGA and EVEREST. Pop. (1981) 57,603.

Dark Ages Period of European history, from the fall of the Roman empire in the 5th century to the 9th or 10th century. The term appears to imply cultural and economic backwardness after the Classical civilization of Greece and Rome, but in fact refers to the paucity of historical evidence.

Darmstadt City in Hesse state, W central Germany. The old town dates from the Middle Ages. The city was severely damaged during World War

2. It is a cultural centre, with a notable international music school. Industries: chemicals, aerospace engineering, steel. Pop. (1990) 140,900.

Darwin, Charles Robert (1809–82) British naturalist, originator of a theory of EVOLUTION based on NATURAL SELECTION. In 1831, he joined a round-the-world expedition on HMS Beagle. Observations of the flora and fauna of South America (especially the GALÁPAGOS ISLANDS) formed the basis of his work on animal variation. The development of a similar theory by A. R. WALLACE led Darwin to present his ideas to the Linnean Society in 1858, and in 1859 he published *The Origin of Species*, one of the world's most influential science books.

Darwinism See EVOLUTION

dasyurus Genus of mainly nocturnal, carnivorous MARSUPIALS found in Australia, New Guinea, and Tasmania. They have large canine teeth, separate digits and long tails. The female's pouch is normally shallow. Family Dasyuridae.

data Information, such as lists of words, quantities or measurements. A computer PROGRAM works by processing data, which may be entered on the keyboard, or stored in code as a data file on a DATABASE, MAGNETIC DISK or tape.

database Collection of DATA produced and retrieved by computer. The data is usually stored on MAGNETIC DISK or tape. A database PROGRAM enables the computer to generate files of data and later search for and retrieve specific items or groups of items. A library database system can list, on screen, all the books on a particular subject and can then display further details of any selected book.

data processing Systematic sequence of operations performed on DATA, especially by a COMPUTER, in order to calculate or revise information stored on MAGNETIC DISK or tape. The main processing operations performed by a computer are arithmetical and logical operations that involve decision-making based on comparison of data.

data protection Measures taken to guard data against unauthorized access. Computer technology now makes it easy to store large amounts of data, such as financial details. Many governments have passed legislation ensuring that such databases are registered and that the information they contain is used only for the purpose for which it was given.

date palm Tree native to the Near East. It has feather-shaped leaves and large flower clusters that produce the popular edible fruit. Height: up to 30m (100ft). Family Arecacae/Palmae.

dating, radioactive (radiometric dating) Any of several methods using the laws of RADIOACTIVE DECAY to assess the ages of archaeological remains, fossils, rocks and of the Earth itself. The specimens must contain a long-lived radioisotope of known HALF-LIFE, which, with a measurement of the ratio of radioisotope to a stable ISOTOPE (usually the decay product), gives the age. In **potassium-argon** dating, the ratio of potassium-40 to its stable decay product argon-40, gives ages over ten million years. In **radiocarbon** dating, the proportion of carbon-14 (half-life 5,730 years) to stable carbon-12 absorbed into once-living matter, such as wood or bone, gives ages up to several thousand years.

David, Saint (d. *c.*600) Patron saint of Wales. He founded a monastery at what is now St Davids. Little is known of his life, but legends abound. His feast day is 1 March.

David (*c.*1000–*c.*962 BC) King of Israel. His career is related in the OLD TESTAMENT. He became a hero by defeating GOLIATH in a duel and was made king of Judah on SAUL's death. He united Judah and Israel and made Jerusalem his capital. God is said to have promised that his dynasty would be eternal (*see* MESSIAH*)*.

David, Gerard (1460–1523) Flemish painter. He was commissioned by the town of BRUGES to paint several works: *The Judgement of Cambyses* and *The Flaying of Sisamnes* warned officials of the retribution for injustice. Other works include *Madonna Enthroned* and *Annunciation*.

David, Jacques Louis (1748–1825) French painter, a leader of NEO-CLASSICISM. David's work was closely tied up with his JACOBIN views and support of Napoleon I. His most famous work is *Oath of the Horatii*. Other masterpieces include *Death of Marat, Madame Recamier* and *Death of Socrates.*

Davies, Sir Peter Maxwell (1934–) British composer. Prolific and eclectic, he has written five operas, including *Taverner* (1972) and *Resurrection* (1988). Much of his work reflects the landscape and culture of his adopted home, the remote Orkney Islands, N Scotland, notably the opera *The Martyrdom of St Magnus* (1977).

Davies, Robertson (1913–95) Canadian novelist, dramatist and journalist. Davies is best known for *The Deptford Trilogy* (1970–75), which exhibits his characteristic mixture of myth, satire and psychological symbolism. Other works include *The Salterton Trilogy* (1951–58), and several plays, including *A Jig for the Gypsy* (1954). His non-fiction is collected in *The Mirror of Nature* (1983).

Da Vinci, Leonardo *See* LEONARDO DA VINCI

Davis, Bette (1908–89) US film actress. She is remembered for her intense character portrayals and tough, fiery screen presence. She won two Best Actress Oscars in *Dangerous* (1935) and *Jezebel* (1938). Other classic films include *Now Voyager* (1942) and *All About Eve* (1950). In 1977 she became the first woman to receive a Life Achievement Award from the American Film Institute.

Davis, Jefferson (1808–89) American statesman, president of the CONFEDERATE STATES during the CIVIL WAR (1861–65). He was elected to Congress in 1845, but resigned to fight in the MEXICAN WAR. He entered the Senate in 1849 and was made secretary of war (1853–57). He resigned when Mississippi seceded from the Union, and became president of the Confederacy. After the war he served two years in prison.

Davis, Miles Dewey (1926–91) US jazz trumpeter, a highly influential modern jazz musician. During the 1940s he played BEBOP with Charlie PARKER. Eager to experiment with diverse musical forms, he recorded the reflective *Birth of the Cool* (1949) and played with John COLTRANE on the seminal *Kind of Blue* (1959). During the late 1960s he switched to electric instrumentation and was a pioneer of jazz-rock. From the 1970s he blended funk, soul, pop and rap with his distinctive jazz tone.

Davy, Sir Humphry (1778–1829) British chemist. He discovered that electrolytic cells produce electricity by chemical means. This led to his isolation of sodium, potassium, barium, strontium, calcium and magnesium. He also proved that all acids contain hydrogen. An investigation into the explosive reaction of firedamp (methane and other gases) and air led to the invention of the miner's safety lamp.

Dayan, Moshe (1915–81) Israeli army officer and politician. He served with the British Army in World War 2. He led the invasion of the Sinai Peninsula in 1956 and, as minister of defence, became a hero of the SIX DAY WAR (1967). Active in Israeli policymaking, he served as foreign minister (1977–79).

Day-Lewis, Cecil (1904–72) British poet and critic. He was associated with the AUDEN circle. His concern for social justice is evident in *Transitional Poem* (1929), *Magnetic Mountain* (1933), *Overtures to Death* (1938) and *Collected Poems* (1954). He was poet laureate from 1968. He wrote detective fiction under the pseudonym Nicholas Blake.

Day-Lewis, Daniel Michael (1957–) Irish actor, b. London. He achieved public recognition for his powerful performance in *My Beautiful Laundrette* (1986). In 1989 he won a Best Actor Oscar for his extraordinary physical role in *My Left Foot*. Other credits include *The Age of Innocence* (1993) and *In the Name of the Father* (1993).

Dayton City at the confluence of the Great Miami and Stillwater rivers, SW Ohio, USA. Settled in 1796, it is a commercial centre of an agricultural region. In 1995 the Dayton Peace Accord ended the Bosnian civil war. Pop. (1990) 182,044.

D-day (6 June 1944) Codename for the Allied invasion of Normandy during WORLD WAR 2. Commanded by General EISENHOWER, Allied forces landed on the French coast between Cherbourg and Le Havre. The largest amphibious operation in history, it involved *c.*5,000 ships. Despite fierce resistance, bridgeheads were established by 9 June. It was the first step in the liberation of Europe.

DDT (dichlorodiphenyltrichloroethane) Organic compound used as an insecticide. It acts as a contact poison, disorganizing the nervous system. Though effective against most insect pests, it proved to have long-lasting toxic effects and many species developed resistance. It is now banned in many countries.

deadly nightshade (belladonna) Poisonous perennial plant native to Europe and W Asia. It has large leaves, purple flowers and black berries.

ALKALOIDS, such as ATROPINE, are obtained from its roots and leaves. Eating its fruit can be fatal. Family Solanaceae; species *Atropa belladonna*.

Dead Sea (Al-Bahr-al-Mayyit) Salt lake in the Jordan valley, Jordan-Israel border. It is fed by the River JORDAN. The surface, 396m (1,302ft) below sea-level, is the lowest point on Earth. One of the world's saltiest waters, it supports no life, and large quantities of salts are commercially extracted.

Dead Sea Scrolls Ancient manuscripts discovered from 1947 in caves at Qumran near the DEAD SEA. Written in Hebrew or Aramaic, they date from the 1st century BC to the 1st century AD. They include versions of much of the OLD TESTAMENT and other types of religious literature. Some are 1,000 years older than other biblical manuscripts.

deafness Partial or total hearing loss. **Conductive** deafness, faulty transmission of sound to the sensory organs, is usually due to infection or inherited abnormalities of the middle EAR. **Perceptive** deafness may be hereditary or due to injury or disease of the COCHLEA, auditory nerve or hearing centres in the brain. Treatment ranges from removal of impacted wax to delicate microsurgery. Hearing aids, sign language and lip-reading are techniques which help the deaf to communicate.

Dean, James (1931–55) US film actor. He played the restless son in the film of John Steinbeck's *East of Eden* (1954) and appeared as a misunderstood teenager in *Rebel Without a Cause* (1955). He was killed in a car crash, a year before the release of his final film *Giant*. He has become a cult hero.

dean Administrative official. In education, a head of administration in a university faculty or medical school. In the Anglican Church, the leader of the chapter in a cathedral or collegiate church. In the Roman Catholic Church, the head of the College of Cardinals is a dean.

death Cessation of life. In medicine, death has traditionally been pronounced on cessation of the heartbeat. However, modern resuscitation and life-support techniques have led to the revival of patients whose hearts have stopped. In a tiny minority of cases, while breathing and heartbeat can be maintained artificially, the potential for life is extinct. In this context, death may be pronounced when it is clear that the brain no longer controls vital functions. The issue is highly controversial.

death cap (deadly amanita) Highly poisonous FUNGUS that grows in woodlands. It has a yellowish-green cap and a white stem with a drooping ring and sheathed base. If eaten, the poison causes great pain, serious liver damage and, in most cases, death. Species *Amanita phalloides*.

Death Valley Desert basin in E California, USA. It is the lowest point in the western hemisphere, 86m (282ft) below sea level. Temperatures can reach 57°C (134°F), the highest in the USA. Gold and silver were mined in the 1850s. It is surrounded by the Panamint mountains (w) and the Armagosa (E). Length: 225km (140mi).

deathwatch beetle Small beetle that tunnels through wood. It makes a faint ticking sound once said to presage death. It is actually the mating signal of the female as it taps its head against the wood. Length: to 0.9cm (0.3in). Family Anobiidae; species *Xestobium rufovillosum*.

De Broglie, Louis Victor *See* BROGLIE, PRINCE LOUIS VICTOR DE

debt, national Public debt of a government. National debt accumulates if governments spend more than they generate through taxation; it consists largely of borrowing from individuals and other governments. Many political groups demand that governments construct balanced budgets.

Debussy, Claude Achille (1862–1918) French composer, exponent of IMPRESSIONISM. Debussy wrote highly individual music that was delicate and suggestive. He explored new techniques of harmony and orchestral colour. Some critics cite his *Prélude à l'après-midi d'un faune* (1894) as the beginning of 20th-century music. Other orchestral works are *Nocturnes* (1899), *La Mer* (1905) and *Images* (1912). His piano works, such as *Suite Bergamasque* (1890) and *Etudes* (1915), are among the most important in the repertoire. His one completed opera was *Pelléas and Mélisande* (1902).

decathlon Sports event comprising ten different track and field activities: 100m, long jump, shot-put, high jump, 400m, 110m hurdles, discus, pole vault, javelin and 1,500m. It is an Olympic event.

Deccan Plateau in central India, S of the Narmada River. In attempting to conquer it in the 17th century, Aurangzeb fatally weakened the MOGUL dynasty. In the late 18th century, the British defeated the French here. On its E and W edges, the Deccan rises to the GHATS. Cotton, cereal, coffee and tea are grown on the plateau's with rich volcanic soil.

decibel Logarithmic unit (symbol dB), one tenth of a bel, used for comparing two power levels and for expressing the loudness of a sound. The faintest audible sound (2×10^{-5} pascal) is given an arbitrary value of 0dB. The human pain threshold is about 120dB. Ordinary conversations occur at 50–60 dB.

deciduous Annual or seasonal loss of all leaves from a tree or shrub. *See also* EVERGREEN

decimal system Commonly used system of writing numbers, using a base ten and the Arabic numerals 0 to 9. It is a positional number system, each position to the left representing an extra power of ten. Thus 6,741 is $(6 \times 10^3) + (7 \times 10^2) + (4 \times 10^1) + (1 \times 10^0)$. Note that $10^0 = 1$. Decimal fractions are represented by negative powers of ten placed to the right of a decimal point.

Declaration of Independence (4 July 1776) Statement of principles, in which the THIRTEEN COLONIES of North America justified the AMERICAN REVOLUTION and separation from Britain as the United States of America. Its blend of idealism and practical statement has ensured its place as one of the world's most important political documents.

175

The Declaration was drafted by a committee that included Thomas JEFFERSON, and was based on the theory of NATURAL RIGHTS, propounded by John LOCKE to justify the GLORIOUS REVOLUTION in England. It was approved by the CONTINENTAL CONGRESS on 4 July . The Declaration states the necessity of government having the consent of the governed, of government's responsibility to its people, and contains the famous paragraph: "We hold these truths to be self-evident, that all men are created equal, that they are endowed by their Creator with certain unalienable Rights, that among these are Life, Liberty, and the Pursuit of Happiness."

Declaration of Rights See BILL OF RIGHTS

Declaration of the Rights of Man and Citizen (1789) Statement of principles of the FRENCH REVOLUTION, adopted by the National Assembly, accepted by Louis XVI and included in the 1791 constitution. Influenced by the American DECLARATION OF INDEPENDENCE and the ideas of Jean Jacques ROUSSEAU, it established the sovereignty of the people and the restrictions for social consideration embodied in "liberty, equality, and fraternity".

decomposition Natural degradation of organic matter into simpler substances, such as carbon dioxide and water. Organisms of decay are usually BACTERIA and FUNGI. Decomposition recycles nutrients by releasing them back into the ECOSYSTEM.

decompression sickness See BENDS

deconstruction In architecture, a term used to describe work dating from the early 1980s that explores ways of reconciling traditional oppositions in building design, such as structure–decoration or abstraction–figuration. Leading designers include Bernard Tschumi, Peter Eisenman, Frank Gehry and the OMA group. Deconstruction is also a literary and philosophical term of critical analysis, pioneered by the work of the French philosopher Jacques Derrida. Patterns of opposition, which form a given text, are broken down and considered. Derrida's key writings include *Writing and Difference* (1967) and *Dissemination* (1972). The process of deconstruction is highly text-centred, and its critics claim that it is ahistorical.

Decorated style Style of English Gothic architecture which flourished *c.*1250–1350. The most exuberant phase of English Gothic, it featured the double-curving ogee ARCH and intricate, curvilinear window tracery. Its French equivalent, the FLAMBOYANT STYLE, came much later. The windows of Exeter Cathedral are excellent examples of Decorated stone carving. *See also* GOTHIC ART AND ARCHITECTURE

deer Long-legged, hoofed, RUMINANT. There are 53 species in 17 genera distributed worldwide. In most species, the male (buck, hart or stag) bears ANTLERS. Only in REINDEER does the female (hind or doe) bear antlers. Deer often gather in herds. They are generally brown, with spotted young (fawns). They eat bark, shoots, twigs and grass. Humans exploit them for their meat (venison), hides and antlers. The deer family Cervidae has existed since the Oligocene epoch. The Chinese water deer is the smallest, measuring 55cm (22in) tall at the shoulder; the ELK at 2m (6.5ft), is the largest.

Defence, Ministry of (MOD) British department of state. First formed in 1940, in 1964 it was reorganized to combine the old War Office, Admiralty and Air Ministry. It is presided over by a secretary of state and two ministers of state.

Defender of the Faith (Lat. *Fidei Defensor*) Title adopted by English monarchs since 1521. The title was first given to Henry VIII by Pope Leo X after the publication of a tract by Henry attacking the protestant Martin LUTHER.

deflation Falling prices, accompanied by falls in output and employment; the opposite of INFLATION. It normally occurs during a RECESSION or DEPRESSION and can be measured by the price index. It is usually caused by excess production capacity. Supply then outstrips demand.

Defoe, Daniel (1660–1731) English journalist and novelist. He championed William III in his first notable poem, *The True-born Englishman* (1701). A politically controversial journalist, he was twice imprisoned, once for *The Shortest Way with the Dissenters* (1702). His reputation now rests on his fiction. His enduringly popular novels include *Robinson Crusoe* (1719), *Moll Flanders* (1722), *Colonel Jack* (1722) and *Roxana* (1724). Defoe is among the most prolific writers in the English language.

De Forest, Lee (1873–1961) US inventor of the audion triode valve (1907), which could amplify signals. Valves became essential in radio, television, and radar systems. They were replaced by the TRANSISTOR in 1947.

deforestation Clearing away forests and their ECOSYSTEMS, usually on a large scale, by humans. It may be done to create open areas for farming or building, or for timber. There is an immediate danger that the vital topsoil will be eroded by wind (such as the DUST BOWL, USA) or, in hilly areas, by rain. Proposals to clear whole regions of the Amazonian rainforests, which play a key role in maintaining the oxygen balance of the Earth, could cause an environmental catastrophe.

Degas, (Hilaire Germain) Edgar (1834–1917) French painter and sculptor. Degas took part in exhibitions of IMPRESSIONISM and shared an interest in scenes of everyday life, especially ballet and horse-racing. A brilliant draughtsman, he found inspiration in Japanese prints and photography. He made sculptures of dancers and horses to master the expression of movement. His subtle use of colour and light became concentrated in his later pastels.

De Gaulle, Charles André Joseph Marie (1890–1970) French general and statesman, first president (1959–69) of the fifth republic. In 1940 De Gaulle became undersecretary of war, but fled to London after the German invasion. He organized French Resistance (Free French) forces, and in June 1944 was proclaimed president of the provisional

French government. In 1958 he emerged from retirement to deal with the war in Algeria. In 1959 a new constitution was signed, creating the French Community. In 1962 De Gaulle was forced to cede Algerian independence. Gaullist foreign policy attempted to reinstate France as a world power. De Gaulle's devaluation of the franc brought relative domestic prosperity. He was re-elected (1965) but resigned following defeat in a 1969 referendum.

degree In mathematics, unit of angular measure equal to 1/360 of a complete revolution. One degree is written 1°, and can be divided into 60 parts called minutes (e.g. 20′), which may in turn be divided into 60 parts called seconds (e.g. 25″). Three hundred and sixty degrees equal 2π radians. In physics and engineering, a degree is one unit on any of various scales, such as the CELSIUS temperature scale.

dehydration Removal or loss of water from a substance or tissue. Water molecules can be removed by heat, catalysts or a dehydrating agent such as concentrated sulphuric acid. Dehydration is used to preserve food. In medicine, excessive water loss is often a symptom or result of injury or illness.

deism System of natural religion, first developed in England in the late 17th century. It affirmed belief in one God, but held that He detached himself from the universe after its creation and made no revelation. Reason was man's only guide. The deists opposed revealed religion in general, and Christianity in particular. Influential deist writings include John Toland's *Christianity not Mysterious* (1696) and Matthew Tindal's *Christianity as Old as the Creation* (1730). Deism was a great influence on the ENLIGHTENMENT. VOLTAIRE, ROUSSEAU and DIDEROT were its chief exponents.

deity God or goddess, or the condition, rank or quality of divinity. Deity is applied broadly to any divine being who is the object of worship, regardless of religious creed. In the 18th century, the DEISTS used the term to signify a supreme being without having to refer to the God of Christianity.

De Klerk, F.W. (Frederik Willem) (1936–) South African statesman, president (1989–94). In 1972 De Klerk became a National Party MP, joining the cabinet in 1978. He replaced P. W. BOTHA as president. De Klerk oversaw the dismantling of APARTHEID, culminating in the constitutional end of white minority rule. In 1993 he shared the Nobel Peace Prize with Nelson MANDELA. Following the 1994 majority rule elections, De Klerk became deputy president in Mandela's government of national unity. In 1996 he resigned and led the Nationalists out of the coalition. In 1997 he retired as leader of the National Party.

de Kooning, Willem (1904–97) US painter, b. Netherlands. In 1948 he became one of the leaders of ABSTRACT EXPRESSIONISM. Unlike POLLOCK, he kept a figurative element in his work and shocked the public with violently distorted images such as the *Women* series (1953). His emphasis on technique became known as ACTION PAINTING.

Delacroix, (Ferdinand Victor) Eugène (1798–1863) French painter, the greatest French artist of ROMANTICISM. Success came at his first Paris salon (1822), when he sold *The Barque of Dante* and, two years later, *The Massacre at Chios*. A visit to Morocco (1832) inspired a rich collection of sketches. In the 1830s, he began to exploit divisionism (placing complementary colours side by side to obtain greater vibrancy).

De la Mare, Walter (1873–1956) British poet, short-story writer and anthologist. His collections of poems include *Songs of Childhood* (1902), *Peacock Pie* (1913), *Winged Chariot* (1951) and the anthology *Come Hither* (1923). His prose includes the novel *Memoirs of a Midget* (1921).

Delaunay, Robert (1885–1941) French painter, co-founder (with his wife Sonia DELAUNAY-TERK) of ORPHISM. He deeply influenced the *Blaue Reiter* group of German expressionist painters. Many of his works are abstract cityscapes; the Eiffel Tower series is his most famous.

Delaunay-Terk, Sonia (1885–1979) French painter, b. Russia. Co-founder (with her husband Robert DELAUNAY) of ORPHISM. Among her most notable works are the lyrical *Simultaneous Contrasts* (1912) and delightful abstract illustrations for the *Prose du Trans-Sibérien* by Blaise Cendrars.

Delaware State in E USA, on the Atlantic coast, occupying a peninsula between Chesapeake and Delaware bays. The capital is DOVER, the largest city is WILMINGTON. Discovered by Henry Hudson in 1609, it was named after the British governor of Virginia, Baron De la Warr. Delaware was settled by Swedes in 1638. The Dutch, under Peter Stuyvesant, conquered the territory by 1655. It was under English control from 1664–1776. It was the first to ratify the Articles of Confederation (1789). Despite being a slave state, it maintained a fragile loyalty to the Union during the CIVIL WAR. It is the second-smallest US state and most of the land is coastal plain. The Delaware River, an important shipping route, forms part of the E boundary. Industries: chemicals, rubber, plastics, metallurgy. Agriculture: cereal crops, soya, dairy produce. Area: 5,328sq km (2,057sq mi). Pop. (1990) 666,168.

Delft City in South Holland province, SW Netherlands. Founded in the 11th century, it was an important commercial centre until the 17th century. It has a 13th-century Gothic church and a 15th-century church. Industries: Delftware pottery, ceramics, china, tiles, pharmaceuticals. Pop. (1994) 91,941.

Delhi Former capital of India, on the River Yamuna, union territory of Delhi, N central India. In the 17th century Delhi was capital of the MOGUL empire. In 1912 it became capital of British India (replacing CALCUTTA) and remained so until independence in 1947. Sites include the Red Fort; the Rajghat, a shrine where GANDHI was cremated; the Jamii Masjid; and the Jai Singh observatory. Industries: cotton textiles, handicrafts, tourism. Pop. (1991) 7,206,704.

Delibes, (Clément Philibert) Léo (1836–91) French composer. He was famous for his ballet music, especially *Coppélia* (1870). He also wrote several operas (such as *Lakmé*, 1883) and sacred and secular choral works.

Delilah Philistine woman in the Old Testament (Judges 16). The mistress of SAMSON, she betrayed him to the Philistines by cutting his hair, the source of his strength, while he slept.

delirium State of confusion in which a person becomes agitated, incoherent and loses touch with reality; often associated with DELUSIONS or HALLU-CINATIONS. It may be seen in various disorders, brain disease, fever, and drug intoxication.

Delius, Frederick (1862–1934) English compos-er. He combined elements of ROMANTICISM with IMPRESSIONISM, most notably in orchestral pieces, such as *Brigg Fair* (1907) and *On Hearing the First Cuckoo in Spring* (1912). His interest in nature is evident in the operas *A Village Romeo and Juliet* (1901) and *Fennimore and Gerda* (1910).

Delphi Ancient city state in Greece, near Mount Parnassus. The presence of the ORACLE of APOLLO made it a sacred city. The Pythian Games were held at Delphi every four years. The Temple of Apollo was sacked in Roman times, and the oracle closed with the spread of Christianity (AD 390).

delphinium (larkspur) Any of about 250 species of herbaceous plants native to temperate areas, with spirally arranged leaves and loose clusters of flowers. Petals form a tubular spur, which contains nectar. Garden delphiniums are varieties of *Del-phinium elatum*. Family Ranunculaceae.

delta Fan-shaped body of ALLUVIUM deposited at the mouth of a river. A delta is formed when a river deposits sediment as its speed decreases while it enters the sea. Most deltas are extremely fertile areas, but are subject to frequent flooding.

delusion False or irrational belief based upon a misinterpretation of reality. Fixed delusions can be a symptom of PARANOIA.

dementia Deterioration of personality and intel-lect that can result from brain disease or damage. It is characterized by memory loss, impaired mental processes, personality change, confusion, lack of inhibition and failing personal hygiene. Dementia can occur at any age, though it is more common in the elderly. *See also* ALZHEIMER'S DISEASE

Demeter In GREEK MYTHOLOGY, the goddess of nature, sister of ZEUS and mother of PERSEPHONE.

De Mille, Cecil B. (Blount) (1881–1959) US film producer and director, noted for his lavish presentations. His debut film, *The Squaw Man* (1913), established Hollywood as the world's film production capital. Much of his best-known work deals with biblical themes, such as *The Ten Com-mandments* (two versions, 1923, 1956) and *King of Kings* (1927). Other major films include *For-bidden Fruit* (1921), *Union Pacific* (1939) and *The Greatest Show on Earth* (1952).

Demirel, Süleyman (1924–) Turkish politi-cian, prime minister (1965–71, 1975–77, 1979–80, 1991–93), president (1993–). He became leader of the centre-right Justice Party in 1964. He was twice ousted as prime minister by military coups (1971 and 1980). He led the Justice Party's successor, the Truth Path Party, 1987–93.

democracy (Gk. *demos kratia*, people authority) Rule of the people, as opposed to rule by one (autocracy) or a few (oligarchy). Ancient GREECE is regarded as the birthplace of democracy, in particu-lar ATHENS (5th century BC). Small Greek city-states enabled direct political participation, but only among its citizens (a small political elite). In a FEU-DAL SYSTEM, the king selected tenants-in-chief to provide counsel. In late 13th-century England, a PARLIAMENT evolved, but remained answerable to the monarchy. Changes in land ownership and the growth of a mercantile class widened the represen-tative base of parliament. The Roundheads' victory in the English CIVIL WAR was, in general terms, a victory for parliamentary sovereignty. A fundamen-tal shift in emphasis was the transition from natural law to NATURAL RIGHTS, as expounded by John LOCKE: in addition to responsibility (to crown or church), people possessed inalienable rights. ROUSSEAU developed these notions into the SOCIAL CONTRACT, which influenced the FRENCH and AMERICAN REVOLUTIONS: government was limited by law from impinging on individual freedoms. During the 19th century, the FRANCHISE was extend-ed. Democratic representation remains a matter of debate or sometimes bloody dispute. Common to modern **liberal democracy** is the principle of free multiparty elections with universal adult suffrage.

Democratic Party US political party, descendant of the ANTI-FEDERALIST PARTY and DEMOCRATIC REPUBLICAN PARTY. From the election of Thomas JEFFERSON (1801) until James BUCHANAN in 1857, the Party was the dominant force in US politics, gathering support from farmers and white-collar workers. The Party was split by the Civil War (1861–65), with support mainly restricted to the South and West. It regained power in 1932 with Franklin D. ROOSEVELT's NEW DEAL. Democratic presidents were in office from 1961–69 (John F. KENNEDY, Lyndon JOHNSON), a period marked by progressive economic and social policy, such as the passing of CIVIL RIGHTS legislation. The 1970s and 1980s were more barren years; only Jimmy CARTER (1977–81) held the presidency. In the 1992 elections, Bill CLINTON recaptured the centre ground of US politics. He was re-elected in 1996.

Democratic Republican Party Early US polit-ical party, and precursor to the modern DEMOCRA-TIC PARTY. It was formed in the late 1790s in oppo-sition to the FEDERALIST PARTY, and led by Thomas JEFFERSON and James MADISON. It opposed strong central government and Alexander Hamilton's economic policies, and advocated a liberal agrarian democracy. It became the Democ-ratic Party in the era of Andrew JACKSON.

democratic socialism Political movement that proposes evolution rather than revolution as the best way to introduce SOCIALISM. Democratic socialism arose in late 19th- and early 20th-century Europe, out of the evolutionary wing of the Second COMMUNIST INTERNATIONAL. Broadly speaking, they committed themselves to the principles of equality, social justice, solidarity, parliamentary government, redistribution of wealth (through progressive taxation), social protection and international cooperation. Democratic socialist parties have held power in most Western European countries, as well as Australia, New Zealand, Canada and some Latin American countries.

Democritus (460–370BC) Greek philosopher and scientist. Only fragments of his work remain. He contributed to the theory of atomism, propounded by his teacher Leucippus, by suggesting that all matter consisted of tiny, indivisible particles.

dendrochronology Means of estimating time by examination of the growth rings in trees. Chronology based on the bristle-cone pine extends back over 7,000 years.

dengue Infectious viral disease transmitted by the *Aedes aegypti* MOSQUITO. Occurring principally in the tropics, it produces fever, headache and fatigue, followed by severe joint pains, aching muscles, swollen glands and a rash. Recovery usually follows, but relapses are common.

Deng Xiaoping (1904–97) Chinese statesman. He took part in the LONG MARCH, served in the Red Army, and became a member of the central committee of the Chinese COMMUNIST PARTY in 1945. After the establishment of the People's Republic (1949), he held several important posts, becoming general secretary of the Party in 1956. During the CULTURAL REVOLUTION he was denounced for capitalist tendencies and dismissed. He returned to government in 1973, was purged by the GANG OF FOUR in 1976, but reinstated in 1977 after MAO ZEDONG's death. Within three years he ousted HUA GUOFENG to become the dominant leader of party and government. He introduced rapid economic modernization, encouraging foreign investment, but without social and political liberalization. Deng officially retired in 1987, but was still essentially in control at the time of the TIANANMEN SQUARE massacre (1989). In 1993 JIANG ZEMIN became president.

De Niro, Robert (1943–) US film star. An intense, powerful player, he first gained critical acclaim in Martin SCORSESE's *Mean Streets* (1973). In 1974 he won an Oscar for best supporting actor in *The Godfather, Part II*. Another critical triumph in *Taxi Driver* (1976) was followed by a nominated role in *The Deer Hunter* (1978). He finally won an Oscar for best actor in *Raging Bull* (1981). He made his directorial debut with *A Bronx Tale* (1993). Other films include *Goodfellas* (1990), *Casino* (1995) and *Heat* (1995).

Denmark Smallest country in Scandinavia; the capital is COPENHAGEN. **Land and climate** It consists of a peninsula, Jutland (which is joined to Germany), and more than 400 islands, 89 of which are inhabited. Copenhagen lies on Sjaelland (the largest island) facing Sweden across a narrow strait, The Sound. To the NW of Denmark lie the self-governing Danish dependencies of GREENLAND and the FARÖE ISLANDS. Bornholm, off the S tip of Sweden, forms a separate administrative region. Denmark is flat and mostly covered by rocks deposited by huge ice sheets during the last Ice Age. The highest point is only 171m (561ft) above sea level. Denmark has a cool but pleasant climate due to North Atlantic Drift. The Sound may freeze over in winter. Summers are warm, and rainfall occurs throughout the year. The wettest seasons are summer and autumn. Much of Denmark consists of green fields, lakes and sandy beaches. Most of the original forests of oak and pine have been felled. Today, planted belts of beech, pine and spruce help to break the strong westerly winds. **Economy** Denmark has few natural resources, apart from North Sea oil and gas. The economy is highly developed, with manufacturing industries employing 27% of the workforce. Products include furniture, electrical goods and textiles. Farms cover about 75% of the land. Farming employs only 4% of the workforce, but is highly technological and productive. Meat and dairy farming are the leading activities. Fishing is also important. Service industries, such as tourism, form the largest sector of the economy, employing 67% of the workforce. **History and politics** In c.2000 BC the Danes developed an advanced Bronze Age culture. During the 9th–11th centuries AD, VIKINGS terrorized W Europe, and Danes were among the invaders who conquered much of England. In the 11th century King CANUTE ruled over Denmark, Norway and England. Queen Margaret unified the crowns of Denmark, Sweden and Norway in 1397. Sweden broke away in 1523, while Norway was lost to Sweden in 1814. Denmark adopted LUTHERANISM as the national religion in the 1530s. Danish culture flourished in the 16th and early 17th centuries. A succession of wars with Sweden, including the THIRTY YEARS WAR (1618–48), weakened Danish aristocratic rule. Serfdom was abolished in 1788. In the late 19th century, the Danes set up cooperatives and improved farming techniques. Denmark was neutral in World War 1. In 1918 ICE-

DENMARK
AREA: 43,070sq km (16,629sq mi)
POPULATION: 5,170,000
CAPITAL (POPULATION): Copenhagen (620,970)
GOVERNMENT: Parliamentary monarchy
ETHNIC GROUPS: Danish 97%
LANGUAGES: Danish (official)
RELIGIONS: Christianity (Lutheran 91%, Roman Catholic 1%)
CURRENCY: Krone = 100 ore

179

LAND was granted independence. During the 1920s Denmark passed much progressive social welfare legislation. In 1940 Germany occupied Denmark, and in 1943 martial law was declared. Many Jews escaped to Sweden. In 1945 Denmark was liberated by British forces. In 1949 Denamark relinquished its traditional neutrality and joined NATO. In 1973 Denmark became a member of the European Economic Community (EEC), the first Scandinavian country to do so. In 1992 it narrowly rejected the MAASTRICHT TREATY, but reversed the decision in a second referendum (1993). Danes enjoy a high standard of living. Problems include pollution and the high cost of social services.

density Ratio of mass to volume for a given substance, usually expressed in SI UNITS as kg/m^3. It is an indication of the concentration of particles within a material. The density of a solid or liquid changes little over a wide range of temperatures and pressures. **Specific gravity** (sg), or relative density, is the ratio of the density of one substance to that of a reference substance (usually water) at the same temperature and pressure.

dentistry Profession concerned with the care and treatment of the mouth, particularly the TEETH and their supporting tissues. As well as general practice, dentistry includes specialities such as oral surgery, periodontics and orthodontics.

dentition Type, number and arrangement of TEETH. An adult human has 32 teeth. In each jaw are four incisors, two canines, four premolars, four molars and, in most adults, up to four wisdom teeth. Children lack the premolars and four molars. The incisors are used for cutting; the canines for gripping and tearing; the molars and premolars for crushing and grinding food. In CARNIVORES unspecialized milk teeth are replaced by specialized adult teeth, which have to last a lifetime. A HERBIVORE has relatively unspecialized teeth that grow throughout life to compensate for wear, and are adapted for grinding.

Denver Capital and largest city of COLORADO state, USA, at the foot of the ROCKY MOUNTAINS. At an altitude of 1,608m (5,280ft), it is nicknamed "Mile High City". Founded in 1860, it became state capital in 1867. Its prosperity was based on the discovery of gold and silver and the building of the Denver Pacific Railroad (1870). Denver is the site of many government agencies, including the US Mint. Other sites include Denver International (the world's largest airport), the Denver Art Museum, and a university (1864). After World War 2, Denver's high altitude and rapid growth led to serious pollution problems. During the 1970s, exploitation of oil fuelled further growth. Its proximity to the Rockies and the ski resort of Aspen make it a major tourist centre. Denver is a processing, shipping and distribution centre and home to many high-technology industries, especially aerospace and electronics. Pop. (1990) 467,610.

deoxyribonucleic acid *See* DNA

Depardieu, Gérard (1948–) French film actor. He has an extraordinary range, equally adroit at playing historical figures such as *Danton* (1982), or a hunchback tax-collector in *Jean de Florette* (1986). His performance as *Cyrano de Bergerac* (1990) was definitive. He made his directorial debut with *Tartuffe* (1984). Other films include *Germinal* (1993).

depression In economics, a period of economic hardship, more severe than a RECESSION. It is usually measured by a fall in output and a rise in unemployment. The most severe and widespread was the GREAT DEPRESSION of the 1930s.

depression In meteorology, a region of low atmospheric pressure with the lowest pressure at the centre. It usually brings unsettled or stormy weather. *See also* CYCLONE

depression Disorder characterized by feelings of guilt, failure or worthlessness. Often stress-related, depression leads to low self-esteem, self-recrimination and obsessive thoughts. Insomnia, loss of appetite and lethargy can be present; in severe cases there is a risk of suicide. *See also* MANIC DEPRESSION

De Quincey, Thomas (1785–1859) English essayist and critic. An associate of WORDSWORTH and COLERIDGE, whom he memorialized in *Recollections of the Lakes and the Lake Poets* (1834–39). He is best known for his famous *Confessions of an English Opium Eater* (1822).

Derby, Edward George Geoffrey Smith Stanley, 14th Earl of (1799–1869) British statesman, prime minister (1852, 1858–59, 1866–68). He entered Parliament as a WHIG in 1827, and acted as chief secretary for Ireland (1830–33). He resigned shortly after becoming colonial secretary (1833), and joined the TORY PARTY. He was colonial secretary under PEEL (1841–45), but resigned over the repeal of the CORN LAWS. From 1846–68, Derby led the Tory protectionists, briefly heading two administrations. His third spell as prime minister saw the introduction of the REFORM ACT (1867). He was succeeded by DISRAELI.

Derby City and county district on the River Derwent, Derbyshire, central England. Industries include railway and aerospace engineering, textiles and ceramics. Rolls-Royce cars are made here. Pop. (1991) 218,802.

Derbyshire County in N central England; the county town is DERBY, other major towns are Chesterfield and Alfreton. Low-lying in the S, it rises to the PEAK DISTRICT in the N, and is drained by the River Trent and its tributaries the Dove, Derwent and Wye. Agriculture is important, including dairy farming, livestock rearing, wheat, oats, and market gardening. There are coal deposits in the E. Industries: steel, textiles, paper, and pottery. Area: 2,631sq km (1,016sq mi). Pop. 887,600.

derivative Rate of change of the value of a mathematical function with respect to a change in the independent VARIABLE. The derivative is an expression of the instantaneous rate of change of the function's value: in general it is itself a function of the variable. An example is obtaining the velocity and acceleration of an object that moves distance x in time t according to the equation $x = at^n$. In such motion the velocity increases with time. The expression dx/dt, called the first derivative of distance with respect to time, is equal to the velocity of the object; in this example it equals $nat^{(n-1)}$. The result is obtained by differentiation. In this example, the second derivative, written d^2x/dt^2, is equal to the acceleration. *See also* CALCULUS; DIFFERENTIAL

dermatitis Inflammation of the skin. In acute form it produces itching and blisters. In chronic form it causes thickening, scaling and darkening of the skin. *See also* ECZEMA

dermatology Branch of medicine that deals with the diagnosis and treatment of skin diseases.

dermis Thick inner layer of the SKIN, which lies beneath the EPIDERMIS. It consists mainly of loose CONNECTIVE TISSUE, richly supplied with BLOOD and lymph vessels, nerve endings, sensory organs and sweat glands.

Derry City and administrative district on the Foyle River, near Lough Foyle, NW Northern Ireland. In AD 546 St Columba founded a monastery here. In 1311 Derry was granted to the earl of Ulster. In 1600 English forces seized the city, and in 1613 James I granted Derry to the citizens of London. It was renamed **Londonderry**, a new city was laid out and Protestant colonization began. In recent years the city has been plagued by sectarian violence. In 1984 its name reverted to Derry. The major industry is clothing manufacture. Area: 347sq km (149sq mi). Pop. (1991) 95,371.

dervish Member of a Muslim fraternity. Communities arose within SUFISM and by the 12th century had established themselves in the Middle East. The Bektashi order, based in KONYA, acted as companions to the Ottoman JANISSARIES, and were suppressed by ATATÜRK. The chief devotion of dervishes is *dhikr* (remembering of God). Its encouragement of emotional display and hypnotic trances has earned dervishes the epithet "whirling".

desalination Extraction of pure water from water containing dissolved salts, usually sea water. The commonest and oldest method is DISTILLATION. Another method is to freeze the salt solution; salt is excluded from the ice crystals which can then be melted. In reverse OSMOSIS, pure water only passes through a semi-permeable membrane against which salt water is pressurized. Other methods include electrodialysis.

Descartes, René (1596–1650) French philosopher and mathematician. Descartes is often regarded as the father of modern philosophy. In 1619, he described an all-embracing science of the universe. His works include *Discourse on Method* (1637), *Meditations on the First Philosophy* (1641) and *Principles of Philosophy* (1644). His methods of deduction and intuition inform modern metaphysics. By doubting all his ideas, he reached one

indubitable proposition: "I am thinking", and from this he concluded that he existed: *cogito ergo sum* (I think, therefore I am). Descartes founded analytic geometry, introduced the CARTESIAN COORDINATE SYSTEM and helped establish the science of optics.

desert Arid region of the Earth, at any latitude, characterized by scant, intermittent rainfall of less than 25cm (10in) per year, and little or no vegetation. Regions with 25–50cm (10–20in) are semi-deserts. Cold deserts, almost permanently covered with ice, extend over 15% of the Earth's surface; and hot deserts over 20%. Most desert regions lie between 20° and 30° N and S of the Equator, where mountains form a barrier to prevailing winds, or where high pressure prevents precipitation. The SAHARA in Africa is the world's largest desert.

desertification Process by which a DESERT gradually spreads into neighbouring areas of semi-desert. The change may result from a natural event, such as fire or climatic change, but occurs most frequently as a result of human activity. Once vegetation is removed (usually by over-grazing or for firewood), the soil is easily eroded and the land rendered infertile. Restoration is a long and slow process.

De Sica, Vittorio (1901–74) Italian film director and actor. He is noted for his contribution to Italian NEO-REALISM, with films such as *Shoeshine* (1946) and *Bicycle Thieves* (1948). Other credits include *Umberto D* (1952), *Indiscretion of an American Wife* (1953), and *A Brief Vacation* (1975).

Des Moines Capital and largest city of Iowa state, USA, near the confluence of the Des Moines and Raccoon rivers. Founded in 1843, it is now an industrial and transport centre for the Corn Belt. Severely flooded in 1954, the city is now protected by a system of dams and reservoirs. Industries: mechanical and aerospace engineering, chemicals. Pop. (1990) 193,187.

Desmoulins, Camille (1760–94) French revolutionary. His popular pamphlets, include *Révolutions de France et de Brabant* (1789). He was responsible for provoking the mob that attacked the BASTILLE in 1789. With Georges DANTON, he played a part in removing the GIRONDINS, but was guillotined during the FRENCH REVOLUTION.

De Soto, Hernando (1500–42) Spanish explorer. After assisting in the conquest of the Incas under Francisco PIZARRO, he became governor of Cuba (1537) with permission to conquer the North American mainland. His expedition landed in Florida (1539) and advanced as far north as the Carolinas and as far west as the Mississippi. The brutal treatment of natives led to the battle at Maubilia (1540).

Des Prés, Josquin *See* JOSQUIN DESPREZ

detergent Synthetic chemical cleansing substance. The most common type is alkyl sulphonate. Detergents have molecules that possess a long hydrocarbon chain attached to an ionized group. This chain attaches to grease and other nonpolar substances, while the ionized group has an affinity for water (so grease is washed away with the water).

determinism Philosophical thesis that every event is the necessary result of its causes. Nothing is accidental. It usually involves the denial of FREE WILL, though Thomas HOBBES and David HUME struggled to reconcile the two ideas. CALVIN's concept of PREDESTINATION is a form of determinism.

Detroit City on the Detroit River, SE Michigan state, USA. Founded as a French trading post (1710), the British captured it in 1760 and used it as a base during the American Revolution. It was lost to Britain in the WAR OF 1812, but retaken by US forces in 1813. The largest city in Michigan, Detroit is a major GREAT LAKES centre, and headquarters of General Motors, Chrysler and Ford. Industries: motor vehicles, steel, pharmaceuticals, machine tools, tyres and paint. Pop. (1990) 1,027,974.

deuterium ISOTOPE (D or H²) of hydrogen whose nuclei contain a neutron in addition to a proton. Deuterium occurs in water as D_2O (heavy water), from which it is obtained by ELECTROLYSIS. Heavy water is used as a moderator in some FISSION reactors. Mass no. 2; at. wt. 2.0144.

Deuteronomy Biblical book, fifth and last of the PENTATEUCH or TORAH. It contains three discourses ascribed to MOSES, which frame a code of civil and religious laws. The book was probably written long after Moses.

De Valera, Eamon (1882–1975) Irish politician, prime minister (1932–48, 1951–54, 1957–59), b. USA. He was active in the Irish independence movement, and after the EASTER RISING (1916) was elected president of SINN FÉIN while imprisoned in England. He opposed William Cosgrave's Irish Free State ministry and founded the FIANNA FÁIL party in 1924. He defeated Cosgrave in 1932 and remained prime minister (with two brief interruptions) until 1959, when he became president of the republic. He retired in 1973.

devaluation Lowering the value of one nation's currency with respect to that of another or to gold. The decision to devalue is made by a central government usually when the nation is having BALANCE OF PAYMENTS problems. Devaluation stimulates the economy by reducing the foreign currency price of exports and raising the domestic price of imports.

developing countries See LESS DEVELOPED COUNTRIES (LDCs)

developmental psychology Study of behaviour through all life stages, from the fetus to old age. Psychologists study normal growth, change, and self-actualization, as well as life-stage related problems. See also CHILD PSYCHOLOGY

Devil Evil spirit considered in many religions to be the arch-enemy of the Supreme being. In Christianity, the Devil is chief of the fallen angels cast out of heaven for their sins. The Devil was named as SATAN, BEELZEBUB or the Prince of Darkness. The biblical account of Christ's temptation leads to the perception of the Devil as the tempter of men's souls. In Islam, Iblis is the name of the devil figure.

Devon County in SW England, bounded by the English Channel (S) and the Bristol Channel (N); the county town is EXETER. There are Bronze and Iron Age remains. During the Middle Ages, tin mining was a major industry. Devon is a hilly region that includes Dartmoor and Exmoor. The principal rivers are the Ex, Tamar, Dart and Teign. Cattle farming is important. Industries: tourism, fishing, dairy products, cider, textiles. Area: 6,711sq km (2,591sq mi). Pop. (1991) 1,009,950.

Devonian Fourth-oldest period of the PALAEOZOIC era, lasting from 408–360 million years ago. Numerous marine and freshwater remains include jawless fishes and forerunners of today's bony and cartilaginous fishes. The first known land vertebrate, the amphibian *Ichthyostega*, appeared at this time. Land animals included scorpions, mites, spiders and the first insects. Land plants consisted of CLUB MOSS, scouring rushes and ferns.

De Vries, Hugo (1848–1935) Dutch botanist. De Vries introduced the concept of MUTATION into the study of GENETICS. He wrote *The Mutation Theory* (1901–03), which influenced concepts of the role of mutation in EVOLUTION.

dew Water droplets formed, usually at night, by condensation on vegetation and other surfaces near the ground.

Dewar, Sir James (1842–1923) Scottish chemist and physicist who researched materials at extremely low temperatures. In 1872, he invented the Thermos flask. He also built a device that could produce liquid oxygen.

Dewey, John (1859–1952) US educator and philosopher. A founder of PRAGMATISM and FUNCTIONALISM, he had a profound impact on US educational practice and the development of applied psychology. His books include *The School and Society* (1899) and *Experience and Education* (1938).

Dewey decimal system Means of classifying books, created by US librarian Melvil Dewey in the 1870s. It is popular because of its subject currency and simplicity.

dew point Temperature at which a vapour begins to condense, for example when water vapour in the air condenses into cloud as the air becomes saturated with vapour.

Dhaka (Dacca) Capital of BANGLADESH, a port on the GANGES delta, in the E of the country. Its influence grew as the 17th century Mogul capital of Bengal. In 1765 it came under British control. At independence (1947) it was made capital of the province of East Pakistan. Severely damaged during the war of independence from Pakistan, it became capital of independent Bangladesh (1971). Sites include the Dakeshwari temple, Lal Bagh fort (1678) and Bara Katra palace (1644). It is in the centre of the world's largest jute-producing area. Industries: engineering, textiles, printing, glass and chemicals. Pop. (1991) 3,397,187.

dharma Religious concept relating to what is true or right, found in the principal religions of India. In HINDUISM, it is the moral law or code governing an individual's conduct in life. In BUDDHISM, dharma is the doctrine of universal truth proclaimed by the BUDDHA. In JAINISM, dharma is moral virtue or The Good and is also the principle that gives beings the power of movement.

diabetes Disease characterized by lack of INSULIN needed for sugar METABOLISM. This leads to HYPER-GLYCAEMIA and an excess of SUGAR in blood. Symptoms include abnormal thirst, over-production of urine and weight loss; degenerative changes occur in blood vessels. Untreated, the condition progresses to diabetic coma and death. There are two forms of the disease. **Type 1** usually begins in childhood and is an autoimmune disease. Those affected owe their survival to insulin injections. Milder **type 2** diabetes mostly begins in middle-age; there is some insulin output but not enough for the body's needs. The disease is managed with dietary restrictions and oral insulin. Susceptibility to *diabetes mellitus* is inherited and more common in males.

diagenesis Physical and chemical processes whereby sediments are transformed into solid rock, usually at low pressure and temperature. Pressure results in compaction, forcing grains together and eliminating air and water.

Diaghilev, Sergei Pavlovich (1872–1929) Russian ballet impresario. He was active in the Russian avant-garde before moving to Paris, where he formed the Ballets Russes (1909). He assembled talented artists, dancers and musicians, such as NIJINSKY, STRAVINSKY and FOKINE.

dialect Regional variety of a language, distinguished by features of pronunciation, grammar and vocabulary. Dialectal differences may be relatively slight (as in the dialects of American English), or so great (Italian) that mutual comprehension becomes difficult or impossible.

dialectic Method of argument through conversation and dialogue; based on the philosophy of SOCRATES, in particular the *Dialogues*. HEGEL went on to argue that ordinary logic, governed by the law of contradiction, is static and lifeless. In the *Science of Logic* (1812–16) he claimed to satisfy the need for a dynamic method, whose two moments of thesis and antithesis are cancelled and reconciled in a higher synthesis. Logic was to be dialectical, or a process of resolution by means of conflict of categories.

dialectical materialism Scientific theory and philosophical basis of MARXISM. It asserts that everything is material, and that change results from the struggle of opposites according to definite laws. Its main application was in the analysis of human history. Karl MARX agreed with HEGEL that the course of history is logically dialectical; true social change can only occur when two opposing views are resolved through a new synthesis, rather than one establishing itself as true. Marx believed that Hegel was wrong to define dialectics as purely spiritual or logical. For Marx, the proper dialectical subject was material experience. According to his theory of historical materialism, history was derived from economic or social realities.

dialysis Process for separating particles from a solution by virtue of differing rates of diffusion through a semipermeable membrane. In the artificial KIDNEY, unwanted molecules of waste products are separated out to purify the blood. Electrodialysis employs a direct electric current to accelerate the process, especially useful for isolating proteins.

diamond Crystalline form of carbon (C). The hardest natural substance known. It is found in kimberlite pipes and alluvial deposits. Its appearance varies according to its impurities. Bort, inferior in crystal and colour, carborondo, an opaque grey to black variety, and other non-gem varieties are used in industry. Industrial diamonds are used as abrasives, bearings in precision instruments, and cutting heads of drills for mining. Synthetic diamonds are made by subjecting GRAPHITE, with a catalyst, to high pressure and temperatures of about 3,000°C (5,400°F). Diamonds are weighed in carats (0.2gm) and points (1/100 carat). The largest producer is Australia. Hardness 10; s.g.3.5.

Diana In Roman religion, the virgin huntress and patroness of domestic animals. She was identified with ARTEMIS. A fertility deity, she was invoked to aid conception and childbirth.

Diana, Princess of Wales (1961–97) Former wife of the heir to the British throne. Diana married CHARLES, Prince of Wales in 1981, and they had two sons. A popular, glamorous figure, she worked for many public health and children's charities and campaigned for humanitarian causes. Their marriage fell apart acrimoniously and publicly, and they divorced in 1996. Her death in a car crash provoked an unprecedented outpouring of public emotion.

diaphragm Sheet of muscle that separates the abdomen from the THORAX. During exhalation it relaxes and allows the chest to subside; on inhalation it contracts and flattens.

diarrhoea Frequent elimination of loose, watery stools, accompanied by cramps and stomach pains. It arises from various causes, such as infection, intestinal irritants or food allergy.

Diaspora (dispersion) Jewish communities outside Palestine. Although there were communities of Jews outside Palestine from the time of the BABYLONIAN CAPTIVITY (6th century BC), the Diaspora essentially dates from the destruction of Jerusalem by the Romans (AD 70). *See also* ZIONISM

diatom Any of a group of tiny microscopic single-celled ALGAE (phylum Bacillariophyta) characterized by a shell-like cell wall made of silica. Diatoms live in nearly all bodies of salt and freshwater, and even soil and tree bark.

Diaz, Bartholomeu (1450–1500) Portuguese navigator, the first European to round the CAPE OF GOOD HOPE. In 1487 Diaz sailed three ships around the Cape, opening the route to India. He took part in the expedition of CABRAL that discovered Brazil, but was drowned when his ship foundered.

Díaz, Porfirio (1830–1915) President of Mexico (1876–80, 1884–1911). After twice failing to unseat President JUÁREZ, he succeeded against Lerdo in 1876. Díaz provided stable leadership for 30 years. Growing opposition crystallized under Francisco MADERO in 1911 and Díaz resigned.

Dickens, Charles John Huffam (1812–70) British novelist. His first success was the series of satirical pieces collected in 1836 as *Sketches by Boz*. They were followed by *The Posthumous Papers of the Pickwick Club* (1836–37), which launched his literary career. Most of his novels first appeared in serial form, such as *Oliver Twist* (1837–39), *Nicholas Nickleby* (1838–39), *The Old Curiosity Shop* (1840–41), and *Martin Chuzzlewit* (1843–44). His great mature novels include *David Copperfield* (1849–50), *Bleak House* (1852–53), *Hard Times* (1854) and *Great Expectations* (1860–61). Dickens' relentless energy also found outlet in journalism, short stories, comic plays, and demanding public reading tours.

Dickinson, Emily Elizabeth (1830–86) US poet. She led an active social life until the age of 23, when she became almost totally reclusive, writing more than 1,700 short, mystical poems. Now considered one of the finest US poets, her rich verse explores the world of emotion and the beauty of simple things. Only seven of her poems were published during her lifetime. *Poems by Emily Dickinson* appeared in 1890 and her collected works were not published until 1955.

dicotyledon Larger of the two subgroups of flowering plants or ANGIOSPERMS, characterized by two seed leaves (COTYLEDONS) in the seed embryo. Other general features of dicotyledons include broad leaves with branching veins; flower parts in whorls of fours or fives; vascular bundles in a ring in the stem and root; and a taproot. There are about 250 families of dicotyledons, such as the ROSE, DAISY and MAGNOLIA.

dictatorship Absolute rule without consent of the governed. In many modern dictatorships, all power resides in the dictator, with representative DEMOCRACY abolished or existing as mere formality. Personal freedom is severely limited, CENSORSHIP is generally enforced, education is tightly controlled, and legal restraints on governmental authority are abolished.

dictionary Book that lists in alphabetical order, words and their definitions. A dictionary may be general or subject oriented. In the former category, Samuel JOHNSON's *A Dictionary of the English Language* (1755) is the pioneering work in English; its two most comprehensive descendants are (in the UK) the *Oxford English Dictionary*, published from 1884, and (in the USA) *Webster's Dictionary*, published from 1828.

Diderot, Denis (1713–84) French philosopher and writer. He was chief editor of the *Encyclopédie* (1751–72), an influential publication of the ENLIGHTENMENT. He broadened the scope of the *Encyclopédie* and with d'ALEMBERT recruited contributors, such as VOLTAIRE. As a philosopher, Diderot progressed gradually from Christianity through DEISM to ATHEISM. His books *On the Interpretation of Nature* (1754) and *D'Alembert's Dream* (1769) reveal his scientific MATERIALISM. *Jacques the Fatalist* (1796) and *Rameau's Nephew* illustrate his DETERMINISM. He also wrote plays and art and literary criticism.

Dido In Greek and Roman legend, Phoenician princess and founder of CARTHAGE. Carthage prospered and Dido's hand was sought by the king of Libya. To escape him she stabbed herself. VIRGIL made Dido a lover of AENEAS, and attributes her suicide to his decision to abandon her.

Dien Bien Phu Fortified village in N Vietnam. In a 1954 battle the French stronghold was captured by the Vietnamese Viet Minh after a siege lasting 55 days. French casualties were *c.*15,000. The resultant ceasefire ended eight years of war.

diesel engine (compression-ignition engine) INTERNAL COMBUSTION ENGINE, invented by Rudolf Diesel (1897). Heat for igniting the light fuel oil is produced by compressing air.

diet Range of food and drink consumed by an animal. The human diet falls into five main groups of nutrients: PROTEIN, CARBOHYDRATE, FAT, VITAMIN and MINERAL. An adult's daily requirement is about one gramme of protein for each kilogramme of body weight. Beans, fish, eggs, milk and meat are important protein sources. Carbohydrates (stored as GLYCOGEN) and fat, are the chief sources of energy and are found in cereals, root vegetables and sugars. Carbohydrates make up the bulk of most diets. Fats aid the absorption of fat-soluble vitamins (vitamins A, D, E and K). Water and minerals such as iron, calcium, potassium and sodium are also essential.

Dietrich, Marlene (1904–92) German film actor and cabaret singer. Her glamorous, sultry image evolved in films directed by Josef von Sternberg, such as *The Blue Angel* (1930) and *Blonde Venus* (1932). Other films include *Destry Rides Again* (1939) and *Rancho Notorious* (1956).

differential calculus *See* CALCULUS

differential In mathematics, small change in the value of a mathematical expression due to a change in a VARIABLE. If $f(x)$ is a function of x, the differential of the function, written d f, is given by $f'(x)$ d x, where $f'(x)$ is the DERIVATIVE of $f(x)$.

differential In mechanics, a set of circular gears that transmits power from an engine to the wheels. When a car is turning a corner, the differential allows the outside drive wheel to rotate faster than the inner one.

diffraction Spreading of a wave, such as a LIGHT beam, on passing through a narrow opening or hitting the edge of an obstacle, such as sound being heard around corners. It is evidence for the wave nature of light. Diffraction provides information on the wavelength of light and the structure of CRYSTALS. All waves are diffracted by obstacles.

diffusion Movement of a substance in a mixture from regions of high concentration to regions of low concentration, due to the random motion of individual atoms or molecules. Diffusion ceases when there is no longer a concentration gradient. Its rate increases with temperature, since average molecular speed also increases with temperature.

digestion Process of the DIGESTIVE SYSTEM, in which food is broken down into smaller molecules that can be readily absorbed by an organism. Digestion occurs mainly by means of chemical agents called ENZYMES.

digestive system (alimentary system) Group of organs of the body concerned with the DIGESTION of foodstuffs. In humans, it begins with the mouth, and continues into the OESOPHAGUS, which carries food into the STOMACH. The stomach leads to the small INTESTINE, which then opens into the COLON. After food is swallowed, it is pushed through the digestive tract by PERISTALSIS. On its journey, food is transformed into small molecules that can be absorbed into the bloodstream and carried to the tissues. CARBOHYDRATE is broken down to sugars, PROTEIN to AMINO ACIDS, and FAT to FATTY ACIDS and GLYCEROL. Indigestible matter, mainly CELLULOSE, passes into the RECTUM, and is eventually eliminated from the body (as faeces) through the ANUS.

Diggers (1649–50) English millenarian social and religious sect, an extreme group of the LEVELLERS. They formed an egalitarian agrarian community at St George's Hill, Surrey. It was destroyed by local farmers. The main Digger theorist, Gerrard Winstanley, proposed communalization of property to establish social equality in *Law of Freedom* (1652).

digital DATA expressed in terms of a few discrete quantities, often associated with a digital COMPUTER. Data is represented as a series of zeros and ones in a BINARY SYSTEM. Digital can also refer to displaying information in numbers, as opposed to continuously varying analogue.

digital audio tape (DAT) Technology for recording sound in DIGITAL form on magnetic TAPE. The original sound signal is encoded to form patterns of equal-strength pulses. These DIGITAL SIGNALS are recorded onto tape. On playback, the patterns are detected and decoded to produce an identical signal.

digitalis Drug obtained from the leaves of the FOXGLOVE (*Digitalis purpurea*), used to treat HEART disease. It increases heart contractions and slows the heartbeat.

digital signal Group of electrical or other pulses in a COMPUTER or COMMUNICATIONS system. They may represent DATA, sounds or pictures. Pulses in a stream of digital signals are represented by zeros and ones in the BINARY SYSTEM.

Dijon City in E France; capital of Côte-d'Or département. In the 11th century it became capital of Burgundy. It was annexed to France (1477). Sites include Dijon University (1722), Cathedral of St Bénigne and the Church of Notre Dame. Exports: wine, cassis, mustard. Pop. (1990) 146,703.

dill Aromatic annual herb native to Europe. Its small oval seeds and feathery leaves are used in cooking. Family Apiaceae/Umbelliferae; species *Anethum graveolens*.

dimensions In mathematics, numbers specifying the extent of an object in different directions. A figure with length only, is one-dimensional; a figure having area but not volume, two-dimensional; and a figure having volume, three-dimensional.

diminishing returns, law of (law of increasing costs) In economics, if more of a variable input, such as labour, is added to the production process, while all other factors are held constant, the addition to total output per unit input begins to decline at some point.

Dinaric Alps (Dinara Planina) Mountain range parallel to the E coast of the Adriatic Sea. Forming part of the E Alps, it extends from the Istrian peninsula (Croatia) to NW Albania, with peaks over 2,400m (7,900ft). Length: 640km (400mi).

Dinesen, Isak (1885–1962) (Karen Blixen) Danish writer. Her best-known work is *Out of Africa* (1937). Her collections of short stories include *Seven Gothic Tales* (1934), *Winter's Tales* (1942) and *Shadows on the Grass* (1960).

dingo Yellowish-brown wild DOG found in Australia; it is probably a descendant of early domestic dogs introduced by Native Australians. It feeds mainly on rabbits and other small mammals. Family Canidae; species *Canis dingo*.

dinosaur Any of a large number of REPTILES that lived during the MESOZOIC era, 225–65 million years ago. They appeared during the Triassic period, survived the Jurassic and became extinct at the end of the Cretaceous. There were two orders: Saurischia ("lizard hips"), included the bipedal carnivores and the giant herbivores; the Ornithiscia ("bird hips") were smaller herbivores. Their posture, with limbs vertically beneath the body, distinguish them from other reptiles. Many theories are advanced to account for their extinction. It is possible that, as the climate changed, they were incapable of swift adaptation. A more catastrophic theory is that they died because of the devastating atmospheric effects from the impact of a large METEOR. *See also* BRONTOSAURUS; DIPLODOCUS; TYRANNOSAURUS

Diocletian (245–313) Roman emperor (284–305). He reorganized the empire to resist the Barbarians, dividing it into four divisions. He ordered the last great persecution of the Christians (303).

diode Electronic component with two electrodes, used as a RECTIFIER to convert alternating current (AC) to direct current (DC). Semiconductor diodes have largely replaced electron-tubes, and allow ELECTRIC CURRENT to flow freely in only one direction; only a small current flows in the reverse direction. A Zener diode blocks current until a critical voltage is reached.

Dionysus Greek god of wine and fertility, identified with the Roman god BACCHUS. Son of ZEUS and Semele, he was reared by nymphs and taught men the secrets of cultivating grapes.

dioxin Any of various poisonous chemicals, most commonly 2,3,7,8-tetrachlorodibenzo-p-dioxin (TCDD), a by-product and impurity in the manufacture of various disinfectants and HERBICIDES. It is also produced in the burning of chlorinated chemicals and plastics. Dioxin causes skin disfigurement and is associated with birth defects, cancer and miscarriages. Accidental release of dioxin from chemical plants have caused major disasters.

dip, magnetic Angle between the direction of the Earth's magnetic field and the horizontal. A freely suspended magnetic needle in London dips, with its north pole pointing down, at an angle of 71.5° to the horizontal.

diphtheria Acute infectious disease characterized by the formation of a membrane in the throat which can cause asphyxiation; there is also release of a toxin which can damage the nerves and heart. Caused by a bacterium, *Corynebacterium diphtheriae*, which often enters through the upper respiratory tract, it is treated with antitoxin and antibiotics.

diplodocus DINOSAUR that lived in N USA during the JURASSIC period. The longest land animal that has ever lived. It had a long slender neck and tail, and was a swamp-dwelling herbivore. Length: 25m (82ft).

diploid CELL that has its CHROMOSOMES in pairs. Diploids are found in almost all animal cells, except GAMETES which are haploid. Cells of flowering plants and gymnosperms are also diploid. Algae and lower plants, such as ferns, have two generations in their life cycle, one diploid, the other haploid. In diploids, the chromosomes of each pair carry the same GENES. *See also* ALTERNATION OF GENERATIONS

dipole Separation of electric charge in a molecule. In a COVALENT BOND, the electron pair is not equally shared. In hydrogen chloride, HCl, electrons are attracted towards the more electronegative chlorine atom, giving it a partial negative charge and leaving an equal positive charge on the hydrogen atom. Dipoles contribute to the chemical properties of molecules.

dipper Bird found near fast-flowing mountain streams, where it dives for small fish and aquatic invertebrates. It has a thin, straight bill, short wings and greyish-brown plumage. Length: to 19cm (7.5in). Family Cinclidae; genus *Cinclus*.

dip pole Either of two imaginary points on the Earth's surface where the direction of the Earth's magnetic field is vertical (downwards at the North Pole, upwards at the South Pole).

direct current (DC) *See* ELECTRIC CURRENT

disarmament Attempts post-1918 (and especially post-1945) to reach international agreements to reduce armaments. The United Nations established the Atomic Energy Commission (1946), and the Commission for Conventional Armaments (1947). In 1952 these were combined into the Disarma-

ment Commission. It produced no results and the Soviet Union withdrew in 1957. The USA and the Soviet Union signed the Nuclear Test Ban Treaty (1963) and the Nuclear Non-Proliferation Treaty (1968). This was followed by a series of STRATEGIC ARMS LIMITATION TALKS (SALT). Intensification of the COLD WAR in the early 1980s froze all disarmament efforts. In 1986 SALT was superseded by START (strategic arms reduction talks), resulting in the Intermediate Nuclear Forces (INF) Treaty (1987), which reduced the superpowers' arsenal of short-range, intermediate missiles by c.2,000 (4% of the total stockpile). The Conventional Forces in Europe Treaty (1990) set limits on equipment and troop levels. Attempts to sign a new comprehensive Test Ban Treaty have been thwarted by China, France, India and Pakistan.

disciple One of the followers of Jesus Christ during his life on earth, especially one of his 12 close personal associates, or APOSTLES.

discontinuity *See* MOHO

discus Field athletics event, in which a wooden and metal disc is thrown by competitors. The thrower rotates in a circle (diameter 2.5m/8.2ft) several times before releasing the discus. Originally an ancient Greek sport, it was revived for the first modern Olympic Games held in Athens (1896).

disease Any departure from health, with impaired functioning of the body. Disease may be **acute**, severe symptoms for a short time; **chronic**, lasting a long time; or **recurrent**, returning periodically. There are many types and causes of disease: infectious, caused by harmful BACTERIA or VIRUSES; hereditary and metabolic; growth and development; IMMUNE SYSTEM diseases; neoplastic (TUMOUR-producing); nutritional; deficiency; ENDOCRINE SYSTEM diseases; or diseases due to environmental agents, such as lead poisoning. Treatment depends on the cause and course of the disease. It may be **symptomatic** (relieving symptoms, but not necessarily combating a cause) or **specific** (attempting to cure an underlying cause). Disease prevention includes eradication of harmful organisms, VACCINES, public health measures and routine medical checks.

disk Form of computer data storage. Disks come in many different forms, some using magnetic methods to store DATA, such as the HARD DISK, while others use optical systems like the COMPACT DISC (CD) and CD-ROM.

disk operating system (DOS) COMPUTER operating system, developed in the early 1980s by Bill GATES and Microsoft for use with early International Business Machines (IBM) personal computers. DOS is the SOFTWARE that governs a computer's data storage and PROGRAM execution. Windows is a relatively DOS-free environment.

Disney, Walt (Walter Elias) (1901–66) US film animator, producer and executive. Disney's first success, *Steamboat Willie* (1928), was the first cartoon to use sound and featured his own voice as Mickey Mouse. Disney's first feature was *Snow*

White and the Seven Dwarfs (1937). A series of popular classics followed: *Pinocchio* (1940), *Fantasia* (1940), *Dumbo* (1941) and *Bambi* (1942). In 1955, Disneyland opened in Anaheim, California.

Disraeli, Benjamin, 1st Earl of Beaconsfield (1804–81) British statesman, prime minister (1868, 1874–80), and novelist. He entered parliament in 1837, and led the land-owning Tory squires, following the Conservative split over repeal of the CORN LAWS (1846). He was chancellor of the exchequer in several governments led by Lord DERBY, and became prime minister on Derby's retirement. A few months later, Disraeli was defeated by GLADSTONE's Liberal Party. His second tenure was noted for British expansion (particularly in India). A conservative at home and an imperialist abroad, Disraeli enacted political and social reforms. His novels include the trilogy *Coningsby*, *Sybil* and *Tancred* (1847).

Dissolution of the Monasteries (1536–40) Abolition of English MONASTICISM in the reign of HENRY VIII. The operation, managed by Thomas CROMWELL, was a result of the break with Rome, but also provided additional revenue, since the monasteries owned *c.*25% of the land in England, all of which passed to the crown. The Dissolution caused social hardship, resentment and revolt, while providing estates for upwardly mobile gentry.

distillation Extraction of a liquid by boiling a solution and cooling the vapour so that it condenses and can be collected. Distillation is used to separate liquids in solution, or liquid solvents from dissolved solids, to yield drinking water, or to produce alcoholic spirit. Fractional distillation, which uses a vertical column for condensation, is used in OIL refining to separate the various fractions of crude oil.

distilling Production of liquor by DISTILLATION, especially of ethyl ALCOHOL. In wine, yeast FERMENTATION produces a maximum alcohol content of *c.*15%. Distillation concentrates alcohol to produce spirits of *c.*40% proof.

distributive law Rule of combination in mathematics, in which an operation applied to a combination of terms is equal to the combination of the operation applied to each individual term. Thus, in arithmetic $3 \times (2+1) = (3 \times 2) + (3 \times 1)$ and, in algebra $a(x + y) = ax + ay$.

District of Columbia Federal district, since 1890 it has been co-extensive with WASHINGTON, D.C. It was created in 1790–91 from the states of Maryland and Virginia. Area: 179sq km (69sq mi).

diuretic Drug used to increase the output of URINE. It is used to treat raised blood pressure and OEDEMA.

dividend Net earnings of a public company that is paid to its stockholders. The dividend is a percentage of the par value of the stock or is calculated on a per share basis. It is a share of the profits.

diving Water sport in which acrobatic leaps are performed off a springboard or highboard. Techniques include tuck, pike, twist and somersault.

diving, deep-sea Underwater activity for commercial or leisure purposes. Deep-sea diving developed with the introduction of the diving-bell and diving-suit. It refers to descents to depths of more than *c.*11m (36ft). Divers need to ascend slowly from such depths to avoid the BENDS. *See also* SCUBA DIVING

divorce Legal dissolution of marriage. In most Western countries, adultery was for many years the only ground for divorce. Desertion, insanity and mental cruelty were added over the years. More recently, irretrievable breakdown, which apportions blame on neither partner is cited. In many contemporary Western societies, more than 1 in 3 marriages end in divorce.

Diwali Festival of lights in HINDUISM. Homes are lit with numerous tiny clay lamps in commemoration of the defeat of Ravana by RAMA. The story is symbolic of the return of light after the monsoon.

Dix, Otto (1891–1969) German painter and engraver. He was a satirist of inhumanity, notably in a series of 50 etchings called *The War* (1924), and his portrayal of prostitutes. He was jailed for an alleged plot to kill Hitler (1939).

Djibouti (Jibouti) Republic on the NE coast of Africa; the capital is DJIBOUTI. **Land and Climate** Djibouti occupies a strategic position around the Gulf of Tadjoura, where the RED SEA meets the Gulf of Aden. Djibouti contains the lowest point on the African continent, Lake Assal, at 155m (509ft) below sea-level. Djibouti has one of the world's hottest and driest climates; summer temperatures regularly exceed 42°C (100°F) and average annual rainfall is 130mm (5in). Nearly 90% of the land is semi-desert, and shortage of pasture and surface water make life difficult. **Economy** Djibouti is a poor country, heavily reliant on food imports. The economy is based mainly on revenue from the capital. A free trade zone, it has no major resources. The only important activity is livestock raising, and 50% of the population are pastoral nomads. **History and politics** ISLAM was introduced in the 9th century. The subsequent conversion of the Afars led to conflict with Christian Ethiopians who lived in the interior. By the 19th century, Somalian Issas had moved N and occupied much of the Afars' traditional grazing land. France gained influence in the late-19th century, and set up French Somaliland (1888). In a referendum (1967), the electorate voted to retain links with France, though most Issas

---

DJIBOUTI
AREA: 23,200sq km (8,958sq mi)
POPULATION: 695,000
CAPITAL (POPULATION): Djibouti (353,000)
GOVERNMENT: Multiparty republic
ETHNIC GROUPS: Issa 47%, Afar 37%, Arab 6%
LANGUAGES: Arabic and French (both official)
RELIGIONS: Islam 96%, Christianity 4%
CURRENCY: Djibouti franc =100 centimes

Djibouti

favoured independence. The country was renamed the French Territory of the Afars and Issas. Full independence as the Republic of Djibouti was achieved in 1977, and Hassan Gouled Aptidon was elected president. He declared a one-party state in 1981. Continuing protests against the Issas-dominated regime forced the introduction of a multiparty constitution in 1992. The Front for the Restoration of Unity and Democracy (FUUD), supported primarily by Afars, boycotted 1993 elections, and Aptidon was re-elected for a fourth six-year term. FUUD rebels continued their armed campaign. In 1996 government and FUUD forces signed a peace treaty, recognizing FUUD as a political party.

Djibouti (Jibouti) Capital of DJIBOUTI, on the S shore of the Gulf of Tadjoura, NE Africa. Founded in 1888, it became capital in 1892. A railway link from ADDIS ABABA provides further trade for the busy port. Pop. (1993 est.) 353,000.

DNA (deoxyribonucleic acid) Molecule found in all cells (and in some viruses) which is responsible for storing the GENETIC CODE. It consists of two long chains of alternating SUGAR molecules and PHOSPHATE groups linked by nitrogenous bases. The whole molecule is shaped like a twisted rope ladder, with the nitrogenous bases forming the rungs. The sugar is deoxyribose, and the four bases are adenine, cytosine, guanine and thymine. A base and its associated sugar are known as a **nucleotide**; the whole chain is a polynucleotide chain. The genetic code is stored in terms of the sequence of nucleotides: three nucleotides code for one specific amino acid and a series of them constitute a GENE. In EUKARYOTE cells, DNA is stored in CHROMOSOMES inside the nucleus. Loops of DNA also occur inside chloroplasts and mitochondria. *See also* RECOMBINANT DNA RESEARCH; RNA

Dnieper (Dnepr) River in E Europe. Rising W of Moscow, it flows S through Belarus and Ukraine to the Black Sea. It is the third longest river in Europe. The Dneproges dam (completed 1932) made the river navigable. It is linked by canal to the Bug River, and has several hydroelectric power stations. Length: 2,286km (1,420mi).

doberman Strong guard dog, bred in late 19th-century Germany. It has a long, wedge-shaped head; its ears are often clipped to a short, erect shape. The smooth coat may be black, red or fawn. Height: to 71cm (28in) at the shoulder.

dock Any of more than 200 species of flowering plants native to N USA and Europe. Curled dock (*Rumex crispus*) has scaly brown flowers and oblong leaves with curly margins. Its leaves are a remedy for nettle stings. Family Polygonaceae.

Doctorow, E.L. (Edgar Lawrence) (1931–) US author. *Ragtime* (1975) is his best known novel. Other works include *Welcome to Hard Times* (1960), *The Book of Daniel* (1971), *Loon Lake* (1980), *Billy Bathgate* (1988), and *The Waterworks* (1994).

Dodecanese (Dhodhekánisos) Group of 20

islands in the SE Aegean Sea, between Turkey and Crete; a department of Greece. The capital and largest island is RHODES. The islands were under Ottoman control (1500–1912), before passing to Greece (1947). The main occupation is agriculture. Area: 2174sq km (839sq mi). Pop. (1991) 163,476.

dodo Extinct, flightless bird that lived on the Mascarene Islands in the Indian Ocean. The last dodo died in c.1790. The true dodo (*Raphus cucullatus*) of Mauritius and the similar Réunion solitaire (*Raphus solitarius*) were heavy-bodied birds with large heads and large hooked bills. Weight: to 23kg (50lb).

Dodoma Capital of Tanzania, central Tanzania. In 1974 Dodoma replaced DAR ES SALAAM as capital. It is in an agricultural region, crops include grain, seeds and nuts. Pop. (1988) 203,833.

dog Domesticated carnivorous mammal, closely related to the jackal, wolf and fox. Typically it has a slender, muscular body; long head with slender snout; small paws, five toes on the forefeet, four on the hind; non-retractile claws; and well-developed teeth. Smell is the dog's keenest sense; its hearing is also acute. The gestation period is 49–70 days. Dogs developed from the tree-dwelling *miacis*, which lived about 40 million years ago, through intermediate forms to *tomarctus*, which lived 15 million years ago. The dog was domesticated c.10–14,000 years ago. There are c.400 breeds, classified in various ways, such as TERRIER, sporting, hound, working and toy. Length: 34–135cm (13–53in); tail 11–54cm (4–21in); weight: 1kg–68kg (2–150lb). Family Canidae; species *Canis familiaris. See also* individual breeds

dogfish SHARK found in marine waters worldwide. Generally greyish with white spots, it lacks a lower tail lobe. Eggs are laid in cases (mermaids' purses). Dogfish are divided into two groups: **spiny**, with a stout, sharp spine in front of each dorsal fin; and **spineless**, without a spine in front of the second dorsal fin. They are sold as rock salmon. Length: spiny, 0.6–1.2m (2–4ft); spineless, 7.3m (24ft). Suborder Squalidae.

dogwood Any of several small trees and shrubs in the genus *Cornus* of the family Cornaceae. Wild flowering dogwoods are found in deciduous forests. They have small flowers, enclosed by four large, petal-like, white bracts.

Doha Capital of QATAR, on the E coast of the Qatar peninsula, in the Persian (Arabian) Gulf. Doha was a small fishing village until oil production began in 1949. It is now a modern city and trade centre. Industries: oil refining, shipping, trade. Pop. (1992 est.) 313,639.

Doisy, Edward Adelbert (1893–1986) US biochemist. He researched BLOOD buffers, VITAMINS and METABOLISM. He also isolated the female sex HORMONES, oestrone (1929) and oestradiol (1935). Doisy shared the 1943 Nobel Prize in physiology or medicine with Henrik Dam, for their analysis of vitamin K.

doldrums Region of the ocean near the EQUA-TOR, characterized by calms, and light and variable winds. It corresponds approximately to a belt of low pressure around the Equator.

Dole, Bob (Robert Joseph) (1923–) US Republican leader. He was seriously injured in World War 2. Elected to the House of Representatives (1960) and the Senate (1969), he was President Gerald FORD's running mate in the unsuccessful Republican campaign (1976). He served as a partisan, conservative Republican leader of the Senate (1984–96). He finally secured the Republican presidential nomination (1996). He ran a lacklustre campaign and lost the election to the incumbent president Bill CLINTON.

dollar Standard monetary unit of the USA since 1792. Divided into a hundred cents, the value of the US dollar was based on the gold price until 1934. Many other countries, such as Australia and New Zealand, have adopted the dollar as their currency.

dolmen Megalithic monument comprising a stone lintel supported by upright stones. Dolmens were originally used as burial chambers and covered by mounds. They are most common in Cornwall, SW England, and Brittany, NW France.

dolomite Carbonate mineral, calcium-magnesium carbonate, $CaMg(CO_3)_2$, found in altered limestone. It is usually colourless or white. A prismatic crystal, it is often found as a gangue mineral in hydrothermal veins. It is also a sedimentary rock, probably formed by the alteration of limestone by seawater. Hardness 3.5–4; s.g. 2.8.

Dolomites (Dolomiti or Dolomiten) Alpine range in NE Italy. The Dolomites are composed of dolomitic limestone, eroded to form a striking landscape. The highest peak is Marmolada, 3,342m (10,964ft) high.

dolphin Family of small-toothed aquatic WHALES, there are salt and freshwater species. The best-known are the common dolphin, the bottle-nosed dolphin and the KILLER WHALE. Larger than a POR-POISE, a dolphin has a distinct beak and slender body, a tail fin for propulsion and a dorsal fin for steering. A dolphin breathes through a single blowhole. It is the fastest and most agile of the whales. Dolphins swim in large schools, feeding on fish and crustacea. They communicate through a complex language and map their environment by ECHOLOCATION. Dolphins have a gestation period of 12 months, the mother nurtures her calf for the first two years of life. Length: to 4m (13ft). Family Delphinidae; species *Tursiops truncatus*.

domain In mathematics, a set of values that can be assigned to the independent VARIABLE in a function or relation; the set of values of the dependent variable is called the range. For example, let the function be $y = x^2$, with x restricted to 0, 1, 2, 3 and -3. Then y takes the values 0, 1, 4, 9 and 9 respectively. The domain is {0, 1, 2, 3, -3} and the range is {0, 1, 4, 9}.

domain In TAXONOMY, the domain is sometimes seen as a higher category than KINGDOM. In this scheme, the two subkingdoms of PROKARYOTAE (ARCHAEBACTERIA and EUBACTERIA) constitute two domains, called Archaea and Bacteria. All other living organisms are included in a third domain, EUKARYOTES. *See also* PHYLOGENETICS; PLANT CLASSIFICATION

Domenichino (1581–1641) Leading painter of the Italian BAROQUE. In 1602 he worked with Annibale Carracci on the FARNESE Palace. His landscape paintings include *The Hunt of Diana* and *Landscape with St John Baptizing*.

Dome of the Rock (Qubbat al-Sakhrah) MOSQUE and shrine built (685–692) by Abd al-Malik on a Jewish temple site in JERUSALEM. The Dome covers the summit of Mount Moriah, where the prophet Muhammad is believed to have ascended to Heaven. According to the Old Testament, the Rock is also where Abraham was to have sacrificed Isaac.

Domesday Book (1085–86) Census of the English kingdom commissioned by WILLIAM I (THE CONQUEROR). Its purpose was to ascertain potential crown revenue. The most complete survey in medieval Europe, it is a vital primary historical source. It lists property and resources manor by manor.

Domingo, Placido (1941–) Spanish tenor, one of the leading opera singers of his generation. He made his debut at Monterrey, Mexico (1961). In the 1990s, he achieved popularity as one of the Three Tenors.

Dominic, Saint (1170–1221) (Domingo de Guzmán) Spanish priest, founder of the DOMINI-CANS. In 1203 Pope Innocent III sent him to S France to preach to the ALBIGENSES. He founded a monastery at Prouille. His feast day is 4 August.

Dominica Independent island nation in the E Caribbean Sea, West Indies; the capital and chief port is ROSEAU. The largest of the WINDWARD ISLANDS, it was named after *dies dominica* (Sunday), the day it was discovered by Christopher Columbus (1493). The original inhabitants were CARIB, but the present population are mainly the descendants of African slaves. Dominica is mountainous and heavily forested, and the climate is tropical. Dominica was awarded to Britain in 1783. It became a British crown colony in 1805, and was a member of the Federation of the West Indies (1958–62). It achieved complete independence in 1978. Dominica is one of the poorest Caribbean countries. Agriculture is the dominant economic sector. Production was severely affected by hurricane damage in 1979 and 1980. Exports: copra, bananas, citrus fruit. Area: 750sq km (290sq mi). Pop. (1994 est.) 74,200.

Dominican Republic Independent nation occupying the E two-thirds of the island of Hispaniola in the West Indies; the capital is SANTO DOMINGO. Dominican Republic is mountainous: the Cordillera Central range includes the highest point in the Caribbean, Duarte Peak, at 3,175m (10,417ft). Hispaniola was visited by Christopher Columbus in 1492, and a Spanish settlement was eventually established at Santo Domingo. In 1697 the w third of the island (now HAITI) was ceded to France. In 1821 the colony declared itself the independent Dominican Republic, but was annexed by Haiti. It won independence a second time in 1844. Its subsequent history was one of anarchy and civil war, punctuated by dictatorships and US military interventions. The most notorious dictator was Rafael Trujillo, who ruled from 1930–61. Mineral deposits are an increasingly important export, though agriculture is still the economic mainstay. Tourism is encouraged. Chief crops: sugar cane, coffee, fruit, cocoa and tobacco. Area: 48,442sq km (18,703sq mi). Pop. (1994 est.) 7,770,000.

Dominicans (officially *Ordo Praedicatorum*, Order of Preachers, O.P.) Roman Catholic religious order, founded by St DOMINIC in 1215 and sanctioned by Pope Honorius III (1216). They are also known as Friars Preachers, or (in England) Black Friars. In France they are called Jacobins. Dominicans are one of the four great mendicant orders of Roman Catholicism. Specially devoted to preaching and study, the order operates worldwide and includes a contemplative order of nuns.

Don River of sw Russia. Rising SE of Tula, it flows s, then sw to the Sea of Azov. Rostov is the major port. The Don is navigable for 1,370km (850mi) and is an important shipping route for grain, timber and coal. It is linked by canal to the River VOLGA. Length: 1,930km (1,200mi).

Donatello (1386–1466) Greatest European sculptor of the 15th century, joint creator of RENAISSANCE ART in Florence. Inspired by HUMANISM, his reliefs and free-standing statues have been likened to "drawing in stone". His middle work, such as the *Cantoria* for FLORENCE Cathedral and the bronze *David*, have a more CLASSICAL feel. His late work, such as *Judith and Holofernes* and his wood carving of *Mary Magdalene* (1455), show even greater emotional intensity. Donatello greatly influenced MICHELANGELO.

Donegal County in NW Republic of Ireland, bounded by Northern Ireland (E) and the Atlantic Ocean (N and W). The county town is Lifford. There is a rocky, indented coastline and much of the county is hilly. The chief rivers are the Finn, Foyle and Erne. Agriculture is the main activity. Tourism and fishing are also important. Area: 4,830sq km (1,865sq mi). Pop. (1991) 128,117.

Donets Basin (Donbas or Donec) Industrial region in E Ukraine and S Russia; the capital is Donetsk. Development of one of the world's most concentrated industrial areas began in *c.*1870. By 1989, it was producing over 200 million tonnes of coal a year. In the 1990s there was a slump in production due to exhausted pits and antiquated technology. Area: *c.*25,900sq km (10,000sq mi).

Donizetti, Gaetano (1797–1848) Italian composer. His operas, characterized by rich harmonies and orchestration, include *L'Elisir d'Amore* (1832), *Lucia di Lammermoor* (1835), *Roberto Devereux* (1837), *La Fille du Régiment* (1840) and *Don Pasquale* (1843).

Don Juan Legendary Spanish philanderer. A medieval folk tale, the earliest printed version is *The Rake of Seville* (1630) by Tirso de Molina. Notable later versions include Molière's play *The Stone Feast* (1665), Mozart's opera *Don Giovanni* (1787), and Byron's poem *Don Juan* (1819–24).

donkey Domesticated ASS, used by humans since well before 3000 BC. Crossed with a horse it produces a MULE.

Donleavy, J.P. (James Patrick) (1926–) Irish author, b. USA. His first novel, *The Ginger Man* (1955), was not published in uncensored form in Britain and the USA until 1963. Other novels include *The Beastly Beatitudes of Balthazar B.* (1968), *The Onion Eaters* (1971) and *That Darcy, That Dancer, That Gentleman* (1991).

Donne, John (1572–1631) English poet and cleric. He became dean of ST PAUL'S Cathedral, London in 1621. His poems fall broadly into two categories: early love poems and satires, such as *Songs and Sonnets*, have the characteristic wit, extravagant imagery and passion of the greatest METAPHYSICAL POETRY; and later religious poems, such as *Holy Sonnets*. Although he achieved recognition in his lifetime, the poems for which he is now famous were not published until 1633. He also wrote religious sermons and prose, including *Devotions Upon Emergent Occasions*.

Doolittle, Hilda (1886–1961) (H.D.) US poet associated with Ezra POUND and IMAGISM. Her verse collections include *Sea Garden* (1916), *The Flowering of the Rod* (1946) and *Collected Poems 1914–1944* (1983). She also wrote prose, such as *Hermione* (1981), a novel of lesbian love.

dopamine Chemical normally found in the corpus striatum region of the brain. Insufficient levels are linked with PARKINSON'S DISEASE. Dopamine is a NEUROTRANSMITTER and a precursor in the production of ADRENALINE and NORADRENALINE.

Doppler effect Change in frequency of a wave when there is relative motion between the wave source and the observer. The amount of change depends on the velocities of the wave, source and observer. With a sound wave, the effect is demonstrated by the drop in pitch of a vehicle's siren as it passes an observer. With light, the velocity of the source or observer must be large for an appreciable effect to occur, such as the RED SHIFT of a rapidly receding galaxy. *See also* NAVIGATION

Dordogne River in sw France. Rising in the AUVERGNE hills, it is formed by the convergence of the Dor and Dogne rivers. It flows sw then w to meet the River Garonne, and forms the Gironde estuary. It has famous vineyards along its 471km (293mi) course and is a source of hydroelectricity.

Doré, Gustave (1832–83) French illustrator,

painter and sculptor. He is best known for his engraved book illustrations, such as *Inferno* (1861), *Don Quixote* (1862) and the Bible (1866).

Dorian Greek-speaking people, who settled N Greece *c.*1200 BC. They displaced the culturally superior MYCENAEAN CIVILIZATION because they mastered the use of iron. Their arrival marks the start of a 400-year "dark age" of ancient Greece.

Doric order One of the ORDERS OF ARCHITECTURE

dormouse RODENT of Eurasia and Africa that hibernates in temperate climates. Most dormice are active at night and sleep by day. They eat nuts, fruit, seeds, insects and other tiny animals. Length: 10–20cm (4–8in), excluding tail. Family Gliridae.

Dorset County on the English Channel, SW England; the county town is Dorchester, other towns include Bournemouth, Poole and Weymouth. Sites include Maiden Castle, an Iron Age hill fort. It is traversed W to E by the North Dorset and South Dorset Downs, and drained by the rivers Frome and Stour. Cereal crops and livestock-raising are important. Industries: tourism, marble quarrying. Area: 2,654sq km (1,025sq mi). Pop. (1991) 361,919.

Dortmund City and port on the Dortmund-Ems Canal, Nordrhein-Westfalen state, NW Germany. In the 13th century Dortmund flourished as a member of the HANSEATIC LEAGUE. It declined in the late 17th century but grew as an industrial centre from the mid-19th century. Industries: iron and steel, brewing, engineering. Pop. (1990) 600,700.

dory Marine fish found worldwide. It is deepbodied with a large mouth. The species *Zeus faber* of the Mediterranean Sea and Atlantic Ocean is a valuable food fish. Length: to 1m (3.3ft). Family Zeidae.

DOS Acronym for DISK OPERATING SYSTEM

Dos Santos, José Eduardo (1942–) Angolan statesman, president (1979–). Dos Santos' accession to the presidency was marked by escalating violence between the government and the National Union for the Total Independence of Angola (UNITA). UNITA leader Jonas SAVIMBI refused to recognize Dos Santos' re-election in 1992 and fighting resumed. The Lusaka Protocol (1994) paved the way for a government of national unity. This government was inaugurated in 1997 with Dos Santos remaining as president.

Dostoevsky, Fyodor Mikhailovich (1821–81) Russian novelist, one of the greatest 19th century authors. After completing *Poor Folk* and *The Double* (both 1846), he joined a revolutionary group, was arrested, and sentenced to death (1849). He was reprieved at the eleventh hour, and his sentence was commuted to four years' hard labour. He returned to St Petersburg in 1859, where he wrote *Notes from the Underground* (1864). After *Crime and Punishment* was published (1866), he left Russia. While abroad, he wrote *The Idiot* (1868–69) and *The Devils* (or *The Possessed*) (1872). His last major work was *The Brothers Karamazov* (1879–80).

Douai Bible English translation (from the Latin Vulgate) of the BIBLE, authorized by the Roman Catholic Church for use after the REFORMATION. The NEW TESTAMENT was published at Reims (1582), the OLD TESTAMENT at Douai (1609–10). It was revised by Richard Challoner (1749–50).

Douala Chief port of Cameroon, on the Bight of Biafra, W Africa. As Kamerunstadt, it was capital of the German Kamerun Protectorate (1885–1901). It became Douala (1907), and was capital of French Cameroon (1940–46). Industries: ship repairing, textiles and palm oil. Pop. (1991 est.) 810,000.

double bass Largest stringed instrument. It has four strings tuned in fourths (E-A-D-G) and sounds one OCTAVE below the musical notation. It resembles a large violin but has sloping shoulders (it was originally a member of the VIOL family). The double bass is held vertically. A bow is generally used for classical music, but the strings are plucked in jazz.

double bassoon (contrabassoon) *See* BASSOON

double star Two stars that appear close together in the sky. There are two types of double star: BINARY STARS and **optical doubles**. Optical doubles are two stars that are quite distant from each other, but appear close as a result of chance alignment.

Douglas-Home, Sir Alec (1903–96) (Lord Home of the Hirsel) British statesman, prime minister (1963–64). Entering Parliament as a Conservative in 1931, he was parliamentary private secretary for Neville CHAMBERLAIN (1937–39). He acted as foreign secretary (1960–63) and was a surprise choice to succeed Harold MACMILLAN. He was replaced as CONSERVATIVE PARTY leader by Edward HEATH and was his foreign secretary (1970–74).

Douro (Duero) River in Spain and Portugal. Rising in N central Spain, it flows W to form part of the Spain-Portugal border. It then turns W through N Portugal to empty into the Atlantic Ocean near OPORTO. Length: 895km (556mi).

dove Cooing, plump-bodied bird found almost worldwide. Doves are related to PIGEONS, and have small heads, short legs and dense, varied plumage. They feed mostly on vegetable matter. Length: 15–83cm (6–33in). Family Columbidae.

Dover Seaport on the Strait of Dover, Kent, SE England. One of the cinque ports, Dover is a resort and cross-Channel ferry port. The nearest point to France on mainland Britain, it was fortified by the Romans. An important naval base, it suffered intensive bombing during World War 2. Its medieval castle contains the remains of a Roman lighthouse and Saxon stronghold. Pop. (1991) 34,322.

Dover Capital of Delaware state, USA, on the St Jones River. Founded in 1683, it became state capital in 1777. It is a shipping and canning centre for the surrounding agricultural region, and is the site of the Dover Air Force Base. Industries: food products, polymers, chemicals. Pop. (1990) 27,630.

Dowell, Anthony (1943–) British ballet dancer. He was principal dancer at the Royal Ballet, London (1966–86) and the American Ballet Theater (1978–80). He acted as director of the Royal Ballet (1986–89).

191

Down District on the Irish Sea coast, SE Northern Ireland; the administrative centre is Downpatrick. A hilly region, the Mountains of Mourne lie in the S. Livestock and crop farming dominate the economy. Industries: agricultural machinery and textiles. Area: 650sq km (250sq mi). Pop. (1991) 58,008.

Downing Street Street in London, off White-hall, named after the diplomat Sir George Downing (1623–84). It includes the official residence of the British prime minister at No. 10, chancellor of the exchequer at No. 11, chief whip at No. 12.

Downing Street Declaration (15 December 1993) Joint declaration issued by the UK prime minister John MAJOR and the Irish *taoiseach* Albert Reynolds. Continuing the momentum of the ANGLO-IRISH AGREEMENT, it set a framework for peace talks in Northern IRELAND. It stated that all democratically mandated political parties (including SINN FÉIN) could be involved in an all-Ireland forum within three months, if they committed themselves to permanently ending paramilitary violence. Both governments also agreed that the status of Northern Ireland could only change with majority consent of its people. On 31 August 1994, the IRISH REPUBLICAN ARMY (IRA) announced an immediate and "complete cessation of military operations". Loyalist paramilitaries followed suit. Disagreements over arms decommissions stalled the process. On 9 February 1996, the IRA declared an end to its cease-fire and a bomb devastated London's Docklands, killing two civilians. Talks resumed in 1997.

Down's syndrome Human condition caused by a chromosomal abnormality. It gives rise to varying degrees of mental retardation, decreased life expectancy, and perhaps physical problems, such as heart and respiratory disorders. The syndrome was first described by a British physician, J.L.H. Down. It is caused by the presence of an extra copy of CHROMOSOME 2l, and detected by counting chromosomes in the cells of the fetus during pre-natal testing. There is evidence that the risk of having a Down's child increases with maternal age.

Doyle, Sir Arthur Conan (1859–1930) British novelist and physician. *A Study in Scarlet* (1887) introduced Sherlock Holmes and Dr Watson. A succession of highly popular Sherlock Holmes stories followed, including *The Adventures of Sherlock Holmes* (1892), *The Memoirs of Sherlock Holmes* (1894) and *The Hound of the Baskervilles* (1902). Other works include a science fiction novel *The Lost World* (1912).

D'Oyly Carte, Richard *See* CARTE, RICHARD D'OYLY

Drabble, Margaret (1939–) British novelist, sister of A.S. BYATT. Her first book was *The Summer Birdcage* (1963). *The Millstone* (1965) was filmed as *A Touch of Love*. Later work includes the trilogy *The Radiant Way* (1987), *A Natural Curiosity* (1989) and *The Gates of Ivory* (1991).

Draco (Dragon) Long, winding N constellation,

representing the dragon slain by Hercules. It extends between URSA MAJOR and URSA MINOR, with the dragon's head near the star Vega.

drag (air resistance) Force opposing the motion of a body through a gas or liquid. Aircraft experience drag as the friction of air over external surfaces. To combat drag, aircraft have streamlined designs.

dragon Mythical scaly lizard. A fire-breathing monster, it is often depicted with wings, talons and a lashing tail. Sometimes, as in the tale of St GEORGE and the dragon, it is used symbolically as the personification of Evil. In China and Japan, the dragon is identified with a beneficent force of nature. It can also refer to lizards, such as the KOMODO DRAGON.

dragonfly Swift-flying insect of the order Odonata. It has a long, slender, often brightly coloured abdomen, and two pairs of large membranous wings. Like the DAMSELFLY, it mates while flying. The carnivorous nymphs are aquatic. Wingspan: to 17cm (7in).

Drake, Sir Francis (1540–96) English mariner. In 1577–80 he circumnavigated the world in the *Golden Hind*, looting Spanish ships and settlements in the Pacific, and claiming California for England. He was knighted by Elizabeth I on his return. His famous raid on CADIZ in 1587 postponed the Spanish ARMADA, which he helped to defeat in 1588. He died during a raid on the Spanish colonies.

Dravidian Family of languages spoken in S India by *c.*10 million people. The four major Dravidian languages are Telugu, Tamil, Kannada (Kanarese) and Malayalam. Tamil is also spoken in Sri Lanka. Brahui is spoken in Pakistan. Dravidian languages are unrelated to Indic languages, such as HINDI, which are a branch of INDO-EUROPEAN LANGUAGES.

dream Mental activity associated with rapid-eye-movement (REM) sleep. It is usually a train of thoughts, scenes and desires expressed in visual images and symbols. On average, a person dreams for a total of 1.5–2 hours in eight hours of sleep. Dream content is often connected with body changes. For centuries, dreams have been regarded as a source of prophecy or visionary insight. In PSYCHOANALYSIS, patients' dreams are often examined to reveal a latent content.

Dreiser, Theodore Herman Albert (1871–1945) US author, a leading exponent of American NATURALISM. His greatest work is *An American Tragedy* (1925), about a man driven to murder by dreams of success. Other works include *Sister Carrie* (1900) and *Jennie Gerhardt* (1911).

Dresden City on the River Elbe, capital of Saxony state, SE Germany. First settled in the 13th century. It was almost total destroyed by Allied bombing in World War 2. Dresden china is in fact manufactured in Meissen. Industries: optical and precision instruments, glass, chemicals. Pop. (1990) 483,400.

Dreyfus Affair French political crisis arising from the conviction of Alfred Dreyfus for treason in 1894. Dreyfus was a Jewish army officer, convicted on evidence that later proved to be false. In 1898, publication of *J'accuse,* an open letter by Emile ZOLA in defence of Dreyfus, provoked a prolonged and bitter national controversy. Dreyfus, initially imprisoned, later received a presidential pardon.

drug In medicine, a substance used to diagnose, prevent or treat disease, or aid recovery from injury. Although many drugs are still obtained from natural sources, scientists are continually developing synthetic drugs which work on target cells or microorganisms, such as ANTIBIOTICS. Some drugs interfere in physiological processes, such as anti-coagulants. Drugs also may be given to make good some deficiency, such as hormone preparations.

drug addiction Psychological or physical dependence on a DRUG. Physical addiction is often manifested by symptoms of withdrawal (such as vomiting and convulsions) if the drug dose is decreased or stopped. Long-term drug use often produces tolerance. Physical dependence on drugs has only been medically proven for NARCOTICS (such as HEROIN), depressants (such as BARBITURATES or ALCOHOL) and some STIMULANTS (such as NICOTINE). Other drugs, such as hallucinogens or hashish, are not thought to be physically addictive, but can produce PSYCHOSIS or PARANOIA. Two of the most common addictions are alcohol and nicotine. Alcohol is physically harmful especially to the brain and liver, and while nicotine addiction is not in itself harmful, the number of smoking-related illnesses and deaths is a major cause of concern. Addiction to "hard" (addictive) drugs (such as HEROIN or CRACK cocaine) is not common, yet drug-related crime makes up a significant percentage of crime statistics in many countries.

druids Pre-Christian Celtic religious leaders of ancient Britain, Ireland and Gaul. Little is known of them but they appear to have been judges and teachers as well as priests. In Britain and Gaul, druidism was suppressed by the Romans, but survived in Ireland until the 5th century.

drum Percussion instrument, generally a hollow cylinder or vessel with a skin stretched across the openings. It is struck with hands or a variety of sticks. Drums were among the earliest musical instruments; examples have been found dating from 6000 BC. Much of African music is percussion-led. Drums first appeared in European CLASSICAL MUSIC in the 18th century, and TIMPANI were standard in 19th century orchestras. In the 20th century, the role of drums in popular music has greatly expanded, especially in forms such as JAZZ. Since the 1980s, electronic drum machines have developed the sound of much contemporary dance music.

drupe (stone fruit) Any FRUIT with a thin skin, fleshy pulp and hard pip enclosing a single seed.

Druze (Druse) Members of a Middle Eastern religious sect. A breakaway group of the ISMAILIS, the Druze originated in the reign of al-Hakim (996–1021), sixth Fatimid CALIPH of Egypt, who claimed to be divine. They are named after al-Darazi, the first to proclaim the cult publicly. Stressing pure MONOTHEISM, they emphasize the possibility of direct communication with divinity as a living presence. There are about 500,000 Druze living in Syria, LEBANON and Israel.

dryads In Greek mythology, nymphs of the woodlands and guardian spirits of trees.

Dryden, John (1631–1700) English poet and playwright. He became known for his *Heroic Stanzas* on Oliver Cromwell's death (1658); diplomatically followed by *Astraea Redux* (1660), praising Charles II. He was poet laureate (1668–88). Other poems include *Annus Mirabilis* (1667), the satires *Absalom and Achitophel* (1681), the allegory *The Hind and the Panther* (1687), and the ode *Alexander's Feast* (1693). Dryden also wrote numerous fine plays, his best-known are *All for Love* (1678) and *Marriage à la mode* (1673).

dry ice Popular term for frozen CARBON DIOXIDE.

drypoint Quick ENGRAVING technique, probably originating in the 15th century, using a sharply pointed tool to draw lines in a metal plate. The drypoint steel can produce different qualities of line according to the amount of pressure.

dualism Doctrine in philosophy and metaphysics that recognizes two basic and mutually independent principles, such as mind and matter, body and soul, or good and evil. Dualism contrasts with MONISM. Both PLATO and DESCARTES were dualists, but modern philosophers, influenced by the discoveries of science, have tended towards monism.

Dubai One of the seven federated states of the UNITED ARAB EMIRATES (UAE), on the Persian (Arabian) Gulf, SE Arabia; the capital is Dubai. It was a dependency of ABU DHABI until 1833. At the end of the 19th century, it became a British protectorate. Dubai was at war with Abu Dhabi from 1945–48. In 1971 it became a founder member of the UAE. Oil was discovered in the early 1960s, and is the largest sector of Dubai's prosperous, export-driven economy. Area: *c.*3,890sq km (1,500sq mi). Pop. (1985) 419,104.

Dubček, Alexander (1921–92) Czechoslovak politician, Communist Party secretary (1968–69). At the start of the PRAGUE SPRING he was elected party leader. His liberal reforms led to a Soviet invasion in August 1968, and Dubček was forced to resign. Following the collapse of communism in 1989, he was publicly rehabilitated, and served as speaker of the Federal Parliament until his death.

Dublin (Baile Átha Cliath) Capital of the Republic of Ireland, at the mouth of the River Liffey on Dublin Bay. In 1014 Brian Boru recaptured it from the Danish. Dublin suffered much bloodshed in nationalist attempts to free Ireland from English rule. Strikes beginning in 1913 finally resulted in the EASTER RISING (1916). Dublin was the centre of the late 19th-century Irish literary renaissance. George Bernard SHAW, James JOYCE and Oscar WILDE were born here. It is now the commercial and cultural centre of the Republic. Notable sites include Christ Church Cathedral (1053), St

193

Patrick's Cathedral (1190), Trinity College (1591) and the ABBEY THEATRE (1904). Industries: brewing, textiles, clothing. Pop. (1992) 915,516.

dubnium *See* ELEMENT 104

Dubrovnik Adriatic seaport, DALMATIA, Croatia. A traditional place of asylum for persecuted peoples, it was devastated by an earthquake (1979), and a 1991 Serbian siege. Sites include a 14th-century mint, Franciscan and Dominican monasteries. Tourism is important. Products: grapes, cheese, olives. Pop. (1981) 66,131.

Dubuffet, Jean (1901–85) French painter and sculptor. Among his best-known works are assemblages of materials (such as glass, sand, rope) arranged into crude shapes, called *pâtes*.

Duccio di Buoninsegna (*c.*1265–1319) Italian painter, first great artist of the Sienese School. He infused the rigid Byzantine style of figure painting with humanity and lyricism. Notable for dramatic depiction of religious subjects, surviving works include *Rucellai Madonna* (1285) and Maestà altarpiece (1308–11).

Duchamp, Marcel (1887–1968) French painter and art theorist. His *Nude Descending a Staircase* outraged visitors to the 1913 Armory Show. He produced few paintings, concentrating on abolishing the concept of aesthetic beauty. He was a leading member of New York DADA, inventing the concept of the "ready-made". His main work, *The Bride Stripped Bare by her Bachelors, Even* (1915–23), is a "definitively unfinished" painting of metal COLLAGE elements on glass.

duck Worldwide waterfowl, related to the SWAN and GOOSE. Most nest in cool areas and migrate to warm areas in winter. All have large bills, short legs and webbed feet. Their colour is varied, and dense plumage is underlaid by down and waterproof feathers. There are two groups: **dabbling** ducks, which feed from the surface, and **diving** ducks. All eat seeds, insects, crustacea and molluscs. Most engage in complex courtship, and lay a large clutch of eggs. There are seven tribes: EIDERS, shelducks, dabbling ducks, perching ducks, pochards, sea ducks and stiff-tailed ducks. There are *c.*200 species. Length: 30–60cm (1–2ft); weight: to 7.2kg (16lb). Family Anatidae.

duck-billed platypus *See* PLATYPUS

Dufy, Raoul (1877–1953) French painter. He was associated with IMPRESSIONISM and FAUVISM, and is famous for his decorative racing and boating scenes.

dugong (sea cow) Large plant-eating aquatic mammal found in shallow coastal waters of Africa, Asia and Australia. Grey and hairless, the dugong has no hind legs, and its forelegs are weak flippers. Length: 2.5–4m (8–13ft); weight: 270kg (600lb). Family Dugongidae.

duiker (duikerbok) Small sub-Saharan African ANTELOPE usually found in scrubland. The female is larger than the male and can bear stunted horns; the horns of the male are short and spiky. Duikers

are grey to reddish-yellow. Height: up to 66cm (26in) at the shoulder; weight: up to 17kg (37lb). Family Bovidae; species *Sylvicapra grimmia*.

Duisburg City at the confluence of the Rhine and Ruhr rivers, Nordrhein-Westfalen state, NW Germany. During World War 2, it was the centre of the German armaments industry, and suffered major bomb damage. Industries: iron, steel, textiles, chemicals. Pop. (1990) 538,300.

Dukas, Paul (1865–1935) French composer. His best-known work, the orchestral scherzo *The Sorcerer's Apprentice* (1897), shows his skilful orchestration and individual style. He also wrote the opera *Ariane et Barbe-Bleue* (1907).

dulcimer Medieval stringed instrument, originally Persian, with a flat, triangular sounding board and ten or more strings struck with hand-held hammers.

Dumas, Alexandre (1802–70) (*père*) French novelist and dramatist. He achieved success with romantic historical plays, such as *La Tour de Nesle* (1832). His swashbuckling popular novels include *The Count of Monte Cristo*, *The Three Musketeers* (1844–45) and *The Black Tulip* (1850).

Dumas, Alexandre (1824–95) (*fils*) French dramatist and novelist, illegitimate son of Alexandre DUMAS (*père*). His first great success was *La Dame aux Camélias* (1852), which forms the basis of Verdi's opera *La Traviata*. His didactic later plays include *Les idées de Madame Aubray* (1867).

Du Maurier, Dame Daphne (1907–89) British novelist. Her romantic novels include *The Loving Spirit* (1931), *Jamaica Inn* (1936), *The Glass Blowers* (1936), *Rebecca* (1938), *Frenchman's Creek* (1941) and *My Cousin Rachel* (1951). She also wrote plays, short stories (including *The Birds*), and a biography of Branwell Brontë.

Dumfries and Galloway Region in SW Scotland, bounded SE by England, S by the Solway Firth; the capital is Dumfries. Major towns include Castle Douglas, Lockerbie and Stranraer. Livestock raising and forestry are important. Sites include the Galloway Hills and the runic Ruthwell Cross. Area: 6,396sq km (2,470sq mi). Pop. (1991) 147,805.

dump In computing, information copied from COMPUTER memory to an output or storage device. It may be the entire contents of a file copied to another DISK, or a print-out of the screen (screen dump).

Dundee City on the N shore of the Firth of Tay, Tayside, E Scotland. A centre of the Reformation in Scotland, Dundee is an important port and has a university (founded 1881). Industries: textiles, confectionery, engineering. Pop. (1991) 165,873.

dune Ridge of wind-blown particles, most often sand. They occur in deserts in many shapes: **barchans** (crescent-shaped) are formed by a constant wind; **seifs** are narrow ridges.

dung beetle Small to medium-sized SCARAB BEETLE. Some species form balls of dung as food for their larvae. Family Scarabaeidae; species *Geotrupes stercorarius*.

Dunkirk (Dunkerque) City on the Strait of Dover,

NW France. It came under French rule in 1662. In World War 2, more than 300,000 Allied troops were evacuated from its beaches between 29 May and 3 June 1940, when the German army broke through to the English Channel. It is a major port and one of Europe's leading iron and steel centres. Industries: oil refining, shipbuilding. Pop. (1990) 70,331.

Duns Scotus, John (1265–1308) Scottish theologian and scholastic philosopher. His main works were commentaries on the writings of the Italian theologian Peter Lombard. He founded a school of SCHOLASTICISM called Scotism.

duodenum First section of the small INTESTINE, shaped like a horseshoe. The pyloric sphincter, a circular muscle, separates it from the STOMACH. Alkaline BILE and pancreatic juices are released into the duodenum to aid the DIGESTION of food.

Du Pré, Jacqueline (1945–87) English cellist. Soon after her London debut (1961), she became widely acknowledged as a remarkable talent. Her interpretation of Elgar, Beethoven and Brahms drew special acclaim. Multiple sclerosis cut short her career in 1973 but she continued to teach.

Duras, Marguérite (1914–96) French novelist and playwright, b. Indochina. Novels include *The Sea Wall* (1950), *The Sailor from Gibraltar* (1952), *Destroy, She Said* (1969), *The Lover* (1984) and *Summer Rain* (1990). Her best-known screenplay is *Hiroshima Mon Amour* (1959).

Durban Seaport on the N of Durban Bay, South Africa. Founded in 1835, the national convention initiating the Union of South Africa was held here. It has the University of Natal (1949) and Natal University College (1960). Industries: shipbuilding, oil refining, and chemicals. Pop. (1991) 1,137,378.

Dürer, Albrecht (1471–1528) German painter, engraver and designer of woodcuts; the greatest artist of the northern RENAISSANCE. His personal synthesis of N and S European traditions deeply affected European art. His album of woodcuts, *The Apocalypse* (1498), established him as a supreme graphic artist. His paintings include *The Feast of the Rose Garlands* (1506) and *Four Apostles* (1526). He is often credited as the founder of etching.

Durham, John George Lambton, 1st Earl of (1792–1840) British statesman. One of the drafters of the Great REFORM ACT of 1832, he led the radical wing of the Whig Party. Governor-general of Canada (1838), he produced a report, which became the basis of British colonial policy.

Durham City and administrative district on the River Wear, NE England; the county town of Co. Durham. Its cathedral (1093) contains the tomb of the Venerable BEDE, and an 11th-century castle is now part of the university (founded 1832). Durham is home to the Gulbenkian Museum of Oriental Art and Archaeology (1960). Industries: textiles, carpet-weaving, engineering. Pop. (1991) 85,800.

Durkheim, Emile (1858–1917) French sociologist. Influenced by the POSITIVISM of Auguste COMTE, Durkheim used the methods of natural science to study human society, and is considered a founder of SOCIOLOGY. In *The Division of Labour in Society* (1893) and the *Elementary Forms of Religious Life* (1912), Durkheim argued that religion and labour were basic organizing principles of society. *The Rules of the Sociological Method* (1895) set out his methodology.

Durrell, Gerald Malcolm (1925–95) British naturalist and author, b. India. Brother of Lawrence DURRELL, his humorous and stylish novels include *My Family and Other Animals* (1956) and *A Zoo in My Luggage* (1960). Other works include *Beasts in the Belfry* (1973) and *The Aye-Aye and I* (1992).

Durrell, Lawrence George (1912–90) British novelist and poet, b. India. Brother of Gerald DURRELL, his major work is the inventive tetralogy, *The Alexandria Quartet: Justine* (1957), *Balthazar* (1958), *Mountolive* (1958) and *Clea* (1960). Other novels include *Avignon Quintet* (1992). His *Collected Poems 1931–74* appeared in 1980.

Dürrenmatt, Friedrich (1921–90) Swiss dramatist, novelist and essayist. Influential in the post-1945 revival of German theatre, his works are ironic and display a nihilistic, black humour. *Woyzeck* (1972) is his most frequently performed play.

Dushanbe (Dušanbe) Capital of Tajikistan, at the foot of the Gissar Mountains, Central Asia. An industrial, trade and transport centre, it was known as Stalinabad from 1929–61. Industries: cotton milling, engineering, leather goods, food processing. Pop. (1991 est.) 592,000.

Düsseldorf Capital of North Rhine-Westphalia, at the confluence of the rivers Rhine and Düssel, NW Germany. Founded in the 13th century, it became part of Prussia in 1815 and was under French occupation 1921–25. It is a cultural centre, with an Academy of Art and an opera house. Industries: chemicals, textiles, iron, steel. Pop. (1990) 577,400.

dust bowl Area of *c*.40.4 million ha (100 million acres) of the GREAT PLAINS, USA. Due to drought, overplanting and mismanagement, much of the topsoil was blown away in the 1930s. Soil conservation programmes have restored productivity.

Dutch Official language of the Netherlands, spoken by almost all of the country's 13 million inhabitants, and also in Netherlands Antilles and Surinam. Dutch is a Germanic language, belonging to the Indo-European family.

Dutch art Before the 16th century, most Netherlandish art was commissioned by the church. Artists such as LUCAS VAN LEYDEN produced elaborate altarpieces. After independence from Spain, the chief patrons were the merchant class. The 17th century was a golden age in portraiture, landscape and genre painting, producing artists such as REMBRANDT, VERMEER, HALS and van RUISDAEL. The 19th-century Hague School rekindled the landscape tradition. Vincent VAN GOGH, though Dutch-born, had closer links with 19th-century FRENCH ART. The main 20th century artistic contributions have come from Piet MONDRIAN and the De STIJL group.

Dutch East India Company See EAST INDIA COMPANY

Dutch East Indies Until 1949 the part of Southeast Asia that is now INDONESIA. An overseas territory of the Netherlands, it comprised the MALAY ARCHIPELAGO. The islands were first colonized by the Dutch in the early 17th century.

Dutch elm disease Infective fungus infection that attacks the bark of elm trees and spreads inwards until it kills the tree. It is spread by beetles.

Dutch Wars Three 17th-century naval conflicts between Holland and England arising from commercial rivalry. The first war (1652–54) ended inconclusively. The second war (1665–67) followed England's seizure of New Amsterdam (NEW YORK). The Dutch inflicted heavy losses, and destroyed Chatham naval base, Kent; England modified its trade laws. The third war (1672–74) arose from English support of a French invasion of the Netherlands. The Dutch naval victory forced England to make peace.

Duvalier, "Baby Doc" (Jean-Claude) (1951–) President of Haiti (1971–86). He succeeded his father as president-for-life. Although he introduced several important reforms and disbanded the *Tonton Macoutes*, he retained his father's brutal methods. Civil unrest forced his exile to France in 1986.

Duvalier, "Papa Doc" (François) (1907–71) President of Haiti (1957–71). He declared himself president-for-life and relied on the feared *Tonton Macoutes*, a vigilante group, to consolidate his rule. Under his ruthless regime, the longest in Haiti's history, Haiti's economy severely declined. He was succeeded by his son "Baby Doc" DUVALIER.

Dvořák, Antonín (1841–1904) Czech composer. He adapted Czech FOLK MUSIC to a classical style. Best known for his orchestral works, which include nine symphonies, two sets of *Slavonic Dances* and several symphonic poems, his Cello Concerto (1895) is one of the supreme achievements of the form. His stay in the USA (1892–95) inspired his most popular work, the Symphony in E minor ("From the New World").

dye Substance, natural or synthetic, used to impart colour to various substances. Natural dyes have mostly been replaced by synthetic dyes, many derived from coal tar. Dyes are classified according to their application: **direct** dyes, such as sulphur and vat dyes, can be applied directly to fabric because they bind to the fibres. **Indirect** dyes, such as ingrain and mordant dyes, require a secondary process to fix the dye.

Dyfed County in sw Wales; the administrative centre is Carmarthen. The Cambrian Mountains extend to the coast. Agriculture is based on livestock rearing and the cultivation of crops. Industries: fishing, timber, woollen textiles and tourism. Area: 5,765sq km (2,226sq mi). Pop. (1990) 343,543.

Dyke, Sir Anthony van See VAN DYCK, SIR ANTHONY

dyke In engineering, a barrier or embankment designed to confine or regulate the flow of water. Dykes are used in reclaiming land from the sea by sedimentation (Dutch *polders*), and also as controls against river flooding. In geology, a dyke (dike) is an intrusion of igneous rock whose surface is different from that of the adjoining material.

Dylan, Bob (1941–) US popular singer and composer. His combination of social protest poetry and FOLK MUSIC attracted a wide following. Dylan's most famous songs include *All Along the Watchtower*, *Blowin' in the Wind* and *The Times They Are A-Changin'*.

dynamics Branch of MECHANICS that studies objects in motion. Its two main branches are: kinematics, which examines motion without regard to cause; and kinetics, which also studies the causes of motion. *See also* INERTIA; MOMENTUM

dynamite Solid, blasting explosive. It contains NITROGLYCERINE incorporated in an absorbent base, such as charcoal or wood pulp. Dynamite is used in mining, quarrying and engineering. Its properties are varied by adding ammonium nitrate or sodium nitrate. It was invented by Alfred NOBEL in 1866.

dynamo (generator) Device that converts mechanical energy into electrical energy by the principle of ELECTROMAGNETIC INDUCTION. In a simple dynamo, a CONDUCTOR, usually an open coil of wire (armature), is placed between the poles of a permanent magnet. This armature is rotated within the magnetic field, inducing an ELECTRIC CURRENT. *See also* ALTERNATOR

dysentery Infectious disease characterized by DIARRHOEA, bleeding and abdominal cramps. It is spread in contaminated food and water, especially in the tropics. **Bacillary dysentery** is caused by BACTERIA of the genus *Shigella*. **Amoebic dysentery** is caused by a type of PROTOZOA. Both are treated with antibacterials and fluid replacement.

dyslexia Impairment in reading ability. Dyslexia is usually diagnosed when difficulty in learning to read is clearly not due to inadequate intelligence, brain damage or emotional problems. It is probably due to a neurological disorder. Symptoms may include difficulty with writing, especially spelling.

dyspepsia (indigestion) Pain or discomfort in the stomach or abdomen arising from digestive upset.

dysprosium Silvery-white metallic rare-earth element (symbol Dy) of the LANTHANIDE SERIES, identified in 1886. Chief ores are monazite and bastnaesite. It is important in nuclear technology. Its compounds are used in lasers. Properties: at.no. 66; r.a.m. 162.5; r.d. 8.54; m.p. 1,409°C (2,568°F); b.p. 2,335°C (4,235°F); most common isotope Dy^{164} (28.18%).

E/e is a vowel and the most frequently used letter in written English. It has various pronounciations depending on its position in a word.

eagle Strong, carnivorous diurnal BIRD OF PREY. True (booted) eagles (*Aquila*) have long hooked bills, broad wings, long curved talons and fully feathered legs. They are usually brownish, black or grey with light or white markings. They nest high on sea coasts or island mountains, building massive stick nests (eyries). One or two light-brown or spotted eggs are laid. Length: 40–100cm (16–40in) Family Accipitridae. *See also* FALCON

Ealing Studios British film studios founded in 1929. Ealing produced a series of classic British comedies, such as *Passport to Pimlico* (1949), *The Lavender Hill Mob* (1951) and *The Ladykillers* (1955). Original screenplays and a nucleus of actors led by Alec GUINNESS assured their success.

ear Organ of hearing and balance. It converts sound waves to nerve impulses, which are carried to the BRAIN. In most mammals it consists of the outer, middle and inner ear. The **outer** ear carries sound to the eardrum. The **middle** ear is air-filled, and has three tiny bones (ossicles) that pass on and amplify sound vibrations to the fluid-filled inner ear. The **inner** ear contains COCHLEA and semicircular canals. Vibrations stimulate tiny hairs in these organs and cause impulses to be sent via the auditory nerve to the brain. The inner ear also contains semicircular canals that maintain orientation and balance.

Earhart, Amelia (1898–1937) US aviator, first woman to fly solo across the Atlantic (1932). In 1937 she attempted to fly around the world, but disappeared in the Pacific Ocean.

Early English (Anglo-Saxon or Old English) ENGLISH language from *c.*450–1100. It constitutes the earliest form of English, directly descended from the Germanic languages of the early ANGLO-SAXONS. It had a vocabulary of *c.*50,000 words.

Early English First phase of English GOTHIC ARCHITECTURE (13th century). It followed NORMAN ARCHITECTURE. In *c.*1250 French-inspired English stonemasons developed a native Gothic idiom: CANTERBURY Cathedral is a very early example. *See also* DECORATED STYLE; PERPENDICULAR STYLE

Earp, Wyatt Berry Stapp (1848–1929) US law officer. In 1879 he became deputy sheriff of Tombstone, Arizona. The Earp brothers and Doc Holliday fought the Clanton gang in the famous gunfight at the O.K. Corral in 1881.

Earth Third major planet from the Sun, and the largest of the four inner, or terrestrial planets. Some 70% of the surface is covered by water. This fact and the Earth's average surface temperature of 13°C (55°F) make it suitable for life. Continental land masses make up the other 30%. The Earth has one natural satellite, the MOON. Like all the terrestrial planets, there is a dense CORE rich in iron and nickel, surrounded by a MANTLE of silicate rocks. The thin, outermost layer of lighter rock is the CRUST, which can vary in depth from between 50km (30mi) – the thickest **continental** crust – to 5km (3mi) – the thinnest **oceanic** crust. The boundary between the crust and the mantle is called the MOHO (Mohorovičić) discontinuity. The solid inner core rotates at a different rate from the molten outer layers, and this, together with currents in the outer core, gives rise to the Earth's MAGNETIC FIELD. The crust and the uppermost mantle together form the **lithosphere**, which consists of tightly fitting slabs called **plates**. The plates, which float on a semi-molten layer of mantle called the **asthenosphere**, move with respect to one another in interactions known collectively as PLATE TECTONICS. Diameter (equatorial): 12,750km. Diameter (polar): 12,714km. *See also* ATMOSPHERE

earthquake Tremor below the surface of the Earth that causes shaking to occur in the crust. Shaking only lasts for a few seconds, but widespread devastation can result. According to PLATE TECTONICS, earthquakes are caused by the movement of crustal plates, which produces FAULT lines. The main earthquake regions are found along plate margins, especially on the edges of the Pacific, such as the SAN ANDREAS FAULT. When the shock takes place, three different waves are created: primary/push (P), secondary/shake (S) and longitudinal/surface (L). The surface point directly above the seismic focus is the epicentre, around which most damage is concentrated. A large earthquake is usually followed by smaller "aftershocks". An earthquake beneath the sea is known as a TSUNAMI. Earthquake prediction is a branch of SEISMOLOGY.

Earth sciences Term used to describe all the sciences concerned with the structure, age, composition and atmosphere of the EARTH. It includes the basic subject of GEOLOGY, with its sub-classifications of GEOCHEMISTRY, GEOMORPHOLOGY, GEOPHYSICS; MINERALOGY and PETROLOGY; SEISMOLOGY and volcanism; OCEANOGRAPHY; METEOROLOGY; and PALAEONTOLOGY.

Earth Summit (June 1992) United Nations Conference on Environment and Development, held in Rio de Janeiro. The Rio Declaration laid down principles of environmentally sound development and imposed limits on the emission of gases, responsible for the GREENHOUSE EFFECT.

earthworm Annelid with a cylindrical, segmented body and tiny bristles. Most worms are red, pink or brown, and live in moist soil. Their burrowing loosens and aerates the soil, helping to make it fertile. Length: 5cm–33m (2in–11ft). There are several hundred species. Class Oligochaeta; genus *Lumbricus*.

earwig Slender, flattened, brownish-black insect found in crevices and under tree bark. There are some 900 winged and wingless species worldwide. All have a pair of forceps at the hind end of the abdomen. Order Dermaptera; genus *Forficula*.

East Anglia Region of E England, made up of the counties of NORFOLK and SUFFOLK, and parts of CAMBRIDGESHIRE and ESSEX. The protection afforded by the fenlands made it one of the most powerful Anglo-Saxon kingdoms of the late 6th century. A fertile agricultural land, farming includes grain, vegetables and livestock-raising. Industries: market-gardening, tourism and fishing.

Easter Feast in celebration of the resurrection of JESUS CHRIST on the third day after his crucifixion. It is the oldest and greatest Christian feast, celebrated on the Sunday following the first full moon between 21 March and 25 April.

Easter Island (Isla de Pascua) Volcanic island in the SE Pacific It was discovered by a Dutch navigator on Easter Day, 1722, and under Chilean administration since 1888. It is famous for the curious hieroglyphs (*rongorongo*) and formidable statues carved in stone, standing up to 12m (40ft) high. Industries: farming and tourism. Area: 163sq km (63sq mi). Pop. (1982) 1,867.

Eastern Cape Province in SE South Africa; the capital is East London. Eastern Cape was created in 1994 from the E part of the former CAPE PROVINCE. Area: 169,600sq km (65,466sq mi). Pop. (1994 est.) 6,436,790

Eastern Orthodox Church (Orthodox Church) Community of *c.*130 million Christians living mainly in E and SE Europe, parts of Asia and the USA. The Church is a federation of groups that share forms of worship and episcopal organization, but each group has its own national head. Although there is no central authority, member Churches recognize the patriarch of Istanbul as titular head. Eastern Orthodox Christians reject the jurisdiction of the Roman pope.

Easter Rising (24 April 1916) Rebellion by Irish nationalists against British rule. Led by Patrick PEARSE and James CONNOLLY, *c.*1,200 men (mainly from the Irish Citizen Army) seized the General Post Office and other buildings in Dublin and proclaimed Ireland a republic. The British crushed the rising within a week and executed 15 of the ringleaders. A wave of nationalist sentiment produced an electoral victory for SINN FÉIN in 1917.

East India Company Name of several organizations set up by European countries in the 17th century to trade E of Africa. The British company was set up in 1600 to compete for the East Indian spice trade, but competition with the Dutch led it to concentrate on India. Although the British government assumed political responsibility (1773), the Company continued to administer the British colony in India until the mutiny (1857). The Dutch Company was founded (1602), with headquarters in Jakarta from 1619. The Company was dissolved in 1799,

and its possessions incorporated into the Dutch empire. The French Company was founded in 1664 and set up colonies on several islands in the Indian Ocean. Established as a trading company in India in the early 18th century, it was defeated by the English Company and abolished in 1789.

East Sussex County of SE England. The county town is Lewes, other major towns include BRIGHTON. Its S border is the English Channel. The chalky South Downs run parallel to the coast. In the N, the Weald plains are drained by the River Ouse. Most of the region was included in the kingdom of WESSEX. In 1066 William the Conqueror met Harold II in the Battle of HASTINGS. The economy is dominated by agriculture, services and tourism. Area: 1,795sq km (693sq mi) Pop. (1991) 670,600.

East Timor *See* TIMOR

Eastwood, Clint (1930–) US film actor and director. After appearing in the television series *Rawhide*, he starred in the "spaghetti westerns" *A Fistful of Dollars* (1964), *For a Few Dollars More* (1965) and *The Good, the Bad and the Ugly* (1967). *Dirty Harry* (1971) and its four sequels were also tough and uncompromising. As a director, he earned praise for *The Outlaw Josey Wales* (1976) and *Bird* (1988). He won Best Picture and Best Actor Oscars for *Unforgiven* (1992).

ebola Virus that causes haemorrhagic fever. Ebola was first identified in humans in Zaïre (1976). It is acquired through contact with contaminated body fluids. The death rate can be as high as 90%.

ebony Hard, fine-grained dark heartwood of various Asian and African trees of the genus *Diospyros* in the ebony family (Ebenaceae). Its major commercial tree is the macassar ebony (*D. ebenum*) of S India and Malaysia.

Ebro River in N Spain. Rising at Fontibre in the Catabrian Mountains, it flows ESE and then SE through Logrono and ZARAGOZA, and into the Mediterranean. It is the longest river whose entire course is in Spain. Length: 910km (565mi).

eccentricity (symbol *e*) One of the elements of an ORBIT. It indicates how much an elliptical orbit departs from a circle. It is found by dividing the distance between the two foci of the ellipse by the length of the major axis. A circle has an eccentricity of 0, a parabola an eccentricity of 1.

Ecclesiastes Old Testament book of aphorisms, compiled under the pseudonym "the Preacher, the son of David". Evidence suggests that the book dates from after the BABYLONIAN CAPTIVITY.

Ecclesiasticus Book of the APOCRYPHA, an example of Jewish WISDOM LITERATURE. The work of a Jewish scribe, Jesus ben Sirach, written in *c.*180 BC. A handbook of practical and moral advice, it found its way into the SEPTUAGINT.

echidna (spiny anteater) MONOTREME related to the PLATYPUS, found in Australia, Tasmania and New Guinea. It is a primitive egg-laying mammal with a CLOACA, spines on the upper body, and an elongated snout. Length: 30–77cm (12–30in).

echinoderm Phylum of spiny-skinned marine invertebrate animals. Radially symmetrical with five axes, they have a skeleton of calcareous plates in their skin. Their hollow body cavity includes a complex, internal fluid-pumping system and tube feet. They reproduce sexually and regeneration also occurs. Species include SEA URCHIN, SEA CUCUMBER and STARFISH.

Echo In Greek mythology, a mountain nymph condemned to speak only in echoes, because her chattering distracted the goddess HERA from the infidelity of ZEUS.

echo Reflected portion of a wave, such as SOUND or RADAR, from a surface so that it returns to the source and is heard after a short interval. High notes provide a better sound echo than low notes. Echoes are useful in NAVIGATION.

echolocation In animals, system of orientation used principally by WHALES and BATS. The animal emits a series of short, high-frequency sounds, and from the returning ECHO it gauges its environment.

eclipse Celestial body completely or partially obscuring another, as seen from the Earth. Eclipses are transitory, the most familiar are solar and lunar eclipses. A **solar** eclipse occurs when the MOON passes between the EARTH and the SUN, so that the Sun's light is blocked from the part of the Earth on which the Moon's shadow (umbra) falls. A **lunar** eclipse is caused by the Earth when it moves between the Sun and Moon, so that the Moon passes into the Earth's umbra, and cannot shine by reflected sunlight. If a solar eclipse happens when the Moon is at its apogee (furthest point from Earth), its apparent size is less than the Sun's, and an annular or ring eclipse results, with the Sun appearing as a bright ring around the dark Moon.

Eco, Umberto (1932–) Italian writer and academic. A SEMIOTICS professor, his best-known work is the philosophical thriller *The Name of the Rose* (1981). Other novels include *Foucault's Pendulum* (1989) and *The Island Before Time* (1994).

ecology Biological study of relationships between organisms, groups of organisms and their ENVIRONMENT.

economics Social science studying the allocation of resources in a society. Methods of PRODUCTION are studied to obtain maximum efficiency in the use of RESOURCES and deciding how material wealth is to be distributed. Developments in economic understanding should help societies plan for the satisfaction of their future needs.

ecosystem Interacting community of organisms and their physical ENVIRONMENT. It includes all organic life in a given area along with the soil, water and other inorganic components of their HABITAT, and all the ecological interactions that take place within and between the organic and inorganic. It is a complete ecosystem only if it can incorporate energy into organic compounds and pass it from organism to organism, and if it recycles elements for re-use.

ecstasy (MDMA) (3,4–methylnedioxymethylamphetamine) AMPHETAMINE-based drug, which raises body temperature and blood pressure by inducing the release of adrenaline and targeting the neurotransmitter, SEROTONIN. Users experience short-term feelings of euphoria, rushes of energy and increased tactility. Some deaths have resulted from using the drug.

ECT Abbreviation of ELECTROCONVULSIVE THERAPY

ectopic Occurrence of a pregnancy outside the UTERUS, such as in the FALLOPIAN TUBE. The EMBRYO cannot develop normally and spontaneous ABORTION often occurs. If not, surgery is necessary to save the mother from serious haemorrhage.

Ecuador Republic in NW South America; the capital is QUITO. **Land and climate** Ecuador straddles the Equator on the W side of South America. Three ranges of the high ANDES Mountains form Ecuador's backbone. The snowcapped Andean peaks include Chimborazo and the world's highest active volcano, Cotopaxi, at 5,896m (19,344ft). Nearly half of Ecuador's population live in the high Andean plateaux. West of the Andes lie the flat coastal lowlands, including Ecuador's largest city and port, GUAYAQUIL. The E lowlands (Oriente) are drained by headwaters of the River Amazon. The GALÁPAGOS ISLANDS form a province of Ecuador, in the Pacific Ocean, c.1,050km (650mi) off its W coast. Coastal temperatures remain 23°–25°C (73°–77°F) throughout the year. Quito, just S of the Equator at 2,500m (8,200ft), experiences temperatures of 14°–15°C (57°–59°F). Rainfall is low in the SW, but the Oriente region is hot and wet. Vegetation in the Andes varies from high snowfields to grassy meadows on the lower slopes. The S coast, bordering Peru, is desert. **Economy** Ecuador is a lower-middle income developing country. Agriculture employs 33% of the workforce. Ecuador is the world's third largest producer of bananas. Cocoa and coffee are also important crops. Fishing is important but disrupted by the EL NIÑO current. Ecuador produces balsa wood and hardwoods. Mining has become increasingly important. Petroleum products from the Oriente are one of Ecuador's leading exports. **History and politics** The INCA conquered the kingdom of Quito in the late 15th century. They introduced their language, QUECHUA, and this

ECUADOR
AREA: 283,560sq km (109,483sq mi)
POPULATION: 10,980,972
CAPITAL (POPULATION): Quito (1,100,847)
GOVERNMENT: Multiparty republic
ETHNIC GROUPS: Mestizo 40%, Native American 40%, White 15%, Black 5%
LANGUAGES: Spanish (official)
RELIGIONS: Christianity (Roman Catholic 92%)
CURRENCY: Sucre = 100 centavos

remains widely spoken. In 1532 Spanish forces, under Francisco Pizarro, defeated the Incas at Cajamarca and established the Spanish viceroyalty of Quito. A revolutionary war, launched in 1809, culminated in the defeat of the Spanish at the battle of Mount Pichincha (1822). Simón Bolívar negotiated the admittance of Quito to the federation of Gran Colombia, along with Colombia and Venezuela. Ecuador seceded in 1830. In the 19th and 20th century, Ecuador suffered from political instability, while successive governments failed to tackle its social and economic problems. Ecuador's border with Peru has long been a source of conflict. Ecuador was defeated in a war with Peru (1941), and was forced to cede 50% of its Amazonian territory in the Treaty of Rio (1942). During the 1970s, Ecuador was mostly under military rule. A multiparty constitution was introduced in 1979. President Ballén's programme of economic and social liberalization provoked civil unrest. In July 1996 Abdala Bucaram was elected president, only to be declared mentally unstable and removed from office in February 1997. Fresh elections are due to be held in August 1998.

ecumenical movement Movement to restore the lost unity of Christendom. In its modern sense, the movement began with the Edinburgh Missionary Conference of 1910 and led to the foundation of the World Council of Churches in 1948.

eczema Inflammatory condition of the skin, a form of dermatitis characterized by dryness, itching, rashes and blister formation. It can be caused by contact with a substance, such as detergent, or a general allergy.

Eddington, Sir Arthur Stanley (1882–1944) British scientist who contributed to mathematics, relativity, cosmology and astronomy. While professor of astronomy at Cambridge University, he researched the structure of stars. He made significant additions to the general theory of relativity.

Eddy, Mary Baker (1821–1910) US founder of Christian Science (1879). She claimed to have rediscovered the secret of primitive Christian healing after an instantaneous recovery from serious injury. She expounded her system in *Science and Health With Key to the Scriptures* (1875).

edelweiss Small perennial plant native to the Alps and other high Eurasian mountains. It has white leaves and small yellow flower heads enclosed in whitish-yellow bracts. Family Asteraceae (Compositae); species *Leontopodium alpinum*.

Eden, Sir Anthony, 1st Earl of Avon (1897–1977) British statesman, prime minister (1955–57). He became a Conservative member of Parliament (1923), and was Britain's youngest foreign secretary (1935). He resigned (1938) in protest against the appeasement policy of Neville Chamberlain. He served again as foreign secretary (1940–45, 1951–55), and succeeded Churchill as prime minister. Ill health and his mishandling of the Suez Canal Crisis forced him to resign.

Eden, Garden of In Genesis 2, garden created by God as the home of Adam and Eve. Adam and Eve lived in the garden and enjoyed its fruits without toil, until they were banished for eating the forbidden fruit from the tree of knowledge. The garden of Eden is also mentioned in the Koran and is popularly equated with paradise.

Edgehill, Battle of (23 October 1642) First encounter of Parliamentarians and Royalists in the English Civil War, near Banbury, Oxfordshire. Despite being outnumbered (11,000 men to the Cavaliers' 13,000), the Royalists secured victory.

Edinburgh Capital of Scotland, in Lothian Region. The city grew steadily when Malcolm III made Edinburgh Castle his residence (11th century). It became the capital of Scotland in the early 15th century. Edinburgh flourished as a cultural centre in the 18th and 19th centuries around figures such as David Hume, Adam Smith, Robert Burns and Sir Walter Scott. The Scottish legislative assembly is based in Edinburgh. The University of Edinburgh was founded in 1583. The city has held an international arts festival since 1947. Industries: brewing, tourism, chemicals, printing and publishing, electrical engineering. Pop. (1991) 418,914.

Edinburgh, Duke of *See* Philip, Prince, Duke of Edinburgh

Edison, Thomas Alva (1847–1931) US inventor. He made many important inventions, such as the telegraph (1877), the first commercially successful electric light (1879), and many improvements to the electricity distribution system. In his lifetime he patented over 1,000 inventions. During World War 1 he worked for the US government. Most of his companies merged into the General Electric Company (GEC) in 1892.

Edmonton Capital city of Alberta province, on the N Saskatchewan River, SW Canada. Founded in 1795, it developed with the arrival of the railway in 1891 and became capital in 1905. Edmonton enjoyed a boom with the discovery of oil after World War 2. Industries: coal mining, natural gas, petrochemicals, oil refining. Pop. (1991) 616,741.

Edo Japanese city, renamed Tokyo when it became the official capital and imperial residence in 1868. Edo was the seat of government under the Tokugawa shogunate (1603–1868).

education Process of acquiring knowledge and skills, leading to the development of understanding, attitudes and values. Individuals learn survival skills in their early years from those in their immediate environment. In later years education is influenced by wider culture and society. The individual experiences a variety of educational activities and opportunities in school. Educational approaches usually reflect predominant social attitudes. Authoritarian states tend to pursue dogmatic teaching methods and curricula, whereas democratic states tend towards more open teaching methods that encourage independent learning. *See also* University

Education, UK Department of (DES) British government department responsible for the promotion of EDUCATION and the fostering of civil science in England. Headed by the secretary of state for education and science, its specific function is the broad allocation of capital resources for education, provision and training of teachers, and the setting of basic educational standards.

Edward I (1239–1307) King of England (1272–1307). He won early influence and fame as a warrior by suppressing the baronial revolt (1263–65) and on crusade (1270–72). He carried out important administrative, judicial and financial reforms, and summoned the MODEL PARLIAMENT (1295). Edward conquered Wales and incorporated it into England (1275–84). He also fought a series of inconclusive wars to conquer Scotland.

Edward II (1284–1327) King of England (1307–27). Edward's weak rule and reliance on French favourites alienated his barons. Renewing his father's campaign against the Scots, he was decisively defeated at BANNOCKBURN (1314). He survived a number of attempts to curb his power, especially by Thomas of Lancaster, but when his estranged queen, Isabella, joined forces with her lover, Roger Mortimer, to invade England in 1326, Edward was forced to abdicate in favour of his son, EDWARD III. He was murdered in Berkeley Castle, Gloucestershire, England.

Edward III (1312–77) King of England (1327–77). He became involved in unsuccessful wars with Scotland at the start of his reign, and his claim to the French throne after 1328 led to the outbreak of the HUNDRED YEARS WAR (1337). Edward led several campaigns to France and won a famous victory at CRÉCY (1346). During his reign, Parliament was divided into two houses and permanently sited at Westminster. In old age, his sons, EDWARD THE BLACK PRINCE and JOHN OF GAUNT, took over government. He was succeeded by RICHARD II.

Edward IV (1442–83) King of England (1461–70, 1471–83). He became the Yorkist candidate for the throne in the Wars of the ROSES on the death of his father, Richard, Duke of York (1460), and became king after the defeat of the Lancastrians at Towton. When the powerful Earl of WARWICK changed sides, he was forced into exile, but returned to defeat Warwick at Barnet (1471). Edward accepted a subsidy to withdraw from a French campaign, encouraged trade, restored order and enforced royal authority. He died leaving two young sons, "the princes in the tower", but the throne was usurped by his brother, RICHARD III.

Edward V (1470–83) King of England for 77 days in 1483. He succeeded his father, EDWARD IV (1483). His uncle, as protector, placed Edward and his younger brother in the Tower of London, taking the throne for himself as RICHARD III. The disappearance of "the Princes in the Tower" was attributed to Richard although some suspect HENRY VII.

Edward VI (1537–53) King of England (1547–53). The only legitimate son of HENRY VIII, he reigned under two regents, the dukes of Somerset (1547–49) and Northumberland (1549–53). During his reign the REFORMATION was consolidated by the introduction of Protestant liturgy. Edward died after willing the crown to Lady Jane GREY, in an attempt to exclude his Catholic sister, MARY I.

Edward VII (1841–1910) King of Great Britain and Ireland (1901–10). The eldest son of Queen VICTORIA. A genial and popular king, he restored court pageantry. He attempted to maintain European peace and contributed to the Entente Cordiale (an Anglo-French alliance). He was less successful with Germany.

Edward VIII (1894–1972) King of Great Britain and Ireland (1936), subsequently Duke of Windsor. Soon after succeeding GEORGE V, he abdicated in order to marry Wallis Simpson. Controversy surrounds his diplomacy with Nazi Germany.

Edward the Black Prince (1330–76) Son and heir of EDWARD III of England. An outstanding military commander, he distinguished himself at the Battle of CRÉCY (1346) and won a famous victory at Poitiers (1356), where he captured the French king.

Edward the Confessor (1002–66) King of England (1042–66). The son of Ethelred II (the Unready), he spent much of his life in Normandy before succeeding to the throne. Renowned for his piety, having taken a vow of chastity, he produced no heir. Though said to have promised the crown to WILLIAM I (THE CONQUEROR) in 1051, he acknowledged Earl HAROLD II as his heir. He is remembered for rebuilding WESTMINSTER ABBEY.

Edward the Elder (d.925) King of Wessex (899–925). He was son and successor to ALFRED THE GREAT and was responsible for the reconquest of the Danelaw in 920. He was considered overlord by the rulers of Northumbria and Wales.

Edward the Martyr (d.978) King of England (975–78). He was murdered, perhaps by his stepmother, after failing to establish control of his kingdom. He was popularly regarded as a saint.

EEC Abbreviation of European Economic Community. *See* EUROPEAN COMMUNITY (EC)

eel Marine and freshwater fish found worldwide in shallow temperate and tropical waters. Eels have snake-like bodies, dorsal and anal fins continuous with the tail, and an air bladder connected to the throat. Length: up to 3m (10ft). Types include freshwater, moray and conger. Order Anguilliformes.

eelworm Tiny, thread-like nematode found worldwide in soil, fresh and saltwater. Most species are parasitic. They can cause extensive damage to crops and have been used to control other animal pests. *See* ROUNDWORM

efficiency Work a MACHINE does (output) divided by the amount of work put in (input). It is usually expressed as a percentage. In mechanical systems there are energy losses, such as those caused by FRICTION. Output never equals input, and the efficiency is always less than 100%.

egg (OVUM) Reproductive cell of female organism. Upon union with the male gamete (SPERM), the ovum's nucleus supplies half the chromosome complement of a future ZYGOTE and almost all the CYTOPLASM. Once fertilized, an animal egg is surrounded as it develops by ALBUMIN, shell, egg case or MEMBRANE, depending on the species. The egg provides a reserve of food for the EMBRYO in the form of yolk. Bird and insect eggs have a large yolk, mammalian eggs a much smaller one.

ego Self or "I" that the individual consciously experiences. According to Sigmund FREUD, it is the **conscious** level of personality, which deals with the external world and mediates the internal demands made by the impulses of the ID and the prohibitions of the SUPEREGO.

egret White HERON of temperate and tropical marshy regions. It is known for its plumes. Egrets are long-legged, long-necked, slender-bodied wading birds with dagger-like bills. They feed on small animals and nest in colonies. Height: 50–100cm (20–40in). Family Ardeidae; genus *Egretta*.

Egypt Country in NE Africa; the capital is CAIRO. **Land and climate** Egypt is Africa's second most populous country (after Nigeria), and Cairo is the continent's largest city. Most of Egypt is desert, and almost all the population live either in the NILE valley and its fertile delta, or along the SUEZ CANAL. On the Sudanese border, s of the ASWAN High Dam, lies Lake Nasser. Egypt has three other, largely uninhabited, regions: the Western and Eastern deserts (parts of the SAHARA), and the SINAI PENINSULA, which contains Egypt's highest peak, Gebel Katherina, at 2,637m (8,650ft). The Nile valley forms a long, green ribbon of fertile farmland, but dry landscape covers 90% of Egypt; the Western Desert alone covers *c.*75%. **Economy** Egypt is Africa's second most industrialized country (after South Africa), but it remains a poor developing country. Farming employs 34% of the workforce. Most peasants grow staple crops. The main cash crop is cotton, and textiles are the second most valuable export after oil. **History and politics** (*See* also EGYPT, ANCIENT) The Egyptian state was formed *c.*3100 BC. The Old Kingdom marked the building of the PYRAMIDS at GIZA. The ruins of the Middle Kingdom's capital at LUXOR bear testament to Egypt's imperial power. In 332 BC it was conquered

by Alexander the Great, and the capital moved to ALEXANDRIA. After CLEOPATRA, the Roman empire was dominant. In AD 642 Egypt was conquered by the UMAYYAD dynasty, then the ABBASIDS. Under the FATIMIDS, Cairo became a centre of SHIITE culture. SALADIN's rule (1169–93) is notable for his defeat of the CRUSADES. His dynasty was overthrown (1250) by Mameluke soldier slaves. In 1517 Egypt was conquered by the OTTOMANS. Egypt was occupied (1798–1801) by Napoleon I. France was expelled by MUHAMMAD ALI, who established the modern Egyptian state. The construction of the Suez Canal (1867) encouraged British imperial ambitions. Britain subdued Cairo (1882) and maintained a military presence even after Egypt became an independent monarchy under Fuad I (1922). Fuad was succeeded by FAROUK (1936–52). The creation of ISRAEL (1948) saw the involvement of Egypt in the first of the ARAB-ISRAELI WARS. In 1953 the monarchy fell, and NASSER headed (1954–70) the new republic. Nasser's nationalization of the Suez Canal (1956) was briefly contested by Israel, Britain and France. In 1958 Egypt, Syria and Yemen formed the short-lived United Arab Republic. Egypt was defeated by Israel in the SIX DAY WAR (1967). Nasser was succeeded by SADAT, who ended Egypt's dependence on Soviet aid. The Yom Kippur War (1973) marked another Egyptian defeat. Sadat signed the CAMP DAVID AGREEMENT (1979) with Israel, and Israel withdrew from Sinai (1982). Egypt was expelled from the Arab League, and Sadat assassinated by Islamic extremists. Sadat's successor, Hosni MUBARAK, has managed to gain Egypt's readmittance to the Arab League (1989) and has improved relations with Israel and the West. Egypt participated in the anti-Iraq coalition during the GULF WAR (1991). Domestically, Mubarak has faced growing fundamentalism and national debt.

Egypt, ancient Civilization that flourished along the Nile River in NW Africa from *c.*3400 BC–30 BC, when Egypt was annexed to Rome. The dynasties are numbered from 1 to 30, and the kingdoms of Upper and Lower Egypt were united *c.*3100 BC by the legendary MENES. The highlight of the **Old Kingdom** was the building of the three PYRAMIDS of GIZA during the 4th dynasty. The Great Pyramid was Khufu's; the other two pyramids were those of his son Khafre and grandson Menkaure. After the death of Pepy II in the 6th dynasty, the central government disintegrated, power devolved to the provinces, and the country was in general chaos. This was the **First Intermediate Period**. Central authority was restored in the 11th dynasty and the capital was moved to Thebes (now LUXOR). The **Middle Kingdom** (*c.*2040–1640 BC) saw Egypt develop into a great power. Amenemhet I, founder of the 12th dynasty (*c.*1991BC), crushed provincial opposition, secured Egypt's borders, and moved to a new city. At the end of this Kingdom, Egypt once again fell into disarray (**Second Intermediate Peri-**

EGYPT

AREA: 1,001,450sq km (386,660 sq mi)
POPULATION: 55,163,000
CAPITAL (POPULATION): Cairo (6,663,000)
GOVERNMENT: Republic
ETHNIC GROUPS: Egyptian 99%
LANGUAGES: Arabic (official), French, English
RELIGIONS: Islam (Sunni Muslim 94%), Christianity (mainly Coptic Christian 6%)
CURRENCY: Pound = 100 piastres

od) and control was seized by the Hyksos. The **New Kingdom** began *c*.1550 BC when the Hyksos were expelled, and the 18th dynasty was founded by Ahmose I. The New Kingdom (18th, 19th and 20th dynasties) brought great wealth. Tombs such as TUTANKHAMUNS's in the Valley of the Kings and massive temples were built. However, wars with the Hittites under RAMSES II weakened Egypt and subsequent ineffectual rulers brought about the decline of the New Kingdom. The 21st to 25th dynasties (**Third Intermediate Period**) culminated in Assyrian domination. The Persians ruled from 525–404 BC, when the Egyptians revolted, and the last native dynasties appeared. Egypt fell to the armies of ALEXANDER THE GREAT in 332 BC, who moved the capital to ALEXANDRIA. After Alexander's death, his general, Ptolemy, became ruler of Egypt as PTOLEMY I. The Ptolemies maintained a powerful empire for three centuries, and Alexandria became a great centre of learning. When Ptolemy XII asked Pompey for aid in 58 BC, it marked the end of Egyptian independence. CLEOPATRA tried to assert her independence through associations with Julius CAESAR and Mark ANTONY, but she was defeated at ACTIUM. Her son, Ptolemy XV, was the last Ptolemy to rule; he was killed by Octavian (AUGUSTUS), and Egypt became a province of Rome.

Egyptology Study of ancient EGYPT, its people and its antiquities. Mystery still surrounds ancient Egyptian art and architecture (such as the significance of the PYRAMIDS) and the primitive religion of its ancient peoples. Important landmarks in the exploration and understanding of Egypt include the discovery of the ROSETTA STONE, the Temple of AMUN and the tomb of TUTANKHAMUN at LUXOR, and the moving of the temple at ABU SIMBEL.

Ehrlich, Paul (1854–1915) German bacteriologist. He shared the 1908 Nobel Prize for physiology or medicine for his work on immunization, which included the development of basic standards and methods for studying toxins and antitoxins, especially DIPHTHERIA antitoxins. His search for a "magic bullet" against disease, and his discovery of salvarsan, a chemical effective against syphilis microorganisms, introduced CHEMOTHERAPY.

eider Sea DUCK of N Europe and North America. Its down is used in pillows and quilts. In the breeding season the male grows striking black and white plumage. Family Anatidae; genus *Somateria*.

Eiffel Tower Landmark built for the Paris *Exposition* of 1889. Designed by Alexandre Gustave Eiffel, the iron-framed tower rises 300m (984ft). Lifts and stairs lead to observation platforms.

Einstein, Albert (1879–1955) US physicist, b. Germany, who devised the famous theories of RELATIVITY. His explanation of BROWNIAN MOVEMENT confirmed the reality of atoms, and his application of QUANTUM THEORY to photoelectricity won him the 1921 Nobel Prize for physics. In 1905 he devised the special theory of relativity, which completely revolutionized physics and led, through its

equivalence of MASS and ENERGY ($E = mc^2$), to the invention of the atomic bomb. In 1916 Einstein produced the general theory of relativity. He also made other fundamental contributions to quantum theory.

einsteinium Radioactive, synthetic metallic element (symbol Es) of the ACTINIDE SERIES. The isotope, Es^{253}, was first identified in 1952 at the University of California at Berkeley; this was after it was found as a decay product of U^{238} produced by the first large hydrogen bomb explosion. Eleven isotopes have been identified. Properties: at.no. 99; most stable isotope Es^{254} (half-life 276 days).

Eire *See* IRELAND, REPUBLIC OF

Eisenhower, Dwight D. (David), "Ike" (1890–1969) 34th US President (1953–61). He was commander-in-chief of Allied forces for the latter half of World War 2, and was responsible for the establishment of NATO. He won an easy victory as Republican candidate in the 1952 US presidential election. Eisenhower enforced a prompt end to the KOREAN WAR and established a vigorously anti-communist foreign policy. The domestic economy suffered under austerity budgets, but Eisenhower was resoundingly re-elected in 1956. In 1957 he ordered Federal troops into Little Rock, Arkansas, to end segregation in schools. His second term was marked by the escalation of the COLD WAR. Eisenhower was succeeded by John F. KENNEDY.

Eisenstein, Sergei (1898–1948) Soviet film director, one of the most influential artists in the history of cinema. He developed a strong political style, enhanced by the use of creative editing for narrative and expressive effect. His films include *The Battleship Potemkin* (1925) and *October* (or *Ten Days That Shook the World*) (1928).

El Alamein Village in N Egypt. In October 1942 the British 8th Army (under General MONTGOMERY) launched a successful attack on Axis forces here, and eventually drove them back to Tunisia. The battle was a turning point in the North Africa campaign of World War 2.

eland Largest living ANTELOPE, native to central and S Africa. Gregarious and slow-moving, elands have heavy, spiralled horns. Height: up to 1.8m (5.8ft) at the shoulder; weight: up to 900kg (1,984lb). Family Bovidae.

elasticity Capability of a material to recover its size and shape after deformation by STRESS and strain. When an external force is applied, a material develops stress, which results in strain (a change in dimensions). If a material passes its elastic limit, it will not return to its original shape.

Elat (Eilat) Seaport town in S Israel, on the Gulf of AQABA. A popular holiday resort, its location close to the SINAI PENINSULA and man-made harbour make it a gateway for Israel's trade with Africa. Industries: fishing, tourism. Pop. (1990 est.) 26,000.

Elba Italian island in the Tyrrhenian Sea; largest of the Tuscan Archipelago; the chief port and town is Portoferraio. The island is mountainous, and a major supplier of iron ore. Napoleon I was exiled here (1814–15). Industries: fisheries, wine, tourism. Area: 223sq km (86sq mi). Pop. (1984 est.) 28,907.

Elbe River in central Europe. It rises on the S slopes of the Riesengebirge in the Czech Republic, flows N and NW through Germany and enters the North Sea at Cuxhaven. Length: 1,167km (725mi).

Elbrus, Mount (Gora El'Brus) Two peaks (extinct volcanoes) in S European Russia, in the Caucasus range, on the border with Georgia. The W peak, at 5,633m (18,481ft), is the highest in Europe. The E peak is 5,595m (18,356ft) high.

elder Shrub or small tree found in temperate and subtropical areas. It has divided leaves and clusters of small white flowers. There are 40 species. Family Caprifoliaceae, genus *Sambucus*.

El Dorado (Sp. The Golden One) Mythical city of fabulous wealth, supposedly located in the interior of South America, the focus of many Spanish expeditions in the 16th century.

Electra Daughter of AGAMEMNON and CLYTEMNESTRA, leader of the Greeks in the Trojan Wars. She helped her brother Orestes avenge their father's murder, by plotting to kill Clyemnestra.

electric charge Quantity of ELECTRICITY. Electric charges (measured in coulombs) are either positive or negative. They can be stored on insulated metal spheres (VAN DE GRAAFF GENERATOR), insulated plates (CAPACITOR) or in chemical solutions (electric BATTERY).

electric current Movement of electric charges, usually the flow of ELECTRONS along a CONDUCTOR or the movement of ions through an ELECTROLYTE. Current (symbol I) flows from a positive to a negative terminal, although electrons actually flow along a wire in the opposite direction. It is measured in AMPERES. Direct current (DC) flows continuously in one direction; alternating current (AC) regularly reverses direction. The frequency of AC current is measured in HERTZ (Hz). *See also* ELECTRICITY

electric field (electrostatic field) Region around an ELECTRIC CHARGE in which any charged particle experiences a force. The strength of the field (E) upon unit charge at a distance r from a charge Q is equal to $Q/4\pi r^2\varepsilon$, where ε is the permittivity (degree to which molecules polarize). A changing MAGNETIC FIELD can also create an electric field. *See also* ELECTROMAGNETISM

electricity Form of energy associated with static or moving charges. Charge has two forms – positive and negative. Like charges repel and unlike attract, as described by Charles COULOMB in Coulomb's law. ELECTRIC CHARGES are acted upon by forces when they move in a MAGNETIC FIELD, this movement generates an opposing magnetic field (FARADAY'S LAWS). Electricity and MAGNETISM are different aspects of ELECTROMAGNETISM. The flow of charges constitutes a current, which in a CONDUCTOR consists of negatively charged ELECTRONS. For an ELECTRIC CURRENT to exist in a conductor there must be an ELECTROMOTIVE FORCE (EMF) or POTENTIAL DIFFERENCE between the ends of the conductor.

If the source of potential difference is a BATTERY, the current flows in one direction as a direct current (DC). If the source is the mains, the current reverses direction twice every cycle, as alternating current (AC). The AMPERE is the unit of current, the coulomb is the unit of charge, the OHM the unit of RESISTANCE and the VOLT is the unit of ELECTROMOTIVE FORCE. OHM'S LAW and the laws of KIRCHHOFF are the basic means of calculating circuit values.

electric motor Machine that converts electrical energy into mechanical energy. In a simple electric motor, an ELECTRIC CURRENT powers a set of electromagnets on a rotor in the MAGNETIC FIELD of a permanent MAGNET. Magnetic forces set up between the permanent magnet and the electromagnet cause the rotor to turn. Electric motors may use alternating current (AC) or direct current (DC).

electrocardiogram (ECG) Recording of the electrical activity of the heart traced on a moving strip of paper by an electrocardiograph. It is used to diagnose heart disease.

electrochemistry Branch of chemistry concerned with the relationship between ELECTRICITY and chemical changes. It includes the properties and reactions of IONS in solution, the CONDUCTIVITY of ELECTROLYTES and the study of the processes occurring in electrochemical cells and in ELECTROLYSIS.

electroconvulsive therapy (ECT) Treatment of mental disturbance by means of an electric current passed via ELECTRODES to the brain to induce convulsions. Given under anaesthesia, it is recommended mainly for severe depression that has failed to respond to other forms of treatment. It can produce unpleasant side-effects, such as confusion, memory loss and headache. There is continuing controversy about its use and effectiveness.

electrode Conductor, usually a wire or rod, through which an ELECTRIC CURRENT flows into or leaves a medium. In ELECTROLYSIS, two electrodes – a positive (ANODE) and a negative (CATHODE) – are immersed in an ELECTROLYTE.

electroencephalogram (EEG) Recording of electrical activity of the brain. Electrodes are attached to the scalp to pick up the tiny oscillating currents produced by brain activity. Electroencephalography is used mainly in the diagnosis and monitoring of EPILEPSY.

electrolysis Chemical reaction caused by passing a direct current (DC) through an ELECTROLYTE. This results in positive IONS migrating to the negative ELECTRODE (CATHODE) and negative ions migrating to the positive electrode (ANODE). Electrolysis is an important method of obtaining chemicals, particularly reactive elements such as sodium, magnesium, aluminium and chlorine. A commercial use is in ELECTROPLATING.

electrolyte Solution or molten salt that conducts ELECTRICITY, as in ELECTROLYSIS. In electrolytes, current is carried by IONS, rather than by ELECTRONS.

electromagnetic force One of the four FUNDAMENTAL FORCES in nature. Within an atom, the electromagnetic force binds the negatively charged electrons to the positively charged nucleus.

electromagnetic induction Use of MAGNETISM to produce an ELECTROMOTIVE FORCE. If a bar magnet is pushed through a wire coil, an ELECTRIC CURRENT is induced in the coil, as long as the magnet is moving. By the same principle, an electric current is induced in the coil if it is rotated around the magnet, as in a DYNAMO or ELECTRIC MOTOR.

electromagnetic radiation Energy in the form of waves. It travels through empty space at the speed of light, nearly 300,000km (186,000mi) per second. In general, electromagnetic waves are set up by electrical and magnetic vibrations that occur universally in ATOMS. These waves, which make up the **electromagnetic spectrum**, range from low-frequency radio waves, through the visible spectrum to very high-frequency gamma rays. They can undergo REFLECTION, REFRACTION, INTERFERENCE, DIFFRACTION and polarization. Other phenomena, such as the absorption or emission of light, can be explained only by assuming the radiation to be composed of PHOTONS rather than waves.

electromagnetism Branch of physics dealing with the interaction or interdependence of ELECTRICITY and MAGNETISM. The region in which the effect of an electromagnetic system can be detected is known as an **electromagnetic field**. When a magnetic field changes, an electric field can always be detected and vice-versa. Either type of energy field is an electromagnetic field. A particle with an electric charge is in a magnetic field if it experiences a force only while moving; it is in an electric field if the force is experienced when stationary.

electromotive force (emf) Potential difference between the terminals in a source of ELECTRIC CURRENT, measured in volts. It is equal to the energy liberated when this voltage drives the current round an electric circuit. *See also* ELECTRICITY

electron Stable elementary particle (symbol e) with a negative charge and a rest mass of 9.1×10^{-31} kg. Identified in 1879 by J.J. THOMSON, electrons are constituents of matter, moving around the NUCLEUS of an atom in orbits. In a neutral atom, the electrons' total negative charge balances the positive charge of the PROTONS in the nucleus. Removal or addition of an atomic electron produces a charged ION.

electronic mail (e-mail) Correspondence sent via a COMPUTER NETWORK. In a simple system, messages produced using word-processing programs are transmitted over a network (which could be a local area network or the INTERNET) and stored in a computer called a mail server. People connected to the network can contact the mail server to collect their mail and transfer it to their own computer.

electronic music Music in which electronic methods are used to generate or modulate sounds. The first pieces produced on tape recorders were composed in the 1920s. The development of tapes after World War 2 stimulated more complex elec-

tronic music. In Paris, Pierre Schaeffer and Pierre Henry experimented with the manipulation of recorded sounds, producing one of the first major works *Symphonie pour un homme seul* (1950). The invention of the SYNTHESIZER, capable of generating required sounds and filtering or modulating other sounds, inspired many composers, particularly Karlheinz STOCKHAUSEN. In the 1960s it became possible to use computers in the manipulation of complex electronic sounds; Yannis Xenakis and Pierre BOULEZ are two of the many composers to have used computers in the compositional process.

electronics Study and use of CIRCUITS based on the conduction of electricity through valves and semiconducting devices. The DIODE valve, invented by John FLEMING, and the triode valve, invented by Lee DE FOREST, provided the basic components for the electronics of radio, television and radar. A major revolution occurred in 1948 when William Shockley produced the first semiconducting TRANSISTOR. Semiconductor devices do not require the high operating voltages of valves and can be miniaturized as an INTEGRATED CIRCUIT (IC). This has led to the production of electronic COMPUTERS and automatic control devices, which have changed the face of both industry and scientific research. *See also* MICROELECTRONICS; PRINTED CIRCUIT

electron microscope MICROSCOPE used for producing an image of a minute object. It "illuminates" the object with a stream of electrons, and the "lenses" consist of magnets that focus the electron beam. These microscopes can magnify from 2,000 to a million times.

electroplating Deposition of a coating of metal on another by making the object to be coated the CATHODE in ELECTROLYSIS. Positive ions in the ELECTROLYTE are discharged at the cathode and deposited as metal. Electroplating is used to produce a decorative or corrosion-resistant layer, as in chromium-plated motor-car parts.

electroscope Instrument for detecting the presence of an ELECTRIC CHARGE or radiation. The commonest type is the gold-leaf electroscope, in which two gold leaves hang from a conducting rod held in an insulated container. A charge applied to the rod causes the leaves to separate.

electrostatics *See* STATIC ELECTRICITY

element Substance that cannot be split into simpler substances by chemical means. All atoms of a given element have the same ATOMIC NUMBER (at.no.) and thus the same number of PROTONS and ELECTRONS. Atoms can have different ATOMIC MASS NUMBERS and a natural sample of an element is generally a mixture of ISOTOPES. The known elements range from hydrogen (at.no. 1) to unnilenium (at.no. 109); elements of the first 95 atomic numbers exist in nature, the higher numbers have been synthesized. *See* PERIODIC TABLE

element 104 (dubnium, Db) Synthetic, radioactive, metallic element, the first of the transactinide series. It has ATOMIC NUMBER 104. The longest-lived of its ten ISOTOPES has a half-life of 70 seconds. Previously named "unnilquodium", "dubnium" was adopted in 1995 over the proposed US name of "rutherfordium" (symbol Rf) and Russia's proposal of "kurchatovium" (symbol Ku). Rutherfordium has now become element 106.

element 105 (hahnium, Ha) Synthetic, radioactive, metallic element of the transactinide series. It has ATOMIC NUMBER 105; six isotopes have been synthesized. It was first reported by a Soviet team at the Joint Institute for Nuclear Research at Dubna. They claimed the isotopes of mass numbers 260 and 261, as a result of bombarding americium with neon ions. In 1970 a team at the University of California at Berkeley claimed the isotope 260, obtained by bombarding californium with nitrogen nuclei.

elementary particle In physics, a SUBATOMIC PARTICLE that cannot be subdivided. Such particles are the basic constituents of matter. There are three groups of elementary particles: QUARKS, LEPTONS (light particles) and gauge BOSONS (messenger particles). All elementary particles have an associated antiparticle.

elephant Largest land animal, the only living member of the mammal family Proboscidea. It is native to Africa (*Loxodonta africana*) and India (*Elephas maximus* or *E. indicus*). A bull elephant may weigh as much as 7,000kg (15,400lb). They are herbivores, and browse in herds, each elephant eating about 225kg (100lb) of forage daily.

Elgar, Sir Edward (1857–1934) English composer. He wrote two symphonies, a violin concerto, a cello concerto and several orchestral and choral works, the grandest of the last being the *Dream of Gerontius* (1900). The *Enigma Variations* is his most frequently played work.

Elgin Marbles Group of sculptures from the Acropolis of Athens, including sculptures of the PARTHENON. They were bought by the 7th Earl of Elgin, sold to the British Government in 1816, and are now on display in the British Museum, London. The Greek government has campaigned for their return.

Elijah Old Testament prophet who appeared in Israel in the 9th century BC and attacked the Phoenician cult of Baal (1 Kings 17, 2 Kings 2). The rites associated with Baal were being promoted at the expense of the native cult of YAHWEH. Elijah, aided by ELISHA, set out to prove that there was no God but Yahweh.

Eliot, George (1819–80) British novelist, b. Mary Ann Evans. Influenced by her relationship with G.H. LEWES, her first fiction publication was the collected stories, *Scenes of Clerical Life* (1858). Her novels, all intensely moral, depict the provincial middle classes, examples are *Adam Bede* (1859), *The Mill on the Floss* (1860), *Silas Marner* (1861), the masterpiece *Middlemarch* (1871–72) and *Daniel Deronda* (1876).

Eliot, T.S. (Thomas Stearns) (1888–1965)

British poet, playwright and critic, b. USA. His poem *The Waste Land* (1922), with its complex language and bleak view of contemporary life, is one of the keystones of literary MODERNISM. Later poems, notably *Ash Wednesday* (1930) and the *Four Quartets* (1935–43), held out hope through religious faith. An influential literary critic, Eliot also wrote verse plays, including *Murder in the Cathedral* (1935) and *The Cocktail Party* (1950). His children's poems, *Old Possum's Book of Practical Cats* (1939), formed the basis for the musical *Cats*. He was awarded the 1948 Nobel Prize for literature.

Elisha Old Testament prophet of Israel, disciple and successor of ELIJAH (2 Kings 2–13). He appeared in the 9th century BC and accomplished the destruction of the Phoenician cult of Baal. Elisha is portrayed as a miracle-worker, healer and fulfiller of God's commissions to his master Elijah.

Elizabeth (1709–62) Empress of Russia (1741–62). The daughter of PETER I (THE GREAT), she came to the throne after overthrowing her nephew, Ivan VI. She reduced German influence in Russia, waged war against Sweden (1741–43), and annexed the southern portion of Finland (1743). A great patron of the arts, she was succeeded by her nephew, Peter III.

Elizabeth I (1533–1603) Queen of England (1558–1603). She was the daughter of HENRY VIII and Anne BOLEYN. During the reigns of EDWARD VI and MARY I, her half-brother and half-sister, she avoided political disputes. Once crowned, she reintroduced Protestantism, and Catholics became increasingly discriminated against. Various plots to murder Elizabeth and place the Catholic MARY, QUEEN OF SCOTS on the throne resulted in Mary's imprisonment and execution. Throughout her reign Elizabeth adhered to a small group of advisers, such as Lord BURGHLEY and Sir Francis WALSINGHAM. The hostility of Catholic Spain eventually resulted in the attack by and defeat of the Spanish ARMADA in 1588. She ruled a country experiencing growing prosperity and a cultural flowering. Despite pressure to marry, Elizabeth remained single. Her death marked the end of the TUDOR dynasty, the throne passing to the STUART, James VI of Scotland (JAMES I of England).

Elizabeth II (1926–) Queen of the UK and head of the Commonwealth of Nations (1952–). Daughter of GEORGE VI, she married Philip Mountbatten, Duke of Edinburgh, in 1947, with whom she had four children, CHARLES, Anne, Andrew and Edward. She has had to contend with criticism of royal wealth and scandals associated with the marriage failures in the royal family, particularly that of Prince Charles and DIANA, PRINCESS OF WALES.

Elizabeth (1900–) (Queen Mother) British queen consort of GEORGE VI. Born Lady Bowes-Lyon, she married George in 1923. They had two children, ELIZABETH II and Margaret (later Princess Royal). In 1936 she unexpectedly became queen when George's brother, EDWARD VIII, abdicated. A popular figure, she continued to perform public duties in her nineties.

Elizabethan drama Drama staged in England during the reign of ELIZABETH I (1558–1603). Drawing on folk, classical and medieval forms, Elizabethan drama is characterized by a spiritual vitality and creativity. Masters of the period include SHAKESPEARE, MARLOWE and JONSON.

elk Name of two different species of DEER: the European elk (*Alces alces*), known in North America as the moose; and the American elk, or wapiti. The elk, found in N Eurasia, is the largest of all deer. Height at the shoulder: to 1.9m (6ft); weight: 820kg (1,800lb). Family Cervidae.

Ellice Islands Former name of TUVALU

Ellington, "Duke" (Edward Kennedy) (1899–1974) US jazz pianist and composer. One of the great figures of jazz, he formed his first band in 1918 and remained influential into the 1970s. His many compositions include piano suites, classic jazz band arrangements and many songs, such as "Mood Indigo" (1930), "Caravan" (1937) and "I Got It Bad" (1941).

ellipse CONIC section formed by cutting a right circular cone with a plane inclined at such an angle that the plane does not intersect the base of the cone. When the intersecting plane is parallel to the base, the conic section is a circle. In rectangular Cartesian coordinates its standard equation is $x^2/a^2 + y^2/b^2 = 1$. Most planetary orbits are ellipses.

Ellis Island Island in Upper New York Bay, near MANHATTAN, SE New York, USA. It acted as the main US immigration centre from 1892–1943. From 1943–54 it was a detention centre for aliens and deportees. It is estimated that over 20 million immigrants entered via Ellis Island. The Ellis Island Immigration Museum was opened in 1990. Area: 11ha (27 acre).

elm Hardy, DECIDUOUS tree of N temperate zones. The simple leaves are arranged alternately along the stem, and the flowers are small and greenish. Species include the American (*Ulmus americana*), English (*U. procera*) and Scotch elm (*U. glabra*). Height: over 30m (100ft). Family Ulmaceae.

El Niño (Sp. child Christ) Warm surface current that sometimes flows in the equatorial Pacific Ocean towards the South American coast. It occurs approximately every 7–11 years around Christmas time. The flow of warm water prevents plankton-rich cold water from the Antarctic rising to the surface off the coasts of Peru and Chile, resulting in a dramatic reduction in fish catches. The current is associated with short-term changes in worldwide climate patterns, and may cause drought in Australia, India, Central America and s Africa; flooding and severe winters in Central and North America; and violent tropical cyclones in the Pacific and Indian oceans.

El Salvador Country in Central America; the capital is SAN SALVADOR. **Land and climate** El Sal-

EL SALVADOR
AREA: 21,040sq km (8,124sq mi)
POPULATION: 5,047,925
CAPITAL (POPULATION): San Salvador (422,570)
GOVERNMENT: Republic
ETHNIC GROUPS: Mestizo 89%, Native American 10%, White 1%
LANGUAGES: Spanish (official)
RELIGIONS: Christianity (Roman Catholic 94%)
CURRENCY: Colón = 100 centavos

vador is the smallest and most densely populated country in Central America. It has a narrow coastal plain along the Pacific Ocean. The majority of the interior is mountainous with many extinct volcanic peaks, overlooking a heavily populated central plateau. Earthquakes are common. The coast has a hot tropical climate. Inland, the climate is moderated by altitude. There is a wet season between May and October. Grassland and some virgin forests are found in the highlands. **Economy** El Salvador is a lower-middle-income developing country. Farmland and pasture account for *c.*60% of land use. El Salvador is the world's 10th-largest producer of coffee. Sugar and cotton are grown on the coastal lowlands. Fishing is important. **History and politics** In 1524–26, the Spanish explorer Pedro de Alvarado conquered the Native American tribes, and the region formed part of the Spanish viceroyalty of Guatemala. Independence was achieved in 1821, and El Salvador joined the Central American Federation (1823). The federation was dissolved in 1839. El Salvador declared its independence in 1841, but was subject to frequent incursions (especially from Guatemala and Nicaragua). El Salvador's coffee plantations were developed. Following a collapse in the world coffee market, Maximiliano Hernández Martínez seized power in a palace coup (1931). His brutal dictatorship was overthrown by a general strike (1944). A period of progressive government was followed by a military junta headed by Julio Adalberto Rivera (1962–67) and Fidel Sánchez Hernández (1967–72). Border tension with Honduras was exacerbated by Honduras' discriminatory immigration laws. The "Soccer War" (1969) broke out following an ill-tempered World Cup qualifying match between the two countries. Within four days, El Salvador had captured much of Honduras. A cease-fire was announced and the troops withdrew. Civil war broke out in 1979 between US-backed government forces and the Farabundo Marti National Liberation Front (FMLN). The 12-year war claimed 75,000 lives. A cease-fire came into effect in 1992, and the FMLN became a recognized political party. In 1993 a UN Truth Commission led to the removal of senior army officers for human rights abuses. FMLN arms were decommissioned. In 1994 Armando Calderón Sol of the ruling ARENA party was elected president.

Elysium In Greek mythology, the Elysian fields. The abode of blessed mortals after their removal from the Earth, it is the realm to which heroes departed to live a life of happiness.

Emancipation Proclamation (January 1 1863) Declaration of Abraham LINCOLN freeing slaves in the CONFEDERATE STATES of America. Lincoln's primary aim was to preserve the union. The Proclamation had little immediate effect, but did establish the abolition of SLAVERY as a Union war aim. Slavery was abolished totally by the 13th Amendment to the Constitution (December 1865).

embolism Blocking of a blood vessel by an obstruction called an embolus, usually a blood clot, air bubble or particle of fat. A cerebral embolism causes a STROKE. *See also* ARTERIOSCLEROSIS

embryo Early developing stage of an animal or plant. In animals, the embryo stage starts at FERTILIZATION, and ends when the organism emerges from the egg or from its mother's UTERUS. In plants, the embryo is found in the seed and the embryo stage ends on GERMINATION. An embryo results when the nuclei of an EGG and a SPERM or male sex cell fuse to form a single cell, called a ZYGOTE (fertilized egg). The zygote then divides into a ball of cells called an embryo. The embryo undergoes rapid changes in which the cells differentiate themselves to form features, such as limbs and organs. *See also* MEIOSIS; MITOSIS

emerald Variety of BERYL, highly valued as a gemstone. The colour varies from light to dark green due to the presence of small amounts of chromium.

Emerson, Ralph Waldo (1803–82) US essayist and poet. He was an exponent of TRANSCENDENTALISM, the principles of which are expressed in his book *Nature* (1836). His belief in the soul, the unity of God with man and nature, self-reliance and hope is articulated in his *Essays* (1841, 1844), *Poems* (1847), *The Conduct of Life* (1860), *Society and Solitude* (1870) and many other influential works.

Emilia-Romagna Region in N central Italy, bordering the Adriatic Sea; the capital is BOLOGNA. It was incorporated in the kingdom of Italy in 1860. The N part of Emilia-Romagna forms a vast plain. In the S lies part of the APENNINES. Agriculture is important; cereals, rice, vegetables and dairy produce. Industries: tourism, motor vehicles, refined petroleum, chemicals. Area: 22,124sq km (8,542sq mi). Pop. (1991) 3,909,512.

Empedocles (490–430 BC) Greek scientist and philosopher. He taught the doctrine of the four elements (earth, water, air and fire), and explained change as being alterations in the proportions of these elements.

emphysema Accumulation of air in tissues. Pulmonary emphysema (occuring in the lungs) is characterized by marked breathlessness, is the result of damage to and enlargement of the ALVEOLUS. It is associated with chronic bronchitis and smoking.

Empire State Building New York skyscraper.

Completed in 1931, it was the world's highest building until 1972. It is 381m (1,250ft) tall, or 449m (1,472ft) to the top of its television mast.

Empire Style Neo-classical style in interior decoration, associated with the reign of NAPOLEON I. It made use of Egyptian decorative motifs and corresponded to the REGENCY STYLE in England.

empiricism Philosophical doctrine that all knowledge is derived from experience. It was developed mainly by a school of British philosophers, LOCKE, HUME and Berkeley, in reaction to the RATIONALISM of DESCARTES, SPINOZA and LEIBNIZ. *See also* LOGICAL POSITIVISM

Empson, William (1906–84) British poet and critic. He expanded the ideas of I.A. Richards in the *Seven Types of Ambiguity* (1930). His close analyses of literary texts became known as the New Criticism. Empson's other works include *The Structure of Complex Words* (1951) and *Milton's God* (1961).

emu Large, dark-plumed, flightless Australian bird. It is a strong runner with powerful legs. Large greenish eggs (8–10) are hatched by the male in a ground nest. Height: 1.5m (5ft); weight: to 54kg (120lb). Species *Dromaius novaehollandiae*.

emulator Computer configured in such a way that it acts like another type of computer. Emulators are often used in the development of new microprocessors, allowing a designer to assess a new design without building an expensive prototype.

enamel Decorative or protective glazed coating produced on metal surfaces, or a type of paint. Ceramic enamels are made from powdered glass and calx, with metal oxides to add colour. Enamel paints consist of zinc oxide, lithopone and varnish.

encephalitis Inflammation of the brain, usually associated with a viral infection; often there is an associated MENINGITIS. Symptoms include fever, headache, lassitude and intolerance of light; in severe cases there may be sensory and behavioural disturbances, paralysis, convulsions and coma.

enclosure In European history, the policy of fencing-in by landlords of common land. Enclosure usually led to increased agricultural productivity at the cost of depriving people of free grazing and firewood. It was a cause of popular rebellions especially in the 16th century. The AGRICULTURAL REVOLUTION produced another spurt of enclosure.

encyclical Letter addressed by the Pope to all members of the Roman Catholic Church. Recent encyclicals have condemned contraception (PAUL VI, 1968) and ecumenism (JOHN PAUL II, 1995).

endangered species Animals or plants threatened with extinction as a result of such activities as habitat destruction and overhunting.

endive (chicory) Annual or biennial plant cultivated for its sharp-flavoured leaves. There are two main types: escarole, with slender, curly leaves and a variety with broad, flat leaves. Family Asteraceae/Compositae; species *Cichorium endivia*.

endocrine system Body system made up of all the endocrine (ductless) glands that secrete HOR-

MONES directly into the bloodstream to control body functions. The chief endocrine glands are the PITUITARY GLAND, the THYROID GLAND, the ADRENAL GLAND, and the sex gland or GONAD (TESTIS in males and OVARY in females).

endometriosis Common gynaecological disorder in which tissue similar to the ENDOMETRIUM is found in other parts of the pelvic cavity. It is treated with analgesics, hormone preparations or surgery.

endometrium Mucous membrane, well supplied with blood vessels, that lines the UTERUS. It is shed each month during menstruation.

endoplasmic reticulum Network of membranes and channels in the CYTOPLASM of EUKARYOTE cells. It helps to transport material inside the CELL. Parts of the endoplasmic reticulum are covered with minute granules called RIBOSOMES.

endorphin NEUROTRANSMITTER that occurs naturally in the HYPOTHALAMUS and PITUITARY GLAND connected to the brain. Endorphins are PEPTIDES that reduce pain by affecting communication between nerve cells. *See also* ANALGESIC

endoscope Instrument used to examine the interior of the body. Generally a light source and lenses are included in a flexible tube. "Keyhole" surgery can be performed using fine instruments passed through the endoscope.

endosperm Tissue that surrounds the developing embryo of a seed and provides food for growth. It is triploid (each cell has three sets of chromosomes), being derived from the fusion of one of the male gametes from the germinated pollen grain and two of the haploid nuclei in the embryo sac. *See also* ALTERNATION OF GENERATIONS

energy In physics, capacity for doing work. It is measured in JOULES. The many forms of energy include POTENTIAL, KINETIC, electrical, NUCLEAR, thermal, light and chemical. Energy undergoes limitless transformations by a vast variety of mechanisms. The law of conservation of energy states that energy cannot be created or destroyed. The concept of energy began with GALILEO and Sir Isaac NEWTON. The idea that MASS is a form of energy was established (1905) by Albert EINSTEIN.

energy sources Naturally occurring substances, processes and phenomena from which we obtain ENERGY. The great majority of energy is derived from the Sun. FOSSIL FUELS are the remains of life that was dependent for growth on SOLAR ENERGY. HYDROELECTRICITY also derives from solar energy, which maintains the Earth's HYDROLOGICAL CYCLE, while wind is generated by uneven heating of the atmosphere and its energy harnessed by wind farms. The movements of the oceans have been used successfully in some regions to create energy. Increasingly, solar energy is being used to heat some domestic water supplies, and for providing electricity from PHOTOELECTRIC CELLS. GEOTHERMAL ENERGY is obtained from underground hot rocks. The radioactive metals URANIUM and PLUTONIUM provide NUCLEAR ENERGY.

Engels, Friedrich (1820–95) German political writer. Engels and Karl MARX formulated the theory of DIALECTICAL MATERIALISM, and co-wrote the *Communist Manifesto* (1848). Engels helped with Marx's research and writings, particularly *Das Kapital* which he subsequently edited. His materialist reorientation of the dialectics of HEGEL is most evident in his *Socialism, Utopian and Scientific* (1882) and *Anti-Dühring* (1878).

engine Machine that produces useful energy of motion from some other form of energy. The term is usually restricted to combustion engines, which burn fuel. These machines include the STEAM ENGINE, DIESEL ENGINE, JET ENGINE and ROCKET engine. Combustion engines are of two main kinds: an external combustion engine burns its fuel outside the chamber in which motion is produced. An INTERNAL COMBUSTION ENGINE burns its fuel and develops motion in the same place.

engineering Application of scientific principles for practical purposes, such as construction and developing power sources. Engineering fields include MECHANICAL, CIVIL, CHEMICAL, electrical and nuclear. *See also* ELECTRONICS

England Largest nation within the UNITED KINGDOM, bounded by the North Sea (E), the English Channel (S), Wales and the Irish Sea (W) and Scotland (N); the capital is LONDON. **Land and economy** In general, the N and W are higher and geologically older than the S and E. The chief rivers are the SEVERN, THAMES, TRENT, Ouse, Humber and Mersey. The principal lakes include WINDERMERE and Derwentwater in the Lake District. The S has low hills and downs, while much of E England is flat fenland. The N is predominantly upland and includes the Pennines, Cheviot Hills, and Cumbrian Mountains. **History** There are traces of PALAEOLITHIC settlements in England. Occupied by the CELTS from *c*.400 BC, England was later conquered by the Romans, whose rule lasted until the 5th century. Germanic tribes began arriving in the 3rd century AD and gradually established independent kingdoms. Christianity was introduced into the country in the 6th century. In the 9th century ALFRED THE GREAT led a united England against the Danes. The NORMAN CONQUEST (1066) brought strong central government and inaugurated the FEUDAL SYSTEM. IRELAND was conquered in the late 12th century, and WALES became a principality of England in 1284. The 13th century saw the foundations of parliamentary government and the development of statute law. During the Middle Ages, England's fortunes continued to be linked with France, as English kings laid claim to French territory. The Wars of the ROSES curbed the power of the nobility. Under the TUDORS, Wales was united politically with England, and became a strong Protestant monarchy. The reign of ELIZABETH I was one of colonial expansion and growing naval power. In 1603 JAMES I merged the English and Scottish crowns. For the subsequent history of

England, *see* UNITED KINGDOM. Area: 130,362sq km (50,333sq mi). Pop. (1991) 47,055,204.

English Language belonging to the Germanic branch of the INDO-EUROPEAN family. It may be said to have come into existence with the arrival of the ANGLO-SAXONS in England in the 5th century AD. It is the mother tongue of *c*.300 million people, and a second language for hundreds of millions more worldwide.

English architecture Between the 6th and the 17th centuries, there were at least five distinctive styles of English architecture, including ANGLO-SAXON, NORMAN, GOTHIC, RENAISSANCE and BAROQUE. England was influenced by European architectural trends towards the end of their development. For example, Inigo JONES brought his revolutionary Renaissance ideas relatively late to the 17th century STUART court, and Christopher WREN introduced Baroque forms to England at the end of his career. The GEORGIAN period (1702–1830) is subdivided into English Baroque, PALLADIANISM and NEO-CLASSICISM. In the 19th century, the Victorian age was marked by earnestness and solidity, while the Great Exhibition (1851) paved the way for MODERNISM. William MORRIS and the ARTS AND CRAFTS MOVEMENT encouraged purity of design in the late 19th century; this continued into the early 20th century with the work of LUTYENS. In the late 20th century, notable English modernist and postmodernist architects include Sir Richard ROGERS and Sir Norman FOSTER.

English art England's earliest artistic traditions were shaped by invading forces. The ANGLO-SAXONS had an enduring influence. Their most notable achievement was the BAYEUX TAPESTRY. In succeeding centuries, the preference for foreign talent hampered the development of a native tradition, which eventually emerged in the 18th century, with William HOGARTH, Thomas GAINSBOROUGH and Joshua REYNOLDS. In the 19th century, England's two most influential artists were J.M.W. TURNER and John CONSTABLE. The work of the PRE-RAPHAELITE BROTHERHOOD bridged ROMANTICISM and SYMBOLISM, while William MORRIS was a seminal influence on the ARTS AND CRAFTS MOVEMENT. The major 20th-century figures were Stanley Spencer and Francis BACON. Modern English sculptors, such as Henry MOORE and Barbara HEPWORTH, have exerted a widespread influence.

English Channel (*La Manche*) Arm of the Atlantic Ocean between France and Britain, joining the North Sea at the Strait of Dover. A cross-channel train-ferry service was started in 1936 and the CHANNEL TUNNEL was completed in 1994. Width: 30–160km (20–100mi); length: 564km (350mi).

English Horn *See* COR ANGLAIS

English literature Body of written works produced in the British Isles in the English language. The earliest surviving works are from the Old English period (AD 475–1000). Mainly poems in the heroic mould, epics such as BEOWULF belong to an oral tradition but were written down in the 7th century. King Alfred began a tradition of English prose by translating a number of Latin works into the vernacular, and initiating the *Anglo Saxon Chronicle*. Norman French replaced Old English as the language of the ruling classes after 1066. French influenced English literature, with numerous romances centred around the stories of Charlemagne and the legends of King Arthur. The native tradition of alliterative poetry re-emerged in the 14th century in the works of Geoffrey CHAUCER, whose talent was not surpassed until the 16th century. Humanism and the innovations of the Renaissance began to influence English writing in the 16th century. SPENSER, SIDNEY, MARLOWE and the colossus of English literature, William SHAKESPEARE, were the central figures of the English Renaissance, a golden age of poetry and drama. John DONNE and METAPHYSICAL poets continued this tradition into the 17th century, and the poetry of MILTON stands out in the 1660s. English prose came of age with the production of the Authorised Version of the Bible in 1611. After the RESTORATION, drama revived in the comedies of CONGREVE; the classical ideals of the Augustan age (*c*.1690–1740) are typified in the satiric prose of SWIFT, the poetry of POPE, and the criticism of Samuel JOHNSON. The novel emerged in the early 18th century, with works by RICHARDSON, DEFOE and Smollett, succeeded by Jane AUSTEN, SCOTT, THACKERAY, the BRONTËS and DICKENS in the 19th century. ROMANTICISM, heralded by BLAKE's poetry, gained full flight with WORDSWORTH, KEATS, BYRON and SHELLEY, and continued into the 19th century with TENNYSON and BROWNING. The wit of SHAW and WILDE at the turn of the century, and the novels of HARDY, gave way to the cynicism of war poets such as Wilfred OWEN, and the modernist poetry of T.S. ELIOT. Great novelists of the 20th century include D.H. LAWRENCE, Graham GREENE, Aldous HUXLEY, Evelyn WAUGH, Anthony BURGESS, Muriel SPARK; dramatists include Noel COWARD, John OSBORNE, Samuel BECKETT, Harold PINTER; and poets, W.B. YEATS, W.H. AUDEN, Dylan THOMAS, Philip LARKIN and Ted HUGHES.

engraving INTAGLIO printing process; it describes various methods of making prints by cutting lines into metal or wood. Variations include ETCHING and AQUATINT. *See also* WOODCUT

Enlightenment Intellectual temper of Western Europe in the 18th century. It developed from the spirit of rational enquiry of the Scientific Revolution and from political theorists of the late 17th-century Age of Reason, such as LOCKE. Its leaders thought that all things could be understood or explained by reason.

Entebbe City on the NW shore of Lake Victoria, S central Uganda, E Africa. Founded in 1893, it was capital of the British protectorate of Uganda (1894–1962). Pop. (1991) 41,638.

entropy Quantity that specifies the disorder of a

physical system; the greater the disorder, the greater the entropy. In THERMODYNAMICS, it expresses the degree to which thermal energy is available for work – the less available it is, the greater the entropy. According to the second law of thermodynamics, a system's change in entropy is either zero or positive in any process.

Enver Pasha (1881–1922) Turkish military and political leader. A leader of the YOUNG TURK uprising (1908), he became virtual dictator after a coup (1913). He was instrumental in bringing Turkey into World War 1 as an ally of Germany. He was killed leading an anti-Soviet expedition in Bukhara.

environment Physical and biological surroundings of an organism. The environment covers non-living factors such as temperature, soil, atmosphere and radiation, and also living organisms such as plants, micro-organisms and animals.

enzyme Protein that functions as a catalyst in biochemical reactions. Enzymes are not altered in these reactions so are effective in tiny quantities. Enzymes only operate within narrow temperature and pH ranges and many require the presence of coenzymes in order to function effectively.

Eocene Second of the five epochs of the TERTIARY period, c.55–38 million years ago. The fossil record shows members of modern plant genera, including beeches, walnuts and elms, and indicates the apparent dominance of mammals, including the ancestors of camels, horses, rodents, bats and monkeys.

Ephesus (Efes) Ancient Ionian city of w Asia Minor (modern Turkey). A prosperous port under the Greeks and Romans, it was a centre of the cult of ARTEMIS (Diana). The Temple of Artemis was the largest Greek temple ever built and was one of the SEVEN WONDERS OF THE WORLD. Ephesus was captured by CROESUS (c.550 BC), CYRUS THE GREAT (c.546 BC) and ALEXANDER THE GREAT (334 BC), falling into Roman hands in 133 BC. Today it is one of the world's major archaeological sites.

epic Long narrative poem in grandiose style. The earliest known form of Greek literature, epics were originally used to transmit history orally. Using highly formalized language, epics tend to involve gods, men and legendary battles. HOMER's epics, the *Iliad* and the *Odyssey*, effectively established the scope and conventions of the form. Later examples include the *Aeneid* by VIRGIL, *Paradise Lost* (1667) by MILTON and *The Faerie Queene* (1589–96) by SPENSER.

Epicureanism School of Greek philosophy founded by Epicurus (341–270 BC). He proposed that the sensations of pleasure and pain were the ultimate measures of good and evil, and that pleasure should be actively pursued. He also embraced a theory of physics derived from the atomism of DEMOCRITUS, and a theology denying the existence of an afterlife.

epidemic Outbreak of an infectious disease rapidly spreading to many people. The study of epidemics, which includes the causes and patterns

of contagion and the methods of containment of disease, is known as **epidemiology**. An epidemic sweeping across many countries, such as the BLACK DEATH, is termed a pandemic.

epidermis In animals, outer layer that contains no blood vessels. In many invertebrates it is only one cell thick, in vertebrates it may comprise several layers, and forms part of the SKIN. In plants, it is the outermost layer of a leaf or of an unthickened stem or root. It is usually coated in a waxy layer, the CUTICLE, which reduces water loss.

epilepsy Disorder characterized by abnormal electrical discharges in the brain which provoke seizures. It is seen both in generalized forms, involving the whole of the CEREBRAL CORTEX, or in partial (focal) attacks arising in one small part of the brain. Attacks are often presaged by warning symptoms, the "aura". Seizure types vary from the momentary loss of awareness seen in *petit mal* attacks ("absences") to the major convulsions of *grand mal* epilepsy.

Epiphany Christian feast celebrated on 6 January. It originated in the Eastern Church as an observance of the baptism of Jesus. In the West it became associated with the manifestation of Christ to the Gentiles, and more particularly it has come to celebrate the coming of the Magi (Three Wise Men).

epiphyte (air plant) Plant that grows on another plant but is not a parasite. Epiphytes usually have aerial roots and produce their own food by PHOTOSYNTHESIS. They are common in tropical forests. Examples are some FERNS, orchids, Spanish moss, and many BROMELIADS.

epistemology Branch of philosophy that critically examines the nature, limits and validity of knowledge and the difference between knowledge and belief. DESCARTES showed that many previously "philosophical" questions would be better studied scientifically, and that what remained of metaphysics should be absorbed into epistemology.

epistles Collection of 20 letters forming most of the middle section of the New Testament. More than half of them are attributed to the apostle St PAUL – the so-called Pauline Epistles.

epoxy resin Group of thermosetting polymers that have outstandingly good mechanical and electrical properties, stability, heat and chemical resistance, and adhesion. Epoxy resins are used as adhesives, in casting and in protective coatings. Popular epoxy resins are sold in two separate components, a viscous resin and a hardener.

Epstein, Sir Jacob (1880–1959) British sculptor, b. USA. His audacious early series of 18 nude figures (1907–08) caused a public outcry with their explicit representation. He scandalized Paris with the angel carved on Oscar Wilde's tomb (1912). His most revolutionary sculpture was *The Rock Drill* (1913–14), an ape that has mutated into a robot. He also produced some religious works, including the bronze *Visitation* (1926), the stone *Ecce Homo* (1934–35) and the alabaster *Adam* (1939).

equation Mathematical statement of variables, equal to some subset of all possible variables. The equation $x^2 = 8 - 2x$ is true only for certain values (solutions) of x ($x = 2$ and $x = -4$). This type of equation is contrasted with an **identity**, such as ($x + 2$)$^2 = x^2 + 4x + 4$, which is true for all values of x. Equations are said to be linear, quadratic, cubic, quartic, and so on, according to whether their degree (the highest power of the variable) is 1, 2, 3, 4, ... *See also* SIMULTANEOUS EQUATIONS

equator Name given to two imaginary circles. The **terrestrial** Equator lies midway between the North Pole and South Pole and is the zero line from which latitude is measured. It divides the Earth into the Southern and Northern Hemispheres. The **celestial** equator lies directly above the Earth's Equator and is used as a reference to determine the position of a star using the astronomical co-ordinate system of right ascension and declination.

Equatorial Guinea (formerly Spanish Guinea) Republic in w central Africa, consisting of a mainland, Mbini (Río Muni), between Cameroon and Gabon, and five islands in the Gulf of Guinea; the largest of which is Bioko (Fernando Póo). The capital is MALABO (on Bioko). **Land and climate** Bioko is a volcanic island with fertile soils, and Malabo's harbour is part of a submerged volcano. Bioko is mountainous, rising to 3,008m (9,869ft), and has heavy rainfall. Mbini (90% of Equatorial Guinea's land area) consists mainly of hills and plateaux behind the coastal plains. Its main river, the Lolo, rises in Gabon. Mbini has a similar climate to Bioko, though rainfall diminishes inland. Dense rainforest covers most of Mbini. Mangrove forests line the coast. **Economy** Agriculture employs 66% of the workforce. The main food crops are bananas, cassava and sweet potatoes. The most valuable export crop is cocoa. Timber and coffee are also exported, but the country has few manufacturing industries. **History** Portuguese navigators reached the area in early 1471. In 1778 Portugal ceded the islands and commercial mainland rights to Spain. Spanish settlers on Bioko were hit by yellow fever and withdrew in 1781: nobody settled on mainland Mbini. In 1827 Spain leased bases on Bioko to Britain, and the British settled some freed slaves. Descendants of these former slaves (*Fernandinos*) remain on the island. Spain returned to the area in the mid-19th century and began to develop plantations on Bioko. Bioko and Mbini attained a degree of self-government (1963) and finally achieved independence (1968). In 1979 the nation's first president, Francisco Macias Nguema, was deposed by a Supreme Military Council, led by Colonel Teodoro Obiang Nguema Mbasogo. **Politics** In 1991, a referendum voted to set up a multiparty democracy, consisting of the ruling Equatorial Guinea Democratic Party (PDGE), led by Mbasogo, and ten opposition parties. In 1996 elections, boycotted by most opposition parties, President Mbasogo claimed 99% of the vote. His regime has been accused of arresting and torturing opponents.

equilibrium In physics, a stable state in which any variety of forces acting on a particle or object negate each other, resulting in no net force. While thought of as a state of balance or rest, an object with constant velocity is also said to be in equilibrium. The term can also be ascribed to a body with a constant temperature; this is known as **thermic equilibrium**.

equinox Either of the two days each year when day and night are of equal duration. They occur on the two occasions when the Sun crosses the celestial EQUATOR, moving in either a northerly or southerly direction.

equity In law, a field of jurisdiction which enables the judiciary to apply principles or morals. It applies to individual cases where a strict adherence to the law would result in unjust sentencing. In a number of legal systems equity (as well as the rules of law) must be considered before the judiciary makes its decision.

Erasmus, Desiderius (1466–1536) Dutch scholar and teacher, considered the greatest of the RENAISSANCE humanists, b. Gerhard Gerhards. His Latin translation of the Greek New Testament revealed flaws in the VULGATE text. He also edited the writings of Saint JEROME and other patristic literature. Among his original works, his *Enchiridion militis* (*Manual of the Christian Knight*) (1503) emphasized simple piety as an ideal of CHRISTIANITY and called for church reform. His works had an early influence on LUTHER and other Protestant reformers, although he sought change from within the Catholic Church and disagreed with the course of the REFORMATION. In *On Free Will* (1524) he openly clashed with Luther. *See also* HUMANISM; LUTHERANISM

erbium Silvery metallic element (symbol Er) of the LANTHANIDE SERIES (rare-earth) group. There are six isotopes naturally occurring, and the chief ores are monazite and bastnaesite. Nine radioactive isotopes have been identified. Soft and malleable, erbium is used in some specialized alloys, and erbium oxide is used as a pink colourant for glass. Properties: at.no. 68; r.a.m. 167.26; m.p. 1,522°C (2,772°F); r.d. 9.045 (25°C); b.p. 2,863°C (5,185°F); most common isotope Er^{166} (33.41%).

erica Genus of more than 500 species of mostly

EQUATORIAL GUINEA

AREA: 28,050sq km (10,830 sq mi)
POPULATION: 420,000
CAPITAL (POPULATION): Malabo (35,000)
GOVERNMENT: Multiparty republic (transitional)
ETHNIC GROUPS: Fang 83%, Bubi 10%, Ndowe 4%
LANGUAGES: Spanish (official)
RELIGIONS: Christianity (mainly Roman Catholic) 89%, traditional beliefs 5%
CURRENCY: CFA franc = 100 centimes

low, evergreen shrubs comprising true heaths and heathers. Most species are native to Africa, but many grow on moors in Britain and other parts of Europe. Blossoms are colourful and tube-shaped or bell-shaped. Family Ericaceae.

Eric the Red (active late 10th century) Discoverer of Greenland. Born in Norway, he settled in Iceland, from which he was banished after a murder. He set off to the west and discovered the land he named Greenland in *c*.981. Returning to Iceland, he organized a party of colonists who set out in *c*.985.

Erie, Lake Great Lake in North America, bordered by Ontario (w), New York (E), Ohio and Pennsylvania (s), and Michigan (sw); part of the GREAT LAKES-ST LAWRENCE SEAWAY. It was the site of a British defeat by the USA in the WAR OF 1812. The second smallest of the lakes, it has been polluted by urban development. Government regulations are now aiding its recovery. Area: 25,667sq km (9,910sq mi). Max. depth: 64m (210ft).

Eritrea Independent state in NE Africa, bordered the Red Sea; the capital is ASMARA. **Land and climate** Much of Eritrea is a continuation of the high Ethiopian plateau, sloping down to plains in the E and w. Unreliable rainfall is a frequent cause of drought. **History** A dependency of Ethiopia until the 16th century, when it became annexed to the Ottoman empire. During the 19th century, control of the region was disputed between Ethiopia, Egypt and Italy. In 1890 it became an Italian colony. From 1941–52 it was under British military administration. In 1952 it was federated with Ethiopia, becoming a province in 1962. Eritrean separatists began a 30-year campaign of guerrilla warfare; over 700,000 refugees fled to SOMALIA. In 1991, the Eritrean People's Liberation Front (EPLF) helped topple Mengistu's Ethiopian government, and won a referendum on independence. Eritrea formally gained independence in 1993. The war-devastated economy is mainly agricultural. Industries: textiles, leather goods and salt. Area: 117,599sq km (45,405sq mi). Pop. (1994 est.) 3,530,000.

ermine Slender mammal, known as a STOAT in Eurasia, or short-tailed WEASEL in North America.

Ernst, Max (1891–1976) German painter and sculptor, founder of Cologne DADA (1919), later influential in SURREALISM. Ernst was a prolific innnovator, and developed ways of adapting COLLAGE, photomontage and other radical pictorial techniques. His most important works include *L'Eléphant Célèbes* (1921) and *Two Children Threatened by a Nightingale* (1924).

Eros In GREEK MYTHOLOGY, god of love, equivalent to the Roman god Cupid. Depicted as a winged boy carrying a bow and arrows, and often blindfold, he was the youngest and most mischievous of the gods. He married PSYCHE.

erosion In geology, alteration of landforms by the wearing away of rock and soil, and the removal of any debris (as opposed to WEATHERING). Erosion is carried out by the actions of wind, water, glaciers

and living organisms. In **chemical** erosion, minerals in the rock react to other substances, such as weak acids found in rainwater, and are broken down. In **physical** erosion, powerful forces such as rivers and glaciers physically wear rock down and transport it. *See also* GEOMORPHOLOGY

erythrocyte Red blood cell, usually disc-shaped and without a nucleus. It contains HAEMOGLOBIN that combines with oxygen and gives blood its red colour. Normal human blood contains an average of five million such cells per cu mm of blood.

escape velocity Minimum velocity required to free a body from the gravitational field of a celestial body or stellar system. Escape velocities are, for the Earth 11.2km/sec (7mi/s) and Moon 2.4km/sec (1.5mi/s). They can be calculated from the formula: $v = (2G\,M/R)^{1/2}$ where G is the gravitational constant, M the mass of the planet or system and R the distance of the rocket from the centre of mass of the system.

Esfahan *See* ISFAHAN

Eskimo (Algonquian, eaters of raw flesh) Native inhabitants of Arctic and sub-Arctic regions of North America, Greenland and Asia. Eskimos originally migrated from Asia *c*.2,000 years ago. Sharing the common language family of Eskimo-ALEUT, Eskimos have adapted well to harsh climates, and are proficient hunters. In some areas, a nomadic existence has been replaced by village settlements and work in the oil and mining industries. *See also* INUIT

ESP Abbreviation of EXTRASENSORY PERCEPTION

Esperanto Language for international communication, devised in 1887. Its spelling and grammar are regular and consistent, and its vocabulary mostly derived from w European languages.

essay (Fr. *essai*, attempt) Usually short, non-fictional prose, written expressing a personal point of view. The essay form originated with the 16th century French writer Montaigne. Famous British essayists include Francis BACON, Henry FIELDING, Dr Samuel JOHNSON, Oliver GOLDSMITH, Matthew ARNOLD, Charles LAMB and William MORRIS.

Essen City on the River Ruhr, Nordrhein-Westfalen state, NW Germany. Lying at the centre of a major coalfield, Essen underwent a huge industrial expansion during the 19th century and is home to the Krupp steelworks. The city was heavily bombed in World War 2. It has a cathedral (begun 11th century). Industries: mining, iron and steel, glass, textiles, chemicals. Pop. (1990) 627,800.

Essex, Robert Devereux, 2nd Earl of (1566–1601) English courtier and soldier. A favourite of ELIZABETH I, he won prestige with an attack on Cadiz in 1596. Following a quarrel with Elizabeth, he was made the reluctant lord lieutenant of a rebellious Ireland. He returned in disgrace six months later, attempted a coup d'état, and was executed for treason.

Essex County in SE England; the county town is Chelmsford. Colonized by the Romans at COLCH-

ESTER, it was invaded by the Anglo-Saxons in the 5th century, and later came under Danish control. Low lying on the E coast, the land rises to the NW providing pasture for dairy and sheep farming. Wheat, barley and sugar-beet are important crops. Industries: machinery and electrical goods. Area: 3,674sq km (1,419sq mi). Pop. (1991) 1,528,577.

ester Any of a class of organic compounds formed by reaction between an ALCOHOL and an ACID.

Estonia Republic on the E coast of the Baltic Sea; the capital is TALLINN. **Land and climate** Estonia is mostly flat, and is dotted with more than 1,500 small lakes. Lake Peipus (Chudskoye Ozero) and the River Narva make up most of Estonia's Russian border. Estonia has more than 800 islands, which together make up *c*.10% of total area; the largest is Saaremaa. Estonia has a fairly mild climate. Rainfall averages from 480 to 580mm (19 to 23in). **Economy** Under Soviet rule, Estonia was the most prosperous of the Baltic states. Chief natural resources are oil shale deposits and forests. Oil shale is used to fuel power plants and in the petrochemical industry. Manufactures include petrochemicals, fertilizers, machinery, processed food and textiles. Agriculture and fishing are important. Barley, potatoes and oats are major crops. Since 1988, the nationalized economy has begun a process of privatization, and Estonia has strengthened its European ties. **History** The original settlers were related to the Finns. The TEUTONIC KNIGHTS introduced Christianity in the 13th century, and by the 16th century German noblemen owned much of the land. In 1561, Sweden took the N part of the country, and Poland the S. In 1625, Sweden assumed complete control, before passing to Russia in 1721. Estonia became independent in 1918. In 1940, Soviet forces occupied Estonia, but were driven out by Germany in 1941. Soviet troops returned in 1944, and Estonia became one of the 15 socialist republics of the Soviet Union. Estonians strongly opposed Soviet rule, and many were deported to Siberia. Political changes in the Soviet Union in the late 1980s led to renewed demands for freedom. In 1990, Estonia declared independence, and the Soviet Union recognized this in September 1991. Estonia adopted a new constitution in 1992 and multiparty elections were held. President Meri was elected and a right-wing coalition government was formed. Russian troops completed their withdrawal in 1993. **Recent Events** In 1995 elections a centre-left government was elected.

estuary Coastal region where a river mouth opens into the ocean and freshwater from the land mixes with saltwater from the sea. Estuaries usually provide good harbours and breeding grounds for many kinds of marine life.

etching Method of INTAGLIO (incised) printing used for black-and-white designs. A metal plate, usually copper, is coated with an acid-proof ground. A design is etched with a needle so that the lines penetrate the ground. The plate is then placed in an acid that eats away the exposed line so that it will hold ink. When the plate is finished, it is rolled with ink and placed in an etching press to be printed.

ethanal (acetaldehyde) Colourless, volatile flammable liquid (CH_3CHO) manufactured now by catalytic oxidation of ethene or ethanol, or catalytic hydration of acetylene. It is used in the breathalyser test and to silver mirrors. Properties: r.d. 0.788; m.p. $-123.5°C$ ($-190.3°F$); b.p. 20.8°C (69.4°F).

ethane Colourless, odourless gas (CH_3CH_3), the second member of the ALKANE series of HYDROCARBONS. It is a minor constituent of natural gas. *See also* SATURATED COMPOUND

ethanoic acid (acetic acid) Colourless, corrosive liquid (CH_3COOH) made by the oxidation of ethanol, either by catalysis or by the action of bacteria. It is the active ingredient in VINEGAR. Properties: r.d. 1.049; m.p. 16.6°C (61.9°F); b.p. 117.9°C (244.4°F).

ethanol (ethyl alcohol) Colourless, flammable and volatile ALCOHOL (C_2H_5OH), produced by the fermentation of sugars, molasses and grains, or by the catalytic hydration of ethylene. Its many uses include alcoholic beverages (such as wine, beer, cider and spirits), cleaning solutions, antifreeze, rocket fuels, cosmetics, and pharmaceuticals. Properties: r.d. 0.789; b.p. 78.5°C (173.3°F).

Ethelbert (d.616) King of Kent (560–616). He was the strongest ruler in England S of the Humber River, and was the first Christian king in Anglo-Saxon England. He allowed AUGUSTINE and his monks to settle and preach in Canterbury.

Ethelred II (the Unready) (968–1016) (Old English, evil *rede* or counsel) King of England (978–1013; 1014–16). Following continuous Danish attacks, he paid off the raiders with money raised by the Danegeld (994). The Danes returned in 997 and 1002, when they were massacred by Ethelred's forces. The Danish King Sweyn retaliated and conquered England (1013). Ethelred was made king again on Sweyn's death, but was succeeded by Sweyn's son CANUTE II.

ethene (ethylene) Colourless gas (CH_2H_4) derived from the cracking of propane and other compounds. Vast quantities are used in polyethylene production.

ether In physics, hypothetical medium that was

ESTONIA
AREA: 44,700sq km (17,300sq mi)
POPULATION: 1,491,583
CAPITAL (POPULATION): Tallinn (490,000)
GOVERNMENT: Multiparty republic
ETHNIC GROUPS: Estonian 62%, Russian 30%, Ukrainian 3%, Belorussian 2%, Finnish 1%
LANGUAGES: Estonian (official)
RELIGIONS: Christianity (Lutheran, with Orthodox and Baptist minorities)
CURRENCY: Kroon = 100 senti

supposed to fill all space and offer no resistance to motion. It was postulated as a medium to support the propagation of electromagnetic radiations, but was disproved.

ether (diethyl ether) Colourless volatile inflammable liquid ($C_2H_5OC_2H_5$) prepared by the action of sulphuric acid on ethanol followed by distillation. It is used as an industrial solvent, fuel additive and decreasing as an anaesthetic. Properties: m.p. $-116.2°C$ ($-177.2°F$;); b.p. $34.5°C$ ($94.1°F$).

Ethiopia Land-locked republic in NE Africa, the capital is ADDIS ABABA. **Land and climate** The dominant feature is the Ethiopian Plateau, a block of volcanic mountains. Its average height is 1,800m–2,400m (6,000ft–8,000ft), and rises to 4,620m (15,157ft), at Ras Dashen. The plateau is bisected by the Great RIFT VALLEY. The Eastern Highlands include the Somali Plateau and the desert of the Ogaden Plateau. The Western Highlands include the Blue Nile (Abbay) and its source, Lake Tana, Ethiopia's largest lake. The Danakil Desert forms Ethiopia's border with ERITREA. The rainfall is generally over 1,000mm (39in), with a rainy season from April to September. The NE and SW lowlands are extremely hot and arid with less than 500mm (20in) annual rainfall and frequent droughts. Grass, farmland and trees cover most of the highlands. Semi-desert and tropical savanna cover parts of the lowlands. Dense rainforest grows in the SW. **Economy** Ethiopia is one of the world's poorest countries, 88% of the population are engaged in agriculture (mostly subsistence) and 67% of exports are food products. Coffee is the main cash crop, shipped through the port of DJIBOUTI. During the 1970s and 1980s, it was plagued by civil war and famine. **History and politics** According to tradition, the Ethiopian kingdom was founded in c.1000 BC by Solomon's son, Menelik I. Coptic Christianity was introduced to the N kingdom of Axum in the 4th century. In the 6th century, Judaism flourished. The expansion of Islam led to the isolation of Axum. The kingdom fragmented in the 16th century. In 1855 Kasa re-established unity, proclaimed himself Emperor Theodore, and founded the modern state. The late 19th century was marked by European intervention, and Menelik II

became emperor with Italian support. He expanded the empire, made Addis Ababa his capital (1889), and defeated an Italian invasion (1895). In 1930 Menelik II's grandnephew, Ras Tafari Makonnen, was crowned Emperor HAILE SELASSIE I. In 1935 Italian troops invaded Ethiopia (Abyssinia). In 1936 Italy combined Ethiopia with Somalia and Eritrea to form Italian East Africa. During World War 2, British and South African forces recaptured Ethiopia, and Haile Selassie was restored as emperor. In 1952, Eritrea was federated with Ethiopia. The 1960s witnessed violent demands for Eritrean secession and economic equality. Following famine in N Ethiopia, Selassie was deposed by a military coup in 1974. The Provisional Military Administrative Council (PMAC) abolished the monarchy. Military rule was repressive and civil war broke out. In 1977, Somalia seized land in the Ogaden Desert. The new PMAC leader, Mengistu Mariam, with Soviet military assistance, recaptured territory in Eritrea and the Ogaden. In 1984–85 widespread famine received global news coverage, and 10,000 FALASHAS were airlifted to Israel. In 1987 Mengistu established the People's Democratic Republic of Ethiopia. In 1991 the Tigrean-based Ethiopian People's Revolutionary Democratic Front (EPRDF) and the Eritrean People's Liberation Front (EPLF) brought down Mengistu's regime. In 1993 Eritrea achieved independence. In 1994 a federal constitution was adopted. In 1995 elections were won by the EPRDF. Negasso Gidada was elected president.

ethnic group In sociology, any social group that shares a complex of characteristics distinguishing it from larger society. Such groups are usually based on national origins, religion, language, culture or race.

ethnography Study of the culture of an ETHNIC GROUP. Ethnographers gather anthropological data by direct observation of a group's economic and social life. *See also* ANTHROPOLOGY; ETHNOLOGY

ethnology Comparative study of cultures. Historical ethnology was developed in the late 19th century in an attempt to trace cultural diffusion.

ethology Study of animal behaviour, especially in the natural environment, first outlined in the 1920s by Konrad LORENZ. Ethologists study natural processes, such as mating and self-defence.

ethylene *See* ETHENE

ethyne (acetylene) Colourless flammable gas (C_2H_2), manufactured by cracking of petroleum fractions. The simplest ALKYNE, it is explosive if mixed with air. When burned with oxygen, it produces extremely high temperatures up to 3,480°C (6,300°F) and is used in oxyacetylene torches. It is polymerized to manufacture plastics, fibres, resins and rubber. It is also used to produce ethanal and ethanoic acid. Properties: r.d. 0.625; m.p. $-80.8°C$ ($-113.4°F$); b.p. $-84°C$ ($-119.2°F$).

Etna Volcanic mountain on the E coast of Sicily, Italy. The first known eruption was in 475 BC, others occurring in 1169, 1669 and 1971. It is the highest

---

ETHIOPIA

AREA: 1,128,000sq km (435,521sq mi)
POPULATION: 55,500,000
CAPITAL (POPULATION): Addis Ababa (1,700,000)
GOVERNMENT: Federation of nine provinces
ETHNIC GROUPS: Oromo (Galla) 40%, Semitic (Amhara and Tigreans) 33%, Shangalla 5%, Somalis 5%, Others 17%
LANGUAGES: Amharic (de facto official)
RELIGIONS: Christianity 53%, Islam 36%, traditional beliefs 11%
CURRENCY: Birr = 100 cents

215

active volcano in Europe and the highest mountain in Italy s of the Alps. The fertile lower slopes are used for agriculture. Height: c.3,340m (10,958ft).

Etruscan Inhabitant of ancient Etruria, central Italy. Etruscan civilization flourished in the first millennium BC. Their sophisticated society was influenced by Greece and organized in city-states. From the 5th to the 3rd century BC they were gradually overrun by the Romans.

Eubacteria Subkingdom of the kingdom PROKARYOTAE, sometimes considered a separate DOMAIN. Eubacteria include all multicellular BACTERIA, including those that photosynthesize, deriving their carbon from the air. They do not have the unique types of cell walls, RIBOSOMES and RNA of ARCHAEBACTERIA. *See also* PHOTOSYNTHESIS

eucalyptus (gum tree) Genus of evergreen shrubs and slender trees, native to Australia and cultivated in temperate regions. They are valuable sources of hardwood and oils. Leaves are blue/white and they bear woody fruits. Height: to 122m (400ft). There are c.600 species. Family Myrtaceae.

Eucharist Central act of Christian worship, in which the priest and congregation partake in Holy Communion – one of the principal SACRAMENTS. The Eucharist is a commemorative re-enactment of the LAST SUPPER. The nature of the Eucharist was at the centre of Reformation theological debate. *See also* TRANSUBSTANTIATION

Euclid (c.330–c.260 BC) Ancient Greek mathematician, who taught at Alexandria, Egypt. He is remembered for his text books on geometry, such as *The Elements* (Lat. pub. 1482) and *Data*. Other works include *Phaenomena* (on astronomy). Several books have been lost.

Eugène of Savoy (1663–1736) French-born prince and Austrian general. Rejected by LOUIS XIV, he fought against the Turks at Vienna (1683) and Zenta (1697). In the War of the SPANISH SUCCESSION (1702–13), he cooperated with the Duke of MARLBOROUGH to defeat the French at BLENHEIM (1704), Oudenarde (1708) and Malplaquet (1709).

eugenics Study of human improvement by selective breeding, founded in the 19th century by Sir Francis Galton. It proposed the genetic "improvement" of the human species through the application of social controls on parenthood: encouraging parents who are above average in certain traits to have more children, while ensuring those who are below average have fewer. As a social movement, eugenics was discredited in the early 20th century owing to its ethical implications and its racist and class-based assumptions. Advances in GENETICS, have given rise to the modern field of genetic counselling, through which people known to have defective genes that could cause physical or mental disorders in offspring are warned of the risks.

euglenophyta Phylum of single-celled ALGAE which includes the genus *Euglena*. Members of this group have both animal and plant characteristics. They swim by means of flagella. Many species contain CHLOROPLASTS and employ PHOTOSYNTHESIS, but some are colourless and feed on BACTERIA and DIATOMS.

eukaryote Organism whose CELLS have a membrane-bound NUCLEUS, with DNA contained in CHROMOSOMES. Making up one of the three DOMAINS, eukaryotes include all ANIMALS, PLANTS, FUNGUS and PROTOCTISTA. They have a complex CYTOPLASM with an ENDOPLASMIC RETICULUM, and most of them possess MITOCHONDRIA. Most plants and algae also possess CHLOROPLASTS. Other structures specific to eukaryotic cells include microtubules, GOLGI BODIES, and membrane-bound flagella. *See also* KINGDOM; PROKARYOTAE

Euler, Leonhard (1707–83) Swiss mathematician. He is best known for his geometric theorem, which states that for any polyhedron (many-sided figure), $V - E + F = 2$, where V is the number of vertices, E the number of edges, and F the number of faces. He published on subjects as diverse as mechanics, algebra, optics and astronomy.

Euphrates (Firat) River of sw Asia. Formed by the confluence of the rivers Murat and Karasu, it flows from E Turkey across Syria into central Iraq, where it joins the River TIGRIS NW of BASRA to form the Shatt Al-Arab, and eventually flows into the PERSIAN GULF. The ancient civilizations of BABYLONIA and ASSYRIA developed along the lower Euphrates, including the cities of BABYLON and UR. Length: 2,800km (1,740mi).

eurhythmics System of musical and dance training which has influenced ballet and acting. Developed by Emile Jaques-Dalcroze during the early 20th century, and also applied by Rudolf STEINER, it evolved from a series of interpretive gymnastic exercises in response to music.

Euripides (480–450 BC) Greek playwright. With AESCHYLUS and SOPHOCLES, one of the three great writers of Greek tragedy. Euripides' plays caused contemporary controversy with their cynical depiction of human motivation. The significance of the CHORUS was reduced. His works, such as *Medea, Electra, Hecuba* and the anti-war satire *Trojan Women* have been radically reassessed. Provocative and iconoclastic, they achieved great posthumous popularity. Only 18 plays are extant.

Europa Smallest of Jupiter's Galilean satellites, with a diameter of 3,138km (1,950mi). Mainly rock, Europa's smooth water-ice crust is crisscrossed by a network of linear markings.

Europe Earth's second-smallest continent, comprising the western fifth of the Eurasian land mass. It is separated from Asia by the Urals (E), Caspian Sea and the Caucasus (SE), Black Sea and Dardanelles (S), and from Africa by the Mediterranean Sea. **Land** Europe is dominated by the Alpine mountain chain, the principal links of which are the PYRENEES, ALPS, CARPATHIAN MOUNTAINS, BALKAN STATES and the CAUCASUS, traversing the continent from W to E. Between the Scandinavian peninsula and the Alpine chain is the great European plain, which extends from the Atlantic coast in France to the Urals. To the S of the Alpine chain are the Iberian, Italian and Balkan peninsulas. Major islands include the British Isles, Sicily, Sardinia, Corsica and Iceland. **Structure and geology** Much of N Europe is made up of large sedimentary plains overlying an ancient PRECAMBRIAN shield. There are also PALAEOZOIC highlands. Many upland areas N of the Alps were formed during the CARBONIFEROUS period, including Ireland, the moorlands of Devon and Cornwall and the PENNINES, England. Southern Europe is geologically younger. Europe's longest river is the VOLGA, other major rivers are the TAGUS, LOIRE, RHÔNE, RHINE, ELBE and DANUBE. The CASPIAN SEA is the world's largest lake. **Climate and vegetation** Europe's climate varies from sub-tropical to polar. The Mediterranean climate of the S is dry and warm. Much of the land is scrub, with some hardwood forests. Further N, the climate is moderated by prevailing W winds and the GULF STREAM. The natural vegetation is mixed forest, but this has been extensively depleted. In SE European Russia, wooded and grass steppe merge into semi-desert. In the far N lies the tundra **Economy** Almost half of European land is unproductive because of climate, relief, soil or urbanization. Nearly 25% is forested. Two-thirds of cultivated land is arable. Cereals are the principal crop: wheat is the most important. Rice is grown with the aid of irrigation. Sheep are grazed on many upland areas, but dairy farming is the most important form of animal husbandry. In Mediterranean areas many fruits, early vegetables and vines (mainly for wine) are cultivated. Fishing is a major industry in countries with Atlantic or North Sea coastlines. Europe produces over a third of the world's coal. Germany, Poland, the Czech Republic and European Russia are the leading producers. Other mineral deposits include bauxite, mercury, lead, zinc and potash. Romania was the largest producer of oil in Europe until North Sea states (especially Britain) began to exploit their offshore resources. Europe is highly industrialized and manufacturing employs a high proportion of the workforce. The largest industrial areas are in W central Europe, in particular N France, the RUHR and around the North Sea ports of ANTWERP, AMSTERDAM, ROTTERDAM and HAMBURG. **History** The Mediterranean region was the cradle of the ancient Greek and Roman civilizations. The collapse of the W Roman empire and the barbarian invasions brought chaos to much of Europe, although Byzantium remained intact until the 15th century. During the Middle Ages, Christianity was a unifying force throughout the continent. The post-medieval period witnessed a fundamental split in the Catholic Church and the emergence of the nation state. European powers began to found vast world empires (*see* COLONIALISM; IMPERIALISM). The FRENCH REVOLUTION ushered in an era of momentous political changes. During the 20th century, a period overshadowed by two World Wars and the rise of COM-

MUNISM, Europe began to lose some of its pre-eminence in world affairs. During the COLD WAR, Europe was divided into two ideological blocs: Eastern Europe, dominated by the Soviet Union, and Western Europe, closely aligned with the USA. The NORTH ATLANTIC TREATY ORGANIZATION (NATO) was established to act as a deterrent to the spread of communism; the WARSAW PACT was its E European counterpart. Several economic organizations, in particular the EUROPEAN COMMUNITY (EC), were working towards closer intra-national cooperation. In 1991 the collapse of Soviet communism added to the momentum for a more closely integrated EUROPEAN UNION (EU). *Area c.*10,360,000sq km (4,000,000sq mi) *Highest mountain* Mount Elbrus (Russia) 5,633m (18,481ft) *Longest river* Volga 3,750km (2,330mi) *Population* (1990 est.) 785,700,000 *Largest cities* MOSCOW (8,881,000); LONDON (6,679,700); ST PETERSBURG (4,952,000); BERLIN (3,419,000)

European Atomic Energy Community (Euratom) Organization that was formed following the second of the Treaties of ROME (1958). Euratom was founded to coordinate non-military nuclear research and production, and provide capital for investment, specialists and equipment. It is administered by the European Commission.

European Community (EC) Economic and political body dedicated to European development. The beginnings of the Community lie in the establishment of the European Coal and Steel Community (ECSC) (1952), following the Treaty of Paris (1951). The purpose of the ECSC was to integrate the coal and steel industries (primarily of France and West Germany) to create a more unified Europe. The success of the ECSC led to the formation of the European Economic Community (EEC) and the EUROPEAN ATOMIC ENERGY COMMUNITY (EURATOM). Established by the Treaties of ROME (1957 and 1958), the aim was to create a common economic approach and to give Western Europe more influence in world affairs. Original members included France, West Germany, Italy, Belgium, Netherlands and Luxembourg; the United Kingdom, Ireland and Denmark joined (1973), Greece (1981), Spain and Portugal (1986), and Austria, Finland and Sweden joined (1995). The Czech Republic, Hungary, Poland, Estonia and Slovenia may have joined by 2003. The Community's institutional structure comprises the **European Commission** (responsible for implementing EC legislation), the **Council of Ministers** (which votes on Commission proposals), the Economic and Social Committee (which advises on draft EC legislation), the European Investment Bank (responsible for all the EC's financial operations), the EUROPEAN PARLIAMENT and the EUROPEAN COURT OF JUSTICE. *See also* EUROPEAN UNION (EU)

European Convention on Human Rights Agreement to protect the rights and freedoms of the individual, signed by the members of the

COUNCIL OF EUROPE in 1950. The Convention listed 12 basic rights, including the right to life, to a fair trial, to peaceful assembly and association, and to freedom of expression and from slavery and torture. An additional protocol provides for the abolition of the death penalty. *See also* HUMAN RIGHTS

European Court of Human Rights Created in 1959, the court decides whether or not an individual's rights have been disregarded by a member state in cases when the two parties have already failed to reach a settlement through the European Commission of Human Rights. The court is located in Strasbourg, E France.

European Court of Justice (officially Court of Justice of the European Communities) Court responsible for the interpretation and implementation of European Community laws. The court will also rule in cases where member states are alleged to have broken EC laws.

European Currency Unit (ECU) Theoretical unit against which the currencies of all European Community countries are valued. Part of the EUROPEAN MONETARY SYSTEM (EMS), the ECU is intended to lead to a single currency.

European Free Trade Association (EFTA) Organization seeking to promote free trade among its European members. Established in 1960, it originally comprised Austria, Denmark, Ireland, Norway, Portugal, Sweden, Switzerland and the UK. By 1995 all but Norway and Switzerland had joined the EUROPEAN UNION (EU). Iceland and Liechtenstein joined EFTA in 1970 and 1991 respectively.

European Monetary System (EMS) System set up in 1979 to bring about monetary stability among members of the EUROPEAN COMMUNITY (EC). There are three parts to the system: the EUROPEAN CURRENCY UNIT (ECU); the EXCHANGE RATE MECHANISM (ERM); and the credit mechanisms. From the start, the ECU had no coins or notes, but was a symbolic unit based on a weighted average of a number of currencies. The ERM sets a central rate of exchange, and each country is required to keep within a certain percentage above or below the rate.

European Monetary Union (EMU) Proposed union of EU member states who will share common economic policies and a common currency. Those member states who meet certain economic criteria will initially relinquish control of their own money supplies. Then, following the creation of a European Central Bank, which would take increasing responsibility for the regulation of the money supply, exchange rates would become fixed and a single European currency, the Euro, created. The "first wave" of the Union is planned for 1999, when international financial transactions will be calculated in Euros, the "second wave", in 2002, will involve the introduction of Euros to the public and its use as an alternative to national currencies.

European Parliament Institution of the EUROPEAN COMMUNITY. The Parliament forms part of the permanent structure of the European Community, along with the Council of Ministers, the Commission, the Court of Justice and the Court of Auditors. It meets in Strasbourg, Brussels and Luxembourg. It has 626 members, representing the 15 member states, elected for five-year terms. It has limited legislative powers.

European Space Agency (ESA) Organization founded by several European nations in 1962 as the European Space Research Agency (ESRO) to promote international cooperation in space research. Australia was admitted in 1965.

European Union (EU) Political entity that was established following the ratification of the MAASTRICHT TREATY in 1993. The EU aims to use the existing framework and institutions of the EUROPEAN COMMUNITY (EC) to implement greater integration of member states, particularly in foreign and security policies, and internal and judicial affairs. *See also* EUROPEAN MONETARY SYSTEM (EMS); EUROPEAN PARLIAMENT

europium Silvery-white metallic rare earth element (symbol Eu) of the LANTHANIDE SERIES. Chief ores monazite and bastnaesite. Used in colour television screens, lasers, and control rods in nuclear reactors. Properties: at.no. 63; r.a.m. 151.96; r.d. 5.25; m.p. 822°C (1,512°F); b.p. 1,597°C (2,907°F); most common isotope Eu^{153} (52.18%).

Eurydice In Greek mythology, the nymph married to ORPHEUS.

euthanasia Inducing the painless death of a person (usually with a terminal illness), often through the administration of a drug. It is illegal in most countries. An associated practice is the withholding of treatment which would prolong life.

eutrophication Process by which a stream or lake becomes rich in inorganic nutrients, such as compounds of nitrogen, phosphorus, iron, sulphur and potassium, by agricultural run-off or other artificial means. These compounds overstimulate the growth of surface ALGAE and microorganisms, which consume all the available dissolved oxygen, killing off most higher organisms.

evangelicalism (Gk. *euangelos*, good news or gospel) Term applied to several, generally Protestant, tendencies within the Christian Church. In a broad sense it has been applied to PROTESTANTISM as a whole because of its claim to base its doctrines strictly on the gospel.

evangelist Person who preaches the gospel, announcing the good news of redemption through Jesus Christ and the hope of everlasting life. The word also applies, by extension, to the authors of the four gospels of the New Testament: Saints MATTHEW, MARK, LUKE and JOHN.

Evans, Dame Edith (1888–1976) British stage and screen actress. A British theatrical legend, her best-remembered roles include Lady Bracknell in *The Importance of Being Earnest*. She was awarded the New York Film Critic's Award for her performance in *The Whisperers* (1967).

evaporation Process by which a liquid or solid

becomes a vapour. The reverse process is CON-DENSATION. Solids and liquids cool when they evaporate because they give up energy (LATENT HEAT) to the escaping molecules.

Eve In the Bible (GENESIS 2), the first woman, created by God from Adam's rib to be his companion and wife in the Garden of EDEN. She succumbed to temptation and disobeyed God by eating the fruit of the tree of the knowledge of good and evil and sharing it with Adam. For this act the couple became mortal and were banished from the garden. She was the mother of CAIN, ABEL and Seth.

evening primrose Any of various plants of the genus *Oenothera*, many of which are native to w North America. They have yellow, pink or white flowers that open in the evening. Height: 1.8m (5.3ft). Family Onagraceae.

Everest, Mount (Nepalese *Sagarmatha*; Tibetan *Chomo-Langma*, Mother Goddess of the World) Highest mountain in the world, in the central Himalayas on the borders of Tibet and Nepal. It is named after George Everest, first surveyor-general of India. Everest was conquered on 29 May 1953, by Sir Edmund HILLARY and Tenzing Norgay. Height: 8,848m (29,029ft).

Everglades Large tract of marshland in s Florida, USA, extending from Lake Okeechobee to Florida Bay; it includes the Everglades National Park. The region is made up of mangrove forests, saw grass and hummocks (island masses of vegetation). It supports tropical animal life, including alligators, snakes, turtles, egrets and bald eagles. Area: *c*.10,000km (4,000sq mi).

evergreen Plant that retains its green foliage, unlike DECIDUOUS plants. Evergreens are divided into two groups: narrow-leaved, or CONIFERS, and broad-leaved. Conifers include fir, spruce, pine and juniper. Among the broad-leaved evergreens are holly and rhododendron. Not all conifers are evergreens; exceptions are the deciduous larch (*Larix*).

Evert, Chris (Christine Marie) (1954–) US tennis player. She won numerous singles titles, including six US Opens between 1975 and 1982, seven French Opens between 1974 and 1986, the Australian Open (1982, 1984) and Wimbledon (1974, 1976 and 1981).

evolution Theory that a species undergoes gradual changes to survive and reproduce in a competitive, and often changing, environment, and that a new species is the result of development and change from the ancestral forms. Early work on evolutionary theory was initiated by Jean LAMARCK, but it was not until Charles DARWIN wrote *The Origin of Species* that the theory was considered worthy of argument. Present-day evolutionary theory is largely derived from the work of Darwin and MENDEL, and maintains that in any population or gene pool, there is VARIATION, including random MUTATION, in genetic forms and characteristics. Most species produce greater quantities of offspring than their environment can support, so only those members best adapted to the environment survive. When new characteristics provide survival advantages those individuals that possess them pass on these characteristics to their offspring. Since more of their offspring are likely to survive, the proportion of the population containing these new characteristics increases down the generations. *See also* ADAPTATION; ADAPTIVE RADIATION; NATURAL SELECTION; PUNCTUATED EQUILIBRIUM

Exchange Rate Mechanism (ERM) System for keeping the currencies of member states of the EUROPEAN UNION (EU) stable, as part of the EUROPEAN MONETARY SYSTEM (EMS). Currency speculation forced UK sterling and Italian lira to leave the system in 1992, because they were unable to keep the value of their currencies above the minimum limit. The ERM was near collapse, and to save it several currencies were allowed to fluctuate by as much as 15% above or below their central rate. *See also* FOREIGN EXCHANGE

exclusion principle Basic law of QUANTUM MECHANICS, proposed by Wolfgang PAULI in 1925, stating that no two ELECTRONS in an atom can possess the same energy and SPIN. More precisely, the set of four QUANTUM NUMBERS characterizing certain ELEMENTARY PARTICLES called FERMIONS must be unique.

excommunication Formal expulsion from the communion of the faithful, from sacraments and from rites of a religious body. Largely abandoned by Protestants, excommunication has been retained by Jewish congregations and by the Roman Catholic Church..

excretion Elimination of materials from the body that have been involved in METABOLISM. Such waste materials, particularly nitrogenous wastes, would be toxic if allowed to accumulate. In mammals these wastes are excreted mainly as URINE, and to some extent also by sweating. Carbon dioxide is excreted through the lungs during breathing.

Exeter City on the River Exe; county town of Devon, sw England. Many ancient buildings remain, notably the Norman cathedral (*c*.1275), the 12th-century Guildhall and the remains of Roman walls. Exeter University was established in 1955. Industries: tourism, textiles, leather goods, metal products, pharmaceuticals. Pop. (1991) 98,125.

existentialism Philosophical movement concerned with individuals and their relationship with a seemingly meaningless universe or with God. Most adherents believe that people are free to create their own destinies and are not constrained by forces outside their control. The beginnings of the modern existentialist movement can be seen in the theological writings of Søren KIERKEGAARD. Later existentialists include Martin HEIDEGGER, Jean-Paul SARTRE and Albert CAMUS.

Exodus Old Testament book of the Bible, the second book of the PENTATEUCH or TORAH. The first part details the flight of the Israelites from Egypt; the second part contains a catalogue of religious instructions that formed the basis of Mosaic law.

exoskeleton Protective skeleton or hard supporting structure forming the outside of the soft bodies of certain animals, notably ARTHROPODS and MOLLUSCS. In arthropods, it consists of a thick horny covering attached to the outside of the body and may be jointed and flexible. The exoskeleton does not grow as the animal grows; instead it is shed periodically and the animal generates a new one.

expansion Change in the size of an object with change in temperature. Most substances expand on heating, although there are exceptions (ice expands on cooling). The expansivity of a substance is its increase in length, area or volume per unit temperature rise. For a gas, the coefficient of expansion is the ratio of the rates of change of volume to temperature (at constant pressure), or of volume to pressure (at constant temperature).

explosives Substances that react rapidly and violently, emitting heat, light, sound and shock waves. Chemical explosives are mostly highly nitrated compounds or mixtures that are unstable and decompose violently with the evolution of much gas. Nuclear explosives are radioactive metals, the atoms of which can undergo nuclear FISSION or FUSION to release radiant energy and devastating shock waves.

exponent Superscript number placed to the right of a symbol indicating its power, e.g. in a^4 ($= a \times a \times a \times a$), 4 is the exponent. Certain laws of exponents apply in mathematical operations. For example, $3^2 \times 3^3 = 3^{(2+3)} = 3^5$; $3^4/3^3 = 3^{(4-3)} = 3^1$; $(3^2)^3 = 3^{(2\times3)} = 3^6$; $3^{-5} = 1/3^5$.

exponential In general a function of x of the form a^x, where a is a constant. The exponential function e^x, where e is the base of natural logarithms, 2.7182818..., can be represented by a power series $1 + x + x^2/2! + x^3/3! + ...$

expressionism Style of art in which conventional methods of naturalism are replaced by distorted and exaggerated images to express intense, subjective emotion. The term is often used in relation to a radical German art movement between the 1880s and c.1905. The inspiration for this new focus came from many different sources, including the work of VAN GOGH, GAUGUIN, MUNCH and SYMBOLISM, as well as from folk art. German expressionism reached its apogee in the work of the *Blaue Reiter* group, which included KANDINSKY, KLEE and MACKE, among others. The term also applies to performance arts, such as the works of STRINDBERG and WEDEKIND.

extensor *See* MUSCLE

extinction Dying out of a species or population. Extinction is part of the process of EVOLUTION in which certain species of plants and animals die out, often to be replaced by others. Extinctions brought about by human impact on the environment do not necessarily involve the replacement of extinct species by others.

extrasensory perception (ESP) Perception that takes place outside the known sensory systems. The term covers alleged parapsychological phenomena such as clairvoyance, telepathy and precognition.

extroversion Personality type characterized by outgoing behaviour; the opposite of INTROVERSION. The term was popularized by Carl JUNG, according to whose theory of PERSONALITY, extroverts are sociable, impulsive, and more interested in the outside world than in their own emotions.

extrusion In geology, the breaking-out of IGNEOUS ROCK from below the Earth's surface. Any volcanic product reaching the surface becomes extrusive material, whether it is ejected through a VOLCANO's cone or through pipe-like channels or fissures in its crust.

Eyck, Jan van (c.1390–d.1441) Flemish painter. His best-known work is the altarpiece for the Church of St Bavon, Ghent, which includes the *Adoration of the Lamb* (1432) and the *Arnolfini Wedding* (1434), both of which display intricate detail. He is said to have perfected the manufacture and technique of oil paint.

eye Organ of vision. It converts light energy to nerve impulses that are transmitted to the visual centre of the brain. Most of the mass of a human eye lies in a bony protective socket, called the orbital cavity, which also contains muscles and other tissues to hold and move the eye. The eyeball is spherical and composed of three layers: the **sclera** (white of the eye), which contains the transparent CORNEA; the **choroid**, which connects with the IRIS, PUPIL and LENS and contains blood vessels to provide nutrients and oxygen; and the RETINA, which contains rods and cones for converting the image into nerve impulses. The aqueous humour (a watery liquid between the cornea and iris) and the vitreous humour (a jelly-like substance behind the lens) both help to maintain the shape of the eye. *See also* SIGHT

eyebright Any of several small annual and perennial plants found in temperate and subarctic regions. They have terminal spikes of white, yellow or purple flowers. Some are hemiparasites, whose roots form attachments to those of other plants. European eyebright (*Euphrasia officinalis*) was formerly used to treat eye diseases. Family Scrophulariaceae.

Eyre, Lake Salt lake in NE South Australia. It is the lowest point on the continent, c.15m (50ft) below sea-level, and the largest salt lake in Australia. Area: 9,324sq km (3,600sq mi). Max. depth: 1.2m (4ft).

Ezekiel Old Testament prophet who was among the Jews deported during the BABYLONIAN CAPTIVITY. He is traditionally considered the author of the Old Testament Book of Ezekiel. He was the third and last of the "greater" Old Testament prophets, the successor of ISAIAH and JEREMIAH.

Ezra In the Old Testament, a continuation of Chronicles I and II. It records Ezra's journey from Babylon to Jerusalem to spread the law of Moses.

F/f is derived from the hook-shaped Semitic letter waw. *In earlier stages of English, f between vowels sounded as v. In Welsh, a single f is regularly pronounced as v.*

Fabian Society British society of non-Marxists founded in 1883, who believed that SOCIALISM should be attained through gradual political change. With George Bernard SHAW and Sidney and Beatrice WEBB as leaders, the Society gained widespread recognition and helped found the Labour Representation Committee (1900), which became the LABOUR PARTY in 1906. The Fabian Society is affiliated to the Labour Party.

facies In geology, all the features of a rock that show the history of its formation. Geologists often distinguish age by facies. The term is also applied to gradations of IGNEOUS ROCK.

factor In mathematics, any number that divides exactly into a given number. For example, the factors of 72 are 1, 2, 3, 4, 6, 8, 9, 12, 18, 24 and 36.

factory farming Intensive rearing of livestock, such as pigs, poultry and calves, in large, densely populated enclosures. Feeding is usually automatically dispensed, and the emphasis is on "mass production" of the food products rather than the well-being of the animals involved. Increasing awareness of ANIMAL RIGHTS has encouraged less factory farming, such as free-range chickens.

Fahrenheit, Gabriel Daniel (1686–1736) German physicist. He invented the alcohol THERMOMETER (1709), the first mercury thermometer (1714) and devised the FAHRENHEIT TEMPERATURE scale. He also showed that the boiling points of liquids vary with changes in pressure and that water can remain liquid below its freezing point.

Fahrenheit temperature scale System for measuring temperature based on the freezing point (32°F) and the boiling point (212°F) of water. The interval between them is divided into 180 equal parts. Although replaced in Britain by CELSIUS, Fahrenheit is still used in the USA for nonscientific measurements. *See also* THERMOMETER

fainting (syncope) Temporary loss of consciousness accompanied by general weakness of the muscles. A faint may be preceded by giddiness, nausea and sweating. Its causes include insufficient flow of blood to the brain and shock.

Fairfax of Cameron, Thomas, 3rd Baron (1612–71) Parliamentary commander in the English CIVIL WAR. He succeeded Essex as commander-in-chief (1645), but in 1650 he refused to march against the Scots and was replaced by Oliver CROMWELL. He later headed the commission to arrange the restoration of Charles II (1660).

Falange Spanish political party founded in 1933 by José Antonio Primo de Rivera. Modelled on other European followers of FASCISM, it was merged with other groups under the FRANCO regime and became the sole legal political party. It was heavily defeated in free elections in 1977.

Falashas Ethnic group of black Jews in Ethiopia, probably descended from early converts to JUDAISM. Their religion relies solely on observance of the OLD TESTAMENT. Israel acknowledged them as Jews in 1975, and, suffering discrimination at home, many migrated to Israel. During the early 1980s, there were about 30,000 Falashas living in Ethiopia, but amid the war and famine that ensued, thousands were airlifted to Israel.

falcon Widely distributed, hawk-like BIRD OF PREY, sometimes trained by man to hunt game. Falcons have keen eyesight, short hooked bills, long pointed wings, streamlined bodies, strong legs with hooked claws, and grey or brownish plumage with lighter markings. The females are much larger than the males. Falcons feed on insects, smaller birds and small ground animals. They can kill on the wing, using their talons. They lay two to five brown-spotted white eggs. Length: 15–64cm (6–25in). Family Falconidae.

Faldo, Nick (Nicholas Alexander) (1957–) English golfer. He has won the British Open (1987, 1990 and 1992) and the US Masters (1989, 1990 and 1996), the only player beside Jack Nicklaus to win in successive years. He was a member of the victorious 1997 European Ryder Cup team.

Falkland Islands (Islas Malvinas) British crown colony in the S Atlantic Ocean, SE of Argentina; the capital is STANLEY (on East Falkland). It includes two large islands (East and West Falkland) and 200 smaller ones. First explored by Europeans in the late 16th century, the Falklands were at various times under Spanish, French and British control. Argentinian denials of British sovereignty led to the FALKLANDS WAR (1982). The main activity is sheep farming; wool and hides are exported. Area: *c.*12,200sq km (4,620sq mi). Pop. (1991) 2,121.

Falklands War (April–June 1982) Military conflict between Great Britain and Argentina on the question of sovereignty over the Falkland (Malvinas) Islands, located *c.*400km (250mi) off the Argentine coast. On 2 April, Argentine forces invaded and occupied the Falklands, South Georgia, and South Sandwich Islands, which had been administered and occupied by Great Britain since the 19th century. UN-backed negotiations failed to secure an Argentine withdrawal. Britain blockaded the islands and staged an amphibious landing at Port San Carlos. They surrounded the Argentine troops at the capital, Port Stanley, and forced them to surrender on 14 June. Losses on both sides were heavy. Britain resumed administration of the islands, but sovereignty remains unresolved.

Falla, Manuel de (1876–1946) Spanish composer. He combined folk songs with modern harmonies. His works include the opera *La Vida Breve*

(1905), *Nights in the Gardens of Spain* (1916) for piano and orchestra, and the ballets *Love the Magician* (1915) and *The Three-Cornered Hat* (1919).

Fallopian tube (oviduct) In mammals, either of two narrow ducts leading from the upper part of the UTERUS into the pelvic cavity and ending near each OVARY. After ovulation, the OVUM enters and travels through the Fallopian tube where FERTILIZATION can occur. The fertilized ovum, or EMBRYO, continues into the uterus where it becomes implanted.

family planning *See* CONTRACEPTION

famine Extreme prolonged shortage of food, produced by both natural and man-made causes. If it persists, famine results in widespread starvation and death. Famine is often associated with drought or climatic change, which lead to crop failure and the destruction of livestock. However, warfare and complex political situations resulting in the mismanagement of resources are equally likely causes.

FAO *See* FOOD AND AGRICULTURE ORGANIZATION

Faraday, Michael (1791–1867) British physicist and chemist. A student of Sir Humphry DAVY, in 1825 he became director of the laboratories at the Royal Institution in London. He liquefied chlorine, discovered benzene and enunciated the laws of electrolysis (FARADAY'S LAWS). He also discovered electromagnetic induction, made the first DYNAMO, built a primitive electric motor, and studied non-conducting materials (dielectrics). The unit of capacitance (the farad) is named after him.

Faraday's laws Two laws of ELECTROLYSIS and three of ELECTROMAGNETIC INDUCTION, formulated by Michael FARADAY. The **electrolysis** laws state that: (1) the amount of chemical change during electrolysis is proportional to the charge passed; and (2) the amount of chemical change produced in a substance by a certain amount of electricity is proportional to the electrochemical equivalent of that substance. Faraday's laws of **induction** state that: (1) an electromagnetic force is induced in a conductor if the magnetic field surrounding it changes; (2) the electromagnetic force is proportional to the rate of change of the field; and (3) the direction of the induced electromagnetic force depends on the field's orientation.

farming *See* AGRICULTURE

Farnese Italian family of the Roman aristocracy. The military skill of Ranuccio Farnese (d. *c.*1460) won the gratitude of Pope Eugenius IV, and his son Alessandro became Pope PAUL III (1534).

Faröe Islands Group of 22 volcanic islands (17 inhabited) in the N Atlantic between Iceland and the Shetland Islands. The largest are Streymoy and Esturoy. Settled in the 7th century, the group was part of Norway from the 11th century until 1380, when it was ceded to Denmark. In 1852 parliament was restored, and since 1948 it has enjoyed a degree of autonomy. Capital and chief port: Tórshavn (Streymoy), pop. (1993) 14,192; Language: Faroese; Industries: fishery, sheep-rearing. Area: 1,339sq km (540sq mi). Total pop. (1993) 45,349.

Farouk (1920–65) King of Egypt (1936–52). Son of King FUAD I, he alienated many Egyptians by personal extravagance and corruption. His ambitious foreign policy ended in defeat in the first ARAB-ISRAELI WAR (1948), and he was overthrown in a military coup.

Farquhar, George (1678–1707) Irish dramatist associated with RESTORATION THEATRE. His comedies were distinguished by their combination of humour and depth of character. Among his plays are *The Constant Couple* (1699), *The Recruiting Officer* (1706) and *The Beaux Stratagem* (1707).

Farrakhan, Louis (1933–) US leader of the Nation of Islam, a black separatist organization. A controversial figure, he was recruited into the BLACK MUSLIMS in the 1950s by MALCOLM X. He formed the Nation of Islam in 1976. In 1995, he organized the USA's largest political demonstration, assembling 400,000 men in a "Million Man March" on Washington D.C.

fascism Political movement founded in Italy by Benito MUSSOLINI (1919), characterized by nationalism, totalitarianism and anti-communism. The term also applied to the regimes of Adolf HITLER in Germany (1933) and Francisco FRANCO in Spain (1936). A reaction to the Russian Revolution (1917) and the spread of COMMUNISM, the movement based its appeal on the fear of financial instability among the middle-class and on a wider social discontent. Basic to fascist ideas were: glorification of the state and total subordination to its authority; suppression of all political opposition; preservation of a rigid class structure; stern enforcement of law and order; the supremacy of the leader as the embodiment of high ideals; and an aggressive militarism aimed at achieving national greatness. It also typically encouraged racist and xenophobic attitudes and policies. Unlike communism, it lacked a consistent philosophy. Discredited by defeat in World War 2, fascism was insignificant in the politics of Western Europe for many years. In the 1990s, far-right nationalist groups have re-emerged in many countries. *See also* NATIONAL SOCIALISM

Fassbinder, Rainer Werner (1946–82) German film director, and leader of modern German cinema. Fiercely political, his films include *The Bitter Tears of Petra von Kant* (1972) and *Veronika Voss* (1982).

fat Semi-solid organic substance made and used by plants and animals to store energy. In animals, fats also serve to insulate the body and protect internal organs. Fats are soluble in organic solvents such as ether, carbon tetrachloride, chloroform and benzene. They are triglycerides: ESTERS, in which one molecule of glycerol is connected to three molecules of FATTY ACIDS (such as palmitic, lauric and stearic acid) each having 12 to 18 carbon atoms. Research indicates that high levels of animal fats in diets can increase the risk of heart disease. Vegetable oils are similar to fats, but are viscous liquids and have a higher proportion of molecules with double carbon–carbon bonds in the chain – that is, they are unsaturated. *See also* LIPID; SOAP

Fates (Gk. *Moirae,* Roman *Parcae*) In Greek mythology, the three goddesses of human destiny. They correspond to the Roman and the Germanic Norns. Clotho spun the thread of life; Lachesis measured it; and Atropos, the inevitable, cut it.

Fatima (606–632) Daughter of the prophet MUHAMMAD, and wife of ALI. She is revered by the SHIITE sect of ISLAM, who honour Ali as the rightful successor to Muhammad.

Fatimid SHIITE dynasty who claimed the caliphate on the basis of their descent from FATIMA. The dynasty was founded by Said ibn Husayn at the close of the 9th century. The Fatimids quickly overthrew the SUNNI rulers in most of NW Africa. By ibn Husayn's death (934), the Fatimid empire had expanded into s Europe, and in 969 they captured Egypt. By the end of the 11th century, Egypt was all that remained of the Fatimid empire.

fatty acids Organic compounds, present in nature as constituents of FAT. They contain a single carboxyl acid group ($-COOH$). Examples of saturated fatty acids (those which lack double bonds in their hydrocarbon chain) are acetic acid and palmitic acid, the latter being a common fat constituent; unsaturated fatty acids (having one or more double carbon–carbon bonds) include oleic acid. Both saturated and non-saturated types have molecules shaped like a long, straight chain. *See also* LIPID

Faulkner, William Cuthbert (1897–1962) US author. The Yoknapatawpha Saga charted the disintegration of traditional Southern US society. He was awarded the 1949 Nobel Prize for literature. His novels, which often employ a "stream-of-consciousness" style, include *Sartoris* (1929), *The Sound and the Fury* (1929), *Sanctuary* (1931), *Absalom, Absalom!* (1936) and *The Reivers* (1962).

fault In geology, a fracture in the Earth's crust along which movement has occurred. The result of PLATE TECTONICS, faults are classified by the type of movement. Vertical movements in the crust cause **normal** and **reverse** faults, while horizontal movements result in **tear** faults. Faults can occur in groups creating **horsts** (block mountains) or **grabens** (rift valleys).

Fauré, Gabriel Urbain (1845–1924) French composer renowned for his intimate, restrained compositions. They include many songs, such as *Clair de lune* (1889); chamber music, such as his *Elégie* (1883); and the *Requiem* (1887). He was director of the Paris Conservatoire (1805–22).

fauvism Expressionist art style based on vivid non-naturalistic colours. MATISSE was the leading figure and, with SIGNAC, exhibited at the Salon d'Automne (1905). A critic described their work as something produced by wild animals (*fauves*). Other later fauvists include VLAMINCK and BRAQUE.

Fawcett, Dame Millicent Garrett (1847–1929) British leader of the suffrage movement. She was president of the National Union of Women's Suffrage Societies (1897–1919). She also founded Newnham College, Cambridge, one of the first women's university colleges in Britain.

Fawkes, Guy (1570–1606) English conspirator in the GUNPOWDER PLOT of 1605. He was enlisted by Roman Catholic conspirators in a plot against JAMES I and Parliament. The plot was betrayed, and Fawkes was arrested in a building adjacent to the House of Lords, surrounded by barrels of gunpowder. He was later executed. Traditionally, an effigy (a "guy") is burned on 5 November, the anniversary of the intended explosion.

fax (facsimile transmission) Equipment by which text, photographs and drawings can be transmitted and received through a TELEPHONE system. The image, on paper, is scanned to translate it into a series of electrical pulses. Inside the fax machine, a MODEM converts the pulses to a form that can be transmitted down a telephone line. At the receiving end, the fax machine's modem converts the signals back into pulses, and prints these as dots to build up a copy of the original document. *See also* SCANNING

FBI *See* FEDERAL BUREAU OF INVESTIGATION

feather One of the skin appendages that make up the plumage of birds. Feathers are composed of KERATIN, and provide insulation and enable flight. They are usually replaced at least once a year.

February Revolution (1848) French insurrection that overthrew the government of LOUIS PHILIPPE. The Revolution began in Paris following the economic crisis of 1847–48 and agitation for parliamentary reform. Led by bourgeois radicals and working-class revolutionaries, it sparked popular uprisings and unrest throughout Europe, and created the short-lived Second Republic in France.

Federal Bureau of Investigation (FBI) US organization that investigates violations of federal law, especially those concerning internal security. Its findings are reported to the ATTORNEY GENERAL and various nationwide attorneys for decisions on prosecution. Established in 1908, its autonomy was strengthened under the directorship of J. Edgar HOOVER. Its headquarters are in Washington, D.C.

federalism Political system that allows states united under a central government to maintain a measure of independence. Examples include the USA, Australia, Canada, Germany, India and Switzerland. Central government has supreme authority, but individual states have considerable autonomy in such matters as education and health.

Federalist Party US political party led by George WASHINGTON, John ADAMS, John Jay and Alexander Hamilton. Formed (1787) to promote ratification of the Constitution, the Federalists were opposed to the states' rights, agrarian philosophy of the DEMOCRATIC REPUBLICAN PARTY.

feedback In technology, process by which an electronic or mechanical control system monitors and regulates itself. Feedback works by returning part of the "output" of the system to its "input". *See also* BIOFEEDBACK

feldspar Group of common rock-forming minerals that all contain aluminium, silicon and oxygen, but with varying proportions of potassium, sodium and calcium. They are essential constituents of IGNEOUS ROCKS. Hardness 6–6.5; s.g. 2.5–2.8.

Fellini, Federico (1920–93) Italian film director, famous for his satirical, often autobiographical, films. He won four Oscars for best foreign language film. Major works include *La Strada* (1954), *La Dolce Vita* (1960), *8½* (1963), *Satyricon* (1969), *Roma* (1972), *Amarcord* (1974), *Casanova* (1977) and *Voices of the Moon* (1990).

felony Indictable criminal offence. In British law until 1967, felonies were distinguished from misdemeanours (crimes of a less serious nature).

feminism Movement that promotes equal rights for women. In both the USA and the UK, the feminist movement became focused during the late 19th century, particularly over women's right to vote (the SUFFRAGETTE MOVEMENT). It gained further impetus during the two World Wars, as women assumed manufacturing and administrative roles previously filled by men, and won the right to vote (in the UK in 1918, and in the USA in 1920). Post-war feminists, such as Simone de BEAUVOIR and Germaine GREER, argued that gender differences are socially conditioned and demanded equal rights. In an attempt to end discrimination in Britain, the Equal Opportunities Commission was set up (1978).

femur Thigh bone, extending from the hip to the knee. It is the longest and strongest bone of the human skeleton.

fencing Sport of swordsmanship, using blunt weapons: the foil, épée and sabre. Fencers wear gloves and wire-mesh masks. In competitions, electronic sensors register hits, which score 1 point each. It has been an Olympic sport since 1896.

Fenian movement (Irish Republican Brotherhood) Irish nationalist organization set up in 1858, which sought independence from Britain by revolution. After several abortive plots, the leaders were arrested in 1867 and the focus of Fenian activity moved to the USA. The movement was superseded by SINN FÉIN.

fennel Tall, PERENNIAL herb of the parsley family, native to s Europe. The seeds and oil are used to add a liquorice flavour to medicines, liqueurs and foods. It grows to 1m (3.2ft). Family Apiaceae/Umbelliferae; species *Foeniculum vulgare*.

Fens Lowland region of E England, including parts of Lincolnshire, Cambridgeshire and Norfolk. About 117km (73mi) long and 56km (35mi) wide, this marshy area was drained in the 17th century and is intensively cultivated for fruit and vegetables.

Ferdinand (1861–1948) Prince (1887–1908) and tsar (1908–18) of Bulgaria. In 1908 he declared Bulgaria independent of the Ottoman empire and himself tsar. He allied Bulgaria with Serbia, Greece and Montenegro in the first BALKAN WAR (1912–13), but Bulgaria's territorial gains were largely lost to its former allies in

the second war (1913). Ferdinand joined the CENTRAL POWERS in World War 1 after which he abdicated in favour of his son Boris III.

Ferdinand II (1578–1637) Holy Roman emperor (1619–37) and HABSBURG king of Bohemia (1617–37) and Hungary (1621–37). Educated by the Jesuits, he opposed the REFORMATION. The Bohemian revolt against him in 1618 precipitated the THIRTY YEARS WAR.

Ferdinand III (1608–57) Holy Roman emperor (1637–57). The son of FERDINAND II, he succeeded Albrecht WALLENSTEIN as commander of the imperial armies in the THIRTY YEARS WAR from 1634. He won the battle of Nordlingen (1634), but later suffered a series of defeats and sought peace, which was achieved after many years' endeavour at WESTPHALIA in 1648. It marked the end of HABSBURG authority in Germany.

Ferdinand V (1452–1516) (Ferdinand the Catholic) King of Castile and León (1474–1504), of Aragon (as Ferdinand II) (1479–1516), of Sicily (1468–1516), and of Naples (as Ferdinand III) (1504–16). He became joint king of Castile and León after marrying Isabella I in 1469, and inherited Aragon from his father, John II, in 1479. After he and Isabella conquered the Moorish kingdom of Granada (1492), they ruled over a united Spain. They sponsored the voyage of Christopher COLUMBUS to the New World (1492), expelled the Jews from Spain, and initiated the Spanish INQUISITION. Under Ferdinand, Spain became involved in the Italian wars against France. After Isabella's death (1504), Ferdinand acted as regent in Castile for their insane daughter, Joanna, and later for her son, Charles I (who succeeded Ferdinand and ruled most of Europe as Holy Roman emperor CHARLES V).

Fermanagh District in sw Northern Ireland; the county town is Enniskillen. During the 17th century English people settled here as part of the Plantation of Ulster. The district is hilly in the NE and SW. Cattle raising is important. Area: 1,876sq km (724sq mi). Pop. (1991) 54,033.

Fermat, Pierre de (1601–65) French mathematician. With Blaise PASCAL, he helped to formulate the theory of probability, and Fermat's principle, that light travels along the shortest optical path, laid the foundation for geometric optics.

Fermat's last theorem Theory that, for all integers $n > 2$, there are no non-zero integers x, y and z that satisfy the equation $x^n + y^n = z^n$. Fermat died without revealing a proof. Attempts at validation enriched algebraic number theory. In 1993 Andrew Wiles announced a proof, but it was found to contain a gap. Further work repaired this, and the proof was widely accepted in 1995.

fermentation Energy-yielding metabolic process by which sugar and starch molecules are broken down to carbon dioxide and ethanol in the absence of air (ANAEROBIC respiration). Catalysed by ENZYMES, it is used for wine- and bread-making, beer-brewing and cheese maturation. The intoxicating effect of fermented fruits has been known since 4000 BC.

Fermi, Enrico (1901–54) US physicist, b. Italy. He worked mainly in the fields of atomic behaviour and structure and QUANTUM THEORY. He discovered NEPTUNIUM and produced the first self-sustaining CHAIN REACTION in uranium. In 1942 he built the world's first nuclear reactor. He worked on the MANHATTAN PROJECT and on developing the hydrogen bomb. For his work with RADIOACTIVITY, Fermi was awarded the 1938 Nobel Prize for physics; the element FERMIUM was named after him.

fermion Any SUBATOMIC PARTICLE that obeys the EXCLUSION PRINCIPLE, and has a half-integer SPIN (such as 0.5, 1.5, or 2.5). Examples are protons, electrons and quarks. *See also* BOSON

fermium Radioactive metallic TRANSURANIC ELEMENT (symbol Fm) of the ACTINIDE SERIES. It was first identified in 1952 as a decay product of U^{255} from the first large hydrogen bomb explosion. Ten isotopes have been identified. Properties: at.no. 100; most stable isotope Fm^{257} (half-life 80 days).

fern Non-flowering plant. Many ferns grow in warm, moist areas; there are about 10,000 species. The best-known genus *Pteridium* (BRACKEN) grows on moorland and in open woodland. Ferns are characterized by two generations: the SPOROPHYTE possesses leafy fronds, stems, RHIZOMES and roots, and reproduces by minute SPORES usually clustered on the leaves; and the inconspicuous GAMETOPHYTE resembles moss and produces sperm and ova. Fronds unroll from curled "fiddle-heads" and may be divided into leaflets. Phylum Filicinophyta.

ferret Semi-domesticated form of the POLECAT. WEASEL-like animals, they have long necks, slender bodies, long tails, short legs and white fur. They are agile killers, used to hunt rats and rabbits. Body length: 36cm (14in); weight: 700g (1.5lb). Family Mustelidae; species *Mustela putorius*.

Ferrier, Kathleen (1912–53) English contralto. She sang the title role in the first performance of Benjamin BRITTEN's *The Rape of Lucretia* (1946) at Glyndebourne, England.

fertility drugs Drugs taken to increase a woman's chances of conception and pregnancy. One of the major causes of female sterility results from insufficient secretion of pituitary hormones, and this can be treated with either human chorionic gonadotropin or clomiphene citrate, although use of the latter has resulted in multiple births. In cases where fertilization occurs, but where the uterine lining is unable to support the developing fetus, the hormone progesterone may be used.

fertilization Impregnation of an EGG nucleus by a SPERM (or male sex cell) nucleus forming a ZYGOTE. Fertilization is the key process in the SEXUAL REPRODUCTION of plants, animals, fungi and protoctists, and includes the penetration of the egg by the sperm, and the fusion of the egg and sperm nuclei. Fertilization can be external (as in most fish, amphibians and plants) or internal (as in reptiles, birds, mammals and most protistas). *See also* EMBRYO; GAMETE

fertilizer Substance added to soil to improve plant growth by increasing fertility. Manure and compost were the first fertilizers. Other natural fertilizers include bone meal, ashes, guano and fish. Modern chemical fertilizers, composed of nitrogen, phosphorus and potassium in powdered, liquid, or gaseous forms, are now widely used.

Fessenden, Reginald Aubrey (1866–1932) US engineer, physicist and inventor. He is thought to have broadcast the first radio programme in 1906. Among his more than 500 patents were AMPLITUDE MODULATION (AM), the high-frequency alternator, the electrolytic detector, the heterodyne system of radio reception and the fathometer.

fetus (foetus) Stage of EMBRYO development in a mammal after the main adult features are recognizable. In humans it dates from about eight weeks after conception.

feudal system Social system that prevailed in most of Europe from the 9th century to the late Middle Ages, based on the tenure of land. The system originated from the need to provide for a permanent group of knights to assist the king in his wars. All land was theoretically owned by the monarch and leased out to his tenants-in-chief in return for their attendance at court and military assistance; and they in turn let out fiefs to knights in return for military service and other obligations. The lowest rank, serfs, worked their lord's land in return for the right to grow their own produce. The system ended in the 16th century in England but lasted until the 18th century in parts of Europe and Russia.

fever Elevation of the body temperature above normal – above 37°C (98.6°F). It is usually caused by bacterial or viral infection and can accompany virtually any infectious disease.

Feydeau, Georges (1862–1921) French playwright. His absurd plots and sparkling dialogue pioneered 19th-century French farce. His major plays were *La Dame de chez Maxim* (1899) and *L'Hôtel du Libre Échange* (1894).

Feynman, Richard Phillips (1918–88) US physicist. He worked on the atom bomb during World War 2, then worked with Hans BETHE on QUANTUM ELECTRODYNAMICS (QED). **Feynman diagrams** greatly facilitated the solution of electromagnetic interactions between ELEMENTARY PARTICLES. He shared the 1965 Nobel Prize for physics. With Murray GELL-MANN, Feynman developed a theory of weak interactions, occurring in the emission of electrons from radioactive nuclei. He also did research on the structure of protons and the properties of liquid helium.

Fez (Fès) City in N central Morocco. Founded *c.*790, it is a former capital of Morocco and a sacred city of Islam containing many mosques. Industries: leather goods, pottery, traditional crafts, metal-working. Pop. (1982) 448,823.

Fianna Fáil (Soldiers of Destiny) Irish political party. Formed in 1926 by those opposed to Irish partition, the party came to power in 1932 under Eamon DE VALERA. It has dominated Irish government since then. It seeks the reunification of Ireland by peaceful means, believes that the government should take an active role in economic development, and has traditionally been the most conservative of the main parties.

Fibonacci, Leonardo (c.1170–c.1240) Italian mathematician. He wrote *Liber abaci* (c.1200), the first Western work to propose the adoption of the Arabic numerical system. He produced a mathematical sequence, in which each term is formed by the addition of the two terms preceding it. The sequence begins 0, 1, 1, 2, 3, 5, 8, 13, 21.... and so on. Many natural forms, such as spiral shells and leaf systems, are delimited by the Fibonacci series.

fibre Any of various materials consisting of thread-like strands. **Natural** fibres can be made into yarn, textiles and other products, including carpets and rope. The fibres consist of long narrow cells. **Animal** fibres are based on protein molecules and include WOOL, SILK, mohair and angora. **Vegetable** fibres are based on CELLULOSE and include COTTON, LINEN, FLAX, JUTE, SISAL and KAPOK. **Regenerated** fibres are manufactured from natural products, modified chemically. RAYON is made from cellulose fibre obtained from cotton or wood. **Synthetic** fibres are made from a molten or dissolved plastic resin by forcing it through fine nozzles. The result is a group of filaments that are wound onto bobbins. These fibres can be used as single-strand yarn, or spun and woven into textiles. Some synthetic fibres are made into rope, carpets and other products. Synthetic fibres include NYLON and other polyamides, polyesters and ACRYLICS. Other synthetic fibres, such as carbon or metals, can be used to reinforce resins to produce extremely strong materials.

fibreglass Spun glass used as a continuous filament in textiles and electrical insulation, and in a fibrous form to reinforce plastics or for sound or heat insulation. Molten glass is drawn through spinnerets or spun through holes in a revolving dish. Combined with layers of resin, fibreglass is a popular material for chassis and containers.

fibre optics Branch of OPTICS concerned with the transmission of data and images by reflecting light through very fine glass OPTICAL FIBRES.

fibrin Insoluble, fibrous protein that is essential to BLOOD CLOTTING. Developed in the blood from a soluble protein (fibrinogen), fibrin is laid down at the site of a wound in the form of a mesh, which then dries and hardens so that the bleeding stops.

fibula Long thin outer bone of the lower leg of four- and two-legged VERTEBRATES, including humans. It articulates with the other lower leg bone, the TIBIA, just below the knee.

Fidei Defensor *See* DEFENDER OF THE FAITH

Fielding, Henry (1707–54) British novelist and playwright. His first work of fiction, *An Apology for*

the Life of Mrs Shamela Andrews (1741), was a parody of *Pamela* (1740) by Samuel RICHARDSON. Later novels include *Joseph Andrews* (1742), *The Life of Mr Jonathan Wild the Great* (1743) and his masterpiece, *Tom Jones* (1749). He was also responsible for the foundation of the Bow Street Runners, the forerunner of the British police force.

Fife Region in E central Scotland between the firths of Tay and Forth; the capital is Glenrothes. The central part is mostly low-lying farmland. Coalfields are situated in the W and E. Along the North Sea coast there are many fishing villages. The Rosyth naval base lies on the N shore of the Firth of Forth. St Andrews is the seat of Scotland's oldest university (1410) and the home of the Royal and Ancient Golf Club. Area: 1,305sq km (504sq mi). Pop. (1991) 341,199.

fig Tree, shrub or climber of the mulberry family, growing in warm regions, especially from the E Mediterranean to India and Malaysia. The common fig (*Ficus carica*) has tiny flowers without petals that grow inside fleshy flask-like receptacles; these become the thick outer covering holding the seeds, the true, edible fruit of the fig tree. Height: to 11.8m (39ft). Family Moraceae, genus *Ficus*.

Fiji Independent nation in the S Pacific Ocean, consisting of more than 800 volcanic islands and islets; the capital is Suva (on Viti Levu). The two largest islands, Viti Levu and Vanua Levu, rise sharply from the fertile, heavily populated coastal region to a mountainous interior. On the wet E side, the islands are covered in dense tropical forest. The W side is mainly dry grassland with some scrub. Settlement of the region dates back to the second millennium BC. Discovered by Abel TASMAN in 1643, the islands became a British crown colony in 1874. Indians were imported to work on the sugar plantations, and by the 1950s outnumbered the native Fijian population. In 1970 Fiji achieved independence within the Commonwealth of Nations. The election of an Indian majority government in 1987 led to a military coup by native Fijians and the proclamation of a republic. Agriculture is the most important sector of the economy: the main products are copra, sugar and rice. Gold and silver are mined and tourism is important. Area: 18,272sq km (7,055sq mi). Pop. (1995 est.) 783,800.

filariasis Group of tropical, infectious diseases caused by a nematode worm, *filaria*. The parasites, which are transmitted by insects, infiltrate the lymph glands, causing swelling and impaired drainage. Drug treatment reduces the symptoms.

Fillmore, Millard (1800–74) 13th US president (1850–53). Fillmore served (1833–43) in the House of Representatives as a member of the Whigs. In 1848 he was elected vice president to Zachary TAYLOR, becoming president on Taylor's death. In an attempt to mediate between proslavery and antislavery factions, Fillmore agreed to the COMPROMISE OF 1850.

filter Porous device for separating solid particles

from a liquid or gas. The process is known as filtration. Most cars have a number of filters, for air, petrol and oil. These operate either by trapping solid particles in porous materials such as paper or meshes, or by circulating the material to be filtered through a maze, the pockets of which trap particles, as in the air filter.

finch Any of a family (Fringillidae) of small or medium-sized birds, such as the SPARROW, CARDINAL, CANARY, BUNTING and GROSBEAK. They are found worldwide, except the Antipodes and the Pacific islands. Most have a cone-shaped bill and feed on seeds, though some eat fruit or insects. Some British "finches", such as the bullfinch and goldfinch, belong to the family Ploceidae.

Fine Gael Irish political party. It was founded in 1933 as a successor to the party under William Cosgrave that had held power since the inception of the Irish Free State. The party has four times held office in coalition with the Labour Party (1948–51, 1954–57, 1973–77, 1994–97).

fingerprint Pattern of ridges in the dermis or deeper skin on the end of the fingers and thumbs. Fingerprints are specific to an individual and remain unchanged in pattern throughout life. They are a useful means of identification.

Finland (Suomi) Republic in N Europe, the capital is HELSINKI. **Land and climate** The Republic of Finland has four geographical regions. In the S and W, on the Gulfs of Bothnia and Finland, is a low, narrow coastal strip, where most Finns live, and the capital is situated. The Åland Islands lie in the entrance to the Gulf of Bothnia. Most of the interior is a beautiful wooded plateau, with over 60,000 lakes. The Saimaa area is Europe's largest inland water system. A third of Finland lies within the Arctic Circle. This "land of the midnight sun" is called *Lappi* (LAPLAND). Finland has short, warm summers. In Lapland the temperatures are lower, and in June the sun never sets. Winters are long and cold; Helsinki's January average is –6°C (21°F). North Atlantic Drift keeps the Arctic coasts free of ice. Forests (birch, pine and spruce) cover 60% of Finland. The vegetation becomes more and more sparse in the N until it merges into Arctic tundra. **Economy** Forests are Finland's most valuable resource. Forestry accounts for *c*.35% of exports. The chief manufactures are wood and paper products. Post-1945 the economy has diversified. Engineering, shipbuilding and textile industries have grown. Farming employs only 9% of the people. Livestock and dairy farming are the chief activities. The collapse of the Soviet bloc led to economic decline and unemployment. Finland's economy is only slowly recovering. **History and politics** In the 8th century, the Lapps were forced N by Finnish-speaking settlers. In the 13th century Sweden conquered the country. Lutheranism was established in the 16th century. Finland was devastated by wars between Sweden and Russia. Following the Northern War (1700–21), Russia gained much Finnish land. In the NAPOLEONIC WARS, Russia conquered Finland and it became a grand duchy (1809). Tsar Nicholas II's programme of Russification (1899–1905) met fierce resistance. Following the Russian Revolution, Finland declared independence. Civil war (January–May 1918) broke out between the Russian-backed Red Guard and the German-backed White Guard, led by MANNERHEIM. The conservative White Guard triumphed, and a republic was established (1919). Territorial disputes with the Soviet Union focused on KARELIA. Finland declared its neutrality at the start of World War 2, but Soviet troops invaded in November 1939, and in March 1940 Finland ceded part of Karelia and Lake LADOGA. In 1941 Finland allied itself with Germany, and in 1944 Soviet troops invaded and forced Finland to sign an armistice. Much of N Finland was destroyed in the ensuing war with Germany. The 1947 Paris Treaty confirmed the 1944 armistice terms. In 1955 Finland joined the UN and the Nordic Council, and maintained a policy of neutrality during the Cold War. Urho Kaleva Kekkonen led Finland (1956–81) through reconstruction. Finland became a member of the European Free Trade Association (EFTA) in 1986 and joined the European Union (EU) in 1995.

Finnish One of the two official languages of Finland and a member of the FINNO-UGRIC group of languages. It is spoken by over 4.5 million people in Finland and by nearly a million people in Sweden, Russia and the USA.

Finno-Ugric Group of related languages spoken by more than 22 million people in Finland and N Norway, Estonia and Karelia, various areas at the N end of the Volga river and each side of the Ural Mountains, and Hungary. The languages are totally unrelated to the Indo-European family. The Finnic branch includes FINNISH, Estonian, Lappish, Mordvinian, Mari, Komi, Votyak, Cheremiss and Zyrian; the Ugric branch comprises HUNGARIAN, Ostyak and Mansi (Vogul). Together with the Samoyed languages, Finno-Ugric makes up the Uralic family.

fir Any of a number of evergreen trees of the PINE family, native to cooler, temperate regions of the world. They are pyramid-shaped and have flat needles and erect cones. Species include the silver and balsam firs. Height: 15–90m (50–300ft). Family Pinaceae; genus *Abies*.

FINLAND
AREA: 338,130sq km (130,552sq mi)
POPULATION: 5,042,000
CAPITAL (POPULATION): Helsinki (508,588)
GOVERNMENT: Multiparty republic
ETHNIC GROUPS: Finnish 93%, Swedish 6%
LANGUAGES: Finnish and Swedish (both official)
RELIGIONS: Evangelical Lutheran 88%
CURRENCY: Markka= 100 penniä

firearm Term used usually to describe a small arm (weapon carried and fired by one person or a small group of people). Firearms were used in Europe in the 14th century. They were, however, ineffective in close combat until *c.*1425, when a primitive trigger to bring a lighted match into contact with the gunpowder charge was invented. These **matchlocks** were heavy and cumbersome. The lighter **flintlock** (which used the spark produced by flint striking steel to ignite the powder) superseded the matchlock in the mid-17th century. During the 19th century there were great changes. In 1805 the explosive properties of mercury fulminate were discovered and, together with the percussion cap invented in 1815, it provided a surer, more efficient means of detonation. It permitted the development by 1865 of both the centre-fire cartridge (the basic ammunition used in firearms ever since) and breech loading. Another major advance was **rifling**; the cutting of spiral grooves inside the barrel in order to make the bullet spin in flight. During the 1830s Samuel Colt perfected the revolver, a PISTOL which could fire several shots without the need to reload. By the 1880s magazine RIFLES were also in use and a bolt action was incorporated after 1889. Development of a weapon that could fire a continuous stream of bullets began with the manually operated GATLING GUN. The first modern MACHINE GUN was the maxim gun, invented in the 1880s, which used the recoil energy of the fired bullet to push the next round into the breech and recock the weapon. Guns of this type dominated the World War 1 trenches. By World War 2 more portable automatic weapons and light machine guns were in use. Newer developments include gas-operated rifles, firearms with several rotating barrels and extremely high rates of fire, and small firearms that use explosive bullets.

fireball (bolides) Exceptionally bright meteor. Fireballs have been loosely defined as meteors brighter than the planets; with the modern estimate of the maximum brightness of Venus, this would mean that all meteors brighter than magnitude –4.7 should be classified as fireballs.

firefly Light-emitting beetle found in moist places of temperate and tropical regions. Organs underneath the abdomen usually give off rhythmic flashes of light that are typical of the species. The luminous larvae and wingless females of some species are called GLOW-WORMS. Length: to 25mm (1in). There are 1,000 species. Family Lampyridae.

Fire of London (2–6 September 1666) Accidental fire that destroyed most of the City of London, England. It started in a baker's shop in Pudding Lane, a site now marked by the Monument. The fire provided an opportunity for rebuilding London on a grand scale, but only the churches of Christopher WREN (including ST PAUL'S Cathedral) were completed.

first aid Action taken by anyone encountering sudden illness or injury in order to save life, mitigate harm or assist subsequent treatment.

First World War *See* WORLD WAR 1

Fischer, Hans (1881–1945) German biochemist who received the 1930 Nobel Prize in chemistry for his structural studies of CHLOROPHYLL and of the red blood pigment haemin. His research indicated the close relationship between the substances. He was able to synthesize haemin and almost completely synthesized one of the chlorophylls.

Fischer-Dieskau, Dietrich (1925–) German baritone. One of the foremost operatic singers of the 20th century, and a major interpreter of *Lieder*.

fish Cold-blooded, aquatic vertebrate animal characterized by fins, gills for breathing, a streamlined body (almost always covered by scales or bony plates onto which a layer of mucus is secreted), and a two-chambered heart. Fish are the most ancient form of vertebrate life, with a history of about 450 million years. They reproduce sexually, and the eggs develop in water or inside the female, according to species. Fish have lateral line organs, which are fluid-filled pits and channels that run under the skin of the body. Sensitive fibres link these channels to the central nervous system and detect changes of pressure in the water and changes of strength and direction in currents. About 75% of all fish live in the sea; the remainder are freshwater species that live in lakes, rivers and streams. A few fish, such as the SALMON and EEL, divide their lives between salt and freshwater habitats. The classification of fish varies. They are usually divided into three classes: Agnatha, which are **jawless fish**, including the hagfish and LAMPREY; Chondrichthyes (**cartilaginous fish**), which includes SHARK, SKATE, RAY and CHIMERA; and the much more numerous Osteichthyes (**bony fish**), including subclasses of softrayed fish (LUNGFISH and lobefin) and the very successful teleost fish, such as salmon and COD. There are some 22,000 species of bony fish, and they represent about 40% of all living vertebrates. They are divided into 34 orders and 48 families.

Fisher, Saint John (1469–1535) English Roman Catholic prelate. Fisher opposed Henry VIII's proposed divorce from Catherine of Aragon in 1529. He was tried and executed for denying that Henry was supreme head of the church under the Act of Supremacy. He was canonized in 1935. His feast day is 9 July.

fishing and **fisheries** Harvesting fish for commercial uses. Fishing boats and fleets employ several methods for catching fish, including: pole and line, purse seine, gill netting, trawling and stunning. About 70% of the fish catch is taken in the Northern Hemisphere, with the greatest hauls between the Philippines and Japan. The most significant Southern Hemisphere grounds are the Pacific coast of Peru and the South African coast. Herring, sardine and anchovy make up the largest percentage of the total catch. Other species caught in large quantities include cod, haddock, hake, redfish, sea bream, mackerel, tuna, salmon and flatfish. The world's eight leading fishing nations are (in order): China, Japan, Peru, Chile, Russia, United States, India, and

Indonesia. Due to increasingly sophisticated and efficient methods of locating and catching fish, by the late 1970s fish stocks were severely depleted. While attempts have been made to restore fish numbers, such as the 1983 United Nations "Law of the Sea" resolution which allowed countries to enforce an exclusive 320km (200mi) limit around their coastlines, stocks are still low. *See also* ANGLING

fission Form of ASEXUAL REPRODUCTION in unicellular organisms. The parent cell divides into two or more identical daughter cells. Binary fission produces two daughter cells (as in bacteria). Multiple fission produces 4, 8, or, in the case of some protozoa, more than 1,000 daughter cells, each developing into a new organism.

fission, nuclear Form of nuclear reaction in which a heavy atomic NUCLEUS splits into two, with the release of two or three NEUTRONS and large amounts of energy. It may occur spontaneously or be made to occur by bombarding certain nuclei with low-energy (slow) neutrons. The neutrons released by the initial splitting may go on to produce further fission in a nuclear CHAIN REACTION. The process is employed in atom bombs and nuclear reactors. *See also* FUSION, NUCLEAR; NUCLEAR ENERGY

Fitzgerald, Ella (1917–96) US jazz singer. Ella was famed for her scat singing. Her smooth style best represented by her interpretations of "standards" by Gershwin, Cole Porter and Jerome Kern.

Fitzgerald, F. Scott (Francis Scott Key) (1896–1940) US author. His debut novel was *This Side of Paradise* (1920). *The Beautiful and Damned* (1922) established him as a chronicler of what he christened the "Jazz Age". Fitzgerald's masterpiece, *The Great Gatsby*, was published in 1925. His last novels were *Tender is the Night* (1934) and the unfinished *The Last Tycoon* (1941).

Fitzgerald, Penelope (Mary) (1916–) British novelist and biographer. After her first novel, *The Golden Child* (1977), she won the Booker Prize for *Offshore* (1979). Other works include *At Freddie's* (1982), *Innocence* (1986) and *The Gate of Angels* (1990).

fjord (fiord) Narrow, steep-sided inlet on a sea coast. They were formed by GLACIERS moving towards the sea, and were flooded when the ice melted and sea levels rose.

flagellate Any single-celled organism that possesses, at some stage of its development, one or several whiplike structures (flagella) for locomotion and sensation. There are two major groups; the phytoflagellates resemble plants, the zooflagellates resemble animals. Most have a single nucleus. Reproduction may be asexual (FISSION) or sexual.

flamboyant style Final phase of French GOTHIC ARCHITECTURE (14th–16th century). The name comes from the flame-like elaborate tracery, such as the w façade of Rouen Cathedral (1370). The English DECORATED STYLE is an equivalent.

flamenco Traditional song, dance and instrumental music, developed in Andalusia, S Spain. Flamen-

co is an improvised form with strict rules. There are three types of song, of which the most demanding is the *cante hondo*. The dances epitomize pride, poise and sensuality. Songs and dances are accompanied by handclaps, finger-snapping and a series of intricate and rhythmic rolls on the guitar.

flamingo Long-necked, long-legged wading bird of tropical and subtropical lagoons and lakes. They have webbed feet and a plumage that varies in colour from pale to deep pink. Their bills have fine, hair-like filters which strain food. Height: to 1.5m (5ft). Family Phoenicopteridae.

Flanders Historic region now divided between Belgium and France. By 1400 it was part of Burgundy, passing to the Habsburgs in 1482, before becoming part of the Spanish Netherlands. It was frequently fought over by France, Spain and later Austria, and was the scene of devastating trench warfare in World War 1.

flare, solar *See* SOLAR FLARE

flat In musical notation, an accidental sign placed before a note or immediately after the clef to indicate that the note it refers to should be sounded a semitone lower.

flatfish Any of more than 500 species of bottom-dwelling, mainly marine fish found worldwide. Most have oval flattened bodies. Both eyes are on the upper side; the lower side is generally white. Examples include the halibut, flounder, plaice, dab, turbot and sole. Order Pleuronectiformes.

flatworm Simple, carnivorous, ribbon-like creature which, having no circulatory system and sometimes no mouth or gut, feeds by absorption through its body wall. The FLUKE and TAPEWORM are both parasites of animals. Order Platyhelminthes.

Flaubert, Gustave (1821–80) French novelist, one of the great 19th-century realists. *Madame Bovary* (1857), his masterpiece, represents the transition from ROMANTICISM to REALISM. Other fiction includes *The Temptation of St Anthony* (1847), *Salammbô* (1862), *A Sentimental Education* (1869) and the short stories *Three Tales* (1877).

flax Slender, erect, flowering plant cultivated for its fibres and seeds. After harvesting, the stems are retted (soaked in water) to soften the fibres and wash away other tissues. The fibres are spun into yarn to make linen. The seeds yield linseed oil. Family Linaceae; species *Linum usitatissium*.

flea Any of 1,000 species of wingless, leaping insects found worldwide. They are external parasites on warm-blooded animals. In moving from one host to another, they can carry disease. Length: to 1cm (0.4in). Order Siphonaptera.

Fleming, Sir Alexander (1881–1955) Scottish bacteriologist, discoverer of PENICILLIN. In 1922 Fleming had discovered lysozyme, a natural antibacterial substance found in saliva and tears. During research on staphylococci in 1928, Fleming noticed that a mould, identified as *Penicillium notatum*, liberated a substance that inhibited the growth of some bacteria. Penicillin became the first antibi-

229

otic. Howard FLOREY and Ernst CHAIN refined the drug's production, and in 1941 it was produced commercially. In 1945 Fleming, Florey and Chain shared the Nobel Prize for physiology or medicine.

Fleming, Ian Lancaster (1908–64) British novelist. Beginning with *Casino Royale* (1952), he wrote 13 escapist spy thrillers about James Bond, secret agent "007". Others include *From Russia with Love* (1957) and *Goldfinger* (1959).

Fleming, Sir John Ambrose (1849–1945) British electrical engineer, inventor of the thermionic valve. Fleming's valve was a RECTIFI-ER, or DIODE, consisting of two electrodes in an evacuated glass envelope. The diode could detect radio signals but could not amplify them.

Fleming's rules In physics, ways of remembering the relationships between the directions of the current, field and mechanical rotation in electric motors and generators. In the **left-hand** rule (for motors), the forefinger represents field, the second finger current, and the thumb, motion; when the digits are extended at right-angles to each other, the appropriate directions are indicated. The **right-hand** rule applies the principles to generators. The rules were devised by John FLEMING.

Flemish One of the two official languages of Belgium (the other being French). It is spoken mainly in the N half of the country, by about 50% of the population. Flemish is virtually the same language as DUTCH.

Flemish art (Netherlandish art) Art from what roughly corresponds to modern-day Netherlands, Belgium and Luxembourg. In the 14th and early 15th centuries, Flemish artists were masters of the International Gothic style, brilliantly characterized by the illuminated manuscripts of the LIMBOURG brothers. Naturalism became a hallmark of Flemish art, such as the portraits and altarpieces of van EYCK and van der WEYDEN and the LANDSCAPE PAINTINGS of BRUEGEL The greatest figures of the next generation were Anthony VAN DYCK and Peter Paul RUBENS, the chief exponent of BAROQUE art in N Europe. After 1650, Flemish art went into decline. In the 19th century, the leading Belgian artist was James Ensor, a precursor of EXPRESSION-ISM. In the 20th century, MAGRITTE and Paul Delvaux both made significant contributions to the SURREALISM movement. *See also* DUTCH ART

Fletcher, John (1579–1625) English dramatist and poet. He collaborated with Francis Beaumont on romantic tragicomedies, such as *Philaster, The Maid's Tragedy* and *A King and No King*. His own plays include *The Faithful Shepherdess* (1608) and *The Chancer* (1623).

flight *See* AERODYNAMICS; AERONAUTICS; AIRCRAFT

flight recorder (black box) Device for automatically recording data during the operation of an aircraft. Investigators analyse the data after a crash or malfunction. A small aircraft may have a simple cockpit voice recorder (CVR), which records all cockpit sounds and all radio contact with air traffic control. Larger aircraft carry a separate flight data recorder (FDR). Control settings, instrument readings and other data are recorded on magnetic wire.

flint Granular variety of QUARTZ (SiO_2) of a fine crystalline structure. It is usually brown or dark grey. It occurs in rounded nodules and is found in chalk or other sedimentary rocks containing calcium carbonate. Of great importance to early humans during the STONE AGE, when struck a glancing blow, flint is flaked, leaving sharp edges appropriate for tools and weapons; two flints struck together produce a spark which can be used to make fire.

Flood, the Primeval deluge, sent by God to devastate the Earth as a punishment for wickedness. As related in the Old Testament (Genesis 6–9), God sent rain upon the Earth for 40 days and nights, destroying everything he had created. Only NOAH, his family, and a pair of every living creature, contained in the Ark, were spared to start creation afresh. Similar myths occur in many cultures, from Native Americans to Native Australians. The Genesis account bears some resemblance to a section of the Mesopotamian Epic of Gilgamesh. The Flood is also mentioned in the Koran.

Florence (Firenze) Capital of Tuscany and Firenze province, on the River Arno, Italy. Initially an Etruscan town, it was a Roman colony from the 1st century BC to 5th century AD. The site of factional power struggles, especially the 13th-century war between the GUELPHS and GHIBELLINES, it nevertheless became the cultural and intellectual centre of Italy. Florence's period of dominance coincided with the rule of the MEDICI family. It became a city-state and one of the leading centres of the RENAISSANCE, with artists such as MICHELANGELO, LEONARDO DA VINCI, RAPHAEL and DONATELLO. In 1569 Florence became the capital of the Grand Duchy of Tuscany. In the late 16th century, it witnessed the development of opera. From 1865–71 Florence was the capital of the kingdom of Italy. Notable sites include the Duomo gothic cathedral (1296); San Lorenzo, Florence's first cathedral rebuilt in 1425 by BRUNELLESCHI; and the monastery San Marco, which holds Fra ANGELICO masterpieces. Major art collections include the Uffizi museum and the Bargello palace. Industries: tourism, craft and fashion. Pop. (1992) 397,434.

Florence, school of Painters and sculptors who flourished in Florence during the RENAISSANCE. Major figures include GIOTTO, Fra ANGELICO, LEONARDO DA VINCI, MICHELANGELO, BOTTICELLI and RAPHAEL.

Florey, Sir Howard Walter (Baron Florey of Adelaide) (1898–1968) British pathologist, b. Australia. He shared, with Alexander FLEMING and Ernst CHAIN, the 1945 Nobel Prize for physiology or medicine for his part in the development of PENICILLIN. Florey's isolation of the antibacterial agent made possible the mass preparation of penicillin.

Florida State in the extreme SE USA, occupying a peninsula between the Atlantic Ocean and the Gulf of Mexico; the capital is TALLAHASSEE. The largest city is JACKSONVILLE. Florida forms a long peninsula with thousands of lakes, many rivers and vast areas of swampland. At the S tip there is a chain of small islands, the FLORIDA KEYS, stretching W. The subtropical climate has encouraged tourism; the biggest attractions are the EVERGLADES, Florida Keys and Disney World. Discovered in 1513, the first permanent settlement in Florida was at St Augustine. Originally Spanish, the land passed to the English (1763), and returned to the Spanish (1783). America purchased Florida in 1819 and, though the state seceded from the Union in 1861, it was little affected by the American Civil War. Florida's historic ties with Cuba are particularly evident in MIAMI, it's second largest city. Industries focus on the John F. Kennedy Space Center at CAPE CANAVERAL. Chief agricultural products are citrus fruits, sugar cane and vegetables. Area: 151,670sq km (58,560sq mi). Pop. (1990) 12,938,000.

flour Finely ground edible part of cereal grains, seeds of leguminous plants, or various nuts. Flour used for baking bread comes from cereals. The degree of whiteness varies according to the bran content. Self-raising flour contains added SODIUM BICARBONATE (baking powder).

flower Reproductive structure of a FLOWERING PLANT. It has four sets of organs set in whorls on a short apex (receptacle). The leaf-like sepals protect the bud and form the calyx. The brightly coloured petals form the corolla. The stamens are stalks (filaments) tipped by anthers (pollen sacs). The carpels form the pistil, with an ovary, style and stigma. Flowers are bisexual if they contain stamens and carpels, and unisexual if only one of these is present. Reproduction occurs when POLLEN is transferred from the anthers to the stigma. A pollen tube grows down into the ovary where FERTILIZATION occurs and a seed is produced. The ovary bearing the seed ripens into a FRUIT and the other parts of the flower wilt and fall.

flowering plant Any of *c*.250,000 species of plants that produce FLOWERS, FRUITS and SEEDS. Such plants include most herbs, shrubs, many trees, fruits, vegetables and cereals. Their seeds are protected by an outer covering and are classified as ANGIOSPERMS. Angiosperms are subdivided into two main groups, MONOCOTYLEDONS and DICOTYLEDONS. Many flowering plants are used for food, timber, and medicine. Phylum Angiospermophyta.

flu Abbreviation of INFLUENZA

fluid Any substance that is able to flow. Of the three common states of matter, GAS and LIQUID are considered fluids, while a SOLID is not.

fluid mechanics Study of the behaviour of liquids and gases. Fluid statics is the study of fluids at rest and includes the study of pressure, density and the principles of PASCAL and ARCHIMEDES. Fluid dynamics is the study of moving fluids and includes the study of streamline flow, BERNOULLI'S LAW and the propagation of waves. Engineers use fluid mechanics in the design of bridges, dams and ships. AERODYNAMICS is a branch of fluid mechanics.

fluke FLATWORM, an external or internal parasite of animals. Flukes have suckers for attachment to the host. Human infection can result from eating uncooked food containing encysted larvae, or from penetration of the skin by larvae in infected waters. The worms enter the liver, lungs and intestines, causing oedema (swelling) and decreased function. Phylum Platyhelminthes, class Trematoda.

fluorescence Emission of radiation, usually light, from a substance when its atoms have acquired excess energy from a bombarding source of radiation, usually ultraviolet light or electrons. When the source of energy is removed, the fluorescence ceases. Mercury vapour is used in motorway lights; television tubes use fluorescent screens.

fluoride Any salt of hydrogen fluoride (HF); more particularly, fluoride compounds added to drinking water or toothpaste in order to build up resistance to tooth decay. Fluoride protection appears to result from the formation of a fluorophosphate complex in the outer tooth layers, making them resistant to penetration by acids made by mouth bacteria.

fluorine Gaseous toxic element (symbol F) of the HALOGEN group, isolated in 1886. Chief sources are fluorspar and cryolite. The pale yellow element, obtained by ELECTROLYSIS, is the most electronegative and reactive nonmetallic element. It is in FLUORIDE in drinking water, and is used in making FLUOROCARBONS and extracting URANIUM. Properties: at.no. 9; r.a.m. 19; m.p. $-219.6\,°C$ ($-363.3°F$); b.p. $-188.1\,°C$ ($-306.6°F$); single isotope F^{19}.

fluorite (fluorspar) Mineral, calcium fluoride (CaF_2). It has cubic system crystals with granular and fibrous masses. Brittle and glassy, it can be yellow, purple or green. It is used as a flux in steel production, and in ceramics and chemical industries. Hardness 4; s.g. 3.1.

fluorocarbon (technically chlorofluoromethanes) Used as propellants in some AEROSOL spray cans and as refrigerants (freons). They are inert gases, yet in the STRATOSPHERE they are broken down by sunlight to release chlorine atoms. These can react with ozone, so reducing the protective OZONE LAYER. *See also* CHLOROFLUOROCARBON (CFC)

flute WOODWIND musical instrument. Air is blown across a mouth-hole near one end of a horizontally held tube. It has a range of three octaves, with a mellow tone in the lower register and a brighter tone in the higher.

flux In ceramics, any substance that promotes vitrification when mixed with clay. When the ware is fired, the flux melts, filling the porous clay form. As the piece cools, it hardens, becoming glossy and non-porous. Fluxes include felspathic rock, silica and borax. In METALLURGY, a flux is added to the charge of a smelting furnace to purge impurities from the ore and lower the melting point of the slag.

fly Any of a large order (Diptera) of two-winged insects. They range in size from midges 1.6mm

(0.06in) long to robber flies more than 76mm (3in) in length. The 60,000–100,000 species are found worldwide. Adult flies have compound eyes and sucking mouthparts. Many are pests and vectors of disease, especially horseflies, mosquitoes and tsetse flies. The common housefly is species *Musca domestica*.

flycatcher Any of several small birds of the order Passeriformes that catch insects in midflight.

flying bomb Popular name for the V1, V2 ROCK-ETS used by the Germans in World War 2.

flying fish Tropical marine fish found worldwide. It is dark blue and silver, and uses its enlarged pectoral and pelvic fins to glide above the water surface for several metres. Length: to 45.7cm (18in). Family Exocoetidae; species *Cypselurus opisthopus*.

flying fox Large fruit-eating bat with a fox-like head that lives in SE Asia. Length: to 40cm (16in); wingspan: to 1.5m (5ft). Genus *Pteropus*.

flying squirrel Small gliding rodent that lives in forests of Eurasia and the USA. It glides by means of furry flaps of skin that stretch out flat and taut on both sides of the body when the limbs are extended. Genus *Pteromys*. The African flying squirrel is of a separate genus (*Anomalurus*).

FM Abbreviation of FREQUENCY MODULATION

Fo, Dario (1926–) Italian playwright and director. Inspired by the traditions of the COMMEDIA DELL' ARTE and the "alienation" techniques of Bertolt BRECHT, Fo's drama incorporates elements of farce and the carnivalesque. His most famous work is *Accidental Death of an Anarchist* (1970). In 1997 he was awarded the Nobel Prize for literature.

focal length Distance from the midpoint of a curved mirror or the centre of a thin lens to the focal point of the system. For converging systems it is given a positive value; for diverging systems, a negative value.

fog (mist) Water vapour in the atmosphere that has condensed around particles of dust at or near the ground, as opposed to water vapour condensed as clouds. Fog forms when moist air is cooled below its DEW POINT.

Fokine, Michel (1880–1942) Russian choreographer. He was chief choreographer for DIAGHILEV and his Ballets Russes in Paris (1909). His best-known works include *Les Sylphides*, *Firebird*, *Petrushka* and *Don Juan*.

fold In geology, bend in a layer of rock. An upfold is an ANTICLINE; a downfold a SYNCLINE. The line around which the rock is folded is the fold axis. The fold system may be symmetrical, asymmetrical, overturned or recumbent (with the axis of the fold horizontal). A single folding line is a monocline.

folic acid Yellow crystalline derivative of glutamic acid, it forms part of the vitamin B complex. Found in liver and green vegetables, it is crucial for growth and is used in the treatment of ANAEMIA.

folklore Traditions, customs and beliefs of the people. The most prevalent form of folklore is the folk tale. In contrast to literature, the folk tale has an oral basis and is transmitted primarily through memory and tradition. Often the tales take the form of myths, fables and fairy tales.

folk music Music deriving from, and expressive of, a particular national, ethnic or regional culture; it is nearly always vocal. Its main theme tends to be the history of a people: folksongs are usually narrative. The musical structure is the simple repetition of a tune (with or without chorus), sometimes with a freedom of rhythm that adheres more to the natural metre of the word than to the more formal requirements of composition. Some writers of popular music, such as Bob DYLAN, have applied the folk idiom to their compositions.

Fonda, Jane (1937–) US film actress. She has won two Best Actress Oscars, for *Klute* (1970) and *Coming Home* (1978). In 1981 she starred opposite her father, Henry Fonda, in *On Golden Pond*.

Fontainebleau Town in the Forest of Fontainebleau, N France. The 16th-century palace was commissioned by Francis I. Built on the site of a previous royal residence, it is a world heritage site and a masterpiece of French Renaissance architecture. It is now a museum and the presidential summer residence.

Fontainebleau School Style of painting associated with a group of artists working at the French court in the 16th century. In a bid to match the magnificence of the Italian courts, Francis I gathered a team of artists to decorate his palace at FONTAINEBLEAU. The group evolved a unique style of MANNERISM, blending sensuality and elegance.

Fonteyn, Dame Margot (1919–91) British ballerina, one of the most exquisite classical dancers of the 20th century. She was a member of the Royal Ballet (1934–59) and a guest artist worldwide. She continued to dazzle audiences late in her career, especially in her appearances with NUREYEV.

food Material taken into an organism to maintain life and growth. Important substances in food include PROTEINS, FATS, CARBOHYDRATES, MINERALS and VITAMINS. *See also* FOOD CHAIN

food additive Substance introduced into food to enhance flavour, to act as a preservative, to effect a better external coloration or appetizing appearance, or to restore or increase nutritional value. Other additives include thickeners, stabilizers and anti-caking agents. The use of food additives is strictly regulated by law and requires prominent labelling.

Food and Agriculture Organization (FAO) Specialized agency of the United Nations (UN), established in 1946. It aims to eliminate hunger and improve world nutrition. Its headquarters are in Rome.

food chain Transfer of energy through a series of organisms, each organism consuming the previous member of the chain. Its main sequence is from green plants (producers) to HERBIVORES (primary consumers) and then to CARNIVORES (secondary consumers). Decomposers, such as bacteria and fungi, act at each stage, breaking down waste and dead matter into forms that can be absorbed by plants. *See also* DECOMPOSITION; PHOTOSYNTHESIS

food poisoning Acute illness caused by consumption of food which is itself poisonous or which has become contaminated with bacteria. Frequently implicated are SALMONELLA bacteria, found in cattle, pigs, poultry and eggs, and listeria, sometimes found in certain types of cheese. Symptoms include abdominal pain, DIARRHOEA, nausea and vomiting. Treatment includes rest, fluids to prevent dehydration and, possibly, medication to curb vomiting. *See also* BOTULISM; GASTROENTERITIS

food preservation Treatment of foodstuffs to prolong the time for which they can be kept before spoiling. Salting, pickling and FERMENTATION preserve food chemically. Chemical preservatives, such as sodium benzoate, can also be added to foods. In **canning**, meats and vegetables are sterilized by heat after being sealed into airtight cans. Cold storage at 5°C (41°F) prolongs the life of foods temporarily, while **deep-freezing** at −5°C (23°F) or below greatly extends the acceptable storage period. In the technique of **freeze-drying**, frozen foods are placed in a vacuum chamber and the water in them is removed as vapour; the foods can be fully reconstituted at a later date. Since the early 1990s, **irradiation** (preservation of food by subjecting them to low levels of radiation in order to kill micro-organisms) has been increasingly used.

food technology Application of scientific techniques to the generation, mass production, packaging and preservation of all types of food. Generating new and better forms of food often involves GENETIC ENGINEERING. The genetic material in edible plants is improved in order to achieve greater yield and resistance to disease. Improving genetic strains is also important in the mass production of forms of meat farming. The scientific provision of an idealized environment can increase the size and quality of vegetables and animals. Animals can be further scientifically bioengineered through the careful introduction of hormones intended to cause effects beneficial to the eventual consumer. Mechanical and electronic machinery for the mass-production of both plant and animal foodstuffs evolves year by year. *See also* BIOENGINEERING; FOOD PRESERVATION

food web *See* FOOD CHAIN

football, American Contact and handling football game, played mainly in the USA. The rules were first drawn up at Princeton College in 1867. It is played over four 15-minute quarters between two teams of 11 players using an oval-shaped ball. Up to 40 substitutes are allowed. The field of play (the "gridiron") is rectangular, 109.7×48.8m (360×160ft), including the end zone behind the goal-lines. Points are scored by touchdown (6), field goal (3), or conversion (1 or 2). A "safety", when an offensive player is caught in possession in his own end zone, is worth 2 points. The team with the ball at the line of scrimmage (confrontational row of defensive and offensive players) has

four chances to move the ball 10 yards forward by running with it or passing it, or lose possession. If 10 yards or more is gained, the ensuing scrimmage ("down") is the "first down" of four. Players protect the ball-carrier by blocking opponents, but he is the only one who may be tackled. Possession of the ball in the opponents' end zone scores a touchdown. The winners of the two US professional leagues, the American Football Conference (AFL) and the National Football Conference (NFL), play off each January for the Super Bowl.

football, association (soccer) Worldwide ball game. It involves 2 teams of 11 players who attempt to force a round ball into their opponents' goal. It is played on a rectangular pitch of maximum size 120×90m (390×300ft), minimum 90×45m (300×150ft). The goals are 7.32m (24ft) wide by 2.44m (8ft) high. Only the goalkeeper may handle the ball, and then only in the penalty area of the goal he is defending. The other players may play the ball in any direction with any other part of the body; essentially it is kicked or headed. A match is played over two 45-minute periods and controlled by a referee. Modern football rules were formulated in 19th-century England, and the Football Association (FA) was founded in 1863. The FA Cup is the world's oldest knockout football competition (established 1872). The introduction of professionalism in 1885 led to the foundation of the Football League Championship (1888). In 1904, FIFA (*Fédération internationale de football association*) was formed to control the sport at world level. Football has been played at the Olympic Games since 1908. The first World Cup was held in 1930. In Europe, the winners of each national league compete for the European Champions Cup (established 1955). In 1992–93 the English FA introduced a "Premier League" of the top 20 clubs, and restructured the First, Second and Third Divisions of the Football League.

football, Australian rules Football popular in Australia and Papua New Guinea. It is played over four 25-minute quarters between two teams of 18 players using an oval-shaped ball on an oval pitch 135–185m (440–600ft) long and 110–155m (345–504ft) wide. The ball may be kicked or punched, and though players can run with the ball, they must bounce it on the ground every 10m (33ft). The object of the game is to score points by kicking the ball between goalposts 6.4m (21ft) apart (6 points). A ball passing between a goal post and one of two other posts, 6.4m (21ft) from each goalpost, scores a *behind* (1 point).

football, Gaelic Sport popular in Ireland and dating from the 16th century. Each side has 15 men who may kick, punch or pass the ball, but not throw it. Players may not pick the ball up from the ground with the hands, but it may be carried for four paces. The pitch is between 128m (420ft) and 146m (480ft) long and 77m (252ft) to 91m (300ft) wide. One point is scored for putting the ball over the crossbar and three for driving it under. The game lasts 60 minutes (except the All-Ireland semi-finals and final which last for 80 minutes) with two halves. A referee and four umpires officiate.

foraminifera Amoeboid protozoan animals that live among plankton in the sea. They have multi-chambered chalky shells (tests), which may be spiral, straight or clustered and vary in size from microscopic to 5cm (2in) across, according to species. Many remain as fossils and are useful in geological dating. When they die, their shells sink to the seabed to form large deposits, the source of chalk and limestone. Order Foraminiferida.

force Push, pull or turn. A force acting on an object may: (1) balance an equal but opposite force or a combination of forces so that it does not move; (2) change the state of motion of the object (in magnitude or direction); or (3) change the shape or state of the object. There are four FUNDAMENTAL FORCES in nature.

Ford, Ford Madox (1873–1939) British novelist, poet and critic, b. Ford Madox Hueffer. His editorship of the *Transatlantic Review* and the *English Review* provided vital support to leading modernist writers. His most remembered works are *The Good Soldier* (1915) and the tetralogy *Parade's End* (1924–28).

Ford, Gerald Rudolph (1913–) 38th US President (1974–77). Ford was elected to the House of Representatives in 1948. A diligent Republican, he was nominated by President NIXON to replace Spiro AGNEW as vice-president (1973). When Nixon resigned, Ford became president, the only man to become president without being elected. As president he was handicapped by conflict with a Democratic Congress. Renominated in 1976, he narrowly lost the election to Jimmy CARTER.

Ford, Henry (1863–1947) US industrialist. He founded Ford Motors in 1903. From 1913 the Model T was produced on an assembly line, drastically reducing production costs. Ford also introduced an eight-hour working day.

Ford, John (1586–1639) English playwright who, with Cyril Tourneur, pioneered post-Jacobean drama. His major plays include *The Broken Heart* (c.1630), *Love's Sacrifice* (c.1630), *'Tis Pity She's a Whore* (c.1633) and *Perkin Warbeck* (1634).

Ford, John (1895–1973) US film director. He won Academy Awards as Best Director for *The Informer* (1935), *The Grapes of Wrath* (1940), *How Green Was My Valley* (1941) and *The Quiet Man* (1952). He made a major contribution to the development of the Western. Other films include *Stagecoach* (1939) and *Cheyenne Autumn* (1964).

foreign exchange Buying and selling national currencies. All currencies have an underlying value relative to the value of gold, registered with the INTERNATIONAL MONETARY FUND (IMF). This value may deviate and governments can control the amount of deviation by tactical trading on foreign exchange markets. Speculators may trade in the hope of profiting from short-term fluctuations in the value, an activity known as arbitrage. International commercial companies may also trade on these markets. *See also* EXCHANGE RATE MECHANISM (ERM)

Foreign Legion Professional military group, created in 1831 to serve in French colonies. In 1962, after fighting in the two World Wars and later French colonial struggles, the Legion moved its headquarters from Algeria to S France.

forensic science (medical jurisprudence) Application of medical, scientific or technological knowledge to the investigation of crimes. Forensic medicine involves examination of living victims and suspects, as well as the pathology of the dead. The cause of death, if there is doubt, is established at an autopsy. Forensic science developed in the early 1900s in England. Modern developments include testing bodily specimens (blood, semen and so on) linked to the crime to provide a DNA "fingerprint" to be compared with the defendant's.

Forester, C.S. (Cecil Scott) (1899–1966) British author. He is most famous for his 12-novel saga about Horatio Hornblower; starting with *The Happy Return* (1937). His other works include *The African Queen* (1935) and *The Gun* (1933).

forestry Managing areas of forest, their waters and clearings. Forestry aims to produce timber, but conservation of soil, water and wildlife is also a consideration. Natural forests once covered nearly 66% of the world's land surface, but DEFORESTATION has reduced this figure to less than 33%.

forget-me-not Any of about 50 species of hardy perennial and annual herbs of the genus *Myosotis* found in temperate parts of Europe, Asia, Australasia and North America. The typical five-petalled flowers are sky blue but may change colour with age. Family Boraganacead (BORAGE)

forging Shaping of metal by hammering or by applying pressure against a shaped die. Blacksmiths forge iron objects, such as horseshoes, by hammering red-hot metal on an anvil. In mass-manufacturing processes, pressure from a hydraulic forging press shape metal parts by forcing them against hard-metal die.

formaldehyde Alternative name for METHANAL
formic acid Alternative name for METHANOIC ACID
Formosa *See* TAIWAN
Forster, E.M. (Edward Morgan) (1879–1970) British novelist. He wrote six novels: *Where Angels Fear to Tread* (1905), *The Longest Journey* (1907), *A Room with a View* (1908), *Howards End* (1910), *A Passage to India* (1924) and the posthumously published *Maurice* (1971). *Aspects of the Novel* (1927) is a collection of literary criticism. *Abinger Harvest* (1936) and *Two Cheers for Democracy* (1951) comprise essays on culture and politics.

forsythia Genus of hardy deciduous shrubs of the OLIVE family Oleaceae, named after the British botanist William Forsyth. They are commonly cultivated in temperate regions. The small yellow flowers look like golden bells and appear in early spring before the leaves. Height: to 3m (10ft).

Fort-de-France Capital of the French overseas department of Martinique. It remained undeveloped until the beginning of the 20th century, when a volcanic eruption destroyed St. Pierre. It is now a popular tourist resort. Exports: sugar cane, rum, cacao. Pop. (1990) 101,540.

Fort Lauderdale City on the Atlantic coast of SE Florida, USA. It was established as a military post in 1838. Port Everglades is one of the world's largest passenger ports. Industries: tourism, computing. Pop. (1990) 149,377.

Fort Sumter Fort in South Carolina, scene of the first hostilities of the American CIVIL WAR. On April 12 1861, the Confederate General BEAUREGARD fired the first shots of the war. The fort fell to the Confederacy within 24 hours.

Fort Worth City in N central Texas, USA. It was settled in 1843. It is famous for its oil and cattle. Industries: aerospace, electronic equipment. Pop. (1990) 447,619.

fossil Direct evidence of the existence of an organism more than 10,000 years old. Fossils document evolutionary change and enable geologic dating. They are original structures, such as bones, shells or wood (often altered through mineralization or preserved as moulds and casts), or imprints, such as tracks and footprints. Leaves can be preserved as a carbonized film outlining their form. Occasionally organisms are totally preserved in frozen soil, peat bogs and asphalt lakes, or trapped in hardened resin (such as insects in amber). Fossil excrement (coprolite) frequently contains recognizable hard parts.

fossil fuels Term to describe COAL, OIL, and NATURAL GAS – FUELS that were formed millions of years ago from the fossilized remains of plants or animals. By their very nature, fossil fuels are a non-renewable energy source.

Foster, Jodie (1962–) US film actress and director. In 1976 she received an Oscar nomination for her role in *Taxi Driver*. She has won two Best Actress Oscars, for *The Accused* (1988) and *The Silence of the Lambs* (1991). *Little Man Tate* (1991) was her directorial debut. Other films include *Sommersby* (1993).

Foster, Sir Norman (1935–) English architect, one of the prime exponents of high-tech modernism. His masterpiece is the Hong Kong Bank building (1986). Striking works in the UK include Stansted airport terminal, Essex (1991).

Foucault, Jean Bernard Léon (1819–68) French physician and physicist who invented the GYROSCOPE. He used a PENDULUM (Foucault's pendulum) to prove that the Earth spins on its axis and devised a method to measure the absolute velocity of light (1850).

Foucault, Michel (1926–84) French philosopher and historian. He examined the social and historical contexts of ideas and institutions. His main theme was how Western systems of knowledge have changed humans into subjects. Works include *Madness and Civilization* (1961), *Discipline and Punish* (1975), *The Order of Things* (1966), and the unfinished three-volume *History of Sexuality*.

Fourier, (François Marie) Charles (1772–1837) French utopian socialist. He set forth detailed plans for the organization of cooperative communities (phalanxes). *See also* UTOPIANISM

four-stroke engine Engine in which the operation of each piston is in four stages, each stage corresponding to one movement of a piston along a cylinder. The stages are: induction, in which the fuel-air mixture enters the cylinder; compression; expansion, in which the exploding mixture forces the piston along the cylinder; and exhaust. This four-stroke (Otto) cycle is used by many INTERNAL COMBUSTION ENGINES.

Fourteen Points Programme presented by US President Woodrow WILSON for a just peace settlement of World War 1 in January 1918. It urged greater liberalism in international affairs and supported national self-determination. It formed the basis for peace and the Treaty of VERSAILLES. The 14th Point called for a LEAGUE OF NATIONS.

fourth estate Name sometimes given to the press. Thomas Babington MACAULAY wrote (1828) of the House of Commons that: "The gallery in which the reporters sit has become a fourth estate of the realm." Th other three estates are the lords spiritual, lords temporal and commons.

Fourth of July US national holiday. It celebrates the signing of the DECLARATION OF INDEPENDENCE, 4 July 1776.

fowl Term applied to domestic species, such as chicken or turkey, and game birds such as PHEASANT and DUCK. *See also* POULTRY

Fowles, John Robert (1926–) British novelist. *The Collector* (1963) was his debut novel. Other works include *The Magus* (1966), *The French Lieutenant's Woman* (1969) and *A Maggot* (1985).

fox Any of several carnivores of the DOG family. The red fox (*Vulpes vulpes*) is typical. Distinguished by its large ears and long bushy tail, it feeds on insects, fruit, carrion and small animals. Height: 38cm (15in) at the shoulder; weight: c.9kg (19.8lb). Family Canidae.

Fox, Charles James (1749–1806) British statesman. He entered Parliament for the Whigs (1768), served as a lord of the Admiralty (1770–72) and as a lord of the Treasury (1773–74). He became foreign secretary (1782) in Rockingham's government and formed a coalition government (1783) with Lord North. Thereafter he led Whig opposition to government of PITT (the Younger), returning to office as foreign secretary in 1806.

Fox, George (1624–91) English religious leader, founder of the QUAKERS. He embarked upon his evangelical calling in 1646 in response to an "inner light". Imprisoned eight times between 1649 and 1673, he travelled to the Caribbean and America to visit Quaker colonists (1671–72).

Foxe, John (1516–87) English Anglican clergyman and historian, whose writings promoted Protestantism. He returned from exile in Elizabeth I's reign and wrote *Actes and Monuments of these latter and perillous Dayes*, better known as *Foxe's Book of Martyrs* (1563).

foxglove Hardy Eurasian biennial and perennial plants of the genus *Digitalis*. They have long, spiky clusters of drooping tubular flowers. The common biennial foxglove (*D. purpurea*), source of the heart stimulant DIGITALIS, is grown for its showy purple or white flowers. Family Scrophulariaceae.

foxhound Medium-sized dog (sporting group) used in fox-hunting. The coat is short and smooth, the ears droop and the tail is carried erect. They are black, tan and white. The American foxhound is slighter than the English variety. Height: 53.3–63.5cm (21–25in) at the shoulder.

fox-hunting Field sport in which a fox is pursued across country by horse riders with hounds, during a season lasting from November to April. In Britain, anti-blood sports campaigners have won widespread public support for a ban on fox-hunting.

fractal Geometrical figure in which an identical motif is repeated on a reducing scale; the figure is "self-similar". "Fractal" was coined by Benoit MANDELBROT and fractal geometry is closely associated with CHAOS THEORY. Fractal objects in nature include shells, cauliflowers, mountains and clouds. Fractals are also produced mathematically.

fraction Quotient written in the form of one number divided by another. A fraction is a/b, where a is the numerator and b the denominator. If a and b are whole numbers, the quotient is a **simple** fraction. If a is smaller than b, it is a **proper** fraction; if b is smaller than a, it is an **improper** fraction. In an **algebraic** fraction the denominator, or the numerator and denominator, are algebraic expressions, e.g. $x/(x^2 + 2)$. In a **composite** fraction, both the numerator and denominator are themselves fractions.

Fragonard, Jean-Honoré (1732–1806) French painter. He is best known for the lighthearted spontaneity of his amorous scenes, rustic landscapes and decorative panels.

franc Monetary unit of France, Belgium, Switzerland and Luxembourg, as well as of the African Financial Community (CFA) and the French Pacific Community. It is divided into 100 centimes.

France Republic in w Europe, the capital is PARIS. **Land and climate** France is Europe's second-largest country (after Ukraine). Almost half of France's 5,500km (3,440mi) of frontier is sea. The PYRENEES form its sw border with Spain. The JURA MOUNTAINS and the ALPS form its E and SE borders with Switzerland and Italy. MONT BLANC is w Europe's highest peak, 4,807m (15,771ft). The RHINE forms part of the German border. The MASSIF CENTRAL, between the RHÔNE-Saône valley and the Aquitaine basin, covers 15% of France. The ÎLE-DE-FRANCE province, w of the LOIRE River, includes the capital, PARIS. The climate in w France is mild, moderated by the effects of the Atlantic Ocean. The E experiences greater seasonal variation. The Mediterranean Sea coast has hot, dry summers and mild, moist winters. The Alps, Jura, and Pyrenees have good snowfall and are popular for winter sports. Fields and meadows cover c.60% of the land. Forests occupy c.27%. **Economy** One of the world's most developed and industrialized nations, France manufactures aircraft, cars, chemicals, electronic products, machinery, steel and textiles. France is the largest producer of farm products in w Europe, and agriculture is highly intensive. Wheat is the leading crop. France is the world's second largest wine producer (after Italy). Fishing and forestry are leading industries. Tourism is also important (1992 receipts, US$ 25,000 million. **History and politics** Julius Caesar completed the Roman conquest of Gaul in 51 BC. The Roman empire began to decline in the 3rd century AD. In 486, the Franks led by CLOVIS I established the MEROVINGIAN dynasty. Following his death, the kingdom fragmented. In 687 the CAROLINGIANS reunited Gaul, and PEPIN III (THE SHORT) overthrew the Merovingians (757). His son, CHARLEMAGNE, was crowned emperor of the West (800). He expanded the empire and provided sound administration. His empire soon disintegrated, and in 843, his grandson, CHARLES II (THE BALD) became ruler. Hugh Capet is often seen as the first king of France (987), and the CAPETIANS gradually subdued the nobility. The NORMAN CONQUEST (1066) marked the start of a long history of Anglo-French rivalry. PHILIP II regained land lost through dowry to the English. In 1328 the first Valois king, PHILIP VI, acceded to the throne. The HUNDRED YEARS WAR (1337–1453) was a series of battles for the French succession. By 1422, England controlled most of France. JOAN OF ARC helped to crush the siege of Orléans (1428), and by 1453 England had been expelled from France. LOUIS XI restored royal authority and crushed the ANGEVINS. FRANCIS I's reign marked the beginning of the Renaissance in France and the struggle with the Habsburgs. The rise of the HUGUENOTS led to the Wars of RELIGION (1562–98). The GUISE faction lost, and Henry IV became the first BOURBON king (1589). Cardinals RICHELIEU and MAZARIN led France to victory in the

---

FRANCE
AREA: 551,500sq km (212,934sq mi)
POPULATION: 57,372,000
CAPITAL (POPULATION): Paris (2,152,423)
GOVERNMENT: Multiparty republic
ETHNIC GROUPS: French 93%, Arab 3%, German 2%, Breton 1%, Catalan
LANGUAGES: French (official)
RELIGIONS: Christianity 90% (Roman Catholic 86%, other 4%), Islam 3%
CURRENCY: Franc = 100 centimes

THIRTY YEARS WAR (1618–48). LOUIS XIV's court at VERSAILLES was the richest in Europe. Yet, the *ancien régime* of LOUIS XV and LOUIS XVI was bankrupted by war and incapable of reform. The FRENCH REVOLUTION (1789–99) saw the execution of the king, and ROBESPIERRE's brutal REIGN OF TERROR. The Directory ended when NAPOLEON I proclaimed himself emperor (1799). The success of the NAPOLEONIC WARS was wiped out at WATERLOO (1815). Napoleon was forced into exile, and the Bourbons restored to the throne. The FEBRUARY REVOLUTION (1848) established a Second Republic. Napoleon I's nephew seized power as NAPOLEON III (1852). His defeat in the FRANCO-PRUSSIAN WAR (1870–71) led to the formation of the Third Republic (1870–1940). The PARIS COMMUNE (1871) was violently suppressed. The DREYFUS Affair polarized France. France was the battleground for most of WORLD WAR 1. CLEMENCEAU and BRIAND led France to peace. Successive prime ministers, Blum and DALADIER, failed to tackle Germany's increasing power. In June 1940 German troops completed the conquest of France, and established the VICHY GOVERNMENT. Charles DE GAULLE became head of a government-in-exile. Paris was liberated in August 1944, and a Fourth Republic was founded (1946). Political instability and colonial war, especially in ALGERIA, slowed the post-war recovery. In 1958 Charles de Gaulle was elected president and established a Fifth Republic. De Gaulle resigned in 1969, replaced first by POMPIDOU, then GISCARD D'ESTAING. François MITTERRAND's presidency was marked by nationalization, civic rebuilding, decentralization, and advocacy of European Union. Following Mitterrand's death, his conservative rival Jacques CHIRAC was elected president (1995). His attempt to meet the criteria for EUROPEAN MONETARY UNION (EMU) and to reform the welfare state has brought strikes and unemployment. In 1997 parliamentary elections, the opposition Socialist Party was victorious and Lionel JOSPIN became prime minister.

France, Anatole (1844–1924) (Jacques Anatole François Thibault) French novelist. He achieved recognition with *The Crime of Sylvester Bonnard* (1881) and *Thaïs* (1890). Other works include the four-volume series *Contemporary History* (1897–1901) and *Penguin Island* (1908). He was awarded the 1921 Nobel Prize for literature.

Francesca, Piero della *See* PIERO DELLA FRANCESCA

Franche-Comté Historic region of E France; its capital was Dôle until 1674 and Besançon thereafter. Founded in the 12th century as the "free county" of the Burgundians, it was finally recognized as part of France in 1678. It covers 16,202sq km (6,254sq mi). Pop. (1991) 1,097,300.

franchise Right or privilege of an individual to vote in public political elections, granted by government. Franchise is conferred according to a set of criteria, which may include age, sex, race and class. In contemporary democracies, the intention is that anyone over a specific age has the right to vote. In Britain, the modern basis of the franchise dates from the 1832 Reform Act and subsequent acts which, by 1918, ensured all men over the age of 21 and women over 30 were entitled to vote (the first country to give women the vote was New Zealand, 1893). By 1928 women aged over 21 were enfranchised, and in 1969 the voting age in Britain was lowered to 18. In the USA, the franchise is granted by each state. The 14th and 15th Amendments to the US Constitution forbid any state to deny voting rights to adult men aged over 21 on the grounds of race, colour or previous servitude. The 19th Amendment (1920) gave women the vote. Grandfather clauses were added to the constitutions of seven Southern States to deprive African-Americans of their voting rights. The 26th Amendment lowered the voting age to 18.

Francis I (1708–65) Holy Roman emperor (1745–65), duke of Lorraine (1729–35) and Tuscany (1737–65). In 1736 he married the Habsburg heiress MARIA THERESA. Her accession (1740) precipitated the War of the AUSTRIAN SUCCESSION.

Francis II (1768–1835) Last Holy Roman emperor (1792–1806) and first emperor of Austria, as Francis I (1804–35). He was forced to accept steady diminution of his territories, culminating in the abolition of the HOLY ROMAN EMPIRE (1806). He preserved Austria by alliance with Napoleon and in 1813 joined the coalition that defeated him. At the Congress of VIENNA, his minister, Prince METTERNICH, restored Austrian dominance in Europe.

Francis I (1494–1547) King of France (1515–47). A leader of the Renaissance, he is best remembered for his contributions to the humanities and arts. Repression of religious reform, centralization of monarchical power and foolish financial policies made him unpopular. A costly struggle with the Emperor CHARLES V over the imperial crown led to a defeat at Pavia (1525). Francis was imprisoned and forced to give up Burgundy (1526). An ensuing war with Charles (1527–29) led to the loss of Italy.

Francis II (1544–60) King of France (1559–60). Eldest son of HENRY II and CATHERINE DE' MEDICI, he was king for less than two years and ruled only in name. Married to MARY, QUEEN OF SCOTS at the age of 14, he was a sickly youth and his kingdom was controlled by two uncles – Charles, cardinal of Lorraine, and Francis, duke of Guise.

Franciscans Friars belonging to an itinerant religious order founded by ST FRANCIS OF ASSISI. The first order, known as the Friars Minor, now comprises three subdivisions: the Observants; the CAPUCHIN; and the Conventual. The second order, the Poor Clares order of nuns, was founded (1212) by St Francis and St CLARE.

Francis of Assisi, Saint (1182–1226) Italian founder of the FRANCISCANS. He renounced his worldly life for one of poverty and prayer in 1205. In 1209 he received permission from Pope Innocent

III to begin a monastic order. In 1212, with St CLARE, he established an order for women, popularly called the Poor Clares, and in 1221 a lay fraternity. Canonized in 1228, his feast day is 4 October.

Francis Xavier, Saint (1506–52) Early JESUIT missionary, often called the Apostle to the Indies. He was an associate of ST IGNATIUS OF LOYOLA, with whom he took the vow founding the Society of Jesus. From 1541 he travelled through India, Japan and the East Indies. His feast day is 3 December.

Franck, César Auguste (1822–90) French composer, b. Belgium. He is best remembered for the *Symphonic Variations* for piano and orchestra (1885), the popular *Symphony in D Minor* (1888) and significant chamber works.

Franck, James (1882–1964) US physicist, b. Germany. Franck and Gustav HERTZ shared the 1925 Nobel Prize for physics for studies on the changes of energy occurring when atoms collide with electrons. He later worked with the MANHATTAN PROJECT (1945) to develop the atom bomb, but opposed its use against Japanese civilians.

Franco, Francisco (1892–1975) Spanish general and dictator of Spain (1939–75). He joined the 1936 military uprising that led to the Spanish CIVIL WAR and assumed leadership of the fascist FALANGE. In 1939, with the aid of Nazi Germany and Fascist Italy, he won the war and formed a dictatorship. He kept Spain neutral in World War 2, and presided over Spain's post-war economic growth, while maintaining rigid control over its politics. In 1947 he declared Spain a monarchy with himself as regent. In 1969 he designated Juan Carlos as heir.

Franco-Prussian War (1870–71) Conflict engineered by the Prussian chancellor BISMARCK. The nominal cause was a dispute over the Spanish succession. Bismarck's aim was to use the prospect of French invasion to frighten the S German states into joining the North German Confederation. The French were defeated at Sedan, NAPOLEON III abdicated, and Paris was besieged. An armistice was agreed in January 1871, and Alsace and Lorraine were ceded to the new German empire.

Frank, Anne (1929–45) German Jew who became a symbol of suffering under the Nazis. She fled with her family to the Netherlands in 1933. The Franks were living in Amsterdam at the time of the German invasion in 1940 and went into hiding from 1942 until they were betrayed in August 1944. Anne died in Bergen-Belsen concentration camp. Her diary was first published in 1947.

Frankfort Capital of Kentucky state, USA, on the Kentucky River, N central Kentucky. First settled in 1779, it was made the state capital in 1792. Industries: tobacco, whisky distilling, textiles, electronic parts, furniture. Pop. (1990) 25,535.

Frankfurt am Main City and port on the River Main, Hesse state, W Germany. One of the royal residences of Charlemagne, the Holy Roman emperors were elected here, and the first German National Assembly met here in 1848. Notable buildings include a Gothic cathedral, an art museum and a university. Frankfurt is Germany's banking centre and a venue for international fairs. Industries: chemicals, electrical equipment, telecommunications, publishing. Pop. (1993 est.) 660,800.

Franklin, Aretha (1942–) US singer, the "Queen of Soul". She rose to stardom in 1966 with *I Never Loved a Man (the Way I Love You)*. Other classics include *Respect* and *Young, Gifted, and Black*.

Franklin, Benjamin (1706–90) US statesman and inventor, one of the founders of the republic. He was a successful printer in Philadelphia and published *Poor Richard's Almanac* (1732–57). He identified the electric nature of lightning. His travelled to England in the 1750s and 1760s to resolve disagreements between Britain and the American colonies. When war broke out, he went to Paris and negotiated a treaty of alliance (1778). He served as ambassador to Paris, was president of Pennsylvania's executive council (1785-88) and a member of the CONSTITUTIONAL CONVENTION.

Franklin, Sir John (1786–1847) British Arctic explorer. He was involved in several Arctic expeditions (1818–27) and was governor of Tasmania (1834–45). Appointed to lead a naval expedition to find the Northwest Passage in 1845, he died with the entire crew of his two ships.

Franks Germanic people who settled in the region of the River Rhine in the 3rd century. Under CLOVIS I in the late 5th century, they established the MEROVINGIAN empire. This was divided into the kingdoms of Austrasia, Neustria and Burgundy, but was reunited by the CAROLINGIANS. The partition of CHARLEMAGNE's empire into the East and West Frankish kingdoms is the origin of Germany and France.

Franz Ferdinand (1863–1914) Archduke of Austria. Nephew of the Emperor FRANZ JOSEPH, he became heir apparent in 1889. On an official visit to Sarajevo, Bosnia-Herzegovina, on 28 June 1914, he and his wife were assassinated by a Serb nationalist. The incident led to the outbreak of WORLD WAR 1.

Franz Josef Land (Zemlya Franca-iosifa) Russian archipelago in the Arctic Ocean, part of Archangel'sk oblast. It was discovered in 1873 and incorporated in the Soviet Union (1926). Area: 20,700sq km (8,000sq mi).

Franz Joseph (1830–1916) Emperor of Austria (1848–1916) and king of Hungary (1867–1916). He quickly brought the revolutions of 1848 under control, defeating the Hungarians under KOSSUTH in 1849. In 1867 he was forced to form the AUSTRO-HUNGARIAN EMPIRE. He died two years before the final collapse of the HABSBURG empire.

Frasch process Method of mining sulphur by pumping superheated water and air into the sulphur deposits, melting the mineral, and forcing it to the surface.

Fraunhofer, Joseph von (1787–1826) German physicist and optician, founder of astronomical spectroscopy. By studying the DIFFRACTION of light through narrow slits, he developed the earliest form of diffraction grating. He observed and began to map the dark lines in the Sun's spectrum (1814), now called **Fraunhofer lines**.

Frazier, Joe (1944–) US boxer. An Olympic heavyweight champion (1964), Frazier won one of the world's heavyweight titles in 1968 and became undisputed champion in 1970. He lost the title to George Foreman (1973). His bouts with Muhammad ALI, whom he defeated in 1971, were his most notable. He retired in 1976.

Frederick I (Barbarossa) (1123–90) Holy Roman emperor (1152–90). Pope ALEXANDER III encouraged the formation of the LOMBARD LEAGUE against Frederick. Frederick set up an antipope, but after his defeat at Legnano (1176), he was reconciled with Alexander and made peace (1183) with the Lombards.

Frederick II (1194–1250) Holy Roman emperor (1215–50) and king of Sicily (1198–1250). Son of Emperor HENRY VI, he devoted himself to Italian affairs. Frederick made his son, Conrad IV, German king. In Sicily, Frederick set up a centralized royal administration. He went on a crusade and was crowned king of Jerusalem (1229). In 1245 Innocent IV deposed him, and civil war ensued in Germany and Italy.

Frederick II (the Great) (1712–86) King of Prussia (1740–86). He made Prussia a major European force. In the War of the AUSTRIAN SUCCESSION (1740–48) he took Silesia from Austria. During the SEVEN YEARS WAR (1756–63), his brilliant generalship preserved the kingdom. In 1760 Austro-Russian forces reached Berlin, but Russia's subsequent withdrawal enabled Frederick to emerge triumphant. He directed Prussia's remarkable recovery from the devastation of war after 1763. Gaining further territory in the first partition of Poland (1772), he renewed the contest against Austria in the War of the Bavarian Succession (1778–79). Artistic and intellectual, he was a friend and patron of Voltaire and built the palace of Sans Souci.

Frederick V (1596–1623) (Winter King) Elector Palatine (1610–20) and king of Bohemia (1619–20). He married the daughter of James I of England (1613). In 1619 he was chosen as king by the Protestant rebels of Bohemia in preference to the Holy Roman emperor FERDINAND II, provoking the outbreak of the THIRTY YEARS WAR. Defeat at the Battle of the White Mountain (1620) resulted in the loss of both Frederick's titles.

Fredericksburg Historic US city on the Rappahannock River, N Virginia. Planned in 1727, it is associated with the American Revolution and Civil War. Many sites are connected to George Washington. The civil war Battle of Fredericksburg (1862) was a one-sided victory for the Confederate army, led by General Robert E. LEE, over the Union Army, led by Major General Ambrose Burnside. Nearly 13,000 Union troops were killed or wounded. Industries: tourism. Pop. (1990) 19,030.

Frederick William (1620–88) (Great Elector) Elector of Brandenburg (1640–88). He inherited a collection of small, disparate and impoverished territories ravaged by the THIRTY YEARS WAR. By the end of his reign his organizational powers had created a unified state with a sound, centralized tax system and a formidable standing army. He acquired Eastern Pomerania at the Peace of WESTPHALIA.

Frederick William III (1770–1840) King of Prussia (1797–1840). Son and successor of Frederick William II, he declared war on France (1806), suffered a disastrous defeat at Jena, and was forced to sign the Treaty of Tilsit (1807). The reorganized Prussian army re-entered the war against Napoleon in 1813 and played a major part in his defeat.

Free Church Any of a number of Protestant churches that are independent of the established church. In England CONGREGATIONALISM, METHODISM, PRESBYTERIANISM and the BAPTIST movements formed a National Council of Evangelical Free Churches.

Free Church of Scotland Grouping of Scottish Presbyterians formed as a result of the secession of nearly one-third of the membership of the established CHURCH OF SCOTLAND in the Disruption of 1843. In 1900 most of this Free Church joined the United Presbyterian Church to become the United Free Church of Scotland. In 1929, following the acceptance of the Church of Scotland's spiritual independence, the United Free Church of Scotland reunited with it. The tiny Presbyterian minority who had opposed union retained their independence and kept the name United Free Church.

Free French Group formed by Charles DE GAULLE on the creation of the VICHY GOVERNMENT in 1940. Its purpose was to continue French opposition to Germany. Operating outside France, the group was aligned with internal Resistance groups and aided the Allies throughout the war, forming a provisional government after the D-DAY invasion.

freemasonry Customs and teachings of the secret fraternal order of Free and Accepted Masons, an all-male secret society with national organizations worldwide. Freemasonry is most popular in the UK and countries once in the British empire. It evolved from the medieval guilds of stonemasons and cathedral builders. The first Grand Lodge was founded in England (1717). Freemasonry teaches morality, charity and law-abiding behaviour. Freemasons believe in God and the immortality of the soul. In recent times, they have incurred criticism because of their strict secrecy, male exclusivity and alleged use of influence within organizations, such as the police or local government, to benefit members. It is estimated that there are c.6 million masons worldwide.

freesia Genus of perennial herbs of the IRIS family, native to South Africa. Species of freesia are widely cultivated for their fragrant yellow, white or pink tubular flowers.

Free State (formerly Orange Free State)

Province in E central South Africa; the capital is Bloemfontein. The Drakensberg Range forms part of its E border with Lesotho. The Orange River forms its S border with Northern Cape. Boers began to settle after the Great Trek (1836). In 1848 the British annexed the region as the Orange River Sovereignty and, in 1854, it achieved independence as Orange Free State. After its involvement in the SOUTH AFRICAN WARS (1899–1902), it was again annexed by Britain. Regaining independence in 1907, the Orange Free State joined the Union of South Africa in 1910. The economy is dominated by agriculture and gold. Pop. (1995 est.) 2,782,500.

freethinkers People whose opinions and ideas, especially on matters of religion, are not influenced by CANON law or dogma. The original freethinkers were part of a post-Reformation movement that sought to assert reason over religious authority. Deists emerged as the chief exponents of freethought during the 17th and 18th centuries. *See also* ATHEISM; DEISM; HUMANISM

Freetown Capital and chief port of Sierra Leone, W Africa. Freetown was founded in 1787 by the British as a settlement for freed slaves from England, Nova Scotia and Jamaica. It was the capital of British West Africa from 1808–74. Freetown was made capital of independent Sierra Leone in 1961. Industries: platinum, gold, diamonds, oil refining and palm oil. Pop. (1985 est.) 469,776.

free trade Commerce conducted between nations without restrictions on imports and exports. In modern history, its origins lie in the 19th-century attack on MERCANTILISM. The repeal of the CORN LAWS (1846) and the Anglo-French free trade treaty (1860) were the hallmarks of the mid-Victorian faith in free trade. Twentieth-century free trade agreements include the EUROPEAN FREE TRADE AGREEMENT (EFTA) (1959) and the NORTH AMERICAN FREE TRADE AGREEMENT (NAFTA) (1994).

free verse Verse with no regular metre and no apparent form, relying primarily on cadence. WHITMAN and RIMBAUD were early users of free verse.

freezing *See* FOOD PRESERVATION

freezing point Temperature at which a substance changes state from liquid to solid. The freezing point for most substances increases with pressure. Melting point is the change from solid to liquid and is the same as freezing point.

Frege, Gottlob (1848–1925) German philosopher. With George BOOLE he was one of the founders of modern symbolic logic. Frege attempted to derive all mathematics from logical axioms in his *Foundations of Arithmetic* (1884).

French Major language, spoken in France and parts of Belgium, Switzerland, Canada, Haiti, Africa and other areas. There are some 80–100 million French speakers worldwide. Descended from Latin, it is one of the Romance languages and part of the INDO-EUROPEAN family. It is one of the six official languages of the United Nations.

French and Indian War (1754–63) Colonial war in North America forming part of the SEVEN YEARS WAR. British and American colonial forces fought French Canadians with Native American nations fighting on both sides. After 1756 British resources improved, forts at Louisburg and Duquesne (1758) were captured. Ticonderoga fell in 1759. The British capture of Quebec was decisive in the conquest of Canada, which passed to Britain in the Treaty of Paris (1763).

French architecture From the 8th to early 19th centuries, French architects were dependent on royal patronage, though the 10th-century Benedictine abbey at Cluny had an influence on church architecture. During the 11th and 12th centuries, cathedrals in the ROMANESQUE style were constructed. In the 13th century Gothic cathedrals, such as Chartres and Notre-Dame, were built. Italian RENAISSANCE ARCHITECTURE inspired kings to construct palaces, such as FONTAINEBLEAU and the LOUVRE. Royal influence climaxed in the 17th century with Louis XIV's VERSAILLES. In the mid-18th century, official architecture turned to NEO-CLASSICISM. In the 19th century, patronage shifted to the bourgeoisie. Baron George-Eugèe Haussman designed the wide boulevards of Paris. The skeletal frame of the EIFFEL TOWER (1889) heralded MODERNISM. ART NOUVEAU faded quickly. In the 1920s and 1930s, BAUHAUS had a large influence, and LE CORBUSIER spearheaded the INTERNATIONAL STYLE.

French art In the 12th century there were several important centres of manuscript illumination, but for many centuries FRENCH ARCHITECTURE was more prominent than the visual arts. During the Renaissance, art was heavily influenced by Italian trends, such as the work of Jean FOUQUET and the FONTAINEBLEAU SCHOOL. In the 17th century, artists such as CLAUDE LORRAIN and Nicolas POUSSIN were masterful exponents of classical landscape painting. The twilight years of the *ancien régime* were celebrated in the light-hearted ROCOCO fantasies of François BOUCHER and Jean-Honoré FRAGONARD. The revolutionary era was dominated by neo-classical painters such as Jacques Louis DAVID. The leading French romantic artist was Eugène DELACROIX. In the later 19th century began with the REALISM of COURBET and culminated in IMPRESSIONISM, POST-IMPRESSIONISM and SYMBOLISM.

French Guiana French overseas department in South America. **Land and Climate** The coastal plain includes cultivated areas, particularly near the capital, CAYENNE. Inland lies a plateau, with low mountains (Sierra Tumucumaque) in the S. The Maroni River forms the border with SURINAM, and the Oyapock River its E border with Brazil. The climate is hot and equatorial, with high annual temperatures. Rainfall is heavy, although August to October is dry. Rainforest covers c.90% of the land and contains valuable hardwood species. **History and Politics** The original inhabitants of the area were Native Americans, but today only a few remain in the interior. Europeans first explored the coast in

1500, and they were followed by adventurers seeking EL DORADO. The French were the first settlers (1604). Initial attempts at colonization failed, and the area changed hands several times before becoming a French colony in the late 17th century. The colony's plantation economy depended on African slaves. Slavery was abolished in 1848, and Asian labourers were introduced. France used the colony as a penal settlement for political prisoners and between 1852–1945 French Guiana was notorious for the harsh treatment of prisoners. In 1946 French Guiana became an overseas department of France and, in 1974, also became an administrative region. An independence movement developed in the 1980s, but most people wanted to retain links with France. **Economy** Despite rich forest and mineral resources, it is a developing country with high unemployment. It depends on France to finance services, and the government is the main employer. Since 1968, Kourou has been the EUROPEAN SPACE AGENCY's rocket-launching site. Industries: fishing, forestry, gold mining and agriculture.

French horn Brass musical instrument. It has a flared bell, long coiled conical tube, three or four valves and a funnel-shaped mouthpiece.

French literature The 12th-century *chansons de geste* celebrated the military exploits of the nobility. The allegorical romances of Chrétien de TROYES gave way to the more intimate style of Francois VILLON. The 16th-century poetic school La PLÉIADE rivalled Renaissance Italy. In prose, the comic genius of RABELAIS contrasted with the pithy originality of the essayist Montaigne. The 17th century was the golden age of French literature, including the dramatic works of CORNEILLE, RACINE and MOLIÈRE, and the philosophical works of DESCARTES and PASCAL. They were succeeded by the writers of the ENLIGHTENMENT, such as ROUSSEAU, DIDEROT, VOLTAIRE and BEAUMARCHAIS. The 19th-century romantic movement included Victor HUGO, Lamartine and DUMAS (*père* and *fils*). STENDHAL, BALZAC, FLAUBERT, MAUPASSANT and ZOLA were leading figures in NATURALISM and REALISM. BAUDELAIRE and RIMBAUD paved the way for SYMBOLISM and modernism, typified by VERLAINE, VALÉRY and APOLLINAIRE. PROUST and GIDE dominated French fiction until 1940. SARTRE, de BEAUVOIR, CAMUS and Maurois produced the finest post-war work. Post-war dramatists include Jean GENET, IONESCO and BECKETT.

French Polynesia French overseas territory in the S central Pacific Ocean, divided into five scattered archipelagos: SOCIETY ISLANDS, MARQUESAS ISLANDS, Tuamotu Archipelago, Gambier Islands, and Tubuai Islands. The capital is Papeete on TAHITI (Society Islands). The larger islands are volcanic with fertile soil and dense vegetation. The more numerous coral islands are low-lying. The climate is tropical. Missionaries arrived at the end of the 18th century, and in the 1840s France began establishing protectorates. During 1880–82, the islands

became part of Oceania. In 1958 they were granted the status of an overseas territory. In the 1960s, the French government began nuclear tests on Mururoa atoll, leading to worldwide protests. In recent years there have been increasing demands for autonomy in Tahiti. In 1995 the French government proposed to grant Polynesia the status of an autonomous overseas territory. Copra and vanilla are the leading agricultural products, and cultured pearls are exported. Tourism is important. Area: 3,265sq km (1,260sq mi). Pop. (1994 est.) 216,600.

French Revolution (1789–99) Series of events that removed the French monarchy, transformed government and society, and established the First Republic. Suggested causes include economic pressures, an antiquated social structure, weakness of royal government and the influence of the ENLIGHTENMENT. In June 1789 the STATES GENERAL met at Versailles. The bourgeoisie demanded reform and proclaimed a National Assembly. Popular resistance, epitomized by the storming of the BASTILLE, forced the government to accede to demands which included the abolition of the aristocracy, reform of the clergy, and a Declaration of the Rights of Man. The Legislative Assembly was installed (October 1791) and, faced with growing internal and external pressure, declared war on Austria (April 1792). It was soon in conflict with most other European states. War hastened political change: LOUIS XVI was deposed (August 1792) and the National Convention met to proclaim a republic (September 1792). After a period of rivalry between JACOBINS and GIRONDINS (November 1792–June 1793), strong central government was imposed during the REIGN OF TERROR and Louis was executed. Social anarchy and runaway inflation characterized the Thermidorean Reaction (July 1794–October 1795), which followed the fall of ROBESPIERRE. Another new constitution imposed a five-man executive called the "Directory" (1795–99). The Consulate (1799–1804) was dominated by NAPOLEON I.

French Revolutionary Wars (1792–1802) Series of campaigns in which the armies of revolutionary France fought various European foes. Fear and hatred of the FRENCH REVOLUTION fuelled the hostility of Austria in particular. The French declared war on Austria and Prussia in 1792. French success provoked other states, including Britain, the Netherlands and Spain, to form the First Coalition (1793). It was no more successful against France's conscript army and Austria made peace at Campo-Formio. Britain remained at war and NELSON won significant naval victories, but a Second Coalition was again unsuccessful on land in 1799–1800, NAPOLEON I winning a notable victory at Marengo. Britain made peace at Amiens in 1802, but it marked only an interval before the NAPOLEONIC WARS.

frequency Rate of occurrence. In statistics, the number of times a numerical value, event, or special property occurs in a population in a given time. In physics, the number of oscillations occurring in a given time (measured in HERTZ), such as sound, light and radio waves, or a swinging PENDULUM. Frequency is the reciprocal of period.

frequency modulation (FM) Form of RADIO transmission. It is the variation of the FREQUENCY of a transmitted radio carrier wave by the signal being broadcast. The technique makes radio reception fairly free from static interference and, though restricted in range, has become the most favoured transmission method. *See also* AMPLITUDE MODULATION (AM)

fresco Method of painting on freshly spread plaster while it is still damp. In *buon fresco*, paint combines chemically with moist plaster. *Fresco secco* involves the application of paint in a water and glue medium to a dry plaster wall. It does not last as well as true fresco.

Fresnel, Augustin Jean (1788–1827) French physicist and engineer. His pioneer work in optics was instrumental in establishing the wave theory of light. He researched the interference phenomena in POLARIZED LIGHT, studied double refraction, and produced circularly polarized light.

Freud, Sigmund (1856–1939) Austrian physician and founder of PSYCHOANALYSIS. With Josef Breuer he developed new methods of treating mental disorders by free association and the interpretation of dreams. These methods derived from his theories of the ID, EGO and SUPEREGO, and emphasized the unconscious and subconscious as agents of human behaviour. He developed theories of neuroses involving childhood relationships to one's parents and stressed the importance of sexuality in behaviour. He believed that each personality had a tripartite structure: the **id**, unconscious desires which may surface in dreams or madness; the **ego**, conscious rationalizing section of the mind; and the **superego**, which may be compared to the conscience. The adoption of a satisfactory superego is dependent on the resolution of the OEDIPUS COMPLEX. His works include *The Interpretation of Dreams* (1900), *The Psychopathology of Everyday Life* (1904) and *The Ego and the Id* (1923).

friar Member of certain religious orders. The four main orders – the DOMINICANS, FRANCISCANS, CARMELITES, and AUGUSTINIANS – were founded in the 13th century. Friars are involved outside the monastery and are centrally organized.

friction Resistance encountered when surfaces in contact slide or roll against each other, or when a fluid flows along a surface. Friction is directly proportional to the force pressing the surfaces together and the surface roughness. When the movement begins, it is opposed by a static friction up to a maximum "limiting friction" and then slipping occurs.

Friedman, Milton (1912–) US economist. An influential supportor of MONETARISM. *A Monetary History of the United States 1867–1960* (1963) is a key book in monetary economics. Other works include *A Theory of the Consumption Function*

(1957) and *Capitalism and Freedom* (1962). He gained the 1976 Nobel Prize in economic science.

Friedrich, Caspar David (1774–1840) German painter. One of the greatest German romantic painters, he created eerie, symbolic landscapes, such as *Shipwreck on the Ice* (1822) and *Man and Woman Gazing at the Moon* (1824).

Friendly Societies Associations established in Britain to provide insurance against sickness, old age and funeral expenses. Started in the 17th century, they acted as an alternative to parish relief and charitable assistance. In the Victorian age, they were the most important form of insurance for the working-class.

Friends, Religious Society of *See* QUAKERS

Frisch, Karl von (1886–1982) Austrian zoologist. He shared the 1973 Nobel Prize in physiology or medicine with K. LORENZ and N. TINBERGEN for his pioneering work in ETHOLOGY. He deciphered the "language" of bees by studying their dance patterns.

Frisch, Max (1911–91) Swiss novelist and dramatist. His early, experimental plays include *The Chinese Wall* (1946), *The Fire Raisers* (1953), and *Andorra* (1961). Other later plays include *Biography* (1968) and *Triptych* (1979).

fritillary Common name for several genera of butterflies including large fritillaries (silverspots) of the genus *Speyeria* and small fritillaries of the genus *Boloria*. The larvae (caterpillars) are largely nocturnal. Family Nymphalidae.

Froebel, Friedrich Wilhelm August (1782–1852) German educator and influential educational theorist. In 1841 he opened the first kindergarten. He stressed the importance of pleasant surroundings, self-directed activity, physical training and play in the development of the child.

frog Tailless AMPHIBIAN, found worldwide. Frogs have long hind limbs, webbed feet and external eardrums behind the eyes. Most begin life as TADPOLES. Some frogs remain aquatic, some terrestrial, living in trees or underground. Most have teeth in the upper jaw and all have long sticky tongues attached at the front of the mouth to capture live food, usually insects. Length: 2.5–30cm (1–12in). Subclass Salientia (or Anura), divided into 17 families; the most typical genus is *Rana*. *See also* TOAD

Frondes (1648–53) Series of rebellions against oppressive government in France. The Fronde of the Parlement (1648–49) began when ANNE OF AUSTRIA tried to reduce the salaries of court officials. It gained some concessions from the regent, Louis XIV. The Fronde of the Princes (1650–53) was a rebellion of the aristocratic followers of CONDÉ, and forced the unpopular Cardinal MAZARIN into temporary exile. Condé briefly held Paris, but the rebellion soon collapsed. Under Louis XIV royal absolutism triumphed.

front In meteorology, the boundary between two air masses of different temperatures or of different densities. **Cold** fronts occur as a relatively cold and dense air mass moves under warmer air. With a **warm** front, warmer air is pushing over colder air and replacing it. An **occluded** front is composed of two fronts: a cold front overtakes a warm or stationary front. In a **stationary** front, air masses remain in the same areas.

frontier In US history, the westernmost region of white settlement. In the 17th century the frontier began at the foothills of the APPALACHIAN Mountains and gradually moved westwards until the late 19th century. Frontier notions of rugged individualism and free enterprise were promoted by Frederick Jackson Turner in *The Significance of the Frontier in American History* (1893).

Frost, Robert Lee (1874–1963) US poet. His first two volumes of lyric poems, *A Boy's Will* (1913) and *North of Boston* (1914), established his reputation. His best-known poems include: *Stopping by Woods on a Snowy Evening, The Road Not Taken* and *Mending Wall*. He received the Pulitzer Prize for poetry (1924, 1931, 1937 and 1943).

frost In meteorology, atmospheric temperatures at Earth's surface below 0°C (32°F). The visible result is usually a deposit of minute ice crystals formed on exposed surfaces from DEW and water vapour.

frostbite Freezing of living body-tissue in sub-zero temperatures. Frostbite is an effect of the body's defensive response to intense cold, which is to shut down blood vessels at the extremities in order to preserve warmth at the core of the body. Consequently, it mostly occurs in the face, ears, hands and feet. Superficial frostbite can be treated by gentle thawing. Deep frostbite, which causes tissue death, requires urgent medical treatment.

fructose (fruit sugar) Simple white monosaccharide $C_6H_{12}O_6$, found in honey, sweet fruits and flower nectar. Sweeter than SUCROSE it is made commercially by the HYDROLYSIS of beet or cane sugar.

fruit Seed-containing mature OVARY of a flowering plant. Fruits serve to disperse plants and are an important food source. They can be classified as simple, aggregate or multiple. **Simple** fruits, dry or fleshy, are produced by one ripened ovary of a single pistil, and include legumes and nuts. **Aggregate** fruits develop from several simple pistils, such as raspberry and blackberry. **Multiple** fruits develop from a flower cluster; each flower produces a fruit which merges into a single mass at maturity, such as pineapple and fig. Though considered fruits in culinary terms, apples and pears are regarded botanically as "false" fruits, as the edible parts are created by the RECEPTACLE and not the carpel walls.

Frunze Former name for BISHKEK

fuchsia Genus of shrubby plants found wild in tropical and subtropical America and parts of New Zealand. They are widely cultivated. They have oval leaves and pink, red or purple, trumpet-shaped, waxy flowers. The 100 or so species include the crimson-purple *Fuchsia procumbens* and *F. speciosa*. Family Onagraceae.

fuel Substance that is burned or otherwise modified to produce energy, usually in the form of heat. Apart from FOSSIL FUELS (coal, oil and gas) and firewood and charcoal, the term also applies to radioactive materials used in nuclear power.

Fuentes, Carlos (1928–) Mexican novelist and short story writer. His first novel was *Where the Air is Clean* (1958). Other fiction includes *Change of Skin* (1967), *The Hydra Head* (1978), *Distant Relations* (1980) and *The Campaign* (1991).

Fugard, Athol (1932–) South African playwright, director and actor. Fugard is best known for his plays *The Blood Knot* (1961), *Sizwe Bandi is Dead* (1972) and *My Children! My Africa* (1990).

fugue In music, a composition of several parts or voices where the same melodic line or theme is stated and developed in each voice so that interest in its overall development becomes cumulative. Generally the theme begins in one part and others are added in sequence. Popular in BAROQUE music, the greatest exponent of fugue was J.S. BACH.

Fujiyama (Mount Fuji) Highest mountain in Japan. An extinct volcano, it is the most sacred mountain in Japan. It is a summer and winter sports area. Height: 3,776m (12,389ft).

Fulani (Fulah or Fulbe) *c.*6 million African people living throughout W Africa. Their language belongs to the NIGER-CONGO group. Originally a pastoral people, they helped the spread of Islam throughout W Africa, establishing an empire that lasted until British colonialism in the 19th century.

Fuller, Richard Buckminster (1895–1983) US architect and engineer. Believing that only technology can solve modern world problems, he invented several revolutionary designs. The most widely used is the GEODESIC DOME. His books include *Operating Manual for Spaceship Earth* (1969).

Fuller, Roy Broadbent (1912–91) British poet and novelist. His verse includes *Collected Poems 1936–61* (1962) and *New and Collected Poems* (1985). Novels include *Image of a Society* (1956), *My Child My Sister* (1965) and *Stares* (1990).

fuller's earth Clay-like substance containing over 50% SILICA. Once used for fulling (removing oil and grease from wool), it is now used to bleach petroleum and refine vegetable oils.

Funchal Capital and chief port of MADEIRA. Founded in 1421, it is now an industrial and resort centre for the Madeira archipelago. Industries: sugar milling, distilling, wine. Pop. (1981) 44,111.

function In mathematics, rule that assigns a unique value to each element of a given set. The given set is the **domain** of the function and the set of values is the **range**. Two or more elements of the domain may be assigned the same value, but a function must assign only one value to each element of the domain. A function f maps each element x of the domain to a corresponding element (or value) y in the range. Here x and y are variables, with y dependent on x through the functional relationship f. The dependent variable y is said to be a function of the independent variable x. For example, the square-root is a function, its domain and range being the non-negative real numbers. *See also* TRIGONOMETRIC FUNCTION

functionalism Sociological and anthropological theory outlined by Emile DURKHEIM. The theory attempts to understand the function of each part of society in relation to each other and to the whole society. It attempts to explain how each separate cultural phenomenon corresponds to social "need".

fundamental forces Four basic forces that exist in physics. The most familiar, and the weakest, is GRAVITATION. The gravitational force between the Earth and an object accounts for an object's WEIGHT. Much stronger is the ELECTROMAGNETIC FORCE, which "binds" particles together. The two other forces operate only on the subatomic level. WEAK NUCLEAR FORCE, associated with the decay of particles, is intermediate in strength between the gravitational and electromagnetic force; whereas STRONG NUCLEAR FORCE associated with the "glue" that holds nuclei together is the strongest natural force. *See also* GRAND UNIFIED THEORY (GUT)

fundamentalism Movement within some Protestant denominations, particularly in the USA, which originated in the late 19th and early 20th centuries as a reaction against biblical criticism and contemporary theories of evolution. The name is derived from *The Fundamentals*, a series of 12 tracts published between 1909–15 by eminent US evangelical leaders. Fundamentalism has been loosely used to refer to any extreme orthodox element within a religion.

fungicide Chemical that kills fungi. For example, creosote is used to prevent dry rot in wood.

fungus Any of a wide variety of organisms of the kingdom FUNGI, which are unable to photosynthesize and which reproduce by means of spores and never produce cells with flagella. They include MUSHROOMS, MOULDS and YEASTS. There are *c*.100,000 species. Fungi have relatively simple structures, with no roots, stems or leaves. Their cell walls contain the polysaccharide CHITIN. The main body of a typical multicellular fungus consists of an inconspicuous network (mycelium) of fine filaments (hyphae), which contain many nuclei and which may or may not be divided into segments by cross-walls. The hypha nuclei are HAPLOID. The mycelia may develop spore-producing, often conspicuous, fruiting bodies, such as mushrooms and TOADSTOOLS. Fungal PARASITES depend on living animals or plants: SAPROPHYTES utilize the materials of dead plants and animals; and symbionts obtain food in a mutually beneficial relationship with plants. Fungi feed by secreting digestive ENZYMES onto their food, then absorbing the soluble products of digestion. Many cause diseases in crops, livestock and humans (athlete's foot). Moulds and yeasts are used in the production of BEER and CHEESE. Some fungi, such as

Penicillium, are sources of ANTIBIOTICS. *See also* KINGDOM

fur Soft, dense hair covering the skin of certain mammals, such as mink, fox and ermine. Many are hunted and killed for their pelts. Some fur-bearing animals are now protected by law because overhunting has threatened extinction.

Furies (Erthyes and Eumenides) In Greek mythology, three hideous goddesses of vengeance.

furnace Enclosed space raised to a high temperature by the combustion of fuels or by electric heating. Most furnaces are used in the extraction of metals or the making of alloys. An **arc** furnace relies on the heat generated by an electric arc (spark), often between two large carbon electrodes, which are slowly consumed. A **resistance** furnace is heated by passing an electric current through a heating element or directly through metallic material. An **induction** furnace uses ELECTROMAGNETIC INDUCTION to cause a current to flow in a metallic charge. The resulting heat is sufficient to melt the metal.

furze *See* GORSE

fuse In electrical engineering, a safety device to protect against overloading. Fuses are commonly strips of easily melted metal placed in series in an electrical circuit such that when overloaded, the fuse melts, breaking the circuit and preventing systemic damage.

fusel oil Poisonous, clear, colourless liquid with a disagreeable smell. It consists of a mixture of amyl alcohols, obtained as a by-product of the fermentation of plant materials containing sugar and starch. It is used as a solvent for waxes, resins, fats and oils and in the manufacture of explosives.

fusion, nuclear Form of nuclear reaction in which nuclei of light atoms (such as hydrogen) combine to form one or more heavier nuclei with the release of large amounts of energy. The process takes place in the Sun and other stars, and has been reproduced on Earth in the HYDROGEN BOMB. In a self-sustaining fusion reaction, the combining nuclei are in the form of a PLASMA. It is the maintenance of this state of matter that has proved difficult in harnessing fusion reaction as a controlled source of NUCLEAR ENERGY. *See also* FISSION, NUCLEAR

futurism Art movement that originated in Italy (1909). It aimed to glorify machines and to depict speed and motion by means of an adapted version of CUBISM. It was violently opposed to the study of art of the past and embraced the values of modernity. Leading futurists include the poet MARINETTI.

Fuzhou (Fuzhou, or Fu-chou) City and port on the Min Chiang river, capital of Fukien province, SE China. Fuzhou was founded in the T'ang dynasty (618–907). It was one of the first treaty ports to be opened to foreign trade (1842) and flourished as China's largest tea-exporting centre. It declined in the early 20th century. Industries: engineering, chemicals, textiles. Pop. (1993 est.) 1,290,000.

G/g is derived from the Greek gamma. *In English a* g *may be hard as in* game, *or soft, as in* page. *A following* h *gives it a variety of sounds, such as* w *in* bough.

G Symbol for the universal constant of GRAVITATION. g is also the symbol for acceleration of free fall due to Earth's gravity. One g is *c*.9.8m/s² (32ft/s²).

Gable, (William) Clark (1901–60) US film actor. His magnetism made him a screen idol for 30 years. His films include *It Happened One Night* (1934), *Gone With the Wind* (1939) and *The Misfits* (1961).

Gabon Equatorial republic on the Atlantic Coast of West Africa; the capital is LIBREVILLE. **Land and climate** Libreville lies on the 800km- (500mi) long coastline. Inland, a narrow coastal plain rises to mountains divided by deep valleys carved by the River Ogooué. Dense rainforest covers about 75% of Gabon, with tropical savanna in the E and S. Gabon has high temperatures and humidity most of the year. Libreville has a dry season between June and August. Gabon has several national parks and wildlife reserves. **Economy** Gabon's abundant natural resources, including forests, oil and gas deposits, manganese and uranium, make it one of Africa's richer countries. Minerals and fuels account for 80% of Gabon's exports. Agriculture employs *c*.75% of the workforce. Crops include bananas, cassava and sugar cane. Cocoa is grown for export. **History and politics** Portuguese explorers reached Gabon's coast in the 1470s and established a slave trade. In 1849 France established the settlement of Libreville for freed slaves. From 1889 to 1904 Gabon was part of the French Congo. From 1910 to 1957 it formed part of French Equatorial Africa. In 1960 it became an independent republic. In 1968 President Omar Bongo established a one-party state. During the 1980s his repressive policies caused increasing unrest. In 1990 he was forced to legalize opposition parties. The ruling Gabonese Democratic Party (PDG) won the 1990 elections. President Bongo, of the PDG, won the 1993 presidential elections. Under the Paris Agreement (1994), parliamentary elections were scheduled to take place in 1996 but were not held until 1997, when the PDG were resoundingly reelected.

Gaborone Capital of Botswana, S Africa. Settled in the 1890s, it was the administrative headquarters of the former Bechuanaland Protectorate. In 1966 it became capital of an independent Botswana.

Gabriel Archangel, mentioned in the Old and New Testaments, and in the Koran. The Christian Church celebrates Gabriel's feast day on 24 March.

Gabrieli Italian composers, uncle and nephew. **Andrea** (*c*.1533–86) was organist at St Mark's, Venice. His compositions developed the antiphonal use of several choirs. His nephew, **Giovanni** (*c*.1553–1612), succeeded him at St Mark's. His output included large works for voices and orchestra. He developed the CONCERTO style and was a major influence on the early BAROQUE.

Gaddafi *See* QADDAFI, MUAMMAR AL-

Gaddi, Taddeo (*c*.1300–*c*.1366) Leading member in a family of Florentine artists. Taddeo's father, **Gaddo di Zanobi** (*c*.1259–*c*.1330), was a noted painter and mosaicist. Taddeo's best-known work is the fresco series *Life of the Virgin* (completed in 1338). Taddeo's son, **Agnolo** (d.1396), also painted frescos; the most famous is the *Legend of the True Cross* (*c*.1380).

gadolinium Silvery-white metallic element (symbol Gd) of the LANTHANIDE SERIES. Chief ores are gadolinite, monazite and bastnaesite. Its uses include neutron absorption and the manufacture of certain alloys. Properties: at.no. 64; r.a.m. 157.25; r.d. 7.898; m.p. 1,311°C (2,392°F); b.p. 3,233°C (5,851°F); most common isotope Gd¹⁵⁸ (24.87%).

Gaelic Language spoken in parts of Ireland and Scotland. The two branches diverged in the 15th century and are mutually unintelligible. The Irish variety is one of the Republic of Ireland's official languages. In Scotland, Gaelic has no official status.

Gagarin, Yuri Alekseyevich (1934–68) Russian cosmonaut, the first man to orbit the Earth. On 12 April 1961 he made a single orbit in 1 hour 29 minutes. He died in a plane crash.

Gaia (Gaea) In Greek mythology, mother goddess of the Earth. Wife (and in some legends, mother) of URANUS, she bore the Titans and the CYCLOPES.

Gaia hypotheses Scientific theory that interrelates the Earth's many and varied processes – chemical, physical and biological. Popular in the 1970s, when it was proposed by James Lovelock, it shows Earth as a single living organism.

Gainsborough, Thomas (1727–88) British portrait and landscape painter. Influenced by Dutch landscape painters, he developed a style remarkable for its characterization and use of colour. His portraits, such as *Viscount Kilmorey* (1768), rivalled those of Sir Joshua Reynolds. Among his best landscapes is *The Watering Place* (1777).

GABON
AREA: 267,670sq km (103,347sq mi)
POPULATION: 1,237,000
CAPITAL (POPULATION): Libreville (418,000)
GOVERNMENT: : Multiparty republic
ETHNIC GROUPS: Fang 36%, Mpongwe 15%, Mbete 14%, Punu 12%
LANGUAGES: French (official)
RELIGIONS: Christianity (Roman Catholic 65%, Protestant 19%, African churches 11%), traditional beliefs 3%, Islam 2%
CURRENCY: CFA franc = 100 centimes

Gaitskell, Hugh Todd Naylor (1906–63) British statesman, Labour Party leader (1955–63). Gaitskill became an MP in 1945. In 1950 he became minister of state for economic affairs and then chancellor of the exchequer (1950–51). In the 1950 leadership elections he led Labour's right wing to victory over Aneurin BEVAN's challenge. A period of consensus between the two main parties, known as "Butskillism", ensued in British politics.

Galápagos Islands (Sp. *Archipiélago de Colón*) Pacific archipelago on the equator; a province of Ecuador, c.1,050km (650mi) w of mainland South America. The capital is Baquerizo Moreno, on San Cristóbal. Other main islands include Santa Cruz, San Salvador and Isabela. The islands are volcanic with sparse vegetation, except for dense forests on the high lava craters. Many animal species are unique to the islands, such as the giant land tortoises. The Galápagos National Park is a world heritage site. In 1835 Charles DARWIN spent six weeks studying the Galápagos fauna. Area: 7,845sq km (3,029sq mi) Pop. (1990) 9,785.

galaxy Huge assembly of stars, dust and gas. There are three main types, as classified by Edwin HUBBLE in 1925. **Elliptical** galaxies are round or elliptical systems, showing a gradual decrease in brightness from the centre outwards. **Spiral** galaxies are flattened, disc-shaped systems in which young stars, dust and gas are concentrated in spiral arms coiling out from a central bulge, the nucleus. **Barred spiral** galaxies are distinguished by a bright central bar from which the spiral arms emerge. **Irregular** galaxies are systems with no symmetry. Current theories suggest that all galaxies were formed from immense clouds of gas soon after the BIG BANG. Galaxies can exist singly or in clusters.

galena Grey metallic mineral, lead sulphide (PbS); the major ore of lead. It is found in hydrothermal veins and as a replacement in limestone and dolomite rocks. Hardness 2.5–2.7; s.g. 7.5.

Galicia Region of SE Poland (Western Galicia) and W Ukraine (Eastern Galicia). The major cities are KRAKÓW (Poland) and LVOV (Ukraine). After passing to Austria in 1772, Galicia became the centre of HASIDISM. After World War 1, Poland seized Western Galicia and was awarded Eastern Galicia at the 1919 Paris Conference. The 1939 partition of Poland between Nazi Germany and the Soviet Union gave most of Eastern Galicia to the Ukraine. During World War 2, almost the entire Galician Jewish population perished in the Holocaust. The region is predominantly agricultural, though there are oilfields. Major products: grain, flax, hops, potatoes, tobacco. Area: 78,500sq km (30,309sq mi).

Galicia Autonomous region in NW Spain, comprising the provinces of La Coruña, Lugo, Orense and Pontevedra; the capital is Santiago de Compostela. It was a centre of resistance to the Moorish invasion, and passed to Castile in the 13th century. Galicia has a mountainous interior. Its economy is based on livestock, fishing and

mining. Area: 29,434sq km (11,361sq mi). Pop. (1991) 2,731,669.

Galilee, Sea of (Lake Tiberius or Yam Kinneret) Freshwater lake in N Israel, fed by the River Jordan. Israel's major reservoir, it is an important fishing ground and the source of water for irrigation of the Negev Desert. The surface is c.215m (705ft) below sea-level. Area: 166sq km (64sq mi).

Galileo (1564–1642) (Galileo Galilei) Italian scientist. He disproved Aristotle's view that falling bodies fall at different rates according to weight. In 1610 he used one of the first astronomical telescopes to discover sunspots, Jupiter's major satellites and the phases of Venus. In *Sidereus Muncius* (1610) he supported the Copernican view of the Universe, with Earth orbiting the Sun. This was declared a heresy, and in 1633 he was brought before the INQUISITION and forced to recant.

gall Abnormal swelling of plant tissue stimulated by an invasion of parasitic or symbiotic organisms, including bacteria, fungi, insects and nematodes.

Galla Hamitic people who make up 40% of the population of Ethiopia, living mainly in the S. They are predominantly nomadic pastoralists and practise Christianity, Islam, and animism.

gall bladder Muscular sac, found in most vertebrates, which stores BILE. In humans it lies beneath the right lobe of the LIVER and releases bile into the DUODENUM by way of the bile duct.

Gallic Wars (58–51 BC) Campaigns in which the Romans, led by CAESAR, conquered GAUL. By 57 BC Caesar had subdued SW and N Gaul. In 56 BC he conquered the Veneti, leaders of an anti-Roman confederation, and in 55–54 BC invaded Germany and Britain. He defeated a Gallic revolt in 52 BC.

Gallipoli (Gelibolu) Peninsula and port in W Turkey, on the European side of the DARDANELLES. Colonized by the Ancient Greeks, it has been of strategic importance in the defence of Istanbul (Constantinople). It was the scene of the GALLIPOLI CAMPAIGN. Pop. (1985) 16,715.

Gallipoli Campaign (1915–16) Allied operation against the Turks during WORLD WAR 1. Some 45,000 British and French and 30,000 ANZAC troops were involved. After eight months of inconclusive fighting and more than 145,000 casualties on both sides, the Allies withdrew.

gallium Grey metallic element (symbol Ga) of group III of the periodic table. Chief sources are bauxite and some zinc ores. The metal, liquid at room temperature, is used in lasers and semiconductors. Properties: at.no. 31; r.a.m. 69.72; r.d. 5.9; m.p. 29.78°C (85.60°F); b.p. 2,403°C (4,357°F); most common isotope Ga^{69} (60.4%).

gallstone (cholelithiasis) Hard mass, usually composed of cholesterol and calcium salts, which forms in the GALL BLADDER. Gallstones may cause severe pain (biliary colic) or become lodged in the common bile duct, causing obstructive JAUNDICE or cholecystitis. Treatment is by removal of the stones themselves or of the gall bladder.

Galsworthy, John (1867–1933) British novelist and playwright. His novels deal with contemporary English upper-middle-class life. The most noted are *The Forsyte Saga* (1906–21), *A Modern Comedy* (1924–28) and *End of the Chapter* (1931–33); plays include *The Silver Box* (1906) and *Justice* (1910). He was awarded the 1932 Nobel Prize for literature.

galvanizing Coating of iron or steel articles with zinc in order to prevent CORROSION. The coating can be applied directly in a bath of molten zinc, electroplated from cold zinc sulphate solutions, or dusted on and baked.

Galway County in Connaught province, W Republic of Ireland; the county town is Galway. Bounded by the Atlantic (W), it has an indented coastline with many islands. It is mountainous in the W, low-lying in the E, and drained by the River SHANNON. It is an agricultural region. Industries: tourism, agriculture, cotton-spinning, sugar-refining, handicrafts. Area: 5,939sq km (2,293sq mi). Pop. (1991) 129,511.

Gama, Vasco da (1469–1524) Portuguese naval commander and navigator. He led an expedition around the Cape of Good Hope (1497), which opened up the sea route to India. In 1502 he led a heavily armed expedition of 20 ships and, employing brutal tactics, secured Portuguese supremacy in the Eastern spice trade.

Gambia Smallest country in mainland Africa; the capital is BANJUL. **Land and Climate** Gambia consists of a narrow strip of land bordering the River Gambia, and is enclosed by Senegal, except along its short Atlantic coastline. Near the ocean, the land is flat and the soil is salty. The middle part of the River Gambia is bordered by terraces (*banto faros*), which are flooded after heavy rains. The upper river flows through a sandstone plateau. Mangrove swamps line the river banks. Tropical savanna has been cleared for farming. The Gambia is rich in animals and birdlife. Gambia has hot, humid summers, and SW winds bring rain. In winter (November to May), dry NE winds predominate, and temperatures drop to *c.*16°C (61°F). **Economy** Agriculture employs 80% of the workforce. Main crops include cassava, millet and sorghum; groundnuts are the leading export. Tourism is becoming important. **History and politics** Portuguese mariners reached Gambia's coast in 1455 when the area was part of the Mali empire. In 1664 the British established a settlement and later founded a colony, Senegambia (1765), which included parts of The Gambia and Senegal. In 1783 this was handed over to France. In 1816 Britain founded Bathurst (now Banjul) as a base for its antislavery operations. The Gambia was a British colony from 1888 until independence in 1965. In 1970 The Gambia became a republic. In 1981 an attempted coup was defeated with the help of Senegalese troops. In 1982 The Gambia and Senegal set up a defence alliance, the Confederation of Senegambia, but this ended in 1989. In July 1994 a military group led by Yahyah Jammeh overthrew

GAMBIA	
AREA:	11,300sq km (4,363sq mi)
POPULATION:	878,000
CAPITAL (POPULATION):	Banjul (146,000)
GOVERNMENT:	Parliamentary
ETHNIC GROUPS:	Mandinka (Mandingo or Malinke) 40%, Fulani (Peul) 19%, Wolof 15%, Dyola 10%, Soninke 8%
LANGUAGES:	English (official)
RELIGIONS:	Islam 95%, Christianity 4%, traditional beliefs 1%
CURRENCY:	Dalasi = 100 butut

the president, Sir Dawda Jawara. In 1996 Jammeh was elected president, and in 1997 legislative elections his Patriotic Alliance for Reorientation and Construction (PARC) was victorious.

gamete Reproductive sex cell that joins with another sex cell to form a new organism. Female gametes (ova) are usually motionless; male gametes (sperm) often have a tail (flagellum) enabling them to swim to the ova. All gametes are HAPLOID.

gametophyte Generation of plants and algae that bears the female and male GAMETES. In flowering plants these are the germinated pollen grains (male) and the embryo sac (female) inside the ovule. *See also* ALTERNATION OF GENERATIONS; FERN

gamma radiation Form of very short wavelength ELECTROMAGNETIC RADIATION emitted from the nuclei of some radioactive atoms. High-energy gamma rays have even greater powers of penetration than X-RAYS They are used in medicine to attack cancer cells and in the food industry to kill microorganisms. *See also* RADIOACTIVITY

Gamow, George (1904–68) US nuclear physicist, b. Russia. He developed the BIG BANG theory, helped decipher the genetic code, developed the quantum theory of radioactivity and proposed the liquid-drop model of atomic nuclei. With Edward TELLER, he established the Gamow-Teller theory of beta decay.

Gandhi, Indira (1917–84) Indian stateswoman, prime minister (1966–77, 1980–84). The daughter of Jawaharlal NEHRU, she served as president of the Indian National CONGRESS PARTY (1959–60), becoming prime minister in 1966. In 1975 she was found guilty of breaking electoral rules in her 1971 re-election. She refused to resign, invoked emergency powers and imprisoned many opponents. When elections took place in 1977, the Congress Party suffered a heavy defeat. In 1980, leading a faction of the Congress Party, she returned to power. In 1984, after authorizing the use of force against Sikh dissidents in the Golden Temple at Amritsar, she was killed by a Sikh bodyguard.

Gandhi, "Mahatma" (Mohandas Karamchand) (1869–1948) Indian political and spiritual leader who led the nationalist movement (1919–47). A lawyer, he practised in South Africa

(1893–1914) where he led equal-rights campaigns, before returning to his native India. Following the massacre at AMRITSAR (1919), he launched a policy of non-violent non-cooperation with the British. Resistance methods included the famous 388km (241mi) protest march against a salt tax (1930). He also strove to raise the status of lower CASTES. After frequent imprisonments, he saw India gain independence in 1947. He was assassinated by a religious fanatic in Delhi.

Gandhi, Rajiv (1944–91) Indian politician and prime minister (1984–89). The elder son of Indira GANDHI, Rajiv Gandhi became prime minister after his mother's assassination. He worked to placate India's Sikh extremists, but his reputation was tarnished by a bribery scandal. Defeated in the 1989 election, Gandhi was assassinated campaigning for re-election in 1991.

Ganesh Elephant-headed Hindu god, son of SHIVA and PARVATI. He is the patron of learning and is said to have written down the MAHABHARATA. His birth festival is in the lunar month Bhadrapada.

Ganges (Ganga) River of N India. It rises in the Himalayas, then flows SE and empties into the Bay of Bengal through the Brahmaputra–Ganges delta. The plains of the Ganges are extremely fertile and support one of the world's most densely populated areas. In Hinduism, it is the earthly form of the Goddess Ganga, and pilgrims purify themselves in its waters. Length: 2,512km (1,560mi).

ganglion Cluster of nervous tissue containing cell bodies and SYNAPSES, usually enclosed in a fibrous sheath. In a VERTEBRATE, most ganglia occur outside the CENTRAL NERVOUS SYSTEM.

Gang of Four Radical faction that tried to seize power in China after MAO ZEDONG's death. In 1976 Mao and Prime Minister ZHOU ENLAI died, leaving a power vacuum. Zhang Chunjao, Wang Hungwen, Yao Wenyuan, and their leader JIANG QING (Mao's widow), attempted a military coup but were arrested for treason by premier HUA GUOFENG. They were sentenced to life imprisonment.

gannet Diving seabird related to the tropical booby. Gannets are heavy-bodied with tapering bills, long pointed wings, short legs and webbed feet. Their plumage is white with black wing tips. Length: 63–100cm (25–40in). Family Sulidae.

Ganymede Largest of Jupiter's Galilean satellites, with a diameter of 5,262km (3,270mi). Its cratered terrain is covered with grooves, suggesting recent geological activity.

gar Primitive freshwater bony fish found in shallow waters of North America. Its body is covered with bony diamond-shaped plates. It has a long snout studded with teeth. Length: to 300cm (10ft); Weight: to 135kg (300lb). Family Lepisosteidae.

Garbo, Greta (1905–90) Swedish film actress. Her aura of mystery and legendary romantic beauty made her an adored screen idol. Her greatest successes were *Grand Hotel* (1932), *Anna Karenina* (1935) and *Ninotchka* (1939). She retired in 1941.

García Lorca, Federico *See* LORCA, FEDERICO GARCÍA

García Márquez, Gabriel (1928–) Colombian novelist. His novel *One Hundred Years of Solitude* (1967) achieves a unique combination of realism, lyricism and mythical fantasy, making it a central text of MAGIC REALISM. Later works include *Love in the Time of Cholera* (1985), and *The General in his Labyrinth* (1989). He was awarded the 1982 Nobel Prize in literature.

Garda, Lake Largest lake in Italy, forming the border between Lombardy and Venetia. It has many tourist resorts. Area: 370sq km (143sq mi)

gardenia Genus of more than 60 species of evergreen shrubs and small trees, native to tropical and sub-tropical Asia and Africa. They have white or yellow fragrant, waxy flowers. Height: to 5.5m (18ft). Family Rubiaceae.

Garfield, James Abram (1831–81) 20th US president (1881). He served in the Civil War until 1863, when he was elected to the House of Representatives. He became Republican leader of the house in 1876. In 1880 he was the compromise presidential candidate. He was assassinated on 2 July 1881, and succeeded by Chester A. Arthur.

Garibaldi, Giuseppe (1807–82) Italian patriot who helped to bring about Italian unification. Influenced by MAZZINI, he participated in a republican rising in 1834, subsequently fleeing to South America. Returning in 1848, he defended the Roman Republic against the French. In 1860 he led his 1,000-strong band of "Red Shirts" against the Kingdom of the Two Sicilies, a dramatic episode in the RISORGIMENTO. He handed his conquests over to King VICTOR EMMANUEL II and they were incorporated into the new kingdom of Italy.

Garland, Judy (1922–69) US singer and film actress, b. Frances Gumm. Her performance in *The Wizard of Oz* (1939) made her a worldwide star. Other films include *Meet Me in St Louis* (1944), *Easter Parade* (1948) and *A Star is Born* (1954). Her daughter is the actress Liza Minnelli.

garlic Bulbous herb native to S Europe and central Asia. It has onion-like foliage and a bulb made up of sections (cloves), which are used for flavouring. Family Liliaceae; species *Allium sativum*.

garnet Two series of orthosilicate minerals found in metamorphic rocks and pegmatites. Some varieties are gemstones. Hardness 6.5–7.5; s.g. 4.

Garrick, David (1717–79) English actor, theatre manager and dramatist. He is credited with replacing the formal declamatory style of acting with easy, natural speech. After playing Shakespeare's *Richard III* in 1741, he stayed at the Drury Lane Theatre from 1742 until his retirement in 1776.

Garter, Order of the Most ancient of chivalric orders in Britain. It was created by Edward III (1348) and held its first meeting the same year. The monarch is the Grand Master and there are usually 25 knights of the order.

Garvey, Marcus (1887–1940) US black nationalist leader, b. Jamaica. In 1914 he founded the Universal Negro Improvement Association (UNIA) designed to "promote the spirit of race pride". Garvey created a "back-to-Africa" movement and established the Black Star Line shipping company. By the 1920s, he was the most influential black leader in the USA, via his *Negro World* newspaper. In 1922 the Black Star Line and the UNIA collapsed. Garvey was convicted of fraud, jailed (1925) and deported to Jamaica (1927). RASTAFARI-ANISM is influenced by his philosophy.

gas State of MATTER in which molecules are free to move in any direction; a gas spreads by DIFFUSION to fill a container of any size. Because of their low densities, most gases are poor conductors of heat and electricity (although at high voltages a gas may be ionized and become electrically conductive). When cooled, gases become liquids. Some, such as carbon dioxide, can be liquefied by pressure alone. All gases follow certain laws, such as Avogadro's law, BOYLE'S LAW, CHARLES' LAW, Graham's law and IDEAL GAS LAWS. *See also* SOLID; LIQUID; PLASMA

Gascony Former province in SW France, bounded by the PYRENEES (S) and the Bay of BISCAY (W). Part of Roman Gaul, it was later overrun by the Visigoths and the Franks. In the 6th century it was conquered by the Vascones. From 1154 to the end of the HUNDRED YEARS WAR in 1453, it was ruled by England. It was finally united to the French crown in the 16th century by HENRY IV.

gas exchange In biology, the uptake and output of gases, especially oxygen and carbon dioxide, by living organisms. In animals and other organisms that obtain their energy by AEROBIC respiration, gas exchange involves the uptake of oxygen and the output of carbon dioxide. In plants, algae and bacteria that carry out PHOTOSYNTHESIS, the opposite may occur, with a carbon dioxide uptake and oxygen output. At the cellular level, gas exchange takes place by DIFFUSION across cell MEMBRANES in solution. *See also* BREATHING; CIRCULATORY SYSTEM; RESPIRATION; RESPIRATORY SYSTEM; VENTILATION

Gaskell, Elizabeth Cleghorn (1810–65) British writer. She explored the problems of the industrial poor in her novels *Mary Barton* (1848) and *North and South* (1855). Other works include *Cranford* (1853), and an acclaimed biography of her friend Charlotte BRONTË (1857).

Gasperi, Alcide de (1881–1954) Italian statesman. In 1921 he entered the Italian parliament as a founder of the Italian People's Party. Opposed to fascism, he was imprisoned during Mussolini's regime. During World War 2, he was active in the resistance and helped to create the Christian Democratic Party. As prime minister (1945–1953), he contributed greatly to Italy's postwar recovery.

gastric juice Fluid comprising a mixture of substances, including PEPSIN and hydrochloric acid, secreted by GLANDS of the stomach. It breaks down proteins into polypeptides during DIGESTION.

gastroenteritis Inflammation of the stomach and intestines causing abdominal pain, diarrhoea and vomiting. It may be caused by infection, food poisoning or allergy. Severe cases cause dehydration.

gastropod Class of MOLLUSCS, which includes the SNAIL, SLUG, WHELK, LIMPET, ABALONE and SEA SLUG. Many possess a single spiral shell that has been produced by chemical precipitation from the mantle. Many types of gastropod live immersed in seawater, breathing through gills. Some freshwater snails, however, have lungs and need to surface for air. Slugs are entirely without shells.

gas warfare *See* CHEMICAL WARFARE

Gates, Bill (1955–) US businessman. In 1975 he co-founded Microsoft Corporation, which in the 1980s became the dominant computer SOFTWARE producer. He is noted for his innovative thinking and aggressive marketing and business tactics.

gatling gun Early MACHINE GUN, invented in 1862 by Richard Gatling. It had several barrels mounted in a cylinder that was rotated manually by a crank so that each barrel fired in turn.

GATT Acronym for the GENERAL AGREEMENT ON TARIFFS AND TRADE

gaucho Colourful COWBOY of the Argentine and Uruguayan grasslands. Originally nomadic, the mixed-blood gauchos became farmhands and superb horse soldiers. They were an important political force in the 18th and 19th centuries.

Gaudi, Antonio (1852–1926) Spanish architect, His work employs bizarre sculptural and sinuous forms, and is often associated with ART NOUVEAU. His works include the Palau Guell (1885–89), the Caso Battlo (1905–07), and the unfinished church of the Sagrada Familia, all in Barcelona.

Gaudier-Brzeska, Henri (1891–1915) French sculptor, who lived in England from 1911. A friend of Ezra POUND, he was part of the VORTICISM movement. Two of his best-known works are *The Dancer* and *Bird swallowing Fish.*

Gauguin, Eugène Henri Paul (1848–1903) French painter. His belief that form and pattern should represent mental images influenced SYMBOLISM. In 1891 he left France for Tahiti, where he was inspired by the art of many different cultures. His paintings, often of South Sea islanders, convey a sense of mystery and myth. His masterpiece is *Where do we come from? What are we? Where are we going?* (1897).

Gaul Ancient Roman name for the region roughly equivalent to modern France, Belgium, N Italy and Germany W of the Rhine. Most of Gaul, which was inhabited by Celts, was conquered (58–51 BC) in the GALLIC WARS. From the 3rd century, it was under attack by Germanic tribes who settled in N Gaul.

gaur (seladang) Species of wild cattle found in forested hilly country in India and Malaysia. Gaurs are dark brown with a white "sock" on each leg. Length: up to 3.8m (12.4ft) long. Family Bovidae; species *Bos gaurus.*

Gauss, Karl Friedrich (1777–1855) German

mathematician and physicist. He studied electricity and magnetism and areas of mathematics, such as number theory and series. The unit of magnetic flux density is named after him.

Gauteng Province in N central South Africa; the capital is JOHANNESBURG. Formed in 1994 from the TRANSVAAL as PWV (PRETORIA - WITWATERSRAND - Vereeniging), the province was renamed Gauteng in 1995. It is South Africa's smallest but most populous province. Area: 18,810sq km (7,260sq mi). Pop. (1995 est.) 7,048,300.

Gautier, Théophile (1811–72) French poet, novelist and critic. His poems, such as *Albertus* (1833), *España* (1845) and *Enamels and Cameos* (1852), exhibit the formalist aesthetic theory of art that influenced SYMBOLISM.

gavial Crocodilian native to N India. It has a long, narrow snout, a brownish back and a lighter belly. It feeds on fish. Length: to 5m (15.4ft). Family Gavialidae; species *Gavialis gangeticus*.

Gay, John (1685–1732) English poet and dramatist. His best-known work is the ballad-opera *The Beggar's Opera* (1728), a political satire and burlesque of Italian opera.

Gaya City on the Phalgu River, Bihar state, NE India. It is a pilgrimage centre sacred to both Hindus and Buddhists. Buddha received enlightenment nearby and the God Vishnu is said to have sacrificed the demon of Gaya. Pop. (1991) 292,000.

Gay-Lussac, Joseph Louis (1778–1850) French chemist and physicist. He discovered the law of combining gas volumes (Gay-Lussac's Law) and the law of gas expansion, often attributed to J.A.C. CHARLES.

Gaza Strip Strip of territory in SW Israel, bordering on the SE Mediterranean Sea. The settlement following the ARAB-ISRAELI WAR (1948–49) made it an Egyptian possession. It subsequently served as a Palestinian Arab refugee centre. Occupied by Israel from 1967, it was the scene of the INTIFADA against Israel in 1988. In 1994, under a peace agreement, its administration was taken over by the Palestinian National Authority. Area: 363sq km (140sq mi). Pop. (1994) 724,500.

gazelle Any of several species of graceful, small-to-medium antelopes native to Africa and Asia, often inhabiting plains. Most are light brown with a white rump and horns. Some can run at up to 80km/h (50mph). Family Bovidae; genus *Gazella*.

Gdańsk (Danzig) City and seaport on the Gulf of Gdańsk, N Poland; capital of Gdańsk county. Settled by Slavs in the 10th century, it was a member of the HANSEATIC LEAGUE. It was taken by Poland in the 15th century but passed to Prussia in 1793. The Treaty of VERSAILLES (1919) established Gdańsk as a free city, and annexation by Germany in 1939 precipitated World War 2. In the 1980s its shipyards became a focus of opposition to Poland's communist rulers. Industries: metallurgy, chemicals, machinery, timber. Pop. (1993) 466,500.

gear Wheel, usually toothed, attached to a rotating shaft. The teeth of one gear engage those of another in order to transmit and modify speed or direction of rotation and TORQUE.

gecko Any of about 650 species of LIZARDS, native to warm regions of the world. They owe their remarkable climbing ability to minute hooks on their feet. They make chirping calls. Length: 3–15cm (1–6in). Family Gekkonidae.

Geiger, Hans Wilhelm (1882–1945) German physicist. With Ernest RUTHERFORD, he devised the Geiger counter (1908), which is used to detect and measure the strength of radiation. In 1909 Geiger and Ernest Marsden studied the deflection of alpha particles by thin metal foil, providing the basis of Rutherford's discovery of the atomic nucleus.

gel Homogeneous mass consisting of minute particles dispersed in a liquid to form a fine network throughout the mass. A gel's appearance can be elastic or jellylike, as in GELATIN, or quite rigid and solid, as in silica gel.

gelatin Colourless or yellowish protein obtained from COLLAGEN in animal cartilages and bones. It is used in photographic film emulsions, capsules for medicines, as a culture medium for bacteria, and in foodstuffs such as jellies.

Gell-Mann, Murray (1929–) US theoretical physicist. He was awarded the 1969 Nobel Prize in physics for his application of group theory to ELEMENTARY PARTICLES, which led to the prediction of the QUARK as the basic constituent of the BARYON and MESON.

gem Any of about 100 minerals valued for their beauty, rarity and durability. Transparent stones, such as DIAMOND, RUBY, EMERALD and SAPPHIRE, are the most highly valued. PEARL, AMBER and CORAL are gems of organic origin.

Gemini (the Twins) Northern constellation, situated on the ecliptic between Taurus and Cancer. The brightest star is Beta Geminorum (Pollux).

gender Any of several categories into which nouns and pronouns can be divided for grammatical purposes. In some languages, adjectives or verbs take different forms to agree with different genders.

gene Unit by which hereditary characteristics are passed on from one generation to another in plants and animals. A gene is a length of DNA that codes for a particular protein or peptide. Genes are usually found along the CHROMOSOMES. In most cell nuclei, genes occur in pairs, one located on each of a chromosome pair. Where different forms of a gene (ALLELES) are present in a population, some forms may be recessive to others and will not be expressed unless present on both members of a chromosome pair. *See also* GENETIC CODE; GENETIC ENGINEERING; HEREDITY

General Agreement on Tariffs and Trade (GATT) United Nations agency of international trade, subsumed into the new WORLD TRADE ORGANIZATION in 1995. Founded in 1948, GATT was designed to prevent "tariff wars" (the retaliatory escalation of tariffs) and to work towards the reduction of tariff levels. Most non-communist states were party to GATT.

General Certificate of Education (GCE) Secondary education qualification gained through examination in the UK, except Scotland. Until 1988, pupils took GCE Ordinary (O-) level examinations around the age of 16; they were replaced by the GENERAL CERTIFICATE OF SECONDARY EDUCATION. GCE Advanced (A-) level examinations are taken by students at around age 18 and are used for higher education entrance.

General Certificate of Secondary Education (GCSE) Secondary education qualification gained through examination in UK, except Scotland. It replaced GCE O-level and the less demanding Certificate of Secondary Education (CSE) in 1988.

generator Device for producing electrical energy. The most common is a machine that converts the mechanical energy of a turbine or internal combustion engine into electricity by employing ELECTROMAGNETIC INDUCTION. There are two types of generators: alternating current (an alternator) and direct current (a dynamo). Each has an armature (or ring) that rotates within a magnetic field, creating an induced ELECTRIC CURRENT.

gene replacement therapy (GRT) Method of treating hereditary disorders that employs GENETIC ENGINEERING. Affected cells are removed and their faulty DNA repaired. The repaired cells are then reintroduced into the patient's body. GRT shows most promise with inherited blood disorders (such as SICKLE-CELL ANAEMIA). *See also* GENE; GENETICS

Genesis First book of the OLD TESTAMENT and of the PENTATEUCH or TORAH. It probably achieved its final form in the 5th century BC, but parts may be much older. It relates the creation of the universe, from ADAM and EVE to ABRAHAM, and from Abraham to JOSEPH and the descent into Egypt.

Genet, Jean (1910–86) French dramatist and novelist. In works such as the novel *Notre Dame des Fleurs* (1944) and *Journal du Voleur* (1949) he records his experiences as a homosexual in brothels and prisons. He employed elements of the fantastical and the bizarre in his work.

genet Cat-like carnivore of the CIVET family, native to W Europe and S and E Africa. Solitary and nocturnal, genets have slender bodies, short legs, grey to brown spotted fur, and banded tails. Length: body to 58cm (22in); tail to 53cm (21in); weight: to 2kg (4.4lb). Family Viverridae; genus *Genetta*.

genetic code Arrangement of information stored in GENES. It is the ultimate basis of HEREDITY and forms a blueprint for the entire organism. The genetic code is based on the genes that are present, which, in molecular terms, depends on the arrangement of nucleotides in the long molecules of DNA in the cell CHROMOSOMES. Each group of three nucleotides specifies, or codes, for an amino acid, or for an action such as start or stop.

genetic engineering Construction of a DNA molecule containing a desired gene. The gene is then introduced into a bacterial, fungal, plant or mammalian cell, so that the cell produces the desired protein. It has been used to produce substances such as human growth hormone, insulin and enzymes for biological washing powder.

genetic fingerprinting Forensic technique that uses genetic material, specifically the DNA within sample body cells, to identify individuals. It is used in paternity suits to detect the true father of a child, and sometimes in rape cases.

genetics Study of HEREDITY. Geneticists study how the characteristics of an individual organism depend on its GENES, how the characteristics are passed down to the next generation, and how changes may occur through MUTATION. A person's behaviour, learning ability and physiology may be explained partly by genetics, although the environment has a considerable influence too.

Geneva City at the S end of Lake Geneva, SW Switzerland. A Roman town, it was taken by the Franks in the 6th century and passed to the HOLY ROMAN EMPIRE in the 12th century. During the REFORMATION, it became the centre of PROTESTANTISM under John CALVIN. It joined the Swiss Confederation in 1814. It was the seat of the LEAGUE OF NATIONS (1919–46), and is the headquarters of the Red Cross and the World Health Organization. Industries: banking, watchmaking and jewellery, precision instruments, tourism, enamelware. Pop. (1992) 169,600.

Geneva, Lake (*Lac de Genève, Lac Léman*) Lake in SW Switzerland and E France. Crescentshaped, it lies between the ALPS and the JURA MOUNTAINS. Its S shore forms part of the French–Swiss border. It is drained to the W by the River Rhône. Length: 72km (45mi). Width: up to 14km (9mi). Area: 580sq km (224sq mi).

Geneva convention Series of agreements, beginning 1864, on the treatment of wounded soldiers and prisoners during war, and on the neutrality of the medical services.

Genghis Khan (1167–1227) Conqueror and founder of the MONGOL empire. He united the Mongol tribes in 1206 and demonstrated his military genius by capturing Peking (1215), annexing Iran, and invading Russia as far as Moscow. He ruled over the largest empire ever known.

Genoa (Genova) Seaport on the Gulf of Genoa, NW Italy; capital of Liguria region. An influential trading power during the Middle Ages, its fortunes declined in the 15th century. It has a university (1471) and an Academy of Fine Arts (1751). Industries: oil refining, motor vehicles, textiles, chemicals, paper, shipbuilding. Pop. (1992) 667,563.

genome Entire complement of genetic material carried within the CHROMOSOMES of a single cell. In effect, a genome carries all the genetic information about an individual; it is coded in sequence by the DNA that makes up the chromosomes. The term has also been applied to the whole range of GENES in a particular species. *See also* GENETICS

genotype Genetic makeup of an individual. The particular set of GENES present in each cell of an organism is distinct from the PHENOTYPE, the observable characteristics of the organism.

genus Group of closely related biological SPECIES with common characteristics. The genus name is usually a Latin or Greek noun. *See also* TAXONOMY

geochemistry Study of the chemical composition of the Earth and the changes that have resulted in it from chemical and physical processes.

geodesic dome Architectural structure of plastic and metal, based, in shape, upon triangular or polygonal facets. It was originated (1947) by R. Buckminster FULLER.

geodesic surveying Method of surveying that covers areas large enough to involve consideration of the Earth's curvature. Geodesic surveying is used to establish features such as national boundaries, and for mapping whole states or countries.

Geoffrey of Monmouth (1100–54) Welsh priest and chronicler, best known for his *History of the Kings of Britain*. Though accepted as reliable until the 17th century, Geoffrey essentially told folk tales. His book was the chief source for the legend of King ARTHUR and his knights, and it was Shakespeare's source for *King Lear* and *Cymbeline*.

geography Science studying the physical nature of the Earth and people's relationship to it. It includes land masses and features, seas, resources, climate and population.

geological time Time scale of the history of Earth. Until recently, only methods of relative dating were possible by studying the correlation of rock formations and fossils. The largest divisions of geological time are called eras, each of which is broken down into periods which, in turn, are subdivided into series or epochs.

geology Study of the materials of the Earth, their origin, arrangement, classification, change and history. Geology is divided into several categories, the major ones being mineralogy (arrangement of minerals), petrology (rocks and their combination of minerals), stratigraphy (succession of rocks in layers), palaeontology (study of fossilized remains), geomorphology (study of landforms), structural geology (classification of rocks and the forces that produced them), and environmental geology (study of use of the environment).

geomagnetism Physical properties of the Earth's magnetic field. Geomagnetism is thought to be caused by the metallic composition of the Earth's core. The gradual movements of magnetic north result from currents within the MANTLE.

geometric mean The geometric mean of n numbers is the nth root of their product. For example, the geometric mean of 8 and 2 is $\sqrt{(8 \times 2)} = 4$.

geometry Branch of mathematics concerned with shapes. **Euclidean** geometry deals with simple plane and solid figures. **Analytic** geometry (coordinate geometry), introduced by DESCARTES (1637), applies algebra to geometry and allows the study of more complex curves. **Projective** geometry, introduced by Jean-Victor Poncelet (1822), is concerned with projection of shapes. More abstraction occurred in the early 19th century with formulations of non-Euclidean geometry by Janos Bolyai and N. I. Lobachevsky, and **differential** geometry, based on the application of calculus. *See also* TOPOLOGY

geomorphology Scientific study of features of the Earth's surface and the processes that have formed them.

geophysics Study of the characteristic physical properties of the Earth as a whole system. It uses parts of CHEMISTRY, GEOLOGY, ASTRONOMY, SEISMOLOGY, METEOROLOGY and many other disciplines. From the study of seismic waves, geophysicists have deduced the Earth's interior structure.

George, Saint (active 3rd–4th century) Early Christian martyr, patron saint of England since the late Middle Ages. According to tradition he was born in Palestine and martyred probably at Lydda some time before 323. Many stories grew up about him, including the 12th-century tale of his killing a dragon to save a maiden. His feast day is 23 April.

George I (1660–1727) King of Great Britain and Ireland (1714–27) and Elector of Hanover (1698–1727). A Protestant, he succeeded Queen Anne as the first Hanoverian monarch. He favoured the WHIGS over the Tories, suspecting the latter of JACOBITE sympathies. As king of England, he preferred his native Hanover and spoke little English. As a result, power passed increasingly to ministers, especially Sir Robert WALPOLE, and Parliament.

George II (1683–1760) King of Great Britain and Ireland and Elector of Hanover (1727–1760). Son of GEORGE I, he was more German than English. Sir Robert WALPOLE dominated politics early in the reign. George survived a JACOBITE revolt (1745) and was the last British king to lead his army in battle, at Dettingen (1746). George witnessed great victories overseas in the SEVEN YEARS WAR.

George III (1738–1820) King of Great Britain and Ireland (1760–1820) and King of Hanover (1760–1820). Grandson of GEORGE II, he was the first thoroughly English monarch of his line. His reign saw the loss of the American colonies, wars with France, and the first stages of the Industrial Revolution. In 1765 he suffered his first attack of apparent insanity, now known to be symptoms of porphyria. In 1811 his son, the future GEORGE IV, was made prince regent.

George IV (1762–1830) King of Great Britain and Ireland (1820–30). He served as regent for his father, GEORGE III, from 1811. Self-indulgent and extravagant, he was bored by government but was a strong patron of the arts. His marriage to Caroline of Brunswick (1795) became a source of scandal and he contracted a legally invalid marriage with Mrs Fitzherbert in 1785.

George V (1865–1936) King of Great Britain and Northern Ireland and Emperor of India (1910–36). The second son of EDWARD VII, he married Princess Mary of Teck in 1893. In 1917 he changed the name of the royal house from the German SAXE-COBURG-GOTHA to Windsor. Honourable and devoted to duty, he maintained the popularity of the monarchy.

George VI (1895–1952) King of Great Britain and Northern Ireland (1936–52) and Emperor of India (1936–47). He became king when his brother, EDWARD VIII, abdicated. In 1923 he married Lady Elizabeth Bowes-Lyon. He refused to move his family away from London during the BLITZ. In 1949 he became head of the newly formed COMMONWEALTH. He was succeeded by ELIZABETH II.

Georgetown Capital and largest city of Guyana, at the mouth of the Demerara River. Founded in 1781 by the British, it was the capital of the united colonies of Essequibo and Demerara and was known as Stabroek during the brief Dutch occupation from 1784. Renamed Georgetown in 1812 by the British, it is the country's major port. Industries: shipbuilding, food processing, brewing and rum distilling. Pop. (1985 est.) 200,000.

Georgia Country in central Europe; the capital is TBILISI. **Land and climate** Georgia contains two autonomous republics (ABKHAZIA and Ajaria), and the province of Tskhinvali (South Ossetia). It has four geographical areas: the CAUCASUS Mountains form its N border with Russia, and include its highest peak, Mount Kazbek, at 5,042m (16,541ft); the fertile Black Sea coastal plain in the w; the E end of the Pontine Mountains forms its s borders with Turkey and Armenia; and a low plateau to the E extends into Azerbaijan. Between the mountains lies the Kura valley and Tbilisi. The climate varies from subtropical in the Black Sea lowlands, to the snow-covered, alpine Caucasus. Tbilisi has moderate rainfall, hot summers and cold winters. Forest and shrubs cover *c*.50% of Georgia. Alpine meadows lie above the tree line. **Economy** Georgia is a developing country, its economy was devastated by civil war and the break-up of the Soviet Union. Agriculture is an important activity, engaging 58% of the workforce, though the rugged terrain makes intensive farming difficult. The E region is famous for its grapes, used to make wine. The coastal lowlands produce large amounts of tea and tropical fruit, and are a major tourist destination. Georgia is rich in minerals, such as barite, coal and copper. These remain relatively unexploited, though manganese is mined relatively extensively. Georgia has potential for generating hydroelectric power, but is dependent on Ukraine, Azerbaijan and Russia for oil. **History** Georgia was an independent kingdom from *c*.4th century BC, and the Georgians formed the two Black Sea states of Colchis and Iberia in *c*.1000 BC. The Persian SASSANIDS ruled during the 3rd and 4th centuries AD. Christianity was introduced in AD 330, and the established church is independent Eastern Orthodox. In the 11th century, independence was won from the Turkish SELJUK empire. The 12th century was Georgia's greatest

---

GEORGIA
AREA: 69,700sq km (26,910sq mi)
POPULATION: 5,456,000
CAPITAL (POPULATION): Tbilisi (1,279,000)
GOVERNMENT: Multiparty republic
ETHNIC GROUPS: Georgian 70%, Armenian 8%, Russian 6%, Azerbaijani 6%, Ossetes 3%, Greek 2%, Abkhazian 2%, others 3%
LANGUAGES: Georgian (official)
RELIGIONS: Christianity (Georgian Orthodox 65%, Russian Orthodox 10%, Armenian Orthodox 8%), Islam 11%
CURRENCY: Lary

---

period of cultural, economic and military expansion. In 1555 Georgia was divided between Persia (w) and Turkey (E). In the early 19th century, it was absorbed into the Russian empire. In 1921 Georgia became a constituent republic of the SOVIET UNION. Russia combined Georgia, Armenia and Azerbaijan into a single republic of TRANSCAUCASIA. This federation was broken up in 1936, and Georgia became a separate Soviet republic. Following violent demonstrations in 1989, Georgia declared its independence (May 1991). By the end of 1991, President Gamsakhurdia's authoritarian regime had led to civil war in Tbilisi. In 1992 Eduard SHEVARDNADZE was elected president. Faced by conflict from Gamsakhurdia's supporters and secessionist movements in Abkhazia and South Ossetia, Shevardnadze called in Russian troops to defeat the rebellion. **Politics** In return for Russian support, Georgia joined the COMMONWEALTH OF INDEPENDENT STATES (CIS) and allowed Russia ultimate economic power. Minority demands for secession continued; in 1995 South Ossetia was renamed Tskhinvali and Abkhazia was granted autonomous status. Conflict continues in the region and CIS peacekeeping forces are deployed in Abkhazia.

Georgia State in SE USA, on the Atlantic Ocean, N of Florida; the capital is ATLANTA. Other major cities are Columbus, Macon and SAVANNAH. First settled in 1732, it was one of the original six states of the Confederacy in the American CIVIL WAR. In the S and E of the state is a broad coastal plain. The central area consists of the Piedmont plateau beyond which, in the N, are the Blue Ridge Mountains and the Appalachian plateau. The area is drained by the Savannah, Ogeechee and Altamaha rivers. Cotton has declined in favour of tobacco, peanuts, livestock and poultry. Chemicals, paper and timber, and the manufacture of ships, aircraft and truck bodies are increasingly significant. Area: 152,488sq km (58,876sq mi). Pop. (1996 est.) 7,193,700.

Georgian architecture Building styles in Britain and its colonies (1714–1830). The name derives from the Hanoverian kings who reigned during this period (George I–IV). The various Georgian styles

253

include PALLADIANISM, ROCOCO, NEO-CLASSICISM, GOTHIC REVIVAL and REGENCY STYLE.

Georgian language Language of GEORGIA. The most important member of the South Caucasian (Kartvelian) language family, it is used by nearly 4 million people south of the Caucasus.

geostationary orbit Location of an artificial satellite so that it remains above the same point on a planet's surface. Communications and remote-sensing satellites are often placed in geostationary orbits.

geothermal energy Heat contained in the Earth's crust. It is produced by RADIOACTIVITY within the Earth's core and by the movement of tectonic plates. It is released naturally by GEYSERS and VOLCANOES, and can be used as a power source for generating electricity. *See also* PLATE TECTONICS

geranium (Pelargonium) Genus of 400 perennial plants. They bear pink, red, purple or white flowers over a long season. Family Geraniaceae.

gerbil Nocturnal rodent native to arid areas of Asia and Africa, also a popular pet. It has long hind legs and a long tail. Its fur may be grey, brown or red. It is a subterranean herbivore. Family Cricetidae.

germ Popular term for any infectious agent. Germs can be bacteria, fungi or viruses. In biology, it denotes a rudimentary stage in plant growth.

German Indo-European language spoken by about 120 million people in Germany, Austria and Switzerland, and by German communities in other countries. High German (*Hochdeutsch*), of s Germany and Austria, is now the standard dialect. Low German (*Plattdeutsch*) was spoken widely in the N but is now declining.

German architecture Architecture of Germany including, in its early days, that of Austria. The earliest surviving buildings date from CHARLEMAGNE. They are in the ROMANESQUE style, at its best in Worms cathedral (built *c.*1180). Romanesque was superseded by GOTHIC, seen in ecclesiastical architecture and provincial buildings such as the *Rathaus* (town hall), typical of NE German towns. There is little RENAISSANCE architecture in Germany, an exception being the rebuilt facade of the *Rathaus* in Bremen. The BAROQUE period extended into the ROCOCO, an example being the elaborate Church of the *Vierzehnheiligen* (Fourteen Saints) (1772) by Balthasar Neuman. Vienna has several examples of such work. In the late 1700s NEOCLASSICISM inspired buildings in Berlin and Munich by Friedrich Schinkel, Leo von Klenze and others. New materials such as cast iron were exploited, as in Vienna's *Dianabad* (baths), by Karl Etzel (1843). Walter GROPIUS and the BAUHAUS dominated the beginning of the 20th century. In the 1930s, MIES VAN DER ROHE exemplified the INTERNATIONAL STYLE, which was replaced by the re-adoption of neoclassicism under HITLER, with "official" Nazi architect Albert Speer. After the destruction of World War 2, most new buildings adopted principles of EXPRESSIONISM or MODERNISM.

German art It dates back to the illuminated manuscripts of the 9th and 10th centuries. By the end of the Middle Ages, a flourishing tradition in wood carving had grown up in the south. In the 16th century, Germany was at the forefront of the Northern Renaissance, led by Albrecht DÜRER and Hans HOLBEIN the Younger. This was a golden age for German painting and, although Caspar FRIEDRICH made an important contribution to ROMANTICISM, it was only in the 20th century that EXPRESSIONISM and BAUHAUS achieved comparable status.

Germanic languages Group of languages, a sub-division of the INDO-EUROPEAN family. One branch (West Germanic) includes English, German, Yiddish, Dutch, Flemish, Frisian and Afrikaans; another (North Germanic) includes Swedish, Danish, Norwegian, Icelandic and Faroese.

germanium Grey-white metalloid element (symbol Ge) of group IV of the PERIODIC TABLE. A by-product of zinc ores or the combustion of certain coals, it is important in semiconductor devices. Properties: at.no. 32; r.a.m. 72.59; r.d. 5.35; m.p. 937.4°C; (1,719°F); b.p. 2,830°C (5,126°F); most common isotope Ge^{74} (36.54%).

German measles (rubella) Viral disease usually contracted in childhood. Symptoms include a sore throat, slight fever and pinkish rash. Women developing rubella during the first three months of pregnancy risk damage to the fetus.

Germany Republic in central Europe; the capital is BERLIN. **Land and climate** Germany is the fifth largest country (by area) in Europe (after Ukraine, France, Spain and Sweden), but the world's 12th most populous country. Germany can be divided into three geographical regions: the N German plain; the central highlands; and the s Central Alps. The fertile N plain is drained by the rivers ELBE, Weser and Oder. It includes the industrial centres of HAMBURG, BREMEN, HANOVER and KIEL. In the E lies the capital, Berlin, and the former East German cities of LEIPZIG, DRESDEN, and MAGDEBURG. NW Germany (especially the RHINE, RUHR and Saar valleys) is Germany's industrial heartland. It includes the cities of COLOGNE, ESSEN, DORTMUND, DÜSSELDORF and DUISBURG. The central highlands

GERMANY	
AREA: 356,910sq km (137,803sq mi)	
POPULATION: 80,569,000	
CAPITAL (POPULATION): Berlin (3,446,000)	
GOVERNMENT: Federal multiparty republic	
ETHNIC GROUPS: German 93%, Turkish 2%, Yugoslav 1%, Italian 1%, Greek, Polish, Spanish	
LANGUAGES: German (official)	
RELIGIONS: Christianity (Protestant, mainly Lutheran 45%, Roman Catholic 37%), Islam 2%	
CURRENCY: Deutschmark = 100 Pfennige	

include the HARZ MOUNTAINS and the cities of MUNICH, FRANKFURT AM MAIN, STUTTGART, NUREMBERG and AUGSBURG. Southern Germany rises to the Bavarian ALPS and Germany's highest peak, Zugspitze, at 2,963m (9,721ft). The BLACK FOREST, overlooking the Rhine valley, is a major tourist attraction. The region is drained by the DANUBE. Germany has a temperate climate. The NW is warmed by the North Sea. The Baltic lowlands in the NE are cooler. In the S, the climate becomes more continental. The North German plain contains large areas of heath. The forests of central and S Germany include pine, beech and oak. **Economy** Germany remains one of the world's greatest economic powers. Services form the largest economic sector. Machinery and transport equipment account for 50% of exports. It is the world's third-largest car producer. Other major products: ships, iron, steel, petroleum, tyres, synthetic rubber. It has the world's second-largest lignite mining industry. Other minerals: copper, potash, lead, salt, zinc, aluminium. Germany has a large agricultural sector. It is the world's second-largest producer of hops and beer, and fifth-largest wine-producer. Other products include cheese and milk, raspberries, barley, rye, pigmeat, sugar beet. **History** In *c*.2000 BC, German tribes began to displace the Celts. In the 5th century AD, they conquered much of the W Roman empire. In 486 CLOVIS I conquered S and W Germany and THURINGIA. His son CHARLEMAGNE expanded the territory and was crowned emperor (800). His empire rapidly fragmented, and the FEUDAL SYSTEM created powerful local duchies. In 918 Henry I began a century of SAXON rule, and his son OTTO I (THE GREAT) established the HOLY ROMAN EMPIRE (first Reich) (962). In 1152 FREDERICK I founded the HOHENSTAUFEN dynasty. FREDERICK II's conflict with the papacy created civil war. In 1273 Rudolf I founded the HABSBURG dynasty. City states formed alliances, such as the HANSEATIC LEAGUE. CHARLES V's reign (1519–58) brought religious and civil unrest, such as the REFORMATION and the PEASANTS' WAR. Catholic and Protestant conflict culminated in the devastating THIRTY YEARS WAR (1618–48). The reign of FREDERICK II (THE GREAT) (1740–86) saw the emergence of the state of PRUSSIA. The NAPOLEONIC WARS (1803–15) were a humiliating defeat. The Congress of VIENNA (1815) created the German Confederation. The 19th century brought growing nationalism. The REVOLUTIONS OF 1848 led to the election of BISMARCK as chancellor (1862–90). Prussian victories in the AUSTRO-PRUSSIAN WAR (1866) and the FRANCO-PRUSSIAN WAR (1870–71) created the second German Reich under the HOHENZOLLERN king, WILLIAM I. Prince von Bülow's imperial ambitions were a cause of WORLD WAR 1 (1914–18). The Treaty of VERSAILLES (1919) placed a heavy price on German defeat. WILLIAM II was forced to abdicate, and the WEIMAR REPUBLIC (1919–33) was created. Mass unemployment, crippling inflation, war reparations, and world depression created the conditions for FASCISM. The leader of the National Socialist Party, Adolf HITLER, was elected (1933) to build a THIRD REICH. NATIONAL SOCIALISM pervaded all areas of society, dissent was crushed by the GESTAPO, opposition parties and elections banned. Hitler as *Führer* became the father of the nation through GOEBBELS' propagandizing. CONCENTRATION CAMPS were set up, and armaments stockpiled. Hitler remilitarized the RHINELAND (1936), aided Franco in the Spanish CIVIL WAR (1936–39), and annexed Austria (1938). The MUNICH AGREEMENT (1938) marked the failure of appeasement, Germany invaded Czechoslovakia (March 1939) and Poland (September 1939), precipitating WORLD WAR 2. Initial success was halted by failure in the Battle of BRITAIN and Hitler's disastrous Soviet offensive (June 1941). The blanket bombing of German cities devastated German industry and morale. Faced with defeat, Hitler committed suicide (April 1945). Germany surrendered (8 May 1945), and leading Nazis faced the NUREMBERG TRIALS. Germany was divided into four military zones. COLD WAR tension increased. Following the Berlin Airlift (1949), American, British and French zones were joined to make the Federal Republic of Germany (West Germany); the Soviet zone formed the German Democratic Republic (East Germany). Berlin was also divided: East Berlin became capital of East German, BONN *de facto* capital of West Germany. Walter ULBRICHT became leader of **East Germany** (1950–71). Economic deprivation led to a revolt in 1953, which Soviet troops subdued. In 1955 East Germany joined the Warsaw Pact. From 1945–61, 4 million people crossed to the west. The BERLIN WALL was built to halt the exodus. Ulbricht was replaced by Erich HONECKER (1971–89). Relations with West Germany thawed. Honecker's refusal to adopt reforms led to civil unrest. In November 1989, a rally of 500,000 people demanded reunification, the Wall was opened, and the regime collapsed. Christian Democrats won the first free elections (March 1990). In July 1990, East and West Germany were formally unified. Konrad ADENAUER was elected as the first chancellor (1949–63) of **West Germany**. He was committed to German reunification. In 1955 West Germany became a member of NATO. The economy grew dramatically under Kiesinger (1963–69). Willy BRANDT's chancellorship (1969–74) was noted for his *Ostpolitik* (establishing better relations with the Soviet bloc). His successor was Helmut SCHMIDT (1974–82). Helmut KOHL's chancellorship (1982–) was more conservative. In December 1990, Kohl was elected in the first all-German elections since 1933. Reunification has meant massive investment to restructure the former East German economy, which has strained federal resources and entailed tax increases. High unemployment, unequal distribution of wealth, crime and the rise of neo-Nazi groups are serious political problems. Germany is a major advocate of greater European cooperation.

germination Growth of the embryo in the seed of a new plant. To germinate, a seed or spore needs favourable conditions of temperature, light, moisture and oxygen. *See also* DICOTYLEDON

Geronimo (1829–1908) Chief of the Chiricahua Apaches. He led his tribe against white settlers in Arizona for over ten years. In 1886 he surrendered his tribe and became a farmer and national celebrity.

Gershwin, George (1898–1937) US popular composer. His brother Ira Gershwin (1896–1983) mostly wrote the lyrics. He wrote scores for several musicals, such as *Lady Be Good* (1924), a jazz opera *Porgy and Bess* (1935), and some orchestral works, such as *Rhapsody in Blue* (1924).

gestalt psychology School of psychology holding that phenomena are perceived as relating to a whole, rather than the sum of their parts. It was developed from the end of the 19th century in Germany by Max Wertheimer, Wilhelm WUNDT, Wolfgang Köhler and Kurt Koffka.

Gestapo (*Geheime Staatspolizei*) State secret police of Nazi Germany. Founded in 1933 by GOERING, it became a powerful, national organization under HIMMLER from 1934, as an arm of the SS. With up to 50,000 members by 1945, it had virtually unlimited powers in suppressing opposition.

Gettysburg Address Speech by US President Abraham LINCOLN on 19 November 1863 at the dedication of the national cemetery on the battlefield of GETTYSBURG. It ended by describing democracy as "government of the people, by the people and for the people".

Gettysburg, Battle of Decisive campaign of the American CIVIL WAR, fought over three days in July 1863 near Gettysburg, Pennsylvania. The Union army of George Gordon Meade checked the invasion of Pennsylvania by the Confederate forces of Robert E. LEE. The heavy casualties prompted Abraham Lincoln's GETTYSBURG ADDRESS.

geyser Hot spring that erupts intermittently, throwing up jets of superheated water and steam, to a height of *c.*60m (197ft), followed by a shaft of steam with a thunderous roar. Geysers occur in Iceland, New Zealand and the USA.

Ghana Republic in w Africa, the capital is ACCRA. **Land and climate** Ghana (formerly the Gold Coast) faces the Gulf of Guinea in West Africa. The densely populated s coastal plains are lined by lagoons. In the sw plateau lies the ASHANTI region, and its capital KUMASI. Ghana's major river is the Volta. The Aksombo Dam (built 1964) created Lake Volta, one of the world's largest artificial lakes. Accra has a tropical climate. Rain occurs throughout the year and is especially heavy in the sw. The winter months (November–March) have a low average rainfall. Tropical savanna dominates the coastal region and the far N. Rainforest covers most of the central region. **Economy** Ghana is a low-income developing country. Agriculture

---

GHANA
AREA: 238,540sq km (92,100sq mi)
POPULATION: 16,944,000
CAPITAL (POPULATION): Accra (949,013)
GOVERNMENT: Republic
ETHNIC GROUPS: Akan 54%, Mossi 16%, Ewe 12%, Ga-Adangame 8%, Gurma 3%
LANGUAGES: English (official)
RELIGIONS: Christianity 62% (Protestant 31%, Roman Catholic 21%), traditional beliefs 21%, Islam 16%
CURRENCY: Cedi = 100 pesewas

---

employs 59% of the workforce, and accounts for over 66% of exports. Ghana is the world's fifth-largest producer of cocoa beans. Other cash crops: coffee, coconuts and palm kernels. Minerals are the second-largest export. Ghana is the world's tenth-largest producer of manganese. The Ashanti Goldfields Corporation is one of the world's largest producers. Timber is also an important export. The economy has grown significantly since 1983. **History and politics** Various African kingdoms existed in the region before the arrival of Portuguese explorers in 1471, who named it the Gold Coast after its precious mineral resource. The Dutch gained control (1642) and the Gold Coast was a centre of the 17th-century slave trade. Following the abolition of slavery (1860s), the European powers withdrew under the advance of Ashanti. In 1874 Britain colonized the region, excluding Ashanti. In 1901 Ashanti was also subdued. The British developed cacao plantations. After World War 2, nationalist demands intensified. In 1951 elections were held and Kwame NKRUMAH became prime minister. In 1957 Ghana became the first African colony to gain full independence. British Togoland was incorporated into the new state. The country was renamed Ghana after a powerful, medieval West African kingdom. In 1960 Ghana became a republic with Nkrumah as president. In 1964 Ghana became a one-party state. The economy slumped, burdened by debt, corruption, and the falling cacao price. Nkrumah was deposed in a military coup (1966). Ghana briefly returned to civilian rule (1969–72). The National Redemptive Council (NRC), led by Colonel Acheampong (1972–78), continued to nationalize industry. In 1979 Flight-Lieutenant Jerry Rawlings overthrew the government and executed opposition leaders. A civilian government was formed. In 1981 this too was toppled by Rawlings. In 1992 a new constitution paved the way for multiparty elections. Opposition parties and voters boycotted the elections, and The National Democratic Council (NDC), led by Rawlings, secured a victory. Rawlings became president in November 1992 and started a second term in 1997.

Ghats Two mountain systems in India, running parallel to the coast on both sides of the Deccan

Plateau. The Western Ghats extend from the Tapti River to Cape Comorin. The Eastern Ghats extend from the Mahānadi River to the Nilgiri Hills. Height: (Western) 900–1,500m (2,950–4,920ft); (Eastern) 600m (1,970ft). Length: (Western) 1,600km (1,000mi); (Eastern) 1,400km (875mi).

Ghent (Gent, Gand) City in NW central Belgium. A major cloth centre in the 13th century, it came under Austrian control in 1714, and was captured by the French in 1792, becoming part of Belgium in 1830. Textile factories revived its prosperity in the 19th century. Industries: plastics, chemicals, steel, electrical engineering. Pop. (1993 est.) 228,490.

Ghibelline Political faction in 13th-century Italy that supported the Hohenstaufen dynasty of the HOLY ROMAN EMPIRE, and opposed the pro-papal GUELPHS. During the struggles between FREDERICK II and the popes in the mid-13th century, Ghibellines came to designate those on the imperial side. They were defeated by the Guelphs in 1268.

Ghiberti, Lorenzo (1378–1455) Italian sculptor, goldsmith, architect, painter and writer. His bronze "Doors of Paradise" for the Baptistery in Florence are considered his masterpiece.

Ghirlandaio, Domenico (1449–94) Florentine painter, best known for his frescoes. He worked on the Sistine Chapel, his major contribution being *Christ Calling the First Apostles* (1482).

Giacometti, Alberto (1901–66) Swiss sculptor and painter, influenced by SURREALISM. He produced emaciated, dream-like figures built of plaster on a wire base.

Giant's Causeway Promontory on the N coast of Northern Ireland in County Antrim. It extends 5km (3mi) along the coast and consists of thousands of basalt columns of varying height.

gibberellin Any of a group of plant HORMONES that stimulate cell division, stem elongation and response to light and temperature.

Gibbon, Edward (1737–94) British historian. His great work is *The Decline and Fall of the Roman Empire* (1776–88).

gibbon Ape, native to forests in SE Asia. It has a shaggy brown, black or silvery coat and is very agile. It has long, powerful arms for swinging from branch to branch. Height: 41–66cm (16–26in). Family Pongidae, genus *Hyloblates*.

Gibbons, Grinling (1648–1721) English wood carver, best known for his carved fruit and flowers. There are examples of his work at St Paul's Cathedral, London, and in many country houses.

Gibbons, Orlando (1583–1625) English composer. He wrote viol fantasies and madrigals, such as *The Silver Swanne*. He composed mostly church music and was a master of POLYPHONY.

Gibbs, James (1682–1754) British architect who was inspired by Sir Christopher WREN. An invididualist, Gibbs' best-known work is the church of St Martin in the Fields, London (1722–26).

Gibraltar British crown colony, a rocky peninsula on the S coast of Spain. The MUSLIM conquest of Spain began in 711, and Gibraltar remained under Moorish control until 1462. In 1704 it was captured by an Anglo-Dutch fleet and was ceded to Britain by the Treaty of UTRECHT (1713). In 1964 it was granted extensive self-government, and a 1967 referendum showed that Gibraltarians wish to remain British. Industries: tourism, re-exportation of petroleum and petroleum products. Area: 6.5sq km (2.5sq mi). Pop. (1993 est.) 28,051.

Gide, André Paul Guillaume (1869–1951) French novelist and playwright. His works show the struggle between puritan and pagan elements. Mature works, such as *Les Faux-monnayeurs* (1926), dramatize a search for spiritual truth. He was awarded the 1947 Nobel Prize in literature.

Gielgud, Sir Arthur John (1904–) British stage and film actor and director. His excellent performances in both modern and classical roles established him as one of the century's finest actors. He played almost every major Shakespearian role. He achieved popular success in many films, such as *Arthur* (1981), *Gandhi* (1982), *The Shooting Party*, (1985) and *Prospero's Books* (1991).

gila monster Poisonous nocturnal LIZARD that lives in deserts of SW USA and N Mexico. It has a stout body, massive head, flat tail and scales of orange, yellow and black. It eats small mammals and eggs. Length: 50cm (20in). Family Helodermatidae; species *Heloderma suspectum*.

Gilbert, William (1544–1603) English physicist and physician to Elizabeth I. He was the first to recognize terrestrial MAGNETISM, and coined the terms magnetic pole, electric attraction and electric force.

Gilbert, Sir W.S. (William Schwenck) (1836–1911) English librettist and playwright. He collaborated with Sir Arthur SULLIVAN on a successful series of 14 comic operettas, nearly all first performed by the D'Oyly CARTE company. Their works include *The Mikado* (1885), *HMS Pinafore* (1878) and *The Pirates of Penzance* (1879).

Gilbert and Ellice Islands Two groups of coral islands in the W Pacific Ocean, 4,000km (2,500mi) NE of Australia. In 1915 the islands became a British colony. Separated from the Ellice Islands in 1975, the Gilbert Islands are now part of KIRIBATI. The Ellice Islands are now called TUVALU.

Gill, (Arthur) Eric (Rowton) (1882–1940) British engraver and sculptor. He designed many typefaces, including Gill sans serif (1927), and produced marvellous carved sculptures.

Gillespie, "Dizzy" (John Birks) (1917–93) US jazz trumpeter and bandleader. One of the central figures in the history of jazz, he helped found BEBOP with Charlie PARKER.

Gillray, James (1757–1815) English caricaturist, whose witty cartoons were famous in Europe. His caricatures include "Farmer George" (George III) and "Temperance Enjoying a Frugal Meal".

gills Organs through which most fish, some larval amphibians, such as tadpoles, and many aquatic invertebrates obtain oxygen from water. When a fish breathes it opens its mouth, draws in water and shuts its mouth again. Water is forced through the gill slits, over the gills, and out into the surrounding water. Oxygen is absorbed into small capillary blood vessels, and at the same time, waste carbon dioxide carried by the blood diffuses into the water.

ginger Herbaceous perennial plant native to tropical E Asia and Indonesia and grown commercially elsewhere. It has tuberous roots and yellow-green flowers. The kitchen spice is made from the tubers of *Zingiber officinale*. Family Zingiberaceae.

ginkgo (maidenhair tree) Oldest living species of GYMNOSPERM, native to temperate regions of China, occurring only rarely in the wild. It dates from the late Permian period. It has fan-shaped leaves, small, foul-smelling fruits and edible, nut-like seeds. Height: to 30m (100ft). Phylum Ginkgophyta; species *Ginkgo biloba*.

Ginsberg, Allen (1926–97) US poet. His work was influenced by ZEN, meditation and drug use. His most famous poems are *Howl* (1956), which established him as the leading poet of the BEAT MOVEMENT, and *Kaddish for Naomi Ginsberg, 1894–1956* (1961), a lament for his mother.

ginseng Either of two perennial plants found in the USA (*Panax quinquefolius*) and E Asia (*P. ginseng*). It has yellow-green flowers and compound leaves. The dried tuberous roots are used in Chinese traditional medicine. Height: to 51cm (20in). Family Araliaceae.

Giorgione, Il (*c*.1478–1510) Italian painter. He was one of the major painters of the Venetian High RENAISSANCE. He had a mysterious romantic style exemplified by *Tempest* (*c*.1505).

Giotto (di Bondone) (1266–1337) Italian painter and architect, an important figure of the early RENAISSANCE. His best work is the *Lives of the Virgin and Christ* (*c*.1305–08) in the Arena Chapel, Padua.

giraffe Herbivorous mammal native to Africa. It has a very long neck, a short tufted mane, and two to four skin-covered horns. The legs are long, slender and bony. Their coats are pale brown with red-brown blotches. Height: to 5.5m (18ft). Family Giraffidae; species *Giraffa camelopardalis.*

Girl Guides Organization founded in England in 1910 by Agnes Baden-Powell, sister of Lord BADEN-POWELL, founder of the BOY SCOUTS. They are divided into three groups, Brownie Guides, Guides and Ranger Guides, according to age.

Girondins Political group in the FRENCH REVOLUTION named after deputies from Gironde, SW France. From 1792 the relatively moderate and middle-class Girondins tried to prevent the execution of LOUIS XVI and reduce the power of Paris. They were expelled from the National Congress by the JACOBINS in 1793, and their leaders executed.

Giscard d'Estaing, Valéry (1926–) French statesman, president (1974–81). He was elected to the National Assembly (1956). In 1974, as the candidate of the right, he defeated François MITTER-

RAND to become president, but lost to him in 1981. In 1988 he was elected leader of the Union for French Democracy (UDF), a centre-right alliance.

Giulio Romano (1492–1546) Italian painter and architect. One of the founders of MANNERISM, he was the chief assistant to RAPHAEL in his youth. His later work was considered pornographic and he had to flee from Rome to Mantua, where in 1526 he began his famous *Palazzo del Tè*.

Giza (Al-Jīzah) City in N Egypt. It is the site of the Great SPHINX, the PYRAMID of Khufu (Cheops) and Egypt's film industry. A suburb of Cairo, it is a resort and agricultural centre, with cotton textiles, footwear and cigarette-manufacturing industries. Pop. (1990 est.) 2,156,000.

glacier Large mass of ice, mainly recrystallized snow, which creeps downslope or outwards in all directions due to the stress of its own weight. The flow terminates where the rate of melting is equal to the advance of the glacier. There are three main types: the **mountain** or **valley** glacier, originating above the snow line in mountain regions; the **piedmont**, which develops when valley glaciers spread out over lowland; and the **ice-sheet** and ICE-CAP.

gladiolus Genus of 250 species of PERENNIAL flowering plants native to Europe and Africa but cultivated widely. A gladiolus passes the dry season as a CORM, which sprouts in spring to produce funnel-shaped flowers and tall, lance-shaped leaves. Height: to 1m (3ft). Family Iridaceae.

Gladstone, William Ewart (1809–98) British statesman, prime minister (1868–74, 1880–85, 1886, 1892–94). He entered Parliament as a Tory (1832), but joined the Whigs and then, under his leadership, the Liberals (1859). He was a social reformer and Christian moralist. His adoption of a policy of home rule for Ireland in 1886 split his party and dominated his fourth ministry.

Glamorganshire (Morganwg) Former county in S Wales, divided into West, Mid and South Glamorgan. The Romans invaded in the 1st century AD. Christianity spread through the region in the 6th century. In Norman times Glamorgan became a border territory owing allegiance to the English crown. In the 15th century it suffered during the rebellion of Owain GLYN DŴR. Created as a county in 1536, it underwent rapid industrialization owing to its coal industry. Area: 2,119sq km (818sq mi).

gland Cell or tissue that manufactures and secretes special substances. There are two basic types. Exocrine glands make such substances as hydrochloric acid, mucus, sweat, sebaceous fluids and ENZYMES, and secrete these through ducts to an external or internal body surface. Endocrine glands secrete HORMONES directly into the bloodstream. *See also* ENDOCRINE SYSTEM

glandular fever (infectious mononucleosis) Acute disease, usually of young people, caused by the Epstein-Barr virus. There are an increased number of white cells (monocytes) in the blood and symptoms include fever, painful enlargement of the

LYMPH nodes and pronounced lassitude. There may be a sore throat, skin rash and digestive disorder.

Glaser, Donald Arthur (1926–) US physicist who invented the BUBBLE CHAMBER, using it to study ELEMENTARY PARTICLES. He won the 1960 Nobel Prize in physics.

Glasgow City and port on the River Clyde, Strathclyde Region, SW central Scotland. Founded in the 6th century, it developed with the American tobacco trade in the 18th century and the cotton trade in the 19th century. Nearby coalfields and the Clyde estuary promoted the growth of heavy industry, chiefly iron and steel, and shipbuilding (now in decline). Industries: shipbuilding, heavy engineering, flour milling, brewing, textiles, tobacco, chemicals, printing. Pop. (1991) 662,853.

glasnost (Rus. openness) Term adopted by Mikhail GORBACHEV to express his more liberal social policy. One result was widespread popular criticism of the Soviet system, leading to the break-up of the Soviet Union. *See also* PERESTROIKA

Glass, Philip (1937–) US composer. The hypnotic repetition of short motifs within a simple harmonic idiom characterizes him as a minimalist composer. In addition to many operas, he has written instrumental and chamber works.

glass Brittle, transparent material. It is made by melting together silica (sand), sodium carbonate (soda) and calcium carbonate (limestone). It can be worked only while hot and pliable. Soda-lime glass is used in the manufacture of bottles and drinking vessels. Flint glass refracts light well and is used in lenses and prisms. Toughened glass (laminated with plastic) is used in car windscreens. Glass is also used in optical fibres.

glass fibre Glass in the form of fine filaments. It is made by forcing molten glass through fine metal nozzles (spinnerets). The resulting continuous filaments are usually bundled together to form strands. These may then be chopped, twisted, or woven. It is used for heat insulation (as glass wool), fabrics, and with a plastic resin to make GRP (glass-reinforced plastic).

glass snake (glass lizard) Legless LIZARD found in North America, Eurasia and Africa. The cylindrical body has a groove along each side and is mostly brown or green. Length: 60–120cm (24–48in). Family Anguidae; genus *Ophisaurus*.

glaucoma Condition in which pressure within the eye is increased due to an excess of aqueous humour, the fluid within the chamber. Most frequently found in the over 40s, the sight-threatening disorder cannot be cured but is managed with drugs and surgery.

Glazunov, Alexander Constantinovich (1865–1936) Russian composer whose works include eight symphonies, chamber music, two violin concertos and the ballets *Raymonda* (1897) and *The Seasons* (1898).

Glendower, Owen *See* GLYN DŴR, OWAIN

Glenn, John Herschel Jr. (1921–) First US astronaut to orbit the Earth (February 20, 1962). He made three orbits in *Friendship 7*. Glenn later became a Democrat senator from Ohio.

gliding Leisure activity involving flight in a glider. The unpowered glider is launched off the ground by a sling mechanism or towed by a small aircraft and then released. Once airborne, gliders descend relative to the surrounding air. If this air is a rising updraught, a glider may gain altitude for a while, thus prolonging the flight. *See also* HANG GLIDING

Glinka, Mikhail (1804–57) Russian composer. His two operas, *A Life for the Czar* (1836) and *Ruslan and Ludmila* (1841), inspired the RUSSIAN FIVE. Later in his life he lived in Italy and Spain, writing songs and orchestral music.

global warming Trend towards higher average temperatures on Earth's surface. During the last few million years, there have been several periods when surface temperatures have been significantly higher or lower than at present. During cold periods (ice ages) much of the land area has been covered by glaciers. The Earth is currently in the middle of a warm period (inter-glacial), which began about 10,000 years ago. Since the 1960s, some scientists have called attention to signs that the Earth is becoming unnaturally warmer as the result of an increased GREENHOUSE EFFECT.

globular cluster Near-spherical cluster of very old stars in the halo of our GALAXY and others. Globular clusters contain anything from 100,000 to several million stars, concentrated so tightly near the centre that they cannot be separately distinguished by ground-based telescopes.

glockenspiel Percussion musical instrument with a bell-like sound. Its tuned metal bars are struck with a hammer, either freehand or from a miniature keyboard.

Glorious Revolution (1688–89) Abdication of JAMES II of England and his replacement with WILLIAM III (OF ORANGE) and MARY II. After James had antagonized powerful subjects by his favour towards Roman Catholics, political leaders invited William to take the throne. William landed in November and James fled to France.

Gloucester County town of GLOUCESTERSHIRE, on the River SEVERN, W England. It was the Roman city of Glevum and capital of Mercia in Saxon times. There is an 11th-century cathedral where Edward II is buried. Industries: agricultural machinery, aircraft components, railway equipment, fishing. Pop. (1991) 101,608.

Gloucestershire County in SW England; the county town is GLOUCESTER. Other towns include Cheltenham and Stroud. There was a strong Roman presence in the county. Later it was a centre for coal mining and the wool industry. The Cotswold Hills sustain dairy and arable farming. The fertile SEVERN valley is devoted to dairying. Sheep are raised in the Forest of Dean and the Wye valley. Industries: engineering, scientific instruments, plastics. Area: 2,642sq km (1,020sq mi). Pop. (1991) 528,370.

glow-worm Any of a number of wingless female BEETLES or beetle larvae of the genus *Lampyris* that possess organs that emit a glow of light, and especially the European beetle *Lampyris noctiluca*. A winged male is known as a FIREFLY. Family Lampyridae.

Gluck, Christoph Willibald von (1714–87) German operatic composer. His early operas were in the Italian tradition. In *Orfeo ed Euridice* (1762) he attempted to unify musical and dramatic components. He turned to the French tradition in *Iphigénie en Tauride* (1779).

glucose (dextrose) Colourless crystalline sugar ($C_6H_{12}O_6$) occurring in fruit and honey. It is the key substance in the METABOLISM of living things. Its polymers include CELLULOSE, GLYCOGEN and STARCH. It is prepared commercially by the hydrolysis of starch. It is used in food and pharmaceuticals.

glue Adhesive made by boiling animal skin, bones, horns and hooves. Vegetable glues are made from starch, rubber, soya beans and other sources.

gluten Main protein substance in wheat flour. Not present in barley, oats or maize, gluten contributes the elasticity to dough.

glycerol (glycerine) Thick, syrupy, sweet liquid (propane-1,2,3,-triol $CH_2OHCH(OH)CH_2OH$) obtained from animal and vegetable fats and oils, or propene. It is used in the manufacture of various products, including plastics, explosives and foods.

glycogen Carbohydrate stored in the body, mainly by the liver and muscles. Glycogen is a polymer of GLUCOSE. When the body needs energy, glycogen is broken down to glucose. *See also* RESPIRATION

Glyn Dwr, Owain (Owen Glendower) (*c*.1359–1416) Welsh leader. A member of the house of Powys, he led a revolt against English rule (1400). Proclaimed Prince of Wales, he won temporary alliances with the Mortimer and Percy families in England and captured Harlech and Aberystwyth castles. He lost both castles by 1409, retreating to the hills to maintain guerrilla warfare against the English until 1412.

GMT Abbreviation of GREENWICH MEAN TIME

gnat Common name for several small flies, mainly of the family Culicidae, the female of which bites human beings. *See also* MOSQUITO.

gneiss METAMORPHIC ROCK with a distinctive layering or banding. The darker minerals are likely to be hornblende, augite, mica or dark feldspar.

Gnosticism Religious movement, embracing numerous sects, based on *gnosis*. This was occult knowledge that released the spiritual part of human beings from the evil bondage of the material world. Gnosticism became widespread by the 2nd century AD and competed with Christianity.

gnu (wildebeest) Large, ox-like African ANTELOPE. The white-tailed gnu (*Connochaetes gnou*) is almost extinct. The brindled gnu (*Connochaetes taurinus*) lives in E and S Africa, where large herds migrate annually. It has a massive, buffalo-like head and a slender body. Both sexes have horns.

Length: up to 2.4m (7.8ft); height: 1.3m (4ft); weight: up to 275kg (600lb). Family Bovidae.

Goa State in SW India, on the Arabian Sea; the capital is Panaji. It was ruled by Hindu dynasties until it came under Muslim domination in the 15th century. Captured by the Portuguese in 1510, it became a flourishing trade centre. It was annexed by India in 1962 and made a Union territory of India. In 1987 Goa was created a separate state. Goa's products include rice, cashews, spices, pharmaceutical products, footwear and pesticides. Area: 3,702sq km (1,429sq mi). Pop. (1991) 1,169,793

goat Horned RUMINANT raised for milk, meat, leather and hair. Closely related to sheep, wild species are nomadic, living in rugged mountains. The five species include the ibex (*Capra ibex*), markhor (*Capra falconeri*) and the pasang (*Capra aegagrus*). Length: to 1.4m (4.5ft); height: to 0.85m (2.8ft). Family Bovidae; genus *Capra*.

goatsucker Common name for various large-mouthed, nocturnal birds of the order Caprimulgiformes. Widely distributed in warm areas, they include the frogmouth, nighthawk, nightjar, potoo and whippoorwill. Length: 15–30cm (6–12in). Family Caprimulgidae.

Gobelins, Manufacture nationale des State-controlled TAPESTRY factory in Paris, founded *c*.1440 by Jean Gobelin. The factory converted from a dyeworks to making tapestry (1601).

Gobi (Sha-moh) Desert area in central Asia, extending over much of S Mongolia and N China. One of the world's largest deserts, it is on a plateau, 900–1,500m (3,000–5,000ft) high. The fringes are grassy and inhabited by nomadic Mongolian tribes who rear sheep and goats. The Gobi has cold winters, hot summers, and fierce winds and sandstorms. Area: *c*.1,295,000sq km (500,000sq mi).

Gobind Singh (1666–1708) Tenth and last Sikh guru, who laid the foundations of Sikh militarism. In 1699 he created the *Khalsa*, a military fraternity of devout Sikhs, which became the basis of the Sikh army he led against the MOGUL empire. The wearing of the turban and the common attachment of Singh ("lion") to Sikh names date from his reign.

God Supernatural, divine, and usually immortal being worshipped by followers of a polytheistic religion such as those of ancient Greece and Rome. Also a single supreme being, creator of the universe, as worshipped by the followers of monotheistic religions such as JUDAISM or ISLAM. ALLAH is God of Islam and YAHWEH is God of Judaism. CHRISTIANITY, a monotheistic religion, conceives of one God with three elements – Father, Son and Holy Spirit. In HINDUISM, BRAHMA is considered the soul of the world, but there are lesser gods. *See also* POLYTHEISM; MONOTHEISM; AGNOSTICISM; ATHEISM; BUDDHISM; DEISM; ZEUS

Godard, Jean-Luc (1930–) French film director whose imaginative flair revolutionized film-making. He produced the respected science-fiction film *Alphaville* (1965), and his political sketches, such as *Weekend* (1968) and *Tout va bien* (1972), transformed film as propaganda.

Goddard, Robert Hutchings (1882–1945) US physicist and pioneer in rocket development. He developed and launched (1926) the first liquid-fuelled rocket.

Godiva, Lady (d. *c*.1080) English benefactress, wife of Leofric, Earl of Mercia. According to tradition, she rode naked through the streets of Coventry in 1040 to persuade her husband to reduce the burden of taxation.

Godthåb *See* NUUK

Godunov, Boris (1551–1605) Tsar of Russia (1598–1605). The chief minister (and brother-in-law) of IVAN IV, he became regent to Ivan's son Fyodor after Ivan's death. He was popularly supposed to have murdered Fyodor's brother and heir, Dmitri, in 1591. Boris gained recognition for the independence of the Russian Orthodox Church.

Goebbels, Joseph (1897–1945) German Nazi leader. When the Nazis came to power in 1933, he became minister of propaganda. He took total control of the media, which he exploited to support Nazi policy. He committed suicide with his entire family in April 1945.

Goering, Hermann Wilhelm (1893–1946) German Nazi leader. As commander of the Luftwaffe (air force) from 1933, and overall director of economic affairs from 1936, he was second to HITLER. Captured in 1945, he was sentenced to death at the NUREMBERG TRIALS but committed suicide.

Goethe, Johann Wolfgang von (1749–1832) German poet. He wrote simple love lyrics, profound philosophical poems and scientific theories. His drama *Götz von Berlichingen* (1773) and his novel *Die Leiden des Jungen Werthers* (1774) are seminal works of ROMANTICISM. His most famous work, the tragic and wide-reaching drama *Faust*, is in two parts: *Part 1* (1808), *Part 2* (1832).

Gogol, Nikolai (1809–52) Russian novelist and dramatist. He made his reputation with stories, such as *The Nose* (1835), and the drama *The Government Inspector* (1836). Later major works include *Dead Souls* (1842) and *The Overcoat* (1842).

Golan Heights Range of hills in sw Syria on the border with Israel. During the Arab-Israeli War of 1967, Israel occupied the area and later annexed it. Of great strategic importance to Israel, it remains a source of conflict between the two countries. Area: 1,150sq km (444sq mi). Pop. (1983 est.) 19,700.

gold Naturally occurring metallic element, symbol Au. Gold is used in jewellery, in electronic equipment, and as a form of money. Gold in the form of a COLLOID is sometimes used in colouring glass. The metal is unreactive, but dissolves in aqua regia, a mixture of nitric and hydrochloric acids. Properties: at. no. 97; r.a.m. 196.9665; s.g. 19.30; m.p. 1,063°C (1,945°F); b.p. 2,800°C (5,072°F).

goldcrest Smallest British bird. Its head is capped with bright orange and a black stripe. Its body is green and its wings are black with a white

stripe. Length: about 8.4cm (3.3in). Family Muscicapidae; species *Regulus regulus*.

Golden Fleece In Greek mythology, fleece of the ram that saved Helle and Phrixus from their stepmother Ino. On arrival in Colchis, Phrixus sacrificed the ram and hung the fleece in a wood guarded by a dragon. The fleece was seized by JASON and the ARGONAUTS.

Golden Horde Name given to the Mongol state established in s Russia in the early 13th century. The state derived from the conquests of GENGHIS KHAN and was extended by his successors, who took over the whole of the Russian state centred on Kiev. It was conquered by Tamerlane in the late 14th century and subsequently split up.

goldfinch Any of various small, seed-eating birds of the genus *Carduelis*. The males of the American goldfinches, such as *C. tristis*, have yellow plumage in the summer. The red-faced European goldfinch (*C. carduelis*) has a brownish body with yellow and black wings. Family Fringillidae.

goldfish Freshwater CARP originally found in China. It was domesticated there *c*.1,000 years ago. The wild form is plain and brownish, but selective breeding has produced a variety of colours. Family Cyprinidae; species *Carassius auratus*.

Golding, Sir William (Gerald) (1911–93) British novelist. He achieved fame with his first novel, *Lord of the Flies* (1954). Other novels include *The Spire* (1964) and the trilogy *The Ends of the Earth* (1991), which incorporates the Booker Prize-winning *Rites of Passage* (1980). He was awarded the 1983 Nobel Prize in literature.

gold rush Rapid influx of population in response to reports of the discovery of gold. The largest gold rush brought about 100,000 prospectors to California (1849–50). Some of the diggers, known as Forty-Niners, went on to Australia (1851–53). There were also gold rushes to the WITWATERSRAND, South Africa (1886), to the Klondike in the Yukon, Canada (1896), and to Alaska (1898).

Goldsmith, Oliver (1730–74) Irish writer. His work includes the essay *The Citizen of the World* (1762), the poem *The Deserted Village* (1770), the novel *The Vicar of Wakefield* (1766) and the play *She Stoops to Conquer* (1773).

Goldwyn, Samuel (1882–1974) US film producer, b. Poland. He was noted for his commercially successful films, including *Wuthering Heights* (1939), *The Best Years of Our Lives* (1946), *Guys and Dolls* (1955), and *Porgy and Bess* (1959). He formed Goldwyn Pictures in 1917 and later merged with Louis B. Mayer to form Metro-Goldwyn-Mayer (1924).

golf Game in which a small, hard ball is struck by a club. The object of the game is to hit the ball into a sequence of holes (usually 18), in the least possible number of shots. The length of each hole varies from *c*.100–500yd (90–450m). Each hole consists of a tee, from where the player hits the first shot; a fairway of mown grass bordered by trees and longer grass, known as the rough; and a green, a putting area of smooth, short grass and the site of the hole. A player may have to circumvent hazards, such as ponds or bunkers. Each hole is given a par – the number of shots it should take to complete it.

golgi body Collection of microscopic vesicles or packets near the nucleus of many living cells. It is a part of a cell's ENDOPLASMIC RETICULUM, specialized for the purpose of packaging and dispatching proteins made by the cell.

Goliath In the OLD TESTAMENT, the PHILISTINE giant slain by the shepherd boy DAVID (1 Samuel 17). David killed Goliath with a slingshot, hitting him between the eyes with a stone.

Gómez, Juan Vicente (1857–1935) Ruler of Venezuela (1908–35). Vice-president under Cipriano Castro, he seized power during Castro's absence abroad and ruled either directly as elected president (1908–15, 1922–29, 1931–35) or through puppet leaders, until his death. His rule was autocratic and intolerant of opposition.

Gomulka, Wladyslaw (1905–82) Polish communist leader. He rose through party ranks to become first secretary and deputy prime minister (1945), but was dismissed during a Stalinist purge (1948). Reinstated (1956), he adopted liberal policies that made him popular at home and were accepted by Moscow. Steep rises in food prices (1970) led to his resignation.

gonad Primary reproductive organ of male and female animals, in which develop the GAMETES, or sex cells. The gonad in the male is a testis and in the female an ovary. Hermaphrodite animals possess both types.

Goncourt, Huot de, Edmond Louis Antoine and **Jules Alfred** French novelists and social historians, Edmond (1822–96) and Jules (1830–70). They wrote in collaboration until Jules died of syphilis. They are famous for *The Journal of the Goncourts* (1836–40). Edmond wrote the novels *La Fille Elisa* (1877) and *Les Frères Zemganno* (1879). In his will, he provided for the *Prix Goncourt*, France's top literary award.

Gondwanaland Southern supercontinent. It began to break away from the single land mass PANGAEA *c*.200 million years ago and formed South America, Africa, India, Australia and Antarctica. The northern supercontinent, which eventually became North America and Eurasia was Laurasia.

gonorrhoea SEXUALLY TRANSMITTED DISEASE caused by the bacterium *Neisseria gonorrhoeae*, giving rise to inflammation of the genital tract. Symptoms include pain on urination and the passing of pus. Some infected women experience no symptoms. The condition is treated with antibiotics. If not treated, it may spread, causing sterility and threatening other organs in the body; there is a risk of blindness in a baby born to an infected mother.

Good Friday Friday before EASTER Day. It is observed by all Christians as marking the day of the crucifixion of Jesus.

goose Widely distributed waterfowl, related to the DUCK and SWAN. Geese have blunt bills, long necks, shortish legs, webbed feet and, in the wild, a combination of grey, brown, black and white dense plumage underlaid by down. They live near fresh or brackish water and spend time on land, grazing on meadow grasses. Wild geese breed in colonies, mate for life, and build grass-and-twig, down-lined nests for 3–12 eggs. There are 14 species. Weight: 1.4–5.9kg (3–13lb). Family Anatidae.

gooseberry Hardy, deciduous, spiny shrub and its edible fruit. The fruit is generally green and hairy. Family Grossulariaceae; species *Ribes grossularia*.

gopher Small, stout burrowing rodent of North and Central America. It has fur-lined external cheek pouches and long incisor teeth outside the lips. It lives underground, digging tunnels to find roots and tubers, and for shelter and food storage. Length: 13–46cm (5–18in). Family Geomyidae.

Gorbachev, Mikhail Sergeyevich (1931–) Soviet statesman, president of the Soviet Union (1985–91). Secretary of the Communist Party from 1985, he embarked on a programme of reform based on two principles: PERESTROIKA and GLASNOST. He agreed to arms limitation treaties with the USA and acquiesced to the demolition of the communist regimes in Eastern Europe (1989–90), effectively ending the COLD WAR. Having strengthened his presidential powers in 1990, he was forced to resign in 1991 by opponents eager to grant independence to the constituent republics of the Soviet Union. He won the Nobel Peace Prize in 1990.

Gordimer, Nadine (1923–) South African author. Her works, critical of apartheid, are concerned with politics and social morality. Her novels include *The Lying Days* (1953), *The Guest of Honour* (1970), *The Conservationist* (1974) and *My Son's Story* (1990). She won the 1991 Nobel Prize for literature.

Gordon, Charles George (1833–85) British soldier and administrator. He fought in the CRIMEAN WAR and OPIUM WAR. He was governor-general of the Sudan (1877–80), and returned to Khartoum in 1884 to evacuate Egyptian forces threatened by the MAHDI. He was killed two days before the arrival of a relief force.

Gordon Riots (1780) Violent demonstrations against Roman Catholics in London, England. Protestant extremists led by Lord George Gordon (1751–93) marched on Parliament to protest against the Catholic Relief Act (1778), which lifted some restrictions on Catholics. The march degenerated into a riot; *c*.450 people were killed or injured.

Gore, Al (Albert Arnold) (1948–) US statesman, vice-president (1993–). A Democratic representative for Tennessee (1977–85) and the Senate (1985–93). Bill CLINTON's re-election in November 1996 saw Gore begin a second term as deputy.

Górecki, Henryk (1933–) Polish composer. His later output is inspired by medieval Polish chants and Renaissance polyphony.

Gorgon In Greek mythology, three monsters named Stheno, Euryale and the mortal MEDUSA. With gold wings and snakes for hair, they turned anyone who looked directly at them to stone. PERSEUS killed Medusa using his shield as a mirror.

gorilla Powerfully built great ape native to the forests of equatorial Africa. The largest primate, it is brown or black, with long arms and short legs. It walks on all fours and is herbivorous. Height: to 175cm (70in); weight: 140–180kg (308–396lb). Family Pongidae; species *Gorilla gorilla*.

Gorky, Maxim (1868–1936) Russian dramatist and writer. He championed the worker in *Sketches and Stories* (1898), in the play *The Lower Depths* (1902) and in the novel *Mother* (1907). He wrote autobiographical volumes (1913–23) and plays. He lived in intermittent exile after 1907.

gorse (furze) Any of several dense thorny shrubs found mainly in European heathland; genus *Ulex*; family Fabaceae/Leguminosae. The common European species, *U. europaea*, bears yellow flowers.

gospel Central content of the Christian faith, the good news (*god spell* in Old English) that human sins are forgiven and that all sinners are redeemed. The first four books of the NEW TESTAMENT are known as the four Gospels.

gospel music African-American vocal church music. It arose in the depression of the 1930s from the fusion of Protestant hymn harmony with African rhythmic and melodic features. It emphasizes the "good news" of revivalist Christianity.

Goths Ancient Germanic people, groups of whom settled near the Black Sea in the 2nd–3rd centuries AD. The **Visigoths** were driven westwards into Roman territory by the HUNS in 376, culminating in their sacking Rome under ALARIC in 410. They settled in sw France, then, driven out by the Franks in the early 6th century, in Spain. Some groups united to create the **Ostrogoths**, who conquered Italy under THEODORIC THE GREAT (489). They held Italy until conquered by the Byzantines.

Gothenburg (Göteborg) City in sw Sweden, at the confluence of the Göta and Kattegat rivers; Sweden's chief seaport and second-largest city. Founded in 1619, it flourished as a commercial centre. Industries: shipbuilding, vehicles, food processing, chemicals, textiles. Pop. (1993) 437,313.

Gothic architecture Architecture of medieval Europe (12th–16th centuries). It is characterized by the pointed arch, ribbed vault, and the introduction of flying buttresses. The style is religious in inspiration and ecclesiastical in nature. Its greatest, most characteristic expression is the cathedral.

Gothic novel Genre of English fiction popular in the late 18th and early 19th centuries; part of the romantic movement. Horace WALPOLE wrote an important prototype, *The Castle of Otranto* (1764). Later examples include *The Mysteries of Udolpho* (1794) by Ann Radcliffe and *Frankenstein* (1818) by Mary SHELLEY.

Gothic revival (neo-Gothic) Architecture based on the Gothic style of the Middle Ages. Beginning in the late 18th century, it peaked in 19th-century Britain and the USA, appearing in many European countries. Notable examples are the Houses of Parliament in London by Pugin and Sir Charles BARRY, and Trinity Church in New York City by Richard Upjohn. *See also* GOTHIC ARCHITECTURE

gouache Watercolour paint made opaque by the addition of white. It lightens in colour when dry and cracks if used thickly. Popular among manuscript illuminators in the Middle Ages, gouache has also been used by 20th-century artists.

Gould, Glenn (1932–82) Canadian pianist. A soloist with the Toronto Symphony Orchestra at the age of 14, he is famous for interpretations of J.S. BACH. He was also a composer.

Gounod, Charles François (1818–93) French composer and organist. He composed church and choral music and is best known for his operas, which include *Faust* (1859) and *Mireille* (1863).

gourd Annual vine and its ornamental, hard-shelled fruit. The fruit range from almost spherical, as in *Cucurbita pepo*, to irregular or bottle-shaped, as in *Lagenaria siceraria*. The rind may be smooth or warty. Family Cucurbitaceae.

gout Form of arthritis, featuring an excess of uric acid crystals in the tissues. More common in men, it causes attacks of pain and inflammation in the joints, most often those of the feet or hands.

Gower, John (1330–1408) English poet. Ranked in his time with CHAUCER, his work includes *Vox Clamantis* (1379–82), an attack on social injustice, and *Confessio Amantis* (1386–93), allegorical tales on the subject of Christian and courtly love.

Goya y Lucientes, Francisco José de (1746–1828) Spanish painter and engraver. A severe illness (1791) provoked a vein of fantastic works, one of which is *Los Caprichos*, a series of 82 engravings published in 1799. Goya enjoyed the patronage of Charles IV despite mercilessly realistic paintings such as *The family of Charles IV* (1800). His bloody scenes, *The Second of May, 1808* and *The Third of May, 1808*, portray Spanish resistance to the French invasion. The nightmare continued in his savage suite of 65 etchings, *The Disasters of War* (1810–14).

Gracchus (153–121 BC) (Gaius Sempronius) Roman statesman. As tribune (123–11 BC) he organized the social reforms of his brother Tiberius (d.133 BC). He sought to check the power of the Senate by reforming agrarian laws to benefit the poor. He was defeated in the election of 121 and killed during the riots that followed.

Grace, W.G. (William Gilbert) (1848–1915) English cricketer. He played for England, Gloucestershire and London County. He scored a total of 54,896 runs (including 126 centuries) and took 2,876 wickets. He led England in 13 of his 22 Test matches (1880–99).

Graces In Greek mythology, three goddesses who represented beauty, grace and charm. Associated especially with poetry, Aglaia, Euphrosyne and Thalia were often linked with the MUSES. They were also described as daughters of ZEUS.

grackle Several species of stout-billed, New World blackbirds within the genera *Quiscalus* and *Cassidix* of the family Icteridae. They have blackish, iridescent plumage. Species of Asian MINA birds of the genus *Gracula* are also called grackles.

Graf, Steffi (1969–) German tennis player. Graf succeeded Martina NAVRATILOVA as the world's No 1 woman tennis player in 1987. In 1988 she completed a Grand Slam of the major tournaments. Graf's powerful serve and forehand play dominated the women's game, despite injury problems.

grafting Method of plant propagation. A twig of one variety, called the scion, is established on the roots of a related variety, called the stock. Most fruit trees are propagated by a similar process called budding, in which the scion is a single bud.

Graham, Billy (William Franklin) (1918–) US evangelist. A charismatic preacher, he led Christian revivalist crusades all over the world.

Graham, Martha (1894–1991) US choreographer and dancer, a leading figure in MODERN DANCE. Breaking with traditional BALLET, she employed individual forms based on natural movement.

Graham, Thomas (1805–69) British chemist best remembered for Graham's law. This law states that the diffusion rate of a gas is inversely proportional to the square root of its density. It is used in separating isotopes by the diffusion method, and has important industrial applications. He also discovered DIALYSIS.

Grahame, Kenneth (1859–1932) British author of children's books. He created the classic *Wind in the Willows* (1908), which formed the basis for the A.A. MILNE play *Toad of Toad Hall* (1929).

grain Fruits of various CEREAL plants, or the plants themselves. The main kinds of grain are wheat, maize and RICE. They are an important food, not only rich in carbohydrates but also containing proteins and vitamins.

Grainger, Percy Aldridge (1882–1961) Australian composer and pianist. His arrangements of *Country Gardens* and *Shepherd's Hey* were both published in 1908. He produced other pieces in the folk tradition and also wrote experimental music.

grammar Nature and structure of language, including the form, sound and meaning of words and the construction of sentences. Traditional rules of grammar were developed in the Middle Ages and were based on Latin. They were later applied to other languages such as English, German and Russian. In the mid-20th century, linguists such as Noam CHOMSKY developed a more scientific approach to analysing language, which did not depend on structural similarities with Latin.

Grampian Region in NE Scotland, bordered by the North Sea, the Grampian Highlands and the CAIRNGORMS; the capital is ABERDEEN. The w of the region is mountainous, rising to 1311m (4,301ft) at Ben Macdhui. The E is drained by the Spey, Dee and Don rivers. Along the banks of the Spey lie many whisky distilleries. Industries: beef farming, fishing, and tourism. Area: 8,707sq km (3,361sq mi). Pop. (1991) 503,900.

Grampians Mountain range in N central Scotland. It is the highest mountain system in Britain, running SW–NE between Glen More and the Scottish Lowlands. Rivers rising in the Grampians include the Spey and Findhorn (flowing N), the Don and Dee (flowing E), and the Tay and Forth (flowing S). Highest peak: BEN NEVIS, 1,343m (4,406ft).

Granada City in Andalusia, s Spain; capital of Granada province. Founded in the 8th century, it became the capital of the independent Muslim kingdom of Granada in 1238. The last Moorish stronghold in Spain, it surrendered to the Christian armies of Ferdinand and Isabella (1492). The central splendour of Granada is the ALHAMBRA. Industries: tourism and textiles. Pop. (1991) 254,034.

Gran Chaco Lowland plain of central South America, stretching across the borders of Argentina, Bolivia and Paraguay. Arid and largely unpopulated, the region is famous for its quebracho trees, a major source of TANNIN. The discovery of oil in the Chaco Boreal, and Bolivia's subsequent need for a route to the sea, led to the Chaco War (1932–35) between Bolivia and Paraguay.

Grand Canyon Deep gorge in NW Arizona, USA, carved by the Colorado River. It is 450km (280mi) long and varies from 6km (4mi) to 18km (11mi) in width. With its magnificent multicoloured rock formations revealing hundreds of millions of years of geological history, the Grand Canyon is one of the great natural wonders of the world.

Grand Remonstrance (November 1641) Statement of grievances by the English Parliament presented to CHARLES I. It listed numerous objections to the royal government and demanded parliamentary approval of ministers. It was passed in the House of Commons by only 11 votes, and Charles rejected it. It hardened the division between the crown and Parliament, which culminated in the English CIVIL WAR.

grand unified theory (GUT) Theory that would demonstrate that three of the four FUNDAMENTAL FORCES are actually different aspects of the same fundamental force. The WEAK NUCLEAR FORCE and ELECTROMAGNETIC FORCE have been incorporated as the electroweak force, as demonstrated by particle accelerator experiments. In order to prove the GUT the electroweak force must be unified with the STRONG NUCLEAR FORCE. If the gravitational force could be incorporated then a UNIFIED FIELD THEORY could be produced.

granite Coarse-grained, light-grey, durable IGNEOUS ROCK, composed chiefly of feldspar and quartz, with some mica or hornblende. It is thought to have solidified from magma.

Grant, Cary (1904–86) US film actor b. Britain. Grant specialized in playing romantic leads, especially in screwball comedies. His films include *The Philadelphia Story* (1937), *Bringing Up Baby* (1938), *His Girl Friday* (1940), *An Affair to Remember* (1957), and *North by Northwest* (1959).

Grant, Duncan (1885–1978) British landscape painter, portraitist and designer, one of the first British artists to be influenced by POST-IMPRESSIONISM. He was a member of the BLOOMSBURY GROUP.

Grant, Ulysses S. (Simpson) (1822–85) US Civil War general and 18th US President (1869–77). In 1864 Abraham LINCOLN gave him overall command of the Union forces. He coordinated the final campaigns and accepted the surrender of Robert E. LEE (1865). As president, he achieved foreign policy successes, but failed to prevent the growth of domestic corruption.

grape Vines that grow in temperate and subtropical climates, producing fruit that is eaten raw, dried, or used for making WINE. The classical European vine (*Vitis vinifera*) had its origins in Asia. The climate, soil, topography and cultivation methods determine the quality of the crop. Family Vitaceae.

grapefruit Evergreen citrus fruit tree of the family Rutaceae; also its yellow edible fruit. The tree, which may reach 6m (20ft), is grown mainly in subtropical climates in the USA, Israel, South Africa and Argentina.

graphical user interface (GUI) Computer PROGRAM enabling a user to operate a COMPUTER using simple symbols. Early personal computers used operating systems that were text based. A GUI replaces these commands with a screen containing symbols called icons, manipulated with a "mouse".

graphite (plumbago) Dark grey, soft crystalline form of CARBON. It occurs naturally in deposits of varying purity and is made synthetically by heating petroleum coke. It is used in pencils, lubricants, electrodes, rocket nozzles and as a moderator in nuclear reactors. Graphite is a good conductor of heat and electricity. Hardness 1–2; s.g. 2.1–2.3.

Grass, Günter Wilhelm (1927–) German novelist, poet and playwright. His prose combines evocative description with historical documentation. He used powerful techniques to grotesque comic effect in *The Tin Drum* (1959) and *Cat and Mouse* (1961). Later works include *The Flounder* (1977) and *The Call of the Toad* (1992).

grass Non-woody plants with fibrous roots that have long, narrow leaves enclosing hollow, jointed stems. The stems may be upright or bent, lie on the ground, or grow underground. The flowers are small, without PETALS and SEPALS. The leaves grow from the base, and so removal of the tips does not inhibit growth, making grass suitable for lawns and pastures. CEREAL grasses, such as rice, millet, maize and wheat, are cultivated for their seeds. Others are grown as food for animals and for erosion control and ornament. There are *c.*8,000 species. Family Poaceae/Gramineae. *See also* MONOCOTYLEDON

grasshopper Plant-eating insect. It is a powerful jumper owing to its enlarged hind legs.

Length: 8–11cm (0.3–4.3in). Order Orthoptera; families Acrididae and Tettingoniidae. *See also* CRICKET; LOCUST

Grattan, Henry (1746–1820) Irish political leader. A compelling orator, he led the movement to free the Irish Parliament from British control, which was finally achieved in 1782. He failed to prevent the merger of the Irish and British Parliaments in the Act of UNION (1801). As a member (1805–20), Grattan fought for CATHOLIC EMANCIPATION.

Graves, Robert von Ranke (1895–1985) British poet, novelist and critic. After publishing his classic World War 1 autobiography, *Goodbye To All That* (1929), he emigrated to Majorca. Other works include the novels *I, Claudius* (1934) and *The Crowning Privilege* (1955). His *Collected Poems* appeared in 1938 and 1975.

gravitation One of the four FUNDAMENTAL FORCES in nature. Gravitation is weak compared with the others, but it is apparent because of the great mass of the Earth. The gravitational force F between two masses m_1 and m_2 a distance d apart was found by Isaac NEWTON to be $F = Gm_1m_2/d^2$, where G is a constant of proportionality called the universal constant of gravitation. A more complete treatment of gravitation was developed by Albert EINSTEIN, who showed in his general theory of RELATIVITY that gravitation is a manifestation of space-time.

Gray, Elisha (1835–1901) US inventor. He patented the telegraphic repeater and the type-printing telegraph. He claimed priority as the inventor of the telephone, but Alexander Graham BELL's patent rights were upheld by the US Supreme Court.

Gray, Thomas (1716–71) English poet. His masterpiece was *Elegy Written in a Country Churchyard* (1751). Other poems include *Ode on the Death of a Favourite Cat* (1748) and *The Descent of Odin* (1768).

gray SI unit of absorbed radiation dose (symbol Gy). One gray is equivalent to supplying 1 joule of energy per kilogram of irradiated material. It superseded the rad (1 gray = 100 rad).

Graz City on the River Mur, SE Austria; capital of Styria. Graz's many historic buildings include the famous *Uhrturm* clock tower (1561) and the Renaissance Landhaus (provincial parliament). Industries: iron and steel, paper, leather, glass, chemicals, textiles. Pop. (1991) 237,810.

Great Barrier Reef World's largest CORAL REEF, in the Coral Sea off the NE coast of Queensland, Australia. It is up to 800m (2,600ft) wide. The reef is separated from the mainland by a shallow lagoon 11–24km (7–15mi) wide. Length: 2,000km (1,250mi). Area: *c.*207,000sq km (80,000sq mi).

Great Bear Lake Lake in Northwest Territories, NW Canada; the largest lake in Canada and fourth largest in North America. It was first explored in 1825 by John FRANKLIN. It is drained in the w by the Great Bear River. Though the lake is one of North America's deepest, it is icebound for eight months of the year. Area: *c.*31,800sq km (12,300sq mi).

265

Great Britain Geographical name for the British Isles, comprising ENGLAND, SCOTLAND and WALES. Wales was united with England in 1536. The Act of UNION (1707) united Scotland with England, and the Act of Union (1801) established the UNITED KINGDOM of Great Britain and Ireland.

great circle Circle on a spherical surface, whose centre is coincident with the centre of the sphere. On the celestial sphere, the EQUATOR is a great circle, as are all MERIDIANS. The shortest distance between any two points on a sphere, great circles are used for mapping aircraft routes.

Great Dane (German mastiff) Large hunting dog. One of the largest dog breeds, it has a narrow head and blunt muzzle. Its deep-chested body is set on long, strong legs. The smooth coat may be various colours. Height: up to 92cm (36in) at the shoulder.

Great Depression Severe economic DEPRESSION that afflicted the USA throughout the 1930s. At the close of the 1920s, economic factors such as over production, stock-market speculation, lack of external markets, and unequal distribution of wealth contributed to the prolonged economic crisis. The stock market collapse in October 1929 saw US$30,000 million wiped off stock values in the first week. Bank failures became commonplace. At the depth of the Depression (1932–33), unemployment stood at 16 million, almost 33% of the total work force. The gross national product (GNP) fell by almost 50%. Franklin D. ROOSEVELT, sensing the national emergency, instituted the NEW DEAL, which helped to mitigate the worst effects of the crisis. The economy only really started to pick up in the 1940s.

Great Dividing Range (Eastern Highlands) Series of mountain ranges along the E coast of Australia. They extend S from the Atherton Tableland in Queensland to the Grampian Mountains in Victoria (S). The highest peak is Mount Kosciusko, 2,230m (7,316ft). Length: 3,703km (2,300 mi).

Greater Antilles Largest of three major island groups in the WEST INDIES, between the Atlantic Ocean and the Caribbean Sea. The group includes CUBA, HISPANIOLA, JAMAICA, PUERTO RICO and the CAYMAN ISLANDS.

Great Exhibition (1851) *See* CRYSTAL PALACE

Great Lakes World's largest expanse of freshwater; five lakes in central North America, between Canada and the USA. They are, from W to E, Lakes SUPERIOR, MICHIGAN, HURON, ERIE and ONTARIO. They are connected by straits, rivers and canals, providing a continuous waterway. They are drained by the ST LAWRENCE River, the deepening of which opened up the lakes to world shipping. Major cities include CHICAGO, TORONTO, DETROIT, BUFFALO, CLEVELAND and MILWAUKEE. Total surface area: *c.*245,300sq km (94,700sq mi).

Great Plains High, extensive region of grassland in central North America. The Great Plains extend from the Canadian provinces of Alberta, Saskatchewan and Manitoba through W central USA to Texas. The plateau slopes down and E from the Rocky Mountains. Most of the land is prairie, and cattle-ranching and sheep-rearing are the main economic activities. The soil is often fertile, and wheat is the principal crop.

Great Salt Lake Large, shallow saltwater lake in NW Utah, USA. It is fed by the Bear, Weber and Jordan rivers, and its depth and area vary with climatic changes. Bonneville Salt Flats, famous for land speed records, lies in the Great Salt Desert. Area: varies from *c.*2,500sq km (960sq mi) to *c.*6,200sq km (2,400sq mi).

Great Schism Division within the Roman Catholic Church resulting in the election of rival popes (1378–1417). An Italian line of popes continued in Rome, and a rival "antipope" line in AVIGNON, France. The SCHISM ended with the Council of CONSTANCE (1414–17), which established MARTIN V as the only pope.

Great Slave Lake Second largest lake in Canada, W Northwest Territories; the deepest lake in North America. It is named after the Slave tribe of Native Americans. The first European discovery was in 1771. Gold is mined on its N shore. It is drained by the Mackenzie River. Area: *c.*28,400sq km (10,980sq mi). Max. depth: 615m (2,015ft).

Great Smoky Mountains Part of the APPALACHIANS, on the North Carolina–Tennessee border, USA. One of the oldest ranges on Earth, it includes the largest virgin forest of red spruce. The highest point is Clingmans Dome, 2,026m (6,643ft). Area: 2,090sq km (806sq mi).

Great Trek (1835–40) Migration of *c.*12,000 BOERS from Cape Colony into the South African interior. They aimed to escape British control and to acquire cheap land. Many settled in what became Orange FREE STATE, TRANSVAAL and NATAL.

Great Wall of China Defensive frontier and world heritage site, *c.*2,400km (1,500mi) long, extending from the Huang Hai (Yellow Sea) to the central Asian desert, N China. Sections of the wall were first built by the Warring States. QIN SHIHUANGDI ordered that they should be joined to form a unified boundary (214 BC). The present wall was mostly built 600 years ago by the MING dynasty. It averages 8m (25ft) high and up to 9m (30ft) thick.

Great Zimbabwe Ruined city and world heritage site, SE Zimbabwe. It was the capital of a Bantu-speaking kingdom (12th–15th century). At the height of its power, the city's population probably numbered more than 15,000. The city's 9m (30ft) tower is a national symbol.

grebe Brown, grey and black freshwater diving bird found worldwide. It flies laboriously and has legs set so far back that it cannot walk. There are six common species of grebes in North America, Britain and W Europe. Length: to 48cm (19in). Family Podicepididae; genus *Podiceps*.

Greco, El (1541–1614) Spanish painter, b. Crete. His early style was influenced by TITIAN. His characteristically elongated and distorted figures disregard normal rules of perspective. His later paintings, such as *Burial of Count Orgasz* (1586), *Agony in the Garden* (1610) and *Assumption* (1613), express his profound religious conviction.

Greece Republic in SE Europe; the capital is ATHENS. **Land and climate** The mountainous, maritime Hellenic Republic can be divided into four geographical regions: Northern Greece includes the historic regions of THRACE and MACEDONIA, and its second-largest city THESSALONÍKI. Central Greece, N of the Gulf of Corinth, includes Athens, and its highest peak, Mount OLYMPUS at 2,917m (9,570ft). Southern Greece is the PELOPONNESOS peninsula, and includes the city of CORINTH. The fourth region is the Greek islands, which constitute *c.*20% of Greece. These include CRETE (the largest) in the Mediterranean Sea, the DODECANESE group (including RHODES), Euboea and Lesbos in the Aegean Sea. Low-lying areas have mild, moist winters and hot, dry summers. The E coast has *c.*50% of the rainfall of the W. The mountains have a much more severe climate. Much of Greece's original vegetation has been destroyed. Some areas are covered by maquis. **Economy** Despite improvements in infrastructure and industry, Greece is one of the poorest members of the European Community. Manufacturing is important. Products: textiles, cement, chemicals and metallurgy. Minerals: lignite, bauxite and chromite. Farmland covers *c.*33% of Greece, grazing land 40%. Major crops: tobacco, fruit (olives, grapes), cotton and wheat. Livestock are raised. Shipping and tourism are major sectors. **History and politics** (*See* GREECE, ANCIENT) Crete was the centre of MINOAN CIVILIZATION, between *c.*3000 and 1450 BC. The Minoans were followed by the MYCENAEAN CIVILIZATION, which prospered until the DORIANS settled *c.*1200 BC. Powerful city-states emerged, such as SPARTA and Athens. Solon established DEMOCRACY in Athens (5th century BC). The revolt of the IONIANS started the PERSIAN WARS (499–79 BC). Athens was defeated in the PELOPONNESIAN WAR (431–04 BC), and Corinth and THEBES gained control. In 338 BC MACEDONIA, led by PHILIP II, became the dominant power. His son, ALEXANDER THE GREAT, ushered in the HELLENISTIC AGE. Greece became a Roman province in 146 BC. Greece formed part of the BYZANTINE EMPIRE from AD 330–1453. In 1456 the Ottomans conquered Greece. The Greek War of Independence (1821–27) was supported by the European powers, and an independent monarchy was established (1832). As king of the Hellenes (1863–1913), George I recovered much Greek territory. In 1913 Greece gained Crete. Greece finally entered World War 1 on the Allied side (1917). In 1923, 1.5 million Greeks from Asia Minor were resettled in Greece. In 1936 Metaxas became premier. His dictatorial regime remained neutral at the start of World War 2. By May 1941, Germany had occupied Greece. Resistance movements

> **GREECE**
> AREA: 131,990sq km (50,961sq mi)
> POPULATION: 10,300,000
> CAPITAL (POPULATION): Athens (3,072,922)
> GOVERNMENT: Multiparty republic
> ETHNIC GROUPS: Greek 96%, Macedonian 2%, Turkish 1%, Albanian, Slav
> LANGUAGES: Greek (official)
> RELIGIONS: Christianity (Eastern Orthodox 97%), Islam 2%
> CURRENCY: Drachma = 100 lepta

recaptured most territory by 1944, and the Germans withdrew. From 1946–49 a civil war raged between communist and royalist forces. In 1951 Greece was admitted to NATO. In 1955 Konstantinos Karamanlis became prime minister; the economy improved, but tension with Turkey over CYPRUS surfaced. In 1964 a republican, George Papandreou, became prime minister. In 1967 a military dictatorship seized power. The "Greek Colonels" imposed harsh controls on dissent. In 1973 the monarchy was abolished and Greece became a presidential republic. Civil unrest led to the 1974 restoration of civilian government, headed by Karamanlis. In 1981 Greece joined the European Community, and Andreas PAPANDREOU became president. A series of scandals saw the re-election of Karamanlis (1990). In 1995 Constantine Stephanopoulos became president.

Greece, ancient Period beginning with the defeat of the second Persian invasion in 479 BC and ending with the establishment of Macedonian power in 338 BC. Warring city-states flourished as centres of trade. ATHENS, the most wealthy and powerful, developed a democratic system under the guidance of PERICLES. Its main rival was the military state of SPARTA. Classical Greece was the birthplace of many ideas in art, literature, philosophy and science – among them those of PLATO and ARISTOTLE. It is traditionally regarded as the birthplace of Western civilization and foundation of Western culture.

Greek INDO-EUROPEAN LANGUAGE spoken in Greece since *c.*2000 BC. In ancient Greece there were several dialects: Attic, spoken in Athens, is the most common in literary records. Greek was widely spoken in the Middle East during the HELLENISTIC AGE. It was the official language of the Byzantine Empire, and began to evolve into its modern form in *c.*1000 AD.

Greek and architecture Greek architecture came into its own in the 6th century BC when stone replaced wood as the building material for civic and temple buildings. Distinct ORDERS OF ARCHITECTURE began to emerge. The earliest remaining Doric temple is the Temple of Hera at Olympia (late 7th century BC), and the most outstanding example is the PARTHENON. Among Ionic temples, the Erectheum is considered the most perfect. The Corinthian mausoleum at Halicarnassus (350 BC) was one of the SEVEN WONDERS OF THE WORLD. Greek art may be divided into four chronological periods: **Geometric** (late 11th–late 8th century BC), **Archaic** (late 8th century–480 BC), **Classical** (480–323 BC) and **Hellenistic** (323–27 BC). Only a few small bronze horses survive from the Geometric period. During the Archaic period, stone sculpture appeared, vase painting proliferated, and the human figure became a common subject. Civic wealth and pride was a feature of the Classical period, and sculpture reached its peak of serene perfection. The Hellenistic period is noted for increasingly dramatic works.

Greek drama First form of DRAMA in Western civilization, which took three forms: TRAGEDY, COMEDY and satyr plays. Tragedy developed from religious festivals, at which a CHORUS sang responses to a leader. AESCHYLUS introduced a second actor, and SOPHOCLES added a third. The other major tragedian was EURIPIDES. Greek tragedy usually dealt with mythical subjects, but sometimes (as in Aeschylus' *The Persians*) used recent history. Greek comedy arose in the 5th century BC. It was often topical and lampooned politics and the conventions of tragedy; its best-known exponent was ARISTOPHANES. Comedy flourished in the Hellenistic Age (323–27 BC), especially in the work of MENANDER. Satyr plays were bawdy works written to accompany tragedies.

Greek literature One of the longest surviving traditions in world literature. The earliest Greek literature took the form of EPIC songs, collected by HOMER in the *Iliad* and the *Odyssey*. It also saw the development of lyric poetry, such as the choric lyrics and odes of PINDAR. Throughout the Classical period (480–323 BC) there was a tradition of fine literature in poetry and prose writing. During the Hellenistic Age (323–27 BC), epic, epigrammatic and didactic poetry flourished. Herodus revitalized the art of MIME. During the Roman period (*c.*27 BC–*c.* AD 330) important figures included PLUTARCH, MARCUS AURELIUS and PTOLEMY. Writing in Greek died out after the Turkish invasions of the 15th century and was revived only after their overthrow in 1828. Prominent among the new generation were Dionysios Solomos and Andreas Kalvos. Modern Greek writers of international stature include KAZANTZAKIS.

Greek mythology Collection of stories mainly concerning the adventures of gods and heroes. In the myths, the gods are not wholly admirable figures: they have similar weaknesses to humans and are capable of great vindictiveness and favouritism.

green algae Large group of marine and freshwater ALGAE (phylum Chlorophyta). They are distinct from other algae by virtue of possessing cup-shaped CHLOROPLASTS that contain chlorophyll b, and by producing cells with flagella at some stage in their lives. *See also* LICHEN

Greenaway, Peter (1942–) Welsh film director and screenwriter. An innovative and painterly film-maker, his breakthrough was *The Draughtsman's Contract* (1983). Other films include *The Cook, the Thief, His Wife and Her Lover* (1989), *Prospero's Books* (1991) and *The Pillow Book* (1996).

Greene, (Henry) Graham (1904–91) British novelist and dramatist. His psychological thrillers are among the most popular and critically acclaimed works of 20th-century fiction. Important novels include *Brighton Rock* (1938), *The Power and the Glory* (1940), *The Heart of the Matter* (1948), *The Quiet American* (1955), the "entertainment" *Our Man in Havana* (1958), *The Honorary Consul* (1973), and *Travels with My Aunt* (1978).

greenhouse effect Raised temperature at a planet's surface as a result of heat energy being trapped by gases in the ATMOSPHERE. As the Sun's rays pass through Earth's atmosphere, some heat is absorbed but most of the short-wave SOLAR ENERGY passes through. This energy is re-emitted by the Earth as long-wave radiation, which cannot pass easily through the atmosphere. More heat is retained if there is a CLOUD layer. In recent centuries, more heat has been retained due to the increased levels of carbon dioxide (CO_2) from the burning of FOSSIL FUELS. Tiny particles of CO_2 form an extra layer, which acts like the glass in a greenhouse. Some scientists argue that the greenhouse effect is contributing to GLOBAL WARMING.

Greenland World's largest island, in the NW Atlantic Ocean, lying mostly within the Arctic Circle. It is a self-governing province of Denmark; the capital is NUUK. More than 85% of Greenland is covered by PERMAFROST, with an average depth of 1,500m (5,000ft). Settlement is confined to the SW coast, which is warmed by Atlantic currents. Most of Greenland's inhabitants are INUIT. Its European discovery is credited to ERIC THE RED, who settled in 982, founding a colony that lasted over 500 years. Greenland became a Danish possession in 1380, and was incorporated into Denmark in 1953. Greenland achieved home rule (1979) and self-government (1981). In 1985 it withdrew from the EU. Greenland's economy is heavily dependent on subsidies from Denmark. Fishing is ther largest sector. Lead and zinc are mined in the NW, and the s has reserves of uranium. Area: 2,175,000sq km (840,000sq mi). Pop. (1993) 55,117.

green movement Campaign to preserve the environment and to minimize pollution or destruction of the Earth's natural habitat. The green movement formed its own active pressure groups GREENPEACE and Friends of the Earth in the early 1970s. It gained political representation shortly afterwards in the form of various European Green Parties.

Green Party Any of a number of European political parties embodying the principles of the GREEN MOVEMENT. Green parties promote sustainable exploitation of natural resources and the use of RENEWABLE ENERGY sources. By the late 1980s, traditional political parties had adopted many Green policies and the Green vote declined.

Greenpeace International pressure group founded in 1971, initially to oppose US nuclear testing in Alaska. Greenpeace promotes environmental awareness and campaigns against environmental abuse. It gains wide media coverage for its active, nonviolent demonstrations against whaling, toxic-waste dumping and nuclear testing.

green revolution Intensive plan of the 1960s to increase crop yields in developing countries by introducing higher-yielding strains of plants and new fertilizers. The scheme began in Mexico in the 1940s and was successfully introduced in parts of India, SE Asia, the Middle East and Latin America.

Greenwich Borough in SE London, England. In Greenwich Park stands the former Royal Observatory (founded 1675). The prime meridian, which passes through Greenwich, forms the basis of GREENWICH MEAN TIME (GMT). Greenwich has a rich maritime history and is home to the Royal Naval College. Pop. (1991) 207,650.

Greenwich Mean Time (GMT) Local time at GREENWICH, London, situated on the prime meridian. It has been used as the basis for calculating standard time in various parts of the world since 1884. GMT corresponds with civil time in Britain during the winter months; British Summer Time (BST) is one hour ahead of GMT.

Greer, Germaine (1939–) Australian feminist author and journalist. Her controversial book *The Female Eunuch* (1970) questioned the institution of marriage and gender stereotypes. Other works include *Sex and Destiny: the Politics of Human Fertility* (1984) and *The Change: Women, Ageing and the Menopause* (1991).

Gregory I, Saint (540–604) (Gregory the Great) Pope (590–604). He devoted himself to alleviating poverty and hunger among the Romans. His reforms included changes in the Mass, and he initiated the conversion of the LOMBARDS. He sent Saint AUGUSTINE OF CANTERBURY to convert the ANGLO-SAXONS. His feast day is 12 March.

Gregory VII (1020–85) Pope (1073–85), b. Hildebrand. He brought about various reforms to counteract abuses in the church and twice excommunicated the Holy Roman Emperor HENRY IV. He increased the papacy's temporal power.

Gregory XIII (1502–85) Pope (1572–85), b. Ugo Buoncompagni. He promoted church reform and sought to carry out the decrees of the Council of TRENT. He is best known for his reform of the Julian CALENDAR (1582).

Grenada Independent island nation in the SE Caribbean Sea, the most southerly of the WINDWARD ISLANDS, *c.*160km (100mi) N of Venezuela. It consists of Grenada and the smaller islands of the Southern Grenadines dependency; the capital is ST GEORGE'S. First sighted in 1498 by Christopher Columbus, the islands were then inhabited by the Carib. It became a permanent British possession in 1783 and a crown colony in 1877. It was a member of the West Indian Federation (1958–62). In 1974 it

became an independent Commonwealth state. In 1979 the New Jewel movement seized power, and in 1983, following a military coup, US forces invaded the island. They were withdrawn in 1985 after the re-establishment of a democratic government. Elections in 1995 were won by the New National Party, led by Dr Keith Mitchell. Grenada is volcanic in origin. It has a tropical climate with occasional hurricanes. The economy is agricultural, based on cocoa, bananas, sugar, spices and citrus fruits. It is also heavily dependent on tourism. Area: 344sq km (133sq mi). Pop. (1995 est.) 96,000.

Grenadines Group of *c.*600 small islands in the S Windward Islands, Caribbean Sea, WEST INDIES. The S Grenadines are included in GRENADA. The N Grenadines form part of ST VINCENT AND THE GRENADINES. Industries: cotton, limes, tourism.

Grenville, Sir Richard (1541–91) English naval commander and hero. He commanded the fleet that carried Sir Walter RALEIGH's colonists to Roanoke, Virginia, in 1585. His adventurous career ended when he was fatally wounded and his ship, *Revenge*, captured in a battle off the Azores.

Grey, Charles, 2nd Earl (1764–1845) British statesman, prime minister (1830–34). During his administration the First REFORM ACT was passed (1832) and slavery was abolished throughout the British empire (1833).

Grey, Lady Jane (1537–54) (Nine-Day Queen) Queen of England (1553). Great-granddaughter of Henry VII, she was married to the son of the Duke of NORTHUMBERLAND, regent for the ailing EDWARD VI. On Edward VI's death she was proclaimed queen, but the rightful heir, MARY I, was almost universally preferred. Lady Jane and her husband were executed.

Grieg, Edvard Hagerup (1843–1907) Norwegian composer. He used Norwegian folk themes in his compositions. Among his best-known works are the two suites *Peer Gynt* (1876) for orchestra, and the Piano Concerto (1868).

Griffith, Arthur (1872–1922) Irish statesman, founder of SINN FÉIN. From 1899 he edited the republican newspaper *United Irishman*. Griffith regarded armed resistance as impractical and took no part in the EASTER RISING (1916). He was elected vice president of the Dáil Éireann (1918), and led the negotiations that created the Irish Free State (1921). When DE VALERA rejected the settlement, Griffith became president.

Griffith, D.W. (David Wark) (1875–1948) US film director, the most influential figure in the development of the cinema in the USA. His Civil War epic *The Birth of a Nation* (1915) is often cited as the most important document in cinematic history, but has also been condemned as racist.

griffon (griffon vulture) Bird of prey of Eurasia and N Africa, with gold or sandy-brown plumage. It is gregarious and nests in large flocks. Length: 1m (3.3ft). Family Accipitridae; species *Gyps fulvus*.

Grimm brothers German philologists and folklorists. Jakob Ludwig Karl (1785–1863) formulated **Grimm's law** relating to the regular shifting of consonants in INDO-EUROPEAN LANGUAGES. He and his brother Wilhelm Karl (1786–1859) are popularly known for their enduring collection of folk tales, *Grimm's Fairy Tales* (1812–15). It was a major text of ROMANTICISM

Gris, Juan (1887–1927) Spanish painter. With PICASSO and BRAQUE, he was a leading exponent of synthetic CUBISM. Later works include collages, architectonic paintings, stage sets and costumes.

grizzly bear Large BEAR, generally considered to be a variety of brown bear (*Ursus arctos*) although sometimes classified as a separate species (*Ursus horribilis*). Once widespread in W North America, the grizzly is now rare except in W Canada, Alaska and some US national parks. Length: to 2.5m (7ft); weight: 410kg (900lb).

Gromyko, Andrei (1909–89) Soviet statesman, foreign minister (1957–85), president (1985–88). Gromyko took part in the Yalta and Potsdam peace conferences (1945). He acted as the permanent Soviet delegate to the United Nations (1946–48). As foreign minister, he was influential in establishing the round of summits between the US and Soviet presidents. GORBACHEV promoted Gromyko to the presidency, but he was forced to retire in 1988.

Groningen City at the confluence of the Hoornse Diep and the Winschoter Diep, NE Netherlands; capital of Groningen province. A member of the HANSEATIC LEAGUE from 1284, it controlled most of Friesland. Groningen remained loyal to the Habsburgs, but was captured by the Dutch in 1594. The surrounding fertile agricultural land makes it one of the country's biggest markets. Industries: shipbuilding, electrical equipment. Pop. (1994) 170,535.

Gropius, Walter (1883–1969) German-American architect, founder of the BAUHAUS (1919–28). Gropius transformed the Weimar School of Art into the Bauhaus, which was relocated to his new buildings in Dessau (1926). He fled Germany (1934) and headed the Harvard school of architecture (1937–52). Gropius pioneered functional design and INTERNATIONAL STYLE in particular.

grosbeak Any of several birds of the FINCH family (fringillidae). They have short, thick, seed-cracking beaks. Found in woodlands of the Americas, Europe and Asia, species include the rose-breasted grosbeak (*Pheucticus ludovicianus*) of North and South America, and the pine grosbeak (*Pinicolor enucleator*) of Canada and N Europe. Length: 18–25cm (7–10in).

gross domestic product (GDP) Total amount of goods and services produced by a country annually. It does **not** include income from investments or overseas possessions. GDP gives an indication of the strength of national industry. *See also* GROSS NATIONAL PRODUCT (GNP)

gross national product (GNP) Total market value of all goods and services produced by a country annually, **plus** net income from abroad.

GNP is a universal indicator of economic performance, and provides an assessment of different economic sectors. GNP is the sum of four types of spending: private consumption, government expenditure, balance of trade, and business investment. *See also* GROSS DOMESTIC PRODUCT (GDP)

groundnut *See* PEANUT

ground squirrel (gopher) Small terrestrial SQUIRREL native to Eurasia and North America. Ground squirrels eat plants, seeds, insects, small animals and sometimes eggs. Most have greyish-red to brown fur and some are striped or spotted. Length: to 40.5cm (16in); weight: 85–1,000g (0.1–2.2lb). Family Sciuridae; genus *Citellus* (and others).

ground water Water that lies beneath the surface of the Earth. It comes chiefly from rain, although some is of volcanic or sedimentary origin. It moves through porous rocks and soil and can be collected in wells. Ground water can dissolve minerals and leave deposits, creating structures such as CAVES, STALAGMITES and STALACTITES. *See also* WATER TABLE

grouper Tropical marine fish found from the coast of Florida to South America, and in the Indian and Pacific oceans. It has a large mouth, sharp teeth, a mottled body and the ability to change colour. Length: to 3.7m (12ft); weight: to 450kg (1,000lb). Family Serranidae; species: giant, *Epinephelus itajara*; Australian, *Epinephelus lanceolatus*.

Group of Eight (G8) (formerly G7) In 1975, the heads of government of the world's seven wealthiest nations met in the first of a series of annual economic summits. The changing world economy has led other countries to seek membership. In 1997, Russia was formally admitted to the group.

grouse Plump gamebird of he Northern Hemisphere. Grouse are fowl-like, but have feathered ankles and toes and brightly coloured air sacs on the neck. Family Tetraonidae. *See also* PRAIRIE CHICKEN

Grozny City in the Caucasus Mountains, SW Russia; the capital of CHECHENYA. Founded in 1818, it has been an oil-producing centre since 1893 and has a pipeline to the Black Sea and the Donets Basin. Grozny was severely damaged in fighting between Russian forces and Chechen rebels from 1994–96, and there were many civilian casualties. Industries: oil, petrochemicals. Pop. (1992) 388,000.

Guadalajara City in SW Mexico; capital of Jalisco state and second-largest city in Mexico. Founded in 1531, it has become a major industrial centre. Noted for its mountain scenery and mild climate, it is a popular health resort. Industries: engineering, textiles, food processing, pottery, glassware. Pop. (1990) 1,650,205.

Guadalcanal Largest of the Solomon Islands, *c.*970km (600 mi) E of New Guinea, W central Pacific Ocean; the capital is Honiara. Guadalcanal was the scene of heavy fighting between Japanese and US troops in World War 2. The chief products are coconuts, fish, fruit and timber. Area: 5,302sq km (2,047sq mi). Pop. (1991 est.) 60,692.

Guadeloupe French overseas département (since 1946), consisting of the islands of Basse-Terre (w), Grande-Terre (E), and several smaller islands in the Leeward Islands, E WEST INDIES. Discovered in 1493 by Columbus, Guadeloupe was settled by the French (1635), briefly held by Britain and Sweden, and reverted to French rule in 1816. Chief crops are sugar cane and bananas. Industries: distilling, tourism. Area: 1,780sq km (687sq mi). Pop. (1990) 378,178.

Guam Southernmost and largest of the MARI-ANA ISLANDS in the w Pacific Ocean; the capital is Agaña. An unincorporated US territory, Guam was discovered by Ferdinand Magellan (1521), and ceded to the USA (1898). Guam was the first US territory to be occupied by the Japanese during World War 2. Industries: oil refining, palm oil, fish products. Area: 541sq km (209sq mi). Pop (1992 est.) 140,200.

Guangxi (Kwangsi) Autonomous region in s China; the capital is Nanning. It was established in 1958 for the Zhuang, China's largest minority nationality. Cultivation is limited by the mountainous terrain. Minerals include manganese, zinc, tin, tungsten and antimony. Industries: oil refining, fertilizers. Area: 220,495sq km (85,133sq mi). Pop. (1990) 21,000,000.

Guangzhou (Canton) Largest city in s China, on the Pearl River; capital of Guangdong province. Since 300 BC it has been a trading port. The birthplace of SUN YAT-SEN, it was the focal point of the nationalist revolution (1911). It is s China's leading industrial and commercial city. Industries: textiles, rubber products, shipbuilding, sugar refining, iron, steel. Pop. (1993 est.) 3,560,000.

Guatemala Republic in Central America; the capital is GUATEMALA CITY. **Land and climate** Guatemala contains a densely populated fertile mountain region, where Guatemala City is situated. The highlands contain many volcanoes. The inactive volcano Tajmulco is the highest peak in Central America, at 4,211m (13,816ft). South of the highlands lie the Pacific coastal lowlands. North of the highlands is the thinly populated Caribbean plain and a vast tropical forest. Guatemala's largest lake, Izabal, drains into the Caribbean Sea. Guatemala lies in the tropics and the lowlands are hot and rainy. The central mountain region is more temperate. Guatemala City, at c.1,500m (5,000ft), has a marked dry season between November and April. Tropical hardwood forests exist in the N, with mangrove swamps on the coast. Much of the land on the Pacific plains is farmed. **Economy** Guatemala is a lower-middle-income developing nation. Agriculture employs 50% of the workforce. Coffee, sugar, bananas and beef are leading exports. Other crops are cardamom and cotton. Maize is the chief food crop, but Guatemala has to import food. Forestry is a major activity. Tourism and manufacturing are growing in importance. **History and politics** Between AD 300 and 900, the

GUATEMALA	
AREA:	108,890sq km (42,042sq mi)
POPULATION:	9,745,000
CAPITAL (POPULATION):	Guatemala City (2,000,000)
GOVERNMENT:	Republic
ETHNIC GROUPS:	Native American 45%, Ladino (mixed Hispanic and Native American) 45%, White 5%, Black 2%, others including Chinese 3%
LANGUAGES:	Spanish (official)
RELIGIONS:	Christianity (Roman Catholic 75%, Protestant 25%)
CURRENCY:	Guatemalan quetzal = 100 centavos

QUICHÉ branch of the MAYA ruled much of Guatemala, but inexplicably abandoned their cities on the N plains. In 1523–24 the Spanish conquistador Pedro de Alvarado defeated the native tribes. In 1821 Guatemala became independent. From 1823–39 it formed part of the Central American Federation. In 1941 Guatemala nationalized the German-owned coffee plantations. After World War 2 Guatemala embarked on further nationalizations. In 1960 the mainly Quiché Guatemalan Revolutionary National Unity Movement (URNG) began a guerrilla war, which killed over 100,000 people. During the 1960s and 1970s, Guatemala was beset by terrorism and political assassinations. In 1976 Guatemala City was devastated by an earthquake. In 1983 Guatemala reduced its claims to BELIZE. Civilian rule was restored in 1984, after the USA withdrew backing for the Guatemalan military. In 1995 an accord was signed recognizing the rights of the indigenous population. Support for the URNG has dwindled and in 1996 the civil war officially ended. In 1996 Alvaro Arzú was elected president.

Guatemala City (Ciudad Guatemala) Capital of Guatemala, on a plateau in the Sierra Madre; the largest city in Central America. Founded in 1776, the city was the capital of the Central American Federation from 1823–39. It was badly damaged by earthquakes in 1917–18 and in 1976. Industries: mining, furniture, textiles, handicrafts. Pop. (1989 est.) 2,000,000.

guava Any of 100 species of fruit-bearing trees or shrubs native to tropical America and the West Indies. The large white flowers produce a berry-like fruit. Family Myrtaceae.

Guayaquil City on the River Guayas, near the Gulf of Guayaquil, w Ecuador; chief port and largest city of Ecuador. Industries: textiles, pharmaceuticals, leather goods, cement, iron products, oil refining, fruit. Pop. (1990) 1,508,444.

gudgeon Freshwater CARP found in rivers from Britain to China. It has an elongated body, variable colour, and a small mouth with barbels. Length: 20cm (8in). Species *Gobio gobio*.

guelder rose Plant of the HONEYSUCKLE family (Caprifoliaceae). It has globular clusters of white or pink flowers. Species *Viburnum opulus*.

Guelph Political faction in medieval Italy, opposed to the GHIBELLINE. The two factions were linked to rival families contending for the HOLY ROMAN EMPIRE in the 12th century. In 1198 OTTO IV (a Guelph) became Holy Roman emperor. In the battle for control of Italy, the Guelphs took the side of the papacy, while the Ghibellines backed the emperor FREDERICK II. The Ghibellines were defeated by the Guelphs at Tagliacozzo in 1268, though the feud lived on.

guenon Any of 10–20 species of long-tailed, slender, medium-sized African MONKEYS found s of the Sahara Desert. Guenons are omnivorous tree-dwellers, living in small troops dominated by an old male. Genus *Cercopithecus*.

Guernsey Second-largest island in the CHANNEL ISLANDS; the capital is St Peter Port. It constitutes a bailiwick with several smaller islands, including Alderney and SARK. Its mild, sunny climate is ideal for dairy farming and horticulture. Tourism is also important. Area: 78sq km (30sq mi). Pop. (1991) 58,867.

guerrilla warfare Small-scale ground combat operations frequently designed to harass, rather than destroy, the enemy. Such tactics are especially suited to difficult terrain and rely on lightning attacks and aid from civilian sympathizers. In the 20th century, guerrilla tactics have been used by many nationalist and communist movements.

Guevara, "Che" (Ernesto) (1928–67) Argentine-Cuban revolutionary leader. He became associated with Fidel CASTRO in Mexico, and returned with him to Cuba in 1956 to conduct guerrilla activities against the BATISTA regime. He disappeared from public view in 1965. Two years later he was captured and killed while trying to establish a communist guerrilla base in Bolivia. His remains were returned to Cuba in 1997.

guided missile Missile controlled during its flight by exterior or interior control systems. There are four types: surface-to-surface, surface-to-air, air-to-air, air-to-surface. The first guided missiles were built in Germany during World War 2. Post-war developments ranged from huge intercontinental ballistic missiles (ICBMs) to small hand-launched anti-tank missiles. The multiple independently targeted re-entry vehicles (MIRVs) – ICBMs with many sub-missiles – were developed in the late 1960s. The CRUISE MISSILE has wings like an aeroplane, making it capable of flying at low altitudes.

guillemot Small, usually black-and-white seabird of the AUK family (Alcidae). It lives on cold Northern Hemisphere coastlines and dives for food. Nesting in colonies, it lays two eggs. Length: *c.* 43cm (17in). Genera *Cepphus* and *Uria*.

guillotine Mechanized device for execution by beheading adopted during the FRENCH REVOLUTION. First used in 1792, *c.*1,400 died under it during the REIGN OF TERROR. It remained in use in France until the abolition of CAPITAL PUNISHMENT in 1981. The term also describes a British parliamentary procedure (first used in 1887) by which a set time is allotted to various stages of a bill in order to speed its passage into law.

Guinea Republic in W Africa; the capital is CONAKRY. **Land and climate** Guinea can be divided into four regions: an alluvial coastal plain, which includes Conakry; the highland region of the Fouta Djallon, the source of one of Africa's longest rivers, the NIGER; the NE savanna; and the SE Guinea Highlands, which rise to 1,752m (5,748ft) at Mount Nimba. Guinea has a tropical climate. Conakry has heavy rains between May and November. During the dry season, hot, harmattan winds blow from the SAHARA. Mangrove swamps grow along parts of the coast. Inland, the Fouta Djallon is largely open grassland. North-eastern Guinea is tropical savanna. Rainforests grow in the Guinea Highlands. **Economy** Guinea is a low-income developing country. It is the world's second-largest producer of bauxite, which accounts for 90% of its exports. Guinea has 25% of the world's known reserves of bauxite. Other natural resources include diamonds, gold, iron ore and uranium. Due to the mining industry, the rail and road infrastructure is improving. Agriculture (mainly at subsistence level) employs 78% of the workforce. Major crops include bananas, cassava, coffee, palm kernels, pineapples, rice and sweet potatoes. Cattle and other livestock are raised in highland areas. **History** The NE Guinea plains formed part of the medieval empire of Ghana. The Malinke formed the Mali empire, which dominated the region in the 12th century, before the advent of the SONGHAI empire. Portuguese explorers arrived in the mid-15th century, and the slave trade began soon afterwards. From the 17th century, other European slave traders became active in Guinea. In the early 18th century, the FULANI gained control of the Fouta Djallon. Following a series of wars, France gained control and made Guinea the colony of French Guinea (1891). France exploited Guinea's bauxite deposits and mining unions developed. In 1958 Guinea voted to become an independent republic. France severed all aid. Its first president, Sékou Touré (1958–84),

---

GUINEA

AREA: 245,860sq km (94,927sq mi)
POPULATION: 6,116,000
CAPITAL (POPULATION): Conakry (705,000)
GOVERNMENT: Multiparty republic
ETHNIC GROUPS: Fulani 40%, Malinke 26%, Susu 11%, Kissi 7%, Kpelle 5%
LANGUAGES: French (official)
RELIGIONS: Islam 85%, traditional beliefs 5%, Christianity 2%
CURRENCY: Guinean franc = 100 cauris

adopted a Marxist programme of reform and embraced Pan-Africanism. Opposition parties were banned and dissent was brutally suppressed. In 1970 Guinea was invaded by Portuguese Guinea (Guinea-Bissau). Conakry acted as the headquarters for independence movements in Guinea-Bissau. A military coup followed Touré's death, and established the Military Committee for National Recovery (CMRN) led by Colonel Lansana Conté (1984). **Politics** Conté improved relations with the West and introduced free-market reforms. Civil unrest forced the introduction of a multiparty system in 1992, and Conté was elected president amid claims of electoral fraud. An attempted military coup in February 1996 proved unsuccessful.

Guinea-Bissau Small republic in West Africa; the capital and chief port is Bissau. **Land and Climate** Guinea-Bissau is mostly low-lying, with a broad, swampy coastal plain and broad river estuaries. The land rises to low plateaus in the E. Guinea-Bissau has a tropical climate, with a dry season (December to May) and a rainy season. Mangrove forests grow along the coasts, and dense rainforest covers much of the coastal plain. Inland, forests merge into tropical savanna, with open grassland on the high ground. **Economy** Guinea-Bissau is a poor country, with agriculture (mostly subsistence) employing over 80% of its workforce. Major crops: rice, coconuts, groundnuts, the last two making up 40% of Guinea-Bissau's exports. Fishing is also important. **History** It was first visited by Portuguese navigators in 1446. Between the 17th and early 19th centuries, Portugal used the coast as a slave trade base. In 1836 Portugal appointed a governor to administer Guinea-Bissau and the Cape Verde Islands, but in 1879 the two territories were separated and Guinea-Bissau became the colony of Portuguese Guinea. In 1956 African nationalists founded the African Party for the Independence of Guinea and Cape Verde (PAIGC). Portugal's determination to keep its overseas territories forced the the PAIGC to begin a guerrilla war (1963), and by 1968 it held 66% of the country. In 1972 a rebel National Assembly in the PAIGC-controlled area voted to form the independent republic of Guinea-Bissau.

GUINEA-BISSAU
AREA: 36,120sq km (13,946sq mi)
POPULATION: 1,006,000
CAPITAL (POPULATION): Bissau (126,900)
GOVERNMENT: Multiparty republic
ETHNIC GROUPS: Balante 27%, Fulani (or Peul) 23%, Malinke (Mandingo or Mandinka) 12%, Mandyako 11%, Pepel 10%
LANGUAGES: Portuguese (official)
RELIGIONS: Traditional beliefs 54%, Islam 38%, Christianity 8%
CURRENCY: Guinea-Bissau peso = 100 centavos

In 1974 it formally achieved independence (followed by Cape Verde in 1975). In 1980 an army coup led by Major João Vieira overthrew the government. The new Revolutionary Council was against unification with Cape Verde; it concentrated on national policies and socialist reforms. In 1991 the PAIGC voted to introduce a multiparty system. The PAIGC won the 1994 elections, and Vieira was re-elected president.

guinea fowl Pheasant-like game bird of Africa and Madagascar. The common domestic guinea hen (*Numida meleagris*) is blue, grey or black with white spots and an ornamental crest. Length: to 50cm (20in). Family Phasianidae.

guinea pig Type of cavy found in South America. The domestic *Cavia porcellus* is a popular pet. It has a large head, soft fur, short legs and no tail. It eats grass and other green plants. *Cavia aperea* is a wild species. Family Caviidae.

Guinness, Sir Alec (1914–) British stage and film actor. Guinness won fame for his performances in the Ealing Studios comedies, such as *The Lavender Hill Mob* (1951) and *The Ladykillers* (1955). He won a Best Actor Oscar for *Bridge on the River Kwai* (1957). Other films include *Lawrence of Arabia* (1962), *Doctor Zhivago* (1965), *Star Wars* (1977), *A Passage to India* (1984), and *Little Dorrit* (1988).

Guise, House of Ducal house of Lorraine, the most powerful family in 16th-century France. Claude, duke of Lorraine (1496–1550), founded the house in 1528. His son François (1519–63) supervised the massacre of Huguenots at Vassy in 1562, precipitating the French Wars of Religion. His brother Charles (1524–74), cardinal of Lorraine, played an important role at the Council of Trent. Their sister, Marie of Scotland, married James V, and their daughter, Mary (later Mary, Queen of Scots), married the future François II of France. François' son, Henri (1550–88), helped organize the Saint Bartholomew's Day Massacre (1572) and led the Holy League, which vehemently opposed Protestantism. Guise power declined when Henry IV acceded to the throne.

guitar Plucked stringed musical instrument. The modern guitar has six or 12 strings. In the 1940s Les Paul invented the electric guitar, now a standard instrument in blues, pop and rock music. Acoustic and semi-acoustic guitars are also widely used in folk and jazz.

Guizhou (Kweichow) Province in s China; the capital is Guiyang. Guizhou became a Chinese province in the Ming dynasty. During World War 2, it served as a military base for Allied forces. It was taken by Chinese communists in 1950. Industries: coal mining, iron ore, mercury. Area: 174,060sq km (67,204sq mi). Pop. (1990) 32,370,000.

Gujarat State in w India, on the Arabian Sea; the capital is Gandhinagar. Absorbed into the Mauryan empire in the 3rd century BC, it was a centre of Jainism under the Maitraka Dynasty (5th–8th centuries AD). In the early 15th century it was an autonomous Muslim sultanate. Under British rule it became a province (1857). After independence it was established as a separate state. It is highly industrialized, with substantial reserves of oil and gas. Industries: cotton textiles, salt mining, electrical engineering, petrochemicals. Area: 195,984sq km (75,669sq mi). Pop. (1994 est.) 44,235,000.

Gujarati (Gujerati) Modern language of N India. It is the official language of GUJARAT. Belonging to the Indic branch of INDO-EUROPEAN LANGUAGES, it began to evolve in c. AD 1000. Gujarati is spoken by more than 30 million inhabitants of Gujarat state and other Asian communities worldwide.

Gulf States Countries around the Persian (Arabian) Gulf, including IRAN, IRAQ, KUWAIT, SAUDI ARABIA, QATAR, Trucial OMAN and the BAHRAIN islands. Since the 1960s, the political and economic importance of the states has been bolstered by the extensive exploitation of oil reserves.

Gulf Stream Relatively fast-moving current of the N Atlantic Ocean. It flows from the straits of Florida, USA, along the E coast of North America, then E across the Atlantic (as the North Atlantic Drift) to the NW European coast. The current warms coastal climates along its course.

Gulf War (16 January 1991–28 February 1991) Military action by a US-led coalition of 32 states to expel Iraqi forces from KUWAIT. Iraqi forces invaded Kuwait (2 August 1990) and claimed it as an Iraqi province. On 7 August 1990, Operation Desert Shield began a mass deployment of coalition forces to protect Saudi oil reserves. Economic sanctions failed to secure Iraqi withdrawal, and the UN Security Council set a deadline of 15 January 1991 for the withdrawal of Iraqi forces. Iraqi president Saddam HUSSEIN ignored the ultimatum, and General Norman SCHWARZKOPF launched Operation Desert Storm. Within a week, extensive coalition air attacks had secured control of the skies. Iraqi ground forces were defenceless against the coalition's superior weaponry. Iraq launched Scud missile attacks on Saudi Arabia and Israel, in the hope of weakening Arab support for the coalition. On 24 February, the ground war was launched. Iraqi troops burned Kuwaiti oil wells as they fled. Kuwait was liberated two days later, and a cease-fire was declared on 28 February. Saddam Hussein remained in power. An estimated 100,000 Iraqi troops were killed, 600,000 wounded, captured or deserted; 300 coalition force soldiers were killed.

gull (seagull) Any of various ground-nesting birds found along coastlines worldwide. They eat carrion, refuse, fish, shellfish, eggs and young birds. The herring gull (*Larus argentatus*) is grey and white with black markings, hooked bill, pointed wings and webbed feet. It grows to 56–66cm (22–26in). The black-headed gull (*L. ridibundus*) is smaller. Family Laridae.

gum Secretions of plants. Gums are chemically complex, consisting mainly of various saccha-

rides bound to organic acids. Common examples are gum arabic, agar and tragacanth. *See also* EUCALYPTUS; RESINS

gun Tubular weapon firing a projectile, usually by force of explosion. The term is now restricted to ARTILLERY pieces with a relatively high muzzle velocity and a flat trajectory. PISTOLS, RIFLES and MACHINE GUNS are usually described as guns; mortars and howitzers are not.

gunpowder Mixture of saltpetre (potassium nitrate), charcoal and sulphur. When ignited, it expands violently due to the almost instantaneous conversion of solid ingredients into gases. It was used extensively in firearms until c.1900, when it was replaced by smokeless powders such as cordite.

Gunpowder Plot (November 1605) Failed Roman Catholic conspiracy to blow up JAMES I of England and his Parliament. The leader of the plot was Robert Catesby, and its chief perpetrator Guy FAWKES. The plotters were arrested on 5 November, a date now celebrated in Britain as Bonfire Night.

Gupta dynasty (c.320–c.550) Ruling house whose kingdom covered most of N India. It was founded by Chandragupta I. The Gupta dynasty embraced Buddhism, and is seen as a golden age. It reached its greatest extent at the end of the 4th century, but declined at the end of the 5th century under concerted attack from the HUNS.

Gurdwara (Sanskrit, Guru's doorway) Sikh temple housing a copy of the *Adi Granth*, the holy scripture of SIKHISM. There are several historically important *gurdwaras*, such as the Golden Temple of AMRITSAR, Punjab.

Gurkha Hindu ruling caste of Nepal since 1768. They speak a SANSKRIT language. The name also denotes a Nepalese soldier in the British or Indian army.

Gustavus I (Vasa) (1496–1560) King of Sweden (1523–60) and founder of the Vasa dynasty. He led a victorious rebellion against the invading Danes in 1520. In 1523 he was elected king and the Kalmar Union was destroyed. During his reign Sweden gained independence.

Gustavus II (Adolphus) (1594–1632) King of Sweden (1611–32). His reign was distinguished by constitutional, legal and educational reforms. He ended war with Denmark (1613) and Russia (1617). He entered the THIRTY YEARS WAR and died in battle.

Gutenberg, Johann (1400–68) German goldsmith and printer, credited with the invention of PRINTING from movable metallic type. He experimented with printing in Mainz in the 1430s. He produced the first printed Bible, known as the *Gutenberg Bible* or *Mazarin Bible* (c.1455).

Guyana (formerly British Guiana) Republic on the Atlantic Ocean, NE South America; the capital is GEORGETOWN. **Land and Climate** Over 80% of Guyana is forested. Its interior includes the valleys of the Essequibo River and the Pakaraima Moun-

GUYANA

AREA: 214,970sq km (83,000sq mi)
POPULATION: 808,000
CAPITAL (POPULATION): Georgetown (188,000)
GOVERNMENT: : Multiparty republic
ETHNIC GROUPS: Asian Indian 49%, Black 36%, Mixed 7%, Amerindian 7%, Portuguese, Chinese
LANGUAGES: English (official)
RELIGIONS: Christianity (Protestant 34%, Roman Catholic 18%), Hinduism 34%, Islam 9%
CURRENCY: Guyana dollar = 100 cents

tains, which rise to 2,772m (9,094ft) at Mount Roraima. The coastal plain is largely reclaimed marshland and mangrove swamp. Guyana has a hot and humid climate. Rainfall is heavy. There are two dry seasons: February to April, and August to November. **Economy** Guyana is a poor, developing country, its economy dominated by mining and agriculture. Principal exports: sugar, rice, bauxite. Diamond and gold mining are important. Fishing, forestry and tourism are expanding. **History** The Dutch settled here in 1581, and the Treaty of Breda (1667) awarded them the area. Plantations began in the 18th century under the control of the Dutch West India Company. Britain gained control in the early 19th century, setting up the colony of British Guiana (1831). Slavery was abolished in 1838. After World War 2, progress towards self-government was achieved with a new constitution (1952) and the election of Dr Cheddi Jagan. British Guiana became independent in 1966, and Forbes Burnham of the socialist People's National Congress (PNC) became the first prime minister. Ethnic conflict between the majority East Indian and African minority marred much of the late 1960s. In 1970 Guyana became a republic. In 1980 Burnham became president, and a new constitution increased his power. After Burnham's death (1985), Desmond Hoyte introduced liberal reforms. Hoyte was defeated in 1992 presidential elections by Jagan. Jagan's People's Progressive Party (PPP) formed the first non-PNC government since independence. On the death of Jagan in 1997, Samuel Hinds became president.

Gwent County in SE Wales; the county town is Cwmbran. It is drained by the Usk and Wye rivers. Dairying is important in the Usk valley. Sheep are reared in upland areas. Industries: aluminium, tin plate, chemicals, textiles, electronics. Area: 1,376sq km (531sq mi). Pop. (1991) 442,212.

Gwynedd County in NW Wales, on the Irish Sea coast; the administrative centre is CAERNARVON. Gwynedd includes most of the Snowdonia National Park. To the N lie the Lleyn peninsula and the island of Anglesey. Industries: slate quarrying, hydroelectric power, tourism. Area: 3,866sq km (1,493sq mi). Pop. (1990) 235,452.

gymnastics Multidisciplined sport requiring suppleness, strength and poise in a variety of regulated exercises. Men perform in six events: vault, parallel bars, horizontal bars, pommel horse, rings and floor exercises. Women perform in four events: vault, balance beam, asymmetrical bars and floor exercises. Exercises are rated in terms of difficulty, and points are awarded for technical skill and artistry.

gymnosperm Seed plant with naked seeds borne on scales, usually cones. Most EVERGREENS are gymnosperms. All living seed-bearing plants are divided into two main groups: gymnosperms and ANGIOSPERMS. In the Five KINGDOMS classification system, gymnosperms comprise three distinct phyla: Coniferophyta (such as PINE, SPRUCE and CEDAR); Ginkgophyta (a single species, the GINKGO); and Gnetophyta (strange plants such as *Welwitschia*, *Ephedra* and *Gnetum*).

gynaecology Area of medicine concerned with the female reproductive organs. Its study and practice is often paired with OBSTETRICS.

gypsum Most common sulphate mineral, hydrated calcium sulphate ($CaSO_4.2H_2O$). Beds of gypsum occur in sedimentary rocks, where it is associated with HALITE. It crystallizes in the monoclinic system. Varieties are ALABASTER, selenite (transparent and foliated) and satin spar (silky and fibrous). It is a source of plaster of Paris. Hardness 2; s.g. 2.3.

gypsy *See* ROMANY

gypsy moth Small tussock MOTH with black zigzag markings; the larger female is a lighter colour. The caterpillar feeds on forest and fruit trees, and can be a serious pest. Length: 5cm (2in). Family Lepidoptera; species *Lymantria dispar*.

gyroscope Symmetrical spinning disc that can adapt to any orientation, being mounted in gimbals (a pair of rings with one swinging freely in the other). When a gyroscope is spinning, a change in the orientation of the gimbals does not change the orientation of the spinning wheel. This means that changes in direction of an aircraft or ship can be determined without external references. A gyrostabilizer is used to stabilize the roll of a ship or aircraft. *See also* AUTOPILOT

H/h is derived from the Semitic letter cheth. It was taken into the Greek alphabet as eta. In its earlier form it passed into the Roman alphabet.

Haarlem City on the River Spaarne, W Netherlands; capital of North Holland province. A centre of Dutch painting in the 16th and 17th centuries, it is famous for its tulip bulbs. Industries: electronic equipment, publishing and printing. Pop. (1994) 150,213.

Haber process Industrial process (invented by Fritz Haber and Carl Bosch) in which nitrogen from the atmosphere is "fixed" by synthesizing ammonia. A mixture of nitrogen and hydrogen is passed over a heated catalyst at a pressure of $c.1,000$ atmospheres. The chemical reaction $N_2+3H_2\rightarrow 2NH_3$ occurs. *See also* NITROGEN FIXATION

habitat Place in which an organism normally lives. A habitat is defined by characteristic physical conditions and the presence of other organisms.

Habsburg (Hapsburg) Austrian royal dynasty, a leading ruling house in Europe from the 13th–19th century. It became a major force when Count Rudolph was elected king of the Germans (1273). From 1438–1806 the Habsburgs ruled the HOLY ROMAN EMPIRE. Under CHARLES V their dominions included the Low Countries, Spain and its empire, and parts of Italy. From 1556 the house was divided into Austrian and Spanish branches. The Spanish branch ended in 1700, and the male line of the Austrian branch ended in 1740. MARIA THERESA, though losing Silesia, re-established the house as that of Habsburg-Lorraine. By 1867 the Habsburg empire was reduced to the AUSTRO-HUNGARIAN EMPIRE. It finally broke up in 1918, when CHARLES I was deposed.

hacker In computing, a person who obtains unauthorized access to a computer DATABASE. A hacker, who usually gains access through the public telephone system using a MODEM, may read or even alter the information in the database.

haddock Marine fish found in cold and temperate waters, primarily in the Northern Hemisphere. Dark grey and silver, it has a large, dark blotch near the pectoral fins. Length: to about 90cm (36in); weight: to 11kg (24.5lb). Family Gadidae; species *Melanogrammus aeglefinus*.

Hades In Greek mythology, the world of the dead, ruled by PLUTO and PERSEPHONE; also another name for Pluto. The dead were ferried to Hades by CHARON across the river STYX. In Hades the virtuous were led to ELYSIUM. The wicked were confined to Tartarus, the bottomless pit.

Hadrian, Publius Aelius (76–138) Roman emperor (117–138). Nephew and protegé of Emperor TRAJAN, he adopted a policy of imperial retrenchment, discouraging new conquests, relinquishing territory hard to defend, and ordering the construction of HADRIAN'S WALL in Britain. He erected Hadrian's Villa, Tivoli, and rebuilt the PANTHEON. The erection of a shrine to Jupiter on the site of the Temple in Jerusalem provoked a Jewish revolt (132–135) which was ruthlessly suppressed.

Hadrian's Wall Defensive fortification in N England. Erected (AD 122–36) on the orders of the Roman Emperor HADRIAN. It extended 118.3km (73.5mi) and was about 2.3m (7.5ft) thick and 1.8–4.6m (6–15ft) high. Forts were built along its length. Extensive stretches of the wall survive.

hadron Group of SUBATOMIC PARTICLES that are influenced by the STRONG NUCLEAR FORCE. Made up of QUARKS, the group can be divided into BARYONS, such as the NEUTRON and PROTON, and MESONS. Over 150 hadrons have been discovered and with the exception of the proton and antiproton they are all unstable. Unlike LEPTONS, they have a measurable size.

haemoglobin Protein present in the ERYTHROCYTES of vertebrates. It carries oxygen to all cells in the body by combining with it to form oxyhaemoglobin. Oxygen attaches to the haem part of the protein, which contains iron; the globin part is a globular PROTEIN.

haemophilia Hereditary blood clotting disorder causing prolonged external or internal bleeding, often without apparent cause. Haemophilia A is caused by inability to synthesize blood factor VIII, a substance essential to clotting. This can be managed with injections of factor VIII. The rarer haemophilia B is caused by a deficiency of blood factor IX. The gene for both types is passed on almost exclusively from mother to son.

haemorrhage Loss of blood from a damaged vessel. It may be external, flowing from a wound, or internal, as from internal injury or a bleeding ulcer. Blood loss from an artery is most serious, causing shock and death if untreated. Chronic bleeding can lead to ANAEMIA. Internal bleeding is signalled by the appearance of blood in the urine or sputum.

hafnium Silvery metallic element (symbol Hf), one of the TRANSITION ELEMENTS. It was discovered in 1923 by Dirk Coster and Georg von Hevesy. Hafnium's chief source is as a by-product in obtaining the element ZIRCONIUM. It is used as a neutron absorber in reactor control rods. Properties: a.n. 72; r.a.m. 178.49; r.d. 13.31; m.p. 2,227°C (4,041°F); b.p. 4,602°C (8,316°F); most common isotope Hf^{180} (35.24%).

Haggadah Story of the Exodus and redemption of the people of Israel by God, read during PASSOVER services. Developed over centuries, it includes excerpts from the Bible, rabbinical writings, psalms, stories and prayers.

Haggai (active 6th century BC) Old Testament prophet. He is probably not the author of the Book of Haggai, the tenth of the 12 books of the Minor

Prophets. The book records four prophesies made by Haggai in 521 BC, in which he urged the Jews to make haste in the rebuilding of the TEMPLE.

Haggard, Sir (Henry) Rider (1856–1925) British novelist. He wrote hugely successful romantic adventure novels, such as *King Solomon's Mines* (1885), *She* (1887) and *Allan Quatermain* (1887).

Hagia Sophia (Aya Sofia) Byzantine church in Istanbul. It was built (532–37) for Emperor JUSTINIAN I. A supreme masterpiece of Byzantine architecture, the interior contains columns of marble and porphyry. The church was converted into a mosque in 1453. The Hagia Sophia now acts as a museum.

Hague, William Jefferson British politician, leader of the Conservative Party (1997–). He became a Conservative MP in 1989. In 1995 he joined John MAJOR's cabinet as secretary of state for Wales. After the Conservatives' defeat in the 1997 general election, Hague emerged as the youngest Tory leader since William Pitt in 1783. He is strongly opposed to the European single currency.

Hague, The ('s-Gravenhage or Den Haag) City in the W Netherlands; capital of South Holland province. It is the seat of the Dutch government. Founded in the 15th century, the city has been an intellectual and political centre since the 17th century. The Hague has been the seat of the International Court of Justice since 1945. Much of the city's economy depends on its diplomatic activities. Industries: textiles, pottery, furniture, chemicals. Pop. (1994) 445,279.

hahnium *See* ELEMENT 105

Hahn, Otto (1879–1968) German chemist. With Fritz Strassmann in 1939, he discovered nuclear fission, for which he won the 1944 Nobel Prize for chemistry. With Lise Meitner, he discovered protoactinium.

Haifa (Hefa) City in NW Israel, on Mount Carmel. It is the centre of the BAHA'I religion and is the seat of Haifa University (1963). It is one of Israel's largest ports. Industries: textiles, chemicals, shipbuilding, oil refining. Pop. (1992) 251,000.

Haig, Douglas, 1st Earl (1861–1928) British general. Soon after the beginning of World War 1, he became commander in chief of the British forces (1915). His policy of attrition produced enormous casualties but he cooperated effectively with Marshal Foch in the last stages of the war.

haiku Japanese poetry form consisting of 17 syllables in five-seven-five pattern, originally evoking a moment in nature. Matsuo Bashō (1644–94) is considered to be the finest exponent of the form, which remains popular in Japan.

hail Precipitation from clouds in the form of balls of ice. Hailstorms are associated with atmospheric turbulence extending to great heights together with warm, moist air nearer the ground.

Haile Selassie I (1892–1975) (Ras Tafari Makonnen) Emperor of Ethiopia (1930–74). When Italy invaded Ethiopia in 1935, he was forced into exile (1936), despite his appeal to the League of Nations for help. He drove out the Italians with British aid in 1941. Subsequently he became a leader among independent African nations, helping to found the ORGANIZATION OF AFRICAN UNITY (OAU) in 1963. Unrest at lack of reforms led to his being deposed by a military coup in 1974. He died while under arrest. *See also* RASTAFARIANISM

Hainan Island off S China, separated from the mainland by the Hainan Strait; the capital is Haikou. It has been under Chinese authority since the 2nd century BC. In 1988 it was designated a special economic zone. Its products include rubber, coffee, rice, timber, tin, copper, iron, steel and bauxite. Area: 33,991sq km (13,124sq mi). Pop. (1990) 6,420,000.

Haiphong Port on the Red River Delta, N Vietnam. Founded in 1874, it became the chief naval base of French Indochina. It was occupied by the Japanese during World War 2, bombed by the French in 1946 during the conflict with the Viet Minh, and heavily bombed by the USA in the Vietnam War. Industries: cement, glass, chemicals, cotton. Pop. (1989) 456,049.

hair Outgrowth of mammalian skin, with insulating, protective and sensory functions. It grows in a follicle, a tubular structure extending down through the EPIDERMIS to the DERMIS. New cells are continually added to the base of the hair; older hair cells become impregnated with KERATIN and die. Hair colour depends on the presence of MELANIN in the hair cells. A small muscle attached to the base of the hair allows it to be erected in response to nerve signals sent to the follicle. Erecting the hairs traps a thicker layer of air close to the skin, which acts as INSULATION. *See also* FUR

hairstreak Any of a group of butterflies of the family Lycaenidae. They are grey and brown and found in open areas on every continent, especially in the tropics. Hairstreaks have a quick erratic flight. Genus *Strymon*.

Haiti Independent nation occupying the W third of the Caribbean island of Hispaniola, and including the islands of Tortuga and Gonâve; the capital is PORT-AU-PRINCE. Much of the country is mountainous, with a humid tropical climate. Discovered by Columbus in 1492, Spanish settlements were established at the E end of the island and within 100 years most of the native Arawaks had died out through disease or ill-treatment. In the 17th century, French corsairs set up plantations in the W part of the island; in 1697 the Spanish recognized the area as French territory. Known as Saint Dominque, the region prospered in the 18th century. The sugar and coffee plantations were worked by African slaves, who soon formed the majority of the population. In 1790 Toussaint L'Ouverture led a slave revolt against the colonial rulers. In 1801, as governor general, he abolished slavery, but he was killed by the French two years later. The country was declared independent in 1804, under the name of Haiti, and Jean Jacques Dessalines became emperor. During the 19th century, Haiti experienced much political instability. From 1915–34 it was virtually governed by the USA. The election of François DUVALIER as president in 1957 inaugurated a period of corruption. Attempts to establish a democratic government in the 1980s and 1990s, after the deposition of the Duvalier family, were frustrated by the army. The democratically elected president Jean-Bertrand Aristide was removed from office by a military coup (1991), but was restored in 1994 with US backing. In 1995 René Préval was elected president. Haiti is the poorest country in the Western Hemisphere. Farming is not sufficient to supply domestic demand. There is some light manufacturing industry. Area: 27,750sq km (10,714sq mi). Pop. (1992 est.) 6,763,746.

Haitink, Sir Bernard (1929–) Dutch conductor, principal conductor of the Amsterdam Concertgebouw Orchestra (1961–88) and the London Philharmonic (1967–79). In 1987 he became musical director of the London Royal Opera House, where he was noted for superb WAGNER performances.

Hajj (Arabic, migration) Pilgrimage to MECCA, made in the 12th month of the Muslim year. All Muslims are required to undertake the Hajj. It is the last of the Five Pillars of ISLAM, the religious duties defined by the KORAN.

hake Marine fish found in cold and temperate waters. Its streamlined body is silver and brown. Length: to 1m (40in); weight: to 14kg (30lb). Family Gadidae or Merluccidae; species Atlantic *Merluccius bilinearis*; Pacific *M. productus*.

Hale, George Ellery (1868–1938) US astronomer who organized a number of observatories, including the Yerkes Observatory, completed in 1897, the Mount Wilson Observatory, completed in 1917, and the Palomar Observatory, which entered regular service in 1949.

half-life Time taken for one-half of the nuclei in a given amount of radioactive ISOTOPE to decay (change into another element or isotope). Only the half-life is measured because the decay is never considered to be total. Half-lives remain constant under any temperature or pressure, but there is a great variety among different isotopes. Oxygen-20 has a half-life of 14 seconds and Uranium-234 of 250,000 years. A radioactive isotope disintegrates by giving off alpha or beta particles, and a measurement of this rate of emission is the normal way of recording decay. The term "half-life" also refers to particles that spontaneously decay into new particles, such as a free neutron being transformed into an electron. *See also* RADIOACTIVITY; DATING, RADIOACTIVE

halibut Flatfish found worldwide in deep, cold to temperate seas. Important commercially, it is brownish on the eye side and white below. Family Pleuronectidae; species, Atlantic *Hippoglossus hippoglossus*, giant Pacific *H. stenolepis*.

Halicarnassus Ancient Greek city in sw Asia

Minor. In the 4th century BC it was a semi-independent state under the Persian governor, Mausolus, whose tomb was one of the SEVEN WONDERS OF THE WORLD.

halide Salt of one of the HALOGENS (elements in group VII of the PERIODIC TABLE), or a compound containing a halogen and one other element; examples are sodium fluoride and potassium chloride. The alkyl halides (haloalkanes) are organic compounds, such as methyl chloride (chloromethane CH_3Cl).

Halifax City and seaport in E Canada, on the Atlantic Ocean; capital of Nova Scotia. Founded in 1749, it developed as an important naval base. Industries: commercial fishing, shipbuilding, oil refining. Pop. (1992) 114,455.

halite Sodium chloride (NaCl), or common (rock) salt. It is found in evaporite sedimentary rocks, and in salt domes and dried lakes. It is colourless, white or grey with a glassy lustre. It has a cubic system of interlocking cubic crystals, granules and masses. It is important as table salt and as a source of CHLORINE. Hardness 2.5; s.g. 2.2.

Hall, Sir Peter (Reginald Frederick) (1930–) British theatrical director. He was director of the ROYAL SHAKESPEARE COMPANY (1961–73). He has directed opera at Glyndebourne and the Royal Opera House and made several films, including *Akenfield* (1974). He was director of the National Theatre of Great Britain (1973–88) and formed his own Peter Hall Company (1987).

Hallé, Sir Charles (1819–95) British conductor and pianist. In 1857 he formed a symphony orchestra in Manchester, England, which subsequently became the Hallé Orchestra. In 1893 he was a founder of the Royal Manchester College of Music.

Halley, Edmond (1656–1742) British astronomer and mathematician. His most famous achievement was to realize that comets could be periodic, following his observation of HALLEY'S COMET. It was Halley who financed Isaac NEWTON to write the *Principia*. He also charted variations in the Earth's magnetic field and established the magnetic origin of the AURORA borealis. He showed that atmospheric pressure decreases with altitude, and studied monsoons and trade winds.

Halley's comet Bright periodic COMET. It takes 76 years to complete an orbit that takes it from within Venus' orbit to outside Neptune's. It was observed by Edmond HALLEY in 1682; later he deduced that it was the same comet as had been seen in 1531 and 1607, and predicted its return in 1758. There are records of every return since 240 BC. In 1986 the Giotto space probe showed the nucleus to be an irregular object measuring 15×8km (9×5mi) and consisting of ice. Hale-Bopp is the brightest comet.

Hallowe'en (hallowed or holy evening) In medieval times, a holy festival observed on 31 October, the eve of All Saints' Day. It was merged with the ancient Celtic festival of Samhain. Today, Hallowe'en is observed as a festival of masquerade.

Hallstatt Small town in W central Austria, believed to be the site of the earliest IRON AGE culture in W Europe. Iron was worked there from c.700 BC. The site contains a large Celtic cemetery and a deep salt mine. Fine bronze and pottery objects have also been discovered.

hallucination Apparent perception of something that is not present. Although they may occur in any of the five senses, auditory hallucinations and visual hallucinations are the commonest. While they are usually symptomatic of psychotic disorders, hallucinations may result from fatigue or emotional upsets and can also be a side-effect of certain drugs.

hallucinogen Drug that causes HALLUCINATIONS. Hallucinogenic drugs, such as MESCALINE, were used in primitive religious ceremonies. Today drugs such as LSD are illicitly taken.

halogens Elements (FLUORINE, CHLORINE, BROMINE, IODINE and ASTATINE) belonging to group VII of the PERIODIC TABLE. They react with most other elements and with organic compounds. They produce crystalline salts (HALIDES) containing negative ions of the type F^- and Cl^-.

halon Any of several organic gases used in fire extinguishers. Chemically halons can be considered as simple HYDROCARBONS that have had some or all of their hydrogen atoms replaced by a HALOGEN. Similar to CHLOROFLUOROCARBONS (CFCs), they are ten times more destructive of the OZONE LAYER.

halophyte Any plant, usually a seed plant, which is able to live in salty conditions.

Hals, Frans (c.1580–1666) Dutch painter. He is best known for his paintings of robust, vital figures, such as the *Laughing Cavalier* (1624), and his group portraits. His more subdued later works have a dignity and strength approaching those of his contemporary, REMBRANDT.

Hamburg City, state and port in N Germany, on the River Elbe. Founded in the 9th century by CHARLEMAGNE, it was a founder of the HANSEATIC LEAGUE. Severely bombed during World War 2, it is now the country's second biggest city. It is a notable cultural centre. Industries: electronics, brewing, publishing, chemicals. Pop. (1990) 1,675,200.

Hamilcar Barca (d.228 BC) Carthaginian commander. Initially successful in the first of the PUNIC WARS, he was defeated in 241 BC. He suppressed a revolt of Carthaginian mercenaries in 238 BC and the following year conquered much of Spain. He was the father of HANNIBAL and Hasdrubal Barca.

Hamilton, James Hamilton, 1st Duke of (1606–49) Scottish political and military leader. He fought in the Thirty Years War. Later, as Charles I's commissioner in Scotland (1638–39), he failed to achieve a compromise with the COVENANTERS and led an army against them in 1639. He fought for Charles in the English CIVIL WAR, though his constant plotting resulted in his imprisonment (1644–45). In 1648 he led Scottish forces in support of the king. He was defeated by CROMWELL at Preston and executed.

Hamilton, Richard (1922–) British artist, a leader of the POP ART movement. He produced collages using images taken from commercial art. His best-known work is *Just what is it that makes today's homes so different, so appealing?* (1956).

Hamilton Capital and chief seaport of Bermuda, on Great Bermuda, at the head of Great Sound. Founded in 1790, it became the capital in 1815 and was made a free port in 1956. Tourism is the major industry. Pop. (1994) 1,100.

Hamilton City in Canada, in SE Ontario, 64km (40mi) SW of Toronto. Founded in 1813, it is an important communication and manufacturing centre. Industries: iron, steel, vehicles, electrical equipment, textiles. Pop. (1991, city) 318,499.

Hamito-Semitic languages See AFRO-ASIATIC LANGUAGES

Hammarskjöld, Dag (1905–61) Swedish diplomat and second secretary-general of the United Nations (1953–61), an office to which he brought great moral force. In 1956 he played a leading part in resolving the Suez Crisis. He sent a UN peace-keeping force to the Congo (now Zaïre) and later died there in an air crash. He was posthumously awarded the 1961 Nobel Peace Prize.

hammer In athletics, men's field event in which a spherical, metallic weight attached to a steel wire is thrown. The "hammer" weighs 7.26kg (16lb) and the wire is 1.2m (3.8ft) long. The thrower stands within a circle 2.13m (7ft) in diameter, and by rotating two or three times, builds up momentum before releasing the hammer. An Olympic event since 1900, the Olympic record stands at 64.09m (212ft 11in).

hammerhead Aggressive SHARK found in tropical marine waters and warmer temperate zones. It can be recognized by its head, which has extended sideways into two hammer-like lobes, with one eye and one nostril located at the tip of each. It is grey above and white below. Length: to 6.1m (20ft); weight: to 906kg (2,000lb). Family Sphyrnidae.

Hammerstein, Oscar, II (1895–1960) US lyricist and librettist. He worked with Jerome KERN on *Show Boat* (1927) and with Richard RODGERS on *Oklahoma!* (1943), *Carousel* (1945), *South Pacific* (1949), *The King and I* (1951), and *The Sound of Music* (1959).

Hammett, Dashiell (1894–1961) US author. Hammett created the hard-boiled, cynical detectives Sam Spade and Nick Charles. His books include *Red Harvest* (1929), *The Maltese Falcon* (1930) and *The Thin Man* (1934).

Hammurabi King of BABYLONIA (r. c.1792–c.1750 BC). By conquering neighbours, such as SUMERIA, he extended his rule in Mesopotamia and reorganized the empire under the Code of HAMMURABI. He was also a good administrator, improving productivity by building canals and granaries.

Hammurabi, Code of Ancient laws compiled under HAMMURABI. A copy of the code is in the Louvre, Paris. It is composed of 282 provisions with harsh penalties for offenders and includes the maxim, "An eye for an eye, a tooth for a tooth".

Hampden, John (1594–1643) English parliamentarian, a leader of the opposition to CHARLES I. As a result of his criticism and his part in drawing up the GRAND REMONSTRANCE, Hampden was one of the five members whom the king tried to arrest in the House of Commons in 1642, an act that precipitated the English CIVIL WAR.

Hampshire County in S England, bordering the English Channel; the county town is Winchester. There are traces of Iron Age hill forts. The area was settled in Roman times, the most notable remains being at Silchester. Predominantly agricultural, Hampshire contains the major port of Southampton and the naval base at Portsmouth. Its coastal resorts and the New Forest woodlands are tourist attractions. Industries: agriculture, oil refining, chemicals, brewing, electronics. Area: 3,782sq km (1,460sq mi). Pop. (1991) 1,541,547.

Hampton Court Palace Palace situated beside the River Thames, 23km (14mi) from Westminster, London. Cardinal WOLSEY began building in 1515, and gave it to HENRY VIII in 1526, hoping to regain his favour. The splendour of its architecture was matched by the garden, famous both for its maze and for the discreet towers which Henry added for liaisons with his mistresses. Christopher WREN rebuilt and extended the palace (1696–1704).

hamster Small, mainly nocturnal, burrowing RODENT native to Eurasia and Africa. It has internal cheek pouches for carrying food. Golden hamsters, popular as pets, are descendants of a single family discovered in Syria in 1930. Length: up to 18cm (7in). Family Cricetidae; species *Cricetus mesocricetus*.

Hamsun, Knut (1859–1952) Norwegian novelist, playwright and poet. A proponent of individualism, his work reflected his suspicion of modern Western culture. In 1920 he won the Nobel Prize in literature for *The Growth of the Soil* (1917). Other important novels include *Hunger* (1890), *Victoria* (1898), and *Vagabonds* (1927).

Han Imperial Chinese dynasty (202 BC–AD 220). It was founded by a rebellious peasant, Liu Pang, who established the capital at Chang'an. Under the Han, CONFUCIANISM became the state philosophy, and China achieved unprecedented power, prosperity, technological invention (paper, porcelain) and cultural growth, especially under the rule of Han Wu Ti in the 2nd century BC. A usurper, WANG MANG, interrupted the dynasty between AD 8 and 25; the dynasty is divided by that period into the Former Han and Later Han.

handball Name given to two games played mostly in Ireland and the USA. One is played indoors or outdoors with a hard, small ball by two or four gloved players on courts of one, three or four walls. A variant of this game that additionally utilizes wooden rackets is called **paddleball**. The other game, sometimes called **team** handball, is

played on a court where, between two goals and two goalkeepers, players catch, pass and throw a ball like a small basketball with the object of hurling the ball past the opposing goalkeeper.

Handel, George Frideric (1685–1759) German composer, who became a British citizen in 1726. One of the greatest composers of the BAROQUE period, his many works include operas (such as *Berenice*, *Serse* and *Semele*), oratorios (including *Samson* and *Judas Maccabaeus*), organ music, and chamber works. His most popular pieces include the *Water Music* (c.1717), *Music for the Royal Fireworks* (1749) and the oratorio *Messiah* (1742).

hang gliding GLIDING using a lightweight craft, usually with a triangular wing, which is stabilized by the weight of the pilot's body underneath. The wing may be rigid, but is usually made of fabric. Take-off is made by running down a slope, assisted by a steady updraught. The pilot hangs from a harness and, by using a control bar to shift body weight, steers the glider.

Hanging Gardens of Babylon One of the SEVEN WONDERS OF THE WORLD. The gardens are thought to have been spectacular, rising in a series of terraces (rather than hanging) and ingeniously irrigated by water pumped up from the Euphrates. They were probably built by NEBUCHADNEZZAR II (king of Babylon, 605–562 BC). Nothing remains of them.

hanging valley Valley that ends high up the face of a larger valley, possibly with a stream running through it and ending in a waterfall. Most hanging valleys result from glacial deepening of the main valley.

Hanks, Tom (1956–) US film star and director. Early films included *Splash* (1984) and *Big* (1988). His performance in *Philadelphia* (1993) won him a Best Actor Oscar. He won a second award for *Forrest Gump* (1994). In 1996 he made his directorial debut with *That Thing You Do!*

Hannibal (247–183 BC) Carthaginian general in the second of the PUNIC WARS, son of HAMILCAR BARCA. One of the greatest generals of ancient times, he fought against the Romans in Spain (221 BC). In 218 BC he invaded N Italy after crossing the Alps with a force of elephants and 40,000 troops. He won a series of victories in Italy, but was unable to capture Rome. In 203 BC he was recalled to Carthage to confront the invasion of SCIPIO AFRICANUS. Lacking cavalry, he was defeated at Zama (202 BC). After the war, as chief magistrate of Carthage, he alienated the nobility by reducing their power. They sought Roman intervention, and Hannibal fled to the Seleucid kingdom of ANTIOCHUS III. He fought under Antiochus against the Romans, was defeated and committed suicide.

Hanoi Capital of Vietnam and its second largest city, on the Red River. In the 7th century the Chinese ruled Vietnam from Hanoi; it later became capital of the Vietnamese empire. Taken by the French in 1883, the city became the capital of

French Indochina (1887–1945). From 1946–54 it was the scene of fierce fighting between the French and the Viet Minh. It was heavily bombed during the VIETNAM WAR. Industries: engineering, vehicles, textiles, rice milling. Pop. (1989) 1,088,862.

Hanover (Hannover) Former kingdom and province of Germany. In 1692 Duke Ernest Augustus, one of the dukes of Brunswick-Lüneberg, was created elector of Hanover; his lands were known thereafter as Hanover. His son George succeeded to the British throne (GEORGE I) in 1714. Divided during the Napoleonic era, Hanover was reconstituted as a kingdom in 1815. Allied with Austria in the AUSTRO-PRUSSIAN WAR (1866), it was annexed by Prussia after Austria's defeat. After World War 2 it was incorporated into the state of Lower Saxony.

Hanover (Hannover) City on the River Leine, N Germany; capital of Lower Saxony. Chartered in 1241, the city joined the HANSEATIC LEAGUE in 1386. In 1636 it became the residence of the dukes of Brunswick-Lüneberg (predecessors of the House of Hanover); GEORGE I was elector of Hanover. Hanover was badly damaged during World War 2, but many old buildings were later reconstructed. Industries: machinery, steel, textiles, rubber, chemicals. Pop. (1990) 520,900.

Hanover, House of German royal family and rulers of Britain from 1714–1901. The electors of Hanover succeeded to the English throne in 1714 under the terms of the Act of Settlement (1701) and the Act of Union (1707). GEORGE I, the first elector also to be king of England, was succeeded in both England and Hanover by GEORGE II, GEORGE III, GEORGE IV, and WILLIAM IV. Salic law forbade Queen Victoria's accession in Hanover; the Hanoverian title was inherited by her uncle, the Duke of Cumberland, and the crowns of Britain and Germany were separated.

Hansard Colloquial name for the daily record of the proceedings of the British Houses of Parliament. Named after Luke Hansard (1752–1828), printer to the Commons, who compiled unofficial reports.

Hanseatic League Commercial union of *c.*160 German, Dutch and Flemish towns established in the 13th century. The League protected its merchants by controlling the trade routes from the Baltic region to the Atlantic. It began to decline in the late 15th century with the opening up of the New World and aggressive trading by the British and Dutch.

Hanukkah (Chanukah or Feast of Lights) Eight-day festival celebrated in JUDAISM. It commemorates the re-dedication of the Jerusalem TEMPLE in 165 BC and the miracle of a one-day supply of oil lasting for eight days.

Hanuman In Hindu mythology, the monkey general who helped RAMA to find and rescue his wife, Sita. His attributes include great strength, agility and wisdom.

haploid Cell that has only one member of each CHROMOSOME pair. All human cells except GAMETES are DIPLOID, having 46 chromosomes. Gametes are haploid, having 23 chromosomes. The body cells of many lower organisms, including many algae and single-celled organisms, are haploid. *See also* MEIOSIS; ALTERNATION OF GENERATIONS

Harare (formerly Salisbury) Capital of Zimbabwe, in the NE part of the country. Settled by Europeans in 1890 as Fort Salisbury, it became capital of Southern Rhodesia in 1902. Harare served as capital of the Federation of Rhodesia and Nyasaland (1953–63) and of Rhodesia (1965–79). Industries: gold mining, textiles, steel, tobacco, chemicals, furniture. Pop. (1992) 1,184,169.

hard disk Rigid MAGNETIC DISK for storing computer PROGRAMS and DATA. The built-in hard disk drive in a typical personal COMPUTER consists of a number of hard platters coated with a magnetic material set on a common spindle. They are housed inside a sealed container, with a motor to spin the stack of platters, a head to write (record) and read (replay) each side of each platter, and associated electronic circuits.

Hardie, (James) Keir (1856–1915) British socialist politician, a founder of the LABOUR PARTY. He founded the newspaper *Labour Leader* and was chairman of the Independent Labour Party (1893–1900, 1913–14). He was the first Labour member of Parliament and for three years (1892–95) the only Labour representative.

Harding, Warren G. (Gamaliel) (1865–1923) 29th US President (1921–23). His campaign for a return to "normalcy" easily defeated the Democratic challenge. While in office, he left government to his cabinet and advisers (the "Ohio Gang"). His administration was one of the most corrupt in US history. The TEAPOT DOME SCANDAL forced a Congressional investigation. Harding died before the worst excesses became public, and he was succeeded by the vice-president, Calvin COOLIDGE.

hardness Resistance of a material to abrasion, cutting or indentation. The Mohs' scale is a means of expressing the comparative hardness of materials, particularly minerals, by testing them against ten standard materials. These range from (1) talc to (10) diamond (the hardest).

hardness of water Reluctance of water to produce a lather with soap, due to various dissolved salts, mainly calcium and magnesium. These salts give rise to an insoluble precipitate, which causes "fur" or "scale" in boilers, pipes and kettles. Lather is inhibited until all the dissolved salts are precipitated as scum, which floats on the surface. Hardness may be temporary (removed by boiling), caused by calcium bicarbonate; or permanent (not affected by boiling), caused by calcium sulphate.

hardware In computing, equipment as opposed to the programs, or software, with which a computer functions. The computer, keyboard, printer and electronic circuit boards are examples of hardware.

Hardy, Thomas (1840–1928) British novelist and poet. His birthplace of Dorset, England, formed the background to most of his writing. He began to write while training as an architect and published his first novel, *Desperate Remedies,* in 1871. His first major success was *Far from the Madding Crowd* (1874). The often tragic tales that followed remain among the most widely read 19th-century novels and include *The Return of the Native* (1878), *The Mayor of Casterbridge* (1886), *Tess of the d'Urbervilles* (1891) and *Jude the Obscure* (1895).

Hare, David (1947–) British playwright and director. Hare founded the Portable Theatre in 1968. He has worked as a dramatist and director for stage, film and television. His plays include *Slag* (1970), *Licking Hitler* (1978), *Pravda* (1985), *Strapless* (1989) and *The Absence of War* (1993).

hare Large member of the RABBIT family (Leporidae). Unlike rabbits, true hares (genus *Lepus*) have ears that are longer than their heads, and their young are born with open eyes and a full coat of fur. Length: to 76cm (30in); weight: to 4.5kg (10lb). Hares include the JACK RABBIT and snowshoe rabbit.

harebell Flowering plant of the bellflower family (CAMPANULACEAE), widespread as a wild flower of pastures and also cultivated in gardens. It has drooping, bell-shaped, mid-blue flowers. Species *Campanula rotundifolia.*

Hare Krishna Hindu religious movement. Members of the sect celebrate the life of KRISHNA, and believe that through a combination of self-denial, meditation, chanting, and reading the Hindu scriptures they will achieve true enlightenment and escape the cycle of reincarnation.

harelip Congenital cleft in the upper lip caused by the failure of the two parts of the palate to unite. It is often associated with a CLEFT PALATE.

harem Women's quarters in a Muslim household. It contained wives, concubines and female servants. The most famous harems were those of the Turkish sultans in Istanbul, which often had several hundred women and were guarded by eunuchs.

Hargreaves, James (1722–1778) British inventor and industrialist. In 1764 he invented the spinning jenny. This machine greatly speeded the spinning process of cotton by producing eight threads at the same time. In 1768 Hargreaves moved to Nottingham and became one of the first great factory owners.

Harlem Residential area of New York City, USA, a political and cultural focus for African-Americans. The Center for Research in Black Culture is located here, next to the Countee Cullen library, an historic meeting place for writers since the 1920s.

Harlem Renaissance Period of creativity, particularly in literature, among African-Americans in the 1920s. Centered in HARLEM, the Renaissance produced many fine writers, such as Countee Cullen, Langston Hughes and Claude McKay.

harmonica (mouth organ) Musical instrument consisting of a metal cassette containing metal reeds. The reeds are vibrated as the player blows or inhales through slots along one edge of the cassette.

harmonics In acoustics, additional notes whose frequencies are multiples of a basic (fundamental) note. When a violin string is plucked, the sounds correspond to vibrations of the string. The loudest sound (note) corresponds to the fundamental mode of vibration. But other weaker notes, corresponding to subsidiary vibrations, sound at the same time. Together these notes make up a harmonic series.

harmony In music, structure of chords and the relationships between them. The diatonic scale (from one C to the next on a piano, for example) is the basis of chord construction, and a harmonic progression from one chord to the next is defined by the KEY. The tonic, dominant and subdominant chords are the primary chords of a key (C, G, and F chords in the key of C) and composers, especially of the 18th and 19th centuries, followed specific rules of harmony.

Harold I (d.1040) (Harold Harefoot) Danish king and ruler of England (1035–40). An illegitimate son of CANUTE II, he claimed the crown, ruling as regent (1035–37). Elected king at Oxford, he disposed of his rival, Alfred the Aethling, and displaced the heir, his half-brother Hardecanute.

Harold II (1022–66) Last Anglo-Saxon king of England (1066). He was elected king following the death of EDWARD THE CONFESSOR, despite having pledged to support William of Normandy's (WILLIAM I) claim to the throne. He was immediately invaded by Harold III of Norway, whom he defeated. Three days later he was defeated and killed by William at the Battle of HASTINGS.

harp Ancient musical instrument consisting of a frame over which strings are stretched. Variations have been found in civilizations as diverse as Egyptian, Greek and Celtic. A modern orchestral harp has a large triangular frame that carries 47 strings. Seven pedals ensure the whole chromatic range is covered by altering the pitch of the strings.

harpsichord Keyboard musical instrument. Its metal strings are mechanically plucked by quill plectrums. Its volume can barely be regulated, although stops may be used to bring extra strings into use. Historic instruments may have had two or, rarely, three keyboards. The harpsichord was the principal keyboard instrument from 1500 to 1750 but was later replaced by the PIANO.

harrier BIRD OF PREY. Active by day, it frequents grasslands where it swoops on small animals. It has a small bill and long wings, legs and tail. Length: 38–50cm (15–20in). Family Accipitridae; genus *Circus.*

Harrisburg Capital of Pennsylvania, USA, in the SE of the state, on the Susquehanna River. Established as a trading post in *c.*1718, by 1785 a town was established, which was the scene of the Harrisburg Convention (1788). It became the state capital in 1812. Industries: textiles, machinery, electronic equipment. Pop. (1992 est.) 53,430.

Harrison, Benjamin (1833–1901) 23rd US President (1889–93). He was a grandson of William Henry HARRISON. He ran as the Republican candidate against President CLEVELAND in 1888. He won with a majority of the electoral votes, although Cleveland had the most popular votes. As president, Harrison signed into law the Sherman Antitrust Act and the McKinley Tariff Act. He was defeated by Cleveland in 1892.

Harrison, William Henry (1773–1841) Ninth US President (1841). He is remembered chiefly for his military career, especially his victory at Tippecanoe over Native Americans (1811). He died one month after taking office.

hartebeest Large ANTELOPE native to African grasslands s of the Sahara Desert. They have sharply rising horns united at the base. Length: up to 200cm (79in); height: to 150cm (59in); weight: up to 180kg (397lb). Family Bovidae.

Hartford State capital of Connecticut, USA, on the Connecticut River. More than 25 insurance companies have their headquarters here. Manufactures include precision instruments and electrical equipment. Pop. (1990) 139,739.

Hartley, L.P. (Lesley Poles) (1895–1972) British novelist, short-story writer and critic. He first won acclaim with his trilogy of novels *The Shrimp and the Anemone* (1944), *The Sixth Heaven* (1946) and *Eustace and Hilda* (1947). *The Go-Between* (1953) was made into a successful film.

Hartmann, Nicolai (1882–1950) German realist philosopher. Although influenced by PLATO and Immanuel KANT, he proposed, in *Outlines of a Metaphysics of Knowledge* (1921), that existence is a prerequisite for knowledge, a reversal of Kant's idea. He finally rejected Kantian ideas in his book *New Ways of Ontology* (1942). *See also* REALISM

Harun al-Rashid (764–809) Most famous of the ABBASID caliphs of Baghdad (786–809). His reign has gained romantic lustre from the stories of the *Thousand and One Nights*.

harvestman ARACHNID with legs that may be several times its body length. It feeds on insects and plant juices. Body length: 2.5–13mm (0.1–0.5in). Family Phalangidae.

Harvey, William (1578–1657) English physician and anatomist who discovered the circulation of the blood. His findings, published in *De Motu Cordis et Sanguinis* (1628), were ridiculed at first. He also studied embryology.

Haryana State in N central India; the capital is Chandigarh. It was formed in 1966 from part of the state of Punjab. The land has been improved by irrigation and fertilization. Industries: machine tools, farming implements, cement, paper. Area: 44,222sq km (17,074sq mi). Pop. (1991) 16,403,648.

Harz Mountains Mountain range in central Germany, extending 96km (60mi) between the Weser and Elbe rivers. The highest peak is the Brocken, 1,142m (3,747ft).

Hašek, Jaroslav (1883–1923) Czech novelist and short-story writer. He wrote the best-selling satirical novel *The Good Soldier Schweik* (1920–23).

hashish Resin obtained from the flowering tops of the hemp plant *Cannabis sativa* and used as a psychotropic drug. When smoked or eaten it generally induces heady sensations and often a feeling of detachment. It is not considered addictive. Possession of the drug is illegal in the UK and the USA. *See also* MARIHUANA

Hasidism Popular pietist movement within JUDAISM founded by Israel ben Eliezer (c.1699–c.1761). The movement, centred in E Europe until World War 2, strongly supports Orthodox Judaism. Its main centres are now in Israel and the USA.

Hassan II (1929–) King of Morocco (1961–), son and successor of Muhammad V. He dissolved the National Assembly in 1965 and introduced a new constitution, which gave him supreme power. He nationalized Moroccan industries (1973) and established claims to much of WESTERN SAHARA.

Hastings, Warren (1732–1818) First British governor general of India (1774–85). He successfully defended British territory against several Indian opponents. He made many enemies and returned to England to face a variety of charges. Though eventually acquitted, his career was ruined.

Hastings, Battle of (14 October 1066) Fought near Hastings, SE England, by King HAROLD II of England against an invading army led by WILLIAM, duke of Normandy. The Norman victory and death of Harold marked the end of the Anglo-Saxon monarchy and produced a social revolution.

Hatshepsut (d.1482 BC) Queen of Egypt (c.1494–1482 BC). Daughter of Thutmose I, she married Thutmose II and after his death (c.1504 BC) ruled, first as regent for her nephew, then in her own right. She was the only woman to rule as pharaoh.

Haughey, Charles (1925–) Irish statesman, prime minister (1979–81, 1982, 1986–92). A controversial figure, Haughey became a Fianna Fáil member of parliament in 1957. He was dismissed from the cabinet in 1970 for alleged conspiracy in IRISH REPUBLICAN ARMY (IRA) gun running, although he was later acquitted. He retired in 1992.

Hauptmann, Gerhart (1862–1946) German dramatist, poet and novelist. His play *Vor Sonnenaufgang* (1889) marked the birth of German naturalist drama. He was awarded the 1912 Nobel Prize for literature.

Hausa Predominantly Muslim people, inhabiting NW Nigeria and s Niger. Hausa society is feudal and based on patrilineal descent. Its language is the official language of N Nigeria and a major trading language of W Africa. Hausa crafts include weaving, leatherwork and silversmithing.

Havana (La Habana) Capital of CUBA, on the NW coast; largest city and port in the West Indies. It was founded by the Spanish explorer Diego Velázquez in 1515. Havana became Cuba's capital at the end of the 16th century. Industries: oil refining, textiles, sugar, cigars. Pop. (1990 est.) 2,096,054.

Havel, Vaclav (1936–) Czech playwright, politician and president (1989–92, 1993–). Havel was imprisoned several times by the communist regime during the 1970s and 1980s, both for his satirical plays and for his work as a human-rights activist. After the Velvet Revolution, Havel became the first post-communist president and tried to preserve a united republic. He resigned in 1992 when break-up became inevitable, but returned as president of the newly formed Czech Republic in 1993.

Hawaii State of the USA in the N Pacific Ocean; the capital is HONOLULU. It consists of eight large and 124 small volcanic islands, many of which are uninhabited. Polynesians established settlements in the 9th century AD. Annexed by the USA in 1898, it was the last state to be admitted to the Union, in 1959. There is an important US naval base at PEARL HARBOR. The economy is based on agriculture and tourism. Exports include bananas, pineapples, sugar, nuts and coffee. Area: 16,705sq km (6,450sq mi). Pop. (1993 est.) 1,171,592.

hawfinch Largest European FINCH, nesting in temperate regions. Its large bill cracks nuts and fruit stones. It has mostly chestnut plumage, with black and white patches. Length: 18cm (7in). Species *Coccothraustes coccothraustes*.

hawk Any of several species of day-active BIRDS OF PREY found in temperate and tropical climates. They have short, hooked bills for tearing meat and strong claws for killing and carrying prey. Hawks have red, brown, grey or white plumage with streaks on the wings. Length: 28–66 cm (11–26in). Order Falconiformes; genera *Accipiter* and *Buteo*.

Hawke, Bob (Robert) (1929–) Australian statesman, prime minister (1983–91). He was elected as a Labor member of parliament in 1980, and became Labor Party leader in 1983. His held office for an unprecedented four terms. A prolonged recession led to the accession of Paul Keating.

Hawking, Stephen William (1942–) British theoretical physicist. Hawking supported the BIG BANG theory of the origin of the Universe and did much pioneering work on the theory of BLACK HOLES. He published a popular account of his work in *A Brief History of Time* (1988).

Hawkins, Sir John (1532–95) English naval commander. With the support of Queen Elizabeth I, he led two lucrative expeditions to Africa and the West Indies (1562–63, 1564–65), but on his third expedition (1567–69) the Spanish destroyed most of his ships. He played an important role in the defeat of the Spanish ARMADA in 1588.

Hawksmoor, Nicholas (1661–1736) English BAROQUE architect who started his career as an assistant to WREN. He also assisted VANBRUGH at Castle Howard and Blenheim Palace. His own buildings are bold and highly original, and include Queen's College, Oxford, and several outstanding London churches, notably St Mary Woolnoth.

hawthorn Any of more than 200 species of thorny deciduous shrubs and trees of the genus *Crataegus*, growing in N temperate parts of the world. Their flowers are white or pink, and small berries are borne in clusters. Family Rosaceae.

Hawthorne, Nathaniel (1804–64) US novelist. He helped to develop the US short story. His reputation was made with *The Scarlet Letter* (1850). Other works include *The House of the Seven Gables* (1851), *The Blithedale Romance* (1852) and *The Snow Image and Other Twice-Told Tales* (1851).

Haydn, Franz Joseph (1732–1809) Austrian composer. One of the greatest classical composers, his mastery of the SONATA form is evident in more than 100 symphonies, such as the *Military*, the *Clock* and the *London* (all 1793–95). He also wrote many string quartets, chamber works, concertos, masses and choral works, notably the oratorios *The Creation* (1798) and *The Seasons* (1801).

Hayek, Friedrich August von (1899–1992) British economist, b. Vienna. A leading critic of Keynesianism and an influence on Thatcherism, he won the 1974 Nobel Prize for economics. His works include *The Road to Serfdom* (1944).

Hayes, Rutherford Birchard (1822–93) 19th US President (1877–81). As governor of Ohio, he was the successful Republican presidential candidate in 1876. Hayes removed all federal troops from the South and tried to promote civil service reform. He retired after one term.

hay fever Seasonal ALLERGY induced by grass POLLENS. Symptoms include ASTHMA, itching of the nose and eyes, and sneezing. Symptoms are controlled with an ANTIHISTAMINE.

hazel Any of about 15 bushes or small trees of the genus *Corylus*, native to temperate regions of Europe, Asia and America. There are separate male and female flowers. The fruit is a hazelnut. Family Betulaceae.

Hazlitt, William (1778–1830) British writer and critic. His works include *Characters of Shakespeare's Plays* (1817) and *Table Talk* (1821–22).

Health, UK Department of UK government department responsible for the administration of the NATIONAL HEALTH SERVICE and local authority social services. It also provides information on public and environmental health, and is responsible for public ambulance services. The head of the Department is the Secretary of State for Health.

Health and Safety Commission British Government body set up in 1974 to instigate and monitor measures to protect people in working environments. It employs officers to inspect working premises in order to prevent accidents.

Heaney, Seamus (1939–) Irish poet and critic, influenced by the history of sectarian violence in Northern Ireland. His works include *Eleven Poems* (1965), *Death of a Naturalist* (1966), *Door to the Dark* (1969), *North* (1975) and *The Spirit Level* (1996). He won the 1995 Nobel Prize for literature.

hearing Process by which sound WAVES are experienced. SOUND waves enter the EAR canal and vibrate the eardrum. The vibrations are transmitted by three small bones to the COCHLEA. In the cochlea, receptors generate nerve impulses that pass via the auditory nerve to the brain, to be interpreted.

heart Muscular ORGAN that pumps BLOOD throughout the body. In humans, the heart is located behind the breastbone between the lower parts of the lungs. Divided longitudinally by a muscular wall, the right side contains only deoxygenated blood, the left side only oxygenated blood. Each side is divided into two chambers, an atrium and a ventricle. The average heart beat rate for an adult at rest is 70–80 beats per minute.

heart attack (myocardial infarction) Death of part of the heart muscle due to the blockage of a coronary artery by a blood clot (thrombosis). It is accompanied by chest pain, sweating and vomiting. Modern drugs treat abnormal heart rhythms and dissolve clots in the coronary arteries. **Heart failure** occurs when the heart is unable to pump blood at the rate necessary to supply body tissues, and may be due to high BLOOD PRESSURE or heart disease. Symptoms include shortness of breath, oedema and fatigue. Treatment is with a DIURETIC and heart drugs. *See also* ANGINA

heat Form of energy associated with the constant vibration of atoms and molecules. Currently accepted KINETIC THEORY holds that the hotness of a body depends on the extent of vibration of its atoms. Heat is distributed in three forms: CONVECTION through fluids, CONDUCTION through solids and RADIATION mainly through space. *See also* TEMPERATURE

heat capacity (thermal capacity) The ratio of the heat supplied to an object to the rise in its temperature. It is measured in joules/kelvin. *See also* SPECIFIC HEAT CAPACITY

Heath, Sir Edward Richard George (1916–) British statesman, prime minister (1970–74). He became a Conservative member of Parliament in 1950, and acted as lord privy seal (1960–63) before becoming Conservative Party leader (1965). As prime minister, he secured Britain's membership of the EUROPEAN COMMUNITY (1973), but poor industrial relations led to a miners' strike and a "Three-Day Week" (1974). Defeated in two general elections in 1974, Heath was replaced as party leader by Margaret THATCHER (1975). He was a major critic of Thatcherism and staunchly pro-Europe.

heath Any of various woody evergreen shrubs of the genus *Erica*, found in Europe, Africa and North America. They generally have bell-shaped blue or purple flowers. Family Ericaceae. The term also applies to land that supports heath.

heather (ling) Evergreen shrub native to Europe and Asia Minor. It has small bell-shaped flowers of pink, lavender or white. Family Ericaceae; species *Calluna vulgaris*. *See also* ERICA

heatstroke Condition in which the body temperature rises above 41°C (106°F). It is brought on by exposure to extreme heat. In mild cases there may be exhaustion and fainting; in severe cases, coma and death may ensue.

heavy metal Metal of high density, such as platinum or lead. The term may also refer to metallic pollutants in soil that restrict plant growth.

heavy water *See* DEUTERIUM

Hebrew Language of the SEMITIC branch of the AFRO-ASIATIC family. Spoken in Palestine from ancient times, it is the language of the OLD TESTAMENT. It declined during the BABYLONIAN CAPTIVITY and was overtaken by ARAMAIC. Hebrew persisted as a literary and liturgical language among Jews. It was revived as an ordinary spoken language in the 19th century and became the official language of ISRAEL (1948).

Hebrews, Epistle to the Part of the NEW TESTAMENT. It contains a letter of encouragement to a group of Jewish Christians and a review of Israel's history and Jesus' place in it. Its author is unknown.

Hebrides (Western Isles) Group of more than 500 islands in the Atlantic Ocean off the w coast of Scotland. They are divided into the Inner Hebrides (including Skye, Rhum, Eigg, Islay, Mull) and the Outer Hebrides (including Lewis with Harris, North and South Uist). From the 3rd century AD the islands were settled by Picts and later by Scots. In the 8th century they were invaded by Vikings and became a Norwegian dependency. In the 13th century they were ceded to Scotland by Norway. Few of the islands are inhabited, and agriculture is limited. There is abundant wildlife. The main occupations are fishing, farming and distilling.

Hebron (El Khalil) City in the Israeli-occupied WEST BANK, almost entirely controlled by the Palestinian National Authority. An ancient city, it came under Arab control in the 7th century AD and was occupied by the Crusaders (12th–13th centuries). In 1948 it was annexed to Jordan, but was occupied by Israel during the SIX DAY WAR (1967). The ISRAELI-PALESTINIAN ACCORD granted Palestinian self-rule to 85% of the city. Israel finally withdrew in January 1997. Hebron is sacred to both Jews and Muslims. The Tomb of the Patriarchs is the traditional burial place of Abraham, Sarah, Isaac, Rebecca, Jacob and Leah. Hebron is surrounded by vineyards and vegetable farms. Pop. (1995 est.) 117,000.

Hecate Goddess in Greek mythology. Associated with ARTEMIS, she bestowed wealth and blessings.

Hector In Greek legend, the greatest of the Trojan heroes, eldest son of PRIAM. He was slain by ACHILLES.

hedgehog Small, nocturnal Eurasian and African mammal of the family Erinaceidae. It has short, sharp spines above, lighter-coloured fur below, and a pointed snout. It feeds on insects and other small animals and defends itself by rolling into a ball with the spines outermost. Genus *Erinaceus*

hedonism Pursuit of pleasure, or any of several philosophical or ethical doctrines associated with it. Aristippus (*c.* 435–*c.* 356 BC) taught that pleasure was the highest good. EPICURUS advocated discrimination in the seeking of pleasure. LOCKE believed

285

that the idea of "good" can be defined in terms of pleasure. BENTHAM and J.S. MILL adapted psychological hedonism in formulating UTILITARIANISM.

Hegel, Georg Wilhelm Friedrich (1770–1831) German philosopher, whose method of dialectical reasoning had a strong influence on Karl MARX. He was professor of philosophy at Heidelberg and subsequently at Berlin, where he developed a metaphysical system that traced the self-realization of spirit by dialectical movements towards perfection. Hegel wrote two major books, *Phenomenology of Spirit* (1807) and *Science of Logic* (1812–16). *See also* DIALECTICAL MATERIALISM

hegemony Leadership or dominance of one state over others. The term originated in ancient Greece where the cities of Athens, Sparta and Thebes held hegemony over Greece in the 5th and 4th centuries BC. Britain was a hegemonic power in the 19th century and the USA since 1945. The term was also employed by the Italian Marxist theorist Antonio Gramsci to refer to the phenomenon of one social class monopolizing the creation and transmission of values.

Heidegger, Martin (1889–1976) German philosopher. A founder of EXISTENTIALISM and a major influence on modern philosophy, his most important work was *Being and Time* (1927). Influenced by hermeneutics, PHENOMENOLOGY and Christian ontology, his central concern was how human self-awareness is dependent on the concepts of time and death. His later work focused on the role of language.

Heidelberg City on the River Neckar, Baden-Württemberg state, SW Germany. Founded in the 12th century, it has the oldest university in Germany (1386) and a medieval castle. Industries: printing machinery, precision instruments, publishing, textiles, leather goods. Pop. (1990) 139,900.

Heimlich manoeuvre First-aid technique for relieving blockage in the windpipe. The rescuer uses their arms to encircle the choking person's chest from behind, positioning one fist in the space just beneath the breastbone and covering it with the other hand. The rescuer then thumps the fist into the person's midriff.

Heine, Heinrich (1797–1856) German poet and prose writer. The *Book of Songs* (1827) is his best-known work. It was followed by the four-volume satirical *Pictures of Travel* (1826–31). SCHUMANN and SCHUBERT both set his lyrics to music.

Heisenberg, Werner Karl (1901–76) German physicist and philosopher, best known for discovering the UNCERTAINTY PRINCIPLE (1927). He won the 1932 Nobel Prize for physics for his contribution to QUANTUM MECHANICS.

Hejaz Region in NW Saudi Arabia, on the Red Sea coast. The centre of ISLAM, it contains the Muslim holy cities of MECCA and MEDINA. Area: 388,500sq km (150,000sq mi).

Hejira (Arab. *Hegira*, breaking off of relations) Flight of MUHAMMAD from MECCA to MEDINA in

AD 622 in order to escape persecution. The Islamic calendar begins from this date.

Helen In Greek legend, the beautiful daughter of LEDA and ZEUS. She married Menelaus, King of Sparta, but was carried off by PARIS, Prince of TROY, thus provoking the TROJAN War.

Helena Capital of Montana state, USA. It was settled by prospectors in 1864. By 1868 the population was 7,500 and US$16 million worth of gold had been mined. In 1875 it was made capital of Montana territory, becoming state capital in 1889. Industries: minerals, ceramics. Pop. (1990) 24,569.

helicopter Aircraft that gains lift from power-driven rotor(s). The helicopter is capable of vertical take-off and landing (VTOL), hovering, and forward, backward and lateral flight.

Helios In Greek mythology, god of the Sun, identified with the Roman god APOLLO. Helios appears driving a four-horse chariot through the sky.

helium Nonmetallic element (symbol He), a NOBLE GAS, discovered in 1868. First obtained in 1895 from the mineral clevite, the chief source today is from natural gas. It is also found in some radioactive minerals and in the Earth's atmosphere (0.0005% by volume). It has the lowest melting and boiling points of any element. It is colourless, odourless and nonflammable. It is used in balloons, scuba diving, semiconductors and lasers. Liquid helium is used in cryogenics (physics dealing with low temperatures). Properties: at.no. 2; r.a.m. 4.0026; r.d. 0.178; m.p. $-272.2°C$ ($-458°F$); b.p. $-268.9°C$ ($-452.02°F$); single isotope He^4.

helix Curve generated when a point moves over the surface of a cylinder so that it traces a path inclined at a constant angle to the cylinder's axis, as in a coil spring.

hellebore Any of about 20 species of poisonous herbaceous plants of the genus *Helleborus*, native to Eurasia. Best known is the Christmas rose, *H. niger*, which bears white flowers from mid-winter to early spring. Family Ranunculaceae.

Hellenistic Age (323–27 BC) Period of Classical Mediterranean history from ALEXANDER THE GREAT to the reign of AUGUSTUS. Alexander's conquests helped to spread Greek civilization over a wide area E of the Mediterranean. The age was distinguished by remarkable scientific and technological advances, especially in ALEXANDRIA, and by more elaborate and naturalistic styles in the visual arts.

Heller, Joseph (1923–) US author. His first novel, *Catch–22* (1961), is one of the satirical masterpieces of the 20th century. Other works include the play *We Bombed in New Haven* (1968), and the novels *Something Happened* (1974), *God Knows* (1984) and *Closing Time* (1994).

Hellespont *See* DARDANELLES

Helmholtz, Hermann Ludwig Ferdinand von (1821–94) German anatomist, physicist and physiologist. He made contributions in ACOUSTICS and OPTICS, expanding Thomas YOUNG's three-colour theory of vision. His experiments on the speed of nerve impulses led him to formulate a principle of conservation of energy.

Helsinki (Helsingfors) Capital of Finland, in the S of the country, on the Gulf of Finland. Founded in 1550 by GUSTAVUS I (VASA), it became the capital in 1812. The administrative centre of Finland, it is also its largest port. Industries: shipbuilding, engineering, ceramics, textiles. Pop. (1993) 508,588.

Helvétius, Claude Adrien (1715–71) French philosopher and educator. His best-known work, *On the Mind* (1758), attacked the religious basis of morality. He claimed that everybody is intellectually equal but some have less desire to learn than others. In *Of Man* (1772) he claimed that all human problems could be solved by education.

hematite One of the most important iron ores, containing mainly ferric oxide, Fe_2O_3. Containing 70% iron by weight, it occurs in several forms and varies in colour from steel-grey to black, but sometimes red. Deposits are found on all continents.

Hemingway, Ernest Millar (1899–1961) US author. A war correspondent in the Spanish Civil War and World War 2, the novel *The Sun Also Rises* (1926) chronicled the "Lost Generation" and established his reputation. Later works include *A Farewell to Arms* (1929), *For Whom the Bell Tolls* (1940) and the novella *The Old Man and the Sea* (1952). He won the 1954 Nobel Prize in literature.

hemlock Poisonous herbaceous plant found in Eurasia. It has a long taproot and clusters of white flowers. The leaf stalks have purple spots. Family Apiaceae/Umbelliferae; species *Conium maculatum*. Hemlock also refers to conifers of the genus *Tsuga*, family Pinaceae.

hemp Herb native to Asia and cultivated throughout Eurasia, North America and parts of South America. It has hollow stems with fibrous inner bark, also called hemp, which is used to make ropes and cloth. Oil from the seeds is used in soap and paint. Some strains, referred to as CANNABIS, produce MARIHUANA and HASHISH. Height: to 16ft (5m). Family Cannabinaceae; species *Cannabis sativa*.

Hendrix, Jimi (James Marshall) (1942–70) Influential and innovative US rock musician. He formed The Jimi Hendrix Experience in 1965 with Mitch Mitchell and Noel Redding. He was renowned for his powerful live performances. Albums include *Band of Gypsies* (1969). He died from a drugs overdose.

henna (Egyptian privet) Small shrub native to the Middle East and N Africa. Since ancient times, people have extracted a red-brown dye from the leaves to colour hair and skin. Family Lythraceae; species *Lawsonia inerma*.

Henrietta Maria (1609–69) Queen consort of CHARLES I of England. Daughter of Henry IV of France, her Catholicism and her support for Charles' absolutist tendencies incurred Parliament's hostility.

Henry III (1017–56) German king (1039–56) and Holy Roman emperor (1046–56). He succeeded his father, Conrad II. Imperial power reached its zenith in his reign as he subdued Saxony and Lorraine and compelled the rulers of Poland, Bohemia, Hungary, and S Italy to pay him homage.

Henry IV (1050–1106) German king (1056–1106) and Holy Roman emperor (1084–1106). Embroiled in controversy with the popes over the lay investiture of clerics, he deposed Pope GREGORY VII and was in turn deposed by the pope (1076). Rebellion in Germany weakened Henry's position. After seeking papal absolution in 1077, he continued the struggle, setting up the antipope Clement III. In 1105 he was deposed by his son, HENRY V.

Henry V (1081–1125) German king (1105–25) and Holy Roman emperor (1111–25). Having deposed his father, HENRY IV, he resumed the quarrel with the papacy over investiture, while antagonizing German princes by the ruthless assertion of his power. He was defeated in Germany and compelled to compromise with the papacy. The Concordat of Worms (1122) ended the investiture conflict.

Henry VI (1165–97) German king (1190–97) and Holy Roman emperor (1191–97). The son of Frederick I, he married (1186) Constance, heiress of Sicily, and much of his reign was devoted to securing that inheritance. Although he failed to secure the succession of the HOHENSTAUFEN line, his son, Frederick II, was accepted as emperor.

Henry I (1068–1135) King of England (1100–35). He rescinded unpopular taxes and married a Scottish princess of Anglo-Saxon descent. He thus won the support that helped him defeat his brother ROBERT II, duke of Normandy, and regain Normandy for the English crown (1106).

Henry II (1133–89) King of England (1154–89). Son of Geoffrey of Anjou and Matilda (daughter of HENRY I). He inherited the ANGEVIN lands and obtained Aquitaine by marrying ELEANOR in 1152. He re-established stable royal government in England and instituted reforms in finance, local government and justice. His efforts to extend royal justice to priests led to his famous quarrel with Thomas à BECKET. His later years were troubled by the rebellions of his sons, RICHARD and JOHN.

Henry III (1207–72) King of England (1216–72). The influence of foreigners on his administration antagonized the nobles. He was forced to accept the Provisions of Westminster (1259), giving more power to his councillors, but renounced them in 1261, provoking the Barons' War. The leader of the barons, Simon de MONTFORT, was defeated at Lewes (1264) by Henry's son, the future EDWARD I, who thereafter ruled on his father's behalf.

Henry IV (1367–1413) King of England (1399–1413). Son of JOHN OF GAUNT, he was exiled in 1399 by RICHARD II. He returned and overthrew Richard. As a usurper he had to overcome revolts, notably by Owen GLYN DŴR and the Percy family.

Henry V (1387–1422) King of England (1413–22). Son of HENRY IV, he renewed the English claims against France of the HUNDRED YEARS

WAR and won a decisive victory at AGINCOURT in 1415. Further conquests in 1417–19 resulted in the Treaty of Troyes (1420), when CHARLES VI of France recognised him as his heir.

Henry VI (1421–71) King of England (1422–61, 1470–71). He succeeded his father, HENRY V, as a baby. His reign was characterized by military disasters in France and by the dynastic conflict known as the Wars of the ROSES. Deposed by the Yorkists (1461), he was restored in 1470 but was again deposed and murdered.

Henry VII (1457–1509) King of England (1485–1509), founder of the TUDOR dynasty. Henry defeated RICHARD III at Bosworth in 1485, and united the warring houses of LANCASTER and YORK by marrying the Yorkist heiress, Elizabeth. His financial acumen restored England's fortunes after the devastation of civil war. He concluded various advantageous foreign treaties and secured the future of his dynasty.

Henry VIII (1491–1547) King of England (1509–47). Second son of HENRY VII, he became heir on the death of his elder brother, Arthur, in 1502. His aggressive foreign policy, administered by Cardinal WOLSEY, depleted the royal treasury. Henry, supported by Thomas CROMWELL, presided over the first stages of the English REFORMATION. It was brought about largely because the pope refused to grant Henry a divorce from his first wife, CATHERINE OF ARAGON, who had failed to produce a male heir. With the legislation in place, Henry divorced Catherine and married Anne BOLEYN (1533). In 1535 Anne was executed for adultery. Thomas MORE (Henry's former chancellor) was also executed for refusing to accept Henry as head of the church. Henry then married Jane Seymour, who died shortly after the birth of the future EDWARD VI. His next marriage, to ANNE OF CLEVES, ended in divorce (1540) and with the execution of Cromwell. Shortly after, he married Catherine HOWARD (executed 1542) and finally Catherine Parr (1543) who survived him. The DISSOLUTION OF THE MONASTERIES (1536–40) brought temporary relief from financial problems but caused social unrest.

Henry II (1519–59) King of France (1547–59). Son and successor of FRANCIS I, he married CATHERINE DE' MEDICI but was dominated by his mistress, Diane de Poitiers, and the rival families of GUISE and Montmorency. After bankrupting the royal government, the war with Spain ended with the peace of Cateau-Cambrésis (1559). Henry died after being accidentally wounded in a tournament.

Henry III (1551–89) King of France (1574–89). He fought against the HUGUENOTS in the Wars of RELIGION, but made peace in 1576, thus antagonizing extremist Roman Catholics, who formed the Catholic League led by the House of GUISE. After the League provoked a revolt in 1588, Henry had its leaders killed and made an alliance with the Huguenot, Henry of Navarre (later HENRY IV). The king was assassinated by a member of the League.

Henry IV (1553–1610) King of France (1589–1610), first of the BOURBON dynasty. He was raised a Protestant and, escaping the St Bartholemew's Day Massacre (1572), he became the leader of the HUGUENOTS. On inheriting the throne, he converted to Roman Catholicism and ended the French Religious Wars by the Edict of NANTES (1598). Henry remained sympathetic to Protestantism, secretly supporting the revolt of the Protestant Netherlands against Spain. During his reign France recovered economic prosperity.

Henry the Navigator (1394–1460) Portuguese prince. A son of JOHN I, he sponsored Portuguese voyages of discovery to the Atlantic coast of Africa, which later led to the discovery of the route to India via the Cape of Good Hope.

Henry I (the Fowler) (c.876–936) King of the Germans (918–36), duke of Saxony. He asserted his authority over the German princes and reconquered Lotharingia (Lorraine, 925). In 933 he defeated the Magyar raiders. He was succeeded by his son, OTTO I, the first Holy Roman emperor.

Henry, Joseph (1797–1878) US physicist whose contribution to ELECTROMAGNETISM was essential for the development of the commercial telegraph. His work on INDUCTION led to the development of the TRANSFORMER. The unit of inductance is named after him.

Henze, Hans Werner (1926–) German composer. Influenced by TWELVE-TONE MUSIC, he has composed in almost every genre and is best known for his operas, such as *Elegy for Young Lovers* (1961).

hepatitis Inflammation of the liver, usually due to a generalized infection. Early symptoms include lethargy, nausea, fever and muscle and joint pains. Five different hepatitis viruses are known: A, B, C, D and E. The most common single cause is the hepatitis A virus (HAV). More serious is infection with the hepatitis B virus (HBV), which can lead to chronic inflammation or complete failure of the liver and, in some cases, to liver cancer.

Hepburn, Audrey (1929–93) US actress, b. Belgium. She won a Best Actress Oscar for her ingénue role in *Roman Holiday* (1953). Other films include *Sabrina* (1954), *Breakfast at Tiffany's* (1959), *Funny Face* (1957) and *My Fair Lady* (1964). She later became involved in humanitarian work.

Hepburn, Katharine (1909–) US stage and film actress. She won her first Best Actress Oscar for *Morning Glory* (1933). She starred opposite Cary Grant in *Bringing up Baby* (1938) and *The Philadelphia Story* (1940). She made nine films with her long-standing partner, Spencer Tracy, including a second Oscar-winning performance in *Guess Who's Coming to Dinner* (1967). She won two further Best Actress Oscars for *The Lion in Winter* (1968) and *On Golden Pond* (1981). Other credits include *The African Queen* (1951).

heptathlon Athletics discipline for women, consisting of seven events contested over 2 days. *See also* DECATHLON

Hepworth, Dame Barbara (1903–76) English sculptor. One of the leading modernist sculptors of 20th-century Britain, she is noted for the simplicity and elegance of her abstract works.

Hera In Greek mythology, queen of the Olympian gods, sister and wife of ZEUS. She appears as a jealous scold who persecuted her rivals but helped heroes such as JASON and ACHILLES.

Heracles In Greek mythology, greatest of the Greek heroes (Roman Hercules). Condemned to serve King Eurystheus, he performed 12 labours: he killed the Nemean lion and the Hydra; caught the Erymanthian boar and the Cerynean hind; drove away the Stymphalian birds; cleaned the Augean stables; caught the Cretan bull and Diomedes' horses; stole the girdle of Hippolyte; killed Geryon; captured Cerberus; and stole the golden apples of Hesperides. After death, he was allowed to ascend as a god to Olympus.

Heraclitus (536–470 BC) Greek philosopher. Heraclitus believed that the outward, unchanging face of the universe masked a dynamic equilibrium in which all things were constantly changing, but with opposites remaining in balance, summed up by the phrase "You cannot step into the same river twice". The elemental substance was fire.

Heraclius (575–641) Byzantine emperor (610–41). An outstanding military leader, he led the Byzantine empire from crisis to unrivalled power. He re-established government and army, and defeated the Persians. At his death, however, the Arabs had conquered much of the empire.

herb Seed-bearing plant, usually with a soft stem that withers away after one growing season. Most herbs are ANGIOSPERMS. The term is also applied to any plant used as a flavouring, seasoning or medicine, such as THYME, SAGE and MINT.

Herbert, George (1593–1633) English poet and churchman. His verse, some of the finest META-PHYSICAL POETRY, was published after his death as *The Temple*. It is remarkable for its devotional tone and technical complexity.

herbicide Chemical substance used to kill weeds and other unwanted plants. There are two kinds: selective herbicides kill the weeds growing with crops, leaving the crops unharmed; non-selective herbicides kill all the vegetation.

herbivore Animal that feeds solely on plants. The term is most often applied to mammals, especially ungulates. Herbivores are characterized by broad molars and blunt-edged teeth, which they use to pull, cut and grind their food. Their digestive systems are adapted to the assimilation of cellulose.

Herculaneum Ancient city on the Bay of Naples, Italy, the site of modern Resina. Devastated in AD 62 by an earthquake, it was buried in AD 79 by the eruption of VESUVIUS. Archaeological excavations unearthed the Villa of the Papyri.

Herder, Johann Gottfried von (1744–1803) Prussian philosopher and historian. He believed human society to be an organic, secular totality that

develops as the result of a historical process. Herder was a founder of German ROMANTICISM and an opponent of KANT. His masterpiece is *Ideas on the Philosophy of History of Humanity* (1784–91).

heredity Transmission of characteristics from one generation of plants or animals to another. The unique combination of characteristics that make up an organism is set out in the organism's GENETIC CODE, passed on from its parents. The first studies of heredity were conducted by MENDEL.

Hereford and Worcester County in W central England, bounded W and SW by Wales; the county town is WORCESTER. It is drained by the Severn, Wye and Teme rivers. The Malvern Hills divide the county into two lowland plains. The fertile Vale of Evesham is used for market gardening. Agriculture and dairy farming are important activities. Area 3,926sq km (1,516sq mi). Pop. (1991) 676,747.

heresy Denial of, or deviation from, orthodox religious belief. The concept is found in most organized religions with a rigid dogmatic system. The early Christian church fought against heresies such as ARIANISM and NESTORIANISM. In the Middle Ages, the Catholic Church set up the INQUISITION to fight heresy. After the REFORMATION, the Catholic Church described Protestants as heretics because of their denial of many papally defined dogmas, while Protestants applied the term to those who denied their interpretation of the major scriptural doctrines.

hermaphrodite Organism that has both male and female sexual organs. Most hermaphrodite animals are invertebrates, such as the EARTHWORM and SNAIL. They reproduce by the mating of two individuals each of which receives SPERM from the other. Some hermaphrodites are self-fertilizing.

Hermes In Greek mythology, god identified with the Roman Mercury. Depicted with winged hat and carrying a golden wand, Hermes was the messenger of the gods and patron of travellers and commerce.

hermit crab Small, crab-like CRUSTACEAN found in tidal pools and shallow water worldwide. It uses sea-snail shells to protect its soft abdomen, changing shells as it grows. Some are terrestrial and do not use shells as adults. Family Paguridae.

hernia Protrusion of an organ, or part of an organ, through its enclosing wall or connective tissue. Common hernias are a protrusion of an intestinal loop through the umbilicus (umbilical hernia) or protrusion of part of the stomach or oesophagus into the chest cavity (hiatus hernia).

Herod Agrippa I (10–44) King of Judaea (41–44). Grandson of HEROD THE GREAT, he attracted the favour of CALIGULA who confirmed him as ruler of most of Palestine. He was a zealous opponent of Christianity.

Herod Agrippa II (27–93) King of Chalcis (50–93) and of Judaea (53–70). Son of HEROD AGRIPPA I and last of the Herodian dynasty, he tried to prevent the Jewish revolt of 66 and afterwards sided with Rome.

Herodotus (c.485–c.425 BC) Greek historian. Regarded as the first true historian, his *Histories* are the first great prose work in European literature. His main theme was the struggle of Greece against the mighty Persian empire in the PERSIAN WARS.

Herod the Great (73–04 BC) King of Judaea (37–04 BC). Supported by Mark ANTONY and AUGUSTUS, he endeavoured to reconcile Jews and Romans and was responsible for the rebuilding of the TEMPLE in Jerusalem. He later became cruel and tyrannical, executing three of his sons and his wife. According to the New Testament, Herod was king of Judaea when JESUS was born.

heroin Drug derived from MORPHINE. It produces similar effects to morphine, but is effective in smaller doses, acts more quickly and is more addictive. It is prescribed to ease pain in terminal illness and severe injuries. It is widely used illegally.

heron Any of several species of wading bird that live near rivers. Herons have white, grey or brown plumage, long neck and legs, and a sharp bill. They feed mainly on fish, and nest in large groups. Height: to 1.8m (6ft). Family Ardeidae.

herpes Infectious disease caused by one of the herpes viruses. Herpes simplex 1 infects the skin and causes cold sores. Herpes zoster attacks nerve ganglia, causing SHINGLES. The same virus is responsible for CHICKENPOX.

Herrick, Robert (1591–1674) English poet, disciple of Ben JONSON. He was ordained in 1623 but was ejected (1647) for royalist sympathies. He regained his position after the RESTORATION. His poems, notably the collection *Hesperides* (1648), have great lyrical freshness.

herring Marine fish found worldwide. One of the most important food fish, various species are canned as PILCHARD or SARDINE or sold fresh, pickled or smoked. Herrings have a deeply forked tail fin. Length: 8–46cm (3–18in). Family Clupeidae; the 190 species include *Clupea harengus*.

Herschel, Sir John Frederick William (1792–1871) English astronomer. In 1834 he undertook a systematic survey of the southern sky, discovering more than 1,200 double stars and 1,700 nebulae and clusters. He combined these and his father, Sir William HERSCHEL's, observations into a *General Catalogue of Nebulae and Clusters*. He made the first good direct measurement of solar radiation, and inferred the connection between solar and auroral activity. His *Outlines of Astronomy* (1849) was a standard textbook for many decades.

Herschel, Sir William (1738–1822) English astronomer, b. Germany. He discovered Uranus (1781) and was appointed astronomer royal (1782). He discovered two SATELLITES of Uranus (1787) and two of Saturn (1789). He observed many double stars and more than 2,000 nebulae and clusters, and published catalogues of them. Herschel realized that the MILKY WAY is the plane of a disk-shaped universe. In 1800 he discovered infrared radiation.

Hertfordshire County in SE England; the county

town is Hertford. Other towns include St Albans (built on the site of a Roman settlement), Watford, Hatfield and Letchworth (the first garden city). The terrain is flat apart from an extension of the Chiltern Hills in the NW. The main rivers are the Lea, Stort and Colne. Agriculture is important. Industries: engineering, electrical equipment, printing. Area 1,636 sq km (631sq mi). Pop. (1994) 1,005,400.

Hertz, Heinrich Rudolf (1857–94) German physicist. He discovered, broadcasted and received the radio waves predicted by James Clerk MAXWELL. He also demonstrated that heat and light are kinds of ELECTROMAGNETIC RADIATION. The unit of frequency is named after him.

hertz SI unit of FREQUENCY (symbol Hz) named after Heinrich HERTZ. A periodic phenomenon with a period of one second (such as one oscillation per second) is equivalent to 1Hz.

Hertzog, James Barry Munnik (1866–1942) South African politican, prime minister (1924–39). He was a general in the Boer forces during the SOUTH AFRICAN WAR (1899–1902). A member of the Union government under Louis BOTHA (1910), he founded the National Party in 1914, becoming prime minister in 1924. He later formed an alliance with SMUTS in the United Party but resigned in protest at South Africa's support for Britain in World War 2.

Hertzsprung-Russell Diagram (HR Diagram) Plot of the absolute MAGNITUDE of stars against their spectral type; this is equivalent to plotting their LUMINOSITY against their surface temperature or colour index. Brightness increases from bottom to top, and temperature increases from right to left. The diagram was devised by Henry Norris Russell in 1913, independently of Ejnar Hertzsprung. The HR diagram reveals a pattern in which most stars lie on a diagonal band, the **main sequence**.

Herzegovina *See* BOSNIA-HERZEGOVINA

Herzl, Theodor (1860–1904) Jewish leader and founder of ZIONISM, b. Budapest. He worked as a lawyer and a journalist. He became president of the World Zionist Organization (1897), which worked throughout Europe to establish a Jewish national home in Palestine.

Hess, Rudolf (1894–1987) German Nazi leader. He joined the Nazi Party (1921) and took part in the abortive MUNICH PUTSCH. Hess was the nominal deputy leader under HITLER from 1933. In 1941 he flew alone to Scotland in a mysterious one-man effort to make peace with the British. He was sentenced to life imprisonment in the NUREMBERG TRIALS in 1945 and spent the rest of his life in Spandau jail, Berlin, for many years its sole inmate.

Hess, Victor Francis (1883–1964) US physicist, b. Austria. As a result of his investigations into the ionization of air, he suggested that cosmic RADIATION comes from space. He shared the 1936 Nobel Prize for physics with Carl Anderson.

Hesse, Hermann (1877–1962) German novelist. Hesse's study of Indian mysticism and Jungian psychology is evident in novels such as *Demian* (1919), *Siddhartha* (1922) and *Steppenwolf* (1927). Other novels include *Narcissus and Goldmund* (1930) and *The Glass Bead Game* (1943). He was awarded the 1946 Nobel Prize in literature.

Hessen Region of central Germany. It was divided by a strip of Prussian territory until 1945. Industries: chemicals, manufacturing, electrical engineering, cereal cropping. Area 21,114sq km (8,150sq mi). Pop. (1993) 5,967,305.

Hestia In Greek mythology, goddess of the burning hearth. She scorned the attentions of Apollo and Poseidon. In Rome, she was worshipped as Vesta. *See also* VESTAL VIRGINS

heterosexuality Attraction of a male or female to members of the opposite sex. The word is used to distinguish such attraction from HOMOSEXUALITY.

heterozygote Organism possessing two contrasting forms (ALLELES) of a GENE in a CHROMOSOME pair. In cases where one of the forms is dominant and one RECESSIVE, only the dominant form will be expressed in the PHENOTYPE. *See also* HOMOZYGOTE

Hewish, Antony (1924–) British radio astronomer. He shared the 1974 Nobel Prize for physics, with Martin Ryle, for his work on PULSARS.

hexagon Six-sided plane figure. Its interior angles add up to 720°. For a regular hexagon, whose sides and interior angles are all equal, each interior angle is 120°.

Heyerdahl, Thor (1914–) Norwegian ethnologist who, with five companions, drifted on the balsa raft *Kon Tiki* c.8,000km (5,000mi) across the Pacific Ocean from Peru to Polynesia (1947) in an attempt to prove that the Polynesians came from South America and not from Southeast Asia.

Hiawatha Native American leader. As chief of the Onondaga, he founded the five-nation Iroquois Confederacy (c.1575) to halt intertribal wars.

hibernation Dormant condition adopted by some animals to survive harsh winters. Adaptive mechanisms to avoid starvation and extreme temperatures include reduced body temperature, and slower heartbeat, breathing rate and metabolism.

hibiscus Genus of plants, shrubs and small trees native to tropical and temperate regions and cultivated worldwide. Their large white, pink, yellow, blue or red bell-shaped flowers have darker or variegated centres. Family Malvaceae.

hickory Deciduous tree of the WALNUT family native to E North America. Hickories are grown for ornament, timber and nuts. Height: 25m (80ft). Family Juglandaceae; genus *Carya. See also* PECAN

hieroglyphics Writing system used in ancient Egypt, ancient Crete, Asia Minor, Central America and Mexico. The Egyptian system of hieroglyphics (pictorial characters or symbols) arose sometime before 3100 BC. At first they were purely picture symbols. In due course, they also came to be used conceptually. Eventually, many symbols were used phonetically. By the 7th century, hieroglyphics were used for business and literary

purposes. As ancient Egyptian was supplanted by Greek, hieroglyphics died out. Most Egyptian texts have been deciphered, thanks to the discovery of the ROSETTA STONE (1799).

High Court of Justice In English law, court established primarily to hear civil cases. It also hears appeals from the magistrates' courts. It consists of three divisions: the Queen's Bench, the CHANCERY and the Family division.

high-definition television (HDTV) Form of television on which the picture is made up of 1,250 or 1,125 scanning lines (instead of 625 or 525). The increased number of scanning lines makes the TV image sharper. It relies on digital transmission along OPTICAL FIBRES rather than the transmission of electronic signals by radio waves. The use of cables increases the total number of available channels.

high jump Track-and-field event in which a competitor attempts to jump over a bar supported between two uprights. An Olympic sport since 1896, a competitor may have up to three attempts to clear each height to which the bar is raised.

Highland Games Series of athletics competitions featuring traditional Scottish events. The term specifically refers to the autumn Royal Braemar Games or Braemar Gathering held annually since 1819. The programme includes highland dancing, bagpipe-playing and the tossing of the caber.

Highlands Scottish mountain and moorland region, lying N of a line running roughly SW to NE from Dumbarton to Stonehaven; the administrative centre is Inverness. The area is split geologically into the Northwest Highlands and the Grampian Highlands (separated by Glen More). Industries: tourism, forestry, fishing. Area: 25,396sq km (9,804sq mi) Pop: (1991) 204,000

high-level language COMPUTER LANGUAGE that is reasonably close to spoken English. The higher the level, the further the language is removed from the BINARY SYSTEM of most computer languages.

Hill, Geoffrey (1932–) British poet. He usually writes on historical and religious themes. His works include *For the Unfallen* (1959), *King Log* (1968), *Mercian Hymns* (1971), *Tenebrae* (1978) and *The Mystery of the Charity of Charles Péguy* (1983).

Hill, Graham (1929–75) English motor racing driver. In 1962 he won his first Grand Prix and the world driver's championship, winning his second title in 1968. In 1972 he became the first Formula 1 world champion to win the Le Mans 24-hour race. His son, **Damon** (1960–), is also a successful Formula 1 driver, becoming world champion in 1996.

Hill, Sir Rowland (1795–1879) British administrator and postal reformer. He invented the "penny post" – the first adhesive, pre-paid postage stamp.

Hillary, Sir Edmund Percival (1919–) New Zealand mountaineer. On 29 May 1953, Hillary and the Sherpa Tenzing Norgay were the first climbers to reach the summit of Mount EVEREST.

Hilliard, Nicholas (1547–1619) English miniaturist and goldsmith. He portrayed many of the leading figures of the time in an exquisitely graceful style.

Himachal Pradesh State in the W Himalayas, NW India; the capital is Simla. It suffered numerous invasions before coming under British rule in the 19th century. The state is mountainous and heavily forested, with highly cultivated valleys. Timber provides the main source of income. Area: 55,673sq km (21,495sq mi). Pop. (1991) 5,170,877.

Himalayas System of mountains in S Asia, extending c.2,400km (1,500mi) N–S in an arc between Tibet and India-Pakistan. The mountains are divided into three ranges: the Greater Himalayas (N), which include Mount EVEREST, the Lesser Himalayas and the Outer Himalayas (S).

Himmler, Heinrich (1900–45) German Nazi leader. In 1929 he became head of the SS. After the Nazis came to power in 1933, he assumed control of the police and of the CONCENTRATION CAMPS. He was captured in 1945 and committed suicide.

Hindemith, Paul (1895–1963) German composer, who emigrated to the USA in 1939. In the 1930s he developed, with Kurt WEILL, *Gebrauchsmusik* (Ger. utility music) written for amateur performance. His best-known work is the symphony derived from his opera *Mathis der Maler* (1934).

Hindi Most widespread language in India, spoken in the north central area by 154 million people. Hindi and English are the official languages of India. It derives from SANSKRIT and belongs to the Indo-European family.

Hinduism Traditional religion of India, characterized by a philosophy and a way of life rather than a dogmatic structure. It was not founded by an individual and has been developing gradually since c.3000 BC, absorbing external influences. There are several schools within Hinduism, but all recognize the VEDAS as sacred, believe that all living creatures have souls, follow the doctrine of TRANSMIGRATION OF SOULS, and consider *moksha* (liberation from the cycle of suffering and rebirth represented by REINCARNATION) as the chief aim in life. One of the features of Hindu society is the CASTE system, but modern Hindu scholars maintain that it is not part of the Hindu religion. In the mid-1990s, Hindus numbered about 800 million worldwide.

Hindu Kush Mountain range in central Asia, a continuation of the Himalayas extending WSW for 800–960km (500–600 mi) from N Pakistan and NE Afghanistan. The highest peak is Tirich Mir, 7,700m (25,260ft).

Hindustani Member of the Indo-Iranian branch of INDO-EUROPEAN LANGUAGES, closely related to HINDI and URDU. More than 300 million people in India and Pakistan are thought to use Hindustani.

hip Joint on each side of the lower trunk, into which the head of the femur fits; the hip bones form part of the PELVIS.

Hipparchus (active 2nd century BC) Greek astronomer. He estimated the distance of the Moon from the Earth and drew the first accurate star map. He developed an organization of the Universe which, although it had the Earth at the centre, provided for accurate prediction of the positions of the planets.

Hippocrates (460–377 BC) Greek physician, often called "the father of medicine". He emphasized clinical observation and provided guidelines for surgery. He is credited with the **Hippocratic oath**, a code of professional conduct still followed by doctors.

Hippolytus In Greek mythology, son of Theseus and Hippolyta. He spurned the advances of his step-mother, Phaedra, and was put to death, but came back to life when his innocence was proved.

hippopotamus Bulky, herbivorous mammal, native to Africa. *Hippopotamus amphibius* has a massive grey or brown body with a large head, short legs and tail. It spends much time in water. Males weigh up to 4.5 tonnes. Pygmy hippopotami (*Choeropsis liberiensis*) are much smaller and spend more time on land. Family Hippopotamidae.

Hirohito (1901–89) Emperor of Japan (1926–89). He persuaded the Japanese government to surrender to the Allies in 1945. Under the new constitution of 1946, he lost power and renounced the traditional claim of the Japanese emperors to be divine.

Hiroshige, Ando (1797–1858) Japanese master of the UKIYO-E (coloured WOODCUT). With HOKUSAI and UTAMARO, he was one of the leading Japanese printmakers of his day. He is best known for his landscapes, which influenced IMPRESSIONISM.

Hiroshima City on the delta of the River Ota, on SW Honshū Island, Japan; the river divides the city into six islands. Founded in 1594, it was a military headquarters in the SINO-JAPANESE and RUSSO-JAPANESE wars. In August 1945 it was the target of the first atomic bomb dropped on a populated area. The city centre was obliterated and more than 70,000 people were killed. Industries: brewing, shipbuilding, motor vehicles, chemicals, engineering. Pop. (1993) 1,072,000.

Hirst, Damien (1965–) British sculptor. He has made his name by exhibiting sculptures of animals preserved in formaldehyde. *Mother and Child Divided* (1993) won him the 1995 Turner Prize.

Hispaniola Island in the West Indies, in the N central Caribbean Sea, between Cuba (W) and Puerto Rico (E). The second-largest island in the West Indies, it was discovered in 1492 by Christopher COLUMBUS. HAITI occupies the W third of the island and the DOMINICAN REPUBLIC the remaining portion. It is a mountainous, agricultural region. Industries: coffee, cacao, tobacco, rice, sugar cane. Area: 76,480sq km (29,521sq mi).

histamine Substance derived from the amino acid histidine, occurring naturally in many plants and in animal tissues, and released on tissue injury. It is implicated in allergic reactions that can be treated with ANTIHISTAMINE drugs.

histology Biological, especially microscopic, study of TISSUES and structures in living organisms.

history Written record of the human past or the events themselves. The Western historical tradition began with the Greek historians HERODOTUS and Thucydides. China has an even older historical tradition in which the past was seen as a source of wisdom with discernible pattern.

Hitchcock, Sir Alfred (1899–1980) British film director, master of the sophisticated suspense thriller. His films include *Blackmail* (1929), *The Thirty-Nine Steps* (1935), *Strangers on a Train* (1951), *Dial M for Murder* (1954), *Rear Window* (1954), *Psycho* (1960) and *Frenzy* (1972).

Hitler, Adolf (1889–1945) German fascist dictator (1933–45), b. Austria. He served in the German army during World War 1 and was decorated for bravery. In 1921 he became the leader of the small National Socialist Workers' Party (Nazi Party). While imprisoned for his role in the failed MUNICH PUTSCH, he set out his extreme racist and nationalist views in *Mein Kampf*. Economic distress and dissatisfaction with the WEIMAR government led to electoral gains for the Nazis and, by forming an alliance with orthodox Nationalists, Hitler became chancellor in January 1933. He made himself dictator of a one-party state in which all opposition was ruthlessly suppressed by the SS and GESTAPO. The race hatred he incited led to a policy of extermination of Jews and others in the HOLOCAUST. Hitler pursued an aggressive foreign policy aimed at territorial expansion in E Europe. The invasion of Poland finally goaded Britain and France into declaring war on Germany in September 1939. Hitler himself played a large part in determining strategy during WORLD WAR 2. In April 1945, with Germany in ruins, he committed suicide.

Hittites People of Asia Minor who controlled a powerful empire in the 14th–13th centuries BC. They founded a kingdom in Anatolia (Turkey) in the 18th century BC. They expanded E and S in the 15th century BC, and conquered N Syria before being checked by the Egyptians under RAMSES II. Under attack from ASSYRIA, the Hittite empire disintegrated in *c*.1200 BC.

hives (urticaria or nettle rash) Transient, itchy, reddish or pale raised skin patches. Hives may be caused by an ALLERGY, by irritants, or by stress.

Hizbollah (Hezbollah) Iranian-backed, Islamic fundamentalist group. It was formed in the early 1980s to encourage the integration of Shiite religious militants into Middle Eastern politics. Hizbollah has been responsible for terrorist and military activities in the Middle East and elsewhere, including missile attacks on Israel from within Lebanon.

Hobart Capital and port of the state of TASMANIA, SE Australia. Founded as a penal colony in the early 1800s, it became capital in 1812. It has one of the best natural harbours in the world. Industries: fruit processing, textiles, zinc. Pop. (1994 est.) 52,900.

Hobbes, Thomas (1588–1679) English social and political philosopher. In *De Corpore* (1655), *De Homine* (1658) and *De Cive* (1642) he argued that matter and its motion comprise the only valid subjects for philosophy. His greatest work, *Leviathan* (1651), argued that man is not naturally social but obeys moral rules in order to maintain society.

Ho Chi Minh (1890–1969) (Nguyen That Thanh) Vietnamese political leader. An agent of the COMMUNIST INTERNATIONAL, he founded the Vietnamese Communist Party in 1930. Forced into exile, he returned to Vietnam in 1941 to lead the VIET MINH against the Japanese. In 1945 he declared Vietnamese independence and led resistance to the French colonial authorities. He was recognized as president of North Vietnam in 1954. He supported the VIET CONG against South Vietnam and committed North Vietnamese forces against the USA in the VIETNAM WAR.

Ho Chi Minh City (Saigon) City at the mouth of the Saigon River, in the Mekong delta, S Vietnam; the largest city in Vietnam. It was an ancient Khmer settlement. Saigon was seized by the French in 1859 and made capital of French Indochina (1887–1902). In 1954 it became capital of independent South Vietnam. During the VIETNAM WAR it served as the military headquarters for US and South Vietnamese forces. Taken by the North Vietnamese in 1975, it was later renamed Ho Chi Minh City. It is the commercial, industrial and transport centre of Vietnam. Industries: shipbuilding, textiles, pharmaceuticals. Pop. (1989) 3,169,135.

hockey (field hockey) Game played by teams of 11 of either sex, in which the object is to use a hooked stick to strike a small, solid ball into the opponents' goal. The field of play classically measures 91.44×54.86m (300×180ft), usually grassed. To score, a player must be within the semi-circle marked out in front of the goal. There are two 35-minute halves, and an indoor version of the game exists. The modern game dates from the mid-19th century and has been an Olympic sport since 1908.

Hockney, David (1937–) British painter, the most acclaimed British artist of his generation. He made his name with witty POP ART paintings such as *Flight into Italy–Swiss Landscape* (1962). In the late 1960s and the 1970s, he developed a more realistic, classical style, with pictures such as *A Bigger Splash* (1967) and portraits in spacious interiors.

Hoddle, Glenn (1957–) English football player and coach. He made 377 appearances for Tottenham and earned 53 international caps. After a brief spell at Monaco, Hoddle became player-manager at Swindon Town and then Chelsea. He succeeded Terry Venables as England coach in 1996. He led England to the 1998 World Cup finals.

Hodgkin's disease Rare type of cancer causing painless enlargement of the LYMPH GLANDS, lymphatic tissue and spleen, with subsequent spread to other areas. Treatment consists of RADIOTHERAPY, surgery, drug therapy or a combination of these. It is curable if caught early.

Hoffman, Dustin (1937–) US film actor, who rose to stardom in *The Graduate* (1967). A dedicated character actor, he played roles ranging from a derelict in *Midnight Cowboy* (1969), to a comedian in *Lenny* (1974), and a transvestite in *Tootsie* (1982). He is committed to the method approach and has won Best Actor Oscars for *Kramer vs Kramer* (1979) and *Rain Man* (1988).

Hoffmann, E.T.A. (Ernst Theodor Amadeus) (1776–1822) German romantic author, musician and music critic. He wrote many fantastic stories, several of which later formed the basis for the opera *The Tales of Hoffmann* (1881) by OFFENBACH. *The Devil's Elixir* (1815–16) and *Leben Ansichen* (1820–22) are his two novels.

Hofstadter, Robert (1915–) US physicist who shared the 1961 Nobel Prize for physics. He proposed that PROTONS and NEUTRONS have a positively charged central core surrounded by a cloud of elementary particles (pions).

hog *See* PIG

Hogan, (William) Ben (Benjamin) (1912–97) US golfer who overcame a near fatal car accident to become one of the world's greatest players. He won four US Open championships (1948, 1950–51, 1953), two PGA titles (1946, 1948), two Masters' (1951, 1953) and the British Open (1953).

Hogarth, William (1697–1764) English painter and engraver. He is best known for his dark portrayals of contemporary English society, expressed most famously in his narrative paintings (later released as engravings), *The Harlot's Progress*, *The Rake's Progress* and *Marriage à la Mode*.

Hogmanay In Scotland, New Year's Eve. Traditionally more festive than Christmas, the Hogmanay celebrations date back to Celtic times.

Hohenstaufen German dynasty that exercised great power in Germany and the HOLY ROMAN EMPIRE from 1138–1254. From Conrad III to Conrad IV, the family occupied the Imperial throne, except for the years 1209–15 (when Otto IV, the leader of their great rivals the GUELPHS, was emperor). The greatest of the dynasty was FREDERICK II.

Hohenzollern German dynasty. The family acquired Brandenburg in 1415 and Prussia in 1618. FREDERICK WILLIAM further expanded their territories. Frederick William I built up the famous Prussian army, and FREDERICK II (THE GREAT) used it to great effect against the HABSBURGS. Germany was finally united in 1871 under the Hohenzollern emperor, WILLIAM I. His grandson WILLIAM II abdicated at the end of World War 1.

Hokkaidō (formerly Yezo) Most northerly and second largest of the main islands of Japan, bounded W by the Sea of Japan and E by the Pacific Ocean; the capital is Sapporo. Until the late 19th century it was the homeland of the Ainu aboriginals. It is mountainous and forested, with some active volcanoes. Linked to HONSHŪ by the Seikan Tunnel, it is Japan's chief farming region and coal-producer, and a winter sports resort. Crops: rice, maize, wheat, soya beans, potatoes, sugar beet. Industries: fishing, forestry, coal min-

ing, natural gas. Area: 83,451sq km (32,212sq mi). Pop. (1992 est.) 5,659,000.

Hokusai, Katsushika (1760–1849) Japanese master of UKIYO-E (coloured WOODCUT), especially famous for his landscapes. He had enormous influence on late 19th-century European painters. His most famous print is *The Wave*.

Holbein, Hans, the Younger (1497–1543) German painter. He gained recognition with three portraits of his friend Erasmus (1523). He settled in London (1532) and was court painter to Henry VIII. Holbein's masterpieces include *The Ambassadors* (1533), *Christina of Denmark, Duchess of Milan* (1538) and *Anne of Cleves* (1540).

Holiday, Billie (1915–59) US blues and jazz singer, nicknamed Lady Day. She became famous in the 1930s with the bands of Count Basie and Artie Shaw. Her melancholic renditions of "My Man, Mean to Me" (1937) and "God Bless the Child" (1941) are legendary in the history of jazz.

Holland Popular name for the NETHERLANDS, but properly referring only to a historic region, divided into two provinces. A fief of the Holy Roman Empire in the 12th century, it passed to Burgundy in 1433 and to the Habsburgs in 1482. In the 16th century, Holland led the Netherlands in their long struggle for independence from Spain.

Hollywood Suburb of LOS ANGELES, California, USA. After 1911 it became the primary centre for film-making in the USA and by the 1930s its studios dominated world cinema.

Holocaust Great massacre, in particular the extermination of European Jews and others by the Nazi regime in Germany (1933–45). Jews, as well as others considered racially inferior to the Nazis, were killed in CONCENTRATION CAMPS such as AUSCHWITZ, BELSEN and DACHAU. Total Jewish deaths are estimated at more than 6 million.

Holocene (Recent epoch) Division of GEOLOGICAL TIME extending from *c.*10,000 years ago to the present. It includes the emergence of humans as settled members of communities; the first known villages date from *c.*8,000 years ago.

holography Process of making a hologram. One or more photographs are formed on a single film or plate by interference between two parts of a split LASER beam. The photograph appears as a flat pattern until light hits the plate in the correct position; it then becomes a 3-D image.

Holst, Gustav (Gustavus Theodore von) (1874–1934) British composer. His early works were often influenced by Hinduism, such as the opera *Sita* (1906), and folksong, as in *Somerset Rhapsody* (1907). Other works include *The Perfect Fool* (1922) and the popular orchestral suite *The Planets* (1914–16).

Holy Alliance Agreement signed by the crowned heads of Russia, Prussia and Austria in 1815. Its purpose was to re-establish the principle of hereditary rule and to suppress democratic and nationalist movements, which had sprung up in the wake of the FRENCH REVOLUTION. The agreement, signed later by every European dynasty except the king of England and the Ottoman Sultan, came to be seen as an instrument of reaction and oppression.

Holy Communion *See* EUCHARIST

Holy Grail In medieval legend, the cup supposedly used by JESUS at the LAST SUPPER and by JOSEPH OF ARIMATHEA at the crucifixion to catch the blood from Jesus' wounds. The quest for the grail, especially by the knights of Arthurian legend, became a search for mystical union with God.

Holy Roman Empire European empire centred on Germany (10th–19th centuries), which echoed the empire of ancient Rome. It was founded in 962 when the German king OTTO I (THE GREAT) was crowned in Rome, although some historians date it from the coronation of CHARLEMAGNE in 800. The emperor, elected by the German princes, claimed to be the temporal sovereign of Christendom, ruling in cooperation with the spiritual sovereign, the pope. However, the empire never encompassed all of western Christendom and relations with the papacy were often stormy. From 1438 the title was virtually hereditary in the HABSBURG dynasty. After 1648, the empire became little more than a loose confederation, containing hundreds of semi-independent states. It was abolished by NAPOLEON I in 1806.

Holy Spirit (Holy Ghost) Third Person of the TRINITY in Christian theology. The Holy Spirit represents the spiritual agent through whom God's grace is given. The NEW TESTAMENT refers to the Holy Spirit as the agent by whom Mary conceived JESUS and as the divine power of the church.

Holy Week Seven-day period preceding EASTER. It begins with Palm Sunday, commemorating Christ's entry into Jerusalem; Maundy Thursday marks his institution of the EUCHARIST; Good Friday marks his betrayal and crucifixion.

Home, Sir Alec Douglas- *See* DOUGLAS-HOME, SIR ALEC

Home Office British department of state, dating from 1782. The Home Office's present duties cover all matters of national administration not entrusted to another minister. The head of the department, the Home Secretary, is a cabinet position; there are separate secretaries of state for Scotland and Wales. There is also a separate Northern Ireland Office.

homeopathy Unorthodox medical treatment that involves administering minute doses of a drug or remedy which causes effects or symptoms similar to those that are being treated. It was popularized in the 18th century by Christian Hahnemann.

homeostasis In biology, processes that maintain constant conditions within a cell or organism in response to either internal or external changes.

homeothermal (endothermic or warm-blooded) Describes an animal whose body temperature does not fluctuate as the temperature of its surroundings fluctuates. Mammals and birds are warm-blooded. They maintain their body temperature through metabolism. *See also* POIKILOTHERMAL

Homer Greek epic poet of the 8th century BC. He is traditionally considered to be the author of the great epics of the Trojan wars, the *Iliad* and the *Odyssey*. Nothing factual is known about Homer, but the works attributed to him represent the foundations of Greek and European literature.

homo Genus to which humans belong. *See* HUMAN EVOLUTION

homology In biology, similarity in essential structure of organisms based on a common genetic heritage. It often refers to organs that now have a different superficial appearance and function in different organisms. For example, a human arm and a seal's flipper are homologues, having evolved from a common origin. *See also* EVOLUTION

homophony In music, the sounding in unison of voices or instruments. It also refers to a musical texture with a predominant melody part and an accompaniment, as opposed to monophony (music in a single part) or POLYPHONY.

homosexuality Emotional or sexual attraction to members of one's own sex. Male and female homosexuals are popularly known as gays and lesbians. Doctors now agree that homosexuality is a normal aspect of sexuality. Gays and lesbians have long sought to gain egalitarian legislation in recognition of their rights. In the UK, gay liberation groups have struggled for an end to discrimination. The issue of homosexuality within the armed forces remains controversial. The threat of AIDS (ACQUIRED IMMUNE DEFICIENCY SYNDROME) has unified much of the gay community into promoting the importance of safe sex, emphasizing the need for greater public awareness and AIDS research.

homozygote Organism possessing identical forms of a gene on a CHROMOSOME pair. It is a purebred organism and always produces the same kind of GAMETE. *See also* HETEROZYGOTE

Honduras Republic in Central America; the capital is TEGUCIGALPA. **Land and climate** Honduras is the second-largest country in Central America (after NICARAGUA). Honduras has two coastlines: along the *c.*600km- (375mi-) long Caribbean N coast are vast banana plantations; the Gulf of Fonseca is a narrow, 80km- (50mi-) long outlet to the Pacific. To the E lies the MOSQUITO COAST. The

HONDURAS
AREA: 112,090sq km (43,278 sq mi)
POPULATION: 5,462,000
CAPITAL (POPULATION): Tegucigalpa (670,100)
GOVERNMENT: Republic
ETHNIC GROUPS: Mestizo 90%, Native American 7%, Garifunas (West Indian) 2%
LANGUAGES: Spanish (official)
RELIGIONS: Christianity (Roman Catholic 85%, Protestant 10%)
CURRENCY: Honduran lempira = 100 centavos

Cordilleras highlands form 80% of Honduras, and include Tegucigalpa. Honduras has a tropical climate. The rainy season is from May to October. The N coastal plains contain rainforest and tropical savanna. The Mosquito Coast contains mangrove swamps and dense forests. **Economy** Honduras is the least industrialized country in Central America, and the poorest developing nation in the Americas. It has very few mineral resources. Agriculture dominates the economy, forming 78% of all exports and employing 38% of the workforce. Bananas and coffee are the leading exports, and maize is the principal food crop. Fishing and forestry are also important activities. Honduras has vast timber resources. **History and politics** From AD 400–900 the MAYA civilization flourished. The magnificent ruins at Copán in w Honduras were discovered by the Spaniards in 1576, but became covered in dense forest and were only rediscovered in 1839. Christopher Columbus sighted the coast in 1502. Pedro de Alvarado founded the first Spanish settlements (1524.) The native population was gradually subdued, and gold and silver mines were established. In 1821 Honduras gained independence, forming part of the Mexican empire. From 1823–38 Honduras was a member of the Central American Federation. Throughout the rest of the 19th century, Honduras was subject to continuous political interference, especially from Guatemala. Britain controlled the Mosquito Coast. In the 1890s, US companies developed the banana plantations and exerted great political influence. Honduras became known as a "banana republic". The Liberal government was overthrown by a military coup in 1963. Honduras' expulsion of Salvadoran immigrants led to the short "Soccer War" (1969) with El Salvador, following an ill-tempered World Cup qualifying match between the two countries. Civilian government was restored in 1982. During the 1980s Honduras acted as a base for the US-backed CONTRA rebels from Nicaragua. Honduras was heavily dependent on US aid. Massive popular demonstrations against the presence of the Contras led to the declaration of a state of emergency (1988). In 1990 the war in Nicaragua ended. In 1992 Honduras signed a treaty with El Salvador, settling the disputed border. The Liberal Party won the 1993 elections, and Carlos Reina became president.

Honecker, Erich (1912–94) East German Communist leader (1971–89). Imprisoned by the Nazis (1935–45), he succeeded Walter ULBRICHT as Communist Party leader, pursuing policies approved by Moscow. With the reforms under Mikhail GORBACHEV and the collapse of European communism, the ailing Honecker resigned.

Honegger, Arthur (1892–1955) French composer. One of a group of Parisian composers known as *Les Six*, he caused a sensation with *Pacific 231* (1923), an orchestral description of a steam locomotive. His other compositions include five symphonies, two operas, and the dramatic psalm *Le Roi David* (1921).

honey Sweet, viscous liquid manufactured by honeybees from nectar. It consists of the sugars laevulose and dextrose, traces of minerals, and about 17% water.

honeyeater (honey sucker) Any of a group of Australian songbirds. They have long tongues for feeding on nectar and fruit, and pollinate the flowers they feed on. Family Meliphagidae

honeysuckle Woody twining or shrubby plant that grows in temperate regions worldwide. It has oval leaves and tubular flowers. A common species in Eurasia, *Lonicera periclymenum*, climbs to 6m (20ft). Family Caprifoliaceae.

Hong Kong (Xianggang Special Administrative Region) Former British crown colony off the coast of SE China; the capital is Victoria, on Hong Kong Island. The colony comprises: Hong Kong Island, ceded to Britain by China in 1842; the mainland peninsula of Kowloon acquired in 1860; the New Territories on the mainland, leased for 99 years in 1898, and some 230 islets in the South China Sea. In 1984 Britain agreed to transfer sovereignty of the whole colony to China on July 1 1997. The Joint Declaration of the British and Chinese governments (1985) assured the retention of Hong Kong's social and economic structure as a special administrative region of China. Deng Xiaoping described this arrangement as "one country, two systems". It remains a free port with its own commercial and financial policies. The last British governor (1992–97), Chris PATTEN, introduced limited democratic reforms, which China promised to reverse. In 1995, elections to the Legislative Council (Legco) were held, in which pro-democracy parties triumphed. In 1996 China arranged the election of a more pro-Chinese provisional legislative council to replace Legco. Elections to replace the provisional council are scheduled for 1998, and, after the handover in 1997, China announced changes to the system, which look likely to limit the number of seats the Democratic Party will be able to win. The climate is subtropical, with hot, dry summers. Hong

---

HONG KONG
AREA: 1,071 sq km (413 sq mi)
POPULATION: 6,000,000
CAPITAL (POPULATION): Victoria (Hong Kong Island, 1,251,000)
GOVERNMENT: Chinese/Hong Kong provisional legislature
ETHNIC GROUPS: Chinese 98%, others 2% (including European)
LANGUAGES: English and Chinese (official)
RELIGIONS: Buddhism majority, Confucism, Taoism, Christianity, Islam, Hinduism, Sikhism, Judaism
CURRENCY: Hong Kong dollar = 100 cents

Kong is an international financial centre, with a strong manufacturing base. Industries: textiles, electronic goods, cameras, plastics, printing

Honolulu Capital and chief port of Hawaii, on SE Oahu Island. It became the capital of the kingdom of Hawaii in 1845 and remained the capital after the annexation of the islands by the USA in 1898. Sites include Iolani Palace, Waikiki Beach and Diamond Head Crater. Tourism is of major importance. Industries: sugar refining, pineapple canning. Pop. (1990) 365,272. *See also* PEARL HARBOR

Honshū Largest of Japan's four main islands, lying between the Sea of Japan (W) and the Pacific Ocean (E). It includes Mount Fuji (FUJIYAMA) and Lake Biwa (Biwa-ko). It is highly industrial and has six of Japan's largest cities, including TOKYO. The majority of the population inhabit the coastal lowlands. Industries: shipbuilding, oil refining, chemicals, textiles, rice, tea, fruit. Area: 230,782sq km (89,105sq mi). Pop. (1990) 82,569,581.

Hooke, Robert (1635–1703) English philosopher, physicist and inventor. Interested in astronomy, he claimed to have stated the laws of planetary motion before Isaac NEWTON. He studied elasticity of solids, which led to HOOKE'S LAW. Among his inventions were a practical telegraph system and the Gregorian (reflecting) microscope.

Hooke's law Law applying to an elastic material when it is stretched. The law states that the stress (internal tension) is proportional to the strain (a change in dimensions). It was discovered in 1676 by Robert HOOKE. *See also* ELASTICITY

hookworm Two species of human parasite. Larvae usually enter the host through the skin of the feet and legs, and attach to the wall of the small intestine. Symptoms can include anaemia, constipation and weakness. Phylum Nematoda; species *Necator americanus* and *Ancyclostoma duodenale*.

hoopoe Striped, fawn-coloured bird that lives in open areas throughout warmer parts of Eurasia. It has a fan-like crest, a long, curved bill, and feeds on small invertebrates. Length: 30cm (12in). Family Upupidae; species *Upupa epops*.

Hoover, Herbert Clark (1874–1964) 31st US President (1929–33). He was secretary of commerce under Republican presidents HARDING and COOLIDGE and easily defeated Alfred E. Smith in the 1928 presidential elections. In 1929, the economy was shattered by the Wall Street crash and the ensuing GREAT DEPRESSION. With his belief in individual enterprise and distrust of government interference, Hoover failed to mobilize government resources to deal with the Depression and was easily defeated by Franklin D. ROOSEVELT in 1932.

Hoover, J. (John) Edgar (1895–1972) Director of the US Federal Bureau of Investigation (FBI) (1924–72). He reorganized the Bureau, compiling a vast file of fingerprints and building a crime laboratory. During the 1930s he fought organized crime. After World War 2 he concentrated on what he saw as the threat of communist subversion in the USA.

hop Twining vine native to Eurasia and the Americas. It has rough stems, heart-shaped leaves and small male and female flowers on separate plants. The female flowers of *Humulus lupulus* are used to flavour BEER. Family Cannabiaceae.

Hopi Shoshonean-speaking tribe of Native North Americans. They are famous for having retained the purest form of pre-Columbian life in the USA today. About 6,000 Hopi people inhabit 11 villages in Coconino county, N Central Arizona. In 1981, 725,000ha (1.8 million acres) in Arizona were partitioned equally between the Hopi and NAVAJO.

Hopkins, Sir Anthony (1937–) Welsh film and stage actor. His film career experienced several false starts before a dramatic resurgence in the 1990s. His hypnotic performance in *The Silence of the Lambs* (1991) won a Best Actor Oscar. He also starred in *Shadowlands* (1993) and *Nixon* (1995). *August* (1995) was his directorial debut.

Hopkins, Gerard Manley (1844–89) British poet and Jesuit priest. He contributed the principle of sprung rhythm to English poetry. Hopkins' writing is most concerned with problems of faith. The sinking of a German ship carrying five nuns inspired *The Wreck of the Deutschland*.

Hopper, Edward (1882–1967) US realist painter. A pupil of Robert Henri, he was greatly influenced by the Ashcan school. His paintings of urban scenes in New England or New York, such as *Early Sunday Morning* (1930), convey a unique sense of melancholic romanticism.

Horace (65–8 BC) Roman poet. His first *Satires* appeared in *c*.35 BC, and were followed by *Epodes* (*c*.30 BC), *Odes* (*c*.23 BC), *Epistles* (*c*.20 BC) and *Ars Poetica* (*c*.19 BC). His simple Latin lyrics provided a vivid picture of the Augustan age.

horizon, celestial GREAT CIRCLE on the CELESTIAL SPHERE. It lies midway between the observer's ZENITH and NADIR.

hormone Chemical substance secreted by living cells. Hormones affect the metabolic activities of cells in other parts of the body. In MAMMALS, hormones are secreted by glands of the ENDOCRINE SYSTEM and are released directly into the bloodstream. They exercise control of physiological functions, regulating growth, development, sexual functioning, METABOLISM and (in part) emotional balance. The secretion and activity of the various hormones maintain a delicate equilibrium that is vital to health. The HYPOTHALAMUS is responsible for overall coordination of the secretion of hormones. Hormones include THYROXINE, ADRENALINE, INSULIN, OESTROGEN, PROGESTERONE and TESTOSTERONE. In plants, hormones control many aspects of metabolism, including cell elongation and division, direction of growth, flowering and development of fruits, leaf fall, and responses to environment. Important plant hormones include AUXIN, GIBBERELLIN and CYTOKININ. *See also* HOMEOSTASIS

hormone replacement therapy (HRT) Use of the female HORMONES progestogen and OESTRO-

GEN in women who are either menopausal or who have had both ovaries removed. HRT relieves symptoms of the MENOPAUSE; it also gives some protection against heart disease and OSTEOPOROSIS. Oestrogen causes a thickening of the lining of the uterus, which may increase risk of cancer of the ENDOMETRIUM. Progestogen causes a regular shedding of the lining, which may lessen this risk.

horn BRASS musical instrument traditionally used in hunting and ceremonies. They appeared in the opera orchestras of 17th-century Europe and in the 19th century with Wagner and Strauss. The modern instrument (French horn) consists of a coiled tube of conical bore that widens to a flared bell; most have three valves. It has a mellow tone.

hornbill Brownish or black-and-white bird, native to tropical Africa and SE Asia. It has a large, brightly coloured bill. The female lays one to six eggs in a concealed hole high up in a tree trunk. The male feeds her. There are several species. Length: 38–152cm (15–60in). Family Bucerotidae.

hornblende Black or green mineral found in IGNEOUS and METAMORPHIC ROCKS. It is the commonest form of AMPHIBOLE, and contains iron and silicates of calcium, aluminium and magnesium. Hardness 5.5; s.g. 3.2.

hornet Large, orange-and-brown wasp native to Europe. They build egg-shaped paper nests with one queen and many nectar-gathering workers. They have a powerful sting, but are less aggressive than the common wasp. Family Vespidae.

horoscope Map of the stars and planets at the time of a person's birth. It shows the position of the celestial bodies in relation to the 12 signs of the ZODIAC and is the basis of ASTROLOGY.

Horowitz, Vladimir (1904–89) US concert pianist, b. Russia. He first performed in public in 1921 and was world-famous by the age of 20 for his virtuoso technique and great sensitivity.

horse Hoofed mammal that evolved in North America but became extinct there during the late Pleistocene epoch. Early horse forms crossed the land bridge across the Bering Strait, dispersed throughout Asia, Europe and Africa, and produced the modern horse family. The only surviving true wild horse is Przewalski's horse. The horse was first domesticated about 5,000 years ago in central Asia and played a crucial role in agricultural and military development. Horses returned to the New World with the Spanish conquistadores in the 1500s. Horses are characterized by one large functional toe, molars joined by ridges for grazing, an elongated skull, and a simple stomach. Fast runners, they usually live in herds. All species in the family can interbreed. Family Equideae; species *Equus caballus*.

horse chestnut Any of 25 species of deciduous trees that grow in temperate regions, especially the common horse chestnut, *Aesculus hippocastanum*. It has large leaves, long flower spikes and round prickly fruits containing inedible nuts. Family Hippocastanaceae. Height: to 30m (100ft).

horsefly Any of several species of flies in the family Tabanidae, especially *Tabanus lineola*. It is a pest to livestock and human beings. The female inflicts a painful bite and sucks blood. Length: to 3cm (1.2in).

horsepower Unit (hp) indicating the rate at which work is done, adopted by James WATT in the 18th century. He defined it as the weight, 250kg (550lb), a horse could raise 0.3m (1ft) in one second. The electrical equivalent of 1 hp is 746 watts.

horse racing Sport in which horses guided by jockeys race over a course of predetermined length. Most popular is thoroughbred racing, although harness racing (in which horses draw a light two-wheeled vehicle) is popular in some countries. Thoroughbred racing includes flat races and steeplechases, in which the course has obstacles such as hurdles, fences and water jumps. Horse racing began in Assyria in about 1500 BC. The oldest current race is the English Derby, first held in 1780. One of the most famous is the Grand National Steeplechase, held annually at Aintree, Liverpool, England, since 1839.

horseradish Perennial plant native to Eastern Europe. Its pungent, fleshy root is used for seasoning. It has lance-shaped, toothed leaves, white flower clusters and egg-shaped seed-pods. Height: 1.25m (4.1ft). Family Brassicaceae/Cruciferae; species *Armoracia rusticana*.

horsetail Any of about 30 species of flowerless, plants that are allied to ferns and grow in all continents except Australasia. The hollow jointed stems have a whorl of tiny leaves at each joint. Spores are produced in a cone-like structure at the top of a stem. Horsetails date from the Carboniferous period. Phylum Sphenophyta, genus *Equisetum*.

Horthy, Miklós Nagybánai (1868–1957) Hungarian statesman, regent (1920–44). He commanded the Austro-Hungarian fleet in World War 1. He took part in the counter revolution that overthrew Béla KUN, becoming effective head of state. His highly conservative regime suppressed political opposition and resisted the return of CHARLES I. Allied with the Axis Powers in 1941, he tried to make peace with the Allies in 1944, but was arrested by the Germans.

horticulture Growing of vegetables, fruits, seeds, herbs, shrubs and flowers on a commercial scale. Techniques employed include propagation by leaf, stem and root cuttings, and by stem and bud grafting. Fruit trees, shrubs and vines are usually propagated by grafting the fruiting stock on to a hardier rootstock. SEED is a major horticultural crop. Close scientific control of POLLINATION is essential for producing crops of specific quality.

Horus In Egyptian mythology, falcon-headed god, son of ISIS and OSIRIS. The pharaohs were considered to be Horus incarnate.

Hosea (Osee) OLD TESTAMENT prophet active in the 8th century BC. The Book of Hosea is the first of the 12 books of the Minor Prophets.

Hospitaller *See* KNIGHTS HOSPITALLERS

Hottentot (Khoikhoi) KHOISAN-speaking peoples of S Africa, many now almost extinct. Traditionally nomadic, many were displaced or exterminated by Dutch settlers. Descendants have mostly been absorbed into the South African population.

Houphouët-Boigny, Félix (1905–93) First President of the Ivory Coast (1960–93). He served in the French colonial government, becoming president on independence. He maintained close relations with France. In the 1980s, recession caused mounting unrest, and he was forced to legalize opposition parties (1990).

House of Commons Lower house of the British PARLIAMENT (the upper house being the unelected HOUSE OF LORDS), dating from the 13th century. It is the major forum for voting on intended legislation and questioning of ministers. Its 659 members are elected by their constituents in a secret ballot, usually in general elections which must be held at least every five years. The prime minister is the leader of the majority party in the Commons, and most members of the CABINET are drawn from the Commons, although some may be from the Lords. Debates and proceedings are controlled by the speaker. Select committees scrutinize legislation.

House of Lords Upper house of the British PARLIAMENT. In its legislative capacity, the Lords is completely subordinated to the HOUSE OF COMMONS. The Parliament Acts of 1911 and 1949 checked virtually all its power, except the right to delay passage of a bill for a year. Life peers, whose titles may not be inherited, and hereditary peers sit in the House. Hereditary peers may resign their titles to run for election to the Commons. There are special "law lords" who sit in judgement when the House acts as Britain's final court of appeal.

House of Representatives Lower house of the US legislature, which together with the SENATE forms the CONGRESS. It has 435 members. Each state has at least one representative; the larger the population of a state the more representatives are allowed. Representatives are directly elected and serve two-year terms. The House considers bills and has exclusive authority to originate revenue bills, initiate impeachment proceedings and elect the president, if the electoral college is deadlocked.

Houses of Parliament (Palace of Westminster) First large-scale public building of the GOTHIC REVIVAL in Britain. After a fire destroyed the old Palace of Westminster, Charles BARRY won a competition for its replacement. Together with PUGIN, he created a building that combined functionalism and modern technology with Gothic detail. The Palace was finished in 1868.

Housman, A.E. (Alfred Edward) (1859–1936) British poet and classical scholar. He is best known for three volumes of poetry, *A Shropshire Lad* (1896), *Last Poems* (1922) and *More Poems* (1936), in which he treats universal themes, such as the brevity of life, in short, subtle lyrics.

Houston City and port in SE Texas, USA, connected to the Gulf of Mexico by the Houston Ship Canal. Founded in 1836, it was capital of the Republic of Texas (1837–39, 1842–45). Its greatest growth came after the building of the canal (1912–14), as the coastal oil fields provided a rich source of income and Houston developed as a deepwater port. The largest city in the state, it is a leading industrial, commercial, and financial centre, with vast oil refineries and a massive petrochemical complex. Industries: space research, shipbuilding, meat-packing, electronics, chemicals, brewing, sugar- and rice-processing. Pop. (1990) 1,630,553.

hovercraft (AIR-CUSHION VEHICLE) Fast, usually amphibious craft, invented by Sir Christopher Cockerell. A horizontal fan produces a cushion of air supporting the craft just above the ground or water. Vertical fans propel the craft. Most hovercraft are powered by diesel or gas turbine engines, similar to those used in aircraft. Hovercraft travel at speeds up to $c.160$km/h (100mph).

Hovhaness, Alan (1911–) US composer. Influenced by Far Eastern music, he gained recognition as an original composer. His works, some of which reflect his Armenian ancestry, include *Mysterious Mountain* (1955), *Magnificat* (1957) and *And God Created Great Whales* (1970). He has written over 60 symphonies.

Howard, Catherine (1520–42) Fifth queen of HENRY VIII. She was brought to Henry's attention by opponents of Thomas CROMWELL. Henry married her in July 1540, but evidence of her premarital indiscretions led to her execution.

Howard, John Winston (1939–) Australian statesman, prime minister (1996–). Howard was elected to the House of Representatives in 1974. He served in Malcolm Fraser's government, before becoming Liberal Party leader in 1985. In 1995 he was appointed leader of the opposition. In 1996 Howard led the Liberal-National coalition to victory against Paul Keating.

Howe, Sir Geoffrey (1926–) British statesman, chancellor of the exchequer (1979–83), foreign secretary (1983–89), deputy prime minister and leader of the House of Commons (1989–90). A leading figure in the Conservative Party, Howe's dramatic resignation, following disagreements on European policy, was partly responsible for the ousting of Margaret THATCHER.

Hoxha, Enver (1908–85) Albanian statesman and general, prime minister (1944–54), first secretary of the Communist Party (1954–85). He was active in the Albanian National Liberation Movement during World War 2. In 1941 he established the Communist Party. Initially allied with TITO of Yugoslavia, he supported the Soviet Union until its rift with China (1960) and later broke with Peking also. His rule was dictatorial and strongly isolationist.

Hoyle, Sir Fred (Frederick) (1915–) English astrophysicist and cosmologist. He developed the

STEADY-STATE THEORY which, although it was subsequently displaced by the BIG BANG theory, sparked important research into NUCLEOSYNTHESIS.

Hua Guofeng (1918–) (Hua Kuofeng) Chinese political leader, premier, chairman of the Military Commission, and chairman of the Chinese Communist Party (1976–81). When DENG XIAOPING was ousted as prime minister in 1976, he was replaced by Hua, a relatively unknown party functionary. After the death of MAO ZEDONG, Hua also became chairman of the party and thus successor to both Mao and ZHOU ENLAI. He resigned and was ousted from the central committee (1982).

Huang Hai (Yellow Sea) Shallow branch of the Pacific Ocean, N of the East China Sea between the China mainland and the Korean peninsula. The HUANG HE, Liao and Yalu drain into it; the yellow loess (fine-grained silt) from these rivers give the sea its popular name. Such deposits, along with shifting sandbanks and fogs, make navigation perilous. Area: c.466,200sq km (180,000sq mi).

Huang He (Huang Ho, or Yellow) River in N central China; China's second longest (after the YANGTZE). It rises in the Kunlun mountains, QINGHAI province, and flows E to LANZHOU. It then takes a "great northern bend" around the Ordos Desert. It turns S through Shanxi province, and then E through Henan and NE through Shandong to enter the HUANG HAI. The river gets its popular name from the huge amounts of yellow silt it collects in its middle course. The silting of the riverbed makes it prone to flooding, but the threat has been reduced by dikes and dams. Length: c.5,500km (3,400mi).

Hubbard, L. Ron (Lafayette Ronald) (1911–86) Science fiction writer of the late 1930s and 1940s and the guiding spirit of the Church of SCIENTOLOGY. His works *Dianetics: The Modern Science of Mental Health* (1950) and *Science and Survival* (1951) formed the basis of scientology.

Hubble, Edwin Powell (1889–1953) US astronomer. He discovered that NEBULAE were resolvable as independent star systems, and attributed the RED SHIFT of spectral lines of galaxies to their recession, and hence to the expansion of the Universe, upon which modern COSMOLOGY is based. *See also* HUBBLE'S LAW

Hubble's law Proposed by HUBBLE (1929), it claimed a linear relation between the distance of galaxies from us and their velocity of recession, deduced from the RED SHIFT in their spectra. The **Hubble constant** (symbol H_0) is the rate at which the velocity of recession of galaxies increases with distance from us. The inverse of the Hubble constant is the **Hubble time**, which gives a maximum age for the Universe on the assumption that there has been no slowing of the expansion.

Hubble Space Telescope (HST) Optical telescope that was placed in Earth orbit by the SPACE SHUTTLE in 1990. Images transmitted back to Earth revealed that the telescope's main mirror was incor-

rectly shaped. A shuttle repair team corrected the fault in 1993, and it was again modified in 1997.

Hudson, Henry (d.1611) English maritime explorer. He made several efforts to find a NORTH-EAST PASSAGE. Employed by the Dutch EAST INDIA COMPANY (1609), he was blocked by ice and crossed the Atlantic to search for a NORTHWEST PASSAGE, becoming the first European to sail up the HUDSON River. In 1610 he embarked on another voyage to discover the Northwest Passage and reached HUDSON BAY. Forced by ice to winter in the Bay, his crew set him adrift to die in an open boat.

Hudson River in E New York state. It rises in the ADIRONDACK MOUNTAINS and flows S to New York Bay, NEW YORK CITY. First explored in 1609 by Henry HUDSON, it has become one of the world's most important waterways, connected to tthe Great Lakes and the St Lawrence River. Length: c.493km (306mi).

Hudson Bay World's largest inland sea, in E Northwest Territories, Canada, bounded by Quebec (E), Ontario (S) and Manitoba (SW). It is connected to the Atlantic by the Hudson Strait (NE) and to the Arctic Ocean by the Foxe Channel (N). Explored in 1610 by Henry HUDSON, the bay contains Southampton, Mansel and Coats Islands. The Churchill and Nelson rivers drain into the bay, which is ice-free from July to October. Area: c.1,243,000sq km (480,000sq mi).

Hudson's Bay Company English company chartered in 1670 to promote trade in the HUDSON BAY region of North America and to seek a NORTHWEST PASSAGE. The Company had a fur trading monopoly and was virtually a sovereign power in the region. Throughout the 18th century, it fought with France for control of the bay. In 1763, France ceded control of CANADA to England, and the North West Company was formed. The companies merged in 1821, with the new company controlling a territory from the Atlantic to the Pacific. After the confederation of Canada (1867), challenges to its monopoly power increased, and in 1869 it was forced to cede all its territory to Canada for £300,000. As the fur trade declined, the company diversified and in 1930 was divided up.

Huerta, Victoriano (1854–1916) Mexican general and president (1913–14). Instructed by President Francisco MADERO to suppress the revolt led by Félix Díaz, Huerta instead joined forces with the rebels. Madero was arrested and killed, and Huerta became president. Defeated by the Constitutionalists led by CARRANZA, Huerta fled to the USA.

Hughes, Howard Robard (1905–76) US industrialist, aviator and film producer. He inherited an industrial corporation (1923) and became a billionaire as head of the Hughes Aircraft Company. In 1935 he set the world speed record of 567km/h (352mph). He occasionally produced films, including *Hell's Angels* (1930) and *The Outlaw* (1943). He is famed for his reclusive lifestyle.

Hughes, Ted (Edward James) (1930–)

British poet. Hughes' work concerns itself with raw nature. Collections include *Hawk in the Rain* (1957), *Lupercal* (1960), *Wodwo* (1967), *Crow* (1970), *Moortown* (1979) and *Wolfwatching* (1989). He was married to Sylvia PLATH (1956–62) and became poet laureate in 1984.

Hughes, Thomas (1822–96) British novelist and political writer. An active member of the Christian Socialist Movement, he is best known for the novel *Tom Brown's Schooldays* (1857). Other works include *The Scouring of the White Horse* (1859) and *The Manliness of Christ* (1879).

Hugo, Victor Marie (1802–85) French poet, dramatist and novelist. A major force in 19th-century French literary life, he received a pension from Louis XVIII for his first collection of *Odes* (1822), and presented his manifesto of ROMANTICISM in the preface to his play *Cromwell* (1827). Later works include the plays *Hernani* (1830) and *Ruy Blas* (1838), and the novels *The Hunchback of Notre Dame* (1831) and *Les Misérables* (1862).

Huguenots French Protestants who arose in Roman Catholic France during the REFORMATION and suffered persecution. In 1559 a national synod of Huguenot congregations met in Paris and adopted a confession of faith and an ecclesiastical structure highly influenced by CALVIN. During the Wars of RELIGION (1562–98), Huguenots continued to face persecution and thousands died. King HENRY IV, a Huguenot, came to the throne in 1589 and, despite converting to Catholicism in 1593, promulgated the Edict of NANTES (1598) which recognized Catholicism as the official religion, but protected Huguenots rights. It was revoked by LOUIS XIV in 1685, and many Huguenots fled France. In 1789 their civil rights were restored, and the *Code Napoléon* (1804) guaranteed religious equality.

Huitzilopochtli Chief deity of the AZTEC, revered as a Sun god, god of war and protector of the fifth era. He is usually shown in armour decorated with hummingbird feathers. His cult required a daily nourishment of human blood. *See also* CENTRAL AND SOUTH AMERICAN MYTHOLOGY

Hull (officially Kingston upon Hull) City and unitary authority in NE England, on the N bank of the Humber estuary. Britain's third largest port, it was founded in the late 13th century and grew around its fishing industry. Hull gained city status in 1897. The decline of the fishing industry has been partly offset by the construction of the Humber Bridge (1981), one of the world's longest single-span suspension bridges. The city is home to the University of Hull (1954) and the University of Humberside (1992). Pop. (1991) 254,117

human Primate MAMMAL of the genus *Homo*, the only living species of which is *Homo sapiens*. When compared with near relatives, the CHIMPANZEE, GORILLA and ORANG-UTAN, humans are distinguishable by a number of features. They walk upright, their body is only patchily hairy, their big toes are not opposable to the other toes, their back-bone is more S-shaped than straight, and their forehead is higher than that of any ape. Microscopically, humans are distinguishable from great apes by the size, number and shape of their chromosomes. Another distinction is the human capacity for language. Socially, humans are similar to lesser primates, preferring a family or other small group.

human body Physical structure of a HUMAN. It is composed of water, PROTEIN and other organic compounds, and some minerals. The SKELETON consists of more than 200 bones, sheathed in voluntary MUSCLE to enable movement. A SKULL surrounds the large BRAIN. The body is fuelled by nutrients absorbed from the DIGESTIVE SYSTEM and oxygen from the LUNGS, which are pumped around the body by the CIRCULATORY SYSTEM. Metabolic wastes are eliminated mainly by EXCRETION. Continuation of the species is enabled by the reproductive system. Overall control is exerted by the NERVOUS SYSTEM, working closely with the ENDOCRINE SYSTEM. The body surface is covered by a protective layer of SKIN.

human evolution Process by which humans developed from pre-human ancestors. The FOSSIL record of human ancestors is patchy and unclear. Some scientists believe that our ancestry can be traced back to one or more species of Australopithecines that flourished in S and E Africa *c*.4–1 million years ago. Other scientists believe that we are descended from some as yet undiscovered ancestor. The earliest fossils that can be identified as human are those of *Homo habilis* (handy people) which date from 2 million years ago. The next evolutionary stage was *Homo erectus* (upright people), who first appeared *c*.1.5 million years ago. The earliest fossils of our own species, *Homo sapiens* (wise people), date from *c*.250,000 years ago. An apparent side-branch, the NEANDERTHALS, *Homo sapiens neanderthalensis* existed in Europe and W Asia some 130,000–40,000 years ago. Fully modern humans, *Homo sapiens sapiens*, first appeared about 50,000 years ago. All human species apart from *Homo sapiens sapiens* are now extinct.

human immunodeficiency virus (HIV) Organism that causes ACQUIRED IMMUNE DEFICIENCY SYNDROME (AIDS). A RETROVIRUS identified in 1983, HIV attacks the IMMUNE SYSTEM, leaving the person unable to fight off infection. There are two distinct viruses: HIV-1, which has now spread worldwide, and HIV-2, which is concentrated almost entirely in West Africa. Both cause AIDS. There are three main means of transmission: from person to person by sexual contact, from mother to baby during birth, and by contact with contaminated blood or blood products (for instance, during transfusions or when drug-users share needles). People can carry the virus for many years before developing symptoms.

humanism Philosophy based on a belief in the supreme importance of human beings and human values. The greatest flowering of humanism came during the RENAISSANCE, spreading from Italy to other parts of Europe. Early adherents included PETRARCH and ERASMUS. From the 15th–18th centuries, humanism represented the revival of classical values in philosophy and art. Modern humanism, as expounded by Bertrand RUSSELL, developed as an alternative to traditional Christian beliefs.

human rights Entitlements that an individual may arguably possess by virtue of being human and in accordance with what is natural. The concept of the inalienable rights of the human being has traditionally been linked to the Greek and Roman idea of natural law. John LOCKE helped to shape ideas of fundamental human rights and liberal DEMOCRACY in *Two Treatises on Government* (1690). The concept of human rights has been most notably formulated in a number of historic declarations, such as the American DECLARATION OF INDEPENDENCE (1776), American CONSTITUTION (1789) and particularly its first amendments in the BILL OF RIGHTS (1791), and the French DECLARATION OF THE RIGHTS OF MAN AND CITIZEN (1789). These documents owed much to the English PETITION OF RIGHT (1628) and BILL OF RIGHTS (1689), which extended the concept of individual freedom proclaimed earlier in the MAGNA CARTA (1215). The responsibility of the international community for the protection of human rights is proclaimed in the Charter of the United Nations (1945) and the Universal Declaration of Human Rights (1948). *See also* CIVIL RIGHTS

Humboldt, Baron Friedrich Heinrich Alexander von (1769–1859) German scientist and explorer. He studied volcanoes, the origins of tropical storms, and the increase in magnetic intensity from the equator towards the poles. His five-volume work *Kosmos* (1845–62) is a comprehensive description of the physical universe.

Hume, David (1711–76) Scottish philosopher. Hume's publications include *A Treatise of Human Nature* (1739–40), *History of England* (1754–63), and various philosophical "enquiries". Widely known for his humanitarianism and philosophical SCEPTICISM, Hume's philosophy was a form of EMPIRICISM that affirmed the contingency of all phenomenal events. His position was that it was impossible to go beyond the subjective experiences of impressions and ideas.

Hume, John (1937–) Northern Irish politician, leader of the SOCIAL DEMOCRATIC LABOUR PARTY (SDLP). He has been a British MP for Foyle (1983–). Hume's nationalist politics and commitment to peace in Northern Ireland saw him enter into negotiations with Gerry ADAMS and Sinn Féin.

humerus Bone in the human upper arm. A depression on the roughened lower end of the humerus provides the point of articulation for the ULNA.

humidity (relative humidity) Measure of the amount of water vapour in air. It is the ratio of the actual vapour pressure to the saturation vapour pressure at which water normally condenses. *See also* HYGROMETER

hummingbird Popular name for small, brilliantly coloured birds of the family *Trochilidae*, found in S and N America. They feed in flight on insects and nectar, usually by hovering in front of flowers. Their speed can reach 100km/h (60mph) and their wings, which beat 50–75 times a second, make a humming sound. Length: 6–22cm (2.2–8.6in).

Humperdinck, Engelbert (1854–1921) German composer. His works include incidental music, songs and seven operas, of which *Hansel and Gretel* (1893) is his most popular. He worked with WAGNER in the preparation of *Parsifal* (1880–81).

humus Dark brown, organic substance resulting from partial decay of plant and animal matter. It improves soil by retaining moisture, aerating and increasing mineral nutrient content and bacterial activity. Types include peat moss, leaf mould and soil from woods.

Hunan Province in SE central China; the capital is Changsha. The region is largely forested, but agriculture is important; rice, tea, rape seed and tobacco are produced. Hunan has valuable mineral resources. Area: 210,570sq km (81,301sq mi). Pop. (1990) 60,600,000.

Hundred Years War Conflict between France and England pursued sporadically between 1337 and 1453. EDWARD III's claim to the French crown sparked the war. Early English successes brought territorial gains in the Peace of Brétigny (1360). The French gradually regained their lost territory and a revival stimulated by JOAN OF ARC led eventually to the expulsion of the English from all of France except Calais.

Hungarian (Magyar) Official language of Hungary, spoken by its 10 million inhabitants, and by *c*.3 million more in parts of Romania, Slovakia and other countries bordering Hungary. It belongs to the Ugric branch of the FINNO-UGRIC languages.

Hungary Land-locked republic in central Europe; the capital is BUDAPEST. **Land and climate** Hungary is mostly low-lying. The DANUBE forms much of its N border with the Slovak Republic. Budapest lies on the river. To the E of the Danube is the Great Hungarian Plain (*Nagyalföld*), drained by the River Tisza and including Hungary's second-largest city, Debrecen. To the E of the Danube is the Little Plain (*Kisalföld*) and the region of Transdanubia, which includes central Europe's largest lake, BALATON. Hungary has a continental climate, with hot summers and cold winters. Much of Hungary's original vegetation has been cleared for farmland. **Economy** Since the early 1990s, Hungary has adopted market reforms and privatization programmes. The economy has suffered from the collapse of the Soviet Union. National debt, unemployment and inflation have all risen. The manufacture of machinery and transport is the most valuable sector. Hungary's natural resources include bauxite, coal and natural gas. Agriculture remains important. Major crops: grapes, maize, potatoes, sugar beet and wheat. Tourism is growing. **History and**

HUNGARY
AREA: 93,030sq km (35,919sq mi)
POPULATION: 10,313,000
CAPITAL (POPULATION): Budapest (2,009,000)
GOVERNMENT: Multiparty republic
ETHNIC GROUPS: Magyar (Hungarian) 98%,
Gypsy, German, Croat, Romanian, Slovak
LANGUAGES: Hungarian (official)
RELIGIONS: Christianity (Roman Catholic 64%,
Protestant 23%, Orthodox 1%), Judaism 1%
CURRENCY: Forint = 100 filler

politics MAGYARS first arrived in the 9th century. In the 11th century, Saint STEPHEN made Roman Catholicism the official religion. In the 14th century, the Angevin dynasty extended the empire. In the Battle of Mohács (1526), Hungary was defeated by the Ottomans. In 1699 LEOPOLD I expelled the Turks and established HABSBURG control. The accession of FRANZ JOSEPH led to war with Austria (1848). Austrian defeat in the Austro-Prussian War (1866) led to the compromise solution of the "dual monarchy" AUSTRO-HUNGARIAN EMPIRE (1867–1918). As defeat loomed in World War 1, nationalist demands intensified. In 1918 independence was declared. In 1919 communists, led by Béla Kun, briefly held power. In 1920 Miklós HORTHY became regent. World War 1 peace terms saw the loss of all non-Magyar territory (66% of Hungarian land). In 1941 Hungary allied with Nazi Germany, gaining much of its lost territory. Virulent anti-semitism saw the extermination of many Hungarian Jews. Hungary's withdrawal from the war led to German occupation (March 1944). The Soviet expulsion of German troops (October 1944–May 1945) devastated much of Hungary. In 1946 Hungary became a republic, headed by Imre NAGY. In 1948 the Communist Party gained control, forcing Nagy's resignation and declaring Hungary a People's Republic (1949). Hungary became a Stalinist state. Industry was nationalized and agriculture collectivized. Economic crisis forced the brief reinstatement of Nagy (1953–55). In 1955 Hungary joined the Warsaw Pact. In 1956 a nationwide revolution led to Nagy forming a government. János Kádár formed a rival government and called for Soviet military assistance. Soviet troops brutally suppressed the uprising. Nagy was executed and 200,000 people fled. Relations with the Catholic Church were gradually restored, and a new economic policy (1968) relaxed the command economy. During the 1980s Hungary began to seek Western aid to modernize its economy. Kádár was ousted in 1988 and the Communist Party disbanded (1989). Multiparty elections were won by the conservative Democratic Forum (1990). The Hungarian Socialist Party (HSP), composed of ex-communists, won the 1994 elections and set up a coalition government with the liberal Alliance of Free Democrats. Gyula Horn of the HSP became prime minister.

Huns Nomadic people of Mongol or Turkic origin who expanded from central Asia into E Europe. Under ATTILA, they overran large parts of the Roman empire in 434–53, exacting tribute, but after his death they disintegrated.

Hunt, (James Henry) Leigh (1784–1859) British critic, journalist and poet. He was instrumental in popularizing the work of SHELLEY and KEATS. He founded the literary periodical *The Examiner*. He published a two-volume memoir of BYRON (1828) and *Poetical Works* (1832).

Hunt, William Holman (1827–1910) British painter who was one of the founders of the PRE-RAPHAELITE BROTHERHOOD in 1848. His works, such as *The Light of the World* (1854) and *The Scapegoat* (1856), combine meticulous precision with heavy, didactic symbolism.

hunting and gathering Practice of small societies in which members subsist by hunting and by collecting plants rather than by agriculture. The groups are always small bands and have sophisticated kinship and ritualistic systems. Today, hunting-gathering societies are most numerous in lowland South America and parts of Africa.

Huntington's disease (formerly Huntington's chorea) Acute degenerative disorder. It is genetically transmitted and usually occurs in early middle life. It is caused by the presence of abnormally large amounts of glutamate and aspartate. Physical symptoms include loss of motor coordination. Mental deterioration can take various forms.

hurling (hurley) One of the national sports of Ireland. It is played by two teams of 15 on a field 137×82m (450×270ft). The object is to score points by propelling the ball between the goal uprights, either above (1 point) or below (3 points) the crossbar. Every player carries a hurley (hooked stick) on which the ball may be balanced as the player runs, or with which it may be hit upfield; the ball may also be kicked.

Huron, Lake Second largest of the GREAT LAKES of North America, forming part of the boundary between the USA and Canada. It drains Lake SUPERIOR and feeds Lake ERIE as part of the Great Lakes–St Lawrence Seaway system and is navigable by ocean-going vessels. Area: 59,596sq km (23,010sq mi). Max. depth: 230m (750ft).

hurricane Wind of Force 12 or greater on the BEAUFORT WIND SCALE; intense tropical cyclone with winds ranging from 120–320km/h (75–200mph), known as a **typhoon** in the Pacific. Originating over oceans around the Equator, hurricanes have a calm central eye, surrounded by inward spiralling winds and cumulonimbus clouds.

Hus, Jan (1369–1415) Bohemian (Czech) religious reformer. Influenced by the English reformer John WYCLIFFE, he became leader of a reform movement, for which he was excommunicated in 1411. In *De Ecclesia* (1412), Hus outlined his case for reform. In 1415 he was burned at the stake as a heretic. His followers were known as HUSSITES.

Hussein I (1935–) King of Jordan (1953–). British educated, he sought to maintain good relations with the West while supporting the Palestinians in the ARAB-ISRAELI WARS. In 1967 he led his country into the SIX DAY WAR and lost the WEST BANK and East JERUSALEM to Israel. In 1970 he ordered his army to suppress PALESTINE LIBERATION ORGANIZATION (PLO) activities in Jordan. In 1974 he relinquished Jordan's claim to the West Bank to the PLO. He supported efforts to secure peace in the Middle East in the 1990s, signing a peace treaty with Israel in 1994.

Hussein, Saddam (1937–) Iraqi statesman, president of Iraq (1979–). In 1957 he joined the Ba'ath Socialist Party. In 1959 he was forced into exile after taking part in an attempt to assassinate the Iraqi prime minister. He returned home in 1963, but was imprisoned in 1964. After his release he played a prominent role in the 1968 Ba'athist coup, which replaced the civilian government with the Revolutionary Command Council (RCC). In 1979 he became chairman of the RCC and state president. His invasion of Iran marked the beginning of the IRAN-IRAQ WAR (1980–88). At home he ruthlessly suppressed all internal opposition, including the gassing of Kurdish villagers. His 1990 invasion of Kuwait provoked worldwide condemnation, and in 1991 a multinational force expelled Iraqi forces from Kuwait (*see* GULF WAR). Further uprisings by KURDS and Iraqi SHIITES were ruthlessly surpressed. Despite strict sanctions against Iraq, which have inflicted severe hardship on the population, Saddam has retained power.

Husserl, Edmund (1859–1938) German philosopher, founder of PHENOMENOLOGY. He studied man's consciousness as it related to objects and the structure of experience. His works include *Ideas: General Introduction to Pure Phenomenology* (1913) and *Cartesian Meditations* (1931).

Hussites Followers of the religious reformer Jan HUS in Bohemia and Moravia in the 15th century. The execution of Hus (1415) provoked the Hussite wars against Emperor Sigismund. Peace was agreed at the Council of Basel (1431), but it was rejected by the radical Hussites, the Taborites, who were defeated at the Battle of Lipany (1434).

Hutton, James (1726–97) Scottish geologist. He sought to formulate theories of the origin of the Earth and of atmospheric changes. Concluding that the Earth's history could be explained only by observing existing forces, he laid the foundations of modern geological science.

Huxley, Aldous Leonard (1894–1963) British novelist, grandson of Thomas HUXLEY. He was a journalist before the appearance of novels such as *Crome Yellow* (1921), *Antic Hay* (1923) and *Point Counter Point* (1928), which satirized the hedonism of the 1920s. His best-known work, *Brave New World* (1932), presents a nightmarish vision of a future society. His later works included *Eyeless in Gaza* (1936) and *The Doors of Perception* (1954).

Huxley, Sir Julian Sorell (1887–1975) British biologist. Grandson of Thomas HUXLEY, his researches were chiefly on the behaviour of birds and other animals in relation to evolution. His books include *The Individual in the Animal Kingdom* (1911) and *Evolutionary Ethics* (1943).

Huxley, Thomas Henry (1825–95) British biologist. Huxley was a champion of DARWIN's theory of evolution. His works include *Zoological Evidences as to Man's Place in Nature* (1863), *Manual of Comparative Anatomy of Vertebrated Animals* (1871) and *Evolution and Ethics* (1893).

Huygens, Christiaan (1629–95) Dutch physicist and astronomer. In 1655 he discovered Saturn's largest satellite, Titan, and explained that Saturn's appearance was due to a broad ring surrounding it. He introduced the convergent eyepiece for telescopes. Huygens' contributions to physics include the idea that light is a wave motion and the theory of the pendulum; he built the first pendulum clock.

hyacinth Bulbous plant native to the Mediterranean region and Africa. It has long, thin leaves and spikes of bell-shaped flowers, which may be white, yellow, red, blue or purple. Family Liliaceae; genus *Hyacinthus*.

hybrid Offspring of two parents of different GENE composition. It often refers to the offspring of different varieties of a species or of the cross between two separate species. Most inter-species hybrids are unable to produce fertile offspring.

hybridization Cross-breeding of plants or animals between different species to produce offspring that differ in genetically determined traits. Changes in climate or in the environment of an organism may give rise to natural hybridization, but most hybrids are the result of human intervention to produce chaeaper or hardier plants or animals.

Hyderabad City in S India, in the Musi River valley; capital of Andhra Pradesh state. Founded in 1589, sites include the Char Minar (1591). Industries: tobacco, textiles. Pop. (1991) 3,145,939.

Hyderabad City on the INDUS River, Sind province, SE Pakistan. Founded in 1768, it was the capital of Sind until captured by the British in 1843. Industries: chemicals, pottery, shoes, furniture and handicrafts. Pop. (1981) 795,000.

hydra Popular name for a group of small, freshwater organisms including the JELLYFISH, CORAL and SEA ANEMONE.

hydrangea Genus of 80 deciduous woody shrubs, small trees and vines, native to the W Hemisphere and Asia. They are grown for their showy clusters of flowers, which may be white, pink or blue. Family Hydrangeaceae.

hydraulics Physical science and technology of the behaviour of fluids in both static and dynamic states. It deals with practical applications of fluid in motion and devices for its utilization and control. *See also* FLUID MECHANICS

hydrocarbon Organic compound containing only CARBON and HYDROGEN. There are thousands of different hydrocarbons, including open-chain compounds, such as the alkanes (paraffins), alkenes (olefins) and acetylenes. Petroleum, natural gas and coal tar are sources of hydrocarbons.

hydrocephalus Increase in volume of cerebrospinal fluid (CSF) in the brain. A condition that exerts dangerous pressure on brain tissue, it can be due to obstruction or a failure of natural reabsorption. In babies it is congenital; in adults it may arise from injury or disease. It is treated by insertion of a system to drain the CSF into the abdominal cavity.

hydrochloric acid Solution of hydrogen chloride (HCl) gas in water. It is obtained by the action of sulphuric acid on common salt, as a by-product of the chlorination of hydrocarbons, or by a combination of HYDROGEN and CHLORINE. Hydrochloric acid is used in industry and is produced by cells in the stomach lining to allow PEPSIN to digest proteins.

hydroelectricity Electricity generated from the motion of water. In all installations this energy of movement, or kinetic energy, is first converted into mechanical energy in the spinning blades of a water turbine, and then into electricity by the spinning rotor of an electric GENERATOR.

hydrofoil Boat or ship whose hull is lifted clear of the water, when moving at speed, by submerged wings. They usually have gas-turbine or diesel engines that power propellers or water jets. Speeds range from 30 to 60 knots.

hydrogen Gaseous nonmetallic element (symbol H), first identified in 1766 by Henry CAVENDISH. Colourless and odourless, hydrogen is the lightest and most abundant element in the universe (76% by mass), mostly found combined with oxygen in water. It is used to manufacture AMMONIA, to harden fats and oils, and in rocket fuels. Properties: at.no. 1; r.a.m. 1.00797; r.d. 0.0899; m.p. $-259.1°C$ $(-434.4°F)$; b.p. $-252.9°C$ $(-423.2°F)$; most common isotope H^1 (99.985%).

hydrogen bomb (H-bomb) NUCLEAR WEAPON developed by the USA in the late 1940s and first exploded in 1952 in the Pacific. The explosion results from nuclear FUSION when hydrogen nuclei are joined to form helium nuclei, releasing great destructive energy and radioactive fallout.

hydrogen peroxide Liquid compound of hydrogen and oxygen (H_2O_2). It is prepared by electrolytic oxidation of sulphuric acid and by the reduction of oxygen. Hydrogen peroxide is used as a bleach, a disinfectant and an oxidizer for rocket fuel and submarine propellant. Properties: r.d. 1.44; m.p. $-0.9°C$ (30.4°F); b.p. 150°C (302°F).

hydrogen sulphide Colourless, poisonous gas (H_2S) with the smell of bad eggs. It is produced by decaying matter, found in crude oil and prepared by the action of sulphuric acid on metal sulphides. Properties: m.p. $-85.5°C$ (-121.9), b.p. $-60.7°C$ $(-77.3°F)$.

hydrological cycle (water cycle) Circulation of water around the Earth. Water is evaporated from the sea; most falls back into the oceans, but some is carried over land. There it falls as precipitation, and (by surface runoff or infiltration and seepage) it gradually finds its way back to the sea. Less than 1% of the world's water is involved in this cycle.

hydrology Study of the Earth's waters, their sources, circulation, distribution, uses and chemical and physical composition. The HYDROLOGICAL CYCLE is the Earth's natural water circulation system. Hydrologists are concerned with the provision of freshwater, building dams and irrigation systems, and controlling floods and water pollution.

hydrolysis Chemical reaction in which molecules are split into smaller molecules by reaction with water, often assisted by a CATALYST. For example, in digestion, ENZYMES catalyse the hydrolysis of CARBOHYDRATES, PROTEINS and FATS.

hydrophyte (aquatic plant) Plant that grows only in water or in damp places. Examples include WATER LILIES, WATER HYACINTH, DUCKWEED and various PONDWEEDS.

hydroponics (soil-less culture or tank farming). Plants are grown with their roots in a mineral solution or a moist inert medium (such as gravel) containing the necessary nutrients, instead of soil.

hydrotherapy Use of water within the body or on its surface to treat disease. It is often used in conjunction with PHYSIOTHERAPY.

hydroxide Inorganic chemical compound containing the group OH, which acts as a BASE. The strong inorganic bases such as potassium hydroxide (KOH) dissociate (break down) in water almost completely to provide many hydroxyl ions.

hydrozoa Class of animals without backbones, all living in water, belonging to the phylum Coelenterata. They vary in shape and size from the large PORTUGUESE MAN-OF-WAR to the simple HYDRA.

hyena Predatory and scavenging carnivore native to Africa and S Asia. The spotted or laughing hyena (*Crocuta crocuta*) of the sub-Sahara is the largest. The brown hyena (*Hyaena brunnea*) is smaller. Weight: 27–80kg (60–176lb). Family Hyaenidae.

hygrometer Instrument used to measure the HUMIDITY of the atmosphere. One type, the psychrometer, compares the wet and dry bulb temperatures of the air; other types measure absorption or condensation of moisture from the air, or chemical or electrical changes caused by that moisture.

Hymen In Greek mythology, god of marriage. Son of APOLLO, he is represented as a youth attending APHRODITE.

hymen In ANATOMY, MEMBRANE that covers the entrance to the VAGINA. Intact at birth, it normally opens spontaneously before PUBERTY or at first penetration during intercourse.

hyperbola Plane curve traced out by a point that moves so that its distance from a fixed point bears a constant ratio, greater than one, to its distance from a fixed straight line. The fixed point is the focus, the ratio is the eccentricity, and the fixed line is the directrix. The curve has two branches and is a CONIC section. Its standard equation in Cartesian coordinates x and y is $x^2/a^2 - y^2/b^2 = 1$.

hyperglycaemia Condition in which blood-sugar level is abnormally high. It occurs most notably in DIABETES. *See also* HYPOGLYCAEMIA

Hyperion In Greek mythology, sometimes said to be the original Sun god. He was one of the TITANS, the son of URANUS and Gaea and the father of HELIOS the Sun, SELENE the Moon, and EOS the dawn. He is the subject of the incomplete epic poem (1818–19) of the same name by KEATS.

hypersensitivity Condition in which a person reacts excessively to a stimulus. Most hypersensitive reactions are synonymous with ALLERGIES, the commonest being HAY FEVER.

hypertension Persistent high BLOOD PRESSURE. It can damage blood vessels and may increase the risk of strokes or heart disease. *See also* HYPOTENSION

hyperthermia Abnormally high body temperature, usually defined as being 41°C (106°F) or more. It is usually due to HEATSTROKE or FEVER.

hyperthyroidism Excessive production of thyroid hormone, with enlargement of the thyroid gland. Symptoms include protrusion of the eyeballs, rapid heart rate, high blood pressure, accelerated metabolism. *See also* HYPOTHYROIDISM

hyperventilation Rapid breathing that is not brought about by physical exertion. It reduces the carbon dioxide level in the blood, producing dizziness, tingling and tightness in the chest; it may cause loss of consciousness.

hypnosis Artificially induced, sleep-like state during which suggestions are readily obeyed. It was first described more than two centuries ago. It is physiologically different from sleep and closer to a state of relaxed wakefulness. There is a reduction of critical faculties, and effects on memory.

hypodermic syringe Surgical instrument for injecting fluids beneath the skin, into a muscle or blood vessel. It comprises a graduated tube containing a piston plunger. *See also* INJECTION

hypoglycaemia Abnormally low level of sugar in the blood. It may result from fasting, excess INSULIN in the blood, or various metabolic and glandular diseases, notably DIABETES. Symptoms include dizziness, headache, sweating and mental confusion. *See also* HYPERGLYCAEMIA

hypotension Condition in which the blood pressure is abnormally low. It is commonly seen after heavy blood loss or excessive fluid loss due to prolonged vomiting or diarrhoea. Temporary hypotension may cause sweating, dizziness and fainting. *See also* HYPERTENSION

hypotenuse Side opposite the right angle in a right-angled triangle. It is the longest side of the triangle.

hypothalamus Region at the base of the brain containing centres that regulate body temperature, fluid balance, hunger, thirst and sexual activity. It is also involved in emotions, sleep and the integration of HORMONE and nervous activity.

hypothermia Fall in body temperature to below 35°C (95°F). Most at risk are newborns and the elderly. Insidious at onset, it can progress to coma and death. Hypothermia is sometimes induced during surgery to lower the body's oxygen demand. It occurs naturally in animals during HIBERNATION.

hypothesis Assumption or proposal made in order to account for or correlate known facts. Consequences inferred from a hypothesis are put to further inquiry, thus enabling the assumption to be tested in a particular situation. A set of hypotheses, logically connected and leading to the prediction of a wide range of events or states, is called a theory.

hypothyroidism Deficient functioning of the THYROID GLAND. Congenital hypothyroidism can lead to cretinism in children. In adults the condition is called myxoedema. More common in women, it causes physical and mental slowness, weight gain, sensitivity to cold and susceptibility to infection. It can be due to a defect of the gland or a lack of iodine. It is treated with the hormone thyroxine.

hyrax Small, rodent-like, herbivorous, hoofed mammal of Africa and sw Asia, with a squat, furry body and short ears, legs and tail. Rock hyraxes (genus *Procavia*) living in deserts and hills are larger than the solitary, nocturnal, tree-dwelling hyraxes (genus *Dendrohyrax*). Length: to 50cm (20in). Family Procaviidae.

hysterectomy Removal of the UTERUS, possibly with surrounding structures. It is performed to treat fibroids or cancer or to put an end to heavy menstrual bleeding.

hysteresis Phenomenon occurring in the magnetic and elastic behaviour of substances in which the strain is greater when the stress is decreasing than when it is increasing because of a lag in the effect. When the stress is removed, a residual strain remains.

hysteria In psychology, a group of disorders characterized by emotional instability, dissociation, hallucinations and the presence of physical symptoms of illness with no physiological cause. Hysteria is no longer used as a diagnostic term. Leading researchers of hysteria have included Jean Martin CHARCOT, Pierre Janet and Sigmund FREUD.

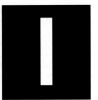

I/i is derived from the Semitic letter yod, meaning hand. It passed through Phoenician unchanged to the Greeks, who called it iota. In the Roman alphabet it was pronounced ee.

Iasi City in NE Romania. Capital of Moldavia from 1562–1861, it remains a commercial and administrative centre. Industries: textiles, machinery, pharmaceuticals, food products. Pop. (1992) 342,994.

Ibadan City in SW Nigeria; capital of Oyo state. It was established in the 1830s as a Yoruba military base. Ibadan is the regional centre of the cacao and cotton trades. Industries: plastics, cigarettes, brewing. Pop. (1992 est.) 1,295,000.

Iberian Peninsula Part of SW Europe occupied by Spain and Portugal, separated from Africa by the Strait of Gibraltar and from the rest of Europe by the Pyrenees Mountains. Area: 596,384sq km (230,264sq mi).

ibex Any of several species of wild Old World GOATS. The long, backward curving horns grow up to 1.5m (5ft) long on the male. Both sexes have yellow-brown hair. Ibexes are renowned for their agility. Height: 85cm (3ft) at shoulder. Family Bovidae.

ibis Tropical lagoon and marsh wading bird with long down-curved bill, long neck and lanky legs. Closely related to the SPOONBILL, it may be black, whitish or brightly coloured. It feeds on small animals, and nests in colonies. Length: 60–90cm (2–3ft). Subfamily: Threskiornithidae.

Ibiza Island of Spain, 130km (80mi) off the E coast, in the W Mediterranean; part of the Balearic group. Ibiza's mild climate and beautiful scenery have made it a major tourist resort. Industries: fishing, salt mining and the cultivation of figs and olives. Area: 572sq km (221sq mi). Pop. (1981) 60,937.

Ibsen, Henrik Johan (1828–1906) Norwegian playwright. He is best known for a dramatic blend of naturalism and symbolism. His plays include *Peer Gynt* (1867), *A Doll's House* (1879), *Ghosts* (1881), *An Enemy of the People* (1882), *Hedda Gabler* (1890) and *The Master Builder* (1892).

Icarus In Greek mythology, the son of DAEDALUS. Daedalus made wings of feathers and wax to effect his escape from Crete. He flew too near the Sun, which melted his wings, and he fell into the sea and drowned.

ice Water frozen to 0°C (32°F) or below, when it forms complex six-sided crystals. It is less dense than water and floats.

Ice Ages Periods in the Earth's history when ice sheets and GLACIERS advance to cover areas previously not affected by ice. There is evidence of at least six ice ages having occurred in the Earth's history. The best-known is the most recent ice age, which began about 2 million years ago and lasted

until the retreat of the ice to its present extent some 10,000 years ago. The present epoch may be a warmer period known as an interglacial.

iceberg Large drifting piece of ice, broken off from a GLACIER or polar ice cap. In the Northern Hemisphere the main source of icebergs is the SW coast of Greenland. In the south, the glacial flow from Antarctica releases huge tabular icebergs.

ice hockey Fast-action sport on an oval ice rink in which two teams of six players wearing ice-skates (and protective clothing) use special hockey sticks to try to propel a vulcanized rubber disc ("puck") into the opponents' goal. The rink is usually 61m (200ft) long by 26m (85ft) wide, and surrounded by walls about 1.2m (4ft) high. It is evenly divided into three, 18.3m (60ft), zones. A game consist of three 20-minute periods of actual timed play. A penalized player may be banished to the "sin-bin" for two or more minutes, and the team remains a player short unless the opponents score. Popular in Canada, the USA, Scandinavia, Britain, and central and eastern Europe, it has been an Olympic sport since 1920.

Iceland Small Scandinavian republic in the North Atlantic Ocean, N Europe; the capital is REYKJAVÍK. **Land and climate** Iceland sits astride the Mid-Atlantic Ridge, which is slowly widening as the ocean is being stretched apart by CONTINENTAL DRIFT. It has *c*.200 volcanoes and eruptions are frequent. Geysers and hot springs are also common features. Ice-caps and glaciers cover *c*.12% of the land, the largest is Vatnajökull in the SE. The only habitable regions are the coastal lowlands. Vegetation is sparse or non-existent on 75% of the land. Deep fjords fringe the coast. **Economy** Iceland has few resources besides its fishing grounds. Fishing and fish processing are major industries, accounting for 80% of Iceland's exports. Barely 1% of the land is used to grow crops, mainly root vegetables and fodder for livestock, and 23% is used for grazing sheep and cattle. Iceland is self-sufficient in meat and dairy products. Vegetables and fruits are grown in greenhouses. Manufacturing products include: aluminium, cement, electrical equipment and fertilizers. Geothermal power is an important energy source and heats Reykjavik. Overfishing is a major economic problem. **History and politics** Norwegian Vikings colonized Iceland in AD 874, and in 930 the settlers founded the world's oldest

---

ICELAND
AREA: 103,000 sq km (39,768 sq mi)
POPULATION: 260,000
CAPITAL (POPULATION): Reykjavik (101,824)
GOVERNMENT: Multiparty republic
ETHNIC GROUPS: Icelandic 94%, Danish 1%
LANGUAGES: Icelandic (official)
RELIGIONS: Christianity (Evangelical Lutheran 92%, other Lutheran 3%, Roman Catholic 1%)
CURRENCY: Króna = 100 aurar

parliament (Althing). Iceland united with Norway in 1262, and when Norway united with Denmark in 1380, Iceland came under Danish rule. In this colonial period Iceland lost much of its population, due to migration, disease and natural disaster. In 1918 Iceland became a self-governing kingdom. During World War 2 Iceland escaped German occupation, largely due to the presence of US forces. In 1944 a referendum decisively voted to sever links with Denmark, and Iceland became a fully independent republic. In 1946 it joined the North Atlantic Treaty Organization (NATO). In 1970 Iceland joined the European Free Trade Association (EFTA). The extension of Iceland's fishing limits in 1958 and 1972 precipitated the "Cod War" with the United Kingdom. In 1977 the UK agreed not to fish within Iceland's 370km (200 nautical mi) fishing limits. The continuing US military presence remains a political issue. Vigdis Finnbogadottir has been president since 1980. In 1995 David Oddson was reelected prime minister, heading a centre right coalition.

Icelandic Official language of Iceland, spoken by virtually all of its 268,000 inhabitants. It belongs to the Germanic family of Indo-European languages and is descended from Old Norse.

Icelandic literature Early Icelandic literature emerged in the 13th century from the oral tradition of Eadic and Skaldic poetry, both of which were based on ancient Icelandic mythology. Other early writings (14th–16th centuries) include the sagas of Norse monarchs. From the 14th–19th centuries the *rímur*, a narrative verse poem, was popular. The late 19th century saw the development of Icelandic realism. Important 20th-century writers include Halldór LAXNESS.

Iceni Ancient British tribe that occupied the area now known as Norfolk and Suffolk. The territory had been ruled by Prasutagus, a client-king, but on his death (AD 60) the Romans attempted to annex it. This led to a widespread revolt led by Prasutagus' queen, BOADICEA. The Iceni sacked Colchester, London and St Albans before they were crushed by the Roman governor, Suetonius Paulinus.

ice skating Winter leisure activity and all-year-round indoor competitive sport in which participants use steel skates to glide on ice. The three disciplines of competition skating are solo and pairs skating and ice dancing. Solo and pairs skating comprise compulsory figure skating, a short programme of compulsory elements and free skating (to the skater's choice of music). The ice dancing competition is structured similarly but based on set styles of dancing. **Speed** skating has two disciplines: international-track and short-track.

ichneumon fly Parasitic insect that attacks other insects and spiders. Found worldwide, they are characterized by an ovipositor that is often longer than the body. They are usually 1cm (0.4in) long. Family Ichneumonidae.

icon Type of religious painting or sculpture, often of Christ, the Virgin and Child or individual saints. The term is particularly used of Byzantine pictures and later Russian imitations.

id In psychoanalytic theory, the deepest level of the personality. It includes primitive drives (hunger, anger, sex) demanding instant gratification. Even after the EGO and SUPEREGO develop, the id is a source of motivation and unconscious conflicts.

Idaho State in NW USA, on the border with Canada; the capital and largest city is BOISE. Idaho remained unexplored until 1805. The discovery of gold (1860) brought many immigrants, and the Native American population was subdued in 1877. Idaho is dominated by the Rocky Mountains and is drained chiefly by the Snake River. The principal crops are potatoes, hay, wheat and sugar beet. Cattle are reared. Silver, lead, antimony and zinc are mined. Industries: food processing, timber. Area: 216,412sq km (83,557sq mi). Pop. (1993 est.) 1,099,096.

ideal gas law Law relating pressure, temperature and volume of an ideal (perfect) gas: $pV = NkT$, where N is the number of molecules of the gas and k is a constant of proportionality. This law implies that at constant temperature (T), the product of pressure and volume (pV) is constant (BOYLE'S LAW); and at constant pressure, the volume is proportional to the temperature (CHARLES' LAW).

idealism Philosophical doctrine that assigns metaphysical priority to the mental over the material. It denies the claim within REALISM that material things exist independently of the mind. Idealism in the West dates from the teachings of PLATO. The term is also applied to denote a rendering of something "as it ought to be" rather than as it actually is.

ideology Collection of beliefs or ideas reflecting the interests and aspirations of a country or its political system. In the 20th century the term has been applied to various political theories, including FASCISM, MARXISM and COMMUNISM.

Igbo (Ibo) Kwa-speaking people of E NIGERIA. Their patrilineal society originally consisted of autonomous village units, but during the 20th century political unity developed in reaction to British colonial rule. In 1967 the Igbo attempted to secede from Nigeria as the Republic of BIAFRA.

Ignatius of Loyola, Saint (1491–1556) Spanish soldier and churchman. In 1534, with FRANCIS XAVIER, he made vows of poverty, chastity and obedience. He founded the JESUITS.

igneous rock Broad class of rocks produced by the cooling and solidifying of molten magma deep within the Earth. Intrusive rocks, such as GRANITE, are formed beneath the Earth's surface by the gradual cooling of molten material; extrusive rocks, such as BASALT, are formed by the rapid cooling of molten material upon the Earth's surface.

iguana Any of numerous species of terrestrial, arboreal, burrowing or aquatic LIZARDS that live in tropical America and the Galápagos Islands. The common iguana (*Iguana iguana*) is greenish-brown, with a serrated dewlap and a crest along its back. Length: to 2m (6.5ft). Family Iguanidae.

ileum Major part of the small INTESTINE, *c.*4m (13ft) long. Its inner wall is lined with finger-like villi, which increase the area for the absorption of nutrients.

Iliescu, Ion (1930–) Romanian statesman, president (1990–). He was banished to Timisoara for his opposition to Nicolae CEAUŞESCU's "cultural revolution" and growing personality cult. Iliescu was one of the first leaders to emerge during the "Christmas Revolution" of 1989, when Ceauşescu was overthrown. He was elected president in May 1990, and re-elected in 1992.

Illinois State in N central USA, on the E bank of the Mississippi River; the capital is SPRINGFIELD. Illinois was explored first by the French in 1673. Ceded to the British in 1763, it was occupied by American troops during the American Revolution. Illinois became a state of the Union in 1818. The land is generally flat and is drained by many rivers flowing SW to the Mississippi. Illinois has fertile soil which supports crops such as hay, oats and barley; livestock farming is also important. CHICAGO (the largest city) is a transport centre and port on Lake MICHIGAN. Area: 146,075sq km (56,400sq mi). Pop. (1993 est.) 11,697,336.

illumination Coloured decorations serving to beautify manuscripts of religious books, the earliest dating from about the 5th century. The style ranges from decoration of initial letters and borders to miniatures and full-page illustrations.

imagism Movement in poetry that flourished in the USA and England from 1912 to 1917. Imagists, such as Ezra POUND, believed that poetry should use the language and rhythms of everyday speech. Amy Lowell, the principal exponent, produced three anthologies called *Some Imagist Poets* (1915–17).

imago Adult, reproductive stage of an insect that has undergone full METAMORPHOSIS. Imagos are the winged insects, such as butterflies and dragonflies, that emerge from PUPAS or develop from NYMPHS.

IMF Abbreviation of INTERNATIONAL MONETARY FUND

Immaculate Conception Roman Catholic belief that the Blessed Virgin MARY was free of all ORIGINAL SIN from the moment of conception. It was defined as a dogma by Pope PIUS IX in 1854.

immune system System by which the body defends itself against disease. It involves many kinds of LEUCOCYTES in the blood, lymph and bone marrow. Some of the cells make ANTIBODIES against invading microbes and other foreign substances, or neutralize TOXINS produced by PATHOGENS, while PHAGOCYTES attack and digest invaders. *See also* MACROPHAGE

immunity Resistance to attack by disease-causing microorganisms. It can be acquired naturally, as from an infection that stimulates the body to produce protective ANTIBODIES. Alternatively, it can be conferred by IMMUNIZATION.

immunization Practice of conferring IMMUNITY against disease by artificial means. **Passive** immunity may be conferred by the injection of an antiserum containing antibodies. **Active** immunity involves vaccination with dead or attenuated (weakened) organisms to stimulate production of specific antibodies and so provide lasting immunity.

immunoglobulin PROTEIN found in the bloodstream that plays a role in the body's immune defences. Immunoglobulins act as ANTIBODIES for specific ANTIGENS. They can be obtained from donor plasma and injected into people at risk of particular diseases.

immunology Study of IMMUNITY and ALLERGY. It is concerned with preventing disease by vaccination.

immunosuppressive drug Any drug that suppresses the body's immune responses to infection or "foreign" tissue. Such drugs are used to prevent rejection of transplanted organs and to treat autoimmune disease and some cancers.

impala (or pala) Long-legged, medium-sized African antelope. Long horns are found only on the males, but both sexes have sleek, glossy, brown fur with black markings on the rump. Length: to 1.5m (5ft); height: to 1m (3.3ft) at the shoulder. Family Bovidae; species *Aepyceros melampus.*

impatiens (Busy Lizzies) Genus of 450 species of succulent annual plants, mostly native to the tropics of Asia and Africa. They have white, red or yellow flowers and seedpods which, when ripe, pop and scatter their seeds. Family Balsaminaceae.

imperialism Domination of one people or state by another. Imperialism can be economic, cultural, political or religious. The 16th century age of exploration saw the establishment of trading empires by major European powers, such as the British, Spanish French, Portuguese and Dutch. They penetrated Africa, Asia and North America: their colonies serving as a source of raw materials and providing a market for manufactured goods. With few exceptions, imperialism imposed alien cultures on native societies. In the 20th century, most former colonies have gained independence.

imperial system Units of measurement developed in the UK. It is based on the foot, pound and the second. *See also* METRIC SYSTEM

impetigo Contagious skin condition caused by streptococcal or staphylococcal infection. It causes multiple, spreading lesions with yellowish-brown crusts and primarily affects exposed areas.

impressionism Major French anti-academic art movement of the later 19th century, gaining its name from a painting by MONET entitled *Impression, Sunrise* (exhibited 1874). Impressionism became widely influential from the late 1880s and spread throughout Europe. DEGAS and PISSARRO were prominent impressionists and CÉZANNE exhibited with them twice. MANET was influenced by, and influenced, impressionism. Other members include RENOIR and SISLEY. In music, the term impressionism refers to a period lasting from *c*.1890 to 1930, and is usually applied to the work of Claude DEBUSSY. *See also* ROMANTICISM

imprinting Form of learning that occurs within a critical period in very young animals. A complex relationship develops between the newborn infant and the first animate object it encounters, which is usually a parent. The future emotional development of the infant depends upon this relationship.

inbreeding Mating of two closely blood-related organisms. It is the opposite of outbreeding and over successive generations causes much less variation in GENOTYPE and PHENOTYPE than is normal in a wild population. A form of GENETIC ENGINEERING, it can be used to improve breeds in domestic plants and animals.

Inca South American people who migrated from the Peruvian highlands into the Cuzco area *c*.AD 1250. The Incas expanded and consolidated their empire until the reigns of Pachacuti (*c*.1438–71) and his son Topa (*c*.1471–93), when Inca dominance extended over most of the continent w of the Andes. The empire collapsed with the Spanish invasion led by PIZARRO (1532).

incandescence Emission of light by a substance at a high temperature. An incandescent object is never at a temperature below about 400°C (750°F).

incest Sexual relations within a family or kinship group, the taboo on which varies between societies. In many countries incest is a crime.

Inchon City and port on the Yellow Sea, NW South Korea. It was first opened to foreign trade in the 1880s. It was the scene of a Russo-Japanese naval battle in 1904, and US forces landed here in the KOREAN WAR (1950). It is one of South Korea's major commercial centres. Industries: iron and steel, textiles, chemicals. Pop. (1990) 1,818,293.

incubation In biology, process of maintaining stable, warm conditions to ensure that eggs develop and hatch. Incubation is carried out naturally by birds and by some reptiles. It is accomplished by sitting on the eggs, making use of volcanic or solar heat, the warmth of decaying vegetation, or by covering the eggs with an insulating layer.

incubation period In medicine, time lag between becoming infected with a disease and the appearance of the first symptoms. In many infectious diseases, the incubation period is quite short – anything from a few hours to a few days.

India Republic in s Asia; the capital is NEW DELHI. **Land and climate** India is the world's seventh largest country, but the second most populous (after China). India can be divided into three geographical regions: N India is dominated by the HIMALAYAS. The rivers BRAHMAPUTRA, INDUS and GANGES rise in the Himalayas and form the fertile, alluvial central plains. A densely populated area, the plains include New Delhi. CALCUTTA lies in the Ganges delta. In the w is the THAR DESERT and India's largest state, RAJASTHAN. Southern India consists of the large DECCAN plateau, bordered by the Western

---

INDIA
AREA: 3,287,590sq km (1,269,338sq mi)
POPULATION: 879,548,000
CAPITAL (POPULATION): New Delhi (301,800)
GOVERNMENT: Multiparty federal republic
ETHNIC GROUPS: Indo-Aryan 72%, Dravidian (Aboriginal) 25%, Other 3%
LANGUAGES: Hindi 30% and English (both official), Telugu 8%, Bengali 8%, Marati 8%, Urdu 5%, and many others
RELIGIONS: Hinduism 83%, Islam (Sunni) 11%, Christianity 2%, Sikhism 2%, Buddhism 1%
CURRENCY: Rupee = 100 paisa

---

and Eastern GHATS. India's largest city is BOMBAY (*see* individual state and city articles). India has three main seasons: a cool season (October–February); a hot season (March–June); and a monsoon season (mid-June–September). The KARAKORAM RANGE in the far N has permanently snow-covered peaks. The E Ganges delta has mangrove swamps. Between the gulfs of Kutch and Cambay are the deciduous forest habitats of the last of India's wild lions. The Ghats are clad in heavy rainforest. **Economy** India has rapidly industrialized, and manufacturing is now its largest export sector. India is rich in mineral resources; it is the world's 3rd largest producer of bituminous coal, yet it is heavily dependent on imported fuel. Agriculture employs 62% of the workforce, and food crops account for 75% of areas under cultivation. India is the world's 2nd greatest producer of rice (after China), and the 3rd largest producer of wheat. It is also the world's largest exporter of tea. In 1991, India abandoned its command economics and introduced free market reforms. Poverty and urban overcrowding remain urgent problems. **History** One of the world's oldest civilizations flourished in the lower Indus valley, *c*.2500–1700 BC. In *c*.1500 BC, Aryans conquered India, and established an early form of HINDUISM. In 327–325 BC, Alexander the Great conquered part of NW India. CHANDRAGUPTA founded the MAURYA EMPIRE. His grandson, ASHOKA, unified India and established BUDDHISM in the 3rd century BC. The CHOLA established a s trading kingdom in the 2nd century AD. In the 4th and 5th centuries AD, N India flourished under the GUPTA DYNASTY. The 7th century is seen as the classical period of India's history. In 1192 the DELHI Sultanate became India's first Muslim kingdom and dominated the region. In 1526 BABUR founded the MOGUL EMPIRE (1526–1857). In the 17th century. India became a centre of ISLAMIC ART AND ARCHITECTURE under SHAH JAHAN (who built the TAJ MAHAL) and AURANGZEB. In the 17th century, the MARATHA successfully resisted European imperial ambitions in the guise of the EAST INDIA COMPANY. Robert CLIVE established the BRITISH EMPIRE (1757–1947). Growing civil unrest culminated in the INDIAN MUTINY

(1857–58). Reforms failed to dampen Indian nationalism, and the CONGRESS PARTY was formed (1885). The MUSLIM LEAGUE was founded (1906) to protect Muslim minority rights. Following World War 1, Mahatma GANDHI began his passive resistance campaigns. The AMRITSAR Massacre (1919) intensified Indian nationalism. In August 1947 British India was partitioned into India and the Muslim state of PAKISTAN. The ensuing mass migration killed over 500,000 people. India became the world's largest democratic republic. Jawaharlal NEHRU became India's first prime minister. Conflict began (1948) with Pakistan over the status of JAMMU AND KASHMIR. In 1965 Nehru's daughter, Indira GANDHI, became prime minister. In 1971 India provided military support to create an independent BANGLADESH. In 1974 India became the world's sixth nuclear power. In 1984, faced with demands for an independent Sikh state, troops stormed the Golden Temple in Amritsar. Indira Gandhi was murdered by her Sikh bodyguards (October 1984), and was succeeded by her son, Rajiv GANDHI, who was assassinated by TAMILS during the 1990 elections. In 1947–96, India has been ruled by the Congress Party (I) for all but four years. In 1996 the United Front formed a coalition government, first under H.D. Deve Gowda (1996) and then Inder Kumar Gujral (1997–).

Indiana State in N central USA, s of Lake Michigan; the capital is INDIANAPOLIS. Indiana was explored first by the French in the early 18th century. It was ceded to the British in 1763 and passed to the USA after the American Revolution. The Native-American population was not subdued until 1811. The state remained a rural area until late 19th-century industrialization. Indiana is regarded as the USA's richest farming region. The development of heavy industry in the NW has made it a leading producer of machinery. Industries: grain, soya beans, livestock, coal, limestone, steel, motor vehicles, chemicals. Area: 93,993sq km (36,291sq mi). Pop. (1993 est.) 5,713,000.

Indianapolis State capital of Indiana, USA, in the centre of Indiana, on the White River. It became the state capital in 1825. The city is the major cereal and livestock market in a fertile agricultural area. Industries: electronics, vehicle parts, pharmaceuticals, meat packing. Pop. (1990) 741,952.

Indian art and architecture Earliest examples of Indian art date from the ancient civilization of the Indus Valley (c.2300–1750 BC). Excavations have revealed complex, fortified cities. Art in the MAURYA EMPIRE (321–185 BC) was intensely Buddhist in motivation. It can be seen in the *chaitya* (shrines) and *vihara* (monastic halls hollowed out of solid rock) at Ajanta. The GUPTA DYNASTY (AD 320–550) was the golden age of Buddhist art. From the 6th century AD, a typical Hindu temple plan developed. In s India in the 7th and 8th centuries AD, a Dravidian style of Hindu temple emerged. ISLAMIC ART AND ARCHITECTURE were introduced after the Muslim conquest (1192). Between the 16th and 18th centuries, during the MOGUL EMPIRE, an Indo-Islamic style evolved, influenced by Persian prototypes. The TAJ MAHAL stands as the most perfect example of Mogul architecture. Persian influence was initially strong in drawing, but by the late 16th century, Indian taste was emerging in brightly coloured and detailed miniatures. Under British rule, most Indian art declined to mere craftsmanship until the early 20th century.

Indian Mutiny (1857–58) Indian rebellion against the British, originating among Indian troops (sepoys) in the Bengal army. It is known in India as the first war of independence. The immediate cause was the introduction of cartridges lubricated with the fat of cows and pigs. A more general cause was resentment at modernization and Westernization. Delhi was captured, and atrocities were perpetrated by both sides. The revolt resulted in the British government assuming control of India from the EAST INDIA COMPANY in 1858.

Indian National Congress *See* CONGRESS PARTY

Indian Ocean Third-largest ocean in the world, bounded by Asia (N), Antarctica (S), Africa (W) and Southeast Asia and Australia (E). Known in ancient times as the Erythraean Sea, the Indian Ocean was the first to be extensively navigated. Branches of the ocean include the Arabian Sea, the Bay of BENGAL, and the Andaman Sea. Its largest islands are MADAGASCAR and SRI LANKA. The average depth is 4,000m (13,000ft) although there is a mid-oceanic ridge, extending from Asia to Antarctica; several of its peaks emerge as islands. The deepest part is the Java Trench, reaching 7,725m (25,344ft). The climate of the nearby land masses is strongly influenced by the ocean's winds and currents. Area: c.73,600,000sq km (28,400,000sq mi).

Indians, American *See* NATIVE AMERICANS

Indian theatre Classical and modern dramatic traditions of the Indian subcontinent, including Sanskrit, Kutiyattam and Kathakali. Sanskrit (Hindu) classical drama, the two great epics of which are the MAHABHARATA and the RAMAYANA, can be traced back as far as the 3rd century BC and survived into the 11th century AD. Sanskrit was followed by a more eclectic tradition that emphasized music, poetry and dance in its performance. This developed in tandem with Indian folk drama. Largely as a result of Western influence, modern drama appeared during the latter half of the 20th century. There is also a strong tradition of puppetry.

India-Pakistan Wars Three conflicts between India and Pakistan. The first (1947–49) arose from a dispute over KASHMIR. Inconclusive fighting continued until January 1949, when the UN arranged a truce, leaving Kashmir partitioned. It remained a source of friction and was the chief cause of a second war (1965). Both sides invaded the other's territory, but military stalemate resulted

311

in a rapid cease-fire. The third war arose out of the civil war between East and West Pakistan in 1971. India intervened in support of East Pakistan (BANGLADESH), to defeat (West) Pakistan.

indicator In chemistry, substance used to indicate acidity or alkalinity. It does this usually by a change of colour. Indicators, such as the dye LITMUS, can detect a change of pH. Universal indicator (liquid or paper) undergoes a spectral range of colour changes from pH 1 to 13.

indigestion *See* DYSPEPSIA

indigo Violet-blue dye traditionally obtained from plants of the genus *Indigofera*, produced synthetically since the 1890s.

indium Silvery-white metallic element (symbol In) of group III in the PERIODIC TABLE. Its chief source is as a by-product of zinc ores. Malleable and ductile, indium is used in semiconductors and mirrors. Properties: at.no. 49; r.a.m. 114.82; r.d. 7.31; m.p. 156.6°C (313.9°F); b.p. 2,080 °C (3,776°F); most common isotope In^{115} (95.77%).

Indochina Peninsula of SE Asia, including BURMA, THAILAND, CAMBODIA, VIETNAM, West MALAYSIA and LAOS. The name refers more specifically to the former federation of states of Vietnam, Laos and Cambodia, associated with France within the French Union (1945–54).

Indo-European languages Family of languages spoken throughout Europe and SW and S Asia, and used in all areas of European colonial settlement. About 50% of the world's population speaks one or other of these languages.

Indonesia Republic in the Malay archipelago, SE Asia; the capital is JAKARTA. **Land and climate** Indonesia is the world's most populous Muslim nation and the fourth most populous nation on Earth. It is also the world's largest archipelago, with 13,677 islands. Three-quarters of its area and population is included in five main islands: the Greater Sunda Islands of SUMATRA, JAVA, SULAWESI and KALIMANTAN; and IRIAN JAYA (W New Guinea). Over 50% of the total population live on Java, site of Jakarta. The Lesser Sunda Islands include BALI, TIMOR and Lombok. Indonesia is mountainous and prone to earthquakes. Indonesia lies on the equator and is hot and humid throughout the year. Rainfall

---

INDONESIA

AREA: 1,904,570sq km (735,354sq mi)
POPULATION: 191,170,000
CAPITAL (POPULATION): Jakarta (7,885,519)
GOVERNMENT: Multiparty republic
ETHNIC GROUPS: Javanese 39%, Sundanese 16%, Indonesian (Malay) 12%, Madurese 4%, more than 300 others
LANGUAGES: Bahasa Indonesian (official)
RELIGIONS: Islam 87%, Christianity 10% (Roman Catholic 6%), Hinduism 2%, Buddhism 1%
CURRENCY: Indonesian rupiah = 100 sen

---

is generally heavy, only the Sunda Islands have a dry season. Mangrove swamps line the coast. Tropical rainforests remain the major vegetation on less populated islands. Much of the larger islands have been cleared by logging and shifting cultivation. **Economy** Indonesia is a developing country. Agriculture employs 56% of the workforce. Oil is its most valuable resource. Indonesia is the world's second-largest exporter of natural gas. Its abundant forests also make it the second-largest exporter of rubber. Coffee and rice production are also important. In an attempt to diversify its economy, manufacturing is increasing, especially on Java. **History and politics** In the 7th and 8th century, the Indian GUPTA DYNASTY was the dominant force, and was responsible for the introduction of Buddhism and the building of Borobudur, Java. In the 13th century Buddhism was gradually replaced by Hinduism. By the end of the 16th century Islam had become the principal religion. In 1511 the Portuguese seized MALACCA. By 1610 the Dutch had acquired all of Portugal's holdings, except East Timor. During the 18th century, the Dutch EAST INDIA COMPANY controlled the region. In 1799 Indonesia became a Dutch colony. Throughout the 19th century, Indonesia fought against European colonialism. In 1883 KRAKATOA erupted, claiming *c*.50,000 lives. In 1927 SUKARNO formed the Indonesian Nationalist Party (PNI). During World War 2, the Japanese expelled the Dutch (1942) and occupied Indonesia. In August 1945 Sukarno proclaimed independence; the Dutch forcibly resisted. In November 1949 Indonesia became a republic, with Sukarno as its first president. During the 1950s, economic hardship and secessionist demands were met with authoritarian measures. In 1962 paratroopers seized Netherlands New Guinea and, in 1969, Netherlands New Guinea formally became part of Indonesia as Irian Jaya. In 1966 General SUHARTO assumed control. The Communist Party was banned and alleged communists executed; up to 750,000 people were killed. In 1968 Suharto was elected president and has continued to rule autocratically. In 1975 Indonesian forces seized East Timor and declared it a province of Indonesia. Resistance to Indonesian rule has killed over 200,000 East Timorese. The UN does not recognize the annexation. In 1997 Indonesia suffered from dangerously high levels of smog caused by forest fires exacerbated by drought.

Indra In Vedic mythology, the ruler of heaven, great god of storms, thunder and lightning, worshipped as rain-maker and bringer of fertility.

inductance Property of an electric circuit or component that produces an ELECTROMOTIVE FORCE (EMF) following a change in the current. The SI unit of inductance is the henry. Self-inductance (symbol L) occurs when current flows through the circuit or component, and mutual inductance (symbol M) when current flows through two circuits or components that are linked magnetically. *See also* ELECTROMAGNETIC INDUCTION; INDUCTION

induction In medicine, initiation of LABOUR before it starts of its own accord. It involves perforating the fetal membranes and administering the hormone oxytocin to stimulate contractions of the UTERUS.

induction In physics, process by which an ELECTROMOTIVE FORCE (EMF) is created in a circuit by a change in the magnetic field around the circuit. The magnitude of the current is proportional to the rate of change of magnetic flux. *See also* ELECTROMAGNETIC INDUCTION; FARADAY'S LAWS; INDUCTANCE

Indus River of S Asia. It rises in the Kailas mountain range in Tibet and flows WNW through the Indian state of Jammu and Kashmir, then SW through Pakistan and into the Arabian Sea. Semi-navigable along its shallow lower part, the river is used chiefly for irrigation and hydroelectric power. Length: *c*.3,060km (1,900mi).

Industrial Revolution Term applied to the profound economic changes that took place in W Europe and the USA in the late 18th and 19th centuries. It was preceded by a rapid increase in population, which was both a cause and result of the AGRICULTURAL REVOLUTION. The STEAM ENGINE was the driving force, leading to huge advances in manufacturing and transport. The Industrial Revolution produced major social changes, in particular the creation of an industrial working class.

inequality Mathematical statement that one expression is less, or greater, than another. The symbols $>$, for "is greater than," and $<$, for "is less than," are used. The symbols $\geqslant$ and $\leqslant$ are also used, for "greater than or equal to" or "less than or equal to," respectively.

inert gases *See* NOBLE GAS

inertia Property possessed by all matter in respect to the way an object resists changes to its state of motion. Isaac NEWTON formulated the first law of motion, sometimes called the law of inertia, stating that a body will remain at rest or in a uniform motion unless acted upon by external forces.

infarction Death of part of an organ caused by a sudden obstruction in an artery supplying it. In a myocardial infarction (HEART ATTACK), a section of heart muscle dies.

infection Invasion of the body by disease-causing organisms that become established, multiply and give rise to symptoms.

infertility Inability to reproduce. In a woman it may be due to a failure to ovulate (release an egg for FERTILIZATION), obstruction of the FALLOPIAN TUBE, or disease of the ENDOMETRIUM; in a man it is due to inadequate sperm production. In plants, it refers to the inability to reproduce sexually. Infertility occurs in a HYBRID between different species, which are unable to produce viable GAMETES.

infinity Abstract quantity that represents the magnitude of an object without limit or end. In geometry, the "point at infinity" is where parallel lines can be considered as meeting. In algebra, $1/x$ approaches infinity as x approaches zero. In set theory, the set of all integers is an example of an infinite set.

inflammation Reaction of body tissue to infection or injury, with resulting pain, heat, swelling and redness. It occurs when damaged cells release a substance called histamine, which causes blood vessels at the damaged site to dilate.

inflation In economics, continual upward movement of prices. Although often associated with periods of prosperity, inflation may also occur during recessions. It usually occurs when there is relatively full employment. Under "cost-push" inflation, prices rise because producers' costs increase. Under "demand-pull" inflation, prices increase because of excessive consumer demand for goods.

inflorescence FLOWER or flower cluster. Inflorescences are classified into two main types according to branching characteristics. A **racemose** inflorescence has a main axis and lateral flowering branches, with flowers opening from the bottom up or from the outer edge inwards. A **cymose** inflorescence has a composite axis, with the main stem ending in a flower and lateral branches bearing additional, later-flowering branches.

influenza Viral infection mainly affecting the airways, with chesty symptoms, headache, joint pains, fever and general malaise. It is treated by bed rest and painkillers. Vaccines are available to confer immunity to some strains.

information technology (IT) Computer and TELECOMMUNICATIONS technologies used in processing information of any kind. Word processing, the use of a DATABASE, and the sending of messages over a COMPUTER NETWORK all involve the use of information technology. Television stations use IT to provide viewers with teletext services.

information theory Mathematical study of the laws governing communication channels. It is primarily concerned with the measurement of information and the methods of coding, transmitting, storing and processing this information.

infrared wave Electromagnetic radiation that produces a sensation of heat emitted by hot objects. Intermediate in energy between visible light and microwaves, its wavelength range is *c*.750nm to 1mm. It has applications in astronomy, medicine and warfare.

Ingres, Jean Auguste Dominique (1780–1867) French neo-classical painter. One of the great figures of early 19th-century French art, he was an outstanding portraitist, especially of women in high society such as *Madame d'Haussonville* (1845). He also produced sensual nudes, such as *Bather of Valpinçon* (1808) and, much later, *The Turkish Bath* (1863). In 1824 Ingres found himself hailed as the leader of the anti-Romantic movement, with DELACROIX as his arch rival.

injection In medicine, use of a syringe and needle to introduce drugs or other fluids into the body to diagnose, treat or prevent disease. Most injections are either intravenous (into a vein), intramuscular (into a muscle), or intradermal (into the skin).

Inkatha South African political organization,

founded in 1975 by Chief BUTHELEZI. Its initial aim was to work towards a democratic, non-racial political system. In the early 1990s, it was involved in violent conflict with the AFRICAN NATIONAL CONGRESS (ANC). It is the third-largest party in South Africa's National Assembly, and its strongest base is in KWAZULU-NATAL.

Innocent III (1161–1216) Pope (1198–1216), b. Lotario di Segni. He increased papal control over civil matters, and set up the courts of INQUISITION. He approved the Franciscan and Dominican orders and backed the crusade against the ALBIGENSES.

Innsbruck City on the Inn River, W Austria; capital of Tirol state. Founded in the 12th century, the city grew because of its strategic position on a historic transalpine route. Innsbruck is a commercial and industrial centre, and an important winter sports resort. Industries: manufacturing, metalworking, textiles, food processing. Pop. (1991) 118,112.

inorganic chemistry See CHEMISTRY

Inquisition Court set up by the Roman Catholic Church in the Middle Ages to seek out and punish heresy. The accused were sometimes interrogated under torture. Punishments ranged from penances to banishment and death. The medieval Inquisition was active in Europe from the 12th to the 15th centuries. A later tribunal, the Spanish Inquisition, was instituted in 1483 at the request of the rulers of Spain and was not formally abolished until 1834.

insect Any of more than a million species of small, invertebrate animals, including the BEETLE, BUG, BUTTERFLY, ANT and BEE. There are more species of insects than all other species combined. Adult insects have three pairs of jointed legs, usually two pairs of wings, and a segmented body with an EXOSKELETON. The head has three pairs of mouthparts, a pair of compound eyes, three pairs of simple eyes, and a pair of antennae. Most insects can detect a wide range of sounds through ultra-sensitive hairs on various parts of their bodies. Some can "sing" or make sounds by rubbing together parts of their bodies. Most insects are plant-eaters, some prey on small animals (especially other insects), and a few are scavengers. There are two main kinds of mouthparts – chewing and sucking. Reproduction is usually sexual. Most insects go through four distinct life stages, in which complete METAMORPHOSIS is said to take place. The four stages are: OVUM (egg), LARVA (caterpillar or grub), PUPA (chrysalis) and adult (IMAGO). Young grasshoppers and some other insects, called NYMPHS, resemble wingless miniatures of their parents. The nymphs develop during a series of moults (incomplete metamorphosis). SILVERFISH and a few other primitive, wingless insects do not undergo metamorphosis. Phylum Arthropoda, class Insecta. See also ARTHROPOD

insectivore Small order of carnivorous MAMMALS (Insectivora), many of which eat insects. Almost worldwide in distribution, some species live underground, some on the ground and some in streams and ponds. Most insectivores have narrow snouts, long skulls and five-clawed feet. Three families are always placed in the order: Erinaceidae (moon rats, gymures, HEDGEHOGS); Talpidae (MOLES, shrew moles, desmans) and Soricidae (SHREWS).

insectivorous plant (carnivorous plant) Any of several plants that have poorly developed root systems and are often found in nitrogen-deficient sandy or boggy soils. They obtain the missing nutrients by trapping, "digesting" and absorbing insects. Some, such as the Venus's fly-trap (*Dionaea muscipula*), are active insect trappers. The sundews (*Drosera*) snare insects with a sticky substance and then enclose them in their leaves. Bladderworts (*Utricularia*) suck insects into their underwater bladders. Other plants have vase-shaped leaves, such as the pitcher plant (*Sarracenia flava*).

insemination, artificial Introduction of donor semen into a female's reproductive tract to bring about fertilization. First developed for livestock breeding, it is now routinely used to help infertile couples. See also IN VITRO FERTILIZATION (IVF)

instinct Behaviours that are innately determined. In the 19th century instincts were often cited to explain behaviour, but the term fell into disrepute with the advent of BEHAVIOURISM.

insulation Technique for reducing or preventing the transfer of heat, electricity, sound or other vibrations. Wool, fibre-glass and foam plastic are good heat-insulating materials because they contain air. This trapped air reduces the transfer of heat by CONDUCTION. Electrical insulation materials include rubber, polythene and glass. Sound insulating materials absorb sound and change it to heat by FRICTION.

insulin HORMONE that controls blood-glucose levels, secreted by the islets of Langherhans in the PANCREAS. Insulin lowers the blood-glucose level by helping the uptake of glucose into cells, and by causing the liver to convert glucose to glycogen. In the absence of insulin, glucose accumulates in the blood and urine, resulting in DIABETES.

intaglio Incised carving on gemstones, hardstones or glass, in which the design is sunk below the surface. In printing, the term is used to describe processes in which ink is applied to incisions and hollows in a printing plate, as in ETCHING.

integer Negative or positive whole number and zero, e.g. -3, -2, -1, 0, 1, 2, 3 .... There is a infinite number of integers. The positive integers are the natural numbers. The existence of negative integers and zero allow any integer to be subtracted from any other integer to give an integer result.

integral calculus In mathematics, the branch of calculus that deals with integration: the finding of a function, one or more derivatives of which are given. It is used to find the areas and volumes of curved shapes. In engineering calculations, differential equations are solved by integral calculus. Its principles are also incorporated in many measuring and control instruments.

integrated circuit (IC) Complete miniature electronic CIRCUIT incorporating semiconductor devices such as the TRANSISTOR and RESISTOR. **Monolithic** integrated circuits have all the components manufactured into or on top of a silicon CHIP. In **hybrid** integrated circuits, components are attached to a ceramic base. Components in both types are joined by conducting film. *See also* PRINTED CIRCUIT

Integrated Services Digital Network (ISDN) High-speed telephone lines designed to carry digital information. An ISDN can carry information more than a thousand times faster than conventional analogue voice lines. ISDN lines connect directly to a computer and do not need a MODEM.

integration *See* INTEGRAL CALCULUS

intelligence General ability to learn and to deal with problems, new situations and abstract concepts. It can be manifest in many different ways, including skills in adaptability, memory and reasoning. Fierce debate has raged over the roles of hereditary and environmental factors in developing intelligence. Intelligence tests measure abstract reasoning and problem-solving abilities.

intelligence quotient *See* IQ

interface Way that a computer PROGRAM or system interacts with its user. The simplest form of computer interface is the keyboard, through which the user controls the computer by typing in commands. The most common type for personal computers is the GRAPHICAL USER INTERFACE (GUI).

interference In physics, the interaction of two or more wave motions, such as those of light and sound, creating a disturbance pattern. Constructive interference is the reinforcement of the wave motion because the component motions are in phase. Destructive interference occurs when two waves are out of phase and cancel each other.

interferometer Instrument in which a wave, especially a light wave, is split into component waves that are made to travel unequal distances to recombine as INTERFERENCE patterns. The patterns have such uses as quality control of lenses and prisms, and the measurement of wavelengths.

interferon Protein produced by body cells when infected with a virus. Interferons can help uninfected cells to resist infection by the virus and also may impede virus replication and protein synthesis. In some circumstances they can inhibit cell growth; human interferon is now produced by GENETIC ENGINEERING for therapeutic use, to treat some cancers, HEPATITIS and MULTIPLE SCLEROSIS.

internal combustion engine Engine in which fuel is burned inside, so that the gases formed can produce motion, widely used in automobiles. They may be TWO-STROKE ENGINES or FOUR-STROKE ENGINES. *See also* DIESEL ENGINE

International Atomic Energy Agency (IAEA) Specialized, intergovernmental agency of the United Nations. It was founded in 1956 to promote peaceful uses of nuclear energy and establish international control of nuclear weapons. The organization's headquarters are in Vienna, Austria.

International Labour Organization (ILO) Specialized, intergovernmental agency of the United Nations. Its aim is to improve industrial relations and conditions of work. It was formed as an agency of the LEAGUE OF NATIONS in 1919, and has a membership comprising government, employer and worker representatives. Its headquarters are in Geneva, Switzerland.

International Monetary Fund (IMF) Specialized, intergovernmental agency of the United Nations, and administrative body of the international monetary system. Its main function is to provide assistance to member states troubled by BALANCE OF PAYMENTS problems and other financial difficulties. The IMF does not actually lend money to member states; rather, it exchanges the member state's currency with its own Special Drawing Rates (SDR) (a "basket" of other currencies) in the hope that this will alleviate balance of payment difficulties. The organization is based in Washington, D.C., USA.

International style (International modern style) Architectural style developed in Europe in the 1920s and 1930s that stresses function and avoids superfluous decoration in design. It characteristically features austere white walls, asymmetrical cubic shapes, and large expanses of glass. LE CORBUSIER and Walter GROPIUS were early exponents.

Internet Worldwide communications system consisting of hundreds of small COMPUTER NETWORKS, interconnected by telephone systems. It is a network of networks, in which messages and data are sent using short local links from place to place around the world. This enables users to send a message to the other side of the world by ELECTRONIC MAIL (E-MAIL) for the cost of a local phone call.

interplanetary matter Material in the space between the planets. It is made up of atomic particles (mainly protons and electrons) ejected from the Sun via the solar wind, and dust particles (mainly from COMETS, but some possibly of cosmic origin) in the plane of the ecliptic.

Interpol (International Criminal Police Organization) Intergovernmental organization. Established in 1923, its main function is to provide member states with information about international criminals and to assist in their arrest. Its headquarters are in Lyon, France.

intestine Lower part of the ALIMENTARY CANAL, beyond the STOMACH. Food is moved through the intestine by PERISTALSIS. It undergoes the final stages of digestion and is absorbed into the bloodstream in the small intestine, which extends from the stomach to the large intestine. In the large intestine (caecum, colon and rectum) water is absorbed from undigested material, which is then passed out of the body through the anus.

Intifada (Arabic, uprising) Campaign of civil disobedience by Palestinians in the Israeli-occupied territories of the WEST BANK and GAZA STRIP. The Intifada began in 1987 and was a sustained attempt to disrupt Israel's heavy-handed policing tactics. By early 1995 the Intifada had claimed over 1,400

315

Palestinian and 230 Jewish lives. It lost momentum following the Israeli-Palestinian Accord.

intravenous drip Apparatus for delivering drugs, blood and blood products, nutrients and other fluids directly into the bloodstream. A hollow needle is inserted into a vein and then attached to a length of tubing leading from a bag containing the solution.

introversion Preoccupation with one's own responses and impressions, coupled with a preference for reflection over action and a dislike of social activity. The term was coined by C.G. Jung as a polar opposite to extroversion.

intrusion In geology, emplacement of rock material that was either forced or flowed into spaces among other rocks. An igneous intrusion consists of magma that never reached the Earth's surface but filled cracks and faults, then cooled and hardened.

Inuit Collective name for the Eskimo people of Alaska, Greenland, and the Northwest Territories, Arctic Quebec and N Labrador areas of Canada. Many still live in remote communities, employing traditional skills of fishing, trapping, and hunting.

invertebrate In zoology, the term for an animal without a backbone. There are more than a million species of invertebrates, divided into 30 major groups. One of these is Arthropoda (joint-legged animals), the largest of all animal phyla in numbers of species. Most are insects, but it also includes crustaceans and arachnids. Molluscs make up the second largest group of invertebrates. *See also* arthropods; crustacea; phylum

in vitro fertilization (IVF) Use of artificial techniques that join an egg with sperm outside a woman's body to help infertile couples to have children of their own. The basic technique of IVF involves removing eggs from a woman's ovaries, fertilizing them in the laboratory and then inserting them into the uterus. In zygote intrafallopian transfer (ZIFT), a fertilized egg is returned to the Fallopian tube, from which it makes its own way to the uterus. In gamete intrafallopian transfer (GIFT), the eggs are removed, mixed with sperm, then both eggs and sperm are inserted into a Fallopian tube to be fertilized in the natural setting.

involuntary muscle One of three types of muscle in the body, so called because, unlike skeletal muscle, it is not under the conscious control of the brain but is stimulated by the autonomic nervous system and by hormones in the bloodstream. It is of two kinds: **smooth** muscle is the muscle of the alimentary canal, blood vessels and bladder. **Cardiac** muscle powers the heart.

Io Large innermost satellite of Jupiter. It was discovered by Galileo in 1609–10 and is larger than the Moon. It is more than 3,600km (2,200mi) in diameter and is 422,000km (262,000mi) above the surface of the planet.

iodine Nonmetallic element (symbol I) that is the least reactive of the halogen group (group VII). The black volatile solid gives a violet vapour and has an unpleasant odour that resembles chlorine.

Iodine was discovered in 1811. Existing in seawater, seaweeds and other plants, it is also extracted from Chile saltpetre and oil-well brine. Iodine is essential for the functioning of the thyroid gland. It is used as a medical antiseptic and in photography. Properties: at.no. 53; r.a.m. 126.9; r.d. 4.93; m.p. 113.5°C (236.3°F); b.p. 184.4°C (363.9°F); most stable isotope I^{127} (100%).

ion Atom or group of atoms with an electric charge resulting from the loss or gain of one or more electrons. Positive ions are called cations and move towards the cathode in electrolysis; negative ions are called anions and move towards the anode. The process of forming ions is called ionization.

Iona Island off the coast of W Scotland in the Inner Hebrides. The island has an abbey, founded in AD 563 by St Columba. Tourism is the main source of income. Area: 13sq km (5sq mi).

Ionesco, Eugène (1912–94) French dramatist in the Theatre of the Absurd. Plays include *The Bald Prima Donna* (1950) and *Rhinoceros* (1959).

Ionia Historic region on the W coast of Asia Minor (Turkey), including neighbouring Aegean islands. Ionia was settled in the 11th and 10th centuries BC. Ephesus was one of its major cities. Ionia was conquered by the Persians in the 6th century BC. After the conquests of Alexander the Great, Ionia was ruled by Hellenistic kings and from the 2nd century BC was part of the Roman empire.

ionic bond (electrovalent bond) Type of chemical bond in which ions of opposite charge are held together by electrostatic attraction.

ionic compound Substance formed by ionic bonding. Salts, bases and some acids are ionic compounds. As crystalline solids, such compounds have high melting and boiling points. As solids, they are also nonconductors of electricity and are usually soluble in water but insoluble in organic solvents. In dissolved and molten states, ionic compounds are good conductors.

Ionic order One of the orders of architecture

ionosphere Wide region of ions or charged particles in the atmosphere. It extends from *c.*60km (37mi) above the Earth to the limits of the atmosphere in the Van Allen radiation belts. Radio waves are deflected in the ionosphere, which makes possible long-distance radio communication.

Iowa State in N central USA, lying between the Missouri and Mississippi rivers; the capital is Des Moines. First explored by Europeans in 1673, the region was sold by France to the USA in the Louisiana Purchase of 1803. Iowa was admitted to the Union in 1846. Originally prairie, the region is known for its fertile farmland. Maize and other cereals are produced and Iowa stands second only to Texas in the raising of prime cattle. Industries: food processing, farm machinery. Area: 145,790sq km (56,290sq mi). Pop. (1995 est.) 2,842,000.

Iphigenia In Greek legend, daughter of Agamemnon and Clytemnestra and sister of Electra and Orestes. She was sacrificed by

Agamemnon to the goddess Artemis in exchange for favourable winds for his journey to Troy.

Ipswich City and port on the Orwell estuary, E England; the county town of SUFFOLK. The wool trade brought it prosperity in the Middle Ages. After a decline, its fortunes were revived in the 19th century with the introduction of light industry. Industries: milling, brewing, printing, agricultural machinery. Pop. (1991) 116,956.

IQ (Intelligence Quotient) Classification of the supposed intelligence of a person. It is computed by dividing assessed "mental age" by actual age, then multiplying by 100. "Mental age" is determined by comparison with the average performance of people of various ages on a standard intelligence test. *See also* APTITUDE TEST

IRA *See* IRISH REPUBLICAN ARMY

Iráklion (Heraklion or Candia) Seaport and largest city on the island of Crete, S Greece; capital of Iráklion prefecture. Founded by the Saracens in the 9th century, it became part of Greece in 1913. The ruins of KNOSSOS are nearby. Tourism is important. Exports: wine, olive oil, almonds, raisins. Pop. (1991) 115,124.

Iran Islamic republic in SW Asia; the capital is TEHRAN. **Land and climate** A barren central plateau covers *c.*50% of Iran: it includes the *Dasht-e-Kavir* (Great Salt Desert) and the *Dasht-e-Lut* (Great Sand Desert). Tehran lies in the Elburz Mountains, N of the plateau, which contain Iran's highest point, Damavand, at 5,604m (18,368ft). To the NE lies Iran's second city of MASHHAD. On the NW edge of the plateau lies the city of QOM. The W of the plateau is bounded by the Zagros Mountains, including the cities of ISFAHAN and Shiraz. In the far NW lies its largest lake, Lake Urmia, and the city of TABRIZ. The Shatt al Arab channel forms part of its border with Iraq. Iran is susceptible to earthquakes. It has hot summers and cold winters. Precipitation is highest in the N, often in the form of winter snow. Forest covers *c.*10% of Iran, mainly in the Elbruz and Zagros mountains. Semi-desert and desert cover most of the country. **Economy** Iran's prosperity is based on oil production. Oil accounts for 95% of its exports, and it is the world's fourth-largest producer of crude oil. The Iran-Iraq war devastated Iran's industrial base. Oil revenue has been used to develop the manufacturing base. Industry now employs 26% of the workforce. Attempts have been made to reduce Iran's dependence on food imports. Agriculture employs 30% of the workforce. Iran is the world's largest producer of dates. Other major crops include wheat and barley. Iran is famous for its fine carpets. Tourism has great potential, but the political situation discourages many visitors. **History** Until 1935 Iran was known as PERSIA. Aryans settled in Persia *c.*2000 BC. The Persian king CYRUS THE GREAT founded the ACHAEMENID dynasty in 550 BC. The Persian empire fell to Alexander the Great in 331 BC. Persian rule was restored by the SASSANIDS in AD 224. Arabs conquered Persia in AD 641 and introduced ISLAM. For the next two centuries Persia was a centre of ISLAMIC ART AND ARCHITECTURE. SELJUK Turks conquered Persia in the 11th century, but in 1220 the land was overrun by the MONGOLS. The SAFAVID dynasty (1501–1722) was founded by Shah ISMAIL, who established the SHIITE theocratic principles of modern Iran. Nadir Shah expelled Afghan invaders. His despotic rule (1736–47) was noted for imperial ambition. The Qajar dynasty (1794–1925) witnessed the gradual decline of the Persian empire in the face of European expansion. Britain and Russia competed for influence in the area. The discovery of oil in SW Iran led to the Russian and British division of Iran (1907). In 1919 Iran effectively became a British protectorate. In 1921 Reza Khan seized power in a military coup, established the Pahlavi dynasty, and was elected shah (1925). He annulled the British treaty and began a process of modernization. In 1941 British and Soviet forces occupied Iran. Reza Shah abdicated in favour of his son, Muhammad Reza Shah PAHLAVI. The 1943 Tehran Declaration guaranteed Iran's independence. In 1951 the oil industry was nationalized. The shah fled Iran, but soon returned with US backing and restored Western oil rights (1953). During the 1960s the shah undertook large-scale reforms, such as land ownership and extending the franchise to women (1963). Discontent surfaced over increasing westernization and economic inequality. Iranian clerics, led by Ayatollah KHOMEINI, openly voiced their disapproval. In 1971 Britain withdrew its troops from the Persian Gulf. Iran became the largest military power in the region. In exile, Khomeini called for the abdication of the shah (1978). In January 1979 the shah fled and Khomeini established an Islamic republic. The theocracy was profoundly conservative and anti-western. In July 1979 the oil industry was renationalized. In September 1980 Iraqi invasion marked the start of the IRAN-IRAQ WAR (1980–88). The war claimed over 500,000 lives. In 1986 the US covertly agreed to supply Iran with arms (*see* IRAN-CONTRA AFFAIR). In June 1989 Khomeini died and was succeeded by RAFSANJANI. Rafsanjani improved relations with the West. Free market reforms were adopted and Iran supported international sanctions against Iraq in 1991. Allega-

IRAN
AREA: 1,648,000sq km (636,293 sq mi)
POPULATION: 59,964,000
CAPITAL (POPULATION): Tehran (6,475,527)
GOVERNMENT: Islamic republic
ETHNIC GROUPS: Persian 46%, Azerbaijani 17%, Kurdish 9%, Gilaki 5%, Luri, Mazandarani, Baluchi, Arab
LANGUAGES: Farsi (or Persian, official)
RELIGIONS: Islam 99%
CURRENCY: Rial = 100 dinars

tions of support for international terrorism and development of a nuclear capability led the USA to impose trade sanctions in 1995. In 1997 elections Rafsanjani was defeated by Muhammad Khatami.

Iran-Contra affair (Irangate) US political scandal (1987–88). It involved a secret agreement to sell weapons to Iran via Israel, in order to secure the release of US hostages held in the Middle East. The profits were diverted to support the Nicaraguan CONTRAS. The affair, negotiated by Colonel Oliver NORTH, was revealed by a congressional investigative committee. North was convicted of obstructing Congress. In 1992 he was controversially pardoned by President BUSH.

Iranian languages Group of languages forming a subdivision of the Indo-Iranian family of INDO-EUROPEAN LANGUAGES. The major Iranian languages are Persian, Pashto, Kurdish, Mazanderani and Gilaki (of Iran), Baluchi (Iran, Pakistan) and Tajik and Ossetic (Tajikistan, South Ossetia and North Ossetia).

Iran-Iraq War (1980–88) Contest for supremacy in the Persian Gulf. The war began when Iraq (partly in response to Iranian support for the Shiites of s Iraq) invaded Iran. Iraq's objective was the Shatt al Arab waterway, but stiff Iranian resistance checked its advance and forced a withdrawal (1982). Prolonged stalemate was punctuated with sporadic Iranian offensives. US-led intervention in 1987 was seen as tacit support for Iraq. A United Nations cease-fire resolution (1987) was accepted by Iraq and, after several Iraqi successes, by Iran also. Estimated total casualties were more than 1 million.

Iraq Republic in sw Asia; the capital is BAGHDAD.
Land and climate Iraq has only a narrow outlet, via the Shatt al Arab delta, to the PERSIAN GULF. Its main port, BASRA, is located here. Part of the Syrian Desert forms most of w Iraq and there are mountains in the NE. Central Iraq is dominated by the valleys of the EUPHRATES and TIGRIS rivers. Baghdad lies in the Tigris valley. Iraq's climate varies from temperate in the N to subtropical in the S and E. There is little rainfall. Dry grassland and shrub grow in the N. The S is predominantly marshland.
Economy Protracted wars, sanctions and financial mismanagement have created economic chaos. Oil traditionally accounts for 98% of revenue and 45% of GNP. Since 1990 a UN embargo has halted oil exports. In 1996, concern about severe hardship suffered by the civilian population led to a UN "oil-for-food" deal, which allowed the annual sale of a certain amount of oil to provide funds for buying humanitarian goods. Farmland covers c.20% of Iraq. Major products include barley, cotton, dates, fruit and livestock, but Iraq is dependent on food imports. Manufacturing is dominated by petroleum products. **History** The ancient region of MESOPOTAMIA roughly corresponds with modern Iraq. SUMERIA was the world's first great civilization, c.3000 BC. In c.2340 BC Sargon I conquered Sumeria. In the 18th century BC, HAMMURABI

IRAQ	
AREA: 438,320sq km (169,235sq mi)	
POPULATION: 19,290,000	
CAPITAL (POPULATION): Baghdad (3,850,000)	
GOVERNMENT: Republic	
ETHNIC GROUPS: Arab 77%, Kurdish 19%, Turkmen, Persian, Assyrian	
LANGUAGES: Arabic (official), Kurdish (official in Kurdish areas)	
RELIGIONS: Islam 96%, Christianity 4%	
CURRENCY: Iraqi dinar = 20 dirhams = 1,000 fils	

established the first empire of BABYLONIA In the 8th century BC, Babylonia fell to ASSYRIA. In the 1st century BC, the Assyrian kings Sargon II, Sennacherib and ASHURBANIPAL added to the splendour of NINEVEH. NEBUCHADNEZZAR extended the New Babylonian empire and was responsible for the BABYLONIAN CAPTIVITY (from 586 BC). In 539 BC Babylon fell to CYRUS THE GREAT, who founded the ACHAEMENID dynasty. Mesopotamia became part of the PERSIAN EMPIRE. ISLAM was introduced via the Arab conquest in AD 637. In the 8th century Baghdad became capital of the ABBASID caliphate (750–1258). Mongols captured Baghdad in 1258. From 1534 Mesopotamia was part of the OTTOMAN EMPIRE. Britain invaded Mesopotamia in 1916. In 1920 it became a British mandated territory. Britain renamed the country Iraq and set up an Arab monarchy. Iraq finally became independent in 1932 and oil was first exported in 1934. Iraq participated in the 1948 ARAB-ISRAELI WAR. By the 1950s, oil dominated Iraq's economy. In 1958 a proposal to form an Arab Union with Jordan precipitated a military coup. A republic was established and the king executed. In 1962 the KURDS of N Iraq demanded autonomy, beginning a protracted war of secession. In 1968 the BA'ATH PARTY emerged as the dominant power. Iraq participated in the 1973 Arab-Israeli War. In 1979 Saddam HUSSEIN became president and purged the Ba'ath Party. Iraq invaded Iran, starting the IRAN-IRAQ WAR (1980–88). The Kurdish rebellion continued and poison gas was used against villagers. On 2 August 1990, Iraqi troops invaded Kuwait (see GULF WAR). **Politics** Following Iraq's forced withdrawal from Kuwait (1991), rebellion broke out in the Kurdish N highlands and Shiite S marshlands. The revolt was brutally suppressed. The UN formed air exclusion zones to protect civilians. In 1994 an autonomous Kurdish administration collapsed. In 1995 weapons inspectors discovered evidence of Iraq's attempts to gain a nuclear capability.

Ireland, John Nicholson (1879–1962) British composer. His works, firmly grounded in ROMANTICISM and often inspired by landscape, include The Forgotten Rite (1913), Mai-Dun (1921), These Things Shall Be (1937) and Satyricon (1946).
Ireland Second-largest island of the BRITISH ISLES.

Ireland is w of Great Britain. The Irish Sea and St Georges Channel run between the two islands. Ireland is divided into two separate countries, the Republic of IRELAND and NORTHERN IRELAND. **Land and climate** Central Ireland is a lowland with a mild, wet climate. This area is covered with peat bogs and sections of fertile limestone. The interior has many lakes and rivers. Most coastal regions are barren highlands. The SHANNON is the longest river in the British Isles. **History** From c.3rd century BC to the late 8th century, Ireland was divided into five kingdoms inhabited by Celtic and pre-Celtic tribes. The Danes invaded in the 8th century BC, establishing trading towns such as DUBLIN. In 1014 Brian Boru defeated the Danes, and for the next 150 years Ireland was free from invasion but subject to clan warfare. In 1171 HENRY II of England established English control. In the late 13th century, an Irish parliament was formed. English dominance was threatened by Scottish invasion (1315). In the late 15th century HENRY VII restored English hegemony and began the plantation of Ireland. Edward Poynings forced the Irish Parliament to pass Poynings Law (1495), stating that future Irish legislation must be sanctioned by the England. Under JAMES I the plantation of ULSTER was intensified. An Irish rebellion (1641–49) was eventually thwarted by Oliver CROMWELL. During the GLORIOUS REVOLUTION Irish Catholics supported JAMES II, while Ulster Protestants supported WILLIAM III. After James' defeat, the English-controlled Irish Parliament passed a series of punitive laws against Catholics. In 1782 Henry GRATTAN forced trade concessions and the repeal of Poynings Law. William PITT's government passed the Act of UNION (1801), which abolished the Irish assembly and created the UNITED KINGDOM of Great Britain and Ireland. In 1829, largely due to Daniel O'CONNELL, the Act of CATHOLIC EMANCIPATION was passed, which secured Irish representation in the British Parliament. A blight ruined the Irish potato crop and caused the Great Potato Famine (1845–49). Nationalist demands intensified. GLADSTONE failed to secure Home Rule, amid mounting pressure from fearful Ulster Protestants. Arthur GRIFFITH founded SINN FÉIN (1905). In 1914 Home Rule was agreed, but implementation was suspended during World War 1. In the EASTER RISING (1916) Irish Nationalists announced the creation of the Republic of Ireland. The British Army's brutal crushing of the rebellion was a propaganda victory for Sinn Féin and led to a landslide victory in Irish elections (1918). During 1918–21 the IRISH REPUBLICAN ARMY (IRA) fought a guerrilla war against British forces. In 1920 a new Home Rule bill established separate parliaments for Ulster and Catholic Ireland. Sinn Féin initially opposed the bill, but the Anglo-Irish Treaty (1921) led to the creation of an Irish Free State in January 1922 and *de facto* acceptance of partition (for history post-1922, *see* IRELAND, NORTHERN; IRELAND, REPUBLIC OF).

Ireland, Northern Part of the UNITED KINGDOM, 26 districts occupying the NE of IRELAND, traditionally divided into the six counties of Antrim, Armagh, Derry, Down, Fermanagh and Tyrone; the capital is BELFAST. Other major towns include DERRY, Coleraine, Ballymena, Lisburn, Newry, Armagh and Enniskillen (for land and climate and pre-1922 history, *see* IRELAND). **Economy** Over 80% of the land is farmed (chief crops are potatoes and barley). Heavy industry is concentrated around the port of Belfast. Industries: shipbuilding, vehicle manufacture, textiles. The majority population is Protestant, Catholics form a significant minority of 38%. The Catholic community has a much higher rate of unemployment. The economy has been devastated by civil war. **History** In 1920 the six counties of Ulster became the self-governing province of Northern Ireland with a separate, Protestant-dominated parliament. The British government affirmed the inclusion of Northern Ireland within the UK under the principle of self-determination. The Irish Free State (now Republic of IRELAND) constitution upheld the unity of the island of Ireland. In 1955 the IRISH REPUBLICAN ARMY (IRA) began a campaign of violence for the creation of an independent, unified Ireland. In 1962 the Republic of Ireland condemned the use of terrorism. Northern Catholics felt aggrieved at discrimination in employment, housing and political representation, and in 1967 the Civil Rights Association was established. In 1968 civil rights marches resulted in violent clashes. Catholic fear of the increasing Protestant-domination of local security forces was compounded when the Royal Ulster Constabulary (RUC) was supplemented by the sectarian Ulster Defence Regiment (UDR). The British Army was brought in to protect the Catholic populations of Belfast and Derry. The IRA and Protestant LOYALIST paramilitary organizations, such as the Ulster Defence Association (UDA), increased their campaigns of sectarian violence. In 1972 the Northern Ireland parliament was suspended, replaced by direct rule from Westminster. Also in 1972 the British Army killed 13 demonstrators in what became known as "Bloody Sunday". The IRA campaign widened to include terrorist attacks on the British mainland and British military bases in Europe. Hunger strikes by IRA prisoners in 1981 gained worldwide attention. In 1985 the ANGLO-IRISH AGREEMENT gave the Republic of Ireland a consultative role in the government of Northern Ireland. In 1986 a Northern Ireland Assembly was re-established, but failed under the Unionists' boycott. In 1993 the DOWNING STREET DECLARATION offered all-party negotiations following a cessation of violence. A cease-fire in 1994 raised hopes of an end to a sectarian conflict that had claimed over 2,700 lives. Disputes over arms decommissions stalled the process and the IRA resumed its terrorist campaign in Great Britain. In July 1997 another cease-fire was agreed, and in October Sinn Féin and Unionists took part in joint peace talks for the first time since partition. Area: 14,121sq km (5,452sq mi). Pop. (1991) 1,573,836.

Ireland, Republic of Country occupying most of the island of Ireland, NW Europe; the capital is DUBLIN. **Land and climate** (for land, climate and pre-1922 history and politics, *see* IRELAND) **Economy** Ireland's economy has benefited greatly from membership of the European Community. Agriculture employs 14% of the workforce. Food and live animals account for over 20% of exports. There is a marked contrast in land use between the poorer W areas and the rich E lowlands of Wicklow and Westford. Major products include cereals, cattle and dairy products, sheep, sugar beet and potatoes. Fishing is also an important economic activity. Industry has greatly expanded and accounts for 35% of GNP. Traditional sectors like brewing, distilling and textiles have been supplemented by high-tech industries, such as electronics. The service sector employs 57% of the workforce and accounts for over 50% of GNP. Tourism is the most important component: receipts from tourism totalled US$1,620 million (1992). Unemployment remains high and economic migration, though decreasing, is common. **History** In January 1922, the Irish Free State was created as a Dominion within the British empire. Civil war ensued between supporters of the settlement and those who refused to countenance the partition of Ireland and the creation of Northern IRELAND. The anti-settlement party SINN FÉIN (led by Eamon DE VALERA) and the IRISH REPUBLICAN ARMY (IRA) (led by Michael COLLINS) were defeated. Collins died in the conflict. In 1926 De Valera formed a separate party, FIANNA FÁIL, and became prime minister (1932). In 1937 a new constitution declared the sovereign nation of Ireland (Eire) to be the whole island of Ireland and abolished the oath of loyalty to the English crown. During World War 2 Eire remained neutral. In 1949 Ireland became a republic outside of the Commonwealth. Its claim to Northern Ireland was reiterated. In 1955 the republic was admitted to the UN. During the 1950s, the IRA was banned by both Irish governments and, as a secret organization, it conducted bombing campaigns in Northern Ireland and England. In 1973 Ireland joined the European Community (EC). During the 1980s a series of short-lived coalition government caused political uncertainty. The ANGLO-

IRISH AGREEMENT (1985) gave Ireland a consultative role in the affairs of Northern Ireland. In 1990 Mary ROBINSON was elected as Ireland's first female president. The DOWNING STREET DECLARATION (1993), signed by John Major and Albert REYNOLDS, continued the search for a peaceful settlement in Northern Ireland. The Republic agreed to relinquish its claim to Northern Ireland, if a majority of the peoples of the North voted to remain in the UK. **Politics** In 1995 John BRUTON's FINE GAEL formed a coalition government. A 1995 referendum saw the legalization of divorce. In 1997 elections Fianna Fáil returned to office, led by Bertie Ahern.

Irian Jaya (West Irian or Irian Barat) Province of E Indonesia, comprising the W half of New Guinea and adjacent islands; the capital is Djajapura. A central mountain range rises to over 5,000m (16,500ft). Much of the region N of the range is covered by tropical rainforest. Irian Jaya is noted for the richness of its flora and fauna. First explored by Europeans in the 16th century, it was formally claimed by the Netherlands in 1828 and became known as Dutch New Guinea. It achieved independence in 1962 and was incorporated into Indonesia in 1963. The economy is mainly agricultural. Chief products are copra, groundnuts, rice and timber. Copper and crude oil are exported. Area: 422,170sq km (162,900sq mi). Pop. (1990) 1,648,708.

iridium Silver-white metallic element (symbol Ir) discovered in 1804. A platinum-type metal, iridium is hard and brittle and the most corrosion-resistant metal. It is used in making surgical tools, scientific instruments, pen tips and electrical contacts. Properties: at.no. 77; r.a.m. 192.22; r.d. 22.42; m.p. 2,410°C (4,370°F); b.p. 4,130°C (7,466°F); most common isotope Ir^{193} (62.6%).

iris Coloured part of the EYE. It controls the amount of light that enters the PUPIL in the centre of the eye by varying the size of the pupil. These changes are effected by muscles in the iris.

iris Genus of about 300 species of monocotyledonous flowering plants widely distributed, mostly in temperate areas. They may have BULBS or RHIZOMES. Height: up to 90cm (3ft). Family Iridaceae. *See also* CROCUS; GLADIOLUS

Irish *See* GAELIC

Irish literature Earliest written works, mainly heroic sagas, date from the 7th to the 12th centuries and were composed in GAELIC. A number of lyric poets were also active during this period. Between the 13th and the 17th centuries, professional poets produced long poems in honour of their wealthy patrons. After a quiet period in the 17th and 18th centuries, the late 19th and early 20th centuries saw a renaissance in Irish literature. Inspired by the movement for self-government, literature and drama prospered, although now largely written in English. Among those involved were W.B. YEATS, J.M. SYNGE and Sean O'CASEY.

Irish Republican Army (IRA) Guerrilla organization dedicated to the reunification of Ireland.

IRELAND, REPUBLIC OF
AREA: 70,280sq km (27,135sq mi)
POPULATION: 3,547,000
CAPITAL (POPULATION): Dublin (915,516)
GOVERNMENT: Multiparty republic
ETHNIC GROUPS: Irish 94%
LANGUAGES: Irish and English (both official)
RELIGIONS: Christianity (Roman Catholic 93%, Protestant 3%)
CURRENCY: Irish pound = 100 new pence

Formed in 1919, the IRA waged guerrilla warfare against British rule. Some members ("irregulars") rejected the Anglo-Irish settlement of 1921, fighting a civil war until 1923. In 1970 the organization split into an "official" wing (which emphasized political activities), and a "provisional" wing (committed to armed struggle). Thereafter, the provisional IRA became committed to terrorist acts in Northern Ireland and Great Britain. It declared a cease-fire in 1994, but in 1996 resumed its campaign. It declared another cease-fire in 1997. *See also* SINN FÉIN

Irish Sea Part of the Atlantic Ocean, lying between Ireland and Britain. It is connected to the Atlantic by the North Channel (N) and the St George's Channel (S). Scotland, Wales and England are on its E shore and Ireland on the W shore. Area: 103,600sq km (40,000sq mi).

iron Common metallic element (symbol Fe), a transition element, known from earliest times. Its chief ores are hematite (Fe_2O_3), magnetite (Fe_3O_4), and iron pyrites (FeS_2). It is obtained in a blast furnace by reducing the oxide with carbon monoxide from coke, using limestone to form a slag. The pure metal – a reactive soft element – is rarely used; most iron is alloyed with carbon and other elements to make STEEL. Properties: at.no. 26; at.wt. 55.847; s.g. 7.86; m.p. 1,535°C (2,795°F); b.p. 2,750°C (4,982°F); most common isotope Fe^{56} (91.66%).

Iron Age Period succeeding the BRONZE AGE, dating from *c.*1100 BC in the Near East, later in N Europe. During this period people learned to smelt iron, although the HITTITES had probably developed an iron industry in Armenia soon after 2000 BC.

irrational number In mathematics, any number that cannot be expressed as the ratio of two integers. An example is $\sqrt{2}$: like other irrational numbers, its expression as a decimal is infinite and non-repeating. Irrational numbers, together with the RATIONAL NUMBERS, make up the set of REAL NUMBERS.

Irrawaddy (Irawadi) River in central Burma (Myanmar), formed by the union of the Mali and Nmai rivers. A vast delta extends 290km (180mi) from Henzada to the Andaman Sea. One of Asia's major rivers, it is at the centre of an important rice-producing region. Length: *c.*2,100km (1,300mi).

irrigation Artificial watering of land for growing crops. Irrigation enables crops to grow in regions with inadequate precipitation. The first irrigation systems date from before 3000 BC in Egypt, Asia and the Middle East. In some regions, freshwater for irrigation is obtained by DESALINATION. Canals, ditches, pumps and pipes are used to convey water.

Isaac Biblical character of the Old Testament, one of the Patriarchs. He was the only son of ABRAHAM and Sarah. As a test of faith in God, Abraham was prepared to sacrifice Isaac as commanded, but at the last minute, Isaac was told to sacrifice a lamb instead. Isaac and his wife Rebecca were the parents of JACOB and Esau.

Isabella I (1451–1504) Queen of Castile (1474–1504), whose marriage (1469) to Ferdinand

II of Aragon (FERDINAND V of Castile and León) led to the unification of Spain and its emergence as a dominant power. She reformed royal administration in Castile and encouraged humanist scholarship. Isabella was also responsible for the Spanish INQUISITION (1487) and the expulsion of Jews (1492). Her support for the voyages of COLUMBUS led to the establishment of Spain's New World empire.

Isaiah (Isaias) (active *c.*8th century BC) Old Testament prophet, who gave his name to the Old Testament Book of Isaiah. The Book of Isaiah was written in both verse and prose. Only part of it is attributed to Isaiah. The book contrasts Judah's perilous present-day state with glimpses into the future, when God shall send a king to rule over his people.

ISDN Abbreviation of INTEGRATED SERVICES DIGITAL NETWORK

Isfahan (Esfahan) City on the Zaindeh River, central Iran. In the late 16th century the SAFAVID dynasty made it their capital and transformed it into one of the most beautiful cities of the age. After its capture by the Afghans in 1722, Isfahan declined. Industries: steel, textiles, carpets and rugs, silverware. Pop. (1986) 986,753.

Isherwood, Christopher William Bradshaw (1904–86) British writer. His novels include *All the Conspirators* (1928) and *Mr Norris Changes Trains* (1935). The musical *Cabaret* (1966) was based on a short story from his *Goodbye to Berlin* (1939). He collaborated on three plays with W.H. AUDEN. He emigrated to the USA in 1939, and became interested in Hinduism.

Ishiguro, Kazuo (1954–) British-Japanese novelist. His first novels, *A Pale View of the Hills* (1982) and *An Artist of the Floating World* (1986), are set in Japan. *The Remains of the Day* (1989) won the Booker Prize. *The Unconsoled* (1995) was a radical departure from his early style.

Ishtar Principal goddess of Assyro-Babylonian mythology. She is the daughter of Anu, the sky god, and Sin, the moon god.

Isis In Egyptian mythology, wife and sister of OSIRIS, and mother of Horus. After Osiris was murdered, Isis put together the dismembered parts of Osiris's body and magically revived him.

Islam (Arabic, submission to God) Monotheistic religion founded by MUHAMMAD in Arabia in the early 7th century. At the heart of Islam stands the KORAN, considered the divine revelation in Arabic of God to Muhammad. MUSLIMS date the beginnings of Islam from AD 622, the year of the HEJIRA. They submit to the will of Allah by five basic precepts (pillars). First, the *shahadah*, "there is no God but Allah, and Muhammad is his prophet". Second, *salah*, five daily ritual prayers. At the MOSQUE a Muslim performs ritual ablutions before praying to God in an attitude of submission, kneeling on a prayer mat facing MECCA with head bowed. Third, *zakat* or alms-giving. Fourth, *sawm*, fasting during RAMADAN. Fifth, HAJJ, the pilgrimage to Mecca. The rapid growth in Islam during the 8th century

321

can be attributed to the unification of the temporal and spiritual. The CALIPH is both religious and social leader. The Koran was soon supplemented by the informal, scriptual elaborations of the Sunna (Muhammad's sayings and deeds), collated as the Hadith. A Muslim must also abide by the SHARIA, religious law. While Islam stresses the importance of the unity of the *summa* (nation) of Islam, several distinctive branches have developed, such as SUNNI, SHIITE and SUFISM. In 1990 it was estimated that there were 935 million Muslims worldwide.

Islamabad Capital of Pakistan, in the N of the country. Construction of a new capital to replace KARACHI began in 1960, and in 1967 Islamabad became the official capital. It lies at the heart of an agricultural region. Pop. (1981) 201,000.

Islamic art and architecture Islamic art developed as a unique synthesis of the diverse cultures of conquered countries from the 7th century. Because of a religious stricture on the representation of nature, Islamic art developed stylized figures, geometrical designs and floral-like decorations (arabesques). The KORAN was the focus for much of the development of calligraphy and ILLUMINATION. Many of the cursive scripts were developed in the 10th century, and the most commonly used script, Nastaliq, was perfected in the 15th century. Muslim secular art included highly ornamented metalwork, which developed in the 13th-century around Mosul, N Mesopotamia. The art of pottery and ceramics was extremely advanced, with excellent glazes and decoration. The Islamic *minai* (enamel) technique reached its zenith in the 16th century in ISFAHAN. Perhaps the best-known art of the Islamic world is that of rug-making. Two of the most impressive surviving examples of early Islamic architecture are the DOME OF THE ROCK (685–92) in Jerusalem and the UMAYYAD Mosque in Damascus (*c*.705). Common architectural forms, such as the DOME, MINARET, *sahn* (courtyard) and the often highly-decorated *mihrab* (prayer niche) and *mimbar* (prayer pulpit) developed in the 9th century. In Spain, Moorish architecture is characterized by its use of the horseshoe arch, faience and stone lattice screens, as seen in the ALHAMBRA. Islamic CAIRO is a world heritage site of Muslim architecture, often derived from Persian innovation. The masterwork of Persian MOSQUES, with their distinctive onion-shaped domes and slender pencil minarets, is the Isfahan Imperial Mosque (1585–1612).

Isle of Man *See* MAN, ISLE OF

Isle of Wight *See* WIGHT, ISLE OF

Ismail (1486–1524) Shah of Persia (Iran) (1501–24), founder of the SAFAVID dynasty. A national and religious hero in Iran, he re-established Persian independence and established SHIITE Islam as the state religion.

Ismailis (Seveners) Smaller of the two SHIITE branches of ISLAM. Ismailis believe that Muhammad, the son of ISMAIL, was the seventh and last IMAM. They are based mainly in India and Pakistan.

isobar Line on a weather map connecting points of equal pressure, either at the Earth's surface or at a constant height above it. The patterns of isobars depict the variation in atmospheric pressure.

isomers Chemical compounds having the same molecular formula but different properties due to the different arrangement of atoms within the molecules. Structural isomers have atoms connected in different ways. Geometric (or cis-trans) isomers, differ in their symmetry about a double bond. Optical isomers are mirror images of each other.

isotope One of two or more atoms with the same ATOMIC NUMBER but a different number of neutrons. Both mass number and mass of the nucleus are different for different isotopes. The atomic mass of an element is an average of the isotope masses. Most elements have two or more naturally occurring isotopes, some of which are radioactive. Radioisotopes are used in medicine, research and industry. Isotopes are also used in radioactive DATING.

Israel Name given in the Old Testament to JACOB and to the nation that the Hebrews founded in Canaan. Jacob was renamed Israel after he had met the mysterious "man" who was either an angel or God (Genesis 32: 28). As a geographical name, Israel at first applied to the whole territory of Canaan occupied by the Hebrews after the Exodus from Egypt. This territory was united under DAVID in the early 10th century BC, with its capital at JERUSALEM. Following the death of David's son SOLOMON, the ten northern tribes seceded, and the name Israel thereafter applied to the kingdom they founded in N Palestine; the remaining two tribes held the southern kingdom of JUDAH.

Israel Republic in SW Asia; the capital is JERUSALEM. **Land and climate** Israel can be divided into four geographical regions: a narrow, fertile coastal plain, site of Israel's main industrial cities, HAIFA and TEL AVIV; the Judaeo-Galilean highlands; the NEGEV Desert occupies the S half of Israel extending to ELAT on the Gulf of AQABA and includes the city of BEERSHEBA; in the E lies part of the Great RIFT VALLEY, including the Sea of GALILEE, the River JORDAN, and the DEAD SEA, the world's lowest point at 396m (1,302ft). Israeli-occupied territories are the GAZA STRIP, the WEST BANK (including East JERUSALEM), and the GOLAN

ISRAEL

AREA: 26,650 sq km (10,290 sq mi)

POPULATION: 4,946,000

CAPITAL (POPULATION): Jerusalem (544,200)

GOVERNMENT: Multiparty republic

ETHNIC GROUPS: Jewish 82%, Arab and others 18%

LANGUAGES: Hebrew and Arabic (both official)

RELIGION: Judaism 82%, Islam 14% Christianity 2%, Druse and others 2%

CURRENCY: New Israeli sheqel = 100 agorat

HEIGHTS. Israel has a Mediterranean climate. The Dead Sea region has only 70mm (2.5in) of annual rainfall, and temperatures rise to 49°C (120°F). Despite reforestation, forests account for only 6% of land use. Farmland covers c.20% of the land, with pasture making up another 40%. **Economy** Israel is a prosperous nation. During the 1950s Israel was reliant on food imports, but it is now self-sufficient and an exporter of fruits and vegetables. Agriculture, which employs 4% of the workforce, is highly scientific. Manufactured goods are the leading export. Major products include chemicals, electronic and military equipment, jewellery, plastics, scientific instruments and textiles. About 66% of the workforce are employed in the service sector. Tourism is a major source of foreign earnings. **History** Israel is part of a historic region that makes up most of the Biblical Holy Lands (for history pre-1947, see PALESTINE). From the late 19th century ZIONISM pressed for a Jewish homeland. In 1947 the United Nations agreed to partition Palestine into an Arab and a Jewish state; the plan was rejected by the Arabs. On 18 May 1948 the State of Israel was proclaimed. Hundreds of thousands of Palestinians fled. Egypt, Iraq, Jordan, Lebanon and Syria invaded in the first of the ARAB-ISRAELI WARS. The Haganah successfully defended the state. An Israeli government was formed with Chaim WEIZMANN as president and David BEN-GURION as prime minister. In 1949 Israel was admitted to the UN, and the capital transferred from Tel-Aviv to Jerusalem. In 1950 the Law of Return provided free citizenship for all immigrant Jews. Following Egypt's nationalization of the SUEZ CANAL, Israel captured Gaza and the SINAI PENINSULA. In 1957 Israel withdrew. In 1963 Ben-Gurion resigned and Levi Eshkol became prime minister (1963–69). In 1967 NASSER blockaded Elat. Israel's defence minister Moshe DAYAN launched a pre-emptive attack against Egypt and Syria. Within six days Israel had occupied the Gaza Strip, the Sinai peninsula, the Golan Heights, the West Bank and East Jerusalem. Eshkol died in 1969 and Golda MEIR became prime minister (1969–74). On 6 October 1973 (YOM KIPPUR), Egypt and Syria attacked Israeli positions in Sinai and the Golan Heights. Recovering from the initial surprise, Israel launched a counter-offensive and retained the 1967 gains. Yitzhak RABIN's government (1974–77) is chiefly remembered for the daring rescue of Israeli hostages at Entebbe. Rabin was succeeded by Menachem BEGIN (1977–83). Begin's hardline government encouraged Jewish settlement on the West Bank and suppressed Palestinian uprisings. Following the CAMP DAVID AGREEMENT, Egypt and Israel signed a peace treaty (1979) in which Egypt recognized the Israeli state and regained Sinai. In 1982 Begin launched a strike against nuclear installations in Iraq and a full-scale invasion of LEBANON (1982–85) to counter the PALESTINE LIBERATION ORGANIZATION (PLO). In 1987 the INTIFADA began in Israeli-occupied territory. From 1989–92 Israel's

population expanded by 10%, due to the immigration of FALASHAS and Soviet Jews. Increasing Jewish settlement inflamed the popular uprising. During the GULF WAR (1991) Israel was the target for Iraqi Scud missiles. In 1992 Rabin was re-elected and began "peace-for-land" negotiations with the PLO. In 1993 Rabin and Yasir ARAFAT signed the ISRAELI-PALESTINIAN ACCORD. In 1994 the Palestinian National Authority (PNA) assumed limited autonomy over the West Bank town of JERICHO and the Gaza Strip. On 4 November 1995 Rabin was assassinated by a Jewish extremist. His successor, Shimon PERES, continued the peace process. **Politics** Peres was narrowly defeated in the 1996 general election by Benjamin NETANYAHU who, while vowing to maintain the process, favoured a more hard-line policy. In January 1997 Israeli troops withdrew from 85% of HEBRON and the process crept forward. However, Jewish settlement on the West Bank intensified, despite US and UN disapproval. In March 1997 the decision to build a Jewish settlement at Har Homa, East Jerusalem, threatened to stall the process.

Israeli-Palestinian Accord Agreement that aimed to end hostilities between Palestinians and Israelis, especially in the WEST BANK and GAZA STRIP. Secret talks began in the mid-1980s. On 13 September 1993 a "Declaration of Principles" was signed by Yitzhak RABIN and Yasir ARAFAT. The PLO recognized Israel's right to exist and renounced terrorism. In return, Israel recognized the PLO as the legitimate representative of Palestinians and agreed to a staged withdrawal of troops from parts of the occupied territories. On 18 May 1994 the Israeli army completed its redeployment in the Gaza Strip and withdrew from JERICHO. The Palestinian National Authority (headed by Arafat) assumed limited autonomy. In September 1995 Rabin agreed to withdraw Israeli troops from six more towns and 85% of HEBRON. The assassination of Rabin and the election of Benjamin NETANYAHU slowed the momentum for peace. See also INTIFADA

Istanbul City and seaport on both sides of the BOSPORUS, partly in Europe and partly in Asia, NW Turkey. The city was founded by Greek colonists in the 7th century BC. It was known as Byzantium until AD 330 when CONSTANTINE I chose it as the capital of the Eastern Roman Empire and renamed it Constantinople. Captured by the OTTOMANS in 1453, the city was largely destroyed by an earthquake in 1509 and rebuilt by Sultan Beyazid II. When the new Turkish Republic was established after World War 1, the capital was moved to ANKARA and Constantinople was renamed Istanbul. Today it is the commercial and financial centre of Turkey. Industries: tourism, shipbuilding, cement, textiles, glass, pottery, leather goods. Pop. (1990) 6,293,397.

Italian Language of Italy, where it is spoken by 58 million inhabitants, and in the canton of Ticino, Switzerland. It is one of the ROMANCE LANGUAGES descended from spoken Latin and so

323

belongs ultimately to the Italic group of INDO-EUROPEAN LANGUAGES. There are many Italian dialects, and the official language is based on those of central Italy, particularly Tuscan.

Italian art and architecture By the 6th century, trade with the Byzantine empire had brought a Byzantine influence to Italian art, which lasted until the 11th century. The chief centres of the Italo-Byzantine style were Venice, Tuscany and Rome. Mosaics and stylized, geometric forms became standard as decorations for GOTHIC cathedrals and churches. Icon panels were the main type of paintings from the 11th to the 13th centuries, with major schools in SIENA and PISA. The RENAISSANCE masters, such as LEONARDO DA VINCI, GHIBERTI, DONATELLO, BOTTICELLI and MICHELANGELO, emphasized balance and harmony. MANNERISM developed in Florence in the late Renaissance, giving way to the BAROQUE style of the 17th century. This was typified by CARAVAGGIO and BERNINI. In the 18th and 19th centuries, the NEO-CLASSICAL movement, such as PIRANESI's engravings, was inspired by classical Roman art. The 20th century saw the birth of FUTURISM, as well as the more tranquil works of MODIGLIANI and DE CHIRICO.

Italian literature Vernacular literature emerged in the 13th century with the SONNETS of the Sicilian poets at the court of Frederick II. Major figures of the 14th century were DANTE, PETRARCH, and BOCCACCIO. The RENAISSANCE produced outstanding poets and philosophers, such as MACHIAVELLI. During the Age of ENLIGHTENMENT, a new literary language was required to reflect modern experience. The poet Carlo Porta employed regional dialects. The lyrical works of Giacomo Leopardi and the novels of Alessandro Manzoni ushered in ROMANTICISM. The 19th-century movement for Italian unification inspired literary figures, such as Gabriele D'ANNUNZIO. Important 20th-century writers include Alberto MORAVIA and Eugenio MONTALE, and more recently Umberto ECO and Italo Calvino.

Italy Republic in S Europe; the capital is ROME.

Land and climate Italy is bordered in the N by the ALPS, which include Italy's highest peak, Gran Paradiso, at 4,061m (13,323ft). In the NE lies Italy's largest lake, LAKE GARDA, framed by the DOLOMITES. A vast, fertile plain is drained by Italy's largest river, the PO. This is Italy's richest industrial and agricultural region. The APENNINES form Central Italy's backbone. Either side of the range are narrow coastal lowlands. On the Tyrrhenian side lies Rome. SICILY is the largest Mediterranean island and includes Mount ETNA (*see* individual gazetteer articles). Italy has a Mediterranean climate, except Sicily, which is subtropical. Alpine winters are long and the frequent snow is ideal for winter sports. **Economy** Italy's main industrial region is the NW triangle of MILAN, TURIN and GENOA. It is the world's 8th largest car and steel producer. Machinery and transport equipment account for 37% of exports. Italy has few mineral resources. Agricultural production is important. Italy is the world's largest producer of wine. Tourism is a vital economic sector, with receipts over US$21,577 million. **History** By tradition ROMULUS and REMUS were the founders of ancient ROME in 753 BC. The ETRUSCANS were overthrown by the Romans, who established a republic (509 BC). In the PUNIC WARS, Rome gained a Mediterranean empire. POMPEY was defeated by Julius CAESAR, whose assassination led to the formation (27 BC) of the ROMAN EMPIRE under AUGUSTUS. DIOCLETIAN divided the empire into Eastern (BYZANTINE EMPIRE) and Western sections. The PAPACY ensured the continuation of Rome's influence. PEPIN III (THE SHORT) expelled the LOMBARDS and enabled the creation of the PAPAL STATES. His son CHARLEMAGNE was crowned emperor of the West (800). In 962 OTTO I conquered Italy and established the HOLY ROMAN EMPIRE. Central and N Italy were controlled by powerful city-states, while the S established a FEUDAL SYSTEM under the HOHENSTAUFEN and ANGEVIN dynasties. The 13th century battle between imperial and papal power divided the cities and nobles into the GUELPH and GHIBELLINE factions. The RENAISSANCE profoundly affected western civilization. ITALIAN ART AND ARCHITECTURE was an informing force across Europe. In the 16th century Spain gained Sicily, Naples and Milan. The FRENCH REVOLUTIONARY WARS failed to bring reunification. Nationalist groups, such as the RISORGIMENTO, emerged. MAZZINI's republicans were defeated by monarchists led by GARIBALDI and the kingdom of Italy was unified under VICTOR EMMANUEL II (1861). The papacy refused to concede the loss of Rome and VATICAN CITY was set up as a sovereign state (1929). The late-19th century was marked by industrialization and empire-building. VICTOR EMMANUEL III's reign (1900–46) saw Italy enter World War 1 on the Allied side (1915). Italian discontent at the post-war settlement culminated in D'ANNUNZIO's seizure of TRIESTE and the emergence of FASCISM. In 1922 Benito MUSSOLINI assumed dictatorial powers. Aggressive foreign policy included the seizure of Ethiopia and Albania. In 1936 Mussolini entered an alliance with Hitler. During World War 2, Italy fought on the Axis side, but after losing its North African empire, Mussolini was dismissed and Italy

ITALY	
AREA:	301,270sq km (116,320sq mi)
POPULATION:	57,782,000
CAPITAL (POPULATION):	Rome (2,775,250)
GOVERNMENT:	Multiparty republic
ETHNIC GROUPS:	Italian 94%, German, French, Greek, Albanian, Slovenian, Ladino
LANGUAGES:	Italian 94% (official), Sardinian 3%
RELIGIONS:	Christianity (Roman Catholic) 83%
CURRENCY:	Lira = 100 centesimi

surrendered (1943). Germany invaded and Italy declared war. Rome fell to the Allies in 1944. The Christian Democrat Party emerged as the dominant post-war political force, with De GASPERI as prime minister. In 1948 Italy became a republic and was a founder member of NATO (1949) and the European Community (1958). Italy has been riven by political instability (50 governments since 1947), corruption (often linked to the MAFIA) and social unrest. **Politics** Popular discontent with traditional politics led to the adoption of a "first-past-the-post" system (1993), and the emergence of the Northern League and anti-corruption parties. The 1996 election was won by the centre-left Olive Tree alliance. Romano Prodi became prime minister. In 1997 there were discussions on constitutional reforms, notably the adoption of a system in which a president is directly elected and has increased powers.

Ivan III (the Great) (1440–1505) Grand Duke of Moscow (1462–1505). He laid the foundations of the future empire of Russia. By 1480 Moscow's northern rivals were absorbed by conquest or persuasion, domestic rebellion crushed, and the Tatar threat ended permanently.

Ivan IV (the Terrible) (1530–84) Grand Duke of Moscow (1533–84) and tsar of Russia. Ivan was crowned tsar in 1547 and married Anastasia, a ROMANOV. At first, he was an able and progressive ruler, reforming law and government. By annexing the TATAR states of Kazan and Astrakhan, he gained control of the River Volga. He established trade with W Europe and began Russian expansion into Siberia. After his wife's death in 1560, he became increasingly unbalanced, killing his own son. He established a personal dominion inside Russia and created a military force to oppose the boyars.

Ives, Charles (1874–1954) US composer. He often used American folk music for his themes, as in the *Variations on America* for organ (1891) and the Symphony No. 2 (1902). He also wrote symphonies and chamber music.

IVF Abbreviation of IN VITRO FERTILIZATION

ivory Hard, yellowish-white dentine of some mammals. The most highly prized variety is obtained from elephant tusks.

Ivory Coast (officially, Côte d'Ivoire) Republic in W Africa; the capital is YAMOUSSOUKRO. **Land and**

IVORY COAST

AREA: 322,460 sq km (124,502 sq mi)
POPULATION: 12,910,000
CAPITAL (POPULATION): Yamoussoukro (106,786)
GOVERNMENT: Multiparty republic
ETHNIC GROUPS: Akan 41%, Kru 17%, Voltaic 16%, Malinke 15%, Southern Mande 10%
LANGUAGES: French (official)
RELIGIONS: Islam 38%, Christianity 28%, traditional beliefs 17%
CURRENCY: CFA franc = 100 centimes

---

climate The SE coast features lagoons enclosed by sandbars, on one of which the former capital and chief port of ABIDJAN is situated. Coastal lowlands give way to a plateau. The NW highlands are an extension of the Guinea Highlands. Ivory Coast has a hot and humid tropical climate. The S has two rainy seasons, while the N only has one. Rainforests once covered the S lowlands, but much of the land has been cleared for farming. Tropical savanna covers the plateau, and forests cover much of the highlands. **Economy** Agriculture employs c.66% of the workforce and makes up c.50% of exports. Ivory Coast is the world's largest producer of cocoa beans and fourth-largest producer of coffee. Other exports include cotton, bananas, palm oil, pineapples and hardwoods. Food crops include cassava, rice, vegetables and yams. Manufactures include fertilizers, refined oil, textiles and timber. **History and politics** European contact dates back to the late 15th century, and trade in ivory and slaves soon became important. French trading posts were founded in the late 17th century, and Ivory Coast became a French colony in 1893. From 1895 Ivory Coast was governed as part of French West Africa, a union that also included modern-day Benin, Burkina Faso, Guinea, Mali, Mauritania, Niger and Senegal. In 1958 Ivory Coast voted to remain within the French Community, but achieved full independence in 1960. Its first president, HOUPHOUËT-BOIGNY, was the longest-serving African head of state. He died after 33 years in office. In 1983 the National Assembly agreed to move the capital from Abidjan to Yamoussoukro, the president's birthplace. Civil unrest continued throughout the 1980s and led to the legalization of opposition parties (1990). Houphouët-Boigny was succeeded by Henri Konan Bédié. Bédié was re-elected in 1995 elections, following an opposition boycott.

ivy Woody, EVERGREEN vine with leathery leaves, native to Europe and Asia. Its long, climbing stems cling to vertical surfaces by aerial roots. The common English ivy (*Hedera helix*) grows in moist shady or sunny areas. Family Araliaceae.

Izetbegović, Alija (1925–) Bosnian statesman, president of BOSNIA-HERZEGOVINA (1992–). Izetbegović was imprisoned (1945–48, 1983–88) by the Yugoslav government for pan-Islamic activities. Elected leader of the Party of Democratic Action (PDA) in 1990, he advocated a multi-faith republic. He led Bosnia's coalition government from 1990 until its declaration of independence (1992). In 1995 he signed the Treaty of Paris, which ended the Bosnian War. He was re-elected in 1996.

Izmir (formerly Smyrna) City and seaport on the Gulf of Izmir, w Turkey. Settled by Greeks at the beginning of the 1st millennium BC, Izmir was part of the Ottoman empire from 1424 to 1919, when it was assigned to Greece. It passed to Turkey under the Treaty of Lausanne (1923). Industries: tourism, tobacco, silk, carpets, cotton and woollen textiles. Pop. (1990) 2,319,188.

J/j evolved from the letter i and was the last to be incorporated into the modern alphabet. The j developed from the tailed form of the i as often written at the beginnings of words.

jabiru STORK found in tropical swamps from Mexico to Argentina. Length: 1.5m (5ft); wingspan: 2m (7ft). Family Ciconiidae, species *Jabiru mycteria*.

jaçana (lily trotter) Long-toed water bird of tropical lakes with a slender body, narrow bill, wrist spurs and tapered claws. It is black or reddish-brown. It feeds on aquatic plants and small animals. Length: to 50.8cm (20in). Family Jacanidae.

jacaranda Genus of trees native to tropical America. The ornamental *Jacaranda mimosifolia* and *J. cuspidifolia* have showy blue flowers and fern-like leaves. There are 50 species. Family Bignoniaceae.

jackal Wild dog that resembles a COYOTE in habits, size and general appearance. It preys on small animals and eats fruit and seeds. The species are distributed throughout Asia and Africa. Length: to 74cm (29.1in). Family Canidae; genus *Canis*.

jackdaw Gregarious black-and-grey bird that frequents open country near buildings, ruins or cliffs. Smaller than its relative, the CROW, it has a grey head and white-rimmed eyes. It lives in colonies. Family Corvidae; species *Corvus monedula*.

jack rabbit Any of several large, slender, long-eared HARES of w North America. They rely on their speed and agility to escape from predators. Most are grey with white underparts. Family Leporidae; genus *Lepus*.

Jackson, Andrew (1767–1845) Seventh US President (1829–37). He became a national hero as a result of his victory over the British at New Orleans (1815). His supporters built a formidable party machine, the basis of the new DEMOCRATIC PARTY. His two terms were marked by controversy over states' rights, the tariff, the forced resettlement of Native Americans and the spoils system.

Jackson, Glenda (1936–) British actress, politician. She has won two Best Actress Academy Awards for *Women in Love* (1969) and *A Touch of Class* (1973). Other films include *Sunday Bloody Sunday* (1971) and *Hedda* (1975). In 1992 she was elected as a Labour MP and retired from acting.

Jackson, Jesse (1941–) US political leader and CIVIL RIGHTS activist. He worked with Martin Luther KING in the Southern Christian Leadership Conference. He mounted unsuccessful campaigns for the Democratic presidential nomination in 1984 and 1988. In 1986 he became president of the National Rainbow Coalition.

Jackson State capital and largest city of Mississippi, USA, on the Pearl River, sw Mississippi. Originally a trading post established in the 1790s, it was chosen as the site of the state capital in 1821. Industries: natural gas, glass. Pop. (1990) 196,637.

Jacksonville Seaport on the St John's River, largest city in Florida, USA. It served as a CONFEDERATE base during the Civil War, developed as a port in the 19th century and was devastated by fire in 1901. It has shipyards and a naval air station. Pop. (1994 est.) 676,718.

Jacob Old Testament figure who was a grandson of ABRAHAM and, by tradition, ancestor of the nation of ISRAEL. He was the second-born son of ISAAC and Rebecca and younger twin brother of Esau. Jacob had 12 sons and one daughter by his two wives, Rachel and Leah, and their respective maids. The descendants of his 12 sons became the 12 tribes of Israel.

Jacobean (Lat. *Jacobus*, James) Term designating the artistic styles of the reign of JAMES I (1603–25). The major literary form was drama, typical examples of which are the works of WEBSTER and the late plays of SHAKESPEARE. METAPHYSICAL POETRY, such as the work of John DONNE, was also a feature of the age. In architecture the major achievement was the work of Inigo JONES.

Jacobins French political radicals belonging to a club that played an important role during the FRENCH REVOLUTION. Begun in 1789 the club split in 1791 when the moderates left it. In 1793–94, the club was an instrument of ROBESPIERRE and became part of the government's administration. It closed soon after Robespierre's downfall in 1794.

Jacobites Supporters of JAMES II of England and his STUART descendants, who attempted to regain the English throne after the GLORIOUS REVOLUTION of 1688. Jacobitism was strong in the Scottish Highlands and parts of Ireland. Several Jacobite rebellions took place, most notably the rising of 1745, in which Prince Charles Edward STUART won Scotland. His Highlanders were decisively defeated at CULLODEN in 1746, and the British government's suppression of the clans ended the Jacobite threat.

Jacob's ladder Any of 50 species of wild and cultivated plants of temperate areas. It has clusters of delicate blue, violet or white flowers and alternate compound leaves. Height: up to 90cm (3ft). Family Polemoniaceae.

jade Semiprecious silicate mineral of two major types: jadeite, which is often translucent; and nephrite, which has a waxy quality. Both types are extremely hard. Jade is found mainly in Burma and comes in many colours, most commonly green and white. Hardness 5–6; s.g. 3–3.4.

Jade, August Personage of In Chinese mythology, the supreme god of heaven and, according to some traditions, the creator of human beings. He concerned himself exclusively with the affairs of the emperor.

jaeger (skua) Gull-like, predatory, fast-flying seabird that breeds in the Arctic and winters in the subtropics. It has a dark, stocky body with pointed wings and long tail feathers. It feeds on small land animals and seabirds. Length: 33–51cm (13–20in). Genus: *Stercorarius*.

Jaffa City and port in w Israel, a suburb of TEL AVIV. It was captured by ALEXANDER THE GREAT in 332 BC. It was taken back by the Jews during the Hasmonean revolt but was destroyed by the Roman emperor Vespasian in AD 68. In the 20th century it became a focus of Palestinian resistance to Jewish settlement. In 1948 Jaffa was settled by Israelis and united with Tel Aviv in 1950.

jaguar Spotted big CAT found in wooded or grassy areas from sw USA to Argentina. It has a chunky body and a yellowish coat with black rosettes. It eats mammals, turtles and fish. Length: body to 1.8m (5.9ft); tail to 91cm (35.8in); weight to 136kg (299.8lb). Family Felidae; species *Panthera onca*.

jaguarundi Small, ground-dwelling CAT found in Central and South America. It is black, brown, grey, or red. Length: to 67cm (26.4in), excluding the tail; weight: to 9kg (19.8lb). Family Felidae; species *Felis yagouaroundi*.

Jainism Ancient religion of India originating as a reaction against BRAHMANISM. It was founded by Mahavira (599–527 BC). Jains do not accept Hindu scriptures, rituals, or priesthood, but they do accept the Hindu doctrine of the TRANSMIGRATION of SOULS. Jainism lays special stress on *ahimsa* – non-injury to all living creatures. Today, the number of Jains is estimated at *c*.4 million.

Jaipur State capital of Rajasthan. Founded in 1727, the walled city of Jaipur is famous for its carpets, jewellery, enamels and printed cloth. Pop. (1991) 1,458,000.

Jakarta Capital of Indonesia, on the NW coast of Java. It was founded (as Batavia) by the Dutch *c*.1619, and it became the headquarters of the Dutch EAST INDIA COMPANY. It became the capital after Indonesia gained its independence in 1949. Industries: ironworking, printing, timber. Exports: rubber, tea, quinine. Pop. (1994 est.) 7,885,519.

Jamaica Independent island nation in the Caribbean, 145km (90mi) s of Cuba; the capital is KINGSTON. Jamaica was discovered by Christopher Columbus in 1494 and remained a Spanish possession until captured by the British in 1655. Its sugar plantations brought prosperity, but the economy declined after the abolition of slavery in 1834. British rule was threatened by a rebellion in 1865. In 1944 Jamaica was granted internal self-government within the Commonwealth, and in 1958 joined the Federation of the WEST INDIES. After the collapse of the Federation, Jamaica achieved full independence in 1962. Many social reforms were introduced, but Jamaica continued to suffer from severe economic problems. It is a largely mountainous country with a tropical maritime climate. Chief crops are sugar cane, bananas and other fruits. The economy is based on light engineering, construction and mining. Tourism is also important. Area: 10,962sq km (4,232sq mi). Pop. (1993 est.) 2,471,600.

James I (1566–1625) King of England (1603–25) and, as James VI, king of Scotland (1567–1625). Son of MARY, QUEEN OF SCOTS, he acceded to the Scottish throne as an infant on his mother's abdication. In 1603 he inherited the English throne and thereafter confined his attention to England. He supported the Anglican Church, at the cost of antagonizing the PURITANS, and sponsored a translation of the Bible, the Authorized, or King James Version (1611). His troubled relationship with Parliament weakened his effectiveness as a ruler.

James II (1633–1701) King of England (1685–88). The second son of CHARLES I, following the Civil War James spent time fighting for the French and Spanish, before returning to become lord high admiral after the RESTORATION (1660). He converted to Roman Catholicism in 1669 and was forced to resign. He eventually succeeded his brother, but his pro-Catholic policies provoked the GLORIOUS REVOLUTION. WILLIAM OF ORANGE assumed the crown and James fled to France. With French aid, he invaded Ireland but was defeated by William at the Battle of the BOYNE (1690).

James I (1394–1437) King of Scotland (1406–37). His father, Robert III, sent him to France for safety but he was intercepted by the English (1406). He was not ransomed until 1424. James then restored royal authority by ruthless methods. He carried out reforms of the financial and judicial systems and encouraged trade. His campaign against the nobility gained him many enemies, and he was assassinated at Perth.

James II (1430–60) King of Scotland (1437–60). Succeeding his father, James I, at the age of six, his minority was dominated by aristocratic factions, particularly the Douglases. During the English Wars of the ROSES, James supported the Lancastrians against the Yorkists, who were allied with the Douglases, and was killed at Roxburgh.

James III (1451–88) King of Scotland, son of JAMES II, whom he succeeded in 1460. James was challenged by his brother Albany, whom Edward IV of England recognized as king in 1482. Peace was arranged, but a new rebellion resulted in James' defeat and his subsequent murder.

James IV (1473–1513) King of Scotland (1488–1513). He succeeded his father, JAMES III, capturing and killing those nobles responsible for his death. He defended royal authority against the nobility and the church and endeavoured to promote peace with England, marrying HENRY VIII's sister, Margaret Tudor. Henry's attack on Scotland's old ally, France, drew him into war (1513), and he was killed at Flodden.

James V (1512–42) King of Scotland (1513–42). He made a French alliance through marriage as a safeguard against HENRY VIII. Failure to gain the support of the nobility contributed to the defeat of his forces by the English at Solway Moss (1542). He was succeeded by his infant daughter, MARY, QUEEN OF SCOTS.

James Edward Stuart See STUART, JAMES FRANCIS EDWARD

James, Henry (1843–1916) US novelist, short-story writer and critic, brother of William JAMES. He settled in England in 1876, and much of his work examines the conflict between the values of American and Old World society, as in *The Portrait of a Lady* (1881). He also wrote plays, short stories and critical works.

James, Jesse Woodson (1847–82) US outlaw. With his brother Frank he fought for the Confederacy during the Civil War. In 1867 they formed an outlaw band and terrorized the frontier, robbing banks and trains.

James, William (1842–1910) US philosopher and psychologist, elder brother of Henry JAMES. He held that emotion is based on the sensation of a state of the body; the bodily state comes first and the emotion follows. As a philosopher, he influenced PRAGMATISM. His most famous works are *The Principles of Psychology* (1890) and *Varieties of Religious Experience* (1902).

James, the Epistle of Book of the New Testament consisting of a letter traditionally attributed to St James, the brother of Jesus. It exhorts Christians to live righteous lives, warning that profession of faith should not take the place of good works.

Jamestown First successful English settlement in America. It was established in 1607 on the James River, Virginia. On the verge of collapse, it was saved by the leadership of Captain John Smith (1608) and the timely arrival of new supplies and colonists (1610).

Jammu and Kashmir State in NW India, bounded N by Pakistan-controlled KASHMIR, W by Pakistan and E by China. The Himalayas tower above the heavily populated valleys of the Indus and Jhelum rivers. The basic economy of the state includes rice cultivation, animal husbandry, silk factories, rice and flour mills, and tourism. The capitals are Srinagar (summer) and Jammu (winter). Area: 100,569sq km (38,845sq mi). Pop. (1994 est.) 8,435,000.

Janáček, Leoš (1854–1928) Czech composer. His compositions include orchestral works such as *Taras Bulba* (1918) and the *Sinfonietta* (1926), two string quartets (1923 and 1928), and the cantata *The Eternal Gospel* (1914). He also wrote a number of operas, including *Jenůfa* (1904), *The Cunning Little Vixen* (1924) and *The Makropoulos Case* (1926).

Jansen, Cornelis (1585–1638) Dutch theologian. He studied problems raised for Catholics by Lutheran and Calvinist doctrine. In his writings he argued for a return to the views of St AUGUSTINE OF HIPPO on grace and salvation.

Jansenism Theological school that grew up in the Roman Catholic Church in the 17th and 18th centuries. It was named after Cornelius JANSEN, but the movement was strongest in France. The Jansenists believed that man is incapable of carrying out the commandments of God without divine "grace", which is bestowed only on a favoured few. French Jansenists incurred the hostility of the Jesuits and the French crown, and were condemned by the pope (1713).

Jansky, Karl (1905–50) US engineer who, in 1931, discovered unidentifiable radio signals from space. He concluded that they were stellar in origin and that the source lay in the direction of SAGITTARIUS. Jansky's discovery is considered to be the beginning of RADIO ASTRONOMY. The unit measuring radio emission is named after him.

Japan Archipelago state in E Asia; the capital is TOKYO. **Land and climate** Japan's four largest islands are (in decreasing order of size): HONSHŪ, HOKKAIDŌ, KYŪSHŪ and SHIKOKU. These constitute 98% of the total land area and enclose the Inland Sea (Sea of Japan). Japan has thousands of other small islands, including the RYUKYU ISLANDS. The four main islands are mostly mountainous. The highest peak is the sacred FUJIYAMA, at 3,776m (12,389ft). Japan has more than 150 volcanoes, 60 of which are active. Volcanic eruptions, earthquakes and TSUNAMI occur frequently. Around the coast are small, densely populated fertile plains covered by alluvium, deposited by the short rivers that rise in the mountains. The Kanto plain stretches from the S coast of Honshū to N Kyūshū and is Japan's industrial heartland. The plain contains Tokio. If YOKOHAMA is included, this is the world's most densely populated area. Other major cities in the area include NAGOYA, KYŌTO, OSAKA, KŌBE, and FUKUOKA. The climate varies greatly from cool temperate in the N to subtropical in the S. Forests and woodland cover *c.*66% of the land. **Economy** Japan is the world's second largest economic power (1993 GDP, US$4,190,399 million). Its success is based on advanced industrial technology, a skilled and committed labour force, vigorous export policies, and comparatively small defence expenditure. The rapid growth of industrial cities has led to high land prices, housing shortages and pollution. An aging workforce also presents problems. Services form the largest sector: Japan has seven of the world's ten largest banks. Despite having to import most of its raw materials and fuel, manufacturing is a vital sector of the Japanese economy. Machinery

JAPAN
AREA: 377,800sq km (145,869sq mi)
POPULATION: 124,336,000
CAPITAL (POPULATION): Tokyo (7,894,000)
GOVERNMENT: Constitutional monarchy
ETHNIC GROUPS: Japanese 99%, Chinese, Korean, Ainu
LANGUAGES: Japanese (official)
RELIGIONS: Shintoism 93%, Buddhism 74%, Christianity 1% (most Japanese consider themselves to be both Shinto and Buddhist)
CURRENCY: Yen = 100 sen

and transport equipment account for over 70% of exports. Japan is the world's leading car, ship and steel producer. It is the world's second largest iron and cement producer. Other important manufactures include electrical and electronic equipment, chemicals and textiles. Japan has the second largest fish catch (after China). Attempts have been made to reduce its whaling. Because Japan is so mountainous only 15% of land is farmed and Japan has to import 30% of its food. Rice is the chief crop, taking up *c*.50% of total farmland. Japan is under increasing pressure to lift its import restrictions and high tariffs. **History** Most Japanese people are descendants of migrants from mainland Asia. One of the earliest groups are the AINU, *c*.15,000 of whom still live on Hokkaidō. According to legend, Japan's first emperor, Jimmu, ascended the throne in 660 BC. The native religion was SHINTO. The Yamato established the Japanese state in the 5th century and made Kyōto the imperial capital. In the 6th century AD BUDDHISM was introduced to Japan, and the Chinese influence on JAPANESE ART AND ARCHITECTURE and JAPANESE LITERATURE was profound. In the 12th century civil war gave way to the power of the shōgun, who ruled in the emperor's name. For the next 700 years Japan was ruled by these warrior-kings. European contact began when Portuguese sailors reached Japan in 1543. Following unsuccessful invasions of Korea and China, the TOKUGAWA shogunate (1603–1867) unified Japan and established their capital at Edo (Tokyo). Through the codes of BUSHIDO, the Tokugawa ensured total loyalty. Japan pursued an isolationalist path. In 1854 Matthew C. PERRY forced the Tokugawa shōgunate to open its ports to Western trade. Western powers plotted the overthrow of the shōgunate and the re-establishment of imperial power (MEIJI RESTORATION, 1868). Emperor MEIJI's reign (1868–1912) was characterized by social and economic modernization, headed by the ZAIBATSU. Japanese nationalism created the desire for empire-building. The first of the SINO-JAPANESE WARS (1894–95) saw Japan acquire Formosa (Taiwan). Japan's decisive victory in the RUSSO-JAPANESE WAR (1904–05) marked its emergence as the dominant regional power. In 1910 Japan annexed Korea. During the 1920s Japan concentrated on building its economy. The 1923 earthquake at Kanto claimed 143,000 lives. Militarists began to dominate Japanese politics, and in 1930 Japan invaded MANCHURIA and set up the puppet state of MANCHUKUO. In 1937 Japan invaded China and precipitated the second Sino-Japanese War. At the start of WORLD WAR 2 Japan signed a pact with Germany and Italy. In 1941, Japan launched an attack on the US naval base at PEARL HARBOR. Japan conquered a huge swathe of Pacific territory, but gradually the Allies regained ground. In 1945 the USA dropped atomic bombs on HIROSHIMA and NAGASAKI and forced Japan's unconditional surrender (14 August 1945). The US occupation of Japan under Douglas MACARTHUR (1945–52) undertook the demilitarization of industry and the adoption of a democratic constitution. Emperor HIROHITO disclaimed his divinity and became a constitutional monarch. The Liberal Democratic Party (LDP) governed Japan almost continuously from 1948 to 1993. In 1951 Japan concluded a security treaty that allowed US bases to be stationed on Japan in return for securing its defences. During the 1960s and early 1970s Japan witnessed popular demonstrations against US interference. Under the prime ministership of Eisaku SATO, the US completed the return of the Ryukyu Islands to Japan (1972). In 1989 Hirohito died and was succeeded by his son, AKIHITO. **Politics** In the early 1990s, Japan was rocked by a series of political corruption scandals. In 1993 the LDP split: the 3 splinter parties formed a short-lived coalition government. In 1994 constitutional changes introduced an electoral system partly based on proportional representation. In 1996 the LDP leader Ryutaro Hashimoto became prime minister.

Japanese Official language of Japan and the native tongue of more than 120 million people in Japan, the Ryukyu and Bonin islands. Some scholars classify Japanese as a member of the Ural-Altaic family, which also includes Finnish, Hungarian and Turkish. Japanese uses a pitch accent. There are at least four different forms of spoken Japanese, and a modern literary style. Japanese writing uses a combination of some 1,850 Chinese characters and tables of syllabic symbols called *kana*.

Japanese art and architecture Earliest surviving examples of **Japanese art** are Jomon pottery figurines (*c*.1000 BC). In the 6th century AD Chinese influence was strong. LACQUER work, sculpture and ink-painting developed during the Nara period (AD 674–794). The later Yamato-e tradition was based on national, rather than Chinese, aesthetic standards. It flowered during the Kamakura military rule (1185–1333). The influence of ZEN Buddhism is particularly apparent in the Muromachi period (1333–1573). Many of the best-known examples of Japanese art were produced in the Edo (TOKUGAWA) period (*c*.1600–1868). The UKIYO-E prints of UTAMARO, HOKUSAI, HIROSHIGE and others date from this period. **Japanese architecture** derives from 6th century Chinese Buddhist structures. Temples have curved wooden columns, overhanging roofs and thin exterior wood and plaster walls. Domestic structures are traditionally built with interior wooden posts supporting the roof. The outer walls are movable panels of wood or rice paper that slide in grooves. The interior is subdivided by screens.

Japanese literature Body of creative writing of Japan. Japanese literature is one of the oldest and richest in the world. The earliest extant works are the *Kojiki* (712) and the *Nihongi* (720), histories written in Chinese characters. The earliest recorded Japanese poetry is in the *Manyoshu* (760), which contains poems dating from the 4th century. The **Heian Period** (794–1185) is noted for the *Kokin-*

shu (905), an anthology of poetry, which provided a pattern for *tanka* (short poems). Classical prose developed during this period: the most significant work was Murasaki Shikibu's *Genji Monogatari* (*c*.1010). During the **Middle Ages** (1185–1603) NO DRAMA was refined. The "war tales" genre of this period are typified by *Heike Monogatari*. In the **Tokugawa Period** (1603–1868) literature, once the preserve of the aristocracy, became the field of the commoners. HAIKU became popular; Matsuo Bashō (1644–94) was the greatest poet of this form. There were developments in puppet theatre and KABUKI THEATRE. In the **Modern Period**, Western literature has had a major influence.

Japanese theatre Various dramatic forms, including NO DRAMA, puppet theatre and KABUKI THEATRE. Japanese theatre descended from ritual dances, and involves music, song and dance in addition to dialogue. Modern drama, known as *shinpa* and *shingeki* (new theatre), was influenced by Western theatre, and developed out of the desire to portray modernity in a more realistic style.

Jarrow March (1936) British protest march of unemployed workers from Jarrow, County Durham, to London. Unemployment was especially high in Jarrow, a small shipbuilding town dependent on one company which closed down in 1933. About 200 people took part in the march.

jasmine Any evergreen or deciduous shrub or vine of the genus *Jasminum*, common in the Mediterranean. It produces fragrant yellow, pink or white flowers, and an oil that is used in perfumes. Height: to 6.5m (20ft). Family Oleaceae.

Jason In Greek mythology, hero and leader of the ARGONAUTS. Sent on a quest for the GOLDEN FLEECE, Jason sailed aboard the *Argo*. After surviving many perils, he found the fleece in Colchis and stole it, with the help of the sorceress MEDEA.

jaundice Yellowing of the skin and the whites of the eyes, caused by excess of BILE pigment in the blood. Mild jaundice is common in newborn babies. In adults jaundice may occur when the flow of bile from the liver to the intestine is blocked by an obstruction such as a GALLSTONE, or in diseases such as CIRRHOSIS, HEPATITIS or ANAEMIA.

Java Indonesian island, between the Java Sea and the Indian Ocean, SE of Sumatra; its largest city is JAKARTA. In the early centuries AD Java was ruled by Hindu kingdoms. Islam began to spread in the 16th century. By the 18th century the island was mainly under Dutch control. It was occupied by the Japanese during World War 2. Java is a mountainous country, with a volcanic belt in the S and an alluvial plain to the N. It is thickly forested and has many rivers. It produces rice, tea, coffee, sugar cane, textiles, tobacco and rubber. Silver, gold and phosphate are mined in the N. Area: 126,501sq km (48,842sq mi). Pop. (1990) 107,581,306.

jay Any of several species of birds related to the MAGPIE and JACKDAW. It has blue wing markings. Length: 34.2cm (13.5in). Family Corvidae.

jazz Style of music that evolved in the USA in the late 19th century out of African and European folk music, popular songs and VAUDEVILLE. It is traditionally characterized by a steady rhythm, prominence of melody, often with elements derived from the BLUES, and improvisation. Early jazz developed in New Orleans in the form of ragtime, blues and Dixieland music. In the 1920s it spread to Chicago and New York City. In the 1930s SWING enjoyed great popularity, as did the BEBOP style of the 1940s. During the late 20th century jazz movements have developed worldwide.

Jeans, Sir James Hopwood (1877–1946) British astrophysicist and writer who popularized astronomy. He investigated stellar dynamics and proposed the tidal theory of planetary origin.

Jedda *See* JIDDAH

Jefferson, Thomas (1743–1826) Third US President (1801–09). An accomplished scholar, Jefferson was the primary author of the DECLARATION OF INDEPENDENCE, the first secretary of state (1789–93) under WASHINGTON, and vice president under John ADAMS, before becoming president. He was also governor of Virginia (1779–81), US minister to France (1785–89) and founder of what became the DEMOCRATIC PARTY. He was a slave owner, although in principle opposed to SLAVERY. His presidency is noted for the LOUISIANA PURCHASE (1803) and the LEWIS AND CLARK EXPEDITION.

Jefferson City State capital of Missouri, on the Missouri River. It was chosen as state capital in 1821. Industries: shoes, clothes, electrical appliances, bookbinding. Pop. (1990) 35,480.

Jeffreys, George, 1st Baron (1648–89) English judge. He became lord chief justice (1683) and lord chancellor (1685). He presided over the "Bloody Assizes" following MONMOUTH's rebellion against JAMES II. After the GLORIOUS REVOLUTION (1688), he was imprisoned in the Tower of London where he died.

Jehovah Latinized representation of YAHWEH

Jehovah's Witnesses Religious sect founded in the 1870s by Charles Taze Russell (1852–1916) of Pittsburgh, Pennsylvania, USA. The sect believes in the imminent end of the world for all except its own members. They hold to the theory of a theocratic kingdom, membership of which cannot be reconciled with allegiance to any country. They deny most of the fundamental Christian doctrines. No member of the sect may give or receive blood transfusions. The sect is active worldwide.

jellyfish Marine COELENTERATE found in coastal waters and characterized by tentacles with stinging cells. The adult is the medusa. It has a bell-shaped body with a thick layer of jelly-like substance between two body cell layers, many tentacles and four mouth lobes around the gut opening. Diameter: 7.5–30.5cm (3in–12in). Class Scyphozoa.

Jenner, Edward (1749–1823) British physician who pioneered VACCINATION. Aware that cowpox seemed to protect people from smallpox, Jenner, in 1796, inoculated a healthy boy with cowpox from the sores of an infected dairymaid. The boy was later found to be immune to smallpox.

jerboa Nocturnal, herbivorous, burrowing RODENT of Eurasian and African deserts, with long hindlegs developed for jumping. It has a satiny, sand-coloured body and a long tail. Length: to 15cm (5.9in), excluding the tail. Family Dipodidae.

Jeremiah (active c.626–c.586 BC) Prophet who gave his name to the Old Testament Book of Jeremiah. He preached that the sinful behaviour of his countrymen would be punished by God. When Babylon invaded Judah (587 BC), Jeremiah saw it as divine judgement.

Jericho Ancient city of Palestine, on the WEST BANK of the River Jordan, N of the Dead Sea. It is one of the earliest known sites of continuous settlement, dating from c.9000 BC. According to the Old Testament, Joshua captured Jericho from the Canaanites (c.300 BC). The city was destroyed and Herod the Great built a new city to the south. In 1993, following the Israel-PLO peace agreement, Jericho was selected as the centre for Palestinian self-rule. It lies in an agricultural area.

Jerome, Saint (347–420) b. Eusebius Hieronymous, scholar and translator of the Bible into Latin. He spent two years of intense study as a hermit in the Syrian desert before being ordained a priest at Antioch. Pope Damasus I commissioned Jerome to prepare a standard text of the gospels for use by Latin-speaking Christians. His work was the basis for what became the authorized Latin text of the Bible. In 384 Jerome left Rome and set up a monastic community in Bethlehem.

Jerome, Jerome K. (Klapka) (1859–1927) British humorist, actor and dramatist. His most successful works include the play *The Passing of the Third Floor Back* (1907) and the novel *Three Men in a Boat* (1889).

Jersey Largest of the CHANNEL ISLANDS, lying c.16km (10mi) off the NW coast of Normandy in France; the capital is St Helier. It is administered as a bailiwick. Fruit and dairy farming form the basis of the economy. Area: 117sq km (45sq mi). Pop. (1991) 84,082.

Jerusalem Capital of Israel, a sacred site for Christians, Jews and Muslims. Originally a Jebusite stronghold (2000–1500 BC), the city was captured by King DAVID after 1000 BC. Destroyed by NEBUCHADNEZZAR c.587 BC, it was rebuilt by HEROD THE GREAT c.35 BC, but was again destroyed by Titus, in AD 70. The Roman colony of Aelia Capitolina was established, and Jews were forbidden within city limits until the 5th century. Christian control was ended by the Persians in AD 614. It was conquered in 1071 by the SELJUKS, whose mistreatment of Christians precipitated the CRUSADES. It was held by the OTTOMAN Turks from 1244–1917, before becoming the capital of the British-mandated territory of Palestine. In 1948 it was divided between Jordan (East) and Israel (West). In 1967 the Israeli army captured the Old City of East Jerusalem. In 1980 the united city was declared the capital of Israel, although this status is not recognized by the UN. Notable monuments within the old city include the DOME OF THE ROCK, the El Aqsa Mosque and the WESTERN WALL. Jerusalem is an administrative and cultural centre, with banking, insurance and public service employment. The main industries are tourism and diamond-cutting. Pop. (1992) 544,200.

Jesuits Members of a Roman Catholic religious order for men officially known as the Society of Jesus, founded by St IGNATIUS OF LOYOLA in 1534. They played a significant role in the COUNTER REFORMATION. The Jesuits were active missionaries. They antagonized many European rulers because they gave allegiance only to their general in Rome and to the pope. In 1773 Pope Clement XIV abolished the order, under pressure from the kings of France, Spain and Portugal, but it continued to exist in Russia. The order was re-established in 1814 and remains an influential international religious organization.

Jesus Christ (c.4 BC–c.AD 30) Hebrew preacher who founded CHRISTIANITY, hailed and worshipped by his followers as the son of God. Knowledge of Jesus' life is based mostly on the biblical gospels of St MATTHEW, St MARK and St LUKE. Jesus' birth occurred near the end of the reign of HEROD THE GREAT in Bethlehem, Judaea. MARY, believed by Christians to have been made pregnant by God, gave birth to Jesus. The birth was said to have taken place in a stable and been attended by the appearance of a bright star and other unusual events. Jesus grew up in Nazareth and may have followed his father, JOSEPH, in becoming a carpenter. In c.AD 26, Jesus was baptized in the River Jordan by JOHN THE BAPTIST. Thereafter he began his own ministry, preaching to large numbers as he wandered throughout the country. He also taught a special group of 12 of his closest disciples, who were later sent out as his APOSTLES to bring his teachings to the Jews. Jesus' basic teaching, summarized in the Sermon on the Mount, was to "love God and love one's neighbour". He also taught that salvation depended on doing God's will rather than adhering to the letter and the contemporary interpretation of Jewish law. Such a precept angered the hierarchy of the Jewish religion. In c.AD 30 Jesus and his disciples went to Jerusalem. His reputation as preacher and miracle-worker went before him, and he was acclaimed as the MESSIAH. A few days later Jesus gathered his disciples to partake in the LAST SUPPER. At this meal, he instituted the EUCHARIST. Before dawn the next day, Jesus was arrested by agents of the Hebrew authorities, accompanied by JUDAS ISCARIOT, and summarily tried by the SANHEDRIN, the Supreme Council of the Jews. He was then handed to the Roman procurator, PONTIUS PILATE, on a charge of sedition. Roman soldiers crucified Jesus at Golgotha. After his death, Jesus' body was buried in a sealed rock tomb. Two days later, according to the gospel accounts, he rose from the dead and appeared to his disciples and to others. Forty days after his resurrection, he is said to have ascended to heaven.

jet engine Engine that derives forward motion by reaction to the rapid discharge of a jet of fluid (gas or liquid) in the opposite direction. In a jet engine, fuel burns in oxygen from the air to produce a fast-moving stream of exhaust gases. These are ejected from the back of the jet engine and produce a forward thrust in accordance with Newton's third law of motion. *See also* NEWTON'S LAWS

jet lag Phenomenon experienced when the body clock is disrupted by a sudden change in time zones, causing adverse effects on physiological and psychological rhythms. Symptoms include fatigue, confusion, irritability and sleep disturbance.

jet stream Narrow, swift winds between slower currents at altitudes of 10–16km (6–10mi) in the upper troposphere or lower stratosphere, principally in the zone of prevailing westerlies.

Jews Followers of JUDAISM, especially those who claim descent from the ancient Hebrews, a Semitic people who settled in Palestine towards the end of the 2nd millennium BC. The word Jew arose in medieval times, derived from the Latin word *Judaea* (Judea), the Romanized name of the region of PALESTINE. From *c.*600 BC, the people of Judah suffered domination by a number of foreign powers, among them the Assyrians, Babylonians, Seleucids, and finally the Romans. After the destruction of Jerusalem by the Romans (AD 70), they were dispersed throughout the world (*see* DIASPORA). The Jews were driven out of England in 1290 and were expelled from Spain in the 15th century. During World War 2 (1939–45), six million Jews were murdered in the HOLOCAUST. In 1948, having struggled against British rule in modern Palestine, a group of Jews finally established the state of ISRAEL, despite opposition from Arab and other Islamic states. About five million Jews live in Israel. Many millions more live in other countries.

Jiang Qing (1914–92) Chinese actress and politician, the third wife of MAO ZEDONG. She became a high-ranking party official and the leader of the CULTURAL REVOLUTION. One of the radical GANG OF FOUR who sought power after Mao's death in 1976, she was arrested in 1977, convicted of treason and imprisoned for life.

Jiangsu (Kiangsu) Province in E China; the capital is NANKING. It was ruled by the Ming dynasty (1368–1644), becoming a separate province in the 18th century. Taken by Japan in 1937, Jiangsu was freed by the Chinese nationalists in 1945 and fell to Chinese communists in 1949. One of China's smallest and most densely populated provinces, it is a fertile region that includes the YANGTZE River delta. It is highly industrialized. SHANGHAI (the largest city) is China's chief manufacturing centre. Industries: silk, oil refining, tex-

tiles, cement. Area: 102,240sq km (39,474sq mi). Pop. (1990) 68,170,000.

Jiang Zemin Chinese politician and statesman. He served on the Communist Party central committee from 1982, was mayor of Shanghai (1985–88) and was appointed to the politburo in 1987. In 1989 he succeeded ZHAO ZIYANG as general secretary of the Chinese Communist Party. Jiang became paramount leader on DENG XIAOPING's death in 1997.

Jiddah (Jedda) Administrative capital and largest port of Saudi Arabia, on the Red Sea, 74km (46mi) w of Mecca. Under Turkish rule until 1916, it was taken in 1925 by Ibn Saud. It acts as a port of entry for the HAJJ. Oil wealth has expanded the city and port. Industries: steel rolling, oil refining, cement, pottery. Pop. (1986 est.) 1,400,000.

jihad (jehad) Religious obligation imposed upon Muslims through the KORAN to spread ISLAM and protect its followers by waging war on non-believers. There are four ways in which Muslims may fulfil their jihad duty: by the heart, by the tongue, by the hand, and by the sword.

Jinnah, Muhammad Ali (1876–1948) Founder of PAKISTAN. He joined the Indian National Congress in 1906, but left in 1920 when his demand for a separate Muslim electorate was rejected. He led the MUSLIM LEAGUE in campaigning for political equality for Indian Muslims. By 1940 he had adopted the aim of a separate Muslim state. This was realized when India was partitioned in 1947.

Joan of Arc (1412–31) (Jeanne d'Arc, Joan of Lorraine or Maid of Orléans) National heroine of France. A peasant girl, she claimed to hear heavenly voices urging her to save France during the HUNDRED YEARS WAR. In early 1429, she led French troops in breaking the English siege of Orléans. She drove the English from the Loire valley and persuaded the indecisive dauphin to have himself crowned as CHARLES VII of France. In 1430 she was captured and handed over to the English. Condemned as a heretic, she was burned at the stake.

Job Old Testament book describing the crises in the life of Job. The main theme is that suffering comes to good and bad people alike.

Jodhpur (Marwar) Walled city on the edge of the Thar Desert, Rajasthan, NW India. Founded in 1459, it was the capital of the former princely state of Jodhpur. Industries: textiles, lacquerware, bicycles. Pop. (1991). 668,000

Jodrell Bank Experimental station, part of the University of Manchester, England, site of one of the world's largest steerable radio telescopes.

Johannesburg City in NE South Africa; capital of GAUTENG province. Founded in 1886, it is now the country's leading industrial and commercial city, and the administrative headquarters for gold-mining companies. Industries: pharmaceuticals, metal, machinery, textiles, engineering, diamond-cutting. Pop. (1991) 1,916,063.

John, Saint (active 1st century AD) (St John the Apostle or St John the Evangelist) Apostle of

JESUS CHRIST, one of the original 12 disciples. He is widely believed to be the author of the fourth GOSPEL and the three New Testament epistles of John. He is also identified with St John the Divine, the author of the Book of REVELATION. John was the brother of another apostle, St James the Greater. His feast day is 27 December.

John XXIII (1881–1963) Pope (1958–63), b. Angelo Giuseppe Roncalli. He served in the papal diplomatic service before his election as pope. He convened the Second Vatican Council to promote reform and renewal within the Church and to encourage moves towards Christian unity.

John (1167–1216) King of England (1199–1216). The youngest son of HENRY II, he ruled during RICHARD I's absence on the Third Crusade. Disgraced for intriguing against Richard, John nevertheless succeeded him as king. The loss of vast territories in France (1204–05) and heavy taxation made him unpopular. In 1215 he was compelled to sign the MAGNA CARTA, and his subsequent disregard of the terms led to the first Barons' War.

John II (the Good) (1319–64) King of France (1350–64). Son of PHILIP VI, he was captured by the English in 1356 at Poitiers in the HUNDRED YEARS WAR and held in captivity in England. He was released on the promise of a large ransom, but when he was unable to provide it he returned to England, where he died.

John III Sobieski (1624–96) King of Poland (1674–96). He conspired with the French against Polish interests, but his successful generalship against the Ottoman Turks gained him election as king. In 1683 he raised the siege of Vienna and liberated Hungary by defeating the Turks. In Poland his rule was frustrated by opposition and revolt.

John I (1357–1433) King of Portugal (1385–1433). After the death of his half-brother, Ferdinand I, he resisted the proposed regency of Ferdinand's daughter, and was elected king. A popular king, his reign marked the start of Portuguese maritime and colonial expansion.

John VI (1767–1826) King of Portugal (1816–26). Owing to the insanity of his mother, Queen Maria, he was effectively sovereign from 1792, officially regent from 1799. In 1807 he fled to Brazil to escape the invading French and did not return to claim the throne until 1822.

John, Augustus Edwin (1878–1961) British portrait and landscape painter. He was an ardent opponent of academicism. Although influenced by the Old Masters and POST-IMPRESSIONISM, his high-toned colour and solidity of line were very much his own. His works include *Galway* (1916) and the portraits *Dorelia* and *Bernard Shaw* (c.1914).

John, Gwen (Gwendolen Mary) (1876–1939) British painter. The direct antithesis of her brother, Augustus JOHN, she created restrained, grey-toned portraits of single figures. Her subtlety in characterization is demonstrated in *Self Portrait* (c.1900) and *Portrait of a Nun* (c.1920–30).

John of Gaunt (1340–99) English nobleman, duke of Lancaster (1362–99). Fourth son of EDWARD III, he acquired the Lancastrian estates through marriage. He spent much of his life campaigning abroad in the HUNDRED YEARS WAR and attempted to enforce a claim to the crown of Castile (1386–88). Protector of John WYCLIFFE and patron of CHAUCER, he was the father of HENRY IV, first king of the Lancastrian dynasty.

John of the Cross, Saint (1542–91) Spanish poet and Carmelite monk. He tried to make the order more austere, and became co-founder of the contemplative order of the Discalced Carmelites. He is best known for his spiritual poems. His feast day is 14 December or 24 November.

John Paul I (1912–78) Pope (1978), b. Albino Luciani. A modest but gregarious man, he was pope for only 34 days.

John Paul II (1920–) Pope (1978–) b. Poland as Karol Wojtyla. Ordained a priest in 1946, he became auxiliary bishop of Kraków (1958), archbishop (1964) and then cardinal (1967). He became the first non-Italian pope in 455 years. Theologically conservative, John Paul II upheld papal infallibility and condemned the use of contraception and the ordination of women as priests.

John, Gospel according to Saint Fourth and last gospel of the New Testament, recounting the life and death of JESUS CHRIST. It is believed to be the work of the Apostle JOHN. It is more concerned with the spiritual meaning of events than with historical facts or even historical sequence.

Johns, Jasper (1930–) US painter, sculptor and printmaker. A leading figure in POP ART and MINIMAL ART, his characteristic style features canvases covered with everyday images, such as *Three Flags* (1958) and *Target With Four Faces* (1955).

Johnson, Amy (1903–41) British pilot, the first woman to fly solo from England to Australia (1930). In 1932 she broke the record for a solo flight to the Cape of Good Hope, South Africa. In World War 2 she was a pilot in the Air Transport Auxillary.

Johnson, Andrew (1808–75) 17th US President (1865–69). A Democrat, he entered politics as a supporter of Andrew JACKSON. He was nominated as vice president with the Republican LINCOLN in 1864 and they were elected on a National Union ticket. He became president when Lincoln was assassinated. Conflict with Congress over Johnson's relatively pro-Southern approach to RECONSTRUCTION led to his impeachment for "crimes and misdemeanours". He was acquitted by one vote.

Johnson, Jack (John Arthur) (1878–1946) US boxer. He was the first African-American to win the world heavyweight title, defeating Tommy Burns (1908). He lost the title to Jess Willard in 1915.

Johnson, Lyndon Baines (1908–73) 36th US President (1963–69). He represented Texas as a Democrat in the House of Representatives (1937–48) and the Senate (1948–60). Elected vice president in 1960, he became president on the assassination of John F. KENNEDY in 1963. He showed considerable skill in securing passage of the CIVIL RIGHTS Act (1964) and was overwhelmingly re-elected in 1964. He carried out an ambitous domestic reform programme, but its success was overshadowed by the escalation of the VIETNAM WAR, which, together with severe race riots in 1965–68, dissuaded him from seeking re-election.

Johnson, "Magic" (Earvin) (1959–) US professional basketball player. He led the Los Angeles Lakers to five National Basketball Association (NBA) championships and was three times (1987, 1989, 1990) voted Most Valuable Player. In 1991 Johnson announced he was HIV-positive and retired. He returned to play in the 1992 US Olympic gold medal-winning "Dream Team".

Johnson, Dr Samuel (1709–84) British lexicographer, poet and critic. Most notable among his prolific array of works is the *Dictionary of the English Language* (1755), which established his reputation. He also produced a collection of essays, *The Idler* (1758–61), and an edition (1765) of the plays of SHAKESPEARE. James BOSWELL's *Life of Johnson* contains invaluable biographical detail.

John the Baptist (active 1st century AD) Prophet who heralded the appearance of JESUS CHRIST and of the coming of the kingdom of God. The son of ZECHARIAH and Elizabeth, he was born in Judaea six months before Jesus. Jesus was one of those who accepted his baptism, an action that marked the beginning of his ministry.

joint In anatomy, place where one BONE meets another. In movable joints, such as those of the knee, elbow and spine, the bones are separated and cushioned from one another by pads of CARTILAGE. In fixed joints, cartilage may be present in infancy but disappear later as the bones fuse together, as in the SKULL. In the movable joints of bony VERTEBRATES, the bones are held together by LIGAMENTS. SYNOVIAL FLUID lubricates the joint.

Joliot-Curie, Irene See CURIE, MARIE

Jolson, Al (1886–1950) US music hall singer and comedian. He is remembered for his sentimental renditions of *Swanee* and *Mammy*. He later starred in *The Jazz Singer* (1927), the first "talkie".

Jonah Fifth of the 12 minor prophets and central character in the Old Testament Book of Jonah. This book is an account of Jonah's adventures, showing God's mercy to non-Jews.

Jones, Inigo (1573–1652) English architect, stage designer and painter. He introduced England to a pure CLASSICAL style based on the work of Andrea PALLADIO. His knowledge of Italian architecture gained him enormous prestige in JACOBEAN and Carolingian England. His most noted buildings include Queen's House, Greenwich (1616–35) and Banqueting House, Whitehall (1619–21).

Jonson, Ben (1572–1637) English dramatist, lyric poet and actor. A friend of SHAKESPEARE, he was popular and influential in Elizabethan and Stuart drama. His comedies include *Volpone* (1606),

The Alchemist (1610) and *Bartholomew Fair* (1614). He also wrote the neoclassical tragedies *Sejanus* and *Catiline*, and several court masques.

Joplin, Scott (1868–1917) US composer. He wrote ragtime piano music such as *Maple Leaf Rag* (1900) and *The Entertainer* (1902.

Jordan, Michael Jeffrey (1963–) US professional basketball player. He led the Chicago Bulls to four National Basketball Association (NBA) championships (1991–93, 1996). Nicknamed "Air Jordan", he was four times voted Most Valuable Player. He played in both the 1984 and 1992 US Olympic gold-medal winning teams.

Jordan Hashemite kingdom in SW Asia; the capital is AMMAN. **Land and climate** Jordan can be divided into three geographical areas. The Transjordan plateau in the E constitutes 90% of the land area and is the most populous region. It includes Amman. Central Jordan forms part of the Great RIFT VALLEY, and contains the River JORDAN and the DEAD SEA. West Jordan (now the WEST BANK) is part of historic PALESTINE and includes the region of SAMARIA. The area is now occupied by ISRAEL. Jordan has a coastline on the Gulf of AQABA. The ancient city of PETRA lies close to Jordan's highest peak, Jebel Ram at 1,754m (5,755ft). Amman has lower rainfall and a longer dry season than the Mediterranean zone. Parts of the W plateau have scrub vegetation. Jordan has areas of dry grassland. The rest of the area is desert or semi-desert. **Economy** Jordan is a developing country. It is the world's seventh-largest producer of phosphates and potash. Less than 56% of the land is farm or pasture land. Major crops include barley, citrus fruits, grapes, olives, vegetables and wheat. It is dependent on aid. Jordan has an oil refinery and produces natural gas. Tourism is developing rapidly and reforms are helping to expand the economy. **History** The region was conquered by the SELEUCIDS in the 4th century BC. In the 1st century BC the Nabatean empire developed their capital at Petra. The Romans, led by Pompey, captured the region in the 1st century AD. In AD 636 Arab armies conquered the territory and introduced Islam. After the First CRUSADE it was incorporated into the Latin Kingdom of Jerusalem (1099). In 1517 the area became part of the Ottoman empire. After the defeat of the Ottoman empire in World War 1, the area E of the River Jordan was included

---

JORDAN

AREA: 89,210sq km (34,444sq mi)
POPULATION: 4,291,000
CAPITAL (POPULATION): Amman 1,300,042)
GOVERNMENT: Constitutional monarchy
ETHNIC GROUPS: Arab 99%, of which Palestinians make up roughly half
LANGUAGES: Arabic (official)
RELIGIONS: Islam 93%, Christianity 5%
CURRENCY: Jordan dinar = 1,000 fils

in the British League of Nations mandate of Palestine. In 1921 the E region was administered separately as Transjordan. In 1928 it became a constitutional monarchy ruled by the Hashemite dynasty. In 1946 Transjordan achieved independence. The creation of Israel (1948) led to the first of the ARAB-ISRAELI WARS (1948–49). Hundreds of thousands of Palestinians fled to Jordan. Under the peace terms, Transjordan annexed the remaining Arab parts of Palestine (West Bank and East Jerusalem). This incensed the Palestinians and King Abdullah was assassinated in 1951. HUSSEIN I acceded in 1953. In 1958 Jordan formed the short-lived Arab Federation with Iraq. The SIX DAY WAR (1967) ended in Israel's occupation of East Jerusalem and the West Bank. Over 1 million Palestinian refugees now lived in E Jordan. Jordan became embroiled in a bloody civil war with Palestinian independence movements (1970). By 1971 Jordan had ejected all guerrillas operating from its soil. In 1974 King Hussein recognized the Palestinian Liberation Organization (PLO) as the legitimate representative of the Palestinian peoples. In 1988 Jordan gave up its claim to the West Bank and approved the creation of an independent Palestine. Jordan sided with Iraq in the IRAN-IRAQ WAR and the GULF WAR. **Politics** Opposition parties were legalized in 1991. Multiparty elections were held in 1993. In October 1994 Jordan and Israel signed a peace treaty, which ended the state of war existing since 1948. The border between ELAT and Aqaba was opened and King Hussein was granted custodial rights of Islamic holy sites in Jerusalem.

Jordan River in the Middle East, rising in the Anti-Lebanon Mountains, it flows S through Israel and the Sea of Galilee and empties into the Dead Sea. Since 1967 the S part of the river has formed a section of the Israel-Jordan border. Length: 320km (200mi).

Joseph, Saint In the New Testament, husband of MARY and legal father of JESUS CHRIST. His feast day is 19 March or 1 May.

Joseph I (1678–1711) Holy Roman emperor (1705–11). His reign was dominated by revolt in Hungary, and by the War of the SPANISH SUCCESSION. He was succeeded by CHARLES VI.

Joseph II (1741–90) Holy Roman emperor (1765–90). Co-ruler until 1780 with his mother, MARIA THERESA, he introduced liberal and humanitarian reforms, while retaining autocratic powers.

Joseph In the Old Testament book of Genesis, 11th of the 12 sons of JACOB. Given a richly woven, multi-coloured coat by his father, Joseph was sold into slavery by his jealous elder brothers. He was taken to Egypt, where he gained the pharaoh's favour by predicting the seven-year famine, thus allowing provisions to to be set aside. He was later reconciled with his brothers.

Joséphine (1763–1814) Consort of NAPOLEON I and empress of the French (1804–09). Her first marriage, to Vicomte Alexandre de Beauharnais,

ended with his death in 1794 during the REIGN OF TERROR. She married Napoleon in 1796. Her inability to bear him a son caused Napoleon to seek and obtain annulment of their marriage in 1809.

Joseph of Arimathea, Saint Prosperous Jew who was a secret follower of JESUS CHRIST. He claimed Christ's body from PONTIUS PILATE after the crucifixion and attended to its burial. His feast day is 17 March in the West, 31 July in the East.

Josephson, Brian David (1940–95) British physicist. In 1962 he predicted that an electric current would flow between two superconductors separated by a thin layer of insulator. Known as the Josephson effect, he shared the 1973 Nobel Prize for physics for its discovery. It has helped in the understanding of SUPERCONDUCTIVITY.

Joshua Heroic figure among the Israelites, who became their commander after the death of MOSES and led them into CANAAN following their exodus from Egypt. His subsequent exploits are recorded in the Old Testament Book of Joshua.

Jospin, Lionel (1937–) French statesman, prime minister (1997–). Jospin became first secretary of the French Socialist Party (PS) in 1981. In 1995 he succeeded MITTERRAND as leader of the PS, but lost the presidential election to CHIRAC. In 1997 prime ministerial elections, Jospin won a surprise victory against the incumbent prime minister, Alain Juppé.

Josquin Desprez (1445–1521) (Josquin Des Prés) Flemish composer. A member of the papal choir in Rome (1486–94), he wrote three books of masses, more than 100 motets and many secular songs. The expressiveness and inventiveness of his music mark him as the most prominent composer of Renaissance Europe.

Joule, James Prescott (1818–89) British physicist. Joule's law (1841) relates the current flowing through a wire to its heat loss. It laid the foundation for the law of conservation of energy.

joule SI unit of energy (symbol J). One joule is the work done by a force of one NEWTON acting over a distance of one metre. It was named after James P. JOULE and replaced the erg.

Joyce, James (1882–1941) Irish novelist. He left Ireland in 1904 to live and work in Europe. One of the most influential figures in 20th-century writing, Joyce's experiments with narrative form place him at the centre of MODERNISM. His principal works are the collection of short stories *Dubliners* (1914); the fictionalized autobiography *A Portrait of the Artist as a Young Man* (1916); and the novels *Ulysses* (1922) and *Finnegan's Wake* (1939).

Juárez, Benito Pablo (1806–72) President of Mexico (1858–62, 1867–72). Elected governor of Oaxaca (1847), he was exiled (1853–55) by SANTA ANNA. As president, he won a victory over conservatives in the "War of Reform", and headed resistance to the French invasion (1862) until the fall of MAXIMILIAN (1867).

Judah Fourth son of JACOB and his first wife Leah, and forefather of the most important of the

12 tribes of ancient ISRAEL. After the Exodus and Joshua's conquest of CANAAN, the tribe of Judah received the region south of JERUSALEM. This territory later became known as Judaea. Israel's greatest kings, DAVID and SOLOMON, belonged to the tribe of Judah, and prophets foretold that the MESSIAH would arise from among its members.

Judaism Monotheistic religion developed by the ancient HEBREWS in the Near East during the third millennium BC and practised by modern JEWS. Tradition holds that Judaism was founded by ABRAHAM, who, in c.20th century BC, was chosen by God to receive favourable treatment in return for obedience and worship. Having entered into this covenant with God, Abraham moved to CANAAN, from where centuries later his descendants migrated to Egypt and became enslaved. God accomplished the Hebrews' escape from Egypt and renewed the covenant with their leader MOSES. Through Moses, God gave the Hebrews a set of strict laws. These laws are revealed in the TORAH, the core of Judaistic scripture. Apart from the PENTATEUCH, the other holy books are the TALMUD and several commentaries. Local worship takes place in a SYNAGOGUE, where the Torah is read in public and preserved in a replica of the ARK OF THE COVENANT. A RABBI undertakes the spiritual leadership and pastoral care of a community. Modern Judaism is split into four large groups: Orthodox, Reform, Conservative and Liberal Judaism. **Orthodox** Judaism, followed by most of the world's 18 million Jews, asserts the supreme authority of the Torah and adheres most closely to traditions, such as the segregation of men and women in the synagogue. **Reform** Judaism denies the Jews' claim to be God's chosen people and is more liberal in its interpretation of certain laws and the Torah. **Conservative** Judaism is a compromise between Orthodox and Reform Judaism, adhering to many Orthodox traditions, but seeking to apply modern scholarship in interpreting the Torah. **Liberal** Judaism, also known as Reconstructionism, is a more extreme form of Reform Judaism, seeking to adapt Judaism to the needs of society.

Judas Iscariot (d. c.AD 30) Disciple who betrayed JESUS CHRIST to the Jewish hierarchy. In the New Testament, he was named as one of the 12 apostles originally chosen by Jesus and served as the group's treasurer. In return for 30 pieces of silver, Judas agreed to assist the chief priests in arresting Jesus.

Jude, Epistle of New Testament book of the Bible. It consists of a letter exhorting all Christians to keep the faith and live righteously. The author calls himself the brother of James, probably the one mentioned in Mark 6:3.

Judges Seventh book of the Old Testament. It covers a 200-year period in the history of ancient ISRAEL, from the death of JOSHUA to the establishment of the first Israelite kingdom (c.11th century BC). The judges are leaders inspired by God to fight battles on behalf of the fledgling nation against neighbouring enemies. The Book of Judges contains some of the oldest material in the Bible.

Judith Heroine of an Old Testament book that is considered to be apocryphal by Protestants and Jews. She heroically rescued the Israelite city of Bethulia from siege by the Assyrians.

judo Form of JUJITSU and one of the most popular of the Japanese martial arts. It places great emphasis on physical fitness and mental discipline. A system of belt colours displays a practitioner's standard. Manoeuvres include holds, trips and falls. Scoring is according to the finality of a throw or hold, at the discretion of two judges and a referee.

jujitsu Method of unarmed self-defence used in hand-to-hand combat. There are c.50 systematized variants (including JUDO, KARATE and aikido) that have been refined over a period of 2,000 years in Japan, China and Tibet. In the early 19th century, when the SAMURAI were forbidden to carry weapons, jujitsu became a form of self-defence.

jujube Either of two species of small thorny trees and their fruit of the genus *Zizyphus*. *Z.jujuba*, native to China, has elliptical leaves and reddish brown, plum-sized fruits, which have a crisp, white, sweet flesh. *Z. mauritania* of India has smaller fruit. Family Rhamnaceae.

Julius Caesar *See* CAESAR, (GAIUS) JULIUS

July Revolution Insurrection in France (1830). The immediate cause was the July Ordinances, which dissolved the chamber of deputies, reduced the electorate and imposed rigid press censorship. CHARLES X was forced to abdicate and LOUIS PHILIPPE was proclaimed king with a more liberal constitution.

Juneau State capital of Alaska, USA; a seaport on the Gastineau Channel, bordering British Columbia. It grew rapidly after the discovery of gold in 1880, was made capital of Alaska territory in 1900 and state capital in 1959. Industries: mining, timber, salmon canning, tourism. Pop. (1990) 26,751.

Jung, Carl Gustav (1875–1961) Swiss psychiatrist. After working with Sigmund FREUD (1906–14), he broke away to found his own school of analytical psychology. Investigations into spirituality and the unconscious led him to his concept of a collective unconscious. He believed INTROVERSION and EXTROVERSION to be basic personality types.

juniper Any evergreen shrub or tree of the genus *Juniperus*, native to temperate regions of the Northern Hemisphere. Junipers have needle-like or scale-like leaves. The aromatic timber is used for making pencils, and the berry-like cones of common juniper for flavouring gin. Family Cupressaceae.

Junkers Landed aristocracy of Prussia. Descendants of the knights who conquered large areas of E Germany in the Middle Ages, they came to dominate the government and army in Prussia and, after 1871, the German Empire. Intensely conservative, their hostility to the WEIMAR REPUBLIC contributed to the success of the Nazis.

Juno Asteroid discovered by Karl Harding in 1804. It is the tenth-largest, with a diameter of 244km (152mi).

Juno In Roman mythology, the principal female deity and consort of Jupiter, depicted as a statuesque, matronly figure.

Jupiter Fifth major planet from the Sun and the largest of the giant planets. It is one of the brightest objects in the sky. Through a telescope, Jupiter's yellowish elliptical disk is seen to be crossed by brownish-red bands, known as belts and zones. The most distinctive feature is the **Great Red Spot (GRS)**, first observed by Robert HOOKE in 1664. Spots, streaks and bands are caused by Jupiter's rapid rotation and turbulent atmosphere. Eddies give rise to the spots, which are cyclones or (like the GRS) anticyclones. Hydrogen accounts for nearly 90% of Jupiter's atmosphere and helium for most of the rest. The pressure at the cloud tops is c.0.5 bar. At 1000km (600mi) below the cloud tops there is an ocean of liquid molecular hydrogen. At a depth of 20,000–25,000km (12,500–15,000mi), under a pressure of 3 million bars, the hydrogen becomes so compressed that it behaves as a metal. At the centre of Jupiter there is probably a massive iron–silicate core surrounded by an ice mantle. The core temperature is estimated to be 30,000K. The deep metallic hydrogen "mantle" gives Jupiter a powerful magnetic field. It traps a large quantity of plasma; high-energy plasma is funnelled into radiation belts. Its magnetosphere is huge, several times the size of the Sun, and is the source of the planet's powerful radio emissions. Jupiter has 16 known SATELLITES, the four major ones being the GALILEAN SATELLITES. Knowledge of the planet owes much to visits by space probes: Pioneers 10 and 11, Voyagers 1 and 2, Ulysses and Galileo. Diameter (equatorial): 142,800km; diameter (polar): 133,500km.

Jupiter King of the Roman gods, identified with the Greek god ZEUS. He could take on various forms: the light-bringer (Lucetius), god of lightning and thunderbolts (Fulgur), and god of rain (Jupiter Elicius).

Jura Mountains Mountain range in E France and NW Switzerland. Forming part of the Alpine system, it extends from the River Rhine at Basel to the River Rhône SW of Geneva. It has several hydroelectric schemes.

Jurassic Central period of the MESOZOIC era, lasting from 213–144 million years ago. In this period there were saurischian and ornithischian DINOSAURS, such as *Allosaurus* and *Stegosaurus*. Plesiosaurs, pterosaurs and ARCHAEOPTERYX date from this period. Primitive mammals had begun to evolve.

jurisprudence Philosophy and science of the law, which dates back to the ancient Greeks.

PLATO and ARISTOTLE attempted to answer the question "What is law?". Jurisprudence seeks to discover the source and justification of the law and its scope and function in a particular society.

jury Group of people summoned to pass judgment under oath. The 12-member jury in criminal trials dates from the mid-12th century, but it was only in the 17th century that jury members ceased to give evidence and simply passed judgment on the basis of evidence heard in court. The basics of the British jury system have been adopted by most Commonwealth and European countries and the USA.

Justinian I (482–565) Byzantine Emperor (527–565), sometimes called the Great. His troops, commanded by Belisarius, regained much of the old Roman empire, including Italy, North Africa and part of Spain. Longer-lasting achievements were the Justinian Code, a revision of the whole body of Roman law, and his buildings in Constantinople. Heavy taxation to pay for wars, including defence against Sassanid Persia, drained the strength of the empire.

Justin Martyr, Saint (100–165) Greek philosopher. He became one of the first Christian apologists in the early church. Raised in a Jewish environment, he was converted to Christianity, probably while studying Platonic and Stoic philosophy at Ephesus. He strongly defended Christian doctrine and was put to death in Rome for his faith. His feast day is 1 June.

jute Natural plant fibre obtained from *Corchorus capsularis* and *C. olitorius*, both native to India. The plants grow up to 4.6m (15ft) tall. The fibre is obtained from the bark by soaking (retting) and beating. Jute is used to make sacking, twine and rope. Family Tileaceae.

Jutes Germanic people who invaded Britain in the 5th century along with Angles, Saxons and others. They settled mainly in Kent and the Isle of Wight.

Jutland, Battle of (1916) Naval battle in the North Sea between the British and Germans in World War 1. The only full-scale engagement of the war involving the two main fleets, it ended indecisively. Although British losses were greater, the German fleet remained in harbour for the rest of the war.

Juvarra, Filippo (1678–1736) Italian architect, one of the finest exponents of the BAROQUE style. His greatest achievements are the Superga (1717–31), just outside Turin, and the Church of the Carmine, Turin (1732).

Juvenal, Decimus Junius (55–140) Roman poet. His satirical poems denounced the immorality of his time. He contrasted decadence in imperial Rome with the virtues of the republic.

K/k is derived from the Semitic letter kaph, possibly from an earlier Egyptian hieroglyph for a hand. In Greek it became kappa, and in that form passed into the Roman alphabet.

K2 Mountain in NE Pakistan, on the border with China. It is the world's second-highest peak, and the highest in the Karakoram range. Height: 8,611m (28,251ft).

Kaaba (Ka'abah or Ka'ba) Central shrine of ISLAM, located in the Great Mosque in MECCA. In prayer, Muslims face the meridian that passes through the Kaaba. Each pilgrim who undertakes the HAJJ circles the shrine seven times, touching the Black Stone for forgiveness.

kabbala Variant spelling of CABBALA

kabuki theatre Stylized mixture of dance and music, mime and vocal performance; a major form of JAPANESE theatre since the mid-17th century. In contrast to NO DRAMA, which originated with the nobility, Kabuki was the theatre of the workers.

Kabul Capital of Afghanistan, on the Kabul River, in the E part of the country. It is strategically located in a high mountain valley in the HINDU KUSH. The capital of Afghanistan since 1776, it was occupied by the British during the 19th-century Afghan Wars. Following the Soviet invasion in 1979, Kabul was the scene of bitter fighting. Unrest continued into the mid-1990s as rival Muslim groups fought for control. Industries: textiles, leather goods, furniture, glass. Pop. (1993 est.) 700,000.

Kaddish Ancient Jewish prayer used particularly at services of mourning for the dead.

Kafka, Franz (1883–1924) German novelist, b. Czechoslovakia. Kafka requested that Max Brod destroy his works after his death. Brod overrode his wishes and published the trilogy for which Kafka is best known today: *The Trial* (1925), *The Castle* (1926) and *Amerika* (1927) are disturbing studies of the alienation of the individual in a bureaucratic society.

Kaifeng City in Henan province, E central China. First settled in the 4th century BC, it served as capital of China from 907 to 1127. Industries: electrical goods, agricultural machinery, chemicals, silk, flour. Pop. (1990) 690,000.

Kalahari Desert region in S Africa, covering parts of BOTSWANA, NAMIBIA and SOUTH AFRICA, between the ORANGE and ZAMBEZI rivers. Thorn scrub and forest grow in some parts of the desert, and it is possible to graze animals during the rainy season. The Kalahari is inhabited by the SAN. Area: *c.*260,000sq km (100,000sq mi).

kale Hardy crop plant related to the CABBAGE. It is short-stemmed and has large, bluish-green, curly-edged leaves. It may reach a height of 61cm

(24in). Family Brassicaceae; (sub)species *Brassica oleracea acephala.*

Kali Hindu goddess of destruction, consort of SHIVA. She represents the all-devouring aspect of Devi, the mother-goddess of India.

Kalimantan Region of Indonesia, forming the S part of the island of BORNEO. In the 17th century, the Dutch gradually established colonial rule over what became part of the Netherlands East Indies. Kalimantan came under Indonesian control in 1950. Products: rice, copra, pepper, oil, coal, industrial diamonds, timber. Area: 539,460sq km (208,232sq mi). Pop. (1990) 9,099,874.

Kalinin, Mikhail Ivanovich (1875–1946) Soviet statesman, first head of state of the SOVIET UNION (1919–46). Prominent in the RUSSIAN REVOLUTION (1917) and founder of the newspaper *Pravda*, he was elected chairman of the Communist Party Central Committee, and joined the Politburo in 1925.

Kaliningrad (Königsberg) City and seaport in Russia, on the Baltic coast; capital of Kaliningrad oblast (self-governing region). Founded in 1255 as Königsberg, the city was a member of the Hanseatic League. It became the residence of the dukes of Prussia in 1525. From 1946–91 it was incorporated into the Soviet Union. Kaliningrad oblast is separated from Russia proper, and shares a border with Poland and Lithuania. Industries: shipbuilding, fishing, motor vehicle parts. Pop. (1993) 411,000.

Kalmykia Republic of the Russian Federation on the Caspian Sea, SE European Russia; the capital is Elista. The region was made an autonomous republic in 1936. In World War 2 its inhabitants were deported to Soviet Central Asia for alleged collaboration with the Germans. They returned in 1957 and Kalmykia was later re-established as an autonomous republic. After the break-up of the Soviet Union, it became a republic within the Russian Federation. Industries: fishing. Area: *c.*75,900sq km (29,300sq mi). Pop. (1994) 320,600.

Kamchatka Peninsula Peninsula in E Siberia, Russia, separating the Sea of Okhotsk (w) from the Bering Sea and the Pacific Ocean (E). The region has several active volcanoes. Mineral resources include oil, coal, gold and peat. Area: 270,034sq km (104,260sq mi).

kamikaze (Jap. divine wind) Name given to crews or their explosive-laden aircraft used by the Japanese during World War 2. Their suicidal method of attack was to dive into ships of the enemy fleet.

Kampala Capital and largest city in UGANDA, on the N shore of Lake Victoria. Founded in the late 19th century on the remains of a royal palace of the kings of Buganda, it replaced Entebbe as capital when Uganda attained independence in 1962. Industries: textiles, food processing, tea blending, coffee, brewing. Pop. (1991) 773,463.

Kampuchea *See* CAMBODIA

Kanchenjunga Third-highest mountain in the world, in the E Himalayas. The highest of its five peaks reaches 8,586m (28,169ft).

Kandahar (Qandahar) City and provincial capital in S Afghanistan. Because of its strategic location, it was occupied by many foreign conquerors before becoming the capital of the independent Afghani kingdom (1747–73). It was the scene of fighting after the Soviet invasion of Afghanistan in 1979 and became the headquarters of the TALIBAN in the 1990s. It is a commercial centre for the surrounding region. Pop. (1988 est.) 225,500.

Kandinsky, Wassily (1866–1944) Russian painter and theorist. From 1911 he was an active member of der BLAUE REITER. His writings, such as *Concerning the Spiritual in Art* (1914), show the influence of Oriental art philosophy. *White Line* (1920) and *In the Black Circle* (1921) demonstrate the beginnings of a refinement of geometrical form that developed at the BAUHAUS (1922–33).

Kandy City in Sri Lanka. Former capital of the ancient kings of Ceylon. The city is a market centre for a region producing tea, rice, rubber and cacao. The chief industry is tourism. Pop. (1981) 97,872.

kangaroo MARSUPIAL found only in Australia, New Guinea and adjacent islands. The three main types are the grey and the red kangaroo, and the wallaroo (euro). The thick, coarse fur is red, brown, grey or black. The front legs are small, the hind legs long and used in leaping. Height: to 1.8m (6ft) at the shoulder; weight: to 70kg (154lb). Family Macropodidae, genus *Macropus*.

Kanpur (Cawnpore) City on the River Ganges, Uttar Pradesh, N India. During the INDIAN MUTINY the entire British garrison in Kanpur was massacred. The city is now a major industrial and commercial centre. Industries: chemicals, leather goods, textiles. Pop. (1991) 1,879,420.

Kansas State in central USA; the capital is TOPEKA. Other major cities are Wichita and KANSAS CITY. Part of the Great Plains, the land rises from the prairies of the E to the semi-arid high plains of the W. The area is drained by the Kansas and Arkansas rivers. First visited by Spanish explorers in the 16th century, the area passed from France to the new United States under the LOUISIANA PURCHASE of 1803. It was Native American territory until 1854, when the Territory of Kansas was created and the area opened up for settlement. It was admitted to the Union as a free state in 1861. Kansas is the leading US producer of wheat. Manufacturing is important. Industries: transport equipment, chemicals, machinery. Area: 213,094sq km (82,276sq mi). Pop. (1993 est.) 2,530,746.

Kansas City City in W Missouri, USA, on the Missouri River, adjacent to KANSAS CITY, Kansas. Established in 1821, it developed with the railroad and the growth in cattle trade. Industries: aerospace equipment, vehicles, chemicals, petroleum products, livestock, grain. Pop. (1990) 435,146.

Kansas City City in NE Kansas, USA, at the confluence of the Kansas and Missouri rivers, adjacent to KANSAS CITY, Missouri. Part of a Native American reservation, it was sold to the US gov-

ernment in 1855. The modern city was established in 1886. Industries: livestock, motor vehicles, metal products, chemicals. Pop. (1990) 149,767.

Kant, Immanuel (1724–1804) German metaphysical philosopher. Kant's philosophy, outlined in *Critique of Pure Reason* (1781), sought to discover the nature and boundaries of human knowledge. Kant's system of ethics, described in the *Critique of Practical Reason* (1790), places moral duty above happiness. His views on aesthetics are embodied in his *Critique of Judgment* (1790).

kaolin (china clay) Fine clay composed chiefly of KAOLINITE, a hydrous silicate of aluminium. It is used in the manufacture of coated paper, ceramics and fine porcelains.

kaolinite Sheet silicate mineral of the kaolinite group, hydrous aluminium silicate $[Al_2Si_2O_5(OH)_4]$. It is a product of the weathering of feldspar and has triclinic system tabular crystals. It is white with a dull lustre. Hardness 2–2.5; s.g. 2.6.

kapok Tropical tree with compound leaves and white or pink flowers. Its seed pods burst to release silky fibres, which are commonly used for stuffing and insulation. Height: to 50m (165ft). Family Bombacaceae; species *Ceiba pentandra*.

Karachi City and seaport on the Arabian Sea, SE Pakistan; capital of Sind province. It was the first capital of Pakistan in 1947 and remains the country's largest city. Karachi is an important trading centre for agricultural produce. Industries: steel, engineering, oil refining, motor vehicle assembly, textiles, chemicals, printing and publishing. Pop. (1981) 5,103,000.

Karadžić, Radovan (1945–) Bosnian Serb leader. On Bosnia-Herzegovina's independence in 1992, he proclaimed a "Serbian Republic of Bosnia and Herzegovina", thus prompting civil war. Serb military aggression, along with its policy of "ethnic cleansing", led to Karadžić being indicted for war crimes in 1996.

Karajan, Herbert von (1908–89) German conductor. He conducted the Berlin State Opera (1938–45) and was director of the Vienna State Opera (1945–1964). As musical director of the Berlin Philharmonic Orchestra (1955–89) and artistic director of the Salzburg festival (1956–60), he dominated the European classical music scene.

Kara-Kalpak Autonomous republic in W Uzbekistan; the capital is Nukus. It became an autonomous region of Kazakstan (1925) and an autonomous republic (1933). In 1936 it became part of the Uzbek Soviet Republic. Crops include alfalfa, rice, cotton, maize and jute. Livestock raising and the breeding of muskrats and silkworms are also important. Area: 165,600sq km (63,940sq mi). Pop. (1990) 1,244,700

Karakoram Range Mountain range in central Asia, extending SE from E Afghanistan to Jammu and Kashmir in India. It includes some of the world's highest mountains, among them K2. Length: *c*.480km (300mi).

karate Martial art popularized in Japan in the 1920s. The technique, which involves a formal method of physical and mental training, includes a variety of blows. In competition, scoring depends on the finality of the blow.

Karelia Republic of the Russian Federation in NW European RUSSIA, bounded by the White Sea to the E and FINLAND to the W; the capital is Petrozavodsk. Split in the 12th century between Sweden and NOVGOROD, it was unified under Swedish rule in the 17th century . The E was returned to Russia in 1721, while the W was part of Finland until 1940. After the 1939–40 Soviet-Finnish War the E sector absorbed 36,000sq km (14,000sq mi) of Finnish land and became a constituent Soviet republic. During World War 2 the Finns occupied most of Karelia but it was returned to the Soviet Union in 1944. It became a constituent republic of the Russian Federation in 1992. Climate restricts farming to the S. Fishing and timber are the chief industries. Area: 172,400sq km (66,564sq mi). Pop. (1994) 794,200.

karma Concept in Indian philosophy that relates one's actions in a past life to one's present and future life experiences. The Vedic principle of karma is directly related to belief in REINCARNATION. Salvation involves cancelling the effects of past evil deeds by virtuous actions in one's present life. *See also* HINDUISM; VEDAS

Karnak *See* LUXOR

Kashmir Region in N India and NE Pakistan; former Indian princely state. When the Indian subcontinent was partitioned in 1947, the maharaja of Kashmir acceded to India, precipitating war between India and Pakistan. A cease-fire agreement left it divided between the Indian-controlled state of JAMMU AND KASHMIR and the Pakistan-controlled areas in the N and W. The N area of Kashmir is ruled directly by the Pakistan government; the W area, Azad Kashmir, is partly autonomous. The Aksai Chin area of Kashmir, on the border with Tibet, is occupied by China. Kashmir includes parts of the Himalayas and the KARAKORAM RANGE. The Vale of Kashmir, in the valley of the River Jhelum, is the most populated area. Wheat and rice are grown. Total area: 222,236sq km (85,806sq mi).

Kasparov, Gary (1963–) Russian chess champion. He beat Anatoly Karpov for the world title in 1985, becoming the youngest world chess champion. After disagreements with FIDE, the international chess organization, Kasparov formed the Grandmasters' Association in 1987. He was defeated by the Deep Blue super-computer in 1997.

Katmandu (Kathmandu) Capital of Nepal, situated *c.*1,370m (4,500ft) above sea-level in a valley of the Himalayas. It was founded in AD 723. Katmandu is Nepal's administrative, commercial and religious centre. Pop. (1991) 419,073.

Katz, Sir Bernard (1911–) British biophysicist. He shared the 1970 Nobel Prize in physiology or medicine with Ulf von Euler and Julius Axelrod for work on the chemistry of nerve transmission.

Katz discovered how the NEUROTRANSMITTER acetylcholine is released by neural impulses.

Kaunda, Kenneth (1924–) Zambian statesman, first president of independent Zambia (1964–91). He was leader of the United National Independence Party (UNIP) in colonial Northern Rhodesia (1960) before becoming president. His government imposed single-party rule in 1972. Kaunda was a strong supporter of African independence and a respected figure among Commonwealth leaders. Economic problems and political unrest led to his defeat in 1991 multiparty elections. He was barred from contesting the 1996 elections.

Kawasaki City in SE Honshū Island, on Tokyo Bay, Japan. The city suffered extensive damage from bombing during World War 2. Industries: iron and steel mills, machinery, motor vehicles, petrochemicals, shipbuilding. Pop. (1993) 1,168,000.

Kazak Turkic-speaking Muslim people who inhabit the Republic of KAZAKSTAN and the adjacent Sinkiang province of China. Traditionally nomadic, in the 20th century they settled within the collective farm system of the former Soviet Union.

Kazakstan Republic in central Asia, the capital is ALMATY. **Land and climate** Kazakstan stretches over 3,000km (2,000mi) from the VOLGA and CASPIAN SEA lowlands in the W to the ALTAI and TIAN SHAN mountains in the E. The Caspian Sea lowlands extend E through the ARAL SEA region and include the Karagiye depression at 132m (433ft) below sea level. Eastern Kazakstan contains several freshwater lakes, the largest of which is Lake BALKHASH. Kazakstan's rivers have been used extensively for irrigation, causing ecological problems: the ARAL SEA has shrunk from 66,900sq km (25,830sq mi) in 1960 to 33,642sq km (12,989sq mi) in 1993. Kazakstan has a continental dry climate. Winters are cold. Kazakstan has very little woodland. Grassy steppe covers much of the N, while the S is desert or semi-desert. Large dry areas between the Aral Sea and Lake Balkhash are irrigated farmland. **Economy** Kazakstan is a developing country. The break-up of the Soviet Union hit Kazak exports. In 1994 it entered into a single market agreement with other Central Asian states. Its post-independence free market reforms have

---

KAZAKSTAN

AREA: 2,717,300sq km (1,049,150sq mi)
POPULATION: 17,038,000
CAPITAL (POPULATION): Almaty (1,515,300)
GOVERNMENT: Multiparty republic
ETHNIC GROUPS: Kazak 40%, Russian 38%, German 6%, Ukrainian 5%, Uzbek, Tatar
LANGUAGES: Kazak (official); Russian, the former official language, is widely spoken
RELIGIONS: Mainly Islam, with a Christian minority
CURRENCY: Tenge

encouraged much inward investment. Industry accounts for 41% of earnings. Kazakstan is rich in minerals. It is the world's ninth largest producer of bituminous coal. Its gas, oil and gold reserves are being increasingly exploited. Agriculture is highly developed. Grain is the principal crop. Cotton and wool are also produced. **History** In 1218 the Mongol emperor GENGHIS KHAN conquered the region. Following his death the empire was divided into khanates. Feudal trading towns emerged beside the oases. In the late 15th century the towns formed a Kazak state, which fought for its independence from the neighbouring khanates. In 1731 Kazakstan acceded to the Russian empire. In the early 19th century, Russia abolished the khanates, and encouraged Russian settlement. In 1920 Kazakstan became an autonomous Soviet republic, and a full constituent republic in 1936. During the 1920s and 1930s the process of Russification increased. Stalin's enforced collectivization of agriculture and rapid industrialization led to great famine. In the 1950s, the "Virgin Lands" project sought to turn vast areas of grassland into cultivated land. The Soviets placed many of their nuclear missile sites in Kazakstan. In 1986 nationalist riots were prompted by the imposition of a Russian to lead the republic. Following the dissolution of the Soviet Union, Kazakstan declared independence (December 1991) and joined the COMMONWEALTH OF INDEPENDENT STATES (CIS). **Politics** A former Communist Party leader, Nursultan Nazarbayev, was Kazakstan's first elected president. He introduced free market reforms and a multiparty constitution. Multiparty elections were held in 1994. In a 1995 referendum Nazarbayev was confirmed as president until 2000. In 1996, the government announced plans to move the capital to AQMOLA by 2000.

Kazan, Elia (1909–) US author and director b. Turkey. He was one of the founders of the ACTORS' STUDIO. He won two Academy Awards for best director, for *Gentleman's Agreement* (1947) and *On the Waterfront* (1954). Other films include *East of Eden* (1955) and *The Last Tycoon* (1976). He also made his novel *The Arrangement* into a film.

Kazan City and port on the River Volga, E European Russia; capital of TATAR REPUBLIC. Founded in the 13th century, Kazan became the capital of the Tatar khanate (1438). Conquered by Ivan IV, it served as the E outpost of Russian colonization. Industries: electrical equipment, engineering, oil refining, chemicals, fur. Pop. (1992) 1,104,000.

Keaton, Buster (1895–1966) US comic silent-film actor and director. *Our Hospitality* (1923), *Seven Chances* (1925) and *The General* (1926) are pre-eminent among the ten full-length features he released before 1928.

Keats, John (1795–1821) Prolific British poet. In 1819 alone he wrote, among other pieces, *The Eve of St Agnes*; *La Belle Dame Sans Merci*; the magnificent odes *On a Grecian Urn*, *To a Nightingale*, *On Melancholy* and *To Autumn*; the

long poem *Lamia*; and the second version of his fragmentary epic *Hyperion*.

Keelung (Chilung) City on the East China Sea, N Taiwan. Under Japanese occupation (1895–1945) Keelung developed rapidly. Today, it is Taiwan's principal naval base. Industries: fishing, chemicals, shipbuilding. Pop. (1992) 355,894.

Keillor, Garrison Edward (1942–) US author and humorist. His poignant stories of Lake Wobegon appear in *Happy To Be Here* (1981), *Leaving Home* (1987) and *We Are Still Married* (1989).

Kellogg-Briand Pact (1928) International peace agreement negotiated by US secretary of state, Frank B. Kellogg, and French foreign minister, Aristide BRIAND. It renounced war as a means of settling international disputes and was subsequently signed by most of the world's governments.

Kelly, Gene (1912–96) US dancer, choreographer, film-star and director. His greatest films, co-directed with Stanley Donen, were *On the Town* (1949), *An American in Paris* (1951) and the hugely popular *Singin' in the Rain* (1951).

kelp Any of several brown SEAWEEDS commonly found on Atlantic and Pacific coasts, a type of brown ALGAE. A source of iodine and potassium compounds, kelps are now used in a number of industrial processes. Giant kelp (*Macrocystis*) exceeds 46m (150ft) in length. Phylum Phaeophyta.

Kelvin, William Thomson, 1st Baron (1824–1907) British physicist and mathematician after whom the absolute scale of temperature is named. The Kelvin temperature scale has its zero point at absolute zero and degree intervals the same size as the degree CELSIUS. The freezing point of water occurs at 273K (0°C or 32°F) and the boiling point at 373K (100°C or 212°F). In THERMODYNAMICS he resolved conflicting interpretations of the first and second laws.

Kemal Atatürk *See* ATATÜRK, KEMAL

Kempis, Thomas à (1380–1471) German Augustinian monk and spiritual writer. Ordained in 1413, he remained in the monastery of the Brethren of the Common Life, near Zwolle, for most of his life. He wrote or edited many treatises on the life of the soul. The most famous work often attributed to him is *Imitation of Christ*. Other works include *Soliloquium Animae* and *De Tribus Tabernaculis*.

Kendall, Edward Calvin (1886–1972) US chemist, who isolated CORTISONE. He shared the 1950 Nobel Prize in physiology or medicine for his work on the biological effects of the hormones of the ADRENAL GLANDS.

Keneally, Thomas Michael (1935–) Australian novelist. His early novels, include *The Place at Whitton* (1964) and *Bring Larks and Heroes* (1967). His best-known work *Schindler's Ark* (1982) won the Booker Prize.

Kennedy, John F. (Fitzgerald) (1917–63) 35th US President (1961–63). He was elected to Congress as a Democrat from Massachusetts in 1946, serving in the Senate from 1953–60. He gained the presidential nomination in 1960 and narrowly defeated Richard NIXON. He adopted an ambitious liberal programme (the "New Frontier"), and embraced the cause of CIVIL RIGHTS, but his planned legislation was often blocked by Congress. In foreign policy, he founded the "Alliance for Progress" to improve the image of the USA. Adopting a strong anti-communist line, he was behind the BAY OF PIGS disaster (1961) and outfaced Khrushchev in the ensuing CUBAN MISSILE CRISIS. He increased military aid to South Vietnam. He was assassinated in Dallas, Texas, on 22 November 1963.

Kennedy, Robert Francis (1925–68) US lawyer and politician. He served (1957–59) on the Senate Select Committee on Improper Activities, where he clashed with the Teamsters' Union president Jimmy Hoffa. In 1960 he managed the campaign of his brother John F. KENNEDY. He became US attorney general (1961–64), vigorously promoting the Civil Rights Act (1964). After his brother's assassination, he left the cabinet and was elected senator for New York in 1964. While a candidate for the Democratic presidential nomination, he was assassinated in Los Angeles in June 1968.

Kennedy Space Center *See* CAPE CANAVERAL

Kent County in SE England, S of the Thames estuary and NW of the Strait of Dover; the county town is Maidstone. Apart from the North Downs, the area is mainly low-lying. It is drained by the rivers Medway and Stour. Cereals, hops, fruit and vegetables are grown. Sheep and cattle are reared. DOVER, Folkestone and Ramsgate are ports. There are Norman cathedrals at CANTERBURY and Rochester. Roman settlement began in AD 43. It later became an Anglo-Saxon kingdom, and remained a separate kingdom until the 9th century. Industries: paper making, shipbuilding, chemicals, brewing. Area: 3,732sq km (1,441sq mi). Pop. (1991) 1,508,873.

Kentucky State in SE central USA; the capital is FRANKFORT. Other major cities include Lexington and Louisville. Ceded to Britain by France in 1763, the territory was admitted to the Union in 1792. Its loyalties were divided during the CIVIL WAR, and the state was invaded by both sides. Most of the area consists of rolling plains. In the SE the Cumberland Mountains dominate a rugged plateau region. The state is drained chiefly by the Ohio and Tennessee rivers. Tobacco is the chief crop. Kentucky is noted for its thoroughbred racehorses. It is also a major producer of coal. Industries: electrical equipment, machinery, chemicals. Area: 104,623sq km (40,395sq mi). Pop. (1990) 3,685,296.

Kenya Republic on the E coast of Africa, the capital is NAIROBI. **Land and climate** Kenya straddles the Equator in East Africa. MOMBASA lies on the narrow coastal plain. Most of Kenya comprises high plains. In the NW is an area of high scrubland around Lake Turkana. In the SW are the Kenyan highlands, including Mount KENYA, the country's highest peak at 5,199m (17,057ft), and Nairobi. The Great RIFT VALLEY cuts through W Kenya. Mom-

---

KENYA

AREA: 580,370sq km (224,081sq mi)
POPULATION: 26,985,000
CAPITAL (POPULATION): Nairobi (1,346,000)
GOVERNMENT: Multiparty republic
ETHNIC GROUPS: Kikuyu 21%, Luhya 14%, Luo 13%, Kamba 11%, Kalenjin 11%
LANGUAGES: Swahili and English (both official)
RELIGIONS: Christianity (Roman Catholic 27%, Protestant 19%, others 27%), traditional beliefs 19%, Islam 6%
CURRENCY: Kenya shilling = 100 cents

---

basa is hot and humid. Inland the climate is moderated by elevation: Nairobi has summer temperatures 10°C (18°F) lower than Mombasa. The coast is lined with mangrove swamps. The inland plains are bushlands. Much of the N is semi-desert. Forests and grasslands are found in the SW highlands. **Economy** Kenya is a developing country. Agriculture employs c.80% of the workforce and accounts for c.50% of exports. Kenya is the world's fourth-largest tea producer. Coffee is also an important cash crop. Many Kenyans are subsistence farmers. The chief food crop is maize. Kenya's wildlife parks attract many tourists. **History and politics** Some of the earliest hominid fossils have been found in S Kenya. Kenya's coast has been a trading centre for more than 2,000 years. In the 8th century, the Arabs founded settlements. Vasco da Gama landed in 1498, and Portuguese traders controlled the area in the 16th century. In 1729 Arab dynasties regained control. Britain gained rights to the coast in 1895. Colonization began in 1903, and land was acquired from the KIKUYU for plantations and farms. The territory was divided into the inland Kenya Colony and the coastal Protectorate of Kenya. European settlement intensified. MAU MAU waged an armed struggle (1952–56) for land rights and independence. Britain declared a state of emergency and imprisoned its leader, Jomo KENYATTA. In 1963 Kenya achieved independence, and became a republic in 1964. Jomo Kenyatta was the first president. Kenyatta's authoritarian regime tried to establish unity. Drought and territorial disputes with Uganda and Tanzania created civil unrest. In 1978 Kenyatta died and was succeeded by Daniel Arap MOI. Moi rejected calls for democracy and cracked down on dissent. Following nationwide riots in 1988, the government agreed to electoral reform. In 1992 multiparty elections saw the re-election of Moi. Independent observers claimed the elections were rigged. In 1997 pro-democracy demonstrators again called for democratic reform.

Kenya, Mount Extinct volcanic mountain in central Kenya. The second-highest mountain in Africa, it was first climbed in 1899. It consists of three peaks, the highest rising to 5,199m (17,057ft).

Kenyatta, Jomo (1893–1978) First president of

Kenya. A KIKUYU, he led the struggle for Kenyan independence from 1946. He was imprisoned by the British in 1953 for MAU MAU terrorism. As leader of the Kenya African National Union, he became Kenya's first post-colonial president in 1964. He suppressed domestic opposition and pursued a pro-Western foreign policy.

Kepler, Johannes (1571–1630) German mathematician and astronomer. He supported the heliocentric Solar System put forward by COPERNICUS. He succeeded Tycho BRAHE as Imperial Mathematician. He concluded that Mars moves in an elliptical orbit and went on to establish the first of his three laws of planetary motion. The *Rudolphine Tables*, based on Brahe's observations and Kepler's laws, appeared in 1627.

Kerala State on the Arabian Sea, SW India; the capital is Trivandrum. One of India's smallest states, it is the most densely populated. Fishing is important. Major products include rubber, tea, coffee, coconuts and cashew nuts. Area: 38,864sq km (15,005sq mi). Pop. (1991) 29,098,518.

keratin Fibrous PROTEIN present in large amounts in SKIN cells, where it serves as a protective layer. Hair, fingernails, horns and feathers are made up of cells filled with keratin.

Kerensky, Alexander Feodorovich (1881–1970) Russian moderate political leader. He became prime minister of the provisional government in July 1917, shortly after the overthrow of the Tsar. Deposed by the BOLSHEVIKS, he fled to France. *See also* RUSSIAN REVOLUTION

kerosene (paraffin) Distilled petroleum product heavier than petrol but lighter than diesel fuel. Kerosene is used in camping stoves, tractor fuels and fuels for jet and turboprop aircraft.

Kerouac, Jack (1922–69) US poet and novelist. He published his first novel, *The Town and the City*, in 1950. *On the Road* (1957) established him as the leading novelist of the BEAT MOVEMENT. Later works include *The Dharma Bums* (1958), *Desolation Angels* (1965) and the posthumously published *Visions of Cody* (1972).

Kerry County in Munster province, SW Republic of Ireland; the county town is Tralee. It is a mountainous region with an indented coastline and many lakes. Oats and potatoes are grown, sheep and cattle raised. Industries: tourism, fishing, footwear. Area: 4,701sq km (1,815sq mi). Pop. (1991) 121,894.

kestrel (windhover) Small FALCON that lives mainly in Europe, and hovers over its prey before attacking. It feeds mainly on rodents, insects and small birds. Length: 30cm (12in). Species *Falco tinnunculus*.

kettledrum *See* TIMPANI

Kew Gardens (Royal Botanic Gardens) Collection of plants and trees in SW London, UK. Founded in 1760 by George III's mother, they were given to the nation by Queen Victoria in 1840. Much plant research is carried out here.

key In music, term used to indicate TONALITY in a composition, based on one of the major or minor scales. The key of a piece of music is indicated by the key signature at the left hand end of the stave. The key of a passage may, however, change by the addition of accidentals before prescribed notes; a change of key is known as a modulation.

keyboard instrument Large group of musical instruments played by pressing keys on a keyboard. Notes are sounded by hitting or plucking a string (as in the PIANO or HARPSICHORD), passing air through a pipe or reed (as in the ORGAN or ACCORDION), or electronically (as in the SYNTHESIZER).

Keynes, John Maynard (1883–1946) British economist. In *The General Theory of Employment, Interest, and Money* (1936), Keynes established the foundation of modern MACROECONOMICS. He advocated the active intervention of government in the economy to stimulate employment and prosperity. He was highly influential as an economic advisor in the BRETTON WOODS CONFERENCE of 1944.

KGB (*Komitet Gosudarstvennoye Bezhopaznosti*, Rus. Committee for State Security) Soviet secret police . In the 1980s, it employed an estimated 500,000 people and controlled all police, security and intelligence operations in the Soviet Union. It also gathered military and political information. Its chief was a leader of the attempted coup against GORBACHEV in 1991. After the break-up of the Soviet Union, it was extensively reformed.

Khachaturian, Aram Ilyich (1903–78) Armenian composer. He wrote a piano concerto (1936) and a violin concerto (1940). His best-known works are the ballets *Gayane* (1942) and *Spartacus* (1953).

Khan, (Niazi) Imran (1952–) Pakistani cricketer and politician. He made his test debut for Pakistan in 1971. He played English county cricket for Worcestershire (1975–77) and Sussex (1978–88). He captained Pakistan for most of the decade 1982–92, and led them to victory in the 1992 World Cup. He took 325 wickets in Test matches and was only the second player to score a century and take ten wickets in a test (1983). His political aspirations were dented in the 1997 Pakistan elections.

Kharkov (Kharkiv) City in NE Ukraine. It was founded in the 17th century to serve as a stronghold for the Ukrainian Cossacks defending Russia's S border. During the 19th century its development was stimulated by nearby coalfields. During 1919–34 it was capital of the Ukrainian Soviet Socialist Republic. Industries: mining machinery, ball bearings, chemicals. Pop. (1991) 1,623,000.

Khartoum Capital of Sudan, at the junction of the Blue NILE and White Nile rivers. Khartoum was founded in the 1820s by MUHAMMAD ALI. In 1885 it was besieged by Mahdists, and General GORDON was killed. In 1898 it became the seat of government of the Anglo-Egyptian Sudan, and from 1956 the capital of independent Sudan. Industries: cement, gum arabic, chemicals, glass, cotton textiles, printing. Pop. (1983) 476,218.

Khayyám, Omar *See* OMAR KHAYYÁM

Khazars Turkic people who first appeared in the lower Volga region *c.*2nd century AD. Between the 8th and 10th centuries their empire prospered and extended from N of the Black Sea to the River Volga and from W of the Caspian Sea to the River Dnieper. In the 8th century, their ruling class was converted to JUDAISM. Their empire was destroyed in 965.

Khmer Language of up to 85% of the inhabitants of Cambodia. It belongs to the Mon-Khmer language group and has given its name to the people who speak it. A Khmer empire was set up between the 9th and 15th centuries AD. Cambodia was renamed the Khmer Republic in 1970. When the Republic fell to the KHMER ROUGE in 1975, the country was renamed Kampuchea; the name Cambodia was restored in 1989.

Khmer Rouge Cambodian communist guerrilla organization. It gained control of Cambodia in 1975. Led by POL POT and Khieu Samphan, it embarked on a forced communist transformation of Cambodian society, during which an estimated 2 to 3 million people died. The regime lost power to the Vietnamese after intense conflict (1977–78). In 1982 the Khmer Rouge joined in a coalition with Prince SIHANOUK (the former Cambodian leader) and the Khmer Peoples National Liberation Front. In 1991 each faction signed a ceasefire agreement, monitored by United Nations (UN) troops. After 1993 elections, in which the Khmer Rouge refused to take part, Prince Sihanouk's parliamentary monarchy was re-established. The Khmer Rouge resumed hostilities and were banned in 1994.

Khoisan Group of South African languages. The Khoikhoi and SAN are the two largest groups of native speakers. The Khoisan languages also include Sandawe and Hadza, spoken by small tribal groups in Tanzania. *See also* CLICK LANGUAGE

Khomeini, Ayatollah Ruhollah (1900–89) Iranian religious leader. An Islamic scholar with great influence over his Shi'ite students, he published an outspoken attack on Riza Shah Pahlavi in 1941 and remained an active opponent of his son, Muhammad Reza Shah PAHLAVI. Exiled in 1964, he returned to Iran in triumph after the fall of the Shah in 1979. His rule was characterized by strict religious orthodoxy, elimination of political opposition, and economic turmoil.

Khrushchev, Nikita Sergeyevich (1894–1971) Soviet politician, first secretary of the Communist Party (1953–64) and Soviet prime minister (1958–64). Noted for economic success and ruthless suppression of opposition in the Ukraine, he was elected to the Politburo in 1939. After Stalin died, he made a speech denouncing him and expelled his backers from the central committee. Favouring detente with the West, he yielded to the USA in the CUBAN MISSILE CRISIS. Economic setbacks and trouble with China led to his replacement by Leonid BREZHNEV and Aleksei Kosygin in 1964.

Khyber Pass Mountain pass in the Safid Kuh range, linking the Kabul valley in Afghanistan (w)

with Peshawar in Pakistan (E). Height: 1,073m (3,520ft). Length: 50km (30mi).

kibbutz Israeli collective settlement, developed from pioneering Jewish settlements in Palestine.

Kidd, William (1645–1701) (Captian Kidd) Scottish pirate. After a successful career as a privateer, he became a pirate in 1696. He was arrested in Boston, Massachusetts, in 1699 and sent to England where he was tried and hanged for piracy.

kiddush Jewish prayer recited before a meal on the eve of the Sabbath or of a festival. The head of the household says the prayer over a cup of wine.

kidney In vertebrates, one of a pair of organs responsible for regulating blood composition and the EXCRETION of waste products. The kidneys are at the back of the abdomen, one on each side of the backbone. The human kidney consists of an outer cortex and an inner medulla with about one million tubules (NEPHRONS). Nephrons contain numerous CAPILLARIES, which filter the blood entering from the renal ARTERY. Some substances, including water, are reabsorbed into the blood. URINE remains, which is passed to the URETER and on to the BLADDER. *See also* HOMEOSTASIS

Kiel City and seaport in N Germany, at the head of the Kiel Canal linking the North Sea and the Baltic Sea; capital of SCHLESWIG-HOLSTEIN state. Today Kiel is a yachting centre. Industries: shipbuilding, textiles, printing. Pop. (1993) 249,100.

Kierkegaard, Søren (Aaby) (1813–55) Danish philosopher and theologian, regarded as the founder of modern EXISTENTIALISM. He believed that the individual must exercise free will. Critical of HEGEL's speculative philosophy, he considered that religious faith was, at its best, blind obedience to an irrational God. His books include *Either/Or* (1843) and *Philosophical Fragments* (1844).

Kieslowski, Krzysztof (1941–96) Polish film director. He gained international praise for the ten-part epic *Dekalog* (1988). He received further acclaim for his final work, the *Three Colours* film trilogy – *Blue* (1993), *White* (1993) and *Red* (1994).

Kiev (Kiyev) Capital of Ukraine and a seaport on the Dnieper River. Founded in the 6th or 7th century, Kiev was the capital of Kievan Russia. It became the capital of the Ukrainian Soviet Socialist Republic in 1934, and of independent Ukraine in 1991. Industries: shipbuilding, machine tools, footwear, furniture. Pop. (1993) 2,600,000.

Kigali Capital of Rwanda, central Africa. A trade centre during the period of German and Belgian colonial administration, it became capital of independent Rwanda in 1962. Industries: tin mining, cotton, textiles and coffee. Pop. (1993) 234,500.

Kikuyu Bantu-speaking people of the highlands of Kenya, E Africa, forming 21% of Kenya's population. British rule strained their political and agricultural system, resulting in the MAU MAU revolt.

Kilauea Volcanic crater in Hawaii, on SE Hawaii Island. It is the world's largest active crater. Height: 1,247m (4,090ft). Depth: 152m (500ft).

Kildare County in Leinster province, E Republic of Ireland; the county town is Naas. A low-lying region, the chief rivers are the Liffey, Boyne and Barrow. Primarily agricultural, Kildare is noted for its breeding of racehorses. Area: 1,694sq km (654sq mi). Pop. (1991) 122,656.

Kilimanjaro Mountain in NE Tanzania, near the border with Kenya. The highest mountain in Africa, it is an extinct volcano with twin peaks joined by a broad saddle. Coffee is grown on the intensely cultivated s slopes. Height: Kibo 5,895m (19,340ft); Mawenzi 5,150m (16,896ft).

Kilkenny County in Leinster province, SE Republic of Ireland; the county town is Kilkenny. Part of the central plain of Ireland, it is drained by the Suir, Barrow and Nore rivers. Farmers grow cereal crops and vegetables, and cattle are reared. The chief industries are brewing and coal mining. Area: 2,062sq km (796sq mi). Pop. (1991) 73,635.

killer whale Toothed marine mammal of the DOLPHIN family that lives in the world's oceans, especially colder regions. A fierce predator, it is black above and white below, with a white patch above each eye. Length: 9m (30ft). Species: *Orcinus orca*.

kilogram SI unit of mass (symbol *kg*) defined as the mass of the international prototype cylinder of platinum-iridium kept at the International Bureau of Weights and Measures near Paris. One kilogram is equal to 1,000g (2.2lb).

Kimberley City in South Africa; capital of Northern Cape province. It was founded in 1871 after the discovery of diamonds nearby. Today it is one of the world's largest diamond centres. Other industries include the processing of gypsum, iron and manganese. Pop. (1991) 167,060.

Kim Il Sung (1912–94) Korean statesman, ruler of North Korea (1948–94). He joined the Korean Communist Party in 1931. In 1950 he led a North Korean invasion of South Korea, precipitating the KOREAN WAR (1950–53). Chairman of the Korean Workers' Party from 1948, his Stalinist regime suppressed all political opposition.

Kim Jong Il (1941–) North Korean statesman, ruler of North Korea (1994–) In 1980 he was officially named as his father's (KIM IL SUNG) successor, finally assuming office on his father's death. His regime was faced with recession and famine.

Kim Young Sam (1927–) South Korean statesman, president (1992–). He was a founder-member of the Democratic Party in 1955 and president of the New Democratic Party (NDP) from 1974. In 1979 he was banned from politics for his opposition to President Park. The ban was lifted in 1985.

kinetic energy Energy that an object possesses because it is in motion. It is the energy (symbol K) given to an object to set it in motion; it depends on the mass (*m*) of the object and its velocity (*v*), according to the equation $K = 1/2 \, mv^2$. On impact, it is converted into other forms of energy such as heat, sound and light. *See also* POTENTIAL ENERGY

kinetics In physics, one of the branches of DYNAM-ICS. In chemistry, a branch of physical chemistry that deals with the rates of chemical reactions.

kinetic theory Theory in physics dealing with matter in terms of the forces between particles and the energies they possess. There are five principles of kinetic theory: matter is composed of tiny particles; these are in constant motion; they do not lose energy in collision with each other or the walls of their container; there are no attractive forces between the particles or their container; and at any time the particles may not all have the same energy.

King, Billie Jean (1943–) US tennis player. She won a record 20 Wimbledon titles, including six singles titles (1966–68, 1972–73, 1975). She also won the US Open women's singles (1967, 1971–72, 1974); Australian Open (1968); and French Open (1972).

King, Martin Luther, Jr (1929–68) US Baptist minister and CIVIL RIGHTS leader. He led the boycott of segregated public transport in Montgomery, Alabama in 1956. As founder (1960) and president of the Southern Christian Leadership Council, he became a national figure. He opposed the Vietnam War and demanded measures to relieve poverty, organizing a huge march on Washington (1963) where he made his famous ("I have a dream....") speech. In 1964 he became the youngest person to be awarded the Nobel Peace Prize. He was assassinated in Memphis, Tennessee.

King, William Lyon Mackenzie (1874–1950) Canadian politician, prime minister (1921–30, 1935–48). His career was marked by the drive for national unity, culminating in the Statute of WESTMINSTER (1931).

kingbird (tyrant flycatcher) New World flycatcher whose habitat is mainly in tropical America. It dives at intruders. It grows to 17cm (6.8in).

kingdom Most widely adopted TAXONOMY for living organisms is the **Five Kingdoms** system, in which the kingdom is the topmost level (taxon). The Five Kingdoms are Animalia (ANIMAL), Plantae (PLANT), Fungi (FUNGUS), PROKARYOTAE and PROTISTA. Two subkingdoms are often recognized within Prokaryotae, ARCHAEBACTERIA and EUBACTERIA, but the bacteria are so diverse that many taxonomists think they comprise more than one kingdom. Some believe that they merit the status of a new, even higher category, DOMAINS. *See also* EUKARYOTE; PLANT CLASSIFICATION

kingfisher Compact, brightly coloured bird with a straight, sharp bill, which dives for fish along rivers, streams and lakes. It nests in a horizontal hole in an earth bank. Length: 12.7–43.2cm (5–17in). Family Alcedinidae.

Kings I and II Two books in the OLD TESTAMENT, the Third and Fourth Kingdoms in the Greek SEPTUAGINT. They recount the history of the kingdom of ISRAEL from the end of the reign of DAVID (*c*.970 BC) to the fall of Judah and the destruction of Jerusalem by the Babylonians in 586 BC.

Kingsley, Charles (1819–75) British author. He

was one of the first clergymen to support Charles DARWIN, whose ideas he partly incorporated into *The Water Babies* (1863). His immensely popular historical novels include *Hypatia* (1843) and *Hereward the Wake* (1866).

king snake Nonpoisonous SNAKE that lives in the USA. It is generally black with white or yellow markings. Length: to 1.3m (4.2ft). Family Colubridae, genus *Lampropeltis*.

Kingston Capital and largest city of Jamaica. It was founded in 1693. It rapidly developed into Jamaica's commercial centre, based on the export of raw cane sugar, bananas and rum. In 1872 it became the capital. Kingston is the cultural heart of Jamaica, the home of calypso and reggae music. In recent years it has been plagued by urban disturbances and armed drug gangs. Pop. (1991) 643,800.

Kingston upon Hull Official name for HULL, NE England.

Kingstown Capital and chief port of St Vincent and the Grenadines, on the SW coast. Exports: cotton, sugar cane, molasses. Pop. (1991) 26,223.

Kinsey, Alfred Charles (1894–1956) US zoologist, noted for his studies of human sexuality, such as *Sexual Behavior in the Human Male* (1948) and *Sexual Behavior in the Human Female* (1953).

Kinshasa (formerly Léopoldville) Capital of Zaïre, a port on the River Congo, on the Zaïre-Congo border. It replaced Boma as the capital of the Belgian Congo in 1923. When Zaïre gained independence in 1960 it continued as the capital, changing its name in 1966. Industries: tanning, chemicals, brewing and textiles. Pop. (1991 est.) 3,804,000.

kinship Relationship by blood or marriage, sometimes extended to cover relations of affinity. It also refers to a complex of rules in society governing descent, succession, inheritance, residence, marriage and sexual relations. *See also* INCEST

Kipling, Joseph Rudyard (1865–1936) British author, b. India. His *Barrack Room Ballads and Other Verses* (1892), including the poem *If*, established his reputation. His novels include *The Light That Failed* (1890) and *Kim* (1901). He also wrote many children's stories, including *The Jungle Book* (1894) and *Just So Stories* (1902). Kipling was the first English writer to be awarded the Nobel Prize in literature (1907).

Kirchhoff, Gustav Robert (1824–87) German physicist. With Robert BUNSEN, he developed the spectroscope, with which they discovered CAESIUM and RUBIDIUM in 1860. He is famous for two laws that apply to multiple-loop electric circuits.

Kirchhoff's laws state that: (1) at any junction the sum of the currents flowing is zero; and (2) the sum of the ELECTROMOTIVE FORCES (EMF) around any closed path equals the sum of the products of the currents and impedances (resistances).

Kirchner, Ernst Ludwig (1880–1938) German painter and printmaker, a leader of Die BRÜCKE. His art was condemned by the Nazis as degenerate and he committed suicide. *See also* EXPRESSIONISM

Kiribati (formerly Gilbert Islands) Independent nation in the W Pacific Ocean, comprising about 33 islands, including the Gilbert, Phoenix and Line Islands, and straddling the Equator; the capital is Bairiki (on Tarawa). They became a British protectorate in 1892. Full independence within the Commonwealth of Nations was granted in 1979. The mining of phosphates dominated the economy until 1980. Agriculture is now the major economic activity. Area: 717sq km (277sq mi). Pop. (1995 est.) 80,000

Kiritimati (Christmas Island) Largest atoll in the world, one of the Line Islands, forming part of KIRIBATI. It was the site of nuclear tests by Britain (1956–62) and the USA (1962). Area: 575sq km (222sq mi). Pop. (1990) 2,537.

Kirov Former name (1934–92) for VYATKA

Kirov Ballet Ballet company founded in 1735 at St Petersburg. Under the direction of PETIPA (1862–1903), the Kirov Ballet was the world's top company, with principal dancers such as PAVLOVA and NIJINSKY. The **Kirov Opera** has also made a distinguished contribution to Russian culture.

Kisangani (formerly Stanleyville) City and port on the River Congo, N central Zaïre. Kisangani was founded in 1883 by the English explorer Henry M. STANLEY. During the 1950s it was the headquarters of the Congolese National Movement led by Patrice LUMUMBA. In 1996 it was at the centre of the Hutu refugee crisis in Zaïre. Pop. (1984) 282,650.

Kissinger, Henry Alfred (1923–) US political scientist and statesman, b. Germany. In 1969 he became President NIXON's assistant for national security and chief adviser on foreign policy. He became secretary of state in 1973 under Nixon, and continued in the post under President FORD. In 1973 he shared the Nobel Peace Prize with Le Duc Tho for his part in ceasefire negotiations in the Vietnam War. He acted as mediator in the Middle East crisis of 1973–74.

Kitchener, Horatio Herbert, Earl (1850–1916) British soldier and statesman. He took part in the relief of Khartoum (1883–85) and achieved the pacification of the Sudan (1898). After service in the South African (Boer) War (1899–1902), and then in India and Egypt, he was appointed Secretary of State for War in 1914.

kite Common name for several diurnal birds of prey, especially the red kite, *Milvus milvus*, which frequents wooded slopes in Europe. It has a hooked bill, long wings and a long forked tail. Length: 60cm (24in). Family Accipitridae.

kiwi Any of three species of flightless, fast-running, forest and scrubland birds of New Zealand; especially the common brown kiwi, *Apteryx australis*. It has a long, flexible bill with which it probes for food in the ground. Family Apterygidae.

Klee, Paul (1879–1940) Swiss painter and graphic artist. Klee evolved his own pictorial language based on correspondences between line, colour and plane. Some of his images are entirely ABSTRACT.

He taught at the BAUHAUS (1920–31). Characteristic works include *Graduated Shades of Red-Green* (1921) and *Revolutions of the Viaducts* (1937).

Klein, Melanie (1882–1960) Austrian psychoanalyst who developed therapy for young children. In *The Psychoanalysis of Children* (1932) she presents play as a symbolic way of controlling anxiety.

Klein, Yves (1928–62) French painter and experimental artist, one of the forerunners of conceptual art. He is best known for hand and body prints in his characteristic colour scheme of bright blue (Klein blue) on white.

Klimt, Gustav (1862–1918) Austrian painter and designer, a founder of the Vienna SEZESSION group and the foremost ART NOUVEAU painter in Vienna. His style considerably influenced the decorative arts in Austria and the work of the painters Egon SCHIELE and Oskar KOKOSCHKA.

Klondike Gold Rush (1896–1904) Migration of gold prospectors to the Klondike region, YUKON TERRITORY, NW Canada. The rich gold deposits discovered in the Klondike River in 1896 brought more than 30,000 prospectors to the territory.

Kneller, Sir Godfrey (1646–1723) Painter, b. Germany. His best-known works include 42 portraits, known as the *Kit Cat series*. He founded the first English Academy of Painting (1711).

knight In medieval Europe, a mounted warrior of intermediate rank. The knight began as a squire and was knighted after a period of trial. Knights were often landholders, owing military service to their overlord. Honorary orders of knighthood, such as the Knights of the Garter (1349), were founded towards the end of the Middle Ages.

Knights Hospitallers Military Christian order founded in the 12th century. They adopted a military role to defend JERUSALEM. After the fall of Jerusalem (1187), they moved to Acre, then Cyprus, then Rhodes (1310), from where they were expelled by the Ottoman Turks (1522). The pope then gave them Malta, where they remained until driven out by Napoleon in 1798. The order still exists as an international, humanitarian charity.

Knights Templar Military religious order established in 1118, with headquarters in the supposed Temple of Solomon in Jerusalem. With the KNIGHTS HOSPITALLERS, the Templars protected routes to Jerusalem during the CRUSADES. The possessions of the Templars in France attracted the envious attention of King PHILIP IV, who urged Pope Clement V to abolish the order in 1312.

Knossos Ancient palace complex in N central Crete, 6.4km (4mi) SE of modern Iráklion. In 1900 Sir Arthur Evans began excavations that revealed that the site had been inhabited before 3000 BC. He discovered a palace from the MINOAN CIVILIZATION (built *c.*2000 BC, rebuilt *c.*1700 BC). Close to the palace were the houses of Cretan nobles. The complex contains many frescos. Knossos dominated Crete *c.*1500 BC but the palace was occupied *c.*1400 BC by invaders from MYCENAE.

knot Unit of measurement equal to one nautical mile per hour – 1 knot equals 1.852km/h (1.15mph). The speeds of ships, aircraft, winds and currents are generally expressed in knots.

Knox, John (1514–72) Leader of the Protestant REFORMATION in Scotland. Ordained a Catholic priest, he was later converted to Protestantism and took up the cause of the Reformation. Captured by French soldiers in Scotland, he was imprisoned in France (1547). In 1559 Knox returned to Scotland, where he continued to promote Protestantism. In 1560, the Scottish Parliament, under Knox's leadership, made PRESBYTERIANISM the state religion. In 1563 he was tried for treason but acquitted.

koala Small marsupial that lives in eucalyptus trees of Australia, eating their leaves. A single offspring is born, nurtured in its mother's pouch until fully formed, then carried on her back for a further six months. Length: 85cm (33in). Species *Phascolarctos cinereus*.

Kōbe City and seaport on the N shore of Osaka Bay, sw Honshū Island, Japan. It is Japan's leading port and a major industrial centre. In 1995 over 5,000 people were killed and 27,000 injured in an earthquake. Industries: shipbuilding, iron and steel, electronics, chemicals. Pop. (1993) 1,468,000.

Kodály, Zoltán (1882–1967) Hungarian composer. With BARTÓK he collected and systematized Hungarian folk music. Among his best-known compositions are the *Psalmus Hungaricus* (1923) and the comic opera *Háry János* (1927).

Koestler, Arthur (1905–83) British novelist and philosopher, b. Hungary. He went to Spain as a journalist to cover the Spanish Civil War. *Darkness at Noon* (1940), his best-known novel, is a biting indictment of Stalinist totalitarianism. His other novels also embody political themes.

Kohl, Helmut (1930–) German statesman, chancellor of West Germany (1982–90), chancellor of reunified Germany (1990–). Kohl rose rapidly through the ranks of the Christian Democratic Union (CDU). He succeeded Helmut SCHMIDT as chancellor. His conservative approach advocated strong support for NATO and closer European integration. He became the first leader of reunified Germany. He was re-elected in 1994.

Kokoschka, Oskar (1886–1980) Austrian painter. He was influenced by KLIMT, but soon developed his own form of EXPRESSIONISM. His work is characterized by forceful, energetic draughtsmanship and restless brushwork.

kolanut (colanut) Fruit of an African tree that bears the same name, from which is extracted an ingredient of cola soft drinks. Family Sterculiaceae; species *Cola acuminata*.

Kollwitz, Käthe (1867–1945) German graphic artist and sculptor. Her best-known works depict suffering, especially of women and children. Her economical style was in the tradition of German EXPRESSIONISM. She achieved fame with the series of etchings, *The Weavers' Revolt*

(1897–98) and *Peasants' War* (1902–08). She also produced lithographs and woodcuts such as *War* (1922–3) and *Death* (1934–35).

Köln *See* COLOGNE

Kommunizma Pik (Communism Peak) Mountain in central Asia, in SE Tajikistan, in the Pamirs region. Known as Mount Garmo until 1933 and Stalin Peak until 1962, it was the highest peak in the former Soviet Union. Height: 7,495m (24,590ft).

komodo dragon Giant monitor lizard that lives on four islands in the E of Java, Indonesia; it is the largest lizard in the world. Length: 3m (10ft). Family Varanidae; species *Varanus komodoensis.*

Königsberg *See* KALININGRAD

Konya City in S central Turkey. It was first settled in the 8th century BC. The capital of the SELJUK sultanate of Rum from 1099, it was annexed by the Ottoman sultan in 1472. It is the religious centre of the whirling DERVISHES. Manufactures include cotton and leather goods, carpets. Pop. (1990) 543,460.

kookaburra (laughing jackass) Large KINGFISHER of Australia, known for its call resembling fiendish laughter. Groups often scream in unison at dawn, midday and dusk. They feed on animals. Species *Dacelo gigas.*

Koran (Quran) Sacred book of ISLAM. According to Muslim belief, the Koran contains the actual word of God (ALLAH) as revealed by the angel GABRIEL to the Prophet MUHAMMAD. Muhammad is said to have received these revelations over two decades beginning *c.*AD 610 and ending in 632, the year of his death. The 114 *suras* (chapters) of the Koran are the source of Islamic belief and a guide for the whole life of the community. The central teachings of the Koran are that there is no God but Allah and all must submit to Him, that Muhammad is the last of His many messengers (which have included Abraham, Moses and Jesus), and that there will come a day of judgment. In addition to these teachings, the Koran contains rules that a Muslim must follow in everyday life.

Korda, Sir Alexander (1893–1956) British film director, b. Hungary, who was noted for his lavish productions. Films include *The Scarlet Pimpernel* (1935), *Lady Hamilton* (1941) and *Anna Karenina* (1948).

Korea Peninsula in E Asia, separating the Yellow Sea from the Sea Of Japan. The Yalu and Tumen rivers form most of its N border with China. **Land and climate** The E seaboard is mountainous, rising in the NE to 2,744m (9,003ft) at Mount Paektu. The mountains descend in the W to coastal lowlands. The traditional capital, SEOUL, lies close to the 38th parallel border between North Korea and South Korea. The Korean Archipelago lies off the S coast, and includes the province of Cheju-do. North Korea experiences long and severe winters: lakes and rivers can remain frozen for up to 4 months a year. Summers are warm. South Korea has a more tropical climate with occasional typhoons in the rainy months (July–August). **History** Korea's cal-

endar starts in 2333 BC. China was a dominant influence. The first native Korean state was established in the 1st century AD, and Korea was unified under the Silla dynasty in the 7th century. Korea was invaded by Mongols in 1231 and eventually surrendered. The Yi dynasty ruled Korea from 1392–1910. Early in the Yi period, Seoul was made the new capital and CONFUCIANISM became the official religion. In the 17th century Korea was a semi-independent state, dominated by the MANCHU dynasty. A long period of isolationism followed. In the late 19th century Korea became more active in foreign affairs, due to the growing power of Japan. After the RUSSO-JAPANESE WAR (1904–05) Korea was effectively a Japanese protectorate and was formally annexed in 1910. Japan's enforced industrialization of Korea caused widespread resentment. Following Japan's defeat in World War 2, Korea was divided into two zones of occupation: Soviet forces N of the 38th parallel, and US forces S of the line. Attempts at reunification failed, and in 1948 two separate regimes were established: the Republic of Korea in the S and the Democratic People's Republic in the N. In June 1950 North Korea invaded South Korea. The ensuing KOREAN WAR (1950–53) resulted in millions of deaths and devastated the peninsula. An uneasy truce has prevailed ever since. Attempts at reunification continue.

Korea, North Republic in E Asia, the capital is PYONGYANG. **Land and climate** The Democratic People's Republic of Korea occupies the N part of the Korean peninsula. North Korea is largely mountainous. Pyongyang lies on the W coastal plain. North Korea's border with South Korea is based on the 38th parallel. (For land, climate and pre-1953 history, *see* KOREA and KOREAN WAR.) **Economy** North Korea has considerable mineral resources, including coal, copper, iron ore, lead, tin, tungsten and zinc. Yet, it is a net consumer of energy and reliant on oil imports. Industries include chemicals, iron and steel, machinery, processed food and textiles. Agriculture employs over 40% of the workforce. Rice is the leading crop. **History** In 1948 North Korea established a communist government led (1948–94) by KIM IL SUNG. Kim Il Sung's Stalinist regime exploited North Korea's rich mineral resources. Industry

---

KOREA, NORTH

AREA: 120,540sq km (46,540sq mi)
POPULATION: 22,618,000
CAPITAL (POPULATION): Pyongyang (2,639,448)
GOVERNMENT: Single-party people's republic
ETHNIC GROUPS: Korean 99%
LANGUAGES: Korean (official)
RELIGIONS: Traditional beliefs 16%, Chondogyo 14%, Buddhism 2%, Christianity 1%
CURRENCY: North Korean won = 100 chon

was nationalized. Heavy industry and arms production greatly increased. Agriculture was collectivized and mechanized. After the Korean War, several million Koreans fled Kim Il Sung's dictatorial regime. North Korea remained largely closed to outside interests. Alliances were formed with China and the Soviet Union, but the collapse of the latter had adverse effects on North Korea's economy. North Korea's emphasis on military industry had a destabilizing effect on regional politics and internal economic planning. Since 1991 Korea's economy has slumped. In 1991 North and South Korea signed a non-aggression pact and agreed on a series of meetings on reunification. The process was halted in 1994 with the death of Kim Il Sung. He was succeeded by his son, KIM JONG IL. **Politics** During the early 1990s North Korea's nuclear weapons building programme gathered momentum. In 1994 North Korea briefly withdrew from the Nuclear Non-proliferation Treaty. They rejoined after agreeing to halt the reprocessing of plutonium, in return for guarantees on energy supplies and the establishment of economic and diplomatic relations with the USA. In 1995 severe flooding caused over US$15 billion of damage and devastated agricultural production. In 1996 the UN sent emergency food aid to relieve famine. Many analysts see North Korea in imminent danger of collapse.

Korea, South Republic in E Asia, the capital is SEOUL. **Land and climate** The Republic of Korea occupies the S part of the Korean peninsula. South Korea is largely mountainous. Seoul lies on the w coastal lowlands. Other major cities include INCHON, TAEGU, and the main port of PUSAN, on the E coast. Cheju-do is the largest island and includes Mount Halla, South Korea's highest peak, at 1,950m (6,398ft). (For land, climate and pre-1953 history, *see* KOREA and KOREAN WAR). **Economy** South Korea is an upper-middle-income developing country. During the late 20th century it has been one of the world's fastest growing industrial economies, with annual growth rates averaging 10% between 1960 and 1980. US aid of over US$6,000 million (1945–78) has played a large part in the economic success story. South Korea's industrial conglomerates (*chaebols*) have benefited from a highly educated workforce and

import controls. From the mid-1980s growth has slowed, and increasing labour costs led to unpopular changes in the labour market. South Korea's protectionist policies are slowly giving way to free market reforms. The largest sector of the economy is services, employing 50% of the workforce. The manufacturing sector has proved South Korea's greatest asset. Manufactured goods, machinery and transport equipment make up 66% of South Korea's exports. South Korea is the world's fifth-largest car producer. It is also a major producer of iron and steel, cement, electrical and electronic products. It is reliant on the importation of raw materials. Agriculture employs 17% of the workforce. South Korea is self-sufficient in grain, and is the world's eighth-largest producer of rice. Fishing is another vital sector, South Korea has the world's tenth-largest fish catch. **History** South Korea's first government, led (1948–60) by Syngman Rhee, was beset by economic problems. South Korea was a predominantly agricultural economy, heavily dependent on the N for energy and resources. South Korea's infrastructure was devastated by the Korean War. Rhee's corrupt and repressive regime became increasingly unpopular. The massacre of student protestors in 1960 sparked nationwide disturbances and a military junta, led by General Park Chung Hee, seized power in 1961. Park's presidency (1963–79) brought rapid economic growth. Helped by US aid, South Korea became a major manufacturer and exporter. In 1972 Park introduced martial law and passed a constitution that gave him almost unlimited powers. In the social and political sphere his regime pursued increasingly authoritarian policies. Park was assassinated in 1979, but the military still dominated the government. Opposition to the political climate continued to grow. In 1987 a new constitution ensured the popular election of the president and reduced the presidential term to five years. In 1988 Seoul hosted the summer Olympic Games. Relations with North Korea continued to improve, and in 1991 the two countries signed a non-aggression pact and established a series of summit meetings on reunification. In 1992 the long-standing opposition leader, KIM YOUNG SAM, became president. His administration was South Korea's first full civilian government in 32 years. **Politics** The death of North Korean president KIM IL SUNG stalled reunification talks, but the momentum had been established. In 1997 preliminary talks were held to discuss the possibility of four-party peace talks involving North and South Korea, China and the USA.

Korean National language of North and South Korea. Some scholars class it as one of the ALTAIC LANGUAGES. It is spoken by over 50 million people. The Korean alphabet developed in the 15th century.

Korean War (1950–53) Conflict between North Korea, supported by China, and South Korea, supported by UN forces dominated by the USA. South

---

KOREA, SOUTH
AREA: 99,020sq km (38,232sq mi)
POPULATION: 43,663,000
CAPITAL (POPULATION): Seoul (10,799,000)
GOVERNMENT: Multiparty republic
ETHNIC GROUPS: Korean 99%
LANGUAGES: Korean (official)
RELIGIONS: Buddhism 28%, Christianity (Protestant 19%, Roman Catholic 6%)
CURRENCY: South Korean won = 100 chon

Korea was invaded by forces of the North in June 1950. The UNITED NATIONS Security Council, during a boycott by the Soviet Union, voted to aid South Korea. Major US forces, plus token forces from its allies, landed under the overall command of General Douglas MACARTHUR. The North Koreans were repelled. When the UN forces advanced into North Korea, China intervened and drove them back, recapturing Seoul. After more heavy fighting, UN forces slowly advanced until virtual stalemate ensued near the 38th Parallel, the border between North and South Korea. Negotiations continued for two years before a truce was agreed in July 1953. Total casualties were estimated at four million.

Kosciusko, Mount Mountain in SE Australia, in the Great Dividing Range, in SE New South Wales. The highest mountain in Australia, it is a winter sports resort. Height: 2,228m (7,310ft).

kosher Ritually correct or acceptable for Jews. A word of Hebrew origin, it is applied to food that conforms to Jewish dietary laws and customs.

Kossuth, Louis (Lajos) (1802–94) Hungarian nationalist leader. Emerging as leader of the Revolution of 1848, he declared Hungarian independence (1849), but Russian intervention led to his defeat. He fled to rouse support for Hungarian independence in Europe and the USA. The compromise of 1867 created the AUSTRO-HUNGARIAN EMPIRE, and put an end to his hopes.

Kosygin, Aleksei Nikolayevich (1904–80) Soviet statesman, prime minister (1964–70). He was elected to the Communist Party Central Committee in 1939 and the Politburo in 1948. He was removed in 1953 but regained his seat in 1960. After KHRUSHCHEV's fall in 1964, he became prime minister, a position he held until his retirement.

Kowloon Peninsula on the SE coast of China, part of HONG KONG. One of the most densely populated areas of the world, it was ceded to Britain by China in 1860. Industries: shipbuilding. Area: 9sq km (3.5sq mi). Pop. (1986) 2,301,691.

Krakatoa Small volcanic island in w Indonesia, in the Sunda Strait between Java and Sumatra. In 1883 one of the world's largest volcanic eruptions destroyed most of the island. The resulting tidal waves caused 50,000 deaths and great destruction. Height: 813m (2,667ft).

Kraków (Cracow) City in s Poland. Founded in the 8th century, it was made a residence of the Polish kings in the 12th century. In 1795 it was ceded to Austria. The city became part of Poland after World War 1. Historic buildings include the Wawel Cathedral. The Jagiellonian University (1364) is one of the oldest in Europe. Today Kraków is a manufacturing centre. Industries: chemicals, metals, machinery, clothing, printing. Pop. (1993) 751,300.

Krasnoyarsk City and port on the w bank of the upper Yenisei River, w Siberian Russia; capital of Krasnoyarsk Kray. Founded in 1628 by the COSSACKS, it underwent rapid development after the discovery of gold in the area. Industries: shipbuild-

ing, heavy machinery, electrical goods, cement, timber, flour milling. Pop. (1992) 925,000.

Krebs, Sir Hans Adolf (1900–81) British biochemist, b. Germany. In 1953 he shared (with F.A Lipmann) the Nobel Prize for physiology or medicine for his discovery of the CITRIC ACID cycle, the process that results in RESPIRATION.

Kremlin (Rus. citadel) Historic centre of Moscow. It is a roughly triangular fortress covering c.36.5ha (90 acres). The Kremlin walls were built of timber in the 12th century. Its first stone walls were added in 1367. Within the walls several cathedrals face on to a central square; the Great Kremlin Palace was the tsar's Moscow residence until the Revolution. In March 1918 the Supreme Soviet established the Kremlin complex as the location of all government offices. Today, the Kremlin is the home of the Russian presidential offices.

Křenek, Ernst (1900–91) US composer, b. Austria, who emigrated to the USA in 1938. From 1920 in Berlin he experimented with atonal music, and after 1930 in Vienna he adopted the TWELVE-TONE MUSIC technique of SCHOENBERG. His most famous work is the jazz opera *Jonny spielt auf* (1925–26).

krill Collective term for the large variety of marine crustaceans found in all oceans. They are strained and used as food by various species of baleen WHALE.

Krishna Most celebrated hero of Hindu mythology. He was the eighth AVATAR (incarnation) of VISHNU and primarily a god of joyfulness and fertility. Many devotional cults grew up around him, as well as legends and poems.

Krishnamurti, Jiddu (1895–1986) Hindu religious leader. He founded the World Order of Star with Annie Besant, and in 1969 founded the Krishnamurti Foundation in Ojai, California.

Kropotkin, Peter Alexeievich (1842–1921) Russian anarchist leader. He was jailed for seditious propaganda in 1874, but escaped into exile in 1876. Living mostly in Britain, he became one of the most important theorists of anarchist socialism, criticizing the centralizing tendencies of Marxism. He argued in *Mutual Aid* (1902) that cooperation rather than competition is the natural order of things.

Kruger, Paul (Stephanus Johannes Paulus) (1825–1904) South African political leader. In 1883 he became the first president of the South African Republic, and won re-election in 1888, 1893 and 1898. He fought in the first of the SOUTH AFRICAN WARS and, during the second, he sought further European support for the BOER cause. Following the British victory, Kruger died in exile.

Kruger National Park Game reserve in Northern Province, South Africa, on the Mozambique border. Founded in 1898 by Paul Kruger as the Sabi Game Reserve, it became a national park in 1926. Area: c.20,720sq km (8,000sq mi).

krypton Gaseous nonmetallic element (symbol Kr), a NOBLE GAS. Discovered in 1898, krypton makes up about 0.0001% of the Earth's atmosphere by volume and is obtained by the fractional distillation of liquid air. It is used in fluorescent lamps, lasers and in electronic heart valves. Properties: at.no. 36; r.a.m. 83.80; density 3.73; m.p. $-156.6°C$; ($-249.9°F$); b.p. $-152.3°C$; ($-242.1°F$); most common isotope Kr^{84} (56.9%).

Kuala Lumpur Capital of Malaysia, in the S Malay peninsula. Founded in 1857, it was made the capital of the Federated Malay States in 1895, of the Federation of Malaya in 1957 and of Malaysia in 1963. It is home to the world's tallest skyscraper, the twin Petronas Towers. A commercial centre; industries include tin and rubber. Pop. (1990) 1,231,500.

Kublai Khan (1215–94) Mongol Emperor (1260–94). Grandson of GENGHIS KHAN, he completed the conquest of China in 1279, establishing the YÜAN dynasty, which ruled until 1368. He conquered the SUNG dynasty and extended into SE Asia. His attempt to invade Japan was thwarted by storms. He conducted correspondence with European rulers and apparently employed Marco POLO.

Kubrick, Stanley (1928–) US film director. An ambitious and sometimes bleak film-maker, his films include *Dr Strangelove* (1963), *2001: A Space Odyssey* (1968), *A Clockwork Orange* (1971), *The Shining* (1980) and *Full Metal Jacket* (1987).

Kuiper, Gerard Peter (1905–73) US astronomer, b. Netherlands. He discovered the satellites Miranda (of Uranus) in 1948 and Nereid (of Neptune) in 1949. He found methane in the atmospheres of Uranus, Neptune and Titan, and carbon dioxide in the atmosphere of Mars.

Ku Klux Klan (KKK) Name of two secret, white, racist, terrorist groups in the USA. The first Ku Klux Klan was organized in the South in 1866. Opposed to RECONSTRUCTION, it attempted to enforce labour discipline in plantations and to maintain white supremacy by preventing blacks from voting. Klansmen dressed in white robes and hoods terrorized black communities. By 1872 the Klan had been suppressed by Federal authorities. A second Ku Klux Klan was founded in 1915, embracing broader-based racism directed also against Catholics, Jews and communists. By 1925 its membership was estimated at four million. It declined thereafter, but there was a minor resurgence in the 1960s and in some Southern states in the 1990s.

Kumasi City in central Ghana; capital of ASHANTI region. The second-largest city in Ghana, it was the capital of the Ashanti kingdom in the 17th and 18th centuries, before being annexed by the British in 1901. It is a commercial centre for a cocoa-growing region. Industries: food processing, handicrafts, timber. Pop. (1984) 376,246.

kung fu Ancient Chinese martial art based on the idea that the best form of defence against violence utilizes actions that combine attack and defence.

Kuomintang Nationalist Party in China, which was the major political force during and after the creation of a republic in 1911. It was first led by SUN YAT-SEN. It cooperated with the Communist Party until 1927 when Sun's successor, CHIANG KAI-SHEK, turned against the communists, initiating a civil war. Cooperation was renewed (1937–45) in order to repel the Japanese, after which the civil war resumed. With the communists victorious, Chiang set up a rump state on the island of Taiwan, where the Kuomintang survives.

Kupka, František (1871–1957) Czech painter, etcher and illustrator active mainly in Paris. He was among the first painters to develop purely abstract painting. His works include *Fugue in Red and Blue* (1912). *See also* ABSTRACT ART

Kurdistan Extensive mountainous and plateau region in SW Asia, inhabited by the KURDS and including parts of E Turkey, NE Iran, N Iraq, NE Syria, S Armenia and E Azerbaijan. Plans for the creation of a separate Kurdish state were put forward after World War 1, but subsequently abandoned. Area: *c*.192,000sq km (74,000sq mi).

Kurds Predominantly rural, Islamic population numbering some 18 million, who live in a disputed frontier area of SW Asia that they call KURDISTAN. Traditionally nomadic herdsmen, they are mainly SUNNI Muslims who speak an Iranian dialect. For 3,000 years they have maintained a unique cultural tradition, though internal division and constant external invasion have prevented them from uniting into one nation. In recent times, their main conflicts have been with Iran and Iraq. After the IRAN-IRAQ WAR (1988), Iraq destroyed many Kurdish villages. Iraq's merciless response to a Kurdish revolt after the Gulf War (1991) caused 1.5 million Kurds to flee to Iran and Turkey. In 1996 Iraqi captured the Kurdish city of Irbil. The USA responded by launching cruise missiles at Iraqi military installations. Currently *c*.8 million Kurds live in E Turkey, 4 million in N Iraq, 500,000 in Syria and 100,000 in Azerbaijan and Armenia.

Kuril Islands (Kurilskie Ostrova) Chain of 30 large and 26 smaller islands in SAKHALIN region, Russia; extending 1,200km (750mi) from the S Kamchatka Peninsula to NE Hokkaido, Japan, and separating the Sea of Okhotsk from the Pacific Ocean. The N islands were settled by Russians, the S islands by Japanese. In 1875 Russia gave the islands to Japan in exchange for full control of SAKHALIN island. After World War 2 the islands were ceded to the Soviet Union. The chief economic activities are sulphur mining and whaling. Area: 15,600sq km (6,023sq mi).

Kurosawa, Akira (1910–) Japanese film director. *Rashomon* (1950) introduced the SAMURAI code to Western audiences. The popularity of this genre was confirmed with *The Seven Samurai* (1954). *Dursu Uzala* (1975) won an Academy Award for Best Foreign Film. Other films include *Kagemusha* (1980), *Ran* (1985) and *Dreams* (1990).

Kursk City in W Russia, at the confluence of the Tuskoc and Seim rivers. Founded in 1095, it was destroyed by the TATARS in 1240 and rebuilt as a frontier post in 1586. Industries: iron and steel, chemicals, synthetic fibres, shoes, electrical equipment. Pop. (1992) 435,000.

Kush Kingdom and former state in NUBIA. Lasting from c.1000 BC to c.AD 350, it conquered Egypt in the 7th–8th centuries BC. It was later defeated by the Assyrians and moved its capital to Meroë in the Sudan. After Roman and Arab attacks in the N, Meroë was captured by the Axumites around AD 350. The Kushites are thought to have fled W.

Kuwait (Al Kuwayt) Independent state in the NE Arabian Peninsula, N of the Persian Gulf. The capital is Kuwait City. Kuwait was founded in the early 18th century. In 1899 it became a British protectorate, becoming fully independent in 1961. It was invaded in 1990 by Iraqi forces, who were ejected the following year by an international coalition led by the USA. Huge oil reserves have made it one of the world's richest countries. Industries: shipbuilding, petrochemicals, fertilizers. Agriculture is being developed. Area: 17,818sq km (6,878sq mi). Pop. (1995) 1,590,013. *See also* GULF WAR

Kwa languages Group of languages making up a branch of the Niger-Congo family of African languages. Kwa languages include Yoruba and Ibo of S Nigeria; Ewe of Ghana, Togo and Benin; Akan of Ivory Coast and Ghana; Gã of Accra city; and Bini of Benin.

KwaZulu-Natal Province in E South Africa, bordered by the Indian Ocean and the Drakensberg Mountains; the capital is Pietermaritzburg. It was created in 1994 from the Zulu homeland, KwaZulu, and the former province of NATAL. Industries: sugar, textiles, tanning and oil refining. Area: 92,180sq km (33,578sq mi). Pop. (1995 est.) 8,713,100.

Kyd, Thomas (1558–94) English dramatist who achieved popular success with *The Spanish Tragedy* (c.1589). Kyd was a member of the literary circles of his day, associating with MARLOWE. In 1593 he was arrested for treasonable activities.

Kyōto City on W central Honshū Island, Japan; capital of Kyōto prefecture. Founded in the 6th century, it was the capital of Japan for over 1,000 years. Industries: porcelain, lacquerware, textiles, precision tools. Pop. (1993) 1,395,000.

Kyrgyz Turko-Mongolian people who inhabit the Republic of KYRGYZSTAN in central Asia. They are Muslim nomadic pastoralists who began to settle in the TIAN SHAN region of KYRGYZSTAN in the 7th century. They were colonized by the Russians during the 19th century. After fighting the BOLSHEVIKS in the civil war (1917–21), many Kyrgyz perished in the ensuing famine.

Kyrgyzstan The Republic of Kyrgyzstan, or Kirghizia as it is also known, is a land-locked country between China, Tajikistan, Uzbekistan and Kazakstan; the capital is BISHKEK. **Land and climate** A mountainous country, the highest mountain, Pik Pobedy, reaches 7,439m (24,406ft) above sea level. The largest of the country's many lakes is Ozero (Lake) Issyk-Kul in the NE. The lowlands of Kyrgyzstan have warm summers and cold winters, but in the mountains, January temperatures plummet to $-28°C$ ($-18°F$). Mountain grassland is the dominant vegetation, with woodland covering only a small area, mainly in the lower valleys. Less than 10% of the land is used for crops. **Economy** Agriculture, especially livestock rearing, is the chief activity. The chief products include cotton, eggs, fruits, grain, tobacco, vegetables and wool. Industries are concentrated around Bishkek, and manufactures include machinery, processed food, metals and textiles. Exports include wool, chemicals, cotton and metals. **History** The area that is now Kyrgyzstan was populated in ancient times by nomadic herders. MONGOL armies conquered the region in the early 13th century. Islam was introduced in the 17th century. China gained control of the area in the mid-18th century, but in 1876 Kyrgyzstan became a province of Russia. In 1916 Russia put down a rebellion and many local people fled to China. In 1922, when the Soviet Union was formed, Kyrgyzstan became an autonomous region. In 1936 it became a Soviet Socialist Republic. Under communism, nomads were forced to live on government-run farms. **Politics** In 1991, following the breakup of the Soviet Union, Kyrgyzstan became an independent country. The Communist Party was dissolved and the government introduced reforms aimed at increasing free enterprise. A constitution was adopted in 1994 and parliamentary and presidential elections were held in 1995.

Kyūshū Island in S Japan; the southernmost of the four principal Japanese islands. The terrain is mountainous, and the irregular coastline has many natural harbours. It is the most densely populated of the Japanese islands. The chief port is NAGASAKI. Products: rice, tea, tobacco, fruit, soya beans. Industries: mining, fishing, timber, textiles, porcelain, metals, machinery. Area: 42,149sq km (16,274sq mi). Pop. (1992 est.) 13,314,000.

Kyzyl Kum (Kizil Kum) Desert of central Asia, in Uzbekistan and S Kazakstan, between the Amudarya and Syrdarya rivers. Cotton and rice are grown in the irrigated river valleys and karakul sheep are raised by tribespeople. Area: c.230,000sq km (89,000sq mi).

KYRGYZSTAN
AREA: 198,520sq km (76,640sq mi)
POPULATION: 4,568,000
CAPITAL (POPULATION): Bishkek (641,400)
GOVERNMENT: Multiparty republic
ETHNIC GROUPS: Kirghiz 52%, Russian 22%, Uzbek 13%, German 2%, Tatar 2%
LANGUAGES: Kirghiz
RELIGIONS: Islam
CURRENCY: Som

L/l can be traced to the Semitic letter lamedh, *which passed into Greek as* lambda. *It became slightly modified in the Roman alphabet and in this form has passed into English.*

labour In childbirth, stages in the delivery of the FETUS at the end of pregnancy. In the first stage, contractions of the UTERUS begin and the CERVIX dilates. In the second stage, the contractions strengthen and the baby is propelled through the birth canal. The third and final stage is the expulsion of the PLACENTA and fetal membranes.

Labour Party Social democratic political party, traditionally closely linked with the trade-union movement. There are Labour Parties in many countries, including Australia, Britain, Canada, Israel and New Zealand. The first British socialist parties, founded in the 1880s, united in the Independent Labour Party (ILP) in 1893, whose president was Keir HARDIE. The ILP created the Labour Representation Committee in 1900, which was renamed the Labour Party in 1906. Labour formed a brief minority government in 1924 under Ramsay MACDONALD and again in 1929–31, but following a coalition with the Liberals in 1931, the party was split and defeated at the polls. Its leader, Clement ATTLEE, was deputy prime minister from 1942, and prime minister (1945–51). Labour won the general election of 1964 under Harold WILSON and continued in power until 1970. From 1974–79 it was in office, mostly as a minority administration. Subsequent leaders were Neil Kinnock (1983–92), John SMITH (1992–94) and Tony BLAIR, who, under the slogan of "New Labour", moved the party markedly to the right, winning the 1997 election.

Labrador Mainland part of NEWFOUNDLAND province, E Canada, bordered W and S by Quebec and E by the Atlantic Ocean. The coast was visited by John CABOT in 1498. It passed to Britain under the Treaty of Paris (1736). Between 1809 and 1827 the boundaries between Newfoundland and Quebec were under dispute. In 1949 Labrador became part of Canada. It is mountainous with an indented coastline. The inland granite plateau is forested, with many lakes and rivers. Industries: timber, fishing, iron ore mining, hydroelectric power. Area: 292,220sq km (112,826sq mi).

labyrinth In architecture, an intricate structure of chambers and passages, generally constructed with the object of confusing anyone within it. In Greek mythology, MINOS had a labyrinth built by DAEDALUS to confine the MINOTAUR.

lac An insect and the sticky substance it secretes on to twigs; the deposit is harvested in Asia for use in shellac and red lac dye. Species *Laccifer lacca*.

lacewing Any of numerous species of neuropteran insects, especially members of the families Chrysopidae and Hemerobiidae, which are found worldwide. Common green lacewings have a slender greenish body, long antennae and two pairs of delicate, lacy, veined wings.

lachrymal gland Organ that produces tears. It is located in the orbital cavity and is controlled by autonomic nerves. It produces slightly germicidal tears that flow through ducts to the surface of the eye to lubricate it.

Laclos, Pierre (Ambroise François) Choderlos de (1741–1803) French novelist and general. His one important work, *Les Liaisons Dangereuses* (1782), caused a sensation and was only belatedly recognized as a great work.

lacquer Varnish used for ornamental or protective coatings; it forms a film by loss of solvent through evaporation. Lacquer is usually composed of a cellulose derivative, such as cellulose nitrate, in combination with a resin.

lacrosse Ball game that originated among the Iroquois Native Americans of Canada and the USA. It is played on field by teams of 10 male or 12 female players. They carry sticks that have a thonged meshwork head like a flexible scoop. The ball may be conveyed, passed or hit with the stick, or kicked, but only the goalkeepers are allowed to handle it.

lactation Secretion of milk to feed the young. In pregnant women, HORMONES induce the breasts to enlarge, and prolactin (a pituitary hormone) stimulates breast cells to begin secreting milk. The milk appears in the breast immediately after the birth of the baby. Its flow is stimulated by suckling, which, in turn, triggers the release of oxytocin, which controls the propulsion of milk out of the breast.

lactic acid Colourless organic acid (2-hydroxy-propanoic acid, $CH_3CHOHCOOH$) formed from LACTOSE by the action of bacteria. It is also produced in muscles when ANAEROBIC respiration occurs, causing muscle fatigue. Lactic acid is used in foods and beverages, in tanning, dyeing, and adhesive manufacture. Properties: r.d. 1.206; m.p. 18°C (64.4°F); b.p. 122°C (251.6°F).

lactose (milk sugar) Disaccharide present in milk, made up of a molecule of GLUCOSE linked to a molecule of galactose. It is important in cheesemaking: lactic bacteria turn it into LACTIC ACID, thus souring the milk and producing cheese curd.

Ladoga (Rus. *Ladozhskoye Ozero*, Finnish, *Laatokka*) Europe's largest lake, in NW Russia, near the Finnish border. It is drained by the River Neva. Area: 17,678sq km (6,826sq mi).

Lady Day Christian feast marking Gabriel's ANNUNCIATION to the Virgin MARY (often referred to as "Our Lady"), traditionally celebrated on 25 March. Before 1753, Lady Day was the beginning of the legal year in England and Wales; it is still one of the financial year's quarter days.

Lafayette, Marie Joseph Gilbert de Motier, Marquis de (1757–1834) French general who fought for the colonists in the AMERICAN REVOLU-

TION. Returning to France, he became a member of the National Assembly during the FRENCH REVOLUTION. In 1791 he lost popular support by ordering his troops to fire on a riotous crowd; he deserted to the Austrians in 1792. He played a symbolic role in the JULY REVOLUTION (1830) in support of Louis Philippe.

La Fontaine, Jean de (1621–95) French poet. His *Fables choisies, mises en vers* (1668–94) consists of 12 books featuring some 240 fables. He was elected to the Académie Française in 1683.

Lagerkvist, Pär Fabian (1891–1974) Swedish author. His works include *Anguish* (1916) and *The Hangman* (1933). International recognition came with *The Dwarf* (1944) and *Barabbas* (1950). In 1951 he was awarded the Nobel Prize in literature.

Lagerlöf, Selma (1858–1940) Swedish novelist. Her greatest novel, *Jerusalem* (1901), was inspired by a visit to Palestine. In 1909 she became the first Swedish writer to be awarded the Nobel Prize in literature.

lagoon Shallow stretch of seawater protected from waves and tides by a strip of land or coral.

Lagos Largest city and chief port of Nigeria, in the S of the country, on the Gulf of Guinea. Lagos grew as a YORUBA settlement from the 17th–19th centuries, coming under British control in 1861. It became the capital of independent Nigeria in 1960, but was replaced by ABUJA in 1982. Industries: brewing, ship repairing, textiles, crafts. Pop. (1992) 1,347,000.

Lagrange, Joseph Louis (1736–1813) French mathematician. He created the calculus of variations, devised a mathematical analysis of perturbations in gravity, and made contributions in many other areas. He wrote *Analytical Mechanics* (1788).

Lagrangian points Five points at which a celestial body can remain in a position of equilibrium with respect to two much more massive bodies orbiting each other.

Lahore City on the River Ravi, NE Pakistan; capital of Punjab province and Pakistan's second-largest city. An important city during the Ghazni and Ghuri sultanates of the 12th–13th centuries, it was used as a royal residence under the MOGUL EMPIRE. It was part of the Sikh kingdom from 1767 and passed to the British in 1849. From 1955–70 it was capital of West Pakistan. It is an important commercial and industrial centre. Industries: iron, steel, textiles, chemicals, rubber, leather, carpets, gold and silver jewellery. Pop. 2,953,000.

Laing, R.D. (Ronald David) (1927–1989) Scottish psychiatrist. He was an exponent of existential psychology and produced radical work on the nature of schizophrenia. He believed that the mentally ill are not necessarily maladapted: a psychotic disorder may be a reasonable reaction to the stresses of the world and of difficult family relationships.

laissez-faire 19th-century economic doctrine. In reaction to MERCANTILISM, the proponents of laissez-faire adopted Adam SMITH's argument that trade and industry would best serve the interests of all if government interference was reduced to a minimum, so that market forces would be allowed to determine production, prices and wages.

lake Inland body of water, generally of considerable size and too deep to have rooted vegetation completely covering the surface.

Lake District Region of Cumbria, NW England, containing the principal English lakes. Its spectacular mountain and lakeland scenery and its literary associations make it a major tourist attraction. Among its 15 lakes are Derwent Water, Grasmere, Buttermere and WINDERMERE. The highest point is SCAFELL PIKE at 978m (3,210ft). Area: 2,243sq km (866sq mi).

Lake Poets Three English poets who lived in the Lake District *c.*1800: William WORDSWORTH (1770–1850), Samuel Taylor COLERIDGE (1772–1834) and Robert SOUTHEY (1774–1843).

Lakshmi (Padma or Sita) In Hindu mythology, the lotus goddess, wife of VISHNU, who existed at the beginning of creation rising from the ocean borne by a lotus. Lakshmi was the goddess of beauty and youth, and was also worshipped as goddess of wealth and good fortune.

Lalique, René (1860–1945) French jewellery designer whose work significantly contributed to the ART NOUVEAU movement.

Lamaism *See* TIBETAN BUDDHISM

Lamarck, Jean-Baptiste Pierre Antoine de Monet, Chevalier de (1744–1829) French biologist. His theories of EVOLUTION, according to which acquired characteristics are inherited by offspring, influenced evolutionary thought throughout the 19th century, until disproved by DARWIN.

Lamb, Charles (1775–1834) British writer. He is best known for his essays, most famously collected as *The Essays of Elia* (1820–23; 1833). His children's books include *Tales from Shakespeare* (1807), on which he collaborated with his sister, Mary (1764–1847).

Lamentations Old Testament book bewailing the destruction of JERUSALEM and the great TEMPLE there in 587 or 586 BC; it is commonly attributed to the author of the Book of JEREMIAH.

Lammas Christian festival of thanksgiving for the harvest celebrated on 1 August in medieval England. It was originally one of the QUARTER DAYS.

Lamming, George (1927–) Caribbean novelist and poet. His native Barbados is the background to his first novel *In The Castle of My Skin* (1953), while *The Emigrants* (1954) describes the problems facing West Indians in England, where he settled in the 1950s. Later novels include *Water with Berries* (1971) and *Natives of My Person* (1972).

lamprey Eel-like, jawless vertebrate found in marine and freshwaters on both sides of the Atlantic and in the Great Lakes of North America. It feeds by attaching its mouth to fish and sucking blood. Length: to 91cm (3ft). Family Petromyzondiae.

Lancashire County in NW England, bordered by

Cumbria (N), North and West Yorkshire (E), Greater Manchester and Merseyside (S), and the Irish Sea (W); the county town is Preston. It was occupied in Roman times and later formed part of an Anglo-Saxon kingdom. From the 16th century, textile manufacturing became important. In the 20th century, cotton and its other traditional industry, coal, sharply declined. It is drained by the rivers Lune and Ribble and its lowland regions are predominantly agricultural. Area: 3,064sq km (1,183sq mi). Pop. (1994) 1,424,000.

Lancaster, Burt (1913–94) US film actor and producer. A former circus acrobat, he made his first film, *The Killers*, in 1946. He played a wide range of roles in films such as *Elmer Gantry* (1960), *Bird Man of Alcatraz* (1962), *The Leopard* (1963) and *Atlantic City* (1980).

Lancaster, Duchy of English estate first given by HENRY III to his son, Edmund, in 1265. The revenues from the duchy passed permanently to the crown in 1399, with the accession of the Lancastrian king HENRY IV.

Lancaster, House of English royal dynasty. The first earl of Lancaster was Edmund "Crouchback" (1245–96), son of HENRY III. In 1361 the Lancastrian title and lands passed to JOHN OF GAUNT via his wife. Their son became HENRY IV in 1399. During the Wars of the ROSES in the 15th century, the rival royal houses of Lancaster and York, both PLANTAGENETS, contended for the crown.

Lancelot of the Lake In Arthurian legend, father of Galahad and one of the most famous knights; he is portrayed as the lover of Guinevere, wife of King ARTHUR.

Landau, Lev Davidovich (1908–68) Soviet physicist. In 1927 he proposed a concept for energy called the density matrix, later used extensively in QUANTUM MECHANICS. He originated the theory that underlies the superfluid behaviour of liquid HELIUM. In 1962 he received the Nobel Prize for physics for his research into condensed matter.

Landor, Walter Savage (1775–1864) British poet and writer. His works include *Gebir: a Poem in Seven Books* (1798) and *Heroic Idylls* (1863), but it is for his prose dialogues, *Imaginary Conversations of Literary Men and Statesmen* (1824–29), that he is chiefly remembered.

landscape gardening Arranging gardens to produce certain effects. Broadly, there are two main traditions: the Sino-English, with its retention of the informality of nature; and the Franco-Italian, with its geometric patterns in which nature is trimmed to art.

landscape painting Art of portraying natural scenery. While landscape painting was central to the art of the East, especially China, the West did not recognize it as a separate genre until the 16th century. Landscape painting came into full flower in 17th-century Holland; Jacob van RUISDAEL is still regarded as the greatest Dutch landscape painter. A different tradition developed in Italy, with the work of Annibale Carracci. In the 19th century, romantic landscapes were created by painters such as FRIEDRICH in Germany and TURNER in Britain, as well as a number of North American artists. COROT and CONSTABLE introduced a more naturalistic approach, which led to the popularity that landscape achieved through IMPRESSIONISM.

Landseer, Sir Edwin Henry (1802–73) British painter and sculptor. He achieved popularity with his sentimental paintings of animals, such as the stag in *Monarch of the Glen* (1851) and the dogs in *Dignity and Impudence* (1839). His best-known sculptures are the lions in Trafalgar Square.

Landsteiner, Karl (1868–1943) US pathologist, b. Vienna. He discovered the four different BLOOD GROUPS. He won the 1930 Nobel Prize for physiology or medicine. In 1940, in collaboration with A. S. Wiener, he identified the rhesus (Rh) factor .

Lang, Fritz (1890–1976) Austrian film director and writer. His first film as a director was *Halbblut* (1919). His best-known works include *Mabuse the Gambler* (1922), *Metropolis* (1927) and *M* (1931). He later moved to Hollywood, where he directed *Fury* (1936), his most admired US film.

Lange, Dorothea (1895–1965) US photographer. Her portraits of urban poor and migrant labourers in California during the GREAT DEPRESSION, and her images of rural America taken for the Farm Security Administration (1935–42), are classics of documentary photography.

Langland, William (1331–99) English poet. His poem *Piers Plowman* is considered one of the most important works of medieval literature.

Langley, Samuel Pierpont (1834–1906) US astronomer who showed that mechanical flight was possible. He did this by building large steam-powered model aircraft in 1896.

language System of human communication. Although there are more than 4,000 different languages, they have many characteristics in common. Almost every human language uses a fundamentally similar grammatical structure, or syntax, even though the languages may not be linked in vocabulary or origin. Families of languages have been constructed, such as the INDO-EUROPEAN family, but their composition and origins are the subject of continuing debate. Historical studies of language are undertaken by the disciplines of ETYMOLOGY and philology. LINGUISTICS as a discipline usually addresses itself to contemporary language.

Languedoc-Roussillon Region of S France, extending from the Rhône valley to the foothills of the Pyrenees; the capital is MONTPELLIER. Languedoc was originally settled by the Romans. It later became part of the CAROLINGIAN empire, before passing to the French crown in 1271. Languedoc-Roussillon is one of the world's major wine-producing regions. Area: 27,736sq km (10,706sq mi). Pop. (1990) 1,926,514.

langur Any of about 15 species of medium to large MONKEYS of SE Asia and the East Indies.

They are slender, with long hands and tails. Gregarious tree dwellers, they are active by day and are found from sea-level to snowy Himalayan slopes up to an elevation of 4,000m (13,000ft). Length: 43–78cm (17–31in). Family Cercopithecidae; genus *Presbytis*.

lantern fish Any of numerous species of marine fish found in Atlantic and Mediterranean waters, especially *Diaphus rafinesquiei*. It is identified by light organs along its sides, and is found in deep water during the day and near the surface at night. Length: 7.5cm (3in). Family Myctophidae.

lanthanide series (lanthanide elements, rare-earth metals) Series of 15 rare metallic elements with atomic numbers from 57–71. They are lanthanum (sometimes not considered a member), cerium, praseodymium, neodymium, promethium, samarium, europium, gadolinium, terbium, dysprosium, holmium, erbium, thulium, ytterbium and lutetium. Their properties are similar and resemble those of lanthanum, from which the series takes its name. The shiny metals occur in monazite and other rare minerals and are placed in group III of the periodic table.

lanthanum Silvery-white metallic element (symbol La) of the LANTHANIDE SERIES, first identified in 1839. Its chief ores are monazite and bastnasite. Malleable and ductile, it is used as a catalyst in cracking crude oil, in alloys and to manufacture optical glasses. Properties: at.no.57; r.a.m. 138.9055; r.d. 6.17; m.p. 920°C (1,688°F); b.p. 3,454°C (6,249°F); most common isotope La^{139} (99.91%).

Laos Land-locked republic in Southeast Asia; the capital is VIENTIANE. **Land and climate** Mountains and high plateaus cover most of Laos. The highest point is Mount Bia, at 2,817m (9,242ft), in central Laos. Most people live on the plains bordering the River MEKONG and its tributaries. Laos has a tropical monsoon climate, with dry, sunny winters. **Economy** Laos is one of the world's poorest countries: the average annual income is only US$290. Agriculture employs *c.*76% of the workforce and accounts for 60% of GDP. Rice is the main crop; timber and coffee are exported. Hydroelectricity is produced at power stations along the Mekong and exported to Thailand. The "Golden Triangle", on the border with Cambodia

and Burma, is the centre for the illegal production of opium. In 1986 Laos began to introduce liberal economic reforms, including the encouragement of private enterprise. Inflation has rapidly reduced and in 1995 the economy grew by 8%. **History** In 1353 Fa Ngoun founded the kingdom of Lan Xang. In 1707 the kingdom divided into the N kingdom of Luang Prabang and the S kingdom of Vientiane. In the early 19th century the kingdoms were controlled by Siam. In 1893 Siam deferred to French power and Laos was ruled as part of French INDOCHINA. In the aftermath of World War 2, Laos gained increasing self-rule and in 1947 became a semi-autonomous constitutional monarchy. In 1953 Laos achieved independence, but was immediately plunged into civil war. The communist Patriotic Front (Pathet Lao) controlled most of N Laos, and royalist forces controlled Vientiane. The North Vietnamese use of the Ho Chi Minh Trail through Laos as a military supply line saw US bombardment of E Laos, and US military and financial support to the Laotian government against the Pathet Lao. By 1974 the Pathet Lao had secured most of Laos. The victory of the Viet Cong in the VIETNAM WAR enabled the final victory of Pathet Lao. The king abdicated and a democratic republic was proclaimed. The 1991 constitution confirmed the Lao People's Revolutionary Party (LPRP) as the only legal political party. President Nouhak Phonmsavan was elected in 1992.

Lao Tzu (604–531 BC) (Laozi) Chinese philosopher, credited as the founder of TAOISM. Tradition says that he developed Taoism as a mystical reaction to the moral-political concerns of CONFUCIANISM. He is said to have been the author of *Tao Te Ching*, the sacred book of Taoism.

La Paz Administrative capital and largest city of Bolivia. Founded by the Spanish in 1548 on the site of an Inca village, it was one of the centres of revolt in the War of Independence (1809–24). Located at 3,600m (12,000ft) in the Andes, it is the world's highest capital city. Industries: chemicals, tanning, flour-milling, electrical equipment, textiles, brewing and distilling. Pop. (1992) 1,126,000.

Laplace, Pierre Simon, Marquis de (1749–1827) French astronomer and mathematician. He used probability theory to apply Newton's gravitational theory to the entire Solar System; this work was summarized in *Celestial Mechanics* (1798–1827). He also did fundamental work in the study of heat, magnetism and electricity.

Lapland Region in N Europe, lying almost entirely within the Arctic Circle and including N Norway, the northernmost parts of Sweden and Finland, and the W part of the Kola Peninsula of Russia. The land is mountainous in Norway and Sweden, but TUNDRA predominates in the NE. The S regions are forested. Industries: hydroelectricity, fishing, mining for iron ore, copper and nickel. Area: *c.*388,500sq km (150,000sq mi).

La Plata, Rio de *See* PLATA, RÍO DE LA

LAOS

AREA: 236,800sq km (91,428sq mi)
POPULATION: 4,469,000
CAPITAL (POPULATION): Vientiane (449,000)
GOVERNMENT: Single-party republic
ETHNIC GROUPS: Lao 67%, Mon-Khmer 17%, Tai 8%
LANGUAGES: Lao (official)
RELIGIONS: Buddhism 58%, traditional beliefs 34%, Christianity 2%, Islam 1%
CURRENCY: Kip = 100 at

lapwing (peewit) Any of several species of birds, especially the Eurasian lapwing, *Vanellus vanellus*, a wading bird with a conspicuous crest. It commonly nests in open agricultural land and defends its young by luring predators away, feigning a broken wing. Length: 30cm (12in). Family Charadriidae.

Lara, Brian Charles (1969–) West Indian cricketer, b. Trinidad. He was captain of Trinidad at the age of 20 and was first selected for the West Indies in 1990. In 1994, as a member of the Warwickshire English county team, he achieved a world first-class record score of 501 (not out) against Durham.

lark Any of several small birds, known for their melodious songs. Most common in Europe are the woodlark (*Lullula arborea*), skylark (*Alauda arvensis*) and shorelark (*Eremophila alpestris*). Length: to 18cm (7in). Family Alaudidae.

Larkin, Philip Arthur (1922–85) British poet. His first collection was *The North Ship* (1945), but he found his characteristic voice with *The Less Deceived* (1955). Other works include *The Whitsun Weddings* (1964) and *High Windows* (1974).

larkspur *See* DELPHINIUM

La Rochefoucauld, François, Duc de (1613–80) French writer renowned for maxims and epigrams. He was involved in an intrigue against Cardinal RICHELIEU and took part in the FRONDES revolts (1648–53). His best-known work is *Réflexions ou Sentences et Maximes Morales* (1665).

La Rochelle Seaport on the Bay of Biscay, w France; capital of Charente-Maritime *département*. An English possession during the 12th–13th centuries, it changed hands several times during the HUNDRED YEARS WAR. In the 16th century it became a HUGUENOT stronghold, but it capitulated to the forces of Cardinal RICHELIEU in 1628. Industries: shipbuilding, oil refining, sawmilling, fish-canning, fertilizers, plastics. Pop. (1990) 71,094.

Larousse, Pierre (1817–75) French lexicographer. He founded the publishing firm Larousse, which produced *The Great Universal Dictionary of the 19th Century* (1866–76), the first of a famous series of dictionaries and encyclopedias.

larva Developmental stage in the life cycle of many invertebrates and some other animals. A common life cycle, typified by the BUTTERFLY, is egg, larva, PUPA, adult. The larva fends for itself and is mobile, but is distinctly different in form from the sexually mature adult. It metamorphoses (or pupates) to become an adult.

larynx (voice box) Triangular cavity located between the trachea (windpipe) and the root of the tongue. Inside it are the vocal cords. These are thin bands of elastic tissue, which vibrate when outgoing air passes over them, setting up resonant waves that are changed into sound by the action of throat muscles and the shape of the mouth.

La Salle, René-Robert Cavelier, Sieur de (1643–87) French explorer of North America. He explored the Great Lakes area and was governor of Fort Frontenac on Lake Ontario (1675). He followed the Mississippi to its mouth (1682), naming the land Louisiana and claiming it for France.

La Scala (Teatro alla Scala) One of the world's greatest opera houses, in Milan, Italy. Designed by Giuseppe Piermarini, it opened in 1776 and has been the scene of many famous premieres, including Verdi's *Otello* and Puccini's *Madame Butterfly*.

Lascaux Complex of caves in the French Pyrenees, discovered in 1940. They contain examples of 13 different styles of PALAEOLITHIC wall paintings, depicting horses, ibex, stags and a reindeer. The caves were closed in 1963 in order to halt the deterioration of the paintings.

laser (acronym for **l**ight **a**mplification by **s**timulated **e**mission of **r**adiation) Optical MASER, source of a narrow beam of intense monochromatic light in the ultraviolet, visible or infrared region, in which all the waves are of the same wavelength and in step with one another. The source can be a solid, liquid or gas. It has applications in medicine, research, engineering, telecommunications and holography.

Laski, Harold Joseph (1893–1950) British political scientist. A prominent figure in the socialist FABIAN SOCIETY, he served on the national executive of the Labour Party (1937–49) and as party chairman (1945–46). As a lecturer and teacher, he influenced a number of people who later became leaders of newly independent third-world countries.

Lassa fever Acute viral disease, classified as a haemorrhagic fever. The virus, first detected in 1969, is spread by a species of rat found only in w Africa. It is characterized by internal bleeding, with fever, headache and muscle pain.

Last Supper (Lord's Supper) Final meal shared by JESUS CHRIST and his disciples in Jerusalem on or just before the Passover, during which Jesus instituted the Christian EUCHARIST. Jesus warned of his imminent betrayal, and blessed and shared bread and wine among them, telling them that these were his body and blood of the Covenant.

Las Vegas Largest city in Nevada, USA. It is a world-famous gambling and entertainment centre with over 13 million visitors per year. The Mormons established a colony on the site in 1855–57. The modern city began with the construction of a railway in 1905. Nevada legalized gambling in 1931 and the city grew rapidly. Its first big gambling casino opened in 1946. Pop. (1990) 258,295.

latent heat Heat absorbed or given out by a substance as it changes its phase at constant temperature. When ice melts, its temperature remains the same until it has been completely transformed into water; the heat necessary to do this is called the latent heat of fusion. Similarly the heat necessary to transform water into steam at constant temperature is called the latent heat of vaporization.

Lateran Councils Five ecumenical councils of the Western Church, held in the Lateran Palace in Rome. The first, held in 1123, confirmed the Concordat of WORMS of 1122. The second, in 1139, promulgated 30 decrees that, among other things, condemned simony and the marriage of the clergy. The third, in 1179, decreed that the pope was to be elected by a two-thirds majority of the College of Cardinals. The fourth council, in 1215, gave a definition of the doctrine of the EUCHARIST, officially using the term "TRANSUBSTANTIATION" for the first time. The fifth, in 1512–17, introduced some minor reforms in the wake of the Protestant REFORMATION.

Lateran Treaty (1929) Agreement between Italy and the VATICAN. The Italian government recognized the Vatican as an independent sovereign state with the pope as its temporal head, and the Vatican surrendered the Papal States and Rome. Roman Catholicism was affirmed as Italy's state religion.

latex Milky fluid produced by certain plants, the most important being that produced by the RUBBER TREE. It is used in paints, special papers and adhesives, and to make sponge rubbers. Synthetic rubber latexes are also produced.

Latin Language of ancient Rome, the Roman empire and of educated medieval European society. It belongs to the family of INDO-EUROPEAN LANGUAGES. Its earliest written records are inscriptions and legal formulas dating from the late 6th century BC. By the 3rd century BC, a literary form of Latin was evolving, which achieved its richest form between 70 BC and AD 18. Latin eventually broke up into numerous dialects, which formed the basis of the ROMANCE LANGUAGES. It remained the language of the church, science, medicine and law, and of education and most written transactions in Europe throughout the Middle Ages. It was still used in some scholarly and diplomatic circles in the 19th century, and Roman Catholic Church services were conducted in Latin until the 1960s.

Latin America Those parts of the Western Hemisphere (excluding French-speaking Canada) where the official or chief language is a ROMANCE LANGUAGE. It usually refers to Brazil (Portuguese), Haiti (French) and the 18 Spanish-speaking republics. It may include islands of the WEST INDIES where Romance languages are the mother tongue.

Latin literature Literature of ancient Rome. The earliest works date from the 3rd century BC and were imitations of Greek plays and epic poetry. The dramatist PLAUTUS wrote in a similar style in the early 2nd century BC. Latin literature reached its stylistic peak in the 1st century BC, with the prose of CICERO, Julius CAESAR and LIVY and the poetry of VIRGIL, HORACE and OVID. This so-called Golden Age ended soon after the death of AUGUSTUS in AD 14. The following century was noted for the writings of Seneca the Elder, TACITUS, PLINY THE ELDER and PETRONIUS. After c.100 AD, Latin literature went into a decline from which it was revived during the 4th century by the writings of Christian authors such as AUGUSTINE OF HIPPO.

latitude Distance N or S of the Equator, measured at an angle from the Earth's centre. All lines of latitude are parallel to the Equator, which is the zero line of latitude. The tropics of Cancer and Capri-

corn are 23.5° away from the Equator, and the Arctic and Antarctic circles are at 66.5°, which is 23.5° away from the poles.

La Tour, Georges de (1593–1652) French painter of religious and genre scenes. He is famous for his nocturnal scenes lit by a single candle. Examples of his work include *Christ and St Joseph in the Carpenter's Shop* (c.1645) and the *Lamentation over St Sebastian* (1645).

Latter Day Saints, Church of *See* MORMONS

Latter Day Saints, Reorganized Church of Jesus Christ of *See* MORMONS

Latvia Baltic republic in NW Europe; the capital is RIGA. **Land and climate** Latvia consists mainly of flat plains separated by low hills. Small lakes and peat bogs are common. Latvia's main river is the Daugava (Western Dvina). Moderate rainfall occurs throughout the year, with light snow in winter. Forests cover about 40% of the county. About 27% of the land is under crops, while 13% is used for grazing livestock. **Economy** In the 1990s Latvia faced problems in transforming its government-run economy into a free market one. The country lacks natural resources. Its industries are varied, with products including electronic goods, farm machinery, fertilizers, processed food, plastics, radios, vehicles and washing machines. Farm products include barley, dairy products, beef, oats, potatoes and rye. **History** The ancestors of most modern Latvians settled in the area about 2,000 years ago. Between the 9th and 11th centuries, the region was attacked by Vikings from the W and Russians from the E. In the 13th century, German invaders took over. From 1561 the area was partitioned between various groups, including Poles, Lithuanians and Swedes. In 1710 Peter the Great took Riga and, by the end of the 18th century, Latvia was under Russian rule. Nationalist movements developed in the 19th century and, just after the end of World War 1, Latvia declared itself independent. In 1939 Germany and the Soviet Union made a secret agreement to divide up parts of E Europe and, in 1940, Soviet troops invaded Latvia, which became part of the Soviet Union. **Politics** In the late 1980s, when reforms were being introduced in the Soviet Union,

LATVIA

AREA: 64,589sq km (24,938sq mi)

POPULATION: 2,632,000

CAPITAL (POPULATION): Riga (910,200)

GOVERNMENT: Multiparty republic

ETHNIC GROUPS: Latvian 53%, Russian 34%, Belorussian 4%, Ukrainian 3%, Polish 2%, Lithuanian, Jewish

LANGUAGES: Latvian (official)

RELIGIONS: Christianity (including Lutheran, Russian Orthodox and Roman Catholic)

CURRENCY: Lats = 10 santimi

Latvia's government relaxed communist laws, allowed press and religious freedom and made Latvian the official language. In 1990 it declared the country to be independent, an act that was finally recognized by the Soviet Union in September 1991. Latvia held its first free elections in 1993. Voting was limited to those who had been citizens of Latvia on 17 June 1940, and their descendants. This meant that about 34% of Latvian residents were unable to vote. In 1994 Latvia adopted a law restricting the naturalization of non-Latvians, including many Russian settlers. Latvia has been seeking to increase its contacts with the West and, in 1995, it joined the Council of Europe and formally applied to join the European Union. In 1997 the ruling coalition collapsed amid corruption allegations and a new government was appointed.

Laud, William (1573–1645) English cleric, Archbishop of Canterbury (1633–45) and religious adviser to CHARLES I. He imposed press censorship, enforced a policy regulating wages and prices, and sought to remove PURITANS from important positions in the church. His attempt to impose the English prayer book upon the Scots was one of the immediate causes of the English CIVIL WAR. Laud was impeached (1640) by the LONG PARLIAMENT.

Lauraceae Large family of flowering plants, mostly evergreen shrubs and trees, including LAUREL, CINNAMON and SASSAFRAS; it is found in warm and temperate regions worldwide. The flowers are generally green and are followed by berries.

laurel Evergreen shrubs and trees native to S Europe and cultivated in the USA. Included is the noble or bay laurel (*Laurus nobilis*) with leathery, oval leaves, yellowish flowers and purple berries. Height: 18–21m (60–70ft). Family LAURACEAE.

Lautrec, Henri Toulouse See TOULOUSE-LAUTREC, HENRI MARIE RAYMOND DE

lava Molten rock or MAGMA that reaches the Earth's surface and flows out through a volcanic vent in streams or sheets. There are three main types of lava: vesicular, such as pumice; glassy, such as obsidian; and even-grained.

Laval, Pierre (1883–1945) French statesman, prime minister (1931–32, 1935–36). His government fell as a result of the unpopular Hoare-Laval Pact, which approved the Italian conquest of Ethiopia. In 1940 he joined the VICHY GOVERNMENT, becoming its head under PÉTAIN. His capitulation to German demands was seen as treason by the FREE FRENCH and he was executed after the war.

Lavoisier, Antoine Laurent (1743–94) French chemist who founded modern chemistry. He demolished the PHLOGISTON theory (which said that phlogiston was lost during combustion) by demonstrating the function of oxygen in combustion. He named oxygen and hydrogen and showed how they combined to form water. In collaboration with Claude Berthollet, he published *Methods of Chemical Nomenclature* (1787), which laid down the modern method of naming substances.

Law, (Andrew) Bonar (1858–1923) British statesman, prime minister (1922–23), b. Canada. He entered Parliament in 1900 and in 1911 became the first leader of the Conservative Party to come from a manufacturing background. He was chancellor of the exchequer (1916–19), before becoming prime minister.

Law, John (1671–1729) French financier, b. Scotland. His banking and stock-market schemes created a boom in France, where he founded a state bank, later named the Banque Générale, in 1716. Appointed controller-general of finance (1720), he merged all his diverse financial interests into one organization. Within months a dip in confidence caused heavy selling and the whole scheme collapsed. Law died in exile, a bankrupt.

law System of rules governing human society, enforced by punishments specified by society itself. The major systems of law are COMMON LAW, ROMAN LAW and EQUITY.

Law and the Prophets Two major divisions of the Old Testament. The Law, or Law of Moses, is the first five books of the Old Testament, known as the TORAH in Hebrew and the PENTATEUCH in Greek. The Prophets consists of several books, grouped differently in Jewish or Christian tradition. The groupings include: (a) Joshua, Judges, I and II Samuel and I and II Kings; (b) Isaiah, Jeremiah and Ezekiel; and (c) Hosea, Joel, Amos, Obadiah, Jonah, Micah, Nahum, Habakkuk, Zephaniah, Haggai, Zechariah and Malachi.

Lawrence, D.H. (David Herbert) (1885–1930) British novelist, short-story writer and poet. His novels include *Sons and Lovers* (1913), *Women in Love* (1920) and *Lady Chatterley's Lover* (privately published 1928). He also wrote numerous short stories, plays, essays and miscellaneous non-fiction

Lawrence, Ernest Orlando (1901–58) US physicist. In 1930 he built the first cyclotron, a subatomic particle ACCELERATOR. He developed larger cyclotrons and received the 1939 Nobel Prize for physics. LAWRENCIUM was named after him.

Lawrence, T.E. (Thomas Edward) (1888–1935) (Lawrence of Arabia) British soldier. He joined the army in World War 1 and in 1916 became a leader of the Arab revolt against the Turks. He published his remarkable account of the Arab revolt, *The Seven Pillars of Wisdom*, in 1926.

lawrencium Radioactive metallic element (symbol Lr), one of the ACTINIDE SERIES. It was first made in 1961 by bombarding CALIFORNIUM with boron nuclei. Properties: at.no. 103; r.a.m. 262; most stable isotope Lr^{256} (half-life 27 seconds).

Law Society Either of two inclusive organizations of solicitors in Britain – the Law Society in England and Wales, and the Law Society of Scotland – as incorporated in 1831 by an Act of Parliament. Each Law Society regulates and enforces the standards by which solicitors operate. It administers legal aid to those entitled to it and retains a fund from which compensation may be made in the case of a solicitor's fraud or negligence.

Laxness, Halldór Kiljan (1902–) Icelandic novelist. He was awarded the 1955 Nobel Prize for literature for his novels about the fishing villages and farms of Iceland. His fiction includes *Independent People* (1934–35), *The Atom Station* (1948) and *Paradise Reclaimed* (1960).

Lazarus Either of two men mentioned in the New Testament. In John 11 Lazarus was the brother of Mary and Martha of Bethany. Four days after his death, Jesus miraculously restored him to life. In Luke 16 Lazarus is the poor man in Christ's parable about a beggar and a rich man.

L-dopa (levodopa) Naturally occurring amino acid used to relieve some symptoms of PARKINSON'S DISEASE.

Leadbelly (1888–1949) Popular name of US composer and blues singer Huddie LEDBETTER.

lead Metallic element (symbol Pb) of group IV of the periodic table, known from ancient times. Its chief ore is GALENA (lead sulphide), from which lead is obtained by roasting. Soft and malleable, it is used as a shield for x-rays and nuclear radiation, and in plumbing, batteries, cable sheaths and alloys such as pewter and solder. Chemically, lead is unreactive and a poor conductor of electricity. Properties: at.no. 82; r.a.m. 207.19; r.d. 11.35; m.p. 327.5°C (621.5°F); b.p. 1,740°C (3,164°F); most common isotope Pb^{208} (52.3%).

leaf Part of a plant, an organ that contains the green pigment CHLOROPHYLL and is involved in PHOTOSYNTHESIS and TRANSPIRATION. It usually consists of a blade and a stalk (petiole), which attaches it to a stem or twig. Most leaves are simple (undivided), but some are compound (divided into leaflets).

leaf insect Any of several species of flat, green insects that bear a resemblance to leaves and are found throughout tropical Asia. Order Phasmida; family Phylliidae. *See also* STICK INSECT.

League of Nations International organization, forerunner of the UNITED NATIONS (UN). Created as part of the Treaty of VERSAILLES (1919) ending World War 1, it was impaired by the refusal of the USA to participate. The threats to world peace from Germany, Italy and Japan caused the League to collapse in 1939. It was dissolved in 1946.

Leakey, Louis Seymour Bazett (1903–72) English archaeologist and anthropologist. He discovered fossils in East Africa that proved humans to be older than had been thought. In 1931 he began to research Olduvai Gorge in Tanzania. Working with his wife **Mary** (1913–96), he found animal fossils and tools. Mary Leakey continued working in East Africa, often with her son **Richard** (1944–), who became director of the National Museums of Kenya.

Lean, Sir David (1908–91) British film director, producer and scriptwriter. His early films include *In Which we Serve* (1942) and *Brief Encounter* (1945). Later works, such as *The Bridge on the*

River Kwai (1957), *Lawrence of Arabia* (1962), *Dr. Zhivago* (1965) and *Ryan's Daughter* (1970), were productions with meticulous historical detail. This style was epitomized by his last film, *A Passage to India* (1984).

Lear, Edward (1812–88) British poet, painter and draughtsman. He is famous for his tragi-comic nonsense verse. He invented such characters as the *Pobble Which Had No Nose* and the *Owl and the Pussycat*.

Leavis, F.R. (Frank Raymond) (1895–1978) British literary critic. His works of criticism include *The Great Tradition* (1948), *The Common Pursuit* (1952) and *D.H. Lawrence, Novelist* (1955). His views on society and education are expounded in *Mass Civilization and Minority Culture* (1933) and *Education and the University* (1943).

Lebanon Republic in SW Asia, the capital is BEIRUT. **Land and climate** Lebanon lies on the E shores of the Mediterranean Sea. A narrow coastal plain contains Beirut and the second-largest city of TRIPOLI. Behind the plain are the rugged Lebanese Mountains. The Anti-Lebanon Mountains form the E border with Syria. Between the two ranges is the Bekaa Valley, a fertile farming area. Coastal regions have a typical Mediterranean climate, with hot, dry summers and mild, wet winters. Onshore winds bring heavy winter rain to the W slopes of the mountains. **Economy** Lebanon is an historically important commerce and trading centre for the Middle East. The civil war devastated its valuable tourism, trade and financial sectors. Manufacturing was also badly damaged. Manufactures include chemicals, electrical goods and textiles. Farm products include fruits, vegetables and sugar beet. **History and politics** In *c.*3000 BC Canaanites founded the city of TYRE and established what became known as PHOENICIA. In 332 Alexander the Great conquered the territory. In 64 BC the region fell to the Romans. Christianity was introduced in AD 325. Arab conquest in the 7th century saw the introduction of Islam, but Christian MARONITES predominated. Lebanon was one of the principal battlefields of the CRUSADES (1100–1300). In 1516 Lebanon became part of the Ottoman empire, and Turkish rule continued until World War 1. After the

---

LEBANON
AREA: 10,400sq km (4,015sq mi)
POPULATION: 2,838,000
CAPITAL (POPULATION): Beirut (1,500,000)
GOVERNMENT: Multiparty republic
ETHNIC GROUPS: Arab (Lebanese 80%, Palestinian 12%), Armenian 5%, Syrian, Kurdish
LANGUAGES: Arabic (official)
RELIGIONS: Islam 58%, Christianity 27%, Druse
CURRENCY: Lebanese pound = 100 piastres

war Lebanon and Syria were mandated to France. In 1926 Lebanon gained a republican constitution. In 1945 it became fully independent. During the 1950s Lebanon's economy grew rapidly and it pursued a pro-Western foreign policy. This infuriated the Arab population and US troops were called in to crush a 1958 rebellion. Lebanon did not participate in the 1967 or 1973 ARAB-ISRAELI WARS. In 1975 civil war broke out between Maronite, SUNNI, SHIITE and DRUZE militias. In 1976 Syrian troops imposed a fragile cease-fire. In 1978 Israel invaded S Lebanon to destroy Palestinian bases. UN peacekeeping forces were called in to separate the factions. In 1982 Israel launched a full-scale attack on Lebanon. The 1983 deployment of US and European troops in Beirut was met by a terrorist bombing campaign. Multinational forces left in 1984, and Israeli troops withdrew to a buffer zone in S Lebanon. In 1987 Syrian troops moved into Beirut to quell disturbances. In 1990 an uneasy truce was called and the government began to disarm the militias. Syria maintained troops in West Beirut and the Bekaa Valley. The Syrian-backed HEZBOLLAH and the Israeli-backed South Lebanon Army (SLA) continued to operate in S Lebanon. In 1996 Israel launched attacks on Hezbollah guerrilla bases in S Lebanon, in retaliation for terrorist strikes in Israel. Hostilities continued in 1997.

Lebed, Aleksander Ivanovich (1950–) Russian general and politician. As commander of the Tula Airborne Troops Division, he stood guard at the Supreme Soviet building during the attempted coup of August 1991. In 1995 Lebed moved into politics, standing against YELTSIN in the 1996 presidential elections. Lebed's level of support was such that Yeltsin offered him a government position in order to win his votes. He was appointed national security adviser but sacked later that year.

LeBrun, Charles (1619–90) French painter. He painted religious, mythological and historical subjects. As chief painter to LOUIS XIV, he created the Galerie d'Apollon at the Louvre (1661) and designed much of the interior of VERSAILLES, including the Galerie des Glaces (1679–84). He became director of the ACADÉMIE FRANÇAISE and the GOBELINS tapestry factory in 1663.

Le Carré, John British writer. His first novel was *Call for the Dead* (1961), which introduced George Smiley, his best-known character. Among his complex and hugely popular stories of espionage are *The Spy Who Came in from the Cold* (1963), *A Small Town in Germany* (1968), *Tinker, Tailor, Soldier, Spy* (1974) and *The Russia House* (1989).

Leclanché cell Electric cell invented by Georges Leclanché, *c*.1865. Its ANODE was a zinc rod and its CATHODE a carbon plate surrounded by packed manganese dioxide. These electrodes were dipped into a solution of ammonium and zinc chlorides. It is the basis of the dry cell or BATTERY.

Le Corbusier (1887–1963) French architect, b. Switzerland as Charles Édouard Jeanneret. His early work exploited the qualities of reinforced concrete in cube-like forms. The style of his Unité d'Habitation, Marseilles (1946–52), was widely adopted for modern mass housing. Later, he evolved a more poetic style, of which the highly sculptural chapel of Notre-Dame-du-Haut at Ronchamp (1955) is the finest example. In the 1950s he laid out the town of Chandigarh, India, and built its supreme courts. His last major work was the Visual Arts Center at Harvard (Boston, Massachusetts, USA, 1963).

Leda In Greek mythology, Queen of Sparta, wife of Tyndareus and mother of CLYTEMNESTRA. She was also the mother of CASTOR AND POLLUX and HELEN by ZEUS. The myth reveals that Zeus came to her in the form of a swan.

Ledbetter, Huddie (1888–1949) ("Leadbelly") US composer and blues singer. He is known as the composer of many classic blues songs including *Goodnight Irene*, *The Midnight Special* and *Rock Island Line*.

Lee, Laurie (1914–97) British author and poet. His collections of poetry include *The Sun My Monument* (1944) and *My Many-Coated Man* (1955). He is best known for his autobiography *Cider with Rosie* (US: *The Edge of Day*) (1959), and his accounts of travels in Spain during the Spanish Civil War, *As I Walked Out One Midsummer Morning* (1969) and *A Moment of War* (1991).

Lee, Robert E. (Edward) (1807–70) Commander of the Confederate forces in the American CIVIL WAR. He successfully defended Richmond and won the Second Battle of Bull Run. Though checked at Antietam, he defeated the Union forces at FREDERICKSBURG and Chancellorsville. His invasion of the North ended in decisive defeat at GETTYSBURG in July 1863. He was finally trapped by Ulysses S. GRANT, who accepted his surrender in April 1865.

Lee, Spike (1957–) US film director, writer and actor. His first feature, *She's Gotta Have It* (1986), was shot in black-and-white, and its unusual camerawork and witty script revealed a promising talent. *Do the Right Thing* (1989) is a bleak portrait of the problems of racial integration. Other films include *Malcolm X* (1992) and *Crooklyn* (1994).

leech Any of numerous species of freshwater, marine and terrestrial annelids found in tropical and temperate regions. Its tapered, ringed body is equipped with a sucking disc at each end. Many species live on the blood of animals. Length: 13–51mm (0.5–2in). Class Hirudinea.

Leeds City and county district on the River Aire, West Yorkshire, N England. Its woollen industry dates from the 14th century, but it was in the 18th–19th centuries that the city became famous for its cloth manufacture; it remains the centre of England's wholesale clothing trade. Other industries: aircraft components, textile machinery, engineering, chemicals, plastics, furniture, paper and printing. Pop. (1994) 529,000.

leek Biennial plant related to the onion; it originated in the Mediterranean region and is cultivated widely for culinary purposes. Family Liliaceae, species *Allium porrum*.

Lee Teng-hui (1923–) Chinese politician, president of Taiwan (1988–). A member of the ruling Nationalist Party (Kuomintang), he became mayor of Taipei in 1979, and vice president of the party (and of Taiwan) in 1984. He became president in 1988 and was largely responsible for the liberalization of Taiwan.

Leeuwenhoek, Anton van (1632–1723) Dutch scientist. He built simple microscopes with a single lens, which were so accurate that they had better magnifying powers than the compound microscopes of his day. He investigated micro-organisms and described various microscopic structures.

Leeward Islands Group of islands in the West Indies, comprising the N section of the Lesser Antilles; it includes the US and British Virgin Islands, Guadeloupe, Anguilla, Antigua and Barbuda, Montserrat, St Kitts-Nevis, and St Martin. Colonization began in the early 17th century. For the next 200 years control of the islands fluctuated with the changing imperial fortunes of Britain and France. The economy is based on agriculture and tourism. Major crops include fruits, sugar, cotton and coffee.

legal aid In Britain, system by which those below a certain income can receive free or subsidized legal representation or advice. In criminal cases it is paid for mainly from public funds; in civil cases its cost may be partly met from the costs awarded by the court. It was introduced in 1949, and is now covered by the Legal Aid and Advice Act, 1974.

Léger, Fernand (1881–1955) French painter. An influential member of the School of Paris, he evolved a form of CUBISM jokingly called "tubism" because of its emphasis on cylindrical, mechanical forms. He designed stage sets for theatre and ballet and also produced ceramics and stained glass.

legion Basic organizational unit of the Roman army until the fall of the empire in the West in the 5th century AD. During the great period of Rome's expansion, a legion was about 6,000 men strong, consisting mainly of heavy infantrymen (legionaries), with some light troops and cavalry in support.

legionnaire's disease Pneumonia-like lung disease caused by the bacterium *Legionella pneumophila*. It takes its name from the serious outbreak that occurred during a convention of the American Legion held in Philadelphia in 1976. The bacterium thrives in water and may be found in defective heating, ventilation and air-conditioning systems. It is inhaled in fine water droplets present in the air.

legislation *See* LAW

legislature Representative assembly whose primary function is the enactment of laws. Legislatures can be either unicameral or bicameral (composed of one or two chambers). In most democracies, including Britain, the "lower" or more directly elected chamber is the more power-

ful, and the "upper" chamber is filled by either government appointees or hereditary members. In the USA, however, the reverse is true, with the SENATE being constitutionally more powerful than the HOUSE OF REPRESENTATIVES, and both houses being elected.

legumes Members of the pea family of flowering plants, including many trees, shrubs, vines and herbs whose roots bear nodules that contain nitrogen-fixing bacteria. The fruit is typically a pod (legume) containing a row of seeds. Food species include the PEA, runner BEAN, SOYA BEAN, LENTIL, broad bean, kidney bean and haricot bean. *See also* NITROGEN CYCLE; NITROGEN FIXATION; ROOT NODULE

Lehár, Franz (1870–1948) Austrian composer, b. Hungary. From 1890 he travelled as a bandmaster in Austria. His first operetta, *Kukuschka*, was written in 1896. He composed more than 30 operettas, of which *The Merry Widow* (1905) is the most popular today.

Leibniz, Gottfried Wilhelm (1646–1716) German philosopher and mathematician. Leibniz made many practical inventions, including a calculating machine (1671). He published his discovery of differential and integral CALCULUS, which was made independently of Sir Isaac NEWTON. He created a rationalist form of metaphysics, according to which the universe comprises a hierarchy of constituents with God at the top asserting a divine plan. Major works include *New Essays Concerning Human Understanding* (1765) and *Monadology* (1898).

Leicester, Robert Dudley, Earl of (1532–88) English courtier. He was the favourite of Queen ELIZABETH I. Elizabeth projected his marriage to MARY, QUEEN OF SCOTS, who rejected him. Leicester unsuccessfully led an English force in the Revolt of the Netherlands against Spain in 1585–87.

Leicester City in central England; county town of Leicestershire. It was founded in the 1st century AD as a Roman town (Ratae Coritanorum). Leicester was conquered by the Danes in the 9th century. The city became famous for the manufacture of hosiery and footwear. Other industries: textiles, engineering. Pop. (1994) 297,000.

Leicestershire County in E central England; the county town is LEICESTER. The area is drained chiefly by the Soar and Wreak rivers. The uplands of the E are devoted to farming, and the W has more industry. Wheat, barley, sheep and dairy cattle are important, and the region is famous for its hosiery, Stilton cheese and Melton Mowbray meat pies. Area: 2,553sq km (986sq mi). Pop. (1994) 916,900.

Leif Ericsson (c.970–1020) Norse explorer. Son of ERIC THE RED, he sailed from Greenland in 1003 to investigate land in the west. Among the places he visited were Helluland (probably Baffin Island), Markland (Labrador) and VINLAND.

Leigh, Mike (1943–) Innovative English film director, playwright and screenwriter. His debut feature, *Bleak Moments* (1971), established his reputation for social realism. *High Hopes* (1988), *Life*

is Sweet (1990), *Naked* (1993) and *Secrets and Lies* (1995) have gained international recognition.

Leigh, Vivien (1913–67) British film and stage actress. She received an Academy Award for her performance as Scarlett O'Hara in *Gone With The Wind* (1939). She also received an Academy Award for her moving portrayal of Blanche du Bois in *A Streetcar Named Desire* (1951). She was married to Laurence OLIVIER from 1937 to 1960.

Leinster Province in E Republic of Ireland, comprising the counties of Carlow, Dublin, Kildare, Kilkenny, Laois, Longford, Louth, Meath, Offaly, Westmeath, Wexford and Wicklow. It is the most populous of Ireland's four provinces, and includes the most fertile farmland in the country. The major city is DUBLIN. Area: 19,635sq km (7,581sq mi). Pop. (1991) 1,860,949.

Leipzig City in E central Germany, at the confluence of the Pleisse, White Elster and Parthe rivers. Founded as a Slavic settlement in the 10th century, it became a commercial centre. It was the scene of the Battle of the Nations in 1813. Industries: printing, textiles, machinery, chemicals. Pop. (1993 est.) 494,200.

Leitrim County in Connacht province, N Republic of Ireland, narrowly bounded on the NW by Donegal Bay; the capital is Carrick-on-Shannon. Hilly in the N, undulating in the S, it is drained by the River Shannon and its tributaries. Although farming is the main occupation, the soil is not highly productive. Area 1,525sq km (589sq mi). Pop. (1991) 25,301.

Lely, Sir Peter van der Faes (1618–80) Dutch portrait painter, active in England. Principal Painter to CHARLES II, he is associated with the Restoration court. He established the tradition of the society portrait. His best-known paintings include two series, *The Windsor Beauties* and the *Admirals*.

Lemaître, Abbé Georges Édouard (1894–1966) Belgian astrophysicist who formulated the BIG BANG theory for the origin of the universe. His book *The Primeval Atom: An Essay on Cosmogony* (1950) describes his theory.

Le Mans City in NW France; capital of Sarthe *département*. It is world-famous as the venue of the Le Mans 24-hour race for sports cars. Pop. (1990) 145,502.

lemming Any of several species of RODENT, native to Arctic regions. They have brown fur, small ears and a short tail. They occasionally migrate in large numbers when numbers are high, and some species in Norway have been known to suffer great losses by drowning while doing so. Family Cricetidae.

Lemon Evergreen tree and its sour, yellow citrus fruit. Grown primarily in the USA and in subtropical regions, it is rarely eaten raw, but is used in cooking and in drinks. Height of tree: to 6m (20ft). Family Rutaceae; species *Citrus limon*

lemur Any of several small, primitive, mainly arboreal (tree-dwelling) and nocturnal, herbivorous PRIMATES that live in Madagascar. It resem-

bles a squirrel, but has grasping monkey-like hands. Family Lemuridae.

Lena River in E central Russia. It rises in the Baikal Mountains, flows generally N through the central Siberian uplands and empties through a wide delta into the Laptev Sea (part of the Arctic Ocean). Yakutsk is only major town on its course. Though navigable for 3,437km (2,135mi) of its 4,400km (2,730mi) route, it is frozen from early autumn to late spring.

Lenard, Philipp Eduard Anton (1862–1947) German physicist, b. Hungary. He was awarded the 1905 Nobel Prize in physics for his studies of CATHODE RAYS. His work was important in the development of ELECTRONICS and NUCLEAR PHYSICS. He also researched ultraviolet light and PHOSPHORESCENCE.

Lendl, Ivan (1960–) Czech tennis player. He led the world rankings list for a record 270 weeks, winning a total of seven Grand Slam singles titles. He is one of the greatest players never to have won Wimbledon.

lend-lease US programme of assistance during World War 2. The Lend-Lease Act was passed in March 1941, before the USA became a combatant. It empowered President Franklin ROOSEVELT to transfer military equipment to other countries in the US national interest. The first beneficiaries were Britain and China. The programme was later extended to other allies, notably the Soviet Union.

Lenin, Vladimir Ilyich (1870–1924) Russian revolutionary. He evolved a revolutionary doctrine, based mainly on MARXISM, in which he emphasized the need for a vanguard party to lead the revolution. In 1900 he went abroad, and founded what became the BOLSHEVIKS (1903). After the first part of the RUSSIAN REVOLUTION of 1917, he returned to Russia. He denounced the liberal republican government of KERENSKY and demanded armed revolt. After the Bolshevik revolution (November 1917), he became leader of the first Soviet government. He withdrew Russia from World War 1 and totally reorganized government and economy. He founded the third COMMUNIST INTERNATIONAL in 1919. His authority was unquestioned until he was crippled by a stroke in 1922.

Leningrad Former name for ST PETERSBURG

Lennon, John (1940–80) British singer and songwriter, a member of the BEATLES. He co-wrote the vast majority of the Beatles' songs with Paul McCARTNEY. A major figure in the peace movement, he married Yoko Ono in 1969. He was shot dead by Mark Chapman in New York.

Le Nôtre, André (1613–1700) French landscape gardener. He became royal gardener in 1637 and, from the 1650s, created formal gardens for some of France's grandest châteaux and palaces, such as VERSAILLES, Chantilly and the Tuileries in Paris.

lens Piece of transparent glass, plastic, quartz or organic matter, bounded by two surfaces, usually both spherical, that changes the direction of a light beam by REFRACTION. A convex lens bends light rays towards the lens axis. A concave lens bends rays away from the axis. The optical image may be right-way-up or inverted, real or virtual, and magnified or reduced in size.

Lent Period in the Christian liturgical year that precedes Easter. In the Western Churches it begins on Ash Wednesday and is 40 days long (Sundays are not included in the count of days); in the Eastern Church it lasts 80 days (neither Saturdays nor Sundays are reckoned as part of Lent). Lent is meant to be a time of fasting, abstinence and penitence in preparation for the remembrance of the crucifixion and resurrection of JESUS CHRIST.

lentil Annual plant of the pea family that grows in the Mediterranean region, SW Asia and N Africa. It has feather-like leaves and is cultivated for its nutritious seeds. Height: to 51cm (20in). Family Fabaceae/Leguminosae; species *Lens culinaris*.

Lenya, Lotte (c.1898–1981) Austrian singer and actress. She became famous in two notable BRECHT plays with musical scores by her husband Kurt WEILL, namely *The Threepenny Opera* (1928) and *The Rise and Fall of the City of Mahagonny* (1930). She emigrated to the USA in 1935.

Leo III (c.750–816) Pope (795–816). With the help of CHARLEMAGNE, Leo imposed his rule on Rome, and crowned Charlemagne emperor on Christmas Day, 800. This historically important act strengthened papal authority in Rome and led to recognition of the pope and emperor as religious and secular leaders of Western Christendom.

Leo X (1475–1521) Pope (1513–21), b. Giovanni de' Medici, son of Lorenzo de' MEDICI. He continued the artistic schemes of his predecessor, Julius II, and presided over the Fifth Lateran Council.

Leonardo da Vinci (1452–1519) Florentine painter, sculptor, architect, engineer and scientist. He was the founder of the High RENAISSANCE style. By the 1470s he had developed his characteristic style of painting figures who seem rapt in a mood of sweet melancholy. In c.1482 he moved to Milan where he worked on an altarpiece, the *Madonna of the Rocks*, and the portrait of Ludovico Sforza's mistress, *Lady with an Ermine*. He painted the *Last Supper* (1495–98) using a new mural technique. In 1499 he left for Florence, where from 1500–06 he created his finest paintings, including the *Mona Lisa* and the *Battle of Anghiari*. One of his last paintings is *St John the Baptist* (c.1515). In 1516 he went to work for Francis I at Amboise, France, where he lived in semi-retirement.

Leoncavallo, Ruggiero (1858–1919) Italian composer, mainly of operas. He worked as an accompanist and composer of music-hall songs. Of his operas, *I Pagliacci* (1892) alone has withstood the test of time.

Leone, Sergio (1921–89) Italian film director. He is known as the creator of the "spaghetti western". He made the "Man With No Name" trilogy of *A Fistful of Dollars* (1964), *For a Few Dollars More* (1965) and *The Good The Bad and The Ugly*

(1966). The epics *Once Upon a Time in the West* (1968) and *Once Upon a Time in America* (1984) were commercially unsuccessful but later reappraised as his masterworks.

leopard Solitary spotted big CAT found throughout Africa and S Asia, sometimes called a panther. It has a round head with a short nose, and a long, thin tail. The coat may be yellow and white with dark spots, or almost completely black, as in the black panther. A good climber and swimmer, it feeds on birds, monkeys, antelopes and cattle. Length: to 2.45m (8ft) including the tail; weight: to 90.6kg (200lb). Family Felidae; species *Panthera pardus*.

Leopold I (1640–1705) Holy Roman emperor (1658–1705). Throughout his reign, he was compelled to defend the extensive HABSBURG dominions against foreign aggression. Leopold joined the European defensive alliances against the France of LOUIS XIV in 1686, 1689 and 1701, but died before the end of the War of the SPANISH SUCCESSION.

Leopold I (1790–1865) First king of independent Belgium (1831–65). He refused the throne of Greece in 1830, but accepted that of Belgium after it declared independence from the Netherlands. He influenced the young Queen VICTORIA, his niece, and was responsible for their marriage to Albert.

Leopold II (1835–1909) King of Belgium (1865–1909). He initiated colonial expansion and sponsored the expedition of Henry STANLEY to the Congo (1879–84). In 1885 he established the Congo Free State (Zaïre).

Leopold III (1901–83) King of Belgium (1934–51). When the Germans invaded Belgium (1940) during World War 2, he declined to accompany the government into exile and surrendered. He remained in Belgium during the war, until removed to Germany in 1944. On his return, he encountered such fierce opposition that he abdicated in favour of his son, Baudouin.

lepidoptera Order of insects that includes MOTHS and BUTTERFLIES; they are found in every continent except Antarctica.

leprosy (Hansen's disease) Chronic, progressive condition affecting the skin and nerves, caused by infection with the micro-organism *Mycobacterium leprae*. Now confined almost entirely to the tropics, leprosy can be treated with a combination of drugs, but the nerve damage is irreversible.

lepton One of a class of ELEMENTARY PARTICLES. There are 12 types, including the ELECTRON and electron-NEUTRINO, muon and muon-neutrino, tau and tau-neutrino, together with their antiparticles (antileptons). Leptons are governed by the WEAK NUCLEAR FORCE, the force involved in radioactive decay. They have no QUARK substructure.

lesbianism Term that describes female HOMOSEXUALITY.

Lesotho (formerly Basutoland) Enclave kingdom within the Republic of South Africa; the capital is MASERU. **Land and climate** The scenic Drakensberg Range forms Lesotho's NE border

COLOUR SECTION CONTENTS

WORLD MAPS

GENERAL REFERENCE

World in Hemispheres: Western Hemisphere

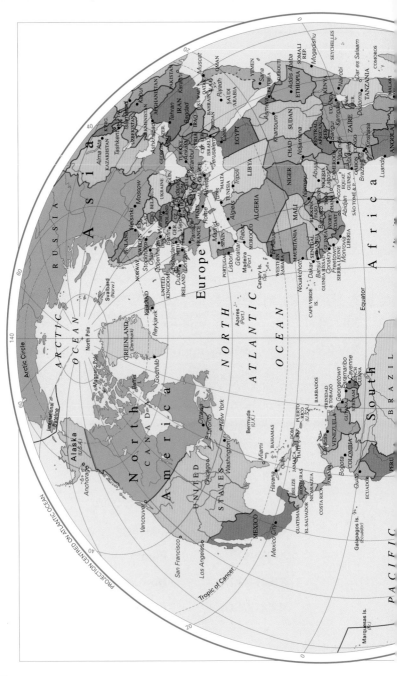

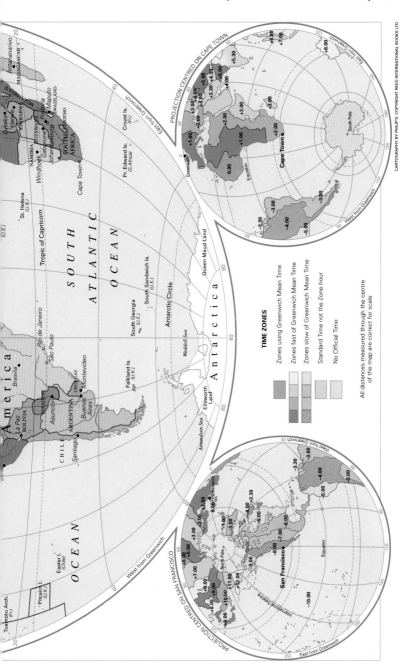

PROJECTION CENTRED ON CAPE TOWN

East from Greenwich

+8.00
+7.00
+8.00
+5.30
+6.00
+3.00
+4.30
+4.00
+2.00
+1.00
+3.00
+3.00
0.00
+2.00
+1.00
Greenwich
Cape Town
Equator
+ South Pole
-3.00
-3.30
-4.00
-5.00

West from Greenwich

CARTOGRAPHY BY PHILIP'S. COPYRIGHT REED INTERNATIONAL BOOKS LTD.

Antananarivo
MADAGASCAR
MOZAMBIQUE
Lusaka
Harare
ZIMBABWE
BOTSWANA
Pretoria
Maputo
Gaborone
SWAZILAND
NAMIBIA
Johannesburg
LESOTHO
Windhoek
SOUTH
AFRICA
St. Helena
(U.K.)
Pt. Edward Is.
(S. African)
Cape Town
Crozet Is.
(Fr.)

Tropic of Capricorn

SOUTH
ATLANTIC
OCEAN

South Georgia
(U.K.)
South Sandwich Is.
(U.K.)
Falkland Is.
(U.K.)

Antarctic Circle

Queen Maud Land

Weddell Sea

A n t a r c t i c a

Ellsworth
Land

Amundsen Sea

Río de Janeiro
São Paulo
A m e r i c a
Brasília
La Paz
BOLIVIA
Asunción
PARAGUAY
Santiago
C H I L E
ARGENTINA
URUGUAY
Montevideo
Buenos
Aires

OCEAN

Easter I.
(Chile)

Tuamotu Arch.
(Fr.)

Pitcairn I.
(U.K.)

TIME ZONES

Zones using Greenwich Mean Time

Zones fast of Greenwich Mean Time

Zones slow of Greenwich Mean Time

Standard Time not the Zone hour

No Official Time

All distances measured through the centre
of the map are correct for scale

PROJECTION CENTRED ON SAN FRANCISCO

West from Greenwich

Greenwich
0.00
-3.00
-4.00
-3.00
-1.00
-3.30
-2.00
-4.00
-3.00
-4.00
-5.00
-3.00
-6.00
-7.00
-8.00
North Pole
-9.00
-8.00
San Francisco
-10.00
-11.00
-12.00
Equator
+6.00
+5.00
+3.00
+7.00
+8.00
+9.00
+8.00
+10.00
+9.00
+11.00
+12.00
International Date Line

East from Greenwich

III

World in Hemispheres: Eastern Hemisphere

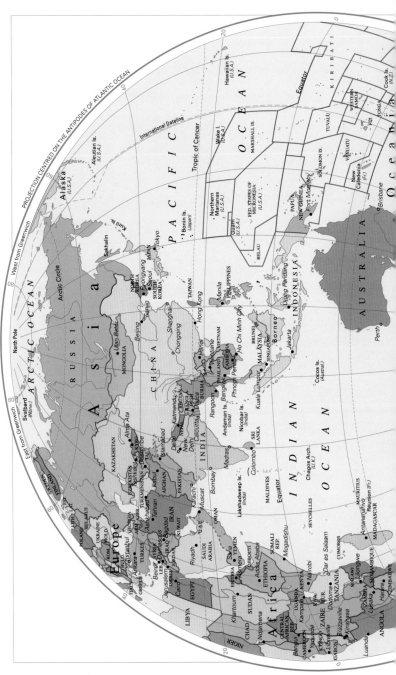

World in Hemispheres: Eastern Hemisphere

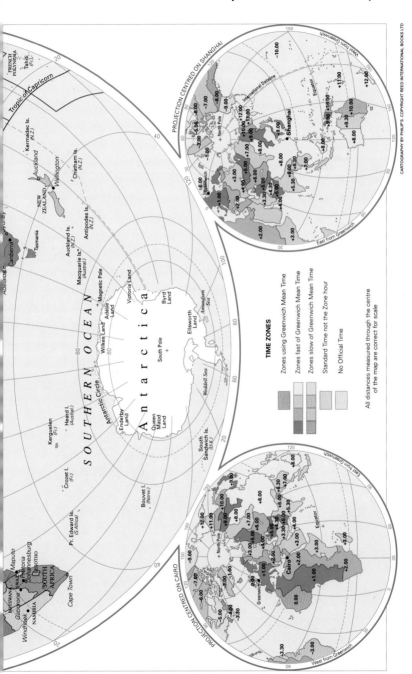

TIME ZONES

Zones using Greenwich Mean Time

Zones fast of Greenwich Mean Time

Zones slow of Greenwich Mean Time

Standard Time not the Zone hour

No Official Time

All distances measured through the centre of the map are correct for scale

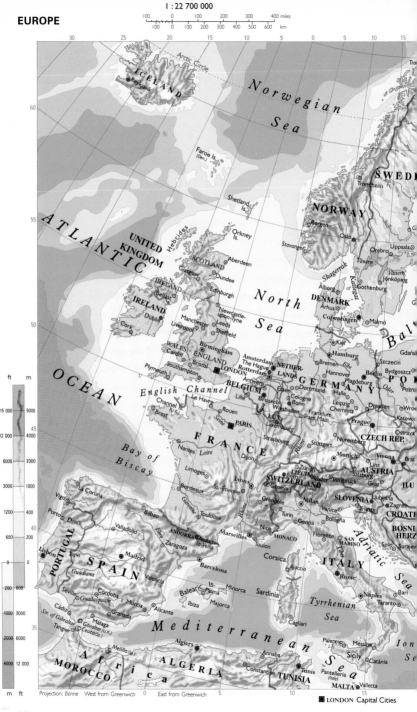

EUROPE

1 : 22 700 000

100   0   100   200   300   400 miles
100   0   100   200   300   400   500   600 km

Arctic Circle

Norwegian Sea

ICELAND
Reykjavik

Faroe Is.
(Den.)

Shetland
Is.

NORWAY
Bergen
Stavanger
Oslo

SWED

Trondheim

Uppsala
Örebro
Vänern

ATLANTIC

UNITED
KINGDOM

Hebrides

Orkney
Is.

Aberdeen
SCOTLAND
Glasgow   Dundee
Edinburgh

N. IRELAND
Belfast

IRELAND
Dublin
Cork

Liverpool
Manchester
Leeds
Sheffield

Newcastle-
upon-Tyne

North Sea

Skagerrak

Göteborg
Jönköping

DENMARK
Ålborg
Århus
Copenhagen   Malmö

Kattegat

Vättern

Balt

WALES
Cardiff
Bristol
ENGLAND
Birmingham

Amsterdam
The Hague
Rotterdam
NETHER-
LANDS

Kiel
Hamburg
Bremen

Gdańsk

OCEAN

Plymouth
Southampton

LONDON
BELGIUM
Antwerp
Brussels
Lille
Le Havre

Dortmund
Essen
Cologne
Bonn
GERMANY
Hannover
Magdeburg
Berlin
PO

Szczecin
Bydgoszcz
Poz

Elbe
Oder

English Channel

Channel Is.
(U.K.)

Brest

Rouen
Seine

PARIS

LUX
Luxembourg
Frankfurt
am Main
Wiesbaden

Halle
Leipzig
Dresden
Chemnitz

Wroc

Katowic
Ostrava

Nantes
Loire
FRANCE
Dijon

Strasbourg
Stuttgart

Prague
CZECH REP.

Nuremberg

Vienna
Brat

*Bay of
Biscay*

Limoges

St-Étienne
Lyons

Munich
Linz
Salzburg
AUSTRIA
Innsbruck   Graz

HU

Bordeaux
Garonne

Toulouse

Zürich
Bern
Geneva
SWITZERLAND
LIECH
Vaduz

Ljubljana
SLOVENIA
Trieste
Zagreb
CROATI

Vigo
La Coruña
Porto   Douro

Bilbao

Grenoble

Milan
Turin
Venice
Bologna
Genoa

BOSNI
HERZ
Split
Sarajev

PORTUGAL
Lisbon
Tagus
Guadiana

Valladolid
Ebro
Zaragoza

ANDORRA   Andorra
la-Vella

Marseilles
Toulon

Nice
MONACO

Florence
SAN
MARINO
(Italy)

Adriatic Sea

SPAIN
Madrid
Valencia

Barcelona

Corsica

Ajaccio

ITALY
Rome

Seville
Córdoba
Guadalquivir
Murcia
Granada

Alicante

Balearic Is.
Palma
Ibiza

Minorca

Majorca

Sardinia

*Tyrrhenian
Sea*

Naples
Bari
Taranto

Cádiz
Málaga
Str. of Gibraltar
Tangier   Ceuta *(Sp.)*
Gibraltar *(U.K.)*

Cágliari

Palermo
Messina
Sicily   Catánia

*Ion
Se*

Melilla *(Sp.)*

Algiers
Annaba

Mediterranean   Sea

Pantelleria
(Italy)

Africa
MOROCCO
ALGERIA
Constantine   TUNISIA
Tunis

MALTA   Valletta

Projection: *Bonne*   West from Greenwich   0   East from Greenwich

■ LONDON Capital Cities

ft   m
15 000   5000
12 000   4000
6000   2000
3000   1000
1200   400
600   200
0   0
200   600
1000   3000
2000   6000
4000   12 000
m   ft

VI

CARTOGRAPHY BY PHILIPS. COPYRIGHT REED INTERNATIONAL BOOKS LTD.

ASIA

1 : 56 800 000

250   0   250   500   750   1000 miles

250   0   500   1000   1500 km

ATLANTIC OCEAN

GREENLAND

ICELAND

Arctic Circle

ARCTIC

Svalbard

Barents Sea

Novaya Zemlya

Kara Sea

UNITED KINGDOM

NORWAY

SWEDEN

FINLAND

Murmansk

Vorkuta

Salekhard

LONDON

North Sea

White Sea

Arkhangelsk

Ob

R   U

FRANCE

PARIS

GERMANY

Berlin

Warsaw

ST.PETERSBURG

Nizhniy Novgorod

Perm

Yekaterinburg

Irtysh

ITALY

Prague

Vienna

UKRAINE

MOSCOW

Kazan

Ufa

Chelyabinsk

Omsk

Rome

Belgrade

Danube

Odessa

Don

Volgograd

Rostov

Volga

Samara

Astrakhan

KAZAKHSTAN

Pavloda

Karaganda

Mediterranean Sea

Athens

İzmir

Konya

Bursa

İSTANBUL

Ankara

Adana

Black Sea

GEORGIA

Tbilisi

Yerevan

ARMENIA

AZERBAIJAN

Baku

Caspian Sea

Aral Sea

Syrdar'ya

L. Balkhash

UZBEKISTAN

Tashkent

Samarkand

Bishkek

KYRGYZSTAN

Alma A

Kashi

TURKEY

Nicosia

CYPRUS

Beirut

Aleppo

Mosul

Tabriz

TURKMENISTAN

Ashkhabad

Mashhad

Dushanbe

TAJIKISTAN

LIBYA

Alexandria

CAIRO

ISRAEL

Damascus

Euphrates

Tigris

Ashkhabad

EGYPT

Suez

LEBANON

'Ammān

JORDAN

IRAQ

Baghdad

Esfahān

IRAN

TEHRĀN

Herāt

Kābul

Islamabad

JAMMU & KASHMIR

Aswân

Nile

Basra

KUWAIT

Kuwait

Shirāz

Zāhedān

Qandahār

Faisalabad

AFGHANISTAN

Lahore

DELHI

New Delhi

Medina

Riyadh

SAUDI ARABIA

BAHRAIN

QATAR

Al Manāmah

Doha

UNITED ARAB EMIRATES

Abu Dhabi

The Gulf

G. of Oman

PAKISTAN

Indus

Jaipur

Lucknow

Kanpur

Varar

Red Sea

Jedda

Mecca

Port Sudan

Khartoum

SUDAN

ERITREA

Sana

YEMEN

Aden

DJIBOUTI

G. of Aden

Muscat

OMAN

Socotra (Yemen)

Arabian Sea

KARACHI

Ahmadabad

Vadodara

Surat

Indore

BOMBAY (MUMBAI)

Pune

Bhopal

Naç

Hyder

INDI

Addis Ababa

ETHIOPIA

SOMALI REP.

Lakshadweep Is. (India)

Bangalore

Madurai

Colombo

UGANDA

KENYA

L. Victoria

Nairobi

Mogadishu

Equator

MALDIVES

Male

INDIAN O

ZAÏRE

TANZANIA

Mombasa

Dar es Salaam

SEYCHELLES

Victoria

Aldabra Is. (Seychelles)

Amirante Is. (Seychelles)

Chagos Arch. (U.K.)

ZAMBIA

MALAWI

Projection: Bonne

Hanoi ● Capital Cities

ft   m

12 000   4000

9000   3000

6000   2000

3000   1000

1500   500

600   200

0   0

200   600

1000   3000

2000   6000

4000   12 000

6000   18 000

8000   24 000

m   ft

VIII

AFRICA

1 : 47 700 000

200 0 200 400 600 800 1000 1200 miles
200 0 200 400 600 800 1000 1200 1400 1600 1800 km

KAZAKHSTAN
TURKMEN.
Aral Sea
RUSSIA
Volgograd
Caspian Sea
TEHRĀN
Eşfahān
IRAN
QATAR
G. of Aden
Socotra (Yemen)
Ras Asir
Berbera
Baku
AZER.
GEORGIA
ARM.
Mosul
Baghdād
IRAQ
Euphrates
Tigris
Basra
KUWAIT
BAHRAIN
Riyadh
SAUDI ARABIA
YEMEN
DJIBOUTI
Djibouti
ERITREA
Asmara
Massawa
Red Sea
Medina
Jedda
Mecca
UKRAINE
Kiev
Odesa
Black Sea
TURKEY
Ankara
CYPRUS
SYRIA
Aleppo
Damascus
LEB.
Beirut
Tel Aviv
Jerusalem
ISRAEL
JORDAN
Syrian Desert
Port Said
Suez
Nile
Aswān
Port Sudan
Wādi Halfa
Atbara
Khartoum
Blue Nile
White Nile
Omdurman
El Obeid
SUDAN
Malakal
Warsaw
POLAND
GERMANY
Prague
CZECH REP.
SLOVA. REP.
Vienna
AUSTRIA
HUNGARY
SLO.
CROATIA
BOS.
HERZ.
SERB.
ROMANIA
BULGARIA
MAC.
ALB.
GREECE
Athens
Crete
Mediterranean Sea
Alexandria
CAIRO
El Faiyûm
Asyût
EGYPT
Al Jawf
Benghazi
LIBYA
Misrātah
Tripoli
Morzuq
Sfax
Sabha
Kufra
NETH.
BELG.
PARIS
FRANCE
SWITZ.
ITALY
Rome
Sardinia
Corsica
Sicily
MALTA
TUNISIA
Tunis
Constantine
Annaba
Adriatic Sea
UNITED KINGDOM
LONDON
B. of Biscay
SPAIN
Madrid
PORTUGAL
Lisbon
Algiers
ALGERIA
In Salah
Agadès
NIGER
L. Chad
CHAD
Ndjamena
Abéché
Sahara
MADEIRA
NORTH
ATLANTIC
OCEAN
Azores (Port.)
Madeira (Port.)
Canary Is. (Sp.)
Casablanca
Rabat
MOROCCO
Marrakech
Fès
Tetouan
Chott Djerid
Tropic of Cancer
Tombouctou
Niger
MALI
Bamako
MAURITANIA
Nouakchott
WESTERN SAHARA
El Aaiún
Dakhla
Fdérik
Ras Nouâdhibou
St-Louis
Dakar
C. Vert
SENEGAL
Senegal
GAMBIA
Banjul
GUINEA BISSAU
Bissau
GUINEA
Conakry
Kano
Maiduguri
NIGERIA
Niamey
Ouagadougou
BURKINA FASO
Bobo Dioulasso
BENIN
CAPE VERDE IS.
Praia
X

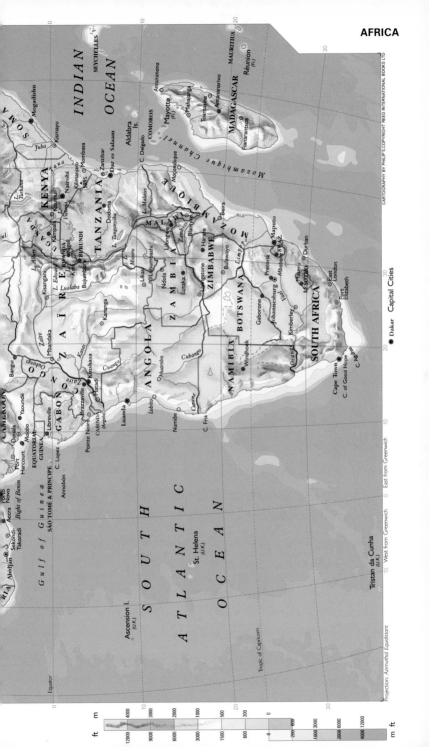

AFRICA

MAURITIUS
Réunion *(Fr.)*

SEYCHELLES

INDIAN

OCEAN

MADAGASCAR

Antsiranana
Mahajanga
Toamasina
Antananarivo
Fianarantsoa

COMOROS
Mayotte *(Fr.)*
Aldabra Is.

Mogadishu

S O M A L I A

Kismayu

Juba

KENYA
Nairobi
Kilimanjaro 5895
Mombasa
Zanzibar
Dar es Salaam

Tana
Turkana

UGANDA
Kampala
L. Victoria
RWANDA
Kigali
BURUNDI
Bujumbura
L. Edward
Kisangani
L. Albert

TANZANIA
Dodoma
L. Tanganyika

MALAWI
L. Malawi
L. Mweru
Lilongwe
Zomba
Blantyre

MOZAMBIQUE
C. Delgado
Mozambique
Mozambique Channel

Lubumbashi
Ndola
ZAMBIA
Lusaka
Kitwe

Z A Ï R E
Zaïre
Lualaba
Kananga
Mbandaka
Kasai
Kwilu

Bangui

CAMEROON
Douala
Yaoundé
GABON
Libreville
C. Lopez
EQUATORIAL GUINEA
Port Harcourt
Bioko
Annobon
SÃO TOMÉ & PRINCIPE

Brazzaville
CONGO
Kinshasa
Matadi
CABINDA *(Angola)*
Pointe Noire

Luanda

ANGOLA
Lobito
Namibe
C. Fria
Cuango
Cuito
Cubango
Huambo
Cunene

Beira
Zambezi
Harare
ZIMBABWE
Bulawayo
Livingstone
Limpopo

BOTSWANA
Gaborone
Maputo
Pretoria
SWAZ.
Mbabane
Johannesburg
LESOTHO
Maseru
Vaal
Kimberley
Orange

NAMIBIA
Windhoek

SOUTH AFRICA
Cape Town
C. of Good Hope
Orange
Port Elizabeth
East London
Durban

Gulf of Guinea
Accra
Sekondi-Takoradi
Abidjan
Porto Novo
Bight of Benin

Ascension I.
(U.K.)

S O U T H

A T L A N T I C

O C E A N

St. Helena
(U.K.)

Tristan da Cunha
(U.K.)

Tropic of Capricorn

Equator

Projection: Azimuthal Equidistant

0 East from Greenwich

10 West from Greenwich

● Dakar Capital Cities

m

ft

ft	m
12000	4000
9000	3000
6000	2000
3000	1000
1500	500
600	200
0	0
	-200 -600
1000 3000	-2000 6000
4000 12000	

NORTH AMERICA

1 : 39 700 000

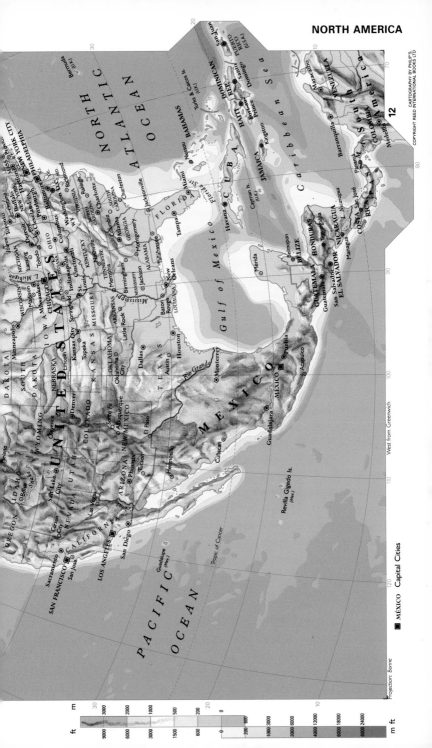

NORTH AMERICA

NORTH ATLANTIC OCEAN

PACIFIC OCEAN

Bermuda (U.K.)

San Juan
PUERTO RICO (U.S.A.)
Santo Domingo
DOMINICAN REP.
HAITI
Port-au-Prince
Turks & Caicos Is. (U.K.)

Maracaibo
VENEZUELA
COLOMBIA
Medellín
South America

Caracas
Barranquilla
Panamá
COSTA RICA
San José
PANAMA

Caribbean Sea

BAHAMAS
Nassau
Kingston
JAMAICA
Cayman Is. (U.K.)

CUBA
Havana
Florida Str.

UNITED STATES

DAKOTA
SOUTH DAKOTA
NORTH DAKOTA
MINNESOTA
Minneapolis
WISCONSIN
Madison
L. Michigan
MICHIGAN
Lansing
Milwaukee
CHICAGO
Detroit
Toronto
Hamilton
Buffalo
ROCHESTER
NEW YORK CITY
MASS. Boston
CONN.
N.J.
PHILADELPHIA
NEW JERSEY
Baltimore
Washington D.C.
Richmond
VIRGINIA
Raleigh
NORTH CAROLINA
Charlotte
SOUTH CAROLINA
Columbia
Charleston
GEORGIA
Atlanta
Savannah
Jacksonville
FLORIDA
Tampa
Miami

OHIO
Cleveland
Pittsburgh
Columbus
Cincinnati
Toledo
INDIANA
Indianapolis
KENTUCKY
WEST VIRGINIA
TENNESSEE
Nashville
Memphis
ALABAMA
Birmingham
Montgomery
MISSISSIPPI
Jackson
Tallahassee

IOWA
NEBRASKA
Lincoln
Kansas City
Topeka
KANSAS
MISSOURI
St. Louis
Springfield
OKLAHOMA
Oklahoma City
ARKANSAS
Little Rock
LOUISIANA
Baton Rouge
New Orleans

WYOMING
Cheyenne
COLORADO
Denver
NEW MEXICO
Santa Fe
Albuquerque
El Paso
TEXAS
Dallas
Austin
Houston

OREGON
IDAHO
Boise
Helena
Salt Lake City
UTAH
NEVADA
Carson City
Las Vegas
CALIFORNIA
Sacramento
SAN FRANCISCO
San José
LOS ANGELES
San Diego
ARIZONA
Phoenix
Tucson

Minneapolis

MEXICO
MÉXICO
Monterrey
Guadalajara
Culiacán
Hermosillo
Chihuahua
Mérida
Puebla
Acapulco
Rio Grande

Revilla Gigedo Is. (Mex.)
Guadalupe (Mex.)

GUATEMALA
Guatemala
BELIZE
Belmopan
HONDURAS
Tegucigalpa
EL SALVADOR
San Salvador
NICARAGUA
Managua
L. Nicaragua

Gulf of Mexico

Tropic of Cancer

20

30

70

80

90

100

110

120

10

20

30

West from Greenwich

Projection: Bonne

12

CARTOGRAPHY BY PHILIP'S
COPYRIGHT REED INTERNATIONAL BOOKS LTD

■ MÉXICO   Capital Cities

m
3000
2000
1000
500
200
0

ft
9000
6000
3000
1500
600
0

m ft
200-600
0
2000 6000
4000 12000
6000 18000
8000 24000
1000 3000

1 : 39 700 000

200   0   200   400   600   800 miles
400   0   400   800   1200 km

Tropic of Cancer

N O R T H

A T L A N T I C

O C E A N

Equator

C. de São Roque
Fortaleza
Natal
RIO G. DO NORTE
PARAÍBA
João Pessoa
Campina Grande
Recife
PERNAMBUCO
ALAGOAS
Maceió
Aracaju
CEARÁ
PIAUÍ
Teresina
São Luís
MARANHÃO
BAHIA
B R A Z I L
Belém
Marajó I.
PARÁ
Tocantins
TOCANTINS
Santarém
Xingu
MATO GROSSO
AMAPÁ
C. Orange
Cayenne
FRENCH GUIANA
Paramaribo
SURINAM
Georgetown
GUYANA
Manaus
Amazon
Madeira
Branco
RORAIMA
Ciudad Guayana
Orinoco
AMAZONAS
RONDÔNIA
Pôrto Velho
Purus
Juruá
ACRE
Madre de Dios
Japurá
Caracas
Valencia
Barquisimeto
VENEZUELA
Maracaibo
C. de la Agula
Cartagena
Barranquilla
G. of
Darién
Medellín
Cúcuta
Bucaramanga
Bogotá
COLOMBIA
Cali
Magdalena
Putumayo
Napo
ECUADOR
Quito
Guayaquil
G. of Guayaquil
Marañón
Iquitos
Ucayali
Huallaga
P E R U
Trujillo
Chimbote
Callao
Lima
Cuzco

NORTH ATLANTIC OCEAN

C U B A
BAHAMAS
Havana
Kingston
JAMAICA
Turks & Caicos Is.
(U.K.)
HAITI
Port-au-Prince
DOMINICAN
REP.
San Juan
PUERTO
RICO
(U.S.A.)
Virgin Is.
(U.K.)
ST. KITTS-
NEVIS
ANTIGUA &
BARBUDA
GUADELOUPE
(Fr.)
Basse-Terre
DOMINICA
Roseau
MARTINIQUE
(Fr.)
Fort-de-France
ST. LUCIA
Castries
BARBADOS
Bridgetown
ST. VINCENT
Kingstown
GRENADA
St. George's
TRINIDAD &
TOBAGO
Port of
Spain
Caribbean Sea
Curaçao
Aruba

BELIZE
GUATEMALA
Guatemala
HONDURAS
Tegucigalpa
EL SALVADOR
San Salvador
NICARAGUA
Managua
COSTA
RICA
San José
PANAMA
Panamá
Gulf of Panama
MEXICO

Galápagos Is.
(Ecuador)

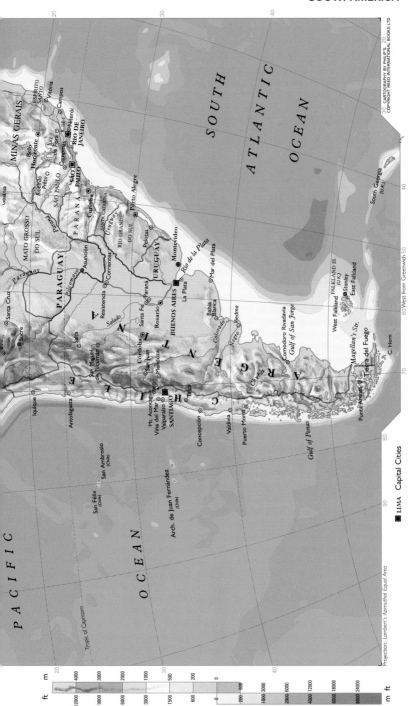

SOUTH AMERICA

SOUTH ATLANTIC OCEAN

PACIFIC OCEAN

MINAS GERAIS

MATO GROSSO DO SUL

PARAGUAY

PARANÁ

SANTA CATARINA

RIO GRANDE DO SUL

URUGUAY

ARGENTINA

CHILE

Tierra del Fuego

Gulf of Peñas

Magellan's Str.

South Georgia (U.K.)

FALKLAND IS. (U.K.)
West Falkland
East Falkland
Stanley

Tropic of Capricorn

Cities labelled on map:
Vitória, Campos, Niterói, RIO DE JANEIRO, Juiz de Fora, Belo Horizonte, Ouro Preto, Ribeirão Preto, SÃO PAULO, Santos, Curitiba, Pôrto Alegre, Pelotas, Montevideo, Río de la Plata, Mar del Plata, La Plata, BUENOS AIRES, Paraná, Santa Fe, Rosario, Corrientes, Resistencia, Asunción, Córdoba, San Miguel de Tucumán, Salta, San Juan, Mendoza, Talca, Mt. Aconcagua 6960, Viña del Mar, Valparaíso, SANTIAGO, Concepción, Valdivia, Puerto Montt, Bahía Blanca, Viedma, Colorado, Negro, Chubut, Comodoro Rivadavia, Gulf of San Jorge, Punta Arenas, C. Horn

Salado, Pilcomayo, Paraguay, Paraná, Uruguay, Santa Cruz, Sucre, Goiânia, Iquique, Antofagasta, San Félix (Chile), San Ambrosio (Chile), Arch. de Juan Fernández (Chile)

60°West from Greenwich 50

30 CARTOGRAPHY BY PHILIP'S 20
COPYRIGHT REED INTERNATIONAL BOOKS LTD

Projection: Lambert's Azimuthal Equal Area

■ LIMA   Capital Cities

m / ft
4000 / 12000
3000 / 9000
2000 / 6000
1000 / 3000
500 / 1500
200 / 600
0 / 0

m / ft
200 / 600
4000 / 12000
6000 / 18000
8000 / 24000

AUSTRALIA AND OCEANIA

1 : 56 800 000

XVI

Two-stroke engine

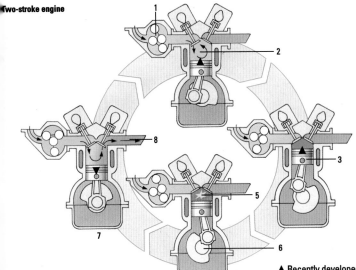

▲ Recently developed two-stroke engines use fans (1) to introduce air under greater pressure into the cyclinder, in an attempt to generate more power. Unlike the four-stroke cycle, combustion occurs every time the piston rises. The cycle starts as air is introduced into the cylinder (2). Fuel is injected and as the piston continues to rise (3) it compresses the mixture. At the top of the piston stroke (4), a spark (5) ignites the fuel, forcing the piston down and turning the crank (6). In the last stage (7), the gases are expelled (8) as more air is pumped through the inlet.

Four-cylinder engine

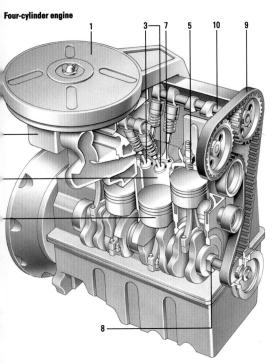

◄ In an in-line, four-cylinder petrol engine air is sucked into the engine through an air filter (1) into the carburettor (2). The air mixes with petrol which enters through the dual inlet valves (3) on each cylinder (4). The spark plug (5) then ignites the mixture forcing the piston (6) down. The burned gases are expelled through the outlet valves (7). The reciprocal motion of the cylinders is converted into rotation by the crankshaft (8). The crankshaft also turns the timing belt (9) which controls the opening of the valves and the firing of the spark plug via the camshaft (10).

Computer

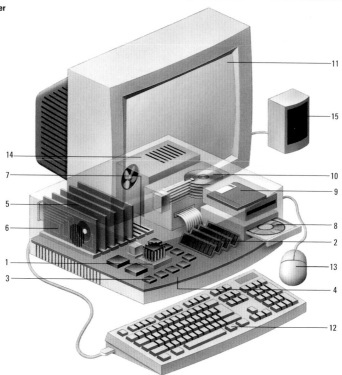

▲ The main components of a computer are the central processing unit (1), RAM (2), BIOS and ROM chips (3), a mother board (4), expansion cards (5), a video card (6), expansion slots (7), an optical disk drive (8), floppy disk drive (9), hard disk (10), monitor (11), keyboard (12), mouse (13), power supply (14) and loudspeaker (15).

Internet

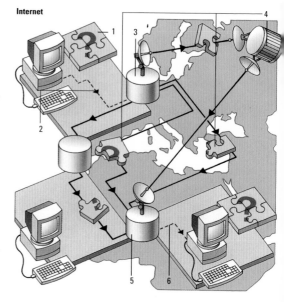

► When information is transported through the Internet it is split into small packages which travel different routes to the end destination. The information (1) travels along the phone network (2) to the local area network (LAN) (3). There it splits and moves by various routes, terrestrial and satellite (4). At the receiver's LAN (5) the message is reassembled in order and again uses the phone network (6) for the final portion of the journey.

Mouse

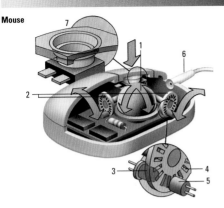

Hard disk

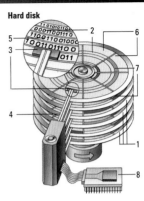

▲ A mouse moves a cursor on a monitor. A ball (1) rotates as the mouse moves. As the ball rolls, spoked wheels (2) turn through horizontal and vertical axes. An LED (3) shines through the spokes (4). The rotation of both wheels is detected by sensors (5) which send information to the computer via a cable (6), moving the cursor appropriately. Buttons at the front (7) are used to click on areas of the screen, or call up menus.

▼ Television screens are cathode-ray tubes. Electron guns (1) fire beams of electrons through vertical and horizontal deflection coils (2) onto a "shadow mask tube" (3) made up of millions of dots (4). The dots glow either red, green or blue when bombarded, making up the colour picture when viewed from a distance. The beams of electrons scan hundreds of lines (5) on the screen, making up the moving images.

▲ A computer hard disk is made of rotating plates (1) each having circular magnetic tracks (2) that are read and written on by a magnetic head (3). The disk spins at about 100 rev/sec. The heads align magnetic particles on the plates' surfaces to represent digital binary code (5). The tracks are divided into sectors (6), and information is stored in different sectors (7). A file allocation table tells a chip (8) where information is held on the plates.

Television screen

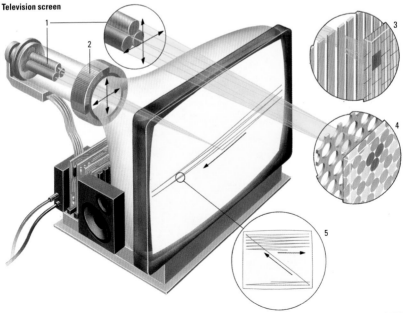

Doric

Ionic

Corinthian

Composite

Etruscan

◄ The five main orders of architecture (A) are Doric (Greek and Roman), Ionic, Corinthian, Composite and Tuscan. Architectural orders were first described in 1st century AD, but the present orders were settled upon during the Renaissance period.

1   2

3   4

▼ Egyptian architecture (B) drew heavily on symbolism. The capitals of the lotus (1), open (2) and budding (3) papyrus, and palm tree (4) symbolize the Nile's fertility. Islamic architectural design (C) is based on geometric patterns, as seen in the examples from the Alhambra in S Spain.

Rococo style

► The Rococo style (1700–50) is characterized with the alternation of doors and windows with decorative panelling known as "boiseries". Square ceiling structures were softened by curved and moulded panelling, minimizing the transition from wall to ceiling.

Vaults

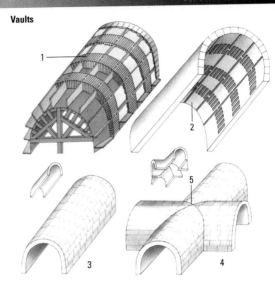

▶ Concrete enabled the Romans to build vaults of a size unequalled until the introduction of steel construction. The vaults were supported on timber centering which was removed after the concrete had set. In some cases vaults were built of brick ribs (1) filled with concrete (2) to lighten the weight on the centering and avoid cracking. The simplest vault was the barrel, wagon or tunnel (3). A prolonged rounded arch, it was used for small spans and simple oblong structures with parallel sides. The cross-vault (4), formed by two barrels intersecting at right angles, was used over square apartments, or over long corridors divided by piers into square bays, each covered with a cross-vault. Their lines of intersection are called "groins" (5).

Gothic

◀ Cologne cathedral, Germany, was begun in 1248, but the present building was completed between 1842 and 1880. It is the largest Gothic church in N Europe. The illustration shows its W facade. The cathedral's grandeur lies predominantly in its highly decorated spiny twin towers, which rise to 152m (502ft). The cathedral tries to emulate the greatest French cathedrals, particularly that of Amiens, and the desire for height is apparent in the choir which features huge arcades.

The basic elements of Gothic – the pointed arch, rib vault and flying buttress – were not original in themselves, but their combination created new aesthetic values. These values can be seen in the soaring towers, which represent a striving to reach God, and the vast areas of stained glass, bathing worshippers in a colourful profusion of light in an attempt to provide a vision of heaven on earth.

▼ Volcanoes form when molten lava (1) from a magma chamber (2) in the Earth's crust forces its way to the surface (3). The classic cone-shaped volcano is formed of alternating layers of cooled lava and cinders (4). Side vents (5) can occur and when offshoots of lava are trapped below the surface, laccoliths (6) form.

When a volcano's lava has a low silica content the lava flows easily, creating a low-angle shield cone. Cinder cones are created by volcanoes that produce ash and cinders not lava during eruptions. The layers of ash and cinders do not have the stability to create the classic cone-shaped volcano. When a magma chamber collapses a caldera is formed as the centre of the volcanic cone follows suit. Lakes (1) often fill the resulting crater and subsequent upsurges of lava can create islands (2).

Low-angle shield cone

Cinder cone

Volcanoes

Cone-shaped volcano

Caldera

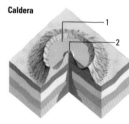

▼ Folds are made by enormous pressures bending rock strata. An anticline is where a fold forces the strata upward (1). A syncline is a depression formed by folding (2). If the pressure is continued an asymmetrical fold can occur (3), and beyond that the forces can push the rock so far the strata double over and fracture, forming a thrust or overthrust fold or fault (4). At the top of an anticline small fractures are common as the rock is bent upwards (5). The fracturing allows greater erosion on higher ground (6) and over long periods of time this weakness can lead to a reversal with the area of the original anticline lower than the syncline (7).

Folding

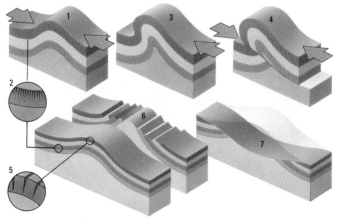

Weathering

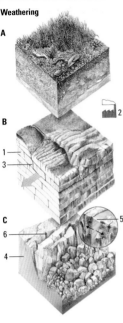

▲ Weathering is the break down (but not transportation) of rock . It occurs in three ways: biologically (A), chemically (B) or physically (C), often in combination. At the surface, plant roots and animals, such as worms, break down rock turning it into soil. In chemical weathering soluble rocks, such as limestone (calcium carbonate, 1), are dissolved by rain, which is a mild solution of carbonic acid. Acid rain caused by sulphate pollution (2) also attacks the rock. The water sinks into the ground along the rock's joints, widening them (3). The acidic water can, over many years, create cave systems. Both heat and cold cause physical weathering. When temperatures drop below freezing, freeze-thaw weathering can split the hardest rocks, such as granite (4). Water that settles in the cracks and joints during the day expands as it freezes at night (5), cleaving the rock along the joints (6). In deserts rock expands and contracts due to the extremes of day and night temperatures, resulting in layers of rock splitting off.

▼ Erosion is the break down and transportation of rock due to the action of an outside agent. It has three main forms: fluvial (rivers), glacial and wind erosion. Rivers (1) erode their channels through the flow of water and the abrasion of the load they are carrying against the banks and riverbed. Erosion is most forceful at the outside of bends (2) where the banks are undercut (3) often creating cliffs or bluffs (4) down which material moves. Flood surges dramatically increase the power of the river and correspondingly magnifies the erosive force. On a smaller scale water in the form of rain will move material down a hillside (5). Particles of soil are carried by rivulets and the impact of raindrops throws soil together. Where the vegetation is removed, as on tracks (6), erosion is accentuated.

In arid conditions, wind erosion can carve distinctive features. Sand and stones blown by the wind (7) have the same effect as shot-blasting. Mushroom-shaped formations called pedestals (8) are often the result. This is due to the height (9) at which the erosive sand is carried by the wind as it bounces across the surface. Above that level (10) the rock is left as before.

Erosion

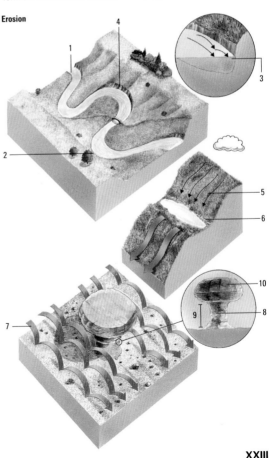

Leaves

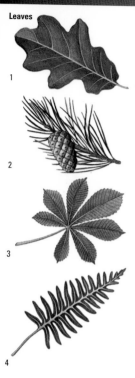

1

2

3

4

◀ Leaves exhibit a wide variety of shapes. The pedunculate oak (1) and the Scots Pine (2) have simple leaves with a single leaf blade, while the horse chestnut (3) and ferns (4) have compound leaves. The leaflets of compound leaves either radiate from one point (palmate) as in the case of the horse chestnut, or are arranged in opposite pairs down the main stalk (pinnate) as is the case with ferns.

Hawthorn

White spruce

▶ Trees fall into two main groups, angiosperms and gymnosperms. Angiosperms, such as the hawthorn, are flowering plants that form ovaries, which contain seeds and develop into fruit. Gymnosperms, such as the white spruce, produce naked seeds rather than seed-containing fruit. The conifers, such as the white spruce, make up the largest order within the gyymnosperm genera. Their seeds are contained in cones.

Tree trunk

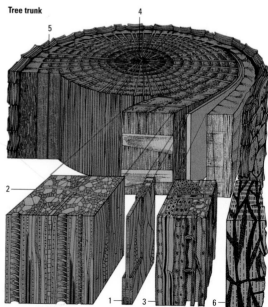

5

4

2

1

3

6

▶ The trunks of trees increase in girth by rings of new wood, produced annually in temperate zones but less often in the tropics. The cambium (1) produces xylem (2) and phloem (3). They are alive but the heartwood (4) is dead. The medullary rays (5) allow the transport of food across the trunk. Bark (6) is a protective outer coating.

Flowers

1

2

3

4

◄ Flowers are adapted to different pollination methods. These are non-specialized simple flowers, such as the buttercup (1), bird-pollinated flowers (2), such as humming-bird pollinated hibiscus, bee-specialized flowers, such as gorse (3), and wind-pollinated catkins (4), such as those found on hazel.

Sugar beet   **Sugar cane**

Tea

Cacoa

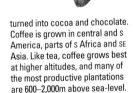

Many plants are grown to be sold rather than for subsistence. Sugar, coffee, tea and cacoa are examples of cash crops. Sugar is obtained through the cultivation and processing of sugar beet (grown mostly in temperate regions) and sugar cane (grown in subtropical areas). Tea is grown extensively in monsoon Asia, notably India, China and Sri Lanka. Cacoa is grown mainly in tropical w Africa, and central and s America, the beans of which are turned into cocoa and chocolate. Coffee is grown in central and s America, parts of s Africa and sE Asia. Like tea, coffee grows best at higher altitudes, and many of the most productive plantations are 600–2,000m above sea-level.

Coffee

Front Skeleton

Front Skeletal Muscles

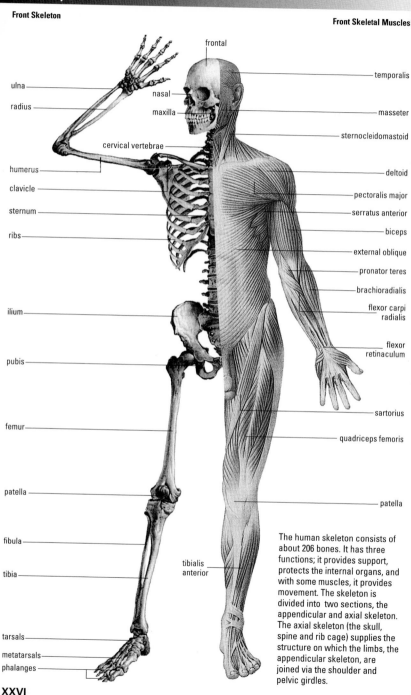

frontal

temporalis

ulna

nasal

radius

maxilla

masseter

sternocleidomastoid

cervical vertebrae

humerus

deltoid

clavicle

pectoralis major

sternum

serratus anterior

ribs

biceps

external oblique

pronator teres

brachioradialis

flexor carpi radialis

ilium

flexor retinaculum

pubis

sartorius

femur

quadriceps femoris

patella

patella

fibula

tibia

tibialis anterior

tarsals

metatarsals

phalanges

The human skeleton consists of about 206 bones. It has three functions; it provides support, protects the internal organs, and with some muscles, it provides movement. The skeleton is divided into two sections, the appendicular and axial skeleton. The axial skeleton (the skull, spine and rib cage) supplies the structure on which the limbs, the appendicular skeleton, are joined via the shoulder and pelvic girdles.

Back Skeleton

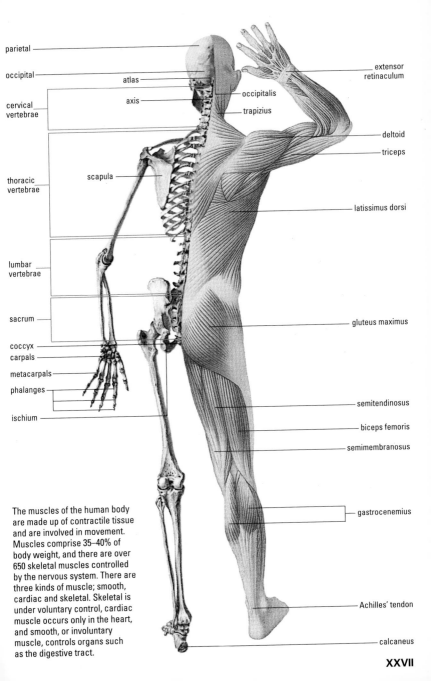

parietal

occipital

atlas

axis

occipitalis

trapizius

cervical
vertebrae

scapula

thoracic
vertebrae

lumbar
vertebrae

sacrum

coccyx

carpals

metacarpals

phalanges

ischium

extensor
retinaculum

deltoid

triceps

latissimus dorsi

gluteus maximus

semitendinosus

biceps femoris

semimembranosus

gastrocenemius

Achilles' tendon

calcaneus

The muscles of the human body
are made up of contractile tissue
and are involved in movement.
Muscles comprise 35–40% of
body weight, and there are over
650 skeletal muscles controlled
by the nervous system. There are
three kinds of muscle; smooth,
cardiac and skeletal. Skeletal is
under voluntary control, cardiac
muscle occurs only in the heart,
and smooth, or involuntary
muscle, controls organs such
as the digestive tract.

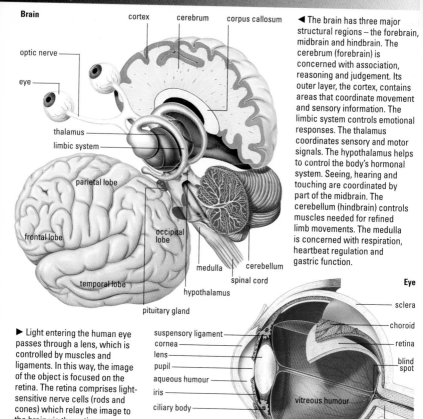

Brain

- cortex
- cerebrum
- corpus callosum
- optic nerve
- eye
- thalamus
- limbic system
- parietal lobe
- frontal lobe
- occipital lobe
- temporal lobe
- medulla
- cerebellum
- spinal cord
- hypothalamus
- pituitary gland

◄ The brain has three major structural regions – the forebrain, midbrain and hindbrain. The cerebrum (forebrain) is concerned with association, reasoning and judgement. Its outer layer, the cortex, contains areas that coordinate movement and sensory information. The limbic system controls emotional responses. The thalamus coordinates sensory and motor signals. The hypothalamus helps to control the body's hormonal system. Seeing, hearing and touching are coordinated by part of the midbrain. The cerebellum (hindbrain) controls muscles needed for refined limb movements. The medulla is concerned with respiration, heartbeat regulation and gastric function.

Eye

- sclera
- choroid
- retina
- blind spot
- suspensory ligament
- cornea
- lens
- pupil
- aqueous humour
- iris
- ciliary body
- conjuctiva
- vitreous humour
- optic nerve

► Light entering the human eye passes through a lens, which is controlled by muscles and ligaments. In this way, the image of the object is focused on the retina. The retina comprises light-sensitive nerve cells (rods and cones) which relay the image to the brain via the optic nerve.

Ear

- ossicles
- stapes
- incus
- malleus
- semicircular canals
- cochlea
- auditory nerve
- tympanic membrane
- oval window
- utricle
- saccule
- ear canal
- Eustachian tube
- pinna

◄ The ear is divided into three sections – the outer, middle and inner ear. The outer consists of the pinna, which funnels sound waves via the ear canal to the ear drum, the tympanic membrane. The sound waves are transmitted, and amplified, by tiny bones, the ossicles, situated in the middle ear. The ossicles cause the oval window to vibrate. This sets the fluids of the inner ear in motion. Hair cells in the structures of the inner ear, the cochlea and the semicircular canals, are stimulated and generate nerve impulses which are interpreted by the brain as sound.

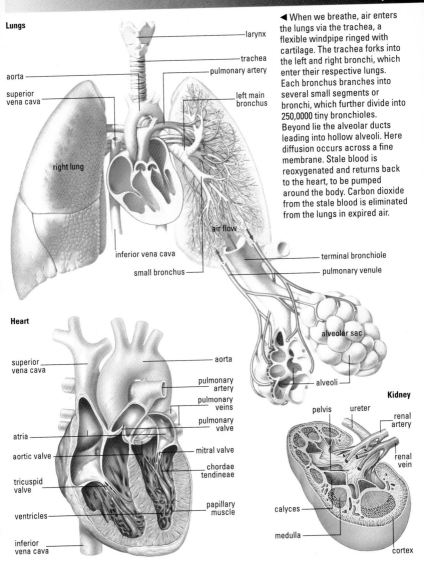

Lungs

larynx

trachea

pulmonary artery

aorta

superior vena cava

left main bronchus

right lung

▲ When we breathe, air enters the lungs via the trachea, a flexible windpipe ringed with cartilage. The trachea forks into the left and right bronchi, which enter their respective lungs. Each bronchus branches into several small segments or bronchi, which further divide into 250,0000 tiny bronchioles. Beyond lie the alveolar ducts leading into hollow alveoli. Here diffusion occurs across a fine membrane. Stale blood is reoxygenated and returns back to the heart, to be pumped around the body. Carbon dioxide from the stale blood is eliminated from the lungs in expired air.

air flow

inferior vena cava

small bronchus

terminal bronchiole

pulmonary venule

alveolar sac

alveoli

Heart

superior vena cava

aorta

pulmonary artery

pulmonary veins

pulmonary valve

atria

mitral valve

aortic valve

tricuspid valve

chordae tendineae

ventricles

papillary muscle

inferior vena cava

Kidney

pelvis

ureter

renal artery

renal vein

calyces

medulla

cortex

▲ The human heart contains four chambers – two atria and two ventricles – and four sets of valves. Blood from the body passes into the right atrium, via the venae cavae. Flow of blood into the right ventricle is controlled by the tricuspid valve. Pulmonary arteries carry blood from the right ventricle to the lungs, while the pulmonary veins carry oxygenated blood back from the lungs to the left atrium. In a similar way, the mitral valve controls the flow of blood between the left atrium and the left ventricle. The aorta conducts the oxygenated blood from the left ventricle to all parts of the body.

▲ The human kidney, enclosed in a fibrous capsule, consists of an outer cortex region, a medulla region with pyramidal-shaped areas, and an inner pelvis region, which leads into the ureter. The pelvis region is divided into calyces, which are lined with connective tissues and smooth muscle bands.

▼ Although not the largest animal kingdom, mammals of which there are some 4,250 species, are perhaps the most familiar. The majority are terrestial, but some such as whales have adapted to an aquatic life, while bats have evolved wings. The African plains are home to a diverse group of herbivorous mammals, such as giraffes (1), elephants (2), eland (3), gereunk (4), black rhino (5), wart hog (6) and dik-dik (7).

Mammals

▼ Some species of mammals spend their entire lives in or around water. While whales and dolphins are totally aquatic, periodically swimming to the surface to take in air, seals, such as the harp seal and the southern fur seal, breed on land. Their forelimbs have evolved into effective paddles, Many marine mammals have an insulating layer of fat (blubber) to protect them from their cooler environment.

Harp seal

Southern fur seal

▼ Some primitive mammals, such as the duck-billed platypus and echidna, are monotremes, they lay eggs rather than give birth to live young. The echidna's egg (1) is soft-shelled and resembles a reptile's egg. Once the egg is laid, the echidna uses its hind limbs to roll it to a special incubation grove (2). The minute hatchling is about 1.25cm (0.5in) long. Other primitive mammals, such as the kangaroo, are marsupials. They give birth to live young but fetal development occurs outside the body, usually in a pouch.

Echidna

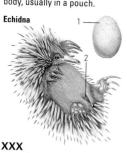

Cheetah

▲ Also known as the hunting leopard, the cheetah is one of the best-adapted carnivorous mammals. It hunts antelope, hares and some species of birds, such as guinea fowl and ostriches. It has long legs, a subtle but strong back, and well-developed eyesight. It is distinguished by its pattern of solid black spots and a striped tail.

▼ Bats are the only mammals that have adapted to fly (although some species of mammal are able to glide). Between the forelimbs, bats evolved a skin membrane which forms a wing. Some bats, such as the large mouse-eared bat, use echolocation to locate their prey. They emit a rapid series of high-pitched squeaks, which when they hit an object rebound. The bat senses the echo, and is able to accurately judge the distance between itself and its prey. Bats also use echolocation to navigate.

Large mouse-eared bat

Frog

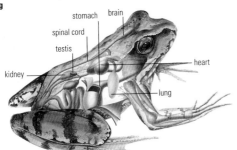

stomach
brain
spinal cord
testis
kidney
heart
lung

▲ The class of amphibians includes frogs, toads, newts, salamanders and caecilians. Their development occurs in two distinct stages. The first, the larval stage is usually aquatic, while the adult stage is spent half on land, half in water.

Lobster

▲ The class of crustaceans, including lobsters, crabs, shrimps, barnacles and woodlice, comprises about 35,000 species. They are arthropods, having jointed limbs and segmented bodies which are covered in a chitinous shell that helps to protect the soft inner organs. Most crustaceans are marine, but there are some freshwater species.

Nile crocodile

▶ There are about 6,000 species of reptiles, including the crocodile, turtles, lizards and snakes. They differ from fish and most amphibians in that fertilization occurs within the female, and their eggs can survive on land.

▶ The surface feathers of birds are vaned and all have a strong, light central shaft, the rachis (1) from which hundreds of barbs (2) extend in one plane to form the vane. Barbules (3) project from the barbs, and those that point away from the bird's body have tiny hooks, hamuli (4) which lock into the hookless barbs. This interlocking construction gives strength and helps the feather to keep its shape. Common types of feathers include the flight feathers (5) and bristle feathers (6). The down feathers (7) provide good insulation. The contour feathers (8) have an interlocking lattice structure. In flying birds they serve as streamlining. Filoplumes (9) are hairlike feathers that are either sensory or decorative. Some birds have body contour feathers (10) with aftershafts (11) that resemble a smaller feather.

Feathers

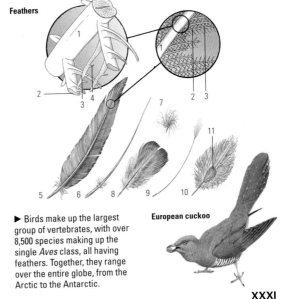

▶ Birds make up the largest group of vertebrates, with over 8,500 species making up the single *Aves* class, all having feathers. Together, they range over the entire globe, from the Arctic to the Antarctic.

European cuckoo

Honey bee

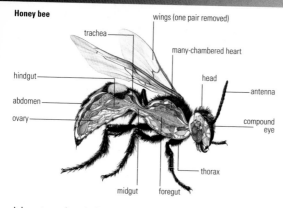

- trachea
- wings (one pair removed)
- many-chambered heart
- head
- antenna
- hindgut
- compound eye
- abdomen
- ovary
- thorax
- midgut
- foregut

▲ Insects, such as the honey bee, make up the largest class in the animal kingdom. There are over a million identified species, adapted to live in just about all the Earth's habitats. Although they vary greatly in size from 0.2–350mm, insects share the same basic body structure. It is divided into three; the head (with a pair of antennae), the thorax (with three pairs of legs, and usually two pairs of wings) and the abdomen.

▼ To reach their adult stage, most insects, such as the European swallowtail butterfly, metamorphose. In this case the adult lays the eggs, which hatch into the first larval stage, the caterpillar (1). The caterpillar moults successively until its skin begins to harden (2–3) forming a chrysalis (4). Inside the case, the caterpillar's body is reorganized into a mature butterfly (5).

European swallowtail butterfly

Cartilaginous fish (shark)

◀ ▼ Fish are divided into two classes; cartilaginous, including sharks and rays, and the true bony fish, mainly those caught for food and game fish. They differ in that bony fish fertilize their eggs outside the body, they have covered gills and a swim bladder to maintain buoyancy. Sharks, however, have open gills, fertilization occurs within the female (some even give birth to live young) and they have no swim bladder.

Bony fish

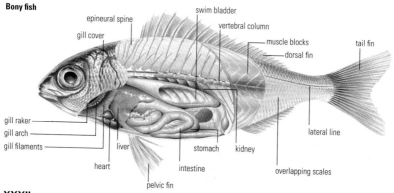

- epineural spine
- swim bladder
- vertebral column
- gill cover
- muscle blocks
- dorsal fin
- tail fin
- gill raker
- gill arch
- gill filaments
- liver
- stomach
- kidney
- lateral line
- heart
- intestine
- overlapping scales
- pelvic fin

LESOTHO
AREA: 30,350sq km (11,718sq mi)
POPULATION: 1,836,000
CAPITAL (POPULATION): Maseru (367,000)
GOVERNMENT: Constitutional monarchy
ETHNIC GROUPS: Sotho 99%
LANGUAGES: Sesotho and English (both official)
RELIGIONS: Christianity 93% (Roman Catholic 44%), traditional beliefs 6%
CURRENCY: Loti = 100 lisente

with KwaZulu-Natal, and includes its highest peak, Thabana Ntlenyana, at 3,482m (11,424ft). Most people live in the w lowlands, site of Maseru, or in the s valley of the River Orange, which rises in NE Lesotho and flows through South Africa to the Atlantic Ocean. All land in Lesotho is held by the king in trust for the Sotho nation. Lesotho's climate is greatly affected by altitude; 66% of the land lies above 1,500m (4,921 ft). Maseru has warm summers and cold winters. Rainfall averages c.700mm (28in). Grassland covers much of Lesotho. Trees and shrubs grow only in sheltered valleys. **Economy** Lesotho is a low-income, less-developed country. It lacks natural resources. Agriculture, mainly at subsistence level, is the main activity. Major farm products include beans, cattle, hides and skins, maize, wool and wheat. Light manufacturing and expatriates' remittances from working abroad (mainly in South African mines) are the other main sources of income. Manufactures include processed food, handicrafts and textiles. Tourism is developing. **History** The early 19th-century tribal wars dispersed the Sotho. In the 1820s a Sotho kingdom was formed by Moshoeshoe I in present-day Lesotho. Moshoeshoe I resisted Boer and British attempts at colonization, but was finally forced to yield to the British, and in 1868 the area became a protectorate. In 1871 it became part of the British Cape Colony, but after British failure to disarm the Sotho, the area fell under direct rule. Sotho opposition to incorporation into the Union of South Africa saw the creation of the independent kingdom of Lesotho in 1966. Moshoeshoe II, great-grandson of Moshoeshoe I, became king. In 1970 Leabua Jonathan suspended the constitution and banned opposition parties. The next 16 years were characterized by civil conflict between government and Basuto Congress Party (BCP) forces. In 1986 a military coup led to the reinstatement of Moshoeshoe II. In 1990 Moshoeshoe II was deposed and replaced by his son, Letsie III. The BCP won the 1992 multiparty elections and the military council was dissolved. **Recent events** In 1994 Letsie III attempted to overthrow the government. In January 1995 Moshoeshoe II was restored to the throne. His death in 1996 saw the reascension of Letsie III. In 1997 the prime minister and former BCP leader,

Ntsu Mokhehle, established a new political party, the Lesotho Congress for Democracy (LCD). A majority of BCP politicians joined the LCD, thus turning the BCP into the official opposition.
less developed countries (LDCs) Those countries, primarily of Africa, Asia and Latin America, that have little or no industrial base. Characteristically, they have high rates of population growth, high infant mortality, short life expectancy, low levels of literacy and poor distribution of wealth.
Lesseps, Ferdinand Marie, Vicomte de (1805–94) French diplomat and engineer. He formed the Suez Canal Company, securing finance from the French government. Digging was begun in 1859 and the canal was opened in November 1869. His scheme to construct the Panama Canal without using a system of locks began in 1879, but was abandoned seven years later with the failure of De Lesseps' company.
Lesser Antilles *See* Antilles
Lessing, Doris May (1919–) British novelist, b. Persia, who was brought up in Rhodesia (Zimbabwe). She came to notice with her first novel, *The Grass Is Singing* (1950). Her commitment to communism and the women's movement informs the five-volume *Children of Violence* series (1952–69) and *The Golden Notebook* (1962).
Lethe In Greek mythology, the river of forgetfulness in Hades. All who drank from it lost their memories of past lives.
leucite Grey or white feldspar mineral, potassium aluminium silicate, $KAl(SiO_3)_2$. Unstable at high pressures, it can be found in potassium-rich lava flows and volcanic plugs. Hardness 5.5–6; s.g. 2.5.
leucocyte White blood cell, a colourless structure containing a nucleus and cytoplasm. There are two types of leucocytes – lymphocytes and phagocytes. Normal blood contains 5,000–10,000 leucocytes per cu mm of blood. Excessive numbers of leucocytes are seen in such diseases as leukaemia.
leukaemia Any of a group of cancers in which the bone marrow and other blood-forming tissues produce abnormal numbers of immature or defective leucocytes. This over-production suppresses output of normal blood cells and platelets, leaving the person vulnerable to infection, anaemia and bleeding. It is potentially curable.
Le Vau, Louis (1612–70) French architect. Inspired by contemporary Italian Baroque buildings, he evolved a classic 17th-century French style, seen most spectacularly in his designs for the Palace of Versailles (1669–85).
Levellers (1645–49) Members of a radical movement in England in the Commonwealth period (c.1645–57). They wanted sweeping parliamentary reform, religious toleration and a fairer, more egalitarian society. Their leaders, including John Lilburne, presented a constitution to Oliver Cromwell in 1647. When their demands were not met, several mutinies broke out in the army, resulting in their suppression.

lever Simple machine used to multiply the force applied to an object, usually to raise a heavy load. A lever consists of a rod and a point (fulcrum) about which the rod pivots.

Leverrier, Urbain-Jean-Joseph (1811–77) French astronomer. He predicted that an unknown planet (Neptune) was responsible for discrepancies between the calculated and observed orbital motion of Uranus.

Levi, Primo (1919–87) Italian writer. A Jew, Levi joined a guerrilla movement in World War 2. He was captured and sent to Auschwitz. His books, such as *If This is a Man* (1947), *The Truce* (1963) and *The Periodic Table* (1984), attempt to deal with his experiences.

Lévi-Strauss, Claude (1908–90) French anthropologist. He was the founder of structural anthropology, which explores the underlying structures of social organization. His books include *The Elementary Structures of Kinship* (1949) and *Structural Anthropology* (1958).

Levites Clan of religious officials in ancient Israel. It is possible that they once constituted one of the 12 tribes of Israel mentioned in the Old Testament, descended from Levi, the third son of JACOB by his first wife Leah. After the building of the TEMPLE of Jerusalem, Levites performed the lesser religious services. By the time of JESUS CHRIST, the Levites ran the entire Temple organization with the sole exception of the actual priesthood.

Leviticus Third book of the PENTATEUCH or TORAH. It is primarily a manual for the instruction of priests on ritual technicalities.

Lewes, George Henry (1817–78) English journalist and critic. He wrote dramatic criticism as well as philosophical works, including *A Biographical History of Philosophy* (1845) and the hugely successful *The Life and Works of Goethe* (1855). Separated from his wife, he lived with George ELIOT, whose work he encouraged and influenced.

Lewis, Carl (Frederick Carlton) (1961–) US track and field athlete. In a glittering career, Lewis won nine Olympic gold medals: 100m, 200m, 4×100m relay and long jump (1984, Los Angeles), equalling Jesse OWENS' feat; 100m and long jump (Seoul, 1988); long jump and 4×100m relay (Barcelona, 1992); and long jump (Atlanta, 1996).

Lewis, C.S. (Clive Staples) (1898–1963) British scholar, critic and author. His scholarly works include *The Allegory of Love* (1936) and *The Discarded Image* (1964). He is best known, however, for the books on religious and moral themes written after his conversion to Christianity, particularly *The Screwtape Letters* (1942) and his autobiography *Surprised by Joy* (1955). He wrote a number of highly acclaimed children's books, including the seven "Narnia" stories, beginning with *The Lion, the Witch and the Wardrobe* (1950).

Lewis, (Harry) Sinclair (1885–1951) US author. He first gained acclaim for *Main Street* (1920). His early work, in particular *Babbitt*

(1922) and the Pulitzer Prize-winning *Arrowsmith* (1925), is generally considered to be his best. In 1930 he became the first US author to be awarded the Nobel Prize for literature.

Lewis, (Percy) Wyndham (1884–1957) British painter, critic and novelist. He was the central figure of the VORTICISM movement. After World War 1 he produced a series of novels and essays, including *The Apes of God* (1930) and *Men Without Art* (1934).

Lewis and Clark Expedition (1804–06) US expedition to seek a route by water from the Mississippi to the Pacific Ocean. Instigated by President JEFFERSON, it was led by army officers Meriwether Lewis and William Clark, with the assistance of a Shoshone woman, Sacajawea. It reached the Pacific at the mouth of the Columbia River and produced valuable information about the country and peoples of the Northwest.

Lexington and Concord, Battles of (April 1775) First battles of the AMERICAN REVOLUTION. British troops marching from Boston to Concord, Massachusetts, were intercepted by Minutemen (militiamen) at Lexington Green. Several minutemen were killed, and the British advanced to Concord and destroyed some military supply stores. During their return to Boston the British were involved in several skirmishes and suffered nearly 300 casualties.

Leyden jar Earliest and simplest device for storing static electricity, developed *c*.1745 in Leyden, Holland. The original electrical condenser (capacitor), it consists of a foil-lined glass jar partly filled with water and closed with a cork through which protrudes a brass rod wired to the foil. To charge the jar, friction is applied to the tip of the rod.

Lhasa Capital of Tibet (Xizang Zizhiqu) Autonomous Region, sw China, on a tributary of the Brahmaputra, at 3,600m (11,800ft) in the N Himalayas. An ancient religious centre, it was occupied by the Chinese in 1951. After the Tibetan revolt against the occupation (1959–60), many of Lhasa's temples and monasteries were closed. The 17th-century Potala Palace was the home of the DALAI LAMA. Today the city is an important trading centre, also manufacturing chemicals and processing gold and copper. Pop. (1992) 124,000.

liana Any ground-rooting woody vine that twines and creeps extensively over other plants for support; it is common in tropical forests. Some species may reach a diameter of 60cm (24in) and a length of 100m (330ft).

Libby, Willard Frank (1908–80) US chemist. From 1941–45 he worked on the separation of isotopes for the atomic bomb. This led to his development of radioactive carbon-14 dating, for which he was awarded the 1960 Nobel Prize for chemistry. He is the author of *Radiocarbon Dating* (1955).

libel Permanent, false statement to a third person containing an untrue imputation against the reputation of another. Publications of any defamatory matter in permanent form (such as an article, picture, film or broadcast statement) are treated as libel. Although usually a civil offence, libel may be considered criminal in certain circumstances.

Liberal Democrats (officially Social and Liberal Democrats) British political party, formed in March 1988 by the merger of the LIBERAL PARTY and the SOCIAL DEMOCRATIC PARTY (SDP). Since 1988 it has been led by Paddy ASHDOWN. The smallest of the main political parties, it has vigorously campaigned for PROPORTIONAL REPRESENTATION. In the 1997 general election, the Liberal Democrats more than doubled their representation in Parliament.

liberalism Political and intellectual belief that advocates the right of the individual to make decisions, usually political or religious, according to the dictates of conscience. Its modern origins lie in the 18th-century ENLIGHTENMENT. In politics it opposes arbitrary power and discrimination against minorities. In British history its greatest influence was exercised in the 19th century.

Liberal Party British political party. It grew out of the early 19th-century WHIG PARTY. The first official use of the name was the National Liberal Federation (1877), founded by Joseph CHAMBERLAIN. The 19th-century party drew its strength from religious dissent and the urban electorate. Its predominant interests were free trade, religious and individual liberty, financial retrenchment and constitutional reform. Its greatest leader was William GLADSTONE. The 1906 government of Campbell-Bannerman legalized TRADE UNIONS, reformed the House of Lords and introduced progressive SOCIAL SECURITY measures. In 1908 Herbert ASQUITH became leader and prime minister. In 1916 LLOYD GEORGE formed a coalition government with the CONSERVATIVE PARTY. Since the fall of that administration, it has never formed a government. It was nevertheless instrumental in keeping the Labour Party in office during two periods of minority government: in the mid-1920s by tacit support, and in 1977 by a formal arrangement (Lib-Lab Pact). After the formation of the SOCIAL DEMOCRATIC PARTY (SDP) in 1980, the Liberal Party entered into an alliance, and then merged with it in 1987. In 1988 the Liberal members and most of the SDP formed the LIBERAL DEMOCRATS.

Liberal Party Canadian political party, formed in 1854 by a union of the more radical elements of the Reformers. Their first administration (1873–78), under Alexander Mackenzie, was anti-railway and advocated free trade. Under the leadership of Wilfrid LAURIER (1896–1911), the Liberals supported ethnic conciliation, independence and immigration. Later, it held power under Lester PEARSON (1963–68), Pierre TRUDEAU (1968–79, 1980–84), John Turner (1984) and Jean CHRÉTIEN (1993–).

Liberia Republic in W Africa on the Atlantic coast; the captial is MONROVIA. **Land and climate** Liberia's coast stretches over 500km (311mi), and is the site of Monrovia, its chief port. A narrow

---

LIBERIA
AREA: 111,370sq km (43,000sq mi)
POPULATION: 2,580,000
CAPITAL (POPULATION): Monrovia (425,000)
GOVERNMENT: Multiparty republic
ETHNIC GROUPS: Kpelle 19%, Bassa 14%, Grebo 9%, Gio 8%, Kru 7%, Mano 7%
LANGUAGES: English (official)
RELIGIONS: Christianity 68%, Islam 14%, traditional beliefs and others 18%,
CURRENCY: Liberian dollar = 100 cents

---

coastal plain rises to a plateau region. Liberia has a tropical climate with high temperatures and humidity. Mangrove swamps and lagoons line the coast, while inland, forests cover nearly 40% of the land. Only 5% of the land is cultivated. **Economy** Civil war has devastated Liberia's economy. Agriculture employs 75% of the workforce, mainly at subsistence level. Chief food crops include cassava, rice and sugar cane. Rubber, cocoa and coffee are grown for export. Timber is also exported. Crude materials, principally iron ore, account for over 90% of Liberia's exports. Liberia also obtains revenue from its "flag of convenience", used by about 15% of the world's commercial shipping. **History** Liberia was founded in 1821 by the American Colonization Society. In 1822 the Society landed African-American former slaves at a coastal settlement, which they named Monrovia. In 1847 Liberia became a fully independent republic. Under the leadership (1944–71) of William Tubman, Liberia's economy grew and social reforms were adopted. Tubman's successor, William R. Tolbert, was assassinated in a military coup in 1980, and Master-Sergeant Samuel Doe led the new military government. In 1990 civil war broke out, and the Economic Community of West African States (ECOWAS) sent a five-nation peacekeeping force. Doe was assassinated and an interim government, led by Amos Sawyer, was formed. **Recent events** In 1995 a cease-fire was agreed and a council of state, composed of formerly warring leaders, was established. Conflict resumed when one faction's leader, Roosevelt Johnson, was dismissed from the council. A further cease-fire was agreed in July 1996. In 1997 parliamentary and legislative elections, former warlord Charles Taylor and his National Patriotic Party (NPP) secured a resounding victory.

libido In PSYCHOANALYSIS, term used by Sigmund FREUD to describe instinctive sexual energy. Freud later enlarged its meaning to include all mental energy (or life energy) that accompanies strong desires.

Libreville Capital and largest city of Gabon, W central Africa, at the mouth of the River Gabon, on the Gulf of Guinea. Founded by the French in 1843 and named Libreville (Fr. Freetown) in 1849, it was initially a refuge for escaped slaves. The

367

city expanded with the development of the country's minerals and is now also an administrative centre. Other industries: timber (hardwoods), palm oil and rubber. Pop. (1993) 418,000.

Libya Republic of N Africa, the capital is Tripoli.
Land and climate Libya consists of three geographical areas: the NW and NE Mediterranean coastal plains are home to the majority of Libya's population. The NE plain includes Tripoli; the NW plain its second-largest city, BENGHAZI. The SAHARA occupies 95% of Libya. The coastal plains have a Mediterranean climate, with hot, dry summers and mild, moist winters. Shrubs and grasses grow on the N coasts. **Economy** The discovery of oil in 1958 transformed Libya's economy. Oil revenue was used to finance welfare services and development projects. Formerly one of the world's poorest countries, it has become Africa's richest in terms of its GDP per capita. Oil accounts for over 95% of exports. **History** The earliest known inhabitants of Libya were the BERBERS. Between the 7th century BC and the 5th century AD, the region came under the rule of Greeks, Carthaginians, Romans and Vandals. Arabs invaded Libya in AD 642 and Islam remains the dominant religion. From 1551 Libya was part of the Ottoman empire. Italy invaded Libya in 1911 and by 1914 had conquered the whole territory. Attempts at colonization were made in the 1930s and in 1939 Libya was formally incorporated into Italy. During World War 2 the country was a battleground for many of the North Africa Campaigns. Following the Allied victory, Libya was placed under UN mandate until 1951, when it became an independent monarchy. In 1953 Libya joined the Arab League, and in 1955 became a member of the UN. In 1969 the king was overthrown in a military coup led by Colonel Muammar al-QADDAFI. A Revolutionary Command Council set about the nationalization of industry, the establishment of an Islamic state, and the reduction of foreign interference. In 1971 Libya entered a Federation with Egypt and Syria. Libya maintained an anti-Israel foreign policy and Qaddafi aided Palestinian guerrilla movements. During the 1980s Libyan and US relations deteriorated further. Following an attack on US forces, the USA placed an oil embargo on Libya. In 1986, following evidence of Libyan support of international terrorism, the USA bombed Tripoli and Benghazi. In 1992 Libya was accused of sheltering the terrorists responsible for the bombing of a domestic airliner over Lockerbie, UK, and has subsequently refused to extradite them to the USA or the UK. Libya has a long-standing territorial dispute with Chad, and sent troops to intervene in the civil war. In 1994 the International Court of Justice dismissed Libya's claim to the Aozou Strip in N Chad. **Politics** Qaddafi has attracted worldwide criticism for his support of revolutionary movements. In 1995 all Palestinians were ordered to leave Libya in protest against the PLO-Israeli peace agreement.

lice See LOUSE

lichen Plant comprising a FUNGUS in which microscopic (usually single-celled) ALGAE are embedded. The fungus and its algae form a symbiotic association in which the fungus contributes support, water and minerals, while the algae contribute food produced by PHOTOSYNTHESIS. See also SYMBIOSIS

Lichtenstein, Roy (1923–97) US painter, sculptor and graphic artist. He experimented with ABSTRACT EXPRESSIONISM and was regarded as a leading exponent of POP ART. Among his best-known paintings are *Whaam!* (1963) and *Good Morning, Darling* (1964).

licorice See LIQUORICE

Lie, Trygve Halvdan (1896–1968) Norwegian statesman, first secretary-general of the UNITED NATIONS (UN) (1946–52). He blamed both sides for the COLD WAR, but antagonized the Soviet Union by his support for UN intervention in the Korean War (1950). He was replaced by HAMMARSKJÖLD.

Liebknecht, Karl (1871–1919) German communist revolutionary. He opposed Germany's participation in World War 1 and was imprisoned (1916–18). With Rosa LUXEMBURG, he was a leader of the communist group known as the Spartacists. After the failure of the Spartacist rising (1919), they were murdered while in police custody.

Liechtenstein Independent principality in W central Europe at the E end of the Alps, between Austria (E) and Switzerland (W); the capital is Vaduz. The principality was formed in 1719 through the merging of Vaduz and Schellenberg. It remained part of the Holy Roman Empire until 1806. A member of the German Confederation from 1815, it gained independent status in 1866. In 1921 Liechtenstein entered into a currency union with Switzerland and, in 1923, a customs union. Until 1990 Switzerland also handled Liechtenstein's foreign policy. In 1990 the principality joined the UN. Liechtenstein has a constitutional and hereditary monarchy. In 1997 the coalition that had ruled Liechtenstein since 1938 collapsed when the Patriotic Union (PU) withdrew. A new government consisting entirely of PU members was formed. It is the fourth-smallest country in the world and one of the richest (1992 GDP per capita, US$34,000). The major part of state revenue is derived from international companies, attracted by the low taxation

---

LIBYA
AREA: 1,759,540sq km (679,358sq mi)
POPULATION: 4,875,000
CAPITAL (POPULATION): Tripoli (990,697)
GOVERNMENT: Single-party socialist state
ETHNIC GROUPS: Libyan Arab and Berber 89%, others 11%
LANGUAGES: Arabic (official)
RELIGIONS: Islam
CURRENCY: Libyan dinar = 1,000 dirhams

rates. Tourism is increasingly important. Area: 157sq km (61sq mi). Pop. (1990) 28,777.

lie detector (polygraph) Electronic device that may be capable of detecting lies when used by a trained examiner. The lie detector monitors such factors as heart rate, breathing rate and perspiration, all of which may be affected when a person lies.

life Feature of organisms that sets them apart from inorganic matter. Life can be regarded as the ability of organisms to obtain energy from the Sun or from food and to use this for growth and reproduction. The current theory on life's origin is that giant molecules, similar to proteins and nucleic acids, reacted together in the watery surface environment of the young Earth that is now commonly called the primordial soup. The evolution and development of cellular life out of this molecular pre-life is yet to be explained fully.

lift In AERODYNAMICS, force that acts upwards on the undersurface of an AEROFOIL, or wing. As it travels forwards, the leading edge of an aerofoil splits the air stream. Because the upper part of the air stream is forced to travel farther, its pressure falls. The lift force is a result of the upward pressure underneath the aerofoil being greater than the downward pressure on the top.

ligament Bands of tough fibrous CONNECTIVE TISSUE that join bone to bone at the joints. In the wrist and ankle joints, for example, they surround the bones like firm inelastic bandages.

light Part of the total electromagnetic spectrum that can be detected by the human eye. Visible light is in the wavelength range from about 400nm (violet) to 770nm (red). Light exhibits typical phenomena of wave motion, such as REFLECTION, REFRACTION, DIFFRACTION, light polarization and INTERFERENCE. The properties of light were investigated in the 17th century by Isaac NEWTON, who believed in a particle theory of light. The wave theory was well-established by the second decade of the 19th century after the work of Thomas YOUNG. At the beginning of the 20th century, experiments on the PHOTOELECTRIC EFFECT and the work of Max PLANCK revived the idea that light can behave like a stream of particles. This dilemma was resolved by the QUANTUM THEORY, according to which light consists of elementary particles called PHOTONS. When light interacts with matter, as in the photoelectric effect, energy is exchanged in the form of photons and so light seems to be particles. Otherwise, it behaves as a wave.

lightning Visible flash of light accompanying an electrical discharge between clouds or between clouds and the surface, most commonly produced in a THUNDERSTORM.

light-year Unit of astronomical distance equal to the distance travelled in free space or a vacuum by light in one tropical year. One light-year is equal to 9.4607×10^{12} km (5.88×10^{12} mi).

lignin Complex non-carbohydrate substance that occurs in woody tissues (especially XYLEM of plants), often in combination with cellulose. It is lignin that gives wood its strength.

Lilburne, John (1614–57) English republican, leader of the LEVELLERS. Imprisoned (1638–40) under CHARLES I, he fought for Parliament during the CIVIL WAR (1642–45). Captured, he escaped execution by the Royalists when Parliament arranged an exchange of prisoners. He left the army in 1645, refusing to sign the SOLEMN LEAGUE AND COVENANT. Demanding greater equality and religious freedom, he led protests against the government of CROMWELL. Often imprisoned, he spent his last years among Quakers.

Lilongwe Capital of Malawi, SE Africa, in the centre of the country, c.80km (50mi) W of Lake Malawi. It replaced Zomba as the capital of Malawi in 1975. It has grown rapidly to become the country's second-largest city. Pop. (1993) 268,000.

lily Any of numerous species of perennial, BULB-producing plants of the genus *Lilium*, from temperate and subtropical regions. They have erect stems and various leaf arrangements. The showy flowers may be almost any colour.

lily of the valley Perennial woodland plant native to Europe, Asia and E USA. It has broad, elongated leaves and bears stalks of tiny, white, bell-shaped fragrant flowers. Family Liliaceae; species *Convallaria majalis*.

Lima Capital and largest city of Peru, on the River Rímac at the foot of the Cerro San Cristóbal. Lima was founded in 1535 by Francisco PIZARRO. It functioned as the capital of the Spanish New World colonies until the 19th century. It is the commercial and cultural centre of Peru. Pop. (1993) 6,386,308.

limbic system Collection of structures in the middle of the brain. Looped round the HYPOTHALAMUS, the limbic system is thought to be involved in emotional responses, such as fear and aggression, the production of mood changes, and the laying down of memories.

limbo In Roman Catholic theology, the abode of souls excluded from HEAVEN but not condemned to any other punishment. According to this concept, which never became doctrine, unbaptized infants go to limbo after death, as did the Old Testament prophets who died before Christ came to redeem the world.

Limbourg, Pol de (active 1380–1416) Franco-Flemish manuscript illustrator. Pol and his brothers, Jan and Hermann, became court painters to Jean, duc de Berry in 1411. Their masterpiece is a Book of Hours known as *Les Très Riches Heures du Duc de Berry* (1413–15). *See also* ILLUMINATION

lime Name for any of the deciduous linden trees that grow throughout the N temperate zone. It has serrated, heart-shaped leaves with small, fragrant, yellowish flowers that are borne in clusters. Family Tiliaceae.

lime Small tropical tree (*Citrus aurantifolia*) of the

rue family (Rutaceae). The trees grow to 2.4–4.6m (8–15ft) and yield small, green, acid fruits. The juice was a valuable commodity in the 18th and 19th centuries for consumption on long sea voyages; the vitamin C helped to ward off SCURVY.

limestone SEDIMENTARY ROCK composed primarily of carbonates, such as calcite $CaCO_3$. Generally formed from deposits of the skeletons of marine invertebrates, it is used to make cement and lime and as a building material.

limpet Primitive gastropod MOLLUSC commonly found fixed to rocks along marine shores. It has a cap-like, rather than coiled, shell and a large muscular foot. Length: to 13cm (5in). Families: Patellacea, Acmaeidae and Fissurellidae.

Limpopo (Crocodile) River in S Africa. It rises in NE South Africa, in the former Transvaal province. It then flows in a great curve N, forming part of the border between South Africa and Botswana, then E as the border of South Africa and Zimbabwe before crossing Mozambique to enter the Indian Ocean NE of Maputo. Length: c.1,770km (1,100mi).

Lin Biao (1907–71) Chinese communist general and political leader. He defeated CHIANG KAI-SHEK in Manchuria (1948), thus helping to secure the victory of the communists in 1949. Lin was a leader of the CULTURAL REVOLUTION (1966–69) and compiled the book of quotations from MAO ZEDONG known as the *Little Red Book*. He was designated Mao's heir in 1969 but, after disagreements with Mao, was said to have died accidentally while fleeing to the Soviet Union.

Lincoln, Abraham (1809–65) 16th US President (1861–65). He served in the US House of Representatives (1847–49) from Illinois and unsuccessfully ran for the Senate for the new REPUBLICAN PARTY in 1858. He was nominated as Republican candidate for president in 1860. Lincoln's victory made the secession of the Southern, slave-owning states inevitable, and his determination to defend FORT SUMTER began the American CIVIL WAR. In September 1862 he issued the EMANCIPATION PROCLAMATION, and in November 1863 delivered his famous GETTYSBURG ADDRESS. Lincoln was re-elected in 1864 and saw the war to a successful conclusion. On 14 April 1865, five days after the surrender of Robert E. LEE, he was shot by John Wilkes BOOTH, a Southern sympathizer. He died the following day.

Lincoln City in E England; the county town of LINCOLNSHIRE. Founded by the Romans as Lindum Colonia, it thrived on its wool trade until the 14th century. The castle was begun in the reign of William I. Lincoln Cathedral (begun c.1073) has one of the original copies of the Magna Carta. Industries: agricultural and automobile parts. Pop. (1991) 81,900.

Lincolnshire County in E England, bordering the North Sea; the county town is LINCOLN. The area was settled by the Romans and an Anglo-Saxon kingdom was later established in Lindsey. In the Middle Ages it was a prosperous farming region. In 1974 part of N Lincolnshire was incorporated into the new authority of Humberside. Apart from the undulating Wolds, the region is flat, drained by the Trent, Welland and Witham rivers. Agriculture is the mainstay of the economy, mainly cereals, sugar beet and sheep. Area 5,886sq km (2,273sq mi). Pop. (1994) 605,800.

Lind, Jenny (1820–87) ("Swedish nightingale") Sweden's most famous operatic soprano. She made her debut in 1838, and after world success in coloratura roles she settled in London (c.1852), where she sang in oratorio and taught at the Royal College of Music.

Lindbergh, Charles Augustus (1902–74) US aviator. He became an international hero when, in *The Spirit of St Louis*, he made the first nonstop transatlantic solo flight, from New York to Paris (1927) in 33 hours 30 minutes. In 1932 his baby son was kidnapped and murdered.

Lindisfarne Gospels Manuscript illuminated in the Hiberno-Saxon style in the late 7th or 8th century. It may have been executed for Eadfrith, Bishop of Lindisfarne (698–721).

linear script Early form of writing, found on clay tablets in Crete and Greece. Linear A was in use during the middle period of the MINOAN CIVILIZATION (c.2100–c.1550 BC). Linear B was an adaptation of Linear A, used by the MYCENAEAN CIVILIZATION of mainland Greece to write their early form of Greek. In 1952 Michael Ventris deciphered Linear B; Linear A defies analysis.

Lineker, Gary Winston (1960–) English footballer. He began his career with Leicester City. He then moved to Everton and in 1986 was the leading scorer at the World Cup finals in Mexico. Further moves took him to Barcelona and in 1989 to Tottenham Hotspur. In 1993 he went to Japan to play for the Nagoya Grampus 8 club, returning to Britain as a sports journalist in 1995.

linen Yarn and fabric made of fibres from the FLAX plant. The fibres are released from the substance that binds them by retting (soaking) the long stems in water. After sorting, the fibres are spun to form yarn, which is then woven.

ling *See* HEATHER

ling Food fish related to the COD found in the Atlantic Ocean. It is brown and silver and has long dorsal and ventral fins. Length: to 2m (7ft); weight: 3.6kg (8lb). Family Gadidae; species *Molva molva*.

lingua franca Language that serves as a medium of communication between people who otherwise lack a common tongue. A lingua franca may be a highly simplified form of the language of the dominant power, such as PIDGIN English, or it may be a hybrid, such as SWAHILI.

linguistics Systematic study of LANGUAGE, its nature, its structure, its constituent elements, and the changes it may undergo. As a discipline, linguistics embraces PHONETICS, phonology (the study of sound systems within languages), GRAM-

MAR (including SYNTAX), SEMANTICS and pragmatics (the study of language use). *See also* LANGUAGE

Linnaeus, Carolus (1707–78) (Carl von Linné) Swedish botanist and taxonomist. His *Systema Naturae*, published in 1735, laid the foundation of the modern science of TAXONOMY by including all known organisms in a single classification system. He was one of the first scientists to define clearly the differences between species, and he devised the system of BINOMIAL NOMENCLATURE, which gave standardized Latin names to every organism.

linseed *See* FLAX

lion Large CAT that lives on African savannas south of the Sahara and in SW Asia. It is golden yellow with light spots under the eyes. The male is instantly recognizable by its deep neck mane, which darkens with age. The female does most of the hunting and preys on antelopes, zebras and bush pigs. Length: to 2.5m (8.5ft) overall. Family Felidae; species *Panthera leo*.

Lipchitz, Jacques (1891–1973) French sculptor, b. Lithuania. He created one of the first cubist sculptures, *Man with Guitar* (1914). After moving to the USA in 1941 his work became more spiritual and more solid in structure. Among his most representative works are *Sailor with a Guitar* (1914), *Harpist* (1928) and *Prayer* (1943). *See also* CUBISM

Li Peng (1928–) Chinese political leader. A protégé of Zhou Enlai, he rose rapidly in the political hierarchy, becoming deputy premier (1983) and a member of the politburo in 1985. He became premier in 1987. During the pro-democracy demonstrations of 1989 he declared martial law, leading to the military intervention against students demonstrating in TIANANMEN SQUARE, Beijing.

lipid One of a large group of fatty organic compounds in living organisms. They include animal fats, vegetable oils and natural waxes. Lipids form an important food store and energy source in plant and animal cells.

Lippi, Filippino (1457–1504) Florentine painter. The son of Fra Filippo LIPPI, he studied with BOTTICELLI. He completed the frescos of MASACCIO in Santa Maria del Carmine (1484). His work is shown to full effect in his fresco cycles in the Caraffa Chapel, Santa Maria sopra Minerva, Rome (1488–93) and the Strozzi Chapel, Santa Maria Novella, Florence. He also painted altarpieces, notably *The Vision of St Bernard* (c.1480, Badia, Florence).

Lippi, Fra Filippo (1406–69) Florentine painter. His most characteristic subject was the Virgin and Child, which he sometimes painted in an innovative circular format. His finest fresco cycle depicts the lives of St Stephen and St John in Prato Cathedral. Lippi was a major influence on the 19th-century PRE-RAPHAELITE BROTHERHOOD.

liquid State of MATTER intermediate between a GAS and a SOLID. A liquid substance has a relatively fixed volume but flows to take the shape of its container. The state that a substance assumes depends on the temperature and the pressure at which it is kept; a substance that is liquid at room temperature, such as water, can be changed into a vapour (its gaseous state, steam) by heating, or into a solid (ice) by cooling.

liquid crystal Substance that can exist half-way between the liquid and solid states with its molecules partly ordered. By applying a carefully controlled electric current, liquid crystals turn dark. They are used in liquid crystal displays (LCDs) to show numbers and letters, as in pocket calculators.

liquorice (licorice) Perennial plant of the pea family, native to the Mediterranean region and cultivated in temperate and subtropical areas. The dried roots are used to flavour confectionery, tobacco, beverages and medicines. Height: to 90cm (3ft). Family Fabaceae/Leguminosae; species *Glycyrrhiza glabra*.

Lisbon (Lisboa) Capital, largest city and chief port of Portugal, at the mouth of the River TAGUS, on the Atlantic Ocean. An ancient Phoenician settlement, the city was conquered by the Romans in 205 BC and, after suffering waves of Teutonic invasions in the 5th century AD, fell to the Moors in 716. In 1147 the Portuguese reclaimed the city, and in 1260 it became the nation's capital. It declined under Spanish occupation from 1580–1640. Modern Lisbon is a busy international port and tourist centre. Industries: steel, shipbuilding, chemicals, oil and sugar refining. Pop. (1991) 2,561,000.

Lister, Joseph, 1st Baron (1827–1912) British surgeon who introduced the principle of antisepsis. Using carbolic acid (phenol) as the antiseptic agent, and employing it in conjunction with heat sterilization of instruments, he brought about a dramatic decrease in post-operative fatalities.

Liszt, Franz (1811–86) Hungarian composer and pianist. He was patron to many great artists of his day, notably Frédéric CHOPIN and Edvard GRIEG. His music influenced subsequent composers including WAGNER, Richard STRAUSS and Maurice RAVEL. Among his compositions are two popular piano concertos, Hungarian rhapsodies and a mass of piano, orchestral and choral music.

literary criticism Discipline concerned with literary theory and the evaluation of literary works. The Western tradition of literary criticism began with PLATO's comments on the role of poets in his *Republic*; ARISTOTLE's response to this, the *Poetics*, represents the first systematic attempt to establish principles of literary procedure. Later contributions to the debate include SIDNEY's *The Defence of Poesie* (1595); DRYDEN's *Of Dramatick Poesie* (1668); WORDSWORTH's preface to *Lyrical Ballads* (1798); SHELLEY's *A Defence of Poetry* (1820) and the critical works of Matthew ARNOLD. The 20th century has seen an explosion of literary critical effort, including the writings of T.S ELIOT, I.A. RICHARDS, William EMPSON and F.R. LEAVIS;

also important are the writings of STRUCTURALISM and post-structuralism, notably BARTHES, FOUCAULT and Jacques Derrida. The late 20th century saw the emergence of critical approaches such as DECONSTRUCTION and feminism.

lithium Common, silvery, metallic element (symbol Li), one of the ALKALI METALS, first isolated in 1817. Ores include lepidolite and spodumene. Chemically it is similar to sodium. The element, which is the lightest of all metals, is used in alloys, and in glasses and glazes; its salts are used in medicine. Properties at.no. 3; r.a.m. 6.941; r.d. 0.534; m.p.180.5°C (356.9°F); b.p. 1,347°C (2,456.6°F); most stable isotope Li^7 (92.58%).

lithography In art, method of printing from a flat inked surface. In traditional lithography, invented in the 1790s, the design is made on a prepared plate or stone with a greasy pencil, crayon or liquid. Water applied to the surface is absorbed where there is no design. Oil-based printing ink, rolled over the surface, sticks to the design, but not to the moist areas. Pressing paper onto the surface produces a print. Today, many magazines, books and newspapers are produced by offset printing, which uses a modern form of lithography.

lithosphere The upper layer of the solid Earth; it includes the CRUST and the uppermost MANTLE. Its thickness varies but is c.60km (40mi); it extends down to a depth of c.200km (125mi). It is rigid, solid and brittle and is made up of a number of tectonic plates that move independently, giving rise to PLATE TECTONICS.

Lithuania Baltic republic in NW Europe; the capital is VILNIUS. **Land and climate** Lithuania is a mostly lowland country, with SE highlands. It has over 2,800 lakes. The longest river is the Neman, which rises in Belarus and flows through Lithuania to the Baltic Sea. Winters are cold and summers warm. Average rainfall is c.630mm (25in). Farmland covers c.75% of Lithuania, and forests only 16%. **Economy** As a Russian republic, Lithuania rapidly industrialized. Since independence it has experienced many problems of transition from a command economy into a more market-oriented one. It lacks natural resources and is dependent on Russian raw materials. Manufacturing is the most valuable export sector: major products include chemicals, electronic goods and machine tools.

LITHUANIA
AREA: 65,200sq km (25,200sq mi)
POPULATION: 3,759,000
CAPITAL (POPULATION): Vilnius (578,000)
GOVERNMENT: Multiparty republic
ETHNIC GROUPS: Lithuanian 80%, Russian 9%, Polish 7%, Belarussian 2%
LANGUAGES: Lithuanian (official)
RELIGIONS: Christianity (mainly Roman Catholic)
CURRENCY: Litas = 100 centai

Dairy and meat farming and fishing are also important activities. **History** The first independent, unified Lithuanian state emerged in 1251, and by the 14th century had expanded E as far as Moscow. In 1386 Lithuania entered into a dynastic union with Poland. The two countries were unified as a Commonwealth in 1569. The final partition of Poland saw Lithuania become part of the Russian empire (1795). In February 1918 Lithuania declared its independence. In 1920 it signed a peace treaty with the Soviet Union, and Poland captured Vilnius. In 1926 a military coup established a dictatorial government. In 1940 the Soviet Union annexed Lithuania as a Soviet republic. Nationalist demands forced the Lithuanian Communist Party to agree to multiparty elections in 1989. The 1990 elections were won by the nationalists, and Lithuania proclaimed its independence. The Soviet Union recognized Lithuania as an independent republic in September 1991. **Politics** The Democratic Labour Party, containing many ex-communists, won 1992 elections. In 1993 Algirdas Brazauskas, a former Communist Party chairman, became president and Soviet troops completed their withdrawal. In 1996 Lithuania signed a treaty of association with the European Union (EU). Presidential elections were held in 1997.

litmus Dye that is purple in neutral aqueous solutions; it is used to indicate acidity (turning red) or alkalinity (turning blue). It is most familiar in the form of litmus paper used as an acid-base indicator. The dye is extracted from lichens. *See also* pH

litre Metric unit (symbol l or L) equal to a cubic decimetre, one thousandth of a cubic metre. A litre is equivalent to 0.22 imperial gallons or 0.264 US gallons.

liturgy Established order of the rituals of public ceremonies and worship, as laid down by the authorities of an organized religion. In Christianity, the term also refers to the Divine Office or to the rites proper to specific days, such as GOOD FRIDAY, or to particular sacraments, such as BAPTISM. In the Eastern Orthodox Church, the Divine Liturgy refers specifically to the celebration of the Eucharist.

Lively, Penelope (1933–) British novelist. She has written numerous children's books, including the award-winning *The Ghost of Thomas Kempe* (1973) and *A Stitch in Time* (1976). She published her first adult novel, *The Road to Lichfield*, in 1977 and won the Booker Prize for *Moon Tiger* in 1987. Other novels include *Passing On* (1989), *City of the Mind* (1991) and *Cleopatra's Sister* (1993).

liver Large organ located in the upper right abdomen of VERTEBRATES. Weighing up to 4.5lbs (2kg) in an adult human, it is divided into four lobes and has many functions. It is extremely important in the control of the body's internal environment (HOMEOSTASIS). It receives nutrients from the intestine and is a site of metabolism of proteins, carbohydrates and fats. It synthesizes BILE and some vitamins, regulates the blood-glucose level, produces blood-clotting factors, breaks down worn-out ERYTHROCYTES and removes toxins from the blood. The many metabolic reactions that go on in the liver are the body's main source of heat, which is distributed around the body by the blood. *See also* INSULIN

Liverpool City and seaport on the N side of the River Mersey estuary, Merseyside, NW England. Liverpool was founded in the 10th century and became a free borough in 1207. The first wet dock was completed in 1715, and the city expanded rapidly to become Britain's largest port. In the early 20th century it was the major embarkation port for emigration to the New World. Liverpool suffered severe bomb damage during World War 2. In the 1980s (after city unemployment reached 28%) inner-city regeneration schemes included the Albert Dock refurbishment. Liverpool Free Port (Britain's largest) was opened in 1984. Pop. (1991) 452,450.

liverwort Any of about 9,000 species of tiny non-flowering green plants, which, like the related mosses, lack specialized tissues for transporting water, food and minerals within the plant body. Liverworts belong to the plant phylum Bryophyta.

Livingstone, David (1813–73) British explorer of Africa. He went to South Africa as a missionary in 1841 and became famous through his account of his journey across the continent from Angola to Mozambique (1853–56). He set off in 1866 to find the source of the Nile. He disappeared and was found in 1871 by Henry Morton STANLEY on Lake Tanganyika.

Livy (59–17 BC) (Titus Livius) Roman historian. One of the greatest Roman historians, he began his *History of Rome* c.28 BC. Of the original 142 books, 35 have survived in full.

lizard Reptile found on every continent; there are 20 families, c.3,000 species. A typical lizard has a scaly cylindrical body with four legs, a long tail and moveable eyelids. Most lizards are terrestrial, and many live in deserts. There are also semi-aquatic and arboreal (tree-dwelling) forms, including the flying dragon. Burrowing species frequently have shortened limbs or are legless. Length: 5cm–3m (2in– 10ft). Order Squamata; suborder Sauria.

Ljubljana (Laibach) Capital and largest city of Slovenia, at the confluence of the Sava and Ljubljanica rivers. Ljubljana was founded as Emona by the Roman emperor Augustus in 34 BC. From 1244 it was the capital of Carniola, an Austrian province within the Habsburg empire. During the 19th century it was the centre of the Slovene nationalist movement. The city remained under Austrian rule until it became part of the Kingdom of Serbs, Croats and Slovenes in 1918. When Slovenia became independent (1991), Ljubljana became capital. Industries: textiles, paper and printing, electronics, chemicals. Pop. (1991) 268,000.

llama Domesticated, South American, even-toed, ruminant mammal. The llama has been used as a beast of burden by Native Americans for more than 1,000 years. It has a long, woolly coat and slender limbs and neck. The smaller alpaca is bred for its superb wool. Family Camelidae; genus *Lama*.

Llewelyn ap Gruffydd (d.1282) (Llewelyn the Last) Prince of Wales. Allied with the rebellious English barons, he gained control of as much territory as his grandfather, LLEWELYN AP IORWERTH. He was recognized as prince of Wales by the Treaty of Montgomery (1267). The accession of EDWARD I brought his ruin. He renewed his rebellion in 1282 and was killed in battle.

Llewelyn ap Iorwerth (1173–1240) (Llewelyn the Great) Prince of Gwynedd. He overcame dynastic rivals, captured Mold from the English (1199) and established his suzerainty in Gwynedd, subsequently gaining control of Powys also. He allied himself with the English barons against John and was recognized as suzerain by all the Welsh princes.

Lloyd George, David (1863–1945) British statesman, prime minister (1916–22). A Welsh Liberal, he sat in the House of Commons from 1890. As chancellor of the exchequer (1908–15), he increased taxation to pay for social measures such as old-age pensions. His "People's Budget" (1909) provoked a constitutional crisis, which led to a reduction of the powers of the House of Lords. He was an effective minister of munitions (1915). In 1916 he joined with Conservatives to dislodge the prime minister, ASQUITH, whom he replaced. He won an easy victory for his coalition government in 1918 and was a leading figure at the peace conference at VERSAILLES. He ended the Irish crisis by the treaty creating the Irish Free State (1921), but then fell from power.

Lloyd's Insurance market in London, dealing especially in marine insurance. Lloyd's began in the 17th century as a coffee house, where businessmen willing to insure shipping gathered. Lloyd's as an institution does not insure anything; it is merely the market where the individual underwriters (known as "names") can meet. Between 1988 and 1993 some syndicates made substantial losses, leading to a change in the regulations of names, allowing some to have limited liability.

Lloyd Webber, Andrew (1948–) British composer. He composed *Joseph and the Amazing Technicolour Dreamcoat* (1967) while still a student. The lyricist, Tim Rice, was also his collaborator on the rock opera *Jesus Christ Superstar* (1971) and on the musical *Evita* (1978). *Cats* (1981), combining Lloyd Webber's music with verse by T.S. Eliot, was a long-running hit, as were *The Phantom of the Opera* (1986) and *Sunset Boulevard* (1993).

lobster Large, long-tailed, marine decapod crustacean. Some species are prized edible shellfish. True lobsters possess enlarged bulbous chelae (claws) and a segmented body.

local government System of regional administration differing in each country. Local government in England developed from the Municipal Reform

373

Act (1835), which first established elected councils in cities; the Local Government Act (1888) set up county councils elsewhere. In 1974 a two-tier system was established in England, Scotland and Wales, with counties subdivided into districts, each with an elected council. Some metropolitan counties were abolished in 1986 and replaced by a single tier of smaller local borough councils.

Locarno Pact (1925) Group of international agreements that attempted to solve problems of European security outstanding since the Treaty of VERSAILLES of 1919. The pact established Germany's w borders and enabled Germany to enter the LEAGUE OF NATIONS. The general peace established at Locarno was soon disturbed by German violations of the Treaty of Versailles under HITLER.

loch Scottish word for "lake". For individual lochs see place name.

Locke, John (1632–1704) English philosopher and exponent of EMPIRICISM. He rejected the concept of "innate ideas" and held that all ideas are placed in the mind by experience. In 1690 he published *Two Treatises on Civil Government*, in which he advocated the social contract, the right to freedom of conscience and the right to property.

lock Structure built into a stretch of inland waterway to raise or lower water levels to correspond with the surrounding countryside. Each lock consists of two sets of lock gates. A vessel enters the lock, the gates are closed, and sluices are opened to admit or release enough water to bring the vessel to the same level as the water beyond the second pair of gates.

lockjaw *See* TETANUS

locomotive Engine that moves under its own power, usually on rails. In 1804 Richard TREVITHICK built the first locomotive, which was steam powered. The first locomotive on a passenger railway was George STEPHENSON's *Locomotion*, built in 1825. Electric locomotives arrived in the late 19th century. Diesel, diesel-electric and gas-turbine locomotives were introduced during the 20th century.

locus In geometry, the path traced by a specified point when it moves to satisfy certain conditions. For example, a circle is the locus of a point in a plane moving in such a way that its distance from a fixed point (the centre) is constant.

locust Insect (a type of GRASSHOPPER) that migrates in huge swarms. Initially, the nymphs (immature insects) move in vast numbers on foot. As they feed, they develop into flying adults. Swarms may contain up to 40,000 million insects, and cover an area of *c*.1,000sq km (386sq mi). Length: 12.5–100mm (0.5–4in). Order Orthoptera; species *Schistocerca gregaria*.

Logan, Mount Peak in the St Elias Mountains, sw Yukon, Canada. At 6,050m (19,849ft), it is the highest peak in Canada and the second-highest in North America. It was first climbed in 1925.

loganberry Biennial, hybrid, red-berried bramble. A cross between the BLACKBERRY and RASPBERRY, it is disease-prone and is grown only in sheltered areas. Family Rosaceae; species *Rubus ursinus loganbaccus*.

logarithm Aid to calculation devised by John NAPIER in 1614 and developed by the English mathematician Henry Briggs. A number's logarithm is the power to which a base must be raised to equal the number, i.e. if $b^x = n$, then $\log_b n = x$, where n is the number, b the base and x the logarithm. Common logarithms have base 10, and so-called natural logarithms have base e (2.71828...).

logic Branch of philosophy that deals with the processes of valid reasoning and argument. Logic defines the way in which one thing may be said to follow from, or be consequent upon, another. This is known as deductive logic. Inductive logic, in which a general conclusion is drawn from a particular fact or facts, is the preserve of science. Although logical systems were devised in China and India, the history of logic in the West began in the 4th century BC with the Greek philosopher ARISTOTLE. Various post-Renaissance scholars, including LEIBNIZ, developed the foundations of modern logic. Symbolic, or mathematical, logic was outlined in the 19th century by George BOOLE and developed by Gottlob FREGE.

logical positivism Early 20th-century school of philosophy whose adherents consider that only empirically verifiable scientific propositions are meaningful. Its roots were in the logic of Gottlob FREGE and Bertrand RUSSELL, the positivism of Ernst Mach and, above all, the claim of Ludwig WITTGENSTEIN that philosophy was the clarification of thought.

Loire Longest river in France. The Loire rises in the Cévennes range, on the SE edge of the MASSIF CENTRAL, and flows N and NW to Orléans. It then turns SW into a wide, fertile basin. The cities of TOURS and Angers lie on its banks. It then flows through the Pays de la Loire to NANTES, emptying into the Bay of BISCAY at St-Nazaire. It is connected by a series of canals to the RHÔNE and SEINE rivers. Length:1,020km (635mi).

Lollards Followers of the 14th-century English religious reformer John WYCLIFFE. They helped to pave the way for the REFORMATION, and challenged many doctrines and practices of the medieval church, including TRANSUBSTANTIATION, pilgrimages and clerical celibacy. They rejected the authority of the PAPACY and denounced the wealth of the church. The first Lollards appeared at Oxford University, where Wycliffe was a teacher (*c*.1377). They went out among the people as "poor preachers", teaching that the Bible was the sole authority in religion. After 1401 many Lollards were burned as heretics, and in 1414 they mounted an unsuccessful uprising in London and then went underground.

Lombard League Defensive alliance of the cities of Lombardy in N Italy (1167). Its purpose was to resist the re-establishment of imperial authority by FREDERICK I. Led by Pope ALEXANDER III, the league defeated the emperor at Legnano (1176). By the Peace of Constance in 1183 the cities retained independence while paying lip service to Frederick's authority. The league was active again in 1226 against FREDERICK II.

Lombards Germanic peoples who inhabited the area E of the lower River Elbe until driven W by the Romans in AD 9. In 568 they invaded N Italy under Alboin and conquered much of the country, adopting Catholicism and Latin customs. The Lombard kingdom reached its peak under Liutprand (d.744). It went into decline after defeat by the Franks under CHARLEMAGNE (775).

Lombardy (Lombardia) Region in N Italy, bordering with Switzerland in the N; the capital is MILAN. Lombardy is Italy's most populous and industrial region. Area: 23,834sq km (9,202sq mi). Pop. (1991) 8,856,074.

Lomé Capital and largest city of the Republic of Togo, W Africa, on the Gulf of Guinea. Made capital of German Togoland in 1897, it later became an important commercial centre. Its main exports are coffee, cocoa, palm nuts, copra and phosphates. Pop. (1991) 590,000.

Lomond, Loch Long, narrow lake in Strathclyde and Central regions, W central Scotland. It is drained by the River Leven into the Firth of Clyde. The largest of the Scottish lochs, it is 37km (21mi) long, with a maximum depth of 190m (625ft). Area: 70sq km (27.5sq mi).

London, Jack (1876–1916) US novelist and short-story writer. He is best known for his Alaskan novels, such as *Call of the Wild* (1903) and *White Fang* (1906). *The Iron Heel* (1907) is a dystopian novel inspired by his socialist beliefs.

London Capital of the United Kingdom, and (after Moscow) the second-largest city in Europe, located on both banks of the River THAMES, 65km (40 mi) from its mouth in the North Sea, SE England. Since 1965 it has been officially called Greater London: comprising the square mile of the City of London and 13 inner and 19 outer boroughs, covering a total of 1,580sq km (610sq mi). Called Londinium, it was the most important Roman town in Britain. By the 3rd century the population numbered c.40,000. After the Romans left Britain, London declined until the 9th century, when ALFRED THE GREAT made it the seat of government. Edward the Confessor built WESTMINSTER ABBEY and made Westminster his capital in 1042. The prosperity of England during the Tudor period firmly established London's wealth and importance. During the 17th century the area between Westminster and the City was built up. The plague of 1665 killed 75,000 Londoners and the FIRE OF LONDON the next year destroyed many buildings. By the end of the 19th century London was the world's biggest city. Much of E London was rebuilt after bomb damage during World War 2, and in the late 1980s the largely

derelict docklands were rapidly developed. Industries: tourism, entertainment, engineering, chemicals, paper, printing and publishing, clothing, brewing. Pop. (1994) 6,966,800.

London, University of University founded in 1836, originally comprising King's College and University College. The university now comprises 14 colleges, 6 medical schools and 11 postgraduate medical institutions, as well as various other academic institutes.

Londonderry *See* DERRY

Longfellow, Henry Wadsworth (1807–82) US poet. Longfellow's escapist poetry was extremely successful in his lifetime. His first book of poetry, *Voices of the Night*, was published in 1839. He is best known for his long narrative poems, such as *Evangeline* (1847), *The Song of Hiawatha* (1855), *The Courtship of Miles Standish* (1858) and *Tales of a Wayside Inn* (1863), which includes "Paul Revere's Ride". *Ballads and Other Poems* (1842) contains two of his most popular shorter poems, "The Wreck of the Hesperus" and "The Village Blacksmith".

longitude Angular measurement around the Earth, usually in degrees E or W of an imaginary N–S line through the prime MERIDIAN. All N–S lines are called either meridians or lines of longitude.

Long March Enforced march of the Chinese RED ARMY in 1934–35, during the war against Nationalist (Kuomintang) forces. Led by Chu Teh and MAO ZEDONG, 90,000 communist troops, accompanied by c.15,000 civilians, broke through a Nationalist encirclement of their headquarters and marched some 10,000km (6,000mi) from Jiangxi province, SE China, to Shanxi province in the NW. Under frequent attack, the communists suffered 45,000 casualties. The march prevented the extermination of the Communist Party by the Nationalists.

Long Parliament English Parliament initially summoned by CHARLES I in November 1640 to raise revenue to combat Scotland in the "Bishop's wars". It followed the SHORT PARLIAMENT, which lasted only weeks. Antagonism between Charles and Parliament resulted in the outbreak of the English CIVIL WAR. The Long Parliament sat, with intervals, for 20 years. Oliver CROMWELL expelled hostile members in PRIDE'S PURGE (1648), and thereafter it was known as the RUMP PARLIAMENT.

long-sight (hypermetropia) Defect of vision that causes distant objects to be seen more clearly than nearby ones. In a long-sighted person, the focusing distance of the eyeball is too short and, as a result, light rays entering the EYE strike the RETINA before they can be properly focused. Long-sightedness is corrected by convex lenses. *See also* MYOPIA

loon (diver) Diving bird of the Northern Hemisphere, known for its harsh call. It has black, white and grey plumage. An excellent swimmer, it often stays submerged while fishing. Length: 88cm (35in). Family Gaviidae.

Loos, Adolf (1870–1933) Czech architect who

pioneered modern building design at the beginning of the 20th century. He hated ART NOUVEAU, the prevailing style of the time, publishing his views in *Ornament and crime* (1908). His most important projects were houses built between 1904–10; Steiner House (Vienna, 1910) was one of the first to use concrete. *See also* MODERNISM

loran (long range navigation) Radio navigational system for guiding ships and aircraft. Pairs of transmitters emit signal pulses that are picked up by a receiver. By measuring the difference in time between the signals reaching the receiver, the vessel's position can be plotted.

Lorca, Federico García (1898–1936) Spanish poet and dramatist. His poetry, ranging from *Gypsy Ballads* (1928) to *The Poet in New York* (1940), was internationally acclaimed. In the theatre, his early farces gave way to tragedies, such as the trilogy *Blood Wedding* (1933), *Yerma* (1935) and *The House of Bernarda Alba* (1936).

Lord Chancellor Head of the British legal system, an office of cabinet rank. The Lord Chancellor's duties include acting as head of the judiciary and as speaker of the House of Lords.

Lord's Prayer Prayer JESUS CHRIST taught his disciples. It is found in Matthew 6:9–13, and slightly differently in Luke 11:2–4. It is also called *Pater Noster* (Lat. Our Father).

Loren, Sophia (1934–) Italian film actress. Her most famous films include *The Black Orchid* (1959), *Two Women* (1960) – for which she won the Best Actress award at the Cannes film festival – and *Marriage Italian Style* (1964).

Lorentz, Hendrik Antoon (1853–1928) Dutch physicist. His early work was concerned with the theory of electromagnetic radiation devised by James Clerk MAXWELL. This led him to the Lorentz transformation and the prediction of the Lorentz-Fitzgerald contraction, both of which helped Albert EINSTEIN to develop his special theory of RELATIVITY. Lorentz also worked on the ZEEMAN EFFECT, for which he and Pieter Zeeman were awarded the 1902 Nobel Prize in physics.

Lorenz, Konrad (1903–89) Austrian pioneer ethologist. He observed that instinct played a major role in animal behaviour, as for example in IMPRINTING. Some of his views are expressed in *On Aggression* (1966). In 1973 he shared, with N. TINBERGEN and K. von FRISCH, the Nobel Prize in physiology or medicine. *See also* ETHOLOGY

loris Any of several species of primitive, tail-less, arboreal, nocturnal PRIMATES of S Asia and the East Indies. They have soft, thick fur and large eyes, and feed mainly on insects. Length: 18–38cm (7– 15in). Family Lorisidae; genera *Loris* and *Nycticebus*.

Lorrain, Claude *See* CLAUDE LORRAIN

Lorraine (Ger. Lothringen) Region of NE France, bounded N by Belgium, Germany and Luxembourg, E by ALSACE, S by Franche-Comté and E by CHAMPAGNE. The capital is Nancy. Lorraine is divided into four départements: Meurthe-et-

Moselle, Meuse, Moselle and Vosges. In 1871, following the Franco-Prussian War, the E part of Lorraine was joined to form the German territory of Alsace-Lorraine. The region was at the heart of Franco-German conflict in World Wars 1 and 2. Industries: brewing and wine-making. It also has rich deposits of iron-ore. Area: 23,547sq km (9,089sq mi) Pop. (1990) 2,305,700

Los Alamos Town in New Mexico, USA, site of a large scientific laboratory. During World War 2 the laboratory was a centre for the MANHATTAN PROJECT, which produced the atomic bomb. After the war, the laboratory developed the HYDROGEN BOMB.

Los Angeles (City of Angels) City in SW California, USA, on the Pacific coast; the second-largest US city (after New York) and the nation's leading manufacturing base. The city was founded in 1781 by Mexican settlers. At the conclusion of the MEXICAN WAR (1848) the USA acquired Los Angeles. The city grew with the completion of the Southern Pacific (1876) and Santa Fe (1885) railways. The discovery of oil (1894), the completion of San Pedro harbour (1914) and the development of the HOLLYWOOD film and television industry encouraged further growth. Los Angeles' rapid growth has brought major social problems. In 1965 five days of riots in the Watts district left 34 dead and $200 million damages. In 1992 the acquittal of four policemen on a charge of beating an African-American suspect sparked off further race riots, which left 58 dead and $1 billion damages. Air pollution is also a major problem. A 1994 earthquake killed 57 people and caused $15–30 billion of damage. Greater Los Angeles sprawls over 1,204sq km (465sq mi) joined by a freeway network. Aerospace is the city's principal industry. Industries: film and television, oil refining, electronic equipment, chemicals, fish canning. It is a major tourist centre. Pop. (1990) 3,489,779.

Lot Biblical character who was living in SODOM at the time when God decided to destroy it (Genesis 11:31–14:16. 19). Lot survived, but his wife disobeyed instructions and looked back at the destruction of the city; she was turned into a pillar of salt.

Lothair II (1070 –1137) Sometimes called Lothair III, "the Saxon", king of the Germans and Holy Roman emperor (1125–37). He secured the throne by successful war against the HOHENSTAUFEN (1125–35). He supported Pope Innocent II against his opponents, invading Italy in 1136–37.

Lothian Region in E central Scotland, bounded N by the Firth of Forth, E by the North Sea and S by the Lammermuir, Moorfoot and Pentland Hills; the capital is EDINBURGH. Industries: coal-mining, engineering, whisky distilling. Area: 1,755sq km (677sq mi). Pop.(1991) 726,000

lotus Common name for any WATER LILIES of the genus *Nelumbo* and several tropical species of the genus *Nymphaea*. The circular leaves and flowers of some species may be 60cm (2ft) across. *Nymphaea* is sacred to the Chinese, Egyptians and

Indians. Family Nymphaeaceae. The genus *Lotus* is made up of the trefoils that belong to the unrelated Fabaceae/Leguminosae family.

loudspeaker Device for converting changing electric currents into sound. The most common type has a moving coil attached to a stiff paper cone suspended in a strong magnetic field. By ELECTROMAGNETIC INDUCTION, the changing currents in the coil cause the cone to vibrate at the frequency of the currents, thus creating sound waves.

Louis, Joe (1914–81) (Joseph Louis Barrow) US boxer. He won the world heavyweight title from James J. Braddock in Chicago in 1937, and retired undefeated in 1949. Louis held the title longer than any other heavyweight.

Louis I (778–840) Emperor of the Franks (814–840), called "the Pious". The only surviving son, he succeeded his father, CHARLEMAGNE. He struggled to maintain Charlemagne's empire, cooperating with the church. The Franks had no law of primogeniture, and Louis's attempts to provide an inheritance for his four sons provoked civil war.

Louis VII (*c.*1120–80) King of France (1137–80). His marriage to Eleanor of Aquitaine extended the French crown's lands to the Pyrenees. As king, he consolidated royal power by cultivating the church and the growing towns. Returning from the Second Crusade, he divorced Eleanor for alleged infidelity. She married HENRY II of England, whose French territories then became greater than those of Louis. Louis retaliated by supporting the rebellions of Henry's sons.

Louis VIII (1187–1226) King of France (1223–26). He invaded England (1216) at the invitation of barons opposing King JOHN but was defeated at Lincoln (1217) and returned to France. He successfully concluded the crusade against the heretical Albigenses in the south of France.

Louis IX (1214–70) King of France (1226–70), later known as St Louis. His mother, Blanche of Castile, was regent from 1226–36 and during his first absence from France (1248–52). Louis defeated the English at Taillebourg (1242) and was a leader of the Sixth Crusade in 1248. He was taken prisoner and did not return to France until 1254. In later years Louis was tolerant, just and peace-loving.

Louis XIII (1601–43) King of France (1601–43). Son of HENRY IV and MARIE DE MÉDICI, he forcibly ended his mother's regency in 1617 and exiled her. During the course of his reign, he increasingly relied on Cardinal RICHELIEU, who exercised total authority from 1624. Louis approved the policy of crushing the Huguenots (Protestants) at home while making alliances with Protestant powers abroad, in opposition to the Habsburgs, during the THIRTY YEARS WAR.

Louis XIV (1638–1715) King of France (1643–1715). The first part of his reign was dominated by Cardinal MAZARIN. From 1661 Louis ruled personally as the epitome of absolute monarchy and became known as the "Sun King" for the luxury of his court. As ministers, he chose men of the junior nobility, such as the able COLBERT, and he reduced the power of the aristocracy in the provinces. After Colbert's death (1683), decline set in. Louis's wars of aggrandisement in the Low Countries and elsewhere drained the royal treasury. His revocation of the Edict of NANTES drove many Huguenots abroad, weakening the economy. In the War of the SPANISH SUCCESSION, the French armies were at last defeated.

Louis XV (1710–74) King of France (1715–74). Grandson and successor of LOUIS XIV, he failed to arrest the slow decline. Disastrous wars, especially the War of the AUSTRIAN SUCCESSION and the SEVEN YEARS WAR, resulted in financial crisis and the loss of most of the French empire. Louis encountered opposition from *parlements* (supreme courts) and conflict with the followers of JANSENISM and court factions. The monarchy became deeply unpopular.

Louis XVI (1754–93) King of France (1774–92). Grandson and successor of LOUIS XV, he married MARIE ANTOINETTE in 1770. Louis' lack of leadership qualities allowed the *parlements* (supreme courts) and aristocracy to defeat the efforts of government ministers to carry out vital economic reforms. The massive public debt forced Louis to convoke the STATES GENERAL in order to raise taxation. His indecisiveness on the composition of the States General led the third (popular) estate to proclaim itself a National Assembly, signalling the start of the FRENCH REVOLUTION.

Louisiana State on the Gulf of Mexico, S central USA; the capital is Baton Rouge. In 1699 the French colony of Louisiana was founded. It was later ceded to Spain but regained by France in 1800. In the LOUISIANA PURCHASE (1803) Napoleon sold the state to the USA. In 1861 it joined the Confederacy, being readmitted to the Union in 1868. The discovery of oil and natural gas in the early 20th century provided a great boost to the economy. Industrial growth was rapid in the 1940s and 1950s. Racial discrimination left the large African-American community (30% of the population) politically powerless until the 1960s. Louisiana consists of two main regions: the MISSISSIPPI alluvial plain and the Gulf coastal plain. The Mississippi Delta is the SE of the state was formed by silt. It covers *c.*33,700sq km (13,000sq mi), about 25% of the state's total area. Nearly 15% of the state is marshland. N of the marshes, rolling prairies stretch to the Texas border. Almost half the state is forested. Louisiana has a mainly subtropical climate. Low-lying land and heavy rainfall (especially in the SE) make it prone to flooding. It is a leading US producer of soybeans, sweet potatoes, rice and sugar cane. Fishing is a major industry, particularly shrimps and crayfish. Louisiana is second only to Texas in US mineral production. Petroleum and coal account for more than 95% of mining income. Area: 125,674sq km (48,523sq mi). Pop. (1992) 4,278,889.

Louisiana Purchase (1803) Treaty in which France conceded the Louisiana Territory to the USA. Extending from the Mississippi River to the Rocky Mountains, the territory encompassed 2,136,000sq km (825,000sq mi), and the price agreed was 60 million francs.

Louis Philippe (1773–1850) King of France (1830–48). He returned to France from exile in 1814 and gained the throne after the JULY REVOLUTION in 1830. Although known as the "Citizen King", he retained much power himself. He abdicated when revolution broke out again and the Second Republic was declared in February 1848. He died in exile in England.

Lourdes Town in SW France, a centre of religious pilgrimage. In 1858 a 14-year-old peasant girl, Bernadette Soubirous, claimed to have had visions of the Virgin Mary in the grotto of Massabielle, where there is an underground spring. In 1862 the Roman Catholic Church declared the visions to be authentic. The waters of the spring, believed to have healing powers, are the focus of pilgrimages.

louse Common name for various small, wingless insects, parasitic on birds and mammals. There are two main groups, classified in different sub-orders of Phthiraptera. The chewing lice (Mallophaga) feed mainly on the feathers of birds. The biting or sucking lice (Anoplura) feed only on the blood of mammals. Both kinds of lice are small, pale and flattened, with leathery or hairy skins.

Louth County in Leinster province, NE Republic of Ireland, bordering Northern Ireland (N) and the Irish Sea (E); the capital is Dundalk. It is a low-lying region, except in the hilly NW and the mountainous N, drained by the rivers Fane, Dee and Castletown. Industries: textiles, footwear, processed food. Area: 821sq km (317sq mi). Pop. (1991) 90,724.

Louvre France's national museum and art gallery in Paris. It holds a collection of more than 100,000 works. The Louvre became a fully fledged museum in the 18th century and opened as the first national public gallery during the Revolution in 1793.

Lovelace, Richard (1618–58) English CAVALIER poet. A flamboyant and ardent royalist, he was imprisoned in 1642 and 1648, during which time he wrote *To Althea, from Prison* and *To Lucasta, Going to the Wars*. Another collection, *Lucasta: Posthume Poems*, appeared in 1659.

Lovell, Sir Alfred Charles Bernard (1913–) British astronomer. From 1951 to 1981 he was director of the JODRELL BANK experimental station for radio astronomy near Manchester, England, and oversaw the construction there of the world's first large steerable radio telescope.

Low Countries Region of NW Europe now occupied by the NETHERLANDS, BELGIUM and LUXEMBOURG. It was the most advanced and prosperous region of N Europe during the Middle Ages and Renaissance, under the dukes of BURGUNDY from 1384 and the HABSBURGS from 1477. The Dutch gained independence as the United Provinces in 1609. The southern Netherlands (Belgium), after a period united with the Dutch (1815–30), became an independent kingdom in 1830. Luxembourg was ruled by the Dutch house of Orange until 1890, when it passed to another branch.

Lowell, Percival (1855–1916) US astronomer. In 1894 he built an observatory at Flagstaff, Arizona. Lowell studied the orbits of Uranus and Neptune and calculated that their orbital irregularities were caused by an undiscovered Planet X. His predictions led to the discovery of PLUTO in 1930. He also observed Mars, producing intricate maps of the "canals".

Lowell, Robert (1917–77) US poet. Lowell was perhaps the most important voice in American poetry to emerge after World War 2. His early work, such as the Pulitzer Prize-winning *Lord Weary's Castle* (1946), is rich in Catholic symbolism. He is best known for his later, more intimate, "confessional" style, best represented by the autobiographical *Life Studies* (1959).

Lower Saxony Region of N Germany, formed in 1946 by the merging of the provinces of Hanover, Brunswick, Oldenberg and Schaumberg–Lippe. The main crops are cereals. Industries: machine construction, electrical engineering. Area 47,606sq km (18,376sq mi). Pop. (1993 est.) 7,648,004.

Lowry, L.S. (Lawrence Stephen) (1887–1976) British painter. He is best known for the highly personal way in which he portrayed cityscapes of his native Salford (Greater MANCHESTER).

Loyalist In Northern Ireland, a person who wishes that province to remain part of the United Kingdom of Great Britain and Northern Ireland. In contrast, a Republican is a person who wishes the province to unite with the neighbouring Republic of Ireland. In US history, the term referred to North American colonists who refused to renounce loyalty to the British crown after the DECLARATION OF INDEPENDENCE (July 1776).

LSD (lysergic acid diethylamide) Hallucinogenic drug, causing changes in mental state, sensory confusion and behavioural changes, resulting from the drug blocking the action of serotonin in the brain. First synthesized in the 1940s, LSD was made illegal in the UK and USA in the mid-1960s.

Luanda Capital, chief port and largest city of Angola, on the Atlantic coast. It was settled by the Portuguese in 1575. Until the abolition of slavery in the 19th century, its economy was based on the shipment of more than 3 million slaves to Brazil. Today it exports crops from the province of Luanda. Industries: oil refining, metal-working, building materials, textiles, paper. Pop. (1990) 1,544,000.

Lucas, George (1944–) US film director and producer. Lucas began his career as an assistant to Francis Ford COPPOLA. *American Graffiti* (1973) was his breakthrough film. Lucas is best known for his science fiction classic *Star Wars* (1977), which was revolutionary in its use of special effects.

Lucas van Leyden (1494–1533) Dutch artist.

His engravings include *Ecco Homo* and *Dance of the Magdalene* (1519). Among his paintings are *Moses Striking Water from the Rock* (1527), *Chess Players* (*c.*1508) and *Last Judgement* (1526).

Lucifer Name given in ancient Roman times to the planet VENUS as seen at dawn. In classical mythology, Lucifer's Greek counterpart was Phosphorus, and both were personified as male torchbearers. In Christian mythology, Lucifer was an epithet of SATAN, used of him before his fall and a symbol of overbearing pride.

Lucretius (c.95–55bc) (Titus Lucretius Carus) Latin poet and philosopher. His long poem, *De rerum natura* (*On the Nature of Things*) is based on the philosophy of EPICURUS.

Luddites Unemployed workers in early 19th-century England who vandalized the machines that had put them out of work. They were chiefly hand-loom weavers made redundant by mechanical looms. The riots started in the Nottingham area in 1811 and spread to Lancashire and Yorkshire.

Ludendorff, Erich (1865–1937) German general. He played a major part in revising the Schlieffen Plan before World War 1. In 1914 he masterminded the victory over the Russians at Tannenberg. In 1916 he and Hindenburg were given supreme control of Germany's war effort. In the 1920s he was a member of the Nazi Party.

Luftwaffe German air force. In English-speaking countries, the term refers specifically to the air force of Nazi Germany. Built up rapidly in the 1930s, it was designed primarily as part of German *Blitzkrieg* tactics and was highly effective in the early stages of the war and during the invasion of the Soviet Union (1941). It was less successful as a high-explosive bombing force in the Battle of Britain (1940).

lugworm Marine WORM that lives in the sand of the sea-bed. With the aid of bristles along its middle portion, it burrows a U-shaped tunnel in sand or mud, from which it rarely emerges. Length: up to 30cm (12in). Genus *Arenicola*.

Lukacs, György (1885–1971) Hungarian literary critic and philosopher. He joined the Communist Party in 1918 and was exiled after the abortive 1919 revolution. He returned to Budapest in 1945 and was a key figure in the 1956 rising. His writings include *History and Class Consciousness* (1923) and *The Historical Novel* (1955).

Luke, Saint Author, according to Christian tradition, of the gospel that bears his name and of the ACTS OF THE APOSTLES in the New Testament. He is said to have been a physician, and to have been able to speak and write Greek, and may have been a non-Jew born in Antioch. He was a co-worker of the apostle St PAUL. Luke is the patron saint of painters. His feast day is 18 October.

Luke, Gospel according to Saint Third book of the New Testament and one of the three SYNOPTIC GOSPELS. It is traditionally attributed to St LUKE. One of its sources is the Gospel according to St

MARK, but it also seems to have relied on another source (now lost), which scholars refer to as "Q".

Lully, Jean-Baptiste (1632–87) French composer, b. Italy, who was an early influence on the development of French opera. After a series of comedy-ballets (1658–64) came *Cadmus and Hermione* (1673), the first French lyrical tragedy. Other operas include *Alceste* (1674), *Proserpine* (1680) and *Acis et Galatée* (1686).

lumbago Pain in the lower (lumbar) region of the back. It is usually due to strain or poor posture. When associated with SCIATICA, it may be due to a slipped disc. *See also* RHEUMATISM

lumen SI unit (symbol lm) measuring the amount of light in a certain area for one second. The light is emitted in a unit solid angle (one steradian) from a source of unit intensity (one CANDELA).

Lumière, Louis Jean and **Auguste** Two brothers, Louis Jean (1864–1948) and Auguste (1862–1954), who were pioneers of CINEMATOGRAPHY. Together they invented an early combination of motion-picture camera and projector called the Cinématographe. Their film *Lunch Break at the Lumière Factory* (1895) is generally considered to be the first motion picture.

luminescence *See* PHOSPHORESCENCE

luminism Art style followed by a group of 19th-century US painters. The Luminists were principally concerned with the depiction of light and atmospheric effects. The leading figures were George Caleb Bingham, Asher Durand and members of the Hudson River School.

luminosity Absolute brightness of a star, given by the amount of energy radiated from its entire surface per second. It is expressed in watts (joules per second), or in terms of the Sun's luminosity.

lumpfish (lumpsucker) Marine fish of the North Atlantic coasts, the pectoral fins of which join to form a sucker, with which it attaches itself to rocks. Length: up to 61cm (2ft); weight 6kg (13lb). Family Cyclopteridae.

lungfish Elongated fish from which AMPHIBIANS developed. It is found in shallow freshwater and swamps in Africa, South America and Australia. It has primitive lungs, and during a dry season various species can breath air or survive total dehydration by burrowing into the mud and enveloping themselves in a mucous cocoon. Order Dipnoi.

lungs Organs of the RESPIRATORY SYSTEM of vertebrates, in which the exchange of gases between air and blood takes place. They are located in the pleural cavity within the ribcage. This cavity is lined by two sheets of TISSUE (the pleura), one coating the lungs and the other lining the walls of the thorax. Between the pleura is a fluid that cushions the lungs and prevents friction. Light and spongy, lung tissue is composed of tiny air sacs, called ALVEOLI, which are served by networks of fine CAPILLARIES. *See also* GAS EXCHANGE; VENTILATION

lupus erythematosus Autoimmune disease affecting the skin and connective tissue. The discoid form causes red patches covered with scales, often on the cheeks and nose. Nine times more common in women than in men, the disease is treated mainly with corticosteroids.

lupus vulgaris Tuberculous infection of the skin. Often starting in childhood, it is characterized by the formation of brownish nodules, leading to ulceration and extensive scarring.

Lusaka Capital and largest city of Zambia, in the s central part of the country, at an altitude of 1,280m (4,200ft). Founded by Europeans in 1905 to service the local lead mining, it replaced Livingstone as the capital of Northern Rhodesia (later Zambia) in 1935. A vital road and rail junction, Lusaka is also the centre of a fertile agricultural region and is a major financial and commercial city. Industries: textiles, shoe manufacture, cement, food processing, car assembly, brewing. Pop. (1990) 982,000.

lute Plucked stringed instrument popular in 16th- and 17th-century Europe. It has an almond-shaped body and fretted neck and originally had 11 gut strings. It was often played to accompany songs and stylized dances and has been revived in recent years as a concert instrument.

Luther, Martin (1483–1546) German Christian reformer, a founder of PROTESTANTISM and leader of the REFORMATION. He was concerned about the problem of salvation, deciding that it could not be attained by good works but was a free gift of God's grace. In 1517 he affixed his 95 Theses to the door of the Schlosskirche in Wittenberg. This document included statements challenging the sale of indulgences, which led to a quarrel between Luther and church leaders. Luther decided that the Bible was the true source of authority and renounced obedience to Rome. He was excommunicated but gained followers among churchmen as well as the laity. After the publication of the Augsburg Confession (1530) he gradually retired from the leadership of the Protestant movement. *See also* LUTHERANISM.

Lutheranism Doctrines and Church structure that grew out of the teaching of Martin LUTHER. The principal Lutheran doctrine is that of justification by faith alone (*sola fide*). Luther held that grace cannot be conferred by the Church but is the free gift of God's love. He objected to the doctrine of TRANSUBSTANTIATION. Instead, he believed in the real presence of Christ "in, with, and under" the bread and wine (consubstantiation). These and other essentials of Lutheran doctrine were set down by Philip MELANCHTHON in 1530 in the AUGSBURG CONFESSION, the basic document of the Lutherans.

Luthuli, Albert John Mvumbi (1898–1967) South African civil-rights leader. He became president of the AFRICAN NATIONAL CONGRESS (ANC) in 1952, during a period of increasing militancy that culminated in the banning of the ANC in 1960. He was the first African to be awarded the Nobel Peace Prize (1960).

Lutoslawski, Witold (1913–94) Polish composer. He gained international recognition with his Concerto for Orchestra (1954). He experimented with serialism, notably in *Funeral Music* (1958), and aleatory techniques, as in *Venetian Games* (1961). He wrote four symphonies.

Lutyens, Sir Edwin Landseer (1869–1944) British architect. He built his reputation on original designs for houses. He developed a talent for more majestic commissions, notably the Cenotaph (1922) in Whitehall, London. His most ambitious project was his plan for the imperial capital of New Delhi (1913–30).

lux SI unit (symbol lx) of illumination, equal to one LUMEN per square metre.

Luxembourg Independent grand duchy in w Europe; the capital is LUXEMBOURG. **Land and climate** Luxembourg is divided geographically into the forested ARDENNES plateau and the fertile Bon Pays in the s. In the E, the Moselle and Sauer river valleys provide fertile farmland. Luxembourg has a temperate climate. Forests cover *c*.20% of Luxembourg, farms 25%, and pasture another 20%. **Economy** There are rich deposits of iron ore, and Luxembourg is a major producer of iron and steel. Other industries include chemicals, tourism, banking and electronics. Farmers raise cattle and pigs. Crops include cereals, fruits and grapes for winemaking. The city of Luxembourg is a major centre of European administration and finance. **History** In the 11th century the county of Luxembourg formed one of the largest fiefs of the Holy Roman Empire. In 1482 it passed to the HABSBURG dynasty, and in the 16th century it was incorporated in the Spanish Netherlands. In 1714 it passed to Austria. It was occupied by France during the Napoleonic Wars and was made a Grand Duchy at the Congress of VIENNA (1815). In 1839 Belgium acquired a large part of the duchy. In 1867 Luxembourg was recognized as an independent state and its neutrality was guaranteed by the European powers. Luxembourg was occupied by Germany in both World Wars. In 1948 it joined NATO. It was one of the six members of the European Community (EC). **Politics** Following 1994 elections, the Christian Social People's Party (CD) and the Luxembourg Socialist Workers'

LUXEMBOURG

AREA: 2,590sq km (1,000sq mi)
POPULATION: 390,000
CAPITAL (POPULATION): Luxembourg (76,446)
GOVERNMENT: Constitutional monarchy (Grand Duchy)
ETHNIC GROUPS: Luxembourger 71%, Portuguese 10%, Italian 5%, French 3%, Belgian 3%, German 2%
LANGUAGES: Letzeburgish (Luxembourgian-official), French, German
RELIGIONS: Christianity (Roman Catholic 95%, Protestant 1%)
CURRENCY: Luxembourg franc = 100 centimes

Party (SOC) formed a coalition government. Jean-Claude Juncker (CD) became prime minister.

Luxembourg Capital of the Grand Duchy of Luxembourg. It was a stronghold in Roman times. The walled town developed around a 10th-century fortress. It is the seat of the European Court of Justice, the Secretariat of the Parliament of the European Union, the European Monetary Fund, the European Investment Bank and the European Coal and Steel Union. Industries: iron and steel, chemicals, textiles, tourism. Pop. (1995) 76,446.

Luxemburg, Rosa (1871–1919) German socialist leader, b. Poland. She was an active revolutionary and anti-nationalist in Russian Poland before acquiring German citizenship by marriage. She founded the radical left-wing Spartacist League in 1916 with Karl LIEBKNECHT. Both she and Liebknecht are thought to have been murdered while under arrest in 1919.

Luxor (El Uqsur) City in E central Egypt, on the E bank of the River Nile; known to the ancient Egyptians as Weset and to the ancient Greeks as Thebes. There are remains of many temples and tombs, dating back nearly 4,000 years. Luxor Temple was linked to the Karnak temple, 2.5km (1mi) N of Luxor, by an avenue of sphinxes. Karnak's temple complex covers 40ha (100ac) and was built over a period of 1,300 years. The Valley of the Kings contains the tombs of many pharaoahs. Pop. (1992) 146,000.

Luzon Largest island of the Philippines; the main cities are QUEZON CITY and the nation's capital, MANILA. Luzon accounts for about one-third of the land mass of the Philippines and over 50% of its population. The coastal areas are mountainous, the highest peak being Mount Pulog at 2,928m (9,606ft). Rice is grown on the central plain and on the mountain terraces. The Bicol peninsula in the SE has coconut plantations. Luzon has mineral deposits, such as gold, chromite and copper. Luzon has been at the epicentre of Philippine nationalism, leading revolts against Spanish rule in 1896 and against US rule in 1899. In 1941 the island was invaded by the Japanese, who were finally expelled in 1945. Several US bases have remained on the island since World War 2. Area: 104,688sq km (40,420sq mi). Pop. (1992 est.) 30,500,000.

Lycopodophyta Taxonomic group (phylum) of about 1000 species of VASCULAR PLANTS related to ferns, which includes the CLUB MOSSES, selaginellas and quillworts. They have branching underground stems (RHIZOMES) and upright shoots supported by roots. Some species are EPIPHYTES.

Lycurgus (active c.625 BC) Semi-mythical lawgiver of ancient Sparta. The author of the political and social system in Sparta, he probably lived at the time of the slave revolt in the mid-7th century BC.

Lydia Ancient kingdom of W Asia Minor. Under the Mermnad dynasty (c.700–547 BC), it was a powerful and prosperous state, the first to issue a coinage, with its capital at Sardis. Its last king was

CROESUS, famous for his wealth, who was defeated by the Persians under CYRUS THE GREAT in 547 BC.

Lyly, John (1553–1606) English poet, dramatist and writer of prose romances. His prose comedies and pastoral romances include *Sappho and Phao* (1584), *Endymion: the Man in the Moon* (1591) and *Midas* (1592). He is best known for the elaborate prose style that he evolved in *Euphues* (1578).

lyme disease Condition caused by a spirochaete transmitted by the bite of a TICK that lives on deer. It usually begins with a red rash, often accompanied by fever, headache and pain in the muscles and joints. Untreated, the disease can lead to chronic arthritis, and there may also be involvement of the nervous system, heart, liver or kidneys.

lymph Clear, slightly yellowish fluid derived from the BLOOD and similar in composition to plasma. Circulating in the LYMPHATIC SYSTEM, it conveys LEUCOCYTES and some nutrients to the tissues.

lymphatic system System of connecting vessels and organs in vertebrates that transport LYMPH through the body. Lymph flows into lymph capillaries and from them into lymph vessels, or lymphatics. These extend throughout the body, leading to LYMPH GLANDS that collect lymph, storing some of the LEUCOCYTES. Lymph glands empty into large vessels, linking up into lymph ducts that empty back into the CIRCULATORY SYSTEM. The lymphatic system plays a major role in the body's defence against disease. At the lymph nodes, MACROPHAGES remove foreign particles, including bacteria.

lymph glands (lymph nodes) Masses of tissue occurring along the major vessels of the LYMPHATIC SYSTEM. They are filters that collect harmful material, notably bacteria and other disease organisms, and become swollen when the body is infected.

lymphocyte Type of leucocyte found in vertebrates. Produced in the bone marrow, they are mostly found in the LYMPH and blood and around infected sites. In human beings lymphocytes form about 25% of leucotyes. There are two main kinds: B-lymphocytes, responsible for producing antibodies; and T-lymphocytes, which maintain immunity.

lyre Ancient stringed musical instrument. Used originally by the Sumerians, it was introduced into Egypt and Assyria in the second millennium BC. In classical Greek times it had seven strings supported by a wooden frame and attached to a sound box at the base; the strings were plucked using a plectrum. In Europe since the Middle Ages they have more commonly been played with a bow. Today the lyre exists in various forms in E Africa.

Lysander (d.395 BC) Spartan general. He was responsible for the victory over Athens during the PELOPONNESIAN WAR (429–404 BC), defeating the Athenian fleet in 406 and 405 and obtaining Persian support for Sparta. He forfeited his popularity by establishing oligarchies under a Spartan governor in cities he liberated from Athens, and lost influence in Sparta after the accession of King Agesilaus II in 399 BC.

M/m is derived from the Semitic letter mem *(meaning water). The corresponding Greek letter was* mu, *which went, via the Etruscan alphabet, to Latin as* m.

Maastricht Capital city of Limburg province, on the River Maas, SE Netherlands. In 1992 the MAASTRICHT TREATY was signed here. Industries: dairy products, paper, leather, glass. Pop. (1994) 118,102.

Maastricht Treaty (7 February 1992) Agreement signed by the leaders of 12 European nations at MAASTRICHT, Netherlands. It turned the EUROPEAN COMMUNITY (EC) into the EUROPEAN UNION (EU), with a view to eventually becoming an integrated federation. The Treaty included a timetable for a single currency; the end of all internal immigration/emigration, customs and excise operations; the full empowerment of the EUROPEAN PARLIAMENT and its Commissions; the social chapter; and measures to set up a common defence policy. The UK Conservative government insisted on retaining an opt-out clause on the social chapter. The succeeding Labour government signed the chapter.

Mabuse (1478–1536) (Jan Gossaert) Netherlandish painter. *Neptune and Amphitrite* (1516) is a classic example of his unique mix of Italianate and Netherlandish styles.

macadamia Genus of Australian trees of the family Proteaceae. Most species have stiff, oblong, lance-like leaves. The edible seeds are round, hard-shelled nuts, covered by thick husks that split when ripe. Height: to 18m (60ft).

macaque Diverse group of omnivorous, medium-sized to large Old World MONKEYS found from NW Africa to Japan and Korea. Most are yellowish brown and are forest dwellers and good swimmers. Weight: to 13kg (29lb). Genus *Macaca. See also* BARBARY APE; RHESUS

MacArthur, Douglas (1880–1964) US general. He became US army chief of staff in 1930 and military adviser to the Philippines in 1935. In 1941 he conducted an unsuccessful defence of the Philippines aginst Japan. As supreme Allied commander in the SW Pacific (1942), he directed the campaigns that led to Japan's defeat. In 1950 he was appointed commander of UN forces in the KOREAN WAR. Autocratic and controversial, he was relieved of his command by President TRUMAN in April 1951.

Macau (Macao) Portuguese overseas province in SE China, 64km (40mi) W of Hong Kong, on the Pearl River estuary; it consists of the 6sq km (2sq mi) Macau Peninsula and the islands of Taipa and Colôane. The city of Santa Nome de Deus de Macau (coextensive with the peninsula) is connected by a narrow isthmus to the Chinese province of GUANGZHOU. The first European discovery was by Vasco da Gama in 1497. The Portuguese colonized the island in 1557. In 1887 the Chinese government recognized Portugal's right of "perpetual occupation". Competition from Hong Kong and the silting of Macau's harbour led to the port's decline towards the end of the 19th century. In 1974 Macau became a Chinese province under Portuguese administration. It is scheduled to be returned to China in 1999. Industries: gambling, tourism, textiles, electronics, plastics. Pop. (1991) 339,464.

Macaulay, Thomas Babington (1800–59) English historian and statesman. He upheld liberal causes in parliament (1830–38) and served on the British governor's council in India (1834–38), where he introduced a Western education system. He spent his later years writing his *History of England* (1849–61).

Macbeth (d.1057) King of Scotland (1040–57). He seized the throne from his cousin Duncan I. English intervention on behalf of Duncan's son (later Malcolm III Canmore) resulted in his defeat by Siward, earl of Northumbria, at Dunsinane Hill, near Scone (1054). Macbeth was eventually killed by Malcolm at Lumphanan. Shakespeare based his tragedy on a 16th-century history of the king.

Maccabees, Books of Four historical books, two of which are included in the Roman Catholic Deuterocanonical books of the Bible and the Protestant APOCRYPHA. These two are modelled on the Old Testament books of CHRONICLES and are a valuable historical source. The other two books of Maccabees are PSEUDEPIGRAPHA.

McCarthy, Joseph Raymond (1908–57) US Senator from Wisconsin, leader of the crusade against alleged communists in US society. Taking advantage of public hysteria in the 1950s COLD WAR, his investigations committee conducted a series of witch-hunts against public figures.

McCarthy, Mary (1912–89) US writer and drama critic. She wrote several novels, including *A Charmed Life* (1955) and *The Group* (1963). Her non-fiction works include *Venice Observed* (1956) and *Memories of a Catholic Girlhood* (1957).

McCartney, Sir Paul (1942–) British singer-songwriter. He was a member of the BEATLES and co-wrote the majority of their songs with John LENNON. Following the break-up of the band (1971), he formed Wings, but they disbanded in 1981. He was part of the reforming of the Beatles project in late 1995, with all the original members except John Lennon. He was knighted in 1997.

McCullers, Carson (1917–67) US writer. A sensitive exponent of the Southern Gothic, she published her remarkable first novel, *The Heart is a Lonely Hunter*, in 1940. Other works include *A Member of the Wedding* (1946) and *The Ballad of the Sad Cafe* (1951).

MacDiarmid, Hugh (1892–1978) Scottish poet and critic, b. Christopher Murray Grieve. He was a dominant voice in 20th century Scottish poetry, and responsible for the revival of Scots as a poetic language. *A Drunk Man Looks at the Thistle* (1926) is regarded as his masterpiece.

Macdonald, Sir John Alexander (1815–91) Canadian statesman, first prime minister of the Dominion of Canada (1867–73, 1878–91). He introduced protective tariffs, encouraged western settlement and acquired the HUDSON'S BAY COMPANY lands (1869). His efforts to organize a transcontinental railway led to the Pacific Scandal and electoral defeat (1873).

MacDonald, (James) Ramsay (1866–1937) British statesman, prime minister (1924, 1929–31, 1931–35). He became leader of the Labour Party in 1911. His opposition to Britain's participation in World War 1 lost him the leadership in 1914 and his seat in 1918. Re-elected in 1922, he became Britain's first Labour prime minister (1924). His government collapsed after the Liberal Party withdrew its support. He became prime minister again in 1929, but the Great Depression led to the collapse of the Labour government. MacDonald, however, remained in office at the head of a Conservative-dominated "National" government. He was succeeded by Stanley BALDWIN.

Macedon Ancient country in SE Europe, roughly corresponding to present-day MACEDONIA, Greek Macedonia and Bulgarian Macedonia. PHILIP II founded the city of THESSALONÍKI (348 BC). His son, ALEXANDER THE GREAT, built a world empire that fragmented after his death (323 BC). Macedon was defeated by the Romans, and in 146 BC Thessaloníki became capital of the first Roman province. In AD 395 Macedonia became part of the Byzantine empire. A brief period of Serbian hegemony was followed by Ottoman rule (14th–19th century). In the late 19th century Macedonia was claimed by Greece, Serbia and Bulgaria. In the First Balkan War, Bulgaria gained much of historic Macedon, but it was defeated in the Second Balkan War and the present-day boundaries were established.

Macedonia Balkan republic in SE Europe, the capital is SKOPJE. **Land and climate** Macedonia is a mountainous country in SE Europe. The land rises to Mount Korab, at 2,764m (9,068ft), on the border with Albania. Most of Macedonia is drained by the River Vardar, and Skopje lies on its banks. In the SW, Macedonia shares the large lakes of Ohrid and Prespa with Albania and Greece. The climate is mainly continental. Mountain forests of beech and oak are common. Farmland covers *c*.30% of Macedonia. **Economy** Macedonia is a developing country. The poorest of the six former republics of Yugoslavia, its economy was devastated by UN trade sanctions against the rump Yugoslav federation and by a Greek embargo. Manufactures dominate its exports. Macedonia mines coal, but imports oil and natural gas. Agriculture employs nearly 17% of the workforce. Major crops include cotton, fruits, maize, tobacco and wheat. **History** (For history pre-1913, *see* MACEDON) The Balkan Wars (1912–13) ended with thousands of Macedonians

MACEDONIA	
AREA: 24,900sq km (9,600sq mi)	
POPULATION: 2,174,000	
CAPITAL (POPULATION): Skopje (440,577)	
GOVERNMENT: Multiparty republic	
ETHNIC GROUPS: Macedonian 65%, Albanian 21%, Turkish 5%, Romanian 3%, Serb 2%	
LANGUAGES: Macedonian	
RELIGIONS: Christianity (mainly Eastern Orthodox, with Macedonian Orthodox and Roman Catholic communities), Islam	
CURRENCY: Denar = 100 paras	

fleeing to Bulgaria. Macedonia was divided between Greece, Bulgaria and Serbia (the largest portion). At the end of World War 1, Serbian Macedonia became part of the Kingdom of the Serbs, Croats and Slovenes (later YUGOSLAVIA). Macedonian nationalists waged an armed struggle against Serbian domination. During 1941–44, Bulgaria occupied all Macedonia, but a peace treaty restored the 1913 settlement. In 1946 President TITO created a federal Yugoslavia and Macedonia became one of its constituent republics. Multiparty elections in 1990 produced a non-communist regional government. The break-up of Yugoslavia led Macedonia to declare independence in September 1991. It renounced all territorial claims to Greek and Bulgarian Macedonia. Under pressure from Greece, the EC refused to recognize its sovereignty, on the grounds that its name, flag and currency were signs of its territorial intentions. A compromise was reached and the country temporarily became known as the Former Yugoslav Republic of Macedonia (FYRM). **Politics** In 1993 the UN accepted the new republic as a member and all the EU members, except Greece, established diplomatic relations. In 1994 Greece imposed a trade embargo. The ban was lifted in 1995, when Macedonia agreed to redesign its flag and remove claims to Greek Macedonia from its constitution. Internal tensions exist between Macedonians and the Albanian minority.

Machaut, Guillaume de (1300–77) French poet, musician and diplomat. His best-known poetry is found in *Le livre de Voir-dit*. A leading figure of the *ars nova*, he was among the first to compose polyphonic settings of poetry and the Mass.

Machiavelli, Niccolò (1469–1527) Florentine statesman and political theorist. He served from 1498–1512 as an official in the republican government of Florence, but lost his post when the Medici family returned to power. His most famous work, *The Prince* (1513), offered advice on how the ruler of a small state might best preserve his power.

machine Device that modifies or transmits a force in order to do useful work. In a simple machine, a force (effort) overcomes a larger force (load). The ratio of the load (output force) to the effort (input force) is the machine's MECHANICAL

ADVANTAGE. The ratio of the distance moved by the load to the distance moved by the effort is the distance or velocity ratio. The ratio of the work done by the machine to that put in it is the EFFICIENCY. The three primary machines are the inclined plane, the LEVER and the WHEEL (which includes the PULLEY and the WHEEL AND AXLE).

machine gun Weapon that loads and fires automatically and is capable of sustained rapid fire. The firing mechanism is operated by recoil or by gas from fired ammunition. The gun may be water- or air-cooled. The first widely used machine gun was invented in 1883. *See also* GATLING GUN

machine tools Power-driven machines for cutting and shaping metal and other materials. Shaping may involve shearing, pressing, rolling, and cutting away excess material using lathes, shapers, planers, drills, grinders and saws. Other techniques include electrical or chemical processes. Advanced machine-tool processes include cutting by means of LASER beams, high-pressure water jets, streams of PLASMA (ionized gas), and ULTRASONICS. Today, computers control many cutting and shaping processes carried out by machine tools and ROBOTS.

Mach number Ratio of the speed of a body or fluid to the local speed of sound. Mach 1 refers to the local speed of sound. An aircraft flying at Mach 1 is said to be subsonic, above it SUPERSONIC.

Machu Picchu Ancient fortified town in Peru. The best-preserved of the INCA settlements, it is situated on an Andean mountain saddle, 2,057m (6,750ft) above sea level. Machu Picchu was discovered in 1911 by Hiram Bingham.

Macke, August (1887–1914) German painter. A member of the *Blaue Reiter* group, he specialized in watercolours. Despite the influence of FAUVISM and ORPHISM, his own work remained expressionist.

Mackenzie River in NW Canada. The longest river in Canada, it flows *c.*1,800km (1,120mi) NW from the Great Slave Lake to the Arctic Ocean. Between the Great Slave and Athabasca lakes, the Mackenzie is called the **Slave River**.

mackerel Fast-swimming, marine food fish related to the TUNNY (tuna) and found in shoals in the N Atlantic, N Pacific and Indian oceans. The mackerel has a streamlined body and powerful tail. Length: 61cm (2ft). Family Scombridae.

McKinley, William (1843–1901) 25th US President (1897–1901). He sat in the House of Representatives as a Republican (1876–90) and was elected governor of Ohio (1891). A strong and effective president, he was largely occupied by foreign affairs. McKinley declared that isolationism was "no longer possible or desirable". He sanctioned US participation in the suppression of the BOXER REBELLION in China (1900). Re-elected in 1900, he was assassinated on 6 September 1901.

McKinley, Mount Peak in S central Alaska, USA, in the Alaska Range, the highest peak in North America. Permanent snowfields cover more than half the mountain. It is included in Mount McKin-

ley National Park (since 1980 known by the Aleutian name of Denali). Height: 6,194m (20,321ft).

Mackintosh, Charles Rennie (1868–1928) Scottish architect, artist and designer. He was one of the most successful and gifted exponents of ART NOUVEAU. His buildings, such as the Glasgow School of Art (1898–1909), were notable for their simplicity of line and skilful use of materials.

McLuhan, (Herbert) Marshall (1911–80) Canadian academic and communications expert. His view that the forms in which people receive information (such as television, radio and computers) are more important than the messages themselves was presented in *Understanding Media* (1964) and *The Medium is the Message* (1967).

McMillan, Edwin Mattison (1907–91) US physicist. In 1951 he shared the Nobel Prize for chemistry with Glenn Seaborg for discovering neptunium and other TRANSURANIC ELEMENTS. McMillan worked on the atomic bomb at Los Alamos, New Mexico, then on the cyclotron with Ernest LAWRENCE. McMillan developed the synchrocyclotron that led to modern nuclear accelerations.

Macmillan, (Maurice) Harold (1894–1986) British statesman, Conservative prime minister (1957–63). In the 1950s he held a number of cabinet posts, such as minister of defence (1954–55) and chancellor of the exchequer (1955–57). He succeeded Anthony EDEN as prime minister. He improved Anglo-American relations after the SUEZ CRISIS, but was unsuccessful in obtaining Britain's entry into the European Economic Community (EEC). He became Earl of Stockton in 1984.

MacNeice, Louis (1907–63) Northern Irish poet. MacNeice was a leading member of a left-wing group of writers of the 1930s, later dubbed the "AUDEN circle". His most outstanding poems are *Autumn Journal* (1939) and *Solstices* (1961).

macroeconomics Study of the economic system as a whole, rather than the study of individual markets (MICROECONOMICS). It involves the determination of items such as GROSS NATIONAL PRODUCT (GNP) and the analysis of unemployment, INFLATION, growth and the BALANCE OF PAYMENTS. *See also* ECONOMICS; KEYNES, JOHN MAYNARD

macrophage Large white blood cell (LEUCOCYTE) found mainly in the liver, spleen and lymph nodes. It engulfs foreign particles and micro-organisms by phagocytosis. Working together with other LYMPHOCYTES, it forms part of the body's defence system.

Madagascar Island republic in the Indian Ocean; the capital is Antananarivo. **Land and climate** Madagascar lies 385km (240mi) off the SE coast of Africa and is the world's fourth-largest island. In the W, a wide coastal plain gives way to a central highland region, mostly between 600m and 1,220m (2,000ft to 4,000ft). This is Madagascar's most densely populated region and site of Antananarivo. The land rises in the N to the volcanic peak of Tsaratanana, at 2,876m (9,436ft). Temperatures are moderated by altitude. Winters are dry, but heavy

MADAGASCAR
AREA: 587,040sq km (226,656sq mi)
POPULATION: 12,827,000
CAPITAL (POPULATION): Antananarivo (802,000)
GOVERNMENT: Republic
ETHNIC GROUPS: Merina 27%, Betsimisaraka 15%, Betsileo 11%, Tsimihety 7%, Sakalava 6%
LANGUAGES: Malagasy (official), French, English
RELIGIONS: Christianity 51%, traditional beliefs 47%, Islam 2%
CURRENCY: Malagasy franc = 100 centimes

rain falls in summer. Grass and scrub grow in the S. Large areas of forest have been cleared for farming, seriously threatening the habitats of its 150,000 unique species of plants and animals. **Economy** Madagascar is one of the world's poorest countries (1992 GDP per capita, US$710). The land has been eroded by deforestation and overgrazing. Farming, fishing and forestry employ *c*.80% of the workforce. Food and live animals form 66% of all exports. The major cash crop is coffee. Madagascar produces two-thirds of the world's natural vanilla. Madsagacar's wildlife encourages eco-tourism. **History** Muslims arrived in the 9th century. In the 17th century Portuguese missionaries vainly sought to convert the native population. By the 1880s the Merina controlled nearly all the island and established a monarchy. In 1896 the French defeated the Merina and Malagasy became a French colony. In 1942 Vichy colonial rule was overthrown by the British and the Free French reasserted control. During 1946–48 a rebellion against French power was brutally dispatched; perhaps as many as 80,000 islanders died. Republican status was adopted in 1958 and full independence achieved in 1960. President Tsiranana's autocratic government adopted many unpopular policies, such as the advocacy of economic ties with South Africa's apartheid regime. In 1972 the military took control. In 1975 Malagasy was renamed Madagascar, and Lieutenant Commander Didier Ratsiraka proclaimed martial law. During the 1980s Madagascar was beset by civil strife and numerous failed coups. In 1991 the opposition forces formed a rival government, led by Albert Zafy. In 1993 multiparty elections Zafy became president. Following the impeachment of Zafy in 1996, presidential elections were held, and in 1997 Ratsiraka became president again.

mad cow disease Popular name for BOVINE SPONGIFORM ENCEPHALOPATHY

Madeira Islands Archipelago and autonomous Portuguese region, off the NW African coast in the Atlantic Ocean; the capital and chief port is FUNCHAL (on Madeira). Madeira (the largest island) and Porto Santo are the only inhabited islands. The region's warm and stable climate makes it a popular European tourist destination. Industries: fortified wine, sugar cane, fruit and embroidery. Area: 794sq km (307sq mi). Pop. (1991) 253,400.

Maderna, Bruno (1920–73) Italian composer, conductor and leader of the Italian avant-garde. In 1955 he was a founder of the electronic music studio of Italian Radio (1955). His use of electronic media was often combined with live performance.

Madero, Francisco Indalecio (1873-1913) Mexican statesman, president (1911–13). Madero organized the armed insurrection that brought down the DÍAZ regime in 1910. He was victorious in the presidential elections that followed but proved a weak administrator. He was murdered in a military coup led by his former general Victoriano HUERTA.

Madhya Pradesh State in central India; the capital is BHOPAL. Lying between the Deccan and Gangetic plains, it is the largest state in India. The economy is dominated by agriculture. Major crops include wheat, rice and cotton. Madhya Pradesh is rich in minerals, such as bauxite, iron ore and manganese. In the 18th century the MARATHAS assumed control. In 1820 it was occupied by the British and during 1903–50 was known as the Central Provinces and Berar. In 1956 Madhya Bharat, Vindhya Pradesh and Bhopal were incorporated into the new state of Madhya Pradesh. Area: 443,446sq km (171,261sq mi). Pop. (1991) 66,181,170.

Madison, James (1751–1836) Fourth US President (1809–17). He was a close adviser to George WASHINGTON until, dismayed by the growing power of the executive, he broke with the FEDERALIST PARTY. He became associated with Thomas JEFFERSON and the DEMOCRATIC REPUBLICAN PARTY. President Jefferson made him secretary of state in 1801 and he succeeded Jefferson as president, in spite of his association with the unpopular Embargo Act (1807). He was unable to avoid the WAR OF 1812 with Britain. The successful conclusion of the war restored national prosperity, and Madison, the "Father of the Constitution", retired.

Madison State capital and second-largest city of Wisconsin, USA; on an isthmus between lakes Mendota and Monona. Founded as the state capital in 1836, it is an educational and manufacturing centre. Industries: agricultural machinery, meat and dairy products. Pop. (1990) 191,262.

Madonna (1958–) (Madonna Louise Veronica Ciccone) US popular singer and actress. She gained notoriety with the documentary *In Bed with Madonna* (1991) and the book *Sex* (1992). She won praise for her role in the film *Evita* (1996).

Madonna Representation in painting or sculpture of the Virgin MARY, usually with the infant Jesus. The early Christians painted the Madonna in their catacombs, and she was a notable feature of many outstanding Byzantine ICONS. The Renaissance saw mass production of less stylized representations.

Madras City on the Bay of Bengal, SE India; capital of Tamil Nadu state. India's second-largest port and fourth-largest city, Madras was founded in 1639 as a British trading post. As Fort St George, it became the seat of the EAST INDIA COMPANY and rapidly developed as a commercial centre. Industries: textiles, Tamil films, railway stock, transport equipment. Pop. (1991) 3,841,396.

Madrid Capital and largest city of Spain, lying on a plain in the centre of the country. It is Europe's highest capital city, at an altitude of 655m (2,149ft). Madrid was founded in the 10th century as a Moorish fortress. It was captured by Alfonso VI of Castile in 1083. In 1561 Philip II moved the capital from Valladolid to Madrid. The French occupied the city during the PENINSULAR WAR (1808–14). The city expanded in the 19th century. During the Spanish CIVIL WAR Madrid remained loyal to the Republican cause and was under siege for almost three years. Its capitulation in March 1939 brought the war to an end. Modern Madrid is a cosmopolitan centre of commerce and industry. Major economic activities include tourism, banking and publishing. Pop. (1991) 2,909,792.

madrigal Form of unaccompanied vocal music originating in 14th-century Italy. Early madrigals featured two or three parts and a highly ornamented upper part. During the 16th and early 17th centuries the style became more contrapuntal and was dominated by Andrea GABRIELI, PALESTRINA and Orlando di LASSO. The late period (*c*.1580–1620) was dominated by Gesualdo, MONTEVERDI, William BYRD, Orlando GIBBONS and Thomas WEELKES.

Maeterlinck, Maurice (1862–1949) Belgian playwright. His plays include *The Princess Maleine* (1889), *Pelléas and Mélisande* (1892) and *The Blue Bird* (1908), first produced by STANISLAVSKY. He won the 1911 Nobel Prize in literature.

Magdalene, Mary *See* MARY MAGDALENE

Magdeburg City on the River Elbe, central Germany; capital of Saxony-Anhalt state. In the 13th century Magdeburg prospered as a leading member of the HANSEATIC LEAGUE. During the 16th century it was a centre of the REFORMATION. During the THIRTY YEARS WAR, Magdeburg was sacked and destroyed by fire (1631). The city suffered heavy bomb damage in World War 2. A major inland port, it is linked to the Rhine and the Ruhr by the Mittelland Canal. Industries: iron and steel, scientific instruments, chemicals. Pop. (1990) 274,000.

Magellan, Ferdinand (1480–1521) Portuguese explorer, leader of the first expedition to circumnavigate the globe. He sailed to the East Indies and may have visited the Spice Islands (Moluccas) in 1511. Subsequently he sought a route to the Moluccas via the New World and the Pacific. He set out with five ships in 1519. He found the waterway near the S tip of South America that is now named Magellan's Strait. After severe hardship, the expedition reached the Philippines, where Magellan was killed. Only one ship, *Victoria*, completed the voyage.

Magellanic Clouds Two small satellite galaxies of the MILKY WAY galaxy, visible in skies around the South Pole as misty stellar concentrations.

Their distance is about 150,000 light-years away. *See also* GALAXY

maggot Name commonly given to the legless LARVA of a fly. It is primarily used to describe those larvae that infest food and waste material.

Maghreb Arabic term for NW Africa, applied to Morocco, Algeria, Tunisia, and sometimes Libya.

Magi Members of a hereditary priestly class of ancient Persia, responsible for certain religious ceremonies and cultic observances. By the time of Christ, the term Magi applied to astrologers, soothsayers and practitioners of the occult. The coming of the Magi to Jesus is marked in the Western Church by the feast of Epiphany. In the East it is celebrated at Christmas.

magic Use or apparent use of natural or spirit forces to produce results that are logically impossible. Belief in magic is associated mainly with primitive societies, though many superstitions persist in highly developed countries. There are two main types of magic: black magic (which makes use of evil spirits) and white magic (used to good purpose). *See also* WITCHCRAFT

magic realism 20th-century school of fiction. Particularly associated with post-1945 Latin American novelists (such as Gabriel GARCÍA MÁRQUEZ), magic realism is characterized by the interweaving of realistic and fantastical or supernatural elements. Márquez's *One Hundred Years of Solitude* (1967) is the greatest example of the genre.

magma Molten material that is the source of all IGNEOUS ROCKS. The term refers to this material while it is still under the Earth's crust. In addition to its complex silicate composition, magma contains gases and water vapour.

Magna Carta "Great Charter" issued by King JOHN of England in June 1215. He was forced to sign the charter by his rebellious barons at Runnymede, an island in the River Thames. The 63 clauses of the Magna Carta were mainly concerned with defining the feudal rights of the king and protecting the privileges of the church.

magnesia Magnesium oxide (MgO), a white, neutral, stable powder formed when magnesium is burned in oxygen. It is used industrially in firebrick and medicinally in stomach powders. Magnesium carbonate, found as magnesite and also used as an antacid, is often also called magnesia.

magnesium Silvery-white metallic element (symbol Mg), one of the ALKALINE-EARTH METALS. Magnesium's chief sources are magnesite and DOLOMITE. Magnesium burns in air with an intense white flame and is used in flashbulbs, fireworks, flares and incendiaries. Magnesium alloys are light and used in aircraft fuselages, jet engines, missiles and rockets. Chemically the element is similar to CALCIUM. Properties: at.no. 12; r.a.m. 24.312; r.d. 1.738; m.p. 648.8°C (1,200°F); b.p. 1,090°C (1,994°F); most common isotope Mg^{24} (78.7%).

magnet Object that produces a MAGNETIC FIELD. Lodestones, which are naturally magnetic, were used as early magnets; strong magnetic materials were later recognized as containing either iron, cobalt, nickel or their mixtures. A typical permanent magnet is a magnetized iron bar. The Earth is a giant magnet, its magnetic lines of force being detectable at all latitudes. An ELECTROMAGNET is stronger than a permanent one and is used for raising heavy steel weights. A superconducting magnet, the strongest of all, has special alloys cooled to very low temperatures. *See also* MAGNETISM

magnetic disk Plastic disk coated with magnetic material and used for storing computer PROGRAMS and DATA as a series of magnetic spots. Most computers contain a HARD DISK unit for general storage. There is also a unit for inserting lower-capacity floppy disks. Hard magnetic disks can store larger amounts of data and come in cartridges that slot into a special drive unit. *See also* CD-ROM

magnetic field Region surrounding a magnet or a conductor through which a current is flowing, in which magnetic effects, such as the deflection of a compass needle, can be detected. A magnetic field can be represented by a set of lines of force (flux lines) spreading out from the poles of a magnet or running around a current-carrying conductor. The direction of a magnetic field is the direction a tiny magnet takes when placed in the field. **Magnetic poles** are the field regions in which MAGNETISM appears to be concentrated. If a bar magnet is suspended to swing freely in the horizontal plane, one pole will point north; this is called the **north pole**. The other pole, **south pole**, will point south. Unlike poles attract each other; like poles repel each other. The Earth's magnetic poles are the ends of the huge "magnet" that is Earth.

magnetic flux Lines of force or of magnetic induction in a MAGNETIC FIELD. These lines can be seen as the closed curves followed by iron filings placed near a magnet. The direction of the flux at any point is the direction of the magnetic field, and the closeness of the flux (number of lines in a given area) is a measure of the magnetic field strength.

magnetic recording Formation of a record of electrical signals on a wire or tape by means of a pattern of magnetization. In an audio tape recorder, plastic tape coated with iron oxide is fed past an electromagnet that is energized by the amplified currents produced by a MICROPHONE. By ELECTROMAGNETIC INDUCTION, variations in magnetization are induced in the particles of iron oxide on the tape. When played back, the tape is fed past a similar electromagnet, which converts the patterns into sound, which is in turn fed to an AMPLIFIER and LOUDSPEAKER.

magnetic resonance Absorption or emission of electromagnetic radiation by atoms placed in a magnetic field. Spectrometers for nuclear magnetic resonance (NMR) use radio frequencies for chemical analysis and research in nuclear physics, and medically to analyse body tissues. Magnetic resonance imaging (MRI) is a medical scanning system for the brain, spinal cord and other body tissues.

magnetism Properties of matter and of electric currents associated with a MAGNETIC FIELD and with a north–south polarity (magnetic poles). All substances possess these properties to some degree because orbiting electrons in their atoms produce a magnetic field; similarly, an external magnetic field will affect the electron orbits. All substances possess weak magnetic (diamagnetic) properties and will tend to align themselves with the field, but in some cases this diamagnetism is masked by the stronger forms of magnetism: paramagnetism and ferromagnetism. Paramagnetism is caused by electron spin and occurs in substances having unpaired electrons in their atoms or molecules. The most important form of magnetism, ferromagnetism, is shown by substances such as iron and nickel, which can be magnetized by even a weak field due to the formation of tiny regions, called domains, that behave like miniature magnets and align themselves with an external field.

magnetite Iron oxide mineral (Fe_3O_4). It is a valuable iron ore, found in igneous and metamorphic rocks. It is black, metallic and brittle. Permanently magnetized deposits are called lodestone. Hardness 6; s.g. 5.2.

magnification Measure of the enlarging power of a MICROSCOPE or TELESCOPE. It is the size of an object's image produced by the instrument compared with the size of the object viewed with the unaided eye. In an astronomical telescope, magnification is equal to the ratio of the FOCAL LENGTH of the objective (the lens or lenses nearest the object) to the focal length of the eyepiece.

magnitude In astronomy, numerical value expressing the brightness of a celestial object on a logarithmic scale. **Apparent** magnitude is the magnitude as seen from Earth, determined by eye, photograph or photometric. It ranges from positive to negative values, the brightness increasing rapidly as the magnitude decreases. **Absolute** magnitude indicates intrinsic luminosity and is defined as the apparent magnitude of an object at a distance of 10 parsecs (32.6 light-years) from the object.

magnolia Any of about 40 species of trees and shrubs of the genus *Magnolia*, native to North and Central America and E Asia. They are valued for their white, yellow, purple or pink flowers. Height: to 30m (100ft). Family Magnoliaceae.

magpie Bird of the CROW family, closely related to the JAY, found mostly in the Northern Hemisphere. The common magpie (*Pica pica*) has a chattering cry, a long greenish-black tail and short wings. It has a clearly defined white underside with black above. Length: 46cm (18in). Family Corvidae.

Magritte, René (1898–1967) Belgian painter. His most characteristic works portrayed ordinary objects in strange juxtapositions. The first of these scenes was *The Menaced Assassin* (1926). Apart from a brief flirtation with NEO-IMPRESSIONISM, he explored these incongruous images for the rest of his life. *See also* SURREALISM

Magyars People who founded the kingdom of HUNGARY in the late 9th century. They adopted Christianity and established a powerful state that included much of the N Balkans, but lost territory to the Ottoman Turks after the battle of Mohács (1526). The remainder of the kingdom subsequently fell to the HABSBURG empire.

Mahabharata (Sanskrit, Great Epic of the Bharata Dynasty) Poem of almost 100,000 couplets, written *c*.400 BC– *c*.AD 200. It is considered one of India's two major Sanskrit epics, the other being RAMAYANA. It incorporates the BHAGAVAD GITA.

Maharashtra State in W India, bordering the Arabian Sea; the capital is BOMBAY. From the 14th–17th centuries the area was under Muslim rule. Britain incorporated Maharashtra into its empire in the early 19th century. India's third-largest state in both area and population, it was formed in 1960. Most of the land lies on the Deccan plateau. The area has rich mineral deposits, including manganese and coal. Industries: textiles, chemicals. Area: 307,762sq km (118,827sq mi). Pop. (1991) 78,707,000.

Mahayana (greater vehicle) One of the two main schools of Buddhism, the other being THERAVADA. Mahayana Buddhism was dominant in India from the 1st to the 12th century and is now prevalent in Tibet, China, Korea, and Japan. Unlike the Theravada school, it conceives of the Buddha as divine.

Mahdi Messianic Islamic leader. The title is usually used to refer to Muhammad Ahmad (1844–85) of the Sudan, who declared himself to be the Mahdi (Rightly Guided One) in 1881. He led the attack on KHARTOUM (1885) during which the British general Charles George GORDON was killed. The Mahdi set up a great Islamic empire with its capital at Omdurman. His reign lasted only six months.

Mahler, Gustav (1860–1911) Austrian composer and conductor. Many of his works combine orchestral and choral parts and contain instrumental effects requiring massive orchestras. His works include ten symphonies (the last left as a full-length sketch at his death), *The Song of the Earth* (1908) for orchestra with contralto and tenor solo, and the song cycle *Songs on the Death of Children* (1902).

mahogany Any of numerous species of tropical American deciduous trees and their wood, valued for furniture making. Mahogany has composite leaves, large clusters of flowers, and winged seeds. Height: to 18m (60ft). Family Meliaceae.

Mailer, Norman (1923–) US novelist. His first novel, *The Naked and the Dead* (1948), is one of the major realistic novels of World War 2. *Armies of the Night* (1968) and *The Executioner's Song* (1979), both of which won Pulitzer Prizes, tread a fine line between fact and fiction. Later novels include *Harlot's Ghost* (1991) and *The Gospel According to the Son* (1997).

Maillol, Aristide (1861–1944) French sculptor.

His work was almost exclusively of the female nude. He turned away from the romanticism of RODIN towards classical ideals. Pieces include *Mediterranean* (1901) and *Night* (1902).

Maimonides, Moses (1135–1204) Jewish philosopher, Hebrew scholar and physician, b. Spain. His *Guide of the Perplexed* is a plea for a more rational philosophy of Judaism. He emigrated to Egypt in 1159. He became court physician to SALADIN and was the recognized leader of Egyptian Jewry. His *Mishneh Torah* is a systematic compilation of Jewish oral law. He is one of the most influential thinkers of the Middle Ages.

Maine State in the extreme NE USA, in NEW ENGLAND; the capital is AUGUSTA. Maine was explored by John Cabot in 1498. Colonization began in the 1620s. Further British settlements were hindered by French and Native American resistance. In 1652 it fell under the administration of the MASSACHUSETTS BAY COMPANY and then of MASSACHUSETTS proper in 1691. In 1820 Maine achieved statehood and became the 23rd state of the Union. Economic development was rapid, based on the trading ports and Maine's timber resources. The land is generally rolling country with mountains in the W and over 2,000 lakes. The chief rivers are the St John, Penobscot, Kennebec and the St Croix. Three-quarters of Maine is forested. The major economic sector is the manufacture of paper and wood products. Economic development has been hampered by poor soil, a short growing season, geographic remoteness and a lack of coal and steel. Lobsters are the economic mainstay of the fishing industry. Tourism is an important sector. Area: 86,026sq km (33,215sq mi). Pop. (1990) 1,127,928.

Mainz City in W Germany, at the confluence of the Rhine and Main rivers; capital of Rhineland-Palatinate. A historic city, it was founded in 1 BC as a Roman camp. In the 15th century, Mainz flourished as a major European centre of learning. Today Mainz is an important transport and commercial centre. Pop. (1990) 183,300.

maize (corn or sweet corn) Cereal plant of the grass family. Originally from Central America, it is the key CEREAL in subtropical zones. Edible seeds grow in rows upon a cob, protected by a leafy sheath. Height: to 5m (16 ft). Species *Zea mays*.

Major, John (1943–) British statesman, prime minister (1990–97). He became a Conservative MP in 1979 and rose rapidly to become chief secretary to the Treasury in 1987. In 1989 he briefly served as foreign secretary before becoming chancellor of the exchequer. When Margaret THATCHER was forced to resign, Major emerged as heir. In 1992 he led the Conservative Party to a surprise general election victory. His administration was faced with prolonged recession and was forced to increase taxes. The pound was suspended from the European EXCHANGE RATE MECHANISM (ERM). The Conservative Party fractured over European Community policy. Continuing allegations of sleaze led to a landslide defeat in the 1997 general election; Major resigned as party leader.

Majorca (Mallorca) Largest of the BALEARIC ISLANDS, in the w Mediterranean, *c*.233km (145mi) off the Spanish coast; the capital is PALMA. The island is administered by Spain. During the Spanish Civil War it served as a base for Italian forces supporting General Franco. The island is fertile, with rolling hills and a mild climate. Agricultural products include olives, figs and citrus fruits. Tourism is the island's economic mainstay. Area: 3,639sq km (1,405sq mi). Pop. (1987 est.) 605,512.

Makarios III (1913–77) Greek-Cypriot leader. Appointed Greek Orthodox archbishop of Cyprus in 1950, he led the movement for ENOSIS (union with Greece), and was deported by the British in 1956. He was elected president when Cyprus became independent in 1959, but was briefly overthrown (1974) by Greek Cypriots still demanding *enosis*. The coup provoked unrest among Turkish Cypriots and Makarios was unable to prevent a Turkish invasion and the partition of Cyprus into Greek and Turkish sections.

Malabo Seaport capital of Equatorial Guinea, on BIOKO island, in the Gulf of Guinea, w central Africa. The city stands on the edge of a volcanic crater that was breached by the Atlantic to create a natural harbour. Industries: fish processing, hardwoods, cocoa, coffee. Pop. (1992) 35,000.

Malacca (Melaka) State in Malaysia, in sw Malay Peninsula, on the Strait of Malacca; the capital is Malacca. The city was founded in 1403. The sultanate became the region's most powerful empire and the centre for the spread of Islam throughout Malaya. In 1511 Malacca was conquered by the Portuguese. In 1641 the Dutch seized the region and fortified the city. In 1824 it was ceded to Britain. In 1957 it became a state of independent Malaya and, in 1963, of Malaysia. Area: 1,658sq km (640sq mi). Pop. (1993 est.) 583,400.

Málaga City and seaport in s Spain, on the coast of Andalusia; capital of Málaga province. It was founded in the 12th century BC by the Phoenicians. In 711 it was captured by the Moors and prospered as a trading port. Modern tourism has swollen Málaga's population and spilled over into the nearby resorts of Torremolinos and Marbella. Industries: wine, beer, textiles. Pop. (1991) 512,136.

Malagasy *See* MADAGASCAR

malaria Parasitic disease caused by infection with one of four species of *Plasmodium* PROTOZOA. Transmitted by the *Anopheles* mosquito, it is characterized by fever and enlargement of the spleen. Attacks of fever, chills and sweating typify the disease and recur as new generations of parasites develop in the blood. Malaria claims two million lives a year.

Malawi Republic in E central Africa, the capital is LILONGWE. **Land and climate** Malawi is dominated by Lake MALAWI, which constitutes 50% of its area. The lake forms most of Malawi's E border with Tanzania and Mozambique, and is drained in the s by the River Shire. Lilongwe lies in a valley of the central plateau. Mountains fringe the w edge of Lake Malawi. The lowlands are hot and humid throughout the year, but the uplands have a pleasant climate. Grassland and tropical savanna cover much of Malawi. **Economy** Malawi is one of the world's poorest countries (1992 GDP per capita, US$820). Over 80% of the workforce are farmers, most at subsistence level. Major food crops include cassava, maize and rice. Chief export crops include tobacco, tea, sugar and cotton. Malawi lacks mineral resources and has few manufacturing industries. Lake fishing is an important activity. **History and politics** In the early 19th century, the area was a centre of the slave trade. In 1891 it became a British protectorate. Slavery was abolished and coffee plantations established. In 1907 it became known as Nyasaland. In 1953 Britain made Nyasaland part of the Federation of Rhodesia (now Zimbabwe) and Nyasaland (the Federation also included present-day Zambia). The Congress Party, led by Dr Hastings BANDA, strongly opposed the Federation. In 1959 a state of emergency was declared. The Federation was dissolved in 1963 and Nyasaland achieved independence as Malawi (1964). Banda became prime minister, and when Malawi became a republic in 1966 he was made president. In 1971, as the newly appointed president-for-life, Banda became the first post-colonial, black African head of state to visit South Africa. Malawi became a shelter for rebels and refugees from the civil war in Mozambique, more than 600,000 were accommodated in the late 1980s. Banda's repression of opposition became more brutal. In 1992 famine relief aid was tied to improvements in human rights and the establishment of multiparty democracy. Elections were held in 1994, and Banda and his Malawi Congress Party were defeated. Bakili Muluzi of the United Democratic Front became president.

Malawi, Lake (formerly Lake Nyasa) Lake in E central Africa, in the Great RIFT VALLEY, bordered by Tanzania (N), Mozambique (E) and Malawi (S and w). The lake was visited by David LIVINGSTONE

MALAWI

AREA: 118,480sq km (45,745sq mi)

POPULATION: 8,823,000

CAPITAL (POPULATION): Lilongwe (268,000)

GOVERNMENT: Multiparty republic

ETHNIC GROUPS: Maravi (Chewa, Nyanja, Tonga, Tumbuka) 58%, Lomwe 18%, Yao 13%, Ngoni 7%

LANGUAGES: Chichewa and English (both official)

RELIGIONS: Christianity (Protestant 34%, Roman Catholic 28%), traditional beliefs 21%, Islam 16%

CURRENCY: Kwacha = 100 tambala

in 1859. Africa's third-largest lake, it is fed chiefly by the River Ruhuhu and drained by the Shire.

Malayalam Language spoken on the W coast of extreme S India, principally in the state of Kerala. It belongs to the Dravidian family of languages and there are about 20 million speakers.

Malay Peninsula Promontory of SE Asia, stretching for c.1,100km (700mi) between the Strait of MALACCA and the South China Sea. The N part of the peninsula is S Thailand and the S part forms Malaya (W MALAYSIA). SINGAPORE lies off its S tip. A mountain range forms the backbone of the peninsula, rising to 2,190m (7,186ft) at Mount Gunong Tahang. Most of the vegetation is dense tropical rainforest. The peninsula is one of the world's largest producers of tin and rubber. Today the peninsula is populated equally by Malays and Chinese. The region was controlled almost continuously from the 8th–13th century by the Buddhist Sailendra dynasty from SUMATRA. In the 15th century the Malaccan empire held sway. For the next three centuries the region came under the control of various European imperial powers. In 1909 Britain assumed control of a majority of the states, and reached a border agreement with Siam (Thailand). Area: c.180,000sq km (70,000sq mi).

Malaysia Federation of SE Asian states; the capital is KUALA LUMPUR. **Land and climate** The Federation of Malaysia consists of two main parts. **West Malaysia** is on the MALAY PENINSULA between the Strait of Malacca and the SOUTH CHINA SEA. It is home to c.80% of the population and includes Kuala Lumpur. **East Malaysia** consists of the states of SABAH and SARAWAK, in N BORNEO. Within Sarawak is the independent nation of BRUNEI. East and West Malaysia consist of coastal lowlands with mountainous interiors. The highest peak is Kinabalu (in Sabah), at 4,101m (13,455ft). Malaysia has a hot and rainy climate. Dense rainforest covers c.60% of Malaysia; only 13% of the land is farmed. **Economy** Malaysia is an upper-middle income developing country. The National Development Policy (1990–2000) is the second stage in its rapid industrialization. During the 1990s economic growth has averaged 8% per annum and many

economists predict it will become one of the leading economic powers in E Asia. Manufactured goods account for 78% of exports. Malaysia is the world's largest producer of palm oil, second-largest producer of tin and third-largest producer of natural rubber. Agriculture is an important activity. Rice is the chief food crop. **History** (For early history, *see* MALAY PENINSULA, SABAH, and SARAWAK) In 1641 the Dutch captured MALACCA, but were expelled by the British in 1795. In 1819 Britain founded SINGAPORE and in 1826 formed the Straits Settlement, consisting of PENANG, Malacca and Singapore. In 1867 the Straits Settlement became a British colony. Sabah and Sarawak became a British protectorate in 1888. In 1896 the states of Perak, Selangor, Pahang, and Negeri Semblian were federated. In 1909 the states of Johor, Kedah, Kelantan, Perlis and Terengganu formed the Unfederated Malay States. Japan occupied Malaysia throughout World War 2. After Japan's defeat, the British expanded the Federation of Malaya (1948) to include the unfederated states, and Malacca and Penang. Communists (largely from the Chinese population) began a protracted guerrilla war, and many Chinese were forcibly resettled. In 1957 the Federation of Malaya became an independent state within the Commonwealth of Nations. In 1963 Singapore, Sabah and Sarawak joined the Federation, which became known as Malaysia. Tension over Chinese representation led to the secession of Singapore in 1965. The New Economic Policy (1970–90) was largely successful in reducing ethnic tension. **Politics** Malaysia is a constitutional monarchy, with a parliamentary democracy. The sovereign is elected every five years by and from the rulers of each state. The United Malays National Organization (UMNO) has held power since independence.

Malcolm X (1925–65) (Malcolm Little) US African-American nationalist leader. While in prison, Malcolm joined the BLACK MUSLIMS and, after his release in 1953, became their leading spokesman. Following an ideological split with the founder of the movement, Elijah MUHAMMAD, he made a pilgrimage to MECCA, became an orthodox Muslim and formed a rival group. His assassination was probably authorized by the Black Muslims.

Maldives Republic in the Indian Ocean, c.640km (400mi) SW of Sri Lanka, consisting of c.1,200 low-lying coral islands grouped into 26 atolls; the largest island and capital is MALE. The islands (200 of which are inhabited) are prone to flooding. The climate is tropical. Coconuts and copra are the primary crop. Fishing is the major industry, and the leading export-earner is the bonito . The chief religion is Sunni Muslim. In 1518 the islands were claimed by the Portuguese. From 1665–1886 they were a dependency of Ceylon (Sri Lanka). In 1887 they became a British protectorate. In 1965 they achieved independence as a sultanate. In 1968 the sultan was deposed and a republic was declared. In 1982 Maldives joined the Commonwealth. An

---

MALAYSIA

AREA: 329,750sq km (127,316sq mi)
POPULATION: 18,181,000
CAPITAL (POPULATION): Kuala Lumpur (1,231,500)
GOVERNMENT: Federal constitutional monarchy
ETHNIC GROUPS: Malay and other indigenous groups 62%, Chinese 30%, Indian 8%
LANGUAGES: Malay (official)
RELIGIONS: Islam 53%, Buddhism 17%, Chinese folk religions 12%, Hinduism 7%, Christianity 6%
CURRENCY: Ringgit (Malaysian dollar) = 100 cents

attempted coup in 1988 was suppressed with the aid of Indian troops. Area: 298sq km (115sq mi). Pop. (1990) 213,215.

Male Largest of the Maldive Islands, in the Indian Ocean. The atoll forms the only urban area in the group, trading in bonito, breadfruit, copra and other coconut products. Pop. (1990) 55,000.

Malenkov, Georgi Maksimilianovich (1902–88) Soviet statesman, prime minister (1953–55). On STALIN's death (1953), he succeeded him as prime minister and leader of the Communist Party. He was soon superseded by KHRUSHCHEV as party leader and in 1955 lost the premiership also. Implicated in an unsuccessful coup against Khrushchev in 1957, he was dispatched to manage a power station in Siberia.

Malevich, Kasimir (1878–1935) Russian painter, a pioneer of geometric ABSTRACT ART. He experimented with the fragmentation and multiplication of images, such as *The Knife Grinder* (1912). He founded the SUPREMATISM movement (1913) and later concentrated on developing CONSTRUCTIVISM.

Mali Republic and largest country in W Africa; the capital is BAMAKO. **Land and climate** Mali is generally flat. Northern Mali is part of the SAHARA. The old trading city of Timbuktu lies on the edge of the desert. The main rivers, the Sénégal and the Niger, are both in S Mali. Bamako lies on the banks of the Niger. Northern Mali has a hot, arid climate. Dry and dusty harmattan winds blow from the Sahara. Over 70% of Mali is desert or semi-desert. Central and SE Mali form part of the SAHEL. In prolonged droughts, the N Sahel dries up and becomes part of the Sahara. Southern Mali, the most densely populated region, is covered by fertile farmland and tropical savanna. **Economy** Mali is one of the world's poorest countries (1992 GDP per capita, US$550). Agriculture, including nomadic pastoralism, employs 85% of the workforce. Farming is hampered by water shortages and only 2% of the land is cultivated. Another 25% is used for grazing animals. Food crops include millet, rice and sorghum. The chief cash crops are cotton, groundnuts and sugar cane. Fishing is an important economic activity. Mali has vital mineral deposits of gold and salt.

MALI
AREA: 1,240,190sq km (478,837sq mi)
POPULATION: 9,818,000
CAPITAL (POPULATION): Bamako (646,000)
GOVERNMENT: Multiparty republic
ETHNIC GROUPS: Bambara 32%, Fulani (or Peul) 14%, Senufo 12%, Soninke 9%, Tuareg 7%, Songhai 7%, Malinke (Mandingo or Mandinke) 7%
LANGUAGES: French (official)
RELIGIONS: Islam 90%, traditional beliefs 9%, Christianity 1%
CURRENCY: CFA franc = 100 centimes

In 1984 Mali rejoined the franc zone, and is a major recipient of international aid to support its free market reforms. **History** The region of Mali has lain at the heart of many of Africa's historic empires. From the 4th to the 11th centuries, the region was part of the Ghana empire. The medieval empire of Mali was one of the world's most powerful and prosperous powers. The 14th-century reign of Emperor Mansa Musa saw the introduction of Islam. Timbuktu became a great centre of learning and for trans-Saharan trade. The SONGHAI empire dominated the region during the 15th century. In the 19th century France gained control. In 1893 the region became known as French Sudan, and in 1898 was incorporated into the Federation of West Africa. In 1958 French Sudan voted to join the French Community as an autonomous republic. In 1959 it joined with SENEGAL to form the Federation of Mali. Shortly after gaining independence, Senegal seceded and in 1960 Mali became a one-party state. In 1963 Mali joined the ORGANIZATION OF AFRICAN STATES (OAS). Economic crisis forced the prime minister, Modibo Keita, to revert to the franc zone and permit France greater economic influence. Opposition led to Keita's overthrow by a military coup in 1968. The army group formed a National Liberation Committee and appointed Moussa Traoré as prime minister. During the 1970s a devastating famine claimed thousands of lives. In 1979 Traoré was elected president. In 1991 Traoré was overthrown in a military coup and in 1992 a new constitution provided for multiparty democracy. **Politics** The Alliance for Democracy in Mali (ADEMA) won the 1992 elections and Alpha Oumar Konaré became president. In 1997 both ADEMA and Konaré were re-elected.

mallard Large freshwater duck. The male is black, white, brown and grey with a green head; the female is mottled brown with blue wing markings. Length: 63cm (28in). Species *Anas platyrhynchos.*

Mallarmé, Stephane (1842–98) French poet, leading exponent of SYMBOLISM and precursor of MODERNISM. Mallarmé's allusive poetic style defies definitive statement in favour of sound associations. His best-known poems are *Hérodiade* (1869) and *L'Après-Midi d'un faune* (1876).

mallow Annual and perennial plants occurring in tropical and temperate regions of the world. The flowers are pink and white. The mallow family includes more than 900 species of plants, including cotton, okra, hollyhock and hibiscus. Family Malvaceae; especially genus *Malva.*

Malory, Sir Thomas (active 1460–70) English author. He wrote *Le Morte d'Arthur*, which recounts the legend of King ARTHUR.

malt Germinated grain, usually BARLEY, used in beverages, beer and foods. The grain is softened in water and allowed to germinate. This activates ENZYMES, which convert the starch to malt sugar (maltose). The grain is then kiln-dried.

Malta Archipelago republic in the Mediterranean

MALTA
AREA: 316sq km (122sq mi)
POPULATION: 359,000
CAPITAL (POPULATION): Valletta (102,571)
GOVERNMENT: Multiparty republic
ETHNIC GROUPS: Maltese 96%, British 2%
LANGUAGES: Maltese and English (both official)
RELIGIONS: Christianity (Roman Catholicism 99%)
CURRENCY: Maltese lira = 100 cents

Sea, *c*.60mi (100km) S of Sicily; the capital is VAL-LETTA (on Malta). **Land and climate** Malta consists of two main islands, Malta (area: 246sq km/95sq mi) and Gozo (67sq km/26sq mi). The small island of Comino is located between the two. The islands are low-lying. Malta island is mostly limestone. Gozo is largely covered by clay, and its landscapes are less arid. The climate is Mediterranean. In spring, the SIROCCO may raise temperatures and damage crops. Arable land makes up 38% of Malta. **Economy** Malta is an upper-middle income developing country. It lacks natural resources. Machinery and transport equipment account for over 50% of exports. Malta's historic naval dockyards are now used for commercial shipbuilding and repair. Manufactures include chemicals, electronic equipment and textiles. The largest economic sector is services, especially tourism. The rocky soil makes farming difficult, and Malta produces only 20% of its food. The main crops are barley, fruits, vegetables and wheat. Malta has a small fishing industry. **History** The Phoenicians colonized Malta in *c*.850 BC. In AD 395 Malta became part of the Byzantine empire. Arab invasion in 870 introduced Islam, but Christian rule was restored in 1091 by Roger I, Norman king of Sicily. In 1530 the Holy Roman Emperor gave Malta to the KNIGHTS HOSPITALLERS. NAPOLEON I took Malta in 1798, but was driven out in 1800. In 1814 Malta became a British colony and strategic naval base. In World War 2 Italian and German aircraft bombed the islands. In recognition of the bravery of the Maltese resistance, George VI awarded the George Cross to Malta in 1942. In 1953 Malta became a NATO base. Malta became independent in 1964 and in 1974 it became a republic. In 1979 Britain's military agreement with Malta expired, and British forces withdrew. In the 1980s Malta declared itself a neutral country. **Politics** In 1990 Malta applied to join the European Union. In the 1996 general election, the Malta Labour Party (MLP) won a surprise victory. It has reversed Malta's application to join the EU.

Malthus, Thomas (1766–1834) British economist and minister, famous for his *Essay on Population* (1798). According to Malthusian theory, population increases geometrically but the food supply increases only arithmetically so that population must eventually overtake it, resulting in famine, war and disease.

maltose (malt sugar) Disaccharide ($C_{12}H_{22}O_{11}$) that contains two molecules of the simple sugar GLUCOSE. It is produced by the hydrolysis of STARCH by the enzyme AMYLASE and by the breakdown of starches and GLYCOGEN during digestion.

mamba Any of several large, poisonous African tree snakes of the cobra family, Elapidae. The deadly black mamba (*Dendroaspis polylepis*) is the largest species. It is grey, greenish-brown or black and is notoriously aggressive; its bite is almost always fatal. Length: to 4.3m (14ft).

mammal Class (Mammalia) of VERTEBRATE animals, characterized by mammary glands in the female and full, partial or vestigial hair covering. Mammals are warm-blooded. They have a four-chambered heart with circulation to the lungs separate from the rest of the body. As a group, mammals are active, alert and intelligent. They usually bear fewer young than other animals and give them longer and better parental care. Most mammals before birth grow inside the mother's body and are nourished by means of a placenta. When born, they continue to feed on milk from the mother's mammary glands. There is a wide range of features among mammals. Mammals include 17 orders of placentals, one MARSUPIAL order – all live-bearing – and an order of egg-laying MONOTREMES. They probably evolved about 180 million years ago from a group of warm-blooded reptiles. Today, mammals range in size from shrews weighing a few grams, to the blue whale, which can weigh up to 150 tonnes.

mammary gland *See* BREAST

mammoth Extinct PLEISTOCENE ancestor of the elephant. Many were covered with long red or brown hair. The prominent tusks were long and curved, sometimes crossing in adult males. The permafrost of Siberia has been known to yield whole specimens that have been frozen for as long as 30,000 years. Genus *Mammuthus*.

man Zoological term for a HUMAN BEING

Man, Isle of Island off the NW coast of England, in the Irish Sea; the capital is Douglas. It has been a British crown possession since 1828 and has its own government (the Tynwald). The basis of the economy is tourism, though agriculture is important. Products include oats, fruit and vegetables. Area: 572sq km (221sq mi). Pop. (1991) 69,788.

Managua Capital of Nicaragua, in the W central part, on the S shore of Lake Managua. It became the capital in 1855. It is the industrial and commercial hub of Nicaragua. Industries: textiles, tobacco, cement. Pop. (1985) 682,111.

Manama (Al-Manamah) Capital of Bahrain, on the N coast of Bahrain Island, in the Persian Gulf. It was made a free port in 1958. It is Bahrain's principal port and commercial centre. Industries: oil refining, banking, boatbuilding. Pop. (1988) 151,500.

manatee Any of three species of large, plant-eating, sub-ungulate, aquatic mammals found primarily in shallow coastal waters of the Atlantic Ocean. It has a tapered body ending in a large rounded flipper; there are no hindlimbs. Length: to 4.5m (14.7ft); weight: 680kg (1,500lb). Family Trichechidae; genus *Trichechus*.

Manchester City on the River Irwell, forming a metropolitan district in the Greater Manchester urban area, NW England. In AD 79 the Celtic town was occupied by the Romans, who named it Mancunium. The textile industry (now in decline) dates back to the 14th century. In 1830 the world's first passenger railway was constructed between LIVERPOOL and Manchester. In 1894 the Manchester Ship Canal opened, providing the city with its own access to the sea. Modern Manchester has a diverse manufacturing base, including chemicals, pharmaceuticals, printing and publishing. It is the major financial centre of N England. Pop. (1991) 404,861.

Manchu Nomadic peoples of MANCHURIA. They established the QING dynasty.

Manchukuo Japanese puppet state in MANCHURIA (1932–45). It was under the nominal rule of the pretender to the QING throne, Henry PU YI. The state of Manchukuo was not recognized by most foreign governments and, after the defeat of Japan in 1945, Manchuria was returned to China.

Manchuria Region of NE China, now included in the provinces of Heilongjiang, Jilin and Liaoning. Manchuria is rich in mineral deposits and is one of China's leading sites for heavy industry. It is also a major agricultural area. The Manchus conquered China in the 17th century. In the late 19th century Russia developed the naval facilities at Port Arthur. In the 1904–05 RUSSO-JAPANESE WAR Japan seized control of S Manchuria and Port Arthur. In 1931 Japan occupied the whole of Manchuria and established the puppet state of MANCHUKUO. In 1948 Chinese communists defeated Manchurian nationalists and reconstruction began. From 1960–90 the region was at the forefront of Sino-Soviet hostilities. Area: c.1,500,000sq km (600,000sq mi).

Manchurian Incident Japanese seizure of MANCHURIA (1931). Japan overran the province, setting up the puppet state of MANCHUKUO.

Mandalay City in central Burma (Myanmar), on the River Irrawaddy; capital of Mandalay division. Founded in 1857, Mandalay was the last capital (1860–85) of the Burmese kingdom before it was annexed to Britain. The city was occupied by the Japanese during World War 2. Pop. (1983) 532,985.

Mandarin Major dialect of CHINESE, the spoken language of about 70% of the population of China. It was originally the language of the imperial court. Mandarin is the basis of modern standard Chinese.

Mandela, Nelson Rolihlahla (1918–) South African statesman, president (1994–). Mandela joined the AFRICAN NATIONAL CONGRESS (ANC) in 1944, and for the next 20 years led a campaign of civil disobedience against South Africa's APARTHEID government. Following the SHARPEVILLE Massacre (1960), Mandela formed *Umkhonte We Sizwe*, a paramilitary wing of the ANC. The ANC was banned. In 1964 Mandela was sentenced to life

imprisonment for political offences. For the next 27 years in prison, Mandela was a symbol of resistance to apartheid. International sanctions forced F.W. DE KLERK to begin dismantling apartheid. In February 1990 Mandela was released to resume his leadership of the newly legalized ANC. In 1993 Mandela and de Klerk shared the Nobel Peace Prize. Mandela gained 66% of the popular vote in South Africa's first democratic general election (1994). A strong advocate of the need for reconciliation, Mandela made de Klerk deputy president (1994–96) in his government of national unity.

Mandelbrot, Benoit B. (1942–) US mathematician, b. Poland. He has made major contributions to CHAOS THEORY. His book *The Fractal Geometry of Nature* contains many examples of natural FRACTALS, such as ferns and trees. The Mandelbrot set, a well-known fractal object, is named after him.

mandolin Stringed musical instrument related to the LUTE. It has four or six paired wire strings, which are played with a plectrum. It is most often used as an accompaniment to folksongs and dances.

mandrake Plant of the potato family, native to the Mediterranean region and used since ancient times as a medicine. It contains the ALKALOIDS hyoscyamine, scopolamin and mandragorine. Leaves are borne at the base of the stem, and the large greenish-yellow or purple flowers produce a many-seeded berry. Height: 40cm (16in); family Solanaceae; species *Mandragora officinarum*.

mandrill Large BABOON that lives in dense rainforests of central W Africa. Mandrills roam in small troops and forage for their food. The male has a red-tipped, pale blue nose, yellow-bearded cheeks and a reddish rump. Height: 75cm (30in); weight: to 54kg (119lb). Species *Mandrillus sphinx*.

Manet, Édouard (1832–83) French painter. Although his name is usually linked with IMPRESSIONISM, he did not consider himself an impressionist. *Le Déjeuner sur l'Herbe* was violently attacked by critics when first exhibited (1863), as was *Olympia*. He achieved recognition with later works, such as *Le Bar aux Folies-Bergères* (1881).

manganese Grey-white metallic element (symbol Mn), first isolated in 1774. Its chief ores are pyrolusite, manganite and hausmannite. The metal is used in alloy steels, ferromagnetic alloys, fertilizers and paints. Properties: at.no. 25; r.a.m. 54.938; r.d. 7.20; m.p. 1,244°C (2,271°F); b.p. 1,962 °C (3,564°F); most common isotope Mn^{55} (100%).

mango Evergreen tree native to SE Asia and grown widely in the tropics for its fruit. It has lanceolate leaves, pinkish-white clustered flowers, and yellow-red fruit. Height: to 18m (60ft). Family Anacardiaceae; species *Mangifera indica*.

mangrove Common name for any of 120 species of tropical trees or shrubs found in marine swampy areas. Stilt-like aerial roots arise from the branches and hang down into the water. Some species also have roots that rise up out of the water. Height: to 20m (70ft). Chief family: Rhizophoraceae.

Manhattan Borough of NEW YORK CITY, in SE New York state, USA; lying mainly on Manhattan Island and bounded w by the HUDSON River. In 1625 the Dutch West India Company began to build New Amsterdam. The British captured the colony in 1664 and renamed it New York. Industries: electrical goods, finance, tourism, entertainment, broadcasting, publishing. Pop. (1990) 1,487,536.

Manhattan Project Codename given to the development of the US atomic bomb during WORLD WAR 2. Work on the bomb was carried out in great secrecy by a team including Enrico FERMI and J. Robert OPPENHEIMER. The first test took place on 16 July 1945, near Alamogordo, New Mexico. In August 1945 bombs were dropped on Japan.

manic depression (bipolar disorder) Mental illness featuring recurrent bouts of DEPRESSION, possibly alternating with periods of mania. Depressive and manic symptoms may alternate in a cyclical pattern, be mixed or separated by periods of remission and disturbances of thought and judgement.

Manichaeism Religious teaching of the Persian prophet Mani (c.216–c.276), based on a supposed primeval conflict between light and darkness. The Manichaean sect, influenced by ZOROASTRIANISM and CHRISTIANITY, spread to Egypt and Rome, where it was considered a heresy, and to Chinese Turkistan, where it survived until the 13th century.

Manila Capital of the Philippines, on Manila Bay, SW Luzon island. It is the industrial, commercial and administrative heart of the Philippines. In 1942 it was occupied by the Japanese. In 1945 a battle between Japanese and Allied forces destroyed the old walled city. Pop. (1990) 1,587,000.

Manitoba Province in S central Canada, bordered by Hudson Bay (NE) and the USA (S); the capital and largest city is WINNIPEG. In 1670 Charles II granted the land to the HUDSON'S BAY COMPANY. In 1869 the Company sold it to the newly created confederation of Canada. Manitoba became a province in 1870. The terrain varies from the prairie country and lake district of the S to the rugged upland of the Canadian Shield of the NE and the tundra of the far N. Manitoba is famous for its wheat fields. There are large oilfields in the SW of the province and extensive timber reserves. Area: 649,947sq km (250,946sq mi). Pop. (1994 est.) 1,131,100.

Mann, Thomas (1875–1955) German novelist. Perhaps the outstanding figure of 20th-century German literature, Mann linked individual psychological problems to the great decline in European culture. His first novel, *Buddenbrooks* (1901), is an epic family saga. Shorter works followed, including the novella *Death in Venice* (1912). *The Magic Mountain* (1924) is widely acclaimed as his masterpiece. He won the 1929 Nobel Prize for literature.

Mannerheim, Carl Gustav Emil von (1867–1951) Finnish general and statesman, president (1944–46). He served in the Russian army and was a general in World War 1. After the Russian Revolution (1917), he returned to Finland and led the anti-Bolshevik forces in the civil war. In 1918–19 he obtained international recognition of Finnish independence. He also planned the fortified Mannerheim Line across Karelia.

mannerism Term applied to the art and architecture of Italy between the High RENAISSANCE and the BAROQUE. The style is typified by PARMIGIANO, Pontormo and Giovanni Lanfranco. Theorists debate the scope of mannerism: it has been extended to include El GRECO, the FONTAINEBLEAU SCHOOL and Romanist painters of the Netherlands.

Mannheim City and river port in central Germany, in Baden-Württemberg state, on the E bank of the River Rhine. Originally a fishing village, it was fortified in 1606 and destroyed by the French in 1689. It was the seat of the Rhine Palatinate (1719–77). Industries: chemicals, oil refining, engineering, paper, textiles. Pop. (1990) 316,900.

Mansfield, Katherine (1888–1923) British short-story writer, b. New Zealand. Her delicate humour and deceptively simple style are best represented in *The Garden Party* (1922) and *The Dove's Nest* (1923).

Mantegna, Andrea (1431–1506) Italian painter and engraver. In 1460 he became court painter to the Gonzaga family in Mantua and decorated the *Camera degli Sposi* in the Duke's Palace. This room contains the first example of illusionistic architecture to have been created since antiquity. Mantegna's other great work was his series of oil paintings, *The Triumph of Caesar* (c.1480–95).

mantis (praying mantis) Any of several species of mantids, insects found worldwide. They have powerful front legs to catch and hold their prey. Length: 25–150mm (1–6in). Family Mantidae.

mantissa Decimal part of a LOGARITHM.

mantle Layer of the Earth between the CRUST and the CORE, which extends to a depth of 2,890km (1,795mi). The mantle forms the greatest bulk of the Earth: 82% of its volume and 68% of its mass. The uppermost part is rigid, solid and brittle and together with the Earth's crust forms the **lithosphere**. From a depth of about 60km (40mi) down to 200km (125mi) the mantle has a soft zone, which is called the **asthenosphere**. Temperature and pressure are in balance so that much of the mantle material is near melting point or partly melted and capable of flowing. The remainder of the mantle is thought to be more solid but still capable of creeping flow. In the lower mantle several changes in seismic velocity can be detected. The chemical constitution of the mantle is uncertain, but it is thought to be made up of iron-magnesian silicates.

Manx Language formerly spoken in the Isle of Man. Closely related to Scottish GAELIC, it was spoken by most of the native inhabitants until c.1700, when English was introduced. By 1900 there were only a few thousand speakers left.

Maori Polynesian population, native inhabitants of New Zealand. Traditionally, Maoris lived by agriculture, hunting and fishing. They retain strong attachments to the Maori language, culture and customs. Maori war chants (*haka*) are still kept alive. Since the 1970s the Maoris have been increasingly politically active, and some of their land has been returned to them.

Maori Wars Two Wars (1845–48, 1860–72) between British settlers and indigenous MAORI tribes in New Zealand. They arose when the settlers broke the agreement in the Treaty of WAITANGI (1840) that guaranteed the Maoris possession of their lands. As a result of the wars, a Native Land Court was established (1865), a Maori school system formed (1867) and the Maoris were given four elected members in the New Zealand legislature.

Mao Zedong (1893–1976) Chinese statesman, founder and chairman (1949–76) of the People's Republic of China. Mao was a founder member of the Chinese COMMUNIST PARTY in 1921. After the nationalist KUOMINTANG, led by CHIANG KAI-SHEK, dissolved the alliance with the communists in 1927, Mao helped to establish rural soviets. The advance of nationalist forces forced Mao to lead the Red Army on the LONG MARCH. In 1937 the civil war was suspended as communists and nationalists combined to fight the second SINO–JAPANESE WAR. The communists' brand of guerrilla warfare gained hold of much of rural China. Civil war recommenced in 1945, and by 1949 the nationalists had been driven out of mainland China. Mao became chairman of the People's Republic and was re-elected in 1954. ZHOU ENLAI acted as prime minister. In 1958 Mao launched the Great Leap Forward, a programme that ended in mass starvation and the withdrawal of Soviet aid. Mao's leadership was challenged. The CULTURAL REVOLUTION was an attempt by Mao and his wife, JIANG QING, to reassert Maoist ideology. The cult of the personality was encouraged, political rivals were dismissed, and Mao became supreme commander of the nation and army (1970).

map Graphic representation of part or all of the Earth's surface. Maps are usually printed on a flat surface using various kinds of projections based on land surveys, aerial photographs and other sources.

maple Genus of deciduous trees native to temperate and cool regions of Europe, Asia and North America. They have yellowish or greenish flowers and winged seeds. The sugar maple is tapped for maple syrup. Height: 4.6–36m (15–120ft). Family Aceraceae; genus *Acer*. *See also* SYCAMORE.

Maputo (Lourenço Marques) Capital and chief port of Mozambique, on Maputo Bay. Visited by the Portuguese in 1502, it was made capital of Portuguese East Africa in 1907. Industries: footwear, textiles, rubber. Pop. (1992 est.) 2,000,000.

Maracaibo City and port in NW Venezuela, between Lake Maracaibo and the Gulf of Venezuela. Founded in 1529, it expanded after the discovery of oil in 1917. Industries: oil processing, coffee, cacao, sugar. Pop. (1990) 1,207,513.

Marat, Jean Paul (1743–93) French revolutionary. A physician, he founded *L'Ami du Peuple*, a vitriolic journal supporting the JACOBINS. His murder by Charlotte Corday, a member of the GIRONDINS, was exploited for propaganda by the Jacobins and contributed to the REIGN OF TERROR.

Maratha (Mahratta) Hindu warrior people of W central India, who rose to power in the 17th century. They extended their rule throughout W India by defeating the MOGUL EMPIRE and successfully resisting British supremacy in India during the 18th century. They were finally defeated in 1818.

marathon Long-distance race. The standard marathon is 42.2km (26.2mi), which was the distance run by the Greek soldier who brought news of the victory at MARATHON to Athens in 490 BC.

Marathon, Battle of (490 BC) Victory of the Greeks, mainly Athenians, during the PERSIAN WARS. The defeat of a much larger Persian army on the Marathon plain NE of Athens secured Attica from the invasion of CYRUS THE GREAT.

marble Metamorphic rock composed largely of recrystallized limestones and dolomites. The colour is normally white, but when tinted by serpentine, iron oxide or carbon can vary to shades of yellow, green, red, brown or black. It has long been a favourite building and sculpting material.

Marche Region in E central Italy, between the Apennines and the Adriatic Sea; the capital is Ancona. Marche is mainly mountainous. Farming is the principal economic activity. Crops include cereals, olives and grapes. Area: 9,692sq km (3,743sq mi). Pop. (1990) 1,435,570.

Marconi, Guglielmo (1874–1937) Italian physicist who developed RADIO. In 1897 Marconi was able to demonstrate radio telegraphy over a distance of 19km (12mi). He established radio communication between France and England in 1899. By 1901 radio transmissions were being received across the Atlantic Ocean. Marconi was awarded the Nobel Prize for physics in 1909.

Marco Polo *See* POLO, MARCO

Marcos, Ferdinand Edralin (1917–89) Philippine statesman, president (1965–86). His presidency was marked by civil unrest, which led to the imposition of martial law in 1972. A new constitution (1973) gave Marcos authoritarian powers. His regime acquired a reputation for corruption and repression. In 1983 his main rival, Benigno Aquino, was assassinated and political opposition coalesced behind Benigno's widow, Cory AQUINO. Allegations of vote-rigging in the 1986 general election forced him into exile. In 1988 US authorities indicted both him and his wife, Imelda, for fraud. Ferdinand was too ill to stand trial and died in Hawaii. Imelda was subsequently acquitted, but in 1993 was sentenced to 18 years imprisonment. She appealed the judgement.

Marcus Aurelius (Antoninus) (121–180) Roman emperor (161–180) and philosopher of the STOIC school. For eight years (161–169) he ruled as co-emperor with his adoptive younger brother

Lucius Aurelius Verus (d.169). His only surviving work, *Meditations*, is a collection of philosophical thoughts and ideas gleaned from his campaigns.

Marcuse, Herbert (1898–1979) US political philosopher, b. Germany. He is noted for his reinterpretations of MARXISM and Freudian analysis of 20th-century industrial society. In the 1920s he was a founder member of the Frankfurt Institute for Social Research. Fleeing Nazi Germany in 1933, he settled in the USA and worked for the US government (1941–50). He held a number of academic posts. His advocacy of civil resistance chimed with the 1960s student protests. Marcuse's books included *Eros and Civilization* (1955) and *One-Dimensional Man* (1964). *See also* ALIENATION

Mare, Walter de la *See* DE LA MARE, WALTER

Margaret of Anjou (1430–82) Wife of HENRY VI of England from 1445. During the Wars of the ROSES she led the cause of Lancaster, raising troops in France. After her only son, Edward, was killed at Tewkesbury (1471), she was taken prisoner. Ransomed by Louis XI of France in 1476, she left England for good.

Margrethe II (1940–) Queen of Denmark, daughter of Frederick IX. In 1972 she became the first queen regent since the Middle Ages and the first democratically appointed sovereign in Denmark's history. In 1967 she married the French Count Henri Laborde Monpezat.

marguerite Perennial plant of the daisy family native to the Canary Islands. It has white-rayed, yellow-centred flower heads about 5cm (2in) across. Height: to 91cm (3ft). Family Asteraceae/COMPOSITAE; species *Argyranthemum frutescens.*

Mariana Islands Volcanic island chain in the W Pacific Ocean, stretching over 800km (500mi) of the Marianas Trench. The group comprises GUAM and the islands of the Northern Marianas: Saipan, Tinian, Rota, Pagan and 11 smaller islands. Discovered by Ferdinand Magellan in 1521, they were taken by US forces in 1944 and in 1947 became part of the US Trust Territory of the Pacific Islands. In 1978 the Commonwealth of the Northern Mariana Islands was formed in association with the USA, and in 1986 the islanders acquired US citizenship. Trusteeship status was ended in 1990. Exports include sugar cane, coconuts and coffee. Tourism is important. Area (excluding Guam): 464sq km (179sq mi). Pop. (1990) 43,345.

Maria Theresa (1717–80) Archduchess of Austria, ruler of the Austrian HABSBURG empire (1740–80). She succeeded her father, Emperor CHARLES VI, and was immediately faced with the War of the AUSTRIAN SUCCESSION (1741–48). She lost Silesia to Prussia, but secured the imperial title for her husband, FRANCIS I. She failed to regain Silesia in the SEVEN YEARS WAR (1756–63).

Marie Antoinette (1755–93) Queen of France. Daughter of Emperor FRANCIS I and MARIA THERESA of Austria, she married the future LOUIS XVI in 1770. Her life of pleasure and extrava-

gance contributed to the outbreak of the FRENCH REVOLUTION in 1789. In 1791 she attempted to escape, but was captured and guillotined.

Marie de Médici (1573–1642) Queen of France. A member of the Medici family, daughter of the Grand Duke of Tuscany, she married HENRY IV of France (1600). He was assassinated the day after she was crowned queen in 1610, possibly with her connivance. As regent for her son, LOUIS XIII, she relied on Italian advisers and reversed Henry's anti-Habsburg policy. She was constantly at odds with Louis after 1614 and antagonized Cardinal RICHELIEU. She was forced to leave France (1631).

marigold Any of several mostly golden-flowered plants, mainly of the genera *Chrysanthemum, Tagetes* and *Calendula*, all of the daisy family (Asteraceae/COMPOSITAE). The most commonly cultivated are the French marigold (*Tagetes patula*) and the African marigold (*T. erecta*).

marihuana NARCOTIC drug prepared from the dried leaves of the Indian hemp plant (*Cannabis sativa*); it is different from HASHISH, which is prepared from resin obtained from the flowering tops of the plant. Possession of the drug is illegal in many countries.

Mariner program Series of US space probes to the planets. Mariner 2 flew past Venus in 1962. Mariner 4 flew past Mars in July 1965, photographing craters on its surface. Mariner 5 passed Venus in October 1967, making measurements of the planet's atmosphere. Mariners 6 and 7 obtained further photographs of Mars in 1969. Mariner 9 went into orbit around Mars in November 1971. It made a year-long photographic reconnaissance of the planet's surface and obtained close views of the two moons. Mariner 10, the last of the series, was the first two-planet mission, passing Venus in February 1974 and then encountering Mercury three times, in March and September 1974 and March 1975.

Marinetti, Filippo Tommaso (1876–1944) Italian poet, novelist, dramatist and founder of FUTURISM. In such works as *Futurismo e Fascismo* (1924), he embraced fascism and advocated the glorification of machinery, speed and war. Collections of poetry include *Destruction* and *War: the Only Hygiene of the World* (1915).

marjoram Perennial herb of the mint family (Lamiaceae/Labiatae), *c.*60cm (24in) tall with purplish flowers. It is native to the Mediterranean region and W Asia and is cultivated as an annual in northern climates. Species *Origanum vulgare*.

Mark, Gospel according to Saint Second GOSPEL in the New Testament, but the earliest in composition. It was written *c.*AD 55–65 and is believed to be one of two reference works (the other being "Q") used by St MATTHEW and St LUKE. It is one of the three SYNOPTIC GOSPELS.

Mark, Saint (active 1st century AD) Apostle and possibly one of the four evangelists of the New Testament. He is identified with John Mark, the cousin of the apostle St BARNABAS. Christian tradition says that he became secretary to St PETER and wrote the first gospel. His feast day is 25 April.

Mark Antony *See* ANTONY, MARK

market economy Economy in which resources are controlled by the operation of free markets (in which the forces of supply and demand operate without interference). The opposite is a controlled economy, in which market forces are under governmental control.

Markova, Dame Alicia (1910–) British ballerina, b. Lilian Alicia Marks. She joined the Vic-Wells Ballet in 1931 and was its first prima ballerina. Classical ballets in which she excelled include *Giselle, Les Sylphides* and *Swan Lake*. She was made a Dame of the British Empire in 1963.

Marlborough, John Churchill, 1st Duke of (1650–1722) English general. After initially supporting James II against MONMOUTH (1685), he switched allegiance in support of the GLORIOUS REVOLUTION (1688). Marlborough led the Allied armies against France in the War of the SPANISH SUCCESSION, winning great victories at Blenheim (1704), Ramillies (1706), Oudenaarde (1708) and Malplaquet (1709).

Marley, Bob (Robert Nesta) (1945–81) Jamaican singer-songwriter. A reggae artist dedicated to RASTAFARIANISM, he achieved worldwide recognition with his group The Wailers. Their albums include *Rastaman Vibrations* (1976), *Exodus* (1977) and *Uprising* (1980).

Marlowe, Christopher (1564–93) English poet and playwright. He played a part in making BLANK VERSE the vehicle of ELIZABETHAN DRAMA. His major plays are *Tamburlaine the Great* (1590), *The Tragical History of Doctor Faustus* (1604) and *The Jew of Malta* (1633). His greatest poems are *Hero and Leander* (1598) and *The Passionate Shepherd* (1599). He was killed in a tavern brawl.

marmoset Diurnal, arboreal MONKEY of tropical America. Among the smallest of the monkeys, they have soft, dense fur and sickle-shaped nails. Family Callitrichidae; typical genus *Callithrix*.

marmot Stocky, terrestrial rodent of the SQUIRREL family, native to North America, Europe and Asia. Most marmots have brown to grey fur, short, powerful legs and furry tails. Length, excluding tail: 30–60cm (12–24in); weight: 3–8kg (6.6–16.5lb). Family Sciuridae.

Maronites Members of a Christian community of Syrian origin, which claims its origins both from St Maron, a Syrian hermit, in the late 4th or early 5th centuries, and St John Maro, a patriarch of Antioch (685–707). Some 400,000 Maronites live in Lebanon, with other smaller groups in Syria, Cyprus, southern Europe, and North and South America. The Maronites have the status of a uniate Church – that is, an Eastern Church in union with Rome but retaining its own rite and canon law.

Marquesas Islands Volcanic island group in the Pacific Ocean, S of the Equator and N of Tuamotu, including Fatu Hiva, Hiva Oa and Nuku Hiva, and forming part of French Polynesia; the capital is Taiohae (on Nuku Hiva). The islands were first discovered by a Spanish navigator in 1595. During the 19th century, European diseases killed many of the native Polynesians. The islands are mountainous, with fertile valleys and several good harbours. Exports include tobacco, vanilla and copra. Area: 1,049sq km (405sq mi). Pop. (1988) 7,538.

Márquez, Gabriel García *See* GARCÍA MÁRQUEZ, GABRIEL

Marrakech City in W central Morocco, at the NW foot of the Atlas Mountains. Founded in 1062 by the ALMORAVIDS, it was Morocco's capital until 1147. Industries: tourism, leather goods. Pop. (1983) 439,728.

marrow Soft tissue containing blood vessels, found in the cavities of BONE. The marrow found in many adult bones is yellowish and functions as a store of fat. The marrow in the flattish bones is reddish and contains cells that give rise eventually to ERYTHROCYTES as well as to most of the LEUCOCYTES, but not LYMPHOCYTES and platelets.

Mars Fourth major planet from the Sun. Mars appears red to the naked eye because of the high iron content of its crust. The atmosphere consists of 95% carbon dioxide, 2.5% nitrogen, and 1.5% argon, with small quantities of oxygen, carbon monoxide and water vapour. Its axial tilt is similar to the Earth's, so it passes through a similar cycle of SEASONS. The surface temperature on Mars varies between extremes of 130K and 290K. The surface of Mars reveals a long and complex history of geological activity. The major difference in terrain is between the smooth, lowland volcanic plains of the N hemisphere and the heavily cratered uplands of the S. The biggest volcanic structure on Mars is Olympus Mons, which is hundreds of kilometres across and 27km (17mi) high. Other geographical features include channels in which rivers once flowed. The variable polar ice caps appear to be composed of solid carbon dioxide with underlying caps of water-ice. Mars has two tiny SATELLITES in close orbits, Phobos and Deimos. In 1996 scientists investigating a meteorite, thought to have originated on Mars, found fossilized micro-organisms, which some believe indicates the presence of primitive life on the planet. In 1997 the US Pathfinder probe reached Mars and launched a small vehicle onto the planet's surface. It analysed the geological formations it encountered, sending information back to Earth. Diameter (equatorial): 6,787km; diameter (polar): 6,752km.

Mars Ancient Roman god of war, often depicted as an armed warrior; one of the three protector-deities (with JUPITER and Quirinus) of the city of Rome.

Marsalis, Wynton (1961–) US jazz musician. Marsalis is one of the few jazz players to crossover successfully into classical music. He is admired for his interpretation of Haydn's trumpet concerto. He has embarked on a revision of jazz history.

Albums include *Black Codes (From the Underground)* (1984) and *Blood on the Fields* (1996).

Marseilles (Marseille) City and seaport in SE France, on the Gulf of Lyon; capital of Bouches-du-Rhône département. The oldest city in France, it was founded in 600 BC. During the CRUSADES, Marseilles was a commercial centre and shipping port for the Holy Land. Industries: flour milling, soap, vegetable oil, cement, sugar refining, chemicals, engineering. Pop. (1990) 800,550.

marsh Flat wetland area, devoid of peat, saturated by moisture during one or more seasons. Typical vegetation includes grasses, sedges, reeds and rushes. Marshes are valuable wetlands and maintain water tables in adjacent ecosystems. Unlike BOGS, they have alkaline soil. *See also* SWAMP

Marshall, George Catlett (1880–1959) US general and politician. He was chief of staff during World War 2. After the war he was secretary of state (1947–49) and defense secretary (1950–51). He inspired the MARSHALL PLAN.

Marshall Islands Republic in the W Pacific Ocean, E of the Caroline Islands, consisting of a group of atolls and coral reefs; the capital is Dalap-Uliga-Darrit (on Majuro Atoll). It consists of two great chains, the Ralik (W) and the Ratak (E). Annexed to Germany in 1885, the group was occupied by Japan in 1914 and by US forces in World War 2. In 1947 the islands became part of the US-administered Trust Territory of the Pacific Islands. In 1991 they became an independent republic. Products: copra, coconuts, tropical fruits, fish. Area: *c.*180sq km (70sq mi). Pop. (1994 est.) 54,000.

Marshall Plan US programme of economic aid to European countries after World War 2. Promoted by the secretary of state, General MARSHALL, its purpose was to restore war damage and promote trade within Europe, while securing political stability. The Soviet Union and Eastern Europe declined to participate. Between 1948 and 1951, 16 countries received a total of $12,000 million under the plan.

Marston Moor Site of a decisive battle (2 July 1644) in the English CIVIL WAR, 11km (7mi) W of York. Royalist forces under Prince RUPERT were defeated by the Parliamentarians under Thomas FAIRFAX.

marsupial Mammal of which the female usually has a pouch (marsupium), within which the young are suckled and protected. At birth, the young are in a very early stage of development. Types include the KANGAROO, KOALA, WOMBAT, TASMANIAN DEVIL, BANDICOOT, and marsupial MOLE. The only marsupials to live outside Australasia are the OPOSSUMS. *See also* MONOTREME

marten Any of several species of carnivorous mammals of the WEASEL family that live in forests of Europe, Asia, North and South America. Martens have long bodies and short legs and are hunted for their fur. The dark brown skins of the SABLE, *Martes zibellina*, are the most valuable. Family Mustelidae.

Martin V (1368–1431) Pope (1417–31), b. Oddone Colonna. After 39 years of schism, he tried to restore papal prestige and church unity through political means. He reorganized the Curia and vainly sought to reopen diplomatic links with the Eastern Orthodox Church in Constantinople.

martin Fast-flying bird closely related to the SWALLOW and native to Europe and North America. Species include the house martin (*Delichon urbica*), purple martin (*Progne subis*) and sand martin (*Riparia riparia*). Family Hirundinidae.

Martineau, Harriet (1802–76) British writer and reformer. Her works include *Illustrations of Political Economy* (9 vols, 1832–34) and *Poor Laws and Paupers Illustrated* (1833–34). An outspoken opponent of slavery, she also wrote *Society in America* (1837).

Martinique Island in the Caribbean, in the Windward group of the Lesser ANTILLES, forming an overseas département of France; the capital is Fort-de-France. Discovered in 1502 by Christopher Columbus, the island became a permanent French possession after the Napoleonic Wars. Of volcanic origin, it is the largest of the Lesser Antilles. The original capital, St Pierre, was destroyed by a volcanic eruption in 1902. Industries: tourism, sugar, rum, fruits, cocoa, tobacco, vanilla, vegetables. Area: 1,079sq km (417sq mi). Pop. (1990) 359,579.

Martins, Peter (1946–) Danish dancer, choreographer, teacher and ballet director. Martins danced with Suzanne Farrell in what is considered one of the greatest ballet partnerships. He officially retired from dancing in 1983 to become Ballet Master in Chief of the New York City Ballet.

Marvell, Andrew (1621–78) English poet and satirist. He is chiefly remembered for his lyric poetry, first collected in 1681 in a volume that included *The Garden, Bermudas* and his best-known poem, *To His Coy Mistress*.

Marx, Karl Heinrich (1818–83) German social philosopher, political theorist and founder (with Friedrich ENGELS) of international COMMUNISM. He produced his own philosophical approach of DIALECTICAL MATERIALISM. He proclaimed that religion was "the opium of the people" and in *The German Ideology* (1845–46), written with Engels, described the inevitable laws of history. In Brussels he formed the Communist League and wrote with Engels the epoch-making *Communist Manifesto* (1848). Marx took part in the revolutionary movements in France and Germany, then went to London (1849), where he lived until his death. His work at the British Museum produced a stream of writings, including *Das Kapital* (3 vols, 1867, 1885, 1894), which became the "Bible of the working class". In 1864 the International Workingmen's Association (the First International) was formed and Marx became its leading spirit. His expulsion of the political philospher Mikhail Bakunin from the Association in 1872 led to its collapse. *See also* MARXISM

Marx Brothers US team of vaudeville and film

comedians. The brothers were Chico (Leonard) (1891–1961), Harpo (Arthur) (1893–1964), Groucho (Julius) (1895–1977), Gummo (Milton) (1894–1977) and Zeppo (Herbert) (1901–79). Their films include *Animal Crackers* (1930), *Duck Soup* (1933) and *A Night at the Opera* (1935).

Marxism School of SOCIALISM that arose from the writings of Karl MARX. According to Marxism, a communist society was historically inevitable. Capitalism, because of its emphasis on profits, would eventually so reduce the condition of workers that they would rebel, overthrow the capitalists and establish a classless society in which the means of production were collectively owned. *The Communist Manifesto* (1848) and *Das Kapital* (1867, 1885, 1894) both contain ideas central to Marxism, which forms the basis of COMMUNISM. *See also* DIALECTICAL MATERIALISM

Mary (Blessed Virgin Mary) (active 1st century AD) Mother of JESUS CHRIST. She figures prominently in the first two chapters of the Gospels according to St MATTHEW and St LUKE. Mary has always been held in high regard in Christendom. In the early church, the principal Marian feast was called the Commemoration of St Mary, from which developed the feast of the ASSUMPTION (15 August). Other Marian feasts are: the Nativity (8 September), the ANNUNCIATION or LADY DAY (25 March), the Purification or Candlemas (2 February), the Visitation (2 July), and (for Roman Catholics) the IMMACULATE CONCEPTION (8 December).

Mary, Queen of Scots (1542–87) Daughter of JAMES V, she succeeded him as queen when one week old. She was sent to France aged six and married the future FRANCIS II of France in 1558. On his death in 1560, she returned to Scotland, where, as a Catholic, she came into conflict with Protestant reformers. Her marriage to Lord Henry Stuart (Lord Darnley) was resented and soon broke down. After Darnley's murder (1567), she married Lord Bothwell, possibly her husband's murderer, which alienated her remaining supporters. She was imprisoned and forced to abdicate in favour of her infant son, James VI (later JAMES I of England). She escaped and raised an army, but was defeated at Langside (1568) and fled to England. She was kept in captivity, but became involved in Spanish plots against ELIZABETH I and was eventually executed.

Mary I (Mary Tudor) (1516–58) Queen of England (1553–58). Daughter of HENRY VIII and CATHERINE OF ARAGON, she acceded to the throne despite a plot to supersede her with Lady Jane GREY. A devout Catholic, she was determined to restore the authority of the pope. Her marriage to the future King PHILIP II of Spain (1554) led to war with France. Under heresy laws, about 300 Protestants were executed during her reign, earning her the nickname "Bloody Mary".

Mary II (1662–94) Queen of England, Scotland and Ireland. Eldest daughter of JAMES II, she was a Protestant who married the Dutch prince WILLIAM III (OF ORANGE) (1677). Following the flight of the Catholic James in the GLORIOUS REVOLUTION (1688–89), she and her husband were invited to England as joint sovereigns.

Maryland State in E USA, on the Atlantic Ocean; the capital is ANNAPOLIS. The largest city is BALTIMORE. The first settlements were founded in 1634. Maryland (one of the 13 original states) was active in the move towards American independence. In 1791 the state ceded land adjacent to the Potomac River to create the District of Columbia, the site of the national capital. During the American CIVIL WAR, Maryland was one of the border states that did not secede from the Union. The W half of the state is part of the Piedmont plateau region. Maryland is dominated by Chesapeake Bay and its coastal marshlands. The rearing of cattle and chickens is the most important farming activity. Maize, hay, tobacco and soya beans are the chief crops. Industries: iron and steel, shipbuilding, primary metals, transport equipment, chemicals, electrical machinery, fishing. Area: 25,316sq km (9,775sq mi). Pop. (1990) 4,781,468.

Mary Magdalene, Saint (active 1st century AD) Early follower of Jesus Christ. According to the gospels, Christ freed her of seven demons. She accompanied Christ on his preaching tours in Galilee, witnessed his crucifixion and burial and was the first person to see him after his resurrection. Her feast day is 22 July.

Masaccio (Tommaso Giovanni di Mone) (1401–28) Italian painter. The first of his three most important surviving works is a polyptych (1426) for the Carmelite Church, Pisa. The second is a fresco cycle in the Brancacci Chapel, Santa Maria del Carmine, Florence (*c*.1425–28). The third is his *Trinity* fresco in Santa Maria Novella, Florence (probably 1428).

Masai African people of Kenya and Tanzania, consisting of several subgroups who speak a Nilotic language. They are characteristically tall and slender. Their patrilineal, egalitarian society is based on nomadic pastoralism. The traditional Masai *kraal* is a group of mud houses surrounded by a thorn fence.

Masaryk, Tomáš (1850–1937) Czechoslovak statesman, first President of Czechoslovakia (1918–35). During World War 1, he travelled in Western countries gaining support for an independent Czech-Slovak state.

Masefield, John (1878–1967) British poet and novelist. He was poet laureate from 1930. His narrative poems include *The Everlasting Mercy* (1911) and *Reynard the Fox* (1919). His most famous poem is "Sea Fever".

maser (acronym for **m**icrowave **a**mplification by **s**timulated **e**mission of **r**adiation) Device using atoms artificially kept in states of higher energy than normal to provide amplification of high-frequency radio signals. The principle was discovered by Charles Townes, for which he shared the 1964 Nobel Prize for physics with Nikolai BASOV and Alexander PROKHOROV. The first maser used electrostatic plates to separate high-energy ammonia atoms from low-energy ones. Radiation of a certain frequency would then stimulate the high-energy ammonium atoms to emit similar radiation and strengthen the signal. *See also* LASER

Maseru Capital of Lesotho, on the River Caledon, near the w border with South Africa. It was capital of British Basutoland protectorate (1869–71, 1884–1966). It remained the capital when the country achieved independence as Lesotho in 1966. It is a commercial, transport and administrative centre. Pop. (1992 est.) 367,000.

Mashhad (Arabic, shrine of martyrdom) City in NE Iran, close to the border with Turkmenistan; capital of Khorasan province. It is a place of pilgrimage for SHIITE Muslims. In 809 the Abbasid Caliph HARUN AL-RASHID was buried here. In the 18th century Mashhad became the capital of Persia. It is famous for its carpet and textile manufacture. Pop. (1986) 1,463,508.

Mason-Dixon Line Border of Pennsylvania with Maryland and West Virginia, USA. It was regarded as the dividing line between slave and free states at the time of the MISSOURI COMPROMISE (1820–21), and became the popular name for the boundary between North and South in the USA.

masque Dramatic presentation that originated in Italy but became popular in the English court during the late 16th and early 17th centuries. The masque consisted of verse, comedy and a dance for a group of masked revellers. The earliest masque text is *Proteus and the Adamantine Rock*, performed at Gray's Inn in 1594 in honour of Elizabeth I.

mass Celebration of the EUCHARIST in the Roman Catholic Church and among some High Church Anglicans. The Catholic rite comprises the Liturgy of the Word and the Liturgy of the Eucharist, which includes the Offertory, the sacrifice of Christ's body and blood under the guise of bread and wine. Following the Second Vatican Council (1962–65), the mass underwent a number of changes .

mass In music, setting of the Roman Catholic religious service in Latin. Composers from all eras have written masses. One of the most famous is J.S. Bach's Mass in B minor. In the 19th century mass settings increased in scale until they were more likely to be performed in concert halls than church services.

mass Measure of the quantity of matter in an object. Scientists recognize two types of mass. The **gravitational** mass of a body is determined by its mutual attraction to a reference body, such as Earth, as expressed in Newton's law of gravitation. Spring balances and platform balances proved a measure of gravitational mass. The **inertial** mass of a body is determined by its resistance to a change in state of motion, as expressed in the second law of motion. INERTIA balances provide a measure of inertial mass. According to EINSTEIN's principle of equivalence, upon which his general theory of RELATIVITY

is based, the inertial mass and the gravitational mass of a given body are equivalent. *See also* WEIGHT

Massachusetts State in NE USA, in NEW ENGLAND, on the Atlantic Ocean; the capital and largest city is BOSTON. The first settlement was made in 1620 at Plymouth on Massachusetts Bay by the Pilgrim Fathers. Boston was founded by English Puritans in 1630 and it became the centre of the MASSACHUSETTS BAY COLONY. The state played a leading role in events leading up to the American Revolution and was the scene of the first battle. Massachusetts achieved statehood in 1788. In the E of the state is a low-lying coastal plain. The principal rivers are the Housatonic, Merrimack and Connecticut. A highly industrialized region, Massachusetts is one of the most densely populated states in the nation. Agricultural produce includes cranberries, tobacco, hay, market garden and dairy products. Industries: electronic equipment, plastics, footwear, paper, machinery, metal and rubber goods, printing and publishing, fishing. Area: 20,300sq km (7,838sq mi). Pop. (1990) 6,016,425.

Massachusetts Bay Company English company chartered in 1629. Its purpose was trade and colonization of the land between the Charles and Merrimack rivers in North America. A group of Puritans led by John Winthrop gained control of the company and founded the Massachusetts Bay Colony in 1630. They took the company's charter with them to Massachusetts and thus enjoyed considerable autonomy. Within 10 years about 20,000 people, mainly English Puritans, had settled in the colony.

Massenet, Jules Émile-Frédéric (1842–1912) French composer. He composed many operas, including *Le Cid* (1885), *Werther* (1892) and *Thérèse* (1909). His two masterpieces are considered to be *Manon* (1884) and *Thaïs* (1894).

Massif Central Extensive mountainous plateau in SE central France. The AUVERGNE Mountains form the core of the region, which also includes the Cévennes (SE) and the Causses (SW). Sheep and goats are grazed on the slopes. Hydroelectric power is generated, and coal and kaolin are mined. The highest peak is Puy de Sancy, rising to 1,886m (6,186ft). Area: c.85,000sq km (32,800sq mi).

Massine, Léonide (1896–1979) US choreographer and ballet dancer, b. Russia. His choreography includes *La Boutique Fantasque* (1919) and *Three Cornered Hat* (1919). He also created symphonic ballets, including *Les Présages* (1933). He performed in the films *The Red Shoes* (1948) and *Tales of Hoffmann* (1951).

mass production Manufacture of goods in large quantities by standardizing parts, techniques and machinery. Eli WHITNEY introduced mass production in 1798 to produce weapons. The assembly line, a conveyor belt carrying the work through a series of assembly areas, was introduced in 1913 by Henry FORD. Many mass-production processes depend on computer control of machines.

mass spectrograph (mass spectrometer) Instrument used in chemical analysis for separating ions according to their charge-to-mass ratio. In the simplest types, the ions are first accelerated by an electric field and then deflected by a strong magnetic field; the lighter the ions the greater the deflection. By varying the field, ions of different masses can be focused in sequence onto a photographic plate and a record of charge-to-mass ratios obtained.

mastectomy In surgery, removal of all or part of the female breast. It is performed to treat cancer. Simple mastectomy involves the breast alone. If the cancer has spread, radical mastectomy may be undertaken, removing also the lymphatic tissue from the armpit.

Masters, William Howell (1915–) US physician who, with his psychologist wife Virginia (née Johnson) (1925–), became noted for studies of physiology and anatomy of human sexual activity. Their works include *Human Sexual Response* (1966) and *Human Sexual Inadequacy* (1970).

mastiff (Old English mastiff) Large fighting dog that was first bred in England more than 2,000 years ago. It has a broad head with a dark muzzle. The wide body is set on strong legs with large feet. The short, coarse coat may be brown or grey. Height: to 84cm (33in) at shoulder; weight: to 95kg (210lb).

mastodon Any of several species of extinct elephantine mammals, all of which existed mainly in the PLEISTOCENE epoch. Mastodons had a long coat of red hair; the grinding teeth were notably smaller and less complex than those of modern elephants, and the males had small tusks on the lower as well as the upper jaw. Genus *Mastodon*.

Mata Hari (1876–1917) Dutch courtesan, b. Margaretha Geertruida Zelle. In 1917 she was arrested in Paris as a German agent and subsequently executed. Few people now believe she was the mysterious secret agent that the French authorities alleged.

materialism System of philosophical thought that explains the nature of the world as dependent on matter. The doctrine was formulated as early as the 4th century BC by DEMOCRITUS. The early followers of BUDDHISM were also materialists. The DIALECTICAL MATERIALISM of Karl MARX is a modern development of the theory.

mathematical induction Method of proving that a mathematical statement is true for any positive integer n by proving: (1) that it is true for a base value, for example 1; and (2) that if it is true for a value k then it is also true for $k + 1$. If (1) and (2) hold, then it follows in a finite number of steps that the statement is true for any positive integer n.

mathematics Study concerned originally with the properties of numbers and space; now more generally concerned with deductions made from assumptions about abstract entities. Mathematics is often divided into pure mathematics, which is purely abstract reasoning based on axioms, and applied mathematics, which involves the use of mathematical reasoning in other fields, such as engineering, physics, chemistry and economics. The main divisions of pure mathematics are GEOMETRY, ALGEBRA and analysis. This last deals with the concept of limits and includes differential and integral CALCULUS. *See also* ARITHMETIC; TRIGONOMETRY

Matisse, Henri Emile Benoît (1869–1954) French painter, sculptor and graphic artist. Having experimented with NEO-IMPRESSIONISM in paintings such as *Luxe, calme et volupte* (1905), he developed the style of painting that became known as FAUVISM. His art is typified by a luminous and sensual calmness. He became ill in later life, but produced one of his greatest works, the design of the Chapel of the Rosary at Vence (1949–51). He also started making coloured paper cut-outs, such as *L'Escargot* (1953). Matisse's most famous sculptures include a series of four bronzes called *The Back* (1909–29).

Mato Grosso State in W central Brazil, bordered S by MATO GROSSO DO SUL, and W and SW by Bolivia; the capital is Cuiabà. It became a state in 1889. There is rainforest in the N and marshland in the SW. The W has good grazing land and cattle rearing is the chief occupation. Rice, maize and sugar-cane are grown. There are extensive mineral deposits, mostly unexploited. Area: 881,000sq km (340,156sq mi). Pop. (1991) 2,020,581.

Mato Grosso do Sul State in SW Brazil, bordered N by MATO GROSSO, W by Bolivia, and W and S by Paraguay; the capital is Campo Grande. Early pioneers exploited the area's gold and diamonds but there was little permanent settlement until the late 20th century. In 1979 it was created a separate state from the S part of Mato Grosso. It has extensive grazing land. There are vast mineral resources, including iron ore and manganese. Agriculture and livestock are important. Area: 350,548sq km (135,347sq mi). Pop. (1991) 1,778,494.

matriarchy Any society or group that is ruled by women. Some matriarchal societies exist in South America. *See also* PATRIARCHY

matrix Rectangular array of numbers in rows and columns. Matrices can be combined (added and multiplied) according to certain rules. They are useful in the study of transformations of coordinate systems and in solving sets of simultaneous equations.

matter Any material that takes up space. Ordinary matter is made up of atoms, which are combinations of ELECTRONS, PROTONS and NEUTRONS. Atoms, in turn, make up elements, an ordered series of substances that have atoms with from one proton in their nuclei (hydrogen) to a hundred or more. All matter exerts an attractive force on other matter, called GRAVITATION. Charged particles exert an attractive or repulsive ELECTROMAGNETIC FORCE that accounts for nearly all everyday phenomena. The strong interaction force is responsible for binding the protons and neutrons in an atomic NUCLEUS, and the weak interaction is responsible for beta decay. *See also* ANTIMATTER; FUNDAMENTAL FORCES; MATTER, STATES OF; MOLECULE

matter, states of Classification of MATTER according to its structural characteristics. Four states of matter are generally recognized: solid, liquid, gas and plasma. Any one ELEMENT or compound may exist sequentially or simultaneously in two or more of these states. SOLIDS may be crystalline, as in salt and metals; or amorphous, as in tar or glass. LIQUIDS have molecules that can flow past one another, but that remain almost as close as in a solid. In a GAS, molecules are so far from one another that they travel in relatively straight lines until they collide. In a PLASMA, atoms are torn apart into electrons and nuclei by the high temperatures, such as those in stars.

Matterhorn (Monte Cervino) Mountain peak in Switzerland, in the Pennine Alps, on the Swiss-Italian border. Height: 4,478m (14,691ft).

Matthew, Saint (active 1st century AD) Apostle and probably one of the four evangelists of the New Testament. In the lists of the disciples given in the SYNOPTIC GOSPELS, Matthew is sometimes called Levi. Before his calling, he was a tax collector for King Herod Antipas. Feast day: 21 September in the West, 16 November in the East.

Matthew, Gospel according to Saint Gospel traditionally placed first in the New Testament but probably written after those of St MARK and St LUKE. Written about AD 70–75, it is traditionally ascribed to St MATTHEW, the tax gatherer who became one of the 12 disciples. The Gospel of St Matthew contains more of the teachings, parables and sayings of Jesus than any other gospel. It is also the only SYNOPTIC GOSPEL written in a Jewish, rather than a Hellenistic, style.

Maugham, (William) Somerset (1874–1965) British novelist, dramatist and essayist. He achieved fame initially as a playwright, and his plays include *Lady Frederick* (1912) and *The Circle* (1921). Among his novels are the semi-autobiographical *Of Human Bondage* (1915), *Ashenden* (1928) and *Cakes and Ale* (1930).

Mau Mau Anti-colonial terrorist group of the KIKUYU of Kenya. Following attacks on Europeans, a state of emergency was declared in 1952 and troops drafted in. Within four years about 100 Europeans and 2,000 anti-Mau Mau Kikuyu were killed. More than 11,000 Mau Mau died before the state of emergency ended in 1960. Kenya achieved independence in 1963, and the former Mau Mau leader Jomo KENYATTA became prime minister.

Mauna Kea (White Mountain) Dormant shield volcano in central Hawaii, USA. Mauna Kea is the highest island mountain in the world at 4,205m (13,796ft). At the snow-capped peak of the volcano stands Mauna Kea Observatory, the world's biggest astronomical site with many large telescopes.

Mauna Loa Active volcano in central Hawaii, USA, s of Mauna Kea. The second highest active volcano in the world, Mauna Loa has many craters. Kilauea is the largest. Mokuaweoweo is the summit crater. The greatest eruption was in

1881. Major eruptions also took place in 1942, 1949, 1975 and 1984. Height: 4,169m (13,678ft).

Maupassant, Guy de (1850–93) French short-story writer and novelist. He produced one of his greatest short stories, *Boule de suif,* for the collection *Les Soirées de Médan* (1880). He wrote more than 300 short stories; a number are collected in *La Maison Tellier* (1881), *Contes de la Bécasse* (1883) and *L'Inutile Beauté* (1890). *Pierre et Jean* (1887) is regarded as the best of his six novels.

Mauritania Republic in NW Africa; the capital is NOUAKACHOTT. **Land and climate** The SAHARA desert covers most of Mauritania. A sandstone plateau runs N to S through the centre of Mauritania. The majority of Mauritanians live in the semi-arid SW region of SAHEL. Tropical savanna covers much of the rainier S. **Economy** Mauritania is a low income developing country (1992 GDP per capita, US$1,650). The chief resource and leading export is iron ore. Agriculture employs 69% of the workforce. Recent droughts have forced many nomadic herdsmen to migrate to urban areas. Farmers in the SE grow crops such as beans, dates, millet, rice and sorghum. **History** Berbers migrated to the region in the first millennium AD. The Hodh basin lay at the heart of the ancient Ghana empire (700–1200); towns grew up along the trans-Saharan caravan routes. In the 14th and 15th century the region formed part of the ancient Mali empire. Portuguese mariners explored the coast in the 1440s, but European colonialism did not begin until the 17th century. France set up a protectorate in 1903. In 1920 the region became a separate colony within French West Africa. In 1958 Mauritania became a self-governing territory in the French Union, before achieving full independence in 1960. Mokhtar Ould Daddah was elected president, and re-elected in 1966 and 1971. Mauritania became a one-party state. Devastating drought increased dissatisfaction with Ould Daddah's regime. In 1973 Mauritania withdrew from the franc zone and joined the Arab League. In 1976 Spain withdrew from Spanish Sahara: Morocco occupied two-thirds of the territory, while Mauritania took the rest. Nationalists, led by the guerrillas of the Popular Front for the Liberation of Saharan Territories (POLISARIO) began an armed struggle for independence, which drained Mauritania's

---

MAURITANIA

AREA: 1,025,520sq km (395,953sq mi)
POPULATION: 2,143,000
CAPITAL (POPULATION): Nouakchott (393,325)
GOVERNMENT: Multiparty Islamic republic
ETHNIC GROUPS: Moor (Arab-Berber) 70%, Wolof 7%, Tukulor 5%, Soninke 3%, Fulani 1%
LANGUAGES: Arabic (official)
RELIGIONS: Islam 99%
CURRENCY: Ouguiya = 5 khoums

resources. In 1978 Ould Daddah was overthrown in a military coup. In 1979 Mauritania withdrew from Western Sahara, and Morocco assumed sole authority (for political developments, *see* WESTERN SAHARA). In 1984 recognition of Western Sahara's independence provoked civil unrest, and Ould Taya came to power. **Recent events** In 1991 Mauritania adopted a new constitution. Ould Taya was elected president in 1992 multiparty elections. Tension continues between the black African minority in S Mauritania and Arabs and Berbers in the N.

Mauritius Republic in the SW Indian Ocean, *c*.800km (500mi) E of Madagascar; the capital is PORT LOUIS (on Mauritius). The country consists of the main island of Mauritius, 20 nearby islets and the dependency islands of Rodrigues, Agalega and Cargados Carajos. The climate is sub-tropical, with up to 5,000mm (200in) of rain a year. Its vast plantations produce sugar cane. Sugar and molasses are the major exports. Tourism and textile production have partly compensated for the decline in the world sugar market. The Dutch began to colonize the island in 1598, and named it after Prince Maurice of Nassau. In 1715 it came under the control of France. The French established the sugar cane plantations and imported African slave labour. In 1810 Britain seized Mauritius and it became a British colony in 1814. In 1833 slavery was abolished. In 1968 Mauritius achieved independence as a member of the Commonwealth. It became a republic in 1992. Area: 2,046sq km (790sq mi). Pop. (1990) 1,058,942.

Maurya empire (321–185 BC) Ancient Indian dynasty and state founded by CHANDRAGUPTA (r. *c*.321–297 BC). All N India was united under ASHOKA (r. *c*.264–238 BC), Chandragupta's grandson. After Ashoka's death the empire broke up, the last emperor was assassinated *c*.185 BC.

mausoleum Impressive tomb. The widow of Mausolus, ruler of Caria, raised a great tomb to his memory at HALICARNASSUS (*c*.350 BC). It became one of the SEVEN WONDERS OF THE WORLD. The best-known mausoleum is the TAJ MAHAL in India.

Mawson, Sir Douglas (1882–1958) British geographer and Antarctic explorer. He accompanied Sir Ernest SHACKLETON on the first expedition to the South Pole (1907–09) and led the Australasian Antarctic expedition (1911–14).

Maximilian I (1459–1519) Holy Roman emperor (1493–1519). He was one of the most successful members of the HABSBURG dynasty. He gained Burgundy and the Netherlands by marriage and defended them against France. He was less successful in asserting control over the German princes and was defeated by the Swiss in 1499. He strengthened the Habsburg heartland in Austria and organized the marriages that made his grandson, CHARLES V, the most powerful 16th-century ruler.

Maxwell, James Clerk (1831–79) Scottish mathematician and physicist who did outstanding theoretical work in ELECTROMAGNETIC RADIATION.

He used the theory of the electromagnetic field for Maxwell's equations, which linked light with electromagnetic waves, established the nature of Saturn's rings, and did work in thermodynamics and statistical mechanics.

Maya Outstanding culture of classic American civilization. Occupying S Mexico and N Central America, it was at its height from the 3rd–9th centuries. They built great temple-cities, with buildings surmounting stepped PYRAMIDS. They were skilful potters and weavers and productive farmers. They worshipped gods and ancestors, and blood sacrifice was an important element of religion. Maya civilization declined after *c*.900, and much was destroyed after the Spanish conquest in the 16th century. The modern Maya, numbering *c*.4 million, live in the same area and speak a variety of languages related to that of their ancestors.

Mayakovsky, Vladimir (1893–1930) Soviet poet and dramatist. The leader of the FUTURISM movement in Russia, he founded the journal *Left Arts Front*. His work includes the poems *A Cloud in Trousers* (1914–15) and *150 Millions* (1919–20), and the plays *Mystery Bouffe* (1917–18) and *The Bedbug* (1928).

Mayan Family of languages spoken on the Yucatán Peninsula of Mexico, and in Guatemala and part of Belize by the MAYA. There are several dozen of these languages, the most important being Yucatec, of Mexico, and Quiché, Cakchiquel, Mam and Kekchi, of Guatemala.

May beetle (June bug) Medium-sized, stout, brownish scarab beetle that feeds on tree foliage. The white grubs that eat roots of various crops are a destructive soil pest. Genus *Phyllophaga*.

May Day First day of May, traditionally celebrated as a festival, the origin of which may lie in the spring fertility rites of pagan times. The Roman festival of Flora was held from 28 April to 3 May. In England, the festivities have centred on the dance round the Maypole. In some countries May Day is a holiday in honour of workers.

Mayflower Ship that carried the PILGRIMS from Plymouth, England to Massachusetts in September 1620. It carried 120 English Puritans, who established the PLYMOUTH COLONY in December that year.

mayfly Soft-bodied insect found worldwide. The adult does not eat and lives only a few days, but the aquatic larvae (NYMPH) may live several years. Adults have triangular front wings, characteristic thread-like tails and vestigial mouthparts; they often emerge from streams and rivers in swarms. Length: 10–25mm (0.4–1in). Order Ephemeroptera.

Mayo County in NW Republic of Ireland, in Connaught province, bounded to the N and W by the Atlantic Ocean; the county town is Castlebar. A largely mountainous region, it has numerous lakes and is drained by the rivers Errif and Moy. Oats and potatoes are the chief crops. Cattle, sheep, pigs and poultry are reared. Woollen milling and toy manufacturing are the main industries. Area: 5,397sq km (2,084sq mi). Pop. (1991) 110,713.

Mayotte (Mahore) French-administered archipelago in the Indian Ocean, E of the COMOROS. The two major islands are Grande Terre and Petite Terre (Pamanzi). Grande Terre includes the new capital, Mamoudzou. Pamanzi is the site of the old capital, Dzaoudzi. Mayotte was a French colony from 1843–1914, when it was attached to the Comoro group. In 1974 the Comoros became independent, while Mayotte voted to remain a French dependency. In 1976 it became an overseas collectivity of France. The economy is primarily agricultural; chief products are bananas and mangoes. Area: 373sq km (144sq mi). Pop. (1991) 94,410.

Mazarin, Jules, Cardinal (1602–61) French statesman, b. Italy. He was the protégé of Cardinal RICHELIEU and chief minister under ANNE OF AUSTRIA from 1643. During the civil wars of the FRONDES, he played off one faction against another and, though twice forced out of France, emerged in full control. He was a skilful negotiator of the treaties ending the THIRTY YEARS WAR.

Mazzini, Giuseppe (1805–72) Italian patriot and political thinker of the RISORGIMENTO. A member of the *Carbonari* (Italian republican underground) from 1830, he founded the "Young Italy" movement in 1831. He fought in the revolution of 1848 and ruled in Rome in 1849, but was then exiled.

Mbabane Capital of Swaziland, in the NW of the country, in the high veld region of S Africa. It is both an administrative and commercial centre, serving the surrounding agricultural region. Tin and iron ore are mined nearby. Pop. (1986) 38,290.

ME (abbreviation of myalgic encephalomyelitis) Extreme fatigue that persists for six months or more and is not relieved by rest. Also known as chronic fatigue syndrome and post-viral fatigue syndrome, it may include many other non-specific symptoms. It ranges in severity from chronic weariness to total physical collapse. The cause is unknown.

Mead, George Herbert (1863–1931) US philosopher and social psychologist. A founder of PRAGMATISM, influenced by John DEWEY, Mead studied the mind, self and society. His studies of the behaviour of individuals and small groups led to the sociological theories of symbolic interactionism.

mean (arithmetic mean) Mathematical average. It is found by adding a group of numbers and dividing by the number of items in the group. Thus, for numbers a, b, c and d, the mean is $(a + b + c + d)/4$.

measles (rubeola) Extremely infectious viral disease of children. The symptoms (fever, catarrh, skin rash and spots inside the mouth) appear about two weeks after exposure. Hypersensitivity to light is characteristic. Complications such as pneumonia occasionally occur, and middle-ear infection is also a hazard. Vaccination produces life-long IMMUNITY.

Mecca (Makkah) Holiest city of ISLAM, in W Saudi Arabia. The birthplace of the prophet MUHAMMAD, only Muslims are allowed in the city. Mecca was originally home to an Arab population of merchants. When Muhammad began his ministry here the Meccans rejected him. The flight (HEJIRA) of Muhammad from Mecca to MEDINA in 622 marked the beginning of the Muslim era. In 630 Muhammad's followers captured Mecca and made it the centre of the first Islamic empire. The OTTOMAN Turks held it (1517–1916), finally losing control after Hussein Ibn Ali secured Arabian independence. Mecca fell in 1924 to the forces of Ibn SAUD, who later founded the Saudi Arabian kingdom. Much of Mecca's commerce depends on Muslim pilgrims undertaking the HAJJ to the Great Mosque enclosing the KAABA. Pop. (1991 est.) 630,000.

mechanical advantage (force ratio) Factor by which any MACHINE multiplies an applied force. It may be calculated from the ratio of the forces involved or from the ratio of the distances through which they move, as with simple machines such as the LEVER and PULLEY. *See also* EFFICIENCY

mechanical engineering Field of ENGINEERING concerned with the design, construction and operation of machinery. Mechanical engineers work in many branches of industry. Achievements in mechanical engineering include the development of wind and water TURBINES, STEAM ENGINES and INTERNAL COMBUSTION ENGINES.

mechanics Branch of physics concerned with the behaviour of MATTER under the influence of FORCES. It may be divided into solid mechanics and fluid mechanics. Another classification is as STATICS – the study of matter at rest – and DYNAMICS – the study of matter in motion. Relativistic mechanics deals with the behaviour of matter at very high speeds, whereas QUANTUM MECHANICS deals with the behaviour of matter at the atomic level. *See also* NEWTON'S LAWS; QUANTUM THEORY; RELATIVITY

Mecklenburg-West Pomerania State in NE Germany, on the Baltic coast; the capital is Schwerin. In 1871 Mecklenburg-Schwerin and Mecklenburg-Güstrow were among the founding members of the German empire. In 1934 the two states were unified. In 1946 they were joined with Pomerania to form a region of East Germany. In 1990 Mecklenburg-West Pomerania became one of the five new states of the reunified Federal Republic. It is a low-lying agricultural state. On the coast are the Baltic ports of Rostock, Wismar and Straslund. Area: 23,170sq km (8,944sq mi). Pop. (1993) 1,843,455

Medawar, Sir Peter Brian (1915–87) British biologist. He shared the 1960 Nobel Prize in physiology or medicine with Sir Frank Macfarlane Burnet for the discovery of acquired immune tolerance. *See also* IMMUNE SYSTEM

Medea Daughter of Aeëtes, King of Colchis, whom she defied to help Jason retrieve the Golden Fleece. Renowned as a sorceress, she lived with JASON for many years in Corinth but fled to Athens after his desertion led her to murder their children, and his new wife, in a jealous rage.

Medellín City in NW central Colombia; capital of

Antioquia department and the second-largest city in Colombia. In recent years it has become the focal point of the country's illegal cocaine trade. Gold and silver are mined in the surrounding region. Industries: food processing, coffee, chemicals, steel. Pop. (1992) 1,581,364.

median In statistics, the middle item in a group found by ranking the items from smallest to largest. In the series, 2, 3, 7, 9, 10, for example, the median is 7. With an even number of items the MEAN of the two middle items is taken as the median. Thus in the series 2, 3, 7, 9, the median is 5.

Medici, Catherine de' See CATHERINE DE' MEDICI

Medici, Cosimo de' (the Elder) (1389–1464) Ruler of Florence (1434–64). He increased the Medici fortune, strengthened Florence by alliance with Milan and Naples, and was a great patron of the scholars and artists of the early Renaissance.

Medici, Cosimo I de' (the Great) (1519–74) Duke of Florence and later grand duke of Tuscany (1537–74). He established the hereditary rule of Tuscany by the Medici. He conquered Siena and unified Tuscany, and was given the title of grand duke by the pope in 1569.

Medici, Lorenzo de' (1449–92) Ruler of Florence. Grandson of Cosimo (the Elder), he succeeded his father, Piero, in 1494. He ruled Florence autocratically. He survived an assassination attempt by the rival Pazzi family, whom he afterwards largely exterminated. A notable poet, he presided over a brilliant Renaissance court, patronizing BOTTICELLI, MICHELANGELO and LEONARDO DA VINCI.

medicine Practice of the prevention, diagnosis and treatment of disease or injury; the term is also applied to any agent used in the treatment of disease. Medicine has been practised since ancient times, but the dawn of modern Western medicine coincided with accurate anatomical and physiological observations first made in the 17th century. By the 19th century practical diagnostic procedures had been developed for many diseases; bacteria had been discovered and research undertaken for the production of immunizing serums in attempts to eradicate disease. The great developments of the 20th century include the discovery of PENICILLIN and INSULIN, CHEMOTHERAPY, new surgical procedures including organ transplants, and sophisticated diagnostic devices such as radioactive TRACERS and various scanners. Alternative medicine, such as osteopathy, homeopathy or acupuncture, some of which have existed for hundreds of years, is becoming increasingly popular.

medieval music Music produced in Europe during the later Middle Ages, c.1100–1400. It was dominated by Christian liturgical CHANTS, which were sung in polyphonic style. Secular songs were transmitted orally by travelling Saxon, French and German troubadours or Minnesingers. In the 14th and 15th centuries, guilds of professional musicians were formed, and musical notation began to become more sophisticated, enabling composers to transmit whole works to later generations. See also MOTET; MUSICAL NOTATION; POLYPHONY

Medina (Arabic, Prophet's city) City in Saudi Arabia, N of MECCA. Originally called Yathrib, the city was renamed Medinat an-Nabi after MUHAMMAD fled Mecca and settled here in 622. Medina became his capital. In 661 the UMAYYAD caliphs moved their capital to DAMASCUS and Medina's importance declined. It came under Turkish rule (1517–1916), after which it briefly formed part of the independent Arab kingdom of the Hejaz. In 1932 it became part of Saudi Arabia. Pop. (1991 est.) 400,000.

Mediterranean Sea Largest inland sea in the world, lying between Europe and Africa and extending from the Strait of Gibraltar in the W to the coast of SW Asia in the E. The Mediterranean was once a trade route for Phoenicians and Greeks, later controlled by Rome and Byzantium. In the Middle Ages, Venice and Genoa were the dominant maritime powers until the rise of the Ottoman Turks. The opening of the Suez Canal in 1869 made the Mediterranean one of the world's busiest shipping routes and the development of the Middle Eastern oilfields further increased its importance. The Mediterranean is connected to the Black Sea via the Dardanelles, the Sea of Marmara and the Bosporus, and to the Red Sea by the Suez Canal. It includes the Tyrrhenian, Adriatic, Ionian and Aegean seas. It receives the waters of several major rivers, including the NILE, RHÔNE, EBRO, TIBER and PO. There are c.400 species of fish in the Mediterranean. In recent years pollution has become a major issue. Area: 2,509,972km (969,100sq mi).

Medusa In Greek mythology one of the three gorgons. Athena sent PERSEUS to decapitate her, and from the wound sprang PEGASUS and Chrysaor, children of POSEIDON.

meerkat (suricate) Any of a number of small carnivorous mammals closely related to the MONGOOSE, native to the bush country of S Africa. It is similar in appearance to the mongoose but without the bushy tail. Length: 47cm (19in). Typical species *Suricata suricatta*.

megalith (lit. huge stone) Prehistoric stone monument. Historians usually apply the term to the gigantic slabs that form many stone circles, half circles and rows in N Europe. These constructions date from the NEOLITHIC and early BRONZE AGE. One of the most well-known and complex examples is the circle at STONEHENGE (c.2100–2000 BC). Megaliths existed long before the first stone buildings of Mycenean Crete. See DOLMEN

Mehta, Zubin (1936–) Indian conductor. He was musical director of the Los Angeles Philharmonic Orchestra from 1961 before moving to the New York Philharmonic in 1978.

Meiji, Mutsohito (1852–1912) Emperor of Japan (1867–1912), whose reign saw the transformation of Japan into a modern industrial state. Mutsuhito introduced sweeping reforms, including the abolition of the feudal system, a western-style constitution, the establishment of state education and the encouragement of industrial growth.

Meiji Restoration Constitutional revolution in Japan (1868). Opposition to the shogunate built up after Japan's isolationism was ended by US Commodore Perry in 1854. Pressure for modernization resulted in a new imperial government, at first dominated by former samurai, with the young Emperor MEIJI as its symbolic leader.

meiosis In biology, process of cell division that reduces the CHROMOSOME number from DIPLOID to HAPLOID. Meiosis involves two nuclear divisions. The first division halves the chromosome number in the two resulting cells; the second division forms four haploid "daughter" cells, each containing a unique configuration of the parent cells' chromosomes. In most higher organisms, the resulting haploid cells are the GAMETES, or sex cells, the OVA and SPERM. In this way, meiosis enables the genes from both parents to combine in a single cell without increasing the overall number of chromosomes. *See also* MITOSIS

Meir, Golda (1898–1978) Israeli stateswoman, prime minister (1969–74), b. Ukraine. She emigrated to the USA in 1906 and to Palestine in 1921. A leading figure in ZIONISM, she became prime minister after the death of Levi Eshkol. She was forced to resign after criticism of the government's lack of preparedness for the 1973 ARAB-ISRAELI WAR.

Mekong River in SE Asia. It rises in Tibet and flows S through Yünnan, China. It forms the Burma-Laos border and part of the Laos-Thailand border and flows S through Cambodia and Vietnam. Its vast delta is one of Asia's most important rice-producing regions. Length: *c.*4,180km (2,600mi).

Melaka *See* MALACCA

Melanchthon, Philip (1497–1560) German theologian. With Martin LUTHER, he was a founder of PROTESTANTISM. Melanchthon wrote the *Confessions of Augsburg* (1530). He also helped Luther with his German translation of the New Testament.

Melanesia Collective term for island groups in the W Pacific Ocean. It includes the Bismarck Archipelago, SOLOMON ISLANDS, New Hebrides and the TONGA group. Melanesia, POLYNESIA and MICRONESIA are subdivisions of OCEANIA.

melanin Dark pigment found in skin, hair and parts of the eye. The amount of melanin determines skin colour. Absence of melanin results in ALBINO.

Melba, Dame Nellie (1861–1931) Australian soprano, b. Helen Porter Mitchell. A high coloratura soprano, she was famous in the roles of Lucia (Donizetti's *Lucia di Lammermoor*) and Gilda (Verdi's *Rigoletto*).

Melbourne, William Lamb, 2nd Viscount (1779–1848) British statesman, prime minister (1834, 1835–41). Melbourne entered Parliament as a Whig in 1805. He joined the House of Lords in 1828. As home secretary (1830–34) in Earl GREY's administration, Melbourne was responsible for the suppression of the TOLPUDDLE MARTYRS. As prime minister he oversaw reform of the POOR LAW (1834), but resisted changes to the CORN LAWS. Melbourne tutored Queen VICTORIA in statecraft.

Melbourne City and port in SE Australia, at the N end of Port Phillip Bay; capital of Victoria state. Founded in 1835, it became the state capital in 1851 and served as the seat of the Australian federal government (1901–27). A major centre of finance, commerce, communications and transport, it exports wool, flour, meat, fruit and dairy produce. Industries: aircraft, motor vehicles, heavy engineering, shipbuilding, textiles, chemicals and agricultural machinery. Pop. (1993 est.) 3,189,200.

melodrama Theatrical form originating in late 18th-century France and achieving its greatest popularity during the 19th century. It relied on simple, violent plots in which virtue was finally rewarded.

melody In music, sequence of notes that makes a recognizable musical pattern. The term is most commonly used of the dominant part or voice, to which harmonic accompaniment is nearly always subordinate. Music featuring several melodies simultaneously is known as POLYPHONY.

melon Annual vine and its large fleshy edible fruit. Melons grow in warm temperate and subtropical climates. The cantaloupe melon, with its rough skin, probably originated in Armenia; the smoother yellow rind honeydew, in SE Asia. The large, dark green watermelon is believed to have come from Africa. Family Cucurbitaceae.

melting point Temperature at which a substance changes from solid to liquid. The melting point of the solid has the same value as the freezing point of the liquid, so the melting point of ice, 0°C (32°F), is the same as the freezing point of water.

Melville, Herman (1819–91) US novelist and sailor. His debut novel was *Typee* (1846). *Moby Dick* (1851), an allegorical story of the search for a great whale, is a classic of US literature. His short story *Billy Budd* (published 1924) was the inspiration for BRITTEN's opera of the same name.

membrane In biology, boundary layer or layers inside or around a living CELL or TISSUE. Cell membranes include the plasma membrane surrounding the cell, the network of membranes inside the cell (endoplasmic reticulum) and the double membrane surrounding the NUCLEUS. The multicellular membranes of the body comprise mucous membranes of the respiratory, digestive and urinogenital passages, synovial membranes of the joints, and the membranes that coat the inner walls of the abdomen, thorax and the surfaces of organs. *See also* EPITHELIUM

memory Capacity to retain information and experience and to recall or reconstruct them in the future. Modern psychologists often divide memory into two types, short-term and long-term. An item in short-term memory lasts for about 10–15 seconds after an experience, but is lost if not used again. An item enters long-term memory if the item is of sufficient importance or is required frequently.

Memphis City and river port in SW Tennessee, USA, on the Mississippi River; largest city in Tennessee. Strategically located on Chickasaw Bluff above the Mississippi, the first permanent settlement was made in 1819. Today it is a major transport centre and livestock market. Industries: timber, farm machinery, cotton, food processing, pharmaceuticals. Pop. (1990) 610,337.

Mencius (*c.*372–289 BC) (Mengzi) Chinese philosopher of the Confucian school. He held that human beings are basically good but require cultivation to bring out the goodness. His teachings are found in the *Book of Mencius*, one of the Four Books in the canonical writings of CONFUCIANISM.

Mendel, Gregor Johann (1822–84) Austrian naturalist. He discovered the laws of HEREDITY and in so doing laid the foundation for the modern science of GENETICS. His study of the inheritance of characteristics was published in *Experiments with Plant Hybrids* (1866).

mendelevium Radioactive metallic element (symbol Md) that is the ninth of the TRANSURANIC ELEMENTS in the ACTINIDE SERIES. It was first synthesized in 1955 by the alpha-particle bombardment of einsteinium-253. Properties: at.no. 101; r.a.m. 258; most stable isotope Md^{258} (half-life 2 months).

Mendeleyev, Dmitri Ivanovich (1834–1907) Russian chemist who devised the PERIODIC TABLE. Mendeleyev demonstrated that chemically similar elements appear at regular intervals if the elements are arranged in order by atomic weight. He classified the 60 known elements and left gaps in the table, predicting the existence and properties of several unknown elements. The radioactive element MENDELEVIUM is named after him.

Mendelssohn (-Bartholdy), (Jakob Ludwig) Felix (1809–47) German composer and conductor. A child prodigy, at 17 he wrote his overture to *A Midsummer Night's Dream*. His orchestral works include a violin concerto (1844) and five symphonies. He also wrote much chamber music. His oratorios, *St Paul* (1836) and *Elijah* (1846), are considered to be among the greatest of the 19th century.

Menem, Carlos Saul (1935–) Argentinian president (1989–). A Perónist, Menem was imprisoned during the 1976 military coup. Released in 1981, he returned as governor of La Rioja (1983–89). He has introduced economic reforms, such as privatization and an austerity programme. Negotiations with the UK over the FALKLAND ISLANDS were reopened. He was re-elected in 1995, but in 1997 the Perónists lost their majority in the lower house. Menem will have to negotiate with the opposition for the remainder of his presidential term.

Menière's disease Chronic condition of the inner EAR affecting hearing and balance. Symptoms are deafness, vertigo and ringing in the ears (tinnitus). Caused by excessive fluid in the inner ear, it occurs in middle age or later life. It is generally treated with ANTIHISTAMINE drugs.

meningitis Inflammation of the meninges (membranes) covering the brain and spinal cord, resulting from infection. Bacterial meningitis is more serious than the viral form. Symptoms include headache, fever, nausea and stiffness of the neck. The disease can vary from mild to lethal.

Mennonites Christian sect founded by the Dutch reformer Menno Simons (1496–1561) and influenced by ANABAPTIST doctrines. They believe in the BAPTISM of adult believers as well as the doctrine of the real presence in the EUCHARIST.

menopause Stage in a woman's life marking the end of the reproductive years, when the MENSTRUAL CYCLE becomes irregular and finally ceases, generally around the age of 50. It may be accompanied by unpleasant effects, such as hot flushes, excessive bleeding and emotional upset. HORMONE REPLACEMENT THERAPY (HRT) is designed to relieve menopausal symptoms.

menorah Sacred seven-branched candelabra that has become a worldwide symbol of Judaism. It is rich in symbolic meaning: some interpret it in terms of the seven planets, the tree of life or the six-day creation of the universe with the centre shaft representing the Sabbath. An eight-branched menorah is used during the HANUKKAH festival.

Menotti, Gian Carlo (1911–) US composer, b. Italy. His operas in modern OPERA BUFFA style have been most successful and include *The Telephone* (1947). Menotti has also composed operas specifically for television such as *Amahl and the Night Visitors* (1951) and *Labyrinth* (1963).

Menshevik Moderate faction of the Russian Social Democratic Labour Party. The Mensheviks ("the minority") split from the more radical BOLSHEVIKS ("the majority") in 1903. They believed in "scientific socialism" and therefore favoured a gradual transformation of society, whereas the Bolsheviks wanted total revolution organized by a small, central group of disciplined revolutionaries. The Mensheviks were suppressed in 1922.

menstrual cycle In humans and some higher primates of reproductive age, the stage during which the body prepares for pregnancy. In humans the average cycle is 28 days. At the beginning of the cycle, HORMONES from the PITUITARY GLAND stimulate the growth of an OVUM contained in a follicle in one of the two OVARIES. At approximately mid-cycle the follicle bursts, the egg is released (ovulation) and travels down the FALLOPIAN TUBE to the UTERUS. The follicle (now called the corpus luteum) secretes two hormones, PROGESTERONE and OESTROGEN, and the ENDOMETRIUM thickens, ready to receive the fertilized egg. Should fertilization (conception) not occur, the corpus luteum degenerates, hormone secretion ceases, the endometrium breaks down and menstruation occurs in the form of blood loss. In the event of conception, the corpus luteum remains and maintains the endometrium with hormones until the PLACENTA is formed. In humans, the onset of the menstrual cycle (menarche) occurs at PUBERTY; it ceases with the MENOPAUSE.

mental handicap Intellectual functioning that is below average, irrespective of cause. It is usually related to congenital conditions but can arise later in life through brain damage. Assuming a normal intelligence quotient or IQ of 90–110, impairment is often described as borderline (IQ 68–85), mild (IQ 52–67), moderate (IQ 36–51), severe (IQ 20–35) and profound (IQ under 20).

mental illness (mental disorder) Any failure of mental health that is severe enough for psychiatric treatment to be appropriate. Some mental disorders can be attributed to injury or organic disease of the BRAIN. Mental disorder may also be the result of a hereditary predisposition. Other disorders are psychogenic, without any clear evidence of any physiological cause. SCHIZOPHRENIA, severe depression and manic-depressive psychoses are the most widespread disorders. Neurotic disorders include persistent anxiety, phobia, obsession and HYSTERIA.

menthol ($C_{10}H_{19}OH$) White, waxy crystalline compound having a strong odour of peppermint. Its main source is oil of peppermint from the plant *Mentha arvensis*. It is an ingredient of decongestant ointments and nasal sprays.

Menuhin, Yehudi, Lord (1916–) US violinists, one of the world's most famous musicians. He gave his first concert aged seven. He was partly responsible for bringing Indian music to Western audiences.

Menzies, Sir Robert Gordon (1894–1978) Longest-serving Australian prime minister (1939–41, 1949–66). He encouraged British and US commitment to the security of Southeast Asia and supported the ANZUS PACT and the SOUTHEAST ASIA TREATY ORGANIZATION (SEATO).

mercantilism 16th–18th century trade policy advocating state intervention in economic affairs, primarily to maximize exports. Foreign trade was publicly controlled to produce the maximum possible surplus in the nation's trade balance, thus increasing the country's store of silver and gold.

Mercator, Gerardus (1512–94) Flemish cartographer. His huge world map of 1569 employed the system of projection now named after him, in which lines of longitude, as well as latitude, appear as straight, parallel lines.

Mercury Smallest planet and the planet closest to the Sun. It has no known satellite. Little was known about Mercury's surface until the MARINER 10 probe made three close approaches to the planet in 1974 and 1975, and returned pictures of nearly half the surface. These showed a heavily cratered, lunarlike world marked by valleys and ridges. Radar mapping of Mercury's polar regions in 1991 and 1992 revealed what may be water-ice on the floors of craters permanently in shadow. There is a very tenuous atmosphere, mainly of helium and sodium and a weak magnetic field. Diameter: 4878km

mercury (quicksilver) Liquid metallic element (symbol Hg), known from earliest times. The chief ore is cinnabar (a sulphide), from which it is extracted by roasting. The silvery element is poisonous and the only metal that is liquid at normal temperatures. Mercury is used in barometers, thermometers, mercury-vapour lamps and mercury cells. Mercury compounds are used in pharmaceuticals. Properties: at.no. 80; r.a.m. 200.59: r.d. 13.6; m.p. $-38.87°C$; ($-37.97°F$); b.p. 356.58°C (673.84°F); most common isotope Hg^{202} (29.8%).

merganser Any of several species of slender, freshwater or marine ducks that dive for food, especially the red-breasted merganser (*Mergus serrator*) which has a hooked bill. The goosander (*M. merganser*) differs in coloration. Family: Anatidae.

meridian Circle that runs through the North and South Poles, at right angles to the Equator. *See also* LONGITUDE.

meristem In plants, a layer of cells that divides repeatedly to generate new tissues. It is present at the growing tips of shoots and roots, and at certain sites in leaves. In monocotyledons the leaf meristem is at the base, explaining why grasses continue to grow when the leaf tips are removed by grazing or mowing. *See also* CAMBIUM

Merovingian (476–750) Frankish dynasty. It was named after Merovech, a leader of the Salian Franks, whose grandson CLOVIS (r. c.481–511) ruled over most of France and converted to Christianity. The last Merovingian king was overthrown by PEPIN, founder of the CAROLINGIAN dynasty.

Merseyside Metropolitan county in NW England, formed in 1974. It lies on both banks of the estuary of the River Mersey. The major town is LIVERPOOL. In the 19th century shipbuilding and ship repair grew in importance, and Liverpool became Britain's leading port. Industries: motor vehicles, chemicals and electrical goods. Area: 655sq km (253sq mi). Pop. (1991) 1,403,642.

mesa Large, broad, flat-topped hill or mountain of moderate height and with steep, cliff-like sides. A mesa is capped with layers of resistant horizontal rocks which may erode to form narrower buttes.

mescaline Psychedelic drug obtained from the dried tops of the peyote cactus, *Lophophora williamsii*. In North America, mescaline is used in some Native American religious rites.

Mesmer, Franz (Friedrich Anton) (1734–1815) Austrian physician. He developed mesmerism, later called HYPNOSIS, in Vienna and Paris, which helped to arouse interest in the therapeutic use of hypnosis.

Mesolithic (Middle Stone Age) In NW Europe the period in human cultural development following the PALAEOLITHIC and preceding the NEOLITHIC. It followed an ice age (c.8000 BC). As the environment changed, scrub gave way to forest and small game proliferated. A nomadic form of life became unnecessary and human settlement was a feature of this period, as were flint tools.

meson Subatomic particle, member of a subgroup of HADRONS, all of which have either zero or integral spin. They include the pions, kaons and eta mesons.

mesophyll Soft tissue located between the two

layers of epidermis in a plant leaf. In most plants, mesophyll cells contain CHLOROPLASTS, which are essential to PHOTOSYNTHESIS.

Mesopotamia Ancient region between the rivers TIGRIS and EUPHRATES in SW Asia, roughly corresponding to modern Iraq. It was the setting of one of the earliest human civilizations, resulting from the development of irrigation in the 6th millennium BC and the extreme fertility of the irrigated land. The first cities were established by the Sumerians c.2500 BC. Sargon conquered the Sumerian cities c.2300 BC. BABYLONIA gained supremacy in the 18th century BC. Later ruled by Assyria, Persia, Greece and Rome, Mesopotamia gradually lost its distinctive cultural traditions. *See also* SUMERIA

Mesozoic Third era of geologic time, extending from c.248–65 million years ago. It is divided into three periods: the TRIASSIC, JURASSIC and CRETACEOUS. For most of the era, the continents are believed to have been joined into one huge landmass called PANGAEA. The period was also characterized by the variety and size of its reptiles.

Messiaen, Olivier (1908–92) French composer and organist. His organ works, such as *L'Ascension* (1933) and *La Nativité du Seigneur* (1935), are an important part of the organ repertoire. Other compositions include the monumental ten-movement *Turangalîla-symphonie* (1949) and an opera on the life of Francis of Assisi.

Messiah (Hebrew, anointed) Saviour or redeemer. Specifically, the Messiah was the descendant of King DAVID expected by Jews of ancient times to become their king, free them from foreign bondage, and establish a golden age of glory, peace and righteousness. It refers to the "idealized" king as having been anointed by God or his representative in the way that David and his successors were. The title "Christ", derived from the Greek version of the Messiah, was applied to Jesus by his followers.

Messina Seaport city in NE Sicily, Italy, on the Strait of Messina; capital of Messina province. It was founded by the Greeks in c.730 BC. The city was conquered by mercenaries, whose backing from Rome led directly to the first of the PUNIC WARS. In 1190 Messina was taken by the Crusaders and was ruled by Spain from 1282 to 1714. In 1860 it was liberated by Giuseppe Garibaldi. In 1908 an earthquake killed over 80,000 people and destroyed most of the city. Exports: wine, citrus fruit, olive oil, chemicals. Industries: chemicals, pharmaceuticals, processed foods. Pop. (1991) 231,693.

metabolism Chemical or physical processes and changes continuously occurring in a living organism. They include the breakdown of organic matter (catabolism), resulting in energy release, and the synthesis of organic components (anabolism) to store energy and build and repair TISSUES.

metal Element that is a good conductor of heat and electricity – the atoms of which are bonded together within crystals in a unique way. Mixtures of such elements (alloys) are also metals. About 75% of the known elements are metals. Most are hard, shiny materials that form oxides. Malleability and ductility are further metallic characteristics. Some metals have very high melting points and various high-temperature applications: TUNGSTEN, with the highest melting point of all at 3,410°C (6,170°F), is employed for incandescent-lamp filaments. ALUMINIUM and IRON are the two most abundant and useful of metals. TITANIUM, although rarely seen as a metal, is more commonly distributed than the more familiar COPPER, ZINC and LEAD. Other metals of economic importance, because they can undergo nuclear FISSION, are URANIUM and PLUTONIUM.

metalloid ELEMENT having some properties typical of metals and some normally associated with non-metals. Metalloids are sometimes called semi-metals or semi-metallic elements. Examples are silicon, germanium and arsenic. Some metalloids are SEMICONDUCTORS.

metallurgy Science and technology concerned with metals. Metallurgy includes the study of methods of extraction of metals from their ores; physical and chemical properties of metals; ALLOY production; and the hardening, strengthening, corrosion-proofing and ELECTROPLATING of metals. *See also* ANODIZING; GALVANIZING

metamorphic rock Broad class of rocks that have been changed by heat or pressure from their original nature – SEDIMENTARY, IGNEOUS, or older metamorphic. The changes characteristically involve new crystalline structure, the creation of new minerals or a radical change of texture. For example, the metamorphic rock slate is made from sedimentary shale.

metamorphosis Change of form during the development of various organisms, such as the changing of a tadpole into a frog. Sometimes the change is gradual, as with a grasshopper, and is known as incomplete metamorphosis. Complete metamorphosis usually involves the distinct stages of LARVA, PUPA and adult.

metaphysical poetry English literary form of the 17th century, characterized by the combination of unlike ideas or images to create new representations of experience, and a reliance on wit and subtle argument. Though this method was by no means new, in the hands of writers such as George HERBERT, Andrew MARVELL and John DONNE it infused new life into English poetry.

metaphysics Branch of philosophy that deals with the first principles of reality and with the nature of the universe. Metaphysics is divided into ontology, the study of the essence of being, and COSMOLOGY, the study of the structure and laws of the universe. Leading metaphysical writers include PLATO, ARISTOTLE, DESCARTES, LEIBNIZ, KANT and A.N. WHITEHEAD.

meteor (shooting star) Brief streak of light in the night sky caused by a meteoroid entering the Earth's upper atmosphere at high speed from space. A typical meteor lasts from a few tenths of a second to a few seconds, depending on the meteoroid's impact speed, which can vary from about 11–70km/s (7–45mi/s). At certain times of the year there are meteor showers.

meteorite That part of a large meteoroid (a small particle or body following an Earth-crossing orbit) that survives passage through the Earth's atmosphere and reaches the ground. Most of a meteoroid burns up in the atmosphere to produce meteors, but about 10% reaches the surface as meteorites and micrometeorites. Meteorites generally have a pitted surface and a fused charred crust. There are three main types: iron meteorites (siderites); stony meteorites (aerolites) and mixed iron and stone meteorites. Some are tiny particles, but others weigh up to 200 tonnes.

meteorology Study of weather conditions, a branch of CLIMATOLOGY. Meteorologists study and analyse data from a network of weather ships, aircraft and satellites in order to compile maps showing the state of high- and low-pressure regions in the Earth's atmosphere. They also anticipate changes in the distribution of the regions and forecast the future weather.

methanal (formaldehyde) Colourless, inflammable, poisonous gas, HCHO, with a penetrating odour. It is the simplest aldehyde and is produced by the oxidation of METHANOL. It was discovered by von HOFMANN in 1867. Most methanal is in the form of formalin. Methanal is used in the manufacture of dyes and plastics. Chief properties: r.d. 0.82; m.p. −92°C (−133.6°F), b.p. −19°C (−2.2°F).

methane Colourless, odourless HYDROCARBON (CH₄), the simplest ALKANE (paraffin). It is the chief constituent of NATURAL GAS, from which it is obtained. It is produced by decomposing organic matter, such as in marshes. In the air, it contributes to the GREEENHOUSE EFFECT and an increase in global temperature. Methane is used in the form of natural gas as a fuel. Properties: m.p. −182.5°C (−296.5°F); b.p. −164°C (−263.2°F).

methanoic acid (formic acid) Colourless, corrosive, pungent, liquid carboxylic acid, HCOOH. It is used to produce insecticides and for dyeing, tanning and electroplating. It occurs naturally in a variety of sources – stinging ants, nettles, pine needles and sweat. The simplest of the carboxylic acids, it can be produced by the action of concentrated sulphuric acid on sodium methanoate. Properties: r.d. 1.22; m.p. 8.3°C (46.9°F); b.p. 100.8°C (213.4°F).

methanol (methyl alcohol) Colourless, poisonous, flammable liquid (CH₃OH), the simplest of the ALCOHOLS. It is obtained synthetically either from carbon monoxide and hydrogen, by the oxidation of natural gas, or by the destructive distillation of wood. It is used as a solvent and to produce rocket fuel and petrol. Properties: m.p. −93.9°C (−137°F); b.p. 64.9°C (148.8°F).

Methodism Worldwide religious movement that began in England in the 18th century. It was originally an evangelical movement within the CHURCH OF ENGLAND, started in 1729 by John and Charles WESLEY. In 1795 the Wesleyan Methodists became a separate body and divided into other sects, such as the Methodist New Connection (1797) and the Primitive Methodists (1811). The United Methodist Church reunited the New Connection with the smaller Bible Christians and the United Methodist Free Churches in 1907; in 1932 these united with the Wesleyans and Primitives. In the USA, the Methodist Episcopal Church was founded in 1784. By the 1990s there were more than 50 million Methodists worldwide.

Methuselah In the Old Testament (Genesis 5:25–27), the longest-lived of all human beings; son of ENOCH and eighth in descent from ADAM and EVE. He is said to have died at the age of 969 and was the father of many children, including Lamech, the father of NOAH.

methylated spirit Industrial form of ETHANOL (ethyl alcohol). It contains 5% METHANOL (methyl alcohol), which is extremely poisonous, and enough pyridine to give it a foul taste. It is dyed purple and used as a solvent and fuel.

metre SI unit of distance (symbol m). Conceived as being a ten millionth of the surface distance between the North Pole and the Equator, it was formerly defined by two marks on a platinum bar kept in Paris. It is now defined as the length of the path travelled by light in a vacuum during 1/299,792,458 of a second. 1 metre equals 39.3701 inches.

metre In poetry, a regular rhythmic pattern. It imposes a regular recurrence of stresses, typically dividing a line into equal units called metrical feet. The most commonly used metrical feet are anapaest, dactyl, iamb and trochee. The metre of a poem is described according to the kind and number of metrical feet per line: for example, iambic pentameters have five iambs per line.

metric system Decimal system of WEIGHTS AND MEASURES based on the METRE (m) and the KILOGRAM (kg). Larger and smaller metric units are related by powers of 10. Devised in 1791, the metric system is used internationally by scientists (particularly as SI UNITS) and has been adopted for general use by most Western countries, though the IMPERIAL SYSTEM is still commonly used in the USA and for certain measurements in Britain.

Metternich, Klemens Wenzel Lothar, Prince von (1773–1859) Austrian statesman, foreign minister (1809–48), chancellor (1821–48). He was the leading European statesman of the post-Napoleonic era. Following Austria's defeat in the NAPOLEONIC WARS (1809), he adopted a conciliatory policy towards France. After Napoleon's retreat from Moscow (1812), he formed the QUADRUPLE ALLIANCE (1813), which led to Napoleon's defeat. He was the dominant figure at the Congress of VIENNA (1814–15) and at subsequent conferences held under the CONGRESS SYSTEM. Thereafter he became increasingly autocratic, pressing for the intervention of the great powers against any revolutionary outbreak. He was driven from power by the REVOLUTION OF 1848.

Metz City on the River Moselle, NE France; capital of Moselle département. After the 8th century the bishops of Metz ruled a vast empire. It was taken by France in 1552, but became part of Germany in 1871. The Treaty of Versailles (1919) restored it to France. Industries: metals, machinery, tobacco, wine, tanning, clothing. Pop. (1990) 119,594.

Mexican Revolution (1910–40) Extended political revolution to improve the welfare of the Mexican underpriviliged. The revolution was prompted by the dictatorial presidency of Porfirio DÍAZ. Díaz was forced to resign in 1911 by MADERO, who became president. Madero was assassinated in 1913 by his former general Victoriano HUERTA. The repressive regime of Huerta caused massive unrest in the peasant community led by Venustiano Carranza, Francisco "Pancho" VILLA and Emiliano ZAPATA. Huerta resigned and Carranza became president (1914). Lázaro Cárdenas (inaugurated 1934) finally introduced sweeping measures, involving land redistribution, support of the labour movement, and improving health and education.

Mexican War (1846–48) War between Mexico and the USA. It broke out following the US annexation of TEXAS (1845). Mexican forces were swiftly overwhelmed, and a series of US expeditions effected the conquest of the SW. The war ended when General Winfield Scott defeated the army of SANTA ANNA and entered Mexico City on 8 September 1847. In the Treaty of Guadalupe-Hidalgo (1848), Mexico ceded sovereignty over California and New Mexico, as well as Texas north of the Rio Grande.

Mexico Mountainous republic in S North America; the capital is MEXICO CITY. **Land and climate** Mexico is the world's largest Spanish-speaking country. The SIERRA MADRE Occidental begins in the NW state of Chihuahua and runs parallel to Mexico's W coast and the Sierra Madre Oriental. Monterrey lies in the foothills of the latter. Between the two ranges lies the Mexican Plateau. The S part of the plateau contains a series of extinct volcanoes, rising to Citlaltépetl, at 5,700m (18,701ft). This region includes many of Mexico's largest cities, including the world's largest city, MEXICO CITY, and GUADALAJARA. The S highlands of the Sierra Madre del Sur include the archaeological sites in OAXACA. Mexico contains two large peninsulas: the mountainous and arid Baja California in the NW; and the lowland YUCATÁN peninsula in the SE. Ciudad Juárez and Nuevo Laredo are important cities on the border with the USA. Mexico's climate varies greatly according to altitude. Most rain occurs between June and September, and rainfall decreases N of Mexico City. Over 70% of Mexico has a desert or semi-desert climate. Irrigation is essential for agriculture. The N deserts are abundant in plants such as cactus, mesquite and yucca. Luxuriant rainforests exist in the S. **Economy** Mexico is an upper-middle-income developing country, faced with problems of unemployment, inflation, inequality and illegal emigration to the USA. Mexico's heavy borrowing on the strength of its oil reserves in the 1970s led to economic depression in the 1980s caused by the drop in oil prices. In June 1993 Mexico joined the Organization for Economic Co-operation and Development (OECD). In 1994 Mexico, the USA and Canada formed the NORTH AMERICAN FREE TRADE AGREEMENT (NAFTA), the world's single largest trading bloc. In late 1994 Mexico was plunged into economic crisis. Only a US$50,000 million loan from the USA prevented it defaulting on its foreign debts. An austerity package of wage freezes, interest rate rises and tax increases was introduced. Remarkably the loan was repaid by 1997. Mexico is the world's fifth-largest producer of crude oil. Machinery and transport equipment account for 32% of exports. Other manufactures include chemicals, clothing, steel and textiles. Many factories near the US border assemble goods for US companies. Agriculture is important, contributing c.8% of GDP and employing 28% of the workforce. Mexico is the world's fifth-largest producer of coffee. Food crops include beans, maize, rice and wheat. Beef and dairy cattle are also raised. Fishing is also an important activity. Forestry and tourism are growing. **History** One of the earliest NATIVE AMERICAN civilizations was the OLMEC (800–400 BC). The MAYA flourished between AD 300 and 900. The TOLTEC empire was dominant between 900 and c.1200. But it was the AZTEC who dominated the central plateau from their capital at Tenochtitlán (modern-day Mexico City). Fernández de Córdoba was the first European to explore Mexico, in 1517. During 1519–21 Spanish *conquistadors*, led by Hernán CORTÉS, captured the capital and the Aztec emperor MONTEZUMA. In 1535 the territory became the viceroyalty of New Spain. Christianity was introduced. Spanish colonial rule was harsh, divisive and unpopular. In 1821 Mexico gained independence and General Augustín de Iturbide became emperor. In 1823 republicans seized power and Mexico became a republic (1824). In 1832 SANTA ANNA became president. War with Texas escalated into the MEXICAN WAR (1846–48) with the USA. In the Treaty of Guadalupe-Hidalgo

---

MEXICO
AREA: 1,958,200sq km (756,061sq mi)
POPULATION: 89,538,000
CAPITAL (POPULATION): Mexico City (15,047,685)
GOVERNMENT: Federal republic
ETHNIC GROUPS: Mestizo 60%, Native American 30%, European 9%
LANGUAGES: Spanish (official)
RELIGIONS: Christianity (Roman Catholic 90%, Protestant 5%)
CURRENCY: New peso = 100 centavosm.

(1848), Mexico lost 50% of its territory. A revolution led to the overthrow of Santa Anna in 1855, and civil war broke out. Liberal forces, led by Benito JUÁREZ, triumphed in the War of Reform (1858–61), but conservatives with support from France installed Maximilian of Austria as emperor in 1864. In 1867 republican rule was restored and Juárez became president. In 1876 an armed revolt gave Porfirio DÍAZ the presidency. Beside the period 1880–84, the Díaz dictatorship lasted until 1910. After an armed insurrection, Francisco MADERO became president in 1911. An ineffectual leader, Madero was toppled by General Victoriano HUERTA in 1913. Huerta's dictatorial regime prolonged the MEXICAN REVOLUTION (1910–40) and led to US intervention. The US-backed forces of Carranza battled with the peasant armies of VILLA and ZAPATA. During the 1920s and 1930s Mexico introduced land and social reforms. After World War 2, Mexico's economy developed with the introduction of liberal reforms. Relations with the USA improved greatly, though problems remain over Mexican economic migration and drug trafficking. **Politics** The Institutional Revolutionary Party (PRI) has ruled Mexico almost continuously since its formation in 1929. In 1994 the Zapatista National Liberation Army (ZNLA) staged an armed revolt in the S state of Chiapas, principally calling for land reforms and recognition of Native American rights. In 1994 Ernesto ZEDILLO of the PRI was elected president. In 1997 mid-term congressional elections, the PRI lost its majority in the Chamber of Deputies for the first time since its formation.

Mexico City Capital of Mexico, largest city in the world, situated in a volcanic basin at an altitude of 2,380m (7,800ft), in the centre of the country. Mexico City is the nation's political, economic and cultural centre. It suffers from overcrowding and high levels of pollution and is vulnerable to earthquakes. The former AZTEC capital, known as Tenochtitlán, was destroyed by Hernán Cortés in 1521. A new city was constructed, which acted as the capital of Spain's New World colonies for the next 300 years. During the MEXICAN WAR, the city was occupied by US troops (1847). In 1863 French troops conquered the city. It was recaptured in 1867 by Benito JUÁREZ's republican forces. In 1914–15, the city was captured and lost three times by the revolutionary forces of ZAPATA and Francisco VILLA. It is a major tourist centre. Pop. (1990) 15,047,685.

mezzo-soprano (middle soprano) Range of the human voice falling between SOPRANO and CONTRALTO. It grew popular with opera composers in the 19th century, when the CASTRATO voice (which had a similar range) became less usual.

Miami City and port on Biscayne Bay, SE Florida, USA. Originally a small agricultural community, it developed quickly after 1895 when the railroad was extended and the harbour dredged. Modern Miami is a popular tourist resort, with luxury hotels and many sporting facilities. Industries:

clothing, concrete, metal products, fishing, printing and publishing. Pop. (1990) 358,548.

mica Group of common rock-forming minerals characterized by a flaky appearance. All contain aluminium, potassium and water; other metals, such as iron and magnesium, may be present. Micas have perfect basal cleavage. Common micas are muscovite and the biotite group. Muscovite is commonly found in coarse-grained acidic rocks, schists and gneisses, and in sedimentary rocks. The biotite micas are found in a wide range of igneous and metamorphic rocks.

Michael, Saint One of the four archangels mentioned in the Bible, the others being GABRIEL, RAPHAEL and Uriel. In the Old Testament, Michael is the guardian of Israel and the highest of the archangels. In the New Testament book of Revelation, he is said to have thrown down the Dragon (Satan). His feast day is 29 September (Michaelmas). He is given prominence also in ISLAM.

Michaelmas Christian feast day of St Michael and All Angels, celebrated on 29 September. Since the Middle Ages, Michaelmas has been one of the four quarter days of the financial year.

Michelangelo Buonarroti (1475–1564) Florentine sculptor, painter, architect and poet. He was one of the outstanding figures of the High RENAISSANCE and a creator of MANNERISM. He spent five years in Rome, where he made his name with a statue of *Bacchus* and the *Pietà* (now in St Peter's). In 1501 he returned to Florence, where he carved the gigantic *David*, which symbolizes the new-found confidence of the Florentine Republic. The vast painting for the Sistine Chapel ceiling was Michelangelo's most sublime achievement. He added *The Last Judgment* later, starting in 1536. Among Michelangelo's other great (unfinished) works are the Medici Chapel and the Biblioteca Laurenziana. For the last 30 years of his life, Michelangelo concentrated on architecture. He created the magnificent cathedral of ST PETER'S, Rome, but died before completing it.

Michelson, Albert Abraham (1852–1931) US physicist, b. Germany. In 1887 he conducted an experiment with Edward Morley to determine the velocity of the Earth through the ETHER, using an INTERFEROMETER of his own design. The negative result prompted the development of the theory of RELATIVITY. In 1907 Michelson became the first US scientist to win a Nobel Prize.

Michigan State in N central USA, bordered by four of the GREAT LAKES; the capital is Lansing. The largest city is DETROIT. First settled by the French in the 17th century, the region was ceded to Britain after the SEVEN YEARS WAR. Michigan became a US territory in 1805, achieving full statehood in 1837. The opening of the Erie Canal in 1825 aided its growth, but the real industrial boom came with the development of the motor vehicle industry in the early 20th century. Michigan is made up of two peninsulas separated by the Straits of Mackinac, which connect lakes Michigan and Huron. On the Upper Peninsula, copper and iron ore and timber are valuable resources. The Lower Peninsula is also forested and mineral deposits include oil, gypsum, sandstone and limestone. The Lower Peninsula has most of Michigan's population and industries, such as motor vehicles, metals, chemicals and food products. Area: 150,544sq km (58,110sq mi). Pop. (1990) 9,295,297.

Michigan, Lake Third-largest of the five GREAT LAKES of North America, and the only one entirely within the USA. Discovered by the French in 1634, it is connected to Lake Huron by the Straits of Mackinac. The St Lawrence Seaway opened up the lake to international trade. Chicago is on the sw shore. Area: 57,757sq km (22,300sq mi).

microbiology Study of microorganisms, their structure, function and significance. Mainly concerned with single-cell forms such as VIRUSES, BACTERIA, PROTOZOA and FUNGI, it has immense applications in medicine and the food industry.

microcomputer Small computer that has its central processing unit (CPU) on an integrated circuit (chip) called a MICROPROCESSOR.

microeconomics Study of individual components of the economic system. It analyses individual consumers and producers, the market conditions and the law of SUPPLY AND DEMAND. It is one of the two major subdivisions of ECONOMICS; the other is MACROECONOMICS.

microelectronics In ELECTRONICS, systems designed and produced without wiring or other bulky components. They allow a high packing density, greatly reducing the size of component assemblies. Following World War 2, the application of new technology such as the TRANSISTOR saw the beginnings of the microelectronics industry. This accelerated with the development of the PRINTED CIRCUIT. Even further reduction in size, or microminiaturization, was achieved with INTEGRATED CIRCUITS. Molecular electronics is a new development that promises to be the ultimate in size reduction.

Micronesia Group of islands located in the w Pacific Ocean, N of Polynesia. Micronesia includes BELAU, KIRIBATI, MARIANA ISLANDS, MICRONESIA, FEDERATED STATES OF, Nauru and Tuvalu.

Micronesia, Federated States of Republic in the w Pacific Ocean, consisting of all the CAROLINE ISLANDS except BELAU; the capital is Palikir (on Pohnpei). The 607 islands of the republic are divided into four states: Kosrae, Pohnpei, Truk and Yap. The islands are widely dispersed. The economy is heavily dependent on US aid. Land use is limited to subsistence agriculture. Japan occupied the archipelago in 1914, and in 1920 was given a mandate to govern by the League of Nations. In 1944 US naval forces captured the islands, and in 1947 they became part of the UN Trust Territory of the Pacific Islands. In 1979 the Federated States of Micronesia came into being, with Belau remaining a US trust territory. In 1986 a compact of free asso-

ciation with the USA was signed. In 1991 Micronesia became a full member of the UN. Area: 705sq km (272sq mi). Pop. (1991) 107,662.

microphone Device for converting sound into varying electric currents of the same frequency. Live music performers often use a moving coil microphone, in which a coil attached to a diaphragm vibrates in a stationary magnetic field. The recording industry prefers the condenser microphone, which employs a CAPACITOR. Crystal microphones use the PIEZOELECTRIC EFFECT.

microprocessor Complex INTEGRATED CIRCUIT (chip) used to control the operation of a computer or other equipment.

microscope Optical device for producing an enlarged image of a minute object. The first simple microscope was made in 1668 by Anton van LEEUWENHOEK. The modern compound microscope has two converging lens systems, the objective and the eyepiece, both of short focal length. The objective produces a magnified image, which is further magnified by the eyepiece to give the image seen by the observer. Because of the nature of the visible spectrum of light, an optical microscope can magnify objects only up to 2,000 times. For extremely small objects, an ELECTRON MICROSCOPE is used.

microsurgery Delicate surgery performed under a binocular microscope using specialized instruments, such as microneedles as small as 2mm long, sutures 20 micrometers in diameter, ENDOSCOPES and LASERS. It is used in a number of specialized areas, including the repair of nerves and blood vessels, eye, ear and brain surgery, and the reattachment of severed parts.

microwave Form of ELECTROMAGNETIC RADIATION having a wavelength between 1mm (0.04in) and 1m (3.3ft) and a frequency range of about 255 to 300,000MHz. Microwaves are used for RADAR, RADIO and TELEVISION broadcasting, high-speed microwave heating and cellular telephones.

Midas Name of several historical Phrygian rulers and one legendary foolish king in classical mythology. As a reward for rendering a service to a god, King Midas asked that everything he touched should become gold. Midas found he was unable to eat or drink because his food, too, was transformed. His story was told by OVID.

Mid-Atlantic Ridge Underwater topographic feature along the margin between the diverging American crustal plate and the European and African plates. It runs for 14,000km (8,700mi) along the middle of the Atlantic Ocean. Iceland is located on the ridge itself and was formed by the outpourings of volcanic lava.

Middle Ages Period in European history covering c.1,000 years between the disintegration of the Roman empire in the 5th century and the RENAISSANCE. The Middle Ages are sometimes divided into Early (up to the 10th century), High (10th–14th centuries), and Late Middle Ages. The Middle Ages were, above all, the age of the Christian church, whose doctrine was universally accepted, and the hegemony of the FEUDAL SYSTEM. In the arts, the Middle Ages encompassed the GOTHIC period (from the 11th century), and in science and learning, the predominance of ISLAM.

Middle English Form of the English language in use from *c.*1100 to *c.*1450. This period saw the borrowing of many words from NORMAN FRENCH. Grammatical gender was superseded by natural gender, and the use of an Anglo-Norman writing system caused radical changes in spellings.

Middlesbrough Port and unitary authority on the River Tees estuary in NE England; the former county town of Cleveland. During the 19th century Middlesbrough developed around its iron industry. Industries: steel, shipbuilding. Pop. (1991) 140,849.

Middlesex Former county of SE England, adjoining LONDON. In 1888 it became an administrative county, losing much of its area to the county of London. In 1965 the county was absorbed into Greater London, SURREY and HERTFORDSHIRE.

Middleton, Thomas (1570–1627) English playwright. Among his comedies are *The Honest Whore* (1604), in collaboration with Thomas Dekker, and the political satire *A Game at Chesse* (1624). His best-known play is *The Changeling* (1621).

Mid Glamorgan County on the Bristol Channel in S Wales; the administrative centre is CARDIFF, in SOUTH GLAMORGAN. Other towns include Merthyr Tydfil, Pontypridd and Bridgend. The region is drained by the Taff, Rhymney and Ogmore rivers. The economy was formerly dominated by the coal mines in the N, particularly the Rhondda Valley. Long-term decline in the coal, iron and steel industries has caused economic and social problems. Area: 1,019sq km (393sq mi). Pop. (1991) 526,500.

Midway Islands Coral atoll in the central Pacific Ocean, *c.*2,000km (1,250mi) WNW of Honolulu, consisting of two small islands, Easter and Sand. They were the scene of the World War 2 Battle of Midway (1942). The islands are now administered by the US Department of the Interior. Area: 5sq km (2sq mi). Pop. (1995 est.) 2,000.

Midwest (Middle West) Imprecise term referring to the interior plains of the USA around the W GREAT LAKES and the upper Mississippi River valley. It usually refers to the states of INDIANA, ILLINOIS, IOWA, KANSAS, MICHIGAN, MINNESOTA, MICHIGAN, NEBRASKA, OHIO and WISCONSIN. Traditionally, the Midwest has been the manufacturing heartland of the USA, but it is also one of the world's richest wheat-growing regions.

migraine Recurrent attacks of throbbing headache, mostly on one side only, often accompanied by nausea, vomiting and visual disturbances. It results from changes in diameter of the arteries serving the brain. More common in women, it is seen usually in young adults and often runs in families. Attacks, which may last anything from two to 72 hours, are often associated with trigger factors, such as diet or fatigue.

migration Any periodic movement of animals or humans, usually in groups, from one area to another, in order to find food, breeding areas or better conditions. Animal migration involves the eventual return of the migrant to its place of departure. Fish migrate between fresh and saltwater or from one part of an ocean to another. Birds usually migrate along established routes. Mammals migrate usually in search of food. For thousands of years the deserts of central Asia widened inexorably and this phenomenon resulted in the human migration of prehistoric tribes to China, the Middle East and Europe. Another type of migration occurred in the 14th century when the Maoris left their overpopulated homes in the islands of central Polynesia.

Milan (Milano) City in NW Italy; capital of Lombardy region. It was powerful Italian state under the Sforza family (1447–1535). It was ruled by Napoleon (1796–1814) and subsequently by the Austrian Habsburgs, before becoming part of Italy in 1860. It is Italy's leading commercial, financial and industrial centre. Industries: motor vehicles, machinery, electrical goods, textiles, clothing, publishing and printing. Pop. (1991) 1,369,231.

mildew External filaments and fruiting structures of numerous mould-like FUNGI. Mildews are PARASITES of plants and cause great damage to crops.

Milhaud, Darius (1892–1974) French composer. *Orestes* (1913–22) was an experiment with polytonality. He included jazz elements in his compositions, notably *La Création du Monde* (1923). His most ambitious work was the opera *Christophe Colombe* (1930).

milk Liquid food secreted from mammary glands by the females of nearly all mammals to feed their young. The milk of domesticated cattle has been used as food by humans since prehistoric times, both directly and to make BUTTER, CHEESE and yogurt. Milk is a suspension of fat and protein in water, sweetened with lactose sugar.

Milky Way Faint band of light visible on clear dark nights encircling the sky along the line of the galactic equator. It is the combined light of an enormous number of stars, in places obscured by clouds of interstellar gas and dust. It is the disc of our GALAXY, viewed from our vantage point within it.

Mill, James (1773–1836) Scottish philosopher. He became a friend of Jeremy BENTHAM and together they evolved UTILITARIANISM. Mill wrote an *Analysis of the Phenomena of the Human Mind* (1829) and a multi-volume history of the East India Company, for which he worked. He was the father of John Stuart MILL.

Mill, John Stuart (1806–73) British philosopher who advocated UTILITARIANISM. His book *On Liberty* (1859) made him famous as a defender of human rights. *System of Logic* (1843) attempted to provide an account of inductive reason.

Millais, Sir John Everett (1829–96) English painter and illustrator, a founder member of the PRE-RAPHAELITE BROTHERHOOD. His pre-Raphaelite works, such as *Christ in the House of his Parents* (1850), show the Brotherhood's liking for righteous subjects. He later started to paint more sentimental subjects, such as *Bubbles* (1886).

millennium In religion, supposed second coming of Christ, when he will reign for 1,000 years. This belief (millenarianism) was popular until the 4th century. It then fell dormant until the REFORMATION, when it was revived by the ANABAPTISTS and the MORAVIAN CHURCH. Since the 19th century, MORMONS and ADVENTISTS have professed millenarian beliefs. Some sects, such as JEHOVAH'S WITNESSES, have forecast the imminence of the millennium.

Miller, (Alton) Glenn (1904–44) US jazz trombonist and bandleader. He led the most popular dance band of all time, featuring *Moonlight Serenade* and *In the Mood* (1939), which Miller composed.

Miller, Arthur (1915–) US dramatist. His Pulitzer Prize-winning *Death of a Salesman* (1949) is a dramatic masterpiece of the 20th century. *The Crucible* (1953) is a dramatic reconstruction of the SALEM witch trials and also a parable of the MCCARTHY era. Miller won a second Pulitzer Prize for *A View From the Bridge* (1955). He was married (1955–61) to Marilyn MONROE, and *After the Fall* (1964) is a fictionalized account of their relationship.

Miller, Henry (1891–1980) US author. Most of his novels were first published in Paris and were banned as obscene in the USA and Britain until the 1960s. They include *Tropic of Cancer* (1934) and *Tropic of Capricorn* (1939). He is also remembered for the trilogy, *Sexus, Plexus* and *Nexus* (1949–60).

millet CEREAL grass that produces small, edible seeds. The stalks have flower spikes and the hulled seeds are white. In Russia, W Africa and Asia it is a staple food. In W Europe it is used mainly for pasture. Height: 1m (39in). Family Poaceae/Gramineae.

millipede Any of numerous species of elongated, invertebrate, arthropod animals with large numbers of legs. Found worldwide, it has a segmented body, one pair of antennae, two pairs of legs per segment and can be orange, brown or black. All species avoid light and feed on plant tissues. Length: 2–280mm (0.2–11in). Class Diplopoda.

Mills, C. (Charles) Wright (1916–62) US sociologist. His works include *From Max Weber* (1946), *The Power Elite* (1956), *The Sociological Imagination* (1959) and *Listen Yankee* (1960).

Milne, A.A. (Alan Alexander) (1882–1956) British essayist, dramatist and author of children's books. He wrote the verses in *When We Were Very Young* (1924) and *Now We Are Six* (1927), and the stories in *Winnie-the-Pooh* (1926) and *The House at Pooh Corner* (1928).

Milošević, Slobodan (1941–) Serbian politician, president of Serbia (1989–97), president of Yugoslavia (1997–). He became head of the Serbian Communist Party in 1986. As Serbian president, he was confronted with the break-up of the

federation of Yugoslavia. After his re-election in 1992, Milošević gave support to the Serb populations in Croatia and Bosnia-Herzegovina, who fought for a Greater Serbia. Milošević gradually distanced himself from the brutal activities of the Bosnian Serb leaders Mladić and KARADŽIĆ. In November 1995 he signed the Dayton Peace Accord with the Bosnian president IZETBEGOVIĆ and the Croatian president TUDJMAN to end the civil war in the former Yugoslavia. In 1996 Milošević refused to recognize oppostion victories in municipal elections. After massive, peaceful demonstrations, he was forced to concede some of these victories in 1997. He was elected president of the Federal Republic of Yugoslavia in 1997.

Milstein, César (1927–) British molecular biologist and immunologist, b. Argentina. In 1975 he helped develop a technique for cloning monoclonal antibodies (MABs), which combat diseases by targeting their sites. He shared the 1984 Nobel Prize for physiology or medicine.

Milton, John (1608–74) English poet. Milton's first major pieces are the masque *Comus* (1634) and the pastoral elergy *Lycidas* (1637). Committed to reform of the Church of England, his pamphlet *Of Reformation in England* (1641) attacked episcopacy. He was the champion of the revolutionary forces in the English CIVIL WAR. His *Areopagitica* (1644) is an argument for freedom of the press. *Paradise Lost*, written in blank verse, is perhaps the greatest epic poem in English. First published in 10 books (1667), in 1674 Milton produced a revised edition in 12 books. Its sequel is *Paradise Regained* (1671).

Milwaukee City and port of entry on the W shore of Lake Michigan, SE Wisconsin, USA. It was founded in 1836. Industries: brewing, diesel and petrol engines, construction and electrical equipment. Pop. (1990) 628,088.

mime In drama, the communication of mood, story and idea through the use of gestures, movements and facial expressions, with no verbal interaction. It derives from Greek and Roman theatrical traditions.

mimosa Genus of plants, shrubs and trees native to tropical North and South America. They have showy, feather-like leaves and heads or spikes of white, pink or yellow flowers. Family Mimosaceae.

mina (myna or mynah) Any of several species of tropical birds of SE Asia, S Africa, Australasia and the Pacific Islands; it is related to the STARLING. A natural mimic, especially the species *Gracula religiosa*, it imitates other birds. It feeds mainly on fruit. Length: to 33 cm (13in). Family Sturnidae.

minaret Tower of a MOSQUE from which the MUEZZIN calls a Muslim to prayer. A mosque may have several minarets. The earliest minarets were built in Egypt *c*.673 as low square towers.

mind Hypothetical faculty postulated to account for the ability of conscious beings to think, feel, will or behave. The mind is considered to control, or consist of, so-called mental processes. Dualist philosophers, such as René DESCARTES, have distinguished between mind and matter as two totally independent entities. IDEALISM suggests that the world is a product of the mind and dependent on experience. MATERIALISM postulates that the mind is not separate from the physical but derives from it.

Mindanao Second-largest island of the Philippines, in the S of the archipelago; Davao is the major port and city. The island is forested and mountainous, rising to the active volcano of Mount Apo, at 2,954m (9,690ft) the highest peak in the Philippines. The jagged coastline features deep bays and islets. Islam arrived in the 14th century. In the 1960s the central government encouraged Philippine colonization of the island, and the dispossessed Moros began to advocate secession. In 1969 the Philippine army began a military campaign that resulted in thousands of deaths. The economy is primarily agricultural. Area: 94,631sq km (36,537sq mi). Pop. (1990) 14,297,000.

mine Excavation from which minerals are extracted. Underground mines are of two main types: shaft mines and drift mines. **Shafts** are sunk vertically in the Earth's crust until they reach the depth of the seams to be exploited, which are then reached by tunnels or galleries. **Drift** mines are generally shallower, the seams being reached by a drift, or gradually sloping shaft, which leads on to a gallery system. In **opencast** or strip mining, the seams are near or on the surface and are exposed by giant dragline machines that dig away the topsoil.

mineralogy Investigation of naturally occurring inorganic substances found on Earth and elsewhere in the Solar System. *See* GEOCHEMISTRY; MINERALS; PETROLOGY

minerals Natural, homogeneous and, with a few exceptions, solid and crystalline materials that form the Earth and make up its ROCKS. Most are formed through inorganic processes, and more than 3,000 minerals have been identified. They are classified on the basis of chemical make-up, crystal structure and physical properties, such as hardness, specific gravity, cleavage, colour and lustre. Some minerals are economically important as ORES from which metals are extracted. *See* individual articles

Minerva Roman goddess of the arts, professions and handicrafts. She was identified with the Greek goddess ATHENA.

Ming Imperial Chinese dynasty (1368–1644). It was founded by a Buddhist monk and peasant leader, Chu Yüan-chang (r.1328–98), who expelled the Mongol YÜAN dynasty and unified China by 1382. Under the despotic rule of the early Ming emperors, China experienced a period of great artistic and intellectual distinction and economic expansion. In 1644 a rebel leader took Beijing. A Ming general summoned aid from the MANCHU, who overthrew the dynasty and established their own.

miniature painting Term that originally meant the art of manuscript ILLUMINATION but was later applied to very small paintings. In Europe, the earliest miniatures were produced in the late 15th century, using the same materials as illuminated manuscripts. During the 18th century miniaturists usually painted in watercolour on ivory or in oils on metal. After the mid-19th century the art of miniature painting declined in the West because of competition from PHOTOGRAPHY. The tradition remained strong in Islamic countries and India.

minimal access surgery Term used to encompass operations that do not involve cutting open the body in the traditional way. Minimal access (keyhole) procedures are performed either by means of an ENDOSCOPE or by passing miniature instruments through a fine catheter into a large blood vessel. The surgical LASER is also used.

minimal art Movement in 20th-century painting and sculpture that used only the most fundamental geometric forms. It originated in the 1950s as a reaction against the chaotic emotions provoked by ABSTRACT EXPRESSIONISM.

minimalism Trend in musical composition, beginning in the 1960s, in which short melodic or rhythmic fragments are repeated in gradually changing patterns, usually in a simple harmonic context. Many minimalist composers, such as Steve REICH and Philip GLASS, were influenced by the repetitive patterns of non-Western music.

mink Small, semi-aquatic mammal of the WEASEL family, with soft, water-repellent hair of high commercial value. Wild mink have dark brown fur with long black outer hair. Ranch mink have been bred to produce fur of various colours. They eat fish, rodents and birds. Length to: 73cm (29in) including the tail; weight: 1.6kg (3.5lb). Family Mustelidae.

Minneapolis City and port on the Mississippi River, SE Minnesota, USA; the largest city in Minnesota. It is an important processing and distribution centre for grain and cattle. Industries: electronics, printing and publishing. Pop. (1990) 368,383.

Minnesota State in N central USA, on the Canadian border; the capital is ST PAUL. The largest city is MINNEAPOLIS. The area E of the Mississippi passed to Britain after the SEVEN YEARS WAR, then to the USA after the American Revolution. The lands W of the Mississippi were acquired from France in the LOUISIANA PURCHASE (1803). Minnesota was organized as a territory in 1849, acquiring statehood in 1858. The terrain varies from the prairies of the S to the forests of the N. The state is drained by the Minnesota, St Croix and Mississippi rivers. Wheat and maize are the major crops, and many farms raise dairy cattle. Manufacturing is the main economic activity. Industries: electronics, machinery, chemicals, printing and publishing. Area: 206,207sq km (79,617sq mi). Pop. (1990) 4,375,099.

minnow Subfamily of freshwater fish found in temperate and tropical regions. It includes shiners, dace, chub, tench and bream. More specifically, the term includes small fish of the genera *Phoxinus* and *Leuciscus*. Length: 4–46cm (1.5–18in). Family Cyprinidae.

Minoan civilization Ancient AEGEAN CIVILIZATION that flourished *c*.3000–*c*.1100 BC on the island of Crete, named after the legendary King Minos. The Minoan period is divided into three: Early (*c*.3000–*c*.2100 BC), Middle (*c*.2100–*c*.1550 BC) and Late (*c*.1550–*c*.1100 BC). Minoan art peaked in the Late period. The prosperity of Bronze Age Crete is evident from the excavations at KNOSSOS.

Minos In Greek mythology, the son of EUROPA and ZEUS, king of Crete. He was consigned at his death to HADES to judge human souls. He angered POSEIDON who, in revenge, caused the king's wife Pasiphaë to give birth to the monstrous MINOTAUR.

Minotaur In Greek mythology, beast with the head of a bull and the body of a man, the issue of Pasiphaë, wife of MINOS, and a bull. He was confined by Minos in the LABYRINTH built by DAEDALUS. The Minotaur was killed by THESEUS.

Minsk Capital of Belarus, on the River Svisloc. During World War 2 Mink's large Jewish population was exterminated by the occupying Germans. In 1991 it became the capital of the newly independent Belarus. Industries: textiles, machinery, motor vehicles, electronic goods. Pop. (1991) 1,633,600.

mint In botany, any species of aromatic herbs, with a characteristic flavour, of the genus *Mentha*. It is commonly used as a flavouring in cooking, confectionery and medicines. Most species have oval leaves and spikes of purple or pink flowers. Family Lamiaceae/Labiatae. *See also* PEPPERMINT

minuet French dance fashionable at the court of Louis XIV from 1650. Graceful and precise, it is danced by couples and played in triple time. It became popular as a dance in the 18th century and was a familiar movement in the SUITES of composers such as HANDEL and MOZART.

Miocene Geological epoch beginning about 25 million and ending about 5 million years ago. It falls in the middle of the TERTIARY period and is marked by an increase in grasslands over the globe, and the development of most of modern mammals.

Mirabeau, Honoré (1749–91) French revolutionary. One of the most capable early leaders of the FRENCH REVOLUTION, he was instrumental in establishing the National Assembly and became its leader. His goal was a parliamentary monarchy, but his plans were frustrated by the obstinacy of the king on the one hand and the assembly on the other.

miracle play *See* MYSTERY PLAY

Miró, Joan (1893–1983) Spanish painter and graphic artist, one of the most versatile of 20th-century artists. Early works are experiments with FAUVISM, CUBISM and DADA. His *Catalan Landscape* (1923) heralds his more mature work and affinity with ABSTRACT ART and PRIMITIVISM. In 1924 he became a member of the surrealist movement. He also worked in murals, ceramics and stained glass.

miscarriage Popular term for a spontaneous ABORTION, the loss of a FETUS from the UTERUS before it is sufficiently developed to survive.

Mishima, Yukio (1925–70) Japanese author. An early novel, *Confessions of a Mask* (1949), is a partly autobiographical study of homosexuality. His final work, the four-volume *The Sea of Fertility* (1965), is an epic of modern Japan. He committed ritual suicide at Tokyo's military headquarters, which he had occupied with his small private army.

Mishna Collection of Jewish legal traditions and moral precepts that form the basis of the TALMUD. The Mishna was compiled in *c*.AD 200. It is divided into six parts: agricultural laws; laws concerning the sabbath, fasts, and festivals; family laws; civil and criminal laws; laws regarding sacrifices; and laws concerning ceremonial regulations.

missile Unmanned and self-propelled flying weapon. Ballistic missiles travel in the outer atmosphere and are powered by rockets. Cruise missiles travel in the lower atmosphere and are powered by jet engines. GUIDED MISSILES carry guidance systems or can be radio-controlled.

Missionary Societies Organizations for the promotion of Christianity among non-Christians. The first such society was established in New England in 1649. In the 18th century both the Baptists and Methodists established societies, and the 19th century saw the emergence of interdenominational and geographically specialized societies. The International Missionary Council was formed in 1921. Today governments or agencies, such as Christian Aid, have taken over much of the Missionary Societies' educational and medical work.

Mississippi State in S central USA, on the Gulf of Mexico; the capital and largest city is JACKSON. The French claimed the region in 1682, but it passed to Britain after the SEVEN YEARS WAR. The Territory of Mississippi was organized in 1798. The state seceded from the Union in 1861. It was a battleground during the American CIVIL WAR. Racial segregation remained in force until the 1960s when the state became a focus of the civil rights movement. The land slopes down from the hills of the NE to the Delta, a fertile plain between the Mississippi and Yazoo rivers. Pine forests cover most of the S of the state as far as the coastal plain. Mississippi is the leading producer of cotton in the USA. Dairy farming is also of great importance. There are valuable reserves of oil and natural gas. Industries: clothing, wood products, chemicals. Area: 123,515sq km (47,689sq mi). Pop. (1990) 2,573,216.

Mississippi Principal river of the USA, second-longest national river (after the MISSOURI), *c*.3,780km (2,350mi) long. It rises in NW Minnesota and flows SE (forming many state boundaries along its course), emptying into the Gulf of Mexico via its huge marshland delta in SE Louisiana. Its chief tributaries include the Missouri, Ohio, Arkansas and Tennessee rivers. A major transport route, it is connected to the GREAT LAKES and the ST LAWRENCE SEAWAY (N) and the Intracoastal Waterway (E). Major ports on the river include MINNEAPOLIS, ST LOUIS, MEMPHIS and NEW ORLEANS. In 1541 Hernando DE SOTO became the first European to discover the river. In 1803 it was acquired by the USA as part of the LOUISIANA PURCHASE. The Mississippi was used as a major transport route by Union forces during the Civil War.

Missouri State in central USA, w of the Mississippi River; the capital is JEFFERSON CITY. The largest cities are St Louis, KANSAS CITY and Springfield. The French were the first to settle the area in the mid-18th century. The USA acquired the region as part of the LOUISIANA PURCHASE of 1803. The Missouri Territory was organized in 1812 and became a main corridor of westward migration. Missouri was admitted to the Union in 1821. During the American CIVIL WAR, the state remained in the Union, but sympathies were bitterly divided. Geographically, it is divided into two parts. To the N of the Missouri River is prairie country, where farmers grow maize and raise livestock; s of the river are the foothills and plateaus of the Ozark Mountains. In the sw is a small wheat-growing area, and in the SE are the cotton fields of the Mississippi floodplain. The chief mineral resources are coal, lead, zinc and iron ore. Missouri's economy is based on manufacturing. Industries: transport equipment, chemicals, printing and publishing, metals, electrical machinery. Area: 178,446sq km (68,898sq mi). Pop. (1990) 5,117,073.

Missouri ("Big Muddy") Longest river of the USA, at *c*.4,120km (2,560mi) long; the major tributary of the MISSISSIPPI. It rises at the confluence of the Jefferson, Madison and Gallatin rivers in the Rocky Mountains, Montana. It turns SE across the Great Plains, passing through Sioux City, Omaha and KANSAS CITY. It joins the Mississippi River near St Louis, Missouri. Sioux City, Iowa, is the head of navigation. Seasonal fluctuation in flow is a major problem and the Missouri has seven major dams along its route. Its major tributaries are the Yellowstone and Platte rivers. The river was used as a trade route by the Native Americans before its discovery by Marquette and Jolliet in 1683.

Missouri Compromise Effort to end the dispute between slave and free states in the USA in 1820–21. Pushed through Congress by Henry Clay, it permitted Missouri to join the union as a slave state at the same time as Maine was admitted as a free state.

mistletoe Any of numerous species of evergreen plants that are semi-parasitic on tree branches. It has small, spatula-shaped, yellowish-green leaves and generally forms a large dense ball of foliage. The mistletoe taps into the branch of its host to sap its food supply, avoiding the necessity of growing roots itself. It also carries out photosynthesis. Families: Loranthaceae and Viscaceae.

mistral Dry, winter WIND prevalent in the NW Mediterranean. It sweeps from the MASSIF CENTRAL down the Rhône valley to the Rhône delta.

mite Minute ARACHNID found worldwide, many as parasites on plants and animals. The adult has four pairs of legs with claws at the tip, and a

fused head and abdomen. Length: 0.5–3mm (0.02–0.1in). Class Arachnida; order Acarina. *See also* CHIGGER; TICK

Mithridates VI (132–63 BC) King of Pontus (120–63 BC). He was overwhelmed by the forces of Sulla in the war of 88–85 BC and lost his kingdom in a second campaign in 83–82 BC. He reconquered it in 74 BC but was defeated by POMPEY in 66 BC.

mitochondrion Structure (organelle) inside a CELL containing ENZYMES necessary for energy production. Mitochondria are found in the cytoplasm of most types of cell (but not in bacteria). *See also* RESPIRATION

mitosis Nuclear division of a CELL resulting in two genetically identical "daughter" cells with the same number of chromosomes as the parent cell. Mitosis is the normal process of TISSUE growth, and is also involved in ASEXUAL REPRODUCTION. *See also* MEIOSIS

Mitra (Mithra or Mithras) God who in different forms was worshipped in India, Persia and then the Roman empire, and whose cult was the basis of Mithraism. In Vedic mythology, Mitra was the spirit of the day, of the rain and of the sun, linked closely with VARUNA. The Persian Mitra was revered by the ACHAEMENIDS as the god of light and power.

Mitterrand, François Maurice Marie (1916–96) French statesman, president (1981–96). He was active in the French Resistance during World War 2, and served in the government of the Fourth Republic. In 1965 he united the parties of the left. He defeated the incumbent president GISCARD D'ESTAING in 1981 and was re-elected in 1988. He introduced reforms, such as the abolition of CAPITAL PUNISHMENT, and favoured state intervention in the economy. In the 1980s he gradually changed course. Nationalization ceased and some industries returned to private ownership. He was forced further to the right after 1986, when he had to cooperate with Gaullist prime minister, Jacques CHIRAC. Mitterrand was a supporter of greater European union and of close Franco-German relations.

mixture In chemistry, two or more substances that retain their specific identities when mixed (such as air containing oxygen, nitrogen and other gases). The identities remain separate no matter in what proportion or how closely the components are mixed. *See also* COMPOUND; SOLUTION

mobile telephone (cellular phone) Portable radio that connects users to the public telephone system. They operate within a network of radio cells. The first generation operated with analogue signals, the second generation with digital signals.

Mobutu Sese Seko (1930–97) Zaïrean political leader, president (1967–97) b. Joseph-Désiré Mobutu. As head of the army, he deposed Patrice Lumumba in 1960. Mobutu became prime minister in 1966. He embarked on a process of "Africanization". Mobutu's autocratic rule was maintained via political repression and wholesale corruption. Zaïre was plunged into poverty, while his personal wealth soared. In 1997 he was forced into exile by rebel forces led by Laurent Kabila.

mockingbird Any of a group of New World birds, known for imitating other birds. The common mockingbird (*Mimus polyglottos*) of the USA is typical; it is about 27cm (11in) long, ashy above with brownish wings and tail marked with white. Family Mimidae.

mock orange (Philadelphus or sweet syringa) Ornamental deciduous shrub native to the Western Hemisphere and Asia. It has solitary, white or yellowish, fragrant flowers. Family Hydrangeaceae; genus *Philadelphus*.

mode Classified scheme developed during the 4th to 16th centuries AD to systematize music. From the scale worked out scientifically by PYTHAGORAS, St Ambrose is thought to have devised (4th century) four "authentic" modes – the Dorian, Phrygian, Lydian and Mixolydian. All the modes comprised eight notes within the compass of an octave. Pope Gregory (6th century) added four "plagal" modes, which were essentially new forms of the Ambrosian modes (such as Hypodorian, Hypophrygian). Glareanus (16th century) added the Aeolian and Ionian modes, the basis of the minor and major scales respectively.

mode In statistics, a measure of central tendency. It is computed by determining the item that occurs most frequently in a data set. It is a quick measure of central tendency, but is not as commonly used as the MEDIAN or MEAN.

Model Parliament English parliament summoned by EDWARD I in 1295. For the first time, knights of the shire and burgesses (representatives of the Commons) dealt with the affairs of the nation with the king and magnates. This enlargement of the Commons' function was held to be the model for the future.

modem (modulator-demodulator) Electronic device for sending and receiving COMPUTER signals through a telephone system. The electrical pulses produced by a computer are fed into a modem, which uses the pulses to modulate a continuous tone (carrier) by a process called FREQUENCY MODULATION (FM). At the other end, another modem extracts the pulses (demodulation), so that they can be fed into a receiving computer. *See also* COMPUTER NETWORK; INTERNET

modern dance Dance style that began to develop during the late 19th century as a protest against classical BALLET. It is often said to have been pioneered by Isadora Duncan.

modernism 20th-century movement in art, architecture, design and literature that, in general, concentrates on space and form, rather than content or ornamentation. In architecture and design, early influences were BAUHAUS (1919–33) and individuals such as Walter GROPIUS and Mies van der Rohe. Modernism developed the use of new building materials, such as glass, steel and concrete. While difficult to define and date precisely, the echoes of literary modernism can still be heard in late-20th-century fiction. The most recognizably distinct form is the STREAM OF CONSCIOUSNESS narrative, used by Virginia WOOLF and in James JOYCE's seminal modernist novel, *Ulysses* (1922). The outstanding example of modernist poetry is the fragmentary *The Wasteland* (1922) by T.S. ELIOT. Literary modernism exhibits an increasing concern with psychological states and the subconscious. Artists such as PICASSO and Marcel DUCHAMP adopted new techniques of representation and worked in previously unexploited media. The movements of DADA and SURREALISM were vital to this new experimentation. In music, composers such as STRAVINSKY challenged previously held notions of tonality. *See also* POST-MODERNISM

Modigliani, Amedeo (1884–1920) Italian painter, sculptor and draughtsman. Many of his sculptures portray elongated heads, inspired by African masks and caryatids. During World War 1 he returned to painting, focusing mainly on erotic female nudes and portraits.

modulation In physics, process of varying the characteristics of one wave system in accordance with those of another. It is basic to RADIO broadcasting. In AMPLITUDE MODULATION (AM), the amplitude of a high-frequency radio carrier wave is varied in accordance with the frequency of a current generated by a sound wave. For short-range broadcasting FREQUENCY MODULATION (FM) is used, in which the carrier wave's frequency is modulated.

Mogadishu Capital and chief port of Somalia, on the Indian Ocean. In the 16th century it was captured by the Portuguese and became a cornerstone of their trade with Africa. In 1871 control passed to the sultan of Zanzibar, who sold (1905) the port to the Italians. Mogadishu was made the capital of Italian Somaliland. In 1960 Mogadishu became the capital of independent Somalia. During the 1980s and early 1990s the city was devastated by civil war, its population swollen by refugees escaping famine and drought in the outlying regions. In 1992 UN troops were flown into Mogadishu to control aid distribution, but withdrew in 1995 after little success. Pop. (1990 est.) 1,200,000.

Mogul empire (1526–1857) Muslim empire in India. It was founded by BABUR, who conquered Delhi and Agra (1526). The Mogul empire reached its height under Akbar (r.1556–1605), Babur's grandson, when it extended from Afghanistan to the Bay of Bengal and as far S as the Deccan. Mogul art and architecture reached a peak under SHAH JAHAN (1627–58), builder of the TAJ MAHAL. By the death of AURANGZEB (1707), the Mogul dynasty was in decline. The last Mogul emperor was deposed by the British in 1858.

Mohammed Alternative spelling of MUHAMMAD

Mohawk Iroquoian-speaking Native North American tribe of the Iroquois confederacy, formerly inhabiting central New York State. Today there are about 2,000 Mohawks.

Mohican (Mahican) Algonquian-speaking tribe of Native North Americans, formerly inhabiting the upper Hudson valley in New York, and the area E of the Housatonic River in Connecticut, USA. They once numbered about 3,000. Today only *c*.525 Mohicans survive.

Moho (Mohorovičić discontinuity) Boundary between the Earth's CRUST and MANTLE, first recognised in 1909. It is identified by a sharp increase in the velocity of seismic waves passing through the Earth. The velocity increase is explained by a change to more dense rocks in the mantle. The depth of the Moho varies from *c*.5km (3mi) to 60km (37mi) below the Earth's surface.

Moholy-Nagy, László (1895–1946) Hungarian designer, painter and sculptor. He was a founder of CONSTRUCTIVISM. He taught at the BAUHAUS (1923–28) before working in Berlin as a stage designer and film-maker. In 1937 he emigrated to the USA and became director of the New Bauhaus.

Moi, Daniel (Torotich) Arap (1924–) Kenyan political leader, president (1978–). He succeeded KENYATTA as president. He continued with liberal economic reforms, but was criticized for his repressive rule. He was re-elected in 1992.

Mojave Desert Arid region with low, barren mountains in S California, USA, surrounded by mountain ranges on the N and W, and the Colorado Desert on the SE. It was formed by volcanic eruptions and deposits from the Colorado River. Area: *c*.38,850sq km (15,000sq mi).

Moldavia Historic Balkan region, between the CARPATHIAN MOUNTAINS in Romania and the DNIEPER River in MOLDAVA. Under Roman rule it formed the major part of the province of Dacia. In 1504 Moldavia was conquered by the Turks and remained part of the Ottoman empire until the 19th century. In 1859 the twin principalities of Moldavia and Wallachia were united under one crown to form ROMANIA. Russia re-occupied S Bessarabia in 1878. In 1924 the Soviet republic of Moldavia was formed, which was enlarged in 1947 to include Bessarabia and N Bukovina. In 1989 the Moldovans asserted their independence by making Romanian the official language. In 1991 Moldavia became the independent republic of MOLDOVA.

Moldova Republic in E Europe; the capital is CHISINAU. **Land and climate** Moldova is a mostly hilly country, except for a large S plain. The main river is the Dniester, which flows through E Moldova. Moldova has warm summers and fairly cold winters. Most rainfall occurs in summer. In the drier S, most of the region is used for farming. **Economy** Moldova is a lower-middle-income developing economy. Agriculture is important. Major products include fruits, grapes for wine-making, maize, sugar beet, tobacco and wheat. Moldova has few natural resources and has to import materials and fuels for its industries. Major manufactures include agricultural machinery and domestic appliances. Leading exports include food, wine, tobacco, tex-

MOLDOVA	
AREA: 33,700 sq km (13,010 sq mi)	
POPULATION: 4,458,000	
CAPITAL (POPULATION): Chisinau (700,000)	
GOVERNMENT: Multiparty republic	
ETHNIC GROUPS: Moldovan 65%, Ukrainian 14%, Russian 13%, Gagauz 4%, Jewish 2%, Bulgarian	
LANGUAGES: Moldovan (Romanian) (official)	
RELIGIONS: Christianity (Eastern Orthodox)	
CURRENCY: Leu	

tiles and footwear. **History** (For history pre-1991, *see* MOLDAVIA) Following independence in 1991, the majority Moldovan population wished to rejoin Romania, but this alienated the Ukrainian and Russian populations E of the Dniester, who declared their independence. War raged between the two, with the Dniester region supported by the Russian army. A cease-fire was declared in August 1992. The former communists of the Agrarian Democratic Party won 1994 multiparty elections, and a referendum rejected reunification with Romania. Parliament voted to join the Commonwealth of Independent States (CIS). **Politics** Under the new 1994 constitution Moldova is a presidential parliamentary republic. In 1995 President Snegur resigned from the Agrarian Democratic Party and, despite promises of greater autonomy, the Dniester region voted in favour of independence in a referendum. Russian troops began to withdraw. In 1996 presidential elections Petru Lucinschi defeated Snegur. Negotiations continued concerning the normalization of relations between Moldova and the breakaway Dnestr Moldovian Republic.

mole SI unit (symbol mol) of amount of substance. A mole is the amount of substance that contains as many elementary units, such as atoms and molecules, as there are atoms in 0.012kg of carbon-12. A mass of one mole of a compound is its relative molecular mass (molecular weight) in grams.

mole Any of several species of small, burrowing, mainly insectivorous mammals that live in various habitats worldwide. The European mole, *Talpa europaea*, has short brown or black fur, a short tail and wide clawed forefeet for digging tunnels. Its eyes are sensitive only to bright light. Length: to 18cm (7in). Family Talpidae.

molecular biology Biological study of the make-up and function of molecules found in living organisms. Major areas of study include the chemical and physical properties of proteins and of nucleic acids such as DNA. *See also* BIOCHEMISTRY

molecule Smallest particle of a substance (such as a compound) that exhibits the properties of that substance. Molecules consist of two or more atoms held together by chemical bonds. Water molecules consist of two atoms of hydrogen bonded to one atom of oxygen (H_2O). A molecule (unlike an ION) has no electrical charge. *See also* MACROMOLECULE

Molière (1622–73) French playwright, b. Jean-Baptiste Poquelin. An accurate observer of contemporary modern manners, he is regarded as the founder of modern French comedy. His best-known comedies include *Tartuffe* (1661), *The Misanthrope* (1667) and *The Miser* (1669). His work found favour with Louis XIV but was unpopular with church leaders. His last play was *The Imaginary Invalid*.

mollusc Any of more than 80,000 species of invertebrate animals in the phylum Mollusca. They include snails, clams, squids, and a host of less well-known forms. Originally marine, members of the group are now also found in freshwater and on land. There are six classes: the GASTROPODS, CHITONS, univalves (slugs and snails), BIVALVES, tusk shells and CEPHALOPODA. The mollusc body is divided into three: the head, the foot and the visceral mass. Associated with the body is a fold of skin (the mantle) that secretes the limy shell typical of most molluscs. The head is well developed only in snails and in the cephalopods. The visceral mass contains the internal organs. The sexes are usually separate but there are many hermaphroditic species.

Molotov, Vyacheslav Mikhailovich (1890–1986) Soviet politician. A loyal ally of STALIN, he was foreign minister (1939–49, 1953–56). He signed the Nazi-Soviet Pact (1939). He lost favour under KHRUSHCHEV and was expelled from the party in 1962, but later readmitted.

Moluccas (Maluku) Island group and province in E Indonesia, between Sulawesi (W) and New Guinea (E); the capital is Ambon. The fabled Spice Islands were originally explored by Magellan in the early 16th century. The Dutch took the islands in the 17th century and monopolized the spice trade. After Indonesian independence the S Moluccas became the focus of a movement for secession. Products: spices, copra, timber, sago. Area: 74,505sq km (28,759sq mi). Pop. (1990) 1,857,790.

molybdenum Silvery-white metallic element (symbol Mo); one of the TRANSITION ELEMENTS. It was first isolated in 1782. Its chief ore is molybdenite. Hard but malleable and ductile, it is used in alloy steels, x-ray tubes, and missile parts; molybdenum compounds are used as catalysts and lubricants. It is one of the essential TRACE ELEMENTS for plant growth. Properties: at.no. 42; r.a.m. 95.94; r.d. 10.22; m.p. 2,610°C (4,730°F); b.p. 5,560°C (10,040°F); most stable isotope Mo^{98} (23.78%).

Mombasa City and seaport on the Indian Ocean, SW Kenya, partly on Mombasa Island and partly on the mainland. From the 11th–16th centuries Mombasa was a centre of the Arab slave and ivory trades. Taken by Zanzibar in the mid-19th century, Mombasa passed to Britain in 1887, when it was made capital of the British East Africa Protectorate. Kenya's chief port, Mombasa exports coffee, fruit and grain. Industries: tourism, glass, oil refining, aluminium products. Pop. (1989) 465,000.

moment of a force *See* TORQUE

moment of inertia For a rotating object, the sum of the products formed by multiplying the point masses of the rotating object by the squares of their distances from the axis of the rotation.

momentum Product of the mass and linear velocity of an object. One of the fundamental laws of physics is the principle that the total momentum of any system of objects is conserved at all times, even during and after collisions.

Monaco Principality in S Europe, on the Mediterranean coast, forming an enclave in French territory near the border with Italy; the capital is Monaco-Ville. Ruled by the Grimaldi family from the end of the 13th century, it came under French protection in 1860. The chief source of income is tourism, attracted by the casinos of MONTE CARLO. Area: 1.9sq km (0.7sq mi). Pop. (1990) 29,972.

Monaghan County in Ulster province, NE Republic of Ireland, on the boundary with Northern Ireland; the county town is Monaghan. The S and E are hilly, but the rest of the county is a fertile plain. The Blackwater and the Finn are the chief rivers. It is primarily an agricultural county and the main crops are potatoes, oats and flax. Beef and dairy cattle are raised. Industries: linen-milling, footwear, furniture. Area: 1,290sq km (498sq mi). Pop. (1991) 51,293.

monasticism Ascetic mode of life followed by men and women who have taken religious vows and belong to a recognized Roman Catholic or Orthodox religious order. Christian monasticism is said to have its origins in the late-3rd-century asceticism of the desert hermits of Egypt, St ANTHONY and St Pachomius. In time, this solitary life was replaced by a communal approach, in which community members followed a strict rule. The earliest such rule in Europe was that laid down by St BENEDICT OF NURSIA in the 6th century. Monasticism still embraces community life of enclosed Christian orders, such as the CISTERCIANS and the reformed CARMELITES. There are many orders that combine asceticism with social welfare work and spiritual guidance. Monasticism is also found in HINDUISM, BUDDHISM, JAINISM, and TAOISM.

Monck, George, 1st Duke of Albemarle (1608–70) English soldier. In the CIVIL WAR he fought for CHARLES I (1643–44), was captured and imprisoned (1644–46), and subsequently changed sides. Under CROMWELL, he served in Ireland and was commander-in-chief in Scotland from 1654. After Cromwell's death he led the movement to restore the monarchy (1660). His troops became the first permanent regiment of the British army, the Coldstream Guards.

Mondrian, Piet (1872–1944) Dutch painter, one of the pioneers of ABSTRACT ART. He co-founded the abstract art review *De Stijl*. In 1940 he moved to the USA where his work, such as *Broadway Boogie-Woogie* (1942–43), became more colourful, reflecting his fascination with jazz and dance rhythms.

Monera *See* PROKARYOTAE

Monet, Claude (1840–1926) French painter.

During the 1860s he studied in Paris where he met RENOIR, Sisley and most of the future impressionists. To record the effect of changing light, he painted the same scene several times, for example *The Gare St-Lazare* (1876–78) and *Rouen Cathedral* (1892–94). In 1874 he exhibited *Impression, Sunrise,* which gave the IMPRESSIONISM movement its name. In 1883 he settled in Giverny and produced the *Water-Lily* series (1906–26).

monetarism Economic and monetary theory that argues changes in monetary stability are the principal causes of changes in the economy. It asserts the importance of controlling the money supply as the means of achieving a non-inflationary, stable economy capable of supporting high employment and economic growth. This theory is associated particularly with the views of Milton FRIEDMAN.

Mongol Nomadic people of E central Asia who overran a vast region in the 13th–14th centuries. The different tribes in the area were united by GENGHIS KHAN in the early 13th century and conquered an empire that stretched from the Black Sea to the Pacific Ocean and from Siberia to Tibet. Genghis Khan's possessions were divided among his sons and developed into four khanates, one of which was the empire of the Great Khan (KUBLAI KHAN), which included China. In the 14th century TAMERLANE conquered the Persian and Turkish khanates, and broke up the GOLDEN HORDE.

Mongolia Republic in central Asia; the capital is ULAN BATOR. **Land and climate** Sandwiched between China and Russia, Mongolia is the world's largest landlocked country. High plateaus cover most of Mongolia, with the highest plateau in the w between the ALTAI and Hangai mountains. The Altai Mountains contain Mongolia's highest peaks, rising to 4,362m (14,311ft). The land descends towards the GOBI desert. Ulan Bator lies on the N edge of a desert plateau. Winter temperatures drop to −50°C (−58°F). Summer temperatures are moderated by altitude. Mongolia has large areas of steppe grassland. **Economy** Mongolia is a lower-middle-income developing country. Traditional nomadic life was disrupted by communism: forced collectivization placed many in permanent settlements. Nomads still exist, however, especially in the Gobi Desert. In the mid-20th century, Mongolia

---

MONGOLIA
AREA: 1,566,500sq km (604,826sq mi)
POPULATION: 2,130,000
CAPITAL (POPULATION): Ulan Bator (601,000)
GOVERNMENT: Multiparty republic
ETHNIC GROUPS: Khalkha Mongol 79%, Kazakh 6%
LANGUAGES: Khalkha Mongolian (official)
RELIGIONS: Tibetan Buddhism was once the main religion; reliable recent information is unavailable
CURRENCY: Tugrik = 100 möngö

---

rapidly industrialized, especially the mining of coal, copper, gold and molybdenum. Minerals and fuels now account for *c.*50% of Mongolia's exports. Livestock and animal products remain important. Economic development is hampered by lack of labour and poor infrastructure. **History** In the 13th century, GENGHIS KHAN united the Mongolian peoples and built up a great empire. Under his grandson, KUBLAI KHAN, the Mongol empire extended from Korea and China to E Europe and Mesopotamia. The empire broke up in the late 14th century, and in the early 17th century, Inner Mongolia came under Chinese control. By the late 17th century, Outer Mongolia also became a Chinese province. In 1924 the Mongolian People's Republic was established (Inner Mongolia remained a Chinese province). The Mongolian Peoples's Revolutionary Party (MPRP) became the sole political party. Changes in land ownership prompted the Lama Rebellion (1932), which saw the migration of thousands of people into Inner Mongolia. From the 1950s, Mongolia supported the Soviets in Sino-Soviet disputes. In 1961 Mongolia was accepted into the United Nations. Popular demonstrations led to mulitparty elections in 1990, which were won by the MPRP. **Politics** In 1992 a new constitution confirmed the process of liberalization, enshrining democratic principles. In 1993 President Ochirbat was re-elected. In 1996 the Democratic Union Coalition formed the first non-communist government for more than 70 years. In 1997 Natsagiyn Bagabandi of the MPRP became president.

mongolism *See* DOWN'S SYNDROME

mongoose Small, agile, carnivorous mammal of the CIVET family, native to Africa, S Europe and Asia. It has a slender, thickly furred body and a long, bushy tail. Mongooses eat rodents, insects, eggs, birds and snakes. Length: 46–115cm (18–45in). Family Viverridae.

monism Metaphysical theory that reduces the multiplicity of things to one fundamental reality, usually either physical or mental/spiritual. The term has come to describe a range of philosophies that stress the unity of reality.

monitor Any of several species of powerful lizards that live in Africa, S Asia, Indonesia and Australia, including the KOMODO DRAGON (*Varanus komodoensis*). Most species are dull-coloured with yellow markings; many are semi-aquatic. Length: to 3m (10ft). Family Varanidae.

monk Member of a monastic community living under vows of religious observance such as poverty, chastity and obedience. *See* MONASTICISM

Monk, Thelonious Sphere (1917–82) US jazz pianist. He was a key figure in the development of BEBOP. In the early 1950s he formed his own band, featuring John COLTRANE. His distinctive, idiosyncratic chord structures and dissonances brought humour to the idiom. His greatest compositions, such as "Round Midnight", "Straight No Chaser" and "Epistrophy" have become jazz standards.

monkey Any of a wide variety of mostly tree-dwelling, diurnal, omnivorous PRIMATES that live in the tropics and subtropics. Most monkeys have flat, human-like faces, relatively large brains and grasping hands. They fall into two broad groups – Old World monkeys (family Cercopithecidae) and New World monkeys (Cebidae). The 60 **Old World** species include MACAQUES, BABOONS, BARBARY APES and LANGUR monkeys. They all have non-prehensile tails. They are found from Japan and N China through S Asia and Africa. The 70 species of **New World** monkeys include CAPUCHIN monkeys, SPIDER MONKEYS and MARMOSETS. They are all tree dwellers, and most have prehensile tails. They live in tropical forests of Central and South America.

monkey puzzle (Chilean pine) Evergreen tree native to the South American Andes mountains. It has tangled branches, with spirally arranged, sharp, flat leaves. The female seeds are edible. Height to 45m (150ft). Family Araucariaceae; species *Araucaria araucana*.

Monmouth, James Scott, Duke of (1649–85) English nobleman, illegitimate son of CHARLES II. He became a general and the champion of the Protestants, opposing the succession of the Catholic Duke of York to the English throne. Exiled in 1679, he returned in 1685 to assert his claim to the throne, but the "Monmouth Rebellion" was defeated at the Battle of Sedgemoor by JAMES II, and Monmouth was executed.

monocotyledon Subclass of flowering plants (ANGIOSPERMS) characterized by one seed leaf (COTYLEDON) in the seed embryo; the leaves are usually parallel-veined. Examples include lilies, onions, orchids, palms and grasses. The larger subclass of plants is DICOTYLEDON.

monomer Chemical compound composed of single molecules, as opposed to a POLYMER, which is built up from repeated monomer units. For example, propene (propylene) is the monomer from which polypropene (polypropylene) is made.

mononucleosis, infectious *See* GLANDULAR FEVER

monopoly Sole supplier or producer of a product or service. A monopoly is able to determine levels of output and prices. In many countries there are regulations to limit or prevent monopolies.

monotheism Belief in the existence of a single God. JUDAISM, CHRISTIANITY and ISLAM are the three major monotheistic religions.

monotreme One of an order of primitive mammals that lay eggs. The only monotremes are the PLATYPUS and two species of ECHIDNA, all native to Australasia. The eggs are temporarily transferred to a pouch beneath the female's abdomen where they eventually hatch and are nourished by rudimentary mammary glands. *See also* MARSUPIAL

Monroe, James (1758–1831) Fifth US President (1817–25). He fought in the American Revolution, served as JEFFERSON's lieutenant in the Continental Congress (1783–86), and was governor of Virginia (1790–94). He helped negotiate the LOUISIANA PURCHASE (1803) and was secretary of state (1811–17) under MADISON. He was elected president in 1816 and re-elected, unopposed, in 1820. His administration is noted for its foreign policy successes, including: agreement on the US–Canadian border; the acquisition of Florida and the MONROE DOCTRINE.

Monroe, Marilyn (1926–62) US film star, b. Norma Jean Baker. Following the success of *Gentlemen Prefer Blondes* and *How To Marry A Millionaire* (both 1953), Monroe married baseball legend Joe DiMaggio. She divorced him during the filming of *The Seven Year Itch* (1955). After the making of *Bus Stop* (1956), she married playwright Arthur MILLER. Her talent for comedy acting was realised in *Some Like It Hot* (1959), and her last film *The Misfits* (1961). Her rags-to-riches life and tragic death from a drug overdose is the stuff of Hollywood legend. Her intimate relationships with President Kennedy and his brother Bobby Kennedy fuelled stories of political conspiracy. Countless biographies and dramatizations have ensured that Monroe lives on a mythic symbol of femininity.

Monroe Doctrine Foreign policy statement made by US President James MONROE to Congress in 1823. It asserted US authority over the American continent and declared that European interference in the western hemisphere would be regarded as "dangerous to peace and safety". It also stated that the USA would not become involved in the internal conflicts of Europe.

Monrovia Capital and chief port of Liberia, West Africa, on the estuary of the St Paul River. It was settled in 1822 by freed US slaves on a site chosen by the American Colonization Society. Monrovia exports latex and iron ore. Pop. (1984) 425,000.

monsoon Seasonal reversal of winds, and their associated abrupt weather changes, that blow inshore in summer and offshore in winter. The monsoon occurs annually in S Africa and E Asia and is centred on the Indian subcontinent where it occurs as a distinct rainy season.

monstera Genus of tropical American, climbing or trailing plants with large glossy leaves that are commonly holed or deeply incised. *Monstera deliciosa* is a popular houseplant; it is often called a Swiss-cheese plant. Family Araceae.

Montana State in NW USA, on the Canadian border; the capital is HELENA. The USA acquired the area in the LOUISIANA PURCHASE of 1803. The discovery of gold in 1852 brought mass immigration and the Territory of Montana was organized in 1864. The opening of the Northern Pacific Railroad in 1883 stimulated growth. The W section of Montana is dominated by the ROCKY MOUNTAINS. The E is part of the GREAT PLAINS, drained by the Missouri and Yellowstone rivers. Sheep and cattle are raised on the plains. The principal crops are wheat, hay, barley and sugar beet. The Rockies have large mineral deposits such as copper, silver, gold, zinc, lead and manganese. Oil, natural gas and coal are found in the SE. Industries: timber, petroleum products. Tourism is important. Area: 381,086sq km (147,137sq mi). Pop. (1990) 799,065.

Mont Blanc Highest peak in the Alps and the second-highest peak in Europe, lying on the border between France and Italy. It was first climbed in 1786. Height: 4,810m (15,781ft).

Monte Carlo Town in N MONACO, on the Mediterranean coast. It was founded in 1858 by Prince Charles III of Monaco. The Casino is a great tourist attraction. Pop. (1982) 13,154.

Montenegro (Crna Gora) Constituent republic of YUGOSLAVIA; the capital is Podgorica (formerly Titograd). By 1500 most of Montenegro had fallen to the Ottoman empire. In 1799 Turkey recognized Montenegro's independence. In 1851 a monarchy was established, and in 1878 the sovereignty of the state was formally recognized. In 1914 King Nicholas I declared war on Austria, and Montenegro was quickly overrun by the Austro-German armies. He was deposed in 1918 and Montenegro was united with SERBIA. In 1946 Montenegro became a republic of Yugoslavia. In 1989 the local communist leadership resigned. In the 1990 elections communists were returned to power in Montenegro, but four of the former six Yugoslav republics voted to secede from the union. Montenegro supported Serbia in the establishment of a new, Serb-dominated federation. In a 1992 referendum Montenegro voted to remain part of the rump Yugoslav federation with Serbia. Tension remains high between pro- and anti-independence factions. Montenegro is a mountainous region. Industries: tobacco, grain, stock raising, bauxite mining. Area: 13,812sq km (5,331sq mi). Pop. (1991) 615,035.

Montessori, Maria (1870–1952) Italian educationalist who believed that pre-school children, given an environment rich in manipulative materials and free from restraint, would develop their creative and academic potential.

Monteverdi, Claudio (1567–1643) Italian composer, the first great opera composer. Many of his operas are lost; the surviving ones include *L'Orfeo* (1607) and *L'Incoronazione di Poppea* (1642). He was one of the greatest MADRIGAL composers.

Montevideo Capital of Uruguay, in the S part of the country, on the River Plate. It became the capital in 1828. One of South America's major ports, it is the base of a large fishing fleet and handles most of the country's exports. Industries: textiles, dairy goods, wine and meat. Pop. (1992 est.) 1,383,660.

Montezuma Name of two AZTEC emperors. Montezuma I (r.1440–69) increased the empire by conquest. Montezuma II (r.1502–20) was captured by Spanish colonizers led by CORTÉS.

Montfort, Simon de, EARL of Leicester (1208–65) French–born leader of the barons' revolt against HENRY III of England. He was forced to flee, but returned as leader of the rebels in the Barons' War in 1263. He won the Battle of Lewes (1264) but was defeated and killed by the future EDWARD I.

Montgolfier, Joseph Michel (1740–1810) and **Jacques Étienne** (1745–99) French inventors of the hot-air balloon. In November 1783 the brothers launched the first balloon to carry humans.

Montgomery, Bernard Law, 1st Viscount Montgomery of Alamein (1887–1976) British general. As commander of the British Eighth Army in World War 2, he led the successful North Africa campaign, beginning with the defeat of ROMMEL at EL ALAMEIN. He led the invasion of Sicily and Italy. He helped plan the Normandy landings (1944), and, under the command of General EISENHOWER, led the Allies in the initial stages. He was Deputy Supreme Allied Commander, Europe, (1951–58).

Montgomery State capital of Alabama, USA, in SE central Alabama. Made state capital in 1847, in 1861 it became the first capital of the Confederate States of America. In the 1950s it was the scene of the beginnings of the civil rights movement. Industries: textiles, fertilizers. Pop. (1990) 187,106.

Montpelier State capital of Vermont, USA, in the N central part of the state. First settled in the 1780s, it became state capital in 1805. Industries: tourism, machinery. Pop. (1990) 8,247.

Montpellier City in S France; capital of Hérault département. In the 1960s the population grew rapidly with an influx Algerian refugees. Industries: textiles, metal goods, wine, printed materials, chemicals. Pop. (1990) 207,996.

Montreal City on Montreal Island and the N bank of the St Lawrence River, S Quebec province, Canada. Montreal is Canada's chief port and second-largest city. The site was settled by the French in 1642. Montreal's growth accelerated with the opening of the Lachine Canal in 1825, connecting it to the Great Lakes. Montreal served (1844–49) as the seat of the Canadian government. Industries: aircraft, electrical equipment, textiles, oil refining, metallurgy, chemicals. Pop. (1990) 1,017,666.

Montserrat British dependent territory in the West Indies, a volcanic island in the Lesser Antilles group; the capital is Plymouth. Discovered in 1493 by Christopher Columbus, it was colonized in 1632 by the British. It formed part of the Leeward Island colony (1871–1956), then became a Dependent Territory. In 1997 increased volcanic activity prompted the British government to offer an aid package to the remaining islanders for rehousing in the N or relocation to neighbouring islands. Cotton is the major product. Area: 102sq km (40sq mi). Pop. (1991) 11,597.

Moon Natural satellite of a planet; in particular the natural satellite of the planet EARTH. Apart from the Sun it is the brightest object in the sky as seen from the Earth because of its proximity, being at a mean distance of only 384,000km (239,000mi). Its diameter is 3,476km (2,160mi). The Earth and Moon revolve around a common centre of gravity. As the Moon orbits the Earth, it is seen to go through a sequence of PHASES, as the proportion of the illuminated hemisphere visible o us changes. An observer on Earth always sees the same side of the Moon because its orbital period around the Earth is the same as its axial rotation period. The surface features may be broadly divided into the darker **maria**, which are low-lying volcanic plains, and the brighter highland regions (sometimes called terrae), which are found predominantly in the southern part of the Moon's nearside and over the entire farside. The origin of the Moon is uncertain. A current theory is that a Mars-sized body collided with the newly formed Earth, and debris from the impact formed the Moon. Lunar rocks are IGNEOUS ROCKS. The Moon has only the most tenuous of atmospheres. The surface temperature variation is extreme, from 100 to 400K. *See also* APOLLO PROGRAM

Moore, Brian (1921–) Canadian novelist, b. Northern Ireland. His works examine the nature of religions and sexual guilt. Novels include *The Lonely Passion of Miss Judith Hearne* (1955), *Lies of Silence* (1990) and *The Statement* (1995).

Moore, Henry (1898–1986) British sculptor and graphic artist. He is acknowledged as one of the greatest sculptors of the 20th century. The most characteristic features of his art are hollowed-out or pierced spaces. He based most of his work on natural forms, such as mother and child. Many of his sculptures are placed in parks rather than galleries.

moorhen (waterhen) Common Old World aquatic bird of the RAIL family, so named because of its liking for rivers and ponds. It has black plumage and a yellow bill, and its long toes lack the webs or lobes typical of other water birds. Length: to 32.5cm (13in). Species *Gallinula chloropus*.

Moors Name given to the predominantly BERBER people of NW Africa. In Europe the name is applied particularly to North African Muslims who invaded Spain in 711 and established a distinctive civilization that lasted nearly 800 years. It was at its height under the Cordoba CALIPHS in the 10th–11th centuries. The Christian rulers of N Spain gradually reconquered the country. GRANADA, the last refuge of the Moors in Spain, fell in 1492.

moose *See* ELK

moraine General term indicating a mound, ridge or other visible accumulation of unsorted glacial drift, predominantly TILL. End moraines are formed when a GLACIER is either advancing or retreating and the rock material is dumped at the glacier's edge. Ground moraines are sheets of debris left after a steady retreat of the glacier.

morality play *See* MYSTERY PLAY

Moravia Region of the CZECH REPUBLIC, bordered N by the Sudetes Mountains, E by the Carpathian Mountains and W by Bohemia. Major cities include BRNO. A fertile agricultural region, Moravia also has abundant mineral resources, such as coal and iron, which have aided rapid industrialization. In the 9th century Moravia built a large empire and adopted Christianity. From the 11th to 16th century, it formed part of BOHEMIA. In 1526 it became Austri-

an HABSBURG territory and a process of Germanification was begun. In 1918 the Habsburgs were deposed and Moravia was incorporated into the new republic of Czechoslovakia. In 1938 s Moravia was annexed by Germany. Following World War 2, Moravia was restored to Czechoslovakia.

Moravia, Alberto (1907–90) Italian novelist. Early novels, such as *The Fancy Dress Party* (1940), were critical of fascism, and he was forced into hiding until 1944. Later works include *The Woman of Rome* (1947), *The Conformist* (1951) and *Two Women* (1957).

More, Sir Thomas (1478–1535) English scholar and statesman. He was a leading exponent of HUMANISM. His most famous work, *Utopia* (1516), portrays an ideal state founded on reason. More succeeded Cardinal WOLSEY as lord chancellor (1529) but, unhappy at HENRY VIII's break with the pope, resigned in 1532. He enraged the king by refusing to subscribe to the Act of Supremacy, and in 1535 he was executed for treason.

Moreau, Gustave (1826–98) French painter and leading practitioner of SYMBOLISM. His pictures are sensuous with jewel-like colours. He was professor at the École des Beaux-Arts, Paris.

Morgan, Thomas Hunt (1866–1945) US biologist who was awarded the 1933 Nobel Prize in physiology or medicine for the establishment of the CHROMOSOME theory of HEREDITY. His discovery of the function of chromosomes through experiments with the fruit-fly (*Drosophila*) is related in his book *The Theory of the Gene* (1926).

Mormons (Church of Jesus Christ of Latter-day Saints) ADVENTIST sect established by Joseph SMITH in 1830 in New York, USA. Believing that they were to found a New Jerusalem, Smith and his followers moved west. They tried to settle in Ohio, Missouri, and Illinois, but were driven out. Joseph Smith was murdered in Illinois in 1844. Brigham YOUNG became leader, and in 1846–47 took the Mormons to UTAH.

Morocco Country in NW Africa; the capital is RABAT. **Land and climate** Morocco is separated from Europe by the narrow Strait of Gibraltar. The majority of the population live on the narrow W coastal plain, which includes Rabat, CASABLANCA (the largest city), TANGIER and AGADIR. The ATLAS mountains dominate central Morocco, and Djebel Toubkal (in the Haut Atlas) is the highest peak in North Africa, at 4,165m (13,665ft). The Rif Atlas lie in the far N. Between the Atlas mountains and the coastal plain lies a broad plateau, which includes the cities of FEZ and MARRAKECH. Southern Morocco forms part of the SAHARA Desert, which continues into the disputed territory of WESTERN SAHARA. The fertile Atlantic coast is cooled by the Canaries Current. Inland, summers are hot and dry. During the mild winters (October to April) SW winds from the Atlantic bring moderate rainfall, and snow on the Haut Atlas. The Sahara is barren. Forests of cedar, fir and juniper swathe the moun-

425

tain slopes. **Economy** The post-independence exodus of Europeans and Jews from Morocco created an economic vacuum. The cost of war in Western Sahara further strained Morocco's scant resources. Morocco is a lower-middle-income developing country (1992 GDP per capita, US$3,370). Its main resource is phosphates: Morocco is the world's fourth-largest producer and processes 75% of the world's phosphate reserves. Agriculture employs 46% of the workforce. In the mountains, most agriculture is undertaken by nomadic pastoralists. The chief commercial farming areas are the Atlantic coastal plains and the inland plateaux. The main crops include barley, beans, fruits, grapes, maize, olives, sugar beet and wheat. Casablanca is the chief manufacturing city and largest port. Tourism contributes over US$1,360 million annual receipts. In 1996 Morocco and Spain agreed to build a tunnel linking the two countries. **History** In c.AD 685 Morocco was invaded by Arab armies, who introduced Islam and Arabic. In 711 Moroccan Muslims (MOORS) invaded Spain. In 788 BERBERS and Arabs were united in an independent Moroccan state. In the mid-11th century the ALMORAVIDS conquered Morocco and established a vast Muslim empire. They were succeeded by the ALMOHAD dynasty. In 1660 the present ruling dynasty, the Alawite, came to power. In 1912 Morocco was divided into French Morocco and the smaller protectorate of Spanish Morocco. Abd al-Krim led a revolt (1921–26) against European rule. In 1947 Sultan Sidi Muhammad called for the reunification of the French and Spanish Morocco. In 1956 Morocco gained independence. In 1957 Morocco became an independent monarchy when Sidi Muhammad changed his title to King Muhammad V. In 1961 Muhammad was succeeded by his son, King HASSAN II. In 1965 Hassan II declared a state of emergency and assumed extraordinary powers. While the 1972 constitution reduced royal influence, the king effectively wields all political power. In 1976 Spain finally relinquished its claim to Spanish Sahara, and the region became known as Western Sahara. Western Sahara was divided between Morocco and Mauritania. In 1979 Morocco assumed full control of the phosphate-rich region. (*See* WESTERN SAHARA for political developments) **Politics** The collapse of several coalition governments in 1993 led to King Hassan's appointment of an administration. In 1994 Morocco restored diplomatic links with Israel. In 1995 Hassan formed a new government of technocrats and independents. In 1996 a referendum approved amendments to the constitution, to allow for the introduction of a bicameral legislature.

Moroni Capital of the COMOROS Islands, on sw Grande Comore. Founded by Arab settlers, it replaced Mayotte as capital in 1958. Exports: coffee, vanilla, cacao, timber. Pop. (1988 est.) 22,000.

morphine White, crystalline ALKALOID derived from OPIUM. It depresses the CENTRAL NERVOUS SYSTEM and is used as an ANALGESIC. An addictive drug, side-effects can include nausea. Morphine was first isolated in 1806. *See also* HEROIN

morphology Biological study of the form and structure of living things. It focuses on the relation between similar features in different organisms.

Morris, William (1834–96) British artist, craftsman, writer, social reformer and printer. In 1861 he founded the ARTS AND CRAFTS MOVEMENT, a collection of decorators and designers influenced by medieval craftsmanship. Morris is perhaps best remembered for his wallpaper designs, which anticipated ART NOUVEAU in their use of the S-curve. In the 1880s he became interested in socialism, writing *The Dream of John Ball* (1886–87) and *News from Nowhere* (1890).

Morrison, Toni (1931–) US writer, b. Chloe Anthony Wofford, one of the most distinguished African-American writers. Her books, which experiment with narrative voice and time, include *The Bluest Eye* (1970), *Song of Solomon* (1977), *Tar Baby* (1981), *Beloved* (1987) and *Jazz* (1992). She was awarded the 1993 Nobel Prize for Literature.

Morse, Samuel Finley Breese (1791–1872) US inventor of the **Morse code**. His receiver was based on an electromagnet. Using a simple system of dots and dashes, he set up the first US telegraph from Washington to Baltimore in 1844.

mosaic Technique of surface decoration using small pieces of coloured material set tightly together in an adhesive to form patterns or pictures. The technique was employed for floor and wall decorations in ancient Mesopotamia and Greece. Roman mosaics often featured a central design or a portrait, surrounded by a decorative geometric border. The art developed rapidly in early Christian times.

Moscow (Moskva) Capital of Russia and largest city in Europe, on the River Moskva. In 1367 the first stone walls of the KREMLIN were constructed and Moscow emerged as the focus of Russian opposition to the Mongols. Moscow was the capital of the Grand Duchy of Russia (1547–1712). In 1812 Napoleon occupied Moscow but was forced to flee when the city burned to the ground. In 1918, following the Bolshevik Revolution, it became the capital of the SOVIET UNION. The failure of the German army to seize the city in 1941 was the Nazis' first major setback in World War 2. The Kremlin is the centre of the city and the administrative heart of

---

MOROCCO

AREA: 446,550sq km (172,413sq mi)
POPULATION: 26,318,000
CAPITAL (POPULATION): Rabat (518,616)
GOVERNMENT: Constitutional monarchy
ETHNIC GROUPS: Arab 70%, Berber 30%
LANGUAGES: Arabic (official)
RELIGIONS: Islam 99%, Christianity 1%
CURRENCY: Moroccan dirham = 100 centimes

Russia. Adjoining it are Red Square, the Lenin Mausoleum and the 16th-century cathedral of Basil the Beatified. Industries: metalworking, oil-refining, motor vehicles, film-making, precision instruments, chemicals, publishing, wood and paper products, tourism. Pop. (1993) 8,881,000.

Moscow Art Theatre Russian theatre, famous for its contribution to naturalistic theatre. It was founded in 1898 by STANISLAVSKY and Nemirovich-Danchenko. The original company was composed of amateur actors from the Society of Art and Literature. It was here that Stanislavsky developed the principles of method acting.

Moses (active *c*.13th century BC) Biblical hero, who as a prophet and leader of the ancient Hebrew people was the central figure in the Jews' liberation from bondage in Egypt and the founding of Israel. His story is recounted in the Old Testament books of Exodus and Numbers. Moses sought to lead the Hebrews out of Egypt, and eventually was permitted to lead the EXODUS. God revealed himself to Moses on Mount Sinai, but made the Israelites wander in the desert for a further 40 years before they entered the promised land of CANAAN.

Moslem *See* MUSLIM

Mosley, Sir Oswald Ernald (1896–1980) British politician, founder of the British Union of Fascists (1932). The black-shirted fascists were virulently anti-Semitic. Mosley's outspoken support of Hitler led to his internment during World War 2.

mosque Islamic place of worship. Mosques are usually decorated with abstract and geometric designs, because ISLAM prohibits the imitation of God's creation. The building's parts include: a DOME, a *mihrab* (prayer niche), which shows the direction of MECCA; a MINARET, from which the muezzin calls the faithful to prayer; and a *sahn* (courtyard) often with a central fountain for ritual ablution. The complex often includes a *madrassa* (school). *See also* ISLAMIC ART AND ARCHITECTURE

Mosquito Coast (Mosquitia) Coastal region bordering on the Caribbean Sea, *c*.65km (40mi) wide, now divided between Nicaragua and Honduras. In 1894 it became part of Nicaragua. International arbitration awarded the N part to Honduras in 1960. The region, which consists mainly of tropical forest, swamp and lagoons, is only thinly populated.

mosquito Long-legged, slender-winged insect, found worldwide. The female sucks blood from warm-blooded animals. Some species carry the parasites of diseases, including MALARIA, YELLOW FEVER, DENGUE, viral ENCEPHALITIS and FILARIASIS. The larvae are aquatic. Adult length: 3–9mm (0.12–0.36in) Family Culicidae.

moss Any of about 14,000 species of small, simple non-flowering green plants that typically grow in colonies, often forming dense carpets. They reproduce by means of SPORES produced in a capsule on a long stalk. The spores germinate into branching filaments, from which buds arise that grow into moss plants. Mosses in a wide variety of land habitats, especially in shady damp places. *See also* ALTERNATION OF GENERATIONS; BRYOPHYTE

motet Musical form prominent in all choral church music from *c*.1200–1600. In the 13th and 14th centuries it consisted of three unaccompanied voice parts. The Renaissance motet, usually in four or five parts, was contrapuntal in style. PALESTRINA composed some of the purest examples of the form.

moth Insect of the order LEPIDOPTERA, found in almost all parts of the world. It is distinguished from a BUTTERFLY mainly by its non-clubbed antennae, though there are a few exceptions. Most moths are nocturnal. Like a butterfly, a moth undergoes METAMORPHOSIS. It has a long coiled proboscis for sipping the nectar of flowers.

motor Mechanism that converts energy into useful work, sometimes applied to the internal combustion ENGINE but more often applied to the ELECTRIC MOTOR. ROCKET engines are motors that can leave the Earth's atmosphere because they carry both fuel and oxidizer. Ion motors for spacecraft are in development. A stream of ions, possibly from a nuclear reactor, is accelerated in a strong electrostatic field to produce a reaction that drives the spacecraft.

motorcycle Powered vehicle, usually with two wheels. Gottlieb DAIMLER is credited with building (1885) the first practical motorcycle. Motorcycles are classified in terms of engine capacity, usually 50cc to 1200cc. Transmission of power to the rear wheel is by chain, shaft or belt. The clutch, accelerator and front brake controls are on the handlebars. Foot pedals control the gears and rear brake.

motorcycle racing Sport in which motorcyclists compete on various surfaces, such as tarmac, cross country (scrambling and trials), or cinder (speedway). Road-racing motorcyclists contest an annual world championship of Grands Prix in Europe, South and North America, and Japan.

motor nerve NERVE carrying messages to the muscles from the BRAIN via the SPINAL CORD. The cell bodies of some motor NERVES form part of the spinal cord. Motor nerves are involved in both reflex action and voluntary muscular control.

mould Mass composed of the spore-bearing mycelia (vegetative filaments) and fruiting bodies produced by numerous fungi. Many moulds live dead organic material. Roquefort and stilton cheeses involve the use of mould. Although many species are pathogenic (disease-causing), PENICILLIN and a few other ANTIBIOTICS are obtained from moulds. *See also* FUNGICIDE; FUNGUS; SLIME MOULD

mountain Part of the Earth's surface that rises steeply at least 380m (1,250ft) higher than the surrounding area. They are identified geologically by their most characteristic features, and are classified as FOLD, volcanic, or fault-block mountains. Mountains may occur as single isolated masses, as ranges or in systems or chains.

mountain lion *See* PUMA

Mountbatten, Louis, 1st Earl Mountbatten of Burma (1900–79) British admiral. He had a distinguished World War 2 naval career. As Allied commander-in-chief in SE Asia, he led operations against the Japanese in Burma. In 1947 he became India's last viceroy, presiding over Britain's evacuation of India. He was murdered by an Irish Republican Army (IRA) bomb.

Mount Rushmore Mountain in the Black Hills, SW South Dakota, USA. The colossal busts of US presidents Washington, Jefferson, Lincoln and Theodore Roosevelt were carved out of the granite face of Mount Rushmore by Gutzon Borglum from 1927. The work was completed by his son.

mouse Any of numerous species of small, common RODENTS found in a variety of habitats worldwide; especially the omnivorous, brown-grey house mouse (*Mus musculus*) of the family Muridae. This prolific nest-builder, often associated with human habitation, is considered a destructive pest and is believed to carry disease-producing organisms. It may grow as long as 20cm (8in). Many species within the family Cricetidae are also called mice, as are pocket mice (Heteromydiae), jumping mice (Zapodidae) and marsupial mice (Dasyuridae).

Mozambique Republic in SE Africa; the capital is MAPUTO. **Land and climate** Mozambique faces the Indian Ocean. The coastline is dotted with the mouths of many rivers, including the LIMPOPO and the ZAMBEZI. The coast is fringed by swamps and offshore coral reefs. The only natural harbour is Maputo. Coastal plains make up 50% of Mozambique's land area. Inland, a savanna plateau rises to highlands at the frontiers with Zimbabwe, Zambia, Malawi and Tanzania. Mozambique has a tropical climate. The warm, south-flowing Mozambique Current gives Maputo hot, humid summers. Winters are mild and fairly dry. Tropical savanna is the most widespread vegetation. **Economy** Mozambique is one of the world's poorest countries (1992 GDP per capita, US$380). Agriculture employs 85% of the workforce, mainly at subsistence level. Crops include cassava, cotton, cashew nuts, rice, sugar cane and tea. Fishing is also important. Shrimps, sugar and copra are exported. Electricity is exported to South Africa. **History and politics** Vasco da GAMA was the first European to discover Mozambique in 1498. During the 16th century Por-

tuguese adventurers built huge, semi-autonomous plantations. In the 18th and 19th centuries, Mozambique was a major centre of the slave trade. In 1910 Mozambique formally became a Portuguese colony. In 1964 the Front for the Liberation of Mozambique (FRELIMO) launched a guerrilla war. In 1975 Mozambique gained independence, and Samora Machel became president. Many Europeans fled the country, taking vital capital and resources. The new FRELIMO government established a one-party Marxist state. FRELIMO's assistance to liberation movements in Rhodesia (now Zimbabwe) and South Africa was countered by these white-minority regimes' support of the Mozambique National Resistance Movement (RENAMO) opposition. Civil war raged for 16 years, claiming tens of thousands of lives. In 1986 Samora Machel died and was succeeded by Joachim Chissano. In 1992, faced with severe drought and famine, a peace agreement was signed between FRELIMO and RENAMO. In 1994 Chissano was elected president. In 1995 Mozambique joined the Commonwealth of Nations.

Mozart, Wolfgang Amadeus (1756–91) Austrian composer. A child prodigy on the piano, he was taken by his father, Leopold, on tours in Europe (1762–65), during which he composed his first symphonies. In the 1770s he worked at the Prince Archbishop's court in Salzburg. Masses, symphonies and his first major piano concerto date from this time. In the 1780s he moved to Vienna, becoming court composer to the Austrian emperor in 1787. In this decade he composed and performed his greatest piano concertos, the last eight of his 41 symphonies and the brilliant comic operas *Le Nozze di Figaro* (1786), *Don Giovanni* (1787) and *Così fan tutti* (1790). In the last year of his life, Mozart wrote the operas *Die Zauberflöte* and *La Clemenza di Tito*, the clarinet concerto and the *Requiem* (completed by a pupil). In all, he composed more than 600 works, perfecting the CLASSICAL style and foreshadowing ROMANTICISM.

Mubarak, Hosni (1928–) Egyptian statesman, president (1981–). Vice president under SADAT (1975–81), he became president on his assassination. He continued Sadat's moderate policies, improving relations with Israel and the West. He gained Egypt's readmission to the Arab League (1989). He has struggled to repress the growth of Islamic fundamentalism.

mucous membrane Sheet of TISSUE (or EPITHELIUM) lining all body channels that communicate with the air, such as the mouth and respiratory tract, the digestive and urogenital tracts, and the various glands that secrete mucus.

Mugabe, Robert Gabriel (1925–) Zimbabwean prime minister (1980–86), president (1987–). He co-founded the Zimbabwe African National Union (ZANU) in 1963. Mugabe was imprisoned in 1964 by Ian SMITH, leader of Rhodesia's white minority regime. Upon his release (1974), he became joint

---

MOZAMBIQUE

AREA: 801,590sq km (309,494sq mi)

POPULATION: 14,872,000

CAPITAL (POPULATION): Maputo (2,000,000)

GOVERNMENT: Multiparty republic

ETHNIC GROUPS: Makua 47%, Tsonga 23%, Malawi 12%, Shona 11%, Yao 4%, Swahili 1%, Makonde 1%

LANGUAGES: Portuguese (official)

RELIGIONS: Traditional beliefs 48%, Christianity (Roman Catholic 31%, others 9%), Islam 13%

CURRENCY: Metical = 100 centavos

---

leader (with Joshua Nkomo) of the Patriotic Front during the war of independence. Mugabe was elected as independent Zimbabwe's first prime minister. Following his re-election (1986) and constitutional changes, Mugabe became executive president. Mugabe was re-elected in 1990 and 1996.

Muhammad (d. *c.*632) Arab prophet and inspirational religious leader who founded ISLAM. He was born in MECCA. Orphaned at the age of six, he went to live with his grandfather and then with his uncle. At the age of 25, he began working as a trading agent for Khadijah, a wealthy widow of 40, whom he married. For 25 years, she was his closest companion and gave birth to several children. Only one bore him grandchildren – his daughter FATIMA, who married his cousin ALI. In *c.*610, Muhammad had a vision while meditating on Mount Hira, outside Mecca. A voice three times commanded him to "recite". Then he heard the first of many revelations that came to him over the next two decades. The revelations came from ALLAH (God), and Muhammad's followers believe that they were passed to him through the angel GABRIEL. At the core of the new religion was the doctrine that there is no God but Allah and His followers must submit to Him. Muhammad gained followers but also enemies among the Meccans. In 622 he fled to MEDINA. MUSLIMS later took this HEJIRA as initiating the first year in their calendar. Thereafter, Muhammad won more followers. He organized rules for the proper worship of Allah and for Islamic society. He also made war against his enemies, and conquered Mecca in 630. In Medina, he married Aishah, the daughter of ABU BAKR. Muhammad is considered an ideal man, but is not held to be divine. His tomb is in the Holy Mosque of the Prophet, in Medina.

Muhammad, Elijah (1897–1975) US African-American nationalist leader, b. Elijah Poole. He became leader of the BLACK MUSLIMS in 1934, following the disappearance of the movement's founder, Wallace D. Fard. The rhetorical skills of MALCOLM X gained the movement national attention, and tensions grew until Malcolm was suspended from the movement. Under Muhammad's leadership, the Muslim doctrines were codified and membership increased.

Muhammad II (1429–81) Ottoman sultan (1451–81), considered to be the true founder of the OTTOMAN EMPIRE. He captured Constantinople (1453) and made it the empire's capital.

Muhammad Ali (1769–1849) Albanian soldier who founded an Egyptian dynasty. In 1798 he took part in an unsuccessful OTTOMAN expeditionary force sent to Egypt to drive out the French. In 1805 he was proclaimed the Ottoman sultan's viceroy. In 1811 he defeated the Mamelukes. He put down a rebellion in Greece in 1821 but his fleet was later destroyed by the European powers at the Battle of NAVARINO in 1827. Muhammad challenged the sultan and began the conquest of Syria in 1831, but the European powers compelled him to withdraw.

Muhammad Riza Pahlavi *See* PAHLAVI, MUHAMMAD REZA SHAH

mulberry Any member of the genus *Morus*, trees and shrubs that grow in tropical and temperate regions. The male flowers are catkins, while the female flowers are borne in spikes. Several species are cultivated for their fleshy, edible fruits.

mule HYBRID offspring of a female horse and a male ass. It has a similar body to a horse, but has the long ears, heavy head and thin limbs of an ass. The mule is often used as a draught or pack animal. It is usually sterile. Height: 1.8m (5.8ft).

mullah Muslim cleric well-versed in the SHARIA. There are no formal qualifications, but he will usually have attended a *madrassa* (religious school).

Muller, Hermann Joseph (1890–1967) US geneticist. He found that he could artificially increase the rate of MUTATIONS in the fruit-fly (*Drosophila*) by the use of x-rays. He thus highlighted the human risk in exposure to radioactive material. For this work he was awarded the 1946 Nobel Prize for physiology or medicine.

mullet (grey mullet) Marine food fish found in shoals in shallow tropical and temperate waters worldwide. Its torpedo-shaped body is green or blue and silver. Size: to about 90cm (3ft); weight: 6.8kg (15lb). Family Mugilidae.

Mulroney, Brian (1939–) Canadian prime minister (1984–93). In 1983 he became leader of the Progressive Conservative Party. As prime minister, he sought to improve US relations and reduce unemployment. He was re-elected in 1988. His popularity declined, due to the prolonged recession, and he resigned as Conservative leader in 1993. He remained prime minister until his successor, Kim Campbell, was elected.

multiple sclerosis Incurable disorder of unknown cause in which there is degeneration of the myelin sheath that surrounds nerves in the brain and spinal cord. Striking mostly young adults (more women than men), it is mainly a disease of the world's temperate zones. Symptoms may include unsteadiness, loss of coordination and speech and visual disturbances. Affected people typically have relapses and remissions over many years.

mummy Human body embalmed and usually wrapped in bandages before burial. The practice was common in ancient EGYPT, where religion decreed that the dead would require the use of their bodies in the afterlife.

mumps Viral disease, most common in children, characterized by fever, pain and swelling of one or both parotid salivary glands (located just in front of the ears). The symptoms are more serious in adults, and in men inflammation of the testes (orchitis) may occur, with the risk of sterility. One attack of mumps generally confers lifelong immunity.

Munch, Edvard (1863–1944) Norwegian painter and printmaker. He was one of the most influential modern artists, inspiring EXPRESSIONISM and the SEZESSION. His tortured, isolated figures and violent colouring caused a scandal when he exhibited in Berlin in 1892. His series of studies of love and death, entitled a *Frieze of Life*, included *The Scream* (1893). Other important works are *Ashes* (1894) and *Virginia Creeper* (1898).

Munich (München) City on the River Isar, s Germany; capital of BAVARIA. Founded in 1158, the city became the residence of the dukes of Bavaria in 1255. From the early 1920s Munich was the centre of the Nazi Party. It sustained heavy bomb damage in World War 2. Industries: chemicals, brewing, pharmaceuticals, motor vehicles, tobacco, precision instruments, tourism. Pop. (1990) 1,241,300.

Munich Agreement Pact agreed in September 1938 by Britain, France, Italy and Germany to settle German claims on Czechoslovakia. Hoping to preserve European peace, Britain and France compelled Czechoslovakia to surrender the SUDETENLAND to Nazi Germany on certain conditions. HITLER ignored the conditions and, six months later, his troops took over the rest of Czechoslovakia, an action that finally ended the policy of APPEASEMENT.

Munich Putsch (Beer-hall Putsch) Attempted coup in 1923 by Adolf HITLER and the Nazi Party to overthrow the republican government of Bavaria. The coup proved abortive and Hitler was arrested and sentenced to five years in the Landsberg fortress. He served only nine months.

Munro, H.H. (Hector Hugh) *See* SAKI

Munster Province in s Republic of Ireland, on the Atlantic coast; largest of Ireland's four provinces. It includes the counties of CLARE, CORK, KERRY, LIMERICK, N and s TIPPERARY and WATERFORD. Area: 24,126sq km (9,315sq mi). Pop. (1991) 1,009,533.

muntjac Small primitive Asian DEER. It is brown with cream markings and has tusk-like canine teeth and short, two-pronged antlers. There are two well known species, the Indian muntjac or barking deer (*Muntiacus muntjak*) and the Chinese muntjac *(M. reevesi)*. Height: to 60cm (24in) at the shoulder; weight: to 18kg (40lb). Family Cervidae.

mural Painting or other design medium applied directly to a wall; a FRESCO is a type of mural. The Egyptians, Greeks and Romans produced murals in TEMPERA as well as fresco. In the Renaissance, mural painting was allied with architecture to create illusions of space. The 20th century has accorded more significance to the exterior mural as exemplified by the works of José Clemente OROZCO and Diego RIVERA. Porcelain and liquid silicate enamels are among the media used in modern murals.

Murcia Autonomous region in SE Spain; the capital is Murcia. It was settled in *c.*225 BC by the Carthaginians, who founded the port of Cartagena and the city of Murcia. In the 11th century Murcia became an independent kingdom, but in the 13th century fell under the control of Castile. Murcia is an arid, rugged province with desert vegetation. Historically, the region has been associated with the production of silk. Area: 11,317sq km (4,368sq mi). Pop. (1991) 1,045,601.

Murdoch, (Jean) Iris (1919–) British novelist and philosopher. Her novels include *Under the Net* (1954), *A Severed Head* (1961), *An Accidental Man* (1971), *The Sea, the Sea* (1978) and *The Philosopher's Pupil* (1983). Her philosophical writings include *Metaphysics as a Guide to Morals* (1992).

Murdoch, (Keith) Rupert (1931–) Australian media tycoon. He quickly made a success of his father's newspaper, *The Adelaide News*, with a recipe of sensationalist journalism. In 1969 he bought the British *News of the World* and in 1970 *The Sun*. He went on to acquire *The Times* and the *Sunday Times*. In 1973 he moved into the US newspaper market, his publications include the *Boston Herald* and the *Star*. In the early 1990s he has diversified his media empire, starting his own satellite television network BSkyB and launching digital cable television.

Murray Longest river in Australia. It flows 2,590km (1,610mi) from the Australian Alps in SE New South Wales through Lake Alexandrina, and empties into the Indian Ocean at Encounter Bay, SE of Adelaide. It forms a large part of the border between New South Wales and Victoria. Its main tributary is the Darling. The Murray valley contains almost all the irrigated land in Australia.

Muscat (Masqat, Maskat) Capital of Oman, on the Gulf of Oman, in the SE Arabian Peninsula. It became the capital in 1741. Industries: fish, dates, natural gas, chemicals. Pop. (1990 est.) 380,000.

muscle Tissue that has the ability to contract, enabling movement. There are three basic types: SKELETAL MUSCLE, smooth muscle and cardiac muscle. **Skeletal** (striped) muscle is the largest tissue component of the human body, comprising *c.*40% by weight. It is attached by TENDONS to the BONES of the SKELETON and is characterized by cross-markings known as striations. **Smooth** muscle lines the digestive tract, blood vessels and many other organs. It is not striated. **Cardiac** muscle is found only in the heart and differs from the other types of muscle in that it beats rhythmically and does not need stimulation by a nerve impulse to contract. *See also* INVOLUNTARY MUSCLE; VOLUNTARY MUSCLE

muscular dystrophy Any of a group of hereditary disorders in which the characteristic feature is progressive weakening and ATROPHY of the muscles. The commonest type, Duchenne muscular dystrophy, affects boys, usually before the age of four. Muscle fibres degenerate, to be replaced by fatty tissue.

muses In classical mythology, nine daughters of the Titan Mnemosyne (memory) and ZEUS. Calliope was the muse of epic poetry, Clio of history, Erato of love poetry, Euterpe of lyric poetry, Polyhymnia of song, Melpomene of tragedy, Terpsichore of choral dance, Thalia of comedy and Urania of astronomy.

mushroom Any of numerous relatively large fleshy fungi, many of which are gathered for food. A typical mushroom consists of two parts: an extensive underground cobwebby network of fine filaments (hyphae), called the mycelium, which is the main body of the fungus, and a short-lived fruiting body (the visible mushroom).

music Sound arranged for instruments or voices, for many purposes, exhibiting a great variety of forms and styles. It can be split into categories, such as ROCK, JAZZ, BLUES, FOLK MUSIC, SOUL MUSIC and COUNTRY AND WESTERN. Within classical music, there are distinct historical periods: MEDIEVAL (1100–1400); RENAISSANCE (1400–1600); BAROQUE (1600–1750); CLASSICAL (1750–c.1800) and Romantic (c.1800–1900) (see ROMANTICISM). In the 20th century, various techniques developed, notably SERIAL MUSIC, TWELVE-TONE MUSIC and IMPRESSIONISM. Composers also experimented with ELECTRONIC MUSIC.

musical Genre of popular dramatic light entertainment, exemplified by firm plot, strong songs and vivacious dance numbers. It developed at the end of the 19th century from elements of light opera, revue and burlesque. The most popular musicals originated in the USA with the work of George GERSHWIN, Jerome Kern, Richard RODGERS, Oscar HAMMERSTEIN and Stephen SONDHEIM. Audiences in the 1970s responded to the works of Andrew LLOYD WEBBER and Tim Rice, such as *Jesus Christ Superstar* (1971) and *Evita* (1978). Lloyd Webber was extremely successful in the 1980s with *Cats* (1981) and *The Phantom of the Opera* (1986). Film musicals, such as *My Fair Lady* (1964) and *The Sound of Music* (1965), are often based on stage originals. Original film musicals include *42nd Street* (1933) and *Singin' in the Rain* (1952).

musical form Structural scheme that gives shape and artistic unity to a composition. The standard forms are binary, ternary, rondo and sonata. Each consists of a number of musical sections or subsections. **Binary** form consists of two sections, which may be contrasted in idea, key or tempo but which complement each other within the musical entity. **Ternary** form consists of a re-statement of the first section after a middle section of contrasted material; an example is the minuet and trio. In **rondo** form, the number of sections varies, but there is at least one restatement of the first section. **Sonata** form evolved with the SONATA and is used most often for the first movement of a sonata or symphony. The exposition states two subjects, which are developed musically in the middle section, before being reworked in the recapitulation.

musical notation Method of writing down music – the language of music. Staff notation defines the absolute and relative pitches of notes; crotchets, quavers and so on indicate their time values.

music hall Stage for popular variety shows devoted to comic song, acrobatics, magic shows, juggling and dancing. The popularity of the music hall was at its height in late Victorian and Edwardian England, but declined with the advent of radio and motion pictures in the 1930s.

musicology Academic study of music. The term embraces various disciplines, such as the study of music history, the analysis of compositions, acoustics and ethnomusicology. The study of music history began in the 18th century. Musicological research in the 20th century is responsible for the development of early music.

musk ox Large, wild, shaggy RUMINANT, related to oxen and GOATS, native to N Canada and Greenland. Its brown fur reaches almost to the ground, and its down-pointing, recurved horns form a helmet over the forehead. Length: to 2.3m (7.5ft); weight: to 410kg (903lb). Family Bovidae; species *Ovibos moschatus*. *See also* OX

muskrat Large, aquatic RODENT (a type of VOLE) native to North America. It is a good swimmer, with partly webbed hind feet and a long, scaly tail. Its commercially valuable fur (musquash) is glossy brown and durable. Length: to 53.5cm (21in); weight: to 1.8kg (4lb). Family Cricetidae; species *Ondatra obscura* and *O. zibethica*.

Muslim (Arabic, one who submits) Follower or believer in ISLAM. A Muslim is one who worships ALLAH alone and holds MUHAMMAD to be the only true prophet. In 1990 it was estimated there were 935 million Muslims worldwide.

Muslim League Political organization (founded 1906) to protect the rights of Muslims in British India. The League initially cooperated with the predominantly Hindu National Congress. In 1940, under the leadership of Muhammed Ali JINNAH, it called for a separate Muslim state, which was achieved when the country was partitioned at independence (1947). The League soon split into rival factions.

mussel Any of several species of bivalve MOLLUSCS with thin oval shells. Marine species of the family Mytilidae are found worldwide in dense colonies on sea walls and rocky shores, where they attach themselves by means of strands called byssus threads. The edible mussel, *Mytilus edulis*, is sometimes cultivated on ropes hanging from rafts. Freshwater mussels of the family Unionidae, found in northern continents only, produce PEARLS.

Mussolini, Benito (1883–1945) Italian fascist dictator, prime minister (1922–43). In 1919 he founded the Italian Fascist movement. The fascists' march on Rome in 1922 secured Mussolini's appointment as prime minister. He imposed one-party government with himself as *Il Duce*, or dictator. His movement was a model for HITLER's Nazi Party, with whom Mussolini formed an alliance in 1936. Imperial ambitions led to the conquest of Ethiopia (1935–36) and the invasion of Albania (1939). Mussolini delayed entering World War 2 until a German victory seemed probable in 1940. A succession of defeats led to his fall from power. He was briefly restored as head of a puppet government in N Italy by the Germans, but in April 1945, fleeing Allied forces, he was captured and killed by Italian partisans.

Mussorgsky, Modest Petrovich (1839–81) Russian composer, one of the "Russian Five" who promoted nationalism in Russian music. His finest work is the opera *Boris Godunov* (1868–69). Other important works include the piano work *Pictures from an Exhibition* (1874, later orchestrated by several composers) and *A Night on the Bare Mountain* (1867). After his death much of his work was edited and revised, mostly by Nikolai RIMSKY-KORSAKOV.

Mustafa Kemal *See* ATATÜRK, KEMAL

mustang Feral HORSE of the Great Plains of the USA, descended from horses that were imported from Spain. The mustang has short ears, a low-set tail and round leg bones. During the 17th century there were 2–4 million mustangs. Today only *c*.20,000 survive in SW USA.

mustard Any of various species of annual and perennial plants, native to the temperate zone. These plants have pungent-flavoured leaves, cross-shaped, four-petalled flowers and carry pods. The seeds of some species are ground to produce the condiment mustard. Height: 1.8–4m (6–13ft). Family Brassicaceae/Cruciferae.

mutation Sudden change in an inherited characteristic of an organism. This change occurs in the DNA of the GENES. Natural mutations during reproduction are rare, occur randomly, and usually produce an organism unable to survive in its environment. Occasionally the change results in the organism being better adapted to its environment and, through NATURAL SELECTION, the altered gene may pass on to the next generation. Natural mutation is therefore one of the key means by which organisms evolve. The mutation rate can be increased by exposing genetic material to ionizing radiation, such as x-rays or UV light, or mutagenic chemicals. *See also* EVOLUTION

Muti, Riccardo (1941–) Italian conductor. He made his debut in 1968. He was principal conductor of the Philadelphia Orchestra (1981–92) and musical director of La Scala, Milan (1986–).

Myanmar Official name of BURMA since 1989

Mycenae Ancient city in Greece, 11km (7mi) N of modern Argos, which gave its name to the MYCENAEAN CIVILIZATION. Dating from the third millennium BC, Mycenae was at its cultural peak *c*.1580–1120 BC. The ruins of the city were discovered by Heinrich SCHLIEMANN in 1874–76.

Mycenaean art Greek art of the Late Bronze Age. The name comes from the fortress-city of MYCENAE and refers to the work of the late Helladic period (*c*.1500–1100 BC). Its greatest achievements came in the fields of architecture, which included both grand fortifications and beehive tombs, and in pottery, precious metalwork and fresco.

Mycenaean civilization Ancient Bronze age civilization (*c*.1580–1120 BC) centred around MYCENAE, S Greece. The Mycenaeans entered Greece from the N, bringing with them advanced techniques, especially in architecture and metal-lurgy. By 1400 BC, having incorporated much of MINOAN CIVILIZATION, the Mycenaeans became the dominant power in the Aegean. It is uncertain why the Mycenaean civilization collapsed. Most likely it was due to the Dorian invasion.

mycology Science and study of FUNGUS

mynah *See* MINA

myopia (short-sightedness) Common disorder of vision in which near objects are seen sharply but distant objects are hazy. It is caused either by the eyeball being too long or the eye's lens being too powerful, so that light rays entering the eye focus in front of the RETINA. It is easily corrected with concave lenses in spectacles or contact lenses.

myrrh Aromatic, resinous, oily gum obtained from thorny, flowering trees such as *Commiphora myrrha* (family Burseraceae). Known and prized since ancient times, it has commonly been used as an ingredient in incense, perfumes and medicines.

myrtle Any of numerous species of evergreen shrubs and trees that grow in tropical and subtropical regions, especially the aromatic shrub, *Myrtus communis*, of the Mediterranean region. Its leaves are simple and glossy; the purple-black berries that follow the white flowers were once dried and used like pepper. Family Myrtaceae.

mystery play (miracle play) Medieval English drama based on a religious theme. Mystery plays were originally used by the clergy to teach their illiterate congregation the principal stories of the Bible. By the 14th century, they had become a popular entertainment. Each year, the plays were performed by the various craft guilds in a town. In England the mystery plays from four towns have survived: Chester, York, Wakefield and Coventry.

mysticism Belief in, or experience of, a perception of reality that is elevated above some normal human understanding. It may involve some form of spiritual search for unity of self with God or the universe. It is found in most major religions, and mystics may experience trances, dreams or visions. In India, mysticism has long been important in HINDUISM and is based on YOGA. Mysticism in Judaism is apparent in HASIDISM and the CABBALA. Mystics in the Far East have mostly been followers of TAOISM or BUDDHISM.

mythology Literally, telling of stories, but usually collectively defined as the myths of a particular culture. A myth occurs in a timeless past, contains supernatural elements and seeks to dramatize or explain such issues as the creation of the world and human beings, the institutions of political power, the cycle of seasons, birth, death and fate. Most mythologies have an established pantheon of gods who are more or less anthropomorphic.

myxoedema Disease caused by deficient function of the THYROID GLAND, resulting in fatigue, constipation, dry skin, a tendency towards weight-gain and, in the later stages, mental dullness. It mostly affects middle-aged women. Treatment involves administration of the thyroid hormone, thyroxine.

N/n is derived from the Semitic letter nun, *which was the pictorial representation of a fish. It was adopted by the Greeks as the letter* nu *and subsequently by the Romans.*

Nabokov, Vladimir (1899–1977) US novelist, b. Russia. A highly imaginative and experimental writer, Nabokov is perhaps best known for his controversial novel *Lolita* (1955). Other works include *Pnin* (1957) and *Ada* (1969).

nadir Point on the CELESTIAL SPHERE vertically below the observer, opposite the zenith.

Nagaland State in NE India; the capital is Kohima. Briefly ruled by Burma in the early 19th century, it gradually came under British control, then became a separate state in 1963. Crops: rice, potatoes, sugar cane. Area: 16,579sq km (6,399sq mi). Pop. (1991) 1,209,546.

Nagasaki Port in SW Japan, W Kyūshū island. In the 16th century it was the first Japanese port to receive Western ships and became a centre of Christian influence. During Japanese isolation (1639–1859) it was the only port open to foreign trade. In August 1945 the inner city was destroyed by a US atomic bomb, and over 70,000 people were killed. Industries: shipbuilding, heavy engineering. Pop. (1993) 439,000.

Nagorno-Karabakh Autonomous region of AZERBAIJAN, between the Caucasus and Karabakh mountains. The capital is Stepanakert. During the 19th century the region was absorbed into the Russian empire. In 1921 it was annexed to the Azerbaijan republic. In 1991 the region declared its independence and Azerbaijan responded by imposing direct rule. The ensuing civil war claimed thousands of lives. In 1993 Armenian troops occupied the enclave and a peace agreement was reached in 1994. The main activities are farming and silk production. Area: 4,400sq km (1,700sq mi). Pop. (1990) 192,400.

Nagoya City and port in central Japan, in central Honshū island, on the Pacific Ocean. Industries: iron and steel, textiles, motor vehicles, aircraft. Pop. (1993) 2,095,000.

Nagpur City in Maharashtra state, W central India. Founded in the 18th century as the capital of the kingdom of Nagpur, it became the capital of Berar state (from 1903) and of Madhya Pradesh state (1947–56). Industries: metal goods, transport equipment, cigarettes, textiles, pottery, glass, leather, brassware. Pop. (1991) 1,624,572.

Nagy, Imre (1896–1958) Hungarian communist statesman, premier (1953–55). As premier, Nagy enacted liberal reforms of the Hungarian economy and society. Under pressure from the Soviet Union, Nagy was dismissed from the Hungarian Commu-

nist Party. The Hungarian Revolution (1956) led to Nagy's reinstatement as premier. Soviet tanks crushed the uprising and handed power to János Kádár. Nagy was tried and executed for treason.

Naipaul, V.S. (Vidiadhar Surajprasad) (1932–) West Indian writer. He was educated in his native Trinidad and at Oxford, but later settled in London. His novels include *A House for Mr Biswas* (1961), the Booker Prize-winning *In a Free State* (1971) and *A Bend in the River* (1979).

Nairobi Capital and largest city of Kenya, in the S central part of the country. Founded in 1899, Nairobi replaced Mombasa as the capital of the British East Africa Protectorate in 1905. Nairobi is also an administrative and commercial centre. Industries: cigarettes, textiles, chemicals, food processing, furniture, glass. Pop. (1989) 1,346,000.

Nakhichevan Autonomous republic of Azerbaijan, bounded N and E by Armenia, S and W by Iran, and W by Turkey; the capital is Nakhichevan. Under Persian domination from the 13th–19th century, it became part of Russia in 1828. In 1924 it was made an autonomous republic within the Soviet Union. In 1991 it became part of the independent republic of AZERBAIJAN, but was subsequently claimed by ARMENIA. Industries: mining, silk textile production, food processing. Area: 5,500sq km (2,120sq mi). Pop. (1994) 315,000.

Namib Desert Coastal desert region of Namibia, between the Atlantic Ocean and the interior plateau. It has less than 1cm (0.4in) of rain a year and is almost completely barren. Diamonds are mined. Length: *c*.1,900km (1,200mi).

Namibia (formerly South West Africa) Republic in SW Africa. **Land and climate** Namibia can be divided into four geographical regions. The arid NAMIB DESERT runs along the entire Atlantic coast. Inland, a central plateau, mostly between 900 and 2,000m (2,950–6,560ft), includes the capital, WINDHOEK. The highest point is Brandberg Mountain, at 2,606m (8,550ft). In the N lies an alluvial plain, which includes the marshlands of the Caprivi Strip. To the E is the W fringe of the KALAHARI. The ORANGE River forms Namibia's S border. Namibia is a warm, arid country. Windhoek has an average annual rainfall of 370mm (15in). The N is the wettest part of Namibia, with *c*.500mm (20in) of annual rain. Grassland and shrub cover much of the interior. **Economy** Namibia is the world's seventh-largest producer of diamonds, and ninth-largest producer of uranium. Minerals make up 90% of exports. Farming employs *c*.40% of the workforce, and is mainly cattle and sheep farming. The chief food products are maize, millet and vegetables. Atlantic fishing is also important. **History** The nomadic SAN inhabited the region *c*.2,000 years ago. They were gradually displaced by various Bantu-speaking peoples. Portuguese navigators arrived in the early 15th century. Colonization began in earnest in the 19th century. In 1884 Germany claimed the region

NAMIBIA
AREA: 825,414sq km (318,694 sq mi)
POPULATION: 1,562,000
CAPITAL (POPULATION): Windhoek (126,000)
GOVERNMENT: Multiparty republic
ETHNIC GROUPS: Ovambo 50%, Kavango 9%,
Herero 7%, Damara 7%, whites 6%, Nama 5%
LANGUAGES: English (official)
RELIGIONS: Christianity 90% (Lutheran 51%)
CURRENCY: Namibian dollar = 100 cents

as a protectorate, and subsumed it into the territory of South West Africa. Local rebellions were brutally suppressed. The discovery of diamonds in 1908 increased European settlement. During World War 1 it was occupied (1915) by South African troops. In 1920 South Africa was granted a mandate. After World War 2 South Africa refused to relinquish control. In 1966 the SOUTH WEST AFRICA PEOPLE'S ORGANIZATION (SWAPO) began a guerrilla war against South Africa. In 1968 the United Nations (UN) called on South Africa to withdraw. In 1971 the International Court of Justice declared that South African rule over Namibia was illegal. South Africa refused to comply and divided Namibia into bantustans. International pressure forced South Africa to promise Namibia independence, but then qualified the terms. Civil war raged from 1977. A UN security council peace settlement was finally implemented in 1989. **Politics** SWAPO won multiparty elections in November 1989. In March 1990 Namibia became an independent republic within the Commonwealth of Nations. Sam NUJOMA became its first president, and was re-elected in 1994. In 1994 South Africa renounced its claim to Walvis Bay and it was incorporated into the state.

Nanak (1469–1539) Indian spiritual teacher, and founder and first guru of SIKHISM. Nanak preached a monotheistic religion that combined elements from both HINDUISM and ISLAM.

Nanking (Nanjing) City on the River Yangtze, E China; capital of Jiangsu province. Founded in the 8th century BC, it served as the capital of China at various times. The Treaty of Nanking (1842) ended the OPIUM WAR with Britain. It was the seat of SUN YAT-SEN's presidency in 1912. In 1937, during the SINO-JAPANESE WAR, Nanking was captured by the Japanese and over 100,000 people were massacred. Industries: iron and steel, oil refining, chemicals. Pop. (1993) 2,430,000.

nanotechnology Micromechanics used to develop working devices the size of a few nanometres. (A nanometre is one-billionth of a metre.)

Nansen, Fridtjof (1861–1930) Norwegian explorer and statesman. After a pioneering crossing of Greenland (1888), he designed a ship to withstand being frozen in ice so that currents would carry it to the North Pole. It did not reach the Pole, but crossed the Arctic Ocean undamaged (1893–96). Nansen and one companion failed to reach the Pole with skis and kayaks. After 1918 Nansen was involved in humanitarian work and was awarded the Nobel Peace Prize in 1922.

Nantes City at the mouth of the Loire River, W France; capital of Loire-Atlantique département. It has been an important trading centre since Roman times. In the 10th century it was captured from Norse invaders by the duke of Brittany. Nantes remained a residence of the dukes until 1524, and their tombs lie in the 15th-century cathedral. By the 18th century it had become France's largest port. It was a centre of French resistance in World War 2. Industries: shipbuilding, sugar refining, food products. Pop. (1990) 244,995.

Nantes, Edict of (1598) French royal decree establishing toleration for HUGUENOTS (Protestants). It granted freedom of worship and legal equality for Huguenots within limits, and ended the Wars of RELIGION. The Edict was revoked by LOUIS XIV in 1685, causing many Huguenots to emigrate.

naphthalene Hydrocarbon ($C_{10}H_8$) composed of two benzene rings sharing two adjacent carbon atoms. A white, waxy solid, naphthalene is soluble in ether and hot alcohol and is highly volatile. It is a constituent of moth balls, dyes and synthetic resins, and occurs in coal tar. Properties: m.p. 80°C (176°F); b.p. 218°C (424°F).

Napier, John (1550–1617) Scottish mathematician. He developed "Napier's bones", a calculating device that he used to invent logarithms (1614) and the present form of decimal notation.

Naples (Napoli) City in S central Italy, on the Bay of Naples; capital of the province of Campania. Founded c.600 BC as a Greek colony, Naples was conquered by Rome in the 4th century BC. It was successively ruled by the Byzantines, Normans, Spanish and Austrians. In 1734 it became the capital of the Kingdom of the Two Sicilies, joining the Kingdom of Italy in 1860. Industries: textiles, leather, steel, shipbuilding, aircraft, telecommunications, tourism. Pop. (1991) 1,067,365.

Napoleon I (1769–1821) (Napoléon Bonaparte) Emperor of the French (1804–15), b. Corsica. He became a brigadier (1793) after driving the British out of Toulon. He was given command in Italy (1796), where he defeated the Austrians and Sardinians. In 1798 he launched an invasion of Egypt. French defeats in Europe prompted his return to Paris (1799), where his coup of 18 Brumaire (9 November) overthrew the Directory and set up the Consulate, headed by himself. He enacted sweeping administrative and legal reforms with the *Code Napoléon*, while defeating the Austrians at Marengo (1800) and making peace with the British at Amiens (1802). In 1804 he crowned himself emperor. Efforts to extend French power provoked renewal of war in 1803. Napoleon's Grand Army shattered his continental opponents but, after TRAFALGAR (1805), Britain controlled the seas.

Napoleon imposed trade sanctions on Britain, which led indirectly to the PENINSULAR WAR in Portugal and Spain. By 1812 he controlled most of continental Europe. His invasion of Russia (1812) ended in the destruction of the Grand Army, encouraging a new coalition against France, which captured Paris in March 1814. Napoleon was exiled to ELBA, but in March 1815 he returned to France. The hundred days of his renewed reign ended with defeat at WATERLOO in June. Napoleon was exiled to St Helena, where he died.

Napoleon III (1808–73) (Louis Napoleon) Emperor of the French (1852–70). The nephew of NAPOLEON I, he twice attempted a coup in France (1836 and 1840). Returning from exile after the FEBRUARY REVOLUTION (1848), he was elected president of the Second Republic. In 1851 he assumed autocratic powers and established the Second Empire (1852), taking the title Napoleon III. His attempt to establish a Mexican empire under the Archduke MAXIMILIAN ended in disaster, and in 1870 he was provoked by BISMARCK into declaring war on Prussia. Defeat at Sedan was followed by a republican rising that ended his reign.

Napoleonic Wars (1803–15) Campaigns by a series of European coalitions against French expansion under NAPOLEON I. Britain declared war in 1803 and formed the Third Coalition with Austria, Russia and Sweden in 1804. Napoleon defeated the Austrians at Ulm and the Russians and Austrians at AUSTERLITZ (1806), but the British won a decisive naval victory at TRAFALGAR (1805). Prussia joined the Fourth Coalition (1806) but was defeated at Jena. Portuguese resistance to French occupation (1807) began the PENINSULAR WAR. The Fifth Coalition (1809) collapsed with the defeat of Austria at Wagram. In 1812 Napoleon invaded Russia. Bitter weather forced his retreat, and much of his army perished. The Sixth Coalition defeated Napoleon at Leipzig. Allied forces entered Paris in 1814. War was renewed during the hundred days of Napoleon's reign in 1815, but ended in his final defeat by WELLINGTON and Blücher at WATERLOO (1815).

Nara City in Japan, in S Honshu island; capital of Nara prefecture. A centre of Japanese Buddhism, Nara was founded in 706. From 710–84 it acted as Japan's first imperial capital. Pop. (1993) 353,000.

narcissus Genus of Old World, bulb-forming, garden flowers. The long, pointed leaves surround yellow, orange or white trumpet-like flowers. Family Amaryllidaceae.

narcotic Any drug that induces sleep and/or relieves pain. The term is used especially in relation to opium and its derivatives. Other narcotics include alcohols and BARBITURATES.

narwhal Small, toothed Arctic WHALE. The male has a twisted horn, half as long as its body, which develops from a tooth and protrudes horizontally through one side of the upper lip. Length: up to 5m (16ft). Species *Monodon monoceros*.

NASA Acronym for NATIONAL AERONAUTICS AND SPACE ADMINISTRATION

Naseby, Battle of Final battle of the first English CIVIL WAR, fought in June 1645. Royalist troops under Prince RUPERT were defeated by the Parliamentarians under CROMWELL and FAIRFAX.

Nash, John (1752–1835) British architect and town planner, an important figure in the REGENCY STYLE. He designed Regent's Park and Regent Street, London, and rebuilt the Royal Pavilion, Brighton (1815–23).

Nash, Ogden (1902–71) US poet. Among his many volumes of humorous and satirical poetry are *Free Wheeling* (1931), *I'm a Stranger Here Myself* (1938) and *Everyone But Me and Thee* (1962).

Nash, Paul (1889–1946) British painter and graphic artist. He was in touch with European modernism. SURREALISM stimulated the poetic, dreamlike style of his landscapes, as in *The Menin Road* (1918) and *Landscape from a Dream* (1938).

Nash, Sir Walter (1882–1968) New Zealand statesman, prime minister (1957–60), b. England. He emigrated to New Zealand in 1909 and entered Parliament in 1929. As finance minister (1935–49), he helped to introduce the Labour Party's wide-ranging social-security scheme.

Nashville Capital of Tennessee, USA, a port on the Cumberland River. Settled in 1779, it became state capital in 1843. Nashville merged with Davidson in 1963. Industries: music, publishing. Pop. (1990) 510,784.

Nassau Capital of the Bahama Islands, West Indies, a port on the NE coast of New Providence Island. Founded in the 1660s, it is a commercial centre and tourist resort. Pop. (1990) 172,000.

Nasser, Gamal Abdel (1918–70) Egyptian soldier and statesman, prime minister (1954–56) and first president of the republic of Egypt (1956–70). In 1942 Nasser founded the Society of Free Officers, which campaigned against British imperialism and domestic corruption. He led the 1952 army coup against King FAROUK. He ousted the nominal prime minister General Muhammad Neguib and assumed presidential powers. Nasser's nationalization of the SUEZ CANAL (1956) prompted an abortive Anglo-French and Israeli invasion. Nasser emerged as champion of the Arab world. He briefly resigned after Israel won the SIX DAY WAR (1967).

Natal Former name (1910–94) of KWAZULU-NATAL province, E South Africa.

National Aeronautics and Space Administration (NASA) US government agency that organizes civilian aeronautical and space research programmes. The Lyndon B. Johnson Space Center in Houston, Texas, controls manned space flights. Space rockets, both manned and unmanned, are launched from the John F. Kennedy Space Center at CAPE CANAVERAL, Florida.

National Association for the Advancement of Colored People (NAACP) US CIVIL RIGHTS organization founded in 1909 "to achieve through peaceful and lawful means, equal citizenship rights for all American citizens by eliminating segregation and discrimination in housing, employment, voting, schools, the courts, transportation and recreation". Early leaders were W.E.B. Du Bois and Booker T. WASHINGTON.

national curriculum Curriculum that is compulsory for all of a country's schools. In the UK a national curriculum for state primary and secondary schools was introduced in 1989. Mathematics, English and science are core subjects to be studied by all pupils from 5 to 16.

national debt *See* DEBT, NATIONAL

National Front (NF) Extreme right-wing British political party founded in the 1960s. It has an essentially racist doctrine, advocating the repatriation of ethnic minorities and strongly opposing immigration. *See also* NATIONAL SOCIALISM

National Health Service (NHS) In Britain, system of state provision of health care established in 1948. The NHS undertook to provide comprehensive coverage for most health services including hospitals, general medical practice and public health facilities. It is administered by the Department of Health. General practitioners (GPs) have registered patients; they may also have private patients and may contract out of the state scheme altogether. They refer patients, when necessary, to specialist consultants in hospitals for outpatient or inpatient treatment. Health visitors such as midwives and district nurses are the third arm of the service. Hospitals are administered by regional boards.

national insurance In Britain, state scheme, founded in 1911, to provide sickness and unemployment benefits and old-age pensions. The scheme is funded by compulsory contributions from employers and employees, and is administered by the Department of Social Security.

nationalization Policy of acquiring for public ownership enterprises formerly privately owned. In the UK, the Labour government (1945–51) nationalized industries such as coal, steel and transport. *See* PRIVATIZATION

national service *See* CONSCRIPTION

National Socialism (Nazism) Doctrine of the National Socialist German Workers' (Nazi) Party, 1921–45. It was biologically racist (believing that the so-called Aryan race was superior to others), anti-Semitic, nationalistic, anti-communist, anti-democratic and anti-intellectual. It placed power before justice and the interests of the state before the individual. These beliefs were stated by the party's leader, Adolf HITLER, in his book *Mein Kampf* (1925). *See also* FASCISM

National Theatre The National Theatre of Great Britain was founded in 1963. With Laurence OLIVIER as artistic director, the first production, *Hamlet*, took place on 22 October 1963, at the OLD VIC theatre. In 1973 Sir Peter HALL succeeded Olivier. New buildings designed by Sir Denys Lasdun were opened in October 1976, and comprise the Lyttelton, Olivier and Cottesloe theatres. Following the departure of Richard Eyre, who succeeded Sir Peter Hall, Trevor NUNN became the new artistic director in 1996.

National Trust British organization formed in 1895 in order to acquire and own buildings and land for permanent preservation. In 1907 the trust was given the power to declare its land inalienable. Today it protects about 471,000 acres, of which it owns 400,000, the rest being covenanted.

Native Americans Aboriginal peoples of the American continent. Native North Americans are believed to be descended from Asian peoples who crossed via the Bering Strait or the Aleutian Islands about 20,000 BC or earlier. Native South Americans derived from North American groups who migrated S. Native Americans of the Andean area developed the highest cultures of the continent. Native Americans of the Amazon Basin are mainly isolated, primitive, agricultural communities of many localized tribes. Native Americans of the pampas successfully resisted Inca and Spaniard alike.

Native Australians Indigenous peoples of Australia. Originally from SE Asia, Native Australians are thought to have colonized Australia 40,000–45,000 years ago. Before the arrival of Europeans (*c*.1788) they probably numbered over 400,000, but many thousands died from European diseases when they were placed in reserves. All the 500 tribal groups led a nomadic life, hunting and gathering. They believe that the land is a religious phenomenon, inhabited by spirits of their ancestors, and these beliefs are celebrated in legends, song, mime, carving and painting. They were granted the right to full Australian citizenship in 1967, and were first included in the census in 1971, when their estimated numbers were 140,000. The Aboriginal Land Rights Act (1976) and the Aboriginal and Torres Islander Heritage Protect Act (1984) have resulted in an increased population approaching 300,000 by the mid-1990s.

Native North American art Traditional art of the indigenous peoples of North America. The INUIT of the Arctic area have been producing ivory carvings since prehistoric times and are also noted for their ceremonial masks (made from driftwood or whalebone). The NW region is best known for its totem poles, while in California, basket-weaving and pottery were specialities. Similar crafts were practised by the PUEBLO people of the SW, who also created remarkable prehistoric wall paintings. The painted decoration of animal hides was popular in the Great Plains, while in the Eastern Woodlands, there was a preference for copper ornaments and stone carvings.

Native North American languages Any of more than 100 languages that are spoken in N and Central America by descendants of the various aboriginal peoples. In the USA and Canada, languages include Algonquin, Athabascan and Sioux. In the USA and Mexico, Uto-Aztecan is the most common; in Mexico, Oto-Manguean; and in Mexico and Guatemala, Mayan. Nahuatl is the most widely spoken of this group.

Native South American languages Any of more than 1,000 languages spoken in South America by between 10 and 12 million people. Among the more important linguistic families are Chibcha, Arawak and Tupian. Widely spoken languages are Quechua and Aymará, found in Peru and Bolivia. Guaraní, of Paraguay, is also important.

nativity Birth of a New Testament figure as marked by a Christian feast. In general, the term refers to the birth of JESUS CHRIST, as described in the GOSPELS. Christians celebrate Jesus' Nativity at the festival of CHRISTMAS on 25 December.

NATO Acronym for NORTH ATLANTIC TREATY ORGANIZATION

natural In musical notation, an accidental sign placed before a note; it cancels a SHARP or FLAT.

natural gas Fossil fuel associated geologically with PETROLEUM. The fossil history of the two fuels is the same, since they were both formed by the decomposition of ancient marine plankton. The main constituent of natural gas is methane, CH_4.

naturalism Late 19th-century literary movement that began in France and was led by Emile ZOLA. An extension of REALISM, it emphasized the importance of documentation. Writers sought to represent unselective reality with all its emotional and social ramifications. The movement declined by the beginning of the 20th century, but influenced the modern US novel and social realist art.

natural rights Concept that human beings possess certain fundamental and inalienable rights, as described by John LOCKE. Among these rights were life, property ownership and political equality.

natural selection In EVOLUTION, theory that advantageous change in an organism tends to be passed on to successive generations. Changes arise out of natural genetic VARIATION, especially MUTATION. Those that give an individual organism a greater capacity for survival and reproduction in a particular environment help it to produce more offspring bearing the same beneficial characteristic or trait. This theory was proposed by Charles DARWIN in his book *The Origin of Species* (1859). It is still regarded as the key mechanism of evolution.

naturopathy System of medical therapy that relies exclusively on the use of natural treatments, such as fresh air, a healthy diet of organically grown foods and herbal remedies.

Nauru Island republic in the W Pacific Ocean, a coral atoll located halfway between Australia and Hawaii, and the world's smallest independent state. Nauru has rich deposits of high-grade phosphate rock, the sale of which accounts for 98% of its exports. Nauru was explored by a British navigator, John Hunter, in 1798. In 1888 the atoll was annexed to Germany. During World War 1 Nauru was occupied by Australian forces, and by the Japanese in World War 2. In 1968 it became an independent republic within the Commonwealth. Area: 21sq km (8sq mi). Pop. (1990) 8,100.

nautilus (chambered nautilus) CEPHALOPOD MOLLUSC found in W Pacific and E Indian oceans at depths down to 200m (660ft). Its large coiled shell is divided into numerous, gas-filled chambers, which give it buoyancy, with the body located in the foremost chamber. Its head has 60–90 retractable, thin tentacles without suckers, and it moves by squirting water from a funnel. Shell size c.25cm (10in). Family Nautilidae; genus *Nautilus*.

Navajo Athabascan-speaking tribe, the largest group of NATIVE AMERICANS in the USA. Their reservation in Arizona and New Mexico is the biggest in the country. In the early 1990s the growing population numbered c.150,000.

Navarino, Battle of (1827) Naval battle off the port of Navarino (Pylos), Greece. The British, French and Russian fleets destroyed the Turkish-Egyptian fleet of Ibrahim Pasha. The battle helped to ensure Greek independence (1829).

Navarre Autonomous region and ancient kingdom in N Spain, stretching from the River Ebro to the W Pyrenees border; the capital is Pamplona. For 400 years Navarre resisted invasion, by the Visigoths, Arabs and Franks. In the 11th century, Sancho III of Navarre ruled over most of Christian Spain. In 1512 S Navarre was annexed by Ferdinand II of Aragon. The N part was incorporated as French crown land in 1589. It is a mountainous, mainly agricultural region producing cattle, grapes, timber, cereals, vegetables and sugar beet. Area: 10,421sq km (4,023sq mi). Pop. (1991) 519,227.

navigation Determining the position of a vehicle and its course. Five main techniques are used: dead reckoning, piloting, celestial navigation, inertial guidance and radio navigation. The last includes the use of radio beacons, LORAN, radar navigation and satellite navigation systems. Instruments and charts enable the navigator to determine position, expressed in terms of LATITUDE and LONGITUDE, direction in degrees of arc from true north, speed, and distance travelled.

Navigation Acts English 17th-century statutes placing restrictions on foreign trade and shipping. The first Navigation Act (1651) declared that English trade should be carried only in English ships. It was the main cause of the first Anglo–Dutch War.

Navratilova, Martina (1956–) US tennis player, b. Czechoslovakia. One of the greatest tennis players ever, she has won 167 singles tournaments, including Wimbledon on 9 occasions.

Nazism *See* NATIONAL SOCIALISM

Ndjamena Capital of Chad, N central Africa, a port on the River Chari. Founded by the French in 1900, it was known as Fort Lamy until 1973. It grew rapidly after independence in 1960. It is an important market for the surrounding region, which produces livestock, dates and cereals. The main industry is meat processing. Pop. (1993) 529,555.

Neagh, Lough Lake in Northern Ireland, the

largest freshwater lake in the British Isles. It has many feeder channels, the largest of which is the River Bann. The lake is noted for its fishing (especially trout and eels). Area: 396sq km (153sq mi).

Neanderthal Middle PALAEOLITHIC variety of human, known from fossils in Europe and Asia. Neanderthals were discovered when a skeleton was unearthed in the Neander Valley in W Germany in 1856. The bones were thick and the skull had a pronounced brow ridge. Neanderthals are now considered a separate species of human, and are not thought to be ancestral to modern humans. *See also* HUMAN EVOLUTION

Nebraska State in W central USA, in the Great Plains; the capital is Lincoln. OMAHA is the largest city. The region was acquired under the LOUISIANA PURCHASE of 1803 and was unexplored until the LEWIS AND CLARK EXPEDITION the following year. The territory of Nebraska was created in 1854. Nebraska was admitted to the union in 1867. The land rises gradually from the E to the foothills of the Rocky Mountains in the W, and is drained chiefly by the Platte River, a tributary of the MIS-SOURI. The E half of the state is farmland, where farmers grow cereal crops and raise cattle and pigs. Nebraska's economy is overwhelmingly agricultural. Industries: food processing, oil, and sand, gravel and stone quarrying. Area: 199,113sq km (76,878sq mi). Pop. (1990) 1,578,385.

Nebuchadnezzar (*c.*630–562 BC) Second and greatest king of the Chaldaean (New Babylonian) empire (605 BC–562 BC) who had a profound effect on the lands of the ancient Middle East. A brilliant military leader, Nebuchadnezzar was also responsible for many buildings in Babylon and, according to legend, built for his Median wife the famous hanging gardens, which became one of the SEVEN WONDERS OF THE WORLD. Biblical accounts of Nebuchadnezzar appear principally in II Kings, Jeremiah, and Daniel.

nebula (Lat. cloud) Region of interstellar gas and dust. There are three main types of nebula. Emission nebulae are bright diffuse nebulae that emit light and other radiation as a result of ionization and excitation of the gas atoms by ultraviolet radiation. In contrast, the brightness of reflection nebulae results from the scattering by dust particles of light from nearby stars. Dark nebulae are not luminous: interstellar gas and dust absorb light from background stars, producing apparently dark patches in the sky.

nectarine Variety of PEACH tree and its sweet, smooth-skinned, fleshy fruit. The tree and stone are identical to those of the peach. Family Rosaceae; species *Prunus persica nectarina.*

Nefertiti (active 14th century BC) Queen of Egypt as wife of AKHNATEN. She was exceptionally beautiful. Her best surviving representation is a bust in the Berlin Museum.

Negev (Hebrew, dry) Desert region in S Israel that extends from Beersheba to the border with Egypt at Eilat, and accounts for over half of Israeli land. An irrigation network has greatly increased cultivation in the region. The area has good mineral resources including copper, phosphates, natural gas, gypsum, ceramic clay and magnesium ore. Area: *c.*13,300sq km (5,130sq mi).

Nehru, Jawaharlal (1889–1964) Indian statesman, first prime minister of independent India. He belonged to the more radical wing of the Indian National Congress and was its president in 1929 and later. Conflicts with the British resulted in frequent spells in prison, but he took a leading part in the negotiations leading to the independence of India and Pakistan and headed the Indian government from 1947 until his death. Internationally he followed a policy of nonalignment, and became a respected leader of the Third World.

Nelson, Horatio, Viscount (1758–1805) Britain's most famous naval commander. He lost an eye in action in 1794 and his right arm in 1797. Having played a notable part in the victory at Cape St Vincent (1797), he again used unorthodox tactics in the Battle of the Nile (Abukir Bay) in 1798. He was killed when he destroyed the combined French and Spanish fleets at TRAFALGAR (1805).

nematode *See* ROUNDWORM

neo-classicism Movement in late 18th- and early 19th-century European art and architecture. Neo-classicism grew out of the Age of ENLIGHT-ENMENT, whose exponents admired the order and clarity of ancient Greek and Roman art. The archaeological discoveries at Herculaneum and Pompeii, Italy, in the 1740s helped to stimulate interest in these ancient civilizations. Many of the movement's pioneers congregated in Rome, notably Johann Winckelmann, CANOVA, John Flaxman, Gavin Hamilton and Bertel Thorvaldsen. The most powerful neo-classical painter was Jacques Louis DAVID, whose work expressed great severity and grandeur. The concurrent **Greek Revival** had more superficial aims, which, in architecture, involved imitating the simplicity of ancient Greek buildings.

neo-Darwinism Development of Darwinism that incorporates the modern ideas of genetic heredity, with DARWIN's ideas of EVOLUTION through NATURAL SELECTION.

neodymium Silver-yellow metallic element (symbol Nd) of the LANTHANIDE SERIES. It is used to manufacture lasers, and neodymium salts are used to colour glass. Properties: at.no. 60; r.a.m. 144.24; r.d. 7.004; m.p. 1,010°C (1,850°F); b.p. 3,068 °C (5,554°F); most common isotope Nd^{142} (27.11%).

neo-fascism Revival of the principles of FASCISM. Neo-fascism surfaced in Germany in the 1980s, feeding on muted social discontent and the presence of many foreign workers. In France some Jewish graves were desecrated and Italian neo-fascism has had moderate electoral success. There are neo-fascist elements in Britain and the USA in certain white supremacist groups.

neo-Impressionism Late 19th-century painting style, originating in France and involving the use of POINTILLISM. The finest exponent was SEURAT.

Neolithic (New Stone Age) Period in human cultural development following the PALAEOLITHIC. The Neolithic began about 8000 BC in W Asia, and about 4000 BC in Britain. It was during this period that people first lived in settled villages, domesticated and bred animals, cultivated cereal crops and practised stone-grinding and flint mining.

neon Gaseous nonmetallic element (symbol Ne), a NOBLE GAS. Colourless and odourless, it is present in the atmosphere (0.0018% by volume) and is obtained by the fractional distillation of liquid air. Its main use is in discharge tubes for advertising signs (emitting a bright red glow while conducting electricity). It forms no compounds. Properties: at.no. 10; r.a.m. 20.179; m.p. $-248.67°C$ ($415.6°F$); b.p. $-246.05°C$ ($-410.89°F$); most common isotope Ne^{20} (90.92%).

Neoplatonism School of philosophy that dominated intellectual thought between about AD 250 and 550. It combined the ideas of PYTHAGORAS, the STOICS, PLATO and ARISTOTLE with strains from JUDAISM, oriental religions and Christianity. Fundamental to Neoplatonism was the concept of the One, something that transcends knowledge or existence but from which are derived intelligence and the Soul. Neoplatonism's influence persisted throughout the Middle Ages.

neo-realism Italian film movement (1945–50) that dealt with the harshness of life and death. Roberto ROSSELLINI directed the first such film, called *Open City* (1945), using non-professionals and real locations.

Nepal Independent kingdom in central Asia, between India (S) and China (N); the capital is KATMANDU. **Land and climate** Nepal comprises three distinct regions. A S lowland area (terai) of grassland, forests and national park is the location of much of Nepal's agriculture and timber industry. The central Siwalik mountains and valleys are divided between the basins of the Ghaghara, Gandak and Kosi rivers. Between the Gandak and Kosi lies Katmandu valley, the country's most populous area and centre for Nepal's greatest source of foreign currency – tourism. The last region is the main section of the Himalayas and includes Mount EVEREST. **Economy** The most important economic activity in the Himalayas is livestock farming (especially yaks) and the growing of medicinal herbs. Nepal is an undeveloped rural country, heavily reliant on Indian trade and cooperation. **History** In 1768 Nepal was united under GURKHA rule. Gurkha expansion into N India ended in conflict with Britain. British victory led Nepal to ratify its present boundaries and accept permanent British representation in Katmandu. From 1846–1951 Nepal was ruled by hereditary prime ministers from the Rana family. In 1923 Britain recognized Nepal as a sovereign state. Gurkha soldiers fought with distinction in the British army during both world wars. In 1951 the Rana government was overthrown and the monarchy restored. In 1959 the first national constitution was adopted and free elections took place. In 1960 King Mahendra dissolved parliament and the democratic constitution was replaced by village councils (*panchayat*). In 1972 King Birendra succeeded. Mass demonstrations in 1990 led to the establishment of a new democratic constitution, with the king retaining joint executive powers. Multiparty elections in 1991 were won by the Nepali Congress Party. **Politics** The United Marxist Leninist Party formed a short-lived minority government in 1994. In 1995 a coalition government was formed, but in 1997 the prime minister was forced to resign, after losing a vote of confidence. A new coalition government was formed.

nephritis (Bright's disease) Inflammation of the KIDNEY. It is a general term, used to describe a condition rather than any specific disease. It may be acute or chronic, often leading to kidney failure.

nephron Basic functional unit of the mammalian KIDNEY. Each of the million nephrons consists of a cluster of tiny blood capillaries, cupped in a structure with an attached long, narrow tubule. Blood enters the kidney under pressure, and water and waste are forced into the tubule. Some water and essential molecules are reabsorbed into the bloodstream; the remaining filtrate, URINE, is passed to the BLADDER for voiding.

Neptune Eighth planet from the Sun. The mass, orbit and position of an unseen planet had been calculated by LEVERRIER and, independently, by British astronomer John Couch Adams (1819–92). It was first observed in 1846 and is invisible to the naked eye. The upper atmosphere is *c*.85% molecular hydrogen and 15% helium. Its blue colour is due to a trace of methane, which strongly absorbs red light. Several different atmospheric features were visible at the time of the fly-by of the Voyager 2 probe in 1989. There were faint bands parallel to the equator, and spots, the most prominent of which was the oval Great Dark Spot (GDS), about 12,500km (8,000mi) long and 7,500km (4,500mi) wide, which is a giant anticyclone. White, cirrus-type clouds of methane crystals cast shadows on the main cloud deck some 50km (30mi) below. There are also the highest wind speeds recorded on any planet, at over 2,000km/h (1,250mi/h) in places. Diameter (equatorial): 49,528km, (polar): 48,686km

Neptune Roman god, originally associated with freshwater but later identified with the Greek god

NEPAL
AREA: 140,800sq km (54,363sq mi)
POPULATION: 21,953,000
CAPITAL (POPULATION): Katmandu (419,073)
LANGUAGES: Nepali
CURRENCY: Nepalese rupee = 100 paisa

POSEIDON and hence the sea. He was often depicted carrying a trident and riding a dolphin.

neptunium Radioactive metallic element (symbol Np), the first of the TRANSURANIC ELEMENTS of the ACTINIDE SERIES. The silvery element is found in small amounts in uranium ores. Properties: at.no. 93; r.a.m. 237.0482; r.d. 20.25; m.p. 640°C (1,184°F); b.p. 3,902 °C (7,056°F); most stable isotope Np^{237} (half-life 2.2 million years).

Nero (37–68) Roman emperor (54–68). One of the most notorious of rulers, he was responsible for the murders of his half-brother, his mother and his first wife. Rome was burned (64), according to rumour, at Nero's instigation. He blamed the Christians and began their persecution. Faced with widespread rebellion, Nero committed suicide.

nerve Collection of NEURONS providing a communications link between the vertebrate NERVOUS SYSTEM and other parts of the body. Afferent or sensory nerves transmit nervous impulses to the CENTRAL NERVOUS SYSTEM; efferent or MOTOR NERVES carry impulses away from the central nervous system to muscles.

nerve cell *See* NEURON

nervous system Communications system consisting of interconnecting nerve cells or NEURONS that coordinate all life, growth and physical and mental activity. The mammalian nervous system consists of the CENTRAL NERVOUS SYSTEM (CNS) and the PERIPHERAL NERVOUS SYSTEM.

Ness, Loch Freshwater lake in N Scotland, running SW to NE along the geological fault of Glen More. It is 38km (24mi) long and 230m (754ft) deep and forms part of the Caledonian Canal. Accounts of a Loch Ness monster date back to the 15th century, but the veracity of the legend has never been established.

Nestorianism Christian heresy according to which JESUS CHRIST, the incarnate God, possesses two separate natures, one divine and the other human, as opposed to the orthodox belief that Christ is one person who is at once both God and man. The heresy was associated with Nestorius (d.*c*.451), Bishop of Constantinople. It was condemned by the Council of CHALCEDON (451). Nestorius was deposed and banished. Nestorians have survived as a small community.

Netanyahu, Benjamin (1949–) Israeli statesman, prime minister (1996–). Netanyahu served as permanent representative to the UN (1984–88), before becoming deputy minister of foreign affairs. In 1993 he became leader of the right-wing Likud Party. Netanyahu defeated Shimon PERES in the elections that followed the assassination of Yitzhak RABIN. His uncompromising stance over Israeli settlement on the West Bank and Likud's opposition to the ISRAELI-PALESTINIAN ACCORD threatened to disrupt the peace process.

netball Seven-a-side ball game played by women. It is a variant of BASKETBALL. Only two players of each team are allowed in the shooting circle at goal, which is the same size and height as basketball but without a backboard. The game dates from the 1880s and is played chiefly in the English-speaking countries and the Commonwealth.

Netherlands Country in NW Europe, the capital is AMSTERDAM. **Land and climate** The Netherlands, Belgium and Luxembourg form the LOW COUNTRIES. Except in the far SE, the Netherlands is flat and *c*.40% lies below sea level. Large areas (*polders*) have been reclaimed from the sea. Dykes prevent flooding and have created Ijsselmeer. The maritime provinces include Amsterdam, the administrative capital THE HAGUE, and the cities of ROTTERDAM, DELFT, HAARLEM, GRONINGEN and Utrecht. The Netherlands has a temperate maritime climate, with mild winters and abundant rainfall. It is very densely populated. About 66% of the land is arable or grazing land. The country is irrigated by a series of canals. **Economy** The Netherlands has prospered through its close European ties. Private enterprise has successfully combined with progressive social policies. Services account for 65% of GDP and industry 30%. It is highly industrialized. Products include aircraft, chemicals, electronics, machinery and textiles. Natural resources include natural gas, but it is a net importer of raw materials. Agriculture is highly intensive and mechanized, employing only 5% of the workforce. Dairy farming is the leading agricultural activity. Major products include cheese, barley, flowers and bulbs. **History and politics** During the 4th–8th century the region was ruled by the Franks, and in the 10th century it became part of the Holy Roman Empire. In the 14th and 15th centuries trade flourished through the HANSEATIC LEAGUE. In 1477 the region passed to the Habsburgs. PHILIP II's attempt to impose the Inquisition met with fierce resistance. The N Protestant provinces, led by William I (the Silent), declared independence in 1581. The foundation of the Dutch EAST INDIA COMPANY in 1602 marked the beginnings of empire. The mercantile class became the patrons of DUTCH ART. Following the THIRTY YEARS WAR, the Peace of WESTPHALIA (1648) recognized the independence of the N and S provinces as the United Provinces. In 1652 Jan de WITT established a republic. Trading rivalry with England led to the DUTCH WARS. The Treaty of Breda (1667) confirmed Dutch imperial possessions. In 1672 France invaded and De Witt was murdered. The House of ORANGE re-established control under WILLIAM III (OF ORANGE). France controlled the Netherlands from 1795 to 1813. In 1815 the former United Provinces, Belgium and Luxembourg united to form the kingdom of the Netherlands under WILLIAM I. Belgium broke away in 1830. In 1890 Luxembourg also seceded, and WILHELMINA began her long reign. The Netherlands was neutral in World War 1. Germany invaded in May 1940; most Dutch Jews were deported to Poland and then murdered. Queen Wilhelmina was exiled during World War 2. In 1948 Wilhelmina abdicated in favour of

NETHERLANDS
AREA: 41,526sq km (16,033sq mi)
POPULATION: 15,178,000
CAPITAL (POPULATION): Amsterdam (724,096)
GOVERNMENT: Constitutional monarchy
ETHNIC GROUPS: Netherlander 95%, Indonesian, Turkish, Moroccan, German
LANGUAGES: Dutch (official)
RELIGIONS: Christianity (Roman Catholic 34%, Dutch Reformed Church 17%, Calvinist 8%), Islam 3%
CURRENCY: Guilder = 100 cents

her daughter, Juliana. In 1949 the Netherlands joined NATO, and Indonesia gained its independence. In 1957 it was a founder member of the European Community, and in 1958 formed the Benelux customs union. It gave Netherlands New Guinea and Surinam independence in 1962 and 1975 respectively. It retains the islands of NETHERLANDS ANTILLES. In 1980 Queen Juliana abdicated in favour of her daughter, Beatrix. Post-1945, the Netherlands has been ruled by a succession of coalition governments. In 1994 Wim Kok was elected prime minister.

Netherlands Antilles Group of five main islands (and part of a sixth) in the WEST INDIES, forming an autonomous region of the Netherlands; the capital is Willemstadt (on CURAÇAO). The islands were settled by the Spanish in 1527 and captured by the Dutch in 1634. They were granted internal self-government in 1954. Industries: oil refining, petrochemicals, phosphates, tourism. Area: 993sq km (383sq mi). Pop. (1992) 189,474.

nettle Any of numerous species of flowering plants of the genus *Urtica*, especially the stinging nettle (*U. dioica*), which is typical of the genus in that it has stinging hairs along the leaves and stem. The "sting" is formic acid. Family Urticaceae.

network *See* COMPUTER NETWORK

Neumann, John von (1903–57) US mathematician, b. Budapest. His contribution to quantum theory was followed by work on the atomic bomb at LOS ALAMOS. He did important work in the early development of computers and was also responsible for the development of GAME THEORY.

neuralgia Intense pain from a damaged nerve, possibly tracking along its course. Forms include trigeminal neuralgia, which features attacks of stabbing pain in the mouth area, and post-herpetic neuralgia following an attack of SHINGLES.

neurology Branch of medicine dealing with the diagnosis and treatment of diseases of the NERVOUS SYSTEM.

neuron (nerve cell) Basic structural unit of the NERVOUS SYSTEM that enables rapid transmission of impulses between different parts of the body. It is composed of a cell body, which contains a nucleus, and a number of trailing processes. The

largest of these is the axon, which carries outgoing impulses; the rest are dendrites, which receive incoming impulses.

neurosis Emotional disorder such as anxiety, depression or various phobias. It is a form of mental illness in which the main disorder is of mood, but the person does not lose contact with reality, as happens in PSYCHOSIS.

neurotransmitter Any one of several dozen chemicals involved in communication between nerve cells or between nerve and muscle cells. When an electrical impulse arrives at a nerve ending, a neurotransmitter is released to carry the signal across the junction (synapse) between the nerve cell and its neighbour. Some drugs work by disrupting neurotransmission. *See also* NERVOUS SYSTEM

neutralization In chemistry, mixing of equivalent amounts of an acid and a base in an aqueous medium until the mixture is neither acidic nor basic (PH of 7).

neutrino Uncharged ELEMENTARY PARTICLE (symbol v) with no mass or a very low mass, spin 1/2 and travelling at the speed of light. Classified as a LEPTON, it has little reaction with matter and is difficult to detect.

neutron Uncharged ELEMENTARY PARTICLE (symbol n) that occurs in the atomic nuclei of all chemical elements except the lightest isotope of HYDROGEN. Outside the nucleus, it is unstable, decaying with a half-life of 11.6 minutes into a PROTON, ELECTRON and antineutrino. Its neutrality allows it to penetrate and be absorbed in nuclei and thus induce nuclear transmutation and fission.

neutron bomb Nuclear weapon that produces a small blast but a very intense burst of high-speed neutrons. The lack of blast means that buildings are not heavily damaged. The neutrons, however, produce intense RADIATION SICKNESS in people located within a certain range of the explosion.

neutron star Extremely small, dense star that consists mostly of neutrons. Neutron stars are formed when a massive star explodes as a SUPERNOVA, blasting off its outer layers and compressing the core so that its component protons and electrons merge into neutrons. They are observed as PULSARS. They have masses comparable to that of the Sun, but diameters of only about 20km (12mi) and average densities of about 10^{15}g/cm^3.

Nevada State in w USA; the capital is CARSON CITY. The USA acquired the region in 1848 at the end of the MEXICAN WAR. When gold and silver were found in 1859, settlers flocked to Nevada. Much of the state lies in the Great Basin, but the SIERRA NEVADA rise steeply from its w edge. Nevada's dry climate and steep slopes have hindered the development of an agricultural economy. Hay and lucerne (alfalfa) are the chief crops; sheep and cattle grazing are important. Most of Nevada's economic wealth comes from its mineral deposits, which include copper, lead, silver, gold, zinc and tungsten. Industries: chemicals, timber, electrical machinery, glass products. It is a tourist area and, in cities such as LAS VEGAS and Reno, gambling provides an important source of state revenue. Area: 286,297sq km (110,539sq mi). Pop. (1990) 1,201,833.

New Age System of philosophy and religion that came to the fore during the late 1980s and traces its origins to a variety of sources, including oriental mysticism and new scientific ideas. The movement embraces diverse issues, including feminism, astrology, ecology, spiritualism and paganism and takes a holistic approach to healing.

New Brunswick Maritime province in E Canada, on the US–Canadian border; the capital is Fredericton. The region was first explored by Jacques CARTIER in 1534. It was ceded to Britain in 1713. Many loyalists entered the region from the American colonies during the AMERICAN REVOLUTION. The province of New Brunswick was established in 1784. In 1867 New Brunswick joined NOVA SCOTIA, QUEBEC and ONTARIO to form the Dominion of CANADA. The chief crops are hay, clover, oats, potatoes and fruit. Industries: timber, leather goods, pharmaceuticals, machinery. There are also valuable mineral deposits. The largest towns are St John and Moncton. Area: 73,437sq km (28,354sq mi). Pop. (1991) 723,900.

New Caledonia (Nouvelle Calédonie) French overseas territory in the SW Pacific Ocean, c.1,210km (750mi) E of Australia, consisting of New Caledonia, Loyalty Islands, Isle des Pins, Isle Bélep and Chesterfield and Huon Islands; the capital is NOUMÉA (New Caledonia). Discovered in 1774 by COOK, the islands were annexed by France in 1853. The group became a French overseas territory in 1946. In the 1980s there was a growing separatist movement. Direct French rule was imposed in 1988. Products: copra, coffee, cotton, nickel, iron, manganese, cobalt, chromium. Area: 18,575sq km (7,170sq mi). Pop. (1989) 164,182.

Newcastle upon Tyne City in NE England, a major port on the River Tyne; administrative centre of Tyne and Wear. The site of a fort in Roman times, Newcastle acquired a Norman castle in the 11th century. It was a major wool-exporting port in the 13th century and later a coal-shipping centre. Its shipbuilding industry is in decline, but heavy engineering is still important. Industries: pharmaceuticals, engineering, aircraft. Pop. (1991) 259,541.

New Deal Programme for social and economic reconstruction in the USA (1933–39) launched by President Franklin D. ROOSEVELT to restore prosperity after the GREAT DEPRESSION. It was based on massive federal intervention in the economy. The New Deal encountered bitter resistance from conservatives and did not avert recession in 1937–38. Industrial expansion, full employment and agricultural prosperity were achieved less by the New Deal than by World War 2. However, the programme laid the basis for future federal management of the economy and provision of social welfare.

New Delhi Capital of India, in the N of the country, on the River Yamuna in Delhi Union Territory. Planned by the British architects Sir Edwin LUTYENS and Herbert Baker, it was constructed 1912–29 to replace Calcutta as the capital of British India. Whereas the old city of DELHI (to the SW) is a commercial centre, New Delhi has an administrative function. Industries: textiles, chemicals, machine tools, plastics, food processing, electrical appliances, traditional crafts. Pop. (1991) 301,800.

New England Region in NE USA, made up of the states of MAINE, NEW HAMPSHIRE, VERMONT, CONNECTICUT, MASSACHUSETTS and RHODE ISLAND. In 1643 the New England Confederation was set up by some of the colonies for the purposes of defence and to establish a common policy towards the Native Americans. New England was the centre of events leading up to the AMERICAN REVOLUTION.

New Forest Region of forest and heathland in S England, in S Hampshire. It was established as a royal hunting ground in 1079 by William I. It is a popular tourist resort. Area: c.383sq km (148sq mi).

Newfoundland Province in E Canada, on the Atlantic Ocean, consisting of the mainland region of LABRADOR and the island of Newfoundland plus adjacent islands; the capital is ST JOHN'S (in Newfoundland). Norsemen are believed to have landed on the coast of Labrador c. AD 1000. John CABOT reached the island in 1497. The region became a British colony in 1824. It remained apart from the rest of Canada until 1949, when it became the country's tenth province. The island of Newfoundland is a plateau with many lakes and marshes. Labrador has tundra in the N. The cold climate and lack of transport facilities have hindered economic development. There are, however, valuable mineral resources. Timber is an important industry, and the Grand Banks is one of the world's best cod-fishing areas. Area 404,420sq km (156,185sq mi). Pop. (1991) 568,474.

New France Area of Canada claimed by France in the 16th–18th centuries. It included the St Lawrence valley, the Great Lakes region and the Mississippi valley. Parts were lost during the Anglo–French wars of the 18th century, and the whole of New France passed to Britain in 1763.

New Guinea Second-largest island in the world, part of the E Malay archipelago, in the W Pacific Ocean. Discovered in the early 16th century, New Guinea was colonized by the Dutch, the Germans and the British during the next two centuries. In 1904 the British-administered part was transferred to Australia and during World War 1 Australian forces seized German New Guinea. The E half eventually achieved independence as PAPUA NEW GUINEA in 1975. The W half, IRIAN JAYA, became a province of Indonesia in 1969. The island has a tropical climate and is mountainous. Products: copra, cocoa, coffee, rubber, coconuts, tobacco. Area: 885,780sq km (342,000sq mi).

New Hampshire State in NE USA, on the Canadian border; the capital is CONCORD. The first settlement was made in 1623. Much of the land is mountainous and forested. The principal rivers are the Connecticut and the Merrimack, and there are more than 1,000 lakes. Farming is restricted by poor soil, and is concentrated in the Connecticut valley. Dairy and market garden produce are the chief products. New Hampshire is highly industrialized. There is abundant hydroelectricity. Industries: electrical machinery, paper and wood products, printing and publishing, leather goods, textiles. Area: 24,097sq km (9,304sq mi). Pop. (1990) 1,109,253.

New Jersey State in E USA, on the Atlantic coast, S of New York; the capital is TRENTON. Other major cities include NEWARK, ATLANTIC CITY and Camden. Settlement began in the 1620s, when the Dutch founded the colony of New Netherland (later New York). When the British took the colony in 1664 the land between the Hudson and Delaware rivers was separated and named New Jersey. The N of the state is in the Appalachian highland region; SE of this area are the Piedmont plains, and more than half the state is coastal plain. A variety of crops are grown, and dairy cattle and poultry are important. New Jersey is industrial and densely populated. Industries: chemicals, pharmaceuticals, rubber goods, textiles, electronic equipment, copper smelting, oil refining. Area: 20,295sq km (7,836sq mi). Pop. (1990) 7,730,188.

Newlands, John Alexander Reina (1837–98) British chemist. In 1864 he announced his law of octaves, which arranged chemical elements in a table of eight columns according to atomic weight. MENDELEYEV included the law in his own PERIODIC TABLE five years later.

Newman, Cardinal John Henry (1801–90) British theologian. As leader of the OXFORD MOVEMENT (1833–45), he had a powerful effect on the Church of England, equalled only by the shock of his conversion to Roman Catholicism (1845). A great literary stylist, he is remembered especially for his autobiography, *Apologia pro vita sua* (1864).

Newman, Paul (1925–) US film actor, director and producer. He is known for his portrayals of wryly humorous anti-heroes in such films as *The Hustler* (1961), *Butch Cassidy and the Sundance Kid* (1969) and *The Sting* (1973). Recent work includes *The Color of Money* (1986; Academy Award) and *The Hudsucker Proxy* (1994).

New Mexico State in SW USA, on the Mexican border; the capital is SANTA FE. The largest city is ALBUQUERQUE. The first permanent Spanish settlement was established at Santa Fe in 1610. The USA acquired the region in 1848 at the end of the MEXICAN WAR. It entered the Union in 1912 as the 47th state. The first atomic bomb was exploded at Alamogordo in 1945. The Sangre de Cristo Mountains in the N flank the Rio Grande, which runs N to S through the state. The terrain includes desert, forested mountains and stark mesa. In the S and SW are semi-arid plains. The S Pecos and Rio Grande rivers are used to irrigate cotton crops; hay, wheat, dairy produce and chili beans are also important. Much of the land is pasture. A large proportion of the state's wealth comes from mineral deposits, including uranium, manganese, copper, silver, turquoise, oil, coal and natural gas. Area: 314,334sq km (121,335sq mi). Pop. (1990) 1,515,069.

New Model Army Reformed Parliamentary army in the English CIVIL WAR. Formed in 1645 by Oliver CROMWELL, it was better organized, trained and disciplined than any comparable Royalist force, and it ensured final victory for Parliament.

New Orleans City and river port in SE Louisiana, USA, between Lake Pontchartrain and the Mississippi River. Founded by the French in 1718, it was ceded to Spain in 1763 and acquired by the USA under the LOUISIANA PURCHASE of 1803. Its industries expanded rapidly in the 20th century after the discovery of oil and natural gas. New Orleans made an important contribution to the development of JAZZ. Industries: food processing, petroleum, natural gas, oil and sugar refining, shipbuilding, tourism, aluminium, petrochemicals. Pop. (1990) 496,938.

Newport City and port in Narragansett Bay, SE Rhode Island, USA. Founded in 1639, it served as joint state capital with Providence until 1900. It is home to music festivals and for many years hosted the America's Cup yachting races. Tourism is the chief industry. Pop. (1990) 28,227.

New South Wales State in SE Australia, on the Tasman Sea; the capital is SYDNEY. Captain COOK first visited the area in 1770, landing at Botany Bay. He claimed the E coast of Australia for Britain, naming it New South Wales. The colony developed in the first half of the 19th century with the growth of the wool industry. New South Wales achieved responsible government in 1855, becoming a state of the Commonwealth of Australia in 1901. The Great Dividing Range separates the narrow coastal lowlands from the W plains that occupy two-thirds of the state. The MURRAY River and its tributaries are used extensively for irrigation. Wheat, wool, dairy produce and beef are the principal agricultural products. The state has valuable mineral deposits. New South Wales is the most populous and most industrialized state in Australia. Steel is the chief product. Area: 801,430sq km (309,180sq mi). Pop. (1991) 5,730,947.

newt Any of numerous species of tailed AMPHIBIANS of Europe, Asia and North America. The common European newt, *Triturus vulgaris*, is terrestrial, except during the breeding season when it is aquatic and the male develops ornamental fins. Its body is long and slender and the tail is laterally flattened. Length: to 17cm (7in). Family Salamandridae.

New Testament Second part of the Bible, consisting of 27 books all originally written in Greek after AD 45 and concerning the life and teachings of JESUS CHRIST. It begins with three SYNOPTIC GOSPELS (MATTHEW, MARK, and LUKE), which present a common narrative of Christ's life and ministry, and a fourth gospel (JOHN), which is more of a theological meditation. The ACTS OF THE APOSTLES follow a history recording the early development and spread of Christianity, and 21 letters (EPISTLES) addressed to specific early Church communities; the New Testament ends with the REVELATION of St John the Divine (as the Apocalypse), which is an interpretation of history designed to demonstrate the sovereignty of God.

Newton, Sir Isaac (1642–1727) English scientist. He studied at CAMBRIDGE and became professor of mathematics there (1669–1701). His main works were *Philosophiae Naturalis Principia Mathematica* (1687) and *Opticks* (1704). In the former, he outlined his laws of motion and proposed the principle of universal GRAVITATION; in the latter he showed that white light is made up of colours of the SPECTRUM and proposed his particle theory of light. He also created the first system of CALCULUS in the 1660s, but did not publish it until Gottfried LEIBNIZ had published his own system in 1684. He built a reflecting telescope in *c.*1671.

newton SI unit (symbol N) of FORCE. One newton is the force that gives a mass of 1kg an acceleration of one metre per second per second.

Newton's Laws Three physical laws of motion formulated by Isaac NEWTON. The first law states that an object remains at rest or moves in a straight line at constant speed unless acted upon by a force. The second law states that force is proportional to the rate of change of MOMENTUM. The third law states that every force has associated with it an equal and opposite force. *See also* MECHANICS

New York State in NE USA, bounded by the Canadian border, the Great Lakes, the Atlantic Ocean and three New England states; the capital is ALBANY. NEW YORK CITY is by far the largest city in the state. Henry HUDSON discovered New York Bay in 1609 and sailed up the river that now bears his name. The New Netherland colony was established in the Hudson valley. In 1664 it was seized by the British and renamed New York. It was one of the 13 original states of the Union. The opening of the ERIE CANAL in 1825 was a stimulus to New York's growth. Much of the state is mountainous, the ADIRONDACK MOUNTAINS (NE) and Catskills (SE) being the principal ranges. The W consists of a plateau sloping down to Lake Ontario and the St Lawrence valley. The HUDSON and its tributary, the Mohawk, are the chief rivers. Agricultural produce is varied. New York is the leading manufacturing and commercial state in the USA. Industries: clothing, machinery, chemicals, electrical equipment, paper, optical instruments. Area: 127,190sq km (49,108sq mi). Pop. (1993 est.) 18,197,154.

New York City City and port in SE New York State, USA, at the mouth of the Hudson River; largest city (by population) in the USA. MANHATTAN Island was bought from the Native Americans in 1626 by the Dutch West India Company, and New Amsterdam was founded at the S end of the

island. In 1664 the British took the colony and renamed it New York. The founding of the Bank of New York by Alexander Hamilton and the opening of the Erie Canal in 1825 made New York the principal US commercial and financial centre. After the CIVIL WAR and in the early 20th century, the city received a great influx of immigrants. It is made up of five boroughs: Manhattan, the Bronx, BROOKLYN, QUEENS and Staten Island. Monuments and buildings of interest include the STATUE OF LIBERTY, the EMPIRE STATE BUILDING and the METROPOLITAN MUSEUM OF ART. It is one of the world's leading ports and an important financial centre. Industries: clothing, chemicals, metal products, scientific instruments, shipbuilding, food processing, broadcasting, entertainment, tourism, publishing. Pop. (1990) 7,322,564.

New Zealand Archipelago state in the S Pacific; the capital is WELLINGTON. **Land and climate** New Zealand consists of two mountainous main islands and several smaller ones, *c.*1,600km (1,000mi) SE of Australia. Much of NORTH ISLAND is volcanic; Ngauruhoe and Ruapehu are active volcanoes. It is noted for its hot springs and geysers. The N has fertile peninsulas and river basins. New Zealand's largest river (Waikato) and largest lake (Taupo) are both on North Island. North Island cities include Wellington and the largest port, AUCKLAND. The Southern Alps extend for almost the entire length of SOUTH ISLAND, rising to Mount COOK at 3,753m (12,313ft). South Island is famed for its glaciers and fjords. The major South Island cities are CHRISTCHURCH and DUNEDIN. Territories include the ROSS DEPENDENCY in Antarctica. COOK ISLANDS and NIUE are associated states. **Economy** During the 1980s New Zealand gradually shifted from a state-controlled economy with a large welfare state to a more capitalist economy, encouraging private sector finance. It has traditionally depended on agriculture, particularly sheep- and cattle-rearing. New Zealand is the world's third-largest producer of sheep – more than 51 million in 1993. Manufacturing now employs twice as many people as agriculture. Tourism is the fastest growing sector of the economy (1992 receipts, US$1,032 million). The climate varies from N to S.

NEW ZEALAND
AREA: 270,990sq km (104,629sq mi)
POPULATION: 3,414,000
CAPITAL (POPULATION): Wellington (329,000)
GOVERNMENT: Constitutional monarchy
ETHNIC GROUPS: New Zealand European 74%, New Zealand Maori 10%, Polynesian 4%
LANGUAGES: English and Maori (both official)
RELIGIONS: Christianity (Anglican 21%, Presbyterian 16%, Roman Catholic 15%, Methodist 4%)
CURRENCY: New Zealand dollar = 100 cents

Auckland has a warm, humid climate throughout the year. Wellington has cooler summers, while in Dunedin, temperatures can dip below freezing in winter. Rainfall is heaviest on the w highlands. Only small areas of original *kauri* forests survive, mainly in the N and s extremities of South Island. Beech forests grow in the highlands, and large plantations are grown for timber. Abundant sunshine is ideal for E coast vineyards. **History and politics** MAORI settlers arrived in New Zealand more than 1,000 years ago. The first European discovery was by the Dutch navigator Abel TASMAN in 1642. The British explorer James COOK landed in 1769. Trade in fur and whaling brought British settlers in the early 19th century. A series of intertribal wars (1815–40) killed tens of thousands of Maoris. In 1840 the first British settlement at Wellington was established. The Treaty of WAITANGI (1840) promised to honour Maori land rights in return for recognition of British sovereignty. In 1841 New Zealand became a separate colony. Increasing colonization led to the Maori Wars (1845–48, 1860–72). In 1893 New Zealand was the first country to extend the franchise to women. In 1907 New Zealand became a self-governing dominion in the British Commonwealth. New Zealand troops fought on the side of the Allies in both World Wars. In 1973 Britain joined the European Community, and New Zealand's exports to Britain shrank. **Recent events** Since the 1980s, New Zealand has pursued a more independent economic and foreign policy. Maori rights and Maori culture remain a political issue. A 1992 referendum voted in favour of proportional representation. John Bolger was re-elected prime minister in 1996.

Niagara Falls Waterfalls on the Niagara River on the border of the USA (w New York state) and Canada (SE Ontario); divided into the Horseshoe, or Canadian, Falls, and the American Falls. The Canadian Falls are 48m (158ft) high and 792m (2,600ft), wide; the American Falls are 51m (167ft) high and 305m (1,000ft) wide.

Niamey Capital of Niger, West Africa, in the sw part of the country, on the River Niger. It became capital of the French colony of Niger in 1926. It grew rapidly after World War 2 and is now the country's largest city and its commercial and administrative centre. Industires: textiles, ceramics, plastics, chemicals. Pop. (1988) 392,169.

Nicaea, Councils of Two important ecumenical councils of the Christian church held in Nicaea (modern Iznik, Turkey). The first was convoked in AD 325 to resolve the problems caused by the emergence of ARIANISM. It promulgated a creed, affirming belief in the divinity of Christ. The Second Council of Nicaea, held in 787, was summoned by the patriarch Tarasius to deal with the problem of the worship of icons.

Nicaragua Republic in Central America; the captial is MANAGUA. **Land and Climate** Nicaragua is the largest country in Central America. The Central Highlands rise in the NW Cordillera Isabella to over 2,400m (8,000ft) and are the source of many of the rivers that drain the E plain. The Caribbean coast forms part of the MOSQUITO COAST. Lakes Managua and Nicaragua lie on the edge of a narrow volcanic region, which contains Nicaragua's major urban areas, including Managua, and the second-largest city of León. This region is highly unstable with many active volcanoes, and is prone to earthquakes. **Economy** Nicaragua faces many problems in rebuilding its shattered economy and introducing free-market reforms. Agriculture is the main activity, employing *c.*50% of the workforce and accounting for 70% of exports. Major cash crops include coffee, cotton, sugar and bananas. Rice is the main food crop. It has some copper, gold and silver, but mining is underdeveloped. Most manufacturing is based in and around Managua. Nicaragua has a tropical climate, with a rainy season from June to October. The Central Highlands are cooler, and the wettest part is the Mosquito Coast, with *c.*4,200mm (165in) of annual rain. Rainforests cover large areas in the E. Tropical savanna is common in the drier w. **History** Christopher COLUMBUS reached Nicaragua in 1502 and claimed the land for Spain. By 1518 Spanish forces had subdued the indigenous population, and Nicaragua was ruled as part of the Spanish Captaincy-General of Guatemala. In the 17th century Britain secured control of the Caribbean coast. In 1821 Nicaragua gained independence and formed part of the Central American Federation (1825–38). In the mid-19th century Nicaragua was ravaged by civil war, and US and British interference. José Santos Zemalya's dictatorial regime gained control of Mosquito Coast and formed close links with the British. Following his downfall, civil war raged once more. In 1912 US marines landed to protect a pro-US regime. In 1933 the US marines withdrew, and set up the National Guard to help defeat the rebels. In 1934 guerrilla leader Auguste Sandino was assassinated by Anastasio SOMOZA, director of the National Guard and official president from 1937. Somoza was succeeded by his sons Luis (1956) and Anastasio (1967).

NICARAGUA
AREA: 130,000sq km (50,193sq mi)
POPULATION: 4,130,000
CAPITAL (POPULATION): Managua (682,111)
GOVERNMENT: Multiparty republic
ETHNIC GROUPS: Mestizo 77%, White 10%, Black 9%, Native American 4%
LANGUAGES: Spanish (official)
RELIGIONS: Christianity (Roman Catholic 91%, others 9%)
CURRENCY: Córdoba oro (gold córdoba) = 100 centavos

Anastasio's diversion of international relief aid following the devastating 1972 Managua earthquake cemented opposition. In 1979 the SANDINISTA National Liberation Front (FSLN) overthrew the Somoza regime. The Sandinista government, led by Daniel Ortega, instigated wide-ranging socialist reforms. The USA, concerned over the Sandinista's relations with Cuba and the Soviet Union, sought to destabilize the government by organizing and funding the CONTRA rebels. A ten-year civil war destroyed the economy, and created dissatisfaction with the Sandinistas. **Politics** In 1990 elections, the Sandinistas lost power to the National Opposition Union coalition of opposition parties. Violeta CHAMORRO became president. Many of Chamorro's reforms were blocked by her coalition partners and the Sandinista-controlled trade unions. In 1996 elections, Chamorro was defeated by the Liberal leader, Arnoldo Aleman.

Nice City in SE France, on the Mediterranean coast; capital of Alpes-Maritimes département. Founded by Phocaean Greeks in the 4th century BC, it was conquered by Rome in the 1st century AD. In the 10th century it passed to the counts of Provence. In 1388 it became a possession of the House of Savoy. It was under French rule from 1792 to 1814, when it was returned to Savoy, becoming permanently part of France in 1860. It is a major centre of the French Riviera. Industries: tourism, olive oil, perfumes, textiles, electronics. Pop. (1990) 342,349.

Nicene Creed Statement of Christian faith named after the First Council of NICAEA (325). Its exact origin is uncertain. The Nicene Creed defends the orthodox Christian doctrine of the TRINITY against the ARIAN heresy. It is subscribed to by all the major Christian Churches and is widely used by them in their celebrations of the EUCHARIST. *See also* APOSTLES' CREED; ATHANASIAN CREED

Nicholas, Saint Patron saint of children and sailors. Traditionally he was Bishop of Myra in Asia Minor in the 4th century. His name in his Dutch dialect, *Sinter Claes*, became SANTA CLAUS.

Nicholas I (1796–1855) Tsar of Russia (1825–55). On ascending the throne, he was immediately confronted by the Decembrist revolt, during which a secret society of officers and aristocrats assembled some 3,000 troops in St Petersburg, demanding a representative democracy. Having crushed the rebels, he ruthlessly suppressed rebellion in Poland and assisted Austria against the Hungarian revolution of 1848. His pressure on Turkey led to the CRIMEAN WAR (1853–56).

Nicholas II (1868–1918) Last Tsar of Russia (1894–1917). Torn between the autocracy of his father, ALEXANDER III, and the reformist policies of ministers such as Count Sergei Witte, he lacked the capacity for firm leadership. Defeat in the RUSSO-JAPANESE WAR was followed by the RUSSIAN REVOLUTION OF 1905. Nicholas agreed to constitutional government but, as danger receded, removed most of the powers of the Duma (parliament). In

World War 1 he took military command (1915) but defeat again provoked revolution (1917). Nicholas was forced to abdicate, and in July 1918 he and his family were executed by BOLSHEVIKS.

Nicholson, Ben (1894–1982) British painter, a champion of ABSTRACT ART in Britain. Influenced by CUBISM and Piet MONDRIAN, he developed a geometric abstract style, which he expressed in austere carved and painted reliefs, such as *White Relief* (1935).

Nicholson, Jack (1937–) US film actor. He first attracted attention in *Easy Rider* (1969). Oscar-nominated several times for films such as *Five Easy Pieces* (1970) and *Chinatown* (1974), he eventually won Academy Awards for *One Flew Over the Cuckoo's Nest* (1975) and *Terms of Endearment* (1983). Other films include *The Shining* (1980), *Batman* (1989) and *Mars Attacks!* (1996).

nickel Silvery-white metallic element (symbol Ni), one of the TRANSITION ELEMENTS. Its chief ores are pentlandite and niccolite. Hard, malleable and ductile, nickel is used in stainless steels, other special alloys, coinage, cutlery, storage batteries and as a hydrogenation catalyst. Properties: at.no. 28; r.a.m. 58.71; r.d. 8.90 (25°C); m.p. 1,453°C (2,647 °F); b.p. 2,732°C (4,950°F); most common isotope Ni^{58} (67.84%).

Nicklaus, Jack William (1940–) US golfer. He has secured 20 major championship wins during 27 playing years. His record in the British Open is unparalleled, with three victories and a top six place in 15 consecutive years. He won the US Masters six times, the last victory being in 1986.

Nicosia (Levkosía) Capital of Cyprus, in the central part of the island. Known to the ancient world as Ledra, the city was later successively held by the Byzantines, French crusaders and Venetians. The Ottoman Turks occupied the city from 1571 to 1878, when it passed to Britain. It is now divided into Greek and Turkish sectors. Manufactures include cigarettes, textiles and footwear. Pop. (1992 est.) 177,451.

nicotine Poisonous ALKALOID obtained from the leaves of TOBACCO, used in agriculture as a pesticide and in veterinary medicine to kill external parasites. Nicotine is the principal addictive agent in smoking tobacco. *See also* CIGARETTE

Nielsen, Carl (1865–1931) Danish composer, known internationally for his six symphonies. He also composed concertos for violin, flute and clarinet, two operas, a woodwind quintet and four string quartets.

Niemöller, Martin (1892–1984) German Protestant minister and theologian. He opposed Hitler's creation of a "German Christian Church" and was arrested in 1938 because of his opposition to the Nazi Party. In 1961 he became President of the World Council of Churches.

Nietzsche, Friedrich Wilhelm (1844–1900) German philosopher who rejected Christianity and the prevailing morality of his time and emphasized people's freedom to create their own values. He presented his notion of the *Übermensch* (super-man), the idealized man, strong, positive, and able to impose his wishes upon the weak and worth-less, in *Thus Spake Zarathustra* (1883–85).

Niger Landlocked nation in NW Africa, the capital is NIAMEY. **Land and climate** The N plateaux lie in the SAHARA. Central Niger contains the rugged, partly volcanic Aïr Mountains, which reach a height of 2,022m (6,634ft) near Agadez. The S con-sists of broad plains, including the Lake CHAD basin in SE Niger, on the borders with Chad and Nigeria. The only major river is the NIGER in the SW. The narrow Niger valley is the country's most fertile and densely populated region, and includes Niamey. Niger is one of the world's hottest coun-tries. The hottest months are March to May, when the HARMATTAN wind blows from the Sahara. Niamey has a tropical climate, with a rainy season from June to September. Rainfall decreases from S to N. Northern Niger is practically rainless. The far S consists of tropical savanna. Most of S Niger lies in the SAHEL region of dry grassland. The Aïr Mountains support grass and scrub. The N deserts are generally barren. **Economy** Niger has been badly hit by droughts, which have caused great suf-fering and food shortages and the destruction of the traditional nomadic lifestyle. Niger's chief resource is uranium and it is the world's second-largest producer. Uranium accounts for over 80% of exports, most of which is exploited by the French Atomic Energy Authority. Some tin and tungsten are also mined. Other mineral resources are unexploited. Despite its resources, Niger is one of the world's poorest countries (1992 GDP per capita, US$820). Farming employs 85% of the workforce, though only 3% of the land is arable and 7% is used for grazing. Food crops include beans, cassava, millet, rice and sorghum. Cotton and groundnuts are leading cash crops. **History and politics** Neolithic remains have been found in the N desert. Nomadic TUAREG settled in the Aïr Mountains in the 11th century AD, and by the 13th century had established a state based on Agadez and the trans-Saharan trade. In the 14th century, the HAUSA settled in S Niger. In the early 16th century the SONGHAI empire controlled much of Niger, but was defeated by the Moroccans at the end of the

century. In the early 19th century the FULANI gained control of much of S Niger. The first French expedition arrived in 1891, but Tuareg resistance prevented full occupation until 1914. In 1922 Niger became a colony within French West Africa. In 1958 Niger voted to remain an autonomous republic within the French Community. Full inde-pendence was achieved in 1960. Hamani Diori became Niger's first president, and maintained close ties with France. Drought in the Sahel began in 1968 and killed many livestock and destroyed crops. In 1974 a group of army officers, led by Lieutenant-Colonel Seyni Kountché, overthrew Hamani Diori and suspended the constitution. Kountché died in 1987 and was succeeded by his cousin General Ali Saibou. **Recent events** In 1991 Tuaregs in N Niger began an armed campaign for greater autonomy. A national conference removed Saibou and established a transitional government. In 1993 multiparty elections, Mahamane Ousmane of the Alliance of Forces for Change (AFC) coali-tion became president. The collapse of the coalition led to further elections in 1995, which were won by the National Movement for a Development Society (MNSD), but a military coup, led by Colonel Ibrahim Bare Mainassara, seized power. A peace accord was signed between the government and the Tuaregs. In 1996 elections, Brigadier-General Mainassara became president.

Niger Major river of W Africa. It rises in the Fouta Djallon plateau in the SW Republic of Guinea and flows NE through Guinea into Mali, where it forms an extensive inland delta. It then flows SW through Niger in a great curve across the border into Nigeria and S into another vast delta before emptying into the Gulf of Guinea. Length: 4,180km (2,600mi).

Niger-Congo languages Group of nearly a thousand languages spoken by more than 300 million people in Africa S of the Sahara. The main ones are BANTU (spoken in S Africa), FULANI (Guinea, Senegal and other W African countries), SWAHILI (E coast), YORUBA (primarily Nigeria) and Malinke (Mali).

Nigeria Republic in W Africa, the capital is ABUJA. **Land and climate** Nigeria is the most populous nation in Africa. It has a sandy coastline, fringed by a belt of mangrove swamps and lagoons, which includes the former capital, LAGOS. The NIGER and Benue rivers meet in cen-tral Nigeria, and run S into the Niger Delta, where BENIN CITY is situated. North of the coastal low-lands is a hilly region of rainforest and savanna. At the foot of the great plateau of Nigeria lies the city of IBADAN. The plateau region includes Abuja. In the extreme NE lies the Lake CHAD basin. In the NW lies the Sokoto plains. The Adamawa High-lands extend along the SE border with Cameroon, and contain Nigeria's highest point, at 2,042m (6,699ft). Lagos has a tropical climate, with high temperatures and rain throughout the year. The N is drier and often hotter than the S, though the

NIGER
AREA: 1,267,000sq km (489,189sq mi)
POPULATION: 8,252,000
CAPITAL POPULATION: Niamey (392,169)
GOVERNMENT: Multiparty republic
ETHNIC GROUPS: Hausa 53%, Zerma-Songhai 21%, Tuareg 11%, Fulani (or Peul) 10%
LANGUAGES: French (official)
RELIGIONS: Islam 98%
CURRENCY: CFA franc = 100 centimes

NIGERIA
AREA: 923,770sq km (356,668sq mi)
POPULATION: 88,515,000
CAPITAL (POPULATION): Abuja (305,900)
GOVERNMENT: Federal republic
ETHNIC GROUPS: Hausa 21%, Yoruba 21%, Ibo (or Igbo) 19%, Fulani 11%, Ibibio 6%
LANGUAGES: English (official)
RELIGIONS: Christianity (Protestant 26%, Roman Catholic 12%, others 11%), Islam 45%
CURENCY: Naira = 100 kobo

highlands are cooler. KANO in N central Nigeria has a marked dry season from October to April. Behind the coastal swa mps are rainforests, though large areas have been cleared by farmers. The plateau contains large areas of tropical savanna with forested river valleys. Open grassland and semi-arid scrub occur in drier areas. To the N lie the dry grasslands of the SAHEL. **Economy** Nigeria is a low-income developing country, with great economic potential. It is the world's 11th-largest producer of crude oil, which accounts for 95% of its exports. The major oilfields are in the Niger delta, and the bights of Benin and Biafra. The drop in the price and production of oil, and mounting foreign debt caused economic recession in the 1980s. Agriculture employs 43% of the workforce. Nigeria is the world's third-largest producer of palm oil and palm kernels, fourth-largest producer of groundnuts, fifth-largest producer of cocoa, and seventh-largest producer of rubber. Cattle rearing is important in the N grasslands, while fishing is a major activity in the S. Manufacturing is diversifying. Major products include chemicals and clothing. Nigeria also has petroleum refineries, vehicle assembly plants and steel mills. **History and politics** Excavations around the Nigerian village of Nok have uncovered some of the oldest and most beautiful examples of African sculpture. The Nok civilization flourished between 500 BC and AD 200. In the 11th century, the Kanem-Bornu kingdom extended s from Lake Chad into Nigeria, and the HAUSA established several city-states. In SW Nigeria, the state of BENIN and the YORUBA kingdom of Oyo flourished in the 15th century. They were renowned for their brass, bronze and ivory sculptures. The SONGHAI empire dominated N Nigeria in the early 16th century. The Portuguese were the first Europeans to reach the Nigerian coast, and they established trading links with Benin in the late 15th century. Nigeria became a centre of the slave trade, with major European powers competing for control. The IGBO established city-states on the wealth of the trade. In the early 19th century, the FULANI captured many of the Hausa city-states. Sokoto retained its independence. The SW began a protracted civil war. In 1807 Britain renounced the slave trade, but other countries continued the prac-

tice. In 1861 Britain seized Lagos, ostensibly to stop the trade. By 1885 Britain controlled all of s Nigeria and gradually extended northwards. By 1906 Britain had conquered all of Nigeria, and divided the country into the Colony (Lagos) and Protectorate of Southern Nigeria and the Protectorate of Northern Nigeria. In 1914 the two were combined. Britain ruled indirectly through colonial officials and local rulers. Cities, infrastructure and industries developed. In 1954 Nigeria was federated into three regions (N, E, and W) plus the territory of Lagos. In 1960 Nigeria gained independence and became a republic in 1963. In 1966 Igbo army officers staged a successful coup, but the regime was rapidly toppled by a Hausa-led coup. In 1967 the Igbo, increasingly concerned for their safety within the federation, formed the independent republic of BIAFRA. For the next three years civil war raged in Nigeria, until Biafra capitulated. The division of Nigeria into 30 states reflects the fact that it contains more than 250 ethnic and language groups, and several religious ones. The early 1970s were more peaceful, as Nigeria expanded its oil industry. Nigeria joined OPEC in 1971. Oil revenue created widespread government corruption and widened the wealth gap. Drought in the SAHEL killed much livestock and led to mass migration to the s. After several military coups, civilian rule was briefly restored in 1979. Following the 1983 elections, the military seized power again. Between 1960 and 1996 Nigeria enjoyed only nine years of civilian government. In 1993 presidential elections, won by Chief Moshood Abiola, were declared invalid by the military government. The army commander-in-chief, General Sanni Abacha, gained power. In 1994 nationwide demonstrations prompted Abiola to form a rival government, but he was swiftly arrested. In 1995 General Abacha was given an open-ended term in office, vowing to restore civilian rule by 1998. His regime has been severely criticized for human rights abuses and the suppression of opposition. In November 1995, after the execution of nine activists, Nigeria was suspended from the Commonwealth of Nations.

Nightingale, Florence (1820–1910) British nurse, b. Italy. She founded modern NURSING and is best known for her activities in the CRIMEAN WAR. In 1854 she took a unit of 38 nurses to care for wounded British soldiers. In 1860 she founded the Nightingale School and Home for nurse training at St Thomas's Hospital, London.

nightingale Migratory Old World songbird of the THRUSH family (Turdidae). The common nightingale of England and Western Europe (*Luscinia megarhynchos*) is ruddy-brown with light grey underparts. Length: *c*.16.5cm (6.5in).

nightjar Insect-eating, nocturnal bird found worldwide. It has a whirring cry. Length: 27cm (10.5in). Family Caprimulgidae.

nightshade Any of various species of poisonous

flowering plants, but especially the DEADLY NIGHT-SHADE (*Atropa belladonna*) and its close relatives.

Nijinsky, Vaslav (1890–1950) Russian dancer, often regarded as the greatest male ballet dancer of the 20th century. Dancing with the Ballets Russes, his most noted roles were in *Petrushka*, *Les Sylphides* and *Scheherazade*. From 1912 he choreographed such ballets as *L'Après-midi d'un faune*, *Jeux* and *Le Sacre du printemps* for DIAGHILEV.

Nile Longest river in the world, flowing *c.*6,700km (4,160mi) from the Kagera headstream, E Burundi, to its Mediterranean delta in NE Egypt. The Kagera empties into Lake VICTORIA. The Victoria Nile flows from Lake Victoria to Lake ALBERT in Uganda. From Lake Albert to the Sudanese border, it is called the Albert Nile. It flows N through the S Sudanese swamps as the Bahr el Jebel. From Malakâl to KHARTOUM the river is called the White Nile. At Khartoum it converges with the Blue Nile. As simply the Nile, it flows N to the Egyptian border. There it flows into Lake Nasser, created by the damming of the river at ASWAN. From Aswan the river flows through LUXOR to Cairo. N of Cairo is the Nile Delta, Egypt's largest agricultural area. The Nile empties into the Mediterranean at Damietta and Rosetta.

Nineveh Capital of ancient ASSYRIA, on the River Tigris (opposite modern Mosul, Iraq). The site was first occupied in the 6th millennium BC. It became the Assyrian capital under Sennacherib (r.704–681 BC). Nineveh was sacked by the Medes in 612 BC, but continued to be occupied until the Middle Ages.

niobium Shiny grey-white metallic element (symbol Nb), a TRANSITION ELEMENT. Its chief ore is pyrochlore. Soft and ductile, niobium is used in special stainless steels and in alloys for rockets and jet engines. Properties: at.no. 41; r.a.m. 92.9064; r.d. 8.57; m.p. 2,468°C (4,474°F); b.p. 4,742°C (8,568°F); most common isotope Nb^{93} (100%).

Nirvana Conception of salvation and liberation from rebirth in the religions of ancient India – HINDUISM, BUDDHISM and JAINISM. To Hindus, *nirvana* is extinction in the supreme being, brought about by internal happiness, internal satisfaction and internal illumination. To Buddhists, it is the attainment of a transcendent state of enlightenment through the extinction of all desires. To Jainists, *nirvana* is a state of eternal blissful repose.

nitrate Salt of NITRIC ACID (HNO_3). Nitrate salts contain the nitrate ion (NO_3^-), and some are important naturally occurring compounds, such as saltpetre (potassium nitrate, KNO_3) and Chile saltpetre (sodium nitrate, $NaNO_3$). Nitrates are used as food preservers, fertilizers, explosives and as a source of nitric acid. They can be an environmental hazzard.

nitric acid Colourless liquid (HNO_3), one of the strongest mineral acids. Nitric acid attacks most metals, resulting in the formation of NITRATES, and is a strong oxidizing agent. It is used in the manufacture of agricultural chemicals, explosives, plastics, dyes and rocket propellants.

nitrogen Common gaseous nonmetallic element (symbol N) of group V of the periodic table. Colourless and odourless, it is the major component of the atmosphere (78% by volume), from which it is extracted by fractional distillation of liquid air. It is necessary for life, being present in all plants and animals. The main industrial use is in the HABER PROCESS. Nitrogen compounds are used in fertilizers, explosives, dyes, foods and drugs. The element is chemically inert. Properties: at. no. 7; r.a.m. 14.0067; r.d. 1.2506; m.p. −209.86°C (−345.75°F); b.p. −195.8°C (−320.4°F); most common isotope N^{14} (99.76%).

nitrogen cycle Circulation of nitrogen through plants and animals in the BIOSPHERE. Plants obtain nitrogen compounds for producing essential proteins. Nitrogen-fixing bacteria in the soil or plant root nodules take free nitrogen from the soil and air to form the nitrogen compounds used by plants to grow. The nitrogen is returned to the soil and air by decay or denitrification.

nitrogen fixation Incorporation of atmospheric NITROGEN into chemicals for use by organisms. Nitrogen-fixing microorganisms (mainly BACTERIA and CYANOBACTERIA) absorb nitrogen gas from the air, from air spaces in the soil, or from water, and build it up into compounds of ammonia. Other bacteria then change these compounds into nitrates, which can be taken up by plants.

nitroglycerine Oily liquid used in the manufacture of explosives. It is also used in medicine (as glyceryl trinitrate) to relieve ANGINA.

nitrous oxide (dinitrogen oxide) Colourless gas (N_2O). It is used as an anaesthetic or analgesic during surgical or dental operations.

Niue Island territory in the S Pacific Ocean, 2,160km (1,340mi) NE of New Zealand; the capital is Alofi. The largest coral island in the world, Niue was first visited by Europeans in 1774. In 1901 it was annexed to New Zealand. In 1974 it achieved self-government in free association with New Zealand. The island is prone to hurricanes. Its economy is agricultural. The major export is coconut. Area: 260sq km (100sq mi). Pop. (1991) 2,239.

Nixon, Richard Milhous (1913–94) 37th US President (1969–74). He was vice president under EISENHOWER (1953–60), but lost the presidential election of 1960 to John F. KENNEDY. He was nominated as presidential candidate again in 1968, defeating the Democrat, Hubert Humphrey. As president, Nixon persevered with STRATEGIC ARMS LIMITATIONS TALKS (SALT) with the Soviet Union. In 1972 he became the first US president to visit communist China. Nixon easily won re-election in 1972. In 1973, following the blanket bombing of North Vietnam, Nixon withdrew US troops from VIETNAM WAR. The WATERGATE AFFAIR revealed that he was personally implicated in the obstruction of justice, and he resigned to avoid impeachment.

Nkrumah, Kwame (1909–72) Ghanaian statesman, prime minister (1957–60), first president of

Ghana (1960–66). Nkrumah was the leading post-colonial proponent of PAN-AFRICANISM. In 1949 he formed the Convention People's Party in the Gold Coast. He was imprisoned (1950) by the British, but released when his party won the general election. He led the Gold Coast to independence (1957), and became prime minister of Ghana. In 1960 it became the Republic of Ghana and Nkrumah was made president. Nkrumah gradually assumed absolute power and, following a series of assassination attempts, Ghana became a one-party state (1964). While on a visit to China, he was deposed in a military coup (1966).

Noah Old Testament patriarch who was the only person righteous enough to be chosen by God to survive (with his family) the destruction of the FLOOD. In Genesis 6–9, Noah built an ARK, in accordance with God's strict instructions, to carry himself, his family and selected animals and birds.

Nobel, Alfred Bernhard (1833–96) Swedish chemist, engineer and industrialist. He invented DYNAMITE in 1866, and patented a more powerful explosive, gelignite, in 1876. With the fortune he made from the manufacture of explosives, he founded the NOBEL PRIZES.

nobelium Radioactive metallic element (symbol No) of the ACTINIDE SERIES. Seven isotopes are known. Properties: at.no. 102, most stable isotope No^{255} (half-life 3 minutes).

Nobel Prize Awards given each year for outstanding contributions in the fields of physics, chemistry, physiology or medicine, literature and economics, and to world peace. The prizes were established in 1901 by the will of Alfred NOBEL.

noble gas (inert gas) Helium, neon, argon, krypton, xenon and radon – the elements (in order of increasing atomic number) forming group 0 of the PERIODIC TABLE. They are colourless, odourless and very unreactive. They have low reactivity because their outer electron shells are complete.

No drama Form of Japanese symbolic drama that developed between the 12th or 13th and the 15th centuries. It was influenced by ZEN, and the actors were originally Buddhist priests. The plots were taken chiefly from Japanese mythology and poetry. The No play seeks to convey a moment of experience or insight. It is highly stylized and uses masks, music, dance and song. No was central to the development of KABUKI THEATRE.

Nolan, Sidney (1917–92) Australian painter. He is famed for a series of paintings (begun in 1946) based on the life of a notorious bushranger, Ned Kelly. He continued painting subjects that portrayed events from Australian history, notably the *Eureka Stockade* series (1949).

Nolde, Emil (1867–1956) German painter and graphic artist who exemplified EXPRESSIONISM. He painted his subjects (often flowers or landscapes) with deep, glowing colours and simplified outlines, bringing the works to the borders of ABSTRACT ART.

nomad Member of a wandering group of people who live mainly by hunting or herding. Nomadism has been regarded as an intermediate state between hunter-gatherer and farming societies. Today, nomadic groups survive only in the more remote parts of Africa, Asia and the Arctic.

nominalism Philosophical theory, opposed to REALISM, that denies the reality of universal concepts. Whereas realists claim that there are universal concepts, such as *roundness* or *dog*, that are referred to by the use of these terms, nominalists argue that such generalized concepts cannot be known, and that the terms refer only to specific qualities common to particular circles or dogs that have been encountered up to now. Nominalism was much discussed by the scholastic philosophers of the Middle Ages.

nonconformism Dissent from or lack of conformity with the religious doctrines or discipline of an established church, especially the CHURCH OF ENGLAND. The term Nonconformist applies to all the sects of British Protestantism that do not subscribe to the principles of the established Anglican Church or the established CHURCH OF SCOTLAND. Movements such as CONGREGATIONALISM and PRESBYTERIANISM, BAPTISTS and QUAKERS proliferated. Nonconformist Churches were eventually granted freedom of worship in 1689 and civil and political rights in 1828. METHODISM and UNITARIANISM were added to their ranks during the 18th century.

nonjurors Clergy in England and Scotland who refused to take the oath of allegiance to WILLIAM III and MARY II in 1689. Anglo-Catholic in sympathy, they included several bishops and *c*.400 priests in England and most of the Scottish episcopal clergy.

Nono, Luigi (1924–90) Italian composer. An early follower of WEBERN, he gained international recognition with the *Canonic Variations* (1950), an orchestral work based on a note series of SCHOENBERG. He composed several political works, including the anti-fascist opera *Intolerance* (1960).

noradrenaline Hormone secreted by nerves in the autonomic nervous system and also by the ADRENAL GLANDS. It slows the heart rate and constricts small arteries, thus raising the blood pressure. It is used therapeutically to combat the fall in blood pressure that accompanies shock.

Nordenskjöld, Nils Adolf Erik, Baron (1832–1901) Swedish explorer and scientist. A geologist by training, he explored the Greenland ice cap and the Arctic Ocean. In 1878 he led the Swedish expedition in the *Vega*, which was the first ship to sail through the NORTHEAST PASSAGE.

Norfolk County of E England; the county town is NORWICH. The region was home to the ICENI tribe in the 3rd century BC. After the departure of the Romans it became part of the ANGLO-SAXON kingdom of East Anglia, but was later subjugated by the Danes. The land is low-lying and is used for agriculture. The region is drained by the Waveney, Yare, Bure and Ouse, and the BROADS. Norfolk produces cereals and root vegetables; poultry farming and fishing are also important. Area: 5,372sq km (2,073sq mi). Pop. (1991) 745,613.

Norfolk Broads *See* BROADS, NORFOLK

Norfolk Island Territory of Australia in the SW Pacific Ocean, c.1,450km (900mi) E of Australia. Visited in 1774 by Captain Cook, it was a British penal colony (1788–1814, 1825–55). Many people living on Pitcairn Island, descendants of the *Bounty* mutineers, were resettled here in 1856. The chief activities are agriculture and tourism. Area: 34sq km (13sq mi). Pop. (1991) 1,912.

Noriega, Manuel (Antonio Morena) (1934–) Panamanian general. He was made chief of military intelligence in 1969. Recruited as a CIA-operative by the USA, Noriega became an important backstage power-broker. During 1983–89 he was effectively Panama's paramount leader, ruling behind puppet presidents. In 1988 he was indicted by a US court on drug-connected charges and accused of murder. In December 1989 US troops invaded Panama and installed a civilian government. Noriega surrendered and was taken to the USA for trial on corruption, drug trafficking, and money laundering. In April 1992 he was sentenced to 40 years in prison.

Norman architecture ROMANESQUE architectural style of the Normans in England, N France and S Italy. Characteristic buildings include the cathedrals at St Étienne and Caen in France and Durham in England. The style was marked by massive proportions, square towers, round arches and little decoration.

Norman Conquest Invasion of England in 1066 by WILLIAM I (the Conqueror), duke of Normandy. William claimed that EDWARD THE CONFESSOR (d.1066) had recognized him as heir to the throne of England, and he disputed the right of HAROLD II to be Edward's successor. William's army defeated and killed Harold at the Battle of HASTINGS, then advanced on London, where William was accepted as king. The ruling class, lay and ecclesiastical, was gradually replaced by Normans, and Norman institutions were imposed.

Normandy Region and former province of NW France, coextensive with the départements of Manche, Calvados, Orne, Eure and Seine-Maritime. Part of the Roman province of Gaul, it was absorbed into the Frankish kingdom of Neustria in the 6th century. In the mid-9th century it was invaded by Vikings. It was the seat of William duke of Normandy (later WILLIAM I), who invaded England in 1066. Normandy was recovered by the French in 1204. It was the site of the landings by the Allies in German-occupied France in June 1944. It is characterized by forests, flat farmlands and rolling hills. The economy is based on livestock rearing, dairy products, fruit, cider and fishing.

Normandy Campaign Allied invasion of German-occupied France, launched on 6 June 1944 (D-Day). Commanded by EISENHOWER, the invasion was the largest amphibious operation in history. The successful landings were the start of the final campaign of WORLD WAR 2 in W Europe.

Norman French Dialect of Old French spoken by the Normans at the time of the conquest of England (1066). In England it coexisted with contemporary MIDDLE ENGLISH for about three centuries.

Normans Descendants of Vikings who settled in NW France in the 9th–10th centuries. They created a powerful state, with a strongly centralized feudal society and warlike aristocracy. In the 11th century, under Robert Guiscard and Robert II, they defeated the Muslims to create an independent kingdom in Sicily. In 1066 Duke William of Normandy conquered England and became WILLIAM I.

Norodom Sihanouk *See* SIHANOUK, NORODOM

Norse literature Literature of the Scandinavian Norsemen, written between the 9th and the 12th century. It consists mainly of mythological poetry and SAGAS. Works survived orally to be recorded in the 12th–14th centuries.

North, Frederick, Lord (1732–92) British statesman and prime minister (1770–82). North's repressive measures against unrest in the North American colonies, particularly the Intolerable Acts designed to punish the colonists for the BOSTON TEA PARTY, have been blamed for their rebellion.

North, Oliver Laurence (1943–) US marine lieutenant colonel. He was recruited as an aide to the National Security Council and was involved in several covert operations. The Congressional committee that investigated the notorious IRAN-CONTRA AFFAIR in 1987 revealed him as the central figure, and he was convicted of three criminal charges.

North America Continent, including the mainland and offshore islands N of and including Panama. **Land** North America extends N of the Arctic Circle and S almost to the Equator. To the W it is bordered by the Bering Sea and the Pacific Ocean, and to the E by the Atlantic Ocean. There are many islands off both coasts, particularly to the N in the Arctic Ocean, and to the SE in the Caribbean Sea. There are two major mountain ranges: the APPALACHIANS in the E and the ROCKY MOUNTAINS in the W. Between these two ranges lie the fertile GREAT PLAINS and the Central Lowlands. In the E, a long coastal plain extends from New England to Mexico. The W coast is more mountainous. **Structure and geology** Much of Canada is an old Precambrian shield area forming a saucer-shaped depression centred in the HUDSON BAY. The Appalachians also have their origins in the Precambrian era. In the W, the complex fold mountains of the Rockies and the Pacific Margin are much younger and continue into South America as the ANDES. **Lakes and rivers** Lake SUPERIOR is the largest lake in North America, and together with MICHIGAN, HURON, ERIE and ONTARIO, makes up the GREAT LAKES. The ST LAWRENCE River forms a navigable link between the Great Lakes and the Atlantic Ocean. The longest river is the combined MISSISSIPPI-MISSOURI system. Other important rivers include the YUKON, MACKENZIE, COLORADO, COLUMBIA, DELAWARE and RIO GRANDE. **Climate and vegetation** Its geographical range means that every climatic zone is represented. In the far N, there are areas of tundra and arctic conditions. In the interior, sheltered by high mountains, there are deserts. Tropical rainforest is found in the lower areas of Central America. On much of the continent the climate is temperate. The Great Plains region is temperate, and the natural vegetation is grass, bordered by mixed and coniferous forests in the mountains to the E, W and N. **People** North America's first settlers probably arrived about 45,000 years ago from Asia by way of Alaska. By the time the Vikings arrived from Europe, around AD 1000, NATIVE AMERICANS occupied the entire continent. European settlement accelerated after Christopher Columbus's voyage in 1492. The Spaniards settled in Mexico and the WEST INDIES. The English and French settled farther N in the USA and Canada. Swedes, Germans and Dutch also formed settlements. Europe's political and economic problems later drove larger numbers to the New World. Descendants of Spanish settlers are predominant in Mexico, Central America and some Caribbean islands. French concentrations exist in Quebec province, Canada, and parts of the West Indies. In Central America and the Caribbean, European descendants are in the minority. **Economy** Much of North America benefits from fertile soil and a climate conducive to agriculture. The North American plains are one of the world's major grain and livestock-producing areas. The S area produces mainly cotton, tobacco, coffee and sugar cane. There is also substantial industrial development. Mining is important, particularly in Canada and Mexico. **Recent history** The early 20th century saw mass emigration to the USA and Canada. The USA has been the dominant economic force on the continent throughout the 20th century. In the Spanish American War (1898) the USA emerged as a world power. In 1903 Theodore ROOSEVELT enforced the construction of the PANAMA CANAL, control of which is due to return to Panama in 1999. The USA and Russia emerged from World War 2 as global superpowers. The ideological battle between CAPITALISM and COMMUNISM created the COLD WAR, and led to US involvement in the KOREAN WAR and the VIETNAM WAR. Since January 1994, Canada, the USA and Mexico have been linked through the NORTH AMERICAN FREE TRADE AGREEMENT (NAFTA). As the USA and Canada have developed a more service-based economy, manufacturing has transferred to Mexico. Economic inequality and instability remain major issues in Mexico. Since World War 2 many Caribbean islands have gained independence. *Highest mountain* Mount McKinley 6,194m (20,321ft) *Longest river* Mississippi-Missouri 6,050km (3,760mi) *Population* 395,000,000 *Largest cities* Mexico City (15,047,685); New York City (7,322,564); Los Angeles (3,489,779) *See also* individual country articles

North American Free Trade Agreement (NAFTA) Treaty designed to eliminate trade barriers between Canada, Mexico and the USA. The agreement was signed in 1992, and NAFTA came into effect on 1 January 1994. Some Latin American countries have also applied to join.

North American mythology Native North Americans displayed a great diversity of languages and cultures, but their mythologies had many common features. Among these was the concept of heroes in the form of animal deities, such as Raven or Coyote, believed to have been the original inhabitants of the land. They brought order into the world by having power over fire, wind and rain, and by establishing laws and institutions. They also created mountains and rivers and other natural features. Native Americans had numerous gods, including the Great Spirit and the Earth Mother of the Algonquins, and the gods of thunder and wind of the Iroquois. Belief in protective or harmful spirits remains universal, and the SHAMAN acts as an intermediary between man and the spirit world.

Northamptonshire County in central England; the county town is Northampton. There are traces of pre-Celtic habitations as well as Roman and Anglo-Saxon settlement. The land is undulating and is drained by the Welland and Nene rivers. Much of the region is devoted to pasture, wheat growing and forestry. Products include cereals, potatoes and sugar beet. There are extensive iron ore deposits and iron and steel industries remain important. Area: 2,367sq km (914sq mi). Pop. (1991) 578,807.

North Atlantic Treaty Organization (NATO) Intergovernmental organization, military alliance of the USA, Canada and 14 European countries. The original treaty was signed in Washington in 1949 by Belgium, Britain, Canada, Denmark, France, Iceland, Italy, Luxembourg, Norway, Portugal, Netherlands and the USA. Since then, Greece, Turkey, Spain and Germany have joined. In July 1997, despite Russian opposition, the Czech Republic, Hungary and Poland were invited to join. NATO's headquarters is in Brussels. During the COLD WAR, it was the focus of the West's defence against the Soviet Union.

North Carolina State in E USA, on the Atlantic coast; the capital is RALEIGH. The first English colony in North America was founded in 1585 on Roanoke Island. Permanent settlers moved into the region from Virginia in the 1650s. It was the last state to secede from the Union. North Carolina's coastal plain is swampy and low-lying. Its W edge rises to rolling hills, and further W are the Blue Ridge and Great Smoky Mountains. It is the leading producer of tobacco in the USA. Important agricultural products are maize, soya beans, peanuts, pigs, chickens and dairy produce. Industries: textiles, timber, fishing, tourism, electrical machinery, chemicals. Mineral resources include phosphate, feldspar, mica and kaolin. Area: 136,523sq km (52,712sq mi). Pop. (1990) 6,628,637.

North Dakota State in N central USA, on the Canadian border; the capital is BISMARCK. French explorers first visited the region in 1738. The USA acquired the W half of the area from France in LOUISIANA PURCHASE (1803), and the rest from Britain in 1818 when the boundary with Canada was fixed. Dakota was divided into North and South Dakota in 1889. The region is generally low-lying and is drained by the Missouri and Red rivers. Wheat, barley, rye, oats, sunflowers and flaxseed are the chief crops. Cattle rearing is the most important economic activity. Area: 183,022sq km (70,665sq mi). Pop. (1990) 638,800.

Northeast Passage Route from the Atlantic to the Pacific via the Arctic Ocean. Attempts were made to find the passage by Dutch and English mariners from the 16th century. The first complete voyage was made by NORDENSKJÖLD in 1878–80.

Northern Cape Province in SW South Africa; the capital is Kimberley. Northern Cape was created in 1994 from the N part of the former CAPE PROVINCE. Area: 361,800sq km (139,650sq mi). Pop (1994) 737,360.

Northern Ireland See IRELAND, NORTHERN

northern lights Popular name for the AURORA borealis.

Northern Province Province in N South Africa; the capital is Pietersburg. In 1994 Northern Transvaal was formed from the N part of the former province of TRANSVAAL. In 1995 it was renamed Northern Province. Area: 123,280sq km (46,970sq mi). Pop. (1994 est.) 5,201,630.

Northern Territory Territory in N central Australia bounded by the Timor and Arafura seas (N), and the states of Western Australia (W), South Australia (S) and Queensland (E); the capital is Darwin. The territory lies mostly within the tropics. The coastal areas are flat with many offshore islands, and the region rises inland to a high plateau, the Barkly Tableland. In the mainly arid south are the Macdonnell Ranges and AYERS ROCK. Manganese ore, bauxite and iron are mined. Area: 1,347,525sq km (520,280sq mi). Pop. (1993) 169,298.

North Island Smaller but more densely populated of the two main islands of New Zealand; separated from SOUTH ISLAND by Cook Strait. Chief cities are WELLINGTON, AUCKLAND and Hamilton. The island contains several mountain ranges, Lake Taupo (New Zealand's largest lake), fertile coastal plains and numerous hot springs. Most of New Zealand's dairy produce comes from North Island. Industries: wood pulp, paper, mining, fishing. Area: 114,729sq km (44,297sq mi). Pop. (1991) 2,553,413.

North Korea See KOREA, NORTH

North Pole Most northerly point on Earth; the N end of the Earth's axis of rotation, 725km (450mi) N of Greenland. Geographic north lies at 90° latitude, 0° longitude. The Arctic Ocean covers the entire area.

North Sea Arm of the Atlantic Ocean, lying between the E coast of Britain and the European mainland and connected to the English Channel by the Straits of Dover. Generally shallow, it is c.960km (600mi) long, with a maximum width of 640km (400mi). It is a major fishing ground, shipping route and an important source of oil and natural gas. Area: c.580,000sq km (220,000sq mi).

Northumberland, John Dudley, Duke of (1502–53) Effectively ruler of England (1549–53). He was one of the councillors named by HENRY VIII to govern during the minority of EDWARD VI. In 1553 he attempted to usurp the succession through his daughter-in-law, Lady Jane GREY, but was thwarted by popular support for the rightful queen, MARY I. He was executed for treason.

Northumberland County in NE England, on the border with Scotland; the county town is Morpeth. In the 2nd century AD HADRIAN'S WALL was built to defend Roman Britain from the northern tribes. In the 7th century the region became part of the Saxon kingdom of Northumbria. The land slopes down from the Cheviot Hills in the NW, and the region is drained by the Tyne, Tweed, Blythe and Coquet rivers. The county is largely rural, the chief farming activities being cattle and sheep rearing. Barley and oats are grown and forestry is important. Coal is mined in the S. Area: 5,033sq km (1,943sq mi). Pop. (1991) 304,694.

Northumbria, Kingdom of Largest kingdom in Anglo-Saxon England. Formed in the early 7th century, it included NE England and SE Scotland up to the Firth of Forth. In the age of the historian BEDE and the LINDISFARNE GOSPELS, Northumbria experienced a blossoming of scholarship and monastic culture. Its power declined in the 8th century.

Northwest Passage Western route from the Atlantic to the Pacific via N Canada. Many European explorers in the 16th–17th centuries tried to find a passage through North America to the Pacific. The effort was renewed in the 19th century. Sir John FRANKLIN'S expedition, which set out in 1845, was lost with all hands, but during the search for survivors, the route was established. First to make the passage in one ship was Roald AMUNDSEN in 1903–06.

North-West Frontier Province Province in NW Pakistan; the capital is PESHAWAR. It is a region of high mountains divided by fertile valleys of the River INDUS. The region is linked by a series of passes with India and Afghanistan, including the KHYBER PASS. Since the 7th century, the PATHANS have fiercely defended the region. Islam was introduced in the 10th century. In 1849 Britain assumed control. For the next 50 years the Pathans resisted British rule. In 1901 Britain divided the PUNJAB and created a separate North-West Frontier Province. In 1947 it joined the new state of Pakistan. The economy is based on agriculture and the principal crop is wheat. Area: 74,521sq km (28,765sq mi). Pop. (1985 est.) 12,287,000.

North-West Province Province in NW South Africa; the capital is Mmabatho. North-West Province was created from the NW part of the former province of TRANSVAAL. Area: 116,190sq km (44,489sq mi). Pop. (1994 est.) 3,252,991.

Northwest Territories Region in N Canada, covering more than 33% of the country and consisting of mainland Canada N of latitude 60°N, and hundreds of islands in the Arctic Archipelago. The capital is Yellowknife. Much of the N and E of the province is tundra, inhabited by INUIT and other native peoples. The HUDSON'S BAY COMPANY acquired the area under a charter from CHARLES II in 1670. In 1869 the Canadian government bought the land from the company. The present boundaries were set in 1912. In 1999 Northwest Territories will become the Inuit land of Nunavut. The Mackenzie district has large tracts of softwoods and rich mineral deposits. Area: 3,426,000sq km (1,320,000sq mi). Pop. (1992) 57,649.

North Yorkshire County in N England; the administrative centre is YORK. Other major towns include Scarborough, Whitby and Harrogate. In the 9th century a thriving culture was destroyed by the Scandinavian invasions. In the Middle Ages the region was noted for its many monasteries. In the W are the PENNINES. In the E are the North Yorkshire Moors. North Yorkshire is mainly agricultural, with dairy farming, cereals and hill sheep farming. There is some manufacturing industry. Area: 8,309sq km (3,208sq mi). Pop. (1991) 702,161.

Norway Scandinavian kingdom in NW Europe, the capital is OSLO. **Land and climate** Norway forms the W part of the mountainous Scandinavian peninsula. Norway's coast is fringed by many islands and long, deep fjords. The distant Arctic islands of SVALBARD and Jan Mayen are Norwegian possessions. Many of Norway's cities lie on or near the fjords, including Oslo, BERGEN and TRONDHEIM. The land rises steeply from the coastal lowlands to a 1,500m (5,000ft) central plateau. Europe's largest glacier field, Josdtedalsbreen, lies W of Galdhøppigen, Norway's highest point at 2,469m (8,100ft). The plateau contains many deep valleys with lakes and fast-flowing rivers, such as the Glåma. North Atlantic Drift gives Norway a mild climate. Most of Norway's seaports remain ice-free throughout the year. Snow covers the land for over three months every year. Large areas of the rugged mountains are bare rock. Forest and woods cover c.27% of Norway, with trees such as birch, pine and spruce. **Economy** Norway has developed rapidly post-1945, and has one of the world's highest standards of living (1992 GDP per capita, US$18,580). Norway's chief exports are oil and natural gas. Oil was discovered in 1969. Norway is the world's eighth-largest producer of crude oil. Per capita, Norway is the world's largest producer of hydroelectricity. Major manufactures include petroleum products, chemicals, aluminium, wood pulp and paper. Farmland covers c.3% of the land. Dairy farming and

NORWAY	
AREA: 323,900sq km (125,050sq mi)	
POPULATION: 4,286,000	
CAPITAL (POPULATION): Oslo (459,292)	
GOVERNMENT: Constitutional monarchy	
ETHNIC GROUPS: Norwegian 97%	
LANGUAGES: Norwegian (official), Lappish, Finnish	
RELIGIONS: Christianity (Lutheran 88%)	
CURENCY: Krone = 100 ore	

meat production are the chief activities, but Norway has to import food. Norway has the largest fish catch in Europe after Russia. **History and politics** Norway's seafaring tradition dates back to the VIKINGS, who raided W Europe between the 9th and 11th centuries. Olaf II introduced Christianity in the early 11th century, but was deposed by King CANUTE II of Denmark. Haakon IV re-established unity in the early 13th century. In 1319 Sweden and Norway were joined. In 1397 Norway, Sweden and Denmark were united in the Kalmar Union. For the next four centuries Norway was subject to Danish rule. Lutheranism became the state religion in the mid-16th century. In 1814 Denmark ceded Norway to Sweden. Norway declared its independence, but Swedish troops forced Norway to accept union under the Swedish crown. An independent monarchy was established in 1905. Norway remained neutral in World War 1. In the 1920s Norway rapidly industrialized. In the 1930s Norway adopted progressive social welfare provisions. In April 1940 German troops invaded. Over 50% of Norway's merchant fleet was destroyed in the resistance. Liberation was achieved in May 1945. Norway joined NATO in 1949. Norway was a co-founder (1960) of the European Free Trade Association (EFTA). In 1972 and 1994 referenda, Norway voted against joining the European Community. In 1977 Gro Harlem Brundtland became Norway's first woman prime minister. She was re-elected in 1993. In 1991 Olav V was succeeded by his son, Harald V. In 1996 Brundtland was succeeded as prime minister by Thorbjoern Jagland. The 1997 general election produced a disappointing result for Jagland's Labour Party, and it was replaced by a centrist government headed by Kjell Magne Bondevik.

Norwegian Official language of Norway, spoken by nearly all the country's four million inhabitants. It belongs to the northern branch of the Germanic family of INDO-EUROPEAN LANGUAGES.

Norwich City and county town of NORFOLK, E England. It was an important market town by the 11th century. There are many fine churches dating from the medieval period, including the Norman cathedral (1096). Industries: textiles, machinery, chemicals, electrical goods, foodstuffs, footwear. Pop. (1991) 120,895.

nose In human beings, other primates and some

vertebrates, prominent structure between the eyes. It contains receptors sensitive to various chemicals (sense of SMELL) and serves as the opening to the respiratory tract, warming and moistening air and trapping dust particles on the MUCOUS MEMBRANES.

Nostradamus (Michel de Nostredame) (1503–66) French seer and astrologer. After practising as a doctor, he began making astrological predictions in 1547. These were published in rhyming quatrains in *Centuries* (1555) and represented one verse for every year from then till the end of the world (in the 1990s). To avoid prosecution as a magician, he changed the order of the verses so that no time sequence was discernible.

notochord In chordates and the early embryonic stages of vertebrates, the flexible, primitive backbone; replaced by the SPINE in mature vertebrates.

Nottingham City and county town of NOTTING-HAMSHIRE, on the River Trent, N central England. Originally a 6th-century Anglo-Saxon settlement, it is the traditional birthplace of ROBIN HOOD. The city grew rapidly in the 19th century, becoming famous for the manufacture of fine lace, cotton and hosiery. It is a centre of communications and transport. Industries: textiles, engineering, bicycles, electronic equipment, pharmaceuticals. Pop. (1991) 263,522.

Nottinghamshire County in central England; the county town is NOTTINGHAM. The land slopes down from the E ridges of the PENNINES in the W to the lowlands of the E. The principal river is the TRENT. Wheat, barley and sugar-beet are the chief crops; beef and dairy cattle are also important. There are rich deposits of coal in the county. Nottinghamshire has long been noted for its textile industries. Area: 2,164sq km (836sq mi). Pop. (1991) 993,872.

Nouakchott Capital of MAURITANIA, NW Africa, in the SW part of the country, *c.*8km (5mi) from the Atlantic Ocean. Originally a small fishing village, it was chosen as capital of Mauritania when it became independent in 1960. Light industries have also been developed and handicrafts are important. Pop. (1988) 393,325.

noun Member of a linguistic class or category consisting of words that serve to name a person, place, thing or concept.

nova Faint star that undergoes unpredictable increases in brightness by several magnitudes, apparently due to explosions in its outer regions, and then slowly fades back to normal. *See also* VARIABLE STAR

Novalis (1772–1801) German romantic poet and novelist, b. Friedrich Leopold, Baron von Hardenberg. He began his major work, the mythical romance *Heinrich von Ofterdingen*, in 1799, but had not completed it by the time of his early death.

Nova Scotia Maritime province in SE Canada, consisting of a mainland peninsula, the adjacent Cape Breton Island and a few smaller islands; the capital is HALIFAX. The first settlement of Nova Scotia was made by the French at Port Royal in 1605. The mainland was awarded to Britain in

1713, and Cape Breton Island was seized from the French in 1758. Nova Scotia joined NEW BRUNSWICK, QUEBEC and ONTARIO to form the Dominion of CANADA in 1867. The land is generally low-lying, rolling country and there are extensive forests. The principal crops are hay, apples, grain and vegetables. There are valuable coal deposits on Cape Breton Island. Fishing is important. Industries: shipbuilding, pulp, paper, steelmaking, food processing. Area: 55,490sq km (21,425sq mi). Pop. (1991) 899,942.

novel Narrative fiction, usually in prose form, that is longer and more detailed than a short story. The roots of the modern novel are generally traced to CERVANTES' *Don Quixote* (1605–15); its development as a major literary form can be seen in 18th-century Britain in Daniel DEFOE's *Robinson Crusoe* (1719) and Samuel RICHARDSON's *Pamela* (1740). The 20th century has seen considerable formal experimentation, with developments such as the STREAM OF CONSCIOUSNESS technique.

novella Short, highly structured prose narrative. The form was developed by Giovanni BOCCACCIO in the *Decameron* (1348–53), and has proved popular since the 18th century. In modern usage, the term broadly denotes a work of prose fiction that is longer than a short story but shorter than a NOVEL.

Novgorod City in NW Russia, on the River Volchov. One of Russia's oldest cities, it was supposedly founded by the Varangian prince RURIK in the 9th century. Its inhabitants were forcibly converted to Christianity in 989. It subsequently became capital of a vast territory. After a long fight for supremacy, the city was forced to submit to Moscow in 1478. In 1570 IVAN IV massacred the inhabitants. It declined in importance after the founding of ST PETERSBURG. During World War 2 it suffered great destruction. Industries: distilling, foodstuffs, electrical engineering, furniture, chinaware. Pop. (1992) 235,000.

Nu, U (1907–95) Burmese political leader. Active in the independence movement, he became first prime minister of independent BURMA (1948–56, 1957–58). He returned to power in 1960, but in 1962 he was ousted in the military coup of U NE WIN. After years of exile, he returned to Burma in 1980 and was later placed under house arrest.

Nuba Name for a group of several unrelated peoples inhabiting a region of S Sudan. Most Nuba peoples are farmers and many tribes cultivate terraces on granite hillsides. Animal husbandry is also practised. The predominant religious rituals are closely linked to agricultural fertility rites.

Nubia Ancient state on the upper Nile in NE Africa. It was closely associated with Egypt. At its height, Nubia extended from Egypt to the Sudan. At first ruled by Egypt, it later controlled Egypt in the 8th and 7th centuries BC. It converted to Christianity in the 6th century AD and became part of Ethiopia in the 14th century.

nuclear disarmament *See* DISARMAMENT; STRATEGIC ARMS LIMITATION TALKS (SALT)

455

nuclear energy ENERGY released during a nuclear reaction as a result of the conversion of mass into energy according to Einstein's equation $E = mc^2$. Nuclear energy is released in two ways: by FISSION and by FUSION. Fission is the process responsibile for the atomic bomb and for NUCLEAR REACTORS now contributing to energy requirements throughout the world. Fusion provides the energy for the Sun and the stars and for the HYDROGEN BOMB. It also offers the prospect of cheap energy once a method has been perfected for controlling fusion reactions. *See also* NUCLEAR WEAPON

nuclear fission *See* FISSION, NUCLEAR

nuclear fusion *See* FUSION, NUCLEAR

nuclear physics Branch of physics concerned with the structure and properties of the atomic NUCLEUS. The principal means of investigating the nucleus is the SCATTERING experiment, carried out in particle ACCELERATORS, in which a nucleus is bombarded with a beam of high-energy ELEMENTARY PARTICLES, and the resultant particles analysed. Study of the nucleus has led to an understanding of the processes occurring inside stars, and has enabled the building of NUCLEAR REACTORS.

nuclear reactor Device in which nuclear FISSION reactions are used for power generation or for the production of radioactive materials. In nuclear power stations, NUCLEAR ENERGY is released as heat for use in electricity generation. In the reactor, the fuel is a radioactive heavy metal: uranium-235, uranium-233 or plutonium-239. In these metals, atoms break down spontaneously, a process known as RADIOACTIVE DECAY. Some NEUTRONS released in this process strike the nuclei of fuel atoms, causing them to undergo fission and emit more neutrons. These cause more fissions to occur. In this way a CHAIN REACTION is set up, and heat is produced in the process. The heat is absorbed by a circulating coolant and transferred to a boiler to raise steam to drive an electricity GENERATOR. Experiments are being undertaken with FUSION reactors.

nuclear waste Residues containing radioactive substances. After URANIUM, PLUTONIUM and other useful fission products have been removed, some long-lived radioactive elements remain, such as caesium-137 and strontium-90. The storage of nuclear waste is a major environmental issue.

nuclear weapon Device whose enormous explosive force derives from nuclear FISSION or FUSION reactions. The first atomic bombs were dropped by the USA on the Japanese cities of HIROSHIMA and NAGASAKI in August 1945. The bombs consisted of two stable sub-critical masses of URANIUM or PLUTONIUM which, when brought forcefully together, caused the CRITICAL MASS to be exceeded, thus initiating an uncontrolled nuclear fission reaction. In such detonations, huge amounts of energy and harmful radiation are released: the explosive force can be equivalent to 200,000 tonnes of TNT. The HYDROGEN BOMB (H-bomb or thermonuclear bomb), first tested in 1952, consists of an atomic bomb that on explosion provides a temperature high enough to cause nuclear fusion in a surrounding solid layer, usually lithium deuteride. The explosive power can be that of several megatons of TNT.

nucleic acid Chemical molecules present in all living cells and in viruses. They are of two types, DNA (deoxyribonucleic acid) and RNA (ribonucleic acid), both of which play fundamental roles in heredity. *See also* GENE; CHROMOSOME

nucleon Any of the particles found within the NUCLEUS of an atom: a NEUTRON or a PROTON.

nucleosynthesis Production of all the various chemical elements that exist in the universe from one or two simple atomic nuclei. It is believed to have occurred by way of large-scale nuclear reactions during cosmogenesis and is still in progress in the Sun and other stars.

nucleus Membrane-bound structure that contains the CHROMOSOMES in most cells. Exceptions include BACTERIA, which, instead of chromosomes, have a naked, circular molecule of DNA in the CYTOPLASM, and mature red blood cells. As well as holding the genetic material, the nucleus is essential for the maintenance of cell processes. Nucleus is also the term for the central part of an ATOM.

Nujoma, Sam (1929–) Namibian politician, president of Namibia (1990–). He was a founder and leader of the guerrilla army the SOUTH WEST AFRICA PEOPLE'S ORGANIZATION (SWAPO) from 1959. He was exiled to Tanzania by the South Africans in 1960. After negotiating Namibia's independence through the United Nations, he returned in 1989 for the first free elections.

Nukualofa Capital of Tonga, SW Pacific Ocean, on the N coast of Tongatabu Island. The chief industry is copra processing. Pop. (1986) 29,018.

numbat (banded anteater) Squirrel-like Australian marsupial that feeds on TERMITES. The female, unlike most marsupials, has no pouch. The numbat has a long snout and lateral white bands on its red-brown coat. Length: 46cm (18in). Species *Myrmecobius fasciatus*.

number Symbol representing a quantity used in counting or calculation. All ancient cultures devised number systems for the practical purposes of counting and measuring. From the basic process of counting we get the natural numbers. This concept can be extended to define INTEGERS, RATIONAL NUMBERS, REAL NUMBERS and COMPLEX NUMBERS. *See also* BINARY SYSTEM; IRRATIONAL NUMBER

Numbers Fourth book of the Bible and of the PENTATEUCH. Its central theme is the events that took place during the Israelites' 40 years of wandering in the desert of the Sinai Peninsula, in search of the Promised Land of CANAAN.

number theory Branch of mathematics concerned with the properties of natural numbers (whole numbers) or special classes of natural numbers such as PRIME NUMBERS.

numeral Symbol used alone or in a group to denote a NUMBER. Arabic numerals are the 10 digits from 0 to 9. ROMAN NUMERALS consist of seven letters or marks.

nun Woman belonging to a female religious order who has taken monastic VOWS (*see* MONASTICISM). Nuns may belong to a closed order or one that encourages its members to work in the world for the welfare of society at large. BUDDHISM, CHRISTIANITY and TAOISM all have monastic orders of nuns. Nuns serve a preparatory period called a novitiate, after which they take their final vows.

Nunn, Trevor (1940–) British stage director. He was appointed artistic director of the ROYAL SHAKESPEARE COMPANY (RSC) (1968). He directed the hit West End musicals *Cats* (1981) and *Starlight Express* (1984). In 1996 he was appointed artistic director of the National Theatre of Great Britain.

Nuremberg (Nürnburg) City in s Germany, in Bavaria. It grew up around an 11th-century castle, later becoming a free imperial city. It was a centre of learning and artistic achievement during the 15th and 16th centuries. During the 1930s it was the location of the annual congress of the Nazi Party, and after World War 2 was the scene of the trials of Nazi war criminals. Today Nuremberg is an important commercial and industrial centre. Industries: textiles, pharmaceuticals, electrical equipment, machinery, publishing and printing, motor vehicles, toys, brewing. Pop. (1990) 498,500.

Nuremberg Trials (1945–46) Trials of Germans accused of war crimes during World War 2, held before a military tribunal. The tribunal was established by the USA, Britain, France and the Soviet Union. Several Nazi leaders were sentenced to death and others to terms of imprisonment.

Nureyev, Rudolf (1938–93) Soviet ballet dancer and choreographer. While on tour in Paris in 1961 he defected from the Soviet Union. Major ballets in which he had leading roles included *Sleeping Beauty, Giselle* and *Swan Lake,* and he regularly partnered Margot FONTEYN.

nursing Profession that has as its general function the care of people who, through ill-health, disability, immaturity or advanced age, are unable to care for themselves. Caring for the sick was particularly emphasized by the early Christian Church; many religious orders performed such "acts of mercy". In the 19th century Florence NIGHTINGALE revealed the need for reforms in nursing; by the end of the century certain of her principles had been adopted in England and the USA. Modern nursing is continually broadening its range of services, with standards laid down by relevant professional bodies.

nut Dry, one-seeded fruit with a hard, woody or stony wall. It develops from a flower that has petals attached above the OVARY (inferior ovary). Examples include ACORNS and HAZEL nuts.

nutation Oscillating movement (period 18.6 years) superimposed on the steady precessional movement of the Earth's axis so that the precessional path of each celestial pole on the CELESTIAL SPHERE follows an irregular rather than a true circle.

It results from the varying gravitational attraction of the Sun and Moon on the Earth. *See* PRECESSION

nutcracker Crow-like bird of evergreen forests of the Northern Hemisphere. A projection inside the bill turns it into a highly efficient seed cracker or nutcracker. The European thick-billed nutcracker (*Nucifraga caryocatactes*) is a typical species. Family Corvidae. Length: 30cm (12in).

nuthatch Bird found mainly in the Northern Hemisphere and occasionally in Africa and Australia. It is bluish-grey above and white, grey or chestnut underneath. It eats nuts, insects and seeds. Length: 9–19cm (3.5–7.5in). Family Sittidae.

nutmeg Evergreen tree native to tropical Asia, Africa and America. Its seeds yield the spice nutmeg; the spice mace comes from the seed covering. Height: up to 18m (60ft). Family Myristicaceae.

nutrition Processes by which plants and animals take in and make use of food substances. The science of nutrition involves identifying the kinds and amounts of nutrients necessary for growth and health. Nutrients are usually divided into PROTEINS, CARBOHYDRATES, FATS, MINERALS and VITAMINS.

Nuuk (Danish *Godthåb*) Capital and largest town of Greenland, at the mouth of a group of fjords on the sw coast. Founded in 1721, it is the oldest Danish settlement in Greenland. Industries: fishing and fish processing, scientific research. Pop. (1993) 12,181.

Nyerere, Julius Kambarage (1922–) Tanzanian statesman, first president of Tanzania (1964–85). In 1954 he founded the Tanganyika African National Union. Following the 1960 election victory, he became chief minister and led Tanganyika to independence (1961). Nyerere negotiated the union between Tanganyika and Zanzibar, which created TANZANIA (1964). He established a one-party state. Under his autocratic but generally benign socialist government, Tanzania made striking progess in social welfare and education. In the 1980s, however, economic setbacks encouraged demands for democracy and Nyerere retired.

nylon Any of numerous synthetic materials consisting of polyamides (with protein-like structures) developed in the USA in the 1930s. It can be formed into fibres, filaments, bristles or sheets. Nylon is characterized by elasticity and strength and is used in yarn, cordage and moulded products.

Nyman, Michael (1944–) English composer. His works include operas, notably *The Man who Mistook his Wife for a Hat* (1986), but he is best known for his film scores, such as *The Draughtman's Contract* (1982) and *The Piano* (1993).

nymph In Greek mythology, female nature spirit said to be a guardian of natural objects.

nymph Young insect of primitive orders that do not undergo complete METAMORPHOSIS. The term is used to designate all immature stages after the egg. The nymph resembles the adult and does so more closely with each successive moulting. Examples are the aquatic nymphs of dragonflies and mayflies.

457

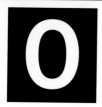

O/o is derived from the Phoenician alphabet. It entered the Greek alphabet as omicron, "short o", and passed unchanged through the Roman alphabet into various languages.

oak Common name of almost 600 species of the genus *Quercus*, which are found in temperate areas of the Northern Hemisphere and at high elevations in the tropics. Most species are hardwood trees that grow 18–30m (60–100ft) tall. Leaves are simple, often lobed and sometimes serrated. The fruit is an acorn, surrounded by a cup.

oarfish Any of several deepwater, marine, ribbon fish. Its long, thin body has a dorsal fin extending along its entire length. Two long oar-like pelvic fins protrude from beneath the head. Length: to 6m (20ft). Genus *Regalecus*.

OAS Abbreviation of the ORGANIZATION OF AMERICAN STATES

OAS (Organisation de l'Armée Secrète) French terrorist group opposed to Algerian independence. It was set up in 1961 by disaffected army officers and French settlers in Algeria when President DE GAULLE negotiated with Algerian nationalists.

oasis Fertile location that has water in an arid landscape. Usually, groundwater is brought to the surface in a well.

oat Cereal plant native to W Europe and cultivated worldwide. The flower comprises numerous florets that produce one-seeded fruits. Mainly fed to livestock, oats are also eaten by humans. Family Poaceae/Gramineae; species *Avena sativa*.

Oates, Titus (1649–1705) English author of the anti-Catholic Popish Plot (1678). He invented the story of a Jesuit plot to depose King CHARLES II. It provoked a hysterical reaction and encouraged efforts to exclude Charles' Catholic brother, the future JAMES II, from the succession. Oates was convicted of perjury in 1685 but pardoned in 1688.

OAU Abbreviation of the ORGANIZATION OF AFRICAN UNITY

Oaxaca (officially Oaxaca de Juárez) City in S Mexico; capital of Oaxaca state. Oaxaca is an agricultural state, and coffee is the principal crop. It was founded by the Aztecs. It is a tourist centre for exploring the nearby archaeological sites, such as Monte Albán. Pop. (1990) 213,985.

Ob River in W Siberia, central Russia. It flows NW then NE through the lowlands of W Siberia, before continuing N and then E to enter the Gulf of Ob on the Arctic Ocean. Length: 3,680km (2,300mi). With its principal tributary, the Irtysh, it is the seventh-longest river in the world: 5,410km (3,360mi).

obelisk Stone monolith that usually has a tapering, square-based column with a pyramid-shaped

Oberammergau Village in upper Bavaria, S Germany, famous for its PASSION PLAY. The performance takes place once every 10 years, in fulfilment of a vow made by the inhabitants in 1634 during an outbreak of the plague.

Oberon In medieval folklore, the king of the fairies and husband of TITANIA. Perhaps the most familiar use of the character is in SHAKESPEARE's *A Midsummer Night's Dream*.

obesity Condition of being overweight, generally defined as weighing 20% or more above the recommended norm for a person's sex, height and build. People who are overweight are at increased risk of disease and have a shorter life expectancy.

oboe WOODWIND musical instrument. It has a slightly flared bell and, like the BASSOON, is a double-reed instrument. The earliest true oboes were used in the mid-17th century.

Obote, (Apollo) Milton (1924–) Ugandan political leader. He was the first prime minister of independent Uganda (1962–66). In 1966 he deposed the king of the old kingdom of Buganda, and became president of a more centralized state. He was ousted by his army chief, Idi AMIN, in 1971, but returned to power after Amin was overthrown in 1979. Obote was again overthrown by an army coup in 1985.

O'Brien, Flann (1911–66) Irish novelist, b. Brian O'Nolan. His first and most ambitious novel was *At Swim-Two-Birds* (1939). He wrote three other novels in English – *The Hard Life* (1961), *The Dalkey Archive* (1964) and *The Third Policeman* (1967) – and one in Gaelic, *An Béal Bocht* (1941).

O'Brien, William Smith (1803–64) Irish nationalist leader. In 1843 he joined Daniel O'CONNELL's Repeal Association against the Act of UNION (1800), but left in 1846 to set up the more militant Repeal League. He was arrested after leading an ineffective insurrection in 1848 and sentenced to death, but his sentence was commuted to transportation.

observatory Location of TELESCOPES and other equipment for astronomical observations. Large optical telescopes are housed in domed buildings and radio observatories are open sites containing one or more large radio telescopes.

obsidian Rare, grey to black, glassy volcanic rock. It is the uncrystallized equivalent of rhyolite and GRANITE. Hardness 5.5; s.g. 2.4.

obstetrics Branch of medicine that deals with pregnancy, childbirth and the care of women following childbirth.

O'Casey, Sean (1880–1964) Irish playwright. His early plays include *Juno and the Paycock* (1924) and *The Plough and the Stars* (1926). His later works, such as *The Silver Tassie* (1929), are in an expressionistic style, very different from the realism of his early plays.

Occam's razor *See* WILLIAM OF OCCAM

ocean Continuous body of saltwater that surrounds the continents and fills the Earth's great depressions. There are five main oceans, the

ATLANTIC, PACIFIC, INDIAN, ARCTIC and Antarctic and they cover 71% of the Earth's surface. The oceans may be divided by region (littoral, pelagic and abyssal) or by depth (CONTINENTAL MARGIN, deep sea plain and deep trenches).

Oceania Collective term applied to the islands in the central and S Pacific Ocean. It includes the islands of MELANESIA, MICRONESIA and POLYNESIA and, sometimes, Australasia (Australia and New Zealand) and the Malay Archipelago.

Oceanic art Mostly objects used in religious rites. Among the most notable examples are the giant figures of EASTER ISLAND, MAORI wood carvings and the carved drums, masks, stools and shields of NEW GUINEA.

oceanic current Movement of seawater between layers of varying temperature and density. Ocean circulation is produced by CONVECTION, with warm currents travelling away from the equator, cooler water moving from the poles. In the Southern Hemisphere the oceanic currents move in an anti-clockwise system, whereas in the Northern the system is clockwise, an effect caused by the Earth's rotation. There are about 50 major currents, including the GULF STREAM of the N Atlantic and the Humboldt (Peru) current off the W coast of South America. *See also* CORIOLIS EFFECT; EL NIÑO

Oceanic mythology Traditional beliefs of the native inhabitants of OCEANIA. The mythological traditions are varied and complex. Among the Polynesians, there are various accounts of the creation of the world by the celestial deity Tangaroa (Ta'aroa). Maui, often thought of as half god and half human, is known for his cunning deeds. In Melanesian creation myths, the beginning of the world is seen as a movement that brings order out of chaos. In Micronesian creation myths, female deities play a prominent part. The worship of ancestors is also an important part of social life. *Mana*, an impersonal supernatural force, is a central concept.

oceanography Science of the marine environment. It studies oceans and seas past and present, the shorelines, sediments, rocks, muds, plants, animals, temperatures, tides, winds, currents, formation and erosion of abyssal depths and heights, and the effect of neighbouring land masses.

ocelot Small cat that lives in S USA, Central and South America. Its valuable fur is yellowish with elongated dark spots. It feeds on small birds, mammals and reptiles. Length: to 1.5m (4.9ft). Family Felidae; species *Felis pardalis*.

O'Connell, Daniel (1775–1847) ("the Liberator") Irish nationalist leader. He led resistance to Britain's remaining anti-Catholic laws and founded the Catholic Association (1823) to unite Irish Catholics. In 1828 he was elected to the British Parliament; the Catholic Emancipation Act (1829) was passed to enable him to take his seat. He tried unsuccessfully to extract reforms from the government.

octane number Indication of the antiknock prop-

erties of a liquid motor fuel. The higher the number, the less likely the possibility of the fuel detonating.

octave In music, the interval between any given note and another one that is exactly twice (or half) the frequency of the first and thus, acoustically, a perfect consonance. In Western music it encompasses the eight notes of the diatonic scale.

Octavian *See* AUGUSTUS

October Revolution *See* RUSSIAN REVOLUTION

octopus Predatory cephalopod mollusc with no external shell. Its sac-like body has eight powerful suckered tentacles. Many of the 150 species are small, but the common octopus (*Octopus vulgaris*) grows to 9m (30ft). Family Octopodidae.

ode Lyric poem of unspecific form but typically of heightened emotion or public address. The first great writer of odes was Pindar. In 17th-century England it was taken up by JONSON, HERRICK and MARVELL and in the 19th century by WORDSWORTH, SHELLEY and KEATS.

Odessa City and port on the Black Sea, S Ukraine. A Tatar fortress was built here in the 14th century and it was brought under Russian control in 1791. Industries: fishing, whaling, shipbuilding and repairing, oil-refining, metalworking, chemicals, heavy machinery. Pop. (1991) 1,101,000.

Odin Principal god in Norse mythology. Identified with the Teutonic god Woden, he is considered to be the god of wisdom, culture, war and death. *See also* VALHALLA

odontology Study of the structure, development and diseases of the teeth. It is closely allied with DENTISTRY.

Odysseus (Ulysses) Greek hero of HOMER's epic poem, the ODYSSEY. King of the city-state of Ithaca, husband of the faithful PENELOPE. It was Odysseus who designed the TROJAN HORSE.

Odyssey, The Epic poem of 24 books attributed to HOMER. The story of ODYSSEUS tells of his journey home from the Trojan Wars after 10 years of wandering and of how he wins back PENELOPE.

oedema Abnormal accumulation of fluid in the tissues; it may be generalized or confined to one part, such as the ankles. It may be due to heart failure, obstruction of one or more veins, or increased permeability of the capillary walls.

Oedipus In Greek mythology and literature, son of Laius (king of Thebes) and Jocasta; father of Antigone, Ismene, Eteocles and Polynices by his own mother. SOPHOCLES told how Oedipus was saved from death as an infant and raised in Corinth. He inadvertently killed his father, solved the riddle of the SPHINX, and became king of Thebes. There he married Queen Jocasta, unaware that she was his own widowed mother. On discovering the truth he made himself blind.

Oedipus complex In psychoanalytic theory, a collection of unconscious wishes involving sexual desire for the parent of the opposite sex and jealous rivalry with the parent of the same sex. Sigmund FREUD argued that children pass through this phase between ages three to five. Carl JUNG coined the term Electra complex for the complex in females.

Oersted, Hans Christian (1777–1851) Danish physicist. He took the first steps in explaining the relationship between electricity and magnetism, thus founding the science of ELECTROMAGNETISM. The oersted unit of magnetic field strength is named after him.

oesophagus (gullet) Muscular tube, part of the ALIMENTARY CANAL (or gut), which carries swallowed food from the throat to the STOMACH. Food is moved down the lubricated channel by the wave-like movement known as PERISTALSIS.

oestrogen Female SEX HORMONE. First produced by a girl at PUBERTY, oestrogen leads to the development of the secondary sexual characteristics: breasts, body hair and redistributed fat. It regulates the MENSTRUAL CYCLE and prepares the UTERUS for pregnancy. *See also* PILL

Offenbach, Jacques Levy (1819–80) French composer. His reputation was founded on the brilliance of his numerous operettas, notably *Orpheus in the Underworld* (1858).

Official Secrets Act Law passed by the British Parliament in 1989 forbidding government employees to disclose information formally classified as secret.

offset Method of PRINTING. In the printing machine, a roller applies ink to the printing plate, which is mounted on a rotating cylinder. The image is then transferred (offset) to a cylinder with a rubber covering, called the blanket. This transfers the image to the paper. Usually, the plates are made by LITHOGRAPHY, and the process is called offset lithography.

O'Flaherty, Liam (1897–1984) Irish novelist and short-story writer. His novels, which often reflect contemporary Irish social conditions, include *The Informer* (1925), *The Puritan* (1931), *Famine* (1937) and *Insurrection* (1950).

Ogdon, John (1937–89) British pianist and composer. He established his international reputation in 1962 when he was joint winner of the Tchaikovsky Competition with ASHKENAZY.

O'Higgins, Bernardo (1778–1842) South American revolutionary leader and ruler of Chile. A member of the revolutionary junta in colonial Chile, he commanded the army against the Spanish. Defeated in 1814, he joined José de SAN MARTÍN in Argentina to defeat the Spanish at Chacabuco (1817). Appointed "supreme director" of Chile, he declared independence in 1818 but resigned in 1823.

Ohio State in E central USA, bounded by Lake Erie in the N; the capital is COLUMBUS. Other cities include CLEVELAND and Toledo. Britain acquired the land in 1763 at the end of the Seven Years' War. It was ceded to the USA after the American Revolution, and in 1787 it became part of the Northwest Territory. Ohio was accepted into the Union in 1803. Ohio's large farms produce hay,

maize, wheat, soya beans and dairy foods, and cattle and pigs are raised. The state is highly industrialized. Ohio produces sandstone, oil, natural gas, clay, salt, lime and gravel. Its lake ports handle large amounts of iron and copper ore, coal and oil. Industries: vehicle and aircraft manufacture, transport equipment, primary and fabricated metals. Area: 106,764sq km (41,222sq mi). Pop. (1990) 10,847,115.

ohm SI unit (symbol Ω) of electrical resistance, equal to the resistance between two points on a conductor when a constant potential difference of one VOLT between them produces a current of one AMPERE.

Ohm's law Statement that the amount of steady current through a material is proportional to the voltage across the material. Proposed in 1827 by the German physicist Georg Ohm (1787–1854), Ohm's law is expressed mathematically as $V = IR$ (where V is the voltage in volts, I is the current in amperes and R is the resistance in ohms).

oil General term to describe a variety of substances, whose chief shared properties are viscosity at ordinary temperatures, a density less than that of water, inflammability, insolubility in water, and solubility in ether and alcohol. Mineral oils are used as fuels. Animal and vegetable oils (fatty oils or fats) are used as food, lubricants, and in soap.

oil painting Method of painting that uses pigments saturated in a drying oil medium. Widely used in Europe since the 16th century.

oil palm Tree grown in humid tropical regions of w Africa and Madagascar, source of oil for margarine and soap. The long, feather-shaped fronds rise from a short trunk. Height: 9–15m (30–50ft). Family Arecaceae/Palmae.

O'Keeffe, Georgia (1887–1986) US painter. Her early works were stylized and associated with ABSTRACT ART. She is best known for her microscopically detailed paintings of flowers, such as *Black Iris* (1926).

Okinawa Largest island of the Okinawa archipelago, sw of mainland Japan, part of the RYUKYU ISLANDS group in the w Pacific Ocean; the major settlement is Naha. The N is mountainous, densely forested and sparsely populated. Economic activity, such as agriculture and fishing, is concentrated in the s. In April 1945 US troops landed here. After fierce resistance and many casualties, Okinawa surrendered in April 1945.

Oklahoma City Capital and largest city of Oklahoma, USA, in the centre of the state on the North Canadian River. The city was made the state capital in 1910, and prospered with the discovery of oil in 1928. It was the site of a terrorist bomb in April 1995, which killed 168 people. Industries: oil refining, grain milling, cotton processing, steel products, electronic equipment, aircraft. Pop. (1990) 404,014.

Oklahoma State in central s USA; the capital is OKLAHOMA CITY. Other important cities are TULSA and Lawton. The Territory of Oklahoma was merged with the Indian Territory to form the state of Oklahoma in 1907. The w of the state is part of the GREAT PLAINS. The E is mountainous. The area is drained chiefly by the Arkansas and Red rivers. Wheat and cotton are the leading crops, but livestock is more important. There are many minerals, but oil and natural gas form the basis of Oklahoma's economic wealth. Area: 181,089sq km (69,918sq mi). Pop. (1990) 3,189,456.

okra (gumbo) Annual tropical plant with red-centred yellow flowers. The green fruit pods are eaten as a vegetable. Height: 0.6–1.8m (2–6ft). Family Malvaceae; species *Hibiscus esculentus*

Okri, Ben (1959–) Nigerian novelist. His first two novels, *Flowers and Shadows* (1980) and *The Landscapes Within* (1981), established his reputation. *The Famished Road* won the Booker Prize in 1991; its sequel is *Songs of Enchantment* (1993).

Old Bailey (Central Criminal Court) Court on Old Bailey Street, London. It became a CROWN COURT in 1971.

Oldcastle, Sir John (1377–1417) English leader of the LOLLARDS. He fought in the army under HENRY IV and earned the respect and liking of the future HENRY V. A fervent supporter of the teachings of John WYCLIFFE, he was a leader of the Lollards and was condemned as a heretic in 1413. He escaped to lead an unsuccessful Lollard rising but was eventually captured and executed.

Old Catholics Religious movement rejecting the dogma of PAPAL INFALLIBILITY, which had been announced by the First Vatican Council of 1870. The Old Catholics set up churches in German- and Dutch-speaking Europe, which later united in the Union of Utrecht in 1889. Since then the Archbishop of Utrecht has been head of the International Old Catholic Congress.

Oldenbarneveldt, Johan van (1547–1619) Dutch political leader in the Revolt of the Netherlands. With William I (the Silent), he was the founder of the Dutch republic. He played an important part in arranging the union of the provinces at Utrecht (1579), and supported Maurice of Nassau as stadtholder when William was assassinated (1584).

Oldenburg, Claes (1929–) US sculptor, a leading member of the POP ART movement. He is famous for his gigantic sculptures based on everyday objects, such as *Lipstick* (1969), and for his "soft sculptures" and pieces representing food.

old red sandstone Geological term for freshwater deposits of the DEVONIAN PERIOD found in Britain. These strata are noted for their fish fossils, among which are jawless fishes (ostracoderms), the first jawed fishes (placoderms), and the first true bony fishes (osteichthyes).

Old Testament First and older section of the BIBLE, originally written in Hebrew or Aramaic, and accepted as religiously inspired and sacred by both Jews and Christians. Among Jews it is known as the Hebrew Bible. It begins with the creation, but the main theme of the Old Testament is the history of the Hebrews. It comprises the PENTATEUCH or TORAH (Genesis to Deuteronomy); the Wisdom Books (Job, Proverbs and Ecclesiastes); the Major Prophets (Isaiah, Jeremiah and Ezekiel); the 12 Minor Prophets (Hosea to Malachi) and the miscellaneous Writings (including Psalms and Song of Songs). The number, order and names of the books of the Old Testament vary between the Jewish and Christian traditions; texts for both are based mainly on the SEPTUAGINT. Parts of the ancient Hebrew text were found among the DEAD SEA SCROLLS. *See also* LAW AND THE PROPHETS

Olduvai Gorge Site in N Tanzania where remains of primitive humans have been found. Louis LEAKEY uncovered four layers of remains dating from *c*.2 million years ago to *c*.15,000 years ago. In 1964 he announced the discovery of *Homo habilis*, whom he believed to have been a direct ancestor of modern man. The gorge, which is 40km (25mi) long and 100m (320ft) deep, runs through the Serengeti Plain.

Old Vic London theatre. It was built in 1818 as the Royal Coburg Theatre, renamed the Royal Victoria in 1833 and became known as the Old Vic. From 1963–1976 it was the home of the National Theatre of Great Britain. The Young Vic was opened in 1970.

oleander Evergreen shrubs of the genus *Nerium*, native to the Mediterranean region. They have milky poisonous sap, clusters of white, pink or purple flowers and smooth leaves. The best known is the rosebay (*N. oleander*). Family Apocynaceae.

oligarchy System of government in which power is concentrated in the hands of a few, who rule without the requirement of popular support and without external check on their authority.

Oligocene Extent of geological time from about 38 to 25 million years ago. It is the third of five epochs of the TERTIARY period. During it, the climate cooled, and many modern mammals evolved, including elephants and an ancestor of the modern horse.

olive Tree, shrub or vine and its fruit, especially the common olive tree, *Olea europaea*, native to the Mediterranean region. It has leathery, lance-shaped leaves, a gnarled and twisted trunk and may live for more than 1,000 years. The fruit is bitter and inedible before processing. Height: to 9m (30ft). Family Oleaceae. *See also* OLIVE OIL

olive oil Yellowish liquid oil, containing oleic acid, obtained by pressing OLIVES. It is used for cooking, as a salad oil, in the manufacture of soap and in medicine.

Olivier, Laurence Kerr, Baron Olivier of Brighton (1907–89) British actor. He was a leading actor by 1928, playing romantic (*Beau Geste*, 1929) and comic parts (*Private Lives*, 1930). In 1937 he joined the OLD VIC. He was director of the NATIONAL THEATRE (1963–73). He won a Best Actor Oscar for the film of *Hamlet* (1948).

olivine Ferromagnesian mineral, $(MgFe)_2SiO_4$, found in basic and ultrabasic IGNEOUS ROCKS. Olivine has orthorhombic system crystals and is usually olive-green. It is glassy and brittle with no cleavage. Hardness 6.5–7; s.g. 3.3.

Olmec Early civilization of Central America, which flourished between the 12th and 4th centuries BC. Its heartland was the S coast of the Gulf of Mexico, but its influence spread more widely. From the 9th century BC the main Olmec centre was La Venta. The OLMEC influenced the MAYA.

Olympia Area in S Greece, the site of an ancient sanctuary and of the original OLYMPIC GAMES. It was not rediscovered until the 18th century. It contained the huge temple of Zeus which housed a giant statue of the god that was numbered among the SEVEN WONDERS OF THE WORLD.

Olympia State capital and port of entry in SW Washington, on S tip of Puget Sound. Development was spurred with the coming of the railroad in the 1880s and its port was expanded during both World Wars. Industries: agriculture, food canning, beer, oysters, lumber. Pop. (1990) 27,447.

Olympic Games World's major international athletic competition, held every four years in two segments – the Summer Games and the Winter Games. The games were first celebrated in 776 BC in OLYMPIA, Greece and were held every four years until AD 393. The modern summer games were initiated by Baron Pierre de Coubertin, and were first held in Athens, Greece, in 1896. Women did not compete until 1912. The games were cancelled during World War 1 and World War 2. Control of the games is vested in the International Olympic Committee, which lays down the rules and chooses venues.

Olympus Mountain range in N Greece, on the border of Thessaly and Macedonia, c.40km (25mi) long. Its peak, Mount Olympus, is the highest point in Greece, at 2,917m (9,570ft). In Greek mythology it was the home of the gods.

Om (Aum) Sacred mystical symbol representing a sound considered to have divine power by Hindus, Buddhists and other religious groups. The sound is chanted at the beginning and end of prayers and is used as a mantra in meditation.

Oman Sultanate on the SE corner of the Arabian peninsula, SW Asia; the capital is MUSCAT. **Land**

OMAN
AREA: 212,460sq km (82,278sq mi)
POPULATION: 1,631,000
CAPITAL (POPULATION): Muscat (250,000)
GOVERNMENT: Monarchy with a consultative council
ETHNIC GROUPS: Omani Arab 74%, Pakistani 21%
LANGUAGES: Arabic (official)
RELIGIONS: Islam 86%, Hinduism 13%
CURRENCY: Omani rial = 100 baizas

---

and climate Oman is 95% desert. On the Gulf of Oman coast lies the fertile plain of Al Batinah, and the city of Muscat. The plain is backed by the Al Hajar mountains. In the S, lies part of the barren and rocky Rub' al Khali desert (the "Empty Quarter"). The sultanate also includes the tip of the Musandam Peninsula, overlooking the Strait of Hormuz, and separated from the rest of Oman by the United Arab Emirates. Oman has a hot tropical climate. Parts of the N mountains have an average annual rainfall of 400mm (16in), but most of Oman has less than 125mm (5in). **Economy** Oman is an upper-middle income developing country. Its economy is based on oil production. Oil was first discovered in 1964 and now accounts for more than 90% of exports. Oil refining and the processing of copper are among Oman's few manufacturing industries. Agriculture supports 50% of the workforce. Major crops include alfalfa, bananas, coconuts, dates, limes, tobacco, vegetables and wheat. Fishing, especially for sardines, is also important, but Oman is reliant on food imports. **History and politics** In ancient times, Oman was an important trading area on the main route between The Gulf and the Indian Ocean. Islam was introduced in the 7th century AD, and Muslim culture remains a unifying force. In 1507 the Portuguese captured several seaports in Oman, including Muscat. Portugal controlled maritime trade until they were expelled by the Ottomans in 1659. Oman set up trading posts in East Africa, including Zanzibar in 1698 and, until the 1860s, was the dominant Arabian power. The Al Said family have ruled Oman since taking power in 1741. British colonial interference and economic inequality led to popular rebellions in the 1950s and 1960s. Insurrectionist forces continued to control much of S Oman. In 1970 Sultan Said bin Taimur was deposed by his son, Qaboos bin Said. In 1971 Oman joined the UN and the Arab League. Qaboos bin Said initiated the modernization of health, education and social welfare. Despite the extension of free education, 65% of the population remained illiterate by 1992. In 1981 Oman was a founder member of the Gulf Cooperation Council (GCC). Relations with the UK and the USA remain strong.

Omar (581–644) (Umar) Second CALIPH, or ruler of ISLAM. He was converted to Islam in 618 and became a counsellor of MUHAMMAD. He chose the first caliph, ABU BAKR, in 632 and succeeded him two years later. Under his rule, Islam spread by conquest into Syria, Egypt and Persia, and the foundations of an administrative empire were laid.

Omar Khayyám (1048–1131) Persian poet, mathematician and astronomer. His fame in the West is due to a collection of verses freely translated by Edward Fitzgerald as *The Rubáyát of Omar Khayyám* (1859).

Omayyads *See* UMAYYADS

ombudsman Official appointed to safeguard citizens' rights by investigating complaints made against the government or its employees.

omnivore Any creature that eats both animal and vegetable foods, for example human beings and pigs. Omnivores have characteristic teeth adapted for cutting, tearing and pulping food.

Omsk City on the Irtysh and Om rivers, W Siberia, Russia. Founded as a fortress town in 1716, it was made the administrative centre of W Siberia in 1824. It is now a major port. Industries: oil refining, chemicals, engineering, agricultural machinery, textiles. Pop. (1992) 1,169,000.

onager Fast-running animal related to the ASS, found in semi-desert areas of Iran and India. The onager is dun-coloured with a dorsal stripe that reaches the tip of the tail. Height at the shoulder: 0.9–1.5m (2.9–4.9ft). Family Equidae; species *Equus hemionus onager.*

onchocerciasis (river blindness) Tropical disease of the skin and connective tissue, caused by infection with filarial worms; it may also affect the eyes, causing blindness. It is transmitted by bloodsucking blackflies found in Central and South America and Africa.

oncogene Gene that, by inducing a cell to divide abnormally, contributes to the development of CANCER. Oncogenes arise from gene mutations (proto-oncogenes), which are present in all normal cells and in some viruses. *See also* GENETICS

oncology In medicine, speciality concerned with the diagnosis and treatment of CANCER.

O'Neill, Eugene Gladstone (1888–1953) US playwright. His first full-length play, *Beyond the Horizon* (1920), won the Pulitzer Prize, as did *Anna Christie* (1921) and *Long Day's Journey into Night* in 1956. In 1936 he was awarded the Nobel Prize for literature. Other plays include *The Iceman Cometh* (1946).

onion Hardy, bulb-forming, biennial plant of the lily family, native to central Asia, and cultivated worldwide for its strong-smelling, edible bulb. It has hollow leaves, white or lilac flowers. Height: to 130cm (50in). Family Alliaceae/Liliaceae.

Ontario, Lake Smallest of the GREAT LAKES, bounded by New York state (S and E) and Ontario province, Canada (S, W and N). Fed chiefly by the Niagara River, the lake is drained to the NE by the St Lawrence River. Forming part of the St Lawrence Seaway, it is a busy shipping route. The chief Canadian cities on Lake Ontario are TORONTO, HAMILTON and Kingston; on the US shore are Rochester and Oswego. Area: 19,684sq km (7,600sq mi).

Ontario Province in SE Canada, bounded to the S by four of the Great Lakes (Superior, Huron, Erie and Ontario) and the USA; the capital is TORONTO. Ontario is Canada's most populous province; other major cities include OTTAWA, HAMILTON, Windsor and London. Trading posts were established in the region during the 17th century by French explorers. The area became part of New France, but was ceded to Britain in 1763. Ontario was known as Upper Canada until 1841, when it joined with QUEBEC to form the province of Canada. In 1867 the Dominion of Canada was created, and the province of Ontario was established. In the N is the forested Canadian Shield, with its lowlands bordering on Hudson and James bays. To the E and S are the lowlands of the ST LAWRENCE River and the Great Lakes, where agriculture and industry are concentrated. Cattle, dairy produce and pigs are important. The chief crops are tobacco, maize, wheat and vegetables. Industries: motor vehicles, transport equipment, metallurgy, chemicals, paper, machinery, electrical goods. Area: 1,068,587sq km (412,582sq mi). Pop. (1994 est.) 10,900,000.

onyx Semi-precious variety of the mineral CHALCEDONY, a form of AGATE. It has straight parallel bands. White and red forms are called carnelian onyx; white and brown, sardonyx. It is found mostly in India and South America.

ooze Fine-grained, deep-ocean deposit containing material of more than 30% organic origin. Oozes are divided into two main types. Calcareous ooze at depths of 2,000–3,900m (6,562–12,792ft) contains the skeletons of animals such as foraminifera and pteropods. Siliceous ooze at depths of more than 3,900m contains skeletons of radiolarians and diatoms.

opal Non-crystalline variety of QUARTZ, found in recent volcanoes, deposits from hot springs and sediments. Usually colourless or white with a rainbow play of colour in gem forms, it is the most valuable of quartz gems. Hardness 5.5–6.5; s.g. 2.0.

op art (optical art) US ABSTRACT ART movement, popular in the mid-1960s. It relies on optical phenomena to confuse the viewer's eye and to create a sense of movement on the surface of the picture. Leading exponents include Bridget Riley, Victor Vasarély and Kenneth Noland.

OPEC Acronym for ORGANIZATION OF PETROLEUM EXPORTING COUNTRIES

opencast mining Stripping surface layers to obtain coal, ores or other minerals. Dragline excavators strip away the surface and mechanical shovels distribute minerals and spoil. The minerals are carried away for grading and processing.

open cluster (galactic cluster) Group of young stars in the spiral arms of our GALAXY, containing from a few tens of stars to a few thousand. They are usually several light-years across. One example is the PLEIADES.

open-hearth process Method of producing STEEL in a furnace heated by overhead flames from gas or oil burners; oxygen may be blown through to raise the temperature. Pig iron, scrap steel and limestone are heated together. Various impurities form slag, which is removed from the surface of the molten metal.

Open University (OU) Form of British higher education chartered in 1969 as a nonresidential alternative to conventional universities with open access. Teaching is carried out through television and radio broadcasts, as well as personal tuition and summer schools.

opera Stage drama that is sung. It combines acting, singing, orchestral music, set and costume design, making spectacular entertainment. Opera began in Italy in about 1600. The classical style evolved in about 1750; its greatest exponent was MOZART. The 19th century was dominated by VERDI and WAGNER. Twentieth-century opera has been marked by a profusion of styles by composers such as PUCCINI, STRAUSS, BERG and BRITTEN. *See also* OPERA BUFFA; OPÉRA COMIQUE; OPERA SERIA

opera buffa Style of Italian comic opera that developed in mid-18th-century Naples. Light and simple in style, it introduced the elaborate finale which influenced the subsequent development of opera. An early example of the style is *La Serva Padrona* (1733) by Giovanni Pergolesi.

opéra comique Style of French opera that began in the late 18th century. Its hallmarks are a witty plot involving some spoken dialogue, romantic subject matter and simple engaging music. The genre can also include tragic works, such as Bizet's *Carmen* and Offenbach's *Tales of Hoffmann*.

opera seria Style of Italian opera in the 17th and early 18th centuries. The plots were usually heroic or tragic. Priority was given to virtuoso vocal display in elaborate arias. The formalism and stylization of such operas prompted a reaction that gave rise to the development of OPERA BUFFA.

operetta Type of light OPERA involving songs, dialogue, dancing and an engaging story. Notable composers were Johann STRAUSS, Arthur SULLIVAN (in association with W.S. GILBERT) and Jacques OFFENBACH.

ophthalmology Branch of medicine that specializes in the diagnosis and treatment of diseases of the eye.

ophthalmoscope Instrument for examining the interior of the eye, invented by Hermann von HELMHOLTZ in 1851.

Ophüls, Max (1902–57) German film director. His contribution was superbly realized in two masterpieces, *Letter from an Unknown Woman* (1948) and *Reckless Moment* (1949). His son, Marcel (1927–), is a documentary-maker and his work includes *The Memory of Justice* (1975).

opium Drug derived from the unripe seed-pods of the opium POPPY. Its components and derivatives have been used as NARCOTICS and ANALGESICS for many centuries. It produces drowsiness and euphoria and reduces pain. MORPHINE and CODEINE are opium derivatives.

Opium Wars (1839–42) Conflict between Britain and China. It arose because Chinese officials prevented the importation of opium. After a British victory, the Treaty of Nanking gave Britain trading rights in certain ports and the grant of Hong Kong. A second similar war was fought by the British and French in 1856–60. When China refused to ratify the Treaty of Tientsin (1858), Anglo-French forces occupied Peking (Beijing).

Oporto City in NW Portugal, a port on the River Douro, 3km (2mi) from the Atlantic Ocean. A Roman settlement, it was occupied by the Visigoths (540–716) and the Moors (716–997) before being brought under Portuguese control in 1092. By the 17th century it was a famous wine centre and its PORT is still exported. Industries: textiles, fishing, fruit, olive oil. Pop. (1991) 310,640.

opossum (possum) New World MARSUPIAL animal. The only marsupial found outside Australasia. Omnivorous tree-dwellers, they have silky grey fur (except on the long prehensile tail), and feign death when in danger. The common opossum, *Didelphis marsupialis*, grows up to 50cm (20in) long, including a 30cm (12in) tail. Family Didelphidae.

Oppenheimer, (Julius) Robert (1904–67) US theoretical physicist. He was appointed director (1943–45) of the Los Alamos laboratory in New Mexico, where he headed the MANHATTAN PROJECT to develop the atomic bomb. In 1949 he opposed the construction of the HYDROGEN BOMB and in 1953 was suspended by the Atomic Energy Commission. He was subsequently reinstated.

optical fibre Fine strand of glass (less than 1mm (0.04in) thick) that is able to transmit digital information in the form of pulses of light. Light entering an optical fibre is conducted, by reflection, from one end of the fibre to the other with very little loss of intensity. Initially used in ENDOSCOPES, their application is spreading to many forms of mass communication.

optics Branch of physics concerned with the study of LIGHT. Fundamental aspects are the physical nature of light, both as a wave phenomenon and as particles (PHOTONS), and the REFLECTION, REFRACTION and polarization of light. Optics also involves the study of mirrors and LENS systems and of optically active chemicals and crystals that polarize light. *See also* POLARIZED LIGHT

optometry Testing of vision in order to prescribe corrective eyewear, such as spectacles or contact lenses. It is distinct from OPHTHALMOLOGY.

Opus Dei International Roman Catholic organization of laymen and a few priests, known for its highly conservative political and religious influence. It was founded in Spain in 1928. Its members seek to put into practice traditional Christian values through their chosen professions.

oracle In ancient Greece, a priest or priestess who gave the answer of a god to questions put by individuals. The most famous was the oracle of Apollo at DELPHI. The god spoke through a priestess (Pythia), whose words were interpreted by priests.

Oran City and seaport on the Gulf of Oran, NW Algeria. Founded in the 10th century, it was taken by Spain from its Arab rulers in 1509. Captured by Ottoman Turks in 1708, it was retaken by Spain in 1732. Under French rule from 1831–1962, it developed as a naval base. It is Algeria's second-largest city. Industries: iron ore, textiles, chemicals, cereals, wine, fruit. Pop. (1987) 609,823.

Orange Longest river of South Africa. It rises in the Drakensberg Mountains in N Lesotho and flows generally w, forming the boundary between FREE STATE and CAPE PROVINCE. It continues w through the Kalahari and Namib deserts, forming South Africa's border with Namibia. It empties into the Atlantic Ocean at Oranjemund. Length: c.2,100km (1,300mi).

orange Evergreen citrus tree and its fruit. There are two basic types. The sweet orange (*Citrus sinensis*) is native to Asia and widely grown in the USA and Israel. The fruit develops without flower pollination and is often seedless. The sour orange (*C.aurantium*) is widely grown in Spain for the manufacture of marmalade. Related fruits include the mandarin, tangerine and satsuma, all varieties of *C. reticulata*. Height: to 9m (30ft). Family Rutaceae; genus *Citrus*.

Orange, House of Royal dynasty of the Netherlands. Orange was a principality in s France, which was inherited by WILLIAM I (THE SILENT) in 1544. He led the successful Dutch revolt against Spain in the late 16th century. WILLIAM III became king of England in 1689. The son of William V became king of the Netherlands in 1815 as WILLIAM I.

Orange Free State Former name (1854–1995) of the FREE STATE province of South Africa.

Orangemen Members of the Orange Society, or Orange Order. It was founded in Ulster in 1795 in response to the Roman Catholic, nationalist United Irishmen, and was named after the Protestant hero, WILLIAM III, prince of Orange. His victory over the Catholic JAMES II at the Battle of the BOYNE (1690) is celebrated on its anniversary, 12 July.

orang-utan Stout-bodied great APE native to forests of Sumatra and Borneo. It has a bulging belly and a shaggy, reddish-brown coat. It swings by its arms when travelling through trees, but proceeds on all fours on the ground. Height: 1.5m (5ft); weight: to 100kg (220 lb). Species *Pongo pygmaeus*. *See also* PRIMATES

oratorio Sacred music for solo voices, chorus and orchestra, which were first presented in oratories (chapels) in 17th-century Italy. An outstanding example is Handel's *Messiah* (1742).

orbit Path of a celestial body in a gravitational field. The path is usually a closed one about the focus of the system to which it belongs, as with those of the planets about the Sun. Most celestial orbits are elliptical, although the ECCENTRICITY can vary greatly. It is rare for an orbit to be parabolic or hyperbolic.

orchestra Group of musicians who play together. During the 17th century string orchestras developed out of viol consorts; in the 18th century some wind instruments were added. The woodwind section was soon established, and by the end of the 19th century the brass section was too. Modern orchestras consist of between 80 and 120 players divided into sections: strings (violin, viola, cello, double bass and harp); woodwind (flute, oboe, clarinet and bassoon); brass (trumpet, trombone, French horn and tuba) and percussion.

orchid Any plant of the family Orchidaceae common in the tropics. There are about 35,000 species. All are perennials and grow in soil or as EPIPHYTES on other plants. Parasitic and saprophytic species are also known. All orchids have bilaterally symmetrical flower structures, each with three sepals. They range in diameter from c.2mm (0.1in) to 38cm (15in).

orders, holy In the Anglican, Roman Catholic, and Orthodox churches, the duties of the clergy, and the grades of hierarchical rank as outlined in the office of ORDINATION. A person is ordained as a subdeacon, deacon, priest or bishop. These ranks are known as the major orders. The minor orders are those of porter, lector, exorcist, and acolyte.

orders of architecture Style and decoration of a column, its base, capital and entablature. Of the five orders, the Greeks developed the Doric, Ionic and Corinthian. The Tuscan and Composite orders were Roman adaptations. A typical **Doric** column has no base, a short shaft with surface fluting and an unornamented capital. The **Ionic** column is slender with 24 flutes and a spiral-scrolled capital. The **Corinthian** is the most ornate: it has a high base, a slim, fluted column and a bell-shaped capital with acanthus-leaf ornament.

ordination Process of consecrating a person as a minister of religion. In Christian Churches organized along episcopal lines, ordination confirms the ordinand (the individual undergoing the process) as a priest or minister in holy ORDERS. In Roman Catholic and Orthodox Churches, the rite of ordination is a SACRAMENT. In Protestant Churches without episcopal organization, ordination is carried out by ministers, ruling elders, or specially selected lay persons.

ordination of women Official recognition of women as priests or ministers by a church. In Christianity, the ban on women as full members of the clergy has persisted in some churches, notably the Roman Catholic Church. During the 20th century many Protestant churches began to admit women first as deacons and later as priests. The first Anglican women priests were ordained in 1994.

Ordovician Second-oldest period of the PALAEOZOIC era, 505 to 438 million years ago. All animal life was restricted to the sea. Numerous invertebrates flourished and included trilobites, brachiopods, corals, graptolites, molluscs, and echinoderms. Remains of jawless fish from this period are the first record of the vertebrates.

ore Mineral or combination of minerals from which metals and non-metals can be extracted. It occurs in veins, beds or seams parallel to the enclosing rock or in irregular masses.

oregano (majoram) Dried leaves and flowers of several perennial herbs of the genus *Oreganum*, native to Mediterranean lands and w Asia. It is a popular culinary herb. Family Lamiaceae/Labiatae.

Oregon State of NW USA, on the Pacific coast; the capital is SALEM. Other major cities include PORTLAND and Eugene. Trading posts were set up in the 1790s, mainly by the HUDSON'S BAY COMPANY. From 1842 the Oregon Trail brought more settlers. Oregon Territory was formed in 1848 and was admitted to the Union in 1859. It is dominated by the forested slopes of the CASCADE and the Coast ranges. Between the two lies the fertile Willamette Valley. The COLUMBIA and the Willamette are the major rivers. Agricultural products include cattle, dairy produce, wheat and market garden products. Oregon produces more than 20% of the nation's softwood timber. Area: 251,180sq km (96,981sq mi). Pop. (1993 est.) 3,038,000.

Orestes In Greek legend, the son of AGAMEMNON and CLYTEMNESTRA, and brother of ELECTRA. He killed his mother and her lover Aegisthus to avenge their murder of his father.

Orff, Carl (1895–1982) German composer. He used deliberately primitive rhythms, for example in *Carmina Burana* (1937).

organ In biology, group of TISSUES that form a functional and structural unit in a living organism. The major organs of the body include the brain, heart, lungs, skin, liver and kidneys. Leaves, flowers and roots are examples of plant organs.

organ KEYBOARD INSTRUMENT. The player sits at a console and regulates a flow of air to ranks of pipes, producing rich tones. The organ was in use in Christian churches in the 8th century. The modern organ dates from the BAROQUE period.

organic chemistry *See* CHEMISTRY

Organization for Economic Cooperation and Development (OECD) International consultative body set up in 1961 by the major Western trading nations. Its aims are to stimulate trade by raising standards of living and coordinating aid to less developed countries. Its headquarters are in Paris and it has 26 member nations.

Organization of African Unity (OAU) Intergovernmental organization. Founded in 1963, the OAU brings together all African states. It aims to safeguard African interests and independence, encourage development and settle disputes. Its headquarters are in Addis Ababa, Ethiopia.

Organization of American States (OAS) Organization of 35 member states of the Americas that promotes peaceful settlements to disputes, regional cooperation in the limitation of weapons, and economic and cultural development. An extension of the 1948 Pan American Union held in Colombia, its charter became effective in 1951. The OAS is affiliated to the UNITED NATIONS (UN).

Organization of Petroleum Exporting Countries (OPEC) Intergovernmental organization established in 1960 by many of the world's major oil producing states to safeguard their interests. Its primary purpose is to set production quotas and coordinate prices among the 12 members. Its headquarters are in Vienna, Austria.

orienteering Sport requiring athletic and navigational skills. Runners, leaving at timed intervals, carry a map and compass with which to locate control points around the usually 10km (6.2mi) course. The fastest to finish the course wins.

original sin Sin committed by ADAM and EVE for which they were expelled from the Garden of EDEN and were made mortal (Genesis 3). The sin was eating from the tree of the knowledge of good and evil against God's instructions. Their guilt has been passed down through all the generations.

Orinoco River in Venezuela, rising in the Sierra Parima Mountains in S Venezuela. It flows NW to Colombia, then N, forming part of the Venezuela-Colombia border, and E into the Atlantic Ocean by a vast delta. Length: *c.*2,062km (1,281mi).

oriole Two unrelated types of songbirds. The Old World oriole (family Oriolidae) is brightly coloured and lays eggs in a cup-shaped nest. The New World oriole (family Icteridae) has similar colouring and builds hanging nests in trees.

Orion Prominent constellation, representing a hunter. Four young stars form a conspicuous quadrilateral containing a row of three other stars representing his belt.

Orissa State in NE India, on the Bay of Bengal; the capital is Bhubaneswar. It was ceded to the Mahrattas in 1751 and occupied by the British in 1803. It was proclaimed a constituent state of India in 1950. Industries: mining, fishing, rice, wheat, sugar cane, oilseeds, forestry. Area: 155,782sq km (60,147sq mi). Pop. (1991) 31,659,736.

Orkney Islands Archipelago of over 70 islands off the N coast of Scotland, which constitute an Islands Area administrative region. Mainland (Pomona) is the largest, and is the seat of the regional capital (Kirkwall). Other principal islands include Hoy and South Ronaldsay. The islands were conquered in 875 by the Viking king Harald I and remained Norwegian territory until 1231. In 1472 the islands were annexed to Scotland. Scapa Flow (between Mainland and Hoy) was the major British naval base in both World Wars. The local economy remains predominantly agricultural. Area: 974sq km (376sq mi). Pop. (1991) 19,612.

Orlando City in central Florida, USA. Orlando is one of the world's most popular tourist destinations, with Disney World and Magic Kingdom theme parks. Industries: citrus-growing, aerospace, electronics. Pop. (1990) 164,693.

Orléans City on the River Loire, N central France; capital of Loiret département. Besieged by the English during the HUNDRED YEARS WAR, it was relieved by JOAN OF ARC in 1429. During the 16th-century Wars of RELIGION, the city was besieged by Catholic forces and held by them until the Edict of NANTES. Industries: tobacco, textiles, fruit and vegetables, chemicals. Pop. (1991) 105,111.

Ormuzd *See* AHURA MAZDAH

ornithology Study of birds. Included in general ornithological studies are classification, structure, function, evolution, distribution, migration, reproduction, ecology and behaviour.

orogenesis Mountain building, especially where the Earth's crust is compressed to produce large-scale FOLDS and FAULTS.

Orpheus In Greek mythology, the son of Calliope by APOLLO, and the finest of all poets and musicians. Orpheus married Eurydice, who died after being bitten by a snake. He descended into the Underworld to rescue her and was allowed to regain her if he did not look back at her until they emerged into the sunlight. He could not resist, and Eurydice vanished forever.

orphism (orphic cubism) Term invented in 1912 by APOLLINAIRE to describe a new art form combining aspects of CUBISM, FUTURISM and FAUVISM. Exponents include Robert and Sonia DELAUNAY, and the BLAUE REITER group.

orthoclase Essential mineral in acidic IGNEOUS rocks and common in METAMORPHIC rocks. It is a potassium aluminium silicate, $KAISi_3O_8$, with monoclinic system crystals. It is usually white but can be pink. Hardness 6–6.5; s.g. 2.5–2.6.

orthodontics *See* DENTISTRY

Orthodox Church (Eastern Orthodox Church) Family of Christian national churches mostly of E Europe. The churches are independent but acknowledge the primacy of the Patriarch of Constantinople. They developed from the Church of the BYZANTINE EMPIRE, which separated from Rome in 1054. The Russian Orthodox Church has the most adherents. *See also* SCHISM

orthopaedics Branch of medicine that deals with diseases, disorders and injuries of bones, muscles, tendons and ligaments.

ortolan Small European bird. It has an olive-green head and chest, black back streaked with brown, yellow throat, and pinkish underparts. Length: 16.4cm (6.5in). Species *Emberiza hortulana*.

Orton, Joe (John Kingsley) (1933–67) British playwright who specialized in black satirical comedies; notably, *Entertaining Mr Sloane* (1964) and *Loot* (1965).

Orwell, George (1903–50) British novelist and journalist, b. Eric Arthur Blair in India. His major works include the autobiographical *Down and Out in Paris and London* (1933); the political polemic *The Road to Wigan Pier* (1937); and the books for which he is most popularly remembered: *Animal Farm* (1945) and *Nineteen Eighty-four* (1949).

oryx (gemsbok) Any of four species of ANTELOPES. The male has a tuft of hair at the throat and both sexes carry long horns ringed at the base. Two species are almost extinct. Height: 1.2m (4ft). Family Bovidae.

Osaka City on Osaka Bay, S Honshū island, Japan; capital of Osaka prefecture. Japan's third-largest city and its principal industrial port, Osaka was intensively bombed during World War 2. It is a major transport hub. Pop. (1993) 2,495,000.

Osborne, John James (1929–95) British

dramatist whose play *Look Back in Anger* (1956) established his reputation as the "ANGRY YOUNG MAN" of the theatre. His other successes included *The Entertainer* (1957) and *Luther* (1961).

Oscar (officially Academy Award) Prize awarded annually for services to the cinema by the US Academy of Motion Picture Arts and Sciences. The gold-plated bronze statuettes stand 25cm (10in) high and are reputed to have been nicknamed after the Academy librarian's uncle Oscar.

oscillating universe theory Variant of the BIG BANG theory in which it is suggested that the universe passes through successive cycles of expansion and contraction (or collapse). The universe would thus oscillate between Big Bang and "Big Crunch" episodes and so be infinite in age.

oscillator In physics, a device for producing sound waves, as in a SONAR or an ultrasonic generator. In electronics, an oscillator circuit converts direct current (DC) electricity into high-frequency alternating current (AC).

oscilloscope Electronic instrument in which a CATHODE-RAY TUBE (CRT) displays how quantities, such as voltage or current, vary over a period of time. The electron beam that traces the pattern on the screen is moved by a time-base generator within the oscilloscope. The result is generally a curve or graph on the screen.

osier Any of various willows, especially *Salix viminalis* and *S. purpurea*, the flexible branches and stems of which are used for wickerwork.

Osiris In Egyptian mythology, the god of the dead, usually depicted wearing a feathered crown and bearing the crook and flail of a king. In the myths, Osiris was killed by his brother SETH. His sister and wife, ISIS, retrieved the corpse, and Osiris' son HORUS avenged his death.

Oslo Capital of Norway, in the SE of the country, at the head of Oslo Fjord. The city was founded in the mid-11th century. Largely destroyed by fire in 1624, it was rebuilt by CHRISTIAN IV, who named it Christiania. In 1905 it became the capital of independent Norway and was renamed Oslo in 1925. Industries: machinery, wood products, food processing, textiles, chemicals, shipbuilding. Pop. (1990) 459,292.

osmium Bluish-white metallic element (symbol Os), one of the TRANSITION ELEMENTS. The densest of the elements, osmium is associated with platinum; the chief source is as a by-product from smelting nickel. Like IRIDIUM, osmium is used in producing hard alloys. It is also used to make electrical contacts and pen points. Properties: at.no.76; r.a.m. 190.2; r.d. 22.57; m.p. 3,045°C (5,513°F); b.p. 5,027°C (9,081°F); most common isotope Os^{192} (41.0%).

osmosis Diffusion of a solvent (such as water) through a selectively permeable MEMBRANE into a more concentrated solution. Osmosis is a vital cellular process. *See also* TURGOR PRESSURE

osprey HAWK that lives beside lakes and in coastal

regions of all continents except Antarctica. It has a short hooked bill, broad ragged wings and a white head; it has brownish-black plumage on its back and a cream breast. Length: 51–61cm (20–24in). Family Pandionidae, species *Pandion haliaetus.*

Ossetia Region of the central Caucasus. The region is divided along the River Terek. **North Ossetia** is an autonomous republic within the Russian Federation, whose capital is Vladikavkaz. **South Ossetia** is an autonomous region of GEORGIA, whose capital is Tshkinvali. Ossetia is a mountainous agricultural region, producing fruit, wine and grain. North Ossetia has rich mineral deposits. In 1922 South Ossetia was made a region within the Republic of Georgia. In 1924 North Ossetia became part of the Russian republic, and in 1936 achieved the status of an autonomous republic. In 1990 Georgia abolished South Ossetia's autonomous status, which was restored in 1995. Area: North Ossetia, 8,000sq km (3,090sq mi); South Ossetia, 3,900sq km (1,505sq mi). Pop. North Ossetia (1990), 638,000; South Ossetia (1990), 99,800.

ossification (osteogenesis) Process of bone formation in vertebrates. Bone is formed through the action of special cells called osteoblasts, which secrete bone-forming minerals that combine with a network of COLLAGEN fibres.

osteomyelitis Infection of the BONE, sometimes spreading along the marrow cavity. Rare except in diabetics, it can arise from a compound fracture, or from infection elsewhere in the body. The condition may be treated with immobilization, ANTIBIOTICS and surgical drainage.

osteopathy System of alternative medical treatment based on the use of physical manipulation. The concept was formulated by US physician Andrew Still in 1874.

osteoporosis Condition where there is loss of bone substance, resulting in brittle bones. It is common in older people, especially in women following the MENOPAUSE; it may also occur in Cushing's syndrome and as a side-effect of prolonged treatment with corticosteroid drugs.

ostrich Largest living bird, found in central Africa. It is flightless and has a small head and long neck. Plumage is black and white in males, brown and white in females. Eggs are laid in holes in the sand. Height: to 2.5m (8ft); weight: to 155kg (345lb). Family Struthionidae; species *Struthio camelus.*

Ostrogoths *See* GOTH

Ostrovsky, Alexsandr Nikolayevich (1823–86) Russian dramatist. He is an important figure in 20th-century Russian theatrical realism. His plays and include *Poverty is no Crime* (1854) and *The Thunderstorm* (1859).

Oswald, Lee Harvey (1939–63) Alleged assassin of US President John F. KENNEDY, on 22 November 1963, in Dallas. Before he could stand trial he was murdered in police custody by Jack Ruby. *See also* WARREN COMMISSION

Oswald, Saint (*c.*605–42) King of Northumbria (633–42). He became a Christian and converted his people with the help of St AIDAN. Oswald became King of Northumbria in 633 and was eventually killed in battle. His feast day is 5 August.

otosclerosis Inherited condition in which overgrowth of bone in the middle ear causes deafness. It is twice as common in women. Surgery can restore the sound conduction mechanism.

Ottawa Capital of Canada, in SE Ontario, on the Ottawa River and Rideau Canal. Founded in 1826 as Bytown, it was named Ottawa in 1854. Queen Victoria chose it as capital of the United Provinces in 1858. In 1867 it became the national capital of the Dominion of Canada. Industries: glass-making, printing, publishing, sawmilling, pulp-making, clocks and watches. Pop. (1991) 313,987.

otter Semi-aquatic carnivore found everywhere except Australia. Otters have narrow, pointed heads with bristly whiskers, sleek furry bodies, short legs with webbed hind feet and long tapering tails. The river otter (genus *Lutra*) is small to medium-sized and spends considerable time on land. Family Mustelidae.

Otto I (the Great) (912–973) King of the Germans (936–973) and first Holy Roman emperor (962–973). He succeeded his father, HENRY I, in Germany and defeated rebellious princes and their ally, Louis IV of France. In 955 he crushed the MAGYARS at Lechfeld. He invaded Italy to aid Queen Adelaide of Lombardy, married Adelaide and became king of Lombardy. In 962 he was crowned as Roman emperor (the "Holy", meaning "Christian", was added later).

Otto IV (1174–1218) (Otto of Brunswick) Holy Roman emperor (1198–1215). A member of the GUELPH family, Otto antagonized the powerful Pope Innocent III by his invasion of Italy against the HOHENSTAUFEN King Frederick I (later Emperor FREDERICK II). With Innocent's support, Frederick was elected king by the German princes (1212) and supported by PHILIP II of France. Otto was defeated by Philip at Bouvines (1214) and forced to retire.

Ottoman empire Former Turkish state that controlled much of SE Europe, the Middle East and North Africa between the 14th and 20th centuries. It was founded by Osman I (r.1290–1326). The struggle with the BYZANTINES ended with the capture of Constantinople (now ISTANBUL), which became the Ottoman capital in 1453. Under SULEIMAN I (THE MAGNIFICENT) (r.1520–66), the Ottoman empire included the Arab lands of the Middle East and North Africa, SE Europe and the E Mediterranean. The decline of Ottoman power began before 1600 and thereafter was reduced in wars with its European neighbours, Austria and Russia. After World War 1 nationalists led by ATATÜRK deposed the last Ottoman sultan and created the modern Turkish republic (1923).

Ouagadougou Capital of Burkina Faso, West Africa. Founded in the late 11th century as capital of the Mossi empire, it remained the centre of

Mossi power until captured by the French in 1896. Industries: handicrafts, textiles, food processing, groundnuts, vegetable oil. Pop. (1985) 442,223.

ouzel (ousel) Heavy-bodied bird found in the mountains of Asia, Europe and the Western Hemisphere. The ring ouzel (*Turdus torquatus*) has black plumage, with a white chest collar. Family Turdidae.

ovary In biology, part of a multicellular animal or a flowering plant that produces egg cells (ova), the female reproductive cells; in vertebrates it also produces female sex hormones. In female humans there is an ovary on each side of the UTERUS. Controlled by the PITUITARY GLAND, each ovary produces OESTROGEN and PROGESTERONE, which control the functioning of the female reproductive system. In flowering plants, the female sex cells are contained within structures called ovules inside the ovary. After fertilization the ovules develop into seeds, and the ovary develops into fruit. *See also* MENSTRUAL CYCLE; HORMONES

Overseas Development Administration (ODA) Department of the British Foreign and Commonwealth Office that assigns development aid to other countries and contributes to the European Development Fund and other aid agencies including charities.

overture Instrumental prelude to an opera or operetta; the term now also includes an orchestral composition, usually lively in character.

Ovid (43 BC–AD 18) (Publius Ovidius Naso) Roman poet. He was a great success in Rome until, aged 50, he was exiled by AUGUSTUS. His works include *Amores*, short love poems; *Ars Amatoria*, amusing instructions on how to seduce women; and *Metamorphoses*, a retelling of Greek myths.

ovule In seed-bearing plants, part of the reproductive organ that contains an egg cell or OVUM and develops into a seed after fertilization. In ANGIOSPERMS, ovules develop inside an OVARY. In GYMNOSPERMS, ovules are borne on the inner surface of the cone without any covering.

ovum (egg cell) Female GAMETE produced in an OVARY. After FERTILIZATION by SPERM it becomes a ZYGOTE, which is capable of developing into a new individual.

Owen, Robert (1771–1858) Welsh industrialist and social reformer. He believed that better conditions for workers would lead to greater productivity. He put these beliefs into practice at his textile mills in Scotland. His ideas provided the basis for the COOPERATIVE MOVEMENT.

Owen, Wilfred (1893–1918) British war poet. His World War I poems are a searing indictment of war. After Owen's death in action, Siegfried SASSOON arranged for their publication.

Owens, Jesse (1913–80) US black athlete. Owens broke several world records for jumping, hurdling and running (1935–36). At the 1936 Olympics in Berlin he won four gold medals, much to the displeasure of Adolf Hitler.

owl Bird that is found worldwide, except at extreme latitudes. Owls have round heads, hooked bills, large eyes and long, curved talons. Most are nocturnal, and feed on small birds and mammals. Order Strigiformes.

ox Domesticated cattle of the genus *Bos*. The term is specifically applied to castrated males used as draught animals.

oxalic acid Poisonous, colourless, crystalline organic acid ($C_2H_2O_4$) whose salts occur naturally in some plants, such as sorrel and rhubarb. It is used for metal and textile cleaning and in tanning. Properties: m.p. 101.5°C (214.7°F).

oxbow Crescent-shaped section of a river channel that no longer carries the main discharge of water. It is formed by contact at the neck of a meander loop, leaving the loop abandoned.

Oxfam British charity formed in 1948. It attempts to alleviate suffering due to poverty or natural disaster in all parts of the world. Nearly 75% of Oxfam's overseas budget is devoted to long-term projects, including agriculture and medicine.

Oxford City and county district in S central England, on the River Thames; the county town of Oxfordshire. Established as a trading centre and fort, it was raided by the Danes in the 10th and 11th centuries. During the English Civil War the city was a Royalist stronghold. Industries: motor vehicles, steel products, electrical goods, printing and publishing. Pop. (1991) 110,113.

Oxford, University of Oldest university in Britain. It developed from a group of teachers and students who gathered in OXFORD in the 12th century. The first colleges, University, Balliol and Merton, were founded between 1249 and 1264. The colleges quickly increased in number and became almost autonomous.

Oxford Movement Attempt by some members of the CHURCH OF ENGLAND to restore the ideals of the pre-REFORMATION Church. It lasted from *c.*1833 to the first decades of the 20th century. The main proponents were John Keble, Edward Pusey and John NEWMAN. The aims and ideals of the movement live on in Anglo-Catholicism.

Oxfordshire County in S central England, bounded in the NW by the COTSWOLDS and in the SE by the Chilterns, and drained by the River THAMES. The county town is OXFORD. It lies mostly within the Thames basin. Its economy is based on agriculture, with sheep and arable farming, dairying and beef production. Industries: motor vehicles, pressed steel, light engineering. Area: 2,611sq km (1,008sq mi). Pop. (1991) 547,584.

oxidation-reduction (redox) Chemical reaction involving simultaneous oxidation (a loss of one or more electrons by an atom or molecule) and reduction (a gain of those electrons by another atom or molecule). Oxidation–reduction reactions are important in many biochemical systems.

oxide Any inorganic chemical compound in which OXYGEN is combined with another element.

oxygen Common gaseous element (symbol O) that is necessary for the RESPIRATION of plants and animals and for combustion. Colourless and odourless, it is the most abundant element in the Earth's crust (49.2% by weight) and is a constituent of water and many rocks. It is also present in the atmosphere (23.14% by weight). It can be obtained by the ELECTROLYSIS of water or fractional distillation of liquid air. It is used in apparatus for breathing (oxygen masks) and resuscitation (oxygen tanks); liquid oxygen is used in rocket fuels. It is chemically reactive, and forms compounds with most other elements (especially by oxidation). Properties: at.no. 8; r.a.m. 15.9994; r.d. 1.429; m.p. $-218.4°C$; $(-361.1°F)$; b.p. $-182.96°C$; $(-297.3°F)$; most common isotope O^{16} (99.759%). *See also* OXIDATION-REDUCTION; OZONE

oxytocin Hormone produced by the posterior PITUITARY GLAND in women during the final stage of pregnancy. It stimulates the muscles of the UTERUS, initiating labour and maintaining contractions during childbirth. It also stimulates lactation.

oyster Edible BIVALVE mollusc found worldwide in temperate and warm seas. The European flat, or edible, oyster *Ostrea edulis* occurs throughout coastal waters. The pearl oyster (*Pinctada fucats*) is used to produce cultured pearls.

oystercatcher Seashore bird with a strikingly marked black-and-white stocky body and bright orange legs and beak. Oystercatchers feed on molluscs, prising them open with their long beaks. Length: 43cm (17in). Family Haematopodidae; typical genus *Haematopus*.

ozone Unstable, pale-blue, gaseous allotrope of OXYGEN, formula (O_3). It has a characteristic pungent odour and decomposes into molecular oxygen. In industry, ozone is used as an oxidizing agent in bleaching, air-conditioning and purifying water. *See also* ALLOTROPY; OZONE LAYER

ozone layer Region of Earth's atmosphere in which OZONE (O_3) is concentrated. It is densest at altitudes of 21–26km (13–16mi). Produced by ultraviolet radiation in incoming sunlight, the ozone layer absorbs much of the ultraviolet, thereby shielding the Earth's surface. Aircraft, nuclear weapons and some aerosol sprays and refrigerants yield chemical agents that can break down high-altitude ozone, which could lead to an increase in the amount of harmful ultraviolet radiation reaching the Earth's surface. *See also* CHLOROFLUOROCARBON (CFC).

P/p descends from the Semitic letter pe, a word meaning "mouth". The letter was modified in shape by the Greeks and taken into their alphabet as pi.

paca (spotted cavy) Shy, nocturnal, tail-less RODENT of South America; it is brown with rows of white spots and has a relatively large head. A burrow-dweller, it feeds mainly on leaves, roots and fruit. Length: to 76cm (30in). Family Dasyproctidae; species *Cuniculus paca*.

pacemaker (sino-atrial node) Specialized group of cells in the vertebrate heart that contract spontaneously, setting the pace for the heartbeat itself. If it fails it can be replaced by an artificial pacemaker.

Pacific Ocean Largest and deepest ocean in the world, covering *c*.33% of the Earth's surface and containing more than 50% of the Earth's seawater. The Pacific extends from the Arctic Circle to Antarctica, and from North and South America in the E to Asia and Australia in the w. The E Pacific region is connected with the Cordilleran mountain chain, and there is a narrow CONTINENTAL MARGIN. The ocean is ringed by numerous volcanoes (the Pacific Ring of Fire). There are a number of large islands in the Pacific, most of which are in the S and w. The principal rivers that drain into the ocean are the COLUMBIA in North America, and the HUANG HE and YANGTZE in Asia. The average depth of the Pacific is 4,300m (14,000ft). The greatest-known depth is the Challenger Deep in the Mariana Trench, at 11,033m (36,198ft). Area: *c*.166,000,000sq km (64,000,000sq mi).

Pacino, Al (Alberto) (1940–) US film actor. He studied method acting at Lee STRASBERG's Actors' Studio, and made his film debut in *Me, Natalie* (1969). He appeared three times (1972, 1974 and 1990) in his famed role as Michael Corleone (in *The Godfather* and its two sequels). He finally won a Best Actor Academy Award for *Scent of a Woman* (1992). Other films include *Serpico* (1973), *Dog Day Afternoon* (1975), *Scarface* (1983) and *Donnie Brasco* (1996).

paddlefish Primitive bony fish related to the sturgeon and found in the basins of the Mississippi and Yangtze rivers. Blue, green or grey, it has a cartilaginous skeleton and a long paddle-like snout. Length: 1.8m (6ft). Family Polyodontidae.

Padua (Padova) City in NE Italy, in Veneto region. It came under Venetian control in 1405 and passed to Austria in 1815. It played a leading part in the movement for Italian independence. Padua is renowned for its art treasures. Industries: motor vehicles, textiles, machinery, electrical goods. Pop. (1991) 215,137.

paediatrics Medical specialty devoted to the diagnosis and treatment of disease and injury in children. Paediatric specialists require a thorough knowledge not only of a wide range of conditions peculiar to children, but also of normal childhood development and the ways in which it may affect treatment and recovery.

Paganini, Niccolò (1782–1840) Italian virtuoso violinist. He enlarged the range of the violin by exploiting harmonics and mastered the art of playing double and triple stops.

pagoda Eastern temple in the form of a multistoreyed, tapering tower. The basic design is either square or polygonal, and each storey is a smaller replica of the one beneath. The storeys often have wide, overhanging roofs. Pagodas originated in India and spread with the diffusion of BUDDHISM.

Pahlavi, Muhammad Reza Shah (1919–80) Shah of Iran (1941–79), who encouraged rapid economic development and social reforms. The westernization of Iran, combined with repression and social inequality caused a theocratic revolution (1979), led by Ayatollah KHOMEINI. He was forced into exile.

pain Unpleasant sensation signalling actual or threatened tissue damage as a result of illness or injury; it can be acute (severe but short-lived) or chronic (persisting for a long time). Pain is felt when specific nerve endings are stimulated. According to the "gate theory", pain signals must pass through a gating mechanism in the SPINAL CORD in order to be transmitted onwards to the brain; this "gate" can be shut by the use of other stimuli that block entry of the pain messages. Pain is treated in a number of ways, most commonly by ANALGESICS.

Paine, Thomas (1737–1809) Anglo–American revolutionary political writer. He emigrated from England to Pennsylvania in 1754. His pamphlet *Common Sense* (1776) demanded independence for the North American colonies. He returned to England in 1787 and published *The Rights of Man* (1791–92), a defence of the French Revolution. Accused of treason, he fled to France and was elected to the National Convention, but later imprisoned (1793–94). He returned to the USA in 1802.

paint Coating applied to a surface for protective, decorative or artistic purposes. Paint is composed of PIGMENT (colour) and a liquid vehicle (binder or medium) that suspends the pigment, adheres to a surface and hardens when dry.

painting Art of using one or more colours, generally mixed with a medium (such as oil or water) and applied to a surface with a brush, finger, or other tool to create pictures. Painting in early civilizations, such as Egypt, was largely a matter of filling in with colour areas outlined by drawing. The Romans were greatly influenced by Greek art, as the fine FRESCO paintings at POMPEII and Herculaneum demonstrate. In the early Christian and Byzantine periods, traditions in mural painting and manuscript ILLUMINATION were established. When the humanist ideals of the RENAISSANCE took root in S Europe, the range of subjects and techniques widened enormously. The period also saw the first use of oil paint on canvas, the beginnings of GENRE PAINTING and pure portraiture. It was also the age of PERSPECTIVE. To this creative legacy the great painters of the BAROQUE period added an unrivalled bravura brushwork and drama of vision. The 17th-century Dutch painters' choice of intimate, everyday subjects was the antithesis of the grand manner characteristic of the Italian masters. By the 18th century British painters had become established in portraiture, animal and landscape painting, although overshadowed by the great Venetian masters. The 19th century opened with the supremacy of NEO-CLASSICISM challenged by the new ROMANTICISM. Both schools were superseded, first by IMPRESSIONISM and then by a succession of new movements in the late-19th and early 20th centuries. Most of these movements – POST-IMPRESSIONISM, SYMBOLISM, FAUVISM, CUBISM, DADA and SURREALISM – originated in Paris. Germany was the cradle of EXPRESSIONISM and Russia contributed SUPREMATISM. In the later 20th century, the USA has produced many original movements, such as ABSTRACT EXPRESSIONISM, POP ART and OP ART.

Pakistan Republic in S Asia; the capital is ISLAMABAD. **Land and climate** Pakistan is divided into the four provinces of BALUCHISTAN, NORTH-WEST FRONTIER PROVINCE, PUNJAB, and SIND. The mountains of the HINDU KUSH extend along the NW border with Afghanistan. In N Pakistan lies the disputed territory of KASHMIR. It contains the world's second highest peak, K2, at 8,611m (28,251ft), in the KARAKORAM range. At the foot of the mountains lie Islamabad and Rawalpindi. The Punjab plains are drained by the River INDUS and its tributaries. LAHORE lies on the border with India. The alluvial plain continues into Sind, which includes HYDERABAD and KARACHI. Baluchistan is an arid plateau region. Most of Pakistan has hot summers and cool winters. Rainfall is sparse, except in the monsoon season (June–October). Forests grow on mountain slopes, but most of Pakistan is covered by dry grassland. **Economy** Pakistan is a low-income developing country (1992 GDP per capita, US$2,890). The economy is based on agriculture, which employs c.47% of the workforce. Pakistan has one of the world's largest irrigation systems. It is the world's third largest producer of wheat. Other crops include cotton, fruits, rice and sugar cane. Pakistan produces natural gas and coal, as well as iron ore, chromite and stone. Major products include clothing and textiles. Small-scale craft industries, such as carpets, are also important. **History and politics** The Indus Valley civilization developed c.4,500 years ago. Waves of invaders later entered the area. The Kushan conquered the entire region in the 2nd century AD. Arabs conquered Sind in 712 and introduced Islam. In 1206 Pakistan became part of the Delhi Sultanate. In 1526 the Sultanate was replaced by the MOGUL EMPIRE, which introduced URDU. In the late 18th century, Ranjit Singh conquered the Punjab, and introduced SIKHISM. The early 19th century saw the emergence of the British EAST INDIA COMPANY. The British conquered Sind (1843) and Punjab (1849). Much of Baluchistan was conquered in the 1850s. Pathans in the NW resisted subjection, and the British created a separate province in 1901. The dominance of Hindus in British India led to the formation of the MUSLIM LEAGUE (1906). In the 1940s the League's leader, Muhammad Ali JINNAH, gained popular support for the idea of a separate state of Pakistan (Urdu, "land of the pure") in Muslim-majority areas. British India achieved independence in 1947, and was partitioned into India and Pakistan. The resulting mass migration and communal violence claimed over 500,000 lives. In 1947 the long-standing war with India over Kashmir began. Jinnah became Pakistan's first governor-general. Muslim Pakistan was divided into two parts: East Bengal and West Pakistan, more than 1,600km (1,000mi) apart. Pakistan was faced with enormous political and administrative problems. In 1955 East Bengal became East Pakistan, and in 1956 Pakistan became a republic within the Commonwealth of Nations. General Muhammad AYUB KHAN led a military coup in 1958, and in 1960 established presidential rule. His dictatorship failed to satisfy East Pakistan's claim for greater autonomy. The pro-independence Awami League won a landslide victory in 1970 East Pakistan elections. In 1971 East Pakistan declared independence as BANGLADESH. West Pakistani troops invaded. The ensuing civil war killed hundreds of thousands of people, and millions fled to India. India sent troops to support Bangladesh. West Pakistan was forced to surrender and Zulfikar Ali BHUTTO assumed control. In 1977 a military coup, led by General Zia-ul-Haq, deposed Bhutto. In 1978 General Zia proclaimed himself president and Bhutto was hanged for murder. During the 1980s Pakistan received US aid for providing a safe haven for Mujaheddin fighters in the war in Afghanistan. In 1985 Zia ended martial law. In 1988 Zia dismissed parliament, but died shortly after in a plane crash. The Pakistan People's Party (PPP) won the ensuing elections and Benazir BHUTTO, daughter of Zulfikar, became president. Charged with nepotism and corruption,

PAKISTAN	
AREA:	796,100sq km (307,374sq mi)
POPULATION:	115,520,000
CAPITAL (POPULATION):	Islamabad (201,000)
GOVERNMENT:	Federal republic
ETHNIC GROUPS:	Punjabi 60%, Sindhi 12%, Pushtun 13%, Baluch, Muhajir
LANGUAGES:	Urdu (official)
RELIGIONS:	Islam 97%, Christianity, Hinduism
CURRENCY:	Pakistan rupee = 100 paisa

she was removed from office in 1990. The ensuing election was won by the Islamic Democratic Alliance, led by Nawaz Sharif. In 1991 Islamic law was given precedence over civil law. Sharif also faced charges of corruption and lost the 1993 election to Benazir Bhutto. In 1994 civil disorder flared in Sind, inspired by a militant campaign for an autonomous Karachi province. Bhutto was again dismissed on corruption charges in 1996, and 1997 elections saw the return of Nawaz Sharif.

palaeobotany Study of ancient plants and pollen that have been preserved by carbonization, water-logging or by freezing. Some plants have been preserved almost intact in frozen soils and in AMBER.

Palaeocene Geological epoch that extended from about 65 to 55 million years ago. It is the first epoch of the TERTIARY period, when the majority of the DINOSAURS had disappeared and the small early mammals were flourishing.

Palaeolithic (Old Stone Age) Earliest stage of human history, from c.2 million years ago until between 40,000 and 10,000 years ago. It was marked by the use of stone tools and the evolution of humans from *Homo habilis* to *Homo sapiens*.

Palaeolithic art Art from the PALAEOLITHIC period. Typical works are realistic cave paintings of bison, deer and hunting scenes. The best-known surviving examples are at ALTAMIRA and LASCAUX.

palaeomagnetism Study of changes in the direction and intensity of Earth's magnetic field through GEOLOGICAL TIME. This is important in the investigation of the theory of CONTINENTAL DRIFT. The Earth's polarity has reversed at least 20 times in the past 4–5 million years. *See also* MAGNETIC FIELD; EARTH

palaeontology Study of the fossil remains of plants and animals. Evidence from fossils is used in the reconstruction of ancient environments and in tracing the evolution of life.

Palaeozoic Second era of geological time, after the PRECAMBRIAN era, lasting from 590 million to 248 million years ago. It is sub-divided into six periods: Cambrian, Ordovician, Silurian, Devonian, Carboniferous and Permian. Invertebrate animals evolved hard skeletons capable of being preserved as fossils in the Cambrian; fish-like vertebrates appeared in the Ordovician; amphibians emerged in the Devonian; and reptiles in the Carboniferous.

palate Roof of the mouth, comprising the bony front part known as the hard palate, and the softer fleshy part at the back, known as the soft palate.

Palermo City and seaport in Italy, in NW Sicily, on the Tyrrhenian Sea; capital of Sicily. The city was founded by the Phoenicians in the 8th century BC. Captured by the Normans in 1072, it later became the capital of the Kingdom of Sicily. Palermo was the scene of the outbreak of the 1848 revolution in Italy and was captured by Giuseppe GARIBALDI in 1860. Industries: shipbuilding, textiles, chemicals, tourism. Pop. (1991) 698,556.

Palestine Territory in the Middle East, on the E shore of the Mediterranean Sea; considered a Holy Land by Jews, Christians and Muslims. Palestine has been settled continuously since 4000 BC. The Jews moved into Palestine from Egypt c.2000 BC but were subjects of the Philistines until 1020 BC, when SAUL, DAVID and SOLOMON established Hebrew kingdoms. The region was then under Assyrian and, later, Persian control before coming under Roman rule in 63 BC. In succeeding centuries Palestine became a focus of Christian pilgrimage. It was conquered by the Muslim Arabs in 640. In 1099 Palestine fell to the Crusaders, but in 1291 they in turn were routed by the Mamelukes. The area was part of the OTTOMAN EMPIRE from 1516–1918, when British forces defeated the Turks at Megiddo. Jewish immigration was encouraged by the BALFOUR DECLARATION. After World War 1 the British held a League of Nations mandate over the land W of the River JORDAN (now once again called Palestine). World War 2 and Nazi persecution brought many Jews to Palestine, and in 1947 Britain, unable to satisfy both Jewish and Arab aspirations, consigned the problem to the United Nations. The UN proposed a plan for separate Jewish and Arab states. This was rejected by the Arabs, and in 1948 (after the first of several ARAB-ISRAELI WARS) most of ancient Palestine became part of the new state of ISRAEL; the GAZA STRIP was controlled by Egypt and the WEST BANK of the River Jordan by JORDAN. These two areas were subsequently occupied by Israel in 1967. From the 1960s, the PALESTINE LIBERATION ORGANIZATION (PLO) led Palestinian opposition to Israeli rule, which included the INTIFADA. In 1993 Israel reached an agreement with the PLO, and in 1994 the Palestine National Authority took over nominal administration of the Gaza Strip and West Bank.

Palestine Liberation Organization (PLO) Organization of Palestinian parties and groups, widely recognized as the representative of the Palestinian people. It was founded in 1964 with the aim of dissolving the state of Israel and establishing a Palestinian state to enable Palestinian refugees to return to their ancestral land. Many of its component guerrilla groups were involved in political violence against Israel and, in the 1970s, in acts of international terrorism, to further their cause. Dominated by the al-Fatah group led by Yasir ARAFAT, in 1974 the PLO was recognized as a government-in-exile by the Arab League and the United Nations. In the early 1990s, PLO representatives conducted secret negotiations with Israel, culminating in a peace agreement signed in 1993. *See also* WEST BANK; GAZA STRIP; PALESTINE

Palestrina, Giovanni Pierluigi da (1525–94) Italian composer who spent most of his life in the service of the church. He wrote masses, magnificats, litanies and about 600 motets in four to eight or twelve parts. The mass *Assumpta est Maria* and the motet *Stabat Mater* are examples of polyphonic and rhythmic mastery, melodic balance and proportion.

473

Palladianism Architectural style based on Roman classicism and especially popular in England, derived from the work of Andrea PALLADIO. Inigo JONES introduced Palladianism to England after visiting Italy (1613–14). There was a revival of interest in Palladianism in the early 18th century.

Palladio, Andrea (1508–80) Italian RENAISSANCE architect. He studied Roman architecture and published his drawings of Roman ruins in *Four Books of Architecture* (1570). *See also* PALLADIANISM

palladium Shiny silver-white metallic element (symbol Pd), one of the TRANSITION ELEMENTS. Discovered in 1803, it is malleable and ductile. It does not tarnish or corrode and is used for electroplating, surgical instruments, jewellery and catalytic converters for cars. Properties: at.no. 46; r.a.m. 106.4; r.d. 12.02; m.p. 1,552°C (2,826F); b.p. 3,140°C (5,684°F); most common isotope Pd^{106} (27.3%).

palm Member of a family of trees found in tropical and subtropical regions. Palms have a woody, unbranched trunk with a crown of large, stiff leaves. The leaves may be palmate or pinnate. Palms are the source of wax, fibres and sugar. Height: 60m (200ft). Family Arecacae/Palmae.

Palma (Palma de Mallorca) City and seaport in W Majorca, Spain; capital of the BALEARIC ISLANDS. Conquered by James I of Aragon in the 13th century, it was finally united with Spain in 1469. Industries: tourism, pottery, glasswork, leather goods, jewellery, wine. Pop. (1991) 296,754.

Palmerston, Henry John Temple, 3rd Viscount (1784–1865) British statesman. He was a dominant influence on foreign affairs, 1830–65. He vigorously upheld British interests abroad, initiating the OPIUM WAR to help British merchants. At the same time he supported liberal and nationalist causes in Europe, such as the RISORGIMENTO in Italy.

Palm Sunday In the Christian year, the Sunday before Easter. Palm Sunday commemorates JESUS CHRIST's triumphal entry into Jerusalem, when the people spread palm branches before him.

Palmyra (Tadmur, City of Palms) Ancient oasis city, in the Syrian Desert. By the 1st century BC it had become a city-state by virtue of its control of the trade route between Mesopotamia and the Mediterranean. In 273 Emperor Aurelian laid waste to the city. Tourists visit its extensive ruins.

Pamirs Mountainous region in central Asia, lying mostly in Tajikistan and partly in Pakistan, Afghanistan and China. The region forms a geological structural knot from which the TIAN SHAN, KARAKORAM, Kunlun and HINDU KUSH mountain ranges radiate. The main activity is sheep herding, and some coal is mined. The highest peak is KOMMUNIZMA PIK, at 7,495m (24,590ft).

pampas grass Species of tall, reed-like GRASS native to South America and cultivated as an ornamental. Female plants bear flower clusters, 91cm (3ft) tall, which are silvery and plume-like. Family Poaceae/Gramineae; species *Cortaderia selloana*.

Pamplona Ancient city in N Spain; capital of

Navarre province. In the 11th century it was made capital of the kingdom of Navarre. In 1512 control of Pamplona passed to Ferdinand of Aragon, who united Navarre with Castile. Industries: rope and pottery manufacture, papermaking, flour and sugar milling. Pop. (1991) 179,251.

Pan In Greek mythology, the god of woods and fields, shepherds and their flocks. He is depicted with the horns, legs and hooves of a goat. A forest dweller, he pursued and loved the DRYADS.

Pan-Africanism Historical political movement for the unification and independence of African nations. It began officially at the Pan-African Congress of 1900 in London, organized by western black leaders. It met five times between 1900 and 1927, and worked to bring gradual self-government to African colonial states. In 1945 the Pan-African Federation convened the Sixth Congress, attended by many future leaders of post-colonial Africa. As independence was gained, the movement broke up and was replaced by the ORGANIZATION OF AFRICAN UNITY (OAU), formed in 1963.

Panama Republic on the Isthmus of Panama, connecting Central and South America; the capital is PANAMA CITY. **Land and climate** The narrowest part of Panama is less than 60km (37mi) wide. The PANAMA CANAL cuts across the isthmus. The Canal has given Panama great international importance, and most Panamanians live within 20km (12mi) of it. Most of the land between the Pacific and Caribbean coastal plains is mountainous, rising to the volcanic Barú at 3,475m (11,400ft). Panama has a tropical climate. The rainy season is between May and December. The Caribbean side of Panama has about twice as much rain as the Pacific side. Tropical forests cover *c*.50% of Panama. Mangrove swamps line the coast. **Economy** The Panama Canal is a major source of revenue. After the Canal, the main activity is agriculture, which employs 27% of the workforce. Rice is the main food crop. Bananas, shrimps, sugar and coffee are exported. Tourism is also important. Many ships are registered under Panama's flag, because of its low taxes. **History** Christopher COLUMBUS landed in Panama in 1502. In 1510 Vasco Núñez de Balboa became the first European to cross Panama and see the Pacific Ocean. The indigenous population were

PANAMA
AREA: 77,080sq km (29,761sq mi)
POPULATION: 2,515,000
CAPITAL (POPULATION): Panama City (584,803)
GOVERNMENT: Multiparty republic
ETHNIC GROUPS: Mestizo 60%, Black and Mulatto 20%, White 10%, Native American 8%, Asian 2%
LANGUAGES: Spanish (official)
RELIGIONS: Christianity (Roman Catholic 84%, Protestant 5%), Islam 5%
CURRENCY: Balboa = 100 cents

soon wiped out and Spain established control. In 1821 Panama became a province of Colombia. The USA exerted great influence from the mid-19th century. After a revolt in 1903, Panama declared independence from Colombia. In 1904 the USA began construction of the Panama Canal and established the Panama Canal Zone. The Canal was opened in 1914. Panama has been politically unstable throughout the 20th century, with a series of dictatorial regimes and military coups. Civil strife during the 1950s and 1960s led to negotiations with the USA for the transfer of the Canal Zone. In 1977 a treaty confirmed Panama's sovereignty over the Canal, while providing for US bases in the Canal Zone. The USA agreed to hand over control of the Canal on 31 December 1999. In 1983 General NOR-IEGA took control of the National Guard, and ruled through a series of puppet governments. In 1987 the USA withdrew its support for Noriega after he was accused of murder, fraud and aiding drug smuggling. In 1989 Noriega made himself president and declared war on the USA. On 20 December 1989 25,000 US troops invaded Panama. Noriega was captured and taken to the USA for trial. Pérez Balladares was elected president in 1994.

Panama Canal Waterway connecting the Atlantic and Pacific oceans across the Isthmus of Panama. The main construction took about ten years to complete, and the first ship passed through in 1914. The 82-km (51-mi) waterway reduces the sea voyage between San Francisco and New York by about 12,500km (7,800mi). Control of the canal passes from the USA to Panama at the end of 1999.

Panama City Capital of Panama, on the shore of the Gulf of Panama, near the Pacific end of the PANAMA CANAL. It was founded by Pedro Arias de Avila in 1519, and was destroyed and rebuilt in the 17th century. It became the capital of Panama in 1903 and developed rapidly after the completion of the Canal in 1914. Industries: brewing, shoe, textile, oil-refining, plastics. Pop. (1990) 584,803.

Panchen Lama Tibetan Buddhist religious leader who is second in importance to the DALAI LAMA. When the Dalai Lama fled to India in 1959, the Chinese government recognized the next Panchen Lama as leader of Tibet. However, in 1964 he was stripped of his power. In May 1995 the Dalai Lama announced the six-year-old successor of the 10th Panchen Lama. The boy immediately disappeared, reportedly detained by the Chinese authorities. In December 1995 another boy, was selected by the Chinese government and enthroned as the 11th Panchen Lama. He is not recognized by the Tibetan government-in-exile. See also TIBETAN BUDDHISM

pancreas Elongated gland lying behind the stomach to the left of the mid-line. It secretes pancreatic juice into the SMALL INTESTINE to aid digestion. Pancreatic juice contains the enzymes AMY-LASE, TRYPSIN and lipase. The pancreas also contains a group of cells known as the islets of Langerhans, which secrete the hormones INSULIN and glucagon, concerned in the regulation of blood-sugar level. See also DIABETES

panda Two mainly nocturnal mammals of the raccoon family. The lesser panda, *Ailurus fulgens*, ranges from the Himalayas to w China. It has soft, thick, reddish brown fur, a white face and a bushy tail. It feeds mainly on fruit and leaves, but is also a carnivore. Length: 115cm (46in) overall. The rare giant panda, *Ailuropoda melanoleuca*, inhabits bamboo forests in China (mainly Tibet). It has a short tail and a dense white coat with black fur on shoulders, limbs, ears and around the eyes. It eats mainly plant material, particularly bamboo shoots. Length: 1.5m (5ft); weight: 160kg (350lb).

Pandora In Greek mythology, the first woman. She was created on ZEUS' orders as his revenge on PROMETHEUS, who had created men and stolen fire from heaven for them. When she opened a box she had been ordered by Zeus not to look into, all the evils of the human race flew out.

Pangaea Name for the single supercontinent that formed about 240 million years ago, and which began to break up at the end of the Triassic period. See also GONDWANALAND

pangolin (scaly anteater) Any of several species of toothless insectivorous mammals, covered with horny overlapping plates, that live in Asia and Africa. It has short, powerful forelegs with which it climbs trees and tears open the nests of tree ants, on which it feeds. Length: to 175cm (70in). Family Manidae; genus *Manis*.

Pankhurst, Emily (Emmeline Goulden) (1858–1928) British leader of the militant movement for women's suffrage, the SUFFRAGETTE MOVEMENT. She set up the Women's Social and Political Union in 1903, supported by her daughters, Christabel (1880–1958) and Sylvia (1882–1960).

pansy Common name for a cultivated hybrid VIO-LET. An ANNUAL or short-lived PERENNIAL, it has velvety flowers, usually in blue, yellow and white, with five petals. Height: to 15–30cm (6–12in). Family Violaceae; species *Viola tricolor*.

pantheism Religious system, contrasted with certain forms of DEISM, that is based on the belief that God (or gods) and the universe are identical. According to this philosophy, all life is infused with divinity. No distinction is recognized between the creator and creatures.

pantheon Ancient Greek and Roman temple for the worship of all the gods. The most famous example is the Pantheon in Rome, originally built by Agrippa (27 BC). The term was later extended to apply to a building honouring public figures.

panther See LEOPARD

Paolozzi, Sir Eduardo (1924–) Scottish sculptor and graphic artist. He created box-like, chromium-plated sculptures evocative of amusement arcades and picture palaces. Since the 1950s he has worked mainly on large-scale ABSTRACT sculptures.

papacy Office, status or authority of the pope as head of both the ROMAN CATHOLIC CHURCH and the

475

VATICAN CITY. The pope is nominated Bishop of Rome and Christ's spiritual representative on Earth. He is elected by the College of Cardinals. Until the REFORMATION the papacy claimed authority over all Western Christendom. Today papal authority extends only over the members of the Roman Catholic Church. *See also* PAPAL INFALLIBILITY

Papal Bull Official letter from the pope, written in solemn style and consisting of a formal announcement. Such a document usually contains a decree relating to doctrine, CANONIZATION, ecclesiastical discipline, or promulgation of INDULGENCES.

Papal infallibility Roman Catholic doctrine according to which the pope, under certain conditions, cannot make a mistake in formal statements on issues of faith or morals. It was defined in its present form, amid great controversy, at the First Vatican Council (1869–70). An essential requirement of the doctrine is that all Roman Catholics must accept any papal statement without question.

Papal States Territories of central Italy under the rule of the popes (756–1870). In the 15th century the papal government displaced the feudal magnates who had ruled the Papal States in the Middle Ages and imposed direct control from Rome. The territory was temporarily lost during the Napoleonic period, restored to the papacy in 1815, and annexed by the Italian nationalists during the RISORGIMENTO. The LATERAN TREATY of 1929 restored the VATICAN CITY in Rome to papal rule.

Papandreou, Andreas (1919–96) Greek statesman, prime minister (1981–89, 1993–96). Papandreou founded the Pan-Hellenic Socialist Movement (PASOK) in the mid-1970s, becoming leader of the opposition in 1977. In 1981 he was elected as Greece's first socialist prime minister and was re-elected in 1985. Implicated in a financial fraud, he resigned in 1989. Cleared of all charges, Papandreou was re-elected in 1993.

papaya (pawpaw) Palm-like tree widely cultivated in tropical America for its fleshy, melon-like, edible fruit. It also produces the ENZYME papain, which breaks down proteins. Height: to 6m (20ft). Family Caricaceae; species *Carica papaya*.

Papeete Capital and chief port of French Polynesia, in the S Pacific Ocean, on the NW coast of Tahiti. It is a trade centre and tourist resort. Exports: copra, mother-of-pearl, vanilla. Pop. (1988) 78,814.

paper Sheet or roll of compacted cellulose fibres with a wide range of uses. Over 5,500 years ago, the Egyptians used PAPYRUS to make sheets of writing material. The modern process of manufacture originated *c.*2,000 years ago in China, and consists of reducing wood fibre, straw, rags or grasses to a pulp by the action of an ALKALI, such as CAUSTIC SODA. The noncellulose material is then extracted and the residue is bleached. After washing and the addition of a filler, the pulp is made into sheets and dried.

paprika Popular, spicy condiment, a red powder ground from the fruit of a sweet PEPPER native to central Europe. Family Solanaceae.

pap smear test Sample of cells from the female genital tract, specially stained to detect malignant or premalignant disease. It is named after its discoverer, George Papanicolaou.

Papua New Guinea Independent Commonwealth island group in Melanesia, SW Pacific, 160km (100mi) NE of Australia; the capital is PORT MORESBY. **Land and climate** Papua New Guinea includes the E part of New Guinea, the Bismarck Archipelago, the N SOLOMON ISLANDS, the Trobriand and D'Entrecasteaux Islands and the Louisiade Archipelago. The land is largely mountainous, rising to Mount Wilhelm at 4,508m (14,790ft), E New Guinea. East New Guinea also has extensive coastal lowlands. Papua New Guinea has a tropical climate, with high annual temperatures. The monsoon season runs from December to April. The dominant vegetation is rainforest. "Cloud" forest and tussock grass are found on the higher peaks. Mangrove swamps line the coast. **Economy** Agriculture employs 75% of the workforce, many at subsistence level. Minerals, notably copper and gold, are the most valuable exports. Papua New Guinea is the world's ninth-largest producer of gold. Other exports include yams, coffee, timber, palm oil, cocoa and lobster. **History and politics** The first European sighting was made by the Portuguese in 1526, although no settlements were established until the late 19th century. In 1828 the Dutch took W New Guinea (now IRIAN JAYA in Indonesia). In 1884 Germany took NE New Guinea as German New Guinea and Britain formed the protectorate of British New Guinea in SE New Guinea. In 1906 British New Guinea passed to Australia as the Territory of Papua. When World War 1 broke out, Australia occupied German New Guinea. In 1921 German New Guinea became the League of Nations mandate Territory of New Guinea under Australian administration. Japan captured the islands in 1942, and the Allies reconquered them in 1944. In 1949 Papua and New Guinea were combined to form the Territory of Papua and New Guinea. In 1973 the Territory achieved self-government as a prelude to full independence as Papua New Guinea in 1975. Post-independence, the government of Papua New Guinea has worked to develop its mineral reserves. One of the most valu-

---

PAPUA NEW GUINEA
AREA: 462,840sq km (178,073 sq mi)
POPULATION: 4,056,000
CAPITAL (POPULATION): Port Moresby (193,242)
GOVERNMENT: Constitutional monarchy
ETHNIC GROUPS: Papuan 84%, Melanesian 1%
LANGUAGES: English (official)
RELIGIONS: Christianity (Protestant 58%, Roman Catholic 33%, Anglican 5%), traditional beliefs 3%
CURRENCY: Kina = 100 toea

able reserves was a copper mine at Panguna on BOUGAINVILLE. Conflict developed when Bougainville demanded a larger share in mining profits. The Bougainville Revolutionary Army proclaimed independence in 1990. In 1992 and 1996 Papua New Guinea launched offensives against the rebels. The use of highly paid mercenaries created unrest in the army. In March 1997 troops and civilians surrounded parliament, forcing the resignation of the prime minister, Sir Julius Chan. In the ensuing elections, Bill Skate became prime minister.

papyrus Stout, perennial water plant, native to S Europe, N Africa and the Middle East, and used by the ancient Egyptians to make a PAPER-like writing material. Height: to 4.5m (15ft). Family Cyperaceae; species *Cyperus papyrus*.

parabola Mathematical curve, a CONIC section traced by a point that moves so that its distance from a fixed point, the focus, is equal to its distance from a fixed straight line, the directrix. It may be formed by cutting a cone parallel to one side. The general equation of a parabola is $y = ax^2 + bx + c$, where a, b and c are constants.

Paracelsus (1493–1541) Swiss physician and alchemist, real name Philippus Aureolus Theophrastus Bombast von Hohenheim. He introduced mineral baths and made opium, mercury, and lead part of the pharmacopoeia.

paracetamol ANALGESIC drug that lessens pain and is also effective in reducing fever. It is used to treat mild to moderate pain, such as headaches, toothaches and rheumatic conditions, and is particularly effective against musculoskeletal pain.

parachute Lightweight fabric device for slowing movement through the air. Parachutes allow people to descend safely from aircraft or are used to drop cargo and supplies.

paraffin (kerosene) Common domestic fuel that is mainly a mixture of ALKANE hydrocarbons. It is a product of the distillation of petroleum. Less volatile than petrol, paraffin is also used as a fuel for jet aircraft. Paraffin wax is a white, translucent substance, consisting of a mixture of solid alkanes, used to make candles, polishes and cosmetics.

Paraguay Landlocked republic in central South America; the capital is ASUNCIÓN. **Land and climate** Paraguay is bisected by the River Paraguay.

PARAGUAY

AREA: 406,750sq km (157,046sq mi)

POPULATION: 4,579,000

CAPITAL (POPULATION): Asunción (637,737)

GOVERNMENT: Multiparty republic

ETHNIC GROUPS: Mestizo 90%, Native American 3%

LANGUAGES: Spanish and Guaraní (both official)

RELIGIONS: Christianity (Roman Catholic 96%, Protestant 2%)

CURRENCY: Guaraní = 100 céntimos

The majority of the population live between the E bank of the River Paraguay and the River PARANÁ. The S has extensive marshes. West of the River Paraguay is part of the GRAN CHACO. The plain rises gradually in the W to the Bolivian border. The S is subtropical. Rainfall is heaviest in the SE Paraná plateau. The Chaco is the driest and hottest part of Paraguay. **Economy** Agriculture and forestry are the leading activities, employing 48% of the workforce. Paraguay has large cattle ranches, and many crops are grown in the fertile soils of E Paraguay. Paraguay is the world's seventh-largest producer of soya beans. Other crops include cassava, cotton and coffee. Raw materials account for 79% of exports. Major exports include timber, coffee, tannin and meat products. In 1973 construction started on the Itaipú Dam on the River Paraná. This is the world's largest dam by volume. Paraguay has no major mineral or fossil fuel resources. **History** The earliest known inhabitants of Paraguay were the Guaraní. Spanish and Portuguese explorers reached the area in the early 16th century. In 1537 a Spanish expedition built a fort at Asunción, which became the capital of Spain's colonies in SE South America. From the late 16th century, Jesuit missionaries worked to protect the Guaraní from colonial exploitation and convert them to Christianity. In 1767 the Spanish king expelled the Jesuits. In 1776 Paraguay was subsumed into the colony of the viceroyalty of Río de la Plata. Paraguayan opposition intensified, and Paraguay declared independence in 1811. Paraguay's post-colonial history has been dominated by dictatorships. The disastrous War of the Triple Alliance (1865–70) against Brazil, Argentina and Uruguay killed over 50% of Paraguay's population and resulted in great loss of territory. Border disputes with Bolivia led to the Chaco War (1932–35) in which Paraguay regained some land. In 1954 General Alfredo Stroessner led a successful military coup. His dictatorial regime suppressed all political opposition. In 1989, shortly after re-election for an eighth successive term, Stroessner was overthrown by General Andrés Rodríguez. In 1993 Juan Carlos Wasmosy became Paraguay's first civilian president since 1954. An attempted military coup was foiled in 1996.

parakeet *See* PARROT

parallax Angular distance by which a celestial object appears to be displaced with respect to more distant objects, when viewed from opposite ends of a baseline. The parallax of a star (annual) is the angle subtended at the star by the mean radius of the Earth's orbit (one astronomical unit); the smaller the angle, the more distant the star. *See also* PARSEC

parallelogram Quadrilateral (four-sided plane figure) having each pair of opposite sides parallel and equal. Both the opposite angles are also equal. Its area is the product of one side and its perpendicular distance from the opposite side. A parallelogram with all four sides equal is called a RHOMBUS.

Paralympic Games Sports meeting held every

four years in conjunction with the OLYMPIC GAMES and in which all competitors are physically handicapped. Much of the full Olympic programme of events is staged.

paralysis Weakness or loss of muscle power; it can vary from a mild condition to complete loss of function and sensation in the affected part. It can be associated with almost any disorder of the NERVOUS SYSTEM, including brain or spinal cord injury, infection, stroke, poisoning, or progressive conditions such as a tumour or motor neurone disease. Paralysis is very rarely total.

Paramaribo Capital of SURINAM, a port on the River Surinam. It was founded in the early 17th century by the French. Industries: bauxite, timber, sugar cane, rice, rum, coffee, cacao. Pop. (1993 est.) 200,970.

Paraná River in SE central South America. It rises in SE Brazil, flows S into Argentina, forming the SE and S border of Paraguay, and joins the River Uruguay to form the Río de la PLATA. Combined Length Paraná/Plata: *c.*4,000km (2400mi).

paranoia Term in psychology for a psychotic disorder characterized by a systematically held, persistent delusion, usually of persecution or irrational jealousy. Paranoia can accompany SCHIZOPHRENIA, manic depression, drug abuse, or brain damage.

paraplegia PARALYSIS of both legs. It is usually due to spinal cord injury, and often accompanied by loss of sensation below the site of the damage.

parapsychology Branch of psychology concerned with research into phenomena that appear inexplicable by traditional science. It involves research into EXTRASENSORY PERCEPTION (ESP), such as TELEPATHY and precognition. Parapsychology is also concerned with physical phenomena such as psychokinesis and the poltergeist phenomenon.

parasite Organism that lives on or in another organism (the host) upon which it depends for its survival; this arrangement may be harmful to the host. Parasites occur in many groups of plants and in virtually all major animal groups. A parasite that lives in the host is called an **endoparasite**; a parasite that survives on the host's exterior is an **ectoparasite**. Many parasites, such as PROTOZOA, FLEAS and WORMS, carry disease or cause sores, which may become infected. In parasitoidism, the relationship results in the death of the host. A hyperparasite is one that parasitizes another parasite.

parathyroid glands Four small endocrine glands, usually embedded in the back of the THYROID GLAND, that secrete a HORMONE to control the level of calcium and phosphorus in the blood. Overproduction of parathyroid hormone causes loss of calcium from the bones to the blood; a deficiency causes tetany. *See also* ENDOCRINE SYSTEM

Paré, Ambroise (1517–90) French physician regarded by some as the founder of modern surgery. He introduced new methods of treating wounds, described in his book *The Method of Treating Wounds Made by Harquebuses and Other Guns* (1545), and revived the practice of tying arteries during surgery instead of cauterizing them.

Paris In Greek legend, the son of PRIAM and Hecuba. Paris chose APHRODITE as the victor in a competition among goddesses, and she helped him to abduct HELEN. This kidnapping sparked the TROJAN WAR, in which Paris slew ACHILLES.

Paris Capital of France, on the River SEINE. When the Romans took Paris in 52 BC, it was a small village on the Ile de la Cité on the Seine. Under their rule it became an important administrative centre. Paris was the capital of the Merovingian Franks in the 5th century but subsequently declined. It was re-established as the French capital by the Capetian kings in the 10th century. Paris expanded rapidly in the 11th and 12th centuries. During the 14th century it rebelled against the Crown and declared itself an independent commune. Paris suffered further civil disorder during the Hundred Years War. In the 16th century it underwent fresh expansion, its architecture strongly influenced by the Italian Renaissance. In the reign of Louis XIII, Cardinal RICHELIEU established Paris as the cultural and political centre of Europe. The FRENCH REVOLUTION began in Paris when the BASTILLE was stormed in 1789. Under Emperor NAPOLEON I the city began to assume its present-day form. The work of modernization continued during the reign of NAPOLEON III, when Baron Haussmann was commissioned to plan the boulevards, bridges and parks that now characterize the city. Although occupied during the Franco-Prussian War (1870–71) and again in World War 2, Paris was not badly damaged. The city proper consists of the Paris département, Ville de Paris. Its suburbs lie in the départements of the Ile-de-France region. Paris remains the hub of France despite attempts at decentralization, and retains its importance as a European cultural, commercial and communications centre. Paris is noted for its fashion industry and for the manufacture of luxury articles. Industries: tourism, motor vehicles, chemicals, textiles, clothing, printing, publishing. Pop. (1990, city) 2,152,423; (conurbation) 9,318,821.

Paris, Treaties of Name given to several international agreements made in Paris. The most notable include: the Treaty of 1763, which ended the SEVEN YEARS WAR; the Treaty of 1783, in which Britain recognized the independence of the USA; the Treaty of 1814, which settled the affairs of France after the first abdication of NAPOLEON I; the Treaty of 1815, after Napoleon's final defeat; the Treaty of 1856, ending the CRIMEAN WAR; and the Treaty of 1898, ending the Spanish-American War and giving the Philippines to the USA.

Paris Commune (18 March–28 May 1871) Revolutionary government in Paris. Anger with the national government provoked Parisians into establishing an independent city government. Besieged by the forces of the national government, the city fell and an estimated 30,000 were slaughtered.

parity In physics, term used to denote space-reflection symmetry. The principle of conservation of parity states that physical laws are the same in a left- and right-handed co-ordinate system. In 1956, Chen Ning YANG and Tsung-Dao Lee showed that parity was transgressed by certain interactions between elementary atomic particles. Parity is also used in information theory to denote a coding method employed in message transmission to detect errors.

Park, Mungo (1771–1806) British explorer. Approaching from the Gambia, he explored *c*.450 km (280 mi) of the Upper Niger, a journey described in his *Travels...* (1799). On a second expedition (1805) he and his companions were ambushed and killed.

Parker, Charlie (Charles Christopher) (1920–55) US jazz alto saxophonist, nicknamed "Bird". He recorded with Dizzy GILLESPIE in the 1940s, and was one of the founders of BEBOP.

Parker, Dorothy (1893–1967) US poet, short-story writer and critic. She wrote three volumes of poetry, including *Enough Rope* (1926). Many of her short stories were collected in *Here Lies* (1939). Her gift for witty, often caustic, epigrams was famed.

Parkinson's disease Degenerative BRAIN DIS-EASE characterized by tremor, muscular rigidity and poverty of movement and facial expression. It arises from a lack of the NEUROTRANSMITTER DOPAMINE. Foremost among the drugs used to control the disease is L-DOPA.

parliament Legislative assembly that includes elected members and acts as a debating forum for political affairs. Many parliamentary systems are based on the British Parliament, which emerged in the late 13th century as an extension of the king's council and has been housed at Westminster since that time. It is the supreme power in the country. Parliament comprises the monarch, in whose name members of the government act, and two Houses: the House of Lords, an upper chamber of hereditary and life peers, bishops and law lords, and the House of Commons. There are 659 members of the Commons (known as "members of Parliament" or MPs), elected in single-member constituencies by universal adult suffrage. The PRIME MINISTER and CABINET are almost always members of the Commons.

Parma City in N Italy; capital of Parma province. Parma is famed for its local food products, such as Parma ham and Parmesan cheese. It was founded by the Romans in 183 BC. In 1545 Pope Paul III established the duchy of Parma, and until 1731 it was controlled by the Farnese family. Despite suffering severe bombing in World War 2, Parma retains many historic sites. Pop. (1991) 170,520.

Parmigiano (1503–40) (Francesco Mazzola) Northern Italian painter, a master of MANNERISM. His best-known works are *Madonna with St Zachary* (*c*.1530), *Vision of St Jerome* (*c*.1527) and *Madonna with the Long Neck* (*c*.1535).

Parnell, Charles Stewart (1846–91) Irish political leader. He entered the British Parliament in 1875, vigorously supporting home rule for Ireland

and rapidly taking over leadership of the Irish group in the Commons. He was imprisoned (1881–82), but his power peaked in 1886, with the introduction of the Home Rule Bill. The bill was eventually defeated. His career collapsed when he was cited as co-respondent in the divorce of William O'Shea.

parrot Common name for many tropical and subtropical birds. Parrots are brightly coloured and have thick, hooked bills. They include BUDGERIGARS, macaws, lories, lorikeets, parakeets, keas and kakapos. Length: 7.5–90cm (3in–3ft). Family Psittacidae.

Parry, Sir (Charles) Hubert Hastings (1848–1918) British composer. His mastery of choral music is best shown in *Blest Pair of Sirens* (1887). He is well known for *Jerusalem* (1916).

parsec (pc) Distance at which a star would have a PARALLAX of one second of arc; equivalent to 3.2616 light years, 206,265 astronomical units, or 3.0857×10^{13} km.

Parsi (Parsee) Modern descendant of a small number of ancient Persian Zoroastrians who emigrated to Gujarat in India from the 10th century onwards. Modern Parsis, concentrated in Bombay, follow a mixture of ZOROASTRIANISM and some Indian beliefs and practices.

parsley Branching biennial herb, native to the Mediterranean region and widely cultivated for its aromatic leaves. It has heads of greenish-yellow flowers. Height: to 0.9m (3ft). Family Apiaceae.

parsnip Biennial vegetable native to Eurasia, widely cultivated for its edible white taproot. The plant has many leaves, deeply and finely lobed. The roots mature quickly in winter. Family Apiaceae.

Pärt, Arvo (1935–) Estonian minimalist composer. Among his best-known works are *Tabula Rasa* (1977), *Cantus in memoriam Benjamin Britten* (1980), and the *St John Passion* (1981).

parthenogenesis Development of a female sex cell or GAMETE without fertilization. Since there is no involvement of a male gamete, it leads to the production of offspring that are genetically identical to the mother. This process occurs naturally among some plants and invertebrates, such as APHIDS.

Parthenon Temple to the goddess ATHENA erected (447–432 BC) by PERICLES on the ACROPOLIS in Athens. The finest example of a DORIC ORDER temple, it was badly damaged by an explosion in 1687. Most of the surviving sculptures were removed by Lord Elgin in 1801–03. *See* ELGIN MARBLES

Parthia Region in ancient Persia, roughly corresponding to the Iranian province of Khurāsān and part of S TURKMENISTAN. It was the seat of the Parthian empire, founded after a successful revolt against the SELEUCIDS (238 BC). Under the Arsacid dynasty, the Parthian empire extended from Armenia to Afghanistan. In AD 224 the Parthians were defeated by the SASSANIDS.

particle accelerator *See* ACCELERATOR, PARTICLE

particle physics Branch of physics that studies SUBATOMIC PARTICLES and interactions between them. Physicists recognize more than 300 different subatomic particles, which can be grouped in various ways, although they are all composed of a few basic building blocks. The indivisible units of matter are known as ELEMENTARY PARTICLES. They are termed the gauge BOSON, LEPTON and QUARK. Other subatomic particles, termed HADRONS, are made up of two or more elementary particles.

partridge Any of several species of gamebirds found worldwide. True partridges of Europe belong to the pheasant family (Phasianidae), and include the common partridge *Perdix perdix*. It lives on heathland and feeds on plants and insects.

Parvati In Hindu mythology, the wife of the god SHIVA in one of her more benevolent aspects as a mountain goddess. Parvati is also the mother of GANESH and Skanda.

Pascal, Blaise (1623–62) French scientist and mystic. With Pierre de FERMAT, he laid the foundations of the mathematical theory of probability. He also contributed to calculus and hydrodynamics, devising Pascal's law in 1647. It states that the pressure applied to an enclosed fluid (liquid or gas) is transmitted equally in all directions and to all parts of the enclosing vessel. The SI unit of pressure is named after him.

Pashto (Pushto) One of the two major languages of Afghanistan, the other being Persian. Pashto is spoken by *c*.12 million people in E Afghanistan and N Pakistan. It is historically the language of the PATHAN tribes and is written in an adapted Arabic alphabet. One of the Iranian languages, it forms part of the INDO-EUROPEAN family of languages.

passion In Christian theology, the suffering of JESUS CHRIST from the time of his praying in the garden of Gethsemane until his death on the cross. Passion Sunday is the fifth Sunday in Lent; PALM SUNDAY then EASTER follow.

passion flower Any plant of the genus *Passiflora*, climbing tropical plants that probably originated in tropical America, especially the widely cultivated blue passion flower, *P. caerulea*. Flowers are red, yellow, green or purple. The leaves are lobed and some species produce edible fruits, such as granadilla and calabash. Family Passifloraceae.

passion play Dramatic presentation of Christ's PASSION, death and resurrection, originally developed in medieval Europe. The best-known example of this tradition is still held every ten years in OBERAMMERGAU, Germany.

Passover (Pesach) Jewish festival of eight days, commemorating the Exodus from Egypt and the redemption of the Israelites. Symbolic dishes are prepared to remind Jews of the haste with which they fled Egypt and, by extension, of their heritage. It is a family celebration, at which the HAGGADAH is read. Christ's Last Supper, at which he instituted the EUCHARIST, was a Passover meal.

Pasternak, Boris (1890–1960) Soviet poet, novelist, and translator. Before the Stalinist purges, he published works such as the poetry col-

lection *My Sister, Life* (1922) and the autobiographical *Safe Conduct* (1931). After the death of Stalin he began work on *Dr Zhivago* (1957), his best-known novel in the West. The book was not published in the Soviet Union until the 1980s. He was also compelled to retract his acceptance of the 1958 Nobel Prize in literature.

Pasteur, Louis (1822–95) French chemist and one of the founders of microbiology. He discovered that micro-organisms can be destroyed by heat, a technique now known as PASTEURIZATION. Pasteur also discovered that he could weaken certain disease-causing microorganisms and then use the weakened culture to vaccinate against the disease.

pasteurization Controlled heat treatment of food to kill bacteria and other micro-organisms, discovered by Louis PASTEUR in the 1860s. Milk is pasteurized by heating it to 72°C (161.6°F), and holding it at that temperature for 16 seconds. Ultrapasteurization is now used to produce UHT (ultra-heat-treated) milk; it is heated to 132°C (270°F) for one second.

pastoral In literature, work portraying rural life in an idealized manner, especially to contrast its supposed innocence with the corruption of the city or royal court. In classical times THEOCRITUS and VIRGIL wrote pastoral poems. The form was revived during the RENAISSANCE by poets such as DANTE, PETRARCH, BOCCACCIO and SPENSER. MILTON and SHELLEY were noted for their pastoral elegies, and William WORDSWORTH and Robert FROST have been loosely referred to as pastoral poets.

pastoralism Form of subsistence agriculture that involves the herding of domesticated livestock. Societies practising this are small, restricted by the large amount of grazing land needed for each animal. Indigenous pastoralism is widespread in N Africa and central Asia, but in the Americas is confined to the Andes. *See also* NOMAD

Patagonia Region in Argentina, E of the Andes Mountains, extending to the Strait of Magellan; the term is sometimes used to include part of S Chile. The area was first visited by MAGELLAN in the early 16th century. It was colonized in the 1880s, many of the settlers being Welsh or Scottish. The present boundaries were set in 1902. Most of Patagonia is arid, windswept plateaux. Until recently sheep rearing was the main source of income. Oil production is now important, and coal and iron ore are mined in the S. Area: 805,452sq km (311,000sq mi).

patella (kneecap) Large, flattened, roughly triangular bone just in front of the joint where the FEMUR and TIBIA are linked. It is surrounded by bursae (sacs of fluid) that cushion the joint.

Pathans (Pashtuns) MUSLIM tribes of SE Afghanistan and NW Pakistan. They speak various dialects of an E Iranian language, PASHTO, and number *c*.10 million. Formerly, they were pastoralists inhabiting the mountainous border regions, but they are now mainly farmers and are more widespread. In their clashes with the British in the 19th century, they gained a reputation as formidable warriors. Their way of life was disrupted during the Soviet occupation (1979–89) and the subsequent civil wars in Afghanistan.

pathogen Microorganism that causes disease in plants or animals. Animal pathogens are most commonly BACTERIA and VIRUSES, while common plant pathogens also include FUNGI.

pathology Study of diseases, their causes and the changes they produce in the cells, tissues and organs of the body.

Paton, Alan Stewart (1903–88) South African novelist and reformer. Strongly opposed to APARTHEID, he helped to found the South African Liberal Party, of which he was president (1958–68). His two best-known novels, *Cry, the Beloved Country* (1948) and *Too Late the Phalarope* (1953), raised awareness of the injustice of apartheid.

patriarch Head of a family or tribe, invested in certain circumstances with the status or authority of a religious leader. In the Old Testament, the term referred either to the ancestors of the human race who lived on Earth before the Flood (as recorded in Genesis 1–11) or more commonly to ABRAHAM, ISAAC, JACOB, and Jacob's 12 sons (Genesis 12–50).

patriarchy Social organization based on the authority of a senior male, usually the father, over a family.

patrician Aristocratic class in the ancient Roman Republic, members of the SENATE. In the early years of the republic, the patricians controlled all aspects of government and society. Over the centuries, the PLEBEIANS achieved a greater share of power and the division between the classes disappeared.

Patrick, Saint (active 5th century AD) Patron saint of Ireland. He was born in Britain into a Romanized Christian family. He was sent to Ireland as a missionary by Pope Celestine I (432), and established an episcopal see at Armagh. His missionary work was so successful that Christianity was firmly established in Ireland before he died. His feast day is 17 March.

Patten, Christopher Francis (1944–) British politician, last British governor of HONG KONG (1992–97). As chairman of the Conservative Party (1990–92), he helped engineer a Conservative victory in the 1992 election, but lost his own seat. Patten sought to preserve Hong Kong's political and economic institutions in the handover to China.

Patton, George Smith, Jr (1885–1945) US general. In World War 1 he served with the American Expeditionary Force (AEF) in France. He commanded a tank corps in North Africa and the 7th Army in Sicily in World War 2. As military governor of Bavaria after the war, he was criticized for leniency to Nazis and was removed to command the US 15th Army.

Paul, Saint (active 1st century AD) Apostle of JESUS CHRIST, missionary, and early Christian theologian. His missionary journeys among the Gentiles form a large part of the ACTS OF THE APOSTLES.

His many letters (epistles) to early Christian communities, recorded in the NEW TESTAMENT, represent the most important early formulations of Christian theology. Named Saul at birth, he was both a Jew and a Roman citizen. He saw the teachings of Jesus as a major threat to JUDAISM, and became a leading persecutor of early Christians. Travelling to Damascus, he suddenly saw a bright light and heard the voice of Jesus addressing him. Following this religious conversion, he adopted the name Paul and thereafter became a committed evangelist and teacher of Christianity. In *c*.60 he was arrested after returning to Jerusalem and taken as a prisoner to Rome, where he was probably executed.

Paul III (1468–1549) Pope (1534–49), b. Alessandro Farnese. As pope he largely initiated the COUNTER-REFORMATION. He sponsored reform, approved the JESUITS, and summoned the Council of TRENT (1545).

Paul VI (1897–1978) Pope (1963–78), b. Giovanni Battista Montini. He earned a reputation as a reformer in the Vatican secretariat (1937–54) and as archbishop of Milan (1954–63). He continued the Second VATICAN COUNCIL, begun by John XXIII, but disappointed liberals by upholding the celibacy of priests, papal primacy, and condemning contraception.

Pauli, Wolfgang (1900–58) US physicist, b. Austria. His work on QUANTUM THEORY led him to formulate (1925) the EXCLUSION PRINCIPLE, which explains the behaviour of electrons in atoms. In 1931 he predicted the existence of the NEUTRINO.

Pauling, Linus Carl (1901–94) US chemist. His early work on the application of WAVE MECHANICS to molecular structure led to the Nobel Prize in chemistry in 1954. He also worked on the structure of PROTEINS. His work on DNA nearly anticipated the findings of Francis CRICK and James WATSON, when he suggested, in the 1950s, that its molecules were arranged in a helical structure. A keen advocate of nuclear disarmament, he was awarded the 1962 Nobel Peace Prize.

Pavarotti, Luciano (1935–) Italian tenor. He made his operatic debut, as Rodolfo in Puccini's *La Bohème*, in 1961. He formed part of the popular open-air concert in Rome called *The Three Tenors*, along with José CARRERAS and Plácido DOMINGO.

Pavlov, Ivan Petrovich (1849–1936) Russian neurophysiologist. His early work centred on the PHYSIOLOGY and NEUROLOGY of digestion, for which he received the 1904 Nobel Prize in physiology or medicine. He is best-known for his studies of conditioning of behaviour in dogs. His major work is *Conditioned Reflexes* (1927).

Pavlova, Anna (1881–1931) Russian ballerina who made her debut in 1899. She left Russia in 1913 to tour with her own company. She excelled in *Giselle*, *The Dragonfly*, *Autumn Leaves* and the *Dying Swan*, choreographed for her by Michel FOKINE in 1905.

pawpaw *See* PAPAYA

Paz, Octavio (1914–) Mexican poet and essayist. His poetry was collected in translation as *The Collected Poems of Octavio Paz, 1957–1987* (1987). He has also written essays and literary criticism, including *The Labyrinth of Solitude* (1950). He was awarded the 1990 Nobel Prize for literature.

pea Climbing annual plant (*Pisum sativum*), probably native to W Asia. It has small oval leaves and white flowers that give rise to pods, whose seeds are a popular vegetable. It grows to 1.8m (6ft). Family Fabaceae/Leguminosae.

peach Small fruit tree (*Prunus persica*) native to China and grown throughout temperate areas. The lance-shaped leaves appear after the pink flowers in spring. The fruit has a thin, downy skin, white or yellow flesh, with a hard "stone" in the middle. Height: to 6.5m (20ft). Family Rosaceae.

peacock (peafowl) Any of several species of birds of Asia and Africa. Strictly speaking, the male is a peacock and the female a peahen. The male has a 150cm (60in) tail, which it can spread vertically as a semicircular fan with a pattern of eye-like shapes. The body of the male may be metallic blue, green or bronze, depending on the species. Hens lack the tail and head ornaments and are brown, red or green. In the wild, peafowl inhabit open, lowland forests, roosting in trees. Eggs are laid in a ground nest. Length of body: 75cm (30in). Family Phasianidae; genera *Pavo* and *Afropavo*.

Peacock, Thomas Love (1785–1866) British writer. Peacock is remembered for his satirical novels, such as *Headlong Hall* (1816), *Melincourt* (1817), *Nightmare Abbey* (1818), *Crotchet Castle* (1831) and *Gryll Grange* (1860–61).

Peak District Plateau area at the S end of the PENNINES, Derbyshire, N central England. The Peak District National Park was established here in 1951. The highest point is Kinder Scout, at 636m (2,088ft). Area: 1,404sq km (542sq mi).

peanut (groundnut) Annual leguminous plant *Arachis hypogaea* of the PEA family. Native to South America, it is now grown in many temperate regions of the world. The seeds (peanuts) are a valuable source of protein and their oil is used in food and in industry. Family: Fabaceae/Leguminosae.

pear Tree and its edible fruit, native to N Asia and S Europe and grown in temperate regions. The tree has white flowers and glossy, green leaves. The fruit, picked unripe and allowed to mature, is eaten fresh or preserved. Height: 15–23m (50–75ft). Family Rosaceae; species *Pyrus communis*.

pearl Hard, smooth, iridescent concretion of calcium carbonate produced by certain marine and freshwater bivalve MOLLUSCS. It is composed of nacre, or mother-of-pearl, which forms the inner layer of mollusc shells. A pearl results from an abnormal growth of nacre around minute particles of foreign matter, such as a grain of sand.

Pearl Harbor US naval base in Hawaii. On 7 December 1941 the base, headquarters of the US Pacific fleet, was bombed by aircraft from a Japanese naval task force. The attack left 2,400 people dead and provoked US entry into WORLD WAR 2.

Pears, Sir Peter (1910–86) British tenor. He was a lifelong friend of Benjamin BRITTEN. Britten composed all the major tenor roles in his operas for him, notably in *Peter Grimes* (1945), *Albert Herring* (1949) and *Death in Venice* (1973).

Pearse, Patrick Henry (1879–1916) Irish author and political figure. He headed the revival of interest in Gaelic culture and led the insurgents in the EASTER RISING (1916), for which he was court-martialled and executed.

Pearson, Lester Bowles (1897–1972) Canadian statesman, prime minister (1963–68). He entered parliament in 1948. His work in settling the Suez Crisis earned him the 1957 Nobel Peace Prize. He became leader of the Liberal Party in 1958. His term as prime minister was marked by health and social welfare reforms.

Peary, Robert Edwin (1856–1920) US Arctic explorer. He made several expeditions to Greenland (1886–92) and in 1893 led the first of five expeditions towards the North Pole. He claimed to have reached the pole in April 1909.

Peasants' Revolt (1381) Rebellion in England. The immediate provocation was a POLL TAX (1380). Fundamental causes were resentment of feudal restrictions and statutory control of wages, which were held down artificially, despite the shortage of labour caused by the BLACK DEATH. Led by Wat TYLER, the men of Kent marched into London, where they were pacified by RICHARD II. Promises to grant their demands were broken.

Peasants' War (1524–25) Rebellion of German peasants, probably the largest popular uprising in European history. The peasants hoped for the support of Martin LUTHER, but he rejected their charter of liberties and the rebellion was savagely suppressed.

peat Dark brown or black mass of partly decomposed plant material. It forms in bogs and areas of high rainfall, and contains a high proportion of water. It is thought to be similar to the first stage in the formation of coal, and its high carbon content makes it suitable for use as a fuel.

peat moss Decomposed organic matter (HUMUS) obtained from disintegrated sphagnum MOSS. The most widely obtainable source of humus, it is dug into soil and added to compost to retain moisture.

pecan North American nut tree whose nut, resembling a small, smooth-shelled WALNUT, is 70% fat. Family Juglandaceae; species *Carya illinoinensis*.

peccary Omnivorous, pig-like mammal native to SW USA and Central and South America. It has coarse, bristly hair, and scent glands on its back. Collared peccaries, or javelinas (*Tayassu taja*), have dark-grey hair with a whitish collar. White-lipped peccaries (*Tayassu pecari*) have brown hair. Weight: 23–30kg (50–66lb). Family Tayassuidae.

Peck, (Eldred) Gregory (1916–) US film star.

He made his debut in *Days of Glory* (1943). Other credits include *Spellbound* (1945), *The Gunfighter* (1950), *Moby Dick* (1956), *To Kill a Mockingbird* (1962, Academy Award for Best Actor), *The Omen* (1976) and *MacArthur* (1977).

pectin Water-soluble POLYSACCHARIDE found in the cell walls and intercellular tissue of certain ripe fruits or vegetables. When fruit is cooked, it yields a gel that is the basis of jellies and jams.

Pedro I (1798–1834) Emperor of Brazil (1822–31). He fled with the rest of the royal family to Brazil in 1807. When his father, JOHN VI, reclaimed the Portuguese Crown (1821), he became prince regent of Brazil and declared it an independent monarchy (1822). Following military failure against Argentina (1825–28) and revolt in Rio de Janeiro (1831), he abdicated and returned to Portugal, where he secured the succession of his daughter, Maria II.

Pedro II (1825–91) Emperor of Brazil (1831–89). He reigned under a regency until 1840. His reign was marked by internal unrest and external threats from Argentina and Paraguay. Slavery was abolished in 1888. Pedro's reforms antagonized the military and the rich planters. He was forced to resign when Brazil became a republic.

Peel, Sir Robert (1788–1850) British statesman, prime minister (1834–35, 1841–46). One of the founders of the CONSERVATIVE PARTY, his Tamworth manifesto (1934) was a statement of emergent conservatism. As TORY PARTY home secretary, he created the first modern police force, the Metropolitan (London) Police, in 1829. He was chiefly responsible for the CATHOLIC EMANCIPATION Act (1829). Peel became converted to FREE TRADE, and the Irish famine convinced him of the need to repeal the CORN LAWS.

peerage British nobility holding any of the following titles: baron, viscount, earl, marquess or duke. Although all titles were originally hereditary, these are now rare, and non-hereditary life peerages are more usually granted. Peers constitute the Lords Temporal section of the HOUSE OF LORDS.

Pegasus In Greek mythology, winged horse. Born out of the blood of MEDUSA, it was tamed by Bellerophon and helped him in his battles. Later, it carried the thunderbolts of ZEUS.

Peking *See* BEIJING

Pelagius (*c*.360–*c*.420) Monk and theologian, probably born in Britain, who preached the heresy of Pelagianism. He maintained that man is master of his own salvation and rejected the idea of original sin. His ideas were denounced by St AUGUSTINE OF HIPPO. He countered criticisms from Augustine and St JEROME in his book *De Libero Arbitrio* in 416. He was excommunicated by Pope Innocent I in 417.

Pelé (1940–) (Edson Arantes do Nascimento) Brazilian soccer player. He led Brazil to three World Cup victories (1958, 1962 and 1970). He made his last international appearance in 1971. Apart from 1975–77, when he played for New York Cosmos, all his club games were played for Santos. He scored a total of 1,281 goals.

pelican Any of several species of stout-bodied, inland water birds, with a characteristic distensible pouch under its bill for scooping up fish. It is generally white or brown and has a long hooked bill, long wings, short thick legs and webbed feet. Length: to 1.8m (6ft). Family Pelecanidae; genus *Pelecanus*.

pellagra Disease caused by a deficiency of nicotinic acid, one of the B group of vitamins. Its symptoms are lesions of the skin and mucous membranes, diarrhoea, and mental disturbance.

Peloponnesian Wars (431–404 BC) Conflict in ancient Greece between ATHENS and SPARTA. Sparta's fear of Athenian hegemony and hostility towards CORINTH provoked the Spartan declaration of war. Having a stronger army, Sparta regularly invaded Attica, while Athens, under PERICLES, relied on its navy. The early stages were inconclusive. The Peace of Nicias (420 BC) proved temporary. Neither side kept to the agreement, and in 415 BC Athens launched a disastrous attack on Syracuse. With Persian help, Sparta built up a navy which, under LYSANDER, defeated Athens in 405 BC.

Peloponnesos (Pelopónnisos) Mountainous peninsula in S Greece, connected to the mainland by the Isthmus of CORINTH. The chief cities are Patras, Corinth, Pirgos and SPARTA. The peninsula was involved in the Persian Wars (500–449 BC), and was the site of many battles between Sparta and Athens during the PELOPONNESIAN WARS (431–404 BC). Held by the Venetians from 1699–1718, then by the Ottoman Turks, the peninsula passed to Greece after independence. Industries: silk, fish, manganese, chromium, fruits, wheat, tourism. Area: 21,756sq km (8,400sq mi). Pop. (1991) 1,077,002.

Peltier effect Phenomenon of the temperature changes at a junction where an electric current passes from one kind of metal to another. The effect was discovered in 1834 by Jean Charles Peltier. *See also* SEEBECK EFFECT

pelvis Dish-shaped bony structure that supports the internal organs of the lower abdomen in vertebrates, and serves as a point of attachment for muscles that move the limbs or fins.

Penang (Pinang) Island of MALAYSIA, off the NW coast of the Malay Peninsula, which (together with a coastal strip on the mainland) comprises a state of Malaysia; the capital is Penang. The island was Britain's first possession in Malaya (1786). In 1826 it united with Singapore and MALACCA, and in 1867 the group became the Straits Settlements colony. Penang joined the Federation of Malaya in 1948. Its products include rice, rubber and tin. The city of Penang is the principal port of Malaysia. Area: 1,040sq km (400sq mi). Pop. (1993 est.) 1,141,500.

Penderecki, Krzysztof (1933–) Polish composer. His reputation was established with *Threnody for the Victims of Hiroshima* (1960). Other pieces include a *Passion According to St Luke* (1963–65).

pendulum Any object suspended at a point so it

483

swings in an arc. A simple pendulum consists of a small heavy mass attached to a string or light rigid rod. A compound pendulum has a supporting rod whose mass is not negligible. The pendulum was first used to regulate clocks in 1673 by Christiaan HUYGENS. Foucault's pendulum, devised by Léon FOUCAULT, demonstrated the Earth's rotation.

Penelope In Greek mythology, wife of ODYSSEUS. As described in HOMER's *Odyssey*, she had been married for only a year when Odysseus left.

penguin Flightless seabird that lives in the Southern Hemisphere and ranges from the Antarctic northwards to the Galápagos Islands. Their wings have been adapted to flippers and they have webbed feet. Although they are awkward on land, they are fast and powerful swimmers, easily able to catch the fish and squid that they feed on. Height: to 1.22m (4ft). Family Spheniscidae.

penicillin ANTIBIOTIC agents derived from moulds of the genus *Penicillium*. The first antibiotic to be discovered (by Sir Alexander FLEMING in 1928), it can now be produced synthetically. It can produce allergic reactions and some microorganisms have become resistant to its action.

Peninsular War (1808–14) Campaign of the NAPOLEONIC WARS in Portugal and Spain. A British force commanded by the future Duke of WELLINGTON supported Portuguese and Spanish rebels against the French. Initally on the defensive, Wellington's forces gradually drove the French out of the Iberian peninsula and, after the victory at Vitoria (1813), invaded s France. Napoleon's abdication (1814) brought the campaign to an end.

penis Male reproductive organ. It contains the URETHRA, the channel through which URINE and SEMEN pass to the exterior, and erectile tissue, which, when engorged with blood, causes the penis to become erect.

Penn, William (1644–1718) English Quaker leader and chief founder of what later became the US state of PENNSYLVANIA. Because of his advocacy of religious freedom, he was imprisoned four times. He persuaded King CHARLES II to honour an unpaid debt by granting him wilderness land in America to be settled by the Quakers and others seeking refuge from religious persecution. The colony was named the Commonwealth of Pennsylvania in his honour.

Pennines Range of hills in N England, extending from the Tyne Gap and Eden Valley on the border with Scotland to the valley of the River Trent. The highlands are dissected by the Tees, Aire and Ribble river valleys. The rearing of sheep is the chief occupation. Tourism and limestone quarrying are also important. The highest peak is Cross Fell, rising to 893m (2,930ft). Length: *c.*260km (160mi).

Pennsylvania State in E USA; the capital is HARRISBURG. The chief cities are PHILADELPHIA and PITTSBURGH. Swedish and Dutch settlements were made along the DELAWARE River in the mid-17th century. By 1664 the area was controlled by the English, and William PENN received a charter from

Charles II in 1681 for what is now Pennsylvania. It was one of the 13 original states of the Union. The DECLARATION OF INDEPENDENCE was signed and the US constitution ratified in Philadelphia, which also acted as the national capital from 1790 to 1800. The Union victory at the Battle of GETTYSBURG in July 1863 was a turning point in the American CIVIL WAR. Apart from small low-lying areas in the NW and SE, the state is composed of a series of mountain ridges and rolling hills with narrow valleys. Farming is concentrated in the SE; the principal crops are cereals, tobacco, potatoes and fruit. Dairy products are important. Pennsylvania has rich deposits of coal and iron ore. The state has long been a leading producer of steel, and today accounts for *c.*25% of the national output. Industries: chemicals, cement, electrical machinery, metal goods. Area: 117,412sq km (45,333sq mi). Pop. (1990) 11,881,643.

Pentagon Headquarters of the US Department of Defense in Washington, D.C. The complex is made up of five concentric buildings and covers 14ha (34 acres). It was completed in 1943.

Pentateuch (Gk. Five scrolls) First five books of the Bible, traditionally attributed to MOSES and in JUDAISM referred to collectively as the *Torah*, or Law. The Pentateuch comprises the five Old Testament books of GENESIS, EXODUS, LEVITICUS, NUMBERS, and DEUTERONOMY. They were probably collected in their present form during the BABYLONIAN CAPTIVITY of the Jews during the 6th century BC.

Pentecost Important religious festival celebrated in May or June. In Judaism, it is a festival held seven weeks after the second day of the PASSOVER, commemorating the giving of the Law to MOSES. In the Christian calendar it is also known as Whit Sunday, falling seven weeks after Easter.

Pentecostal Churches Fellowship of revivalist Christian sects, inspired by the belief that all Christians should seek to be baptized with the Holy Spirit, as Jesus' disciples were, and to experience events such as speaking in tongues. Pentecostalists believe in the literal truth of the Bible, and many abstain from alcohol and tobacco and disapprove of dancing, theatre and other pleasures. The Pentecostal movement began in the USA at Topeka, Kansas, in 1901. It became an organized movement in Los Angeles in 1906. The Pentecostal Churches now have a world membership of *c.*10 million.

Penzias, Arno Allan (1933–) US astrophysicist, b. Germany, who together with Robert Wilson discovered the cosmic background radiation emanating from outer space, which scientists agree supports the BIG BANG theory. They shared the 1978 Nobel Prize in physics with Peter Kapitza.

peony PERENNIAL plant native to Eurasia and North America. It has glossy, divided leaves and large white, pink or red flowers, and is frequently cultivated in gardens. Height: to 0.9m (3ft). Tree peonies grow in hot, dry areas and have brilliant blossoms of many colours. Height: to 1.8m (6ft). Family Paeoniaceae; genus *Paeonia*.

Pepin III (the Short) (*c*.714–768) First CAROLIN-GIAN king of the Franks (750–768). Pepin deposed the last Merovingian king. He changed Carolingian policy by supporting the papacy against the LOM-BARDS, and defeated them in 754 and 756. He ceded the conquered territories (the future PAPAL STATES) to the papacy in what was known as the Donation of Pepin. He was the father of CHARLEMAGNE.

pepper (capsicum) PERENNIAL woody shrub native to tropical America. The fruit is a many-seeded, pungent berry whose size depends on the species. Included are bell, red, cayenne and CHILLI peppers. They all belong to the NIGHTSHADE fami-ly, Solanaceae; genus *Capsicum*.

peppermint Common name for *Mentha piperita*, a PERENNIAL herb of the MINT family (Lamiaceae/Labiatae) cultivated for its ESSEN-TIAL OIL, which is distilled and used in medicine and as a flavouring.

pepsin Digestive ENZYME secreted by GLANDS of the STOMACH wall as part of the GASTRIC JUICE. In the presence of hydrochloric acid it catalyzes the splitting of PROTEINS in food into polypeptides.

peptide Molecule consisting of two or more linked AMINO ACID molecules. Peptides containing several amino acids are called polypeptides. PRO-TEINS consist of polypeptide chains with up to sev-eral hundred amino acids.

Pepys, Samuel (1633–1703) English diarist. His *Diary* (1660–69) describes his private life and contemporary English society. It includes a vivid account of the RESTORATION, the 1661 coronation, the PLAGUE and the Great FIRE OF LONDON (1666). Written in shorthand, it was not published until 1815, and not in complete form until 1983.

percentage Quantity expressed as the number of parts in 100 (considered to be a whole). Fractions can be expressed as a percentage by multiplying by 100, i.e. 3/4 becomes 75%.

perch Freshwater food fish found in Europe and the USA east of the Rocky Mountains. Weight: 1.0–2.7kg (2.2–6lb). Family Percidae.

percussion Term for any of several musical instruments that produce sound when struck with a beater or the hand. They are divided into two groups: **ideophones**, in which the whole object vibrates when struck (such as CYMBALS and XYLO-PHONES); and **membranophones**, in which a stretched skin vibrates a column of air (all DRUMS).

Percy, Sir Henry (1364–1403) English noble-man, known as "Hotspur" for his zeal in guarding the border with Scotland. Son of the Earl of Northumberland, he backed the deposition of Richard II (1299), but quarrelled with the new king, Henry IV. In 1403 he and his father, in alliance with Owain GLYN DŴR, launched a rebellion. They were defeated at Shrewsbury, where Percy was killed.

peregrine falcon Crow-sized, grey, black and white bird of prey. It inhabits craggy open country or rocky coastlines and marshes or estuaries. The largest breeding FALCON in Britain, it flies swiftly with prolonged glides. Length: to 48cm (19in). Family Falconidae; species *Falco peregrinus*.

perennial Plant with a life cycle of more than two years. It is a common term for flowering herbaceous and woody plants. They include the LILY, DAISY and IRIS. *See also* ANNUAL; BIENNIAL

Peres, Shimon (1923–) Israeli statesman, prime minister (1986–88, 1995–96) b. Poland. Elected to the Knesset in 1959, he was a founder of the Labour Party (1968), becoming its leader (1977). He held ministerial posts under Golda MEIR and Yitzhak RABIN. In 1992, losing the party leadership to Rabin, he played a vital role in the Palestine peace process. On Rabin's assassination (1995), he returned as prime minister but was defeated in 1996 elections by Benjamin NETANYAHU.

perestroika (Rus. reconstruction) Policy adopt-ed by Soviet prime minister, Mikhail GORBACHEV in 1986, *perestroika* was linked with GLASNOST. The restructuring included reform of government and bureaucracy, decentralization and abolition of the Communist Party monopoly.

Pérez de Cuéllar, Javier (1920–) Peruvian diplomat, fifth secretary-general of the UN (1982–91). He emerged as a compromise candi-date in 1981, following opposition to the re-elec-tion of Kurt WALDHEIM. His two terms as secre-tary-general are considered highly successful.

performance art Events that take place before an audience, but which defy the traditional definitions of DRAMA and MUSIC. It is often visually oriented and tends to be multi-disciplinary and improvised.

perfume Substance that produces a pleasing fra-grance. The scents of plants, such as rose, citrus, lavender and sandalwood, are obtained from their essential oils. These are blended with a fixative of animal origin, such as musk, ambergris or civet. Liquid perfumes are usually alcoholic solutions containing 10–25% of the perfume concentrate; colognes contain *c*.2–6% of the concentrate.

Pergamum Ancient city-state on the site of mod-ern BERGAMA, W Turkey. It was founded by Greek colonists under licence from the Persian emperors in the 4th century BC. At its peak in the 3rd–2nd centuries BC, it controlled much of Asia Minor. In 133 BC it was bequeathed to Rome by Attalus III.

Pergolesi, Giovanni Battista (1710–36) Ital-ian composer. Despite his early death, he produced an intermezzo *La Serva Padrona* (1733), which became a model for Italian OPERA BUFFA, and a *Stabat Mater* (1730), which is one of the finest examples of religious Baroque music.

perianth Outer region of a flower. The perianth includes all the structures surrounding the reproduc-tive organs and usually consists of an outer whorl of sepals (calyx) and an inner whorl of petals (corolla).

pericarp In seed plants, the wall of a ripened fruit that is derived from the ovary wall. The tissues of the pericarp may be fibrous, stony or fleshy.

Pericles (490–429 BC) Athenian statesman. He dominated Athens from *c*.460 BC to his death. He is associated with achievements in art and literature, including the building of the PARTHENON, while strengthening the Athenian empire and government. He initiated the PELOPONNESIAN WARS (431–404 BC) but died of plague at its outset.

peridot Gem variety of transparent green OLIVINE, a silicate mineral. Large crystals are found on St John's Island in the Red Sea and in Burma.

peridotite Term derived from PERIDOT. It is a heavy IGNEOUS ROCK of coarse texture composed of OLIVINE and pyroxene with small flecks of mica or hornblende. It alters readily into SERPENTINE.

perigee Point in the orbit about the Earth of the Moon, or an artificial satellite at which the body is nearest the Earth.

perihelion Point in the orbit of a planet, asteroid, comet or other body (such as a spacecraft) moving around the Sun at which the body is nearest the Sun.

periodic table Arrangement of the chemical elements in order of their ATOMIC NUMBERS in accordance with the periodic law first stated by Dmitri MENDELEYEV in 1869. In the modern form of the table, the elements are arranged into 18 vertical columns and seven horizontal periods. The metallic TRANSITION ELEMENTS are arranged in the middle of the table between groups II and III. ALKALI METALS are in group I and ALKALINE EARTH-METALS in group II. Metalloids and non-metals are found from groups III to VII, with the halogens in group VII and the NOBLE GASES (inert gases) collected into group 0. The elements in each group have the same number of VALENCE electrons and accordingly have similar chemical properties. Elements in the same horizontal period have the same number of electron shells (*see* illustration).

peripheral nervous system All parts of the nervous system that lie outside the CENTRAL NERVOUS SYSTEM (brain and spinal cord). It comprises the 12 pairs of cranial nerves, which principally serve the head and neck region, and 31 pairs of spinal nerves with their fibres extending to the farthermost parts of the body.

periscope Optical instrument consisting of a series of mirrors or prisms that allows a person to view the surroundings from a concealed position by changing the direction of the observer's line of sight. Since World War 1, the periscope has been most commonly associated with SUBMARINES.

peristalsis Series of wave-like movements that propel food through the gut or digestive tract. It is caused by contractions of the smooth INVOLUNTARY MUSCLE of the gut wall. The reverse process, antiperistalsis, produces vomiting.

peritoneum Strong membrane of CONNECTIVE TISSUE that lines the body's abdominal wall and covers the abdominal organs. *See also* PERITONITIS

peritonitis Inflammation of the PERITONEUM. It may be caused by bacterial infection or chemical irritation or it may arise spontaneously in certain diseases. Symptoms include fever, abdominal pain, distension and shock.

periwinkle Any of several species of trailing or erect evergreen plants. Family Apocynaceae.

periwinkle (winkle) Any of several marine snails, gastropod molluscs that live in clusters along marine shores. A herbivore, it nestles in cracks among rocks. Many are edible. Length: to 2.5cm (1in). Family Littorinidea; genus *Littorina*.

permafrost Land that is permanently frozen, often to a considerable depth. The top few centimetres generally thaw in the summer, but the meltwater is not able to sink into the ground because of the frozen subsoil. If the landscape is fairly flat, surface water lies on the ground throughout the summer. *See also* TUNDRA

Permian Geological period of the PALAEOZOIC era, lasting from 286 to 248 million years ago. There was widespread geologic uplift and mostly cool, dry climates with periods of glaciation in the southern continents. Many groups of marine invertebrate animals became extinct.

Perón, Eva Duarte de (1919–52) Argentine political leader known as "Evita", first wife of President Juan PERÓN. She administered the country's social welfare agencies and was Argentina's chief labour mediator. Her popularity contributed to the longevity of her husband's regime.

Perón, Juan Domingo (1895–1974) President of Argentina (1946–55, 1973–74). He took part in the military coup of 1943 and became leader of the junta (1944–46). He gained the support of trade unions and the poor by social reforms, greatly assisted by his wife, Eva PERÓN. Briefly ousted in 1945, he won the presidential election (1946) and was re-elected in 1952. Economic recession and the death of his wife reduced Perón's popularity after 1951, and he was eventually overthrown. He retired to Spain, but returned to regain the presidency. His second term was marked by violence.

perpendicular style Final period of English Gothic architecture, from *c.*1330 to the mid-16th century. Named after the strong vertical lines of its window tracery and panelling, it is characterized by fan vaulting and flattened arches.

Perry, Fred (Frederick John) (1909–95) British table tennis and tennis player. World table tennis champion in 1929, he won three successive Wimbledon tennis singles titles (1934–36). He also won the US, French and Australian titles.

Persephone In Greek mythology, goddess of spring. She was the daughter of ZEUS and DEMETER. When Persephone was abducted by HADES, famine spread over the Earth. To prevent catastrophe, Zeus commanded Hades to release her. He did so, and thus, each year, spring returns to the Earth. Persephone was known as Proserpine to the Romans.

Persepolis City of ancient Persia (Iran). c.60km (35mi) NE of Shiraz. It was the capital (539–330 BC) of the ACHAEMENID empire, and was renowned for its splendour. It was destroyed by the forces of ALEXANDER THE GREAT in 330 BC.

PERIODIC TABLE

KEY

atomic number	43
atomic symbol	Tc
name of element	Technetium
atomic weight	[97]
(most stable isotope in brackets)	

GROUP I	II											III	IV	V	VI	VII	0
1 **H** Hydrogen 1.00794																	2 **He** Helium 4.0026
3 **Li** Lithium 6.941	4 **Be** Beryllium 9.0122											5 **B** Boron 10.81	6 **C** Carbon 12.011	7 **N** Nitrogen 14.0067	8 **O** Oxygen 15.9994	9 **F** Fluorine 18.998	10 **Ne** Neon 20.179
11 **Na** Sodium 22.9898	12 **Mg** Magnesium 24.305											13 **Al** Aluminium 26.9815	14 **Si** Silicon 28.086	15 **P** Phosphorus 30.9738	16 **S** Sulphur 32.06	17 **Cl** Chlorine 35.453	18 **Ar** Argon 39.948
19 **K** Potassium 39.098	20 **Ca** Calcium 40.06	21 **Sc** Scandium 44.956	22 **Ti** Titanium 47.90	23 **V** Vanadium 50.941	24 **Cr** Chromium 51.996	25 **Mn** Manganese 54.9380	26 **Fe** Iron 55.847	27 **Co** Cobalt 58.9332	28 **Ni** Nickel 58.70	29 **Cu** Copper 63.546	30 **Zn** Zinc 65.38	31 **Ga** Gallium 69.72	32 **Ge** Germanium 72.59	33 **As** Arsenic 74.9216	34 **Se** Selenium 78.96	35 **Br** Bromine 79.904	36 **Kr** Krypton 83.80
37 **Rb** Rubidium 85.4678	38 **Sr** Strontium 87.62	39 **Y** Yttrium 88.906	40 **Zr** Zirconium 91.22	41 **Nb** Niobium 92.906	42 **Mo** Molybdenum 95.94	43 **Tc** Technetium [97]	44 **Ru** Ruthenium 101.07	45 **Rh** Rhodium 102.905	46 **Pd** Palladium 106.4	47 **Ag** Silver 107.868	48 **Cd** Cadmium 112.40	49 **In** Indium 114.82	50 **Sn** Tin 118.69	51 **Sb** Antimony 121.75	52 **Te** Tellurium 127.75	53 **I** Iodine 126.9045	54 **Xe** Xenon 131.30
55 **Cs** Caesium 132.905	56 **Ba** Barium 137.34	57–71 Lanthanide Series	72 **Hf** Hafnium 178.49	73 **Ta** Tantalum 180.948	74 **W** Tungsten 183.85	75 **Re** Rhenium 186.207	76 **Os** Osmium 190.2	77 **Ir** Iridium 192.22	78 **Pt** Platinum 195.09	79 **Au** Gold 196.9665	80 **Hg** Mercury 200.59	81 **Tl** Thallium 204.37	82 **Pb** Lead 207.2	83 **Bi** Bismuth 208.98	84 **Po** Polonium [209]	85 **At** Astatine [210]	86 **Rn** Radon [222]
87 **Fr** Francium [223]	88 **Ra** Radium [226]	89–103 Actinide Series	104 **Rf** Dubnium [261]	105 **Db** Dubnium [262]	106 **Hn** Hahnium [263]	107 **Uns** Unnilseptium [262]	108 **Uno** Unniloctium [265]	109 **Une** Unnilennium [266]									

LANTHANIDE SERIES (rare earth elements)	57 **La** Lanthanum 138.9055	58 **Ce** Cerium 140.12	59 **Pr** Praseodymium 140.9077	60 **Nd** Neodymium 144.24	61 **Pm** Promethium [145]	62 **Sm** Samarium 150.36	63 **Eu** Europium 151.96	64 **Gd** Gadolinium 157.25	65 **Tb** Terbium 158.9254	66 **Dy** Dysprosium 162.50	67 **Ho** Holmium 164.9308	68 **Er** Erbium 167.26	69 **Tm** Thulium 168.9342	70 **Yb** Ytterbium 173.04	71 **Lu** Lutetium 174.97
ACTINIDE SERIES (radioactive rare earth elements)	89 **Ac** Actinium [227]	90 **Th** Thorium 232.0381	91 **Pa** Protactinium 231.0359	92 **U** Uranium 238.029	93 **Np** Neptunium 237.0482	94 **Pu** Plutonium [244]	95 **Am** Americium [243]	96 **Cm** Curium [247]	97 **Bk** Berkelium [247]	98 **Cf** Californium [251]	99 **Es** Einsteinium [254]	100 **Fm** Fermium [257]	101 **Md** Mendelevium [256]	102 **No** Nobelium [254]	103 **Lr** Lawrencium [256]

Perseus In Greek mythology, son of Danaë and ZEUS. Perseus beheaded the snake-haired gorgon MEDUSA, turned ATLAS to stone and rescued ANDROMEDA from being sacrificed to a sea monster.

Persia Former name of IRAN, in SW Asia. The earliest empire in the region was that of Media (c.700–549 BC). It was overthrown by the Persian king, CYRUS THE GREAT, who established the much larger ACHAEMENID dynasty (c.550–330 BC), destroyed by ALEXANDER THE GREAT. Alexander's successors, the SELEUCIDS, were replaced by people from PARTHIA in the 3rd century BC. The Persian SASSANID dynasty was established by Ardashir I in AD 224. Weakened by defeat by the Byzantines under HERACLIUS, it was overrun by the Arabs in the 7th century.

Persian art Earliest manifestations of art in Persia (Iran), prior to the 7th century development of ISLAMIC ART AND ARCHITECTURE. The oldest pottery and engraved seals date back to c.3500 BC. However, the greatest achievements of Persian art occurred during the rule of the ACHAEMENID (c.550–330 BC) and SASSANID (AD 224–642) dynasties. The former is best represented by the low relief carvings and massive gateway figures executed for the palace of Darius at PERSEPOLIS. The Sassanians excelled at metalwork and sculpture.

Persian Gulf (Arabian Gulf) Arm of the Arabian Sea between Arabia and the Asian mainland, and connected to it by the Strait of Hormuz and the Gulf of Oman. European powers began to move into the region in the 17th century. Britain had achieved supremacy in the Gulf by the mid-19th century. The discovery of oil in the 1930s increased its importance, and (after the British withdrawal in the 1960s) both the USA and the Soviet Union sought to increase their influence. Tension was heightened by the IRAN-IRAQ WAR (1980–88) and the GULF WAR (1991). It remains a major shipping and oil supply route. Area: c.240,000sq km (93,000sq mi).

Persian (Farsi) Official language of IRAN. It is spoken by nearly all of Iran's population as a first or second language. It is also widely used in Afghanistan. Persian belongs to the Indo-Iranian family of INDO-EUROPEAN LANGUAGES. Since the spread of ISLAM to Iran during the Middle Ages, Persian has incorporated many borrowings from ARABIC. It is also written in the Arabic script.

Persian mythology, ancient Beliefs of the Persian people c.500 BC. The oldest Persian deity was Mithra, who was identified with the sun. He was a god of courage and enlightenment. He was associated with Anahita, the goddess of water and of fertility. In the Zoroastrian period Mithra became subordinate to AHURA MAZDAH, who was worshipped by the ACHAEMENID kings of Persia as the creator and ruler of the world. Ahura Mazdah was engaged in an eternal conflict with Ahriman, the principle of evil. Later, both Ahura Mazdah and Ahriman were regarded as the twin offspring of Zurvan (Time).

Persian Wars (499–479 BC) Conflict between the ancient Greeks and Persians. In 499 BC the IONIAN cities of Asia Minor rebelled against Persian rule. Having crushed the rebellion, the Persian emperor, DARIUS I, invaded Greece but was defeated at MARATHON (490 BC). In 480 BC his successor, XERXES, burned Athens but withdrew after defeats at Salamis and Plataea (479 BC). Under Athenian leadership, the Greeks fought on, until the outbreak of the PELOPONNESIAN WARS (431 BC).

persimmon Any of several types of tree of the genus *Diospyros* that produces reddish-orange fruit. Species include the North American persimmon (*D.virginiana*) and the Japanese persimmon (*D. kaki*). Family Ebenaceae.

personality Emotional, attitudinal and behavioural characteristics that distinguish an individual. Psychologists use the term to refer to enduring, long-term characteristics of a person. Influential theories of personality include Sigmund FREUD's PSYCHOANALYSIS and JUNG's theories of personality types.

perspective Method of showing three-dimensional objects and spatial relationships in a two-dimensional image. The linear perspective system is based on the idea that parallel lines converge at a vanishing point as they recede into the distance.

perspiration *See* SWEATING

Perth City on the Swan River, SW Australia; capital of Western Australia. Founded in 1829, the city grew rapidly after the discovery of gold in the 1890s, the development of the port at Fremantle and the construction of railways in the early 20th century. Industries: textiles, cement, food processing, motor vehicles. Pop. (1993 est.) 1,221,200.

Peru Republic in W South America; the capital is LIMA. **Land and climate** Peru is divided into three geographical areas. Along the Pacific coast lies a narrow strip of desert. Peru's major urban areas, such as Lima, are sited beside oases. The centre is dominated by three ranges of the ANDES Mountains. In the foothills of the Cordillera Occidental lies Peru's second-largest city, AREQUIPA. The range includes Peru's highest peak, Mount Huascarán, at 6,768m (22,205ft). The Cordillera Central merges into the Cordillera Oriental, site of CUZCO and the INCA ruins of MACHU PICCHU. Between the E and W ranges lies the Altiplano Plateau site of many lakes,

PERU
AREA: 1,285,220sq km (496,223sq mi)
POPULATION: 22,454,000
CAPITAL (POPULATION): Lima (6,386,308)
GOVERNMENT: Transitional republic
ETHNIC GROUPS: Quechua 47%, Mestizo 32%, White 15%, Aymara 5%
LANGUAGES: Spanish and Quechua (both official)
RELIGIONS: Christianity (Roman Catholic 93%, Protestant 6%)
CURRENCY: New sol = 100 centavos

including Lake TITICACA. In the E lie forested highlands and the lowlands of the AMAZON basin. Lima has an arid climate. EL NIÑO brings infrequent violent storms. Inland, there is more frequent precipitation. The high Andes are permanently snowcapped. The coastal desert oases form Peru's major growing region. The E is a region of *selva* (tropical rainforest), where the major crop is coca. **Economy** Peru is a lower-middle-income developing country. Agriculture employs 35% of the workforce. Major crops include beans, maize, potatoes and rice. Coffee, cotton and sugar cane are major exports. Peru lands the world's third largest fish catch and is the world's eighth-largest producer of copper ore. Since 1990 Fujimori's regime has instigated free-market reforms that have significantly reduced inflation and foreign debt, and created economic growth. Inequality remains the greatest economic problem. **History and politics** Native American civilizations developed over 10,000 years ago. By *c.*AD 1200, the INCA had established a capital at CUZCO. In 1532 the Spanish conquistador Francisco PIZARRO captured the Inca ruler ATAHUALPA. By 1533 Pizarro had conquered most of Peru; he founded Lima in 1535. In 1544 Lima became capital of Spain's South American empire. Spain's rule caused frequent native revolts. In 1820 José de SAN MARTÍN captured coastal Peru. In 1821 Peru declared independence. Spain still held much of the interior, and Simón BOLÍVAR completed liberation in 1826. In 1836 Peru and Bolivia formed a short-lived confederation. In the War of the Pacific (1879–84), Peru lost some of its S provinces to Bolivia. The early 20th century was characterized by dictatorship and the growing gap between a wealthy oligarchy and the poverty of the native population. From 1968–80 a military junta failed to carry out democratic reforms. Austerity measures, introduced by the civilian government during the 1980s, caused civil unrest. *Sendero Luminoso* (Shining Path) and the Tupac Amaru Revolutionary Movement (MRTA) have waged an insurgency campaign that has claimed over 30,000 lives. Alberto Fujimori was elected in 1990, and began a series of anti-terrorist measures. In 1992 he suspended the constitution and dismissed parliament. The guerrilla movements leaders were captured. A new constitution was adopted in 1993. Fujimori was re-elected in 1995. In December 1996 MRTA guerrillas mounted a siege of the Japanese embassy in Lima, which lasted for four months before the army intervened. Despite successfully ending the hostage crisis, Fujimori has lost popularity amid allegations of corruption and authoritarianism.

Perugino, Pietro Vannucci (1445–1523) Italian painter, a notable fresco artist of the early Renaissance. His *Christ Delivering the Keys to St Peter*, painted for the Sistine Chapel in Rome, did much to establish his reputation.

Peshawar City in NW Pakistan, 16km (9mi) E of the KHYBER PASS. An ancient settlement, the city has always had great strategic importance. Brought under Muslim rule in the 10th century, Peshawar fell to the Afghans in the 16th century. Conquered by Sikhs in 1834, it was annexed by Britain in 1849. In 1948 it became part of Pakistan. In the 1980s and 1990s it was a base for rebels operating in Afghanistan. The modern city is famous for handicrafts, carpets and leather goods. Industries: textiles, chemicals, paper. Pop. (1981) 555,000.

pesticide Chemical substance that is used to kill pests. Pesticides are often harmful chemicals, and an important factor in their manufacture is that they should decompose. *See also* FUNGICIDE; HERBICIDE

Pétain, Henri Philippe (1856–1951) French statesman and general. In World War 1 his defence of VERDUN (1916) made him a national hero. With the defeat of France in 1940, he was recalled as prime minister. He signed the surrender and became head of the collaborationist VICHY regime. He was charged with treason after the liberation of France in 1945 and died in prison.

petal Part of a flower. The petals of a flower are together known as the corolla. Surrounded by SEPALS, flower petals are often brightly coloured and may secrete nectar and perfume to attract the insects and birds necessary for cross-pollination.

Peter, Saint (d. *c.*64) APOSTLE of JESUS CHRIST. He was born Simon and was a fisherman on the Sea of Galilee. He and his brother ANDREW were called by Jesus to be disciples. Jesus gave Simon the name Peter (John 1:42). Peter was one of Jesus' closest and most loyal associates. With James and John, he witnessed the Transfiguration. While Jesus was on trial before the SANHEDRIN, Peter denied knowing him three times, just as Jesus had predicted. After Jesus' ascension, Peter was the first publicly to preach Christianity in Jerusalem. He took Christianity to Samaria. Imprisoned by King Herod, he was allegedly rescued by an angel. In his final years, he seems to have left Jerusalem and undertaken a missionary journey. Roman Catholic theology accepts him as the first head of the Church and the first bishop of Rome. His feast day is 29 June.

Peter I (the Great) (1672–1725) Emperor of Russia (1682–1725), regarded as the founder of modern Russia. After ruling jointly with his half-brother Ivan from 1682, he gained sole control in 1689. He employed foreign experts to modernize Russia. He compelled the aristocracy and the church to serve the interests of the state. In the Great Northern War, Russia replaced Sweden as the dominant power in N Europe and gained lands on the Baltic, where Peter built his new capital, ST PETERSBURG. In the E, he warred against Turks and Persians and initiated the exploration of Siberia.

Peter I (1844–1921) King of Serbia (1903–21). He was brought up in exile while the Obrenović dynasty ruled Serbia. He was elected king when Alexander Obrenović was assassinated. In 1918 he became the first king of the new Kingdom of Serbs, Croats and Slovenes (Yugoslavia).

Peter II (1923–70) Last king of Yugoslavia (1934–41). He succeeded to the throne at the age of 11. The actual ruler was his uncle, Prince Paul, who was deposed in 1941 by a military coup. Peter ruled for a month until the invasion of the AXIS POWERS, when he fled to London. After the monarchy was abolished in 1945 he settled in the USA.

Peterloo Massacre (1819) Violent suppression of a political protest in Manchester, England. A large crowd demonstrating for reform of Parliament was dispersed by soldiers. Eleven people were killed and 500 injured.

petition of right Means by which an English subject could sue the crown; in particular, the statement of grievances against the crown presented by Parliament to CHARLES I in 1628. It asserted that the crown acted illegally in raising taxation without Parliament's consent, imprisoning people without charge, maintaining a standing army, and quartering soldiers. It led to the dissolution of Parliament and Charles' period of untrammelled rule.

Petra Ancient city in what is now sw Jordan. It was the capital of the Nabataean kingdom from the 4th century BC. It was captured by the Romans in the 2nd century AD. Many of its remarkable ruined houses, temples, theatres and tombs were cut from the high, pinkish sandstone cliffs that protected it.

Petrarch, Francesco (1304–74) Italian lyric poet and scholar. Most of his lyric poems, *Rime sparse*, have as their subject "Laura", a woman idealized in the style of earlier poets but seen in a more realistic and human light.

petrel Any of several small oceanic birds related to the ALBATROSS. Most of them nest in colonies and fly over open water, feeding on squid and small fish. They have webbed feet and tubular nostrils. Length: to 42cm (16in). Order Procellariiformes.

petrochemical Chemical substances derived from PETROLEUM or NATURAL GAS. The refining of petroleum is undertaken on a large scale not only for fuels but also for a wide range of chemicals. These chemicals include ALKANES, ALKENES, BENZENE, TOLUENE, NAPHTHALENE and their derivatives.

petrol (gasoline) Major HYDROCARBON fuel, a mixture consisting mainly of hexane, octane and heptane. One of the products of oil refining, petrol is extracted from crude oil (PETROLEUM). Frequently other fuels and substances are added to petrol to alter its properties.

petrol engine Most common type of INTERNAL COMBUSTION ENGINE

petroleum (crude oil) Fossil fuel that is a complex chemical mixture of HYDROCARBONS. It accumulates in underground deposits and probably originated from the bodies of long-dead organisms, particularly marine plankton. Most petroleum is extracted via oil wells from reservoirs in the Earth's crust sealed by upfolds of impermeable rock or by salt domes that form traps. *See also* NATURAL GAS; PETROL

petrology Study of rocks, including their origin,

chemical composition and location. Formation of the three classes of rocks – IGNEOUS (of volcanic origin); SEDIMENTARY (deposited by water); and METAMORPHIC (either of the other two changed by temperature or pressure) – is studied.

petunia Genus of flowering plants of the NIGHTSHADE family that originated in Argentina, and the common name for any of the varieties that are popular as bedding plants. Most varieties derive from the white flowered *P. axillaris* and the violet-red *P. integrifolia*. The bell-shaped flowers have five petals. Family Solanaceae.

Pevsner, Antoine (1886–1962) French sculptor, b. Russia. He was initially influenced by CUBISM, but later became a leading exponent of CONSTRUCTIVISM, creating works in bronze and other materials. In the 1930s he concentrated on NON-FIGURATIVE structures such as *Projections in Space*.

pewter Any of several silver-coloured, soft alloys that consist mainly of TIN and LEAD. The most common form has about four parts of tin to one of lead, combined with small amounts of antimony and copper.

pH A numerical scale that indicates the acidity or alkalinity of a solution. The pH value measures the concentration of hydrogen ions. The scale runs from 0 to 14, and a neutral solution, such as pure water, has a pH of 7. A solution is acidic if the pH is less than 7 and alkaline if greater than 7.

phaeophyta Taxonomic division (phylum) of the Kingdom Protoctista that consists of the brown ALGAE. Classified by some biologists as plants, the organisms belonging to this group are mostly marine, found mainly in the intertidal zone of rocky shores. They include familiar seaweeds such as *Fucus* (wracks) and *Ascophyllum* (bladder wrack).

phagocyte Type of LEUCOCYTE or white blood cell able to engulf other cells, such as bacteria. It digests what it engulfs in the defence of the body against infection. Phagocytes also act as scavengers by clearing the bloodstream of the remains of the cells that die as part of the body's natural processes.

phalanger (possum) Any of about 45 species of mainly nocturnal arboreal MARSUPIALS of Australasia. It has opposable digits for grasping branches and the tail is long and prehensile. Family Phalargeridae.

pharaoh Title of the rulers of ancient EGYPT. The title was only adopted during the New Kingdom. He was considered an incarnation of HORUS.

Pharisees Members of a conservative Jewish religious group, prominent in ancient Palestine from the 2nd century BC to the time of the destruction of the second Temple in JERUSALEM (AD 70). They constituted a political party opposed to the pagan Greek and Roman conquerors, but by New Testament times they were largely non-political. They were the founders of orthodox JUDAISM and were often in conflict with the SADDUCEES.

pharmacology Study of the properties of drugs and their effects on the body.

pharmacopoeia Reference book listing drugs and other preparations in medical use. Included are details of their formulae, dosages, routes of administration, known side-effects and precautions.

Pharos Mediterranean island, off the coast of Alexandria, N Egypt; connected to the mainland by a causeway built by ALEXANDER THE GREAT. A lighthouse was completed by Ptolemy II in c.280 BC and was considered one of the SEVEN WONDERS OF THE WORLD. It was c.135m (450ft) tall, and was destroyed by an earthquake in 1346.

pharynx Cavity at the back of the nose and mouth that extends down towards the OESOPHAGUS and TRACHEA. Inflammation of the pharynx, usually caused by viral or bacterial infection, is known as pharyngitis.

phase Proportion of the illuminated hemisphere of a body in the Solar System as seen from Earth. The phase of a body changes as the Sun and the Earth change their relative positions. All the phases of the Moon (new, crescent, half, gibbous, and full) are observable with the naked eye.

phase In physics, a stage or fraction in the cycle of an oscillation, such as the wave motion of light or sound. This is usually measured from an arbitrary starting point or compared with another motion of the same frequency. Two waves are said to be "in phase" when their maximum and minimum values happen at the same time. If not, there is a "phase difference", as seen in INTERFERENCE phenomenon. It can also refer to any one of the states of MATTER.

pheasant Gamebird of the genus *Phasianus* originally native to Asia, introduced into Europe and North America. PEACOCKS and GUINEA FOWL belong to the same family. Males are showy, with brownish green, red and yellow feathers; females are smaller and brownish. Length: up to 89cm (35in). Family Phasianidae.

phenol Aromatic compound whose members each have an attachment of a hydroxyl group to a carbon atom forming part of a BENZENE ring. The simplest of the family is also called phenol or carbolic acid (C_6H_5OH). Phenols are colourless liquids or white solids at room temperature. They are used by industry for products such as aspirin, fungicide, explosive and as a starting material for nylon and epoxy resin.

phenomenology School of philosophy that arose with the work of Edmund HUSSERL. Husserl rejected causal explanations of experience in favour of direct description of experienced phenomena.

phenotype Physical characteristics of an organism resulting from HEREDITY. Phenotype is distinct from GENOTYPE, since not all aspects of genetic make-up manifest themselves.

pheromone Substance secreted externally by certain animals that influences the behaviour of members of the same species. Common in mammals and insects, these substances are often sexual attractants. They may be a component of body products such as urine, or secreted by specific glands.

Phidias (490–430 BC) Sculptor of ancient Greece. During his lifetime he was best known for two gigantic chryselephantine (gold and ivory) statues, one of Athena for the PARTHENON and the other of Zeus for his temple at Olympia. The Zeus was one of the SEVEN WONDERS OF THE WORLD. He also worked on the PARTHENON friezes.

Philadelphia City and port at the confluence of the Delaware and Schuylkill rivers, SE Pennsylvania, USA. The city was founded by William PENN in 1681. By 1774 it was a major commercial, cultural and industrial centre of the American colonies. The DECLARATION OF INDEPENDENCE was signed here in 1776, and Philadelphia served as capital of the USA from 1790–1800. Industries: shipbuilding, textiles, chemicals, clothing, electrical equipment, vehicle parts, metal products, publishing and printing, oil refining. Pop. (1990) 1,585,577.

Philip, Saint (active 1st century AD) One of the original 12 APOSTLES of JESUS CHRIST. Philip came from Bethsaida, on the Sea of Galilee. Later Christian tradition says he preached in Asia Minor and met a martyr's death. His feast day is 3 May (in the West) or 14 November (in the East).

Philip II (1165–1223) (Philip Augustus) King of France (1180–1223). Greatest of French medieval kings, he increased the royal domain by marriage, feudal rights, and war. His main rival was HENRY II of England. Philip supported the rebellions of Henry's sons, fought a long war against RICHARD I and, during the reign of JOHN, occupied Normandy and Anjou. English efforts to regain them were defeated at Bouvines in 1214. Philip persecuted Jews and Christian heretics, and opened the crusade against the Albigenses in S France.

Philip IV (the Fair) (1268–1314) King of France (1285–1314). Partly to pay for wars against Flanders and England, he expelled the Jews (1306), confiscating their property. Claiming the right to tax the clergy involved him in a bitter quarrel with Pope Boniface VIII. He used assemblies (later called the STATES GENERAL) to popularize his case. After the death of Boniface (1303) Philip secured the election of a French pope, Clement V, based at Avignon.

Philip VI (1293–1350) King of France (1328–50) First of the house of Valois, he was chosen to succeed his cousin, Charles IV, in preference to EDWARD III of England. After the outbreak of the HUNDRED YEARS WAR (1337), many of his vassals supported Edward. Philip suffered serious defeats at the battles of Sluys (1340) and CRÉCY (1346).

Philip II (382–336 BC) King of Macedonia (359–336 BC). He conquered neighbouring tribes and gradually extended his rule over the Greek states, defeating the Athenians at Chaeronea in 338 BC and gaining reluctant acknowledgment as king of Greece. He was preparing to attack the Persian empire when he was assassinated, leaving the task to his son, ALEXANDER THE GREAT.

Philip II (1527–98) King of Spain (1556–98), King of Portugal (1580–98). From his father, CHARLES V, he inherited Milan, Naples and Sicily, Netherlands, as well as Spain and its New World empire. War with France ended at Château-Cambrésis (1559), but the revolt of the Netherlands began in 1566. A defender of Roman Catholicism, Philip launched the unsuccessful ARMADA of 1588 to crush the English who, as fellow Protestants, aided the Dutch. The Ottoman Turks presented a continuing threat, in spite of their defeat at Lepanto (1571).

Philip V (1683–1746) King of Spain (1700–46). Because he was a possible successor of LOUIS XIV of France, his accession to the Spanish throne provoked the War of the SPANISH SUCCESSION. By the Treaty of UTRECHT (1713), he kept the Spanish throne at the price of exclusion from the succession in France and the loss of Spanish territories in Italy and the Netherlands.

Philip, Prince, Duke of Edinburgh (1921–) Husband of Queen ELIZABETH II of Britain and Prince Consort. He was born in Corfu, the son of Prince Andrew of Greece, and educated in Britain. He became a naturalized British citizen and took the surname Mountbatten. In 1947 he married Elizabeth after becoming the Duke of Edinburgh. He was created a prince in 1957.

Philippines Southeast Asian republic in the SW Pacific Ocean; the capital is MANILA. **Land and climate** The Philippines consists of over 7,000 islands, of which 1,000 are inhabited. LUZON and MINDANAO islands constitute over 66% of land area. Around Manila Bay (Luzon), lies Manila and the second-largest city, QUEZON CITY. The islands are mainly mountainous with several active volcanoes, one of which is the highest peak, Mount Apo, at 2,954m (9,692ft). Narrow coastal plains give way to forested plateaux. Earthquakes are common. Philippines has a tropical climate, with high annual temperatures. The dry season runs from December to April, but the rest of the year is wet. Much of the rainfall is due to typhoons. Over 33% of the land is forested. Much of the land is fertile. **Economy** The Philippines is a lower-middle income developing country. The economy is beginning to recover from the mismanagement of the Marcos' years. Agriculture employs 45% of the workforce. It is the world's second-largest producer of rice (after China) and the world's fourth-largest producer of bananas. The raising of livestock, forestry and fishing are also important activities. Manufacturing is increasing. **History and politics** Islam was introduced in the late 14th century. In 1521 Ferdinand MAGELLAN landed near Cebu. In 1571 the Spanish founded Manila, and named the archipelago *Filipinas*, after Philip II. It became a vital trading centre, subject to frequent attack from pirates. In 1896 the Filipinos revolted against Spanish rule and declared independence. In the Spanish-American War (1898), the USA defeated the Spanish navy in Manila Bay. Filipinos seized Luzon. Manila was captured with US help. In the Treaty of Paris (1898) the islands were ceded to the USA. From 1899 to 1902 Filipinos fought against US control. The Commonwealth of the Philippines was established in 1935. Manuel Luis Quezon became the first president. In 1941 the Japanese invaded and captured Manila by 1942. General MACARTHUR was forced to withdraw and US forces were ousted from Bataan. In 1944 the USA began to reclaim the islands. In 1946 the Philippines became an independent republic. The USA were granted a 99-year lease on military bases (subsequently reduced to 25 years from 1967). In 1965 Ferdinand MARCOS became president. Marcos' response to mounting civil unrest was brutal. In 1972 he declared martial law. In 1981 Marcos was re-elected amid charges of electoral fraud. In 1983 the leader of the opposition, Benigno Aquino, was assassinated. His widow, Cory AQUINO, succeeded him. Marcos claimed victory in 1986 elections, but faced further charges of electoral fraud. Cory Aquino launched a campaign of civil disobedience. The USA withdrew its support for the regime and Marcos was forced into exile. Aquino's presidency was marred by attempted military coups. **Recent events** In 1992 Fidel Ramos succeeded Aquino as president. The USA closed its military bases at the end of 1992. In 1996 an agreement was reached with the Moro National Liberation Front, ending 24 years of rebellion on Mindanao. It allows the creation of an autonomous Muslim state.

Philistine Member of a non-Semitic people who lived on the S coast of modern Israel, known as Philistia, from *c.*1200 BC. They clashed frequently with the Hebrews.

philodendron Genus of house plants native to tropical America. Philodendrons have shiny, heart-shaped leaves, which are sometimes split. Height: 10cm–1.8m (4in–6ft). Family Araceae.

philosophy Study of the nature of reality, knowledge, ethics and existence by means of rational enquiry. The oldest known philosophical system is the Vedic system of India, which dates back to the 2nd millennium BC. Like other Eastern philosophies, it is founded upon a largely mystical view of the universe and is integrated with India's main religion, HINDUISM. From the 6th century BC, Chinese philosophy was largely dominated by CONFU-

PHILIPPINES
AREA: 300,000sq km (115,300sq mi)
POPULATION: 64,259,000
CAPITAL (POPULATION): Manila (1,587,000)
GOVERNMENT: Multiparty republic
ETHNIC GROUPS: Tagalog 30%, Cebuano 24%, Ilocano 10%, Hiligaynon Ilongo 9%, Bicol 6%, Samar-Leyte 4%
LANGUAGES: Pilipino (Tagalog) and English (both official)
RELIGIONS: Christianity (Roman Catholic 84%, Philippine Independent Church or Aglipayan 6%, Protestant 4%), Islam 4%
CURRENCY: Philippine peso = 100 centavos

CIANISM and TAOISM. Also in the 6th century, Western philosophy began among the Greeks with the work of THALES of Miletus. Later pre-Socratic philosophers included PYTHAGORAS, EMPEDOCLES, HERACLITUS, ZENO OF ELEA and DEMOCRITUS. Greek philosophy reached its high point with SOCRATES (who laid the foundations of ethics), PLATO (who developed a system of universal ideas), and ARISTOTLE (who founded the study of LOGIC). ZENO OF CITIUM evolved the influential philosophy of stoicism, which contrasted with the system of EPICUREANISM, founded by Epicurus. A dominant school of the early Christian era was NEOPLATONISM, founded by Plotinus in the 3rd century AD. The influence of Aristotle and other Greeks pervaded the thought of Muslim philosophers, such as AVICENNA and AVERRÖES, and the Spanish-born Jew, Moses MAIMONIDES. In the work of scholastic philosophers such as ABÉLARD, Saint Thomas AQUINAS and WILLIAM OF OCCAM, philosophy became a branch of Christian theology. Modern scientific philosophy began in the 17th century, with the work of DESCARTES. His faith in mathematics was taken up by LEIBNIZ. In England, HOBBES integrated materialism with social philosophy. The 18th-century empiricists included George Berkeley and HUME. The achievements of KANT in Germany and the French Encyclopedists were also grounded in science. In the 19th century, a number of diverging movements emerged, among them the classical idealism of HEGEL, the dialectical materialism of MARX and ENGELS, the POSITIVISM of COMTE, and the work of KIERKEGAARD and NIETZSCHE, which emphasized the freedom of the individual. In the 20th century, dominant movements included EXISTENTIALISM, LOGICAL POSITIVISM, PHENOMENOLOGY and vitalism. *See also* AESTHETICS; EPISTEMOLOGY; METAPHYSICS

phlebitis Inflammation of the wall of a vein. It may be caused by infection, trauma, underlying disease, or by the presence of VARICOSE VEINS. Symptoms include localized swelling and redness. Treatment includes rest and anticoagulant therapy.

phloem Vascular tissue for distributing dissolved food materials in plants. Phloem tissue contains several types of cells. The most important are long, hollow "sieve-tube" cells. Columns of sieve tubes are joined end to end, allowing ACTIVE TRANSPORT from cell to cell. Phloem may also contain fibres, which help to support the tissue. *See also* XYLEM

phlogiston Odourless, colourless and weightless material believed by early scientists to be the source of all heat and fire. Combustion was believed to involve the loss of phlogiston. The phlogiston theory was proved erroneous when the true nature of combustion was explained by Antoine LAVOISIER.

Phnom Penh (Phnum Pénh) Capital of Cambodia, in the S of the country, a port at the confluence of the Mekong and Tonle Sap rivers. Founded in the 14th century, the city was the capital of the Khmers after 1434. Occupied by the Japanese during World War 2, it was extensively damaged during the Cambodian civil war. After the communists took over in 1975 many of its inhabitants were forcibly removed to rural areas. Industries: rice-milling, brewing, distilling, fish processing, cotton. Pop. (1994 est.) 920,000.

phobia Irrational and uncontrollable fear that persists despite reassurance or contradictory evidence. Psychoanalytic theory suggests that phobias are actually symbolic subconscious fears and impulses.

Phoenicia Greek name for an ancient region bordering the E Mediterranean coast. Famous as merchants and sailors, the Phoenicians never formed a single political unit. Throughout the Bronze Age, Phoenician city-states, such as Tyre, Sidon and Byblos, prospered on the Mediterranean trade. They founded colonies in Spain and North Africa, notably CARTHAGE.

Phoenician mythology Beliefs current in the Phoenician city-states of the E Mediterranean *c.*500 BC. The most ancient god was El. Closely related to the Hebrew YAHWEH, he was revered as the father of all gods and the creator of man. Baal, the storm god and the god of fertility, occupied an important place in the divine hierarchy. With lightning as his weapon, he defended the divine order against the ever-present menace of Chaos. Anath, the goddess of love and war, was the consort of Baal.

Phoenix Capital of Arizona, USA, on the Salt River. Founded in 1870, it became the capital in 1889. Phoenix is a popular winter sports resort. Industries: computers, aircraft, metals, machinery, textiles, clothing. Pop. (1990) 983,403.

pholidota Small order of mammals, containing only one genus, *Manis*, in the family Manidae; its members are called PANGOLINS. Some species are entirely toothless and feed on ants and termites.

phonetics Study of the sounds of speech, divided into three main branches: **articulatory** phonetics (how the speech organs produce sounds); **acoustic** phonetics (the physical nature of sounds, mainly using instrumental techniques); and **auditory** phonetics (how sounds are received by the ear and processed). Linguists have devised notation systems to allow the full range of human speech sounds to be represented. *See also* LINGUISTICS

phosphate Chemical compounds derived from phosphoric acid (H_3PO_4). The use of phosphates as fertilizers can cause environmental damage.

phosphor Substance capable of luminescence (storing energy and later releasing it as light). They are used to coat the inside of cathode-ray tubes and fluorescent lamps.

phosphorescence Form of luminescence in which a substance emits light of one wavelength. Unlike FLUORESCENCE, it may persist for some time after the initial excitation. In biology, phosphorescence is the production of light by an organism without associated heat, as with a glow-worm. In warm climates, the sea often appears phosphores-

493

cent at night, as a result of the activities of millions of microscopic algae.

phosphoric acid Group of ACIDS, the chief forms of which are tetraoxophosphoric acid (H_3PO_4), metaphosphoric acid (HPO_3) and heptaoxodiphosphoric acid ($H_4P_2O_7$). Tetraoxophosphoric acid is a colourless liquid obtained by the action of sulphuric acid on phosphate rock, and used in fertilizers, soaps and detergents. Metaphosphoric acid is obtained by heating tetraoxophosphoric acid and is used as a dehydrating agent. Heptaoxodiphosphoric acid is formed by moderately heating tetraoxophosphoric acid or by reacting phosphorus pentoxide (P_2O_5) with water, and is used as a catalyst and in metallurgy.

phosphorus Common nonmetallic element (symbol P) of group V of the periodic table, discovered by Hennig Brand in 1669. It occurs, as PHOSPHATES, in many minerals; apatite is the chief source. The element is used in making PHOSPHORIC ACID for detergents and fertilizers. Small amounts are used in insecticides and in matches. Phosphorus exhibits ALLOTROPY. Properties: at.no. 15; at.wt. 30.9738; s.g. 1.82 (white), 2.34 (red); m.p. 44.1°C (111.38°F) (white); b.p. 280°C (536°F) (white); most common isotope P^{31} (100%).

photocopying Reproduction of words, drawings or photographs by machine. In a photocopying machine, a light shines on the item to be copied, and an optical system forms an image of it. Various techniques may be used to reproduce this image on paper. In a modern plain-paper copier, the image is projected onto an electrically charged drum, coated with light-sensitive selenium. Light makes the selenium conduct electricity, so bright areas of the drum lose their charge. The dark areas, which usually correspond to image detail, retain their charge, and attract particles of a fine powder called toner. Electrically charged paper in contact with the drum picks up the pattern of toner powder. A heated roller fuses the powder so that it sticks to the paper and forms a permanent image.

photoelectric cell (photocell) Device that produces electricity when light shines on it. Nearly all modern photocells are made using two electrodes separated by light-sensitive semiconductor material. Photoelectric cells are used in electric eyes, burglar alarms, light meters and solar cells.

photoelectric effect Liberation of electrons from the surface of a material when light, ultraviolet radiation, x-rays or gamma rays fall on it. The effect can be explained only by the QUANTUM THEORY: PHOTONS in the radiation are absorbed by atoms in the substance and enable electrons to escape by transferring energy to them.

photography Process of obtaining a permanent image of an object, either in black and white or in colour, on treated paper or film. In black and white photography, a CAMERA is used to expose a film to an image of the object to be photographed, for a set time. The film is covered on one side with an emulsion containing a silver halide (silver bromide or silver chloride). Exposure makes the silver compound easily reduced to metallic silver when treated with a developer. The action of the developer is to produce a black deposit of metallic silver particles on those parts of the film that were exposed to light, thus providing a "negative" image. After fixing in "hypo" (thiosulphate) and washing, the negative can be printed by placing it over a piece of sensitized paper and exposing it to light so that the silver salts in the paper are affected in the same way as those in the original film. The dark portions of the negative let through the least light, and the image on the paper is reversed back to a positive.

photon Quantum of ELECTROMAGNETIC RADIATION, such as a "particle" of LIGHT. The energy of a photon equals the frequency of the radiation multiplied by PLANCK's constant. Absorption of photons by atoms and molecules can cause excitation or ionization. A photon may be classified as a stable elementary particle of zero rest mass, zero charge and spin 1, travelling at the velocity of light. It is its own antiparticle. Virtual photons are thought to be continuously exchanged between charged particles and are carriers of ELECTROMAGNETIC FORCE.

photoperiodism Biological mechanism that governs the timing of certain activities in an organism by reacting to the duration of its daily exposure to light and dark. For example, the start of flowering in plants and the beginning of the breeding season in animals are determined by day length. *See also* BIOLOGICAL CLOCK

photosphere Visible surface of the SUN. It is a layer of highly luminous gas *c.*500km (300mi) thick and with a temperature of *c.*6,000K, falling to 4,000K at its upper level. The photosphere is the source of the Sun's visible spectrum. The lower, hotter gases produce the continuous emission spectrum, while the higher, cooler gases absorb certain wavelengths. Sunspots and other visible features of the Sun are situated in the photosphere.

photosynthesis Chemical process occurring in green plants, algae and many bacteria, by which water and carbon dioxide are converted into food and oxygen using energy absorbed from sunlight. The reactions take place in the CHLOROPLASTS. During the first part of the process, light is absorbed by CHLOROPHYLL and splits water into hydrogen and oxygen. The hydrogen attaches to a carrier molecule and the oxygen is set free. The hydrogen and light energy build a supply of cellular chemical energy, adenosine triphosphate (ATP). Hydrogen and ATP convert the carbon dioxide into sugars, including glucose and starch.

phototropism Growth of a plant in response to the stimulus of light, which increases cell growth on the shaded side of the plant, resulting in curvature towards the source of light. Auxin hormones are involved in this process.

Phrygia Historic region of w central Anatolia. A prosperous kingdom was established by the Phrygians early in the 1st millennium BC, with its capital at Gordion. MIDAS was a legendary Phrygian king. In the 6th century BC Phrygia was taken over by Lydia, then by Persia and later empires.

phylloxera Small, yellowish insect of the order Homoptera that is a pest on grape plants in Europe and W USA. It attaches itself to the leaves and roots and sucks the plant's fluids, resulting in the eventual rotting of the plant. Family Phylloxeridae; species: *Phylloxera vitifoliae*.

phylogenetics Study of the evolutionary relationships between organisms. In molecular phylogeny, the evolutionary distances between organisms are analysed by comparing the DNA sequences of specific GENES. At the most fundamental level, molecular phylogeny has revealed that all known organisms evolved from a common ancestor and can be grouped into five KINGDOMS.

phylum In the systematic categorization of living organisms, a major group within the animal KINGDOM. It comprises a diverse group of organisms with a common fundamental characteristic. In plant classification, the analogous category is sometimes called division. *See also* TAXONOMY

physical chemistry Study of the physical changes associated with chemical reactions and the relationship between physical properties and chemical composition. The main branches are THERMODYNAMICS, concerned with the changes of energy in physical systems; chemical kinetics, concerned with rates of reaction; and molecular and atomic structure. Other topics include ELECTROCHEMISTRY, SPECTROSCOPY and some aspects of NUCLEAR PHYSICS.

physical units Units used in measuring physical quantities. Units are of two types: **base** units that, like the kilogram, have fundamental definitions; and **derived** units that are defined in terms of these base units. Various systems of units exist, founded on certain base units. They include Imperial units (foot, pound, second), CGS units (centimetre, gram, second) and MKS units (metre, kilogram, second). For scientific purposes, SI UNITS have been adopted.

physics Branch of science concerned with the study of MATTER and ENERGY. Physics seeks to identify and explain their many forms and relationships. Modern physics recognizes four FUNDAMENTAL FORCES in nature: GRAVITATION, which was first adequately described by Isaac NEWTON; ELECTROMAGNETIC FORCE, codified in the 19th century by MAXWELL's equations; WEAK NUCLEAR FORCE, which is responsible for the decay of some subatomic particles; and STRONG NUCLEAR FORCE, which binds together atomic nuclei. The latter is some 10^{12} times stronger than the weak force. Branches of physics include PARTICLE PHYSICS, geophysics, BIOPHYSICS, ASTROPHYSICS and NUCLEAR PHYSICS. Physics may also be divided into six fundamental theories: MECHANICS, THERMODYNAMICS, ELECTROMAGNETISM, STATISTICAL MECHANICS, RELATIVITY and QUANTUM MECHANICS.

physiology Branch of biology concerned with the functions of living organisms, as opposed to their structure (anatomy).

physiotherapy (physical therapy) Use of various physical techniques to treat disease or injury. Techniques include massage, manipulation, heat, hydrotherapy, ultrasonics and electrical stimulation.

pi (π) Symbol used for the ratio of the circumference of a circle to its diameter. It is an IRRATIONAL NUMBER, and an approximation to five decimal places is 3.14159.

Piaget, Jean (1896–1980) Swiss psychologist, who developed a comprehensive theory of the intellectual growth of children in the 1920s and 1930s. He wrote several influential books, including *The Child's Conception of the World* (1926), *The Origin of Intelligence in Children* (1954) and *The Early Growth of Logic in the Child* (1964).

piano (pianoforte) Musical instrument whose sound is made with strings struck by hammers that are moved from a keyboard. Its invention (*c*.1709) is attributed to Bartolomeo Cristofori. Its name, from the Italian *piano* (soft) and *forte* (strong or loud), was adopted because its range of volume (as of tonal quality) far exceeded that of earlier instruments. The modern grand piano, much larger, louder and more resonant than the 18th-century piano, was developed in the early 19th century.

Picardy Region and former province of N France, on the English Channel; includes Somme, and parts of Pas-de-Calais, Oise and Aisne départements. Picardy was the scene of heavy fighting during WORLD WAR 1. The area is made up of the plateau to the N of Paris, where wheat and sugar-beet are grown; the valley of the Somme, where industrial centres such as Amiens are located; and the coast, where fishing is important. Area: 19,399sq km (7,488sq mi) Pop. 1,810,700.

Picasso, Pablo (1881–1973) Spanish painter, sculptor, graphic artist, designer and ceramicist. Art historians often divide his work into separate periods. During his "Blue" and "Rose" periods (1900–07), he turned from portrayals of the poor and outcasts to representations of harlequins, acrobats and dancers in warmer colours. *Les Demoiselles d'Avignon* (1907) is now seen as a watershed in the development of contemporary art. The fragmentary forms in the painting heralded CUBISM. In the 1920s he produced solid classical figures but at the same time he was exploring SURREALISM. He started creating more violent and morbid works, which culminated in *Guernica* (1937). Picasso's sculpture ranks as highly as his painting. He was one of the first to use assembled rather than modelled or carved materials. The most famous example is his *Head of a Bull, Metamorphosis* (1943), which consists of a bicycle saddle and handlebars.

Piccard, Auguste (1884–1962) Swiss physicist who explored the STRATOSPHERE and deep seas. In 1931, a hydrogen balloon carried Piccard and an assistant, to an altitude of *c*.15,800m (51,800ft); the first ascent into the stratosphere. From 1948, he experimented with designs for a diving vessel called a bathyscaphe. In the Pacific Ocean in 1960, Piccard descended in the bathyscaphe *Trieste* to a record depth of 10,900m (35,800ft).

piccolo WOODWIND musical instrument of the FLUTE family. About half the size of the flute, it is pitched one octave higher.

Picts Ancient inhabitants of E and N Scotland. By the 8th century they had a kingdom extending from Caithness to Fife, and had adopted Christianity. To the w and s of the Picts, invaders from Ireland had established the kingdom of Dalriada; in 843 its king, Kenneth I, also became king of the Picts, uniting the two kingdoms into the kingdom of Scotland.

pidgin Simplified form of a language, differing from other LINGUA FRANCAS by comprising a very limited vocabulary and being used for communication between people who do not speak the same language. The Pidgin English of Papua New Guinea (Tok Pisin) is an official national language.

Piedmont (Piemonte) Region of NW Italy, bounded to the N, W and s by mountains, and to the E by the Po Valley; it comprises the provinces of Alessandria, Asti, Cuneo, Novara, Torino and Vercelli. Under the influence of Savoy from the early 15th century, it became part of the kingdom of Sardinia in 1720. In the early 19th century it was the focus of the movement for Italian independence, joining a united Italy in 1861. The Po Valley has some excellent farmland. Products: grain, vegetables, fruit, dairy. Industries: wine-making, motor vehicles, textiles, glass, chemicals. Area: 25,400sq km (9,807sq mi). Pop. (1991) 4,302,565.

Pierce, Franklin (1804–69) 14th US President (1853–57). He represented New Hampshire in the US House of Representatives (1833–37) and the Senate (1837–42). He gained the Democratic presidential nomination as a compromise candidate. His presidency is noted for his endorsement of the Kansas-Nebraska Act (1854), which resulted in near-civil war between pro- and antislavery settlers.

Piero della Francesca (1415–92) (Piero dei Francheschi) Italian painter. His most important work is the FRESCO series depicting the *Legend of the True Cross* (finished *c*.1465) for the choir of San Francesco, Arezzo. He later embraced HUMANISM at Federico da Montefeltro's court at Urbino.

Pierre Capital of South Dakota, USA, on the Missouri River opposite Fort Pierre. It became the state capital in 1904. Its economy is based on government services and agriculture. Pop. (1990) 12,906.

Pietism Influential Christian spiritual movement within Protestantism founded in the late 17th century by the German Lutheran minister, Philipp Spener. Its aim was to revitalize evangelical Christianity.

piezoelectric effect Creation of positive electric charge on one side of a nonconducting crystal and a negative charge on the other when the crystal is squeezed. The pressure results in an electric field that can be detected as voltage between the opposite crystal faces. The effect has been used in record player stylii, microphones and cigarette lighters.

pig Any of numerous species and varieties of domestic and wild swine of the family Suidae. The male is generally called a boar; the female, a sow. A castrated boar is usually known as a hog. It is usually a massive, short-legged omnivore with a thick skin bearing short bristles. Wild pigs include the warthog, wild BOAR, bush pig and babirusa.

pigeon (dove) Any of a large family of wild and domestic birds found throughout temperate and tropical regions. Pigeons have small heads, short necks, plump bodies and scaly legs and feet. Plumage is loose but thick. Length: to 46cm (18in). Family Columbidae; typical genus, *Columba*.

Piggott, Lester (1935–) British jockey. Piggott was champion jockey 11 times. Closely associated with the Epsom Derby, he rode a record 9 winners. By his retirement (1995), he had won 4,493 races.

pigment Coloured, insoluble substance used to impart colour to an object and added for this purpose to paints, inks and plastics. They generally function by absorbing and reflecting light, although some luminescent pigments emit coloured light.

pigmentation In biology, a natural chemical that gives colour to TISSUES. In humans, the skin, hair and iris are coloured by the pigments MELANIN and carotene, together with the HAEMOGLOBIN in ERYTHROCYTES (red blood cells), which also acts as a pigment.

pika Any of 12 species of short-haired relatives of the RABBIT. They live in cold regions of Europe, Asia and w USA. Length: to 20cm (8in). Genus *Ochotona*.

pike Predatory, freshwater fish found in E North America and parts of Europe and Asia. It has a shovel-shaped mouth and a mottled, elongated body. Length: to 137.2cm (54in); weight: 20.9kg (46lb) Family Esocidae; genus *Esox*.

pike perch Freshwater food and game fish of Central Europe, where it includes the zander, and of North America, where it is related to the walleye and sauger. A dark olive, mottled fish, it has an elongated body and large head and mouth. Length: to 91.4cm (3ft); weight: to 11.3kg (25lb). Family Percidae; species *Stizostedion vitreum*.

pilchard Marine food fish resembling a herring, found in shoals along most coasts except those of Asia. They are caught in millions and support a huge canning industry. The young are sometimes called SARDINES. Length: less than 45.7cm (18in). Family Clupeidae; species *Sardina pilchardus*.

pilgrimage Religiously motivated journey to a shrine or other holy place in order to gain spiritual help or guidance, or for the purpose of thanksgiving. A Muslim should make the pilgrimage (HAJJ) to MECCA at least once in his life. Since the second century, Christians have made pilgrimages, including those to Palestine, to the tomb of the Apostles Peter and Paul in Rome, and to that of James in Santiago de Compostela in Spain.

Pilgrims (Pilgrim Fathers) Group of English Puritans who emigrated to North America in 1620. After fleeing to Leiden, Netherlands, in 1608, to escape persecution in England, they decided to look for greater religious freedom by founding a religious society in America. They sailed from Plymouth, England, on the MAYFLOWER and founded the PLYMOUTH COLONY in present-day Massachusetts.

pill, the Popular term for oral contraceptives based on female reproductive hormones. They work by preventing ovulation. Two types of synthetic hormone, similar to OESTROGEN and PROGESTERONE, are generally used, although the former alone is effective in preventing ovulation, the latter helps to regulate the menstrual cycle. Possible side-effects include HYPERTENSION, weight-gain, and a slightly increased risk of THROMBOSIS. See CONTRACEPTION

Pilsudski, Józef (1867–1935) Polish general and statesman. During World War 1 he led Polish forces against Russia, hoping to establish a Polish state. After independence, Pilsudski became head of state. His attempt to create a larger Polish state during the Polish-Soviet War failed, although he inflicted a remarkable defeat on the invading Russians in 1920. He retired in 1923, but seized power again in 1926 and established an authoritarian personal rule that lasted until his death.

pimpernel Small, trailing ANNUAL plant of the genus *Anagallis*, native to Britain and the USA. The single, small, five petalled flowers are scarlet, white or blue. The yellow pimpernel, a creeping European plant is *Lysimachia nemorum*. Family Primulaceae.

pine Any of various evergreen, cone-bearing trees of the genus *Pinus*, most of which are native to cooler temperate regions of the world. The reproductive organs may be catkins or cones. Many species are valued for soft wood, wood pulp, oils and resins. Family Pinaceae.

pineal body Small gland attached to the undersurface of the vertebrate brain. In human beings, it has an endocrine function, secreting the hormone melatonin, which is involved in daily rhythms. See also ENDOCRINE SYSTEM

pineapple Tropical herbaceous perennial plant and its fruit that is cultivated in the USA, South America, Asia, Africa and Australia. The fruit is formed from the flowers and bracts and grows on top of a short, stout stem bearing stiff, fleshy leaves. Height: to 1.2m (4ft). Family Bromeliaceae; species *Ananas comosus*.

pinna Flap of skin and cartilage that comprises the visible, external part of the EAR. It helps to collect sound waves and direct them into the ear canal.

Pinochet Ugarte, Augusto (1915–) Ruler of Chile (1973–89). He led the military coup that overthrew Salvador ALLENDE and headed a four-man junta, taking the title of president under a new constitution (1981). His policies were pursued by ruthless means. After a referendum (1988) in which a majority voted against extending his presidency, he permitted free elections and accepted civilian rule, while retaining, until 1998, command of the armed forces.

Pinter, Harold (1930–) British playwright. His first play, *The Room* (1957), met with critical disapproval, but he followed it with successes such as *The Birthday Party* (1958), *The Caretaker* (1960) and *No Man's Land* (1975). His recent plays include *Party Time* (1991) and *Moonlighting* (1993). In most of his plays, ordinary characters and settings are presented in an atmosphere of mystery and fear.

Pinyin System of phonetic spelling used to transliterate Chinese characters into the Roman alphabet. It was officially adopted by China in 1958.

pipefish Any of numerous species of marine fish found in the shallow, warm and temperate waters of the Atlantic and Pacific oceans. Closely related to the seahorse, it has a pencil-like body covered with bony rings. Its mouth is at the end of a long snout. Length: to 58.4cm (23in). Family Syngnathidae.

pipit (fieldlark, titlark) Any of more than 50 birds that resemble LARKS. They are found worldwide. The plumage is a streaked brown or greyish colour, with a long, white-edged "wag" tail. Length: 15cm (6in). Family Motacillidae; genus *Anthus*.

Piraeus Seaport city in SE Greece, 8km (5mi) SW of Athens; largest Greek port. Piraeus was planned c.490 BC and rapidly developed into the major sea outlet. It was destroyed by Sulla in 86 BC and fell into decline. In the 19th century, following Greek independence, a process of reconstruction led to the creation of the modern naval and commercial port. Industries: shipbuilding, oil-refining, textiles, chemicals. Pop. (1991) 182,671.

Pirandello, Luigi (1867–1936) Italian dramatist, novelist and short-story writer. Among his plays are *Six Characters in Search of an Author* (1921) and *As You Desire Me* (1930). His novels include *The Late Mattia Pascal* (1923). He won the 1934 Nobel Prize for literature.

Piranesi, Giovanni Battista (1720–78) Italian engraver and architect. He is best known for his *Vedute* (1745), 137 etchings of Rome.

piranha (piraya) Tropical, freshwater, bony fish that lives in rivers in South America. It is an aggressive predator with sharp teeth. Piranhas usually travel and attack in shoals and can pose a serious threat to much larger creatures. Length: to 24in (61cm). Family Characidae; genus *Serrasalmus*.

Pisa City on the River Arno, Tuscany, W central Italy. Already an important Etruscan town, Pisa prospered as a Roman colony from c.180 BC. In the Middle Ages it was a powerful maritime republic but later came under Florentine domination. Industries: tourism, textiles. Pop (1992 est.) 108,000.

Pisanello (c.1395–c.1455) (Antonio Pisano) Italian painter and medallist. Working in the International Gothic style, he drew detailed studies of birds, people and costumes. His medals of important people of his time are of historic value.

Pisano, Nicola (1225–84) Italian sculptor. In

497

Pisa he executed his first masterpiece, the pulpit for the Baptistry (1260). In his work on the cathedral pulpit in Siena (1265–68) he was aided by his son, **Giovanni** (*c*.1250– *c*.1320), whose decoration was influenced by the French Gothic style. Giovanni executed two other pulpits: Sant' Andrea, Pistoia (1298–1301) and Pisa cathedral (1302–10).

Pisces (the Fishes) Inconspicuous equatorial constellation situated on the ecliptic between Aquarius and Aries; it is the 12th sign of the Zodiac.

Pissarro, Camille (1830–1903) French painter who adopted IMPRESSIONISM and tried POINTILLISM. In the 1880s he experimented with the pointillist theories of Georges SEURAT but abandoned them in the 1890s for a freer interpretation of nature. His works include *Louvre from Pont Neuf* (1902).

pistachio Deciduous tree native to the Mediterranean region and E Asia. It is grown commercially for the edible greenish seed (the pistachio nut) of its wrinkled red fruit. Height: to 6m (20ft). Family Anacardiaceae; species *Pistacia vera*.

pistil Female organ located in the centre of a flower. It consists of an OVARY, a slender STYLE and a STIGMA, which receives POLLEN.

pistol Firearm held and fired in one hand. The first were matchlocks, in which a glowing fuse ignited the charge; by the end of the 16th century, wheel-locks and the cheaper flintlocks were also in use. The invention of the percussion cap in 1815 enabled pistol technology to advance rapidly, and Samuel Colt's revolver of 1835 was the first reliable repeating firearm.

Pitcairn Island Volcanic island in the central S Pacific Ocean, part of a British crown colony. First sighted in 1767, Pitcairn was settled in 1790 by mutineers from HMS *Bounty*. Some of their descendants still live on Pitcairn. The principal economic activity is the growing and exporting of fruit. Area: 4.6sq km (1.7sq mi). Pop. (1994) 56.

pitch Quality of sound that determines its position in a musical scale. It is measured in terms of frequency (measured in hertz) – the higher the frequency, the higher the pitch. It also depends to some extent on loudness and timbre.

pitchblende *See* URANINITE

pitcher plant Any of several species of INSECTIVOROUS PLANT of the tropics and sub-tropics. Insects are trapped in the vase-shaped leaves, which are lined with bristles. Trapped insects decompose and are absorbed as nutrients by plant cells. The flower is usually red. Height: 20–61cm (8–24in). Family Sarraceniacea; genera *Sarracenia* and *Nepenthes*.

Pitt, William, the Younger (1759–1806) British statesman, prime minister (1783–1801, 1804–06). The second son of William Pitt, earl of Chatham, he became chancellor of the exchequer in 1782 and shortly after became Britain's youngest prime minister, aged 24. He resigned in the face of GEORGE III's refusal to consider CATHOLIC EMANCIPATION. He returned to power in 1804 and died in office. His reputation rests chiefly on his financial and com-

mercial reforms of the 1780s, which restored British prosperity and prestige after the AMERICAN REVOLUTION. During his administrations, the India Act (1784), the Constitutional Act (1791) dividing Canada into French and English provinces, and the Act of Union with Ireland (1800) were passed.

Pittsburgh City and port at the confluence of the Allegheny and Monongahela rivers, SW Pennsylvania, USA. Under French control, it was captured from the French by the British in 1758 and renamed Fort Pitt. Pittsburgh grew as a steel manufacturing centre in the 19th century (the industry is now in decline). Industries: glass, machinery, petroleum products, electrical equipment, publishing, coal mining, oil and natural gas. Pop. (1990) 369,379.

pituitary gland Major gland of the ENDOCRINE SYSTEM, located at the base of the BRAIN. In human beings it is about the size of a pea and is connected to the HYPOTHALAMUS. It produces many HORMONES, some of which regulate the activity of other endocrine glands, while others control growth.

Pius V, Saint (1504–72) Pope (1568–72), b. Antonio Ghislieri. He was an energetic reformer of the Church and enemy of Protestantism. He excommunicated Queen ELIZABETH I of England in 1570. During his reign, he tightened the rules of INQUISITION and succeeded in eliminating Protestantism from Italy. He was canonized in 1712.

Pius VII (1742–1823) Pope (1800–23), b. Barnaba Gregorio Chiaramonti. After NAPOLEON I took Rome in 1808 and annexed the PAPAL STATES in 1809, Pius excommunicated him and was removed and imprisoned until 1814. On his restoration he encouraged the reform of religious orders.

Pius IX (1792–1878) Pope (1846–78), b. Giovanni Maria Mastai-Ferretti. He was driven from Rome (1848–50), but restored by NAPOLEON III. The PAPAL STATES were seized by Italian nationalists in 1860. In 1869 Pius convened the First VATICAN COUNCIL, which proclaimed the principle of PAPAL INFALLIBILITY. In 1870 Pius refused to accept the incorporation of Rome into the kingdom of Italy.

Pius XII (1876–1958) Pope (1939–58), b. Eugenio Pacelli. Fearing reprisals, he failed to denounce Nazism and the persecution of Jews during World War 2. He was more openly hostile to communism.

Pizarro, Francisco (1471–1541) Spanish *conquistador* of the INCA empire of Peru. He served under CORTÉS and led expeditions to South America (1522–28). Having gained royal support, he led 180 men to Peru in 1530. They captured and later murdered the Inca ATAHUALPA, and took Cuzco, the capital (1534). Pizarro acted as governor, founding Lima in 1535.

placenta Organ in mammals (except monotremes and marsupials) that connects the FETUS to the UTERUS of the mother. Part of the placenta contains tiny blood vessels through which oxygen and food are carried from the mother to the fetus via the umbilical cord and wastes are carried from the fetus to the mother's bloodstream to be excreted.

The placenta secretes hormones that maintain pregnancy and is discharged from the mother's body as the afterbirth, immediately after delivery.

plagioclase Type of FELDSPAR. Plagioclase minerals occur in IGNEOUS and METAMORPHIC rocks. Off-white, or sometimes pink, green or brown, they are composed of varying proportions of the silicates of sodium and calcium with aluminium. They show an oblique cleavage and have triclinic system crystals. Hardness 6–6.5; s.g. 2.6.

plague Acute infectious disease of man and rodents caused by the bacillus *Yersinia pestis*. In man it occurs in three forms: **bubonic** plague, most common and characterized by vomiting, fever and swellings of the lymph nodes called "buboes"; **pneumonic** plague, in which the lungs are infected; and **septicaemic** plague, in which the bloodstream is invaded. Treatment is the administration of vaccines, bed rest, antibiotics and sulpha drugs. *See also* BLACK DEATH

plaice Marine flatfish found along the W European coast. An important food fish, it is brown or grey with orange spots. Length: to 90cm (3ft); weight: to 11.8kg (26lb). Family Pleuronectidae; species *Pleuronectes platessa*.

Plaid Cymru (Party of Wales) Welsh nationalist political party, founded in 1925. Its first MP was elected in 1966. It advocates Welsh independence (from the UK) within the European Union.

plainsong (plainchant) Collection of unharmonized liturgical melodies of the Western Church, performed unaccompanied and in unison. The chants use free rhythms and melodic cells derived from the MODES of ancient Greek music.

Planck, Max Karl Ernst Ludwig (1858–1947) German theoretical physicist whose revolutionary QUANTUM THEORY helped to establish modern physics. In 1900 he came to the conclusion that the frequency distribution of BLACK BODY radiation could only be accounted for if the radiation was emitted in separate "packets" (quanta) rather than continuously. Planck's constant indicates wave and particle behaviour on the atomic scale. His equation, relating the energy of a quantum to its frequency, is the basis of quantum theory. He won the 1918 Nobel Prize for physics.

plane In mathematics, a flat surface such that a straight line joining any two points on it lies entirely within the surface. Its general equation is $ax + by + cz = d$, where a, b, c and d are constants.

planet Large, non-stellar body in orbit around a star, shining only by reflecting the star's light. In our SOLAR SYSTEM there are nine major planets, as opposed to the thousands of ASTEROIDS or minor planets. *See also* MERCURY; VENUS; EARTH; MARS; JUPITER; SATURN; URANUS; NEPTUNE; PLUTO

planetarium Domed building in which a projector displays an artificial sky in order to demonstrate the positions and motions of the Sun, Moon, planets and stars relative to the Earth. The projector was invented in 1913 by Walter Bauersfeld.

plankton All the floating or drifting life of the ocean, especially that near the surface. The organisms are very small and move with the currents. There are two main kinds: **phytoplankton**, floating plants such as DIATOMS and dinoflagellates; and **zooplankton**, floating animals such as radiolarians, plus the larvae and eggs of larger marine animals. They are a vital part of the food chain.

plant Multicellular organism whose cells have cellulose walls and contain CHLOROPLASTS or similar structures (plastids). They develop from DIPLOID embryos and have a regular alternation of HAPLOID and diploid generations in their life cycles. Most plants are green and make their own food by PHOTOSYNTHESIS. A few are colourless PARASITES or SAPROPHYTES. Simple plants reproduce by means of SPORES, whereas more advanced plants produce SEEDS and FRUITS. Plants show a wide range of biochemistry; some produce chemicals such as ALKALOIDS or NARCOTICS. Plants are classified on the basis of their morphology (shape and structure). The most important phyla (divisions) are the BRYOPHYTES (mosses and liverworts); LYCOPODOPHYTA, or CLUB MOSSES; Sphenophyta (HORSETAILS); Filicinophyta (FERNS); Cycadophyta (CYCADS); Ginkgophyta (GINKGO); Coniferophyta (CONIFERS); and Angiospermophyta (ANGIOSPERMS).

Plantagenet English royal dynasty (1154–1485). The name encompasses the ANGEVINS (1154–1399) and the houses of LANCASTER and YORK. They are descended from Geoffrey of Anjou and Matilda, daughter of HENRY I. The name was adopted by Richard, duke of York and father of EDWARD IV, during the Wars of the ROSES.

plantain Plant with a rosette of basal leaves and spikes of tiny, greenish-white flowers; it grows in temperate regions and was used for medicinal purposes. Family Plantaginaceae; genus *Plantago*. It also refers to a tropical banana plant, cultivated throughout the tropics. Its green fruit is eaten cooked. Height: to 10m (33ft). Family Musaceae; species *Musa paradisiaca*.

plant classification System devised to group PLANTS according to relationships among them. Plants are known by common names that often vary from area to area, but have only one correct scientific name. *See* TAXONOMY

plant genetics Science of heredity and variation in plants. Research in GENETICS since 1900 has supplied the principles of plant breeding, especially HYBRIDIZATION. The development of consistently reliable and healthy first-generation crosses (F1 hybrids) has revolutionized the growing of food crops and bedding plants. Genetic engineers grow cell and TISSUE CULTURES by replication or cloning. They also concentrate on isolating individual GENES with the aim of producing new colour varieties, improving the flavour of crops, breeding resistance to pests and herbicides, and lengthening the shelf-life of crops. *See also* GENETIC ENGINEERING

plaque Abnormal deposit building up on a body

surface, especially the film of saliva and bacteria that accumulates on teeth. Dental plaque leads to tooth decay and gum disease.

plasma In physics, an ionized gas that contains roughly equal amounts of positive and negative IONS. Plasma, often described as the fourth state of MATTER, occurs at enormous temperatures, as in the interiors of the Sun and other stars and in fusion reactors.

plastic Synthetic material composed of organic molecules, often in long chains called POLYMERS, that can be shaped and hardened. The structure of the molecules determines the properties of a given compound. Plastics are synthesized from common materials, mostly petroleum. CELLULOSE comes from cotton or wood pulp, CASEIN from skimmed milk. Thermoset plastics, such as BAKELITE, stay hard once set; thermoplastics, such as polyethylene, can be resoftened. Biodegradable plastics are environmentally friendly because they decompose.

plastid Type of organelle found in the cells of plants and green algae. CHLOROPLASTS and leucoplasts are two examples of plastids, which have a double membrane and contain DNA.

Plata, Río de la (River Plate) Estuary in SE South America formed by the junction of the PARANÁ and Uruguay rivers at the border between Argentina and Uruguay. BUENOS AIRES and MONTEVIDEO lie on its S and N shores respectively. It is 270km (170mi) long, and 190km (120mi) wide at its mouth. Area: c.35,000sq km (13,500sq mi).

platelet Colourless, usually spherical structures found in mammalian BLOOD. Chemical compounds in platelets, known as factors and cofactors, are essential to blood clotting. The normal platelet count is c.300,000 per cu mm of blood.

plate tectonics Theory or model to explain the distribution, evolution and causes of the Earth's crustal features. It proposes that the Earth's CRUST and part of the upper MANTLE (LITHOSPHERE) are made up of several separate, rigid slabs (plates) that move independently, forming part of a cycle in the creation and destruction of crust. The plates collide or move apart at the margins, and produce zones of earthquake and volcanic activity. Three types of plate boundary can be identified: constructive, destructive and conservative. Plate movement is thought to be driven by convection currents in the mantle. *See also* SEAFLOOR SPREADING

Plath, Sylvia (1932–63) US poet. Her verse includes *The Colossus* (1960) and *Ariel* (1965). The latter was published after her suicide, as were *Crossing the Water* (1971), *Winter Trees* (1971) and *Collected Poems* (1981). She wrote one novel, *The Bell Jar* (1963). Her most effective work is characterized by intensely personal, confessional elements. She was married to Ted HUGHES.

platinum Lustrous, silver-white metal (symbol Pt), one of the TRANSITION ELEMENTS. Discovered in 1735, it is chiefly found in certain ores of nickel. Malleable and ductile, it is used as a CATALYST in catalytic converters for car exhausts. It is chemically unreactive and resists tarnishing and CORROSION. Properties: at.no. 78; r.a.m. 195.09; r.d. 21.45; m.p. 1,772°C (3.222°F); b.p. 3,800°C (6,872°F); most common isotope Pt^{195} (33.8%).

Plato (427–347 BC) Ancient Greek philosopher and writer who formulated an ethical and metaphysical system based upon philosophical IDEALISM. From c.407 BC Plato was a disciple of SOCRATES. Following the trial and execution of Socrates in 399 BC, he travelled extensively. Plato sought to educate Dionysius II as a philosopher-king and set up an ideal political system, but the venture failed. In Athens, Plato set up his famous Academy (c.387 BC). In the Academy he taught ARISTOTLE. In Plato's dialogues, SOCRATES genially interrogates another person, demolishing their arguments. All of Plato's 36 works survive. His greatest work was the *Republic*.

platypus MONOTREME mammal of Australia. It is amphibious, lays eggs and has webbed feet, a broad tail and a soft duck-like bill. The male has a poison spur on the hind foot. It is 60cm (24in) long and eats small invertebrates. Family Ornithorhynchidae; species *Ornithorhynchus anatinus*.

plebeian General body of Roman citizens, as distinct from the small PATRICIAN class. In the early years of the Republic they were barred from public office and from marrying a patrician. The gulf between the two classes gradually closed.

Pléiade, La Group of seven 16th-century French poets. They were Pierre de Ronsard, Joachim du Bellay, Jean-Antoine de Baïf, Rémy Belleau, Estienne Jodelle, Pontus de Tyard and Jean Dorat. They advocated French as a literary language.

Pleiades Young OPEN CLUSTER in the constellation Taurus, popularly called the Seven Sisters. Although only six or seven stars are visible to the naked eye, there are in fact over a thousand embedded in a reflection NEBULA.

Pleistocene Geological epoch that began about 2 million years ago, during which humans and most forms of familiar mammalian life evolved. Episodes of climatic cooling in this epoch led to widespread glaciation in the Northern Hemisphere, and the Pleistocene is the best-known ice age. It ended c.8,000 BC.

pleura Double membrane that lines the space between the lungs and the walls of the chest. The fluid between the pleura lubricates the two surfaces to prevent friction during breathing movements.

pleurisy Inflammation of the PLEURA. It is nearly always due to infection, but may arise as a complication of other diseases.

Plimsoll, Samuel (1824–98) British social reformer. As a radical MP (1868–80), he was chiefly responsible for the Merchant Shipping Act (1876), which required merchant ships to have a line painted on their hulls to indicate loading limits.

Pliny the Elder (23–79) (Gaius Plinius Secundus) Roman author of *Historia Naturalis* (*Natural*

History). His only major surviving work, it covers a vast range of subjects.

Pliny the Younger (62–114) (Gaius Plinius Caecilius Secundus) Roman administrator. The nephew and adopted son of PLINY THE ELDER, he is best known for his correspondence with the Emperor TRAJAN.

Pliocene Last era of the TERTIARY period that lasted from 5 to 2 million years ago and preceded the PLEISTOCENE. Animal and plant life was not unlike that of today.

PLO *See* PALESTINE LIBERATION ORGANIZATION

Plotinus (205–270) Ancient philosopher, the founder of NEOPLATONISM. He opened a school in Rome in *c*.244. In essence, he conceived of the universe as a hierarchy proceeding from matter, through soul and reason, to God. God was pure existence, without form. His pupil and biographer Porphyry compiled and edited Plotinus' writings into the *Enneads*.

plover Any of several species of wading shorebirds, many of which migrate from Arctic breeding grounds to Southern Hemisphere wintering areas. It has a large head, a plump grey, brown or golden speckled body and short legs. Length: to 28cm (11in). Family Charadriidae; genera include *Charadrius* and *Pluvialis*.

Plowright, Joan Anne (1929–) British actress. She often appeared in classical pieces opposite her husband Laurence OLIVIER. She performed in the first performances of John OSBORNE's *The Entertainer* (1957) and Arnold WESKER's *Roots* (1959).

plum Fruit tree, mostly native to Asia and naturalized in Europe and North America, widely cultivated for its fleshy, edible fruit, which has a hard "stone" at the centre. The most common cultivated plum of Europe and Asia is *Prunus domsetica*; in North America, the Japanese plum (*Prunus salicina*) is crossed with European varieties to give several cultivated strains. Family Rosaceae.

pluralism In politics, theory that state power is wielded by a number of groups with conflicting interests, none of which is able to establish absolute authority. In philosophy, pluralism is the name given to the theory that there are many ultimate substances, rather than one (as in MONISM).

Plutarch (46–120) Greek biographer and essayist. His best-known work is *The Parallel Lives*, which consists of biographies of soldiers and statesmen. Lesser known, but also of great interest, are Plutarch's *Moralia*, which comprise essays and dialogues on ethical, literary and historical subjects.

Pluto Smallest and outermost planet of the Solar System. The last planet in our Solar System to be discovered. Independently, William H. Pickering and Percival LOWELL calculated the possible existence of Pluto. The planet was eventually located in 1930 by Clyde Tombaugh within 5° of Lowell's predicted position. Pluto seems to have a mottled surface with light and dark regions, and signs of polar caps. The surface is covered with icy deposits consisting of 98% nitrogen, with traces of methane, and also probably water, carbon dioxide, and carbon monoxide. Pluto has a single moon, Charon, which is so large that some astronomers consider Pluto/Charon as a double planet. Diameter: 2,300km.

Pluto Roman god of the underworld, equivalent to the Greek god HADES. He ruled over the land of the dead and was also a god of wealth, since his realm contained all underground mineral riches.

plutonium Silver-white radioactive metallic element (symbol Pu) of the ACTINIDE SERIES. It was first synthesized in 1940 by Glenn Seaborg and associates at the University of California at Berkeley by deuteron (heavy hydrogen) bombardment of URANIUM. It is found naturally in small amounts in uranium ores. Pu^{239} (half-life 24,360 years) is made in large quantities in breeder reactors. It is a fissile element used in NUCLEAR REACTORS and nuclear weapons. The element is very toxic and absorbed by bone, making it a dangerous radiological hazard. Properties: at.no. 94; r.d. 19.84; m.p. 641°C (1,186°F); b.p. 3,232°C (5,850°F); most stable isotope Pu^{244} (half-life 25,000 years). *See also* TRANSURANIC ELEMENTS

Plymouth City and port on the Tamar estuary, Devon, SW England. In 1588 Sir Francis DRAKE set out from Plymouth to attack the Spanish ARMADA, and the MAYFLOWER sailed for America from here in 1620. Plymouth was severely damaged by bombing in World War 2. It has a naval base and ferry links with France and Spain. Industries: China clay, machine tools. Pop. (1991) 243,373.

Plymouth Brethren Strictly Puritan sect of evangelical Christians, founded in Ireland in the late 1820s by J.N. Darby. In 1849 they split into the "Open Brethren" and the "Exclusive Brethren".

Plymouth Colony First colonial settlement in New England (founded 1620). The settlers were a group of about 100 Puritan Separatist PILGRIMS, who sailed on the MAYFLOWER and settled on what is now Cape Cod Bay, Massachusetts. Lacking a royal charter, government was established by the "Mayflower Compact". During the first winter nearly half the settlers died. Plymouth Colony became part of Massachusetts in 1691.

pneumonia Inflammation of the LUNG tissue, most often caused by bacterial infection. The commonest form is pneumococcal pneumonia, caused by the bacterium *Streptococcus pneumoniae*. Symptoms include fever, chest pain, coughing and the production of rust-coloured sputum. Treatment is with ANTIBIOTICS.

pneumothorax Presence of air in the pleural space between the lungs and the chest wall. It may arise spontaneously or be caused by injury or disease. The lung is liable to collapse because it is prevented from expanding normally.

Po Italy's longest river, in N Italy. It rises in the Cottian Alps near the French border, and flows E to empty into the Adriatic Sea. The Po valley is an important industrial and agricultural region. Length: 650km (405mi).

Pocahontas (1595–1617) Native American princess and early colonial heroine. According to legend, she saved the life of John Smith, leader of the JAMESTOWN colonists, when he was about to be killed by her father, Powhatan.

podiatry Treatment and care of the foot. Podiatrists treat such conditions as corns and bunions and devise ways to accommodate foot deformities.

Poe, Edgar Allan (1809–49) US poet and short-story writer. Much of his finest poetry, such as *The Raven* (1845), deals with fear and horror in the tradition of the GOTHIC NOVEL. Other works include the poem *Annabel Lee* (1849), and the stories *The Fall of the House of Usher* (1839), *The Murders in the Rue Morgue* (1841) and *The Pit and the Pendulum* (1843).

poet laureate Title conferred by the British monarch on a poet whose duty is then to write commemorative verse on important occasions. The position has been held by, among others, WORDSWORTH (1843–50), TENNYSON (1850–92), John MASEFIELD (1930–67) and Sir John BETJEMAN (1972–84). Ted HUGHES was made poet laureate in 1984.

poetry Literary medium that employs the line as its formal unit, and in which the sound, rhythm and meaning of words are all equally important. Until the modern introduction of the concept of FREE VERSE, poetry was characteristically written in regular lines with carefully structured METRES, often with rhymes. *See also* PROSE

poikilothermal (ectothermic or cold-blooded) Animal whose body temperature fluctuates with the temperature of its surroundings. Reptiles, amphibians, fish and invertebrates are cold-blooded. They can control their body temperature only by their behaviour – by moving in and out of the shade, or orientating themselves to absorb more or less sunlight. *See also* HOMEOTHERMAL

Poincaré, (Jules) Henri (1854–1912) French mathematician. He worked on CELESTIAL MECHANICS, winning an award for his contribution to the theory of orbits. In 1906, independently of EINSTEIN, he obtained some of the results of the special theory of RELATIVITY. His works include *The Value of Science* (1905) and *Science and Method* (1908).

poinsettia Showy house plant native to Mexico. It has tapering leaves and tiny yellow flowers centred in leaf-like red, white or pink bracts. In its natural environment, the tree grows to about 5m (16ft). Height: to 60cm (2ft) when potted. Family Euphorbiaceae; species *Euphorbia pulcherrima*.

pointer Smooth-coated sporting and gun dog. It can be trained to indicate the direction in which game lies by standing motionless, aligning its muzzle, body and tail. The strong lean body is set on muscular legs. The short dense coat can be white with black, or brown markings. Height: to 63cm (25in); weight: to 27kg (60lb).

pointillism (Fr. *pointiller*, to dot) Technique of painting in regular dots or small dashes of pure colour, developed from NEO-IMPRESSIONISM by Georges SEURAT. When looked at from a distance, the dots create a vibrant optical effect.

poison ivy North American shrub that causes a severe, itchy rash on contact with human skin. It has greenish flowers and white berries. Species *Rhus radicans* and *R. toxicodendron*. Family Anarcardiaceae.

Poland Republic in central Europe; the capital is WARSAW. **Land and climate** Poland is mostly lowland. The N, lagoon-lined, Baltic Sea coast includes the ports of GDAŃSK and Szczecin, and the mouths of the VISTULA and Oder rivers. There are many lakes. The central plains include the cities of Warsaw, POZNAŃ, Lódz and Lublin. Poland's best farmland is in the SE uplands. Beyond the cities of Katowice and KRAKÓW, the land rises to Mount Rysy, at 2,499m (8,199ft), in the CARPATHIAN Mountains. In the SW lies the region of Silesia, and its capital Wroclaw. Poland has a continental climate, with warm summers and bitterly cold, snowy winters. Forests cover *c.*30% of Poland. Nearly 50% of the land is arable. **Economy** Before World War 2, Poland had a mainly agricultural economy. Under communism, industry expanded greatly. Today, 27% of the workforce are employed in agriculture and 37% in industry. Upper Silesia is the richest coal basin in Europe. Copper ore is also a vital mineral resource. Manufacturing accounts for *c.*24% of exports. Poland is the world's fifth-largest producer of ships. Agriculture remains important. Major crops include barley, potatoes and wheat. The transition to a market economy has doubled unemployment and increased foreign debt. Economic growth is slowly returning. **History** In the 9th century AD Slavic tribes unified the region. The Piast dynasty came to power. Boleslav I became the first king of Poland (1025), but the kingdom disintegrated in the 12th century. Ladislas I reunified Poland in 1320, but the dynasty collapsed under the might of the TEUTONIC KNIGHTS. The 16th-century rule of the Jagiello dynasty is regarded as Poland's "golden age". In 1569 Poland and Lithuania were united. In John II's reign, Poland was plundered by Sweden, Russia and Turkey. JOHN III SOBIESKI restored some prestige, but his death brought divi-

POLAND	
AREA: 312,680sq km (120,726sq mi)	
POPULATION: 38,356,000	
CAPITAL (POPULATION): Warsaw (1,653,300)	
GOVERNMENT: Multiparty republic	
ETHNIC GROUPS: Polish 98%, Ukrainian 1%	
LANGUAGES: Polish (official)	
RELIGIONS: Christianity (Roman Catholic 94%, Orthodox 2%)	
CURRENCY: Zloty = 100 groszy	

sion. Following the War of Succession (1733–35) Russia dominated Polish affairs. In 1772 and 1793 Poland was partitioned between Austria, Prussia and Russia. The defeat of a Polish revolt in 1795 led to further partition, and Poland ceased to exist. The Congress of Vienna (1814–15) established a small, semi-independent Polish state based on Kraków. Polish uprisings in 1848 and 1863 against Russian dominance led to more impositions. In World War 1 Poland initially fought with Germany against Russia, but Germany occupied Poland. Poland regained its independence in 1918. In 1920 Poland recaptured Warsaw from Russia. In 1921 Poland became a republic. The 1920s and 1930s were a period of dictatorship and military rule. In September 1939, Germany invaded and Poland was partitioned between the Soviet Union and Germany. Britain declared war. Following the German invasion of the Soviet Union, all of Poland fell under German rule. The Nazis established concentration camps, such as Auschwitz. Over 6 million Poles perished. Only 100,000 Polish Jews, from a pre-war community of over 3 million, survived the Holocaust. Polish resistance intensified. In 1944 a provisional government was established. In August 1944 the Warsaw uprising was ruthlessly crushed by the Germans. In 1945 Poland regained its independence. It lost land in the E to the Soviet Union, but gained sections of Prussia from Germany. In 1949 Poland joined the Council for Mutual Economic Assistance (COMECON). In 1952 Poland became a people's republic, modelled on the Soviet constitution. In 1955 it was a founder member of the Warsaw Pact. Uprisings in 1956 led to the formation of a more liberal administration, led by Wladislaw Gomulka. The collectivization of agriculture was reversed, and restrictions on religious worship were relaxed. Inflation and recession during the 1970s led to further riots and political protests. In 1980 striking dockers in Gdańsk, led by Lech Walesa, formed a trade union called Solidarity, which gained popular support. In 1981 General Jaruzelski declared martial law, Solidarity was banned and its leaders arrested. Continuing recession and civil unrest led to the lifting of martial law in 1983. Following reforms in the Soviet Union, Solidarity was legalized and won free elections in 1989. In 1990 the Communist Party was disbanded and Walesa became president. **Politics** In 1995 elections, Walesa was defeated by the Democratic Left Alliance, led by Aleksander Kwasniewski. In 1996 Poland joined the Organization for Economic Cooperation and Development (OECD). In 1997 it was invited to join NATO. Parliamentary elections in 1997 were won by a centre-right coalition.

Polanski, Roman (1933–) Polish actor and director. His first full-length film, *Knife in the Water* (1962), was followed by *Repulsion* (1965) and *Cul de-Sac* (1966). Other credits include *Rosemary's Baby* (1968), *Chinatown* (1974) *Tess* (1980), *Bitter Moon* (1992) and *Death and the Maiden* (1994).

polar bear Large white bear that lives on Arctic coasts and ice floes. It spends most of its time at sea on drifting ice. It preys chiefly on seals and is hunted for fur and meat. Length: 2.3m (7.5ft); weight: to 405kg (900lb). Species *Thalarctos maritimus*.

Polaris See Pole Star

polarized light Light waves that have electromagnetic vibrations in only one direction (ordinary light vibrates in all directions perpendicular to the direction of propagation). Scientists distinguish between three types: plane-polarized, circularly polarized and elliptical-polarized light, each depending on the net direction of the vibrations.

Pole, Reginald (1500–58) English cardinal, the last Roman Catholic archbishop of Canterbury. He opposed Henry's divorce of Catherine of Aragon and moved to Italy during the Reformation, returning to England in 1554 as papal legate to Queen Mary I. She made him archbishop in 1556.

pole Generally either of the two points of intersection of the surface of a sphere and its axis of rotation. The Earth has four poles: the North and South geographic poles, where the Earth's imaginary axis meets its surface; and the North and South magnetic poles, where the Earth's magnetic field is most concentrated. A bar magnet has a north pole, where the magnetic flux leaves the magnet, and a south pole, where it enters. A pole is also one of the terminals (positive or negative) of a battery, electric machine or circuit.

polecat Any of several species of small, carnivorous, nocturnal mammals that live in wooded areas of Eurasia and N Africa; especially *Mustela putorius*, the common polecat. It has a slender body, long bushy tail, anal scent glands, and brown to black fur (fitch). It eats small animals, birds and eggs. Length: 45.7cm (18in). Family Mustelidae.

Pole Star (Polaris, North Star) Important navigational star, nearest to the N celestial star. It is in the constellation Ursa Minor and always marks due N.

police Body of people concerned with maintaining civil order and investigating breaches of the law. Britain's first regular professional force was the Marine Police established in 1800. The Metropolitan Police was created by Sir Robert Peel in 1829.

poliomyelitis Acute viral infection of the nervous system affecting the nerves that activate muscles. Often a mild disease with effects limited to the throat and intestine, it is nonetheless potentially serious, with paralysis occurring in 1% of patients. It becomes life-threatening only if the breathing muscles are affected. It has become rare in developed countries since the introduction of vaccination in the mid-1950s.

Polish National language of Poland, spoken by virtually all of the country's 39 million people. It belongs to the Slavonic family of Indo-European languages. Polish is written in the Roman alphabet, but with a large number of diacritical marks to represent Slavonic vowels and consonants.

politics Sphere of action in human society in

503

which power is sought in order to regulate the ways in which people live together. A political society accepts the need for perpetually changing the rules in order to make them accord with altered circumstances.

Polk, James Knox (1795–1849) 11th US President (1845–49). During his administration, California and New Mexico were acquired following US victory in the MEXICAN WAR (1846–48). He also gained Oregon through the Oregon Treaty (1846).

pollen Yellow, powder-like SPORES that give rise to the male sex cells in flowering plants. Pollen grains are produced in the anther chambers of the STAMEN. When the pollen lands on the STIGMA of a compatible plant, it germinates, sending a long pollen tube down through the STYLE to the OVARY. During this process, one of its nuclei divides, giving rise to two male nuclei (the equivalent of male sex cells or GAMETES), one of which fuses with a female sex cell in fertilization. The other sex cell fuses with two more of the female nuclei to form a special tissue, the endosperm. In many species, this tissue develops into a food store for the embryo in the seed. *See also* POLLINATION; ALTERNATION OF GENERATIONS

pollination Transfer of POLLEN from the STAMEN to the STIGMA of a flower. Self-pollination occurs on one flower and cross-pollination between two flowers on different plants. Incompatability mechanisms in many flowers prevent self-pollination. Pollination occurs mainly by wind and insects.

Pollock, Jackson (1912–56) US painter. A leading figure in ABSTRACT EXPRESSIONISM. He began experimenting with ABSTRACT ART in the 1940s. In 1947 he began pouring paint straight onto the canvas. Instead of brushes he used sticks or knives to create the surface patterns. This method has been called ACTION PAINTING.

poll tax Tax of a fixed sum imposed on all liable individuals. Such taxes were occasionally levied by medieval governments: one provoked the PEASANTS' REVOLT (1381) in England. Southern US states after the Civil War made the right to vote dependent on payment of a poll tax, a device to disenfranchise poor blacks. A poll tax (Community Charge), introduced in Britain in 1989, was withdrawn after civil disobedience.

pollution Spoiling of the natural environment, generally by industrialized society. Pollution is usually a result of an accumulation of waste products, although excess of noise or heat that has adverse effects on the surrounding ecology is also considered as pollution.

Polo, Marco (1254–1324) Venetian traveller in Asia. In 1274 he accompanied his father and uncle on a trading mission to the court of KUBLAI KHAN, the MONGOL emperor of China. According to his account, *The Description of the World,* he remained in the Far East more than 20 years, becoming the confidant of Kublai Khan and travelling throughout China and beyond.

polo Field game played on horseback. Two teams of four players, on a field up to 182m (600ft) by 273m (900ft), each try to hit a small ball into a goal using mallets. A game consists of four, six or eight chukkas (periods), each 7.5 minutes long. Polo originated in Persia in ancient times, and spread throughout Asia. It was revived in India in the 19th century and was taken up by British army officers.

polonium Rare radioactive metallic element (symbol Po) of group VI of the PERIODIC TABLE, discovered in 1898 by Marie CURIE. It is found in trace amounts in uranium and may be synthesized. Properties: at.no. 84; density 9.40; m.p. 254°C (489°F); b.p. 962°C (1764°F); most stable isotope Po^{209}.

Pol Pot (1928–) Cambodian ruler. He became leader of the KHMER ROUGE, which overthrew the US-backed government of Lon Nol in 1975. He instigated a reign of terror in Cambodia (renamed Kampuchea). The intellectual elite were massacred, and city-dwellers driven into the countryside. Estimates suggest that 1–4 million died. Pol Pot's regime was overthrown by a Vietnamese invasion in 1979. He continued to lead the Khmer Rouge until after the Vietnamese withdrawal (1989). In 1997 it was reported that Pol Pot had been sentenced to life imprisonment by a Khmer Rouge court for the murder of a Khmer Rouge comrade.

polyanthus Any of a group of spring-flowering, perennial primroses of the genus *Primula*. They occur mainly in the N temperate zone. They have basal leaves and disc-shaped flowers, branching from a common stalk to form a ball-like cluster. Height: to 15cm (6in). Family Primulaceae.

polychlorinated biphenyl (PCB) Any of several stable mixtures – liquid, resinous or crystalline – of organic compounds. They are fire-resistant and are used as lubricants and heat-transfer fluids. The use of PCBs has been restricted since 1973 because their toxicity and resistance to decomposition in streams and soils poses a threat to wildlife.

polyester Class of organic substance composed of large molecules arranged in a chain and formed from many smaller molecules through the establishment of ester linkages. Polyester fibres are resistant to chemicals and are made into ropes and textiles.

polyethylene POLYMER of ETHENE. It is a partially crystalline, lightweight, thermoplastic RESIN, with high resistance to chemicals, low moisture absorption and good insulating properties.

polygamy Marriage in which more than one spouse is permitted. More often it is used to denote polygyny (several wives) than polyandry (several husbands). Polygamy is legal and commonplace in many Muslim and African countries.

polygon Plane geometric figure having three or more sides intersecting at three or more points (vertices). They are named according to the number of sides: triangle (three-sided), quadrilateral (four-sided), hexagon (six-sided). A regular polygon is equilateral (sides equal in length) and equiangular (equal angles).

polygraph *See* LIE DETECTOR

polyhedron In geometry, three-dimensional solid figure whose surface is made up of polygons. These are called the faces of the polyhedron, and the points at which they meet are the vertices.

polymer Substance formed by the union from two to several thousand simple molecules (monomers) to form a large molecular structure. Some, such as cellulose, occur in nature; others form the basis of plastics and synthetic resins.

polymerase chain reaction (PCR) Chemical reaction, speeded up by an ENZYME, that is used to make large numbers of copies of a specific piece of DNA, starting from only one or few DNA molecules. It enables scientists to make large enough quantities of DNA to be able to analyse or manipulate it. PCR is extremely important in GENETIC ENGINEERING and GENETIC FINGERPRINTING.

Polynesia One of the three divisions of OCEANIA, and the general term for the islands of the central Pacific Ocean; MICRONESIA and MELANESIA lie to the w. The principal islands in Polynesia are the Hawaiian Islands, Phoenix Islands, Tokelau Islands, the Samoa group, Easter Island, Cook Islands and French Polynesia. Because of their Maori population, the two larger islands of New Zealand are also included. The islands are mostly coral or volcanic in origin.

polynomial Sum of terms that are powers of a variable. For example, $8x^4 - 4x^3 + 7x^2 + x - 11$ is a polynomial of the fourth degree (the highest power four). In general a polynomial has the form $a_0 x^n + a_1 x^{n-1} + a_2 x^{n-2} + \ldots + a_{n-2} x^2 + a_{n-1} x + a_n$, although certain powers of x and the constant term a_n may be missing. The values a_n, a_{n-1}, etc., are the coefficients of the polynomial.

polyp Body type of various species of animals within the phylum Cnidaria. It has a mouth surrounded by extensible tentacles and a lower end that is adapted for attachment to a surface. It is distinct from the free-swimming medusa. It may be solitary, as in the SEA ANEMONE, but is more often an individual of a colonial organism such as CORAL.

polyp In medicine, swollen mass projecting from the wall of a cavity lined with mucous membrane, such as the nose. Although usually benign, some growths can be cancerous.

polyphony Vocal or instrumental part music in which the compositional interest centres on the "horizontal" aspect of each moving part rather than on the "vertical" structure of chords. The golden age of polyphony was the 16th century. Masters included Giovanni PALESTRINA and William BYRD.

polysaccharide Any of a group of complex CARBOHYDRATES made up of long chains of monosaccharide (simple-sugar) molecules. GLUCOSE is a monosaccharide, and the polysaccharides STARCH and CELLULOSE are both POLYMERS of glucose. Higher carbohydrates are all polysaccharides that will decompose by HYDROLYSIS into a large number of monosaccharide units. Polysaccharides function both as food stores (starch in plants and

GLYCOGEN in animals) and as structural materials (cellulose and PECTIN in the cell walls of plants, and CHITIN in the protective skeleton of insects).

polystyrene Synthetic organic POLYMER, composed of long chains of the aromatic compound styrene. It is a strong thermoplastic RESIN, acid- and alkali-resistant, non-absorbent and an excellent electrical insulator.

polytheism Belief in or worship of many gods and goddesses. The ancient Egyptian, Babylonian, Greek and Roman religions were all polytheistic. HINDUISM is a modern polytheistic religion. *See also* ANCESTOR WORSHIP; ANIMISM; MONOTHEISM

polyunsaturate Type of FAT or OIL that has molecules of long CARBON chains with many double bonds. Polyunsaturated fats exist in fish oils and most vegetable oils. At room temperature, unsaturated oils are liquids and SATURATED FATS are solids. Polyunsaturates, which have low or no CHOLESTEROL content, are widely used in margarines and cooking oils. They are considered to be healthier than saturated fats.

polyvinyl chloride (PVC) White, tough, solid thermoplastic that is a polymer of vinyl chloride. PVC can be softened and made elastic with a plasticizer. Easily coloured and resistant to weather and fire, PVC is used in the production of fibres, windows, electrical insulation, pipes, vinyl flooring, audio discs, raincoats and upholstery.

Pombal, Sebastião José de Carvalho e Mello, Marquês de (1699–1782) Portuguese statesman, minister for foreign affairs (1750–56). Pombal was virtual ruler of Portugal until the death of King Joseph in 1777. He increased royal power at the expense of the old nobility, the INQUISITION and the JESUITS, whom he expelled in 1759.

pomegranate Deciduous shrub or small tree native to w Asia. It has shiny, oval leaves and orange-red flowers. The round fruit has a red, leathery rind and numerous seeds coated with edible pulp. Family Punicaceae; species *Punica granatum.*

Pompeii Ancient Roman city in SE Italy, buried by volcanic eruption in AD 79. Pompeii was founded in the 8th century BC. The eruption of Mount VESUVIUS was so sudden and violent that about 2,000 died and the city was swiftly covered by volcanic ash, preserving whole houses intact until excavation began in the 18th century.

Pompey (106–48 BC) (Gnaeus Pompeius Magnus) Roman general. He fought for SULLA in 83 BC and campaigned in Sicily, Africa and Spain. He was named consul with CRASSUS in 70 BC and fought a notable campaign against MITHRIDATES VI of Pontus in 66 BC. In 59 BC he formed the first triumvirate with Crassus and his great rival, Julius CAESAR. After the death of Crassus, Pompey joined Caesar's enemies, and civil war broke out in 49 BC. Driven out of Rome by Caesar's advance, Pompey was defeated at Pharsalus in 48 BC and fled to Egypt, where he was murdered.

Pompidou, Georges Jean Raymond

(1911–74) French statesman, premier (1958–68), president (1969–74). He served on DE GAULLE's staff and was a member of the council of state (1946–57) before becoming premier. He succeeded De Gaulle as president and died in office.

pondweed Any of numerous species of a family of aquatic, perennial, flowering plants of the genus *Potamogeton*, found mostly in temperate regions in freshwater lakes, but also in brackish and saltwater. Most pondweeds have spike-like flowers that stick out of the water, and submerged or floating leaves. Family Potamogetonaceae.

pontifex Priest of ancient Rome, a member of the college of priests who organized Rome's state religion. Since the 5th century AD, the title *Pontifex Maximus* has been in use in a Christian context as a designation for the pope.

Pontius Pilate (active 1st century AD) Roman prefect or procurator of Judaea at the time when JESUS CHRIST was crucified. Pilate was made procurator of Judaea in AD 26 and earned a reputation for arrogance and cruelty. He died after AD 36.

Pontus Ancient kingdom of NE Anatolia (Turkey). The coastal cities were colonized by Greeks in the 6th–5th centuries BC and retained virtual autonomy under the Persian empire. The kingdom of Pontus reached the height of its power under MITHRIDATES VI, the Great, who conquered Asia Minor, gained control of the Crimea and threatened Rome. After his defeat by POMPEY (65 BC), the country was divided up but maintained its prosperity.

pony Any of several breeds of small horses, usually solid and stocky. They are commonly used as a children's saddle horse. Types include the hardy Shetland pony; the Dartmoor and Exmoor ponies of Cornwall, Somerset and Devon; the grey Highland pony; the Welsh pony and the Welsh Cob. Height: 115–45cm (45– 57in) at the shoulder.

Pony Express (1860–61) US relay mail service that operated between Saint Joseph, Missouri, and Sacramento, California. The scheduled time for the 3,200-km (1,800-mi) journey was ten days, less than half the time taken by stagecoach. The service was gradually replaced by the telegraph.

poodle Breed of dog believed to have originated in Germany. It has a rounded skull and long straight body, and a high-set tail, often docked. The thick, wiry coat is commonly clipped. The main sizes are standard, miniature and toy. Height: (standard) more than 38cm (15in) at the shoulder.

poor laws English legislation designed to prevent begging and vagrancy. Introduced in the 16th century and consolidated in the Poor Law Act of 1601, they required individual parishes to provide for the local poor. Later, workhouses were established. Poor-law amendments of 1834 sought to provide uniform assistance by a system of national supervision, but relief was maintained at a low level.

pop art Movement inspired by consumerist images and popular culture that flourished in Britain and the USA from the late 1950s to the early 1970s. Richard HAMILTON described pop art as "popular, transient, expendable, low-cost, mass-produced, young, witty, sexy, gimmicky, glamorous and Big Business".

Pope See PAPACY

Pope, Alexander (1688–1744) British poet. He wrote lyric and elegiac poetry and published fine translations of HOMER (1720 and 1726) and *Imitations of Horace* (1733). Among his finest work are the satires *The Rape of the Lock* (1714), *The Dunciad* (1728) and *An Epistle to Dr Arbuthnot* (1735).

poplar Any of a number of deciduous, softwood trees of the genus *Populus*, native to cool and temperate regions. The oval leaves grow on stalks, and flowers take the form of catkins. Height: to 60m (197ft). Family Salicaceae.

Popocatépetl Snow-capped, dormant volcano in central Mexico, 72km (45mi) SE of Mexico City. The crater contains sulphur deposits. Height: 5,452m (17,887ft).

Popper, Sir Karl Raimund (1902–94) British philosopher of natural and social sciences, b. Austria. He proposed his theory of falsification in *The Logic of Scientific Discovery* (1934), saying scientific "truth" cannot be absolutely confirmed. Other works include *The Poverty of Historicism* (1957), *Conjectures and Refutations* (1963) and *Objective Knowledge* (1972).

poppy Any of about 100 species of annual or perennial plants of the genus *Papaver*. They have bright red, orange or white flowers, often with dark centres, with four thin, overlapping petals and two thick sepals; all produce the milky sap, LATEX. The unripe capsules of the Asian opium poppy are used to produce the drug OPIUM.

popular front Alliance of left-wing political parties. In Europe, such alliances were formed in the 1930s, partly in reaction to threats from the extreme right and with the encouragement of the Soviet Union. A popular-front government came to power in France, under Léon BLUM (1936–37), and in Spain (1936), where it provoked a civil war.

porcelain White, glass-like, non-porous, hard, translucent ceramic material. Porcelain is widely used for tableware, decorative objects, laboratory equipment and electrical insulators. It was developed by the Chinese in the 7th or 8th century. True or hard-paste porcelain is made of kaolin (white china clay) mixed with powdered petuntse (FELDSPAR) fired at *c*.1,400°C (2,550°F).

porcupine Short-legged, mostly nocturnal herbivorous rodent with erectile, defensive quills in its back. Old World porcupines of the family Hystricidae have brown to black fur with white-banded quills and are terrestrial. New World porcupines of the family Erethizontidae are smaller with yellow to white quills and are arboreal.

porphyria Group of rare genetic disorders in which there is defective METABOLISM of one or more porphyrins, the breakdown products of HAEMOGLOBIN. It can produce a wide range of effects, includng intestinal upset, HYPERTENSION, weakness, abnormal skin reactions to sunlight and mental disturbance. A key diagnostic indicator is that the patient's urine turns reddish-brown. There is no specific remedy and treatment tends to be supportive.

porpoise Small, toothed whale with a blunt snout. The best known is the common porpoise of the Northern Hemisphere. Its body is black above and white below. Length: to 1.5m (5ft). Family Delphinidae; species *Phocaena phocaena*.

port Fortified wine produced in the Douro Valley in N Portugal. It may be white, tawny, or red, and contains 17–20% alcohol.

Port-au-Prince Capital of Haiti, a port on the SE shore of the Gulf of Gonâve, on the w coast of Hispaniola. It was founded by the French in 1749, becoming the capital in 1770. Industries: tobacco, textiles, coffee, sugar. Pop. (1992) 1,255,078.

Porter, Cole (1891–1964) US composer and lyricist. His hugely successful musicals include *Gay Divorcee* (1932), *Anything Goes* (1934), *Kiss me Kate* (1948) and *High Society* (1956). Among his most popular songs are "Night and Day", "Let's Do It" and "Begin the Beguine".

Porter, Katherine Anne (1890–1980) US author. She won acclaim with her first collection of short stories, *Flowering Judas* (1930). Subsequent works include *Pale Horse, Pale Rider* (1939), *The Leaning Tower* (1944), and her best-known work, *Ship of Fools* (1962).

Portland City and port on the Willamette River, NW Oregon. First settled in 1845, it developed as a major port after 1850. It was a supply station for the California goldfields and the Alaska gold rush (1897–1900). It is Oregon's largest city. Industries: shipbuilding, timber, wood products, textiles, metals, machinery. Pop. (1990) 437,319.

Port Louis Capital of Mauritius, a seaport in the NW of the island. It was founded by the French in 1735. Taken by the British during the Napoleonic Wars, it grew in importance as a trading port after the opening of the Suez Canal. The main export is sugar. Pop. (1993) 144,250.

Port Moresby Capital of Papua New Guinea, on the SE coast of New Guinea. Settled by the British in the 1880s, its sheltered harbour was the site of an important Allied base in World War 2. Exports: gold, copper, rubber. Pop. (1990) 193,242.

Port of Spain Capital of Trinidad and Tobago, on the NW coast of Trinidad. Founded by the Spanish in the late 16th century, it was seized by Britain in 1797. From 1958–62 it was the capital of the Federation of the West Indies. It is a major Caribbean tourist and shipping centre. Pop. (1990) 58,400.

Porto-Novo Capital of Benin, West Africa, a port on the Gulf of Guinea. Settled by 16th-century Portuguese traders, it later became a shipping point for slaves to America. It was made the capital of independent Benin in 1960, but COTONOU is assuming increasing importance. Exports: palm oil, cotton, kapok. Pop. (1982) 208,258.

Portsmouth City and seaport in Hampshire, S England; Britain's principal naval base. First settled in the late 12th century, it was already a base for warships when the naval dockyard was laid down in 1496. Industries: engineering, ship repairing, electronics. Pop. (1991) 174,697.

Portugal Republic on the w of the Iberian Peninsula, SW Europe, the capital is LISBON. **Land and climate** Portugal lies on the w side of the IBERIAN PENINSULA. The Atlantic coastal plain includes Lisbon and OPORTO. In the S lies the ALGARVE. In central Portugal, the Serra da Estrela contains Portugal's highest peak, at 1,991m (6,352ft). The TAGUS and DOURO river valleys support most of Portugal's agriculture. Portugal also includes the autonomous islands of the AZORES and MADEIRA. The overseas territory of MACAU will return to China in 1999. Compared to other Mediterranean lands, summers are cooler and winters are milder. Forests cover *c*.36% of Portugal. It is the world's leading producer of cork. **Economy** Portugal joined the European Exchange Rate Mechanism in 1992. Manufacturing accounts for 33% of exports. Textiles, footwear and clothing are major exports. Portugal is the world's fifth-largest producer of tungsten. Agriculture and fishing remain important. Portugal is the world's eighth-largest producer of wine. Olives, potatoes, and wheat are also grown. Tourism is a rapidly growing sector (1992 receipts, US$3.7 million). **History and politics** Visigoths conquered the region in the 5th century AD. In 711 they were ejected by the Moors. In 1139 Alfonso I defeated the Moors. Portugal's independence was recognized by Spain in 1143. The reconquest was completed in 1249, when the Moors were removed from the Algarve. JOHN I founded the Aviz dynasty in 1385 and launched Portugal's colonial and maritime expansion. His son, HENRY THE NAVIGATOR, captured the Azores and Madeira. The reign of Manuel I was Portugal's "golden age". By 1510 Portugal had established colonies in Africa, Asia and South America. The fall of the Aviz dynasty brought PHILIP II of Spain to the throne. For the next 60 years, Portugal was subject to Spanish control. JOHN IV established the BRAGANZA dynasty (1640–1910). In the 18th century Marquês de POMBAL reformed Portugal's institutions and rebuilt Lis-

---

PORTUGAL
AREA: 92,390sq km (35,670sq mi)
POPULATION: 9,846,000
CAPITAL (POPULATION): Lisbon (2,561,000)
GOVERNMENT: Multiparty republic
ETHNIC GROUPS: Portuguese 99%, Cape Verdean, Brazilian, Spanish, British
LANGUAGES: Portuguese (official)
RELIGIONS: Christianity (Roman Catholic 95%, other Christians 2%)
CURRENCY: Escudo = 100 centavos

bon. JOHN VI was forced to flee to Brazil during the PENINSULA WAR (1808–14). His son, PEDRO I, declared Brazilian independence in 1722. In 1910 Portugal became a republic. In 1926 a military coup overthrew the government. Antonio de Oliveira SALAZAR became prime minister in 1932. The terms of the 1933 constitution enabled Salazar to become Western Europe's longest-serving dictator. The *Estado Novo* (New State) was repressive and the economy stagnated. In 1968 Salazar was replaced by Marcello Caetano. Failure to liberalize the regime and the cost of fighting liberation movements in its African colonies led to a military coup in 1974. In 1975 many Portuguese colonies gained independence. In 1976 a new liberal constitution was adopted. In 1986 Portugal joined the European Community and Marco Soares became president. The Portuguese economy emerged from recession. In 1996 Soares was replaced by Jorge Sampaio.

Portuguese National language of both Portugal and Brazil, spoken by about 10 million people in the former and 100 million in the latter. Another 15 million people speak it in Angola, Mozambique and other former Portuguese colonies. A ROMANCE LANGUAGE, it is closely related to Spanish.

Portuguese man-of-war Colonial COELENTERATE animal found in marine subtropical and tropical waters. It has a bright blue gas float and long, trailing tentacles with poisonous stinging cells. It is not a true jellyfish: the tentacles are a cluster of several kinds of modified medusae and POLYPS. Length: to 18m (60ft). Class Hydrozoa; genus *Physalia*.

Poseidon In Greek mythology, god of all waters, and brother of Zeus and Hades, identified with the Roman god NEPTUNE. Poseidon controlled the monsters of the deep, created the horse (he was the father of PEGASUS) and sired Orion and Polyphemus. He is always represented holding a trident.

positivism Philosophical doctrine asserting that "positive" knowledge (definite or scientific facts) can be obtained through direct experience. Positivism was first proposed by Auguste COMTE and was a dominant system of 19th-century philosophy. LOGICAL POSITIVISM was developed in the 20th century, initially by the philosophers of the Vienna Circle, as an attempt to link "positive knowledge" to the strict application of logic.

positron Particle that is identical to the ELECTRON, except that it is positively charged, making it the antiparticle of the electron. It was observed in 1932 in cosmic RADIATION by Carl Anderson. It is also emitted from certain radioactive nucleii. Electron-positron pairs can be produced when GAMMA RADIATION interacts with matter. *See also* ELEMENTARY PARTICLE

positron emission tomography (PET) Medical imaging technique (used particularly on the brain) that produces three-dimensional images. Radioisotopes, injected into the bloodstream prior to imaging, are taken up by tissues where they emit POSITRONS that produce detectable photons.

possum Popular name for any of the PHALANGERS of Australasia.

post-impressionism Various movements in painting that developed (*c*.1880–*c*.1905), especially in France, as a result of or reaction to IMPRESSIONISM. Roger Fry, the British painter and theorist, invented the term when he organized the exhibition *Manet and the post-impressionists* in London (1910). SEURAT was an important member of the post-impressionists, although his style is more accurately described as NEO-IMPRESSIONISM. A common characteristic is the rejection of impressionist NATURALISM.

post-modernism Originally, an architectural movement that started in the 1970s in reaction to the monotony of international MODERNISM. Its exponents sought new ways to merge anthropomorphic details or traditional design elements with 20th-century technology. The term is no longer restricted to architecture. In literature, post-modernism is characterized by works that refer to their own fictionality. In the early 1980s the concept of post-modernism exploded into popular culture. *See also* DECONSTRUCTION

post-natal depression Mood disorder, characterized by intense sadness, which may develop in a mother shortly after childbirth. It ranges from the "baby blues", which are usually short-lived, to the severe depressive illness known as puerperal psychosis.

Post Office UK public corporation formed in 1969 from the General Post Office (GPO). Mail delivery, its sole function until the 19th century, is still a Post Office monopoly. Private post, at rates related to distance, was first delivered in 1635; HILL's penny post of 1840 standardized the rate.

post-traumatic stress disorder Anxiety condition that may develop in people who have been involved in or witnessed some horrific event. It is commonly seen in survivors of battles or major disasters. The condition is characterized by repeated flashbacks to distressing events, hallucinations, nightmares, insomnia, edginess and depression. It usually recedes over time, but as many as 10% of sufferers are left with permanent disability.

potash Any of several potassium compounds, especially potassium oxide (K_2O), potassium carbonate (K_2CO_3) and potassium hydroxide (KOH). Potash is mined for use as fertilizer because potassium is an essential element for plant growth. Potassium carbonate is used for making soap and glass, and potassium hydroxide for soap and detergents.

potassium Common metallic element (symbol K) first isolated in 1807 by Sir Humphry DAVY. Its chief ores are sylvite, carnallite and polyhalite. Chemically it resembles sodium. Potassium in the form of POTASH is used as a fertilizer. The natural element contains a radioisotope K^{40} (half-life 1.3×10^9 yr), which is used in the radioactive dating of rocks. Properties: at. no. 19; at. wt. 39.102; density 0.86; m.p. 63.65°C (146.6°F); b.p. 774°C

(1,425°F); most common isotope K^{39} (93.1%). *See also* ALKALI METALS

potato Plant native to Central and South America and introduced into Europe in the 16th century. Best grown in a moist, cool climate, it has oval leaves and violet, pink or white flowers. The potato is an edible TUBER. The leaves and green potatoes contain the alkaloid solanine and are poisonous if eaten raw. Family Solanaceae; species *Solanum tuberosum.*

potential difference Difference in electric potential between two points in a circuit or electric field, usually expressed in volts. It is equal to the work done to move a unit electric charge from one of the points to the other. *See also* ELECTROMOTIVE FORCE (EMF)

potential energy Type of ENERGY an object possesses because of its vertical position in the Earth's gravitational field; also the energy stored in a system such as a compressed spring, or in an oscillating system (pendulum). An object on a shelf has potential energy mgh, where m is mass, g the acceleration due to gravity, and h the height of the shelf.

Potsdam Conference (July–August 1945) Summit meeting of Allied leaders in World War 2 held in Potsdam, Germany. The main participants were US President TRUMAN, Soviet leader STALIN and the British prime minister, at first CHURCHILL, later ATTLEE. It dealt with problems arising from Germany's defeat, including the arrangements for military occupation and the trial of war criminals, and issued an ultimatum to Japan demanding surrender.

Potter, Beatrix (1866–1943) British children's author who created the characters of Peter Rabbit, Jemima Puddleduck, Squirrel Nutkin and others. Her first books were *The Tale of Peter Rabbit* (1901) and *The Tailor of Gloucester* (1902).

Potter, Dennis (1935–94) British playwright. He is best known for his television plays, notably *Brimstone and Treacle* (1976), *Pennies from Heaven* (1978), *Blue Remembered Hills* (1979) and *The Singing Detective* (1986). His unusual approach to dramatic form and his use of direct language often aroused controversy.

pottery Objects shaped of clay and hardened by fire or dried in the sun. The making of pottery is dependent on the plasticity and durability of clay after firing. The finished object can be divided into three categories: earthenware, baked at 700°C (1,292°F) or lower; stoneware, fired at up to 1,150°C (2,102°F); and PORCELAIN, fired at 1,400°C (2,552°F).

potto Slow-moving African primate with large eyes and a pointed face; it is nocturnal and arboreal. The common potto has sturdy limbs, a short tail and small spines formed by the neck vertebrae. Its woolly fur is grey-red. Length: 37cm (15in), excluding the tail. Species *Perodicticus potto.*

Poulenc, Francis (1899–1963) French composer. Spontaneity characterizes his works, which include ballets, notably *Les Biches* (1923), orchestral works, chamber music, piano music and songs.

poultry Collective term for domestic fowl reared as a source of meat and eggs. Chickens are the most important domesticated bird in the world. They are the major source of eggs and an important meat source. Males are known as cocks; females as hens; and castrated males as capons. Species *Gallus domesticus*. Other forms of poultry are DUCK, GOOSE, GUINEA FOWL and TURKEY.

Pound, Ezra Loomis (1885–1972) US poet and critic. He spent much of his life in Europe where his earliest works, *Exultations* (1909) and *Personae* (1909), attracted critical acclaim. From 1924 he made his home in Italy and on the outbreak of war between the USA and Italy supported the Italians. He was later arrested for treason, but was judged unfit to stand trial and confined to a mental hospital (1946–58). His major works include *Homage to Sextus Propertius* (1917) and *Cantos* (1925–60).

pound Imperial unit of weight equal to 0.453kg. It became a unit of currency when a pound weight of silver was divided into 240 pennies. Sterling has been the English currency since the Middle Ages.

Poussin, Nicolas (1594–1665) French painter who worked mainly in Rome. At first inspired by MANNERISM, he later specialized in mythological subjects. In the late 1630s he turned to more elaborate Old Testament and historical themes. Notable works include *The Seven Sacraments* (1648).

Powell, Anthony Dymoke (1905–) British novelist. He is best known for *A Dance to The Music of Time*, a series of 12 novels that portray the snobbish world of the English upper classes after World War 1. His later work includes *The Fisher King* (1986).

Powell, Cecil Frank (1903–69) British physicist. During the 1930s, he developed a technique to record SUBATOMIC PARTICLES directly onto film. In 1947 he used this method at high altitude to investigate cosmic RADIATION and discovered a new particle, the pi MESON. Powell subsequently discovered the antiparticle of the pion and the decay process of K mesons. He was awarded the 1950 Nobel Prize for physics.

Powell, Michael and **Pressburger, Emeric** Powell (1905–90) and Pressburger (1902–88) were one of the most influential director/screenwriter partnerships in cinema history. Their collaboration began with *The Spy in Black* (1939). Their wartime films, such as *The Life and Death of Colonel Blimp* (1943), *A Canterbury Tale* (1944) and *A Matter of Life and Death* (1946), were intended as propaganda pieces. Other classics include *Black Narcissus* (1946) and *The Red Shoes* (1948).

power In physics, rate of doing work or of producing or consuming energy. It is a measure of the output of an engine or other power source. James WATT was the first to measure power; he used the unit called HORSEPOWER. The modern unit of power is the WATT.

Powys County in E central Wales; the administrative centre is Llandrindod Wells. There are Iron

Age and Roman remains. Offa's Dyke and the later Norman castles were built as border defences by the Welsh and English. Powys is drained by the Usk, Wye and Taff rivers. Agriculture and forestry are the main occupations. Area: 5,077sq km (1,960sq mi). Pop. (1991) 117,647.

Poznań City on the Warta River, W Poland. One of the oldest Polish cities, it became the seat of the first Polish bishopric in 968. The Grand Duchy of Poznań was created in 1815 as part of Prussia, but the area reverted to Poland in 1919. Industries: metallurgy, agricultural machinery, electrical equipment, chemicals, textiles. Pop. (1993) 589,700.

pragmatism Philosophical school holding the view that the truth of a proposition has no absolute standing but depends on its practical value or use. It was first proposed by C. S. PEIRCE and was adopted by William JAMES and John DEWEY.

Prague (Praha) Capital of the Czech Republic, on the River Vltava. Founded in the 9th century, it grew rapidly after Wenceslaus I established a German settlement in 1232. In the 14th century it was the capital of BOHEMIA. Prague was the capital of the Czechoslovak republic (1918–93). It was occupied throughout World War 2 by the Germans and liberated by Soviet troops in 1945. Prague was the centre of Czech resistance to the Soviet invasion in 1968. It is an important commercial centre. Industries: engineering, iron and steel, chemicals, glass, furniture, printing. Pop. (1990) 1,215,000.

Prague Spring (1968) Short-lived political and social reorganization in Czechoslovakia. From 1945 Czechoslovakia was subject to hardline Soviet communism. In January 1968 Alexander DUBČEK gained power and initiated reforms intended to create "socialism with a human face". Political prisoners were freed, censorship abolished, the power of central bureaucracy curbed and non-communist parties legalized. In August, Soviet tanks imposed a Soviet occupation on a powerless populace.

prairie Region of treeless plain. The prairies of North America extend from Ohio through Indiana, Illinois and Iowa to the Great Plains, and N into Canada. The pampas of S South America, the llanos of N South America and the steppes of central Europe and Asia are also prairies.

praseodymium Silver-yellow metallic element (symbol Pr) of the LANTHANIDE SERIES. It was first isolated in 1885. Its chief ores are monazite and bastnasite. Soft, malleable and ductile, praseodymium is used in carbon electrodes for arc lamps, and its green salts are used in coloured glasses, ceramics and enamels. Properties: at.no.59; r.a.m. 140.9077; r.d. 6.77; m.p. 931°C (1,708°F); b.p. 3,512°C (6,354°F); only one isotope Pr^{141} (100%).

prawn Any of numerous species of edible crustaceans in the order Decapoda; it is generally larger than a SHRIMP but smaller than a LOBSTER. Typical genera include *Penaeus*, *Pandalus*, *Crangon* and *Nephrops*, which includes the Dublin bay prawn or Norway lobster. Large prawns are called scampi.

prayer Act of thanking, adoring, conferring with or petitioning a divine power; also the form of words used for this purpose. In some religions, it is customary to kneel in prayer, while in others people stand, sit or lie prone while praying. Muslims recite prayers while facing in the direction of MECCA. In Christianity, the service book of the Anglican Communion is known as the Book of COMMON PRAYER. Among Roman Catholics, such regulated forms are found in a missal. Prayer can also be the private devotional act of an individual.

praying mantis *See* MANTIS

Precambrian Oldest and longest era of Earth's history, lasting from the formation of the Earth c.4,600 million years ago to the beginning of a good fossil record c.590 million years ago. Precambrian fossils are extremely rare. Primitive bacteria and CYANOBACTERIA have been identified in deposits more than 3,000 million years old.

precession Wobble of the axis of a spinning object. It occurs as a result of the torque on the spin axis, which increases as the angle of precession increases. The Earth precesses about a line through its centre and perpendicular to the plane of the ECLIPTIC extremely slowly (a complete revolution taking 25,800 years) at an angle of 23.5°. The motion of a GYROSCOPE is another consequence of precession.

precipitate Formation of an insoluble solid in a liquid either by direct reaction or by varying the liquid composition to diminish the solubility of a dissolved compound.

precipitation In meteorology, all forms of water particles, whether liquid or solid, that fall from the atmosphere to the ground. Distinguished from cloud, fog, dew and frost, precipitation includes rain, drizzle, snow and hail.

pre-Columbian art and architecture Arts of Mexico, Central America and the Andean region of South America before colonization. In the MAYA period, beginning c.200 AD, many cities or ceremonial centres were built in Central America. Their pyramid temples were succeeded by TOLTEC and AZTEC civilizations in the post-classical period (AD 900–1300). In the Andean region, the INCA constructed rich temples in the 14th century.

predestination Doctrine that a person's ultimate spiritual salvation or condemnation by God has been ordained in advance. As possible solutions to the problem of how this doctrine affects free will, three propositions have been put forward: the first is to refute the doctrine altogether (Pelagianism); the second is to state that God never intended to save everybody (Predestinaranism); and the third is to qualify the premise by seeing God's prevision subject to possible revision depending on the will and spirituality of the individual. This last position is the solution to which most Christians adhere. The concept is also found in ISLAM.

pregnancy Period of time from conception until birth, in humans normally about 40 weeks (280 days). It is generally divided into three 3-month periods called trimesters. In the first trimester, the EMBRYO grows into a FETUS *c*.7.6cm (3in) in length. At the beginning of the second trimester movements are first felt and the fetus grows to about 36cm (14in). In the third trimester the fetus attains its full body weight. *See also* LABOUR

prehistory Term to describe the period of human cultural development before the invention of writing. *See* BRONZE AGE; IRON AGE; MESOLITHIC; NEOLITHIC; PALAEOLITHIC; STONE AGE

premature birth Birth of a baby prior to 37 weeks' gestation or weighing less than 2.5kg (5.5lb). Premature babies are more at risk than those born at full term and often require special care.

Pre-Raphaelite Brotherhood (PRB) Name
adopted in 1848 by a group of young English painters who joined forces to revitalize British art. The most prominent members of the PRB were Dante Gabriel ROSSETTI, John Everett MILLAIS and William Holman HUNT. They attracted fierce criticism for their rejection of RAPHAEL but were helped by John RUSKIN. By 1853 the PRB had largely dissolved but Rossetti maintained the name, and under his influence a second wave of Pre-Raphaelite painting began in the 1860s, which lasted well into the 20th century. *See also* MORRIS, WILLIAM

Presbyterianism Major form of Protestant Christianity that became the national CHURCH OF SCOTLAND in 1690. It arose in the mid-16th century from the teachings of John CALVIN in Switzerland, and was taken to Britain by the Scottish religious reformer John KNOX. In 1972 the Presbyterian Church of England (formed 1876) united with the CONGREGATIONAL Church of England and Wales. There are Presbyterian Churches all over the world, particularly in North America.

Prescott, John Leslie (1938–) British politician, deputy prime minister and secretary of state for transport and the environment (1997–). Prescott became a Labour MP in 1970; from 1975–79 he simultaneously served as a member of the European Parliament. He became deputy leader of the Labour Party when Tony BLAIR succeeded John Smith as leader (1994).

Presley, Elvis (1935–77) US singer who dominated rock and roll for a decade after his first recordings in 1953. "Jailhouse Rock", "Hound Dog", "Heartbreak Hotel" and "Love Me Tender" are among his most successful songs. He also starred in films, such as *Love Me Tender* (1956) and *Follow That Dream* (1962).

pressure In physics, the force on an object's surface divided by the area of the surface. The SI unit is the pascal (symbol Pa); 1 pascal is equal to the pressure exerted by a force of 1 newton on an area of $1m^2$. In meteorology, the millibar (symbol mb), which equals 100 pascals, is commonly used.

Prester John Legendary ruler of a Christian kingdom in Asia in the Middle Ages. European Christians hoped to make an alliance with him against the Muslims in the CRUSADES.

Pretoria City in Gauteng province, South Africa. It was founded in 1855 by Marthinus Pretorius. It became the capital of the Transvaal in 1860 and of the South African Republic in 1881. The Peace of Vereeniging, which ended the Boer War, was signed here in 1902. In 1910 it became the capital of the Union of South Africa. Pretoria is an important communications centre. Industries: steel, cars, railway engineering, diamonds. Pop. (1990) 1,080,187.

Previn, André George (1929–) US conductor, pianist and composer, b. Germany. His early career was as a jazz pianist and musical director of Hollywood film scores. He was principal conductor of the London Symphony Orchestra (1968–79). He became music director of the Los Angeles Philharmonic Orchestra in 1986.

Prévost d'Exiles, Antoine François (1697–1763) (L'abbé Prévost) French novelist who lived as, alternately, a Jesuit novice, soldier and forger. His most famous work, *Manon Lescaut* (1731), is the seventh novel of a series *Mémoires et aventures d'un homme de qualité* (1728–31).

Priam In Greek legend, the king of Troy at the time of the war with Greece. He had been installed as king by HERACLES, but by the time of the Ten Years' War was an old man. His sons HECTOR and PARIS were killed by the Greeks. He was killed by Neoptolemus, the son of ACHILLES.

prickly heat Skin rash caused by blockage of the sweat glands in hot, humid weather. It occurs most often in infants and obese people.

prickly pear CACTUS with flat or cylindrical joints. It grows in North and South America and has been introduced into Europe, Africa and Australia. The jointed pads have tufts of bristles, and the edible fruit is red and pulpy. Family Cactaceae; genus *Opuntia*.

Pride's purge (1648) Expulsion of *c*.140 members from the English LONG PARLIAMENT. It was carried out by Colonel Thomas Pride (d.1658) on the orders of the army council. The aim was to rid Parliament of members still anxious to negotiate with CHARLES I. The remnant, known as the RUMP PARLIAMENT, voted to put Charles on trial.

Priestley, J.B. (John Boynton) (1894–1984) British author and literary critic. His novels include *The Good Companions* (1929), *Angel Pavement* (1930) and *Bright Day* (1946). Among his plays are *Time and the Conways* (1937) and *An Inspector Calls* (1945), both of which explore his theories of time, and *The Glass Cage* (1957).

Priestley, Joseph (1733–1804) British chemist and clergyman who discovered OXYGEN in 1774. He also discoved a number of other gases, including AMMONIA and oxides of NITROGEN. He studied the properties of CARBON DIOXIDE. Priestley was an advocate of the later discredited phlogiston theory.

primary school School providing elementary education for children from compulsory school age.

In the UK, primary school education starts at five, and children progress to secondary schools at 11 or 12. Primary schools cater for children throughout key stages 1 and 2 of the National Curriculum.

primates Order of mammals that includes MONKEYS, APES and HUMAN beings. Primates, native to most tropical and sub-tropical regions, are mostly herbivorous, diurnal, or arboreal animals. Their hands and feet, usually with flat nails instead of claws, are adapted for grasping. Most species have opposable thumbs, and all but humans have opposable big toes. They have a poor sense of smell, good hearing and acute binocular vision. The outstanding feature of primates is a large complex brain and high intelligence. Primate characteristics are less pronounced in the relatively primitive prosimians (including BUSHBABIES, LORISES and TARSIERS) and are most pronounced in the more numerous and advanced anthropoids (such as human beings).

prime minister Chief executive and head of government in a country with a parliamentary system. He or she is usually the leader of the largest political party in PARLIAMENT. The office evolved in Britain in the 18th century, along with the CABINET system and the shift of power away from the crown towards the House of Commons.

prime number Positive or negative integer, excluding one and zero, that has no FACTORS other than itself or one. Examples are 2, 3, 5, 7, 11, 13 and 17. The integers 4, 6, 8,... are not prime numbers because they can be expressed as the product of two or more primes.

primitivism Russian form of EXPRESSIONISM. It developed c.1905–20 and was influenced by Russian folk art, FAUVISM and CUBISM. It was characterized by simplified forms and powerful colour, used principally to depict scenes from working-class life. MALEVICH worked in the style early in his career.

Primo de Rivera, Miguel (1870–1930) Spanish dictator (1923–30). He staged a coup in 1923 with the support of King ALFONSO XIII. He dissolved parliament and established a military dictatorship. He restored order, stimulated economic improvement and helped to end the revolt of Abdel-Krim in Morocco (1926).

primrose Any of numerous species of herbaceous, generally perennial plants of the genus *Primula*, which grow in the cooler climates of Europe, Asia, Ethiopia, Java and North America. It has a tuft of leaves rising from the rootstock and clustered flowers of pale yellow to deep crimson. In Britain, it refers to *Primula vulgaris*. Family Primulaceae.

Prince Edward Island Province in E Canada, an island in the Gulf of St Lawrence off the coast of New Brunswick and Nova Scotia; the capital is Charlottetown. The island was discovered by Jacques CARTIER in 1534. Ceded to Britain in 1763, it became a province of Canada in 1873. Fishing and agriculture are the most important economic activities. Area: 5,657sq km (2,184sq mi). Pop. (1993 est.) 131,600.

printed circuit Network of electrical conductors chemically etched from a layer of copper foil on a board of insulating material such as plastic, glass or ceramic. It interconnects components such as capacitors, resistors and integrated circuits (CHIPS). The printed circuit board (PCB) represents one stage in the miniaturization of electronic circuits.

printing Technique for multiple reproduction of images, such as text and pictures. In ancient China and Japan carved wooden blocks were inked to print pictures. From the 10th century, the Chinese used separate pieces of type. Metal type made by casting first appeared in Korea around 1403. In Europe, GUTENBERG and CAXTON developed the use of letterpress in the 1400s. Printing expanded rapidly in the 1700s and 1800s. LITHOGRAPHY enabled printers to produce impressive colour prints. For text, stereotype printing plates were cast from the pages of type, so that the type could be reused for setting other pages. TYPESETTING machines speeded up the process of setting up pages. The invention of photography in the 1820s led to the development of new techniques for reproducing photographs, such as the HALFTONE PROCESS. More recently, production speeds have greatly increased with the use of photosetting, in which the type is set photographically on sheet film, and OFFSET printing. Today, many publications are produced using desktop publishing (DTP) programs, which allow text and pictures to be arranged on screen. The computer data is used to print sheet film, and the film images are transferred to printing plates.

prion Infective agent that appears to consist simply of a protein. Prions are thought to cause diseases such as CREUTZFELD-JAKOB DISEASE (CJD) in humans, BOVINE SPONGIFORM ENCEPHALOPATHY (BSE) in cattle, and SCRAPIE in sheep. It is not yet understood how prions work.

prism In mathematics, a solid geometrical figure whose ends are congruent (most commonly triangles) and perpendicular to the length, with the other faces rectangles. The volume of a prism is equal to the area of the end multiplied by the length of the prism. In physics, a prism is a piece of transparent material, such as glass, plastic or quartz, in which light is refracted and split into its component colours (spectrum) by dispersion.

privateer Privately owned vessel with a government commission to capture enemy shipping. Their government licences, called letters of marque, distinguished privateers from pirates. Crews were unpaid but were allowed to keep the booty. Privateering was at its height from the 16th to the 18th century. It was outlawed by most European powers in the Declaration of Paris (1856).

privatization Transfer of state-run enterprises to private ownership. It is the opposite of NATIONALIZATION. In the 1980s policy-makers in some European countries, as well as Canada, Japan and New Zealand, maintained that economic growth would best be encouraged by governments selling nationalized industries to private enterprises, which were then free to respond to market forces and create a more competitive company. By the late 1980s and early 1990s the trend was taken up by many former Eastern Bloc countries.

Privy Council Group of leading advisers to the British monarch. It developed in the Middle Ages out of the King's Council (Curia Regis). As the CABINET system of government developed, the Privy Council became increasingly restricted in its powers. Its Judicial Committee, established by legislation in 1833, is the final appeal court for most Commonwealth countries.

probability Number representing the likelihood of a given occurrence. The probability of a specified event is the number of ways that event may occur divided by the total possible number of outcomes, assuming that each possibility is equally likely.

probation In Britain, sentence of a court of law on a person aged 17 or over that allows the offender to remain at liberty subject to certain conditions and under the supervision of a probation officer. It is not regarded as a conviction. The sentence may last from one to three years, and breach of probation is an offence.

production In economics, methods by which wealth is produced. It is one of the basic principles of economics. The factors of production are land, labour and capital.

progesterone Steroid HORMONE secreted mainly by the corpus luteum of the mammalian OVARY and by the PLACENTA during pregnancy. Its principal function is to prepare and maintain the inner lining (endometrium) of a UTERUS for pregnancy. Synthetic progesterone is one of the main components of the contraceptive PILL.

program (SOFTWARE) Set of instructions that enables a COMPUTER to carry out a task. A typical computer can carry out many tasks, such as word processing, calculating, drawing, and providing games. Programs can be written in a variety of COMPUTER LANGUAGES and are usually stored on a magnetic DISK. To make a computer perform a particular task, a program is loaded into the computer's RAM.

programme music (illustrative music) Music that aims to describe a scene or tell a story. It may be contrasted with absolute music. Programme music is an essential concept in the music of the romantic period; perhaps the earliest example from this time is BEETHOVEN's 6th Symphony (The Pastoral). See also ROMANTICISM

progressive education Movement that began in the late 19th century in Europe and the USA, as a reaction to formal traditional education. In Europe FROEBEL and MONTESSORI were influential in the movement, which aimed to educate "the whole child". In the USA the movement owed much to the philosophy of John DEWEY. It led in some cases to what critics termed laxness, and produced a backlash in the form of the "back to basics" movement.

prohibition (1919–33) Period in US history when the manufacture, sale and transport of alcoholic drinks were prohibited. It was instituted by the 18th amendment of the US constitution, confirmed by the Volstead Act. Smuggling, corruption of civil servants and police, and the growth of organized crime financed by BOOTLEGGING made it a failure. Prohibition was repealed by the 21st amendment.

projector Instrument with a lens system, used to cast images onto a screen from an illuminated flat object. An **episcope** is a projector for opaque objects such as a printed page; it uses light that is reflected from the object. A **diascope** is a projector for transparent objects such as photographic slides; it uses light transmitted through the object. An **epidiascope** can project images from both transparent and opaque objects. A motion-picture or **cine** projector produces moving images from many frames (pictures) on a transparent film.

Prokaryotae (formerly Monera) Biological KINGDOM that includes BACTERIA and CYANOBACTERIA (formerly blue-green algae). They have more simple cells than other organisms. DNA is not contained in chromosomes in the NUCLEUS, but lies in a distinct part of the CYTOPLASM called the nucleoid. They have no distinct membrane-surrounded structures (organelles). Cell division is simple and in the rare cases where SEXUAL REPRODUCTION occurs, genetic material is simply transferred from one partner to another; there are no separate sex cells. In photosynthetic prokaryotes, PHOTOSYNTHESIS takes place on the cell membrane. At present two subkingdoms are recognized: ARCHAEBACTERIA and EUBACTERIA. See also ASEXUAL REPRODUCTION; EUKARYOTE; SYMBIOSIS

Prokofiev, Sergei (1891–1953) Russian composer. His style is characterized by biting dissonances within rich harmony, and brilliant orchestration. His most popular works include the ballets *Romeo and Juliet* (1935) and *Cinderella* (1944); the *Classical* (first) Symphony (1918); *Peter and the Wolf* (1936); and the comic opera *The Love for Three Oranges* (1921). He also wrote film scores.

prolapse Displacement of an organ due to weakening of supporting tissues. It most often affects the rectum, due to bowel problems, or the UTERUS following repeated pregnancies.

Prometheus In Greek mythology, the fire-giver. He created humans, provided them with reason, and stole fire from the gods. For this theft, ZEUS had him chained to a rock where an eagle consumed his liver. In some myths he was rescued by HERACLES.

promethium Radioactive metallic element (symbol Pm) of the LANTHANIDE SERIES. It was made in 1941 by particle bombardment of NEODYMIUM and PRASEODYMIUM. Promethium occurs in traces in uranium ores. The isotope Pm^{147} is used in phosphorescent paints, x-rays and nuclear-powered batteries for space vehicles. Properties: at.no. 61; m.p. 1,080°C (1,976°F); b.p. 2,460°C (4,460°F); most stable isotope Pm^{145} (half-life 17.7 years).

pronghorn Only extant member of the family

Antilocapridae, related to the ANTELOPE. It is a horned, hoofed, herbivorous animal of w USA and N Mexico. The swiftest North American mammal, it is said to be capable of up to 80km/h (50mph). Height: 3ft (90cm); weight: 45kg (100lb).

propaganda Systematic manipulation of public opinion through the media. Although examples are found in ancient and early modern writings, the most effective propagandists in the 20th century have been totalitarian governments of industrialized states, who are able to control all means of public communication. Many political, economic and social organizations, and pressure groups of all kinds employ some kind of propaganda.

propane Colourless, flammable gas (C_3H_8), the third member of the ALKANE series of HYDROCARBONS. It occurs in natural gas, from which it is obtained; it is also obtained during petroleum refining. Propane is used as bottled gas, as a solvent and in the preparation of many chemicals. Properties: m.p. $-190°C$ ($-310°F$); b.p. $-42°C$ ($-43.6°F$).

propanol (propyl alcohol) Colourless ALCOHOL used as a solvent and in the manufacture of various chemicals. It exists as two ISOMERS. Normal propanol, $CH_3CH_2CH_2OH$, is a by-product of the synthesis of METHANOL. Isopropanol (isopropyl alcohol), $(CH_3)_2CHOH$, is a secondary alcohol that is easily oxidized into acetone.

propene (propylene) Colourless, aliphatic hydrocarbon, C_3H_6, manufactured by the cracking of ETHENE. It is used in the making of various chemicals, such as vinyl and acrylic resins. Properties: b.p. $-48°C$ ($-54.4°F$); m.p. $-185°C$ ($-301°F$).

prophet Individual who is thought to be a divinely inspired messenger from a god, or is believed to possess the power to foretell future events. The classic examples of prophets were the holy men who preached by the authority of YAHWEH in the Old Testament kingdoms of ISRAEL and JUDAH. It also applied to ABRAHAM, MOSES and SAMUEL. JOHN THE BAPTIST fulfilled the role of a New Testament prophet, predicting the coming of the Messiah. In ancient Greece and Rome, divinely inspired prophetesses made oracular pronouncements. Among Muslims, MUHAMMAD is held to be a prophet, the last of a long line of God's messengers, who included ADAM, Abraham, Moses and JESUS CHRIST. Many prophets have occurred in HINDUISM.

proportion Mathematical relation of equality between two ratios, having the form a/b = c/d. A continued proportion is a group of three or more quantities, each bearing the same ratio to its successor, as in 1:3:9:27:81.

proportional representation (PR) System of electoral representation in which the allocation of seats reflects the proportion of the vote commanded by each candidate or party. The main contrast is with a system in which representatives are elected for each of numerous single constituencies.

propylene See PROPENE

prose In LITERATURE, a relatively unstructured form of language. Unlike the metrical discipline of POETRY, prose is more closely connected with the rhythms of everyday speech. With the rise of 18th-century realism and the establishment of the modern novel as a distinctive literary form, prose embedded itself in the nature of fiction as a genre.

Proserpine Roman equivalent of PERSEPHONE

prostaglandin Series of related fatty acids, with hormone-like action, present in SEMEN, liver, brain and other tissues. Their biological effects include the lowering of blood pressure and the stimulation of contraction in a variety of smooth-muscle tissues, such as the UTERUS.

prostate gland Gland in the male reproductive tract surrounding the URETHRA. It secretes specific chemicals that mix with sperm cells and other secretions to make up SEMEN.

prosthesis Artificial substitute for a missing organ or part of the body. Until the 17th century, artificial limbs were made of wood or metal, but innovations in metallurgy, plastics and engineering have enabled lighter, jointed limbs to be made. More recent prosthetic devices include artificial heart valves made of silicone materials.

protactinium Rare radioactive metallic element (symbol Pa) of the ACTINIDE SERIES, first identified in 1913. Its chief source is URANINITE. Properties: at.no. 91; at.wt. 231.0359; s.g. 15.4; m.p. 1,200°C (2,192°F); b.p. 4,000°C (7,232°F); most stable isotope Pa^{231} (half-life $3.25x10^4$ yr).

Protectorate In English history, the period in which Oliver CROMWELL ruled as lord protector (1653–58), followed by his son Richard (1658–59).

protein Organic compound containing many AMINO ACIDS linked together by PEPTIDE bonds. Living cells use about 20 amino acids, which are present in varying amounts. The order of amino acids in proteins is controlled by the cell's RNA. The most important proteins are ENZYMES, which determine all the chemical reactions in the cell, and ANTIBODIES, which combat infection.

Protestantism Branch of Christianity formed in protest against the practices and doctrines of the old ROMAN CATHOLIC CHURCH. Protestants sought a vernacular Bible to replace the Latin VULGATE, and to express individual elements of nationalism. The movement is considered to have started when Martin LUTHER nailed his 95 theses to a Wittenberg church door. His predecessors included John WYCLIFFE and Jan HUS. Later supporters included Ulrich ZWINGLI and John CALVIN, whose interpretation of the Bible and concept of PREDESTINATION had great influence. The Protestants held the EUCHARIST to be a symbolic celebration, as opposed to the Roman Catholic dogma of TRANSUBSTANTIATION, and claimed that because Christ is the sole medium between God and man, his function cannot be displaced by priests. See also ANGLICANISM

Proteus In Greek mythology, a sea god, son of Oceanus and Tethys. Proteus possessed the gift of prophecy and the ability to alter his form at will.

Protista Former name of PROTOCTISTA kingdom

Protoctista Proposed classification of certain unicellular and simple multicellular organisms, including PROTOZOA, ALGAE, BACTERIA and FUNGI. The term was introduced to overcome the difficulty of distinguishing such organisms from the true plant and animal KINGDOMS (Plantae and Animalia). This kingdom may include organisms with many nuclei within one cell wall (coenocytes).

proton Stable ELEMENTARY PARTICLE (symbol p) with a positive charge equal in magnitude to the negative charge of the ELECTRON. It forms the nucleus of the lightest isotope of HYDROGEN, and with the NEUTRON is a constituent of the nuclei of all other elements. It is made up of three QUARKS. The proton is a BARYON with a mass 1836.12 times that of the electron. The number of protons in the nucleus of an element is equal to its ATOMIC NUMBER. Protons also occur in primary cosmic rays.

protoplasm Living contents of a plant or animal CELL. It includes both the NUCLEUS and the CYTOPLASM of cells.

protozoa Phylum of unicellular organisms found worldwide in marine or freshwater. These microscopic animals have the ability to move (by CILIA or pseudopodia) and have a nucleus, cytoplasm and cell wall; some contain CHLOROPHYLL. Reproduction is by FISSION or encystment. Length: 0.3mm (0.1in). The 30,000 species are divided into classes: Flagellata, Cnidospora, Ciliophora and Sporozoa.

Proudhon, Pierre Joseph (1809–65) French journalist and philosopher. His anarchist theories of liberty, equality and justice conflicted with the communism of Karl MARX. In *Qu'est-ce que la propriété?* (1840), he argued that "property is theft".

Proust, Marcel (1871–1922) French novelist whose *À la recherche du temps perdu* (1913–27) is regarded as one of the great works of literature. Proust was involved in the DREYFUS AFFAIR (1897–99), but ill-health caused him to withdraw from society and devote himself to writing.

Provençal Variety of the Occitan language, spoken in PROVENCE, SE France. It is a ROMANCE LANGUAGE belonging to the family of INDO-EUROPEAN LANGUAGES. It enjoyed a literary flowering in the Middle Ages as the language of the TROUBADOURS. Today, it is largely a spoken language.

Provence Region and former province of SE France, roughly corresponding to the present départements of Var, Vaucluse and Bouches-du-Rhône, and parts of Alpes-de-Haute-Provence and Alpes-Maritimes. The coastal area was settled *c.*600 BC by the Greeks, and the Romans established colonies (2nd century BC). The region came under Frankish control in the 6th century AD. It retained its distinctive identity and language (PROVENÇAL), and was the focus of a revival of secular literature and music in the Middle Ages. It was finally united with France in 1481. Tourism is the major industry.

Proverbs Book of the Old Testament, probably the oldest existing example of Hebrew WISDOM LITERATURE. The book's subtitle attributes its authorship to King SOLOMON, but scholars believe that it contains material from later periods.

Providence Capital of Rhode Island, USA, a port on Providence Bay in NE Rhode Island. The city was founded in 1636 as a refuge for religious dissenters from Massachusetts and played an active role in the American Revolution. Industries: jewellery, electrical equipment, silverware, machine tools, rubber goods. Pop. (1990) 160,728.

Proxima Centauri Nearest star to the Sun, slightly closer than the nearby star ALPHA CENTAURI. It was long thought to be part of the Alpha Centauri system, but some astronomers now believe it to be an unrelated star making a close approach.

prozac One of a small group of antidepressants, known as selective serotonin re-uptake inhibitors (SSRIs). They work by increasing levels of serotonin in the brain. Serotonin, or 5-hydroxytryptamine (5-HT), is a NEUROTRANSMITTER involved in a range of functions. Low levels of serotonin are associated with DEPRESSION. *See also* DRUG

Prussia Historic state of N Germany. The region was conquered by the TEUTONIC KNIGHTS in the 13th century. The duchy of Prussia, founded in the 15th century, passed to the electors of BRANDENBURG in 1618. Under FREDERICK WILLIAM I and FREDERICK II in the 18th century, Prussia became a strong military power, absorbing SILESIA and parts of Poland. After defeats as the NAPOLEONIC WARS, Prussia emerged again as a powerful state at the Congress of VIENNA (1815). In the 19th century Prussia displaced Austria as the leading German power and, under BISMARCK, led the movement for German unity, accomplished in 1871. Comprising 65% of the new German empire, it was the leading German state until World War 1. It ceased to exist as a political unit in 1945.

Przewalski's horse (Mongolian wild horse) Only surviving species of the original wild HORSE, found only in Mongolia and Sinkiang. It is small and stocky with an erect black mane. Height: to 1.5m (4.8ft) at the shoulder. Family Equidae; species *Equus caballus przewalskii*.

Psalms, Book of Book of the Old Testament, consisting of 150 hymns, lyric poems and prayers. The works were collected over a very long period, at least from the 10th to the 5th centuries BC, and probably achieved their final form before the 2nd century BC. Many were collected by King DAVID.

Pseudepigrapha Jewish writings of the period 200 BC–AD 200 that have been falsely attributed to a biblical author. They follow the style and content of authentic Old Testament works. The term refers more widely to almost all ancient Jewish texts that have not been accepted as canonical by the Christian Church. *See also* APOCRYPHA

pseudomorphism In mineralogy, chemical or structural alteration of a mineral without change in shape. It is exemplified by petrified wood: the wood has been gradually replaced by silica.

515

psittacosis (parrot fever) Disorder usually affecting the respiratory system of birds. Caused by a bacterium, it can be transmitted to human beings, producing pneumonia-like symptoms. Treatment is with ANTIBIOTICS.

psoriasis Chronic recurring skin disease featuring raised, red, scaly patches. The lesions frequently appear on the chest, knees, elbows and scalp. Treatment is with tar preparations, steroids and ultraviolet light. Psoriasis is sometimes associated with a form of ARTHRITIS.

psychiatry Analysis, diagnosis and treatment of mental illness and behavioural disorders. It includes research into the cause and prevention of mental disorders, and the administering of treatment, usually carried out by physical means such as drugs and electroconvulsive therapy.

psychoanalysis Method of therapy devised by FREUD and Josef Breuer in the 1890s for treating behaviour disorders, particularly NEUROSIS. It is characterized by its emphasis on the unconscious and on the treatment of mental disorder by the use of free association and the therapist's interpretation.

psychology Study of mental activity and behaviour. It includes the study of perception, thought, problem solving, personality, emotion, mental disorders and the adaptation of the individual to society. It overlaps with many other disciplines, including PHYSIOLOGY, PHILOSOPHY, ARTIFICIAL INTELLIGENCE and social ANTHROPOLOGY. Central areas of psychology include COGNITIVE PSYCHOLOGY, SOCIAL PSYCHOLOGY and DEVELOPMENTAL PSYCHOLOGY. Applied psychology aims to use the discipline's insights into human behaviour in practical fields such as education and industry.

psychopharmacology Study of how DRUGS affect behaviour. Drugs are classified according to their effect: sedative hypnotics, such as barbiturates and alcohol; stimulants, such as amphetamines; opiate narcotics, such as heroin; and psychedelics and hallucinogens, such as LSD.

psychosis Serious mental illness in which the patient loses contact with reality, in contrast to NEUROSIS. It may feature extreme mood swings, delusions or hallucinations, distorted judgement and inappropriate emotional responses. Organic psychoses may spring from brain damage, advanced SYPHILIS, senile dementia or advanced EPILEPSY. Functional psychoses include SCHIZOPHRENIA and manic-depressive psychosis.

psychotherapy Treatment of a psychological disorder by nonphysical methods. It is carried out either with individuals or groups and usually involves some sort of "talking cure" and the development of a rapport between patient and therapist. Psychotherapy is often based on PSYCHOANALYSIS.

ptarmigan Any of three species of northern or alpine grouse; especially the Eurasian ptarmigan, *Lagopus mutus*. The wings and breast are white in colder months, but in spring they become a mottled grey-brown. It inhabits high barren regions, feeding on leaves and lichens. Length: to 36cm (14in). Family Tetraonidae.

pteridophyte Commonly used name for any of a group of spore-bearing VASCULAR PLANTS. At one time pteridophytes were taken to include CLUB MOSSES, HORSETAILS and FERNS. These plants have similar life cycles but in other respects are quite distinct and are now classified as separate phyla (divisions). *See also* TRACHEOPHYTE

pterodactyl Any of several species of small pterosaurs. Almost tail-less, it had a large toothed beak and flimsy membranous wings. Fossil remains show a lack of muscular development and the absence of a breast keel. It is therefore believed that pterodactyls were gliders, incapable of sustained flapping flight.

PTFE (polytetrafluoroethylene) Chemically inert, solid plastic. PTFE is used as a heat-resistant material for heat-shields on spacecraft, as a non-stick coating on cooking utensils and as a lubricant. PTFE is stable up to about 300°C (572°F).

Ptolemy I (367–283 BC) (Ptolemy Soter) King of ancient Egypt, first ruler of the Ptolemaic dynasty. A Macedonian general of ALEXANDER THE GREAT, he was granted Egypt in the division of Alexander's empire upon the latter's death in 323 BC. He assumed the title of king in 305 BC. He made his capital at Alexandria, where he created the famous library. He abdicated in 284 BC in favour of his son.

Ptolemy (90–168) (Claudius Ptolemaeus) Greek astronomer and geographer. He worked at the library of Alexandria, Egypt, a great centre of Greek learning. His main works were *Almagest*, which described an Earth-centred universe, and *Geography*, which included a world map.

puberty Time in human development when sexual maturity is reached. The reproductive organs take on their adult form, and secondary sexual characteristics, such as the growth of pubic hair, start to become evident. Girls develop breasts and begin to menstruate; in boys there is deepening of the voice and the growth of facial hair. Puberty may begin at any time from about the age of ten, usually occurring earlier in girls than in boys. The process is regulated by HORMONES.

public limited company (plc) Company with limited liability whose shares are quoted on a stock exchange. Most companies have limited liability, which means that their owners are responsible only for the money originally invested, and not for the whole of the company's debts. Unlike a private limited company, a public limited company may have any number of shareholders.

public sector borrowing requirement (PSBR) Amount a government needs to borrow to cover its expenditure. If it has to spend more than the amount raised by taxes and excise duties, it must raise the rest by borrowing. To do this, it issues short- and long-term stocks and BONDS. These form part of the national DEBT.

Puccini, Giacomo (1858–1924) Italian composer of operas. Among his best-known works are *La Bohème* (1896), *Tosca* (1900), *Madam Butterfly* (1904) and the incomplete *Turandot* (1926).

Pueblo Generic name for several Native American tribes inhabiting the Mesa and Rio Grande regions of Arizona and New Mexico.

Puerto Rico Self-governing island commonwealth (in union with the USA) in the West Indies; the most easterly island of the Greater Antilles; the capital is San Juan. First visited by Columbus in 1493, the island remained a Spanish colony until 1898, when it was ceded to the USA. In 1952 it was proclaimed a semi-autonomous commonwealth. The decline in the sugar industry in the 1940s created considerable unemployment. Many Puerto Ricans emigrated to the USA. The island is of volcanic origin, and much of the land is mountainous and unsuitable for agriculture. The principal crops are sugar, tobacco, coffee, pineapples and maize. Industries: tourism, textiles, electronic equipment, petrochemicals. Area: 8,870sq km (3,425sq mi). Pop. (1993 est.) 3,552,039.

puff adder Widely distributed African VIPER. Its skin pattern varies, but it usually has yellow markings on brown. It hunts large rodents and its poisonous bite can be fatal to humans. Up to 80 young are born at one time. Length: to 1.2m (4ft). Family Viperidae; species *Bitis arietans*.

puffball Any of a large order of MUSHROOMS (Lycoperdiales) whose SPORE masses become powdery at maturity and are expelled in "puffs" when the case is pressed. Puffballs are stemless, and some species, but not all, are edible.

puffin Small diving-bird of the AUK family (Alcidae), found in large colonies in the Northern Hemisphere. The Atlantic puffin (*Fratercula arctica*) has a short neck, a triangular bill with red, yellow and blue stripes, and reddish legs and feet. The puffin lays a single egg in a burrow *c.*1–2m (3.3–6.6ft) deep on a cliff. Length: *c.*30cm (12in)

pug Small dog that probably originated in China. It has a large head, a blunt muzzle and facial wrinkles. The wide-chested, short body is set on strong legs. The short coat may be grey, light brown or black with a characteristic black face. Height: to 28cm (11in) at the shoulder; weight: to 8kg (18lb).

Pugin, Augustus Welby Northmore (1812–52) British architect who helped to design the Houses of Parliament with Sir Charles BARRY. His *True Principles of Pointed or Christian Architecture* (1841) helped promote the GOTHIC REVIVAL.

Puglia (Apulia) Region in SE Italy, consisting of the provinces of Bari, Brindisi, Foggia, Lecce and Taranto; the capital is Bari. Colonized by the Greeks, it was taken by the Romans in the 3rd century BC. The region became part of Italy in 1861. Products: wheat, almonds, figs, tobacco, wine, salt. Industries: petrochemicals, iron and steel. Area: 19,357sq km (7,472sq mi). Pop. (1992 est.) 4,049,972.

Pulitzer Prize Annual US awards presented for outstanding achievement in journalism, letters and music. The first prize was awarded in 1917. There are prizes for fiction, drama, US history, biography, poetry and musical composition.

pulley Simple machine used to multiply force or to change the direction of its application. A simple pulley consists of a wheel, often with a groove, attached to a fixed structure. Compound pulleys consist of two or more such wheels, some movable, that allow a person to raise objects much heavier than he or she could lift unaided.

pulsar Object emitting radio waves in pulses of great regularity. They were first noticed in 1967 by the British radioastronomer Jocelyn Bell. Pulsars are believed to be rapidly rotating NEUTRON STARS. A beam of radio waves emitted by the rotating pulsar sweeps past the Earth and is received in the form of pulses. More than 500 pulsars are known, "flashing" at rates from *c.*4 seconds to 1 millisecond.

pulse Regular wave of raised pressure in arteries that results from the flow of blood pumped into them at each beat of the HEART. The pulse is usually taken at the wrist, though it may be observed at any point where an artery runs close to the body surface. The average adult pulse rate is about 70 per minute.

pulse Any leguminous plant of the pea family with edible seeds, such as the bean, lentil, pea, peanut and soya bean (soybean). The term may also refer to the seed alone. Pulses are a valuable human food crop. They are also used for oil production. Family Papilionaceae/Leguminosae. *See also* LEGUME

puma (mountain lion, cougar) Large cat found in mountains, swamps and jungles of the Americas. It has a small, round head, erect ears and a heavy tail. The coat is tawny with dark brown on the ears, nose and tail; the underparts are white. It preys mainly on deer and small animals. Length: to 2.3m (7.5ft), including the tail; height: to 75cm (30in) at the shoulder. Family Felidae; species *Felis concolor*.

pumice Light rock formed when molten LAVA is blown to a low-density rock froth by the sudden discharge of gases during a volcanic action. It is used as a light abrasive.

pump Device for raising, compressing, propelling or transferring fluids. The lift pump, for raising water from a well, and the bicycle pump are reciprocating (to-and-fro) pumps. In many modern pumps, a rotating impeller (set of blades) causes the fluid to flow. Jet pumps move fluids by forcing a jet of liquid or gas through them.

pumpkin Orange, hard-rinded, edible garden fruit of a trailing annual VINE found in warm regions of the Old World and the USA; a variety of *Cucurbita pepo*. Family Cucurbitaceae.

punctuated equilibrium Theory, expounded by Stephen Jay Gould and Niles Eldridge in 1972, that is strongly sceptical of the notion of gradual change in the EVOLUTION of the natural world, as advocated by Charles DARWIN. Fossil records rarely document the gradual development of a new SPECIES, rather showing its seemingly sudden appearance. Darwin explains this is due to gaps in the fossil records. Punctuated equilibrium explains this by invoking a different model of evolution. Each species is predominantly in a steady state (equilibrium), which is punctuated by brief but intense periods of sudden change that give rise to new species.

Punic Wars (264–146 BC) Series of wars between Rome and Carthage. In the First Punic War (264–241 BC), Carthage was forced to surrender Sicily and other territory. In the Second (218–201 BC), the Carthaginians under HANNIBAL invaded Italy and won a series of victories. They were forced to withdraw, and the Romans invaded North Africa and defeated Hannibal. The Third Punic War (149–146 BC) ended in the destruction of Carthage.

Punjab State in N India, bounded W and NW by Pakistan; the capital is CHANDIGARH. Other major cities include AMRITSAR. In the 18th century Sikhs wrested part of the region from Mogul rule and established a kingdom. In 1849 it was annexed by the British. In 1947 the Punjab was split between India and Pakistan, the smaller E part going to India. In 1966 this was further reorganized into two states, HARYANA and Punjab, which is now the only Indian state with a Sikh majority. Punjab is mainly a flat plain. Much of the land is irrigated and agriculture is important. Industries: textiles, electrical goods, fertilizers, cereals, cotton, sugar. Area: 50,376sq km (19,450sq mi). Pop. (1991) 20,281,969.

Punjab Province in NE Pakistan, bounded E and S by India; the capital is LAHORE. It was subject to a succession of foreign conquerors, including Aryans, Greeks and the British. The province was formed in 1947, acquiring its present boundaries in 1970. The area lies on an alluvial plain and most of the land under cultivation is irrigated. Agriculture is the chief source of income, with wheat and cotton the major crops. Industries: textiles, machinery, electrical appliances. It is Pakistan's most heavily populated province. Area: 206,432sq km (79,703sq mi). Pop. (1985 est.) 53,840,000.

Punjabi (Panjabi) Language spoken by 50 million people in the PUNJAB. It belongs to the Indo-Iranian family of INDO-EUROPEAN LANGUAGES and is one of the 15 languages recognized by the Indian Constitution. It has similarities to HINDI, but possesses very few borrowings from Persian and Arabic.

punk Term used to describe music and fashion of the mid-1970s, characterized by raw energy and iconoclasm. Heavily influenced by US bands, such as New York Dolls, punk was pioneered in Britain by the Sex Pistols and the Clash. Often anti-establishment, the associated fashions in dress, hair and make-up were also designed to shock.

pupa Non-feeding, developmental stage during which an insect undergoes complete METAMORPHOSIS. It generally occurs as part of a four-stage life cycle from the egg, through LARVA, to pupa, then adult. Most pupae consist of a protective outer casing inside which the tissues of the insect undergo a drastic reorganization to form the adult body. Insects that undergo pupation include the many different kinds of BUTTERFLY and BEETLE and many kinds of FLY. The pupa is often called a CHRYSALIS in butterflies and moths.

pupil In the structure of the EYE, circular aperture through which light falls onto the LENS; it is located in the centre of the IRIS. Its diameter changes by reflex action of the iris to control the amount of light entering the eye.

Purcell, Henry (1659–95) English composer and organist of the Baroque period. It is his church music for which he is most famous; much of it is still performed. His only opera, *Dido and Aeneas* (1689), is regarded as an early operatic masterpiece. Other works include *The Fairy Queen* (1692).

purgatory Place or state intermediate between HEAVEN and HELL where a soul that has died in a state of grace is purged of its sins before entering heaven. In the teachings of the Roman Catholic Church, souls that die with unforgiven venial and forgiven mortal sins go to purgatory.

Purim Ancient Jewish celebration of thanksgiving, held on the 14th day of the Jewish month of Adar (February or March). It commemorates the deliverance of the Jews of Persia from a plot to destroy them. The story, which appears in the Old Testament Book of ESTHER, is recited in all synagogue services. The gift of alms to the poor is obligatory, and it is associated with a carnival atmosphere.

Puritans British Protestants who were particularly influential during the 16th and 17th centuries. They originated in the reign of ELIZABETH I as a faction within the CHURCH OF ENGLAND; their chief aim was to make it a truly Protestant Church, rather than an Anglo-Catholic one. Following the ideas of CALVIN, they were initially opposed to Anglicanism because of its preoccupation with what they considered to be "popish" practice. However, they later demanded the setting up of PRESBYTERIANISM. Many of the parliamentary opponents of JAMES I and CHARLES I were Puritans. Among them were religious separatists who emigrated to America. The English CIVIL WAR (1642–49) resulted from attempts by Puritan parliamentarians to block Charles I's policies on religious grounds. After the war, the Puritans' zenith was reached when Oliver CROMWELL assumed full executive power in 1653. The authority of the Church of England as an Anglican institution was re-established in 1660, although 30 years later Presbyterianism was accepted as the state-supported form of Christianity in Scotland. In England, the Puritans lived on as Dissenters and Nonconformists.

pus Yellowish fluid forming as a result of bacterial infection. It comprises blood serum, LEUCOCYTES, dead tissue and living and dead BACTERIA. An ABSCESS is a pus-filled cavity.

Pusan City on the Korea Strait, SE South Korea. It has thrived through its trading links with Japan. The Japanese modernized Pusan's harbour facilities during their occupation of Korea (1905–45).

In the Korean War Pusan acted as the United Nations' supply port. Pusan is Korea's leading port and second-largest city. Industries: shipbuilding, iron and steel. Pop. (1990) 3,798,000.

Pushkin, Alexander Sergeievich (1799–1837) Russian poet and novelist. In 1820 he was exiled for his political beliefs and his folk poem *Ruslan and Lyudmila* was published. *The Prisoner of the Caucasus* (1822) is his response to the beauty of the Crimea and the Caucasus; and the tragedy *Boris Godunov* (1826) reveals the influence of BYRON. Pushkin's masterpiece was the verse novel *Eugene Onegin* (1833).

Pu Yi, Henry (1906–67) Last Emperor of China (1908–11). His reign name was Hsuan Tung. Deposed after the formation of the Chinese republic, he was temporarily rescued from obscurity to become president, later "emperor", of the Japanese puppet state of MANCHUKUO in 1932. Captured by Soviet forces (1945), he was delivered to Mao Zedong and imprisoned (1949–59).

PVC *See* POLYVINYL CHLORIDE (PVC)

pyelitis Inflammation of the pelvis of the KIDNEY, where urine collects before draining into the URETER. It is usually caused by bacterial infection. Treatment is with ANTIBIOTICS and copious fluids.

Pym, John (1584–1643) English leader of the parliamentary opposition to King CHARLES I. In the LONG PARLIAMENT (1640) he initiated proceedings against Charles' advisers, Strafford and LAUD, and took part in drafting the GRAND REMONSTRANCE (1641). He was one of the five members whom Charles tried to arrest in the House of Commons (1642), and he helped to arrange the alliance with the Scots in the English CIVIL WAR.

Pynchon, Thomas (1937–) US novelist whose works are noted for their offbeat humour and inventiveness. His books include *V* (1963), *The Crying of Lot 49* (1966), *Gravity's Rainbow* (1973), *Vineland* (1990) and *Deadly Sins* (1993).

Pyongyang Capital of North Korea, in the W of the country, on the River Taedong. An ancient city, in the 16th and 17th centuries it came under both Japanese and Chinese rule. Pyongyang's industry developed during the Japanese occupation (1910–45). It became the capital of North Korea in 1948. During the KOREAN WAR it suffered considerable damage. Industries: cement, iron and steel, chemicals, machinery. Pop. (1984) 2,639,448.

pyramid In geometry, a solid figure having a polygon as one of its faces (the base), the other faces being triangles with a common vertex. Its volume is one-third of the base area times the vertical height.

Pyramids Monuments on a square base with sloping sides rising to a point. They are associated particularly with ancient EGYPT, where some of the largest have survived almost intact. They served as burial chambers for pharaohs. The earliest Egyptian pyramid was a step pyramid (ZIGGU-RAT), built *c*.2700 BC for Zoser. Pyramid building in Egypt reached its peak during the 4th dynasty, the time of the Great Pyramid at GIZA. The largest pyramid in the world, it was built *c*.2500 BC, and stands 146m (480ft) high with sides 231m (758ft) long at the base. The largest New World ziggurat pyramid was built in TEOTIHUACÁN, Mexico, in the 1st century AD; it was 66m (216ft) high.

Pyrenees Range of mountains in S France and N Spain, extending from the Mediterranean Sea to the Bay of Biscay. They were formed in the Tertiary era. The Pyrenees contain deposits of marble, gypsum and oil, and there are extensive forests. Sheep and goat grazing is the chief farming activity. The highest point is Pico de Aneto, 3,406m (11,168ft). Length: 435km (270mi).

Pyrenees, Peace of the (1659) Treaty between France and Spain after the THIRTY YEARS WAR. France gained territory in Artois and Flanders, and Philip IV of Spain reluctantly agreed to his daughter's marriage to LOUIS XIV. She was to renounce her claim to the Spanish throne in exchange for a subsidy. Because Spain could not pay the subsidy, the renunciation became void, giving Louis a claim on the Spanish Netherlands and resulting in the War of Devolution.

pyrite (fool's gold) Widespread sulphide mineral, iron sulphide (FeS_2), occurring in all types of rocks and veins. It is a brass-yellow colour. It crystallizes as cubes and octahedra, and also as granules and globular masses. It is opaque, metallic and brittle. Hardness 6.5; s.g. 5.0.

pyroxene Important group of rock-forming, silicate minerals. They are usually dark greens, browns and blacks. Crystals are usually short prisms with good cleavages. Hardness 2.3–4; s.g. 5.5–6.

Pyrrhus (*c*.319–272 BC) King of Epirus (307–302, 295–272 BC). An able general, he fought several battles against Rome. Although he won, the cost was so heavy that victory was useless, hence the term "pyrrhic victory".

Pythagoras (*c*.580–500 BC) Greek philosopher and founder of the Pythagorean school. The Pythagoreans believed in the TRANSMIGRATION OF SOULS and that numbers and their interrelationships constitute the true nature of things in the universe. Pythagoras is credited with many advances in mathematics and geometry, medicine and philosophy. The theorem that the square of the hypotenuse of a right-angled triangle equals the sum of the squares of the other two sides is named after him.

python Name of more than 20 species of non-poisonous snakes of the BOA family (Boidae), found in tropical regions. Like boas, pythons kill their prey by squeezing them in their coils. Unlike boas, pythons lay eggs. The reticulated python (*Python reticulatus*) of SE Asia vies with the anaconda as the world's largest snake, reaching up to about 9m (30ft). Subfamily Pythoninae.

Q/q is the 17th letter of the English alphabet and a letter employed in the alphabets of other w European languages. It is a consonant and is descended from the Semitic letter qoph.

Qaddafi, Muammar al- (1942–) Libyan political leader. He led the coup that toppled King Idris I in 1969. As commander-in-chief of the army and chairman of the Revolutionary Command Council, he effectively became head of state. An Arab nationalist, he closed US and British bases, nationalized petroleum assets and encouraged a return to Islamic principles. Qaddafi's sponsorship of worldwide revolutionary and terrorist groups infuriated the US and led to air strikes and trade embargoes.

Qatar Sheikhdom on the Qatar peninsula in the Persian Gulf; the capital is DOHA. The low-lying land is mostly stony desert, with some barren salt flats. Qatar's territory includes several offshore coral islands. The climate is hot and humid. Qatar is heavily dependent on food imports. Qatar's high standard of living derives from its oil and gas reserves. Oil was first discovered in 1939 and today accounts for c.90% of exports and 80% of income. The economy is heavily dependent on an immigrant workforce, many from India or Pakistan. Forty percent of Qatar's population are Sunni Muslim, though only 25% are native Qataris. Once a part of the Ottoman empire, Qatar was a British protectorate from 1916–71, when it achieved independence. Sheikh Khalifa bin Hamad Al-Thani became Emir after a coup in 1972. During the 1980s Qatar's status was threatened by the regional dominance of Iran and Iraq and a territorial dispute with BAHRAIN. In the 1991 GULF WAR, Allied coalition forces were deployed on Qatar's territory. In 1995 the Emir was overthrown and replaced by his son, Sheikh Hamad bin Khalifa Al-Thani. Area: 11,437sq km (4,415sq mi). Pop. (1986) 369,079.

Qin (formerly Ch'in) Imperial dynasty of China (221–206 BC) which emerged after the collapse of the ZHOU dynasty; its founder was QIN SHIHUANG-DI. The first centralized imperial administration was established. The GREAT WALL took permanent shape during this period.

Qing (formerly Ch'ing) Imperial Manchurian dynasty of China (1644–1911). It was established following the collapse of the MING dynasty. By 1800 the dynasty exercised control over an area stretching from Siam (Thailand) and Tibet to Mongolia and the Amur River. The dynasty weakened in the 19th century, following internal struggles, such as the TAIPING REBELLION, and with the increase of foreign influence, particularly after the OPIUM WARS. It ended with the abdication of PU YI in 1911 and the establishment of the Chinese republic.

Qinghai (Tsinghai) Mountainous province in NW China; the capital is Xining (Sining). It became a province of China in 1928. Qinghai is the source of the HUANG HE, YANGTZE and MEKONG rivers. It is famous for its horses. Iron ore, coal, oil, and salt are extracted. Area: 721,280sq km (278,486sq mi). Pop. (1990) 4,430,000.

Qin Shihuangdi (259–210 BC) Emperor of China (221–210 BC). The first emperor of the QIN dynasty. Excavations of his tomb on Mount Li (near XIAN) during the 1970s revealed, among other treasures, an "army" of c.7,500 life-size terracotta guardians.

Qom City in w central Iran. The burial place of FATIMA, it is a pilgrimage site for SHIITE Muslims. Industries: textiles, pottery. Pop. (1986) 543,139.

quadrant In plane geometry, a quarter of a circle, bounded by radii at right angles to each other and by the arc of the circle. In analytic geometry it is one of the four sections of a plane divided by an x axis and a y axis. A quadrant is also a device for measuring angles, based on a 90° scale.

quadratic equation Algebraic equation in which the highest exponent of the variable is 2; an equation of the second degree. A quadratic equation has the general form $ax^2 + bx + c = 0$, where a, b and c are constants. It has, at most, two solutions (roots), given by the formula $x = [-b \pm \sqrt{(b^2 - 4ac)}]/2a$.

Quadruple Alliance Alliance among four states, in particular three alliances in Europe in the 18th and 19th centuries. The first (1718) consisted of Britain, France, Netherlands, and the Holy Roman Empire against PHILIP V of Spain. The second (1814) consisted of Austria, Britain, Prussia and Russia against NAPOLEON I. After Napoleon's defeat the four partners created the CONGRESS SYSTEM. The third Alliance (1834) consisted of Britain and France in support of Portugal and Spain.

quail Any of a group of Old World gamebirds. The European quail (*Coturnix coturnix*), a small, short-tailed bird with a white throat and mottled brownish plumage, is found throughout Europe, Asia and Africa. The Australian quail (*Turnix velox*) is a stocky, brownish bird. Mainly ground-living birds, they scrape for fruits and seeds and nest on the ground. The Japanese quail (*C. coturnix japonica*) is used as a source of meat and eggs.

Quakers (officially Society of Friends) Christian sect that arose in England in the 1650s, founded by George Fox. The name derived from the injunction given by early Quaker leaders that their followers tremble at the word of the Lord. Quakers rejected the episcopal organization of the CHURCH OF ENGLAND, believing in the priesthood of all believers and a direct relationship between man and God. Quakers originally worshipped God in meditative silence unless someone was moved to testify. Since the mid-19th century, their meetings have included hymns and readings. The largest national Quaker Church is in the USA, where it began with the founding of a settlement by William PENN in (1681). There are c.200,000 Quakers worldwide.

qualitative analysis Identification of the chemical elements or ions in a substance or mixture. *See also* QUANTITATIVE ANALYSIS

quango (acronym for **Qu**asi-Autonomous **N**on-**G**overnmental **O**rganization) Any of a number of bureaux set up in Britain with government funds. They are responsible for regulating or monitoring various aspects of industrial, political, financial and social welfare. They are not directly elected, but report on their operational findings. There is much public debate about these bodies resulting from their expense and lack of accountability.

quantitative analysis Identification of the amount of chemical constituents in a substance or mixture. Chemical methods use reactions such as precipitation, NEUTRALIZATION and OXIDATION, and measure volume (volumetric analysis) or weight (gravimetric analysis). Physical methods measure qualities such as density and refractive index.

quantum chromodynamics Study of the properties of QUARKS in which, to explain permissible combinations of quarks to form various ELEMENTARY PARTICLES, each is assigned a colour. Quarks are given one of the three primary colours: red, green and blue. When three quarks combine to form BARYONS, the resulting colour is always white. Antiquarks are given one of the three complementary colours: cyan, magenta and yellow. When a quark combines with an antiquark to form a MESON, the resulting colour is also white.

quantum electrodynamics (QED) Use of QUANTUM MECHANICS to study the properties of ELECTROMAGNETIC RADIATION and how it interacts with charged particles. For example, the theory predicts that a collision between an ELECTRON and a PROTON should result in the production of a PHOTON of electromagnetic radiation, which is exchanged between the colliding particles.

quantum mechanics Use of QUANTUM THEORY to explain the behaviour of ELEMENTARY PARTICLES. Louis de BROGLIE suggested in 1924 that particles have wave properties, the converse having been postulated in 1905 by Albert EINSTEIN. Erwin SCHRÖDINGER used this hypothesis in 1926 to predict particle behaviour on the basis of wave properties, but a year earlier Werner HEISENBERG had produced a mathematical equivalent to Schrödinger's theory without using wave concepts at all. In 1928 Paul DIRAC unified these approaches while incorporating RELATIVITY. The complete modern theory of quantum mechanics was derived by Richard FEYNMAN in the 1940s. *See also* QUANTUM NUMBERS

quantum numbers In physics, a set of four numbers used to classify electrons and their atomic states. The principal quantum number (symbol n) gives the electron's energy level; the orbital quantum number (l) describes its angular momentum; the magnetic quantum number (m) describes the energies of electrons in a magnetic field; and the SPIN quantum number (m_s) gives the spin of the individual electrons. *See also* QUANTUM THEORY

quantum theory Together with the theory of RELATIVITY, the foundation of 20th-century physics. It is concerned with the relationship between matter and energy at the elementary or subatomic level and with the behaviour of ELEMENTARY PARTICLES. According to the theory, all radiant energy is emitted and absorbed in multiples of tiny "packets" or quanta. The idea that energy is radiated and absorbed in quanta was proposed in 1900 by Max PLANCK. Using Planck's work, Albert EINSTEIN quantized light radiation and in 1905 explained the PHOTOELECTRIC EFFECT. In 1913 Niels BOHR used quantum theory to explain atomic structure and the relationship between the energy levels of an atom's electrons and the frequencies of radiation emitted or absorbed by the atom. *See also* QUANTUM MECHANICS; QUANTUM NUMBERS

quark Any one of six ELEMENTARY PARTICLES and their antiparticles (antiquarks); the constituents of the HADRON group of SUBATOMIC PARTICLES. They occur in one of six "flavours": up, down, top, bottom, charmed and strange. Antiquarks have similar flavours but their charge is opposite that of their corresponding quark. Quarks always exist in combination; free quarks cannot exist.

quartz Rock-forming mineral, the natural form of silicon dioxide (silica), SiO_2. It is widely distributed, occurring in igneous and metamorphic rocks (notably granite and gneiss), clastic sediments, and mineral veins. It forms six-sided crystals. Pure quartz is clear and colourless but the mineral may be coloured by impurities. The most common varieties are colourless quartz (rock crystal), rose, yellow, milky and smoky. The most usual cryptocrystalline varieties, whose crystals can be seen only under a microscope, are CHALCEDONY and FLINT. Quartz crystals exhibit the PIEZOELECTRIC EFFECT and are used to keep time. Hardness 7; s.g. 2.65.

quartzite METAMORPHIC ROCK usually produced from sandstone, in which the quartz grains have recrystallized. Quartzite is a hard and massive rock. It is usually white, light grey, yellow or buff.

quasar (quasi-stellar object) In astronomy, an object that appears to be a massive, highly compressed, extremely powerful source of radio and light waves, characterized by a large red shift. If such red shifts are due to the DOPPLER EFFECT, it can be deduced that quasars are more remote than any other objects previously identified; many are receding at velocities greater than half the speed of light. Their energy may result from the gravitational collapse of a GALAXY or from many SUPERNOVAS exploding in quick succession.

Quaternary period Most recent period of the CENOZOIC era, beginning *c*.2 million years ago and extending to the present. It is divided into the PLEISTOCENE epoch, characterized by a periodic succession of great ice ages, and the HOLOCENE epoch, which started some 10,000 years ago.

quattrocento (It. fourteen hundred) Art history term applied to the 15th-century Italian RENAIS-

SANCE. Venice was its centre. It includes the painters Fra ANGELICO, Fra Filippo LIPPI, MASACCIO and UCCELLO; the architects BRUNELLESCHI and ALBERTI; and the sculptors DONATELLO and GHIBERTI.

Quebec (Québec) Province in E Canada; the largest province in area and second-largest in population; the capital is QUEBEC and the largest city is MONTREAL. Jacques CARTIER discovered the E coast of Canada in 1534. The French settled in Québec in 1608. The region became a British colony in 1763. With the establishment of the Dominion of Canada in 1867, Quebec became a province. In the late 20th century Quebec's French-speaking inhabitants demanded greater autonomy in recognition of their separate cultural heritage. In a 1995 referendum a tiny majority of the population voted against independence. Most of the state is on the Canadian Shield and is relatively uninhabited. The lowlands by the ST LAWRENCE River are the centre of industry and agriculture. The province yields vast quantities of hydroelectric power and timber. Copper, iron, asbestos and gold are mined. Area: 1,540,687sq km (594,860sq mi). Pop. (1991) 6,895,963.

Quebec (Québec) City and seaport on the St Lawrence River, S QUEBEC province, Canada; capital of Quebec province. Samuel de Champlain established a French trading post on the site of Quebec in 1608. Captured by the British in 1629, the city was returned to France and became the capital of New France in 1663. It was ceded to Britain in 1763. The city served as the capital of Lower Canada (1791–1841) and of the United Provinces of Canada (1851–55, 1859–65), before becoming capital of Quebec province in 1867. Quebec has in recent years become a focal point for Canada's French-speaking separatists. Industries: shipbuilding, paper, leather, textiles, machinery, canned food, tobacco, chemicals. Pop. (1991) 167,517.

Queen Anne style Art history term applied to a British style of decorative arts (especially furniture) popular during the reign (1702–14) of Queen Anne. Curved cabriole legs are a distinctive feature, as are inlay, veneering and lacquerwork.

Queen Mother See ELIZABETH

Queens Largest borough of NEW YORK CITY, on the W end of Long Island, SE New York State, USA. It was created a borough of Greater New York in 1898. Queens has La Guardia and John F. Kennedy International airports and St John's University (1870). It is a residential and industrial area. Area: 280sq km (108sq mi). Pop. (1990) 1,951,598.

Queensberry, John Sholto Douglas, Marquess of (1844–1900) British nobleman who sponsored the **Queensberry rules** – the basis of the rules for modern boxing. The rules were standardized in 1889. In 1895 Queensberry publicly insulted Oscar WILDE because of Wilde's association with his son, Lord Alfred Douglas. Wilde unsuccessfully sued Queensberry for libel and was convicted of homosexual practices.

Queensland State in NE Australia; the capital is BRISBANE. Queensland was originally part of New South Wales and served as a penal colony from 1824–40. It became a colony in 1859 and a separate state in 1901. The GREAT DIVIDING RANGE separates the fertile coastal strip from the interior plains. Its chief crops are sugar cane, wheat, cotton and tropical fruits. The main industry is mining. Area: 1,727,530sq km (667,000sq mi). Pop. (1993 est.) 3,155,400.

quetzal Forest bird of Central America. The male is bright green above and crimson below with iridescent green tail plumes forming a 60cm (2ft) train. The Aztec and Maya regarded the quetzal as sacred. The duller female lays two eggs, which are incubated by both parents. Family Trogonidae; species *Pharomachrus mocinno*.

Quetzalcóatl God of CENTRAL AND SOUTH AMERICAN MYTHOLOGY, a principal deity of the TOLTECS, MAYA and AZTECS. He took the form of a feathered serpent. He created the human race by fertilizing bones with his own blood, and was associated with agriculture and the arts.

Quezon City City on LUZON island, adjacent to MANILA, N Philippines. Second-largest city in the Philippines, it was capital of the Philippines from 1948–76. Pop. (1990) 1,632,000.

Quiché Mayan group of Native South Americans located in the highlands of W Guatemala. Archeological remains show large pre-conquest population centres and an advanced civilization.

quicksilver See MERCURY

quietism Mystical Christian movement begun by Miguel de Molinos in the 17th century. It was a great influence on the Wesleyan movement of 18th-century Britain. Its adherents believed that only in a state of absolute surrender to God was the mind able to receive the saving infusion of grace.

quince Shrub or small tree native to the Middle East and central Asia. Its greenish-yellow fruit is used in preserves. Height: to 6.1m (20ft). Family Rosaceae; species *Cydonia oblonga*

Quine, Willard Van Orman (1908–) US philosopher and mathematical logician. His work focused on language as a logical system. His writings include *A System of Logistics* (1934), *Mathematical Logic* (1940), *Word and Object* (1960) and *Philosophy of Logic* (1969).

quinine White, crystalline substance isolated in 1820 from the bark of the cinchona tree. It was once widely used in the treatment of MALARIA but has been largely replaced by drugs that are less toxic.

Quito Capital of Ecuador, in the N central part of the country; it lies almost on the Equator and at 2,850m (9,260ft) above sea level. The site was settled by Quito Native Americans, and captured by the INCAS in 1487. It was taken by Spain in 1534, and liberated from Spanish rule in 1822 by Antonio José de SUCRE. A cultural and political centre, the 17th-century cathedral is the burial place of de Sucre. Products: textiles and handicrafts. Pop. (1990) 1,100,847.

R/r is the 18th letter of the English alphabet and is used in the alphabets of other w European languages, It is a consonant and is descended from the Semitic letter resh, meaning head.

Ra (Re) In Egyptian mythology, Sun god of Heliopolis and lord of the dead. He is usually depicted as falcon-headed, with a solar disc on his head.

Rabat Capital of Morocco, in the N of the country, on the Atlantic coast. The fortified city was founded in the 12th century by the ALMOHAD ruler, Abd al-Mumin. In 1912 it became capital of the French protectorate of Morocco. Notable sites include the 12th-century Hassan Tower. Industries: handwoven rugs, textiles. Pop. (1982) 518,616.

rabbi Person qualified through study of the Hebrew Bible and the TALMUD to be the chief religious leader of a Jewish congregation and the person responsible for its education and spiritual guidance. Modern Israel has a rabbinic council with two chief rabbis, one representing the SEPHARDIC tradition, the other representing the ASHKENAZI rite.

rabbit Long-eared, herbivorous mammal of the family Leporidae, including the European common rabbit and the American cotton-tail. The common rabbit is *Oryctolagus cuniculus* and has thick, soft, greyish-brown fur. Domesticated rabbits are also of this species. Length: 35–45cm (14–18in); weight: 1.4–2.3kg (3–5lb). *See also* HARE

Rabelais, François (1494–1553) French humanist and satirist. He is famed for his classic series of satires *Gargantua and Pantagruel*. The series consists of *Pantagruel* (1532), *Gargantua* (1534), *Le Tiers Livre* (1546), *Le Quart Livre* (1552) and *Le Cinquième Livre* (1564). Although condemned as obscene, the books were widely popular.

rabies (hydrophobia) Viral disease of the central nervous system. It can occur in all warm-blooded animals, but is especially feared in dogs due to the risk of transmission to human beings. The incubation period varies from a week to more than a year. It is characterized by severe thirst, fever, muscle spasms and delirium. Once the symptoms have appeared, death usually follows within a few days. Anyone bitten by a rabid animal may be saved by prompt injections of rabies vaccine and antiserum.

Rabin, Yitzhak (1922–95) Israeli statesman, prime minister (1974–77, 1992–95). He was army chief of staff (1964–68) during the SIX DAY WAR (1967). Rabin succeeded Golda MEIR as prime minister, but resigned in favour of Shimon PERES. As minister of defence (1984–90), he had to deal with the Palestinian INTIFADA. In 1992 he won a second term in office. In 1993 he reached an agreement with the PALESTINE LIBERATION ORGANIZATION, promising progress towards Palestinian autonomy in the occupied territories. On 4 November 1995 he was assassinated by an Israeli extremist.

race Informal classification of the human species according to hereditary (genetic) differences. Different racial characteristics arose among geographically separated populations partly through environmental adaptation across many generations. However, because there is no evidence of genetic racial distinctions, anthropologists reject the term.

Rachmaninov, Sergei (1873–1943) Russian composer and pianist. Composing in the late romantic tradition of Tchaikovsky, Rachmaninov's works are typically lyrical and melancholy. Among his most popular works are the Piano Concerto No.2 (1901), *Rhapsody on a Theme of Paganini* (1934) and Symphony No.2 (1907).

Racine, Jean Baptiste (1639–99) French classical dramatist whose early plays, such as *La Thebaïde* (1664) and *Alexandre le Grand* (1665), were influenced by contemporaries such as CORNEILLE. His other plays include *Britannicus* (1669), *Mithridate* (1673) and *Phèdre* (1677).

racism Doctrine advocating the superiority of one human RACE over some or all others. From time to time it has been the avowed policy of certain countries and regimes which, as a result, sanctioned slavery and discriminatory practices, such as the APARTHEID system practised in South Africa. Racism was defined by UNESCO in 1967 as "anti-social beliefs and acts which are based on a fallacy that discriminatory inter-group relations are justifiable on biological grounds".

racoon (raccoon) Stout-bodied, omnivorous, mostly nocturnal mammal of North and Central America. Racoons have a black, mask-like marking across their eyes and a long, black-banded tail. Seven species include the North American *Procyon lotor*. Length: 40–61cm (16–24in); weight: 10–22kg (22–48lb). Family Procyonidae.

radar (acronym for **ra**dio **d**etecting **a**nd **r**anging) System for determining the direction and distance of objects. Developed during World War 2, it works by the transmission of pulses of RADIO waves to an object. The object reflects the pulses, which are detected by an antenna. By measuring the time it takes for the reflected waves to return, the object's distance may be calculated, and its direction ascertained from the alignment of the receiving antenna.

radar astronomy Branch of astronomy in which radar pulses, reflected back to Earth from celestial bodies in the solar system, are studied for information concerning their distance from Earth, their orbital motion, and large surface features. Techniques developed for radar mapping of planetary surfaces have proved particularly important for cloud-covered VENUS.

radian Angle formed by the intersection of two radii at the centre of a circle, when the length of the arc cut off by the radii is equal to one radius in length. Thus, the radian is a unit of angle equal to $c.57.295°$, and there are 2π radians in $360°$.

radiation Transmission of energy by SUBATOMIC PARTICLES or electromagnetic waves. *See* ELECTROMAGNETIC RADIATION

radiation, cosmic (cosmic rays) Streams of SUBATOMIC PARTICLES from space that constantly bombard the Earth at velocities approaching the speed of light. Primary cosmic rays are high-energy RADIATION that comes from the Sun and other sources in outer space. They consist mainly of atomic nuclei and PROTONS. When primary cosmic rays strike gas molecules in the upper atmosphere they yield showers of secondary cosmic rays, which consist of energetic protons, NEUTRONS and pions. Further collisions yield muons, ALPHA PARTICLES, POSITRONS, ELECTRONS, GAMMA RADIATION and PHOTONS.

radiation, heat Energy given off from all solids, liquids or gases as a result of their temperature. The energy comes from the vibrations of atoms in an object and is emitted as ELECTROMAGNETIC RADIATION, often in the form of INFRARED WAVES.

radiation, nuclear Particles or ELECTROMAGNETIC RADIATION emitted spontaneously and at high energies from atomic nuclei. Possible causes include RADIOACTIVE DECAY, which yields ALPHA PARTICLES, BETA PARTICLES, GAMMA RADIATION and, more rarely, POSITRONS. It can also result from spontaneous FISSION of a nucleus.

radio Method of communication between a transmitter and a receiver of radio waves (*see* ELECTROMAGNETIC RADIATION). The term most often refers to the receiver of a sound broadcast. A radio signal of fixed FREQUENCY (the carrier wave) is generated at the transmitter. The sound to be broadcast is converted by a MICROPHONE into a varying electrical signal that is combined with the carrier by means of MODULATION. This is passed to an AERIAL from which it is transmitted into the atmosphere. At the receiver, an aerial intercepts the signal, and it undergoes "detection", the reverse of modulation, to retrieve the sound signal. TELEVISION uses radio waves to send sound and picture signals, and RADAR transmits pulses of radio waves. New technology has enabled DIGITAL SIGNALS to be carried via radio waves. *See also* AMPLITUDE MODULATION (AM); BROADCASTING; FREQUENCY MODULATION (FM)

radioactive decay Process by which a radioactive ISOTOPE (radioisotope) loses SUBATOMIC PARTICLES from its nucleus and so becomes a different element. The disintegration of the nuclei occurs with the emission of ALPHA PARTICLES (helium nuclei) or BETA PARTICLES (electrons), often accompanied by GAMMA RADIATION. The two processes of alpha decay or beta decay cause the radioisotope to be transformed into a chemically different atom. Alpha decay results in the nucleus losing two protons and two neutrons; beta decay occurs when a NEUTRON changes into a PROTON, with an ELECTRON (beta particle) being emitted in the process. Thus the ATOMIC NUMBER changes in both types of decay, and an isotope of another element is produced, which might also be radioactive. In a large collec-

tion of atoms there is a characteristic time (the HALF-LIFE) after which one-half of the total number of nuclei would have decayed. This time varies from millionths of a second to millions of years, depending on the isotope concerned. The activity of any radioactive sample decreases exponentially with time. *See also* CARBON DATING

radioactivity Spontaneous emission of RADIATION from an atomic nucleus. The process by which a radioactive nucleus disintegrates is known as RADIOACTIVE DECAY.

radio astronomy Study of radio waves (ELECTROMAGNETIC RADIATION with wavelengths from about 1mm to many metres) that reach the Earth from objects in space. Observations can be made using a RADIO TELESCOPE. Radio noise from the Milky Way was discovered in 1931 by Karl JANSKY. The number of radio sources increases with distance, demonstrating that the Universe has been evolving with time. This, combined with the discovery at radio wavelengths of the cosmic microwave background, is strong evidence in favour of the BIG BANG theory.

radio galaxy GALAXY that emits strong ELECTROMAGNETIC RADIATION of radio frequency. These emissions seem to be produced by the motion of ELEMENTARY PARTICLES in strong magnetic fields.

radiography Use of X-RAYS to record the interiors of opaque bodies as photographs. Industrial x-ray photographs can show assembly faults and defects in metals. In medicine and dentistry, radiography is invaluable for diagnosing bone damage, tooth decay and internal disease. Using modern scanning techniques, cross-sectional outlines of the body can show organs, blood vessels and diseased parts.

radiology Medical speciality concerned with the use of RADIATION and radioactive materials in the diagnosis and treatment of disease. *See also* RADIOGRAPHY; RADIOTHERAPY

radio telescope Instrument used to collect and record radio waves from space. The basic design is the large single dish or parabolic reflector, up to 100m (330ft) in diameter. Radio waves are reflected by the dish via a secondary reflector to a focus, where they are converted into electrical signals. The signals are amplified and sent to a main control room for further amplification before analysis and recording. *See also* RADIO ASTRONOMY; TELESCOPE

radiotherapy In medicine, the use of RADIATION to treat tumours or other pathological conditions. It may be done by: implanting a pellet of a radioactive source in the part to be treated; dosing a patient with a radioactive isotope; or exposing a patient to precisely focused beams of radiation from an x-ray machine or particle accelerator. Synthesized radioisotopes are the most effective; cobalt-60 is often used as it produces highly penetrating gamma radiation. In the treatment of CANCERS, radiation slows down the proliferation of the cancerous cells.

radish Annual garden vegetable developed from a wild plant native to the cooler regions of Asia. Its leaves are long and deeply lobed; the fleshy root, which may be red, white or black, is eaten raw. Family Brassicaceae; species *Raphanus sativus*.

radium White, radioactive, metallic element (symbol Ra) of the ALKALINE-EARTH METALS, first discovered in 1898 by Pierre and Marie CURIE; the metal is present in uranium ores. It is used in RADIOTHERAPY. Radium has 16 isotopes, which emit alpha, beta and gamma radiation, and heat. RADON gas is a decay product. Properties: at.no. 88; r.a.m. 226.025; r.d. 5.0; m.p. 700°C (1,292°F); b.p. 1,140°C (2,084 °F); most stable isotope Ra^{226} (half-life 1,622 years).

radius In anatomy, one of the two forearm bones, extending from the elbow to the wrist. The radius rotates around the ULNA, permitting the hand to rotate and be flexible.

radon Radioactive gaseous element (symbol Rn), a NOBLE GAS. It was first discovered in 1899 by Ernest RUTHERFORD. The 20 known isotopes, which are alpha particle emitters, are present in the Earth's atmosphere in trace amounts. Radon is mainly used in medical RADIOTHERAPY. Though inert, it forms fluoride compounds. Properties: at.no. 86; r.d. 9.73; m.p. −71°C (−95.8°F); b.p. −61.8°C (−79.24 °F); most stable isotope Rn^{222} (half-life 3.8 days).

RAF *See* AIR FORCE, ROYAL

rafflesia Parasitic plant native to Sumatra and Java. It grows as a PARASITE on the roots of jungle vines and has no stem or leaves. The foul-smelling, reddish-brown flowers are 1m (3.25ft) in diameter, the world's largest flowers. Family Rafflesiaceae; species *Rafflesia arnoldii*.

Rafsanjani, Hojatoleslam Ali Akbar Hashemi (1934–) Iranian cleric and politician, president (1989–97). After KHOMEINI's return from exile in 1979, Rafsanjani became speaker of the Iranian parliament. During the Iran-Iraq War, Rafsanjani was acting commander of the armed forces (1988–89). Following Khomeini's death, he became president. His tenure witnessed a slight thawing of relations with the West.

ragwort Any of several plants with daisy-like flowers, such as the common ragwort (*Senecio jacobaea*). Height: to 1.3m (4ft). Family Asteraceae/Compositae.

rail Slender, long-legged marsh bird. Rails are shy, generally nocturnal and often emit melodious calls. They lay 8–15 eggs in ground nests. Length: 10–45cm (4–18in). Family Rallidae. Genus *Rallus*.

railway (railroad) Form of transport in which carriages run on a fixed track, usually steel rails. Railways date from the 1500s, when mining wagons were drawn by horses along tracks. Richard TREVITHICK built the first steam LOCOMOTIVE in 1804. In 1825 George STEPHENSON's *Locomotion* became the first steam locomotive to pull a passenger train, on the Stockton and Darlington Railway. The first passenger-carrying railway, the Liverpool and Manchester Railway, opened in 1830, using Stephenson's *Rocket*. The growth of rail fed the Industrial Revolution. The world's first UNDERGROUND RAIL-

way to carry passengers was the City and South London Railway in 1890. Steam locomotives are still used in India, but most countries use electric, diesel or diesel-electric locomotives. Modern developments include high-speed trains, such as the French TGV (*Train à Grande Vitesse*), that travel at average speeds of *c*.300km/h (185mph).

rain Water drops that fall from the Earth's atmosphere to its surface, as opposed to fog or dew which drift as suspensions, and snow or hail which fall as ice particles. Warm air passing over the sea absorbs water vapour and rises in thermal currents, or on reaching a mountain range. The water vapour condenses and forms CLOUDS, accounting for the usually heavier annual rainfall on windward, compared to leeward, mountain slopes. *See also* PRECIPITATION; HYDROLOGICAL CYCLE

rainbow Multicoloured band, usually seen as an arc opposite to the Sun or other light source. The primary bow is the one usually seen. A secondary bow, in which the order of the colours is reversed, is sometimes seen beyond the primary bow. The colours are caused by reflection of light within spherical drops of falling rain, which cause white light to be dispersed into its constituent wavelengths. The colours usually seen are those of the visible SPECTRUM: red, orange, yellow, green, blue, indigo and violet.

rainforest Dense forest of tall trees that grows in hot, wet regions near the Equator. The main rainforests are in Africa, central and S America, and SE Asia. They comprise 50% of the Earth's timber and house 40% of the world's animal and plant species. They also, through PHOTOSYNTHESIS, supply most of the world's oxygen. This is why the present rapid destruction of the rainforests (up to 20 million ha are destroyed annually) is a cause of great concern. Also, clearing rainforest contributes to the GREEN-HOUSE EFFECT and may lead to GLOBAL WARMING. There are many species of broad-leaved evergreen trees in rainforest, which grow up to 60m tall. The crowns of other trees, up to 45m tall, form the upper canopy of the forest. Smaller trees form the lower canopy. Climbing vines interconnect the various levels, providing habitats for many animals. Very little light penetrates the forest floor, which consequently has few plants. Rainforest trees provide many kinds of food and other useful materials, such as Brazil nuts, cashews and figs, as well as fibrous kapok and the drugs quinine and curare.

Rainier, Mount Peak in W central Washington, USA; the highest point in the Cascade Range. The summit of this ancient volcano is the centre of the greatest single-peak glacier system in the United States. Height: 4,395m (14,410ft).

Rajasthan State in NW India, on the border with Pakistan; the capital is JAIPUR. Other major cities include UDAIPUR, and JODHPUR. Rajasthan was the homeland of the RAJPUTS. Rajasthan state was formed in 1950. The THAR DESERT in the W is home to pastoral nomads. The E is part of the DEC-

525

CAN plateau. Wheat, millet and cotton are grown. Coal, marble, mica and gypsum are mined. Industries: handicrafts, cotton milling. Area: 342,266sq km (132,149sq mi). Pop. (1991) 44,005,990.

Rajput Predominantly Hindi, warrior caste from NW India. In the 7th century AD they formed the region of Rajputana. During the colonial period much of Rajputana retained its independence under local princely rule. After Indian independence in 1947 most of the princes lost their powers. *See also* RAJASTHAN

Raleigh, Sir Walter (1552–1618) English soldier, explorer and writer. A favourite of ELIZABETH I, he organized expeditions to North America, including the failed attempt to found a colony in Virginia (now North Carolina). On JAMES I's accession, he was imprisoned for treason (1603–1616), and wrote his *History of the World*. He gained release in order to lead an expedition to Guiana in search of EL DORADO, but was betrayed to the Spanish. At Spanish insistence, he was returned to prison and later executed for treason.

Raleigh Capital of North Carolina, USA, in the E central part of the state. Founded in 1792 as state capital, it was named after Sir Walter Raleigh. It is a market centre for cotton and tobacco. Industries: food processing, textiles. Pop. (1990) 207,951.

RAM (**r**andom **a**ccess **m**emory) INTEGRATED CIRCUITS (chips) that act as a temporary store for computer PROGRAMS and DATA. To run a program on a computer, the program is first transferred from a MAGNETIC DISK, or other storage device, to the RAM. The RAM also holds documents produced when the program is used. Another part of the RAM stores the images to be displayed on the screen. The contents of the RAM are lost when the computer is switched off.

Rama Hero of the RAMAYANA. He is considered to be the seventh incarnation of VISHNU.

Ramadan Ninth month of the Islamic year, set aside for fasting. Throughout Ramadan, the faithful must abstain from food, drink and sexual intercourse between sunrise and sunset. They are also encouraged to read the whole of the KORAN in remembrance of the "Night of Power", when MUHAMMAD received his first revelation.

Ramayana (Romance of Rama) Great epic poem of ancient India. Written *c*.300 BC along with the MAHABHARATA, it comprises 24,000 couplets in seven books on the adventures of RAMA and Sita.

Rambert, Dame Marie (1888–1982) British ballet dancer, teacher and choreographer, b. Poland. She was a member of DIAGHILEV's Ballets Russes (1912–13) and advised NIJINSKY in the first performance of Stravinsky's *The Rite of Spring* (1913). She founded her own school in 1920.

Rameau, Jean Philippe (1683–1764) French composer and musical theorist. His most famous opera is *Castor et Pollux* (1737).

Ramsay, Allan (1713–84) Scottish portrait painter. The Scottish counterpart of GAINSBOR-

OUGH and REYNOLDS, he settled in London where, during 1760, he was appointed painter to George III in preference to his rival Reynolds. His style, graceful and Italianate, lent itself especially well to female portraiture, such as *The Artist's Wife* (1755).

Ramsay, Sir William (1852–1916) British chemist. Working with Lord RAYLEIGH, he discovered ARGON in air. Later he discovered HELIUM, NEON and KRYPTON. He was knighted in 1902 and awarded the 1904 Nobel Prize for chemistry.

Ramses II Egyptian king of the 19th dynasty (r.1290–1224 BC). He reigned during a period of unprecedented prosperity and power. His efforts to confirm Egypt's dominance in Palestine and regain Syria led to a major clash with the HITTITES at Kadesh in 1285 BC. He built the sun temple at ABU SIMBEL.

Rand *See* WITWATERSRAND

Rangoon (Yangon) Capital of Burma (Myanmar), a seaport on the Rangoon River. The site of an ancient Buddhist shrine, Rangoon was made capital of Burma in 1886. The scene of fighting between British and Japanese forces in World War 2, it is the country's chief trade centre. Industries: oil refining, timber, rice, iron ores. Pop. (1983) 2,458,712.

Ranjit Singh (1780–1839) Indian maharaja, founder of the Sikh kingdom of the Punjab. In 1799 he established his capital at Lahore. In 1803 he took possession of the Sikh holy city of Amritsar. His kingdom collapsed after his death.

Ransome, Arthur Mitchell (1884–1967) British writer. He wrote very successful children's novels, including *Swallows and Amazons* (1930) and *Peter Duck* (1933).

rape Plant grown for animal fodder and for its small, black seeds, which yield rape oil, used industrially as a lubricant. It has curly, blue-green leaves, small, yellow flowers and slender seed pods. Family Brassicaceae; genus *Brassica*.

Raphael Biblical archangel who, with MICHAEL, GABRIEL and Uriel, serves as a messenger of God. According to the Book of Tobit and the Second Book of Enoch, he is one of the seven holy angels who present the prayers of the saints to God.

Raphael (1483–1520) (Raphael Sanzio or Raphael Santi) Italian painter, one of the finest artists of the High RENAISSANCE. One of his most important commissions was the decoration of the four rooms in the Vatican. He only completed two of these but the first, the *Stanza della Segnatura*, contains two large FRESCOS, the *School of Athens* and the *Disputà*, both of which show Raphael's mastery of PERSPECTIVE. After BRAMANTE's death he became architect to St Peter's, Rome.

rare earth *See* LANTHANIDE SERIES

raspberry Fruit grown in polar and temperate regions of Europe, North America and Asia. The fruit may be black, purple or red. Canes, rising from perennial roots, bear fruit the second year. Family Rosaceae; species *Rubus idaeus*.

Rasputin, Grigori Yefimovich (1872–1916)

Russian peasant mystic. He exercised great influence at the court of NICHOLAS II but attracted suspicion because of his advocacy of sexual ecstasy as a means of religious salvation. He was poisoned by nobles, and when this failed, was shot and drowned.

Rastafarianism West Indian religion focusing on veneration of Ras Tafari (HAILE SELASSIE I). The movement was started in Jamaica in the 1920s by Marcus GARVEY. He advocated a return to Africa in order to overcome black oppression. Followers of Rastafarianism follow a strict diet and are forbidden various foods including pork, milk and coffee.

rat Any of numerous small RODENTS found worldwide. Most species are herbivorous. The best-known are the black rat (*Rattus rattus*) and brown rat (*R. norvegicus*), both of the family Muridae. They carry diseases and destroy or contaminate property and food.

ratio Number relating two numbers or two quantities of the same kind, such as two prices or two lengths, that indicates their relative magnitude. Ratios, as of the numbers 3 and 4, can be written as a fraction 3/4, or with a colon (3:4).

rationalism Philosophical theory that reason alone, unaided by sense experience, can arrive at basic truths. Associated with this theory is the doctrine of innate ideas and the method of deducing truths from self-evident premises. Eminent rationalists included DESCARTES, LEIBNIZ, and SPINOZA.

rational number Number representing the ratio of two integers, the second of which is not zero. Thus, 1/2, 18/11, 0, −2/3 and 12 are all rational numbers. Any rational number can be represented as a terminating decimal (such as 1.35) or a recurring decimal (such as 18/11 = 1.636363....). *See also* IRRATIONAL NUMBERS

ratite Group of large, usually flightless birds with flat breastbones instead of the keel-like prominences found in most flying birds. Ratites include the OSTRICH, RHEA, CASSOWARY, EMU, KIWI and the unusual flying tinamou.

rattan Climbing PALM native to the East Indies and Africa. Its stems grow to 152m (500ft). They are used for making ropes and furniture. Family Arecaceae/Palmae; genus *Calamus*.

rattlesnake Any of about 30 species of venomous New World pit vipers characterized by a tail rattle of loosely connected segments of unshed skin. It ranges from Canada to South America. Most are blotched with dark diamonds, hexagons or spots. They feed mostly on rodents. Length: 30cm–2.5m (1–8ft). Family Viperidae. *See also* SNAKE

Ravel, (Joseph) Maurice (1875–1937) French composer, a leading exponent of IMPRESSIONISM. His piano compositions include *Jeux d'eau* (1901), *Gaspard de la nuit* (1908), *Le Tombeau de Couperin* (1917) and two concertos. Among his orchestral works are *Rhapsodie espagnole* (1907) and *Boléro* (1927). He also composed the ballet *Daphnis and Chloe* (1912).

raven Large bird of the crow family found in the Northern Hemisphere. It has a long, conical bill, shaggy throat feathers, a wedge-shaped tail and black plumage with a purple sheen. It eats carrion or any other animal food. Length: to 68cm (27in). Family Corvidae.

Ray, Man (1890–1976) US photographer, painter, sculptor and film-maker, the founder of the New York DADA movement with Marcel DUCHAMP. He is best known for photographs produced without a camera by placing objects on light-sensitive paper and exposing them to light.

Ray, Satyajit (1921–92) Indian film director. He is best-known for the classic Apu Trilogy: *Pather Panchali* (1955), *The Unvanquished* (1956) and *The World of Apu* (1959). Other films include *The Big City* (1963) and *The Lonely Wife* (1965).

ray Any of several species of cartilaginous, mostly marine fish related to the SKATE, SHARK and CHIMAERA. The ray's flattened body extends sideways into large, wing-like pectoral fins that are "flapped" while swimming. The tail is narrow and may be whip-like or bear poisonous spines. Electric (torpedo) rays stun their prey with electrical charges of up to 200 volts. Length: 1.5m (5ft).

Rayleigh, John William Strutt, Lord (1842–1919) British physicist. He was awarded the 1904 Nobel Prize in physics for his discovery (with William RAMSAY) of the noble gas ARGON and for work on gas densities.

rayon Fine, smooth fibre made from solutions of CELLULOSE. It was the first synthetic textile. Viscose rayon, the most common, is spun-dried and has a strength approaching NYLON. Acetate rayon is made of filaments of cellulose ACETATE.

razor-billed auk (razorbill) Stocky, penguin-like seabird that lives along coastlines in the cold parts of the Northern Hemisphere. It is black and white with a white-ringed, narrow bill. Length: 41cm (16in). Species *Alca torda*.

Reagan, Ronald Wilson (1911–) 40th US President (1981–89). A well-known film actor, he joined the Republican Party (1962) and became governor of California (1966–74). In the 1980 presidential elections he defeated Jimmy CARTER. Surviving an assassination attempt (1981), he introduced large tax cuts and reduced public spending, except on defence. By the end of his second term, budget and trade deficits had reached record heights. Fiercely anti-communist, he adopted a tough foreign policy, invading Grenada (1983) and undermining the SANDINISTA regime in Nicaragua. While pursuing his Strategic Defence Initiative ("Star Wars"), he reached arms control agreements with GORBACHEV (1987). His last years in office were tainted by the IRAN-CONTRA AFFAIR.

realism Broad term in art history, often interchangeable with NATURALISM. It often refers to the faithful representation of objects without emotional bias. It is also used to denote a movement in 19th-century French art, led by COURBET, that focused on unidealized scenes of modern life. Superrealism is a 20th-century movement, in which real objects are depicted in very fine detail so that the overall effect appears unreal. *See also* SOCIALIST REALISM

realism Philosophical doctrine in which universal concepts, as well as tangible objects, exist in their own right, outside the human mind. The idea developed from a medieval view that "universals" are real entities rather than simply names for things. Realism was thus opposed to NOMINALISM. Some philosophers rejected this view in favour of moderate realism, which held that "universals" exist only in the mind of God. *See also* IDEALISM

real number Any number that is a RATIONAL NUMBER or an IRRATIONAL NUMBER. Real numbers exclude imaginary numbers (the square roots of negative quantities). *See also* COMPLEX NUMBER

receptacle Biological structure that serves as a container for reproductive cells or organs in plants. In flowering plants, the receptacle is the enlarged end of a stalk to which the flower is attached. In ferns, it is the mass of tissue that forms the spore-bearing organ. In some seaweeds, it is the part that seasonally becomes swollen and carries the reproductive organs.

recession In economics, phase of the business cycle associated with a declining economy. Its manifestations are rising unemployment, contracting business activity and decreasing consumer spending. Government policy, such as cuts in government spending or taxes, may be used to stimulate and expand the economy during a recession. If a recession is not checked, it can lead to a DEPRESSION.

Recife City and port on the Atlantic coast, NE Brazil; the capital of Pernambuco state. Settled by the Portuguese in the 1530s, it was under Dutch occupation in the 17th century. It is now a major port and shipping centre. Pop. (1991) 1,290,149.

reciprocal Quantity equal to the number 1 divided by a specified number. The reciprocal of 2 is $\frac{1}{2}$, and the reciprocal of $\frac{1}{2}$ is 2.

recombinant DNA research Branch of GENETIC ENGINEERING involving the transferral of a segment of DNA from a source organism into a host organism (typically a microbe). The transferred segment is spliced into the host's overall DNA structure, thus altering the information contained in its GENETIC CODE. When the host undergoes asexual cell division, each product cell carries a replica of the new DNA. In this way numerous clones of the new cell can be made.

Reconstruction In US history, the process of restoring the former Confederate states to the Union after the CIVIL WAR. The relatively pro-Southern approach of President Andrew JOHNSON led to his impeachment. The Republicans were determined to establish the political and civil rights of African-Americans, and they succeeded in imposing Radical Reconstruction over presidential veto. It alienated many Southern whites, and growing violence in the 1870s required the presence of federal troops. When Rutherford B.

HAYES became president (1877), he withdrew the troops, Southern Republican governments collapsed, and Reconstruction was abandoned.

recorder Simple WOODWIND musical instrument, popular in Europe since the 15th century. It comprises an end-blown straight tube with eight finger-holes. Modern recorders include soprano, descant, tenor and bass instruments.

recording Storing of signals that represent sound or images. In disc recording, the sounds or images being recorded are electronically modified and converted into movements of a stylus. The stylus cuts an original lacquer disc, which is then electroplated to make a master negative for pressing out plastic copies. In magnetic recording, sound is recorded on tape with a TAPE RECORDER; a VIDEO RECORDING machine records sound and vision. Recent advancements in technology include the COMPACT DISC (CD) and the DIGITAL AUDIO TAPE (DAT).

rectangle Four-sided geometric figure (quadrilateral). The interior angles are right angles and each pair of opposite sides is of equal length and is parallel. It is a special case of a PARALLELOGRAM.

rectifier Component of an electric CIRCUIT that converts alternating current (AC) into direct current (DC). The rectifier is usually a semiconductor DIODE. *See also* ELECTRIC CURRENT

recycling Natural and man-made processes by which substances are broken down and reconstituted. In nature, elemental cycles include the CARBON CYCLE, NITROGEN CYCLE and HYDROLOGICAL CYCLE. Natural cyclic chemical processes include the metabolic cycles of living organisms. Man-made recycling includes the use of bacteria to break down organic wastes. Large quantities of inorganic waste, such as metal, glass and plastic are recycled.

red admiral Distinctive European butterfly with red bars on the wings and black wing-tips spotted with white. The caterpillar is dark with light side-stripes and branching spikes. Family Nymphalidae; species *Vanessa atalanta*.

red algae PHYLUM of reddish ALGAE, the Rhodophyta. They are numerous in tropical and subtropical seas. Most are slender, branching seaweeds that form shrub-like masses. Some become encrusted with calcium carbonate and are important in reef formation. Rhodophytes have red and purplish pigments, which help to absorb light for photosynthesis. They also have CHLOROPHYLL. They have complex life cycles with two or three distinct stages, involving ALTERNATION OF GENERATIONS.

red blood cell *See* ERYTHROCYTE

Red Cross International organization that seeks to alleviate human suffering, particularly through disaster relief and aid to war victims. It is composed of more than 150 independent national societies, with central headquarters in Geneva, Switzerland. It is staffed largely by volunteers. Its symbol is a red cross on a white background. It was awarded the Nobel Peace Prize in 1917 and 1944. It is known as the Red Crescent in Muslim countries.

redcurrant Widely cultivated shrub and its small, round, red, edible fruit; it is closely related to the blackcurrant. Family Grossulariaceae; species *Ribes silvestre*.

red dwarf Star at the lower end of the main sequence. Red dwarfs have masses of between 0.8 and 0.08 of a solar mass. They are of small diameter, relatively low surface temperature (2500–5000K) and low absolute magnitude.

Redford, Robert (1937–) US film actor, director and producer. He shot to fame appearing opposite Paul NEWMAN in *Butch Cassidy and the Sundance Kid* (1969) and *The Sting* (1974). Other acting credits include *The Great Gatsby* (1974) and *All the President's Men* (1976). In 1980 he won an Academy Award as Best Director for his debut feature *Ordinary People* (1980) and launched the Sundance Institute for independent film-makers.

Red Guards Chinese youth movement active in the CULTURAL REVOLUTION (1966–68). The Red Guards attacked revisionists, westerners and alleged bourgeois influences. Originally encouraged by Mao, they caused severe social disorder and were suppressed after 1968.

Red Sea Narrow arm of the Indian Ocean between NE Africa and the Arabian Peninsula, connected to the Mediterranean Sea by the Gulf of Suez and the Suez Canal. Its maximum width is about 320km (200mi). Area: 438,000sq km (169,000sq mi).

redshank Eurasian wading bird of the SANDPIPER family. It has a long slender bill, mottled grey, brown and white plumage, and characteristic slender red legs. Length: to 28cm (11in). Family Scolopacidae; species *Tringa totanus*.

red shift (z) Lengthening of the wavelength of light or other ELECTROMAGNETIC RADIATION from a source, caused either by the DOPPLER EFFECT or by the expansion of the Universe. It is defined as the change in the wavelength of a particular spectral line, divided by the rest wavelength of that line. The Doppler effect results from motion through space; cosmological red shifts are caused by the expansion of space, stretching the wavelengths of light.

reduction See OXIDATION-REDUCTION

redwood See SEQUOIA

Reed, Sir Carol (1906–76) British film director. He won an Academy Award as Best Director for *Oliver!* (1968). Other credits include *The Fallen Idol* (1948), *The Third Man* (1949), *Outcast of the Islands* (1952) and *The Man Between* (1956).

reed Aquatic GRASS native to wetlands worldwide. The common reed (*Phragmites communis*) has broad leaves, feathery flower clusters and stiff smooth stems. Height: to 3m (10ft). Family Poaceae/Gramineae.

reed instrument Musical instrument that produces sound when an air current vibrates a fibre or metal tongue. In a CLARINET, a beating reed vibrates against a hole at the end of the tube. The OBOE and BASSOON have double-reed mouthpieces, the two tongues vibrating against each other when blown.

reef Rocky outcrop lying in shallow water, especially one built up by CORALS or other organisms.

reflection Change in direction of part or all of a WAVE. When a wave, such as light or sound, encounters a surface separating two different media, it is bounced back into the original medium. The incident wave (striking the surface), reflected wave and the normal (line perpendicular to the surface) all lie in the same plane; the incident wave and reflected wave make equal angles with the normal.

reflex camera Camera that allows the user to view and focus through the lens of the camera. A plane mirror and prism reflect the scene through the lens on to a ground glass screen. When the photographer presses the shutter on a **single-lens reflex** (SLR) camera, the mirror flips back and light reaches the film.

reflexor See MUSCLE

Reform Acts British acts of Parliament extending the right to vote. The Great Reform Bill (1832) redistributed seats in the House of Commons to include large cities that were previously unrepresented. It also gave the vote to adult males occupying premises worth at least £10 a year. The second Reform Act (1867) extended the FRANCHISE to include better-off members of the working class. The acts of 1884 and 1885 gave the vote to most adult males. Women over 30 gained the vote in 1918, and the Representation of the People Act (1928) introduced universal adult suffrage.

Reformation Sixteenth-century European movement that sought reform of the universal Catholic Church and resulted in the development of PROTESTANTISM. It also represented a protest by many theologians and scholars against the interference of the church in politics and the activities of the clergy in the sale of INDULGENCES and holy relics. The influence of Martin LUTHER during the 1520s was significant. The effect of the Reformation was felt first in Germany, then in Switzerland (with John CALVIN), England, Scotland and Scandinavia, and finally in parts of France. In England, the Reformation was at first more political than religious: King HENRY VIII, angry over the refusal of Pope CLEMENT VII to grant him a divorce, passed an Act of Supremacy (1534) rejecting papal authority and making himself head of the Church of England. It became known as the ANGLICAN CHURCH, developing its own liturgy in the English language. *See also* COUNTER-REFORMATION

Reformed church Any Christian denomination that came into being during the REFORMATION by separating, as a congregation, from the old universal Catholic Church (the Western Church). More specifically, Reformed churches are those churches that adopted CALVINISM rather than LUTHERANISM.

refraction Bending of a wave, such as light or sound, when it crosses the boundary between two media, such as air and glass, and undergoes a change in velocity. The incident wave (striking the surface), refracted wave and the normal (line perpendicular to the surface) all lie in the same plane. The incident wave and refracted wave make an angle of incidence, i, and an angle of refraction, r, with the normal. The index of refraction for a transparent medium is the ratio of the speed of light in a vacuum to its speed in the medium. It is also equal to sin i/sin r. Snell's law states that this ratio is constant for a given interface.

refrigeration Process by which the temperature in a refrigerator or air-conditioner is lowered. In a domestic refrigerator, a refrigerant gas such as AMMONIA or freon is first compressed by a pump and cooled in a condenser where it liquefies. It is then passed into an evaporator where it expands and boils, absorbing heat from its surroundings and thus cooling the refrigerator. It is then passed through the pump again to be compressed.

Regency style Style of art and architecture fashionable when the future George IV was Prince Regent (1811–20) and during his reign. It generally denotes designs that are elegant and refined.

regeneration Biological ability of an organism to replace one of its parts if it is lost. Regeneration also refers to a form of ASEXUAL REPRODUCTION in which a new individual grows from a detached portion of a parent organism.

Reich, Steve (1936–) US composer. His minimalist works are characterized by transforming musical patterns. Many of his works, such as *Drumming* (1971), are written for percussion ensembles.

Reich, Wilhelm (1897–1957) Austrian psychoanalyst and clinical assistant to FREUD (1922–28). He theorized the existence of "orgone" energy, a primal force in the atmosphere. The function of sexual orgasm was to discharge this energy. Reich marketed an orgone box, which would release this energy. He was imprisoned for fraud and died in jail.

Reign of Terror Phase of the FRENCH REVOLUTION (June 1793–July 1794). It began with the overthrow of the GIRONDINS and the ascendancy of the JACOBINS under ROBESPIERRE. Against a background of foreign invasion and civil war, opponents were ruthlessly persecuted and c.1,400 executed by the GUILLOTINE. The Terror ended with a coup on 27 July 1794. Robespierre and leading Jacobins were arrested and executed.

Reims City on the River Vesle, NE France. CLOVIS I was baptized and crowned here in 496, and it was the coronation place of later French kings. Reims is the centre of the champagne industry. Industries: woollen goods, metallurgy. Pop. (1990) 180,620.

reincarnation Passage of the soul through successive bodies, causing the rebirth of an individual and the prolonging of existence on Earth. In HINDUISM and BUDDHISM, an individual's KARMA determines the condition into which one is born in the next life.

reindeer (caribou) Large DEER, which ranges from Scandinavia across Siberia to North America. It has thick fur and broad hoofs. It stands up to 1.4m (4.6ft) tall at the shoulders, and feeds on grasses and saplings in the summer and lichens it finds under the snow in the winter. It is domesticated for meat and as a pack animal by the Lapps. Both sexes have antlers. Species *Rangifer tarandus*.

relative atomic mass (r.a.m.) (formerly atomic weight) Mass of an atom of the naturally occurring form of an element divided by 1/12 of the mass of an atom of carbon-12. The naturally occurring form may consist of two or more isotopes, and calculation of the r.a.m. must take this into account.

relative density (formerly specific gravity) Ratio of the DENSITY of a substance to the density of water. The relative density of gold is 19.3, thus it is over 19 times denser than an equal volume of water.

relative molecular mass (formerly molecular weight) Mass of a molecule, the sum of the relative atomic masses of all its atoms. It is the ratio of the average mass per molecule of an element or compound to 1/12 of the mass of an atom of carbon-12. The molecular masses of reactants (elements or compounds) must be known in order to make calculations about yields in a chemical reaction.

relativity Theory, proposed by Albert EINSTEIN, based on the postulate that the motion of one body can be defined only with respect to that of a second body. This led to the concept of a four-dimensional space-time continuum in which the three space dimensions and time are treated on an equal footing. The **special theory** (1905) is limited to the description of events as they appear to observers in a state of uniform relative motion. The consequences of the theory are: (1) that the velocity of light is absolute, that is, not relative to the velocity of the observer; (2) that the mass of a body increases with its velocity, although only appreciably at velocities approaching that of light; (3) that mass (m) and energy (E) are equivalent, that is, $E = mc^2$, where c is the velocity of light (this shows that when mass is converted to energy, a small mass gives rise to large energy); (4) the **Lorentz-Fitzgerald** contraction, that is bodies contract as their velocity increases, again only appreciably near the velocity of light; and (5) an object's sense of elapsed time expands, "time dilation". The **general theory** of relativity (1915) is applicable to observers not in uniform relative motion. This showed the relation of space and GRAVITATION. The presence of matter in space causes space to "curve", forming gravitational fields; thus gravitation becomes a property of space itself. The existence of black holes is postulated as a consequence of this.

religion Code of beliefs and practices formulated in response to a spiritual awareness of existence. It may involve either faith in a state of existence after earthly death, or a desire for union with an omnipotent spiritual being, or a combination of the two. Polytheism entails the worship of many distinct gods or personifications of nature. HINDUISM classifies deities into a pantheon or hierarchy. Some religions, such as BUDDHISM and TAOISM, incorporate belief in a state of existence after death as a system of ethical philosophy, concentrating on metaphysical contemplation. Common to **monotheism** (JUDAISM, CHRISTIANITY and ISLAM) is the worship of a single omnipotent force, beyond the physical plane occupied by humans. The ancient Hebrews were among the first people to worship a single omniscient and omnipotent being, YAHWEH. He gave them His protection in return for their total faith and obedience. In many religions, both monotheistic and polytheistic, sacrifice to an individual god or God is an important element, either in propitiation, or to redeem the faithful from some wrongdoing, or in thanksgiving.

Religion, Wars of (1562–98) Series of religious conflicts in France. At stake was freedom of worship for HUGUENOTS (Protestants). The conflicts ended with the defeat of the extremist Catholic Holy League by HENRY IV. The Edict of NANTES (1598) extended toleration to the Huguenots.

Remarque, Erich Maria (1898–1970) German novelist. A World War 1 veteran, his best-known novel, *All Quiet on the Western Front* (1929), is a savage indictment of war. The sequel *The Road Back* (1931) concerns Germany's post-war collapse and readjustment.

Rembrandt Harmenszoon van Rijn (1606–69) Dutch painter and graphic artist. During 1625–31 he painted many self-portraits. He settled in Amsterdam (1631–32), becoming highly regarded as a painter of group portraits such as the *Anatomy Lesson of Dr Tulp* (1632). By 1636 he was painting in the richly detailed BAROQUE style typified by the *Sacrifice of Abraham* (1636). In 1642 he finished his famous group portrait, *The Corporalship of Captain Frans Banning Cocq's Civic Guards* (or *The Night Watch*). His late masterpieces include *Jacob Blessing the Sons of Joseph* (1656) and *The Jewish Bride* (late 1660s). He completed more than 300 paintings, 300 etchings and 1,000 drawings.

remote sensing Any method of obtaining and recording information from a distance. The most common sensor is the CAMERA, which is used in aircraft, satellites and space probes to collect and transmit information back to Earth (often by radio). The resulting photographs provide information, such as weather data. MICROWAVE sensors use radar signals that can penetrate cloud. Infra-red sensors can measure temperature differences over an area. Data from sensors can be processed by computers.

Remus *See* ROMULUS AND REMUS

Renaissance (Fr. rebirth) Period of European history lasting roughly from the mid-l5th century to the end of the 16th century. The word was used by late 15th-century Italian scholars to describe the revival of interest in classical learning. It was helped by the fall of Constantinople to the Ottoman Turks in 1453, which resulted in the transport of classical texts to Italy. In Germany, the invention of a PRINTING press with moveable type assisted the diffusion of the new scholarship. In religion, the spirit of questioning led to the REFORMATION. In politics, the Renaissance saw the rise of assertive sovereign states and the expansion of Europe, with the building of trading empires in Africa, the East Indies and America. The growth of a wealthy urban merchant class led to a tremendous flowering of the arts. *See also* RENAISSANCE ARCHITECTURE; RENAISSANCE ART; RENAISSANCE MUSIC

Renaissance architecture Architectural style that began as a revolt against GOTHIC ARCHITECTURE in 15th century Italy and spread throughout Europe until the advent of MANNERISM and the BAROQUE. In Italy, BRUNELLESCHI and ALBERTI studied Roman ruins. In France, Lescot was commissioned by Francis I to work on the Louvre (1546). In other European countries, classical forms were integrated with medieval motifs.

Renaissance art Style that emerged in Italy in the 15th century, heavily influenced by classical Greek or Roman models and by HUMANISM. In painting, the decisive differences between Gothic and Renaissance painting emerged in Florence in the early 15th century. These differences included: the development of PERSPECTIVE; a new interest in composition and colour harmonies; the increasing use of secular subjects; the rise of portraiture; experimentation to develop new skills; and a growing concern for individual expression. The creators of High Renaissance painting were LEONARDO DA VINCI, MICHELANGELO and RAPHAEL. The ideas of the Italian artists were taken to France and N Europe and emulated with national variations.

Renaissance literature found an early exponent in PETRARCH; other Italian Renaissance literary figures include DANTE and MACHIAVELLI. By the 16th century the Renaissance literary movement had reached N Europe, where it inspired much poetry and history writing and the dramas of Shakespeare.

Renaissance music Music composed in Europe from *c*.1400–1600. It was mainly religious vocal POLYPHONY, usually MASSES and MOTETS. Non-religious music was mainly in the form of songs – Italian and English MADRIGALS, French *chansons*, German *Lieder* – and some instrumental music for organ, clavier, lute, or for small ensembles. Composers of this period include PALESTRINA, LASSO, BYRD and GABRIELI.

renewable energy (alternative energy) ENERGY from a source that can be replenished or that replenishes itself, and is more environmentally friendly than traditional energy forms such as COAL, GAS or NUCLEAR ENERGY. SOLAR ENERGY harnesses the rays of the Sun. TIDAL POWER stations use the gravitational force of the Sun and Moon. Wave power harnesses the natural movement of the sea. The power of rivers and lakes can be tapped by damming the flow and using turbines to generate HYDROELECTRICITY. WIND POWER schemes have existed for centuries in the form of WINDMILLS. GEOTHERMAL ENERGY is produced in the Earth's crust.

rennet Substance used to curdle milk in cheese-making. It is obtained as an extract from the inner lining of the fourth stomach of calves and other young ruminants, and is rich in rennin, an ENZYME which coagulates the casein (protein) of milk.

Renoir, Pierre Auguste (1841–1919) French impressionist painter. In 1874 he contributed to the first exhibition of IMPRESSIONISM and masterpieces of the period include *La Loge* (1874) and *Le Moulin de la Galette* (1876). In the early 1880s he became interested in the human figure with such works as *Bathers* (1884–87) and *After the Bath* (*c*.1895).

Representatives, House of *See* HOUSE OF REPRESENTATIVES

repression Process by which unacceptable thoughts or memories are kept in the UNCONSCIOUS so that they cannot cause guilt or distress. In Freudian psychology, it is part of the function of the ego, whereby it controls the primal and instinctual urges of the id. Repressed desires find an outlet in dreams, and are believed to cause various neurotic disorders.

reproduction Process by which living organisms create new organisms similar to themselves. Reproduction may be sexual or asexual, the former being the fusion of two special reproductive cells from different parents, and the latter being the generation of new organisms from a single organism. ASEXUAL REPRODUCTION is the more limited, found mainly in PROTOZOA, some INVERTEBRATES and many plants. By contrast, almost all living organisms have the capacity for SEXUAL REPRODUCTION. In the majority of cases the species has two kinds of individuals – male and female – with different sex functions. Male and female sex cells (in animals, sperm and egg) fuse to produce a new cell, the ZYGOTE, which contains genetic information from both parents, and from which a new individual develops. Alternatively, organisms may be HERMAPHRODITES, each individual having male and female functions, so that when two of them mate each individual fertilizes the other's eggs. Sexually reproducing plants (or generations) are called GAMETOPHYTE; ones which reproduce asexually, SPOROPHYTE. *See also* ALTERNATION OF GENERATIONS; POLLEN

reptile Any one of about 6,000 species of VERTEBRATES distributed worldwide. Reptiles are cold-blooded. Most lay yolky eggs on land. Some species (particularly SNAKES) carry eggs in the body and bear live young. The skin is dry and covered with scales or embedded with bony plates. Their limbs are poorly developed or non-existent. Those with limbs usually have five clawed toes on each foot. There are now four living orders: Chelonia (TURTLES); Rhynchocephalia (TUATARA); Squamata (scaly reptiles such as snakes and LIZARDS); and Crocodilia (ALLIGATORS and CROCODILES).

Republican Party US political party. It was organized in 1854. Its first successful presidential candidate was Abraham LINCOLN (elected 1860). During the 20th century, the Republicans were generally the minority party to the DEMOCRATIC PARTY in Congress, especially in the House of REPRESENTATIVES. From the 1970s, however, the party shifted rightwards and gained substantial support. Despite President CLINTON being a Democrat, the Senate and House of Representatives remain in Republican control.

resin (rosin) Artificial or natural POLYMER that is generally viscous and sticky. Artificial resins include polyesters and epoxies, used as adhesives and binders. Natural resins are secreted by various plants. Oleoresin, secreted by conifers, is distilled to produce turpentine.

resistance Property of an electric conductor (symbol R), calculated as the ratio of the voltage applied to the conductor to the current passing through it. The SI unit of resistance is the OHM. *See also* RESISTOR

resistivity Electrical property (symbol ρ) of materials. Its value is given by $\rho = AR/l$, where A is the cross-sectional area of a conductor, l is its length and R is its RESISTANCE. Resistivity is generally expressed in units of ohm-metres and is a measure of the resistance of a piece of material of given size.

resistor Electrical CIRCUIT component with a specified RESISTANCE. Resistors limit the size of the current flowing. Electronic circuit resistors usually consist of carbon particles mixed with a ceramic material and enclosed in an insulated tube. Resistors for larger currents are coils of insulated wire.

resonance Increase in the amplitude of vibration of a mechanical or acoustic system when it is forced to vibrate by an external source. It occurs when the FREQUENCY of the applied force is equal to the natural vibrational frequency of the system. Large vibrations can cause damage to the system.

respiration Series of chemical reactions by which food molecules are broken down to release energy in living organisms. These reactions are controlled by ENZYMES, and are an essential part of METABOLISM. There are two main types of respiration: AEROBIC and ANAEROBIC. In **aerobic** respiration, oxygen combines with the breakdown products and is necessary for the reactions to take place. **Anaerobic** respiration takes place in the absence of oxygen. In most living organisms, the energy released by respiration is used to convert adenosine diphosphate (ADP) to adenosine triphosphate (ATP), which transports energy around the cell. At the site where energy is needed, ATP is converted back to ADP, with the aid of a special enzyme, and energy is released. The first stages of respiration take place in the cytoplasm and the later stages in the MITOCHONDRIA.

respiratory system System in air-breathing animals concerned with GAS EXCHANGE. The respiratory tract begins with the nose and mouth. The air then passes through the LARYNX and into the TRACHEA. The trachea at its lower end branches into two bronchi, each BRONCHUS leads to a LUNG. The bronchi divide into many bronchioles, which lead in turn to bunches of tiny air sacs (ALVEOLI), where the exchange of gases between air and blood takes place. Exhaled air leaves along the same pathway.

Restoration In English history, the re-establishment of the monarchy in 1660. After the death of Oliver CROMWELL, his son and successor, Richard, was unable to prevent growing conflict or restrain the increasing power of the army. He resigned (1659), and the crisis was resolved by the march of General MONCK from Scotland. Army leaders backed down and a new Parliament was elected. From exile, CHARLES II issued the Declaration of Breda (1660), promising an amnesty to opponents (except those directly responsible for the execution of CHARLES I), payment of army wage arrears, and religious toleration. He was invited by a new Parliament to resume the throne. In French history, it refers to the restoration of the BOURBONS (1814–30) after the defeat of Napoleon.

Restoration drama Plays and performances following the restoration of CHARLES II, when the theatres were reopened. The drama, principally comedies, reflected the laxity of court morals. Major playwrights included DRYDEN and CONGREVE.

resurrection Rising of the dead to new life, either in heaven or on Earth. JUDAISM, CHRISTIANITY and ISLAM all hold that at the end of the world there will come a Day of Judgement on which those worthy of eternal joy will be allowed to draw near to God. The term also applies to the rising of JESUS CHRIST from the dead on the third day after his crucifixion.

resuscitation Measures taken to revive a person who is on the brink of death. The most successful technique available to the layman is mouth-to-mouth resuscitation. Medical staff provide cardiopulmonary resuscitation (CPR), which involves specialized equipment and drugs to save patients.

retina Inner layer of the EYE, composed mainly of different kinds of NEURONS, some of which are the visual receptors of the eye. Receptor cells, known as cones and rods, are sensitive to light. Cones respond to the spectrum of visible colours; rods respond to shades of grey and to movement. The rods and cones connect with sensory neurons, which in turn connect with the optic nerve, which carries the visual stimuli to the brain.

retrovirus Any of a large family of VIRUSES (Retroviridae) that, unlike other living organisms, contain RNA (ribonucleic acid) rather than the customary DNA (deoxyribonucleic acid). In order to multiply, retroviruses make use of a special enzyme to convert their RNA into DNA, which then becomes integrated with the DNA in the cells of their hosts. Diseases caused by retroviruses include ACQUIRED IMMUNE DEFICIENCY SYNDROME (AIDS).

Réunion Volcanic island in the Indian Ocean, in the Mascarene group, *c.*700km (435mi) E of Madagascar, forming an overseas *département* of France; the capital is St Denis. Discovered in 1513, it was claimed by France in 1638. The island became an overseas *département* in 1948. Exports: sugar, rum, maize, tobacco. Area: 2,510sq km (969sq mi). Pop. (1994 est.) 645,000.

Revelation (Apocalypse) Last book of the NEW TESTAMENT. It was written perhaps as late as AD 95 by St John the Divine. In highly allegorical and prophetic terms, it concentrates on depicting the end of Creation, the war between good and evil, the Day of Judgment and the ultimate triumph of good.

Revere, Paul (1735–1818) American silversmith and patriot, famous for his ride from Charlestown to Lexington, Massachusetts. Revere made his ride on the night of 18 April 1775 to warn the colonists of Massachusetts of the approach of British troops at the start of the AMERICAN REVOLUTION.

reversible reaction Chemical reaction in which the products can change back into the reactants. Thus nitrogen and hydrogen can be combined to give ammonia (as in the HABER PROCESS) and ammonia may be decomposed into nitrogen and hydrogen. Such processes yield a CHEMICAL EQUILIBRIUM.

revolution Movement of a planet or other celestial object around its orbit, as distinct from ROTATION of the object on its axis. A single revolution is the planet's or satellite's "year".

Revolutions of 1848 Series of revolutions in European countries. The general cause was the frustration of liberals and nationalists, against a background of economic depression. The risings began with the FEBRUARY REVOLUTION against LOUIS PHILIPPE in France and resulted in the foundation of the Second Republic. It inspired revolts in Vienna (forcing the resignation of METTERNICH), and among the national minorities under Austrian rule. In Germany, liberals forced FREDERICK V to summon a constitutional assembly.

Revolutions of 1989 Popular risings in East European states against communist governments. Long-suppressed opposition to Soviet-dominated rule erupted in most Soviet satellite states. In November 1989 the Berlin Wall came down. Within months, Communist Parties throughout Eastern Europe were driven from power. They were followed by the withdrawal of the constituent republics of the Soviet Union and President GORBACHEV resigned after a failed hardline coup.

Reykjavík Capital of Iceland, a port on the SW coast. Founded *c.*870, it was Iceland's first permanent settlement. It became the capital in 1918. During World War 2 it served as a British and US air base. Industries: fishing, textiles, metallurgy, printing, publishing, shipbuilding. Pop. (1993) 101,824.

Reynolds, Sir Joshua (1723–92) English portrait painter and writer on art. The first president of the ROYAL ACADEMY OF ARTS (RA) (1768), he espoused the principles of the "Grand Manner" style in his *Discourses*. These writings describe how painting, through allusions to classical, heroic figures, can be a scholarly activity.

rhapsody Musical term applied in the 19th and 20th centuries to orchestral works, usually performed in one continuous movement and most often inspired by a nationalist or romantic theme.

rhea Either of two species of large, brownish,

533

flightless, fast-running South American birds resembling a small OSTRICH. They feed mostly on vegetation and insects. Height: to 1.5m (5ft). Family Rheidae.

rhenium Silver-white metallic element (symbol Re), one of the TRANSITION ELEMENTS, which have incomplete inner electron shells. Discovered in 1925, rhenium is found in molybdenite and PLATINUM ores. It is used in alloys in thermocouples, flashlights and electronic filaments, and is also a useful catalyst. Properties: at. no. 75; r.a.m. 186.2; r.d. 21.0; m.p. 3,180°C (5,756°F); b.p. 5,627°C (10,160°F); most common isotope Re^{187} (62.93%).

rheostat Variable RESISTOR for regulating an electric current. The resistance element may be a metal wire, carbon or a conducting liquid. Rheostats are used to adjust generators, to dim lights and to control the speed of electric motors.

rhesus Medium-sized, yellow-brown MACAQUE monkey of India. Short-tailed, it has a large head with large ears and closely spaced, deep-set eyes. Height: 60cm (2ft). Species *Macaca mulatta*.

rheumatic fever Inflammatory disorder characterized by fever and painful swelling of the joints. Rare in the modern developed world, it mostly affects children and young adults. An important complication is possible damage to the heart valves, leading to rheumatic heart disease in later life.

rheumatism General term for a group of disorders whose symptoms are pain, inflammation and stiffness in the bones, joints and surrounding tissues. Usually some form of ARTHRITIS is involved.

Rhine (Rhein, Rhin or Rijn) River in W Europe. It rises in the Swiss Alps and flows N, bordering on or passing through Switzerland, Austria, Liechtenstein, Germany, France and Netherlands to enter the North Sea at Rotterdam. The Rhine is navigable to ocean-going vessels as far as Basel, Switzerland. Length: c.1,320km (820mi).

Rhineland Region in W Germany along the W bank of the River Rhine. It includes Saarland and Rhineland-Palatinate, and parts of Baden-Württemberg, Hesse and North Rhine-Westphalia. It was the scene of heavy fighting in the later stages of World War 2.

rhinoceros (rhino) Massive, herbivorous mammal native to Africa and Asia. Rhinos have thick skin and poor eyesight, and are solitary grazers or browsers. In the heat of the day they like to wallow in muddy pools. Now rare except in protected areas, rhinos are illegally hunted for their horns. Weight: 1–3.5 tonnes. Family Rhinocerotidae.

rhizoid Fine hair-like growth used for attachment to a solid surface by some simple organisms, such as certain fungi and mosses. The rhizoid lacks the conducting TISSUES of a root.

rhizome Root-like underground stem of certain plants. It usually grows horizontally, is rich in accumulated starch, and can produce new roots and stems asexually. Rhizomes differ from roots in producing buds and leaves. *See also* TUBER

Rhode Island State in NE USA, on the Atlantic coast in New England; the smallest state in the USA; the capital is PROVIDENCE. The region was first settled in 1636. Much of the land is forested, but there is some dairy farming. Industries: textiles, metals, machinery and tourism. Area: 3,144sq km (1,214sq mi). Pop. (1993 est.) 1,000,012.

Rhodes, Cecil John (1853–1902) South African political leader, prime minister of Cape Colony (1890–96), b. Britain. He emigrated in 1870 and made a fortune in diamonds and gold, founding the De Beers Company. Through his British South Africa Company (founded 1889), he controlled a vast area of S Africa, including Rhodesia (now Zambia and Zimbabwe).

Rhodes (Ródhos) Greek island in the SE Aegean Sea; the largest of the Dodecanese archipelago. It was colonized by the Dorians c.1000 BC. The island was captured in 1310 by the KNIGHTS HOSPITALLERS. It was taken by Ottoman Turks in 1522. Ceded to Italy in 1912, it was awarded to Greece in 1947. The chief city is Rhodes. Products: wheat, tobacco, cotton, olives, fruits, vegetables. Area: 1,400sq km (540sq mi). Pop. (1981) 88,000.

Rhodesia Former name of a territory in S central Africa. The area was developed by Cecil RHODES. In 1923 Southern Rhodesia became a self-governing British colony, and in 1924 Northern Rhodesia was made a British protectorate. In 1953 the two were united with Nyasaland (now MALAWI) in the Central African Federation. When the federation was dissolved in 1963, Northern Rhodesia achieved independence as ZAMBIA. The name Rhodesia was used by Southern Rhodesia until the country achieved independence as ZIMBABWE in 1980.

rhodium Silver-white metallic element (symbol Rh), one of the TRANSITION ELEMENTS. Discovered in 1803, it is associated with PLATINUM and is a by-product of NICKEL smelting. It resists corrosion and is used in hard platinum alloys and jewellery. Properties: at. no. 45; r.a.m. 102.906; r.d. 12.4; m.p. 1,966°C (3,571°F); b.p. 3,727°C (6,741°F); most common isotope Rh^{103} (100%).

rhododendron Large genus of shrubs and small trees that grow in the acid soils of cool temperate regions in North America, Europe and Asia. Primarily evergreen, they have leathery leaves and bell-shaped white, pink or purple flowers. Family Ericaceae. *See also* AZALEA

rhodophyta *See* RED ALGAE

rhombus Plane figure with all of its sides equal in length but no right angles. A rhombus is a type of PARALLELOGRAM whose diagonals bisect each other at right angles.

Rhône River in W Europe. It rises in the Rhône Glacier in S Switzerland, flows W to Lake Geneva and then crosses the French border. It continues S through LYON and AVIGNON to Arles, where it branches into the Grand Rhône and the Petit Rhône, which both enter the Mediterranean W of Marseilles. Length: 813km (505mi).

rhubarb Perennial herbaceous plant native to Asia and cultivated in cool climates worldwide for its edible leaf stalks. It has large poisonous leaves and small white or red flowers. Height: to 1.2m (4ft). Genus *Rheum*.

rib Long, curved bones that are arranged in pairs, extending sideways from the backbone of vertebrates. In fish and some reptiles they extend the length of the spine; in mammals they form the framework of the chest, and protect the lungs and heart. There are 12 pairs of ribs in humans.

Ribbentrop, Joachim von (1893–1946) German diplomat and politician. He initiated the Nazi-Soviet Pact (1939), but lost influence during World War 2. At the NUREMBERG TRIALS (1946), he was convicted of war crimes and hanged.

Ribera, José (1591–1652) Spanish painter and graphic artist. His early work, like that of CARAVAGGIO, used dark shadows. His late paintings are richly coloured, such as *The Clubfooted Boy* (1642).

riboflavin VITAMIN B_2 of the B complex, lack of which impairs growth and causes skin disorders. It is a co-enzyme important in transferring energy within cells. Soluble in water, riboflavin is found in milk, eggs, liver and green vegetables.

ribonucleic acid *See* RNA

ribosome Tiny structure in the CYTOPLASM of EUKARYOTE cells, involved in synthesizing PROTEIN molecules. Proteins are made up of specific sequences of AMINO ACIDS, and segments of DNA, called GENES, contain the instructions for individual proteins. The DNA molecule is too large to escape from the CELL nucleus into the cytoplasm, but a "copy" is made in the form of messenger RNA, and this travels to the ribosomes. Ribosomes attach themselves to the messenger RNA, then assemble the amino acids in the correct sequence to form a particular protein. Ribosomes are made up of proteins and ribosomal RNA. *See also* GENETIC CODE

Ricardo, David (1772–1823) British political economist. He advocated minimal state interference and a free market. His labour theory of value (that the price of commodities reflects the labour involved in their production) advanced in *Principles of Political Economy and Taxation* (1817), had a strong influence on Karl MARX.

rice Plant native to SE Asia and Indonesia, cultivated in many warm humid regions. It provides a staple diet for half the world's population. It is an annual grass; the seed and husk is the edible portion. It is usually grown in flooded, terraced paddies with hard subsoil. Species *Oryza sativa*.

Richard I (1157–99) King of England (1189–99), known as Richard the Lion-Heart, or *Coeur de Lion*. He succeeded his father HENRY II. A leader of the Third CRUSADE (1189–92), he won several victories but failed to retake Jerusalem and was held prisoner (1192–94). During this period, his brother JOHN conspired against him in England. The revolt in England was contained, and Richard returned to try and restore the ANGEVIN empire in France.

Richard II (1367–1400) King of England (1377–99). Son of EDWARD THE BLACK PRINCE, he succeeded his grandfather, EDWARD III. His uncle, JOHN OF GAUNT, controlled the government until 1381 and opposed Richard's supporters. The struggle for power reached a climax with the invasion of the exiled Henry Bolingbroke, son of John of Gaunt, who overthrew Richard and became King HENRY IV. Richard died in captivity.

Richard III (1452–85) King of England (1483–85). As Duke of Gloucester, he supported his brother, EDWARD IV. When Edward died, Richard became protector and had the young King EDWARD V declared illegitimate and took the crown. Edward and his younger brother, the "Princes in the Tower", subsequently disappeared. Richard's enemies supported the invasion of Henry Tudor (HENRY VII) in 1485. Richard was killed in battle.

Richardson, Samuel (1689–1761) English novelist and printer. He wrote his first novel *Pamela* in 1740–41. It was followed by two more novels of letters, *Clarissa* (1747–48) and *Sir Charles Grandison* (1753–54). His work prompted FIELDING's parodies *An Apology for the Life of Shamela Andrews* (1741) and *Joseph Andrews* (1742).

Richardson, Tony (1928–91) British film and stage director. His first stage and film production was *Look Back in Anger*. In the early 1960s he had a string of successful films, such as *The Entertainer* (1960) and *A Taste of Honey* (1961). He won a Best Director Academy Award for *Tom Jones* (1963).

Richelieu, Armand Jean du Plessis, Duc de (1585–1642) French cardinal and statesman. A protégé of MARIE DE MÉDICI, he became chief of the royal council in 1624. He suppressed the military and political power of the HUGUENOTS, but tolerated Protestant religious practices. He alienated many aristocratic Catholics by the primary role he accorded to the state, and survived several plots against him. In the THIRTY YEARS WAR, he formed alliances with Protestant powers against the HABSBURGS. His more scholarly interests resulted in the foundation of the ACADÉMIE FRANÇAISE (1635).

Richmond Capital of Virginia, USA, in E Virginia, and a port on the James River. Settled in 1637, Richmond became state capital in 1779. During the US Civil War it was the capital of the CONFEDERATE STATES (1861) until it fell to Union forces in 1865. Industries: metal products, tobacco, textiles, clothing, chemicals. Pop. (1990) 203,056.

Richter, Burton (1931–) US physicist. He discovered (1974) a new subatomic particle (which he named psi); it is a type of MESON. For this work Richter shared the 1976 Nobel Prize for physics.

Richter scale Classification of earthquake magnitude set up in 1935 by the American geologist Charles Richter. The scale is logarithmic – each point on the scale increases by a factor of ten – and is based on the total energy released by an earthquake, as opposed to a scale of intensity that measures the damage done at a particular place.

rickets Disorder in which there is defective growth of bone in children; the bones fail to harden sufficiently and become bent. Due either to a lack of VITAMIN D in the diet or to insufficient sunlight to allow its synthesis in the skin, it results from the inability of the bones to calcify properly.

Ridley, Nicholas (1500–55) English bishop and Protestant martyr. He was made bishop of Rochester (1547) and of London (1550). As chaplain to Thomas CRANMER he helped to compile the BOOK OF COMMON PRAYER (1549). In 1553 he supported the Protestant Lady Jane GREY against the Catholic MARY I (MARY TUDOR). Convicted of heresy under Mary, he was burned at the stake.

Riemann, Georg Friedrich Bernhard (1826–66) German mathematician who laid the foundations for much of modern mathematics and physics. He worked on integration, variable functions, and differential and non-Euclidean geometry, later used in the general theory of RELATIVITY.

rifle FIREARM with spiral grooves (rifling) along the inside of the barrel to make the bullet spin in flight, thereby greatly increasing range and accuracy over that of a smoothbore weapon. Not until the Minié rifle of 1849 were rifles widely used. During the 19th century, breech-loading and magazine rifles were developed.

rift valley Depression formed by the subsidence of land between two parallel faults. Rift valleys are believed to be formed by thermal currents within the Earth's MANTLE that break up the CRUST into large blocks of rock, which then become fractured.

Rift Valley (Great Rift Valley) Steep-sided, flat-floored valley in SW Asia and E Africa. It runs from N Syria, through the Jordan Valley and the Dead Sea, and then continues as the trough of the Red Sea through E Africa to the lower valley of the Zambezi River in Mozambique. Lake TANGANYIKA lies on its floor. Length: c.6,400km (4,000mi).

Riga Capital of Latvia, on the Gulf of Riga. In 1282 it joined the Hanseatic League. It was taken by Peter the Great in 1710. In 1918 it became the capital of independent Latvia. In 1940, when Latvia was incorporated into the Soviet Union, thousands of its citizens were deported or executed. Under German occupation from 1941, the city reverted to Soviet rule in 1944. In 1991 it resumed its status as capital of an independent Latvia. Industries: shipbuilding, engineering, electronics. Pop (1991) 910,200.

rigor mortis Stiffening of the body after death brought about by chemical changes in muscle tissue. Onset is gradual from minutes to hours, and it disappears within about 24 hours.

Rilke, Rainer Maria (1875–1926) German lyric poet, b. Prague. His first volume was *The Book of Hours* (1899–1903). In *New Poems* (1907–08), he developed the "object poem". Both *Sonnets to Orpheus* and his existential masterpiece *Duino Elegies* appeared in 1922.

Rimbaud, Arthur (1854–91) French anarchic poet, who influenced SYMBOLISM. He had a stormy relationship with Paul VERLAINE, under whose tutelage he wrote *The Drunken Boat* (1871). In 1873 they separated and *A Season in Hell* appeared. Rimbaud abandoned poetry for travel. *Les Illuminations* was published by Verlaine in 1886 as the work of the late Arthur Rimbaud.

Rimsky-Korsakov, Nikolai Andreievich (1844–1908) Russian composer, one of the RUSSIAN FIVE. His operas include *The Snow Maiden* (1881) and *The Golden Cockerel* (1907). His popular orchestral works include *Sheherazade* (1888), *Capriccio espagnole* (1887) and *The Flight of the Bumblebee* from the opera *Tsar Saltan* (1900).

ringworm Fungus infection of the skin, scalp or nails. The commonest type of ringworm is athlete's foot (*tinea pedis*).

Rio de Janeiro City on Guanabara Bay, SE Brazil. Discovered by Europeans in 1502, by the 18th century it had become a leading port for gold export and the seat of the viceroy. During 1834–1960 it was Brazil's capital. The second-largest city in Brazil, it is the commercial and industrial centre and a popular tourist resort. There are large shanty towns surrounding the city. Industries: coffee, sugar refining, shipbuilding. Pop. (1991) 5,336,179.

Rio Grande River in North America. It rises in the San Juan Mountains of SW Colorado state, and flows generally S through New Mexico. It forms the border between Texas and Mexico, and empties into the Gulf of Mexico. The river is largely unnavigable. Length: c.3,035km (1,885mi).

Risorgimento (It. resurgence) Nationalist movement resulting in the unification of Italy (1859–70). With the restoration of Austrian and Bourbon rule in 1815, MAZZINI's Young Italy movement called for a single, democratic republic. Mazzini's influence was at its peak in the REVOLUTIONS OF 1848. In Sardinia-Piedmont (the only independent Italian state), the aim of the chief minister, CAVOUR, was a parliamentary monarchy under the royal house of Savoy. Securing the support of Napoleon III against Austria, he acquired much of N Italy in 1859. In 1860 GARIBALDI conquered Sicily and Naples. Garibaldi cooperated with Cavour, and the kingdom of Italy was proclaimed in 1861 under Victor Emmanuel II of Savoy. Rome was seized when the French withdrew in 1870.

river Large natural channel containing water which flows downhill under gravity. A river system is a network of connecting channels. It can be divided into tributaries which collect water and sediment, the main trunk river, and the dispersing system at the river's mouth where much of the sediment is deposited. The discharge of a river is the volume of water flowing past a point in a given time. The velocity of a river is controlled by the slope, its depth and the roughness of the river bed. Rivers transport sediment as they flow, by the processes of traction (rolling), saltation (jumping), suspension (carrying) and solution. Most river sediment is transported during flood conditions, but as a river returns to normal flow it deposits sediment. This can result in the erosion of a river channel or the building up of flood plains. All rivers tend to flow in a twisting pattern, even if the slope is relatively steep, because water flow is naturally turbulent. Over time, on shallow slopes, small bends grow into large meanders. The current flows faster on the outside of bends eroding the bank while sedimentation occurs on the inside of bends where the current is slowest. This causes the curves to exaggerate, forming loops. Flood risk can be reduced by straightening the channel, dredging sediment or making the channel deeper. *See also* DELTA; OXBOW

Rivera, Diego (1886–1957) Mexican mural painter, married to fellow artist Frida Kahlo. He used symbolism and allegory to depict historical events. His work adorns buildings in Mexico City.

Riviera Region of SE France and NW Italy, on the Mediterranean Sea, extending 370km (230mi) from Cannes, France, to La Spezia, Italy. Its spectacular scenery and mild climate make it a leading tourist centre. Resorts include NICE and CANNES in France and MONTE CARLO in Monaco. Products: flowers, olives, grapes and citrus fruits.

Riyadh Capital of Saudi Arabia, in the E central part of the country. In the early 19th century it was the domain of the Saudi dynasty, becoming capital of Saudi Arabia in 1932. The chief industry is oil refining. Pop. (1994 est.) 1,500,000.

RNA (ribonucleic acid) Chemical that controls the synthesis of PROTEIN in a cell and is the genetic material in some viruses. The molecules of RNA in a cell are copied from DNA and consist of a single strand of nucleotides, each containing the sugar ribose, phosphoric acid, and one of four bases: adenine, guanine, cytosine or uracil. **Messenger** RNA carries the information for protein synthesis from DNA in the cell NUCLEUS to the RIBOSOMES in the CYTOPLASM. **Transfer** RNA brings amino acids to their correct position on the messenger RNA. Each AMINO ACID is specified by a sequence of three bases in messenger RNA.

roach European freshwater carp. Colours include silver, white and green. Length: to 40cm (16in). Family Cyprinidae; species *Rutilus rutilus*.

road runner Fast-running desert cuckoo that lives in SW USA. It has a crested head, streaked brownish plumage, long, strong legs and long tail. Family Cuculidae; species *Geococcyx californianus*.

Robbe-Grillet, Alain (1922–) French novelist and theoretician, a founder of the experimental fiction form, the *nouveau roman*. His novels include *The Erasers* (1953), *Jealousy* (1957), *Topology of a Phantom City* (1976) and *Djinn* (1981).

Robert I (the Bruce) (1274–1329) King of Scotland (1306–29). He swore fealty to EDWARD I of England (1296) but joined the Scottish revolt against the English in 1297. He later renewed his allegiance to Edward. In 1306 he was crowned king of Scotland, but was defeated by the English and fled. Returning on Edward's death (1307),

the Bruce renewed the struggle. In 1314 he secured Scottish independence by defeating the English at BANNOCKBURN.

Robespierre, Maximilien François Marie Isidore de (1758–94) French revolutionary leader. Elected to the National Assembly in 1789, he became leader of the JACOBINS, and gained credit when his opposition to war with Austria was justified by French defeats. With the king and the GIRONDINS discredited, Robespierre led the republican revolution of 1792 and was elected to the National Convention. His election to the Committee of Public Safety (June 1793) heralded the REIGN OF TERROR. Robespierre was arrested in the coup of 9th Thermidor (27 July) 1794 and executed.

robin Small Eurasian bird with a characteristic red breast. Length: to 14cm (5.5in). Family Turdidae; species *Erithacus rubecula*. The much larger American robin (*Turdus migratorius*) is a member of the thrush family and is *c.*25cm (10in) long.

Robin Hood Legendary English outlaw, traditionally a displaced nobleman and head of an outlaw band in Sherwood Forest, near Nottingham. Robin robbed the rich and gave to the poor, fighting a running battle with the sheriff of Nottingham.

Robinson, Mary (1944–) Irish stateswoman, president of the Republic of Ireland (1990–97), UN High Commissioner for Human Rights (1997–). Robinson entered politics as a senator in 1969. She is known for her stand on human rights, and, as president, she supported the campaign to liberalize laws on abortion and divorce.

robot Automated machine used to carry out various tasks. Robots are often computer-controlled, the most common type having a single arm that can move in any direction. Such robots are used to carry out various tasks in car manufacturing.

Rob Roy (1671–1734) Scottish outlaw. A member of the proscribed clan MacGregor, he took part in the JACOBITE rising of 1715 and was engaged in a long feud with the Duke of Montrose. He was twice captured and twice escaped, before making his peace with the government in 1722.

rock Solid material that makes up the Earth's crust. Rocks are classified by origin into three major groups: IGNEOUS ROCKS; SEDIMENTARY ROCKS; and METAMORPHIC ROCKS.

rock Form of popular music characterized by amplified guitars and singing, often with repetitive lyrics and driving rhythms. Rock extended from 1950s rock and roll and rhythm and blues, and drew on earlier BLUES and FOLK MUSIC to become a major form of cultural expression in the 1960s. Its offshoots include heavy metal, grunge and PUNK.

Rockefeller, John Davison (1839–1937) US industrialist and philanthropist. In 1870 Rockefeller formed the Standard Oil Company of Ohio. On retirement, he donated *c.*US$550 million to charity. In 1913 he founded the Rockefeller Foundation.

rocket Missile or craft powered by a rocket engine. Most of its volume contains fuel; the remainder is the payload (such as an explosive, scientific instruments or a spacecraft). **Liquid-fuelled** rockets use a fuel (such as liquid hydrogen) and an oxidizer (usually liquid oxygen), which are burnt together in the engine. **Solid-fuelled** rockets have both fuel and oxidizer in a solid mixture. Rockets can be single-stage or multi-stage. They are the only known propulsion systems that can function in a vacuum and so are essential for space exploration.

Rocky Mountains Major mountain system in W North America. Extending from Mexico to the Bering Strait, the mountains form the continental divide. The highest point is Mount Elbert.

rococo Playful, light style of art, architecture and decoration that developed in early 18th-century France. It soon spread to Germany, Austria, Italy and Britain. Rococo brought swirls, scrolls, shells and arabesques to interior decoration. It was also applied to furniture, porcelain and silverware.

rodent Any member of the vast order Rodentia, the most numerous and widespread of all mammals, characterized by a pair of gnawing incisor teeth in both the upper and lower jaws. Numbering c.2,000 species, including rats, mice, squirrels, beaver, dormice, porcupines and guinea pigs, rodents live worldwide. Most are small and light.

Rodgers, Richard Charles (1902–79) US composer of Broadway musicals. He worked with Oscar HAMMERSTEIN on many musicals, such as *Oklahoma!* (1943), *Carousel* (1945), *South Pacific* (1949), *The King and I* (1951) and *The Sound of Music* (1959).

Rodin, Auguste (1840–1917) French sculptor, one of the greatest European artists. His first major work, *The Age of Bronze* (exhibited in 1878), caused a scandal because the naked figure was so naturalistic. His next great project was *The Gates of Hell*, unfinished studies for a bronze door for the *Musée des arts décoratifs*. Further great sculptures include *The Thinker* (1880), *The Kiss* (1886) and *Fugit Amor* (1897). Perhaps his most extraordinary work is the full-length bronze of Balzac (1897).

Roethke, Theodore (1908–63) US poet. His first book of verse, *Opera House*, appeared in 1941. Other collections include *The Waking: Poems 1933–53* (1953), which won a Pulitzer Prize.

Rogers, Richard (1933–) British architect. His best-known buildings include the Pompidou Centre, Paris (co-designed with Renzo Piano, 1971–77) and the Lloyds Building, London (1978–80). He designs his buildings "inside-out" to allow for servicing without disrupting the interior. *See also* COMMUNITY ARCHITECTURE; MODERNISM

Rolling Stones, The British ROCK group, formed in 1962 around vocalist Mick Jagger (1943–), guitarist Keith Richards (1943–), bassist Bill Wyman (1941–) and drummer Charlie Watts (1942–). Their rebellious posturing courted great controversy and publicity. Early hit singles included "Satisfaction" (1965), "Paint it Black" (1966) and "Jumpin' Jack Flash" (1968). Million-selling albums include *Beggar's Banquet* (1968) and *Exile on Main Street* (1972).

ROM (Read-Only Memory) INTEGRATED CIRCUITS (chips) that act as a permanent store for DATA (information) required by a computer. The contents of ordinary ROM chips are set by the manufacturer and cannot be altered by the user. The stored data is available to the computer's MICROPROCESSOR whenever the computer is switched on.

Roman art and architecture Classical art and architecture of ancient ROME. Prior to 400 BC, Roman art was largely ETRUSCAN art, after this Greek influence became dominant. The best surviving examples of later Roman painting are found in POMPEII. Floors and walls were decorated in elaborate geometric mosaics, but they also depicted everyday scenes, or gods and goddesses. In sculpture the Romans excelled in portrait busts and reliefs. In architecture, notable features include their adoption of the ARCH, VAULT and dome. Fine examples include the Pantheon and Colosseum in Rome.

Roman Britain Period of British history from the Roman invasion in the reign of CLAUDIUS I (AD 43) until c.410. The occupation included Wales but not Ireland nor most of Caledonia (Scotland). Its N frontier was marked by HADRIAN'S WALL from c.130. Only the English lowlands were thoroughly Romanized. Britain was ruled as a province under Roman governors. Roman power disintegrated in the 3rd century. Local Romano-British kings held out for more than 100 years before lowland Britain was overrun by the ANGLO-SAXONS.

Roman Catholic Church Christian denomination that acknowledges the supremacy of the pope (*see* PAPACY; PAPAL INFALLIBILITY). An important aspect of the doctrine is the primacy given to the Virgin MARY, whom Roman Catholics believe to be the only human born without sin (IMMACULATE CONCEPTION). Before the REFORMATION, the word "Catholic" applied to the Western Church as a whole, as distinguished from the Eastern ORTHODOX CHURCH based at Constantinople. The Reformation led to a tendency for the Roman Catholic Church to be characterized by rigid adherence to doctrinal tradition from the 16th to the early 20th century. The desire for a reunited Christendom led to a more liberal attitude. Today, there are some 600 million Roman Catholics worldwide, with large numbers in S Europe, Latin America and the Philippines. The government of the Church is episcopal, with archbishops and bishops responsible for provinces and dioceses. The centre of the Roman Catholic liturgical ritual is the MASS or EUCHARIST. Since the second Vatican Council (1962–65), the Roman Catholic Church has undergone marked changes, notably the replacement of Latin by the vernacular as the language of the liturgy.

romance (Old French *romanz*, vulgar tongue) Literary form, typically a heroic tale or ballad usually in verse. The form derives from the medieval narratives of troubadours. The romance spread throughout Europe during the 12th century, and was used in English by CHAUCER.

Romance languages Indo-European languages that evolved from LATIN. They include Italian, French, Spanish, Portuguese, Romanian, Catalan, Provençal and Romansh (a language spoken in parts of Switzerland).

Roman empire Mediterranean empire established after the assassination of Julius CAESAR (27 BC), whose power centre was ancient ROME. The Romans adopted the culture of ancient Greece, but their empire was based on military power and ROMAN LAW. By the death of AUGUSTUS, the first emperor (AD 14), the empire included most of Asia Minor, Syria, Egypt and the whole North African coast. In the 1st–2nd centuries AD Britain was conquered. The empire was at its greatest extent at the death of TRAJAN (AD 117), when it included all the lands around the Mediterranean and extended to N Britain, the Black Sea and Mesopotamia. HADRIAN (r.117–138) called a halt to further expansion. In the 3rd century AD pressure from Germanic tribes and the Persians, plus economic difficulties, contributed to the breakdown of government. Armies in the provinces broke away from Rome. DIOCLETIAN restored order, and divided the empire into E and W divisions. CONSTANTINE founded an E capital at Constantinople (330). By 500 the Roman empire in the W had ceased to exist. The Eastern or BYZANTINE EMPIRE survived until 1453.

Romanesque Architectural and artistic style that spread throughout W Europe during the 11th and 12th centuries. English Romanesque architecture includes ANGLO-SAXON and NORMAN styles.

Romania Balkan republic in SE Europe; the capital is BUCHAREST. **Land and climate** Romania is dominated by a central plateau. The CARPATHIAN MOUNTAINS frame the region of TRANSYLVANIA. E and S Romania form part of the DANUBE river basin; the site of Bucharest. The Danube delta, near the Black Sea, is an important wetland. The port of CONSTANŢA lies on the Black Sea coast. The W lowlands include the city of Timişoara. Romania is one of the sunniest places in Europe. Arable land accounts for c.66% of Romania. **Economy** Communism's overconcentration on heavy industry devastated Romania's economy. Today, industry accounts for 40% of

GDP. Oil, natural gas and antimony are the main mineral resources. Agriculture employs 29% of the workforce and constitutes 20% of GDP. Romania is the world's second-largest producer of plums and ninth-largest producer of wine. Other major crops include maize and cabbages. Economic reform is slow. Unemployment and foreign debt remain high. **History and politics** Modern Romania roughly corresponds to ancient Dacia, which was conquered by the Romans in AD 106. The Dacians assimilated Roman culture and language, and the region became known as Romania. In the 14th century, the principalities of Wallachia (S) and MOLDAVIA (E) were formed. In the 18th century the Ottoman empire dominated Romania. Russia captured Moldavia and Wallachia in the Russo-Turkish War (1828–29). Romanian nationalism intensified, and the two provinces were united in 1861. The Congress of Berlin (1878) ratified Romania as an independent state, and in 1881 CAROL I became king. Neutral at the start of World War 1, Romania joined the Allies in 1916, but was occupied by German forces in 1917. The Allied victory led to Romania acquiring large regions, such as Transylvania. In 1927 Michael became king, but surrendered the throne to his father, CAROL II, in 1930. Political instability and economic inequality led to the growth of fascism and anti-semitism. At the start of World War 2, Romania lost territory to Bulgaria, Hungary and the Soviet Union. In 1940 Michael was restored. Ion Antonescu became dictator and, in June 1941, Romania joined the German invasion of the Soviet Union. Over 50% of Romanian Jews were exterminated during World War 2. In 1944 Soviet troops occupied Romania, Antonescu was overthrown and Romania surrendered. In 1945 a communist-dominated coalition assumed power, led by Gheorghe Gheorghiu-Dej. In 1947 Romania became a people's republic. Industry was nationalized and agriculture collectivized. In 1955 Romaina became a member of the Warsaw Pact. In 1965 Gheorghiu-Dej was succeeded by Nicolae CEAUŞESCU. Rapid industrialization and political repression continued. In December 1989 Ceauşescu and his wife were executed. May 1990 presidential elections were won by the former communist Ion ILIESCU. In 1995 Romania applied to join the European Union. In 1996 presidential and legislative elections, Emil Constantinescu and his centre-right coalition were victorious.

Romanian Official language of Romania, spoken by up to 25 million people in Romania, Macedonia, Albania and N Greece. It is a language belonging to the Romance branch of the Indo-European family. Originally written in CYRILLIC characters, Romanian has used the Roman alphabet since 1860.

Roman law System of CIVIL LAW developed between 753 BC and the 5th century AD, which forms the basis of civil law in many parts of the world. Roman law was enacted originally by the PATRICIANS, then, increasingly after 287 BC, by the

---

ROMANIA
AREA: 237,500sq km (91,699sq mi)
POPULATION: 23,185,000
CAPITAL (POPULATION): Bucharest (2,350,984)
GOVERNMENT: Multiparty republic
ETHNIC GROUPS: Romanian 89%, Hungarian 7%, Romany (Gypsy) 2%
LANGUAGES: Romanian (official)
RELIGIONS: Christianity (Romanian Orthodox 87%, Roman Catholic 5%, Greek Orthodox 4%)
CURRENCY: Romanian leu = 100 bani

PLEBEIAN assemblies. From 367 BC magistrates (*praetors*) proclaimed the legal principles (*edicta*) which became an important source of law known as *jus honorium*. By the mid-2nd century AD the emperor became the sole creator of laws. Roman law can be divided into two parts: *jus civile* (civil law), which applied only to Roman citizens and was codified in the TWELVE TABLES of 450 BC; and *jus gentium*, which gradually merged into *jus civile*, originally applying to non-citizens. Roman law was codified by the Emperor JUSTINIAN I (r.527–64).

Roman numeral Letter used by the ancient Romans and succeeding European civilizations to represent numbers before the adoption of Arabic numerals. There were seven individual letters: I (1), V (5), X (10), L (50), C (100), D (500) and M (1,000). Combinations were used to represent the numbers. From 1 to 10 they ran: I, II, III, IV, V, VI, VII, VIII, IX and X. The tens ran: X, XX, XXX, XL, L and so on up to XC, which represented 90. The ancients used Roman numerals for commerce and mathematics. Modern applications include numbering the preliminary pages of a book.

Romanov Russian imperial dynasty (1613–1917). Michael, the first Romanov tsar, was elected in 1613. His descendants, especially PETER I (THE GREAT) and CATHERINE II (THE GREAT) transformed Russia into the world's largest empire. The last Romanov emperor, NICHOLAS II, abdicated in 1917 and was later murdered by the BOLSHEVIKS.

Romans In the New Testament, a letter by St PAUL to the Christians of Rome, written *c*.57 AD. In it, he declares the universality of the saving power of God realized in the life, death and resurrection of Jesus.

romanticism Late 18th- and early 19th-century cultural movement. Its exponents valued individual experience and intuition, rather than the orderly, concrete universe of CLASSICAL artists. For this reason, romantics and classicists are often seen as opposites, but in fact they shared a belief in IDEALISM, as opposed to the exponents of REALISM and RATIONALISM. An emphasis on nature rather than science was also a characteristic. Leading literary romantics include GOETHE, SHELLEY, BYRON, KEATS and SCHILLER. William BLAKE was both a romantic poet and artist. Other artists include DELACROIX, Caspar David FRIEDRICH, GÉRICAULT and TURNER.

romanticism Period of music history lasting from *c*.1800–1910. It is characterized by the primacy of emotional expression and imagination, in contrast to the restraint of CLASSICAL MUSIC. Orchestras expanded as composers experimented with unusual and colourful orchestration to express extra-musical influences. Leading romantic composers include WAGNER, BERLIOZ, MENDELSSOHN, SCHUMANN, CHOPIN and LISZT.

Romany (Gypsy) Nomadic people and their language. Romanies are believed to have originated in N India. They first appeared in Europe in the 15th century. Their nomadic lifestyle has aroused prejudice, often resulting in persecution. The Romany language originated in N India, and like HINDI and SANSKRIT to which it is related, it belongs to the Indo-Iranian branch of the family of INDO-EUROPEAN LANGUAGES.

Rome (Roma) Capital of Italy, on the River Tiber, W central Italy. Founded in the 8th century BC, it was probably an Etruscan city-kingdom in the 6th century. By the 3rd century BC, Rome ruled most of Italy and began to expand overseas. In the 1st century AD, Rome was transformed as successive emperors constructed grand civil buildings. It remained the capital of the Roman empire until 330 AD. In the Middle Ages Rome became the seat of the papacy. Rome began to flourish once more in the 16th and 17th centuries. Italian troops occupied it in 1870, and in 1871 it became the capital of unified Italy. The 1922 fascist march on Rome brought MUSSOLINI to power, and he did much to modernize Rome. It is also home to the VATICAN CITY. Industries: tourism, pharmaceuticals, chemicals, oil refining, engineering, textiles, films, printing and publishing, banking and finance. Pop. (1991) 2,775,250.

Rome, ancient Capital of the Roman republic. According to tradition, Rome was founded in 753 BC by ROMULUS AND REMUS. By 509 BC the Latin-speaking Romans had thrown off the rule of ETRUSCAN kings and established an independent republic dominated by an aristocratic elite. Its history was one of continual expansion, and by 340 BC Rome controlled Italy S of the River Po. By the 3rd century BC the PLEBEIAN class had largely gained political equality. The PUNIC WARS gave it dominance of the Mediterranean in the 2nd century BC. The republican constitution was strained by social division and military dictatorship. SPARTACUS' slave revolt was crushed by POMPEY, who emerged as SULLA's successor. Pompey and Julius CAESAR formed the First Triumvirate (60 BC). Caesar emerged as leader and greatly extended Rome's territory and influence. His assassination led to the formation of the ROMAN EMPIRE under AUGUSTUS (27 BC).

Rome, Treaties of (1957) Two agreements establishing the European Economic Community, now the EUROPEAN COMMUNITY (EC), and the EUROPEAN ATOMIC ENERGY COMMISSION (EURATOM). The 1957 treaty was extensively amended by the Single European Act (1986) and the MAASTRICHT TREATY (1992), but still forms the basis of the EUROPEAN UNION (EU).

Rommel, Erwin (1891–1944) German general. He commanded tanks in France in 1940 and later led the AFRIKA KORPS in a victorious campaign in North Africa, until defeated by the British at EL ALAMEIN (1942). Transferred to France in 1943, he was unable to repel the invasion of NORMANDY and was wounded. Implicated in the plot against Hitler in July 1944, he committed suicide.

Romulus and Remus In Roman mythology, founders of ROME. Twin bothers, they were said to be sons of Mars. Amulius ordered the babies to be drowned in the Tiber. They survived and were suckled by a wolf. They built a city on the site of their rescue. Romulus later killed Remus.

Röntgen, Wilhelm Konrad (1845–1923) German physicist. In 1895 he discovered X-RAYS, for which he was awarded the first Nobel Prize for physics in 1901. He also did important work on electricity, the specific heats of gases and the heat CONDUCTIVITY of crystals.

röntgen Former unit (symbol R) used to measure X-RAY or gamma-ray RADIATION. One röntgen causes sufficient ionization to produce a total electric charge of 2.58×10^{-4} coulombs on all the ions in one kilogram of air. The unit has been replaced by the SI unit, the GRAY (symbol Gy).

rook Large European bird of the CROW family. It has glossy black plumage, but commonly loses the feathers from about its face. It feeds on grain and insects, and has a characteristic raucous cry. Family Corvidae; species *Corvus frugilegus*.

Roosevelt, Franklin D. (Delano) (1882–1945) 32nd US President (1933–45). He served as assistant secretary of the navy under Woodrow WILSON (1913–20) and was vice-presidential candidate in 1920. In 1921 he lost the use of his legs as a result of polio. He was governor of New York (1928–32) and won the Democratic candidacy for president. He defeated the incumbent president, Herbert HOOVER. To deal with the GREAT DEPRESSION, he embarked upon his NEW DEAL, designed to restore the economy through direct government intervention. He was re-elected in 1936 and won an unprecedented third term in 1940 and a fourth in 1944. When World War 2 broke out in Europe, he gave as much support to Britain as a neutral government could, until the Japanese attack on PEARL HARBOR ended US neutrality. He died in office and was succeeded by Harry S. TRUMAN.

Roosevelt, Theodore (1858–1919) 26th US President (1901–09). He was the organizer of the Rough Riders in the Spanish-American War (1898). He became Republican governor of New York (1899), and vice president (1901). The assassination of President McKINLEY made him president, and he was re-elected in 1904. Roosevelt moved to regulate monopolies through anti-trust legislation. He reversed isolationist US foreign policy and gained the PANAMA CANAL. His mediation after the RUSSO-JAPANESE WAR won him the Nobel Peace Prize (1905). After retiring in 1909, he challenged his successor, President TAFT, for the presidency in 1912 as leader of his National Progressive Party (Bull Moose Party). The Republican split resulted in a Democratic victory.

root Underground portion of a VASCULAR PLANT that serves as an anchor and absorbs water and minerals from the soil. Some plants, such as the dandelion, have taproots with smaller lateral branches. Other plants, such as the grasses, develop fibrous roots with lateral branches.

root In mathematics, fractional power of a number. The SQUARE ROOT of a number, x, is written as either $\sqrt{x}$ or $x^{\frac{1}{2}}$. The fourth root of x may be written in radical form as $4\sqrt{x}$ or in power form as $x^{\frac{1}{4}}$. For example, the fourth root of 16 is 2 since $2 \times 2 \times 2 \times 2 = 16$.

root nodule Small swelling in the roots of various plants, such as LEGUMES, that contain nitrogen-fixing bacteria. *See also* NITROGEN CYCLE

Rorschach test (ink-blot test) In psychology, test used to analyse a person's motives and attitudes when these are projected into ambiguous situations. The individual is presented with 10 standardized ink blots and interpretation is based on the description of them.

rose Wild or cultivated flowering shrub of the genus *Rosa*. Most roses are native to Asia, several to America, and a few to Europe and NW Africa. The stems are usually thorny, and flowers range in colour from white to yellow, pink, crimson and maroon; many are fragrant. There are about 150 species. Family Rosaceae.

Roseau Capital of Dominica, in the Windward Islands, a port on the SW coast at the mouth of the Roseau River. Roseau was burnt by the French in 1805, and virtually destroyed by a hurricane in 1979. Tropical vegetables, oils, spices, limes and lime juice are exported. Pop. (1991) 15,853.

Rosebery, Archibald Philip Primrose, 5th Earl of (1847–1929) British political leader. Foreign secretary under GLADSTONE, he succeeded him as prime minister (1894) and as leader of the divided Liberal Party, which was defeated in the election of 1895. He became further alienated from his party by his strongly imperialist views.

rosemary Perennial evergreen herb of the mint family. It has small, needle-like leaf clusters of small pale-blue flowers. Sprigs of rosemary are commonly used as a flavouring. Family Lamiaceae/Labiatae; species *Rosmarinus officinalis*.

Roses, Wars of the (1455–85) English dynastic civil wars. They are named after the badges of the rival royal houses of York (white rose) and Lancaster (red rose). Both houses were descended from EDWARD III. The Lancastrian king, HENRY VI, was challenged by Richard, Duke of York, who gained brief ascendancy after the battle of St Albans (1455). The Lancastrians recovered control, but in 1460 Richard, supported by the Earl of WARWICK, forced Henry to recognize him as heir. Richard was killed soon after, but the Yorkist victory at Towton (1461) put his son on the throne as EDWARD IV. In 1469 Warwick changed sides and Edward was deposed, but returned to win a decisive victory at Tewkesbury (1471). In 1483 RICHARD III seized the throne. He was defeated and killed at BOSWORTH, when Henry Tudor (HENRY VII) won the crown.

Rosetta Stone Slab of black basalt inscribed with the same text in Egyptian HIEROGLYPHICS, demotic (a simplified form of Egyptian hieroglyphs) and Greek script. By comparing the three versions, first Thomas YOUNG (1818) and later Jean-François

Champollion (1822) deciphered the hieroglyphs, leading to a full understanding of the signs.

rosewood Any of several kinds of ornamental hardwoods derived from various tropical trees. The most important are Honduras rosewood (*Dalbergia stevensoni*) and Brazilian rosewood (*D. nigra*). It varies from a deep, ruddy brown to purplish and has a black grain. Family Fabiaceae/Leguminose

Rosh ha-Shanah Jewish New Year and first day of the month of Tishri (generally in September). It is the day on which a ceremonial ram's horn (*shofar*) is blown to call sinners to repentance (the Day of Judgement or of Remembrance). It begins the Ten Days of Penitence that end with YOM KIPPUR.

Rosicrucians Esoteric, secret, worldwide society using supposedly magical knowledge drawn from ALCHEMY. The name comes from pamphlets published (*c.*1615) by Christian Rosenkreutz, of whom there is no other record. The modern movement has splintered into several factions.

Ross Dependency Region of Antarctica that includes Ross Island, the coast along the Ross Sea and nearby islands. It has been under the jurisdiction of New Zealand since 1923. Area: land mass, *c.*415,000sq km (160,000sq mi); ice shelf, *c.*450,000sq km (174,000sq mi).

Rossellini, Roberto (1906–77) Italian film director and producer. His post-war films, such as *Open City* (1945), were landmarks in post-war NEO-REAL-ISM. During the 1950s he made a series of films with his wife Ingrid BERGMAN, such as *Stromboli* (1949).

Rossetti, Christina Georgina (1830–94) British poet, the sister of Dante Gabriel ROSSETTI. Her most enduring works are *Goblin Market and Other Poems* (1862) and *The Prince's Progress and Other Poems* (1866). Many of her poems are religious, and she was influenced by the OXFORD MOVEMENT.

Rossetti, Dante Gabriel (1828–82) British poet and painter. A founding member of the PRE-RAPHAELITE BROTHERHOOD, he later developed a distinctive style of medieval romanticism. He painted his wife (Elizabeth Siddal) many times. He also worked with William MORRIS, but became a recluse and died of drug and alcohol addiction. Perhaps his best-known poem is *Blessed Damozel* (1850).

Rossini, Gioacchino Antonio (1792–1868) Italian opera composer. His comic operas, such as *The Barber of Seville* (1816) and *Cinderella* (1817), demonstrate his wit and sense of melody. His serious operas include *William Tell* (1829).

Rosso, Il (1495–1540) (Giovanni Battista Rosso) Italian painter and decorative artist. He worked with Primaticcio in decorating FONTAINEBLEAU palace and helped to found the FONTAINEBLEAU SCHOOL.

Rostand, Edmond (1868–1918) French poet and dramatist. His major verse plays include *Cyrano de Bergerac* (1897) and *L'Aiglon* (1900).

Rostropovich, Mstislav Leopoldovich (1927–) Soviet musician, who established a reputation as one of the century's best cellists. Leading composers, such as SHOSTAKOVICH, PROKOFIEV and BRITTEN, dedicated works to him.

rotation Turning of a celestial body about its axis. In the Solar System, the Sun and all the planets, with the exception of Uranus and Venus, rotate from W to E.

Roth, Philip (1933–) US novelist and short-story writer. He established his name with the collection *Goodbye Columbus* (1959). His later works, including *Operation Shylock* (1993), *Sabbath's Theater* (1995) and *American Pastoral* (1997), are overshadowed by the success of his best-known novel *Portnoy's Complaint* (1969).

Rothko, Mark (1903–70) US painter, b. Russia. He developed a highly individual style featuring large, rectangular areas of thinly layered, pale colours arranged in parallel. Rothko later introduced darker colours, such as the paintings *Black on Maroon* and *Red on Maroon* from the late 1950s.

rotifer (wheel animacule) Microscopic metazoan found mainly in freshwater. Although it resembles ciliate PROTOZOA, it is many-celled with a body structure similar to that of a simple WORM. Rotifers may be elongated or round, and are identified by a crown of cilia around the mouth. Class Rotifera.

Rotterdam City at the junction of the Rotte and the New Meuse rivers, W Netherlands; chief port and second-largest city in the Netherlands. Founded in the 14th century, it became accessible to ocean-going vessels in the mid-19th century. In 1940 the centre was devastated by German bombing. The building of Europoort harbour (1966) made Rotterdam one of the world's largest ports. Industries: shipbuilding and ship repairing, petrochemicals, electronics, textiles, cars. Pop. (1994) 598,521.

Rouault, Georges (1871–1958) French painter, printmaker and designer. Studying under Gustave MOREAU with MATISSE, he became acquainted with FAUVISM. He designed book illustrations, ceramics and tapestries as well as the sets for Diaghilev's ballet, *The Prodigal Son* (1929). After 1940 Rouault concentrated exclusively on religious art.

Rouen City in NW France, a port on the River Seine; capital of Seine-Maritime département. By the 10th century Rouen was capital of Normandy. Under English rule (1066–1204, 1419–49), it was the scene of Joan of Arc's trial and burning in 1431. Badly damaged in World War 2, it was later rebuilt. Industries: textiles, flour milling, iron, petrochemicals, perfumes, leather goods. Pop. (1990) 102,723.

Roundheads Name given to Puritans and other supporters of Parliament during the English CIVIL WAR. It was originally a derogatory nickname for Puritans who cut their hair short, in contrast to the ringlets of the CAVALIERS (Royalists).

roundworm Parasite of the class Nematoda, which inhabits and breeds in the intestine of mammals. The larva bores through the intestinal wall, is carried to the lungs in the bloodstream and crawls to the mouth, where it is swallowed. Length: 15–30cm (6–12in).

Rousseau, Henri (1844–1910) French painter, greatest of all naïve painters. Rousseau is best known for his scenes from an imaginary tropical jungle, such as *Surprised! (Tropical Storm with Tiger)* (1891) and *The Dream* (1910).

Rousseau, Jean Jacques (1712–78) French philosopher of the Age of Reason, whose social theories informed the French Revolution. He was born a Protestant in Geneva, Switzerland, and became a Roman Catholic in the 1730s. Later in his life he reconverted to Protestantism in order to regain his citizenship rights in Geneva. In 1740 Rousseau moved to Paris. He contributed articles on music to DIDEROT's *Encyclopédie* in the 1740s, and finally won fame for his essay, *Discourses on Science and the Arts* (1750). In *The Social Contract* (1762), he argued that man had been corrupted by civilization. His ideas on individual liberation from the constraints of society were developed in the novel *Émile* (1762). He described his early, wandering life in *Confessions*, published posthumously in 1782.

rowing Using oars to propel a boat; the first activity and a sport. It has been a full Olympic event since 1904. Modern racing events include pairs, fours or eights, each crew member using both hands to pull one oar (to use two oars is sculling). A coxswain steers for eights and directs the crew; pairs and fours may or may not have a coxswain.

Royal Academy of Arts (RA) British national academy of the arts, founded by George III in 1768 and based in London. Members aimed to raise the status of the arts by establishing high standards of training and organizing annual exhibitions.

Royal Greenwich Observatory UK national astronomical observatory, founded at Greenwich, London, in 1675. After World War 2 the observatory moved to Sussex, and to Cambridge in 1990.

Royal Navy Fighting force that defends Britain's coastal waters and its merchant shipping. The first naval fleet in Britain was built by ALFRED THE GREAT in 878 to fight off the Viking raids. In the 16th century Henry VII built the first specialist naval ships and established the first dockyards. The following centuries saw a struggle for naval supremacy between Britain, France and The Netherlands, culminating in the Battle of TRAFALGAR. The British victory heralded the supremacy of the Royal Navy, which lasted into the 20th century. Since World War 2 the Royal Navy has diminished.

Royal Shakespeare Company (RSC) State-subsidized British theatrical repertory company, based in Stratford upon Avon. It received a royal charter in 1961. In 1960 it established a second base in London and presented Shakespearean plays alongside other pieces. The RSC also tours widely.

Royal Society British society founded in 1660 and incorporated two years later. Its aim was to accumulate experimental evidence on a wide range of scientific subjects, including medicine and botany as well as the physical sciences.

Royal Society for the Prevention of Cruelty to Animals (RSPCA) British organization established in 1824 to prevent cruelty and promote kindness to animals. The RSPCA has its headquarters at Horsham, Sussex. Its inspectors investigate cases of cruelty to animals and, if necessary, bring offenders to court.

rubber Elastic solid obtained from the latex of the RUBBER TREE. Natural rubber consists of a POLYMER of cis-isoprene and is widely used for vehicle tyres and other applications, especially after VULCANIZATION. Synthetic rubbers are polymers tailored for specific purposes.

rubber plant Evergreen FIG native to India and Malaysia. Tree-sized in the tropics, juvenile specimens are grown as houseplants in temperate regions. Once cultivated for its white LATEX to make india-rubber, it has large, glossy, leathery leaves and a stout, buttressed trunk. Height: to 30m (100ft). Family Moraceae; species *Ficus elastica*.

rubber tree Any of several South American trees whose exudations can be made into RUBBER; especially *Hevea brasiliensis* (family Euphorbiaceae), a tall softwood tree native to Brazil but introduced to Malaysia. The milky exudate, called LATEX, is obtained from the inner bark by tapping and then coagulated by smoking over fires or chemically.

rubella See GERMAN MEASLES

Rubens, Peter Paul (1577–1640) Flemish painter, engraver and designer, most influential BAROQUE artist of N Europe. He gained an international reputation with his huge, vigorous triptychs, *Raising of the Cross* (1610–11) and *Descent from the Cross* (1611–14). His most notable commissions included 25 paintings of Marie de' Medici; a series of scenes depicting the life of James I for the Banqueting House, London; and over 100 mythological paintings for Philip IV of Spain.

rubidium Silver-white metallic element (symbol Rb) of the ALKALI METALS (group I of the periodic table). It was discovered in 1861 by Robert BUNSEN and Gustav KIRCHHOFF. The element has few commercial uses; small amounts are used in photoelectric cells. Chemically it resembles SODIUM but is more reactive. Properties: at. no.37; r.a.m. 85.4678; r.d. 1.53; m.p. 38.89°C (102°F); b.p. 688°C (1,270°F); most common isotope Rb^{85} (72.15%).

Rubinstein, Arthur (1887–1982) US pianist, b. Poland. He made his debut with the Berlin Symphony Orchestra in 1901. He was famed for his interpretations of CHOPIN and Spanish composers.

ruby Gem variety of the mineral CORUNDUM (aluminium oxide), whose characteristic red colour is due to impurities of chromium and iron oxides. The traditional source of rubies is Burma. Synthetic rubies are widely used in industry.

rudd (red eye or pearl ROACH) Fish related to the MINNOW. Found in Europe, N America and Asia, it is a large, full-bodied fish with reddish fins. Length: to 40.6cm (16in); weight: to 2kg (4.5lb). Family Cyprinidae; species *Scardinius erythrophthalmus*.

Rudolf I (1218–91) German king (1273–91), founder of the HABSBURG dynasty. He set out to restore monarchical order, and won the duchies of Austria, Styria and Carniola from Ottokar II of Bohemia (1278). He was never crowned emperor, and failed to persuade the electors to confirm his son, Albert I, as his successor.

Rudolf II (1552–1612) Holy Roman emperor (1576–1612). Son and successor of Maximilian II, he moved the imperial capital to Prague. His opposition to Protestantism caused conflict in Bohemia and Hungary. A Hungarian revolt was suppressed by his brother and eventual successor, Matthias, to whom he ceded Hungary, Austria, Moravia (1608) and Bohemia (1611).

ruff Bird of the SANDPIPER family (Scolopacidae). The male is noted for a collar of long feathers about its neck, and for its bizarre courtship performances. The female is called a reeve. Species *Philomachus pugnax*.

rugby Ball game for two teams in which an oval ball may be handled as well as kicked. There are two codes, union and league, but the purpose is the same: to touch the ball down in the opposition ingoal area for a try, which allows a kick at the H-shaped goal (a conversion). Kicks must pass over the crossbar between the line of the posts. Players may not pass or knock the ball forward when attempting to catch it. The field of play is rectangular, 100m (330ft) long and 55–68m (180–225ft) wide, and play consists of two 40-minute halves. Rugby union is a 15-a-side game, which used to be restricted to amateurs. It is most popular in Britain, France, South Africa, New Zealand and Australia. Rugby league is a 13-a-side game for professionals and amateurs. Recent developments are bringing about an integration of the two codes.

Ruhr River in Germany; its valley is Germany's manufacturing heartland. The River Ruhr rises in the Rothaargebirge Mountains and flows w for 235km (146mi) to join the River Rhine at Duisburg. Major cities on its banks include Essen, Dortmund and Mülheim. In the 19th century, the region's coal was intensively mined and massive steelworks developed. During 1923–25 France and Belgium occupied the Ruhr in order to compel Germany to pay the agreed war reparations. During World War 2 its armaments factories marked it out as a major Allied target and more than 75% of the region was destroyed. The post-war shift to light industry saw the region regain its prosperity.

Ruisdael, Jacob van (*c.*1628–82) Dutch landscape painter who brought an unusual breadth and accuracy to his paintings of the flat northern landscape. Among his many works are *Wooded Landscape* (*c.*1660) and *Windmill at Wijk* (*c.*1670).

Rumi (1207–73) Persian poet, b. Jalāl ad-Dīn ar-Rūmī. His huge body of work (some 30,000 couplets and numerous *rubaiyat* or quatrains) was inspired by SUFISM. His main work is *Mathnawi*.

ruminant Cud-chewing, even-toed, hoofed mammal. They include the DEER, GIRAFFE, ANTELOPE, CATTLE, SHEEP and GOAT. All except the chevrotain have four-chambered stomachs, and re-chew food previously swallowed and stored in one of the chambers.

Rump Parliament (1648–53) Name given to the LONG PARLIAMENT in England after 140 members were expelled. Unrepresentative and quarrelsome, it was dissolved by CROMWELL in 1653. It was recalled after the collapse of the PROTECTORATE in 1659, and expelled members were reinstated.

runes Angular characters or letters of an alphabet used by Germanic peoples in early medieval times. Also called *futhark* after its first six letters (*f*, *u*, *th*, *a*, *r*, and *k*), the runic alphabet may have been developed from a N Italian alphabet.

runner In botany, a long, thin stem that extends along the surface of the soil from the axil of a plant's leaf, and serves to propagate the plant. At nodes along its length, a runner has small leaves with buds that develop shoots and roots, and turn into small independent plants as the runner dies.

Rupert, Prince (1619–82) British military commander, b. Bohemia. His uncle Charles I made him commander of the cavalry in the English CIVIL WAR. He was undefeated until MARSTON MOOR (1644). He was dismissed after the Royalist defeat at NASEBY (1645) and surrendered at Bristol. He led raids against English shipping during the Protectorate period and, after the Stuart restoration, served as an admiral in the Dutch wars.

rush Any of about 700 species of PERENNIAL tufted bog plants found in temperate regions. It has long, narrow leaves and small flowers crowded into dense clusters. The most familiar rush is *Juncus effusus*, found in Europe, Asia, North America, Australasia. It has brown flowers and ridged stems. Height: 30–152cm (1–5ft). Family Juncaceae.

Rushdie, Salman (1947–) British novelist, b. India. His early works, including the Booker Prize-winning *Midnight's Children* (1981), were eclipsed by the controversy surrounding the *Satanic Verses* (1988). This novel incited the condemnation of Islamic extremists who perceived the book as BLASPHEMY, and he was forced into hiding by the imposition of a death sentence by the Ayatollah KHOMEINI. Subsequent works include *Haroun and the Sea of Stories* (1990) and *The Moor's Last Sigh* (1995).

Ruskin, John (1819–1900) British author, artist and social reformer. A strong religious conviction was the basis for his advocacy of Gothic naturalism. His ideas are outlined in his books on architecture: *The Seven Lamps of Architecture* (1849) and *The Stones of Venice* (three vols., 1851–53). His five-volume work *Modern Painters* (1834–60) championed the paintings of J.M.W. TURNER and he also supported the PRE-RAPHAELITE BROTHERHOOD.

Russell, Bertrand Arthur William, 3rd Earl (1872–1970) British philosopher, mathematician and social reformer, b. Wales. His most famous work, the monumental *Principia Mathematica* (1910–13), written in collaboration with A.N. WHITEHEAD, set out to show exactly how mathematics was grounded in logic. He also wrote various philosophical works, including the best-seller *History of Western Philosophy* (1946). Russell was a lifelong pacifist and a constant campaigner for educational and moral reforms. From 1949 he increasingly advocated nuclear disarmament. He won the 1950 Nobel Prize for literature.

Russell, George William (1867–1935) Irish poet, essayist, journalist and painter, who wrote under the pen name A.E. A leading figure of the Irish literary renaissance, he published many collections of romantic and mystical poetry, such as *The Divine Vision* (1904) and *Midsummer Eve* (1928).

Russell, John, 1st Earl (1792–1878) British statesman, prime minister (1846–52, 1865–66). He entered the cabinet in 1830. He was a supporter of Roman Catholic emancipation and parliamentary reform and moved the Whig Party in the direction of liberalism. The defeat of his Reform Bill (1866) caused his resignation.

Russia Federation in E Europe and N Asia; the capital is MOSCOW. **Land and climate** The Russian Federation is the world's largest country. The URALS form a natural border between European and Asian Russia (SIBERIA). About 25% of Russia lies in Europe, W of the Urals. European Russia contains about 80% of Russia's population, and includes Moscow. It is predominantly a vast plain. The CAUCASUS Mountains form Russia's SW border with Georgia and Azerbaijan, and include Europe's highest peak, Mount ELBRUS, at 5,633m (18,481ft). GROZNY, capital of CHECHENYA, lies close to the Georgian border. The port of ASTRAKHAN lies on the shore of the CASPIAN SEA, the world's largest inland body of water. ST PETERSBURG, Russia's second-largest city, is a Baltic seaport. ARCHANGEL is the major White Sea port. European Russia's major rivers are the DON and the VOLGA (Europe's longest river). Volgograd lies on its banks. SIBERIA is a land of plains and plateaus, with mountains in the E and S. It is drained by the OB, YENISEI and LENA rivers. The

industrial centre of Novosibirsk lies on the River Ob. Close to the Mongolian border lies Lake BAIKAL (the world's deepest lake). On its shores lies Irkutsk. VLADIVOSTOCK is the major port on the Sea of Japan. SAKHALIN and the KURIL ISLANDS have often been a source of conflict with Japan. The KAMCHATKA PENINSULA contains many active volcanoes. The climate varies from N to S and from W to E. Moscow has a continental climate with cold, snowy winters and warm summers. Siberia has a much harsher and drier climate. In Northern Siberia winter temperatures often fall below $-46°C$ ($-51°F$). The far N is tundra. To the S is the taiga, a vast region of coniferous forest. South-central Russia contains large areas of former steppe, most of which is now under the plough; its dark chernozem soils are among the world's most fertile. **Economy** Under Soviet rule, Russia was transformed from an essentially agrarian economy into the world's second greatest industrial power (after the USA). By the 1970s, concentration on the military-industrial complex and the creation of a bloated bureaucracy had caused the economy to stagnate. Gorbachev's policy of PERESTROIKA was an attempt to correct this structural weakness. Yeltsin sped up the pace of reform. In 1993 the command economy was abolished, private ownership was re-introduced and mass privatization began. By 1996, 80% of the Russian economy was in private hands. Inflation remains high, but the biggest problem is the size of Russia's foreign debt (1995, US$120,000 million). Industry employs 46% of the workforce and contributes 48% of GDP. Mining is the most valuable activity. Russia is rich in resources; it is the world's leading producer of natural gas and nickel, and the world's third-largest producer of crude oil, lignite and brown coal. It is the world's second-largest manufacturer of aluminium and phosphates. Consumer manufactures are growing in importance. Most farmland is still government-owned or run as collectives. Russia is the world's largest producer of barley, oats, rye and potatoes. It is the world's second-largest producer of beef and veal. **History** Traditionally, the Varangian king, Rurik, established the first Russian state in *c.*AD 862. His successor, Oleg, made KIEV his capital and the state became known as Kievan Rus. VLADIMIR I adopted Greek Orthodox Christianity as the state religion in 988. Vladimir and Kiev vied for political supremacy. In 1237–40 the Mongol TATARS conquered Russia and established the GOLDEN HORDE. Saint ALEXANDER NEVSKI became Great Khan of Kiev. The Grand Duchy of Moscow was established in 1380. IVAN III (THE GREAT) greatly extended the power of Moscow, began the construction of the KREMLIN, and completed the conquest of the Golden Horde in 1480. In 1547 IVAN IV (THE TERRIBLE) was crowned tsar of all Russia. He conquered the Tatar khanates of KAZAN (1552) and Astrakhan (1556), gaining control of the Volga River, and

RUSSIA
AREA: 17,075,000sq km (6,592,800sq mi)
POPULATION: 149,527,000
CAPITAL (POPULATION): Moscow (8,881,000)
GOVERNMENT: Federal multiparty republic
ETHNIC GROUPS: Russian 82%, Tatar 4%, Ukrainian 3%, Chuvash 1%, more than 100 other nationalities
LANGUAGES: Russian (official)
RELIGIONS: Christianity (mainly Russian Orthodox, with Roman Catholic and Protestant minorities), Islam, Judaism
CURRENCY: Russian rouble = 100 kopecks

545

began the conquest of Siberia. Following the death of Boris GODUNOV (1605), Russia was subject to foreign incursions. In 1613 Michael founded the ROMANOV dynasty, which ruled Russia until 1917. The reign (1696–1725) of PETER I (THE GREAT) marked the start of the westernization and modernization of Russia: central governmental institutions were founded, and the church was subordinated to the crown. Russia expanded w to the Baltic Sea, and St Petersburg was founded in 1703. Peter made it his capital in 1712. In 1762 CATHERINE II (THE GREAT) became empress. Under her authoritarian government, Russia became the greatest power in continental Europe, acquiring much of Poland, Belarus and Ukraine. Alexander I's territorial gains led him into direct conflict with NAPOLEON I. Napoleon captured Moscow in 1812, but his army was devastated by the harsh Russian winter. The Decembrist Conspiracy (1825) unsuccessfully tried to prevent the accession of NICHOLAS I. At the end of Nicholas' reign, Russia became embroiled in the disastrous CRIMEAN WAR (1853–56). ALEXANDER II undertook much-needed reforms, such as the emancipation of the serfs. Alexander III was succeeded by the last Romanov tsar, NICHOLAS II. In the 1890s, drought caused famine in rural areas and there was much discontent in the cities. Defeat in the RUSSO-JAPANESE WAR (1904–05) precipitated the RUSSIAN REVOLUTION OF 1905. Nicholas II was forced to adopt a new constitution and establish an elected duma (parliament). The democratic reforms were soon reversed, revolutionary groups were brutally suppressed, and pogroms were encouraged. In 1912 the Russian Social Democratic Labor Party, secretly founded in 1898, split into BOLSHEVIK and MENSHEVIK factions. Russia's support of a Greater Slavic state contributed to the outbreak of World War 1. Russia was ill-prepared for war and suffered great hardship. The RUSSIAN REVOLUTION (1917) had two main phases. In March, Nicholas II was forced to abdicate (he and his family were executed in July 1918), and a provisional government was formed. In July, KERENSKY became prime minister, but failed to satisfy the radical hunger of the soviets (revolutionary workers' councils). In November 1917, the Bolsheviks, led by LENIN, seized power and proclaimed Russia a Soviet Federated Socialist Republic. In 1918 the capital was transferred to Moscow. Under the terms of the Treaty of BREST-LITOVSK (1918), Russia withdrew from World War 1, but was forced to cede much territory to the Central Powers. For the next five years, civil war raged between the Reds and Whites (monarchists and anti-communists), complicated by foreign intervention. The Bolsheviks emerged victorious, but Russia was left devastated. In 1922 Russia was united with Ukraine, Belarus and Transcaucasia (Armenia, Azerbaijan and Georgia) to form the Union of Soviet Socialist Republics (USSR). (for history 1922–91, see SOVIET UNION)

In June 1991 Boris YELTSIN was elected President of the Russian Republic. In August 1991 communist hardliners arrested the Soviet president Mikhail GORBACHEV and attempted to capture the Russian parliament in Moscow. Democratic forces rallied behind Yeltsin, and the coup was defeated. On 25 December 1991, Gorbachev resigned as president, and on 31 December, the Soviet Union was dissolved. The Russian Federation became a co-founder of the COMMONWEALTH OF INDEPENDENT STATES (CIS), composed of former Soviet Republics. In March 1992, a new Federal Treaty was signed between the central government in Moscow and the autonomous republics within the Russian Federation. Chechenya refused to sign, and declared independence. Yeltsin's reforms were frustrated by institutional forces, forcing him to dissolve parliament in September 1993. Parliamentary leaders formed a rival government, but the coup failed. In December 1993 a new democratic constitution was adopted. **Politics** Yeltsin's progress in the democratization of political institutions and reform of the social economy has been slow. A central problem is the representation of Russia's diverse minorities. Many ethnic groups have demanded greater autonomy within the Federation. In 1992 direct rule was imposed in Ingush and North Ossetia. From 1994–96 Russia was embroiled in a costly civil war in the secessionist state of Chechenya. In May 1996, despite concern about his ill-health, Yeltsin was re-elected. In 1997 Yeltsin's biggest problem was the bad state of the economy, and there were nationwide protests about wage arrears.

Russian Official language of the Russian Federation and several other republics. It is the primary language of c.140 million people and used as a second language by millions more. It is the most important of the Slavic languages, which form a subdivision of the family of INDO-EUROPEAN LANGUAGES. It is written in the CYRILLIC alphabet.

Russian architecture Architectural style that began as a regional variety of Byzantine architecture in the 10th century with the Christianization of Russia. Important centres of architectural activity developed at Kiev, Novgorod and Pskov. Early churches were built of wood. The Cathedral of Sancta Sophia, Kiev (1018–37) was the first stone construction. The distinctive onion-shaped dome was introduced in the 12th century at the Cathedral of Sancta Sophia, Novgorod. Although the Byzantine influence remained strong, during the 15th century Russia was subject to a series of western European trends, and Italian architects built the KREMLIN in a Renaissance style. Peter the Great and Catherine brought ROCOCO and neoclassical principles to St Petersburg. In the 19th century a revival of medieval Russian architecture occurred.

Russian art Paintings and sculpture produced in Russia after c.1000 AD, as distinct from the earlier SCYTHIAN art. In the Middle Ages, Russian art carried on BYZANTINE ART traditions, and was primarily religious. After the fall of Constantinople (1453), Russia regarded itself as the spiritual heir of Byzantium. In the late 19th century, Ilya Repin and the Wanderers breathed new life into Russian art. In the early 20th century, Russia was at the heart of MODERNISM, SUPREMATISM and CONSTRUCTIVISM.

Russian Five Group of Russian composers, active in St Petersburg during the 1860s and 1870s, who hoped to create a truly Russian style of music. They were Alexander BORODIN, Modest MUSSORGSKY, Nikolai RIMSKY-KORSAKOV, Mily Balakirev and César Cui.

Russian literature Literary works of Russia until 1917, then of the Soviet Union until 1991. Thereafter the literature properly belongs to the individual republics. Russian literature has its origins in religious works dating from c.1000 AD, when Christianity came to Russia. The ROMANTICISM of writers such as Alexander PUSHKIN (*Boris Godunov*, 1825), gave way to the realism of Leo TOLSTOY (*War and Peace*, 1869), Fyodor DOSTOEVSKY, Anton CHEKHOV (*Uncle Vanya*, 1899) and Maxim GORKY (*The Lower Depths*, 1902). The early 20th-century revolutionary movements had their counterparts in the arts. Major literary figures included the symbolist poet Alexander Blok, and post-symbolists such as Vladimir MAYAKOVSKY. After the Russian Revolution (1917), many writers fled overseas to escape censorship. Authors who remained had to depict favourable images of the Soviet Union. The major authors of this period include Boris PASTERNAK. Criticism of the regime was published, however, in works by novelists such as Alexander SOLZHENITSYN (*One Day in the Life of Ivan Denisovich*, 1962).

Russian Orthodox Church See ORTHODOX CHURCH

Russian Revolution Events of 1917 in Russia that resulted, first, in the founding of a republic (March) and, second, in the seizure of power by the BOLSHEVIKS (November). Widespread discontent, a strong revolutionary movement, and the hardships of World War 1 forced Tsar NICHOLAS II to abdicate in March. A provisional government was formed by liberals in the Duma (parliament), which represented only the middle classes. Its aim was to make Russia into a liberal democracy and to defeat Germany. Workers and peasants had a different agenda: greater social and economic equality and an end to the war. The provisional government faced a challenge from the powerful socialist soviet in Petrograd (St Petersburg), which in May formed a coalition government that included Alexander KERENSKY, prime minister from July, and other socialists. The launching of a new military offensive combined with disappointing reforms, discredited the government and the socialist parties associated with it. Meanwhile, soviets sprang up in many cities; in the countryside, peasants seized land from the gentry; at the front, soldiers deserted. In the cities, the Bolsheviks secured growing support in

the soviets. In November, at the order of LENIN, they carried out a successful coup in Petrograd. The Kerensky government folded, but a long civil war ensued before Lenin and his followers established their authority throughout Russia.

Russian Revolution of 1905 Series of violent strikes and protests against tsarist rule in Russia. It was provoked mainly by defeat in the RUSSO-JAPANESE WAR (1904–05). It began on Bloody Sunday (22 January), when a peaceful demonstration in St Petersburg was fired on by troops. Strikes and peasant risings spread, culminating in a general strike in October, which forced the tsar to institute a democratically elected duma (parliament). By the time it met in 1906, the government had regained control. Severe repression followed.

Russo-Japanese War (1904–05) Conflict arising from the rivalry of Russia and Japan for control of Manchuria and Korea. The war opened with a Japanese attack on Port Arthur. Russian forces suffered a series of defeats, culminating in the Battle of Mukden (February–March 1905) and the annihilation of the Baltic fleet at Tsushima (May). Russia was forced to surrender Korea, the Liaotung Peninsula and S Sakhalin to Japan.

rust In botany, group of fungi that live as PARASITES on many kinds of higher plants. Rusts damage cereal crops and several fruits and vegetables. They have complex life cycles that involve growth on more than one host plant.

rust Corrosion of iron or its alloys by a combination of air and water. Carbon dioxide from the air dissolves in water to form an acid solution that attacks the iron to form iron (II) oxide. This is then oxidized to reddish-brown iron (III) oxide. Rusting may be prevented by GALVANIZING.

Ruth Eighth book of the Old Testament. It tells of Ruth's fidelity to Naomi, her Hebrew mother-in-law; her decision to leave her own land and settle in Israelite territory; and her eventual marriage to the wealthy Boaz, whereby she becomes the great-grandmother of Israel's greatest leader, King DAVID.

Ruth, "Babe" (George Herman) (1895–1948) US baseball player. He held the career home-run record (714) until 1974, when it was surpassed by Hank Aaron. Ruth's record of 60 home runs in one season (154 games) was not topped until the season was extended to 162 games. He played for three teams: the Boston Red Sox (1914–19), New York Yankees (1920–34) and Boston Braves (1935). He was elected to the Baseball Hall of Fame in 1936.

ruthenium Silver-white metallic element (symbol Ru), one of the TRANSITION ELEMENTS. It was discovered in 1827. Ruthenium is found in PLATINUM ores. It is used as a catalyst, and its alloys are used in electrical contacts and to colour glass and ceramics . Properties: at.no. 44; r.a.m. 101.07; r.d. 12.41; m.p. 2,310°C (4,190°F); b.p. 3,900°C (7,052°F); most common isotope Ru^{102} (31.61%).

Rutherford, Ernest, Lord (1871–1937) British physicist, b. New Zealand, who pioneered modern

NUCLEAR PHYSICS. He discovered and named alpha and beta radiation, named the nucleus, and proposed a theory of the radioactive transformation of atoms for which he received the 1908 Nobel Prize for chemistry. Under J.J. THOMSON, he discovered uranium radiations. At Manchester (1907) he devised the nuclear theory of the atom and, with Niels BOHR, the idea of orbital electrons. In 1919 his research team became the first to split an atom's nucleus. He predicted the existence of the NEUTRON.

rutile Black to red-brown oxide mineral, titanium dioxide (TiO_2), found in igneous and metamorphic rocks and quartz veins. It occurs as long, prismatic crystals in the tetragonal system and as granular masses. It has a metallic lustre, is brittle and is used as a gemstone. Hardness 6–6.5; s. g. 4.2.

Rwanda Nation in E central Africa; the capital is KIGALI. **Land and climate** The Republic of Rwanda is Africa's most densely populated country. It is a small state in the heart of Africa, bordered by Uganda (N), Tanzania (E), Burundi (S) and Zaïre (W). The W border is formed by Lake Kivu and the Ruzizi River. Rwanda has a rugged landscape, dominated by high, volcanic mountains, rising to Mount Karisimbi, at 4,507m (14,787ft). Kigali stands on the central plateau. East Burundi consists of stepped plateaux, which descend to the lakes of the Kagera National Park. Rwanda's climate is moderated by altitude. Rainfall is abundant. The lush rainforests in the W are one of the last refuges for the mountain gorilla. Many forests have been cleared; 35% of the land is now arable. Despite contour ploughing, heavy rain has caused severe soil erosion. **Economy** Rwanda is a low-income developing country (1992 GDP per capita, US$710). Most people are subsistence farmers. Crops include bananas, beans, cassava and sorghum. Some cattle are raised, mainly by Tutsis. Rwanda's most valuable crop is coffee, accounting for over 70% of exports. **History and Politics** Twa pygmies were the original inhabitants of Rwanda, but c.1,000 AD, Hutu farmers began to settle, gradually displacing the Twa. In the 15th century, Tutsi cattle herders began to dominate the Hutu. By the late 18th century, Rwanda and Burundi formed a single Tutsi-dominated state, ruled by a king (*mwami*). In 1890 Germany conquered the area and subsumed it into German East Africa. Dur-

ing World War 1, Belgian forces occupied (1916) both Rwanda and Burundi. In 1919 it became part of the Belgian League of Nations mandate territory of Ruanda-Urundi (which in 1946 became a UN trust territory). The Hutu majority became more vociferous in their demands for political representation. In 1959 the Tutsi *mwami* died. The ensuing civil war between Hutus and Tutsis claimed over 150,000 lives. Hutu victory led to a mass exodus of Tutsis. The 1960 elections were won by the Hutu Emancipation Movement, led by Grégoire Kayibanda. In 1961 Rwanda declared itself a republic. Belgium recognized independence in 1962. Kayibanda became president. Rwanda was subject to continual Tutsi incursions from Burundi and Uganda. In 1973 Kayibanda was overthrown in a military coup, led by Major General Habyarimana. In 1978 Habyarimana became president. During the 1980s, Rwanda was devastated by drought. Over 50,000 refugees fled to Burundi. In 1990 Rwanda was invaded by the Tutsi-dominated Rwandan Patriotic Front (RPF), who forced Habyarimana to agree to a multiparty constitution. UN forces were drafted in to oversee the transition. In April 1994 Habyarimana and the Burundi president were killed in a rocket attack on their aircraft. The Hutu army and militia launched a premediated act of genocide against the Tutsi minority, killing between 500,000 and 1 million Tutsis within three months. In July 1994 an RPF offensive toppled the government and created 2 million Hutu refugees. A government of national unity, comprising both Tutsis and moderate Hutus, was formed. Over 50,000 people died in refugee camps in E Zaïre before aid arrived. Hutu militia remained in control of the camps, and their leaders faced prosecution for genocide. Refugees remained fearful of Tutsi reprisals. The number of refugees (1995, 1 million in Zaïre and 500,000 in Tanzania) destabilized regional politics and the "ethnic cleansing" that dominated the region in the 1990s continued.

rye Hardy cereal grass originating in SW Asia and naturalized worldwide. It grows in poorer soils and colder climates than most other cereals. It has flower spikelets that develop one-seeded grains. It is used for flour, as a forage crop and for making alcoholic drinks. Height: to 0.9m (3ft). Family Poaceae/Gramineae; species *Secale cereale*.

Ryle, Sir Martin (1918–84) British physicist and pioneer of RADIO ASTRONOMY. He catalogued radio sources, which led to his discovery of QUASARS.

Ryukyu Islands Japanese archipelago in the W Pacific Ocean, extending c.965km (600mi) between Kyūshū in S Japan and Taiwan; it separates the East China Sea (W) from the Philippine Sea (E). The islands were relinquished by China to Japan in 1879. After World War 2 they were administered by the USA, being restored to Japan in 1972. The group includes OKINAWA. Agriculture and fishing are the chief occupations. Area: c.2,200sq km (850sq mi). Pop. (1984 est.) 1,161,000.

RWANDA

AREA: 26,340sq km (10,170sq mi)
POPULATION: 7,526,000
CAPITAL (POPULATION): Kigali (234,500)
GOVERNMENT: Republic
ETHNIC GROUPS: Hutu 90%, Tutsi 9%, Twa 1%
LANGUAGES: French and Kinyarwanda (both official)
RELIGIONS: Christianity 74% (Roman Catholic 65%), traditional beliefs 17%, Islam 9%
CURRENCY: Rwanda franc = 100 centimes

S/s is the 19th letter of the English alphabet and a letter employed in the alphabets of other w European languages. It is descended from the Semitic letter sin or shin, meaning tooth.

Saarland State in SW Germany on the borders with France (S) and Luxembourg (W); the capital is Saarbrücken. Belonging intermittently to France, the Saar was finally ceded to Prussia after the defeat of Napoleon I in 1815. France administered the region after both world wars. Saarland finally gained the status of a West German state in 1967. The valley of the River Saar is occupied by blast furnaces and steel works, which exploit local coal and nearby iron ore. There is little agriculture and some market gardening. Area: 2,570sq km (992sq mi). Pop. (1989 est.) 1,054,000.

Sabah, Sheikh Jabir al Ahmad al- (1928–) (Jabir III) Emir of Kuwait (1977–). A member of the ruling family of Al-Sabah, he succeded Sabah III al Salim. When Iraq invaded Kuwait (1990), Jabir took refuge in Saudia Arabia and set up a government in exile. He returned to Kuwait in 1991.

Sabah (North BORNEO) State of MALAYSIA and one of the four political subdivisions of the island of Borneo. Ceded to the British in 1877, it remained the British Protectorate of North Borneo until 1963, when it became an independent state of the Malaysian Federation. The terrain is mountainous and forested. The capital is Kota Kinabalu (1990 pop. 208,484). The main products include oil, timber, rubber, coconuts and rice. Area: 76,522sq km (29,545sq mi). Pop. (1990) 1,736,902.

Sabbath Seventh day of the week, set aside as a sacred day of rest. For Jews, the Sabbath runs from sunset on Friday for sunset on Saturday. Christians set aside Sunday for their Sabbath, making it a day of worship and rest from labour.

sable MARTEN native to Siberia. It has been hunted almost to extinction for its thick, soft, durable fur, which is dark brown, sometimes flecked with white. Length: to 60cm (24in). Family Mustelidae; species *Martes zibellina*.

sabre-toothed tiger Popular name for a prehistoric member of the CAT family (Felidae) that existed from the OLIGOCENE period to the PLEISTOCENE period. It had extremely long canine teeth adapted to killing large herbivores. Subfamily Machairodontinae, genus *Smilodon*.

saccharide Organic compound based on SUGAR molecules. Monosaccharides include GLUCOSE and FRUCTOSE. Two sugar molecules join together to make a disaccharide, such as LACTOSE or SUCROSE. POLYSACCHARIDES have more than two sugar molecules. *See also* CARBOHYDRATE

saccharin Synthetic substance used as a substitute for SUGAR. It is derived from TOLUENE. Formula: $C_7H_5NO_3S$.

Sackville-West, Vita (Victoria Mary) (1892–1962) British poet and novelist. Her best-known works include *The Edwardians* (1930), *All Passion Spent* (1931) and *The Land* (1926).

sacrament Symbolic action in which the central mysteries of a religious faith are enacted and which, on some accounts, confers divine grace upon those to whom it is given. For Protestants there are two sacraments: BAPTISM and the Lord's Supper (*see* LAST SUPPER). In the Roman Catholic and Eastern Orthodox Churches, the sacraments are baptism, CONFIRMATION, the EUCHARIST, holy ORDERS, matrimony, penance, and the anointing of the sick.

Sacramento State capital and inland port of central California, USA, on the Sacramento River. A 69km (43mi) channel links it to an arm of San Francisco Bay, and the city has a large US Army depot and the McClellan Air Base. Industries: missile development, transport equipment, food processing, bricks. Pop. (1992) 382,816.

Sadat, (Muhammad) Anwar (al-) (1918–81) President of Egypt (1970–81). A close associate of NASSER, he was vice president (1964–66, 1969–70), and succeeded him as president. After the costly ARAB-ISRAELI WARS of 1973, he sought peace with ISRAEL. He signed a peace treaty in 1979. He was assassinated by Muslim fundamentalists.

Sade, Donatien Alphonse François, Marquis de (1740–1814) French novelist and playwright. Imprisoned for sexual offences, he wrote novels renowned for their licentiousness, among them *Justine* (1791) and *Juliette* (1797).

Safavid Persian dynasty (1501–1722) that established the territorial and SHIITE theocratic principles of modern Iran. The founder, Shah ISMAIL, claimed descent from a Shiite SUFISM order. His successor, ABBAS I, accepted the Ottoman occupation of W Iran. His death created a power vacuum and Iran's borders contracted. Shah Husayn's concentration on the capture of BAHRAIN enabled Afghan troops to overrun the country. His forced abdication in 1722 marked the end of Safavid rule.

safflower Annual plant with large, red or orange flower heads that are used in making dyestuffs. The seeds yield oil, used in cooking and in the manufacture of MARGARINE. Family Asteraceae/Compositae; species *Carthamus tinctorius*.

saffron (autumn CROCUS) Perennial crocus, native to Asia Minor and cultivated in Europe. It has purple or white flowers. The golden, dried stigmas of the plant are used as a flavouring or dye. Family Iridaceae; species *Crocus sativus*.

sage Common name for a number of plants of the MINT family (Lamiaceae/Labiatae) native to the Mediterranean region. The best-known is *Salvia officinalis*, an aromatic perennial herb used widely for seasoning. Height: 15–38cm (6–15in).

Sagittarius (the archer) Southern constellation between Scorpio and Capricorn. Rich in stellar

CLUSTERS, this region of the sky also contains much interstellar matter. In astrology, it is the ninth sign of the zodiac, represented by a centaur firing a bow and arrow. The Sun is in Sagittarius from 22 November to 21 December.

sago palm (fern palm) Feather-leaved PALM tree native to swampy areas of Malaysia and Polynesia. Its thick trunk contains sago, a starch used in foodstuffs. Height: 1.2–9.1m (4–30ft). Family Arecaceae/Palmae; species *Metroxylon sagu*.

Sahara World's largest desert, *c*.9,065,000sq km (3,500,000sq mi), covering nearly a third of Africa's land area. It consists of Algeria, Niger, Libya, Egypt and Mauritania, the S parts of Morocco and Tunisia, and the N parts of Senegal, Mali, Chad and Sudan. Annual rainfall is less than 10cm (4in). Two-thirds of the Sahara is stony desert, and the topography ranges from the Tibesti Massif (N Chad) at 3,350m (11,000ft) to the Qattara Depression (Egypt) at 133m (436ft) below sea-level. The numerous oases act as vital centres for the Sahara's 2 million inhabitants. The two main ethnic groups are the Tuareg and the Tibu. Mineral deposits include salt, iron ore, phosphates, oil and gas.

Sahel Band of semi-arid scrub and savanna grassland in Africa, S of the SAHARA. It extends through Senegal, S Mauritania, Mali, Burkina Faso, N Benin, S Niger, N Nigeria and S central Chad. Over the past 30 years the Sahara has encroached on the N Sahel in a notorious example of DESERTIFICATION.

Saigon *See* HO CHI MINH CITY

sailing *See* YACHT

saint Person who has manifested exceptional holiness and love of God. In the Roman Catholic and Eastern Orthodox churches, individual saints are regarded as having a special relationship with God and are therefore venerated for their perceived role as intercessors. *See also* CANONIZATION

Saint Bartholomew's Day Massacre (24 August 1572) Mass murder of HUGUENOTS (French Protestants) on St Bartholomew's feast day. The Huguenot leaders had gathered in Paris for the marriage of Henry of Navarre (later HENRY IV). On orders from CATHERINE DE' MÉDICI, a bungled attempt was made on the life of Gaspard de Coligny. With the support of the king, CHARLES IX, the massacre began when soldiers killed Coligny and other Huguenot leaders. It soon spread and continued in the provinces until 3 October; *c*.70,000 people died.

St Bernard Swiss mountain and rescue dog with excellent scenting abilities; from the 17th century it has been used to find people lost in deep snow. It has a massive head with a short deep muzzle, and a dense white and red coat. Height: to 74cm (29in) at the shoulder; weight: to 77kg (170lb).

St George's Capital of GRENADA, West Indies. Founded in 1650 as a French settlement, it was capital of the British WINDWARD ISLANDS (1885–1958). Industries: rum distilling, sugar processing, tourism. Pop. (1989) 35,742.

St Helena Rocky island in the S Atlantic, 1,920km (1,190mi) from the coast of W Africa; its capital is Jamestown (1992 pop. 1,500). It was the place of Napoleon I's exile. Discovered by the Portuguese in 1502, it was captured by the Dutch in 1633. It passed to the British East India Company in 1659, becoming a British crown colony in 1834. It is now a UK dependent territory and administrative centre for the ASCENSION and TRISTAN DA CUNHA islands. It services ships and exports fish and handicrafts. Area: 122sq km (47sq mi). Pop. (1992) 5,700.

St Helens, Mount Volcanic peak in the Cascade Range, SW Washington. Dormant since 1857, it erupted on 18 May 1980, killing 60 people. The 2,950m (9,578ft) summit was reduced to 2,560m (8,312ft), with a deep horseshoe crater. It is predicted to erupt in the early 21st century.

St John of Jerusalem, Knights Hospitallers of *See* KNIGHTS HOSPITALLERS

St John's Port and capital of Antigua, in the Leeward Islands, West Indies. During the 18th century, St John's was the headquarters of the Royal Navy in the West Indies. Industries: tourism, rum, sugar, cotton. Pop. (1992) 38,000.

St Kitts-Nevis Self-governing state in the Leeward Islands, West Indies. The state includes the islands of Saint Kitts (Saint Christopher), Nevis and Sombrero. BASSETERRE (on Saint Kitts) is the capital. The islands were discovered in 1493 by COLUMBUS, and settled by the English (1623) and the French (1624). Anglo-French disputes over possession were settled in Britain's favour in 1783 by the Treaty of Paris, and the islands achieved self-government in 1967. Industries: tourism, sugar, cotton, salt, coconuts. Area: 311sq km (120sq mi). Pop. (1991) 40,618.

St Lawrence Canadian river, in SE Ontario and S Quebec provinces, flowing from the NE end of Lake Ontario to the Gulf of St Lawrence. The river forms the boundary between the USA and Canada for *c*.184km (114mi) of its total of 1,244km (760mi). Since the completion of the ST LAWRENCE SEAWAY in 1959, the river has been navigable to all but the very largest vessels. Length: 1,050km (650mi).

St Lawrence Seaway Waterway in Canada and the USA. Built in the 1950s, it connects the GREAT LAKES with the Atlantic Ocean. The St Lawrence Seaway extends about 750km (470mi) from N of Montreal down to Lake Erie. The main part of the waterway consists of a series of canals and locks that bypass the rapids along the St Lawrence River and the Niagara Falls. The St Lawrence Seaway allows ocean-going vessels to reach industrial lakeside ports of central North America.

St Lucia Volcanic island in the Windward group, West Indies; the capital is Castries (1992 pop. 53,883). The island changed hands 14 times between France and Britain before being ceded to Britain in 1814. It finally achieved full self-government in 1979. Mountainous, lush and forested, its tourist income is growing rapidly. The principal export crop is bananas. Area: 616sq km (238sq mi). Pop. (1991) 133,308.

St Mark's BASILICA in Venice. Begun in 829 to enshrine the remains of the city's patron saint, St Mark, it was restored after a fire in 976. It was rebuilt in the 11th century in the BYZANTINE style.

St Paul US state capital and port of entry, on the E bank of the Mississippi River, E MINNESOTA. In 1849 St Paul was made capital of Minnesota territory. Modern-day St Paul is a major manufacturing and distribution centre. Pop. (1992) 268,266.

St Paul's Anglican cathedral in London, built 1675–1710 on the site of a medieval cathedral that had been destroyed in the Great FIRE OF LONDON. It was designed by WREN in the Classical style.

St Peter's Great Christian BASILICA in the VATICAN CITY. In 1506 Pope Julius II laid the foundation stone on the site of an earlier structure over the grave of St Peter. The church was completed in 1615 during the reign of Pope Paul V, under the supervision of Carlo Maderno (1556–1629).

St Petersburg (formerly Petrograd and Leningrad) Second-largest city in RUSSIA and a major Baltic seaport at the E end of the Gulf of Finland, on the delta of the River Neva. Founded in 1703 by PETER I (THE GREAT), the city was the capital of Russia from 1712 to 1918. Renamed Petrograd in 1914, it was a centre of the political unrest that culminated in the RUSSIAN REVOLUTION. The city was renamed Leningrad (1924). It suffered extensive damage during World War 2 and has been massively rebuilt. Renamed St Petersburg (1991) following the break-up of the Soviet Union, it enjoys federal status within the Russian Republic. Industries: shipbuilding, heavy engineering, brewing, electronics, chemicals. Pop. (1994) 4,883,000.

St Pierre and Miquelon Group of eight small islands in the Gulf of St Lawrence, SW of Newfoundland, Canada. The capital is St Pierre (pop. 5,000) on the island of the same name; Miquelon is the largest island. The group was claimed for France in 1535 and since 1985 has been a "territorial collectivity". Fishing is the most important activity. Area 242sq km (93sq mi). Pop. (1990) 6,392.

Saint-Saëns, Charles Camille (1835–1921) French composer, pianist and organist. He composed prolifically in all forms and is best remembered for his opera *Samson and Delilah* (1877), the Third Symphony (1886), the *Carnival of the Animals* (1886) and the *Danse Macabre* (1874).

St Vincent and the Grenadines Island state of the WINDWARD ISLANDS, West Indies. The capital is KINGSTOWN. It comprises the volcanic island of St Vincent and five islands of the Grenadine group, including Mustique. St Vincent remained uncolonized until British settlement in 1762. It was part of the British Windward Islands colony from 1880–1958 and of the West Indies Federation 1958–62. Self-government was granted in 1969, followed by full independence within the Commonwealth in 1979. Agriculture dominates the econo-

my. Major crops: arrowroot, bananas and coconuts. Area: 388sq km (150sq mi). Pop. (1991) 106,499.

Sakhalin (Jap. *Karafuto*) Island off the E coast of Russia, between the Sea of Okhotsk and the Sea of Japan. The capital is Yuzhno-Sakhalinsk (1992 pop. 174,000). Settled by Russians and Japanese, it was finally ceded to Russia in 1945. Sakhalin's chief importance lies in its deposits of coal and iron ore. Industries: timber, fishing, canning. Area: 76,400sq km (29,500sq mi). Pop. (1989) 709,000.

Sakharov, Andrei Dimitrievich (1921–89) Soviet physicist. His work in nuclear FUSION was instrumental in the development of the Soviet HYDROGEN BOMB. An outspoken defender of civil liberties, he created the Human Rights Committee in 1970 and received the 1975 Nobel Peace Prize.

Saki (1870–1916) (Hector Hugh Munro) Scottish writer. His reputation rests on his short stories, among them the collections *Reginald* (1904) and *Beasts and Superbeasts* (1914).

Saladin (1138–93) Muslim general, founder of the Ayyubid dynasty. A soldier and administrator, he was appointed grand vizier in 1169. He overthrew the FATIMIDS in 1171 and made himself sultan. He gathered widespread support for a JIHAD to drive the Christians from Palestine (1187). He reconquered Jerusalem, provoking the Third Crusade (1189). His rule restored Egypt as a major power.

salamander Any of 320 species of amphibians found worldwide, except in Australia and polar regions. It has an elongated body, a long tail and short legs. Most species lay eggs, but some give birth to live young. The largest European species, the fire salamander (*Salamandra salamandra*), may reach a length of 28cm (11in). Order Urodela.

Salazar, António de Oliveira (1889–1970) Portuguese statesman, dictator (1932–68). He became prime minister and assumed dictatorial powers (1932). Imposing a semi-fascist constitution (1933), he held power with a powerful army and secret police, enforcing law and order at the cost of economic progress. He was sympathetic to FRANCO in Spain and remained neutral in World War 2.

Salem State capital of Oregon, USA, on the Willamette River. Founded in 1840 by Methodist missionaries, it became state capital in 1859. Industries: timber, food canning, meat packing, high-technology equipment. Pop. (1990) 112,050.

Salem City on Massachusetts Bay, NE Massachusetts, USA. First settled in 1626, Salem achieved notoriety for its witchcraft trials (1692), when 19 people were hanged. Industries: electrical products, leather goods, textiles, tourism. Pop. (1990) 38,090.

Salieri, Antonio (1750–1825) Italian composer. As court composer in Vienna, he composed operas, sacred music, vocal and orchestral works.

Salinger, J.D. (Jerome David) (1919–) US novelist. He achieved fame with his first book and only novel, *Catcher in the Rye* (1951). Other works are collections of short stories, including *Franny and Zooey* (1961) and *Raise High the Roof Beam* (1963).

Salisbury, Robert Arthur Talbot Gascoyne-Cecil, 3rd Marquess of (1830–1903) British statesman and diplomat. A Conservative, he served in DISRAELI's administration (1874–80). On Disraeli's death (1881), he became leader of the Conservative Party and served three terms (1885–86, 1886–92, 1895–1902) as prime minister. His policy of "splendid isolation" left England with few friends during the SOUTH AFRICAN WARS.

saliva Fluid secreted into the mouth by the salivary glands. In vertebrates, saliva is composed of about 99% water with dissolved traces of sodium, potassium, calcium and the ENZYME amylase. Saliva softens and lubricates food to aid swallowing, and amylase starts the digestion of starches.

salmon Marine and freshwater fish of the Northern Hemisphere. The Atlantic salmon (*Salmo salar*) is a marine trout that spawns in rivers on each side of the Atlantic Ocean and then returns to the sea. The Pacific salmon (*Oncorhynchus*) hatches, spawns and dies in freshwater, but spends its adult life in the ocean. Weight: to 36kg (80lb). Family Salmonidae.

Salmond, Alex (Alexander Elliott Anderson) (1954–) Scottish politician, leader of the SCOTTISH NATIONAL PARTY (SNP) from 1990. In 1987 he was elected member of Parliament for Banff and Buchan, becoming the SNP's National Convener in 1990. Despite pressing for full Scottish independence, he agreed to participate in a devolved assembly for Scotland.

salmonella Several species of rod-shaped bacteria that cause intestinal infections in human beings and animals. *Salmonella typhi* causes TYPHOID FEVER; other species cause GASTROENTERITIS. The bacteria are transmitted by carriers, particularly flies, and in food and water.

Salome (active 1st century AD) Daughter of Herodias and stepdaughter of Herod Antipas. She conspired with her mother to have JOHN THE BAPTIST executed.

salsa Cuban-inspired music; the term was first used in the early 1970s of the Latin music being produced in New York. Salsa is a percussive and brass-led big band music. It embraces dance forms, including rumba, mambo and guaracha.

salt Ionic compound formed, along with water, when an ACID is neutralized by a BASE. The hydrogen of the acid is replaced by a metal or ammonium ion. Salts are typically crystalline compounds. They usually dissolve in water to form a solution that can conduct electricity.

Salt Lake City State capital of Utah, USA, 21km (13mi) E of the Great Salt Lake. Founded in 1847 by the MORMONS under Brigham YOUNG, it grew rapidly. Salt Lake City is the world headquarters of the Mormon Church. Zinc, gold, silver, lead and copper are mined nearby. Other industries: missiles, rocket engines, oil-refining, tourism, printing and publishing. Pop. (1992) 165,835.

Salvador (Bahia) Seaport city in E central Brazil, capital of Bahia state. Founded by the Portuguese in 1549 as Bahia, it was the capital of Brazil until 1763. Industries: oil refining, petrochemicals, tobacco, sugar, coffee, industrial diamonds. Pop. (1991) 2,056,000.

Salvador, El *See* EL SALVADOR

Salvation Army Christian society devoted to the propagation of the gospel among the working classes. Its origin was the Christian Revival Association, founded in 1865 in London by William BOOTH. In 1867 it became the East London Christian Mission and in 1878 the Salvation Army; members were given ranks and led by "General" Booth.

Salzburg City on the River Salzach, NW Austria, capital of the alpine Salzburg state. It grew around a 7th-century monastery and was ruled by the archbishops of Salzburg for more than 1,000 years. Mozart's birthplace and the home of several music festivals, its major industry is tourism. Pop. (1991) 144,000.

Samaria Ancient region and town of central Palestine. It was built as the capital of the northern kingdom of Israel in the 9th century BC. Conquered by Shalmaneser in 722–21 BC, Samaria was later destroyed by John Hyrcanus I and rebuilt by HEROD THE GREAT. *See also* SAMARITANS

Samaritans Descendants of those citizens of SAMARIA who escaped deportation after their kingdom was overrun by the Assyrians in 722–21 BC. The Jews to the south rejected them. Their sole religious scripture is the TORAH.

samarium Grey-white metallic element (symbol Sm) of the LANTHANIDE SERIES. First identified in 1879, its chief ores are monazite and bastnasite. Samarium is used as a neutron absorber in NUCLEAR REACTORS and as a catalyst. Properties: at.no. 62; r.a.m. 150.35; r.d. 7.52; m.p. 1,072°C (1,962°F); b.p. 1,791°C (3,256°F); most common isotope Sm^{152} (26.72%).

Samoa Volcanic island group in the S Pacific, comprising the independent state of WESTERN SAMOA and the US-administered AMERICAN SAMOA. Extending *c.*560km (350mi), the islands are predominantly mountainous and fringed by coral reefs. The majority of the population is indigenous Polynesian.

Sampras, Pete (1971–) US tennis player, the youngest man ever to win the US Open (1990) and the youngest to be ranked world no.1 (1993). He won Wimbledon (1993–95), the US Open (1990, 1993, 1995) and the Australian Open (1994).

Samson Israelite judge and Old Testament hero renowned for his great strength. Samson was a Nazarite, whose strength lay in his long hair. When his mistress DELILAH discovered this, she had his hair cut off while he slept and handed him over to his enemies, the PHILISTINES. Samson regained his strength as his hair regrew, and when called upon to display his strength in the Philistine Temple of Dagon, he pulled down its central pillars and roof, killing himself and thousands of his captors.

Samurai Member of the elite warrior class of feudal Japan. Beginning as military retainers in the 10th century, the samurai came to form an aristocratic ruling class.

San (Bushmen) Khoisan-speaking people of S Africa. They have lived in the region for thousands of years and until recently had a hunting and gathering culture. About half still follow the traditional ways, mostly in the Kalahari region of Botswana and Namibia.

Sana'a (San'a) Capital and largest city of Yemen. Situated on a high plateau at 2,286m (7,500ft), it claims to be the world's oldest city, founded by Shem, eldest son of Noah. In 1918 it became capital of an independent Yemen Arab Republic, and in 1990 capital of the new, unified Yemen. It is noted for its handicrafts. Agriculture (grapes) and industry (iron) are also important. Pop. (1988) 427,502.

San Andreas fault Geological FAULT line extending more than 965km (600mi) through California. PLATE TECTONIC movement causes several thousand EARTHQUAKES each year, though only a few are significant. The most destructive earthquake occurred in 1906: it horizontally displaced land around the fault by up to 6.4m (21ft) and killed 503 people.

Sand, George (1804–76) French novelist, b. Amandine-Aurore-Lucie Dupin. Her novels, such as *Lélia* (1833) and *Mauprat* (1837), advocate women's right to independence. Her later work includes the novels of rural life with which she is often associated, as well as an autobiography.

sand Mineral particles worn away from rocks by EROSION, individually large enough to be distinguished with the naked eye. Sand is composed mostly of QUARTZ, but black sand (containing volcanic rock) and coral sand also occur.

sandalwood Any of several species of Asian trees of the genus *Santalum*, many of which are PARASITES on the roots of other plants. The fragrant wood is used in carving and joss sticks. The distilled oil is used in perfumes and medicines. Height: to 10m (33ft). Family Santalaceae.

Sandburg, Carl (1878–1967) US poet. His first volume of poetry, *Chicago Poems*, appeared in 1916. Other collections include *Cornhuskers* (Pulitzer Prize, 1918) and *Good Morning, America* (1928). Sandburg also won Pulitzer Prizes for *Complete Poems* (1950) and the second volume of his biography of Abraham Lincoln (1939).

sand hopper (sand flea) Any of several species of small, terrestrial crustaceans. The nocturnal European sand hopper (*Talitrus saltator*) lives on beaches, emerging to feed on organic debris. Length: to 1.5cm (0.6in). Order Amphipoda; family Talitridae.

San Diego City in S California, USA. It was founded in 1769 as a mission. It is an important centre for scientific research (especially oceanography). Industries: aerospace, electronics, fishing and fish canning, shipbuilding, tourism. Pop. (1992) 1,148,851.

Sandinista (Sandinista National Liberation Front) Revolutionary group in Nicaragua. They took their name from Augusto Cesar Sandino, who opposed the dominant SOMOZA family and was killed in 1934. The Sandinistas overthrew the Somoza regime in 1979 and formed a government led by Daniel Ortega Saavedra. In power they were opposed by right-wing guerrillas, the CONTRA, supported by the USA. The conflict ended when the Sandinista agreed to free elections. They lost, but the Contra were disbanded and the Sandinista remain an influential political force.

sandpiper Wading bird that breeds in cold regions and migrates long distances to winter in warm areas, settling in grass or low bushes near water. It nests in a grass-lined hole in the ground. Length: 15–60cm (6–24in). Family Scolopacidae.

sandstone SEDIMENTARY ROCK composed of sand grains cemented in such materials as SILICA or calcium carbonate. Its hardness depends on the character of the cementing material.

San Francisco Port in W California, USA, on a peninsula bounded by the Pacific Ocean (W) and San Francisco Bay (E), which are connected by the Golden Gate Strait. Founded by the Spanish in 1776, it was acquired by the USA in 1846. Devastated by an earthquake and fire in 1906, it was quickly rebuilt and prospered with the opening of the PANAMA CANAL. Industries: tourism, shipbuilding, oil refining, aircraft, fishing, printing and publishing. Pop. (1992) 728,921.

Sanger, Frederick (1918–) British biochemist, the first person to win two Nobel Prizes in chemistry. He was awarded the first in 1958 for finding the structure of INSULIN. His second prize came in 1980 (shared with Walter Gilbert and Paul Berg) for work on the chemical structure of nucleic acids.

Sanhedrin Ancient Jewish religious council, prominent in Jerusalem during the period of Roman rule in Palestine. The Great Sanhedrin is believed to have served as a legislative and judicial body on both religious and political issues. JESUS CHRIST appeared before the Sanhedrin after his arrest.

San José Capital and largest city of Costa Rica. Founded c.1736, it became the centre of a prosperous coffee trade. Products: coffee, sugar cane, cacao, fruit, tobacco. Pop. (1992) 303,000.

San Jose City in W California, USA. Founded in 1777, it was California's capital from 1849–1851. It is the centre of a fruit-growing region, but is best known as the focal point of "Silicon Valley", the hub of the computer industry. Pop. (1992) 801,331.

San Juan Capital, largest city and major port of PUERTO RICO. It has one of the finest harbours in the West Indies. Founded in 1508, the port prospered during the 18th and 19th centuries. It is the commercial centre of Puerto Rico. Exports: coffee, tobacco, fruit, sugar. Industries: cigars and cigarettes, sugar refining, metal products, pharmaceuticals, tourism. Pop. (1990) 437,745.

San Marino World's smallest republic and perhaps Europe's oldest state, near the Adriatic Sea, NE

Italy. According to legend, it was founded in the 4th century AD. Its mountainous terrain has enabled it to retain a separate status, becoming an independent commune in the 13th century. The economy is largely agricultural, but tourism is important. While San Marino has its own currency and stamps, Italian and Vatican City equivalents are widely used. It possesses its own legislative assembly. There are two towns: Serravalle (1991 pop. 7,264) and the capital San Marino (1993 pop. 4,335). Area: 61sq km (24sq mi). Pop. (1993) 24,003.

San Martín, José de (1778–1850) South American revolutionary. After defeating the Spaniards in Argentina, he took them by surprise in Chile (1817–18) by crossing the Andes, and won Peru (1821) with an unexpected naval attack. He surrendered his effective rule of Peru to Simón BOLÍVAR in 1822 and retired to Europe.

San Salvador Capital and largest city of El Salvador, in central El Salvador. Founded in 1524 near the volcano of San Salvador, which rises to 1,885m (6,184ft) and last erupted in 1917, the city has been damaged frequently by earthquakes. The main industry is the processing of coffee grown on the rich volcanic soils of the area. Other manufactures include beer, textiles and tobacco. Pop. (1992) 422,570.

Sanskrit Classical language of India, the literary and sacred language of HINDUISM, and a forerunner of the modern Indo-Iranian languages spoken in N India, Pakistan, Nepal and Bangladesh. Sanskrit was the language in which the VEDAS were written. It is an INDO-EUROPEAN LANGUAGE and has been designated one of India's national languages.

Santa Anna, Antonio López de (1794–1876) Mexican general and dictator. He was the dominant political figure in Mexico from 1823–55, sometimes as president, sometimes unofficially as the result of a coup. After his failure in the MEXICAN WAR (1846–48), he went into exile. He returned to power in 1853, but was overthrown in 1855.

Santa Claus Variant of the Dutch name *Sinte Klaas*, itself a version of the name Saint NICHOLAS, who was Bishop of Myra sometime during the 4th century. Santa Claus has become associated with the feast of Christmas and is identified with Father Christmas in North America, the UK and some former Commonwealth countries.

Santa Cruz de Tenerife Capital of the CANARY ISLANDS and largest city in TENERIFE. Founded in 1494, it has a fine harbour and exports fruit, vegetables and sugar cane. Its industries include oil refining and tourism. Pop. (1991) 189,317.

Santa Fe State capital of New Mexico, USA. The oldest US capital city, it was founded in *c*.1609 by the Spanish and acted as a centre for Spanish–Native American trade for more than 200 years. In 1846 US troops captured the city, and in 1850 the region became US territory, achieving statehood in 1912. Today it is an administrative, tourist and resort centre. Pop. (1992) 59,004.

Santer, Jacques (1937–) Luxembourg politician and president of the European Union (1994–). He was prime minister of Luxembourg (1984–94), when he became president of the EU.

Santiago Capital of Chile, in central Chile on the Mapocho River. Founded in 1541, it was destroyed by an earthquake in 1647. It is the nation's administrative, commercial and cultural centre. Industries: textiles, pharmaceuticals, food processing, footwear. Pop. (1992) 4,385,381.

Santo Domingo (formerly Ciudad Trujillo, 1936–61) Capital and chief port of the Dominican Republic, on the S coast of the island, on the Ozama River. Founded in 1496, the city is the oldest continuous European settlement in the Americas. It was the base for the Spaniards' conquering expeditions. It houses more than a third of the country's population, many of whom work in the sugar industry. Pop. (1991) 2,055,000.

São Paulo City on the Tietê River, SE Brazil, capital of São Paulo state, located almost exactly on the Tropic of Capricorn. Founded by the Jesuits in 1554, it grew as the base for expeditions into the interior in search of minerals. It expanded in the 17th century as a trading centre for a large coffee region. It is the world's fastest-growing metropolis. Pop. (1991) 9,646,185. São Paulo state houses up to 60% of Brazil's industry and most of its sugar production. Pop. (1991) 31,588,925.

São Tomé and Príncipe Country in the Gulf of Guinea, 300km (186mi) off the W coast of Africa. The capital is São Tomé. The republic consists of two main islands, São Tomé (the largest) and Príncipe. The islands are volcanic, the vegetation predominantly tropical rainforest. In 1522 the islands became a Portuguese colony. The Dutch controlled the island from 1641–1740, but the Portuguese regained control and established plantations. The islands became independent in 1975, ushering in 16 years of Marxist rule. Cocoa, coffee, bananas and coconuts are grown on plantations and their export provides the republic's only serious source of income. Area: 1,001sq km (387sq mi). Pop. (1995) 131,100.

sap Fluid that circulates water and nutrients through plants. Water is absorbed by the roots and carried, along with minerals, through the XYLEM to the leaves. Sap from the leaves is distributed throughout the plant.

sapphire Transparent to translucent gemstone variety of CORUNDUM. It has various colours produced by impurities of iron and titanium, the most valuable being deep blue.

Sappho (active early 6th century BC) Greek poet. Her passionate love poetry, written on the island of Lesbos, was regarded by PLATO as the expression of "the tenth Muse".

saprophyte Plant that obtains its food from dead or decaying plant or animal tissue. Generally it has no CHLOROPHYLL. Included are most fungi and some flowering plants.

Saracens Name applied by the ancient Greeks and Romans to the Arab tribes who threatened their borders. The name was later extended to include all Arabs and eventually all Muslims. As a term similar to "Moors", it was used particularly by medieval Christians to denote their Muslim enemies.

Sarajevo Capital of Bosnia-Herzegovina, on the Miljacka River. It fell to the Turks in 1429 and became a flourishing commercial centre in the Ottoman empire. Passing to the AUSTRO-HUNGARIAN EMPIRE in 1878, the city was a centre of Serb and Bosnian resistance to Austrian rule. On 28 June 1914 the Austrian Archduke Franz Ferdinand and his wife were assassinated here by a Serbian nationalist (an act that helped to precipitate World War 1). In 1991 during the bloody civil war between Croatian, Bosnian and Serbian forces, the city endured a long and devastating siege. After the 1995 peace agreement (the Dayton Accord), it effectively became a Bosnian city, with the 1991 population figure of 526,000 drastically reduced as many Serbs fled.

Sarasvati In Hindu mythology, goddess of the arts, sciences and eloquent speech. Depicted as a beautiful young woman, she is credited with the invention of the Sanskrit language. She became the consort of BRAHMA.

Sarawak Largest state of Malaysia, in NW Borneo, comprising a highland interior and swampy coastal plain; the capital is Kuching City. Ruled as an independent state by Britain after 1841, it was made a British protectorate in 1888 and a Crown colony in 1946. Sarawak became a part of Malaysia in 1963, triggering a dispute with Indonesia. Oil is an important modern product alongside the traditional coconuts, rice, rubber and sago. Area: 124,449sq km (48,050sq mi). Pop. (1990) 1,648,217.

sarcoma Cancerous growth or TUMOUR arising from muscle, fat, bone, blood or lymph vessels or connective tissue. *See also* CANCER

sardine Small marine food fish found throughout the world. It has a large toothless mouth and oily flesh. Length: to 30cm (1ft). Species include the California *Sardinops caerulea*, South American *Sardinops sagax* and the European sardine, or PILCHARD, *Sardina pilchardus*. Family Clupeidae.

Sardinia Mountainous island of Italy, 208km (130mi) W of the Italian mainland, separated by the Tyrrhenian Sea. The capital is Cágliari. A trading centre for the Phoenicians, Greeks, Carthaginians and Romans, Sardinia became a kingdom in 1720. Farming and fishing are the chief occupations. Wheat, barley, grapes, olives and tobacco are grown, and sheep and goats are reared. Salt extraction is important; other minerals include coal, lead, magnesium, manganese and zinc. Area 24,090sq km (9,302sq mi). Pop. (1992) 1,651,902.

Sargasso Sea Area of calm, barely moving water in the N Atlantic between the West Indies and the Azores. It takes its name from the floating seaweed (*Sargassum*) covering its surface.

Sark One of the CHANNEL ISLANDS of the UK, divided into Great Sark and Little Sark, which are connected by a causeway. Sark is part of the Bailiwick of GUERNSEY, with a feudal organization dating from the 17th century. There are no cars and the residents pay no income tax. The population swells in the summer with tourists. Area: 5.5sq km (2.1sq mi). Pop. (1991) 575.

sarsaparilla Tropical perennial vine of the genus *Smilax*, native to central and S America. Its roots are the source of a chemical used to give an aromatic flavour to medicines and drinks. The main species used are *S. aristolochiaefolia*, *S. regelii* and *S. febrifuga*. Family Liliaceae.

Sartre, Jean-Paul (1905–80) French philosopher and writer who was instrumental in the popularization of EXISTENTIALISM. His works include *Nausea* (1939), *Being and Nothingness* (1943), and the trilogy *The Roads to Freedom* (1945–49). He also wrote a number of plays. He refused the 1964 Nobel Prize in literature on "personal" grounds, but is later said to have accepted it.

Saskatchewan Province in W central Canada, the S half on the fertile Great Plains and the N half in the lake-strewn Canadian Shield. Principal cities are Saskatoon (1991 pop. 186,058), Regina (the capital and largest city, pop. 179,178), Prince Albert (34,181), and Moose Jaw (33,593). The cultivation of wheat is the most important agricultural activity, but oats, barley, rye, flax and rapeseed are also grown. The province's rich mineral deposits include uranium, copper, zinc, gold, coal, oil, natural gas and potash. Most industries process raw materials, and steel is also manufactured. Area: 570,113sq km (251,700sq mi). Pop. (1991) 988,928.

Sassanid (Sassanian) Royal dynasty of Persia (AD 224–651). Founded by Ardashir I (r.224–241), the Sassanids revived the native Persian traditions of the ACHAEMENIDS, confirming ZOROASTRIANISM as the state religion. There were about 30 Sassanid rulers, the most important after Ardashir being Shapur II (309–379), Khoshru I (531–579) and Khoshru II (590–628), whose conquest of Syria, Palestine and Egypt marked the height of the dynasty's power. The Sassanids were overthrown by the Arabs.

Sassoon, Siegfried (1886–1967) British poet and author. His disillusionment with military service in World War 1 inspired his most memorable poetry. The trilogy *The Complete Memoirs of George Sherston* (1937) includes his most famous novel *Memoirs of a Fox-hunting Man* (1928).

Satan Name for the DEVIL. Satan first appeared in the Old Testament as an individual angel, subordinate to God. Gradually, however, Satan took on a more sinister role. In the New Testament, he was the devil who tempted JESUS CHRIST. Satan emerged in medieval Christian theology as the chief devil, ruler of hell and source of all evil.

satellite Celestial body orbiting a planet or star, also called a moon. In the Solar System, planets with satellites are the Earth (1), Mars (2), Jupiter (13), Saturn (10), Uranus (5) and Neptune (2). Those of the Earth and Mars are rocky. The satellites of the others are believed to consist of ice or frozen methane and ammonia.

satellite, artificial Spacecraft placed in orbit around the Earth or other celestial body. Communications satellites relay microwave signals from one part of the Earth to another. Navigation satellites transmit radio signals that enable navigators to determine their positions.

satellite television Television services transmitted to viewers via communications satellites in orbit around the Earth. Television companies beam their signals to the satellites from ground stations. The satellites retransmit the signals back to viewers' dish-shaped receiving aerials.

Satie, Erik (1866–1925) French composer. Rebelling against Wagnerian ROMANTICISM, he developed a deceptively simple style in piano pieces such as *Trois Gymnopédies* (1888). He also composed the ballets *Parade* (1917) and *Relâche* (1924), and a choral work, *Socrate* (1918).

satire Literary work in which human foibles and institutions are mocked, ridiculed and parodied. In the Middle Ages it often took the form of *fabliaux* or bestiaries, using animal characters to illustrate typical human failings. Dramatists have often employed the form, as in the plays of ARISTOPHANES, JONSON, MOLIÈRE, WILDE and BRECHT.

Sato, Eisaku (1901–75) Japanese statesman, prime minister (1964–72). He restored Japan's prominence in international affairs for the first time since World War 2. In 1974 he was awarded the Nobel Peace Prize.

saturated compound In organic chemistry, compounds in which the carbon atoms are bonded to one another by single COVALENT BONDS, not by the more reactive double or triple bonds. For this reason, they tend to be unreactive.

saturated fat Organic fatty compounds, the molecules of which contain only saturated FATTY ACIDS combined with GLYCEROL. These acids have long chains of carbon atoms that are bound together by single bonds only. *See also* SATURATED COMPOUNDS

saturated solution In chemistry, SOLUTION containing so much of a dissolved compound (SOLUTE) that no more will dissolve at that temperature.

Saturn Sixth planet from the Sun and second-largest in the SOLAR SYSTEM. Viewed through a telescope it appears as a golden yellow disk encircled by white rings. The rings are made up of particles ranging from dust to objects a few metres in size, all in individual orbits. The main rings are only a kilometre or so thick. Saturn has an internal heat source, which probably drives its weather systems. It is assumed to be composed predominantly of hydrogen, and to have an iron–silicate core about five times the Earth's mass, surrounded by an ice mantle of perhaps twenty Earth masses. The upper atmosphere contains 97% hydrogen

and 3% helium, with traces of other gases. Diameter (equatorial): 120,536km (polar): 107,100km

Saudi Arabia Arabic kingdom on the Arabian Peninsula, sw Asia, the capital is RIYADH. **Land and climate** The Kingdom of Saudi Arabia occupies *c.*75% of the Arabian peninsula. Desert constitutes over 95% of the land. The Gulf of AQABA and the RED SEA lie off the w coast. The Hejaz (boundary) plain in the NW includes the cities of MECCA and MEDINA, and Saudi Arabia's main port, JIDDAH. In the sw is the Asir (inaccessible) region, which contains the country's highest point, Sawda, at 3,133m (10,279ft). The Tihama is a narrow, fertile sw coastal plain. In the centre lies the Najd (plateau), which contains Riyadh. The plateau descends E to the Al Hasa lowlands. This region is the centre of the Saudi oil industry. In the N is the Nafud Desert. The s of Saudi Arabia is dominated by the Rub' al Khali (Empty Quarter), the world's largest expanse of sand. Saudi Arabia has a hot, dry climate. Summer temperatures in Riyadh often exceed 40°C (104°F). The Asir highlands have an average rainfall of 300–500mm (12in–20in). The rest of the country has less than 100mm (4in). Grass and shrub provide pasture on the w highlands and parts of the central plateau. **Economy** Saudi Arabia is the world's largest producer and exporter of crude oil. It has *c.*25% of the world's known oil reserves and in 1994 supplied over 13% of world demand. Oil and oil products make up 85% of its exports. Oil revenue has been used to develop education, services, light industry, farming and purchasing of military hardware. The construction of desalination plants has improved the supply of freshwater. Agriculture employs 48% of the workforce, although only 1% of the land is fertile. Crops grown in Asir and at oases include dates and other fruits, vegetables and wheat. Some nomadic livestock herders remain. Mecca is visited by more than 1.5 million pilgrims a year, making this a vital addition to state revenue. **History** In the 18th century, the Wahhabi (a strict Islamic sect) gained the allegiance of the Saud family, who formed an independent state in Nejd. The Wahhabi rapidly conquered most of the Arabian peninsula. In the 1810s the region was conquered by Turkey. Abdul Aziz ibn Saud laid the foundations of the modern state of Saudi Arabia. In

---

SAUDI ARABIA
AREA: 2,149,690sq km (829,995sq mi)
POPULATION: 15,922,000
CAPITAL (POPULATION): Riyadh (1,500,000)
GOVERNMENT: Absolute monarchy
ETHNIC GROUPS: Arab (Saudi 82%, Yemeni 10%, other Arab 3%)
LANGUAGES: Arabic (official)
RELIGIONS: Islam 99% (almost exclusively Sunni), Christianity 1%
CURRENCY: Saudi riyal = 100 halalah

1902 Ibn Saud captured Riyadh, and by 1906 had taken the whole of the Nejd. In 1913 the Turkish province of Al Hasa also fell. In 1920 Ibn Saud captured the Asir, and by 1925 he had conquered the Hejaz. In 1932 the territories were combined to form Saudi Arabia. Ibn Saud became king, ruling in accordance with the sharia of Wahhabi Islam. Oil was discovered in 1936. In 1945 Saudi Arabia joined the Arab League. In 1953 Ibn Saud died and was succeeded by his eldest son, King Saud, who ruled with the aid of Crown Prince Faisal. In 1964 Saud was overthrown, and Faisal became king. In 1971 British troops withdrew from the Gulf. Faisal supported the creation of the United Arab Emirates and sought to increase national ownership of Saudi's oil wealth. In 1975 King Faisal was assassinated, and Crown Prince Khalid became king. Khalid's conservativism was challenged by the growth of Islamic fundamentalism. In 1979 Shiite fundamentalists captured the Great Mosque in Mecca. The rebellion was suppressed. Saudi Arabia's support for Iraq in the IRAN-IRAQ WAR led to Iranian attacks on Saudi shipping. In 1982 Khalid died and was succeeded by Prince Fahd. In 1990 over 1,400 pilgrims died in a stampede during the HAJJ. When Iraq invaded Kuwait in 1990, King Fahd invited coalition forces to protect it against possible Iraqi aggression. Saudi forces played a significant role in the Allied victory in the GULF WAR. **Politics** The king retains supreme authority, assisted by a 60-man Consultative Council. Saudi Arabia has no formal constitution. It attracts international criticism for human rights abuses, especially for its state executions and treatment of women.

Saul First king of the Hebrew state of ancient ISRAEL (r.c.1020–c.1000 BC). He was the son of Kish, a member of the tribe of Benjamin. He was anointed by the prophet SAMUEL and acclaimed by all Israel. Saul's story is contained in the First Book of Samuel, the ninth book of the Old Testament.

Saussure, Ferdinand de (1857–1913) Swiss linguist, founder of modern linguistics. For Saussure, language was a system of signs whose meaning is defined by their relations to each other. His work laid the foundation for STRUCTURALISM and semiotics.

savanna Plain with coarse grass and scattered tree growth, particularly the wide plains of tropical and subtropical regions.

Savannah City and port on the Savannah River, E Georgia, USA. Founded in 1733, it became the seat of the colonial government in 1754. During the American Revolution it was held by the British 1778–82. During the Civil War it remained a confederate stronghold until December 1864. Today it is a major port whose exports include tobacco, cotton and sugar. Pop. (1992) 138,908.

Savimbi, Jonas (1934–) Angolan political leader. Prominent in the struggle for independence, he formed the National Union for the Total Independence of Angola (UNITA) in 1966. After inde-

pendence (1975), Savimbi mounted a guerrilla war against the government. In 1991 President DOS SANTOS and Savimbi signed a peace agreement. Savimbi refused to recognise the 1992 re-election of Dos Santos and civil war resumed. UNITA's deteriorating support forced Savimbi to accept the Lusaka Protocol (1994), paving the way for a government of national unity. This was inaugurated in 1997 but Savimbi refused the vice presidency. UNITA retained military control of c.50% of Angola and fighting continued. In 1997 the UN imposed sanctions on UNITA for failing to comply with the Lusaka Protocol.

Savoy Area of SE France, bounded by Lake Geneva (N), the River Rhône (W), the Dauphiné (S) and the Alps of Italy and Switzerland (E); it includes the départements of Haute Savoie and Savoie. It was part of the first Burgundian kingdom and, in the 11th century, the Holy Roman Empire. It was part of the kingdom of Sardinia after 1713. Savoy was annexed by France in 1792, returned to Sardinia in 1815, and finally ceded to France in 1860.

sawfish Any of several species of shark-like, flat-bodied RAYS that live in tropical marine and brackish waters. It has a grey or black-brown body with a saw-toothed snout resembling a flat blade. Length: to 5m (16ft). Family Pristidae; genus *Pristis*.

sawfly Any of 400 species of primitive, plant-feeding WASPS that lack a narrow waist between thorax and abdomen. Most sawflies are included in the family Tenthredinidae. Length: to 20mm (0.8in). Order Hymenoptera.

Saxe-Coburg-Gotha Duchy in Saxony, Germany, whose ruling dynasty intermarried with many royal families. After Prince Albert married the English Queen VICTORIA, Saxe-Coburg-Gotha became the name of the English royal house until it was changed to Windsor in 1917.

saxifrage Perennial plant of the genus *Saxifraga* native to temperate and mountainous regions of Europe and North America. The branched clusters of small flowers are white, pink, purple or yellow. Height: to 61cm (2ft). Family Saxifragaceae.

Saxons Ancient Germanic people. They appear to have originated in N Germany and S Denmark. By the 5th century they were settled in NW Germany, N Gaul and S Britain. In Germany they were subdued by CHARLEMAGNE. In Britain, together with other Germanic tribes, known collectively as ANGLO-SAXONS, they evolved into the English.

Saxony Federal state and historic region in E central Germany; the capital is DRESDEN. It successively became a duchy, a collection of fiefdoms, an electoral region, a duchy again and finally (from 1815–71) comprised the Prussian province of Saxony and the kingdom of Saxony. From 1871–1918 the kingdom of Saxony was part of the German Empire. In the aftermath of World War 1, the kingdom was made a state of the Weimar Republic. After World War 2, it joined the German Democratic Republic (East Germany). Following

German reunification in 1991, it became a state in the Federal Republic of Germany. Area: 18,409 sq km (7,106 sq mi). Pop: (1993 est.) 4,608,000.

Saxony-Anhalt Federal state in s Germany; the capital is MAGDEBURG. The history of the region coincides with that of SAXONY until 1871, when it became a state of the German empire. After World War 2, the Red Army briefly occupied the region and the district was abolished in 1952. Following German reunification in 1991, Saxony-Anhalt was reformed as a federal state of Germany. Major manufactures: machine and transport equipment. Area: 20,445sq km (7,892sq mi). Pop: (1994) 2,759,213.

saxophone Musical instrument with single reed, conical metal tube and finger keys. It was invented by Adolphe Sax in the 1840s. Four members of the saxophone family are commonly used today: the soprano (in B flat), the alto (in E flat), the tenor (in B flat) and the baritone (in E flat).

Sayers, Dorothy L. (Leigh) (1893–1957) British novelist and playwright, best known for detective fiction. Her first novels featured Lord Peter Wimsey, a detective who appeared in 10 books including *Whose Body?* (1923) and *Gaudy Night* (1935).

scabies Contagious infection caused by a female mite, *Sarcoptes scabiei*, which burrows into the skin to lay eggs. It can be seen as a dark wavy line on the skin and is treated with antiparasitic creams.

Scafell Pike Highest peak in England at 978m (3,210ft) high, part of the Scafell range in the LAKE DISTRICT, NW England.

scalar Mathematical quantity that has only a magnitude, as opposed to a VECTOR, which also has direction. Mass, energy and speed are scalars.

scale In biology, small hard plate that forms part of the external skin of an animal. It is usually a development of the SKIN layers. In most fish, scales are composed of bone in the dermal skin layer. The scales of reptiles and those on the legs of birds are horny growths of the epidermal skin layer and are composed mostly of the fibrous protein KERATIN.

scale In music, term for the ordered arrangement of intervals that forms the basis of musical composition. There are many types of scale. In Western music the most important has been the seven-note diatonic scale, both in its major and minor forms. The 12-note CHROMATIC scale has a regular progression of semitones.

scallop Edible BIVALVE mollusc. One shell, or valve, is usually convex and the other almost flat. The shell's surface is ribbed (scalloped). Most scallops have a row of eyes that fringe the fleshy mantle. Width: 2.5–20cm (1–8in). Family Pectinidae.

Scandinavia In physical geography, the N European peninsular countries of SWEDEN and NORWAY. In a broader, cultural sense it also includes DENMARK, FINLAND, ICELAND and the FARÖE ISLANDS. The largest cities are STOCKHOLM and GOTHENBURG in Sweden; OSLO in Norway; COPENHAGEN in Den-

mark, and HELSINKI in Finland. Area: c.1,258,000sq km (485,250sq mi). *See also* EUROPE

scandium Silver-white, metallic element (symbol Sc) of group III of the periodic table, discovered in 1897. It is found in thortveitite and, in small amounts, in other minerals. Scandium is a soft metal used as a radioactive tracer and in nickel alkaline storage batteries. Chemically it resembles the metals of the LANTHANIDE SERIES. Properties: at.no. 21; r.a.m. 44.956; r.d. 2.99; m.p. 1,539°C (2,802°F); b.p. 2,832°C (5,130°F); most common isotope Sc^{45} (100%).

scanning In medicine, use of a non-invasive system to detect abnormalities of structure or function in the body. Detectable waves (x-rays, gamma rays, ultrasound) are passed through the part of the body to be investigated and the computer-analyzed results are displayed as images on a viewing screen.

scarab beetle Any of several different species of broad beetles distributed worldwide. Most, including the June bug, Japanese beetle and rhinoceros beetle, are leaf chafers. A smaller group, including the DUNG BEETLE, are scavengers. Family Scarabaeidae.

Scarlatti, Alessandro (1660–1725) Italian BAROQUE composer. His genius is displayed in his dramatic music and he is known as the founder of OPERA SERIA.

Scarlatti, (Giuseppe) Domenico (1685–1757) Italian composer, son of Alessandro Scarlatti. He is primarily known for his harpsichord sonatas, of which he composed more than 500. He is considered the founder of modern keyboard technique.

scarlet fever (scarlatina) Acute infectious disease, usually affecting children, caused by BACTERIA in the *Streptococcus pyogenes* group. It is characterized by a bright red body rash, fever, vomiting and a sore throat. It is treated with ANTIBIOTICS.

scattering In physics, deflection of the path of SUBATOMIC PARTICLES by atoms. It is the means by which the structure of atoms was discovered. Our knowledge of ELEMENTARY PARTICLES has been obtained by scattering experiments carried out in particle ACCELERATORS.

Scheele, Karl Wilhelm (1742–86) Swedish chemist who discovered OXYGEN. Publication of his discovery was delayed and the credit went to Joseph PRIESTLEY. His other important discoveries included CHLORINE, GLYCEROL and a number of organic acids.

Schiele, Egon (1890–1918) Austrian painter, one of the greatest exponents of EXPRESSIONISM. His paintings typically portray anguished naked figures whose distorted bodies reflect their mental pain.

Schiller, Johann Christoph Friedrich von (1759–1805) German dramatist, historian and philosopher. He wrote blank verse STURM UND DRANG plays, including *Don Carlos* (1787), *Wallenstein* (1800), *Mary Stuart* (1801), *Maid of Orleans* (1801) and *William Tell* (1804).

schism Split or division within a church, sect or

other religious organization, or a breakaway from a church. Before the Protestant REFORMATION, there were two other important schisms within Christianity. A series of disputes culminated in a complete break between the Eastern (ORTHODOX) Church and the Western (ROMAN CATHOLIC) Church in 1054. The so-called GREAT SCHISM occurred in the 14th and 15th centuries and involved a split within the Roman Catholic Church itself.

schist Large group of METAMORPHIC ROCKS that have been made cleavable, causing the rocks to split into thin plates leaving a wavy, uneven surface.

schizophrenia One of a group of psychotic disorders marked primarily by disturbances of cognitive functioning, particularly thinking and speech. As well as the charcteristic loss of contact with reality, symptoms include hallucinations and delusions, and muffled or inappropriate emotions.

Schleswig-Holstein Federal state and historic region, in NW Germany; the capital is KIEL. In the early 12th century, the duchy of Holstein was created as part of the Holy Roman Empire, while Schleswig was made a fiefdom independent of Danish control. They were twice united under the Danish crown, but not incorporated into the Danish state. In 1848 Frederick VII proclaimed the complete union of Schleswig with Denmark, the predominantly German population of both duchies rebelled, and the German Confederation occupied the two duchies. The 1852 Treaty of London reestablished the duchies' personal union with Denmark. In 1863 Demark once more tried to incorporate Schleswig into the state proper. Prussia and Austria declared war. In 1865 Schleswig was administered by Prussia, and Holstein by Austria. The resulting tension led to the Austro-Prussian War (1866); the Prussian victory created the state of Schleswig-Holstein. In 1920 the N part of Schleswig was returned to Denmark. In 1937 the city of Lübeck was incorporated into the German state of Schleswig-Holstein. The land is mainly flat and fertile. Principal economic activities: shipping and fishing. Area: 15,738sq km (6,075sq mi). Pop. (1993 est. 2,695,000)

Schliemann, Heinrich (1822–90) German archaeologist. In 1871 he began excavations in Hisarlik, Turkey, which he believed to be the site of the Homeric city of TROY. He uncovered nine superimposed towns; later excavations indicated that the seventh layer was probably the Homeric Troy.

Schmidt, Helmut (1918–) Chancellor of West Germany (1974–82). He became chairman of the Social Democratic Party (SDP) in 1967. He succeeded Willy BRANDT as chancellor and was re-elected in 1976 and 1980. He was forced to resign in 1982 when the Free Democrats, coalition partners of the SDP, withdrew their support.

Schoenberg, Arnold (1874–1951) Austrian composer and theorist who abandoned traditional tonality for a method drawn from the 12-tone scale. He reached atonality in *Erwartung* (1909) and

twelve-note serialism in his Suite for Piano (1923). *See also* SERIAL MUSIC; TWELVE-TONE MUSIC

scholasticism Medieval philosophy that attempted to join faith to reason by synthesizing theology with classical Greek and Roman thought. Scholasticism was first explored by John Scotus Erigena in the 9th century and by ANSELM OF CANTERBURY in the 11th century. Its greatest thinkers were Albertus Magnus, Thomas AQUINAS and DUNS SCOTUS.

Schopenhauer, Arthur (1788–1860) German philosopher whose exposition of the doctrine of the will opposed the idealism of HEGEL and influenced NIETZSCHE, WAGNER and others. Schopenhauer's system, described in *The World as Will and Idea* (1819), was an intensely pessimistic one.

Schrödinger, Erwin (1887–1961) Austrian physicist who formulated a quantum mechanical wave equation. He founded the science of quantum WAVE MECHANICS and shared the 1933 Nobel Prize for physics with Paul Dirac. The wave equation was based on a suggestion by Louis de BROGLIE that moving particles have a wave-like nature.

Schubert, Franz Peter (1797–1828) Austrian composer and leading figure of ROMANTICISM. Among his most popular works are his symphonies, especially the Eighth ("Unfinished", 1822). He wrote more than 600 songs to the lyrics of such poets as Heine and Schiller; these include the cycles *Die schöne Müllerin* (1823) and *Winterreise* (1827). He also composed much chamber music.

Schumacher, Michael (1969–) German racing driver. He entered Formula 1 racing in 1991. He won his first Grand Prix in 1992. He won the drivers' championship in 1994 and 1995 with Bennetton, before moving to Ferrari in 1996. In 1997 he was fined for shunting Jacques Villeneuve in the deciding race of the drivers' championship.

Schumann, Clara Josephine Wieck (1819–96) German pianist, composer and wife of Robert SCHUMANN. She was an outstanding interpreter of the works of her husband and of their friend BRAHMS. She composed chamber music.

Schumann, Robert Alexander (1810–56) German composer and leading figure of ROMANTICISM. His piano compositions include *Kinderszenen* (1838) and *Waldscenen* (1848–49). His best-known song cycle is *Frauenliebe und Leben* (1840). His Piano Concerto (1841–45) and "Spring" Symphony (1841) are among his best orchestral works.

Schwarzkopf, Dame Elisabeth (1915–) German soprano known for her versatility in recitals, oratorios and opera. She specialized in Richard Strauss, Mozart, Schubert and Wolf.

Schwarzkopf, H. Norman (1934–) US general. As supreme commander of the Allied forces in the Gulf War (1991), he liberated Kuwait from the Iraqi occupation.

sciatica Pain in the back and radiating down one or other leg, along the course of the sciatic nerve. It is usually caused by inflammation of the sciatic nerve or by pressure on the spinal nerve roots.

science fiction Literary genre in which reality is subject to certain transformations in order to explore man's potential and his relation to his environment; these transformations are usually technological and the stories set in the future or in imaginary worlds. Until the 1960s most science fiction involved adventure stories set in space. Some writers, such as Isaac ASIMOV, explored the paradoxes contained in purely scientific ideas; others, including Ray BRADBURY, stressed the moral implications of their stories.

scientology (officially Church of Scientology) "Applied religious philosophy" based on a form of psychotherapy called dianetics. It advocates confrontation with painful experiences from the past to achieve true mental health. Founded by L. Ron HUBBARD in California in 1954, it has aroused controversy over its methods of recruiting members.

Scilly, Isles of Archipelago of more than 140 rocky isles in the Atlantic Ocean off the coast of Cornwall, SW England; 45km (28mi) SW of Land's End. The combination of mild climate and heavy rainfall makes the islands a good environment for growing flowers and spring vegetables. Tourism is an important industry. Only five of the islands are inhabited: St Mary's (the largest), Tresco, St Martin's, St Agnes and Bryher. The capital, Hugh Town, is on St Mary's. Total pop. (1991) 2,900.

Scipio Africanus Major (236–183 BC) (Publius Cornelius Scipio) Roman general in the second of the PUNIC WARS. He defeated the Carthaginian forces in Spain in 209 BC. Elected consul in 205, he invaded North Africa with a volunteer army and defeated HANNIBAL at Zama in 202 BC.

Scipio Africanus Minor (185–129 BC) (Publius Cornelius Scipio Aemilianus) Roman general of the third of the PUNIC WARS. He took the name of his grandfather by adoption, SCIPIO AFRICANUS MAJOR. He destroyed Carthage in 146 BC, bringing the Punic wars to an end.

sclerosis Degenerative hardening of tissue, usually due to scarring following inflammation or as a result of ageing. It can affect the brain and spinal cord, causing neurological symptoms, or the walls of the arteries.

scorpion Any of numerous species of ARACHNIDS that live in warmer regions throughout the world. It has two main body sections, two eyes, a pair of pedipalps (pincers) and a long slender tail ending in a curved, poisonous sting. Length: to 17cm (7in). Class Arachnida; order Scorpionida.

Scorsese, Martin (1942–) US film director. His first major film was *Mean Streets* (1973). Success followed with *Alice Doesn't Live Here Anymore* (1975), *Taxi Driver* (1976), *Raging Bull* (1980), *The King of Comedy* (1983) and *After Hours* (1985). He has also directed *Goodfellas* (1990), *Cape Fear* (1991), *The Age of Innocence* (1993) and *Casino* (1995).

Scotland Northern part of the main island of Britain, and a constituent of the United Kingdom of Great Britain and Northern Ireland; the capital i EDINBURGH. The largest city is GLASGOW. Scotlan is administratively divided into nine regions an three island authorities. Its jagged coastline feature many islands (including the ORKNEY and SHETLAN ISLANDS), lochs (including LOMOND and NESS) an firths. Major Scottish rivers include the TAY, CLYDE Dee and Forth. Scotland can be broadly divided int three geographical regions: the Southern Uplands immediately N of the English border; the Centra Lowlands, where the majority of the population live; and the HIGHLANDS including BEN NEVIS. I prehistory Scotland was inhabited by the PICTS Kenneth I united the lands of the Picts and th SCOTS in 843 AD. In 1174, with the development c feudalism, Scotland was made a fiefdom of Eng land. In 1189 Richard I granted Scottish freedom but the enmity between England and Scotland (i alliance with France) continued. Edward I force the Scots to submit, only for William WALLACE t lead a Scottish revolt. ROBERT I (THE BRUCE) recap tured much Scottish land and defeated the Englis at the Battle of Bannockburn (1314); this led t England's recognition of Scottish independence i 1328. The 15th century was characterized by inter nal factionalism and weak government. JAMES I and many Scottish nobles were killed at the Battl of Flodden (1513). The Protestant REFORMATIO quickly took root in Scotland via the preaching o John KNOX. In 1513 JAMES V cemented the Frenc alliance by marrying Mary of Guise, a Frenc Catholic. When her daughter, MARY, QUEEN O SCOTS, assumed the throne in 1561, England sup ported the Scottish Protestants, and France backe the Catholics. The Protestant faction forced Mary t relinquish the throne in 1567. Her son, James V assumed the Scottish crown, and in 1601 he wa also crowned JAMES I of England, thereby unitin the English and Scottish thrones. The Scot opposed Charles I in the English CIVIL WAR but th King's concessions to PRESBYTERIANISM won th support of the COVENANTERS. The GLORIOUS REVO LUTION reestablished Presbyterianism as the Scot tish national church. The massacre of the Macdon ald clan by WILLIAM III at Glencoe in 169 tarnished enthusiasm for his rule and the JACOBIT agitation prompted the constitutional union of th two crowns in the Act of UNION (1707). At CULLO DEN Moor (1746) the Jacobite insurgency was final ly suppressed with the defeat of the Highlanders le by Prince Charles Edward STUART. (*See* UNITE KINGDOM for additional subsequent history.) Th principal agricultural activity is the rearing of live stock; oats and potatoes are the chief crops. Coa mining and heavy industry dominated the econom of the central lowlands by the end of the 19th centu ry, but declined in the 1980s. The discovery c North Sea oil and natural gas in the 1970s benefite the Scottish economy. Other important industrie textiles, whisky, beer and fishing. The SCOTTISH NATIONAL PARTY (SNP) gained support during th

1970s, but a 1979 referendum for a separate Scottish assembly was defeated. In the 1990s there were renewed calls for devolution. A 1997 referendum saw Scotland gain its own legislative assembly, with tax-varying power. Scotland has its own church, education and legal system. Area: 77,167sq km (29,797sq mi). Pop. (1991) 4,998,567.

Scotland Yard Name given to the headquarters in London of the Metropolitan Police and synonymous with the CRIMINAL INVESTIGATION DEPARTMENT (CID). Originally located in Scotland Yard, off Whitehall, it was moved to New Scotland Yard in 1890 and to further new premises in 1967.

Scots Originally a Gaelic-speaking Celtic people from N Ireland. Their raids on the W coast of Roman Britain from the 3rd to the 5th century failed to establish independent settlements. In the 5th century, however, they established the kingdom of Dalriada in Pictish territory.

Scott, Sir George Gilbert (1811–78) British architect, prominent figure in the GOTHIC REVIVAL. In London, he designed the Albert Memorial, the Foreign Office and St Pancras Station.

Scott, Sir Giles Gilbert (1880–1960) British architect. He designed the new Anglican Cathedral in Liverpool, the last major example of the GOTHIC REVIVAL. Other important works include the New Bodleian Library, Oxford.

Scott, Robert Falcon (1868–1912) British Antarctic explorer. He led the expedition of 1901–04, which established a record for advancing farthest south. On a second expedition (1910–12), he reached the South Pole but found that Roald AMUNDSEN had reached it a month earlier. On the return journey Scott's party was trapped by blizzards and all died within 18km (11mi) of safety.

Scott, Sir Walter (1771–1832) Scottish novelist and poet. His first novel, the anonymously published *Waverley* (1814), was an immediate success and was followed by a series of Scottish novels, including *Rob Roy* (1817) and *The Heart of Midlothian* (1818). Later novels are *Ivanhoe* (1819), *Kenilworth* (1821) and *Quentin Durward* (1823).

Scottish (Scots) Dialect of English traditionally spoken in Scotland and regarded by some experts as a distinct GERMANIC language. It developed from the Northumbrian dialect of EARLY ENGLISH before AD 700. Over the following 600 or 700 years, it spread throughout Scotland. Before the union of the English and Scottish crowns in 1603, the Scottish language was both a national language and an official court language. The language continues as a spoken dialect in many areas.

Scottish National Party (SNP) UK political party, founded in 1928. It elected its first member of Parliament in a byelection in 1945. It expanded its support base significantly in the late 1960s, gaining around 20% of the Scottish vote in general elections since then. It advocates Scotland's independence (from the UK) within the European Union.

Scouts *See* BOY SCOUTS and GIRL GUIDES

scrapie Fatal disease of sheep and goats that affects the central nervous system, causing staggering and itching. It is caused by a slow-acting, virus-like, microscopic particle called a PRION. The disease is thought to be related to BOVINE SPONGIFORM ENCEPHALOPATHY (BSE) and CREUTZFELDT-JAKOB DISEASE (CJD).

scree (talus) Heap of rock waste lying at the bottom of a cliff. It is made up of particles that have been loosened from the cliff rock by weathering.

screening In medicine, test applied either to an individual or to groups of people who, although apparently healthy, are known to be at risk of developing a particular disease. It is used to detect treatable diseases while they are still in the early stages.

Scriabin, Alexander Nicolas (1872–1915) Russian composer whose works are harmonically experimental. His most significant works include ten piano sonatas, *The Poem of Ecstasy* (1908), three symphonies and numerous short piano pieces.

scriptures Sacred writings of a religion. In Christianity, they are the books of the OLD TESTAMENT and NEW TESTAMENT, with or without those of the APOCRYPHA. Scripture, in the singular, is a collective term for biblical writings in general. It is possible to refer of the KORAN as the scripture of ISLAM and the VEDAS as the scriptures of HINDUISM.

scuba diving Diving with the use of self-contained underwater breathing apparatus, or scuba. The equipment consists of tanks of compressed air connected to a demand regulator, which controls the air flow to the mouth.

sculpture Art of creating forms in three dimensions, either in the round or in relief. Techniques include carving (in wood, stone, marble, ivory, etc.), modelling (in clay, wax, etc.), or casting (in bronze and other metals). The history of sculpture parallels that of PAINTING. The early civilizations of Egypt, Mesopotamia, India and the Far East were rich in sculpture. The Greeks developed a style of relief and free-standing sculpture. Roman sculptors were influenced by the Greeks. Medieval European sculpture was a feature of ROMANESQUE and GOTHIC churches, many of which were covered with carvings. The Florentine RENAISSANCE was enriched by the works of GHIBERTI, DONATELLO and MICHELANGELO. High BAROQUE sculpture is exemplified in the works of BERNINI in Rome. Puget was the movement's leading exponent in France where, in the 18th century, it was superseded by NEO-CLASSICISM. This extended into the 19th century, when it was rivalled and replaced by a movement of realist sculpture, such as that of RODIN. African, Aztec and other ethnic and ancient sculpture have stimulated great modern sculptors such as PICASSO, MODIGLIANI, BRANCUSI and MOORE.

scurvy Disease caused by a deficiency of VITAMIN C (ascorbic acid), which is contained in fresh fruit and vegetables. It is characterized by weakness, painful joints and bleeding gums.

Scythians Nomadic people who inhabited the

steppes N of the Black Sea in the 1st milennium BC. In the 7th century BC their territory extended into Mesopotamia, the Balkans and Greece. Powerful warriors, their elaborate tombs contain evidence of great wealth. Pressure from the Sarmatians confined them to the Crimea (*c*.300 BC) and their culture eventually disappeared.

SDLP Abbreviation of SOCIAL DEMOCRATIC LABOUR PARTY

SDP Abbreviation of SOCIAL DEMOCRATIC PARTY

sea anemone Sessile, polyp-type COELENTERATE animal found in marine pools and on rocky shores. It has a cylindrical body with tentacles around its mouth. Height: to 20cm (8in). Class Anthozoa; genera include *Tealia, Anemonia* and *Metridium*.

sea cow *See* DUGONG

sea cucumber Marine ECHINODERM found in rocky areas. It has a cylindrical, fleshy body in five parts around a central axis; it has branched tentacles around the mouth. Species include the cottonspinners (*Holothuria* spp). Class Holothuroidea.

seafloor Floor of the oceans, which includes a variety of different landforms. The major features of the seafloor are the continental shelf, the continental rise, the abyssal floor, seamounts, oceanic trenches and oceanic ridges. The abyssal floor is about 3km (1.8mi) deep and is mostly made of basaltic rock covered with fine-grained (pelagic) sediment consisting of dust and the shells of marine organisms. Oceanic trenches are up to 11km (7mi) deep, typically 50–100km (30–60mi) wide and may be thousands of kilometres long. Oceanic ridges are long, linear volcanic structures that tend to occupy the middle of seafloors and they are the sites of crustal spreading. *See also* OCEAN; CONTINENTAL MARGIN; SEAFLOOR SPREADING

seafloor spreading Theory that explains how continental drift occurs. It proposes that ocean floor is moved laterally as new basalt rock is injected along mid-ocean ridges and so the ocean floor becomes older with increasing distance from the ridge. *See also* PLATE TECTONICS

sea horse Marine fish found in shallow tropical and temperate waters. It swims in an upright position and has an outer bony skeleton of plate-like rings, a mouth at the end of a long snout, and a curled, prehensile tail with which it clings to seaweed. The male incubates the young in a brood pouch. Length: 3.8–30.5cm (1.5–12in). Family Syngnathidae.

seal Any of several species of carnivorous, primarily marine, aquatic mammals. It feeds on fish, crustaceans and other marine animals; various species are hunted for meat, hides, oil and fur. Species of true, earless seals such as the leopard seal (*Hydrurga leptonyx*) are included in the family Phocidae. They swim with powerful strokes of their hind flippers and sinuous movements of the whole trunk. Members of the eared family Otariidae have longer fore flippers, used for propulsion, and use all four limbs when moving on land. They include fur seals (genera *Callorhinus* and *Arctocephalus*) and species of SEA LION. Order Pinnepedia.

sea lion Any of five species of SEALS that live in coastal waters of the Pacific and feed on fish and squid. They have streamlined bodies and long fore flippers for propulsion. The males of all species, except the California sea lion (*Zalophus californianus*), have manes. The largest species is the Steller sea lion (*Eumetopias jubata*); it may reach 3.3m (11ft) in length. Order Pinnepedia; family Otariidae.

sea slug (nudibranch) Any of numerous species of marine gastropod molluscs, related to snails and found worldwide. They have no shells, quills or mantle cavities, frequent shallow water and feed primarily on sea anemones. Order Nudibranchia.

seasons Four astronomical and climatic periods of the year based on differential solar heating of the Earth as it makes its annual revolution of the Sun. The Northern Hemisphere receives more solar radiation when its pole is aimed towards the Sun in summer and less in winter when it is aimed away; the opposite holds for the Southern Hemisphere. The seasons begin at the vernal (spring) and autumnal EQUINOXES and the winter and summer SOLSTICES.

SEATO Acronym for SOUTHEAST ASIA TREATY ORGANIZATION (SEATO)

Seattle City and seaport in W Washington, USA. Settled in 1851, it developed with the construction of the railway. It is an important shipping point for Alaska and the Far East. Industries: aerospace, shipbuilding, precision instruments, timber, fishing, tourism. Pop. (1992) 519,598.

sea urchin Spiny ECHINODERM animal found in marine tidal pools. Round with radiating (often poisonous) moveable spines, its skeletal plates fuse to form a perforated shell. Class Echinoidae.

seaweed Any of numerous species of brown, green or red ALGAE, found in greatest profusion in shallow waters on rocky coasts. KELPS are the largest forms. Many species are important for the manufacture of fertilizers or food, or as a source of chemicals such as iodine. Kingdom Protista.

sebaceous gland Gland in the skin producing the oily substance sebum, which is secreted onto the skin and hair, making them water-repellent and supple.

secant In TRIGONOMETRY, ratio of the length of the hypotenuse to the length of the side adjacent to an acute angle in a right-angled triangle. The secant of angle A is usually abbreviated to sec A, and is equal to the reciprocal of its COSINE.

second SI unit of time (symbol s) defined as the time taken for 9,192,631,770 periods of vibrations of the electromagnetic radiation emitted by a caesium-133 atom. It is commonly abbreviated as 1/60 of a minute. *See also* PHYSICAL UNITS

secondary school Schools providing education for pupils after primary school. The ages at which pupils transfer from primary to secondary schools in the UK vary in different education authorities.

second coming Christian belief that JESUS CHRIST will one day return to Earth. He will sweep away the present world order, establish his kingdom, deal with his enemies and reward those who have been faithful to him.

Second World War *See* WORLD WAR 2

secretary bird Bird of prey found in Africa, S of the Sahara. It is pale grey with black markings and has quill-like feathers behind its ears, large wings, and long legs and tail. It feeds on reptiles, eggs and insects, and lays its eggs in a tree nest. Height: 1.2m (4ft). Species *Sagittarius serpentarius*.

secretion Production and discharge of a substance, usually a fluid, by a cell or a GLAND. The substance so discharged is also known as a secretion. Secretions include ENZYMES, HORMONES, saliva and sweat.

sedative Drug used for its calming effect, to reduce anxiety and tension; at high doses it induces sleep. Sedative drugs include NARCOTICS, BARBITURATES and benzodiazepines.

sedge Any of numerous species of grass-like perennial plants, especially those of the genus *Carex*, widely distributed in mountain regions, usually on wet ground. Cultivated as ornamental plants, they have narrow leaves and spikes of brown, green or greenish-yellow flowers. Family Cyperaceae.

Sedgemoor, Battle of (1685) Defeat of the English rebellion led by the Duke of MONMOUTH against JAMES II. An attempt to launch a surprise night attack by the rebel forces ended in disaster.

sedimentary rock Type of rock formed of mineral or organic particles that have been moved by the action of water, wind or glacial ice (or have been chemically precipitated from solution) to a new location. Following a process of compaction and cementation, the particles usually form layers of sedimentary rock.

Seebeck effect Thermoelectric effect important in the thermocouple for temperature measurement. If wires of two different metals are joined at their ends to form a circuit, a current flows if the junctions are maintained at different temperatures. *See also* PELTIER EFFECT

seed Part of a flowering plant that contains the embryo and food store. It is formed in the ovary by FERTILIZATION of the female GAMETE (*see* POLLEN). Food may be stored in a special tissue called the endosperm, or it may be concentrated in the swollen seed leaves (COTYLEDONS). Seeds are the unit of dispersal of flowering plants and conifers. *See also* GERMINATION

Segovia, Andrés (1893–1987) Spanish guitarist. He created many new techniques of guitar playing, adapting the instrument to the complex music of modern composers and transcribing early contrapuntal music.

Seine River in N central France. It rises in Langres Plateau near DIJON and flows NW through PARIS to enter the English Channel near LE HAVRE. It is connected to the rivers LOIRE, RHÔNE, Meuse, Schelde, Saône and Somme by a network of canals. With its main tributaries (Aube, Marne, Oise, Yonne, Loing and Eure), the Seine drains the entire Paris Basin. The most important river of N France, it is navigable for most ocean-going vessels as far as ROUEN, 560km (350mi) of its full course of 776km (482mi).

seismology Study of seismic waves, the shock waves produced by earthquakes. The velocity of seismic waves varies according to the material through which they pass. Primary (P) and secondary (S) waves are transmitted by the solid Earth. Only P waves are transmitted through fluid zones. The movement of seismic waves is detected and recorded by instruments called seismographs. *See also* EARTHQUAKE

Selassie, Haile *See* HAILE SELASSIE

selenium Grey METALLOID element of group VI of the periodic table, discovered in 1817. Its chief source is a by-product in the electrolytic refining of copper. It is used in PHOTOELECTRIC CELLS, SOLAR CELLS, XEROGRAPHY and red pigments. Properties: at.no. 34; r.a.m. 78.96; r.d. 4.79; m.p. 217°C (422.6°F); b.p. 684.9°C (1,265°F); most common isotope Se^{80} (49.82%).

Seles, Monica (1973–) US tennis player, b. Yugoslavia. At the age of 16, she won the French Open. She repeated this success in 1991, when she also took the US Open and the Australian Open. In 1992 and 1993 she again won the Australian Open. Her career was halted in 1993 when she was stabbed by a follower of her rival Steffi GRAF. She resumed competitive play late in 1995. She reclaimed her Australian title early in 1996.

Seleucids Hellenistic dynasty founded by SELEUCUS I, a former general of ALEXANDER THE GREAT, in 306–281 BC. Centred on Syria, it included most of the Asian provinces of Alexander's empire, extending from the E Mediterranean to India. War with the Ptolemies of Egypt and, later, the Romans, steadily reduced its territory. In 63 BC its depleted territory became the Roman province of Syria.

Seleucus Name of two kings of Syria. Seleucus I (*c.*355–281 BC) was a general of ALEXANDER THE GREAT and founder of the SELEUCID dynasty. He was on the brink of restoring the whole of Alexander's empire under his rule when he was murdered. Seleucus II (r.247–226 BC) spent his reign fighting Ptolemy III of Egypt and Antiochus Hierax, his brother and rival, losing territory to both.

Seljuk Nomadic tribesmen from central Asia who adopted Islam in the 7th century and founded the Baghdad sultanate in 1055. Their empire included Syria, Mesopotamia and Persia. They laid the organizational basis for the future Ottoman administration. In the early 12th century the Seljuk empire began to disintegrate, and the Seljuk states were conquered by the MONGOLS in the 13th century.

Sellers, Peter (1925–80) English comedy film actor. His success began in radio comedy with *The Goon Show* (1951–59). During the 1950s, he starred in various English black comedies such as *The Ladykillers* (1955). International recognition came with *Lolita* (1962), *Dr Stangelove* (1963) and *The Pink Panther* series. Sellers won an Academy Award nomination for *Being There* (1979).

semantics Branch of LINGUISTICS and PHILOSOPHY concerned with the study of the meaning of words. In historical linguistics, it generally refers to the analysis of how meanings change over time. In modern linguistics and philosophy, semantics seeks to assess the contribution of word-meaning to phrases, sentences and the relationship among and between words.

semen Fluid in a male that contains sperm from the TESTES and the secretions of various accessory sexual glands.

semiconductor Substance with electrical CONDUCTIVITY between that of a CONDUCTOR and an insulator. A semiconductor consists of elements, such as GERMANIUM and SILICON, or compounds, such as aluminium phosphide. At normal temperatures, some electrons break free and give rise to *n*-type (negative) conductivity with the electrons as the main carriers of the electric current. The holes (electron deficiencies) left by these electrons give rise to *p*-type (positive) conductivity with the holes as the main carriers. Impurities are usually added to the semiconductor material in controlled amounts to add more free electrons or create more holes. A semiconductor junction is formed when there is an abrupt change along the length of the crystal from one type of impurity to the other. Such a *p-n* junction acts as a very efficient RECTIFIER and is the basis of the semiconductor DIODE. Semiconductors are used in transistors and photoelectric cells.

Semites Peoples whose native tongue belongs to the SEMITIC LANGUAGES group. They originally inhabited an area in Arabia and spoke a common language, Proto-Semitic, from which the Semitic languages descend. Among the modern Semites are Arabs, native Israelis and many Ethiopians.

Semitic languages Group of languages spoken by peoples native to N Africa and the Middle East and forming one of the five branches of the Afro-Asiatic language family. The Semitic languages are divided into three sub-branches: North West Semitic (including Hebrew, Aramaic and Eblaite); North East Semitic (consisting of Akkadian); and Central and Southern Semitic (including Arabic, South Arabian and Ethiopic). Only Hebrew and Arabic have survived to develop modern forms.

Senate Upper house of the US legislature, which together with the HOUSE OF REPRESENTATIVES forms the CONGRESS. It is composed of two senators from each state, who are elected for six-year terms. The approval of a simple majority of the Senate is necessary for major presidential appointments, and a two-thirds majority for treaties.

Senate, Roman Chief governing body of the Roman republic. Senators were chosen for life by the CENSORS and at first were mainly former CONSULS. PLEBEIANS gained entry in the 4th century BC. Under the empire, the emperor's control of military and civil officials gradually restricted the senate to judicial matters and to the city government in Rome. Under the late empire, senatorial status was extended to the landowning elite.

Seneca (4–65) Roman STOIC philosopher, a major influence on European literature. He wrote 12 books of *Moral Essays* and numerous philosophical letters. His tragedies, based on Greek models, included *Phaedra*. Seneca fell from Nero's favour in AD 62 and committed suicide.

Senegal Republic in the extreme W of Africa, the capital is DAKAR. **Land and climate** Senegal contains the continent's most westerly point, the volcanic Cape Verde, on which Dakar stands. It entirely surrounds The Gambia. Plains cover most of Senegal. The N forms part of the SAHEL. The main rivers are the Sénégal, which forms the N border, and the Casamance in the S. The River Gambia flows from Senegal into The Gambia. Dakar has a tropical climate, with a rainy season between June and September. Temperatures are higher inland. Rainfall is greatest in the S. Desert and semi-desert cover NE Senegal. In central Senegal, dry grasslands predominate. Mangrove swamps border parts of the S coast. The far S is a region of tropical savanna, though large areas have been cleared for farming. **Economy** Senegal is a lower-middle-income developing country (1992 GDP per capita, US$1,750). Agriculture employs 81% of the workforce, mainly at subsistence level. Food crops include cassava, millet and rice. Senegal is the world's sixth-largest producer of groundnuts, its major cash crop and export. Phosphates are Senegal's chief mineral resource, but it also refines oil. Fishing is an important activity. **History and politics** During the 6th–10th centuries Senegal formed part of the empire of ancient Ghana. The ALMORAVID dynasty of Zenega Berbers introduced Islam, and it is from the Zenega that Senegal got its name. In 1444 Portuguese sailors became the first Europeans to reach Cape Verde. In the 17th century, Portugal's influence was replaced by France and the Netherlands. By 1763 Britain had expelled the French from Senegal and, in 1765, set up Senegambia, the first

---

SENEGAL
AREA: 196,720sq km (75,954sq mi)
POPULATION: 7,736,000
CAPITAL (POPULATION): Dakar (1,729,823)
GOVERNMENT: Multiparty republic
ETHNIC GROUPS: Wolof 44%, Fulani-Tukulor 24%, Serer 15%
LANGUAGES: French (official)
RELIGIONS: Islam 94%, Christianity (mainly Roman Catholic) 5%, traditional beliefs and others 1%
CURRENCY: CFA franc = 100 centimes

British colony in Africa. France had regained control of the region by 1783. In 1895 Senegal became a French colony within the federation of French West Africa. In 1902 the capital of this huge empire was transferred from St Louis to Dakar. In 1959 Senegal joined French Sudan (now Mali) to form the Federation of Mali. Senegal withdrew in 1960, and became an independent republic within the French community. Léopold Sédar Senghor became Senegal's first post-colonial president. During the 1960s, Senegal's economy deteriorated, and a succession of droughts caused starvation and civil unrest. In 1974 Senegal was a founding member of the West African Economic Community. In 1981 Senghor was succeeded by Abdou Diouf, and Senegalese troops put down an attempted coup in The Gambia. In 1982 the two countries were joined in the Confederation of Senegambia, but the union was dissolved in 1989. From 1989–92 Senegal was at war with Mauritania. In 1993 presidential elections Diouf secured his third victory.

senna Plants, shrubs and trees of the genus *Senna*, native to warm and tropical regions; some species grow in temperate areas throughout the world. They have rectangular, feathery leaves and yellow flowers. Family Fabaceae/Leguminosae.

senses Means by which animals gain information about their environment and physiological condition. The five senses, SIGHT, HEARING, TASTE, SMELL and TOUCH, all rely on specialized receptors on or near the external surface of the body.

Seoul (Kyongsong) Capital of South Korea, on the Han River. The political, commercial, industrial and cultural centre of South Korea, it was founded in 1392 as the capital of the Yi dynasty. From 1910–45 it developed rapidly under Japanese governorship. After World War 2, Seoul was the headquarters for the US army of occupation. Following the 1948 partition, it became capital of South Korea. Seoul's capture by North Korean troops precipitated the beginning of the KOREAN WAR, and the following months witnessed the city's virtual destruction. In March 1951 it became the headquarters of the UN command in Korea, and a rebuilding programme was started. By the 1970s it was the hub of one of the most successful economies of Southeast Asia. Seoul was the scene of violent student demonstrations for reunification with North Korea in 1996. Pop. (1994) 10,799,000.

sepal Modified leaf that makes up the outermost portion of a flower bud. Although usually green and inconspicuous, once the flower is open, in some species the sepals look like the petals.

Sephardim Descendants of the Jews of medieval Spain and Portugal and others who follow their customs. Iberian Jews followed the Babylonian rather than the Palestinian Jewish tradition. After the expulsion of the Jews from Spain (1492), many settled in parts of the Middle East and North Africa.

Sepoy Rebellion Alternative name for the INDIAN MUTINY

septicaemia Medical term for widespread sepsis or BLOOD POISONING.

Septuagint Earliest surviving Greek translation of the Hebrew Bible (the OLD TESTAMENT), made for the Greek-speaking Jewish community in Egypt in the 3rd and 2nd centuries BC. It contains the entire Jewish CANON plus the APOCRYPHA.

sequoia Two species of giant evergreen conifer trees native to California and S Oregon: the giant sequoia (*Sequoiadendron giganteum*) and the Californian redwood (*Sequoiasempervirens*). Their height, up to 100m (330ft), has made them a natural wonder of the USA. Family Taxodiaceae.

Serbia Balkan republic that, combined with the smaller republic of MONTENEGRO, forms the rump federal state of YUGOSLAVIA. The republic is bounded by Hungary (N), Romania and Bulgaria (E), S by Macedonia, SW by Albania and Montenegro, W by BOSNIA-HERZEGOVINA and NW by CROATIA. The capital is BELGRADE, other major cities include Niš (Serbia), Novi Sad (Vojvodina) and Priština (Kosovo). The republic can be divided geographically between the mountainous S and the fertile N plain drained by the Danube, Sava, Tisza and Morava rivers. Vojvodina is the principal agricultural area, producing fruit and grain. Serbia is the principal industrial area, with mining and steel manufacture. Kosovo is a poor region with large coal deposits. The area was settled by Serbs in the 7th century AD, and they adopted Orthodox Christianity under BYZANTINE rule. Serbia became the leading Balkan power until, in 1389, it was defeated by the OTTOMAN Turks. The 18th-century decline of the Ottoman empire encouraged Serbian nationalism. In 1878 Turkey granted Serbia complete independence. In 1903 King Alexander Obrenović was assassinated, and PETER I became king. When Austro-Hungary annexed Bosnia and Herzegovina in 1908, Serbia responded by forming the Serbian League. The expansion of Serbian territory in the Balkan Wars antagonized Austria, and the assassination of the Austrian Archduke FRANZ FERDINAND led to the outbreak of World War 1. In 1918 Serbia became the leading partner of the kingdom of the Serbs, Croats and Slovenes, renamed YUGOSLAVIA in 1929. During World War 2, Yugoslavia was occupied and divided by the German army. Resistance was two-fold: TITO led the Yugoslav communist partisans, and Mihajović led the Serbian nationalists. In 1946 Serbia became an autonomous republic within Tito's neo-communist Yugoslavia. In 1987 President Slobodan MILOŠEVIĆ restated nationalist claims for a Greater Serbia, including Vojvodina, Kosovo and Serb-populated areas in Croatia, Bosnia-Herzegovina and Macedonia. In 1989 Serbian troops were sent to suppress Albanian nationalism in Kosovo. In 1991 Serbia prevented Croatia from assuming presidency of the federation. Croatia and SLOVENIA responded by declaring independence, and the Serbian-controlled Yugoslav army invaded. In 1991 the army withdrew from

Slovenia. In 1992 a UN-brokered cease-fire was agreed between Serbia and Croatia, allowing Serbia to keep the territory it had captured. Serbian troops quickly seized nearly 75% of the newly recognized republic of Bosnia-Herzegovina and pursued a policy of "ethnic cleansing". The UN imposed sanctions on the Serbian regime, but atrocities continued on both sides. In 1995 Bosnian Serb troops captured UN protected areas, and Western governments and NATO launched air-strikes against Serb targets. Bosnia-Herzegovina and Croatia launched a new offensive against Serbia and reclaimed much lost territory. The US-brokered Dayton Peace Accord was signed in November 1995 dividing Bosnia-Herzegovina into provinces; Ratko Mladić and Radovan KARADŽIĆ were charged with genocide. Democratic elections were held in September 1996, but Milošević refused to recognize opposition victories. Massive, peaceful demonstrations were held in Belgrade, and Milošević was forced to recognize some of the Zajedno coalition's victories. In 1997 Milošević resigned the Serbian presidency in order to become president of Yugoslavia.

Serbs Slavic people who settled in the Balkans in the 7th century and who became Christians in the 9th century. They were distinguished from Croats and Slovenes by their use of the Cyrillic, not the Roman, alphabet. Most of them now live in Serbia, but there are Serb minorities in Bosnia and Croatia.

serial music Technique of musical composition in which a work is structured on a fixed series of notes; the series is repeated in various permutations for the duration of the work. TWELVE-TONE MUSIC is a form of serial music.

serotonin Chemical found in cells of the gastrointestinal tract, blood platelets and brain tissue, concentrated in the midbrain and HYPOTHALAMUS. It is a vasoconstrictor and has an important role in the functioning of the nervous system and in the stimulation of smooth muscles.

serpentine Group of sheet silicate minerals, hydrated magnesium silicate ($Mg_3Si_2O_5(OH)_4$). Serpentine minerals come in various colours, usually green, although sometimes brownish, with a pattern of green mottling. They are commonly used in carving; fibrous varieties are used in asbestos cloth. Hardness 2.5–4; s.g. 2.5–2.6.

serum Clear fluid that separates out if blood is left to clot. It is essentially of the same composition as plasma, but without fibrinogen and clotting factors.

serval (bush cat) Orange and black spotted cat found in grassy areas of sub-Saharan Africa. It has a narrow head and long legs, neck and ears. Length: body 70–100cm (30–40in); weight: 6.8–11.3kg (15–25lb). Family Felidae; species *Felis serval*.

servomechanism Device that provides remote control to activate a mechanism. An input signal, such as a radio impulse or mechanical movement, is converted into a mechanical output, such as a lever movement or amplified hydraulic force. The device usually forms part of a control system.

sesame Tropical plant native to Asia and Africa. It is also cultivated in Mexico and sw USA for its oil and seeds, both used in cooking. An annual, it has oval leaves, small pink or white flowers, and seed capsules along the stem. Height: 61cm (2ft). Family Pedaliaceae; species *Sesamum indicum*.

Seth Egyptian god. Although a beneficent god in predynastic Egypt, Seth became associated with darkness and was later identified as a god of evil and the antagonist of HORUS.

Seth, Vikram (1952–) Indian novelist and poet. He came to attention with his award-winning 1983 travelogue, *From Heaven Lake*. His epic *A Suitable Boy* (1993) is one of the century's longest English novels. His volumes of poetry include *All You Who Sleep Tonight* (1990).

sets In mathematics, a defined collection of objects. The objects are the elements or members of the set. The number of members can be finite or infinite, or even be zero (the empty set). Various relations can exist between two sets, A and B: A equals B if both sets contain exactly the same members; A is a subset of B if all members of A are members of B; disjoint sets have no members in common; overlapping sets have one or more common members. Operations on sets produce new sets: the union of A and B contains the members of both A and B; the intersection of A and B contains only those members common to both sets.

set theory Branch of mathematics concerned with the properties of SETS, which can be applied to most other branches of mathematics.

Settlement, Act of (1701) English parliamentary statute regulating the succession to the throne. The purpose of the act was to prevent the restoration of the Catholic STUART monarchy, the last surviving child of Queen ANNE having died. It settled the succession on SOPHIA of Hanover, granddaughter of James I, and her heirs, providing they were Protestants. The crown was inherited (1714) by Sophia's son, who became GEORGE I of England.

Seurat, Georges Pierre (1859–91) French painter and founder of NEO-IMPRESSIONISM. From 1876–84 he developed his theory of colour vision known as POINTILLISM, which was based on the juxtaposition of pure colour dots. His paintings include *Bathing at Asnières* (1883–84) and *Sunday in Summer on the Island of La Grande-Jatte* (1886).

Sevastopol (Sebastopol) Black Sea port on the sw of the Crimean Peninsula, Ukraine. The city became home to the Russian Black Sea fleet and was the major strategic objective of the CRIMEAN WAR. During World War 2 the city was besieged for eight months before surrendering to the Germans in July 1942. In 1995 Ukraine agreed to allow the Russian fleet to maintain its Sevastopol base in return for Ukrainian ownership of 19% of the fleet. Pop. (1993) 366,000.

Seventh-day Adventists Christian denomination whose members expect JESUS CHRIST to return to earth in person. They hold the SABBATH on Saturday and accept the BIBLE literally as their guide for living. The sect was formally organized in the USA in 1863 and is the largest ADVENTIST denomination.

Seven Wonders of the World Group of fabled sights that evolved from the various ancient Greek lists. They were, in chronological order: the PYRAMIDS of EGYPT; the HANGING GARDENS OF BABYLON; the statue of ZEUS by PHIDIAS at OLYMPIA; the temple of ARTEMIS at EPHESUS; the MAUSOLEUM at HALICARNASSUS; the COLOSSUS OF RHODES; and the PHAROS at ALEXANDRIA.

Seven Years War (1756–63) Major European conflict. The war was a continuation of the rivalries involved in the War of the AUSTRIAN SUCCESSION (1740–48). Britain and Prussia were allied, with Prussia undertaking nearly all the fighting in Europe, against Austria, Russia, France and Sweden. FREDERICK II (THE GREAT) of Prussia fought a defensive war against superior forces. Only his brilliant generalship and the withdrawal of Russia from the war in 1762 saved Prussia from being overrun. Overseas, Britain and France fought in North America, India and West Africa, with the British gaining major victories. At the end of the war, the Treaty of PARIS (1763) confirmed British supremacy in North America and India, while the Treaty of Hubertusberg left Prussia in control of Silesia.

Severn Longest river in the UK, flowing 290km (180mi) through Wales and W England. Major tributaries include the rivers Vyrnwy, Teme and Stour. The Severn Road Bridge (1966) is one of the world's longest suspension bridges. A second road bridge opened in 1996.

Severus, Lucius Septimius (146–211) Roman emperor (193–211). Of North African background, he was proclaimed emperor by his troops, who marched on Rome and persuaded the Senate to confirm him. In Britain from 208, he divided the country into two provinces and launched a campaign to conquer Scotland. Repulsed, he died at York.

Seville Port on the River Guadalquivir, sw Spain, capital of Seville province. It exports fruit (notably oranges) and wine from the fertile area. Industries: agricultural machinery, shipbuilding, chemicals, spirits, tourism. Pop. (1991) 659,126.

Sèvres, Treaty of (1920) Peace treaty between Turkey and its European opponents in World War 1 that imposed harsh terms on the Ottoman sultan. It was not accepted by the Turkish nationalists led by ATATÜRK, who fought a war for Turkish independence (1919–22). The treaty, never ratified, was replaced by the Treaty of Lausanne (1923).

sex Classification of an organism into male or female, denoting the reproductive function of the individual. In mammals the presence of sex organs, OVARIES in the female, TESTES in the male, are primary sexual characteristics. Secondary sexual characteristics such as size, colouration, and hair growth are governed by the secretion of SEX HORMONES. In flowering plants, the female sex organs are the carpel, including the ovary, STYLE and STIGMA, and

the male organs the STAMENS. Male and female organs may occur in the same flower or on separate flowers or plants. *See also* SEXUAL REPRODUCTION

sex hormones Chemical "messengers" secreted by the gonads (TESTES and OVARIES). They regulate sexual development and reproductive activity and influence sexual behaviour. In males they include TESTOSTERONE; in females they include OESTROGEN and PROGESTERONE.

sextant Optical instrument for finding LATITUDE (angular distance N or S of the Equator). The sextant consists of a frame with a curved scale marked in degrees, a movable arm with an ordinary mirror at the pivot, a half-silvered glass, and a telescope. The instrument measures the angle of a heavenly body above the horizon, which depends on the observer's latitude. A set of tables gives the corresponding latitude for various angles measured.

sexually transmitted disease (STD) Any disease that is transmitted by sexual activity involving the transfer of body fluids. It encompasses a range of conditions that are spread primarily by sexual contact, although they may also be transmitted in other ways. These include ACQUIRED IMMUNE DEFICIENCY SYNDROME (AIDS), pelvic inflammatory disease, cervical cancer, viral HEPATITIS, SYPHILIS and GONORRHOEA.

sexual reproduction Biological process of reproduction involving the combination of genetic material from two parents. It occurs in different forms throughout the plant and animal kingdoms. This process gives rise to variations of the GENOTYPE and PHENOTYPE within a species. GAMETES, HAPLOID sex cells produced by MEIOSIS, contain only half the number of CHROMOSOMES of their parent cells (which are DIPLOID). At fertilization, the gametes, generally one from each parent, fuse to form a ZYGOTE with the diploid number of chromosomes. The zygote divides repeatedly and the cells differentiate to give rise to an EMBRYO and, finally, a fully formed organism.

Seychelles Republic consisting of over 100 islands in the Indian Ocean, *c.*970km (600mi) N of Madagascar. Seychelles comprises two geologically distinct island groups: the volcanic **Granitic** group are to the NE, and include the three principal, inhabited islands of Mahé, Praslin and La Digue. Mahé is home to over 80% of the republic's people; Seychelles' capital, Victoria, lies on its NE coast. To the SW lie the **Outer** group of coral islands. In 1502 Vasco da Gama explored the islands. The islands were colonized by the French in 1756, who established spice plantations worked by slaves from Mauritius. In 1794 the archipelago was captured by the British during the Napoleonic Wars and, in 1814, became a dependency of Mauritius. In 1903 the Seychelles became a separate crown colony. In 1976 they achieved full independence within the Commonwealth of Nations. In 1977 a coup established Albert René as president. In 1981 South African mercenaries attempted to overthrow the government. Continued civil unrest, and another failed coup in 1987, led to the first multiparty elections in 1991. In 1993 René was elected for a fourth term. Tourism is the largest industry; exports include coconuts and tuna. Area: 453sq km (175sq mi). Pop. (1993 est.) 72,250

Sezession Radical movement (est. 1897) of Austrian artists who defied traditional organizations and aligned themselves with progressive European contemporaries. The first president was Gustav KLIMT.

Shackleton, Sir Ernest Henry (1874–1922) Irish Antarctic explorer. He led an expedition (1907–09) that approached to within 155km (97mi) of the South Pole. On his second expedition (1914–16), his ship was crushed by ice and his men marooned on a small island before being rescued.

shad Saltwater food fish of the HERRING family that swims upriver to spawn. Deep-bodied, they have a notch in the upper jaw for the tip of the lower jaw. Length: to 75cm (30in). Family Clupeidae.

Shaffer, Peter (1926–) British dramatist. After establishing his reputation as a playwright with *Five Finger Exercise* (1960), he wrote a double-bill *The Private Ear and The Public Eye* (1962). Other works include *The Royal Hunt of the Sun* (1964), *Black Comedy* (1965) and *Equus* (1973).

Shaftesbury, Anthony Ashley Cooper, 1st Earl of (1621–83) English political leader. A member of the council of state under the COMMONWEALTH, he was among those who invited CHARLES II to return to England at the RESTORATION (1660). His determination to prevent the succession of the Catholic JAMES II drove him to lead the parliamentary opposition to the court (1673) as a founder of the WHIG PARTY. Accused of treason (1682), he fled.

Shah Jahan (1592–1666) MOGUL emperor of India (1628–58), third son of Jahangir. His campaigns expanded the Mogul dominions and accumulated great treasure. Though relatively tolerant of Hinduism, he made Islam the state religion. Shah Jahan was responsible for building the TAJ MAHAL, and the vast ornamental chambers of the Red Fort at DELHI, which he made his capital.

Shaka (1787–1828) King of the ZULU. He claimed the throne *c.*1816 and reorganized the Zulu, forming a powerful army and extending his control over all of what is now KwaZulu-Natal.

Shakespeare, William (1564–1616) English poet and dramatist, b. Stratford upon Avon. By 1592 he was established in London, having already written the three parts of *Henry VI*. By 1594 he was a member of the Lord Chamberlain's Men and in 1599 a partner in the Globe Theatre (now rebuilt), where many of his plays were presented. He retired to Stratford upon Avon around 1613. His 154 *Sonnets*, which were first published in 1609, stand among the finest works of English poetry. The plays can be divided into four groups – the historical plays, the comedies, the tragedies and the late romances – and their plots are generally drawn from existing sources.

SHAKESPEARE'S PLAYS

Histories: (date written) *Henry VI (part I)* (1589–90), *Henry VI (part II)* (1590–91), *Henry VI (part III)* (1590–91) *Titus Andronicus* (1590–94), *Richard III* (1592–93), *King John* (1595–97), *Richard II* (1595), *Henry IV (part I)* (1596), *Henry IV (part II)* (1597), *Henry V* (1599), *Julius Caesar* (1599), *Troilus and Cressida* (1601–02), *Timon of Athens* (1605–09), *Antony and Cleopatra* (1606–07), *Coriolanus* (1607–08), *Henry VIII* (1613)

Comedies: *The Comedy of Errors* (1590–94), *Love's Labour's Lost* (1590–94), *The Two Gentlemen of Verona* (1592–93), *The Taming of the Shrew* (1592), *A Midsummer Night's Dream* (1595), *The Merchant of Venice* (1596–98), *The Merry Wives of Windsor* (1597), *Much Ado About Nothing* (1598) *As You Like It* (1599), *Twelfth Night* (1600–02), *All's Well That Ends Well* (1602–03), *Measure for Measure* (1604–05)

Tragedies: *Romeo and Juliet* (1595–96), *Hamlet* (1600–01), *Othello* (1604), *King Lear* (1605–06), *Macbeth* (1605–06)

Late Romances: *Pericles* (1607–08), *Cymbeline* (1609–10) *The Winter's Tale* (1611), *The Tempest* (1613)

shale Common SEDIMENTARY ROCK formed from mud or clay. Characterized by very fine layering, it may contain various materials such as fossils, carbonaceous matter and oil.

shallot Perennial plant native to W Asia and cultivated in temperate climates. It has thin, small leaves and clustered bulbs, which have a mild, onion-like flavour. Family Liliaceae; species *Allium cepa*.

shaman Tribal witch doctor or medicine man believed to be in contact with spirits or the supernatural world, and thought to have magical powers. Shamanism is found among the ESKIMOS and NATIVE AMERICANS and in Siberia.

shamrock Plant with three-part leaves, usually taken to be *Trifolium repens* or *T. dubium*, the national emblem of Ireland. Other plants called shamrock include *Oxalis acetosella* and *Medicago lupulina*. Family Fabiaceae/Leguminosae.

Shang (Yin) Chinese dynasty (*c.*1523–*c.*1027 BC). The Shang was based in the valley of the Huang He (Yellow River). During the Shang period, the Chinese written language was perfected, techniques of flood control and irrigation were practised, and artefacts were made in cast bronze.

Shanghai Largest city and port in China, 22km (13mi) from the Yangtze (Changjiang) delta, SE China. By the Treaty of Nanking (1842), the city was opened to foreign trade, which stimulated economic growth. Occupied by the Japanese in 1937, it was was restored to China at the end of World War 2. Industries: textiles, steel, chemicals, publishing, farm machinery, shipbuilding, pharmaceuticals, financial services. Pop. (1993) 8,760,000.

Shankar, Ravi (1920–) Indian musician. He was responsible for popularizing the SITAR and Indian music in general in the West.

Shannon Longest river in the Republic of Ireland and the British Isles. It rises on Cuilcagh Mountain in NW County Cavan and flows S through loughs Allen, Ree and Derg, then S across the central plain of Ireland to Limerick, and w to enter the Atlantic Ocean. Length: 370km (230mi)

Shapley, Harlow (1885–1972) US astronomer who provided the first accurate model of the MILKY WAY. By observing CEPHEID VARIABLE stars in globular clusters, he calculated the distance to each cluster in the galaxy, obtaining a picture of its shape and size.

share Document representing money invested in a company in return for membership rights in the ownership of that company. Shares are expressed in monetary units. Shareholders regularly receive payment of dividends that depend on the net profit of the company. **Stocks** are usually fixed-interest securities such as those issued by government.

sharia Traditional law of ISLAM, believed by Muslims to be the result of divine revelation. It is drawn from a number of sources, including the KORAN and a collection of teachings and legends about the life of MUHAMMAD known as the *Hadith*.

shark Torpedo-shaped, cartilaginous fish found in subpolar to tropical marine waters. They have well-developed jaws, bony teeth, usually 5 gill slits on each side of the head and a characteristic, lobe-shaped tail with a longer top lobe. Sharks are carnivorous and at least 10 species are known to attack humans. There are about 250 living species. Order Selachii. *See also* DOGFISH; HAMMERHEAD; WHALE SHARK; WHITE SHARK

sharp In musical notation, an accidental sign placed before a note or immediately after the clef to indicate that the note it refers to should be sounded a semitone higher.

Sharpeville Black township, N of Vereeniging, South Africa, scene of a massacre by security forces in March 1960. A large gathering of local people demonstrating against the pass laws, failed to obey orders to disperse. The police opened fire, killing 67 people and wounding 186. The massacre led to greater militancy in the struggle against APARTHEID and focused international attention on South Africa.

Shaw, George Bernard (1856–1950) Irish dramatist, critic and member of the FABIAN SOCI-ETY. His first publicly performed play was *Arms and the Man* (1894). Later plays include *Candida* (1897), *Man and Superman* (1905), *Major Barbara* (1905), *Pygmalion* (1913) and *Saint Joan* (1923). Shaw received the 1925 Nobel Prize for literature.

Shearer, Alan (1970–) English footballer. In 1992 he joined Blackburn Rovers, and the following season he became the first player to score 100 goals in the Premier League. In 1996 he was the leading scorer in the European Championship, and moved to Newcastle for a world-record transfer fee of £15 million.

shearwater Seabird related to the ALBATROSS and PETREL. Most species are brown or black with pale underparts. Shearwaters live most of their lives on the ocean; they feed on fish and squid, and burrow nests in coastal cliffs. Length: 19–56cm (7.5–22in). Family Procellariidae.

Sheba (Saba) Ancient kingdom of S Arabia celebrated for its trade in gold, spices and precious stones. According to the Bible, the Queen of Sheba visited Jerusalem to hear the wisdom of SOLOMON in the 10th century BC.

sheep Ruminants of the genus *Ovis*, and those of the less numerous genera *Pseudois* and *Ammotragus*. Domestic sheep, *O. aries*, are now bred for WOOL, fur (karakul) and meat. Wild species are found in the mountains of Europe, Asia, Africa and North America. All are of the Family Bovidae.

Sheffield City and county district in South Yorkshire, N England. A hilly city, it lies at the confluence of the River Don and its tributaries, the Sheaf, Rivelin and Lordey. It is an industrial centre, noted for steel and steel products. Pop. (1991) 501,202.

shell In biology, the hard protective case of various MOLLUSCS. The case is secreted by the epidermis of the mollusc and consists of a protein matrix strengthened by calcium carbonate.

Shelley, Mary Wollstonecraft (1797–1851) British novelist. She eloped with Percy Bysshe SHELLEY in 1814 and married him in 1816. Her later works of fiction, which include *The Last Man* (1826) and *Lodore* (1835), have been eclipsed by her first novel, the Gothic *Frankenstein* (1818).

Shelley, Percy Bysshe (1792–1822) English ROMANTIC poet. His poems include *Queen Mab* (1813), "Ode to the West Wind" (1819), "To a Skylark" (1820) and *Adonais* (1821). *Prometheus Unbound* (1820), a four-act lyrical drama, is often regarded as his masterpiece.

shellfish Common name for edible shelled MOLLUSCS and CRUSTACEA. Shelled molluscs include CLAMS, MUSSELS, OYSTERS and SCALLOPS; crustaceans include SHRIMPS, LOBSTERS and CRABS.

Shenyang Capital of Liaoning province, NE China. Once capital of the QING dynasty, it is the centre of a group of communes that grow rice, cereals and vegetables under intensive cultivation. Industries: aircraft, machine tools, heavy machinery, cables and cement. Pop. (1993) 3,860,000.

Sheridan, Richard Brinsley (1751–1816) British dramatist and politician. He excelled in comedies of manners, such as *The Rivals* (1775) and *The School for Scandal* (1777). Entering Parliament as a member of the WHIGS in 1780, he became one of the most brilliant speakers of his time.

sherry Fortified wine. It has a characteristic raisiny flavour produced by a special method of vinification and blending. True sherry comes from Jerez, Spain.

Sherwood Forest Ancient royal hunting ground in Nottinghamshire, central England. Famous as the home of the legendary ROBIN HOOD, some of the original forest remains.

Shetland Islands Group of *c.*100 islands NE of the Orkneys, 210km (130mi) off the N coast of Scotland, constituting an administrative region. Settled by Norse invaders in the 9th century, the islands were seized by Scotland in 1472. The principal islands are Mainland (which has the main town of Lerwick), Yell, Unst, Whalsay and Bressay. The islands are rocky with thin soils, but oats and barley are grown in places. Fishing and livestock are important, and the islands are famous for SHETLAND PONIES. More recently, oil and tourism have become major industries. Area: 1,433sq km (553sq mi) Pop. (1991) 22,522.

Shetland pony One of the smallest types of light horse. Originating in the SHETLAND ISLANDS, it has been introduced to most parts of the world. It has been used for draught work and makes an ideal child's mount. Height: typically 71cm (28in) at the shoulder; weight: 169kg (350lb).

Shevardnadze, Eduard Ambrosievich (1928–) Georgian political leader. Head of the Georgian Communist Party, he was made Soviet foreign minister (1985) by Mikhail GORBACHEV. He resigned in 1990, warning that Gorbachev was becoming authoritarian. In 1992 he became head of state in newly independent Georgia. With Russian help, he overcame supporters of the deposed leader, Zviad Gamsakhurdia. He escaped an assassination attempt in 1995, and later that year won a sweeping victory in elections.

Shiite (Arabic, *shiat Ali*, supporter of Ali) Second-largest branch of ISLAM. Shiites believe that the true successor of MUHAMMAD was ALI, whose claim to be CALIPH was not recognized by SUNNI Muslims. It rejects the *Sunna* (the collection of teachings outside the KORAN) and relies instead on the pronouncements of a succession of holy men called IMAMS. One of the principal causes of the Iranian revolution was Shah PAHLAVI's attempt to reduce clerical influence on government. Ayatollah KHOMEINI's Shiite theocracy stressed the role of Islamic activism in liberation struggles. After the 1991 Gulf War, the Iraqi Shiite opposed the oppressive regime of Saddam Hussein, but were defeated. The ISMAILIS of the Indian subcontinent are the other major Shiite grouping.

Shikoku Smallest of the four main islands of Japan, S of Honshū and E of Kyushu. The interior is mountainous and extensively forested, and most settlements are on the coast. The principal cities are Matsuyama, Takamatsu and Tokushima. Products: rice, tea, wheat, timber, fish, tobacco, fruit, soya beans, camphor, copper. Area 18,798sq km (7,258sq mi). Pop. (1995) 4,183,000.

shingles (herpes zoster) Acute viral infection of sensory nerves. Groups of small blisters appear along the course of the affected nerves, and the condition can be very painful.

Shinto (Jap. way to the gods) Indigenous religion of Japan. Originating as a primitive cult of nature worship, it was shaped by the influence of CONFUCIUS and, from the 5th century, BUDDHISM. A revival of the ancient Shinto rites in the 17th century contributed to the rise of Japanese nationalism in the late 19th century. Shinto has many deities in the form of spirits, souls and forces of nature.

ship Vessel for conveying passengers and freight by sea. The earliest sea-going ships were probably Egyptian, making voyages to the E coast of Africa in c.1500 BC. In c.200 AD extensive sea voyages were being made by Chinese ships that carried more than one mast and featured a rudder, some 1,200 years before such ships appeared in Europe. In the Mediterranean region, the galleys of the Greek, Phoenician and Roman navies combined rows of oars with a single square sail, as did the Viking longboats, which were capable of withstanding violent seas. By the 14th and 15th centuries, carracks and galleons were being developed to fulfil the exploration of the New World. Fighting ships of the 17th and 18th centuries included frigates of various designs. Sailing freighters culminated in the great clippers of the late 19th century, some of which had iron hulls. A century or so earlier, the first steamships had been built. They were powered by wood or coal-burning steam engines that drove large paddle wheels. In 1819 the first Atlantic crossing was made by "steam-assisted sail" and this crossing became a regular service. In the mid-19th century, steamships, such as Brunel's *Great Britain* (1844), were driven by propellers. Marine steam TURBINES were developed at the turn of the 19th century and gradually replaced reciprocating (back-and-forth cranking) steam ENGINES for large vessels. Oil, rather than coal, soon became the favoured fuel for large marine engines. Diesel engines were developed in the early 1900s, but did not replace steam turbines until the 1970s. Some of the newest military ships and icebreakers are fitted with nuclear engines in which heat from a NUCLEAR REACTOR raises steam in boilers to drive steam turbines. *See also* AIRCRAFT CARRIER; SUBMARINE

Shiva (Siva) Major god of HINDUISM. A complex god who transcends the concepts of good and evil, Shiva represents both reproduction and destruction. He periodically destroys the world in order to create it once more. He takes little part in the affairs of humanity, although his wife, known variously as KALI and Uma, is actively involved in them.

shoebill stork (whale-headed stork) Tall, wading bird found in papyrus marshes of tropical NE Africa. It has a shoe-shaped bill with a sharp hook, a short neck, darkish plumage and long legs. It feeds at night on small animals, including lungfish, frogs and turtles. Height: to 1.4m (4.6ft). Family Balaenicipitidae; species *Balaeniceps rex*.

shōgun Title of the military ruler of Japan, first conferred upon Yoritomo in 1192. The Minamoto (1192–1333), Ashikaga (1338–1568) and TOKUGAWA (1603–1868) shōgunates effectively ruled feudal Japan, although an emperor retained ceremonial and religious duties. The shōgunate ended with the MEIJI RESTORATION in 1868.

Sholokhov, Mikhail Alexandrovich (1905–84) Soviet novelist, famous for his novel about his native land, *Tikhy Don* (1928–40), translated as *And Quiet Flows the Don* (1934) and *The*

Don Flows Home to the Sea (1940). Sholokhov was awarded the 1965 Nobel Prize for literature.

Shona Bantu-speaking people of E Zimbabwe. Shona society is based on subsistence agriculture and is centred on small villages, abandoned when local resources are exhausted.

shooting Competitive sport involving firearms, in which a competitor, or team of competitors, fires at stationary or moving targets. The three main types of shooting are rifle, pistol and clay-pigeon shooting. In 1997 all handguns were banned in the UK.

Short Parliament (1640) English Parliament that ended 11 years of personal rule by CHARLES I. Charles was forced to summon Parliament to raise revenue through taxation for war against Scotland. When it refused, he dissolved it, but had to summon the LONG PARLIAMENT a few months later.

Shoshone (Shoshoni) Native North Americans of the Uto-Aztecan language group. They occupy reservations in California, Idaho, Nevada, Utah and Wyoming. They were divided into the COMANCHE, the Northern, the Western and the Wind River Shoshone. They now number *c*.9,500.

Shostakovich, Dmitri Dmitrievich (1906–75) Russian composer. His use of contemporary western musical developments in his compositions did not meet with official approval. His opera *The Lady Macbeth of the Mtsenk District* (1934) received international acclaim but was later criticized in *Pravda*. Other works were deliberately more conventional. He composed 15 symphonies, 13 string quartets, ballets, piano music and film music.

shot put Athletics field event in which a competitor throws a heavy metal ball. Throughout the put, the athlete must remain inside the throwing circle. Men throw a 7.3kg (16lb) shot; women a 4kg (8lb 13oz) shot. The shot is an Olympic event.

shoulder In human anatomy, mobile joint at the top of the arm. It consists of the ball-and-socket joint between the upper arm bone (HUMERUS) and the shoulder blade (scapula).

shrew Smallest mammal, found throughout the world. It is an active, voracious insectivore that eats more than its own weight daily. Family Soricidae.

shrike (butcherbird) Small, perching bird found worldwide, except in South America and Australia. It dives at its prey – insects, small birds, mice – hitting them with its bill and then impaling them on a sharp fence post, twig or thorn. Family Laniidae

shrimp Mostly marine, swimming crustacean. Its compressed body has long antennae, stalked eyes, a beak-like prolongation, a segmented abdomen with five pairs of swimming legs and a terminal spine. Large edible shrimps are often called PRAWNS or scampi. Length: 5–7.5cm (2–3in).

Shropshire (Salop) County in W England; the county town is Shrewsbury. The county is crossed by the River SEVERN. To the N the land is low-lying, and to the S it rises to the Welsh hills. Part of Mercia in Anglo-Saxon history, after the Norman Conquest it became part of the Welsh Marches. The economy

is primarily agricultural. Mineral deposits include coal; industries include metal products. Area: 3,490sq km (1,347sq mi). Pop. (1991) 406,387.

Shrove Tuesday Day before Ash Wednesday, which is the first day of LENT. In many countries, it is associated with celebrations symbolizing the final self-indulgence before the Lenten period of self-denial. Pancakes are a traditional feast.

shrub Woody, perennial plant of limited height, usually less than 10m (30ft) high. Instead of having a main stem, it branches at or slightly above ground level into several stems.

sial In geology, uppermost of the two main rock-classes in the Earth's crust. Their main constituents are silicon and aluminium. They make up the material of the continents and overlay the SIMA.

Siam *See* THAILAND

Siamese twins Identical twins who are born physically joined together, sometimes with sharing of organs. Surgical separation can be possible.

Sian *See* XIAN

Sibelius, Jean Julius Christian (1865–1957) Finnish composer whose works represent the culmination of nationalism in Finnish music. He is best known for his orchestral works, including seven symphonies, a violin concerto (1903–05) and the tone poems *En Saga* (1892) and *Finlandia* (1899).

Siberia (Sibir) Extensive region of Asian Russia, extending E to W from the Ural Mountains to the Pacific Ocean, and N to S from the Arctic Ocean to Kazakstan and Mongolia. Siberia can be divided into five geographical areas: (1) the W Siberian plain, between the Urals and the Central Plateau; (2) the Central Siberian plateau, between the Yenisei and Lena river; (3) the NE Siberian mountains to the E of the Lena; (4) the mountains of the S Trans-Baikal region, close to Lake BAIKAL; and (5) the volcanic and mountainous KAMCHATKA peninsula. Settlement on a large scale in Siberia came after the construction of the TRANS-SIBERIAN RAILWAY; Siberia's population doubled between 1914 and 1946. Economic development was rapid. The 1960s witnessed the development of vast hydro-electric schemes in the Trans-Baikal region. Being such a geographically diverse area, agriculture and industry vary enormously, from reindeer breeding, fishing and seal-hunting in the far N to dairy farming on the W plain and mining of aluminium, gold and diamonds on the central plateau. Area 13,807,000sq km (5,331,000sq mi). Pop. (1994) 35,605,000.

Sichuan (Szechwan) Province in SW China; the capital is Chengdu. The E part of the region comprises the large, heavily populated Red Basin, the most prosperous area of China. Sichuan is China's leading producer of rice, maize and sweet potatoes, while soya beans, barley and fruit are also grown. Livestock, including cattle, pigs, horses and oxen, are reared. Salt, coal and iron are mined; other products include rapeseed-oil and silk. Area: 569,215sq km (219,774sq mi). Pop. (1990) 106,370,000.

Sicily Largest and most populous island in the

Mediterranean Sea, off the SW tip of the Italian peninsula, comprising (with nearby islands) an autonomous region of Italy. The capital is PALERMO; other major cities include MESSINA. It is separated from Italy by the narrow Strait of Messina. Mostly mountainous, Sicily's Mount ETNA, at 3,340m (10,958ft), is the highest volcano in Europe. Strategically situated between Europe and Africa, from the 5th–3rd centuries BC it was a battleground for the rival Roman and Carthaginian empires and, following the first PUNIC WAR in 241 BC, became a Roman province. At the end of the 11th century, the island and S Italy were conquered by the Normans. In 1266 the throne passed to Charles of Anjou, whose unpopular government caused the Sicilian Vespers revolt of 1282 and the election of an Aragónese king. In 1302 peace terms led to Aragón keeping Sicily, while S Italy became the Angevin kingdom of Naples. In 1735 the two regions were reunified under the rule of the Bourbon Don Carlos (Charles III of Spain). Centuries of centralization under Spanish imperial rule led to the crowning of Ferdinand I as King of Two Sicilies in 1816. Sicilian independence revolts of 1820 and 1848–49 were ruthlessly suppressed. In 1860 Garibaldi liberated the island and it was incorporated into the new, unified state of Italy. Agriculture is Sicily's economic mainstay. Grain, olives, wine and citrus fruits are the principal products; tourism is also important. Sicily is one of the poorest local economies in Europe. Area: 25,706sq km (9,925sq mi). Pop. (1992) 4,997,705.

sickle-cell anaemia Inherited blood disorder featuring an abnormality of HAEMOGLOBIN. The haemoglobin is sensitive to a deficiency of oxygen and it distorts erythrocytes, causing them to become rigid and sickle shaped. Sickle cells are rapidly lost from the circulation, giving rise to anaemia and jaundice.

Siddhartha Gautama *See* BUDDHA

sidereal period Orbital period of a planet or other celestial body with respect to a background star. It is the true orbital period. **Sidereal time** is local time reckoned according to the rotation of the Earth with respect to the stars. The sidereal day is 23 hours, 56 minutes and 4 seconds of mean solar time, nearly 4 minutes shorter than the mean solar day. The sidereal year is equal to 365.25636 mean solar days.

sidewinder (horned rattlesnake) Nocturnal RATTLESNAKE found in deserts of SW USA and Mexico. It has horn-like scales over the eyes and is usually tan with a light pattern. It loops obliquely across the sand, leaving a J-shaped trail. Length: to 75cm (30in). Family Viperidae; species *Crotalus cerastes*. The term is also used to describe desert-dwelling snakes of the Old World that move in a similar way.

Sidney, Sir Philip (1554–86) English poet, diplomat and courtier. His works include the intricate pastoral romance *Arcadia* (1590), and the sonnet sequence *Astrophel and Stella* (1591). *The Defence of Poesie* is a milestone of English literary theory.

Siemens German brothers associated with the electrical engineering industry. **Ernst Werner von** Siemens (1816–92) developed an electric telegraph system in 1849. With **Karl** (1829–1906) he set up subsidiaries of the family firm in London, Vienna and Paris. **Friedrich** (1826–1904) and **Karl Wilhelm** (later William) (1823–83) developed a regenerative furnace that was used extensively in industry. In 1843 Karl Wilhelm introduced an ELECTROPLATING process to Britain.

Siena Capital of Siena province, Tuscany, central Italy. It is one of Italy's foremost tourist attractions. Founded by the Etruscans, Siena became a commune in the 12th century. During the 13th century, it rapidly expanded to rival Florence, and was the centre of the Ghibelline faction. In the mid-16th century, it fell under the control of the Medici. In art history, it is famed for the Sienese School of painting (13th–14th centuries). Pop. (1990) 58,278

Sierra Leone Republic on the W coast of Africa; the capital is FREETOWN. **Land and climate** The coast contains several deep estuaries in the N, with lagoons in the S, but the most prominent feature is the mountainous Freetown (or Sierra Leone) peninsula.Behind the coastal plain, the land rises to mountains, with the highest peak, Loma Mansa, reaching 1,948m (6,391ft). Sierra Leone has a wet, tropical climate. Swamps cover large areas near the coast. Inland, much of the original rainforest has been destroyed and replaced by low bush and coarse grassland. **Economy** Sierra Leone has a low-income economy. Agriculture employs 70% of the people, many at subsistence level. Chief food crops include cassava, maize and rice, the staple food, and export crops include cocoa and coffee. The most valuable exports are minerals, including diamonds, bauxite and rutile (titanium ore). **History and politics** Portuguese sailors reached the coast in 1460; in the 16th century the area became a source of slaves. In 1787 Freetown was founded as a home for freed slaves. In 1808 the settlement became a British crown colony. In 1896 the interior was made a protectorate. In 1951 the protectorate and colony were united. In 1961 Sierra Leone gained independence within the Commonwealth of Nations. In 1971 it became a republic. In 1978 the All People's Congress became the sole political party. A 1991 refer-

---

SIERRA LEONE
AREA: 71,740sq km (27,699sq mi)
POPULATION: 4,376,000
CAPITAL (POPULATION): Freetown (469,776)
GOVERNMENT: Transitional
ETHNIC GROUPS: Mende 35%, Temne 37%, Limba 8%
LANGUAGES: English (official)
RELIGIONS: Traditional beliefs 51%, Islam 39%, Christianity 9%
CURRENCY: Leone = 100 cents

endum voted for the restoration of multiparty democracy, but in 1992 a military group seized power. A civil war began between the government and Revolutionary United Front (RUF). The RUF fought to end foreign interference and to nationalize the diamond mines. Following multiparty elections in February 1996, the military government made way for an administration led by Ahmad Tejan Kabbah. In November 1996 Kabbah and the RUF signed a peace agreement ending the war, which had claimed more than 10,000 lives. A military coup soon followed, however, ending Sierra Leone's brief period of civilian rule. The leader of the coup, Major Johnny Paul Koroma, was installed as president in 1997.

Sierra Madre Principal mountain range in Mexico, from the US border to SE Mexico and extending S into Guatemala. The ranges enclose the central Mexican plateau. The main range is 2,400km (1,500mi) long and *c*.16–480km (10–300mi) wide. The highest peak is Orizaba (Giltaltepetl) in the Sierra Madre Oriental, at 5,700m (18,700ft).

Sierra Nevada Mountain system in E California, USA. In the E it rises steeply from the Great Basin, while the W edge slopes more gently down to the Central Valley of California. The rivers are used for irrigation and to provide hydroelectric power. Mount WHITNEY, 4,418m (14,495ft), is the highest peak. The range is 650km (400mi) long.

sight Sense by which form, colour, size, movement and distance of objects are perceived. It is the detection of light by the EYE, enabling the formation of visual images.

Signac, Paul (1863–1935) French painter. Signac was the main theoretical writer of NEO-IMPRESSIONISM, especially in *D'Eugène Delacroix au néo-impressionisme* (1899).

Sihanouk, Norodom (1922–) Cambodian political leader. As king (1941–55, 1993–), prime minister (1955–60) and head of state (1960–70, 1975–76, 1991–93), he was a leading political figure in Cambodia for nearly half a century. Following a right-wing coup by Lon Nol in 1970, he established a government in exile in China. He returned to Cambodia when the KHMER ROUGE took over in 1975, but was soon put under house arrest. He formed another government in exile after the Vietnamese invasion in 1979. He returned to Cambodia in 1991 after an agreement providing for the end of the civil war. In 1993 he became Cambodia's constitutional monarch. His son, Prince Ranariddh, was ousted by his co-premier, Hun Sen, in 1997.

Sikhism Indian religion founded in the 16th century by NANAK, the first Sikh guru. Combining HINDU and MUSLIM teachings, it is a MONOTHEISTIC religion whose adherents believe that their one God is the immortal creator of the universe. Sikhs believe in REINCARNATION and seek spiritual guidance from their guru or leader. Begun in Punjab as a pacifist religion, Sikhism became an activist military brotherhood and a political force. Since Indian indepen-

dence, Sikh extremists have periodically agitated for an independent Sikh state, called Khalistan. In 1984 the leader of a Sikh fundamentalist revival, Sant Jarnail Singh Bhindranwale (1947–84), was killed by government forces at the Golden Temple of AMRITSAR, and in retaliation Indira GANDHI was assassinated by her Sikh bodyguard.

Sikh Wars Two wars (1845–46, 1848–49) between the Sikhs and the British in NW India. After the death of RANJIT SINGH in 1839, disorder affected the Sikh state in the PUNJAB. When Sikh forces, including many non-Sikhs, crossed the frontier on the River Sutlej, the British declared war. After several battles, with heavy casualties on both sides, the British advanced to Lahore where peace was agreed (1846). The conflict was renewed two years later, but superior British artillery led to a heavy Sikh defeat at Gujrat (1849). The Sikhs surrendered and the Punjab was annexed to British India.

Sikkim State in N India, bounded by Tibet, China (N and NE), Bhutan (SE), India (S) and Nepal (W), with its capital at Gangtok (1991 pop. 25,024). The terrain is mountainous, rising to Mount KANCHEN-JUNGA, at 8,591m (28,185ft). The original inhabitants were the Lepchas, but after the 17th century Sikkim was ruled by the rajas of Tibet. It had come under British influence by 1816, and after British withdrawal from India in 1947, Sikkim became independent. Political unrest led to the country becoming an Indian protectorate (1950), and it was made an associate state (1975). Agriculture is the main source of income, tourism is growing. Area: 7,096sq km (2,734sq mi). Pop. (1991) 406,457.

silica Silicon dioxide, a compound of SILICON and oxygen (SiO_2). It occurs naturally as QUARTZ and chert. Silica and silicate minerals are the main constituents of 95% of all rocks and account for 59% of the Earth's crust. Silica is used in the manufacture of glass, ceramics and SILICONE.

silicon Common, grey, nonmetallic element (symbol Si) of group IV of the periodic table. Silicon is found only in combinations such as SILICA and silicate. It is the second most abundant element in the Earth's crust (27.7% by weight). Silicon "chips" are extensively used in microprocessors. Properties: at.no. 14; r.a.m. 28.086; r.d. 2.33; m.p. 1,410°C (2,570°F); b.p. 2,355°C (4,271°F); most common isotope Si^{28} (98.21%).

silicone Odourless and colourless polymer based on SILICON. Silicones are stable at high temperatures, and are used in lubricants, varnishes, adhesives, water repellents and artificial heart valves.

silk Natural fibre produced by many creatures, notably the SILKWORM. Almost all silk is obtained from silkworms reared commercially; a single cocoon can provide between 600–900m (2,000–3,000ft) of filament. China is the largest producer of raw silk.

Silk Road (Silk Route) Ancient trade route linking China with Europe, the major artery of all Asian land exploration before AD 1500. For 3,000 years the manufacture of silk was a secret closely guarded by the Chinese. Silk fetched extravagant prices in Greece and Rome, and the trade became the major source of income for the Chinese dynasties. The silk trade began to decline in the 6th century, when the SILKWORM's eggs were smuggled to Constantinople and the secret exposed. During the 13th century, European merchants travelled along the Silk Road. In the 14th century trade became possible via a sea route to the Far East.

silk-screen printing (serigraphy) Means of producing a print, generally on paper. A screen composed of a mesh of silk or man-made fibres is stretched over a frame; a design is "stopped out" (painted) on the mesh, using glue, varnish, gelatin or a paper stencil. To make the print, ink is taken across the screen with a squeegee; the pressure of this pushes the ink through the unstopped areas of the mesh.

silkworm Moth CATERPILLAR that feeds chiefly on MULBERRY leaves. The common domesticated *Bombyx mori* is raised commercially for its SILK cocoon. Length: 7.5 cm (3in). Family Bombycidae.

Sillitoe, Alan (1928–) British novelist and short-story writer. His best-known novel is *Saturday Night and Sunday Morning* (1958). *The Loneliness of the Long-distance Runner* (1959) is his most celebrated novella. More recent novels include *Leonard's War* (1991) and *Snowdrops* (1993).

Silurian Third-oldest period of the PALAEOZOIC era, 438 to 408 million years ago. Marine invertebrates resembled those of ORDOVICIAN times, and jawless fish began to evolve. The earliest land plants (psilopsids) and first land animals (archaic mites and millipedes) developed.

silver White, metallic element (symbol Ag) one of the TRANSITION ELEMENTS. It occurs in argentite (a sulphide) and horn silver (a chloride), and is obtained as a by-product in the refining of copper and lead. Silver ores are scattered worldwide, Mexico being the major producer. Silver is used on some PRINTED CIRCUITS. Other uses include jewellery, coinage, and silver salts for light-sensitive materials used in photography. Properties: at.no. 47; r.a.m. 107.868; r.d. 10.5; m.p. 961.93°C (1,763°F), b.p. 2,212°C (4,104 °F); most common isotope Ag^{107} (51.82%).

silverfish (bristletail) Primitive, grey, wingless insect found throughout the world. It lives in cool, damp places feeding on starchy materials such as food scraps and paper. Length: 13mm (0.5in). Family Lepismatidae; species *Lepisma saccharina*.

sima In geology, undermost of the two main rock-classes that make up the Earth's crust, so called because its main constituents are silicon and magnesium. It underlies the SIAL of the continents.

Simenon, Georges (1903–89) French novelist. He published more than 500 novels and many more short stories. His character Maigret, a Parisian police inspector, is one of the best-known creations in 20th-century detective fiction.

simile Figure of speech comparing two things. It differs from ordinary comparisons in that it compares things usually considered dissimilar and sharing only one common characteristic.

Simon, Neil (1927–) US playwright. His plays include *Come Blow Your Horn* (1961), *Barefoot in the Park* (1963), *The Odd Couple* (1965), the musical *Sweet Charity* (1966), *They're Playing Our Song* (1979) and *Little Me* (1982).

Simpson, O.J. (Orenthal James) (1947–) US American football player. He made his name as a running back with Buffalo in the National Football League from 1969, and set a single season rushing record in 1973 with 1,831m (2,003yd). In 1994 he was arrested on a charge of murdering his wife and her male friend. The jury found him not guilty, but in 1997 a civil jury found him liable for wrongful death and he was fined US$30 million.

simultaneous equations Two or more equations that can be manipulated to give common solutions. In the simultaneous equations $x + 10y = 25$ and $x + y = 7$, the problem is to find values of x and y, such that those values are solutions of both the equations simultaneously. This can be done by subtracting the two equations to give a single equation in y, which can then be solved. Substituting the value of y in either equation gives the value of x.

Sinai peninsula Peninsula constituting a protectorate of Egypt, bounded by the Gulf of Suez and the Suez Canal (w), the Gulf of Aqaba and the Negev Desert of Israel (E), the Mediterranean Sea (N) and the Red Sea (S). It is a barren plateau region, sandy in the N, rising to granite ridges in the S, and still inhabited chiefly by nomads. The peninsula is the site of Jabal Musa (Mount Sinai). After being occupied by the Israelis in 1967, it was returned to Egypt in 1982. Area: 58,714sq km (22,671sq mi). Pop: (1991 est.) is 264,000.

Sinatra, Frank (Francis Albert) (1915–) US popular singer and actor. He was immensely popular during the 1940s for such songs as "Night and Day". He later became a film actor and won an Academy Award for a supporting role in *From Here to Eternity* (1953).

Sind Province in S Pakistan, bounded by India (E and S) and the Arabian Sea (SW). KARACHI is the national and provincial capital. The region is hot and arid. It was captured by the British in 1843. An autonomous province from 1937 until partition in 1947, Sind received many Muslim refugees after the creation of Pakistan. The major economic activity is agriculture. Grain, cotton, sugar cane, fruits and tobacco are grown. Area: 140,914sq km (54,428sq mi). Pop. (1985 est.) 21,682,000.

Sindhi Language of Pakistan and India, spoken by about 15 million people in the province of SIND, S Pakistan, and across the border in India. It is related to Sanskrit and Hindi, belonging to the Indic branch of the INDO-EUROPEAN LANGUAGES.

sine In a right-angled triangle, ratio of the length of the side opposite an acute angle to the length of the hypotenuse. The sine of angle *A* is usually abbreviated to sin *A*.

Singapore Archipelago republic at the s end of the MALAY PENINSULA, SE Asia; the capital is Singapore City. **Land and climate** Singapore consists of the large Singapore Island, and 59 small islets, 20 of which are inhabited. Singapore Island is linked to the peninsula by a 1,056m- (3,465ft-) long causeway. The land is mostly low-lying; the highest point, Bukit Timah, is only 176m (577ft) above sea level. Singapore has a hot, humid equatorial climate, with temperatures averaging 30°C (86°F). Total average annual rainfall is 2,413mm (95in). Rain occurs (on average) 180 days each year. Rainforest once covered Singapore, but forests now cover only 5% of the land. Most of Singapore is urban land. Farmland covers 4% of the land and plantations of permanent crops make up 7%. **Economy** Singapore is a high-income economy (1992 GDP per capita, US$18,330). It is one of the world's fastest growing (tiger) economies. Historically, Singapore's economy has been based on transshipment, and this remains a vital component. It is one of the world's busiest ports. The post-war economy has diversified. The service sector employs 65% of the workforce. Manufacturing is the largest export sector. Industries include computers, electronics, telecommunications, chemicals, machinery, scientific instruments, ships and textiles. It has a large oil refinery. **History** According to legend, Singapore was founded in 1299. It soon became a busy trading centre within the Sumatran Srivijaya kingdom. Javanese raiders destroyed it in 1377. Subsumed into Johor, Singapore became part of the powerful MALACCA sultanate. In 1819 Sir Thomas Stamford Raffles of the British EAST INDIA COMPANY leased the island from Johor, and the Company founded the city of Singapore. In 1826 Singapore, Penang and Malacca formed the Straits Settlement. Singapore soon became the most important British trading centre in Southeast Asia, and the Straits Settlement became a Crown Colony in 1867. Japanese forces seized the island in 1942, but British rule was restored in 1945. In 1946 the Straits Settlement was dissolved and Singapore

became a separate colony. In 1959 Singapore achieved self-government. Following a referendum, Singapore merged with Malaya, SARAWAK, and SABAH to form the Federation of MALAYSIA (1963). In 1965 Singapore broke away from the Federation to become an independent republic within the Commonwealth of Nations. **Politics** The People's Action Party (PAP) has ruled Singapore since 1959. Its leader, Lee Kuan Yew, served as prime minister from 1959 until 1990, when he resigned and was succeeded by Goh Chok Tong. Under the PAP, the economy has expanded rapidly. The PAP has been criticized by human rights groups for its authoritarian social policies and suppression of political dissent. Goh Chok Tong and the PAP were decisively re-elected in 1997.

Singer, Isaac Bashevis (1904–91) US novelist and short-story writer, b. Poland. His novels of Jewish life, written in Yiddish, include *The Family Moskat* (1950), *The Magician of Lublin* (1960), *The Slave* (1962) and *The Penitent* (1983). He was awarded the 1978 Nobel Prize for literature.

Sinhalese People who make up the largest ethnic group of Sri Lanka. They speak an INDO-EUROPEAN LANGUAGE and practise THERAVADA Buddhism.

Sinn Féin (Gaelic, Ourselves Alone) Irish republican, nationalist party founded in 1905 by Arthur GRIFFITH. It seeks to bring about a united IRELAND. Sinn Féin became a mass party after the EASTER RISING (1916) and established an alternative, republican government in 1918, winning 75% of the Irish vote in elections that year. It was divided by the Irish Free State Agreement (1921), which accepted the partition of Ireland. In the Irish Free State it remained a minority party, rejecting the Dublin government and allying itself with the outlawed IRISH REPUBLICAN ARMY (IRA). It became active in NORTHERN IRELAND, especially during the period of communal strife that began in 1968. In 1969 two groups emerged that mirrored the factions of the Provisional and Official IRA. Sinn Féin has won seats at Westminster Parliament (1981, 1983, 1987 and 1997), but has refused to assume the positions. Gerry ADAMS has been president of Sinn Féin since 1983.

Sino-Japanese Wars Two wars between China and Japan, marking the beginning and the end of Japanese imperial expansion on the Asian mainland. The first (1894–95) arose from rivalry for control of Korea. China was forced to accept Korean independence and ceded territory including Taiwan and the Liaotung peninsula. The latter was returned after European pressure. The second war (1937–45) developed from Japan's seizure of Manchuria (1931), where it set up the puppet state of MANCHUKUO. Further Japanese aggression led to war, in which the Japanese swiftly conquered E China, driving the government out of Peking (Beijing). US and British aid was despatched to China (1938) and the conflict merged into World War 2, ending with the final defeat of Japan in 1945.

SINGAPORE

AREA: 618sq km (239 sq mi)

POPULATION: 3,003,000

CAPITAL (POPULATION): Singapore City (2,812,000)

GOVERNMENT: Multiparty republic

ETHNIC GROUPS: Chinese 78%, Malay 14%, Indian 7%

LANGUAGES: Chinese, Malay, Tamil and English (all official)

RELIGIONS: Buddhism, Taoism and other traditional beliefs 54%, Islam 15%, Christianity 13%, Hinduism 4%

CURRENCY: Singapore dollar = 100 cents

---

sinus Hollow space or cavity, usually in bone. Most often the term refers to the paranasal sinuses, any of the four sets of air-filled cavities in the skull near the nose.

Sioux (Dakota) Group of seven NATIVE AMERICAN tribes inhabiting Minnesota, Nebraska, North and South Dakota and Montana. The tribes concluded several treaties with the US government during the 19th century, and finally agreed in 1867 to settle on a reservation in sw Dakota. The discovery of gold in the Black Hills and the rush of prospectors brought resistance from Sioux chiefs. The last confrontation resulted in the massacre of more than 200 Sioux at the Battle of Wounded Knee in 1890. By the late 1990s, the Sioux numbered more than 50,000.

siren Aquatic, tailed AMPHIBIAN of North America. The adult is neotenic (reaches sexual maturity while retaining the larval physical form). These eel-like animals have external gills, tiny forelegs and minute eyes. They have no hind legs. Length: to 92cm (36in). Family Sirenidae. *See also* SALAMANDER

Sirius (Alpha Canis Majoris) Brightest star visible from Earth, in the northern constellation of Canis Major. Its luminosity is 23 times that of the Sun.

sirocco Wind that arises over the Sahara Desert, picks up moisture from the Mediterranean Sea, and brings hot, rainy weather to the Mediterranean coast of Europe.

sisal (sisal hemp) Plant native to Central America and cultivated in Mexico, Java, E Africa and the Bahamas. Fibres from the leaves are used for rope, matting and twine. Family Agavaceae; species *Agave sisalana*. *See also* AGAVE

Sistine Chapel Private chapel of the popes in the VATICAN, painted by some of the greatest artists of RENAISSANCE Italy. It was built between 1473 and 1481 for Pope Sixtus IV. The side walls were decorated with FRESCOS by PERUGINO, Pinturicchio, BOTTICELLI, GHIRLANDAIO and Signorelli. Its most celebrated features are the ceiling, window lunettes and altar wall painted by MICHELANGELO.

Sisulu, Walter (1912–) South African civil rights activist, who was fiercely opposed to apartheid. A leading member of the AFRICAN NATIONAL CONGRESS (ANC), he became its secretary-general in 1949. When the ANC was declared illegal in 1960, Sisulu and other prominent members were harassed and arrested. In 1964 Sisulu, MANDELA and six others were sentenced to life imprisonment for their membership of the ANC. In 1989 Sisulu was finally released as part of the reforms of F.W. DE KLERK and, after the legalization of the ANC in 1990, became its deputy president (1991–94).

sitar Indian stringed musical instrument with a gourd-like body and long neck. It has three to seven strings, tuned in fourths or fifths, and a lower course of 12 strings. SHANKAR is one of its greatest players.

Sitting Bull (1831–90) North American SIOUX leader. With others, he led the attack on CUSTER'S US cavalry at the Battle of Little Bighorn (1876).

Sitwell, Dame Edith (1887–1964) English poet. Her anthology *Wheels* (1916) encouraged experimentalism in British verse. She contributed the words to WALTON's *Façade* (1922). She also wrote a biography of Alexander POPE (1930) and the *English Eccentrics* (1933).

SI units (Système International d'Unites) Internationally agreed system of units, derived from the mks (metre, kilogram and second) system. They are used for many scientific purposes and have replaced the fps (foot, pound and second) and cgs (centimetre, gram and second) systems. The basic units are the METRE (m), KILOGRAM (kg), SECOND (s), AMPERE (A), KELVIN (K), MOLE (mol) and CANDELA (cd).

Six Day War (1967) Episode of the ARAB-ISRAELI WARS. Israeli forces defeated the four Arab states (Egypt, Jordan, Syria and Iraq). Israel gained control of the old city of Jerusalem, Jordanian territory on the WEST BANK, the GOLAN HEIGHTS and the SINAI PENINSULA, including the GAZA STRIP.

skate Flattened food fish belonging to the RAY family, living mainly in shallow temperate and tropical waters. The pectoral fins are greatly expanded to form wing-like flaps. Length: to about 2.5m (8ft). Family Rajidae.

skeletal muscle In human beings and other mammals, the most plentiful of the three types of MUSCLE comprising the bulk of the body. It is also known as **voluntary muscle** because it is under conscious control, or as striated muscle because of its characteristic striped appearance. *See also* INVOLUNTARY MUSCLE

skeleton Bony framework of the body of a VERTEBRATE. It supports and protects internal organs, provides sites of attachment for muscles and a system of levers to aid locomotion. *See also* EXOSKELETON

skiing Method of "skating" on snow using flat runners (skis) made of various materials, attached to ski-boots; the skier may use hand-held poles to assist balance. The principal forms of competitive skiing are Alpine skiing, ski jumping, cross-country skiing and freestyle skiing. They are all Olympic sports.

skin Tough, elastic outer covering of invertebrates. It protects the body from injury and from the entry of some micro-organisms and prevents dehydration. Nerve endings in the skin provide the sensations of touch, warmth, cold and pain. It helps to regulate body temperature through sweating, regulates moisture loss and keeps itself smooth and pliable with an oily secretion from the SEBACEOUS GLANDS. Structurally the skin consists of two main layers: an outer layer (EPIDERMIS) and an inner layer (DERMIS).

skink Common name for any of more than 600 species of LIZARDS of tropical and temperate regions. They have cylindrical bodies, cone-shaped heads and tapering tails. They live in various habitats and eat vegetation, insects and small invertebrates. Length: to 66cm (26in). Family Scincidae.

Skopje Capital of Macedonia, on the River Vardar. Founded in Roman times, it became the capital of the Serbian empire in the 14th century, fell to the Ottoman Turks in 1392 and was incorporated into Yugoslavia in 1918. Most of the city was destroyed in a 1963 earthquake. Industries: metals, textiles, chemicals, glassware. Pop. (1994) 440,577.

skull (cranium) In vertebrates, brain case that supports and protects the brain, eyes, ears, nose and mouth.

skunk Nocturnal, omnivorous mammal that lives in the USA and Central and South America. It has powerful anal scent glands, which eject a foul-smelling liquid, used in defence. It has a slender, thickly furred body with a large bushy tail. The coat is black with bold white warning markings along the back. The most common species is the striped skunk, *Mephitis mephitis*. Length: to 38cm (15in); weight: 4.5kg (10lb). Family Mustelidae.

Skye Largest island in the Inner Hebrides, off the NW coast of Scotland, with the chief town of Portree. The Cuillin Hills and the many lochs give Skye spectacular scenery and make it a popular holiday destination. A bridge to the mainland was opened in 1996. Occupations include rearing livestock, weaving and fishing. Area 1,735sq km (670sq mi). Pop. (1991). 8,139.

slate Grey to blue, fine-grained, homogeneous METAMORPHIC ROCK, which splits into smooth, thin layers. It is formed by the metamorphosis of SHALE, and is valuable as a roofing material.

Slav Largest ethnic and linguistic group of peoples in Europe. Slavs are generally classified in three main divisions: the East Slavs, the largest division, include the Ukrainians, Russians and Belorussians; the South Slavs include the Serbs, Croats, Macedonians and Slovenes (and frequently also the Bulgarians); the West Slavs comprise chiefly the Poles, Czechs, Slovaks and Wends.

slavery Social system in which people are the property of their owner. Slavery was common to practically all ancient societies and to most modern societies until the 19th century. By the early 19th century slavery had been abolished in much of Europe; it was declared illegal in Britain in 1807 and outlawed in 1833. Most South American states abolished it soon after gaining independence. In the USA, slavery was one cause of the CIVIL WAR and was formally ended by the EMANCIPATION PROCLAMATION (1863). Isolated cases of slavery were discovered in China and some areas of Africa in 1990.

Slavic languages (Slavonic languages) Group of languages spoken in E Europe and the former Soviet Union, constituting a major subdivision of the family of INDO-EUROPEAN LANGUAGES. The main ones in use today are Russian, Ukrainian and Belorussian (East Slavic); Polish, Czech, Slovak and Sorbian or Lusatian, a language spoken in E Germany (West Slavic); and Bulgarian, Serbo-Croat, Slovenian and Macedonian (South Slavic). Some Slavic languages are written in the Cyrillic alphabet, others in the Roman.

sleep Periodic state of unconsciousness from which a person or animal can be roused. During an ordinary night's sleep there are intervals of deep sleep associated with rapid eye movement (REM) sleep. It is during this REM sleep that dreaming occurs. Studies have shown that people deprived of sleep become disturbed. Sleep requirement falls in old age. Difficulty in sleeping is called INSOMNIA.

sleeping sickness (trypanosomiasis) Disease of tropical Africa caused by a parasite transmitted by the TSETSE FLY. It is characterized by fever, headache, joint pains and anaemia. Ultimately it may affect the brain and spinal cord, leading to profound lethargy and sometimes death.

slime mould Any of a small group of strange, basically single-celled organisms that are intermediate between the plant and animal kingdoms. During their complex life cycle they pass through several stages. These include a flagellated swimming stage, an amoeba-like stage, a stage consisting of a slimy mass of protoplasm with many nuclei, and a flowering sporangium stage.

slipped disc (prolapsed intervertebral disc) Protrusion of the soft inner core of an intervertebral disc through its covering, causing pressure on spinal nerve roots. It is caused by a sudden mechanical force on the spine. It causes stiffness and SCIATICA.

sloe *See* BLACKTHORN

sloth Any of several species of slow-moving, herbivorous Central and South American mammals. It has long limbs with long claws and spends most of its time climbing in trees, where it generally hangs upside down. Length: to 60cm (2ft); weight: to 5.5kg (12lb). Family Brachipodidae.

Slovak Official language of the Slovak Republic, spoken by about 5 million people. It is closely related to Czech, and is considered distinct largely for political reasons.

Slovak Republic Republic in central Europe; the capital is BRATISLAVA. **Land and climate** The Slovak Republic (Slovakia) is dominated by the CARPATHIAN MOUNTAINS. The Tatra range on the N border include the republic's highest peak, Gerlachovka, at 2,655m (8,711ft). To the S is a fertile lowland, drained by the River DANUBE, on whose banks stands Bratislava. The Slovak Republic has a

SLOVAK REPUBLIC
AREA: 49,035sq km (18,932sq mi)
POPULATION: 5,297,000
CAPITAL (POPULATION): Bratislava (440,421)
GOVERNMENT: Multiparty republic
ETHNIC GROUPS: Slovak, Hungarian, with small groups of Czechs, Germans, Gypsies, Poles, Russians and Ukrainians
LANGUAGES: Slovak (official)
RELIGIONS: Christianity (Roman Catholic 60%, Protestant 6%, Orthodox 3%)
CURRENCY: Slovak koruna

continental climate, with cold, dry winters and warm, wet summers. Forests cover 41% of the Slovak republic. Arable land covers another 31%. **Economy** Pre-1948, the economy was primarily agrarian. Communism developed heavy industry. Post-independence governments have attempted to diversify industrial ownership and production. The transition was painful, and in 1995 the privatization programme was suspended. Bratislava and Kosîce are the chief industrial cities. Major products include ceramics, machinery and steel. Farming employs 12% of the workforce. Crops include barley and grapes. The economy is slowly improving. **History** Slavic peoples settled in the region in the 5th and 6th centuries AD. In the 9th century the area formed part of the empire of MORAVIA. In the 10th century it was conquered by the MAGYARS, and for nearly 900 years the region was dominated by Hungary. At the end of the 11th century, it was subsumed into the kingdom of Hungary. In the 16th century, the Ottoman empire conquered much of Hungary, and Slovakia was divided between the Turks and the Austrians. From 1541–1784 Bratislava served as the Habsburg capital. The joint rule of MARIA THERESA and JOSEPH II pursued a policy of Magyarization, which increased nationalist sentiment. The AUSTRO-HUNGARIAN EMPIRE was formed in 1867; it continued the suppression of native culture. Many Slovaks fled to the USA. During World War 1, Slovak patriots fought on the side of the Allies. After the defeat of Austro-Hungary (1918), Slovakia was incorporated into CZECHOSLOVAKIA as an autonomous region. The Czechs dominated the union, and many Slovaks became dissatisfied. Following the MUNICH AGREEMENT (1938), part of Slovakia became an independent state, while much of S Slovakia (including Kosîce) was ceded to Hungary. In March 1939 Slovakia gained nominal independence as a German protectorate. In August 1939 Hitler invaded Czechoslovakia. In 1944 Soviet troops liberated Slovakia, and in 1945 it returned to Czechoslovakia. The dramatic collapse of Czech communism in 1989 spurred calls for independence. Elections in 1992 were won by the Movement for a Democratic Slovakia, led by Vladimir Mečiar. The federation was dissolved on 1 January 1993, and the Slovak Republic became a sovereign state, with Mečiar as prime minister. **Politics** Mečiar was re-elected in 1994 elections. The Slovak Republic has maintained close relations with the Czech Republic. In 1996 the Slovak Republic and Hungary ratified a treaty enshrining their respective borders and stipulating basic rights for the 560,000 Hungarians in the Slovak Republic.

Slovenia Mountainous republic in SE Europe; the capital is LJUBLJANA. The Republic of Slovenia was one of the six republics that made up the former YUGOSLAVIA. **Land and Climate** Much of the land is mountainous, rising to 2,863m (9.393ft) at Mount Triglav in the Julian Alps in the NW. Central and E Slovenia contain hills and plains drained by the

SLOVENIA
AREA: 20,251sq km (7,817sq mi)
POPULATION: 1,996,000
CAPITAL (POPULATION): Ljubljana (268,000)
GOVERNMENT: Multiparty republic
ETHNIC GROUPS: Slovene 88%, Croat 3%, Serb 2%, Bosnian 1%
LANGUAGES: Slovene
RELIGIONS: Christianity (mainly Roman Catholic)
CURRENCY: Tolar = 100 stotin

Drava and Sava rivers, while w Slovenia contains the Karst region, an area of limestone landscapes. The coast has a mild Mediterranean climate, but inland the climate is more continental. The mountains are snowcapped in winter and most of Slovenia has cold winters and hot summers. Rain occurs throughout the year. Farmland covers about 35% of the land and forests about 50%. **Economy** The transformation of a centrally planned economy and the fighting in other parts of former Yugoslavia have caused problems for Slovenia. It is an upper-middle-income developing country. Manufacturing is the leading activity. Major manufactures include chemicals, machinery, transport equipment, metal goods and textiles. Agriculture employs 8% of the workforce and fruit, maize, potatoes and wheat are major crops. **History** The ancestors of the Slovenes, the w branch of the South Slavs, settled in the area around 1,400 years ago. For most of the time from the 13th century until 1918, Slovenia was ruled by the Habsburgs. In 1918 Slovenia became part of the Kingdom of the Serbs, Croats and Slovenes, which was renamed Yugoslavia in 1929. During World War 2, Slovenia was invaded and partitioned between Italy, Germany and Hungary, but after the war, Slovenia again became part of Yugoslavia. From the late 1960s, some Slovenes demanded independence, but the central Yugoslav government opposed the break-up of the federation. In 1990, elections were held and a non-communist coalition government was established. Slovenia then declared itself independent, which led to brief fighting between Slovenes and the federal army. The European Community recognized Slovenia's independence in 1992. Further elections were held and a coalition government led by the Liberal Democrats (LDS) was set up in January 1993. In 1996 Slovenia applied to join the European Union (EU). In 1996 legislative elections, no party achieved an overall majority, and a new coalition-government (still led by the LDS) was formed.

slow-worm (blind-worm) European snake-like, legless lizard of grassy areas and woodlands. It is generally brownish; the female has a black underside. It has pointed teeth and feeds primarily on slugs and snails. Length: to 30cm (12in). Family Anguidae; species *Anguis fragilis*.

slug Mostly terrestrial gastropod MOLLUSC, identi-

fied by the lack of shell and uncoiled viscera. It
secretes a protective slime, which aids locomotion.
Length: to 20cm (8in). Class Gastropoda; subclass
Pulmonata; genera *Arion, Limax*. *See also* SEA SLUG

small intestine Part of the DIGESTIVE SYSTEM
that, in humans, extends – about 6m (20ft) coiled
and looped – from the STOMACH to the large INTES-
TINE. Its function is the digestion and absorption of
food. *See also* DUODENUM; ILEUM

smallpox Formerly a highly contagious viral disease characterized by fever, vomiting and skin
eruptions. It remained endemic in many countries
until the World Health Organization (WHO) campaign, launched in the late 1960s; global eradication was achieved by the early 1980s.

smell (olfaction) Sense that responds to airborne
molecules. The olfactory receptors in the nose can
detect even a few molecules per million parts of air.

smelt Small, silvery food fish related to SALMON
and TROUT. It lives in the N Atlantic and Pacific
oceans and in North American inland waters.
Family Osmeridae.

smelting Heat treatment for separating metals
from their ORES. The ore, often with other ingredients, is heated in a furnace to remove non-metallic
constituents. The metal produced is later purified.

Smetana, Bedřich (1824–84) Czech composer.
His masterpiece, *The Bartered Bride* (1866), is
one of the greatest folk operas. Among other popular works by Smetana is the cycle of symphonic
poems *Má Vlast* (My Country, 1874–79), which
includes the *Vltava*.

Smith, Adam (1723–90) Scottish philosopher,
regarded as the founder of modern economics. His
book *The Wealth of Nations* (1776) was influential
in the development of Western capitalist society.
Smith formulated the doctrine of *laissez–faire*: that
governments should not interfere in economic
affairs and that free trade increases wealth.

Smith, Ian Douglas (1919–) Rhodesian statesman, prime minister (1964–78). Smith founded
the Rhodesia Front Party (1961) and sought independence from Britain. In 1965 his white minority
regime issued a unilateral declaration of independence (UDI). By 1980 international sanctions,
combined with guerrilla warfare, had forced his
government to accept free elections. Smith was
defeated by Robert MUGABE's Zimbabwe African
National Union. Smith continued to lead white
opposition to Mugabe.

Smith, John (1938–94) British politician, b.
Scotland. Smith served in James CALLAGHAN's
Labour government and in opposition was chief
spokesman on Treasury and Economic affairs
from 1987. He was elected leader of the Labour
Party in 1992. His sudden death from a heart
attack prompted the election of Tony BLAIR.

Smith, Joseph (1805–44) US religious leader,
founder of the MORMON Church of Jesus Christ of
the Latter Day Saints (1830). His *Book of Mormon*
(1830) was based on sacred writings he claimed

were given to him by a heavenly messenger. In
1844 Smith was jailed for treason at Carthage, Illinois, where he was murdered by a mob.

smooth muscle *See* INVOLUNTARY MUSCLE

smut Group of plant diseases caused by parasitic
fungi that attack many cereals. The diseases are
named after the sooty black masses of reproductive
spores produced by the fungi. *See also* PARASITE

Smuts, Jan Christiaan (1870–1950) South
African statesman. He was a guerrilla commander
during the SOUTH AFRICAN WARS (1899–1902),
but afterwards worked for the union (established
1910). During World War 1, he suppressed a pro-
German revolt, commanded British forces in East
Africa, and became a member of the British war
cabinet. He was South African prime minister in
1919–24 and 1939–48.

Smyrna *See* IZMIR

snail Terrestrial, marine or freshwater gastropod
mollusc. It has a large fleshy foot, antennae on its
head and a coiled protective shell encasing an
asymmetric visceral mass. It may breathe through
gills (aquatic species) or through a kind of air-
breathing lung (terrestrial species), and has a radu-
la – a rasping organ in its mouth. Some species,
such as the Roman snail (*Helix pomatia*), are edible. Length: to 35cm (14in). Class Gastropoda.

snake Any of some 2,700 species of legless, elongated REPTILES forming the suborder Serpentes of
the order Squamata (which also includes LIZARDS).
There are 11 families. They range in length from
about 10cm (4in) to more than 9m (30ft). There are
terrestrial, arboreal (tree-dwelling), semi-aquatic
and aquatic species; one group is entirely marine;
many are poisonous. They have no external ear
openings, eardrums or middle ears; sound vibrations are detected through the ground. Their eyelids
are immovable and their eyes are covered by a
transparent protective cover. The long, forked, pro-
tractile tongue is used to detect odours. Their bodies are covered with scales. Poisonous snakes have
hollow or grooved fangs, through which they inject
venom into their prey. *See also* SNAKEBITE

snakebite Result of an injection of potentially
lethal SNAKE venom into the bloodstream. There
are three types of venomous snake: the Viperidae,
subdivided into true VIPERS and pit vipers, whose
venom causes internal haemorrhage; the Elapidae
(including COBRAS, MAMBAS, kraits), whose venom
paralyzes the nervous system; and the Hydrophi-
dae, Pacific sea snakes with venom that disables
the muscles. Treatment is with anti-venoms.

snapdragon Any of several species of perennial
plants of the genus *Antirrhinum*, with sac-like, two-
lipped, purple or red flowers. The common snapdragon (*A. majus*) is a popular garden plant. Height:
15–91cm (0.5–3ft). Family Scrophulariaceae.

snapper Marine food fish found in tropical
waters of the Indo-Pacific and Atlantic oceans.
Length: to 90cm (3ft); weight: 50kg (110lb). The
250 species include the red snapper (*Lutianus*

campechanus), yellowtail (*Ocyurus chrysurus*) and Atlantic grey *L. griseus*. Family Lutjanidae.

snipe Any of several species of migratory, long-billed, wading shorebirds found in swampy grasslands and coastal areas throughout the world. It is generally mottled brown and buff. Length: 30cm (12in). Family Scolopacidae; genus *Gallinago*.

snooker Game usually for two players, played on a billiards table, using 15 red balls, 6 coloured balls – yellow, green, brown, blue, pink, black – and 1 white cue ball. Each player in turn attempts to knock a red ball into a pocket; if successful, the player may then try to pot a coloured ball; if successful again, the player may go on to another red, and another colour. The turn ends when no ball is potted or when a penalty is incurred. Colours potted are returned to their original positions on the table until all the reds have been potted; the colours are then potted in ascending order of values and remain off the table.

Snow, C.P. (Charles Percy), Baron (1905–80) British novelist, scientist and civil servant. He is especially remembered for his lecture *The Two Cultures and the Scientific Revolution* (1959), which diagnosed a radical divide between scientists and literary intellectuals, and for his 11-volume novel sequence, known collectively as *Strangers and Brothers* (1940–70).

snow Flakes of frozen water that fall from clouds to the Earth's surface. Snowflakes are symmetric (usually hexagonal) crystalline structures.

Snowdon Mountain in Gwynedd, NW Wales. Much of the area is included in the Snowdonia National Park, established in 1951. Snowdon has five peaks, one of which, at 1,085m (3,560ft), is the highest in England and Wales.

snowdrop Low-growing perennial plant of the Mediterranean region, widely cultivated as a garden ornamental. The drooping, green and white, fragrant flowers appear early in spring. The common snowdrop (*Galanthus nivalis*) has narrow leaves; height: to 15cm (6in). Family Amaryllidaceae.

soap Cleansing agent made of salts of fatty acids, used to remove dirt and grease. Common soaps are produced by heating fats and oils with an alkali, such as sodium hydroxide or potassium hydroxide. Soap consists of long-chain molecules, one end of the chain attaches to grease while the other end dissolves in the water, causing the grease to loosen and form a floating scum. *See also* DETERGENT

soccer *See* FOOTBALL, ASSOCIATION

Social and Liberal Democrats (SLDP) Official name of the LIBERAL DEMOCRATS.

social democracy Political ideology concerning the introduction of socialist ideals without an overhaul of the prevailing political system. Before 1914, MARXIST parties of central and eastern Europe termed themselves social democrats. Contemporary social democracy, however, has been invoked by those wishing to distinguish their socialist beliefs from the dogmas of Marxist parties. *See also* CHRIS-TIAN DEMOCRATS; SOCIAL DEMOCRATIC LABOUR PARTY (SDLP); SOCIAL DEMOCRATIC PARTY (SDP)

Social Democratic Labour Party (SDLP) Political party in Northern Ireland that leans towards SOCIALISM. It favours eventual unification of the province with the Republic of Ireland. Founded in 1970, its leader from 1983 was civil rights activist John Hume.

Social Democratic Party (SDP) Political party in England (1981–90), centrist in political outlook. The SDP was formed by the "Gang of Four", (Shirley Williams, David Owen, Roy Jenkins and William Rodgers), a group of disaffected Labour Party ex-ministers. At the general elections of 1983 and 1987, the party joined forces with the Liberal Party to create the Liberal-SDP Alliance. By the second election the two parties were in the process of merging to form the LIBERAL DEMOCRATS.

socialism System of social and economic organization in which the means of production are owned not by private individuals but by the community, in order that all may share more fairly in the wealth produced. Modern socialism dates from the late 18th–early 19th centuries. With the REVOLUTIONS OF 1848, socialism became a significant political doctrine in Europe. Karl MARX, whose *Communist Manifesto* was published in that year, believed that socialism was to be achieved only through the class struggle. Thereafter, a division appeared between the revolutionary socialism of Marx and his followers, later called COMMUNISM or Marxism-Leninism, and more moderate doctrines that held that socialism could be achieved through education and the democratic process. In Russia, the revolutionary tradition culminated in the RUSSIAN REVOLUTION of 1917. From the moderate wing, social-democratic parties, such as the British Labour Party, emerged. They were largely instrumental in mitigating the effects of the market economy in W Europe through political measures.

socialist realism State policy on the arts, promoted by the Soviet Union from the 1930s–80s. It asserted that all the arts should appeal to ordinary workers and should be inspiring and optimistic in spirit. Art that did not fulfil these precepts was effectively banned.

social psychology Field that studies individuals interacting with others in groups and with society. Topics include attitudes and how they change, prejudice, rumours, aggression, altruism, group behaviour, conformity and social conflict

social security Public provision of economic aid to help alleviate poverty and deprivation. In 1909 the UK adopted an old-age pension scheme, and in 1911 LLOYD GEORGE drafted the National Insurance Act to provide health and unemployment insurance. In 1946 the National Insurance Act and the National Health Service Act were passed. In 1948 the National Assistance complemented these, and the WELFARE STATE and the NATIONAL HEALTH SERVICE (NHS) were born.

Social Security, UK Department of UK government department responsible for the payment of universal benefits (such as child benefit), the means-testing of other benefits, and collection of NATIONAL INSURANCE contributions. It also administers the social fund and the legal aid scheme. *See also* SOCIAL SECURITY

social work Community assistance and/or care. Social workers monitor the well-being of families known to have problems, and sometimes have the power to remove children from parents deemed to be dangerously violent or abusive. They may be asked to assist the police in dealing with juvenile suspects. They also help various handicapped, homeless or unemployed people.

Society Islands South Pacific archipelago, part of FRENCH POLYNESIA; the capital is PAPEETE on TAHITI. The archipelago is divided into two groups of volcanic and coral islands. Only eight are inhabited. The larger **Windward** group includes the islands of Tahiti, Moorea, Maio, and the smaller Mehetia and Tetiaroa. The **Leeward** group includes Raiatéa (the largest and site of the chief town, Uturoa), Tahaa, Huahine, Bora-Bora and Maupiti. Tourism is the most important industry. Area: 1,446sq km (558sq mi). Pop. (1992) 165,000.

Society of Jesus *See* JESUITS

sociobiology Study of how genes can influence social behaviour. A basic tenet of biology is that physical characteristics, such as structure and physiology, evolve through natural selection of those traits that are most likely to guarantee an organism's survival. Sociobiologists hold the controversial view that this selection process applies to social behaviours.

sociology Scientific study of society, its institutions and processes. It examines areas such as social change and mobility, and underlying cultural and economic factors. Auguste COMTE invented the term "sociology" in 1843, and since the 19th century numerous complex and sophisticated theories have been expounded by Herbert Spencer, Karl MARX, Emile DURKHEIM, Max WEBER and others.

Socrates (469–399 BC) Greek philosopher, b. Athens, who laid the foundation for an ethical philosophy based on the analysis of human character and motives. The son of a sculptor, he fought in the PELOPONNESIAN WARS. His opposition to the tyranny that took over in Athens after it lost the war, led to his trial on charges of impiety and corrupting the young. Condemned to death, he drank the poisonous draft of hemlock required by law.

soda Any of several SODIUM compounds, especially sodium carbonate (Na_2CO_3). The anhydrous form is known as soda ash; washing soda is hydrated sodium carbonate ($Na_2CO_3,10H_2O$)

sodium Common, silvery-white metallic element (symbol Na), one of the ALKALI METALS, first isolated in 1807. It occurs in the sea as salt (sodium chloride) and in many minerals. Its chief source is sodium chloride, from which it is extracted by

electrolysis. A soft, reactive metal, it is used as a heat-transfer medium in nuclear reactors. Properties: at.no. 11; r.a.m. 22.9898; r.d. 0.97; m.p. 97.81°C (208.05°F); b.p. 882°C (1,620°F).

sodium bicarbonate (sodium hydrogen carbonate, $NaHCO_3$, popularly known as bicarbonate of soda) White, crystalline salt that decomposes in acid or on heating to release carbon dioxide gas. It has a slightly alkaline reaction and is an ingredient of indigestion medicines.

sodium carbonate *See* SODA

sodium chloride Common salt (NaCl). It is the major mineral component of seawater, making up 80% of its dissolved material. Sodium chloride is also the major ELECTROLYTE of living cells, and the loss of too much salt, through evaporation from the skin or through illness, is dangerous. It is used as a seasoning, to cure and preserve foods, and in the chemical industry.

Sofia (Sofija) Capital of Bulgaria and Sofia province, in W central Bulgaria, at the foot of the Vitosha Mountains. The city was founded by the Romans (as Serdica) in the 2nd century AD for its hot mineral springs. It was ruled by the Byzantine Empire (as Triaditsa) from 1018 to 1185. Sofia passed to the second Bulgarian empire (1186–1382), and then to the Ottoman empire (1382–1878). The city was taken by Russia in 1877 and chosen as the capital of Bulgaria by the Congress of Berlin. Industries: steel, machinery, textiles, rubber, chemicals, metallurgy, leather goods, food processing. Pop. (1990) 1,141,142.

softball Game similar to BASEBALL in which a lighter bat, a larger and softer ball, and a smaller field are used. It is played by two teams of nine or ten people. The rules are close to those of baseball except for the pitching delivery (underhand) and the number of innings (seven instead of nine).

software COMPUTER PROGRAM and any associated data file. The term software is used to distinguish these coded instructions and data from computer HARDWARE, or equipment. *See also* CD-ROM; MAGNETIC DISK

soil Surface layer of the Earth, capable of supporting plant life. It consists of undissolved minerals produced by the weathering and breakdown of surface rocks, organic matter, water and gases.

solar cell Device that converts sunlight directly to electricity. It normally consists of a *p*-type (positive) silicon crystal and an *n*-type (negative) one. Light radiation causes electrons to be released and creates a POTENTIAL DIFFERENCE so that current can flow between electrodes connected to the two crystals. The cells are about 10% efficient. Solar cells are often used to power small electronic devices such as calculators. Several thousand cells may be used in panels to provide power of a few hundred watts.

solar energy Heat and light from the Sun consisting of ELECTROMAGNETIC RADIATION, including heat (infrared rays), light and radio waves. About 35% of the energy reaching the Earth is absorbed;

most is spent evaporating moisture into clouds, and some is converted into organic chemical energy by PHOTOSYNTHESIS in plants. All forms of energy (except NUCLEAR ENERGY) come ultimately from the Sun. *See also* SOLAR CELL

solar flare Sudden and violent release of matter and energy from the Sun's surface, usually from the region of an active group of SUNSPOTS. A flare can cause material to be ejected in bulk in the form of prominences. When energetic particles from flares reach the Earth, they may cause radio interference, magnetic storms and more intense aurorae.

Solar System SUN and all the celestial bodies that revolve around it: the nine PLANETS, together with their SATELLITES and ring systems, the thousands of ASTEROIDS and COMETS, meteoroids, and other interplanetary material. The boundaries of the Solar System lie beyond the orbit of Pluto to include the Kuiper Belt and the Oort Cloud of comets.

solar wind Particles accelerated by high temperatures of the solar CORONA to velocities great enough to allow them to escape from the Sun's gravity. The solar wind deflects the tail of the Earth's magnetosphere and the tails of comets away from the Sun.

sole Marine flatfish found in the Atlantic Ocean from NW Africa to Norway, especially *Solea solea*. It is green-grey or black-brown with dark spots. Length: to 60cm (24in). Family Soleidae.

Solemn League and Covenant (September 1643) Agreement between the LONG PARLIAMENT and the Scots during the English CIVIL WAR. In return for Parliament's promise to reorganize the established church on a PRESBYTERIAN basis, the Scots agreed to raise an army in the North of England against CHARLES I. The Scottish help led directly to the Parliamentary victory over the Royalists at MARSTON MOOR.

solid State of MATTER in which a substance has a relatively fixed shape and size. The forces between atoms or molecules are strong enough to hold them in definite locations (about which they vibrate) and to resist compression. *See also* GAS; LIQUID; PLASMA

Solidarity Polish organization that provided the chief opposition to the communist regime during the 1980s. The National Committee of Solidarity was founded in 1980 among shipyard workers in GDAŃSK led by Lech WALESA. Solidarity organized strikes and demanded economic improvements, but soon acquired a political, revolutionary character. Banned from 1981, it re-emerged as a national party, winning the free elections of 1989 and forming the core of the new democratic government.

solid-state physics Physics of SOLID materials. From the study of the structure, binding forces, electrical, magnetic and thermal properties of solids has come the development of the SEMICONDUCTOR, MASER, LASER and SOLAR CELL.

Solomon (d.922BC) King of Israel (*c.*972–922 BC), son of DAVID and Bathsheba. His kingdom prospered, enabling Solomon to build the TEMPLE in Jerusalem. His reputation for wisdom reflected his interest in literature, although the works attributed to him, including the Song of Solomon, were probably written by others.

Solomon Islands Melanesian archipelago and nation in the SW Pacific Ocean, SE of New Guinea, the capital is Honiara (on Guadalcanal). Solomon Islands include several hundred islands scattered over 1,400km (900mi) of the Pacific Ocean. The principal islands are volcanic, mountainous and covered by equatorial rainforest. The largest island is Guadalcanal. The majority of the population are indigenous Melanesians. The main languages are Melanesian dialects, but English is official. The first European discovery of the islands was by the Spanish in 1568. The islands resisted colonization until the late 19th century. In 1893 the S islands became a British protectorate and the N was controlled by the Germans from 1895. In 1942 the S islands were occupied by Japanese troops. After heavy fighting, particularly on Guadalcanal, the islands were liberated by US troops in 1944. In 1976 the Solomons became self-governing and, in 1978, achieved full independence within the Commonwealth. The National Unity, Reconciliation and Progressive Party has been in power since 1994. The coastal plains are used for subsistence farming. Coconuts are the major products, tuna is the biggest export earner and lumber is the main industry. Area: *c.*27,900sq km (10,770sq mi). Pop. (1993) 349,500.

solstice Either of the two days each year when the Sun is at its greatest angular distance from the celestial equator, leading to the longest day and shortest night (summer solstice) in one hemisphere of the Earth, and the shortest day and longest night (winter solstice) in the other hemisphere. In the Northern Hemisphere the summer solstice occurs on about 21 June and the winter solstice on about 22 Dec.

solubility Mass (grams) of a SOLUTE that will saturate 100 grams of SOLVENT under given conditions to give a SATURATED SOLUTION. Solubility generally rises with temperature, but for a few solutes, such as calcium sulphate, increasing temperature decreases solubility in water.

solute Gaseous, liquid or solid substance that is dissolved in a SOLVENT to form a SOLUTION. Many solids dissolve in water. Liquids can dissolve in liquids, and some gases, such as hydrogen chloride (HCl), are soluble in water.

solution Liquid (the SOLVENT) into which another substance (the SOLUTE) is dissolved, or a liquid consisting of two or more chemically distinct compounds, inseparable by filtering. The amount of a solute dissolved in a solvent is called the concentration. *See also* MIXTURE; SATURATED SOLUTION

solvent Liquid that dissolves a substance (the SOLUTE) without changing its composition. Water is the most universal solvent, and many inorganic compounds dissolve in it. Ethanol, ether, acetone and carbon tetrachloride are common solvents for organic substances. *See also* SOLUTION

Solzhenitsyn, Alexander (1918–) Russian novelist. Sentenced to a forced labour camp in 1945 for criticizing Stalin, he was subsequently exiled to Ryazan but was officially rehabilitated in 1956. His novels include *One Day in the Life of Ivan Denisovich* (1962), *The First Circle* (1968), *Cancer Ward* (1968) and *August 1914* (1971). He was awarded the 1970 Nobel Prize for literature. Criticism of the Soviet régime in *The Gulag Archipelago* (1974) led to his forced exile to the West, from which he returned to Russia only in 1994.

Somalia Republic in extreme E Africa, the capital is MOGADISHU. **Land and climate** Somalia occupies part of the E Horn of Africa. A narrow, mostly barren, coastal plain borders the Indian Ocean and the Gulf of Aden. In the interior, the land rises to a plateau, nearly 1,000m (3,300ft) high. In the N is a highland region. The S contains Somalia's only rivers: the Scebeli and the Giuba. Rainfall is light throughout Somalia; the wettest regions are in the far S and N highlands. Drought is a persistent problem. Temperatures on the plateaux and plains regularly reach 32°C (90°F). Much of Somalia is dry grassland or semi-desert. **Economy** Somalia is a low-income developing country, shattered by drought and civil war (1992 GDP, US\$1,1000). Many Somalis are nomadic herdspeople. Live animals, hides and skins are the major exports. Bananas are grown in the S. **History and politics** In the 7th century, Arab traders established coastal settlements and introduced Islam. Mogadishu was founded in *c.*900 as a trading centre. The interest of European imperial powers increased after the opening of the Suez Canal (1869). In 1887 Britain established a protectorate in what is now N Somalia. In 1889 Italy formed a protectorate in the central region, and extended its power to the S by 1905. In 1896 France established a colony in modern-day Djibouti. In 1936 Italian Somaliland was united with the Somali regions of Ethiopia to form Italian East Africa. During World War 2, Italy invaded (1940) British Somaliland. British forces reconquered the region in 1941 and captured Italian Somaliland. In 1950 Italian Somaliland returned to Italy as a UN trust territory. In 1960 both Somalilands gained independence and joined to become the United Republic of Somalia. Somalia was faced with pan-Somali irredentists, calling for the creation

of a "Greater Somalia" to include the Somali-majority areas in Ethiopia, Kenya and Djibouti. The failure of reunification forced a successful military coup, led by Major General Siad Barre. The country became the Somali Democratic Republic. During the 1970s, Somalia and Ethiopia fought for control of the Ogaden Desert, inhabited mainly by Somali nomads. Ethiopia forced Somalia to withdraw in 1978, but internal resistance continued. Drought and civil war led to nearly a million refugees fleeing to Somalia. In 1991 Barre was overthrown and the United Somali Congress (USC), led by General Muhammad Farah Aydid, seized power. Somalia disintegrated into civil war between rival clans. The Somali National Movement gained control of NW Somalia, and declared a separate state of Somaliland Republic. The new state has not gained international recognition. Mogadishu was devastated by an attack from the Somali National Alliance (SNA). Civil war and drought combined to create a devastating famine, which claimed thousands of lives. The UN was slow to provide relief, and when aid arrived was unable to secure distribution. US marines led a task force to secure food distribution, but became embroiled in conflict with Somali warlords. Following the deaths of US troops, US marines withdrew in 1994. Somalia remains without an effective government, subject to factional strife. In January 1997, a National Salvation Council was formed.

Somerset County on the Bristol Channel, SW England. The county is divided into five districts, with the administrative centre at Taunton (1991 pop. 93,969). Other major towns include Yeovil and Bridgewater. The region is low-lying in the centre and is drained by the rivers Avon, Exe and Parrett. Much of the land is given over to agriculture. Dairy farming and fruit growing are important economic activities and the region is noted for Cheddar cheese and cider. Limestone is mined. Area: 3,452sq km (1,332sq mi). Pop. (1991) 460,368.

Somme, Battle of the Major WORLD WAR 1 engagement in N France along the River Somme. It was launched by Douglas HAIG on 1 July 1916. On the first day the British suffered 60,000 casualties in an attempt to break through the German lines. A trench war of attrition continued until the offensive was abandoned on 19 November 1916.

Somoza García, Anastasio (1896–1956) Central figure in Nicaraguan politics from 1936. Somoza created both a dictatorial government and a political dynasty; he was succeeded in office by his two sons. The Somoza dynasty was overthrown by the SANDINISTA in 1979.

sonar (Acronym for **so**und **na**vigation **and ra**nging) Underwater detection and navigation system. It emits high-frequency sound that is reflected by underwater objects and detected on its return.

sonata Musical composition, usually instrumental, in several movements. In the BAROQUE era, sonatas were usually written for two melodic

---

SOMALIA

AREA: 637,660sq km (246,201sq mi)

POPULATION: 9,204,000

CAPITAL (POPULATION): Mogadishu (1,200,000)

GOVERNMENT: Transitional

ETHNIC GROUPS: Somali 98%, Arab 1%

LANGUAGES: Somali and Arabic (both official), English, Italian

RELIGIONS: Islam 99%

CURRENCY: Somali shilling = 100 cents

parts, a bass part and a continuo. In the CLASSICAL period, the sonata became a more clearly defined form for one or two instruments. The first movement of a sonata is usually in sonata form, a widely used MUSICAL FORM. The second movement is generally slow in tempo and the third and perhaps fourth movements faster (allegro or presto).

Sondheim, Stephen (1930–) US composer and lyricist. Sondheim made his mark on Broadway in 1957 with the lyrics for *West Side Story*. His first success as a lyricist-composer was in 1962 with *A Funny Thing Happened on the Way to the Forum*. His reputation was enhanced with works such as *A Little Night Music* (1972), *Sunday in the Park with George* (1984) and *Assassin* (1991).

Songhai West African empire, founded *c.* AD 700. In 1468 Sonni Ali captured the market city of Timbuktu and the Songhai empire acquired control of most of the trade in w Africa. Sonni was succeeded by Askia Muhammad I, who further increased their stranglehold on trade routes. The empire began to disintegrate on because of factional in-fighting.

sonnet Poem of 14 lines, often in iambic pentameter and usually employing Petrarchan or Shakespearean rhyme schemes. The Petrarchan consists of an octet and a sextet, usually with an *abbaab-bacdecde* rhyme scheme. The Shakespearean, having a final rhyming couplet, is *ababcdcdefefgg*.

Sophia (1630–1714) Electress of Hanover. A granddaughter of JAMES I and the widow of the elector of Hanover, she was recognized as heir to the English throne by the Act of SETTLEMENT (1701), to ensure a Protestant succession and prevent the return of the Catholic Stuarts. When she died, her son became king as GEORGE I.

Sophists Professional Greek teachers of the 5th–4th centuries BC. Although not a formal school, they emphasized the intellectual and rhetorical skills needed to succeed in ancient Greek society, and regarded law and ethics as convenient human inventions with no basis in natural law. Serious philosophers, such as PLATO, disapproved of them.

Sophocles (496–406 BC) Greek playwright. Of his 100 plays, only seven tragedies and part of a Satyr play remain. These include *Ajax*, *Antigone* (*c.*442–441 BC), *Electra* (409 BC), *Oedipus Rex* (*c.*429 BC) and *Oedipus at Colonus*.

soprano Highest singing range of the human voice. The normal range may be given as two octaves upwards from middle C, although exceptional voices may reach notes considerably higher. Sopranos have always been important in opera, with various types of soprano (dramatic, lyric or coloratura) taking different types of roles.

sorghum Tropical cereal grass native to Africa and cultivated worldwide. Varieties that are raised for grain, such as *Sorghum vulgare*, have leaves coated with white waxy blooms and flower heads that bear up to 3,000 seeds. They yield meal, oil, starch and dextrose (a sugar). Height: 0.5–2.5m (2–8ft). Family Poaceae/Gramineae.

sorrel (dock) Herbaceous perennial plant native to temperate regions. It has large leaves that can be cooked as a vegetable and small green or brown flowers. Height: to 2m (6ft). Family Polygonaceae; genus *Rumex*, especially *Rumex acetosa*.

Sotho Major cultural and linguistic group of s Africa. It includes the Northern Sotho of TRANSVAAL, South Africa, the Western Sotho (better known as the Tswana) of BOTSWANA, and the Southern Sotho (Basotho or Basuto) of LESOTHO.

Soto, Hernando de *See* DE SOTO, HERNANDO

soul music Form of popular music. The term designates black music that developed in the 1960s from rhythm and blues. Soul is also used generically to describe music that possesses a certain "soulful" quality. Its influence has extended into many popular musical styles.

sound Physiological sensation perceived by the brain via the EAR, caused by an oscillating source, and transmitted through a material medium as a sound wave. The velocity at which a sound wave travels through a medium depends on the ELASTICITY of the medium and its density. If the medium is a gas, the sound wave is longitudinal and its velocity depends on the gas temperature. The velocity of sound in dry air at standard temperature and pressure (STP) is 331m/sec (741mph) and depends on the height above sea level. Pure sounds are characterized by PITCH, TIMBRE and intensity (the rate of flow of sound energy).

sound barrier Name for the cause of an aircraft's difficulties in accelerating to a speed faster than that of sound. When approaching the speed of sound, an aircraft experiences a sudden increase in drag and loss of lift, caused by the build-up of sound waves to form shock waves at the front and back of the aircraft. The problems were solved by designing aircraft with smaller surface area, swept-back wings and more powerful engines.

Sousa, John Philip (1854–1932) US composer and bandmaster. He composed about 100 marches, including *Semper Fidelis* (1888) and *The Stars and Stripes Forever* (1896).

sousaphone Largest BRASS musical instrument of the TUBA family. It was introduced by John SOUSA to fortify the bass section of US military bands.

South Africa Republic in s Africa; the legislative capital is CAPE TOWN, the administrative capital is PRETORIA. **Land and climate** South Africa is the southernmost African country. A narrow coastal margin includes: the Indian Ocean port of DURBAN; the dry s tablelands, Little and Great Karoo; CAPE TOWN on the CAPE OF GOOD HOPE; and part of the NAMIB DESERT. The interior forms part of the African plateau. The plateau rises in the E to an escarpment over 2,000m (6,000ft) high, on the fringe of which lies BLOEMFONTEIN. SOWETO, JOHANNESBURG and Pretoria all lie on the N of the escarpment. In the N, lies part of the KALAHARI Desert. In the NE, are the WITWATERSRAND goldfields. KIMBERLEY has the largest diamond mines.

The longest river is the ORANGE. Most of South Africa is subtropical. The SW has a Mediterranean climate. Much of the plateau is arid. Grassland covers much of the high interior, with tropical savanna in lower areas. Forest and woodland cover only 3% of the land. **Economy** Mining forms the base of Africa's most industrialized economy. South Africa is the world's leading producer of gold, and fifth-largest producer of diamonds. Chromite, coal, copper, iron ore, manganese, platinum, silver and uranium are also mined. Sanctions, falling gold price, civil and industrial strife created prolonged recession. Unemployment stands at 45% (1995). Major manufactures include chemicals, iron and steel. Agriculture employs over 33% of the workforce. Major products include fruits, grapes for winegrowing, maize, meat and sugar cane. **History and politics** The indigenous people of South Africa are the SAN. The first European settlement was not until 1652, when the Dutch EAST INDIA COMPANY founded a colony at Table Bay. Dutch AFRIKANERS (Boers) established farms, employing slaves. From the late 18th century, conflict with the XHOSA intensified, as the Boers trekked inland. In the early 19th century, Britain gained control of the Cape. Following Britain's abolition of slavery in 1833, the Boers began the GREAT TREK. They met with fierce resistance, particularly from the ZULU kingdom. The Boer republics of TRANSVAAL and Orange FREE STATE were established in 1852 and 1854. The discovery of diamonds and gold in the 1870s and 1880s increased the pace of colonization, and Britain sought to gain control of Boer- and Zulu-held areas. The British defeated the Zulu in the ZULU WAR (1879), and Zululand was annexed to Natal (1897). In 1890 Cecil RHODES became governor of Cape Colony. Britain defeated the Boers in the SOUTH AFRICAN WARS (1880–81, 1899–1902). The Union of South Africa was formed in 1910, with Louis BOTHA as prime minister. In 1912 the AFRICAN NATIONAL CONGRESS (ANC) was founded. During World War 1, South Africa captured NAMIBIA (1915), and after the war it was mandated to the Union. In 1919 Jan SMUTS succeeded Botha as prime minister. In 1931 Smuts' successor and Nationalist Party founder (1914), James HERTZOG, realized Afrikaner ambitions as South Africa achieved full independence within the Commonwealth of Nations. Smuts regained power in 1939, and South Africa joined the Allies in World War 2. The Nationalist Party won the 1948 election, advocating a policy of APARTHEID. The ANC began a campaign of non-violent resistance, but after the Sharpeville massacre (1960), Nelson MANDELA formed a military wing. In 1961, faced by international condemnation, Nationalist prime minister Verwoerd established South Africa as a republic. In 1964 Mandela was jailed. Verwoerd was assassinated in 1966, and was succeeded by VORSTER. Vorster involved South African forces in attempts to prevent black majority rule in South Africa's neighbouring states. The crushing of the 1976 Soweto uprising marked a new wave of opposition. In 1977 Steve Biko died in police custody. In 1978 P.W. BOTHA was elected prime minister. During the 1970s, four bantustans (homelands) gained nominal independence. External economic sanctions forced Botha into reform. In 1984 a new constitution gave Indian and Coloured minorities some parliamentary representation; black Africans were still excluded. From 1985–90, South Africa was in a state of emergency. Archbishop Desmond TUTU called for further sanctions. In 1989 President F. W. DE KLERK began the process of dismantling apartheid. In 1990 Mandela was released and reassumed leadership of a newly legalized ANC. Clashes continued between the ANC and Chief BUTHELEZI's Zulu Inkatha movement. In 1994 the ANC won South Africa's first multi-racial elections, and Mandela became president. De Klerk remained as vice president in a coalition government until 1996. The homelands were reintegrated, and South Africa was divided into nine provinces. In 1995 a Truth and Reconciliation Commission was set up to investigate political crimes committed under the apartheid system.

South African Wars Two wars between the Afrikaners (Boers) and the British in South Africa. The first (1880–81) arose from the British annexation of the Transvaal in 1877. Under Paul KRUGER, the Transvaal regained autonomy, but further disputes, arising largely from the discovery of gold and diamonds, provoked the second, greater conflict (1899–1902), known to Afrikaners as the Second War of Freedom and to the British as the Boer War. It was also a civil war between whites; black Africans played little part on either side. In 1900 the British gained the upper hand, defeating the Boer armies and capturing Bloemfontein and Pretoria. Boer commandos fought a determined guerrilla campaign but were forced to accept British rule in the peace treaty signed at Vereeniging (1902).

South America Fourth-largest continent, the southern of the two continents of America, in the Western Hemisphere, connected to North America

SOUTH AFRICA
AREA: 1,219,916sq km (470,566sq mi)
POPULATION: 39,790,000
CAPITAL (POPULATION): Cape Town (legislative, 2,350,157); Pretoria (administrative, 1,080,187); Bloemfontein (judicial, 300,150)
GOVERNMENT: Multiparty republic
ETHNIC GROUPS: Black 76%, White 13%, Coloured 9%, Asian 2%
LANGUAGES: Afrikaans, English, Ndebele, North Sotho, South Sotho, Swazi, Tsonga, Tswana, Venda, Xhosa, Zulu (all official)
RELIGIONS: Christianity 68%, Hinduism 1%, Islam 1%
CURRENCY: Rand = 100 cents

by the isthmus of PANAMA. **Land** Off the N coast lies the Caribbean Sea, off the E the Atlantic Ocean, and the W the Pacific Ocean. It is politically divided into 12 independent nations: BRAZIL and ARGENTINA (the two largest), BOLIVIA, CHILE, COLOMBIA, ECUADOR, GUYANA, PARAGUAY, PERU, SURINAM, URUGUAY and VENEZUELA, plus the French overseas département of FRENCH GUIANA. It is c.7,640km (4,750mi) long (Punta Gallinas, Colombia to Cape Horn, Chile), and at its widest (near the Equator) c.5,300km (3,000mi). **Structure and geology** South America's W edge towers above the rest of the continent, which slopes downwards towards the Atlantic Ocean, except for the Guiana and Brazilian Highlands. These form the continental shield. The middle of the continent is marked by a series of lowlands. The ANDES, which stretch from Colombia to Chile, contain the highest peaks of the Americas, and Aconcagua (Argentina) is the tallest mountain outside Asia, at 6,960m (22,834ft). The ATACAMA DESERT, a coastal strip in N Chile, is the driest place on Earth. PATAGONIA is a semi-arid plateau. **Lakes and rivers.** Excluding Lake MARACAIBO (13,512sq km/5,217sq mi) as an extension of the Gulf of Venezuela, the largest lake in South America is Lake TITICACA, on the Peru-Bolivia border, covering 8,290sq km (3,200sq mi). Lengthy rivers combine to form three major systems that reach the Atlantic. At 6,430km (3,990mi) the AMAZON is the world's second-longest river (after the Nile). With its many substantial tributaries, it drains by far the biggest of the world's river basins. Flowing S is the PARAGUAY-PARANÁ system and NE is the ORINOCO. **Climate and vegetation** Except in the mountains and the S, the climate remains generally warm and humid. Much of the N supports tropical RAINFOREST, while lowlands in the extreme N and the central region have a cover of tropical grass. The Pampas, S of the Tropic of CAPRICORN, produce temperate grasslands, but vegetation is scarce to the far SE of the mountains. In the S, pine and other temperate forests grow along the W coast. **People** Some Incas (QUECHUAS) still remain in the Andes, as do some Mapucho (Araucanians) of Chile. But the majority of the population is mestizo (of dual Indian and European descent), except in Argentina, S Brazil, Chile and Uruguay, whose population is primarily European. Latin American Spanish and Portuguese are the dominant continental languages and Roman Catholicism is the major religion. **Economy** About 30% of the workforce are employed in subsistence farming, working 15% of the land, most of which is owned by Europeans. Chief exports include cash-crops such as coffee, bananas, sugarcane and tobacco. The drugs industry is also important: Peru and Colombia are major cultivators of coca leaves, and Colombia supplies over 50% of the world's illegal trade in cocaine. Industrial development and mineral exploitation have been dominated by Europe and the USA. Since 1945 South American countries have sought greater economic independence, yet reliance on banking finance has often led to a burden of debt. Another drawback has been the scarcity of continental coal reserves and the dependence on petroleum, especially in Venezuela's MARACAIBO region. The Guiana and Brazilian Highlands have large deposits of iron ore and the Andes range has many copper reserves. Bolivia has large tin mines, and Brazil reserves of manganese. However, despite the industrialization of some countries, particulary Brazil, Venezuela and Argentina, most countries remain industrially underdeveloped. During the 1970s and 1980s, the rush for economic growth and industrialization was often at the expense of the continent's rainforests. Worldwide treaties in the 1990s have attempted to slow down the deforestation, but with little success. Industrialization has also often been seen to exacerbate the continent's high inflation and huge debt crises. **Recent history** The early 1900s saw a number of conflicts within and between countries of the region. Notable among these were the territorial Chaco Wars (1928–30, 1932–35) between Bolivia and Paraguay. South American republics failed to become world powers until the end of World War 2, helped by the formation of the United Nations in 1945 and the ORGANIZATION OF AMERICAN STATES (OAS) in 1948, which gave them influence in international affairs. Many countries of South America have swung between military dictatorships and democratic governments, mainly caused by wildly fluctuating economic fortunes, which in turn have brought about extremes of wealth and poverty, leading to unrest and instability. During the 1980s and 1990s, international pressure, particularly from the USA, has also been brought to bear on those governments, notably Bolivia and Colombia, who are either unwilling or unable to control the production and export of vast quantities of cocaine. Total area: c.17,793,000sq km (6,868,000sq mi); *Highest mountain* Aconcagua 6,960m (22,834ft) *Longest river* Amazon 6,430km (3,990mi) *Population* 299,000.000 *Largest cities* São Paulo 16,567,317; Buenos Aires 11,652,050; Rio de Janeiro 5,336,179

Southampton Port and county district in Hampshire, S England. At the head of Southampton Water and a port since Roman times, the city is Britain's principal passenger port and a major commercial port. Industries: shipbuilding, engineering, oil refining. Pop. (1994) 214,000.

South Australia State in S central Australia, on the Great Australian Bight. The capital is ADELAIDE, home to 60% of the state's population. Other major cities include Salisbury and Elizabeth. The S coast of Australia was visited by the Dutch in 1627, the first English colonists arrived in 1836, and the region was federated as a state in 1901. The area is hilly in the E (Flinders Ranges) and the N (Musgrave Ranges), and in the W are the E parts of the Great Victoria Desert and the Nullarbor Plain. The MURRAY in the SE is the only important river, and farming is mainly confined to this area. Barley, oats, wheat, rye and grapes are the chief crops, and livestock are grazed in the N. Mineral deposits include iron ore, uranium, silver, lead, salt, gypsum, opals, coal and natural gas. Industries: heavy metals, transport equipment. Whyalla has the largest shipyards in Australia. Area: 984,380sq km (379,760sq mi). Pop. (1994) 1,471,000.

South Carolina State on the Atlantic Ocean, SE USA; the capital and largest city is COLUMBIA. The main port is Charleston. The land rises from the coastal plain to the rolling hills of the Piedmont plateau to the Blue Ridge Mountains in the NW. The region is drained by many rivers including the Savannah. From 1633 the English were the first to settle the area permanently. South Carolina became a royal province in 1729, and a plantation society evolved based on rice, indigo and cotton. Major crops include tobacco, soya beans, maize, sweet potatoes and groundnuts. Timber and fishing are still sources of employment, but tourism is now the state's second-biggest source of income after textiles and clothing. Area: 80,432sq km (31,055sq mi). Pop. (1992) 3,602,854.

South China Sea Part of the Pacific Ocean, surrounded by SE China, Indochina, the MALAY PENINSULA, Borneo, the Philippines and Taiwan; connected to the East China Sea by the Formosa Strait. The world's largest "sea", its chief arms are the Gulf of Tonkin and Gulf of Thailand. The Si, Red, Mekong and Chao Phraya rivers flow into it. Area: 2,300,000sq km (848,000sq mi). Average depth: 1,140m (3,740ft).

South Dakota State in N central USA, on the GREAT PLAINS. The capital is PIERRE; the largest cities are Sioux Falls and Rapid City. The land rises gradually from the E to the Black Hills (featuring MOUNT RUSHMORE) in the W and the Badlands in the SW, with the Missouri River bisecting the state. West of the river is semi-arid plain, inhabited mainly by Native Americans, and large cattle and sheep ranches. East of the Missouri, livestock rearing is important and wheat, maize, oats, soya beans and flax are also grown. Meatpacking and food processing are the most important industries. South Dakota is the largest producer of gold in the USA, but tin, beryllium, stone, sand and gravel are also mined. French trappers claimed the region for France in the 1740, and the USA acquired part of the land in the LOUISIANA PURCHASE of 1803. Trading and military posts were the only settlements until the 1850s. Dakota Territory was formed in 1861, and the discovery of gold in the Black Hills in 1874 led to an increase in population and the territory was divided into the states of North and South Dakota Area: 199,551sq km (77,047sq mi). Pop. (1992) 708,411.

Southeast Asia Region bounded by India, China and the Pacific Ocean, and comprising BURMA, THAILAND, MALAYSIA, CAMBODIA, LAOS, VIETNAM, PHILIPPINES, SINGAPORE and INDONESIA. Area: approx. 4,506,600sq km (1,740,000sq mi).

Southeast Asia Treaty Organization (SEATO) Regional defence agreement signed by Australia, New Zealand, France, Pakistan, the Philippines, Thailand, Britain and the USA in Manila in 1954. It was formed in response to communist expansion in Southeast Asia. With administrative headquarters in Bangkok, SEATO had no standing forces. Some members were unwilling to support the USA in the VIETNAM WAR, and SEATO was abandoned in 1977. The nonmilitary aspects of the treaty were replaced by the ASSOCIATION OF SOUTHEAST ASIAN NATIONS (ASEAN).

Southey, Robert (1774–1843) British poet and prose writer, poet laureate (1813–43). His long epic poems include *Thalaba the Destroyer* (1801), *Madoc* (1805) and *Roderick the Last of the Goths* (1814).

South Georgia Island in the S Atlantic Ocean, about 1,750km (1,100mi) E of Tierra del Fuego. Mountainous and barren, it rises to 2,934m (9,626ft). A British dependency administered from the Falklands, the island has a research station and garrison but no permanent population.

South Glamorgan County on the Bristol Channel, S Wales. The capital is CARDIFF. The county is divided into two districts, Cardiff and the Vale of Glamorgan. The Vale of Glamorgan is fertile agricultural land. Cardiff is an industrial district. Industries: engineering, steel. Area: 416sq km (161sq mi). Pop. (1991) 383,000.

South Island Larger of the two principal islands that comprise NEW ZEALAND. Its chief cities are CHRISTCHURCH, Dunedin and Invercarguill. The Southern Alps separate the thickly forested W coast from the Canterbury Plains in the E. Cereal growing, sheep and cattle rearing, and dairying are important on the Plains, and tourism is a valuable source of income in most parts. Area: 150,461sq km (58,093sq mi). Pop. (1991) 881,540.

South Pole Southernmost geographical point on the Earth's surface. The magnetic south pole is located c.2,400km (1,500mi) from the geographical South Pole. It lies 2,992m (9,816ft) above sea level, c.480km (300mi) S of the Ross Ice Shelf.

South Sea Bubble (1720) Speculation in the shares of the English South Sea Company ending in financial collapse. The South Sea Company was founded in 1711 for trade in the Pacific. Shares sold so well and interest was so high that in 1720 the company volunteered to finance the national debt. The result was intensive speculation with a 900% rise in the price of shares, until the bubble burst in September 1720, bankrupting investors and closing banks. Credit for saving the company and the government was given to Robert WALPOLE.

South West Africa *See* NAMIBIA
South West Africa People's Organization (SWAPO) Political organization, formed in 1960 in South West Africa (now NAMIBIA). Swapo's aim was to achieve independence for Namibia and to this end declared itself at war with South Africa.

Soon after ANGOLA gained independence in 1975, SWAPO established guerrilla bases there. In 1978 these bases were attacked by South Africa. Truce talks in Geneva in 1981 failed, and in 1984 SWAPO refused to cooperate with the rival Multi-Party Conference (MCP) in drawing up a timetable for independence. When independence was achieved, SWAPO fought a general election in 1989 and gained 57% of the votes and 75% of the seats in the constituent assembly. In 1990 SWAPO leader Sam NUJOMA became president.

South Yorkshire Metropolitan county in N central England. The county is divided into four districts, with Barnsley its administrative centre. South Yorkshire's only city is SHEFFIELD, but other other major towns include Doncaster and Rotherham. The area includes the PEAK DISTRICT National Forest and the western Pennine moors. The River Don flows E across the county. Following the Industrial Revolution, the county's prosperity depended on its heavy industry, and its major industries still include iron, steel and coal mining. Area: 1,561sq km (603sq mi). Pop. (1991) 1,249,300.

Soviet Union (officially, Union of Soviet Socialist Republics) Former federal republic, successor to the Russian empire and the world's first communist state. The Soviet Union was formed on 30 December 1922 and, when dissolved on 31 December 1991, was the largest country in the world. The BOLSHEVIK regime led by LENIN, came to power in the 1917 RUSSIAN REVOLUTION. Lenin's government survived civil war and famine (1918–22) by instituting a centralized command economy. In 1921 the New Economic Policy (NEP) marked a return to a mixed economy. In 1922 a treaty of union was signed by the republics of RUSSIA, UKRAINE, Belorussia and Transcaucasia. In 1923 a new constitution was adopted establishing the supremacy of the COMMUNIST PARTY OF THE SOVIET UNION (CPSU) and the Supreme Soviet as the highest legislative body. Lenin died in January 1924 and a power struggle ensued between TROTSKY and STALIN. Stalin emerged the victor and Trotsky was expelled in 1927. In 1928 the first Five-Year Plan was adopted. It transformed Soviet agriculture and industry. Collective and state farms were imposed on the peasantry, and industrialization was accelerated. The urban population rapidly doubled. The collectivization schemes directly led to the 1932–34 Ukraine famine, which claimed over seven million lives. State control infiltrated all areas of society, and was sometimes brutally imposed by the secret police. The systems of state control led to the creation of a massive bureaucratic administration. The murder of Sergei Kirov in 1934 led to the Stalinist purges and the wave of terror in 1936–38. Supposed dissidents within the government, party and army were sentenced to death or sent to the Siberian gulags. The purges also targeted Soviet Jews and ethnic groups. In 1936 Transcaucasia was divided into the republics of GEORGIA, ARMENIA and AZER-BAIJAN. In August 1939 Stalin concluded a non aggression pact with Hitler. Germany and the USSR invaded Poland and divided up the country In 1940 Soviet expansion incorporated the Baltic states of LITHUANIA, LATVIA and ESTONIA into the Union. A costly war with Finland led to the formation of the Karelo-Finnish republic. On 22 June 1941 Germany invaded Russia. The 1943 failure of the siege of Stalingrad led to the surrender of 330,000 Axis troops, and was a decisive turning-point in WORLD WAR 2. The Red Army launched a counter-offensive that liberated much of E Europe. World War 2 devastated the Soviet Union. It is estimated that 25 million Soviet lives were lost.

The Soviet Union and the USA emerged as the two post-war superpowers. Their antagonistic ideologies and ambitions led to the COLD WAR. Not only had Soviet territory increased, but its European sphere of influence extended into Albania, Bulgaria, Czechoslovakia, East Germany, Hungary, Poland and Romania. In 1948 the Soviet army attempted to blockade the western sectors of BERLIN. In 1949, when NATO was formed, the Soviet Union exploded its first atomic bomb. In March 1953 Stalin died and a collective leadership was installed. In 1955 the WARSAW PACT was established as the Communist counterpart to NATO. In 1956, at the 20th CPSU Congress, KHRUSHCHEV made his famous secret speech denouncing Stalin as a dictator. In October 1956 a Hungarian uprising against Moscow domination was crushed by Soviet troops. In 1958 Khrushchev won the battle for succession. He began a policy of liberalization. Economic decentralization entailed a reduction in the bloated bureaucracy. Huge areas of "virgin land" were opened to grain cultivation in order to prevent further famine. New alliances were formed with worldwide anti-colonial movements, and Khrushchev formulated a policy of peaceful coexistence with the West. The Cold War shifted into a technological battle to produce more powerful weapons of mass destruction and a Space Race. In 1957 the Soviet Union launched *Sputnik 1*, the world's first artificial satellite and, in 1961, Yuri GAGARIN became the first man in space. Also in 1961 the Berlin Wall was built to divide East from West Berlin, and Khrushchev went further in his attacks on the Stalin regime. In 1962 the CUBAN MISSILE CRISIS shattered the Cold War stand-off and the world stood at the brink of nuclear war. Khrushchev agreed to remove Soviet missiles and catastrophe was avoided. In October 1964 Khrushchev was removed from office by a conservative collective leadership headed by BREZHNEV and KOSYGIN. They were determined to reverse his liberal reforms and improve the Soviet economy. Brezhnev ruled by consensus and brought close political associates such as ANDROPOV (KGB chief) and GROMYKO (Foreign Minister) into his politburo. Brezhnev instituted cautious economic reforms and agricultural production increased dramatically. In foreign affairs, the "Brezhnev doctrine" preserved the right of the Soviet Union to intervene in Communist states to preserve international communism. On 21 August 1968 the doctrine was invoked to stem the liberalization of Czechoslovakia and Warsaw Pact troops invaded to crush the "Prague Spring". Internal dissent was not tolerated. Leading dissident scientists and intellectuals, such as SOLZHENITSYN and SAKHAROV, were sent to prison or forced into exile. Many Soviet Jews emigrated in the early 1970s. The Cold War created a series of indirect conflicts between the USA and the USSR in Asia and Africa.

In 1969 an era of superpower détente began with a series of STRATEGIC ARMS LIMITATION TALKS (SALT) resulting in the signing of SALT I by Brezhnev and Nixon in 1972. In 1975 the Helsinki Accords recognized the post-war European borders. In 1977 Brezhnev was elected president and a new constitution was formed. In 1979 SALT II was signed but the Soviet invasion of Afghanistan ended the period of détente and the treaty was never ratified by the USA. In 1980 the USA led a boycott of the Moscow Olympics and the USA placed new, intermediate range Pershing II missiles on European soil. The Soviet economy stagnated with the stabilization of oil prices and its outdated manufacturing technology. Brezhnev died in 1982 and Andropov was elected leader. He began a series of far-reaching economic reforms targeting centralization, corruption, inefficiency and alcoholism. He promoted a series of advisors, including GORBACHEV, to implement the reforms. His tenure was short, he died after a mere 15 months in office. He was replaced by a hardline Brezhnevite, Konstantin Chernenko. Chernenko died 13 months later and, in March 1985, Mikhail Gorbachev became CPSU General Secretary.

Gorbachev began a process of economic restructuring (PERESTROIKA) and political openness (GLASNOST). The 1986 CHERNOBYL disaster provided the first test of glasnost. Dissidents were released and restraints on emigration were lifted. Gorbachev began a new détente initiative, focusing on nuclear DISARMAMENT. A series of meetings with Ronald Reagan led to the Intermediate Nuclear Forces (INF) Treaty, which agreed to scrap intermediate-range nuclear missiles. The Soviet Union agreed to halt the disastrous war in Afghanistan and all its troops withdrew by February 1989. Perestroika continued the process begun by Andropov by reducing bureaucracy and allowing a more mixed economy. The restructuring was hampered by opposition from conservatives (anxious to prevent change) and radicals led by Boris YELTSIN, urging more far-reaching policies. In 1988 Gorbachev convened a conference of the CPSU (the first since 1941) at which parliamentary elections were approved. In March 1989 the first pluralist elections since 1917 were held, and Gorbachev was elected state president. The tide of reform swept over Eastern Europe, by the close of 1989 every communist leader in the Warsaw Pact had been overthrown. The constituent republics of the Soviet Union began to clamour for secession. In 1989 Gorbachev and Bush declared an end to the Cold War and the West promised economic support to the Soviet Union.

In 1990 the political and economic situation worsened. The Baltic republics, KAZAKSTAN and GEORGIA demanded independence and ARMENIA and AZERBAIJAN fought for control of NAGORNO-KARABAKH. In March 1990, the newly elected Soviet parliament authorized the private ownership of the means of production. The central economic principle of Marxism was removed and the CPSU fractured. Boris Yeltsin resigned his membership. Amid the breakdown in federal government structures, the economy declined by 4%. In December 1990 Gorbachev gained emergency presidential powers and the conservatives demanded action to prevent the disintegration of the Union of Soviets. Paratroopers were sent to LATVIA and LITHUANIA to prevent secession. Miners went on strike, calling for Gorbachev's resignation. SHEVARDNADZE resigned and went on to form the Democratic Reform Movement. In June 1991 a new Union Treaty was drafted which devolved power to the republics and reconstituted the federal government. It was approved by nine republics, but Armenia, the Baltic states, Georgia and MOLDOVA refused to cooperate. Also in June 1991, Boris Yeltsin was elected president of the Russian republic. In July 1991 Gorbachev attended the Group of Seven (G7) summit and signed the Strategic Arms Reduction Treaty (START), reducing the number of long-range missiles. On 18 August 1991 a coup was launched against Gorbachev by hardliners. Gorbachev was kept under house arrest, while the coup leaders assumed control of the media and sent tanks into Moscow to capture the Russian parliament and Boris Yeltsin. The coup failed and Gorbachev was reinstated on 22 August 1991. The republics seized the opportunity to declare independence from federal control. Yeltsin emerged as the new political power-broker. He banned the CPSU and seized its assets, took control of the Russian armed forces and forced Gorbachev to suspend the Russian Communist Party. Gorbachev resigned as General Secretary of the CPSU.

In September 1991 the Baltic States of ESTONIA, Latvia and Lithuania were formally granted independence. On 8 December 1991 Russia, UKRAINE and BELARUS formed the COMMONWEALTH OF INDEPENDENT STATES (CIS). By the end of December, the republics of Armenia, Azerbaijan, Kazakstan, KYRGYZSTAN, Moldova, TAJIKISTAN, TURKMENISTAN and UZBEKISTAN had all joined the CIS. On 25 December 1991 Gorbachev resigned as president of the USSR and, on 31 December, the Soviet Union was officially dissolved.

Soweto (South-West Township) Group of black townships of more than a million people on the outskirts of JOHANNESBURG, South Africa. Soweto attracted international attention in June 1976, when a student demonstation against the compulsory teaching of Afrikaans in Bantu schools sparked a series of riots against the APARTHEID regime. The police brutally suppressed the disturbances, killing 618 people. Comprising mostly sub-standard government housing, it remained a focus of protest. Pop. (1991) 597,000.

soya bean Annual plant native to China and Japan. It has oval, three-part leaves and small lilac flowers. Grown internationally for food, forage, green manure and oil, its seed is an important source of PROTEIN. Height 60cm (24in). Family Fabaceae/Leguminosae; species *Glycine max*.

space Open expanse between matter. RELATIVITY states that space and time are aspects of one thing. More usually, space is taken to mean the Universe beyond the Earth's atmosphere, the vast region in which the density of matter is low.

space exploration Using spacecraft to investigate outer space and heavenly bodies. *Sputnik 1*, launched into Earth orbit by the Soviet Union on 4 October 1957, was the first artificial satellite. Soviet cosmonauts, and their American equivalents, astronauts, orbited the Earth soon after. Unmanned space probes crash-landed on the Moon, sending back pictures to Earth during the descent. Then came soft landings, and probes made to orbit the Moon showed its hidden side for the first time. By 1968 Soviet space scientists had developed techniques for returning a Moon orbiter safely to the Earth. The Americans, in 1969, were first to land men on the Moon and return them safely to the Earth. By that time, probes had already been to Venus and Mars. Recent events: Clementine probe (1994) thought to have discovered water-ice deposits in craters of the Moon; SOHO (launched 1995) to probe Sun's interior; Mars Pathfinder (1997) deployed a six-wheel rover to explore Mars' surface; Cassini space probe (1997) launched towards Saturn on a journey that will take seven years.

space shuttle Re-usable, rocket-powered US spacecraft. The main part of the shuttle, called the **orbiter** (of which four were built, *Columbia, Challenger, Discovery* and *Atlantis*), looks like a bulky jet aircraft with swept-back wings. It takes off attached to a large fuel tank, using its own three rocket engines, assisted by two booster rockets. The boosters are jettisoned about two minutes after launch and are later recovered. Six minutes later, the external fuel tank is dumped. Manoeuvring engines then put the craft into the required orbit. When it is time to return to Earth, these engines provide reverse thrust. As a result, the craft slows down and descends into the atmosphere. It glides down and lands on a runway. The first shuttle, *Columbia*, was launched on 12 April 1981.

space station Orbiting structure in space for use by astronauts and scientists. Space laboratories, such as *Skylab* and *Mir*, are space stations built for

scientists to carry out a variety of experiments, study the Solar System and observe distant parts of the Universe. They are capable of supporting astronauts for many months.

space-time In the RELATIVITY theory, central concept that unifies the three space dimensions with time to form a four-dimensional frame of reference. In 1907 the German mathematician Hermann Minkowski explained relativity theory by extending three-dimensional geometry to four dimensions. A line drawn in this space represents a particle's path both in space and time.

spadix In some flowering plants, a spike of small flowers; it is generally enclosed in a sheath called a SPATHE. A familiar example is the CUCKOOPINT (*Arum maculatum*).

Spain Kingdom on the E Iberian Peninsula, the capital is MADRID. **Land and climate** Spain occupies 80% of the Iberian peninsula. The central Spanish regions of ARAGÓN, CASTILE-LA MANCHA, and CASTILE-LEÓN form part of a vast plateau (the *Meseta*), in the centre of which lies Madrid. The plateau is drained by the EBRO and TAGUS rivers. The Cantabrian Mountains lie between León and the N coastal regions of GALICIA and ASTURIAS. Bilbao and PAMPLONA are the major cities in BASQUE COUNTRY. The PYRENEES form a natural border with France. The *Meseta* has hot summers and cold winters. The S coast has Europe's mildest winters. Winter snowfall is heavy on the high mountains. Forests cover 32% of Spain, mostly in the mountainous regions. Grassland and scrub cover much of the *Meseta*, but 30% of land is arable. **Economy** Spanish economic revival began in the 1950s, based on tourism (1992 receipts, US$21,181) and manufacturing. It has rapidly transformed from a largely poor, agrarian society into a prosperous industrial nation. Agriculture now employs only 10% of the workforce. Spain is the world's third-largest wine producer. Other crops include citrus fruits, tomatoes and olives. Sheep are the main livestock. Spain is the world's sixth-largest car producer. Other manufactures include ships, chemicals, electronics, metal goods, steel and textiles. It lacks mineral resources. Unemployment remains high (1997, 22%). **History** Iberians and BASQUES were Spain's early inhabitants. In the 9th century BC, the Phoenicians estab-

---

SPAIN
AREA: 504,780sq km (194,896sq mi)
POPULATION: 39,085,000
CAPITAL (POPULATION): Madrid (3,121,000)
GOVERNMENT: Constitutional monarchy
ETHNIC GROUPS: Castilian Spanish 72%, Catalan 16%, Galician 8%, Basque 2%
LANGUAGES: Castilian Spanish (official), Catalan, Galician, Basque
RELIGIONS: Christianity (Roman Catholic 97%)
CURRENCY: Peseta = 100 céntimos

lished trading posts on the s coast. In c.600 BC Greek merchants set up colonies. In c.237 BC the Carthaginian general HAMILCAR BARCA conquered most of the peninsula. By the 1st century AD, most of Spain had fallen to the Romans; it became a prosperous province. From c.AD 400, Germanic tribes swept into Spain. During the 5th–8th centuries, Visigoths controlled s Spain. In 711 the MOORS defeated the Visigoths. Spain was rapidly conquered (except Asturias and the Basque Country) and an independent Muslim state founded (756). The Basques established an independent kingdom of Navarre. Asturias acted as the base for the Christian reconquest. The reconquest of Granada (1492) saw FERDINAND V and ISABELLA I become rulers of all Spain. The INQUISITION was used to ensure Catholic supremacy through persecution and conversion. Columbus' discovery of America (1492) led to Spain becoming the leading imperial power. In 1519 Charles I became CHARLES V, Holy Roman emperor. The supremacy of the HABSBURGS was established. The extension and centralization of power was continued by PHILIP II, who gained Portugal (1580). Spanish naval power was dented by the defeat of the Spanish ARMADA (1588). During the 17th century, Spain's political and economic power declined. The War of the SPANISH SUCCESSION (1701–14) resulted in the accession of PHILIP V, and the establishment of the BOURBON dynasty. CHARLES III brought the church under state control. Charles IV's reign ended in French occupation, and the appointment of Joseph BONAPARTE as king. Spanish resistance led to the restoration of the Bourbons in 1813. Many of Spain's New World colonies gained independence. The accession of Isabella II resulted in prolonged civil war with the CARLISTS. A short-lived constitutional monarchy and republic was followed by a further Bourbon restoration under ALFONSO XII and XIII. Spain remained neutral during World War 1. From 1923–30, Spain was ruled by the dictator PRIMO DE RIVERA. He was forced to resign and a second republic was proclaimed. The Popular Front won 1936 elections, and conflict between republicans and nationalists, such as the FALANGE, intensified. With the backing of the Axis powers, the nationalists led by General FRANCO emerged victorious from the Spanish CIVIL WAR (1936–39), and Franco established a dictatorship. Spain did not participate in World War 2. Spain joined the UN in 1955. During the 1960s most of Spain's remaining colonies gained independence. In 1975 Franco died, and a constitutional monarchy was established under Juan Carlos. Spain began a process of democratization and decentralization of power. Spain joined NATO (1982) and the European Community (1986). **Politics** Throughout much of its history there has been tension between central government and the regions. Basque independence has been a constant feature. Since 1959 the militant Basque organization ETA has waged a campaign of terror. In 1977 the Basque

Country (*Pais Vasco*), Catalonia and Galicia gained limited autonomy. In 1996 elections, after 13 years in office, the Spanish Socialist Workers' Party was defeated. The centre-right Popular Party, led by José María Aznar, formed a minority government.

spaniel Any of several breeds of sporting dogs that may be trained to locate and flush game, to drop for the hunter's shot and to retrieve on command. Land spaniels include the springer, cocker and toy breeds. Water spaniels are usually RETRIEVERS.

Spanish Major world language, spoken as an official language in Spain, most of South America (except Brazil, French Guiana, Guyana and Surinam), all of Central America, Mexico, Cuba, the Dominican Republic and Puerto Rico. It is also spoken in a number of other countries, notably the USA and former Spanish dependencies such as the Philippines. Its total number of speakers is more than 200 million. Spanish is a member of the Romance group of INDO-EUROPEAN LANGUAGES but its vocabulary contains a large number of words of Arabic origin, the result of Moorish domination of Spain for many centuries.

Spanish Armada *See* ARMADA, SPANISH

Spanish art Artistic tradition beginning with the Palaeolithic cave paintings at Altamira. Successively occupied by the Romans, Visigoths and Moors, Spain's earliest native traditions were the Mozarabic and Mudéjar styles, which blended Moorish and Christian elements. As the country was reconquered from the Moors, Spain drew closer to artistic developments in the rest of Europe. By the 16th century, it was the most powerful force on the continent, and this period coincided with the career of its first true genius, El GRECO b. Crete. The most glittering era in Spanish art occured in the next century, with Diego VELÁZQUEZ, José RIBERA and Francisco de Zurbarán. In later years, Francisco GOYA was one of the greatest of the ROMANTICISM movement and Pablo PICASSO was the dominant figure in 20th-century art.

Spanish literature One of the major early works is the epic poem *Cantar de Mío Cid* (c.1140). Major figures of the 14th and 15th centuries include the poet Juan Ruiz (c.1283–1350), the Marqués de Santilla and Juan de Mena. The most important work of fiction of the 15th century was the novel *La Celestina* (1499). French and Italian influences predominated until the 16th century when a truly Spanish literature emerged. The late-16th and 17th centuries are known as the Golden Age, with the work of Miguel de CERVANTES (whose *Don Quixote de la Mancha* is still seen as an influential masterpiece of European literature), the poet Luis de Góngora y Argote, Lope de VEGA CARPIO, and the dramatist Pedro Calderón de la Barca. The 18th century witnessed a decline in Spanish writings, saved by the rise of ROMANTICISM. *Costumbrismo* (sketches of life and customs) flourished in the 19th century. In the early 20th century the writers of the Generation of '98 re-examined Spanish traditions.

The Spanish Civil War (1936–39) drove many Spanish writers into hiding, and its reverberations can be seen in the grim realism of much of the work that followed. The theories of MODERNISM exerted an influence on technique and narrative style; the Generation of 1927 group of poets were also inspired by SURREALISM. The most important Spanish writer of the 20th century, however, was Federico García LORCA.

Spanish Sahara Former name, from 1958 to 1975, of the WESTERN SAHARA.

Spanish Succession, War of the (1701–14) Last of the series of wars fought by European coalitions to contain the expansion of France under LOUIS XIV. It was precipitated by the death of the Spanish king, Charles II, without an heir. He willed his kingdom to the French Philip of Anjou (PHILIP V), Louis's grandson. England and the Netherlands supported the Austrian claimant to the Spanish throne, the Archduke Charles (later Emperor CHARLES VI). The ensuing war marked the emergence of Britain as a maritime and colonial power. The Spanish succession was settled by a compromise in the Peace of UTRECHT, with Philip attaining the Spanish throne on condition that he renounced any claim to France, and Britain and Austria receiving substantial territorial gains.

Spark, Dame Muriel (1918–) British novelist, short-story writer and poet. She is best known for her novels, which include *Memento Mori* (1959), *The Ballad of Peckham Rye* (1960), *Girls of Slender Means* (1963), *The Mandelbaum Gate* (1965) and *Symposium* (1990). *The Prime of Miss Jean Brodie* (1961) is a portrait of a charismatic schoolmistress.

sparrow Any of a number of small FINCH-like birds that live in or around human settlements. Sparrows feed, roost and dust-bathe in noisy, twittering flocks. Basically seed-eaters, with a preference for grain, they are widely regarded as pests. They also eat fruit, worms and household scraps. Length: 14.5cm (5.75in). Family Ploceidae

Sparta City-state of ancient Greece, near the modern city of Spárti. Founded by Dorians after *c*.1100 BC, Sparta conquered Laconia (SE Peloponnese) by the 8th century BC and headed the Peloponnesian League against Persia in 480 BC. In the PELOPONNESIAN WARS (431–404 BC) it defeated its great rival, ATHENS, but was defeated by THEBES in 371 BC and failed to withstand the invasion of PHILIP II of Macedon. In the 3rd century BC Sparta struggled against the Achaean League, subsequently joining it but coming under Roman dominance after 146 BC. The ancient city was destroyed by Alaric and the Goths in AD 395.

Spartacus (d.71 BC) Thracian gladiator in Rome who led a slave revolt known as the Third Servile (Gladiatorial) War (73–71 BC). His soldiers devastated the land and then moved S towards Sicily, where they were eventually defeated by CRASSUS with POMPEY's aid. Spartacus died in battle.

spasm Sustained involuntary muscle contraction. It may occur in response to pain, or as part of a generalized condition, such as spastic paralysis or TETANUS.

spathe Broad leaf-like organ that spreads from the base of, or enfolds, the SPADIX of certain plants.

spearmint Common name of *Mentha spicata*, a hardy perennial herb of the MINT family (Lamiaceae/Labiatae). Its leaves are used for flavouring, especially in sweets. Oil distilled from spearmint is used as a medicine. The plant has pink or lilac flowers that grow in spikes.

Special Branch Department within every British police force that is technically affiliated to MI5, the intelligence bureau within the Home Office. Its duties are to investigate and deter all activities against the interests of the state, to protect visiting foreign rulers and dignitaries, and to monitor the immigration and naturalization of foreign nationals.

species Group of physically and genetically similar individuals that interbreed to produce fertile offspring under natural conditions. Each species has a unique two-part Latin name, the first part being the GENUS name. So far, more than 1.5 million plant and animal species have been identified. *See also* TAXONOMY, BINOMIAL NOMENCLATURE

specific gravity *See* RELATIVE DENSITY

specific heat capacity Heat necessary to raise the temperature of 1kg of a substance by 1K (1°C). It is measured in J/kgK (J equals joule).

spectroscopy Branch of OPTICS dealing with the measurement of the wavelength and intensity of lines in a SPECTRUM. The main tool in this study is the spectroscope. It produces a spectrum and a spectrograph photographs it. An analysis of the spectrogram can reveal the substances causing the spectrum by the position of emission and absorption lines and bands. A spectrometer is a calibrated spectroscope capable of precise measurements.

spectrum Arrangement of ELECTROMAGNETIC RADIATIONS ordered by wavelength or frequency. The visible light spectrum is a series of colours: red, orange, yellow, green, blue, indigo and violet. Each colour corresponds to a different wavelength of light. A spectrum is seen in a rainbow or when white light passes through a PRISM. This effect, also seen when visible light passes through a DIFFRACTION grating, produces a continuous spectrum in which all wavelengths (between certain limits) are present. Spectra formed from objects emitting radiations are called emission spectra. These occur when a substance is strongly heated or bombarded by electrons. An absorption spectrum, consisting of dark regions on a bright background, is obtained when white light passes through a semi-transparent medium that absorbs certain frequencies. A line spectrum is one in which only certain wavelengths or "lines" appear. *See* SPECTROSCOPY

speedwell Common name applied to herbaceous plants of many species of the genus *Veronica* found throughout the world. Germander speedwell, *V. chamaedrys*, is a common British wild flower. Family Scrophulariaceae.

Spence, Sir Basil (1907–76) Leading British architect. He was famous for his modernist design for the new Coventry Cathedral (1951, consecrated in 1962). Other works include the Household Cavalry Barracks (1970) at Knightsbridge, London, and the British Embassy in Rome (1971).

Spender, Stephen Harold (1909–95) British poet. His best verse includes the often anthologized *I Think Continually of Those Who Were Truly Great*. His autobiography *World Within World* (1951) is a powerful evocation of his time. His *Collected Poems 1928–1985* appeared in 1985.

Spenser, Edmund (1552–99) English poet. His poetry includes the pastoral *The Shepheardes Calender* (1579); the sonnet sequence *Amoretti*, published with *Epithalamion* in 1595; *Four Hymns* and *Prothalamion* (both 1596). His life's work, however, was *The Faerie Queene* (1589–96).

sperm (spermatozoon) Motile male sex cell (GAMETE) in sexually reproducing organisms. It corresponds to the female OVUM. The head of the sperm contains the genetic material of the male parent, while its tail or other motile structure provides the means of moving to the ovum to carry out FERTILIZATION.

spermatophyte Seed-bearing plant, including trees, shrubs and herbaceous plants. It has a stem, leaves, roots and well-developed vascular system. The dominant generation is the SPOROPHYTE.

sperm whale Largest of the toothed whales. It has a squarish head and feeds on squid and cuttlefish. Species *Physeter catodon. See also* WHALE

sphalerite (blende) Sulphide mineral composed of zinc sulphide (ZnS). It is an important source of zinc. Hardness 3.5–4; s.g. 4.

sphere 3-D geometric figure formed by the locus in space of points equidistant from a given point (the centre). The distance from the centre to the surface is the radius, *r*. The volume is $(4/3)\pi r^3$ and the surface area is $4\pi r^2$.

spherical trigonometry Branch of mathematics that deals with the sides, angles and areas of spherical triangles, that is, portions of the surface of a sphere bounded by three arcs or great circles. *See also* TRIGONOMETRY

sphinx Mythical beast of the ancient world, usually represented with the head of a man or woman and the body of a lion. In Greek mythology, the riddle of the Sphinx of Thebes was solved by OEDIPUS, so destroying her evil power. Although found throughout the Middle East, images of sphinxes were especially popular in Egypt, where thousands were built.

spice Food flavouring consisting of the dried form of various plants. Spices were used in medieval times to disguise the taste of food decaying, and as preservatives. They also had medicinal and religious functions.

spider Any of numerous species of terrestrial, invertebrate, ARACHNID arthropods found throughout the world in a wide variety of habitats. Spiders have an unsegmented **abdomen** attached to a **cephalothorax** by a slender **pedicel**. There are no antennae; sensory hairs are found on the appendages (four pairs of walking legs). Most species have spinnerets on the abdomen for spinning silk to make egg cases and webs.

spider monkey Medium-sized, arboreal (tree-dwelling), MONKEY found from S Mexico to SE Brazil. It has long, spidery legs, a fully prehensile tail, and is an agile climber, using the tail as a fifth limb. It eats mainly fruit and nuts. Genera *Ateles* and *Brachyteles.*

Spielberg, Steven (1947–) US film director and producer. The success of *Jaws* (1975), established his reputation as a money-maker. *Close Encounters of the Third Kind* (1977) earned him an Academy Award nomination. The *Indiana Jones* trilogy began in 1981 with the Academy Award-nominated *Raiders of the Lost Ark*. Spielberg's mastery of special effects was confirmed by *E.T. The Extra-Terrestrial* (1982). In 1984, he founded an independent production company. *Jurassic* (1993) made over $200 million within 23 days of its US release. He won a Best Director Academy Award for *Schindler's List* (1993).

spin In QUANTUM MECHANICS, intrinsic angular momentum possessed by some SUBATOMIC PARTICLES, atoms and nuclei. This may be regarded by analogy as the spinning of the particle about an axis within itself. Spin (symbol *s*) is one of the quantum numbers by which a particle is specified.

spina bifida Congenital disorder in which the bones of the SPINE do not develop properly to enclose the SPINAL CORD. Surgery to close the defect is usually performed soon after birth but this may not cure the disabilities caused by the condition.

spinach Herbaceous, annual plant cultivated in areas with cool summers. Spinach is used as a culinary herb and as a vegetable. Family Chenopodiaceae; species *Spinacia oleracea.*

spinal cord Tubular, central nerve cord, lying within the SPINE. With the brain, it makes up the CENTRAL NERVOUS SYSTEM. It gives rise to the 31 pairs of spinal nerves, each of which has sensory and motor fibres.

spine (vertebral column) Backbone of VERTEBRATES, extending from the skull to the tip of the tail and enclosing the SPINAL CORD. The human spine consists of 26 vertebrae interspersed with discs of CARTILAGE. It articulates with the SKULL, ribs and hip bones and provides points of attachment for the back muscles.

spinet Early musical instrument of the harpsichord family with one keyboard and one string to each note. The strings were plucked with a quill or leather plectrum.

spinning Process of making thread or yarn by twisting fibres together. The fibres may be of animal, vegetable or synthetic origin.

593

Spinoza, Baruch (1632–77) Dutch-Jewish rationalist philosopher, also known as Benedict de Spinoza. Spinoza argued that all mind and matter were modes of the one key substance, which he called either God or Nature. In *Ethics* (1677), he held that free will was an illusion that would be dispelled by man's recognition that every event has a cause.

spiny anteater *See* ECHIDNA

spiraea Genus of flowering, perennial shrubs native to the Northern Hemisphere. They have small flat leaves and clusters of small white, pink or red flowers. Many of the 100 species are grown as ornamentals. Height: 1.5m (5ft). Family Rosaceae.

spiritualism Belief that, at death, the personality of an individual is transferred to another plane of existence, with which communication from the world of the living is believed to be possible. The channel of such communication is a receptive living person called a medium.

spleen Organ located on the left side of the abdomen, behind and slightly below the stomach. It is important in both the lymphatic and blood systems, helping to process LYMPHOCYTES, destroying worn out or damaged erythrocytes and storing iron. Removal of the spleen (splenectomy) is sometimes necessary following trauma or in the treatment of some blood disorders.

Split Major port in Croatia on the Dalmatian coast of the Adriatic Sea. Split was held by Venice from 1420–1797, when it passed to Austria. It became part of the Kingdom of Serbs, Croats and Slovenes (later Yugoslavia) in 1918. Croatia's second-largest city, its industries include shipbuilding, textiles, chemicals, timber, wine and tourism, which was severely disrupted by the wars that followed the break-up of Yugoslavia. Pop. (1991) 189,388.

Spock, Dr Benjamin McLane (1903–) US paediatrician and writer whose *The Common Sense Book of Baby and Child Care* (1946) reversed the trend in child-rearing by calling for parental warmth and understanding.

Spode, Josiah (1754–1827) British potter. He gave his name to Spode porcelain, which became the standard English bone china.

sponge Primitive, multicellular aquatic animal. Its extremely simple structure is supported by a skeleton of lime, silica or spongin. There is no mouth, nervous system or cellular coordination, nor are there any internal organs. Sponges reproduce sexually and by asexual budding. There are about 5,000 species, including the simple sponge genus *Leucosolenia*. Length: 1mm–2m (0.4in–6ft). Phylum Porifera.

spoonbill Any of several species of wading birds, each with a long bill that is flat and rounded at the tip; species are found in tropical climates throughout the world. It has large wings, long legs, a short tail, and white or pinkish plumage; it feeds on small plant and animal matter. Length: 90cm (3ft). Family Threskiornithidae.

spore Small, reproductive body that detaches from the parent organism to produce new offspring. Mostly microscopic, spores may consist of one or several cells (but do not contain an embryo) and are produced in large numbers. Some germinate rapidly, others "rest", surviving unfavourable environmental conditions. Spores are formed by FERNS, HORSETAILS, MOSSES, FUNGI and BACTERIA.

sporophyte DIPLOID stage in the life cycle of a plant or alga. Usually, the sporophyte gives rise to HAPLOID SPORES, which germinate to produce a haploid generation (the GAMETOPHYTE stage), which will produce the GAMETES. In ferns, horsetails, conifers and flowering plants the diploid sporophyte is the dominant phase of the life cycle, the plant body we usually see. *See also* ALTERNATION OF GENERATIONS

sprat (brisling) Small herring-like commercial fish found in the N Atlantic Ocean. It is slender and silvery. Length: to 12.5 cm (5in). Family Clupeidae; species *Clupea sprattus*.

springbok (springbuck) Small, horned ANTELOPE native to S Africa; the national emblem of South Africa. The reddish-brown colour on the back shades into a dark horizontal band just above the white underside. Height: to 90cm (3ft) at the shoulder. Family Bovidae; species *Antidorcas marsupialis*.

spruce Various evergreen trees, related to firs, native to mountainous or cooler temperate regions of the Northern Hemisphere. Pyramid-shaped and dense, they have angular rather then flattened needles and pendulous cones. Height: to 52m (170ft). Family Pinaceae; genus *Picea*.

sputnik World's first artificial satellite, launched by the Soviet Union on 4 October 1957. Weighing 83.5kg (184lb) and with a radio transmitter, *Sputnik 1* circled the Earth for several months.

square In geometry, rectangle with four sides of the same length. In arithmetic or algebra, a square is the result of multiplying a quantity by itself: the square of 3 is 9, and the square of x is x^2.

square root Number or quantity that must be multiplied by itself to give a specified number or quantity. The square root of 4 is 2, i.e. $\sqrt{4} = 2$. A negative number has imaginary square roots.

squash Ball game played with small round-headed rackets by two (or occasionally four) people on a rectangular, four-walled court. The wall at the front of the court is marked with three horizontal lines at different heights. The ball from the serve must land above the middle line (the cut line). Balls hitting the wall above the third line are out. The hollow rubber ball may bounce off front, side, and back walls, but may bounce only once on the floor before it is struck. The object of each point is to make it impossible for the opponent to return the ball. Only the server scores, and the first player to score 9 points wins the game.

squid Any of numerous species of marine, cephalopod MOLLUSCS that have a cylindrical body with an internal horny plate (the pen) that serves as a skeleton. It has eight short, suckered tentacles surrounding the mouth, in addition to which there are two longer, arm-like tentacles that can be shot out to seize moving prey. Several species of giant squid (genus *Architeuthis*) may reach 20m (65ft) in length. Class Cephalopoda; order Teuthoidea.

squint *See* STRABISMUS

squirrel Any of numerous species of primarily arboreal, diurnal rodents found throughout the world. Most species feed on nuts, seeds, fruit, insects, and some eat eggs and young birds. Most have short fur and bushy tails. Family Sciuridae.

squirrel monkey Either of at least two species of small, diurnal, arboreal MONKEYS of tropical South America; it has thick, dark fur and a long, heavy tail. *Saimiri sciureus* has a cap of greyish fur; *S. oerstedi* has a black cap and reddish fur on its back. Both are gregarious and live on fruit. Length: to 40cm (16in); tail: 47cm (19in). Family Cebidae.

Sri Lanka State in the Indian Ocean, the capital is COLOMBO. **Land and climate** Sri Lanka (formerly Ceylon) is a pear-shaped island, separated from SE India by the Palk Strait. A chain of coral islands (Adam's Bridge) almost joins the two countries. Most of Sri Lanka is low-lying. A coastal plain is fringed by cliffs and lagoons. On the sw coast lies the capital, Colombo. The s central core of Sri Lanka is a highland region. The highest peak is Pidurutalagala, at 2,524m (8,281ft). Western Sri Lanka has high temperatures and heavy rainfall. The monsoon season is between May and October. The N and E are drier. Over 30% of Sri Lanka is tropical rainforest or woodland. **Economy** Sri Lanka is a low-income developing country (1992 GDP per capita, US$2,850). Agriculture employs 50% of the workforce. Sri Lanka is the world's third-largest producer of tea It is also a leading producer of coconuts and rubber. Manufacturing has increased rapidly and contributes 67% of exports. Products include ceramics, textiles and clothes. Tourism is also important. **History and politics** The native Veddahs were forced into the mountains *c.*2,400 years ago by SINHALESE settlers from N India. Some Veddahs remain in remote regions. The Sinhalese founded Anuradhapura in 437 BC, which acted as their capital and a centre of THERAVADA Buddhism, until the arrival of the Tamils in the 8th

century AD. The Chola dynasty conquered the island in the 11th century. The Sinhalese were gradually forced s. The Portuguese landed in 1505 and formed coastal settlements. In 1658 Portuguese lands passed to the Dutch EAST INDIA COMPANY. In 1796 the British captured the Dutch colonies, and in 1802 Ceylon became a crown colony. In 1815 Britain captured Kandy. Colonialism developed the plantations. In 1948 Ceylon achieved self-government within the Commonwealth of Nations. In the late 1950s, following the declaration of Sinhalese as the official language, communal violence flared between Tamils and Sinhalese. In 1958 Prime Minister Solomon BANDARANAIKE was assassinated. His widow, Sirimavo BANDARANAIKE, became the world's first woman prime minister (1960). Following a brief period in opposition, she was re-elected in 1970. In 1972 Ceylon became the independent republic of Sri Lanka (resplendent island). The new republic was faced with resurgent demands for a separate Tamil state in N and E Sri Lanka. In 1978 a new constitution provided for a presidential form of government. In 1983 secessionist demands spiralled into civil war between government forces and the TAMIL TIGERS. In 1987 the Sri Lankan government called for Indian military assistance. Unable to enforce a peace settlement, Indian troops withdrew in 1989. In 1993 President Ranasinghe Premadasa was assassinated. In 1994 Prime Minister Chandrika Bandaranaike Kumaratunga was elected president, and her mother, Sirimavo Bandaranaike, became prime minister for the third time. Military offensives against the Tamil Tigers led to the recapture of Jaffna in 1995. The Tamil Tigers refused to accept devolution and the war, which has claimed over 40,000 lives, continued.

SS (*Schutzstaffeln*, guards unit) Chief paramilitary force of Nazi Germany. It was originally Hitler's bodyguard but expanded under HIMMLER after 1928 to become the Nazi Party militia and internal police force. With its distinctive black uniform, the SS controlled the GESTAPO and the SD (security organization). It ran the CONCENTRATION CAMPS and, from 1936, controlled the police. After the outbreak of war it formed its own fighting units, notorious for their ferocity, known as the Waffen SS.

Staël, (Anne-Louise-Germaine), Madame de (1766–1817) French writer. One of the most influential intellectual figures of her time, she published two proto-feminist novels, *Delphine* (1802) and *Corinne* (1807), but is best known for her works of social and aesthetic philosophy. They include *A Treatise on the Influence of the Passions upon the Happiness of Individuals and of Nations* (1796), a key text of ROMANTICISM.

Staffordshire County in w central England. The terrain is composed of rolling hills with moorlands in the N. The region is drained chiefly by the River Trent. The county is primarily industrial. It includes the Potteries around STOKE-ON-TRENT and the Black Country, one of the great industrial

---

SRI LANKA

AREA: 65,610sq km (25,332sq mi)
POPULATION: 17,405,000
CAPITAL (POPULATION): Colombo (684,000)
GOVERNMENT: Multiparty republic
ETHNIC GROUPS: Sinhalese 74%, Tamil 18%, Sri Lankan Moor 7%
LANGUAGES: Sinhala and Tamil (both official)
RELIGIONS: Buddhism 69%, Hinduism 16%, Islam 8%, Christianity 7%
CURRENCY: Sri Lankan rupee = 100 cents

hubs of England. Stafford (1991 pop. 117,800) is the county town. Area 2,716sq km (1,049sq mi). Pop. (1991) 1,031,035.

stag beetle Large, brown or black BEETLE of Eurasian oak forests; the male bears large antler-like mandibles. The larvae feed on rotten wood. Length: to 8cm (3in). Family Lucanidae; species *Lucanus cervus.*

stainless steel Group of iron alloys that resist corrosion. Besides carbon, contained in all steels, stainless steels contain from 12% to 25% chromium. This makes the steel stainless by forming a thin, protective oxide coating on the surface. Most also contain nickel. Other metals and non-metals may be added to give the steel particular properties.

stalactite Icicle-like formation of CALCIUM CARBONATE found hanging from the roofs of caves. It is made by the precipitation of LIMESTONE out of water that has seeped into limestone caves.

stalagmite Deposit of crystalline CALCIUM CARBONATE rising from the floor of cavern, and formed by dripping water that has seeped into limestone caves.

Stalin, Joseph (1879–1953) (Vissarionovich Dzhugashvili) Leader of the Soviet Union (1924–53). He supported LENIN and the BOLSHEVIKS from 1903, adopting the name Stalin ("man of steel") while editing *Pravda*, the party newspaper. Exiled to Siberia (1913–17), he returned to join the RUSSIAN REVOLUTION (1917) and became secretary of the central committee of the party in 1922. On Lenin's death in 1924, he achieved supreme power through his control of the party organization. He outmanoeuvred rivals such as TROTSKY and BUKHARIN and drove them from power. From 1929 he was virtually dictator. He enforced collectivization of agriculture and intensive industrialization, brutally suppressing all opposition, and, in the 1930s, he exterminated all possible opponents in a series of purges of political and military leaders. During World War 2 Stalin controlled the armed forces and negotiated skilfully with the chief Allied leaders, Churchill and Roosevelt. After the war he reimposed severe repression and forced puppet communist governments on the states of Eastern Europe.

stamen Pollen-producing male organ of a flower. It consists of an anther, in which POLLEN is produced, on the end of a stalk-like **filament**. The arrangement and number of stamens is important in the classification of flowering plants.

standard deviation In statistics, a measure of dispersion or deviation of scores from the average or MEAN of the scores. It is written as either ø or *s*. In a list of numbers, the deviation is found by calculating the difference from the mean of each score in the list. The value of each differing score is then squared, and the mean calculated. The deviation of the resultant mean is the square root of that number.

standard temperature and pressure (STP) (normal temperature and pressure [NTP]) In chemistry and physics, standard conditions for measurements, especially when comparing the volumes of gases. It is a temperature of 273K–0°C (32°F)–and a pressure of 1 standard atmosphere (101,325 pascals).

Stanford-Binet scale Most commonly used English-language intelligence test for measuring children's IQ.

Stanislavsky, Konstantin (1863–1938) (Konstantin Sergeyevich Alekseyev) Russian actor, director and teacher. His theory of drama, described in *My Life In Art* (1924), stressed a naturalistic approach and the value of the ensemble, with actors making emotional contact with their characters.

Stanley, Sir Henry Morton (1841–1904) US explorer of Africa. He was born in Wales as John Rowlands, emigrated to the USA at 16 and took the name of a cotton merchant who adopted him. He became a journalist and was commissioned by the *New York Herald* to lead an expedition in search of David LIVINGSTONE in E Africa. They met at Ujiji in 1871. On a second expedition, Stanley led a large party from the E African lakes down the Congo (Zaïre) River to the w coast. He returned to the area (1880) as agent for King LEOPOLD II . In 1887–89 he led an expedition supposedly to rescue Emin Pasha from the Sudan, and pressed on, with heavy losses, to the Indian Ocean.

Stanley (Port Stanley) Capital and chief port of the FALKLAND ISLANDS, on East Falkland. Originally called Port William, it became capital of the Falkland Islands in 1843. In 1982 it was captured by the Argentinians, precipitating the FALKLANDS WAR. Since 1983 the British army have maintained a base there. Pop. (1991) 2,121

staphylococcus Spherical bacterium that grows in grape-like clusters and is found on the skin and mucous membranes of human beings and other animals. Pathogenic staphylococci cause a range of local or generalized infections, including PNEUMONIA and SEPTICAEMIA. They may be destroyed by ANTIBIOTICS.

star Self-luminous ball of gas whose radiant energy is produced by FUSION reactions, mainly the conversion of hydrogen into helium. The temperatures and luminosities of stars are prescribed by their masses. Large stars are very luminous and hot, and therefore appear blue. Medium-sized stars like the Sun are yellow, while small stars are a dull red. The smallest stars contain less than one-twentieth of a solar mass. *See also* BINARY STAR

starch CARBOHYDRATE stored in many plants and providing about 70% of human food in such forms as potatoes and cereals. Animals and plants convert it to GLUCOSE for energy (RESPIRATION). It is made commercially from cereals, maize, potatoes and other plants, and used in the manufacture of adhesives and foods.

Star Chamber English court of the 15th–17th centuries, named after its meeting place in Westminster. It arose as a judical branch of the royal council, which received petitions from subjects and tried offences against the crown. It was used by CHARLES I to attack his oppponents. It was dissolved by Parliament in 1641.

starfish Any of numerous species of marine ECHINODERMS, with a central disc body and a five-rayed symmetry resulting in 5 to 40 radiating arms. The mouth is on the underside of the disc and the stomach can be extruded to take in other echinoderms and shellfish. Calcareous spines are embedded in the skin. Starfish move by means of tube feet, which they may also use for pulling open the bivalve molluscs on which they feed. Class Asteroidea.

Stark, Dame Freya Madeline (1893–1993) British explorer and writer. She travelled widely in the Middle East, especially Arabia, and gained esteem through her many books, regarded as classics of travel literature.

starling Any of several species of small, aggressive birds found throughout the world. The common Eurasian starling, *Sturnus vulgaris*, is mottled black and brown. It feeds on the ground on insects and fruit, often damaging crops. Length: to 36cm (14in). Family Sturnidae.

Star of David (Shield of David) Six-pointed device formed by opposing two equilateral triangles. Known in Hebrew as *Magen David* or *Mogen David*, it was used as an emblem or magic sign by pagans, Christians and Muslims, and gradually found its way into JUDAISM as a kabbalistic sign. It appears on the flag of the modern state of ISRAEL.

States General National assembly composed of separate divisions, or 'estates', each historically representing a different social class. In France the Assembly was divided into three estates – clergy, nobility and commoners – before the FRENCH REVOLUTION. The Dutch parliament still retains the name Estates-General.

static electricity ELECTRIC CHARGES at rest. Electrically charged objects have either too many or too few ELECTRONS. COULOMB's law describes the forces that charged objects have on each other and relates the force to their charge and the distance between them. Static electricity can be produced by friction. Electrons may then jump off as a spark, shocking anyone touching the object. Lightning is a larger result of static electricity. This form of electricity is studied in **electrostatics**.

statics Branch of MECHANICS that deals with the action of forces on objects at rest. Its topics include finding the resultant (net) of two or more forces; centres of gravity; moments; and stresses and strains. *See also* DYNAMICS

statistical mechanics Branch of physics that studies large-scale properties of matter based on the statistical laws of large numbers. The large number of molecules in such a system allows the use of STATISTICS to predict the probability of finding the system in any state.

statistics Science of collecting and classifying numerical data. Statistics can be **descriptive** (summarizing the data obtained) or **inferential** (leading to conclusions or inferences about larger numbers of which the data obtained are a sample). Inferential statistics are used to give a greater degree of confidence to conclusions, because statistics make it possible to calculate the probability that a conclusion is in error.

Statue of Liberty Large copper statue of a woman, standing on Liberty Island in New York Harbour. A symbol of US democracy, it was a gift from France and built to commemorate the 1876 centenary of US independence. It was designed by BARTHOLDI on an iron framework designed and built by Gustave Eiffel.

steady-state theory Cosmological theory put forward by Hermann Bondi and Thomas Gold in 1948, and further developed by Fred HOYLE and others. According to this theory, the Universe has always existed; it had no beginning and will continue forever. Although the Universe is expanding, it maintains its average density (steady-state) through the continuous creation of new matter. Most cosmologists now reject the theory.

stealth technology Methods used to render an aircraft near invisible primarily to radar and heat detection. To achieve "invisibility", a stealth aircraft must have sympathetic airframe design (all radar-reflecting "hard" edges smoothed away), engine exhaust dampers that mask and disperse jet efflux, and radar absorbent material that "holds" electronic emissions rather than reflecting them.

steam engine Engine powered by steam. In some engines, the steam forces pistons to move along cylinders. This results in a reciprocating (to-and-fro) motion. A mechanism usually changes this into rotary motion. Steam turbines are engines that produce rotary motion directly by using the steam to turn sets of fan-like wheels. The first steam engine was a form of pump, used to remove water from mines invented in 1689 by English inventor Thomas Savery. In 1712 Thomas Newcomen invented a steam-operated pump with pistons in Britain. From the 1760s, Scottish engineer James WATT produced more efficient steam engines. This led to the use of steam engines to power machinery in factories. British engineer Charles Parsons invented the first practical steam TURBINE in 1884.

Steel, Sir David (Martin Scott) (1938–) British politician. Liberal member of Parliament since 1965, he was elected leader of the Liberal Party in 1976. He encouraged an alliance with the Social Democratic Party in 1981, which resulted in a total merger and the creation of the SOCIAL AND LIBERAL DEMOCRATS in 1988. He resigned the leadership that year. He remained an MP, retiring before the 1997 general election.

steel Group of iron alloys containing a little carbon. The great strength of steel makes it an extremely important material in construction and manufacturing. The most common type is called plain carbon steel, because carbon is the main alloying material. This kind of steel usually contains less than 1% of carbon by weight. Alloy steels contain some carbon but owe their special properties to the presence of manganese, nickel, chromium, vanadium or molybdenum.

Steele, Sir Richard (1672–1729) British essayist and dramatist. He helped set the tone of public debate in his various publications, including most notably *The Tatler* (1709–11), which he founded and edited under the pseudonym Isaac Bickerstaff.

Stein, Gertrude (1874–1946) US author and critic. Her prodigious output includes the novel *Three Lives* (1909) and *The Autobiography of Alice B. Toklas* (1933), a fictionalized account of her life.

Steinbeck, John (1902–68) US novelist. He first came to notice with *Tortilla Flat* (1935), the success of which was consolidated by the novella *Of Mice and Men* (1937). Later novels include *Cannery Row* (1945), *East of Eden* (1952), and his masterpiece, *The Grapes of Wrath* (1939), which earned him a Pulitzer Prize and a National Book Award. He was awarded the 1962 Nobel Prize for literature.

Steiner, Rudolf (1861–1925) Austrian philosopher and educationalist who helped to found the German THEOSOPHY movement.

stem Main, upward-growing part of a plant that bears leaves, buds and flowers or other reproductive structures. In VASCULAR PLANTS the stem contains conducting tissues (XYLEM and PHLOEM). In flowering plants this vascular tissue is arranged in a ring (in DICOTYLEDONS) or scattered (in MONOCOTYLEDONS). They may be modified into underground structures (RHIZOMES, TUBERS, CORMS, BULBS). Stems vary in shape and size from the thread-like stalks of aquatic plants to tree-trunks.

Stendhal (1783–1842) (Marie Henri Beyle) French novelist. His first novel, *Armance*, appeared to critical scorn in 1827. In 1830 he published the first of his two great novels *The Red and the Black*, whose ironic tones satirized Parisian contemporary society. *The Charterhouse of Parma* came out in 1839.

Stephen, Saint (977–1038) Stephen I of Hungary (r.1000–38), the first king of the Árpád dynasty. His chief work was to continue the Christianization of Hungary begun by his father, by endowing abbeys, inviting in foreign prelates, and suppressing paganism. He was canonized in 1083.

Stephen (1097–1154) King of England (1135–54). A nephew of HENRY I, he usurped the throne on Henry's death in spite of an earlier oath of loyalty to Henry's daughter, Matilda. A long civil war (1139–48) began when Matilda's forces invaded. Stephen received support from most of the English barons, who were unwilling to accept a female sovereign. He was captured in 1141 but exchanged for the Duke of Gloucester, Matilda's half-brother. After the death of his son, Eustace, in

1153, Stephen accepted Matilda's son, the future HENRY II, as heir to the throne.

Stephenson, George (1781–1848) English engineer, regarded as the father of the locomotive. He built his first locomotive, *Blucher*, in 1814. His most famous locomotive, *Rocket*, was built in 1829. It ran on the Liverpool to Manchester line, one of the many railway lines that he engineered.

Stephenson, Robert (1803–59) English engineer, son of George STEPHENSON. From 1827 Robert Stephenson managed his father's locomotive works. He built several railway lines and tubular bridges, including the Britannia Bridge over the Menai Strait, Wales.

stereoscope Optical device that produces an apparently three-dimensional image by presenting two slightly different plane images, usually photographs, to each eye. Some modern devices use POLARIZED LIGHT to project images that are viewed through polarized filters.

sterilization Surgical intervention that terminates the ability of a human or other animal to reproduce. In women, the usual procedure is tubal ligation: sealing or tying off the FALLOPIAN TUBES so that fertilization can no longer take place. In men, a VASECTOMY is performed to block the release of sperm. The term is also applied to the practice of destroying micro-organisms in order to prevent the spread of infection. Techniques include heat treatment, irradiation and the use of disinfecting agents.

Sterne, Laurence (1713–68) British novelist, b. Ireland. He became famous following the publication of the first two volumes of *Tristram Shandy* (1760–67), a forerunner of MODERNISM in literature. *A Sentimental Journey Through France and Italy* appeared in 1768, and *The Sermons of Mr Yorick* from 1760–1769.

sternum (breastbone) Flat, narrow bone extending from the base of the front of the neck to just below the diaphragm in the centre of the chest. The top is attached by ligaments to the collarbones and the centre part is joined to the ribs by seven pairs of costal cartilages.

steroid Class of organic compounds widely distributed in animals and plants, the most abundant being the sterols, such as cholesterol. Another important group are the steroid HORMONES, including the corticosteroids, secreted by the adrenal cortex, and the sex hormones (OESTROGEN, PROGESTERONE and TESTOSTERONE). Synthetic steroids are widely used in medicine. Some athletes illegally abuse steroids to increase their muscle mass, strength and stamina.

stethoscope Instrument that enables an examiner to listen to the action of various parts of the body, principally the heart and lungs. It consists of two earpieces attached to flexible rubber tubes that lead to either a disc or a cone.

Stevenson, Robert Louis (1850–94) Scottish novelist, essayist and poet. His novels include such classic adventure stories as *Treasure Island* (1883) and *Kidnapped* (1886), and historical novels such as *The Black Arrow* (1888) and *The Master of Ballantrae* (1889), as well as the psychological novel *The Strange Case of Dr Jekyll and Mr Hyde* (1886). *A Child's Garden of Verses* appeared in 1885.

Stewart, Jackie (John Young) (1939–) Scottish Formula 1 motor racing driver. He retired from racing in 1973 after winning what was then a record 27 Grand Prix. In 1997 he established his own Formula 1 racing team.

Stewart, James Maitland (1908–97) US film actor famed for his slow drawl. His notable films include *Mr Smith Goes to Washington* (1939), *The Philadelphia Story* (1940, Academy Award), *Harvey* (1950), *Vertigo* (1958), *Anatomy of a Murder* (1959), *The Man who Shot Liberty Valance* (1962), *Shenandoah* (1965) and *The Shootist* (1976).

stick insect Any of numerous species of herbivorous insects of the order Phasmida, which resemble the shape and colour of the twigs upon which they rest. Some lay eggs that resemble seeds. Length: to 32cm (11in). *See also* LEAF INSECT

stickleback Small fish found in fresh, brackish and salt water. It is usually brown and green, and may be identified by the number of spines along its sides and back. The male builds a nest of water plants and drives the female into it. He then watches the eggs and cares for the young. Length: 8–11cm (3–4.5in). The 12 or so species include the threespine *Gasterosteus aculeatus*. Family Gasterosteidae.

stigma In botany, the free upper part of the STYLE of the female organs of a flower, to which pollen grains adhere before FERTILIZATION.

Stijl, De Group of modern artists that originated in the Netherlands in 1917. They were associated with the art periodical of the same name founded by Theo van Doesburg. De Stijl ideas were representative of the AVANT-GARDE movement as a whole.

stimulant Substance that increases mental alertness and activity. There are a number of stimulants that act on the CENTRAL NERVOUS SYSTEM, notably drugs in the amphetamine group. Many common beverages, including tea and coffee, contain small quantities of the stimulant caffeine.

stingray Any of several species of bottom-dwelling elasmobranch fish that live in marine waters and in some rivers in South America. It has a flattened body, with wing-like fins around the head. It has a long, slender tail which can inflict a venomous sting to stun prey, and can cause injury to humans. Width: to 2.1m (7ft). Family Dasyatidae.

stinkhorn Any of several species of foul-smelling Basidiomycete fungi. At first it resembles a small, whitish "egg", which contains the unripe fruit body (receptacle). When ripe, the receptacle elongates to 10–20cm (4–8in) in height, rupturing the egg. It carries with it a glutinous brownish spore mass, which attracts the flies that disperse the spores. Genus *Phallus*.

stoat Carnivorous mammal of the WEASEL family. Its slim body is about 30cm (12in) long, including the tail, and it has short legs and moves sinuously. It preys upon rabbits and smaller animals in many temperate and northern parts of the world. In the latter regions its fur turns from red-brown and white to white in winter, when it is known as ermine. Family Mustelidae; species *Mustela ermina*.

stock (gilliflower) Annual plant native to S Europe, South Africa and parts of Asia, cultivated as a garden plant. It has oblong leaves and pink, purple or white flower clusters. Height: to 80cm (30in). Family Brassicaceae/Cruciferae; species *Matthiola bicornis*.

stock *See* SHARES

stock exchange Market in which stocks and SHARES are bought and sold. There are exchanges in major cities throughout the world, the largest in New York and London.

Stockhausen, Karlheinz (1928–) German composer and theorist, the most successful exponent of ELECTRONIC MUSIC. An example of his work is *Kontakte* (1960), which uses instruments with tape. He began his seven-part opera, *Licht*, in 1977.

Stockholm Port and capital of Sweden, on Lake Mälar's outlet to the Baltic Sea. Founded in the mid-13th century, it became a trade centre dominated by the HANSEATIC LEAGUE. GUSTAVUS I (VASA) made it the centre of his kingdom and ended the privileges of Hanseatic merchants. The city became the capital of Sweden in 1436. Industrial development dates from the mid-19th century. Industries: textiles, clothing, paper and printing, rubber, chemicals, shipbuilding, beer, electronics, metal, machine manufacturing. Pop. (1994) 1,708,502.

Stoics Followers of the school of philosophy founded by ZENO OF CITIUM in *c*.300 BC. Founded on the premise that virtue is attainable only by living in harmony with nature, stoicism stressed the importance of self-sufficiency and of equanimity in adversity.

Stoke-on-Trent City and county district in NW STAFFORDSHIRE, W central England. On the river Trent, the city is the centre of the Potteries and is noted for its manufacture of china and porcelain. Pop. (1991) 244,637.

Stoker, Bram (Abraham) (1847–1912) Irish novelist. He wrote several novels and a memoir of the actor Henry Irving (1906), but he is best remembered for the classic horror novel *Dracula* (1897).

stomach J-shaped organ, lying to the left and slightly below the DIAPHRAGM in human beings; one of the organs of the DIGESTIVE SYSTEM. It is connected at its upper end to the gullet (OESOPHAGUS) and at the lower end to the SMALL INTESTINE. The stomach itself is lined by three layers of muscle and a folded mucous layer containing gastric glands. These GLANDS secrete hydrochloric acid, which destroys some food bacteria and makes possible the action of pepsin, the ENZYME that digests PROTEINS. Gastric gland secretion is controlled by the sight, smell and taste of food, and by hormonal stimuli, chiefly the HORMONE gastrin. As the food is digested, it is churned by muscular action into a thick liquid state called chyme, at which point it passes into the small intestine.

stomata In botany, pores found mostly on the undersides of leaves that allow atmospheric gases to pass in and out for RESPIRATION and PHOTOSYN-THESIS. Surrounding each stoma are two guard cells that can close to prevent excessive loss of water vapour. *See also* GAS EXCHANGE, TRANSPIRATION

Stone Age Period of human evolution defined by the use of stone tools. The Stone Age dates from the earliest identifiable broken-pebble tools made by human ancestors about 2.5 million years ago. The period is generally considered to have ended when metal tools first became widespread during the BRONZE AGE. The Stone Age is usually subdivided into the PALAEOLITHIC, MESOLITHIC and NEOLITHIC.

stonechat Small thrush found in open heath and scrubland of Europe, Africa and Asia. The plumage of the male is black, white and rust-brown. Stonechats feed on the ground on insects. Species *Saxicola torquata*.

stonecrop Any plant of the genus *Sedum* of the family Crassulaceae, especially creeping sedum (*S. acre*), a succulent, low-growing plant of European origin with pungent, fleshy leaves and yellow flowers, found in rocky areas.

stonefish Bottom-dwelling, marine fish that lives in tropical waters of the Indo-Pacific Ocean. It has a warty, slime-covered body and sharp dorsal spines with which it can inflict a painful, sometimes deadly, sting to human beings. Length: to 33cm (13in). Family Synancejidae; species *Synanceja verrucosa*.

stonefly (salmon fly) Soft-bodied insect with long, narrow front wings and chewing mouthparts, found throughout the world. The aquatic nymphs have branched gills, and the adults, used as bait by anglers, are brown to black. Length: 5–60mm (0.2–2.5in). Order Plecoptera.

Stonehenge Circular group of prehistoric standing stones within a circular earthwork on Salisbury Plain, S England, 13km (8mi) N of Salisbury. The largest and most precisely constructed MEGA-LITH in Europe, Stonehenge dates from the early 3rd millennium BC, although the main stones were erected *c*.2000–1500 BC.

Stopes, Marie Charlotte Carmichael (1880–1958) British pioneer of birth control. She campaigned for a more rational and open approach to contraception, establishing the first birth control clinic in Britain in 1921.

Stoppard, Tom (1937–) British dramatist, b. Thomas Straussler. His reputation was established with *Rosencrantz and Guildenstern are Dead* (1966); other plays include *Jumpers* (1972) and *Travesties* (1974). He wrote *Artist Descending a Staircase* (1973) as a radio play and *Professional Foul* (1977) for television.

stork Long-legged wading bird that lives along rivers, lakes and marshes in temperate and tropical regions, often nesting in colonies in trees. Usually black, white and grey, storks have straight bills, long necks, robust bodies and long broad wings. They are diurnal and feed on small animals and sometimes carrion. Length: 0.8–1.5m (2.5–5ft). Family Ciconiidae.

storm and stress *See* STURM UND DRANG

Stowe, Harriet Beecher (1811–96) US novelist. A prolific writer, she is best known for *Uncle Tom's Cabin* (1851–52), a powerful anti-slavery novel.

STP *See* STANDARD TEMPERATURE AND PRESSURE (STP)

strabismus (squint) Condition in which the eyes do not look in the same direction. It may result either from disease of or damage to the eye muscles or their nerve supply, or an error of refraction within the eye.

Stradivari, Antonio (1644–1737) Italian violin-maker. Originally an apprentice to Nicolo AMATI, Stradivari perfected violin design. His instruments remain unsurpassed in brilliance of tone.

Strasberg, Lee (1901–82) US theatrical director. One of the founders of the Group Theatre (1931), he began teaching the method approach based on STANISLAVSKY's teachings. Later he was one of the founders of the ACTORS' STUDIO (1947) with Elia KAZAN, and became its artistic director (1950).

Strasbourg City in E France, on the River Ill, capital of Bas-Rhin département and the commercial capital of the Alsace region. Known in Roman times as Argentoratum, the city was destroyed by the Huns in the 5th century. It became part of the HOLY ROMAN EMPIRE in 923 and developed into an important commercial centre, becoming a free imperial city in 1262. Strasbourg was a centre of medieval German literature and of 16th-century Protestantism. The city was seized by France in 1681, regained by Germany after the FRANCO-PRUSSIAN WAR, but recovered by France at the end of World War 1. German troops occupied the city during World War 2. Industries: metallurgy, oil and gas refining, machinery, food processing. Its river port on the Rhine, with its good canal connections, is France's chief grain outlet. Pop. (1990) 252,338 (city).

Strategic Arms Limitation Talks (SALT) Two phases of talks between the USA and the Soviet Union to limit the expansion of nuclear weapons. The talks began in 1969 between Lyndon JOHNSON and Leonid BREZHNEV. In 1972, NIXON and Brezhnev signed SALT I. This agreement limited anti-ballistic missiles systems and produced an interim accord on intercontinental ballistic missiles (ICBMs). A second phase began in 1973 with meetings between Gerald FORD and Brezhnev and, in 1974, they agreed to limit ballistic missile launchers. SALT II, signed in Vienna between CARTER and Brezhnev, banned new ICBMs and limited other launchers. In 1986 SALT was superseded by **START (Strategic Arms Reduction Talks)** between GORBACHEV and REAGAN. This began a process of DISARMAMENT.

Stratford upon Avon Town in Warwickshire, central England, the birthplace of William SHAKESPEARE and home of the ROYAL SHAKESPEARE COMPANY (RSC). Industries: tourism, engineering, boatbuilding, textiles. Pop. (1992) 22,800.

Strathclyde Region in W Scotland, bounded N by the Highlands, S by the Southern Uplands and W by the Atlantic Ocean. Strathclyde is divided into 19 districts. The capital is GLASGOW; other major towns include Paisley, Kilmarnock, Clydebank and Motherwell. The industrial heartland of Scotland, it contains half of Scotland's population. Sites include Loch LOMOND, Glencoe and Mull, Arran and Bute. Industries: shipbuilding, engineering. Area: 13,529sq km (5,222sq mi) Pop: (1991) 2,248,700

Strauss, Johann (the Younger) (1825–99) Austrian composer and conductor. He became popular for his waltzes, such as *The Blue Danube*, *Tales from the Vienna Woods* and *Wine, Women and Song*. He also composed two popular operettas, *Die Fledermaus* (1874) and *The Gypsy Baron* (1885).

Strauss, Richard (1864–1949) German composer and conductor. His SYMPHONIC POEMS, such as *Don Juan* (1888), *Till Eulenspiegel* (1895) and *Also sprach Zarathustra* (1896), use brilliantly coloured orchestration for characterization. His early operas, such as *Salome* (1905) and *Elektra* (1909), were among the most progressive of the time.

Stravinsky, Igor Feodorovich (1882–1971) Russian composer, one of the most important of the 20th century. Stravinsky wrote in a great variety of styles. His early ballets *The Firebird* (1910) and *Petrushka* (1911) earned him popularity. *The Rite of Spring* (1913) established him as a major composer. Late in life, he developed a personal style of SERIAL MUSIC, as in *Agon* (1957).

strawberry Fruit-bearing plant of the rose family, common in Europe and Asia. It has three-lobed leaves and clusters of white or reddish flowers. The large fleshy fruit is dotted with seeds (pips). Family Rosaceae; genus *Fragaria*.

stream of consciousness Literary style in which the thought processes of characters are presented in the disconnnected, illogical, chaotic or seemingly random way they might come to them, without the usual literary regard for narrative continuity or linear sequence.

streptococcus Genus of gram-positive spherical or oval BACTERIA that grow in pairs or bead-like chains. They live mainly as parasites in the mouth, respiratory tract and intestine. Some are harmless but others are pathogenic, causing SCARLET FEVER and other infections. Treatment is with ANTIBIOTICS.

stress In medicine and psychology, mental or physical strain brought on by pressures from the environment. Stress caused by frustrating and difficult work, family or social situations may be a factor in many mental and physical disorders.

stress In physics, internal tension in a material. Tensile stress stretches an object, compressive stress squeezes it and shearing stress twists it. Fluid stresses are called PRESSURE.

Strindberg, Johan August (1849–1912) Swedish dramatist and novelist, whose work influenced George Bernard SHAW among others. Many of his plays relied on SYMBOLISM for their dramatic impact. He is best known for *The Father* (1887), *Miss Julie* (1888) and *A Dream Play* (1902).

stroboscope (strobe) Device that emits regular flashes of light. Stroboscopes usually have a calibrated scale from which the number of flashes per minute can be read. They are used in photography to make multiple exposures of moving subjects and in engineering to "slow down" or "stop" moving objects for observation.

stroke (apoplexy) Interruption of the flow of blood to the brain. It is caused by blockage or rupture of an artery and may produce a range of effects from mild impairment to death. Conditions that predispose to stroke include atherosclerosis and HYPERTENSION. Many major strokes are prevented by treatment of risk factors, including surgery and the use of anticoagulant drugs.

strong nuclear force One of the four FUNDAMENTAL FORCES in nature. The strongest of the four forces, it binds together protons and neutrons within the NUCLEUS of an atom. Like the WEAK NUCLEAR FORCE it operates at very short distances (a millionth of a millionth of a centimetre) and therefore occurs only within the nucleus. *See also* GRAND UNIFIED THEORY (GUT)

strontium Silvery-white, metallic element (symbol Sr) of the alkaline-earth metals in group II of the periodic table. Resembling CALCIUM physically and chemically, it occurs naturally in strontianite and celestite and is extracted by electrolysis. The isotope Sr^{90} (half-life 28 years) is a radioactive element present in fallout, from which it is absorbed into milk and bones; it is used in nuclear generators. at.no. 38, r.a.m. 87.62, r.d. 2.554, m.p. 769°C (1,416°F), b.p. 1,384°C (2,523°F).

structuralism 20th-century school of critical thought. It stresses the arbitrary nature of the relationship between the **signifier** (sound or image) and the **signified** (concept). Language is seen as a structure of relationships. One of the century's most influential critical movements, it is particularly associated with the analysis of a literary text as a system of signs and structural relationships. Structuralism has also developed as a mode of analysis of cultural institutions and products. *See also* DECONSTRUCTION

strychnine Poisonous ALKALOID obtained from the plant *Strychnos nux-vomica*. In the past it was believed to have therapeutic value in small doses as a tonic. Strychnine poisoning causes symptoms similar to those of TETANUS, with death occurring due to SPASM of the breathing muscles.

Stuart, Charles Edward (1720–88) Scottish

prince, known as "Bonnie Prince Charlie" or the "Young Pretender". A grandson of the deposed JAMES II, he led the JACOBITES in the rebellion of 1745 ("the '45") on behalf of his father, James, the "Old Pretender". Landing in the Scottish Highlands without the hoped-for backing of France, he gained the support of many clan chiefs, defeated government troops at Prestonpans, E central Scotland, and marched on London. Lacking widespread support in England, he turned back at Derby. The following year his largely Highland force was decimated in the battle of CULLODEN. He escaped to the continent and lived in exile until his death.

Stuart, James Francis Edward (1688–1766) British claimant to the throne, called the "Old Pretender". He was the only son of JAMES II, and was proclaimed king of England by the JACOBITES on the death of his father (1701). He made two attempts to regain the throne (1708 and 1715), landing in Scotland where support for the Stuart dynasty was greatest. On both occasions the cause was lost before James arrived. His son was Charles STUART.

Stuart, Mary *See* MARY II

Stuarts (Stewarts) Scottish royal house, which inherited the Scottish crown in 1371 and the English crown in 1603. Robert II became the first Stuart king in 1371. The crown descended in the direct male line until the death of James V (1542), who was succeeded by his infant daughter, MARY, QUEEN OF SCOTS. Her son, James VI, succeeded ELIZABETH I of England in 1603 as JAMES I. His son, CHARLES I, was executed in 1649 following the CIVIL WAR, but the dynasty was restored with the RESTORATION of Charles II in 1660. His brother, James II, lost the throne in the GLORIOUS REVOLUTION (1685) and was replaced by the joint monarchy of William III and Mary II, James' daughter. On the death of ANNE, James' second daughter, who died in 1714 without an heir, the House of HANOVER succeeded. The male descendants of James II made several unsuccessful attempts to regain the throne, culminating in the JACOBITE rebellion of 1745.

Stubbs, George (1724–1806) British painter and engraver. He made his name with the book *The Anatomy of the Horse*, which contained his own engravings.

sturgeon Large, primitive, bony fish found in temperate fresh and marine waters of the Northern Hemisphere. The ovaries of the female are the source of CAVIAR. It has five series of sharp-pointed scales along its sides, fleshy whiskers and a tapering, snout-like head. Family Acipenseridae; species Atlantic sturgeon (*Acipenser sturio*) length: to 3.3m (11ft), weight: to 272kg (600lb). The Eurasian freshwater sturgeon is also called beluga.

Sturm und Drang (Ger. Storm and Stress) Name of a German literary movement associated principally with the early writings of Johann Gottfried von HERDER, Johann Wolfgang von GOETHE and Friedrich SCHILLER, and seen as an anticipa-

tion of ROMANTICISM. Characteristic elements of Sturm und Drang writings include medieval knights, sieges and battles, family hostilities, and situations of passion and revenge.

Stuttgart Capital of Baden Württemberg, SW Germany, on the River Neckar. Now the eighth largest city in Germany, it was founded in *c.*950 when a German duke, Liutolf, set up a *stuttgarten* (stud farm). The capital of the kingdom of Württemberg from 1495–1806, its industrial base expanded rapidly during the 19th century. Historically it is associated with motor vehicle construction, and the Daimler-Benz factory is the world's oldest car-plant (1890). Additional industries include electronics, photographic equipment, publishing, wine and beer. Pop. (1993) 598,000.

style In botany, part of a flower – the tube that connects the pollen-receiving STIGMA at its tip to the ovary at its base.

Styx In Greek mythology, the river across which the souls of the dead were ferried by Charon on their journey from the world of the living to the underworld.

subatomic particles Particles that are smaller than ATOMS or are of the types that make up atoms. They can be divided into two groups: the HADRONS, such as protons and neutrons, which can be further subdivided, and ELEMENTARY PARTICLES, such as quarks and electrons, which cannot be further divided.

sublimation Direct change from solid to gas, without an intervening liquid phase. Most substances can sublimate at certain pressures, but usually not at atmospheric pressure. *See also* CONDENSATION; EVAPORATION

submarine Seagoing warship capable of travelling both on and under the water. Experimental submarines were used in warfare from the late 18th century. Early submarines were essentially surface ships with a limited ability to remain submerged. Once underwater, they depended on battery-powered electric motors for propulsion and, with a limited air supply, were soon forced to surface. Submerging is accomplished by letting air out of internal ballast tanks; trimming underwater is done by regulating the amount of water in the ballast tanks with pumps; and surfacing is accomplished by pumping ("blowing") the water out of the tanks. The most modern submarines use nuclear power, which eliminates the need to surface while on operations.

submersible Small craft for underwater exploration, research or engineering. Modern submersibles have evolved from simple divices. A device called the bathysphere, invented in the 1930s, was a spherical observation chamber. The bathyscaphe, invented in the 1940s by Swiss scientist Auguste Piccard, had a spherical chamber attached to a much larger hull, which was used as a buoyancy control device. A new generation of submersibles has evolved since the late 1950s for engineering and research work. A typical craft has a spherical passenger capsule capable of withstanding water pressure down to about 3,600m (12,000ft). Attached to this is a structure containing batteries, an electric motor with propeller, lighting, a mechanical arm for gathering samples, and other technical equipment. A specially designed support ship launches and retrieves the submersible. Some submersibles are unmanned and operated by remote control from the surface.

substitution reaction Chemical reaction in which one atom or group of atoms replaces (usually in the same structural position) another group in a molecule or ion.

succession Orderly change in plant and animal life in a biotic community over a long time period. It is the result of modifications in the community environment. The process ends in establishment of a stable ECOSYSTEM (climax community).

succulent Plant that stores water in its tissues to resist periods of drought. Usually PERENNIAL and evergreen, they have bodies mostly made up of water storage cells, which give them a fleshy appearance. A well-developed CUTICLE and low rate of daytime TRANSPIRATION also conserve water. Succulent plants include CACTUS, LILY and STONECROP.

sucker Any of several species of freshwater fish found mainly from N Canada to the Gulf of Mexico. A bottom-feeder similar to minnows, it has a thick-lipped mouth for feeding by suction. Length: to 66cm (26in); weight: to 5.4kg (12lb). Family Catostomidae.

Sucre City in S central BOLIVIA and the legal capital of Bolivia, the seat of government being La Paz. Known successively as La Plata, Chuguisaca and Charcas, Sucre was renamed in 1839 after the revolutionary leader and first president of Bolivia, Antonio José de SUCRE. It is a commercial and distribution centre for the surrounding farming region. Industries: cement, oil refining. Pop. (1992) 103,952.

sucrose Common white crystalline sugar, a disaccharide SUGAR ($C_{12}H_{22}O_{11}$) consisting of linked GLUCOSE and FRUCTOSE molecules. It occurs in many plants, but its principal commercial sources are SUGAR CANE and SUGAR BEET. It is widely used for food sweetening and making preserves.

Sudan Republic and Africa's largest country in NE Africa, the capital is KHARTOUM. **Land and climate** Sudan extends from the arid SAHARA in the N to an equatorial swamp region (the *Sudd*) in the S. Much of the land is flat, but there are mountains in the NE and SE; the highest point is Kinyeti, at 3,187m (10,456ft). The River NILE (*Bahr el Jebel*) runs S–N, entering Sudan as the White Nile, converging with the Blue Nile at Khartoum, and flowing N to Egypt. The climate ranges from the virtually rainless N deserts to the swamplands in the S. Khartoum is prone to summer dust storms (*haboobs*). From the bare deserts of the N, the land

merges into dry grasslands and savanna. Dense rainforests grow in the S. **Economy** Sudan is a low-income economy. Agriculture employs 62% of the people. The leading crops are cotton, millet, wheat and sesame. Nomadic herders raise livestock. Mineral resources include chromium, gold, gypsum and oil. Manufacturing industries produce cement, fertilizers and textiles. The main exports are cotton, gum arabic and sesame seeds. **History and politics** The ancient state of NUBIA extended into N Sudan. In c.2,000 BC it became a colony of EGYPT. From the 8th century BC to c.350 AD, it was part of the KUSH kingdom. N Sudan came under Muslim control and Islam became its dominant religion. In 1821 MUHAMMAD ALI's forces occupied Sudan. Anglo-Egyptian forces, led by Charles George GORDON, attempted to extend Egypt's influence into the S. Muhammad Ahmad led a MAHDI uprising, which briefly freed Sudan from Anglo-Egyptian influence. In 1898 KITCHENER's forces defeated the Mahdists, and in 1899 Sudan became Anglo-Egyptian Sudan, governed jointly by Britain and Egypt. Opposition to colonial rule continued until independence in 1956. The S Sudanese, who are predominantly Christians or followers of traditional beliefs, revolted against the dominance of the Muslim N, and civil war broke out. In 1958 the civilian government was overthrown in a coup; re-established in 1964, it was overthrown again in 1969, when Gaafar Muhammad Nimeri seized control. In 1972 S Sudan was given considerable autonomy but unrest continued. The imposition of strict Islamic law in 1983 sparked further conflict with the Sudan People's Liberation Army (SPLA) in the S. Nimeri was deposed in 1985, and a civilian government came to power in 1986. In 1989 it was overthrown by Omar Hassan Ahmed al Bashir, who established a Revolutionary Command Council. In 1996 Bashir was re-elected, though there had been no serious rival. The National Islamic Front (NIF) dominates the government and is believed to have strong links with Iranian terrorist groups. In 1996 the UN imposed sanctions on Sudan. Civil war between various SPLA factions and government forces continues in the S. By 1994 much of the area was government-controlled, but in 1995 and 1996 the SPLA gained ground. In 1996 a peace

---

SUDAN

AREA: 2,505,810 sq km (967,493 sq mi)
POPULATION: 26,656,000
CAPITAL (POPULATION): Khartoum (476,218)
GOVERNMENT: Military regime
ETHNIC GROUPS: Sudanese Arab 49%, Dinka 12%, Nuba 8%, Beja 6%, Nuer 5%, Azande 3%
LANGUAGES: Arabic (official)
RELIGIONS: Islam 73%, traditional beliefs 17%, Christianity (Roman Catholic 4%, Protestant 2%)
CURRENCY: Dinar = 10 Sudanese pounds

treaty, which involved the relinquishment of the fight for southern independence, was signed by the government and by some SPLA factions. Rejected by other factions, civil war continues. Food shortages and the displacement of people from areas of unrest have added to Sudan's economic difficulties.

sudden infant death syndrome (SIDS) (cot death) Unexpected death of an apparently healthy baby, usually during sleep. The peak period seems to be around two months of age, although it can occur up to a year or more after birth. Claiming more boys than girls, it is more common in winter. The cause is unknown, but a number of risk factors have been identified, including prematurity and respiratory infection.

Suez Canal Waterway in Egypt linking Port Said on the Mediterranean Sea with the Gulf of Suez and the Red Sea. The 169km (105mi) canal was planned and built in the period 1859–69 by the Suez Canal Company under the supervision of Ferdinand de LESSEPS. In 1875 the British government became the major shareholder in the company. After Egypt nationalized the canal in 1956, Israeli and British forces attacked Egypt, and the canal was closed from 1956–57 while repairs were carried out. It was again closed during the ARAB-ISRAELI WAR of 1967. The canal reopened in 1975. In the intervening period many new ships, especially oil tankers, were too large to pass through the canal. Loss of revenue forced Egypt to clear and widen the waterway.

Suffolk County in E England, on the North Sea coast; the county town is IPSWICH. The land is mainly low-lying and flat, rising in the SW. The principal rivers are the Orwell, Stour and Waveney. The economy is mainly agricultural, growing cereal crops and sugar beet and rearing sheep, pigs and poultry. Fishing along the coast (especially at Lowestoft, Britain's easternmost point) is in decline. Industries: food processing, farm machinery, fertilizers, finance. Area 3,807sq km (1,470sq mi). Pop. (1991) 632,266.

suffrage *See* FRANCHISE

suffragette movement Women's campaign in Britain in the late 19th and early 20th centuries to win the right to vote. It began in the 1860s, and developed until the founding of the National Union of Women's Suffrage Societies in 1897. Emmeline PANKHURST founded the Women's Social and Political Union in 1903. Women of the age of 30 and over were given the vote in 1918.

Sufism Mystic philosophical movement within ISLAM that developed among the SHIITE communities in the 10th and 11th centuries. Sufis stress the capability of the soul to attain personal union with God. *See also* DERVISH

sugar Sweet-tasting, soluble, crystalline monosaccharide or disaccharide CARBOHYDRATE. The common sugar in food and beverages is SUCROSE. This is also the main sugar transported in plant tissues. The main sugar transported around the

bodies of animals to provide energy is GLUCOSE. *See also* SACCHARIDE

sugar beet Variety of BEET grown commercially for its high SUGAR content, which is stored in its thick, white roots. Family Chenopdiaceae; species *Beta vulgaris*.

sugar cane Perennial GRASS cultivated in tropical and subtropical regions throughout the world. After harvesting, the stems are processed in factories, and are the main source of SUGAR. Most cultivated canes are *Saccharum officinarum*. Height: to 4.5m (15ft). Family Poaceae/Gramineae.

Suharto, Raden (1921–) Indonesian military and political figure, president (1968–). Suharto seized power from President SUKARNO, averting an alleged communist coup, in 1966. Elected president in 1968, he has been re-elected at regular intervals, despite criticism of his authoritarian rule.

Suhrawardi, as- (1155–91) Islamic philosopher and theologian, b. Persia (Iran). He was the founder of the Ishraqi (Illuminationist) school of thought, which embraced elements from many sources, including Orphism, Hellenism, ZOROASTRIANISM, SUFISM and SHIITE Islam. His thinking is still in evidence in Iran today among mystical sects, such as the Nuyah. His principal work is *Kitab Hikmat al-ishraq* (*The Wisdom of Illumination*).

suite Musical form popular in the BAROQUE period, comprising a number of instrumental dances, which differ in metre, tempo and rhythm but are generally all in the same key. By the 18th century the dances had become standardized: a prelude, allemande, courante, saraband and gigue. There was some flexibility, and the minuet, gavotte, bourrée and rondeau were often added.

Sukarno, Achmad (1901–70) First president (1947–67) of independent Indonesia. Founder of the Indonesian Nationalist Party (1927), he led opposition to Dutch rule and was frequently imprisoned or exiled (1933–42). At the end of World War 2 he declared Indonesian independence and became president of the new republic. In the 1950s his rule became increasingly dictatorial. He dissolved the parliament, declared himself president for life (1963) and aligned himself with the communists. He was forced out of power by the generals, led by SUHARTO, who eventually replaced him as president.

Sukkoth (Sukkat) Jewish Feast of Tabernacles, or Feast of Booths, an autumn festival that lasts for seven days. It commemorates the wandering of the Jews in the desert and their salvation through God. A *sukkat*, or simple tent of branches, is raised in the synagogue.

Sulawesi (formerly Celebes) Large island in E Indonesia, separated from Borneo by the Makasar Strait, with Ujung Pandang (formerly Makasar, 1990 pop. 913,196) the main port and largest city. A largely mountainous and volcanic island, the highest peak is Mount Rantekombola at 3,455m (11,335ft). The first European discovery was by the

Portuguese in 1512. The Dutch assumed control in the early 17th century and successfully waged war against the native population in the 1666–69 Makasar War. In 1950 it became a province of the Indonesian republic, and it is made up of four separate provinces: Utara, Tengah, Selatan and Tenggara. The population is primarily Malayan. Industries: fishing, agriculture. Area: 189,216sqkm (73,031sq mi). Pop. (1990) 12,520,711

Suleiman I (the Magnificent) (1494–1566) Ottoman sultan (1520–66). He succeeded his father, Selim I. He captured Rhodes from the KNIGHTS HOSPITALLERS and launched a series of campaigns against the Austrian HABSBURGS, defeating the Hungarians at Mohács (1526) and subsequently controlling most of the country. His troops besieged Vienna (1529), and Suleiman's admiral, BARBAROSSA, created a navy that dominated the Mediterranean and ensured Ottoman control of much of the North African coastal region. In the east he won victories against the Safavids of Persia and conquered Mesopotamia.

Sullivan, Sir Arthur Seymour (1842–1900) British composer famous for a series of operettas written with the librettist W.S. GILBERT. They included *H.M.S. Pinafore* (1878), *The Pirates of Penzance* (1879) and *The Mikado* (1885). Sullivan also composed one opera, *Ivanhoe* (1881), and oratorios, cantatas, and church music.

sulphate Salt of SULPHURIC ACID (H_2SO_4). Common sulphates include copper (II) sulphate ($CuSO_4$) and iron (II) sulphate ($FeSO_4$).

sulphonamide drug Any of a group of DRUGS derived from sulphanilamide, a red textile dye, that prevent the growth of bacteria. Introduced in the 1930s, they were the first antibacterials, prescribed to treat a range of infections. They were replaced by less toxic and more effective ANTIBIOTICS.

sulphur Nonmetallic element (symbol S) in group VI of the periodic table, known since prehistory (the biblical brimstone). It may occur naturally as a free element or in sulphide minerals such as GALENA and iron pyrites, or in sulphate minerals such as GYPSUM. The main commercial source is native (free) sulphur, extracted by the Frasch process. It is used in the VULCANIZATION of rubber and in the manufacture of drugs, matches, dyes, fungicides, insecticides and fertilizers. Properties: at.no. 16; r.a.m. 32.064; r.d. 2.07; m.p. 112.8°C (235.0°F); b.p. 444.7°C (832.5°F). Most common isotope S^{32} (95.1%).

sulphuric acid Colourless, odourless liquid (H_2SO_4), one of the strongest acids known. It is produced by the oxidation of sulphur dioxide (SO_2). Sulphuric acid is a major industrial chemical, used in the manufacture of many acids, fertilizers, detergents, drugs and a wide range of chemicals. Properties: r.d. 1.84; m.p. 10.3°C (50.5°F); b.p. 330°C (626°F).

Sumatra (Sumatera) Island in W Indonesia – the world's sixth-largest island. The W coast is rugged and mountainous, the Barisan Mountains rising to 3,810m (12,500ft), and nearly 60% of the lowland area is jungle. The Portuguese landed on the island in the 16th century and the Dutch followed a century later. Britain held certain parts of the island briefly in the 18th and 19th centuries, and Sumatra became part of newly independent Indonesia in 1950. The principal cities (1990 figures) are Medan (1,685,972), Palembang (1,084,483) and Padang (477,344). The main products are oil, timber, rubber, tin, tobacco, palm oil, tea, coffee, sisal and rice. Mining and farming were the chief occupations, but the N is being rapidly industrialized. Sumatra now accounts for around 75% of Indonesia's total income. Area 425,000sq km (164,000sq mi). Pop. (1990) 36,505,703.

Sumeria World's first civilization, dating from before 3000 BC, in S MESOPOTAMIA. The Sumerians are credited with inventing cuneiform writing, many familiar socio-political institutions and a money-based economy. Major cities were UR, Kish and Lagash. During the third millennium it built up a large empire. In c.2340 BC, the Semitic peoples of Akkadia conquered Mesopotamia, and by c.1950 BC the civilization had disintegrated.

sumo wrestling Traditional and popular sport of Japan. Pairs of wrestlers, who usually weigh more than 159kg (350lb), attempt to force each other out of a ring. The technique employs holds, trips, pushes and falls. A referee monitors the brief bout and keeps score.

Sun Star at the centre of the Solar System, around which all other Solar System bodies revolve in their orbits. The Sun is a typical, average star. It consists of about 70% hydrogen (by weight) and 28% helium, with the remainder mostly oxygen and carbon. Its temperature, pressure and density increase towards the centre. Like all stars, the Sun's energy is generated by nuclear fusion reactions taking place under the extreme conditions in the core. The temperature at the surface is 5,700K (5,470°C), while at the core it reaches 14 million K (14 million°C). The core is about 400,000km (250,000mi) across. Energy released from the core passes up through the radiative zone, which is about 300,000km (nearly 200,000mi) thick, then passes through the 200,000km (125,000mi) thick convective zone to the surface, the PHOTOSPHERE, from where it is radiated into space. Most of the Sun's visible activity takes place in the 500km (300mi) thick photosphere. Above the photosphere lies the chromosphere, which consists of hot gases and extends for thousands of kilometres. Extending outwards from the chromosphere for millions of kilometres is the CORONA, which emits the SOLAR WIND. The solar wind and the Sun's magnetic field dominate a region of space called the heliosphere, which extends to the boundaries of the Solar System.

sunbird Tropical, nectar-feeding songbird of the Old World, often considered a counterpart of the

New World hummingbird. The males are usually brightly coloured. Length: 9–15cm (3.5–6in). Family Nectariniidae.

Sunderland County district in SE TYNE AND WEAR, NE England at the mouth of the River Wear. Once renowned for coal-mining and the biggest shipbuilding centre in the world, it now has chemicals, vehicles, glass, electronics and furniture among its many industries. Pop. (1991) 289,040.

sundew Any INSECTIVOROUS PLANT of the genus *Drosera*, native to temperate swamps and bogs. Sundews have hairy basal leaves that glisten with a sticky dew-like substance that attracts and traps insects. The leaves then fold over the insect, and secrete ENZYMES to digest it. Family Droseraceae.

sunfish North American freshwater fish. A popular angler's fish, similar in appearance to PERCH, it has a continuous dorsal fin containing spiny and soft rays. The 30 species range in size from the blue spotted *Enneacanthus gloriosus* (length: 8.9cm; 3.5in) to the large-mouth bass *Micropterus salmoides* (length: 81.3cm; 32in; weight: 10kg; 22lb). Family Centrarchidae.

sunflower Any of several ANNUAL and PERENNIAL plants of the genus *Helianthus*, native to North and South America. The flower heads resemble huge daisies with yellow ray flowers and a centre disc of yellow, brown or purple. The seeds yield a useful oil. The common sunflower (*H. annuus*) has 30cm (1ft) leaves and flower heads more than 30cm across; height: to 3.5m (12ft). Family Asteraceae/Compositae.

Sung (960–1279) Chinese imperial dynasty (960–1279). The period is divided into the Northern (960–1126) and, after the north was overrun by Jurchen tribes, the Southern (1127–1279) Sung. The Sung dynasty was notable for a deliberate reduction in military might, after the initial conquests of Chao K'uang-yin, and the development of a powerful civil service. The Southern Sung, with its capital at Hangzhou, was overrun by the Mongols.

Sunni Traditionalist orthodox branch of ISLAM, whose followers are called *Ahl as-Sunnah* ("People of the Path"). It is followed by 90% of Muslims. Sunnis accept the *Hadith*, the body of orthodox teachings based on Muhammad's spoken words outside the KORAN.

sunspot Region in the Sun's PHOTOSPHERE that is cooler than its surroundings and appears darker. Sunspots vary in size from *c*.1,000–50,000km (600–30,000mi), and occasionally up to *c*.200,000km (125,000mi). Their duration varies from a few hours to a few weeks, or months for the very biggest. Sunspots occur where there is a local strengthening of the Sun's magnetic field.

Sun Yat-sen (1866–1925) Chinese nationalist leader, first president of the Chinese Republic (1911–12). After the revolution of 1911 he became provisional president, but soon resigned in favour of the militarily powerful Yüan Shih-k'ai. When

Yüan turned autocratic, Sun gave his support to the KUOMINTANG, or Nationalist Party, formed to oppose Yüan.

superconductivity Electrical behaviour in metals and alloys that are cooled to very low temperatures. In a superconducting circuit, an electric current flows indefinitely because there is no electrical resistance. High-temperature superconductivity has been observed in certain systems; research continues into the theory of this.

superego In PSYCHOANALYSIS, level of personality that acts as a conscience or censor. It develops as a child internalizes the standards of behaviour defined by the rewards and punishments of parents and society. *See also* ID; EGO

superfluidity Property of a liquid that has no viscosity and therefore no resistance to flow. Helium II – liquid helium at temperatures less than 2K, or −271°C (−456°F) – was the first known superfluid. Helium II apparently defies gravity by flowing up slopes. *See also* CRYOGENICS; HELIUM

Superior, Lake Lake in the USA and Canada, the largest freshwater lake in the world, bordered on the W by Minnesota, on the N and E by Ontario and on the S by Michigan and Wisconsin. The most westerly of the five GREAT LAKES, it is connected to Lake HURON and the ST LAWRENCE SEAWAY by the St Mary's River and the Soo (Sault Ste Marie) canals. A centre for commercial and recreational fishing, the lake is also a major commercial transportation route, particularly for grain and iron ore. Area: 82,413sq km (31,820sq mi). Maximum depth: *c*.400m (1,300ft).

supernova Stellar explosion in which virtually an entire star is disrupted. For a week or so, a supernova may outshine all the other stars in its galaxy. After a couple of years the supernova has expanded so much that it becomes thin and transparent. A supernova is about 1,000 times brighter than a NOVA.

superposition, law of In geology, law that states that in undisturbed layers of sedimentary deposits, younger beds overlie older ones.

supersonic speed Speed greater than that of the local speed of sound. In dry air at 0°C (32°F), this speed is about 330m/s (1,080ft/s) or 1,188km/h (736mph). Its magnitude is usually expressed as a MACH NUMBER.

supply-side economics Policies designed to reduce the role of governments in economic matters. The theory of supply-side economics is that production of goods and services can be stimulated by reducing taxes, thereby increasing the supply of money for investment. It also promotes governmental expenditure that generates industrial activity.

suprematism Abstract art movement launched in Russia in 1915 by Kasimir MALEVICH. Epitomized by the stark geometrical forms of Malevich's painting *White on White* (1919), suprematism had a profound influence on the development of geometrical ABSTRACT ART and CONSTRUCTIVISM.

Surabaja Port in NE Java, second-largest city in Indonesia and capital of East Java province. An important naval base occupied by Japan in World War 2, the city remains Indonesia's primary naval centre. It is a fishing and industrial port with shipyards, textile mills, car assembly plants and oil refining. Pop. (1990) 2,421,016.

surfing Water sport in which a person lies or stands on a specially designed wooden or fibreglass board, usually 1.2–1.8m (4–6ft) long, and is propelled by the crest of a wave towards the shore.

surgery Branch of medical practice concerned with treatment by operation. Traditionally it has mainly involved open surgery: gaining access to the operative site by way of an incision. However, the practice of using ENDOSCOPES has enabled the development of "keyhole surgery", using minimally invasive techniques. Surgery is carried out under sterile conditions, using ANAESTHESIA.

Surinam Independent nation in NE South America, on the Atlantic Ocean, bordered by Brazil (S), French Guiana (E), and Guyana (W). Its capital is PARAMARIBO. Surinam is made up of the Guiana highlands plateau, a flat coastal plain, and a forested inland region. Its many rivers serve as a source of hydroelectric power. The region was discovered in 1499 by Spanish explorer Alfonso de Ojeda, but it was the British who founded the first colony (1651). In 1667 it was ceded to Holland in exchange for New Amsterdam (later New York), and in 1815 the Congress of Vienna gave the Guyana region to Britain and reaffirmed Dutch control of "Dutch Guiana". It became officially autonomous in 1954, and in 1975, as Surinam, gained full independence from the Netherlands and membership of the United Nations. In 1980 the military seized control, imposing martial law and banning political parties. Guerrilla warfare disrupted the economy. In 1987 a new constitution provided for a 51-member National Assembly, with powers to elect the president. Rameswak Shankar was elected president in 1988, but was overthrown by another military coup in 1990. In 1991 the New Front for Democracy and Development won the majority of seats in the National Assembly and their leader, Ronald Venetian, became president. The constitution was amended in 1992 to limit the power of the military. In the 1996 National Assembly elections, the New Front did not win enough seats to elect the president, and a coalition government was formed. Jules Wijdenbosch of the National Democracy Party was elected president. Surinam's economy depends greatly on the export of bauxite, of which it is one of the world's largest producers. The chief agricultural products are rice, bananas, sugar cane, coffee, coconuts, lumber and citrus fruits.

surrealism Influential movement in 20th-century art and literature; it evolved in the mid-1920s from Dadaism. Taking inspiration from Freudian theories of the subconcious, the surrealists used bizarre imagery and strange juxtapositions to surprise and shock viewers. Important surrealist writers include Louis Aragon, Georges Bataille, Paul Éluard and Benjamin Peret, while painters include Jean ARP, Max ERNST, René MAGRITTE, Salvador DALI, Joan MIRÓ and Paul KLEE. *See also* DADA

Surrey County in SE England, bordering Greater London. From E to W are the North Downs, which slope down to the Thames Valley. The Wey and the Mole are the principal rivers. Much of the land in the W is devoted to farming, with dairy and market-garden produce, wheat and oats the chief products. Guildford (1991 pop. 122,378) is the county town, but the county council is in Kingston-upon-Thames (132,996), a Greater London borough no longer in Surrey. Area 1,679sq km (648sq mi). Pop. (1991) 1,018,003.

surveying Accurate measurement of the Earth's surface. It is used in establishing land boundaries, the topography of landforms and for major construction and civil engineering work. For smaller areas, the land is treated as a horizontal plane. Large areas involve considerations of the Earth's curved shape and are referred to a geodetic surveys.

suspension Liquid (or gas) medium in which small solid (or liquid) particles are uniformly dispersed. The particles are larger than those found in a COLLOID and will settle if the suspension stands undisturbed.

Sussex Former county in SE England, on the English Channel, since 1974 divided into the counties of EAST SUSSEX and WEST SUSSEX. Area: 3,773sq km (1,457sq mi).

Sussex Kingdom of Anglo-Saxon England, settled by the South Saxons under Aelle (*c.* AD 477). It was allegedly the last Anglo-Saxon kingdom to adopt Christianity (*c.*680). A number of kings of Sussex are known from the 7th–8th centuries, but at various times they were under the dominance of Mercia. Sussex was absorbed by WESSEX in the early 9th century. *See also* EAST SUSSEX; WEST SUSSEX

Sutherland, Graham (1903–80) English painter, draughtsman and printmaker. During World War 2 he was employed as an official artist to record the effects of bomb damage. After the war he concentrated on religious themes and creat-

---

SURINAM

AREA: 163,270sq km (63,069 sq mi)
POPULATION: 438,000
CAPITAL (POPULATION): Paramaribo (200,970)
GOVERNMENT: Multiparty republic
ETHNIC GROUPS: Indian 37%, Creole, 31%, Indonesian 14%, Black 9%, Native American 3%, Chinese 3%, Dutch 1%
LANGUAGES: Dutch (official)
RELIGIONS: Christianity (Roman Catholic 23%, Protestant 19%), Hinduism 27%, Islam 20%
CURRENCY: Surinam guilder = 100 cents

ed the celebrated tapestry *Christ in Glory* (1962) for Coventry Cathedral. His controversial portrait of Winston Churchill (1954) was destroyed by Lady Churchill on her husband's behalf.

Sutton Hoo Archaeological site in Suffolk, SE England. The 1939 excavation of the cenotaph of Raedwald, a Saxon King of East Anglia (d.625), was Britain's richest archaeological find. The digs revealed a Saxon rowing boat 27m (90ft) long. In the centre of the boat lay a wooden funeral chamber, containing silver plate, gold jewellery and coins and bronze armour.

Suva Seaport on the SE coast of Viti Levu Island, in the SW Pacific Ocean, capital of the Fiji Islands. It is the manufacturing and trade centre, with an excellent harbour. Exports include tropical fruits, copra and gold. Pop. (1992) 73,500.

Suzhou (Soochow, Su-chow) City on the Grand Canal, Jiangsu province, E central China. Capital of Wu kingdom in the 5th century BC, its famous silk industry developed under the Sung dynasty in the 12th century. It has been noted since 100 BC for its many gardens, temples and canals. Industries: silk, cotton, embroidery, chemicals. Pop. (1991) 706,000.

Suzman, Helen (1917–) South African politician. Suzman was an outspoken opponent of the apartheid regime in South Africa for 40 years. Elected to parliament in 1953, she formed the Progressive Party in 1959, and for the next 12 years was the only member. She retired from parliament shortly after the election of Nelson MANDELA.

Svalbard Archipelago in the Arctic Ocean, *c*.640km (400 mi) N of Norway, to which it has officially belonged since 1925. There are nine main islands, of which by far the largest is Spitsbergen. The administrative centre and largest settlement is Longyearbyen on Spitsbergen. The islands are an important wildlife refuge, and protective measures have saved certain mammals from extinction. Animals include polar bear, walrus and whale. Large coal deposits were found on Spitsbergen at the end of the 19th century, and the area was mined by Norway, Russia and Sweden. In 1925 the islands became a sovereign territory of Norway (although over half the population is Russian), in return for allowing mining concessions to other nations. Area: 62,000sq km (24,000sq mi). Pop. (1994) 2,906.

Swahili BANTU language of the Niger-Congo family of African languages. It developed as a lingua franca and trading language in most of E Africa, becoming the official language of Tanzania in 1967 and of Kenya in 1973. It is also in use in parts of central Africa. It has a large body of literature.

swallow Any of 75 species of graceful and agile birds with long, tapering wings and a long, forked tail. The common swallow (*Hirundo rustica*), known as the barn swallow in North America, is grey-blue with a light brown underside and red throat markings; it feeds primarily on insects,

which it catches in flight. Length: 20cm (8in) Family Hirundinidae.

swamp Low-lying wetland area, found near large bodies of open water. Swamps are characterized by numerous plants and animals, including rushes and sedge in N regions, and species of trees, such as the swamp cypress, in warmer S areas. Swamps can prevent flooding by absorbing flood waters from rivers and coastal regions. *See also* BOG; MARSH

swan Any of several species of graceful, white or black waterfowl that nest in N Northern Hemisphere and migrate S for winter. Three species, including the Australian Black swan, live in the Southern Hemisphere. Most have broad, flat bills, long necks, plump bodies and dense plumage. They dip their heads under water to feed on plant matter. Length: to 2m (6.5ft). Family Anatidae; genus *Cygnus*.

Swansea (Abertawe) City and county district on Swansea Bay at the mouth of the River Tawe, West Glamorgan, S Wales. The second-largest Welsh city, it is the administrative centre of West Glamorgan and an industrial city that grew with the export of coal in the 19th century. Formerly noted for its production of steel, it is now dominated by light industry. Pop. (1991) 181,906.

SWAPO Acronym for SOUTH WEST AFRICA PEOPLE'S ORGANIZATION

Swaziland Small, landlocked and mountainous kingdom in S Africa, bounded by South Africa (N, W, S) and Mozambique (E); its capital is MBABANE.
Land and climate There are four land regions. In the W, the Highveld, with an average height of 1,200m (3,950ft), makes up 30% of Swaziland. The Middleveld, between 350 and 1,000m (1,150–3,300ft), covers 28% of the country, while the Lowveld, with an average height of 270m (890ft), covers another 33%. The Lebombo Mountains, the fourth region, reach 800m (2,600 ft) along the E border. The Lowveld is almost tropical, with an average temperature of 22°C (72°F) and a low rainfall of about 500mm (20in) a year. The altitude moderates the climate in the W and Mbabane has a climate typical of the Highveld with warm summers and cool winters. Meadows and pasture cover about 65% of Swaziland. Arable land covers 8% of the land and forests only 6%.
Economy Swaziland is classified as a lower-mid-

SWAZILAND
AREA: 17,360sq km (6,703 sq mi)
POPULATION: 792,000
CAPITAL (POPULATION): Mbabane (38,290)
GOVERNMENT: Monarchy
ETHNIC GROUPS: Swazi 84%, Zulu 10%, Tsonga 2%
LANGUAGES: Siswati and English (both official)
LANGUAGES: Christianity (Protestant 37%, indigenous African churches 29%, Roman Catholic 11%), traditional beliefs 21%
CURRENCY: Lilangeni = 100 cents

le-income developing country and agriculture employs 74% of the workforce. Farm products and processed foods, including sugar, wood pulp, citrus fruits and canned fruit, are the leading exports, though many farmers live at subsistence level. Mining has declined in importance in recent years. Swaziland's high-grade iron ore reserves were used up in 1978, while the world demand for its asbestos has fallen. Swaziland is heavily dependent on South Africa and the two countries are linked through a customs union. **History** According to tradition, a group of Bantu-speaking people, under the Swazi chief Ngwane II, crossed the Lebombo range and united with local African groups to form the Swazi nation in the 18th century. Under attack from Zulu armies, the Swazi people were forced to seek British protection in the 1840s. Gold was discovered in the 1880s and many Europeans sought land concessions from the king, who did not realize that in doing this he was losing control of the land. In 1894 Britain and the Boers of South Africa agreed to put Swaziland under the control of the South African Republic (the Transvaal). At the end of the second SOUTH AFRICAN WAR (1899–1902), Britain took control of the country. In 1968 Swaziland became fully independent as a constitutional monarchy, with King Sobhuza II as head of state. **Politics** In 1973 Sobhuza suspended the constitution. He took over supreme power in 1976, and banned political parties in 1978. The bicameral legislature consists of a Senate and a House of Assembly; the king appoints 10 of the 65 members of the House of Assembly and 20 of the 30 members of the Senate. Sobhuza died in 1982, and in 1983 one of his sons, Prince Makhosetive (b. 1968), was chosen as his heir. In 1986 he was installed as king, taking the name Mswati III. In 1993 Swaziland held its first ever multiparty elections. Pro-democracy demonstrations were held in 1996, resulting in a promise from Mswati to reconsider the ban on political parties. A Constitutional Review Committee was established.

sweating (perspiring) Loss of water, salts and urea from the body surface of many mammals as a result of the action of certain glands (sweat glands). Sweat glands are situated in the dermis of the skin, and open onto the surface through tiny pores. In humans, they are found all over the body, but in some mammals they are found only on the soles of the feet. Sweating is controlled by the nervous system and forms an important part of the body's temperature control mechanism.

swede Root vegetable belonging to the mustard family (Brassicaceae/Cruciferae). The large, swollen taproot may be eaten cooked as a vegetable or fed to animals as fodder. Height: *c.* 30cm (12in). Species: *B. napus napobrassica*.

Sweden Kingdom on the E half of the Scandinavian peninsula, N Europe, the capital is STOCKHOLM. **Land and climate** Sweden is the largest of the SCANDINAVIAN countries in both area and population. Most of N Sweden is mountainous; its highest point is Kebnekaise in LAPLAND, at 2,117m (6,946ft). The S lowlands contain Sweden's largest cities, Stockholm and GOTHENBURG, and two of Europe's largest lakes, Vänern and Vättern. The climate of S Sweden is moderated by the Gulf Stream. Further N the climate becomes more severe. Forest and woodland cover *c.*68% of Sweden. Arable land makes up 7% and grass only 1%. **Economy** Sweden is a highly developed industrial country. It has rich iron ore deposits, but other industrial materials are imported. Steel is a major product and is used to manufacture aircraft, cars, machinery and ships. Forestry and fishing are important. Farmland covers 10% of the land and livestock and dairy farming are valuable activities; crops include barley and oats. **History and politics** The earliest inhabitants of the area were the Svear, who merged with the Goths in the 6th century AD. Christianity was introduced in the 9th century. Swedes are thought to have been among the VIKINGS who plundered areas to the S and E between the 9th and 11th centuries. Swedes (Varangians), led by Rurik, also penetrated Russia as far as the Black Sea. In 1319 Sweden and Norway were united under Magnus VII. In 1397 Sweden, Denmark and Norway were united by the Danish Queen Margaret in the Kalmar Union. Her successors failed to control Sweden, and in 1520 Gustavus Vasa led a successful rebellion. He was crowned king, as GUSTAVUS I, of an independent Sweden in 1523. (Southern Sweden remained under Danish control until 1660.) Known as the founder of modern Sweden, Gustavus made the monarchy hereditary within the Vasa dynasty and made Lutheranism the state religion. Sweden's power was strengthened by John III's marriage to the king of Poland's sister. Their son, Sigismund III, a Roman Catholic, came to the throne in 1592 but was deposed (because of his religion) by Charles IX in 1599. Charles' son, GUSTAVUS II, won territory in Russia and Poland; further victories in the THIRTY YEARS WAR established Sweden as a great European power. CHARLES XII fought brilliant campaigns in Denmark, Poland, Saxony and Russia, but his eventual defeat in Russia (1709) seriously weakened Sweden. The 18th century was marked by internal friction. Gustavus IV (r.1792–1809) brought Sweden into the NAPOLEONIC WARS.

SWEDEN
AREA: 449,960sq km (173,730sq mi)
POPULATION: 8,678,000
CAPITAL (POPULATION): Stockholm (692,594)
GOVERNMENT: Constitutional monarchy
ETHNIC GROUPS: Swedish 91%, Finnish 3%
LANGUAGES: Swedish (official), Finnish
RELIGIONS: Christianity (Lutheran 89%, Roman Catholic 2%)
CURRENCY: Swedish krona = 100 ore

Charles XIII (r.1809–18) lost Finland to Russia in 1809, but the Congress of VIENNA granted Norway to Sweden as compensation. Industry grew during the late 19th century. In 1905 the union between Sweden and Norway was dissolved. Under Gustavus V (r.1907–50), Sweden was neutral in both World Wars. In 1946 it joined the United Nations (UN). Sweden has wide-ranging welfare services, but many people are concerned about the high taxes necessary to fund these services. In 1991 the Social Democratic Party, which had built up the welfare state, was defeated by a coalition of centre and right-wing parties, which favoured cuts in government spending on welfare. In 1994 the Social Democratic Party returned to power, forming a minority government. In 1995 Sweden joined the European Union.

Swedish National language of Sweden, spoken by virtually all the country's 8.7 million people. It is also spoken by many people in Finland. Closely related to Norwegian and Danish, it is a member of the northern branch of the Germanic family of INDO-EUROPEAN LANGUAGES.

sweet pea Climbing, annual plant native to Italy. Widely cultivated as an ornamental, it has fragrant, butterfly-shaped flowers of white, pink, rose, lavender, purple, red or orange. Height: to 1.8m (6ft). Family Fabaceae/Leguminosae; species *Lathyrus odoratus*.

sweet potato Trailing plant native to South America and cultivated as a vegetable in Japan, Russia, USA and the Pacific. Its funnel-shaped flowers are pink or violet. The orange or yellow, tuber-like root is edible. Family Convolvulaceae; species *Ipomoea batatas*.

Swift, Jonathan (1667–1745) Irish satirist and poet. His early works include *The Battle of the Books* (1704) and *A Tale of a Tub* (1704). His best-known work, *Gulliver's Travels* (1726), is a satire on human follies. He wrote numerous works criticizing England's treatment of Ireland, including *A Modest Proposal* (1729).

swift Any of several species of fast-flying, widely distributed birds. They have hooked bills, wide mouths, long narrow wings and darkish plumage. They typically feed on insects, which they catch in flight, and build nests of plant matter held together with saliva. Length: to 23cm (9in). Family Apodidae.

swimming Self-propulsion through water, a leisure activity or as a competitive sport. The National Swimming Association was formed in England in 1837; the Fédération Internationale de Natation Amateur (FINA), the world governing body, was formed by 1908. There are four main strokes – breaststroke, front crawl, backstroke and butterfly. Recognized race distances for men and women range from 100m to 1,500m; there are also relay and medley races. Synchronized swimming also features at the Olympic Games and at the four-yearly world championships, as does DIVING.

Swimming is one of the disciplines of the triathlon and the modern pentathlon.

Swinburne, Algernon Charles (1837–1909) British poet and critic. *Atalanta in Calydon* (1865) brought him fame, and his *Poems and Ballads* (1866) also won praise. Two further series of *Poems and Ballads* appeared in 1876 and 1889.

swing Form of JAZZ, prevalent in the USA during the 1930s and 1940s. It originated in the music of small groups who played a rhythm of four even beats to the bar, as opposed to the two beats to the bar of the New Orleans style.

Switzerland Small, landlocked republic in central Europe, the capital is BERN. **Land and climate** The Swiss Confederation is a mountainous, landlocked country in central Europe. The Jura Mountains lie on the w border with France. The Swiss Alps make up about 60% of the country. Switzerland's highest peak is Monte Rosa, at 4,634m (15,217ft). The plateau contains the cities of ZÜRICH, BASEL, Lausanne and BERN, and lakes GENEVA and Constance. The climate varies with altitude. The plateau has warm summers and cold, snowy winters. Grassland covers *c.*30% of the land and arable land *c.*10%. Forests cover *c.*32% and help to reduce the destructiveness of avalanches. **Economy** Despite lacking natural resources, Switzerland is wealthy and industrialized. Manufactures include chemicals, electrical equipment, machinery, precision instruments, watches and textiles. Livestock raising, notably dairy farming, is the chief agricultural activity. Tourism is important, and Swiss banks attract worldwide investment. **History and politics** Originally occupied by Celtic Helvetii people, the region was taken by Romans in 58 BC. Ruled by FRANKS in the 6th century AD; it was later divided between Swabia and Burgundy. United within the HOLY ROMAN EMPIRE, it came under HABSBURG rule in the 13th century. In 1291 the cantons, Schwyz, Uri and Unterwalden, united against the Habsburgs. Traditionally led by William TELL, the Swiss League expanded and defeated the Habsburgs (1386, 1388). The defeat of Emperor MAXIMILIAN in 1499 brought partial independence.

SWITZERLAND
AREA: 41,290sq km (15,942sq mi)
POPULATION: 6,905,000
CAPITAL (POPULATION): Bern (135,600)
GOVERNMENT: Federal republic
ETHNIC GROUPS: German 64%, French 19%, Italian 8%, Yugoslav 3%, Spanish 2%, Romansch 1%
LANGUAGES: French, German, Italian and Romansch (all official)
RELIGIONS: Christianity (Roman Catholic 46%, Protestant 40%)
CURRENCY: Swiss franc = 100 centimes

Defeated by the French in 1515, the Swiss adopted neutrality. The REFORMATION caused religious divisions in Switzerland, but the confederation survived to achieve formal independence in 1648. The French Revolutionary Wars led to the overthrow of the oligarchy and the establishment of the Helvetic Republic (1798–1803). In 1815 the federation was fully re-established. The Congress of VIENNA expanded it to 22 cantons and guaranteed its neutrality. A brief civil war led to the constitution of 1848, turning Switzerland into one federal state. In 1979 Jura, the 23rd canton, was created. A 1986 referendum rejected Swiss membership of the UN to avoid compromising its neutrality. In 1992 EC membership was similarly rejected. In 1995 the ruling coalition of Radical Democrats, Christian Democrats, Social Democrats and the Swiss People's Party was re-elected.

swordfish (broadbill) Marine fish found worldwide in temperate and tropical seas. A popular food fish, it is silvery-black, dark purple or blue. Its long flattened upper jaw, in the shape of a sword, is one-third of its length and used to strike at prey. Length: to 4.50m (15ft); weight: 530kg (1,180lb). Family Xiphiidae; species *Xiphias gladius*.

sycamore Deciduous tree of the MAPLE family, native to central Europe and w Asia but widely naturalized. Also known as the great maple or false plane, it has deeply toothed, five-lobed leaves, greenish yellow flowers and winged brown fruit. Height: to 33m (110ft). Family Aceraceae; species *Acer pseudoplatanus*.

Sydney State capital of New South Wales, SE Australia, on Port Jackson, an inlet on the Pacific Ocean. Sydney is the oldest and largest city, the most important financial, industrial and cultural centre and the principal port in Australia. The city was founded in 1788 on a natural harbour as the first British penal colony in Australia. Industries: shipbuilding, textiles, motor vehicles, oil refining, building materials, chemicals, brewing, tourism, clothing, paper, electronics. The city will host the Olympic Games in the year 2000. Pop. (1994) 3,738,500.

symbiosis Relationship between two or more different organisms that is generally mutually advantageous. It is more accurately referred to as mutualism. *See also* PARASITE

symbolism European art and literary movement. Symbolism had its origins in France in the 1880s when it arose as a reaction against the pragmatic REALISM of COURBET and IMPRESSIONISM. Its exponents wanted to express ideas or abstractions rather than simply imitate the visible world. The most powerful tendency in the movement stemmed from GAUGUIN and Émile Bernard (*c.*1888). In literature, the movement included a group of poets active in the 19th century who were followers of VERLAINE and BAUDELAIRE such as MALLARMÉ and RIMBAUD in France and writers in English such as POE and SWINBURNE.

symmetry In biology, anatomical description of body form or geometrical pattern of a plant or animal. It is used in the classification of living things (TAXONOMY), and to clarify relationships. In mathematics a symmetrical figure is one that has an exact correspondence of shape about a point, line or plane.

symphonic poem (tone poem) Orchestral piece of the late-romantic period that describes in music a poem, story, or other extra-musical programme. The term was first used by Franz LISZT. *Till Eulenspiegel* and *Also sprach Zarathustra* by Richard STRAUSS are perhaps the best-known examples of the genre. *See also* PROGRAMME MUSIC

symphony Large-scale musical work for orchestra. It has evolved steadily since the 18th century, when it received its first classical definition in the works of HAYDN and MOZART. A symphony usually has four movements and, in the classical tradition, has its first movement in SONATA form. The first symphonies were scored almost exclusively for stringed instruments of the violin family, but in the early 19th century the use of brass and woodwind sections had become general. Later composers of symphonies include BEETHOVEN, SCHUBERT, SCHUMANN, BRAHMS, BRUCKNER, TCHAIKOVSKY, MAHLER, SIBELIUS and SHOSTAKOVICH.

synagogue Place of assembly for Jewish worship, education and cultural development. Synagogues serve as communal centres, under the leadership of a RABBI, and house the ARK OF THE COVENANT. The first synagogue buildings date from the 3rd century BC, but may go back to the destruction of Solomon's Temple in Jerusalem in 586 BC.

synapse Connection between the nerve ending of one NEURON and the next or between a nerve cell and a muscle. It is the site at which nerve impulses are transmitted using NEUROTRANSMITTERS.

syncline Downward FOLD in rocks. When rock layers fold down into a trough-like form, it is called a syncline. (An upward arch-shaped fold is called an anticline.)

syncope *See* FAINTING

Synge, John Millington (1871–1909) Irish dramatist and poet who was important in the Irish Literary Renaissance. He was one of the organizers of the Abbey Theatre in 1904 and his works include *Riders to the Sea* (1904), *The Well of the Saints* (1905) and *The Playboy of the Western World* (1907). *See also* IRISH LITERATURE

synovial fluid Viscous, colourless fluid that lubricates the movable joints between bones. It is secreted by the synovial membrane. Synovial fluid is also found in the **bursae**, membranous sacs that help to reduce friction in major joints such as the shoulder, hip or knee.

syntax Branch of grammar that encompasses the body of rules governing the ways in which words are put together to form phrases, clauses and sentences in a language. The word syntax also

611

describes the structure of a sentence or of an utterance produced by a writer or speaker.

synthesizer In music, an electronic instrument capable of producing a wide variety of different sounds, pitches and timbres. The modern instrument was invented by Robert Moog in 1964. Computer technology is now used to control the instrument's different functions, enabling synthesizers to replicate non-electronic sounds.

syphilis Sexually transmitted disease caused by the bacterium *Treponema pallidum*. Untreated, it runs in three stages. The first symptom is often a hard, painless sore on the genitals, appearing usually within a month of infection. Months later, the second stage features a skin rash and fever. The third stage, often many years later, brings the formation of growths and serious involvement of the heart, brain and spinal cord, leading eventually to blindness, insanity and death. The disease is treated successfully with ANTIBIOTICS.

Syria Republic in the Middle East, the capital is DAMASCUS. **Land and climate** Syria lies in the N Middle East. It is divided into two regions. The smaller, densely populated W region comprises a narrow coastal plain and several mountain ranges. The Jabal an Nusayriyah range drops sharply to the Great RIFT VALLEY in the E. In the SW, the Anti-Lebanon range contains Syria's highest peak, Mount Hermon (2,184m, 9,232ft). Damascus and ALEPPO lie in fertile valleys. Eastern Syria is mainly grassy plain and contains the valley of the River EUPHRATES. In the SE is the Syrian desert. The coast has a Mediterranean climate. To the E, the land becomes drier. Only 4% of Syria is forested. Farmland covers c.30% of Syria, grassland makes up 44%. **Economy** Syria is a lower-middle-income developing country. Its main resources are oil, hydroelectricity, and its fertile agricultural land. Petroleum and its products accounted for 56% of 1994 exports, but Syria also exports farm products, textiles and phosphates. Agriculture employs 23% of the workforce. The chief crops are cotton and wheat. Syria is rapidly diversifying its industrial base. **History** Syria's location on the trade routes between Europe, Africa and Asia has made it a desired possession of many rulers. The area, including what is now Lebanon and some of modern-day Jordan, Israel, Saudi Arabia and Iraq, was ruled by the HITTITES and by EGYPT during the 15th–13th centuries BC. Under the PHOENICIANS (13th–10th centuries BC), trading cities on the Mediterranean coast flourished. From the 10th century BC, Syria suffered invasions by ASSYRIANS and Egyptians. The ACHAEMENID empire provided stability. From the 3rd century BC, the SELEUCIDS controlled Syria, often challenged by Egypt. PALMYRA flourished as a city-state. The Romans conquered the region in AD 63. Christianity was introduced via Palestine. When the ROMAN EMPIRE divided in the 4th century, Syria came under BYZANTINE rule. Arabs invaded in AD 637, and most of the population converted to Islam. The UMAYYADS and ABBASID dynasties followed. In the 11th century, Syria was a target of the CRUSADES, but at the end of the 12th century SALADIN triumphed. MONGOL and Mameluke rule followed Saladin's death. In 1516 the area became part of the OTTOMAN EMPIRE. European interest in the region grew in the 19th century. During World War 1, Syrian nationalists revolted and helped Britain defeat the Turks. After the war, Syria, now roughly its present size, became a French mandate territory. It achieved independence in 1944. Syria has supported the Arab cause in the Middle East and has been involved in the ARAB-ISRAELI WARS. In 1967 it lost the GOLAN HEIGHTS to Israel, and in 1973 tried unsuccessfully to reclaim them. A UN-patrolled buffer zone was established in the area. It continues to be a source of considerable tension. Since independence, Syria has suffered from political instability, with many coups. In 1958 Syria joined the United Arab Republic with Egypt and North Yemen. Egypt's increasing power led to Syrian withdrawal from the UAR and the formation of a Syrian Arab Republic in 1961. The BA'ATH PARTY has been the ruling party since 1963. In 1970 Hafez al-ASSAD took power through a coup, and was re-elected in 1971. A new constitution was adopted in 1973, declaring Syria to be a democratic, popular socialist state. Assad's stable but repressive regime has attracted international criticism. In the 1991 GULF WAR, Syria supported the coalition against Iraq. In 1994 Syria and Israel held talks over the Golan Heights. These talks, part of an attempt to establish a peace settlement for the entire region, received a setback when a right-wing coalition won the 1996 Israeli elections.

Szechwan *See* SICHUAN

Szent-Györgyi, Albert von (1893–1986) US biochemist, b. Hungary. He was awarded the 1937 Nobel Prize for physiology or medicine for his work on biological OXIDATION processes and the isolation of vitamin C. He studied the biochemistry of MUSCLE, discovering the muscle protein actin.

SYRIA
AREA: 185,180sq km (71,498sq mi)
POPULATION: 12,958,000
CAPITAL (POPULATION): Damascus (1,497,000)
GOVERNMENT: Multiparty republic
ETHNIC GROUPS: Arab 89%, Kurd 6%
LANGUAGES: Arabic (official)
RELIGIONS: Islam 90%, Christianity 9%
CURRENCY: Syrian pound = 100 piastres

T/t is the 20th letter of the alphabet, derived from the Semitic letter taw *(meaning mark) and the Greek letter* tau. *The Roman letter had the same form as the modern T.*

table tennis Table sport played by two or four people, who use a rubber-covered, wooden bat to hit a small, celluloid ball back and forth across a net 15.2cm (6in) high. The table is 2.7m (9ft) long and 1.5m (5ft) wide. After the serve, the ball must bounce only on the far side of the net. If the ball misses the table or fails to clear the net, a point is scored by the opponent. The winner is the first player to score 21 points with two clear points.

Tabriz (formerly Tauris) Capital of East Azerbaijan province, NW Iran. From 1295 it was the administrative centre for the Persian empire. It was occupied by the Ottoman Turks and later held by the Russians. Tabriz's proximity to Turkey and the Commonwealth of Independent States makes it an important trading centre. Manufactures: carpets, shoes, soap, textiles. Pop. (1986) 971,482.

tachycardia Increase in heart rate beyond the normal. It may occur after exertion or because of excitement or illness, particularly during fever; or it may result from a heart condition.

Tacitus, Cornelius (55–120) Roman historian. His crisp style and reliability make him one of the greatest of Roman historians. His books include the *Annals* and *Histories* of which large parts are lost.

tadpole Aquatic larva of a TOAD or FROG; it has a finned tail and gills, and lacks lungs and legs. The tadpoles of most species are herbivores, feeding on algae and other aquatic plants. During META-MORPHOSIS legs are grown, the tail is reabsorbed and internal lungs take the place of gills.

Taegu City in S central South Korea; capital of North Kyŏngsang province and the country's third-largest city. Successfully defended by UN troops during the KOREAN WAR, it is the trading centre for a large apple-growing area. The main industries are textiles, including silk and synthetic fabrics. Pop. (1990) 2,228,834.

tae kwon do Korean martial art. It is a form of unarmed combat developed over 2,000 years in Korea and is characterized by high standing and jump kicks as well as punches. It is practised both for sport and for spiritual development.

Taft, William Howard (1857–1930) 27th US President (1909–13). After a distinguished legal career, he gained great credit as governor of the Philippines (1901–04) and entered the cabinet of Theodore ROOSEVELT. He won the Republican nomination for president and was elected in 1908. His lack of political experience and his tendency to side with the conservatives in the Republican Party

against the progressives caused increasing dissension. In 1912 Roosevelt set up his own Progressive Party. With the Republican vote split, the Democrat, Woodrow WILSON, won the election. Taft taught at Yale Law School until 1921, when he was appointed chief justice of the supreme court.

Tagore, Rabindranath (1861–1941) Indian poet and philosopher. Immensely influential in the West and in India, he combined the traditions of both cultures, writing novels, essays, plays and poetic works. He won the Nobel Prize for literature in 1913 for *Gitanjali*.

Tagus (Tajo, Tejo) Longest river on the Iberian peninsula, flowing *c*.1,000km (620mi). The Tagus rises in the Sierra de Albarracin in Teruel, E central Spain. It flows SW for 785km (488mi), passing through Toledo, to the Spain-Portugal border. It then winds S to meet the Atlantic at Lisbon. The estuary is one of the world's finest natural harbours.

Tahiti Island in the S Pacific Ocean, in the Windward group of the SOCIETY ISLANDS, the largest in FRENCH POLYNESIA and accounting for over half its population. Charted in 1767 by the British navigator Samuel Wallis and explored by Captain COOK, it was colonized by France in 1880. Tahiti is mountainous, rising to 2,237m (7,339ft), but also fertile, producing tropical fruits, copra, sugar cane and vanilla. Industries: tourism, pearl-fishing, phosphates. Paul GAUGUIN lived and painted here (1891–93, 1895–1901). Area: 1,058sq km (408sq mi). Pop. (1988) 115,820.

Tai Chi Neo-Confucian concept of the Supreme Ultimate, the intrinsic energy of the universe (Chi). A philosophic system was developed in the work of Chou Tun-i (1017–73) and Chu Hsi (1130–1200). *Tai Chi* also refers to the most popular form of exercise in China – a martial arts-based series of slow, flowing movements designed to enhance the effective flow of Chi around the body.

Taipei Capital and largest city of Taiwan, at the N end of the island. A major trade centre for tea in the 19th century, the city was enlarged under Japanese rule (1895–1945) and became the seat of the Chinese Nationalist government in 1949. Industries: textiles, chemicals, fertilizers, metals, machinery. The city expanded from 335,000 people in 1945 to 2,653,000 in 1993.

Taiping Rebellion (1851–64) Revolt in China against the Manchurian QING dynasty, led by a Hakka fanatic, Hung Hsiu-ch'uan. The fighting laid waste to 17 provinces of China and resulted in more than 20 million casualties. The Manchus never recovered their full ability to govern China.

Taiwan (officially the Republic of China) Pacific island, separated from the SE coast of the Chinese mainland by the 160km (100mi) Taiwan Strait. The republic comprises the main island of Taiwan, several islets and the Pescadores group. The terrain is mostly mountainous and forested, and the highest peak is Yu Shan at 3,997m (13,113ft). The climate is semi-tropical and subject to typhoons. Agriculture, fishing and forestry are important economic activities, and rice is the principal crop. Spectacular economic growth from the mid-1950s was achieved through low-cost, export-led manufacture of textiles, electrical goods, machinery and transport equipment. In 1590 the Portuguese visited the island, but in 1641 the Dutch assumed full control of the island. They in turn were forced to relinquish control to the MING dynasty. The ruling Chinese QING dynasty captured Taiwan in 1683 and immigration increased. It was ceded to Japan in 1895 after the first SINO-JAPANESE WAR. Following the 1949 mainland victory of the Chinese Communist Party, the vanquished Nationalist KUOMINTANG government (led by CHIANG KAI-SHEK) and 500,000 troops fled to Taiwan. The new Chinese regime claimed sovereignty over the island, and in 1950, a Chinese invasion was prevented by the US Navy. The Nationalists, with continued US military and financial support, remained resolute. By 1965 the economic success of Taiwan had removed the need for US aid. In 1975 Chiang Kai-shek died and a gradual process of liberalization began. Immediately prior to the 1996 Taiwanese elections, China dispatched missiles close to the island's coast, reminding the world community of its territorial claims. Lee Teng-hui has been president since 1988.

Tajik Native speaker of Tajiki, an Iranian language spoken in Tajikistan and (with some TURKIC elements) in Afghanistan, S Russia and much of central Asia. Tajiks constitute a minority of 30% within Tajikistan.

Tajikistan Republic in central Asia, the capital is DUSHANBE. **Land and climate** Tajikistan lies in SE Central Asia. In the N is the westernmost part of the TIAN SHAN range. In the E lie the snow-capped PAMIRS, including KOMMUNIZMA PIK at 7,495m (24,590ft). Dushanbe lies at the foot of the central Gissar-ALTAI range. In the NW lies part of the Fergana valley on the ancient route to Samarkand. In the SW, a plain extends from Dushanabe to the River Amudarya border with Afghanistan and Uzbekistan. Summers are hot and dry in the lowlands, but winters are long and cold in the mountains. Much of the country is arid, but the SE has heavy snowfalls. Much of Tajikistan consists of desert or rocky mountain landscapes capped by snow and ice. The country is prone to earthquakes. **Economy** The poorest of the former Soviet republics, Tajikistan is a low-income developing country (1992 GDP per capita, US$1,740). It has faced enormous problems in the transition to a market economy. The cost of civil war devastated a fragile economy. In 1994 Tajikistan ceded much of its economic sovereignty to Russia in return for financial and military assistance. Agriculture is the main activity. Cotton is the chief product. Livestock-rearing is also important. Tajikistan is rich in resources, such as hydroelectricity, oil, uranium and gold. Aluminium is the major manufactured export. Textiles are also important. **History and politics** The Tajiks are descendants of Persians who settled in the area c.2,500 years ago. ALEXANDER THE GREAT conquered the region in the 4th century BC. In the 7th century AD Tajikistan was conquered by Arabs, who introduced Islam. In the 9th century it fell to the Persian empire. The Tajik cities of BUKHARA and Samarkand were vital centres of trade and Islamic learning. In the 13th century Tajikistan was overrun by the Mongol hordes. From the 16th to the 19th centuries, Uzbeks ruled the area as the khanate of Bukhara. The fragmentation of the region aided Russian conquest from 1868. Following the RUSSIAN REVOLUTION (1917), Tajikistan rebelled against Russian rule. Though Soviet troops annexed N Tajikistan into Turkistan in 1918, the Bukhara emirate held out against the Red Army until 1921. In 1924 Tajikistan became an autonomous part of the republic of Uzbekistan. In 1929 Tajikistan achieved full republican status, but Bukhara and Samarkand remained in the republic of Uzbekistan. During the 1930s, vast irrigation schemes greatly increased agricultural land. Many Russians and Uzbeks were settled in Tajikistan. As reforms accelerated in Russia, many Tajiks began to demand independence. In 1990 the Tajik parliament declared itself the supreme sovereign group. In 1991 Tajikistan became an independent republic within the COMMONWEALTH OF INDEPENDENT STATES (CIS). In 1992, tension between the new government (consisting mainly of former communists) and an alliance of Islamic and democratic groups spiralled into full civil war. The government called for Russian military assistance, and by 1993 the Islamic-Democratic rebels had retreated into Afghanistan. Imamali Rakhmonov was elected president by the Supreme Soviet. Fighting continued along the Afghan border, and the rebels made frequent incursions into Tajikistan. In 1994 a brief cease-fire enabled elections to take place. Rakhmonov was elected president amid an opposition boycott. In 1995 the civil war resumed, and the Russian airforce attacked rebel bases in Afghanistan. Further elections in 1995 saw the return of the former communist People's Party of Tajikistan, amid charges of electoral corruption and another opposition boycott. In 1997 a peace agreement was signed formally ending the five-year civil war.

Taj Mahal Muslim MAUSOLEUM near Agra, India, built (1632–54) by the Mogul emperor SHAH JAHAN at his favourite wife, Mumtaz Mahal. With its bulb-shaped dome, intricate inlays of semi-precious stones and rectangular reflecting pool, it ranks among the world's most beautiful buildings.

takahe Rare, flightless New Zealand bird, related to the RAIL and gallinule. Turkey-sized, it has a heavy, curved bill, a reddish shield on the forehead and bright, blue-green plumage. Family Rallidae; species *Notornis mantelli*.

Talbot, William Henry Fox (1800–77) British scientist. Talbot improved on the work of Niepce and DAGUERRE by inventing the first photographic process capable of producing any number of positive prints from an original negative.

talc Sheet silicate mineral, hydrous magnesium silicate, $Mg_3Si_4O_{10}(OH)_2$. It occurs as rare tabulate crystals in a monoclinic system and as masses. It is used as base for talcum powder and in ceramics. Hardness 1; s.g. 2.6.

Taliban (Persian "students") Radical SUNNI political movement in Afghanistan. From their headquarters in Kandahar, SW Afghanistan, Taliban militia launched themselves on Afghan society in 1996, vowing to spread SHARIA (Islamic law) throughout the country. They soon captured Kabul.

Tallahassee State capital of Florida, USA. First discovered by Europeans in 1539, it became the capital of Florida Territory in 1824. Industries: chemicals, timber, paper, food processing, tourism. Pop. (1992) 130,357.

Tallinn (Talin) Capital and largest city of Estonia, on the Gulf of Finland, opposite Helsinki. Founded in 1219 by the Danes, it became a member of the Hanseatic League (1285). It passed to Sweden in 1561 and was ceded to Russia in 1721. Developed in the 19th century for Russia's Baltic Fleet, it remains a major port and industrial centre. Industries: machinery, cables, paper, textiles, oilfield equipment. Pop. (1994) 490,000.

Tallis, Thomas (1505–85) English composer famous for his church music. In 1575 he and William BYRD published the *Cantiones Sacrae*, a set of motets. His church music includes a setting of Lamentations, two masses and a number of anthems. His contrapuntal skill shows in his 40-part motet, *Spem in alium*, probably written in 1573.

Talmud Body of Jewish religious and civil laws and learned interpretations of their meanings. Study of the Talmud is central to orthodox Jewish faith. The Talmud consists of two elements: the *Mishna* and the *Gemara*. The MISHNA is the written version of a set of oral laws that were handed down from the time of MOSES (c.1200 BC); the written version was completed by c.200. The

Gemara, the interpretation and commentary on the Mishna, was completed by c.500.

tamarind Tropical tree native to Asia and Africa. It has divided, feather-like leaves and pale yellow flowers, streaked with red. The fruit pulp is used in beverages, food and medicines. Height: 12–24m (40–80ft). Family Fabaceae/Leguminosae; species *Tamarindus indica*.

tamarisk Any of a group of deciduous shrubs found in semi-arid areas. They have slender branches covered with blue-green, scale-like leaves and clusters of small, white or pink flowers. Height: to 9.1m (30ft). Family Tamaricaceae; genus *Tamarix*.

tambourine PERCUSSION musical instrument much used by wandering musicians in Europe in the Middle Ages. It comprises a narrow circular frame, made of wood, with a single parchment drumhead and metal jangles attached to the sides.

Tamerlane (1336–1405) (Turkish *Timur Leng*, Timur the Lame) Mongol conqueror, b. Uzbekistan. By 1369 Tamerlane had conquered present-day Turkistan and established Samarkand as his capital. He extended his conquests to the region of the GOLDEN HORDE between the Caspian and Black Seas. In 1398 he invaded NW India and defeated the Delhi Sultanate. He then turned toward the Mameluke empire, capturing Syria and Damascus. In 1402 he captured the Ottoman sultan Beyazid I at Angora. Tamerlane died leading a 200,000-strong invasion force of China.

Tamil Language spoken chiefly in the state of Tamil Nadu, SE India, by up to 50 million people. There are also about 3 million speakers in N SRI LANKA and about 1 million distributed throughout Malaysia, Singapore, Fiji, Mauritius and Guyana.

Tamil Tigers Militant TAMIL group in Sri Lanka that seeks independence from the SINHALESE majority. Located mainly in the N and E of the island, the 3 million Tamils are Hindus, unlike the Buddhist Sinhalese. In the 1980s the Tamil Tigers embarked on a campaign of civil disobedience and terrorism. Autonomy for the Tamils was agreed by India and Sri Lanka in 1986, but no date fixed. The Indian army was sent in 1987 but withdrew in 1990, having failed to stop the violence.

tanager Small, brightly coloured, American forest bird with a cone-shaped bill. The scarlet tanager (*Piranga olivacea*) of E North America has black on its wings and tail. Family Emberizidae.

T'ang Chinese imperial dynasty (618–907). The early period was a golden age for China. Armies carried Chinese authority to Afghanistan, Tibet and Korea. Trade expanded, and new ideas and foreign influences were freely admitted. During the 8th century the dynasty succumbed to civil conflicts.

Tanganyika, Lake Second-largest lake in Africa and the second-deepest freshwater lake in the world. It lies in E central Africa, on the borders of Tanzania, Zaïre, Zambia and Burundi, in the RIFT VALLEY. Area: 32,893sq km (12,700sq mi); depth 1,437m (4,715ft).

tangent In TRIGONOMETRY, the ratio between the length of the sides opposite and adjacent to an acute angle within a right-angle triangle.

Tangier (Tanger) Port on the Strait of Gibraltar, N Morocco. An ancient Greek, Phoenician and then Roman port, it was later occupied by Moors and taken by the Portuguese in 1471. Tangier was passed to England in 1662, but was abandoned to the Sultan of Morocco in 1684. Under international control from 1904 to 1956, it became part of Morocco in 1956. Industries: rugs, pottery, shipping, fishing, tourism. Pop. (1990) 420,000.

Tanizaki, Junichiro (1886–1965) Japanese novelist and dramatist. He was influenced by classical Japanese literature and by BAUDELAIRE. His works include *Some Prefer Nettles* (1928–29) and *The Makioka Sisters* (1943–48).

tank Tracked, armoured vehicle mounting a single primary weapon, usually an artillery piece, and one or more machine guns. First used at the Battle of the SOMME in 1916, modern battle tanks weigh from 35 to 50 tonnes.

tannin (tannic acid) Any of a group of complex organic compounds derived from tree bark, roots and galls, unripe fruit, tea and coffee. Tannin is used in tanning to cure hides and make leather, in inks and dyes, and as an astringent in medicine.

tansy Any of several mostly perennial plants characterized by fern-like, aromatic leaves and clusters of yellow, button-like flower heads. Height: to 91cm (3ft). Family Asteraceae/Compositae.

tantalum Rare, blue-grey metallic element (symbol Ta). Its chief ore is columbite-tantalite. Hard but malleable, it is used as wire and in electrical components, chemical equipment and medical instruments. Properties: at.no. 73; r.a.m. 180.948; r.d. 16.6; m.p. 2,996°C (5,425°F); b.p. 5,425 °C (9,797°F); most common isotope Ta^{181} (99.988%).

Tantrism Collective term for religious systems within BUDDHISM, JAINISM and HINDUISM that are based on esoteric practices recorded in sacred texts called Tantras. For Hindus and Jains, the Tantras are post-Vedic (VEDAS) texts that give instruction on how to fulfil worldly desires and attain spiritual experiences. For Buddhists, the Tantras are a set of writings attributed to BUDDHA explaining how the believer may attain enlightenment.

Tanzania Republic in E Africa, the capital is DODOMA. **Land and climate** The United Republic of Tanzania consists of the mainland republic of Tanganyika and the island republic of ZANZIBAR. A narrow plain borders the Indian Ocean, and includes the largest city, DAR ES SALAAM. The interior is dominated by a plateau between 900 and 1,500m (2,950ft to 4,900ft). The capital, DODOMA, lies in the centre of Tanzania. The plateau is broken by the Great RIFT VALLEY, the W arm of which contains Lake TANGANYIKA. The E arm runs through central Tanzania to meet the W arm near Lake MALAWI. The Serengeti Plain lies on the E shore of Lake VICTORIA. In the NE lies Africa's highest peak,

Mount KILIMANJARO, at 5,896m (19,344ft). The coastal region is hot and humid. The plateau and mountains are much less humid. Mount Kilimanjaro is permanently snow-covered. Mangrove swamps and palm groves line the coast. The plateau is vast, open savanna grass or woodland (*miombo*). Tanzania's rich wildlife is protected in national parks, which cover over 12% of the land. Only 5% of land is cultivated. **Economy** Tanzania is one of the world's poorest countries (1992 GDP per capita, $US620). Agriculture employs 85% of the workforce, mainly at subsistence level. Tanganyika's main export crops are coffee, cotton, tea and tobacco, while Zanzibar is the world's largest producer of cloves. Diamonds are the principal mineral resource. Manufacturing is mostly small scale. **History and politics** OLDUVAI GORGE is the site of early human remains. In 1498 Vasco da Gama became the first European to land on the Tanzanian coast. For the next 200 years, the Portuguese controlled coastal trade. In 1698 the Portuguese were expelled with the help of Omani Arabs. During the 18th century, ZANZIBAR was the principal centre of the E African ivory and slave trade. In 1841 the sultan moved his capital to Zanzibar. The interior was opened up by caravan routes bringing slaves and ivory to the coast. In the European scramble for Africa, Tanganyika was subsumed into German East Africa (1887), and the sultanate of Zanzibar became a British protectorate (1890). Resistance to German colonial rule was fierce. The Germans established plantations, built railroads, and missionaries encouraged the spread of Christianity. During World War 1, British and Belgian troops occupied German East Africa (1916), and in 1919 Tanganyika became a British mandate. The British ruled indirectly, via local leaders. In 1961 Tanganyika became the first East African state to gain independence. Julius NYERERE became the first post-colonial president. In 1963 Zanzibar gained independence, and in 1964 Tanganyika and Zanzibar merged to form Tanzania, though Zanzibar retained economic sovereignty. Despite promises of decentralization, Tanzania became a one-party state. In 1977 Tanganyika and Zanzibar's ruling parties

---

TANZANIA

AREA: 945,090sq km (364,899sq mi)
POPULATION: 27,829,000
CAPITAL POPULATION: Dodoma (203,833)
GOVERNMENT: Multiparty republic
ETHNIC GROUPS: Nyamwezi and Sukuma 21%, Swahili 9%, Hehet and Bena 7%, Makonde 6%, Haya 6%
LANGUAGES: Swahili and English (both official)
RELIGIONS: Christianity (mostly Roman Catholic) 34%, Islam 33% (99% in Zanzibar), traditional beliefs and others 33%
CURRENCY: Tanzanian shilling = 100 cents

merged to form the Party of the Revolution (CCM). In 1978 Uganda occupied N Tanzania. In 1979 Tanzania and Ugandan rebels counter-attacked and overthrew the Ugandan president Idi AMIN. In 1985 Nyerere retired, and was succeeded by Ali Hassan Mwinyi. In 1992 Mwinyi endorsed multiparty elections and in 1995 Benjamin Mkapa became the first president to be elected in a multiparty system.

Taoism Chinese philosophy and religion considered as being next to CONFUCIANISM in importance. Taoist philosophy is traced to a 6th-century BC classic of LAO TZU, the *Tao Te Ching*. Taoist ethics emphasize patience, simplicity and the harmony of nature, achieved through the proper balance of the *yin*, or female principle, and *yang*, or male principle. As a religion, Taoism dates from AD 142.

tape, magnetic Thin strip of plastic, coated on one side with a layer of iron or chromium oxide, used in audio and video tape recorders and computers. During recording, the oxide layer is magnetized by the recording head in a pattern corresponding to the input signal. During playback, the magnetized oxide particles induce an electric current almost identical to the one that produced them.

tape recorder Device which records and plays back sound on magnetically treated tape. Sound is transformed into electric current and fed to a TRANSDUCER, which converts it into the magnetic variations that magnetize the particles on the treated tape. *See also* TAPE, MAGNETIC; DIGITAL AUDIO TAPE (DAT)

tapestry Hand-woven, plain weave fabric. Used for wall decoration, tapestry is an ancient craft and a few fragments survive from 15th-century BC Egypt. The first great French woollen tapestry came from Arras in the 14th century. The most famous designs came from the GOBELINS factory in Paris.

tapeworm Parasite of the genus *Taenia* that colonizes the intestines of vertebrates, including human beings. Caught from eating raw or undercooked meat, it may cause serious disease.

tapioca *See* CASSAVA

tapir Any of several species of nocturnal, plant-eating, hoofed mammals native to forests of tropical South America and Malaysia. The tapir has a large head, a long, flexible snout, a heavy body, short legs and a tiny tail. Length: to 2.5m (7.5ft). Family Tapiridae; genus *Tapirus*.

tar Black or dark brown, complex liquid mixture of HYDROCARBON compounds, derived from wood, coal and other organic materials. Tar, from PETROLEUM oil, is a major source of hydrocarbons for the synthesis of pharmaceuticals, pesticides and plastics; cruder tar compounds such as pitch are used for road surfacing and protecting timber against rot and pests. Wood tar yields creosote and paraffin.

tarantula Large, hairy wolf spider of S Europe. It spins no web, but chases and pounces on its prey. Length of body: to 2.5cm (1in). Family Lycosidae; species *Lycosa tarentula*. The name is also applied to the sluggish, dark, hairy spiders of SW USA,

Mexico and South America. Length of body: to 5cm (2in). Family Theraphosidae; genera *Aphonopelma* and *Eurypelma*.

Tarawa Town on an atoll of the same name in the W Pacific Ocean, capital of KIRIBATI. Located in the N central part of the group, it is the main trade centre for the islands. Copra, fish and fish products are its principal exports. Pop. (1990) 29,000.

tariff Tax placed on imports, calculated either as a percentage of the value of the item (ad valorem tariff) or per unit (specific duty). Tariffs may be used to discourage the import of certain types of goods.

Tarim Basin Basin in XINJIANG region, NW CHINA, between the TIAN SHAN and Kunlun mountain ranges. Taklamakan Shamo, a desert, covers most of the region, and Turfan depression, China's lowest point, at 154m (505ft), is in the extreme E.

taro Large, tropical plant native to the Pacific Islands and SE Asia and cultivated in other parts of the world for its edible tuberous root. Family Araceae; species *Colocasia esculenta*. *See also* LILY

tarpon Tropical, marine game fish. Blue and bright silver, it has a long, forked tail. Length: to 180cm (6ft); weight: to 150kg (300lb). Species include the small Pacific *Megalops cyprinoides* and the large Atlantic *M. atlanticus*.

tarragon Perennial plant with liquorice-flavoured leaves used fresh or dried in salads, pickles and other food. Family Asteraceae/Compositae; species *Artemisia dracunculus*.

tarsier Any of several species of nocturnal PRIMATES of Indonesia. They are small, squat animals with large eyes, long tails and monkey-like hands and feet. Family Tarsiidae; genus *Tarsius*.

tartan Cloth, usually woollen, with a pattern of stripes crossing at right angles. The cross-bars are of different colours and widths. The patterned cloth is now associated mainly with the Highlands of Scotland.

Tartars *See* TATARS

Tasaday Small group of isolated aboriginal people of the rainforests of S Mindanao in the Philippines. They are food-gathering cave dwellers with a STONE AGE culture.

Tashkent Largest city and capital of Uzbekistan, in the Tashkent oasis in the foothills of the TIAN SHAN mountains, watered by the River Chirchik. It was ruled by the Arabs from the 8th until the 11th century. The city was captured by TAMERLANE in 1361 and by the Russians in 1865. The modern city is a terminus for road, rail and air routes and is the economic centre of the region. Industries: textiles, chemicals, mining machinery, paper, porcelain, clothing, leather, furniture. Pop. (1990) 2,094,000.

Tasman, Abel Janszoon (1603–59) Dutch maritime explorer who made many discoveries in the Pacific. On his voyage of 1642–43 he discovered Tasmania. He reached New Zealand, but was attacked by Maoris in Golden Bay, and landed on Tonga, Fiji and Papua New Guinea.

Tasmania Island state of Australia, separated

from Victoria by the Bass Strait. The chief cities are HOBART, the state capital in the S, and Launceston in the N. Tasmania is mountainous and forested, with a temperate maritime climate. The first European discovery was made by Abel TASMAN in 1642 and it was named Van Diemen's Land. Captain COOK visited it in 1777 and claimed it for the British, who established a penal colony there. Tasmania became a separate colony in 1825 and it was federated as a state of the Commonwealth of Australia in 1901. Mineral deposits include copper, tin and zinc. The development of hydroelectric power has stimulated the growth of manufacturing, with metallurgy and textiles the main industries. Area 68,332sq km (26,383sq mi). Pop. (1991) 452,837.

Tasmanian devil Carnivorous marsupial with a bear-like appearance; it is found only in the forest and scrub of Tasmania. It feeds mainly on a wide variety of animal food, including carrion. Length: to 80cm (31in). Species *Sarcophilus harrisii*.

Tasmanian wolf (thylacine) Largest carnivorous marsupial. It became extinct on the mainland of Australia, but a few specimens are believed to have survived in forested areas of Tasmania. It has a wolflike appearance, but its coat is marked with transverse dark stripes on the back, hindquarters and tail. Species *Thylacinus cynocephalus*.

Tasso, Torquato (1544–95) Italian poet and prose writer. He was a member of the court at Ferrara from 1565. His masterpiece, *Jerusalem Delivered* (1575), an epic of the First Crusade, became a model for later writers.

taste One of the five SENSES responding to the chemical constituents of anything placed in the mouth. In human beings the taste buds of the tongue differentiate four qualities: sweetness, saltiness, bitterness and sourness.

Tatar Republic Autonomous region in the Russian Federation populated mainly by TATARS. Tatar nationalism originated in the Crimean Autonomous Socialist Republic, founded in 1921. The Republic was dissolved and the entire population deported by Stalin in 1945. After the break-up of the Soviet Union in 1991, many of the 300–400,000 exiled Tatars began to return to the Crimea.

Tatars (Tartars) Turkic-speaking people of central Asia. They originated in E Siberia and were converted to Islam in the 14th century. They became divided into two groups, one in S Siberia, which came under Russian rule, the other in the Crimea, which was part of the Ottoman empire until annexed by Russia in 1783.

Tate Gallery UK national collection of modern art. The gallery's main building at Millbank, London, was constructed in 1897. It started as a collection of British painting and sculpture and now covers the mid-16th century to the present day. The Tate Gallery of Modern Art, located in the old Bankside Power Station, is due to open in 2000.

Tatlin, Vladimir Evgrafovitch (1885–1953) Russian sculptor. In 1913, influenced by CUBISM

and FUTURISM, he instigated the ABSTRACT ART style CONSTRUCTIVISM. He is best known for his three-dimensional constructions known as *Reliefs*.

Taurus (the Bull) In astronomy, N constellation on the ecliptic between Aries and Gemini. It contains the Pleiades and Hyades stellar clusters and the Crab Nebula. The brightest star is Alpha Tauri.

Tavener, John Kenneth (1944–) English composer. He achieved early success with his biblical cantata *The Whale* (1966). His conversion to the Eastern Orthodox Church in 1977 was accompanied by a move towards a more austere and spiritual musical style, as in *The Protecting Veil* (1987).

Taverner, John (*c.*1490–1545) English composer. Most of his surviving works date from 1526–30. He composed mostly church music.

taxation Compulsory payments of various kinds made by members of society to the state. Taxes are levied both on individuals and on corporations and are of two chief kinds: direct taxes are levied on income; indirect taxes are levied on commodities and services. The fundamental purpose of taxation is to fund government expenditure. Taxation is also used to reduce wealth inequalities in a community.

taxonomy Organization of organisms into categories based on similarities of genetic sequences, appearance, structure or evolution. The categories, from the most inclusive to the exclusive, are: KINGDOM, phylum, class, order, family, GENUS, SPECIES and sometimes variety. There are also subphyla, subfamilies, and so on, in some categories. *See also* PHYLOGENETICS; PLANT CLASSIFICATION

Tay River in central Scotland, rising in the Grampians and flowing SE to enter the North Sea at the Firth of Tay near Dundee. At 193km (120mi) it is the longest river in Scotland. The Tay Bridge (1883–88) crosses the firth at Dundee.

Taylor, Zachary (1784–1850) 12th US President (1849–50). He fought in both the WAR OF 1812 and the MEXICAN WAR. He emerged as a popular hero, winning the Whig nomination for president and the subsequent election (1848). He died suddenly after only 16 months in office.

Tayside Region in E Scotland, bounded N and W by the Grampians and E by the North Sea. The capital is DUNDEE, and other major cities include Perth, Arbroath and Montrose. The N is mountainous and the S is low-lying farmland. It is drained by the Rivers Tay, Isla and Earn. The mainly agricultural economy produces beef and dairy products. Area: 7,502sq km (2,896sq mi). Pop. (1991) 383,848.

Tbilisi (Tiflis) Largest city and capital of Georgia, on the River Kura. It was founded in the 5th century AD and ruled successively by the Persians, Byzantines, Arabs, Mongols and Turks, before coming under Russian rule in 1801. An important stop on the trade route between the Black Sea and Caspian Sea. It is the economic centre of modern Transcaucasia. Industries: chemicals, petroleum products, locomotives, electrical equipment, beer, wine, spirits. Pop. (1991) 1,279,000.

Tchaikovsky, Peter Ilyich (1840–93) Russian composer. His gift for melody is apparent in all his works, which include nine operas, four concertos, six symphonies, three ballets, and numerous other pieces. His ballets include *Swan Lake* (1876), *The Sleeping Beauty* (1889) and *The Nutcracker* (1892); operas include *Eugene Onegin* (1879) and *The Queen of Spades* (1890).

tea Family of trees and shrubs with leathery, undivided leaves and five-petalled blossoms. Among the 500 species is *Camellia sinensis*, the commercial source of tea. Cultivated in moist, tropical regions, tea plants can reach 9m (30ft) in height, but are kept low by frequent picking of the young shoots for tea leaves. The leaves are dried immediately to produce green tea and are fermented before drying for black tea. Family Theaceae.

teak Tree, native to s India, Burma and Indonesia, valued for its hard, yellowish-brown wood. Teak wood is water-resistant and takes a high polish; it is widely used for furniture and in shipbuilding. Height: 45m (150ft). Family Verbenaceae; species *Tectona grandis*.

teal Small, widely distributed river duck; many species have bright plumage. Teal dabble for food at the water surface. Family Anatidae, genus *Anas*.

tears Salty fluid secreted by glands to moisten the surface of the eye. It cleanses and disinfects the surface of the eye and brings nutrients to the CORNEA.

teasel Any of several species of plants that grow in Europe, the Middle East and the USA. They are prickly plants, with cup-like leaf bases that trap water. Family Dipsacaceae.

technetium Silver-grey, radioactive, metallic element (symbol Tc), one of the TRANSITION ELEMENTS. Technetium is found in the fission products of uranium and is present in some stars. It is used in radioactive tracer studies. There are 16 known isotopes. Properties: at.no. 43; r.a.m. 98.9062; r.d. 11.5; m.p. 2,172°C (3,942°F); b.p. 4,877°C (8,811°F); most stable isotope Tc^{99} (half-life 2.6 x 10^6 years).

technology Systematic study of the methods and techniques employed in industry, research, agriculture and commerce. More often the term is used to describe the practical application of scientific discoveries to industry.

tectonics Deformation within the Earth's CRUST and the geological structures produced by deformation including folds, faults and the development of mountain chains. *See also* PLATE TECTONICS

teeth Hard, bone-like structures embedded in the jaws of vertebrates, used for chewing food, defence or other purposes. Mammalian teeth have an outer layer of hard enamel. A middle layer consists of dentine, a bone-like substance that is capable of regeneration. The core of a tooth contains pulp, which is softer and has a blood supply and nerves. *See also* DENTITION

Tegucigalpa Largest city and capital of HONDURAS, in the Cordilleras. Founded in the 16th century by the Spanish as a mining town, it became the national capital in 1880. Industries: sugar, textiles, chemicals, cigarettes. Pop. (1991) 670,100.

Tehran Capital of Iran, 105km (65mi) s of the Caspian Sea, in a strategic position on the edge of the plains in the foothills of the country's highest mountains. It replaced ISFAHAN as the capital of Persia in 1788. Tehran is now the economic, administrative and cultural centre of the country. Its manufactures include cement, textiles, chemicals, and, most famously, carpets. Pop. (1991) 6,475,527.

Teilhard de Chardin, Pierre (1881–1955) French JESUIT philosopher and palaeontologist. He worked in China (1923–1946) and shared in the discovery of Peking Man (a fossilized, Stone Age human). His best-known work is *The Phenomenon of Man* (1938).

Tel Aviv City and port in Israel, on the Mediterranean Sea, *c.*50km (30mi) w of Jerusalem. The economic, cultural and tourist centre of Israel, it was founded in 1909. During the British administration of Palestine (1923–48), the town grew rapidly as Jews fled persecution in Europe. It served as the seat of the transitional government and legislature of the new state of Israel (1948–49), until the capital was moved to JERUSALEM. In 1950 it was merged with Jaffa. Industries: construction, textiles, clothing. Pop. (1994) 355,200.

telecommunications Technology involved in the sending of information over a distance. The information comes in a variety of forms, such as digital signals, sounds, printed words or images. The sending is achieved through TELEGRAPH, TELEPHONE or RADIO, and the medium may be wires, FIBRE OPTIC cables, or electromagnetic (radio) waves. There are two basic types of message: DIGITAL and ANALOGUE.

telegraph Any communications system that transmits and receives visible or audible coded signals over a distance. The first, optical, telegraphs were forms of semaphore. Credit for the electric telegraph and its code is generally given to Samuel MORSE (1844).

Telemann, Georg Philipp (1681–1767) German composer. He wrote more than 40 operas, 600 overtures and 44 settings of the Passion.

telepathy Form of extrasensory perception involving the transmission and reception of thoughts without using the usual sensory channels. Telepathy has not been conclusively proved.

telephone Instrument that communicates speech sounds over a distance using wires or radiowaves. In 1876 Alexander Graham BELL invented the prototype, which relied on eletromagnetism. Modern telephones employ solid-state electronics.

telephoto lens Camera lens with a long focal length. For a 35mm camera, any lens with a focal length of more than about 80mm may be regarded as a telephoto lens.

telescope Instrument for enlarging a distant object or studying electromagnetic radiation from a distant source. Optical telescopes can use lenses (refracting telescopes) or mirrors (reflecting telescopes); catadioptric telescopes use both in combination. Earth-bound astronomical telescopes have limitations because the incoming radiation has to pass through the Earth's atmosphere. This ceases to be a problem with telescopes in Earth orbit, such as the HUBBLE SPACE TELESCOPE. Orbiting telescopes can also detect other types of electromagnetic radiation more easily, such as infra-red rays, ultraviolet rays, x-rays and gamma rays. Radio telescopes are complex electronic systems that detect and analyse radio waves from beyond the Earth.

television System that transmits and receives visual images by RADIO waves or cable. A television camera converts the images from light rays into electrical signals. The electrical signals are amplified and transmitted as VERY HIGH FREQUENCY (VHF) or ULTRA HIGH FREQUENCY (UHF) radio waves. The receiver (TV set) operates in reverse to the camera. On reception, the signals are converted to light again in a CATHODE-RAY TUBE.

Telford, Thomas (1757–1834) Scottish civil engineer who built roads, bridges, canals, docks and harbours. His most notable achievements were the Caledonian Canal in Scotland and the 177m (580ft) Menai Strait suspension bridge, connecting Anglesey with mainland Wales.

Tell, William Legendary Swiss hero, leader in the 14th-century war of liberation against Austria. For refusing to salute the cap of Albert I's steward, Gessler, he was made to shoot an arrow through an apple placed on his son's head.

Teller, Edward (1908–) US physicist, b. Hungary. During World War 2, he contributed to atomic bomb research under Enrico FERMI and was then involved in the MANHATTAN PROJECT. He was also a central figure in developing and testing (1952) the HYDROGEN BOMB.

tellurium Silver-white, metallic element (symbol Te). It occurs naturally in sylvanite, and its chief source is a by-product of the electrolytic refining of copper. The brittle element is used in semiconductor devices, as a catalyst in petroleum cracking and as an additive to increase the ductility of steel. Properties: at.no. 52; r.a.m. 127.60; r.d. 6.24; m.p. 449.5°C (841.1°F); b.p. 989.8°C (1,814°F).

tempera Painting medium used extensively during the Middle Ages, made of powdered pigments mixed with an organic gum or glue, usually of egg white or yolk. It began to be replaced by the more flexible medium of oil painting in the 15th century.

temperature In biology, intensity of heat. In warm-blooded (HOMEOTHERMAL) animals, body temperature is maintained within narrow limits regardless of the temperature of their surroundings. In humans, the normal body temperature is about 36.9°C (98.4°F), but this may vary with degree of activity. In cold-blooded (POIKILOTHERMAL) animals, body temperature varies depending on the temperature of the surroundings.

temperature Measure of the hotness or coldness of an object. Two objects of different temperatures placed in thermal contact exchange heat energy until they have thermal equilibrium and the same temperature. *See also* ABSOLUTE ZERO; HEAT

temple Place of worship for Jews and members of many other religions. Temples were a focal point in the religion of ancient Egypt and the Near East. In Mesopotamia, they took the form of towers called ZIGGURATS. Greek and Roman temples were houses fit for the gods. In Judaism, the term refers specifically to the first and second temples built in Jerusalem. Temples also exist as places of worship for Muslims, Hindus, Buddhists and Sikhs. Some Evangelical Christian sects and the Mormon Church use the term.

Temple, Jerusalem Most significant shrine of the Jews in East Jerusalem. There have been three temples on the site. The first was built in the 10th century BC by order of SOLOMON. It was destroyed by NEBUCHADNEZZAR in 587 BC. A second temple was completed in 515 BC by Jewish exiles who had returned from Babylon. Between 19 and 9 BC, this was replaced by a more elaborate structure under HEROD the Great. Destroyed by the Romans in AD 70, it was never rebuilt but part of its ruins remain as the WAILING WALL. Part of the ancient temple site is occupied by the Muslim DOME OF THE ROCK.

tench Freshwater food and sport fish of Europe and Asia, belonging to the carp family Cyprinidae. It has a stout, golden yellow body with small scales. Length: to 71cm (28in). Species *Tinca tinca*.

Ten Commandments (Decalogue) Code of ethical conduct held in Judaeo-Christian tradition to have been revealed by God to MOSES on Mount Sinai during the Hebrew exodus from Egypt (c.1200 BC). They represent the moral basis of the Covenant made by Yahweh (God) with Israel.

tendon Strong, flexible band of CONNECTIVE TISSUE that joins muscle to bone.

tendril Coiling part of stem or leaf, a thread-like structure used by climbing plants for support.

Tenerife Largest of the Canary Islands, Spain, in the Atlantic Ocean, 64km (40mi) WNW of Grand Canary Island. It is a mountainous island with Pico de Teide, 3,718m (12,198ft), its highest peak. Products include dates, sugarcane, palms and cotton. Tourism is the mainstay of the economy. The main town is SANTA CRUZ DE TENERIFE. Area 2,059sq km (795sq mi). Pop. (1991) 725,815.

Tennessee State in SE central USA. The capital is NASHVILLE. Other cities include MEMPHIS, CHATTANOOGA and Knoxville. The first European discovery was by Hernando DE SOTO in 1540. The French followed a century later, but their claim was ceded to Britain in 1763 and the first permanent settlement was established (1769). During the American CIVIL WAR, the state was the site of some of the bloodiest battles. In the E are the GREAT SMOKY MOUNTAINS and the Cumberland Plateau. Central Tennessee is a BLUEGRASS region famed for its horse-breeding and livestock rearing; W Tennessee has fertile floodlains, drained by the Tennessee River, that produce cotton, tobacco and soybeans. Mineral deposits include zinc, stone and coal. Industries: chemicals, electrical equipment, foods. Area 109,411sq km (42,244sq mi). Pop. (1992) 5,025,621.

tennis Racket and ball game played on a variety of surfaces by either two (singles) or four (doubles) players. The game is played on a court 23.8m (78ft) by 8.2m (27ft) for singles. The doubles court is widened to 11m (36ft). It is bisected by a net 0.9m (3ft) high. The ball is put into play by a server, who is allowed two attempts to hit it into the opposite service court. Play continues back and forth until a player fails to return the ball legally, conceding the point. The ball must be hit before its second bounce and land in the opponent's court. A match is played as the best of three or five sets. Each set is divided into games, consisting of individual points. Service alternates at the end of each game. Modern tennis evolved from real tennis in England in the 1860s.

Tennyson, Alfred, 1st Baron (1809–92) (Alfred Lord Tennyson) British poet. He became poet laureate in 1850. His body of work includes *Ode on the Death of the Duke of Wellington* (1852), *The Charge of the Light Brigade* (1855) and *In Memoriam* (1850). Other notable works include the Arthurian epic *Idylls of the King* (1872–73).

tenor Range of the human voice, falling below CONTRALTO and above baritone. It is the highest natural male voice apart from the COUNTERTENOR.

Teotihuacán Ancient AZTEC city of Mexico, about 48km (30mi) N of Mexico City. It flourished between c.100 BC and c.AD 700. It contained huge buildings, notably the Pyramid of the Sun. At its height, c.AD 600, the city housed at least 100,000 people and was the centre of a large empire.

terbium Silver-grey, metallic element (symbol Tb) of the LANTHANIDE SERIES. It is found in such minerals as monazite, gladolinite and apatite. The soft element is used in semiconductors; sodium terbium borate is used in lasers. Properties: at.no. 65; r.a.m. 158.9254; r.d. 8.234; m.p. 1,360°C (2,480°F); b.p. 3,041°C (5,506°F). Single isotope Tb159.

Teresa, Mother (1910–97) (Agnes Gonxha Bojaxhiu) Roman Catholic missionary, b. Skopje, Yugoslavia. Her Order of the Missionaries of Charity was established in India in 1950 to tend to the homeless, starving and sick in Calcutta's slums. She was subsequently extended to other countries. She was awarded the first Pope John XXIII Peace Prize in 1971 and the Nobel Peace Prize in 1979.

terminal velocity Maximum velocity attainable by a falling body or powered aircraft. It is dependent upon the shape of the body, the resistance of the air through which it is moving, and (in the case of aircraft) the thrust of the engines.

termite Insect found worldwide in subterranean nests and above-ground mounds. They have a caste system, with a king and queen guarded and tended by soldiers, workers and nymphs. Wood is a common component of their diet, which is digested with the help of symbiotic protozoa or bacteria. Length: 0.2–2.25mm (0.08–0.9in). Order Isoptera.

tern (sea swallow) Any of several species of graceful seabirds that live throughout the world. The tern is usually white and grey, and has a pointed bill, long pointed wings, a forked tail and webbed feet. It dives for fish and crustaceans. Length: to 55cm (22in). Family Laridae; genus *Sterna*.

terrapin Any of several species of aquatic TURTLES that live in fresh or brackish water in the USA and South America, especially the diamondback terrapin (*Malaclemys terrapin*). Length: to 23cm (9in). Family Emydidae.

terrier Any of several breeds of dog. Originally trained to dig out game, they have been used to hunt other animals. Separate breeds include fox and Manchester terriers. Larger breeds such as the Airedale and Irish terriers are used as guard dogs.

territory In animal behaviour, the restricted life space of an organism. An area selected for mating, nesting, roosting, hunting or feeding, it may be occupied by one or more organisms and defended against others of the same, or a different, species.

terrorism Use of violence, sometimes indiscriminately, against persons and property for the nominal purpose of making a political statement. Terrorists act in an attempt to empower political minorities, and to publicize perceived political grievances.

Tertiary Earlier period of the CENOZOIC era, lasting from 65 million to c.2 million years ago. It is divided into five epochs, starting with the PALAEOCENE, followed by the EOCENE, OLIGOCENE, MIOCENE and PLIOCENE. Early Tertiary times were marked by great mountain-building activity. Mammals diversified greatly and archaic forms of carnivores and herbivores flourished, along with primitive primates, bats, rodents and early whales.

Tesla, Nikola (1856–1943) US electrical engineer and inventor, b. Croatia, who pioneered the applications of high-voltage electricity. He developed arc lighting, the first generator of alternating current (AC) and the high-frequency Tesla coil.

Test Ban Treaty (1963) Agreement signed in Moscow by the Soviet Union, the USA and Britain to cease most tests of nuclear weapons. Nearly 100 other states eventually signed the treaty, although France and China continued to conduct tests in the atmosphere and underwater.

testis (plural testes) Male sex GLAND, occurring, in humans, as a pair located in a pouch, the scrotum, external to the body. The testes are made up of seminiferous tubules in which SPERM form and mature, after which they drain into ducts and are stored in the epididymis prior to being discharged.

testosterone Steroid HORMONE secreted mainly by the mammalian TESTIS. It is responsible for the growth and development of male sex organs and male secondary sexual characteristics, such as voice change and facial hair.

tetanus (lockjaw) Life-threatening disease caused by the toxin secreted by the anaerobic bacterium *Clostridium tetani*. The symptoms are muscular spasms and rigidity of the jaw, which then spreads to other parts of the body, culminating in convulsions and death. The disease is treated with anti-tetanus toxin and ANTIBIOTICS.

tetracyclines Group of antibiotics that are effective against a wide range of bacterial infections.

Teutonic Knights German military and religious order, founded in 1190. During the 13th century the knights waged war on non-Christians, especially in Prussia. They were defeated in 1242 by ALEXANDER NEVSKI and, in 1410, by the Poles and Lithuanians.

Teutonic mythology Traditional beliefs of the Germanic peoples. The creation mythology of pre-Christian Germany and Scandinavia is preserved in two Icelandic works, the Eddas. ODIN and his brothers founded the race of gods, created the world and made the first man and woman from pieces of trees. Odin was the head of the AESIR (heroic gods), next in importance was THOR. Other members of the Teutonic pantheon included the handsome Balder and Loki, the son of a giant. *See also* VALHALLA

Texas State in central S USA, bounded by the Gulf of Mexico (SE) and the Rio Grande (SW). Major cities are HOUSTON, DALLAS, AUSTIN (the state capital) and FORT WORTH. It became part of the Spanish colony of Mexico in the 17th century. By Mexican independence in 1821, many Americans had settled in Texas. They revolted against Mexican rule and in 1836, after defeating the Mexican army, established the Republic of Texas. Eight years later Texas was admitted to the Union. E Texas has pine-covered hills and cypress swamps; cotton and rice are the main crops and the timber industry is important. Cattle are raised on the plains of the Rio Grande valley, and the land rises to the Guadalupe Mountains in the W and the Great Plains area of the Texas Panhandle in the N. Oilfields are the mainstay of the state's economy. Industries: oil refining, food processing, aircraft, electronics. Area 692,405sq km (267,338sq mi). Pop. (1992) 17,682,538.

textiles Fabrics, especially those produced by WEAVING yarn. The yarn is made by SPINNING natural or artificial FIBRES. Textiles are used to make clothing, curtains, carpets, sheets, blankets, towels and many other products.

Thackeray, William Makepeace (1811–63) British novelist and satirist, b. India. *Vanity Fair* (1847–48) is his best-known work. His other novels include *Barry Lyndon* (1844), *Pendennis* (1848–50), *Henry Esmond* (1852), *The Newcomes* (1853–55) and *The Virginians* (1857–59).

Thai National language of Thailand, spoken by most of the population. It is closely related to Lao, spoken across the border in Laos. It belongs to the Tai family, possibly a sub-family of the SINO-TIBETAN LANGUAGES group.

Thailand Kingdom in Southeast Asia; the capital is BANGKOK. **Land and climate** Central Thailand is a fertile plain, drained mainly by the Chao Phraya. A densely populated region, it includes Bangkok.

THAILAND
AREA: 513,120sq km (198,116sq mi)
POPULATION: 57,760,000
CAPITAL POPULATION: Bangkok (5,572,712)
GOVERNMENT: Constitutional monarchy
ETHNIC GROUPS: Thai 80%, Chinese 12%, Malay 4%, Khmer 3%
LANGUAGES: Thai (official)
RELIGIONS: Buddhism 94%, Islam 4%, Christianity 1%
CURRENCY: Thai Baht = 100 stangs

To the NE lies the Khorat plateau, which extends the MEKONG River border with Laos. The NW mountainous, and includes the second-largest cit CHIANGMAI. The S forms part of the MALAY PENI SULA. Thailand has a tropical climate. The monsoo season lasts from May to October. The N include many valuable hardwood trees, which are bein rapidly exploited. The S has many rubber plant tions. Grass, shrub and swamp make up 20% land. Arable land, especially rice fields, covers ov 33%. **Economy** Thailand is a rapidly industriali ing, developing nation. It was a founder (1967) the ASSOCIATION OF SOUTHEAST ASIAN NATIO (ASEAN). Manufacturing and services have grow rapidly, but agriculture still employs 66% of t workforce. Thailand is the world's largest produc of pineapples and natural rubber. It is also t fourth-largest producer of rice, buffalo and cassav Thai silk is among the world's finest. Touris drawn by the island beaches, are a vital source revenue (1992 receipts, US$ 4,829 million). 1997 economic crisis led to the devaluation of t currency and the intervention of the Internation Monetary Fund. **History and politics** The Mong capture (1253) of a Thai kingdom in SW Chin forced the Thai people south. A new kingdom w established around Sukhothai. In the 14th centur the kingdom expanded and the capital moved Ayutthaya. The first European contact was in t early 16th century. In the late 17th century, the kin dom was briefly held by the Burmese. Europe desire to acquire the brilliance of the Thai cou resulted in their expulsion for over a century, a Thailand remained the only Southeast Asian natio to resist colonization. In 1782 a Thai Gener became King Rama I, establishing the Chakk dynasty, which has ruled ever since. The count became known as Siam, and Bangkok acted as capital. From the mid-19th century, Siam began gradual process of westernization. In World War Siam supported the Allies. In 1932 Thaila became a constitutional monarchy. In 1938 Pib Songgram became premier, and changed the cou try's name to Thailand. In 1941 Pibul invited Japa ese forces into Thailand. Military coups and sho lived civilian governments are characteristic post-war Thai politics. In 1950 Bhumib

Adulyadej acceded to the throne as Rama IX. In return for economic and technical aid, Thailand supported US military action in Korea and Vietnam. In 1957 Pibul was overthrown in a military coup. Public pressure forced elections in 1992, which saw the return of civilian rule. The coalition's collapse led to 1995 elections, and a new coalition led by the militarist Chart Thai party. In 1996 this was replaced by a coalition led by the National Aspiration Party.

thalamus One of two ovoid masses of grey matter located deep on each side of the forebrain. Sometimes called the sensory-motor receiving areas, they fulfil relay and integration functions in respect of sensory messages reaching the BRAIN.

thalassemia Group of hereditary disorders characterized by abnormal bone marrow and erythrocytes (red blood cells). The predominant symptom is ANAEMIA, requiring frequent blood transfusions.

Thales (636–546 BC) Greek scientist and philosopher. He made discoveries in geometry, such as the equality of the angles at the base of an isosceles triangle. He predicted the eclipse of the Sun that took place in 585 BC.

thalidomide Drug originally developed as a mild hypnotic, but whose use by women in early pregnancy until the early 1960s came to be associated with serious birth deformities. It is still used in the treatment of LEPROSY and ACQUIRED IMMUNE DEFICIENCY SYNDROME (AIDS).

thallium Shiny metallic element (symbol Tl) of group III of the periodic table. Soft and malleable, it is a by-product of processing zinc or lead sulphide ores. It is used in electronic components, infrared detectors and optical and infrared glasses. Thallium is toxic, and thallium sulphide is used as a rodent and ant poison. Properties: at.no. 81; r.a.m. 204.37; r.d. 11.85; m.p. 303.5°C (578.3°F); b.p. 1,457°C (2,655°F); most common isotope Tl^{205} (70.5%).

Thames Longest river in England. It rises in the Cotswold Hills, E Gloucestershire, then flows E across S England and through London to enter the North Sea at The Nore. The river is tidal up to Teddington. Above London it is used mainly by pleasure craft and for recreational purposes. The river is navigable for ocean-going vessels below Tilbury. Length: 338km (210mi).

Thant, U (1909–74) Burmese diplomat, third secretary-general of the United Nations (UN) (1962–72). He helped to settle the civil wars in the Congo (Zaïre) in 1963 and Cyprus in 1964.

Thatcher, Margaret Hilda (1925–) British stateswoman. As prime minister (1979–90), she was perhaps the most influential British political leader since CHURCHILL. Her government embarked on a radical free-market programme. Her monetarist policies, especially cuts in public spending, contributed to a recession, but her popularity was restored by victory in the FALKLANDS WAR (1982). Privatization of national utilities boosted government revenue in a period when incomes rose rapidly, except among the poor. Thatcher's determination to curb trade union power provoked a bitter miners' strike (1983–84). A poll tax introduced in 1989 was widely seen as unfair. After increasingly frequent clashes with senior party colleagues, she was forced to resign as party leader and prime minister in 1990.

Thebes City-state of ancient Greece, the dominant power in Boeotia. It was allied with Persia during the PERSIAN WARS, and during the 5th century BC was in continual conflict with Athens. It reached its height in the 4th century BC. The city was largely destroyed by ALEXANDER THE GREAT in 336 BC.

Thebes Greek name for the ancient capital of Upper Egypt, roughly corresponding to the present-day town of LUXOR.

theism Any of various philosophical and theological systems that profess belief in the existence of one supreme being, who is the creator of the universe. *See also* MONOTHEISM; POLYTHEISM

theocracy Government by religious leaders in accordance with divine law. Theocracies were common in non-literate societies and existed in ancient Egypt and the Orient.

Theocritus (310–250 BC) Greek poet. He is regarded as the father of pastoral poetry. His work, which influenced generations of later writers from VIRGIL to Matthew ARNOLD, is noted for its vivid expression and perceptive portrayal of rural life.

Theodoric the Great (454–526) King of the Ostrogoths and ruler of Italy. He drove Odoacer from Italy (488) and attempted to recreate the Western Roman empire. His kingdom was destroyed by JUSTINIAN after his death.

theology Systematic study of God or gods. In its narrowest sense, it is the investigation or expression of the beliefs and precepts of a religion. In a much broader sense, theology is intricately related to philosophical and historical studies and strives to achieve an understanding of various beliefs.

theosophy Religious philosophy that originated in the ancient world but was given impetus in 1875 when the Theosophical Society was founded. The main aims of the Society are to promote a spiritual brotherhood of all humanity; to encourage the comparative study of religions, philosophy and science; and to develop latent spiritual powers.

Theravada ("Doctrine of the Elders") Older of the two major schools of BUDDHISM. It developed early in the Buddhist history as a contrast to MAHAYANA ("greater vehicle"). Theravada Buddhism stresses that sorrow and suffering can be conquered only by the suppression of desire. This type of Buddhism is widespread in Sri Lanka and SE Asia.

thermal Small-scale, rising current of air produced by local heating of the Earth's surface. Thermals are often used by gliding birds.

thermionics Study of the emission of electrons or ions from a heated conductor. This is the principle on which electron tubes (valves) work. The heated conductor is the CATHODE and the emitted electrons are attracted to the ANODE.

thermodynamics Branch of physics that studies heat and how it is transformed to and from other forms of ENERGY. The three existing laws of thermodynamics are calculated from statistical and quantum mechanical principles. The first law states that the change in a system's internal energy is equal to zero, because heat and mechanical work are mutually convertible. The second law says that if a system is left alone, its ENTROPY tends to increase. The third law states that a system at absolute zero would have an entropy of zero.

thermometer Instrument for measuring TEMPERATURE. A MERCURY thermometer depends on the expansion of mercury, which is held in a glass bulb connected to a narrow, graduated tube. Temperatures can also be measured by a gas thermometer and by a resistance thermometer. Common scales are the CELSIUS, FAHRENHEIT and KELVIN.

Theseus In Greek mythology, a hero of many adventures, the son of Aethra by Aegeus, King of Athens, or by POSEIDON. His most famous exploit was the vanquishing of the MINOTAUR of Crete.

Thessaloníki (Salonica) Port on the Gulf of Thessaloníki, Greece, the country's second-largest city and capital of Greek Macedonia. Founded c.315 BC, it flourished under the Romans after 148 BC as the capital of MACEDON. The city was part of the Ottoman empire until 1913, when it was conquered by Greece. Industries: oil refining, textiles, metals, engineering, chemicals. Pop. (1991) 383,967.

thiamine VITAMIN B_1 of the B complex, required for carbohydrate metabolism. Its deficiency causes the disease beriberi. Thiamine is found in grains and seeds, nuts, liver, yeast and legumes.

Third Reich Official name of Nazi Germany (1933–45). The first *Reich* (empire) was the Holy Roman Empire, the second the German empire of 1871–1918.

Third World Former term for LESS DEVELOPED COUNTRIES. First and Second world countries were those of the Western and Eastern blocs respectively.

Thirteen Colonies English colonies in North America that declared independence from Britain (1776) and became the USA. They were: Connecticut, Delaware, Georgia, Maryland, Massachusetts, New Hampshire, New Jersey, New York, North Carolina, Pennsylvania, Rhode Island, South Carolina and Virginia. *See also* AMERICAN REVOLUTION

Thirty Years War (1618–48) Conflict fought mainly in Germany, arising out of religious differences. It began with a Protestant revolt in Bohemia against the HABSBURG emperor, FERDINAND II. Both sides sought allies and the war spread to much of Europe. The Peace of WESTPHALIA was concluded in 1648, but war between France and Spain continued until the Peace of the PYRENEES (1659). The chief loser in the war, apart from the German peasants, was FERDINAND III, who lost control of Germany. Sweden was established as the dominant state in N Europe, while France replaced Spain as the greatest European power.

thistle Any of numerous species of plants with thorny leaves and yellow, white, pink or purple flower heads with prickly bracts. The heraldic thistle is the national emblem of Scotland. Family Asteraceae/Compositae.

Thomas, Dylan Marlais (1914–53) Welsh poet and short-story writer. His flamboyant public persona contributed to the popularity of his powerful, meticulously crafted, but often wilfully obscure, verse. His *Collected Poems* was published in 1953. Many of his best short stories appear in *Portrait of the Artist as a Young Dog* (1940) and *Adventures in the Skin Trade* (1955). The "play for voices" *Under Milk Wood* (1952) is perhaps his best-known work.

Thomas, R.S. (Ronald Stuart) (1913–) Welsh poet and clergyman. *Song at the Year's Turning* (1955) collected his early verse; it embodies his characteristic concerns with Wales and its working people, and with the implications of his faith. His later work evinces a distrust of the modern world.

Thomas, Saint One of the original 12 APOSTLES or disciples of JESUS CHRIST. He is called "Doubting Thomas" because, after the RESURRECTION of Christ, he refused to believe that the Lord had appeared to the other disciples (John 20). Only when Jesus appeared to him and allowed him to touch his wounds did he believe it. His feast day is 3 July.

Thomas à Kempis *See* KEMPIS, THOMAS À

Thomism Philosophy of Saint Thomas AQUINAS, one of the major systems in SCHOLASTICISM. Aquinas blended the philosophy of ARISTOTLE with Christian theology. Using Aristotle's concept of matter and form, he conceived a hierarchy in which spirit is higher than matter, soul higher than body, and theology above philosophy.

Thomson, James (1700–48) Scottish poet. His most famous poem, *The Seasons*, was published in four parts: *Winter* (1726), *Summer* (1727), *Spring* (1728) and *Autumn* (1730). It was used by HAYDN for his oratorio of the same name (1801).

Thomson, Sir George Paget (1892–1975) British physicist, the son of Sir Joseph THOMSON. He shared the 1937 Nobel Prize for physics with Clinton Davisson for their independent work in diffracting ELECTRONS. This confirmed the wave nature of particles predicted by Louis de BROGLIE.

Thomson, Sir Joseph John (1856–1940) British physicist. He discovered the ELECTRON (1897) and won the 1906 Nobel Prize for physics for his study of the electrical conductivity of gases.

Thomson, Virgil (1896–1989) US critic and composer. Influenced by Erik SATIE, his works include the operas *Four Saints in Three Acts* (1928) and *The Mother of Us All* (1947).

Thor In TEUTONIC MYTHOLOGY, god of thunder and lightning, corresponding to JUPITER. The eldest and strongest of ODIN's sons, he was represented as a handsome, red-bearded warrior, benevolent towards humans but a mighty foe of evil. Thursday is named after him.

thorax In animal anatomy, part between the neck

and the abdomen. In mammals it is formed by the rib cage and contains the lungs, heart and oesophagus. In insects it consists of several segments to which legs and other appendages are attached.

thorium Radioactive metallic element (symbol Th) of the ACTINIDE ELEMENTS, first discovered in 1828. The chief ore is monazite (phosphate). It is used in photoelectric and thermionic emitters. One decay product is RADON-220. Thorium is sometimes used in radiotherapy, and is increasingly used for conversion into uranium-233 for nuclear fission. Properties: at.no. 90; r.a.m. 232.0381; s.g. 11.72; m.p. 1,750°C (3,182°F); b.p. 4,790°C (8,654°F); most stable isotope Th^{232}(1.41×10^{10} yrs).

thorn apple Plant of the genus *Datura*, especially Jimson weed (*D. stramonium*), a poisonous, annual weed of tropical American origin. It has foul-smelling leaves, large white or violet flowers and round prickly fruits. Family Solanaceae.

Thrace (Thráki) Ancient SE European country, now divided between Bulgaria, Greece and European Turkey. From 1300–600 BC the Thracian lands extended W to the Adriatic and N to the Danube. By c.600 BC Thrace had lost much of its E lands to the Illyrians and Macedonians, and the Greeks established the colony of Byzantium. In 342 BC Philip II of Macedon conquered the country. After 100 BC it became part of the Roman Empire. In the 7th century AD the N of the region was conquered by the Bulgarians, and by 1300 they controlled all Thrace. From 1361–1453 the region was disputed between the Bulgarians and the emerging Ottoman empire, eventually falling to the Turks. In 1885 Bulgaria annexed N Thrace. The regions either side of the Maritsa River became known as Eastern Thrace (Bulgaria) and Western Thrace (Turkey). After World War 1, Bulgaria ceded S and most of E Thrace to Greece. The Treaty of LAUSANNE (1923) restored E Thrace to Turkey forming the current boundaries. Its economy is mainly agricultural.

threadworm Small ROUNDWORM of the phylum Aschelminthes. It is common in moist tropical regions and resembles a short length of hair or thread. It may inhabit the intestines of human beings and other animals, but can live and breed freely in soil. Species *Oxyurus vermicularis*.

thrip Any of numerous species of slender, sucking insects found throughout the world. Most feed on plants and some carry plant diseases. Length: to 8mm (0.3in). Order Thysanoptera.

throat *See* PHARYNX

thrombophlebitis Inflammation of the walls of veins associated with THROMBOSIS. It can occur in the legs during pregnancy.

thrombosis Formation of a blood clot in an artery or vein. It causes loss of circulation and carries the risk of EMBOLISM.

thrush Any of numerous species of small songbirds of the family Turdidae. The European song thrush (*Turdus philomelos*) is mottled brown with a lighter, speckled breast. Length: to 30cm (12in).

thrush (candidiasis) Fungal infection of the mucous membranes, usually of the mouth but also sometimes of the vagina. Caused by the fungus *Candida albicans*, it is sometimes seen in people taking broad-spectrum ANTIBIOTICS.

thrust Driving force resulting from operation of a propeller, jet engine or rocket engine. An aircraft propeller forces air backwards, and jet and rocket engines expel gases backwards. Thrust is produced in the forward direction in accordance with the third of NEWTON'S LAWS of motion.

thulium Lustrous, silver-white, metallic element (symbol Tm) of the LANTHANIDE SERIES. Its chief ore is monazite but thulium is as rare as gold. Soft, malleable and ductile, it combines with OXYGEN and the HALOGENS. It is used in arc lighting and portable x-ray units. Properties: at.no. 69; r.a.m. 168.9342; r.d. 9.31 (25°C); 1,545°C (2,813°F); b.p. 1,947°C (3,537°F); most stable isotope Tm^{169} (100%).

thunderstorm Electrical storm caused by the separation of electrical charges in clouds. Water drops are carried by updraughts to the top of a cloud, where they become ionized and accumulate into positive charges – the base of the cloud being negatively charged. The electrical discharge between clouds, or between a cloud and the ground is seen as LIGHTNING. Heat expands the air explosively and causes it to reverberate and produce sounds and echoes called thunder.

Thuringia Historic region of central Germany. Its rulers became powerful princes with the HOLY ROMAN EMPIRE in the 11th century. Thuringia was reconstituted as a state in 1920 under the WEIMAR REPUBLIC, but lost its separate identity in 1952. The main economic activities are manufacturing and cereal cropping. Area: 16,176sq km (6,244sq mi). Pop. (1992) 2,545,808.

thyme Aromatic garden herb of the MINT family (Lamiaceae/Labiatae), used as an ornamental plant and in cooking. It yields an oil from which the drug thymol is prepared. It has purple flowers. Height: 15–20cm (6–8in). Genus *Thymus*.

thymus gland One of the endocrine GLANDS, located in the upper chest in mammals. In childhood it controls the development of lymphoid tissue and the immune response to infection. Disorder of the thymus may be associated with autoimmune diseases (those caused by the body's own antibodies). *See also* ENDOCRINE SYSTEM

thyroid gland H-shaped gland of the ENDOCRINE SYSTEM. It lies in the base of the neck, straddling the trachea below the Adam's apple. It secretes hormones, principally THYROXINE.

thyroxine Hormone secreted by the THYROID GLAND. It contains iodine and helps regulate the rate of metabolism; it is essential for normal growth and development.

Tiananmen Square World's largest public square, covering 40ha (98 acres) in Beijing, China. In April 1989 a series of nationwide pro-democracy demonstrations culminated in the occupation of the square by thousands of protesters. On 4 June tanks and troops stormed the square. Official casualties were put at over 200, but eyewitnesses reported thousands of deaths. The government imposed martial law for a year and executed student leaders.

Tianjin (Tientsin) Port and industrial city on the Hai River, NE China. It is China's third-largest city and the most important international port in N China. Founded in *c*.300 BC, it grew in the late 18th century because of its strategic position en route to Manchuria. In 1860, the British and French obtained the right to use Tianjin as a treaty port. In 1900 the city came under European occupation. It remains the trading centre for N China with excellent transport links. Industries: iron, steel, heavy machinery, transport equipment, textiles. The city is administered as a special economic zone to encourage inward investment. Pop. (1993) 4,970,000.

Tian Shan (Tien Shan, "Celestial Mountains") Mountain range in central Asia, 2,415km (1,500mi) long, forming the border between Kyrgyzstan and Xinjiang, NW China. At their W edge, they divide the Tarim and Junggar Basins. The range then rises to 7,439m (24,406ft) at Peak Pobeda, on the Chinese border with Kazakstan and Kyrgyzstan.

Tiber (Tevere) River in central Italy. It rises in the Etruscan Apennines, flows S then SW through Rome and empties into the Tyrrhenian Sea at Ostia. The silting of the river is causing the delta to expand; the ancient coastal port of Ostia Antica now lies 6km (4mi) inland. Length: 404km (251 mi).

Tiberius (42 BC–AD 37) (Tiberius Julius Caesar Augustus) Roman emperor (AD 14–37). He was the stepson of AUGUSTUS, who adopted him as his heir (AD 4). Initially, his administration was just and moderate, but he became increasingly fearful of conspiracy and had many people executed for alleged treason. He left Rome and spent his last years in seclusion on Capri.

Tibet (Xizang) Autonomous region in SW China. The capital and largest city is LHASA. Tibet is the highest region on earth, with an average altitude of 4,875m (16,000ft). An historically inaccessible area, Tibet is surrounded by mountains on three sides. The Tibetan HIMALAYAS include the world's highest mountain, EVEREST. Many of Asia's greatest rivers, including the YANGTZE, MEKONG, HUANG HE, INDUS and GANGES have their source in Tibet, though its major river is the BRAHMAPUTRA. The area has scant rainfall, and the Brahmaputra valley is the only agricultural area and the location of the major cities. Many of the people remain nomadic pastoralists. Tibet is rich in mineral resources, such as gold, copper and uranium. The principal religion is TIBETAN BUDDHISM. Until 1959, a large percentage of the urban male population were Buddhist monks (Lamas). From the 7th century, the spiritual leaders of Lamaism (the DALAI LAMA and the PANCHEN LAMA) also acted as the country's temporal rulers. Tibet flourished as an independent kingdom in the 7th century, and in the 8th century Pad-

masambhava developed the principles of MAHAYANA Buddhism and founded Lamaism. In 1206 Genghis Khan conquered the region, and it remained under nominal Mongol rule until 1720, when the Chinese QING dynasty claimed sovereignty. At the close of the 19th century the Tibetan areas of Ladakh and Sikkim were incorporated into British India, and in 1906 Britain recognized Chinese sovereignty over Tibet. In 1912 the fall of the QING dynasty prompted the Tibetans to reassert their independence. China, however, maintained its right to govern, and in 1950 the new communist regime sent its forces to invade. In 1951 Tibet was declared an autonomous region of China, nominally governed by the Dalai Lama. The Chinese government began a series of repressive measures principally targeting the Buddhist monasteries. In March 1959 a full-scale revolt against Chinese rule was suppressed by the Chinese army. The Dalai Lama managed to flee to N India (Christmas Day 1959), and he established a government-in-exile at Dharamsala. In 1965 China formally annexed Tibet as an autonomous region. The CULTURAL REVOLUTION banned religious practice and 4,000 monasteries were destroyed. Thousands of Tibetans fled into exile from the brutal communist regime. Despite the restoration of some of the desecrated monasteries and the reinstatement of Tibetan as an official language, human rights violations continued. Pro-independence rallies in 1987–9 were violently suppressed by the Chinese army. Area: 1,222,070sq km (471,841sq mi). Pop. (1993) 2,290,000.

Tibetan art Virtually all art in Tibet is religious in character, designed to serve the elaborate rituals of TIBETAN BUDDHISM. Artworks are anonymous and mostly undated. Paintings come in two forms – wall-paintings and *thangkas* (banners), usually displayed in temples or carried in processions. *Thangkas* generally depict scenes from the life of a deity or *mandalas* (patterns used for meditation).

Tibetan Buddhism Distinctive blend of Mahayana BUDDHISM and Bonism (a pre-Buddhist shamanism). It mixes meditative monasticism with indigenous folk religion and involves a system of reincarnating lamas (monks). Spiritual and temporal authority reside with the DALAI LAMA. The Bon priests opposed Buddhist ways, and Buddhism was not thoroughly introduced into Tibet until the 8th century. From the 11th-century, four major sects emerged in Tibetan Buddhism. Of these, the Gelugpa order was politically dominant from the 17th century. There are now two Gelugpa sects, the Red and Yellow monks. The Dalai Lama, a member of the latter, became revered as the "Living Buddha". Each new Dalai Lama is believed to be a reincarnation of his predecessor. The PANCHEN LAMA heads the Red monks.

tibia (shinbone) Inner and larger of the two lower leg bones. It articulates with the FEMUR at the knee and extends to the ankle. *See also* FIBULA

tick Any of numerous species of wingless, blooducking ARACHNIDS, the most notable of which are ctoparasites of vertebrates and invertebrates. Many species carry diseases (some fatal) in wild and domesticated animals and in humans Length: o 3mm (0.1in). Class Arachnida; order Acarina.

tidal power Energy harnessed from tidal movement of the Earth's oceans and used by man. It is economic only where the tidal range is greater than about 4.6m (15ft). Modern schemes involve the use of turbo-generators driven by the passage of water through a tidal barrage.

tide Periodic rise and fall of the surface level of the oceans caused by the gravitational attraction of the Moon and Sun. Tides follow the Moon's cycle of 28 days, arriving at a given spot 50 minutes later each day. When the Sun and Moon are in conjunction or opposition, the greatest tidal range occurs (spring tides). When they are in quadrature, when the Moon is half-full, tidal ranges are lowest (neap tides).

Tiepolo, Giovanni Battista (1696–1770) Italian painter. His pictures are full of action, using sunny colours. The peak of his career came in the 1750s when he decorated the Kaisersaal and grand staircase of the Prince Archbishop's Palace, Würzburg.

Tierra del Fuego (Sp. Land of Fire) Archipelago separated from mainland S South America by the Magellan Strait. It consists of one large island and other smaller islands. At the S extremity of the islands lies Cape Horn. The main island is politically divided between Argentina and Chile. The first European discovery was by Ferdinand MAGELLAN in 1520. The islands were settled in the 1880s, when the discovery of gold and later oil attracted Europeans, Argentinians and Chileans to the area. The indigenous population was killed by diseases brought by settlers. The mountainous terrain and harsh climate limit economic activity to sheep rearing and oil exploration. Area: 73,746sq km (28,473sq mi). Pop. (1991) 69,450.

Tiffany, Louis Comfort (1848–1933) US painter, designer and a leader of the ART NOUVEAU style. In 1878 he formed an interior decorating firm, which became known as Tiffany Studios.

tiger Large, powerful cat found (in decreasing numbers) throughout Asia, mainly in forested areas. It has a characteristic striped coat of yellow, orange, white and black, with the chin and underparts white. Relying on keen hearing, it hunts for birds, deer, cattle and reptiles. The largest is the Siberian tiger. Length to 4m (13ft) overall; weight: to 230kg (500lb). Family Felidae; species *Panthera tigris*.

Tigris River in SW Asia. It rises in the Taurus Mountains of E Turkey and flows SE through Iraq, joining the River Euphrates to form the Shatt Al-Arab Waterway. The river is liable to sudden flooding, but there are flood-control schemes and the river irrigates more than 300,000ha (750,000 acres). Length: c.1,900km (1,180mi).

till In geology, sediment consisting of an unsorted mixture of clay, sand, gravel and boulders that is deposited directly by the ice of GLACIERS.

timbre Characteristic of a musical sound determined by the number and intensity of the overtones (harmonics) produced as well as the principal (fundamental) note. Musical instruments of different types make characteristic sounds because of the different harmonics produced.

time Perception of a sequential order in all experience; also the interval perceived between two events. A consideration of time falls within the disciplines of physics, psychology, philosophy and biology. Until the theory of RELATIVITY was devised by Albert EINSTEIN, time was conceived of as absolute – a constant one-direction (past to future) flow. Since then the concept of time linked with distance ("space-time") has connected time with the relative velocities of those perceiving it.

time scale *See* GEOLOGICAL TIME

time zone One of 24 divisions of the Earth's surface, each 15° of longitude wide, within which the time of day is reckoned to be the same. Standard time in each successive zone westwards is one hour behind that in the preceding zone. *See also* GREENWICH MEAN TIME (GMT)

Timor Largest of the Lesser Sunda Islands in the Malay archipelago; part of INDONESIA. The chief towns are Kupang in the W and Dili in the E. The East Timor independence movement FRETILIN has maintained resistance to Indonesian rule amid widespread reports of human rights violations. A mountainous island, its produces rice, coconuts, coffee and tobacco. Area: 33,857sq km (13,074sq mi). Pop. (both provinces) (1990) 4,015,394.

timpani (kettledrums) Principal percussion instruments in a symphony orchestra. They are hemispherical vessels of copper or brass with single skins, tuned by pedals or screws and struck with sticks with hard felt heads.

Timur *See* TAMERLANE

tin Metalloid element (symbol Sn) of group IV of the periodic table, known from ancient times. Its chief ore is cassiterite. Soft, malleable and resistant to corrosion, tin is used as a protective coating for other metals, and in such alloys as solder, bronze and type metal. Properties: at.no. 50; r.a.m. 118.69; r.d. 7.29; m.p. 232°C (449.6°F); b.p. 2,270°C (4,118°F); most common isotope Sn^{118} (24.03%).

Tintoretto (1518–94) (Jacopo Robusti) Italian painter. Among his notable works are *The Finding of the Body of St Mark* (1562) and *The Last Supper* (1592–94). Some of his finest paintings are in the series depicting the life of Christ (1565–87).

Tipperary County in central S Republic of Ireland, in Munster province. The region is part of the central plain of Ireland but there are hills in the S; the Suir and Shannon are the principal rivers. The soil is fertile and Tipperary is one of the country's best farming regions. The county town is Clonmel. Area 4,255sq km (1,643sq mi). Pop. (1991) 132,772.

Tippett, Sir Michael Kemp (1905–) British composer. His music includes symphonies and other orchestral pieces such as *Fantasia on a*

627

Theme of Corelli (1953), piano and chamber music, the oratorios *A Child of our Time* (1941) and *The Mask of Time* (1982) and several operas including *The Midsummer Marriage* (1952), *King Priam* (1962), and *New Year* (1989).

Tirana (Tiranë) Capital of Albania, on the Ishm River in central Albania. It was founded in the early 17th century by the Ottoman Turks and became Albania's capital in 1920. In 1946 the communists came to power and the industrial sector of the city was developed. Industries: metal goods, agricultural machinery, textiles. Pop. (1991) 251,000.

Tirol (Tyrol) Federal state in W Austria, bordered N by Germany and S by Italy. The capital is INNSBRUCK. The Romans conquered the region in 15 BC, and the Franks held it during the 8th century. In 1363 the province was taken by the Habsburgs. In 1805 Napoleon I awarded Tirol to Bavaria in return for its support. In 1810 Napoleon gave S Tirol to the Italians, but the Congress of Vienna (1815) reunited Tirol with Austria. After World War I, when S Tirol was awarded to Italy, a process of Italianization was resisted by the German-speaking inhabitants. After World War 2, S Tirol was made an autonomous Italian region. An Alpine region, its economy is now dominated by tourism. Other economic activities are mainly agricultural. Area: 12,647sq km (4,882sq mi). Pop. (1994) 654,753.

tissue Material of a living body consisting of a group of similar, often interconnected cells. Tissues vary greatly in structure and complexity. In animals they may be loosely classified by function into epithelial, connective, skeletal, muscular, nervous and glandular tissues.

tissue culture In biology, artificial cultivation of living TISSUE in sterile conditions. Tissue culture in laboratories is used for biological research or to help in the diagnosis of diseases. It is also used as a means of propagating plant CLONES. *See also* GENETIC ENGINEERING

Titania In folklore, queen of the fairies and wife of OBERON. In the writing of OVID she represents DIANA at the head of her nymphs. In Shakespeare's *A Midsummer Night's Dream* she quarrels with her husband over a changeling boy.

Titanic British passenger liner that sank on her maiden voyage (14–15 April 1912). The largest vessel of her time, she was sailing from Southampton to New York when she struck an iceberg in the N Atlantic. About 1,500 people were drowned. In 1985 the wreck was located on the ocean floor.

titanium Lustrous, silver-grey, metallic element (symbol Ti) of the TRANSITION ELEMENTS. A common element, it is found in many minerals, chief sources being ilmenite and RUTILE. Resistant to corrosion and heat, it is used in steels and other alloys, especially in aircraft, spacecraft and guided missiles where strength must be combined with lightness. Properties: at.no. 22; r.a.m.. 47.90; r.d. 4.54; m.p. 1,660°C (3,020°F); b.p. 3,287°C (5,949°F); most common isotope Ti^{48} (73.94%).

Titian (1485–1576) (Tiziano Vecellio) Venetian painter. He evolved a brilliant, worldly style demonstrated in three magnificent altarpieces, *The Assumption*, *Pesaro* and *St Peter Martyr*. He combined the balance of High RENAISSANCE composition with a new dynamism, which heralded the BAROQUE. Between 1518 and 1523 he produced some of his finest mythological paintings, the *Worship of Venus*, *Bacchanal* and *Bacchus and Ariadne*. His last work was the astonishingly powerful *Pietà*, which he designed for his own tomb.

Titicaca Lake in the Andes on the Peru-Bolivian border, draining S through the River Desaguadero into Lake Poopó. It is the highest navigable body of water in the world at 3,810m (12,500ft). The lake is famed for its totora reeds, from which the Uru make their floating island homes and distinctive fishing rafts. Area: 8,290sq km (3,200sq mi).

titmouse (tit, chickadee) Small, stubby-bodied and large-headed bird of open woodlands and wooded parks of the Northern Hemisphere and Africa. Family Paridae; genus *Parus*.

Tito, Josip Broz (1892–1980) Yugoslav statesman. He helped to organize the Yugoslav Communist Party, and led the successful campaign of the Partisans against the Germans in Yugoslavia during World War 2. In 1945 he established a communist government, holding the office of prime minister (1945–53) and thereafter president, although virtually a dictator. Soviet efforts to control Yugoslavia led to a split between the two countries in 1948. As later events confirmed, his greatest achievement was to hold the Yugoslavia federation together.

titration Method used in analytical chemistry to determine the concentration of a compound in a solution by measuring the amount needed to complete a reaction with another compound. A solution of known concentration is added in measured amounts to a known volume of a liquid of unknown concentration until the reaction is complete. The volume added enables the unknown concentration to be calculated.

TNT (2,4,6–trinitrotoluene) Explosive organic compound ($C_7H_5N_3O_6$) made from TOLUENE by using sulphuric and nitric acids. Its resistance to shock makes it one of the safest high explosives.

toad Any of numerous species of tail-less amphibians found worldwide, except Australasia. Most are short and rotund and move with a crawling or hopping gait. Length: 2–25cm (1–10in). Order Anura; family Bufonidae. *See also* TADPOLE

toadstool Popular name for the fruiting body of a FUNGUS of the class Basidiomycetae. The name usually refers to inedible species and describes the stool-like appearance of the reproductive organ. It consists of a stem and a cap, on which the spores are borne on gills or in tubes.

tobacco Herb native to the Americas but cultivated throughout the world for its leaves, which are dried and smoked. It has large leaves with no stalk, and white, pink, or red flowers. *Nicotiana tabacum* is the principal cultivated species. Family Solanaceae (NIGHTSHADE). Height: 0.6–2m (2–6ft).

Tobago *See* TRINIDAD AND TOBAGO

Togo Small republic in w Africa; the capital is LOMÉ. It is divided geographically into four regions. The coastal plain is sandy; N of the coast is an area of fertile, clay soil. N again is the Mono Tableland, which reaches an altitude of *c*.450m (1,500ft), and is drained by the Mono River. The Atakora Mountains are the fourth region; N of the mountains is a plateau region. The vegetation is mainly open grassland. The historic region of Togoland comprised what is now the Republic of Togo and Ghana. From the 17th–19th centuries, the Ashantis raided Togoland, seizing the indigenous inhabitants, the Ewe, and selling them to Europeans as slaves. As a German protectorate from 1884, it developed economically and Lomé was built. At the start of World War 1, Britain and France captured Togoland from Germany. In 1922 it was divided into two mandates, which, in 1942, became UN trust territories. In 1957 British Togoland became part of Ghana. In 1960 French Togoland became independent as the Republic of Togo. In 1961 Slyvanus Olympio became the first president, but he was assassinated in 1963. Nicolas Grunitzky became president, but was overthrown in a coup in 1967. Ghansimgbe Eyadéma, leader of the military coup, became president in 1972. The constitution of 1979 confirmed Togo as a single-party state, the sole legal party being the Rassemblement du Peuple Togolais (RPT). Re-elected in 1972 and 1986, Eyadéma was forced to resign in 1991 after pro-democracy riots. Kokou Koffigoh was elected prime minister. Unrest continued with troops loyal to Eyadéma attempting to overthrow Koffigoh. In 1992 a new multi-party constitution was introduced and Eyadéma regained some power. In 1993 a rigged election, boycotted by opposition parties, was won by Eyadéma. Elections to the National Assembly were won by an opposition alliance, with whom Eyadéma formed a coalition government in 1994. The economy is mainly agricultural with cocoa, coffee and cotton the chief cash crops and palm oil and phosphates the principal exports. Manufacturing is on a small scale.

Tokugawa Japanese family that controlled Japan

TOGO

AREA: 56,790sq km (21,927sq mi)
POPULATION: 3,763,000
CAPITAL (POPULATION): Lomé (590,000)
GOVERNMENT: Multiparty republic
ETHNIC GROUPS: Ewe-Adja 43%, Tem-Kabre 26%, Gurma 16%
LANGUAGES: French (official), Ewe, Kabiye
RELIGIONS: Traditional beliefs 50%, Christianity 35%, Islam 15%
CURRENCY: CFA franc = 100 centimes

---

through the SHŌGUN (1603–1867). The Tokugawa shōgunate was established by Ieyasu Tokugawa (1543–1616), who completed the unification of Japan. The Tokugawa banned Christianity and Western trade and isolated Japan internationally. The regime declined during the 19th century as their isolationist policy began to crack under Western pressure. The last Tokugawa shōgun was overthrown before the MEIJI RESTORATION (1868).

Tokyo (Jap. eastern capital) Capital of Japan, on E central Honshū, at the head of Tokyo Bay. The modern city is divided into distinct districts: Kasumigaseki, Japan's administrative centre; Marunouchi, its commercial centre; Ginza, its shopping and cultural centre; the w shore of Tokyo Bay (including Kawasaki and Yokohama seaport), its industrial centre. Modern Tokyo is the country's educational centre with over 100 universities. Founded in the 12th century as Edo, it became capital of the TOKUGAWA shōgunate in 1603. In 1868 the Japanese Reformation re-established imperial power. Emperor Meiji renamed the city Tokyo and it replaced Kyōto as the capital of Japan. The 1923 earthquake and subsequent fire claimed over 150,000 lives and necessitated the city's reconstruction. In 1944–45 US bombing destroyed over half the city, and another restoration programme began. Industries: electronic equipment, cameras, automobile manufacture, metals, chemicals, textiles. Pop. (1994) 7,894,000.

Tolkien, J.R.R. (John Ronald Reuel) (1892–1973) English scholar and novelist. A respected academic, Tolkien is now remembered chiefly for the imaginative epic trilogy, *The Lord of the Rings* (1954–55).

Tolpuddle Martyrs Name given to six British farm labourers in Dorset, S England, who were sentenced to transportation for forming a trade union (1834). As unions were not illegal, the Dorset men were charged with taking a seditious oath. After a public outcry, they were pardoned in 1836.

Tolstoy, Leo Nikolaievich, Count (1828–1910) Russian novelist and philosopher. After serving in the army during the CRIMEAN WAR (1853–56), he wrote his masterpieces *War and Peace* (1865–69) and *Anna Karenina* (1875–77).

Toltec (Nuhuatl, master-builder) Ancient Native American civilization, whose capital was Tollán (Tula), Mexico. The Toltec were the dominant people in the region from AD 900 to 1200. Their architecture is characterized by PYRAMID building. Although a polytheistic culture, images of QUETZALCÓATL predominate. In the 12th century the Toltec were gradually supplanted by the AZTEC.

toluene (methylbenzene) Aromatic hydrocarbon ($C_6H_5CH_3$) derived from coal tar and petroleum. It is a colourless, flammable liquid widely used as an industrial solvent and in aircraft and motor fuels. Toluene is also used in the manufacture of TNT. Properties: r.d. 0.87; m.p. −94.5°C (−138.1°F); b.p. 110.7°C (231.3°F).

tomato Fruit plant native to the Americas. The plant was cultivated as an ornament in Europe as early as 1544. It was not widely eaten until the 19th century because it was believed to be poisonous. Species *Lycopersicum esculentum*. Family Solanaceae.

tomography Technique of X-RAY photography in which details of only a single slice or plane of body tissue are shown.

tonality Harmonic system that underpins most Western music from the 17th century to the 20th, using the twelve major and minor scales. The notes of the scale, and their corresponding chords and harmonies, have their own hierarchy around the central KEY note.

tone poem *See* SYMPHONIC POEM

Tonga (Friendly Islands) South Pacific island kingdom, *c*.2,200km (1,370mi) NE of New Zealand. The archipelago consists of nearly 170 islands in five administrative groups. Only 36 of the islands are inhabited. They are mainly coral atolls, but the W group are volcanic, with some active craters. The largest island is Tongatapu, the seat of the capital, NUKUALOFA, and home to 66% of the population. The N islands were discovered by Europeans in 1616, and the rest by Abel TASMAN in 1643. During the 19th century, British missionaries converted the indigenous population to Christianity. In 1900 Tonga became a British protectorate. In 1970 the country achieved independence. The economy is dominated by agriculture; the chief crops are yams, tapioca and fish. Area: 748sq km (289sq mi). Pop. (1991) 103,000.

tongue Muscular organ usually rooted to the floor of the mouth. The tongue contains the TASTE buds and helps to move food around the mouth for chewing and swallowing; animals also use it for lapping fluids and for grooming. In human beings the tongue is vital for the production of speech. *See also* SENSES

tonsillitis Acute or chronic inflammation of the TONSILS caused by bacterial or viral infection. It is signalled by fever, sore throat and difficulty in swallowing. Chronic tonsillitis is often treated by surgical removal of the tonsils (tonsillectomy).

tonsils Two masses of LYMPH tissue located at the back of the throat. They have a pitted surface that easily becomes infected (TONSILLITIS).

tooth *See* TEETH

topaz Transparent, glassy mineral, aluminium fluosilicate, $Al_2SiO_4(F,OH)_2$, found in pegmatites. Its crystals are orthorhombic system columnar prisms. Topaz is colourless, white, blue or yellow; some large crystals are gem quality. Hardness 8; s.g. 3.5.

tope Small shark that lives in British waters. It has a grey-brown body and is often found in schools, or near the bottom where it feeds on small fish. Length: to 2m (6.5ft). Family Carcharinidae; species *Galeorhinus galeus*.

Topeka State capital of Kansas, USA, on the Kansas River, 90km (55mi) W of Kansas City. It was founded in 1854 by settlers from New England and became the state capital in 1861. Topeka is a major transport centre for cattle and wheat. Industries: printing, rubber goods, steel products, footwear. Pop. (1992) 120,257.

topology Branch of mathematics concerned with those properties of geometric figures that remain unchanged after a continuous deformation process such as stretching or twisting. The number of boundaries of a surface is such a property.

Torah (Hebrew, law) Hebrew name for the PENTATEUCH, the first five books of the Old Testament. The Torah is the body of written Jewish laws contained within these five books. The Torah also describes the complete Jewish Bible.

tornado Funnel-shaped, violently rotating storm extending downwards from the cumulonimbus cloud in which it forms. At the ground its diameter may be only about 100m (310ft). Rotational wind speeds range from 160–480km/h (100–300mph). Tornadoes occur in deep low pressure areas, associated with FRONTS or other instabilities.

Toronto Capital of Ontario province and Canada's largest city, on the N shore of Lake Ontario. It is Canada's main banking, financial and manufacturing centre. In 1787 the British purchased the site from Native Americans and the settlement of York was founded in 1793. During the WAR OF 1812 the city was twice captured by US troops. In 1834 it was renamed Toronto (meeting place) and it became the capital of Ontario province in 1867. Its development as a major distribution centre was spurred by the 1959 opening of the ST LAWRENCE SEAWAY. Toronto produces over half of all Canada's manufacturing products. Industries: electrical equipment, brewing, printing and publishing, iron and steel, meat packing, aircraft and motor vehicle manufacture. Pop. (1991) 635,395.

torpedo Self-propelled underwater missile used by submarines, small surface warships and aircraft. Modern torpedoes often have internal electronic equipment for guiding the missile to the target.

torpedo ray *See* RAY

torque Turning effect of a force. The output of a rotary engine, such as a four-stroke engine or an electric motor, is rated by the torque it can develop. The unit of measurement is Nm (newton metre).

Torquemada, Tomás de (1420–98) Spanish churchman and grand inquisitor. A DOMINICAN priest and confessor to King FERDINAND V and Queen ISABELLA I, he was appointed head of the Spanish INQUISITION (1483). He was noted for the severity of his judgments and the harshness of his punishments.

Torricelli, Evangelista (1608–47) Italian physicist. Assistant to GALILEO, he is credited with the first man-made VACUUM (Torricellian vacuum) and the invention of the mercury BAROMETER (1643).

tort In British law, wrongful act or omission that can give rise to a civil action at law, other than concerning breach of contract. The law of tort includes negligence, libel, slander, trespass, false imprisonment and nuisance.

tortoise Terrestrial or freshwater reptile of the order Chelonia. All tortoises are heavily armoured and enclosed within a domed, bony, carapace (shell). When disturbed, tortoises pull their legs, head and tail into the shelter of the shell. They live in tropical and subtropical regions, and hibernate in temperate countries. They are slow movers, feed almost entirely on plants and live to a great age. Length: usually to 30cm (1ft). A giant species, up to 1.9m (5ft) long, lives in the GALÁPAGOS ISLANDS.

Tory Party Alternative name for the British CONSERVATIVE PARTY. The name Tory, originally meaning an Irish bandit, was applied insultingly in the 1680s to those who did not oppose a Catholic monarchy. It became the name of the political party that represented the interests of landowners and the Anglican Church in the 18th century. The name Conservative was adopted in 1832.

Toscanini, Arturo (1867–1957) Italian conductor who became music director at LA SCALA, Milan, in 1898. He conducted the New York Philharmonic Orchestra (1928–36) and founded the NBC Symphony Orchestra in New York in 1937.

totalitarianism Form of government in which the state tries to acquire total control of every aspect of social and individual activity or thought, by means of controlling the mass media, suppression of opposition and the often violent use of police or army. The term arose in the 1920s to describe Italian FASCISM and has since been applied to Nazi Germany, the Soviet Union under Stalin and many other states.

totemism Complex collection of ideas held by certain primitive societies about the relationships between human beings and the animals or plants around them. The natural objects or people with which many tribal societies believe they have a kinship or mystical relationship are called totems.

toucan Any of 35 species of colourful, gregarious birds of the forests of tropical America, characterized by a large, colourful bill. The plumage is generally red, yellow, blue, black or orange. It feeds on fruit and berries. Length: 60cm (2ft). Family Ramphastidae.

touch One of the five SENSES, functioning by means of specialized nerve receptors in the skin.

Toulon Capital of Var département, on the Mediterranean coast, SE France. Toulon is France's leading naval base and its second-largest Mediterranean port after Marseilles. Originally known as Telo Martius, the city was a Roman naval base and an important port of embarkation for the Crusaders. During the 17th century, LOUIS XIV and Cardinal RICHELIEU improved the port's fortifications. In 1942 the French navy was scuttled there to prevent German capture. Industries: shipbuilding and naval repairs. Pop. (1990) 167,619.

Toulouse City on the River Garonne, S France, capital of Haute-Garonne département. The capital of the Visigoths in the 5th century, it became part of the French crown lands in 1271. The city is the centre of the country's aeronautic industry. Other industries: paper, textiles, chemicals, fertilizers, armaments. Pop. (1990) 358,688.

Toulouse-Lautrec, Henri Marie Raymond de (1864–1901) French painter and graphic artist. At first he depicted sporting subjects, but in around 1888 he began to illustrate the theatres, cabarets, music-halls, cafes and brothels of Paris. His prints, depicting powerfully simplified forms, helped to establish the poster as a respected art form.

Tour de France Premier professional road cycling race in Europe. Raced over three weeks from the end of June, it travels over all types of terrain in a series of timed stages. It mostly circles France, occasionally venturing into neighbouring states, and ends in Paris.

Tourette's syndrome Rare movement disorder. It is a lifelong affliction that starts in childhood with tics and involuntary grimaces. Involuntary sounds also frequently occur. Its cause is unknown.

tourmaline Silicate mineral, sodium or calcium aluminium borosilicate, found in IGNEOUS and METAMORPHIC rocks. Its crystals are hexagonal system and glassy, either opaque or transparent. Some are prized as gems. Hardness 7.5; s.g. 3.1.

Tower of London English royal castle. It was begun by William the Conqueror in 1078 and was extended by later monarchs. It has served various functions throughout the centuries, but is associated especially with the imprisonment and execution (on Tower Hill) of traitors, alleged or real.

toxicology Study of poisonous substances and their effects on living things.

toxic shock syndrome Potentially fatal condition in which there is a dangerous drop in blood pressure and rapid onset of fever, diarrhoea, vomiting and muscular pains. It is caused by SEPTICAEMIA (blood poisoning) caused by toxins put out by normally present and harmless bacteria. The syndrome is most common in young women using tampons.

toxin Poisonous substance produced by a living organism. The unpleasant symptoms of many bacterial diseases are due to toxins released by BACTERIA. Many MOULDS, some larger FUNGI and seeds of some higher plants produce toxins. The venoms of many snakes contain powerful toxins.

toxoplasmosis Disease caused by the protozoan *Toxoplasma gondii*, which is transmitted from animals to human beings. It produces symptoms that are generally flu-like in adults, but it can damage the nervous system, eyes and internal organs.

trace elements Chemical elements that are essential to life but normally obtainable from the diet only in small quantities. They are essential to the reactions of ENZYMES and HORMONES.

tracer, radioactive Radioactive substance that is introduced into the body so that its progress can be tracked by special diagnostic equipment. It may aid diagnosis of conditions such as thyroid disease.

631

trachea (windpipe) Airway that extends from the larynx to about the middle of the breastbone. Reinforced with rings of CARTILAGE, it is lined with hair-like CILIA that prevent dirt and other substances from entering the lungs.

tracheophyte In certain classification systems, any VASCULAR PLANT of the phylum Tracheophyta. Within this phylum are: psilopsids (leafless, rootless primitive forms, such as whisk fern); sphenopsids (such as HORSETAIL); lycopsids (such as CLUB MOSS); pteropsids (such as FERN); GYMNOSPERMS and flowering plants.

trachoma Chronic eye infection caused by the microorganism *Chlamydia trachomatis*, characterized by inflammation of the cornea and pus formation. A disease of dry, tropical regions, it is the major cause of blindness in the developing world.

Tractarianism *See* OXFORD MOVEMENT

trademark Distinguishing mark, such as a name, symbol or word, attached to goods, which identifies them as made or sold by a particular manufacturer. A trademark must be registered at the patent office to establish an exclusive right to it.

Trades Union Congress (TUC) Permanent association of UK trade unions. The TUC was founded in 1868 and holds an annual assembly of delegates to discuss common problems. It had more than 8,000,000 members in the mid-1990s.

trade union Group of workers organized for the purpose of improving wages and conditions of work. The first trade unions were founded in Britain during the INDUSTRIAL REVOLUTION. They were given restricted legality in Britain in 1825. The Trades Union Act (1871) put the unions on a firm legal basis, and over the next 150 years, the movement grew steadily. Their rights were curbed in the 1980s under a series of laws sponsored by the Conservative government under Margaret THATCHER.

trade winds Steady winds that blow westwards towards the equator from subtropical high pressure zones between latitudes 30° and 40° N and S.

Trafalgar, Battle of (1805) British naval victory over the French and Spanish fleets off Cape Trafalgar, Spain. It ended NAPOLEON I's plans for an invasion of England. The victory was secured by the skilful tactics of the British commander, Lord NELSON, who was killed in the battle.

tragedy Form of drama in which a noble hero (the protagonist) meets a fate inherent in the drama's action. *Oedipus Rex* by SOPHOCLES is an early example, which was unmatched until the tragedies of Christopher MARLOWE. ARISTOTLE's *Poetics* systematized tragedy. *See also* AESCHYLUS; EURIPIDES; GREEK DRAMA; SHAKESPEARE

Trajan (53–117) Roman emperor (98–117), b. Spain. He distinguished himself as a general and administrator and became emperor on Nerva's death. He pursued major campaigns in DACIA (101–102, 105–106) and PARTHIA (113–117), enlarging the Roman empire to its greatest extent.

tram Passenger carriage that runs on rails, which are usually sunk into the road. With increasing concern over pollution, electric trams are attracting renewed interest.

trampolining Leisure pursuit and competitive sport that involves the performance of acrobatic manoeuvres while bouncing on a canvas sheet stretched across a tightly sprung rigid frame.

tranquillizers Drugs prescribed to reduce anxiety or tension and generally for their calming effect. They are used to control the symptoms of severe mental disturbance, such as schizophrenia or manic depression. They are also prescribed to relieve depression. Prolonged use of tranquillizers can produce a range of unwanted side-effects.

Transcaucasia Former Soviet Republic, corresponding to the three constituent republics ARMENIA, AZERBAIJAN and GEORGIA. Created in 1918 after the RUSSIAN REVOLUTION, it was granted full republic status in 1924. Georgia, Azerbaijan and Armenia were re-established as separate republics in 1936 and became independent nations on the break-up of the SOVIET UNION in 1990.

transcendentalism School of philosophy that traced its origin to the idealism of Immanuel KANT. It was concerned not with objects, but with our mode of knowing objects. It spread from Germany to England, where Samuel COLERIDGE and Thomas CARLYLE came under its influence. In general, it emphasized individual (as opposed to collective) moral and spiritual responsibilities and rejected materialism.

transcendental meditation (TM) Meditation technique based partly on Hindu practice. The Maharishi Mahesh Yogi introduced the technique to the West. Those who practise TM concentrate on and repeat a MANTRA over and over in order to become relaxed and achieve self-understanding.

transducer Device for converting any nonelectrical signal, such as sound or light, into an electrical signal, and vice versa. Examples include microphones, loudspeakers and various measuring instruments used in ACOUSTICS.

transformer Device for converting alternating current at one voltage to another voltage at the same frequency. It consists of two coils of wire coupled together magnetically. The input current is fed to one coil (the primary), the output being taken from the other coil (the secondary).

transform fault Special class of strike-slip fault characteristic of mid-ocean ridges. Because of the transform faults, which are at right-angles to the ridge itself, the MID-ATLANTIC RIDGE does not run in a straight line but in offset steps.

transfusion, blood *See* BLOOD TRANSFUSION

transistor Electronic device made of SEMICONDUCTOR material that can amplify electrical signals. First developed in 1948 by John BARDEEN, Walter BRATTAIN and William SHOCKLEY, they made possible many technological advances.

transition elements Metallic elements that have incomplete inner electron shells. They are characterized by variable valencies (combining power) and the formation of coloured ions. *See also* PERIODIC TABLE

translocation In VASCULAR PLANTS, the movement of food materials in solution through the tissues from one part of the plant to another.

transmigration of souls Belief that the soul is reborn in one or more successive mortal bodies; a form of REINCARNATION. A tenet of Asian religions such as BUDDHISM, it is common in tribal religions such as that of the South African Venda.

transpiration In plants, the loss of moisture as water vapour from leaf surfaces or other plant parts. Most of the water entering plant roots is lost by transpiration. The flow of water from the roots to the STOMATA is called the transpiration stream.

transplant Surgical operation to introduce organ or tissue from one person (the donor) to another (the recipient); it may also refer to the transfer of tissues from one part of the body to another, as in grafting of skin or bone. Organs routinely transplanted include the kidneys, heart, lungs, liver and pancreas. Many other tissues are commonly grafted, including heart valves, bone and bone marrow. The oldest transplant procedure is corneal grafting, undertaken to restore the sight of one or both eyes.

transsexuality Act of permanently changing one's sex, or the desire to do so. It may be accomplished partly through hormone treatment or through surgery, and in some countries the change can be accompanied by a legal change of status.

Trans-Siberian Railway Russian railway from Moscow to Vladivostok. The world's longest railway, the main part, E from Chelyabinsk, was built in 1891–1905, linking Russia to the Pacific via the Chinese Eastern Railway in Manchuria. The total length is *c*.9,000km (5,750mi).

transubstantiation Belief accepted by the Roman Catholic Church that, during the prayer of consecration at the MASS (the EUCHARIST), the "substance" of the bread and wine is changed into the "substance" of the body and blood of JESUS CHRIST, while the "accidents" (the outward forms of the bread and wine) remain unchanged.

transuranic elements Those elements with atomic numbers higher than that of URANIUM (92). The best known are members of the ACTINIDE SERIES (atomic numbers 89 to 103). All transuranic elements are radioactive. Only NEPTUNIUM and PLUTONIUM occur naturally in minute amounts but all can be synthesized. The only commercially important element in the group is plutonium, which is used in NUCLEAR WEAPONS and as a nuclear fuel.

Transvaal Former province of South Africa. In 1994–95 Transvaal was divided into NORTHERN PROVINCE, Mpumalanga, GAUTENG and NORTH-WEST PROVINCE. The indigenous population are the Bantu-speaking Venda and Sotho peoples. In the 1836 GREAT TREK, the BOERS crossed the River Vaal and began to settle the region. In 1857 the South African Republic was formed. In 1877 the British annexed the republic. After a Boer revolt, the Transvaal was again granted internal self-government in 1881, under the new president, Paul KRUGER. The 1886 discovery of gold in Witwatersrand attracted vast numbers of Britons and Germans. The Boers imposed heavy taxation and denied political rights to the newcomers. In 1895 Leander Starr JAMESON launched an incursion into the Transvaal. The "Jameson Raid" failed to ignite a full-scale rebellion, but the resultant tension between the Boers and the British led to the SOUTH AFRICAN WARS. In the 1902 Treaty of Vereeniging, the Transvaal became a British crown colony. In 1907 the region was again allowed self-government, and in 1910 it became a founding province in the Union of South Africa. In 1995 Transvaal ceased to exist as a political entity and was split into four of South Africa's nine new provinces.

Transylvania (Romanian, beyond the forest) High plateau region in central and NW Romania, separated from the rest of Romania by the CARPATHIAN MOUNTAINS and the Transylvanian Alps. Its major cities are Cluj-Napoca, Braşov and Sibiu. It became part of the Roman province of DACIA in AD 107. It was conquered by Hungary at the beginning of the 11th century. In 1526 the ruler of Transylvania, John Zapolya, defeated the Hungarian army, and claimed the Hungarian throne as John I. His claim was supported by the Turks who, following Zapolya's death in 1540, occupied Transylvania on the pretext of ensuring his son's succession. For the next two centuries Transylvania retained a semi-independent status as it played off the competing imperial claims of Turkey and Austria. During the 17th century, it flourished as Hungary's cultural centre, but in 1765 it became an Austrian province. Hungarian supremacy was re-established in 1867. After World War 1 Hungary ceded the territory to Romania, which embarked on land redistribution and forced assimilation of other nationalities. Hungary annexed part of Transylvania in World War 2, but was forced to return it in 1947. Transylvania is the legendary home of vampires, publicized in the West by Bram STOKER's *Dracula*.

Trappists Popular name for the CISTERCIANS of the Strict Observance, a religious order of monks and nuns. The order originated in La Trappe Abbey, France, in 1664. They maintain complete silence and practise vegetarianism.

trauma Any injury or physical damage caused by some external event such as an accident or assault. In psychiatry, the term is applied to an emotional shock or harrowing experience.

treason Offence against the state or the sovereign. Treason is the most serious criminal offence and is punishable by death in many countries. In Britain, treason is defined to include the infliction of death or injury on the monarch, violation of members of the royal family, levying war against the government, or giving assistance to the enemy.

Treasury UK government department responsible for national finance and monetary policy. Dating from the Norman Conquest, when the chancellor and barons exercised control of royal revenues, the Treasury developed from the office of the chancellor of the exchequer. It became a separate ministry in the 19th century.

tree Woody PERENNIAL plant with one main stem or trunk and smaller branches. The trunk increases in diameter each year, and the leaves may be evergreen or DECIDUOUS. The largest trees, SEQUOIAS, can grow more than 110m (420ft) tall.

tree creeper Brownish, agile bird that scurries up and down trees in cooler areas of the Northern Hemisphere. It uses its long, slightly down-curved bill to probe for insects under the bark. Length: 13cm (5in). Species *Certhia familiaris*.

tree fern Tree-like FERN of the family Cyatheaceae. Tree ferns grow in tropical and subtropical regions, particularly moist mountainous areas. Height: 3–25m (10–80ft). There are 600 species. Phylum Filicinophyta; genus *Cyathea*.

trefoil Any of numerous plants, such as CLOVER, with leaves divided into three parts. Bird's-foot trefoil (*Lotus corniculatus*) is a perennial, used as hay and forage. Family Fabaceae/Leguminosae.

Trent River in central England, at 274km (170mi) the country's third-longest. It rises on Biddulph Moor, Staffordshire, and flows SE through the POTTERIES, and then NE across central England to join the OUSE. Linked by canals to many industrial towns, it provides water for cooling power stations.

Trent, Council of (1545–63) Nineteenth ecumenical council of the Roman Catholic Church, which provided the main impetus of the COUNTER-REFORMATION in Europe. It met at Trent, N Italy, in three sessions under three popes (Paul III, Julius III, Pius IV). It clarified Catholic doctrine and refused concessions to the Protestants, while also instituting reform of many of the abuses that had provoked the REFORMATION.

Trevithick, Richard (1771–1833) British engineer and designer of steam engines. In 1801 he built a steam-powered road vehicle. The following year, he patented a high-pressure steam engine. In 1803 Trevithick built the first steam railway LOCOMOTIVE.

triad Chinese secret society. It existed in S China from the earliest days of the Qing empire in the 17th century. Today triads are said to control Chinese organized crime throughout the world, their chief centre being in Hong Kong.

trial by jury Trial by a number of people (usually 12), who are sworn to deliver a verdict in a court of law on the evidence presented. It is the main method of trying criminal and some civil cases at common law in the Western world. *See also* JURY

Triassic First period of the MESOZOIC era, lasting from 248 to 13 million years ago. Many new kinds of animals developed. On land, the first DINOSAURS roamed. Mammal-like reptiles were common, and by the end of the period the first true MAMMALS existed. In the seas lived the first ichthyosaurs, placodonts and nothosaurs. The first frogs, turtles, crocodilians and lizards also appeared. Plant life consisted mainly of primitive gymnosperms.

Trieste City on the Gulf of Trieste, at the head of the Adriatic Sea, NE Italy. It was an imperial free port from 1719 to 1891 and became an Austrian crown land in 1867. It was ceded to Italy in 1919, occupied by Yugoslavia in 1945, but was returned to Italy in 1954. It is an important industrial and commercial centre with large shipyards. Industries: steel, textiles and petroleum. Pop. (1992) 228,398.

triggerfish Any of several tropical marine fish found in warm shallow Pacific waters, identified by a dorsal fin spine that can be erected to lodge the fish in a coral cavity, as a protection against predators. Length: to 60cm (24in). Family Balistidae; typical genus *Balistoides*.

triglyceride *See* LIPID

trigonometric function Six ratios of the sides of a right-angled triangle containing a given acute angle – they are the SINE, COSINE, TANGENT, COTANGENT, SECANT and COSECANT of the angle. These functions can be extended to cover angles of any size using a system of rectangular coordinates.

trigonometry Use of ratios of the sides of a right-angled triangle to calculate lengths and angles in geometrical figures. If three sides, or two sides and the included angle, or one side and two angles of a triangle are known, then all the other sides and angles may be found.

trilobite Any of an extinct group of ARTHROPODS found as fossils in marine deposits, ranging in age from CAMBRIAN through PERMIAN times. The body was mostly oval, tapering towards the rear and was covered by a chitinous skeleton. Transverse divisions show segmentation and bear pairs of jointed limbs. Most species lived in shallow water. Length: 6mm (0.25in) to 75cm (30in).

Trinidad and Tobago Republic composed of the two southernmost islands of the Lesser ANTILLES, in the SE Caribbean; the capital is PORT OF SPAIN on Trinidad. The larger island of Trinidad lies only 11km (7mi) off the Venezuelan coast. It is mainly low plains with coastal mangrove swamps. The Spanish colonized the island in the 16th century, but it was ceded to Britain in 1802. Tobago lies 30km (19mi) NE of Trinidad. The island, dominated by a mountain ridge, is heavily forested. Scarborough is the principal town. Tobago was initially settled by the British in 1616. After Spanish, Dutch and French rule, in 1803 the island became a British possession. Trinidad and Tobago were integrated into a single crown colony in 1883, becoming an independent state in 1962 and a republic in 1976. In 1990 the prime minister, Arthur Robinson, was captured and later released in an attempted coup. After 1995 elections, a coalition government of the United National Congress and the Alliance for Reconstruction came to power, with Basdeo Panday as prime minister. The economy is dominated by oil and gas, asphalt mining and tourism. Area: 5,128sq km (1,980sq mi). Pop. (1990) 1,169,600.

Trinity Central doctrine of Christianity, according to which God is three persons: the Father, the Son and the HOLY SPIRIT or Holy Ghost. There is only one God, but he exists as "three in one and one in three". The nature of the Trinity is held to be a mystery that cannot be fully comprehended. It was stated in early Christian creeds to counter heresies such as GNOSTICISM. *See also* APOSTLES' CREED; ATHANASIAN CREED; JESUS CHRIST; NICENE CREED

Triple Alliance Name given to several international alliances involving three states. They included the anti-French alliance of Britain, the Netherlands and Sweden of 1668, and the alliance of Britain, France and the Netherlands of 1717, directed against Spanish ambitions in Italy. The most recent was the Triple Alliance of 1882, when Italy joined the Dual Alliance of Austria-Hungary and Germany. In South America, Argentina, Brazil and Uruguay formed a triple alliance in the war against Paraguay (1865–70).

Triple Entente Name given to the alliance of Britain, France and Russia before World War 1. It developed from the Franco-Russian Alliance (1894) formed to counterbalance the threat posed by the TRIPLE ALLIANCE of Germany, Austria and Italy. In 1904 Britain became allied with France in the *Entente Cordiale*, and the Anglo-Russian Convention of 1907 completed the Triple Entente.

triple jump In athletics, similar to the long jump with the exception that from the take-off line a contestant takes two extended leaps on alternate legs to launch into the final jump.

Tripoli Capital and chief port of LIBYA, on the Mediterranean Sea. The city was founded as Oea in the 7th century BC by the Phoenicians and was developed by the Romans. From the 7th century AD the Arabs developed Tripoli as a market centre for the trans-Saharan caravans. In 1551 it was captured by the Ottoman Turks. In the 17th century, Tripoli was a base for pirates. In 1911 it was made the capital of the Italian colony of Libya, and during World War 2 it was a base for Axis forces. Following Allied bombing, the city was captured by the British in 1943. In 1986 Tripoli was bombed by the US Air Force in retaliation for Libya's alleged support of worldwide terrorism. The city is the commercial, industrial, transport and communications centre of Libya. The oases comprise the most fertile agricultural area in N Africa. Pop. (1984) 990,697.

Tripoli Mediterranean port and second-largest city in LEBANON. Tripoli was an important city of the Seleucid and Roman empires. Captured in AD 638 by the Arabs, in 1109 the city was conquered by the Crusaders, who developed the fortifications. In 1289 Tripoli returned to Islamic rule under the Mamelukes. The Turks held the city until the arrival of the British in 1918, and in 1920 it passed to Lebanon. The city remains an major trade centre between Syria and Lebanon, and is the terminus of the oil pipeline from Iraq. Industries: oil refining, textiles, food processing. Pop. (1991) 203,000.

Tristan da Cunha Group of four islands in the S Atlantic Ocean, located midway between S Africa and South America. The group was discovered in 1506 by the Portuguese and annexed by Britain in 1816. In 1961 Tristan, the only inhabitable island, suffered a volcanic eruption that caused a temporary evacuation. A British dependency, it is administered from ST HELENA. Area of Tristan: 98sq km (38sq mi). Pop. (1988) 313.

Triton In Greek mythology, a sea god, son of POSEIDON and Amphitrite. He was half man and half fish, with a scaled body, claws, and a forked fish tail. He had power over the waves.

trogon Brilliantly coloured bird of dark tropical forests in America, Africa and Asia. Trogons nest in holes in trees and feed on fruit and some insect larvae. Length: about 30cm (12in). Family Trogonidae; typical genus *Trogon*.

Trojan horse Colossal, hollow wooden horse built by the Greeks in the final days of the siege of TROY. Thinking it was a peace offering, the Trojans dragged the horse through the gates, and in the night Greek soldiers who had been hiding within, emerged and opened the city gates to their army.

Trollope, Anthony (1815–82) British novelist. The best known of his novels are the Barsetshire chronicles, which include *The Warden* (1855), *Barchester Towers* (1857) and *Doctor Thorne* (1858), and his novels of the Palliser family, including *Can You Forgive Her?* (1864–65) and *The Way We Live Now* (1874–75).

trombone BRASS musical instrument with a cylindrical bore, cupped mouthpiece and flaring bell. It is usually played with a slide. It is a regular member of the orchestra, and is found in jazz, brass and military bands.

Trondheim City on the S shore of Trondheim fjord, central Norway, the third-largest city in Norway. Founded as Nidaros in 997, the city was the political and religious capital of medieval Norway. Industries: fish canning, brewing, electronics, shipbuilding, soap, hardware. Pop. (1990) 137,846.

tropical diseases Diseases predominantly associated with tropical climates. Major ones are MALARIA, leishmaniasis, trypanosomiasis (SLEEPING SICKNESS), lymphatic filariasis and schistosomiasis (bilharzia). The infectious agents of tropical diseases include viruses, bacteria, protozoa, fungi and worms of various kinds. Many of these microbes are spread by insect vectors, such as mosquitoes.

tropism (tropic response) Response in growth and orientation of a plant or a part of it in relation to a directional, external stimulus, such as light or water.

Trotsky, Leon (1879–1940) Russian revolutionary leader and theoretician, b. Lev Davidovich Bronstein. A Marxist revolutionary, he headed the workers' soviet (revolutionary council) in St Petersburg in the RUSSIAN REVOLUTION OF 1905. Arrested, he escaped abroad and embarked on the work that made him, with LENIN, the leading architect of the RUSSIAN REVOLUTION of 1917. Trotsky returned to Russia after the March revolution (1917) and joined the BOLSHEVIKS. As chairman of the Petrograd (St Petersburg) Soviet, he set up the Military Revolutionary Committee to seize power, ostensibly for the Soviet, actually for the Bolsheviks. After the Bolshevik success, he negotiated the peace of BREST-LITOVSK, withdrawing Russia from World War 1. As commissar of war (1918–25), he created the Red Army, which won the civil war and secured the Bolshevik revolution. He criticized the lack of democracy in the party and the failure to expand industrialization. He disapproved of Lenin's dictatorial tendencies and fiercely objected to Stalin's adoption of a policy of "socialism in one country", rather than the world revolution in which Trotsky believed. He was driven from power, from the party and eventually from the country. In exile his prolific writings, though rejected in the Soviet Union, were extremely influential. In 1936 he settled in Mexico, where he was assassinated by a Stalinist agent.

trough In meteorology, area of low atmospheric pressure, usually an extension to a DEPRESSION.

trout Any fish of the salmon family (Salmonidae). There are three types of the single species of European trout (*Salmo trutta*), each with a different name. The brown or river trout is small and dark, and does not migrate. The lake trout, of rivers and lakes, is a larger, paler version, and is sometimes migratory. The large, silvery sea trout is definitely migratory and salmon-like. Length: to 1m (3ft); weight: to 13.5kg (30lb).

Troy (Ilium) Ancient city at what is now Hissarlik, Turkey, familiar chiefly through the *Iliad* of HOMER. Archaeological excavation, begun by Heinrich SCHLIEMANN in the 1870s, suggests that the legend of the Trojan war may be based on an actual episode. Nine cities have been detected in the archaeological strata, dating from *c.*3000 BC.

Trudeau, Pierre Elliott (1919–) Canadian prime minister (1968–79, 1980–84). He promoted the economic and diplomatic independence of Canada, reducing US influence. Aided by his French-Canadian origins, he resisted QUEBEC separatism, imposing martial law to combat separatist terrorism in 1970. Autonomy for Quebec was rejected in a referendum (1980), and Trudeau succeeded in winning agreement for a revised constitution (1981).

True Levellers *See* DIGGERS

Truffaut, François (1932–84) French film director. His first feature film was *The 400 Blows* (1959). His other films include *Jules and Jim* (1961) and *Pocket Money* (1976). *Day for Night* (1973) won an Academy Award for Best Foreign Language Film.

truffle Any of several species of ascomycete FUNGI that grow underground, mostly among tree roots. Most are edible and are highly prized delicacies. Found in Europe, particularly France, and in parts of the USA, they are hunted with trained pigs and dogs that can scent them out. Family Tuberaceae.

Truman, Harry S. (1884–1972) 33rd US President (1945–53). He approved the use of the atomic bomb to force Japanese surrender (1945), ending World War 2, and adopted a robust policy towards the Soviet Union during the COLD WAR that followed. He approved the MARSHALL PLAN (1947) and the creation of NATO (1949). He declined to run for a second full term in 1952.

trumpet BRASS instrument of ancient origin. It has a cylindrical bore in the shape of a flattened loop and three piston valves. An important ceremonial instrument from the 15th century, by the late 17th century it had become standard in the orchestra.

trunkfish Marine fish that lives in temperate and tropical waters. It is almost triangular when seen from the front, with a broad flat ventral region tapering to a narrow dorsal region. Length: to 50cm (20in). Family Ostraciontidae; genus *Lactophrys*.

trypsin Digestive enzyme secreted by the pancreas. It is secreted in an inactive form that is converted into active trypsin by an enzyme in the small intestine. It breaks down peptide bonds on the amino acids lysine and arginine. *See also* ALIMENTARY CANAL; DIGESTION; DIGESTIVE SYSTEM

tsar Name of the rulers of Russia, first adopted by Ivan the Terrible in 1547. It is an adaptation of the Latin *caesar*. In 1721 Peter I changed the official title to "emperor", but "tsar" or "czar" continued to be used in popular language until 1917.

tsetse fly Any of several species of blood-sucking African flies. Larger than a housefly, it is grey and yellow or brown. Females transmit a cattle disease. Males carry SLEEPING SICKNESS by biting humans. Length: to 16mm (0.6in). Order Diptera; family Muscidae; genus *Glossina*.

Tsiolkovsky, Konstantin Eduardovich (1857–1935) Russian scientist who provided the theoretical basis for space travel. In 1898 he was first to stress the importance of liquid propellants in ROCKETS. He also proposed the idea of using multistage rockets to overcome GRAVITATION.

tsunami (seismic sea wave) Ocean wave caused by a submarine EARTHQUAKE, subsidence, or volcanic eruption. Tsunamis spread radially from their source in ever-widening circles. Tsunamis can travel across oceans at speeds up to 400km/h (250mph) and reach heights of 10m (33ft).

Tuareg Fiercely independent BERBERS of Islamic faith, who inhabit the desert regions of N Africa. Their matrilineal, feudal society is based on nomadic pastoralism. Tuareg males wear blue veils, while the women are unveiled.

tuatara Nocturnal, lizard-like reptile of New Zealand; the sole surviving member of the order Rhynchocephalia. It is brownish and has a well-developed PINEAL BODY on its head. Length: to 70cm (2.3ft). Species *Sphenodon punctatus*.

tuba Family of BRASS musical instruments, the lowest of the orchestral brass instruments. The tuba has a conical bore and a cupped mouthpiece and usually has four or five valves.

tuber In plants, the short, swollen, sometimes edible underground stem, modified for the storage of food, as in the potato, or as a swollen root. They enable the plant to survive an adverse season (winter or dry season), providing food for the later development of new shoots and roots.

tuberculosis (TB) Infectious disease caused by the bacillus *Mycobacterium tuberculosis*. It most often affects the lungs (pulmonary tuberculosis), but may involve the bones and joints, skin, lymph nodes, intestines and kidneys. The BCG vaccine against tuberculosis was developed in the 1920s and the first effective treatment drug, streptomycin, became available in 1944. However, the bacillus is showing increasing resistance to drugs and some strains are multi-resistant.

Tubman, William Vacanarat Shadrach (1895–1971) President of Liberia (1944–71). A descendant of US black colonists, he ruled unchallenged until his death, preserving Liberia's close connections with the USA.

TUC *See* TRADES UNION CONGRESS

Tucson City on the Santa Cruz River, S Arizona, USA. The presidio fort of Tucson was built by the Spanish in 1776 and the city was state capital from 1867–77. Today it is a foothills resort with a dry, sunny climate. It is a shipping point for cotton and cattle. Industries: textiles, meat-packing, copper smelting, aircraft parts, electronics, optical instruments. Pop. (1992) 415,079.

Tudjman, Franjo (1922–) Croatian statesman, president of Croatia (1990–). He was twice imprisoned by the Yugoslavian government for nationalist activities. In 1989 he founded the Croatian Democratic Union (HDZ) party, which won Croatia's first democratic elections (1990). He was elected president of newly independent Croatia in 1992, retaining this position during the ensuing civil war. He was re-elected in 1997.

Tudors English royal dynasty (1485–1603). Of Welsh origin, they were descended from Owen Tudor (d.1461), who married the widow of HENRY V. Owen Tudor's grandson defeated RICHARD III at Bosworth in 1485 to win the English throne as HENRY VII. The dynasty ended with the death of ELIZABETH I in 1603.

tulip Hardy, bulb-forming plant of the genus *Tulipa*, native to Europe, Asia and North Africa. Tulips have long, pointed leaves growing from the base and elongated, cup-shaped flowers that can be almost any colour or combination of colours. Family Liliaceae; genus *Tulipa*.

Tull, Jethro (1674–1741) British agriculturalist. He influenced agricultural methods through his innovations and his writings. He invented a mechanical drill for sowing in 1701 and advocated the use of manure and thorough tilling.

tumbleweed Plant of prairie and steppe regions that breaks off near the ground in autumn and is rolled along by the wind. Height: to 51cm (20in). Family Amaranthaceae; genus *Amaranthus*.

tumour Any uncontrolled, abnormal proliferation of cells, often leading to the formation of a lump. Tumours are classified as either benign (non-cancerous) or malignant.

tuna *See* TUNNY

tundra Treeless, level or gently undulating plain characteristic of arctic and subarctic regions. It is marshy with dark soil that supports mosses, lichens and low shrubs, but not trees. It has a permanently frozen subsoil known as PERMAFROST.

tungsten (wolfram) Silvery-grey, hard, metallic element (symbol W), one of the TRANSITION ELEMENTS. Tungsten has the highest melting point of all metals and is used for lamp filaments and in special alloys. Chemically tungsten is fairly unreactive; it oxidizes only at high temperatures. Properties: at.no. 74; r.a.m. 183.85; r.d. 19.3; m.p. 3,410°C (6,170°F); b.p. 5,660°C (10,220°F); most common isotope W^{184} (30.64%).

Tunis Capital and largest city of Tunisia, N Africa. Tunis became the capital in the 13th century under the Hafsid dynasty. Seized by Barbarossa in 1534 and controlled by Turkey, it attained infamy as a haven for pirates. The French assumed control in 1881. Products include olive oil, carpets, textiles and handicrafts. The ruins of CARTHAGE are nearby. Pop. (1994) 674,100.

Tunisia Republic in N Africa, the capital is Tunis. **Land and climate** Tunisia is the smallest country in North Africa. The NW mountain ranges are an extension of the ATLAS Mountains. In the centre is a depression, containing the Chott Djerid salt lake. In the S lies part of the SAHARA desert. The fertile coastal lowlands include Mediterranean ports, such as Bizerte and the capital, TUNIS. Coastal regions have dry summers and mild winters with moderate rainfall. Rainfall decreases and temperatures increase to the S. Cork oak forests grow in the N mountains. The S plateaus are covered by steppe with coarse grasses. The Sahara is barren, except around oases. **Economy** Tunisia is a middle-income developing country (1992 GDP per capita, US$5,160). The world's sixth-largest producer of phosphates, it also exports crude oil. Agriculture employs 26% of the workforce. Tunisia is the world's fourth-largest producer of olives. Other major crops include barley, dates, grapes and wheat. Fishing and livestock-raising are also impor-

TUNISIA
AREA: 163,610sq km (63,170sq mi)
POPULATION: 8,410,000
CAPITAL POPULATION: Tunis (674,100)
GOVERNMENT: Multiparty republic
ETHNIC GROUPS: Arab 98%, Berber 1%, French and other
LANGUAGES: Arabic (official)
RELIGIONS: Islam 99%
CURRENCY: Dinar = 1,000 millimes

tant, and tourism is vital. It has been an associate of the EC since 1969. **History and politics** In tradition, the Phoenician Queen Dido founded Carthage in 814 BC. The Romans destroyed the city in 146 BC, and the region was subsumed into the Roman empire. The Arabs invaded in AD 640. The Berbers slowly converted to Islam and Arabic became the principal language. In 1159 the Almohad dynasty conquered Tunisia. From 1230–1574 Tunisia was ruled by the Hafsids. Spain's capture of much of Tunisia's coast led to the intervention of the Ottoman empire, and the rule of the Turkish governors (beys) continued into the 20th century. In the 16th century Tunisia's harbours were a refuge for Barbary pirates. France invaded in 1881 and Tunisia became a French protectorate (1883). French rule aroused strong nationalist sentiment, and Habib Bourguiba formed the Destour Socialist Party (PSD) in 1934. Tunisia was a major battleground in World War 2. In 1956 it gained independence. In 1957 the bey was deposed and Tunisia became a republic, with Bourguiba as president. Bourguiba pursued a moderate foreign policy and modernizing domestic policies. The first multiparty elections were held in 1981. Bourguiba's failing health created a succession crisis in the 1980s, and in 1987 he was deposed by Zine el Abidine Ben Ali. The PSD became the Constitutional Democratic Rally (RCD), and Ben Ali won a landslide victory in 1989. He was re-elected in 1994.

tunny (tuna) Large marine fish related to MACKEREL, found in tropical and temperate seas. An important commercial fish, it has a blue-black and silvery streamlined body with a large tail. Length: to 4.3m (14ft); weight: to 810kg (1,800lb).

turbine Rotary device turned by a moving fluid (liquid or gas). The modern form of water turbine is like a many-bladed propeller and is used to generate HYDROELECTRICITY. In power stations that burn fuels to produce electricity, energy is harnessed by the blades of steam turbines. As they spin, the turbines turn GENERATORS that produce electricity. Modern wind generators produce electricity when the wind turns their rotors. In gas turbines, hot gases from burning fuel turn turbines that can operate generators or other machinery.

turbocharger Device that boosts the performance of an internal combustion engine. A TURBINE driven by exhaust gases compresses the fuel/air mixture before it passes through the inlet valve.

turbot Scaleless, bottom-dwelling, European marine FLATFISH. It has a broad flat body with both eyes on its grey-brown, mottled upper surface. Length: to 1m (3.3ft). Family Scophthalmidae; species *Scophthalmus maximus*.

turgor pressure Hydrostatic pressure generated in cells of plants and bacteria as a result of the uptake of water by OSMOSIS. Water diffuses through the semi-permeable membrane of the cell, causing the cell to swell. When water is lost, a plant's cells collapse and it wilts.

638

Turin (Torino) City on the River Po, NW Italy, the country's fourth-largest city and capital of Piedmont (Piemonte) region. A Roman town under Augustus, Turin became a Lombard duchy from 590 to 636. From 1720 to 1861 it was capital of the Kingdom of Sardinia and a centre of the RISORGIMENTO. Damaged during World War 2, Turin remains an important industrial centre. Industries: electronic equipment, chemicals, machinery, rubber, paper, leather goods, pharmaceuticals, wines. Pop. (1992) 952,736.

Turing, Alan Mathison (1912–54) British mathematician. In 1936 he gave a precise description of a theoretical computing device, which foreshadowed the digital computer. During World War 2 he helped to break the German "Enigma" codes. After the war he supervised the design and construction of the ACE electronic digital computer.

Turin shroud Sheet of very old linen kept in Turin Cathedral, by tradition the cloth in which the body of Christ was wrapped after the Crucifixion. In 1988 results of carbon dating tests revealed that the shroud had in fact been made sometime between AD 1260 and 1390.

Turkey Republic in SE Europe and Asia, the capital is ANKARA. **Land and climate** Turkey straddles Europe and Asia. European Turkey (THRACE) is a small, fertile region, separated from Asia by the DARDANELLES, the BOSPORUS, and the Sea of Marmara. ISTANBUL lies on both continents. Anatolia (ASIA MINOR) is mainly mountainous, rising to 5,165m (16,945ft) at Mount ARARAT in the E. The plateau region of Central Anatolia includes the capital, Ankara. The Mediterranean coast is a popular tourist destination. Central Turkey has hot, dry summers and cold winters. Western Turkey has a Mediterranean climate. The Black Sea coast has cooler summers. **Economy** Turkey is a lower-middle income developing country. Agriculture employs 47% of the workforce. Turkey is a leading producer of citrus fruits, barley, cotton, wheat, tobacco and tea. Sheep-rearing is also important. Turkey is a major producer of chromium and phosphate fertilizers, and tourism is vital. **History and politics** EPHESUS is one of the many ruins of the ancient Anatolian kingdoms of IONIA and PONTUS. In AD 330 Byzantium (Constantinople) became capital of the Roman empire; thence capital of the

TURKEY
AREA: 779,450sq km (300,946sq mi)
POPULATION: 58,775,000
CAPITAL (POPULATION): Ankara (2,541,899)
GOVERNMENT: Multiparty republic
ETHNIC GROUPS: Turkish 86%, Kurdish 11%, Arab 2%
LANGUAGES: Turkish (official)
RELIGIONS: Islam 99%
CURRENCY: Turkish lira = 100 kurus

BYZANTINE EMPIRE (398). In the 11th century, the SELJUKS introduced Islam, and the capital moved to KONYA. In 1435 Constantinople was captured by MUHAMMAD II, and it served as capital of the vast OTTOMAN EMPIRE. Defeat in World War 1 led to the sultan signing the harsh Treaty of SÈVRES (1920). Nationalists, led by Mustafa Kemal (ATATÜRK), launched a war of independence. In 1923 Turkey became a republic, with Kemal as its president. Kemal's 14-year dictatorship created a secular, Westernized state. In 1938 Atatürk died and was succeeded by Ismet Inönü. Turkey remained neutral throughout most of World War 2. A major post-war recipient of US aid, Turkey joined NATO in 1952. The first multiparty elections were held in 1950. An army coup in 1960 led to the creation of a second republic. In 1965 Süleyman DEMIREL became prime minister. In 1974 Turkey invaded Northern CYPRUS; tension with Greece increased. In 1980 a military coup led to martial law. In 1987 martial law was lifted and Turkey applied to join the EC. In 1993 Demirel was elected president, and Tansu Çiller became Turkey's first woman prime minister. Following 1995 elections, the Islamist Welfare Party (RP) formed a coalition government, with Necmettin Erbakan as prime minister. In 1997 tension increased between the pro-Islamic government and the military, over what the military perceived to be a drift towards radical Islam. Erbakan resigned, and a new coalition, led by Mesut Yilmaz of the secular Motherland Party (ANAP), was appointed by Demirel. Conflict with Kurdish nationalists in E Turkey is a persistent problem, and Turkish authorities have been accused of human rights violations.

turkey North American game bird now domesticated worldwide. The common wild turkey (*Meleagris gallopavo*) was overhunted and is now protected. The male, or gobbler, is often bearded. Length: 125cm (50in). Family Meleagrididae.

Turkic languages Six or seven separate subclasses that form a branch of the ALTAIC family. They are remarkable for their grammatical uniformity and their relative lack of linguistic change over time. The most important is Turkish.

Turkistan (Turkestan) Historic region of central Asia, inhabited by Turkic-speaking peoples. Western (Russian) Turkistan now consists of the republics of TURKMENISTAN, UZBEKISTAN, TAJIKISTAN, KYRGYZSTAN and S KAZAKSTAN. It mainly comprises the deserts of KYZYL KUM and Kara Kum. Eastern (Chinese) Turkistan comprises the Chinese region of XINJIANG and includes the TIAN SHAN mountains. Southern Turkistan consisted of part of N Afghanistan. For nearly two centuries Turkistan was a trade bridge between East and West. The first imperial power to control the region was PERSIA in 500 BC, but in *c.*330 BC ALEXANDER THE GREAT defeated the Persians and for the next few centuries the region was disputed between Bactria, PARTHIA and China. In the 8th century the Arabs conquered the region and the local popula-

---

TURKMENISTAN
AREA: 488,100sq km (188,450 sq mi)
POPULATION: 3,714,000
CAPITAL (POPULATION): Ashgabat (or Ashkhabad, 412,200)
GOVERNMENT: Single party republic
ETHNIC GROUPS: Turkmen 72%, Russian 10%, Uzbek 9%, Kazak 3%, Tatar
LANGUAGES: Turkmen (official)
RELIGIONS: Islam
CURRENCY: Manat

---

tion converted to Islam. During the 13th century, the region was controlled by the Mongols, but then broke into small, independent khanates. In 1867 the Russian empire imposed military rule, and in 1918 Turkistan became an autonomous region within the SOVIET UNION. In 1924 the S part of Turkistan was divided into the republics of Uzbekistan and Turkmenistan; in 1929 Tajikistan became a republic and Kyrgyzstan followed in 1936. The N part of Russian Turkistan was incorporated into the Kazak republic, and Russian Turkistan became known as **Soviet Central Asia**.

Turkmenistan Republic in central Asia. The capital is ASHGABAT. Originally part of the Persian empire, it was overrun by Arabs in the 8th century AD. GENGHIS KHAN invaded in the 13th century, and it subsequently became part of TAMERLANE's vast empire. With the breakup of the Timurid dynasty, Turkmenistan came under Uzbek control. In the 19th century, Russia became increasingly dominant, and in 1899, Turkmenistan became part of Russian Turkistan. In 1925 it was absorbed into the SOVIET UNION. It became independent in 1991 and a full member of the Commonwealth of Independent States (CIS) in 1993. President Niyazov (elected 1990) is head of state; his autocratic government prevents any political opposition to the ruling Democratic Party (formerly Communist Party). In a 1994 referendum Niyazov's term of presidency was extended to 2002. Almost 90% of Turkmenistan is covered by the Kara Kum desert. The chief crop is cotton and there are reserves of natural gas and oil.

Turks and Caicos Islands Two island groups of the British West Indies, including more than 40 islands, eight of them inhabited. Discovered in 1512 by Ponce de León, the islands were British from 1766, administered via Jamaica (1873–1959), and a separate crown colony from 1973. Exports include salt, sponges and shellfish, but the main sources of income are tourism and offshore banking. The capital is Cockburn Town on Grand Turk Island. Area: 430sq km (166sq mi). Pop (1990) 12,350.

Turku (Åbo) Finland's largest port, at the mouth of the Aurajoki River on the Baltic Sea. A Swedish settlement was established in 1157 and in 1220 it became the seat of the first Finnish diocese. It was the national capital until 1812. Industries: steel, shipbuilding, engineering, textiles, clothing. Pop. (1994) 162,370.

turmeric Herbaceous, perennial plant originally native to India and cultivated in SE Asia. The dried RHIZOME is powdered for use as seasoning, a yellow dye and in medicines. Family Zingiberaceae; species *Curcuma longa*.

Turner, Joseph Mallord William (1775–1851) British landscape painter. His paintings were revolutionary in their representation of light, especially on water. His style changed dramatically in his late works, such as *The Slave Ship* (1840) and *Rain, Steam and Speed* (1844).

Turner's syndrome Hereditary condition in females, in which there is only one X chromosome instead of two. It results in short stature, infertility and developmental defects.

turnip Garden vegetable best grown in cool climates. The edible leaves are large and toothed with thick midribs. A biennial, it has an edible, white or yellow, fleshy root. Diameter: 8–15cm (3–6in). Height: to 55cm (20in). Family Brassicaceae/Cruciferae; species *Brassica rapa*.

turnstone Either of two species of migratory shore birds that use their curved bills to turn over pebbles in search of food; they nest on the Arctic TUNDRA. The vividly marked ruddy turnstone (*Arenaria interpres*) ranges widely in winter. Family Scolopacidae.

Turpin, Dick (1706–39) English highwayman. He engaged in many forms of robbery and was hanged for murder. He became a largely fictional hero; his famous ride to York on Black Bess was performed by an earlier highwayman.

turquoise Blue mineral, hydrated copper aluminium phosphate, found in aluminium-rich rocks in deserts. Its crystal system is triclinic and it occurs as tiny crystals and dense masses. Its colour ranges from sky-blue and blue-green to a greenish grey. It is a popular gemstone. Hardness 6; s.g. 2.7.

turtle REPTILE found on land or in marine and fresh waters. Turtles have the most ancient lineage of all reptiles, preceding even the dinosaurs. They have a bony, horn-covered, boxlike shell (carapace) that encloses shoulder and hip girdles and all internal organs. All lay eggs on land. Terrestrial turtles are usually called TORTOISES, and some edible species found in brackish waters are called TERRAPINS. Marine turtles usually have smaller, lighter shells. Length: 10cm–2m (4in–7ft). Order Chelonia.

Tuscany Region in central Italy between the Mediterranean coast and the Apennine Mountains; the capital is FLORENCE. Other cities include SIENA and PISA. Tuscany is mostly mountainous with fertile valleys. Agriculture remains the most important activity, with cereals, olives and grapes among the main products. Carrara marble is quarried in the NW, and there is mining for lead, zinc, antimony and copper in the SW. Industries: tourism, woollens, chemicals, steel, motor-scooters. Area: 22,992sq km (8,877sq mi). Pop (1990) 3,528,735.

Tutankhamun (active *c.*1350 BC) Egyptian pharaoh of the New Kingdom's 18th dynasty. The revolutionary changes introduced by his predecessor, AKHNATEN, were reversed during his reign. The capital was re-established at LUXOR and worship of AMUN reinstated. Tutankhamun's tomb, the only royal tomb of ancient Egypt not stripped by robbers, contained magnificent treasures.

Tutu, Desmond Mpilo (1931–) South African ecclesiastic. Tutu trained as a teacher before becoming an Anglican priest in 1960. He was a prominent anti-apartheid campaigner, and he won the Nobel Peace Prize in 1984. He was appointed Archbishop of Cape Town in 1986. In 1995 he became the leader of the Truth and Reconciliation Committee.

Tuvalu (formerly Ellice Islands) Independent republic in W Pacific Ocean, S of the equator and W of the International Date Line. None of the cluster of nine low-lying coral islands rises more than 4.6m (15ft) out of the Pacific, making them vulnerable to predictions of rising sea levels. Poor soils restrict vegetation to coconut palms, breadfruit and bush. The population survive by subsistence farming, raising pigs and poultry, and by fishing. Copra is the only significant export crop. The first European to discover the islands (1568) was the Spanish navigator Alvaro de Mendaña. The population was reduced from about 20,000 to just 3,000 in the three decades after 1850 by Europeans abducting workers for other Pacific plantations. The British assumed control in 1892, and it was subsequently administered with the nearby Gilbert Islands (now KIRIBATI). Tuvalu became a separate self-governing colony, achieving full independence within the Commonwealth in 1978. Area: 24sq km (9.5sq mi). Pop. (1991) 10,090.

Twain, Mark (1835–1910) US writer, journalist and lecturer, b. Samuel Langhorne Clemens. He was among the first to write novels in the American vernacular, such as *The Adventures of Tom Sawyer* (1876) and *The Adventures of Huckleberry Finn* (1884). Although usually considered a humorist, his later books, such as *The Mysterious Stranger* (1916) are frequently bitter and pessimistic.

twelve-tone music (twelve-note music) SERIAL MUSIC in which the series contains all twelve notes of the CHROMATIC scale. Its introduction, in the early 20th century, is credited to Arnold SCHOENBERG.

two-stroke engine Engine in which the operation of each piston is in two stages. In the two-stroke cycle, a piston moves up a cylinder to compress a fuel-air mixture in the top. At the same time, more of the mixture is sucked in below the piston. A spark ignites the compressed mixture, causing an explosion. This sends the piston back down the cylinder. The piston forces the fresh fuel-air mixture out from beneath it and along a transfer port leading to the top part of the cylinder. The mixture forces the exhaust gases out from the top of the cylinder. The process then repeats.

Tyler, John (1790–1862) Tenth US President (1841–45). The Whigs chose him as vice-presidential candidate with William H. HARRISON and he succeeded to the presidency on Harrison's death (1841). He came into conflict with the nationalistic Whigs in Congress, repeatedly vetoing legislation to create a national bank. His determination to annex TEXAS bore fruit after he had left office.

Tyler, Wat (d.1381) English leader of the PEASANTS' REVOLT. He was chosen as leader of the rebels in Kent, SE England, and led their march on London. He was eventually killed by the lord mayor of London while parleying with RICHARD II.

Tyndale, William (c.1494–1536) Religious reformer and Bible translator. He started printing an English version of the New Testament in Cologne, Germany, in 1525. After this, Tyndale began translating the Old Testament. He was burned at the stake as a heretic. His translation provided a basis for the Authorized Version of the English Bible.

Tyne River in NE England. It is formed at the confluence of the North Tyne (which rises in the S Cheviot Hills) and the South Tyne (which rises in Cumbria) and flows E for 48km (30mi) through Newcastle to enter the North Sea near Tynemouth. It was made fully navigable at the end of the 19th century.

Tyne and Wear Metropolitan council in NE England, formed in 1974 from parts of the former counties of NORTHUMBERLAND and DURHAM, and including the former county borough of NEWCASTLE-UPON-TYNE, its administrative centre. A highly industrialized area, its staple industries of coalmining, iron and steel production and shipbuilding declined after the 1920s. There were signs of a recovery in the 1990s based on various light industries. Area: 537sq km (207sq mi). Pop. (1991) 1,095,152.

typhoid fever Acute, sometimes epidemic communicable disease of the digestive system. Caused by *Salmonella typhi*, which is transmitted in contaminated water or food, it is characterized by bleeding from the bowel and enlargment of the spleen. Symptoms include fever, headache, constipation, sore throat, cough and skin rash.

typhoon Name given in the Pacific Ocean to a HURRICANE, a violent tropical cyclonic storm.

typhus Any of a group of infectious diseases caused by rickettsiae (small bacteria) and spread by parasites of the human body such as lice, fleas, ticks and mites. Epidemic typhus, the result of infection by *Rickettsia prowazekii*, is the most serious manifestation. Associated with dirty, overcrowded conditions, it is mainly seen during times of war or famine.

typography Practice of designing typefaces and type styles mainly for use in printed texts. Typography is widely used in experimental, progressive art and design as well as conventional publishing. Movements that have revolutionized typography include FUTURISM, Dadaism and SURREALISM. Individuals include Eric GILL and MOHOLY-NAGY. The term also refers to the art of fine PRINTING itself. *See also* DADA

tyrannosaurus Any of several species of large, bipedal, carnivorous, theropod DINOSAURS that lived during late CRETACEOUS times. Its head, 1.2m (4ft) long, was armed with a series of dagger-like teeth. The hind legs were stout and well developed, but the forelegs may have been useless except for grasping at close range. The best-known species is *T. rex*. Length: 14m (47ft); height: 6.5m (20ft).

Tyre Historic city on the coast of modern Lebanon. Built on an island, it was a major commercial port of ancient PHOENICIA. It established colonies, including CARTHAGE, around the E Mediterranean. Tyre was never successfully besieged until ALEXANDER THE GREAT built a causeway linking the island to the mainland (332 BC). Ruled by successive empires, including the Romans, it was captured by the Arabs in AD 638 and destroyed by the Mamelukes in 1291. It never regained its former eminence. Pop. (1991) 70,000.

tyre Air-filled rubber and fabric cushion that fits over the wheels of vehicles to grip the road and absorb shock. The pneumatic tyre was invented in 1845 but was not commonly used until 1900. It consists of fabric surrounded by a thick layer of rubber treated with chemicals to increase durability.

Tyrol *See* TIROL

Tyrone Largest of the six counties of Northern Ireland, in the SW of the province. The county town is Omagh. Mainly hilly with the Sperrin Mountains in the N and Bessy Bell and Mary Gray in the S, the region is drained by the Blackwater and Mourne rivers. Cereals and root crops are grown and dairy cattle are raised. Industries: linen, whiskey, processed food. Area 3,263sq km (1,260sq mi). Pop. (1990) 153,000.

Tyson, Mike (1966–) US boxer. In 1986 he became the youngest heavyweight champion in boxing history. Known for his devastating punching power, in 1987 he became the first undisputed heavyweight champion for a decade. In 1992 Tyson was convicted of date rape and sentenced to prison. He was released in 1995, and the following year regained his WBC heavyweight championship by stopping Frank Bruno. He was defeated in 1996 by Evander Holyfield.

Tz'u Hsi (1835–1908) Empress Dowager of China. As mistress of the Emperor Hsi'en Feng and mother of his only son, she became co-regent in 1861 and remained in power until her death by arranging for the succession of her infant nephew in 1875 and displacing him in a palace coup in 1898. Ruthless, extravagant and reactionary, she abandoned the modernization programme of the "Hundred Days of Reform" and supported the BOXER REBELLION (1900).

U/u is the 21st letter of the English alphabet and is included in the alphabets of several w European languages. Like f, v, w and y, it was derived from the Semitic letter vaw meaning hook.

Uffizi (It. offices) Chief public gallery in Florence, housing one of the greatest collections of Italian paintings. The palace was built in the 16th century by VASARI for the Grand Duke Cosimo I de' Medici and once housed government offices.

UFO Abbreviation of UNIDENTIFIED FLYING OBJECT

Uganda Republic in E central Africa, the captial is KAMPALA. **Land and climate** Most of Uganda consists of part of the African plateau. In the w lies an arm of the Great RIFT VALLEY, which contains Lake ALBERT and the Albert NILE. Highland pockets lie in the sw and E. Much of s Uganda is made up of Lake VICTORIA, on the shores of which lie Kampala and Entebbe. Uganda's equatorial climate is moderated by altitude. The wettest regions are the w mountains. Nearly 20% of Uganda is covered by lakes or swamps. Wooded savanna covers central and N Uganda. **Economy** Civil strife greatly damaged Uganda's economy. It is one of the world's poorest countries (1992 GDP per capita, US$860). Agriculture employs 86% of the workforce. Coffee accounts for 90% of exports, Cotton, sugar cane and tea are also exported. **History and politics** In c.1500 the Nilotic-speaking Lwo people formed various kingdoms in sw Uganda, including Buganda ("kingdom of the Ganda") and Bunyoro. During the 18th century, the Buganda kingdom expanded and trade flourished. The conversion activities of Christian missionaries led to conflict with Muslims. The *kabaka* (king) came to depend on Christian support. In 1894 Uganda became a British protectorate. African political representation remained minimal until after World War 2. In 1962 Uganda gained independence. Milton OBOTE became prime minister. In 1971 Major General Idi AMIN established a personal dictatorship, and launched a war against foreign interference. It is estimated that Amin's regime was responsible for the murder of over 250,000 Ugandans. In 1976 Amin declared himself president-for-life. In 1978 Uganda annexed the Kagera region of NW Tanzania. In 1979 Tanzanian troops helped the Uganda National Liberation Front (UNLF) to overthrow Amin. Elections were held in 1980 and Obote was swept back into office. Amid charges of electoral fraud, the National Resistance Army (NRA) began a guerrilla war. Over 200,000 Ugandas sought refuge in Rwanda and Zaïre. In 1986 the NRA captured Kampala, and Yoweri Museveni became president. Museveni began to rebuild the domestic economy and improve foreign relations. In 1996 Museveni won Uganda's first direct presidential elections. AIDS is one of the greatest issues facing Uganda; it has the highest number of reported cases in Africa.

Ugarit Ancient city in NW Syria. Inhabited as early as the 7th millennium BC, it was a great commercial power, trading with Mesopotamia and Egypt. Excavations have revealed a vast palace from the 14th century BC, and many large houses filled with treasures and artefacts.

UHF Abbreviation of ULTRA HIGH FREQUENCY

Ujjain City on the River Sipra, Madhya Pradesh, w central India. It is one of the seven holy cities of India, and a Hindu pilgrimage centre. Pop. (1991) 362,000.

ukiyo-e Japanese paintings and woodblock prints that were prevalent in the Edo period (1615–1867). Their subject matter included people engaged in everyday activities as well as Kabuki actors. Famous ukiyo-e printmakers include HIROSHIGE, HOKUSAI and UTAMARO.

Ukraine Independent state in E Europe, the capital is KIEV. **Land and climate** Ukraine ("Borderland") is the second largest country in Europe (after Russia). The coastal lowlands include the Black Sea port of ODESSA. CRIMEA is a peninsula region, and contains the vital port of SEVASTOPOL. The DNIEPER River divides Ukraine into E and w. In the w, the CARPATHIAN MOUNTAINS rise to 2,061m (6,762ft). The fertile central plateau is among the world's largest producers of wheat and barley. In the E, the DONETS BASIN is one of the world's greatest industrial powerhouses. Ukraine's continental climate is moderated by proximity to the Black Sea. In the N, around the Pripet marshes, are large woodlands. Pine forests swathe the slopes of the Carpathian and Crimean mountains. **Economy** Ukraine was plunged into economic crisis by the rapid dismantling of the former Soviet command economy. Agriculture is important and Ukraine has been called "the breadbasket of Europe". It is the world's leading producer of sugar beet and the second-largest producer of barley. It is also a major producer of wheat. Other crops include maize, potatoes, sunflowers and tobacco. Ukraine has

---

UGANDA
AREA: 235,880sq km (91,073sq mi)
POPULATION: 18,592,000
CAPITAL (POPULATION): Kampala (773,463)
GOVERNMENT: Republic in transition
ETHNIC GROUPS: Ganda 18%, Banyoro 14%, Teso 9%, Banyan 8%, Basoga 8%, Bagisu 7%, Bachiga 7%, Lango 6%, Acholi 5%
LANGUAGES: English and Swahili (both official)
RELIGIONS: Christianity (Roman Catholic 40%, Protestant 29%), traditional beliefs 18%, Islam 7%
CURRENCY: Uganda shilling = 100 cents

UKRAINE
AREA: 603,700sq km (233,100sq mi)
POPULATION: 52,140,000
CAPITAL (POPULATION): Kiev (2,600,000)
GOVERNMENT: Multiparty republic
ETHNIC GROUPS: Ukrainian 73%, Russian 22%, Jewish 1%, Belarussian 1%, Moldovan, Bulgarian, Polish
LANGUAGES: Ukrainian (official)
RELIGIONS: Christianity (mostly Ukrainian Orthodox)
CURRENCY: Hryvna

---

extensive raw materials. The Donets Basin is the world's eighth-largest producer of bituminous coal. Krivoy Rog mines are the world's fourth-largest producer of iron ore, and Nikopol is the world's leading manganese ore producer. **History** In ancient history the area was successively inhabited by Scythians and Sarmatians, before invasions by the Goths, Huns, Avars and Khazars. The first Ukrainian Slavic community originates from this period. In the 9th century, the N regions were united by the Varangians as Kievan Rus. The empire disintegrated under the onslaught of the Mongol hordes. In the late 14th century, Ukraine became part of Lithuania and passed to Poland following the Poland-Lithuania union in the 16th century. In 1648 refugees from Polish rule (COSSACKS) completed Ukraine's liberation. A succession of wars resulted (1775) in the division of Ukraine into three Russian provinces. In 1918 (following the Russian Revolution) Ukraine declared independence and was invaded by the Red Army, who were repulsed with the support of the Central Powers. After the World War 1 armistice, a unified, independent Ukraine was once more proclaimed. The Red Army invaded again, this time with greater success. In 1921 W Ukraine was ceded to Poland, and in 1922 E Ukraine became a constituent republic of the Soviet Union. After 1945 all Ukrainian land was unified into a single Soviet republic. In 1954 the Crimea was annexed to the Ukraine. Ukraine became one of the most powerful republics in the Soviet Union. In 1986 the CHERNOBYL disaster contaminated large areas of Ukraine. Ukraine proclaimed its independence in August 1991. In December 1991 the former communist Leonid Kravchuk was elected president and Ukraine joined the COMMONWEALTH OF INDEPENDENT STATES (CIS). A 1992 treaty with Russia eased tensions over the Black Sea fleet, control of nuclear weapons and oil and gas reserves. Crimea was refused independence. In 1994 Leonid Kuchma became president. Kuchma sped up the pace of market reforms and improved relations with the West. Direct rule was imposed on Crimea for four months in 1995. Disputes continue over the extent of the powers of the Crimean legislature.

ukulele (ukelele) Small guitar, which developed in Hawaii from the Portuguese guitar. It is shaped like a classical guitar with a wooden body, round sound-hole and fretted fingerboard.

Ulan Bator (Ulaanbaatar, formerly Urga) Capital of MONGOLIA, on the River Tola. Ulan Bator dates back to the founding of the Lamaistic Temple of the Living Buddha in 1639. It was later a focus for the Mongolian autonomy movement. It became the capital in 1921. Industries: textiles, building materials, leather, paper, alcohol, food products, carpets, glassware. Pop. (1992) 601,000.

Ulbricht, Walter (1893–1973) East German statesman, leader of East GERMANY (1950–71). A founder of the German Communist Party, Ulbricht spent World War 2 in exile in the Soviet Union. In 1949 he became deputy premier of the newly created German Democratic Republic (East Germany). In 1950 he became general secretary of the Communist Party. Ulbricht established close links with the Soviet Union. The repressive nature of his regime led to a rebellion in 1953 and the building of the BERLIN WALL. In 1971 he was replaced as general secretary by Erich HONECKER.

ulcer Any persistent sore or lesion on the skin or on a mucous membrane, often associated with inflammation. Ulcers may be caused by infection, chemical irritation or mechanical pressure.

ulna Long bone of the inner side of the forearm. At its upper end it articulates with the HUMERUS and the RADIUS.

Ulster Most northerly of Ireland's four ancient provinces, consisting of nine counties. Since 1922, six of these counties have been in Northern IRELAND, while Cavan, Donegal and Monaghan form Ulster province in the Republic of IRELAND. Area: 8,012sq km (3,092sq mi). Pop. (1991) 232,000).

Ulster Unionists Political party in Northern Ireland, which arose in the late 19th century to defend the six northern provinces of Ulster from Irish home rule and to maintain the union with Britain. Almost exclusively Protestant, it was the ruling party in Northern Ireland from 1922 until the imposition of direct rule from Westminster in 1972.

ultra high frequency (UHF) Radio waves in the frequency band 300–3,000MHz. UHF waves have a wavelength of $c.1$m (3ft) or less and are used for TELEVISION broadcasting.

ultrasonics Study of sound waves with frequencies beyond the upper limit of human hearing (above 20,000Hz). In medicine, ultrasonics are used to locate tumours, produce fetal images and to treat certain neurological disorders. Other applications of ultrasonics include the agitation of liquids to form emulsions and the detection of flaws in metals.

ultraviolet radiation Type of ELECTROMAGNETIC RADIATION of shorter wavelength and higher frequency than visible light. Wavelengths range from 4–400nm (nanometres). Sunlight contains ultraviolet rays, most of which are filtered by the OZONE LAYER. If the ozone layer is weakened, enough ultraviolet can reach the ground to harm living things. Excessive exposure to sunlight can cause sunburn and skin cancer in people with fair skins. Ultraviolet is used medically to sterilize equipment. *See also* LIGHT; RADIATION

Ulysses *See* ODYSSEUS

Umayyads (Omayyads) Dynasty of Arabian Muslim caliphs (661–750). From their capital at DAMASCUS, the Umayyads ruled a basically Arab empire, which stretched from Spain to India. They made little effort to convert conquered peoples to Islam, but there was great cultural exchange, and ARABIC became established as the language of Islam. They were overthrown by the ABBASIDS.

umbelliferae Family of flowering plants, all of which have many small flowers borne in umbrella-like clusters (umbels) at the ends of stalks. Umbellifers are mainly herbs and shrubs. Many species are edible, including CARROT, PARSLEY, CELERY, PARSNIP, FENNEL and DILL.

umbilical cord Long cord that connects a developing FETUS with the PLACENTA. At birth, the cord is cut from the placenta, leaving a scar on the baby's abdomen known as the navel.

Umbria Region in central Italy comprising the provinces of Perugia and Terni; the capital is PERUGIA. The only land-locked region of Italy, it is traversed by the APENNINES and drained by the River TIBER. Cereal crops, grapes and olives are grown, and cattle and pigs are raised. The medieval hill towns attract tourists. Industries: iron and steel, chemicals, textiles, confectionery. Area: 8,456sq km (3,265sq mi). Pop. (1992) 814,796.

UN *See* UNITED NATIONS

Un-American Activities Committee, House (HUAC) Committee of the US House of Representatives, established in 1938 to investigate political subversion. Created to combat Nazi propaganda, it began investigating extremist political organizations. After World War 2, encouraged by Senator MCCARTHY, it attacked alleged communists in HOLLYWOOD and in the federal government. It was abolished in 1975.

uncertainty principle In subatomic physics, principle stating that it is not possible to know both the position and the momentum of a particle at the same time, because the act of measuring would disturb the system. It was established by Werner HEISENBERG.

unconformity In geology, break in the time sequence of rocks layered one above the other. The gap may be caused by interruptions in the deposition of sediment, ancient erosion, earth movements, or other activity.

unconscious Term in psychology for that part of mental life believed to operate without the individual's immediate awareness or control. It includes memories that the person is not actually thinking about, and the organizing processes underlying speech and reading. In FREUD's system, it is the area containing the desires and conflicts of the ID. JUNG believed that part of the unconscious (the

collective unconscious) contains inherited concepts, shared by all other human beings.

Underground Railroad Name given to a secret network in the USA organized by free blacks and other abolitionists before the CIVIL WAR to assist slaves escaping from the South.

underground railway Transport system used in urban areas. The world's first underground railway was opened in London in 1863. It was steam-powered and carried passengers between Farringdon and Paddington.

unemployment Inability of workers who are ready, able, and willing to work to find employment. Unemployment is usually expressed as a percentage of the labour force. **Cyclical** unemployment exists when the level of aggregate demand in the economy is less than that required to maintain full employment. People are laid off, and their jobs simply disappear. **Structural** unemployment exists when jobs are available and workers are seeking jobs, but they cannot fill vacancies for some reason (for example, they lack proper training, or live too far away). **Technological** unemployment exists when workers are replaced by machines faster than they can find alternative employment. **Seasonal** unemployment occurs when workers are unable to find jobs at certain seasons of the year. **Underemployment** is inefficient use of labour.

UNESCO Acronym for UNITED NATIONS EDUCATIONAL, SCIENTIFIC AND CULTURAL ORGANIZATION

ungulate MAMMAL with hoofed feet. Most ungulates, including cattle, sheep, pigs and deer, are members of the order Artiodactyla (with an even number of toes). The order Perissodactyla (ungulates with an odd number of toes) consists of horses, tapirs and rhinoceroses. The orders Proboscidea and Hyracoidea, collectively known as sub-ungulates, contain elephants and hyraxes.

UNICEF *See* UNITED NATIONS CHILDREN'S FUND

unicorn In mythology and heraldry, a magical animal resembling a graceful horse or a young goat with one thin conical or helical horn on its forehead.

unidentified flying object (UFO) Any flying object that cannot readily be explained as a man-made craft or a natural phenomenon. Reports of UFOs have been documented since ancient times. With the development of aeronautics and astronautics the number of sightings has increased.

Unification Church International religious movement founded in South Korea in 1954 by Sun Myung Moon. Its adherents are popularly known as **Moonies**. The movement aims to re-establish God's rule on Earth through the restoration of the family. It is known for its mass weddings and has been accused of cult-like practices.

unified field theory Attempt to extend the general theory of RELATIVITY to give a simultaneous representation of both gravitational and electromagnetic fields. A more comprehensive theory would also include the strong and weak nuclear forces. Although some success has been achieved in unifying the electromagnetic and weak nuclear forces, the general problem is still unsolved. *See also* GRAND UNIFIED THEORY (GUT)

Uniformity, Act of (1662) Act of the English Parliament regulating the form of worship in the CHURCH OF ENGLAND after the RESTORATION of the monarchy. It required all ordained clergy to follow the Book of COMMON PRAYER. The act also required the clergy to repudiate the SOLEMN LEAGUE AND COVENANT, to forswear the taking up of arms against the Crown, and to adopt the liturgy of the Church of England.

Union, Acts of Series of acts uniting England with WALES (1536) and SCOTLAND (1707), and Britain with IRELAND (1800). Also, the 1841 Act of Union united French-speaking Lower Canada with English-speaking Upper Canada. The Welsh acts incorporated Wales within the kingdom of England, provided Welsh parliamentary representation and made English the official language. The Scottish act united the kingdoms of England and Scotland forming Great Britain. Scotland retained its own legal system and Presbyterian Church. The Irish act abolished the Irish legislature, and Ireland was given 32 peers and 100 seats in the British Parliament. The established churches of the two countries were united, and free trade was introduced.

Union of Soviet Socialist Republics Official name for the SOVIET UNION

Unitarianism Version of Christianity that denies the TRINITY, accepts God as the father, and rejects the divinity of JESUS CHRIST. Originally considered a heresy, it flourished in Poland in the 16th century. John Biddle (1615–62) first preached Unitarianism in England in the 1640s. Unitarianism in the 20th century has an increasingly humanist point of view.

United Arab Emirates (UAE) Federation of seven independent sheikhdoms of ABU DHABI, DUBAI, Sharja, Ajman, Ras al-Khaimah, Fujairah and Umm al-Qaiwain. It is bordered by the Persian Gulf (N), Oman (E), Saudi Arabia (W and S) and Qatar (NW). The terrain is flat, consisting mainly of desert. The economy is dominated by crude oil and natural gas production, accounting for about half of its GDP. Formerly known as the Trucial States, the area was a British protectorate from 1892. In 1971 British troops withdrew from the Persian Gulf and the United Arab Emirates was formed. Abu Dhabi is more than six times the size of the other states put together. It has the largest population, is the biggest oil producer and provides the federal capital, the city of Abu Dhabi. The other significant populations are Dubai and Sharjah. The population

is almost exclusively Muslim (mostly SUNNI), though the great majority of inhabitants are expatriate workers. Area: 83,600sq km (32,280sq mi). Pop. (1993 est.) 2,083,000.

United Kingdom (UK) Kingdom on the British Isles; the capital is LONDON. The United Kingdom of Great Britain and Northern IRELAND, is a union of four countries in the British Isles. Great Britain is composed of ENGLAND, SCOTLAND and WALES. The Isle of MAN and the CHANNEL ISLANDS are self-governing UK dependencies. In 1536 England and Wales were formally united. Scotland and England were unified in the 1707 Act of UNION. (For land, climate, vegetation and separate history, *see* individual country articles). **Economy** The UK is a major industrial and trading nation. Despite being a major producer of oil, petroleum products, natural gas, potash, salt and lead, the UK lacks natural resources and has to import raw materials. In the early 20th century, the UK was a major exporter of ships, steel and textiles. The economy has become more service-oriented, and high-technology industries have grown in importance. The UK produces only 66% of the food it needs and is reliant on food imports. Agriculture employs only 2% of the workforce. Major crops include hops for beer, potatoes, carrots, sugar beet, strawberries, rapeseed and linseed. Sheep are the leading livestock and wool is a leading product. Poultry, beef and dairy cattle are important. Cheese and milk are major products. Fishing is another major activity. Financial services bring in much-needed revenue. Historic and cultural attractions make tourism a vital income source. **History** In the 17th century England's development of empire was combined with a financial revolution, which included the founding of the BANK OF ENGLAND (1694). Great Britain emerged from the SEVEN YEARS WAR (1756–63) as the world's leading imperial power. GEORGE III's conception of absolute monarchy and resistance to colonial reform led to conflict with parliament and contributed to the AMERICAN REVOLUTION (1776–83). William PITT (THE YOUNGER) oversaw the creation of the United Kingdom of Great Britain and Ireland (1801). The AGRICULTURAL REVOLUTION was both a cause and effect of the doubling of the population from 1801 to 1861. The INDUSTRIAL REVOLUTION brought profound socio-economic changes. The 1820s and 1830s saw a huge body of new reform legislation including: the Act of CATHOLIC EMANCIPATION (1829); the abolition of SLAVERY (1833); harsh new POOR LAWS (1834); and the extension of the franchise to the middle class in the REFORM ACTS. Sir Robert PEEL's repeal of the CORN LAWS (1846) marked the beginnings of FREE TRADE and the emergence of the CONSERVATIVE PARTY from the old TORY PARTY. The LIBERAL PARTY similarly evolved out of the old WHIG PARTY. CHARTISM witnessed the beginnings of a working-class movement. The reign of VICTORIA saw the development of the second British empire, spurred on by the

UNITED ARAB EMIRATES
AREA: 83,600sq km (32,278 sq mi)
POPULATION: 2,083,000
CAPITAL (POPULATION): Abu Dhabi (or Abu Zaby, 670,125)

UNITED KINGDOM
AREA: 243,368sq km (94,202sq mi)
POPULATION: 58,780,000
CAPITAL (POPULATION): London (6,966,800)
GOVERNMENT: Constitutional monarchy
ETHNIC GROUPS: White 94%, Indian 1%, Pakistani 1%, West Indian 1%
LANGUAGES: English (official)
RELIGIONS: Christianity (Anglican 57%, Roman Catholic 13%, Presbyterian 7%, Methodist 4%, Baptist 1%), Islam 1%, Judaism, Hinduism, Sikhism
CURRENCY: Pound sterling = 100 pence

imperial ambitions of Lord PALMERSTON. The historic importance of trade to the UK economy was firmly established. Between 1868 and 1880, UK politics was dominated by DISRAELI and GLADSTONE. Between 1908–16 Herbert ASQUITH and David LLOYD GEORGE enacted a range of progressive social welfare policies, such as NATIONAL INSURANCE and state pensions. Germany's invasion of Belgium (4 August 1914) brought the UK into WORLD WAR 1. Anti-German sentiment persuaded GEORGE V to change the name of the British royal family from Saxe-Coburg to Windsor. The Allies victory (1918) was at the cost of nearly one million British lives. The Anglo-Irish Treaty (1921) confirmed the partition of Ireland. The Irish Free State was formed in 1922, and the UK officially became known as the United Kingdom of Great Britain and Northern Ireland. Neville CHAMBERLAIN's policy of APPEASEMENT toward Nazi Germany ended in failure. In 1924 Ramsay MACDONALD formed the first LABOUR PARTY government. The COMMONWEALTH OF NATIONS was founded in 1931. In 1936 EDWARD VIII was forced to abdicate in favour of GEORGE VI. On 3 September 1939, following the German invasion of Poland, Britain declared war. From May 1940 Winston CHURCHILL led a coalition government, which lasted throughout WORLD WAR 2. Many UK cities were devastated in the Battle of BRITAIN (1940). Britain lost over 420,000 lives in the war, and its economy was devastated. In 1945 elections, the Labour Party was swept back into power, with Clement ATTLEE as prime minister. Attlee began a radical programme of nationalization and increased welfare provision. In 1948 the NATIONAL HEALTH SERVICE (NHS) was created. The British empire was gradually dismantled, beginning with India in 1947. Most newly independent nations joined the Commonwealth. In 1949 the UK joined NATO. In 1951 Churchill returned to power and partly reversed the process of nationalization. In 1952 ELIZABETH II succeeded George VI. Sir Anthony EDEN led Britain into the disastrous SUEZ CRISIS (1956) and was succeeded by Harold MACMILLAN. In 1959 the UK was a founder member of the European Free Trade Agreement (EFTA).

In the 1964 election Harold WILSON narrowly defeated Sir Alec DOUGLAS-HOME. In 1968 the British Army was deployed in Northern Ireland to prevent the violent sectarian conflict that had followed civil rights marches. In 1971, under Edward HEATH, the UK adopted a decimal currency. In 1972 the British parliament assumed direct control of Northern Ireland. In 1973 the UK joined the EUROPEAN COMMUNITY (EEC). Deep recession led to the introduction of a three-day working week. A miners' strike forced Heath to resign, and Wilson resumed office. The discovery of North Sea oil and natural gas decreased Britain's dependence on coal and fuel imports. James CALLAGHAN's inability to control labour unrest led to his defeat in 1979 elections. Margaret THATCHER became Britain's first woman prime minister. Thatcher introduced MONETARISM and PRIVATIZATION. Unemployment grew as Britain attempted to switch to a more service-centred economy. The FALKLANDS WAR (1982) contributed to Thatcher's re-election in 1983. Urban decay, economic inequality (especially between North and South), and an unpopular POLL TAX forced Thatcher to resign in 1990. John MAJOR signed the MAASTRICHT TREATY and won a surprise victory in the 1992 general election. He was soon forced to remove the pound from the EUROPEAN MONETARY SYSTEM (EMS). His administration was dogged by division over Europe and allegations of sleaze. In the 1997 general election, Tony BLAIR's modernized Labour Party formed the first Labour government for 18 years. The Bank of England rapidly gained independence from central government in the setting of interest rates. In September 1997 referenda on devolution saw Scotland and Wales gain their own legislative assemblies.

United Nations (UN) International organization set up to enable countries to work together for peace and mutual development. It was established by a charter signed in San Francisco in June 1945 by 50 countries. In 1996 the UN had 185 members, essentially all the world's sovereign states except for North and South Korea and Switzerland.

United Nations Children's Fund (UNICEF) Intergovernmental organization, agency of the United Nations. Founded in 1946 it assists children and adolescents worldwide, particularly in war-devastated areas and developing countries.

United Nations Educational, Scientific and Cultural Organization (UNESCO) Intergovernmental organization, agency of the United Nations. Founded in 1945, it aims to promote peace by improving the world's standard of education and by bringing together nations in cultural and scientific projects. It also gives aid to developing countries.

United Nations Peacekeeping Forces Military personnel and their equipment placed at United Nations' disposal by member states. The function of the forces is to keep the peace between warring factions anywhere in the world, as requested by the UNITED NATIONS SECURITY

COUNCIL. The first UN Peacekeeping Forces were deployed in the Sinai peninsula and in Beirut in June 1948. The conflict in Bosnia (1992–95) saw the greatest-ever deployment of UN forces.

United Nations Security Council Council responsible for taking action against any nation or faction considered to represent a threat to the security or continued wellbeing of a member state. Such action can be political, economic or, as a last resort, military. The Council also has the power to hold a formal investigation into matters of common concern. There are five permanent member states: the USA, UK, France, Russia and China.

United States of America (USA) Federal republic of North America, the world's fourth-largest country; the capital is WASHINGTON, D.C. **Land and climate** The United States of America is made up of a federal district (Washington, D.C.) and 50 states (48 of which form a large block of land between Canada and Mexico). The other two states are ALASKA and the North Pacific archipelago of HAWAII. On the NE border with Canada are the GREAT LAKES. CHICAGO lies on the shore of Lake MICHIGAN. The densely populated E seaboard includes the major cities of BOSTON, NEW YORK, PHILADELPHIA and Baltimore. The major rivers of the E are the HUDSON, Delaware, and Potomac. Florida lies on a peninsula between the Atlantic and the Gulf of Mexico, and includes the city of MIAMI. The coastal plain is backed by the APPALACHIANS, including the Blue Ridge Mountains. The central lowlands are drained by the MISSISSIPPI-MISSOURI river system, which forms an enormous delta near NEW ORLEANS. The GREAT PLAINS gently rise to the ROCKY MOUNTAINS, which form the continental divide. The COLUMBIA and COLORADO rivers flow into the Pacific Ocean. Between the Rockies and the Pacific coast lie plateaus, basins and ranges. The GRAND CANYON was carved out from the Colorado plateau by the Colorado River. The Great Basin includes SALT LAKE CITY and desert regions including LAS VEGAS and DEATH VALLEY, the lowest point in the western hemisphere, 86m (282ft)

below sea level. The Pacific seaboard, including the cities of SAN FRANCISCO, LOS ANGELES and SAN DIEGO, is fringed by mountain ranges such as the SIERRA NEVADA, which includes Mount WHITNEY (the highest peak outside Alaska). The NW CASCADE RANGE contains active volcanoes, such as Mount ST HELENS. SEATTLE lies in the foothills of the range. Of the 48 states, winters are cold and snowy in the N, but mild in the S. The S states have long, hot summers. Rainfall is heaviest in the NW, lightest in the SW. In the N states are extensive forests. In the E, the original deciduous forests only remain in protected areas. Large areas of the SW are desert. **Economy** The USA is the world's largest manufacturing nation (1992 GDP per capita, US$23,760) and is the world's largest farm producer. Major products include poultry, beef and dairy cattle. Leading crops include cotton, hops for beer, fruits, groundnuts, maize, potatoes, soya beans, tobacco and wheat. Fishing is important. The USA's chief natural resources include oil, natural gas and coal. Timber and paper manufacture are important. Major industries include cars, chemicals, machinery, computers and printing. Services form the largest sector, including finance and tourism (1992 receipts, US$53,361 million). **History and politics** NATIVE AMERICANS arrived perhaps 40,000 years ago from Asia. Vikings, led by LEIF ERICSSON, probably reached North America 1,000 years ago, but did not settle. European exploration did not begin until the discovery of the New World by Christopher COLUMBUS in 1492. The first permanent European settlement was founded by Spain in 1565 at St Augustine, Florida. The French also formed settlements in LOUISIANA, but the first major colonists were the British, who founded JAMESTOWN, Virginia, in 1607. In 1620 PURITANS landed at Cape Cod, MASSACHUSETTS and founded the PLYMOUTH COLONY. The economic success of Massachusetts encouraged further colonization along the E coast. In 1681 William PENN founded PENNSYLVANIA. In the southern colonies, SLAVERY was used to develop plantations. During the 18th century, British MERCANTILISM (especially the NAVIGATION ACTS) restricted commercial growth. The defeat of the French in the FRENCH AND INDIAN WAR (1754–63) encouraged independence movements. Benjamin FRANKLIN'S failure to win concessions from the British led to the AMERICAN REVOLUTION (1775–83), which ended British rule in the THIRTEEN COLONIES. George WASHINGTON, commander-in-chief of the Continental Army, became the first president. The ARTICLES OF CONFEDERATION (1777) produced weak central government, and were superseded by the CONSTITUTION OF THE UNITED STATES (1787). US politics became divided between the Federalist Party and the Democratic-Republican Party (later simply the DEMOCRATIC PARTY). In 1803 Thomas JEFFERSON negotiated the LOUISIANA PURCHASE (1803), which nearly

---

UNITED STATES OF AMERICA
AREA: 9,372,610sq km (3,618,765sq mi)
POPULATION: 259,681,000
CAPITAL (POPULATION): Washington, D.C. (585,221)
GOVERNMENT: Federal republic
ETHNIC GROUPS: White 80%, African-American 12%, other races 8%
LANGUAGES: English (official), Spanish, more than 30 others
RELIGIONS: Christianity (Protestant 53%, Roman Catholic 26%, other Christian 8%), Islam 2%, Judaism 2%
CURRENCY: US dollar = 100 cents

doubled the size of the USA. James MADISON led the USA into the WAR OF 1812. The MISSOURI COMPROMISE (1820) papered over the growing conflict between the commercial, industrial North and the cotton plantations of the pro-slavery South. Andrew JACKSON's presidency furthered the westward expansion of the FRONTIER. The march to the Pacific became the "manifest destiny" of the USA. The 1848 discovery of gold in California prompted a rush of settlers. Territorial expansion was achieved at the expense of Native Americans, who were forced onto reservations. The repeal of the Missouri Compromise led to the founding of the anti-slavery REPUBLICAN PARTY (1854). In 1861 Abraham LINCOLN became the first Republican president. The southern states seceded as the CONFEDERATE STATES OF AMERICA. The American CIVIL WAR (1861–65) claimed over 600,000 lives and devastated the country. The Union victory resulted in the abolition of slavery. The enforced RECONSTRUCTION of the South was highly unpopular. Ulysses S. GRANT's administration was plagued by corruption. In 1867 the USA bought Alaska from Russia. The late 19th century was the era of the railroad, which sped industrialization and urban development. Millions of European immigrants were attracted to the USA. The Spanish-American War (1898) heralded the emergence of the USA as a major world power. Hawaii was annexed. Construction of the PANAMA CANAL began in 1902. In 1917 Woodrow WILSON led the USA into World War 1. The economic boom and PROHIBITION of the 1920s was followed by the GREAT DEPRESSION of the 1930s. Franklin D. ROOSEVELT's NEW DEAL attempted to restore prosperity. The Japanese bombing of PEARL HARBOR (7 December 1941) prompted US entry into WORLD WAR 2. Rearmament fuelled economic recovery. Harry S. TRUMAN became president on Roosevelt's death in 1945, and ordered the use of atomic bombs to force Japan's surrender. The USA was a founder member of NATO. Post-war tension with the Soviet Union led to the COLD WAR and spurred the space race. In order to stem the spread of communism, US forces fought in the KOREAN WAR (1950–53). In 1955 Martin Luther KING launched the civil rights movement. The start of John F. KENNEDY's presidency was marred by the CUBAN MISSILE CRISIS (1962). Kennedy's assassination (22 November 1963) shocked the nation. Lyndon JOHNSON led the USA into the VIETNAM WAR (1965–73). Anti-Vietnam protests were coupled with civil unrest. On 20 July 1969 Neil ARMSTRONG became the first man on the Moon. In 1974 Richard NIXON was forced to resign by the WATERGATE SCANDAL. The CAMP DAVID AGREEMENT crowned Jimmy CARTER's foreign policy initiatives. The start of Ronald REAGAN's presidency (1981–89) marked the deepest recession since the Great Depression. Reagan's loosening grip on power was highlighted by the

IRAN-CONTRA AFFAIR (1987–88). Despite the success of the GULF WAR (1991), domestic recession led to George BUSH's electoral defeat in 1992. Bill CLINTON's reform programme was largely blocked by a Republican-dominated SENATE. Despite allegations of financial and personal scandal, economic recovery led to Clinton's re-election in 1996.

universal time System of time reckoning based on the mean solar day, the average interval between two successive transits of the Sun across the GREENWICH (0°) meridian.

universe Aggregate of all matter, energy and space. On a large scale, the universe is considered uniform: it is identical in every part. It is believed to be expanding at a uniform rate, the galaxies all receding from one other. Recent developments in astronomy imply a finite universe, as postulated in the BIG BANG theory. *See also* COSMOLOGY; STEADY-STATE THEORY

university Institution of higher learning. Universities grew from the *studia generalia* of the 12th century, which provided education for priests and monks and were attended by students from all parts of Europe. Bologna became an important centre of legal studies in the 11th century. Other *studia generalia* were founded in the mid-12th century at Paris, OXFORD and CAMBRIDGE. The first Scottish university was at St Andrews *c.*1412, the first Irish university at Dublin (Trinity College) in 1591.

unsaturated compound In organic chemistry, compound in which two or more carbon atoms are linked, or bonded together, with double or triple bonds. Simple examples are ETHENE and ETHYNE.

untouchables Fifth and lowest *varna* (class) of the Indian CASTE system, making up *c.*20% of India's population. The term arises from the belief among higher castes that to touch *panchamas* amounts to ritual pollution or defilement. Although their pariah status and the resultant social injustice were legally abolished in India (1949) and Pakistan (1953), much discrimination remains.

Upanishads (Sanskrit, session) Texts of HINDUISM, constituting the final stage of Vedic literature. Written in prose and verse, they take the form of dialogues between teacher and pupil. They are of uncertain authorship and date from *c.*650 BC or earlier. Often referred to as the VEDANTA, the *Upanishads* speculate on reality and man's salvation. *See also* BRAHMANISM

Updike, John Hoyer (1932–) US writer. Updike is best known for his lyrical chronicles of Rabbit Angstrom, whose relationship crises often reflect contemporary social pressures. The tetralogy began with *Rabbit Run* (1960) and *Rabbit Redux* (1971). *Rabbit is Rich* (1981) won a Pulitzer Prize. The series was completed by *Rabbit at Rest* (1990). Other novels include *Couples* (1968) and *The Witches of Eastwick* (1984, filmed 1987).

Upper Volta Former name (until 1984) of BURKINA FASO

Ur (Ur of the Chaldees) Ancient city of SUMERIA,

s MESOPOTAMIA. Ur flourished in the 3rd millennium BC, but in *c*.2340 BC it was conquered by SARGON I. The Akkadian period witnessed the integration of Semitic and Sumerian cultures. In *c*.2060 BC the great ZIGGURAT was built by King Ur-Nammu. In *c*.2000 BC much of the city was destroyed by the invading Elamites. In the 6th century BC NEBUCHADNEZZAR briefly restored Ur as a centre of Mesopotamian civilization, but by the 5th century BC it had fallen into terminal decline.

Urals Range of mountains in Russia, traditionally marking the boundary between Europe and Asia. The range extends 2,400km (1,500mi) from the Arctic in the N to the Ural River and the Kazakstan frontier in the S. The mountains are extensively forested and the timber industry is important. The Urals' chief importance lies in their mineral deposits, which include iron ore, oil, coal, copper, nickel, gold, silver, zinc and many precious stones.

uraninite (pitchblende) Dense, radioactive mineral form of uranium oxide, UO_2. It is the chief ore of uranium and the most important source for uranium and radium. The blackish, lustrous ore occurs as a constituent of quartz veins. Hardness 5–6; s.g. 6.5–8.5.

uranium Radioactive, metallic element (symbol U), one of the ACTINIDE SERIES. It was discovered in 1789 and is now used in NUCLEAR REACTORS and bombs. The ISOTOPE U^{238} makes up more than 99% of natural uranium. Chemically, uranium is a reactive metal; it oxidizes in air and reacts with cold water. U^{235} is fissionable and will sustain a neutron chain reaction as a fuel for reactors. Uranium is used to synthesize the TRANSURANIC ELEMENTS. Properties: at.no. 92; r.a.m. 238.029; r.d. 19.05; m.p. 1,132°C (2,070°F); b.p. 3,818°C (6,904°F); most stable isotope U^{238} (half-life 4.51×10^9 years).

Uranus Seventh planet from the Sun, discovered (1781) by Sir William HERSCHEL. Like all the giant planets, it possesses a ring system and a retinue of SATELLITES. Like Pluto, Uranus's axis of rotation is steeply inclined, and its poles spend 42 years in sunlight, followed by 42 years in darkness. The fly-by of the Voyager 2 probe in 1986 provided most of our current knowledge of the planet. The upper atmosphere is *c*.83% molecular hydrogen, 15% helium, and the other 2% mostly methane. Voyager discovered 10 more satellites of Uranus. All the 15 satellites are regular, orbiting close to Uranus' equatorial plane. Diameter (equatorial): 51,118km (polar): 49,947km

Uranus In Greek mythology, the god of the sky, and the husband and son of GAIA, with whom he was father to the TITANS and the CYCLOPES.

Urban II (*c*.1035–99) Pope (1088–99), b. Odo of Châtillon-sur-Marne. Urban carried on the reforms begun by Pope GREGORY VII. In 1095, at the Council of Clermont, he launched the idea of the First CRUSADE. His work as a reformer encouraged the development of the CURIA ROMANA and the formation of the College of Cardinals.

Urban V (*c*.1310–70) Pope (1362–70), b. Guillaume de Grimoard. Crowned at AVIGNON, he tried in 1367 to return the papacy from Avignon to Rome. Insurrections at Rome and the Papal States forced him back to Avignon in 1370. As pope he made a fruitless attempt to unite the Roman and Orthodox Churches.

Urban VI (1318–89) Pope (1378–89), b. Bartolomeo Prignano. The College of Cardinals declared his election invalid and appointed an ANTIPOPE, Clement VII, beginning the GREAT SCHISM. Urban VI's papacy was marked by confusion and financial losses in the papal states.

Urdu Language belonging to the Indic group of the Indo-Iranian sub-family of INDO-EUROPEAN LANGUAGES. It is the official language of Pakistan, but is used as a first language by less than 10% of the population. It is also spoken by most Muslims in India. Urdu has virtually the same grammar as HINDI, the chief difference being that Urdu is written in the Arabic script. Both derive from Sanskrit.

urea Organic compound ($CO(NH_2)_2$), white, crystalline solid excreted in URINE. Most vertebrates excrete their nitrogen wastes as urea. Because it is so high in nitrogen, urea is a good fertilizer.

ureter In vertebrates, the long, narrow duct that connects the KIDNEY to the urinary BLADDER. It transports URINE from the kidney to the bladder.

urethra Duct through which URINE is discharged from the bladder in mammals. In males the urethra is also the tube through which SEMEN is ejaculated.

urine Fluid filtered out from the bloodstream by the KIDNEY. It consists mainly of water, salts and waste products such as UREA. From the kidneys it passes through the URETERS to the BLADDER for voiding by way of the URETHRA.

urinogenital system Organs comprising the body's urinary and reproductive systems. The urinary system consists of the KIDNEYS, URETERS, the BLADDER and URETHRA. In males, the reproductive system consists of paired TESTES located in the scrotum; accessory glands; and the PENIS. In females, the reproductive system consists of: paired OVARIES; FALLOPIAN TUBES, which provide a passage from the ovaries to the UTERUS; the CERVIX; and the VAGINA.

Ursa Major (Great Bear) Northern constellation, whose main pattern, consisting of seven stars, is known as the **Plough** or **Big Dipper**. Five of the Plough stars make up a CLUSTER.

Ursa Minor Constellation that contains the north celestial pole. Its brightest star is Alpha, the POLE STAR. The constellation's seven main stars make a pattern resembling a faint and distorted plough.

urticaria *See* HIVES

Uruguay Republic in South America; the capital is MONTEVIDEO. **Land and climate** The land consists of low-lying plains and hills. The major river is the Río Negro. The River Uruguay, which forms the country's w border, flows into the Río de la Plata, a large estuary leading into the South Atlantic Ocean.

URUGUAY
AREA: 177,410sq km (68,498 sq mi)
POPULATION: 3,116,802
CAPITAL (POPULATION): Montevideo (1,383,660)
GOVERNMENT: Multiparty republic
ETHNIC GROUPS: White 86%, Mestizo 8%, Mulatto or Black 6%
LANGUAGES: Spanish (official)
RELIGIONS: Christianity (Roman Catholic 66%, Protestant 2%), Judaism 1%
CURRENCY: Uruguay peso = 100 centésimos

Uruguay has a mild climate with rain throughout the year. Grasslands cover 77% of Uruguay and arable land about 7%. Such trees as acacia, aloe, eucalyptus and willow grow along the river valleys. Uruguay also has commercial tree plantations. **Economy** Agriculture employs only 5% of the workforce, but farm products, notably hides and leather goods, beef and wool, are the leading exports. The main crops include maize, potatoes, sugar beet and wheat. The leading manufacturing industries, situated mainly in and around Montevideo, are concerned with processing farm produce. Other manufactures include beer, cement, textiles and tyres. Tourism is important. **History** The original Native American inhabitants of Uruguay have largely disappeared. Many were killed by Europeans, others died of European diseases, while some fled into the interior. The first European to arrive in Uruguay was a Spanish navigator in 1516, but few Europeans settled here until the late 17th century. By the late 18th century, Spaniards had settled in most of the country, and Uruguay became part of a colony called the Viceroyalty of La Plata, which also included Argentina, Paraguay, and parts of Bolivia, Brazil and Chile. In 1820 Brazil annexed Uruguay. In 1825 Uruguayans, supported by Argentina, began a struggle for independence and finally, in 1828, Brazil and Argentina recognized Uruguay as an independent republic. Social and economic development were slow in the 19th century, with many revolutions and counter-revolutions. From the 1950s, economic problems caused unrest. Terrorist groups, notably the Tupumaros, carried out murders and kidnappings. The army crushed the Tupumaros in 1972, and then took over the government in 1973. Repressive military rule continued until 1984. However, economic difficulties and high foreign debts continued to threaten stability. Julio María Sanguinetti, who had led Uruguay back to civilian rule in the 1980s, was re-elected in 1994.

USA *See* UNITED STATES OF AMERICA

USSR (Union of Soviet Socialist Republics) *See* SOVIET UNION

Ustinov, Peter Alexander (1921–) British actor and dramatist. His plays include *The Love of Four Colonels* (1951) and *Romanoff and Juliet* (1956). He has acted in many films, including *Billy Budd* (1962), which he also directed. In recent years he has won a reputation as an entertaining raconteur.

usury Lending of money at an excessive or unlawful rate of interest. Before the Middle Ages any payment for the use of money was regarded as usury by Christians. In the late Middle Ages reasonable interest on a loan became acceptable when the lender risked capital.

Utah State in the w USA, in the Rocky Mountains. The state capital is SALT LAKE CITY; other cities include Provo and Ogden. The region was ceded to the USA at the end of the MEXICAN WAR in 1848, and Utah was admitted to the Union in 1896. The influence of the MORMON Church is strong in the the state, and in 1857–58 there were conflicts between federal troops and the Mormons. In the N, the Wasatch Range separates the mountainous E from the GREAT BASIN, which includes the GREAT SALT LAKE. The arid climate hinders agriculture, but hay, barley, wheat, beans and sugar beet are grown using irrigation. The chief farming activity is stock raising. Mining is also important: there are rich deposits of copper, petroleum, coal, molybdenum, silver, lead and gold. With many national parks and monuments, tourism is vital to the economy. Area: 84,915sq mi (219,931sq km). Pop. (1992) 1,811,215.

Utamaro, Kitagawa (1753–1806) Japanese master of the UKIYO-E woodblock colour print, the first Japanese artist to become famous in the West. He excelled in depicting birds, flowers and feminine beauty. His works were strongly erotic, precise, graceful and immensely popular.

uterus (womb) Hollow, muscular organ located in the pelvis of female mammals. It protects and nourishes the growing FETUS until birth. The upper part is broad and branches out on each side into the FALLOPIAN TUBES. The lower uterus narrows into the CERVIX, which leads to the VAGINA. Its muscular walls are lined with mucous membrane (ENDOMETRIUM), to which the fertilized egg attaches itself. *See also* MENSTRUAL CYCLE

utilitarianism Branch of ethical philosophy. It holds that actions are to be judged good or bad according to their consequences. An action is deemed to be morally right if it produces good results. Utilitarianism was developed during the late 18th and 19th centuries by the English philosophers Jeremy BENTHAM and James MILL.

Utopianism (Gk. no place) Projection of ideal states or alternative worlds, which are ordered for the benefit of all and where social ills have been eradicated. Sir Thomas MORE's *Utopia* (1516) outlines his notion of an ideal commonwealth based entirely on reason. Enlightenment philosophers, such as Jean Jacques ROUSSEAU, portrayed a vision of a pre-feudal European Golden Age. Karl MARX and Friedrich ENGELS valued the satirical social insights of utopianism but rejected its unscientific analysis of political and economic realities. By the late 19th century, the utopian novel had become an established literary genre. The spread of TOTALITARIANISM in Europe during the 1930s encouraged **dystopian** novels, such as *Brave New World* by Aldous Huxley and *1984* by George Orwell.

Utrecht, Peace of (1713–14) Series of treaties that ended the War of the SPANISH SUCCESSION. It confirmed the BOURBON King PHILIP V on the Spanish throne on condition that he renounced any claim to the throne of France. Austria received the Spanish Netherlands and extensive Italian territories; Britain gained Gibraltar, Minorca and provinces of E Canada.

Uttar Pradesh State in N India, bordering Nepal and Tibet; its capital is LUCKNOW. It is the hub of India's Hindi-speaking region, and is by far the most populous Indian state. The region has the foothills of the Himalayas to the N and hills in the S, enclosing a low-lying plain drained by the GANGES and its tributaries. The economy is based on agriculture, mainly cereals, sugar cane, rice and pulses, and the mining of coal, copper, bauxite and limestone. Industries: cotton and sugar processing. Area 294,413sq km (113,673sq mi). Pop. (1991) 139,112,287.

Uzbekistan Republic in central Asia; the capital is TASHKENT. **Land and climate** Uzbekistan comprises plains in the W and highlands in the E. The main rivers, the Amu Darya and Syr Darya, drain into the ARAL SEA. So much water has been diverted from these rivers to irrigate farmland that the Aral Sea has shrunk from 66,900sq km (25,830sq mi) in 1960 to 33,642sq km (12,989sq mi) in 1993. The dried-up area has become desert like much of the rest of the country. Uzbekistan has a continental climate, with cold winters and hot summers. The W is extremely arid, with an average annual rainfall of *c*.200mm (8in), but parts of the highlands in the E have three times as much rain. **Economy** Uzbekistan is a lower-middle income developing country. The government controls most economic activity. Uzbekistan produces coal, copper, gold, oil and natural gas, while manufactures include agricultural machinery, chemicals and textiles. Agriculture is important, with cotton the main crop. Other crops include fruits, rice and vegetables and cattle, sheep and goats are also raised. Uzbekistan's exports include cotton, gold, textiles, chemicals and fertilizers. **History and politics** Turkic people first settled in the area *c*.1,500 years ago and

---

UZBEKISTAN
AREA: 447,400sq km (172,740sq mi)
POPULATION: 21,206,800
CAPITAL (POPULATION): Tashkent (2,094,300)
ETHNIC GROUPS: Uzbek 71%, Russian 8%, Tajik 5%, Kazak 4%, Tatar 2%, Kara-Kalpak 2%, Crimean Tatar, Korean, Kyrgyz, Ukrainian, Turkmen
LANGUAGES: Uzbek (official)
RELIGIONS: Islam
CURRENCY: Som

Islam was introduced in the 7th century AD. MONGOLS invaded the land in the 13th century and, in the late 14th century, TAMERLANE ruled a great empire from SAMARKAND. Turkic Uzbek people invaded in the 16th century and gradually the area was divided into states (khanates). Russia controlled the area in the 19th century, and following the Russian Revolution of 1917, the communists took over, establishing the Uzbek Soviet Socialist Republic in 1924. Under communism, all aspects of Uzbek life were controlled; religious worship was discouraged, but education, health, housing and transport were improved. The mass production of cotton caused great environemntal damage. In the 1980s, when reforms were being introduced in the Soviet Union, the Uzbeks demanded more freedom. In 1990 the government stated that its laws overruled those of the Soviet Union. In 1991, following the break-up of the Soviet Union, Uzbekistan became independent. It retained links with Russia through the Commonwealth of Independent States (CIS). On 29 December 1991, Islam Karimov, leader of the People's Democratic Party (formerly the Communist Party), was elected president. In 1992 and 1993 many opposition leaders were arrested. Karimov asserted that economic reform would be gradual to avoid destabilization. A 1995 referendum extended Karimov's term in office until 2000.

Uzbeks Turkic-speaking people, originally of Persian culture, who form two thirds of the population of the Republic of UZBEKISTAN. They took their name from Uzbeg Khan, a chief of the GOLDEN HORDE who died in 1340. By the end of the 16th century, the Uzbeks had extended their rule to parts of Persia, Afghanistan and Chinese TURKISTAN. Their empire was never united and in the 19th century its various states were absorbed by Russia.

V/v is derived from the Semitic letter vaw, *meaning hook. It was identical to* u *in the Greek and Roman alphabets, and was not differentiated from* u *in English until the Middle Ages.*

V1, V2 rockets Abbreviation for *Vergeltungswaffen* (Vengeance Weapons). The V-1s, popularly known as **doodlebugs**, **flying bombs** or **buzz bombs**, were pilotless aircraft, powered by a pulse-jet engine, with a guidance system composed of a distance-measuring device, a gyrocompass and an altimeter. Launched by the LUFTWAFFE against SE England in June 1944, they carried about a tonne of high explosive. Later the same year, England was subjected to attacks by the V-2, a long-range, ballistic missile carrying a 1-tonne warhead to a range of 320km (200mi), with an altitude of 95–110km (60–70mi).

vaccine Agent used to give IMMUNITY against various diseases without producing symptoms. A vaccine consists of modified disease organisms, such as live, weakened VIRUSES, or dead ones that are still able to induce the production of specific ANTIBODIES within the blood. *See also* IMMUNE SYSTEM

vacuole Membrane-bound, fluid-filled cavity within the CYTOPLASM of a CELL. Vacuoles perform various functions including the discharge of wastes from cell metabolism.

vacuum Region of extremely low pressure. Interstellar space is a high vacuum, with an average density of less than 1 molecule per cubic centimetre; the highest man-made vacuums contain less than 100,000 molecules per cubic centimetre.

vagina Portion of the female reproductive tract, running from the CERVIX of the UTERUS to the exterior of the body. Tube-like in shape, it receives the PENIS during sexual intercourse. Its muscular walls enable it to dilate during childbirth.

valence (valency) "Combining power" of a particular element, equal to the number of single chemical bonds one atom can form or the number of electrons it gives up or accepts when forming a compound. Hydrogen has a valency of 1, carbon 4 and sulphur 2, as seen in compounds such as methane (CH_4), carbon disulphide (CS_2) and hydrogen sulphide (H_2S).

Valencia City in E Spain, capital of the province of Valencia, situated on the Turia River. The region of Valencia comprises the provinces of Alicante, Castellón and Valencia. Originally settled by the Romans, the city was conquered by the MOORS in the 8th century, eventually becoming capital of the independent Moorish kingdom of Valencia. In the Spanish CIVIL WAR it was the last Republican stronghold to fall to Nationalist forces. It is an agricultural, industrial and communications centre. Industries: electrical equipment, chemicals, textiles, shipbuilding, vehicles, machinery, fruit, wine. Tourists are drawn by the city's many fine buildings. Pop. (1991) 752,909.

Valentine, Saint Name traditionally associated with two legendary saints of the 3rd century. Little is known about either of them. The martyrdom of both is commemorated on 14 February. The custom of lovers exchanging cards on St Valentine's Day possibly has its roots in the pagan Roman festival of Lupercalia.

Valentino, Rudolph (1895–1926) US silent-film star, b. Italy. He exemplified the mysterious Latin lover, and his films include *The Sheik* (1921) and *The Eagle* (1925).

valerian (garden heliotrope) Plant native to Europe and N Asia and naturalized in the USA. It has pinkish or pale purple flower clusters. Height: to 1.2m (4ft). Family Valerianaceae; species *Valeriana officinalis*.

Valéry, Paul (1871–1945) French poet and critic. He was influenced by MALLARMÉ, and his poems, which include *The Young Fate* (1917) and *Charmes* (1922), are characterized by lyricism and abstract thought. He was elected to the Académie Française (1925).

Valhalla In Norse mythology, the Hall of the Slain, where chosen warriors enjoyed feasts with the god ODIN. It is depicted as a glittering palace, with golden walls and a ceiling of burnished shields.

Valkyries In Norse mythology, warlike handmaidens of the god ODIN, who selected and conducted to VALHALLA those slain heroes who merited a place with him.

Valletta Port and capital of Malta, on the NE coast of the island. It was founded in the 16th century. Industries: shipbuilding and repairs, transshipment, tourism. Pop. (1995) 102,571.

valley Elongated, gently sloping depression of the Earth's surface. It often contains a stream or river that receives the drainage from the surrounding heights. A U-shaped valley was probably formed by a glacier, a V-shaped one by a stream. The term may also be applied to a broad, generally flat area that is drained by a large river.

Valois, Dame Ninette de (1898–) Irish ballerina and choreographer, b. Edris Stannus. She danced with Diaghilev's BALLETS RUSSES (1923–26). In 1931 she founded the Sadler's Wells Ballet School, which later became the Royal Ballet.

value-added tax (VAT) Indirect tax imposed in most European countries. Introduced in Britain in 1971, it consists of a series of taxes (calculated as a percentage) levied on goods (or services) in the various stages of their manufacture until the point of sale.

valves In anatomy, structures that prevent the backflow of blood in the HEART and VEINS. Heart valves separate and connect the two atria and ventricles, the right ventricle and the pulmonary artery, and the left ventricle and the aorta.

vampire bat Small, brown bat that lives in tropical and subtropical America. It uses its sharp teeth to slice the skin of resting animals (including human beings) and then laps up their blood. Length: 7.6cm (3in); wingspan 30cm (12in). Family Desmodontidae; species *Desmodus rotundus*.

vanadium Silver-white, metallic element (symbol V), one of the TRANSITION ELEMENTS. Discovered in 1801, the malleable and ductile metal is found in iron, lead and uranium ores and in coal and petroleum. It is used in steel alloys to add strength and heat resistance. Chemically, vanadium reacts with oxygen and other nonmetals at high temperature. Properties: at.no. 23; r.a.m. 50.9414; r.d. 6.1 at 18.7°C; m.p. 1,890°C (3,434°F); b.p. 3,380°C (6,116°F); most common isotope V^{51} (99.76%).

Van Allen radiation belts Two rings of radiation trapped by the Earth's magnetic field in the upper atmosphere. The belts contain high-energy, charged particles.

Vanbrugh, Sir John (1664–1726) English BAROQUE architect and dramatist, who worked with and was influenced by Sir Christopher WREN. He took London by storm with his witty RESTORATION comedies, *The Relapse* (1696) and *The Provok'd Wife* (1697), before turning to architecture. Blenheim Palace (1705–20) and Castle Howard (1699–1726) are among Vanbrugh's architectural masterpieces.

Van Buren, Martin Eighth US President (1837–41). Elected to the US Senate in 1821, he became Andrew JACKSON's secretary of state. Jackson's support gained him the Democratic presidential nomination in 1836. As president, he supported states' rights on the slavery issue, embarked on the Seminole Wars and declined federal intervention in the economic depression (1837). He was heavily defeated when he stood for re-election in 1840.

Vancouver City on the S shore of Burrard Inlet, S British Columbia, Canada. It is Canada's third-largest city and principal Pacific port. The building of the Canadian Pacific Railway allowed it to grow into the largest city on the Canadian W coast. Its excellent sea and air links make it a leading centre for transport and communication with countries of the Pacific Rim. Industries: tourism, timber, oil refining, shipbuilding, fish-processing. Pop. (1991) 471,844 (conurbation 1,602,502).

Vandals Germanic tribe who attacked the Roman empire in the 5th century AD. Defeated by the GOTHS, they moved south and invaded North Africa (429), establishing a kingdom from which they controlled the W Mediterranean. They sacked Rome in 455. The Vandal kingdom was destroyed by the Byzantine general Belisarius in 533–534.

Van de Graaff generator Machine that generates high voltages by concentrating electrical charges on the outside of a hollow conductor. Positive or negative charges are sprayed onto a vertically moving belt that carries them up to a large hollow metal sphere where voltage builds up. An applied voltage of about 50,000 volts can generate up to 10 million volts.

Van der Waals, Johannes Diderik (1837–1923) Dutch physicist. He was awarded the 1910 Nobel Prize for physics for his work on gases and the gas equation that he derived. The Van der Waals equation takes into account intermolecular attraction and repulsion, which were ignored by the KINETIC THEORY of gases.

Van der Waals Forces Weak forces of mutual attraction that contribute towards cohesion between neighbouring ATOMS or MOLECULES. They are named after Johannes VAN DER WAALS.

Van Dyck, Sir Anthony (1599–1641) Flemish portrait and religious painter. He worked in RUBENS' studio before travelling abroad. His many depictions of English aristocrats greatly influenced future English portrait painting.

Vane, Sir Henry (1613–62) English parliamentary leader during the CIVIL WAR. A Puritan, he was governor of Massachusetts (1636–37). He returned to England to become a leader of parliamentary opposition to Charles I. Although not a regicide, Vane was executed after the RESTORATION (1660).

Van Gogh, Vincent (1853–90) Dutch painter, a leading proponent of POST-IMPRESSIONISM and a formative influence on modern art. His early works were often sombre pictures of peasants. In 1886 he went to Paris, where his work underwent a transformation. Two years later he went to Arles, Provence, where he painted in a frenzy of prolific activity interspersed with bouts of mental illness, which ended in suicide. His paintings were executed with heavy brushwork in heightened, flame-like colour, with passionate expression of light and emotion. To this period belong *The Bridge at Arles* (1888), *Starry Night* (1889) and his sunflower paintings.

vanilla Climbing orchid native to Mexico. The vines bear greenish-yellow flowers that produce seed-pods 20cm (8in) long, which are the source of the flavouring vanilla. Family Orchidaceae; species *Vanilla planifolia*.

Vanuatu Volcanic island group in the SW Pacific Ocean, *c*.2,300km (1,430mi) E of Australia. The group consists of 13 large islands and 70 islets, the majority of them mountainous, which form a chain *c*.725km (450mi) in length. The main islands are Espiritu Santo, Efate (which has the capital Vila, 1992 pop. 19,750), Malekula, Pentecost, Malo and Tanna. Discovered in 1606 by Pedro Fernandez de Queiros, the group was settled by the English and French in the early 1800s. The islands became an independent parliamentary republic in 1980. The inhabitants live mainly by fishing, farming and mining. Area: 12,190sq km (4,707sq mi). Pop. (1996 est.) 160,000.

Van Vleck, John (Hasbrouck) (1899–1980) US mathematician and physicist. He studied the behaviour of electrons in non-crystalline, magnetic materials. In the 1930s, Van Vleck was the first

653

scientist to use QUANTUM MECHANICS to explain the phenomenon of MAGNETISM. For this work, Van Vleck shared the 1977 Nobel Prize in physics.

vaporization (volatilization) Conversion of a liquid or solid into its vapour, such as water into steam.

vapour pressure Pressure exerted by a vapour when it evaporates from a liquid or solid. When as many molecules leave to form vapour as return (in an enclosed space), this equilibrium is termed a saturated vapour pressure.

Varanasi (Benares, Banoras) City on the River Ganges, Uttar Pradesh state, N India. Varanasi is considered by Hindus to be their holy city. Each year it attracts millions of pilgrims who bathe in the river. BUDDHA is reputed to have preached his first sermon nearby. Silk brocade, brassware and jewellery are among the city's specialist industries. Pop. (1991) 1,026,000.

Varèse, Edgard (1885–1965) French composer, a leading advocate of 20th-century experimental music. He experimented with new rhythms and timbres and dissonant harmonies in his works, which include *Hyperprism* (1923) for wind instruments and percussion and *Déserts* (1954) for tape-recorded sound.

variable In mathematics, symbol used to represent an unspecified quantity. Variables are used to express a range of possible values. For example, in the expression $x^2 + x + 1$, the quantity x may be assigned the value of any real number; here x is said to be an independent variable. If y is defined by $y = x^2 + x + 1$, then y is a dependent variable because its value depends on the value of x

variable star Star whose brightness varies with time. Intrinsic variables are stars that vary because of some inherent feature. In extrinsic variables, external factors, such as eclipses or obscuring dust, affect the amount of light reaching us from the star.

variation In biology, differences between members of the same SPECIES. Variation occurs naturally due to heredity and to differences in the environment during development. *See also* ADAPTATION; EVOLUTION

variation In music, a variety of treatments upon a single theme. Successive statements of the theme are altered by such means as simple elaboration, change of KEY or change of time signature.

Varuna In ancient Hindu mythology, the supreme ruler and possessor of universal power. He is worshipped as the upholder of moral order, and is closely identified with the Moon.

Vasari, Giorgio (1511–74) Italian painter, architect and biographer. His fame now rests on his history of Italian art, *The Lives of the most excellent Painters, Sculptors and Architects* (1550). In architecture he is noted for his design for the UFFIZI.

Vasco da Gama *See* GAMA, VASCO DA

vascular bundle Strand of conductive tissue that transports water and dissolved mineral salts and nutrients throughout a VASCULAR PLANT. They extend from the roots, through the stem, and out to the leaves. They consist of two types of tissue XYLEM and PHLOEM.

vascular plant Plant with vessels to carry water and nutrients within it. All higher plants have a vascular system.

vasectomy Operation to induce male sterility, in which the tube (vas deferens) carrying sperm from the testes to the penis is cut. A vasectomy is a form of permanent CONTRACEPTION, although in some cases the operation is reversible.

vasoconstrictor Any substance that causes constriction of blood vessels and, therefore, decreased blood flow. Examples include NORADRENALINE, angiotensin and the hormone vasopressin.

vasodilator Any substance that causes widening of the blood vessels, permitting freer flow of blood. Vasodilator drugs are mostly used to treat HYPERTENSION and ANGINA.

VAT *See* VALUE-ADDED TAX

Vatican, The Short name for the VATICAN CITY or the Vatican Palace. The **Vatican Palace** is the residence of the pope within the Vatican City. A building of well over 1,000 rooms clustered around a number of courtyards, it contains the papal apartments, the offices of the Vatican City state secretariat, state reception rooms, the Vatican Museums, the Vatican Archive and the Vatican Library.

Vatican City Independent sovereign state, existing as a walled enclave on the w bank of the River TIBER, within the city of ROME. It is the official home of the PAPACY and an independent base for the Holy See (governing body of the ROMAN CATHOLIC CHURCH). The first papal residence was established here in the 5th century and it has been the papal home ever since, apart from a brief spell at AVIGNON in the 14th century. Vatican City did not achieve full independence until 1929. The Commission, appointed to administer the Vatican's affairs, has its own radio service, police and railway station and issues its own stamps and coins. Area: 0.44sq km (0.17sq mi).

Vatican Council, First (1869–70) 20th ecumenical council of the Roman Catholic Church. Convened by Pope PIUS IX to rebut various contemporary ideas associated with the rise of liberalism and materialism, it is chiefly remembered for its declaration of PAPAL INFALLIBILITY.

Vatican Council, Second (1962–65) 21st ecumenical council of the Roman Catholic Church. It was convened by Pope JOHN XXIII to revive and renew Christian faith. Among the most significant results were the introduction of the Mass in the vernacular, a greater role for lay people, and a greater tolerance for other sects and other religions.

Vaughan, Henry (1622–95) Welsh poet. His poetry belongs to the tradition of METAPHYSICS. Vaughan's best work draws on his religious experience, most notably in *Silex Scintillans* (1650, revised 1655).

Vaughan Williams, Ralph (1872–1958) British composer. His interest in English folk music is apparent in his three *Norfolk Rhapsodies* (1905–07) and his instrumental arrangement *Fantasia on Greensleeves*. He also used elements of English Tudor music in his *Mass in G Minor* (1923) for unaccompanied chorus. He wrote nine symphonies, the best known of which are the Sixth Symphony (1947) and the *Sinfonia Antarctica* (1952).

vault Curved roof or ceiling usually made of stone, brick or concrete. The simple "barrel" vault is semi-cylindrical; the "groin" vault consists of two barrel vaults intersected at right-angles; the "ribbed groin" is the same as the ordinary groin vault except that it has ribs to give the edges extra support; the so-called Gothic vault has four pointed compartments; the "fan" vault has a delicate, fan-like appearance.

Veblen, Thorstein Bunde (1857–1929) US sociologist and economist. He wrote *The Theory of the Leisure Class* (1899), in which he introduced the idea of conspicuous consumption. A perceptive critic of US capitalist society, he founded the institutionalist school, believing that economics must be studied in the context of social change.

vector In mathematics, a quantity that has both a magnitude and a direction, as contrasted with a SCALAR, which has magnitude only. For example, the VELOCITY of an object is specified by its speed and the direction in which it is moving.

Vedanta (Sanskrit, conclusion of the VEDAS) Best known and most popular form of Indian philosophy; it forms the foundation for most modern schools of thought in HINDUISM. *See also* UPANISHADS

Vedas Ancient and most sacred writings of HINDUISM. They consist of series of hymns and formulaic chants that constituted a Hindu LITURGY. There are four Vedas: *Rig Veda*, containing a priestly tradition originally brought to India by ARYANS; *Yajur Veda*, consisting of prayers and sacred formulas; *Sama Veda*, containing melodies and chants; and *Atharva Veda*, a collection of popular hymns, incantations and magic spells. The Vedas were composed over a long period, probably between *c.*1500 and 1200 BC.

Vega Carpio, Félix, Lope de (1562–1635) Spanish poet and Spain's first great dramatist. A prolific writer, he produced epics, pastorals, odes, sonnets and novels. About 300 of his major works survive; the authentic oeuvre includes the plays *Peribáñez and the Commander of Ocaña* (*c.*1610) and *All Citizens Are Soldiers* (*c.*1613).

vegetable As opposed to ANIMAL, a form of life that builds up its tissues by means of growth using the energy of sunlight, carbon dioxide from the air, and the green pigment CHLOROPHYLL. This process is known as PHOTOSYNTHESIS.

vegetarianism Practice of abstaining from eating meat and fish. A minority of vegetarian purists, known as vegans, further exclude from their diet all products of animal origin, such as butter, eggs, milk and cheese. Vegetarianism has a religious basis in many cultures, particularly among various Jain, Hindu and Buddhist sects.

vegetative reproduction Form of ASEXUAL REPRODUCTION in higher plants. It involves an offshoot or a piece of the original plant (from leaf, stem or root) separating and giving rise to an entire new plant. It may occur naturally, as in strawberries reproducing by runners, or artificially, as in a house plant cutting yielding a new plant.

vein In mammals, vessel that carries deoxygenated blood to the heart. An exception is the pulmonary vein, which carries oxygenated blood from the lungs to the left upper chamber of the heart. *See also* ARTERY; VENA CAVA

Velázquez, Diego Rodriguez de Silva y (1599–1660) Spanish painter. He painted religious works and dignified genre paintings, notably *The Old Woman Cooking Eggs* (1618). During the 1630s and 1640s he produced a striking series of royal and equestrian portraits. A trip to Italy resulted in the superb portrait of *Pope Innocent X* (1650). Towards the end of his life, Velázquez continued to paint with dazzling brushwork, culminating in *The Maids of Honour* (*c.*1656).

velocity Rate of motion of a body in a certain direction. Its symbol is v. Velocity is a VECTOR (magnitude and direction), whereas speed, which does not specify direction, is a scalar.

vena cava Main VEIN of vertebrates. It supplies the HEART with deoxygenated blood, emptying into its right atrium.

venereal disease (VD) Any of the diseases transmitted through sexual contact, chief of which are SYPHILIS, GONORRHOEA and chancroid.

Venetian School School of Italian painting that flourished in the 15th, 16th and 18th centuries. It was noted for the sumptuousness and radiance of its colour. Early Venetian masters included the BELLINI and Vivarini families, who were followed by its greatest exponents, TITIAN and GIORGIONE. TINTORETTO and VERONESE represent the transition from RENAISSANCE to BAROQUE, while TIEPOLO and CANALETTO revived Venetian painting in the 18th century.

Venezuela Republic in N South America, the capital is CARACAS. **Land and climate** The w part of the Republic of Venezuela contains the MARACAIBO lowlands, which surround the the oil-rich Lake Maracaibo. Arms of the ANDES mountains extend across most of N Venezuela. A low-lying region, drained by the ORINOCO River, lies between the N mountains and the Guiana Highlands in the SE. The Guiana Highlands contain ANGEL FALLS, the world's highest waterfall. Venezuela has a tropical climate. About 34% of Venezuela is forested, with dense rainforest in the Orinoco basin and in the Guiana Highlands. Tropical savanna covers the lowlands; mountain grassland occurs in the highlands. Only *c.*4% of the land is cultivated. **Economy** Industry employs 17% of the workforce, with the chief industry being petro-

VENEZUELA
AREA: 912,050sq km (352,143sq mi)
POPULATION: 21,378,000
CAPITAL (POPULATION): Caracas (1,824,892)
GOVERNMENT: Federal republic
ETHNIC GROUPS: Mestizo 67%, White 21%,
Black 10%, Native American 2%
LANGUAGES: Spanish (official)
RELIGIONS: Christianity (Roman Catholic 94%)
CURRENCY: Bolívar = 100 céntimos

leum refining; other industries include aluminium and steel production. Oil accounts for 80% of the exports. Other exports include bauxite, aluminium and iron ore. Agriculture employs 13% of the workforce. Major crops include bananas and other fruits, coffee, maize, rice and sugar cane. **History** The original inhabitants of Venezuela were the Arawak and Carib Native Americans. The first European to arrive was Christopher COLUMBUS, who sighted the area in 1498. In 1499 Amerigo VESPUCCI explored the coastline and nicknamed the country Venezuela (little Venice). Venezuela became part of the Spanish colonial administrative area of New Granada. In the late 18th century, uprisings against Spanish rule were led by Francisco de Miranda. Simón BOLÍVAR liberated Venezuela (1821) and it became part of Greater Colombia, a republic that also included Colombia, Ecuador and Panama. In 1830 Venezuela became a separate state. The mid- to late-19th century was marked by political instability and civil war, with the country ruled by a series of dictators. Juan Vicente GÓMEZ's long and autocratic rule (1908–35) provided the stability for Venezuela to pay off its debts, helped by international interest in its rich oil-fields. In 1945 a pro-democracy military junta gained control. In 1948 Rómulo Gallegos was elected president, but a military coup the same year re-established a dictatorship. Popular uprisings in 1958 brought a return to democracy. Venezuela became increasingly prosperous, but left-wing uprisings, notably two communist revolts in 1962, led to much violence. **Politics** In 1976 Venezuela nationalized its oil industry, using the money to raise living standards. A slump in oil prices in the 1980s damaged the economy. In 1989 Carlos Andrés Pérez of the Democratic Action Party became president. He introduced free-market economic reforms, but despite an improved economy, inflation and unemployment rose. In 1994 Rafael Caldera became president, promising to moderate the economic reforms that had led to recession. Caldera's austerity measures have provoked unrest and demonstrations.

Venice (Venezia) City on the Gulf of Venice, at the head of the Adriatic Sea, N Italy, capital of Venetia region. It is built on 118 islands, separated by narrow canals, in the Lagoon of Venice. It is joined by

causeway to the mainland. Settled in the 5th century, it became a vassal of the Byzantine empire until the 10th century. After defeating Genoa in 1381, Venice became the most important European seapower. Its importance declined in the 16th century, and it was ceded to Austria in 1797, becoming part of Italy in 1866. Tourism imposes a massive strain on a city already suffering from erosion, subsidence and pollution. Industries: glass-blowing, textiles, petrochemicals. Pop. (1992) 305,617.

Venn diagram In mathematics, diagrammatical representation of the relations between mathematical SETS or logical statements, named after the British logician John Venn (1834–1923). The sets are drawn as geometrical figures that overlap whenever different sets share some elements.

ventilation In biology, the process by which air or water is taken into and expelled from the body of an animal and passed over a surface across which GAS EXCHANGE takes place. BREATHING is a ventilation mechanism, as are the movements of the floor of a fish's mouth, which, coupled with those of its GILL covers, draw water across the gills.

ventricle Either of the two lower chambers of the HEART.

venture capital Outside capital provided for a business. Venture capital is often needed to start up new businesses or to expand existing businesses. It is provided by merchant banks or investment and private investors.

Venturi, Robert (1925–) US modernist architect. His buildings seem utilitarian, but they are more subtle and witty than they first appear. His controversial publications include *Complexity and Contradiction in Architecture* (1966) and *Learning from Las Vegas* (1972). His radical approach has prevented his work from entering the mainstream. *See also* MODERNISM

Venus Second planet from the Sun, it is almost as large as the Earth. Visible around dawn or dusk as the so-called **morning star** or **evening star**, it is the most conspicuous celestial object after the Sun and Moon. Most of the surface features are volcanic in origin. The atmosphere consists of 96% carbon dioxide and 3.5% nitrogen, with traces of helium, argon, neon and krypton. Venus has no satellites. Diameter: 12,104km

Venus Roman goddess originally associated with gardens and cultivation, but also with the ideas of charm, grace and beauty. She became identified with the Greek goddess APHRODITE, and hence also personified love and fertility.

verb Linguistic category (part of speech) found in all languages, consisting of words typically denoting an action, an event or a state (for example, in English, *to run, to snow, to depend*). Typical verbs are associated with one or more "arguments", such as subject and direct object. In English, verbs may be intransitive or transitive; intransitives have one argument (*she sneezed*) and transitives two or, rarely, more (*she* played *snooker, she* taught *him Russian*). A list of all forms of a verb is called its paradigm, and this may be regular (predictable by a rule) or irregular (unpredictable). The most irregular verbs in a language are often those in most frequent use and with the most general meaning.

Verdi, Giuseppe (1813–1901) Italian composer, one of the supreme operatic masters of the 19th century. Up to 1853 his masterpieces were *Rigoletto* (1851), *Il trovatore* (1853) and *La traviata* (1853). *Aïda* (1867) shows a richer and more imaginative orchestration. With Verdi's last three operas, *Don Carlos* (1884), *Otello* (1887) and *Falstaff* (1893), Italian opera reached its greatest heights. Among other compositions are several sacred choral works, including the *Requiem* (1874).

Verdun, Battle of Campaign of WORLD WAR 1, February–December 1916. A German offensive in the region of Verdun made initial advances, but was checked by the French under General PÉTAIN. After a series of renewed German assaults, the Allied offensive on the SOMME drew off German troops and the French regained the lost territory. Total casualties were estimated at one million.

Verlaine, Paul (1844–96) French poet. His early poetry, *Poèmes Saturniens* (1866) and *Fêtes Galantes* (1869), was influenced by BAUDELAIRE. While in jail (1874–75), he wrote *Songs Without Words* (1874), an early work of SYMBOLISM. His later poetry deals with the conflict between the spiritual and the carnal. His critical work includes the famous study *The Accursed Poets* (1884).

Vermeer, Jan (1632–75) Dutch painter. Early mythological and religious works gave way to a middle period featuring the serene and contemplative domestic scenes for which he is best known. He treated light and colour with enormous delicacy, as in the superb landscape, *View of Delft* (*c.*1660). Towards the end of his life, Vermeer began to paint in a heavier manner.

Vermont State in New England, NE USA, on the Canadian border. The state capital is MONTPELIER. The Green Mountains dominate the terrain. Most of the W border of the state is formed by Lake Champlain. Samuel de CHAMPLAIN discovered the lake in 1609, but the region was not settled permanently until 1724. In 1777 Vermont declared its independence, retaining this unrecognized status until it was admitted to the Union in 1791. The region is heavily forested and arable land is limited. Dairy farming is the most important farming activity. Mineral resources include granite, slate, marble and asbestos. Industries: pulp and paper, food processing, computer components and machine tools. Area: 24,887sq km (9,609sq mi). Pop. (1992) 571,334.

Verne, Jules (1828–1905) French author. He is chiefly remembered for his imaginative adventure stories, and he is often considered one of the founding fathers of science fiction. His popular novels include *Journey to the Centre of the Earth* (1864),

Twenty Thousand Leagues Under the Sea (1869) and *Around the World in Eighty Days* (1873).

Verona City on the River Adige, NE Italy, capital of Verona province. The city was captured by Rome in 89 BC. It prospered under the Della Scala family in the 13th and 14th centuries, and was held by Austria from 1797–1866, when it joined Italy. Industries: textiles, chemicals, paper, printing, wine. Pop. (1992) 255,492.

Veronese, Paolo Caliari (1528–88) Italian painter and decorative artist. A prominent member of the VENETIAN SCHOOL, he excelled at painting large scenes featuring flamboyant pageants. He also painted religious and mythological themes. He ran into trouble with the Inquisition for his irreverent treatment of *The Last Supper* (1573) and had to rename it *The Feast in the House of Levi*. Other celebrated works are his decorative FRESCOS for the Villa Barbaro near Treviso, and his ceiling, *Triumph of Venice*, for the Doge's Palace.

Versailles City in N France, 16km (10mi) WSW of Paris, capital of Yvelines département. It is famous for its former royal palace. The architects Louis LE VAU, Jules Hardouin-Mansart and Robert de Cotte built the monumental palace for LOUIS XIV in a French classical style. The interior was designed by Charles LEBRUN. The magnificent gardens were landscaped by André LE NÔTRE. The park also contains the Grand and Petit Trianon palaces. It was the scene of the signing of several peace treaties. Pop. (1990) 91,030.

Versailles, Treaty of (1919) Peace agreement concluding WORLD WAR 1, signed at VERSAILLES. The treaty represented a compromise between US President Wilson's FOURTEEN POINTS and the demands of the European allies for heavy penalties against Germany. German territorial concessions included Alsace-Lorraine to France and the loss of its colonies. The Rhineland was demilitarized, strict limits were placed on German armed forces, and extensive reparations for war damage were imposed. The treaty also established the LEAGUE OF NATIONS. It was never ratified by the USA, which signed a separate treaty with Germany in 1921.

vertebra One of the bones making up the SPINE (vertebral column). The human backbone is composed of 26 vertebrae (the 5 sacral and 4 vertebrae of the coccyx fuse together to form two solid bones), which are held together by ligaments and intervertebral discs.

vertebrate Animal with individual discs of bone or cartilage called VERTEBRA, which surround or replace the embryonic NOTOCHORD to form a jointed backbone enclosing the spinal column. The principal division within vertebrates is between FISH and partly land-adapted forms (AMPHIBIANS), and the wholly land-adapted forms (REPTILES, BIRDS and MAMMALS). Phylum CHORDATA; subphylum Vertebrata.

vertigo Dizziness often accompanied by nausea. It is due to disruption of the sense of balance and may be produced by ear disorder, reduced flow of blood to the brain caused by altitude or emotional upset.

vervet monkey *See* GUENON

very high frequency (VHF) Range or band of radio waves with frequencies between 30 and 300MHz and wavelengths between 1 and 10m (3–33ft). This band is used for TELEVISION and FREQUENCY MODULATION (FM) radio broadcasts to provide high-quality reception.

Vespasian (AD 9–79) (Titus Flavius Vespasianus) Roman emperor (69–79). A successful general and administrator, he was leading the campaign against the Jews in Palestine when he was proclaimed emperor by his soldiers. He proved a capable ruler, extending and strengthening the empire, rectifying the budget deficit, widening qualifications for Roman citizenship and adding to the monumental buildings of Rome.

Vespucci, Amerigo (1454–1512) Italian maritime explorer. He was possibly the first to realize that America constituted a new continent, which was named after him by the German cartographer Martin Waldseemüller in 1507.

Vesta In Roman religion, goddess of fire and purity, supreme in the conduct of religious ceremonies. Her priestesses were the vestal virgins. Vesta was the guardian of the hearth and the patron goddess of bakers.

Vesuvius (Vesuvio) Active volcano on the Bay of Naples, S Italy. The earliest recorded eruption was in 79 AD, when POMPEII and HERCULANEUM were destroyed. The height of the volcano changes with each of the 30 or so eruptions recorded since Roman times.

veterinary medicine Medical science that deals with diseases of animals. It was practised by the Babylonians and Egyptians some 4,000 years ago. In the late 18th century schools of veterinary medicine were established in Europe.

VHF Abbreviation of VERY HIGH FREQUENCY (VHF)

vibraphone PERCUSSION musical instrument with metal bars of different lengths that are struck with sticks or mallets to produce various notes. Tubes beneath the bars vibrate at the same frequency as the bar above and magnify the sound.

viburnum Genus of flowering shrubs and small trees, native to North America and Eurasia. All have small, fleshy fruits containing single flat seeds. There are about 120 species. Family Caprifoliaceae.

vicar Priest in the CHURCH OF ENGLAND who is in charge of a PARISH. In the ROMAN CATHOLIC CHURCH, the term "vicar" is used to mean "representative". A **vicar general** is appointed by and represents a bishop in the administration of a diocese. *See also* CURATE

Vichy Government During WORLD WAR 2, regime of SE France after the defeat by Germany in June 1940. Its capital was the town of Vichy, and it held authority over French overseas possessions as well as the unoccupied part of France.

After German forces occupied Vichy France in November 1942, it became little more than a puppet government.

Vico, Giambattista (1668–1744) Italian philosophical historian. In his *New Science* (1725, revised 1730 and 1744), he advanced the arguments of historicism: that all aspects of society and culture are relevant to the study of history, and that the history of any period should be judged according to the standards and customs of that time and place. Since the 19th century he has been regarded as one of the greatest philosophers of history.

Victor Emmanuel II (1820–78) King of Italy (1861–78). From 1852, guided by his able minister, CAVOUR, he strengthened his kingdom, formed a French alliance, and consequently defeated Austria (1859–61). In 1861 he assumed the title of king of Italy. Rome became his new capital after French troops withdrew (1870).

Victor Emmanuel III (1869–1947) King of Italy (1900–46). He appointed Benito MUSSOLINI prime minister in 1922. The king retained the power to dismiss him, and eventually did so in 1943. He abdicated in 1946.

Victoria (1819–1901) Queen of Great Britain and Ireland (1837–1901) and empress of India (1876–1901). A granddaughter of GEORGE III, she succeeded her uncle, WILLIAM IV. In 1840 she married her first cousin, Prince Albert of SAXE-COBURG-GOTHA. During her reign, the longest in English history, the role of the monarchy was established as a ceremonial, symbolic institution, with virtually no power but much influence. Among later prime ministers, she maintained excellent terms with DISRAELI, but was on frosty terms with GLADSTONE. She reigned over an empire containing 25% of the world's people and 30% of its land.

Victoria State in SE Australia, bounded by the Indian Ocean, the Bass Strait and the Tasman Sea. The capital is MELBOURNE (home to over 65% of the state population); other major cities are Geelong, Ballarat and Bendigo. The population increased rapidly after 1851, when gold was discovered. Victoria became part of the Commonwealth of Australia in 1901.Irrigation is used extensively to grow wheat, oats, barley, fruit and vegetables, while sheep and dairy cattle are also important. Brown coal, natural gas and oil are the chief resources. Industries: motor vehicles, textiles, food processing. Area: 227,620sq km (87,813sq mi). Pop. (1991) 4,487,000.

Victoria (Victoria Nyanza) Lake in E central Africa, bordered by Uganda, Kenya and Tanzania. The second-largest freshwater lake in the world, it is the chief reservoir of the River Nile. Area: 68,000sq km (26,000sq mi).

Victoria Falls Waterfalls on the Zambezi River, on the border of Zimbabwe and Zambia. The first European discovery was in 1855 by David LIVINGSTONE. Maximum drop: 108m (355ft); width over 1,700m (5,580ft).

vicuña Graceful, even-toed, hoofed South American mammal. The smallest member of the CAMEL family, it is humpless and resembles the LLAMA. Its silky coat is tawny brown. Vicuña wool is expensive and rare. Height: 86cm (34in) at the shoulder; weight: 45kg (100lb). Family Camelidae; species *Vicugna vicugna*.

Vidal, Gore (1925–) US novelist, playwright and essayist, b. Eugene Luther Vidal. His first novels draw on his experience of army life in World War 2. Other works include the satirical *Myra Breckinridge* (1968) and its sequel *Myron* (1974). A number of his novels satirize the American political establishment, beginning with *Washington DC* (1967) and continuing with a series on US historical figures. Vidal is also the author of critical essays, plays and screenplays, including *Suddenly Last Summer* (1958). His recent works include *Hollywood* (1990) and *Golgotha* (1992).

video disc Vinyl disc coated with a reflective, metallic surfacing. On one side of the reflective surface is etched a spiral of microscopic pits corresponding to digital information that can be picked up by a laser scanner and converted electronically to video pictures and sound. Since the late 1980s video discs have been almost entirely superseded by the smaller, more comprehensive type of COMPACT DISC (CD) called a CD-ROM.

videotape recording Recording and reproducing sound and moving pictures using magnetic tape. The video recorder developed from the audio magnetic tape recorder, from which it differs significantly in two respects: video tape is wider to accommodate the picture signals; and the relative speed at which the tape passes the magnetic head is greater in order to deal with the larger amount of information necessary for recording and reproducing pictures. *See also* MAGNETIC RECORDING

videotext General term for the different methods by which information can be brought to a television screen. Information that is transmitted in parallel with the ordinary TV signals is known as **teletext**. The system that brings information to the screen from a computer databank via a telephone landline is called **videotex**.

Vienna (Wien) Capital of Austria, on the River DANUBE. Vienna became an important town under the Romans. The first HABSBURG ruler was installed in 1276 and the city was the seat of the HOLY ROMAN EMPIRE from 1558–1806. As the capital of the AUSTRO-HUNGARIAN EMPIRE, it was the cultural and social centre of 19th-century Europe. It suffered an economic and political collapse following World War 1. After World War 2, it was occupied (1945–55) by joint Soviet-Western forces. Industries: chemicals, textiles, furniture, clothing. Vienna is the third-largest German-speaking city (after Berlin and Hamburg). Pop. (1993) 1,589,052.

Vienna, Congress of (1814–15) European conference that settled international affairs after the NAPOLEONIC WARS. It attempted, as far as possible, to restore the Europe of pre-1789. Among steps to prevent future European wars, it established the CONGRESS SYSTEM and the German Confederation.

Vientiane (Viangchan) Capital and chief port of Laos, on the Mekong River, close to the Thai border, in central Laos. The city became part of French INDOCHINA in 1893 and in 1899 became the capital of the French protectorate. Industries: textiles, brewing, cigarettes, hides, wood products. Pop. (1992) 449,000.

Viet Cong Nickname for the Vietnamese communist guerrillas who fought against the US-supported regime in South Vietnam during the VIETNAM WAR. After earlier, isolated revolts against the government of Ngo Dinh Diem, the movement was unified (1960) as the National Liberation Front (NLF), modelled on the VIET MINH.

Viet Minh Vietnamese organization that fought for independence from the French (1946–54). It resisted the Japanese occupation of French INDOCHINA during World War 2. After the war it began operations against the colonial forces.

Vietnam Republic in SE Asia, the capital is HANOI. **Land and climate** The Socialist Republic of Vietnam occupies an S-shaped strip of land in Southeast Asia. The coastal plains include two densely populated river delta regions: in the N, the Red River delta is the site of Hanoi and HAIPHONG; in the S, the MEKONG delta contains HO CHI MINH CITY. In the NW, the highlands extend into Laos and China. Vietnam has a tropical climate. Forests cover *c.*30% of Vietnam and include teak and ebony trees. About 17% of the land is farmed. **Economy** Agriculture employs 67% of the workforce. The main crop is rice, of which it is the world's fifth-largest producer. Other crops include bananas, coffee, groundnuts and rubber. Vietnam also produces oil, phosphates and coal; natural gas resources have been found. **History and politics** In 111 BC China seized Vietnam, naming it ANNAM. In 939 it became independent. In 1558 it split into two parts: Tonkin in the N, ruled from Hanoi; and Annam in the S, ruled from Hué. In 1802, with French support, Vietnam was united as the empire of Vietnam. The French took Saigon in 1859 and by 1887 had formed INDOCHINA from the union of Tonkin, Annam and Cochin China. Japan conquered Vietnam during World War 2. After the war the nationalist VIET MINH, led by HO CHI MINH, set up a Vietnamese republic. In 1946 the French tried to reassert control and war broke out. Despite aid from the USA, the French were finally defeated at DIEN BIEN PHU. In 1954 Vietnam was divided along the 17th parallel, with North Vietnam under the communist government of Ho Chi Minh and South Vietnam under the French-supported Emperor Bao Dai. In 1955 Bao Dai was deposed and Ngo Dinh Diem was elected president. Diem's rule was recognized as the legal gov-

VIETNAM
AREA: 331,689sq km (128,065sq mi)
POPULATION: 72,500,000
CAPITAL (POPULATION): Hanoi (1,088,862)
GOVERNMENT: Socialist republic
ETHNIC GROUPS: Vietnamese 87%, Tho (Tay), Chinese (Hoa), Tai, Khmer, Muong, Nung
LANGUAGES: Vietnamese (official)
RELIGIONS: Buddhism 55%, Christianity (Roman Catholic 7%)
CURRENCY: Dong = 10 hao = 100 xu

ernment of Vietnam by many western countries, despite his authoritarian rule. North Vietnam, supported by China and the Soviet Union, extended its influence into South Vietnam, mainly through the VIET CONG. The USA became increasingly involved in what they perceived to be the fight against communism. The conflict soon escalated into the VIETNAM WAR. After US forces were withdrawn in 1975, Ho Chi Minh's nationalist forces overran South Vietnam and it surrendered. In 1976 the reunited Vietnam became a Socialist Republic. In the late 1970s Vietnam invaded Cambodia, defeating the KHMER ROUGE government. It withdrew its troops in 1989. Vietnam's weak economy was improved in the late 1980s and 1990s with the introduction of free-market economic reforms, known as Doi Moi. In 1995 it became a member of ASEAN.

Vietnam War (1954–75) Conflict between US-backed South Vietnam and insurgents known as the VIET CONG, who had the support of communist North Vietnam. It followed the partition of Vietnam in 1954 and was fuelled by the USA's fear of the spread of communism. North Vietnam was supplied by China and the Soviet Union. As fighting intensified, US troops were committed in increasing numbers. In spite of US technological superiority and command of the air, military stalemate ensued. The war was highly unpopular in the USA. A peace agreement was signed in Paris in 1973. The country was united under communist rule.

Vignola, Giacomo Barozzi da (1507–73) Italian architect who succeeded MICHELANGELO as architect of ST PETER'S (1567–73). His Gesú church, Rome (1568), with its revolutionary design uniting clergy and congregation more closely, has been widely copied. .

Vigny, Alfred de (1797–1863) French poet, dramatist and novelist. His work often emphasizes the lonely struggle of the individual in a hostile universe, as in Chatterton (1853). His best poems are found in Poems Ancient and Modern (1826), and his fiction includes the pioneering French historical novel Cinq-Mars (1826).

Vigo, Jean (1905–34) French film director. His anarchic debut feature, Zéro de Conduite (1933), was banned in France until 1945. Atalante (1934),

his second and last feature, is an elegant amalgam of social realism and poetic lyricism.

Vikings Scandinavian, seaborne marauders, traders and settlers, who spread throughout much of Europe and the North Atlantic region in the 9th–11th centuries. Expansion seems to have been caused by rapid population growth and consequent scarcity of good farming land, as well as the desire for new sources of wealth. It was made possible by their advanced maritime technology. Although they first appeared in their greatly feared "longships" as raiders on the coasts of NW Europe, later groups came to settle. Swedes, known as Varangians, founded the first Russian state at Novgorod. Danes conquered much of N and E England. Norwegians created kingdoms in N Britain and Ireland, founding Dublin (c.840) and other cities; they also colonized Iceland and established settlements in Greenland. Viking expansion declined from the 10th century.

Viking space mission US space project to investigate conditions on MARS (1976). Two spacecraft, Viking 1 and Viking 2 made the first successful landings on Mars. They transmitted much information to Earth, including dramatic photographs of the surface. See also SPACE EXPLORATION

Villa, "Pancho" (Francisco) (1877–1923) Mexican revolutionary leader. He began as an outlaw and later joined the revolutionary forces of Francisco MADERO (1909) during the MEXICAN REVOLUTION. He sided with Venustiano Carranza for some time, but later supported Emiliano ZAPATA. Angered by US recognition of Carranza's government, Villa murdered US citizens in N Mexico and New Mexico. In 1920 he was granted a pardon in return for agreeing to retire from politics. He was assassinated three years later.

Villa-Lobos, Heitor (1887–1959) Brazilian composer and conductor. He was influenced by Native South American folk music and the music of Claude Debussy. His range of works includes operas, ballets, symphonies, religious and chamber music.

villi In anatomy, small, finger-like projections of a MUCOUS MEMBRANE such as that which lines the inner walls of the SMALL INTESTINE. They increase the absorptive surface area of the gut. In digestion, intestinal villi absorb most of the products of food broken down in the STOMACH, DUODENUM and ILEUM.

Villon, François (1430–1463) French lyric poet, b. François de Montcorbier or François des Loges. He wrote the famous Ballad of a Hanged Man while awaiting execution in 1462 (the sentence was later commuted to banishment). Among his other major works are Le Petit Testament, a satirical will in verse, and the more subtle Le Grand Testament, which is in part a lament for lost youth.

Vilnius Capital of Lithuania, on the Neris River. Founded in 1323 as the capital of the grand duchy of Lithuania, the city declined after the union of

Lithuania-Poland. After World War 1 it was made capital of an independent Lithuania. In 1939 Soviet troops occupied the city. During World War 2 the city was occupied by German troops, and its Jewish population was all but exterminated. Despite World War 2 bombing, the old city retains many of its historic synagogues, churches and civic buildings. Industries: engineering, chemicals, textiles, food processing. Pop. (1994) 578,700.

vine Plant with a long, thin stem that climbs rocks, plants and supports. To aid their climb, vines develop modifications such as tendrils, disc-like holdfasts, adventitious roots and runners. Examples are tropical LIANA, wild GRAPE and morning glory.

vinegar Any of various types of liquid condiment and preservative based on a weak solution of ETHANOIC ACID. It is produced commercially by the fermentation of alcohol.

viol Fretted stringed instrument that is played with a bow. It is held on or between the knees and, in its most usual shape, has sloping shoulders and a flat back. The six strings are tuned in fourths (unlike members of the violin family, which are tuned in fifths).

viola Stringed instrument of the VIOLIN family. It is slightly larger than the violin and its four strings are tuned a fifth lower. It is the tenor member of a string quartet.

violet Any of about 400 species of herbs and shrublets of the genus *Viola*, found worldwide. Violets may be annual or perennial. Family Violaceae.

violin Stringed instrument. It is thought to have derived from the *lira da braccio*, a Renaissance bowed instrument, and the rebec. It was perfected in Italy by the AMATI, STRADIVARI and Guarneri families between 1650 and 1740.

violoncello *See* CELLO

viper Any of 150 species of poisonous SNAKES characterized by a pair of long, hollow, venom-injecting fangs in the front of the upper jaw. The common adder (*Vipera berus*) of Europe and E Asia has a dark, zigzag band along its back. Length: to 3m (10ft). Family Viperidae.

Virgil (70–19 BC) (Publius Vergilius Maro) Roman poet. He gained a high literary reputation in Rome with the *Eclogues* (42–37 BC) and the *Georgics* (37–30 BC), a pastoral but instructive work on farming and country life. His greatest work was the *Aeneid*, which relates the adventures of the Trojan hero AENEAS, and echoes the themes of Homer's *Odyssey* and *Iliad*.

virginal Musical instrument of the HARPSICHORD family. The strings, a single set running nearly parallel to the keyboard, are plucked by quills. Two keyboards, differing in size and pitch, were sometimes incorporated into the same case. Virginals were particularly popular in 16th- and 17th-century England.

virgin birth Christian doctrine teaching that JESUS CHRIST was conceived by the Blessed Virgin MARY through the power of the HOLY SPIRIT and without the involvement of a human male.

Virginia State in E USA, on the Atlantic coast; the capital is RICHMOND. The coastal plain is low-lying. To the W the Piedmont Plateau rises to the Blue Ridge Mountains, and there are extensive forests. The first permanent British settlement in North America was at JAMESTOWN (1607). Virginia evolved an aristocratic plantation society based on vast tobacco holdings. Virginia's leaders were in the forefront of the American Revolution. During the CIVIL WAR, Richmond acted as the Confederate capital, and Virginia was the main battleground of the war. Virginia was readmitted to the Union in 1870. Farming is an important part of Virginia's economy, and the chief crops include tobacco, peanuts, grain, vegetables and fruits. Dairying and poultry are also widespread. Industries: chemicals, shipbuilding, fishing, transport equipment. Coal is the most important mineral deposit. Stone, sand and gravel are also quarried. Area: 105,710sq km (40,814sq mi). Pop. (1992) 6,394,481.

Virgin Islands, British British colony in the West Indies. It is a group of 36 islands, which form part of the ANTILLES group between the Caribbean Sea and the Atlantic Ocean; the capital is Road Town (on Tortola, the main island). The chief economic activity is tourism. Area: 130sq km (59sq mi). Pop. (1993 est.) 17,000.

Virgin Islands, US Group of 68 islands in the Lesser ANTILLES, in the West Indies. They are administered by the USA with the status of an "unincorporated territory". The chief islands are St Croix and St Thomas, which includes the capital Charlotte Amalie. Spanish from 1553, the islands were Danish in 1917, when they were bought by the USA to protect the northern approaches to the PANAMA CANAL. Tourism is the biggest money earner. Area 344sq km (133sq mi). Pop. (1990) 101,809.

Virgin Mary *See* MARY

virology Study of VIRUSES. The existence of viruses was established in 1892 by D. Ivanovski, a Russian botanist, who found that the causative agent of tobacco mosaic disease could pass through a porcelain filter impermeable to BACTERIA. The introduction of the electron microscope in the 1940s made it possible to view viruses.

virtual reality Use of computer graphics to simulate a three-dimensional environment that users can explore as if it were real.

virus Submicroscopic infectious organism. Viruses vary in size from 10 to 300 nanometres and contain only genetic material in the form of DNA or RNA. Viruses are incapable of independent existence: they can grow and reproduce only when they enter another cell because they lack energy-producing and protein-synthesizing functions. Control of viruses is difficult because harsh measures are required to kill them. Where the specific agent can be isolated, VACCINES can be developed, but some viruses change so rapidly that vaccines become ineffective.

Visconti, Luchino (1906–76) Italian film director. He made his film debut in 1942 with *Ossessione*, which pioneered the Italian NEO-REALISM school. His other films include *Senso* (1953), *Rocco and His Brothers* (1960), *Death in Venice* (1971) and *Conversation Piece* (1975). His later work was characterized by a more opulent, grander style. He also received acclaim for his theatre and opera work.

viscosity Resistance to flow of a FLUID because of internal friction. The more viscous the fluid, the slower it flows. Viscosity is large for liquids and extremely small for gases.

Vishnu Major god of HINDUISM; one of the supreme triad of gods, along with BRAHMA and SHIVA. In mythology, Vishnu is worshipped as a preserver and restorer. According to Hindu tradition, he reigns in heaven with his wife LAKSHMI, the goddess of wealth. From time to time, he comes into the world to fight evil, assuming a different incarnation each time. His incarnations have included RAMA and KRISHNA.

Visigoths *See* GOTH

vision *See* SIGHT

Vistula (Wisala) Longest river in Poland. It rises in the Carpathian Mountains of w Poland and flows NW through Warsaw, then NW through Toruń to enter the Gulf of Danzig at Gdańsk. Canals link it with other important rivers both E and W. Length: 1,090km (675mi).

vitamin Organic compound that is essential in small amounts to the maintenance and healthy growth of all animals. Vitamins are classified as either water-soluble (B and C) or fat-soluble (A, D, E and K). They are usually taken in the diet, but today most can be made synthetically. Some are synthesized in the body. Many vitamins act as coenzymes, helping ENZYMES in RESPIRATION and other metabolic processes. Lack of a particular vitamin can lead to a deficiency disease.

Vitruvius (active early 1st century AD) Roman architect and engineer. His encyclopedic *De Architectura* (before AD 27) covers almost every aspect of ancient architecture, including town planning, types of buildings and materials. It is the only work of its type to survive from the ancient world.

Vitus, Saint (active 4th century) Italian martyr. Secretly raised as a Christian by his nurse, he was put to death during the persecutions of DIOCLETIAN. He is the patron saint of actors.

Vivaldi, Antonio (1675–1741) Italian composer. A master of the CONCERTO and a virtuoso violinist, he helped to standardize the three-movement concerto form and to develop the *concerto grosso* (a concerto for two or more solo instruments). His best-known work is *The Four Seasons* (1725).

viviparity (vivipary) Process or trait among animals of giving birth to live young. Placental mammals show the highest development of viviparity,

in which the offspring develops inside the body, within the mother's UTERUS.

vivisection Dissection of living bodies for experimental purposes. Work with laboratory animals in testing drugs, vaccines and pharmaceuticals frequently involves such dissections. The ethical issue of experimenting on living animals is a matter of controversy.

Vladimir I (the Great) (956–1015) Grand Duke of Kiev and first Christian ruler of Russia (980–1015). Vladimir raised an army of VIKING mercenaries in 979 and conquered Polotsk and Kiev. Proclaimed prince of all Russia, he extended Russian territories, conquering parts of Poland and Lithuania. He established the Greek Orthodox faith in Russia.

Vladivostock Main port, naval base and cultural centre of SIBERIA, Russia, located around a sheltered harbour on the Pacific coast, 50km (30mi) from the Chinese border. Founded in 1860 as a military post, the city developed as a naval base after 1872. Vladivostock is the main E terminus of the TRANS-SIBERIAN RAILWAY. The harbour is kept open in winter by ice-breakers and is a major base for fishing fleets. Industries: ship repairing, oil refining, metal-working, timber products, food processing. Pop. (1994) 637,000.

Vlaminck, Maurice (1876–1958) French painter, graphic artist and writer. One of the leading exponents of FAUVISM, he painted with colours squirted straight from the tube, producing exuberant landscapes. In 1908 he began using darker colours in an attempt to give his painting more weight.

vocal cords *See* LARYNX

volcano Vent from which molten rock or LAVA, solid rock debris and gases issue. Volcanoes may be of the central vent type, where the material erupts from a single pipe, or of the fissure type, where material is extruded along an extensive fracture. Volcanoes are usually classed as active, dormant, or extinct.

vole Short-tailed, small-eared, prolific RODENT that lives in the Northern Hemisphere. Most voles are greyish-brown, herbivorous ground-dwellers and are small. Length: to 18cm (7in). Family Cricetidae.

Volga Europe's longest river, at 3,750km (2,330mi), in E European Russia. The river rises in the Valdai Hills, then flows E past Rzhev to Kazan, where it turns S. It continues SW to Volgograd, and then SE to enter the Caspian Sea below Astrakhan. Many dams and hydroelectric power stations have been constructed along its course. Navigable for around 3,540km (2,200mi), it carries about two-thirds of Russia's river freight traffic.

volleyball Game in which a ball is volleyed by hand over a net across the centre of a court by two six-a-side teams. The object of the game is to get the ball to touch the ground within the opponents' half of the court, or to oblige an opponent to touch the ball before it goes directly out of court. Volleyball has been in the Olympic Games since 1964.

volt SI unit (symbol V) of electric potential and ELECTROMOTIVE FORCE (EMF). It is the POTENTIAL DIFFERENCE between two points on a conducting wire carrying a current of one ampere when the power dissipated is 1 watt.

Voltaire (1694–1778) (François Marie Arouet) French philosopher, historian, playwright and poet; the outstanding figure of the French Enlightenment. He spent much of his life combating intolerance and injustice. He became a strong opponent of the Roman Catholic Church, and towards the end of his life made his home a refuge for victims of injustice and religious persecution. A prolific writer, Voltaire wrote several tragedies and the philosophical novel *Candide* (1759), his best-known work. He contributed to the *Encyclopédie* of Diderot and outlined his view of morality in *Essay on Morals* (1756).

voltmeter Instrument for measuring the voltage (POTENTIAL DIFFERENCE) between two points in an electrical CIRCUIT. Voltmeters are always connected in parallel with the components whose voltages are being measured. A voltmeter has a high internal resistance compared with the resistance across which it is connected. *See also* AMMETER.

volume Amount of space taken up by a body. Volume is measured in cubic units, such as cm³ (cubic centimetres).

voluntary muscle Muscle that is under conscious control. *See* SKELETAL MUSCLE

Von Braun, Wernher (1912–77) US engineer, b. Germany. In World War 2 he was responsible for building the V-2 rocket. In 1945 he went to the USA, where he developed the Jupiter rocket that took the first US satellite, Explorer 1, into space (1958). Von Braun joined the NATIONAL AERONAUTICS AND SPACE ADMINISTRATION (NASA) in 1960 and developed the Saturn rocket that took astronauts to the Moon.

Vonnegut, Kurt, Jr (1922–) US novelist. He often draws on the conventions of fantasy to satirize the horrors of the 20th century. His books, which regularly involve innovative experimention with time sequences and narrative, include *Player Piano* (1952), *Slaughterhouse-Five* (1969) and *Hocus Pocus* (1991).

voodoo Religious belief of African origin. It is prevalent in parts of Africa, but is best known as the national religion of Haiti. Adherents believe in the reincarnate qualities of Loa, which include deified ancestors, local gods and Roman Catholic saints. Loa possesses believers during dreams or ceremonies, including dancing and hypnotic trances.

Vorster, Balthazar Johannes (1915–83) South African statesman, prime minister (1966–78). Imprisoned during World War 2 as a Nazi sympathizer, he succeeded Hendrik Verwoerd as leader of the Nationalist Party and prime minister. He upheld APARTHEID, although some aspects of strict racial segregation were beginning to break down. He became president for a few months in 1978 before charges of financial corruption forced his resignation (1979).

vortex Eddy or whirlpool observed in FLUID motion. Vortices cannot occur in ideal (nonviscous) fluid motion, but they are important in the study of real fluids.

vorticism British art movement derived from CUBISM and Italian FUTURISM. It was originated in 1913 by Wyndham LEWIS in an attempt to express the spirit of the time in harsh angular forms derived from machinery.

Voyager program SPACE EXPLORATION programme to study JUPITER, SATURN, URANUS and NEPTUNE, using two unmanned craft launched in 1977. They beamed back close-up pictures of Jupiter in 1979. The probes then passed Saturn, and showed the structure of the planet's rings. Voyager II went on to study Uranus in 1986 and Neptune in 1989. Both probes have now left the Solar System.

Vulcan (Volcanus) Roman god of fire and volcanoes, identified with the Greek god Hephaestus. Often invoked to avert fires, he was associated with thunderbolts and the Sun.

vulcanization Chemical process, discovered 1839, of heating SULPHUR or its compounds with natural or synthetic RUBBER in order to improve the rubber's durability and resilience.

Vulgate Oldest surviving version of the complete BIBLE, compiled and translated, mostly from Greek, into Latin by St JEROME from 382. The text was revised several times and was used universally in the Middle Ages. In 1546 it was promoted as the official Latin translation by the Council of TRENT.

vulture Large, keen-sighted, strong-flying bird that feeds on carrion. New World vultures, found throughout the Americas, include the CONDOR, turkey BUZZARD and king vulture; family Cathartidae. Old World vultures, related to eagles, are found in Africa, Europe and Asia, and include the Egyptian vulture and the griffon vulture; family Accipitridae.

Vyatka (formerly Kirov) City and river port on the Vyatka River, W Russia; capital of Kirov region. Founded as Khlynov in 1174, it was annexed by Ivan III in 1489. The city was renamed Vyatka in 1780 and then known as Kirov from 1934 to 1992. It has a 17th-century cathedral. Industries: metal products, agricultural machinery, meat processing, timber, leather, furs. Pop. (1992) 493,000.

W/w is the 23rd letter of the English alphabet and is included in the alphabets of several w European languages. Like f, u, v and y, it was derived from the Semitic letter vaw, meaning hook.

Wagner, Richard (1813–83) German composer. His works consist almost entirely of operas, for which he provided his own libretti. His early operas include *Der fliegende Holländer* (1843) and *Lohengrin* (1850). With *Tristan and Isolde* (1865) and the four-part *The Ring of the Nibelung* (1851–76) the genius of Wagner is fully displayed. His rich, chromatic style gives the music great emotional depth, and the complex web of *leitmotifs* propels the drama. Other operas include *The Mastersingers of Nuremberg* (1868) and *Parsifal* (1882).

wagtail Any of several species of mainly Old World birds that live near streams; it wags its long tail while foraging for insects. Family Motacillidae.

Wailing Wall *See* WESTERN WALL

Waitangi, Treaty of (1840) Pact between Britain and several New Zealand MAORI tribes. The agreement protected and provided rights for Maoris, guaranteeing them possession of certain tracts of land, while permitting Britain formally to annex the islands and purchase other land areas.

Wake Island Largest of three small coral islands, known collectively as Wake Island, enclosing a lagoon in the w Pacific Ocean. It was annexed by the USA (1898) and became a naval base, captured by the Japanese (1941) and recaptured in 1945.

Walcott, Derek (1930–) Caribbean poet and playwright. He has written numerous plays, including *Henri Christophe* (1950), *Drums and Colours* (1961), *O Babylon* (1978) and *Viva Detroit* (1992), but he is perhaps best known as a poet. He was awarded the 1992 Nobel Prize for literature.

Waldemar IV (1320–75) (Waldemar Atterday) King of Denmark (1340–75). He restored the Danish kingdom after a century of disintegration by a mixture of force and diplomacy. In 1367 his enemies, including the HANSEATIC LEAGUE, combined to drive him from the country. He regained the throne in 1371 with the peace of Stralsund (1370).

Waldenses Small Christian sect founded in the 12th century, originally the followers of Peter Waldo of Lyons. The Waldenses renounced private property and led an ascetic life. They repudiated many Roman Catholic doctrines and practices, such as indulgences, PURGATORY and MASS for the dead, and denied the validity of SACRAMENTS administered by unworthy priests. The movement flourished in the 13th century, but persecution extinguished it except in the French and Italian Alps.

Waldheim, Kurt (1918–) Austrian president (1986–92), fourth secretary-general of the United Nations (1972–81). He succeeded U THANT as secretary general, but proved to be a weak appeasor of the major powers. His tenure was tainted by revelations of his Nazi war record.

Wales Constituent member of the UNITED KINGDOM, occupying a broad peninsula in w Great Britain; the capital is CARDIFF. Other major cities include SWANSEA. **Land and climate** In the N lies Wales' highest peak, SNOWDON, at 1,085m (3,560ft). Anglesey lies off the NW coast. The Black Mountains lie in the SE. The border regions and coastal plains are lowlands. The principal rivers are the SEVERN and Dee. On average, Cardiff experiences twice as much annual rainfall as London. **Economy** North Wales is predominantly agricultural, with the world's greatest density of sheep. Dairy farming is also important. The s valleys and coastal plain are Wales' industrial heartland. The late 20th-century decline of its traditional heavy industries of coal and steel has been only partly offset by investment in light industries, such as electronics. Unemployment remains high (1996, 8.3% of the workforce). **History** The Celtic-speaking Welsh stoutly resisted Roman invasion in the first centuries AD. St DAVID introduced Christianity in the 5th century. In the 10th century, political power was centralized. In the 11th century, the English conquered the border counties and established the Welsh Marches. In 1282 Wales was conquered by the English Norman King EDWARD I, and in 1301 Prince Edward (later EDWARD II) became Prince of Wales. In the early 15th century, Owain GLYN DWR led resistance to English rule. The accession of the Welsh TUDOR dynasty to the English throne paved the way for the Act of UNION (1536) of England and Wales. In the late 19th century, Wales became the world's leading producer of coal. Rapid industrialization brought social problems, such as unemployment and poverty. The Welsh nationalist party (PLAID CYMRU) was founded in 1926 and gained its first seat in the House of Commons in 1966. A 1979 referendum voted against devolution. The maintenance of a distinct Welsh culture has been strengthened by the teaching of Welsh in schools and a Welsh-language television channel (1982). A 1997 referendum approved the establishment of a separate Welsh Assembly in Cardiff. Area: 20,761sq km (8,016sq mi). Pop. (1994) 2,913,000.

Wales, Prince of *See* CHARLES (PRINCE OF WALES)

Walesa, Lech (1943–) Polish labour leader and president (1990–95). In August 1980 he organized SOLIDARITY, an independent trade union. Walesa became a symbol of the workers' determination to have a greater voice in government affairs. After the government outlawed Solidarity (1981), he was interned until late 1982. In 1983 he was awarded the Nobel Peace Prize. Following reforms in the Soviet Union, Solidarity was legalized and won free elections in 1989. In 1990 the Communist Party was disbanded and Walesa became president.

wallaby Any of various medium-sized members of the KANGAROO family of MARSUPIAL mammals, found chiefly in Australia. All species are herbivorous. They move fast in a series of leaps, using both strong hind legs simultaneously, balanced by the tail. Length: head and body 45–105cm (18–41in); tail 33–75cm (13–30in). Family Macropodidae.

Wallace, Alfred Russel (1823–1913) British naturalist and evolutionist. Wallace developed a theory of NATURAL SELECTION independently of but at the same time as Charles DARWIN. He wrote *Contributions to the Theory of Natural Selection* (1870) explaining the theory of EVOLUTION.

Wallace, Sir William (1270–1305) Scottish nationalist leader. He led resistance to the English king, EDWARD I. He defeated an English army at Stirling Bridge (1297) and pursued them over the border, where he was defeated at Falkirk in 1298. He was eventually captured (1305) and executed.

Wallenstein, Albrecht Eusebius Wenzel von (1583–1634) German general. During the THIRTY YEARS WAR (1618–48) he was commander of the armies of the Holy Roman Empire, winning a series of victories in the late 1620s but losing the battle of Lützen in 1632. He was later convicted of treason, dismissed and then assassinated.

Waller, Fats (1904–43) US jazz and blues pianist and composer, b. Thomas Waller. His best-known tunes include *Honeysuckle Rose* and *Ain't Misbehavin'*.

wallflower Any of several species of perennial plants of the genera *Cheiranthus* and *Erysimum*, commonly cultivated in Europe and the USA. They are usually sweet-scented. Height: to 90cm (36in). Family Brassicaceae/Cruciferae.

Wallis, Sir Barnes Neville (1887–1979) British aeronautical engineer, best known for his invention of the bouncing bomb during World War 2. After the war he designed the first swing-wing aircraft.

Wallis and Futuna French territory in the S Pacific Ocean, W of Samoa. It is made up of two small groups of volcanic islands, the Wallis Islands and the Hoorn Islands. The principal islands are Uvea, Futuna and Alofi, with Uvea containing 60% of the population and the capital of Mata-Utu. Timber is the main export. The islands' economy is based on subsistence agriculture of copra, cassava, yams, taro and bananas. Pop. (1993 est.) 14,400.

Walloons French-speaking people of S Belgium, as opposed to the Flemish-speaking people of the N. They inhabit chiefly the provinces of Hainaut, Liège, Namur and S Brabant. In the 1990s they numbered about 3,000,000.

walnut DECIDUOUS tree native to North and South America, Europe and Asia. It is grown for timber, ornament and nuts. Height: to 50m (165ft). Family Juglandaceae; genus *Juglans*.

Walpole, Horace, 4th Earl of Orford (1717–97) British writer. His Gothicization of his house near London represents a milestone in architectural taste; his bizarre novel *The Castle of Otranto* (1764) established a parallel fashion for the Gothic in literature.

Walpole, Sir Robert, 1st Earl of Orford (1676–1745) British politician. Although he resigned as chancellor of the exchequer in 1717, after developing the first sinking fund, he restored order after the SOUTH SEA BUBBLE crisis in 1720. He returned as chancellor and first lord of the Treasury in 1721. He was forced to resign in 1742 because of opposition to his foreign policy.

walrus Arctic mammal; it has a massive body and a large head. Its tusks, developed from upper canine teeth, may reach 1m (39in) in length and are used to rake up the seafloor in search of molluscs and to climb on to ice floes. Length: to 3.7m (12ft). Family Odobenidae; species *Odobenus rosmarus*.

Walsingham, Sir Francis (1532–90) English statesman, a leading minister of ELIZABETH I. A zealous Protestant, he set up an intelligence system, based on bribery, to detect Catholic conspiracies. He produced the evidence that led to the conviction and execution of MARY, QUEEN OF SCOTS.

Walter, Hubert (d.1205) English statesman. As bishop of Salisbury, he joined RICHARD I on the Third CRUSADE and later negotiated his ransom. Appointed archbishop of Canterbury and chief justiciar (1193), he was virtual ruler of England in Richard's absence.

Walther von der Vogelweide (1170–1230) German poet, one of the greatest MINNESINGER of the Middle Ages. He produced poems of enduring immediacy, such as the popular *Unter den Linden*.

Walton, Ernest Thomas Sinton (1903–95) British physicist. He shared the 1951 Nobel Prize for physics with John COCKCROFT for the development, in 1929, of the first nuclear particle accelerator. In 1931 they produced the first artificial nuclear reaction without radioactive isotopes, using high-energy protons to bombard lithium nuclei.

Walton, Sir William Turner (1902–83) British composer. His orchestral works include *Portsmouth Point* (1926) and *Scapino* (1941). His most widely known works are the jazz-oriented *Façade* (1923), the oratorio *Belshazzar's Feast* (1931) and the opera *Troilus and Cressida* (1954).

waltz Graceful ballroom dance performed by couples to music in triple time. It came into fashion in the early 19th century, having developed from south German folk dances, such as the *Ländler*.

Wang Mang (33 BC – AD 23) Emperor of China. A usurper, he overthrew the HAN dynasty and proclaimed the Hsin (New) dynasty in AD 8. Opposition from landowners and officials forced him to withdraw his reforms, and his one-emperor dynasty ended with his assassination.

Wankel rotary engine Petrol engine with rotors instead of pistons. German engineer Felix Wankel invented this engine in the 1950s. Each triangular rotor turns inside a close-fitting casing. Gaps between the casing and rotor form three crescent-shaped combustion chambers. Each chamber goes through a sequence of events similar to those in a FOUR-STROKE ENGINE with pistons.

war Military combat between large communities, nations and/or groups of nations. All-out (nuclear) war between major powers using modern weapons would undoubtedly result in what is known as "mutually assured destruction" (aptly abbreviated to MAD). Other forms of war include civil war, in which factions within one state or community struggle for supremacy, and guerrilla war, in which partisan forces harass occupying or government troops by making surprise attacks and immediate strategic withdrawals.

warbler Numerous birds of two families, one in the Old World (Sylviidae) and the other in the New World (Parulidae). Old World warblers include the hedge sparrow and tailorbird. Most New World warblers have brighter plumage.

war crimes Violations of international laws of WAR. The modern conception of war crimes followed the atrocities committed in the era of World War 2, which was followed by the NUREMBERG TRIALS. *See also* GENEVA CONVENTION.

Warhol, Andy (1928–87) US painter, printmaker and film-maker, innovator of POP ART. He achieved fame with his stencil pictures of Campbell's soup cans and his sculptures of Brillo soap pad boxes (1962). In 1965 he gave up art to manage the rock group "The Velvet Underground".

warlords Rulers who hold local authority by force of arms. The term is applied, in particular, to regional military leaders in China in the late 19th and early 20th centuries.

warm-blooded *See* HOMEOTHERMAL

War of 1812 (1812–15) Conflict between the USA and Britain. The main source of friction was British maritime policy during the NAPOLEONIC WARS, in which US merchant ships were intercepted. Difficulties on the border with Canada also contributed. The US invasion of Canada failed, although Britain suffered defeats on Lake Erie and on the W frontier. The end of the Napoleonic Wars (1814) freed more British forces. They imposed a naval blockade and captured Washington, D.C., burning the White House. A US naval victory on Lake Champlain ended the British threat to New York, and New Orleans was saved by the victory of Andrew JACKSON.

warrant Legal document of three main kinds. It may be a writ conferring some title or authority upon a person, a command delivered to an officer to arrest an offender, or a citation or summons.

Warren, Robert Penn (1905–89) US poet, novelist and critic. In his fiction, which includes the Pulitzer Prize-winning novel *All the King's Men* (1946), Warren concentrated on Southern themes and characters. He was awarded the prize twice more, for the poetry collections *Promises* (1957) and *Now and Then* (1978).

Warren Commission US presidential commission that investigated the assassination of President KENNEDY. It was headed by Supreme Court Justice Earl Warren. After taking evidence from 552 witnesses, it concluded that the act had been committed by Lee Harvey OSWALD, acting alone, but denial of a conspiracy was not universally accepted.

Warsaw Capital and largest city of Poland, on the River VISTULA. Its first settlement dates from the 11th century. In 1596 it became Poland's capital and developed into the country's main trading centre. From 1813–1915 it was controlled by Russia, and during World War 1 it was occupied by German troops. The 1939 German invasion and occupation of Warsaw marked the beginning of World War 2. In 1940 the Germans isolated the Jewish ghetto. In January 1945, when the Red Army liberated Warsaw, they found only 200 surviving Jews. After the end of World War 2, the old town was painstakingly reconstructed. Warsaw is a major transport and industrial centre. Industries: steel, cars, cement, machinery. Pop. (1993) 1,653,300.

Warsaw Pact Agreement creating the Warsaw Treaty Organization (1955), a defensive alliance of the Soviet Union and its communist allies in Eastern Europe. It was founded after the admission of West Germany to the NORTH ATLANTIC TREATY ORGANIZATION (NATO), the equivalent organization of Western Europe. Its headquarters were in Moscow and it was effectively controlled by the Soviet Union. Attempts to withdraw by Hungary (1956) and Czechoslovakia (1968) were forcibly denied. It was officially dissolved in 1991 after the collapse of the Soviet Union.

wart Small growth on the outer surface of the skin caused by the human papillomavirus. It is usually painless unless in a pressure area, as with a verruca (a form of wart on the sole of the foot).

wart hog Wild, tusked PIG, native to Africa. It has brownish-black skin with a crest of thin hair along the back. Height: about 76cm (2.5ft) at shoulder; weight: 90kg (200lb). Family Suidae; species *Phacochoerus aethiopicus*.

Warwick, Richard Neville, Earl of (1428–71) English magnate, known as "the Kingmaker", who held the balance of power during the Wars of the ROSES. Breaking with Richard's son, EDWARD IV, Warwick changed sides and restored HENRY VI to the throne in 1470. Edward returned with fresh troops and Warwick was defeated and killed at the Battle of Barnet.

Warwickshire County in central England. The county town is Warwick (1992 pop. 116,299). The land is gently rolling, rising to the Cotswold Hills in the S, and is drained chiefly by the River Avon. Cereals are the principal crops and dairy cattle and sheep are raised. There is light industry near Nuneaton, Rugby and Leamington. STRATFORD UPON AVON draws many tourists. Area: 1,981sq km (765sq mi). Pop. (1991) 484,287.

Washington, Booker T. (Taliaferro) (1856–1915) US black educator. Born a slave, he gained an education after the Civil War and became a teacher. He advocated self-help, education and economic improvement as preliminaries to the achievement of equality for blacks, and believed in compromise with white segregationists. Expressing these views in a famous speech in Atlanta, Georgia, in 1895, he gained considerable influence among whites as a spokesman for black causes.

Washington, George (1732–99) Commander of the colonial forces during the AMERICAN REVOLUTION and first president of the USA (1789–97). He was chosen by the CONTINENTAL CONGRESS as commander in chief. With victory achieved, he resigned (1783), but was recalled from retirement to preside over the CONSTITUTIONAL CONVENTION. In 1789 he was elected, unopposed, as president of the new republic and re-elected in 1793. He declined a third term as president.

Washington State in NW USA, bounded by British Columbia, Canada (N), Idaho (E), Oregon (S) and the Pacific Ocean (W). The state capital is OLYMPIA and the largest city is SEATTLE. In the NW is the Puget Sound, along which lie Washington's major industrial and commercial cities. The CASCADE RANGE crosses the state from N to S. The coastal region W of the range is one of the wettest areas of the USA and has dense forest; the region to the E is treeless plain with low rainfall. An important wheat-producing area, the plateau is dependent on irrigation schemes. The COLUMBIA RIVER is one of the world's best sources of hydroelectricity, and is also used for irrigation. The Spanish discovered the mouth of the Columbia River in 1775, and in 1778 Captain COOK established the area's fur trading links with China. In 1792 George Vancouver mapped the Puget Sound and Robert Gray sailed down the Sound and established the US claim to the region. The claim was strengthened by the LEWIS AND CLARK EXPEDITION and the establishment of an American Fur Company trading post by John Jacob Astor (1811). From 1821–46 the region was administered by the HUDSON'S BAY COMPANY. In 1846 a treaty with the British fixed the boundary with Canada, and in 1847 most of present-day Washington state became Oregon Territory. In 1853 Washington Territory was created. It was admitted to the Union in 1889. Large mineral deposits of magnesium and aluminium ores exist. Industries: timber, aerospace, computer technologies. Area: 172,431sq km (66,581sq mi). Pop. (1992) 5,142,746.

Washington, D.C. Capital of the USA, on the E bank of the POTOMAC River, covering the District of Columbia and extending into the neighbouring states of Maryland and Virginia. The site was chosen as the seat of government in 1790, and the city was planned by the French engineer Pierre Charles L'Enfant. Construction of the WHITE HOUSE began in 1793 and of the Capitol the following year. During the WAR OF 1812 the city was occupied by the British and many public buildings were burned (1814). Despite its role, Washington has severe social problems; many of its large black population live in slum housing. Pop. (1992) 585,221.

Washington, Treaty of (1871) Agreement settling a number of disputes involving the USA, Britain and Canada. The most serious was the question of the Alabama claims, which was submitted to international arbitration. US–Canadian disputes over fisheries and the border were also resolved.

wasp Any insect of the stinging Hymenoptera order that is neither a bee nor an ant. The common wasp (*Vespa vulgaris*) has a yellow body ringed with black. Adults feed on nectar, tree sap and fruit. Length: to 3cm (1.2in). Family Vespidae.

water Odourless, colourless liquid (H_2O) that covers *c.*70% of the Earth's surface and is the most widely used solvent. Essential to life, it makes up *c.*60–70% of the human body. It is a compound of hydrogen and oxygen with the two H–O links of the molecule forming an angle of 105°. This asymmetry results in polar properties and a force of attraction between opposite ends of neighbouring water molecules. These forces maintain the substance as a liquid, in spite of its low molecular weight, and account for its unusual property of having its maximum density at 4°C (39.2°F). Properties: r.d. 1.000; m.p. 0°C (32°F); b.p. 100°C (212°F).

waterbuck (waterbok) Large, gregarious, coarse-haired ANTELOPE, native to Africa S of the Sahara, and the Nile Valley. There are six species. Length: 1.4–2.1m (4.5–7ft); height: 1.1–1.5m (3.6– 4.9ft) at the shoulder. Family Bovidae; genus *Kobus*.

water buffalo (caraboa) Large OX, widely domesticated in much of the tropical world; it is feral in some parts of India. Height: to 1.8m (6ft) at the shoulder. Family Bovidae; species *Bubalus bubalis*.

watercolour Paint made from a pigment ground up with a water-soluble gum, such as gum arabic; also a painting rendered in this medium.

watercress Floating plant found in running or spring waters. The succulent leaves, divided into small, oval leaflets, have a pungent flavour and are used in salads and soups. The clustered flowers are white. Height: 25.4cm (10in). Family Brassicaceae/Cruciferae; species *Nasturtium officinale*.

water cycle See HYDROLOGICAL CYCLE

water flea Any of many species of small, chiefly freshwater branchiopod crustaceans, especially those within the genus *Daphnia*, common worldwide. Order Cladocera. *See also* CRUSTACEA

Waterford County in Munster province, S Republic of Ireland, on the Atlantic Ocean. It is a mountainous region, drained chiefly by the rivers Blackwater and Suir. The raising of beef and dairy cattle and sheep is the chief agricultural activity. Industries: fishing, food processing, tanning, glassware. The county town of Waterford (1991 pop. 40,300) is an important port serving the whole of S Ireland. Area: 1,838sq km (710sq mi). Pop. (1991) 91,624.

waterfowl Aquatic birds, including species of DUCK, GOOSE and SWAN, found throughout most of the world. Large flocks migrate from cool nesting grounds to warm winter homes. All have short bills, short legs, and dense plumage underlaid by down. Undomesticated species are known as wildfowl in Britain. Order Anseriformes.

Watergate scandal (1972–74) US political scandal that led to the resignation of President NIXON. It arose from an attempted burglary of the Democratic Party's national headquarters in the Watergate building, organized by members of Nixon's re-election committee. Evidence of the involvement of the administration provoked investigations by the Senate and the justice department, which ultimately implicated Nixon. He was pardoned by his successor, Gerald FORD, but his closest advisers were prosecuted and convicted.

water lily Any of about 90 species of freshwater plants, widely distributed in temperate and tropical regions. They have leaves that float at the surface, and showy flowers of white, pink, red, blue or yellow. Family Nymphaeaceae; genera *Nymphaea*, *Nuphar*, *Nelumbo* and *Victoria*.

Waterloo, Battle of (1815) Final engagement of the NAPOLEONIC WARS, fought *c*.20km (12mi) from Brussels, Belgium. Allied forces were commanded by the Duke of WELLINGTON against Napoleon's larger French forces. Fighting was even until the Prussians arrived to overwhelm the French flank, whereupon Wellington broke through the centre. The battle ended Napoleon's HUNDRED DAYS.

watermelon Trailing annual VINE, native to tropical Africa and Asia and cultivated in warm areas worldwide. Its edible fruit has a greenish rind, red flesh and many seeds. Family Cucurbitaceae; species *Citrullus lanatus*. *See also* GOURD

water mill Machinery powered by the flow of water past a waterwheel. Water mills were invented about 2,000 years ago to grind grain into flour.

water moccasin (cottonmouth) Venomous, semi-aquatic SNAKE, native to SE USA. It is a pit VIPER, closely related to the COPPERHEAD. It vibrates its tail and holds its white mouth open when threatened. Length: to 1.2m (4ft). Family Viperidae; species *Ancistrodon piscivorus*.

water polo Game devised as an aquatic form of FOOTBALL. It is played by two teams of seven people in a pool. At each end of the pool is a net-enclosed goal defended by one player per team. The game has been an Olympic event since 1900.

water power *See* HYDROELECTRICITY

water table In geology, level below which the rock is saturated. The height of the water table gradually changes, moving up or down depending on the recent rainfall. Water located below the water table is called GROUND WATER.

Watson, James Dewey (1928–) US geneticist, known for his role in the discovery of the molecular structure of deoxyribonucleic acid (DNA). He shared the 1962 Nobel Prize in physiology or medicine with Francis CRICK and Maurice Wilkins. Watson helped to break the GENETIC CODE of the DNA base sequences and found the

ribonucleic acid (RNA) messenger that carries the DNA code to the cell's protein-forming structures.

Watson, John Broadus (1878–1958) US psychologist, founder of BEHAVIOURISM in the USA. His work did much to make psychological research more objective, and his point of view was continued in the work of B. F. SKINNER.

Watson-Watt, Sir Robert Alexander (1892–1973) British physicist. He was a major influence in the rapid development of RADAR in World War 2. In 1941 he helped to establish the US radar system.

Watt, James (1736–1819) Scottish engineer. In 1765 Watt invented the condensing STEAM ENGINE. In 1782 he invented the double-acting engine, in which steam pressure acted alternately on each side of a piston. With Matthew Boulton, Watt coined the term "horsepower". The unit of power is called the WATT in his honour.

watt Unit of power in the SI system of units. A machine consuming one JOULE of energy per second has a power output of one watt. One horse-power corresponds to 746 watts. A watt is also a unit of electrical power, equal to the product of voltage and current.

Watteau, Jean-Antoine (1684–1721) French painter. Watteau's early work was influenced by the Flemish genre painter David Teniers, as seen in his early painting *La Marmotte*. He is best known for his *fêtes galantes*, notably his masterpiece *Departure for the Islands of Cythera* (1717), an early example of ROCOCO.

Watts, George Frederick (1817–1904) British painter and sculptor. He produced complicated, moralistic allegories such as *Hope* (1886). Watts' best-known sculpture is an equestrian statue called *Physical Energy* (1904).

Waugh, Evelyn Arthur St John (1903–66) British novelist. *Vile Bodies* (1930), *A Handful of Dust* (1934) and *Put Out More Flags* (1942) reflect British, upper-class life, while *Brideshead Revisited* (1945) is informed by the Roman Catholicism to which he was converted in 1928.

wave In oceanography, moving disturbance travelling on or through water that does not move the water itself. Wind causes waves by frictional drag. Waves not under pressure from strong winds are called swells. Waves begin to break on shore or "feel bottom" when they reach a depth shallower than half the wave's length. When the water depth is about 1.3 times the wave height, the wave front is so steep that the top falls over and the wave breaks.

wave In physics, carrier of energy from place to place. Waves are caused by disturbances that result in some sort of oscillation. These oscillations then spread out (propagate) as waves. The velocity depends on the type of wave and on the medium. ELECTROMAGNETIC waves, such as light, consist of varying magnetic and electric fields vibrating at right angles to each other and to the direction of motion; they are transverse waves. Sound waves are transmitted by the vibrations of the particles of the medium itself, the vibrations being in the direction of wave motion; they are longitudinal waves. Both types of waves can undergo REFLECTION, REFRACTION and give rise to INTERFERENCE phenomena. A wave is characterized by its WAVELENGTH and FREQUENCY, the VELOCITY of wave motion being the product of wavelength and frequency.

wave amplitude Peak value of a periodically varying quantity. This peak value may be either positive or negative, as the quantity varies either above or below its zero value.

wave dispersion Alteration of the refractive index of a medium with wavelength. It occurs with all electromagnetic waves but is most obvious at visible wavelengths, causing light to be separated into its component colours. Dispersion is seen when a beam of light passes through a refracting medium, such as a glass PRISM, and forms a SPECTRUM. Each colour has a different wavelength, and so the prism bends each colour in the light a different amount. *See also* REFRACTION

wave frequency Number of oscillations or wave cycles produced in 1 second, measured in HERTZ. It can be calculated from the wave VELOCITY divided by WAVELENGTH. By QUANTUM THEORY, the frequency of any ELECTROMAGNETIC RADIATION is proportional to the energy of the component photons.

wavelength Distance between successive points of equal phase in a WAVE. Wavelength is equal to the wave VELOCITY divided by the WAVE FREQUENCY.

wave mechanics Version of QUANTUM MECHANICS developed in 1926 by Erwin SCHRÖDINGER. It explains the behaviour of electrons in terms of their wave properties. Although quickly superseded by a more complex formulation by Paul DIRAC, it is still widely used in calculations.

wax Solid, insoluble substance of low melting point. It is mouldable and water-repellent. Animal and vegetable waxes are simple LIPIDS consisting of esters of fatty acids. Mineral waxes include PARAFFIN wax made from petroleum. Synthetic waxes are of diverse origins and include POLYETHYLENES. Waxes are used in the manufacture of lubricants, polishes, cosmetics and candles and to waterproof leather and coat paper.

waxwing Any of a few species of small, greybrown birds, which have black markings on the head, a small crest, and red or red-and-yellow waxy tips on the secondary wing feathers. They are found in the forests of Eurasia and North America and feed on berries and fruit. Length: to 20cm (8in). Family Bombycillidae; genus *Bombycilla*.

Wayne, John (1907–79) US film actor, b. Marion Michael Morrison. His first major success was in *Stagecoach* (1939). He made many more films, including *She Wore a Yellow Ribbon* (1949), *The Man Who Shot Liberty Valance* (1962), *True Grit* (1969) and *The Shootist* (1976).

weak nuclear force (weak interaction) One of the four FUNDAMENTAL FORCES in physics. It caus-

es radioactive decay. The weak nuclear force can be observed only in the subatomic realm, being of very short range. It is weaker than the ELECTROMAGNETIC FORCE and the STRONG NUCLEAR FORCE (the strongest of the forces) but stronger than GRAVITATION.

weasel Any of several species of small, carnivorous mammals of Eurasia, N Africa, the USA and South America. Most species have small heads, long necks, slender bodies, short legs and long tails. Weasels are fierce predators. Length: 50cm (20in) overall. Family Mustelidae; Genus *Mustela*.

weathering Breakdown and chemical disintegration of rocks and minerals at the Earth's surface. In **physical weathering** in cold, wet climates water seeping into cracks in the rock expands on freezing, so causing the rock to crack further and to crumble. Extreme temperature changes in drier regions, such as deserts, also cause rocks to fragment. **Chemical weathering** can lead to a weakening of the rock structure by altering the minerals of a rock, changing their size, volume and ability to hold shape. Unlike EROSION, weathering does not involve transportation.

weaving Process of making fabric by intertwining two sets of threads. A loom is threaded with a set of warp threads. The weft thread is wound round a shuttle and passed between the warp threads, which are separated according to the desired pattern.

Webb, Beatrice (née Potter) (1858–1943) and **Sidney** (1859–1947) British social historians and politicians. Sidney Webb was one of the founders of the FABIAN SOCIETY. The Webbs founded the London School of Economics (1895) and helped to found the *New Statesman* magazine (1913).

Weber, Carl Maria von (1786–1826) German composer and conductor. He helped to establish a German national style in his operas *Der Freischütz* (1821) and *Euryanthe* (1823). He also composed piano and chamber music, concertos and the popular *Invitation to the Dance* (1819).

Weber, Max (1864–1920) German sociologist. He advanced the concept of "ideal types", which were generalized models of social situations, as a method of analysis. In his work *The Protestant Ethic and the Spirit of Capitalism* (1904–05) he put forward the idea that CALVINISM was influential in the rise of capitalism.

Webern, Anton von (1883–1945) Austrian composer. His *Passacaglia* (1908) was written using late-romantic tonality; soon afterwards, however, he adopted atonality (the *Six Bagatelles*, 1913) and then TWELVE-TONE MUSIC.

Webster, John (1580–1634) English dramatist whose reputation rests upon two great tragedies, *The White Devil* (c.1612) and *The Duchess of Malfi* (1614). Both plays explore the theme of revenge using macabre language.

Wedekind, "Frank" (Benjamin Franklin) (1864–1918) German dramatist whose use of theatre anticipated that of EXPRESSIONISM and influenced BRECHT. His plays include *Spring Awakening* (1906) and *Lulu*, which appeared in two parts: *Earth-Spirit* (1902) and *Pandora's Box* (1905).

wedge In mechanics, an example of the inclined plane. It is used to multiply an applied force while changing its direction of action. For example, if a metal or wooden wedge is driven into a block of wood, a force is exerted by the wedge at right angles to the applied force and greater than it.

Wedgwood, Josiah (1730–95) British potter. He pioneered the large-scale production of pottery at his works near Stoke-on-Trent and became famous for his creamware. He is best known for his jasper ware, which gave expression to the contemporary interest in the revival of classical art.

Weelkes, Thomas (*c*.1575–1623) English madrigal composer and organist. Almost 100 of his madrigals have survived, the finest being sets of five- and six-part madrigals.

weever Any of four species of small fish that commonly bury themselves in sand in European and Mediterranean coastal waters. Poison spines on the dorsal fin and gill covers can inflict a painful sting. Family Trachinidae; genus *Trachinus*.

weevil Any of numerous species of beetles that are pests to crops, especially the numerous snout beetles (time weevils), with long, down-curved beaks for boring into plants. Family Curculionidae, the largest in the animal kingdom.

Wegener, Alfred Lothar (1880–1930) German geologist, meteorologist and Arctic explorer. In *The Origin of Continents and Oceans* (1915) he was the first to use scientific argument in support of a theory of CONTINENTAL DRIFT.

weight Force of attraction on a body due to GRAVITATION. An object's weight is the product of its MASS and the gravitational field strength at that point. Mass remains constant, but weight depends on the object's position on the Earth's surface, decreasing with increasing altitude.

weightlessness Condition experienced by an object when the force due to GRAVITATION is neutralized. Such an object is said to have zero gravity and no weight; it floats and cannot fall. Weightlessness can be experienced in space and during a free fall. The adverse effects on the human body of prolonged weightlessness include decreased circulation of blood, less water retention in tissues and the bloodstream, and loss of muscle tone.

weightlifting Exercise or sport in which weights at the end of a bar are lifted over the head. Competitions are conducted according to weight classes that range from bantamweight to heavyweight. In a weightlifting competition, each participant uses three standard lifts known as two-hand press, clean-and-jerk, and snatch. The competitor who lifts the greatest combined total of weights wins. It has been an Olympic event since 1920.

Weil, Simone (1909–1943) French philosopher and writer. Several mystical experiences drew her to the Roman Catholic Church. During World War

2, she became an activist in the French Resistance. Her works include *Gravity and Grace* (1947) and *Waiting for God* (1951).

Weill, Kurt (1900–50) German composer. He first became known for his satirical opera *Der Protagonist* (1926). His collaboration with BRECHT began with the *Rise and Fall of the City of Mahagonny* (1927). *The Threepenny Opera* (1928) was a modern version of John Gay's *Beggar's Opera*, again with libretto by Brecht.

Weimar City in the state of Thuringia, E central Germany. Founded in 975 and chartered in 1348, the city was capital of the Saxe-Weimar duchy from 1547–1918. It reached its zenith in the 18th century as the continent's literary capital. In 1919 the German National Assembly convened here to establish the WEIMAR REPUBLIC. Pop. (1991) 59,100.

Weimar Republic (1919–33) Popular name for the republic of Germany created after World War 1. It was hampered by economic difficulties. The Weimar constitution was suspended after Adolf HITLER became chancellor and the republic was superseded by the THIRD REICH.

Weinberg, Steven (1933–) US physicist who in 1967, independently of Abdus Salam, proposed a theory that unifies the ELECTROMAGNETIC and WEAK NUCLEAR FORCES between subatomic particles – now known as the electroweak force. In 1979 he shared the Nobel Prize in physics with Sheldon Glashow, who had earlier proposed a similar theory. *See also* GRAND UNIFIED THEORY

Weiss, Peter (1916–82) Swedish dramatist, b. Germany. His reputation was established with *The Persecution and Assassination of Jean-Paul Marat as Performed by the Inmates of the Asylum of Charenton Under the Direction of the Marquis de Sade* (1964), more commonly known as *Marat/Sade*. Other plays include *The Investigation* (1965) and *Trotsky in Exile* (1970).

Weizmann, Chaim (1874–1952) Zionist leader, first president of Israel (1948–52). He was born in Russia and became a naturalized British subject in 1910. He played the chief part in securing the BALFOUR DECLARATION (1917). He was president of the World Zionist Organization (1920–31, 1935–46), provisional president of Israel (1948) and was elected president from 1949.

welding Technique for joining metal parts, usually by controlled melting. In fusion welding, the parts to be joined are heated together until the metal starts to melt. On cooling, the molten metal solidifies to form a permanent bond between the parts. In arc welding, an electric arc heats the work and filler metal. In oxyacetylene welding, the heat is provided by burning ethyne gas in oxygen. In resistance or spot welding, the heat is generated by passing an electric current through the parts. In brazing and soldering, the temperature used is sufficient to melt filler metal, but not the parts that it joins.

welfare state Description of a state that takes responsibility for the health and subsistence of its citizens. Limited forms of welfare were introduced by Western governments, such as that of BISMARCK in Germany, in the late 19th century. Comprehensive policies covering the whole of society were introduced after World War 2, particularly in Scandinavian countries and the UK, an influential example being the NATIONAL HEALTH SERVICE (NHS). *See also* SOCIAL SECURITY

well Shaft sunk vertically in the Earth's CRUST through which water, oil, natural gas, brine, sulphur or other mineral substances can be extracted. Artesian wells are sunk into water-bearing rock strata, the AQUIFERS, from which water rises under pressure in the wells to the surface.

Welles, (George) Orson (1915–85) US actor and director. His first film, *Citizen Kane* (1940), earned him an Academy Award. After further successes with *The Third Man* (1949) and *Touch of Evil* (1958), Welles went into self-imposed exile from the USA, directing European productions, including *The Trial* (1963), *Chimes at Midnight* (1966) and *The Immortal Story* (1968).

Wellington, Arthur Wellesley, Duke of (1769–1852) British general and politician, prime minister (1828–30). He commanded allied forces in the PENINSULAR WAR (1808–14) against Napoleon I. He represented Britain at the Congress of VIENNA (1814–15). Together with the Prussian General von Blücher, he defeated Napoleon at the Battle of WATERLOO in 1815.

Wellington Capital of New Zealand, in the extreme s of North Island, on Port Nicholson, an inlet of Cook Strait. First visited by Europeans in 1826, it was founded in 1840. In 1865 it replaced Auckland as capital. Wellington's excellent harbour furthered its development as a transport and trading centre. Pop. (1994) 329,000.

Wells, H.G. (Herbert George) (1866–1946) British author. His reputation was established with his science fiction novels *The Time Machine* (1895), *The Invisible Man* (1897) and *The War of the Worlds* (1898). Later novels include *Love and Mr Lewisham* (1900), *Kipps* (1905), *Tono-Bungay* (1909) and *The History of Mr Polly* (1910).

Welsh (*Cymraeg*) Language of Wales. It is spoken natively by less than 19 per cent of the Welsh population, chiefly in the rural N and W. It belongs to the Brittonic sub-branch of the Celtic family of INDO-EUROPEAN LANGUAGES, and is closely related to BRETON and CORNISH. It survives more strongly than most other CELTIC LANGUAGES.

Welsh National Party *See* PLAID CYMRU

Wembley Complex of sports stadiums in Wembley, NW London. The outdoor Empire Stadium, with its twin towers, built for the 1924 Empire Exhibition, is used for the finals of the FA Cup, Football League Cup and Rugby League Cup, as well as England's home international football matches. In the nearby Empire Pool, a covered arena, ice shows and pop concerts share the facilities with other sports. In 1996 Wembley was granted funding for a complete rebuild to make it the official National Sports Stadium.

Wenceslas, Saint (907–29) Prince of Bohemia and patron saint of the Czechs. In *c*.925 he overthrew his mother who, as regent, persecuted Christians. He continued the Christianization of the country, which, together with his submission to the Germans, aroused opposition. He was killed by his brother and successor, Boleslav I.

Wenceslaus (1361–1419) King of the Germans (1378–1400) and king of Bohemia (1378–1419) as Wenceslaus IV. He succeeded his father, the Emperor CHARLES IV, but was never crowned emperor and was deposed in 1400.

Wentworth, William Charles (1793–1872) Australian journalist and politician. In 1824 he founded the *Australian* newspaper, which he used to promote the cause of self-government for the Australian colonies. His activism was the most important factor leading to the granting of self-government by the British Parliament in 1842.

werewolf In folklore, a person who metamorphoses into a wolf at night but reverts to human form by day. Some werewolves can change form at will; in others the change occurs involuntarily, under the influence of a full moon.

Werner, Alfred (1866–1919) Swiss chemist He was awarded the 1913 Nobel Prize in chemistry for his coordination theory of VALENCE in which he correctly suggested that metals have coordinate bonds which make ISOMERS possible in inorganic compounds.

Wesker, Arnold (1932–) British playwright and director. His plays have socialist themes, and his reputation was established with the trilogy *Chicken Soup with Barley* (1958), *Roots* (1959) and *I'm Talking about Jerusalem* (1960). Other works include *Chips with Everything* (1962), *The Friends* (1970), *The Old Ones* (1972) and *Love Letters on Blue Paper* (1978).

Wesley, Charles (1707–88) English evangelist and hymn-writer, brother of John WESLEY. He was ordained in 1735 and in 1738 he underwent a evangelical conversion. He wrote nearly 6,000 hymns, including "Hark! the herald angels sing" and "Love divine, all loves excelling".

Wesley, John (1703–91) British theologian and evangelist who founded METHODISM. With his brother Charles WESLEY, he founded the Holy Club at Oxford in 1729. He underwent a personal, religious experience during a Moravian meeting in 1738 and this laid the foundation upon which he built the Methodist movement.

Wessex Anglo-Saxon kingdom established in Hampshire, sw England. Traditionally founded by Cerdic (r.519–534), by the beginning of the 9th century it had extended its territory to include much of s England. Egbert became overlord of all England, but his successors relinquished much of their kingdom to the invading Danes. ALFRED THE GREAT managed to resist further Danish encroachment and Wessex was the only English kingdom to escape Danish conquest.

West, Benjamin (1738–1820) US painter. After studying in Italy for three years, he settled in Britain (1763), where he became historical painter to George III and a leader of NEO-CLASSICISM. Two of his best-known paintings are *Death of Wolfe* (1771) and *Penn's Treaty with the Indians* (1772).

West, Mae (1893–1980) US actress and film star. Her first film was *Night After Night* (1932) and others include *She Done Him Wrong* (1933) and *My Little Chickadee* (1940). She is known for the overt sexuality and spicy wit of her characterizations.

West, Dame Rebecca (1892–1983) British novelist and critic, b. Cicily Isabel Fairfield. She is best known for her first novel, *The Return of the Soldier* (1918), the story of a shell-shock victim. Her political works include *The Meaning of Treason* (1949) and *A Train of Powder* (1955). She also wrote psychological novels such as *Birds Fall Down* (1966).

West Bank Region W of the River JORDAN and NW of the Dead Sea. Under the United Nations plan for the partition of Palestine (1947), it was designated an Arab district. It was administered by Jordan after the first ARAB-ISRAELI WAR (1948) but captured by Israel in the SIX DAY WAR of 1967. In 1988 Jordan surrendered its claim to the Israeli-occupied West Bank to the PALESTINE LIBERATION ORGANIZATION (PLO) led by ARAFAT. Under the agreement of 1994 between Arafat and the Israeli government of RABIN, limited autonomy in the West Bank was conceded to the newly formed Palestinian National Authority (PNA). Difficulties created by the growth of Israeli settlements, security disputes and the accession (1996) of a less conciliatory government in Israel threatened to disrupt progress towards total Israeli withdrawal.

Western Type of popular fiction and film, native to the USA, featuring "cowboys" and "Indians" in a Wild West setting. It first appeared in the form of short stories and novels in the "pulp" magazines of the late 19th century.

Western Australia State in Australia, bordered by the Timor Sea (N), the Indian Ocean (W and S), South Australia state and the Northern Territory (E). The capital is PERTH; other significant cities are Mandurah, Kalgoorlie, Bunbury and Fremantle, Perth's ocean port. Settlement began in 1826, when a penal colony was founded. The first free settlement was in 1829. By far the country's largest state, it became a state of the Commonwealth of Australia in 1901. The climate is mainly tropical or sub-tropical and over 90% of the land is desert or semi-desert. Only the SW, which enjoys a temperate climate, is permanently settled. The raising of sheep and cattle is the principal agricultural activity. Western Australia is the country's major gold-producing state, and there is also mining for iron ore, coal, nickel, uranium, bauxite, phosphates, mineral sands, oil and natural gas. Industry is still expanding, and wine became a

major earner during the 1980s. Area: 2,525,500sq km (975,095sq mi). Pop. (1991) 1,586,393.

Western Cape Province in SW South Africa, bounded by the Indian Ocean (S) and Atlantic Ocean (W). The capital is CAPE TOWN. Other major towns include Simonstown and Stellenbosch. Formerly part of CAPE PROVINCE, Western Cape was founded in 1994. The main economic activity is agriculture, with fruit and tobacco growing, dairy farming and sheep rearing. There is also an important fishing industry, and an offshore gas field is exploited in Mossel Bay. Industries: chemicals, machinery, metal goods, textiles. Area: 129,390sq km (50,500sq mi). Pop. (1993) 3,620,200.

Western Isles Administrative area of Scotland (consisting of the Outer HEBRIDES) and a general term for all the Hebridean islands. The largest island is Lewis. Stornoway (1981 pop. 8,640) is the administrative capital. Area: 2,898sq km (1,120sq mi). Pop. (1994) 29,600.

Western Sahara (formerly Spanish Sahara) Desert territory on the Atlantic coast of NW Africa, bordering with Morocco (N), Algeria (NE) and Mauritania (E and S); the capital is El Aaiún. The territory comprises two districts; Saguia el Hamra in the N and Río de Oro in the S. The population is composed of Arabs, BERBERS and pastoral NOMADS, most of whom are SUNNI Muslims, and agriculture is dominated by livestock-rearing. The area remained unexploited by Europeans until the 19th century, and even then Spain controlled only the coastal area. In 1957 a nationalist movement temporarily overthrew the Spanish. In 1973 *Frente Polisario* (the Polisario Front) began a guerrilla war, eventually forcing Spanish withdrawal in 1976, and within a month Morocco and Mauritania had partitioned the country. Polisario (backed by Algeria) continued to fight for independence. In 1979 Mauritania withdrew and Morocco assumed full control. In 1982, as the Saharawi Republic, it was granted membership of the Organization of African Unity (OAU). Fragile cease-fires were agreed in 1988 and 1991. A promised referendum failed to materialize and *c.*200,000 Saharawis continue to live in refugee camps. Talks between Moroccan and Western Saharan government delegations took place in 1997. Area: 266,769sq km (102,680sq mi). Pop. (1993 est.) 214,000.

Western Samoa (Samoa) Independent island republic in the S Pacific Ocean, encompassing the W half of the SAMOA island chain. It comprises two large islands of Savai'i and Upolu, the smaller islands of Manono and Apolima, and several uninhabited islets. The capital, Apia (on Upolu), has 66% of the total population. The cradle of Polynesian culture, the islands became a German protectorate under the terms of an 1899 treaty, but in 1914 New Zealand seized them and they were administered by New Zealand from 1920–61. In 1962, Western Samoa became an independent state within the Commonwealth. Under a friendship treaty, New Zealand handles relations with governments and nations outside the Pacific zone. The Polynesian population is employed mainly in subsistence agriculture, and the chief exports are coconut oil, taro and copra. Area: 2,840sq km (1,097sq mi). Pop. (1991) 161,298.

Western Wall (Wailing Wall) Place in JERUSALEM sacred to all Jews. It is a remnant of a wall of the great TEMPLE destroyed by the Romans in AD 70. It is the focus of many pilgrimages.

West Glamorgan County in s Wales on the Bristol Channel; the administrative centre is SWANSEA. Now divided into four districts (Lliw Valley, Neath, Port Talbot and Swansea), the area has been renowned for its metallurgical industry since the 18th century. In the 20th century, anthracite mining and oil refining became important industries. Tourists are attracted by the Gower Peninsula. Area: 820sq km (317sq mi). Pop. (1991) 361,428.

West Indies Chain of islands encircling the Caribbean Sea and separating it from the Atlantic Ocean. They extend from Florida to Venezuela. Geographically they are divided into three main groups: the BAHAMAS, and the Greater and Lesser ANTILLES. Most islands are now independent, but were formerly British, Spanish, French or Dutch possessions. *See* individual country articles

Westmeath County in Leinster province, N central Republic of Ireland, bounded by the counties of Meath, Cavan, Roscommon and Offaly. It is mainly low-lying, with many lakes or loughs, and is drained by the rivers SHANNON, Inny and Brosna. The main economic activity is cattle raising, and the county town is Mullingar. Area 1,763sq km (681sq mi). Pop. (1991) 61,880.

West Midlands Metropolitan county in central England. It is divided into seven council districts: BIRMINGHAM (the administrative centre), COVENTRY, Dudley, Sandwell, Solihull, Walsall and Wolverhampton. Area: 899sq km (347sq mi). Pop. (1991) 2,551,671.

Westminster, City of Part of the LONDON borough of Westminster since 1965. Westminster was the site of a monastery from 785, and is where EDWARD THE CONFESSOR built WESTMINSTER ABBEY. Pop. (1991) 174,718.

Westminster, Statutes of English acts of the reign of EDWARD I. The first (1275) and second (1285) statutes enshrined Edward's extensive overhaul of medieval English law. A further statute of 1290 is sometimes called the third statute of Westminster. The Statute of Westminster of 1931 granted autonomy to the dominions in the British empire.

Westminster Abbey Church in London where most English monarchs have been crowned, and many buried, since WILLIAM THE CONQUEROR. The first church was built by EDWARD THE CONFESSOR in 1050. HENRY III began work on the present structure in 1245. Various additions were made later.

Westphalia Historic region of W Germany between the rivers Rhine and Weser. From 1180 it

was a duchy under the archbishops of Cologne. Briefly a kingdom during the NAPOLEONIC WARS, it became a province of Prussia in 1816.

Westphalia, Peace of (1648) Series of treaties among the states involved in the THIRTY YEARS WAR. Peace negotiations began in 1642 in cities of Westphalia, leading to the final settlement. In Germany, the peace established the virtual autonomy of the German states. The peace also established the ascendancy of France, the power of Sweden in N Europe, and the decline of Spain.

West Sussex Non-metropolitan county in SE England. It is divided into seven districts: Chichester (the county town), Adur, Arun, Crawley, Horsham, Mid-Sussex and Worthing. Area: 2,016sq km (778sq mi). Pop. (1991) 702,290.

West Virginia State in the Appalachian Mountain region, E central USA. The capital is Charleston. Settlers from Virginia crossed the Appalachian and Allegheny Mountains in the 1700s, settling the Ohio Valley. The region was then part of Virginia, but political and economic disagreements arose between the new settlements and those in the E. When Virginia seceded from the Union in May 1861 there was opposition in the W, and it was admitted to the Union as West Virginia in 1863. Hay, tobacco, maize and apples are the principal crops. West Virginia has rich mineral deposits and is the leading US producer of bituminous coal. Some 65% of the land is forested, much of it with valuable hardwoods. Industries: glass, chemicals, steel, machinery, tourism. Area 62,629sq km (24,181sq mi). Pop. (1992) 1,808,860.

West Yorkshire Metropolitan county in N central England. It is divided into five districts: BRADFORD, Calderdale, Kirklees, LEEDS and Wakefield (the county town). Area: 2,036sq km (786sq mi). Pop. (1991) 2,013,693.

Wexford County in Leinster province, SE Republic of Ireland. The land is mostly low-lying but rises to the Blackstairs Mountains in the w. The chief river is the Slaney. Wexford is primarily an agricultural county; wheat is the chief crop, and cattle raising is important. The county town is Wexford (1991 pop. 9,500), a fishing port at the mouth of the Slaney. Area 2,351sq km (908sq mi). Pop. (1991) 102,069.

Weyden, Rogier van der (1400–64) Netherlandish painter. In 1436 he became official painter to the city of Brussels. His finest works include *Deposition* (before 1443).

whale Any of several species of large aquatic mammals; it has a fish-like body with paddle-like flippers, and a tail flattened horizontally into flukes for locomotion. It spends its whole life in water. Two main groups exist: toothed whales and baleen whales. Toothed whales (Odontoceti) have simple teeth and feed primarily on fish and squid. They include the bottle-nosed whale, SPERM WHALE and BELUGA. Baleen whales (Mysticeti), including the right whale, BLUE WHALE and California grey whale, have no teeth but carry comb-like plates of

673

horny material (baleen or whalebone) in the roof of the mouth. These form a sieve, through which the whales strain krill on which they feed. Order Cetacea. The order also includes DOLPHINS and PORPOISES. *See also* WHALING

whale shark Largest species of shark; it lives throughout the world in tropical waters. Brownish to dark grey with white or yellow spots and stripes, this docile, egg-laying fish often travels near the surface. Length: 9m (30ft). Family Rhincodontidae; species *Rhincodon typus*.

whaling Industry involved in pursuing and catching whales for their oil and flesh. The modern whaling era began in the 1850s with the development of harpoons with explosive heads. Since that time most larger whale species have been hunted to near-extinction. In 1986 the International Whaling Commission (IWC) agreed a moratorium on commercial whaling. Whaling for "scientific purposes", by Japan, Iceland and Norway, continued.

Wharton, Edith Newbold (1862–1937) US novelist. She is best known for *Ethan Frome* (1911), a grim portrait of New England farm life, and her polished anatomies of New York society, *The House of Mirth* (1905) and *The Age of Innocence* (1920), for which she became the first woman to be awarded a Pulitzer Prize.

wheat CEREAL grass originating in the Middle East. Cultivated there since 7000 BC, it is now grown worldwide. It is used for BREAD, PASTA, cake and pastry flour. Wheat is also used in the preparation of MALT, dextrose and ALCOHOL. Family Poaceae/Gramineae.

Wheatstone, Sir Charles (1802–75) British physicist and inventor. In 1843, with William Cooke, he improved the Wheatstone bridge, a device for measuring electrical resistance. In 1837 they patented an electric TELEGRAPH. Wheatstone also invented the harmonica and concertina.

wheel Circular structure that revolves around a central axis. Before the wheel was invented, heavy loads were sometimes moved by rolling them on logs or on rounded stones. More than 5,000 years ago, sections of tree trunks were cut to form the first wheels for carts. Spoked wheels were introduced several hundred years later.

wheel and axle Machine based on the principle that a small force applied to the rim of a wheel will exert a larger force on an object attached to the axle. The MECHANICAL ADVANTAGE, or force ratio, is the ratio of the radius of the wheel to that of the axle.

whelk Edible marine GASTROPOD distributed worldwide on seashores. It has a coiled shell, with a smooth rim and a notch at the end. Family Buccinidae. Length: 13–18cm (5–7in).

Whig Party Semi-formal parliamentary grouping in the UK from the late 17th to the mid-19th century. The word Whig was used by the TORY supporters of JAMES II for politicians who wished to exclude the Duke of York from the throne. The Whig Party thus became those people who promot-ed the GLORIOUS REVOLUTION of 1688 and applauded the Hanoverian succession of 1714. Whiggism became the party of religious toleration, parliamentary reform and opposition to slavery. From the appointment of PITT as prime minister in 1783 until 1830, the Whigs remained in opposition (with one brief exception). They returned to office under Lord GREY, passing the Great Reform Act of 1832. By the mid-19th century they had come to be replaced by, or known as, the Liberal Party.

whinchat Small Eurasian THRUSH that commonly inhabits grassy coastal areas in England. It has a brown, mottled back with a white rump and distinctive red breast. The dark head is clearly marked by a white eye-stripe. Length: to 13cm (5in). Species *Saxicola rubetra*.

whip UK government officer whose duty is to see that government supporters attend debates and vote in divisions. It is also the name for the notices that they send to members of Parliament. There are also opposition whips.

whippet Sporting dog that was originally bred in England for racing and hare coursing. It is capable of running at speeds of 56km/h (35mph). Height: to 56cm (22in) at the shoulder; weight: to 11kg (24lb).

whippoorwill *See* NIGHTJAR

whirligig beetle Medium-sized, dark-coloured water beetle, often seen resting or gyrating on the surface of a still pool. They prey on small insects. Family Gyrinidae.

whirling dervish *See* DERVISH

whirlpool Circular motion of a fluid. Whirlpools in rivers occur in regions where waterfalls or sharp breaks in topographic continuity make steady flow impossible. *See also* VORTEX

whisky (Irish or US whiskey) Alcoholic spirit made by distilling fermented cereal grains. Scotch whisky and Irish whiskey are distilled from barley that has been allowed to sprout, then roasted, and finally "mashed" and distilled. After distillation refined whisky spirit is 70–85% alcohol by volume; all whiskies are therefore heavily diluted.

whist Card game for four people, playing as two pairs of partners. The aim is to accumulate "tricks" – sets of cards, one from each player, in which the player of the highest-value card "takes the trick". The object of ordinary whist is to amass more tricks than any other player.

Whistler, James Abbott McNeill (1834–1903) US painter and etcher who lived mainly in England. His pictures, such as *Nocturne in Black and Gold* (1877), are characterized by serenity. He was an accomplished and prolific etcher, and produced some 400 plates.

Whitby Coastal town in N Yorkshire, England, at the mouth of the River Esk. St Hilda founded an abbey here in 657, which was destroyed by the Danes in the 9th century. The abbey, rebuilt in the 13th century, today lies in ruin. An important medieval port and former whaling town, Whitby has historic links with Captain COOK, who had his ship *Endeavour* built in Whitby shipyard. Pop. (1981) 13,380.

White, Patrick Victor Martin Sale (1912–90) Australian novelist, b. Britain. His novels, concerned with the nature of the Australian experience, include *The Tree of Man* (1955), *Riders in the Chariot* (1961), *The Vivisector* (1970), *The Eye of the Storm* (1973), *A Fringe of Leaves* (1976) and *The Twyborn Affair* (1979). In 1973 he became the first Australian to win a Nobel Prize for literature.

White, T.H. (Terence Hanbury) (1906–64) British author. His autobiographical *England Have My Bones* attracted notice in 1936, but he is best known for his Arthurian tetralogy, *The Once and Future King*, collectively published in 1958.

white ant *See* TERMITE

whitebait Young of several types of European HERRING. Length: to 5cm (2in). The name is also given to a tropical marine fish found in Australian waters. This fish, *Galaxias attenuatus*, is elongated with its dorsal fin set far back. Family Galaxiidae. Length: to 10cm (5in).

white blood cell *See* LEUCOCYTE

white dwarf star High-density type of star about the size of the Earth, but with a mass about that of the Sun. White dwarfs are of low luminosity and gradually cool down to become cold, dark objects.

whitefish (cisco, lake herring) Any of several species of freshwater food fish that live, often in deep waters, in Eurasia and the USA. It is silvery, with large scales and a small mouth. Length: to 150cm (59in); weight: to 29kg (63lb). Family Salmonidae.

White Friars *See* CARMELITES

Whitehead, Alfred North (1861–1947) British philosopher and mathematician. In his "philosophy of organism" he attempted a synthesis of modern science and metaphysics. The system is presented in his *Process and Reality* (1929). His three-volume *Principia Mathematica* (1910–13), written in collaboration with Bertrand RUSSELL, proved an enduring influence on contemporary philosophy.

White House Official residence of the US president, in WASHINGTON, D.C. It was designed in the neo-classical style by James Hoban in 1792 and completed in 1800. After being burned down during the British invasion in 1814, it was rebuilt and the porticoes were added in the 1820s.

white shark (great white shark) Aggressive SHARK found throughout the world in tropical and subtropical waters. It has a heavy, solid body, a crescent-shaped tail and saw-edged triangular teeth; it is grey, blue or brown with a white belly. Length: to 11m (36ft); weight: to 2,180kg (7,000lb). Family Isuridae; species *Carcharodon carcharias*.

whitethroat Small bird of the Old World WARBLER family (Sylviidae). It breeds in undergrowth in W Eurasia and NW Africa and winters in Africa and India. It has drab brown plumage with red-brown wing patches, a long white-edged tail and a white throat. Length:13cm (5in). Genus *Sylvia*.

white whale *See* BELUGA

whiting Several unrelated food fish. The European whiting (*Merlangus merlangus*) is a haddock-like fish of the COD family, Gadidae. It is found primarily in the North Sea, where it feeds on invertebrates and small fish. It is silver with distinctive black markings at the base of the pectoral fin. Length: to 70cm (28in). Other fish commonly called whitings include the kingfish (*Menticirrhus saxatilis*) and the freshwater WHITEFISH (*Coregonus clupeaformis*).

Whitman, Walt (Walter) (1819–92) US poet and essayist. His collection of poems *Leaves of Grass* (1855) is now considered a classic of US literature. *Drum Taps* (1865), which draws on his experience of medical service in the American Civil War, and *Sequel to Drum-taps* (1865), which includes his famous elegies to Abraham Lincoln, "When Lilacs Last in the Dooryard Bloom'd" and "O Captain! My Captain!", were both incorporated into the much-expanded 1867 edition of *Leaves of Grass*.

Whitney, Eli (1765–1825) US inventor and manufacturer. He invented the COTTON GIN (1793), which revolutionized cotton picking in the South and turned cotton into a profitable export. After 1798 he manufactured muskets at a factory in New Haven, Connecticut, which was one of the first to use mass-production methods.

Whitney, Mount Highest peak in the USA (excluding Alaska), at 4,418m (14,495ft). Situated on the E edge of Sequoia National Park, it is part of the Sierra Nevada range in E California.

Whitsun *See* PENTECOST

Whittington, Dick (Richard) (1358–1423) English merchant. The son of a knight, he became wealthy dealing in fine cloths and was lord mayor of London on several occasions (1397–1420). He made loans to Henry IV and Henry V and endowed many charitable institutions. He is, however, best known as the subject of a legend about a poor boy who makes his fortune with the aid of his cat.

whooping cough (pertussis). Acute, highly contagious childhood respiratory disease. It is caused by the bacterium *Bordetella pertussis* and is marked by spasms of coughing, followed by a long-drawn intake of air, or "whoop".

Whorf, Benjamin Lee (1897–1941) US structural linguist. He formed the Whorf hypothesis (also called the Sapir-Whorf hypothesis), which states that "the structure of language influences thought processes and our perception of the world around us".

whortleberry *See* BILBERRY

Wicklow County in Leinster province, E Republic of Ireland. Wicklow is the county town. The terrain is dominated by the Wicklow Mountains, but there are fertile lowland areas. The Liffey, Slaney and Avoca are the chief rivers. Sheep and cattle are reared and cereals grown. Low-grade copper ores

675

are mined and the scenery attracts many tourists. Area 2,025sq km (782sq mi). Pop. (1991) 97,265.

widgeon River duck with mainly brownish plumage. It feeds on the surface of the water and engages in complex courtship displays. Species include the North American *Mareca americana* and European *Mareca penelope*.

Wieland, Christoph Martin (1733–1813) German novelist and poet. His works include prose translations of 22 of Shakespeare's plays – the first in German – and the novels *Agathon* (1766–67), *Peregrinus Proteus* (1791) and *Aristipp* (1800–01). He also wrote the verse epic *Oberon* (1780).

Wieland, Heinrich Otto (1877–1957) German chemist who was awarded the 1927 Nobel Prize for chemistry for his research into BILE acids. He showed them to have a STEROID skeleton and thus found that they were structurally related to CHO-LESTEROL. He also did research into oxidation reactions occurring in living tissues and discovered that they involved the removal of hydrogen, not the addition of oxygen.

Wiener, Norbert (1894–1964) US mathematician and originator of CYBERNETICS. He contributed to the study and development of the COMPUTER and to the understanding of feedback systems that control the behaviour of humans and machines.

Wiesbaden City on the River Rhine at the foot of the Taunus Mountains, W central Germany; the capital of Hessen lande. Founded in the 3rd century BC and later a Roman spa town, the city is still famous for its mineral springs. Industries: metal goods, chemicals, cement, plastics, tourism, publishing. Pop. (1993) 269,600.

Wiesel, Elie (1928–) Novelist, b. Romania. After surviving Nazi concentration camps during World War 2, he lived in France and the USA, becoming a US citizen in 1963. His first novel was written in Yiddish and translated as *Night* (1958). Later work includes *The Town Beyond the Wall* (1962), *A Beggar in Jerusalem* (1968), *The Fifth Son* (1983) and *The Forgotten* (1989). He won the Nobel Peace Prize in 1986.

Wight, Isle of Island and non-metropolitan county off the S coast of England, separated from the mainland (Hampshire) by the Solent. Newport is the county town. The island's mild climate and attractive coastal scenery make it a popular tourist destination. Cowes is a famous yachting centre. Area: 318sq km (147sqmi). Pop. (1991) 124,577.

Wigner, Eugene Paul (1902–95) US physicist, b. Hungary. He worked during World War 2 on the MANHATTAN PROJECT. Wigner was the first physicist to apply group theory to QUANTUM MECHANICS. With this technique, he discovered the law of conservation of parity. For his work on the structure of the atomic nucleus, Wigner shared the 1963 Nobel Prize for physics with Hans Jensen and Maria Goeppert-Mayer.

Wilberforce, William (1759–1833) British social reformer, leader of the campaign in Britain to end the slave trade. His impassioned speeches helped to effect the legal abolition of the trade in 1807.

wild boar Tusked, cloven-hoofed mammal of the PIG family that lives wild in forested areas of Eurasia and Africa. Length: to 1.8m (6ft); weight: to 200kg (450lb). Family Suidae; species *Sus scrofa.*

Wilde, Oscar (1854–1900) (Oscar Fingal O'Flahertie Wills) Irish dramatist, poet, prose writer and wit. He wrote one novel, *The Picture of Dorian Grey* (1891), but most characteristic of his gift for dramatizing serious issues with epigrammatic wit are his plays, including *Lady Windermere's Fan* (1892), *A Woman of No Importance* (1893), *An Ideal Husband* (1895) and his masterpiece *The Importance of Being Earnest* (1895). He was convicted of homosexual practices in 1895 and sentenced to two years' hard labour. While in prison he wrote *The Ballad of Reading Gaol* (1898).

wildebeest *See* GNU

Wilder, Billy (1906–) US film director and screenwriter, b. Germany. His creative partnership with Charles Brackett began with comedy scripts, such as *Ninotchka* (1939). Wilder won Academy Awards for best director, best picture and shared the best screenplay prize with Brackett for *The Lost Weekend* (1945). Wilder's solo career proved just as successful with films such as *The Seven Year Itch* (1955) and *Some Like it Hot* (1959). Wilder won further Academy Awards for best picture and best director for *The Apartment* (1960).

Wilder, Thornton Niven (1897–1975) US novelist and playwright. He received the Pulitzer Prize for his novel *The Bridge of San Luis Rey* (1927). He is perhaps best known for his plays, which include *Our Town* (1938) and *The Skin of Our Teeth* (1942), for which he also won Pulitzer Prizes.

Wilhelmina (1880–1962) Queen of the Netherlands (1890–1948). She helped to keep the country neutral in World War 1 and often intervened in political affairs. During World War 2, she led the government in exile in England and became a symbol of Dutch independence.

Wilkes, John (1727–97) British radical politician and journalist. He was expelled from Parliament for his savage criticism of GEORGE III and his government in the political journal *North Briton* (1763). His prosecution under a general warrant was condemned in the courts, a landmark in civil liberty. The refusal of Parliament to readmit him after he had been elected three times encouraged the movement towards parliamentary reform.

Wilkinson, Sir Geoffrey (1921–) British chemist. His work on organometallic sandwich compounds earned him a Nobel Prize for chemistry in 1973, which he shared with Ernst Fischer, who worked independently on the same subject.

will In law, a clear expression of intent by a person (the testator) concerning the disposal of his or her effects after death. The testator must be of sound mind and legal age, and the will must be witnessed by two competent people who are not beneficiaries. It may be altered or revoked by the testator at any time, with due legal process.

William I (1797–1888) King of Prussia (1861–88) and emperor of Germany (1871–88). He was regent for his brother, Frederick William IV, from 1858. His suppression of revolution in 1848–49 earned him his reputation as a reactionary, but as king he displayed sensible pragmatism and followed the advice of his minister, BISMARCK. He supported the unification of Germany, but accepted his proclamation as emperor reluctantly, fearing a reduction in Prussia's status.

William II (1859–1941) Emperor of Germany (1888–1918). Clashing with BISMARCK, he dismissed him in 1890 and assumed leadership of the government himself. His aggressive foreign policy antagonized Britain, France and Russia. Many historians regard his policies as largely responsible for the outbreak of World War 1 (1914). During the war, William was exclusively concerned with military matters. He abdicated after the armistice (November 1918).

William I (the Conqueror) (1027–87) King of England (1066–87) and Duke of Normandy (1035–87). Supported initially by Henry I of France, he consolidated his position in Normandy against hostile neighbours. On the death of EDWARD THE CONFESSOR, he claimed the English throne, having allegedly gained the agreement of King HAROLD II in 1064. He defeated and killed Harold at the battle of HASTINGS (1066) and subsequently enforced his rule over the whole kingdom. He invaded Scotland (1072), extracting an oath of loyalty from Malcolm III Canmore, and Wales (1081), although he spent much of his reign in France. He ordered the famous survey known as the DOMESDAY BOOK (1086).

William II (Rufus) (1056–1100) King of England (1087–1100). He was the second surviving son of WILLIAM I (THE CONQUEROR). His elder brother, Robert Curthose (Robert II), was Duke of Normandy, and William had to crush revolts by Anglo-Norman lords in Robert's favour. He invaded the duchy twice, and in 1096 Robert mortgaged it to him to raise cash for the First Crusade. He invaded Scotland, later killing Malcolm III (1093), annexed Cumbria and subdued Wales (1097).

William III (of Orange) (1650–1702) Prince of Orange and king of England, Scotland and Ireland (1689–1702). He married Mary, daughter of JAMES II of England in 1677 and, following the GLORIOUS REVOLUTION (1688), he and Mary (as MARY II), strong Protestants, replaced the Catholic James II. They ruled jointly until her death in 1694. After crushing JACOBITE revolt in Scotland and Ireland (1690), William devoted himself to his lifelong task of resisting the forces of Louis XIV of France. He forced the exhausted French to sign the Peace of Ryswick (1697). In 1699 he organized the alliance that was to defeat the French in the War of the SPANISH SUCCESSION. William

approved the BILL OF RIGHTS (1689) and other measures that diminished the royal prerogative.

William IV (1765–1837) King of Great Britain and Ireland and elector of Hanover (1830–37). Third son of GEORGE III, he succeeded unexpectedly aged 65 after a long career in the navy. Nicknamed "Silly Billy", he was well-meaning though unkingly. He assisted the passage of the Great Reform Bill (1832), by creating new peers to give the government a majority in the House of Lords.

William I (1772–1843) King of the Netherlands (1815–40) whose kingdom included Belgium and Luxembourg. His forceful government offended liberals and Roman Catholics, and a revolution in Belgium (1830) was followed by Belgian independence (1839). Compelled to accept a constitution restricting his powers, he abdicated in favour of his son, William II.

William I (the Lion) (1143–1214) King of Scotland (1165–1214). He succeeded his brother Malcolm IV and forged what was later called the "Auld Alliance" with France. Captured by the English during an attempt to regain Northumbria, he was forced to swear fealty to HENRY II (1174). He bought back his kingdom's independence from RICHARD I in return for a cash payment towards the Third Crusade in 1189.

William of Occam (1285–1349) English scholastic philosopher and theologian. Contributing to the development of formal logic, he employed the principle of economy known as Occam's Razor. As a Franciscan monk, he upheld Franciscan ideas of poverty against Pope John XXII and was excommunicated.

Williams, Ralph Vaughan See VAUGHAN WILLIAMS, RALPH

Williams, Tennessee (Thomas Lanier) (1911–83) US playwright. Many of his plays are set in the American South; an oppressive climate often reflects the characters' smouldering passions. His first Broadway play, *The Glass Menagerie* (1945), was awarded the New York Drama Critic's Circle Award. He received Pulitzer Prizes for *A Streetcar Named Desire* (1947) and *Cat on a Hot Tin Roof* (1955). His other plays include *Suddenly Last Summer* (1958) and *Sweet Bird of Youth* (1959).

Williams, William Carlos (1883–1963) US poet. His most monumental achievement was *Paterson* (1946–58), his five-volume epic of American life as seen in the microcosm of a New Jersey town. His *Pictures from Brueghel* (1962) won a posthumous Pulitzer Prize.

Williamson, Malcolm (1931–) Australian composer, pianist and organist. He has composed operas, ballets, film scores, orchestral and keyboard works. Among his operas are *Our Man in Havana* (1963) and *The Winter Star* (1973).

will-o'-the-wisp (Jack-o'-lantern) Mysterious light sometimes seen at night in marshy areas. It is thought to be due to the spontaneous combustion of marsh gas (METHANE).

willow Deciduous shrub and tree native to cool or mountainous temperate regions. It has long, pointed leaves, and flowers borne on catkins. Species include the weeping willow (*Salix babylonica*) and pussy willow (*S. caprea*). Family Salicaceae.

willowherb Any of several species of perennial plants with willow-like leaves, especially *Epilobium angustifolium*, the fireweed or rosebay willowherb. It has a long, unbranched stem with narrow leaves and purple-red flowers. Height: to 1m (3ft). Family Onagraceae; genus *Epilobium*.

Wilson, August (1945–) African-American playwright. His plays, the most well known of which include *Joe Turner's Come and Gone* (1986) and *The Piano Lesson* (1988), draw extensively from Wilson's own experiences. *Fences* won the Pulitzer Prize in 1987.

Wilson, Charles Thomson Rees (1869–1959) British physicist who invented the Wilson cloud chamber used to study radioactivity, x-rays and cosmic rays. It uses water droplets to track ions left by passing radiation. For this invention, he shared the 1927 Nobel Prize for physics.

Wilson, Sir (James) Harold (1916–95) (Baron Wilson of Rievaulx) British statesman, prime minister (1964–70, 1974–76). Wilson entered Parliament in 1945. In 1951 he resigned from ATTLEE's cabinet over the imposition of medical prescription charges. In 1963 Wilson succeeded GAITSKELL as Labour leader (1963). He won a narrow election victory (1964). His administration was faced with a foreign policy dilemma when Rhodesia's white-minority government unilaterally declared independence. Faced with domestic economic crisis, he was forced to impose strict price and income controls and devalue the currency. In the 1970 general election Wilson was defeated by Edward HEATH. Conflict between Labour's left- and right-wings over nationalization and membership of the European Economic Community (EUROPEAN COMMUNITY) threatened to divide the party. Nevertheless, in 1974 Wilson returned to power at the head of a minority Labour government. In 1976 he unexpectedly resigned and was succeeded by CALLAGHAN.

Wilson, (Thomas) Woodrow (1856–1924) 28th US President (1913–21). In 1912 he gained the Democratic presidential nomination. The split in the Republican vote between TAFT's REPUBLICAN PARTY and Theodore ROOSEVELT's Progressive Party handed Wilson the presidency. Several amendments to the US CONSTITUTION were introduced, including PROHIBITION (18th, 1919) and the extension of the FRANCHISE to women (19th, 1920). The MEXICAN REVOLUTION brought instability to the S border of the States and Wilson ordered John Pershing's intervention. Wilson's efforts to maintain US neutrality at the start of WORLD WAR 1 aided his re-election in 1916. The failure of diplomacy and attacks on US shipping forced Wilson to declare war on Germany (April 1917). His FOURTEEN POINTS (January 1918) represented US war aims and became the basis of the peace negotiations at VERSAILLES (1919). He was forced to compromise in the final settlement, but succeeded in securing the establishment of the LEAGUE OF NATIONS.

wilt Any of a group of plant diseases characterized by yellowing and wilting of leaves and young stems, often followed by death of the plant. Wilt diseases are caused by bacteria or fungi that grow in the sapwood and plug water-conducting tissues or disrupt the plant's water balance in some other way.

Wiltshire County in central S England. Trowbridge is the county town. Dominated by Salisbury Plain and the Marlborough Downs, much of this rural county is given over to agriculture. Industry is becoming increasingly important to the local economy. The chief industries are textiles, farm machinery, food processing and electrical goods. Tourists are attracted by the county's many historic sites, including STONEHENGE. Wiltshire was an important centre of Saxon culture. Area: 3,481sq km (1,344sq mi). Pop. (1991) 564,471.

Wimbledon Popular name for the All England Lawn Tennis Championships played annually at the All England Club, Wimbledon, a SW suburb of London. It is the world's foremost championship played on grass. It was first held in 1877 and was open only to amateurs until 1968. The championships have been held at the present ground since 1922.

Winchester County town of Hampshire, S central England, on the River Itchen. Known as Venta Belgarum by the Romans, it became capital of the Anglo-Saxon kingdom of WESSEX in 519 AD. During the reign of ALFRED THE GREAT, it was capital of England. Winchester retained its importance as a centre of learning and religion throughout the medieval period. Much of the old city remains. Pop. (1991) 96,386.

wind Air current that moves rapidly parallel to the Earth's surface. (Air currents in vertical motion are called updraughts or downdraughts.) Wind direction is indicated by wind or weather vanes, wind speed by ANEMOMETERS and wind force by the BEAUFORT WIND SCALE. Steady winds in the tropics are called TRADE WINDS. MONSOONS are seasonal winds that bring rains in Asia. SIROCCOS are hot, humid Mediterranean winds.

Windermere Largest lake in England, in the LAKE DISTRICT, Cumbria. It is linked to Morecombe Bay by the River Leven; the town of Windermere lies on the E shore of the lake. Length: *c.*17km (10mi); Max. width 1.6km (1mi).

Windhoek Capital and largest city of Namibia, situated *c.*300km (190mi) inland from the Atlantic at a height of 1,650m (5,410ft). Originally serving as the headquarters of a Nama chief, in 1892 it was made the capital of the new German colony of South-West Africa. In 1990 it became capital of independent Namibia. Industries: diamonds, copper, meat-packing, Pop. (1992) 126,000.

windmill Machine powered by the wind acting on sails or vanes. Windmills were built in the Middle

East in the 7th century. The idea spread to Europe in the Middle Ages. Their use was widespread during the INDUSTRIAL REVOLUTION, but declined with the development of the STEAM ENGINE in the 19th century. *See also* RENEWABLE ENERGY

windpipe *See* TRACHEA

wind power Harness of wind energy to produce power. Since the 1970s, advanced aerodynamic designs have been used to build wind turbines that generate electricity. Individual turbines are often grouped in strategic locations (wind farms) to maximize the generating potential. Wind power is a cheap form of RENEWABLE ENERGY, but cannot as yet provide a realistic alternative to fossil fuel and nuclear power stations. *See also* WINDMILLS

Windsor, Duke of *See* EDWARD VIII

Windsor Castle English royal residence, 32km (20mi) w of London. It was founded by WILLIAM I to defend the Thames valley. The castle underwent much extension, reconstruction and restoration, but retains the appearance of a medieval fortress. Besieged by rebellious barons in the reign of JOHN, it was never captured, although it was occupied by parliamentary forces during the English CIVIL WAR.

wind tunnel Chamber in which scale models and even full-size aircraft and road vehicles are tested in a controlled airflow. Some wind tunnels can reproduce extreme conditions of wind speed, temperature and pressure. Models of bridges and other structures are tested in wind tunnels to check that winds cannot set up destructive vibrations.

Windward Islands Southern group of the Lesser ANTILLES islands, SE West Indies. They extend from the Leeward Islands to the NE coast of Venezuela. The principal islands are MARTINIQUE, GRENADA, DOMINICA, ST LUCIA, ST VINCENT AND THE GRENADINES group. The islands, volcanic in origin, are generally mountainous and forested. Tropical crops are grown, including bananas, spices, limes and cacao, but for most of them tourism is the leading industry. The islands were inhabited by the indigenous Carib until colonization began in the 17th century. The next two centuries witnessed a struggle for control between France and Britain. Britain eventually controlled all the islands, with the exception of Martinique.

wine Alcoholic beverage made from the fermented juice (and some solid extracts) of fruits, herbs and flowers – but classically from the juice and skins of grapes. The three standard grape wine colorations are white, red and rosé, depending on the grape used and whether, and for how long, the grape skins are left on. For white wine the grapes are fermented without the skin; for red wine the whole grape is used; for rosé wine the skins are removed after fermentation has begun. Dry wines are fermented until all the sugar has turned to alcohol; sweet wines are fermented for less time so that some sugar remains.

wings In biology, specialized organs for flight, which are possessed by most birds, many insects

and certain mammals and reptiles. The forelimbs of a bird have developed into such structures. Bats have membranous tissue supported by the digits ("fingers") of the forelimbs. Insects may have one or two pairs of veined or membranous wings.

Winnebago Native American tribe that in the 1820s and 1830s ceded its tribal lands in SW Wisconsin and NW Illinois to the US government. The tribe's 3,000 members live mostly in reservations in Nebraska and Wisconsin.

wire Strand of metal, made by drawing a rod through progressively smaller holes in metal dies. The drawing process toughens steel, so that a rope or cable made from steel wire is much stronger than an undrawn steel rod of the same diameter.

wireworm Long, cylindrical larva of the click beetle of N temperate woodlands. It is generally brown or yellow and is distinctly segmented. Most species live in the soil, and may cause serious damage to the roots of cultivated crops. Family Elateridae. The name also refers to any of the smooth-bodied MILLIPEDES of the family Paraiulidae.

Wisconsin State in N central USA, SW of the GREAT LAKES and E of the River Mississippi. MADISON is the state capital and MILWAUKEE the largest city. The land is rolling plain that slopes gradually down from the N. There are numerous glacial lakes. The French claimed the region in 1634, Britain took it in 1763 and it was ceded to the USA in 1783. Settlement of the region was slow. The Territory of Wisconsin was established in 1836 and admitted to the Union in 1848. Wisconsin is the leading US producer of milk, butter and cheese, and the chief crops are hay, maize, oats, fruit and vegetables. The state's most valuable resource is timber: 45% of the land is forested. Mineral deposits include zinc, lead, copper, iron, sand and gravel. Industries: farm machinery, brewing, tourism. Area: 145,438sq km (56,154sq mi). Pop. (1992) 4,992,664.

wisdom literature Collection of writings and sayings in the Hebrew Bible. From the Old Testament it includes the Books of Proverbs, Ecclesiastes and Job, and the Song of Solomon, and from the Apocrypha it includeds the Books of Ecclesiasticus and the Wisdom of Solomon.

wisent *See* BISON

wisteria Genus of hardy, woody vines, native to North America, Japan and China. They have showy, fragrant, pendulous flower clusters of purplish-white, pink or blue. Family Fabaceae/Leguminosae.

witchcraft Exercise of supernatural occult powers, usually due to some inherent power, rather than to an acquired skill such as sorcery. In Europe it originated in pagan cults and in mystical philosophies such as GNOSTICISM, which believed in the potency of both good and evil in the universe. In some societies the belief in spirits is associated with attempts to control them through witchcraft for harmful or beneficial ends.

witch hazel Shrubs and small trees of the genus

Hamamelis, native to temperate regions, mostly in Asia. They bloom in late autumn or early spring. The common witch hazel (*Hamamelis virginiana*) has yellow flowers. Family Hamamelidaceae.

Witt, Jan de (1625–72) Dutch political leader. A republican and opponent of the House of Orange, he became effectively head of government in 1653. He defeated the English in the second of the DUTCH WARS (1665–67). In 1672 Witt resigned after a French invasion, the accession of WILLIAM OF ORANGE as stadholder (which he had long resisted), and an attempt on his life.

Wittenberg Town on the River Elbe, Sachsen-Anhalt state, E central Germany. Founded by Frederick III, Wittenberg's university became the cradle of the Protestant REFORMATION during the period when Martin LUTHER and Philip MELANCHTHON were teaching there. Today Wittenberg is primarily a mining and industrial centre, producing chemicals, rubber goods, machinery and foodstuffs. Pop. (1993) 47,200.

Wittgenstein, Ludwig (1889–1951) Philosopher, b. Austria. His masterwork, *Tractatus Logico-philosophicus* (1921), influenced LOGICAL POSITIVISM, arguing the strict relationships between language and the physical world. After 1929 he criticized this hypothesis and his second thoughts were posthumously published in *Philosophical Investigations* (1953), in which he claimed that language was only a conventional "game", in which meaning was affected more by context than by formal relationships to reality.

Witwatersrand (Rand) Series of parallel mountain ranges over 1,500m (5,000ft) high, forming a watershed between the Vaal and Olifant rivers, in S former TRANSVAAL, NE South Africa. Gold was discovered in 1884. Witwatersrand still produces about one-third of the total world output of gold. Silver is recovered as a by-product of gold refining. Coal and manganese are also mined and there are many ancillary industries in the region.

woad (dyerswoad) Biennial or perennial herb once grown as a source of blue dye. A native of Eurasia, it bears small four-petalled, yellow flowers. Height: 90cm (3ft). Family Brassicaceae/Cruciferae; species *Isatis tinctoria*.

Wodehouse, P.G. (Sir Pelham Grenville) (1881–1975) British novelist, short-story writer, playwright and lyricist. He wrote over 100 humorous books. His best-known creations are Bertie Wooster and his valet Jeeves, who feature in a number of books from 1917–71. During World War 2, Wodehouse's ill-advised radio broadcasts from Berlin outraged British public opinion, and he became an US citizen in 1955.

Woden *See* ODIN

Wöhler, Friedrich (1800–82) German chemist who first isolated ALUMINIUM and BERYLLIUM and discovered calcium carbide. In 1828 his synthesis of UREA was the first synthesis of an organic chemical compound from an inorganic one.

wolf Wild, dog-like carnivorous mammal, once widespread in the USA and Eurasia, especially the grey wolf (*Canis lupus*), which is now restricted to the USA and Asia. It is powerfully built with a wide head and neck, muscular limbs and a deep-chested body; the tail is long and bushy. Length: to 2m (6.6ft), including the tail. Family Canidae.

Wolf, Hugo (1860–1903) Austrian composer, generally regarded as one of the finest composers of *Lieder* (a type of song). He produced five "songbooks", setting poems by Mörike (1888), Eichendorff (1888–89), Goethe (1888–89), Spanish authors (1889–90) and Italian poets (1891, 1896).

Wolfe, James (1727–59) British general. He commanded the force that captured Quebec by scaling the cliffs above the St Lawrence River and defeating the French, under Montcalm, on the Plains of Abraham (1759). This victory resulted in Britain's acquisition of Canada. Wolfe's death in action made him an almost legendary hero.

Wolfe, Thomas Clayton (1900–38) US writer. His reputation rests on his sequence of four sprawling autobiographical novels, *Look Homeward, Angel* (1929), *Of Time and the River* (1935), *The Web and the Rock* (1939) and *You Can't Go Home Again* (1940).

Wolfe, Tom (Thomas Kennerley) (1931–) US journalist and novelist. Wolfe established his reputation in the 1960s with essays on American counter-culture such as *The Electric Kool-Aid Acid-Test* (1968). His novel *The Bonfire of the Vanities* (1987) demonstrates a sharp observation that encapsulates the spirit of the age.

wolfram *See* TUNGSTEN

wolframite Black to brown mineral, iron-manganese tungstate, $(Fe,Mn)WO_4$. It is the chief ore of the metal TUNGSTEN. It occurs as crystals in the monoclinic system, or as granular masses. It is found in quartz veins and pegmatites associated with granitic rocks, and also in high temperature hydrothermal veins in association with other minerals. Hardness 5–5.5; s.g. 7–7.5

Wolfram von Eschenbach (1170–1220) German poet. His only complete work is the Middle High German epic *Parzival*. A masterpiece of medieval literature, it introduced the Grail legend into German.

Wollstonecraft, Mary (1759–97) British author. Her *Vindication of the Rights of Women* (1792) was the first great work of FEMINISM. She was the mother of Mary Wollstonecraft SHELLEY.

Wolsey, Thomas (1475–1530) English cardinal and statesman, lord chancellor (1515–29). After the accession of HENRY VIII in 1509, Wolsey acquired major offices of church and state. He became archbishop of York (1514) and then cardinal and lord chancellor (1515). As chancellor, he controlled virtually all state business. Wolsey's attempt to place England at the centre of European diplomacy ended in failure. Despite becoming papal legate (1518) Wolsey's ambition to become pope was never realized. Domestically, his method of raising taxes through forced loans made powerful enemies. Wolsey's failure to obtain the king a divorce from CATHERINE OF ARAGON brought about his ruin. Charged with high treason, he died before his trial.

womb See UTERUS

wombat Either of two species of large, rodent-like marsupial mammals of SE Australia and Tasmania. Both species are herbivorous, primarily nocturnal and live in extensive burrows. The common wombat (*Vombatus ursinus*) has coarse black hair and small ears. The hairy-nosed wombat (*Lasiorhinus latifrons*) has finer, grey fur and large ears. Length: to 1.2m (4ft). Family Vombatidae.

women's rights movement Broad term for the international movement that began in the early 19th century to promote and work for the equality of women. Originally concentrating on women's suffrage, the movement has since worked for equality of employment opportunity and pay, freedom from unjust social, political and theological expectations within society, and an awakening of physical, intellectual and emotional awareness for women. See also FEMINISM; SUFFRAGETTE MOVEMENT

Wonder, Stevie (1950–) US SOUL singer and songwriter, b. Steveland Judkins Morris. Born blind, Wonder was a precocious polymath, playing the harmonica, keyboard, guitar and drums. In 1961 he joined MOTOWN Records. His first album *Little Stevie Wonder: A 12-year-old Musical Genius* was an instant hit. Consistently successful, his albums include *Talking Book* (1972), *Innervisions* (1973) and *Songs in the Key of Life* (1976). *Hotter Than July* (1980) was an enormous popular success.

Wood, Sir Henry Joseph (1869–1944) British conductor. He conducted the Promenade Concerts in London from 1895–1944.

wood Hard substance that forms the trunks of trees; it is the XYLEM that comprises the bulk of the stems and roots, supporting the plant. It consists of fine cellular tubes arranged vertically within the trunk; this accounts for the grain found in all wood. The two chief types are softwoods, from CONIFERS such as PINE, and hardwoods from a deciduous species such as OAK. Wood is commonly used as a building material, fuel, to make some types of PAPER, and as a source of CHARCOAL, CELLULOSE, essential oil, LIGNIN, tannins and dyes.

woodcock Any of five species of reddish-brown shorebirds that nest in cool parts of the Northern Hemisphere and winter in warm areas. Both the Eurasian *Scolopax rusticola* and American *Philohela minor* insert their long, sensitive, flexible bills into swampy ground to find worms. Length: to 34cm (14in). Family Scolopacidae.

woodcut Oldest method of printing using designs carved into wood. The carving produces a negative image, the carved areas representing blank spaces while the flat areas retain the ink. Woodcuts were invented in China in the 5th century AD and became popular in Europe in the Middle Ages.

wood engraving Print made by incising a design on the flat, polished (cross-grain) transverse section of a block of hardwood. Textural and linear effects can be achieved by varying the pressure and direction of the cutting strokes. This technique developed from the less-sophisticated WOODCUT in 18th-century England.

woodlouse (sowbug) Terrestrial, isopod crustacean found throughout the world, living under damp logs and stones, and in houses. It has an oval, segmented body, feeds mainly on vegetable matter, and retains its eggs in a brood pouch. Length: 20mm (0.75in). Order Isopoda; Genus *Oniscus*.

woodpecker Tree-climbing bird found nearly worldwide. Woodpeckers have strong pointed beaks and long, protrudable tongues, which in some species have harpoonlike tips for extracting insect larvae. They have two toes pointing forward, and black, red, white, yellow, brown or green plumage; some are crested. The tail is stiff and helps to support the bird's body when pressed against a tree trunk. Family Picidae.

Woodstock Name given to a music festival held between 15 and 17 August 1969, near Bethel, SW of Woodstock, New York State, USA. Forced to shift from the original Woodstock location because of residents' protests, *c.*450,000 people arrived for the free outdoor concert. The event was a celebration of both the music and aspirations of the hippy generation.

woodwind Family of musical wind instruments that are traditionally made of wood but now often metal. They are played by means of a mouthpiece containing one or two reeds. The FLUTE and PICCOLO are exceptional in that they are played by blowing across a hole. Other woodwind instruments include the CLARINET (single reed) and the OBOE, COR ANGLAIS and BASSOON (all double reed). SAXOPHONES are also included in the woodwind family.

woodworm (furniture beetle) Larva of various species of beetles that burrow in wood. When present in large numbers woodworms can cause extensive damage. Their presence can be detected by holes in the wood from which the adult beetles have emerged; treatment involves the use of poisons. Genera include *Anobium* and *Lyctus*.

wool Soft, generally white, brown or black animal fibre that forms the fleece (coat) of sheep. Wool is also the name of the yarns and textiles made from the fibres after spinning, dyeing and weaving. The fibres are treated to remove a fat called lanolin, which is used in some ointments.

Woolf, Virginia (1882–1941) British novelist and critic. A member of the BLOOMSBURY GROUP, her first novel, *The Voyage Out*, appeared in 1915. Her mature novels, which often use the STREAM OF CONSCIOUSNESS style associated with MODERNISM, include *Mrs Dalloway* (1925), *To the Lighthouse* (1927), *Orlando* (1928) and her most experimental novel, *The Waves* (1931). Her long essay *A Room of One's Own* (1929) is a key text of feminist criticism.

Wordsworth, William (1770–1850) British poet, a leading figure of ROMANTICISM. He collaborated with COLERIDGE to produce the *Lyrical Ballads* (1798). His preface to the second edition (1800) outlined the aims of English romanticism, which through the use of everyday language enabled "the spontaneous overflow of powerful feelings". Critics derided his style. In 1799 he moved to the Lake District. *The Prelude*, a long autobiographical poem, was completed in 1805 but only published posthumously in 1850. After *Poems in Two Volumes* (1807), which includes "Ode: Intimations of Immortality", his creativity declined. In 1843 he succeeded SOUTHEY as POET LAUREATE.

work In physics, energy transferred in moving a force. It equals the magnitude of the force multiplied by the distance moved in the direction of the force. If the force opposing movement is the object's weight m g (where m is the object's mass and g is the acceleration due to gravity), the work done in raising it a height h is m g h. This work has been transferred to the object in the form of POTENTIAL ENERGY; if the object falls a distance, the KINETIC ENERGY at the bottom of the fall equals the work done in raising it.

workhouse Former English institution for the unemployed. Workhouses originated from the houses of correction provided for vagabonds by the POOR LAW of 1601, but officially they date from 1696, when workhouses were established by the Bristol corporation. In 1723 a general act denied relief to those people who refused to enter a workhouse. Workhouses declined in the late 18th century, but were revived by the Poor Law of 1834. With the advent of welfare reforms, workhouses fell into disuse by the early 20th century.

Works Progress Administration (WPA) US National project created by Congress in 1935 under Franklin ROOSEVELT'S NEW DEAL policy to stimulate national economic recovery. Billions of dollars were contributed to the scheme in which work programmes provided jobs for the unemployed. About two million people were registered on WPA rolls at any one time between 1935 and 1941.

World Bank Popular name for the International Bank for Reconstruction and Development (IBRD). It is an intergovernmental organization established in 1944, and has been a specialized agency of the UNITED NATIONS since 1945, based in Washington D.C. Its role is to make long-term loans to member governments to aid their economic development. The major part of the Bank's resources are derived from the world's capital markets.

World Council of Churches International fellowship of Christian churches formed in 1948. Its aim is to work for the reunion of all Christian churches and to establish a united Christian presence in the world. The headquarters of the council are in Geneva, Switzerland. Its membership consists of some 300 churches.

World Health Organization (WHO) Intergovernmental agency of the UNITED NATIONS. Founded in 1948, it collects and shares medical and scientific information and promotes the establishment of international standards for drugs and vaccines. Its headquarters are in Geneva, Switzerland.

World Meteorological Organization (WMO) Intergovernmental agency of the UNITED NATIONS. Founded in 1950, it promotes international cooperation through the establishment of a network of meteorological stations throughout the world, and by the mutual exchange of weather information. Its headquarters are in Geneva, Switzerland.

world music Generic term used to describe ethnic or ethnically influenced music. As part of a growing interest during the 1980s in non-Western music, many artists, such as Peter Gabriel and Paul Simon, began to draw particularly on the traditions of African culture, bringing together a variety of diverse styles and musicians.

World Service Department of BBC Radio, based in London, that transmits daily news, cultural and entertainment programmes in English worldwide, and on a regular basis in more than 30 other languages relayed to specific countries and regions. The first broadcasts overseas began in 1932.

World Trade Organization Body sponsored by the UNITED NATIONS to regulate international trade. The WTO was established on 1 January 1995 to replace the GENERAL AGREEMENT ON TARIFFS AND TRADE (GATT). The WTO took over GATT's rules with increased powers, and brought agriculture, clothing and textiles, intellectual property rights and services also under its control.

World War 1 (1914–18) (Great War) International conflict precipitated by the assassination of the Austrian Archduke Franz Ferdinand by Serbs in Sarajevo (28 June 1914). Austria declared war on Serbia (28 July), Russia mobilized in support of Serbia (from 29 July), Germany declared war on Russia (1 August) and France (3 August), and Britain declared war on Germany (4 August). It resulted from growing tensions in Europe, exacerbated by the rise of the German empire since 1871 and the decline of Ottoman power in the Balkans. The chief contestants were the Central Powers (Germany and Austria) and the Triple Entente (Britain, France and Russia). Many other countries were drawn in. Ottoman Turkey joined the Central Powers in 1914, Bulgaria in 1915. The Western Allies were joined by Italy in 1915, Romania in 1916 and, decisively, the USA in 1917. Russia withdrew following the RUSSIAN REVOLUTION of 1917. In Europe fighting was largely static. After the initial German advance through Belgium was checked at the Battle of Marne, the Western Front settled into a war of attrition, with huge casualties but little movement. On the Eastern Front the initial Russian advance was checked by the Germans, who overran Poland before stagnation set in. Campaigns were also fought outside Europe, against the Turks in the Middle East and the German colonies n Africa and the Pacific. The naval blockade of Germany caused severe food shortages and helped to end the war. An armistice was agreed in November 1918 and peace treaties were signed at VERSAILLES (1919). Casualties were high: c.10 million people were killed.

World War 2 (1939–1945) International conflict arising from disputes provoked by the expansionist policies of Germany in Europe and Japan in the Far East. During the 1930s APPEASEMENT failed to check the ambitions of the HITLER regime in Germany. Having made a defensive pact with the Soviet Union (August 1939), Germany invaded Poland, whereupon Britain and France declared war (3 September). In 1940 German BLITZ tactics resulted in the rapid conquest of Denmark, Norway, the Low Countries and France (June). Inability to gain command of the air prevented a German invasion of Britain (*see* BATTLE OF BRITAIN). Italy, under MUSSOLINI, having annexed Albania (1939) and invaded Greece (1940), joined Germany in 1941. Germany invaded Greece and Yugoslavia. In June the Germans, violating the pact of 1939, invaded the Soviet Union, advancing to the outskirts of Moscow and Leningrad (St Petersburg). Italian defeats by the British in North Africa also drew in German troops, who threw back the British. In the Pacific the Japanese attack on PEARL HARBOR (December 1941) drew the USA into the war. Japan rapidly overran SE Asia and Burma, but the battle of MIDWAY (June 1942) indicated growing US naval and air superiority. From 1942 the tide in Europe turned against Germany. Defeat at STALINGRAD (January 1943) was followed by a Soviet advance that drove the Germans out of the Soviet Union by August 1944. Defeats in North Africa in 1942–43 led to the Allied invasion of Italy, forcing the Italians to make peace (September 1943). German troops then occupied Italy where they resisted the Allied advance until 1945. In June 1944 Allied forces invaded NORMANDY, liberated France and advanced into Germany, linking up with the Soviets on the River Elbe (April 1945). Germany surrendered in May. Japan continued to resist, but surrendered in August after atomic bombs were dropped on Hiroshima and Nagasaki. Estimates of the numbers killed in World War 2 exceed 50 million. The great majority of the dead were civilians, many murdered in Nazi death camps. Politically, two former allies, the USA and the Soviet Union, emerged as the dominant world powers.

Worldwide Fund for Nature (WWF) International organization, established in Britain in 1961 as the World Wildlife Fund. It raises voluntary funds for the conservation of endangered wild animals, plants and places. Its headquarters are in Switzerland.

worm Any of a large variety of wriggling, limbless creatures with soft bodies. Most worms belong to one or other of four main groups: ANNELIDS, FLATWORMS, nematodes (ROUNDWORMS), and ribbon worms.

Worms, Concordat of (1122) Agreement between the Holy Roman emperor Henry V and Pope Calixtus II settling the investiture conflict, a struggle between the empire and the papacy over the control of church offices. The emperor agreed to the free election of bishops and abbots, and surrendered his claim to invest them with the spiritual symbols of ring and staff. They were, however, to pay homage to him as feudal overlord for their temporal possessions.

Worms, Diet of (1521) Conference of the Holy Roman Empire presided over by Emperor CHARLES V. Martin LUTHER was summoned to appear before the Diet to retract his teachings. Luther refused to retract them, and the Edict of Worms (25 May 1521) declared him an outlaw. The Diet was one of the most important confrontations of the early REFORMATION.

wormwood Genus (*Artemisia*) of aromatic bitter shrubs and herbs, including common wormwood (*A. absinthium*), a European shrub that yields a bitter, dark green oil used to make absinthe. Family Asteraceae/Compositae.

Wounded Knee, Massacre at (1890) Last engagement in the conflict between Native Americans and US forces. Fearing a rising by the Sioux, US troops made mass arrests and brought a group of Native Americans to Wounded Knee, South Dakota. A shot was fired and the troops opened fire. About 300 people were killed.

Wren, Sir Christopher (1632–1723) English architect, mathematician and astronomer. He designed more than 50 new churches in the city of London based on syntheses of CLASSICAL, RENAISSANCE and BAROQUE ideas; the greatest of these is ST PAUL'S Cathedral. Among his many other works are Chelsea and Greenwich hospitals, London, and the Sheldonian Theatre, Oxford.

wren Small, insect-eating songbird of temperate regions of Europe, Asia and most of the New World. Many species have white facial lines. The typical winter wren (*Troglodytes troglodytes*) has a slender bill, rounded wings, upright tail and dark brownish plumage; length: to 10cm (4in). Family Troglodytidae.

wrestling Sport in which two opponents try to throw each other to the ground or secure each other in an unbreakable hold, by means of body grips, strength and adroitness. The two major competitive styles are Greco-Roman (most popular in continental Europe), which permits no tripping or holds below the waist, and free-style, which permits tackling, leg holds and tripping, and is most popular in Britain and the USA. A match consists of three periods of three minutes each; points are awarded for falls (pinning both shoulders to the mat) and other manoeuvres. Competitive wrestling originated in ancient Greece, where it was regarded as the next most important event after discus-throwing in the Olympic Games. Wrestling has been an Olympic event since 1904.

Wright, Frank Lloyd (1869–1959) US architect, regarded as the leading modernist designer of private housing. His distinctive "organic" style of low-built, prairie-style houses was designed to blend in with natural contours and features. Influenced by JAPANESE ART AND ARCHITECTURE, Wright's open-plan approach to interiors was highly influential. Notable buildings include: Robie House, Chicago (1909); "Falling Water", Bear Run, Pennsylvania (1936–37); and the Guggenheim Museum, New York (1946–59).

Wright, Joseph (1734–1797) English painter. He made a speciality of industrial and scientific subjects, most notably in *An Experiment on a Bird in the Air Pump* (1768).

Wright, Richard (1908–60) US novelist. His novels include *Native Son* (1940), which describes the life of an African-American youth in white-dominated Chicago; and *Black Boy* (1945), an account of the author's boyhood in the South. He also wrote short stories and non-fiction.

Wright brothers Wilbur (1867–1912) and Orville (1871–1948), US aviation pioneers. They assembled their first aircraft in their bicycle factory. In 1903 Orville made the first piloted flight in a power-driven plane at Kitty Hawk, North Carolina. This flight lasted just 12 seconds, and attracted little attention.

writing Process or result of making a visual record for the purpose of communication by using symbols to represent the sounds or words of a language. Writing systems fall into the following categories: ideographic (using signs or symbols that represent concepts or ideas directly rather than the sound of words for them); pictographic (in which a picture or sign represents the meaning of a word or phrase); syllabic (in which signs represent groups of consonants and vowels); and alphabetic (in which symbols stand for individual speech sounds or certain combinations of sounds).

Wundt, Wilhelm (1832–1920) German psychologist. He established the first laboratory for experimental psychology in 1879 at Leipzig, and did much to convince psychologists that the mind could be studied with objective methods.

Wyatt, Sir Thomas (1503–42) English poet and courtier, a pioneer of the English sonnet. He was popular at Henry VIII's court although, as an alleged former lover of Anne BOLEYN and a friend of Thomas CROMWELL, he was briefly imprisoned in 1536 and 1541.

Wycliffe, John (1330–84) English religious reformer. Under the patronage of JOHN OF GAUNT, he attacked corrupt practices in the church and the authority of the pope, condemning in particular the church's landed wealth. His criticism became increasingly radical, questioning the authority of the pope and insisting on the primacy of scripture, but he escaped condemnation until after his death.

His ideas were continued by the LOLLARDS in England and influenced Jan HUS in Bohemia.

Wyeth, Andrew Newell (1917–) US painter, known for his naturalistic portraits. His best-known painting is *Christina's World* (1948). He was trained by his father, the illustrator N.C. Wyeth. His son James (1946–) is also a noted painter and artist.

Wyler, William (1902–81) US film director. Wyler won three best director and best picture Academy Awards for *Mrs Miniver* (1942), *The Best Years of Our Lives* (1946) and *Ben-Hur* (1959). Other credits include *Jezebel* (1938), *Wuthering Heights* (1939), *The Little Foxes* (1941) and *Roman Holiday* (1953).

Wyndham, John (1903–69) British novelist. He is known for science-fiction "disaster" novels, of which *The Day of the Triffids* (1951) is best known. Other works include *The Kraken Wakes* (1953), *The Chrysalids* (1955) and *The Midwych Cuckoos* (1957).

Wyoming State in NW USA, bounded N by Montana, E by South Dakota, S by Colorado, SW by Utah and W by Idaho; the state capital is CHEYENNE. Other major cities are Jasper and Laramie. Wyoming has the nation's smallest state population. The landscape is dominated by mountains and four million hectares (10 million acres) of forest. The ROCKY MOUNTAINS cross the state from NW to SE. To the E of the Rockies lie the rolling grasslands of the GREAT PLAINS, and the centre of the state is also high plains country. The N of the state is primarily tall grass plain, which is fertile farmland and cattle ranch country. YELLOWSTONE NATIONAL PARK is the oldest and largest US national park, occupying the entire NW corner of Wyoming. Many rivers flow down from the mountains, including the North Platte and the Snake. Tourism is a vital industry, with the state's natural beauty attracting over seven million annual visitors. While cattle ranching, sheep and wheat farming remain important to the economy, Wyoming is primarily an oil-producing state. Other important mineral resources include coal and uranium. Following the LOUISIANA PURCHASE (1803), the USA had by 1846 acquired the entire territory through treaties. Nineteenth-century development was linked to the fur trade and westward migration along the Oregon Trail. The 1860s marked the first dramatic arrival of new settlers: the Bozeman Trail was opened (1864), and the railway was completed (1868). By the end of the 1870s, the Native American population had been placed on reservations. The next 20 years were marked by a rise of vigilante groups to deal with cattle rustlers and outlaws, and in 1890 Wyoming became the 44th state of the Union. Area: 253,596sq km (97,913sq mi). Pop. (1992) 464,736.

Wyszynski, Cardinal Stefan (1901–81) Polish Roman Catholic cardinal. In the late 1970s and early 1980s, as leader of Poland's Roman Catholics, he played an active mediating role between the workers and government authorities.

X/x is the 24th letter of the English alphabet and is included in the alphabets of several w European countries. It is thought to have developed from a Semitic character called samekh.

x-chromosome One of the two kinds of sex-determining CHROMOSOME; the other is the Y-CHROMOSOME. In many organisms, including humans, females carry two x-chromosomes in their DIPLOID cell nuclei, while males carry one x- and one y-chromosome. Non-sexual characteristics are also carried on the x-chromosome, for example the genes for one form of colourblindness and for haemophilia. *See also* GENETICS; HEREDITY

xenon Gaseous nonmetallic element (symbol Xe), one of the NOBLE GASES. Discovered in 1898, xenon is present in the Earth's atmosphere (about one part in 20 million) and is obtained by fractionation of liquid air. Colourless and odourless, it is used in light bulbs, lasers and arc lamps for cinema projection. The element, which has 9 stable isotopes, forms some compounds, mostly with FLUORINE. Properties: at.no. 54; r.a.m. 131.30; r.d. 5.88; m.p. $-111.9°C$ ($-169.42°F$); b.p. $-107.1°C$ ($-160.8°F$); most common isotope Xe^{132} (26.89%).

Xenophon (430–354 BC) Greek historian. He studied with SOCRATES, whose teaching he described in *Memorabilia. Anabasis*, an account of his march with a Greek mercenary army across Asia Minor in 401–399 BC in support of a pretender to the Persian throne, is his best-known work. Other works include a history of Greece from 411 to 362 BC.

xerography Most common process used for PHOTOCOPYING.

xerophyte Any plant that is adapted to survive in dry conditions, in areas subject to drought or in physiologically dry areas such as salt marshes and acid bogs, where saline or acid conditions make the uptake of water difficult. Succulents, such as a CACTUS, have thick fleshy leaves and stems for storing water. Other adaptations include the ability to reduce water loss by shedding leaves during drought, having waxy or hairy leaf coatings or reduced leaf area.

Xerxes I (519–465 BC) King of Persia (486–465 BC). Succeeding his father, DARIUS I, he regained Egypt and crushed a rebellion in Babylon before launching his invasion of Greece (480 BC). After his fleet was destroyed at the Battle of Salamis, he retired, and the defeat of the Persian army in Greece at the Battle of Plataea ended his plans for conquest. He was later assassinated by one of his own men. *See also* PERSIAN WARS

Xhosa (XOSA) Group of related BANTU tribes. The Xhosa moved from E Africa to the vicinity of the Great Fish River, S Africa, in the 17th–18th century. They were defeated by the Europeans in 1835. In culture they are closely related to the ZULU. The 2.5 million Xhosa live in the Eastern Cape and form an important part of South Africa's industrial and mining workforce. Xhosa is the most widely spoken African language in South Africa.

Xiamen Seaport city in Fujian province, SE China. As Amoy, it flourished in the 19th century after being declared an open port by the Treaty of Nanking (1842). It gained extra strategic importance after the communists took control of the Chinese mainland (1949), and in 1981 it was granted the status of special economic zone, accelerating its role as the centre of growing "unofficial" trade between China and Taiwan. Pop. (1993) 470,000.

Xian (Sian, formerly Changan) Capital of Shaanxi province at the confluence of the Wei and HUANG HE rivers, NW China. Inhabited since 6000 BC, from 255–206 BC it was the site of Xianyang, the capital of the QIN dynasty. The elaborate tomb of the dynastic founder, emperor QIN SHIHUANGDI, is a world heritage site and major tourist attraction. It was the focus for the introduction of Buddhism to China. In the following centuries it became a major centre for other religious missionaries. The Great Mosque was built in 742. At the start of the 10th century, Changan was the world's largest city. It has been known as Xian since the MING dynasty (1368–1644). In the Xian Incident (1936), CHIANG KAI-SHEK was held hostage until he agreed to a united Nationalist-Communist Chinese front against the Japanese. It is an important commercial centre of a grain-growing region. Industries: cotton, textiles, steel, chemicals. Pop. (1993) 2,360,000.

Xingu Brazilian river, rising in central Mato Grosso state. It flows N for 1,980km (1,230mi) and empties into the Amazon River at its delta. It courses through rainforest and is navigable only in its lower reaches. International attention was focused on the plight of Native Americans when a government proposal to dam the Xingu meant the flooding of tribal land. The scheme was completed in December 1994 at a cost of US$3.2 billion.

Xinjiang (Mandarin, "new frontier"; Sinkiang or Chinese Turkistan) Autonomous region in NW China, bordered by Tajikistan, Kyrgyzstan and Kazakstan (N and W), Mongolia (E) and Kashmir and Tibet (S). The capital is Ürümqi. The region includes the Dzungarian Basin to the E and the Tarim Basin to the W. The Altai, Kunlun and TIAN SHAN mountains frame the region to the N, S and W respectively. First conquered by the Chinese in the 1st century BC, from the 13th–18th centuries it was loosely controlled by the Mongols. In 1756 the QING dynasty became the leading power in the region. It was made a Chinese province in 1881. It is a predominantly agricultural region, growing wheat, cotton, maize, rice, millet, vegetables and fruit, and livestock rearing (particularly sheep) is also important. The area is rich in minerals including oil, copper, zinc, gold and silver. Industries: iron and steel, chemicals, textiles. Area: 1,647,435sq km (636,075sq mi). Pop. (1990) 15,370,000.

x-ray Electromagnetic ray of shorter wavelength, or higher frequency, than visible light, produced when a beam of electrons hits a solid target. X-rays were discovered in 1895 by the German physicist Wilhelm RÖNTGEN. They are normally produced for scientific use in x-ray tubes. Because they are able to penetrate matter that is opaque to light, x-rays are used to investigate inaccessible areas, especially of the body. *See also* RADIOGRAPHY

x-ray astronomy *See* ASTRONOMY

x-ray crystallography Use of X-RAYS to discover the molecular structure of CRYSTALS. It uses the phenomenon of x-ray diffraction (scattering of an x-ray beam by the atomic structure of a crystal) and has been used to show that DNA can produce crystals.

xylem Transport TISSUE of a plant, which conducts water and minerals from the roots to the rest of the plant and provides support. The most important cells are long, thin tapering cells called **xylem vessels**. These cells are dead and have no cross-walls; they are arranged in columns to form long tubes, up which water is drawn. As water evaporates from the leaves (TRANSPIRATION), water is drawn across the leaf by OSMOSIS to replace it, drawing water out of the xylem. This suction creates a tension in the xylem vessels, and the side walls are reinforced with rings or spirals of LIGNIN, a rigid substance, to prevent them collapsing. Tiny holes in the walls of the xylem vessels, called pits, allow water to cross from one tube to another. In trees, the xylem becomes blocked with age, and new xylem forms towards the outside of the trunk to replace it. The core of dead, non-functioning xylem remains an essential part of the support system. *See also* VASCULAR BUNDLE, PHLOEM

xylophone Tuned PERCUSSION instrument. It is made of hardwood bars arranged as in a piano keyboard and played with mallets. The modern xylophone normally has a range of four octaves, extending from middle C upwards.

Y/y is the 25th letter of the English alphabet and is included in the alphabets of several w European languages. It was derived (as were f, u, v and w) from the Semitic letter vaw.

yacht Boat used for sport and recreation, powered by sail or motor. Sailing yachts, which are usually fore and aft rigged, vary from 6m (20ft) to over 30m (98ft) long and include cutters, schooners, ketches, sloops and yawls. Those fitted with diesel or petrol engines are usually classified as cruising, or motor, yachts. Yachting has been an international sport since 1851, when the Royal Yacht Squadron (formed at Cowes, England, in 1812) offered a prize for a race around the Isle of Wight. The race was won by the schooner *America*, owned by members of the New York Yacht Club (organized 1844), and has since been known as the America's Cup. The *Observer Single-Handed Transatlantic Race* has been held every four years since 1960.

Yahweh Personal name of the God of the ancient Israelites of the Old Testament. God revealed His name to MOSES when He called to him out of the burning bush at Mount Horeb (Sinai) (Exodus 3:14). In Hebrew, it was made up of four consonants, YHWH, and was apparently related to the Hebrew verb "to be". Most English translations render it as "I am".

yak Large, powerful, long-haired ox, native to Tibet, with domesticated varieties throughout central Asia; it inhabits barren heights up to 6,000m (20,000ft). Domesticated varieties are generally smaller and varied in colour; they breed freely with domestic cattle. Wild yaks have coarse, black hair, except on the tail and flanks, where it hangs as a long fringe. The horns curve upward and outward. Height: to 1.8m (6ft) at the shoulder. Family Bovidae; species *Bos grunniens*.

Yakutia (officially Republic of Sakha) Constituent republic of the Russian Federation, in NE Siberia; the capital is Yakutsk. The region is bounded by the Laptev and East Siberian Seas (N) and the Stanovoy Range (S). It is the largest Russian republic and one of the coldest inhabited regions, with more than 40% of the territory within the Arctic Circle. The principal rivers are the LENA, Yana, Indirka and Kolyma. A third of the population is Yakut, a Turkic-speaking people who settled in the Lena basin from the 13th–15th centuries. The area was colonized by Russia during the 17th century, and many Yakuts were forcibly converted from shamanism to Christianity. A republic of the former Soviet Union from 1922–91, Yakutia became a member of the new Russian Federation in 1992. Agriculture is only possible in the S. The major industry is diamond mining and processing. Other

important minerals include gold, silver, lead and coal. Timber is an important industry in the taiga regions. Area: 3,103,200sq km (1,200,000sq mi) Pop: (1994) 1,060,700

Yalow, Rosalyn (1921–) US biochemist. In the 1950s Yalow found that some people who received INSULIN injections developed antibodies against the hormone. She discovered that insulin, labelled with radioactive iodine, combined with the antibodies; from this she developed radio-immunological tests to detect and measure the amount of insulin present. She shared the 1977 Nobel Prize for physiology or medicine for her development of a method of detecting peptide HORMONES in the blood.

Yalta Conference (February 1945) Meeting of the chief Allied leaders of World War 2 at Yalta in the Crimea, S Ukraine. With victory over Germany imminent, ROOSEVELT, CHURCHILL and STALIN met to discuss the final campaigns of the war and the post-war settlement. Agreements were reached on the foundation of the UNITED NATIONS; the territorial division of Europe into "spheres of interest"; the occupation of Germany; and support for democracy in liberated countries. Concessions were made to Stalin in the Far East in order to gain Soviet support against Japan.

yam Any of several species of herbaceous vines that grow in warm and tropical regions and the large, tuberous roots of several tropical species, which are edible. The plant is an annual with a long, climbing stem, with lobed or unlobed leaves and small clusters of greenish, bell-shaped flowers. The SWEET POTATO is also sometimes called a yam. Family Dioscoreaceae; genus *Dioscorea*.

Yamoussoukro Capital of IVORY COAST since 1983. Originally a small Baouké tribal village and birthplace of Ivory Coast's first president, Félix HOUPHOUËT-BOIGNY, it has developed rapidly into the administrative and transport centre of Ivory Coast. Yamoussoukro's Our Lady of Peace Cathedral (consecrated by Pope John Paul II in 1990) is the world's largest Christian church. Pop. (1988) 106,786.

Yamuna (Jumna) River in N central India. It rises in the Himalayas and flows S and SE. The Yamuna's confluence with the GANGES at ALLAHABAD is one of the most sacred Hindu sites. The TAJ MAHAL at AGRA lies on its bank. Navigable for almost its entire length, the Yamuna was once an important trade route and is now primarily used for irrigation. Length: *c*.1,380km (860mi).

Yangtze (Chang Jiang) River in China, the longest in Asia and third longest in the world. Rising in the Kunlun Mountains in NE Tibet, it flows 6,300km (3,900mi) through the central Chinese provinces to the East China Sea near Shanghai. It was joined to the HUANG HE by the Grand Canal in 610. Navigation becomes difficult at the spectacular Yangtze Gorges, between CHUNGKING and Yichang, but after Yichang (site of the huge

Gezhouba Dam) it enters the fertile lowlands of Hubei province. The Yangtze and its main tributaries traverse one of the world's most populated areas, providing water for irrigation and hydro-electricity, and it is China's most economically important waterway. The Chinese government's controversial Three Gorges dam scheme E of Fengjie, destined to take 15 years to complete, will create a reservoir about 600km (375mi) long, displacing some 1.2 million people.

Yaoundé Capital of Cameroon, W Africa. Located in beautiful hills on the edge of dense jungle, it was founded by German traders in 1888. During World War 1 it was occupied by Belgian troops, and from 1921–60 acted as capital of French Cameroon. Since independence it has grown rapidly as a financial and administrative centre with strong Western influences. Yaoundé also serves as a market for the surrounding region, notably in coffee, cacao and sugar. Pop. (1991) 750,000.

Yaroslavl (Jaroslavl') City and river port on the Volga, W central Russia. It is the capital of Yaroslavl oblast. The oldest town on the Volga (founded 1010 by Yaroslavl the Great), it was capital of Yaroslavl principality when absorbed by Moscow in 1463. From March to July 1612 it served as Russia's capital, and still boasts many historic buildings. It is a major rail junction. Industries: linen, diesel engines, construction equipment, oil refining, petrochemicals, plastics, dyes, clothes. Pop. (1994) 631,000.

yaws (framboesia) Contagious skin disease found in the humid tropics. It is caused by a spirochete (*Treponema pertenue*) related to the organism causing SYPHILIS. Yaws, however, is not a SEXUALLY TRANSMITTED DISEASE, but is transmitted by flies and by direct skin contact with the sores. It may go on to cause disfiguring bone lesions.

y-chromosome One of the two kinds of sex-determining CHROMOSOME, the other is the X-CHROMOSOME. Many male organisms have one x- and one y-chromosome in their DIPLOID cell nuclei. SPERM cells contain either an x- or a y-chromosome, and since female ova always contain an x-chromosome, the resulting offspring is either XY (male) or XX (female). The y-chromosome is smaller than the x- and contains fewer GENES.

yeast Any of a group of single-celled microscopic FUNGI found in all parts of the world in the soil and in organic matter. Yeasts reproduce asexually by BUDDING or FISSION. Yeasts are also produced commercially for use in baking, brewing and wine-making. They occur naturally as a bloom (white covering) on grapes and other fruit.

Yeats, W.B. (William Butler) (1865–1939) Irish poet and dramatist. Often cited as the greatest English language poet of the 20th century, Yeats was awarded the 1923 Nobel Prize for literature. He and Lady Gregory founded (1904) the Abbey Theatre, Dublin, as an Irish national theatre. Yeats' plays *On Baile's Strand* (1905) and *Cathleen Ni Houlihan* (1902) were on the first bill, the latter often regarded as the beginning of the renaissance in IRISH LITERATURE. Yeats' early poetry, collected in *The Wanderings of Oisin, and Other Poems* (1889), betrays the influence of mysticism. *Responsibilities* (1914) was more direct; the poetry acting as contemporary commentary. Following the creation of the Irish Free State, Yeats served (1922–28) as a senator. Yeats' mature poetry was often based on his own symbolic system and the adoption of dramatic voices ("masks") outlined in *A Vision* (1925). Works from this second phase include *Michael Robartes and the Dancer* (1921, which contains "The Second Coming" and "Easter 1916") and *The Tower* (1928, which contains "Sailing to Byzantium").

yellow fever Acute infectious disease marked by sudden onset of headaches, fever, muscle and joint pain, jaundice and vomiting; the kidneys and heart may also be affected. It is caused by a VIRUS transmitted by mosquitoes in tropical and subtropical regions. It may be prevented by vaccination.

Yellowstone National Park Park in NW Wyoming and reaching into Montana and Idaho, USA. Established in 1872, it is the oldest and one of the largest US national parks. Formed by volcanic activity, the park contains almost 10,000 hot springs and 200 geysers (the most famous of which is "Old Faithful"). Other scenic attractions include the Yellowstone River and petrified forests. In 1988 large-scale forest fires devastated much of the park. Area: 900,000ha (2.22 million acres)

Yeltsin, Boris Nikolayevich (1931–) Russian statesman, first democratically elected president of the Russian Federation (1991–). He was Communist Party leader in Ekaterinburg before joining the government of Mikhail GORBACHEV (1985), also becoming Party chief in Moscow. His blunt criticism of the slow pace of PERESTROIKA led to demotion in 1987, but his immense popularity gained him election as president of the Russian Republic in 1990. His prompt denunciation of the attempted coup against Gorbachev (August 1991) established his ascendancy. Elected president of the Russian Federation, he presided over the dissolution of the Soviet Union and the termination of Communist Party rule. Economic disintegration, rising crime and internal conflicts, notably in CHECHNYA, damaged his popularity, and failing health reduced his effectiveness, but he was re-elected in 1996.

Yemen Republic on SE tip of the Arabian Peninsula; the capital is SANA'A. **Land and climate** Yemen lies on the S tip of the Arabian peninsula. A narrow plain borders the Red Sea and the Arabian Sea coasts, and includes ADEN, the former capital of South Yemen. The W plain is backed by highlands, which rise to over 3,600m (12,000ft) near Sana'a. The Arabian coastal plain includes the fertile Hadramaut valley, which runs through a lower mountain range. Much of Yemen's interior forms part of the Rub al Khali desert. The desert is bisected by a central plateau. Most of Yemen is hot and rainless, except during the monsoon month of

YEMEN
AREA: 527,970sq km (203,849sq mi)
POPULATION: 11,282,000
CAPITAL POPULATION: Sana'a (427,502)
GOVERNMENT: Multiparty republic
ETHNIC GROUPS: Arab 96%, Somali 1%
LANGUAGES: Arabic (official)
RELIGIONS: Islam
CURRENCY: Yemen rial = 100 fils

August. The highlands are the wettest part of Arabia and the temperature is moderated by altitude. Palm trees grow along the coast. Plants such as acacia and eucalyptus flourish in the interior. Thorn shrubs and mountain pasture are found in the highlands. The Rub al Khali (Empty Quarter) is a barren desert. **Economy** Civil strife has devastated Yemen's economy, seriously damaging the country's infrastructure, such as the oil refinery at Aden. Yemen is a low-income developing nation (1992 GDP per capita, US$2,410). In 1995 high inflation and unemployment forced Yemen to borrow from the International Monetary Fund. Agriculture employs 63% of the workforce, mainly at subsistence level. The major economic activity is livestock-raising, principally sheep. Crops include sorghum, wheat and barley. Oil extraction began in the NW in the 1980s. Natural gas is also exploited. **History and politics** The ancient kingdom of SHEBA flourished in present-day s Yemen between *c*.750 BC and 100 BC. The kingdom was renowned for its advanced technology and wealth, gained through its strategic location on important trade routes. The region was invaded by the Romans in the 1st century BC. Islam was introduced in AD 628. The Rassite dynasty of the Zaidi sect established a theocratic state, which lasted until 1962. The FATIMIDS conquered Yemen in *c*.1000. In 1517 the area became part of the OTTOMAN EMPIRE, and largely remained under Turkish control until 1918. In the 19th century the Saudi Wahhabi sect ousted the Zaidi imams, but were in turn expelled by Ibrahim Pasha. In 1839 Aden was captured by the British. Following the defeat of the Ottomans in World War 1, Yemen was ruled by Imam Yahya of the Hamid al-Din dynasty. In 1937 Britain formed the Aden Protectorate. In 1945 Yemen joined the Arab League. In 1948 Yahya was assassinated. Crown Prince Ahmed became imam. From 1958–61 Yemen formed part of the United Arab Republic (with Egypt and Syria). A 1962 army revolution overthrew the monarchy and formed the Yemen Arab Republic. Civil war ensued between republicans (aided by Egypt) and royalists (aided by Saudi Arabia and Jordan). Meanwhile, the Aden Protectorate became part of the British Federation of South Arabia. In 1967 the National Liberation Front forced the British to withdraw from Aden and founded the People's

Republic of South Yemen. Marxists won the ensuing civil war in South Yemen and renamed it the People's Democratic Republic of Yemen (1970). Border clashes between the two countries were frequent throughout the 1970s, and erupted into full-scale war (1979). Following lengthy negotiations, the two Yemens merged to form a single republic in 1990. Yemen's support for Iraq in the Gulf War (1991) led to the expulsion of 800,000 Yemeni workers from Saudi Arabia. A coalition government emerged from 1993 elections, but increasing economic and political tensions between North and South led to civil war in 1994. The South's brief secession from the union ended with victory for the Northern army. In 1995 agreement was reached with Saudi Arabia and Oman over disputed boundaries, but Yemen clashed with Eritrea over the Hanish Islands in the Red Sea. Presidential elections are due in 1999.

Yenisei (Yenesey) River in central Siberia, Russia. Formed by the confluence of the Bolshoi Yenisei and the Maly Yenisei at Kyzyl, it flows for 4,090km (2,540mi) W then N through the Sayan Mountains and across Siberia, forming the W border of the central Siberian plateau, emptying into the Yenisei Gulf on the Kara Sea. A large hydroelectric station has been built at Krasnoyarsk. The river is a source of sturgeon and salmon. A shipping route, some of its sections are frozen in winter. When the Yenisei is combined with the Angara (its major tributary) it is the world's fifth-longest river at 5,550km (3,445mi).

Yerevan Capital of Armenia, on the River Razdan, s CAUCASUS. One of the world's oldest cities, it was capital of Armenia as early as the 7th century (though under Persian control), a crucial crossroads for caravan routes between India and Transcaucasia. It is the site of a 16th-century Turkish fortress and is a traditional wine-making centre. Industries: chemicals, plastics, cables, tyres, metals, electrical appliances, vodka. Pop. (1994) 1,254,000.

Yevtushenko, Yevgeny (1933–) Russian writer. During the 1960s, Yevtushenko headed a new wave of nonconformist, modern Soviet poetry. Explicitly rejecting SOCIALIST REALISM, Yevtushenko's rhetorical poetry anticipated GLASNOST in its examination of Soviet history. His most famous work, *Babi Yar* (1961), was a direct indictment of Soviet anti-semitism. Other works include *Precocious Autobiography* (1963) and *The Bratsk Station* (1965).

yew Any of a number of evergreen shrubs and trees of the genus *Taxus*, native to temperate regions of the Northern Hemisphere. They have stiff, narrow, dark green needles, often with pale undersides, and red, berry-like fruits. Height: to 25m (80ft). Family Taxaceae.

Yiddish Language spoken by JEWS living in central and E Europe and other countries (including the USA) with Jewish communities. It first developed in W Europe in the 10th and 11th centuries and was taken E with migrating Jews. It is a variety of German, with many Hebrew, Aramaic, French, Italian and Slavic words added. It is written using the Hebrew alphabet.

Yin Alternative transliteration for the SHANG dynasty

yin and yang Interaction of two complementary forces in the universe, as described in the Chinese philosophy of TAOISM. *Yin* and *yang* are two cosmic energy modes comprising the Tao or the eternal, dynamic way of the universe. Earth is *yin*, or the passive, dark, female principle; heaven is *yang*, or the active, bright, male principle. All the things of nature and society are composed of combinations of these two principles of polarity, which maintain the balance of all things. The hexagrams of the *I Ching* embody *yin* and *yang*.

YMCA Abbreviation of YOUNG MEN'S CHRISTIAN ASSOCIATION

yoga (Sanskrit, union) Term used for a number of Hindu disciplines to aid the union of the soul with God. Based on the *Yoga-sutras* of Patañjali (written at about the time of Christ), the practice of yoga generally involves moral restraints, meditation and the awakening of physical energy centres through specific postures (*asanas*) or exercises. Devoted to freeing the soul or self from earthly cares by isolating it from the body and the mind, these ancient practices became popular in the West during the second half of the 20th century as a means of relaxation, self-control and enlightenment.

Yogyakarta (Jogjakarta) City in S Java, Indonesia. Founded in 1749, it is the cultural and artistic centre of Java. Capital of a Dutch-controlled sultanate from 1755, it was the scene of a revolt against colonial exploitation (1825–30). During the 1940s it was the centre of the Indonesian independence movement and, in 1949, acted as the provisional capital of Indonesia. Its many visitors are drawn by the 18th-century palace, the Grand Mosque, the religious and arts festivals, and its proximity to the Borobudur temple. The major industry is handicrafts. Pop. (1990) 412,392.

Yokohama Port and major industrial city on the W shore of Tokyo Bay, SE Honshu, Japan. Japan's main port for many years, it is now its second largest city. It grew from a small fishing village to a major Japanese port after opening to foreign trade in 1859. It served as Tokyo's deep-water harbour and was a vital silk-exporting centre. Yokohama has been rebuilt twice: once, after the devastating earthquake in 1923, and again following intensive Allied bombing during World War 2. Many of the modern port and industrial facilities have been built on land reclaimed from the sea. Industries: iron, steel, shipbuilding. Pop. (1994) 3,265,000.

yolk Rich substance found in the eggs or ova of most animals except those of placental mammals. It consists of fats and proteins and serves as a store of food for the developing embryo.

yolk sac Membranous sac-like structure in the eggs of most animals. It is attached directly to the ventral surface or gut of the developing embryo in the eggs of birds, reptiles and some fish, and contains YOLK. The term also refers to an analogous sac-like membrane that develops below the mammalian embryo. It contains no yolk but is connected to the umbilical cord.

Yom Kippur (Day of Atonement) Most solemn of Jewish feasts. It is the last of the Ten Days of Penitence that begin the New Year. On this day, set aside for prayer and fasting, humanity is called to account for its sins and to seek reconciliation with God. Yom Kippur is described as the SABBATH of Sabbaths, because the break from work is almost complete, and Jews must abstain from food, drink and sex.

York City and county district in NORTH YORKSHIRE, N England. Located at the confluence of the Ouse and Foss rivers, it was an important Roman military post, an Anglo-Saxon capital, a Danish settlement and then the ecclesiastical centre of the North of England; York Minster cathedral dates from the 13th century. Its old buildings and museums make tourism important. Industries: engineering (including rail workshops), confectionery, precision instruments. Pop. (1991) 98,745.

York, Archbishop of Second-highest office of the Church of England. The acts of the Council of Arles (314) mention a bishop of York, but the early Christian community in York was destroyed by Saxon invaders. The uninterrupted history of the present see began with the consecration of Wilfrid as bishop of York in 664. York was raised to the dignity of an archbishopric in 735, when Egbert was given the title Primate of the Northern Province. The archbishop is now called the Primate of England (the Archbishop of CANTERBURY is Primate of all England).

York, House of English royal house, a branch of the PLANTAGENETS. During the Wars of the ROSES, rival claimants from the houses of York and LANCASTER contended for the crown. The Yorkist claimant, Richard, duke of York, was a great-grandson of EDWARD III. His son gained the crown as EDWARD IV. The defeat of Edward's brother, RICHARD III, by HENRY VII in 1485 brought the brief Yorkist line to a close.

Yorkshire *See* NORTH YORKSHIRE, SOUTH YORKSHIRE and WEST YORKSHIRE

Yorkshire terrier Small, long-haired dog originally bred in Lancashire and Yorkshire, England, in the 19th century. It has a small head with a short muzzle and small V-shaped erect ears. The compact body has a short, straight back and is set on short legs, which are hidden under the coat. The tail is commonly docked. The straight, fine, silky coat is generally blue-grey and tan. Height: to 20cm (8in) at the shoulder; weight to 3 kg (7lb).

Yoruba People of SW Nigeria. Most are farmers, growing crops such as yams, maize and cocoa. Many live in towns built around the palace of an *oba* (chief) and travel daily to outlying farms.

Yosemite National Park Spectacular national park in the Sierra Nevada range of central California, USA. Yosemite means "grizzly bear", and the park was named after the river that runs through it. Established in 1890, it is a mountainous area of glacial gorges and granite cliffs rising to the 3,990m (13,090ft) of Mount Lyell. Yosemite Falls, the highest waterfall in North America, drops 739m (2,425ft) in two stages. Other features include Half Dome Mountain and the vertical rock-face of El Capitan. Area: 308,335ha (761,320 acres).

Young, Brigham (1801–77) US religious leader, founder of SALT LAKE CITY. An early convert to the Church of Jesus Christ of Latter-Day Saints (MORMONS), Young took over the leadership when Joseph SMITH, the founder, was killed by a mob in 1844. Young held the group together and led their westward migration (1846–47) to Utah, where he organized the settlement that became Salt Lake City. He was governor of Utah Territory (1850–57).

Young, Thomas (1773–1829) British physicist and physician. He revived the wave theory of light first put forward in the 17th century by Christiaan HUYGENS. He helped present the Young-Helmholtz theory of colour vision and detailed the cause of astigmatism. He studied elasticity, giving his name to the tensile elastic (Young's) modulus. Young was also an Egyptologist who helped decipher the Rosetta stone.

Young Men's Christian Association Christian association for young men established in London (1844) by George Williams. Its aim is to develop Christian morals and leadership qualities in young people. Clubs were soon formed in the USA and Australia, and the world alliance of the YMCA was formed in Geneva in 1855. Women were accepted as members in 1971. *See also* YOUNG WOMEN'S CHRISTIAN ASSOCIATION

Young Turks Group of Turks who wished to remodel the OTTOMAN EMPIRE and make it a modern European state with a liberal constitution. The movement began with unrest in the army and in universities during the 1880s. In 1908 a Young Turk rising, led by ENVER PASHA and Kemal ATATÜRK, deposed Sultan Abdul Hamid II and replaced him with his brother, Mohammed V. Following a 1913 coup d'etat Enver Pasha became a virtual dictator. Under Kemal Atatürk, the Young Turks merged into the Turkish Nationalist Party.

Young Women's Christian Association Christian association for young women, the counterpart of the YMCA. Two groups were founded simultaneously in 1855 in different parts of England; the associations merged in 1877. The YWCA provides accommodation, education, recreation facilities, and welfare services to young women and has local branches in more than 80 countries.

Ypres, Battles of Several battles of World War 1 around the Belgian town of Ypres. The first (October–November 1914) stopped the German "race to the sea" to capture the Channel ports but resulted in the near destruction of the British Expeditionary Force. The second (April–May 1915), the first battle in which poison gas was used, resulted in even greater casualties without victory to either side. The third (summer 1917) was a predominantly British offensive culminating in the Passchendaele campaign, which continued until November, the costliest campaign in British military history.

ytterbium Silver-white, metallic element (symbol Yb) of the LANTHANIDE SERIES of the periodic table. First isolated in 1828, ytterbium's chief ore is monazite. The shiny, soft element is malleable and ductile, and is used to produce steel and other alloys. Properties: at.no. 70: r.a.m. 173.04; r.d. 6.97; m.p. 824°C (1,515°F), b.p. 1,193°C (2,179°F); most common isotope Yb^{174} (31.84%).

yttrium Silver-grey, metallic element (symbol Y) of group III of the PERIODIC TABLE. First isolated in 1828, it is found associated with lanthanide elements in monazite sand, bastnasite and gadolinite, and resembles the lanthanides in its chemistry. Yttrium was found in lunar rock samples collected by the Apollo 11 space mission. Its compounds are used in phosphors and communications devices, such as colour televison picture tubes and superconducting ceramics. Properties: at.no. 39; r.a.m. 88.9059; r.d. 4.47; m.p. 1,523°C (2,773°F); b.p. 3,337°C (6,039°F); most common isotope Y^{89} (100%).

Yüan (1271–1368) MONGOL dynasty in China. Continuing the conquests of GENGHIS KHAN, KUBLAI KHAN established his rule over China, eliminating the last SUNG claimant in 1279. He returned the capital to BEIJING and promoted construction and commerce. Chinese literature took new forms during the Yüan dynasty. Native Chinese were excluded from government, and foreign visitors, including merchants such as Marco POLO, were encouraged. Among the Chinese people, resentment of alien rule was aggravated by economic problems, including runaway inflation. The less competent successors of Kublai were increasingly challenged by rebellion, culminating in victory for the MING dynasty.

Yucatán State in the N part of the Yucatán Peninsula, SE Mexico. Its capital is Mérida. The terrain is low-lying, covered in places with scrub and cactus thickets. Once the centre of the MAYA civilization, Yucatán was conquered by the Spanish in the 1540s. The region is a major producer of henequen (sisal hemp used for cordage). Other products: tobacco, sugar, cotton, tropical fruits. Fishing is important along the coast. Area: 38,508sq km (14,868sq miles). Pop. (1990) 1,362,940.

yucca Genus of *c.*40 species of succulent plants native to S USA, Mexico and the West Indies. Most species are stemless, forming a rosette of leaves, or have a trunk. The flowers grow in clusters and are white, tinged with yellow or purple. The leaves are poisonous. Height: to 10m (33ft). Family Liliaceae.

YUGOSLAVIA
AREA: 102,173sq km (39,449sq mi)
POPULATION: 10,469,000
CAPITAL (POPULATION): Belgrade (1,168,454)
GOVERNMENT: Federal republic
ETHNIC GROUPS: Serb 62%, Albanian 17%,
Montenegrin 5%, Hungarian, Muslim, Croat
LANGUAGES: Serbo-Croatian (official)
RELIGIONS: Christianity (mainly Serbian
Orthodox, with Roman Catholic and
Protestant minorities), Islam
CURRENCY: Yugoslav new dinar = 100 paras

Yugoslavia Balkan federal republic in SE Europe; the capital is BELGRADE. **Land and climate** The Federal Republic of Yugoslavia now consists of SERBIA and MONTENEGRO. The rump Yugoslav federation has not gained international recognition as the successor to the Socialist Federal Republic of Yugoslavia created by Josip TITO. In 1991 the federation began to disintegrate when SLOVENIA, CROATIA and MACEDONIA declared independence. In 1992 BOSNIA-HERZEGOVINA followed suit. A narrow coastal strip on the Adriatic Sea includes Montenegro's capital, Podgorica. The interior of Montenegro consists largely of barren karst, including parts of the DINARIC ALPS and the Balkan Mountains. Kosovo is a high plateau region. Serbia is dominated by the fertile lowland plains of the DANUBE, on whose banks lie the capital Belgrade, and the N city of Novi Sad. (*see* individual country/republic articles for pre-1918 history and post-independence events) The coastal Mediterranean climate gives way to the bitterly cold winters of the highlands. Belgrade has a continental climate. Forests cover about 25% of the republic, while farmland and pasture cover more than 50%. **Economy** Yugoslavia's lower-middle income economy has been devastated by civil war and economic sanctions (1992 GDP per capita, US$4,000). Hyperinflation is one of the greatest economic problems (1994 monthly inflation, 300 million per cent). The war has also caused a collapse in industrial production. Natural resources include bauxite, coal and copper. Oil and natural gas are exploited from the N Pannonian plains and the Adriatic Sea. Under Tito, the manufacturing sector was greatly expanded, especially around Belgrade. Manufactures include aluminium, cars, machinery, plastics, steel and textiles. Agriculture remains important. Crops include fruits, maize, potatoes, tobacco and wheat. **History** Serbian-led demands for the unification of South Slavic lands were a major contributing factor to the outbreak of World War 1. In 1918 the "Kingdom of Serbs, Croats and Slovenes" was formed under the Serbian king, PETER I. He was succeeded by Alexander I in 1921. In 1929 Alexander formed a dictatorship, and renamed the country Yugoslavia. PETER II's reign was abruptly halted by German occupation

(1941) in World War 2. Yugoslav resistance to the fascist puppet regime was stout. The main resistance groups were the communist partisans led by Tito and the royalist *chetniks*. In 1945 Tito formed the Federal People's Republic of Yugoslavia. In 1948 Yugoslavia was expelled from the Soviet-dominated Cominform. Tito adopted an independent foreign policy. In domestic affairs, agricultural collectivization was abandoned (1953), and new constitutions (1963, 1974) devolved power to the constituent republics in an effort to quell unrest. Following Tito's death in 1980, Yugoslavia's underlying ethnic tensions began to re-surface. In 1986 Slobodan MILOŠEVIĆ became leader of the Serbian Communist Party. In 1989 Milošević became president of Serbia and called for the creation of a "Greater Serbia". Federal troops were used to suppress demands for autonomy in Albanian-dominated Kosovo. In 1990 elections, non-communist parties won majorities in every republic, except Serbia and Montenegro. Serbian attempts to dominate the federation led to the formal secession of Slovenia and Croatia in June 1991. The Serb-dominated Federal army launched a campaign against the Croats, whose territory included a large Serbian minority. A cease-fire was agreed in January 1992. The EC recognized Slovenia and Croatia as separate states. Bosnia-Herzegovina's declaration of independence in March 1992 led to a brutal civil war between Serbs, Croats and Bosnian Muslims. In April 1992 Serbia and Montenegro announced the formation of a new Yugoslav federation, and invited Serbs in Croatia and Bosnia-Herzegovia to join. Serbian military and financial aid to the Bosnian Serb campaign of "ethnic cleansing" led the United Nations to impose economic sanctions on Serbia. The threat of further sanctions prompted Milošević to sever support for the Bosnian Serbs. In 1995 Milošević signed the Dayton Peace Accord, which ended the Bosnian war. In 1996 local elections, the Serbian Socialist (formerly Communist) Party was defeated in many areas. In early 1997 massive and prolonged public demonstrations forced Milošević to acknowledge the poll results. In 1997 he resigned the presidency of Serbia in order to become president of Yugoslavia. In Montenegro, tension remains high between pro- and anti-independence factions.
Yukawa, Hideki (1907–81) Japanese physicist. In the 1930s he proposed that there was a nuclear force of very short range (less than 10^{-15} m) strong enough to overcome the repulsive force of protons and which diminished rapidly with distance. He predicted that this force manifested itself by the transfer of particles between neutrons and protons. In 1947 Yukawa's theory was confirmed by the discovery of the pion (pi meson) by Cecil POWELL. In 1949 he was awarded the Nobel Prize for physics for his prediction of the existence of the MESON.
Yukon River Fourth-longest river in North America, deriving its name from an Indian word meaning "great". It rises at Lake Tagish on the

border of British Columbia, Canada, and flows N and NW through Yukon Territory across the border into Alaska. It then flows SW to enter the Bering Sea. The lower course of the river was explored by Russians in 1836–37, the upper course by Robert Campbell in 1843. It was a major transportation route during the KLONDIKE GOLD RUSH. It is navigable for *c*.2,858km (1,775mi) of its 3,185km (1,980mi) course, but is ice-bound from October to June. The river teems with salmon, which spawn in the clear Yukon water.

Yukon Territory Small territory in the extreme NW of Canada, bounded by the Arctic Ocean (N), Northwest Territories (E), British Columbia (S) and Alaska (W). The capital and largest town is Whitehorse. In the N the region consists of Arctic waste and is virtually uninhabited. Further S there is spectacular mountain scenery with lakes and coniferous forests. The region is drained chiefly by the YUKON and MACKENZIE rivers. The climate is harsh, with freezing winters and short summers, though more temperate than Northwest Territories. In 1991 the Canadian government recognized the land claim of the indigenous Yukon (First Nation) Native Americans. From 1840, the region, then part of Northwest Territories, was explored by fur traders from the HUDSON'S BAY COMPANY. In the 1890s the KLONDIKE GOLD RUSH brought over 30,000 prospectors. Farming is extremely limited, but a few cereal crops and vegetables are grown in the valleys. The principal activity is mining, with major deposits including lead, zinc and gold. There is also a healthy forestry industry. With a small manufacturing base, tourism plays an important part in the economy. Area: 483,450sq km (186,675sq mi). Pop. (1991) 27,797.

Yunnan (South of the Clouds) Province in SW China, bounded by Laos and Vietnam (S) and Burma (W); the capital is Kunming. Yunnan's remote, mountain location enabled it to retain an independent status until conquered by the Mongols in 1253. In 1659 it became a province of China and was captured by Chinese communist forces in 1950. Yunnan is divided along ethnic lines into eight autonomous districts, which are home to many of China's minority nationalities. It is renowned for the rich diversity of its wildlife, particularly rare plant species. Agriculture is restricted to a few plains, with rice the major crop. Its valuable mineral resources include deposits of tin, tungsten, copper, gold, silver. Yunnan has road links with Vietnam and Burma. Mining and timber are the main industries. Area: 436,200sq km (168,482sq mi). Pop. (1990) 36,750,000.

YWCA Abbreviation of YOUNG WOMEN'S CHRISTIAN ASSOCIATION

Z

Z/z is the 26th and last letter of the English alphabet and a letter also included in the alphabets of many other w European languages. It is derived from the Semitic letter zayin.

Zacharias, Saint (d.752) (Zachary) Pope (741–52). He strengthened the Holy See, and during his papacy he achieved a 20-year truce with the LOMBARDS. He established cordial relations with the FRANKS by supporting the accession of PEPIN III (THE SHORT) to the Frankish throne.

Zacharias Variant spelling of ZECHARIAH

Zagreb Capital of Croatia, on the River Sava. Founded in the 11th century, it became capital of the Hungarian province of Croatia and Slavonia during the 14th century. The city was an important centre of the 19th-century Croatian nationalist movement. In 1918 it was the meeting place of the Croatian diet, which broke all ties with Austria-Hungary. It later joined a new union with Serbia in what was to become Yugoslavia. Following the break-up of Yugoslavia in 1992, Zagreb remained capital of the newly independent state of Croatia. It is the industrial and manufacturing heart of Croatia. Industries: steel, cement, machinery, chemicals. Pop. (1991) 726,770.

zaibatsu Large, industrial conglomerates in Japan formed after the MEIJI RESTORATION (1868). Headed by powerful families such as Mitsui and Mitsubishi, they came to dominate the Japanese economy in the early 20th century.

Zaïre (officially Democratic Republic of Congo) Republic in w central Africa; the capital is KINSHASA. **Land and climate** The Congo basin is the world's second-largest drainage system. Behind a narrow Atlantic coastline, on the opposite bank of the Congo from Brazzaville, lies Kinshasa. North-central Zaïre consists of a high plateau, 1,000–1,400m (3,300–4,600ft) high, and includes

---

ZAÏRE

AREA: 2,344,885sq km (905,365 sq mi)
POPULATION: 42,552,000
CAPITAL (POPULATION): Kinshasa (3,804,000)
GOVERNMENT: Transitional
ETHNIC GROUPS: Luba 18%, Kongo 16%, Mongo 14%, Rwanda 10%, Azande 6%, Bandi and Ngale 6%, Rundi 4%, Teke, Boa, Chokwe, Lugbara, Banda
LANGUAGES: French (official)
RELIGIONS: Christianity (Roman Catholic 48%, Protestant 29%, indigenous Christian churches 17%), traditional beliefs 3%, Islam 1%
CURRENCY: Zaïre = 100 makuta

---

the city of KISANGANI. In the E, the plateau rises to 5,109m (16,762ft) in the Ruwenzori Mountains. Lakes ALBERT and Edward form much of Zaïre's NE border with Uganda. Lake Kivu lies along its border with Rwanda. Lake TANGANYIKA forms the entire border with Tanzania. All the lakes lie in an arm of the Great RIFT VALLEY. The S highland province of Shaba (Katanga) includes Zaïre's second-largest city, Lubumbashi. Much of Zaïre has an equatorial climate, with high temperatures and heavy rainfall throughout the year. Dense equatorial rainforests grow in N Zaïre. The S plateau is an area of savanna and swamps. **Economy** Zaïre is a low-income developing country (1992 GDP per capita, US$523). Zaïre is the world's leading producer of cobalt and the second-largest producer of diamonds (after Australia). Copper is the major export. Zaïre has enormous potential for hydroelectricity; the Inga dam, near Kinshasa, is one of the world's largest. A major economic problem is an inadequate infrastructure. Agriculture employs 71% of the workforce, mainly at subsistence level. Palm oil is the most vital cash crop. Other cash crops include cocoa, coffee, cotton and tea. Food crops include bananas, cassava, maize and rice. Corruption and hyperinflation are major obstacles to economic growth. **History and politics** By *c.*1000 AD, Bantu-speakers had largely displaced the native pygmy population. From the 14th century large Bantu kingdoms began to emerge. In 1482 a Portuguese navigator became the first European to reach the mouth of the Congo. In the 19th century slave and ivory traders formed powerful states. Henry Morton STANLEY's explorations (1874–77) into the interior established the route of the Congo. In 1878 King LEOPOLD II of Belgium employed Stanley to found colonies along the Congo. In 1885 Leopold proclaimed the foundation of the Congo Free State. Sir Roger CASEMENT's denunciation of the inhuman exploitation of the native population resulted in international criticism. In 1908 Belgium responded by establishing direct control as the colony of Belgium Congo. European companies exploited African labour to develop the copper and diamond mines. In 1958 the French offered the Congo a free vote on independence. Nationalists in Belgium Congo demanded similar elections. In June 1960 independence was granted as the Republic of the Congo. Patrice Lumumba became prime minister. Belgium had not properly secured institutional changes and the state rapidly fractured. The mineral-rich province of Katanga demanded independence. Belgian troops, sent to protect its citizens and mining interests, were replaced by UN troops. In September 1960 Joseph MOBUTU, commander-in-chief of the Congolese National Army, seized power. Lumumba was imprisoned and later murdered. In 1963 UN and government forces combined to force Katanga to drop its demands for secession. Following the withdrawal of UN troops in 1964, the country was again plunged into civil war. Belgian troops once more intervened. In 1965 Mobutu proclaimed himself president. Mobutu began a campaign of "Africanization": Leopoldsville became Kinshasa (1966); the country and river renamed Zaïre (1971); Katanga became Shaba (1972); and Mobutu adopted the name Mobutu Sese Seko. Mobutu was re-elected in uncontested elections in 1974 and 1977. Political repression and endemic corruption led to renewed civil war in Shaba (1977–78). Secessionist forces were again defeated with European aid. An ailing Mobutu came under increasing pressure to reform. In 1990 he was forced to allow the formation of opposition parties. National elections were repeatedly deferred and a succession of transitional governments remained under Mobutu's control. In 1995 millions of Hutus fled from RWANDA into E Zaïre to escape possible Tutsi reprisals. In 1996 rebel forces, led by Laurent Kabila, launched a successful offensive against Mobutu's regime. Mobutu was forced into exile. Kabila's presidency held out the hope of democratic reforms.

Zaïre, River *See* CONGO

Zambezi River in S Africa. Rising in NW Zambia, it flows in a rough "S" shape through E Angola and W Zambia. It turns E to form part of the Zambian border with Namibia and the entire border with Zimbabwe (including the VICTORIA FALLS). It crosses the widest part of Mozambique and turns SE to empty into the Indian Ocean. There is great potential for the generation of hydroelectricity along the river's course, and it has two of Africa's biggest dams: Kariba (Zambia-Zimbabwe) and Cabora Bassa (Mozambique). Length: 2,740km (1,700mi).

Zambia The Republic of Zambia is a landlocked country in S Africa. **Land and climate** Most of Zambia consists of a highland plateau between 900m and 1,500m (2,950ft and 4,920ft) high. The highest peak, 2,067m (6,781ft), lies close to the Lake TANGANYIKA border with Tanzania. Lake Mweru lies on the border with Zaïre. The ZAMBEZI forms Zambia's entire S border with Botswana and Zimbabwe. The spectacular VICTORIA FALLS and the man-made Lake Kariba lie on its banks. Although Zambia lies in the tropics, temperatures and humidity are moderated by altitude. The rainy

---

ZAMBIA

AREA: 752,614sq km (290,586 sq mi)
POPULATION: 9,196,000
CAPITAL (POPULATION): Lusaka (982,000)
GOVERNMENT: Multiparty republic
ETHNIC GROUPS: Bemba 36%, Maravi (Nyanja) 18%, Tonga 15%
LANGUAGES: English (official)
RELIGIONS: Christianity (Protestant 34%, Roman Catholic 26%, African Christians 8%), traditional beliefs 27%
CURRENCY: Kwacha = 100 ngwee

---

season lasts from November to March. Rainfall is greatest in the N. Grassland and wooded savanna cover much of Zambia. There are also several swamps. Evergreen forests exist in the drier SW. **Economy** Zambia is the world's fifth-largest producer of copper ore, which accounts for 80% of exports. It is the second-largest producer of cobalt ore. Zambia also mines lead, zinc and silver. Zambia's dependence on mineral exports constitutes a structural imbalance. The Movement for Multiparty Democracy (MMD) has introduced free market reforms and privatization, leading to a large influx of aid and the reduction of national debt. Agriculture employs 38% of the workforce. Maize is the chief food crop. Cassava, coffee, sugar cane and tobacco are cash crops. **History and politics** In c.800 AD Bantu-speakers migrated to the area. By the late 18th century, Zambia was part of the copper and slave trade. The British explorer David LIVINGSTONE made the first European discovery of Victoria Falls in 1855. In 1890 the British South Africa Company, managed by Cecil RHODES, made treaties with local chiefs. The area was administratively divided into NW and NE Rhodesia. Local rebellions were crushed. In 1911 the two regions were joined to form Northern Rhodesia. In 1924 Northern Rhodesia became a British Crown Colony. The discovery of further copper deposits increased European settlement and the migration of African labour. In 1953 Britain formed the federation of Rhodesia (including present-day Zambia and Zimbabwe) and Nyasaland (now Malawi). In 1963, following a nationwide campaign of civil disobedience, the federation was dissolved. In 1964 Northern Rhodesia achieved independence within the Commonwealth of Nations as the republic of Zambia. Kenneth KAUNDA became Zambia's first president. Following his re-election in 1968, Kaunda established state majority holdings in Zambian companies. Zambia supported the imposition of economic sanctions on Rhodesia. In 1972 Kaunda banned all opposition parties, and won the uncontested 1973 elections. In 1990 a new multiparty constitution was adopted. The MMD won a landslide victory in 1991 elections. The MMD leader, Frederick Chiluba, became president. In 1993 Chiluba declared a state of emergency. Legislation excluded Kaunda from contesting the 1996 presidential elections. Chiluba was resoundingly re-elected. The government faced charges of electoral fraud. In 1997 a military coup was crushed.

Zanzibar Island region of TANZANIA, in the Indian Ocean, off the E coast of Africa; the capital is Zanzibar. In the late 17th century it came under the control of the Omani Arabs, and developed into the major centre of the East African ivory and slave trade. In 1890 the sultanate of Zanzibar was made a British protectorate. In 1963 it became an independent state and a member of the Commonwealth. In 1964 Zanzibar and Tanganyika merged to form the United Republic of Tanzania. Zanzibar retained control over domestic affairs. During the 1980s and 1990s, conflict developed between secessionist and mainland centralist forces. In 1993 a regional parliament for Zanzibar was established. The chief export is cloves and the biggest industry is fishing. Area: 1,660sq km (641sq mi). Pop. (1988) 375,539.

Zapata, Emiliano (1880–1919) Mexican revolutionary leader. He became leader of the growing peasant movement in 1910. His demands for radical agrarian reform led to the MEXICAN REVOLUTION. In pursuit of "Land and Liberty", he opposed Porfirio DÍAZ, Francisco MADERO, Victoriano HUERTA and (with Pancho VILLA) Venustiano Carranza. The guerrilla campaign ended in his murder.

Zaporizhzhya (Ukrainian, Beyond the rapids) City on the River DNIEPER, SE UKRAINE. Zaporizhzhya consists of the old city and the new industrial area, development of which began in the 1930s with the construction of the Dneproges dam. It is now one of Ukraine's leading industrial complexes, producing aluminium, iron and steel, motor vehicles and chemicals. Pop. (1991) 897,000.

Zaragoza (Saragossa) City on the Ebro River, NE Spain; capital of Zaragoza province and Aragón region. Zaragoza was taken by the Romans in the 1st century BC and by Moors in the 8th century. In 1118 it was captured by Alfonso I of Aragón, who made it his capital. It was the scene of heroic resistance against the French in the Peninsular War (1808–09). At the heart of an agricultural region, it acts as a distribution point for wine, olives and cereal. Industries: heavy machinery, textiles. Pop. (1991) 586,219

Zarathustra *See* ZOROASTER

Zealots Jewish sect, active in opposition to Roman rule at the time of JESUS CHRIST and after. They refused to agree that Jews could be ruled by pagans, led resistance to the Roman census of AD 6, pursued a terrorist campaign, and played an important role in the rising of AD 66. Their activities continued into the 2nd century.

zebra Any of three species of strikingly patterned, striped, black-and-white, equine mammals of the grasslands of Africa. It has long ears, a tufted tail and narrow hooves. Height: to 140cm (55in) at the shoulder. Family Equidae; genus *Equus*.

zebu (Brahman cattle) Numerous, domestic varieties of a single species of OX, native to India. Zebu have been used extensively in Asia and Africa, and have been introduced to the New World as livestock. Species *Bos indicus*.

Zechariah (Zachariah) Any of several biblical personalities. One of the most significant was a Jewish prophet of the late 6th century BC. He prophesied the rebuilding of the TEMPLE in JERUSALEM by the Jews who had returned from exile in BABYLON. The other important Zechariah was the priest mentioned in the GOSPEL according to St LUKE as the father of St JOHN THE BAPTIST. According to the New Testament (Luke 1), Zechariah was visited by the angel GABRIEL, who foretold the birth of John. For doubting Gabriel's prophecy, Zechariah was struck dumb until the time of John's circumcision.

Zedillo, Ernesto (1951–) Mexican statesman, president (1994–). He promised to combat unemployment and tackle the failing economy. Within a few months, however, he was forced to devalue the peso, despite his earlier successes in government finance. Dissatisfaction with Zedillo's government became apparent in 1997 elections, when his Institutional Revolutionary Party (PRI) lost its majority in the Chamber of Deputies

Zeeman effect In physics, effect produced by a strong magnetic field on the light emitted by a radiant body; it is observed as a splitting of its spectral lines. It was first observed in 1896 by Pieter Zeeman. The effect has been useful in investigating the charge/mass ratio and magnetic moment of an ELECTRON.

Zeffirelli, Franco (1923–) Italian theatre, opera and film director. Renowned for his sumptuous production values, his films include *The Taming of the Shrew* (1966), *Romeo and Juliet* (1968) and *Brother Sun and Sister Moon* (1973). His major success was the television series *Jesus of Nazareth* (1978).

Zemin, Jiang *See* JIANG ZEMIN

Zen Japanese school of BUDDHISM, initially developed in China, where it is known as Ch'an. Instead of doctrines and scriptures, Zen stresses mind-to-mind instruction from master to disciple in order to achieve *satori* (awakening of Buddha-nature). There are two major Zen sects. **Rinzai** (introduced to Japan from China in 1191) emphasizes sudden enlightenment and meditation on paradoxical statements. The **Soto** sect (brought from China in 1227) advocates quiet meditation. In its secondary emphasis on mental tranquillity, fearlessness and spontaneity, Zen has had a great influence on Japanese culture. In recent decades, a number of Zen groups have emerged in Europe and the USA.

Zend-Avesta (Avesta) Sacred book of ZOROASTRIANISM. Most of the original was apparently lost when ALEXANDER THE GREAT burned Persepolis in 331 BC. The Gathas, the oldest part, originated with ZOROASTER. The other remaining parts are the Yashts, Yasna and Vendidad and prayers. Together they contain the world picture, law and liturgy of Zoroastrianism.

zenith In astronomy, point on the CELESTIAL SPHERE that is directly overhead. The zenith distance of a heavenly body is the angle it makes with the zenith. It is diametrically opposite the NADIR.

Zenobia Queen of PALMYRA (r.c.267–272). She ruled as regent for her son after the death of her husband. Palmyra was an ally of Rome, but Zenobia made it so powerful, conquering Egypt in 269, that the Romans resolved to crush her. AURELIAN defeated her in Syria, capturing Palmyra in 272.

Zeno of Citium (c.334–c.262 BC) Greek philosopher and founder of the STOICS. Proceeding from the CYNIC concept of self-sufficiency, he stressed the unity of the universe and the brotherhood of men living in harmony with the cosmos. He claimed virtue to be the only good, and wealth, illness and death to be of no human concern.

Zeno of Elea (495–430 BC) Greek philosopher. A disciple of Parmenides, he sought to reveal logical absurdities in theories of motion and change using paradoxical arguments.

zeolite Group of alumino-silicates that contain sodium, calcium or barium and loosely held water that can be continuously expelled on heating. Some zeolites occur as fibrous aggregates, while others form robust, non-fibrous crystals. Zeolites vary in hardness from 3 to 5 and in specific gravity from 2 to 2.4. They include analcime, $NaAlSi_2O_6.H_2O$, stilbite, $NaCa_2(Al_5Si_{13})O_{36}.14H_2O$, and natrolite $Na_2Al_2Si_3O_{10}.2H_2O$.

Zephaniah (active c.630 BC) OLD TESTAMENT prophet. He was named as the author of the Book of Zephaniah, the ninth of the 12 books of the Minor Prophets. He condemned Israel's religious and political corruption and stressed the certainty of God's judgment against Israel.

Zeppelin, Ferdinand, Count von (1838–1917) German army officer and inventor. He served in the armies of Württemburg and Prussia. In 1900 he invented the first rigid airship, which was called Zeppelin after him.

Zeus In Greek mythology, the sky god, lord of the wind, clouds, rain and thunder. He is identified with the Roman god, JUPITER. Zeus was the son of Rhea and Kronos, who he deposed. Zeus was the supreme deity of the Olympians. He fathered huge numbers of children.

Zhao Ziyang (1918–) Chinese politician who played a leading part in China's economic modernization. In 1938 he joined the Communist Party, and after the establishment of the communist regime in China in 1949, he became Guangdong province's first party secretary. He was dismissed during the CULTURAL REVOLUTION, but was rehabilitated and restored to his post in 1971. In 1975 he was appointed first party secretary of Sichuan province. He introduced radical economic reforms, which vastly improved industrial and agricultural production. Zhao achieved rapid promotion, becoming a full member of the Politburo in 1979. In 1980 he was appointed premier and, in 1987, general secretary. He began to move China towards a market economy. He was dismissed from office in 1989 after his sympathy for the student pro-democracy movement in TIANANMEN SQUARE.

Zhejiang (Chekiang) Province in SE China, S of the Yangtze River and on the East China Sea; the capital is Hangzhou. It was the centre of the Sung dynasty in the 12th and 13th centuries. A mountainous region, it is one of China's most populous areas and includes the Zhoushan Archipelago. The province was designated a special economic zone to encourage inward capital investment. The major river is the Qiantang. The chief crops are rice and tea. Major industries include silk produc-

tion and fishing. Area: 101,830sq km (39,300sq mi). Pop. (1990) 40,840,000.

Zhou Chinese dynasty (1030–221 BC). After the nomadic Zhou overthrew the SHANG dynasty, Chinese civilization spread to most parts of modern China, although the dynasty never established effective control over the regions. The Late Zhou, from 772 BC, was a cultural golden age, marked by the writings of CONFUCIUS and LAO TZU, and a period of rising prosperity. As the provincial states grew in power, the Zhou dynasty disintegrated.

Zhou Enlai (1898–1976) Chinese statesman. Educated in Japan and Europe, he worked for the nationalist KUOMINTANG (1924–27), before joining the Communist Party. He participated in the LONG MARCH, and acted as second-in-command to MAO ZEDONG. He negotiated the eventual communist victory, and became prime minister (1949–76) and foreign minister (1949–58). He was China's chief international spokesman until his death.

Zhu De (1886–1976) Chinese communist military leader. In 1911 he helped to overthrow the MANCHU dynasty. He joined MAO ZEDONG in 1928 and was a leader during the LONG MARCH (1934–35). Chief military planner of the final communist victory in China, he later served in government and party posts.

Zhukov, Georgi Konstantinovich (1896–1974) Soviet military commander and politician. In World War 2 he led the 1941 defence of Moscow, broke the German sieges of Stalingrad and Leningrad and, in 1945, led the final assault on Berlin. He became defence minister in 1955, but lost all government and party posts in 1957. He was rehabilitated in the 1960s, receiving the Order of Lenin in 1966.

Ziegler, Karl (1898–1973) German chemist. He shared the 1963 Nobel Prize in chemistry with Giulio Natta for research into POLYMERS. Ziegler discovered a technique that used a resin with metal ions attached as a catalyst in the production of POLYETHYLENE.

ziggurat Religious monument originating in BABYLON and ASSYRIA. It was constructed as a truncated, stepped PYRAMID, rising in diminishing tiers, usually square or rectangular. The shrine at the top was reached by a series of ramps. Ziggurats date from 3000–600 BC.

Zimbabwe The Republic of Zimbabwe is a landlocked country in S Africa. **Land and climate** It mainly consists of a plateau 900–1,500m (2,950–4,920ft) high, between the ZAMBEZI and LIMPOPO rivers. The principal land feature is the High Veld, a ridge running from NE to SW. HARARE lies on the NE edge of the ridge. BULAWAYO lies on the SW edge. The Middle Veld is the site of many large ranches. Below 900m (2,950ft) is the Low Veld. Highlands lie on the E border with Mozambique. The Low Veld is much warmer and drier than the High Veld. November to March is mainly hot and wet. Wooded savanna covers much of

ZIMBABWE
AREA: 390,579sq km (150,873sq mi)
POPULATION: 10,583,000
CAPITAL (POPULATION): Harare (1,184,169)
GOVERNMENT: Multiparty republic
ETHNIC GROUPS: Shona 71%, Ndebele 16%, other Bantu-speaking Africans 11%, Europeans 2%
LANGUAGES: English (official)
RELIGIONS: Christianity 45%, traditional beliefs 40%
CURRENCY: Zimbabwe dollar = 100 cents

Zimbabwe. The Eastern Highlands and river valleys are forested. There are many tobacco plantations. Bantu-speakers migrated to the region in AD 300. **Economy** Zimbabwe is a low income developing country. The post-independence emigration of most of the white population removed vital capital. The government's redistribution of land to the African population via compulsory purchase schemes, has been tainted by government corruption. Agriculture employs 70% of the workforce. Zimbawe is one of the world's largest exporter of tobacco. Other cash crops include cotton, sugar and beef. Maize is the main food crop. It has valuable mineral resources, especially around the Great Dyke, a low ridge that crosses the High Veld. Mining accounts for 20% of exports. Zimbabwe is the world's fourth-largest producer of asbestos and fifth-largest producer of chromium ore. Gold and nickel are mined. In 1990 the government began to introduce free-market reforms. The restructuring of the command economy has resulted in high unemployment. The servicing of national debt remains an economic problem. **History and politics** Bantu-speakers migrated to the region in AD 300. By 1200 the SHONA had established a kingdom in Mashonaland, E Zimbabwe. GREAT ZIMBABWE was the capital of this advanced culture. In 1837 the Ndebele displaced the Shona from W Zimbabwe and formed Matabeleland. In 1888 Matabeleland became a British protectorate. In 1889, the British South Africa Company (under Cecil RHODES) was granted a charter to exploit the region's mineral wealth. Native revolts were crushed and the area became Southern Rhodesia (1896). In 1923 it became a British crown colony. European settlers excluded Africans from participation in the government and economy. In 1953 Southern Rhodesia, Northern Rhodesia (now Zambia) and Nyasaland (Malawi) became a federation. In 1961 Joshua NKOMO formed the Zimbabwe African People's Union (ZAPU). In 1963 the federation dissolved and African majority governments were formed in Zambia and Malawi. Southern Rhodesia became simply Rhodesia. Robert MUGABE formed the Zimbabwe African National Union (ZANU). In 1964 the white nationalist leader Ian SMITH became prime minister. Nkomo and Mugabe were imprisoned. In 1965 Smith made a unilateral declaration of independence (UDI) from Britain. The UN imposed economic sanctions. In 1969 Rhodesia became a republic. In 1974 Nkomo and Mugabe were released. Smith's refusal to implement democratic reforms intensified the guerrilla war. The 1979 Lancaster House Agreement established a timetable for full independence. ZANU won a decisive victory in February 1980 elections and Robert Mugabe became prime minister. In 1987 ZANU and ZAPU merged. The post of prime minister was abolished as Mugabe became executive president. In 1996 Mugabe was elected for a fourth term.

zinc Bluish-white, metallic element (symbol Zn) of group II of the periodic table, known from early times. Chief ores are SPHALERITE, smithsonite and calamine. Zinc is a vital trace element, found in erythrocytes. It is used in many alloys, including brass, bronze, nickel and soft solder. It is corrosive-resistant and used in galvanizing iron. Zinc oxide is used in cosmetics, pharmaceuticals, paints, inks, pigments and plastics. Zinc chloride is used in dentistry and to manufacture batteries and fungicides. Properties: at.no. 30; r.a.m. 65.38; r.d. 7.133; m.p. 419.6°C (787.3°F); b.p. 907°C (1,665°F); most common isotope Zn^{64} (48.89%).

Zinnemann, Fred (1907–97) US film director, b. Austria. His major films include *The Seventh Cross* (1944) and *High Noon* (1952). He won two Best Director Academy Awards: for *From Here to Eternity* (1953) and *A Man For All Seasons* (1966).

Zinoviev, Grigori Evseyevich (1883–1936) Russian revolutionary. He joined the BOLSHEVIKS in 1903 and was active in the RUSSIAN REVOLUTION OF 1905. He was a close collaborator of LENIN in exile (1908–17). In the RUSSIAN REVOLUTION (1917), he voted against seizing power but remained a powerful figure in ST PETERSBURG and was appointed head of the COMMUNIST INTERNATIONAL in 1919. Though he sided with STALIN against TROTSKY in 1922, he was later expelled from the party and eventually executed. The "Zinoviev letter" (1924), urging the British Communist Party to revolt, may have contributed to the electoral defeat of the Labour government, but was probably a forgery.

Zion Hill in E Jerusalem, Israel. Zion was originally the hill on which a Jebusite fortress was built. It now refers to the hill on which the TEMPLE was built. It is a centre of Jewish spiritual life and symbolic of the Promised Land.

Zionism Jewish nationalist movement advocating the return of Jews to the land of Zion (Palestine). Though it represents a desire expressed since the Jewish DIASPORA began in the 6th century BC, the modern Zionist movement dates from 1897, when Theodor HERZL established the World Zionist Congress at Basel, Switzerland. In 1917 it secured British approval for its objective in the BALFOUR DECLARATION, and Jewish immigration to Palestine increased in the 1920s and 1930s. In 1947 the United Nations voted to partition Palestine between Jews and Arabs, leading to the foundation of the state of ISRAEL.

zircon Orthosilicate mineral, zirconium silicate ($ZrSiO_4$), found in IGNEOUS and METAMORPHIC rocks and in sand and gravel. It displays prismatic crystals. It is usually light or reddish brown but can be colourless, grey, yellow or green. It is used widely as a gemstone because of its hardness and high refractive index. Hardness 7.5; s.g. 4.6.

zirconium Greyish-white, metallic element (symbol Zr), one of the TRANSITION ELEMENTS. Zirconium was first discovered in 1789 by the German chemist Martin Klaproth, and its chief source is ZIRCON. Lunar rocks collected during the Apollo space missions show a higher content of zirconium than Earth does, and zirconium exists in meteorites and stars, including the Sun. Chemically similar to titanium, it is used in ceramics and in alloys for wire and absorption of neutrons in nuclear reactors. Properties: at.no. 40; r.a.m. 91.22; r.d. 6.51; m.p. 1,852°C (3,366°F); b.p. 4,377°C (7,911°F); most common isotope Zr^{90} (51.46%).

zither Stringed instrument. It consists of a resonator in the form of a wooden box with 30 to 45 strings stretched over it. A few of the strings are stretched over a fretted board for melody; the rest are used for accompaniment. The melody strings are plucked with the fingers or a plectrum.

zodiac (Gk. circle of animals) Belt on the celestial sphere that forms the background for the motions of the Sun, Moon and planets (except Pluto). The zodiac is divided into twelve **signs**, which are named after the constellations they contained at the time of the ancient Greeks: Aries, Taurus, Gemini, Cancer, Leo, Virgo, Libra, Scorpio, Sagittarius, Capricorn, Aquarius and Pisces. The constellations inside the Zodiac do not now correspond to those named by the ancients, because PRECESSION of the Earth's axis has meanwhile tilted the Earth in a different direction. To modern astronomers the zodiac has only historical significance. *See also* ASTROLOGY; ASTRONOMY

Zola, Émile Edouard Charles Antoine (1840–1902) French novelist. He became widely known following the publication of his third book, the novel *Thérèse Raquin* (1867). For the next quarter of a century he worked on what became the Rougon-Macquart sequence (1871–93), a 20-novel cycle telling the story of a family during the Second Empire; it established his reputation as the foremost exponent of the naturalistic school of fiction. The sequence includes his famous novels *The Drunkard* (1877), *Nana* (1880), *Germinal* (1885) and *The Human Animal* (1890). In 1898 he wrote a famous letter, beginning "*J'Accuse*", which denounced the punishment of Alfred Dreyfus. This led to a brief exile in England and, after the vindication of Dreyfus, a hero's return. *See also* DREYFUS AFFAIR

Zollverein German customs union formed in 1834 by 18 German states under Prussian leadership. By reducing tariffs and improving transport, it promoted economic prosperity. Nearly all other German states joined the Zollverein by 1867, despite Austrian opposition. It represented the first major step towards the creation of the German empire (1871).

zoo (zoological gardens) Public or private institution in which living animals are kept and exhibited. Wild animals have been kept in captivity since the beginning of recorded history. Organized public zoos, sometimes called menageries or aquariums (for fish), have been operating for more than 500 years in Europe. Today non-profit-making organizations or zoological societies run most zoos in a scientific manner. The emphasis is on conservation of endangered species and exhibiting animals in natural settings.

zoology Study of animals; combined with BOTANY, it comprises the science of BIOLOGY. It is concerned with the structure of the animal and the way in which animals behave, reproduce and function, their evolution and their role in interactions and their environment. There are various subdivisions of the discipline, including TAXONOMY, ECOLOGY, PALAEONTOLOGY, ANATOMY and zoogeography (the distribution of animals). ANTHROPOLOGY is an extension of zoology. *See also* EMBRYOLOGY; GENETICS; MORPHOLOGY

zoonosis Any infection or infestation of VERTEBRATES that is transmissible to human beings.

zooplankton Animal portion of the PLANKTON. It consists of a wide variety of micro-organisms, including copepod and larval forms of higher animals. It is an important constituent of the ocean's food chain. There are few levels or areas of the ocean that have no zooplankton.

Zoroaster (*c*.628–*c*.551 BC) (Zarathustra) Ancient Persian religious reformer and founder of ZOROASTRIANISM. At the age of 30, he saw the divine being AHURA MAZDAH in the first of many visions. Unable to convert the petty chieftains of his native region, Zoroaster travelled to E Persia, where he converted the royal family. By the time of Zoroaster's death (tradition says that he was murdered while at prayer), his new religion had spread to a large part of Persia. Parts of the ZEND-AVESTA, the holy scripture of Zoroastrianism, are believed to have been written by Zoroaster himself.

Zoroastrianism Religion founded by ZOROASTER in the 6th century BC. It was the state religion of PERSIA from the middle of the 3rd century AD until the mid-7th century. Viewing the world as being divided between the spirits of good and evil, Zoroastrians worship AHURA MAZDAH as the supreme deity, who is forever in conflict with Ahriman, the spirit of evil. They consider fire sacred. The rise of Islam in the 7th century led to the virtual disappearance of Zoroastrianism in Persia. Today the PARSI comprise most of the adherents of Zoroastrianism, which has its centre in BOMBAY, India.

Zulu Bantu people of South Africa, most of whom live in KwaZulu-Natal. They are closely related to the Swazi and the Xhosa. The Zulus have a patriarchal, polygamous society with a strong militaristic tradition. Traditionally cereal farmers, they possessed large herds of cattle, considered to be status symbols. Under their leader Shaka, they fiercely resisted 19th-century colonialism. The predominant religion is now Christianity, although ethnic religions are still common. They are organized politically into the Inkatha movement under Chief Mangosutho Buthelezi.

Zululand Historic region of South Africa, now part of KwaZulu-Natal

Zulu War (1879) Conflict in South Africa between the British and the Zulu. Fearing a Zulu attack, the Afrikaners of Transvaal requested British protection. The British high commissioner demanded that the Zulu king, Cetewayo, disband his army. He refused, and the Zulu made a surprise attack at Isandhlwana, killing 800 British. Lacking modern weapons, the Zulu were checked at Rorke's Drift and decisively defeated at Ulundi.

Zürich City on the River Limmat, at the NW end of Lake Zürich, in the foothills of the Alps, N Switzerland; the country's largest city. Conquered by the Romans in 58 BC, the city later came under Alemanni and then Frankish rule. It became a free imperial city in 1218 and joined the Swiss Confederation in 1351. In the 16th century it was a focal point of the Swiss Reformation. Ulrich Zwingli founded Swiss Protestantism at Zürich Cathedral in 1523. In the 18th and 19th centuries the city developed as a cultural and scientific centre. Zürich is the commercial hub of Switzerland and has numerous banking and financial institutions. Industries: motor vehicles, machinery, paper, textiles, electrical products, printing and publishing, tourism. Pop. (1991) 840,000.

Zwingli, Ulrich (1484–1531) Swiss Protestant theologian and reformer. He was ordained as a Roman Catholic priest in 1506, but his studies of the New Testament in Erasmus' editions led him to become a reformer. By 1522 he was preaching reformed doctrine in Zürich. More radical than Luther, he saw communion as mainly symbolic and commemorative. He died while serving as a military chaplain with the Zürich army during a battle against the Catholic cantons at Kappel.

Zworykin, Vladimir Kosma (1889–1982) US physicist and inventor, b. Russia, a pioneer of television. In 1929 he joined the Radio Corporation of America (RCA), becoming its director of electronic development and in 1947 a vice president. Zworykin and his colleagues developed the iconoscope, the forerunner of the modern television camera tube, and the kinescope (a cathode-ray tube for TV sets). In 1928 he patented a colour television system. He also invented the electron microscope. In 1967 Zworykin received the National Medal of Science for his inventions and contributions to medical research.

zygote In sexual reproduction, a cell formed by fusion of a male and a female gamete. It contains a diploid number of chromosomes, half contributed by the sperm, half by the ovum. Through successive cell divisions, the zygote will develop into an embryo.

Zyuganov, Gennady (1944–) Russian politician. He moved up the Soviet Communist Party hierarchy in the 1970s and 80s. In 1993 he became chairman of the executive committee of the reconstituted Russian Communist Party and was elected to the Duma (lower house of the Russian parliament). In 1995 parliamentary elections, the Communist Party gained the largest number of votes and now control c.30% of the seats in the Duma. Zyuganov mounted a strong challenge in the 1996 presidential elections, but was defeated by a coalition of Boris Yeltsin and Aleksander Lebed.